This book is dedicated
to Don Zminda,
who has been a wonderful friend to me
and to this book.

— Bill James

For my parents,
Jerry and Sherry Henzler,
who imparted a love of
baseball, history and numbers.

— Jim Henzler

Acknowledgments

I have had more help in writing this book than Cecil B. DeMille had extras. I don't know where to start, guys; I had more help than a dog has fleas. I guess I'll start with Don Zminda, to whom this book has been dedicated. The first thing I realized, after I had the idea to do this book, was that I could not do it by myself. I approached STATS Publishing—Don Zminda at that time was head of STATS Publishing—to see whether they would be interested in working with me, and Don said "sure," and appointed Jim Henzler as the point man for the project.

Jim Henzler—I have to acknowledge his help, although he is listed as a co-author; Jim did his part of the work, and then he helped with mine. I've had more help than Nolan Ryan had strikeouts. Don and Jim and John Dewan; those are the guys I have to start with.

For many years, whenever I had a crackpot idea, I would bring it to STATS, Inc. to see if they would like to crack a few with me. They always said "Yes;" almost always. John Dewan was such a talented businessman he could take a crackpot idea and make money out of it sometimes.

Oh, I've had help; I've had more help with this book than Ramses had building that pyramid. I've had more help than Miss Cleo has phone lines. After STATS—meaning John and Don and Jim—had agreed to help me with the book, I wrote up a short version of the project, and I sent that to friends to allow them to comment. I'm not sure I can remember everybody that I gave copies of the book to, but I'll try. . . there was Don and John and Jim, and Rob Neyer, and John Sickels, and Craig Wright, and Dick Cramer, maybe Allen Barra, I'm not sure, and Eddie Epstein, and maybe Michael McCambridge, not sure. This was years ago, sometime in the last millennium. I've had more help than O.J. had alibis.

Most of these people responded and tried to be helpful, but I have to single out one who was especially helpful: Craig Wright. Many of my other friends were nice about the book, and tried to find helpful and supportive things to say, but Craig took a different tack: He pointed out to me the things that needed fixing. I hadn't paid enough attention to the biases in fielding statistics created by left- and right-handed pitching, for example, and I had been using league averages in a lot of places where there were better alternatives available, adjusting for innings differentials and strikeouts. Craig took the time to pound a lot of these things into my thick skull, and I appreciate this.

John Dewan and Dick Cramer, former directors of this company, used to have some serious differences, and one time I went to St. Louis to talk to Dick, trying to smooth some things out. That discussion wandered off track, and it was in that process, talking to Dick in a St. Louis restaurant, that the mathematical construct which underlies this effort suddenly became clear to me, and so I thank Dick Cramer for that conversation.

I've had more help with this book than Disneyland has visitors. I've had more help than Madonna has had lovers. . . well, it would be close, anyway. Mike Webber, for example. . . Mike works with me now, and helped me to finish the book. . . I think he was in kindergarten when I started it. As my father used to say, I've had more help than Carter has little liver pills. John Sickels worked with me at the time I began this project; gotta remember him.

So many people. . . I have had more help than Miller Field has bricks; heck, I've had more help than Shaquille has bricks from the free throw line. Tony Nistler has become the final editor of this project. Marc Elman was involved at one point, sometime in the past; he helped to get the thing re-started after it had stalled out. I've had more help than the old lady who flooded her engine right in front of the fire station. I'd like to thank my dear friend Morton Grove and his wife Lehigh, and all their associates. Ryan Balock has worked in that area, and Marc Carl, and Walter Lis, and Thom Henninger. I've had more help than Bartlett has quotations. I'm not in Morton's office. . . I'm sure I am missing some people who helped out on his end. Alan Leib and Steve Byrd; thanks for your help. Bob Meyerhoff.

I've had more help than a one-armed man delivering pizzas to a starving army. My other editor, Bill Rosen, who works for another company, encouraged me to stick with this project and work it through before I finished the other book, even though this meant the book I owed him would be a couple of years late.

I've had more help than Stephen King has nightmares. My son Isaac helped. . . one time we sat and talked about this book all weekend, a terrific act of patience on his part, particularly since I later learned that, the whole time, he thought I was saying "Win Chairs." Didn't even make any sense; kid just kept nodding and asking questions. I've had more help than Oprah has compassion. My other kids are Reuben, age 8, and Rachel, age 16; they've helped, too, but Reuben is too young to understand the system and Rachel is too old to pretend that she's interested. I've had more help than the Super Bowl has commercials. I've had more help than Marlon Brando has had candy bars.

My wife, Susan McCarthy, has been helpful and supportive, as always. I've had more help than Sinatra had comebacks. In 2001 I decided to take this project to the SABR convention, speak about it there, and get feedback from the 200-odd people who attended my presentation. Neal Pease was helpful to me in arranging that, and I thank him. The comments I got from the people who attended that talk were very helpful to me, and I thank each one of them. I have had more help than Enron had sleazeballs. George Hodak of *Playboy* Magazine has written supportively about what we are doing here, and I thank him for that.

All acknowledgments sections are written with a sense of dread, in the near-certain wariness that someone who should be thankyoued will be overlooked. In writing this book, I have had more help than a topless woman drowning in two feet of water on a crowded beach. I don't imagine I got everybody here, and to those of you I may have missed, I send instead my apologies.

Bill James

CONTENTS

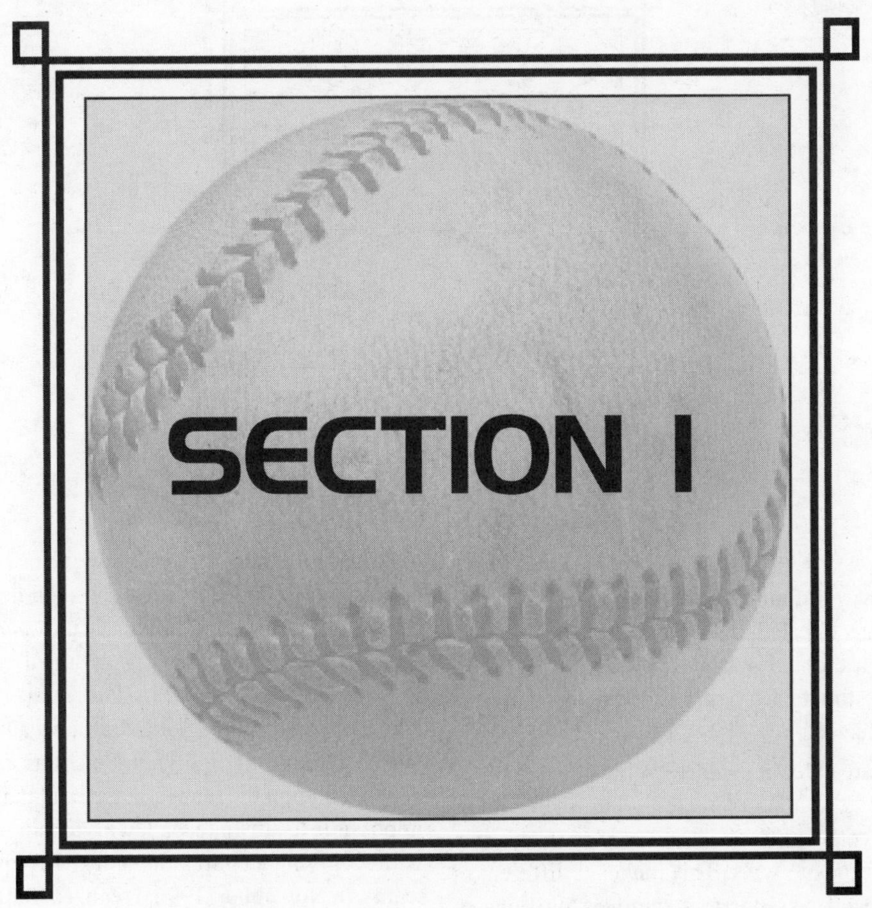

Introduction
(explaining the concept)

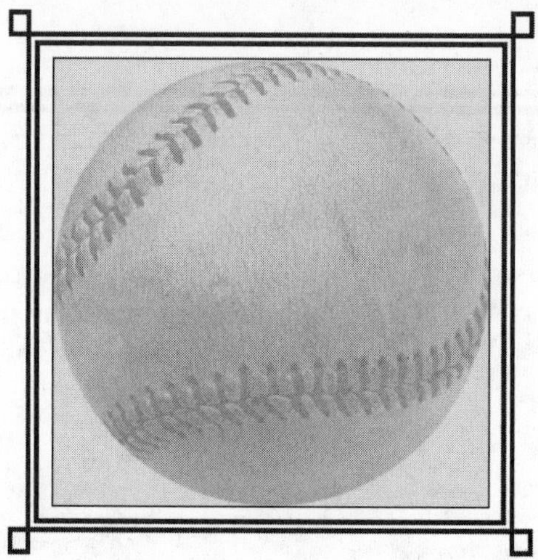

What is a Win Share?

Well, are you familiar with the concept of Runs Created? Runs Created is any formula by which we take the singles, doubles, triples, walks, etc., for each hitter, and estimate from that how many runs the player has created.

Win Shares are, in essence, Wins Created. . . or actually, thirds of a Win Created. Win Shares takes the concept of Runs Created and moves it one step further, from runs to wins. This makes it different in essentially two ways. First, it removes illusions of context, putting a hitter from Yankee Stadium on equal footing with a hitter from Colorado, and putting a hitter from 1968 on equal footing with a hitter from 2000. Second, the Win Shares system attempts to state the contributions of pitchers and of fielders in the same form as those of hitters.

There are two questions that always occur at this point, which are:

1. Why do you do thirds of a win, rather than wins or tenths of a win, and

2. Why did it take you 25 years to move from Runs Created to Wins Created?

Addressing the second question first, the reason I didn't move from Runs to Wins twenty years ago is that, for many years, I assumed that it was impossible to do this. As many of you know, wins by a team are not directly proportional to runs scored; rather, wins by a team are proportional to the *square* of runs scored. For twenty years, I assumed that this fact would make it impossible to state a player's individual win contribution in a global form, because I assumed that this meant the individual's contribution to wins depended upon the team context, and that it would be impossible to attribute team wins to individual players without giving an unfair advantage to players on good teams. In November, 1996, I realized that this assumption was false, and from that I was able to move to an individual player win figure.

As to the first question, we credit a team with three Win Shares for each Win. If a team Wins 100 games, the players on that team are credited with 300 Win Shares, absolutely and without exception.

Why three to one, rather than one to one or ten to one? Three to one is an interval that works. If one player in this system is credited with 20 Win Shares and another with 18, we can state with a fair degree of confidence that the one player contributed more to his team than the other. . . not that we are always right; there will always be anomalies and there will always be limitations to the data, but I would be confident that we had it right a high percentage of the time.

If we awarded ten Win Shares for each win, I would lose that confidence in the meaning of one or two Win Shares. One player then might have 20 Win Shares and another 18, but I wouldn't feel confident in saying that the player with 20 was actually better than the player with 18. A ten-to-one ratio would be, in essence, awarding one Win Share for every run—thus stating that every one-run separation was a meaningful distinction between players. The limitations of baseball statistics do not, in many cases, allow us to make fine estimates with any confidence.

Stated another way, if I were to list here a group of players with 15 Win Shares and a group of players with 13 Win Shares, and you were to guess which group was which, 99% of you would get it right, because, unless the groups were atypical, you would be able to "see" that the one group was better than the other. If we used a ten-to-one ratio (or a one-to-one ratio with a decimal point) and did the same experiment, frankly you wouldn't have a clue which group was which.

If you award one Win Share for one team Win, you have the opposite problem: real and fairly obvious differences between players are rounded out of existence. A player who hits .270 with 12 homers and a teammate who hits .255 with 10 homers would often score exactly the same, simply because the differences between them would often fail to account for a full Win. We use three to one because three to one is an interval that works. Two to one would work, I guess; Four to one would work. Ten to one doesn't work, and one to one doesn't.

For many years, I have wanted to have a system to summarize each player's value each season into a simple integer. Willie Mays' value in 1954 is 40, in 1955, 40, in 1956, 27, while Mickey Mantle in the same three years is 36, 41, 49. If we had an analytical system *in which we had confidence*, and which delivered results in that simple a form, it would open the door to researching thousands of questions which are virtually inaccessible without such a method. It would reduce enormously the time and effort required to research other questions, which can be accessed by other methods, but only with great difficulty.

Player comparisons are only the tip of the iceberg here, but let's start there. Al Kaline and Roberto Clemente. Who was a better player?

I have thought about this issue for thirty years, and I do not know. They had almost the same hit total, 3,000 versus 3,007. Clemente got his three grand with 700 fewer at bats, giving him a batting average twenty points higher, but on the other hand, Kaline scored 200 more runs and drove in almost 300 more runs. Kaline's secondary average, based on his power and his walks, is 90 points higher, more than off-setting the difference in batting average.

The two biggest differences in their career statistics are that:

1. Kaline drew more than twice as many walks,

and

2. Kaline hit almost twice as many homers.

But on the other hand, Clemente played in a tough home run park, Forbes Field, while Kaline played in a good home run park, Tiger Stadium. Kaline hit 226 homers in his home park, while Clemente hit only 101. In road games, Kaline out-homered Clemente by only 20% (173-139). The power difference is a park illusion, and as for Kaline's walks, what about Clemente's throwing arm?

Well, yes, but Tiger Stadium wasn't actually a good hitter's park; it was just a good home run park. And Forbes wasn't actually a poor hitter's park; it is merely a poor home run park. In fact, Forbes may have been a better place for a hitter than Tiger Stadium. Kaline's advantage isn't just in home runs, but in runs scored and RBI.

And as for the throwing arm. . . well, Kaline won ten Gold Gloves, and is considered by many to be one of the best defensive outfielders in baseball history. Granted, Clemente won twelve Gold Gloves, and Clemente did have 96 more assists than Kaline, but Kaline still had an excellent arm and an excellent assists total. Clemente committed almost twice as many errors as Kaline (140 to 73).

And so it goes; Clemente answers, Kaline answers. Of course, there are millions of fans who "know" that Clemente was better, because they saw him play, and there are millions more who "know"

Roberto Clemente

Al Kaline

that Kaline was better for the same reason. I don't want to "know" that way. I want reasons.

There are dozens of comparisons like that which have troubled me over the years. Billy Herman and Buddy Myer. Their stats in terms of games played, batting average, runs scored and RBI are almost identical, playing the same position (second base) in the same era. The differences seem to be minor, and off-setting. Herman had a hundred more doubles, but Myer had 200 more walks, and more stolen bases. In the 1930s there were far more runs scored in the American League than in the National. Myer played in the hitter's league but in pitcher's parks; Herman played in the pitcher's league but in hitter's parks. Herman has spectacular defensive stats at second base, but Myer has good stats at second, plus Myer put in some time at the more difficult defensive positions of shortstop and third base.

They seem the same, but were they? Herman is in the Hall of Fame; Myer isn't. Is this a mistake, or is it justified by subtle differences between them?

I could give you a hundred of them—Mickey Cochrane and Bill Dickey, Mike Schmidt and George Brett, Wally Berger and Hack Wilson, Willie Randolph and Bill Mazeroski, Ted Williams and Stan Musial, Dwight Evans and Dave Parker, Ken Boyer and Ron Santo, Dave Concepcion and Pee Wee Reese, Roger Maris and Bob Allison. One that twists my mind like a pretzel is Norm Cash versus Gil Hodges. At first glance, Cash and Hodges have very similar stats—377 homers for Cash, 370 for Hodges, a .271 average for Cash, .273 for Hodges, .488 slugging percentage for Cash, .487 for Hodges. We estimate that Cash created 1235 runs; Hodges, 1236.

Most baseball fans of my generation, if asked to compare, would assume that Hodges was a better player. When you make objective comparisons, you are pushed rapidly in the other direction. Cash, because he walked more often, had substantially more runs created per 27 outs, 6.52 to 6.13. Cash did this in the 1960s, when runs were scarce; Hodges did it in the 1950s, when runs were more plentiful. Cash's 6.52 Runs per Game are compared to a league norm of 4.02; Hodges is 6.13 over 4.46. Hodges is 37% better than league; Cash is 62% better than league.

Factoring in park effects will probably push Cash a little bit further ahead. Their home/road home run breakdowns are almost the same (213/164 for Cash, 210/160 for Hodges), but Ebbets Field was probably a little bit better hitter's park, all things considered, than Tiger Stadium.

Why, then, the perception that Hodges is better than Cash? Many reasons. Hodges played in seven World Series, Cash in only two, and in one of those only as a pinch hitter. A great many more writers grew up in Brooklyn in the 1950s than grew up in Detroit in the 1960s. Hodges, batting after Reese, Robinson and Snider, had more RBI opportunities than Cash. Hodges stayed in the game after his playing career, managing one of the most celebrated teams of all time. Cash, after his playing career, unwisely confessed to using a corked bat, which he should have taken along as a life preserver.

All of those things would tend to cause Hodges to be over-rated and Cash to be under-rated, but a more subtle factor may be the most important. Cash had eight seasons in his career in which he had 440 to 510 at bats, plus four more seasons in which he had 350 to 440 at bats—altogether, 12 seasons of not-quite-regular playing time, due to injuries and platooning. Nothing is more certain to cause a player to be under-rated than giving him 475 at bats a year. Take any comparable player from the modern era—Eddie Murray, Will Clark, Rafael Palmeiro, Jim Thome, Eric Karros—and scale him back to 475 at bats a year. It's amazing what it does to the way he looks in the record books. The player will consistently miss the magic numbers which bring respect. He will have 80 RBI a year rather than 110, 25 homers rather than 33, 75 runs scored rather than 100. Paul Sorrento was like that. Sorrento's career batting average, on-base percentage, slugging percentage and RBI rate were in the same general range as Karros and Lee May. But because Sorrento got 450 at bats a year rather than 600, he was never perceived as a hitter of the same quality.

Sometimes it may be that what I lack is not a clear idea of who is better, but the confidence to assert it. At times, it seems fairly clear to me that Juan Marichal had a better career than Sandy Koufax. But the perception that Koufax was far better than Marichal is so deeply rooted that trying to dislodge this opinion without a comprehensive analysis which explains why is like trying to dig up an oak tree with a spoon. Comprehensive—there's the point I should have made earlier. We have dozens of methods to compare players. We have piecemeal ways to put those together. What we lack is a way of tying them all into a coherent analysis. We need a comprehensive system, in which we have confidence, which has a place for all of the things we must think about when trying to assess value—productivity, park illusions, defense, playing time, contributions to winning teams. Everything.

Comparing two contemporary pitchers, or comparing two players who have almost the same career batting totals in different leagues with overlapping careers—those are relatively simple tasks. As players move apart in time and job description, it gets harder. How does Chuck Klein really compare to a slugging outfielder of comparable career length who may not have had the good fortune to play in the Baker Bowl in a time when the league batting average was around .300? Chuck Klein versus Tony Oliva, for example—who actually contributed more to his teams? Klein, Oliva, Carl Furillo, Sherry Magee, Ben Chapman, Sam Thompson, Larry Walker, Dolph Camilli, Cy Williams, Kenny Williams, Hugh Duffy, Del Ennis, Indian Bob Johnson and Chili Davis—if you told me that any one of those players was the best of the group, I would have to believe you because I can't prove that he wasn't.

That's a list of players with similar skills in different eras. But what about players with different skills in the same era, like Lou Brock vs. Willie Stargell, or Hoyt Wilhelm vs. Jim Bunning, or Jim Hegan vs. Hank Sauer, or Rickey Henderson vs. Cal Ripken?

Total Baseball tells us that Kaline was better than Clemente, that Billy Herman was three times the player Buddy Myer was, and that Cash was twice as valuable as Gil Hodges. Unfortunately, *Total Baseball* also tells us that Kal Daniels was a better player than Luis Aparicio, that Billy Consolo was better than Julian Javier, that Jerry Dybzinski was much better than Larry Bowa, that Bump Wills was a better player than Vada Pinson, that Don Mincher was better than Heinie Manush, that Frank Quilici was better than Bobby Richardson, that John Romano was better than Elston Howard, that Bob Cerv was better than Steve Garvey, that Randy Milligan was better than Ted

Kluszewski and that Glenn Hubbard was better than Brooks Robinson.

I have a few more of those if you want them (Tom Henke had a better career than Sandy Koufax). Of course, many of *Total Baseball*'s rankings are quite reasonable. It is essential to have confidence in the system; otherwise you don't know whether this is one of the times the system is right, or one of the times it's goofy. A rating system that works 70% of the time is like an airplane that lands safely 70% of the time.

If, however, one truly had confidence in the system, then one could use such a system to "score" trades, in baseball pre-1980, or free agent signings in the modern era. Who won the trade, and by how much? Just add up the values.

If we could use the system to accurately score trades, we would then be able to analyze the overall impact of trading strategies. If we could reliably evaluate past free agent signings, we could state the dollars-to-return ratio in simple, clear terms: this was a better free agent investment than that.

This has wide practical implications for a modern front office. One could use such a system to analyze whether or not it is true that championship teams are strong up the middle. One could use such a system to measure consistency, which is a hard thing to measure without a value clamp. One could use such a system to evaluate the role of racial prejudice in award voting, if there is such an impact.

One could use such a system to analyze aging, in hundreds of ways. If you have a 28-year-old slugging outfielder and a 28-year-old defense-first infielder of the same value, which is likely to be of more value in three years? Is there a difference in the value pattern of a right-handed pitcher versus a left-handed pitcher? A starter versus a reliever? A power pitcher versus a control pitcher?

One could use such a system to determine whether players today age differently than players of 20, 30, or 70 years ago. Forming groups of hundreds of players, one can assess aging patterns within the group by simply adding together the values. One could evaluate the future of any player, a free agent at the current time, by simply forming a group of players with the same characteristics, and adding up the season values.

One could use such a system (in fact, I once did) to evaluate amateur draft picks, and thus, drafting strategies. One could use such a system to evaluate scouts. One could use such a system to try to understand the role of the farm system in producing pennant winners in modern baseball, where the players produced are normally retained by the system for only a few years. Evaluating farm system production over a period of years becomes not a matter of opinion, but a subject capable of objective analysis.

Of course, such a system would also be useful in what could be called the drive-time radio disputes—who's the MVP, who should go into the Hall of Fame, and which third baseman should be added to the All-Star team. But we *have* systems to analyze those questions; that's not what I'm talking about. I'm talking about. . . well, salaries. What is the right salary for Doug Glanville in 2002? If you had such a system, it would be a simple matter to identify 20 players who had value patterns in the years 1997-2000 substantially identical to Glanville's value pattern in the years 1998-2001, and thus a simple matter to find out, objectively, what Glanville's salary in 2002 should be.

For such a system to be useful, for it to be adopted by baseball researchers, it must be fair to players of all types:

1. It must deal fairly with pitchers and position players.

2. It must be fair to hitters, and to glove men.

3. It must be fair to starters, and to relievers.

4. It must be fair to players who play in big-hitting eras, like 1894 and 1930, and to players who play in pitching eras like 1906 and 1968. It must be fair, specifically, to *pitchers* in big-hitting eras, and to hitters in pitching-dominated eras.

5. It must be fair to players who play on good teams, and players who play on bad teams. It would not be acceptable for the system to discriminate against a player because his teammates were not good.

6. It must be fair to infielders and outfielders, to catchers and to shortstops and to designated hitters.

7. It must be fair to part-time players who play well, but it must also be fair to ordinary players who play well enough to keep their jobs.

8. For careers, it must be fair to players who have 4,000-at bat careers, and it must be fair to players who have 10,000-at bat careers.

There are probably many others like that. The system has to be fair to power hitters and .300 hitters, it has to be fair to fast guys and slow guys, etc. Those aren't too problematic, because we've been studying offenses for many years, and there is a solid consensus about how to evaluate hitters, with marginal issues still in dispute. Evaluating pitchers is relatively easy. But when it comes to fielders, we're still feeling our way along.

Suppose you have a team which plays in a run-starved environment, like the 1965 Dodgers. The '65 Dodgers played in the worst hitter's park in baseball in the middle of a pitching-dominated era. They scored only 608 runs, but won 97 games and a World Championship because they allowed only 521 runs.

Predictably, the casual fan thinks that the Dodgers front-line pitchers were incredible, but that their hitters were nothing much. The Dodgers' 1965 pitching and batting stats, like 1960s hairstyles and clothes, give the appearance of their time and place. Statistics preserve baseball history much as artists preserve that which they paint. I take it to be obvious that there is an underlying reality which is, if not truly independent of its time and place, certainly distinct from it, as a naked man is distinct from the customs in which he is painted. If you put the 1965 Dodgers in another park (the Baker Bowl) and in another era (1930)—they might score 900 runs and allow 750—but they would still be an outstanding team.

We need, in essence, to strip the team naked, and see what is underneath. We need to evaluate Sandy Koufax (and Willie Davis) exactly the same as we would evaluate them if they had pitched (or played) in 1930, and in a hitter's park. We must not be misled by the peculiarities of time and place.

If the system fails any of these tests, that will limit its use. The Linear Weights method, while it is largely successful on points 1-6 above, is limited because it fails the seventh and eighth tests, which relate to differences in playing time.

In the past I have advocated a method, called the Value Approximation Method, which could be used to analyze these types of questions. But the Value Approximation Method was ultimately undermined by the fact that there was no logic behind it. The system consisted of arbitrary cutoffs. If you hit 20 homers, that was a point; if you didn't, that was no point. I argued at the time that the utility of the output was such that we should accept the approximate nature of the value-numbers themselves, because we weren't interested in the value-numbers themselves, but in the conclusions which could be reached by forming groups of seasons. One player's approximation might be a little low, another's a little high, but when you are dealing with groups of seasons, that doesn't matter. We're not interested in whether Orlando Cepeda in 1960 should be at 17 or 23; we're interested in all of the groups to which Cepeda contributed—San Francisco Giants, 23-year-old superstars, players from Puerto Rico, first basemen, right-handed sluggers, etc.

The Value Approximation Method fell by the wayside for two reasons. The lesser problem was that, whether or not people *should* be willing to accept the approximate nature of the season-value estimates, some people weren't. Some people, long in the habit of focusing on season ratings as end products, were unwilling to make use of a system which delivered only approximate numbers on that level, for the purpose of moving beyond that level. And, of course, when you're figuring salaries, you really can't have approximations; you need an accurate measure.

The greater problem was that while the Value Approximation Method was conceptually simple, the Book of Values didn't actually exist. I always wanted to have a volume which contained the Approximate Values for every major league player every year, but I never actually did. Since the values didn't exist, then in order to study anything involving hundreds of seasons, one had to start by figuring the approximate values for hundreds of seasons. The sheer work involved in using it limited its use.

This time, with the indulgence of Don Zminda and STATS, Inc. and the programming wizardry of Jim Henzler, we have actually been able to conjure the book of values into existence, so that we can actually look up Rip Collins' value in 1922 or Paul Blair's value in 1970 in just a few seconds. A researcher now, if he trusts the book of values, can start his research with the second step. In the fourth section of this book, I will apply those values to study a few of the questions outlined above.

I need to say a few words up front about the Linear Weights method. Pete Palmer, more than 15 years ago, undertook the immense task of designing a player values system which would evaluate every major league player in baseball history, and place them all along a single scale.

Evaluating baseball players purely by their statistics, given the severe limitations of those statistics, is like playing football in a minefield. Every time you think you've got a clear lane to run in, something blows up underneath you. I was writing books when Pete first published his evaluations, but I was certainly not ready, at that time, to respond to the challenge of evaluating every player every season, with as much accuracy as possible. Even if you have a solid structural concept for the evaluation (and at that time, I didn't), there are a million places that the analysis can go astray. It is a daunting task.

Pete Palmer's Linear Weights have represented the state of the art in baseball player evaluation for many years now. I certainly hope that no one reading this thinks that I don't respect Pete Palmer's work—or, worse yet, that I don't admire Pete Palmer. I quite certainly do.

But it is not the nature of research—good research or bad—to stand back and admire. In a living science, nothing represents the state of the art for more than a few years—not Palmer's methods, not mine, not anybody's. I am trying to move the chains.

And to do that, at times, it is necessary to comment on the failures and limitations of the Linear Weights method, to describe why this isn't the best way to do this. I'm not comparing my system to his because his system was a failure. I'm comparing my system to his because his system has been the industry standard for a good many years.

In some ways, Pete's Linear Weights system is not a parallel system to Win Shares. Palmer's method, like almost all analytical systems in baseball, is oriented toward producing player ratings as an end product. However well it does that, it provides no access to the level of questions which I am trying to study.

Suppose, for example, that one were to use Linear Weights to score a trade. The Linear Weights system scores anyone who is below average as being of negative value. Well, 70% of the players in baseball history are below average over the course of their careers. Most pitchers have losing records. Same thing with batters' records. Nobody could possibly be as bad as Willie Mays was good, so there have to be more losers than winners. Even many of the players who play in the major leagues for many years, who play 1500 or more games, are rated as below-average players.

So, in the Linear Weights analysis, if you trade a nobody, a player who never plays in the major leagues, and you only get some guy who plays 1500 major league games and hits .260 with 180 homers—not an *average* outfielder—well, Linear Weights would say that you've made a bad trade. You may also be challenged by the accuracy of the system. Among players regarded as below average by Linear Weights, thus sub-zero, are Carney Lansford, Lee May, Wally Moon, Keith Moreland, Don Mueller, Pete O'Brien, Tony Taylor and Bobby Richardson. If you trade nothing and you get any one of those players, in the view of Linear Weights, that's a bad trade. The system views Bill Madlock as an average player and an average player as having no value; therefore, if you give away a player like Bill Madlock in a trade, nothing has happened.

This is an insurmountable problem with using Linear Weights on some issues. The Tigers in 1970 traded Denny McLain and some loose change for Joe Coleman, Aurelio Rodriguez and Ed Brinkman. While McLain was out of baseball and on his way toward becoming a career criminal within a few months, Coleman won 20 games for the Tigers in 1971, 19 more in 1972, 23 more in 1973, 14 more in

1974. Brinkman was the Tigers shortstop for four years, and Aurelio Rodriguez manned third base for the Tigers for nine years.

A great trade for the Tigers, right? Analyzed by the Linear Weights system, the Tigers LOST the trade. By Linear Weights, Coleman was +10 in 1971, +8 in '72 and +9 in '73, but -22 in 1974 and -40 in 1975, so he's hurting the team. Both Rodriguez and Brinkman are analyzed as good fielders but bad hitters, which of course is correct, and as being worse at the bat than they are good in the field, therefore below average, therefore of negative value. So as Linear Weights sees it, if you trade away nothing and you only get three guys like Joe Coleman, Eddie Brinkman and Aurelio Rodriguez, that's a bad trade.

I'm not saying that Linear Weights is a bad system. It simply is not designed to analyze trades, and it won't. Win Shares is designed to do that, and it will.

If you used Linear Weights to analyze draft picks, same problem. If you use a draft pick and you only get a player as good as Joe Pepitone, Jimmy Piersall, Cookie Rojas or Deron Johnson, Linear Weights will score that as a negative contribution. A player who never plays in the majors at all is a zero, Bill Russell is -5.7, so if one team drafts a guy who never plays in the majors and the next team drafts Bill Russell, who made the better pick?

You can't use Linear Weights to analyze draft picks, so you can't use them to analyze or evaluate scouts. Since an average player is zero, by Linear Weights an average scout is going to be zero. By such a method, a scout who works for forty years and never finds anybody who plays a game in the major leagues. . . well, he's average. He's plus or minus zero, right in the center of the chart. The scout who signs 50 players who go on to play in the majors is as likely as not to have them total up to negative 358 runs, thus ranking him among the worst scouts of all time.

If you used Linear Weights to analyze salaries, you would have to shuffle to avoid the conclusion that 70% of the players should be giving money back. If you have one player who plays one game and strikes out four times, and a second player who plays 162 games and hits .270 with 12 homers, they would probably be almost exactly equal, since they're both going to score at about -1. But, of course, they're not going to be equal the next winter, when they are negotiating salaries.

If you used Linear Weights to do the free agent analysis that I suggested earlier, almost every group of players would have an average value near zero.

The Linear Weights system simply will not work for analyzing any of these types of questions. It's a good system in a lot of ways, an ambitious method that tackles a behemoth, and delivers reasonable numbers most of the time. But it's not designed to do what we're trying to do here, and it won't. This is an entirely different animal.

I could have called it Wins Created. As the name suggests, The Win Shares System is essentially a method of taking a team's win total, and assigning Shares of the Wins to individual players. Each team has 3.0 Win Shares for each win, a 3-to-1 ratio being established as the basis of the system.

This is the only analytical system I am aware of which is team-based, rather than derived from individual stats. Most analysis builds up from the performance of individuals. This analysis breaks down the performance of the team.

Now, having said that, I want to stress that the Win Shares system DOES NOT discriminate against players on weak teams. No player is or should be marked down because his teammates can't play. A player who hits .300 with 30 home runs on a bad team should rate exactly the same as a player who hits .300 with 30 homers on a good team, other things being equal. A pitcher who pitches 200 innings with a 3.50 ERA is going to rate just the same on a bad team as he does on a good team, other things being equal. There are two articles addressing this issue in Section IV, the articles "Good Teams, Bad Teams" and "Comparable Pitchers on Good Teams and on Bad Teams," but for now, I'll just have to ask you to accept that.

Anyway, if a team wins 80 games, then the players on that team will be assigned a total of 240.0 Win Shares. If they win 100 games, the players will be assigned a total of 300.0 Win Shares. If they win 60, the players will be assigned 180.0 Win Shares.

Win Share assignments from team to player take place in six stages, which reflect the logic of the method.

First, Win Shares are divided between Offense and Defense. (Defense broadly defined, to include both pitching and fielding.)

Second, those Win Shares assigned to the Offense are divided among the team's hitters, on the basis of runs created and outs made.

Third, those Win Shares assigned to the Defense are divided between those assigned to Pitching, and those assigned to Fielding.

Fourth, those Win Shares assigned to the pitchers are divided among the pitchers on the basis of innings pitched and runs allowed (with an adjustment to recognize the contribution of the closer).

Fifth, those Win Shares assigned to fielding are assigned to *defensive positions* (that is, to third base, to second base, to the outfield, etc.)

Sixth, those Win Shares assigned to defensive positions are then assigned to individual fielders.

Win Shares are divided on the basis of "claim points." Everything good that a player does creates claim points for that player, and the Win Shares are then divided in the same ratio as the claim points.

Overall: 48% of Win Shares are assigned to hitters/baserunners, 35% are assigned to pitchers, and 17% are assigned to fielders.

However, these numbers are not locked in place for each team, or even for each league. If a team's offense is better than its pitching and defense, obviously, more Win Shares go to the hitters, and less to the pitchers and fielders.

In modern baseball, where strikeouts are higher, a few more Win Shares are assigned to pitchers. In earlier times, when strikeouts were lower, a few more Win Shares went to fielders.

In the same way, Win Shares are divided between pitchers and fielders based on pitching and fielding numbers. If a team has lots of strikeouts, few walks, and few home runs allowed, obviously that reflects well on the pitchers. On the other hand, if they have a high fielding percentage and turn lots of double plays, that reflects well on the fielders. These credentials are balanced against one another in the third stage of the analysis, as outlined above.

We have been studying offenses for 20 years, and we're pretty comfortable with our methods for doing that. Win Shares are assigned to hitters on the basis of marginal runs created, which is a simple, straightforward process.

Assigning Win Shares to individual pitchers is an essentially simple process, since we have records of innings pitched and runs allowed.

So all of the complexity is in one-sixth of the points, the 16% which are devoted to fielding. There is a potential for error in the third stage of the process, which divides Win Shares between pitchers and fielders. The potential error results from the facts that (a) fielding statistics were never well designed to start with, and (b) we don't have much experience doing this. The logic of it still needs to be thought through in more detail. I'm sure that I'm making some mistakes there that I don't see yet, which will become evident over the next ten years, as more people get a chance to study the method. But the real complexity is in stages Five and Six, where Win Shares are assigned to fielders. The potential for error is limited somewhat because the other areas (hitting and pitching) are much larger, but fielding is where all the work has to be done, and that's what we'll spend most of the book sorting through.

I hope I will not be found guilty by my readers of being over-optimistic about what I have accomplished, or, worse yet, of hyping my work. I know many other people have worked hard on their own fielding systems, and I know they are as proud of their systems as I am of mine. The last seven months, when I have been working on this system every day, have been among the most rewarding months of my professional life. I honestly feel that this is the best sabermetric work that I have done in ten years, maybe twenty.

Twenty years ago, I think that several of us were able to do some good work which helped to build a consensus understanding of how offenses work and what hitting statistics really mean. But from then until now, fielding statistics have remained essentially an enigma.

Quite certainly, the work that I have done here will not put fielding statistics on the same level as hitting statistics. Testing my system, I still find places where it tells me things that I know to be wrong. I know that, in developing this system, I have made some assumptions which were not well founded, and which will have to be replaced.

At the same time, I hope that I have finally found a way to start the process, to get the mud away from the tires and send the truck rumbling down the road. I feel that I have made some minor breakthroughs in the understanding of fielding records, and further, that they are the best kind of breakthroughs: breakthroughs which will certainly lead, when other people see the work that I have done and apply their own abilities to the issues I have raised, to even more and even larger advances.

There are three keys to this approach. One is using a design for fielding performance which incorporates the assumption of value, rather than the assumption of no value; there will be an article later which explains what I mean by this. The second is the understanding that all individual fielding statistics are not "hard stats," like home runs and batting average, but rather, "fuzzy stats," like RBI, which are only meaningful in context.

But I knew those two things going into this process; that isn't what has made the last few months so exciting for me. What has fueled my progress is an absolute accident, something that I did not anticipate until it started to happen. That is the realization that fielding statistics make vastly more sense if you look at them from the top down than they do if you look at them from the bottom up.

On the top level you've got the team, on the second level the role on the team, on the third level, the individual who fills that role. We are in the habit of dealing with statistics from the bottom up. If you think about the 1927 Yankees, you think about what Babe Ruth accomplished, what Lou Gehrig did, what Tony Lazzeri did, what Earle Combs did, what Herb Pennock did. When you put them all together, then you have a concept of the team: the 1927 Yankees were a fantastic team because they had put all of these great players together.

But the same habit of thought doesn't always work with fielding statistics. To make sense of fielding statistics, sometimes you have to start with what the team accomplished, then ask how they accomplished that, and only then work toward the question of which player gets credit for that success.

You're not going to understand what I am talking about when you first read this. But later, after you have read through the system, after you've seen the specific points that I have to make, you'll understand what I'm saying.

There is a poem that religious people use. . . I don't know the poem or where to find it, but the effect is that our lives are like the back side of a tapestry. The pattern is on the other side of the cloth, where we can't see it. Our lives may seem random and pointless now, but later, when we get to the other side, we will see the pattern there, and we will come to understand why things had to be the way they were.

Well, fielding statistics are like that: there are patterns in fielding statistics that you will never see if you look at individuals, rather than teams. These patterns are not subtle, like those vision tricks in the Sunday newspaper, where if you stare at something long enough and catch the light just right, you can see a racehorse made up of little dots. They're obvious patterns, clear to anybody. Many of the things that I have "discovered" in recent months are so obvious that, in all honesty, I am embarrassed not to have discovered them years ago.

Let's get to work. First, we have to explain the details of the Win Shares system. That's Section II, and it's a deadly dull business that won't help you very much to understand why I feel the way I do about this work. I hope that, by the time you finish Section IV, you'll come to see things more my way.

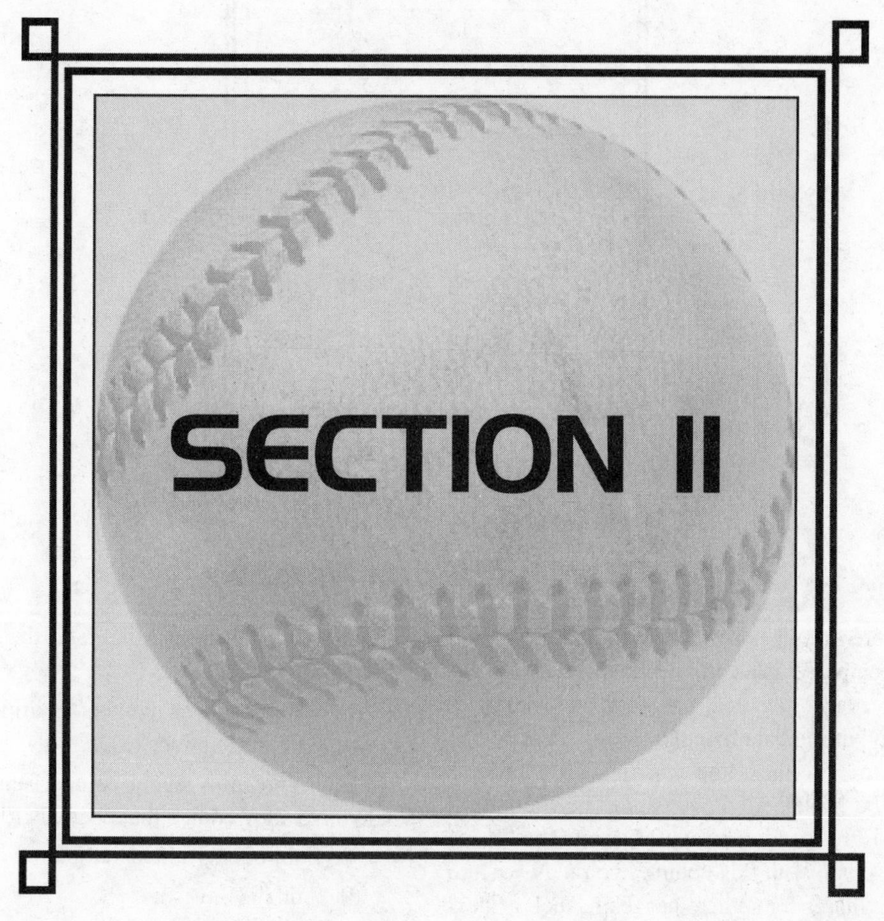

The Win Shares System

(explaining the details)

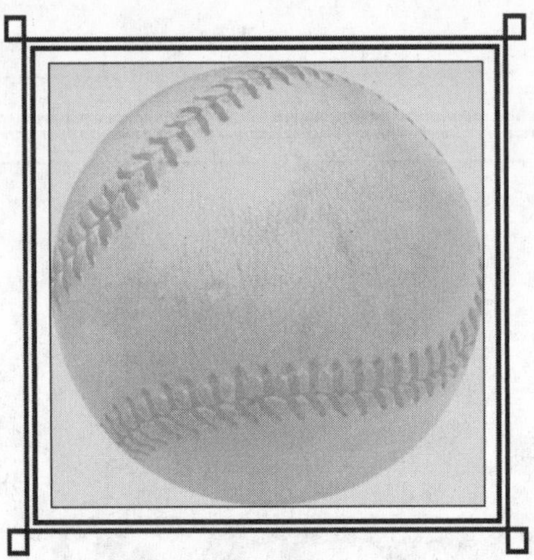

The Short-Form Method

To figure *exactly* how many Win Shares we will credit to each player is a complicated process involving almost every statistical category and countless formulas to put the data together. However, one can get approximately the same results with a process which can be explained in one page. The short-form method is useful for two reasons. Despite the "Book of Values" given with this volume, you may wish to figure Win Shares for some other team, such as next year's San Diego Padres, as of the All-Star break, or your son's little-league team. More significantly, understanding the short-form process gives you an essential understanding of the more detailed process.

This, then, is the one-page version of the Win Shares method:

1. Figure the Runs Created for all of the players on a team.

2. Figure the Outs Made by each hitter.

3. Divide the Outs by 12, and subtract that from the Runs Created.

4. Divide by three. The result is each hitter's batting Win Shares (but not less than zero).

5. For pitchers as hitters, do the same except don't subtract the outs.

6. For pitchers as pitchers, multiply the league ERA by 1.50 and subtract 1.00.

7. Figure how many earned runs the pitcher would have allowed had that been his ERA.

8. Subtract his actual earned runs allowed.

9. Add his Saves.

10. Divide by three. The result is his pitching Win Shares (again, not less than zero).

11. For fielders, give the player one Win Share for every 24 games at catcher, one for every 76 games at first base, one for every 28 games at second base, every 38 games at third base, one for 25 games at shortstop, and one for every 48 games in the outfield.

12. Figure the team total, and then adjust all totals upward or downward so that the team total matches three times the team's wins.

13. Round them off into integers.

Generally, the short-form Win Shares will match actual Win Shares fairly well. For the 1961 Yankees, the short-form method pegs the top three players as

Mickey Mantle (48), Roger Maris (37), and Elston Howard (28). It's actually Mantle 48, Maris 36, and Howard 29. For one or two players per team, the short-form method will miss by three points. These errors are predictable; the short-form estimate over-rates hitters in hitter's parks, over-rates poor defensive players and under-rates good defensive players.

On the 2000 Colorado Rockies, for example, Todd Helton hit .372 with 59 doubles, 42 homers and 147 RBI, while pitcher Brian Bohanon went 12-10 but with an ERA of 4.68. Without looking at park effects, the short-form Win Shares system would credit Helton with 38 Win Shares, and Bohanon with only 8. When the effects of playing in Coors Field are taken into account, Helton drops to 29 Win Shares, while Bohanon goes up to 13. In a pitcher's park, the opposite happens; the short-form Win Shares system will over-rate the pitchers and under-rate the hitters.

You can build in a protection against that by using the team runs scored and allowed per game, rather than the league average, or by using a half-way point between the league average and the team's figures. But that's sort of creating a longer version of the short form, the value of which would be debatable. Coors Field, of course, is an extreme case, and the short-form estimates are rarely off by that much. In Section III (Page 116), I'll present a chart which compares the Short-Form to the actual Win Shares for all members of the 2000 Cleveland Indians and 2000 Atlanta Braves, to give you a better sense of the accuracy of the short form.

Jacobs Field is a little bit hitter-friendly, which causes Manny Ramirez and Jim Thome to be over-valued a little bit in the short-form version, and Chuck Finley to be under-valued. Other things happen. . . Jason Bere is evaluated as worthless by the short-form method because he posted a 6.63 ERA in 11 starts for the 2000 Cleveland Indians. However, despite the lousy ERA, Bere did go 6-3 in those 11 starts, six wins. The longer version of the Win Shares system thinks that this should be taken into account, and thus credits Bere with two Win Shares.

For the 2000 Atlanta Braves, Andruw Jones does better in the longer version because:

a) Turner Field is a little bit pitcher-friendly, and

b) Jones is an exceptional defensive outfielder.

John Rocker posted a 2.89 ERA and saved 24 games, thus earns 12 Win Shares in the short-form version. The longer version of the system focuses on the additional information that Rocker walked 48 men in 53 innings and allowed 8 runs that were scored as un-earned, and thus concludes that he was not nearly as effective as the 2.89 ERA would suggest.

Through baseball history up to the year 2000, there have been 60,796 player seasons in major league history which have value of at least one Win Share. Of these, 16,881, or 28%, have exact matches between short-form and actual Win Shares. The average discrepancy is 1.56 Win Shares—1.27 since 1920, much higher in the early years. In history, 28% of all Win Shares estimated by this manner are exactly right, 37% are off by one, 16% off by two, and 8% off by three. The other 11% are off by four or more Win Shares, and one-half of one percent are off by more than ten, although almost all of those were pre-1920.

Intro to the Long Method

In concept, Win Shares are magnificently simple. Win Shares for a team are three times wins. From there, Win Shares are assigned to individuals on the basis of runs created, quality innings pitched, and fielding excellence.

In its execution, the Win Shares system is almost incomprehensibly complicated. It involves not merely the use of almost every category of every player's batting, pitching or fielding record in a large set of formulas, but also the creation of numerous "background" categories such as the team/league putout percentage, the Left-handed Innings Plus or Minus count, and an array of park effects. These background numbers evaluate outside influences on the statistics, and thus enable us to remove or adjust for biases which make the statistics misrepresent the underlying skills.

The long method is essentially the same as the short-form method, except that, in the actual method, we worry about the small stuff. We decided, in making Win Shares, to worry about *everything*; we decided that there was no factor so small that it wasn't worth worrying about. The complexity results from that decision.

In figuring Win Shares, we remove a few "background runs," at a level which varies depending on the league and park, as well as the outs made by the hitter. In the short form, we just take out one run for each 12 outs.

In the full study, we figure the "zero value level" for pitchers in consideration of the league ERA, the park, and an array of fielding and pitching statistics. In the short form, we just use 1.5 times the league ERA, minus one.

In the long study, pitchers are evaluated not only on ERA, but also on un-earned runs allowed, wins, losses, saves and Component ERA. In the short version, we just use ERA and saves.

In the full study, Win Shares for fielders are "claimed" by fielding performance. In the short form, we just assign points to fielding positions.

The next six groups of articles will outline the six stages that I mentioned before:

1. Dividing Win Shares between Offense and Defense
2. Dividing Offensive Win Shares among the Team's Hitters
3. Dividing Win Shares between Pitchers and Fielders
4. Assigning Win Shares to Individual Pitchers
5. Assigning Win Shares to Defensive Positions
6. Assigning Win Shares to Individual Fielders

Mixed in with these, and at the end of the section, will be miscellaneous articles explaining other details and notes about the system.

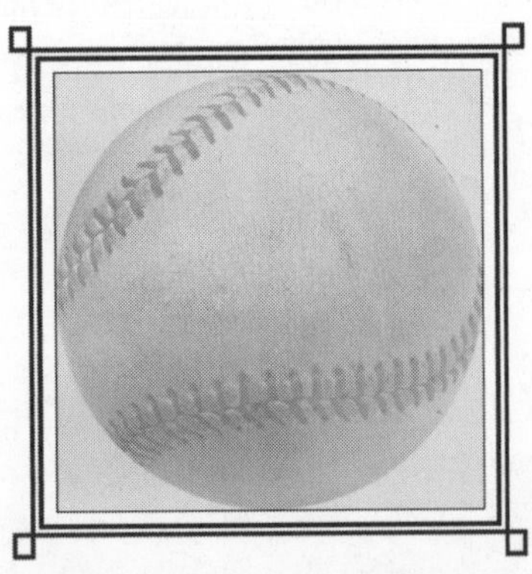

Dividing Win Shares between Offense and Defense

The Win Shares system is based on marginal runs. Suppose that you have a league in which the average team scores and allows 800 runs. Suppose that, in that league, there are three teams which all play in neutral parks.

Team A scores 700 runs and allows 900.
Team B scores 800 runs and allows 800.
Team C scores 900 runs and allows 750.

We know from the Pythagorean Method that the won-lost record of these teams will be, more or less:

	Runs	OR	W-L
Team A	700	900	61-101
Team B	800	800	81-81
Team C	900	750	96-66

Suppose that we consider marginal runs to be:

a) All Runs Scored by the team *minus one-half the league average*, and

b) All Runs Allowed by the team *less than 1.5 times the league average*.

In this league, since the average runs are 800, marginal runs are all runs scored by the team in excess of 400, and all runs allowed by the team *less than* 1200.

Team A has 600 marginal runs—
300 on offense, 300 on defense.
Team B has 800 marginal runs—
400 on offense, 400 on defense.
Team C has 950 marginal runs—
500 on offense, 450 on defense.

Compare the ratios of marginal runs to the wins and losses.

Team A has 600 marginal runs, and 61 wins.
Team B has 800 marginal runs, and 81 wins.
Team C has 950 marginal runs, and 96 wins.

In other words, *the ratio of marginal runs to pythagorean wins is almost exactly the same, regardless of whether you are looking at a good team or a bad team!* What does that mean? That means that Wins can be projected from marginal runs. In fact, an analysis of marginal runs will project wins and losses with almost the same accuracy as the Pythagorean Method.

In a real-data example, take the best team in the American League in 2000, Chicago (95-67), and the worst, Minnesota (69-93). The league average was 855.933 runs/162 games. Without making park adjustments, Chicago, with 978 runs scored and 839 allowed, has a total of 995 marginal runs—550 on offense and 445 pitching and defense. As follows:

Offense 978 minus 428 = 550
Defense 1284 minus 839 = 445

Thus, with 95 wins and 995 marginal runs, each win is purchased at a cost of 10.47 marginal runs.

Minnesota, with 748 runs scored and 880 allowed, has 724 marginal runs, 69 wins, which means that each win is purchased at a cost of 10.49 marginal runs—almost the same ratio.

Of course, these ratios are not exactly the same for every team; in the American League in 2000 the cost of a win ranges from 9.75 marginal runs (Toronto) to 11.00 (Cleveland). Toronto scored only 861 runs and allowed 908, but finished over .500 (83-79). Unusually efficient, the Blue Jays were purchasing a win with each 9.75 marginal runs.

When we evaluate their players, this makes a substantial difference. But it is an appropriate difference, because the Blue Jays won more games than we would expect them to win based on their runs and runs allowed. To make their values consistent with the team's wins, we have to give them a little bit more credit, run for run.

This realization—that there is an almost constant relationship between team wins and marginal runs—is the foundation of the Win Shares system. I was working on another system to accomplish the goals outlined in the first part of this manuscript when I realized that this was true. I had been working on that system for two months when I stumbled across this fact. I had to throw it away and go back to page one, because I realized immediately that this relationship, this straight-line relationship between wins and marginal runs, provided the basis for a much more logical and straightforward way to attribute Win Shares to individual players.

Let's go back to the six stages of the attribution. In the first stage of the process, Win Shares are divided between Offense and Defense (Defense broadly defined, to include both pitching and fielding).

Well, that's easy: they are divided in the same ratio as marginal runs. Suppose that, in the league above in which an average team scored and allowed 800 runs, one team scored 700 runs and allowed 700. That's 300 marginal runs on offense, 500 on defense. 37.5% of the team's Win Shares are allocated to hitters, 62.5% to pitchers and fielders.

Suppose that a team had 900 runs scored and 900 allowed. That's 500 marginal runs on offense, 300 on defense—thus, the opposite ratio.

Actually, that's not exactly right. This outline assumes that 50% of success is attributed to hitting, 50% to pitching and defense. Actually, we attribute 48% to hitting, 52% to pitching and defense.

Why? Basically two reasons:

a) I am convinced that it is as logical to do this as it is to not do it, and

b) it causes problems if you don't.

I'll explain all of that at more length in Section III, in the article "Why 52?" (page 117). Right now, I'm explaining the system, rather than the "why" of the system. Anyway, if the league average is 800 runs per team, we use cutoffs of 416 runs (800 * .52) and 1216 runs (800 * 1.52), rather than 400 and 800. Thus, we attribute 52% of the success of the average team to pitching and defense, 48% to offense.

I have not, as yet, explained how we deal with Park Effects. I'll explain that in a series of articles near the end of Section II, Park Factors (pages 86 to 89). The vast majority of teams (84%) will attribute between 40% and 56% of their Win Shares to the hitters, and 44% to 60% to pitching and defense. In the article "Extreme Teams" (Section IV), I'll list the teams with the best pitching staffs, the best offenses, the most extreme splits among them, etc.

While I explain the process, I will work through the data for three teams to make sure you understand what we're doing. The three teams I've chosen are the 1998 St. Louis Cardinals (the team for which Mark McGwire hit 70 home runs), the 1932 Philadelphia Athletics (a team for which Jimmie Foxx had a monster year) and the 1890 New York Giants of the Players League (whose first baseman, Roger Connor, was perhaps the Most Valuable Player in that league).

First, we take the number of runs scored in the league, and divide by the league's innings pitched:

League:	1998 NL	1932 AL	1890 PL
Runs:	11932	6436	7278
Innings:	23240	11004.667	9268.667
Runs/Inning:	.513425	.584843	.785226

Second, we park-adjust this. A later article will explain the park factors, but the park factor for St. Louis in 1998 is 1.001 (meaning that Busch Stadium increased runs scored by one-tenth of one percent), which results in a park run *adjustment* of 1.00045 (since only one-half of the Cardinals games were played in Busch Stadium). We multiply the league runs per inning by the Park Run Adjustment to get each team's expected runs per inning:

	1998 Cards	1932 Phil. A's	1890 NY Giants
Lg Runs/Inning:	.513425	.584843	.785226
Park Factor:	1.0010	1.1104	1.1718
Park Run Adjust:	1.000450	1.04732	1.07365
Exp Runs/Inning:	.513657	.612516	.843056

To get the team's expected runs *allowed*, we simply multiply this by their team innings pitched:

	1998 Cards	1932 Phil. A's	1890 Giants
Exp Runs/Inning:	.513657	.612516	.843056
Innings:	1469.67	1386	1172.33
Expected Runs Allowed:	754.90	848.95	988.34

I'm carrying more decimals in my spreadsheet than I'm displaying for you, if you're working along with me and find that you have tiny discrepancies. Anyway, to figure expected runs *scored*, we first have to establish offensive innings. Offensive innings are estimated as:

1. Innings pitched

2. Minus Wins at home (Since a team normally does not bat in the ninth innings when they win a home game)

3. Plus Losses on the road (Since a team normally has an extra at bat, with no inning pitched, when they lose a road game)

For these three teams:

	1998 Cards	1932 Phil. A's	1890 Giants
Innings:	1469.67	1386	1172.33
Wins At Home:	48	51	47
Losses on the Road:	45	34	38
Estimated Off. Innings:	1466.67	1369	1163.33

We then multiply Estimated Offensive Innings by the Expected Runs Per Inning to establish Expected Runs Scored:

	1998 Cards	1932 Phil. A's	1890 Giants
Estimated Off. Innings:	1466.67	1369.00	1163.33
Exp Runs/Inning:	.513657	.612516	.843056
Expected Runs Scored:	753.36	838.53	980.75

Having established each team's expected runs scored and expected runs allowed, we are in position to divide credit for the team's success between their offense, and their pitching/defense.

This system gives credit based on *marginal* runs, with marginal runs by the offense defined as runs scored in excess of .52 times expected runs, and marginal runs for the defense defined as runs allowed below the level of 1.52 times expected runs. The 1998 St. Louis Cardinals scored 810 runs; this makes 418.251 marginal runs on offense:

	1998 Cards	1932 Phil. A's	1890 Giants
Expected Runs Scored:	753.36	838.53	980.75
Times .52:	391.75	436.04	509.99
Actual Runs Scored:	810	981	1018
Marginal Offense:	418.25	544.96	508.01

The 1998 Cardinals allowed 782 runs; this makes 365.4540 marginal runs credited to pitching and defense:

	1998 Cards	1932 Phil. A's	1890 Giants
Expected Runs Allowed:	754.90	848.95	988.34
Times 1.52:	1147.45	1290.40	1502.28
Actual Runs Allowed:	782	752	875
Marginal Defense:	365.45	538.40	627.28

Credits for the team's Win Shares are then divided among offense and defense in the same proportions as the marginal offense and the marginal defense:

	1998 Cards	1932 Phil. A's	1890 Giants
Marginal Offense:	418.25	544.96	508.01
Marginal Defense:	365.45	538.40	627.28
Offensive Percentage:	.53368	.50303	.44747

The 1998 St. Louis Cardinals won 83 games, which means that they will have 249 Win Shares as a team. Of these 249, .53368 will be attributed to offense, and .46632 to pitching/defense:

	1998 Cards	1932 Phil. A's	1890 Giants
Offensive Percentage:	.53368	.50303	.44747
Team Wins:	83	94	74
Wins Times Three:	249	282	222
Offensive Wins:	132.89	141.85	99.34
Defensive Wins:	116.11	140.15	122.66

Thus, in evaluating the hitters on the 1998 St. Louis Cardinals, we will have 132.89 Win Shares to divide among them. In evaluating their pitchers and fielders, we will have 116.11 Win Shares to allocate.

The article "Extreme Teams," on page 128, discusses further these team splits.

Dividing Offensive Win Shares among a Team's Hitters

In the second stage of the analysis, those Win Shares assigned to the Offense are divided among the team's hitters, on the basis of runs created and outs made.

Again, this is dead simple in concept, while it may get complicated in practice. Each player earns 1 claim point for each run created in excess of 52% of the league norm, park adjusted. We will start here with the Runs Created and Outs Made by each hitter. If you are really curious about how we figure Runs Created, you can look that up in "How We Figure Runs Created," an article that begins on page 90. For the present, we start with the Runs Created and Outs Made by each hitter. For the players on the 1998 St. Louis Cardinals, that data is:

	Runs Created	Outs Made
Juan Acevedo	1	16
Manny Aybar	1	22
Royce Clayton	33	293
Delino DeShields	68	322
J D Drew	12	26
Gary Gaetti	42	239
Ron Gant	60	299
Shawn Gilbert	1	1
David Howard	11	82
Brian Hunter	8	97
Brian Jordan	97	413
Pat Kelly	13	126
Tom Lampkin	27	174
Ray Lankford	113	390
Mark Little	1	12
John Mabry	39	296
Eli Marrero	26	201
Joe McEwing	1	18
Willie McGee	25	212
Mark McGwire	165	369
Kent Mercker	2	52
Matt Morris	1	34
Luis Ordaz	10	129
Tom Pagnozzi	10	133
Lance Painter	1	1
Mark Petkovsek	3	17
Placido Polanco	10	88
Todd Stottlemyre	3	47
Fernando Tatis	27	154
Bobby Witt	1	9

There were other players who batted for the Cardinals in 1998, but did not create any runs. Those players are not our problem right now. At the moment we are concerned with giving credit for winning ballgames. If you don't create any runs, you don't get any credit.

From the Runs Created by each player, we remove the "background runs" or "sub-marginal" runs created by each player. To find those, you:

1. Take the player's Outs Made
2. Multiply by the league average of Runs Per Out
3. Multiply by the Park Adjustment Factor
4. Multiply that by .52

For Mark McGwire, that is:

1		369
2	X	.170389
3	X	1.00045
4	X	.52

Which is 32.71. For McGwire, 32.71 of his 165 Runs Created will not count toward his Win Shares.

Figures 2 (the league average of runs per out), 3 (the Park Adjustment) and 4 (.52) are the same for all members of the 1998 Cardinals. For all members of the 1998 Cardinals, the background runs are as follows:

	Runs Created	Outs Made	Background Runs
Juan Acevedo	1	16	1.42
Manny Aybar	1	22	1.95
Royce Clayton	33	293	25.97
Delino DeShields	68	322	28.54
J D Drew	12	26	2.30
Gary Gaetti	42	239	21.19
Ron Gant	60	299	26.50
Shawn Gilbert	1	1	.09
David Howard	11	82	7.27
Brian Hunter	8	97	8.60
Brian Jordan	97	413	36.61
Pat Kelly	13	126	11.17
Tom Lampkin	27	174	15.42

	Runs Created	Outs Made	Back-ground Runs
Ray Lankford	113	390	34.57
Mark Little	1	12	1.06
John Mabry	39	296	26.24
Eli Marrero	26	201	17.82
Joe McEwing	1	18	1.60
Willie McGee	25	212	18.79
Mark McGwire	165	369	32.71
Kent Mercker	2	52	4.61
Matt Morris	1	34	3.01
Luis Ordaz	10	129	11.43
Tom Pagnozzi	10	133	11.79
Lance Painter	1	1	.09
Mark Petkovsek	3	17	1.51
Placido Polanco	10	88	7.80
Todd Stottlemyre	3	47	4.17
Fernando Tatis	27	154	13.65
Bobby Witt	1	9	0.80

Ten of these 30 players created less than the "background" number of runs. Five of these were pitchers (Todd Stottlemyre, Manny Aybar, Juan Acevedo, Matt Morris and Kent Mercker). For those guys, the runs that they failed to create, up to this minimal-competence level, will be charged against them as pitchers. Hitting by a pitcher is credited as "contributing to the offense" if it is above this level, and as "just doing your job" up to this level. If you don't hit at least this well, the system regards that as not doing your job, and charges you runs. That way, all runs created by pitchers are counted, whether they are above this level or below (since there are a significant number of pitchers who fail to meet even this minimum-competence level).

Among position players even the worst hitters, given a little playing time, will exceed this minimum-competence level. There is no such thing as a major league player (non-pitcher) whose offense does not exceed this level in his normal season. The last such player was Bill Bergen (1901-1911). In limited playing time, some players will fail to meet this level, although the shortfall is almost always (as it is in all of these cases) less than two runs. Hitters who fail to meet this level are zeroed out, counted as simply not contributing to the offense. On the 1998 Cardinals Mark Little, Luis Ordaz, John McEwing, Brian Hunter and Tom Pagnozzi are zeroed out, regarded as non-contributing offensive players. Tom Pagnozzi, for example, played 51 games for the 1998 Cardinals, batting 160 times. He hit .219 with 1 home run, 10 RBI, a .280 on-base percentage, a .294 slugging percentage. He created 10 runs. To be regarded as contributing to the offense, he would have needed to create at least 12 runs. He missed his mark by 1.79 runs—the largest shortfall of any offensive player on this team who was zeroed out.

Mark McGwire created 165 runs, 32.71 of which are regarded as below the level that will actually help to win any games. The other 132.29 runs are "claim points" for McGwire, for which he will be rewarded with Win Shares. This total was by far the highest among the 1998 Cardinals—indeed, by far the highest in the National League. These are the Claim Points for the 20 St. Louis Cardinal players who contributed to the offense:

	Runs Created	Outs Made	Back-ground Runs	Claim Points
Royce Clayton	33	293	25.97	7.03
Delino DeShields	68	322	28.54	39.46
J D Drew	12	26	2.30	9.70
Gary Gaetti	42	239	21.19	20.81
Ron Gant	60	299	26.50	33.50
Shawn Gilbert	1	1	.09	0.91
David Howard	11	82	7.27	3.73
Brian Jordan	97	413	36.61	60.39
Pat Kelly	13	126	11.17	1.83
Tom Lampkin	27	174	15.42	11.58
Ray Lankford	113	390	34.57	78.43
John Mabry	39	296	26.24	12.76
Eli Marrero	26	201	17.82	8.18
Willie McGee	25	212	18.79	6.21
Mark McGwire	165	369	32.71	132.29
Lance Painter	1	1	.09	.91
Mark Petkovsek	3	17	1.51	1.49
Placido Polanco	10	88	7.80	2.20
Fernando Tatis	27	154	13.65	13.36
Bobby Witt	1	9	0.80	.20

The "Claim Points" for the 1998 St. Louis Cardinals total up to 445—actually, 444.96017 if you carry a few more decimal points somewhere.

Mark McGwire's Win Shares as a hitter, then, are 132.29/444.96017 of those Win Shares attributed to the 1998 St. Louis Cardinals. The Cardinals, we established in the last stage, had 132.89 Win Shares attributed to their offense. McGwire's Win Shares are:

His Claim Points	132.29
Divided by the Team Total Claim Points	444.96017
Times The Team's Win Shares	132.89

This equals 39.51 Win Shares. Offensive Win Shares for all the members of the 1998 Cardinals (other than zero) were:

	Claim Points	Win Shares
Royce Clayton	7.03	2.10
Delino DeShields	39.46	11.78
J D Drew	9.70	2.90
Gary Gaetti	20.81	6.22
Ron Gant	33.50	10.00
Shawn Gilbert	0.91	0.27
David Howard	3.73	1.11
Brian Jordan	60.39	18.04
Pat Kelly	1.83	0.55
Tom Lampkin	11.58	3.46
Ray Lankford	78.43	23.42
John Mabry	12.76	3.81
Eli Marrero	8.18	2.44
Willie McGee	6.21	1.85
Mark McGwire	132.29	39.51
Lance Painter	.91	0.27
Mark Petkovsek	1.49	0.45
Placido Polanco	2.20	0.66
Fernando Tatis	13.35	3.99
Bobby Witt	.20	0.06

The 1998 St. Louis Cardinals won 83 games, which means they have 249 Win Shares as a team.

Of those 249, 132.89 are credited to their ability to score runs.

Of those 132.89, 39.51 are credited to Mark McGwire as an individual.

These are the NL's most win-productive hitters of 1998:

Player	Team	Win Shares
Mark McGwire	St. Louis	39.51
Sammy Sosa	Chicago	31.78
Barry Bonds	San Francisco	31.53
John Olerud	New York	29.46
Craig Biggio	Houston	28.92

McGwire's 39.51 Win Shares are the highest total in the major leagues since Barry Bonds had 44.02 in 1993.

Jimmie Foxx in 1932 hit .364 with 58 homers, 169 RBI. We estimate that he created 188 runs, while making 379 batting outs. From this, we first remove the "background runs." To do that, just as we did for McGwire, we:

1. Take the player's Outs Made
2. Multiply by the league average of Runs per Out
3. Multiply by the Park Adjustment Factor
4. Multiply that by .52

For Foxx, that is:

1		379
2	X	.19781
3	X	1.04732
4	X	.52

For Foxx, this is 40.83 runs. Of Foxx' 188 runs created, 40.83 are background runs, and 147.17 are Claim Points.

The 1932 Philadelphia Athletics hitters have, as a team, 568.74 Claim Points. As we determined in the last stage of this analysis, the '32 A's have 141.85 Win Shares to split among their hitters. Foxx' Win Shares, then, are:

His Claim Points	147.17
Divided by the Team Total Claim Points	568.74
Times The Team's Win Shares	141.85

This equals 36.71 Win Shares. Offensive Win Shares for the members of the 1932 Philadelphia Athletics were:

	Outs Made	Runs Created	Claim Points	Win Shares
Jimmie Foxx	379	188	147.17	36.71
Al Simmons	456	134	84.88	21.17
Mickey Cochrane	370	115	75.14	18.74
Mule Haas	415	93	48.29	12.04
Boob McNair	406	88	44.26	11.04
Maxie Bishop	310	74	40.60	10.13
Jimmy Dykes	420	84	38.75	9.67
Doc Cramer	260	66	37.99	9.48
Bing Miller	221	49	25.19	6.28

	Outs Made	Runs Created	Claim Points	Win Shares
Dib Williams	163	28	10.44	2.60
Ed Coleman	48	13	7.83	1.95
Johnny Heving	57	10	3.86	0.96
George Earnshaw	76	10	1.81	0.45
Eddie Rommel	14	3	1.49	0.37
Joe Bowman	0	1	1.00	0.25
Sugar Cain	9	1	0.03	0.01

The 1932 Philadelphia Athletics won 94 games, which means they have 282 Win Shares as a team. Of those 282, 141.85 are credited to their ability to score runs. Of those 141.85, 36.71 are credited to Jimmie Foxx as an individual.

These are the American League's most win-productive hitters of 1932:

Player	Team	Win Shares
Jimmie Foxx	Philadelphia	36.71
Lou Gehrig	New York	35.80
Babe Ruth	New York	34.16
Heinie Manush	Washington	24.63
Earl Averill	Cleveland	23.51

The 1932 Philadelphia Athletics have, as a team, sixteen players who earn Win Shares for their hitting. Foxx' 36.71 Win Shares that season are the fifth-highest figure of the 1930s, behind Lou Gehrig, 1930 (37.27), Foxx himself in 1933 (37.49), Lou Gehrig in 1934 (38.81), and Joe Medwick in 1937 (36.85).

Now, the 1890 New York Giants. Their star first baseman was Hall of Famer Roger Connor. Connor in 1890 created 155 runs, making 315 batting outs. From this, we first remove the "background runs." To do that, we:

1. Take the player's Outs Made
2. Multiply by the league average of Runs Per Out
3. Multiply by the Park Adjustment Factor
4. Multiply that by .52

For Connor, that is:

1		315
2	X	.260842
3	X	1.07365
4	X	.52

For Connor, that is 45.87 runs. Of Connor's 155 runs created, 45.87 are background runs, and 109.13 are Claim Points.

The 1890 New York Giants (PL) hitters have, as a team, 514.33 Claim Points. As we determined in the last stage of this analysis, the '90 Giants have 99.34 Win Shares to split among their hitters. Connor's Win Shares, then, are:

His Claim Points	109.13
Divided by the Team Total Claim Points	514.33
Times The Team's Win Shares	99.34

This equals 21.08 Win Shares. Offensive Win Shares for the members of the 1890 Players League New York Giants are:

	Outs Made	Runs Created	Claim Points	Win Shares
Roger Connor	315	155	108.13	21.08
Jim O'Rourke	306	131	86.44	16.69
George Gore	272	120	80.39	15.53
Buck Ewing	233	106	72.07	13.92
Mike Slattery	285	89	47.50	9.17
D. Richardson	393	86	28.77	5.56
Gil Hatfield	207	53	22.86	4.41
Willard Brown	166	41	16.83	3.25
Ed Crane	100	30	15.44	2.98
Art Whitney	345	61	10.76	2.08
Dick Johnston	232	42	8.21	1.59
Dan Shannon	254	45	8.01	1.55
Farmer Vaughn	122	25	7.23	1.40
Fred Dunlap	2	1	0.71	0.14

The 1890 New York Giants won 74 games, which means they have 222 Win Shares as a team.

Of those 222, 99.34 are credited to their ability to score runs.

Of those 99.34, 21.08 are credited to Roger Connor as an individual.

These are the Players League's most win-productive hitters:

Player	Team	Win Shares
Pete Browning	Cleveland	22.37
Roger Connor	New York	21.08
Hugh Duffy	Chicago	19.88
Jake Beckley	Pittsburgh	19.20
Billy Shindle	Philadelphia	18.00
Dan Brouthers	Boston	18.00

All Hall of Famers except the Louisville Slugger and the pest control man.

Babe Ruth in 1923 created 193 runs with 341 outs, in a league that averaged 4.90 runs/27 outs.

With park adjustments, we make that 4.89 runs/27 outs.

52% of that is 2.54 runs/27 outs, which would be 32 runs created for 341 outs (32.13).

Ruth is credited with 161 marginal runs—193, minus 32.

All of the Yankee hitters of 1923, figured as individuals, are credited with 461 marginal runs. Ruth is credited with 35% of those.

The 1923 Yankees won 98 games, which means 294 claim points.

We attribute 47.28% of their success to their offense.

That means 139.00 Win Shares for hitters.

Ruth gets 35% of those.

Ruth's 1923 value, not counting defense, is 48.48 Win Shares.

As seen in the chart below, this is the highest total of Babe Ruth's career, and the second-highest total of all time:

	Player, Tm	Year	Age	RC	Outs	MR	Win Shares
1.	Honus Wagner, Pit	1908	34	131	381	107	49.21
2.	Babe Ruth, NYY	1923	28	193	341	161	48.48
3.	Babe Ruth, NYY	1920	25	192	305	163	47.88
4.	Babe Ruth, NYY	1921	26	208	353	172	47.65
5.	Mickey Mantle, NYY	1957	25	155	312	131	46.06
6.	Ted Williams, Bos	1946	27	165	350	136	45.11
7.	Barry Bonds, SF	1993	28	160	388	129	44.02
8.	Mickey Mantle, NYY	1956	24	173	355	142	43.79
9.	Mickey Mantle, NYY	1961	29	156	360	126	42.96
10.	Rogers Hornsby, StL	1922	26	179	400	140	42.86
11.	Babe Ruth, NYY	1928	33	165	376	132	42.69
12.	Babe Ruth, NYY	1926	31	167	330	137	42.60
13.	Stan Musial, StL	1948	27	176	400	141	42.37
14.	Babe Ruth, NYY	1924	29	178	348	144	41.67
15.	Tris Speaker, Bos	1912	24	163	365	129	41.94
16.	Ty Cobb, Det	1915	28	153	402	120	41.56
17.	Ted Williams, Bos	1942	23	160	350	131	41.50
18.	Lou Gehrig, NYY	1927	24	182	395	145	41.45
19.	Ty Cobb, Det	1911	24	172	354	136	41.28
20.	Will Clark, SF	1989	25	141	409	111	41.12
21.	Ted Williams, Bos	1947	28	160	359	129	41.11
22.	Stan Musial, StL	1946	25	151	405	119	40.86
23.	Babe Ruth, NYY	1927	32	176	368	141	40.47
24.	Nap Lajoie, Cle	1910	35	135	385	106	40.41
25.	Ty Cobb, Det	1917	30	144	379	116	40.31
26.	Ty Cobb, Det	1910	23	137	329	112	40.02

Among the 26 seasons in which a player has earned 40.00 Win Shares or more, there are seven seasons by Babe Ruth, four by Ty Cobb, three by Mickey Mantle, three by Ted Williams, two by Stan Musial, and one each by Honus Wagner, Barry Bonds, Rogers Hornsby, Tris Speaker, Lou Gehrig, Will Clark and Nap Lajoie. (This list was compiled during the 2001 season. Barry Bonds has since changed the list.)

Broken down by generation, there are none from the 1800s (the top season of the 1800s scoring at 36.51, by Ed Delahanty in 1899). There is one season from the first decade of the 20th century, six from the 1910s, nine from the Twenties, none from the Thirties, five from the Forties, two from the Fifties, one from the Sixties, none from the Seventies, and one each from the Eighties and Nineties.

All 26 of the players who earned 40.00 Win Shares hit at least .300. Of the 26, two players hit .400, eight hit .380 or better, sixteen hit .360 or better, 22 hit .340 or better, and 25 hit .320 or better. The lowest batting averages in the group were .317, by Mickey Mantle in 1961, and .323, by Babe Ruth in 1928.

Ruth and Mantle hit 54 homers apiece. Among the 26 players, six hit 50 homers or more, twelve hit 40 homers or more, and seventeen hit 30 homers or more.

Twenty-one of the 26 players drove in 100 or more runs. Thirteen of the 26 led the league in homers, 13 led in RBI, and 11 led in batting average. Four of the players won the Triple Crown.

Twenty-five of the 26 players played for teams which finished over .500, the one exception being Nap Lajoie in 1910. Eighteen of the 26 played for teams winning 90 or more games, and eight played for teams winning 100 or more games. Fourteen of the 26 played for teams which won the pennant.

Twelve of the 26 players played in leagues in which there was an MVP Award which the player could have won. Nine of the 12 players won the Award, the three exceptions being Ted Williams in 1947, Mickey Mantle in 1961, and Will Clark in 1989.

Lajoie in 1910 was also the oldest player to make this list; he was 35 at the time. Ted Williams in 1942 and Ty Cobb in 1910 were the youngest players on the list, at 23. Fourteen of the 26 players were between 25 and 29 years of age, although only two of them were 27.

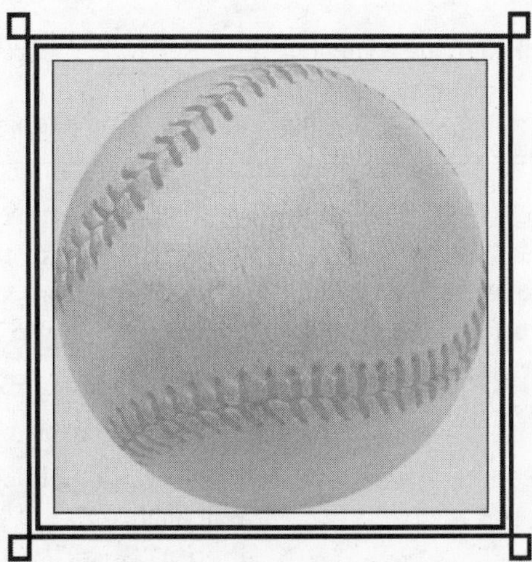

Dividing Win Shares between Pitchers and Fielders

In the third stage of this analysis, the Win Shares assigned to the Defense are divided between those assigned to Pitching, and those assigned to Fielding. In Stage One, we divided Win Shares between Offense and Defense, with Pitching and Fielding both included in Defense. How do we determine how many to assign to pitching, and how many to fielding?

We decide in this stage that the success of the pitching and defense is X% pitching, and (1 - X)% fielding. In a typical case, 67.5% of a team's "defense" is assigned to pitching, 32.5% to fielding. In the 2000 season, pitching percentages ranged from 72% for the Atlanta Braves and 71.5% for Oakland down to 62.7% for the Kansas City Royals and 63.2% for the Cubs.

We consider six factors in making that determination—three which count for the pitchers, two for the fielders, and one which is considered to be shared. The "pitchers" variables are strikeouts, walks, and home runs allowed (park-adjusted).

The "fielders" factors are double plays (compared to *expected* double plays) and fielding percentage.

The shared factor is a kind of short-form version of Defensive Efficiency Record, an estimate of the batting average against the team excluding strikeouts and home runs, also park adjusted.

All of these things except strikeouts are compared to league norms. Strikeouts are allowed to range up and down, not normalized to the league, since, if the league strikeout rate goes up, this does, in effect, transfer responsibility away from the fielders and toward the pitchers.

Each of these six factors is converted into "Claim Points." The original idea was that an *average* team should have 700 Claim Points for pitchers, 300 Claim Points for fielders, distributed as follows:

Strikeouts—200 points
Walks—200 points
Home Runs Allowed—200 points
Fielding Average—100 points
Double Plays—100 points
Short-form Defensive Efficiency—
100 points each way

A typical team would have 70% of their claim points for pitchers—700 out of a thousand.

This was later modified, in struggling with the data to get reasonable answers, in two ways. First, we put in a "bias" so that a team with very strong pitching-and-defense will tend to attribute a higher percentage thereof to pitching than a team with weak pitching-and-defense. Second, we changed the system so that a typical team attributes 32.5% of defensive success to fielders, rather than 30%.

I will label the claim points from the six factors above, as we go through, CL-1, CL-2, etc. Altogether there are 11 procedures in this step, which are:

1. Figuring the Defensive Efficiency Record
2. Park-Adjusting the Defensive Efficiency Record
3. Converting the Park-Adjusted Defensive Efficiency Record into Claim Points
4. Converting the Team's Strikeouts into Claim Points
5. Converting Walks into Claim Points
6. Park-Adjusting Home Runs Allowed
7. Converting Park-Adjusted Home Runs Allowed into Claim Points
8. Converting Fielding Percentage (actually, Errors and Passed Balls) into Claim Points
9. Figuring Expected Double Plays
10. Converting Double Plays into Claim Points
11. Combining the Claim Points to produce Win Shares

I'll explain these all as if they were separate steps, since that seems to be the easiest way to handle it.

1. Figuring the Defensive Efficiency Record

Data Needed:
BFP (Batters Facing Pitcher) by the team
Hits Allowed
Walks Allowed
Strikeouts
Hit Batsmen
Home Runs Allowed

We're using the short-form DER here, the formula for which is:

$$\frac{BFP - H - BB - SO - HB}{BFP - HR - BB - SO - HB}$$

For the 1998 Cardinals, the data is:

BFP	6392
H	1513
BB	558
SO	972
HB	54
HR	151

Which makes a DER of .708:

$$\frac{6392 - 1513 - 558 - 972 - 54}{6392 - 151 - 558 - 972 - 54}$$

This is 3295/4657, which is .707537041.

What this means, essentially, is that when a ball is put into play against the Cardinal defense, the defense turns that ball into an out approximately 70.75% of the time, and allows the ball to become a hit approximately 29.25% of the time.

The short-form DER for the 1932 Philadelphia Athletics was .7166874. For the 1890 New York Giants (PL), it was .71452788.

2. Park-Adjusting the DER

Data Needed:
The team's DER and the Park-S adjustment

1. Subtract the team's DER from 1.000.
2. Divide by the Park-S adjustment.
3. Subtract the result from 1.000.

The Park-S Adjustment is explained in Section II, beginning on page 88, where we explain the various Park Factors used in this process. If a park increases offense, it decreases defense, and vice versa; thus, a high Park-S factor must be turned upside down so that it will reduce the DER. This method turns it upside down.

For the 1998 Cardinals, this is:

1 - .707537041 = .292462959
.292462959 / .9935716 = .2943552.
1 - .2943552 = .7056448.

The Park-Adjusted DER for the 1998 St. Louis Cardinals is .7056448.

The Park-Adjusted DER for the 1932 Philadelphia Athletics is .7163786.

The Park-Adjusted DER for the 1890 New York Giants (PL) is .7244175.

3. Converting the Park-Adjusted DER into Claim Points

Data Needed:
The team's (park-adjusted) DER
The league DER

The Claim Points awarded for DER are:

100 + (Team Park-Adjusted DER - League DER) * 2500

We'll call the resulting figure "CL-1."

First of all, we need to figure the National League DER for 1998. The formula for that was:

$$\frac{BFP - H - BB - SO - HB}{BFP - HR - BB - SO - HB}$$

Which is:

$$\frac{100162 - 23279 - 8743 - 17552 - 821}{100162 - 2585 - 8743 - 17552 - 821}$$

Which is .7063056. The league norm in 1998 was .7063056. Thus, the park-adjusted DER for this team (the 1998 Cardinals) was almost exactly the league norm (a low .706 vs. a high .706), and will score at slightly lower than 100 on this 200-point scale. The formula for that, as I said a moment ago, is:

100 + (Team Park-Adjusted DER - League DER) * 2500, which is
100 + (.7056448 - .7063056) * 2500, which is
100 + (- .0006608) * 2500, which is
100 + (- 1.652), which is
100 - 1.652, which is
98.348

The St. Louis Cardinals CL-1 figure will be 98.348.

The Philadelphia A's 1932 Park-Adjusted DER was .716379 vs. a league norm of .713511, which makes a CL-1 of 107.1697.

The 1890 New York Giants (PL) Park-Adjusted DER was .7244175 against a league norm of .7041450, which makes a CL-1 of 150.6814.

4. Converting the Team's Strikeouts into Claim Points

Data Needed:
The team's Strikeouts and Innings Pitched

1. Figure the team's strikeouts per 9 innings.
2. Add 2.50.
3. Divide by 7.00.
4. Multiply by 200.

We'll call the Result CL-2.

The 1998 St. Louis Cardinals had 972 strikeouts in 1469.2 innings, which is 5.952 strikeouts/9 innings. This makes 241.496 Claim Points. We will call this CL-2. This figure is NOT league-adjusted. It's the same regardless of what the league norms are.

The 1932 A's had 595 strikeouts in 1386 innings, which is 181.818 Claim Points. The 1890 New York Giants had 449 strikeouts in 1172.1 innings, which makes 169.913 Claim points as CL-2.

5. Converting Walks into Claim Points

Data Needed:
The team's Walks, Hit Batsmen and Innings Pitched
The league Walks, Hit Batsmen and Innings Pitched

1. Figure the league average of walks/inning (counting Hit Batsmen by pitchers as if they were walks).
2. Multiply that by the team's innings.
3. Subtract the walks and hit batsmen by this team.
4. Add 200.

In other words, the claiming formula for walks is 200, plus one for each walk or hit batsman that the team is better than average. We'll call this CL-3.

For the St. Louis Cardinals in 1998. . . the league average was .4115 walks and hit batsmen per inning. The Cardinals pitched 1,469.2 innings, so that's 604.81 expected walks and hit batsmen.

The Cardinals actually walked 558 batters and drilled 54, a total of 612, so they were 7.19 walks worse than average. Adding 200, this makes a score of 192.81 on this scale. The 1998 Cardinals CL-3 figure is 192.81.

The 1932 A's had excellent control, 529 walks and hit batsmen against a league average of 576, so they have a CL-3 figure of 246.83, well above average.

The 1890 New York Giants had below-average control, and so score at 175.51 on this scale.

6. Park-Adjusting Home Runs Allowed

Data Needed:
The team's Home Runs Allowed
The Park Home Run Adjustment

I guess this is obvious. . . the team's park-adjusted home runs allowed are their home runs allowed, divided by the park home run adjustment, which is explained near the end of Section II.

For the 1998 St. Louis Cardinals, this is 151 (home runs allowed) divided by 1.028, the park home run adjustment. That makes 146.84059 (park-adjusted) home runs allowed.

For the 1932 Philadelphia A's, this is 112 (home runs allowed) divided by 1.298, the park home run adjustment. That makes 96.273667 (park-adjusted) home runs allowed.

For the 1890 New York Giants (PL), this is 37 (home runs allowed) divided by 1.082, the park home run adjustment. That makes 34.195933 (park-adjusted) home runs allowed.

7. Converting the Park-Adjusted Home Runs Allowed into Claim Points

Data Needed:
The Park-Adjusted Home Runs Allowed by the team
Their Innings Pitched
The league average of Home Runs/Inning

The Claim Points for Home Runs allowed are 200, plus five points for each home run allowed *less than* expected. We will call this CL-4.

The National League average in 1998 was .1112306 home runs/inning. With 1469.2 innings, that makes an expectation of 163.47196 home runs allowed.

The Cardinals actually allowed 151 home runs—which, we figured a moment ago, should be park-adjusted to 146.84059. Thus, they allowed 16.63137 home runs *less than* the league average, park-adjusted.

Multiplying that by five and adding 200, the Cardinal pitchers receive 283.157 Claim Points (CL-4) for allowing less home runs than expected.

The 1932 A's receive 213.85 Claim Points for their home runs allowed. The 1890 New York Giants receive 228.87.

8. Converting Errors and Passed Balls into Claim Points

Data Needed:
Errors
Passed Balls
Innings Pitched for the team and for the league

1. Count each passed ball as one-half of an error.
2. Figure the league average of errors (including one-half passed balls) per inning.
3. Figure the expected errors for this team.
4. Subtract their actual errors.
5. Claim points are 100, plus one for each error *less than* expected.

We will call this CL-5.

The National League in 1998 committed 1850 errors and was charged with 188 passed balls. We count this as 1944 errors, which is .0836489 errors/inning. Since the Cardinals had 1469.2 innings, we would expect the Cardinals to commit 122.93597 errors. The Cardinals in 1998 had 142 actual errors, 6 passed balls—thus, 145 "errors." The Cardinals had 20.06 errors more than expected—thus, 77.94 Claim Points on this scale:

100 + 122.94 - 145 = 77.94

CL-5 for the Philadelphia A's in 1932 was 161.72 (100+192.22-130.5). For the 1890 New York Giants it was 148.19 (100+533.19-485).

9. Figuring Expected Double Plays

Data Needed:
Innings
Hits Allowed
Home Runs Allowed
Walks Allowed
Hit Batsmen
Sacrifice Hits Allowed
Wild Pitches
Balks
Passed Balls
Assists (Fielding)
Double Plays (for the *team* and also for the *league*)
Number of *singles* hit (for the league only)

First, figure for the *league as a whole* the percentage of all non-home runs (H-HR) that were singles.

Second, use this figure to estimate as accurately as possible the number of opposition baserunners on first base: Hits allowed minus home runs allowed, times the league percentage of non-home runs which were singles, plus walks, plus hit batsmen, minus sacrifice hits allowed, minus wild pitches, minus balks, minus passed balls.

Third, calculate the same figure for the league as a whole.

Fourth, figure the *league* percentage of baserunners removed by double plays (Double Plays, divided by the figure above).

Multiply the second figure above, times the fourth. This is a first estimate of expected double plays.

Figure the league average of assists per inning.
Figure the team average of assists per inning.
Divide the team average by the league average.

Multiply the "first estimate," above, by that figure.

For the 1998 Cardinals, the data is:

	Cardinals	League
Innings	1469.2	23240
Hits Allowed	1513	23279
Home Runs Allowed	151	2585
Walks Allowed	558	8743
Hit Batsmen	54	821
Assists (Fielding)	1781	27513
Double Plays	160	2415
Singles	1054	15703
Sacrifice Hits	92	1163
Passed Balls	6	189
Wild Pitches	42	835
Balks	14	143

First, figure for the *league as a whole* the percentage of all non-home runs (H-HR) that were singles. That's 15703/(23279 - 2585), which is .758819. So 75.9% of all league hits which were not home runs were singles.

Second, use this figure to estimate as accurately as possible the number of opposition baserunners on first base: Hits allowed minus home runs allowed, times the league percentage of non-home runs which were singles, plus walks, plus hit batsmen, minus passed balls, wild pitches, sacrifice hits and balks. For the Cardinals, this is (1513- 151) * .7588 + 558 + 54 - 92 - 6 - 42 - 14, which is 1491.5115.

Third, figure the same figure for the league as a whole. That's 15703 + 8743 + 821 - 1163 - 189 - 835 - 143, which is 22937.

Fourth, figure the *league* percentage of these baserunners removed by double plays. Since there were 2415 Double Plays in the National League in 1998, that's 2415/22937, which is .1052884.

Multiply the second figure above (1491.5115), times the fourth (.1052884). This is a first estimate of expected double plays. For the Cardinals, that's 1491.5115 times .1052884, which is 157.03885.

Figure the team average of assists per inning. For the Cardinals, that's 1781/1469.2, or 1.2118394 assists per inning.

Figure the league average of assists per inning. That's 27513/23240, or 1.1838640 assists per inning.

Figure the ratio between the two. That's 1.0236306. In other words, since the St. Louis Cardinals have slightly more assists/inning than an average team, we expect them to also have more double plays.

Multiply the "first estimate," above, by that figure.

That's 157.03885 times 1.0236306, which is 160.74977.

We expect the St. Louis Cardinals in 1998 to turn 160.74977 double plays.

Philadelphia, 1932. First, figure for the *league as a whole* the percentage of all non-home runs (H-HR) which were singles. That percentage, for the American League in 1932, is .747213 (8445/11302).

Second, use this figure to estimate as accurately as possible the number of opposition baserunners on first base: Hits allowed minus home runs allowed, times the league percentage of non-home runs which were singles, plus walks, plus hit batsmen, minus sacrifice hits allowed, minus wild pitches, minus balks, minus passed balls.

For Philadelphia, 1932, this is 1477 (opposition hits allowed), minus 112 (opposition home runs allowed) for 1365, times .7472129 (single percentage) for 1019.9456, plus 511 (walks allowed) for 1530.9456, plus 18 (hit batsmen) for 1548.9456, minus 75 (sac hits allowed) for 1473.9456, minus 21 (wild pitches) for 1451.9456, minus 1 (balk) for 1451.9456, minus 15 (passed balls) for 1436.9456.

Third, figure the same figure for the league as a whole. This figure is 12,026 (you can take my word for it. Please, I'm beggin' ya.)

Fourth, figure the *league* percentage of baserunners removed by double plays (Double Plays, divided by the figure above). There were 1197 double plays in the league, for a percentage of .099534342.

Multiply the second figure above, times the fourth. (1436.9456 times .0995343, which is 143.02543). This is a first estimate of expected double plays.

Figure the league average of assists per inning (14368 divided by 11004.667), which is 1.30563 per inning.

Figure the team average of assists per inning (1736 in 1386, which is 1.2525253).

Divide the team average by the league average (.95933).

Multiply the "first estimate," above, by that figure (.95933 times 143.02543, which is 137.21).

We expect the Philadelphia A's in 1932 to turn 137.21 double plays.

New York, 1890. First, figure for the *league as a whole* the percentage of all non-home runs (H-HR) which were singles. That percentage, for the Players League in 1890, is .7740766 (7901/10207).

Second, use this figure to estimate as accurately as possible the number of opposition baserunners on first base: Hits allowed minus home runs allowed, times the league percentage of non-home runs which were singles, plus walks, plus hit batsmen, minus sacrifice hits allowed, minus wild pitches, minus balks, minus passed balls.

For New York, 1890, this is 1216 (opposition hits allowed), minus 37 (opposition home runs allowed) for 1179, times .7740766 (single percentage) for 912.6363, plus 569 (walks allowed) for 1481.6363, minus 70 (passed balls) for 1411.6363. (There is limited data for 1890 on Hit Batsmen, Wild Pitches, Balks or Sacrifice Hits. We shouldn't have used any of it, but unfortunately our data set threw us a curve, and used a little bit of data that we probably shouldn't have. We'll fix this the next time we run the data.

Our historical data set is the best in the world, but it is not perfect. Occasionally it will include things like HBP, CS or WP for some teams in a league, but not for all, and when it does so, there is a risk that it will foul the calculations, by using imbalanced and distorted data. We look for these places, and we program around them, but we keep finding more of them. We wish we could tell you that we had found them all and fixed them all, but. . . we didn't. Sometimes league sacrifice flies hit don't equal league sacrifice flies allowed. We worked as hard as we possibly could to deal with those type of things, but historical data in baseball contains problems, some of which can never be fixed. Realistically, the only way you can stop finding errors in your data is to stop looking.)

Third, figure the same figure for the league as a whole. This figure is 11897 (including hit batsmen and wild pitches for some teams).

Fourth, figure the *league* percentage of baserunners removed by double plays (Double Plays, divided by the figure above). There were 841 double plays in the league, for a percentage of .07069009.

Multiply the second figure above, times the fourth (1411.6363 times .07069009), which is 99.7887. This is a first estimate of expected double plays.

Figure the league average of assists per inning (13892 divided by 9268.667), which is 1.4988132 per inning.

Figure the team average of assists per inning (1708 in 1172.33), which is 1.4569 per inning.

Divide the team average by the league average (1.4569 divided by 1.4988 is .9720514).

Multiply the "first estimate," above, by that figure (.9720514 times 99.7887), which is 96.99975.

We expect the New York Giants in 1890 to turn 97.00 double plays.

10. Converting Double Plays into Claim Points

Data Needed:
Actual Double Plays by the Team (A)
Expected Double Plays by the Team (B)

The formula is 100 + [(A-B) * 4/3]. We will call this CL-6.

The St. Louis Cardinals in 1998 had 160 actual double plays. That makes this factor, for them:

100 + [(160 - 160.74977) * 4/3]
100 + [(-0.74977) * 4/3]
99.00030

The St. Louis Cardinals have 99.00030 Claim Points on this scale. We will call this CL-6.

The 1932 Philadelphia A's have 106.38895 Claim Points on this scale.

The 1890 New York Giants of the Players League have 96.0003 Claim Points on this scale.

11. Combining the Claim Points to produce Win Shares

We determine the percentage of Win Shares that will go to the *pitchers* on a team by the following formula:

$$\text{Pitcher's \%} = \frac{\text{CL-1} + \text{CL-2} + \text{CL-3} + \text{CL-4} + 650 + (405 * \text{TmWPct})}{2*\text{CL-1} + \text{CL-2} + \text{CL-3} + \text{CL-4} + \text{CL-5} + \text{CL-6} + 1097.5 + (405 * \text{TmWPct})}$$

The Cardinals' winning percentage in 1998 was .512 (they were 83-79); 405 times that is 207.5. This figure is used in both the numerator and the denominator above; I guess we could call it CL-7.

For the St. Louis Cardinals, the numerator of the above equation is 1673.316.

CL-1	98.348
CL-2	241.496
CL-3	192.815
CL-4	283.157
CL-7	207.5
	650
Total	1673.316

The denominator is 2396.100:

CL-1 * 2	196.696
CL-2	241.496
CL-3	192.815
CL-4	283.157
CL-5	77.936
CL-6	99.000
CL-7	207.5
	1097.5
Total	2396.100

And 1673.316 divided by 2396.1 is .698 3498. Thus, 69.83% of St. Louis Cardinal pitching-and-defense Win Shares will be attributed to pitchers, and 30.17% will be attributed to fielders.

For the 1932 Philadelphia A's, 66.68% of defensive Win Shares will be attributed to pitchers, 33.32% to fielders. For the 1890 New York Giants, 65.57% will go to pitchers, 34.43% for fielders.

In the first stage of this analysis, we determined that the 1998 St. Louis Cardinals would have 116.1126 Win Shares for Pitching and Defense. Multiplying this by .698 3497, we now decide that 81.09 of these Win Shares will go to the Cardinal pitchers, and 35.03 of them to the fielders.

We established in stage one that the 1932 Philadelphia A's had 140.1460 Win Shares attributable to Pitching and Defense. Multiplying this by .6668 (excuse me, God. . . this time that's just the number), we can now fix the A's Pitching Win Shares at 93.45, their Fielding Win Shares at 46.70.

We established in stage one that the 1890 New York Giants had 122.6616 Win Shares attributable to Pitching and Defense. Multiplying this by .6557, we can now fix the Jints Pitching Win Shares at 80.43, their Fielding Win Shares at 42.23.

The percentage of Pitching and Defense which is assigned to pitchers (as opposed to fielders) is bounded by 60% and 75% (although those boundaries can be overridden if this would cause the team's fielding Win Shares to exceed or fall short of certain numbers). These barriers have almost no practical impact, since teams would virtually never range outside them, anyway; they just impact the evaluations of a few odd half-assed teams that couldn't really play baseball. Of slightly more impact is a similar constraint, a rule which says that the Defensive Win Shares of a team cannot be less than .16375 per game played, nor more than .32375 per game played.

An average team attributes .675 of pitching-and-defense to pitchers, 32.5% to fielders. Thus, an average major league team has the following split:

Hitting: 48%
Pitching: 35.1%
Fielding: 16.9%

Assuming that an average team wins 81 games, that makes, for an average team:

Hitting: 116.64 Win Shares
Pitching: 85.293 Win Shares
Fielding: 41.067 Win Shares

Assigning Win Shares to Individual Pitchers

In the fourth stage of the analysis, those Win Shares assigned to pitching will be divided among the pitchers.

I'll give you an overview of the system first. The number of Win Shares to be given to all of the pitchers on a team is now a fixed number, a number determined in the previous stage—for the St. Louis Cardinals in 1998, 81.0872.

Those 81.0872 Win Shares will be "claimed" by individual pitchers based on the followings markers of individual accomplishment:

1. Runs Allowed, below a "zero value" level which is different for every team
2. Wins, Losses and Saves
3. Save-Equivalent Innings, and
4. The pitcher's performance as a hitter

The largest factor, by far, is the first one—the number of runs allowed by the pitcher, below the level of a guy who can't really pitch. The other factors are generally just "stuff we shouldn't forget about." We will explain these four factors in seven articles, which are:

1. Establishing the Zero-Value Level for a team
2. Crediting Claim Points (PCL-1) for Runs Not Allowed
3. Crediting Claim Points (PCL-2) for Wins and Losses
4. Figuring Save-Equivalent Innings
5. Crediting Claim Points (PCL-3) for Save-Equivalent Innings
6. Deducting Claim Points for failure to hit even a little bit (PCL-4), and
7. Adding it up and dividing the Win Shares

1. Establishing the Zero-Value Level for a team

First, then, we need to establish for each team a cutoff point, at which runs allowed begin to count. Let's use St. Louis, 1998, data as we explain the method:

Start with the National League run average:	4.6208262
Apply the park adjustment (1.0004508):	4.6229088
Multiply times 1.52:	7.0268213
Subtract the team Runs Allowed:	4.7888410
Difference:	2.2379803

The Cardinals allowed 2.238 runs per game *fewer* than the upper boundary, which I call the contextual max. We attribute .6983497 of those to the pitchers, .3016503 to the fielders.

Multiply the fielder's percentage:	.3016503
Times the run margin:	2.2379803
Produces	.6750874
Subtracted from the upper boundary:	7.0268313
Produces	6.3517342

St. Louis Cardinal pitchers receive credit for any runs that they allow (or don't allow) *less than* 6.352 runs per nine innings.

Let's do the 1932 Philadelphia A's:

Start with the American League run average:	5.2635852
Multiply times the park adjustment (1.047):	5.5126454
Multiply times 1.52:	8.3792210
Subtract the team Runs Allowed:	4.8831169
Produces	3.4961041
Multiply by the fielder's percentage:	.3332015
Produces	1.1649071
Subtracted from the upper boundary (8.38):	7.2143138

Lefty Grove and friends will receive credit for any runs that they allow ***less than*** 7.214 per nine innings.

Pitchers on the 1890 New York Giants of the Players League will receive credit for any runs allowed less than 9.875 1373 per nine innings.

There is a rule, which probably affects about three teams in history and all of those before 1890, which says that the zero-value point must be at least 1.00 run per game greater than the team's runs allowed per game. It's just a weird-data rule. Don't worry about it.

2. Crediting Claim Points (PCL-1) for Runs Not Allowed

Each run allowed below the zero-value level is one claim point. On the 1998 St. Louis Cardinals, for example, Curtis King pitched 51 innings and allowed 20 runs. Had he allowed 6.352 runs per nine innings, he would have allowed 36 runs—actually, 35.993160. He thus has 15.993160 claim points for the space between his actual runs allowed and the point of zero value.

King allowed no *un*-earned runs, but what if he had?

In the Win Shares system, we hold the pitcher to be 50% responsible for un-earned runs scored while he is on the mound—in other words, we give him one-half of one claim point for each run charged to him that is scored as un-earned. Suppose you have two pitchers who pitch 18 innings apiece, one giving up 7 runs, all earned, and the other giving up 8 runs, but only 6 earned runs. In the Win Shares system, they're the same, since the pitcher is held 50% responsible for the un-earned runs.

Why 50%? Well, we're explaining the system right now, not defending it, but the other option would be to excuse the pitcher from responsibility for un-earned runs. This is absurd, since, in almost all cases, the pitcher has contributed to the run. Doc Gooden had an inning when he was a rookie in which he gave up, as I recall, 2 hits and 3 walks, committed a balk and hit a batter, and five runs scored, but all of the runs resulting were un-earned because of one error. That's absurd to say that the one error caused ALL of the runs. It may be true that, without the error, the runs would not have scored, but it is also true that, without the walks, hits and hit batsmen, they wouldn't have scored, either.

This is an extreme example, but it is almost always true that when an un-earned run scores, the pitcher has contributed to it somehow. Lacking better details, we value the pitcher's contribution at 50%, the fielder's at 50%.

These are the innings, runs and earned runs for all the pitchers on the 1998 St. Louis Cardinals:

	Inn	Runs	ER
Kent Mercker	161.2	99	91
Todd Stottlemyre	161.1	74	63
Kent Bottenfield	133.2	72	66
Matt Morris	113.2	37	32
Mark Petkovsek	105.2	63	56
Juan Acevedo	98.1	30	28
John Frascatore	95.2	48	44
Donovan Osborne	83.2	42	38
Manny Aybar	81.1	58	54
Darren Oliver	57.0	31	27
Rick Croushore	54.1	31	30
Curtis King	51.0	20	20
Jeff Brantley	50.2	26	25
Lance Painter	47.1	24	21
Bobby Witt	47.1	32	26
Mike Busby	46.0	23	23
Cliff Politte	37.0	32	26
Jose Jimenez	21.1	8	7
Brady Raggio	7.0	12	12
Bryan Eversgerd	6.0	7	6
Sean Lowe	5.1	9	9
Braden Looper	3.1	4	2
Gary Gaetti	1.0	0	0

Kent Mercker pitched 161.2 innings. Had he allowed 6.352 runs/9 innings, that would have been 114.0960 runs allowed. He actually allowed "only" 99 runs to score, so he gets 15.0960 claim points for that. He is also partially excused from the eight un-earned runs that were charged to him, giving him another 4 claim points. He ranks first on the team in innings pitched, but sixth in claim points:

	Inn	Runs	ER	PCL-1
Matt Morris	113.2	37	32	45.7200
Todd Stottlemyre	161.1	74	63	45.3607
Juan Acevedo	98.1	30	28	40.3986
Kent Bottenfield	133.2	72	66	25.3350
John Frascatore	95.2	48	44	21.5166
Kent Mercker	161.2	99	91	19.0960
Donovan Osborne	83.2	42	38	19.0476
Curtis King	51.0	20	20	15.9932
Mark Petkovsek	105.2	63	56	15.0741
Darren Oliver	57.0	31	27	11.2276
Lance Painter	47.1	24	21	10.9054
Jeff Brantley	50.2	26	25	10.2579
Mike Busby	46.0	23	23	9.4644
Rick Croushore	54.1	31	30	7.8457
Jose Jimenez	21.1	8	7	7.5560
Bobby Witt	47.1	32	26	4.4054
Manny Aybar	81.1	58	54	1.4009
Gary Gaetti	1.0	0	0	0.7057
Braden Looper	3.1	4	2	-.6475
Bryan Eversgerd	6.0	7	6	-2.2655
Cliff Politte	37.0	32	26	-2.8873
Sean Lowe	5.1	9	9	-5.2360
Brady Raggio	7.0	12	12	-7.0598

If players are in the negative when we finish counting the claim points, we will wash our hands of them and move on, but for the moment, we'll carry the negative numbers.

3. Crediting Claim Points (PCL-2) for Wins and Losses

The second thing we will give the pitchers credit for is their won-lost records. To figure claim points awarded in this way:

Multiply each pitcher's wins by 3
Subtract his losses
Add his saves
Divide the total by 3

Juan Acevedo in 1998 was 8-3 with 15 saves; that's 12 Claim Points—8 times three is 24, plus 15 is 39, minus 3 is 36, divided by three is 12.00:

	W	L	Sv	PCL-2
Juan Acevedo	8	3	15	12.00
Kent Mercker	11	11	0	7.33
Todd Stottlemyre	9	9	0	6.00
Mark Petkovsek	7	4	0	5.67
Matt Morris	7	5	0	5.33
Lance Painter	4	0	1	4.33
Mike Busby	5	2	0	4.33
Manny Aybar	6	6	0	4.00
Donovan Osborne	5	4	0	3.67
Kent Bottenfield	4	6	4	3.33
Jeff Brantley	0	5	14	3.00
Jose Jimenez	3	0	0	3.00
Curtis King	2	0	2	2.67
Darren Oliver	4	4	0	2.67
John Frascatore	3	4	0	1.67
Rick Croushore	0	3	8	1.67
Cliff Politte	2	3	0	1.00
Brady Raggio	1	1	0	.67
Bobby Witt	2	5	0	.33
Bryan Eversgerd	0	0	0	.00
Gary Gaetti	0	0	0	.00
Braden Looper	0	1	0	-.33
Sean Lowe	0	3	0	-1.00

You will notice that the numbers for PCL-2 are much smaller than the numbers for runs (not) allowed (PCL-1). On an average team (as on this team), the claim points awarded based on innings and runs allowed are four times greater than the claim points awarded for won-lost records. In the typical case, the impact of these points is less than that, because, in most cases, the pitcher's won-lost record reflects his innings and his ERA, anyway. But in the odd case where a pitcher may pitch a lot of innings with a good ERA but finish 7-16, while a teammate may pitch fewer innings with a worse ERA but finish 11-8, it seems to me appropriate to take some notice of this fact, and make some allowance in the values for the payoff categories, wins and losses.

4. Figuring Save-Equivalent Innings

Under the system as it has been outlined so far, a team's relief ace will rarely rank among the top pitchers on the team (although the 1998 Cardinals are atypical in this respect. Juan Acevedo already leads the 1998 Cardinals in claim points, but this is very unusual, and occurs mostly because the Cardinals didn't have even one starting pitcher who pitched enough innings to qualify for the league lead in ERA.) Anyway, in the typical case the values for relief aces will be low, because the number of innings pitched by these pitchers is so small that the number of runs saved by them is very small compared to starting pitchers.

Relief pitchers don't pitch lots of innings; they pitch crucial innings. The value of a relief ace is greater than the relative number of runs that he saves, of course, because the relief ace prevents runs at moments of the game when the impact would be greater than normal. How do you adjust for that?

The "saves" element of the won-lost adjustment doesn't do that; that just allows the relief pitchers to tread water while the won-lost records are considered. A starting pitcher who goes 20-9 gets 17 Claim Points; a reliever who saves 45 games gets 15. Those save points are a way of holding the reliever unharmed while the starting pitcher gets credit for his won-lost record.

The credit for pitching crucial innings (save innings) in this system is figured in the following way:

1. Multiply the reliever's saves by 3.00. The result is called "Save Equivalent Innings."
2. Save Equivalent Innings cannot exceed .90 times the pitcher's *actual* innings pitched.
3. Add 1.00 for each "Hold."

In other words, Mariano Rivera in 1999 pitched 69 innings and was credited with 45 Saves. He could, thus, be credited with pitching 135 Save Equivalent Innings. Uhn-un. Pitching 69 innings, his Save Equivalent Innings are capped at 62.1.

The reason for this limitation is that studies I have done, attempting to measure the extent to which runs saved by relief aces have disproportionate impact on the won-lost record, have led me to believe that, while there is no doubt that the impact of those runs saved is greater than 1.00 relative to other runs, it is NOT greater than 2.00. A run saved by a relief ace is NOT five times as valuable as a run saved by a starting pitcher, in general, nor is it four times as valuable, nor three times as valuable. One run saved by a relief ace is, at most, a little less than twice as valuable as one run saved by a starting pitcher, in terms of its impact on the team's won-lost record. Thus, in giving credit for the "special impact" of the runs saved by relievers, we limit that impact in this way.

5. Crediting Claim Points (PCL-3) for Save-Equivalent Innings

1. Figure the pitcher's "Component ERA." If you don't know how to figure the pitcher's Component ERA, that explanation is given on page 98 (the next-to-last article in Section II). Better yet, just take the pitcher's Component ERA out of the *STATS Major League Handbook*, published annually, or the *All-Time Major League Handbook.*
2. Add .56 (to adjust the Component ERA to include un-earned runs).
3. Figure the margin between this number and the team cutoff.
4. Multiply the save-equivalent innings times the margin.
5. Award one claim point for each run.

Juan Acevedo in 1998 had a Component ERA of 2.87 (actual ERA, 2.56). To this, we add .56, which makes 3.43. The Cardinals cutoff was 6.35 runs per nine innings—a difference of 2.92 runs per nine innings.

Acevedo had 15 saves and 3 holds, which makes 48 save-equivalent innings. Thus, we credit him with 15.60 Claim Points for his half-season as the Cardinal closer—48, times 2.92, divided by nine.

Jeff Brantley in 1998 had a Component ERA of 3.60 (actual ERA, 4.44). To this 3.60 we add .56, making 4.16.

The difference between 4.16 and 6.35 is 2.19 runs per nine innings.

Brantley had 14 saves, 3 holds, which makes 45 Save-Equivalent innings. Thus, Brantley is credited with 10.96 Claim Points for his half-season as the Cardinal closer—45, times 2.19, divided by nine.

If the reliever's component ERA is 1.68 or less, then divide it by .75, rather than adding 0.56. If a reliever's component ERA is 0.75, his adjusted run average is 1.00, rather than 1.31.

We use Component ERA, rather than actual runs allowed, because a relief pitcher's ERA is kind of flakey. A relief pitcher, often entering the inning with one or two out, can, at times, have his ineffectiveness charged off to other pitchers; you all know this. On the other hand a relief pitcher, pitching so few innings, may have his ERA blown out of the water by bad outings. Juan Acevedo in 1998 posted an ERA of 2.56, Rick Croushore of 4.97—yet in terms of hits per innings, walks per innings, and home runs per innings, they're really not all that different. Acevedo's Component ERA, 2.87, is higher than his actual ERA; Croushore's Component ERA, 3.70, is lower than his. In most cases ERAs and Component ERAs are closely matched, but we use actual runs charged to the pitcher in the main analysis, but use Component ERA in this reliever's sub-routine, so that we're looking at the question both ways.

6. Deducting Claim Points for failure to hit even a little bit (PCL-4)

For those pitchers whose hitting was below the level of one-half the league norm, we will subtract a few claim points for their inability to hit their hat size. Runs Created and "Background Runs" for all Cardinal players who created at least one run, including pitchers, were given earlier, on pages 20-21. Repeating the data just for the guys who pitched, and adding to the chart the pitchers who created zero runs, we have:

	Runs Created	Outs Made	Back-ground Runs
Juan Acevedo	1	16	1.42
Manny Aybar	1	22	1.95
Kent Bottenfield	0	36	3.19
Jeff Brantley	0	1	0.09
Mike Busby	0	3	0.27
Rick Croushore	0	2	0.18
Bryan Eversgerd	0	0	0.00
John Frascatore	0	6	0.53
Gary Gaetti	42	239	21.19
Jose Jimenez	0	8	0.71
Curtis King	0	6	0.53
Braden Looper	0	0	0.00
Sean Lowe	0	2	0.18
Kent Mercker	2	52	4.61
Matt Morris	1	34	3.01
Darren Oliver	0	21	1.86
Donovan Osborne	0	29	2.57
Lance Painter	1	1	.09
Mark Petkovsek	3	17	1.51
Cliff Politte	0	15	1.33
Bryan Raggio	0	1	.09
Todd Stottlemyre	3	47	4.17
Bobby Witt	1	9	0.80

If the pitcher creates *more* runs, as a hitter, than his "background level" expectation, then we will ignore him now; we have earlier given him credit for his contributions to the team as a hitter. If he creates *less* runs than the background level, then we subtract one claim point for each run that he is below the background level. Juan Acevedo, for example, created one run, but needed to create 1.42 runs to match the background level. We thus subtract 0.42 runs from his claim point total.

As to why we handle pitcher's hitting this way. . . it is essentially an accounting problem. When we remove "background runs" from players, we (almost) never get negative numbers for players who bat more than a few times. If we get negative numbers, they're trivial negative numbers, numbers you can throw away and not worry too much about them, like 7/100 of a run. Ignoring these "negative" runs has essentially no impact on the relative comparison of one outfielder to another, since only terrible outfielders playing in only a few games have negative runs, anyway.

However, if you ignore the sub-marginal or background runs for pitchers, the same is not true, since there are many pitchers who fail to hit even at the level of 52% of the league norm. If you ignore those runs, you are often ignoring more runs for one pitcher than you are for another, which is undesirable. Thus, we consider pitchers hitting up to the level of .52 times the contextual norm to be "just doing your job," and pitchers hitting above that level to be "contributing to the offense." That way, all runs created by pitchers as hitters have an impact on the relative comparison of one pitcher to another.

7. Adding it up and dividing the Win Shares

We total up the Claim Points that we have awarded as PCL-1, PCL-2, PCL-3 and PCL-4, and we then divide the Win Shares credited to the team's pitchers in the same proportion as the Claim Points.

The number one pitcher on the 1998 St. Louis Cardinals—this seems fairly obvious—was Juan Acevedo, who began the season as the last man on the Cardinal staff. Acevedo spent the first two months buried in the Cardinal bullpen, doing little to distinguish himself, but earned a start in late May when the Cardinal starting rotation began to disintegrate. In nine starts, Acevedo pitched 50 innings and was 4-1 with a 2.34 ERA. By early August, however, the Cardinals were bleeding heavily from their bullpen, and so Acevedo was moved into the closer role. Over the last two months, Acevedo pitched 21 times, saving 13 games, winning 3 others, and posting a 0.38 ERA. He ranks as easily the best Cardinal pitcher of 1998:

Pitcher	(Runs) CL-1	(W-L) CL-2	(Saves) CL-3	(Batting) CL-4	Total
Acevedo	40.40	12.00	15.60	-0.42	67.58
Stottlemyre	45.36	6.00	0.00	-1.17	50.19
Morris	45.72	5.33	0.00	-2.01	49.04
Bottenfield	25.34	3.33	3.58	-3.19	29.06
Frascatore	21.52	1.67	2.46	-0.53	25.11
Brantley	10.26	3.00	10.96	-0.09	24.13
Mercker	19.10	7.33	0.00	-2.61	23.82
Petkovsek	15.07	5.67	0.24	—	20.98
Osborne	19.05	3.67	0.00	-2.57	20.14
King	15.99	2.67	1.70	-0.53	19.83
Painter	10.91	4.33	3.28	—	18.52
Croushore	7.85	1.67	6.97	-0.18	16.31
Busby	9.46	4.33	1.12	-0.27	14.65
Oliver	11.23	2.67	0.00	-1.86	12.03
Jimenez	7.56	3.00	0.00	-0.71	9.85
Witt	4.41	0.33	0.00	—	4.74
Aybar	1.40	4.00	0.00	-0.95	4.45
Gaetti	0.71	0.00	0.00	—	0.71
Looper	-0.65	-0.33	0.00	—	-0.98
Eversgerd	-2.27	0.00	-0.84	—	-3.10
Politte	-2.89	1.00	0.00	-1.33	-3.22
Lowe	-5.24	-1.00	0.00	-0.18	-6.41
Raggio	-7.06	0.67	0.00	-.09	-6.48

The guys who are in the red ink are Braden Looper (0-1, 2 blown saves, 4 runs allowed in 3 1/3 innings), Bryan Eversgerd (7 runs allowed in 6 innings), Cliff Politte (6.32 ERA in 8 starts), Brady Raggio (15.43 ERA in 7 innings), and Sean Lowe (0-3, 15.19 ERA in 5 and a third innings). None of these players might accurately be said to have contributed anything to the Cardinal cause, and thus, when we're dividing up credit for the Cardinal Wins, they're not going to get any. They're zeroed out.

The other 18 people who pitched for the 1998 Cardinals, however, have 411.13 Claim Points among them. We then divide the Win Shares in the same proportions as the Claim Points. Since the 1998 Cardinals have 81.0872 Win Shares assigned to their pitchers, this means that each Claim Points is worth .197228 Win Shares (81.0872/411.13). Applying that to individuals, we have:

	Claim Points	Win Shares
Juan Acevedo	67.58	13.33
Todd Stottlemyre	50.19	9.90
Matt Morris	49.04	9.67
Kent Bottenfield	29.06	5.73
John Frascatore	25.11	4.95
Jeff Brantley	24.13	4.76
Kent Mercker	23.82	4.70
Mark Petkovsek	20.98	4.15
Donovan Osborne	20.14	3.97
Curtis King	19.83	3.91
Lance Painter	18.52	3.65
Rick Croushore	16.31	3.22
Mike Busby	14.65	2.89
Darren Oliver	12.03	2.37
Jose Jimenez	9.85	1.94
Bobby Witt	4.74	0.93
Manny Aybar	4.45	0.88
Gary Gaetti	0.71	0.14

These are their Win Shares as a pitcher only; some will also have Win Shares as a hitter, and one—Gary Gaetti—has Win Shares in the same season as a hitter, a third baseman, a first baseman, and a Chicago Cub.

This was, not to put too fine a point on it, one sorry-ass pitching staff. 13.33 Win Shares—that's a decent enough season, but it ain't going to put you in the Hall of Fame if you have twenty seasons like that, and it's a pretty pathetic figure for a staff leader. If your top pitcher earns 25 Win Shares, I would guess that you would have at least a 25% chance to win the pennant. If your top pitcher earns 13 Win Shares, you've got a 99% chance of not winning anything. *At least* a 99% chance.

The Claim Points and Win Shares for the 1932 Philadelphia A's pitchers are as follows:

Pitcher	Inn	W-L	ERA	Claim Points	Win Shares
Lefty Grove	291.2	25-10	2.84	165.40	32.94
Rube Walberg	272	17-10	4.73	75.46	15.03
George Earnshaw	245.1	19-13	4.77	72.82	14.50
Tony Freitas	150.1	12-5	3.83	61.02	12.15
Roy Mahaffey	222.2	13-13	5.09	51.18	10.19
Lew Krausse	57	4-1	4.58	18.74	3.73
Eddie Rommel	65.1	1-2	5.51	12.93	2.57
Sugar Cain	45	3-4	5.00	11.74	2.34
Tim McKeithan	12.2	0-1	7.11	—	0.00
Joe Bowman	11	0-1	8.18	—	0.00
Jimmie DeShong	10	0-0	11.70	—	0.00
Irv Stein	3	0-0	12.00	—	0.00

A few notes:

1. The 1932 Philadelphia A's had a starting rotation, as opposed to a long list of pitchers pitching 140 innings apiece. Lefty Grove was vastly better than anyone else on either team, but the A's second and third starters still had better seasons than anyone on the 1998 Cardinals.

2. The 1932 A's used 12 pitchers during the season; the '98 Cardinals, 23.

3. The ratio of Claim Points to Win Shares on the two teams was almost the same, about five to one. This ratio for most teams is basically the inverse of the league runs scored per game.

4. Several of the '32 pitchers hit well enough to avoid losing claim points as hitters. Most of the '98 Cardinals did not—probably because the game simply got tougher in the intervening 66 years.

Lefty Grove

5. Both teams have a young pitcher (Tony Freitas and Matt Morris) who pitched well, but didn't last a full season, got hurt, and basically disappeared. Freitas went back to the Pacific Coast League, and would win over 300 games as a minor league pitcher. Morris probably will not.

The 1890 Giants:

Pitcher	Inn	W-L	ERA	Claim Points	Win Shares
Hank O'Day	329	22-13	4.21	183.10	23.11
John Ewing	267.1	18-12	4.24	149.43	18.86
Tim Keefe	229	17-11	3.38	147.15	18.57
Ed Crane	330.1	16-19	4.63	147.11	18.57
Gil Hatfield	7.2	1-1	3.52	5.38	0.68
Buck Ewing	9	0-1	4.00	5.04	0.64

Notes on these teams:

1. I will note again that the Win Shares by each pitcher essentially match his Wins.

2. The 1890 Giants, like the 1998 Cardinals, used a third baseman (Gil Hatfield) as an emergency pitcher.

3. The Giants catcher, Buck Ewing, also pitched a little, and later made the Hall of Fame. The Cardinals catcher, Eli Marrero, did not and will not.

4. The Giants top pitcher, as an umpire, made the most famous umpire's ruling in the history of baseball. The 1932 A's also had a pitcher, Eddie Rommel, who had a long career as a major league umpire.

The top pitchers in the National League in 1998, by this method, were:

1.	Kevin Brown	25.37
2.	Greg Maddux	24.94
3.	Tom Glavine	23.31
4.	Curt Schilling	22.38
5.	Al Leiter	21.09

The pitcher perceived by this system as third-best in the league, Tom Glavine, actually won the Cy Young Award, but the difference between Glavine and the other pitchers is slight, and the vote for Glavine certainly is reasonable.

The top pitchers in the American League in 1932 were:

1.	Lefty Grove	32.94
2.	General Crowder	30.23
3.	Wes Ferrell	26.02
4.	Red Ruffing	23.38
5.	Mel Harder	20.60

There was no Cy Young Award in 1932 to confirm or rebut this evaluation. In the 1890 Players League:

1.	Silver King	44.48
2.	Mark Baldwin	41.95
3.	Old Hoss Radbourn	33.22
4.	Gus Weyhing	32.09
5.	Harry Staley	27.14

The highest-valued seasons of all time include two of the same names, in different seasons. The top five of all time are:

1.	Old Hoss Radbourn	1884	83.12
2.	Tim Keefe	1883	66.48
3.	Silver King	1888	66.26
4.	Guy Hecker	1884	62.24
5.	John Clarkson	1889	60.38

There is an obvious reason why all of the top figures were posted in the 1880s, when pitchers routinely pitched 500 to 650 innings per season. As a list of the greatest pitchers/seasons ever, this has certain esthetic drawbacks. The top figures since 1900:

1.	Jack Chesbro	1904	51.80
2.	Walter Johnson	1913	50.28
3.	Ed Walsh	1908	46.62
4.	Walter Johnson	1912	44.12
5.	Pete Alexander	1915	43.32
6.	Joe McGinnity	1904	42.30
7.	Pete Alexander	1916	41.95
8.	Lefty Grove	1931	41.83
9.	Joe McGinnity	1903	40.45
10.	Cy Young	1901	40.44

There are twelve seasons since 1900 over 40.00—the ten above plus Joe Wood, 1912, and Steve Carlton, 1972.

This list, however, is dominated by pitchers from the dead-ball era (1900-1920), for the same reason the previous list was dominated by the 1880s: these guys still pitched a bunch of innings. The most Win Shares by a pitcher since 1920:

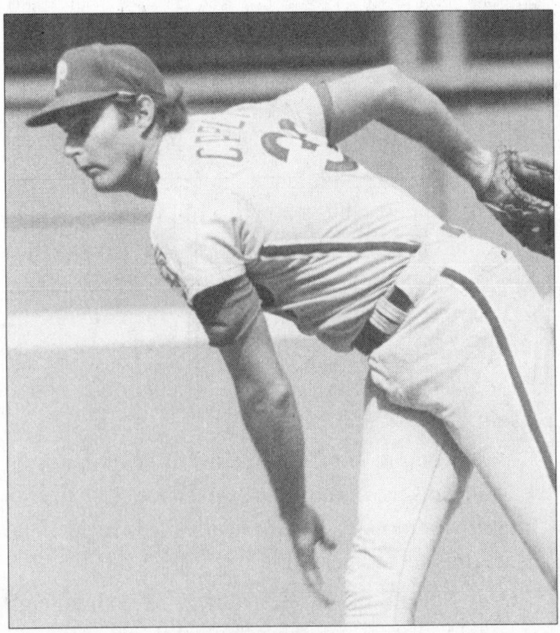

Steve Carlton

1.	Lefty Grove	1931	41.83
2.	Steve Carlton	1972	40.38
3.	Gaylord Perry	1972	39.04
4.	Dolf Luque	1923	38.97
5.	Dizzy Trout	1944	38.12
6.	Dizzy Dean	1934	37.46
7.	Lefty Grove	1930	37.08
8.	Hal Newhouser	1945	37.04
9.	Red Faber	1921	37.02
10.	Carl Hubbell	1936	36.88

That list is still dominated by pitchers pre-1950, so here's a post-1950 list:

1.	Steve Carlton	1972	40.38
2.	Gaylord Perry	1972	39.04
3.	Bob Gibson	1968	36.36
4.	Sandy Koufax	1966	35.12
5.	Robin Roberts	1953	35.03
6.	Fergie Jenkins	1971	34.66
7.	Wilbur Wood	1971	33.36
8.	Sandy Koufax	1965	33.19
9.	Denny McLain	1968	33.08
10.	Bobby Shantz	1952	32.70

That list is dominated by pitchers pre-1975, but what the hell, we have to stop sometime. Well, OK, you talked me into it. . . the best seasons since 1975:

1.	Dwight Gooden	1985	32.65
2.	Roger Clemens	1997	31.66
3.	Jim Palmer	1975	31.33
4.	Ron Guidry	1978	31.18
5.	Phil Niekro	1978	30.29
6.	Greg Maddux	1995	29.87
7.	Catfish Hunter	1975	28.95
8.	Pedro Martinez	2000	28.81
9.	Roger Clemens	1986	28.79
10.	Jim Palmer	1977	28.74

In final version these totals will be rounded to the nearest integer, and may also include some contributions by these pitchers as hitters (if they were decent hitters). In this form, the distinctions between pitchers represent pieces of wins too small to be credible.

Point 0h-one of a Win Share is one three-hundredth of a win, which is like one-twelfth of a single or something. One-twelfth of a single would be about one-eighth of a walk, which is one-half of a pitch. Baseball records don't really allow us to be as precise as we are pretending to be here.

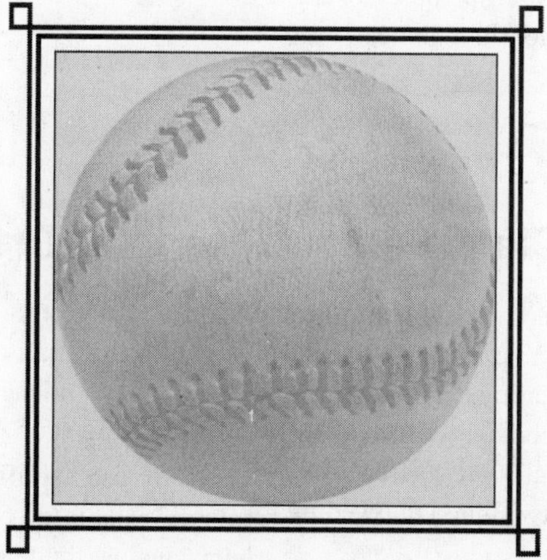

Assigning Win Shares to Defensive Positions

In the Fifth Stage of the Win Shares Analysis, we take the Win Shares assigned to Fielding, and assign those to defensive positions—that is, to third base, to shortstop, etc.

The defensive stats at each position are evaluated on four defensive standards. These evaluations are then converted into "rating percentages" for each defensive position.

Once each position has a rating percentage, based on those four standards, then those rating percentages will be applied to the intrinsic weights, to produce the claim points for the position. The Win Shares assigned to the team's defense will then be split in the same proportions as the Claim Points.

Before we can do that, however, we first have to establish the claim formulas for each position.

How the Rating Percentages are Determined (Overview)

The rating percentage at each position is determined by four factors, each of which is evaluated on a scale.

My original plan was to have, at each position, a 40-point scale, a 30-point scale, a 20-point scale, and a 10-point scale. The most important indicator of defensive excellence at the position would be the 40-point scale, the second-best indicator would be the 30-point scale, etc., with the points on this scales weighted in such a way that a one-run difference in players should have the same impact on one scale as it did on another.

In practice, the available data doesn't always fit into packages of these sizes, so I had to adjust the package sizes at catcher and in the outfield. At catcher, for example, the number one indicator is the percentage of opposing base stealers caught stealing. The third-best indicator is. . . well, gee, I guess it's passed balls.

But passed balls, as a rule, are not one-half as important as caught stealing, and would not be even if they were reliably attributable to the catcher himself. A system which weights caught stealing percentage at 40% and passed balls at 20% is difficult to scale so that a base lost one way has the same impact as a base lost another way. So for catchers, we have a 50-point scale, a 30-point scale, and two 10-point scales.

Anyway, we divide up the points credited on the four scales, divide by 100, and the result is the Claim Percentage for that position. We'll start with catchers.

Determining Claim Percentages for a Team's Catchers

For catchers, we have a 50-point scale, a 30-point scale, and two 10-point scales. (You just said that. . .) The 50-point scale is Caught Stealing Percentage, the 30-point scale is Fielding Percentage (adjusted for strikeouts), and the 10-point scales are Passed Balls and the number of Sacrifice Hits (Bunts) allowed by the team.

If the team matches the league average, the team will place in the middle of the scale. If their catchers throw out the same percentage of base stealers as the league average, the team's catchers will receive 25 Points for that, half of the 50 available. If the team's catchers have a league average fielding percentage, that will score at 15 points on the 30-point scale.

Why use sacrifice hits allowed to evaluate the catcher's defense? Sacrifice hits are the number of bunts against the team. One of a catcher's defensive responsibilities is to field a bunt—thus, a low Sac Hit total may indicate a quick catcher, while a high Sac

Hit total may indicate a slow-moving catcher unable to field a bunt.

If you want to argue that this is an oblique and speculative measure of a catcher's defensive quickness, you are of course correct. We're doing the best we can with very imperfect data. I would have a hard time arguing that fielding bunts is 10% of a catcher's defensive responsibility—but on the other hand, I would have a hard time arguing that throwing out baserunners is 50% of a catcher's defensive responsibility, or that "not making errors" is 30% of a catcher's defensive responsibility, or that "avoiding passed balls" is 10% of a catcher's defensive responsibility. This is what we've got to work with. If you've got a better idea, speak up.

We can't use catcher's ERA, on the team level, because that would be circular definition. The catcher's ERA for the team would just be the team ERA.

At some positions, like this one, we are starved for data, and the best we can hope for is what might be considered a well-organized fishing expedition. At other positions, like second base, we have enough data to make a good evaluation if we do it right.

To create each "scale" there is an A Factor, a B Factor (which is normally the league average in this area), and a formula that combines the A and the B into the Points, which become the rating percentage. The Formulas for Team Catcher's Rating Points (post-1987) are:

50-Point Scale (Caught Stealing)

A Factor	Caught Stealing Percentage
B Factor	League Caught Stealing Percentage
Formula	25 + [(A - B) * 150]

If the league caught stealing percentage is .30 and the team caught stealing percentage (not counting pitcher pickoffs) is .40, this will make 40 on a 50-point scale.

25 + [(.40-.30)*150)]
25 + [.10 * 150]
25 + 15

This figure, however, cannot be greater than 50 nor less than zero.

The 1998 St. Louis Cardinals threw out 35 of 127 opposing base stealers, not counting nine runners thrown out by pitchers. This is .27559. The National League average was .27188. The Cardinals thus receive 25.5566 Claim Points on this scale, figured as follows:

25 + [(.27559 - .27188) * 150)]
25 + [.00371 * 150]
25 + .5567
25.5567

30-Point Scale (Error Percentage, adjusted for team strikeouts)

The Error Percentage is the complement of the fielding percentage, 1.000 minus the Fielding Percentage. If the team fielding percentage at catcher is .995, that's an error percentage of .005.

We use error percentage to get the data to spread out. If the league fielding percentage at a position is .990 and the team fields .995, then the team fielding percentage is less than 1% better than the league norm, although they have committed only one-half as many errors (at the position) as the average team.

The more serious adjustment is the removal of strikeouts from catcher's putouts before the error percentage is figured. We do this because the failure to do it biases the category in favor of a catcher on a high-strikeout team. This issue is discussed in Section IV, in the article "Left-Handed Pitching and Other Things that Screw up Fielding Statistics."

A Factor	Team Error Percentage at Catcher Not Counting Strikeouts
B Factor	League Error Percentage at Catcher Not Counting Strikeouts
Formula	30 - 15 * (A/B)

The exact formula for adjusted error percentage is:

1 - [(cPO + cA - tmK) / (cPO + cA - tmK + cEr)]

Where cPO is Catcher's Putouts, cA is Catcher's Assists, tmK is Team Strikeouts, and cEr is Catcher's Errors.

The St. Louis Cardinals in 1998 receive 12.6 claim points on this 30-point scale (actually, 12.5831).

This is figured as follows: The Cardinals had 1016 catcher's putouts, 66 assists, and 14 errors. Their pitchers had 972 strikeouts. Thus, the fielding percentage of their catchers, not counting strikeouts, was .887 and the error percentage was .113 (actually, .11290).

In the National League in 1998 there were 18067 catcher's putouts, 17552 strikeouts, 1314 catcher's assists, and 197 catcher's errors. That makes a fielding percentage, not counting strikeouts, of .903 (.90276), which is an error percentage of .09724. The formula, then, is:

30 - 15 * (.11290 / .09724)
30 - 15 * 1.16113
30 - 17.417
12.583

10-Point Scale (Passed Balls)

A Factor	Team Passed Balls
B Factor	League Passed Balls Times the Team/League Putout Percentage
Formula	5 + (B - A) / 5

As to what the Team/League Putout Percentage is, that will be explained on Page 100, in the article "What in the Hell is the Team/League Putout Percentage?"

If an average team has 15 passed ball and this team has 10, that will produce 6 Points on a 10-point scale. This data, for the 1998 St. Louis Cardinals, is:

Passed Balls:	6
League Passed Balls:	188
Team/League Putout Percentage:	.06588

This makes 6.27721 Claim Points on this scale:

5 + [(188 * .06588) - 6] / 5
5 + [12.38606 - 6] / 5
5 + 6.38606 / 5
5 + 1.27721
6.27721

The points awarded for passed balls cannot be less than zero or more than 10. This category is "capped" throughout this process, here at zero and 10, and later at zero and 15.

10-Point Scale (Sacrifice Hits Allowed)

A Factor	Team Sacrifice Hits Allowed
B Factor	League Sac Hits Allowed Times the Team/League Putout Percentage
Formula	10 - ((A/B) * 5)

If the average team has 40 Sac Hits Allowed and this team has 24, that produces 7 points on a 10-point scale.

For the 1998 St. Louis Cardinals, this data is:

Sac Hits Allowed	92
League Sac Hits Allowed	1163
Team/League Putout Percentage	.06588

Which produces 3.9965:

10 - [92 / (1163 * .06588)] * 5
10 - [92 / 76.622] * 5
10 - [1.20070 * 5]
10 - 6.0035
3.9965

For the 1998 St. Louis Cardinals, then, we have:

25.5567 on the 50-point scale
12.583 on the 30-point scale
6.2772 on the passed ball 10-point scale
3.9965 on the sac hit 10-point scale

Adding those up, we have 48.4135 points out of 100 possible. The Claim Percentage for St. Louis Cardinal catchers in 1998 is .484.

Hold On a Minute

The method above relies on information that does not exist uniformly throughout baseball history. The method relies on caught stealing data, which we have in an organized form only since 1987, and on Sacrifice Hits allowed, which we don't have reliable, consistent data on until 1931.

Before we're done here, we'll have four distinct methods to figure Claim Points for a team's catchers:

1. 1987-2000
2. 1931-1986
3. 1900-1930
4. 1876-1899

Part II: 1931-1986

For Catchers, Years 1931 to 1986, the categories are Error Percentage (40%), Assists (30%), Sacrifice Hits Allowed (15%), and Passed Balls (15%). The formulas are as follows:

40-Point Scale (Error Percentage)

A Factor	Team Error Percentage at catcher Subtracting Team Strikeouts
B Factor	League Error Percentage at catcher Subtracting League Strikeouts
Formula	40 - 20 * (A/B)

If the league fielding percentage at catcher is .990 and the team fielding percentage at catcher is .994 and the team strikeouts are average, this will produce 28 Points on a 40-point scale.

The 1932 Philadelphia A's catchers had 767 putouts, 106 assists and 5 errors. The Athletics pitchers had 595 strikeouts. This makes a fielding percentage, independent of strikeouts, of .98233, and an error percentage of only .01767 (which is exceptional).

The American League averages in 1932 were .94809 (fielding percentage by catchers, without strikeouts) and .05191 (error percentage by catchers, without strikeouts). This makes 33.193 points for the 1932 A's on this 40-point scale.

30-Point Scale (Assists)

A Factor	Assists by the Team's Catchers Plus Two Times Double Plays by catchers Plus Team Wins
B Factor	League Assists by Catchers Plus Two Times DP Times the Team/League Putout Percentage Plus .5 times Team Decisions
Formula	15 + (A - B) / 4

If the average team has 70 catcher's assists and this team has 90, and the team plays .500 ball, that makes 20 points on the 30-point scale. The points awards for assists cannot be more than 30, nor less than zero.

As part of this project, I undertook a substantial research effort to determine the relationship between catcher's assists per game and caught stealing percentage. First, I can report that there is a positive correlation between catcher's assists and catcher's caught stealing percentages. The catchers who have the higher assists totals tend, on average, to have better ratios of base stealers caught stealing. An analysis of data from the 1990s showed that 71% of catchers who had above-average assists/game averages also had above-average caught stealing percentages, and 71% of catchers who were below average in assists/game were also below average in the percentage of opposing base stealers thrown out.

This, however, is not so reliable a generalization that we may place great weight on it. If we had any really good information by which to rate catchers, I would be happy to reduce assists to a 10% category.

There are (at least) three problems with using assists to evaluate catcher's throwing. One is that opposing base stealers will attempt to run less often against a catcher with a good throwing arm than against a catcher with a weak arm, which reduces the difference between the two if measured in assists. Suppose that you have two catchers, one of whom throws out 20% of opposing base stealers; the other, 40%. Teams will run at least 20% less often against the good-throwing catcher, which means rather than having 100% more assists from caught stealing, he will have about 60% more.

A 60% advantage is still significant and fairly obvious in the stats, except. There is a second and related cross-correlation effect, which is *that good teams allow fewer stolen base attempts than weak teams*, because teams are more reluctant to steal when they are behind than when they are ahead.

If you have a strong-throwing catcher who plays on a great team, then you combine these effects, and the result may very probably be that the outstanding throwing catcher will have a below-average assists total, while a rag-arm catcher who plays on a bad team may well have an above-average assists total. The Linear Weights method rates Johnny Bench and Wally Schang as being poor defensive catchers and Ron Hassey as being good, primarily for this reason.

Total Baseball has Johnny Kling rated as a poor defensive catcher until the end of his career, when he went to a bad team and his assists total shot up, making him, in their evaluation, a much better defensive catcher.

I thus used team wins as an element in evaluating the impact of an assists total, to adjust for this cross-correlation. This is not a good policy; it's not something you'd want to do a lot of. There is a risk of circular definition. In this case I decided it was necessary.

Incidentally, assists by outfielders are also inversely related to team wins. Bad teams have more outfield assists than good teams.

Beyond that, you still have the problems created by the fact that 40% of catcher's assists result from plays other than caught stealing. The result is that while it is true that good throwing catchers have more assists than poor throwing catchers, it is true only 71% of the time in modern baseball, and probably less than that before 1970. Thus, assists can be used to evaluate a catcher's defense, but should be used carefully.

For the 1932 Philadelphia A's, the relevant data is:

Assists by Catchers	106
Double Plays by Catchers	20
Wins by team	94
League Assists by Catchers	789
League Double Plays by C	108
Team Decisions	154
Team/League Putout Percentage	.122956

This figures, with the formula, as 24.857 Claim Points.

A Factor	106 + (2* 20) + 94
B Factor	[789 + (2 * 108)] * .122956 + (154 / 2)
Formula	15 + (A - B) / 4

15-Point Scale (Passed Balls)

A Factor	Team Passed Balls
B Factor	League Passed Balls Times the Team/League Putout Percentage
Formula	7.5 + (B - A) / 5

For the 1932 Philadelphia A's, the data is:

Team Passed Balls	15
League Passed Balls	63
Team/League Putout Percentage	.122956

This produces a result of 6.049.

15-Point Scale (Sacrifice Hits Allowed)

A Factor	Team Sacrifice Hits Allowed
B Factor	League Sacrifice Hits Allowed Times the Team/League Putout Percentage
Formula	15 - ((A/B) * 7.5)

For the 1932 Philadelphia A's, this data is:

Team Sac Hits Allowed	75
League Sac Hits Allowed	714
Team/League Putout Percentage	.122956

Using the formula, this figures as 8.593.

Having figured all four elements of the catcher's claiming formula relating to the 1932 Philadelphia Athletics, we can now figure their claiming percentage. Those four are:

33.193 on the 40-point scale (Error Percentage)
24.857 on the 30-point scale (Assists)
6.049 on the 15-point scale (Passed Balls)
8.593 on the 15-point scale (Sac Hits Allowed)

These total up to 72.692 of the 100 possible points. Thus, the claim percentage for the 1932 Philadelphia A's catchers is .727. This figure is extremely high, which we would expect, since the A's catcher was Mickey Cochrane.

Part III: 1900-1930

Sacrifice Hits have been a part of baseball's statistical record for many years, but prior to 1931, several different definitions of what was a sacrifice hit were used. This renders the sacrifice hit category, which frankly is not *terribly* useful for evaluating catchers at its best, completely useless.

Fortunately, there is something else that, working backward in time, actually becomes more interesting. That is independent putouts by catchers—catcher's putouts which aren't strikeouts. There is an article about them in Section IV, which you can refer to for more information. For catchers from 1876 to 1930, the second 15-point factor, replacing Sacrifice Hits Allowed, is independent putouts by catchers:

A Factor	Putouts By Catchers Minus Team Strikeouts
B Factor	League Total of Same * TLPOP
Formula	7.5 + (A - B) / 10

The 1930 Yankees (Bill Dickey) had 744 putouts by catchers. Their pitchers had 572 strikeouts. That makes 172 independent putouts for the Yankee catchers—highest in baseball that year (actually Pittsburgh, with Rollie Hemsley, also had 172).

The league totals were 5234 catcher's putouts, 4081 strikeouts; that makes 1153 independent putouts by league catchers. The Yankees Team/League Putout Percentage was .123, which creates a B factor of 141.5.

Combining these with the formula, we get 10.55:

7.5 + (172 - 141.5) / 10
7.5 + (30.5) / 10
10.55

The rest of the Claiming Formula is the same for the years 1900-1930 as it is for the years 1931-1986.

Part IV: 1876-1899

For catchers from 1876 to 1899, the numbers of passed balls are so high that they basically swamp the system. In 1980 there were 4,210 team games in the major leagues, and 294 passed balls—11 passed balls per 162 games. In 1880 there were only 680 games, but 753 passed balls—179 passed balls per 162 games. This causes the passed balls to take over the catcher rating system, making everything else irrelevant.

To control this, we change the passed ball formula for nineteenth century catchers. The scale was this:

15-Point Scale (Passed Balls)

A Factor	Team Passed Balls
B Factor	League Passed Balls Times the Team/League Putout Percentage
Formula	7.5 + (B - A) / 5

We just change that last "5" there to a "10"—one point for each ten passed balls, rather than one point for each five. The rest of the system is the same as it is for the years 1900 to 1930, except for a small adjustment to the application of the Error Percentage formula.

I'll retrace the whole system for the 1890 New York Giants of the Players League:

40-Point Scale (Error Percentage)

A Factor	Team Error Percentage at catcher Subtracting Team Strikeouts
B Factor	League Error Percentage at catcher Subtracting League Strikeouts
Formula	35 - 15 * (A/B)

1890 Giants Fielding Pct. (Not Counting Strikeouts)	.837
1890 League Average	.811
Giants Error Percentage	.163
League Error Percentage	.189
Claim Points	22.034

30-Point Scale (Assists)

A Factor	Assists by the Teams Catchers Plus Two Times Double Plays by catchers Plus Team Wins
B Factor	League Assists by Catchers Plus Two Times DP Times the Team/League Putout Percentage Plus .5 times Team Decisions
Formula	15 + (A - B) / 4

1890 Giants Assists by Catchers	164
1890 Giants Double Plays	11
1890 Giants Wins	74
1890 League Assists by Catchers	1270
1890 League DP by Catchers	114
Team/League Putout Percentage	.123593
Giants Team Decisions	131
Claim Points	17.340

15-Point Scale (Passed Balls)

A Factor	Team Passed Balls
B Factor	League Passed Balls Times the Team/League Putout Percentage
Formula	7.5 + (B - A) / 10

1890 Giants Passed Balls	70
League Total	467
Team/League Putout Percentage	.123593
Claim Points	6.272

15-Point Scale (Independent Putouts)

A Factor	Putouts By Catchers Minus Team Strikeouts
B Factor	League Total of Same * TLPOP
Formula	7.5 + (A - B) / 10

1890 New York Giants Catchers Putouts	598
1890 NYG Pitchers Strikeouts	449
League Putouts by Catchers	4399
League Strikeouts	2986
Team/League Putout Percentage	.123593
Claim Points	4.936

Having figured all four elements of the Catcher's Claiming formula relating to the 1890 New York Giants of the Players League, we can now figure their claiming percentage. Those four are:

22.034 on the 40-point scale (Error Percentage)
17.340 on the 30-point scale (Assists)
6.272 on the 15-point scale (Passed Balls)
4.936 on the 15-point scale (Independent Putouts)

These total up to 50.582 of the 100 possible points. Thus, the claim percentage for the 1890 New York Giants catchers is .506.

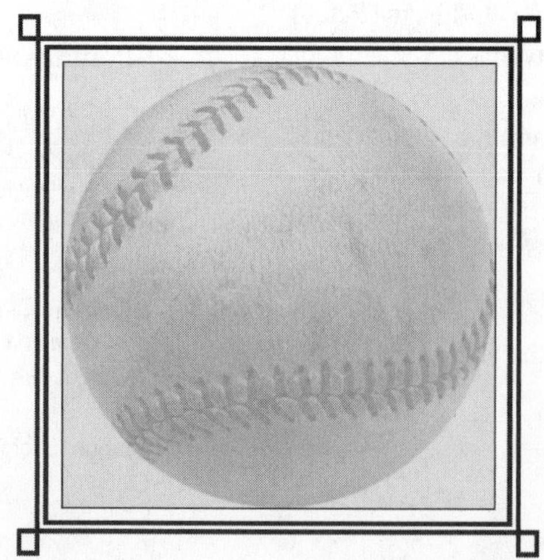

Claim Percentages for First Basemen

The Claim Percentages at First Base are based on four elements, which are:

1. Plays Made (40%)
2. Error Percentage (30%)
3. Arm Rating (20%)
4. Errors by the Team's Shortstops and Third Basemen (10%)

Plays Made (40%)

This process is obscenely complicated, and for that I apologize. We make two initial estimates of first base un-assisted putouts. One of those relies upon an estimate of runners on first base. That estimate of runners on first base, very slightly different from the one we used earlier, is:

Team Hits Allowed
Minus Home Runs Allowed
Times the League % of Non-Home Runs which are singles
Plus Walks
Plus Hit Batsmen
Minus Wild Pitches
Minus Balks
Minus Passed Balls

This is the same as the estimate of runners on first used to adjust double plays, except that we don't remove Sac Hits. (Apparently there is some sort of interaction between SH and 1B Putouts. In any case, removing SH from the data does not improve the accuracy of the estimate, and since the changing definition of this category screws up a formula which would otherwise hold back to 1876, I have chosen not to remove sacrifice hits from this estimate.)

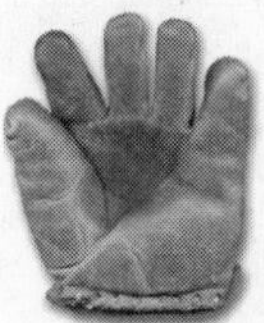

Anwyay, for the 1998 St. Louis Cardinals, this data is:

Hits Allowed	1513	
Minus Home Runs Allowed	151	makes 1362
Times the League % of non-HR which are singles	.7588190	makes 1033.5115
Plus Walks	558	makes 1591.5115
Plus Hit Batsmen	54	makes 1645.5115
Minus Wild Pitches	42	makes 1603.5115
Minus Balks	14	makes 1589.5115
Minus Passed Balls	6	makes 1583.5115

The 1998 Cardinals have 1,584 estimated opposition runners on first base. The 1932 Philadelphia A's have:

Hits Allowed	1477	
Minus Home Runs Allowed	112	makes 1365
Times the League % of non-HR which are singles	.7472129	makes 1019.9456
Plus Walks	511	makes 1530.9456
Plus Hit Batsmen	18	makes 1548.9456
Minus Wild Pitches	21	makes 1527.9456
Minus Balks	1	makes 1526.9456
Minus Passed Balls	15	makes 1511.9456

We estimate that the 1932 Philadelphia A's have 1,512 opposition baserunners on first base. The 1890 New York Giants of the Players League have:

Hits Allowed	1216	
Minus Home Runs Allowed	37	makes 1179
Times the League % of non-HR which are singles:	.7740766	makes 912.6363
which I will round off to	913	
Plus Walks	569	makes 1482
Plus Hit Batsmen	(no data)	
Minus Wild Pitches	(no data)	
Minus Balks	(no data)	
Minus Passed Balls	70	makes 1412

We estimate that the 1890 Giants have 1,412 opposition runners on first base.

With that number in hand, we can make our estimates of the first basemen's un-assisted putouts by each team. The first estimate of first basemen's un-assisted putouts is made as follows:

Putouts by the team's first basemen
Minus .70 times assists by the team's pitchers
Minus .86 times assists by the team's second basemen
Minus .78 times assists by the team's third basemen
Minus .78 times assists by the team's shortstops
Plus .115 times Estimated Runners on First Base
Minus .0575 times Balls In Play against the defense

The 1998 St. Louis Cardinals (regular first baseman, Mark McGwire) had 1465 putouts by first basemen. They had 219 assists by pitchers, 466 by second basemen, 325 by third basemen, and 554 by shortstops. They had an estimated 1584 baserunners on first base.

Balls in Play against the defense are innings pitched times three, minus strikeouts. For the Cardinals, 1998, this is 3437. For the 1998 Cardinals, this calculates as:

		1465
-.70 * 219	=	1311.7
-.86 * 466	=	910.94
-.78 * 325	=	657.44
-.78 * 554	=	225.32
+.115 * 1584	=	407.48
-.0575 * 3437	=	209.85

We have Cardinal first basemen making an estimated 209.85 un-assisted putouts at this point. We will refer to this later as Estimate A.

The second estimate, Estimate B, is much, much simpler. It is:

Balls In Play Against the Defense
Times .1
Minus First Base Assists

Estimate B has the functions of:

a) reducing the standard deviation of Estimate A, and

b) reducing the estimated first base putouts of teams which have a lot of assists by first basemen, since first base assists and first base un-assisted putouts are competitive outcomes.

The second estimate for St. Louis, 1998, is:

(3437 * .1) - 112 = 231.7

We put the two estimates together by weighting Estimate A, the complicated one, at two-thirds, and Estimate B at one-third.

For St. Louis, 1998, this makes 217 estimated un-assisted putouts by first basemen:

Team	EstA	EstB	Combined	Rounded
St. Louis	209.85	231.7	217.13	217

Now, for the 1998 Cardinals, it happens, we have an actual count of un-assisted putouts by first basemen. The actual number was 218. I don't mean to mislead anyone; the estimating system is not *that* accurate, and it is not common for these estimates to be within one of the actual figure. However, since we have the actual figure in this case (as for all teams, post-1987) we will use the actual number, rather than the estimate.

Not complicated enough for you? Relax; we're just getting started. In order to evaluate the Cardinal first basemen, we will need to figure the same for the National League as a whole. In the National League as a whole there were:

22465 Putouts by first basemen
3220 Assists by Pitchers
7556 Assists by Second Basemen
5194 Assists by Third Basemen
7744 Assists by Shortstops
24102 Estimated Runners on First Base
52168 Balls in Play, and
1955 Assists by First Basemen

The first estimate of un-assisted putouts by league first basemen, then, is 3393.27:

League Putouts by First Basemen	22465
Minus .70 * 3220	20211
Minus .86 * 7556	13712.84
Minus .78 * 5194	9661.52
Minus .78 * 7744	3621.20
Plus .115 * 24102	6392.93
Minus .0575 * 52168	3393.27

The second estimate is 3261.80:

League Balls in Play	52168
Times .100	5216.8
Minus 1955 (Assists)	3261.8

Combining these two estimates, we then estimate that National League First Basemen had 3349.45 unassisted putouts by first basemen in 1998. (The actual figure was 3311. Again, since we have the actual figure here, we'll use it.)

We convert the Estimated First Base Un-assisted Putouts into Claim Points by the following formula:

A Factor	Est1BUnPO + 1B Assists + .0285 LHP+/-
B Factor	(Lg Est1BUnPO + 1B Assists) TIMES the Team/League Putout Percentage
Formula	20 + (A - B)/5

The 1998 St. Louis Cardinals LHP+/- is -27. (This is explained in an article in Section IV, "Figuring Excess Batters Faced by LHP.") National League first basemen in 1998 had 1,955 assists, and the Team/League Putout Percentage, which we have used before, was .06588.

Figuring this for the Cardinals, then:

A Factor	218 + 112 - 0.77 =	329.23
B Factor	(3311 + 1955) * .06588 =	346.94
Formula	20 + (-17.71) / 5 =	16.46

We estimate, in essence, that Mark McGwire had somewhat below-average range for a first baseman.

I probably should have explained this. A team with lots of innings by left-handed pitchers will tend to have relatively few balls hit to first base. For each 35 extra batters' balls in play against left-handed pitchers, there will be a loss of one defensive play initiated by first basemen. We offset this in the evaluation process by giving the first basemen credit for extra batters faced by left-handed pitchers.

The reason for this, if it's not obvious, is that more left-handed pitching means more right-handed hitting by the opposition, which means more balls hit to the left side of the infield (shortstop and third base) rather than the right side of the infield.

I did two separate studies, using radically different approaches, which showed that this was true. The first study, which was fairly primitive, used scattered seasons, and established that left-handed pitching created more fielding opportunities at third base, fewer at first base, about one per ten innings. The second study, more comprehensive, is reported in Section IV, in the article "Left-Handed Pitching and Other Things that Screw Up Fielding Statistics."

The 1932 Philadelphia A's (regular first baseman, Jimmie Foxx) had 1458 putouts by first basemen. They had 285 assists by pitchers, 517 by second basemen, 269 by third basemen, and 447 by shortstops. They had an estimated 1512 baserunners on first base.

Balls in Play against the defense is innings pitched times three, minus strikeouts. For the A's, 1932, this is 3563. For the 1932 A's, this calculates as 224.52:

	1458
-.70 * 285 =	1258.5
-.86 * 517 =	813.88
-.78 * 269 =	604.06
-.78 * 447 =	255.40
+.115 * 1512 =	429.28
-.0575 * 3563 =	224.41

This is Estimate A. The second, simpler estimate is:

Balls In Play Against the Defense
Times .1
Minus First Base Assists
Which is, for Philadelphia in 1932, 272.3:
(3563 * .1) - 84 = 272.3

We put the two estimates together by weighting Estimate A at two-thirds and Estimate B at one-third. For Philadelphia this makes 240 estimated un-assisted putouts by first basemen:

Team	EstA	EstB	Combined	Rounded
Philadelphia	224.41	272.3	240.45	240

The computer program which figures these things does not round them off; I just like to present it that way. Anyway, in order to evaluate the Athletic first basemen, we will need to figure the same for the American League as a whole. In the American League in 1932 there were:

11685 Putouts by first basemen
2229 Assists by Pitchers
4147 Assists by Second Basemen
2346 Assists by Third Basemen
3802 Assists by Shortstops
12744 Estimated Runners on First Base
29002 Balls in Play, and
758 Assists by First Basemen

The first estimate of un-assisted putouts by league first basemen, then, is 1560.785:

League Putouts by First Basemen		11685
Minus .70 * 2229	(1560.3)	10124.7
Minus .86 * 4147	(3566.42)	6558.28
Minus .78 * 2346	(1829.88)	4728.4
Minus .78 * 3802	(2965.56)	1762.84
Plus .115 * 12744	(1465.56)	3228.40
Minus .0575 * 29002	(1667.615)	1560.785

The second estimate is much higher:

League Balls in Play	29002
Times .100	2900.2
Minus Assists by 1B (758)	2142.2

Combining these two estimates, we then estimate that American League First Basemen had 1754.59 un-assisted putouts by first basemen in 1932.

We convert the Estimated First Base Un-assisted Putouts into Claim Points by the following formula:

A Factor	Est1BUnPO + 1B Assists + .0285 LHP+/-
B Factor	Lg Est1BUnPO + 1B Assists * the Team/League Putout Percentage
Formula	20 + (A - B)/5

The 1932 A's LHP+/- is +914. (They had lots of left-handed pitching.) American League first basemen in 1932 had 758 assists, and the Team/League Putout Percentage was .122956. Figuring this for the Athletics, then:

A Factor	240.37 + 84 + 26.05 =	350.42
B Factor	(1754.59 + 758) * .122956 =	308.94
Formula	20 + (41.48 / 5) =	28.30

In other words, we believe that Jimmie Foxx in 1932 had very good range, compared to the other American League first basemen of his era.

The 1890 New York Giants (regular first baseman, Roger Connor) had 1432 putouts by first basemen. They had 266 assists by pitchers, 436 by second basemen, 268 by third basemen, and 429 by shortstops. They had an estimated 1412 baserunners on first base.

Balls in Play against the defense are innings pitched times three, minus strikeouts. For the Giants, 1890, this is 3068. For the 1890 Giants, this calculates as:

	1432
-.70 * 266 =	1245.8
-.86 * 436 =	870.84
-.78 * 268 =	661.80
-.78 * 429 =	327.18
+.115 * 1412 =	489.56
-.0575 * 3068 =	313.15

We have Giant first basemen making an estimated 313.15 un-assisted putouts as Estimate A. The second estimate is:

Balls In Play Against the Defense
Times .1
Minus First Base Assists, which is:
(3068 * .1) - 84 = 222.8

We put the two estimates together to form an overall estimate of 283.03 un-assisted putouts by Giant first basemen:

Team	EstA	EstB	Combined	Rounded
New York	313.15	222.8	283.03	283

In order to evaluate the Giant first basemen, we will need to figure the same for the Players League as a whole. In the Players League there were:

10526 Putouts by first basemen
2411 Assists by Pitchers
3284 Assists by Second Basemen
2302 Assists by Third Basemen
3508 Assists by Shortstops
11627 Estimated Runners on First Base
24820 Balls in Play, and
525 Assists by First Basemen

The first estimate of un-assisted putouts by league first basemen, then, is 1392.22:

League Putouts by First Basemen	10526
Minus .70 * 2411	8838.3
Minus .86 * 3284	6014.06
Minus .78 * 2302	4218.50
Minus .78 * 3508	1482.26
Plus .115 * 11627	2819.365
Minus .0575 * 24820	1392.215

The second estimate is 1957.0:

League Balls in Play:	24820
Times .100	2482.0
Minus 525	1957.0

Combining these two estimates, we then estimate that Players League First Basemen had 1580.48 un-assisted putouts.

We convert the Estimated First Base Un-assisted Putouts into Claim Points by the following formula:

A Factor	Est1BUnPO + 1B Assists + .0285 LHP+/-
B Factor	Lg Est1BUnPO + 1B Assists * the Team/League Putout Percentage
Formula	20 + (A - B)/5

However, for teams before 1915, we ignore the LHP+/-, since the tendency of left-handed pitchers to reduce plays made by first basemen is due to platooning, and teams prior to 1915 did not platoon (much). Players League first basemen had 525 assists, and the Team/League Putout Percentage is .1235928. Figuring this for the Giants:

A Factor	283.03 + 84 =	367.03
B Factor	(1580 + 525) * .1235928 =	260.22
Formula	20 + (106.81) / 5 =	41.36

In other words, we believe that Roger Connor had outstanding range in 1890, and have actually credited him with 41 points on a 40-point scale.

With the better fielding data now becoming available from Project Retrosheet and other efforts, students of sabermetrics will soon devise better ways of estimating the range of all defensive players, especially first basemen. I look forward to this system I have created here to evaluate first basemen's range being surpassed and supplanted by better research.

Error Percentage (30%)

The error percentage, of course, is the complement of fielding percentage. The formula is:

A Factor	First Base Error Percentage
B Factor	League Average
Formula	30 - 15 * (A/B)

The data for these three teams is found at the bottom of the page.

Arm Rating (20%)

A Factor	Assists by the First Basemen Plus one-half Double Plays by the Team's Shortstops Minus Putouts by the Pitchers Minus one-half Double Plays by the Second Basemen Plus .015 * LHP+/-
B Factor	League average Of same
Formula	10 + (A - B) / 5

An explanation of why we do this can be found in the article "Arm Ratings for First Basemen," near the end of Section II. For the first two teams and leagues we are tracking, this is the data:

Yr	Tm/Lg	1BA	DPSS	POPt	DP2B	LHP+/-	TLPOP
1998	StL	112	109	101	104	-27	.0658833
1998	NL	1955	1598	1550	1707		
1932	Phi	84	98	59	99	+914	.1229565
1932	AL	758	784	506	817		

Year	Team	A Factor	B Factor	Claim Points
1998	StL	13.095	23.092	8.00
1932	Phi	38.210	28.956	11.85

Year	Team	PO	A	E	EPct	LgPO	LgA	LgE	LgEPct	Claim Points
1998	StL	1465	112	12	.00755	22465	1955	169	.00687	13.52
1932	Phi	1458	84	12	.00772	11685	758	135	.01073	19.21
1890	NYG	1432	84	26	.01686	10526	525	307	.02703	20.64

For teams in the years 1900-1914, the "LHP+/-" is zero, and we ignore the double plays by shortstops and second basemen, due to unreliability in the data. Finally, for the years 1876-1899, we throw up our arms in despair, and enter the "Arm Rating" for all teams as "10." There are two reasons for this:

1. In the beginning of major league baseball, second basemen played very close to second and made almost all plays at second base, and

2. At the beginning of major league baseball, pitchers routinely handled defensive responsibilities (such as catching pop outs and covering bases) which have since moved to other players.

These things change the defensive statistics of early teams in ways that cause this "arm rating" not to work. This period did not end suddenly, but rather some teams (and some second basemen) made the adjustment at one time, and some later on, so that the ratio of second base to shortstop double plays is different for different teams. This had evened out by the early twentieth century, when the modern methods of positioning had evolved, and pitchers had mostly stopped catching pop outs and covering bases.

An article, beginning on page 83, explains and defends the Arm Rating as an element of the first base evaluation.

Errors by Third Basemen and Shortstops (10%)

A Factor	Errors by the teams third basemen and shortstops
B Factor	League total of Same Times the Team/League Putout Percentage
Formula	10 - 5 * (A / B)

In other words, if the team was charged with 20% more errors on third basemen and shortstops than an average team, they'll score at 4 on this 10-point scale.

This, of course, embodies something that we often hear said. Any third baseman during the course of the season is likely to say that his first baseman has saved him 15 or 20 errors by pulling low throws out of the dirt, while any shortstop who *does* make errors is likely to be defended by fans who put the blame for two-thirds of those errors on the first baseman.

As a practical matter, it is hard to know what relationship there is between the fielding of the first baseman and errors on other infielders. I thought it was a reasonable choice for the 10% factor.

For these three teams, the data is as follows:

Yr	Tm	3BE	SSE	Lg3BE	LgSSE	TLPOP	Claim Pts
1998	StL	21	34	314	392	.0658833	4.09
1932	Phi	10	38	192	396	.1229565	6.68
1890	NYG	75	105	643	826	.1235928	5.04

Putting the First Base Elements Together

As in the last cycle, the Claim Percentages for first basemen come from adding these four elements together and dividing by 100:

Yr	Tm	40-Pt	30-Pt	20-Pt	10-Pt	Claim %
1998	StL	16.46	13.52	8.00	4.09	.421
1932	Phi	28.30	19.21	11.85	6.68	.660
1890	NYG	41.36	20.64	10.00	5.04	.770

These claim percentages are consistent with the figures posted by the teams for which these men were the primary first baseman throughout their careers. Although Mark McGwire has always enjoyed a good defensive reputation, and has won one Gold Glove, every team for which he has played, with the sole exception of the 1991 Oakland Athletics, has had a claim percentage at first base below .500. Although the .660 Claim Percentage of 1932 is the highest of any Jimmie Foxx team, his teams had first base Claim Percentages over .500 every year (when he was a regular) except 1938 and 1939, and were .640 or better on two other occasions. And, although Connor never again matched the exceptional .770 Claim Percentage of 1890, his teams were over .500 every year from 1884 through 1896 except in 1892, and were over .600 in 1885, 1886, 1887, 1888 and 1891. Our system evaluates Connor as a consistently outstanding defensive first baseman, Foxx as a good defensive first baseman having an outstanding year, and McGwire as a below-average defensive first baseman.

Claim Percentages for Second Basemen

The scales for evaluating second base play are Team Double Plays Vs. Expected Double Plays (40%), Assists as a percentage of the team total (30%), Error Percentage (20%), and Putouts as a Percentage of the team Total (10%). The Formulas are:

40-Point Scale (Double Plays vs. Expected Double Plays)

A Factor	Team Double Plays
B Factor	Expected Double Plays Calculated as explained earlier
Formula	20 + (A - B) / 3

In other words, if the team matches their expected double plays, that's 20 points on a 40-point scale. If they do better than that, each additional double play moves them up by one-third of a point.

The 1998 Cardinals had 160.75 Expected Double Plays (which we explained in detail earlier). They actually turned 160 double plays. This scores at 19.75 on this 40% factor for second basemen:

Formula	20 + (A - B) / 3
	20 + (160 - 160.75) / 3
	20 + (-.75) / 3
	20 - .25
	19.75

The 1932 Philadelphia Athletics had 142 actual double plays, 137.21 expected. This scores at 21.60 on the 40-point scale.

The 1890 New York Giants turned 94 double plays, but had 97.00 expected double plays. This scores at 19.00.

30-Point Scale (Assists as a Percentage of Team Total)

A Factor	Second Base Assists minus second base double plays
B Factor	League Second Base Assists minus league second base double plays times the Team/League Putout Percentage minus 1/35 of LHP+/-
Formula	15 + (A - B) / 6

Second basemen on the 1998 St. Louis Cardinals were credited with 466 assists, and participated in 104 double plays; that leaves them with an "A" factor of 362.

National League second basemen in 1998 were credited with 7556 assists, and participated in 1707 double plays. The Team/League Putout Percentage was .065883. This creates a "B" factor of 385.3514. From this we subtract negative 27, divided by 35 (adjusting the expected assists at second base for the left/right bias of the pitching staff). This is the same as adding 27/35, which increases the B factor above to 386.1228. (Since left-handed pitchers get more ground balls to the third base side of the infield, the expected assists by a second baseman *decrease* as innings pitched by left-handed pitchers *increase*.)

This scores at 10.98 on this 30-point scale.

Second basemen on the 1932 Philadelphia Athletics were credited with 517 assists, and participated in 99 double plays; that leaves them with an "A" factor of 418.

American League second basemen in 1932 were credited with 4147 assists, and participated in 817 double plays. The Team/League Putout Percentage was .1229565. This creates a "B" factor of 409.445, until we subtract 914/35, making the adjustment for the fact that the 1931 A's had lots of left-handed pitching. That makes a "B" Factor of 383.331, which scores at 20.778 on this 30-point scale.

Second basemen on the 1890 New York Giants were credited with 436 assists, and participated in 56 double plays; that leaves them with an "A" factor of 380.

Players League second basemen were credited with 3284 assists, and participated in 521 double plays. The Team/League Putout Percentage was .1235928. This creates a "B" factor of 341.49.

This scores at 21.42.

20-Point Scale (Error Percentage)

A Factor	Team Error Percentage at Second Base
B Factor	League average of same
Formula	24 - 14 * (A/B)

St. Louis Cardinal second basemen in 1998 had a fielding percentage of .980942, which is an error percentage of .019058. Second basemen in the league as a whole had a fielding percentage of .982140, which is an error percentage of .017860. Thus, the Cardinal second basemen receive 9.06 Claim Points on this scale.

Philadelphia A's second basemen in 1932 had a fielding percentage of .974359, which is an error percentage of .025641. Second basemen in the league as a whole had a fielding percentage of .968471, which is an error percentage of .031529. Thus, the Athletic second basemen receive 12.61 Claim Points on this scale.

New York Giant second basemen in 1890 had a fielding percentage of .914842, which is an error percentage of .085158. Players League second basemen had a fielding percentage of .912903, which is an error percentage of .087097. Thus, the Giant second basemen receive 10.31 Claim Points on this scale. In modern baseball, one error by a second baseman has more impact on the evaluation of the position than one play of any other kind. The points awarded on this scale cannot be less than zero or more than 20.

10-Point Scale (Putouts as a Percentage of the Team)

A Factor	Team Putouts at Second Base
B Factor	Expected Putouts at Second Base
Formula	5 + (A - B) / 12

Expected Putouts at Second Base are established as follows:

Team Putouts
Minus Strikeouts
Times the League Percentage of non-K putouts which are made by second basemen
+ 1/13 of walks above (or below) the league average (per inning)
Plus 1/32 of the LHP+/-

In the National League in 1998, .107096 of non-K putouts are recorded by second basemen. For the 1998 Cardinals, this figures as:

Team Putouts		4409
Minus 972 Strikeouts	4409 - 972	3437
Times .107096		368.0900
Plus (558 - [(8743/23240) * 1469.667])/13)		368.4826
Plus	(-27/32)	367.6389

The Cardinals would be expected to have 367.64 putouts by second basemen. They actually had 409, so that scores at 8.45 on this 10-point scale:

5 + (409 - 367.64) / 12 = 8.45

The 1932 Philadelphia A's had 357 actual putouts at second base, 410.445 expected putouts, and thus score at 0.55 on this scale.

The 1890 New York Giants had 316 putouts by second basemen, 364.09 expected putouts. They score at 0.99 on this scale.

The points awarded on this scale cannot be less than zero or more than 10.

Putting the Second Base Elements Together

To get the claim percentage for each team's second basemen, we total up the claim points on all four scales, and divide by 100. For the 1998 St. Louis Cardinals, those are:

40-point scale (Double Plays)	19.75
30-point scale (Assists)	10.98
20-point scale (Errors)	9.06
10-point scale (Putouts)	8.45
Total	48.24
Claim Percentage:	482

A claim percentage of .482.

For the 1932 Philadelphia Athletics, the elements are:

40-point scale (Double Plays)	21.60
30-point scale (Assists)	20.78
20-point scale (Errors)	12.61
10-point scale (Putouts)	0.55
Total	55.54
Claim Percentage:	.555

A claim percentage of .555.

The Claim Percentage for the 1890 New York Giants is .517:

40-point scale (Double Plays)	19.00
30-point scale (Assists)	21.42
20-point scale (Errors)	10.31
10-point scale (Putouts)	0.99
Total	51.72
Claim Percentage:	.517

Claim Percentages for Third Basemen

At third base we're going to use a 50-30-10-10 system. The 50-point scale is Assists by third basemen:

50-Point Scale (Assists)

A Factor	Assists by Third Basemen
B Factor	Expected Assists by Third Basemen
Formula	25 + (A - B) / 4
(Bounded at zero and fifty)	

To get expected assists by the team's third basemen:

1. Take the team assists total
2. Multiply that by the league percentage of assists which are recorded by third basemen
3. Add 1/31 of the LHP+/- (but no adjustment for the LHP+/- before 1915)

In the 1998 National League, .1887835 of assists were recorded by third basemen:

League Assists	27513
League Assists by third basemen	5194

For the 1998 Cardinals, expected assists at third base would be 335.352:

The Team Assists total	1781
Times .1887835 =	336.223
Plus Negative 27 divided by 31 =	335.352

Cardinal third basemen actually had 325 assists in 1998. This scores at 22.412 on this 50-point scale:

25 + (325 - 335.352) / 4 = 22.412

In the 1932 American League, .1632795 of assists were recorded by third basemen:

League Assists	14368
League Assists by third basemen	2346

For the 1932 Athletics, expected assists at third base would be 312.937:

The Team Assists total	1736
Times .1632795 =	283.453
Plus 914 divided by 31 =	312.937

Philadelphia third basemen actually had only 269 assists in 1932. This scores at 14.016 on this 50-point scale:

25 + (269 - 312.937) / 4 = 14.016

In other words, we believe that Philadelphia third basemen in 1932 had relatively poor range. The 35-year-old Jimmy Dykes, who had a chronic weight problem, was the A's regular third baseman.

In the 1890 Players League, .1657069 of assists were recorded by third basemen:

League Assists	13892
League Assists by third basemen	2302

For the New York Giants, expected assists at third base would be 283.027:

The Team Assists total	1708
Times .1657069 =	283.027

We don't make an adjustment for the LHP+/-, because teams in 1890 didn't platoon.

Giant third basemen actually had 268 assists in 1890. This scores at 21.243 on this 50-point scale:

25 + (268 - 283.027) / 4 = 21.243

30-Point Scale (Third Base Errors)

A Factor	Errors at Third Base
B Factor	Expected Errors at Third Base
Formula	15 + (B - A) / 2

(Bounded at zero and thirty)

Expected errors at third base are established as Plays Made by the team's third basemen (Putouts and Assists), divided by the league fielding percentage at third base, minus the Plays Made.

St. Louis Cardinal third basemen in 1998 had 325 assists, 104 putouts, thus 429 plays made. The league fielding percentage at third base was .9573601. Thus, we would expect Cardinal third basemen to be charged with 19.107 errors—429, divided by .9573601, minus 429.

Cardinal third basemen were actually charged with 21 errors. Thus, the Cardinal third basemen score at 14.054 on this 30-point scale:

15 + (19.107 - 21) / 2 = 14.054

This construction is slightly non-parallel from the "error percentage" element of the previous positions, although it amounts to about the same thing. Had I used the "error percentage" construction here parallel to the one used at the previous positions, I would have gotten a slightly different result here, although not different enough to make a very large difference in the final outcome. I can't really explain why I decided to switch the form, except that, in designing this system, I felt a need to orient myself about the relative cost of one error as opposed to the value of one assist or one double play.

The 1932 Philadelphia A's had 269 assists, 152 putouts, thus 421 plays made. The league fielding percentage at third base was .9498302. Thus, we would expect A's third basemen to be charged with 22.237 errors—421, divided by .9498302, minus 421.

Philadelphia third basemen were actually charged with only 10 errors. Thus, the A's third basemen score at 21.1186 on this 30-point scale:

15 + (22.237 - 10) / 2 = 21.1186

New York Players League Giants third basemen in 1890 had 268 assists, 175 putouts, thus 443 plays made. The league fielding percentage at third base was .8534640. Thus, we would expect New York third basemen to be charged with 76.0611 errors—443, divided by .8534640, minus 443.

Giant third basemen were actually charged with 75 errors. Thus, the New York third basemen score at 15.531 on this 30-point scale:

15 + (76.0611 - 75) / 2 = 15.531

First 10-Point Scale (Sacrifice Hits Allowed)

A Factor	Sac Hits Allowed by team, Divided by (Games Plus Losses)
B Factor	League average of the same
Formula	10 - ((A/B) * 5)

(Bounded by zero and ten, and all teams prior to 1931 receive 5.000 points on this scale)

Let's do the 1963 Orioles, for a change. The Orioles allowed 79 Sacrifice Hits, and lost 76 games. That makes Baltimore's figure .3319 (79/238). The league average is .2954. Thus, the Orioles score 4.38 on this 10-point scale:

10 - ((.3319 / .2954) * 5) = 4.381

The 1998 Cardinals allowed 92 sacrifice bunts (second-highest in the league), played 163 games, and lost 79. Thus, their "A" factor is .3801653—92, divided by 242.

The league data is 1163 sacrifice hits allowed, 2596 games played, and 1299 losses. Thus, the "B" factor is .2985879.

Thus, the 1998 Cardinals receive 3.63395 points on this ten-point scale:

10 - ((.3801653 / .2985879) * 5) = 3.63395

The 1932 A's allowed 75 sacrifice bunts (second-lowest in the league), played 154 games, and lost 60. Thus, their "A" factor is .35404673 (75, divided by 214).

The league data is 714 sacrifice hits allowed, 1230 games played, and 612 losses. Thus, the "B" factor is .3876222.

Thus, the 1932 A's receive 5.4793 points on this ten-point scale:

10 - ((.35404673 / .3876222) * 5) = 5.4793

The 1890 Giants, and all teams prior to 1931, score at 5.000 on this scale, since prior to 1931 the definition of a sacrifice hit is inconsistent, and I really don't know of anything else to replace the data.

As an explanation, we decided not to use third base putouts as an element of the third base claim percentage system, since I was unable to determine that there was any relationship of any kind between the number of third base putouts and quality defensive play. This will be explained in an article later in the book.

Once we lost putouts, which were the 20-point element in the third base system until I realized that they didn't mean squat, we faced the question of what to replace them with. I thought we might be able to use Sacrifice Hits allowed, since it is, to a significant degree, a third baseman's responsibility to field bunts. A problem here is that Sacrifice Hits increase significantly as losses increase. How much?

Sacrifice Hits allowed are essentially proportional to Games Played plus losses. If you compare a 90-72 team to a 72-90 team, the 72-90 team will have about 8% more Sacrifice Hits allowed. But are sacrifice hits, adjusted for this, an indicator of skill at third base?

I did a study in which I compared the defensive statistics at third base of (a) teams with Gold Glove third basemen, (b) teams which had defensive problems at third base, and (c) teams chosen at random. Of the 50 teams with Gold Glove third basemen, 31 were better than average in this category. Among teams with third base problems, 27 of 50 were below average.

Well, that's *something*, I guess—certainly it is better than the same data regarding third base putouts—but it's not sufficient to make Sac Hits allowed, even adjusted, the 20% factor in third base claim points.

I decided on a 50-30-10-10 split at third base, a system based 50% on third base assists, 30% on fielding percentage, 10% on sacrifice hits allowed, 10% on double plays, because I thought third base putouts were meaningless, and sacrifice hits allowed, while marginally meaningful, were not significant enough to do 20% of the work of evaluating the position.

Second 10-Point Scale (Double Plays)

A Factor	Double Plays by Third Basemen
B Factor	Expected Double Plays at Third Base
Formula	5 + (A - B)/2

Expected Double Plays at third base are established by:

1. The team's expected double plays, figured earlier

2. Multiplied by the league percentage of double plays in which third basemen participate

In the National League in 1998, third basemen participated in 471 of 2415 double plays, or .195031. The Cardinals expected double plays were 160.7498, thus the Cardinal expected double plays at third base are 31.3512.

Cardinal third basemen actually participated in only 23 double plays, well below expectation. Thus, they receive only 0.824 Claim Points on this ten-point scale:

5 + (23 - 31.3512) / 2 = 0.824.

In the 1932 American League, third basemen participated in 207 of 1197 double plays, or .1729323. The Athletics expected double plays were 137.2083, thus the A's expected double plays at third base are 23.727749.

Philadelphia third basemen actually participated in 21 double plays. Thus, they receive 3.636 Claim Points on this ten-point scale:

5 + (21 - 23.727749) / 2 = 3.636.

In the Players League, third basemen participated in 186 of 841 double plays, or .221165. The Giants expected double plays were 96.99975, thus the Giants expected double plays at third base are 21.452976.

New York third basemen actually participated in 16 double plays. Thus, they receive 2.2735 Claim Points on this ten-point scale:

5 + (16 - 21.452976) / 2 = 2.2735

Combining the Third Base Elements into Claim Percentages

To form the Claim Percentage at third base, we add together these four elements and divide by 100. For the 1998 Cardinals, this makes a claim percentage of .409:

50-point factor (Assists)	22.412
30-point factor (Errors)	14.054
10-point factor (Sac Hits Allowed)	3.634
10-point factor (Double Plays)	0.824
Total	40.924
Claim Percentage	.409

All four elements of the claim percentage for Cardinal third basemen are relatively poor. For the 1932 A's, we have a claim percentage of .442:

50-point factor (Assists)	14.016
30-point factor (Errors)	21.119
10-point factor (Sac Hits Allowed)	5.479
10-point factor (Double Plays)	3.636
Total	44.250
Claim Percentage	.442

Our belief, in other words, is that while the 35-year-old Dykes was still pretty good at fielding bunts and made relatively few errors, his lack of range still made him a below-average third baseman.

For the 1890 New York Giants (third baseman: Art Whitney), we have almost the same third base claim percentage, .440:

50-point factor (Assists)	21.243
30-point factor (Errors)	15.531
10-point factor (Sac Hits Allowed)	5.000
10-point factor (Double Plays)	2.274
Total	44.047
Claim Percentage	.440

Claim Percentages for Shortstops

The scales for Shortstops are Assists vs. Expected Shortstop Assists (40%), Double Plays (30%), Error Percentage (20%), and Putouts as a percentage of the team total (10%).

The Rating Percentage systems for Shortstops and Second Basemen are largely the same. For second basemen, we have a 40-point scale for double plays and a 30-point scale for assists, whereas for shortstops it is the other way around. I made assists the 40-point factor at shortstop and double plays the 40-point factor at second because it is my perception that a shortstop is evaluated first of all by his range, while a second baseman is evaluated first of all by his ability to turn the double play. Also, the standard deviation of double plays by second basemen (figured on a team level) is substantially larger than the standard deviation of double plays by shortstops, whereas the standard deviation of assists is slightly larger at short than at second.

The Formulas for Shortstop Rating Points are:

40-Point Scale (Assists)

A Factor	Shortstop Assists
B Factor	Expected Shortstop Assists
Formula	20 + (A - B) / 4

Expected Shortstop Assists are figured as:
The Team Assists Total
Times the League Percentage of Assists which are by shortstops
Plus 1/100 of the LHP+/-

For example, the 1956 Cincinnati Reds (shortstop, Roy McMillan). The Reds had 1722 team assists. For the league as a whole, .27658 of assists were recorded by shortstops. This creates an (initial) expectation of 476.28 assists by Cincinnati shortstops.

The Reds LHP+/- in 1956 was -2. Dividing that by 100 reduces the Reds expected shortstop assists to 476.26. The Reds actually had 527 shortstop assists that year, 50.74 more than expected. Their points on this scale are:

20 + (527 - 476.26) / 4

Which gives them 32.69 points on this 40-point scale.

On the other hand, the 1953 Detroit Tigers (shortstop, Harvey Kuenn) had 1783 team assists. For the league, .28422 of assists were by shortstops; this creates an expectation of 506.76 assists.

The Tigers LHP+/- was +230, so we add 2.30 to this figure, making an expectation of 509.06 assists. The Tigers actually had 450 assists by shortstops that year, 59.06 fewer than expected. Their points on this scale are:

20 + (450 - 509.06) / 4

Which gives them 5.24 points on this 40-point scale. This large difference will eventually, several steps down the road, cause Roy McMillan to rate as a very good shortstop, and Harvey Kuenn as a very poor one.

The 1998 St. Louis Cardinals (shortstop, Royce Clayton) had 1781 team assists. For the league as a whole, .2814669 of assists were recorded by shortstops (7744 of 27513). This creates an initial expectation of 501.29 assists by St. Louis shortstops.

The Cards LHP+/- in 1956 was -27. Dividing that by 100 reduces the Cardinals expected shortstop assists to 501.02. The Cardinals actually had 554 shortstop assists that year, 52.98 more than expected. Their points on this scale are:

20 + (554 - 501.02) / 4 = 33.244

Which gives them 33.244 points on this 40-point scale.

The 1932 Philadelphia A's (shortstop, Eric McNair) had 1736 team assists. For the league, .26462 of assists were by shortstops; this creates an expectation of 459.37 assists.

The A's LHP+/- was +914, so we add 9.14 to this figure, making an expectation of 468.51 assists. The A's actually had 447 assists by shortstops that year, 21.51 fewer than expected. Their points on this scale are:

20 + (447 - 468.51) / 4

Which gives them 14.622 points on this 40-point scale.

The 1890 New York Giants of the Players League (shortstop, Danny Richardson) had 1708 team assists. For the league as a whole, .2525194 of assists were recorded by shortstops (3508 of 13892). This creates an expectation of 431.30 assists by New York shortstops.

Since teams in 1890 did not platoon, we won't worry about the left/right bias of the pitching staff in this case. The Giants actually had 429 shortstop assists that year, 2.30 less than expected. Their points on this scale are:

20 + (429 - 431.30) / 4

Which gives them 19.4242 points on this 40-point scale.

30-Point Scale (Double Plays vs. Expectation)

A Factor	Double Plays by the Team
B Factor	Expected Double Plays
Formula	15 + (A - B) / 4

The 1998 Cardinals had 160 double plays, 160.7498 expected double plays; we've already run through the math on that. Thus, they receive 14.81 Claim Points on this 30-point scale. In chart form:

Year	Team	DP	Ex DP	Claim Points
1998	Cardinals	160	160.74979	14.81256
1932	Athletics	142	137.22083	16.19793
1890	Giants	94	96.99975	14.25006

20-Point Scale (Error Percentage)

The same for Shortstops as for Second Basemen.

A Factor	Team Error Percentage at Shortstop
B Factor	League average of same
Formula	20 - 10 * (A/B)

The 1998 Cardinal shortstops had 554 assists, 259 putouts, 34 errors, an error percentage of .0401417. The league data was 7744 assists, 3937 putouts and 392 errors, an error percentage of .0324691. This makes 7.64 points on this 20-point scale:

Year	Team/League	A	PO	E	Error Pct
1998	Cardinals	554	259	34	.0401417
1998	National League	7744	3937	392	.0324691

A divided by B	1.2363022
A divided by B times 10	12.363022
Twenty minus that	7.636978

For the 1932 Philadelphia A's, whose shortstop fielding percentage was better than the league average, we get a figure of 11.40:

Year	Team/League	A	PO	E	Error Pct
1932	Philadelphia	447	267	38	.0505319
1932	American League	3802	2540	396	.0587711

A divided by B	.8598082
A divided by B times 10	8.598082
Twenty minus that	11.401918

The shortstops for the 1890 New York Giants committed 105 errors, which was almost the league average at that time, and results in 9.83 points on this 20-point scale:

Year	Team/League	A	PO	E	Error Pct
1890	NY Giants	429	247	105	.134443
1890	Players League	3508	1916	826	.13216

A divided by B	1.0172747
A divided by B times 10	10.172747
Twenty minus that	9.827253

10-Point Scale (Putouts as a Percentage of Team)

Again, this is the same for Shortstops as it is for Second Basemen, except that the adjustments are different.

A Factor	Team Putouts at Shortstop
B Factor	Expected Putouts at Shortstop
Formula	5 + (A - B) / 15

Expected Putouts at Shortstop Are Established as:

Team Putouts
Minus Strikeouts
Times the League Percentage of non-K putouts which are made by shortstops
+ 1/14 of walks above (or below) the league average (per inning)
Minus 1/64 of the LHP+/-

For the 1947 St. Louis Cardinals (Marty Marion), this figures as:

4192 Putouts by team	4192
Minus 642 K	3550
Times .085125	302.19
Plus (495 - [(4476/10967.33)*1397.67])/14	296.81
Minus (376/64)	290.93

The Cardinals would be expected to have 290.9 putouts by shortstops. They actually had 350, so that scores at 8.94 on this 10-point scale:

5 + (350 - 290.8) / 15 = 8.94

For the 1998 Cardinals, this works out as follows:

Team Putouts	(4409)	4409
Minus Strikeouts (972)	4409 - 972 =	3437
Times the League Percentage of non-K Putouts which are made by Shortstops	(3937 of 52168, .0754677) =	259.38255
+1/14 of walks above (or below) the league norm	558 - 552.895 = 5.104 / 14 =	.3646
which makes		259.74715
Minus 1/64 of the LHP+/-	-27/64 = + .421875 =	260.16902

We expect the 1998 Cardinal shortstops to be credited with 260.16902 putouts. They were actually credited with 259. This makes 4.92 points on this ten-point scale:

5 + (259 - 260.16902) / 15 = 4.922 065

For the 1932 Philadelphia A's, we have 294.93 expected putouts:

Team Putouts	(4160)	4160
Minus Strikeouts	595 =	3565
Times the League Percentage of non-K Putouts which are made by Shortstops	(2540 of 28994, .0876043) =	312.30944
+1/14 of walks above (or below) the league norm	511 - 554.41679 = -43.41679 / 14 =	-3.10120
which makes		309.20824
Minus 1/64 of the LHP+/-	-914/64 = 014.28125 =	294.9270

We expect the 1932 Philadelphia shortstops to be credited with 294.927 putouts. They were actually credited with 267. This makes 3.1382004 points on this ten-point scale:

5 + (267 - 294.9269) / 15 = 3.1382004

For the 1890 New York Giants, we have 239.66 expected putouts:

Team Putouts	3512	3512
Minus Strikeouts	449 =	3063
Times the League Percentage of non-K Putouts which are made by Shortstops	(1916 of 24783, .077311) =	236.80378
+1/14 of walks above (or below) the league norm	569 - 528.95397 = +40.04603 / 14 =	+2.86043
which makes		239.66421

Again, we don't worry about the left/right stuff in 1890. We expect the 1890 Giant shortstops to be credited with 239.66421 putouts. They were actually credited with 247. This makes 5.489053 points on this ten-point scale:

5 + (247 - 239.66421) / 15 = 5.489053

Combining the Shortstop Elements into Claim Percentages

To form the Claim Percentage at shortstop, we add together these four elements and divide by 100. For the 1998 Cards, this makes a claim percentage of .606:

40-point factor (Assists)	33.244
30-point factor (Double Plays)	14.813
20-point factor (Error Percentage)	7.637
10-point factor (Putouts)	4.922
Total	60.616
Claim Percentage	.606

In English, our conclusion is that the Cardinal shortstops, primarily Royce Clayton, were ordinary at turning the double play and a little bit error-prone; nonetheless, because they had excellent range, well above average defensively. For the 1932 A's, we have a claim percentage of .454:

40-point factor (Assists)	14.622
30-point factor (Double Plays)	16.198
20-point factor (Error Percentage)	11.402
10-point factor (Putouts)	3.138
Total	45.360
Claim Percentage	.454

Our belief, in other words, is that while McNair was not error-prone and was OK on the double play, he was not a particularly good shortstop because his range was limited. McNair, who hit 47 doubles and 18 homers in 1932, began converting to second base and third base the following season, suggesting that the A's also regarded him as perhaps not having the range of a top-flight shortstop.

For the 1890 New York Giants (shortstop Danny Richardson and others), we have an almost-average claim percentage, .490:

40-point factor (Assists)	19.424
30-point factor (Double Plays)	14.250
20-point factor (Error Percentage)	9.827
10-point factor (Putouts)	5.489
Total	48.991
Claim Percentage	.490

Claim Percentages in the Outfield

Outfield Claim Percentages post-1954 are based on a 40-30-20-10 system. The 40-point scale in derived from outfield putouts, the 30-point scale from the team's (park-adjusted) DER, the 20-point scale from what I call Arm Elements, and the 10-point scale from errors.

Prior to 1954 there is no data (or sporadic data) on Sacrifice Flies allowed by teams. This makes the Arm Elements less interesting and less useful, and for that reason, pre-1954, the Arm Elements are reduced to a 10-point (10 percent) factor in the analysis.

To compensate, the park-adjusted DER points will be, at that time, increased from a 30-point (30 percent) factor into a second 40-point factor, so that the system will continue to total up to 100 points.

40-Point Scale (Outfield Putouts)

A Factor	Outfield Putouts Divided by (Team Putouts Minus Strikeouts and Assists)
B Factor	League Average of same
Formula	20 + (A - B) * 100

(Bounded by 40 and zero)

The 1998 Cardinals had 4409 putouts, 972 strikeouts and 1781 assists, thus had 1656 putouts which were neither assisted nor strikeouts. Of these 1656, 1055 were recorded by outfielders. Thus, Cardinal outfielders accounted for .6370773 of the team's unassisted, non-K putouts.

In the National League as a whole there were 69,720 putouts, 17,552 strikeouts, and 27,513 assists—thus, 24,655 putouts unaccounted for. Of those, 16,258 were recorded by outfielders. This is .6594200.

Under the formula above, the St. Louis Cardinal outfielders thus receive 17.77 points on this scale:

20 + (.6370773 - .6594200) * 100
20 + (-.0223427) * 100
20 - 2.23427 = 17.76573

In other words, the St. Louis Cardinals made a relatively low percentage of their putouts in the outfield, which may indicate that they did not have outstanding range in their outfielders. (Their regular outfielders were Ron Gant, Ray Lankford and Brian Jordan.)

The data for the other two teams and leagues:

Yr	Tm /Lg	PO	SO	A	PO-SO-A	OFPO	OF PO Pct
1932	Phil	4160	595	1736	1829	1100	.6014215
1932	AL	33006	4012	14368	14626	8621	.5894298
1890	NY	3512	449	1708	1355	687	.5070111
1890	PL	27769	2986	13892	10891	6094	.5595446

This produces 21.19918 Claim Points for Philadelphia, 14.74665 for New York.

Earlier in the process of researching this book, I made note of a previously un-noticed shift in fielding statistics over time, which is the disappearance over time of 80% or more of catchers' putouts other than strikeouts.

Here we note a possibly related phenomenon, which is an increasing concentration, over time, of pop outs and fly balls into the outfield. In 1890, players other than outfielders caught about 44% of popouts and fly balls. By 1932, this percentage had declined to 41%; by 1998, to 34%. Apparently, over time, it has become less and less common for hitters to pop out.

30/40-Point Scale (Park-Adjusted DER)

This formula post-1954:

A Factor	DER Points (CL-1) from Stage 3
Formula	(A * .24) - 9

(Bounded by 30 and zero)

In stage three we used the team's park-adjusted Defensive Efficiency Record (DER) as an element in the determination of the percentage of defensive Win Shares that should belong to the pitchers, as opposed to the fielders.

The St. Louis Cardinals CL-1 figure was 98.348. Multiplying this by .24 and subtracting 9, we have 14.6035.

Pre-1954, we change the formula to this:

Formula	(A * .29) - 9

The Philadelphia A's 1932 CL-1 points were 107.1697. Multiplying this by .29 and subtracting nine, we then have 22.079210 Claim Points.

The 1890 New York Giants (PL) had a CL-1 of 150.6814, which is extremely high. Multiplying this by .29 and subtracting nine, we thus have 34.6976 Claim Points.

There is a logical problem with using Defensive Efficiency Records to evaluate outfielders, which is this. The Defensive Efficiency Record is a measure of a team's overall success at preventing hit baseballs from dropping in for hits. We are now measuring the relative contribution of outfielders to the success of the defense, and we are using the overall success of the defense to measure the value of the outfielders. We are perilously near, then, to circular definition—that is, concluding that the defensive outfield on a good team is always good because we all know that you can't win without a good defensive outfield.

I decided to go with it anyway, for three reasons. First, we are starved for data with which to evaluate outfielders. We need a lot more than we have. Second, it has long been my observation—informal, not supported by research—that when a team has a fast outfield, they tend to have a good Defensive Efficiency Record. Third, it is not illogical to argue that certain markers of defensive excellence may be tied to certain positions. If a team allows few stolen bases, we assume that they have good defensive catchers. If a team turns double plays, we credit this to the shortstops and second basemen. It is equally reasonable, when a team has a high DER, to associate this more with one defensive position than with another.

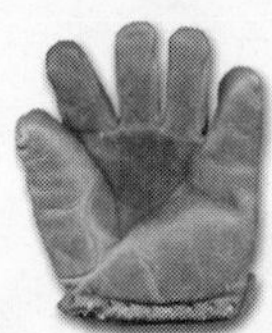

20-Point Scale (Arm Elements—1954 and on)

A Factor	Outfield Assists + Outfield Double Plays - Sacrifice Flies Allowed
B Factor	League Total of the same Times the TLPOP
Formula	10 + (A - B)/5

The 1998 Cardinals had 39 assists, and 15 double plays. The team allowed 45 Sacrifice Flies. This makes an "A Factor" of 9 (39 plus 15, minus 45).

In the National League as a whole there were 530 outfield assists, including 115 double plays. There were 684 Sacrifice Flies allowed in the league. This makes a league total in this category of -39.

The Cardinals Team/League Putout Percentage was .0658833. Multiplying this by -39, we then have a "B Factor" of -2.5694487. This yields a result of 12.31:

10 + (9 - (-2.5694487)) / 5
10 + (11.5694487) / 5
10 + 2.3138897 = 12.3138897

In other words, since this factor is larger than 10.00, we believe, based on the data, that the St. Louis outfielders in 1998 threw relatively well. Their total was positive; the league total was negative. They're better than average.

10-Point Scale (Assists Plus Double Plays—used prior to 1954)

A Factor	Outfield Assists Plus Double Plays B Factor
B Factor	League Total of the Same Times the TLPOP
Formula	5 + (A - B)/5

Lacking data on Sacrifice Flies Allowed, we reduce the significance attached to this category, making it a 10-point scale rather than a 20-point scale.

The 1932 Athletics had 28 Outfield Assists, and 9 Double Plays. This makes an "A Factor" of 37.

In the American League as a whole there were 297 outfield assists, including 70 double plays. This makes a league total in this category of 367.

The Athletics Team/League Putout Percentage was .1229565. Multiplying this by 367, we then have a "B Factor" of 45.125026. This yields a result of 3.374995:

5 + (37 - 45.125035) / 5
5 + (-8.125026) / 5
5 - 1.625005 = 3.374995

In other words, based on their relatively low assists totals, we are inclined to believe that the 1932 Philadelphia outfielders did not throw particularly well. However, since we are missing the key contrasting data of sacrifice flies allowed, we place relatively little weight on this.

The 1890 New York Giants had 61 Outfield Assists, and 10 Double Plays. This makes an "A Factor" of 71.

In the Players League as a whole there were 592 outfield assists, including 121 double plays. This makes a league total in this category of 713.

The Giants Team/League Putout Percentage was .1235928. Multiplying this by 713, we then have a "B Factor" of 88.12166. This yields a result of 1.57567:

5 + (71 - 88.12166) / 5 = 1.57567

10-Point Scale (Outfield Error Percentage)

A Factor	Outfield Error Percentage
B Factor	League average of same
Formula	10 - 5 * (A/B)

For the 1998 Cardinals, this would be:

A Factor:	32 / (1055 + 39 + 32)
B Factor:	348 / (16258 + 530 + 348)
Formula	10 - 5 * (A/B)
A Factor:	.0284192
B Factor:	.0203081
Formula	10 - 5 * (.0284192 / .0203081)

Which is 3.003001.

The 1932 Philadelphia Athletics had an Outfield Error Percentage of .0182768, against an American League average of .0334887. Under the formula before, this yields an output of 7.271202.

The 1890 New York Giants had an Outfield Error Percentage of .0966184, against a Players League average of .0963644. Under the formula before, this yields an output of 4.986822.

Combining the Outfield Elements into Claim Percentages

As we did at the other positions, we add up these four scales, and divide by a hundred. For the 1998 St. Louis Cardinal outfielders, this produces a claim percentage of:

40-point factor (Putouts)	17.7657
30-point factor (DER)	14.6035
20-point factor (Arm Elements)	12.3139
10-point factor (Error Percentage)	3.0030
Total	47.6862
Claim Percentage	.477

In other words, we believe that the 1998 Cardinal outfield was slightly below average defensively.

For the 1932 A's, we have a claim percentage of .539:

40-point factor (Putouts)	21.1992
Second 40-point factor (DER)	22.0792
10-point factor (Arm Elements)	3.3750
10-point factor (Errors)	7.2712
Total	53.9246
Claim Percentage	.539

In other words, we believe that the 1932 Athletics had a relatively good defensive outfield—but not quite as good as that of the 1890 New York Giants:

40-point factor (Putouts)	14.7466
Second 40-point factor (DER)	34.6976
10-point factor (Arm Elements)	1.5757
10-point factor (Errors)	4.9868
Total	56.0067
Claim Percentage	.560

Converting the Claim Percentages into Fielding Win Shares

So far, in the last six articles, we have figured a Claim Percentage for every position for each team. But to reach our goal of assigning Win Shares to each individual season, there are still three things we must do:

1. Convert the Claim Percentages into Claim Points
2. Convert the Claim Points into Win Shares
3. Assign the Win Shares to individual fielders

To convert the Claim Percentages into Claim Points, we do two things:

1. Subtract .200 from each Claim Percentage, and
2. Multiply the Claim Percentage (-.200) for each position by the intrinsic weight assigned to that defensive position.

The intrinsic weights in modern baseball are:

Catcher	38 points	(19%)
First Base	12 points	(6%)
Second Base	32 points	(16%)
Third Base	24 points	(12%)
Shortstop	36 points	(18%)
Outfield	58 points	(29%)

The rating percentage for each position, minus .200, is multiplied by the intrinsic weight of the position to produce the claim points for that position.

Suppose that there were a team on which every position had a rating percentage of .500. On that team, the claim points for catchers would be 11.4 and the total claim points for the team's fielders would be 60.00. The catchers would thus receive 19% of the Win Shares allocated to that's team's fielders—11.4, divided by 60. The first basemen would receive 6%, the second basemen would receive 16%, etc.; each position would receive the percentage of Win Shares which are intrinsic to the position.

On the 1998 St. Louis Cardinals, the Claiming Percentages by position are:

Catcher	First Base	Second Base	Third Base	Shortstop	Outfield
.484	.421	.482	.409	.606	.477

From those, we subtract .200, producing:

Catcher	First Base	Second Base	Third Base	Shortstop	Outfield
.484	.421	.482	.409	.606	.477
.284	.221	.282	.209	.406	.277

These figures we then multiply by the intrinsic weights, producing:

Catcher	First Base	Second Base	Third Base	Shortstop	Outfield
.484	.421	.482	.409	.606	.477
.284	.221	.282	.209	.406	.277
X 38	X 12	X 32	X 24	X 36	X 58
10.79	2.65	9.02	5.02	14.61	16.06

The "Claim Points" for these six positions total up to 58.17. The Win Shares assigned to the 1998 Cardinal fielders, back on page 32, were 35.0254. Thus, for each Claim Point, we award .602163 Win Shares, producing:

Catcher	First Base	Second Base	Third Base	Shortstop	Outfield
.484	.421	.484	.409	.606	.477
.284	.221	.284	.209	.406	.277
X 38	X 12	X 32	X 24	X 36	X 58
10.79	2.65	9.09	5.02	14.61	16.06
X .602	X.602	X .602	X .602	X .602	X .602
6.50	1.60	5.43	3.02	8.80	9.67

St. Louis catchers in 1998 will be credited with 6.50 Win Shares, their first basemen with 1.60, their second basemen with 5.43, etc.

A few small points by way of explanation:

1. The Intrinsic Weights have changed only once in baseball history. Prior to 1930, the intrinsic weight for second base was 26 points; for third base,

30. In the 1930s the intrinsic weight shifted to 28 points for each position, and beginning in 1946, to 32 points for second base, 24 for third. There is an article in Section IV which discusses why the defensive spectrum jumped, and documents that it did.

2. You may wonder why the intrinsic weight given to catchers is greater than the intrinsic weight given to shortstops. The answer is, I tried it the other way, not once but repeatedly, and it simply doesn't work.

Catchers don't play nearly as many innings as shortstops. For this reason, even with more weight being given to catchers than to shortstops, the most valuable defensive player on most teams is the regular shortstop. If you give as much weight to shortstop as you do to catcher, it becomes extremely rare for the regular catcher to receive as many defensive Win Shares as the regular shortstop.

3. The effective distribution of Win Shares in the outfield, at the completion of the fifth stage, is about 1-2-1, center fielders receiving about twice as many defensive Win Shares as left or right fielders. Thus, center fielders in this system are rated just slightly behind second basemen, receiving about 14% of the team's Win Shares, while left and right fielders tend to receive 7% each—a little bit more than first basemen.

4. Before multiplying the Claim Percentage for each position times the inherent weight of the position, we subtract .200 from the Claim Percentage (but do not reduce it below .000, for those very rare cases where the claim percentage at a position is below .200).

This was a very late change to the Win Shares system; the system was designed to work without this reduction (-.200), and then at the last minute that was inserted. The effect of the change is to de-centralize the Win Shares, giving more Win Shares to the best defensive players on a team, and fewer to the weaker players on the team. This, in effect, reduces the advantage of playing on a good defensive team, and allows a good defensive player on a poor defensive team to move up closer to the good defensive players on good teams.

This adjustment is logically consistent with the rest of the analytical structure, in that it assumes that performance has to exceed a certain level of competence before it can be said to have value. A player who creates 2.00 runs per 27 outs in a league where the norm is 4.00 runs per 27 outs is not considered to have one-half the value of an average hitter. His offense is zeroed out. This assumes that an offensive winning percentage of .200 is equivalent to zero value, since a player who creates runs at a level one-half the league norm has an offensive winning percentage of .200.

Intuitively, we would assume that a player who creates 50 runs while making 400 outs does not have one-half the offensive value of a player who creates 100 runs with 400 outs. Basically, that would be assuming that Dal Maxvill (offensive winning percentage: .257) has one-half the offensive value of an average hitter (Hubie Brooks or Terry Pendleton, both of whom had career offensive winning percentages of .500). In the same way, it is awkward to assume that a player who has a defensive winning percentage of .250 has one-half the value of a player who has a defensive winning percentage of .500, since this assumes that a terrible defensive player has one-half the value of an average defensive player.

But the alternative bothered me for a long time, because of the way that we have to figure claim percentages, on the team level. If we zero out a position, we zero out everybody who played the position for that team, even if *one* of the people who played the position was actually pretty good. That bothered me, plus a lot of our analysis of defensive play is new. We haven't worked with it for 20 years, as we have hitters, and I just didn't have a lot of confidence that, if we made this change, we would actually be helping the best defensive players.

My thinking on this issue turned around, however, when I searched for real cases in which a good defensive player would be zeroed out by the incompetence of the other people who played the position for the same team—and concluded that there was not a single such case, in all of baseball history. There aren't very many teams, in all of baseball history, which have had claim percentages below .200 at a position—I think there are five teams in baseball history which are below .200 at a position (2 at catcher, 2 at shortstop, 1 outfield). None of those are really problematic. The *most* problematic of the five are the catchers for the 1987 Rangers, who were all poor defensive catchers.

The 1932 A's. . . in the 1930s, the distribution of inherent weights are as follows:

Catcher	38 points	(19%)
First Base	12 points	(6%)
Second Base	28 points	(14%)
Third Base	28 points	(14%)
Shortstop	36 points	(18%)
Outfield	58 points	(29%)

The same as now except at second and third base. For the 1932 A's, the Claiming Percentages by position are:

Catcher	First Base	Second Base	Third Base	Short-stop	Outfield
.727	.660	.555	.442	.454	.539

These Claiming Percentages work against a total of 46.6968 Win Shares, which are to be distributed to the 1932 Philadelphia fielders. Working through the system as explained before, we arrive at this:

Catcher	First Base	Second Base	Third Base	Short-stop	Outfield
.727	.660	.555	.442	.454	.539
.527	.460	.355	.242	.254	.339
X 38	X 12	X 28	X 28	X 36	X 58
20.03	5.52	9.94	6.78	9.14	19.66
X .657	X .657	X .657	X .657	X .657	X .657
13.16	3.63	6.53	4.45	6.01	12.92

Prior to 1930, the distribution of inherent weights is as follows:

Catcher	38 points	(19%)
First Base	12 points	(6%)
Second Base	26 points	(13%)
Third Base	30 points	(15%)
Shortstop	36 points	(18%)
Outfield	58 points	(29%)

Still the same except at second and third. For the 1890 New York Giants of the Players League, the Claiming Percentages by position are:

Catcher	First Base	Second Base	Third Base	Short-stop	Outfield
.506	.770	.517	.441	.490	.560

These Claiming Percentages work against a total of 42.2284 Win Shares, which are to be distributed to the 1890 New York fielders. Working through the system as explained before, we arrive at this:

Catcher	First Base	Second Base	Third Base	Short-stop	Outfield
.506	.770	.517	.440	.490	.560
.306	.570	.317	.240	.290	.360
X 38	X 12	X 26	X 30	X 36	X 58
11.63	6.84	8.24	7.20	10.44	20.88
X .647	X .647	X .647	X .647	X .647	X .647
7.53	4.43	5.34	4.66	6.76	13.52

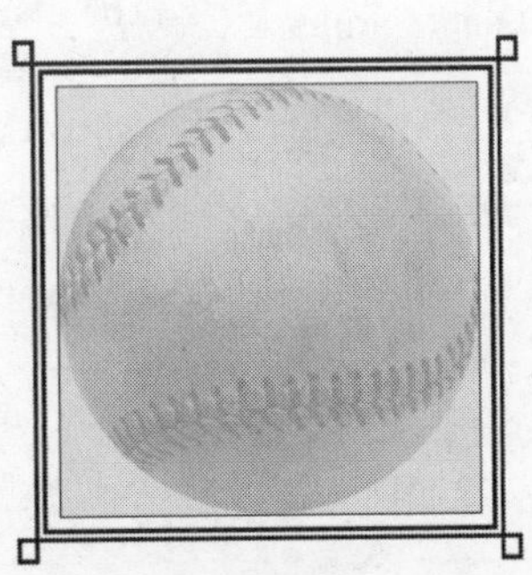

Assigning Win Shares to Individual Fielders

At this point we have assigned Win Shares to each fielding *position* in the history of baseball—that is, to the third basemen on the 1932 Athletics, to the third basemen on the 1890 New York Giants, to the third basemen on the 1998 Cardinals. . . to the third basemen on every team in baseball history, to the players at every position on every team. We still need to assign those Win Shares from teams to individual players.

This process is relatively simple, at least compared to the endless formulas used to assign Win Shares from teams to fielding positions. It has to be simple because basic defensive statistics—putouts, assists, errors and double plays—are not all that complicated, and there just isn't that much you can do with them.

These basic defensive statistics are converted into claim points, and the claim points are used to assign Win Shares to individuals. We'll start, again, with the catchers.

Catchers—Pre-1900

The claim formula for catchers pre-1900 is this:

2PO + 4A - 3E - PB + 4DP

Where PO is putouts, A is assists, E is errors, PB is passed balls, and DP is double plays.

In the last stage of this analysis, we determined that the catchers for the 1890 New York Giants (of the Players League) would receive 7.53 Win Shares for their defense. The three catchers on that team were Buck Ewing (sometimes cited as the greatest player in 19th century baseball), Willard Brown and Farmer Vaughn. This is their data:

Player	PO	A	E	PB	DP
Ewing	372	107	26	43	7
Brown	124	38	18	17	1
Vaughn	102	19	17	10	3

For Ewing, we multiply his putouts (372) by two, making 744. We multiply his assists (107) by four, making 428, for a total of 1172. We multiply his errors (26) by three, making 78, reducing the total to 1094. We subtract his Passed Balls (43), making 1051. We multiply his Double Plays (7) by four, making 28, bringing us back up to 1079. Ewing has 1079 Claim Points against the Giants total of 7.52 Win Shares:

Player	PO	A	E	PB	DP	Claim Points
Ewing	372	107	26	43	7	1079
Brown	124	38	18	17	1	333
Vaughn	102	19	17	10	3	231

Ewing, who has 62% of the putouts by Giants catchers, has 66% of the claim points, because his ratio of "good numbers" to "bad numbers" is better than the other catchers. The three Giant catchers have 1643 Claim Points among them, so each catcher's Win Shares can be determined by multiplying his Claim Points by 7.53—the Win Shares available—and dividing by 1643:

Player	Claim Points	Win Shares
Ewing	1079	4.94
Brown	333	1.53
Vaughn	231	1.06

Buck Ewing has 4.94 Win Shares for his work as the Giants catcher in 1890.

Catchers—1900 to 1930

The claim formula for catchers 1900 to 1930 is this:

PO + 2A - 4E - 2PB + 4DP

The 1925 Cleveland Indians had two catchers, Glenn Myatt (who was a good hitter but a poor fielder), and Luke Sewell (who was an outstanding fielder but an inconsistent hitter). They also had a couple of backup catchers, Frank McCrea and Roxy Walters, who played a few innings. This is the data for their four catchers, and the Claim Points resulting:

Player	G	PO	A	E	PB	DP	Claim Points
Myatt	98	273	53	9	4	6	359
Sewell	66	222	54	8	4	13	342
Walters	5	8	7	0	0	1	26
McCrea	1	4	0	0	0	0	4

In the last stage of this analysis, we determined that the catchers for the 1925 Indians would receive 4.80 Win Shares for their defense (a low total). Dividing the Win Shares in the same proportions as the Claim Points, we wind up with 2.36 Win Shares for Myatt, 2.24 for Sewell, .17 for Walters, and .03 for McCrea. Per inning, Sewell ranks ahead in 1925, as he did throughout his career:

Player	Estimated Defensive Innings	Win Shares	Win Shares Per 1000 EDI
Sewell, 1925	592	2.24	3.79
Sewell, career	13121	74.45	5.67
Myatt, 1925	742	2.36	3.17
Myatt, career	5220	23.39	4.48
Walters, 1925	32	0.17	5.33
Walters, career	3914	23.60	6.03

Walters had an eleven-year career as a backup catcher despite a career slugging percentage—not batting average, *slugging percentage*—of .259; thus, the evaluation of him as an outstanding defensive catcher seems reasonable.

You may wonder why the formula needs to change over time. Well, the catchers for the 1876 Philadelphia Athletics, who were working without a mask, shin guards, a chest protector or a glove, were charged with 110 errors and 109 passed balls in 66 games. If you applied any modern formula to those catchers, they would all wind up with negative totals. This is realistic in a sense, since any modern catcher who had error and passed ball rates even one-third or one-fourth that high would be considered too horrible defensively to actually put on the field. But it doesn't work in evaluating those catchers, since, with negative numbers, additional Win Shares would be "claimed" with additional errors. Modern catchers are expected to have an extremely high ratio of putouts to errors.

But conversely, the 1870s formula doesn't work for 1990, either, because, in order to make a 1870s formula work, we have to reduce the cost of an error (relative to a putout) so low that the errors become essentially meaningless. So we have to use different formulas for different eras.

Catchers—1931 through 1986

In 1900 the fielding percentage for catchers was about .950; by 1930 it was up to about .980. For the years 1931 through 1986, the claim formula we will use is:

PO + 4A - 8E - 4PB + 6DP

In essence, we have increased the value of the "skill elements" relative to the value of putouts, which are essentially a meter on the catcher's playing time.

The catchers for the 1932 Philadelphia A's were Mickey Cochrane (about 1,177 innings), Johnny Heving (about 151 innings) and Ed Madjeski (about 58 innings). This is their data and resulting claim points:

Player	G	PO	A	E	PB	DP	Claim Points
Cochrane	137	652	94	5	11	15	1034
Heving	28	85	5	0	3	2	105
Madjeski	8	30	7	0	1	3	72

In the last stage of this analysis, we determined that the catchers for the 1932 A's would be credited with 13.16 Win Shares (an enormous number). Splitting the Win Shares in the same proportions as the Claim Points, Cochrane receives 11.24 Win Shares, Heving receives 1.14, and Madjeski receives .78. Cochrane's 1932 total is the sixth-highest season total of all time, and the second-highest season rated without modern (post-1987) data.

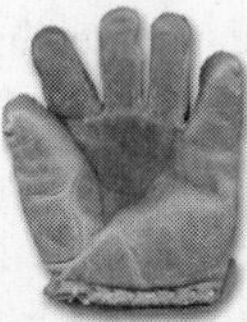

Catchers—1987 to Now

Since 1987, when STATS began tracking every pitch of every major league game, we have a great deal of data which we do not have for most of the game's history. Two elements of this—stolen base/caught stealing data and catcher ERAs—will change the way that we evaluate catchers in this stage. The new formula is:

Putouts	
Plus 2 times	(Assists minus opponents caught stealing)
Minus 8	X Errors
Plus 6	X Double Plays
Minus 4	X Passed Balls
Minus 2	X Stolen Bases Allowed
Plus 4	X Caught Stealing
Plus 2	X Runs Saved

Runs Saved are figured from the team ERA and the catcher ERA in a straightforward way. If the team's ERA is 4.00, but this catcher has caught nine innings with only three earned runs allowed in those nine innings, that is one run saved. If five runs are scored in those nine innings, the "runs saved" are negative one.

For the 1998 St. Louis Cardinals there were three catchers—Eli Marrero, Tom Lampkin and Tom Pagnozzi. This is their data:

Catcher	G	PO	A	E	DP	PB	SB	CS	IC	ER
Eli Marrero	73	426	30	4	3	1	32	12	613	256
Tom Lampkin	62	331	19	5	5	4	30	13	482.1	258
Tom Pagnozzi	44	259	17	5	5	1	30	10	374.1	189

Marrero gets 426 claim points for his putouts, and 36 for his 18 assists which did not result from caught stealing; that's 462 so far. He loses 32 claim points for his errors, reducing him to 430, but gets 18 for his double plays, bringing him back to 448. His passed ball costs him four points; that's 444. His 32 stolen bases allowed cost him 64 points, reducing him to 380, but his 12 runners caught stealing give him 48 back, pushing him back to 428.

The Cardinals on the season allowed 703 earned runs in 1469.2 innings. Since Marrero caught 613 innings, we would expect opponents to score 293.222 earned runs with Marrero catching. They actually allowed only 256, a difference of 37.222. Marrero gets two points for each run saved, giving him 74.445 additional points, for a total of 502.445. Summarizing the data for Eli and both Toms:

Catcher	PO	A	E	DP	PB	SB	CS	RS	Total
Eli Marrero	426	36	-32	18	-4	-64	48	74.44	502.44
Tom Lampkin	331	12	-40	30	-16	-60	52	-54.56	254.44
Tom Pagnozzi	259	14	-40	30	-4	-60	40	-19.88	219.12

Runs Saved are a zero-sum category for a team as a whole. In the last stage of this analysis, we determined that St. Louis catchers would be credited with 6.50 Win Shares in 1998. Dividing the Win Shares in the same proportions as the claim points, we have:

Catcher	Claim Points	Win Shares
Marrero	502.44	3.35
Lampkin	254.44	1.69
Pagnozzi	219.12	1.46

Eli Marrero receives 3.35 Win Shares for his work as the Cardinal catcher in 1998. The system interprets Marrero as being by far the best of the three Cardinal catchers (defensively) in that season.

You may wonder why, in this system, a catcher is charged eight points for an error, four for a passed ball, but is charged only two points for a run allowed. Isn't a run allowed more damaging than a passed ball or an error, you might ask, and shouldn't it be given more weight?

Yes, but there are a lot of things that go into a run scored that a catcher can't do anything about. When a catcher is charged with an error, we can assume that the catcher is largely responsible for that. When a run is scored against him, most of the time, there really wasn't anything he could have done about it. If a catcher has a good ERA in his innings caught, we consider that to be an *indication* that he is a good defensive catcher, but not clear proof.

Stating the same thing in another way. . . if we gave, let's say, ten points for each run saved, that would swamp the system. The number of points credited on this basis would be so large that nothing else would really count very much; the catcher with the best catcher ERA would be considered the best defensive catcher on the team, no matter what the rest of the data was. The catcher's ERA is interesting, but it does not justify that level of attention. It deserves to be considered as simply one factor among others.

Passed Balls are like "weak errors;" they're errors, but they don't (normally) make an on base/out distinction, just a base distinction. Also, the catcher really is not fully responsible for the Passed Ball in many cases; the PB is charged to the catcher, but it varies the pitcher as much or more than it does with the catcher.

First Base

The claiming formula for individual first basemen, from 1876 to the present, is this:

PO + 2A - 5E

Couldn't be any easier—or, if you prefer to look at it that way, any more primitive. For the first basemen on the 1998 St. Louis Cardinals, the data is as follows:

Player	PO	A	E	Claim Points
Mark McGwire	1326	97	12	1460
John Mabry	93	11	0	115
Brian Hunter	23	1	0	25
Gary Gaetti	15	0	0	15
Willie McGee	2	2	0	6
Tom Lampkin	5	0	0	5
Eli Marrero	1	1	0	3
Delino DeShields	0	0	0	0
Team Total				1629

In the previous stage of this analysis, we determined that Cardinal first basemen would be credited with 1.60 Win Shares for their defense. Dividing the Win Shares in the same proportions as the claim points, this makes 1.43 Win Shares for the regular first baseman, Mark McGwire:

Player	Claim Points	Win Shares
Mark McGwire	1460	1.43
John Mabry	115	.11
Brian Hunter	25	.02
Gary Gaetti	15	.01
Willie McGee	6	.01
Tom Lampkin	5	.00
Eli Marrero	3	.00
Delino DeShields	0	—
Team Total	1629	1.58

A rounding discrepancy of .02—kind of unusual, but it happens. We don't actually round these off at this stage of the analysis, which might, once in a blue moon, cause a discrepancy between Win Shares as displayed here and those as calculated elsewhere in the book.

For the first basemen on the 1932 Philadelphia Athletics, the data is as follows:

Player	PO	A	E	Claim Points
Jimmie Foxx	1,328	79	9	1441
Oscar Roettger	130	5	3	125
Team Total				1566

In the last stage we determined that A's first basemen would be credited with 3.63 Win Shares. Dividing the Win Shares in the same proportions as the claim points, this makes 3.34 Win Shares for the regular first baseman, Jimmie Foxx, and 0.29 for the backup, Oscar Roettger.

For the first basemen on the 1890 New York Giants, the data is as follows:

Player	PO	A	E	Claim Points
Roger Connor	1335	80	21	1390
Willard Brown	97	4	5	80
Team Total				1470

Giant first basemen are to be credited with 4.43 Win Shares. Dividing those in the same proportions as the claim points, that makes 4.19 for Connor, 0.24 for Brown.

Third Base (And Explanation of Range Bonus Plays)

The claim formula for third basemen is this:

PO + 2A - 5E + 2RBP

RBP stands for "Range Bonus Play." We give third basemen (and also second basemen, shortstops and outfielders) credit for range plays when it is clear *by any interpretation of the data* that one player is making more plays per inning than his teammates.

To explain first with a theoretical example, suppose that on a team there are two second basemen who play 100 games each. The team as a whole plays 162 games, but the two second basemen are credited with playing 100 games at second, meaning that each man played in 100 games at second base. There are 38 "shared defensive games"—200, minus 162.

Suppose that one player makes 360 successful plays (putouts and assists) at second base, and the other has 450. Would the player with the 450 plays get a range bonus?

No, he would not. He would not because it is *possible*, within the data—indeed, it is not improbable—that the player with 360 plays made may have made more plays per inning than the player with 450 plays made. It is not unlikely that the player with 450 plays made has played 850 defensive innings, while the player with 360 plays made has played the same number of games, but only 600 defensive innings. This is what would happen, in fact, if the second player was a superior defensive player, and thus was used as a late-inning defensive replacement—the first player would get "games" of eight innings each, while the second player would get "games" or one inning. The data would *suggest* that the player playing eight innings a game had better range, but it would not *prove* this. We're not willing to give credit for superior range unless the evidence is more clear than that.

When *would* we give the range bonus play? Well, suppose that, in this example, each player had 87 games played, rather than 100. The number of shared defensive games drops from 38 to 12, making the players' actual range more clear. We'll call the first player, with 450 plays made, Mr. 450, and the other guy Mr. 360. Even if Mr. 450 has played all nine defensive innings in all of his 87 games, that still is only 792 innings. His plays per nine innings are *at least* 5.11 while the team average is 5.00. Thus, by any (normal) possibility, Mr. 450 has made more plays per nine innings than his teammates—and deserves a range bonus.

Switching now to third base, and to a real-data example. . . the 1962 New York Mets. The Mets used nine third basemen in 1962, only one of whom (Don Zimmer) could actually play third worth a damn. The data for the nine New York Met third basemen in 1962 is:

Player	G	PO	A	E	DP	FPct
Mantilla	95	76	179	14	22	.948
Kanehl	30	15	40	8	4	.873
Cook	16	14	21	5	2	.875
Zimmer	14	12	37	2	3	.961
Neal	12	6	31	3	1	.925
Thomas	10	7	19	4	1	.867
Herrscher	6	3	7	2	1	.833
Drake	6	3	5	1	0	.889
Chacon	1	0	0	0	0	—

These nine players, as a group, made 475 plays (136 putouts, 339 assists) in 161 games, which is 2.95 plays per game. This figure is derived, let me note, by using the games played by the team—NOT the games played at third base. The Mets had 190 games played at third base, because of shared defensive games.

Of the nine third basemen, only two (Don Zimmer and Charlie Neal) made more than 2.95 plays per game. Zimmer made 49 plays in 14 games, 3.50 per game, and Neal made 37 plays in 12 games, 3.08 per game.

In this system, we give players credit for range only if that player had better range than the other men who played the position by any interpretation of the data. In other words, we don't estimate defensive innings, and then theorize based on that that some players must have had better range than others. We say instead that "We don't know who played how many defensive innings at third base. But no matter what that data is, it is clear that Zimmer and Neal made more plays per game than the other players."

Persisting along this line, in the fear that I am still not clear and in the vain hope that I can make myself clearer. . . Frank Thomas played 10 games at third base and made 26 successful plays, 2.60 per game. If you total up all data for all third basemen on the team, there are 190 games and 475 plays—exactly 2.50 plays per game. Thomas does better than that; he's at 2.60.

However, what if Thomas played 10 full games at third base, without any split games? What if he had 90 defensive innings at third?

If he did, then Thomas would have made *less* plays per full game than the typical Met third baseman, that standard being 2.95. Thus, because it is *possible* that Thomas had less than average range for a Met third baseman that year, we don't credit him with any range bonus.

A third baseman making 2.95 plays/game in 14 games would have 41.3 plays at third base. Don Zimmer beat that by 7.7 plays—thus, he is credited with 7.7 Range Bonus Plays. Neal, by the same method, gets credit for 1.6 RBP.

For each RBP, the player gets two additional claim points. The formula for third base claim points, as I said above, is PO + 2A - 5E + 2RBP. Don Zimmer thus has 91.4 claim points for his play at third base—12 for his 12 putouts, 74 for his 37 assists, minus 10 for his two errors, plus 15.4 for his Range Bonus. Prior to 1900, a different formula is used for third base claim points, that formula being: (2PO + 3A - 5E + 2RBP).

In the previous level of the analysis, we attributed 3.72 Win Shares to New York Met third basemen in 1962. All nine Met third basemen have a total of 638 Claim Points (actually, 637.6). Don Zimmer thus gets 0.53 Win Shares for his play at third base with that team—91.4, divided by 638, times 3.72. This is the data for all nine players:

Player	G	PO	A	E	RBP	Claim Points	Win Shares
Mantilla	95	76	179	14	0	364	2.12
Zimmer	14	12	37	2	7.7	91.4	0.53
Neal	12	6	31	3	1.6	56.2	0.33
Kanehl	30	15	40	8	0	55	0.32
Cook	16	14	21	5	0	31	0.18
Thomas	10	7	19	4	0	25	0.15
Drake	6	3	5	1	0	8	0.05
Herrscher	6	3	7	2	0	7	0.04
Chacon	1	0	0	0	0	0	—

Zimmer, on a per-game basis, ranks quite a bit better than the other third basemen on the team.

One other note before we move on. If a player comes out negative, zero him out before you figure the team total. It's a rare event, but occasionally somebody will have two plays and boot one of them or something. Just list those guys at zero.

Range Bonuses with Modern Data

In modern data, post-1987, we have actual defensive innings for each player.

When we have actual defensive innings, then we figure range based on actual defensive innings, and we give the range bonus to all players who make more plays/inning than the position total, rather than those who make more plays/game. The effect of this is that rather than about 15% of the players who play the position getting the "range bonus," about 50% will get the bonus. But the system is exactly the same; we don't actually change anything. It just becomes more accurate when we have more data.

Second Base and Shortstop

At second base and shortstop, the claim formula for individual fielders is:

PO + 2A - 5E + 2RBP + DP

Let's do the shortstops and second basemen on the 1966 Pittsburgh Pirates:

Second Base

Player	G	PO	A	E	DP	FPct
Mazeroski	162	411	538	8	161	.992
Pagan	3	1	2	0	0	1.000
Michael	2	1	1	0	0	1.000

Shortstop

Player	G	PO	A	E	DP	FPct
Alley	143	235	472	15	128	.979
Pagan	18	23	50	6	8	.924
Michael	8	9	19	3	7	.903
Rodgers	5	8	13	2	5	.913

That makes 1608 claim points for Mazeroski, 411 for putouts, plus 1076 for assists, -40 for errors, plus

161 for double plays. Gene Michael had 3 claim points and Jose Pagan had 5, making a total of 1616 at the position. Nobody gets the range bonus.

On the previous level, we had determined that Pittsburgh second basemen in 1966 would receive 10.81 Win Shares. Mazeroski claims 99.5% of those, which gives him 10.76 Win Shares, with Pagan claiming 0.03 and Michael 0.02.

Again, you will note that it really doesn't make much difference, at this stage, what the formula is. At this point, anything you do will give Mazeroski 99.5% of the Win Shares. We try to use claiming formulas that make sense, but if you weighted each assist at 25 points and each double play at negative 4, it really wouldn't make much difference. The real work, in this case, was done in the last stage, when Pittsburgh second basemen were assigned a Claiming Percentage of .778, which caused them to get the very high total of 10.76 Win Shares. Mazeroski in 1966 is the sixth-highest valued second baseman of all time, and easily the best in baseball in that season.

At shortstop, with 8.96 Win Shares in play, Gene Alley gets 7.88 Win Shares (fourth in the National League), Pagan gets 0.65, Michael 0.25 and Andre Rodgers gets 0.19.

Outfield

The distribution formula in the outfield is:

PO + 4A - 5E + 2RBP

There is an additional wrinkle here, which is that all outfielders' stats are in a common pool, which thus represents three defensive positions, not one. Thus, to establish the range factor for the team's outfielders, you have to divide the plays made by outfielders by three times the team's games played (or three times innings), rather than just dividing by team games played as we do at third base, second base, and shortstop.

Let's do the 1954 New York Giants. These are the defensive stats for the team's outfielders:

Player	G	PO	A	E	DP	FPct
Mays	151	448	13	7	9	.985
Mueller	153	263	14	6	5	.979
Irvin	128	274	7	7	0	.976
Rhodes	37	62	1	1	0	.984
Taylor	9	6	0	0	0	1.000
Lockman	2	4	0	0	0	1.000
Evers	4	4	0	0	0	1.000
Rodin	3	3	0	0	0	1.000
Thompson	1	0	1	0	0	1.000

Monte Irvin was the team's regular left fielder, Willie Mays the center fielder, Don Mueller the right fielder. Dusty Rhodes was a pinch hitter who played some in left, Bill Taylor and Eric Rodin were young players trying to catch on, Hoot Evers was an old player trying to hang on, and Whitey Lockman and Hank Thompson were infielders who played a little bit in the outfield.

The nine outfielders made 1064 putouts and had 36 assists, a total of 1100 plays. The Giants played 154 games, so that is 2.38 plays per outfielder per game (1100 divided by 154 divided by 3).

The only player on the team who made more than 2.38 plays per game was Willie Mays, who exceeded this standard by 101.5 plays. This is common, for the regular center fielder to be the only outfielder on the team who gets the points for Range Bonus Plays. It is not particularly unusual for the center fielder to make a hundred extra plays. The Range Bonus Plays have a special function, in the outfield, unlike their work in the infield: they recognize the center fielder. The regular center fielder on most teams will claim about one-half of the Win Shares attributed to the team's outfield, as Mays does on the 1954 Giants. Mays has 668 claim points—448 for putouts, 52 for assists, minus 35 for errors, plus 203 for Range Bonus Plays. Mueller has 289 claim points, Irvin has 267, Rhodes 61, Taylor 6, Lockman 4, Evers 4, Rodin 3, and Hank Thompson 4, for a total of 1306.

Giants outfielders, in previous levels of this analysis, were assigned 17.34 Win Shares to divide among them—an exceptionally high total. This makes

Willie Mays

the Win Shares for the Giant outfielders:

Player	G	PO	A	E	DP	Claim Points	Win Shares
Mays	151	448	13	7	9	668	8.87
Mueller	153	263	14	6	5	289	3.84
Irvin	128	274	7	7	0	267	3.55
Rhodes	37	62	1	1	0	61	0.8
Taylor	9	6	0	0	0	6	0.08
Lockman	2	4	0	0	0	4	0.05
Thompson	1	0	1	0	0	4	0.05
Evers	4	4	0	0	0	4	0.05
Rodin	3	3	0	0	0	3	0.04

Mays' 8.87 Win Shares in 1954 are the highest total in the National League that season, the highest total in the National League during the 1950s (although bested twice in the American League, by Jimmy Piersall in '55 and '56). The National League Gold Glove outfield in 1954, as seen by Win Shares:

1. Willie Mays 8.87
2. Richie Ashburn 7.98
3. Bill Bruton 5.52

Historically, Mays' 1954 season ranks as the sixteenth best of all time, between Tris Speaker, 1914 (8.90) and Andruw Jones, 2000 (8.85). But this, of course, is a silly distinction, since this distinguishes among players on the basis of decimal points which represent impossibly small pieces of runs.

The formula for outfield claim points before 1900 is:

2PO + 4A - 4E + 2RBP.

This completes the sequential explanation of the Win Shares method. We have left a fair number of threads hanging, however, and we will need to re-attach those before we can close off this section. Starting with Making Integers of the Win Shares. . .

Making Integers

For each team, we total up each player's Batting Win Shares, his Pitching Win Shares, and his Fielding Win Shares at every position at which he has value. These totals, for all members of the team, will sum up to three times the team's wins.

However, we figure Offensive Win Shares in decimals, Pitching Win Shares in decimals, and Fielding Win Shares in decimals, and add them up. Then we have to convert them to integers.

If we just rounded off to the nearest integer, sometimes the totals would add up wrong; we might have a team with 80 wins that would wind up with 241, possibly 242, even 243 Win Shares. I don't want that; I want a system in which every win is allocated to three individuals.

To cause that to happen:

1. Take the exact shares for each individual,
2. Round that *down* in all cases, but save the rounded-off figures, the "partials,"
3. Add up the whole numbers,
4. Subtract that from the team's desired Win Shares,
5. Arrange the players top-to-bottom in order of their partials, and
6. Give one additional Win Share to each player at the top of the list, until the desired total is reached.

I'm sure some people will object to this, but here's the way I see it:

1. I want an absolutely fixed relationship between the wins of a team and the Win Shares of the players.

2. At least 98% of the players are going to round off the same way.

3. The occasional player who rounds off differently is the player who is near .50 anyway.

4. Rounding 13.47 to 13 is not significantly more accurate than rounding it to 14.

5. Given the inherent limitations of baseball statistics, this particular gain in accuracy is not worth sacrificing the hard-and-fast relationship between team wins and player Win Shares.

Figuring Excess Batters Faced by LHP

When figuring claim percentages for (team) first basemen, claim percentages for second basemen, third basemen and shortstops, we will need to adjust fielding stats for the number of left-handers on the pitching staff. This article will explain how to calculate the number, Excess Batters Faced by Left-Handed Pitchers, which will be the basis of those adjustments. I may refer to it as LHP+/- for shorthand.

We start with four numbers for each team, which are:

a) the innings pitched by left-handed pitchers,

b) the team strikeouts by left-handed pitchers,

c) the team innings, and

d) the team strikeouts.

We use this data for each team and for each league. I'll figure the Washington Senators, 1952 and 1954, as examples. The data is:

	Innings	Strikeouts
1952 Washington Lefties	59	23
1952 Washington Team	1429.2	574
1952 American League Lefties	3529	1706
1952 American League total	11178.1	5154

For each group, we multiply the innings by three and subtract the strikeouts, thus deriving the balls put in play (BIP) against each group of pitchers. Given this data, that creates:

	BIP
1952 Washington Lefties	154
1952 Washington Team	3715
1952 American League Lefties	8881
1952 American League total	28381

For the American League as a whole, .31292 of all balls in play were put in play against left-handed pitchers. Applying this number to the Washington team, we would expect the Senators to have 1163 balls in play against lefties—3715, times .31292. In fact, they had only 154 balls in play against lefties—1009 fewer than expected. Thus, the 1952 Washington Senators LHP+/- is -1009.

Looking now at 1954:

	Innings	Strikeouts
1954 Washington Lefties	793	332
1954 Washington Team	1383.1	562
1954 American League Lefties	3071.2	1532
1954 American League total	11105	5129

Which creates:

	BIP
1954 Washington Lefties	2047
1954 Washington Team	3588
1954 American League Lefties	7683
1954 American League total	28186

In 1954, .2725821 of all balls in play were put in play against left-handed pitching. We would expect the Washington Senators, who had 3588 balls in play, to have had 978 balls in play against left-handed pitchers. In fact, they had 2047. Thus, the 1954 Washington Senators LHP+/- is +1069.

To give you an idea how strange this is, the 1952 Senators are the only major league team 1946-1960 which is -1000. The 1954 Senators are the only team in those 15 years which is +1000. Anyway, that's the method. We'll use this number repeatedly in the next four stages of this process.

For the 1998 Cardinals, the data is:

	Innings	Strikeouts
1998 St. Louis Cardinals LHP	355.2	204
1998 Cardinal Team	1469.2	972
1998 National League Lefties	6021.1	4552
1998 National League total	23240	17552

For each group, we multiply the innings by three and subtract the strikeouts, thus deriving the balls put in play against each group of pitchers. Given this data, that creates:

	BIP
1998 Cardinal Lefties	863
1998 Cardinal Team	3437
1998 National League Lefties	13512
1998 National League total	52168

In 1998, .259009 of all balls in play were put in play against left-handed pitching. We would expect the St. Louis Cardinals, who had 3437 balls in play, to have had 890 balls in play against left-handed pitchers. In fact, they had 863. Thus, the 1998 Cardinals LHP+/- is -27.

For the 1932 Philadelphia A's, the data is:

	Innings	Strikeouts
1932 Philadelphia A's Lefties	714	315
1932 Athletic Team	1386	595
1932 American League Lefties	2835	1072
1932 American League total	11004.2	4012

For each group, we multiply the innings by three and subtract the strikeouts, thus deriving the balls put in play against each group of pitchers. Given this data, that creates:

	BIP
1932 A's Lefties	1827
1932 A's Team	3563
1932 American League Lefties	7433
1932 American League total	29002

In 1932, .256293 of all balls in play were put in play against left-handed pitching. We would expect the Athletics, who had 3563 balls in play, to have had 913 balls in play against left-handed pitchers (actually, 913.17). In fact, they had 1827. Thus, the 1932 A's LHP+/- is +914.

For the 1890 New York Giants, as for all teams before 1915, the LHP+/- is entered as zero, since there was no platooning at that time.

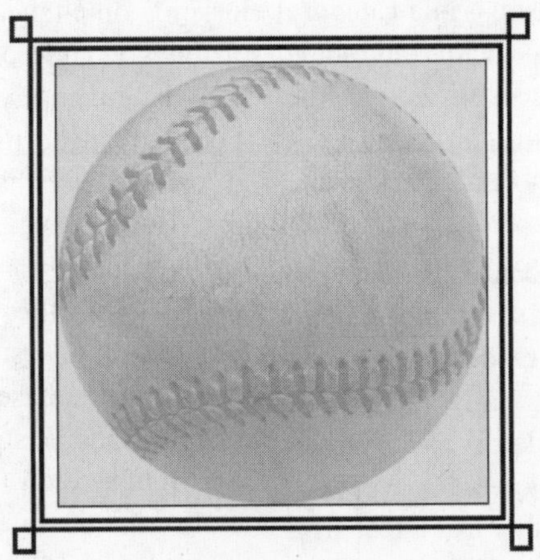

Estimated Un-Assisted Putouts at First Base (Buckner and Garvey)

The defensive range of a first baseman, when not dismissed as utterly beyond the reach of statistics, is usually evaluated by assists. This is troublesome. At one point in the construction of this analysis, I was faced with the question of whether I should make Assists or Fielding Percentage the number one factor in the evaluation of a first baseman.

This is a choice of two bad options. It's hard to say that fielding percentage is the key element, because first basemen in modern baseball field about .993, on the average, which means that a regular major league first baseman makes only about ten errors a year. While "not making errors" is certainly important, if we base a ranking 40% on fielding percentage, we are saying that there is a large difference between a first baseman who makes eight errors in a season and a first baseman who makes thirteen errors in a season. That's hard to justify, because no matter how you slice it, it's only five plays. The standard deviation of errors at first base is 4.5.

On the other hand, basing a rating on assists is problematic, because assists by a first baseman are largely discretionary. A hundred times a year, a ground ball to first can result in either an un-assisted putout (3 un-assisted) or an assist (3-1), based solely on how the first baseman chooses to play it. That's a hundred discretionary plays a season—in a category where the season norm is 120. Some teams (and some first basemen) place a big emphasis on getting the pitcher over there to cover; other organizations don't stress it, and some first basemen just don't like to make the throw unless they have to.

The mishandling of this issue can lead to indefensible ratings of first basemen. Perhaps the best illustration is a comparison of the two Dodgers who competed for the first base job in the early 1970s, Bill Buckner and Steve Garvey. Buckner was a minor league outfielder, but he had bad knees. Garvey was a minor league third baseman, but he had a bad arm. This pushed them both to first base, where they competed for one job.

There is a general agreement that Steve Garvey was a far better first baseman than Bill Buckner. Buckner was a good player and not a hopeless first baseman, but his knees left him unable to spring quickly after a ball. Garvey's arm wasn't all that critical at first base, and he was a four-time Gold Glove first baseman.

Steve Garvey had a very low assists rate throughout his career—just under .5 assists per game, career—and season totals as low as 55 in 160 games in 1977. Bill Buckner's assist rates started out high, and got higher and higher as he aged. At one time he held the single-season assists record both in the American League (184, with Boston in 1985) and the National League (161, with the Cubs in 1983). The National League record has since been broken.

The reason for this difference is obvious. Baseball fundamentals require that the pitcher cover first base on any ground ball to the right side, so that the first baseman is free to go after the ball. Buckner was taught, as all young first basemen are taught, that the way to handle this play is to flip to the pitcher, because if you don't, the pitchers will get lax about covering first base, and you'll lose a game sometime because a pitcher fails to cover first base on a key play. Buckner took this instruction to heart, and was rigorous about insisting on pitchers covering first. The pitchers a lot of times would go about halfway to first base, with body language saying "you can get that, can't you? You don't need me to go all the way to first for a ground ball like that, do you?" I can still see Buckner in my mind's eye, fielding the ball with the glove on his right hand, pointing vigorously to first base with his left, telling the pitcher to stop lollygagging and get his butt over to first base. If the ball was grounded four feet from first base, he would still flip to the pitcher covering, and he still expected the pitcher to be there. If the pitcher didn't cover, Buckner went immediately to the mound to remind him that he should have covered. As he got older, got to where he could hardly

Steve Garvey

move, he became ever more insistent on pitchers covering.

Garvey, on the other hand, preferred to make the play himself. Garvey's thinking, as I understand it, was "Why make a throw if you don't have to? Sure, it's the pitcher's job to cover—but it is the first baseman's job to make certain that the play is made. Why risk making a throw when you have the ball in your hand, and you have time to step on the base?"

Total Baseball interprets the assists to show that Bill Buckner was a great defensive first baseman, Garvey a poor one. But while there is a general correlation between a first baseman's range and his assists, there are many examples of first basemen with limited range who had high assists totals, including Dick Stuart (Dr. Strangeglove), who had one of the highest ratios of assists/game of any first baseman ever, Zeke Bonura, a famous oaf of the 1930s whose assists rates were almost as high as Stuart's, and Marvelous Marv Throneberry (see article in Section IV, Throneberry and White).

The Linear Weights evaluation of first basemen rests on only two statistics, assists and errors, and gives each assist twice as much weight as each error. Thus, comparing Bill Buckner, 1985 (184 assists), and Steve Garvey, 1977 (55 assists). . . in order to off-set the assists and rank the same as Garvey, as I understand their system, Buckner would have to make 258 errors in a season. This two-to-one weighting, I think, is extremely questionable. Errors represent plays which are absolutely not made. Assists by occasionally represent plays not made, but very often they simply represent plays made in a different way.

Also, the standard deviation of errors at first base is 4.5. The standard deviation of assists at first base (among teams) is almost twenty. Thus, if you rate one assist equal to one error, assists will determine about 82% of the rating, and errors about 18%. If you weight each assist at two and each error at one, then your system is 90% determined by the assists. A much more representative ratio, I would suggest, would be to weight each error about three times as heavily as each assist. Then, in order to rate even with Garvey, Buckner would have to make only 43 additional errors.

Total Baseball says that putouts for first basemen "are eliminated (because they) require so little skill in all but the odd case." But what if there was some way to estimate the un-assisted putouts by a first baseman? These are the other side of the discretionary plays, the plays that Steve Garvey makes himself, while Bill Buckner flips to the pitcher, plays that the first baseman makes all by himself.

When you get to the point of asking that question, this turns out to be a fairly simple problem. What happens when the first baseman has an un-assisted putout? The first baseman gets a putout, but nobody gets an assist.

I entered data for about 100 teams into a spreadsheet, data including the number of putouts by the team's first basemen, and the number of assists by the second basemen, the third basemen, the shortstops and the pitchers. Then I added together the assists from the other infielders, and compared the total to the putouts of the first basemen.

It was immediately apparent that this was the solution to the problem.

The 1985 Boston Red Sox, the Bill Buckner team, had 154 more assists by other infielders than putouts at first base. The 1977 Dodgers, the Steve Garvey team, were one of four teams in the study to have more putouts at first base than assists by other infielders. The Buckner team was third from the bottom of the list, ahead of the 1962 Pirates, whose regular first baseman was Dick Stuart, and the 1977 Baltimore Orioles, whose regular first baseman was the 34-year-old Lee May, in his last season before moving to DH. The Garvey team was second from the top of the list, behind the 1985 Texas Rangers, whose regular first baseman, Pete O'Brien, was, like Steve Garvey, an outstanding defensive player, but a player who had few assists that season (although he had high assists totals most of his career). It was obvious that we could, in fact, estimate the un-assisted putouts of the first basemen by studying this relationship.

Working with the data, I made an estimate that about 16% of assists by other infielders go somewhere other than first base, which implies that a typical major league team has about 175 un-assisted putouts by first basemen in a season, or slightly more than one per game.

We can estimate the number of un-assisted putouts by a team's first basemen, then, by:

1. Adding together the assists by the second basemen, shortstops, third basemen and pitchers,

2. Multiplying that total by .84, and

3. Subtracting that from the putouts of the first basemen.

When I did this, and added together the assists by teams' first basemen, and the estimated putouts by teams' first basemen, an amazing thing happened. Teams whose regular first basemen were Keith Hernandez, Steve Garvey, Vic Power, George Scott, Tom McCraw, Wes Parker and Pete O'Brien went to the top of the list. Teams whose regular first basemen were Willie Aikens, Boog Powell and Dick Stuart fell to the bottom of the list, where they were joined by a large number of 38-year-old power hitters. It was very obvious that one can, in fact, measure the defensive range of a first baseman.

Not that the measure is *perfect*; it certainly isn't. We refined it more, working with STATS data, and we can make it better yet when more people get interested in the problem. Ron Fairly in 1962, recognized as an outstanding glove man, rates near the bottom of the list, as does Eddie Murray in 1980 (although Murray in other seasons is near the top). There are some players who appear to be out of line.

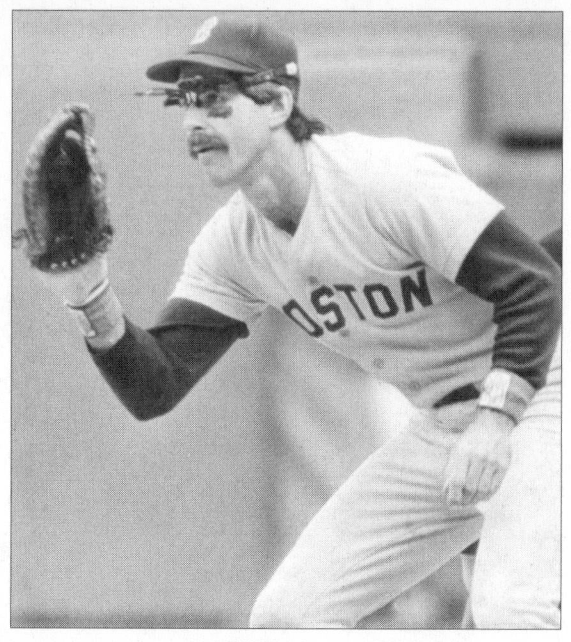

Bill Buckner

But at the same time, I have no doubt that this estimate does in fact measure what it attempts to measure. Why? Three reasons:

1. When we add together the assists and the un-assisted putouts, the concentration of the best defensive players (or their teams) at the top of the list is obvious.

2. There is, in the data, a strong inverse relationship between first basemen's assists and our new estimates of their un-assisted putouts. The first basemen who have the most assists, like Bill Buckner, tend to have the fewest un-assisted putouts. This makes sense, of course—if we are in fact measuring what we are attempting to measure. But if we're not actually measuring that, then why would that be true?

3. There is an inverse relationship between innings pitched by left-handed pitchers and plays made at first base. Those teams which had the most innings pitched by left-handed pitchers tend to have the fewest plays made at first base. The relationship measured in this study was the same as the relationship measured in an earlier study, but on the other side of the infield.

For each ten innings pitched by left-handed pitchers, we can expect one less play to be made by the first basemen.

This makes sense, again—but only if we are in fact measuring what we are intending to measure. The combination of these three factors leaves me 99% satisfied that the method does in fact measure what it attempts to measure.

Arm Ratings for First Basemen

The 20-point factor in evaluating first basemen is the Arm Rating, the formula for which is:

Double Plays by the Team's Shortstops
Plus Assists by the First Basemen
Minus Double Plays by the Second Basemen
Minus Putouts by the Pitchers
Plus or Minus an adjustment for
left-handed pitching

At first glance, this probably seems like an odd and convoluted formula which (you will probably suspect) doesn't actually measure a damn thing. I hope I can convince you otherwise. Odd as it looks, it is, in fact, a simple common sense combination of hard facts, which makes a valuable measure of a first baseman's defensive ability. Although I made it only the 20-point factor in evaluating a team's first basemen, I am inclined to believe that it may be, in fact, a better measure of the performance of a team's first basemen than the 40- and 30-point factors.

When I was trying to think through the problem, "How do we evaluate a first baseman's throwing arm?", I came up with two theories about how we might get some insight into the subject. I checked them out and, to my great surprise, both of them seemed to work. This method puts the two together into one.

My first idea was to compare the double play totals of a team's shortstops and their second basemen. When a first baseman starts a double play, how does that play go? It goes 3-6-3 or 3-6-1, of course. Double Plays started by the first baseman normally involve the shortstop, but not the second baseman.

Thus, if a first baseman is good at starting the double play, this should create more double plays involving the shortstop, rather than the second baseman. Conversely, if a first baseman has a poor arm or is too slow to start the double play, this should create a poor ratio of double plays for the team's shortstops as opposed to their second basemen. Looking at old data, it seems pretty clear that this is true. If you look back at 1990, for example, the highest number of double plays at short as opposed to second were for the Cubs (Mark Grace was their regular first baseman), the Yankees (Don Mattingly), and the Rangers (Rafael Palmeiro), while the lowest totals were for the Angels, Twins and White Sox. The Angels' first baseman, Wally Joyner, was out half the season with an injury, leaving the position to be played by Lee Stevens. The Twins had Kent Hrbek at first; the White Sox had Carlos Martinez and, late in the season, Frank Thomas.

If you go back to 1980, the highest differentials are for Boston in the American League (Tony Perez) and St. Louis in the National (Keith Hernandez), while the lowest ratios were for Baltimore (Eddie Murray) and Philadelphia (Pete Rose).

(Just days before this material went to the publisher, information was distributed on the SABR-L list about this subject. Mike Emeigh, studying data from Project Retrosheet, reported that, in the years 1979-1983, Keith Hernandez fielded a ground ball with a runner on first/less than two out 206 times, and started 49 3-6-3 or 3-6-1 double plays—twenty more than any other first baseman. Hernandez started double plays in 24% of those situations, while Steve Garvey, fielding 113 ground balls in that situation over the five years, started only three 3-6-3 double plays—2.7%. Pete Rose, at 7%, was near the bottom of the list, consistent with our data here, while Perez and Murray were both perched in the middle of the list, over the five-year period. I think this is quite wonderful data, and I am looking forward to more such information emerging over the next few years.)

Anyway, going back to 1970, the highest differential in the American League was for Boston (Carl Yastrzemski and George Scott), while the lowest was for Washington (Mike Epstein). In the National League the highest ratio was for Montreal (Ron Fairly), while the lowest ratio was for Houston, who split playing time at first base among several players.

So I was satisfied with that, and I would have been happy to make that ratio the 20-point factor in evaluating first basemen, if the other thing hadn't worked. The other idea was an outgrowth of this problem about first basemen's "optional assists." Some first basemen will get 75 or 100 easy, optional assists in the course of a season by flipping the ball to the pitcher; see article, Estimated Un-assisted Putouts at First Base.

There are two recorded entries for that play—an assist by a first baseman, and a putout by a pitcher. What if you looked at assists by first basemen which didn't involve a putout by the pitcher?

Tell me if there is something wrong with this logic, but if you think about it, *when a first baseman gets an assist which ISN'T to the pitcher, it's almost always an important play, and it is almost always a skill play*. If the play doesn't go 3-1, how does it go?

Well, it could go 3-2. That happens when a first baseman cuts down a runner at home plate. That's certainly an important play.

The play could go 3-4. That's normally the first baseman fielding a bunt, and throwing to the second baseman covering first. That's an important play, too, because some first basemen can really pounce on a bunt, like Keith Hernandez, while many first basemen absolutely can't play a bunt at all; the only thing they can do is cover first and let somebody else chase the ball. It's an obvious variable among first basemen.

The play could go 3-5. That's rare, but certainly, when a first baseman fires the ball across the infield and gets an out at third base, that's a big money play.

Or the play could go 3-6; probably most assists by first basemen which *aren't* 3-1 are 3-6. But that's a huge play, over the course of a season, because that's the play that keeps the runner on first base, out of scoring position. 3-6 means an out at second; 3 un-assisted on the same play means the runner is in scoring position.

So think what that means: *almost all assists by first basemen which AREN'T 3-1 tend to be significant plays*.

Well, for each team, we have a count of how many assists the first basemen have, right? And we have a count of how many putouts the pitchers have, which is a statistic which has a very high correlation with first basemen's assists. So if we subtract the one from the other (subtract pitcher's putouts from first base assists), shouldn't we get a statistic which is something like a count of the number of significant assists by the team's first basemen?

It's worth a look. In 1995, the highest number in this category (First Base Assists minus Pitcher's Putouts) was 45, for the Houston Astros (Jeff Bagwell). The highest total in the American League was 30, by the Yankees (Don Mattingly) and the Blue Jays (John Olerud). The others near the top of the list were the Mets (Rico Brogna), the Reds (Hal Morris), and the Rockies (Andres Galarraga).

The lowest total in 1995 was 2, by the White Sox (Frank Thomas). The lowest total in the National League was 16, by the Phillies (Dave Hollins and Greg Jefferies, both of whom were battling injuries). There are some exceptions and some anomalies, but in general, I am satisfied that the teams at the top of the list had the best defensive first basemen in the major leagues, while the teams at the bottom had first basemen who didn't throw well.

Let's look back at 1985. The highest total in the major leagues in 1985 was 42, by the New York Mets (Keith Hernandez). The highest total in the American League was 37, by Cleveland (Pat Tabler). The lowest totals in baseball were -3, by the Royals (Steve Balboni) and their World Series opponents, the Cardinals

(Jack Clark). Steve Balboni, although he made a good effort at first and was as nice a man as ever played a major league inning, had an extremely poor throwing arm. Jack Clark was certainly not a good defensive first baseman. Next to them at the bottom of the list are Seattle (Alvin Davis) and San Diego (Steve Garvey). Again, there's no question but that those rankings correlate strongly with the actual throwing of the first basemen involved.

Let's look back to 1975. These are the top and bottom teams and their first basemen:

1.	Montreal	47	Mike Jorgensen
2.	White Sox	46	No Regular
3.	Milwaukee	44	George Scott
4.	Boston	39	Carl Yastrzemski
21.	Pittsburgh	7	Willie Stargell
21.	Los Angeles	7	Steve Garvey
22.	Kansas City	6	John Mayberry
23.	Cleveland	5	Boog Powell
24.	Atlanta	-4	Earl Williams

Again, there is an obvious relationship between the lists and the throwing ability of the first basemen. Mike Jorgensen had a 17-year major league career, based almost entirely on his defensive ability. Scott won eight Gold Gloves, although I think he was over-rated at that time. At the bottom of the list we've got two old guys (Stargell and Powell), plus Garvey and Mayberry, who were good first basemen but not strong throwers, and Earl Williams, who had an outstanding throwing arm, but thought that having to play defense was a nuisance.

Going back to 1965, we have one more player who is +40: Wes Parker. Six Gold Gloves. At the bottom of the list is Willie McCovey.

Our 20-point formula simply combines these two approaches into one. One method, which I believe correlates somewhat with throwing ability at first base, is Shortstops Double Plays minus Second Base Double Plays. A second approach is First Base Assists Minus Pitcher's Putouts. This category puts them together into one rating: Shortstops Double Plays, Plus First Base Assists, Minus Second Base Double Plays, Minus Pitcher's Putouts.

Does it work? Well, let's look at Keith Hernandez' teams. An average figure for a team in this respect is about +20. Keith Hernandez was the regular first baseman for the Cardinals from 1976 through 1982. The totals for the Cardinals, beginning in 1976, are +69, +42, +40, +42, +66, +29 and +31—an average of +46 in Hernandez' seven seasons as the Cardinals first baseman.

The New York Mets, in those years, used a long string of first basemen—Ed Kranepool, Joe Torre, John Milner, Willie Montanez, Lee Mazzilli, Mike Jorgensen and Dave Kingman. Some of these were OK defensive first basemen; some weren't. During those years, the Mets totals were +12, +14, +31, +4, +31, +13 and +18—an average of +18.

Then Hernandez was traded from St. Louis to New York, in mid-1983. In the next four years St. Louis used a number of first basemen—David Green, Jack Clark, and whoever was filling in for the injured Jack Clark. The Cardinals totals in those years were +22, -13, +2, and +0—an average of +3. The Mets totals, with Hernandez, were +40, +40, +41 and +30.

Of course, this doesn't prove that it works for all teams; it only proves that it works for Keith Hernandez. But it also works for Vic Power, for Wes Parker, for Jim Spencer, for Don Mattingly—for all of the recognized defensive standouts at first base of my lifetime, except J.T. Snow, David Segui and Steve Garvey.

Garvey still ranks as a good first baseman, because our system also looks at range, errors, and the performance of the team. But we're also trying to look at the arm, and I believe that this method helps us to do that.

Park Factors

Part I—The Park Factors

How do we determine the park factor for a team? This is one of those issues about which, if you think you know how to do it, you don't understand the problem. There isn't any right way to figure Park Effects, because all the alternatives have a down side. Let's use the 1927 New York Yankees to illustrate.

The Yankees in 1927 played 77 games at Yankee Stadium, scoring 479 runs and allowing 267 at home. That's 9.688 runs per game. On the road, they played 78 games, scoring 496 runs and allowing 332. That's 10.615 runs per game. They scored and allowed 8.7% fewer runs in their home park. Thus, we could set their park factor at .913.

The problem is that if you figure park factors in this manner, they're going to bounce around from season to season, simply because the data samples are not large enough to be stable. Sometimes a park will show a park factor of .90 one season, 1.05 the next, when nothing actually has changed; it's just a matter of some pitchers having a good day in that park one year, and some hitters having a good day there the next.

Well, not to make the issue simpler than it is. . . it might also be a legitimate differential: the weather. It might be that one year, the team played 20 games in cold weather, and the next year, they didn't play any. That's an actual park factor: the park really is different one year than it is the next, even though nothing was intentionally changed. Fewer runs are scored when the weather is cold.

Anyway, at the other extreme, you could base your park factor for Yankee Stadium on all games played in Yankee Stadium between 1922 and 1973, when the park was closed for renovations. That doesn't work, either. That doesn't work because things change over time. Even when Yankee Stadium doesn't change over a period of time, the other parks do. What we need to find is not an absolute figure, but a comparative figure, comparing Yankee Stadium to the other parks in the league. This comparison is different if the other park is the Oakland Coliseum, rather than Sportsman's Park.

You could compare the park to other parks only in the period when the "other parks" were the same, if there were such a period. There isn't, because *something* changes, somewhere in the league, every year—somebody moves a fence, or somebody moves into a new park, or somebody has some ceiling tiles fall off the roof and they have to play twenty extra games on the road, or something.

We are caught between two risks: the risk of using too short a time frame, and thereby treating random events as park factors, and the risk of using too long a time frame, and thereby including inappropriate information in our comparison. On the continuum from short to long, there is no place at which either risk is eliminated—thus, there is no right answer. You just have to pick a method and go with it.

My chosen poison is a five-year standard, with the "focus year" weighted to equal the other four years. In other words, for the 1927 Yankees, one half of the relevant park data is from 1927, one-eighth is from 1925, one-eighth from 1926, one-eighth from 1928, and one-eighth from 1929. This is the actual five-year data:

	In Yankee Stadium			On the Road		
Year	G	R	OR	G	R	OR
1925	79	354	356	77	352	418
1926	75	417	326	80	430	387
1927	77	479	267	78	496	332
1928	77	400	301	77	494	384
1929	77	463	362	77	436	413
Sub-Total	385	2113	1612	389	2208	1934
Plus 1927	77	479	267	78	496	332
Plus 1927	77	479	267	78	496	332
Plus 1927	77	479	267	78	496	332
Total	616	3550	2413	623	3696	2930

The Yankees scored and allowed 9.68 runs per game in Yankee Stadium, 10.64 on the road, creating a park factor of .910166.

This method creates a unique park factor for each team each season, but basing each one on a moving five-year average, so that the number changes a little bit every year, but (normally) only a little bit; the Yankees figure was .93 in 1925, .93 in 1926, .91 in 1927, .85 in 1928, and .91 in 1929. Of course, if a team moves into a new park or moves their fences or something, we don't use the data for all of the surrounding seasons. Since the Yankees played in Shea Stadium in 1974 and 1975, the only relevant data for those seasons is the 1974-75 seasons.

For years prior to 1909, the park factors are based on only one year of data and are stabilized by adding 100 runs and 10 games to both the home and road figures.

Part II—The Park Run Adjustment

A team doesn't play all of their games in their home park, so the park run adjustment is not the same as the park factor. You could just figure that they play half their games in their home park, so the park factor for Yankee Stadium, 1927, would be 1.910166 divided by two, which is .955083. The problem with that is it assumes that everybody's "road" parks are the same, which they aren't. The Yankees don't play in Yankee Stadium as a road park. To adjust for that, we figure that the Yankees, in an eight-team league, play 14 sets of games, 7 at home and 7 on the road. The seven at home are represented by seven times the park factor:

7 X .910 166 = 6.37116

The seven on the road are represented by 8.00 (the total of eight average parks) minus the Yankee park factor:

8 - .910 166 = 7.08983

We add these two together and divide by 14, creating a Park Run Adjustment, for Yankee Stadium in 1927, of .961500. If they were in a fourteen-team league, we'd be dividing by 26.

Let me run the data for the St. Louis Cardinals in 1998, for the sake of the illusion of consistency:

	In Busch Stadium			On the Road		
Year	G	R	OR	G	R	OR
1996	81	391	326	81	368	380
1997	81	345	325	81	344	383
1998	82	432	381	81	378	401
1999	80	383	433	81	426	405
2000	81	438	392	81	449	379
Sub-Total	405	1989	1857	405	1965	1948
Plus 1998	82	432	381	81	378	401
Plus 1998	82	432	381	81	378	401
Plus 1998	82	432	381	81	378	401
Total	651	3285	3000	648	3099	3151

That makes 9.6544 runs per game at home, 9.6451 per game on the road, which is a park factor of 1.000966. A park factor of 1.000966 in a sixteen-team league makes a Park Run Adjustment of 1.00045. The factor for Philadelphia, 1932, is 1.1104, a Park Run Adjustment of 1.04732. For the Giants of the Players League in 1890, the park factor is 1.1718, which makes a Park Run Adjustment of 1.07365.

The Park Adjustment is used to divide the Win Shares between the offense and the defense, in Step One of the Win Shares process, and also to establish base lines at which runs become marginal.

There are, however, three more park factors which will also be needed later in the process. Those are, in order:

The Park Home Run Factor
The Park Home Run Adjustment
The Park Non-Home Run Adjustment
(which is referred to as the Park-S Adjustment)

Part III—Figuring the Park Home Run Factor

The data needed to figure the Park Home Run Factor is:
Games Played at Home by the team during the focus year, each of the two previous years, and each of the two subsequent years
Home Runs Hit at Home each year of the five-year period
Home Runs Allowed at Home each year of the five-year period
Home Runs Hit on the Road each year of the five-year period
Home Runs Allowed on the Road each year of the five-year period

The Park Home Run Factor is figured, from the park home run data, in exactly the same way as the park run factor: (A) is the home runs hit and allowed per game at home, weighting the focus year at four times the surrounding seasons. (B) is the home runs hit and allowed per game on the road, weighting the focus year at four times the surrounding seasons.

The home run factor is (A) divided by (B).

For seasons prior to 1909, the home run factors are based on one year of data, without any additional factors in the formula.

For the 1998 St. Louis Cardinals, that is:

	In Busch Stadium			On the Road		
Year	G	R	OR	G	R	OR
1996	81	68	59	81	76	65
1997	81	70	81	81	72	92
1998	82	113	83	81	110	68
1999	80	104	83	81	90	78
2000	81	124	105	81	111	91
Total	405	479	411	405	459	394
Plus 1998	82	113	83	81	110	68
Plus 1998	82	113	83	81	110	68
Plus 1998	82	113	83	81	110	68
Total	651	818	660	648	789	598

Home Runs Per Game at Home: 2.27035

Home Runs Per Game on the Road: 2.14043

Park Home Run Factor: 1.06070

The Home Run Factor for St. Louis in 1998 was 1.0607.

Part IV—Figuring the Park Home Run Adjustment (PHRA)

The data needed to figure the Park Home Run Adjustment is:
The Park Home Run Factor (PHRF)
The number of teams in the league (N)

The Park Home Run Adjustment is figured by:

$$PHRA = \frac{(N-1) * PHRF + (N - PHRF)}{2 * (N - 1)}$$

The Park Home Run Adjustment for the 1998 St. Louis Cardinals then becomes:

$$\frac{15 * 1.06070 + (16 - 1.06070)}{30}$$

Which is 1.028326. The Park Home Run Adjustment for the 1998 St. Louis Cardinals is 1.028326. Busch Stadium in 1998 increased home runs, in the games played there as opposed to road games, by 6.07%. However, since this applies *only* to the home games, and also because the Cardinals set of "road" stadiums is slightly different than any other team's set of road stadiums, we don't adjust the Cardinal home run totals by 6.07%, but by 2.83%.

Part V—Figuring the Park-S Adjustment

What is the Park-S Adjustment, you asked?

The Park-S Adjustment is an estimate of the Park's effects on offense *other than* home runs.

The data needed to figure this is:
The Park Home Run Adjustment (PHRA)
The Park Run Adjustment (PRA)
The league total of runs scored
The league total of home runs

First, figure the percentage of league runs which were home runs.

Second, multiply that by 1.50. This is the league percentage of runs which scored on home runs, assuming that each home run accounts for about 1.50 runs.

Third, subtract that from 1.000, thus figuring the percentage of runs which scored *without* home runs (LR%-NHR).

Fourth, multiply the percentage of runs which scored by home runs by the park home run adjustment.

Fifth, subtract that from the park *run* adjustment.

Sixth, divide that by the league percentage of runs scored without home runs (LR%-NHR).

Seventh, take the square root of that.

This figure is the Park-S adjustment.

I'll do the 1998 St. Louis Cardinals again.

First, figure the percentage of league runs which were home runs. There were 11932 runs scored in the NL that year, and there were 2565 home runs. That's .214968 of league runs.

Second, multiply that by 1.50. This is the league percentage of runs which scored on home runs, assuming that each home run accounts for about 1.50 runs. 1.50 times .214968 is .322452. About 32.2% of National League runs in 1998 were accounted for by home runs.

Third, subtract that from 1.000, thus figuring the percentage of runs which scored *without* home runs (LR%-NHR). For the 1998 National League, that figure is .677548.

Fourth, multiply the percentage of runs which scored by home runs by the park home run adjustment. For the St. Louis Cardinals, that is .322452 times 1.028326, which is .331586.

Fifth, subtract that from the park *run* adjustment. The Cardinals Park Run Adjustment is 1.000450. Subtracting .331586, we have .668864.

Sixth, divide that by the league percentage of runs scored without home runs (LR%-NHR). This is .987183.

Seventh, take the square root of that. For the Cardinals, this is .9935716. The Park-S Adjustment for the 1998 Cardinals is .9935716.

Let me see if I can explain these steps in plain English. What we are looking for is the park's effect on runs, *other than* home runs. To figure that, we first figure the park's effect on home runs, and then compare that with the park's *overall* run effect.

If the increase in runs resulting from home runs is larger than the overall increase in scoring in the park, that implies that the park is, *apart from home runs*, a pitcher's park. If the increase in runs resulting from home runs is *less* than the overall increase in scoring in the park, that means that the effect of the park on "other offense" is still positive, still larger than one. That is what we are figuring here: whether the increase in scoring overall is greater or lesser than the increase resulting from home runs alone.

Why the square root, rather than the raw number? Three reasons. First, we're deriving the impact on *runs*, but we're applying it to *hits*. A 10% increase in hits will yield a greater-than-10% increase in runs allowed.

Second, we're making some guesses here. When you're applying an adjustment which you're not certain is *exactly* right, it is best to be conservative. It is better to understate the park's effect, rather than overstate it.

Third, using the square root and applying it to the DER as we do in this system causes the Park-S adjustment to *reduce* the standard deviation of the Defensive Efficiency Record. That is, using the square root, the standard deviation of park-adjusted DER is less than the standard deviation of DER, not adjusted. This is what we would expect to be true. One would assume that the spread of DERs among teams is created in part by defensive play, and in part by park effects—thus, that the standard deviation of non-adjusted DER would be greater than the standard deviation of "true" DER.

But if you use the "full impact" S adjustment, this doesn't happen. What happens then is that the DERs are scrambled—some teams go from better than average to worse—but the standard deviation is as large after making the park adjustment as before. I'm just more comfortable using the more conservative adjustment.

The Park-S adjustment for the 1932 Philadelphia A's is .9989112. For the 1890 New York Giants (PL), it is 1.0358863.

How We Figure Runs Created

A hitter's job is to create runs. For many years I have developed and refined formulas to estimate how many runs each player created. There is a basic runs created formula, which is this:

Hits Plus Walks
Times Total Bases
Divided by Plate Appearances
Equals Runs

On a team level, this formula works pretty well. It ignores stolen bases and caught stealing, it ignores hit batsmen and grounding into double plays, it ignores clutch hitting, it ignores strikeouts, and it ignores many other things even smaller or more elusive, but it still works, in a general way. Pick any team, figure their runs created by the formula above, and their actual runs scored will usually be within 5% of the estimate.

If you figure the above for Mark McGwire in 1998, when he hit 70 home runs, you will get the estimate that McGwire created 177 runs:

(152 + 162)
Times 383
Divided by 681
Equals 177

That is a *reasonable* estimate, but my goal has always been to figure runs created as accurately as possible. By working harder at it, we can make a better estimate. There are dozens of variations of the runs created formula. The current runs created formula that I use is explained, sort of, in the *All-Time Major League Handbook (Second Edition)*, published by STATS, Inc., a book which also gives Runs Created for every major league player in history for every season through 1999.

I have had complaints, from some readers, that we did not thoroughly explain in that book how we actually figured the Runs Created. I intended to make a thorough explanation, but I have been told that I fell short, and I accept the criticism. This article is written to repair the shortcoming, to give an absolutely thorough explanation of how we figure runs created, no matter how long-winded and boring this might be.

This is a complicated process, and it would be impossibly time-consuming to do this without computers. But for illustration, I will set this up as a kind of IRS-type fill-in-the-blanks form, and I'll use the data for Mark McGwire, 1998. When we get to the end of the process, I'll explain in a general way what we have done, and then repeat the process for a couple more players:

A1	Enter the player's Hits		152 (for McGwire)	
A2	Add his Walks	+ 162 =	314	
A3	Add his Hit by Pitch	+ 6 =	320	
A4	Subtract his GIDP	- 8 =	312	
A5	Subtract Caught Stealing	- 0 =	312	
A6	The result is the player's "A" factor			312
B1	Take the player's Walks		162	
B2	Minus Intentional Walks	- 28 =	134	
B3	Plus Hit by Pitch	+ 6 =	140	
B4	Multiply by .24	140 X .24 =	33.60	
B5	Take his Stolen Bases		1	
B6	Multiply by .62	1 X .62 =	.62	
B7	Take his Sacrifice Hits	0		
B8	Add his Sacrifice Flies	4 =	4	
B9	Multiply that by .50	4 X .50 =	2.00	

B10	Add together B4, B6 and B9		36.22	
B11	Take his Strikeouts	155		
B12	Multiply by .03	155 X .03 =	4.65	
B13	Subtract that from B10		31.57	
B14	Take his Total Bases		383.00	
B15	Add that to line B13		414.57	
B16	The result is the player's "B" factor			414.57
C1	Take the player's At Bats		509	
C2	Add his Walks	+ 162 =	671	
C3	Add his Hit Batsmen	+ 6 =	677	
C4	Add his Sacrifice Hits	+ 0 =	677	
C5	Add his Sacrifice Flies	+ 4 =	681	
C6	The result is the player's "C" factor			681
D1	Take the player's "C" factor		681	
D2	Multiply by 2.4		1634.40	
D3	Add in the player's "A" factor	+ 312 =	1946.40	
D4	Take the "C" factor again		681	
D5	Multiply by 3.0		2043	
D6	Add in the player's "B" factor	+ 414.57 =	2457.57	
D7	Take the "C" factor again		681	
D8	Multiply by 9	X 9 =	6129	
D9	Multiply D3 Times D6	=	4783414.248	
D10	Divide by D8	=	780.45591	
D11	Take the "C" factor again		681	
D12	Multiply by .90	X 90 =	612.90000	
D13	Subtract D12 from D10		167.55591	
D14	The result is our first Runs Created estimate			167.55591
E1	Take the player's At Bats with men in scoring position		115	
E2	Multiply by his Batting Average	X .29862 =	34.34185	
E3	Find the player's Hits with men in scoring position		32	
E4	Subtract E2 from E3	32 - 34.34185 =	-2.34185	
E5	Take At Bats with runners on base		223	
E6	Multiply by his Home Runs	X 70 =	15610	
E7	Divide by his At Bats	/ 509 =	30.66798	
E8	That is his "expected Home Runs with men on base"		30.66798	
E9	Take his actual HR with men on base		37	
E10	Subtract line E8	- 30.66798 =	6.33202	
E11	Add together lines E4 and E11	=	3.99018	
E12	Add that to line D14	167.55591 + 3.99018 =	171.54608	
E13	The result is our second Runs Created estimate			171.54608

We're back to 172 runs created for McGwire, five less than we started with; so far we've gone through Milwaukee and Jerusalem to get back to high school. Now comes the hard part:

F1	Repeat this process for every member of the player's team			
F2	Total them up. In this case, the result is		844.09778	
F3	Take the actual runs scored by the team		810	
F4	Divide F3 by F2	810 / 844.09773 =	.959604	
F5	Multiply E13 by F4	171.54608 X .959604 =	164.6305	
F6	Round that off		165	
F7	The result is the player's Runs Created estimate			165

Mark McGwire created about 165 runs created in 1998, as best I am capable of estimating it.

Now, you may well ask, why in the hell did we do all of those things, and what did all of that mean?

All runs created formulas have an "A" factor, a "B" factor, and a "C" factor. The A factor always represents times on base. The B factor always represents the things a player has done to advance or score baserunners. The C factor always represents opportunities. These things are true in the simplest Runs Created formula, which showed Mark McGwire creating 177 runs, and they are true in the most complicated Runs Created formula, which showed him creating "only" 165 runs.

Lines A1 through A6, then, make a detailed accounting of the player's times on base.

Lines B1 through B16 make a detailed accounting of the things the player has done to advance or drive in runners.

Lines C1 through C6 make a detailed accounting of the player's plate opportunities.

In the simplest Runs Created formulas, we simply multiply A times B, and divide by C. For 95% of players, this produces an accurate estimate of the player's runs created. There is, however, a flaw in that method which manifests itself acutely in some few cases, such as Mark McGwire (who would have an estimated 190 Runs Created if we did that with these estimates for A, B and C).

The flaw is that this method evaluates the player's offensive contributions as if they were interacting with one another. In other words, in the simplest formulas, Mark McGwire's home runs interact with McGwire's walks—as if McGwire was on base when he hit his home runs. This is not true, of course, and the consequence of this is that when you figure runs created for all of the members of a team and add them up, you will wind up with more runs created than the runs actually scored by the team.

Mark McGwire

How to fix that?

Twenty-five years ago, there were three of us who had our own runs created formulas, all of us writing about them in SABR publications and other obscure venues. I had the basic Runs Created formula. Pete Palmer had the Linear Weights system, which assessed a player's offense by placing a discrete value on each offensive accomplishment. Dick Cramer had the Batter Run Average, which was essentially a Runs Created formula, but with a twist. Cramer figured runs contributed by figuring how many runs the *league* had created, and then figuring how many runs the *league would* have created, had it not been for this hitter.

All three methods, it now seems to me, were flawed. My method was flawed because it presented the player as if his offensive elements were interacting with one another. Pete's method was flawed, I believe, because it presented the player as if he were playing in a vacuum, in which the value of the offensive elements was fixed, and did not vary with respect to the other offensive elements. Cramer, I now believe, was the closest of the three of us to having it right, but Cramer's method was flawed because it placed the player in a *league* context, when in reality he does not play in a league context, but in a team context. Cramer, in other words, evaluated the player's singles, doubles and triples as if they were interacting with the singles, doubles and triples of other teams as well as with those of his teammates.

A player's offensive contributions do not interact with those of players on other teams, but they do interact with those of his teammates. What about the option, then, of evaluating the player's offense by figuring the runs created by his team, and the runs that would have been created by the team if the player had not been there?

Well, that will work, but there are problems with that, too. The runs created formula attempts to evaluate the player *as an individual.* If you evaluate the player by figuring his team's runs created with and without him, the player may rate different on a good team than he would on a poor team.

Now, in truth, this is almost a purely theoretical objection. In practice, the difference between the best team and the worst team is not large enough to significantly impact the runs created by an individual, if the individual was figured in this way. The difference between the best *player* and the worst *player* is large enough to cause this problem, but the difference between the best team and the worst team is not.

However, there is a second theoretical problem with the practice of evaluating the player in the context of his team. Evaluating the player in the context of a *league* is improper, I believe, because it artificially dilutes the player's offensive impact by placing him in a much larger context than the context in which he has actually competed. But what about a player who has played, let us say, 10 games of a 162-game schedule? Same problem. The player's offensive impact is artificially diluted by placing him in the context not only of the ten games he actually played, but in the context of the 152 games which he did not play.

One cannot, to figure runs created for Fred Kendall in 1969, when he played ten games for the San Diego Padres, go back and find the Padres' stats for those ten games, and figure how many runs the Padres created in those ten games, and how many they would have created without Kendall. That's impractical, and anyway, even if you could, you would still have the problem of bias created by unequal teams.

What, then, is the appropriate context in which to evaluate the player?

I have decided to evaluate each player *as if he played in a context of eight other players of average skill, each having the same number of plate appearances*. What represents average skill?

Well, as I said earlier, it doesn't really matter; you're going to get the same answer at the end of the day regardless of what numbers you select to represent the rest of the team. Suppose, however, that in a period of 80 plate appearances, a player had 19 hits, 5 walks, and 30 total bases. That would be a reasonably typical hitter. His batting average would be .253, his on-base percentage .300, his slugging percentage .400.

These particular numbers have an advantage, which is that, when aggregated, they round out nicely. Eight players of this caliber would create 72 runs—192 times 240, divided by 640. Nine players of the same caliber would create 81 runs—216 times 270, divided by 720. Thus, the number of runs created by *eight* of these players—72—is exactly one-tenth of the *plate appearances* you would have with *nine* of these players—720.

Thus, what we do is, we create an offensive context in which there are nine players, each of whom has the same number of plate appearances. One of those players is the individual whose runs created we are measuring. The other eight are the theoretically typical players outlined above—the .253 hitters with .300 on-base percentages and .400 slugging percentages. The runs created by these nine players are then calculated, and the runs created by the "other eight" are removed.

This is what we are doing in the "D" section of the runs created routine above.

In lines D1 to D3, we are modifying the "A" element of the runs created formula by adding in eight other players with .300 on base percentages (Eight times .3 equals 2.4).

In lines D4 to D6, we are modifying the "B" element of the runs created formula by adding in eight other players who get three total bases for each eight at bats (3/8 times 8 equals 3). In lines D7 and D8, we are modifying the "C" element by adding in eight other players who have the same number of plate appearances as the player being tested.

In lines D9 and D10, we are figuring the runs created by these nine players—the individual studied, and the eight theoretically average players.

In lines D11 through D13, we are removing the runs created by the other eight players. Since the runs created by eight of the typical players are 10% of the plate appearances of nine of them, the runs created by the other players are therefore .90 times the plate appearances of the individual. These numbers are used because they are easy to put in, and easy to take back out. What we have done, in lines D1 through D14, is simply put the player in a theoretical offensive context, and then take his individual runs created back out.

Since I last published a full explanation of the Runs Created method, we have added three stages to the system, which we could call the "D Stages," the "E stages" and the "F stages." The E stages are based on the detailed records of every major league game, which have been maintained by STATS, Inc. since the mid-1980s.

I am skeptical whether there is, in baseball, any such thing as "clutch" ability, an ability to get a hit at a key moment of the game. However, within a season, there are deviations in performance in clutch situations. Suppose that there are two players who have identical statistics—.300 with 30 home runs apiece—but one of the two players hit .350 with runners in scoring position (49 for 140), while the other has hit .250 with runners in scoring position (35 for 140), and one hits 20 of his 30 home runs with men or mice on base, and the other hits 20 of his 30 home runs with the bases empty. Would the runs actually created by these two players be the same, or would they be different? Obviously, they would be different.

I took the detailed STATS batting records of a couple hundred major league teams, and studied them to see how performance in key situations affected the runs scored by the team. I found two things:

1. Teams that hit well with runners in scoring position had a gain of essentially one run scored for each extra hit, and vice versa.

2. Teams that hit home runs with men on base had a gain of essentially one run scored for each extra home run, and vice versa.

For the sake of clarity, two points. First, there *might be* any number of other "clutch" performances that also increase or decrease runs scored. I looked at a lot of other things, including extra base hits with men on first base and reaching base leading off an inning. I was unable to find anything else which predicted increases or decreases in runs scored significantly enough to justify adjustments to the runs created estimates. This does not mean that there is nothing else there; I just didn't find it. In theory, one would suppose that all deviations of actual runs scored from theoretical runs created must be explained by some sort of clutch performance or some other as yet unmeasured offensive skill. When I know more, I'll be able to build in better adjustments for clutch performance. This is just where I am today.

Second, the adjustments made for clutch performance are pro-rated for clutch opportunities. Thus, there is no advantage given here to players who have disproportionate chances in RBI situations.

In lines E1 through E4, we figure the player's expected hits with runners in scoring position, and compare that to his actual hits with runners in scoring position.

In lines E5 through E10, we figure the player's expected home runs with runners on base, and compare that to his actual home runs with runners on base.

In lines E11 through E13, we adjust the player's runs created estimate for his performance in these two clutch situations.

Finally, in lines F1 through F7, we reconcile the team's runs created estimates to their actual runs scored. Suppose that there are two teams of players, each of which totals up to 800.00 runs created, by the best estimates that we can make. One team of players, however, actually scored 820 runs. The other team actually scored 780 runs. Are the players on the two teams equal, or are they unequal?

Obviously, they are unequal. We don't know *why* one team scored more runs than the other, but there obviously has to be some reason for it. Until we have perfect data and perfect runs created formulas to assess the data, the best that we can do is to hold all of the players on the team equally responsible for the performance shortfall, or give them equal credit for the team's unexplained accomplishments.

Not everybody thinks that these adjustments are appropriate, and I understand that. Here's how I see it. Our goal is to evaluate as accurately as possible how many runs were created by every major league player in the history of the game. If we estimate that the players on a team created only 800 runs when the team actually scored 850 runs, we *know* that our estimates are wrong. We have to do the best we can, given the information available, to make the estimates right. This is the best we can do.

The statistics available have changed throughout the history of baseball, and so we have a different runs created formula for each era of baseball history. A full accounting of the 24 formulas that we use can be found in the *All-Time Major League Handbook*, by myself, STATS, Inc. and others including John Dewan, Don Zminda, Neil Munro and Jim Callis.

I think that, with the explanation above and the formulas in the book, you can figure the Runs Created for any player in major league history as accurately as I could. Now that you may understand what all of those calculations are and why they are set up the way they are, I will adapt the outline above, and walk you through the calculations for Jimmie Foxx, 1932, and Roger Connor, 1890. First, Foxx:

A1	Enter the player's Hits		213	
A2	Add his Walks	+ 116 =	329	
A3	Add his Hit by Pitch	+ 0 =	329	
A4	Subtract Caught Stealing	- 7 =	322	
A5	The result is the player's "A" factor			322
B1	Take the player's Walks		116	
B2	Plus Hit by Pitch	+ 0 =	116	
B3	Multiply by .23	116 X .23 =	26.68	
B4	Take his Stolen Bases		3	
B5	Add his Sacrifice Hits	+ 0 =	3	
B6	Multiply the total by .50	3 X .50 =	1.50	
B7	Add together B3 and B6		28.18	
B8	Take his Strikeouts		96	
B9	Multiply by .06	96 X .06 =	5.76	
B10	Subtract that from B7		22.42	
B11	Take his Total Bases		438.00	
B12	Add that to line B10		460.42	
B13	The result is the player's "B" factor			460.42

C1	Take the player's At Bats		585	
C2	Add his Walks	+ 116 =	701	
C3	Add his Hit Batsmen	+ 0 =	701	
C4	Add his Sacrifice Hits	+ 0 =	701	
C5	The result is the player's "C" factor			701

D1	Take the player's "C" factor		701	
D2	Multiply by 2.4		1682.40	
D3	Add in the player's "A" factor	+ 322 =	2004.40	
D4	Take the "C" factor again		701	
D5	Multiply by 3.0		2103	
D6	Add in the Player's "B" factor	+ 460.42 =	2563.42	
D7	Take the "C" factor again		701	
D8	Multiply by 9	X 9 =	6309	
D9	Multiply D3 Times D6	=	5138119.048	
D10	Divide by D8	=	814.41101	
D11	Take the "C" factor again		701	
D12	Multiply by .90	X .90 =	630.90000	
D13	Subtract D12 from D10		183.51101	
D14	The result is our first Runs Created estimate			183.51101

We don't have situational data for Foxx, so the "E stages" of the Runs Created analysis are not germane here. We proceed to the team reconciliation:

F1	Repeat this process for every member of the player's team			
F2	Total them up. In this case, the result is		955.82489	
F3	Take the actual runs scored by the team		981	
F4	Divide F3 by F2	981 / 955.82489 =	1.02634	
F5	Multiply D14 by F4	183.51101 X 1.02634 =	188.34444	
F6	Round that off		188	
F7	The result is the player's Runs Created estimate			188

Jimmie Foxx created about 188 runs created in 1932, as best I am capable of estimating it. This is one of the highest totals of the twentieth century.

Now Roger Connor, 1890:

A1	Enter the player's Hits		169	
A2	Add his Walks	+ 88 =	257	
A3	Add his Hit by Pitch	+ 1 =	258	
A4	The result is the player's "A" factor			258

B1	Take the player's Walks		88	
B2	Plus Hit By Pitch	+ 1 =	89	
B3	Multiply by .34	89 X .34 =	30.26	
B4	Take his Stolen Bases		22	
B5	Multiply by .70	22 X .70 =	15.40	
B6	Take his At Bats		484	
B7	Subtract his Strikeouts		32	
B8	Multiply that by .04	452 X .04 =	18.08	
B9	Take his Total Bases		265	
B10	Multiply by 1.10	265 X 1.1 =	291.50	
B11	Add together B3, B5, B8 and B10		355.24	
B12	The result is the player's "B" factor			355.24
C1	Take the player's At Bats		484	
C2	Add his Walks	+ 88 =	572	
C3	Add his Hit Batsmen	+ 1 =	573	
C4	The result is the player's "C" factor			573
D1	Take the player's "C" factor		573	
D2	Multiply by 2.4		1375.20	
D3	Add in the player's "A" factor	+ 258 =	1633.20	
D4	Take the "C" factor again		573	
D5	Multiply by 3.0		1719	
D6	Add in the Player's "B" factor	+ 355.24 =	2074.24	
D7	Take the "C" factor again		573	
D8	Multiply by 9	X 9 =	5157	
D9	Multiply D3 Times D6	=	3387648.768	
D10	Divide by D8	=	656.90300	
D11	Take the "C" factor again		573	
D12	Multiply by .90	X .90 =	515.70000	
D13	Subtract D12 from D10		141.20300	
D14	The result is our first Runs Created estimate			141.20300
F1	Repeat this process for every member of the player's team			
F2	Total them up. In this case, the result is		925.08972	
F3	Take the actual runs scored by the team		1018	
F4	Divide F3 by F2	1018 / 925.08972 =	1.10044	
F5	Multiply D14 by F4	141.20300 X 1.10043 =	155.38455	
F6	Round that off		155	
F7	The result is the player's Runs Created estimate			155

Roger Connor created about 155 runs in 1890. This was the highest total in the Players League.

I hope that this is a full explanation of the Runs Created estimates which we use here. You could take this system, if you wanted, and calculate Runs Created for every player and every season in major league history. The data for each season can be found in the *All-Time Major League Handbook*, while the situational hitting stats needed can be found in each season's edition of the *Player Profiles*, also from STATS, Inc. You will find a couple of problems:

1. It will take you, if you work at it full time, about eight years to figure every player in major league history.

2. You will occasionally find one-run discrepancies between your calculations and the results printed in the *All-Time Major League Handbook*.

The reason for these discrepancies is that STATS, in figuring the Runs Created for the *All-Time Major League Handbook*, has been rounding off the data within the process. This was inappropriate, and I would hope that, if there are future editions of the *Handbook*, this would not be done.

How We Figure Component ERA

A pitcher's Component ERA is, in essence, *the ERA which we would expect a pitcher to have, given his walks, hits, hit batsmen and home runs allowed per nine innings*. It is a "second look" at the pitcher's effectiveness, not *more* important than ERA, but a second look, which is useful in case there is something hinkey about the ERA.

To figure Component ERA, what we do, in essence, is to estimate the "runs created" against the pitcher. Like all runs created formulas, this one has an A factor, a B factor, and a C factor, which are put together in the usual way—A times B, divided by C equals runs.

In this case, the A factor is:

Hits
Plus Walks
Plus Hit Batsmen

The B factor is:

Hits minus Home Runs
Times 1.255
Plus 4 times Home Runs
The sum of that, times .89
Plus Walks minus Intentional Walks, times .56
Plus Hit Batsmen times .56

The C factor is Batters Facing Pitcher.

The result of that will be an estimate of the runs created against the pitcher. To convert that to an ERA equivalent, you multiply by nine, divide by innings pitched, and subtract .56 (to adjust for the un-earned runs). If the expected runs allowed/9 innings is less than 2.24, then multiply it by .75, rather than subtracting 0.56.

Since Kent Mercker led the 1998 Cardinals in innings pitched, let's use Kent Mercker, 1998, to illustrate the process. Mercker allowed 199 hits, 53 walks and 3 hit batsmen; thus, his A factor is 255.

Mercker allowed 199 hits including 11 home runs; that means 188 non-home runs. Multiplying that by 1.255, we have 235.94. Adding 44 for the 11 home runs, we have 279.94.

Multiply that by .89; that makes 249.1466.

Next we take his walks (53), subtract his intentional walks (4), and add his hit batsmen (3). That's 52; we multiply that by .56, and add the result to the 249.1466. It makes a total of 278.27. Mercker's B factor is 278.27.

Mercker faced 716 batters in 1998; his C factor is just 716. We multiply his A factor (255) by his B factor (278.27) and divide by C (716). The result is 99.103. We thus estimate that Mercker would allow 99.103 runs. (He actually allowed 99.) We multiply this figure (99.103) by nine, and divide by his innings pitched (161.67). The result is 5.52.

We then subtract .56, yielding a result of 4.96. This is Kent Mercker's Component ERA for 1998—4.96. His actual ERA was 5.07.

To figure a pitcher's Component ERA, you need seven pieces of information about him:

1. His Innings Pitched
2. His Hits Allowed
3. His Home Runs Allowed
4. His Walks
5. His Intentional Walks
6. His Hit Batsmen
7. His Batters Facing Pitcher

You don't *need* the pitcher's runs allowed and earned runs allowed, but we'll include those anyway as we chart the 1998 Cardinals:

	Inn	R	ER	H	HR	BB	IBB	HB	BFP
Kent Mercker	161.2	99	91	199	11	53	4	3	716
Todd Stottlemyre	161.1	74	63	146	20	51	0	4	674
Kent Bottenfield	133.2	72	66	128	13	57	3	4	578
Matt Morris	113.2	37	32	101	8	42	6	3	468
Mark Petkovsek	105.2	63	56	131	9	36	3	8	476
Juan Acevedo	98.1	30	28	83	7	29	2	4	394
John Frascatore	95.2	48	44	95	11	36	3	3	415
Donovan Osborne	83.2	42	38	84	11	22	2	1	358
Manny Aybar	81.1	58	54	90	6	42	1	2	369
Darren Oliver	57.0	31	27	64	7	23	1	0	256
Rick Croushore	54.1	31	30	44	6	29	2	4	243
Curtis King	51.0	20	20	50	5	20	4	3	218
Jeff Brantley	50.2	26	25	40	12	18	3	1	209
Lance Painter	47.1	24	21	42	5	28	3	4	207
Bobby Witt	47.1	32	26	55	7	20	1	2	217
Mike Busby	46.0	23	23	45	3	15	0	5	202
Cliff Politte	37.0	32	26	45	6	18	0	1	172
Jose Jimenez	21.1	8	7	22	0	8	0	0	94
Brady Raggio	7.0	12	12	22	1	3	0	1	43
Bryan Eversgerd	6.0	7	6	9	1	2	0	1	31
Sean Lowe	5.1	9	9	11	1	5	0	0	31
Braden Looper	3.1	4	2	5	1	1	0	0	16
Gary Gaetti	1.0	0	0	2	0	0	0	0	5

Todd Stottlemyre, the only other Cardinal pitcher to pitch 140 or more innings, has an A factor of 201, a B factor of 242.7357, and a C factor of 674. We would thus expect him to allow 72.39 runs with the Cardinals in 1998 (not counting his work with Texas, after the mid-season trade). He actually allowed 74 runs.

Multiplying the 72.39 times 9, dividing by innings and subtracting .56, this makes a Component ERA for Stottlemyre of 3.48. His actual ERA was 3.51.

These are the A, B and C factors, the "runs created against," the actual runs allowed, and the Component and actual ERAs of all the Cardinal pitchers:

	A	B	C	RC	RA	ERC	ERA
Kent Mercker	255	278.27	716	99.10	99	4.96	5.07
Todd Stottlemyre	201	242.74	674	72.39	74	3.48	3.51
Kent Bottenfield	189	207.21	578	67.76	72	4.00	4.44
Matt Morris	146	154.20	468	48.10	37	3.25	2.53
Mark Petkovsek	175	191.27	476	70.32	63	5.43	4.77
Juan Acevedo	116	127.17	394	37.44	30	2.87	2.56
John Frascatore	134	153.14	415	49.45	48	4.09	4.14
Donovan Osborne	107	132.46	358	39.59	42	3.70	4.09
Manny Aybar	134	139.26	369	50.57	58	5.04	5.98
Darren Oliver	87	100.91	256	34.29	31	4.85	4.26
Rick Croushore	77	81.16	243	25.72	31	3.70	4.97
Curtis King	73	78.70	218	26.35	20	4.09	3.53
Jeff Brantley	59	82.95	209	23.42	26	3.60	4.44
Lance Painter	74	75.37	207	26.94	24	4.56	3.99
Bobby Witt	77	90.29	217	32.04	32	5.53	4.94
Mike Busby	65	68.79	202	22.14	23	3.77	4.50
Cliff Politte	64	75.56	172	28.12	32	6.28	6.32
Jose Jimenez	30	29.05	94	9.27	8	3.35	2.95
Brady Raggio	26	29.26	43	17.69	12	22.18	15.43
Bryan Eversgerd	12	14.18	31	5.49	7	7.67	9.00
Sean Lowe	16	17.53	31	9.05	11	14.71	15.19
Braden Looper	6	8.59	16	3.22	4	8.14	5.40
Gary Gaetti	2	2.23	5	0.89	0	7.48	0.00

Perhaps the most interesting player here is Matt Morris, who posted a 2.53 ERA in a half-season's work as a Cardinal starter. The Component ERA suggests that Morris pitched well—better than any of the other Cardinal starting pitchers—but not *that* well; his 2.53 ERA may reflect a bit of luck.

Suppose that you have two pitchers, each of whom has a 4.00 ERA. One pitcher, however, has a Component ERA of 3.50; the other, of 4.50. Common sense would suggest that, in future years, the pitcher with the better Component ERA might post better actual ERAs, as their luck evens out in terms of how run elements are combined into runs. However, no research that I am aware of confirms this—or, for that matter, refutes it. I don't believe that the issue has ever been studied.

The Component ERA formula changes a little bit for earlier pitchers (pre-1955), for whom intentional walk totals are not available. However, this is almost completely irrelevant to the earlier teams, because the Component ERA is used only to evaluate "Save Equivalent Innings," and earlier pitchers have very few saves.

For these pitchers, you will note, we have no count of their intentional walks. For pitchers for whom intentional walks are missing, we change one element of the formula. One part of the formula is (TBB - IBB + HBP) * .56. We change that now to (TBB + HBP) * .475. Otherwise, the formula still works.

What in the Hell Is the Team/League Putout Percentage?

The Team/League Putout Percentage, or TLPOP for short, is just:

(Team Putouts - Strikeouts) divided by

(League Putouts - Strikeouts)

The Team/League Putout Percentage is often used in this system in lieu of the league average for a team, because the league average for a team would often be misleading for one reason or another. In the extreme case, there were some 19th-century teams which folded after playing only a few games. For those teams, you obviously cannot compare them to the league average. . . you could not, for example, compare the walks issued by the 1884 Richmond Virginians, who played only 46 games, to the league average per team, since the other teams in the league played about 110 games each.

Even setting aside those odd cases, the numbers of innings played by different teams in a league are all different, due to rainouts, extra-inning games, and other factors. If team A has 1100 strikeouts and team B has 800, team A has 300 more fielding chances than team B. The Team/League Putout Percentage is used to build in a kind of "automated adjustment" for this.

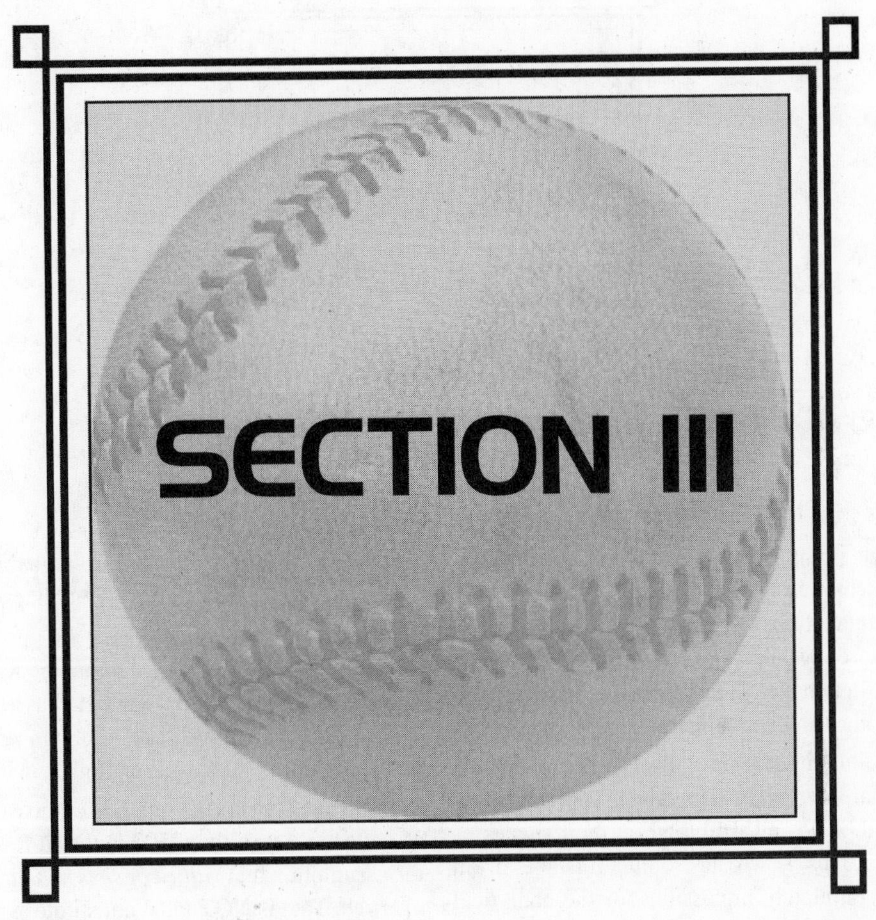

Whys and Wherefores

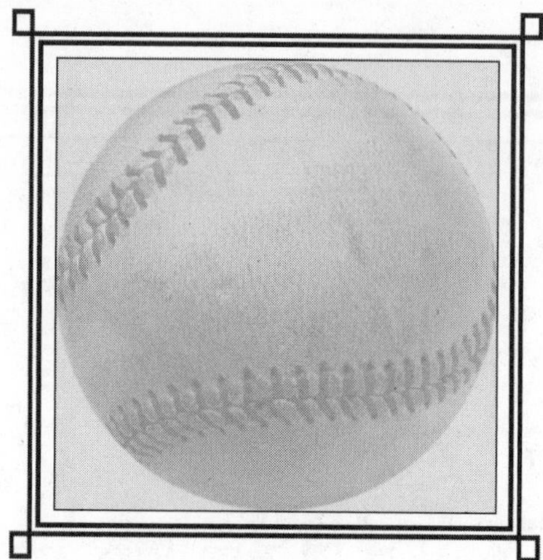

At some point, I need to address the broader question of why this system is designed the way it is. The basic explanation is that I believe that this design embodies more reasonable assumptions about value, particularly defensive value, than the assumptions underlying other analytical methods.

Many value models start all players out at .500, assuming that everybody is average, and then push them upward or downward based on their successes and failures. This is a catastrophic mistake, from which it is completely impossible for the analytical system to recover. If one is resourceful in analyzing the data from that point onward, and if one supports one's system with other methods, then it is possible to delay the point at which this mistake will catch up to you. If you're extremely clever, as Pete Palmer is in designing the Linear Weights method, then it is possible to get a lot of good, valid information out of the system, despite the initial mistake. But sooner or later, if you make that mistake, it is going to undermine your structure.

Why? It is impossible to build a solid analytical structure based on the assumption that teams start out at .500 for the same reasons that it is impossible to build a 17-room mansion on top of a flagpole. You've got no foundation. The assumption underlying the method is simply, flatly and un-arguably false, and sooner or later the structure will collapse because of that.

Baseball teams do not start out the season with 81 wins, and go up or down from there based on how well they play. Teams start the season with zero wins, and go up when they play well enough to win.

The fatal error in the method of measuring players as better or worse than .500 is that it forces one into the assumption that *value consists in being better than average*. That is NOT what constitutes value in baseball. What constitutes value in baseball is *being good enough to play at this level*. What constitutes value is being good enough to help the team win some games.

In a plus/minus system, below-average players have no value. In real baseball, near-average players have tremendous value. What gives them value?

The fact that you'll lose if you don't have them.

Look, every year, pennant races are lost because *teams can't find a .500 pitcher when they need one*. They can't find .500 pitchers, so they send bad pitchers to the mound, and they lose.

Or they can't find an outfielder who will hit .260 with an occasional home run.

Or they can't find a second baseman who can actually play second base.

In view of the fact that teams lose pennant races every year because they can't find average players, in view of the fact that teams pay very average players $2.5 million a year, it would be preposterous to argue that an average player has no value.

So long as the method deals only with players who are above average, so long as it deals only with players who are above average in all phases of their game, so long as it deals only with players who are above average in each season of their careers, so long as it deals only with players of comparable career length or comparable playing time within the season, a "plus/minus" system may be able to make accurate comparisons between two players.

But when a plus/minus system gets outside of any of those parameters, it becomes disoriented, and begins to point in unreliable directions. Suppose that you have a ".510" player—a player who is just a little bit better than average—and a ".501" player—a player who is just a tiny, tiny bit better than average.

If their playing time is equal, a plus/minus system will say that the .510 player has ten times the value of the .501 player, because he is ten times further above average. This is simply not an accurate comparison. The real "floor" on value isn't .500; it's somewhere under .300:

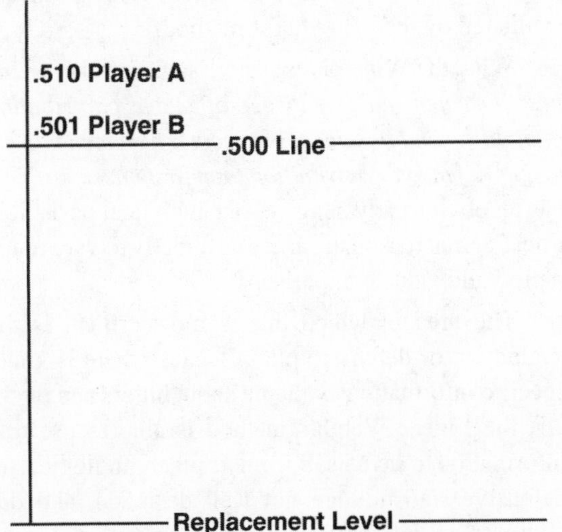

Player A is not ten times as valuable as Player B; rather, he is something more like three percent more valuable, if their playing time is even.

That's the *easy* case. But what if their playing time is not equal? What if the .501 player has played regularly all year, while the .510 player has played only one-third of the games?

The plus/minus system will still find that Player A is more valuable than Player B. The plus/minus system will argue that Player A is ten times as valuable per game, in one-third the playing time, so he is three times as valuable.

But, of course, he is not. In reality, Player B is roughly 97% as valuable, per game, as Player A. With three times the playing time, Player B is 2.9 times as valuable overall, or thereabouts.

This is still a relatively simple case. Suppose that one of the players is not at .501, but at .490—a slightly below-average player. Here, the plus/minus system goes even further off-course. It will insist that a player who is just above average in a third of a season (or in a short career) is far more valuable than a player who is just below average, but in a full season.

This is still a relatively simple case. Suppose that a player is above-average offensively, but below-average defensively. How do you put those together?

Suppose that a player is above-average in some seasons, but below average in others. What then?

Suppose that a player plays two defensive positions, and is great at one but poor at the other. What then?

With a plus/minus system oriented at .500, it is completely impossible to deal with these complications.

Let me back off and try this again. . .

The ".500 line" in baseball is a theoretical construct. It has no real meaning in a player's career. If a player is a .520 player one year and a .480 player the next, it makes only the slightest difference to him or anyone else. He'll get basically the same raise one year that he did the other. His agent will treat him exactly the same, his team will treat him exactly the same, if he was a regular one year he'll be a regular the next. There is no meaningful difference between "just above average" and "just below average."

On the other hand, being better or worse than the replacement level is a critical difference. There is all the difference in the world between being just above that line, and just under it. If you're above it, you're employed. If you're beneath it, you're released. If you're above it, you're in the majors. If you're below it, you're in the minors.

And the reason for that is, *.500 players are not freely available*. They're not easy to find. Shortage creates value—not only economic value, but win value. If you're above replacement level, even if you're below average, you're helping your team win. .500 players are almost as difficult to find as .550 players.

Because the Linear Weights system starts with a false assumption about what constitutes value, it is forced to make other false assumptions later on, to try to re-orient itself. Let me give you a realistic example. Suppose that there is a league in which the average first baseman creates 100 runs, while the average second baseman creates 60 runs. On this team there are two regulars, a first baseman who hits .290 with 25 homers, creating 95 runs, and a second baseman who hits .270 with 12 homers, creating 70 runs. Each of these players is average defensively at his own position.

A plus/minus system, to evaluate these two players, must do one of two things:

1. It must say that, in this league, the first basemen are better players than the second basemen, or

2. It must adjust everything again, comparing the hitting of the first baseman to the hitting of other first basemen and the hitting of the second baseman to the hitting of other second basemen.

Any serious analyst, unhappy with a universe in which the second basemen are just bad players, will choose the second option.

But the second option, again, presents problems. Who is the better hitter, the first baseman who creates 95 runs, or the second baseman who creates 70? The plus/minus system, having made these adjustments, is forced to argue that the second baseman who creates 70 runs is a better hitter than the first baseman who creates 95. He is a better hitter *because he plays second base*.

Well, of course he is not a better hitter. This manner of speaking has become so ingrained in the conversation, from years of using *Total Baseball* as a resource, that the inherent absurdity of it is being lost. A second baseman who hits .270 with 12 homers is not a better hitter than a first baseman who hits .290 with 25 homers—nor, for that matter, is an average defensive first baseman as good a fielder as an average defensive shortstop. I am certain that I will receive the requisite ten letters telling me that I am under-valuing the defense of first basemen, but it is absurd to argue that the Mo Vaughns and Mark Graces of the world are as valuable on defense, on the average, as the Omar Vizquels and Neifi Perezes. They are simply not.

The Linear Weights system, having its foundation in mid-air, is forced to prop itself up with additional false assumptions, in the same way that a man building a 17-story mansion on top of a flagpole would be forced to try to prop the thing up with additional poles and wires, forestalling the project's inevitable collapse. The Win Shares system is not forced to make these adjustments. Nobody hits as a first baseman; everybody hits as a hitter. What defensive position a player plays has nothing to do with how his offense is evaluated by the Win Shares method.

What the Win Shares system says, instead, is that *first basemen make a larger offensive contribution than do second basemen, but second basemen make a larger defensive contribution than first basemen*. This has an obvious advantage, as an analytical basis: it is true. For that reason, it carries us directly toward much more valid value comparisons.

The area in which this is most critical is the evaluation of defensive play. Because there is good, specific information available about hitters and pitchers, the Linear Weights method is able to use that information to save itself from its inherent illogic. But defensive statistics are not well designed, and our ability to get information out of the statistics at some positions is limited. Deprived of that ability, the Linear Weights system is thrown back on its underlying logic—and it collapses.

Take the case of two catchers, one of whom catches 1600 games in the major leagues and is the starting catcher for five teams which reach the World Series, and the other of whom catches 500 games in his career and plays mostly for bad teams. We'll call these two guys, just for the heck of it, Carlton Fisk and Doc Edwards. We could also call them Johnny Kling and Gary Alexander, or Wally Schang and Dick Brown; you get the idea.

The Linear Weights Method starts with the *assumption* that everybody is plus or minus zero as a defensive player, and forces the catchers to prove that they are better than that—without any reference to the won-lost record of their teams. This is impossible for them to do, because good data on catchers' defensive ability just doesn't exist until STATS comes along in the mid-1980s.

The result is that in the Linear Weights method, Johnny Bench rates at -80, one of the worst defensive catchers of all time, Carlton Fisk rates at -44, Bill Freehan at -38, and John Roseboro at -22, while Tim Blackwell rates at +40, George Mitterwald is at +40, Jerry May is at +21, Jeff Newman is at +9, Doc Edwards is at +17, and Jeff Torborg is +79.

I'm not saying that our system will never make any mistakes. What I'm saying is, our system will never make any mistakes of that magnitude. Our system may well rank Johnny Bench below Tony Pena and Yogi Berra, when there is good, documented evidence that Bench was one of the greatest defensive catchers of all time. Our system may well rank Johnny Bench below Gary Carter and Bill Dickey, when he perhaps should rate ahead of those guys.

But there is no way in hell that our system will rank Johnny Bench below Tim Blackwell or Jerry May. It can't.

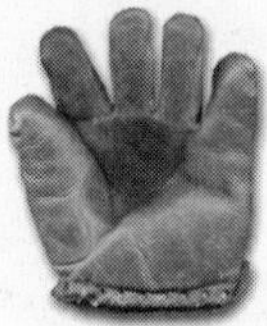

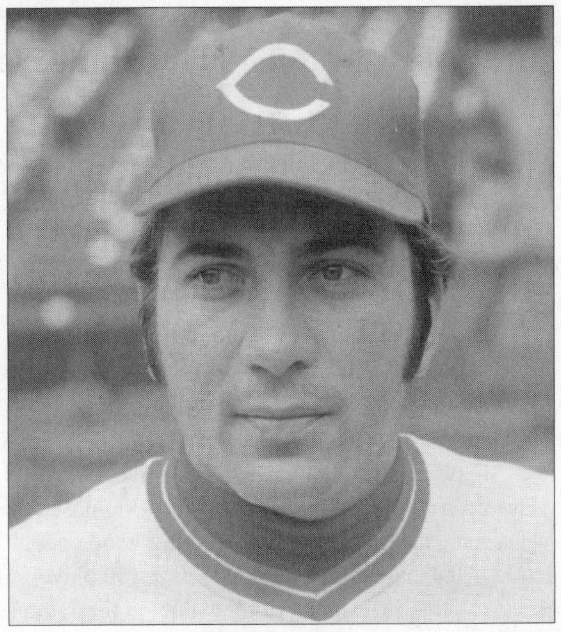

Johnny Bench

When a team wins 100 games, our system assumes that the starting catcher on that team can most probably play defense, just as it assumes that the second baseman can probably play second base and the shortstop can probably play shortstop. Based on that assumption, our system creates a "space" for the defense of the catcher, a space for the defense of the second baseman, etc. That space is larger if the team wins 100 games than if the team wins 60 games, and it is larger if the team allows few runs than it is if the team allows lots of runs.

If our system fails—if we can't find the evidence that Johnny Bench is a good defensive catcher—then Bench winds up *below the usual standard of a player catching 140 games a season for a great team.* If the Linear Weights system fails, he winds up below zero, which means he winds up behind Jerry Moses. That's a big difference. It is the difference between a system which recognizes the obvious, and a system which fails to recognize the obvious.

The Baseball Player as an Iceberg

A baseball player is like an iceberg: 90% of his value is below water.

Suppose that we start with this question: what percentage of a player's value is in being better than average, and what percentage is in being average (or less than average)?

Since players are arrayed around .500, one might think, intuitively, that 50% of value consists in being average, and 50% consists in being better than average. This is far from true.

Suppose that you have three players: a .400 player, a .500 player, and a .600 player. Suppose that we assume that value consists of being good enough to play, and that one has to be at least a .150 player in order to play. How much of the value on these three players, then, is derived from being average (or worse), and how much is derived from being better than average?

Well, the .600 player has a value of about .450 (.600 minus .150)—.350 from being average, and .100 from being better than average.

The .500 player has a value of about .350—all of it based on being average.

The .400 player has a value of about .250—all of it based on being less than average.

Totaling up the three players, then, 90% of the value is in being average:

For the .600 player, 350 of 450
For the .500 player, 350 of 350
For the .400 player, 250 of 250

The total value of the three players is 1050 points—950 from being average, and 100 from being better than average.

Suppose that you articulate the group a little better, make it resemble more closely a real distribution of players. Suppose that you have a universe consisting of one player who has a .400 effective winning percentage, two players who have .450 winning percentages, four players who have .500 winning percentages, two players at .550, and one player at .600. What then?

If you use those assumptions, and the same method outlined above, then you will find that 95% of the value of the ten players is derived from being average, 5% from being better than average.

Of course, the real distribution of player effective winning percentages is much more complicated, and each player's winning percentage is difficult to fix. But as you make the test group more complicated, the same result persists, more or less: about 90% of player value is derived from being average or below average.

That is why a value system based on the assumption that a player's value starts at .500 can't possibly succeed. The .500 assumption doesn't misrepresent *some* of a player's value; it ignores or misrepresents *almost all* of a player's value. It is always the part of the iceberg below water that sinks the ship.

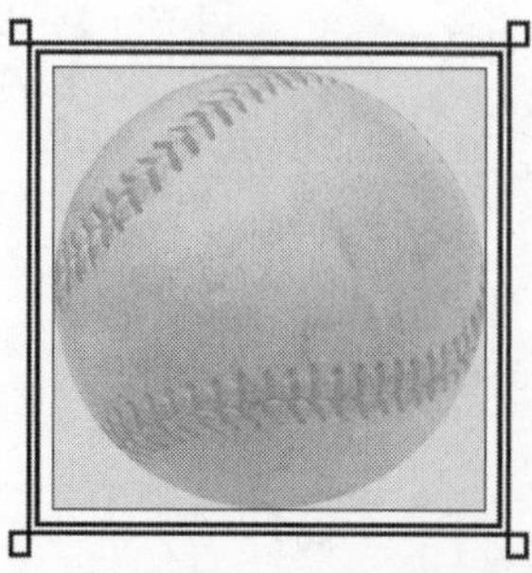

Win Shares and Replacement Level (Or. . . Pandora, shut your trap)

For many years, I have argued that "value" for a baseball player consists of being better than a replacement-level player. In fact. . . I hope I am not confusing the record here, but I think this was one of my ideas, this "replacement level" concept for measuring a player's value. If somebody else was writing about this first, I apologize, but I think it was mine.

Anyway, the Win Shares system operates on an entirely different theory of value—that value consists in winning games. Two distinct theories:

1. That value consists in being better than replacement level,

2. That value consists in winning games for your team.

Because I have in the past advocated theory (1), or because there is a "marginal" concept within Win Shares, or for some other reason, some people have assumed, incorrectly, that Win Shares are a way of measuring *marginal* win contributions, or contributions above replacement level. Not isolated people—lots of people. There has been discussion of Win Shares on bulletin boards and in similar forums, much of which assumes that Win Shares represent marginal win contributions, and debates the system based on that assumption.

No, no, no. . . this doesn't have anything to do with marginal win contributions. There is no "replacement level" contemplated within this system. Our theory here is that value consists in winning games.

In all candor, I myself was confused about this issue when I began working on the system, and I may have written something, or said something in an interview, which contributed to other people's confusion. But if you think about it, our system obviously cannot be measuring *marginal* win contributions, because *this system attributes to an individual all of a team's wins*. If a team wins 100 games, our system credits 300 Win Shares—not 250, not 275. ALL of a team's wins are attributed to individuals, which could not be true if we were measuring just the *marginal* wins.

Let me be a little bit more specific. . . some people have said that the Win Shares system assumes that the replacement level is a .100 player, and other people have said that it assumes a replacement level of .200. Since our system treats runs as marginal runs above a level of one-half the league norm (actually, .52 times the league norm), this could be represented as a winning percentage of .200 (if you assume a 1-2 ratio between runs scored and runs allowed), or as a winning percentage of .100 (if you assume a 1-3 ratio). But both answers are wrong, because the "marginal run level" in the Win Shares system is not a replacement level; it's assumed to be a zero-win level.

Now, this opens up a Pandora's box—a Pandora's box with three lids, if you like. First, *couldn't one argue that both theories of value are true, measure win contributions, and then remove from that win contributions which represent performance below replacement level?* Yes, absolutely; both theories of value could perfectly well be true, and it may well be that the best measure of value will eventually be not Win Shares, or marginal win contributions, but rather, some system which combines features of both. One could perfectly well measure each player's Win contribution, and then find some way to eliminate that portion which is below replacement level.

Opening the second lid. . . haven't we, in fact, confused a player with a very low winning percentage (let's say .100) with a player with a winning percentage of zero?

Yes, in fact, we have; we are pretending here that a certain very low level of performance doesn't contribute *anything* to the team's ability to win, when in fact it contributes *something*, albeit not much. Now, why are we pretending that near-zero performance is absolute zero performance? Because: *a) it is terribly useful to have a statement of how many games a player has won, and b) the distortions involved are trivial.*

Measuring how many games a player has won is something akin to the holy grail of sabermetrics. "How many games did he win?" is the fundamental question about a *player* in the same way that "How many runs did he create?" is the fundamental question about a *hitter*.

Actually, there are two fundamental questions about a hitter: How many runs did he create, and how many outs did he make? And, of course, there are two fundamental questions about a player: How many games did he win, and how many games did he lose?

This opens up the third lid of Pandora's Box. . . Why then, when you were measuring Win Shares, didn't you also measure Loss Shares? I didn't run Loss Shares because I simply could not figure out how to do it, but more on that in a moment. I have wanted for many years to be able to figure how many games were "won" by each player. I always thought that it was impossible to figure this. I was wrong.

Look, the ratio between a team's wins and losses is the same as the ratio between the square of their runs scored and the square of their runs allowed. Thus, an increase of ten percent in runs scored will yield an increase of 21% in wins relative to each loss.

This means that, if you graph wins against runs scored, you get not a straight line, but a line curving upward. Like this:

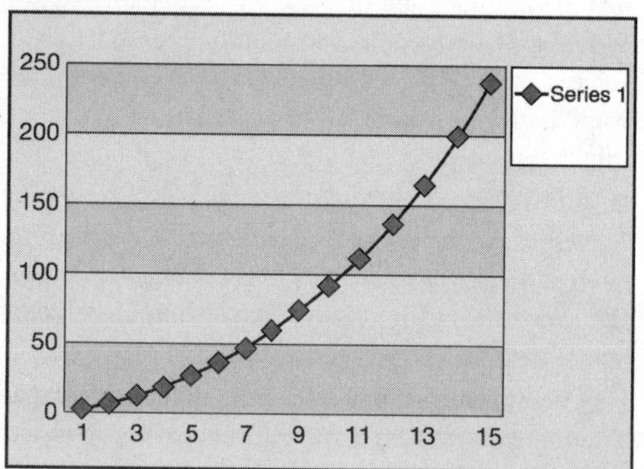

I believed, for many years, that the fact that this line curved upward meant that one could not infer wins from runs created for an individual player, because the answer you would get would depend on where the player was along the line, which means that the number of actual wins delivered by the player would depend on the specific context in which the player performed.

But I eventually realized that this wasn't a real problem, because, while the line describing the win impact of the player's run contribution was not *truly* straight, it was *virtually* straight within the limited range which describes the differences between actual teams. The line only *actually* curved very much in the range where there were no teams at all, and virtually no players—the range of teams creating less than one-half the league average of runs per game. One could make a straight-line representation of the graph that worked well within the critical range. Like this:

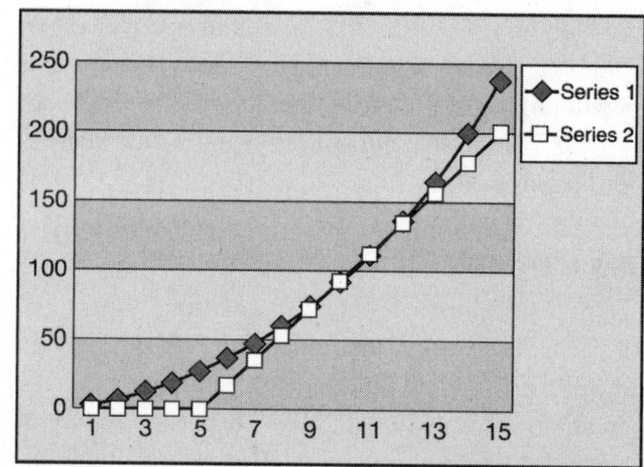

Yes, the line intersects zero at the wrong point, but. . . so what? All the *real* teams are in the range, on the chart above, from about 7 to 13—30% better or worse than the league average. The context in which each player plays is not far enough from the norm that the curvature of the line makes any real difference. Within the range where the teams are clustered, a linear representation of value works perfectly well—exactly as Pete Palmer has always insisted that it did. The curvature of the line would matter if there were teams that created almost no runs, or if there were players who created almost no runs. Since there are neither, it matters very little.

What I realized, which makes this system different from the things we have done in the past, is two things:

1. That this fact could be used not merely to compare players to the average, but that—accepting limited distortions in the way that Palmer had always urged—it could be used to estimate accurately the total win contribution of each player, and

2. That one could extend that structure to create a kind of "exoskeleton," within which we could build a better structure for fielding analysis.

I tried several times to figure Loss Shares, and *some* of the logic of how one would do this is obvious. But some of the logic is tricky, and I kept running into roadblocks. This system, as it is, took me four years to develop and Christ-knows-how-many formulas to explain. I couldn't see waiting another year, two years, three years and tacking on another 150 formulas while trying to figure out whether it is actually possible to do Loss Shares.

And even if I knew how to figure Loss Shares, this wouldn't be the end of the process. . . this would simply lead on to another set of questions. For example, what exactly *is* the replacement level?

Look, I acknowledge that there is some difference between "Wins" (or Win Shares) and "Value." In the other book, the *New Historical Abstract*, I didn't *always* rate the players according to their Career Win Shares. Win Shares are like Wins. Paul Splittorff won more games in his career than Sandy Koufax. Nobody believes that this makes Paul Splittorff a greater pitcher than Sandy Koufax. You have to consider Win Shares, Loss Shares, big-impact seasons, impact on pennant races, special contributions, etc.

I haven't suggested that Win Shares are the end of the discussion. What I have suggested is that Win Shares are an awfully useful thing to know, in order to conduct the discussion intelligently.

I didn't try to fit together Win Shares and replacement level, because there are a tangle of issues involved in putting them together, and frankly, I don't have the vaguest notion how to untangle them all. Let me outline some of the problems.

First, we have no firm idea what "Replacement Level" is, even given an older, established theoretical concept to analyze the game. Exactly what "replacement level" is is difficult to establish, because the distribution curve of actual baseball players simply tails away into a gas on the left end of the spectrum, the sub-.500 side. Nobody really has come up with any good way to establish what is a "replacement level" player.

Second, we have the problem of the distortion created by treating a player who creates less than one-half the league average of runs/plate appearance as if his win contribution was zero, when in reality it is merely near-zero. I think this is a minor problem, and I'm not really sure that it will be *any* problem. But on the other hand, I'm not sure that it isn't, either.

Third, there is a semantic or quasi-semantic problem with stating winning percentages for a theoretical player. You know that brain cramper we all get into trying to figure out why a team which is 51-49 is two games over .500, but only one game ahead of a team which is 50-50? There is a similar problem here. I once theorized that a replacement-level player should be about a .300 to .350 player, but this was assuming that a player who created runs at 70.7% of the league norm should be considered a .333 player (.707 squared divided by one plus .707 squared = .333). But if a team was 71% of league norm offensively and also 71% of the league norm defensively, their likely winning percentage wouldn't be .333, it would be .200. Does performing at a level of 71% of the league norm, measured in runs, represent a winning percentage of .333, or .200? Nobody really knows.

Fourth, the "replacement level winning percentage" *might* be very different, if stated in Win Shares and Loss Shares, than it is if stated in a pythagorean equivalent.

Unsnarling this mass of problems is simply a matter of thinking them through, one at a time. We will eventually get there, although I think it may be several years before we do, and it may be several years after that until there is something like a consensus on the issue.

I suspect that, once the point is reached that we have Win Shares and Loss Shares for each player each year, the issue of replacement level will then be a great deal easier to grab ahold of. We should be able to ask, at that point. . . of 200 players who had Win Share Winning Percentages between .250 and .260, how many were in the major leagues in the following season? By asking these kind of questions, we should be able to reach some sort of consensus about what the replacement level really is.

The Last Hard Fact

Suppose that you have two first basemen who are the same, except that one of them hits 20 home runs more than the other. Would it be reasonable to rate the first baseman who hits more home runs ahead of the first baseman who hits fewer home runs?

Of course it would, because if one first baseman hits more home runs and everything else is even, then his team will score more runs, and there is a well-founded expectation that his team will win more games. Of course one can do this.

Suppose that you have two pitchers who are the same, except that one of them allows just one run fewer than the other. Would it be reasonable to rate the pitcher who allowed one run less ahead of the other pitcher?

Of course it would, for the same reason. It would be reasonable to rate him ahead because there is a well-founded expectation that his team might win an extra game because of that one run. Team wins are the sun of the statistical solar system.

But suppose that you have two second basemen who are otherwise the same, except that one of them makes 50 more assists than the other. Would it be reasonable to rate the second baseman who makes 50 more assists ahead of the other one, based on those assists?

Well, here we run into a problem, which prevents fielders from being evaluated in the same straightforward way that pitchers and hitters are evaluated. If you compare teams on which the second basemen make 450 assists to teams on which the second basemen make 400 assists, you will not find that the teams on which the second basemen make more assists win any more games. In fact, you will find that they win, on average, slightly less games as the assists of the second basemen increase.

This happens because every team has to record 27 defensive outs per game, one way or another. If they record more defensive outs at second base, this simply means that they have recorded fewer outs in some other way—fewer strikeouts, or fewer putouts in the outfield, or something.

All fielding systems, in one way or another, tend to give preference to fielders who make more plays, rather than fielders who make fewer plays. But how can we justify rating one second baseman ahead of another based on extra assists, when research shows that making extra assists at second base is not a characteristic of successful teams? Aren't we rewarding something which is known to be irrelevant to success?

Defensive statistics are a kind of a squirrel cage, which take the energy intended to move forward, but use it instead to move the wheel around the squirrel. No matter how fast the squirrel runs, the cage isn't going anywhere—and no matter how many putouts the second baseman records, the team isn't going to win any more games.

The argument for giving credit for extra assists (or extra putouts) is that while making extra plays at second base is not a characteristic of excellence in the team, it is nonetheless characteristic of excellence *in the individual*. What making extra plays at second base shows, the argument goes, is not that this is a good team, but that *this is a team on which the second basemen make relatively more of a defensive contribution than the other fielders*. "Relatively" is the key word: relative to the other fielders on his team.

If you rush directly from that point to a rating system, without making team adjustments, this implies *that the relationship that the player bears to the league is the same as the relationship that he bears to his team*. And this implies, in turn, that *we are assuming that all defensive teams are equal*. Making 5.08 plays for one defense is the same as making 5.08 plays for another defense.

Well, are all defensive teams, in fact, equal?

Of course they are not. We know very well that all defensive teams are not equal— indeed, I tend to believe that the experience of being a baseball fan teaches us that defense is one of the things which is *most* unequal in a comparison of good and bad teams. So the question I would ask is, why in the world would we assume something which we know to be untrue?

Evaluating a fielder by the number of plays he makes afield is valid, I believe—if one also adjusts for the quality of the team defense. If you compare the player to his teammates *and also compare the team to the league*, then you have a basis for comparing players on different teams. But if you skip that crucial stage, and simply evaluate the player's range relative to his teammates, then you have no basis for a player-to-league comparison.

This is why, I believe, it is absolutely essential to incorporate an evaluation of the team's defensive performance into an evaluation of the player. I do not believe that any accurate defensive system can be developed without this step. I believe that the failure to do this is one of the critical missed steps which undermines the Linear Weights defensive measures, and many other systems as well.

Traditional defensive analysis (including my own, before this) begins with the player's fielding stats in the same way that traditional offensive analysis begins with the player's hitting stats. It's a habit.

But while this seems natural, the problem is that *we have no hard fact as a foundation to the system.* One may proceed from hitters' stats to value statements because a hitter's accomplishments are hard facts, which bear a clear relationship to team wins. One may not proceed from fielder's stats in the same way because fielding stats are "contextual" stats which bear no clear relationship to teams wins.

I chose to begin the defensive Win Shares system with the team wins because team wins are *the last tangible fact in the logical chain leading toward the player's defense*. Everything else achieves significance from the relationship it bears to team wins.

Are there better ways to do many of the things I have done? Of course; I'm certain that there must be.

Are there some inaccuracies in the method that I use to attribute Win Shares to a team's defensive performance?

Of course there are.

But if I have to choose between assuming that the 1975 Baltimore Orioles were 40% better defensively than the 1951 St. Louis Browns, or 60% better, or 80% better, I will choose any of those, rather than assuming that the two teams are even defensively. The assumption that the two teams are defensively even is the one thing that I know is false. My estimate may be off—but it is certainly closer to the truth than assuming that the two teams are defensively equal. I would rather make the best estimate I can and then worry about how to improve it, rather than continuing to use an assumption which I know to be incorrect. A defensive analysis, to approach accuracy, has to proceed not from the theory that all defenses are equal, but from the certain fact that they are not.

Adjusted Range Factors

I have, in the past, urged evaluating fielders by range factors. Range factors are simply plays made (Putouts and Assists) per game.

I have always understood in concept the limitations of this approach. I have, I confess, always underestimated the practical implications of this. While I now see the error of my ways, I am still in the habit of evaluating fielders by range factors, as I suspect that many of you are. Is there some way to redeem range factors from the arguments I have made against them in this book?

We can try. Let's use Jerry Lumpe and Bobby Richardson, 1961, as a test case. Richardson had a much better defensive reputation; Lumpe had a much better range factor. Jerry Lumpe in 1961 had 403 putouts and 426 assists in 147 games, a range factor of 5.64 (829 divided by 147). This is superficially outstanding.

Bobby Richardson had 413 putouts that same season, but only 376 assists, playing 161 games. This is only 4.90 plays per game.

Moving to the "innings" level, Lumpe must have played about 1281 innings in the field, or 142.3 full games. This would make his range factor, on a per-inning basis, an even-more outstanding 5.82. Richardson played about 1395 innings at second base—86 more than Lumpe—so when we adjust his range factor to full games, he winds up at 5.09. Lumpe has moved further ahead.

There is, however, a problem with this. Bobby Richardson won the Gold Glove in 1961. Gold Gloves are sometimes given to the wrong men, but Lumpe and Richardson competed for the Yankee second base job for several years. Lumpe was a better hitter—but Richardson won the contest. If Lumpe had better range than Richardson as well as a better bat, would that have happened?

Lumpe benefits from some illusions. The 1961 A's were not much of a defensive team. They lost 100 games, and led the league in hits allowed and runs allowed. They didn't have many strikeouts by pitchers. That means they had more balls in play against them than the Yankees did.

We can adjust for the strikeouts by simply taking the strikeouts out of the team's putouts, as the Linear Weights system does. The A's had 703 strikeouts among 4,260 putouts, which makes 3557 (PO - K).

We also need to adjust for the balls in play that *weren't* fielded. Those would be Hits allowed minus Home Runs (H - HR), which for Kansas City in 1961 would be 1519 minus 141, or 1378. That makes 4935 balls in play (3557 + 1378), which is 31.38 per nine innings. Lumpe's range factor, then, is 5.83 over 31.38—his individual plays per nine innings, divided by the team balls in play per nine innings.

If you work through the same math for the league, you will find that for the league as a whole there were 29.56 balls in play per nine innings. We can adjust Lumpe's range factor, then, by multiplying his range factor by the ratio of the league average to the Kansas City opportunities per nine innings. That ratio is 29.56 divided by 31.38, which is .942. Lumpe's adjusted range factor for 1961, then, is 5.49.

Making the same adjustments for Bobby Richardson. . . Richardson's raw range factor is 4.90, but on an estimated-innings basis it is 5.09. Putting this in team context, this would be 5.09 over 28.82, which would create an adjusted range factor of 5.22.

In other words, Lumpe's adjusted range factor in 1961 remains superior to Richardson's, but not very much superior. Whereas Lumpe's raw range factor is 74 points better than Richardson's (5.64 to 4.90), his adjusted range factor is only 27 points better (5.49 to 5.22). When we incorporate Richardson's superior ability on the double play, we might still conclude that Richardson was the better defensive second baseman.

By the use of this method, we could easily make adjusted range factors for every player every year. There are, however, unresolved problems. We could also normalize them all-time—that is, adjust everybody to a historic norm, rather than to a league norm. We *could* do that, but should we? I don't know. We could also adjust, for example, for the number of left-handed innings on the staff, or for the ground ball tendencies of the staff.

I think a little more research might be in order before we start doing those things. I think that, as raw measures of defensive ability, range factors may have about outlived their usefulness—but that, if we want to save them, we probably can. Sometime we'll figure out all the things we "should" adjust for, and do an Encyclopedia of normalized fielding statistics.

Ashburn and Hamner

This, to me, is one of the most interesting things that I have found in the years that I have been working on this system, and I hope it is of some interest to you, as well. This is one of those cases where it has taken me 30 years to discover something which is blindingly obvious.

Let's start where I started, which is with Richie Ashburn and Granny Hamner. I am certain that you are all aware of Richie Ashburn's outstanding fielding record. Of the top ten seasons in baseball history for putouts by an outfielder, Ashburn recorded six. He had 538 putouts in 1951, second-highest total ever, and 514 in 1949, third-highest total ever. He had 495 or more putouts six times; everybody else in baseball history did it four times. He led the National League in putouts three other years, in addition to those top six. His defensive statistics, interpreted in a traditional manner, are almost certainly the best of any outfielder in baseball history.

Ashburn's defensive record is beyond well known; it is one of the most discussed, cited, argued about and analyzed facts in the world of baseball statistics. The problem is that Ashburn, while he was certainly a good outfielder, was never regarded, while active, as a transcendent defensive star. When Gold Gloves were introduced in 1957, Richie Ashburn led all major league outfielders in putouts, with 502, in assists, with 18, and in double plays, with 7—but did *not* win a Gold Glove. The closest major league outfielder in putouts was Willie Mays, who trailed him by 80—yet the Gold Gloves went to Mays, Minnie Minoso, and Al Kaline.

Richie Ashburn

In 1958 Ashburn again led all major league outfielders in putouts, this time by a margin of 66. Willie Mays, again, was in second place—but the National League Gold Gloves went to Mays, Hank Aaron, and Frank Robinson. Ashburn, his career winding down, was never to win a Gold Glove.

There is another side to this story which is less well known: Granny Hamner. Hamner, five weeks younger than Richie, was Ashburn's teammate from 1948 until 1959. Well, actually longer than that; they were also teammates, and roommates, at Utica in 1947, and in 1946 they were members of the same U.S. Army team.

As players they were regarded, while active, as more or less equals. This may be generous to Ashburn. When *Sport* magazine rated all the National League players in February, 1955, they rated Ashburn the fifth-best center fielder in the league—and Hamner the second-best second baseman. Hamner was an exceptional hitter for a shortstop/second baseman, hitting as many as 39 doubles in a season, as many as 11 triples, and as many as 21 homers. He drove in 80+ runs in 1950, 1952, 1953 and 1954.

In many ways, they were exact opposites as players. Ashburn was a left-handed hitter; Hamner, a right-handed hitter. Ashburn was an outfielder; Hamner, an infielder. Ashburn walked a lot but had exceptionally little power for an outfielder of his time. Hamner walked very little but had unusual power for a middle infielder.

Hamner's defensive statistics are as bad as Ashburn's are good. In Linear Weights, while Ashburn kicks Ash, Hamner comes out as Hamburger—minus

283 runs, combining offense and D. *Total Baseball* doesn't give any lists of the worst players ever, but Hamner must rank, in their analysis, among the worst players in major league history. Isn't it possible, I wondered, that these two things are two sides of the same coin— that Hamner rates as inexplicably bad for the same external reasons that Ashburn's defensive numbers are inexplicably good? Isn't it more reasonable to think that, rather than Ashburn being an extraordinary defensive outfielder (which nobody noticed) and Hamner being an unusually bad defensive infielder (which nobody noticed), this was simply a team which had lots of fly balls, and very few ground balls?

If only we had counts of the numbers of ground balls and fly balls allowed by each team, maybe we could estimate that. . .

Why it took me thirty years to reach that point, I don't know, but when you reach that point, you discover that this actually is too easy. We didn't find it, I guess, because it's too obvious.

Look, more than 90% of outs are accounted for by one of three things—strikeouts, ground balls, and balls hit into the air. Right?

We count strikeouts, so that's easy.

The number of ground balls by a pitching staff is very simple to estimate accurately. When you have a ground ball, in the vast majority of cases, you have an Assist.

When you have an Assist, in the vast majority of cases, you have had a ground ball.

So the team assist total, while it is not *precisely* the same as the number of ground ball outs, is so closely related to it that the team assist total can easily be used as a stand-in for the number of ground balls.

If you want to refine it a little, you can take out the assists by catchers and the assists by outfielders. That's unnecessary, but that will make assists even closer to ground balls. . .

If you're not happy with that, you've still got an option: Putouts by the first basemen. Putouts by the first basemen, like Assists, are mostly the result of ground balls. And *most* ground ball outs, certainly something over 80%, are going to include a putout by the first baseman.

So the team total of ground ball outs, far from being elusive, is relatively obvious. Outs in the air? That's easy, too. If you take putouts, subtract strikeouts, and subtract assists, what do you have left? If a putout isn't a strikeout and isn't assisted, isn't it extremely likely that it's a fly ball or a pop out? Of course it is.

Well, let's look at the Phillies in the Hamner-Ashburn era. How many ground balls, fly balls and strikeouts did they have?

Their strikeouts are pretty much average. But the 1957 Philadelphia Phillies had only 1,437 assists, as a team. This was the lowest team assist total in the major leagues in 1957. It was the lowest team assist total in the major leagues in the 1950s. In fact, it is the lowest team assist total in the major leagues in the 20th century, except for the strike-shortened 1981, 1994 and 1995 seasons. It is lower than any total posted in the war-shortened 1918 season, or in any of the seasons early in the century when teams played 140 or fewer games.

If you draw up a list of the teams with the lowest assist totals in the major leagues between 1919 and 1960, that list is entirely dominated by the Ashburn-Hamner teams. The 1957 Phillies had the fewest assists, followed by the 1955 Phillies and the 1956 Phillies. Another team sneaks in there, and then we have the 1958 Phillies in fifth place. Only five teams in that long era recorded fewer than 1500 assists—four of those being the Phillies teams of 1955 to 1958.

If you stretch the list to the bottom 40 teams, you'll get the 1948, 1951, 1953, 1954, and 1959 Phillies.

So the solution to this riddle was right in front of our noses the whole time. Ashburn wasn't a spectacular fielder, at all, nor was Hamner terrible. It was simply a team whose pitching staff, led by Robin Roberts, recorded historically low numbers of ground ball outs, and historically high numbers of fly balls.

This, of course, also affects the team double play total, to a great extent. The Phillies in the mid-Fifties were far below the league average in double plays turned—a fact that counts against Hamner in most analyses of their defense:

Year	NL Avg	Phillies
1954	161	133
1955	155	117
1956	149	140
1957	150	117
1958	161	136
Total	776	643

In fact, the Phillies were last in the National League in double plays in all of these seasons except 1956, when they were tied for last. But when *Sport* magazine rated the National League players again in September, 1957, they specifically cited Hamner as being outstanding on the double play. This is their comment:

> Hamner, whose physical condition has been unsound for the past couple of years, gives the Phils one of the best infields in the league when he is in there. He is especially good on the double play.

Plagued by injuries, Hamner had slipped to sixth in the rankings, but Hamner and Bill Mazeroski were the only second base regulars who were cited for their excellence on the double play.

Earlier, I explained how to figure expected double plays. Here is the chart above, but with *expected* double plays added in:

Year	NL Avg	Phillies	Phillies Expected
1954	161	133	134
1955	155	117	127
1956	149	140	132
1957	150	117	120
1958	161	136	141
Total	776	643	654

The Phillies low double play totals are 90% attributable to the fly ball nature of the staff, rather than to the infielders.

How do we know that this system works?

We know that this system works because *groups of teams have a very strong tendency to match their expected double plays*. If you look at the teams which are "expected" to turn 170 double plays, you will find that, on average, they turn 170 double plays. If you look at the teams which are expected to turn 140 double plays, 180 double plays, whatever... individually they may turn more double plays than expected or fewer, but in the aggregate, they'll approximately match it. If the system didn't work, that wouldn't be true.

In most cases, as in this one, a substantial portion a team's double play deviation from the norm is *not* a function of defensive performance, but is a natural outcome of runners on base and ground balls. I don't know whether these factors explain 40% of the variation or 70%, but I know that it's substantial. The 1997 Chicago White Sox, who turned only 131 double plays (lowest in the league) did so, in the main, because the pitching staff just didn't throw ground balls. The team had only 135 expected double plays. The Boston Red Sox, who led the league in double plays with 179, had an expectation of 173.

An exception of note is the 1966 Pirates. The 1966 Pirates, with the double play combination of Bill Mazeroski and Gene Alley, turned 215 double plays, a National League record. In that case, the outcome isn't a product of the circumstances, to a significant degree. That team's expected double plays are only a little bit above average. Their double plays are genuinely created by the excellence of Mazeroski and Alley.

So in my analysis, Granny Hamner isn't viewed as a defensive liability; in fact, he emerges as the outstanding defensive shortstop that he was. Hamner at short is credited with 6.11 Win Shares per 1,000 defensive innings. Among the 285 players in history logging 3,000 or more innings at shortstop, Hamner rates 34th in Win Shares per 1,000 EDI—just missing the top 10%.

Ashburn makes the top 10%. Even adjusting for the fly ball tendency of the staff, Ashburn remains outstanding, although he drops below Willie Mays. Among 930 players putting in 3,000 or more innings in the outfield, Ashburn rates 66th, at 3.95 Win Shares per 1,000 estimated defensive innings. To me, it seems clear that this is a more accurate analysis.

Comparison of Short-Form to Actual Win Shares

2000 Cleveland Indians

	Short Form	Actual
Manny Ramirez	31	29
Travis Fryman	24	23
Kenny Lofton	19	19
Roberto Alomar	19	18
Jim Thome	19	17
Omar Vizquel	17	15
Chuck Finley	14	16
Bartolo Colon	14	15
Dave Burba	11	13
Steve Karsay	11	11
David Justice	11	10
Sandy Alomar	10	9
David Segui	7	6
Paul Shuey	6	8
Justin Speier	6	7
Richie Sexson	6	4
Bob Wickman	6	4
Einar Diaz	5	6
Russ Branyan	5	4
Wilfredo Cordero	4	4
Jolbert Cabrera	4	3
Steve Reed	3	4
Jaret Wright	3	3
Enrique Wilson	3	2
Ricky Rincon	2	3
Tom Martin	2	2
Ricky Ledee	2	2
Jamie Brewington	1	2
Steve Woodward	1	2
Scott Kamieniecki	1	1
Brian Williams	1	1
Andrew Lorraine	1	1
Jacob Cruz	1	1
Cam Cairncross	1	1
Jason Bere	0	2
Sean DePaula	0	1
Jim Brower	0	1

2000 Atlanta Braves

	Short Form	Actual
Chipper Jones	26	25
Greg Maddux	25	24
Andruw Jones	24	28
Tom Glavine	20	21
Javy Lopez	18	17
Rafael Furcal	17	16
Andres Galarraga	16	15
Brian Jordan	15	16
Quilvio Veras	13	13
John Rocker	12	8
Wally Joyner	10	9
Mike Remlinger	9	12
Kevin Millwood	9	10
Keith Lockhart	9	8
Kerry Ligtenberg	8	8
Reggie Sanders	7	7
Bobby Bonilla	7	6
Terry Mulholland	6	7
John Burkett	6	7
Andy Ashby	6	6
Walt Weiss	4	4
Bruce Chen	4	4
B J Surhoff	3	2
Rudy Seanez	2	2
Trenidad Hubbard	2	2
Scott Kamieniecki	1	1
Greg McMichael	1	1
Mark DeRosa	1	1
Kevin McGlinchy	1	1
Luis Rivera	1	1
Fernando Lunar	1	1
Jason Marquis	1	1
Steve Sisco	1	0
Paul Bako	0	1

Why 52?

Why do we credit 52% of a team's success to pitching and defense, 48% to offense? Basically for two reasons:

a) I am convinced that it is as logical to do this as it is to not do it, and

b) it causes problems if you don't.

If we used a 50/50 split, the values for pitchers and fielders would be so low that they would cause all kinds of problems. Even as it is, even giving 52% of the value to pitching and defense, our values for pitchers and fielders still seem low. Picking a distant era to lessen emotional reactions. . . In 1942 Mort Cooper was voted the Most Valuable Player in the National League. In the Win Shares system, his teammate Enos Slaughter is perceived as significantly more valuable (37 to 29). In 1943 Spud Chandler won the American League MVP Award. His teammate, Charlie Keller, is again perceived by Win Shares as significantly more valuable (36 to 29).

In 1944 a shortstop, Marty Marion, won the National League MVP Award, based mostly on his glovework. The Win Shares system, while acknowledging Marion as one of the best defensive shortstops of all time, still perceives several of his teammates as having more overall value, led by Stan Musial (38 Win Shares, 20 for Marion).

In 1950 Jim Konstanty was voted National League MVP. Win Shares sees two position players on his team, and ten in the league, as being more valuable. In 1952 Bobby Shantz was voted the Most Valuable Player in the American League. The Win Shares system thinks that Larry Doby was more valuable (34 to 33).

For the Hall of Fame, the effective standard of a Hall of Fame career for a position player (other than a catcher) is about 320 Win Shares. For a pitcher, it is closer to 250 Win Shares. Our system, in its finished form, still evaluates pitchers more conservatively in relation to position players than do fans, sportswriters, managers or general managers (as reflected in salaries).

On defense. . . the Win Shares system sees Ozzie Smith as being the greatest defensive shortstop in baseball history, a decision that I suppose that many of you would agree with. But what is the relative value of Ozzie Smith's defense and his hitting? Many of you, I suspect, would argue or assume that 70% or 80% or 90% of Ozzie's value is in his fielding. The Win Shares system believes that 57% of his value is in his offense. In part, this is because Ozzie was a better hitter than a lot of people realize. There are many shortstops whose value *is* mostly in their glovework; Ozzie just isn't one of them. But in large part, this reflects the relative scarcity of Win Shares to be credited to defensive stars.

There are still *some* pitchers, in the era of four-man rotations and 70% complete games, who show as the Most Valuable Players in the league—Lefty Grove, 1931, Carl Hubbell in 1936, Bob Gibson in 1968. If we used a 50/50 split, even those guys would slip off their pedestals. Other MVP/Pitchers might slip to little more than half the value of the best position players. It will be difficult enough to gain general acceptance of the method as it is; I don't want or need to battle through those arguments as well.

That explains (b), why it is necessary to use a 52/48 split, rather than 50/50. But what is the logic for so doing?

Let's start here. . . the projection of Winning percentages by Marginal Runs assumes that the "floor" on offense is one-half of the league norm for hitters, 1.5 times the league norm for pitchers. Arizona in the year 2000 scored 792 runs and allowed 754, in a league in which the norm was 812 runs per 162 games. We would thus project for them a winning percentage of .523, which is figured in this way:

Runs Scored
Minus .5 League Norm
Plus 1.5 League Norm
Minus Runs Allowed
Divided By twice the league average
of runs scored

This can be written in formula as:

((R - .5 Lg) + (1.5 Lg - RA)) / (2 Lg)

For Arizona 2000, this figures as:

((792 - 406) + (1218 - 754)) / 1624 = .523

We would thus expect them to win 85 games, which they did. The average error for this formula in 2000 was 2.64 wins, whereas the average error for the Pythagorean approach was 2.58 wins.

However, this formula can be simplified to this:

(R - RA + Lg) / 2 Lg

When we change the boundaries to .52 and 1.52, rather than .50 and 1.50, the formula becomes:

((R - .52 Lg) + (1.52 Lg - RA)) / 2 Lg

This simplifies to exactly the same formula as the original—Runs minus runs allowed plus league average, divided by twice the league average. This approach yields exactly the same expected winning percentage for the Arizona Snakes, and for every other team; it is the same formula. Thus, the use of .52 rather than .50 does *not* make the formula less accurate in predicting wins from marginal runs.

Of course, since .52 receives the same answer as .50, so would .60, .70, or 2.00, or 25.00. But using a figure *radically* different from .50 would cause other logical problems, which kick in about .58, when you begin to have actual teams which would register as having negative offenses, or perhaps even lower than that, when we began encountering a few regular players who register as having negative offense. Using .52 only causes those problems to a limited extent.

In addition to the facts that using .52 rather than .50 is not illogical and eases the problem of perceptually inadequate values for pitchers and fielders, there is an affirmative reason to make the switch. This has to do with variance out of range. There is a famous illustration of this problem, which many of you are familiar with, having to do with size and NFL offensive linemen.

If you studied the weights and skills of offensive linemen in the NFL, you might very well find that size was irrelevant to success within the group. All of the linemen would weigh 290 to 350 pounds, but those who weighed 350 pounds might very well tend to be no more successful than those who weighed 290. Thus, you might very well find that the correlation between size and success for NFL linemen was zero. You could conclude from that that size was irrelevant to success as an NFL lineman.

You could conclude that, but you would be wrong. Size is obviously important in an NFL lineman; it's just that most of the variance which would occur with size has been eliminated by pre-screening (not allowing players who weigh "only" 250 or 260 to play this position at this level), and the remaining variance is disguised by internal biases ("small" linemen—those weighing less than 300 pounds—can play only because they have exceptional skills, while gigantic linemen may be able to hold on to their jobs even if their skills are more marginal). If you started using 185 pound players as offensive linemen, you would quickly find that size *did* matter.

This is a similar problem. Yes, it's true that the correlation of pitching and defensive success with team wins is no higher than the correlation of offensive success with team wins. The baseball universe *appears* to be symmetrical. But this is only true, it seems to me, because of pre-screening of the talent pool. If you started taking people off the street and putting them in the major leagues, or even if you started using AA and college players in the major leagues, you would quickly find that the baseball universe is *not* symmetrical. It cannot be, because it is bounded on one side by zero, while the other side is open.

Suppose that the league ERA is 4.00, which used to be a normal league ERA. If you brought up outfielders from AA ball or college, the number of runs they would create could not be less than zero. If you brought up pitchers from AA, the number of runs they could allow is virtually unlimited.

While the effects of this asymmetry are *largely* eliminated by pre-screening the players so that they are all major leaguers, they are not *totally* eliminated. Suppose that you evaluated every pitcher's ERA, in baseball history, by stating it as relative to the league ERA—that is, half the league ERA is .50, the league ERA is 1.00, etc. If the baseball universe were symmetrical, the number of innings pitched by pitchers with ERAs under .50 would be the same as those pitched by pitchers with ERAs over 1.50. In fact, it is *not* symmetrical; the number of innings pitched by pitchers with ERAs over relative 1.50 is many times larger than the number of innings pitched by pitchers under relative .50. I'm not sure, but I think that the "over 1.50" group is about 12 times larger than the "under .50" group in a normal year, although you will have years when, because of a Pedro Martinez-type season, the "under .50" group will actually be larger.

This asymmetry does have some practical effects in major league baseball, other than the obvious fact that the fear of being caught short of pitchers is greater than the fear of being caught short of outfielders. If you study good teams, you will find that they are as good on offense as they are on defense; if you study bad teams, you will find that they are as bad on offense as they are on defense. But if you study *very* bad teams, the bottom 3%, you will in fact find that they are worse in pitching and defense than they are on offense.

Given this underlying reality, I decided that it was appropriate, in rating players, to make the baseball universe very slightly asymmetrical.

Now, here's the tough question: How do I know that the correct balance point is .52/1.52, rather than .53/1.53, .54/1.54, or something quite different like .5/1.7?

Answer: I don't. I needed a cutoff point; I have no compelling logic to tell me exactly what that cutoff point should be. There *is* an answer to this question. Perhaps I will one day find it; perhaps one day my son will find it, or Mat Olkin will, or Stefan Kretschmann will. This is where we are today.

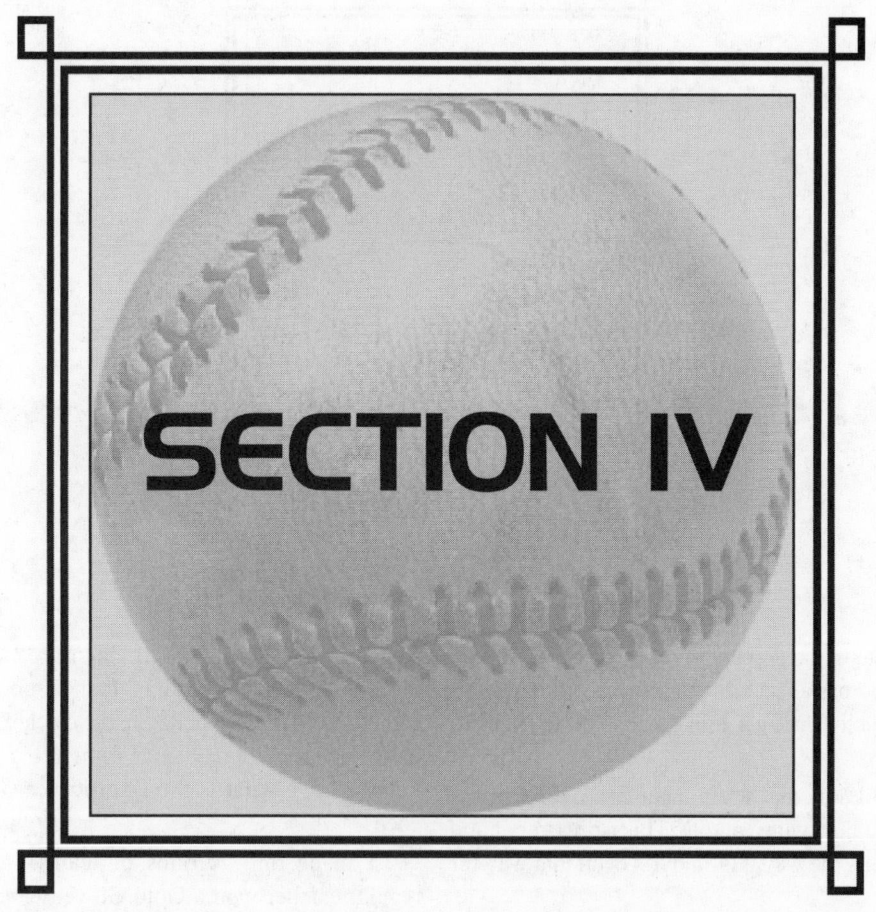

Random Essays

(reporting research and conclusions)

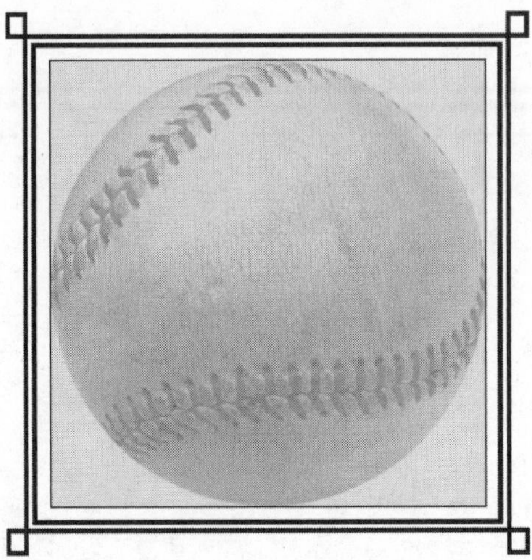

Independent Putouts by Catchers

Very late in the process of researching this book, I stumbled across a fact which I think is quite intriguing, but which frankly I don't know quite what to make of.

You all know that when a batter strikes out, the catcher is credited with a putout. This isn't a very good idea, but that's the way it is, and it's been that way for 130 years.

However, catchers also sometimes record putouts in other ways—tag plays or force plays at home plate, for example, or pop outs, or by covering another base. These putouts, the putouts by catchers that are *not* strikeouts, are called independent putouts.

For individual catchers, there is no official record of independent putouts, and no record at all prior to STATS' data-collection efforts beginning in 1987. For a *team*, however, we can figure the independent putouts by catchers by simply taking the team's putouts by catchers, and subtracting the strikeouts by pitchers.

Searching for better ways to rate defensive performance by catchers, I latched on to this question: Are independent putouts by catchers indicative of catching skill? Will a good defensive catcher record more independent putouts than a poor defensive catcher? Will a mobile defensive catcher record more independent putouts than an immobile catcher? How many more? What is the significance of this difference?

I made three groups of teams—teams whose regular catcher won a Gold Glove, teams which finished under .500 and had catchers with poor defensive reputations (my subjective judgment) and teams chosen at random from the same leagues. The teams which had Gold Glove catchers averaged 67 independent putouts by catchers, the teams with poor catchers averaged 62, the "random" teams 63. Weak, but vaguely connected to defensive performance.

When I have more time, I'll do more studies of that nature—comparing winning teams to losing teams, Hall of Fame catchers to non-Hall of Fame catchers, etc.

I decided not to wedge this into the system post-1931, but there was an opening for it pre-1931—and an interesting other fact, one of those accidental discoveries that makes this type of research worth doing.

The interesting thing is that independent putouts by catchers have declined rather astonishingly over a sustained period of time. At the beginning of the study period (1958) an average team had about 90 independent putouts per season by catchers. Now it's about 30. Two-thirds of putouts by catchers, other than strikeouts, have disappeared. If you go back further, the numbers are even higher. If you go back to 1930, the average was about 140 per team per season—almost one per game. Twenty years before that, the average was about 165 per season. In 1895, the average was about 180 per team per season—in a shorter schedule.

In 1876, the first year of major league baseball, strikeouts accounted for less than one-fourth of putouts by catchers—589 of 2,400. In 2000, strikeouts accounted for 97% of catcher putouts.

Why has this happened? You have any idea? Are pop outs to catchers disappearing? If so, why? Is somebody else catching them? Did baseball used to have that many more contact plays at home plate? Did catchers used to cover other bases more often? What were those 150 putouts a season by catchers which have disappeared over the last century? Where did they go?

My best guess is that the declining numbers in the last thirty years are related to:

1. the disappearance of the high strike, and
2. the thin-handled bats.

With research, we can figure it out. The high strike is making a comeback as I write this (during the 2001 season), so perhaps the post-season data will tell us something.

Not to hype it, but my instinct is that this is important. Why? First, the numbers are huge. Essentially, one full play per game—1/27th of all putouts—have moved, over time, away from catchers to other fielders. That's a significant change in the game, and it's completely undocumented. Second, when you have a trend that remains in motion for more than a hundred years, something has to be driving it. This statistical change has to be connected, somehow, to some powerful underlying force that is re-shaping baseball over time. It could be, for example, that in each generation we have more and more pitchers who throw very hard, which necessitates less and less tolerance by umpires for high fastballs, which (when thrown well) are nearly un-hittable. Or it could be that as more and more pitchers become able to focus pitches on a smaller target area, the expectations of umpires shrink in accordance, thus evaporating the high strikes that result in popouts near home plate.

But whatever it is, it ain't random. I would like to know—and eventually I will know—why this is happening.

Since independent putouts were more common in earlier baseball, this also justifies their use as a rating element for catchers—and, in fact, if you read stories about old baseball players, one of the things which is very often said about a good defensive catcher is that he was good at chasing popups.

Scrambled Second Basemen

Pete Palmer has one way of evaluating defensive players, I have another, but how different are they, really? How often do the two systems actually reach different conclusions?

I took the 100 players who have played the most innings at second base, in all the history of baseball. I put their defensive Win Shares at second base into a spreadsheet, and entered beside them Pete's "Fielding Runs" at second base, as best I could tell what those were from the last edition of *Total Baseball.*

Obviously, there is a degree of agreement between the two systems. Bill Mazeroski, who ranks first in Win Shares/1000 Defensive Innings, ranks second in Pete's analysis. I sorted the 100 players by how I had ranked them. The top 30 players in Win Shares/1000 Defensive Innings were credited by Pete as being an average of 69.8 runs better than average, while the bottom 30 were regarded by Pete as being defensive liabilities:

Group	James	Same Players in Palmer
Top 30	5.35	+69.8
Middle 40	4.56	+18.8
Bottom 30	3.75	-38.3

However, the degree of agreement between the two systems could easily be over-stated. When the 100 second basemen are rated top to bottom, there are 32 who rank at least 20 spots higher in our system than in his system, and 24 more who rank at least 20 spots lower in our system thus, 56 of the 100 players are rated 20 or more spots different in one system than in the other. Bobby Avila, rated by my system as the twelfth-best second baseman in the group, is rated by Pete at negative 64 runs (81st in the group). Maxie Bishop, rated 22nd in my group, is negative 56 in his (78th). Felix Millan, rated a little above average in my study, is listed at negative 129 runs in *Total Baseball* (94th), while Del Pratt, listed 80th in my group, is credited by Pete with being 91 runs better-than-league.

There are many differences between the two rating systems, but most of those are innocuous, and would not really cause players to rate differently. From where do the differences really come?

Two things. First, Palmer rates the earlier second basemen as being better than the more recent second basemen; I rate the second basemen post-1930 as better than the second basemen pre-1930. I arranged the 100 second basemen in chronological order, and then figured group averages:

Group	James	Palmer
First 30	4.18	+66.1
Middle 40	4.72	+ 4.5
Last 30	4.70	-15.5

Pete's rating the earlier second basemen higher than modern second basemen is, to the best of my understanding, an accident or a design flaw; I don't believe he intended to get this outcome. My system, in any case, deliberately gives higher ratings to players playing post-1930, for reasons I have explained elsewhere in the book. It is clear to me that second base became a more critical defensive position once the lively ball era began, and double plays became much more common than they had been before.

Thus, when we identify the players who rate much higher in my system than in his, all of the top ten players are post-1930, whereas when we identify the players who rate much higher in his system than in mine, they are all pre-1930:

Rate Better In Win Shares	Rate Better In Linear Weights
Bobby Avila	Rogers Hornsby
Maxie Bishop	Miller Huggins
Felix Millan	Del Pratt
Jerry Remy	Cub Stricker
Junior Gilliam	Bucky Harris
Julian Javier	George Cutshaw
Frank Bolling	Jimmy Williams
Willie Randolph	Billy Wambsganss
Bret Boone	Hobe Ferris
Rennie Stennett	Cupid Childs

The year of birth is one of two things that split the list. The other is the quality of the teams for which these men played.

Fielding analysis is complicated by what I call the False Normalization of Fielding Stats. The fielding statistics of a good team, on average, are not any better than the fielding stats of a bad team. The batting stats of a good team are much better than the batting stats of a bad team. The pitching stats of a good team are much better than the pitching stats of a bad team. Even irrelevant stats—tiny, incidental stuff that doesn't have any real impact on the won-lost record (like balks), still tends to be much better for good teams than for bad teams, because good teams tend, on average, to do everything better than bad teams.

Fielding stats, however, hide this "good team's advantage" behind a series of screens. The number of plays made per game by a defense is exactly the same for a bad team as it is for a good team, 27 per game either way. There are some little advantages for good teams—higher fielding percentages, fewer passed balls—but there are also some significant disadvantages for good teams. Bad teams tend to make more double plays than good teams, a few more, because bad teams have more people on base against them. Catchers and outfielders on bad teams tend to have more assists. Good teams make more putouts at first base (which are difficult to account for in fielding systems), whereas bad teams make more putouts at second base (which are easier to account for). Adding everything up, the fielding stats of bad teams tend to be slightly better, on average, than the fielding stats of good teams—not because they can actually field the ball as well, but because of the nature of the statistics. This is the False Normalization of Fielding Stats.

The False Normalization of Fielding Stats is the other thing that splits the lists above. The ten second basemen who did better in the Linear Weights system than in Win Shares were major league regulars for a total of 91 seasons (using 800 innings with one team to be the standard of a regular). Of those 91 teams, 49 had winning or .500 records, and 42 had losing records.

The ten second basemen who did better in Win Shares, on the other hand, were regular second basemen for 86 seasons. Their teams had winning or .500 records in 68 of those 86 seasons (79%).

More remarkably, the ten second basemen who rated better in Linear Weights played regularly for 14 teams which won 90 or more games, 13 teams which lost 90 or more games—a more or less even split. The ten second basemen who rated better in Win Shares, on the other hand, played regularly at second base for 35 teams that won 90 or more games—and NONE which lost 90 or more. This is the data player by player, just in case someone might be inclined to think I'm making this up:

Player	Years as Regular	90W	W>L	L>W	90L
Bobby Avila	7	5	6	1	0
Max Bishop	9	6	9	0	0
Felix Millan	9	1	6	3	0
Jerry Remy	6	1	2	4	0
Jim Gilliam	7	6	7	0	0
Julian Javier	10	4	9	1	0
Frank Bolling	11	0	8	3	0
Willie Randolph	15	8	13	2	0
Bret Boone	7	1	4	3	0
Rennie Stennett	5	3	4	1	0
Group Totals	86	35	68	18	0
Rogers Hornsby	9	2	6	3	1
Miller Huggins	11	0	4	7	3
Del Pratt	11	1	3	8	4
Cub Stricker	7	1	2	5	1
Bucky Harris	9	2	5	4	0
George Cutshaw	10	1	6	4	1
Jimmy Williams	9	2	5	4	0
Bill Wambsganss	7	2	5	2	1
Hobe Ferris	7	2	5	2	2
Cupid Childs	11	1	8	3	0
Group Totals	91	14	49	42	13

The players in "my" group rate better because the Win Shares system builds in credit for the quality of the team's defense.

Perhaps the players who best summarize this are two Hall of Famers who didn't make the lists above: Nap Lajoie and Joe Morgan. Lajoie, rated as a defensive superstar by Linear Weights, is an early player who played for a lot of lousy teams; Morgan, rated as a wretched defensive second baseman by Linear Weights, is a more recent player who played for great teams. The Win Shares system agrees that Lajoie was a better second baseman than Morgan, but thinks that Linear Weights has overstated the difference by miles and miles. Lajoie was a very good defensive second baseman; Joe Morgan was a pretty good defensive second baseman.

Perhaps a more puzzling comparison is Bill Mazeroski and Willie Randolph. . .

Mazeroski and Randolph

Linear Weights lists Bill Mazeroski at +362 Fielding Runs for his career, Willie Randolph at +/- zero. Thus Mazeroski is, apparently, 362 runs better, as a second baseman, than Willie Randolph. In the Win Shares system Bill Mazeroski was credited with 112.24 Win Shares for his defense at second base (an all-time record), while Randolph is credited with 97.44—a difference of 14.80 Win Shares, or about 50 runs. Let's look a little more closely at these numbers.

These are their career fielding stats at second base:

	Innings	PO	A	E	DP	FPct
Willie Randolph	18648	4858	6336	234	1547	.980
Bill Mazeroski	18301	4974	6685	204	1706	.983

Randolph played a few more innings, so we need to adjust for that before we do any serious calculatin':

	Innings	PO	A	E	DP	FPct
Willie Randolph	18301	4768	6218	230	1518	.980
Bill Mazeroski	18301	4974	6685	204	1706	.983

Mazeroski has advantages of 206 putouts, 467 assists, 26 errors and 188 double plays—a total of 887 plays, except that there is a lot of double-counting in there. At least a couple hundred plays have been double-counted. Randolph has 26 more errors, but what would those errors be if he hadn't fumbled them? They would be assists or putouts, of course—you can charge him with making errors or failing to make plays, but not BOTH. Same thing with most of Maz's double plays; when he makes an extra double play and he was genuinely amazing on the pivot—that also makes an extra assist. You can credit him with the extra double play or the extra assist, but not both as if they were separate events.

So Mazeroski is about 700 "plays" ahead, more or less, and you can see how 700 extra plays could legitimately be translated into 300-some extra runs, if the extra plays result from Mazeroski's defensive excellence, and not from illusions of context.

Let's look at the context. There are at least four elements of the team's defensive context to consider, which are:

1. Pitcher's strikeouts,
2. Team Hits allowed,
3. Opposition runners on base, and
4. Ground balls.

I created a "Defensive Context Record" for Mazeroski and for Randolph by taking the relevant elements of the team's fielding and pitching records for each season of their careers, and multiplying those by the player's playing time. In other words, since Mazeroski played about 1334 of the Pirates' 1362 defensive innings in 1961, and the Pirates struck out 759 opposing batters that season, we estimate that the Pirate pitchers struck out about 743 batters while Mazeroski was in the field. This is the full Defensive Context Record for both players:

	Mazeroski	Randolph
Defensive Innings	18301	18648
Batters Faced	77160	78560
Hits Allowed	17939	18036
Bases On Balls	5997	6263
Intentional Walks	912	412
Home Runs Allowed	1443	1631
Strikeouts	10700	11201
Hit Batsmen	376	320
Wild Pitches	514	547
Balks	51	104
Sacrifice Hits	931	748

	Mazeroski	Randolph
Sacrifice Flies	478	629
Putouts	54903	55946
Assists	23743	22281
Passed Balls	194	169

There is a bombshell buried in that data, but, being the meticulous bastard that I am, I am going to sift through the data like a kid playing in a sandbox before I set off the landmine. . . perhaps the worst mixed metaphor of my career. Anyway, most of that data isn't helpful; I just included it because I was carried away with the exercise, and it raises interesting questions. Is the fact that Mazeroski allowed only an estimated 478 sacrifice flies while he was in the field, as opposed to 629 for Randolph. . . is that because of Clemente's throwing arm? How much of it is because of Clemente's throwing arm? Is the fact that Mazeroski's teams issued 500 more intentional walks due in part to the fact that they were using the intentional walk to set up double plays, or is it just the difference between the National League in the 1960s and the American League in the 1970s? There were 183 extra bunts recorded with Mazeroski in the field. Was that because opposing managers bunted to stay away from the double play with Maz in the field? Who knows? Somebody will study the data and figure it out.

Focusing on the stuff which is relevant to the current discussion. . . Mazeroski's teams issued fewer walks, but despite that probably had very slightly *more* opposition runners on first base, as best I can figure that (8.47 opposition runners on first base per nine innings for Mazeroski, 8.44 for Randolph. This is figured as hits minus home runs, times .76, plus walks, plus hit batsmen, minus wild pitches, balks, sac hits and passed balls). That difference is nothing, and I'm not going to worry about it.

However, Randolph's teams also had more strikeouts and fewer hits allowed, which means that there were fewer balls in play when he was on the field. How many fewer? While Randolph was in the field there were about:

55,946 Putouts
11,201 Strikeouts
18,036 Hits Allowed, and
1,631 Home Runs Allowed

Thus, there were about 61,150 balls in play while Randolph was in the field—55,946, minus 11,201, plus 18,036, minus 1,631. Since Randolph played about 18,648 innings, there were 29.51 balls in play per nine innings, as best we can figure that.

The parallel figures for Mazeroski are:

54,903 Putouts
10,700 Strikeouts
17,939 Hits Allowed, and
1,443 Home Runs Allowed
60,699 Balls in Play
29.85 Balls in Play per nine innings

In other words, Mazeroski had slightly more than a 1% advantage in terms of balls in play while he was in the field. Mazeroski's edge in fielding statistics is based on the fact that he made about 6% more plays per inning in the field. Thus, about one-sixth of this advantage could be attributed simply to balls in play, without worrying about whether those were ground balls or fly balls.

This, however, is the smaller part of Mazeroski's advantage. Look at the assists. Assists, remember, are an outstanding indicator of a team's ground ball tendency. *Mazeroski's teams averaged 11.68 assists per nine innings. Randolph's teams averaged 10.75—an 8.6% advantage for Mazeroski.*

How significant is that? Mazeroski's great advantage in the field is that he recorded more assists. But Mazeroski recorded 7.5% more assists per inning than Randolph did—while the teams that he played for averaged 8.6% more assists per nine innings. *Relative to the ground balls of his team, Randolph actually recorded more assists than Mazeroski did.* Randolph recorded 3.06 assists per nine innings, playing for teams that recorded 10.75 assists per nine innings. That's 28.4%. Mazeroski recorded 3.29 assists per nine innings, but playing for teams that recorded 11.68 assists per nine innings. That's 28.1%.

Thus, I am reasonably confident that Bill Mazeroski was not, in fact, 362 runs better in the field than Willie Randolph. He *was* great on the double play, and he did make fewer errors than Randolph; I am willing to credit him with those things. But his advantage is proportional to the number of weeks in a year—not to the number of days.

Extreme Teams

By the Win Shares method, what was the greatest offense of all time?

The Win Shares method does not identify the greatest team or teams of all time, because the Win Shares system simply assumes that a Win is a Win. . . actually it assumes that a Win is three Wins, but you get the point. The team with the most Win Shares is simply the team with the most Wins, in all cases, and the team with the fewest Win Shares is the team with the fewest Wins.

When we split the Win Shares between offense and defense, we begin to get interesting lists. What was the greatest offense of all time? According to this analysis, the 1932 New York Yankees won more games with their bats than any other team in baseball history. The top 20 are:

1932	New York Yankees	185.37
1913	Philadelphia A's	185.10
1928	New York Yankees	181.45
2001	Seattle Mariners	181.04
1930	New York Yankees	179.70
1933	New York Yankees	178.89
1962	Los Angeles Dodgers	178.36
1976	Cincinnati Reds	178.09
1964	Milwaukee Braves	177.92
1982	Milwaukee Brewers	177.57
1927	New York Yankees	175.74
1914	Philadelphia A's	174.72
1954	New York Yankees	174.68
1953	Brooklyn Dodgers	174.58
1975	Cincinnati Reds	173.20
1931	New York Yankees	172.82
1998	New York Yankees	171.46
1962	San Francisco Giants	170.10
2000	San Francisco Giants	169.76
1986	New York Mets	169.56

This list is dominated, as lists of the best-hitting teams often are, by the Gehrig/Ruth Yankees. The 1932 Yankees won 107 games, and destroyed the Cubs in four straight in the World Series. We all know that those teams put up phenomenal offensive numbers every year. What many people do not know is that they did so despite playing in what was, at that time, one of the two worst hitter's parks in the American League.

Other than the Gehrig/Ruth Yankees, what do we have here? The 1913 and '14 White Elephants—again, a team almost always cited as among the greatest of all time. The 1975 and '76 Big Red Machine. . . no surprise there. Harvey's Wallbangers (the 1982 Brewers). . . again, everybody knows that was a great offense. The Boys of Summer (the '53 Dodgers), the 1998 Yankees. . . everybody knows these were great offenses.

The interesting teams, or at least somewhat surprising teams on this list, are the 1962 Dodgers, the 1964 Milwaukee Braves, the '62 Giants, the 2000 Giants, and the 1986 New York Mets. Looking at them one at a time:

1962 Dodgers. One of the most interesting teams of all time. Maury Wills broke the stolen base record, Tommy Davis hit .346 and drove in 153 runs, Frank Howard hit 31 homers and drove in 119, while Junior Gilliam, Ron Fairly, Wally Moon and Willie Davis all chipped in important contributions. Koufax got hurt, the Dodgers played .500 ball the last two months, and they lost at the wire.

I have pointed out in several books that this team scored more runs than the 1961 Yankees. I point this out because it is surprising to people who don't read my books, and I probably should stop mentioning it because it is well known to people who do. The 1962 season was the first year for Dodger Stadium, which was, of course, a great pitcher's park, and one of the primary causes of the hitting dearth of the 1960s. At the time, few people realized what a great offense this was, for that exact reason: that few people realized what they were battling against in Dodger Stadium. Dodger Stadium at that time favored the pitchers so much that sportswriters assumed that the Dodgers had incredible pitching. In Dodger Stadium, the '62 Dodgers scored and allowed only 8.41 runs per game. On the road, it was 10.26.

1964 Braves. Few people remember them as a great offense because, like the Dodgers, they:

a) played in a pitcher's era,

b) played in a pitcher's park, and

c) didn't win.

They didn't win, but they scored 803 runs, a huge total under the circumstances. Catcher Joe Torre hit .321 with 20 homers, 109 RBI, shortstop Denis Menke hit .283 with 20 homers, rookie outfielder Rico Carty hit .330 with 22 homers, Henry Aaron hit .328 with 24 homers, Lee Maye hit .304 and led the league in doubles, and Eddie Mathews had a secondary average of .353.

1962 Giants. Beat the Dodgers at the wire. I wrote an article in another book about what a great, unappreciated team that was, so I'm obviously not surprised to see them make the list.

2000 Giants. In some ways reminiscent of the 1962 Dodgers. Like the Dodgers, they were playing in a brand new park, Pac Bell Park, and their offense was somewhat underappreciated for the same reason—that people have not yet understood the park. Jeff Kent and Barry Bonds were two of the three best hitters in the league.

1986 Mets. Gary Carter, Keith Hernandez, Ray Knight, Darryl Strawberry, Lenny Dykstra and Kevin Mitchell led the way to 108 wins.

Like almost all of the teams on the list, the 1986 Mets played in a pitcher's park, Shea Stadium. This brings up a question: Why do historically great offenses tend to occur only in pitcher's parks? Three explanations occur:

1. It could be coincidence. A group of 20 wouldn't prove anything if it was 20 out of 20, which it isn't, and it's really less than 20 because we have the same teams appearing repeatedly.

2. There could be a flaw in the logic of park adjustments which undercuts the teams in hitter's parks. I have no reason to believe that there is such a flaw and don't believe there is, but one should always be alert to the possibility.

3. It could be—and in fact I believe it is—the Fenway Phenomenon. Twenty years ago, when Fenway Park was the best hitter's park in baseball, I argued that the Red Sox had always tended to overrate their offense, because they played in a park which inflated their hitters' numbers, and that because of that they often had mediocre offenses. If a third baseman hit .260 with 11 home runs, they'd figure he was doing alright and they'd leave him alone. In another park, the same player might hit .235 with 8 home runs; in a pitcher's park he might hit .225 with 6 home runs. His value is the same in a pitcher's park, but the chance that he'll lose his job is greater. A team which plays in a pitcher's park will tend to have a better offense because they are less tolerant of failure. In a list of extreme teams, even a faint bias often shows up in brilliant colors.

I would like to be able to present a list of the *worst* offenses of all time, but the list you get depends mostly on who you deem to be eligible among a patchwork of strike-shortened and war-shortened seasons, differing schedule lengths, and 19th century teams which folded after a season or two or, in some cases, a win or two. So, moving along, let's look at the greatest pitching staffs ever. First, we're looking at pitching and fielding combined, greatest "defense," broadly defined.

The team which won more games with pitching and defense than any other, according to Win Shares, was the team which won more *games* than any other: Frank Chance's Cubs. The top 20:

1907	Chicago Cubs	188.62
1906	Chicago Cubs	185.48
1943	St. Louis Cardinals	184.22
1892	Boston Beaneaters	183.61
1969	New York Mets	183.24
1993	Atlanta Braves	181.80
1931	Philadelphia A's	181.09
1954	Cleveland Indians	180.66
1991	Toronto Blue Jays	177.84
1985	Toronto Blue Jays	176.45
1997	Atlanta Braves	173.63
1940	Cincinnati Reds	173.25
1969	Baltimore Orioles	172.90
1999	Atlanta Braves	172.80
1996	Atlanta Braves	172.64
1979	Baltimore Orioles	172.29
1909	Chicago Cubs	171.89
1998	Atlanta Braves	171.85
1954	New York Giants	171.48
1913	New York Giants	171.27

Again, mostly not a surprising list... the wartime Cardinals, when Branch Rickey's farm system was at its zenith, the Miracle Mets (Koosman, Seaver, Gentry, McGraw, Nolan Ryan), the 1954 Indians, and five teams from the Atlanta Braves of the 1990s. The 1892 Boston Beaneaters, Frank Selee's first great team, were led by Kid Nichols (35-16) and Jack Stivetts, (33-16). Other than that, I don't see that there is any team here that needs explanation.

Now, let's focus on "pure pitching," with the contributions of fielders taken out.

Year	Team	
1907	Chicago Cubs	138.44
1906	Chicago Cubs	135.30
1892	Boston Beaneaters	134.40
1943	St. Louis Cardinals	133.39
1931	Philadelphia A's	131.66
1969	New York Mets	130.79
1954	Cleveland Indians	130.16
1993	Atlanta Braves	129.35
1991	Toronto Blue Jays	126.49
1996	Atlanta Braves	126.07
1999	Atlanta Braves	125.55
1997	Atlanta Braves	124.87
1985	Toronto Blue Jays	124.33
1940	Cincinnati Reds	123.07
1998	Atlanta Braves	122.90
1995	Atlanta Braves	122.70
1985	Kansas City Royals	122.38
1888	St. Louis Browns	122.23
1966	Los Angeles Dodgers	122.00
1909	Chicago Cubs	121.70

Essentially the same list, with an additional Braves team. The '66 Dodgers, with three Hall of Famers in the rotation, climb onto the ladder, as do the World Champion Royals of '85 (Bret Saberhagen, Charlie Leibrandt, Bud Black, Mark Gubicza, Danny Jackson, Dan Quisenberry. Didn't have to look that one up). The 1888 Browns, Comiskey's last great team, were led by Silver King (45-21, 1.64 ERA), Nat Hudson (25-10, 2.54), and Icebox Chamberlain (11-2, 1.61).

Now, we could do a list of teams with the most extreme splits in history—that is, teams with very good offenses but weak pitching, or the opposite. Here we have to start with a caveat—worse yet, a caveat requiring a long explanation.

In dividing Win Shares between offenses and defenses, I was required to put in place a rule saying that the percentage of success attributed to offense could not exceed 78% and could not be less than 22%, in any case. This restriction has nothing to do with any modern team, and it has nothing to do with any team that can actually play major league baseball; it just "steers" the data in certain very unusual cases which occurred a long time ago, when the game was not really mature. Since 1890, there are three teams which have been affected by this rule—the 1890 Pittsburgh Innocents of the Players League (who finished 23-113), the 1899 Cleveland Spiders (20-134), and the 1915 Philadelphia A's (43-109).

Why is this rule necessary in those cases (and others, prior to 1890, which are even worse)? Well, the system operates on *marginal* runs; it measures every player by how far he is above the margin. Suppose that on a team you had only two pitchers, one of whom was 15 runs better than the margin, but the other of whom was 15 runs worse than the margin. The team, as a whole, would be zero runs better than the margin. Because the team would be zero runs better than the margin, there would be no credit available to be assigned to *anyone*, including the one pitcher who was 15 runs better-than-margin. Everybody would be rated at zero, even if one player was outstanding.

Real major league teams don't have any players who are sub-marginal, except the "tryout" guys who play only a few games, and occasionally a player who may play 50 or 70 games or pitch 50 or 75 innings at a sub-marginal level because the team is absolutely convinced that he isn't really this bad, and will get going pretty quick here. But the real life case in which this problem does occur is, for example, with John Wyckoff and the 1915 Philadelphia A's.

Connie Mack

After the 1914 season, as 99.7% of you know, Connie Mack was unable to meet the salary demands of his star players. The Federal League, a rival major league, was offering bonuses to major league players who were willing to defect, and this was inflating the salary structure of the game. Connie Mack, owner/manager of the best team in baseball, was unable to meet the new salaries, and so sold off his best players. His other good players, the second-tier stars, defected to the Federal League. He was left with a minor league club, including a pitching staff of teenagers and 20- to 22-year-old kids, most of whom were not really major league pitchers.

However, one of those kids, 23-year-old John Wyckoff, was actually pretty decent. But because the other pitchers on the team are so terrible, unless we reserve some share of the team's overall Win Shares for pitching and defense, there are no Win Shares available to credit him for what he did.

The Win Shares system is essentially an accounting structure. Throughout that structure, it is always the terrible teams that cause problems, that test the limits of the system and force us to impose arbitrary rules. The good teams, no matter how good, never strain the structure; it is always the dreadful teams that wreak havoc. And that is a nuisance, as opposed to a real problem, because:

a) there isn't any real talent *on* these teams to be accounted for, and

b) in general, we don't care very much about them. We are interested in Hall of Fame debates, awards, and in questions about how championship teams are built. All of these things are almost wholly irrelevant to teams like the 1890 Pittsburgh Innocents of the Players League.

End of caveat and long explanation. Setting aside real terrible teams that played before 1920, the most unusual offense/defense splits in history are the following:

1997	San Diego Padres	71.3% Offense
1930	New York Yankees	69.7% Offense
1942	Washington Senators	69.4% Offense
1977	San Diego Padres	67.8% Offense
1964	Milwaukee Braves	67.4% Offense
1998	Tampa Bay Devil Rays	75.4% Defense
1981	Toronto Blue Jays	74.7% Defense
1927	Brooklyn Dodgers	72.0% Defense
1942	Detroit Tigers	70.7% Defense
1943	Boston Braves	69.2% Defense

You will note that, with one exception, all of the teams which had some offense but *no* pitching played in pitcher's parks, while all of the teams which had some pitching but *no* offense played in hitter's parks. These are the Park Factors for the ten teams listed above:

			Park Run Factor
1997	San Diego Padres	71.3% Offense	.86
1930	New York Yankees	69.7% Offense	.84
1942	Washington Nationals	69.4% Offense	.96
1977	San Diego Padres	67.8% Offense	.82
1964	Milwaukee Braves	67.4% Offense	.98
1998	Tampa Bay D Rays	75.4% Defense	1.09
1981	Toronto Blue Jays	74.7% Defense	1.17
1927	Brooklyn Robins	72.0% Defense	.98
1942	Detroit Tigers	70.7% Defense	1.19
1943	Boston Braves	69.2% Defense	1.01

This has to be explained, I believe, by the Fenway Phenomenon. The top group of teams developed wretched pitching staffs, in part, because the parks in which they played disguised their pitching problems until those problems became critical. Similarly, the teams which had no offense but some pitching got into that position, I believe, because Park Factors conspired to cover up the problems with the offense.

I would also provide here a list of the teams with the most and fewest Win Shares awarded for fielding. . . This would be the place to do that. But this list is not really useful, because, again, I placed limits on the category: no team can be credited with defensive value less than .16375 Win Shares per game played, nor greater than .32375.

Why? Well, I have somewhat limited confidence in the system used to divide Win Shares between Pitchers and Fielders. I did the best I could with the system; I designed a system that makes sense to me. There is no way to cross-check the system, and know whether the results are on target or off. When you have a system that is somewhat speculative, it seems to me to be best to be suspicious of exceptional or outlying results. I put limits on the system to avoid results that I might not trust.

In the *New Historical Abstract*, I printed some data comparing expected to actual double plays. The best double play combinations of all time, comparing expected to actual double plays, were the Gordon/Rizzuto Yankees:

Rank	Team	DP	XDP	Diff.	2B	SS	Won-Lost
1.	1942 Yankees	190	136.2	53.8	Gordon	Rizzuto	103-51
2.	1941 Yankees	196	145.3	50.7	Gordon	Rizzuto	101-53
3.	1966 Pirates	215	166.1	48.9	Mazeroski	Alley	92-70
4.	1943 Cardinals	183	135.6	47.4	Klein	Marion	105-49
5.	1946 Reds	192	146.5	45.5	Adams	Miller	67-87
6.	1944 Cardinals	162	118.2	43.8	Verban	Marion	105-49
7.	1911 Pirates	131	87.5	43.5	Miller	Wagner	85-69
8.	1907 Indians	137	93.6	43.4	Lajoie	Turner	85-67
9.	1956 Yankees	214	171.2	42.8	Martin	McDougald	97-57
10.	1928 Reds	194	152.0	42.0	Critz	Ford	78-74

Other than one appearance by Nap Lajoie, none of the top fifteen second basemen of all time appears anywhere on this list. The next appearance by a top second baseman, after Lajoie, is at the 25th spot on the list—the 1920 White Sox (Eddie Collins and Swede Risberg).

The *worst* Double Play combinations of all time were an eccentric mix of short-term regulars on really bad teams, with one good team:

Rank	Team	DP	XDP	Diff.	2B	SS	Won-Lost
1.	1926 Dodgers	95	146.8	51.8	Fewster	Butler	71-82
2.	1974 Padres	126	172.2	46.8	Thomas	Hernandez	60-102
3.	1939 Browns	144	188.6	44.6	Berardino	Heffner	43-111
4.	1935 Braves	101	143.1	42.1	Mallon	Urbanski	38-115
5.	1979 A's	137	178.4	41.4	Edwards	Picciolo	54-108
6.	1998 Cubs	107	147.9	40.9	Morandini	Blauser	90-73
7.	1930 Phillies	169	209.8	40.8	Thompson	Thevenow	52-102
8.	1996 Tigers	157	196.9	39.9	Lewis	Cedeno	53-109
9.	1954 Pirates	136	175.6	39.6	Roberts	Allie	53-101
10.	1896 Browns	73	112.0	39.0	Dowd	Cross	40-90

Marvelous

Marvelous Marv Throneberry, first baseman of the 1962 Mets, is one of the most celebrated inept fielders in the annals of baseball. On his 29th birthday in 1962, Casey Stengel told him "We woulda give you a cake, but we was afraid you'd drop it."

The National League's Gold Glove first baseman in 1962 (and in six other seasons) was Bill White. Reviewing the defensive rankings in *Total Baseball*, I happened to notice that *Total Baseball* had Throneberry listed for the season as a better defensive player (+4 runs) than White (+1). We're not bragging, however; our system does better comparing Throneberry and White (0.74 Win Shares for Throneberry—a very low total—and 2.05 for White)—but gives the National League Gold Glove for 1962 to Orlando Cepeda. Cepeda ran well at that time and threw well, but he was awkward and did not have good hands. Citing him as the best defensive first baseman in the league is not something we would point to with pride.

Total Baseball bases the defensive rankings of first basemen on two statistics—Assists and Errors. Since assists are weighted twice as heavily as errors, and since the variation in assists among different players is much greater than the variation in errors, the result is a system which is 90% determined by the first baseman's assists rate.

Throneberry's assists total in 1962 is influenced by a park effect. The Polo Grounds, where the Mets played in 1962, was a horseshoe-shaped stadium, which caused the fences to pinch the first base line. As a consequence of this, New York Giant first basemen (and Mets, in the two years they played there) often played 20 or 30 feet behind first base when the bases were empty, and well off the foul line—a long way from first base. There was relatively little foul ground that they could reach anyway, and a hard-hit ground ball that in another park would skip over first base and into the corner would often hit the wall just past first base and make a left turn, heading to center field. The first baseman, by playing deep and off the line, could sometimes pick up a ball that would be a double in any other park, and turn it into a ground out. That's one reason the Polo Grounds, although it was a great home run park, was not a good hitter's park overall, for most hitters.

Anyway, New York Giant (and early Met) first basemen almost always had very high assists totals, because they were often playing a long way from first base, forcing the pitcher or occasionally the second baseman to cover first on anything other than a ground ball right at first base. Everybody who played there—Lockman, Mize, Bill Terry, George Kelly, even Zeke Bonura—always had a high assists total. Johnny Mize, playing in St. Louis before the war, never had a hundred assists in a season, and never led the league in assists—but playing in the Polo Grounds in 1947-48, he had 118 and then 111 assists, leading the league both years.

Our thinking about defense is so primitive that we have little ability to deal with park effects for fielders. There are probably many such effects. Artificial turf probably reduces assists for infielders. A large foul territory certainly increases putouts for third basemen. Whoever plays left field for the Red Sox will probably have a low putout total, just because there isn't much ground there for them to cover. Because the study of fielding has not progressed apace with the evaluation of hitting and pitching, we have done little to document these effects.

Gold Glovers

Marvelous Marv got me to wondering what kind of a match there was between the players who rate well at first base in our defensive scheme, and the players who win the Gold Glove. I took the data for all first basemen since Gold Gloves began in 1957, and graded them all "A," "B," "C," "D" and "F" based on their career Win Shares/1000 estimated defensive innings. If a first baseman had earned 2.00 Win Shares per 1000 defensive innings, he was graded an "A" in our system; with 1.67 to 1.99, a "B," 1.33 to 1.66, a "C," 1.00 to 1.32, a "D," and less than 1.00, an "F."

There were 277 players who have played 1,000 or more innings at first base in the years 1957-2000. Of those 277:

34	or 12%	were graded A
92	or 33%	were graded B
112	or 40%	were graded C
39	or 14%	were graded D
10	or 4%	were graded F

Throneberry was in the "D" class; the ten who came in as "Fs" were Dave Kingman, Pedro Guerrero, Carlos Martinez, Dick Stuart, Frank Thomas of the White Sox, Ron Blomberg, Brad Fullmer, and three players from other positions who each played barely over a thousand innings at first base. The better fielders at first also played more innings at the position; the "A" first basemen were 12% of the total, but played 17% of the innings:

A fielders	12% of total	17% of innings
B fielders	33% of total	36% of innings
C fielders	40% of total	39% of innings
D fielders	14% of total	6% of innings
F fielders	4% of total	2% of innings

There have been 87 first base Gold Gloves through the year 2000—one in 1957, and two each year from 1958 to 2000. Of those 87, 53 have gone to fielders identified by our system as "A" first basemen:

A fielders	12% total	17% innings	53 Gold Gloves
B fielders	33% total	36% innings	20 Gold Gloves
C fielders	40% total	39% innings	14 Gold Gloves
D fielders	14% total	6% innings	0 Gold Gloves
F fielders	4% total	2% innings	0 Gold Gloves

(At the end of the article I will update the Gold Glove counts post-2001.)

I should point out: we have given ourselves a fairly easy test here. There are all kinds of ways that our defensive evaluations could be compared to Gold Glove voting. In this study, we ask whether the players recognized by Gold Glove voters are also recognized as good fielders by our system, over the course of their careers. A tougher test would be whether our system could identify a Gold Glove first baseman on one season's data. Also, I have no idea how any other rating system would do. It is possible, for all I know, that Linear Weights would rate 97% of the Gold Glove first basemen as outstanding defensive players.

However, that having been said. . . clearly our system has succeeded in identifying good defensive first basemen, in a general way, in a manner consistent with the evaluations of Gold Glove voters. The first basemen identified by Win Shares as "A" defensive first basemen won eight times as many Gold Gloves, per inning played, as the other first basemen.

The lowest ranking first baseman ever to win a Gold Glove, in our system, was Mark McGwire, who won one Gold Glove (American League, 1990) although he has a career rating of 1.36 Win Shares per 1000 defensive innings (a low C). The other "C" first basemen who have earned Gold Gloves are George Scott, Will Clark, Andres Galarraga, and Cecil Cooper, all of whom are near the top of the "C" range (1.57 or above).

There are eight first basemen in history who have won four or more Gold Gloves—Wes Parker, Vic Power, Mark Grace, Steve Garvey, Bill White, Don Mattingly, Keith Hernandez and George Scott. All of these players except Scott are identified by our system as "A" fielders at first base.

This got me to wondering what the same results would be for other positions, except that, at the other positions, I didn't figure the total innings played by each group of players, because frankly that was a waste of time. There have been 307 catchers since 1957 who have caught 1,000 or more innings in the major leagues. Of those 307, 40 earned 6.30 Win Shares/1000 innings or more, which we designated as "A" defensive play. Those 40 catchers won 59 Gold Gloves. In chart form:

A Level	6.30 WS/1000	40 catchers	59 Gold Gloves
B Level	5.30 WS/1000	97 catchers	26 Gold Gloves
C Level	4.30 WS/1000	104 catchers	2 Gold Gloves
D Level	3.30 WS/1000	57 catchers	0 Gold Gloves
F		9 catchers	0 Gold Gloves

The worst catcher ever to win a Gold Glove, in our analysis, was Joe Torre in 1965. Torre rates at 4.72 Win Shares/1000 innings for his career, a little below average (5.10), but he is the only below-average defensive catcher to win a Gold Glove. The worst fielders to win Gold Gloves are usually great hitters. Occasionally you will hear it said that somebody "won the Gold Glove with his bat," meaning that, there being no consensus about who the best defensive player at a position was, the voters just passed the trophy to the guy they were most familiar with. Occasionally, I think that does happen.

At second base, the match between our analysis and winning the Gold Glove is not as good:

A Level	5.25 WS/1000	41 players	33 Gold Gloves
B Level	4.50 WS/1000	72 players	38 Gold Gloves
C Level	3.75 WS/1000	109 players	16 Gold Gloves
D Level	3.00 WS/1000	51 players	0 Gold Gloves
F		13 players	0 Gold Gloves

The match is not as good here because:

a) the only two second basemen in history who won nine Gold Gloves (Roberto Alomar and Ryne Sandberg) are both graded by our math as "B+" second basemen, not "A," and

b) two players perceived by our system as more or less average, Joe Morgan and Bobby Richardson, won five Gold Gloves apiece.

I don't know if our system for second basemen isn't as good, or the data isn't as good, or the voting isn't as good, or what. . . I'm not commenting on that right now; I'm just charting the matches. The weakest second baseman to win a Gold Glove, in the opinion of the method, was Davey Lopes in 1978.

When we get fewer innings, we get less reliable results. Our system sees Bill Mazeroski as an "A" second baseman, which is good, and Pokey Reese, and Mark Lemke, and Fernando Vina, and Bobby Grich, and Red Schoendienst, and Frank White, and Nellie Fox, and Jose Lind, and Manny Trillo. I don't think anybody would argue about those. But among the 41 second basemen who score as "A" defensive players, we also have Lance Blankenship and Keith Lockhart. Lockhart is one of my favorite players—I love those guys who spend eight years in the minor leagues, but battle through it and prove they can play—but still, I don't think he is generally regarded as a glove wizard, nor was Blankenship. This article seems to establish that our system does a good job of matching general perceptions of defensive excellence—given enough innings to work with. Given fewer innings, it is a lot less reliable.

At third base, the "A" fielders have won 60% of the Gold Gloves:

A Level	4.20 WS/1000	28 players	52 Gold Gloves
B Level	3.40 WS/1000	80 players	33 Gold Gloves
C Level	2.60 WS/1000	121 players	2 Gold Gloves
D Level	1.80 WS/1000	44 players	0 Gold Gloves
F		4 players	0 Gold Gloves

The "C" third basemen who have taken Gold Gloves are Ken Reitz (3.11 per 1000 innings) and Jim Davenport (3.29). Reitz was an extremely reliable third baseman, rarely made a mistake, but had little range.

At shortstop we have almost exactly one-half the Gold Glove winners as "A" shortstops:

A Level	5.80 WS/1000	36 shortstops	44 Gold Gloves
B Level	5.00 WS/1000	77 shortstops	34 Gold Gloves
C Level	4.20 WS/1000	92 shortstops	9 Gold Gloves
D Level	3.40 WS/1000	59 shortstops	0 Gold Gloves
F		13 shortstops	0 Gold Gloves

Gold Glove fielders are basically either "A's" or "B's," with an occasional "C." Belanger, Concepcion, Ozzie Smith, Barry Larkin, and Roy McMillan are seen by our system as "A" fielders. But Luis Aparicio and Omar Vizquel, owners of 17 Gold Gloves between them, are seen as "B" fielders. The lowest-ranking shortstops to have won a Gold Glove are Ernie Banks and Don Kessinger, both "C's."

At no infield position, in other words, has any player perceived by Win Shares as a genuinely bad defensive player ever won a Gold Glove. In the outfield, although the situation is a little bit different, we do have a true anomaly: Dave Winfield.

Outfielders are different, because "outfield" is really three defensive positions which, due to the laziness of 19th century statisticians, we are compelled to treat as one. This creates data problems of all kinds, one of which is that a player who rates as outstanding for a left/right fielder—let's say, 2.6 Win Shares per 1000 innings—would still rank below the norms for a center fielder, since the center fielder is assigned a larger defensive responsibility. There are players who are regarded as very good defensive right fielders, who do not rate well when they are compared to center fielders, just as top-flight third basemen probably would not rate so well if compared to shortstops.

There have been 262 Gold Glove outfielders—87 times three, plus there was one tie in the voting, so the American League in 1985 gave four Gold Gloves in the outfield. Of these 262 Gold Gloves, a little more than half have gone to players regarded by our system as "A" fielders:

A Level	3.30 WS/1000	116 outfielders	136 Gold Gloves
B Level	2.70 WS/1000	195 outfielders	79 Gold Gloves
C Level	2.10 WS/1000	310 outfielders	39 Gold Gloves
D Level	1.50 WS/1000	147 outfielders	8 Gold Gloves
F		10 outfielders	0 Gold Gloves

Dave Winfield won seven Gold Gloves, and won Gold Gloves in both leagues, although he is perceived by our system as a poor defensive outfielder. He is the only player in history to have been a regular member of the Gold Glove team despite poor defensive evaluations by the Win Shares method. At 1.92 Win Shares per 1000 innings, Winfield comes in at a "D+." The only other "D" fielder to win even one Gold Glove is Jay Buhner, who rates a little better than Winfield, at 2.04.

At all positions except pitcher, there have been a total of 377 Gold Gloves awarded to "A" fielders, 320 to "less than A" fielders:

A fielders	377 Gold Gloves
B fielders	230 Gold Gloves
C fielders	82 Gold Gloves
D fielders	8 Gold Gloves
F fielders	ain't happening

Updating this post-2001 as promised. . . these are 2001 Gold Glove winners, and their letter grades as fielders, based on career statistics through 2001:

Position	Lg	Player	WS/1000	Grade
Catcher	NL	Brad Ausmus	6.71	A-
Catcher	AL	Ivan Rodriguez	8.29	A+
First Base	NL	Todd Helton	2.39	A+
First Base	AL	Doug Mientkiewicz	2.19	A
Second Base	NL	Fernando Vina	5.49	A-
Second Base	AL	Roberto Alomar	5.06	B+
Third Base	NL	Scott Rolen	4.23	A-
Third Base	AL	Eric Chavez	3.46	B-
Shortstop	NL	Orlando Cabrera	6.59	A+
Shortstop	AL	Omar Vizquel	5.10	B-
Outfield	NL	Andruw Jones	6.47	A+
Outfield	NL	Jim Edmonds	4.02	A+
Outfield	NL	Larry Walker	3.63	A-
Outfield	AL	Mike Cameron	4.51	A+
Outfield	AL	Torii Hunter	4.88	A+
Outfield	AL	Ichiro Suzuki	3.82	A

So we had a pretty good year in terms of those matches. Andruw Jones, as you will note, rates ridiculously far above the "A+" standard for an outfielder. . . in terms of Win Shares per 1000 defensive innings, Andruw is vastly better than anyone else in baseball history, granted that this is the first part of his career, and his data will probably normalize somewhat over time.

One thing leads to another. . . I got into this because I was interested in Marv Throneberry, and now, having done this analysis, I have created a set of charts to convert statistical rankings into letter grades. That seems kind of interesting, too, so I'll share those with you.

Win Shares Defensive Rankings Expressed as Letter Grades

In the last article, I constructed a system to express any player's rate of Win Shares per 1000 innings as a letter grade, A through F. In the charts below, I will present those "grades" for all players in history who have 5,000 innings at a position (through 2000).

To repeat myself in case anybody missed it, we do not claim that our defensive rankings are accurate 100% of the time. Jimmy Archer, near the top of the first chart, was alleged to be a great defensive catcher—yet we have him evaluated as a "B." His reputation may have become inflated over the years—or our evaluation may simply be wrong. Whenever there is a player who is supposed to be a standout who is rated by us as a "C+" fielder, then his fielding reputation may be undeserved, or our evaluation of him may be wrong. We don't claim that we're batting 1.000.

We *do* claim:

a) that we have worked very hard to solve the riddles of fielding statistics, and

b) that our system works far better, and errs far less, than any other systematically published data.

However, there are some twists and turns in fielding statistics that, as of yet, no one has figured out how to follow.

Catchers

Player	First - Last	Grade
Eddie Ainsmith	1910 - 1924	B-
Sandy Alomar Jr.	1989 - 2000	B-
Jimmy Archer	1904 - 1918	B
Alan Ashby	1973 - 1989	C
Brad Ausmus	1993 - 2000	A-
Joe Azcue	1960 - 1972	B
Ed Bailey	1953 - 1965	C+
Johnny Bassler	1913 - 1927	B-
John Bateman	1963 - 1972	D+
Earl Battey	1955 - 1967	A-
Johnny Bench	1967 - 1983	A-
Bruce Benedict	1978 - 1989	A-
Charlie Bennett	1878 - 1893	A
Bill Bergen	1901 - 1911	A-
Yogi Berra	1946 - 1965	A
Charlie Berry	1925 - 1938	D
Bob Boone	1972 - 1990	B
Pat Borders	1988 - 1999	C+
Frank Bowerman	1895 - 1909	B+
Bob Brenly	1981 - 1989	C
Roger Bresnahan	1900 - 1915	C+
Smoky Burgess	1949 - 1966	C
Doc Bushong	1876 - 1890	B+
Roy Campanella	1948 - 1957	A
Chris Cannizzaro	1960 - 1974	D+
Bill Carrigan	1906 - 1916	B
Gary Carter	1974 - 1992	A
Paul Casanova	1965 - 1974	C-
Rick Cerone	1975 - 1992	C+
Boileryard Clarke	1893 - 1905	C
Jack Clements	1884 - 1900	C+
Mickey Cochrane	1925 - 1937	A
Walker Cooper	1940 - 1957	C
Clint Courtney	1951 - 1961	D+
Del Crandall	1949 - 1966	A
Lou Criger	1896 - 1912	A
Clay Dalrymple	1960 - 1971	B-
Harry Danning	1933 - 1942	A
Darren Daulton	1983 - 1995	C
Jody Davis	1981 - 1990	B+
Spud Davis	1928 - 1945	C+
Rick Dempsey	1969 - 1992	A-
Gene Desautels	1930 - 1946	B+
Bo Diaz	1977 - 1989	B
Bill Dickey	1928 - 1946	A
Red Dooin	1902 - 1916	C+
Brian Downing	1973 - 1981	B
Dave Duncan	1964 - 1976	D+
Duffy Dyer	1968 - 1981	A
Jake Early	1939 - 1949	D+
Johnny Edwards	1961 - 1974	A-
Andy Etchebarren	1962 - 1978	C
Buck Ewing	1880 - 1893	A+
Duke Farrell	1888 - 1905	A-
Joe Ferguson	1970 - 1983	B
Rick Ferrell	1929 - 1947	B-
Carlton Fisk	1969 - 1993	B+
Mike Fitzgerald	1983 - 1992	D+
John Flaherty	1992 - 2000	C
Darrin Fletcher	1989 - 2000	D
Silver Flint	1878 - 1889	B

Player	First - Last	Grade
Barry Foote	1974 - 1982	B
Ray Fosse	1967 - 1979	B
Bill Freehan	1961 - 1976	A-
Rich Gedman	1980 - 1992	B-
George Gibson	1905 - 1918	B-
Joe Girardi	1989 - 2000	B-
Mike Gonzalez	1912 - 1932	B
Johnny Gooch	1921 - 1933	C+
Hank Gowdy	1911 - 1930	A-
Jerry Grote	1963 - 1981	B
Tom Haller	1961 - 1972	B+
Bubbles Hargrave	1913 - 1930	C
Brian Harper	1984 - 1995	D-
Gabby Hartnett	1922 - 1941	A+
Ron Hassey	1978 - 1991	B
Frankie Hayes	1933 - 1947	D+
Ray Hayworth	1926 - 1945	B
Mike Heath	1978 - 1991	C
Jim Hegan	1941 - 1960	A
Rollie Hemsley	1928 - 1947	B+
Ed Herrmann	1967 - 1978	B
Shanty Hogan	1926 - 1937	B
Chris Hoiles	1989 - 1998	C+
Elston Howard	1955 - 1968	A-
Randy Hundley	1964 - 1977	B
Todd Hundley	1990 - 2000	D
Charles Johnson	1994 - 2000	A+
Ron Karkovice	1986 - 1997	A+
Fred Kendall	1969 - 1980	D+
Jason Kendall	1996 - 2000	C+
Terry Kennedy	1978 - 1991	C-
Bill Killefer	1909 - 1921	A+
Malachi Kittridge	1890 - 1906	B-
Johnny Kling	1900 - 1913	B
Chad Kreuter	1988 - 2000	C
Hobie Landrith	1950 - 1963	C
Mike LaValliere	1984 - 1995	A-
Sherm Lollar	1946 - 1963	B+
Ernie Lombardi	1931 - 1947	D+
Stan Lopata	1948 - 1960	C
Al Lopez	1928 - 1947	B
Javy Lopez	1992 - 2000	B
Mike Macfarlane	1987 - 1999	C+
Connie Mack	1886 - 1896	C+
Gus Mancuso	1928 - 1945	B
Kirt Manwaring	1987 - 1999	B+
Buck Martinez	1969 - 1986	B
Phil Masi	1939 - 1952	B-
Milt May	1971 - 1984	B

Player	First - Last	Grade
Brent Mayne	1990 - 2000	C+
Tim McCarver	1959 - 1979	B-
Clyde McCullough	1940 - 1956	C+
Ed McFarland	1893 - 1908	B+
Deacon McGuire	1884 - 1912	C+
Larry McLean	1903 - 1915	C+
Chief Meyers	1909 - 1917	C+
Doggie Miller	1884 - 1896	C-
Otto Miller	1910 - 1922	B
Jocko Milligan	1884 - 1893	B
George Mitterwald	1966 - 1977	B
Charlie Moore	1973 - 1987	C+
Pat Moran	1901 - 1914	A-
Les Moss	1946 - 1957	D+
Ray Mueller	1935 - 1951	A
Thurman Munson	1969 - 1979	B-
Glenn Myatt	1920 - 1936	C-
Greg Myers	1987 - 2000	C-
Russ Nixon	1957 - 1968	D+
Matt Nokes	1985 - 1995	C-
Charlie O'Brien	1985 - 2000	B+
Jack O'Connor	1887 - 1910	B-
Bob O'Farrell	1915 - 1935	B+
Joe Oliver	1989 - 2000	C
Mickey O'Neil	1919 - 1927	B-
Steve O'Neill	1911 - 1928	C+
Mickey Owen	1937 - 1954	B-
Jim Pagliaroni	1955 - 1969	D+
Tom Pagnozzi	1987 - 1998	A-
Lance Parrish	1977 - 1995	A
Heinie Peitz	1892 - 1913	B
Tony Pena	1980 - 1997	A-
Cy Perkins	1915 - 1931	B
Mike Piazza	1992 - 2000	C+
Val Picinich	1916 - 1933	C+
Darrell Porter	1971 - 1987	C
Frankie Pytlak	1932 - 1946	A
Dave Rader	1971 - 1980	C-
Bill Rariden	1909 - 1920	C+
Jeff Reed	1984 - 2000	C
Del Rice	1945 - 1961	A-
Wilbert Robinson	1886 - 1902	C
Bob Rodgers	1961 - 1969	B
Ellie Rodriguez	1968 - 1976	C+
Ivan Rodriguez	1991 - 2000	A+
John Romano	1958 - 1967	B+
Phil Roof	1961 - 1977	C
Buddy Rosar	1939 - 1951	A-
John Roseboro	1957 - 1970	B+

Player	First - Last	Grade
Muddy Ruel	1915 - 1934	A-
Manny Sanguillen	1967 - 1979	C+
Benito Santiago	1986 - 2000	B-
Ray Schalk	1912 - 1929	A
Wally Schang	1913 - 1931	C+
Walter Schmidt	1916 - 1925	B
Ossee Schreckengost	1897 - 1908	A+
Pop Schriver	1886 - 1901	B
Mike Scioscia	1980 - 1992	B+
Andy Seminick	1943 - 1957	C
Scott Servais	1991 - 2000	B-
Hank Severeid	1911 - 1926	B-
Luke Sewell	1921 - 1942	B
Ted Simmons	1968 - 1988	C
Don Slaught	1982 - 1997	D+
Earl Smith	1919 - 1930	C+
Hal W. Smith	1955 - 1964	C-
Frank Snyder	1912 - 1927	B+
Pop Snyder	1876 - 1891	A+
Al Spohrer	1928 - 1935	C-
Oscar Stanage	1906 - 1925	D-
Mike Stanley	1986 - 1997	F
John Stearns	1974 - 1984	B-
Terry Steinbach	1986 - 1999	B-
Joe Sugden	1893 - 1905	B
Billy Sullivan	1899 - 1916	B
Jim Sundberg	1974 - 1989	A
B.J. Surhoff	1987 - 1995	B-
Jeff Sweeney	1908 - 1919	C
Bob Swift	1940 - 1953	B
Eddie Taubensee	1991 - 2000	D
Zack Taylor	1920 - 1935	B+
Birdie Tebbetts	1936 - 1952	B
Gene Tenace	1969 - 1983	C
Mickey Tettleton	1984 - 1995	C
Bob Tillman	1962 - 1970	D
Al Todd	1932 - 1943	C+
Joe Torre	1961 - 1970	C
Mike Tresh	1938 - 1949	C+
Alex Trevino	1978 - 1990	C-
Gus Triandos	1953 - 1965	C
Dave Valle	1984 - 1996	B+
Ozzie Virgil	1980 - 1990	C+
John Warner	1895 - 1908	B+
Wes Westrum	1947 - 1957	A-
Sammy White	1951 - 1962	B-
Ernie Whitt	1976 - 1991	B
Rick Wilkins	1991 - 2000	A
Art Wilson	1909 - 1921	C+
Dan Wilson	1992 - 2000	B+
Jimmie Wilson	1923 - 1940	C+
Ivy Wingo	1911 - 1929	C-
Butch Wynegar	1976 - 1988	C+
Steve Yeager	1972 - 1986	A-

First Basemen

Player	First - Last	Grade
Joe Adcock	1950 - 1966	B+
Dale Alexander	1929 - 1933	C-
Dick Allen	1969 - 1977	C
John Anderson	1896 - 1908	B+
Cap Anson	1879 - 1897	B-
Jeff Bagwell	1991 - 2000	B-
Steve Balboni	1981 - 1990	C+
Ernie Banks	1961 - 1971	B
Jake Beckley	1888 - 1907	B
Dave Bergman	1977 - 1992	C
Del Bissonette	1928 - 1933	C+
Lu Blue	1921 - 1933	B-
Bruce Bochte	1974 - 1986	B-
Zeke Bonura	1934 - 1940	B+
Jim Bottomley	1922 - 1937	C+
Ed Bouchee	1956 - 1962	C
Kitty Bransfield	1898 - 1911	C+
Sid Bream	1983 - 1994	B
Greg Brock	1982 - 1991	C+
Rico Brogna	1992 - 2000	A-
Dan Brouthers	1879 - 1904	B-
Bill Buckner	1970 - 1990	B
George Burns	1914 - 1929	B-
Jack Burns	1930 - 1936	C-
Dolph Camilli	1933 - 1945	B-
Rod Carew	1970 - 1985	C-
Norm Cash	1959 - 1974	A-
Danny Cater	1964 - 1975	C+
Phil Cavarretta	1934 - 1955	C-
Orlando Cepeda	1958 - 1972	C+
Chris Chambliss	1971 - 1986	B-
Frank Chance	1898 - 1914	B
Hal Chase	1905 - 1919	C
Will Clark	1986 - 2000	C+
Tony Clark	1995 - 2000	C
Donn Clendenon	1962 - 1972	C-
Nate Colbert	1968 - 1976	B
Greg Colbrunn	1992 - 2000	B
Gordy Coleman	1959 - 1967	A-
Ripper Collins	1931 - 1941	B

Player	First - Last	Grade
Charlie Comiskey	1882 - 1894	A-
Roger Connor	1881 - 1897	A
Cecil Cooper	1971 - 1986	C+
Babe Dahlgren	1935 - 1946	B-
Jake Daubert	1910 - 1924	B+
Alvin Davis	1984 - 1992	C
Glenn Davis	1984 - 1993	A-
Harry Davis	1895 - 1915	B+
Carlos Delgado	1995 - 2000	C-
Jiggs Donahue	1901 - 1909	B
Jack Doyle	1892 - 1905	C+
Dan Driessen	1973 - 1987	B-
Walt Dropo	1949 - 1961	C+
Mike Epstein	1966 - 1974	C-
Nick Etten	1938 - 1947	F
Darrell Evans	1973 - 1989	B-
Ferris Fain	1947 - 1955	B-
Ron Fairly	1961 - 1978	B+
Sid Farrar	1883 - 1890	B
Cecil Fielder	1985 - 1998	C-
Elbie Fletcher	1934 - 1949	B
Dee Fondy	1951 - 1958	B-
Jack Fournier	1912 - 1927	C-
Dave Foutz	1885 - 1896	A+
Jimmie Foxx	1927 - 1945	A
Andres Galarraga	1985 - 2000	C+
Chick Gandil	1910 - 1919	B+
John Ganzel	1898 - 1908	A+
Steve Garvey	1972 - 1987	A
Lou Gehrig	1923 - 1939	B-
Jim Gentile	1957 - 1966	C+
Dick Gernert	1952 - 1962	C+
Mark Grace	1988 - 2000	A
Hank Greenberg	1933 - 1947	A-
Charlie Grimm	1918 - 1936	A-
Mike Hargrove	1974 - 1985	C+
Buddy Hassett	1936 - 1942	C
Keith Hernandez	1974 - 1990	A-
Doc Hoblitzell	1908 - 1918	C+
Gil Hodges	1948 - 1963	B
Walter Holke	1914 - 1925	B-
Kent Hrbek	1981 - 1994	A-
Don Hurst	1928 - 1934	C
Frank Isbell	1898 - 1909	A+
Deron Johnson	1961 - 1976	B
Doc Johnston	1909 - 1922	C
Tom Jones	1902 - 1910	B-
Buck Jordan	1929 - 1938	C+
Mike Jorgensen	1968 - 1985	B

Player	First - Last	Grade
Wally Joyner	1986 - 2000	B
Joe Judge	1915 - 1934	B-
Eric Karros	1991 - 2000	B+
George Kelly	1915 - 1932	A-
Harmon Killebrew	1960 - 1975	B
Ted Kluszewski	1947 - 1961	C+
Ed Konetchy	1907 - 1921	A-
Ed Kranepool	1962 - 1979	C+
John Kruk	1986 - 1995	B-
Joe Kuhel	1930 - 1946	B+
Candy LaChance	1894 - 1905	A-
Henry Larkin	1887 - 1893	D-
Sam Leslie	1931 - 1938	C
Whitey Lockman	1951 - 1960	B-
Dale Long	1951 - 1963	D+
Fred Luderus	1909 - 1920	B-
Tony Lupien	1940 - 1948	C
Tino Martinez	1990 - 2000	A+
Don Mattingly	1982 - 1995	A-
Lee May	1966 - 1982	B-
John Mayberry	1968 - 1982	C
Frank McCormick	1934 - 1948	A
Willie McCovey	1959 - 1980	C-
Tom McCraw	1963 - 1975	B
Dan McGann	1898 - 1908	B+
Fred McGriff	1986 - 2000	C+
Mark McGwire	1987 - 2000	C-
Stuffy McInnis	1911 - 1927	B+
George McQuinn	1936 - 1948	A-
Fred Merkle	1907 - 1926	B
Dots Miller	1910 - 1921	A-
Don Mincher	1960 - 1972	B-
Johnny Mize	1936 - 1953	B
Willie Montanez	1966 - 1982	C
Eddie Morgan	1928 - 1934	D
John Morrill	1876 - 1890	B
Hal Morris	1989 - 2000	B
Eddie Murray	1977 - 1996	B-
Stan Musial	1946 - 1960	A-
Pete O'Brien	1982 - 1993	A+
John Olerud	1989 - 2000	A+
Al Oliver	1969 - 1985	D-
Dave Orr	1883 - 1890	B
Rafael Palmeiro	1987 - 2000	A
Wes Parker	1964 - 1972	A+
Joe Pepitone	1962 - 1973	B-
Tony Perez	1964 - 1986	B-
Gerald Perry	1983 - 1995	D+
Bill Phillips	1879 - 1888	C+

Player	First - Last	Grade
Wally Pipp	1913 - 1928	A
Boog Powell	1962 - 1977	C-
Vic Power	1954 - 1965	A+
John Reilly	1880 - 1891	B-
Eddie Robinson	1942 - 1957	C+
Pete Rose	1968 - 1986	B
Vic Saier	1911 - 1919	C
Ray Sanders	1942 - 1949	C
George Scott	1966 - 1979	C+
David Segui	1990 - 2000	B+
Earl Sheely	1921 - 1931	B-
Norm Siebern	1959 - 1968	B
Dick Siebert	1932 - 1945	C
Roy Sievers	1952 - 1965	B-
George Sisler	1915 - 1930	C-
Bill Skowron	1954 - 1967	C+
J.T. Snow	1992 - 2000	B
Paul Sorrento	1989 - 1999	C
Jim Spencer	1968 - 1982	B+
Jake Stahl	1904 - 1912	C-
Willie Stargell	1963 - 1982	C-
Joe Start	1876 - 1886	B
George Stovall	1904 - 1915	A-
Dick Stuart	1958 - 1969	F
Gus Suhr	1930 - 1940	B-
Patsy Tebeau	1892 - 1899	A+
Fred Tenney	1894 - 1911	B+
Bill Terry	1923 - 1936	A+
Frank Thomas	1990 - 2000	F
Jason Thompson	1976 - 1986	B-
Andre Thornton	1973 - 1984	B+
Phil Todt	1924 - 1931	B+
Earl Torgeson	1947 - 1961	C+
Joe Torre	1963 - 1977	B-
Hal Trosky	1933 - 1946	B-
Tommy Tucker	1887 - 1899	C+
Willie Upshaw	1978 - 1988	C+
Mo Vaughn	1991 - 2000	D-
Mickey Vernon	1939 - 1959	B-
Eddie Waitkus	1941 - 1955	A-
Greg Walker	1983 - 1990	C-
Bob Watson	1967 - 1984	C+
Perry Werden	1890 - 1897	A
Vic Wertz	1954 - 1963	C+
Bill White	1956 - 1969	A-
Carl Yastrzemski	1968 - 1983	A-
Rudy York	1937 - 1948	A-
Kevin Young	1992 - 2000	C-

Early Second Basemen (1876-1930)
Average 3.55 Win Shares/1000 Innings

Player	First - Last	Grade
Lou Bierbauer	1886 - 1898	A-
Max Bishop	1924 - 1935	A+
Jack Burdock	1876 - 1891	B
Cupid Childs	1888 - 1901	B+
Eddie Collins	1906 - 1928	A-
Hughie Critz	1924 - 1935	A+
Jack Crooks	1889 - 1898	B-
George Cutshaw	1912 - 1923	B
Tom Daly	1887 - 1903	C+
Larry Doyle	1907 - 1920	C+
Fred Dunlap	1880 - 1891	A-
Jimmy Dykes	1918 - 1938	B+
Dick Egan	1908 - 1916	B-
Johnny Evers	1902 - 1929	A-
Jack Farrell	1879 - 1888	B-
Hobe Ferris	1901 - 1909	A-
Hod Ford	1920 - 1932	B-
Frankie Frisch	1919 - 1937	A+
Joe Gerhardt	1876 - 1891	A-
Billy Gilbert	1901 - 1909	B+
Kid Gleason	1889 - 1912	C+
George Grantham	1923 - 1933	C
Bill Hallman	1888 - 1903	C+
Bucky Harris	1919 - 1931	B
Rogers Hornsby	1916 - 1937	C
Miller Huggins	1904 - 1916	B-
Otto Knabe	1907 - 1916	B+
Nap Lajoie	1898 - 1916	A-
Frank LaPorte	1905 - 1915	C-
Bobby Lowe	1891 - 1906	A-
Freddie Maguire	1922 - 1931	A+
Marty McManus	1921 - 1934	B-
Bid McPhee	1882 - 1899	A+
Dots Miller	1909 - 1921	B-
Ray Morgan	1912 - 1918	C+
Danny Murphy	1900 - 1915	B-
Al Myers	1884 - 1891	C
Dick Padden	1896 - 1905	B-
Fred Pfeffer	1882 - 1897	A-
Del Pratt	1912 - 1924	B
Joe Quinn	1886 - 1901	B-
Johnny Rawlings	1914 - 1926	B-
Bill Regan	1926 - 1931	C-
Heinie Reitz	1893 - 1899	A-
Danny Richardson	1886 - 1894	A+

Player	First - Last	Grade
Hardy Richardson	1881 - 1892	A
Claude Ritchey	1897 - 1909	B+
Yank Robinson	1884 - 1892	D
Germany Schaefer	1901 - 1918	B-
Pop Smith	1880 - 1891	B
Cub Stricker	1882 - 1893	C
Fresco Thompson	1925 - 1931	D-
Bill Wambsganss	1914 - 1926	B-
Aaron Ward	1918 - 1928	A-
Jimmy Williams	1901 - 1909	B
Ralph Young	1915 - 1922	C

Depression Era Second Basemen

Average 3.76 Win Shares/1000 Innings

Player	First - Last	Grade
Jimmy Bloodworth	1937 - 1951	B+
Pete Coscarart	1938 - 1945	C+
Tony Cuccinello	1930 - 1944	C+
Bobby Doerr	1937 - 1951	A
Lonny Frey	1935 - 1948	A+
Charlie Gehringer	1924 - 1942	B
Joe Gordon	1938 - 1950	A
Don Gutteridge	1942 - 1947	C-
Jackie Hayes	1928 - 1940	B
Billy Herman	1931 - 1947	B+
Alex Kampouris	1934 - 1943	C
Tony Lazzeri	1926 - 1939	C
Ray Mack	1938 - 1947	C
Ski Melillo	1926 - 1937	A
Buddy Myer	1927 - 1941	B-
Burgess Whitehead	1933 - 1946	A+

Post-War Second Basemen

Average 4.28 Win Shares/1000 Innings

Player	First - Last	Grade
Jerry Adair	1958 - 1970	A
Luis Alicea	1988 - 2000	D+
Bernie Allen	1962 - 1973	C
Roberto Alomar	1988 - 2000	B+
Sandy Alomar	1965 - 1978	B-
Mike Andrews	1966 - 1973	C-
Bobby Avila	1949 - 1959	A-
Wally Backman	1980 - 1993	C
Carlos Baerga	1990 - 1999	B-
Marty Barrett	1982 - 1991	A-
Glenn Beckert	1965 - 1974	C+
Tony Bernazard	1979 - 1991	C-
Craig Biggio	1991 - 2000	B-

Player	First - Last	Grade
Don Blasingame	1955 - 1966	B-
Frank Bolling	1954 - 1966	B-
Bret Boone	1992 - 2000	B-
Jack Brohamer	1972 - 1980	B-
Rod Carew	1967 - 1983	C
Dave Cash	1969 - 1980	B+
Horace Clarke	1965 - 1974	B+
Joey Cora	1987 - 1998	D-
Julio Cruz	1977 - 1986	B+
Rich Dauer	1976 - 1985	C+
Delino DeShields	1990 - 2000	C-
Bill Doran	1982 - 1993	C+
Denny Doyle	1970 - 1977	C+
Ray Durham	1995 - 2000	D
Damion Easley	1993 - 2000	C+
Scott Fletcher	1981 - 1995	A-
Doug Flynn	1975 - 1985	C+
Nellie Fox	1947 - 1965	A
Julio Franco	1985 - 1997	C-
Tito Fuentes	1965 - 1978	C
Jim Gantner	1978 - 1992	B+
Damaso Garcia	1978 - 1989	B
Billy Gardner	1954 - 1963	B+
Phil Garner	1974 - 1987	B-
Jim Gilliam	1953 - 1966	B+
Billy Goodman	1948 - 1962	C
Dick Green	1963 - 1974	B+
Bobby Grich	1970 - 1986	A
Doug Griffin	1970 - 1977	C
Tommy Helms	1965 - 1977	B
Tom Herr	1979 - 1991	C+
Glenn Hubbard	1978 - 1989	A+
Ron Hunt	1963 - 1974	D+
Julian Javier	1960 - 1972	B-
Dave Johnson	1965 - 1978	B-
Jeff Kent	1992 - 2000	D+
Chuck Knoblauch	1991 - 2000	C+
Bobby Knoop	1964 - 1972	A-
Don Kolloway	1940 - 1952	C
Duane Kuiper	1974 - 1984	C
Mike Lansing	1993 - 2000	A-
Jim Lefebvre	1965 - 1972	B-
Mark Lemke	1988 - 1998	A+
Jose Lind	1987 - 1995	A-
Davey Lopes	1972 - 1985	C
Jerry Lumpe	1959 - 1967	C
Billy Martin	1950 - 1961	B-
Bill Mazeroski	1956 - 1972	A+
Dick McAuliffe	1962 - 1974	C

Player	First - Last	Grade
Mark McLemore	1986 - 2000	B-
Cass Michaels	1945 - 1954	D+
Felix Millan	1966 - 1977	B-
Mickey Morandini	1990 - 2000	C
Joe Morgan	1963 - 1984	C
Danny Murtaugh	1941 - 1951	C
Charlie Neal	1956 - 1963	B+
Danny O'Connell	1953 - 1962	B
Ron Oester	1980 - 1990	B-
Jorge Orta	1972 - 1984	F
Tony Phillips	1983 - 1999	C
Jerry Priddy	1941 - 1953	B
Willie Randolph	1975 - 1992	B+
Johnny Ray	1981 - 1990	C+
Jody Reed	1987 - 1997	A+
Jerry Remy	1975 - 1984	B+
Harold Reynolds	1983 - 1994	B-
Bobby Richardson	1955 - 1966	C+
Billy Ripken	1987 - 1998	C+
Jackie Robinson	1948 - 1956	A+
Cookie Rojas	1962 - 1977	B-
Pete Rose	1963 - 1979	C+
Pete Runnels	1952 - 1963	C-
Connie Ryan	1942 - 1953	C
Juan Samuel	1983 - 1998	D-
Ryne Sandberg	1981 - 1997	B+
Steve Sax	1981 - 1994	D+
Red Schoendienst	1945 - 1962	A
Ted Sizemore	1969 - 1980	A-
Eddie Stanky	1943 - 1953	B+
Rennie Stennett	1971 - 1981	A-
Snuffy Stirnweiss	1943 - 1951	A-
Pete Suder	1942 - 1955	C-
Gary Sutherland	1968 - 1978	D-
Tony Taylor	1958 - 1976	C
Johnny Temple	1952 - 1963	C-
Wayne Terwilliger	1949 - 1960	B-
Tim Teufel	1983 - 1993	C
Robby Thompson	1986 - 1996	C+
Manny Trillo	1973 - 1989	A-
Quilvio Veras	1995 - 2000	B+
Emil Verban	1944 - 1950	C+
Fernando Vina	1993 - 2000	A
Lou Whitaker	1977 - 1995	B-
Frank White	1973 - 1990	A
Rob Wilfong	1977 - 1987	A-
Bump Wills	1977 - 1982	B
Bobby Young	1951 - 1958	D
Eric Young	1992 - 2000	C

Early Third Basemen

Average 4.12 Win Shares/1000 Innings

Player	First - Last	Grade
Jimmy Austin	1909 - 1929	C
Home Run Baker	1908 - 1922	B
Les Bell	1925 - 1931	D+
Tony Boeckel	1917 - 1923	D+
Bill Bradley	1899 - 1915	B+
Tom Burns	1880 - 1892	A
Bobby Byrne	1907 - 1917	C+
Hick Carpenter	1879 - 1892	C
Doc Casey	1898 - 1907	C-
Jimmy Collins	1895 - 1908	A+
Wid Conroy	1901 - 1911	C
Bill Coughlin	1899 - 1908	C
Lave Cross	1891 - 1907	A+
Charlie Deal	1912 - 1921	A-
Jerry Denny	1881 - 1894	C+
Art Devlin	1904 - 1913	A+
Jim Donnelly	1884 - 1898	D+
Joe Dugan	1919 - 1931	C
Jimmy Dykes	1918 - 1939	C+
Eddie Foster	1912 - 1923	B
Larry Gardner	1908 - 1924	B+
Eddie Grant	1907 - 1915	C+
Heine Groh	1912 - 1927	A-
Sammy Hale	1920 - 1930	B
Frank Hankinson	1878 - 1888	B
Andy High	1922 - 1934	C-
Charlie Irwin	1894 - 1902	B+
Bob Jones	1917 - 1925	C+
Bill Joyce	1890 - 1898	F
Willie Kamm	1923 - 1935	A
Bill Kuehne	1883 - 1892	B+
Arlie Latham	1883 - 1896	A-
Tommy Leach	1898 - 1914	A+
Freddy Lindstrom	1924 - 1935	B
Hans Lobert	1903 - 1917	D+
Harry Lord	1907 - 1915	F
Denny Lyons	1885 - 1897	C-
John McGraw	1892 - 1906	B+
Marty McManus	1920 - 1934	B
George Moriarty	1903 - 1916	B
Mike Mowrey	1905 - 1917	B-
Joe Mulvey	1883 - 1895	C
Billy Nash	1884 - 1898	A
Frank O'Rourke	1912 - 1930	C-
George Pinckney	1885 - 1893	C+

Player	First - Last	Grade
Babe Pinelli	1918 - 1927	A
Billy Shindle	1887 - 1898	A
Red Smith	1911 - 1919	C
Harry Steinfeldt	1898 - 1911	B-
Milt Stock	1914 - 1925	C
Ezra Sutton	1876 - 1888	B+
Lee Tannehill	1904 - 1912	A+
Pie Traynor	1921 - 1937	B
Terry Turner	1901 - 1919	A-
Ossie Vitt	1912 - 1921	A
Deacon White	1876 - 1890	C-
Art Whitney	1880 - 1891	A-
Ned Williamson	1878 - 1890	A
Harry Wolverton	1898 - 1912	C+
Heinie Zimmerman	1908 - 1919	C+

Depression Era Third Basemen

Average 3.86 Win Shares/1000 Innings

Player	First - Last	Grade
Ossie Bluege	1922 - 1939	B
Harlond Clift	1934 - 1945	B
Wally Gilbert	1928 - 1932	B+
Stan Hack	1932 - 1947	B-
Lee Handley	1936 - 1947	C+
Mike Higgins	1930 - 1946	D
Ken Keltner	1937 - 1950	B
Whitey Kurowski	1941 - 1949	C+
Cookie Lavagetto	1935 - 1947	C
Buddy Lewis	1935 - 1941	C+
Pinky May	1939 - 1943	B+
Marv Owen	1931 - 1940	C+
Lew Riggs	1935 - 1946	B-
Red Rolfe	1934 - 1942	B-
Joe Sewell	1928 - 1933	B+
Joe Stripp	1928 - 1938	B
Jim Tabor	1938 - 1947	D+
Johnny Vergez	1931 - 1936	C-
Bill Werber	1930 - 1942	A-
Pinky Whitney	1928 - 1939	B

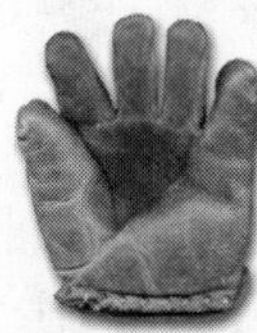

Post-War Third Basemen

Average 3.27 Win Shares/1000 Innings

Player	First - Last	Grade
Bobby Adams	1946 - 1958	B-
Dick Allen	1963 - 1972	C
Max Alvis	1962 - 1970	C
Bob Aspromonte	1960 - 1971	C+
Bob Bailey	1962 - 1978	C
Sal Bando	1966 - 1981	C+
Buddy Bell	1972 - 1989	A-
Wade Boggs	1982 - 1999	B
Bobby Bonilla	1986 - 2000	C-
Clete Boyer	1955 - 1971	A+
Ken Boyer	1955 - 1968	B+
George Brett	1973 - 1992	B
Tom Brookens	1979 - 1990	C+
Scott Brosius	1991 - 2000	A-
Steve Buechele	1985 - 1995	B
Enos Cabell	1973 - 1986	C-
Ken Caminiti	1987 - 2000	B
Andy Carey	1952 - 1962	B
Vinny Castilla	1992 - 2000	B
Ron Cey	1972 - 1987	B-
Ed Charles	1962 - 1969	B-
Jeff Cirillo	1994 - 2000	B+
Billy Cox	1948 - 1955	A-
Jim Davenport	1958 - 1970	C+
Doug DeCinces	1973 - 1987	B-
Bob Dillinger	1946 - 1951	D
Bob Elliott	1942 - 1953	B-
Darrell Evans	1969 - 1989	A-
Joe Foy	1966 - 1971	C+
Gene Freese	1955 - 1966	C-
Travis Fryman	1990 - 2000	B
Gary Gaetti	1981 - 1999	A-
Phil Garner	1973 - 1988	B-
Wayne Garrett	1969 - 1978	A-
Jim Gilliam	1958 - 1966	B-
Wayne Gross	1977 - 1986	C-
Kelly Gruber	1984 - 1993	B
Toby Harrah	1971 - 1984	D+
Jim Ray Hart	1963 - 1973	C
Grady Hatton	1946 - 1956	B-
Charlie Hayes	1988 - 2000	B-
Richie Hebner	1969 - 1985	D+
Don Hoak	1954 - 1963	B
Butch Hobson	1975 - 1981	D
Dave Hollins	1990 - 1998	D

Player	First - Last	Grade
Bob Horner	1978 - 1985	C+
Jack Howell	1985 - 1999	B-
Roy Howell	1974 - 1984	C-
Randy Jackson	1950 - 1959	B-
Brook Jacoby	1981 - 1992	C-
Bill Johnson	1943 - 1953	B
Howard Johnson	1982 - 1995	D+
Chipper Jones	1995 - 2000	D
Puddin' Head Jones	1947 - 1961	B
George Kell	1943 - 1957	B
Harmon Killebrew	1955 - 1971	D
Ray Knight	1974 - 1988	C+
Carney Lansford	1978 - 1992	C
Vance Law	1980 - 1991	D+
Bill Madlock	1973 - 1987	C-
Hank Majeski	1939 - 1955	B+
Frank Malzone	1955 - 1966	B+
Eddie Mathews	1952 - 1968	C
Ken McMullen	1963 - 1977	B-
Bill Melton	1968 - 1977	C-
Paul Molitor	1978 - 1990	B
Don Money	1970 - 1983	B
Graig Nettles	1968 - 1988	A-
Ken Oberkfell	1978 - 1991	C+
Mike Pagliarulo	1984 - 1995	B
Dean Palmer	1989 - 2000	D-
Larry Parrish	1974 - 1987	C-
Terry Pendleton	1984 - 1998	A-
Tony Perez	1967 - 1971	B-
Rico Petrocelli	1966 - 1976	B+
Bubba Phillips	1955 - 1964	C+
Jim Presley	1984 - 1991	C-
Doug Rader	1967 - 1977	B
Joe Randa	1995 - 2000	C
Ken Reitz	1972 - 1982	C
Brooks Robinson	1955 - 1977	A-
Aurelio Rodriguez	1967 - 1983	B+
Scott Rolen	1996 - 2000	B+
Rich Rollins	1961 - 1970	C-
Pete Rose	1966 - 1979	C
Al Rosen	1947 - 1956	B
Chris Sabo	1988 - 1996	C+
Luis Salazar	1980 - 1992	C+
Ron Santo	1960 - 1974	B-
Paul Schaal	1964 - 1974	D-
Mike Schmidt	1972 - 1989	A
Kevin Seitzer	1986 - 1997	B-
Charley Smith	1960 - 1968	C
Eric Soderholm	1971 - 1980	B+

Player	First - Last	Grade
Ed Sprague	1991 - 2000	C-
Hank Thompson	1949 - 1956	B-
Robin Ventura	1989 - 2000	A-
Tim Wallach	1981 - 1996	A
Don Wert	1963 - 1971	B
Matt Williams	1987 - 2000	B
Eddie Yost	1944 - 1962	C-
Todd Zeile	1990 - 1999	C-

Shortstops

Player	First - Last	Grade
Bob Allen	1890 - 1900	A+
Gene Alley	1963 - 1973	B
Ruben Amaro	1958 - 1969	C
Luis Aparicio	1956 - 1973	B
Luke Appling	1930 - 1950	B
Dave Bancroft	1915 - 1930	A
Ernie Banks	1953 - 1961	C
Jack Barry	1908 - 1915	C+
Dick Bartell	1927 - 1943	B+
Mark Belanger	1965 - 1982	A+
Jay Bell	1987 - 1999	C+
Rafael Belliard	1982 - 1998	C-
Jeff Blauser	1987 - 1999	C-
Mike Bordick	1990 - 2000	B-
Lou Boudreau	1939 - 1952	A+
Larry Bowa	1970 - 1985	C
Eddie Bressoud	1956 - 1967	C-
Al Bridwell	1905 - 1914	C+
Ed Brinkman	1962 - 1975	B
Larry Brown	1963 - 1974	B+
Don Buddin	1956 - 1962	D
Rick Burleson	1974 - 1986	A+
Donie Bush	1908 - 1921	C
Bert Campaneris	1964 - 1981	B
Leo Cardenas	1960 - 1975	B+
Chico Carrasquel	1950 - 1959	A-
Ray Chapman	1912 - 1920	B
Royce Clayton	1991 - 2000	B
Dave Concepcion	1970 - 1988	A+
Tommy Corcoran	1890 - 1906	A
Joe Cronin	1926 - 1942	A-
Frankie Crosetti	1932 - 1948	A-
Monte Cross	1892 - 1907	C
Deivi Cruz	1997 - 2000	B-
Bill Dahlen	1891 - 1911	A+
Al Dark	1946 - 1959	B-
George Davis	1890 - 1908	B

Player	First - Last	Grade
Ivan DeJesus	1974 - 1988	D+
Joe DeMaestri	1951 - 1961	D+
Bucky Dent	1973 - 1984	A-
Gary DiSarcina	1989 - 2000	C+
Mickey Doolan	1905 - 1916	A+
Frank Duffy	1970 - 1978	B-
Shawon Dunston	1985 - 2000	C
Leo Durocher	1928 - 1943	A
Kid Elberfeld	1899 - 1914	A-
Kevin Elster	1986 - 2000	A-
Bones Ely	1890 - 1902	A
Woody English	1927 - 1938	B-
Frank Fennelly	1884 - 1890	B
Felix Fermin	1987 - 1996	C
Chico Fernandez	1956 - 1963	B+
Tony Fernandez	1983 - 1997	A
Art Fletcher	1909 - 1922	A+
Scott Fletcher	1981 - 1995	C+
Tim Foli	1970 - 1985	B
Davy Force	1876 - 1886	B+
Hod Ford	1919 - 1933	B-
Julio Franco	1982 - 1987	D
Jim Fregosi	1961 - 1973	C
Shorty Fuller	1888 - 1896	B
Greg Gagne	1983 - 1997	A
Chick Galloway	1919 - 1928	C-
Nomar Garciaparra	1996 - 2000	B-
Charlie Gelbert	1929 - 1940	A+
Wally Gerber	1914 - 1929	B
Jack Glasscock	1880 - 1895	A-
Bill Gleason	1882 - 1889	D+
Chris Gomez	1993 - 2000	D
Alex S. Gonzalez	1994 - 2000	B+
Alfredo Griffin	1976 - 1993	B-
Dick Groat	1952 - 1967	A-
Mark Grudzielanek	1995 - 2000	D+
Ozzie Guillen	1985 - 2000	B+
Ricky Gutierrez	1993 - 2000	D+
Granny Hamner	1944 - 1959	A
Ron Hansen	1958 - 1972	A
Toby Harrah	1969 - 1986	C-
Bud Harrelson	1965 - 1980	B+
Enzo Hernandez	1971 - 1978	D+
Charlie Hollocher	1918 - 1924	C+
Rudy Hulswitt	1899 - 1910	D-
Arthur Irwin	1880 - 1894	B+
Sonny Jackson	1963 - 1973	D+
Travis Jackson	1922 - 1936	B+
Hughie Jennings	1891 - 1907	A+

Player	First - Last	Grade
Derek Jeter	1995 - 2000	D+
Ernie Johnson	1912 - 1925	B+
Eddie Joost	1936 - 1955	B-
Billy Jurges	1931 - 1947	B+
Buddy Kerr	1943 - 1951	B-
Don Kessinger	1964 - 1979	C-
Bill Knickerbocker	1933 - 1942	C
Mark Koenig	1925 - 1936	B+
Larry Kopf	1914 - 1923	F
Red Kress	1927 - 1940	B-
Tony Kubek	1957 - 1965	A
Harvey Kuenn	1952 - 1961	D
Eddie Lake	1939 - 1950	D-
Hal Lanier	1964 - 1973	A-
Barry Larkin	1986 - 2000	A
Lyn Lary	1929 - 1940	B-
Doc Lavan	1913 - 1924	B-
Johnnie LeMaster	1975 - 1987	D
Johnny Lipon	1942 - 1953	B-
Johnny Logan	1951 - 1963	B+
Herman Long	1889 - 1903	A+
Rabbit Maranville	1912 - 1931	A+
Marty Marion	1940 - 1952	A+
Dal Maxvill	1962 - 1975	A+
Dick McAuliffe	1960 - 1974	C
George McBride	1901 - 1920	A
Ed McKean	1887 - 1899	F
Roy McMillan	1951 - 1966	A-
Eric McNair	1929 - 1942	C-
Pat Meares	1993 - 2000	C-
Denis Menke	1962 - 1974	D+
Lennie Merullo	1941 - 1947	C-
Roger Metzger	1970 - 1980	C-
Gene Michael	1966 - 1975	C
Eddie Miller	1936 - 1950	B+
Willie Miranda	1951 - 1959	B+
Billy Myers	1935 - 1941	C+
Skeeter Newsome	1935 - 1947	B-
Jose Offerman	1990 - 1996	F
Charley O'Leary	1904 - 1913	C
Ivy Olson	1911 - 1924	C-
Rey Ordonez	1996 - 2000	A-
Spike Owen	1983 - 1995	C+
Jose Pagan	1959 - 1968	C
Freddy Parent	1901 - 1910	B
Freddie Patek	1968 - 1981	B
Roger Peckinpaugh	1910 - 1927	A
Johnny Pesky	1942 - 1954	A-
Rico Petrocelli	1963 - 1976	A

Player	First - Last	Grade
Rafael Ramirez	1980 - 1992	C-
Pee Wee Reese	1940 - 1958	A-
Edgar Renteria	1996 - 2000	C
Craig Reynolds	1975 - 1989	B+
Topper Rigney	1922 - 1927	D
Cal Ripken Jr.	1981 - 1997	B+
Luis A. Rivera	1986 - 1998	C-
Phil Rizzuto	1941 - 1956	A+
Andre Rodgers	1957 - 1967	D
Alex Rodriguez	1994 - 2000	C+
Billy Rogell	1925 - 1940	A+
Jack Rowe	1881 - 1890	F
Bill Russell	1970 - 1986	B-
Rey Sanchez	1991 - 2000	A-
Heinie Sand	1923 - 1928	D
Rafael Santana	1983 - 1990	B
Dick Schofield	1983 - 1996	B
Dick Schofield	1953 - 1971	C
Everett Scott	1914 - 1926	A+
Joe Sewell	1920 - 1928	A-
Roy Smalley	1975 - 1987	B
Roy Smalley	1948 - 1958	D
Germany Smith	1884 - 1898	A+
Ozzie Smith	1978 - 1996	A+
Chris Speier	1971 - 1989	B
Vern Stephens	1941 - 1953	B
Kurt Stillwell	1986 - 1996	D-
Kevin Stocker	1993 - 2000	B
George Strickland	1950 - 1960	B+
Jackie Tavener	1921 - 1929	B+
Frank Taveras	1972 - 1982	C-
Garry Templeton	1976 - 1991	B-
Tommy Thevenow	1924 - 1938	B
Dickie Thon	1979 - 1993	B
Joe Tinker	1902 - 1916	A+
Alan Trammell	1977 - 1996	B-
Cecil Travis	1936 - 1947	C
Terry Turner	1904 - 1919	A-
Billy Urbanski	1931 - 1936	D
Jose Uribe	1984 - 1993	B
Jose Valentin	1992 - 2000	B
Arky Vaughan	1932 - 1943	B+
Zoilo Versalles	1959 - 1971	B-
Tom Veryzer	1973 - 1984	C
Jose Vizcaino	1989 - 2000	B-
Omar Vizquel	1989 - 2000	B-
Heinie Wagner	1902 - 1916	B-
Honus Wagner	1901 - 1917	A+
Bobby Wallace	1899 - 1918	B
Monte Ward	1881 - 1891	A+
Rabbit Warstler	1930 - 1940	C
U.L. Washington	1977 - 1987	C+
Buck Weaver	1912 - 1920	A
Walt Weiss	1987 - 2000	B-
Maury Wills	1959 - 1972	B+
Bobby Wine	1960 - 1972	B+
Glenn Wright	1924 - 1933	A-
Robin Yount	1974 - 1984	B-

Before running the data for outfielders, I will repeat the caveat that this data mixes up left and right fielders, who typically earn about 2.00 Win Shares/1000 innings, with center fielders, who typically earn about 3.00. A rating can be outstanding for a left fielder, but unimpressive compared to center fielders. But it's what we can do with the data we have.

Outfielders

Player	First - Last	Grade
Hank Aaron	1954 - 1976	C+
Tommie Agee	1962 - 1973	A+
Ethan Allen	1926 - 1938	A-
Bob Allison	1958 - 1970	C+
Mel Almada	1933 - 1939	A+
Felipe Alou	1958 - 1974	C+
Jesus Alou	1963 - 1979	C
Matty Alou	1960 - 1974	B-
Moises Alou	1990 - 2000	B-
George Altman	1959 - 1967	C
Brady Anderson	1988 - 2000	B-
Garret Anderson	1994 - 2000	B
John Anderson	1894 - 1908	C-
Ed Andrews	1885 - 1891	A+
Tony Armas	1976 - 1989	B+
Richie Ashburn	1948 - 1962	A+
Earl Averill	1929 - 1941	A+
Harold Baines	1980 - 1997	B-
Dusty Baker	1968 - 1986	B-
Jesse Barfield	1981 - 1992	A-
Jimmy Barrett	1899 - 1908	A
Shad Barry	1899 - 1908	D
Kevin Bass	1982 - 1995	C+
Johnny Bates	1906 - 1914	C-
Hank Bauer	1948 - 1961	C
Frankie Baumholtz	1947 - 1956	C+
Harry Bay	1901 - 1907	A
Don Baylor	1970 - 1986	C-

Player	First - Last	Grade
Ginger Beaumont	1899 - 1910	B+
Beals Becker	1908 - 1915	C
Rich Becker	1993 - 2000	B+
Beau Bell	1935 - 1941	D-
Derek Bell	1991 - 2000	D+
George Bell	1981 - 1992	C-
Gus Bell	1950 - 1962	C-
Albert Belle	1989 - 2000	C-
Juan Beniquez	1974 - 1988	B
Wally Berger	1930 - 1940	A-
Ken Berry	1962 - 1975	A+
Bob Bescher	1908 - 1918	C-
Dante Bichette	1988 - 2000	C+
Carson Bigbee	1916 - 1926	A-
Joe Birmingham	1906 - 1914	A+
Ray Blades	1922 - 1932	C
Paul Blair	1964 - 1980	A+
Ping Bodie	1911 - 1921	B+
Barry Bonds	1986 - 2000	C
Bobby Bonds	1968 - 1981	B-
Bobby Bonilla	1986 - 2000	D+
Barry Bonnell	1977 - 1986	B
Daryl Boston	1984 - 1994	B
Phil Bradley	1983 - 1990	D
Jackie Brandt	1956 - 1967	A-
Rube Bressler	1918 - 1932	B-
John Briggs	1964 - 1975	D+
Lou Brock	1961 - 1979	C-
Steve Brodie	1890 - 1902	A+
Eddie Brown	1920 - 1928	D+
Ollie Brown	1965 - 1977	C
Tom Brown	1882 - 1898	C+
George Browne	1901 - 1911	D+
Pete Browning	1883 - 1894	C+
Tom Brunansky	1981 - 1994	B-
Bill Bruton	1953 - 1964	A-
Bill Buckner	1970 - 1984	C+
Jay Buhner	1987 - 2000	D+
Al Bumbry	1972 - 1985	A-
Eddie Burke	1890 - 1897	A
Jesse Burkett	1890 - 1905	B
Ellis Burks	1987 - 2000	B
Jeromy Burnitz	1993 - 2000	C
George Burns	1911 - 1925	B-
Oyster Burns	1884 - 1895	D+
Jeff Burroughs	1970 - 1984	D-
Jim Busby	1950 - 1962	A+
Brett Butler	1981 - 1997	B+
Ivan Calderon	1984 - 1993	C+

Player	First - Last	Grade
Johnny Callison	1958 - 1973	B-
Bruce Campbell	1930 - 1942	D+
Jose Canseco	1985 - 2000	D+
Bernie Carbo	1970 - 1979	B+
Jose Cardenal	1963 - 1980	B-
Max Carey	1910 - 1929	A+
Cliff Carroll	1882 - 1893	B-
Joe Carter	1983 - 1998	C+
Rico Carty	1964 - 1976	D+
George Case	1937 - 1947	C
Cesar Cedeno	1970 - 1986	A-
Ben Chapman	1931 - 1945	B
Sam Chapman	1938 - 1951	B+
Gino Cimoli	1956 - 1965	C+
Jack Clark	1975 - 1989	C-
Fred Clarke	1894 - 1915	A-
Roberto Clemente	1955 - 1972	B-
Gil Coan	1946 - 1955	B-
Ty Cobb	1905 - 1928	B+
Rocky Colavito	1955 - 1968	C
Vince Coleman	1985 - 1997	C
Dave Collins	1975 - 1990	C+
Shano Collins	1910 - 1925	B-
Earle Combs	1924 - 1935	C+
Adam Comorosky	1926 - 1935	C+
Tony Conigliaro	1964 - 1971	C-
Jeff Conine	1992 - 2000	D+
Duff Cooley	1893 - 1905	C
Johnny Cooney	1923 - 1944	A-
Pop Corkhill	1883 - 1892	A+
Wes Covington	1956 - 1966	D-
Al Cowens	1974 - 1986	B
Doc Cramer	1929 - 1948	A
Gavy Cravath	1908 - 1920	D+
Sam Crawford	1899 - 1917	C
Willie Crawford	1964 - 1977	C+
Birdie Cree	1908 - 1915	C+
Warren Cromartie	1974 - 1991	B-
Walton Cruise	1914 - 1923	C-
Jose Cruz	1970 - 1988	B-
Roy Cullenbine	1938 - 1946	C
Chad Curtis	1992 - 2000	C+
Kiki Cuyler	1921 - 1938	B
Abner Dalrymple	1878 - 1891	A
Johnny Damon	1995 - 2000	B-
Kal Daniels	1986 - 1992	C-
Vic Davalillo	1963 - 1979	B
Chili Davis	1981 - 1994	C-
Eric Davis	1984 - 2000	B

Player	First - Last	Grade	Player	First - Last	Grade
Mike Davis	1980 - 1989	D+	Buck Freeman	1898 - 1907	D+
Tommy Davis	1960 - 1972	D+	Carl Furillo	1946 - 1960	B
Willie Davis	1960 - 1979	A	Augie Galan	1935 - 1949	B
Andre Dawson	1976 - 1996	B	Oscar Gamble	1969 - 1984	C-
Rob Deer	1984 - 1996	C-	Ron Gant	1989 - 2000	C+
Ed Delahanty	1888 - 1903	B-	Ralph Garr	1969 - 1980	D+
Jim Delsing	1948 - 1960	C	Cito Gaston	1967 - 1978	D+
Frank Demaree	1932 - 1944	C	Gary Geiger	1958 - 1970	B+
Don Demeter	1956 - 1967	B-	Cesar Geronimo	1969 - 1983	A-
Bob Dernier	1980 - 1989	B-	Doc Gessler	1903 - 1911	D
Mike Devereaux	1987 - 1998	B+	Kirk Gibson	1979 - 1995	C
Dom DiMaggio	1940 - 1952	A+	Bernard Gilkey	1990 - 2000	C
Joe DiMaggio	1936 - 1951	A+	Pete Gillespie	1880 - 1887	C+
Vince DiMaggio	1937 - 1946	A+	Dan Gladden	1983 - 1993	B-
Larry Doby	1948 - 1959	A	Doug Glanville	1996 - 2000	A+
Cozy Dolan	1895 - 1906	C-	Juan Gonzalez	1989 - 2000	D-
Mike Donlin	1899 - 1912	C	Luis Gonzalez	1991 - 2000	C+
Patsy Donovan	1890 - 1907	D+	Tony Gonzalez	1960 - 1971	B-
Mike Dorgan	1877 - 1890	C	Wilbur Good	1908 - 1918	C
Patsy Dougherty	1902 - 1911	C	Ival Goodman	1935 - 1944	C
Taylor Douthit	1923 - 1933	A+	Tom Goodwin	1991 - 2000	B+
Tommy Dowd	1891 - 1901	D+	Sid Gordon	1941 - 1955	D+
Brian Downing	1973 - 1987	D+	George Gore	1879 - 1892	A+
Hugh Duffy	1888 - 1905	A+	Goose Goslin	1921 - 1938	C+
Pat Duncan	1915 - 1924	B	Jack Graney	1910 - 1922	C
Lenny Dykstra	1985 - 1996	A	Danny Green	1898 - 1905	C+
Jim Edmonds	1993 - 2000	A+	Lenny Green	1957 - 1968	B-
Jim Eisenreich	1982 - 1998	C+	Shawn Green	1993 - 2000	C
Del Ennis	1946 - 1959	D+	Mike Greenwell	1985 - 1996	C
Dwight Evans	1972 - 1991	B-	Rusty Greer	1994 - 2000	D-
Steve Evans	1908 - 1915	D-	Ken Griffey Sr.	1973 - 1991	C-
Carl Everett	1993 - 2000	A-	Ken Griffey Jr.	1989 - 2000	A-
Hoot Evers	1941 - 1956	A-	Mike Griffin	1887 - 1898	A
Ron Fairly	1958 - 1977	C	Tommy Griffith	1913 - 1925	D+
Bibb Falk	1920 - 1931	C	Marquis Grissom	1989 - 2000	A+
Happy Felsch	1915 - 1920	A+	Greg Gross	1973 - 1989	C-
Steve Finley	1989 - 2000	B+	Johnny Groth	1946 - 1960	B+
Lou Finney	1931 - 1946	C	Johnny Grubb	1972 - 1987	C-
Max Flack	1914 - 1925	C+	Tony Gwynn	1982 - 2000	C-
Ira Flagstead	1917 - 1930	A-	Mule Haas	1925 - 1938	A
Elmer Flick	1898 - 1910	C	Chick Hafey	1924 - 1937	C
Curt Flood	1958 - 1971	A+	Jimmie Hall	1963 - 1970	A-
Jim Fogarty	1884 - 1890	A+	Mel Hall	1981 - 1996	D+
Dan Ford	1975 - 1984	D+	Billy Hamilton	1888 - 1901	A-
George Foster	1969 - 1986	C+	Darryl Hamilton	1988 - 2000	B+
Bob Fothergill	1922 - 1933	D	Ned Hanlon	1880 - 1892	B-
Pete Fox	1933 - 1945	B-	Dick Harley	1897 - 1903	F
Tito Francona	1956 - 1970	C-	George Harper	1916 - 1929	C
Johnny Frederick	1929 - 1934	C+	Tommy Harper	1963 - 1976	C+

Player	First - Last	Grade
Topsy Hartsel	1898 - 1911	C+
Billy Hatcher	1984 - 1995	A-
Von Hayes	1981 - 1992	C+
Jeff Heath	1936 - 1949	C-
Cliff Heathcote	1918 - 1931	B
Emmett Heidrick	1898 - 1908	A-
Harry Heilmann	1914 - 1930	D
Charlie Hemphill	1899 - 1911	C
Dave Henderson	1981 - 1994	B+
Ken Henderson	1965 - 1980	B-
Rickey Henderson	1979 - 2000	C
Steve Henderson	1977 - 1988	D
George Hendrick	1971 - 1988	C
Tommy Henrich	1937 - 1949	C+
Babe Herman	1926 - 1945	C-
Larry Herndon	1974 - 1988	C+
Mike Hershberger	1961 - 1971	B-
Jim Hickman	1962 - 1973	C
Bobby Higginson	1995 - 2000	D
Glenallen Hill	1989 - 2000	F
Bill Hinchman	1905 - 1918	C+
Paul Hines	1876 - 1891	A-
Chuck Hinton	1961 - 1971	C-
Larry Hisle	1968 - 1979	D+
Myril Hoag	1931 - 1945	C
Danny Hoffman	1903 - 1911	B
Solly Hofman	1903 - 1916	A+
Bug Holliday	1889 - 1898	B+
Ducky Holmes	1895 - 1905	B+
Tommy Holmes	1942 - 1952	B+
Harry Hooper	1909 - 1925	C+
Johnny Hopp	1940 - 1952	A-
Joe Hornung	1879 - 1890	A-
Willie Horton	1963 - 1978	D+
Pete Hotaling	1879 - 1888	C
Frank Howard	1958 - 1972	D+
Dummy Hoy	1888 - 1902	B+
Brian L. Hunter	1994 - 2000	B
Pete Incaviglia	1986 - 1998	C
Monte Irvin	1949 - 1956	C+
Darrin Jackson	1985 - 1999	A-
Joe Jackson	1908 - 1920	C+
Reggie Jackson	1967 - 1987	C-
Baby Doll Jacobson	1915 - 1927	A-
Dion James	1983 - 1996	D+
Charlie Jamieson	1915 - 1932	C+
Stan Javier	1984 - 2000	C+
Jackie Jensen	1950 - 1961	B-
Woody Jensen	1931 - 1939	B-
Alex Johnson	1964 - 1976	D+
Bob Johnson	1933 - 1945	C
Lance Johnson	1987 - 2000	A
Roy Johnson	1929 - 1938	C
Dick Johnston	1884 - 1891	A+
Jay Johnstone	1966 - 1984	B-
Andruw Jones	1996 - 2000	A+
Charley Jones	1876 - 1888	C+
Cleon Jones	1963 - 1976	C+
Davy Jones	1901 - 1915	B
Fielder Jones	1896 - 1915	A+
Mack Jones	1961 - 1971	D+
Ruppert Jones	1976 - 1987	B+
Brian Jordan	1992 - 2000	B+
Felix Jose	1988 - 2000	B-
Wally Judnich	1940 - 1949	B+
David Justice	1989 - 2000	B+
Al Kaline	1953 - 1973	B-
Benny Kauff	1912 - 1920	A-
Willie Keeler	1893 - 1910	C+
Charlie Keller	1939 - 1952	C+
Joe Kelley	1891 - 1908	A-
King Kelly	1878 - 1893	B+
Pat Kelly	1968 - 1981	C
Roberto Kelly	1987 - 2000	C+
Steve Kemp	1977 - 1988	D+
Bob Kennedy	1942 - 1957	C
Ralph Kiner	1946 - 1955	C-
Jim King	1955 - 1967	C+
Dave Kingman	1971 - 1983	C
Willie Kirkland	1958 - 1966	C
Chuck Klein	1928 - 1944	C-
Mike Kreevich	1931 - 1945	A+
Harvey Kuenn	1956 - 1966	C-
Chet Laabs	1937 - 1947	C-
Lee Lacy	1975 - 1987	C+
Jim Landis	1957 - 1967	A
Ken Landreaux	1977 - 1987	B-
Bill Lange	1893 - 1899	A+
Ray Lankford	1990 - 2000	B
Rudy Law	1978 - 1986	B+
Matt Lawton	1995 - 2000	C+
Freddy Leach	1923 - 1932	D+
Tommy Leach	1900 - 1918	A+
Hal Lee	1930 - 1936	C
Ron LeFlore	1974 - 1982	B-
Hank Leiber	1933 - 1942	C+
Nemo Leibold	1913 - 1925	B
Chet Lemon	1975 - 1990	A

Player	First - Last	Grade
Jim Lemon	1950 - 1963	D-
Jeffrey Leonard	1977 - 1990	C-
Buddy Lewis	1940 - 1949	C-
Darren Lewis	1990 - 2000	A+
Duffy Lewis	1910 - 1921	B+
Sixto Lezcano	1974 - 1985	C+
Johnny Lindell	1943 - 1953	A-
Danny Litwhiler	1940 - 1951	C
Don Lock	1962 - 1969	B-
Whitey Lockman	1945 - 1959	C
Kenny Lofton	1991 - 2000	A+
Hector Lopez	1956 - 1966	C
Bris Lord	1905 - 1913	B-
John Lowenstein	1970 - 1985	C+
Peanuts Lowrey	1942 - 1955	B
Mike Lum	1967 - 1981	B-
Harry Lumley	1904 - 1910	D-
Greg Luzinski	1972 - 1980	D
Jerry Lynch	1954 - 1966	D
Fred Lynn	1974 - 1990	B+
Shane Mack	1987 - 1998	B+
Elliott Maddox	1970 - 1980	B-
Garry Maddox	1972 - 1986	A+
Sherry Magee	1904 - 1919	B-
Candy Maldonado	1981 - 1995	C-
Billy Maloney	1901 - 1908	B
Les Mann	1913 - 1928	B-
Jack Manning	1876 - 1886	F
Rick Manning	1975 - 1987	B-
Mickey Mantle	1951 - 1966	B+
Heinie Manush	1923 - 1939	C
Roger Maris	1957 - 1968	C+
Mike Marshall	1981 - 1991	C-
Willard Marshall	1942 - 1955	D+
Al Martin	1992 - 2000	D-
Jerry Martin	1974 - 1984	B
Pepper Martin	1928 - 1944	C+
Dave Martinez	1986 - 2000	B-
Gary Matthews	1972 - 1987	D+
Charlie Maxwell	1950 - 1963	C+
Carlos May	1968 - 1977	D+
Dave May	1967 - 1978	B
Lee Maye	1959 - 1971	C-
Willie Mays	1951 - 1973	A+
Lee Mazzilli	1976 - 1989	C
Jimmy McAleer	1889 - 1902	A+
Bake McBride	1973 - 1983	B+
Jack McCarthy	1893 - 1907	B-
Tommy McCarthy	1884 - 1896	A-

Player	First - Last	Grade
Mike McCormick	1940 - 1951	A
Barney McCosky	1939 - 1952	A
Tom McCreery	1895 - 1903	C
Oddibe McDowell	1985 - 1994	A
Jack McGeachey	1886 - 1891	C
Willie McGee	1982 - 1999	B
Matty McIntyre	1901 - 1912	B
Brian McRae	1990 - 1999	A
Kevin McReynolds	1983 - 1994	B-
Jim McTamany	1885 - 1891	B+
Joe Medwick	1932 - 1948	B-
Sam Mele	1947 - 1956	C+
Mike Menosky	1914 - 1923	C+
Sam Mertes	1896 - 1906	B+
Catfish Metkovich	1943 - 1954	B
Bob Meusel	1920 - 1930	C-
Irish Meusel	1914 - 1927	C-
Clyde Milan	1907 - 1922	B+
Bing Miller	1921 - 1936	B-
Dusty Miller	1889 - 1899	B+
Rick Miller	1971 - 1985	B+
Ward Miller	1909 - 1917	C+
Eddie Milner	1981 - 1988	A+
Minnie Minoso	1949 - 1964	B-
Dale Mitchell	1946 - 1956	C
Kevin Mitchell	1986 - 1998	D
Mike Mitchell	1907 - 1914	C
Danny Moeller	1907 - 1916	C+
Rick Monday	1966 - 1984	B
Raul Mondesi	1993 - 2000	B-
Wally Moon	1954 - 1965	C
Gene Moore	1931 - 1945	B+
Johnny Moore	1929 - 1937	B-
Jo-Jo Moore	1930 - 1941	D+
Terry Moore	1935 - 1948	A+
Jerry Morales	1969 - 1983	C-
Herbie Moran	1908 - 1915	C
Keith Moreland	1980 - 1988	D
Omar Moreno	1975 - 1986	A+
Walt Moryn	1954 - 1961	C+
Lloyd Moseby	1980 - 1991	A
Wally Moses	1935 - 1951	C
Johnny Mostil	1921 - 1929	A+
Manny Mota	1962 - 1979	C
Don Mueller	1948 - 1958	D+
Pat Mullin	1940 - 1953	C
Jerry Mumphrey	1974 - 1988	B-
Bobby Murcer	1969 - 1980	B-
Dale Murphy	1980 - 1993	B-

Player	First - Last	Grade
Danny Murphy	1908 - 1915	C+
Dwayne Murphy	1978 - 1989	A-
Red Murray	1906 - 1917	C
Stan Musial	1941 - 1963	B
Hi Myers	1909 - 1925	A+
Greasy Neale	1916 - 1924	C
Bill Nicholson	1936 - 1953	D+
Hugh Nicol	1881 - 1890	A+
Bob Nieman	1951 - 1962	D+
Otis Nixon	1983 - 1999	A+
Irv Noren	1950 - 1960	A
Bill North	1971 - 1981	A-
Ron Northey	1942 - 1956	D+
Jim Northrup	1964 - 1975	C+
Rebel Oakes	1909 - 1915	B-
Darby O'Brien	1887 - 1892	B-
Lefty O'Doul	1919 - 1934	D
Rowland Office	1972 - 1983	B-
Ben Oglivie	1971 - 1986	D+
Rube Oldring	1907 - 1918	C+
Troy O'Leary	1993 - 2000	B
Tony Oliva	1962 - 1972	B-
Al Oliver	1968 - 1985	B+
Paul O'Neill	1985 - 2000	C+
Tip O'Neill	1883 - 1892	A
Jim O'Rourke	1876 - 1893	C+
Joe Orsulak	1983 - 1997	C-
Amos Otis	1967 - 1984	A+
Mel Ott	1926 - 1946	C-
Tom Paciorek	1970 - 1987	D+
Andy Pafko	1943 - 1959	B
Dave Parker	1973 - 1989	C+
Dode Paskert	1907 - 1921	A-
Albie Pearson	1958 - 1966	B
Gary Pettis	1982 - 1992	A
Dave Philley	1941 - 1962	B
Tony Phillips	1984 - 1999	C-
Ollie Pickering	1896 - 1908	B
Jimmy Piersall	1950 - 1967	A+
Lou Piniella	1968 - 1984	C+
Vada Pinson	1958 - 1975	A-
Luis Polonia	1987 - 2000	C
Dick Porter	1929 - 1934	C
Wally Post	1949 - 1964	C-
Jake Powell	1930 - 1945	C
Ray Powell	1913 - 1924	C+
Kirby Puckett	1984 - 1995	A+
Terry Puhl	1977 - 1991	B
Blondie Purcell	1879 - 1890	F
Rip Radcliff	1934 - 1943	C-
Paul Radford	1883 - 1894	C+
Tim Raines	1980 - 1999	B-
Manny Ramirez	1993 - 2000	C+
Gary Redus	1982 - 1994	B-
Rick Reichardt	1964 - 1973	C-
Pete Reiser	1940 - 1952	A+
Rip Repulski	1953 - 1961	C-
Merv Rettenmund	1968 - 1979	B
Carl Reynolds	1927 - 1939	B
Harry Rice	1924 - 1933	C+
Jim Rice	1974 - 1988	C+
Sam Rice	1916 - 1934	B-
Gene Richards	1977 - 1984	D+
Lance Richbourg	1924 - 1932	C
Jim Rivera	1952 - 1961	A
Mickey Rivers	1970 - 1984	A-
Leon Roberts	1974 - 1984	D
Dave Robertson	1912 - 1922	D
Bill Robinson	1966 - 1983	C+
Floyd Robinson	1960 - 1968	C
Frank Robinson	1956 - 1976	C+
Henry Rodriguez	1992 - 2000	D+
Gary Roenicke	1976 - 1988	B-
Pete Rose	1963 - 1984	B-
Chief Roseman	1882 - 1890	C-
Braggo Roth	1914 - 1921	D
Jack Rothrock	1928 - 1937	B
Edd Roush	1913 - 1931	A-
Johnny Rucker	1940 - 1946	D-
Joe Rudi	1967 - 1982	C
Jim Russell	1942 - 1951	B
Babe Ruth	1918 - 1935	C-
Jimmy Ryan	1885 - 1903	B+
Tim Salmon	1992 - 2000	C+
Billy Sample	1978 - 1986	C+
Reggie Sanders	1991 - 2000	C+
Hank Sauer	1941 - 1959	C+
Fred Schulte	1927 - 1937	A+
Wildfire Schulte	1904 - 1918	B-
Tony Scott	1973 - 1984	A
Emmett Seery	1884 - 1892	C-
Kip Selbach	1894 - 1906	C-
George Selkirk	1934 - 1942	B-
Socks Seybold	1899 - 1908	B-
Cy Seymour	1896 - 1913	A
Orator Shaffer	1877 - 1890	B+
Howard Shanks	1912 - 1925	A
Spike Shannon	1904 - 1908	C

Player	First - Last	Grade
Jimmy Sheckard	1897 - 1913	A
Gary Sheffield	1994 - 2000	D
John Shelby	1981 - 1991	B
Pat Sheridan	1981 - 1991	B-
Burt Shotton	1909 - 1922	C
Ruben Sierra	1986 - 1998	C-
Roy Sievers	1949 - 1962	D
Al Simmons	1924 - 1944	A
Ken Singleton	1970 - 1982	C
Bob Skinner	1954 - 1965	C
Jimmy Slagle	1899 - 1908	A
Enos Slaughter	1938 - 1959	B-
Al Smith	1953 - 1964	C
Elmer Smith	1886 - 1901	B
Elmer Smith	1914 - 1925	C
Jack Smith	1915 - 1929	D+
Lonnie Smith	1978 - 1994	C-
Reggie Smith	1966 - 1980	A-
Homer Smoot	1902 - 1906	C-
Duke Snider	1947 - 1964	A-
Fred Snodgrass	1909 - 1916	A-
Cory Snyder	1986 - 1994	C+
Russ Snyder	1959 - 1970	C
Moose Solters	1934 - 1943	C+
Joe Sommer	1880 - 1890	B+
Sammy Sosa	1989 - 2000	C
Billy Southworth	1913 - 1929	B-
Al Spangler	1959 - 1970	D+
Tris Speaker	1907 - 1928	A+
Stan Spence	1940 - 1949	B-
Chick Stahl	1897 - 1906	A-
Mickey Stanley	1964 - 1978	A-
Lee Stanton	1970 - 1978	C-
Willie Stargell	1962 - 1974	C-
Jigger Statz	1919 - 1928	A+
Rusty Staub	1963 - 1985	D+
Casey Stengel	1912 - 1925	B-
Jake Stenzel	1890 - 1899	B+
Riggs Stephenson	1922 - 1934	C
George Stone	1905 - 1910	C-
John Stone	1928 - 1938	C+
Harry Stovey	1880 - 1893	B+
Darryl Strawberry	1983 - 1998	C-
Amos Strunk	1908 - 1924	C+
Homer Summa	1920 - 1930	C-
B.J. Surhoff	1988 - 2000	C
Ed Swartwood	1881 - 1892	C-
Ron Swoboda	1965 - 1973	C+
Danny Tartabull	1986 - 1997	D

Player	First - Last	Grade
White Wings Tebeau	1887 - 1895	B
Frank Thomas	1951 - 1965	C+
Gorman Thomas	1973 - 1984	B-
Roy Thomas	1899 - 1911	A-
Milt Thompson	1984 - 1996	B+
Sam Thompson	1885 - 1906	C-
Bobby Thomson	1947 - 1960	B
Mike Tiernan	1887 - 1899	C
John Titus	1903 - 1913	C-
Jack Tobin	1914 - 1927	C
Bobby Tolan	1965 - 1979	B
Cesar Tovar	1965 - 1976	B
Tom Tresh	1962 - 1969	C+
Thurman Tucker	1942 - 1950	A+
Bill Tuttle	1952 - 1963	B+
Larry Twitchell	1886 - 1894	D
Ted Uhlaender	1965 - 1972	B
Del Unser	1968 - 1982	B
Ellis Valentine	1975 - 1985	C
Elmer Valo	1940 - 1961	D+
George Van Haltren	1887 - 1903	B
Andy Van Slyke	1983 - 1995	A-
Greg Vaughn	1989 - 2000	C
Bobby Veach	1912 - 1925	B
Bill Virdon	1955 - 1968	A+
Joe Vosmik	1930 - 1944	B
Leon Wagner	1958 - 1969	D
Curt Walker	1920 - 1930	C+
Dixie Walker	1931 - 1949	B
Gee Walker	1931 - 1945	B-
Harry Walker	1940 - 1955	B+
Larry Walker	1989 - 2000	A
Tilly Walker	1911 - 1923	C+
Lloyd Waner	1927 - 1945	A+
Paul Waner	1926 - 1944	B
Gary Ward	1979 - 1990	B-
Claudell Washington	1974 - 1990	C-
George Watkins	1930 - 1936	C
Roy Weatherly	1936 - 1950	B
Farmer Weaver	1888 - 1894	D+
Mitch Webster	1983 - 1995	B
Curt Welch	1884 - 1893	A+
Frank Welch	1919 - 1927	C-
Jimmy Welsh	1925 - 1930	B+
Vic Wertz	1947 - 1955	C-
Sammy West	1927 - 1942	A+
Wally Westlake	1947 - 1955	C+
Zack Wheat	1909 - 1927	B-
Devon White	1985 - 2000	A

Player	First - Last	Grade
Jo-Jo White	1932 - 1944	B
Rondell White	1993 - 2000	A+
Roy White	1965 - 1979	C
Mark Whiten	1990 - 2000	C
Possum Whitted	1913 - 1921	B+
Bernie Williams	1991 - 2000	A+
Billy Williams	1959 - 1976	C
Cy Williams	1912 - 1930	B
Gerald Williams	1992 - 2000	A
Ken Williams	1915 - 1929	B-
Ted Williams	1939 - 1960	C
Walt Wilmot	1888 - 1898	B
Chief Wilson	1908 - 1916	B+
Glenn Wilson	1982 - 1993	B
Hack Wilson	1923 - 1934	C+
Mookie Wilson	1980 - 1991	A-
Willie Wilson	1976 - 1994	A+
Dave Winfield	1973 - 1994	D+
Whitey Witt	1917 - 1926	B-
Jim Wohlford	1973 - 1986	B-
Chicken Wolf	1882 - 1892	B
George Wood	1880 - 1892	C+
Gene Woodling	1943 - 1962	C
Taffy Wright	1938 - 1949	C
Jimmy Wynn	1963 - 1977	B-
Marvell Wynne	1983 - 1990	B-
Johnny Wyrostek	1942 - 1954	C
Carl Yastrzemski	1961 - 1983	C+
Tom York	1876 - 1885	A-
Joel Youngblood	1976 - 1989	C-
Ross Youngs	1917 - 1926	C
Robin Yount	1976 - 1993	A-
Al Zarilla	1943 - 1953	D+
Gus Zernial	1949 - 1959	D+
Richie Zisk	1971 - 1980	C+

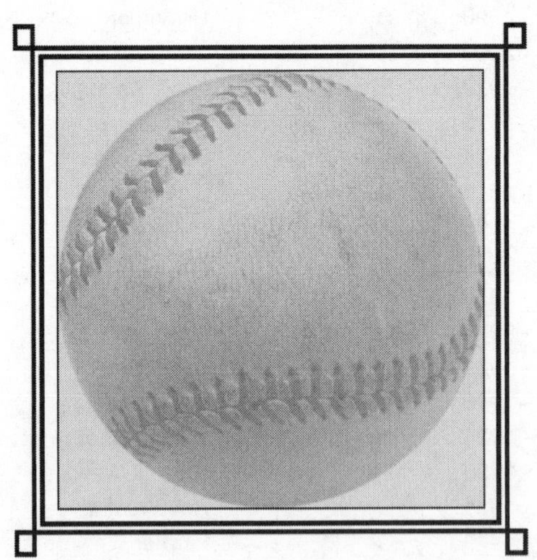

Estimated Defensive Innings

My best advice about estimating defensive innings is: Don't. There are two reasons I say this:

1. It is difficult to estimate defensive innings at a position accurately, and

2. It is far, far, worse to estimate defensive innings inaccurately than it is not to estimate them at all.

What I mean is not really "don't do it," but rather, "Don't put yourself in a position of depending too much on the accuracy of your estimates." We have estimated defensive innings for every player for every season, and those estimates become prominent in *reporting* the data. But they play no role at all in *calculating* the data.

Total Baseball uses estimates of defensive innings, but never fully explains how they are derived. All the book says (that I have found, anyway) is that "we estimate the number of innings for each player at each position based upon each player's entire fielding record and his number of plate appearances." I understand about 90% of their system, and I'm tempted to actually explain it to you in terms you can understand, but:

a) it's not my place to do that, and

b) there are a couple of wrinkles I don't quite get.

However—and I really don't wish to be unkind, because I think the world of Pete Palmer—his estimated defensive innings system, whatever it is, does not work reliably, and this leads to hundreds of fantastically screwy ratings for half-time and part-time players. I would venture to say that, of all the holes in the Linear Weights defensive system, the estimated defensive innings leads to more suspect ratings than any other.

A good example, as a starting point, would be the young Steve Garvey. Garvey came to the major leagues as a third baseman, sort of. His ability as a third baseman can be summarized in a few quotes from his autobiography, *Garvey*, with Skip Rozin:

> In 1970, 1971 and especially 1972, I was making so many errors that I didn't want the ball to be hit to me. I didn't want the onus of the Dodgers losing a game because of an error that I made.
>
> I became tentative—I was just stabbing at the ball. . . the routine plays were the tough ones. I'd have enough time to think about throwing the ball away, and I would.
>
> It wasn't just the weakness of my arm; somehow the weakness had gotten to my head. I had this arm I couldn't rely on, and it plagued me.
>
> To this day I get criticized about my throwing—for not making a bunt play at second, or not trying to make a double play when there might be a chance.

He had suffered a shoulder separation, and the Dodgers were hoping his arm would come back enough to allow him to play third base. It didn't. He was a wretched third baseman, fielding .939 at third base in 1971, and .902 in 1972, after which he never played another inning at third. Playing just 85 games at third base in 1972, Garvey led all major league third basemen in errors, with 28.

Total Baseball ranks Garvey as a brilliant defensive third baseman: +19 runs in 1971, +13 more in 1972. Plus 19 runs in 79 games. . . Brooks Robinson never approached that level of performance. The +19 runs in 1971 made him the best third baseman in the league. Brooks had only three seasons in his career when he was +19, and he had to play twice as many games to accomplish it. Even +13 runs in 85 games (1972) represents a fairly astonishing level of performance. *Total Baseball* has Garvey rated as a better third baseman in his career (+39 runs) than Pie Traynor (+36), George Kell (-17), George Brett (-2) or Don Wert (-22).

Not wishing to be unkind, it is hard to imagine how in the hell you could reach a conclusion like that. A contributing factor is that the Dodgers had a huge number of innings pitched by left-handed pitchers, and Dodger third basemen did lead the National League in assists in 1971, with 388, and 1972, with 359. They had no regular third baseman, using Garvey, Dick Allen, Bobby Valentine, Billy Grabarkewitz, Jim Lefebvre, Bill Sudakis and Maury Wills there in 1971, and adding Ron Cey to the mix in 1972.

But most of the explanation for the anomalous rating of Garvey as a third baseman is that the Linear Weights sub-structure tried to estimate Garvey's defensive innings—and missed. Go back to what *Total Baseball* says about how they estimate defensive innings: "we estimate the number of innings for each player at each position based upon each player's entire fielding record and his number of plate appearances." In a situation like this, that means that you've got to figure out Garvey's 1971 defensive innings in concert with those of Dick Allen, who played 67 games at third base but also 60 in the outfield and 28 at first base, and also Bob Valentine, who played 23 games at third base and also 37 at shortstop, 21 at second base and 11 in the outfield, Billy Grabarkewitz, who played 10 games at third base but also 13 at second base and 1 at shortstop, Bill Sudakis, who drags the catchers and first basemen into the equation, and Maury Wills, the regular shortstop. How in the world can you possibly balance all of those factors in order to estimate how many innings Garvey played at third base?

This is not a rhetorical question; I have the answer for you. You can't. It can be done, but it can't be done accurately. Also, while I'm on the subject, if you're going to *try* to do that, you really need to leave the plate appearances out of it. You'll understand if you think about what you are doing, in contrast to what *managers* are doing.

Suppose that a manager has two third basemen, one of whom is a good hitter but a brutal defensive player, and the other of whom doesn't hit but can pick it and pitch it. This is the most common situation in which players split playing time, because after all, if one player were better offensively and defensively, he would obviously be the regular.

The manager will try to use the two players in such a way that one player will have as many plate appearances as he can get and as few defensive innings, while the other will have as few plate appearances as possible while putting in as many innings in the field as possible. The manager thinks "if I bat the good hitter second and put in the glove man after the hitter bats in the top of the fifth, maybe I can get three at bats out of my hitter but five innings of defense out of my glove man." If a statistician comes along after the fact and assumes that the two players' defensive innings are consistent with their plate appearances, he's just going to be wrong, because *the manager has deliberately managed his team in such a way as to ensure that their offense/defense ratios are NOT the same*. A good defensive player but a weak hitter simply will *not* have the same ratio of plate appearances to defensive innings that a strong hitter/weak fielder will.

For different reasons than that, Garvey in 1971 had a low ratio of plate appearances to games, while sharing a position with several other players who had higher ratios of plate appearances to games played. The result is that Garvey's estimated defensive innings are squeezed downward.

Garvey in fact probably played about 599 innings at third base in 1971. *Total Baseball* estimates that Garvey played about 514 innings at third base—almost 100 innings off. The Linear Weights system then believes that Garvey has extraordinary range, and credits him with making about 54 plays that an "average" defensive third baseman would not make, with 47 of those 54 being assists, which are "doubly weighted."

The Dodgers' two most used third basemen in 1971 were Garvey and Dick Allen. Garvey had 53 putouts, 161 assists; Allen had 36 putouts, 133 assists—yet the Linear Weights system, working off their plate appearances, estimates that Garvey played about 514 innings at third base, and Allen about 580.

But when you think about it, isn't it obvious that *a player's defensive plays at a position are a better indicator of how many innings he has played at the position than his plate appearances*? When player A has 214 putouts plus assists at a position and player B has 169, it is unlikely that player B has played more innings at the position than player A.

Meanwhile, back in the real world, Garvey fails as a third baseman and is sent across the infield to first base, where:

a) he wins four consecutive Gold Gloves, 1974-1977, and

b) he is rated by *Total Baseball* as one of the worst defensive first basemen of all time.

He shows as negative ten to sixteen runs every year, but I've already beat up on Pete for that in another article. No, I love Pete; I just think we can do better in evaluating fielders.

I'm getting off the subject, which is defensive innings for part-time players in *Total Baseball*. If you look up almost any player who has a fifteen-year career in the majors and is a regular for ten years or so, you will almost always find that his defensive ratings in his years as a part-time player are out of line with his ratings as a regular. Take Yogi Berra. From 1950 to 1956, a period in which Berra won three MVP Awards, he never rates better than +7 as a defensive player; on average he is +2.

However, in 1962, when Elston Howard had taken over the catching chores and Berra caught only 31 games, he rates at +6, and in 1963, catching only 35 games, he rates at +8. On a per-game basis, this would make him a historic defensive player. The highest-rated catcher's season of this century, according to *Total Baseball*, is +24 runs, by George Mitterwald in 1970. No, I'm not kidding; you can look it up. On a per-game basis, the 38-year-old Berra (in 1963) is outperforming even the immortal George Mitterwald. It's an astonishing claim, and you wonder how they reached this conclusion, since Berra's defensive stats in 1962 and 1963 *look* so ordinary. The only possible explanation is that they tried to estimate his defensive innings and missed badly, causing all of their defensive calculations to misfire.

Jack Reed, Mickey Mantle's caddy, is rated in 1961 at -9 runs. This is difficult to explain, since Reed had only 13 at bats on the season, probably didn't play 50 innings on defense, and it would be questionable if the other teams even scored 9 runs when he was in the field, let alone 9 more than they would have scored with a better center fielder. Reed, who had a three-year career in which he was used almost exclusively as a pinch runner and defensive replacement, is listed at -53 defensive runs for his career—an absolutely fantastic conclusion, in that Reed probably played no more than 600 innings in his career. It is difficult to imagine that Ray Charles could kick away runs at that rate.

Third baseman Fred Hatfield, on the other hand, makes Steve Garvey look like a piker. In 1951 Hatfield played just 49 games at third base, fielding .959 with a range factor not notably different from those of his teammates. Despite this, Hatfield rates at a phenomenal +21 runs in 49 games. It's mind-boggling.

Johnny Ray, a good-hitting second baseman but not much of a fielder, is rated at negative 15 runs as Pittsburgh's regular second baseman in 1985 (probably a pretty good estimate)—but +12 runs as a part-time player for California in 1990.

Carlton Fisk, catching part-time for the White Sox in 1989, led the American League in fielding percentage—but is rated at negative 15 runs.

Luis Gomez, a Minnesota Twins utility infielder, is listed as the American League's best defensive shortstop in 1974 (+18 runs) despite a fielding percentage below the league norm, and despite playing only 82 games, batting only 168 times. In 1975, batting only 72 times all year, Gomez actually improves to +19, although Belanger manages to slip ahead of him for the league title. Gomez was a good shortstop, but the obvious explanation for this amazing rating is that Gomez had very few plate appearances, because he couldn't hit. *Total Baseball* guessed that his innings in the field must have been proportional to his plate appearances, and therefore thought that Gomez was making an incredible number of plays per nine innings.

Tito Fuentes, playing just 13 games for Oakland in 1978 and committing only 2 errors, is rated at negative 12 runs.

Wally Gerber, as a regular American League shortstop from 1919 to 1927, never rated higher than +9 runs. But as a part-time player for Boston in 1928, the 36-year-old Gerber suddenly vaulted to +34 runs.

Joe Koppe, playing 55 games at shortstop in 1960 and fielding .956, is rated at -12 runs. But in 1964, playing only 31 games and fielding .945, he is rated at +14 runs.

One of my favorites is Gene Leek. I had a baseball card of Gene Leek. He was a Cleveland Indians farmhand who got a chance to play with the expansion Angels, but disappeared after hitting .221 in 77 games, with 9 career walks and 67 strikeouts.

Total Baseball, however, thinks that Leek was an above-average player, which means that they rate him as better than Bobby Richardson, Cookie Rojas, Tony Taylor, etc. Same reason: they tried to estimate his defensive innings, and they missed, leading them to believe that he had fantastic range at third base.

Pete Palmer has done a lot of outstanding work in constructing the Linear Weights system. But the defensive component of the system does not work, and one of the three largest reasons it doesn't work is that:

a) their structure forces them to rely on their estimates of defensive innings, and

b) their estimates of defensive innings are terrible.

(The other big reasons the defensive system doesn't work are (1) the assumption that value resides in being better than average, which is false across the boards, is peculiarly damaging in the way that it applies to defense, and (2) the failure to adjust for differences in team defensive performance, resulting in the false assumption that a player will make the same number of plays playing for a bad team that he would make if he played for a good team.)

One more question: If you *have* to estimate defensive innings, how do you do it?

The best thing to do is just to assume that each player's defensive innings at a position are proportional to his plays made at the position, unless:

a) this would imply that he was playing more than 9 innings per game, or

b) this would imply that he was playing less than 3 innings per game.

In modern baseball we have actual records of defensive innings, published annually by STATS, Inc. This makes it possible to test the accuracy of an estimated-innings approach. Let's take Cleveland second basemen in 1997. The Indians had seven players there, who made 333 putouts, had 514 assists, and were charged with 18 errors—a total of 865 chances. (This was actually current data when I wrote this, just to show you how long I have been working on this damned book.)

Tony Fernandez, their most-regular second baseman, had 514 total chances. The team had 1425.2 innings pitched. If you simply assume that Tony Fernandez had the same percentage of innings afield as plays made, you'll estimate that Fernandez played 847 innings in the field.

In fact, Fernandez played 840.1 innings at second base—only one percent different from our estimate. The Indians used seven second basemen in 1997. The data for all seven and the team is:

	Total Chances	Estimated Innings	Actual Innings
Cleveland, 1997	865	—	1425.2
Tony Fernandez	514	847.16	840.1
Julio Franco	180	296.67	288.2
Jeff Branson	73	120.32	147.0
Bip Roberts	59	97.24	93.1
Casey Candaele	35	57.69	43.1
Enrique Wilson	4	6.59	10.0
Damian Jackson	0	0	3.0

Except that Damian Jackson played one game, so we automatically estimate that he played at least three defensive innings, which he did. All of the estimates are pretty accurate except the one for Jeff Branson, which is off by about 27 innings.

That's about how accurate the system is overall. The 147 major league second basemen in 1997 played an average of 275 defensive innings. The standard error of these estimates is 9.94 innings. The worst percentage error for any second baseman who played 100 or more games is 3.6%, for Luis Alicea of Anaheim, who is estimated to have played 922 innings, but actually played only 890.

You can improve the estimates a little bit by using the "Games" category. Look carefully at the Oakland A's 1997 second basemen. If you just base the playing time estimates on plays made, you'll estimate that:

Scott Spiezio played 1220.97 innings.
Mark Bellhorn played 175.67 innings.
Tilson Brito played 19.13 innings.
Rafael Bournigal played 13.91 innings.
Tony Batista played 10.44 innings.
Scott Sheldon played 5.22 innings.

This is not a particularly good estimate for the regular second baseman, Scott Spiezio. He actually played 1,256 innings, 35 more than we have estimated in our first shot.

However, Mark Bellhorn played only 17 games at second base. This means that we will assume he played no more than 153 innings, not 175.67.

Tilson Brito played only 2 games at second base. This means that we will assume that he played no more than 18.00 innings, not 19.13.

Tony Batista played only one game at second base. We will assume that he played no more than 9 innings, not 10.44 innings.

When you re-figure the team, the extra innings for Batista, Bellhorn and Brito are tossed back into the pot, to be claimed by the remaining second basemen. Almost all of them are claimed by Scott Spiezio, which increases his estimated defensive innings to 1239—only 17 less than he actually played. So actually, this simple "system" can be fairly accurate.

The down side of not figuring defensive innings, I can hear you saying, is that we're losing the range numbers for individuals, if they're different from the team total. We're assuming that everybody who plays the position for one team has the same range.

Let's assume for a moment that this is true. It is far, far better to lose the "comparative range" information than it is to make off-the-wall estimates of defensive innings which give us range "information" which is nutty 40% of the time. If you use inaccurate information, you'll get screwball results. If you use the conservative assumption that everybody is the same, you may be a little bit off, but you won't get range estimates that are weird and indefensible.

And second, it isn't really true that we're losing the range estimates, in many cases. It's only true if the team has a large number of "shared defensive games."

Many times, even in modern baseball, teams will have few shared defensive games at a position. Suppose that two players split a position, but never split a game. One player might play 97 games, and the other player might play 65 games. Regardless of how the plays are divided, there's only one way to split the innings without getting somebody over 9.00 innings per game. As long as a team has relatively few shared defensive games, then a player with good range will still show up with good range, because if you give him too many innings he will go over 9.00 innings per game, forcing a re-calculation. You lose the range information only when there are a substantial number of shared defensive games—which means that you lose the range information only when it is highly speculative anyway.

Suppose that we had an exactly parallel problem with *batting* records for some set of players. Suppose that there was a team, a 19th century team or something, which had four players who appeared in the #4 spot in the batting order; we'll call them Mr. Black, Mr. White, Mr. Brown and Mr. Green. Suppose that we had, for this team, a record of the number of *games* each player had appeared in the four spot, and a record of the number of *hits* which each player had recorded—but no record of individual at bats. We know that these four players had 168 hits among them and we can reconstruct the information that they must have had 600 at bats among them (a .280 average). I'll chart the information that we have:

Player	Games	At Bats	Hits	Bat Avg
Black	108	Unknown	55	Unknown
White	64	Unknown	54	Unknown
Brown	33	Unknown	16	Unknown
Green	25	Unknown	43	Unknown
Total	(154)	600	168	.280

The team played 154 games, but had 230 games at this position because of shared playing time.

What *Total Baseball* has done in this situation, essentially, is to say "we can find each player's batting average by estimating his at bats." We don't have at bats, but we do have games played, so we will assume that each player has about the same ratio of at bats per game.

"We have 230 player games at the position and 600 at bats, so the best we can do is to assume that each player must have about 2.61 at bats per game. This means that we believe the data to be:"

Player	Games	Estimated At Bats	Hits	Estimated Bat Avg
Black	108	282	55	.195
White	64	167	54	.323
Brown	33	86	16	.186
Green	25	65	43	.662
Total	(154)	600	168	.280

If this leads us to the conclusion that Mr. Green is a fantastic player and the regular, Mr. Black, is inept. . . well, that's just where the data leads us, and if it doesn't make any sense, I'm sorry.

What I'm saying is that, rather than do that, it is much better to start with the assumption that all four players probably hit about .280. That makes the data, on a first cut:

Player	Games	Estimated At Bats	Hits	Estimated Bat Avg
Black	108	196	55	.281
White	64	193	54	.280
Brown	33	57	16	.281
Green	25	154	43	.279
Total	(154)	600	168	.280

This creates a problem, however, which is that we are now assuming that Mr. Green played 25 games but had 154 at bats, which is all but impossible, since nobody has more than 4.5 at bats per game. To correct for this, we will assume that Mr. Green had only 112 at bats, which changes the estimated batting average for the other three players to .256. This makes the data:

Player	Games	Estimated At Bats	Hits	Estimated Bat Avg
Black	108	215	55	.256
White	64	211	54	.256
Brown	33	62	16	.258
Green	25	112	43	.384
Total	(154)	600	168	.280

It might not be right, but it's a more reasonable guess. It is possible that if we knew exactly what the Linear Weights method is, we could combine that method and this simple method to make compromise estimates which are more accurate than either independent method. Since we have defensive innings in modern baseball, we would be able to study the issue until we reached a resolution. But until the issue has been thoroughly studied, my advice about estimating defensive innings remains: don't. It's a situation in which inaccurate estimates are far worse than no estimates at all. And if you have to do it, make your estimates based on the most conservative assumptions possible.

Nap Lajoie's Defense

Another player whose defensive contribution I interpret somewhat differently from the Linear Weights method is Napoleon Lajoie.

Craig Wright says that Lajoie had "a tremendous defensive reputation in his (own) era." Let's assume this to be correct. Over time, his reputation was lost, until he came to be regarded, in the words of *Total Baseball*, as "an overlarge, out-of-position defensive liability who made his name with the bat."

In the Linear Weights analysis, however, Lajoie battles Bill Mazeroski for the distinction of being not only the greatest defensive second baseman of all time, but actually the greatest defensive *player* of all time, at any position. Mazeroski ranks as the greatest ever in terms of "Fielding Wins," with Lajoie a close second, but Lajoie is first and Mazeroski second in "Fielding Runs." With his obvious ability as a hitter, this defensive evaluation makes Lajoie, in the view of *Total Baseball*, the third-greatest baseball player of all time, behind only Babe Ruth and Willie Mays.

Lajoie does have extremely unusual defensive statistics for the era in which he played. Cleveland second basemen in 1908 had 453 putouts, 544 assists, and 78 double plays. These are phenomenal raw numbers. The St. Louis Browns were second in the league in putouts at second base, with 361. They were a lot closer to being last than they were to being first. All the other teams in the league are in a group between 293 and 361 putouts; Cleveland's up there at 453.

In assists, everybody else is between 424 and 509; Cleveland leads by 35. In double plays at second base, Cleveland has almost 50% more than any other team in the league, leading by a score of 78 to 53. If it was a circular track, the Indians would have lapped the field.

In the previous year, 1907, the Cleveland second basemen had only 367 putouts (5th in the league), but had 576 assists (79 more than any other team) and turned 95 double plays—more than twice as many as the second basemen of five American League teams, and 37 more than any other team in the league.

Lajoie is the individual most responsible for those eye-popping numbers. He played 156 of 157 games for Cleveland at second base in 1908, 128 of 158 in 1907. *Total Baseball* ranks him at +49 in 1908, meaning 49 runs better than an average American League second baseman, and also +46 in 1907, +40 in 1903, +30 in 1900, +30 in 1916, +29 in 1902, and +29 in 1901, a figure which was still good enough to lead the American League in that season.

But while I agree that Lajoie was a good second baseman, I am not convinced that he was a defensive superstar in the class of Mazeroski, Ozzie Smith or Ivan Rodriguez. I am more inclined to think that he was a great hitter and a good defensive player, like Ryne Sandberg, or Joe Cronin, or Cal Ripken.

There are three specific points on which my analysis of Lajoie's defensive contribution diverges from *Total Baseball*'s. Those three are:

1. The role of a second baseman in turn-of-the-century baseball, as opposed to modern baseball,
2. The evaluation of Lajoie's 1916 season, and
3. The significance of Lajoie's extremely high putout totals.

Taking those one at a time. . .

1. *The role of a second baseman in turn-of-the-century baseball, as opposed to modern baseball.* Second base in 1900 was a *hitter's* position—not exclusively, of course, but certainly to a greater extent than it is in modern baseball. Until 1930, teams tended to emphasize hitting at second base, and fielding at third base, rather than the other way around.

Look at the facts. Between 1900 and 1930, 48 major league second basemen scored 100 runs in a season. Only 23 third basemen scored 100.

In the same years, 21 second basemen drove in 100 runs. Only 19 third basemen drove in 100.

In the same years, 17 major league second basemen hit 15 or more homers. Only four third basemen did.

From 1900 to 1930, 113 major league second basemen hit .300 in 400 or more plate appearances, and 19 hit .350. Only 89 third basemen hit .300, and only five hit .350, four of those in the last three years of the era, when the defensive spectrum was beginning to shift.

Second basemen won twelve batting titles. Third basemen won one.

Twenty-one second basemen had 200 hits in a season. Only ten third basemen had 200 hits.

If you want more systematic data, there's an article later on entitled "Why Did the Defensive Spectrum Jump?"

Focusing on the defense, rather than offense, a typical second baseman in the dead-ball era might turn 40 or 50 double plays a season. That's very different from modern second basemen, who hit much less than third basemen, but are expected to turn 90 or more double plays in a full season.

In our system, we recognize this distinction, and we adjust for it by considering the defensive assignment of the second baseman to be larger after 1930 than before—as it is. Thus, we consider Bill Mazeroski's defensive assignment to be larger than Nap Lajoie's, which seems reasonable when you consider that Mazeroski was turning 60% more double plays than Lajoie, regardless of how they compare to the league. Thus, Mazeroski should tend to accumulate more defensive Win Shares per season than Lajoie.

Of course, not every second baseman post-1930 rates better than every second baseman pre-1930. But if Mazeroski is 30% better than a typical second baseman in his era, and Lajoie is 30% better than a typical second baseman in his era, this *doesn't* make them even in my book. In a sense, it's the "Gavy Cravath" argument, applied to fielding. If Gavy Cravath is the best home run hitter of 1915 and Babe Ruth is the best home run hitter of 1925, is Gavy Cravath equal to Babe Ruth? No, he isn't, because 20 homers are not the same as 50, no matter how many home runs anybody else in the league may have hit. The same thing with fielding: if Nap Lajoie leads the league in double plays one year with 78, and Bill Mazeroski leads the league another year with 161, does this make Lajoie equal to Bill Mazeroski with era adjustments? No, it doesn't, because 78 double plays are not the same as 161, no matter how many double plays anybody else in the league may have turned. It is different because *the game has changed.*

Nap Lajoie

Linear Weights, having assumed that an average player is always at zero, cannot deal with this distinction. After all, Linear Weights considers an average defensive *first baseman* or left fielder to have the same defensive value (zero) as an average second baseman. Of course, this is nonsense—an average defensive first baseman does not have the same value as an average defensive second baseman—but having assumed that he does, the system is then in no position to say that a first baseman is the same as a second baseman, but a second baseman in 1995 is different from a second baseman in 1900. The system is trapped in its initial false assumption.

2. *The evaluation of Lajoie's 1916 season.* Nap Lajoie in 1916 was 41 years old. He hit .246 and, playing 113 games, scored only 33 runs. The team for which he was playing finished with one of the worst records in baseball history, 36-117, which incidentally was the third consecutive season that Lajoie's team had finished last with 100+ losses; the 1915 Philadelphia A's also finished 43-109, and in 1914 Lajoie had been waived by Cleveland after the team lost 102 games.

In spite of these things, the Linear Weights system evaluates Lajoie in 1916 as a spectacular defensive second baseman, 30 runs better than average. This, to me, is simply not a credible evaluation. Our system credits Lajoie with only 1.36 Win Shares—a very low total for a second baseman playing 100+ games.

The defensive records of the A's second basemen in 1916 are very ordinary. They are near the league average in putouts, assists, and fielding percentage, although they did lead the league in double plays. Lajoie's records, including his range numbers, are clearly much better than those of the A's other second basemen that year, Otis Lawry and Roy Grover.

But even if Lajoie *did* have exceptional range numbers, what would this prove? It would prove only that Lajoie had exceptional range *compared to the other fielders on the team.* Somebody on the team has to account for 27 outs per game, no matter how dreadful the team was. Lajoie was surrounded by teenagers, minor league veterans, and old men. This team had a catcher in the outfield (Wally Schang) and an outfielder at shortstop (Whitey Witt). What would it mean to say that Lajoie had better range relative to his position than the other players on the team?

Lajoie in 1916 made 5.51 plays per game, an outstanding figure. In the Linear Weights system, having an outstanding range number is considered to be proof of superior performance, just like hitting 35 homers, hitting .350, winning 20 games, or pitching 250 innings with a 2.70 ERA. But in fact it is not like these accomplishments, for this reason: that *somebody on every team HAS to have a good range number,* since somebody has to record the outs. Every team doesn't have to have somebody who hits 35 homers. Every team doesn't have to have somebody who hits .350, or somebody who wins 20 games, or somebody who pitches 250 innings with a 2.70 ERA—but every team has to have somebody with a good range factor. It's not the same.

But if you want to insist that maybe the 41-year-old Lajoie could have been a brilliant defensive second baseman who just happened to be playing for a dreadful team... well, OK, maybe he could have been. The problem is, *the Linear Weights system credits Lajoie with saving runs that were never actually saved.* The runs that Lajoie supposedly saved—where are they?

The runs that batters are credited with by Linear Weights—those runs actually exist. Suppose that you take a team which scores 100 runs more than an average team in the league. *Total Baseball* will credit the hitters on the team, in sum, with +100 Batter Runs, more or less. It will do this, because the Linear Weights Batter Runs method essentially makes sense, and essentially works in practice. If you add up the "Batter Runs" for all members of the 1961 Yankees, you get a total of +128 runs. This is a very reasonable number. The '61 Yankees scored 827 runs, the league average was 734, and it's a pitcher's park; under the circumstances, +128 runs is about right.

Suppose that a team *allows* 100 runs fewer than average. *Total Baseball* will credit them with 100 Pitcher Runs, because their method just gives run credit for ERA, park-adjusted. It makes sense, and it works.

But *where are the runs for the defense*? Suppose that the defensive players on a team total up to 75 runs saved. If the batters account for runs scored above average, which they do, and the pitchers accounts for runs scored below average, which they do, where do these 75 runs for defense come from?

There are four possibilities that I can see:

a) defensive runs could represent the *un*earned runs,

b) these could be runs which are credited to pitchers, but which are *also* credited to fielders,

c) all teams could be presumed to be defensively average, or

d) they're not anywhere. They're just made up, free-floating runs which are utterly disconnected from the rest of the analysis.

The answer is (d). If you wanted to defend the system, what you would have to say, I think, is that all teams are presumed to be defensively average. Except that, in practice, they're not. Specifically, the 1916 Philadelphia Athletics are not. According to *Total Baseball*, they're not average, they're much *better* than average—33 runs better to be specific. I'm not joking; Nap Lajoie is +30, and the rest of the team is +3.

I remember in 1978, when Butch Hobson fielded .899, I pulled out *The Baseball Encyclopedia*, and figured out that the last major league regular to field less than .900 in a full season was Charlie Pick, who was a member of this same team, the 1916 Philadelphia Athletics; it was his only season as a major league third baseman. But researching this article, I was amazed to discover that *Total Baseball* had rated Pick as a *good* defensive third baseman, despite the .899 fielding percentage. He's +4 runs. I don't understand that one, either.

Anyway, this is an incredible claim, that the 1916 Philadelphia A's are actually a good defensive team. That's amazing. The one thing that we definitely know here is that the 1916 Philadelphia Athletics were a dreadful team overall. They were outscored by their opponents by 329 runs, which means that they were 329 runs worse than an average team. Still, I suppose they *could be* +33 on defense, if their pitching and batting total up to negative 362 runs.

I went through *Total Baseball* and added up the Batting Runs, the Pitching Runs, and the Fielding Runs for everybody who played on the team. The Batting Runs for all 48 players on the team, including pitchers, total up to -27 runs, 27 runs below average. The pitching runs total up to -135. That makes a total of -162 runs. Oddly enough, we are off by *exactly* 200 runs.

Two hundred runs! If you are using a run-accounting system, and you misplace 200 runs on one team, you have made a serious mistake.

The problem with the Linear Weights defensive analysis is, *there is no bottom line*. The system isn't locked in place by any logic. A team can be arbitrarily credited with saving any number of "Fielding Runs," based on who has how many assists and who has how many errors and who has how many estimated defensive innings, and how some combination of these things work out. Nap Lajoie can be credited with 30 runs which don't exist, and it's no problem, because the system never faces any requirement that things add up.

Well, I don't know where those 200 runs are, but I can tell you real quick where about 40 of them are. Lajoie wasn't 30 runs better than average in the field in 1916. He was at least 10 runs *worse* than average. And that 40-run miscalculation makes a very significant difference in how we should evaluate his career.

3. *The significance of Lajoie's extremely high putout totals.* All of the elements of Nap Lajoie's fielding record are good—his double plays are good, his assists/game are good, his fielding percentage is good, his putouts/game are good. . . everything's good. He was a good second baseman.

However, among these elements, the one which is *most* exceptional is his putout total. Lajoie's assists totals are exceptional in some seasons—1903, 1906 through 1910, and 1913. But in his first year at second base, 1898, his Phillies team was last in the National League in assists by second basemen, 416 (406 by Lajoie). The A's were just average in 1901, and Cleveland second basemen were near the league average in assists, or below average, in the other years that Lajoie was their second baseman.

Now, it *can* be debated whether Lajoie's assists records actually show him to have superior range, or whether they are merely a consequence of the teams that he played for. The Naps/Indians, as a team, did have ground ball staffs for most of Lajoie's tenure in Cleveland. In 1907 Cleveland second basemen had 576 assists, an astonishing total—112 more than the American League average, 79 more than any other American League team. Lajoie played 128 games and had 461 assists. The team had two other second basemen, Harry Hinchman and Pete O'Brien. Between them, they played 32 games, exactly one-fourth as many as Lajoie, and had 115 assists, exactly one-fourth as many as Lajoie, rounded off. In other words, the Cleveland Indians in 1907 had the same exceptional assists rate at second base whether Lajoie was in the lineup or whether he wasn't.

This is not a one-year phenomenon. In 1904, Lajoie played 95 games at second base for Cleveland and had 255 assists, 2.68 per game. Charles Hickman, Elmer Flick and George Stovall played 60 games at second base for the same team—and had 3.20 assists per game. Flick was an outfielder, Stovall was a first baseman, and Hickman was called "Piano Legs"; it doesn't seem that likely that any of them was an exceptional second baseman.

In 1909, Cleveland second basemen had 485 assists, second-most in the American League. Nap Lajoie played 120 games there, making 373 assists, 3.11 per game. But Terry Turner and George Perring played 30 games there between them, and had 107 assists—3.57 per game.

In fact, if you look at all Cleveland second basemen from 1901 through 1919. . . there were sixteen men who had 50 or more assists at second base for Cleveland in the dead-ball era. Those sixteen men, and their assists rates, are:

Rank	Player	G	A	A/G
1.	Harry Hinchman	15	60	4.00
2.	Smoky Joe Wood	19	67	3.53
3.	Ivan Howard	69	233	3.38
4.	Elmer Flick	15	50	3.33
5.	Pete O'Brien	17	55	3.24
6.	Piano Legs Hickman	56	177	3.16
7.	Nick Kahl	30	94	3.11
8.	Billy Wambsganss	469	1449	3.09
9.	Ivy Olson	45	139	3.09
10.	Erve Beck	132	404	3.06
11.	Terry Turner	233	708	3.04
12.	Nap Lajoie	1385	4183	3.02
13.	Neal Ball	137	401	2.93
14.	Ray Chapman	49	135	2.76
15.	Frank Bonner	34	89	2.62
16.	George Stovall	78	186	2.38

If you add up the other 15 players, they played 1,398 games at second for Cleveland, and had 4,247 assists—essentially the same totals as Lajoie.

As an aside, I ran comparable lists for several of the other all-time great second basemen—Gehringer, Doerr, Gordon, Sandberg, Frank White, etc. They were all at or near the top of their lists. Bill Mazeroski made 3.19 assists per game, ranking him number one on a 19-man list of players who played second base for the Pirates between 1950 and 1975. Gehringer made 3.20 assists/game, ranking him second on a list of 17 Detroit Tiger second basemen between 1920 and 1945. Frank White made 2.91 assists per game, which ranks first on a list of 19 Royals second basemen between 1969 and 1990. Bobby Doerr recorded 3.08 assists/game, which ranks first on a list of 14 players who played second base for the Red Sox in the years 1935 to 1955. Joe Gordon made 3.19 assists/game in his years with the Yankees, which ranks first on a list of ten Yankee second basemen between 1935 and 1955, even though the other second basemen are mostly pretty good.

Lajoie has assists/game numbers above league average for his era, but not all that much above league average. What drives Lajoie's range numbers through the roof are his putouts. Looking at the putouts per game of the same Cleveland second basemen between 1901 and 1919:

Rank	Player	G	PO	PO/G
1.	Nap Lajoie	1385	3641	2.63
2.	Ivy Olson	45	114	2.53
3.	Smoky Joe Wood	19	47	2.47
4.	Erve Beck	132	310	2.35
5.	Neal Ball	137	316	2.31
6.	Billy Wambsganss	469	1034	2.20
7.	Elmer Flick	15	33	2.20
8.	Ray Chapman	49	99	2.02
9.	Nick Kahl	30	60	2.00
10.	Frank Bonner	34	67	1.97
11.	Terry Turner	233	457	1.96
12.	George Stovall	78	143	1.83
13.	Piano Legs Hickman	56	99	1.77
14.	Pete O'Brien	17	28	1.65
15.	Ivan Howard	69	112	1.62
16.	Harry Hinchman	15	25	1.60

Linear Weights gives twice as much credit for an assist as for a putout, explaining that "assists are doubly weighted because more skill is generally required to get one than to record a putout." In on-line discussions I have seen people second-guess this decision, arguing that "I don't care how much 'skill' you may think was required to make the play. What I care about is how many plays the guy made."

But in fact this decision—to weight assists more heavily than putouts—is pretty much inevitable. Think about it: If you're going to make one putout the same as one assist, without regard to the skill required, then why aren't first basemen regarded as the most valuable defensive infielders? After all, first basemen make far more putouts/game than any other infielder.

A first baseman gets a putout whenever he is able to catch the ball—not that I minimize catching the ball, but it is not equivalent to turning a double play, or picking up a hard-hit ground ball and making a 140-foot on-target throw. We largely ignore putouts by first basemen because they don't say much about the player's skill. But what some people don't think about is that some putouts by second basemen are exactly the same thing, involving nothing more than catching a ball and stepping on the bag after somebody else has made a play.

How many? We don't know. Assists by a second baseman result primarily from ground balls. Probably more than 90% of second base assists result either directly from a ground ball, or from a relay throw to first in the middle of a double play. But putouts can, in ordinary cases, be any of five things:

1. Line drives caught in the air,
2. Short popups/soft line drives which loop toward the outfield,
3. High Popups,
4. Forceouts, or
5. Runners Caught Stealing.

Plays (1) and (2) above are Do-or-Die plays, like ground balls, which are either going to be made by the second baseman or not made at all. But Plays (3), (4), and (5) are "Discretionary" plays, which in most cases can be made by either the second baseman or the shortstop.

Linear Weights implicitly assumes that if a second baseman makes an extra play, this is a play which otherwise would not be made. Range factor makes the same implicit assumption. It ain't necessarily so. These *could* be plays which otherwise would not be made, but they could be plays which would otherwise be made by the shortstop.

Was Lajoie's putout total bolstered by "range" plays, or by plays which were taken away from the Cleveland shortstops? Let's look at the data. Cleveland second basemen in 1908 made 453 putouts, which was far more than any other team in the league.

And their shortstops made 256 putouts, which was far *less* than any other team in the league.

Cleveland second basemen led the league in putouts in 1902, with 364. And their shortstops were last in the league in putouts in 1902, with 244.

Cleveland second basemen led the league in putouts in 1903, with 416. And their shortstops were last in the league in 1903, with 249.

Cleveland second basemen led the league in putouts in 1904, with 385. And their shortstops were last in the league again, with 277.

In the thirteen years that Lajoie was in Cleveland, Cleveland second basemen were above the league average in putouts every year except 1905 and 1907, when they were just a hair under the average. But Cleveland shortstops were below average in putouts every single year.

Doesn't it seem likely, to you, that rather than reflecting exceptional range on the part of Lajoie, what the putout totals actually show is that Lajoie was handling all or almost all of the discretionary putouts at second base—the force plays at second, and the runners caught stealing? Remember, teams at this time probably had about 150 to 200 opposition runners a year caught stealing, far more than we have now. That's a lot of putouts for the second baseman, if the second baseman always chooses to make the play.

Nap Lajoie was not only the team's superstar, after 1905 he was also the manager. He was more than that—hell, the team was actually called the "Naps" in his honor, as if Lajoie *was* the team. If Lajoie was in the habit of covering second base on every play, the shortstop certainly wasn't in any position to say "Hey, some of those are mine."

In modern baseball, we assume that the shortstop will cover second base on a stolen base attempt with a left-handed hitter at the plate, but this is not *always* true. Even in modern baseball, the second baseman sometimes takes the throw with a left-handed hitter at the plate. In modern baseball, we assume that the shortstop will take the throw to the bag on any ball hit to first base or to the pitcher, although, again, this is not *always* true.

But is there any reason to assume that the Cleveland team handled these plays in the same way? In fact, it seems very clear, to me, that they *didn't* handle these plays the same way. Lajoie took everything at second base.

Which wouldn't have been unusual, fifteen years earlier. See, Nap Lajoie actually *doesn't* have unusually high putout totals. He has unusually high putout totals *for his own era*. If you look back to 1880, second basemen made an average of 3.11 putouts per team game, and second basemen made 2.7 times as many putouts as shortstops. How could this be? Easy: second basemen played very near to second base, and second basemen handled all plays at second base. Shortstops rarely were credited with putouts.

In the early 1880s Charles Comiskey, or somebody, decided to pull his fielders off the bag. By 1890, putouts by second basemen had declined to 44% more than putouts by shortstops. By 1900, putouts by second basemen were only 10% more than the putouts of shortstops.

The ratio of putouts by second basemen to putouts at shortstop continued to flatten out until 1909, when major league shortstops actually made 2% more putouts than major league second basemen. Beginning in 1910, the relationship between putouts by second basemen and putouts by shortstops turned around, and headed back up. By 1920, second basemen were again making 14% more putouts than shortstops. By 1950, second basemen were again making 42% more putouts than shortstops.

Lajoie's career, then, spans the trough in this graph. In Lajoie's prime years, the relationship between second base putouts and shortstop putouts was flatter than at any other time in baseball history—for most teams. Not for Cleveland, but for almost everybody else. Lajoie's career average of 2.70 putouts/game is not unusual. Nellie Fox averaged 2.65 putouts/game, Bid McPhee averaged 3.08, Bobby Doerr averaged 2.66, Billy Herman averaged 2.64, Fred Pfeffer averaged 3.07, Bucky Harris averaged 2.71, and Jerry Priddy averaged 2.74.

The fundamental question we have to ask, to evaluate the impact of Lajoie's putout numbers on the success of his team, is whether these were plays which otherwise would not have been made, or plays which otherwise would have been made by someone else.

I'm not suggesting that we should throw away the data. I'm not suggesting that we should give him zero credit for making extra plays.

But in the thirteen seasons that Lajoie played in Cleveland, Cleveland second basemen made 537 more putouts than an average American League team. Their shortstops made 460 fewer putouts than an average American League team. I suspect that the net advantage to his team was closer to 77 extra plays than to 537. And, for that reason as well as others, I am skeptical of the idea that Nap Lajoie was a defensive player of historic stature.

Second Base Putouts

In the period 1880 to 1909, as I discussed in the Lajoie article, the number of putouts per game by second basemen was in sharp decline, as second basemen moved off the bag, and began to share responsibility for making plays at second base with the shortstops.

One of the peculiarities of "trend changes" like this is that they are often adopted more rapidly by younger players than by older players. Thus it is that throughout this era, older players tended to dominate the league leaders in putouts at second base, while younger players normally started out well down the lists, and gradually worked their way toward the top.

In 1890 the major league leaders in putouts at second base was Fred Pfeffer, then 30 years old. Pfeffer led again in 1891, followed by the 32-year-old Cub Stricker. In 1892 Bid McPhee, another 32-year-old, led the National League in putouts by a margin of 66 (451-385), while the 24-year-old Cupid Childs, playing one more game than McPhee, had only 357 putouts.

In 1893 the 33-year-old McPhee led the National League in putouts again by 41 (396-355); in second place was another 33-year-old, Fred Pfeffer. In 1894 the 34-year-old Bid McPhee had 389 putouts, leading the National League by almost 50. Tom Daly, then only 28, was sixth in the league in putouts, and Cupid

Childs, then only 26, was seventh (both were full-time regulars).

In 1895 the 35-year-old McPhee, limited to 115 games at second base, was finally passed—by the 30-year-old Joe Quinn.

By 1899 Kid Gleason, now 32, had worked his way to the top of the putout list, followed by Tom Daly, now 33, and Bobby Lowe, now 30.

By 1900 Bobby Lowe, now 31, and Cupid Childs, now 32, had worked their way to the top of the list, followed by the 33-year-old Kid Gleason. In 1902 Heinie Smith, age 30, led the major leagues in putouts, followed by Bobby Lowe (now 33) and Kid Gleason (now 35).

In 1904 Kid Gleason, now 37, missed by only two of leading the National League in putouts. In 1905, age 38, he did lead the league in putouts.

It's not that these players made more putouts as they aged; in fact, they made less. But they moved up the list, as they aged, because the older guys dropped off the top of the list, and the younger guys didn't make as many putouts.

Nap Lajoie is an exception to this rule: he led the league in putouts as a first-year second baseman in 1898. But the fact that the category is so much dominated by older players powerfully suggests, to me, that it is not a "range" indicator, in that era. A player's range at any position does not generally improve as he grows older.

Good Teams, Bad Teams

The Win Shares system is, of course, based on team wins. For this reason, many of you will suspect that the system discriminates against players who play on poor teams, and in favor of players who happen to play on better teams.

This is not true. Teams which win more games do so because they have better players. The player who plays on a better team is drawing from a larger pool of Win Shares—but, because he has stronger teammates, he draws a smaller share. He'll work out just the same, regardless of how good or how bad his teammates might be.

This is an important issue, because I want the Win Shares system to be accepted by baseball fans as a useful tool. If people *believe* that the system discriminates against players on poor teams, rightly or wrongly, they will reject the system. This overlong, redundant article is written to try to persuade the last skeptic that that suspicion is unfounded, and that players on bad teams do get a fair shake.

Suppose that you had two players who had identical statistics and identical conditions otherwise, but one of whom played for a bad team and the other for a good team. The key question would be, does the system rate the two players even, or does it give extra credit to the player who had better teammates?

Of course, there are no two players whose stats are identical or whose playing conditions are identical (except teammates), but we can find many examples of players who had very similar stats, playing on teams of different quality. In 1957 Roy Sievers became one of the few players in history to lead the league in RBI (114) while playing for a last-place team—probably the only one to do it in a pitcher's park surrounded by seven guys who couldn't hit.

Sievers in 1957 hit .301 with 23 doubles, 5 triples, and 42 homers. Gil Hodges in 1954 hit .304 with an exact match in doubles, triples and homers:

Player	G	AB	R	H	2B	3B	HR	RBI	BB	SO	SB	Avg	OBP	SLG
Sievers	152	572	99	172	23	5	42	114	76	55	1	.301	.388	.579
Hodges	154	579	106	176	23	5	42	130	74	84	3	.304	.373	.579

Two of the best-matched seasons in baseball history, for hitters of that quality. Hodges did this for a team that won 92 games; Sievers, for a team that finished 55-99.

Obviously, if the Win Shares system favored a player on a better team, Hodges would rank as a better player than Sievers. Hodges has been credited with 29 Win Shares—Sievers, with 32.

Why does Sievers rank ahead of Hodges, based on the same hitting stats? A combination of things. . . Sievers was hit with pitches a few times and grounded into fewer double plays, putting him ahead by 10 runs created (126-116). Sievers played in a neutral park in a league averaging 4.24 Runs Per Game; Hodges played in a hitter's park in a league averaging 4.59 Runs Per Game. Hodges gets some of the difference between them back by his defense—but the ability of their teammates doesn't have anything to do with how they rate.

In 1966 Sandy Koufax went 27-9 with a 1.73 ERA. In 1972 Steve Carlton had a very similar season:

Pitcher	G	IP	W	L	Pct	H	SO	BB	ERA
Koufax	41	323	27	9	.750	241	317	77	1.73
Carlton	41	346	27	10	.730	257	310	87	1.97

Koufax did this for a very good team, which won 95 games. Carlton did this for a terrible team, which lost 97 games. Despite this, Koufax earns 35 Win Shares for this season. Carlton earns 40.

Why is Carlton ahead of Koufax? Similar things. Carlton pitched 7% more innings, and his ERA is actually quite a bit better if you look at the league ERA and the parks they were playing in. But the basic point is that Carlton, drawing from a pool of 177 Win Shares, is not adversely affected in comparison to Koufax, drawing from a pool of 285 Win Shares.

Another set of players who illustrate this point are Bobby Richardson and Irv Hall. Irv Who?

Irv Hall, wartime major leaguer. In 1961, Bobby Richardson had about the same stats that Hall had in 1945:

Player	G	AB	R	H	2B	3B	HR	RBI	BB	SO	SB	Avg	OBP	SLG
Richardson	162	662	80	173	17	5	3	49	30	23	9	.261	.295	.316
Hall	151	616	62	161	17	5	0	50	35	42	3	.261	.307	.309

Richardson played for a team which won 109 games. Hall played for a team that finished 52-98—yet they rate almost exactly even as hitters, as fielders, and as complete players:

	Hall	Richardson
Hitting	5.43	5.44
Fielding	6.26	6.33
Total	11.69	11.77
Win Shares	12	12

In 1947 Ralph Kiner and Johnny Mize tied for the National League lead in homers, hitting 51 apiece:

Player	G	AB	R	H	2B	3B	HR	RBI	BB	SO	SB	Avg	OBP	SLG
Mize	154	586	137	177	26	2	51	138	74	42	2	.302	.384	.614
Kiner	152	565	118	177	23	4	51	127	98	81	1	.313	.417	.639

Kiner, playing for a last-place team (62-92), claimed 30 Win Shares. Mize, playing for a much better team (81-73), earned 32 Win Shares.

Tommy Davis in 1967 had almost the same numbers that George Hendrick had in 1979:

Player	G	AB	R	H	2B	3B	HR	RBI	BB	SO	SB	Avg	OBP	SLG
Davis	154	577	72	174	32	0	16	73	31	71	9	.302	.342	.440
Hendrick	140	493	67	148	27	1	16	75	49	62	2	.300	.359	.456

Davis did this for a team which finished 61-101, thus a team with only 183 Win Shares to divide. Davis claims 19 of those. Hendrick's team finished 86-76, leaving them to divide 258 Win Shares, of which Hendrick claims 17. Davis' total is higher because he did this in the Sixties, when runs were scarce.

Another thing we can do is establish a range of ability, and show a group of players having comparable seasons. All of the following players were first basemen: Dale Long in 1956, Bill Skowron in 1961, Joe Pepitone in 1963, Tony Horton in 1969, Bob Oliver in 1970, Deron Johnson in 1970, Nate Colbert in 1971, Lee May in 1977, Kent Hrbek in 1986, Bob Horner in 1986, Greg Walker in 1987, Glenn Davis in 1987, Eddie Murray in 1988, and Fred McGriff in 1995. And they all had about the same numbers:

Player	Year	G	AB	R	H	2B	3B	HR	RBI	BB	SO	SB	Avg	OBP	SLG
Long	1956	148	517	64	136	20	7	27	91	54	85	1	.263	.326	.485
Skowron	1961	150	561	76	150	23	4	28	89	35	108	0	.267	.318	.472
Pepitone	1963	157	580	79	157	16	3	27	89	23	63	3	.271	.304	.448
Horton	1969	159	625	77	174	25	4	27	93	37	91	3	.278	.319	.461
Oliver	1970	160	612	83	159	24	6	27	99	42	126	3	.260	.309	.451
Johnson	1970	159	574	66	147	28	3	27	93	72	132	0	.256	.338	.456
Colbert	1971	156	565	81	149	25	3	27	84	63	119	5	.264	.339	.462
May	1977	150	585	75	148	16	2	27	99	38	119	2	.253	.296	.426
Hrbek	1986	149	550	85	147	27	1	29	91	71	81	2	.267	.353	.478
Horner	1986	141	517	70	141	22	0	27	87	52	72	1	.273	.336	.472
Walker	1987	157	566	85	145	33	2	27	94	75	112	2	.256	.346	.465
Davis	1987	151	578	70	145	35	2	27	93	47	84	4	.251	.310	.458
Murray	1988	161	603	75	171	27	2	28	84	75	78	5	.284	.361	.474
McGriff	1995	144	528	85	148	27	1	27	93	65	99	3	.280	.361	.489

Makes you dizzy, looking at all those parallel numbers, don't it? Some of these players did this with good teams, even great teams. Some of them did it with average teams, some with terrible teams.

Of course, they don't *all* claim the same number of Win Shares. There are differences in parks, leagues, and playing time, and there are some differences in these players' stats, with batting averages ranging from .251 to .284, on-base percentages from .296 to .361. Their Win Shares range from 14 to 21.

But those who play on good teams, on the average, don't score any different from those on bad teams. Joe Pepitone in 1963, playing for a team that won 104 games, earned 18 Win Shares. Deron Johnson in 1970, playing for a bad team, earned 19.

Dale Long in 1956, playing for a bad team, is credited with only 15 Win Shares. But Lee May in 1977, playing for a very good team, is credited with only 14.

Bill Skowron in 1961, playing for the '61 Yankees, is credited with 17 Win Shares. But Tony Horton in 1969, playing for the unforgettable '69 Indians, is credited with 19.

Eddie Murray claims the most Win Shares in the group, 21; he did this playing for a team that lost 107 games. He does have the best season, if you look carefully. But if the Win Shares system gave an edge to players on good teams, obviously this would not be true.

Jeff Blauser had a fine year in 1993, playing for an Atlanta team that won 104 games. Robin Yount had almost the same season in 1984, playing for a team that won only 67 games:

Player	G	AB	R	H	2B	3B	HR	RBI	BB	SO	SB	Avg	OBP	SLG
Blauser	161	597	110	182	29	2	15	73	85	109	16	.305	.401	.436
Yount	160	624	105	186	27	7	16	80	67	67	14	.298	.362	.441

When these stats are put into the context of their teams, Blauser emerges with 29 Win Shares—Yount, with 27.

Dick Kokos was an outfielder with the St. Louis Browns in 1950, who lost 96 games. Fred Lynn had a very similar year with the Red Sox in 1977, when they won 97:

Player	G	AB	R	H	2B	3B	HR	RBI	BB	SO	SB	Avg	OBP	SLG
Kokos	143	490	77	128	27	5	18	67	88	73	8	.261	.375	.447
Lynn	129	497	81	129	29	5	18	76	51	63	2	.260	.327	.447

Kokos, with a bad team, was credited with 17 Win Shares; Lynn, on a good team, with 15.

Danny O'Connell earned 16 Win Shares in 1953 as the star player on a Pittsburgh Pirate team that lost 104 games. Omar Vizquel had an essentially similar season in 1996 with a Cleveland team that won 99 games:

Player	G	AB	R	H	2B	3B	HR	RBI	BB	SO	SB	Avg	OBP	SLG
O'Connell	149	588	88	173	26	8	7	55	57	42	3	.294	.361	.401
Vizquel	151	542	98	161	36	1	9	64	56	42	35	.297	.362	.417

Vizquel, despite the brilliance of his teammates, is credited with 16 Win Shares—the same as O'Connell.

John Olerud in 1992 had a season similar to Billy Williams in 1974:

Player	G	AB	R	H	2B	3B	HR	RBI	BB	SO	SB	Avg	OBP	SLG
Olerud	138	458	68	130	28	0	16	66	70	61	1	.284	.375	.450
Williams	117	404	55	113	22	0	16	68	67	44	4	.280	.382	.453

Olerud's team won 96 games; Williams' team lost 96—but the two players rate even, with 16 Win Shares apiece.

Olerud had a teammate, catcher Pat Borders, who just about matched the numbers of the catcher for the 1975 Detroit Tigers:

Player	G	AB	R	H	2B	3B	HR	RBI	BB	SO	SB	Avg	OBP	SLG
Borders	138	480	47	116	26	2	13	53	33	75	1	.242	.290	.385
Freehan	120	427	42	105	17	3	14	47	32	56	2	.246	.306	.398

The Blue Jays won 96 games; the Tigers lost 102 games—yet Freehan is credited with 13 Win Shares, one more than Borders.

A useful team in this context is the 1960 Pittsburgh Pirates, who won the World Series. The Pirates had few stars, but a very large number of players having good, productive seasons, but still what could be called "historically common" seasons. Almost everybody on the team can be matched against a comparable player from a poor team. The catcher, Smoky Burgess, just about matches Biff Pocoroba in 1977, playing for a team that lost 101 games:

Player	G	AB	R	H	2B	3B	HR	RBI	BB	SO	SB	Avg	OBP	SLG
Burgess	110	337	33	99	15	2	7	39	35	13	0	.294	.356	.412
Pocoroba	113	321	46	93	24	1	8	44	57	27	3	.290	.394	.445

Burgess had many years better than this; Pocoroba had none—a meaningless distinction in the current context. Pocoroba couldn't throw; neither could Burgess. Burgess was credited with 15 Win Shares; Pocoroba, with 14.

I'll spare you the chart, but the third baseman for the 1960 Pirates, Don Hoak, had similar numbers to Buddy Bell in 1982, playing third base for a team that finished 64-98. Hoak is credited with 23 Win Shares; Bell, with 25. Bill Mazeroski, playing second for the 1960 Pirates, had similar numbers to Ron Hunt in 1963, playing second for a team that staggered to 111 losses. Mazeroski is credited with 21 Win Shares; Hunt, with 19. Bill Virdon, playing center field for the 1960 Pirates, had similar numbers to Dwayne Murphy in 1979, playing center for a team that lost 108 games. Virdon is credited with 14 Win Shares; Murphy, with 16.

Roberto Clemente, superstar right fielder for the 1960 Pirates, had a season for which we can find a good many matches on bad teams, including Joe Christopher in 1964 and Chuck Hinton in 1962:

Player	G	AB	R	H	2B	3B	HR	RBI	BB	SO	SB	Avg	OBP	SLG
Clemente	144	570	89	179	22	6	16	94	39	72	4	.314	.357	.458
Christopher	154	543	78	163	26	8	16	76	48	92	6	.300	.360	.466
Hinton	151	542	73	168	25	6	17	75	47	66	28	.310	.361	.472

Christopher and Hinton both played on teams which lost more than 100 games. Clemente is credited with 20 Win Shares, Christopher, with 21, and Hinton, with 17.

Of course, players who have similar stats don't *always* wind up with the same or even about the same Win Shares. Due to defense, differences in the run environment and other factors, players with similar stats may have divergent values—and that divergence *may* favor the player on the better team. Or it may favor the player on the worse team. Mitchell Page in 1977 had numbers very much like the group above (Clemente, Christopher and Hinton), yet he earned 30 Win Shares—playing with a bad team. Sandy Alomar in 1996 had numbers similar to Freehan in '75 and Borders in '92, and played on a great team, but was credited with only 8 Win Shares. George Scott in 1977, playing for a good team, had very similar numbers to Willie Montanez in 1971, playing with a bad team—yet Montanez earned 20 Win Shares, Scott only 15.

Mike Pagliarulo in 1991 (9 Win Shares with a World Championship team) matches the stats of Jesse Gonder in 1964 (9 Win Shares with a terrible team):

Player	G	AB	R	H	2B	3B	HR	RBI	BB	SO	SB	Avg	OBP	SLG
Pagliarulo	121	365	38	102	20	0	6	36	21	55	1	.279	.322	.384
Gonder	131	341	28	92	11	1	7	35	29	65	0	.270	.329	.370

David Concepcion in 1970, with a 102-win team, had a season similar to that of Jose Baez in 1977, with a first-year expansion team:

Player	G	AB	R	H	2B	3B	HR	RBI	BB	SO	SB	Avg	OBP	SLG
Concepcion	101	265	38	69	6	3	1	19	23	45	10	.260	.324	.317
Baez	91	305	39	79	14	1	1	17	19	20	6	.259	.305	.321

Concepcion was credited with 5 Win Shares; Baez, with 6.

Brooks Robinson, playing on a 109-win team in 1969, had similar numbers to Sal Bando in 1977, playing for a team that lost 95 games:

Player	G	AB	R	H	2B	3B	HR	RBI	BB	SO	SB	Avg	OBP	SLG
Robinson	156	598	73	140	21	3	23	84	56	55	2	.234	.298	.395
Bando	159	580	65	145	27	3	17	82	75	89	4	.250	.336	.395

Bando and Brooksie were credited with 17 Win Shares apiece.

Well, I still have a file of comparable players here, but I suppose I'd better stop; I'm beating a dead horse, and the dead jackass beside him who has amazingly similar hoof prints. If you won't believe it, you won't believe it, but the Win Shares system does NOT discriminate against a player on a bad team.

Win Shares for Pitchers with Identical Won-Lost Records

I thought it would be kind of fun to identify all of the pitchers in history who have a given won-lost record, and check to see how they compare by Win Shares. Actually, I wound up doing a group of nine of these. First, I identified all the pitchers in history who had one of these won-lost records:

22-10
21-10
20-10
19-10
18-10
20-8
20-9
20-11
20-12

I collected only data on pitchers who posted one of these won-lost records *with one team*, ignoring pitchers who may have gone 18-7 with one team and 2-4 with another team in the same season, and it is possible that I may have missed somebody. . . which doesn't really matter.

Anyway, the nine won-lost records form a kind of cross-hatch pattern:

		20-8		
		20-9		
18-10	19-10	20-10	21-10	22-10
		20-11		
		20-12		

There are 219 pitchers in history who have posted one of these nine won-lost records. The most common of the nine has been 20-9; the least common have been 20-8 and 19-10. In history, there are:

34 pitchers who have gone 20-9
33 pitchers who have gone 20-12
29 pitchers who have gone 18-10
24 pitchers who have gone 20-11
22 pitchers who have gone 21-10
21 pitchers who have gone 22-10
20 pitchers who have gone 20-10
18 pitchers who have gone 20-8
18 pitchers who have gone 19-10

Probably just a random arrangement, except for the fact that the lower winning percentages are more common than the higher winning percentages. The chart below gives the average record for each of these nine sets of pitchers:

G	IP	W-L	Pct.	SO	BB	ERA	GS	CG
38	278	22-10	.688	139	84	2.79	34	21
39	263	21-10	.677	128	79	2.92	32	20
36	260	20-10	.667	142	66	3.03	34	16
37	263	19-10	.655	126	72	3.14	34	19
35	242	18-10	.643	125	73	3.38	32	14
35	252	20-8	.714	143	73	2.77	32	15
37	259	20-9	.690	148	77	3.05	34	16
36	260	20-10	.667	142	66	3.03	34	16
37	273	20-11	.645	144	75	2.92	35	18
38	274	20-12	.625	133	77	3.13	34	20

I also figured the shutout averages, but that turned out to be "3" for all the groups except 22-10, for whom it was a low four. Anyway, that demonstrates the stability of the data. . . the best ERAs go with the best winning percentages, in general, and you can see innings increasing as decisions increase.

Win Shares. . . oh, yeah; I'm supposed to be writing about Win Shares. All the groups of pitchers averaged 1 to 3 more Win Shares than Wins:

22-10 averaged 25 Win Shares
21-10 averaged 22 Win Shares
20-10 averaged 22 Win Shares
19-10 averaged 20 Win Shares
18-10 averaged 19 Win Shares

20-8 averaged 22 Win Shares
20-9 averaged 21 Win Shares
20-10 averaged 22 Win Shares
20-11 averaged 23 Win Shares
20-12 averaged 22 Win Shares

Basically, 20-game winners averaged about 22 Win Shares regardless of how many losses were attached to the package. On the other line, pitchers with ten losses increased by about one Win Share for each additional win, ignoring the little hiccup at the top of the chart. I also charted the "Runs Saved Against Average, park adjusted". . . actually, I charted that because I was entering the data from the *Sabermetric Encyclopedia*, and this is the summary stat that they used, so I just carried it over. Similar data:

22-10 averaged 25 Win Shares and 25 Runs Saved
21-10 averaged 22 Win Shares and 20 Runs Saved
20-10 averaged 22 Win Shares and 24 Runs Saved
19-10 averaged 20 Win Shares and 17 Runs Saved
18-10 averaged 19 Win Shares and 17 Runs Saved
20-8 averaged 22 Win Shares and 26 Runs Saved
20-9 averaged 21 Win Shares and 21 Runs Saved
20-10 averaged 22 Win Shares and 24 Runs Saved
20-11 averaged 23 Win Shares and 23 Runs Saved
20-12 averaged 22 Win Shares and 24 Runs Saved

I should clarify. . . the fact that these numbers tend to be parallel in this case is kind of a coincidence. If you studied pitchers who averaged 10 Win Shares, they probably would be about +/- zero versus the league average, rather than +10.

All of this has been about these pitchers as groups. What is perhaps more interesting is the pitchers as individuals. Below are the records of the 21 pitchers who have posted won-lost records of 22-10:

Player	Year	Team	W	L	Pct.	IP	SO	BB	ERA	WS
Charlie Ferguson	1887	Phillies	22	10	.688	297.1	125	47	3.00	36
Dazzy Vance	1928	Dodgers	22	10	.688	280.1	200	72	2.09	32
Bucky Walters	1940	Reds	22	10	.688	305.0	115	92	2.48	32
Dick Ellsworth	1963	Cubs	22	10	.688	291.0	185	75	2.10	32
Bob Lemon	1949	Indians	22	10	.688	280.0	138	137	2.99	31
Harry Staley	1892	Braves	22	10	.688	299.2	93	97	3.03	29
Hippo Vaughn	1918	Cubs	22	10	.688	290.0	148	76	1.74	28
Whit Wyatt	1941	Dodgers	22	10	.688	288.0	176	82	2.34	28
Lon Warneke	1934	Cubs	22	10	.688	291.0	143	66	3.22	26
Dave McNally	1968	Orioles	22	10	.688	273.0	202	55	1.95	26
Eppa Rixey	1916	Phillies	22	10	.688	287.0	134	74	1.85	24
Hank Wyse	1945	Cubs	22	10	.688	278.0	77	55	2.69	24
Bob Rhoads	1906	Indians	22	10	.688	315.0	89	92	1.80	23
Pat Malone	1929	Cubs	22	10	.688	267.0	166	102	3.57	23
Early Wynn	1959	White Sox	22	10	.688	256.0	179	119	3.16	23
Bob Porterfield	1953	Senators	22	10	.688	255.0	77	73	3.35	21
Jack McDowell	1993	White Sox	22	10	.688	256.2	159	69	3.37	21
Mike McCormick	1967	Giants	22	10	.688	262.0	150	81	2.85	20
Monte Weaver	1932	Senators	22	10	.688	234.0	83	112	4.08	19
Mike Cuellar	1974	Orioles	22	10	.688	269.0	106	86	3.11	19
Sammy Ellis	1965	Reds	22	10	.688	264.0	183	104	3.78	14

Charlie Ferguson in 1887 also played 27 games at second base and some in the outfield and hit .337 in 284 at bats; that's why he has the most Win Shares in the group, because he also gets credit for his hitting and playing other positions. Other than Ferguson, the best pitchers to finish a season 22-10 are Dazzy Vance in 1928, Bucky Walters in 1940, and Dick Ellsworth in 1963. All pitched around 300 innings with ERAs in the low twos.

The weakest pitcher to finish 22-10 was Sammy Ellis in 1965, who finished with that record although his ERA was worse-than-league, and about the league average park-adjusted. Ellis, an effective reliever in 1964, had insisted on moving to the rotation in 1965. I remember verbatim something I read in a spring preview the next year, although I have no idea who wrote it. "Ellis kept shouting that he wanted to start," reported the writer. "He won 22 games, which proves that he knew whereof he was shouting, but he had some long dry spells in there, too." At the time (I was a kid) I thought the writer was silly, second-guessing Ellis' move to the starting rotation after he had had such a great season. He never had another good one, though.

Among pitchers who have gone 21-10, Warren Spahn was the best—and also, oddly enough, the worst:

Player	Year	Team	W	L	Pct.	IP	SO	BB	ERA	WS
Warren Spahn	1947	Braves	21	10	.677	290.0	123	84	2.33	32
Babe Adams	1913	Pirates	21	10	.677	314.0	144	49	2.15	29
Pete Alexander	1927	Cardinals	21	10	.677	268.0	48	38	2.52	28
Howie Pollet	1946	Cardinals	21	10	.677	266.0	107	86	2.10	27
Wes Ferrell	1929	Indians	21	10	.677	243.0	100	109	3.59	25
Jim Palmer	1972	Orioles	21	10	.677	274.1	184	70	2.07	25
Eddie Cicotte	1920	White Sox	21	10	.677	303.0	87	74	3.27	24
Bill Sherdel	1928	Cardinals	21	10	.677	249.0	72	56	2.86	24
Boo Ferriss	1945	Red Sox	21	10	.677	265.0	94	85	2.95	24
Jack Chesbro	1901	Pirates	21	10	.677	287.2	129	52	2.38	23

Player	Year	Team	W	L	Pct.	IP	SO	BB	ERA	WS
Ed Willett	1909	Tigers	21	10	.677	293.0	89	76	2.33	21
Eddie Rommel	1925	A's	21	10	.677	261.0	67	95	3.69	21
Chief Bender	1913	A's	21	10	.677	237.2	135	59	2.20	20
Joey Jay	1961	Reds	21	10	.677	247.0	157	92	3.53	20
Jerry Koosman	1976	Mets	21	10	.677	247.1	200	66	2.69	20
Don Sutton	1976	Dodgers	21	10	.677	267.2	161	82	3.06	20
Tommy Bridges	1935	Tigers	21	10	.677	274.0	163	113	3.51	19
Vic Raschi	1949	Yankees	21	10	.677	275.0	124	138	3.34	19
Jack Coombs	1912	A's	21	10	.677	262.1	120	94	3.29	18
Jose Lima	1999	Astros	21	10	.677	246.0	187	44	3.59	18
Vic Raschi	1951	Yankees	21	10	.677	258.0	164	103	3.28	17
Warren Spahn	1960	Braves	21	10	.677	268.0	154	74	3.49	16

It was hard to identify all the Warren Spahn seasons that should be in our data here, because, when you look at his records, it looks like he belongs *every* year. 21-10, 20-11, 20-12. . . when *didn't* Spahn post one of those records? Spahn's '47 season was a near-match for Dick Ellsworth's 1963 season. Could Ellsworth, with better luck and better handling, have gone on to a career like Spahn's? Who knows.

Tom Seaver in 1971 went 20-10, but with 289 strikeouts and a 1.76 ERA. Ray Caldwell in 1920 was 20-10, but with twice the runs allowed and a third of the strikeouts:

Player	Year	Team	W	L	Pct.	IP	SO	BB	ERA	WS
Tom Seaver	1971	Mets	20	10	.667	286.1	289	61	1.76	32
Rick Reuschel	1977	Cubs	20	10	.667	252.0	166	74	2.79	26
Johnny Allen	1936	Indians	20	10	.667	243.0	165	97	3.44	25
Jim Palmer	1970	Orioles	20	10	.667	305.0	199	100	2.71	25
Greg Maddux	1993	Braves	20	10	.667	267.0	197	52	2.36	25
Urban Shocker	1920	Browns	20	10	.667	246.0	107	70	2.71	24
Roger Wolff	1945	Senators	20	10	.667	250.0	108	53	2.12	24
Pat Hentgen	1996	Blue Jays	20	10	.667	265.2	177	94	3.22	24
Nixey Callahan	1898	Cubs	20	10	.667	274.1	73	71	2.46	23
Lou Fette	1937	Braves	20	10	.667	259.0	70	81	2.88	23
Lew Burdette	1958	Braves	20	10	.667	275.0	113	50	2.91	23
Ben Cantwell	1933	Braves	20	10	.667	255.0	57	54	2.61	21
Dick Donovan	1962	Indians	20	10	.667	251.0	94	47	3.59	20
Jack McDowell	1992	White Sox	20	10	.667	260.2	178	75	3.18	20
Art Nehf	1921	Giants	20	10	.667	261.0	67	55	3.62	17
Chris Short	1966	Phillies	20	10	.667	272.0	177	68	3.54	17
Bill Monbouquette	1963	Red Sox	20	10	.667	267.0	174	42	3.81	16
Brad Radke	1997	Twins	20	10	.667	239.2	174	48	3.87	16
Mike Scott	1989	Astros	20	10	.667	229.0	172	62	3.10	15
Ray Caldwell	1920	Indians	20	10	.667	238.0	80	63	3.86	14

But focusing on the gulf between Caldwell and Seaver could obscure a more obvious point: that there normally *isn't* too much difference in value between pitchers with the same record. Of the 20 pitchers with 20-10 records, 60% were between 20 and 25 Win Shares.

Tom Seaver had a similar season two years later, and just misses being the best 19-10 pitcher as well:

Player	Year	Team	W	L	Pct.	IP	SO	BB	ERA	WS
Ben Sanders	1888	Phillies	19	10	.655	275.1	121	33	1.90	35
Tom Seaver	1973	Mets	19	10	.655	290.0	251	64	2.08	29
Frank Tanana	1976	Angels	19	10	.655	288.1	261	73	2.43	27
Eddie Plank	1909	A's	19	10	.655	265.1	132	62	1.76	22
Ed Reulbach	1909	Cubs	19	10	.655	263.0	105	82	1.78	21
Schoolboy Rowe	1936	Tigers	19	10	.655	245.0	115	64	4.52	21
Jim Bunning	1962	Tigers	19	10	.655	258.0	184	74	3.59	21
Lee Meadows	1927	Pirates	19	10	.655	299.0	84	66	3.40	20
Lew Burdette	1956	Braves	19	10	.655	256.0	110	52	2.71	20
Johnny Antonelli	1959	Giants	19	10	.655	282.0	165	76	3.10	20
Jack Billingham	1973	Reds	19	10	.655	293.1	155	95	3.04	19
Burt Hooton	1978	Dodgers	19	10	.655	236.0	104	61	2.71	19
Billy Rhines	1895	Reds	19	10	.655	267.2	72	76	4.81	18
Lee Meadows	1925	Pirates	19	10	.655	255.0	87	67	3.67	18
Ed Figueroa	1976	Yankees	19	10	.655	256.2	119	94	3.02	16
Fred Klobedanz	1898	Braves	19	10	.655	270.2	51	99	3.89	15
Dick Newsome	1941	Red Sox	19	10	.655	214.0	58	79	4.12	14
Brooks Lawrence	1956	Reds	19	10	.655	219.0	96	71	3.99	14

Seaver is bumped off the top of this list by Ben Sanders, who, like Charlie Ferguson one year earlier, also played in the field when not pitching, adding to his value. Here, again, 61% of the seasons are valued between 18 and 22 Win Shares.

The best pitcher ever to go 18-10 was Mike Scott, who went 18-10 with 306 strikeouts for the Astros in 1986:

Player	Year	Team	W	L	Pct.	IP	SO	BB	ERA	WS
Mike Scott	1986	Astros	18	10	.643	275.1	306	72	2.22	27
George Mullin	1911	Tigers	18	10	.643	234.1	87	61	3.07	23
Mike Witt	1986	Angels	18	10	.643	269.0	208	73	2.84	23
Bret Saberhagen	1987	Royals	18	10	.643	257.0	163	53	3.36	23
Jesse Tannehill	1901	Pirates	18	10	.643	252.1	118	36	2.18	22
Fred Hutchinson	1947	Tigers	18	10	.643	220.0	113	61	3.03	22
Mel Parnell	1950	Red Sox	18	10	.643	249.0	93	106	3.61	22
Mickey McDermott	1953	Red Sox	18	10	.643	206.0	92	109	3.01	22
Don Sutton	1973	Dodgers	18	10	.643	256.1	20	56	2.42	22
Vida Blue	1978	Giants	18	10	.643	258.0	171	70	2.79	22
Larry Gura	1980	Royals	18	10	.643	283.1	113	76	2.95	22
Ray Kremer	1924	Pirates	18	10	.643	259.0	64	51	3.20	21
Teddy Higuera	1987	Brewers	18	10	.643	261.2	240	87	3.85	20
Jack Quinn	1920	Yankees	18	10	.643	253.0	101	48	3.20	19
Rick Sutcliffe	1987	Cubs	18	10	.643	237.1	174	106	3.68	19
Chan Ho Park	2000	Dodgers	18	10	.643	226.0	217	124	3.27	18
Al Milnar	1940	Indians	18	10	.643	242.0	99	99	3.27	17
Eddie Plank	1913	A's	18	10	.643	242.2	151	57	2.60	16
Guy Bush	1934	Cubs	18	10	.643	209.0	75	54	3.83	16
Jim Perry	1960	Indians	18	10	.643	261.0	120	91	3.62	16
Ron Reed	1969	Braves	18	10	.643	241.1	160	56	3.47	16

Player	Year	Team	W	L	Pct.	IP	SO	BB	ERA	WS
Harry Staley	1893	Braves	18	10	.643	263.0	61	81	5.13	15
Ray Kremer	1929	Pirates	18	10	.643	222.0	66	60	4.26	15
Bobby Shantz	1951	A's	18	10	.643	205.0	77	70	3.95	15
Bob Lemon	1955	Indians	18	10	.643	211.0	100	74	3.88	15
Jim Lonborg	1976	Phillies	18	10	.643	222.0	118	50	3.08	15
Casey Patten	1901	Senators	18	10	.643	254.1	109	74	3.93	14
Jimmie DeShong	1936	Senators	18	10	.643	224.0	59	96	4.62	14
Andy Benes	1996	Cardinals	18	10	.643	230.1	160	77	3.83	14

Scottie won the Cy Young Award that year over two twenty-game winners, Mike Krukow (who will make the 20-9 list) and Fernando Valenzuela (21-11). And deserved it, obviously. . . that's one time the voters figured it out.

I ought to check out the "next season" records of the pitchers on the bottom of these lists. I'm sure it is about .500. Andy Benes was 10-7 following his 18-10 adventure, but Jimmie DeShong was 14-15, Casey Patten 17-16. Brooks Lawrence and Dick Newsome, the weakest of the 19-10 pitchers, are rarely mentioned in Hall of Fame debates.

Tell me within ten seconds: which pitcher makes both the list above and the one below?

Player	Year	Team	W	L	Pct.	IP	SO	BB	ERA	WS
Harry Staley	1891	Braves	20	8	.714	252.1	114	69	2.50	29
Jim Bunning	1957	Tigers	20	8	.714	267.0	182	72	2.70	26
Spud Chandler	1946	Yankees	20	8	.714	257.0	138	90	2.10	25
Jack Pfiester	1906	Cubs	20	8	.714	250.2	153	63	1.51	24
Allie Reynolds	1952	Yankees	20	8	.714	244.0	160	97	2.07	24
Dennis Eckersley	1978	Red Sox	20	8	.714	268.1	162	71	2.99	24
Mark Gubicza	1988	Royals	20	8	.714	269.2	183	83	2.70	24
Jake Weimer	1903	Cubs	20	8	.714	282.0	128	104	2.30	23
Gary Peters	1964	White Sox	20	8	.714	274.0	205	104	2.50	22
Dutch Leonard	1939	Senators	20	8	.714	269.0	88	59	3.55	21
Jimmy Dygert	1907	A's	20	8	.714	261.2	151	85	2.34	20
Jesse Haines	1928	Cardinals	20	8	.714	240.0	77	72	3.19	19
Pat Dobson	1971	Orioles	20	8	.714	282.0	187	63	2.90	19
Tom Glavine	1992	Braves	20	8	.714	225.0	129	70	2.76	19
Scott McGregor	1980	Orioles	20	8	.714	252.0	119	58	3.32	18
Scott Erickson	1991	Twins	20	8	.714	204.0	108	71	3.18	18
David Wells	2000	Blue Jays	20	8	.714	229.2	166	31	4.11	18
John Smiley	1991	Pirates	20	8	.714	207.2	129	44	3.08	14

It's Harry Staley, the number one guy. Different sources use different won-lost records, which often don't match for the years before 1910, and don't match in either case for Staley. I don't really know anything about Staley, by the way. . . he's pretty much a cipher as far as I know, but he also made the 22-10 list.

There are more 20-9 pitchers than any other kind in our group, and they come in all shapes, from Herb Score and Jim Maloney to guys who just put the ball over the plate and took their chances:

Player	Year	Team	W	L	Pct.	IP	SO	BB	ERA	WS
Dean Chance	1964	Angels	20	9	.690	278.0	207	86	1.65	32
Early Wynn	1956	Indians	20	9	.690	278.0	158	91	2.72	28
Roger Clemens	1987	Red Sox	20	9	.690	281.2	256	83	2.97	28
Pat Luby	1890	Cubs	20	9	.690	267.2	85	95	3.19	27
Harvey Haddix	1953	Cardinals	20	9	.690	253.0	163	69	3.06	27
Cliff Melton	1937	Giants	20	9	.690	248.0	142	55	2.61	25
Herb Score	1956	Indians	20	9	.690	249.0	263	129	2.53	25
Pat Malone	1930	Cubs	20	9	.690	272.0	142	96	3.94	24
Howie Pollet	1949	Cardinals	20	9	.690	231.0	108	59	2.77	24
Deacon Phillippe	1902	Pirates	20	9	.690	272.0	122	26	2.05	23
Hod Eller	1919	Reds	20	9	.690	248.0	137	50	2.40	23
Jim Maloney	1965	Reds	20	9	.690	255.0	244	110	2.54	23
Mel Stottlemyre	1965	Yankees	20	9	.690	291.0	155	88	2.62	23
Jim Palmer	1971	Orioles	20	9	.690	282.0	184	106	2.68	22
Hugh Bedient	1912	Red Sox	20	9	.690	231.0	122	55	2.92	21
Don Newcombe	1951	Dodgers	20	9	.690	272.0	164	91	3.28	21
Billy Pierce	1956	White Sox	20	9	.690	276.0	192	100	3.33	21
Bob Wicker	1903	Cubs	20	9	.690	246.2	110	74	3.03	20
Carl Mays	1924	Reds	20	9	.690	226.0	63	36	3.15	20
Vern Law	1960	Pirates	20	9	.690	272.0	120	40	3.08	20
Ray Herbert	1962	White Sox	20	9	.690	237.0	115	74	3.27	20
Joe Coleman	1971	Tigers	20	9	.690	286.0	236	96	3.15	20
Al Downing	1971	Dodgers	20	9	.690	262.0	136	84	2.68	19
Mike Torrez	1975	Orioles	20	9	.690	270.2	119	133	3.06	19
Ed Figueroa	1978	Yankees	20	9	.690	253.0	92	77	2.99	19
Freddie Fitzsimmons	1928	Giants	20	9	.690	261.0	67	65	3.69	18
Mike Cuellar	1971	Orioles	20	9	.690	292.0	124	78	3.08	18
Tom Browning	1985	Reds	20	9	.690	261.1	155	73	3.55	18
Darryl Kile	2000	Cardinals	20	9	.690	232.1	192	58	3.91	17
Steve Carlton	1971	Cardinals	20	9	.690	273.1	172	98	3.56	16
Mike Krukow	1986	Giants	20	9	.690	245.0	178	55	3.05	16
Vida Blue	1973	A's	20	9	.690	263.2	158	105	3.28	15
Bill Gullickson	1991	Tigers	20	9	.690	226.1	91	44	3.90	14
Lee Meadows	1926	Pirates	20	9	.690	227.0	54	52	3.96	13

I believe that Lee Meadows is the only guy who makes one of these lists three straight years, going 19-10 in 1925, 20-9 in '26, and 19-10 again in '27. He was a good pitcher, pitching with a good team. There are also two pairs of teammates on this list—Early Wynn and Herb Score, both 20-9 with the '56 Indians, and Jim Palmer and Mike Cuellar, both 20-9 with the '71 Orioles. Palmer also makes the 20-11 list at the top of the following page:

Player	Year	Team	W	L	Pct.	IP	SO	BB	ERA	WS
Orval Overall	1909	Cubs	20	11	.645	285.0	205	80	1.42	30
Jim Palmer	1977	Orioles	20	11	.645	319.0	198	99	2.91	29
Jim Turner	1937	Braves	20	11	.645	257.0	69	52	2.38	27
Greg Maddux	1992	Cubs	20	11	.645	268.0	199	70	2.18	27
Robin Roberts	1950	Phillies	20	11	.645	304.0	146	77	3.02	26
Tex Hughson	1946	Red Sox	20	11	.645	278.0	172	51	2.75	25
Teddy Higuera	1986	Brewers	20	11	.645	248.1	207	74	2.79	25
Bob Shawkey	1919	Yankees	20	11	.645	261.0	122	92	2.72	24
Warren Spahn	1956	Braves	20	11	.645	281.0	128	52	2.79	24
Jouett Meekin	1897	Giants	20	11	.645	303.2	83	99	3.76	23
Bob Feller	1947	Indians	20	11	.645	299.0	196	127	2.68	23
Camilo Pascual	1962	Twins	20	11	.645	258.0	206	59	3.31	23
Mike Boddicker	1984	Orioles	20	11	.645	261.1	128	81	2.79	23
Tom Glavine	1991	Braves	20	11	.645	246.2	192	69	2.55	23
Hooks Wiltse	1909	Giants	20	11	.645	269.0	119	51	2.01	22
Claude Osteen	1972	Dodgers	20	11	.645	252.0	100	69	2.64	22
Dave Goltz	1977	Twins	20	11	.645	303.0	186	91	3.36	22
Old Hoss Radbourn	1889	Braves	20	11	.645	277.0	99	72	3.67	21
Amos Rusie	1898	Giants	20	11	.645	300.0	114	103	3.03	19
Fritz Peterson	1970	Yankees	20	11	.645	260.0	127	40	2.91	19
Dennis Leonard	1980	Royals	20	11	.645	280.1	155	80	3.79	18
Paul Splittorff	1973	Royals	20	11	.645	262.0	110	78	3.98	17
Ross Grimsley	1978	Expos	20	11	.645	263.0	84	67	3.05	16
Ray Sadecki	1964	Cardinals	20	11	.645	220.0	119	60	3.68	15

Odd thing I remember about that Ray Sadecki season. . . Sadecki had a lousy April that year, did not win a game and had some disagreements with his manager; there were rumors he was about to drop out of the rotation. "I don't care about that now," said Sadecki. "All I want is to win four games in May, four games in June, four games in July, four games in August and four in September." As it turned out, that was almost exactly what he did; he had a five-win month and a three-win month, but otherwise won four each month.

At 20-12 we start out with Sudden Sam McDowell:

Player	Year	Team	W	L	Pct.	IP	SO	BB	ERA	WS
Sam McDowell	1970	Indians	20	12	.625	305.0	304	131	2.92	30
Al Orth	1901	Phillies	20	12	.625	281.2	92	32	2.27	29
Lefty Grove	1935	Red Sox	20	12	.625	273.0	121	65	2.70	29
Lefty Stewart	1930	Browns	20	12	.625	271.0	79	70	3.45	28
Randy Jones	1975	Padres	20	12	.625	285.0	103	56	2.24	28
Bob Shawkey	1922	Yankees	20	12	.625	300.0	130	98	2.91	27
Mel Harder	1934	Indians	20	12	.625	255.0	91	81	2.61	27
Bob Gibson	1965	Cardinals	20	12	.625	299.0	270	103	3.07	26
Bill Singer	1969	Dodgers	20	12	.625	316.0	247	74	2.34	26
Jack Stivetts	1893	Braves	20	12	.625	283.2	61	115	4.41	25
Addie Joss	1905	Indians	20	12	.625	286.0	132	46	2.01	25
Rube Walberg	1931	A's	20	12	.625	291.0	106	109	3.74	24
Paul Derringer	1940	Reds	20	12	.625	297.0	115	48	3.06	24
Dennis Leonard	1977	Royals	20	12	.625	292.2	244	79	3.04	24
Sam Gray	1928	Browns	20	12	.625	263.0	102	86	3.18	23

Player	Year	Team	W	L	Pct.	IP	SO	BB	ERA	WS
Red Ruffing	1936	Yankees	20	12	.625	271.0	102	90	3.85	23
Dizzy Trout	1943	Tigers	20	12	.625	247.0	111	101	2.48	23
Watty Clark	1932	Dodgers	20	12	.625	273.0	99	49	3.49	22
Ned Garver	1951	Browns	20	12	.625	246.0	84	96	3.73	22
Ferguson Jenkins	1972	Cubs	20	12	.625	289.1	184	62	3.20	22
George Suggs	1910	Reds	20	12	.625	266.2	91	48	2.40	20
Jim Colborn	1973	Brewers	20	12	.625	314.0	135	87	3.18	20
Frank Viola	1990	Mets	20	12	.625	249.2	182	60	2.67	20
Hippo Vaughn	1915	Cubs	20	12	.625	270.0	148	77	2.87	19
Urban Shocker	1923	Browns	20	12	.625	277.0	109	49	3.41	19
Bill Doak	1920	Cardinals	20	12	.625	270.0	90	80	2.53	18
Guy Bush	1933	Cubs	20	12	.625	264.0	84	68	2.69	18
Billy Pierce	1957	White Sox	20	12	.625	257.0	171	71	3.26	18
Alex Kellner	1949	A's	20	12	.625	245.0	94	129	3.75	17
Dave Boswell	1969	Twins	20	12	.625	256.0	190	99	3.23	16
Ray Kremer	1930	Pirates	20	12	.625	276.0	58	63	5.02	15
Jim Merritt	1970	Reds	20	12	.625	234.0	136	53	4.08	15
Joe Niekro	1980	Astros	20	12	.625	256.0	127	79	3.55	14

McDowell had a 2.92 ERA in a hitter's park (133 Run Factor) in a league with a 3.71 ERA; Joe Niekro had the same record ten years later but with a much higher ERA, in a pitcher's park (92 Run Factor) in a league with a 3.60 ERA. McDowell went 20-12 for a sub-.500 team; Niekro for a championship team.

Lefty Grove in 1935 is on the list above, at 20-12. The *Sabermetric Encyclopedia*, listing pitchers by RSAA (Runs Saved Against Average), ranks Lefty Grove in 1935 as not only the best of the 20-12 pitchers (64 runs better-than-league) but as the best pitcher on any of these nine lists. That's OK, but. . . playing in a high-run context inflates Grove's value, stated in runs. Grove was a terrible hitter; you have to factor that in somewhere, and 20-12 is not 22-10 or 20-8. He was *among* the best pitchers in the group, but I don't think he was the best.

Who is the best of these 219 pitchers? Our method doesn't really say. Charlie Ferguson has 36 Win Shares and Ben Sanders 35, but those numbers include their contributions as position players. Other than those two, we have a bunch of pitchers at 32 Win Shares, no one of them better than the others.

We are, after all, looking at pitchers who were pretty much alike, not pitchers who were very different.

Why Did the Defensive Spectrum Jump?

The nine defensive positions may be arrayed on a spectrum, which traditionally goes, from left to right: first base, left field, right field, third base, center field, second base, shortstop, catcher, pitcher. As you move rightward on the spectrum (away from first basemen, toward pitchers) players are evaluated more on their defensive contribution, and less on their offense. First basemen hit the most; pitchers hit the least—but pitchers are expected to make the largest contribution toward preventing the other team from scoring.

"Pitcher" and "catcher" are really so far off to the right that they're usually not considered to be a part of the defensive spectrum. Using the rest of the spectrum, first base to shortstop, there are many implications for a player's career, including:

1. As players age, they move leftward on the spectrum. Third basemen are never converted to shortstop as they age; shortstops, if they can hit, are converted to third basemen. Aging first basemen are not moved to the outfield; aging outfielders are moved to first base.

2. As players move through the minors, they move leftward on the spectrum. Minor league shortstops become major league second basemen. Minor league third basemen, if they hit enough, may move to left field. It rarely works the other way.

This defensive spectrum has shifted only once in major league history. In the early part of the 20th century, third base was considered a *more* demanding defensive position than second base. If you look at the data in 1905 or 1915 or 1925, you'll find that second basemen were better hitters than third basemen. About 1935, the spectrum shifted. The hitters moved to third base; the defensive specialists moved to second base.

Let me document that change. This is a little bit tricky, because some players will play both second base and third base in any season, some players will play third base and the outfield, some players will play second base and shortstop, etc. It is hard to say what the average offensive productivity of a major league second baseman in any season is, unless you have modern STATS-type data.

I figured the runs created/27 outs of all players who had 2000 plate appearances in any decade, and whose primary position was second base or third base. In other words, to represent "Second base, 1900-1909," I generated a list of all players who were primarily second basemen and who had at least 2000 plate appearances in the years 1900 to 1909. As the data shows, from 1900 to 1930, second basemen were better hitters than third basemen:

Second Base	1900-1909:	4.54 Runs Created/Game
Third Base	1900-1909:	4.30 Runs Created/Game
Second Base	1910-1919:	4.68 Runs Created/Game
Third Base	1910-1919:	4.40 Runs Created/Game
Second Base	1920-1929:	5.78 Runs Created/Game
Third Base	1920-1929:	4.75 Runs Created/Game

Some of you who are particularly alert will suspect that this effect is created by two players, Nap Lajoie and Rogers Hornsby. It is not. If you look at the 1920s, you'll find six second basemen (Hornsby, Eddie Collins, Tony Lazzeri, George Grantham, Charlie Geh-ringer and Frankie Frisch) who were better hitters than the best-hitting third baseman, Pie Traynor. On the other end of the scale, there are third basemen in each decade, like Lee Tannehill and Babe Pinelli, who are weaker hitters than any regular second baseman who was able to hold a job.

The defensive spectrum began to move about 1930. In the 1930s, there is no real difference between the two:

Second Base	1930-1939:	5.31 Runs Created/Game
Third Base	1930-1939:	5.38 Runs Created/Game

Since 1940, third basemen have been better hitters than second basemen:

Second Base	1940-1949:	4.34 Runs Created/Game
Third Base	1940-1949:	5.25 Runs Created/Game
Second Base	1950-1959:	4.77 Runs Created/Game
Third Base	1950-1959:	5.52 Runs Created/Game
Second Base	1960-1969:	3.87 Runs Created/Game
Third Base	1960-1969:	4.57 Runs Created/Game

To understand why this happened, start with this question: If you take the double play out of baseball, which is the more difficult defensive position: third base or second?

Obviously, it's third. Third basemen need quicker reactions, since they are nearer the batter, and they need a stronger arm, since they are further from first base. Without the double play, third base is obviously the more demanding position.

The defensive spectrum shifted, essentially, because double plays became more common than errors. In 1880 there were 2,950 errors in the major leagues, and only 411 double plays—more than seven times as many errors as double plays.

Over time, errors became less common, and double plays more common. By 1900, the ratio of errors to double plays was about three to one. By 1920, the ratio was about 9 to 5; by 1930, about 6 to 5.

Those lines actually crossed in 1947. In 1947, and in every year since 1947 except 1963 and 1975, there have been more double plays than errors. In modern baseball there are about 30% more double plays than errors, and that ratio is still expanding, although very slowly.

Third basemen have always made more errors than second basemen, as a percentage of their opportunities (although not always more as a raw total). In 1890 the fielding percentage of major league third basemen was .867; of second basemen, .921.

Since then, both of these have generally increased:

Year	Second	Third
1890	.921	.867
1900	.938	.896
1910	.949	.931
1920	.963	.947
1930	.966	.947
1940	.967	.942
1950	.975	.954
1960	.976	.952
1970	.979	.947
1980	.981	.945

But while the ratio of error rates between the two positions has been reasonably stable, the raw numbers of errors have changed dramatically. Third baseman Bill Joyce made 107 errors in 1890. Twenty-six other 19th century third basemen made 70 or more. Early in the 20th century, third basemen would often make more than 50 errors a season. Since 1940, only three major league third basemen (Butch Hobson in 1978, Dick Allen in 1964 and Sibby Sisti in 1941) have made even 40 errors, with the highest total being 43.

As errors have become less common, managers have naturally become less worried about them, more willing to risk defensive mistakes to get a bat in the lineup. Since third basemen make more errors than second basemen, this has more impact on expectations for third basemen than it does for second basemen.

At the same time, double plays have become more common. In 1904, the first season of the 154-game schedule with 16 major league teams, major league second basemen turned an average of 46 double plays per team. By 1910 this number was up to 62 per team; by 1930, to 105 per team; by 1950, to 127 per team.

Conversely, as double plays became more common, major league managers became more willing to sacrifice offense in order to get a second baseman who could turn the double play. About 1935, these forces wrenched the established defensive spectrum out of alignment. Since 1935, major league third basemen have hit better than second basemen. The gap has increased for most of that time. This is the only realignment of the defensive spectrum to have occurred in the twentieth century.

There is a shift in the language which reflects the change in the game. In the dead-ball era, second basemen were commonly referred to as "keystone men" or keystone players. This has been almost entirely replaced by the term "pivot men," referring, of course, to the pivot on the double play. The DP pivot has become the defining function of a second baseman.

In the 19th century. . . well, it's hard to say. The defensive spectrum only makes sense in a highly organized structure. Major league baseball in 1876 wasn't that organized.

In little league ball, the best hitter is usually the pitcher or the shortstop. This is still true more often than not in high school, and it is often true even in good college baseball, where the best athletes still sometimes dominate all phases of the game. The defensive spectrum in college baseball is hard to figure; you do have some big strong first basemen and DHs who are good hitters but terrible fielders, but to an extent, you still have the best hitters clustered at the key defensive positions, where they started out in little league.

Major league baseball in 1876 was much like college baseball today: the defensive spectrum, if there was one, is difficult to pin down. The best hitters in 1876 were a second baseman (Ross Barnes) and a shortstop (George Wright). For purposes of the current analysis, I have assumed that the defensive spectrum was the same throughout the late nineteenth century as it was in 1900, but this is an area in which we could benefit from additional research.

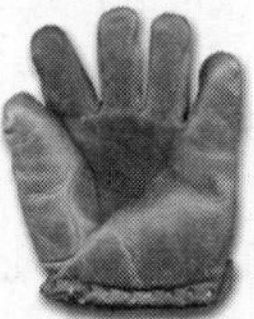

Fuzzy Stats

There are three core reasons why the defensive analysis here is able to reach credible value estimates, to a greater extent than my previous efforts. One of those reasons is the realization that fielding stats are not "hard stats," from which strict mathematical inferences may be made, but rather "fuzzy stats" which should be taken as indications of the nature of the underlying reality.

In the simplest analysis of baseball stats, there are "reliable" stats and "meaningless" stats. Fuzzy stats are stats which lie somewhere between these two. Pitcher's wins, for example, are a fuzzy stat. Certainly no one would doubt that a pitcher's won-lost record does reflect, to some extent, his own performance. If you've got a choice between a 20-8 pitcher and a 12-19 pitcher, and this is the only information you have, who are you going to choose? You'll choose the 20-8 pitcher, and you will have a reasonable expectation that you might get the better pitcher by doing that. At the same time, certainly none of us would doubt that the won-lost log also reflects the quality of the team behind the pitcher, and, to an equally large extent, simple luck.

A mathematical analysis which tried to proceed directly from won-lost records to a statement of the pitcher's true value would, often as not, reach utterly absurd conclusions. In 1952 Warren Spahn finished 14-19 despite posting a 2.98 ERA in 290 innings. Another left-handed pitcher, the same age as Spahn, was Jim Hearn. In the same league the same year, Hearn posted a 3.78 ERA—but finished 14-7. If one reasoned from this to their value, one would have to conclude that Hearn was contributing far more than Spahn.

Any analysis based directly on pitcher's wins would deal roughly with the truth, because pitcher's wins are a fuzzy stat. RBI are a fuzzy stat. If we had to reason directly from RBI to a hitter's value, we would miss the mark. If one had to say "This player had 100 RBI; a typical left fielder in this number of plate appearances would have had 70 RBI, therefore this player is worth 30 runs," one would simply be wrong most of the time. This is what Linear Weights attempts to do with fielding stats, and this is what I had attempted to do for many years.

But suppose that fuzzy stats were all that we had, or perhaps we might have fuzzy stats and some marginally relevant hard stats. Suppose that *the only things we had* to evaluate hitters were RBI, runs scored, walks and strikeouts. Would we still be able to reach reasonable conclusions about the value of the players, based on those four numbers?

Well, in fact we would—but not by strict mathematical analysis. What we would have to do is say "this player drove in a lot of runs. That may be taken as an *indication* that he has some power." By putting the indications together and weighting each as appropriate, we could come up with a good estimate of what each player had contributed to the team.

This is the situation we must deal with, to make sense of fielding stats: we must realize that these stats *suggest* much more than they *prove*. We must deal with them as indications of ability, but look elsewhere for absolute proof.

In our system, the won-lost record of the team is taken to be the absolute proof, the rock-solid foundation of the analysis. The number of runs allowed, relative to league and park, is taken as proof of the overall quality of the pitching and defense.

The *indicators* are then reconciled against the hard truth of the team's performance. This is what makes the system credible, I believe: that it *has* to add up. It is not forced to show that all teams' defensive performance is precisely proportional to their overall success; there are other variables. But neither is our system permitted to reflect a world in which "team defense" is randomly aligned against team success.

Linear Weights risks attributing players with defensive success which never actually existed. Our system may mis-attribute success, but never invents it. We may give credit to the second baseman for what was actually done by the shortstop. But we will never give a team credit for things that the team didn't actually do.

Roy Smalley

Another player whose defense I would interpret differently now than I would have before developing the Win Shares system is Roy Smalley Jr.

Roy Jr. was the shortstop for the Minnesota Twins in the late 1970s, playing for his uncle, Gene Mauch. He led the American League in assists in 1977 (504), 1978 (527), and 1979 (572), the last figure establishing an American League record, since broken by Cal Ripken. He also led in putouts in 1978 (287) and 1979 (296), and in double plays all three of those seasons (116, 121, 144). The 144 double plays in 1979 was a major league record at the time, and remains today the second-highest total in major league history, that record having been claimed by Rick Burleson.

In spite of this, Smalley was not generally regarded as a top-flight defensive shortstop. The Gold Gloves in Smalley's best years went to Mark Belanger (1977-78) and Rick Burleson (1979). His reputation as a defensive player, never great, turned sour in the early 1980s when Smalley:

a) began having back trouble, and

b) was traded to the Yankees.

Smalley suffered from spondylolysis, a congenital back problem. It had troubled him in college, but then hadn't bothered him for years in Minnesota. Trying to play shortstop for the Yankees, he found himself unable to twist or turn without pain. Of course, what he did in New York was twenty times more visible than what he had done in Minnesota, and so Smalley developed the reputation of being an inadequate defensive shortstop.

For years, I defended Smalley as a shortstop, trying to say to people that "the Roy Smalley you saw in New York wasn't the real player. In his prime, Roy Smalley was a great defensive shortstop."

But based on recent research, I have to admit that while Smalley was a good shortstop, he was never as good as I used to say that he was. It is clear that the aging Mark Belanger and Rick Burleson were better.

If we compare Smalley to the 33-year-old Belanger in 1977, Smalley at first appears to have the edge:

	G	PO	A	Er	DP	Range	FPct
Smalley	150	255	504	33	116	5.06	.958
Belanger	142	244	417	10	82	4.65	.985

Smalley's range appears to outweigh Belanger's reliability. But if you look at the total defensive statistics of *all of the team's shortstops*, you get a different picture:

	G	PO	A	Er	DP	Range	FPct
Minnesota	164	289	547	35	132	5.16	.960
Baltimore	208	323	571	19	125	5.52	.979

Minnesota shortstops (90% Smalley) had 289 assists, 547 putouts, and 35 errors. Baltimore shortstops (75% Belanger) had 323 putouts, 571 assists, 19 errors—58 more plays made, about half as many errors. Smalley looks better because the Twins had only two "shared defensive games" at shortstop—164 games played at shortstop in a 162-game season. Baltimore, pinch hitting for Belanger, had 47 shared defensive games at shortstop, which drives Belanger's range number down.

Plus, Baltimore was a much better defensive *team* than Minnesota, which has to count in Belanger's favor, since defensive statistics implicitly compare the player to his teammates. Both teams, oddly enough, had 737 pitcher's strikeouts, but Baltimore pitchers allowed 1,414 hits, one of the lowest figures in the league, while Minnesota allowed 1,546, one of the highest figures in the league. Obviously, if Belanger is playing in the middle of a bunch of other guys who can also go after the ball, that drives his fielding opportunities down, and makes his range advantage even wider.

Belanger's adjusted range factor (see article: Adjusted Range Factors) was 5.55. Smalley's was 5.07, still better than the league average (4.83).

If you look ahead to 1978, Belanger was losing some playing time, but you've got essentially the same picture. Comparing Smalley to Belanger as individuals:

	G	PO	A	E	DP	Range	FPct
Smalley	157	287	527	25	121	5.18	.970
Belanger	134	184	409	9	76	4.43	.985

But comparing Minnesota shortstops to Baltimore shortstops:

	G	PO	A	E	DP	Range	FPct
Minnesota	164	293	547	27	123	5.19	.969
Baltimore	210	271	584	24	111	5.31	.973

The range factors here, for obvious reasons, are based on the team games. Minnesota, again, had two shared defensive games at shortstop; Baltimore had 49.

If you factor in the other elements, again, the Baltimore shortstops are going to move further ahead. Baltimore pitchers had 754 strikeouts; Minnesota had 703, giving Minnesota fielders an extra 51 chances. Baltimore allowed 1,340 hits; Minnesota allowed 1,468, meaning that there were another 128 fielding opportunities in the Minnesota pool. The adjusted range factors in 1978 are almost a repeat of 1977: Belanger, 5.56, Smalley, 5.12, League Average, 4.92.

By 1979, Smalley's best defensive season, Belanger was 35 years old and not playing all that much. That was the season in which Smalley established an American League record for assists by a shortstop and a major league record for double plays by a shortstop. I think a careful analysis would still show that his defensive work was not remarkable.

That Minnesota pitching staff was entirely composed of ground ball pitchers—Jerry Koosman, Dave Goltz, Geoff Zahn, Paul Hartzell, and Mike Marshall out of the bullpen. They had more assists in 1979, as a team, than any other American League team of the 1970s. Minnesota shortstops had 581 assists, 572 of those by Smalley, but New York Yankee shortstops the same year had 608 assists, and Boston had 570. More significantly, Minnesota's shortstops accounted for 581 of the team's 2007 assists, which was the seventh-highest percentage in the league:

	SS	Team	SS%	Regular Shortstop
New York	608	1970	.309	Bucky Dent
Boston	570	1853	.308	Rick Burleson
Cleveland	503	1642	.306	Tom Veryzer
California	480	1608	.299	Jim Anderson
Seatle	554	1879	.295	Mario Mendoza
Milwaukee	557	1905	.292	Robin Yount
Minnesota	581	2007	.28949	Roy Smalley
Chicago	529	1831	.2889	Greg Pryor
Toronto	542	1878	.2886	Alfredo Griffin
League	**7271**	**25462**	**.286**	
KC	485	1778	.273	Patek/Washington
Oakland	468	1718	.272	Rob Picciolo
Baltimore	475	1764	.269	Kiko Garcia
Detroit	471	1767	.266	Trammell
Texas	448	1862	.241	Nelson Norman

When Ozzie had 621 assists for San Diego in 1980, that also was a ground ball staff, but San Diego shortstops had 32.3% of the team assist total. When Ozzie had 549 assists for St. Louis in 1985, that was *not* a ground ball staff, and St. Louis shortstops had 31.9% of the St. Louis team assist total. When Cal Ripken broke Smalley's American League record with 583 assists in 1984, Baltimore shortstops had 30.5% of the team total. Smalley's contribution to his team, while good, was not in that neighborhood.

Assists totals are like RBI counts. A player gets lots of RBI if:

a) he plays a lot,

b) he hits with lots of men on base, and

c) he hits well.

A player gets lots of assists if:

a) he plays a lot,

b) he plays behind a ground ball staff, and

c) he has good range.

Smalley's assist total in 1979, like Joe Carter's RBI in 1997, are largely explained by (a) and (b), as opposed to (c).

In 1979 Smalley's adjusted range factor was 5.27, better than Belanger's (5.05) and better than the league average (5.01)—but still not as good as the Gold Glove winner, Rick Burleson (5.34), or New York's Bucky Dent (5.38).

The Twins defense in 1979 allowed 1,590 hits, almost leading the American League. They allowed *more than three hundred more hits* than Baltimore, 1590-1279. Naturally, if you have a team which allows that many hits, you're going to get some double plays. If you have a ground ball staff, you're going to get even more double plays.

The Win Shares system compares the team double play total to their expected double plays, based on their baserunners allowed and ground balls. The Twins in Smalley's years still come out as a good double play team. In 1977, when the league double play average was 153, the Twins had an expectation of 169, but actually turned 184. That makes them +15, which is good.

In 1978, when the American League average was again 153, the Twins had an expectation of 166, and actually turned 171, making them +5.

In 1979, when the average went up to 166, the Twins led the league in double plays, with 203. But they also have an expectation of 184. They're +19, which is good.

But Baltimore, in the same years, is +33, +12, and +23.

I still regard Smalley as a pretty good shortstop, a B- shortstop. But even in his mid-thirties, Mark Belanger was better.

The Snider/Mays Dilemma

One situation in which the Win Shares system makes an attribution which seems intuitively wrong, although I believe it is logical and appropriate, can be illustrated with respect to Duke Snider and Willie Mays, 1954. The two players' numbers are unusually well matched, for two players competing for the MVP Award: Mays hit .345 with 41 homers, 110 RBI, while Snider hit .341 with 40 homers, but drove in 130 runs. Mays played center field for the New York Giants, who won the pennant, while Snider played center for the Brooklyn Dodgers, who finished second. Mays won the MVP Award; Snider finished fourth in the voting, but *Sport* magazine, doing their periodic player ratings that fall, rated Snider as the best center fielder in the league. The players' numbers are well matched all down the line: 33 doubles vs. 39 (Mays listed first), 13 triples vs. 10, 8 stolen bases vs. 6, 119 runs scored vs. 120, 195 hits vs. 199, 12 GIDP apiece, etc. Snider has a few more walks (84-66), and Snider is estimated to have created one more run (140 to 139), but Mays made 16 fewer outs.

There is, however, an obvious difference: ballparks. Mays played in the Polo Grounds, an essentially neutral park with a slight tendency to favor the pitcher, while Snider played in Ebbets Field, which was a pretty good hitter's park.

When we factor this in, Mays moves a hair ahead of Snider, 104 marginal runs to 103. OK, no problem; the MVP has the highest Win Shares after all.

Well, not quite. Marginal Runs are not the end of the process. We move on from Marginal Runs to Wins. And in this particular case, the two teams have significantly different ratios of marginal runs to wins.

The Giants finished five games ahead of the Dodgers that year, 97 wins to 92. The problem is that, based on their runs scored and runs allowed, the Dodgers shouldn't even have been in the race. Based on runs scored and allowed, the Giants should have won 98 games. The Dodgers, who outscored their opponents by only 38 runs (778 to 740), could have been expected to win only 81. The Dodgers overachieved by a tremendous margin, +11 games. Thus, when we translate marginal runs into Win Shares, a run for the Dodgers means more than a run for the Giants, because there are more Wins resulting from each Run. The Dodger players have an advantage, because their runs count more. They *have* to count more, because they created more wins, one to one.

Now, this *seems* all wrong, because Mays' team won more games than Snider's team did. It seems counter-intuitive to give Snider an advantage for the wins of his team, when Mays' team won the pennant. It is not a small advantage, either; it is much, much larger than the park factor, in this particular case, and that pushes Snider back ahead in the MVP race, giving him 34.56 Win Shares (as a hitter) to Mays' 31.56. In your mental calculations of the MVP vote, you want to give a nod to Willie because his team won, while this system makes the opposite adjustment, based on something that you're not likely to focus on when you're trying to think through your MVP vote.

But while this seems intuitively wrong, it is logically inescapable. All of the team's Wins have to be explained by Runs. If we didn't attribute this advantage to the Dodger players, who would we attribute it to? The problem is, *the Dodger team in 1954 is better than their statistics*. If you just make APBA or Strat-O cards and replay the season, the Giants are going to win easy. The Dodgers on paper shouldn't have been able to hang with them—but they did. And that means that there is "hidden value" there somewhere. When Snider gets his share of the hidden loot, he winds up as the best hitter in the league that year.

But not the best *player*. Fortunately, there is one more adjustment to come: defense. Snider was an OK center fielder; Mays was a defensive wonder. When we add in the defense, Mays will move back ahead. This is a case where the MVP in the league was, as the Win Shares system sees it, actually the best player in the league. There are several other seasons in which Mays is evaluated by Win Shares as the best player in the league, but *didn't* win the MVP Award.

This is a peculiar situation, not something that happens very often. It is not very common for teams which only outscore their opposition by 38 runs to finish 30 games over .500. A parallel situation to the Mays/Snider dilemma is the comparison of Mike Piazza and Tony Gwynn, 1997. Although Gwynn and Piazza don't have closely matched statistics like Snider and Mays, they both had great seasons in the same league, Gwynn hitting .372 with 17 homers, 136 runs created, and Piazza hitting .362 with 40 homers, 137 runs created.

Both played in pitcher's parks, and they are dead even in terms of Marginal Runs, 105 each. Then the same thing happens as in Snider/Mays. Although Piazza's team won 88 games, while Gwynn's won only 76, the Dodgers actually under-achieved by 4.6 games, given their runs scored and runs allowed, while the Padres over-achieved by 4.2 games. That makes the runs-to-wins ratio markedly better on the Padres than on the Dodgers, which pushes Gwynn ahead of Piazza—until you get to defense. When you factor in defense, Piazza moves back to even.

Another case where this will come into play, but one in which it seems intuitively right, is the '69 Mets. That team outscored their opponents by only 91 runs (632-541), but won a hundred games because they won their close games. When we figure Win Shares, that will make all of the players on that team look better than you might expect them to. Ken Boswell, a part-time second baseman who hit .279 with 3 homers, 32 RBI in 362 at bats, winds up with 13 Win Shares—a decent total for a player with 562 at bats, outstanding for a player with 362. Cleon Jones, with good but hardly Ruthian numbers, snares 30 Win Shares.

But in that case, it seems OK, because after all, we know what this team accomplished. We all understand that this isn't the usual case. But in the Win Shares system, we follow the logic that whatever is accomplished by the team is credited to the players, wherever that leads us.

Klein and Yastrzemski

I thought it would be interesting to compare Chuck Klein, 1930, to Carl Yastrzemski, 1967. Our runs created method, in the *All-Time Major League Handbook* shows Klein with 171 runs created, 411 outs. It shows Yastrzemski with 148 runs created, 409 outs.

I picked these two players because they have vaguely similar stats, and tremendously impressive stats, at or near the far ends of the runs per game spectrum. Klein hit .386 with 40 homers, but in a league which hit .303 and scored 5.68 runs per team per game. Yaz won the Triple Crown, but in a league which hit .236 and scored only 3.70 runs per team per game.

I had never realized that these two players and teams had as much in common as they actually do. Although one of them had his season at the peak of a hitting era and the other near the center of a pitcher's era, both players played in hitter's parks. Although Yaz played for a championship team and Klein for a last-place team, both teams were somewhat inefficient in terms of wins versus expected wins, Philadelphia more seriously inefficient than Boston.

Carl Yastrzemski

And, although both played in hitter's parks, both teams were offensively oriented, even when you adjust for the park. Many teams which play in hitter's parks tend to have relatively poor offenses, and many teams which play in pitcher's parks tend to have relatively poor pitching but good offenses. Not these teams. Thus, although a couple of obvious things are very different, many of the adjustments that we make here will actually be parallel.

OK, Klein played in a league which scored an average of 5.68 runs/game, and played in a park which inflated runs scored by an average of 27.34% in the five-year period 1928 to 1932. A park inflation rate of 1.2734 in an eight-team league yields a park adjustment of 1.1172, which increases the contextual average for runs/game to 6.35, or 990 runs per season, since Philadelphia played 156 games.

This means that the Phillies offense, in 1930, produced 429 marginal runs, 429 runs more than 52% of the runs by an average team in that context. An average team would score 990; 52% of that is 515, the Phillies scored 944.

An average *player*, in that context, is expected to create 6.35 runs per 27 outs. 52% of that is 3.30, which is .122 per out. The 1930 stats don't account for quite all of the outs, which drives the runs/out up from .122 to .129, or 53 runs per 411 outs.

Klein created 171 runs. Thus, Klein contributed 118 marginal runs.

Yaz played in a league which scored an average of 3.70 runs/game, and played in a park which inflated runs scored by an average of 24.34% in the five-year period 1965 to 1969. A park inflation rate of 1.2434 in a ten-team league yields a park adjustment of 1.108, which increases the contextual average for runs/game to 4.10, or 664 runs per 162 games.

This means that the Red Sox offense, in 1967, produced 377 marginal runs, figured as 722 (their actual runs scored) minus 345 (52% of 664).

An average hitter, in that context, is expected to create 4.10 runs per 27 outs. 52% of that is 2.132 runs/27 outs, or .079 runs per out, which is 32 runs per 409 outs.

Yaz created 148 runs. Thus, Yaz contributed 116 marginal runs—two fewer than Klein.

In this analytical structure, Klein has two disadvantages—first, that the replacement level is higher, and second, that a marginal run has less value when expressed as a part of a win. In this system, the Phillies have 52 wins and 735 marginal runs, a ratio of 14.13 marginal runs per win. To the best of my knowledge, this is the highest win cost of the 20th century. The figure is driven higher by the fact that the team won only 52 games with runs scored and runs allowed totals that we would expect to yield 58 wins.

Anyway, that isn't exactly how we get to the answer in this system; there's a shorter method of getting there, without figuring marginal run value. The Phillies in 1930 won 52 games, which means that we are going to credit all of their players with 156 Win Shares. The team had 735 marginal runs, 432 of them on offense and 303 on defense. Including the decimals, this means that 58.8% of the team's success is attributable to their offense, 41.2% to the pitching and defense. (Without making park adjustments, we would have attributed 80% of their marginal runs to the offense.) 156 Win Shares times .5880 means that we are attributing 91.72 Win Shares to the offense, 64.28 to the pitching and defense.

The team has 432 marginal runs on offense. Klein, as we calculated earlier, has 118 marginal runs on offense. This means that Klein receives credit for 27% of the team's marginal runs on offense. And 27% of 91.72 is 25.04. Thus, Chuck Klein in 1930 claims 25.04 Win Shares as a hitter.

Except that, because of sub-marginal performance by some hitters, it doesn't work out precisely that way when the team is figured as a series of individuals. . . Klein winds up with 24.09 Win Shares, actually. I should explain better, I guess. I stated that the 1930 Phillies had 432 marginal runs created by hitters. This is what the figure would be if there were no sub-marginal hitters on the team. However, since there are some sub-marginal hitters in the mix, the number of "background runs" removed by ignoring the runs created up to the margin is less than we have allowed for—thus, the pot of runs created to be divided into Win Shares is larger than we have allowed for, and thus, Klein's Win Shares, as a hitter, are 24.09, rather than 25.03.

The 1967 Red Sox had 772 marginal runs, 379 on offense and 393 on defense. This means that 49.0% of the team's success is attributable to their offense.

The Red Sox in 1967 won 92 games, which creates 276 Win Shares for their players. 49.0% of those go to hitters, which means that all of the Red Sox hitters have a total of 135.67 Win Shares in 1967.

The team had 379 marginal runs on offense. Yaz, as we calculated earlier, has 116 marginal runs on offense. This means that Yaz receives the credit for 30.6% of the team's marginal runs on offense (116 divided by 379). 30.6% of 135.67 is 41.45.

Except that, because of the marginal/sub-marginal runs glitch, this figure, again, is not exactly right. The actual figure is 38.18. Carl Yastzemski in 1967 has a value of 38.18 Win Shares, plus defense.

Thus, Yastrzemski's season in 1967 is worth about 60% more than Klein's in 1930, 38.18 vs. 24.09.

Klein's season is still outstanding. Including defense, we have Klein with 28 Win Shares for 1930. There are a lot of guys who have won MVP Awards with less. It isn't his best season. Klein also won a Triple Crown, in 1933; that earns him 30 Win Shares, and that isn't his best season, either. His best season was 1932, when he is credited with 31 Win Shares, and was voted the MVP. Yastrzemski including defense is credited with 42 Win Shares—easily the best total in the American League in 1967, and an outstanding season even for an MVP.

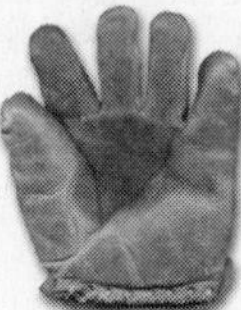

Tresh and Delahanty

Ed Delahanty in 1894 hit .407, driving in 131 runs and scoring 147 runs in just 114 games. Tom Tresh in 1966 hit just .233, driving in 68 runs in 151 games. While both men were basically outfielders, both played some third base that season.

Who was more valuable, in context, Tresh in 1966 or Delahanty in 1894? Being the astute reader that you are, you have smelled a rat by now, and you suspect that I am about to argue that Tresh in 1966 was more valuable, despite his .233 average, than Ed Delahanty, hitting .407. Actually, I am not. I am going to argue that their value was the same.

How can this be? Four things to remember—secondary offense, league context, park context and defense.

1. *Batting Average is not all of offense.* Tresh in 1966 hit .233, but had 27 homers and drew 86 walks, giving him a secondary average of .358. Delahanty also had good secondary offensive skills—he hit 39 doubles and 18 triples, drew 60 walks and stole 21 bases—but his secondary average, .344, was not as good as Tresh's. That narrows the gap between them, although Delahanty did create 144 runs, while Tresh created "only" 82. 82 runs created is a damn good total for 1966.

2. *1894 is not 1966.* The National League batting average in 1894 was .309, and the league averaged 7.36 runs per game. The American League batting average in 1966 was .240, and the league averaged 3.89 runs per game.

Delahanty, creating 144 runs, accounted for all of the runs a team would normally score in slightly less than 20 games. Tresh created 82 runs, accounting for all of the runs a team would normally score in 21 games, although, since Tresh made far more batting outs than Delahanty, Big Ed actually is still ahead at this point of the analysis.

3. *Yankee Stadium was not the Philadelphia Baseball Grounds.* Yankee Stadium in 1966 was the second-worst park for a hitter in the American League, which means that the 82 runs created by Tresh have even more impact. The Philadelphia Baseball Grounds were also somewhat pitcher-friendly, but still, the top four outfielders on the Phillies that year all hit .400. Sliding Billy Hamilton scored 192 runs in 129 games, while Sam Thompson, Delahanty and fourth outfielder Tuck Turner all drove in *and scored* more than one run per game—yet the Phillies still finished fourth. Isn't that pretty compelling evidence that this was a set of conditions in which runs were cheap?

4. *Tresh was playing center field and third base.* We credit Delahanty in 1894 with 2.44 Win Shares for his defense, which is a very good total for a left fielder playing 88 games (plus some games at first base and a few at third). But Tresh, playing 64 games at third base that season and playing center field sometimes when not in the infield, is credited with 4.73.

Adding it all up, I have Delahanty in 1894 with 22 Win Shares—and Tresh with 22.

Trying not to be misunderstood, Delahanty over the course of his career was a far better player than Tresh. Tresh had five seasons over 20 Win Shares, and a peak of 29 (1963). Delahanty had ten seasons over 20 Win Shares, five seasons over 30 Win Shares, and a peak of 41 (1899). In raw Win Shares, Delahanty ranks even with Dan Brouthers and Goose Goslin. Tresh rates even with Dave Henderson, Dutch (Emil) Leonard, Cecil Fielder, Clete Boyer, Fred Luderus, Buck Freeman, Jorge Orta, Mike Garcia, Gene Garber and Jack Coombs. But those guys were good players, and Tresh was a good player, and I just thought it was an interesting comparison.

Steve and Milt versus the Dodger Dons

Sometimes what you would assume to be true may not be, and then, sometimes it may be. In 1984, when Don Drysdale was selected to the Hall of Fame, Modest Milt Pappas pointed out that many of *his* career statistics were nearly the same as Drysdale's. Drysdale won 209 games in his career, lost 166, while Pappas won 209 and lost 164. Pappas pitched 43 shutouts in his career—only six fewer than Drysdale—and nearly matched him in many career categories.

Even closer is the career match between another Dodger Don, Don Sutton, and Steve Carlton. Sutton's career won-lost mark was 324-256; Carlton's, 329-244. Sutton pitched 1% more innings than Carlton with basically the same ERA, 3.26 to 3.22.

Nonetheless, few people ever thought of Sutton as comparable to Steve Carlton, and nobody but Modest Milt himself ever compared Pappas to Drysdale. Drysdale started at 21% in Hall of Fame voting, and went on to win election in his tenth year on the ballot, while Pappas peaked in the polls at one percent. Carlton got 96% of the vote his first year on the ballot; Sutton had to go back for a few more tries before being elected in 1998.

Hall of Fame voters aren't *always* right, but in this case, at least according to the Win Shares system, they were on to something. Pappas had 209 career wins, but 211 Win Shares—a normal ratio. Drysdale had 209 wins, but 258 Win Shares, an unusual ratio.

Sutton and Carlton, same thing. Sutton had 324 wins but 318 Win Shares, a fairly normal ratio. Carlton had 329 wins but 370 Win Shares, an unusual ratio.

As the Win Shares system sees it, Pappas and Sutton are fairly represented by their career win totals. Sutton won 300+ games, and deserved about as many. Pappas won 209 games, which is about what he deserved. Drysdale and Carlton were exceptional players who dragged their teams to victory, and could have won more than they did.

In another book, I argued that Don Drysdale did *not* deserve Hall of Fame selection. I'll stick with that conclusion, I guess; 258 Win Shares is pretty marginal for a Hall of Famer. Drysdale rates even with Jim Bottomley and Joe Tinker, who were Hall of Famers, but also with Larry Gardner, Bucky Walters, Gus Weyhing, Buddy Myer and Rick Monday, who were not. Still, if Don Drysdale was not Walter Johnson, neither was he Milt Pappas. Give the Hall of Fame voters some credit. Even when the bottom lines looked almost the same, they knew the difference between brass and gold.

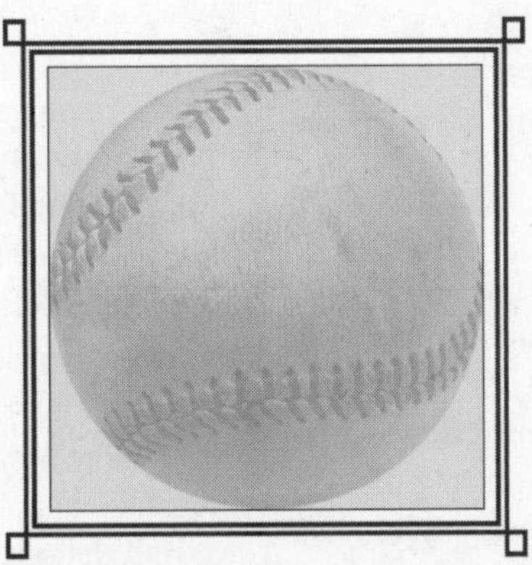

Biases in MVP Voting

Is there a bias, in MVP voting, for players who play on New York teams? Many sportswriters assume that there is, and will state blankly that there is such a bias.

In fact, it is relatively obvious that there is no such bias. This can be pointed up by two simple facts:

1. No member of the New York Mets has ever won the MVP Award, and

2. Since the MVP Award began, perhaps the best player who never won it is Mel Ott.

Mel Ott, or Eddie Mathews. Also, I have studied the issue before, in other ways, and found no bias, but I bring it up here, because this is a relatively simple issue, and I wanted to use a simple issue to explain how Win Shares can be used to examine biases in MVP voting.

From 1931 through 2000 there have been 43 major league players who have been credited with 40 or more Win Shares in a season. Twenty of those 43, or 47%, have won the MVP Award.

In the same period there have been 78 players who have been credited with 37 to 39 Win Shares in a season. Twenty-one of those 78, or 27%, have won the MVP Award.

Picking up the data from there in chart form produces the following figures:

	Players	MVPs	Pct
Group 1 (40 or more Win Shares)	43	20	47%
Group 2 (37 to 39 Win Shares)	78	21	27%
Group 3 (34 to 36 Win Shares)	125	24	19%
Group 4 (32 or 33 Win Shares)	161	21	13%
Group 5 (30 or 31 Win Shares)	201	17	8%

From this, we can estimate with a fair degree of confidence that players who earn 28 or 29 Win Shares probably have a 6% chance of winning the MVP Award, and players who earn 26 or 27 Win Shares probably have a 4% chance of winning the award, not that it matters to us one way or another. 26% of MVP Awards have been won by players earning less than 30 Win Shares, but there are an awful lot of players who earn less than 30 Win Shares. Including them in the study would have made the study 50% better but 5,000% more difficult and more time-consuming to run, and so we didn't.

Given this base of information, and given a population of players having seasons of 30 or more Win Shares, we can figure how many Most Valuable Player Awards can be expected from that population. We could also figure them, of course, by simply looking at the best player in each league each year, and assuming that the best player "should" win the MVP Award. . . there wouldn't be anything clearly wrong with doing it that way, either. But that would be looking for a "particular" bias against a particular player in a particular season. Here we are looking at generalized groups. . . within this group of players, is there evidence of bias *somewhere*?

We'll start with New York players, first dividing the world into New Yorkers and Rubes. Since 1931 there have been 25 New York players who have earned 30 or 31 Win Shares in a season. We would expect 2.1 MVP Awards in that population of players. In fact, four of these players won MVP Awards—Joe Gordon in 1942, Joe DiMaggio in 1947, Yogi Berra in 1951, and Roger Maris in 1960.

If this were all the data there were, we would have to conclude that there might be a New York bias in the voting, since the New Yorkers won more MVP Awards than we would expect. However, taking *all* of the data, New Yorkers in fact have won *fewer* MVP Awards than we would expect, three fewer (19 vs. 22.0). Among players in Group 2, 36 to 39 Win Shares, only 2 of 22 New York players won the MVP Award, both of those in 1936 (Gehrig and Hubbell). Among Rubes having similar seasons, more than a third won MVP Awards (19 of 56).

We also need to look at these things by era, because things change. . . the number of players with 40 or more Win Shares has decreased slightly over time, for example. When we study the patterns by eras, we find that in what we call the second era of MVP voting (1947-1963), New Yorkers won markedly more MVP Awards than we would have expected based on their performance, 12 to 8.0. However, in the other three eras, New York players won *fewer* MVP Awards than expected—6 vs. 6.9 in the years 1931-1946, none vs. 1.6 in the years 1964-1980, and 1 vs. 3.0 in the years 1981-2000. Either way you figure their expectation—by individual eras or by the group norms—they fail to meet expectations. New York players do not have an advantage in MVP voting.

The second thing we'll look at here is race, because, again, it's a pretty simple issue, and also because race *always* comes up quickly when you are looking for evidence of bias. Henry Aaron, in explaining the fact that he won only one MVP Award, is prone to cite racial bias in 1950s sportswriters as the cause of this. This argument could hardly be more silly. Look at the people who won the Most Valuable Player Award in Aaron's first nine years in the National League: Willie Mays in 1954, Roy Campanella in 1955, Don Newcombe in '56, Aaron in '57, Ernie Banks in '58 and '59, Dick Groat in '60, Frank Robinson in '61, Willie Mays in '62. This is racial bias, one white guy in nine years?

In that era (1947-1963; we dated the era from Jackie Robinson to the passage of the landmark Civil Rights Act), black players did *better* in MVP voting than white players of the same quality. Since 1964, black players *have* done slightly worse in MVP voting than comparable white players, but not by a margin large enough to draw any conclusion, but overall, black players (with 30 or more Win Shares) have won 30 MVP Awards, against an expectation of 31.5.

Suppose you compare that data with the data for a *real* bias. We compared the data for players on championship teams with the data for players on non-championship teams. (For recent seasons, we considered any team which reached post-season play to have won some sort of a championship.)

Of the 608 players with 30 or more Win Shares 1931-2000, 215 played for teams which won some sort of pennant, whereas 393 played for other teams. These two groups were not equal in quality; those who played for championship teams were also better players, and thus those 215 had an expectation of winning 38.8 MVP Awards, whereas the "others" had an expectation of winning 64.3, a slightly lower percentage.

However, the players on pennant-winning teams won over two-thirds of the MVP Awards in the group, 70 of 103. Here it is in chart form:

	Players	MVPs	Expected	Pct
On Pennant-Winning Teams	215	70	38.8	180%
Not	393	33	64.3	51%

A player on a pennant-winning team is 3.51 times as likely (251% more likely) to win the MVP Award than the same player playing on a non-championship team.

How about a team which plays well, has a surprisingly good season, but doesn't win the pennant? Here the data was a surprise to me. I had always been under the impression that players who played on teams which did surprisingly well had almost as much of an edge in MVP voting as players who played on championship teams. This turns out to be untrue.

I defined "teams which did surprisingly well" as "all teams which won at least 10 games more than they had won in either of the two previous seasons." I made no adjustment for strike seasons, and counted the "previous years" for expansion teams as 70 wins. There were 172 such teams from 1931 through the year 2000—about two per year before expansion, about three per year now.

Of the 608 star players in our study, 97 played on teams which had surprisingly good seasons, by our definition. Of those 97, 28 won the MVP Award, against an expectation of 17.6 awards. This is the data:

	Players	MVPs	Expected	Pct
On Surprise Teams	97	28	17.6	159%
Not	511	75	85.4	88%

Thus, a player on a "surprise" team was 81% more likely to win an MVP Award than a player not on a surprise team—a significant edge.

However, most of that edge is created by the fact that surprise teams also tended to be pennant-winning teams. Most of the 81% edge for players on surprise teams is simply derived from the fact that winning ten games more than either of the previous two seasons often makes a team a pennant-winner. Although playing for a team which exceeds expectations certainly *is* a factor in MVP calculations, it is nowhere near as large a factor as I had always believed it to be.

Sticking with the "surprise season" theme, I have long noted that players who have their *first* outstanding season are more likely to win an MVP Award than equally good players who have been performing at that level for years. Whatever is moving attracts the eye; a player who plays well every year is not a moving object. Steve Garvey won an MVP award when he had his first outstanding season in 1974. For years after that, Garvey posted almost identical statistics every season—yet never again was he the MVP. Why not? When Dale Murphy hit .281 with 36 homers in 1982 and had similar numbers in '83, he was the MVP both years—but when he posted almost the exact same numbers in '84 and '85, he dropped down the list. By 1987, when he hit .295 with 44 homers, he had dropped out of the top 10 in MVP voting. When Barry Bonds hit .301 with 33 homers in '90, he was the MVP, but then, we didn't really know him yet.

When Sandy Koufax went 25-5 with a 1.88 ERA in 1963 to lead the Dodgers to the pennant, he won the MVP award—but when he had essentially the same season again in 1965 and again in 1966 (actually, he was even a little bit better), leading the Dodgers to two more pennants, he didn't win either award. When Willie Mays had his *first* great season in 1954, he won the MVP award—but then, although he was equally great in '55, in '58 and in '62, he didn't win again until 1965, when he was even better. When Henry Aaron hit .320 with 44 homers the *first* time, in 1957, he won the MVP Award, but he never won another one, although he had five other seasons as good or better (and incidentally almost identical). When Frank Robinson had his first truly great season in '61 he won the award—but then, when he was even better the next season, he didn't win.

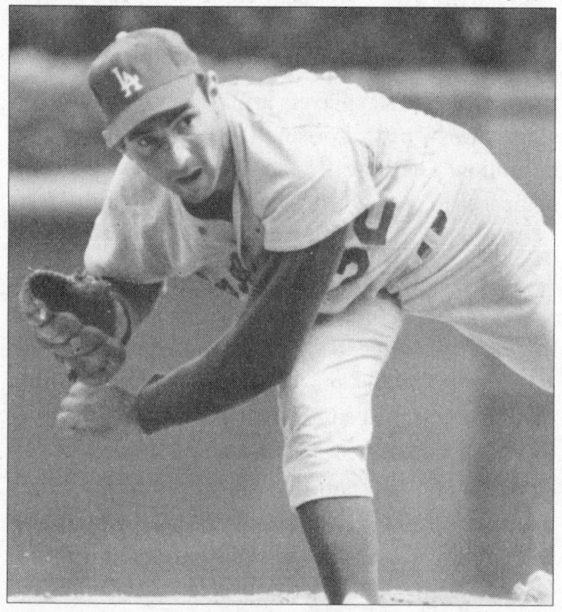

Sandy Koufax

The 2000-2001 AL MVP races reflect this. Ichiro Suzuki wasn't actually the *best* American League player in 2001. Suzuki was great, but Roberto Alomar, Alex Rodriguez and Jason Giambi were every bit as good, maybe a little better. Why did Suzuki win the award?

Because Suzuki was news. The other guys had done this before; they were great, but they weren't news. Giambi was as great in 2001 as he had been in 2000, when he was the MVP. His team won 11 games more in 2001 than they had won in 2000. If he was the MVP in 2000, why wasn't he the MVP in '01?

In every case there are different factors and there is different competition, of course, but I thought it would be fun to compare the performance in MVP voting of players who had their *first* 30-Win Share season with equally qualified players who had had a previous season of that quality. This is the data:

	Players	MVPs	Expected	Pct
First 30-Win Share season	260	47	40.05	117%
Previous 30	348	56	62.95	89%

A player is 32% more likely to win an MVP award having his *first* outstanding season, as opposed to a player having an equally good season with a history of success. I had expected the bias to be larger.

Of course, we haven't *exactly* measured the effect we were trying to focus on here. What I'm trying to assert is that a player's chance of winning an MVP improves substantially when he reaches a new level of success in his career. Jason Giambi in 2000 (his MVP season) had actually had a previous 30-Win

Share season (1999), so he counts in the "previous 30" category above, even though he is really an example of what I'm talking about. Barry Bonds—same thing. Of course, Bonds has been reaching the 30-Win Share standard regularly for years, and he could have won the MVP award in '96, '97, '98 or 2000—but he got back to the MVP stand in 2001 only because he had a season that was *better* than his previous bests.

There are a million studies like this that one could do. . . for example, comparing players who drive in runs with equally good players who are not RBI men, or comparing players who play shortstop with equally good players who play the outfield. There are a million studies like this that one could do, and actually, I have half-done about 40 of them, intending to write them up and report them at this spot in the book. I've run out of time, however; it's time to send this book to the publisher. I'll get back to you.

The Greatest Offense/Defense Seasons

What are the greatest combined offensive and defensive seasons of all time? What I am looking for here is not the greatest seasons, combining offensive and defensive value—that's what we do all the time—but rather, the greatest seasons in the sense of combining both tremendous offense and tremendous defense?

I constructed this list by simply multiplying each player's offensive Win Shares in each season by his fielding Win Shares in each season. The greatest seasons ever, it turns out, are from the dead-ball era:

Player	Year	Hitting	Fielding	Product
1. Honus Wagner	1908	49.21	9.74	479.31
2. Tris Speaker	1912	41.57	9.90	411.54
3. Honus Wagner	1906	34.20	11.32	387.14
4. Honus Wagner	1905	36.75	9.60	352.80
5. Tris Speaker	1914	36.48	8.90	324.67
6. Honus Wagner	1909	33.07	9.38	310.20
7. Babe Ruth	1923	48.48	6.23	302.03
8. Willie Mays	1965	34.99	8.11	283.77
9. Hughie Jennings	1896	23.53	11.99	282.12
10. Joe Morgan	1975	36.24	7.76	281.22

Numbers 11 and 12 will be two more Honus Wagner seasons, leaving us to ask: do we really believe this?

I do, at least. In that era, without many strikeouts and without many home runs, games were decided by fielders to a greater extent than they have been since 1920. Also, with few slow-moving sluggers in the game, many of the greatest hitters tended also to be the greatest fielders. I think it is likely that Wagner and Speaker *were* the greatest offense/defense packages in the history of the game.

Picking up from there, I am going to list the seasons but not the numbers, since I don't think you're all going to be studying those anyway:

11. Honus Wagner	1907
12. Honus Wagner	1912
13. Willie Mays	1954
14. Eddie Collins	1910
15. Ryne Sandberg	1984
16. Joe Cronin	1931
17. Luke Appling	1943
18. Eddie Collins	1909
19. Phil Rizzuto	1950
20. Ty Cobb	1915

It occurs to me, following up on the theme of the previous article, that this odd way of combining offensive and defensive value, which essentially pretends that fielding is as important as hitting, would probably be a pretty good predictor of the MVP Award. Most of this list is of players before the modern MVP Awards, but there are five players on this list since 1950—all five of them MVPs. The highest-rated post-1950 player who didn't win the MVP award was Cal Ripken, 1984, who didn't win the award in part because he had won it the previous year:

21. Cal Ripken 1984
22. Jackie Robinson 1951
23. Arky Vaughan 1937
24. Eddie Collins 1920
25. Mike Schmidt 1974
26. Cal Ripken 1983
27. Bill Freehan 1968
28. Frankie Frisch 1927
29. Rico Petrocelli 1969
30. Nap Lajoie 1910

31. Ty Cobb 1911
32. Eddie Collins 1915
33. Johnny Pesky 1946
34. Joe Cronin 1930
35. Gary Carter 1985
36. Joe Tinker 1908
37. Art Devlin 1906
38. Joe Cronin 1933
39. Babe Ruth 1921
40. Snuffy Stirnweiss 1944

Cal Ripken

Or not. . . we seem to be losing the "MVP effect" here. This is the list I was trying to get here—an eccentric list of great seasons that nobody thinks about as great seasons, because they combine real good offense with real good defense, rather than combining real good offense with even more real good offense. Freehan, Petrocelli, Art Devlin, Johnny Pesky, Snuffy Stirnweiss. . . those kind of guys. Then we have some more MVP types:

41. Johnny Bench 1970
42. Joe Morgan 1973
43. Mickey Mantle 1955
44. Tris Speaker 1915
45. Mickey Mantle 1957
46. Ozzie Smith 1987
47. Ryne Sandberg 1991
48. Bill Dickey 1937
49. Eddie Joost 1949
50. Craig Biggio 1997

Everybody on our list played an "up the middle" defensive position except Babe Ruth, 1921 and 1923, Mike Schmidt, 1974, and Art Devlin, 1906 (a third baseman).

(Late note: Jim Henzler informs me that Alex Rodriguez' 2000 season should have made the list of the top 50 seasons. I am sure he is correct. . . sorry, Alex. My error.)

Aging Patterns Among Great Players

Win Shares, of course, could be used to study aging patterns among groups of players at any length one wished to study the issue (unlike "center-based" value systems, which cannot be used to study aging at all, because they simply show that the average player at every age is about average). Anyway, I'm just going to stick my toe into that area here, studying aging patterns among the greatest players in baseball history.

Of course, in some respects studying aging patterns among great players may give you atypical answers, because great players in certain respects are not typical. For example, one-fourth of the players in this study were still active at age 41. Well, obviously this is not a typical figure; the proportion of major league players who are still active at 41 isn't one in 40, let alone one in four. The ratio is different because these players are so good that, as they lose ability, they are able to remain in the major leagues. Typical players, as soon as they lose a couple of steps along the road to first base, are released, which I think means, as best as I understand these things, that they are put on a train to Idaho, where they are secretly executed. 99% of players are released; these are the guys who "retire."

But in other respects—in fact, in *most* respects—great players are actually the *best* players to study for aging patterns, because *great players are the only players who have "clean" careers with a full opportunity*. Studying aging in baseball players is a complicated, messy business, because, for one thing, the cast of characters changes so much. If you study all 23-year-old major league players and then you study all 33-year-old major league players, you'll find that you are looking at different groups of men. Most of the guys who play in the majors at 23 are gone long before age 33, and many or most of the players who are in the majors at 33 weren't there when they were 23. Controlling for this constantly shifting cast of characters, depending on exactly what questions you are asking and what you are trying to find out, is often a nightmarish problem.

With great players, you don't have that problem; great players get to the majors early, and they stay late. Great players don't have their careers run off-track by injuries a whole lot; if they did, they wouldn't have been great players. In many ways, if you want a "clean" study of aging patterns among baseball players, the *only* guys you can really study are the great players.

Anyway, I created a database of the year-by-year Win Shares of:

a) all players in major league history,

b) who earned 280 Win Shares or more,

c) but who earned less than 10 Win Shares as pitchers, and

d) who were not active in 2001.

In other words, I got rid of active players and pitchers, including guys like Babe Ruth who were partially pitchers. George Sisler, however, did make the group, because he had only 8.33 Win Shares as a pitcher.

This gave me a group of 148 players, who ranged in value from Ty Cobb at the top to Ron Cey, Fred Lynn, Bert Campaneris and Earl Averill at the bottom.

I guess, to start with, I'll present the total Win Shares of the group, by age:

Group	# in Majors	Win Shares	Relative to Peak
Age 17	1	2	0%
Age 18	9	18	0%
Age 19	27	126	3%
Age 20	62	590	16%
Age 21	101	1390	37%
Age 22	129	2179	58%
Age 23	139	2925	77%
Age 24	141	3227	85%
Age 25	141	3575	94%
Age 26	144	3784	100%
Age 27	145	3741	99%
Age 28	146	3675	97%
Age 29	145	3567	94%
Age 30	145	3635	96%
Age 31	146	3523	93%

Group	# in Majors	Win Shares	Relative to Peak
Age 32	145	3394	90%
Age 33	146	3089	82%
Age 34	142	2723	72%
Age 35	137	2453	65%
Age 36	126	2071	55%
Age 37	107	1411	37%
Age 38	85	966	26%
Age 39	69	690	18%
Age 40	49	468	12%
Age 41	35	292	8%
Age 42	18	131	3%
Age 43	10	43	1%
Age 44	4	29	1%
Age 45	2	3	0%
Age 46	1	0	0%

After that we wander off into Minnie Minoso land, where you get occasional data points, but they're just a damn nuisance. The youngest player to have value, in this study, was Mel Ott; the oldest was Pete Rose. (Cap Anson has been excluded from the study somehow... not sure how. I probably cut him because he played several years in other leagues before the National League was re-organized in 1876.)

The average value of an active player in this group was 10 Win Shares at age 20, actually just south of 10. This figure increases to 20 (actually, 21) at age 23, reaches a peak of 26 at ages 26 and 27, drops back below 20 at age 34, and is back to ten at age 39.

I tried to develop a simple formula to predict changes in value among a group of players as the players age. The best formula that I could come up with, granting that what seems like a simple formula to me might not seem like a simple formula to everybody, was this:

The average value of a group of players
we'll call V
Their age this year we will call A
Their age next year we will call A+1
Their expected value next year we will call XV

The formula, then, is:

XV (A+1) = V * (54.2/(A+27)) * (A+1)/A

In other words, suppose that you have a group of players who are 33 years old and whose average value is 20 Win Shares. What would you expect their average value to be at age 34?

That would be:

20 * (54.2/61) * 34/33

Which would be 18.3. We would expect the average value of this group of players to be about 18.3 at age 34, 16.5 at age 35, and 14.6 at age 36. I'm sure there are better "aging formulas" that can be written, but that's just what I could come up with, working on it for a couple of hours.

In this group of players, the total Win Shares were slightly higher at age 26 than at age 27, an unexpected result, but the group is too small to draw any conclusion from that. The number of players having their best seasons, however, did peak at age 27:

Number of Players Having Their Best Years

Group	At this Age	By this Age
Age 20	1	1
Age 21	3	4
Age 22	4	8
Age 23	3	11
Age 24	13	24
Age 25	14	38
Age 26	16	54
Age 27	20	74
Age 28	19	93
Age 29	8	101
Age 30	10	111
Age 31	12	123
Age 32	9	132
Age 33	4	136
Age 34	3	139
Age 35	3	142
Age 36	5	147
Age 37	1	148

Summarizing that data in groups, we get the following results:

Up to 24	24 players having their best seasons
Ages 25-29	77 players having their best seasons
Ages 30-34	38 players having their best seasons
Ages 35 and up	9 players having their best seasons

Sixty percent of players had their best seasons between the ages of 25 and 30, and exactly 50% of the great players had their best season by age 27. Almost 90% of players had their best season by age 32.

The one great player who had his best season at age 20 was Al Kaline, while Joe Jackson, Cesar Cedeno and Eddie Mathews had their best seasons at 21. The player whose value peaked (I wouldn't say he had his best season) at age 37 was Indian Bob Johnson, while Fred Clarke, Zack Wheat, Luke Appling, Jake Beckley and Fielder Jones had peak value at age 36. Almost all of the players who had their best seasons as old men are weird-data cases, in which the players didn't post numbers as good as they had earlier, but the league offensive levels contracted so rapidly that the player's win contribution actually increased, even though his numbers decreased. Zack Wheat, of course, was the opposite.

The average career value of players who peaked young is higher than the average career value of players who peaked later. The 24 players who had their best season by age 24 had an average career value of 375 Win Shares, as opposed to 366 for those whose peak seasons were at age 25-29, and 353 for those whose peak seasons were at or after 30.

This fits in with a theory I have, which is that it *might* be true that players would peak earlier and higher if they reached the majors younger. Since it is probably impossible to learn to play major league baseball at the optimal level while playing against minor league competition, and since young players are more receptive and more adaptable than older players, it would seem to follow that, if you got capable players to the majors earlier, they might reach higher performance peaks. I believe that to be true, but I am also mindful that:

a) there are negative effects to putting immature players in the major leagues, and

b) there are practical obstacles to advancing players too rapidly, in that in many cases it simply takes time to evaluate and sort through the candidates.

Another question I was interested in was whether *defensive* value—fielding Value—would deteriorate more rapidly than hitting performance. Intuitively, one would expect that it would. There are a lot of guys in their mid-thirties who can still hit, but who are no longer able to play the field as they once could.

The answer is that defensive value *does* peak earlier than hitting value, and defensive value does account for a larger percentage of the player's value when he is young than when he is older, but that the difference is not as large as I would have expected. In this study, players up to age 24 accounted for 19.5% of their total value as fielders, while players ages 35 and up accounted for 17% of theirs (as shown in the chart at the bottom of the page).

A common theory is that aging patterns of ballplayers have changed in recent years, due to strength training and the immense popularity of the Jane Fonda workout tapes. That may well be true, that there has been a change in aging patterns in recent years, but it is beyond the scope of the present study. There's just no way to get at that with this data file.

Another thing I was very interested in is the relationship between a player's peak season and his career expectation. In other words, if you have a player whose best season is 30 Win Shares, what would you expect his career value to be? There has to be some sort of predictable relationship there, and I'd like to know what it is.

This data file proved unsuitable for examining that question in depth, although useful for the very top-end players. The formula is something like this. . . take the player's Win Shares in his peak season, and reduce that number to the power .45. Multiply that by two, and then multiply that by the player's peak season. The outcome will be the player's expected career Win Shares.

Suppose that a player's best season is 40 Win Shares. Forty to the power .45 is 5.26, so we double that (10.52) and multiply that by 40. Thus, we expect him to earn about 421 Win Shares in his career.

Up to age 24	Hitting:	8408 Shares	Fielding:	2042 Shares	.195
Ages 25-29	Hitting:	15108 Shares	Fielding:	3208 Shares	.175
Ages 30-34	Hitting:	13511 Shares	Fielding:	2827 Shares	.173
Ages 35 up	Hitting:	7101 Shares	Fielding:	1444 Shares	.169

In chart form:

Peak Season	Expected Career Win Shares
40	421
35	347
30	277
25	213
20	154
15	101
10	56
5	21
4	15
3	10
2	5
1	2

As a player's peak gets higher, his career tends to get longer. The actual chart would be similar to that above, but I can't exactly tell with this database, because this data file only includes players with 280 or more Win Shares, which distorts the data base. There are players in our data (Chili Davis and Luis Aparicio) whose best season is 22 Win Shares, but if your best season is 22 Win Shares, the only way you can qualify for this data set is to have a very long career.

Defensive Contexts for Other Players

Earlier in the book, you will remember, I created a "career defensive context record" for Bill Mazeroski and for Willie Randolph. This work was done about four months ago, and since then I have come to think of it as a happy accident, and to believe that it might be very useful to have defensive context records like that for more players. It's not all that much work to create a defensive context record, and so, I thought, why don't we do a few more of those?

I decided to create defensive context records for Frank White, Glenn Hubbard, Chuck Hiller, Jeff Treadway, Tim Flannery, Paul Molitor and Dave Nelson. Frank White seemed like an obvious choice in that, reading the Mazeroski/Randolph article, I didn't understand why I hadn't included him in that discussion. Hubbard was an obvious choice, because he has unusual defensive records, with very high range numbers, and I have always wondered whether there might be some sort of subtle illusion of context operating there. The other five guys were included to represent a sort of "standard of normalcy" for second basemen. White, Mazeroski, Randolph. . . these guys are not your everyday second basemen. Comparing them one to another with no idea what the record of an "ordinary" second baseman would look like is sort of like evaluating a blind date by asking your buddy, "Is she better looking than Carmen Electra?" There is no such thing as an average defensive second baseman who plays 18,000 innings at second base, so I thought I would do some short-career guys, 3500 to 4500 innings, as a basis for comparison.

I created these records by the same method explained before. OK, at the top of the following pagge is the first part of the data, the "pitching context" records:

Player	Innings	BFP	Hits	TBB	IBB	HR	SO	HBP	WP	Bk	SH	SF
Randolph	18648	78560	18036	6263	412	1631	11201	320	547	104	748	629
Mazeroski	18301	77160	17939	5997	912	1443	10700	376	514	51	93	478
White	17853	71238	17667	5963	479	1478	9531	378	529	91	668	626
Hubbard	11195	47912	11188	4205	437	988	6458	215	326	106	590	339
Hiller	4273	18158	4103	1454	154	416	2644	85	122	21	202	93
Treadway	4103	17417	3987	1448	161	349	2699	71	145	52	228	130
Flannery	3955	16761	3798	1442	166	374	2201	71	114	16	209	111
Nelson	3637	15603	3524	1437	121	307	2234	106	131	10	132	140
Molitor	3517	14974	3712	1015	75	335	1549	70	99	12	119	134

The second part of this context record is the team fielding context record, combined with the player's own fielding statistics:

	Team Context				Individual Fielder					
Player	PO	A	PB	A/9	Games	PO	A	E	DP	FPct
Randolph	55946	22281	169	10.75	2152	4858	6336	234	1547	.9795
Mazeroski	54860	23743	194	11.68	2094	4974	6685	204	1706	.9828
White	53557	22080	141	11.13	2150	4739	6246	178	1381	.9841
Hubbard	33587	14720	97	11.83	1332	2795	4444	127	975	.9828
Hiller	12828	5013	40	10.56	546	1102	1349	84	296	.9669
Treadway	12309	4970	39	10.90	556	1014	1382	61	290	.9752
Flannery	11864	4835	31	11.00	544	1046	1287	42	268	.9823
Nelson	10905	4334	28	10.72	466	1016	1151	53	278	.9761
Molitor	10553	4570	20	11.69	400	926	1274	48	279	.9786

All I'm doing so far is just reporting records, and all of this is really just a big pile of numbers. But to direct your attention to one number, we will note that the Assists per nine innings for Glenn Hubbard's teams are higher than those for any other second baseman under scrutiny—a fact which contributes to the remarkable defensive evaluations of Hubbard which we have all seen.

Now, at this point we know that Willie Randolph recorded 4,858 putouts in his career, and we have estimated that his team recorded 55,946 putouts while he was in the field—an estimate which, in my opinion, rests on very solid ground. There simply isn't any way that the actual data *could* be very much different from that. It is, then, a simple and non-speculative step to divide the one by the other, and conclude that Willie Randolph accounted for 8.7% of his team's putouts while he was in the field—4,858, divided by 55,946.

However, we also know (or have estimated reliably) how many strikeouts there were while Randolph was in the field—plays on which a second baseman cannot ordinarily record a putout. So it's a fairly simple matter to take the strikeouts out of the equation—4,858, divided by (55,946 minus 11,201). Not counting strikeouts, Randolph accounted for about 10.9% of his team's putouts while he was at second base.

There is one other non-speculative calculation that we can make at the same time, which has to do with his assists. Randolph was credited with 6,336 assists in his career. It is likely that his teams recorded about 22,281 assists while he was at second base. Thus, it is a small and relatively safe step to conclude that Randolph accounted for about 28.4% of his team's assists while he was in the field:

Player	Pct TPO	Pct PO/No K	Pct Tm Assists
Randolph	.098	.109	.284
Mazeroski	.091	.113	.282
White	.088	.108	.283
Hubbard	.083	.103	.302
Hiller	.086	.108	.269
Treadway	.082	.106	.278
Flannery	.088	.108	.266
Nelson	.093	.117	.266
Molitor	.088	.103	.279

A quick synopsis: the putout data for the good second basemen (the top four) seems pretty much the same as for the "ordinary" second basemen (the bottom five). The assists percentages, however, are higher for the good second basemen than the other guys—about .015 higher. That suggests that the good second basemen are making about 20 to 25 plays a year that the less-good second basemen aren't getting to, projecting it out to regular status. Interesting thing to know.

Now, departing into the realm of the more speculative. . . assists, generally speaking, represent ground balls. It would be another interesting thing to know, in evaluating a fielder, whether he played behind ground ball pitchers or fly ball pitchers.

All outs may be summarized as one of three things: ground balls, fly balls and strikeouts. . . not really, of course; there are runners put out on the bases all the time, but beggars can't be choosers. This is the data we got. We know how many assists the team had when Randolph was in the field; we know how many strikeouts they had, and we know how many putouts they had.

If we assume that "assists" represent ground balls, then fly balls are simply putouts, minus strikeouts, minus assists. And the ground ball percentage is simply team assists, divided by putouts minus strikeouts. For Randolph:

Team Putouts	55946
Team Strikeouts	11201
Putouts Minus K	44745
Assists (Ground Balls)	22281
Fly Balls	22464
Ground Ball Percentage	.498

We're not deeply into the speculation yet.

What I *really* want to know, in evaluating a fielder, is *what percentage of the plays he made, compared to the balls in play, and particularly the ground balls in play*. Given the data we have developed here, we can make an estimate of the balls in play which, while not perfect, is better than anything we have had before. Again using Willie Randolph as a model, we can estimate the balls in play while he was in the field:

Batters Facing Pitcher	78560
Minus Home Runs Allowed	1631
Minus Walks	6263
Minus Strikeouts	11201
Minus Hit Batsmen	320

There were approximately 59,145 balls in play while Randolph was at second base. If we assume that .498 of those were *ground* balls, that would imply that there were about 29,452 ground balls while Randolph was in the field.

Randolph recorded 6,336 assists during his career. Thus, we estimate that Randolph fielded about 21.5% of all the ground balls hit while he was in the field—6,336, divided by 29,452.

This is the parallel data for the nine second basemen in our study:

Player	GB%	Balls in Play	Ground Balls in Play	% Fielded
Randolph	.498	59145	29452	.215
Mazeroski	.538	58644	31530	.212
White	.502	53888	27026	.231
Hubbard	.543	36046	19558	.227
Hiller	.492	13559	6674	.202
Treadway	.517	12850	6646	.208
Flannery	.500	12673	6341	.203
Nelson	.500	11519	5758	.200
Molitor	.508	12005	6093	.209

In other words, following this line of analysis, we reach two conclusions: That all of the long-term second basemen in our study had better range than any of the short-term second basemen, and that among the long-term second basemen, Frank White had the best range.

Now, the key question: Do you believe it or not?

I have frankly acknowledged that this is a somewhat speculative line of analysis. I can't tell you with a straight face that this approach "proves" or "reveals" that Frank White had better range than Bill Mazeroski. Until we study it in more detail, run data for more players, we're really not in position to say whether we are or are not on the trail of a better way to evaluate an infielder's range.

But I will say this: that I believe it. It makes sense to me.

Look, Bill Mazeroski was terrific at turning the double play. There's no doubt about that, and he should get credit for it. But Bill Mazeroski did *not* have tremendous range at second base. He just didn't. Frank White did. These hundreds of runs that Mazeroski is supposed to have saved for his team. . . it's a pure fiction.

This would be an interesting experiment: ask Freddie Patek what he thinks. Patek played three seasons at short for the Pirates, probably played about 250 games as Bill Mazeroski's double-play partner. Later on, he played the same role with Frank White, probably about 500 games. Ask him what he thinks. I haven't done it—but I'd bet that he would say that White had far, far better range than Mazeroski.

We have been reading statistical analysis which tells us that Mazeroski had super range for so long that, for many people, I am sure that is a fixed opinion. But that analysis was never based on a thorough and systematic review of the data. It was based on a quick and dirty system, the same sort of analysis that makes people who don't know any better think Chuck Klein was a better hitter than Mike Schmidt. No statistics can be read accurately without looking carefully at the conditions under which they were compiled.

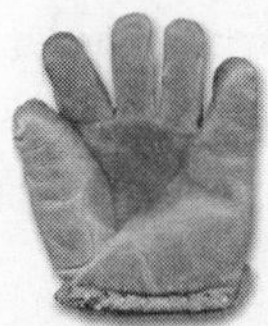

Balanced Teams and Front-Line Talent

Recently at a book signing, I was asked a question which was something of a surprise to me. The question was, "What do you think is the best team of all time, top to bottom?" I was surprised to be asked this because. . . well, I thought the answer was too obvious to miss: the 1998 Yankees may or may not be the greatest team of all time, but they have to be the greatest team ever top to bottom, don't they? Nobody on that team was great; what made them great was everybody on the team was real good.

Later, though, it occurred to me that we could use the Win Shares system to get an objective answer to this question, in a fairly straightforward manner. Let's assume that a baseball team consists of fifteen "slots" of value—one for each position, five starting pitchers, a relief ace, a setup man. You can measure the extent to which a team wins by *depth*, rather than by front-line talent, by taking the value of the top fifteen players on the team, multiplying the value of the number one man by one, the second man by two, the third man by three, etc. . . the value of the 15th-best player on the team is multiplied by 15. This method puts a premium on having many good players, rather than one outstanding player.

Conversely, one can measure the extent to which a team wins by front-line talent, rather than talent depth, by reversing the process: multiply the value of the team's best player by 15, of their second-best player by 14, etc. . . the 15th-best player on the team has his value multiplied by one. Then, by comparing these two figures, one can make a near-perfect statement of the *balance* of the team. If there were a team which was perfectly balanced top to bottom—that is, if the 15th best player was as good as the best player—they would have a "Team Balance Percentage" of 1.000. If a very high percentage of a team's talent is concentrated in a few players, its team balance percentage is low.

For illustration, let's compare the 2001 San Francisco Giants, who won 90 games, and the St. Louis

Cardinals, who won 93. These are the Win Shares for all players on the two teams:

San Francisco		St. Louis	
B.Bonds	54	J.Edmonds	30
R.Aurilia	33	A.Pujols	29
J.Kent	27	J.Drew	22
R.Ortiz	15	F.Vina	22
R.Nen	14	D.Kile	18
F.Rodriguez	12	M.Morris	17
M.Benard	11	P.Polanco	14
B.Santiago	10	E.Renteria	13
A.Rios	10	S.Kline	12
R.Martinez	9	C.Paquette	12
K.Rueter	7	M.McGwire	8
C.Murray	7	M.Matheny	8
S.Estes	7	W.Williams	8
A.Galarraga	7	R.Lankford	8
J.Snow	6	D.Hermanson	8
L.Hernandez	5	D.Veres	7
T.Worrell	5	M.Matthews	7
J.Schmidt	5	E.Marrero	7
S.Dunston	4	G.Stechschulte	5
A.Fultz	3	M.Timlin	5
B.Estalella	3	B.Smith	5
J.Vander Wal	3	K.Robinson	4
J.Christiansen	2	L.Hackman	2
R.Davis	2	M.Cairo	2
C.Zerbe	2	J.Christiansen	2
R.Jensen	2	T.Mathews	1
M.Gardner	1	B.Bonilla	1
B.Boehringer	1	M.James	1
E.Guzman	1	J.Karnuth	1
E.Davis	1		
Y.Torrealba	1		

The total Win Shares for the two teams, because they won about the same number of games, are about the same—270 for San Francisco, 279 for St. Louis. But obviously, the Giants won more by front-line talent; the Cardinals won more by team depth. The Giants had one player having a historic season, Bonds, and two other guys having MVP-candidate type seasons, Aurilia and Kent. The Cardinals had two guys about even with Aurilia and Kent. But after you get by the front three, the Cardinals had a better team.

Barry Bonds

Our method takes these obvious facts, and makes them into statistical statements. To get the "Front-Line Talent" measurement, we multiply Bonds' value by 15, Aurilia's by 14, Kent's by 13, Ortiz' by 12, etc. The Giants' Front-Line talent is 2484; the Cardinals', 2280. To get the "Team Depth" measurement, we reverse the process. We multiply Bonds' value by 1, Aurilia's by 2, Kent's by 3, Ortiz' by 4, etc., stopping with J. T. Snow, whose value (6) is multiplied by 15. The Cardinals' Team Depth is 1384; the Giants', 1180.

You can measure the team's "Balance," then, by dividing the second figure by the first. The Cardinals' team balance is .607; the Giants', .475. The Cardinals' .607 figure is below average in modern baseball, while the Giants' .475 figure was the lowest in the majors since 1972 (the Phillies).

I figured the "team balance percentages" for every team in baseball history. Don't applaud; if this was as hard as it sounds I wouldn't have done it. In theory, this study enables us to identify four lists of unusual teams:

1. The strongest teams of all time top to bottom,

2. The strongest teams of all time in terms of front-line talent,

3. The most balanced teams ever, and

4. The least balanced teams ever.

Let's look at those one at a time:

1. The strongest teams of all time top to bottom

Actually, according to this method at least, the 1998 Yankees *weren't* the strongest team of all time top-to-bottom. The strongest team of all time, in terms of strength at positions one through 15, was the 1906 Cubs:

Team, Lg	Year	Depth
Chicago, NL	1906	2164
Chicago, NL	1907	2092
New York, NL	1905	2030
New York, NL	1912	1915
Pittsburgh, NL	1909	1894
New York, AL	1961	1879
Baltimore, AL	1971	1872
New York, AL	1998	1866
New York, NL	1904	1854
New York, NL	1913	1843
Philadelphia, AL	1911	1838
Philadelphia, AL	1929	1835
New York, AL	1977	1828
Chicago, NL	1910	1827
Seattle, AL	2001	1823
New York, AL	1939	1820
New York, AL	1963	1814
San Francisco, NL	1962	1813
St. Louis, NL	1931	1798
New York, AL	1936	1798
Los Angeles, NL	1974	1797
New York, NL	1911	1793
St. Louis, NL	1943	1792
Brooklyn, NL	1942	1791
St. Louis, NL	1944	1791

This is a surprising conclusion, so let's compare the top 15 players on those two teams, the 1906 Cubs and the 1998 Yankees.

Pos	Players	Value	Contr.		
1.	Three Finger Brown	35	35		
	Bernie Williams			27	27
2.	Frank Chance	35	70		
	Derek Jeter			27	54
3.	Harry Steinfeldt	33	99		
	Scott Brosius			27	81
4.	Jimmy Sheckard	25	100		
	Paul O'Neill			26	104
5.	Jack Pfiester	24	120		
	Chuck Knoblauch			22	110
6.	Wildfire Schulte	24	144		
	Tino Martinez			21	126
7.	Ed Reulbach	23	161		
	David Wells			18	126
8.	Johnny Kling	21	168		
	David Cone			17	136
9.	Johnny Evers	20	180		
	Jorge Posada			15	135
10.	Jimmy Slagle	19	190		
	Mariano Rivera			14	140
11.	Carl Lundgren	19	209		
	Chad Curtis			14	154
12.	Joe Tinker	17	204		
	Andy Pettitte			13	156
13.	Jack Taylor	14	182		
	Orlando Hernandez			13	169
14.	Orval Overall	13	182		
	Ramiro Mendoza			12	168
15.	Solly Hofman	8	120		
	Hideki Irabu			12	180
	Totals		2164		1866

You may not be entirely persuaded by this comparison, and actually, I'm not, either, but let's move on.

2. The strongest teams of all time in terms of front-line talent

Nineteenth-century and early 20th-century teams were dominated by their stars to a much greater extent than modern baseball teams, and so all of the highest values for front-line talent came from teams that played a long time ago.

Team, Lg	Year	Front-Line Talent
Boston, NL	1892	3291
St. Louis, AA	1886	3288
St. Louis, AA	1887	3282
Boston, AL	1912	3168
New York, AL	1927	3163
Boston, NL	1898	3150
Chicago, NL	1906	3116
St. Louis, AA	1888	3064
Providence, NL	1884	3055
New York, NL	1904	3042
Pittsburgh, NL	1909	3034
Philadelphia, AL	1931	3033
New York, AL	1961	3033
New York, NL	1905	2994
Chicago, NL	1886	2982
Pittsburgh, NL	1908	2974
New York, AL	1928	2962
Brooklyn, AA	1889	2960
Philadelphia, AL	1930	2959
Chicago, NL	1885	2957
New York, NL	1885	2951
Boston, AL	1946	2949
Chicago, AL	1920	2946
Philadelphia, AL	1929	2933
Detroit, AL	1915	2921

The only team in the last fifty years to make this list is the '61 Yankees. The 19th century is rife with pitchers who won 30, 35, 40, 45, 50 games. The 1892 Boston Beaneaters, the No. 1 team on the list, had two pitchers who won 35 games apiece. The 1886 St. Louis Browns had two pitchers who won 71 games between them, but also played the outfield when not pitching, and were among the best hitters on the team. Those players are *so* significant to the team that, figured by front-end talent, early teams have to score higher than more recent teams.

The 1912 Red Sox, the highest-scoring team since 1900, had Smokey Joe Wood, who went 34-5 with a 1.91 ERA—and *wasn't* the Most Valuable Player on his own team. The MVP on the team was Tris Speaker, a Gold Glove center fielder who hit .383, and was voted the league's MVP (the Chalmers Award). Wood finished fifth in the league-wide vote.

We all knew anyway that modern baseball teams are much more balanced top to bottom than early teams. But this study, again, gives us a statistical handle on what we already knew. *How much* more balanced are modern teams than early teams?

I figured the "Average Team Balance" for every 10th season since 1880. This is the chart:

Year	Average Team Balance Percentage
1880	.321
1890	.493
1900	.589
1910	.593
1920	.593
1930	.588
1940	.601
1950	.622
1960	.634
1970	.613
1980	.650
1990	.653
2000	.633

3. The most balanced teams ever

And, because balance has increased over time, the most balanced teams ever tend mostly to come from the last fifty years:

Team, Lg	Year	Depth/Front	Balance
Cleveland, AL	1964	1377/1743	.790
Oakland, AL	1989	1643/2085	.788
Boston, AL	1920	1197/1523	.786
St. Louis, NL	1931	1798/2298	.782
St. Louis, NL	1930	1586/2046	.775
Kansas City, AL	1957	946/1230	.769
Cincinnati, NL	1946	1147/1493	.768
Baltimore, AL	1963	1571/2045	.768
San Diego, NL	1985	1525/1995	.764
Minnesota, AL	1999	1019/1333	.764
Baltimore, AL	1973	1720/2264	.760
California, AL	1985	1479/1945	.760
Pittsburgh, NL	1976	1623/2137	.759
Cincinnati, NL	1990	1553/2047	.759
Texas, AL	1988	1275/1685	.757
Chicago, AL	1990	1576/2088	.755
San Francisco, NL	1987	1417/1879	.754
Los Angeles, NL	1967	1313/1743	.753
New York, AL	1977	1828/2428	.753
Cincinnati, NL	2000	1326/1762	.753

Team, Lg	Year	Depth/Front	Balance
Detroit, AL	1980	1407/1873	.751
Chicago, AL	1932	878/1170	.750
Chicago, AL	1986	953/1271	.750
Boston, AL	1952	1124/1500	.749
New York, NL	1986	1822/2434	.749

I had expected, when I began to compile this list, that it would be dominated either by good teams or by bad teams. I assumed that team balance for good teams would either by measured as higher or lower than that for bad teams. Bad teams *might* have higher "team balance percentages" than good teams, I reasoned, for the simple reason that it is easier to balance mediocrity than it is to balance strength. If you don't have any good players, by definition, you're balanced: everybody stinks. It must be easier to balance a team at the bottom than it is at the top.

On the other hand, most bad teams have at least one or two pretty good players. . . the difference in the quality of teams might be not so much in front-line quality as in depth, and therefore the good teams *might* be more balanced than the bad teams.

The actual list (of the most balanced teams) is a mix of good teams and bad teams, with a few mediocre teams included. Making a quick study of this issue, I found no evidence that good teams were either more balanced or less balanced than bad teams. Some good teams are balanced; some are imbalanced. Some bad teams are balanced; some are imbalanced. It's an individual-team thing. . . there may be *some* correlation between team balance and team success, going one way or the other, but the correlation, if there is one, is so slight as to be almost undetectable.

I was also interested in the issue of whether balance would be predictive of future movement. Suppose you have two bad teams of equal quality, one of which has "imbalanced" talent—that is, it has some star players, but gaping holes in their roster—and one of which has "balanced" talent—that is, they have quite a few pretty decent players, but no stars. From the 2001 season, a good match would be the Detroit Tigers (66-96, with a fairly balanced roster), and the Montreal Expos (68-94, with an extremely imbalanced roster). It would seem reasonable that there *might* be a difference in how these teams would perform in subsequent seasons. The team with the imbalanced roster might be expected to have a better chance to improve substantially in the next season than a team with a balanced roster.

My studies of this issue produced no evidence that this was true. I took, for example, all of the teams since 1960 which won exactly 70 games (in a season of 150 or more games). There are 21 such teams. The *most* balanced of those teams were the 1988 Texas Rangers (70-91) and the 1984 Cincinnati Reds (70-92). The least balanced teams in the group were the 1963 Los Angeles Angels (70-91) and the 1992 Philadelphia Phillies (70-92). All four of those teams improved dramatically in the following season—the most balanced, and the least balanced. Overall, balanced teams were neither more likely nor less likely to improve in the following season, nor was I able to document any other reliable relationship between team balance and next-season performance. Good teams which were balanced were neither more likely nor less likely to collapse in the following season than good teams which were imbalanced.

Also, I thought it possible that, in post-season play, there might be an advantage either to the more balanced team, or to the team with more front-line talent. Through 1949, however, there had been 46 World Series played—23 won by the team with the higher Team Balance Percentage, and 23 by the team with the lower Team Balance Percentage. I concluded that there probably was no predictive value to this for post-season play, and called off the study at that point.

Oh, I should say something about Cleveland in '64. The Indians in '64 weren't a bad team. . . they missed .500 by just a couple of wins. The best players on the team were Dick Howser, a shortstop who hit .256 and couldn't field, and Leon Wagner, an outfielder who hit .253 and *really* couldn't field. Howser walked a lot, so he scored 100 runs, and Wagner had power, so he drove in a hundred. The best pitchers on the team were Jack Kralick (12-7) and a couple of kids who started the season at Portland and got called up in mid-season, Sam McDowell and Luis Tiant. But the team almost finished .500 because they had *some* talent everywhere. . . everybody on the team, like

Howser and Wagner, could play a little. The most balanced team ever, top to bottom.

4. The least balanced teams ever

The least balanced teams ever are all teams that played before 1900. These are the Win Shares for Louisville in 1877:

J.Devlin	60
G.Hall	8
O.Shaffer	7
J.Gerhardt	6
B.Crowley	6
P.Snyder	6
J.Latham	5
B.Craver	4
B.Hague	3

Not exactly balanced top to bottom, is it? This is the team, of course, which sold out. . . Devlin decided to work for himself, rather than those crummy teammates, and began throwing games late in the pennant race.

Louisville has a "Team Balance Percentage" of .201, which is not technically a record low. . . St. Paul of the Union Association in 1884 has a figure of .157, but that team played only nine games and won only two, so that hardly counts. All of the lowest figures ever were posted before 1890, at which point it ceases to be of much general interest who else would be at the bottom of the list.

Now, I have a confession. My "Team Balance Analysis" doesn't *exactly* work the way I intended it to. . . there is something wrong with the system. I probably should have used 20 slots to represent the team, or 25 even, rather than 15.

Look, what makes the Win Shares system valuable, in my opinion, is that it creates value statements which are vastly more amenable to being used in derivative analysis—secondary systems set up to use the Win Shares output. The ratings of the top 100 players that I did in the *New Historical Abstract*. . . that rating system is not Win Shares; it's a derivative of Win Shares. That's what I am doing in this section of the book: I am demonstrating the value of Win Shares in analyzing a range of questions by derivative systems.

But not all of those derivative systems are going to work right away, and this one isn't quite ready for prime time. The reason the '98 Yankees don't rate as deeper than the 1906 Cubs is that they are *too* deep for the system. Too much of their talent comes from guys not among the 15 top players on the team. That's not logical, when your team is too deep to be rated as having depth.

Also, compare the 2001 Cardinals and Houston Astros, who tied for the NL Central Division Championship with records of 93-69 each. The Astros rate as having more front-line talent than the Cardinals (2364-2280), but they also rate as having more depth than the Cardinals (1396-1384). That doesn't seem right. If two teams are equal overall and one of them has more front-line talent, it would seem logical that the other should be measured as having more depth. Something doesn't *exactly* work about the system that I have constructed. But even a failure can occasionally be interesting, and I thought I would report upon this, at least to establish a baseline if the issue is to be studied again.

Dee Aitch

Let me begin here by making two statements which are so obviously true, outside the context of the debate which follows, that I need not defend them:

1. The Designated Hitter Rule increases the value of a slugger who has limited defensive ability, and

2. We evaluate ballplayers by what they accomplish, not by what they might have accomplished in different circumstances.

An issue has arisen as to how we should deal with the Designated Hitter Rule, in rating players by use of the Win Shares Method. In the other book, the *New Historical Abstract*, I argued that, if you compare Craig Biggio to Ken Griffey Jr., Biggio has contributed more to the success of his teams in almost every season than Griffey has.

A reader objects, however, that this comparison is unfair to Griffey because I have made no adjustment for the Designated Hitter Rule. Craig Biggio competes in a context of eight hitters, or eight-and-a-half if you want to count the pitcher's batting as a half. Ken Griffey, for most of his career, competed in a context of *nine* hitters. The fact that Biggio created more runs relative to his context, the reader argues, is misleading because the context is different.

This is how I see the issue. First, we evaluate ballplayers by how much good they do for their teams, which means that we evaluate them by how many games they win for their team, or how many pennants they win for their team, or something along that line. . . I am, at the moment, trying to figure out how many games each player has won for his team.

If you add an extra hitter to each lineup, that hitter will win some games for his team—but each team will win no more games. The implication of this could not be any more clear: it means that the other eight hitters will win *fewer* games.

But, replies another reader, I am just not happy with a baseball universe in which Cal Ripken's value is diminished, compared to that of Barry Larkin, because Ripken has to compete with an extra hitter. Well, hell, I'm not *happy* about it, either. I don't *like* the fact that Cal Ripken's value is diminished compared to a National League shortstop because of a rule which is a relic of an incomprehensibly distant time when baseball felt that it needed more offense.

But the fact that I'm not happy about it has nothing to do with anything. I'm not happy about the fact that my home state has no mountains and a death penalty—but that doesn't mean that, in preparing a report on the state of Kansas, I can pretend that we have no death penalty and big ones out west.

Second, it is crystal clear that the Designated Hitter Rule reduces the number of games that are won by each hitter. Therefore, if one *does* choose to "adjust" the Designated Hitter Rule out of existence, in rating players by use of the Win Shares method, the place where that has to be done is not within the calculation of Win Shares, but as a part of the derivative analysis used to convert Win Shares into ratings.

How players should be rated (or ranked) is a question inevitably involving subjective judgments. There is not and can never be any perfectly satisfactory way to rate players, because there is not and can never be any definitive answer to such questions as "How much weight should be given to peak value, how much to career value?", "How steep is the slope of history?", "What credit do you give to leadership?" and "How do you compare players between eras when the roles assigned to those players are radically different?" These questions have no answers, and thus there is no absolutely correct way to rate players. If you choose to adjust for all kinds of things that might have happened differently, knock yourself out.

But I don't want any part of it. To me, this argument hearkens back to a discussion we had about park effects in the pre-history of sabermetrics, back in the 1970s when the only thing we had was a few guys exchanging letters. There were some of us who thought, for a time, that we should adjust for park effects on an *individual* basis—in other words, that we should bring Todd Helton down to earth by adjusting for Colorado's effects on Todd Helton as an individual, rather than by adjusting for its effects on offense.

Todd Helton was a toddler then, and Coors Field a gleam in an architect's beer mug, but you're missing the point.

Take Elston Howard and Bill Dickey, both Yankee catchers, but affected in dramatically different ways by Yankee Stadium. Dickey was enormously HELPED by Yankee Stadium; Howard was tremendously HURT by the same. There was a time when some of us thought that, to adjust for park effects, we needed to make Howard better and Dickey worse, even though both men had played in the same park, and what we now call the park factors were basically the same.

But that position eventually lost the argument, because what we all eventually realized was that the relevant question was not what Todd Helton's value *would be* if he played in another park, but rather, what Todd Helton's value *is* in the circumstances under which he performs. And it's exactly the same here: the relevant question isn't what Cal Ripken's value *would have been* if it wasn't for that nasty rule, but rather, what Cal Ripken's value *was*. The designated hitter rule increases the value of a slugger who has limited defensive ability—this was the innocent premise with which we began—and that value isn't pulled out of the atmosphere. It is taken away from other players. I don't like it, either, but get over it.

If you want to evaluate a player not by what his value *is* under his real playing conditions, but by what it might have been under different conditions, there are any number of absolutely true statements that will demand your attention. It is absolutely true that Elston Howard would have been a more valuable hitter had he played in almost any other park. It is absolutely true that Elston Howard would have become a regular seven to 10 years before he did had he been white and purchased by a team that needed a catcher, rather than being black and a Yankee behind Yogi Berra. It is absolutely true that Roger Cedeno would have been a more valuable player had he played in the 1970s, when we had real big parks with artificial turf, than he is 25 years later. It is absolutely true, in my judgment, that Tommy Thomas (a 1920s starting pitcher) could have had a hell of a career if he had been used like Goose Gossage. It is absolutely true that Trevor Hoffman would have earned more Win Shares than he has if he had pitched more than one inning at a time.

To me, saying that Ken Griffey Jr. *would have been* more valuable than Craig Biggio, but for the Designated Hitter Rule, is exactly like that: it is an invitation to a What-If Ball. And here is the danger in going to that dance. . .

In the *New Historical Abstract*, I argued that Roy White, who has as much chance of being elected to the Hall of Fame as Pat Robertson does of being elected President of Yemen, was actually a better player than Jim Rice. Roy White created 94 runs per season, but did so in a context of about 3.65 runs per game; thus, White created all the runs a team would normally score in about 26 games per season. Rice created 115 runs per season—a lot more—but did so in a league and park where a "game" was about 4.73 runs; thus, Rice's runs represent a team's normal production for only 24 games per season.

"Ahah!" shouts an alert reader. "You forgot to adjust for the Designated Hitter Rule! If you adjust for the Designated Hitter Rule, Rice is actually better."

But the problem with that analysis is, that it adjusts for the Designated Hitter Rule as if the Designated Hitter rule was *hurting* Jim Rice, when in reality, the Designated Hitter rule was obviously *helping* Jim Rice. Remember, the Designated Hitter Rule *increases* the value of a slugger who has limited defensive ability—I said that twice, and you didn't object either time. Jim Rice was a slugger who had limited defensive ability. More than one-fourth of Rice's career games were as a Designated Hitter. He was able to use the Designated Hitter Rule to stay in the lineup when he had minor injuries, and he was able to use the Designated Hitter Rule to stay in the majors at the end of his career. It is utterly irrational to adjust for the Designated Hitter Rule as if the DH rule was *hurting* Jim Rice compared to Roy White, when the obvious reality is that the DH rule was *helping* Jim Rice as compared to Roy White. If you're going to adjust the DH rule out of existence on the one end, don't you *have* to adjust it out of existence on the other end?

That's why you don't do that, guys. That's why, in general, we don't go to the What-If Ball: because it is impossible to sort out all the conditions that would apply under theoretically different circumstances. Every what-if that we can construct always has another side to it, and you never *really* know what that other side is. Elston Howard *might* have been a 15-year regular if he were white and had signed with the Detroit Tigers—and he might have gotten hurt the second year. Sabermetrics is not about What-Ifs; it is about what actually happened. Do your own ratings; do them your own way—but just for myself, I have no doubt and no conflicts about how I should deal with the Designated Hitter Rule.

Will Clark

By anyone's standards, Will Clark in 1989 had a very good season. Clark hit .333 with 38 doubles, nine triples, 23 homers, scored 104 runs, drove in 111—a terrific year, but a dozen people every year have numbers that look as good or better. Clark led the San Francisco Giants to the National League championship, but his teammate, Kevin Mitchell, won the MVP Award, although:

1. Clark was regarded as a better defensive player, and

2. Clark was much better liked by reporters.

Their numbers were of comparable stature—Mitchell hit .291 with 47 homers, 125 driven in—and Mitchell benefited from what could be called the Sally Field effect: nobody expected *him* to be great. Everybody knew Clark was a great player anyway; nobody expected a big effort from Mitchell.

Anyway, when I developed the Win Shares system, I was surprised to see that Clark's 1989 season with the bat actually ranks as not only better than Mitchell's, but actually better than any other major league season of the 1980s.

Why? Basically, Clark starts out with MVP-type numbers, and everything you look at tends to make him look a little bit better. He grounded into only six double plays, and he was 8-for-11 as a base stealer; those things make him a little bit better.

The National League in 1989 was a pitcher's league, relative to the seasons surrounding it. The league ERA was just 3.50, one of the lowest ERAs in the last 20 years (the National League was a hair lower in 1981 and 1988). If you compare him to hitters at the turn of the 21st century, he is competing in a league with 30 to 40% fewer runs.

Clark played in a pitcher's park. The park factor for Candlestick was always low; the number I use for 1989 is .9110; this, again, makes Clark a little bit better than he looks.

In the version of runs created introduced in the *All-Time Handbook*, and used to figure Win Shares, we also consider the player's batting performance in two "run sensitive" game situations: batting average with runners in scoring position, and home runs with men on base. Clark hit .389 with men in scoring position, so we credit him with an additional eight runs created for that. He hit 13 of his 23 home runs with men on base, three more than you would expect given his plate appearances, so we credit him with three more runs created for that.

Clark starts out fairly near the head of the pack, and when each additional consideration is factored in, he edges forward just a little bit. When we get to the end of the race, the best (hitter's) season of the 1980s is not Wade Boggs in 1987 or Don Mattingly in 1986 or George Brett in 1985, although those are all great performances. The best hitter's season of that era was by Will Clark in 1989.

Comparable Pitchers on Good Teams and on Bad Teams

In theory, how a player rates in this system is not affected by whether he plays on a good team or a bad team. A player is supposed to rate just the same whether his teammates are good players or bad players. But in theory, Enron was making money hand over fist. It is periodically necessary to check and see whether your theory works.

One thing we can do to see whether our theory works is to identify sets of pitchers with very comparable innings pitched and ERAs, but on mismatched teams—one on a good team, one on a bad team. When we have identified the matched sets, we can check to see whether their Win Shares are the same, or different.

In order to identify the best possible sets or matches, I focused on all leagues since World War II in which the league ERA was within a range of 3.90 to 4.10. There were 27 such leagues—the National League in 1947, 1948, 1949, 1951, 1954, 1955, 1958, 1959, 1961, 1962, 1970, 1977, 1987 and 1993, and the American League in 1953, 1955, 1961, 1962, 1977, 1980, 1982, 1983, 1984, 1988, 1990, 1991 and 1992.

From those 27 leagues, I identified all the pitchers who pitched 200 or more innings with a team whose winning percentage was:

a) .580 or higher, or

b) .420 or lower.

I ignored any pitcher who split time between two teams, or who pitched for a team with a winning percentage between .421 and .579—that is, in a 162-game schedule, between 69-93 and 93-69.

There were, as it turned out, 195 qualifying pitchers in the 27 leagues—126 who pitched for good teams, and 69 who pitched for poor teams (since poor teams have many fewer pitchers who pitch 200 or more innings).

For each of those 195 pitcher/seasons, I entered into a spreadsheet seven bits of information:

1. The year
2. The league
3. The league ERA
4. His innings pitched
5. His ERA
6. His team's wins
7. His team's losses

From these, I calculated an eighth item, the margin between the pitcher's ERA and the league ERA. I then systematically compared all of the pitchers on bad teams to all of the pitchers on good teams, to identify pitchers with very comparable records. The similarity of any two records was defined as:

1000,
Minus 1 point for each .01 difference in the league ERAs,
Minus 3 points for each difference of 1 inning pitched,
Minus 2.5 points for each .01 difference in the pitcher's ERA,
Minus 2.5 points for each .01 difference in the pitcher's ERA, compared to the league ERA.

For illustration, in 1982 Pete Vuckovich pitched 223.2 innings with an ERA of 3.34, in a league in which the league ERA was 4.07. In 1958, Jim Owens pitched 221 innings with a 3.22 ERA, in a league in which the league ERA was 3.95. This scores as a similarity of 950:

1000,
Minus 12 points for the 0.12 difference in the league ERAs,
Minus 8 points because there is a difference of 2.2 in their innings pitched,
Minus 30 points because there is a difference of 0.12 in their ERAs.

Since each pitcher's ERA was 0.73 better than the league norm, those figures were considered identical, and there was no deduction for that comparison.

Each of the 69 pitchers on bad teams could be compared to each of the 125 pitchers on good teams, creating 8,763 possible matches. I found 32 matched sets of pitchers, which we will detail in a moment. I considered pitchers matched if their similarity score was 950 or better—thus, the Owens/Vuckovich match was the worst match to qualify for the study. (For the sake of clarity, there were more than a hundred "matches" that scored at 950 or better. However, most of these involved duplicate use of the same pitchers, and were eliminated, as each pitcher/season was used only once in the study.)

There were two matches which scored at 1000—Paul Splittorff, 1980, with Frank Tanana, 1980, and Ross Grimsley, 1977, with Paul Minner, 1954. Both Splittorff and Tanana pitched 204 innings with a 4.15 ERA in a league in which the ERA was 4.03. Both Grimsley and Minner pitched 218 innings with a 3.96 ERA in leagues in which the ERA was 4.07. This is a full listing of the 32 matches, in declining order of similarity. . . in all cases the pitcher who pitched for a good team is listed first.

Pitchers, Year/Lg	Lg ERA	IP	ERA	Similarity
Paul Splittorff, 1980 AL	4.03	204	4.15	
Frank Tanana, 1980 AL	4.03	204	4.15	1000

Pitchers, Year/Lg	Lg ERA	IP	ERA	Similarity
Ross Grimsley, 1977 AL	4.07	218	3.96	
Paul Minner, 1954 NL	4.07	218	3.96	1000

Pitchers, Year/Lg	Lg ERA	IP	ERA	Similarity
Jerry Reuss, 1977 NL	3.91	208	4.11	
Tim Leary, 1990 AL	3.92	208	4.11	997

Pitchers, Year/Lg	Lg ERA	IP	ERA	Similarity
Scott McGregor, 1980 AL	4.03	252	3.32	
Jim Clancy, 1980 AL	4.03	251	3.30	987

Pitchers, Year/Lg	Lg ERA	IP	ERA	Similarity
Bob Lemon, 1955 AL	3.96	211	3.88	
Marion Fricano, 1953 AL	4.00	211	3.88	986

Pitchers, Year/Lg	Lg ERA	IP	ERA	Similarity
Dennis Leonard, 1980 AL	4.03	280	3.79	
Vida Blue, 1977 AL	4.07	280	3.83	986

Pitchers, Year/Lg	Lg ERA	IP	ERA	Similarity
Al Brazle, 1949 NL	4.04	206	3.19	
Jim Archer, 1961 AL	4.02	205	3.20	985

Pitchers, Year/Lg	Lg ERA	IP	ERA	Similarity
Ron Guidry, 1980 AL	4.03	220	3.56	
Jim Slaton, 1977 AL	4.07	221	3.58	983

Pitchers, Year/Lg	Lg ERA	IP	ERA	Similarity
Bert Blyleven, 1977 AL	4.07	235	2.72	
Dutch Leonard, 1947 NL	4.07	235	2.68	980

Pitchers, Year/Lg	Lg ERA	IP	ERA	Similarity
Dennis Martinez, 1982 AL	4.07	252	4.21	
D. Lemancyzk, 1977 AL	4.07	252	4.25	980

Pitchers, Year/Lg	Lg ERA	IP	ERA	Similarity
Bob Lemon, 1953 AL	4.00	287	3.36	
K. Raffensberger, 1949 NL	4.04	284	3.39	977

Pitchers, Year/Lg	Lg ERA	IP	ERA	Similarity
Bob Purkey, 1961 NL	4.03	246	3.73	
Dave Stieb, 1980 AL	4.03	243	3.70	976

Pitchers, Year/Lg	Lg ERA	IP	ERA	Similarity
Danny Jackson, 1993 NL	4.05	210	3.77	
Don Sutton, 1984 AL	3.99	212	3.77	972

Pitchers, Year/Lg	Lg ERA	IP	ERA	Similarity
Jack McDowell, 1990 AL	3.92	205	3.82	
Eric Show, 1987 NL	3.99	206	3.84	972

Pitchers, Year/Lg	Lg ERA	IP	ERA	Similarity
Joe Hatten, 1947 NL	4.07	225	3.64	
Bobby Castillo, 1982 AL	4.07	218	3.66	971

Pitchers, Year/Lg	Lg ERA	IP	ERA	Similarity
Jim Palmer, 1980 AL	4.03	224	3.98	
Howie Fox, 1949 NL	4.04	215	3.98	970

Pitchers, Year/Lg	Lg ERA	IP	ERA	Similarity
Rick Rhoden, 1977 NL	3.91	216	3.75	
Randy Johnson, 1992 AL	3.95	210	3.77	969

Pitchers, Year/Lg	Lg ERA	IP	ERA	Similarity
Mike Flanagan, 1982 AL	4.07	236	3.97	
Charlie Hough, 1982 AL	4.07	228	3.95	966

Pitchers, Year/Lg	Lg ERA	IP	ERA	Similarity
Ralph Branca, 1951 NL	3.96	204	3.26	
Matt Young, 1983 AL	4.06	203	3.27	964

Pitchers, Year/Lg	Lg ERA	IP	ERA	Similarity
Bob Turley, 1955 AL	3.96	247	3.06	
Turk Farrell, 1962 NL	3.94	242	3.01	963

Pitchers, Year/Lg	Lg ERA	IP	ERA	Similarity
Doug Rau, 1977 NL	3.91	212	3.44	
Bennie Daniels, 1961 AL	4.02	212	3.44	962

Pitchers, Year/Lg	Lg ERA	IP	ERA	Similarity
S. Sanderson, 1990 AL	3.92	206	3.88	
Alex Kellner, 1953 AL	4.00	202	3.92	959

Pitchers, Year/Lg	Lg ERA	IP	ERA	Similarity
Tommy Greene, 1993 NL	4.05	200	3.42	
Dwight Gooden, 1993 NL	4.05	208	3.45	959

Pitchers, Year/Lg	Lg ERA	IP	ERA	Similarity
L. Christenson, 1977 NL	3.91	219	4.07	
Art Mahaffey, 1961 NL	4.03	219	4.11	958

Pitchers, Year/Lg	Lg ERA	IP	ERA	Similarity
Mike Caldwell, 1982 AL	4.07	258	3.91	
Don Cardwell, 1961 NL	4.03	259	3.82	958

Pitchers, Year/Lg	Lg ERA	IP	ERA	Similarity
Jimmy Key, 1992 AL	3.95	216	3.53	
Jerry Koosman, 1977 NL	3.91	227	3.49	955

Pitchers, Year/Lg	Lg ERA	IP	ERA	Similarity
Mike Garcia, 1955 AL	3.96	211	4.01	
Glenn Abbott, 1980 AL	4.03	215	4.10	954

Pitchers, Year/Lg	Lg ERA	IP	ERA	Similarity
Storm Davis, 1988 AL	3.97	201	3.70	
Vern Law, 1955 NL	4.04	201	3.81	953

Pitchers, Year/Lg	Lg ERA	IP	ERA	Similarity
Mike Flanagan, 1980 AL	4.03	251	4.12	
Jerry Garvin, 1977 AL	4.07	245	4.19	953

Pitchers, Year/Lg	Lg ERA	IP	ERA	Similarity
Ron Guidry, 1977 AL	4.07	211	2.82	
Bob Friend, 1955 NL	4.04	200	2.83	951

Pitchers, Year/Lg	Lg ERA	IP	ERA	Similarity
Whitey Ford, 1955 AL	3.96	254	2.62	
Johnny Schmitz, 1948 NL	3.95	242	2.64	951

Pitchers, Year/Lg	Lg ERA	IP	ERA	Similarity
Pete Vuckovich, 1982 AL	4.07	223	3.34	
Jim Owens, 1959 NL	3.95	221	3.22	950

In sum, the 32 pitchers on good teams pitched 7,250 innings, allowing 2,919 earned runs, a 3.62 ERA. The 32 pitchers on poor teams pitched 7,200 innings, allowing 2,905 earned runs, a 3.63 ERA. The tiny difference reflects what is known as "quality leakage." Whenever you do a matched-set study, one group of players will normally be better than the other in characteristics which are not controlled, and some differences in the quality of the players will tend to leak into the data, despite your efforts to exclude them.

As you would expect, the pitchers on good teams had far better won-lost records than the similar pitchers on bad teams. The 32 pitchers on good teams had an aggregate won-lost record of 505-324, a .609 winning percentage, three points better than the winning percentage of their teams (.606). The pitchers of nearly identical effectiveness on bad teams had an aggregate record of 381-463, a .451 winning percentage, but 61 points better than their teams (.390). In other words, having (nearly) identical starting pitching eliminated only one-fourth of the winning percentage differential between these two groups of pitchers, reducing the margin from 216 points (.606 to .390, the difference between the teams) to 158 points (.609 to .451, the difference between the pitchers).

On bad teams:

- 9 pitchers had winning records
- 4 were at .500, and
- 19 had losing records.

Of the equal pitchers on good teams:

- 29 had winning records,
- 1 was at .500, and
- 2 had losing records.

There were four pitchers on bad teams who had as good or better won-lost records than the comparable pitchers on good teams. Two of those were knuckleballers, and three of the four were veteran pitchers with a lot of innings under their belt; whether this is meaningful or not, I don't know. The four matchups in which the pitcher on a bad team posted a won-lost mark as good or better were:

Bert Blyleven, 1977	14-12 on a good team
Dutch Leonard, 1947	17-12 on a bad team
Mike Garcia, 1955	11-13 on a good team
Glenn Abbott, 1980	12-12 on a bad team
Mike Flanagan, 1982	15-11 on a good team
Charlie Hough, 1982	16-13 on a bad team
Danny Jackson, 1993	12-11 on a good team
Don Sutton, 1984	14-12 on a bad team

On the other hand, Jim Palmer in 1980 went 16-10. Howie Fox in 1949, with the same ERA, went 6-19. Art Mahaffey with the Phillies in 1961 went 11-19—actually a pretty good won-lost record with that team, which won only 47 games. By 1977 the Phillies were considerably better, and helped Larry Christenson, with comparable stats, to a record of 19-6.

Conclusions (Win Shares for these Pitchers)

On the basis of this study, there is no evidence of a problem in the system. The performance of the team does not appear to unduly influence the evaluation of the pitcher.

The 32 pitchers on good teams in this study were credited with a total of 462 Win Shares. The 32 pitchers with nearly identical performance, pitching on bad teams, were credited with 460 Win Shares. The pitchers on bad teams pitched 99.3% as many innings as those on good teams (7200/7250), and earned 99.6% as many Win Shares (460/462).

In individual cases, there are some differences in the Win Shares credited to pitchers with comparable innings and ERAs. Park Effects are the largest reason for that; other factors include the pitcher's hitting ability, un-earned runs allowed, the fielding performance of the team behind him, the pitcher's won-lost record, whether the pitcher has any saves, perhaps his ERA components, and the won-lost performance of the team relative to their runs scored and runs allowed.

As I have mentioned many times, a starting pitcher's Win Shares tend to match his actual wins. In this study, the pitchers on good teams had 505 actual wins, 462 Win Shares, making them -43. The pitchers on bad teams had 381 actual wins, 460 Win Shares, making them +79. Taken together, the 64 pitchers had 886 Actual Wins, 922 Win Shares—a ratio of 1 to 1.04.

In individual matchups, the largest Win Shares discrepancy is between Scott Sanderson, 1990, and Alex Kellner, 1953. Despite winning 17 games, Sanderson was credited with only 9 Win Shares—an unusual ratio. Sanderson worked in an exceptionally good pitcher's park. The Park Run Factor for the Oakland Coliseum in 1990 was .84, easily the lowest in baseball in that particular season. The defense behind Sanderson was outstanding. In spite of these advantages, Sanderson posted a 3.88 ERA, barely better than the league norm of 3.91. Thus, it is our opinion that Sanderson's value was significantly less than is suggested by his 17 Wins.

Kellner pitched for the same team, the A's, but two stops back up the road. Shibe Park was a hitter's park, with a 1953 Run Index of 109, and the A's at that time were not a good defensive team. Despite this, Kellner posted a 3.93 ERA, seven points better-than-league, and also made some contribution with his bat, hitting a little over .200. Kellner, with 11 actual wins, is credited with 15 Win Shares—six more than Sanderson.

There are two other cases in which one pitcher was credited with four more Win Shares than a pitcher with comparable innings and ERAs. Those two were:

Pitcher, Year	IP	Won-Lost	ERA	Win Shares
Mike Caldwell, 1982	258	17-13	3.91	12
Don Cardwell, 1961	259	15-14	3.82	16

Pitcher, Year	IP	Won-Lost	ERA	Win Shares
Dennis Leonard, 1980	280	20-11	3.79	18
Vida Blue, 1977	280	14-19	3.83	14

Park effects, again, are the largest factor in these discrepancies. In 17 of the 32 matched sets, however, the two pitchers have either the same credited Win Shares, or are separated by one Win Share. Art Mahaffey in 1961 went 11-19, Larry Christenson in 1977 went 19-6—but each man was credited with 11 Win Shares.

On balance, the system appears to be fair to pitchers on bad teams, and to pitchers on good teams.

Are Rookies of the Year Slipping?

Has the quality of rookie seasons dropped in recent years?

A friend suggested to me that he believed that the "gap" between the quality of play in the major leagues and the quality of play in the top minor leagues had increased in recent years. If that were true, I responded, we would expect the quality of rookie seasons to decline, as players would, we might assume, experience added difficulties in adjusting to the major league standard.

But it has, he responded; rookies today don't post the big numbers they did at one time. Well, maybe the numbers are just as big, because all the other numbers are bigger, but relative to the game, he argued, we don't have rookies now making the impact that they did 20 or 30 years ago.

Is that true, I wondered? Has the quality of Rookie of the Year seasons declined, for example?

There have now been 106 Rookie of the Year Awards—one per season, 1947-1948, and two per season, 1949-2000 (two votes in the 1970s ended in a tie). I listed those 106 players, and looked up their Win Shares, and then sorted them into four time periods: 1947 to 1961, 1962 to 1974, 1975 to 1987, and 1988 to 2000. (I'll add a post-2001 note at the end. . . be patient.)

Conclusion? The average quality of a Rookie of the Year season probably has not changed, although there may have been a slight slip at the beginning of the free agent era. The average Win Shares for a Rookie of the Year were 18.5 in the first era, 21.7 in the second, 18.8 in the third, and 18.5 in the most recent era. There has been no real change, except that the number of exceptional rookie seasons did click upward in the 1962-1974 era.

Actually, the quality of Rookies of the Year was also high in the first two or three years of the 1975-1987 period; the average for the whole period 1962 to 1976, which includes Fred Lynn and Mark Fidrych, was 22.0. One could, then, segregate the data to begin the modern era in 1977 or 1978, and argue that the numbers show that the quality of rookie seasons *did* slip in the late 1970s. But it seems to me more likely that the 1962-1977 average is just a blip in the data—a few exceptional rookie seasons driving up the average—and that there has been no real change in the quality of Rookie of the Year campaigns from the time the award was first given.

Rookies of the Year are worth, on average, slightly more than one-half as much as Most Valuable Players.

(Post-season 2001 note. . . the 2001 Rookies of the Year, Suzuki and Pujols, were the strongest pair of rookie award winners since 1964, Dick Allen and Tony Oliva. This appears to firmly dispel any suggestion that the quality of the top rookies is slipping.)

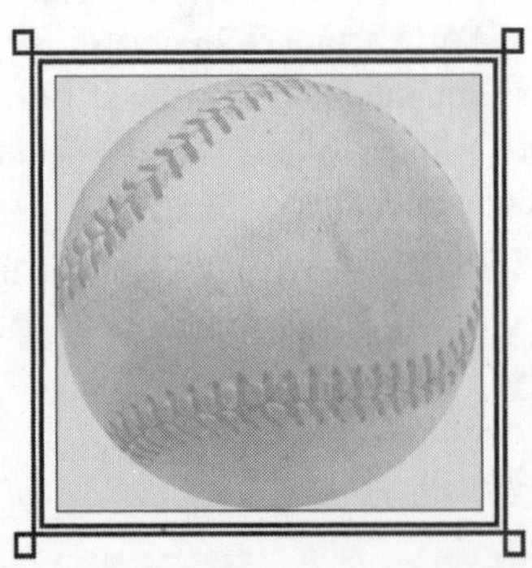

Left-Handed Pitching And Other Things that Screw Up Fielding Statistics

As a part of this effort to develop Win Shares, I compiled a data base of the complete defensive statistics for 240 teams, all major league teams in the years 1946 to 1960. The data consisted of each team's wins, their runs allowed, strikeouts, their fielding totals, the fielding totals for each position on the team, and some miscellaneous data. That is, the data for "first base, Pittsburgh, 1960" was not the data for Dick Stuart in 1960, but the data for all Pittsburgh Pirate first basemen in 1960—Stuart, Rocky Nelson, and RC Stevens combined.

My main purpose was to study the effects of left-handed pitching on the fielding statistics at each position. I entered a category for each team, "left-handed innings." The team with the most left-handed innings in that era was, surprisingly, the 1951 Boston Red Sox, who had five left-handers pitching 113 or more innings, and who nonetheless went 50-25 in Fenway Park. They had 794 innings of left-handed work, 57% of their total innings. Every team in that era had at least one left-handed pitcher on their staff, but the 1947 Philadelphia A's had only seven innings by left-handed pitchers (one start by Lou Brissie), and the 1946 A's had only 37 innings of left-handed pitching, the second-lowest total. One other note: the 1952 Washington Senators were fourth-lowest on the list, with only 59 innings of left-handed pitching, but by 1954 the Senators had added four left-handed starters pitching 179 or more innings apiece (Dean Stone, Johnny Schmitz, Chuck Stobbs and Mickey McDermott), and missed by only one inning of tying the '51 Red Sox for the top spot on the left-handed list.

As a general conclusion, left-handed pitching changes all of the fielding statistics on a team, but most of them not very much. It's a real factor at first base and at third base; otherwise, it's a close call whether it's worth worrying about or not, in a complex environment in which there are many influences on every statistic which cannot be precisely pinned down.

My approach was to compare the fielding statistics of the teams with the most left-handed innings to the fielding statistics of the teams with the fewest left-handed innings. The 48 teams with the most left-handed pitching in the 1946-1960 era had an average of 615 innings of left-handed pitching. The 48 teams (20%) with the least left-handed pitching had an average of 174 innings of left-handed work, and the overall average was 388 innings.

At catcher, there were notably fewer putouts by teams with more left-handed pitching:

Catchers

	PO	A	E	DP	PB	FPct
High Group	732	80	13	13	10	.985
Overall	768	79	13	13	12	.985
Low Group	775	79	12	13	12	.986

Most catcher's putouts are strikeouts, and left-handed pitchers have less of a tendency to be strikeout pitchers. The teams with the most left-handed pitching had an average of 616 strikeouts, and 576 walks. The teams with the least left-handed pitching (the most right-handed pitching) had more strikeouts, 690, and fewer walks, 527. This happens because left-handedness is an advantage to a pitcher, and as such acts as a selection mechanism which off-sets other advantages. The left-handed pitchers were more likely to be ground ball pitchers.

At first base, more left-handed pitching means fewer assists:

First Basemen

	PO	A	E	DP	FPct
High Group	1390	101	15	149	.990
Overall	1384	107	15	140	.990
Low Group	1373	112	16	138	.990

More left-handed pitching means more right-handed hitting on the other team, which means fewer balls hit to first base. There is also a large effect on the "new" categories for first basemen, estimated un-assisted putouts and Arm Rating, but I'll get to that later on.

At second base, more left-handed pitching means more putouts, somewhat fewer assists, significantly more double plays:

Second Basemen

	PO	A	E	DP	FPct
High Group	417	439	20	121	.977
Overall	399	445	21	112	.976
Low Group	376	452	21	108	.975

I made a decision, early on in this, not to adjust for these effects. Later I had to recant, incorporate adjustments for these effects, and re-write a bunch of formulas. The effects are not terribly large when measured against the central tendency—that is, the top group has just 4.5% more putouts than the overall group—and they tend to be off-setting. There is a larger effect measured from top to bottom, but since each putout counts approximately one-half as much as each assist, and since there is a spread of 41 putouts but 13 assists going the other way, the overall effect is not large. But we adjusted for it, anyway.

There's a large effect on second basemen's double plays, but I don't use the second baseman's double play total anyway; I use the team's double plays above or below expectation. The double play effect is caused largely by the tendency of left-handers to be ground ball pitchers, accentuated somewhat by the fact that more left-handed pitchers means more right-handed hitters. This also tends to shift double plays from the shortstop to the second baseman, in part because the second baseman has more of a tendency to cheat toward second with a right-hander at the plate. This is among the reasons I think it is better to use the team double play total, rather than the second base double play total. We are interested in whether an additional double play was made, not so much in who participated in that extra play.

Left-handed pitching has a very substantial impact on the fielding statistics of a team's third basemen:

Third Basemen

	PO	A	E	DP	FPct
High Group	163	341	25	35	.953
Overall	166	319	24	31	.952
Low Group	166	302	22	28	.954

The "high group" had an average of 615 innings by left-handers, which was 441 more than the "low group." This led to an increase of 39 assists by third basemen, essentially one additional assist for each ten additional innings. Obviously, it was appropriate to build in an adjustment for this, in evaluating the defensive play of third basemen.

At shortstop, on the other hand, the effect is not large:

Shortstops

	PO	A	E	DP	FPct
High Group	295	486	30	107	.963
Overall	297	479	32	103	.961
Low Group	309	471	32	105	.960

Shortstops had 15 more assists working behind left-handed pitchers, but 14 more putouts working behind right-handers. If you're using a "range factor" type of analysis, or if you're weighting a putout as equal to an assist, then obviously no adjustment would be necessary for shortstops, as to how much left-handed pitching the team had. We adjusted, anyway, just because we were trying to adjust for everything, no matter how small.

In the outfield, the effect of left-handed pitching on overall fielding totals is not discernable:

Outfielders

	PO	A	E	DP	FPct
High Group	1060	37	23	8	.979
Overall	1052	37	24	8	.979
Low Group	1058	36	23	7	.980

There is no increase in putouts in the outfield as left-handed pitching increases, apparently because the decrease in strikeouts is entirely offset by increased ground balls, rather than fly outs.

The largest effects on team totals, with increased left-handed pitching, are an increase in assists and an increase in double plays:

Team Totals

	PO	A	E	DP	FPct
High Group	4126	1733	141	168	.977
Overall	4143	1703	142	159	.976
Low Group	4139	1677	139	156	.977

Before we leave the subject of left-handed pitching's effect on fielding stats, however, let me note the impact on the new statistics devised here to rate first basemen, which are Estimated Un-assisted Putouts at first base, and Arm Rating. As noted before, first basemen playing behind little left-handed pitching had an average of 112 assists, whereas the first basemen playing behind the most left-handed pitching had an average of 101. However, we also estimated first basemen's un-assisted putouts, by taking the first basemen's putouts and subtracting 84% of assists by pitchers and other infielders. This estimate averages 117 for first basemen playing behind lots of left-handed pitching, and 156 for first basemen playing behind little left-handed pitching:

First Base Plays Made

	A	Estimated Un-assisted PO	Total
High Group	101	117	218
Overall	107	141	248
Low Group	112	156	268

Thus, the increase of 441 innings by left-handed pitchers led to a decrease of 50 plays made by first basemen, essentially consistent with the one-play-per-ten-innings estimate used on the other side of the diamond. I built in an adjustment for this, in evaluating the first basemen.

The Arm Ratings of first basemen playing behind left-handed pitchers also suffer. First basemen playing behind the most left-handed pitching had an average arm rating of 17. Those playing behind the least left-handed pitching had an average arm rating of 27. The difference is approximately one play for each 45 innings of left-handed pitching.

Since I had built this big, hairy database to study left-handed pitchers, it was a pretty simple matter to study some other things. I also studied, for example, the effects of strikeout pitching on fielding stats.

The biggest effect, obviously, is on the statistics of catchers, who for some inane reason are credited with a putout on every strikeout. The "high strikeout group" had an average of 821 strikeouts per team. The low strikeout group had an average of 515 per team, and the overall average was 660 per team:

Catchers

	PO	A	E	DP	PB	FPct
High Group	916	73	12	12	13	.988
Overall	768	79	13	13	12	.985
Low Group	636	85	14	13	12	.980

There are two things about this which are quite striking. First, I had never realized—just blind, I guess—that the effect of strikeouts on catcher's fielding percentages would be as dramatic as it is. Catchers working behind non-strikeout pitchers had an "error percentage" of .020; behind strikeout pitchers, of .012. Thus, the strikeouts of the pitching staff can be a huge factor in where a catcher rates in terms of fielding percentage relative to his peers. It's something we basically have to adjust for, as I did. Johnny Bench, for example, has fielding percentages only a little better than the league average. But since he played almost all of his career for teams with relatively few strikeouts, he's actually well above the league average, when you make the adjustment.

Removing strikeouts from catcher's putouts reduces the fielding percentage of catchers, in modern baseball, from about .990 to about .920. It may also make the fielding percentage of the catcher into a better estimate of his throwing ability. But there's another effect here, which, to be honest, I just don't know what to make of. As you will note above, the catchers on low-strikeout teams had an average of 85 assists per team. The catchers on high-strikeout teams had an average of 73 assists per team.

Now, I am very interested in catcher's assists totals, because I'm trying to figure some way to tease a good estimate of caught stealing percentages out of the catchers' data, or any other data that I can find. But why would catchers have substantially fewer assists when there are more strikeouts? I would have assumed that the opposite would be true, because of the plays that go K (2-3). It doesn't seem to make any sense. I'm asking for help here.

The other real question is whether the decline in fielding plays as strikeouts increase is uniform, applying equally to all positions, or whether it affects some positions more than others. High strikeout totals influence the fielding statistics of outfielders more than infielders, but in general, the effects are fairly uniform, and fairly predictable:

First Basemen

	PO	A	E	DP	FPct
High Group	1355	108	15	134	.990
Overall	1384	107	15	140	.990
Low Group	1389	107	15	142	.990

Nothing noteworthy there.

Second Basemen

	PO	A	E	DP	FPct
High Group	377	435	20	108	.976
Overall	399	445	21	112	.976
Low Group	414	457	25	112	.972

An increase of 306 strikeouts means an overall decrease in fielding putouts of 7.2%, from 3596 per team to 3337. Second basemen show a decrease of 9% in putouts, 5% in assists—thus, an overall effect consistent with the team.

Third basemen, on the other hand, have (almost) no decrease in assists, but a sharp decline in putouts:

Third Basemen

	PO	A	E	DP	FPct
High Group	157	315	23	30	.953
Overall	166	319	24	31	.952
Low Group	176	317	26	32	.950

There's an 11% decrease in third basemen's putouts. I'm not sure what to make of that, but I don't see it as anything especially noteworthy.

Shortstops had a 7% decline in putouts, 3% in assists:

Shortstops

	PO	A	E	DP	FPct
High Group	286	465	31	98	.961
Overall	297	479	32	103	.961
Low Group	308	480	35	104	.958

Am I boring you with all this? Sorry; I feel the need to put the data on record, whether or not it is of any general interest.

Outfielders had the largest effect:

Outfielders

	PO	A	E	DP	FPct
High Group	986	33	21	6	.980
Overall	1052	37	24	8	.979
Low Group	1116	40	27	8	.977

So 42% of the plays "lost" by increased strikeouts were fly balls to the outfield, leading to a 12% decline in outfielder putouts. Team totals:

Team Totals

	PO	A	E	DP	FPct
High Group	4158	1649	134	151	.977
Overall	4143	1703	142	159	.976
Low Group	4111	1730	156	161	.974

The low-strikeout pitchers benefited from 10 more double plays, but suffered from 22 additional errors.

I also sorted the data by strikeouts relative to league. Some of that data is a little bit different, but not different enough to warrant extending this discussion so late at night. Basically, some of the effects noted before are emphasized very slightly by other changes which took place in the major leagues between 1946 and 1960. The "high strikeout" group above is disproportionately composed of teams from the latter part of the era.

I sorted the data by walks, but the teams which had the most walks also tended to have significantly fewer strikeouts than the low-walk teams, so that created some exceptionally annoying cross-correlation effects. To remove those, I created a category called "Walks Minus .16 Strikeouts," to give us a high-walk group and a low-walk group with equal strikeouts.

This doesn't show a lot. In the high-walk group, the catchers have a few more assists, because there are more opposing runners on base. The high-walk group had 168 double plays on average, whereas the low-walk group had 151; there was an increase of one double play for each 12 additional walks. We've already adjusted for that, by figuring expected double plays.

The largest effect is that walks, for obvious reasons, move a certain number of putouts from first base to second, third, or short. With an increase of 211 walks (from 456 to 657), there was a decrease of 33 putouts at first base, but an increase of 11 putouts by second basemen, eight putouts by shortstops, and four putouts by third basemen. There were corresponding decreases in assists by other infielders (-9 at second base, -4 at shortstop, -6 at third base), indicating that walks tend to create a certain number of situations in which plays to first (4-3) are replaced by forceouts (4 un-assisted). Again, I did not feel it appropriate to make any adjustments for this in the system, except that the walks push up the expected double plays.

Sorting the data by Team Wins shows that good teams have higher fielding percentages than poor teams at every position, and also that good teams, in this era, turned more double plays than bad teams (which is not true in some eras). The 48 teams with the most wins had an average DP/Error ratio of 169-130; the 48 teams with the fewest wins had an average ratio of 157-156. The good teams had more strikeouts, thus more putouts at catcher, fewer putouts in the outfield, but essentially the same number of putouts in the infield. The most noteworthy effect on a specific position is that the third basemen on the best teams had an average of 163 putouts, 324 assists. The third basemen on the worst teams had an average of 173 putouts, 313 assists—in other words, about ten assists per season became forceouts on bad teams.

Sorting the data by runs allowed shows more of the same stuff, except that the correlation between Wins and Double Plays does not work the same way. Teams which allowed more runs actually turned more double plays (162-159) than teams which allowed few runs. Teams which allow more runs have more putouts in the outfield and fewer at catcher, but about the same number in the infield.

I sorted the data by the team assists total. This was more interesting. The teams with the most assists had an average of 1817; the teams with the fewest, 1581. The teams with fewer assists, obviously, tended to have more putouts by catchers:

Catchers

	PO	A	E	DP	PB	FPct
High Group	728	83	12	13	11	.986
Overall	768	79	13	13	12	.985
Low Group	823	74	13	12	12	.986

Of the 236 additional assists, 151 resulted in an additional putout at first base:

First Basemen

	PO	A	E	DP	FPct
High Group	1459	114	15	150	.991
Overall	1384	107	15	140	.990
Low Group	1308	103	15	131	.990

But the ground ball teams, the high-assist teams, also had more putouts at second base:

Second Basemen

	PO	A	E	DP	FPct
High Group	409	472	21	121	.977
Overall	399	445	21	112	.976
Low Group	383	422	21	106	.975

Second basemen on the high-assist teams had an average range factor of 5.72; on the low-assist teams, it was 5.23. But at third base, the high-assist teams (the ground ball teams) had a decrease of 20 putouts:

Third Basemen

	PO	A	E	DP	FPct
High Group	155	346	26	33	.951
Overall	166	319	24	31	.952
Low Group	175	291	23	29	.953

Shortstops on ground ball teams had the largest gain in assists, an average of 63 assists, but with no real effect on their putouts:

Shortstops

	PO	A	E	DP	FPct
High Group	299	507	33	110	.960
Overall	297	479	32	103	.961
Low Group	295	444	30	97	.960

On a percentage basis, the gain in assists increases as you go left across the infield. First basemen had an 11% increase in assists, second basemen, a 12% gain, shortstops, a 14% gain, and third basemen, a 19% increase. The gain in putouts decreases as you make the same journey. First basemen on ground ball teams have 12% more putouts than on strikeout/fly ball teams, but second basemen have 7% more, shortstops only 1% more, and third basemen have 11% less.

The outfielders on high-assist teams declined in putouts, but actually not by all that much, as more of the ground balls apparently replaced strikeouts:

Outfielders

	PO	A	E	DP	FPct
High Group	1026	37	23	8	.979
Overall	1052	37	24	8	.979
Low Group	1076	35	23	7	.980

The most noteworthy thing about the Team Totals is that the increase in double plays was in essentially the same proportion as the increase in assists. The high-assist group had 15% more assists, 14% more double plays:

Team Totals

	PO	A	E	DP	FPct
High Group	4158	1817	144	170	.976
Overall	4143	1703	142	159	.976
Low Group	4132	1581	138	149	.976

I sorted the data by pitchers' putouts. This shows the expected—that pitchers' putouts run on the same track as first basemen's assists:

	Pitcher Putouts	First Base Assists
High Group	102	127
Overall	77	107
Low Group	55	89

But also, this data suggests that there is some significant interaction between pitchers' putouts and second base putouts:

	Pitcher Putouts	Second Base Putouts
High Group	102	390
Overall	77	399
Low Group	55	418

There are some plays in baseball on which the second baseman covers first base—on a bunt, for example, but also sometimes on a ground ball. This data suggests that this may be an interaction which should be studied further. (As an afterward to the Lajoie comment, let me note that in the years 1902-1914, the Cleveland Indians also had 55 fewer putouts by pitchers than the American League average, 798 vs. 853.) Otherwise, this data is bland. There is no interaction at all between pitchers' putouts and shortstops' fielding numbers, and nothing else noteworthy in this data.

I sorted the data by catchers' assists, because I'm still interested in trying to figure out how to make something more reliable out of catchers' assists. This data sort shows, as we knew anyway, that catcher's assists are inversely related to team wins, but not so closely related that it does anything to explain why catchers' assists are tied to strikeouts:

	Catcher Assists	Team Wins
High Group	97	71
Overall	79	77
Low Group	63	79

The increase of 34 assists by catchers was accompanied by an increase in putouts by both second basemen (+15) and shortstops (+15):

	Catcher Assists	2B Putouts	SS Putouts
High Group	97	407	303
Overall	79	399	297
Low Group	63	392	288

This is interesting, but it may or may not turn out to be useful information with regard to catcher's throwing. My guess is that it won't. There are so many things that can increase the putouts of a second baseman that an above-average putout total at second base probably has almost no value as an indicator of runners caught stealing. With that exception, this data set is also bland.

As a general conclusion, this study shows:

1. that there are many things which give shape to fielding statistics,

2. that we have limited understanding of those,

3. that it is probably beyond our ability to adjust for all of the interactions which influence defensive statistics at any given position.

For this reason, I would suggest that we should be extremely cautious about attempting to translate defensive statistics into runs saved or hits saved estimates. There is an awful lot here that we just don't know, or can't deal with systematically.

Let us take, for example, the case of two teams, one of which has two left-handed flame throwers and two right-handed junkballers, and the other of which has two right-handed flame throwers, and two left-handed junkballers.

By all of the indicators that we use to predict defensive statistics, the two teams would probably look very much the same. Their strikeouts would be about the same, their left-handed innings would be about the same.

But in fact, the out distribution on the two teams could be radically different. One team, with two right-handed junkballers who were easy to pull and two left-handed flame throwers who were all but impossible to pull, would probably have a huge number of ground balls hit to second base and first base. The other team, with right-handed power pitchers and left-handers throwing slop, might have ground balls hit to shortstop and third base.

If you come along after the fact and try to infer runs saved from the defensive statistics, it is very possible that you might conclude that one team was 30 runs better at third base, while the other was 40 runs better at second base. There might be absolutely no foundation to these estimates.

If the league average is 300 assists by third basemen and one team has 350 assists, this may indicate that the third baseman has made 50 plays that another third baseman would not have made. It may also indicate that this is a team that gets a lot of ground balls to third base. We simply don't know, and we can't know. And for that reason, individual fielding statistics can never be the foundation of a solid evaluation. What we *can* do is to take the real accomplishments of the team's defense—winning games and preventing runs from scoring—and assign credit for that to individual players.

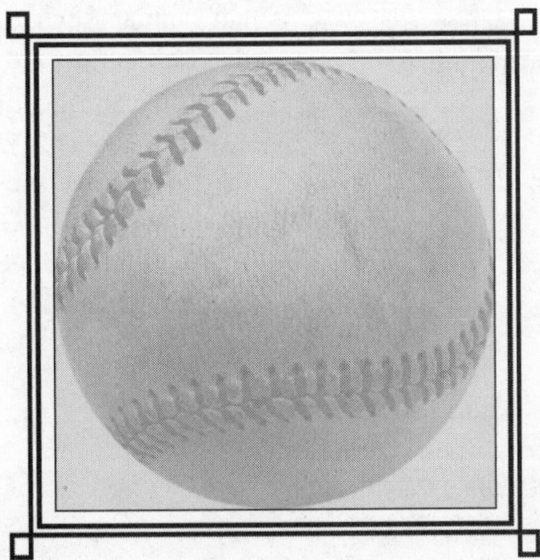

Ed Yost
(Or, "Why, yes, I DID write the same thing in the other book.")

The effects of the failure to adjust for left-handed pitching in evaluating third basemen can be seen by looking at Ed Yost's Fielding Runs in *Total Baseball.* In 1952, when the Senators had only 59 innings of left-handed pitching, Yost ranks at -35 runs—in words, as a truly dreadful defensive performer. In 1954, when the Senators had 793 innings of left-handed pitching, Yost rates at +3—an above average third basemen.

This immense swing in Yost's fielding rating (38 runs—roughly equivalent to 12 Win Shares) was probably created entirely by left-handed pitching. In both seasons, Yost played almost every inning at third base for the Senators. In both seasons, he led the American League in putouts at third base (212 in 1952, 170 in 1954). His fielding percentages were .962 and .968. But whereas Yost had only 248 assists in 1952, when the Senators had almost no left-handed pitching, he had 347 assists in 1954, when the Senators had four left-handed starting pitchers.

In fact, Yost played almost every inning at third base for the Senators from 1950 through 1954. His Linear Weights fielding ratings in each season are tied directly to the Senators' left-handed innings:

Year	Left-Handed Innings	Yost's FR
1950	508	-2
1951	251	-26
1952	59	-35
1953	387	-13
1954	793	+3

The 1954 season, when the Senators had the most left-handed pitching, is evaluated as Yost's best defensive campaign in the era. 1950, when they had the second-most left-handed pitching, is evaluated as his second-best season, and so on down the line. There are 120 ways to put these five seasons in order. *Total Baseball* puts them in the exact same order as the team's number of innings by left-handed pitchers.

The Win Shares system would essentially agree with the Linear Weights analysis that there is little evidence that Yost was a quality defensive third baseman. Among third basemen with 10,000 career innings, he ranks as the third-worst ever, ahead of Richie Hebner and Pinky Higgins (although Dean Palmer, who is far worse, will cross the 10,000 inning mark early in the 2002 season). But we see Yost as essentially the same fielder every year, crediting him with 3.98, 3.53, 4.32, 3.77 and 3.66 Win Shares in the five seasons.

The Win Shares system is vastly more conservative in measuring the differences among third basemen, or players at any defensive position, than is Linear Weights. Linear Weights in 1952 rates Ed Yost at -35 runs, while rating Fred Hatfield of Detroit, who played behind 706 innings of left-handed pitching, at +19 runs. I think it is better not to assert that there is a 54-run difference between two third basemen—a 40-homer difference—without very solid evidence that such a huge gulf actually exists. I mean, I know I have said things like this myself in the past, and I'm not faulting anyone for making the same argument that I myself used to make.

But a 54-run difference would be equivalent to a swing of about 17 Win Shares. I do not now believe that this is a realistic estimate of the defensive impact of a third baseman. Our system would normally evaluate the difference between the league's best defensive third baseman and the worst at something more like four to five Win Shares.

Edwin Peter

In the early 1980s there were three of us who were trying to make a living writing about baseball statistics—myself, Edwin Peter Palmer, and an organization that I will say little about, because there is no point in dredging up 20-year-old hostilities.

When the *Baseball Abstract* hit the best-seller lists, the third group launched their own competitor, the main purposes of which were to:

a) make money,

b) steal all of my ideas, and

c) make as many disparaging comments as possible about me.

So that was a lot of fun. To bring the story up to date, what I didn't realize at the time was that the things which made the third group so obnoxious to me were ultimately self-punishing—and thus, no real cause to dislike them. They weren't hurting me; they were just hurting themselves by trying to harm me.

Anyway, while I had this very difficult relationship on one side of me, on the other side was Pete Palmer. Pete Palmer was everything that the Alias Boys were not. He was as open as they were closed, as generous as they were selfish, as gracious as they were creepy, as friendly as they were hostile, as creative as they were obstructionist, as wise as they were narrow.

Pete's a very unique man, a wonderful man. If you write a letter to me, you might get an answer; you might not. It depends, more or less, on how hard I'm working. If I'm in the middle of book crunch, I wouldn't answer a letter from Steven Spielberg. Not that I've ever gotten a letter from Spielberg or expect to, you understand, but what I'm saying is, when I'm in my work, I'm in my work, and I ain't leaving for anything.

If you write a letter to Pete Palmer, on the other hand, Pete answers you—quickly, graciously, and in detail. Pete is the kind of man who remembers every favor you've ever done for him, and forgets every affront. Unlike me, he does not allow his obsessive interest in the analysis of baseball statistics to override his good nature.

For many years, long before sabermetrics became popular, Pete did amazing work with baseball statistics, particularly with home and road records. He continues to do this work today—hard work, line by line research, compiling day-by-day hitting logs of Joe Gordon and Harlond Clift and hundreds of others into home and road records, and searching for somebody who has pitch-by-pitch scoresheets from the 1982 post-season. He did this kind of work for many years, for no real reason other than that he wanted to know the answers to certain questions. Having found those answers, he was always happy to share what he knew.

In explaining this system, I have found it necessary to dismantle Pete's system, Linear Weights, at great length. The *Total Baseball* rankings are what the public knows. If I want people to understand more than that, get beyond that stage, I have to uproot the assumption that this method actually works.

This is necessary, but it's painful. I do not want to hurt Pete Palmer's feelings or his reputation in the field, for in truth, there is nothing bad to be said about the man. It's not personal; it's just research. I hope that everybody understands that.

Putouts By Third Basemen

In rating fielders, I use basically every available statistic, with one exception. The one thing I don't use, except in oblique ways, is putouts by a third baseman. Why? Because putouts by third basemen don't bear any identifiable relationship to fielding excellence—good, bad or otherwise.

This realization came about, as knowledge often does, when research backfired on me. At one point in the process of developing the Win Shares system—one of the 357 times when I thought I was almost done—I was embarrassed to discover that I had Jim Ray Hart ranked as the number one third baseman in the National League in 1966. I was looking for ways to improve the system for third basemen, and I focused on the fact that Giants third basemen in 1966 had very few putouts. Perhaps, I thought, I over-rated Hart because I under-rated this fact. Perhaps, to make the third base ratings work better, I should devise some way to predict putouts at third base as accurately as possible based on a team's strikeouts, assists, left-handed pitching, etc. I thought that perhaps, when I had done this, there would be an obvious relationship between the ability of the third baseman and the deviation from the team's expected putouts at third base—like, a lot more putouts for teams which had good defensive third basemen.

I pulled up the spreadsheet which has full defensive stats for every team 1946-1960, and I started working on formulas to predict expected putouts at third base. Predicting expected putouts at third base was easy; the problem was with the theory that the deviation from expected putouts would be meaningful.

The number one team on the list was the 1952 Philadelphia Phillies, who had 225 putouts at third base as opposed to 174 expected putouts. Well, that's OK, I guess; Willie Jones was a good third baseman. Number two was OK, Handsome Ransom Jackson of the 1951 Cubs. I mean, it's not Brooks Robinson and Mike Schmidt, but we're off to an OK start here.

But going down the list, there were just all kinds of problems. The 1956 Kansas City A's were fourth on the list. Their regular third baseman, Hector Lopez, was one of the most famous inept fielders of the 1950s. The 1952 Pirates were on the list; they lost 112 games. The 1952 White Sox were near the top of the list (a one-year player named Hector Rodriguez), the 1948 Phillies (Putsy Caballero), the 1959 Kansas City A's (no regular third baseman), the 1960 Cincinnati Reds (no regular third baseman). There were teams which had good defensive third basemen who also had a lot of putouts at third base—but there were at least an equal number of teams who had very good defensive third basemen who were on the "bad list," the list of teams with far fewer putouts at third base than expected. On that list we had the 1948 and 1949 Cleveland Indians (Ken Keltner), the 1948 Brooklyn Dodgers (Billy Cox), the 1947 and 1948 Boston Braves (Bob Elliott), and the 1947 and 1950 New York Yankees (Billy Johnson).

I checked the most famous defensive third basemen of that era—George Kell, Ken Boyer, Frank Malzone, Andy Carey, Keltner, Cox, etc. Nothing. I couldn't see any pattern of the teams which had these players being above expectation. Gold Gloves started at the end of this era, so I checked the seven teams which had Gold Glove third basemen. Four of the seven teams were above expectation, but two of those were +1 and +3, and two of the others were -11 and -18. The bottom team on the list was the 1958 Chicago White Sox (-46; Billy Goodman), followed by the 1956 Cleveland Indians (Al Rosen), the 1953 Cardinals (Ray Jablonski), the 1947 Braves (Bob Elliott), and the 1948 Indians (Keltner). The only one noted as a bad third baseman was Jablonski, who was only a regular for three years, and one of his teams, the 1956 Reds, was +12 in putouts at third base.

That was another problem—there didn't seem to be any consistency in who rated where on the list. Teams would be +16 one year and -12 the next. The only teams to make the top 25 in consecutive seasons were the 1956-57 Kansas City A's (Hector Lopez) and the 1953-54 Yankees, whose third baseman was Gil McDougald one year and Andy Carey the next. I mean, one assumes that if you are measuring a real skill, as opposed to a random fluctuation, then the people who have that skill one year will tend to have that same skill the next year.

After staring at the data for several hours, looking at it this way and that way and trying to see patterns in who was over and who was under, I was unable to see that there was any skill component whatsoever in the third base putouts. I could see various elements in the data. You have putouts at third base if you have few strikeouts, few ground balls, large foul territory, and a bad team. (Third Base Putouts increase as losses increase.) But adjusting for those things, what is the role played by the skill of the third baseman?

If you perform the same operations for third base assists, you get data that makes at least some sense. There are puzzles in that data; there are teams which have many more assists than expected or many fewer, and you can't always see any good reason for that, but the teams that boast the seven Gold Glove winners from the tag end of the era are all at least +20 in third base assists. Only 18% of the teams are +20; all 7 of the teams with Gold Glove third basemen are in that top 18%.

Well, I thought, I'm not going to figure it out with this data set. What is the information I need to understand this? I decided to do a study based on three groups of 50 teams each.

The A group was all the teams with Gold Glove third basemen, 1965 through 1990, except 1981.

For the C group, I wanted teams with third base problems, but not bad third basemen as identified by their statistics, since their statistics were what I wanted to study. I decided to choose the one team from each league which had no regular at the position—in other words, whichever team had the lowest number of games played by any one third baseman. The third basemen for the San Francisco Giants in 1972 were Al Gallagher (69 games), Dave Kingman (59 games), Jim Ray Hart (20 games), Damaso Blanco (19 games) and Chris Arnold (17 games), a high of 69. Everybody else in the league had a third baseman playing more than 69 games, so for the 1972 National League, the Giants were it.

The B group was 50 teams selected at random, one from each league each season, 1965 through 1990 except 1981. I had the computer assign every team in that era a random number, and then for each league whoever had the highest random number was the B group team (unless they had already been selected as the A group team or the C group team). So we had, then, an A group which had Gold Glove third basemen, a C group which had third base as a problem area, and a B group which was a control group.

For each of these 150 teams, I entered eleven statistics into a spreadsheet, actually ten with the eleventh being a calculation from three others. The data was:

Team Wins
Team Losses
Runs Allowed by the team
Strikeouts by the team
Sacrifice Hits allowed by the team
Defensive Games at third base
Putouts by third basemen
Assists by third basemen
Errors by third basemen
Double plays by third basemen
Fielding Percentage at third base

In all of these areas except Strikeouts and Third Base Putouts, the data was markedly different between the three groups. The teams with Gold Glove third basemen (the A Group) had an average won-lost record of 86-75; the C Group, an average of 75-87. The A group teams allowed an average of 644 opposition runs; the C group, 692. The A group teams had an average of 174 defensive games at third base (12 shared defensive games), while the C group teams had an average of 198 (36 shared defensive games).

The A group teams had an average of 367 assists at third base, 20 errors, and a .962 fielding percentage. The C group teams had an average of 338 assists, 28 errors, and a .943 fielding percentage.

But in putouts, there was hardly any difference among the three groups:

Group A	136 putouts
Group B	134 putouts
Group C	133 putouts

A difference of three putouts, top to bottom. This is the full data for the three groups:

	Won	Lost	OR	SO	SH	DG	PO	A	E	DP	FPct
A Group	86	75	644	876	65	174	136	367	20	32	.962
B Group	83	78	668	876	68	189	134	332	24	27	.951
C Group	75	87	692	861	72	198	133	338	28	30	.943

Look, guys, I am anything but anxious to be throwing away data. I am struggling to find all of the meaningful data that I can possibly find to help us make accurate evaluations of defensive players. Declaring information that we have been using to be meaningless and unusable is real low on my list of things that I want to do today.

But having studied this issue as well as I know how to study it, I just can't find any reason to believe that putouts at third base are (or can be made into) a meaningful indicator of a third baseman's fielding ability. I mean, you can find a little bit of skill input here, if you look at it just right. But even then, the skill input is a third the size of the random variance, and a tenth the size of the variance in the category which can be attributed to other known biases. That's useless; that's like weighing a fly by trapping him in the cab of a truck, weighing the truck with the fly and without the fly. If that's all that we can do, we're better off to admit defeat than to pretend that this is a victory.

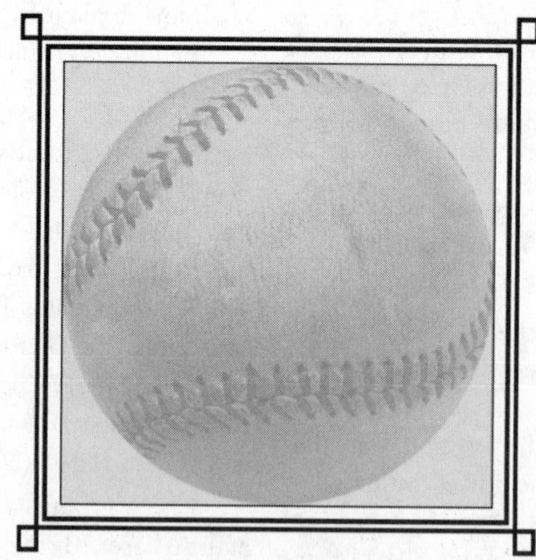

Team Star Power

I don't have any research about this one, and no real point. . . just something that sounds like a fun idea.

What would be the greatest team ever, in terms not merely of playing well, but in terms of *having great players who played well*? Suppose that we compared teams by taking the Win Shares by each player on each team, and multiplying them by the player's *career* Win Shares. What would you have then?

Well, I don't know, because I haven't done the research, but one way of looking for great teams is to look not merely at what the players did that year, but to look at teams which had legitimately great players having good years. In 1950, for example, the five best players in the major leagues were:

1.	Phil Rizzuto	35
2t.	Yogi Berra	32
2t.	Earl Torgeson	32
2t.	Stan Musial	32
5t.	Larry Doby	30
5t.	Eddie Stanky	30

However, while Earl Torgeson may have played as well as Yogi Berra and Stan Musial in 1950, nonetheless Earl Torgeson was not as great a player as Yogi Berra or Stan Musial. On the other hand, these are the five greatest players active in 1950 (by Career Win Shares):

1.	Stan Musial	604
2.	Ted Williams	555
3.	Warren Spahn	412
4.	Joe DiMaggio	387
5.	Luke Appling	378

However, while Luke Appling was certainly a great player, he was, in 1950, a 43-year-old man who hit .234 in 50 games. While Ted Williams was certainly among the greatest players of all time, he was injured in 1950, and missed the second half of the season. What we are interested in here is not either of these lists, but something in between them—great players, having great seasons. We can get that by multiplying the one value by the other.

That list, the ten greatest players having good seasons in 1950, is as follows:

Player	Season	Career	Product
1. Stan Musial	32	604	19328
2. Yogi Berra	35	375	12000
3. Joe DiMaggio	29	387	11223
4. Ted Williams	19	555	10545
5. Duke Snider	29	352	10208
6. Robin Roberts	26	339	8814
7. Warren Spahn	21	412	8652
8. Phil Rizzuto	35	231	8085
9. Larry Doby	30	268	8040
10. Bob Elliott	27	287	7749

Stan Musial is the only guy who makes both of the other top lists—thus, the brightest star of 1950.

On a team level, here's the top and bottom teams of 1950:

1.	New York Yankees	59969
2.	Boston Red Sox	51235
3.	Cleveland Indians	51146
4.	Brooklyn Dodgers	49908
16.	St. Louis Browns	13052
15.	Philadelphia A's	17065
14.	Pittsburgh Pirates	18589
13.	Chicago White Sox	18869

All four of the bottom teams rank below Stan Musial as an individual.

Does this *mean* anything? I don't know; I haven't done the research. Probably not. It might be that there is some sort of connection between having star power on your team, and winning the World Series. . .

I will note that, in the 1950 World Series, the New York Yankees, with three of the top ten players and the highest team total, crushed the Philadelphia Phillies, with one of the top ten players and the majors' sixth-best total. Team star power probably tracks attendance, I'm guessing, and thus might be useful for studying attendance. The two lowest teams on the list, the Browns and A's, were among the first teams to pick up and move to other cities—surely not a coincidence.

Baseball's supposed to be fun. Baseball research doesn't *have* to mean anything.

Using Win Shares For Better Team Age Analysis

Another thing which we could do with Win Shares is an annual analysis of each team's age. By multiplying the age of each player by his Win Shares and dividing the total by the team Win Shares, we can derive a better estimate of the team's liabilities to age. For example, Houston vs. St. Louis, 2001:

Team Age			29.39
	WS	Age	Input
Houston	279		8199
L.Berkman	32	25	800
J.Bagwell	30	33	990
C.Biggio	25	35	875
M.Alou	21	34	714
R.Hidalgo	17	25	425
W.Miller	17	24	408
R.Oswalt	15	23	345
B.Wagner	13	29	377
V.Castilla	12	33	396
O.Dotel	12	25	300
B.Ausmus	10	32	320
S.Reynolds	10	33	330
J.Lugo	9	25	225
N.Cruz	6	28	168
M.Jackson	6	36	216
D.Ward	5	26	130
T.Eusebio	5	34	170
O.Merced	4	34	136
J.Vizcaino	4	33	132
D.Mlicki	4	33	132
J.Powell	3	29	87
C.Truby	3	27	81
P.Astacio	2	31	62
C.Hernandez	2	21	42
M.Williams	2	32	64
R.Villone	2	31	62
T.Redding	2	23	46
T.McKnight	1	24	24
M.Lopez	1	26	26
S.Linebrink	1	24	24
R.Stone	1	26	26
G.Barker	1	30	30
C.Hayes	1	36	36

Team Age			28.47
	WS	Age	Input
St. Louis	279		7944
J.Edmonds	30	31	930
A.Pujols	29	21	609
J.Drew	22	25	550
F.Vina	22	32	704
D.Kile	18	32	576
M.Morris	17	26	442
P.Polanco	14	25	350
E.Renteria	13	25	325
S.Kline	12	28	336
C.Paquette	12	32	384
M.McGwire	8	37	296
M.Matheny	8	30	240
W.Williams	8	34	272
R.Lankford	8	34	272
D.Hermanson	8	28	224
D.Veres	7	34	238
M.Matthews	7	27	189
E.Marrero	7	27	189
G.Stechschulte	5	27	135
M.Timlin	5	35	175
B.Smith	5	21	105
K.Robinson	4	27	108
L.Hackman	2	26	52
M.Cairo	2	27	54
J.Christiansen	2	31	62
T.Mathews	1	31	31
B.Bonilla	1	38	38
M.James	1	33	33
J.Karnuth	1	25	25

I thought, before doing the research, that Houston was a very old team, St. Louis a relatively young team. It turns out that Houston, with significant contributions from Berkman, Hidalgo, Miller and Oswalt, isn't all that old—Team Age of 29.4—and St. Louis isn't all that young, with a Team Age of 28.5.

I used to do something like this in the annual *Abstracts*, and I suspect that somebody probably picked it up and still does it, I don't know. . . my only point was that Win Shares could be used to do it somewhat more precisely.

Years ago, when I was writing annual books, the team age had significant value as a predictor of future performance. . . old teams tended to get worse, young teams tended to get better. In modern baseball, I would be surprised if that was *as* true as it was in the 1980s. In modern baseball, young teams tend to get raped by the Yankees. Veteran baseball teams in 2002 are like vampires; they live forever on the blood of the young. In any case, given the kind of computerized information that we have now, it would be a fairly simple matter for a sophisticated programmer to figure the "team age" for every team in baseball history, to track the movement up or down for teams within different age groups, and to see whether that indicator still functions as well as it once did.

There is a more sophisticated and more interesting analysis which could be done, but not as easily. Suppose that you have a 28-year-old player who earns 20 Win Shares. That player, based on that knowledge, has to have an actuarial expectation for future Win Shares, right? It would be somewhere around 180 expected future Win Shares. A 28-year-old player with 15 Win Shares would have an expectation of about 125 future Win Shares; a 28-year-old with 25 Win Shares would probably have an expectation around 250 future Win Shares. . . I'm just guessing.

By studying past player records, we could establish a chart of actuarial expectations for each current player. By so doing, we could measure the intact resources of each team, at any point during the winter. The Atlanta Braves trade for Gary Sheffield. . . Sheffield was 32 years old in 2001 and earned 30 Win Shares, which means he has an actuarial expectation of earning something like 140 future Win Shares. The Kansas City Royals signed Chuck Knoblauch (Whoa, Doggies!!), who was also 32 years old in 2001, and earned 11 Win Shares, giving him a career Win Share expectation of something like 25, 30 future Win Shares. Each team has a "talent pool." When teams add players or lose them, we add or subtract from their talent pool.

Of course, there is more that should go into establishing the expectation than simply the player's age and his Win Shares. A player who earns 10 Win Shares at age 30 could be a player who earns 10 Win Shares every year, or he could be a player who normally earns 30 Win Shares a season, but was injured most of the season. The expected future Win Shares could be better established by studying multi-year Win Share patterns.

The expectation for a 26-year-old pitcher who earns 20 Win Shares would probably be different than the expectation for a 26-year-old outfielder who does the same. On a more subtle level, the expectation for a 26-year-old power pitcher would certainly be different from the expectation for a 26-year-old finesse pitcher. The expectation for a 26-year-old reliever would probably be different than the expectation for a 26-year-old starter. The expectation for a 26-year-old outfielder with power would probably be different from the expectation for a 26-year-old outfielder who hits singles and steals bases. I am quite certain, from previous studies, that the expectation for a 26-year-old black player would be higher than the expectation for a 26-year-old white player who appeared in all other respects to be statistically identical. The expectation for a player in 2002 is probably different than it was for a similar player fifty years ago.

A rule of science is that all studies are vastly more complicated than you think they are when you plan them. It is common for simple studies, which I think will take me an hour, to wind up requiring two or three weeks. This actuarial stuff doesn't even *sound* simple. It's complicated. It's a book-length project. But it could be done, and the knowledge one would gain from doing these studies might be of immense value in studying baseball teams and baseball players.

Old Gold Gloves

One of the fun things about this research is that it produces a list of who would have won or should have won Gold Gloves over the years, so that if you are really into the 1938 season, you can go to that section and look up who should have been the Gold Glove team in each league in 1938, and get actual reasonable answers most of the time. It would not be a productive use of our time or space to list all of these Gold Gloves and comment upon them, but I thought it might be fun to do a few of them. . . let's say, one league every 12 years. These are the players who Win Shares says should have won these awards:

1880 National League

Pos	Player	Comment
C	Silver Flint	That's good
1B	Cap Anson	Cap would agree with us
2B	Fred Dunlap	Probably right
3B	George Bradley	Who knows?
SS	Arthur Irwin	A solid choice
OF	Paul Hines	Certainly would have won
OF	George Gore	Certainly would have won
OF	Abner Dalrymple	So/so defensive rep—no one is clearly better for third spot

1892 National League

Pos	Player	Comment
C	Chief Zimmer	Sounds right
1B	Dan Brouthers	Did not have good defensive reputation
2B	Bid McPhee	A reasonable guess
3B	Billy Nash	Probably right
SS	Germany Smith	Renowned glove wizard
OF	Jimmy McAleer	Often cited as best outfielder of his generation
OF	Mike Griffin	A reasonable option
OF	Hugh Duffy	Yes

1904 American League

Pos	Player	Comment
C	Deacon McGuire	Very suspect in view of his age (40)
1B	Candy LaChance	He was a good first baseman, certainly
2B	Hobe Ferris	I agree, and I think he would have won
3B	Lee Tannehill	See note
SS	Freddy Parent	Got good reviews, but Bobby Wallace would probably have won the award
OF	Fielder Jones	No doubt
OF	Dave Fultz	Grave doubt
OF	Emmett Heidrick	Who? What?

At third base, Jimmy Collins absolutely would have won, based on his reputation. The ratings for Collins and Tannehill are both very, very high, and Tannehill played 153 games despite a .229 average with no homers, suggesting that he must have been contributing in the field. The outfield Gold Gloves would probably have gone to Fielder Jones, Chick Stahl and Sam Crawford, I'm guessing.

1916 National League

Pos	Player	Comment
C	Hank Gowdy	Absolutely no doubt
1B	Ed Konetchy	Had good glove rep, but Hal Chase would have won the vote
2B	George Cutshaw	Quite certainly would have won
3B	Mike Mowrey	Don't know anything about him
SS	Dave Bancroft	Sure. . . Bancroft and Maranville are close.
OF	Max Carey	Would certainly have won
OF	Cy Williams	An OK choice. He was young and a center fielder.
OF	Zack Wheat	It's *possible* that he might have won, but doubtful.

1928 American League

Pos	Player	Comment
C	Mickey Cochrane	Can't argue with the Hall of Famer
1B	Lu Blue	Would not have won the award
2B	Max Bishop	Not sure. . . Bucky Harris might have won it on reputation
3B	Willie Kamm	Would probably have won—Kamm or Bluege
SS	Joe Sewell	Questionable. There isn't a good option, though.
OF	Fred Schulte	Good choice
OF	Johnny Mostil	Absolutely
OF	Bing Miller	Probably wouldn't have gotten the award

1940 National League

Pos	Player	Comment
C	Harry Danning	Not great, but seems to be the best available option
1B	Frank McCormick	One of the greatest glove men ever at first base
2B	Lonny Frey	Close call between Frey and Herman
3B	Billy Werber	As good a pick as any
SS	Marty Marion	Among the most famous glove men ever
OF	Dixie Walker	Doubt that he would have won
OF	Terry Moore	Certainly
OF	Harry Craft	A good choice

1952 American League

Pos	Player	Comment
C	Yogi Berra	Jim Hegan probably would have won the vote
1B	Mickey Vernon	Sure. Would have won the award easily.
2B	Nellie Fox	Sure. This is easy.
3B	Hector Rodriguez	One-year regular; obviously would not have won the vote
SS	Pete Runnels	A bad pick. Rizzuto would have won the award, and probably deserved to.
OF	Jim Busby	Yes
OF	Jim Rivera	Yes. Jungle Jim was famous for circus catches and inappropriate conduct with minors.
OF	Dave Philley	Yes, but Dom DiMaggio would likely have gotten one of the three slots

For the rest of our seasons, we'll have actual Gold Gloves for comparison, making it unnecessary for me to speculate on who might have won the award. If our selection matches the actual Gold Glove, I'll just note that with a + sign. If not, I'll show a "-" and tell you who actually won:

1964 National League

Pos	Player		Comment
C	Johnny Edwards	+	
1B	Bill White	+	
2B	Bill Mazeroski	+	
3B	Ron Santo	+	
SS	Leo Cardenas	-	Ruben Amaro, but Cardenas won in '65.
OF	Curt Flood	+	
OF	Willie Mays	+	
OF	Willie Davis	-	Roberto Clemente was the third outfielder.

1976 American League

Pos	Player		Comment
C	Jim Sundberg	+	
1B	George Scott	+	
2B	Bobby Grich	+	
3B	Graig Nettles	-	Aurelio Rodriguez. Nettles won in '77 and '78.
SS	Mark Belanger	+	
OF	Ron LeFlore	-	Joe Rudi
OF	Mickey Rivers	-	Rick Manning
OF	Juan Beniquez	-	Dwight Evans

1988 National League

Pos	Player		Comment
C	Tony Pena	-	Benito Santiago won that one, but I'm OK with it.
1B	Glenn Davis	-	See note
2B	Jose Lind	-	Ryne Sandberg won. Lind was terrific.
3B	Tim Wallach	+	
SS	Ozzie Smith	+	
OF	Gerald Young	-	Eric Davis
OF	Andy Van Slyke	+	
OF	John Shelby	-	Andre Dawson

Keith Hernandez won the 1988 Gold Glove at first base, despite injuries which kept him under 100 games played. Hernandez wasn't a great choice; Davis probably isn't, either. Mark Grace, Andres Galarraga, Sid Bream and Will Clark were all regulars in the league.

2000 American League

Pos	Player		Comment
C	Brad Ausmus	-	Ivan Rodriguez won it despite injuries
1B	John Olerud	+	
2B	Randy Velarde	-	Alomar. OUCH. Pretend you didn't see this one.
3B	Tony Batista	-	Travis Fryman. OUCH!! Man, I'm dyin' here.
SS	Alex Rodriguez	-	Omar Vizquel. Alex got the money.
OF	Carl Everett	-	Jermaine Dye
OF	Chris Singleton	-	Darin Erstad. Erstad is fourth by our system.
OF	Bernie Williams	+	

For the four seasons above in which we have actual Gold Gloves for comparison, we matched 15 of the 32 votes, which I think is our normal percentage. . . I think since the Gold Glove votes started, Win Shares has matched about 50% of them. Obviously Randy Velarde and Tony Batista are not good picks, although Batista is such a weird player I never know what to make of him, and these selections punctuate the fact that defensive statistics, no matter how carefully analyzed, sometimes simply do not match up with observable defensive excellence.

Win Shares And MVP Voting

Let us offer a similar, but more extensive, report on Most Valuable Players. As a frame of reference, I sometimes use the following terms:

30-40 Win Shares	MVP-type Seasons
20-30 Win Shares	All-Star Seasons
10-20 Win Shares	Solid Regulars
0-10 Win Shares	Bench Players

However, there have been MVPs who had 20 Win Shares or less, and there have been bench players who had 20 Win Shares or more.

Since 1931, 58 of 142 Most Valuable Players, or 41%, have had or have shared the highest Win Share totals in their leagues. An additional 13 MVPs missed the distinction of being first in their league by only one or two Win Shares, meaning that exactly one-half of all MVPs have been within two points of leading their leagues in Win Shares. I'll put on record here the year-by-year Most Valuable Players, as seen by our analysis, and as seen by the BBWAA voters. The numbers are, of course, the Win Shares for each player, and I'll break in occasionally to comment:

1931 AL Win Shares MVP Lefty Grove (42)
1931 AL Actual MVP Lefty Grove (42)

1931 NL Win Shares MVP Wally Berger (31)
1931 NL Actual MVP Frankie Frisch (21)

1932 AL Win Shares MVP Jimmie Foxx (40)
1932 AL Actual MVP Jimmie Foxx (40)

1932 NL Win Shares MVP O'Doul and Ott (33)
1932 NL Actual MVP Chuck Klein (31)

Another thing I would like to study, when I get time, is the effect of playing in a hitter's park. Obviously hitters who play in hitter's parks, like Klein, are likely to steal an MVP Award once in awhile.

1933 AL Win Shares MVP Jimmie Foxx (41)
1933 AL Actual MVP Jimmie Foxx (41)

1933 NL Win Shares MVP Wally Berger (36)
1933 NL Actual MVP Carl Hubbell (33)

Berger deserved two MVP Awards and was close in two other seasons. Unfortunately, he played for a bad team in a pitcher's park. . .

1934 AL Win Shares MVP Lou Gehrig (41)
1934 AL Actual MVP Mickey Cochrane (23)

This ties with one other Award (1944 NL) as the worst MVP selections, in view of the Win Shares system. However, most of the "worst" MVP selections in this view are of catchers; the Win Shares system rarely sees catchers as the best player in the league. I think the only catcher to *earn* the MVP Award, in our view, was Johnny Bench in 1970, and many of the catchers who have won the Award are not seen by our system as being viable candidates. But it is not unreasonable to give catchers a fair shot at the Award, even though they may not bat 650 times.

1934 NL Win Shares MVP Mel Ott (38)
1934 NL Actual MVP Dizzy Dean (37)

1935 AL Win Shares MVP Wes Ferrell (35)
1935 AL Actual MVP Hank Greenberg (34)

Dick Thompson will be *so* pleased. . .

1935 NL Win Shares MVP Arky Vaughan (39)
1935 NL Actual MVP Gabby Hartnett (26)

1936 AL Win Shares MVP Lou Gehrig (38)
1936 AL Actual MVP Lou Gehrig (38)

1936 NL Win Shares MVP Carl Hubbell (37)
1936 NL Actual MVP Carl Hubbell (37)

1937 AL Win Shares MVP Joe DiMaggio (39)
1937 AL Actual MVP Charlie Gehringer (30)

1937 NL Win Shares MVP Joe Medwick (40)
1937 NL Actual MVP Joe Medwick (40)

1938 AL Win Shares MVP Foxx and Greenberg (34)
1938 AL Actual MVP Jimmie Foxx (34)

1938 NL Win Shares MVP Mel Ott (36)
1938 NL Actual MVP Ernie Lombardi (24)

The third time Ott got stiffed.

1939 AL Win Shares MVP Joe DiMaggio (34)
1939 AL Actual MVP Joe DiMaggio (34)

1939 NL Win Shares MVP Bucky Walters (38)
1939 NL Actual MVP Bucky Walters (38)

1940 AL Win Shares MVP Bob Feller (34)
1940 AL Actual MVP Hank Greenberg (31)

1940 NL Win Shares MVP Johnny Mize (33)
1940 NL Actual MVP Frank McCormick (27)

1941 AL Win Shares MVP Ted Williams (42)
1941 AL Actual MVP Joe DiMaggio (41)

One of the most famous MVP races. . . it's actually too close to call.

1941 NL Win Shares MVP Pete Reiser (34)
1941 NL Actual MVP Dolph Camilli (29)

This is an interesting vote. It is one of about a dozen times when a player has lost the award to an arguably less deserving teammate. I would bet that everybody who was a Dodger fan that season (and is still alive) now remembers Reiser as the better player—but Camilli's winning the award is consistent with the history of the vote, which usually goes to the RBI leader if there is any way that it can.

1942 AL Win Shares MVP Ted Williams (46)
1942 AL Actual MVP Joe Gordon (31)

Ted's still mad about that one.

1942 NL Win Shares MVP Enos Slaughter (37)
1942 NL Actual MVP Mort Cooper (29)

1943 AL Win Shares MVP Luke Appling (40)
1943 AL Actual MVP Spud Chandler (29)

1943 NL Win Shares MVP Stan Musial (39)
1943 NL Actual MVP Stan Musial (39)

1944 AL Win Shares MVP Dizzy Trout (42)
1944 AL Actual MVP Hal Newhouser (35)

1944 NL Win Shares MVP Stan Musial (38)
1944 NL Actual MVP Marty Marion (20)

Can't give it to Stan *every* year.

1945 AL Win Shares MVP Hal Newhouser (38)
1945 AL Actual MVP Hal Newhouser (38)

1945 NL Win Shares MVP Stan Hack (34)
1945 NL Actual MVP Phil Cavaretta (30)

Noted again: the MVP Award doesn't like leadoff men.

1946 AL Win Shares MVP Ted Williams (49)
1946 AL Actual MVP Ted Williams (49)

1946 NL Win Shares MVP Stan Musial (44)
1946 NL Actual MVP Stan Musial (44)

1947 AL Win Shares MVP Ted Williams (44)
1947 AL Actual MVP Joe DiMaggio (30)

A famous controversy.

1947 NL Win Shares MVP Spahn and Mize (32)
1947 NL Actual MVP Bob Elliott (29)

1948 AL Win Shares MVP Ted Williams (39)
1948 AL Actual MVP Lou Boudreau (34)

1948 NL Win Shares MVP Stan Musial (46)
1948 NL Actual MVP Stan Musial (46)

1949 AL Win Shares MVP Ted Williams (40)
1949 AL Actual MVP Ted Williams (40)

Stan Musial

1949 NL	Win Shares MVP	Stan Musial (40)
1949 NL	Actual MVP	Jackie Robinson (36)

The 1940s featured very politicized voting, people using the MVP races to grind their axes. Only six of the twenty Awards went to the players seen by our system as the most deserving—the lowest percentage of any decade.

1950 AL	Win Shares MVP	Phil Rizzuto (35)
1950 AL	Actual MVP	Phil Rizzuto (35)
1950 NL	Win Shares MVP	Earl Torgeson and Musial (32)
1950 NL	Actual MVP	Jim Konstanty (23)
1951 AL	Win Shares MVP	Ted Williams (34)
1951 AL	Actual MVP	Yogi Berra (31)
1951 NL	Win Shares MVP	Stan Musial (39)
1951 NL	Actual MVP	Roy Campanella (33)
1952 AL	Win Shares MVP	Larry Doby (34)
1952 AL	Actual MVP	Bobby Shantz (33)
1952 NL	Win Shares MVP	Stan Musial (37)
1952 NL	Actual MVP	Hank Sauer (28)

That's eight for Stan, if you're counting. Willie takes over now.

1953 AL	Win Shares MVP	Al Rosen (42)
1953 AL	Actual MVP	Al Rosen (42)
1953 NL	Win Shares MVP	Eddie Mathews (39)
1953 NL	Actual MVP	Roy Campanella (33)
1954 AL	Win Shares MVP	Mickey Mantle (36)
1954 AL	Actual MVP	Yogi Berra (34)
1954 NL	Win Shares MVP	Willie Mays (40)
1954 NL	Actual MVP	Willie Mays (40)
1955 AL	Win Shares MVP	Mickey Mantle (41)
1955 AL	Actual MVP	Yogi Berra (24)

Berra was an RBI man *and* a catcher. Therefore, by definition, he *had* to be the MVP.

1955 NL	Win Shares MVP	Willie Mays (40)
1955 NL	Actual MVP	Roy Campanella (28)
1956 AL	Win Shares MVP	Mickey Mantle (49)
1956 AL	Actual MVP	Mickey Mantle (49)
1956 NL	Win Shares MVP	Duke Snider (34)
1956 NL	Actual MVP	Don Newcombe (27)
1957 AL	Win Shares MVP	Mickey Mantle (51)
1957 AL	Actual MVP	Mickey Mantle (51)
1957 NL	Win Shares MVP	Henry Aaron (35)
1957 NL	Actual MVP	Henry Aaron (35)
1958 AL	Win Shares MVP	Mickey Mantle (39)
1958 AL	Actual MVP	Jackie Jensen (27)

Jensen played in a hitter's park and led the league in RBI.

1958 NL Win Shares MVP Willie Mays (40)
1958 NL Actual MVP Ernie Banks (31)

1959 AL Win Shares MVP Mantle and Fox (30)
1959 AL Actual MVP Nellie Fox (30)

1959 NL Win Shares MVP Henry Aaron (38)
1959 NL Actual MVP Ernie Banks (33)

1960 AL Win Shares MVP Mickey Mantle (36)
1960 AL Actual MVP Roger Maris (31)

1960 NL Win Shares MVP Mathews and Mays (38)
1960 NL Actual MVP Dick Groat (25)

1961 AL Win Shares MVP Mickey Mantle (48)
1961* AL Actual MVP Roger Maris (36)

1961 NL Win Shares MVP Henry Aaron (35)
1961 NL Actual MVP Frank Robinson (34)

1962 AL Win Shares MVP Mickey Mantle (33)
1962 AL Actual MVP Mickey Mantle (33)

Mickey Mantle

1962 NL Win Shares MVP Mays and Frank Robinson (41)
1962 NL Actual MVP Maury Wills (32)

1963 AL Win Shares MVP Yastrzemski and Tresh (29)
1963 AL Actual MVP Elston Howard (28)

1963 NL Win Shares MVP Henry Aaron (41)
1963 NL Actual MVP Sandy Koufax (32)

1964 AL Win Shares MVP Mickey Mantle (34)
1964 AL Actual MVP Brooks Robinson (33)

1964 NL Win Shares MVP Dick Allen (41)
1964 NL Actual MVP Ken Boyer (28)

Allen or Callison would have won the award if the Phillies hadn't tanked.

1965 AL Win Shares MVP Tony Oliva (33)
1965 AL Actual MVP Zoilo Versalles (32)

1965 NL Win Shares MVP Willie Mays (43)
1965 NL Actual MVP Willie Mays (43)

1966 AL Win Shares MVP Frank Robinson (41)
1966 AL Actual MVP Frank Robinson (41)

1966 NL Win Shares MVP Willie Mays (37)
1966 NL Actual MVP Roberto Clemente (29)

1967 AL Win Shares MVP Carl Yastrzemski (42)
1967 AL Actual MVP Carl Yastrzemski (42)

1967 NL Win Shares MVP Ron Santo (38)
1967 NL Actual MVP Orlando Cepeda (34)

The winner gets the Hall of Fame. . .

1968 AL Win Shares MVP Carl Yastrzemski (39)
1968 AL Actual MVP Denny McLain (33)

1968 NL Win Shares MVP Bob Gibson (36)
1968 NL Actual MVP Bob Gibson (36)

1969 AL Win Shares MVP Reggie Jackson (41)
1969 AL Actual MVP Harmon Killebrew (34)

But we might get a different answer in this year if we had scoresheets.

1969 NL	Win Shares MVP	Willie McCovey (39)
1969 NL	Actual MVP	Willie McCovey (39)
1970 AL	Win Shares MVP	Carl Yastrzemski (36)
1970 AL	Actual MVP	Boog Powell (31)
1970 NL	Win Shares MVP	Johnny Bench (34)
1970 NL	Actual MVP	Johnny Bench (34)
1971 AL	Win Shares MVP	Bobby Murcer (38)
1971 AL	Actual MVP	Vida Blue (30)
1971 NL	Win Shares MVP	Joe Torre (41)
1971 NL	Actual MVP	Joe Torre (41)
1972 AL	Win Shares MVP	Dick Allen (40)
1972 AL	Actual MVP	Dick Allen (40)
1972 NL	Win Shares MVP	Steve Carlton (40)
1972 NL	Actual MVP	Johnny Bench (37)
1973 AL	Win Shares MVP	Reggie Jackson (32)
1973 AL	Actual MVP	Reggie Jackson (32)
1973 NL	Win Shares MVP	Joe Morgan (40)
1973 NL	Actual MVP	Pete Rose (34)
1974 AL	Win Shares MVP	Jeff Burroughs (33)
1974 AL	Actual MVP	Jeff Burroughs (33)
1974 NL	Win Shares MVP	Mike Schmidt (39)
1974 NL	Actual MVP	Steve Garvey (27)
1975 AL	Win Shares MVP	Lynn, Singleton and Mayberry (33)
1975 AL	Actual MVP	Fred Lynn (33)

A three-way tie here. We could "break" the tie by looking at the underlying data, but I want to do as much as possible to discourage that. One of the worst habits of baseball statisticians is to focus on percentages—this player is at 33.17 and that one is at 33.11, therefore A is better than B—and ignore fundamental questions, like, "Is the difference between .17 and .11 real and meaningful?" Which it clearly is not. . . all distinctions of less than 3 Win Shares are of questionable validity, given the nature of baseball statistics.

1975 NL	Win Shares MVP	Joe Morgan (44)
1975 NL	Actual MVP	Joe Morgan (44)
1976 AL	Win Shares MVP	George Brett (33)
1976 AL	Actual MVP	Thurman Munson (24)
1976 NL	Win Shares MVP	Joe Morgan (37)
1976 NL	Actual MVP	Joe Morgan (37)
1977 AL	Win Shares MVP	Rod Carew (37)
1977 AL	Actual MVP	Rod Carew (37)
1977 NL	Win Shares MVP	Schmidt and Parker (33)
1977 NL	Actual MVP	George Foster (32)
1978 AL	Win Shares MVP	Jim Rice (36)
1978 AL	Actual MVP	Jim Rice (36)
1978 NL	Win Shares MVP	Dave Parker (37)
1978 NL	Actual MVP	Dave Parker (37)
1979 AL	Win Shares MVP	Fred Lynn (34)
1979 AL	Actual MVP	Don Baylor (29)
1979 NL	Win Shares MVP	Schmidt and Winfield (33)
1979 NL	Actual MVP	Hernandez (29) and Stargell (18)

Despite concluding on this dismal note, the 1970s were the most successful decade in terms of matching the MVP Award to the most deserving candidates, as we see them. Eleven of the 20 awards went to the player earning the most Win Shares.

1980 AL	Win Shares MVP	George Brett (36)
1980 AL	Actual MVP	George Brett (36)
1980 NL	Win Shares MVP	Mike Schmidt (37)
1980 NL	Actual MVP	Mike Schmidt (37)

1981 AL Win Shares MVP Rickey Henderson (27)
1981 AL Actual MVP Rollie Fingers (17)

1981 NL Win Shares MVP Mike Schmidt (30)
1981 NL Actual MVP Mike Schmidt (30)

1982 AL Win Shares MVP Robin Yount (39)
1982 AL Actual MVP Robin Yount (39)

1982 NL Win Shares MVP Mike Schmidt (37)
1982 NL Actual MVP Dale Murphy (32)

1983 AL Win Shares MVP Cal Ripken Jr. (35)
1983 AL Actual MVP Cal Ripken Jr. (35)

1983 NL Win Shares MVP Mike Schmidt (35)
1983 NL Actual MVP Dale Murphy (32)

1984 AL Win Shares MVP Cal Ripken Jr. (37)
1984 AL Actual MVP Willie Hernández (24)

1984 NL Win Shares MVP Ryne Sandberg (38)
1984 NL Actual MVP Ryne Sandberg (38)

1985 AL Win Shares MVP Rickey Henderson (38)
1985 AL Actual MVP Don Mattingly (32)

RBI man beats the table-setter once again. Brett's in there, too. . .

1985 NL Win Shares MVP Raines and McGee (36)
1985 NL Actual MVP Willie McGee (36)

1986 AL Win Shares MVP Wade Boggs (37)
1986 AL Actual MVP Roger Clemens (29)

The pitchers stopped winning MVP Awards right about here. . . mostly because they stopped deserving them.

1986 NL Win Shares MVP Tim Raines (32)
1986 NL Actual MVP Mike Schmidt (31)

Two for Raines. . . another leadoff man gets the short end of the stick. Let's see: Schmidt steals one from Raines, Murphy stole two from Schmidt. . . as I see it, Dale Murphy owes Tim Raines a trophy. . .

1987 AL Win Shares MVP Alan Trammell (35)
1987 AL Actual MVP George Bell (26)

1987 NL Win Shares MVP Tim Raines (34)
1987 NL Actual MVP Andre Dawson (20)

Two more MVP Awards for the league RBI leaders. . .

1988 AL Win Shares MVP Jose Canseco (39)
1988 AL Actual MVP Jose Canseco (39)

1988 NL Win Shares MVP Will Clark (37)
1988 NL Actual MVP Kirk Gibson (31)

1989 AL Win Shares MVP Yount and Sierra (34)
1989 AL Actual MVP Robin Yount (34)

1989 NL Win Shares MVP Will Clark (44)
1989 NL Actual MVP Kevin Mitchell (38)

1990 AL Win Shares MVP Rickey Henderson (39)
1990 AL Actual MVP Rickey Henderson (39)

The first AL leadoff man to win the Award since Phil Rizzuto in 1950.

Rickey Henderson

1990 NL	Win Shares MVP	Barry Bonds (41)
1990 NL	Actual MVP	Barry Bonds (41)
1991 AL	Win Shares MVP	Ripken and Frank Thomas (34)
1991 AL	Actual MVP	Cal Ripken (34)
1991 NL	Win Shares MVP	Sandberg and Bonds (37)
1991 NL	Actual MVP	Terry Pendleton (27)
1992 AL	Win Shares MVP	Roberto Alomar (34)
1992 AL	Actual MVP	Dennis Eckersley (18)
1992 NL	Win Shares MVP	Barry Bonds (41)
1992 NL	Actual MVP	Barry Bonds (41)
1993 AL	Win Shares MVP	John Olerud (37)
1993 AL	Actual MVP	Frank Thomas (32)
1993 NL	Win Shares MVP	Barry Bonds (47)
1993 NL	Actual MVP	Barry Bonds (47)
1994 AL	Win Shares MVP	Frank Thomas (25)
1994 AL	Actual MVP	Frank Thomas (25)
1994 NL	Win Shares MVP	Jeff Bagwell (30)
1994 NL	Actual MVP	Jeff Bagwell (30)
1995 AL	Win Shares MVP	Edgar Martinez (32)
1995 AL	Actual MVP	Mo Vaughn (24)
1995 NL	Win Shares MVP	Barry Bonds (36)
1995 NL	Actual MVP	Barry Larkin (30)
1996 AL	Win Shares MVP	Alex Rodriguez (34)
1996 AL	Actual MVP	Juan Gonzalez (21)
1996 NL	Win Shares MVP	Jeff Bagwell (41)
1996 NL	Actual MVP	Ken Caminiti (38)
1997 AL	Win Shares MVP	Frank Thomas (39)
1997 AL	Actual MVP	Ken Griffey Jr. (36)
1997 NL	Win Shares MVP	Piazza and Gwynn (39)
1997 NL	Actual MVP	Larry Walker (33)
1998 AL	Win Shares MVP	Albert Belle (37)
1998 AL	Actual MVP	Juan Gonzalez (25)
1998 NL	Win Shares MVP	Mark McGwire (41)
1998 NL	Actual MVP	Sammy Sosa (35)
1999 AL	Win Shares MVP	Alomar, M. Ramirez and Jeter (35)
1999 AL	Actual MVP	Ivan Rodriguez (28)
1999 NL	Win Shares MVP	Jeff Bagwell (37)
1999 NL	Actual MVP	Chipper Jones (32)
2000 AL	Win Shares MVP	Jason Giambi (38)
2000 AL	Actual MVP	Jason Giambi (38)
2000 NL	Win Shares MVP	Jeff Kent (37)
2000 NL	Actual MVP	Jeff Kent (37)
2001 AL	Win Shares MVP	Jason Giambi (38)
2001 AL	Actual MVP	Ichiro Suzuki (36)
2001 NL	Win Shares MVP	Barry Bonds (54)
2001 NL	Actual MVP	Barry Bonds (54)

. . . I should have mentioned this before now. . . occasionally the Win Shares in this book may not match those in the *Historical Abstract*, just because we have continued to tinker with the system since the *Historical Abstract* was finished.

The average Win Shares for an MVP through history have been 33.4; for the league leader in Win Shares, 37.6. If you split the list in half, pre- and post-expansion, the averages are almost exactly the same in each half.

I'm not going to chart out all the Cy Young leaders in this way. . . you can, if you want to. I think we match the Cy Young vote a little better than the MVP vote, just because there tend to be 2 or 3 good candidates for a Cy Young award, and 3 to 5 for the MVP award. But I shouldn't say that, because I haven't checked what the match is with the new data.

Rookies Redux

The Rookie of the Year Award is awarded for some nebulous combination of performance and potential, with the general understanding being that it is 90% performance. The award is given mostly to the rookie who has the best year, but if two players have about the same seasons, one of them is a 22-year-old kid who can fly, the other is a 27-year-old player who has little room for growth, some people are going to vote for the 22-year-old. This brings up a question: If you give the award 90% for performance but keep one eye on long-term potential, how many eyes do you have?

Anyway, it occurred to me that there was another way to look at old Rookie of the Year awards—not who "should" have won the award, but who was the Rookie of Destiny, so to speak. Taking advantage of the passage of time, knowing all that we know now, who *was* the best rookie in each class? Did the player who won the award go on to be the best player in the class? How often does that happen? Did the player who perhaps should have won the award go on to be the best player in the class? How often does that happen?

I went to the years 1947-1995, and re-visited all of the Rookie of the Year awards in those seasons. There are a total of 96 of them—one per year 1947-1948, two per year since 1949. These 96 Awards can be sorted into four sets of conditions:

1. Clean Sweeps,
2. The Voters Knew Something,
3. The Win Shares System Knows Something,

and

4. Nobody knew nothing.

Willie Mays in 1951 won the National League Rookie of the Year Award. The Win Shares system endorses this selection, also picking Willie Mays as the best player eligible for the award, and Willie (of course) went on to be the best player in his class in terms of career value. That's a Clean Sweep: Willie is the Rookie of the Year no matter how you look at it.

The concept of "The Voters Knew Something" can be best illustrated by the Rookie of the Year votes for 1977, in both leagues. In the American League, the Win Shares system sees the most valuable rookie as being Mitchell Page of Oakland, with 30 Win Shares, followed by Eddie Murray, with 22 Win Shares. When their careers were over, the best rookie in the group was: Eddie Murray. The voters were right.

The same thing happened in the National League. The Win Shares system sees the most valuable rookie as Gene Richards of San Diego, but the award went to Andre Dawson of Montreal. When their careers were over and we could look back at what they had done, the voters were right: Dawson *was* the best player in the group.

But the next category, "The System Knows Something," can be illustrated by the National League vote in the next season, 1978. The top candidates for the Rookie of the Year award were Bob Horner, Don Robinson and Ozzie Smith. The Win Shares system sees Ozzie as easily the best player of the three (20 Win Shares), Robinson second (15), Horner third (14). Horner won the vote, but the Win Shares system was "right" in the long run, in the same sense that it was wrong the previous year. Ozzie *was* the best player in the group.

If the best player in the rookie group, long-term, is *neither* the Rookie of the Year nor the Win Shares Rookie of the Year, then that's Category Four: Nobody Knew Nothin'.

In the 96 Awards, there have been 20 Clean Sweeps. Those are:

1951 National League	Willie Mays
1953 American League	Harvey Kuenn
1956 National League	Frank Robinson
1958 National League	Orlando Cepeda
1961 National League	Billy Williams
1963 National League	Pete Rose
1964 National League	Dick Allen
1967 American League	Rod Carew
1967 National League	Tom Seaver
1968 National League	Johnny Bench

1972 American League	Carlton Fisk
1979 National League	Rick Sutcliffe
1981 American League	Dave Righetti
1982 American League	Cal Ripken Jr.
1986 American League	Jose Canseco
1987 American League	Mark McGwire
1991 National League	Jeff Bagwell
1993 American League	Tim Salmon
1993 National League	Mike Piazza
1994 National League	Raul Mondesi

Some of these clean sweeps come with a big dirty asterisk, but I'll explain those when I walk through these one at a time.

In the history of the award there have been only six times when we would have to say, in retrospect, that the voters were on to something. In the National League in 1953 Jr. Gilliam had a terrific rookie season with the Dodgers, hitting .278 with 31 doubles, 17 triples, 100 walks, 125 runs scored; he won the Rookie of the Year Award, and we credit him with 25 Win Shares. However, Harvey Haddix had what we think is an even better rookie season; he won 20 games, 20-9 with a 3.06 ERA, and for good measure he also hit .289 with 3 triples and 21 runs scored of his own. We credit Haddix with 27 Win Shares.

In the long run, however, the voters were right: Gilliam had the better career. The six "Voters Knew Something" awards are:

1953 National League	Jim Gilliam over Harvey Haddix
1956 American League	Luis Aparicio over Rocky Colavito
1959 National League	Willie McCovey over. . . Joe Koppe?
1977 American League	Eddie Murray over Mitchell Page
1977 National League	Andre Dawson over Gene Richards
1983 National League	Darryl Strawberry over Billy Doran

The "Win Shares System Knows Something" awards might more properly be called "The Voters Missed It." In 1965 two fine second basemen, Joe Morgan and Jim Lefebvre, competed for the Rookie of the Year Award. Morgan obviously should have won the award. He hit for a higher average, hit more doubles, more triples and more homers, drew more walks, and stole seven times as many bases. He had one of the best rookie seasons in history, with 30 Win Shares, but Lefebvre, playing in Los Angeles and playing for a championship team, won the award. The voters just missed it. Since then there have been have been six other times when the voters just missed it:

1965 National League	Joe Morgan over Jim Lefebvre
1978 National League	Ozzie Smith over Bob Horner
1981 National League	Tim Raines over Fernando Valenzuela
1988 National League	Roberto Alomar over Chris Sabo
1989 National League	Craig Biggio over Jerome Walton
1992 American League	Kenny Lofton over Pat Listach
1995 National League	Chipper Jones over Hideo Nomo

How the BBWAA voters picked Chris Sabo over Roberto Alomar as the best rookie of 1988 I don't really understand, but if they don't make me explain Joe Koppe, I guess I won't ask them to explain Chris Sabo. Overall, the Win Shares system has a slightly better record at picking the best player in the group, hitting 27 to the writers' 26.

However, in nearly two-thirds of all races, the correct answer has been: neither. In 63 of 96 rookie classes, the eventual best player in the group was *neither* the Rookie of the Year nor the player who would have been chosen for that award by the Win Shares system, but somebody else entirely.

The prototypical case in this respect is the National League 1966 rookie race. In terms of one-year performance, it was a weak season, and the award went to Tommy Helms, who was credited with only 12 Win Shares. The system thinks that a better answer would have been Sonny Jackson—Joe Morgan's double play partner, oddly enough—who we credit with 19 Win Shares. Jackson was hurt in '67 and never came back, so his career was even less impressive than that of Tommy Helms. Helms and Jackson were 1-2 in the Rookie of the Year voting, which also featured votes for Tito Fuentes, Randy Hundley, Cleon Jones and Larry Jaster—but included not a single mention for any of the three future Hall of Famers in the class. Pitchers Don Sutton, Ferguson Jenkins and Steve Carlton were all rookies in the National League in 1966. Among them they won 21 games, lost 23, and impressed nobody as being the equal of Tito Fuentes or Larry Jaster.

That's extreme, but that in a sense is the common history of rookie classes: the best player in the group usually doesn't have a big season as a rookie. Yogi Berra didn't in '47, Duke Snider didn't in '48, Nellie Fox didn't in '49, Hank Aaron didn't in '54. These 63 cases may be broken down into two groups:

a) The BBWAA voters and the Win Shares method agree on who was the best rookie in the class, but somebody else had a better career, and

b) The BBWAA and the Win Shares method have different Rookie of the Year candidates, but neither player was the eventual star of the class.

There are 40 (a) cases in the 63, in which the player chosen by the BBWAA as the best rookie in the league either had or tied for the class lead in Win Shares as well. There are 23 cases in which there is a difference of opinion, although usually the difference is trivial (three Win Shares or less). Altogether, the Win Shares system and the voters have agreed on 60 of the 96 Rookie of the Year votes, split on the other 36.

In the chart/commentary below, the first line represents the player who actually won the Rookie of the Year award. The second line is claimed by the "Win Shares Rookie of the Year"—the player who we think *should* have won the award. The third line is for the rookie within that rookie class who went on to accumulate the highest career Win Shares total:

1947 (Unified) Jackie Robinson (21-257)
Jackie Robinson (21-257)
Yogi Berra (11-375)

The "21" next to Jackie Robinson means that he is credited with 21 Win Shares for the 1947 season; the "257" after the dash means that he earned 257 Win Shares in his career. Yogi Berra earned 11 Win Shares as a rookie in 1947, 375 in his career.

The standards for who is and ain't eligible for the Award have changed over time. . . I generally understand these but not always, and I'm probably wrong occasionally about whether a player was or was not eligible for the award, since this fact is not recorded systematically anyplace where it would be very easy to look up. Anyway, with those situations, ties in the voting and ties in the Win Shares, it is sometimes surprisingly complicated knowing how to fill out the chart:

1948 (Unified) Al Dark (20-226)
Gene Bearden (22-46)
Duke Snider (5-352)

1949 American Roy Sievers (15-231)
Mike Garcia (21-160)
Nellie Fox (6-304)

1949 National Don Newcombe (21-176)
Don Newcombe (21-176)
Willie Jones (15-189)

Of course, in this case it is merely arguable, as opposed to clear, that Willie (Puddin' Head) Jones was actually the best player of the group. Jones' career total is a little higher because Newcombe lost time to military service and lost the second half of his career to alcholism, but Newcombe was a brilliant performer in his good years. Del Crandall (6-179) is also in this mix:

1950 American Walt Dropo (21-92)
Irv Noren (22-107)
*Al Rosen (29-185)
Whitey Ford (11-261)

Walt Dropo won the American League Rookie of the Year Award in 1950, hitting .322 with 34 homers, 144 RBI. The Win Shares system thinks that Irv Noren, who didn't receive a vote, was actually a hair better (22 to 21) as an all-around player, although it is not anything you would want to start an argument about.

Noren hit .295 with 14 homers, 98 RBI, also 27 doubles and 10 triples, and did this in a park with a home run factor of .36. . . in road games Dropo hit 10 home runs, Noren 8, plus Noren drew 50% more walks and played center field. Sportswriters in 1950 had almost no understanding of park effects, and even modern BBWAA voters would unquestionably be thrown off-course by park effects of this magnitude. In any case, neither Noren nor Dropo ever had another season as good, and both had relatively disappointing careers.

Al Rosen hit 37 homers in 1950, and might well have taken the Rookie of the Year award away from Dropo, but he was not eligible under the standards of the time, although he was clearly a rookie by the standards we use now. Whitey Ford, who went 9-1 as a rookie and finished second in the Rookie of the Year voting, went on to have the best career of the group.

1950 National — Sam Jethroe (22-61)
Sam Jethroe (22-61)
Joe Adcock (9-236)

1951 American — Gil McDougald (23-194)
Minnie Minoso (25-283)
Mickey Mantle (13-565)

1951 National — Willie Mays (19-642)
Willie Mays (19-642)
Willie Mays (19-642)

1952 American — Harry Byrd (18-42)
Harry Byrd (18-42)
Jimmy Piersall (5-162)

1952 National — Joe Black (20-33)
Joe Black (20-33)
Eddie Mathews (19-450)

This was an interesting year, in that the National League had a sensational rookie class, while the American League class was weak. Black was pushed for the Rookie of the Year award by Hoyt Wilhelm (18-256) and Eddie Mathews, both Hall of Famers. Dick Groat (5-225) was also mentioned in the voting.

1953 American — Harvey Kuenn (19-223)
Harvey Kuenn (19-223)
Harvey Kuenn (19-223)

A vote for somebody named Tommy Umphlett prevented Kuenn from a unanimous victory. It wasn't the strongest class in history.

1953 National — Jim Gilliam (25-247)
Harvey Haddix (27-153)
Jim Gilliam (25-247)

1954 American — Bob Grim (13-53)
Jim Finigan (21-43)
Al Kaline (7-443)

1954 National — Wally Moon (20-175)
Wally Moon (20-175)
Hank Aaron (13-643)

Ernie Banks (15-332) was also in the mix.

1955 American — Herb Score (19-58)
Herb Score (19-58)
Harmon Killebrew (1-371)

Harmon doesn't exactly have any rookie season. . . we could cite Elston Howard (11- 203) in that slot.

1955 National — Bill Virdon (14-157)
(See Note)
Roberto Clemente (7-377)

The best rookie in the National League in 1955 was probably Dale Long (17-92), who would be considered a rookie by modern standards, but was not eligible for the award by the standards in use at that time. Other than Long, who was not exactly Albert Pujols himself, no National League rookie met the usual standards of Rookie of the Year performance, although it eventually turned out to be a strong rookie class. Virdon, with 14 Win Shares as a rookie and a decent subsequent career, had a teammate, Ken Boyer, who also earned 14 Win Shares and went on to an outstanding career—yet did not draw a mention in the Rookie of the Year voting, although he was a pure rookie with no previous experience. Sam Jones, who also had 14 Win Shares, 14 actual wins and led the National League in strikeouts with 198, also did not receive a vote, although he may not have been eligible under the standards of the time; I'm not sure.

Finishing second and third in the Rookie of the Year voting were Jack Meyer of Philadelphia (11-30) and Don Bessent of Brooklyn (7-19), although numerous National League rookies had better seasons and better careers. These include Gene Freese (13-88), Jim

King (10-91), Hal Smith (10-73), Luis Arroyo (10-44), and Larry Jackson (9-225) as well as Ken Boyer (14-279).

1956 American — Luis Aparicio (14-293)
Rocky Colavito (16-273)
Luis Aparicio (14-293)

Jim Bunning (4-257) should also be mentioned.

1956 National — Frank Robinson (26-519)
Frank Robinson (26-519)
Frank Robinson (26-519)

Robinson dominates a strong class including Don Drysdale (9-258), Bill Mazeroski (5-219), Bill White (16-209), Lindy McDaniel (6-186), Jackie Brandt (12-122) and Sandy Koufax (3-194).

1957 American — Tony Kubek (14-120)
Tony Kubek (14-120)
Brooks Robinson (2-356)

Frank Malzone (18-135) was not technically eligible for the award, although somebody voted for him, anyway.

1957 National — Jack Sanford (20-115)
Ed Bouchee (27-71)
Don McMahon (7-135)

1958 American — Albie Pearson (15-104)
Albie Pearson (15-104)
Milt Pappas (6-210)

1958 National — Orlando Cepeda (20-310)
Orlando Cepeda (20-310)
Orlando Cepeda (20-310)

The Giants had one of the best rookie classes of all time, with Cepeda, Felipe Alou (5-241), Leon Wagner (10-155), Jim Davenport (11-116) and Willie Kirkland (13-98).

1959 American — Bob Allison (18-203)
Bob Allison (18-203)
Norm Cash (4-315)

1959 National — Willie McCovey (12-408)
Joe Koppe (13-41)
Willie McCovey (12-408)

This situation is such a mess I'm almost unsure how to report on it. Vada Pinson (27-321) was obviously the best rookie in the National League in 1959, and he went on to a distinguished career, but was ineligible for the award due to poorly created standards. Jim Owens of Philadelphia (12-12, 3.21 ERA) was the next-best rookie, but he was also ineligible, for similar reasons.

Joe Koppe of Philadelphia (13-41) played regularly and was OK, hitting .261 with 7 homers, 7 triples. However, Willie McCovey was called up July 30 and was sensational for two months, thus winning the award unanimously—and justifying it with a Hall of Fame career.

This, however, obscures the fact that the National League had a wonderful rookie class, in the long run. Doing little as rookies were Bob Gibson (5-317), Ron Fairly (5-269) and Maury Wills (5-253).

1960 American — Ron Hansen (24-145)
Ron Hansen (24-145)
Jim Kaat (0-268)

The Orioles had the five best rookies in the American League based on that season's performance—Hansen, Jim Gentile (21-125), Marv Breeding (16-29), Chuck Estrada (15-37) and Steve Barber (12-116). Hansen won 22 of 24 Rookie of the Year votes, Gentile and Estrada the other two.

1960 National — Frank Howard (13-297)
Pancho Herrera (15-25)
Ron Santo (6-324)

Although Ron Hansen was by far the best rookie of 1960, five National Leaguers went on to better careers—Howard, Santo, Tommy Davis (9-207), Juan Marichal (6-263) and Tony Gonzalez (9-183).

1961 American — Don Schwall (15-39)
Dick Howser (20-74)
Carl Yastrzemski (12-488)

Six players were mentioned in the American League Rookie of the Year voting—but Yaz, despite driving in 80 runs, was not among them.

1961 National — Billy Williams (15-374)
Billy Williams (15-374)
Billy Williams (15-374)

Joe Torre (13-315) and Willie Davis (10-322) were also in the mix.

1962 American — Tom Tresh (25-160)
Tom Tresh (25-160)
Boog Powell (8-282)

1962 National — Ken Hubbs (9-21)
Tom Haller (16-179)
Lou Brock (9-348)

Haller did not draw a vote, and may not have been eligible for the award at the time; I'm not sure. In any case, several other rookies are seen by the math as better players than Hubbs. Hubbs had 661 at bats and a long and much-publicized errorless streak, which tended to obscure the fact that he really didn't do anything very well. Including navigate.

1963 American — Gary Peters (25-133)
Peters or Pete Ward (25-117) or Max Alvis (25-98)
Bill Freehan (10-267)

1963 National — Pete Rose (19-547)
Rose or Ron Hunt (19-191)
Pete Rose (19-547)

Rose and Hunt, both second basemen at the time, had very similar rookie seasons—but the writers picked up strongly on the fact that Rose was actually a better player.

1964 American — Tony Oliva (27-245)
Tony Oliva (27-245)
Tommy John (2-289)

1964 National — Dick Allen (41-342)
Dick Allen (41-342)
Dick Allen (41-132)

1965 American — Curt Blefary (26-108)
Curt Blefary (26-108)
Jim Palmer (4-312)

Blefary, Rookie of the Year and deserving of the honor, had two rookie teammates who went on to better careers—Palmer and Paul Blair.

1965 National — Jim Lefebvre (23-106)
Joe Morgan (30-512)
Joe Morgan (30-512)

1966 American — Tommie Agee (28-139)
Tommie Agee (28-139)
Roy White (7-263)

1966 National — Tommy Helms (12-114)
Sonny Jackson (19-60)
Steve Carlton (3-366)

1967 American — Rod Carew (19-384)
Carew or Reggie Smith (19-325)
Carew or Reggie Jackson (2-444)

It is hard to know what to do with Reggie Jackson.

Reggie Jackson

Under the standards of the time he was considered a rookie in 1967, but he earned only two Win Shares. . . if considered a rookie in 1967 he would be the best long-term rookie in the class. By modern standards he would be considered a rookie in 1968, which would mean that (a) he should have won the award, since he was a better player than Stan Bahnsen, and (b) he was also the best player in the group.

1967 National	Tom Seaver (21-388)
	Tom Seaver (21-388)
	Tom Seaver (21-388)

1968 American	Stan Bahnsen (23-130)
	Bahnsen or Reggie Jackson (25-444)
	Reggie or Joe Rudi (1-173)

1968 National	Johnny Bench (24-356)
	Johnny Bench (24-356)
	Johnny Bench (24-356)

1969 American	Lou Piniella (16-164)
	Ken Tatum (20-36)
	Graig Nettles (5-321)

Bobby Murcer (20-277) was not technically a rookie. . . more on that in a moment.

1969 National	Ted Sizemore (17-130)
	Richie Hebner (20-219)
	Al Oliver (13-305)

1970 American	Thurman Munson (26-206)
	Thurman Munson (26-206)
	Bert Blyleven (10-339)

1970 National	Carl Morton (21-91)
	Billy Grabarkewitz (29-43)
	Ted Simmons (6-315)

I'm not sure whether Grabarkewitz was or was not eligible for the award at the time. If not, Win Shares would give the award to Bernie Carbo, who finished second in the voting, and didn't go on to a Hall of Fame career, either.

1971 American	Chris Chambliss (11-221)
	Bill Parsons (15-21)
	Toby Harrah (7-287)

1971 National	Earl Williams (19-85)
	Willie Montanez (20-141)
	Darrell Evans (9-363)

Ralph Garr (25-147) was obviously the best rookie in the National League in 1971, but again was not eligible for the award due to standards that were still evolving.

1972 American	Carlton Fisk (33-368)
	Carlton Fisk (33-368)
	Carlton Fisk (33-368)

1972 National	Jon Matlack (22-156)
	Jon Matlack (22-156)
	Rick Reuschel (10-240)

A few words of explanation. In 1961-62 the schedule was lengthened from 154 to 162 games. Also in the 1960s, double-headers began to disappear. . . from the 1920s into the 1950s, teams played 25 to 30 double-headers a season, as a matter of course. By 1970 those numbers were down, and dropping faster than Enron stock.

These effects were pushing the end of the season backward. However, the "callup date" after which minor leaguers could be added to the major league roster remained the same, September 1. As a result of this, these September callups were playing more games than they had before.

The Rookie of the Year standards were playing catchup with this new reality. The BBWAA moved the standards several times, but they continued to miss. Thus, in this era, the best rookies frequently—one might almost say *normally*—were not eligible for the Rookie of the Year award, because they had played too many games in the previous September.

Thus, in the National League in 1972, neither the best actual rookie, Dusty Baker (23-245) nor the best long-term rookie, Greg Luzinski (16-247) was considered a rookie at the time—just as Vida Blue and Ralph Garr had not been the previous season, just as Reggie Jackson was not in 1968 and Bobby Murcer was not in 1969. This is a nuisance. History is messy.

1973 American	Al Bumbry (17-169)
	Doc Medich (18-110)
	Darrell Porter (16-222)

Once more, the American League's best actual rookie, Bill North (25-143) and its best long-term rookie, George Hendrick (13-237) are both excluded from consideration by a poorly written rule.

1973 National	Gary Matthews (21-257)
	Gary Matthews (21-257)
	Mike Schmidt (10-467)
1974 American	Mike Hargrove (20-212)
	Mike Hargrove (20-212)
	George Brett (9-432) or Robin Yount (8-423)

I know that 432 is more than 423, but it doesn't seem right to leave out a player like Robin Yount.

1974 National	Bake McBride (22-132)
	Bake McBride (22-132)
	Bill Madlock (16-242)
1975 American	Fred Lynn (33-280)
	Fred Lynn (33-280)
	Dennis Eckersley (17-301)
1975 National	John Montefusco (20-92)
	John Montefusco (20-92)
	Gary Carter (18-337)

Carter finished a close second in the Rookie of the Year voting. And, as Tommy Lasorda once said about John Montefusco, "I'd like to buy him for what I think he's worth and sell him for what he thinks he's worth."

1976 American	Mark Fidrych (27-36)
	Mark Fidrych (27-36)
	Willie Randolph (17-312)
1976 National	Butch Metzger (12-21) and Pat Zachry (14-60)
	Pat Zachry (14-60)
	Garry Templeton (5-209)
1977 American	Eddie Murray (21-437)
	Mitchell Page (30-70)
	Eddie Murray (21-437)
1977 National	Andre Dawson (18-340)
	Gene Richards (21-122)
	Andre Dawson (18-340)
1978 American	Lou Whitaker (17-351)
	Whitaker or Carney Lansford (17-244)
	Paul Molitor (12-414)
1978 National	Bob Horner (14-140)
	Ozzie Smith (20-325)
	Ozzie Smith (20-325)
1979 American	John Castino (9-70) or Alfredo Griffin (14-134)
	Alfredo Griffin (14-134)
	Rickey Henderson (10-530)
1979 National	Rick Sutcliffe (16-153)
	Rick Sutcliffe (16-153)
	Rick Sutcliffe (16-153)
1980 American	Joe Charboneau (15-17)
	Doug Corbett (24-59)
	Harold Baines (8-307)

Charboneau had the poorest career of any Rookie of the Year Award winner.

1980 National	Steve Howe (11-76)
	Lonnie Smith (13-190) or Dave Smith (13-106)
	Pedro Guerrero (9-246)
1981 American	Dave Righetti (10-137)
	Dave Righetti (10-137)
	Dave Righetti (10-137)
1981 National	Fernando Valenzuela (17-168)
	Tim Raines (18-390)
	Tim Raines (18-390)
1982 American	Cal Ripken Jr. (23-427)
	Cal Ripken Jr. (23-427)
	Cal Ripken Jr. (23-427)
1982 National	Steve Sax (18-198)
	Johnny Ray (19-153) or Chili Davis (19-285)
	Tony Gwynn (7-398)

1983 American	Ron Kittle (19-76) Ron Kittle (19-76) Tony Phillips (12-268) or Don Mattingly (7-263)
1983 National	Darryl Strawberry (18-252) Bill Doran (22-193) Darryl Strawberry (18-252)
1984 American	Alvin Davis (27-153) Alvin Davis (27-153) Roger Clemens (8-352)

Clemens, of course, is still active. I guess I won't mark active players, because I honestly don't know which ones of these guys might play next year.

1984 National	Dwight Gooden (18-187) Carmelo Martinez (21-88) Joe Carter (7-240)
1985 American	Ozzie Guillen (15-148) Ozzie Guillen (15-148) Mickey Tettleton (7-184)

Mickey Tettleton, interesting enough, is the exact opposite of Ozzie Guillen. If you look up "Ozzie Guillen" in the dictionary, it says "Antonyms: Mickey Tettleton, Gene Tenace, Darren Daulton."

1985 National	Vince Coleman (20-138) Vince Coleman (20-138) Lenny Dykstra (8-201)
1986 American	Jose Canseco (21-272) Jose Canseco (21-272) or Mark Eichorn (21-83) or Wally Joyner (21-253) Jose Canseco (21-272)
1986 National	Todd Worrell (19-105) Todd Worrell (19-105) Barry Bonds (15-523)
1987 American	Mark McGwire (30-342) Mark McGwire (30-342) Mark McGwire (30-342)
1987 National	Benito Santiago (15-159) Benito Santiago (15-159) Rafael Palmeiro (7-334) or Greg Maddux (1-317)

An interesting year. The American League's top five rookies, in order, were McGwire (30), Kevin Seitzer (23), Matt Nokes (20), Mike Greenwell (17) and Devon White (17). The voting put them in the same order—McGwire, Seitzer, Nokes, Greenwell, White.

The National League's best rookie—again, there was agreement—was Benito Santiago, but Santiago earned only 15 Win Shares, and thus would have finished sixth in the American League voting, assuming that the voters and the system continue to see things the same way. Well, tied for sixth; the American League actually had two rookie catchers (Terry Steinbach and B.J. Surhoff) and an outfielder (Ellis Burks) who were as good as Santiago, but were ignored in the American League voting because there were better players available. Nine of the top ten rookies in 1987 were in the American League.

But in the long run, the National League rookie class was actually very good; it was just full of guys who didn't come to the surface until later. It was one of the best years ever for rookies, with thirteen players so far reaching 200 career Win Shares:

1.	Mark McGwire	342
2.	Rafael Palmeiro	334
3.	Greg Maddux	317
4.	Fred McGriff	316
5.	Paul O'Neill	259
6.	Jay Bell	243
7.	Ken Caminiti	242
8.	Tom Glavine	236
9.	Ellis Burks	234
10.	Devon White	207
11.	B.J. Surhoff	206
12.	David Cone	205
13.	Chuck Finley	204

1988 American	Walt Weiss (15-123) Walt Weiss (15-123) Brady Anderson (3-214)
1988 National	Chris Sabo (17-104) Roberto Alomar (22-345) Roberto Alomar (22-345)
1989 American	Gregg Olson (18-99) Craig Worthington (20-32) Ken Griffey Jr. (14-313)
1989 National	Jerome Walton (17-40) Craig Biggio (18-342) Craig Biggio (18-342)

Seven players were mentioned in the National League Rookie of the Year voting in 1989. Craig Biggio was not among them, and I'm not absolutely certain that he was eligible for the award. If he wasn't, then (a) Walton deserved the award, and (b) the league's best long-term player in the rookie class was Gregg Jefferies (14-162).

The American League in 1989 had a long list of rookies who had better careers than Jefferies, including Griffey (313), Gary Sheffield (6-276), Edgar Martinez (4-264), Sammy Sosa (2-246), Albert Belle (6-243), Randy Johnson (5-226), Steve Finley (5-222), Kevin Brown (13-211), Greg Vaughn (6-197), Dante Bichette (2-168), and Omar Vizquel (3-166).

1990 American	Sandy Alomar (15-100) Sandy Alomar or Robin Ventura (15-236) Frank Thomas (13-308)
1990 National	David Justice (20-222) David Justice (20-222) Larry Walker (12-240)
1991 American	Chuck Knoblauch (20-229) Chuck Knoblauch (20-229) Bernie Williams (10-233)
1991 National	Jeff Bagwell (23-318) Jeff Bagwell (23-318) Jeff Bagwell (23-318)
1992 American	Pat Listach (21-41) Kenny Lofton (24-202) Kenny Lofton (24-202)
1992 National	Eric Karros (13-157) Moises Alou (15-179) Jeff Kent (10-197)
1993 American	Tim Salmon (24-187) Tim Salmon (24-187) Tim Salmon (24-187)
1993 National	Mike Piazza (31-255) Mike Piazza (31-255) Mike Piazza (31-255)
1994 American	Bob Hamelin (12-30) Hamelin, Rusty Greer (12-130) or Jose Valentin (12-117) Manny Ramirez (11-192)
1994 National	Raul Mondesi (15-156) Raul Mondesi (15-156) Raul Mondesi (15-156)
1995 American	Marty Cordova (17-70) Marty Cordova (17-70) Alex Rodriguez (2-185) or Jason Giambi (5-167)
1995 National	Hideo Nomo (17-77) Chipper Jones (20-186) Chipper Jones (20-186)

Flukes

Another thing which can be done with Win Shares is to establish a statistical method to define a fluke season. Initially, I had defined a fluke season as *any season in which a player has a value of at least 15 Win Shares, and a value at least 10 Win Shares higher than his value in any other season.*

Going back only to 1900—I am never sure whether it is better to treat 19th century baseball with disinterest or contempt—but going back to 1900 with this initial definition, I came up with a list of about 400 qualifying seasons, many or most of which didn't exactly seem to be what I wanted. For example, at the time of the Federal League, I had lots of guys like Charlie Hanford, Ed Lafitte and Benny Meyer, who were "flukes" in the sense that they got to play in the "major leagues" in flukey circumstances.

I amended the definition: A fluke season is any season in which a player *who plays at least 400 Career Games* has a season of at least 15 Win Shares which is at least 10 Win Shares higher than his value in any other season, and is now retired.

At this time I had about 250, 300 names on the list, but 70 or 80% of them were pitchers. Pitchers have a lot of fluke seasons, for various reasons. . . let's just focus on innings pitched. Your average regular player, he plays 150, 160 games a year; there is no way he can go out one year and play 200. But your average regular pitcher, he pitches 200 innings a year, but when he gets a new manager he may suddenly pitch 280. This creates spikes in the value chart for a pitcher. There are several other things which contribute to this, too. Identify the weakest players in career value who have won MVP Awards. They're all pitchers—Jim Konstanty, Bobby Shantz, Willie Hernandez. So I gave up on pitchers, took them off the list.

This gave me a list of about 80 players, but there was still a problem. Sometimes a player's value spikes upward, even though his performance is much the same—like Honus Wagner in 1909 or Luke Appling in 1943. Those two shortstops in those seasons did the same things they always did, but were able to do them in extremely run-scarce environments.

I eliminated from the list any season in which a player had a similarity score of 900 or greater to an adjacent season. This, then left me with a list of 69 qualifying fluke seasons. Many of these—most of them, actually—are still not exactly what I originally went looking for, but the definition of a fluke season is losing conceptual clarity as I add detail. There appears to be about one "true fluke season" every ten years:

Player	Fluke Year	WS	2nd Best	Comment
George Barclay	1902	20	4	401 major league games
Cy Seymour	1905	42	25	A true and classic fluke
George Stone	1906	38	28	Had injuries after 1906
Harry Lumley	1906	36	19	Got fat
Art Devlin	1906	35	25	Just had a good year
Harry Steinfeldt	1906	34	24	Was motivated that one year
Matty McIntyre	1908	34	23	
Hans Lobert	1908	32	21	
John Knight	1910	23	13	Averaged jumped 76 points
Bill Rariden	1915	23	13	Federal League
Ollie O'Mara	1915	17	7	412 major league games

Player	Fluke Year	WS	2nd Best	Comment
Austin McHenry	1921	25	13	Brain tumor
Jigger Statz	1923	25	15	8,000 games in the PCL
Andy High	1924	29	19	No relation to Bobby Lowe
Dick Burrus	1925	21	9	.185, .340, .270
Al Wingo	1925	22	9	.370 in only season as regular
Les Bell	1926	26	15	A true fluke season
Doc Farrell	1927	17	5	Avg fell 101 points in '28
Johnny Hodapp	1930	26	13	Pretty numbers
Earl Webb	1931	25	15	Still holds doubles record
Chet Ross	1940	24	5	Only season as a regular
Cecil Travis	1941	34	22	Left for war that winter
Les Fleming	1942	29	14	'41—Nashville; '43—War work
Jim Russell	1944	30	20	Wartime
Johnny Lindell	1944	26	14	Switched to the mound
Mark Christman	1944	19	9	Only season as a regular
Goody Rosen	1945	29	16	Wartime
Luis Olmo	1945	22	9	Wartime
Hank Edwards	1946	22	11	Post-War breakout
Stan Rojek	1948	22	9	Highly motivated season
Earl Torgeson	1950	32	20	Led league in runs scored
Monte Irvin	1951	29	18	Missing a lot of years
Al Rosen	1953	42	32	Missing years on both ends
Stan Lopata	1956	27	17	Late getting his chance
Bob Cerv	1958	28	15	Even later
Ken Aspromonte	1960	18	5	Only season as a regular
Marv Breeding	1960	16	4	Only season as a regular
Norm Cash	1961	42	27	One of the most famous flukes
Jim Gentile	1961	32	21	First full season
Chuck Hiller	1962	19	9	Iron glove, lost job
Chuck Essegian	1962	16	6	Minor league vet
Roman Mejias	1962	15	4	Minor league vet, expansion
Joe Christopher	1964	21	8	
Sam Bowens	1964	17	3	Only regular season
Zoilo Versalles	1965	32	19	Motivated season
Sonny Jackson	1966	19	9	Had injuries
Ken Harrelson	1968	28	18	Played excited in Fenway
Rico Petrocelli	1969	36	26	A good player's best season

Player	Fluke Year	WS	2nd Best	Comment
Wes Parker	1970	29	19	
Billy Grabarkewitz	1970	29	3	Injured in spring of '71
Jim Hickman	1970	24	13	
Cito Gaston	1970	24	10	Minor league vet
Joe Torre	1971	41	28	Got rid of the catching gear
Paul Schaal	1971	26	16	Put it together
Carlos May	1972	29	15	
Leron Lee	1972	18	6	.264, .300, .237
Danny Thompson	1972	17	6	Only season as a regular
Joe Ferguson	1973	29	19	Yeager brought better D
Dave W. Roberts	1973	18	8	
Elliott Maddox	1974	23	11	
Von Joshua	1975	19	7	First chance to play
Larry Parrish	1979	28	18	Numbers just exploded
Rick Cerone	1980	20	9	
Miguel Dilone	1980	21	7	
Tom Herr	1985	32	19	Only team to have two. . .
Willie McGee	1985	36	21	. . . players having fluke years
Larry Sheets	1987	18	8	Game had only one dimension
Pat Listach	1992	21	8	
Chris Hoiles	1993	26	14	

Ken Caminiti (1996) will be added to the list as soon as he retires.

Of these 70 seasons (including Caminiti's), there are about 12 that I would regard as true flukes, as opposed to odd circumstances or situations in which a player who had waited a long time to get a chance to play had a breakthrough year, then wasn't able to follow up due to injuries or some other cause. Those 12 true fluke seasons were by Cy Seymour, Les Bell, Johnny Hodapp, Norm Cash, Joe Christopher, Wes Parker, Jim Hickman, Dave Roberts, Rick Cerone, Miguel Dilone, Willie McGee and Ken Caminiti.

Five players (and several other pitchers) have won MVP Awards with what were essentially fluke seasons—Al Rosen, Zoilo Versalles, Joe Torre, Willie McGee and Ken Caminiti.

Two Great Pitchers

The 2001 Arizona Diamondbacks won the World Series on the Diamond Backs of the two best pitchers in baseball, Randy Johnson and Curt Schilling.

This caused me to ask a series of questions. . .

How common is it for a baseball team to have the two best pitchers in the league?

Do these teams automatically win the pennant?

Do these teams tend to do well in World Series play?

Are Johnson and Schilling the greatest one-two punch in history?

Etc., etc. . . there are more questions, but we'll get to the essential ones in the course of reviewing these four:

How common is it for a baseball team to have the two best pitchers in the league?

Astonishingly common, at least to me. It has happened 30 times in baseball history, evaluating pitchers by Win Shares, including five times in the last ten years.

Those 30 cases, in chronological order with the #1 pitcher listed first, are as follows:

1889 American Assoc.	St. Louis	Silver King Icebox Chamberlin
1890 Players League	Chicago	Silver King Mark Baldwin
1894 National League	Giants	Amos Rusie Jouett Meekin
1896 National League	Cleveland	Cy Young Nig Cuppy
1901 National League	Braves	Vic Willis Kid Nichols
1903 National League	Giants	Joe McGinnity Christy Mathewson
1904 National League	Giants	Joe McGinnity Christy Mathewson
1905 American League	A's	Rube Waddell Eddie Plank
1914 National League	Braves	Bill James Dick Rudolph
1915 Federal League	St. Louis	Dave Davenport Eddie Plank
1920 American League	Indians	Jim Bagby Stan Coveleski
1925 National League	Reds	Pete Donohue Dolf Luque
1927 American League	White Sox	Ted Lyons Tommy Thomas
1927 National League	Cardinals	Jesse Haines Pete Alexander
1931 American League	A's	Lefty Grove George Earnshaw
1935 American League	Red Sox	Wes Ferrell Lefty Grove
1939 National League	Reds	Bucky Walters Paul Derringer
1942 National League	Cardinals	Mort Cooper Johnny Beazley
1944 American League	Tigers	Dizzy Trout Hal Newhouser
1951 American League	Indians	Early Wynn Mike Garcia
1953 American League	White Sox	Virgil Trucks Billy Pierce
1954 American League	Indians	Early Wynn Mike Garcia
1956 American League	Indians	Early Wynn Herb Score
1960 American League	Tigers	Jim Bunning Frank Lary
1977 National League	Cubs	Bruce Sutter Rick Reuschel
1993 American League	Royals	Kevin Appier Jeff Montgomery
1995 National League	Braves	Greg Maddux Tom Glavine
1999 American League	Red Sox	Pedro Martinez Derek Lowe
2000 American League	Red Sox	Pedro Martinez Derek Lowe
2001 National League	Zona	Randy Johnson Curt Schilling

Do these teams automatically win the pennant?

Far from it. Ten of the thirty teams won the pennant, eleven if you count the 1894 New York Giants, who won a half-assed post-season competition which gave them some claim on the championship.

This, to me, was the most surprising thing, that so many of these teams with two outstanding pitchers did not finish on top.

Do these teams tend to do well in World Series play?

Not so's you'd notice it. Of these ten teams, one (the 1904 Giants) chickened out of the World Series, declined to play. Of the other nine, five won the World Series, four did not.

Interestingly enough, the other four times that one of these teams *did* win the World Series, the scenario was much like it was in 2001: the pitcher who *didn't* start the first game wound up providing the punch that got the team over the top, and then there was considerable media comment on the effectiveness of these one-two punches. But while these four cases, like 2001, gave vent to tons of ink about the irresistible force of a team with two great pitchers, the reality is that these 30 teams have won just five World Series, six if you count 1894. That leaves an awful lot of years in which this irresistible force has been resisted.

Johnson and Schilling were not only the two best pitchers in the league; according to the Win Shares system they were the two best pitchers in baseball. That's much more rare. Not counting the 1890s, when there was only one league, this has happened only five times (1903, 1925, 1931, and 1944). Two of those other four teams didn't make it to the World Series, and the other two lost the World Series.

The 1925 Cincinnati Reds were the only team in major league history which had the three best pitchers in baseball—Pete Donohue, Dolf Luque and Eppa Rixey. They were first, second and third in the league in innings pitched, and first, second and fourth in ERA, interrupted by a guy who pitched 145 innings. Rixey and Donohue won 21 games apiece. But the Reds had no offense—they were last in the league in runs scored—and so finished third.

There are two other very good matches for that team: the 1901 Boston Braves, and the 1993 Kansas City Royals. The 1901 Braves had the three best pitchers in the National League (Vic Willis, Kid Nichols and Bill Dineen), but had the league's worst offense, and finished at .500, 69-69. . . I wrote about that team in the *New Historical Abstract*.

The 1993 Royals had the best pitcher in the American League (Kevin Appier, 18-8, 2.56) and the best reliever in baseball (Jeff Montgomery, 45 saves with a 2.27 ERA). Their second starter, David Cone, was the fourth-best pitcher in the league, behind those two and Randy Johnson. But, like the other two teams, they were last in their league in runs scored, and thus struggled to stay above .500, finishing 84-78.

The 1977 Chicago Cubs had the league's best starting pitcher (Rick Reuschel) and the best reliever (Bruce Sutter); they finished at .500. Two of the 30 teams didn't manage to do that. The 1927 White Sox, with Ted Lyons and Tommy Thomas, finished 70-83. The 1960 Detroit Tigers, with Jim Bunning and Frank Lary, beat them by a half a game, 71-83.

An interesting team, those Tigers. . . Bunning, whom we allege to have been the best pitcher in the league, finished 11-14, while Lary finished 15-15. But oddly enough, I don't think many people would argue with me about those two being the best two pitchers in the league. . . Bunning is a Hall of Famer, and Lary went 23-9 the next year, as the Tigers won 101 games. Also, there was a pronounced shortage of front-line starting pitchers in the American League at that time. . . with Whitey Ford having an off season, the league's third-best starting pitcher was Ray Herbert, who went 14-15 for Kansas City.

Still, most of these teams did *well*, if not as well as I would have expected. Twenty-six of the thirty teams posted winning records, two were at .500, two were under .500. . . I guess I've just been focusing on the exceptions. The overall winning percentage of these 30 teams was .588, which projects to 95-67 for a 162-game season.

In addition to the 1901 Braves and 1925 Reds, there was one other team which had the *three* best pitchers in the league—the 1931 Philadelphia A's, with Grove, Earnshaw and Walberg. The Cleveland Indians had three of the four best pitchers in the league in 1954 (Wynn, Garcia and Lemon) and again in 1956 (Wynn, Herb Score and Lemon). The 1995 Atlanta Braves were the only team in baseball history to have four of the top five pitchers in the league—Maddux, Glavine, John Smoltz and Mark Wohlers.

Are Johnson and Schilling the greatest one-two punch in history?

Probably not, but there's an argument for them.

The most surprising omission from the 1-2 punch list was the 1965 Dodgers, with Koufax and Drysdale. Koufax was the best pitcher in the league, but Drysdale misses the top five, since the list I was using doesn't give him credit for his contributions as a hitter. . . he had a big year as a hitter. That was a heck of a one-two punch, though.

Setting that combination aside, J&S appear to be the best combination since the 1950s, at least. Pedro Martinez and Derek Lowe rated one-two in the American League in both 1999 and 2000—but nobody noticed, and this will be a surprise to even the Red Sox fans reading this. Martinez was *so* good, in both seasons, that nobody thought to put Derek Lowe in the same group with him, even though Lowe was excellent.

In terms of won-lost records and ERA, the 1951-54-56 Cleveland Indians, headed by Early Wynn, had impressive credentials:

1951	Early Wynn	20-13	3.02
1951	Mike Garcia	20-13	3.15
1954	Early Wynn	23-11	2.73
1954	Mike Garcia	19-8	2.64
1956	Early Wynn	20-9	2.72
1956	Herb Score	20-9	2.53
2001	Randy Johnson	21-6	2.49
2001	Curt Schilling	22-6	2.98

Still, one can argue that Johnson and Schilling were better. You can't make *that* argument about the 1944 Tigers:

1944	Hal Newhouser	29-9	2.22
1944	Dizzy Trout	27-14	2.12

But that's wartime, and we don't *have* to accept wartime credentials.

If you get back before the war. . . well, it's a different game. Johnson and Schilling certainly rank *among* the greatest one-two combinations ever put together.

Life Moves On, Or At Least That's the Rumor

You know, I didn't realize it could take this long to write a book.

The realization which is the key to the Win Shares system came to me suddenly in November, 1996. In the other book, I wrote that it was November, 1997, but that was a mistake; it was actually 1996. I know that now because, over the last month, I have been reviewing all the old files on my computers, trying to collect the things I have written about this project over the years which are worth saving.

I worked on Win Shares for several months, and then, in the summer of 1997, I went to STATS, Inc. and asked for their help to produce the book and the reams of data which support it. STATS agreed to help, and I did two things:

1. I wrote up the work I had done up to that time, and sent it out to friends and colleagues, asking for their reactions, and

2. I began work with Jim Henzler to produce the data.

This was a new thing for me, to ask other people for reactions to my work well before I published it. I have one thing to say about this process: I am *never* going to do that again.

No, seriously, the feedback I got from the people who read my manuscript in '97 and '98 was absolutely invaluable to me. Without their input, I could never have thought through satisfactorily all the implications of the method; I would have missed many, many things. Without the programming talents of Jim Henzler, I would have had no way of creating the data that I have used to study these last thirty or forty issues, or any of the hundreds of issues which are yet to be studied.

And seriously, I am never, ever going to do that again. This was a once-in-a-lifetime opportunity for me, to do a comprehensive evaluation of major league history—every player, every team, every facet of his game. I have wanted to do that for many years. Hell,

I have been *doing* it for many years. My younger son is eight years old. When I started on this, he was a little tiny fellow. He doesn't remember that far back.

I have been working on this book for nearly as many years as the national publication of the original *Abstract* series (1982-1987). And believe me, it seems like it. One time, after I had been working on this book for what seemed like an eternity, I compiled a to-do list to finish this book, about twenty things that I had to do to get this project behind me and get on with my life. I found that list, when I was tying up the loose ends. It was written four years ago. I found e-mails that I had sent to Jim Henzler before that, saying that we were on the downhill slope now; all the hard stuff was behind us. Can you imagine what it is like to spend four years trying to tie up the loose ends of a project which is nearly finished?

What I didn't understand was that the process of opening up the book for input from other people would make the book so immensely difficult to close. Don't get me wrong; the input from other people was indispensable to what I was trying to do. If I was starting *this* project now, I would do the same thing now I did then—I would send copies of it to Rob Neyer, and Craig Wright, and Eddie Epstein, and Don Zminda, and John Dewan, and Dick Cramer, and several other people, and I would nag them and goad them until they gave me some kind of reactions to it. I would speak about the system to groups of knowledgeable people, to get their reactions. I *needed*, for this project, to see the flaws and limitations in what I was doing. And then, I would try to get Jim Henzler to work with me to convert the vision into real numbers.

I have tried, in writing up the Win Shares system, to pause occasionally and give the reader an overview, a picture of where we were in the process and what exactly we were trying to do at the moment. Still, the calculations are bewilderingly complex, and I know that most of you will think, on first reading, that there is no way you can follow the twists and turns of the mathematical analysis. Believe me, you can. . . if you read it a couple of times, you can make sense of what we have done.

That complexity is a result of the immense task we undertook, but it is also a result of the fact that a lot of people looked the system over before we published this book. A lot of people had the opportunity to tell us what our system wasn't doing that it should have been doing. Jim Henzler and I have been, for four years, spotting and fixing glitches in the system, the problem being that every mistake we found and fixed would pitch us into another cycle of re-running the data and studying it again, at which time we would find more glitches and more mistakes and more results that we were just not quite happy with. After living for years in that cycle, we lost track of where the exit was.

I hope that I have not worked on this project all these years in vain, and yet I must say this: that if this really is the end of the Win Shares project, then it has been in vain. The purpose of figuring Win Shares was not to wrap up any discussion; rather, the purpose was to open up many more issues, to make additional topics and additional issues more accessible to research. The original idea of Win Shares was not that people would read it and say, "Oh, well, that answers that question." Exactly the opposite; what I wanted was for people to say "Oh, I can use that to study this. I can use these Win Shares to study. . . " whatever it is you want to study. Whether teams which have ground-ball pitching staffs also tend to have good double-play combinations.

So Win Shares were never meant to have an end, and they damned near didn't. The publication of this book is the beginning of a new life for me, and, I hope, the beginning of something new and different in the world of baseball research. We'll see. I appreciate your reading.

Bill James

January 18, 2002

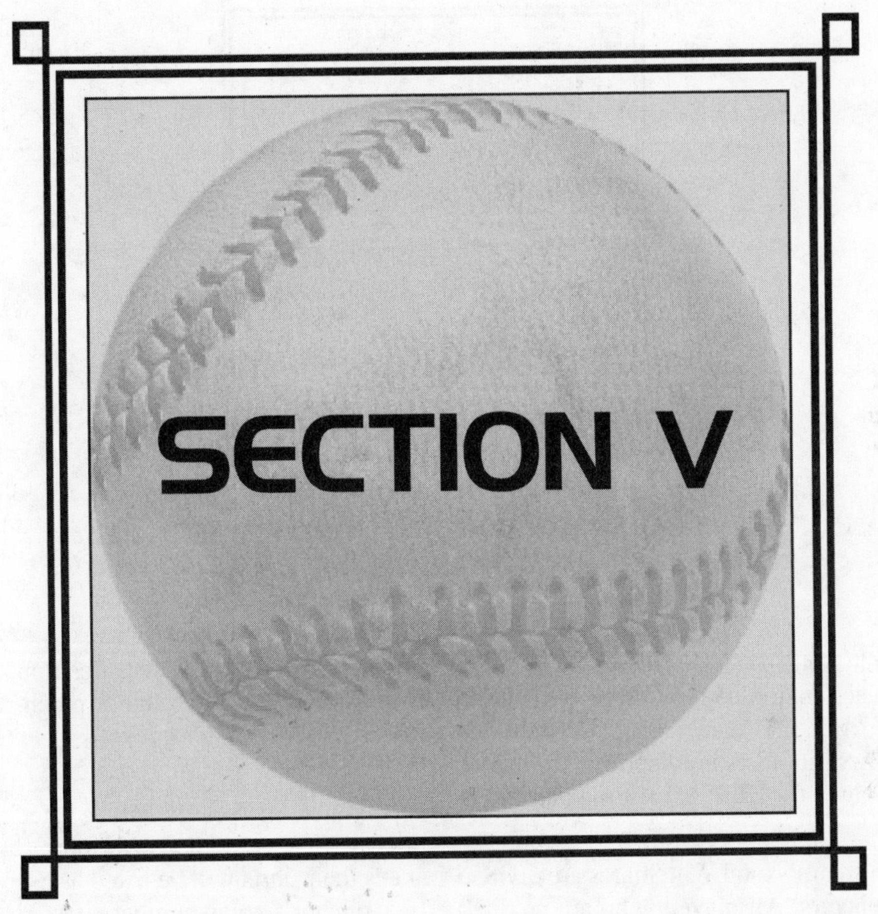

SECTION V

Reference

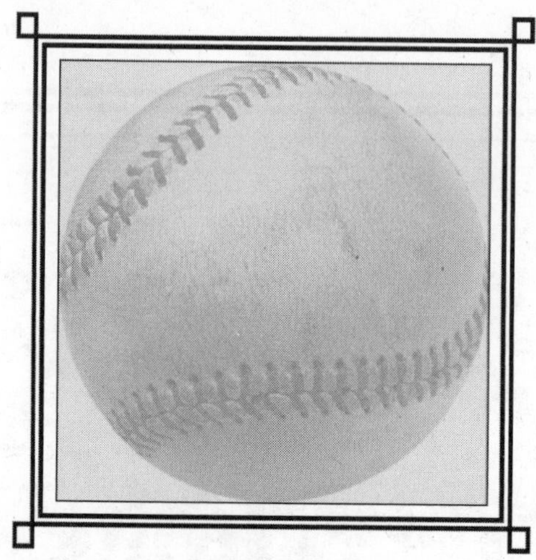

Win Shares by Team

The following pages break down the Win Shares for each major league club between 1876 and 2001. After the team name and won-lost record, the first numbers provided are the team's total Win Shares for Hitting, Fielding and Pitching.

Then the team's total Win Shares are divided among its players. All players who are credited with at least one full Win Share are listed in order of their Win Shares totals, with their primary position provided.

Multiple positions are listed if a player has more than one primary position with the same number of games played at each one. If a player has no games played at a position, he will be listed as a pinch-hitter and/or pinch-runner (PH-PR).

A pitcher who collects more starts than relief appearances in a season will be listed as a starting pitcher (SP). A pitcher with more relief appearances than starts will be listed as a reliever (RP). If a pitcher's total number of starts and relief appearances in a season are equal, he will have both designations (SP-RP).

If a player plays for more than one team in a season, he is listed with each of his teams. The Win Shares given are only those he accumulated for that particular team.

1876 National League

Boston (39-31)	WS
Hitting	**74.3**
Fielding	**14.3**
Pitching	**28.4**
J. Manning, OF	19
J. O'Rourke, OF	17
G. Wright, SS	17
J. Borden, SP	10
A. Leonard, OF	10
T. Murnane, 1B	10
F. Bradley, SP	9
J. Morrill, 2B	8
H. Schafer, 3B	8
L. Brown, C	5
F. Whitney, OF	3
T. Nichols, SP	1

Chicago (52-14)	WS
Hitting	**77.1**
Fielding	**21.4**
Pitching	**57.5**
A. Spalding, SP	57
R. Barnes, 2B	20
C. McVey, 1B	16
C. Anson, 3B	14
D. White, C	13
P. Hines, OF	12
J. Peters, SS	12
J. Glenn, OF	8
B. Addy, OF	3
F. Andrus, OF	1

Cincinnati (9-56)	WS
Hitting	**21.1**
Fielding	**2.4**
Pitching	**3.6**
C. Jones, OF	9
A. Booth, C-3B	4
D. Dean, SP	3
C. Gould, 1B	3
H. Kessler, SS	3
C. Fisher, SP	2
W. Foley, 3B	1
D. Pierson, C	1
D. Williams, SP	1

Hartford (47-21)	WS
Hitting	**53.4**
Fielding	**22.3**
Pitching	**65.3**
T. Bond, SP	47
C. Cummings, SP	22
D. Higham, OF	13
J. Remsen, OF	11
T. York, OF	10
B. Ferguson, 3B	9
J. Burdock, 2B	8
T. Carey, SS	8
D. Allison, C	5
E. Mills, 1B	5
B. Harbridge, C	2
J. Cassidy, OF	1

Louisville (30-36)	WS
Hitting	**19.8**
Fielding	**22.3**
Pitching	**47.9**
J. Devlin, SP	53
C. Fulmer, SS	6
J. Gerhardt, 1B	6
S. Hastings, OF	5
J. Ryan, OF	5
P. Snyder, C	4
E. Somerville, 2B	4
B. Hague, 3B	3
J. Clinton, OF	2
A. Allison, OF	1
B. Holbert, C	1

New York (21-35)	WS
Hitting	**35.1**
Fielding	**9.3**
Pitching	**18.6**
B. Mathews, SP	18
J. Hallinan, SS	12
J. Start, 1B	9
J. Holdsworth, OF	7
N. Hicks, C	5
B. Craver, 2B	4
F. Treacey, OF	3
E. Booth, OF	2
A. Nichols, 3B	2
J. Maloney, OF	1

Philadelphia (14-45)	WS
Hitting	**32.8**
Fielding	**3.7**
Pitching	**5.5**
G. Hall, OF	10
L. Meyerle, 3B	7
W. Fisler, OF	5
L. Knight, SP	5
E. Sutton, 1B	5
D. Eggler, OF	3
D. Force, SS	2
G. Zettlein, SP	2
W. Coon, OF	1
F. Malone, C	1
W. Ritterson, C	1

St. Louis (45-19)	WS
Hitting	**62.6**
Fielding	**20.7**
Pitching	**51.7**
G. Bradley, SP	57
L. Pike, OF	17
J. Battin, 3B	15
J. Clapp, C	14
N. Cuthbert, OF	8
M. McGeary, 2B	8
J. Blong, OF	7
D. Mack, SS	5
H. Dehlman, 1B	2
D. Pearce, SS	2

1877 National League

Boston (42-18)	WS
Hitting	**58.9**
Fielding	**19.7**
Pitching	**47.4**
T. Bond, SP	47
D. White, 1B	16
J. O'Rourke, OF	15
L. Brown, C	9
E. Sutton, SS	9
A. Leonard, OF	8
G. Wright, 2B	8
J. Morrill, 3B	6
T. Murnane, OF	4
H. Schafer, OF	2
W. White, SP	2

Chicago (26-33)	WS
Hitting	**45.0**
Fielding	**11.3**
Pitching	**21.7**
G. Bradley, SP	19
C. McVey, C	14
C. Anson, 3B	11
J. Peters, SS	9
P. Hines, OF	6
A. Spalding, 1B	5
D. Eggler, OF	3
J. Glenn, OF	3
L. Reis, SP	3
R. Barnes, 2B	2
J. Hallinan, OF	2
C. Jones, OF	1

Cincinnati (15-42)	WS
Hitting	**35.1**
Fielding	**4.0**
Pitching	**5.9**
C. Jones, OF	8
J. Manning, SS	8
L. Pike, OF	7
B. Addy, OF	4
L. Meyerle, SS	4
J. Hallinan, 2B	3
A. Booth, SS	2
C. Cummings, SP	2
C. Gould, 1B	2
B. Mitchell, SP	2
W. Foley, 3B	1
B. Mathews, SP	1
H. Smith, C	1

Hartford (31-27)	WS
Hitting	**49.1**
Fielding	**14.8**
Pitching	**29.1**
T. Larkin, SP	31
J. Cassidy, OF	13
J. Start, 1B	11
T. York, OF	10
B. Ferguson, 3B	7
J. Burdock, 2B	6
T. Carey, SS	6
J. Holdsworth, OF	5
B. Harbridge, C	3
D. Allison, C	1

Louisville (35-25)	WS
Hitting	**27.0**
Fielding	**19.7**
Pitching	**58.3**
J. Devlin, SP	60
G. Hall, OF	8
O. Shaffer, OF	7
B. Crowley, OF	6
J. Gerhardt, 2B	6
P. Snyder, C	6
J. Latham, 1B	5
B. Craver, SS	4
B. Hague, 3B	3

St. Louis (28-32)	WS
Hitting	**29.3**
Fielding	**19.2**
Pitching	**35.5**
T. Nichols, SP	24
J. Blong, OF	14
J. Clapp, C	10
M. Dorgan, OF	10
D. Force, SS	8
M. McGeary, 2B	6
J. Remsen, OF	4
J. Battin, 3B	3
A. Croft, 1B	3
H. Dehlman, 1B	1
D. Pearce, SS	1

1878 National League

Boston (41-19)	WS
Hitting	**45.0**
Fielding	**19.4**
Pitching	**58.6**
T. Bond, SP	60
J. O'Rourke, OF	12
J. Burdock, 2B	11
G. Wright, SS	8
A. Leonard, OF	7
J. Manning, OF	7
E. Sutton, 3B	7
P. Snyder, C	6
J. Morrill, 1B	5

Chicago (30-30)	WS
Hitting	**46.8**
Fielding	**14.2**
Pitching	**29.0**
T. Larkin, SP	34
B. Ferguson, SS	11
J. Start, 1B	10
C. Anson, OF	9
B. Harbridge, C	6
J. Cassidy, OF	5
F. Hankinson, 3B	5
J. Remsen, OF	5
J. Hallinan, OF	2
B. McClellan, 2B	2
L. Reis, SP	1

Cincinnati (37-23)	WS
Hitting	**56.7**
Fielding	**17.8**
Pitching	**36.5**
W. White, SP	30
C. Jones, OF	12
C. McVey, 3B	11
D. White, C	11
J. Gerhardt, 2B	10
K. Kelly, OF	8
B. Mitchell, SP	7
B. Geer, SS	6
L. Pike, OF	6
B. Dickerson, OF	5
C. Sullivan, 1B	5

Indianapolis (24-36)	WS
Hitting	**37.1**
Fielding	**11.9**
Pitching	**23.0**
T. Nolan, SP	15
O. Shaffer, OF	13
J. Clapp, OF	10
J. McCormick, SP	6
N. Williamson, 3B	6
S. Flint, C	5
T. Healey, SP	4
R. McKelvy, OF	4
J. Quest, 2B	4
F. Warner, SS	4
A. Croft, 1B	1

Milwaukee (15-45)	WS
Hitting	**16.1**
Fielding	**10.0**
Pitching	**18.9**
S. Weaver, SP	18
A. Dalrymple, OF	8
J. Peters, 2B	5
W. Foley, 3B	4
C. Bennett, C	2
M. Golden, OF	2
J. Goodman, 1B	2
B. Redmond, SS	2
G. Creamer, 2B	1
B. Holbert, OF	1

Providence (33-27)	WS
Hitting	**56.3**
Fielding	**13.9**
Pitching	**28.8**
M. Ward, SP	24
P. Hines, OF	15
T. York, OF	13
L. Brown, C	12
D. Higham, OF	12
T. Carey, SS	5
T. Murnane, 1B	4
D. Allison, C	3
B. Hague, 3B	3
H. Wheeler, SP	3
F. Corey, SP	1
T. Healey, SP	1
T. Nichols, SP	1
L. Pike, 2B	1
C. Sweasy, 2B	1

1879 National League

Boston (54-30)	WS
Hitting	**79.1**
Fielding	**27.2**
Pitching	**55.7**
T. Bond, SP	50
C. Jones, OF	21
J. O'Rourke, OF	17
C. Foley, SP	12
P. Snyder, C	12
S. Houck, OF	11
J. Morrill, 3B	11
E. Cogswell, 1B	9
J. Burdock, 2B	8
E. Sutton, SS	8
B. Hawes, OF	1
L. Richmond, SP	1
J. Tyng, SP	1

Buffalo (46-32)	WS
Hitting	**45.0**
Fielding	**25.6**
Pitching	**67.4**
P. Galvin, SP	61
B. McGunnigle, OF	12
H. Richardson, 3B	12
J. Clapp, C	9
C. Fulmer, 2B	9
J. Hornung, OF	9
B. Crowley, OF	8
O. Walker, 1B	8
D. Force, SS	5
D. Eggler, OF	4
J. Rowe, C	1

Chicago (46-33)	WS
Hitting	**59.4**
Fielding	**26.9**
Pitching	**51.7**
T. Larkin, SP	39
N. Williamson, 3B	17
F. Hankinson, SP	16
S. Flint, C	13
O. Shaffer, OF	12
C. Anson, 1B	9
A. Dalrymple, OF	9
G. Gore, OF	8
J. Peters, SS	7
J. Quest, 2B	5
J. Remsen, OF	2
L. Brown, 1B	1

Cincinnati (43-37)	WS
Hitting	**80.6**
Fielding	**15.0**
Pitching	**33.4**
W. White, SP	33
K. Kelly, 3B	20
D. White, C	17
B. Dickerson, OF	14
P. Hotaling, OF	14
C. McVey, 1B	13
R. Barnes, SS	10
J. Gerhardt, 2B	4
W. Foley, 3B	2
M. Burke, SS	1
B. Purcell, OF	1

Cleveland (27-55)	WS
Hitting	**25.0**
Fielding	**18.5**
Pitching	**37.5**
J. McCormick, SP	33
C. Eden, OF	9
T. Carey, SS	7
B. Phillips, 1B	7
D. Kennedy, C	6
B. Mitchell, SP	6
F. Warner, 3B	5
J. Glasscock, 2B	4
J. Allen, 3B	1
B. Gilligan, C	1
B. Riley, OF	1
G. Strief, OF	1

Providence (59-25)	WS
Hitting	**95.6**
Fielding	**26.5**
Pitching	**54.9**
M. Ward, SP	51
P. Hines, OF	22
J. O'Rourke, OF	17
G. Wright, SS	16
B. Mathews, SP	14
T. York, OF	14
J. Start, 1B	12
M. McGeary, 2B	10
L. Brown, C	8
E. Gross, C	8
B. Hague, 3B	4
J. Farrell, 2B	1

Syracuse (22-48)	WS
Hitting	**33.5**
Fielding	**11.6**
Pitching	**20.8**
H. McCormick, SP	19
M. Dorgan, 1B	9
J. Farrell, 2B	9
B. Purcell, OF	9
J. Macullar, SS	4
J. Richmond, OF	4
B. Holbert, C	3
M. Mansell, OF	3
H. Carpenter, 1B	2
J. McGuinness, 1B	2
G. Creamer, 2B	1
R. Woodhead, 3B	1

Troy (19-56)	WS
Hitting	**33.8**
Fielding	**9.3**
Pitching	**13.9**
G. Bradley, SP	14
E. Caskin, SS	6
D. Brouthers, 1B	5
J. Evans, OF	5
A. Hall, OF	5
A. Clapp, 1B	4
B. Ferguson, 3B	3
C. Nelson, SS	3
H. Doscher, 3B	2
F. Goldsmith, SP	2
T. Hawkes, 2B	2
T. Mansell, OF	2
C. Reilley, C	2
H. Salisbury, SP	2

1880 National League

Boston (40-44)	WS
Hitting	**79.2**
Fielding	**14.1**
Pitching	**26.7**
T. Bond, SP	21
C. Foley, SP	18
Ji. O'Rourke, OF	17
Jo. O'Rourke, OF	13
C. Jones, OF	12
J. Burdock, 2B	11
J. Morrill, 1B	10
E. Sutton, SS	8
J. Richmond, SS	3
S. Trott, C	3
J. Bergh, C	1
S. Dignan, OF	1
D. O'Leary, OF	1
P. Powers, C	1

Buffalo (24-58)	WS
Hitting	**47.5**
Fielding	**9.8**
Pitching	**14.7**
P. Galvin, SP	14
H. Richardson, 3B	11
B. Crowley, OF	10
J. Hornung, OF	10
J. Rowe, C	8
M. Moynahan, SS	5
D. Esterbrook, 1B	4
D. Force, 2B	3
O. Walker, 1B	3
S. Wiedman, SP	2
D. Mack, SS	1
B. McGunnigle, SP	1

Chicago (67-17)	WS
Hitting	**103.5**
Fielding	**27.8**
Pitching	**69.6**
L. Corcoran, SP	52
F. Goldsmith, SP	24
G. Gore, OF	24
A. Dalrymple, OF	23
C. Anson, 1B	20
K. Kelly, OF	16
T. Burns, SS	15
N. Williamson, 3B	12
J. Quest, 2B	8
S. Flint, C	5
T. Poorman, OF	2

Cincinnati (21-59)	WS
Hitting	**28.1**
Fielding	**13.6**
Pitching	**21.3**
W. White, SP	17
J. Clapp, C	12
B. Purcell, OF	12
H. Carpenter, 3B	5
D. White, OF	4
P. Smith, 2B	3
A. Leonard, SS	2
J. Manning, OF	2
M. Mansell, OF	2
L. Say, SS	2
C. Reilley, OF	1
J. Reilly, 1B	1

Cleveland (47-37)	WS
Hitting	**59.2**
Fielding	**27.5**
Pitching	**54.2**
J. McCormick, SP	54
F. Dunlap, 2B	17
O. Shaffer, OF	14
J. Glasscock, SS	10
B. Phillips, 1B	10
P. Hotaling, OF	9
N. Hanlon, OF	8
F. Hankinson, 3B	6
D. Kennedy, C	5
B. Gilligan, C	3
M. McGeary, 3B	3
G. Gardner, SP	2

Providence (52-32)	WS
Hitting	**65.1**
Fielding	**28.2**
Pitching	**62.8**
M. Ward, SP	51
G. Bradley, 3B	24
P. Hines, OF	19
J. Farrell, 2B	13
E. Gross, C	12
J. Start, 1B	12
M. Dorgan, OF	9
J. Peters, SS	7
S. Houck, OF	4
T. York, OF	4
M. McGeary, 3B	1

Troy (41-42)	WS
Hitting	**54.8**
Fielding	**22.7**
Pitching	**45.6**
M. Welch, SP	42
R. Connor, 3B	17
T. Keefe, SP	11
P. Gillespie, OF	10
B. Ferguson, 2B	9
J. Cassidy, OF	8
E. Caskin, SS	7
E. Cogswell, 1B	7
J. Evans, OF	4
B. Holbert, C	4
B. Dickerson, OF	2
B. Harbridge, C	2

Worcester (40-43)	WS
Hitting	**45.6**
Fielding	**26.0**
Pitching	**48.4**
L. Richmond, SP	42
A. Irwin, SS	13
H. Stovey, OF	13
F. Corey, OF	10
G. Wood, OF	8
A. Whitney, 3B	7
C. Bennett, C	6
B. Dickerson, OF	5
L. Knight, OF	5
C. Sullivan, 1B	4
D. Bushong, C	3
G. Creamer, 2B	3
S. Dignan, OF	1

1881 National League

Boston (38-45)	WS
Hitting	**51.0**
Fielding	**21.1**
Pitching	**41.9**
J. Whitney, SP	42
E. Sutton, 3B	12
J. Morrill, 1B	11
R. Barnes, SS	9
J. Hornung, OF	8
J. Burdock, 2B	6
B. Crowley, OF	6
J. Fox, SP	4
J. Richmond, OF	4
P. Snyder, C	4
P. Deasley, C	3
F. Lewis, OF	2
B. Mathews, OF	2
T. Bond, SP	1

Buffalo (45-38)	WS
Hitting	**69.1**
Fielding	**19.3**
Pitching	**46.6**
P. Galvin, SP	36
D. Brouthers, OF	15
H. Richardson, OF	15
J. O'Rourke, 3B	14
J. Rowe, C	12
D. White, 1B	12
J. Lynch, SP	8
B. Purcell, OF	8
C. Foley, OF	7
D. Force, 2B	5
J. Peters, SS	3

Chicago (56-28)	WS
Hitting	**87.0**
Fielding	**27.2**
Pitching	**53.8**
L. Corcoran, SP	30
F. Goldsmith, SP	25
C. Anson, 1B	22
K. Kelly, OF	16
A. Dalrymple, OF	15

G. Gore, OF	15
N. Williamson, 3B	14
T. Burns, SS	12
S. Flint, C	11
J. Quest, 2B	6
H. Nicol, OF	2

Cleveland (36-48)	WS
Hitting	**47.2**
Fielding	**21.0**
Pitching	**39.8**
J. McCormick, SP	34
F. Dunlap, 2B	15
J. Glasscock, SS	10
T. Nolan, SP	9
J. Clapp, C	8
B. Phillips, 1B	8
O. Shaffer, OF	8
G. Bradley, 3B	5
D. Kennedy, C	5
M. Moynahan, OF	2
J. Remsen, OF	2
B. Taylor, OF	2

Detroit (41-43)	WS
Hitting	**55.2**
Fielding	**23.3**
Pitching	**44.5**
G. Derby, SP	34
C. Bennett, C	15
G. Wood, OF	11
N. Hanlon, OF	10
S. Houck, SS	10
S. Wiedman, SP	10
L. Knight, OF	8
M. Powell, 1B	8
J. Gerhardt, 2B	6
A. Whitney, 3B	3
L. Brown, 1B	2
D. Troy, 3B	2
M. Dorgan, OF	1
J. Leary, SP-OF	1
C. Reilley, C	1
S. Trott, C	1

Providence (47-37)	WS
Hitting	**77.4**
Fielding	**20.4**
Pitching	**43.2**
M. Ward, OF	27
O. Radbourn, SP	24
T. York, OF	17
P. Hines, OF	16
J. Start, 1B	16
J. Farrell, 2B	13
E. Gross, C	9
J. Denny, 3B	8
B. Gilligan, C	4
B. Mathews, SP	3
L. Brown, OF	2
B. McClellan, SS	2

Troy (39-45)	WS
Hitting	**48.3**
Fielding	**24.0**
Pitching	**44.7**
M. Welch, SP	25
T. Keefe, SP	23
B. Ferguson, 2B	12
R. Connor, 1B	11
B. Ewing, C	10
P. Gillespie, OF	9
J. Evans, OF	6
B. Holbert, C	6
E. Caskin, SS	5
J. Cassidy, OF	5
F. Hankinson, 3B	5

Worcester (32-50)	WS
Hitting	**46.1**
Fielding	**16.0**
Pitching	**33.9**
L. Richmond, SP	26
B. Dickerson, OF	12
F. Corey, OF	10
P. Hotaling, OF	10
H. Stovey, 1B	9
D. Bushong, C	8
A. Irwin, SS	5
H. Carpenter, 3B	4
M. Dorgan, 1B	4
H. McCormick, SP	3
C. Nelson, SS	3
G. Creamer, 2B	2

1882 National League

Boston (45-39)	WS
Hitting	**61.1**
Fielding	**24.5**
Pitching	**49.3**
J. Whitney, SP	40
B. Mathews, SP	21
J. Hornung, OF	14
J. Morrill, 1B	12
P. Hotaling, OF	9
E. Sutton, 3B	9
E. Rowen, OF	8
J. Burdock, 2B	7
P. Deasley, C	7
S. Wise, SS	6
C. Buffinton, OF	2

Buffalo (45-39)	WS
Hitting	**70.1**
Fielding	**21.8**
Pitching	**43.1**
P. Galvin, SP	29
D. Brouthers, 1B	20
O. Daily, SP	14
C. Foley, OF	12
J. O'Rourke, OF	11
B. Purcell, OF	11
H. Richardson, 2B	11
D. White, 3B	10
J. Rowe, C	9
D. Force, SS	7
T. Dolan, C	1

Chicago (55-29)	WS
Hitting	**86.5**
Fielding	**26.0**
Pitching	**52.5**
F. Goldsmith, SP	29
L. Corcoran, SP	28
C. Anson, 1B	18
G. Gore, OF	17
A. Dalrymple, OF	16
K. Kelly, SS	16
N. Williamson, 3B	16
T. Burns, 2B	10
S. Flint, C	10
H. Nicol, OF	3
J. Quest, 2B	2

Cleveland (42-40)	WS
Hitting	**58.4**
Fielding	**23.5**
Pitching	**44.1**
J. McCormick, SP	42
J. Glasscock, SS	19
F. Dunlap, 2B	14
M. Muldoon, 3B	12
B. Phillips, 1B	10
F. Briody, C	6
O. Shaffer, OF	6
G. Bradley, SP	5
D. Esterbrook, OF	5
D. Rowe, OF	3
H. Doscher, 3B	2
J. Kelly, C	1
J. Richmond, OF	1

Detroit (42-41)	WS
Hitting	**47.5**
Fielding	**25.5**
Pitching	**53.0**
S. Wiedman, SP	35
C. Bennett, C	19
G. Derby, SP	19
G. Wood, OF	13
N. Hanlon, OF	11
J. Farrell, 3B	6
L. Knight, OF	5
M. Powell, 1B	5
M. McGeary, SS	3
S. Trott, C	3
D. Troy, 2B	3
A. Whitney, 3B	2
B. Casey, 3B	1
W. Kinzie, SS	1

Providence (52-32)	WS
Hitting	**61.5**
Fielding	**27.2**
Pitching	**67.3**
O. Radbourn, SP	50
M. Ward, OF	31
P. Hines, OF	18
J. Start, 1B	14
T. York, OF	13
J. Farrell, 2B	11
J. Denny, 3B	10
B. Gilligan, C	5
G. Wright, SS	2
C. Carroll, OF	1
S. Nava, C	1

Troy (35-48)	WS
Hitting	**57.9**
Fielding	**15.3**
Pitching	**31.8**
T. Keefe, SP	24
R. Connor, 1B	19
B. Ewing, 3B	13
M. Welch, SP	12
B. Ferguson, 2B	9
P. Gillespie, OF	8
C. Roseman, OF	6
F. Pfeffer, SS	5
B. Holbert, C	4
J. Egan, OF	3
J. Smith, 1B	2

Worcester (18-66)	WS
Hitting	**35.3**
Fielding	**7.5**
Pitching	**11.2**
L. Richmond, SP	13
H. Stovey, 1B	10
J. Hayes, OF	7
F. Corey, SS	6
G. Creamer, 2B	5
A. Irwin, 3B	4
F. Mountain, SP	3
J. Evans, OF	2
D. Bushong, C	1
J. Clarkson, SP	1
F. Mann, 3B	1
J. Smith, 1B	1

1882 American Assoc.

Baltimore (19-54)	WS
Hitting	**30.6**
Fielding	**10.6**
Pitching	**15.8**
D. Landis, SP	10
E. Whiting, C	10
C. Householder, 1B	9
T. Brown, OF	8
J. Shetzline, 3B	6
M. Cline, OF	3
E. Geis, SP	2
H. Myers, SS	2
H. Jacoby, 3B	1
J. Leary, SP	1
T. Nichols, SP	1
G. Pierce, 2B	1
N. Scharf, OF	1
C. Waitt, OF	1
B. Wise, SP	1

Cincinnati (55-25)	WS
Hitting	**68.1**
Fielding	**25.9**
Pitching	**71.0**
W. White, SP	54
H. McCormick, SP	20
H. Carpenter, 3B	18
J. Sommer, OF	16
P. Snyder, C	13
C. Fulmer, SS	11
H. Wheeler, OF	9
J. Macullar, OF	8
B. McPhee, 2B	8
E. Stearns, 1B	5
H. Luff, 1B	2
P. Powers, C	1

Louisville (42-38)	WS
Hitting	**64.9**
Fielding	**20.7**
Pitching	**40.4**
T. Mullane, SP	36
P. Browning, 2B	20
G. Hecker, 1B	17
C. Wolf, OF	12
J. Reccius, OF	10
D. Sullivan, C	10
B. Schenck, 3B	8
L. Maskrey, OF	6
D. Mack, SS	3
J. Strick, C	2
C. Bohn, SP-OF	1
G. Pierce, 2B	1

Philadelphia (41-34)	WS
Hitting	**51.5**
Fielding	**24.1**
Pitching	**47.4**
S. Weaver, SP	33
J. O'Brien, C	14
J. Birchall, OF	10
J. Latham, 1B	10
B. Sweeney, SP	10
J. Dorgan, C	7
C. Stricker, 2B	7
L. Say, SS	6
B. Blakiston, OF	5
F. Mountain, SP	5
B. Kienzle, OF	3
F. Mann, 3B	3
J. Mansell, OF	2
J. Richmond, OF	2
J. Say, SS	2
B. Greenwood, OF	1
D. Landis, SP	1
P. Smith, 3B	1
G. Snyder, SP	1

Pittsburgh (39-39)	WS
Hitting	**61.3**
Fielding	**17.9**
Pitching	**37.8**
H. Salisbury, SP	19
D. Driscoll, SP	17
E. Swartwood, OF	16
M. Mansell, OF	12
B. Taylor, C	12
J. Peters, SS	10
J. Leary, 3B	7
G. Strief, 2B	5
J. Battin, 3B	4
C. Morton, OF	3

J. Goodman, 1B	2
J. Keenan, C	2
R. Kemmler, C	2
C. Lane, 1B	2
B. Morgan, OF	2
H. Arundel, SP	1
M. Critchley, SP	1

St. Louis (37-43)	WS
Hitting	**61.7**
Fielding	**15.3**
Pitching	**34.1**
J. McGinnis, SP	26
B. Gleason, SS	16
J. Gleason, 3B	12
O. Walker, OF	12
C. Comiskey, 1B	9
N. Cuthbert, OF	7
H. McCaffery, OF	7
J. Schappert, SP	6
B. Smiley, 2B	4
B. Dorr, SP	3
E. Fusselback, C	3
G. Seward, OF	3
M. Critchley, SP	1
E. Hogan, SP	1
S. Sullivan, C	1

1883 National League

Boston (63-35)	WS
Hitting	**88.6**
Fielding	**31.7**
Pitching	**68.7**
J. Whitney, SP	57
C. Buffinton, OF	28
E. Sutton, 3B	21
J. Morrill, 1B	20
J. Burdock, 2B	19
J. Hornung, OF	16
S. Wise, SS	14
M. Hines, C	5
M. Hackett, C	4
P. Radford, OF	2
E. Smith, OF	2
L. Brown, 1B	1

Buffalo (52-45)	WS
Hitting	**83.0**
Fielding	**23.2**
Pitching	**49.8**
P. Galvin, SP	47
D. Brouthers, 1B	24
J. O'Rourke, OF	17
H. Richardson, 2B	17
O. Shaffer, OF	12
D. White, 3B	12
J. Rowe, C	11
D. Force, SS	6
C. Foley, OF	3
J. Lillie, OF	3
E. Cushman, SP	2
D. Eggler, OF	2

Chicago (59-39)	WS
Hitting	**87.0**
Fielding	**28.3**
Pitching	**61.7**
L. Corcoran, SP	38
F. Goldsmith, SP	27
G. Gore, OF	22
T. Burns, SS	16
N. Williamson, 3B	16
C. Anson, 1B	15
A. Dalrymple, OF	13
K. Kelly, OF	13
S. Flint, C	9
F. Pfeffer, 2B	8

Cleveland (55-42)	WS
Hitting	**47.8**
Fielding	**32.4**
Pitching	**84.8**
J. McCormick, SP	40
O. Daily, SP	34
F. Dunlap, 2B	16
J. Glasscock, SS	14
T. York, OF	12
W. Sawyer, SP	11
P. Hotaling, OF	10
J. Evans, OF	7
B. Phillips, 1B	7
M. Muldoon, 3B	5
D. Bushong, C	4
F. Briody, C	3
G. Bradley, SS	1
B. Crowley, OF	1

Detroit (40-58)	WS
Hitting	**66.0**
Fielding	**18.8**
Pitching	**35.3**
C. Bennett, C	18
S. Wiedman, SP	17
G. Wood, OF	17
S. Houck, SS	12
D. Shaw, SP	12
M. Powell, 1B	11
J. Farrell, 3B	9
N. Hanlon, OF	8
S. Trott, 2B	5
J. Jones, SP	4
J. Quest, 2B	3
D. Burns, OF	2
T. Mansell, OF	1
F. McIntyre, SP	1

New York (46-50)	WS
Hitting	**61.8**
Fielding	**25.2**
Pitching	**51.0**
M. Welch, SP	31
M. Ward, OF	28
R. Connor, 1B	19
B. Ewing, C	17
P. Gillespie, OF	15
E. Caskin, SS	7
F. Hankinson, 3B	7
T. O'Neill, SP	5
M. Dorgan, OF	3
D. Troy, 2B	3
M. Allen, SP	1
J. Clapp, C	1
J. Humphries, C	1

Philadelphia (17-81)	WS
Hitting	**39.8**
Fielding	**4.5**
Pitching	**6.7**
J. Coleman, SP	8
E. Gross, C	8
J. Manning, OF	7
B. Purcell, 3B	7
B. McClellan, SS	5
B. Ferguson, 2B	4
S. Farrar, 1B	3
B. Harbridge, OF	3
A. Hagan, SP	1
F. Lewis, OF	1
J. Mulvey, 3B	1
F. Ringo, C	1
E. Smith, SP-OF	1
F. Warner, 3B	1

Providence (58-40)	WS
Hitting	**79.9**
Fielding	**31.7**
Pitching	**62.4**
O. Radbourn, SP	60
J. Farrell, 2B	18
P. Hines, OF	17
J. Denny, 3B	15
A. Irwin, SS	13
J. Start, 1B	10
L. Richmond, OF	9
C. Sweeney, SP	9
C. Carroll, OF	7
J. Cassidy, OF	7
B. Gilligan, C	7
S. Nava, C	2

1883 American Assoc.

Baltimore (28-68)	WS
Hitting	**38.8**
Fielding	**15.7**
Pitching	**29.5**
J. Clinton, OF	12
H. Henderson, SP	12
B. Emslie, SP	10
J. Fox, SP	6
J. McCormick, 3B	6
D. Rowe, OF	6
L. Say, SS	6
E. Stearns, 1B	6
G. Gardner, OF	5
T. O'Brien, 2B	3
P. Baker, C	2
T. Manning, 2B	2
J. Neagle, SP	2
B. Reid, 2B	2
D. Eggler, OF	1
B. Gallagher, OF	1
J. Kelly, C	1
R. Sweeney, C	1

Cincinnati (61-37)	WS
Hitting	**84.7**
Fielding	**31.7**
Pitching	**66.6**
W. White, SP	51
C. Jones, OF	18
J. Reilly, 1B	18
H. Carpenter, 3B	16
C. Fulmer, SS	13
J. Sommer, OF	13
B. McPhee, 2B	11
R. Deagle, SP	10
H. McCormick, SP	10
P. Snyder, C	9
P. Corkhill, OF	8
P. Powers, C	3
B. Traffley, C	2
J. Macullar, OF	1

Columbus (32-65)	WS
Hitting	**65.3**
Fielding	**12.3**
Pitching	**18.4**
F. Mountain, SP	18
P. Smith, 2B	15
J. Richmond, SS	14
T. Brown, OF	12
F. Mann, OF	10
B. Kuehne, 3B	7
J. Field, 1B	6
R. Kemmler, C	4
J. Valentine, SP	4
H. Wheeler, OF	4
E. Dundon, SP	2

Louisville (52-45)	WS
Hitting	**83.8**
Fielding	**23.0**
Pitching	**49.2**
G. Hecker, SP	36
S. Weaver, SP	24
P. Browning, OF	20
J. Gerhardt, 2B	13
J. Gleason, 3B	13
C. Wolf, OF	13
E. Whiting, C	12
J. Latham, 1B	9
L. Maskrey, OF	6
J. Leary, SS	4
T. McLaughlin, SS	3
D. Sullivan, C	3

New York (54-42)	WS
Hitting	**48.9**
Fielding	**31.4**
Pitching	**81.7**
T. Keefe, SP	70
J. Lynch, SP	15
C. Nelson, SS	15
J. O'Rourke, OF	10
S. Brady, 1B	9
D. Esterbrook, 3B	9
B. Holbert, C	8
C. Roseman, OF	8
S. Crane, 2B	6
E. Kennedy, OF	6
D. Orr, 1B	3
C. Reipschlager, C	3

Philadelphia (66-32)	WS
Hitting	**111.8**
Fielding	**24.5**
Pitching	**61.7**
B. Mathews, SP	30
H. Stovey, 1B	25
M. Moynahan, SS	24
G. Bradley, 3B	22
J. O'Brien, C	19
F. Corey, 3B	18
L. Knight, OF	15
J. Birchall, OF	11
C. Stricker, 2B	11
B. Blakiston, OF	5
J. Jones, SP	5
E. Rowen, C	5
J. Bakely, SP	4
B. Crowley, OF	3
A. Hubbard, C-SS	1

Pittsburgh (31-67)	WS
Hitting	**62.8**
Fielding	**12.1**
Pitching	**18.1**
E. Swartwood, 1B	19
M. Mansell, OF	11
D. Driscoll, SP	10
J. Hayes, C	9
B. Taylor, OF	9
G. Creamer, 2B	8
B. Barr, SP	7
J. Battin, 3B	7
B. Dickerson, OF	6
D. Mack, SS	2
T. Nolan, SP	2
F. McLaughlin, SS	1
B. Morgan, SS	1
J. Neagle, SP	1

St. Louis (65-33)	WS
Hitting	**67.6**
Fielding	**31.7**
Pitching	**95.7**
T. Mullane, SP	55
J. McGinnis, SP	42
B. Gleason, SS	16
C. Comiskey, 1B	14
H. Nicol, OF	14
A. Latham, 3B	12
F. Lewis, OF	8
T. Mansell, OF	7
P. Deasley, C	6
T. Dolan, C	6
G. Strief, 2B	6
C. Hodnett, SP	4
J. Quest, 2B	2
N. Cuthbert, OF	1
J. Gleason, OF	1
S. Sullivan, C	1

1884 National League

Boston (73-38)	WS
Hitting	**97.7**
Fielding	**37.6**
Pitching	**83.7**
C. Buffinton, SP	62
J. Whitney, SP	37
E. Sutton, 3B	28
J. Hornung, OF	18
B. Crowley, OF	14
J. Morrill, 1B	14
J. Burdock, 2B	13
S. Wise, SS	12
J. Manning, OF	9
M. Hackett, C	6
M. Hines, C	3
J. Connor, SP	2
T. Gunning, C	1

Buffalo (64-47)	WS
Hitting	**92.6**
Fielding	**32.8**
Pitching	**66.6**
P. Galvin, SP	57
J. O'Rourke, OF	25
D. Brouthers, 1B	22
D. White, 3B	21
H. Richardson, 2B	19
J. Rowe, C	19
B. Serad, SP	9
D. Force, SS	8
J. Lillie, OF	6
C. Collins, 2B	2
D. Eggler, OF	2
G. Myers, C	2

Chicago (62-50)	WS
Hitting	**106.3**
Fielding	**22.4**
Pitching	**57.4**
L. Corcoran, SP	37
K. Kelly, OF	21
C. Anson, 1B	19
F. Pfeffer, 2B	19
N. Williamson, 3B	19
A. Dalrymple, OF	17
G. Gore, OF	16
J. Clarkson, SP	11
T. Burns, SS	7
F. Goldsmith, SP	7
S. Flint, C	4
J. Brown, OF	2
G. Crosby, SP	2
F. Andrus, SP	1
J. Hibbard, SP	1
W. Kinzie, SS	1
T. Lee, SP	1
B. Sunday, OF	1

Cleveland (35-77)	WS
Hitting	**31.7**
Fielding	**25.1**
Pitching	**48.2**
J. McCormick, SP	26
J. Harkins, SP	17
J. Glasscock, SS	8
B. Phillips, 1B	8
P. Hotaling, OF	7
S. Moffett, OF	7
J. Evans, OF	6
M. Muldoon, 3B	6
G. Smith, 2B	6
D. Bushong, C	4
G. Pinckney, 2B	4
F. Briody, C	2
E. Burch, OF	1
J. Henry, SP	1
M. Moynahan, 2B	1
W. Murphy, OF	1

Detroit (28-84)	WS
Hitting	**35.5**
Fielding	**18.7**
Pitching	**29.8**
C. Bennett, C	11
N. Hanlon, OF	11
F. Meinke, SS	11
G. Wood, OF	10
D. Shaw, SP	9
C. Getzien, SP	7
M. Scott, 1B	7
J. Farrell, 3B	6
S. Wiedman, OF	5
H. Jones, 2B	2
F. Brill, SP	1
H. Buker, SS	1
F. Cox, SS	1
E. Gastfield, C	1
B. Geiss, 2B	1

New York (62-50)	WS
Hitting	**100.0**
Fielding	**28.2**
Pitching	**57.8**
M. Welch, SP	46
R. Connor, 2B	23
B. Ewing, C	21
M. Dorgan, OF	16
M. Ward, OF	16
A. McKinnon, 1B	14
P. Gillespie, OF	11
F. Hankinson, 3B	11
E. Caskin, SS	10
E. Begley, SP	9
D. Richardson, OF	7
J. Humphries, C	2

Philadelphia (39-73)	WS
Hitting	**85.8**
Fielding	**12.5**
Pitching	**18.7**
J. Manning, OF	19
C. Ferguson, SP	16
B. McClellan, SS	15
B. Purcell, OF	13
S. Farrar, 1B	10
J. Fogarty, OF	7
J. Mulvey, 3B	7
E. Andrews, 2B	6
J. Coleman, OF	6
J. Crowley, C	5
B. Vinton, SP	5
T. Lynch, C-OF	3
J. Clements, C	1
B. Hoover, OF	1
J. Knight, SP	1
J. McElroy, SP	1
J. Remsen, OF	1

Providence (84-28)	WS
Hitting	**97.9**
Fielding	**36.9**
Pitching	**117.2**
O. Radbourn, SP	89
C. Sweeney, SP	32
P. Hines, OF	28
C. Carroll, OF	17
J. Denny, 3B	16
A. Irwin, SS	14
J. Start, 1B	14
B. Gilligan, C	13
J. Farrell, 2B	11
P. Radford, OF	7
E. Conley, SP	4
H. Arundel, SP	2
C. Miller, SP	2
S. Nava, C	2
C. Bassett, 3B	1

1884 Union Assoc.

Altoona (6-19)	WS
Hitting	**7.6**
Fielding	**4.1**
Pitching	**6.3**
J. Murphy, SP	5
G. Smith, SS	3
J. Brown, OF	2
J. Moore, C	2
C. Cross, 3B	1
C. Dougherty, 2B	1
J. Grady, 1B	1
F. Harris, 1B	1
H. Koons, 3B	1
T. Shaffer, OF	1

Baltimore (58-47)	WS
Hitting	**77.0**
Fielding	**30.8**
Pitching	**66.2**
B. Sweeney, SP	49
Y. Robinson, 3B	24
E. Seery, OF	21
E. Fusselback, C	13
D. Phelan, 2B	10
T. Lee, SP	9
L. Say, SS	9
C. Levis, 1B	7
A. Atkinson, SP	6
B. Graham, OF	5
R. Sweeney, C	5
J. Ryan, SP	3
N. Cuthbert, OF	2
J. O'Brien, OF	2
E. Smith, SP	2
H. Wheeler, OF	2
J. Battin, 3B	1
H. Oberbeck, OF	1
J. Schoeneck, 1B	1
Scott, OF	1
T. Suck, C	1

Boston (58-51)	WS
Hitting	**81.4**
Fielding	**28.4**
Pitching	**64.2**
D. Shaw, SP	31
W. Burke, SP	24
E. Crane, OF	22
T. O'Brien, 2B	18
T. Bond, SP	17
J. Irwin, 3B	13
W. Hackett, SS	12
L. Brown, C	10
T. Murnane, 1B	7
M. Slattery, OF	6
T. McCarthy, OF	4
K. Butler, OF	3
F. Tenney, SP	2
E. Callahan, OF	1
C. Daniels, SP	1
J. Flynn, C	1
E. Peak, OF	1
P. Scannell, OF	1

Chicago (34-39)	WS
Hitting	**44.2**
Fielding	**18.7**
Pitching	**39.1**
O. Daily, SP	31
J. Schoeneck, 1B	13
J. Ellick, OF	7
E. Gross, C	7
B. Krieg, C	7
C. Householder, 3B	6
S. Matthias, SS	6
A. Atkinson, SP	5
W. Foley, 3B	3
G. Gardner, OF	3
P. Horan, SP	3
C. Cady, SP	2
F. McLaughlin, 2B	2
H. Wheeler, OF	2
C. Briggs, OF	1
C. Fisher, 3B	1
M. Hengle, 2B	1
C. Miller, SP	1
T. Suck, C	1

Cincinnati (69-36)	WS
Hitting	**91.8**
Fielding	**34.0**
Pitching	**81.2**
D. Burns, OF	41
G. Bradley, SP	28
J. McCormick, SP	27
J. Glasscock, SS	14
B. Harbridge, OF	13
L. Sylvester, OF	13
B. Hawes, OF	10
J. Jones, SS	9
M. Powell, 1B	7
E. Cleveland, 3B	6
S. Crane, 2B	6
J. Kelly, C	6
C. Barber, 3B	5
F. Briody, C	5
M. McQuery, 1B	4
D. O'Leary, OF	4
J. Crotty, C	3
B. Schwartz, C	3
F. McLaughlin, SS	2
E. Kennedy, 3B	1

Kansas City (16-63)	WS
Hitting	**37.4**
Fielding	**4.2**
Pitching	**6.3**
B. Black, OF	7
J. Gorman, 1B	5
B. McLaughlin, OF	4
F. McLaughlin, 2B-OF	4
C. Berry, 2B	3
J. Sweeney, 1B	3
K. Baldwin, C	2
P. Veach, OF	2
H. Wheeler, OF	2
F. Wyman, OF	2
J. Bakely, SP	1
C. Bastian, 2B	1
D. Blaisdell, SP	1
E. Callahan, SS	1
C. Cross, SS	1
A. Dwight, C	1
E. Hickman, SP	1
H. Oberbeck, 3B	1
L. Say, SS	1
E. Seery, OF	1
T. Shaffer, OF	1
P. Sullivan, 3B	1
T. Sullivan, OF	1
J. Turbidy, SS	1

Milwaukee (8-4)	WS
Hitting	**6.4**
Fielding	**3.9**
Pitching	**13.7**
E. Cushman, SP	7
H. Porter, SP	6
L. Baldwin, OF	3
C. Broughton, C	2
A. Myers, 2B	2
S. Behel, OF	1
T. Griffin, 1B	1
E. Hogan, OF	1
T. Sexton, SS	1

Philadelphia (21-46)	WS
Hitting	**49.1**
Fielding	**5.5**
Pitching	**8.3**
B. Hoover, OF	13
J. McCormick, 3B	8
B. Kienzle, OF	7
J. Clements, OF	6
J. Bakely, SP	5

J. Flynn, OF	5
H. Easterday, SS	3
H. Luff, OF	3
J. McGuinness, 1B	3
G. Fisher, SP	2
E. Peak, 2B	2
S. Weaver, SP	2
D. Drew, RP-2B-SS	1
B. Geer, SS	1
T. Gillen, C	1
C. Rickley, SS	1

Pittsburgh (7-11)	WS
Hitting	**4.6**
Fielding	**5.6**
Pitching	**10.8**
O. Daily, SP	6
A. Atkinson, SP	4
G. Gardner, OF	2
B. Krieg, C	2
J. Battin, 3B	1
J. Ellick, SS	1
C. Householder, OF	1
J. Schoeneck, 1B	1
G. Strief, 2B	1
T. Suck, C	1
H. Wheeler, OF	1

St. Louis (94-19)	WS
Hitting	**143.2**
Fielding	**36.9**
Pitching	**101.8**
B. Taylor, SP	41
F. Dunlap, 2B	38
C. Sweeney, SP	35
O. Shaffer, OF	28
H. Boyle, OF	25
D. Rowe, OF	22
J. Gleason, 3B	20
P. Werden, SP	15
C. Hodnett, SP	13
B. Dickerson, OF	12
J. Quinn, 1B	10
M. Whitehead, SS	8
G. Baker, C	6
J. Brennan, C	5
T. Dolan, C	2
J. Cattanach, SP	1
F. Lewis, OF	1

St. Paul (2-6)	WS
Hitting	**1.3**
Fielding	**1.6**
Pitching	**3.1**
J. Brown, SP	2
B. O'Brien, 3B	2
S. Dunn, 1B	1
L. Galvin, SP	1

Washington (47-65)	WS
Hitting	**71.0**
Fielding	**21.8**
Pitching	**48.2**
B. Wise, SP	30
H. Moore, OF	22
C. Geggus, SP	15
P. Baker, 1B	13
A. Powell, OF	12
A. Voss, SP	10
T. Evers, 2B	9
C. Fulmer, C	7
J. Deasley, SS	3
J. McCormick, 3B	3
F. Tenney, OF	3
D. Drew, SS	2
J. Gunson, C	2
G. Alberts, SS	1
O. Daily, SP	1
J. Halpin, SS	1
P. Joy, 1B	1
J. Kelly, C	1
Larkin, 3B	1
M. Lehane, SS	1
M. Lockwood, SP-OF	1
E. McKenna, C	1
J. Shoupe, OF	1

Wilmington (2-16)	WS
Hitting	**1.3**
Fielding	**1.9**
Pitching	**2.8**
T. Nolan, SP	2
C. Bastian, 2B	1
Da. Casey, SP	1
T. Lynch, C-OF	1
J. Murphy, SP	1

1884 American Assoc.

Baltimore (63-43)	WS
Hitting	**95.3**
Fielding	**30.0**
Pitching	**63.6**
H. Henderson, SP	32
B. Emslie, SP	31
J. Clinton, OF	18
J. Sommer, 3B	17
J. Macullar, SS	15
S. Trott, C	12
T. York, OF	12
E. Stearns, 1B	11
T. Manning, 2B	10
O. Burns, OF	9
G. Gardner, OF	7
D. Casey, OF	5
B. Traffley, C	3
B. Dickerson, OF	2
F. Goldsmith, SP	2
P. Burns, 1B	1
J. McLaughlin, SP-OF	1
J. Roxburgh, C	1

Brooklyn (40-64)	WS
Hitting	**54.8**
Fielding	**20.3**
Pitching	**44.9**
A. Terry, SP	29
S. Kimber, SP	16
B. Geer, SS	14
J. Cassidy, OF	10
O. Walker, OF	10
C. Householder, 1B	8
J. Remsen, OF	8
B. Greenwood, 2B	5
F. Warner, 3B	5
I. Benners, OF	3
J. Corcoran, C	3
J. Conway, SP	2
J. Hayes, C	2
J. Knowles, 1B	2
T. Wilson, OF	2
J. Farrow, C	1

Cincinnati (68-41)	WS
Hitting	**105.0**
Fielding	**35.1**
Pitching	**63.9**
W. White, SP	33
C. Jones, OF	27
J. Reilly, 1B	25
B. Mountjoy, SP	21
B. McPhee, 2B	18
P. Corkhill, OF	16
P. Snyder, C	13
H. Carpenter, 3B	12
G. Shallix, SP	10
F. Fennelly, SS	9
T. Mansell, OF	6
J. Peoples, SS	4
P. Powers, C	3
B. West, OF	3
F. Berkelbach, OF	1
R. Deagle, SP	1
C. Fulmer, SS	1
G. Miller, C	1

Columbus (69-39)	WS
Hitting	**92.4**
Fielding	**35.6**
Pitching	**79.0**
E. Morris, SP	44
F. Mountain, SP	36
F. Mann, OF	20
T. Brown, OF	18
P. Smith, 2B	18
J. Richmond, SS	16
B. Kuehne, 3B	15
F. Carroll, C	14
J. Field, 1B	11
E. Dundon, OF	5
R. Kemmler, C	4
J. Cahill, OF	3
A. Bauer, SP	1
T. Mansell, OF	1
T. Sullivan, SP	1

Indianapolis (29-78)	WS
Hitting	**49.5**
Fielding	**15.0**
Pitching	**22.5**
L. McKeon, SP	17
M. Phillips, SS	11
J. Keenan, C	10
J. Morrison, OF	6
P. Weihe, OF	6
P. Callahan, 3B	5
J. Peltz, OF	5
J. Dorgan, OF	4
J. Donnelly, 3B	3
J. Kerins, 1B	3
A. McCauley, SP	3
J. Aydelott, SP	2
B. Barr, SP	2
C. Collins, 2B	2
C. Robinson, C	2
B. Butler, OF	1
M. MacArthur, SP	1
E. Merrill, 2B	1
J. Sneed, OF	1
J. Tray, C	1
B. Watkins, 3B	1

Louisville (68-40)	WS
Hitting	**91.6**
Fielding	**35.6**
Pitching	**76.8**
G. Hecker, SP	74
P. Browning, 3B	23
C. Wolf, OF	20
M. Cline, OF	18
T. McLaughlin, SS	13
P. Reccius, 3B	13
J. Gerhardt, 2B	11
L. Maskrey, OF	11
R. Deagle, SP	5
D. Sullivan, C	5
D. Driscoll, SP	4
E. Whiting, C	4
W. Andrews, 1B	1
B. Dickerson, OF	1
J. Latham, 1B	1

New York (75-32)	WS
Hitting	**111.2**
Fielding	**36.3**
Pitching	**77.5**
T. Keefe, SP	47
J. Lynch, SP	36
D. Orr, 1B	27
D. Esterbrook, 3B	26
C. Nelson, SS	23
C. Roseman, OF	21
D. Troy, 2B	14
S. Brady, OF	13
C. Reipschlager, C	7
B. Holbert, C	6
E. Kennedy, OF	4
B. Becannon, SP	1

Philadelphia (61-46)	WS
Hitting	**85.9**
Fielding	**31.5**
Pitching	**65.5**
B. Mathews, SP	31
B. Taylor, SP	24
H. Stovey, 1B	22
S. Houck, SS	18
F. Corey, 3B	16
L. Knight, OF	13
H. Larkin, OF	12
J. Milligan, C	11
A. Atkinson, SP	10
C. Stricker, 2B	7
J. O'Brien, C	6
J. Birchall, OF	4
B. Blakiston, OF	4
J. Coleman, OF	2
C. Hilsey, SP-OF	1
M. Mansell, OF	1
E. Rowen, C	1

Pittsburgh (30-78)	WS
Hitting	**39.9**
Fielding	**18.0**
Pitching	**32.1**
F. Sullivan, SP	16
E. Swartwood, OF	16
J. Neagle, SP	14
C. Eden, OF	5
B. White, SS	5
D. Miller, OF	4
G. Creamer, 2B	3
T. Forster, SS	3
J. Knowles, 1B	3
A. Whitney, 3B	3
J. Battin, 3B	2
E. Colgan, C	2
C. Doyle, OF	2
J. Faatz, 1B	2
J. Hayes, C	2
J. Fox, SP	1
J. Gorman, SP-OF	1
J. McDonald, 3B	1
B. Nelson, SP	1
J. Quest, 2B	1
B. Reid, OF	1
F. Smith, C	1
L. Taylor, OF	1

Richmond (12-30)	WS
Hitting	**22.1**
Fielding	**5.6**
Pitching	**8.3**
D. Johnston, OF	5
M. Mansell, OF	5
P. Meegan, SP	5
B. Nash, 3B	5
J. Powell, 1B	4
E. Dugan, SP	3
E. Glenn, OF	3
T. Larkin, 2B	2
J. Hanna, C	1
M. Quinton, C	1
B. Schenck, SS	1
A. Swan, 1B	1

St. Louis (67-40)	WS
Hitting	**91.7**
Fielding	**35.6**
Pitching	**73.7**
J. McGinnis, SP	28
A. Latham, 3B	23
T. O'Neill, OF	21
D. Foutz, SP	19
B. Gleason, SS	19
F. Lewis, OF	18
H. Nicol, OF	17
D. Davis, SP	13
B. Caruthers, OF	10

C. Comiskey, 1B	9
P. Deasley, C	6
J. Quest, 2B	6
T. Dolan, C	5
G. Strief, OF	4
C. Krehmeyer, OF	1
J. Lavin, OF	1
H. Wheeler, OF	1

Toledo (46-58)	WS
Hitting	**46.0**
Fielding	**30.1**
Pitching	**61.9**
T. Mullane, SP	58
S. Barkley, 2B	21
H. O'Day, SP	16
J. Miller, SS	11
C. Welch, OF	9
T. Poorman, OF	6
F. Walker, C	4
C. Lane, 1B	3
C. Morton, 3B	2
F. Olin, OF	2
T. Arundel, C	1
D. McGuire, C	1
T. McSorley, 1B	1
G. Meister, 3B	1
J. Moffett, 1B	1
W. Walker, OF	1

Washington (12-51)	WS
Hitting	**28.1**
Fielding	**3.2**
Pitching	**4.8**
F. Fennelly, SS	12
F. Olin, 2B	5
B. Barr, SP	4
T. Hawkes, 2B	4
W. Prince, 1B	3
W. Murphy, OF	2
T. Farley, OF	1
W. Goldsby, OF	1
J. Hamill, SP	1
Jones, OF	1
J. Kiley, OF	1
E. Yewell, 2B	1

1885 National League

Boston (46-66)	WS
Hitting	**70.9**
Fielding	**21.0**
Pitching	**46.1**
C. Buffinton, SP	28
J. Whitney, SP	24
E. Sutton, 3B	22
S. Wise, SS	19
J. Morrill, 1B	14
J. Manning, OF	6
D. Davis, SP	4
T. Poorman, OF	4
P. Dealy, C	3
T. Gunning, C	2
M. Hackett, C	2
D. Johnston, OF	2
B. Nash, 3B	2
J. Burdock, 2B	1
W. Hackett, 2B	1
M. Hines, OF	1
J. Hornung, OF	1
B. Purcell, OF	1
B. Stemmeyer, SP	1

Buffalo (38-74)	WS
Hitting	**77.5**
Fielding	**14.6**
Pitching	**21.9**
D. Brouthers, 1B	26
H. Richardson, 2B	19
J. Rowe, SS	15
D. White, 3B	12
P. Galvin, SP	8
B. Crowley, OF	5
J. Lillie, OF	5
B. Serad, SP	5
P. Conway, SP	4
G. Myers, C	4
P. Wood, SP	4
D. Force, 2B	3
E. Crane, OF	2
J. McCauley, C	1
E. Stearns, SS	1

Chicago (87-25)	WS
Hitting	**136.0**
Fielding	**36.6**
Pitching	**88.4**
J. Clarkson, SP	62
G. Gore, OF	30
A. Dalrymple, OF	25
K. Kelly, OF	24
C. Anson, 1B	23
N. Williamson, 3B	21
J. McCormick, SP	19
T. Burns, SS	18
F. Pfeffer, 2B	18
L. Corcoran, SP	5
S. Flint, C	5
B. Sunday, OF	5
T. Kennedy, SP	4
J. Ryan, SS	1
S. Sutcliffe, C	1

Detroit (41-67)	WS
Hitting	**61.6**
Fielding	**19.1**
Pitching	**42.3**
C. Bennett, C	15
L. Baldwin, SP	14
N. Hanlon, OF	14
S. Wiedman, SP	14
C. Getzien, SP	13
G. Wood, OF	11
S. Thompson, OF	10
M. McQuery, 1B	7
D. Casey, SP	4
J. Dorgan, OF	4
S. Crane, 2B	3
J. Donnelly, 3B	3
J. Manning, SS	2
D. McGuire, C	2
J. Quest, 2B	2
M. Scott, 1B	2
C. Morton, 3B	1
M. Phillips, SS	1
F. Ringo, C-3B	1

New York (85-27)	WS
Hitting	**112.5**
Fielding	**36.3**
Pitching	**106.2**
M. Welch, SP	57
T. Keefe, SP	42
R. Connor, 1B	30
J. O'Rourke, OF	24
B. Ewing, C	19
M. Dorgan, OF	16
P. Gillespie, OF	15
D. Richardson, OF	14
M. Ward, SS	12
D. Esterbrook, 3B	11
P. Deasley, C	7
J. Gerhardt, 2B	5
L. Corcoran, SP	3

Philadelphia (56-54)	WS
Hitting	**65.8**
Fielding	**34.2**
Pitching	**68.0**
C. Ferguson, SP	41
E. Daily, SP	35
J. Fogarty, OF	15
J. Manning, OF	15
J. Mulvey, 3B	15
E. Andrews, OF	14
S. Farrar, 1B	11
C. Bastian, SS	8
A. Myers, 2B	5
J. Clements, C	2
T. Lynch, OF	2
B. Vinton, SP	2
T. Cusick, C	1
C. Ganzel, C	1
T. Nolan, SP	1

Providence (53-57)	WS
Hitting	**73.3**
Fielding	**28.3**
Pitching	**57.4**
O. Radbourn, SP	39
D. Shaw, SP	23
P. Hines, OF	17
J. Start, 1B	15
P. Radford, OF	13
C. Carroll, OF	12
J. Denny, 3B	9
C. Daily, C	8
B. Gilligan, C	8
J. Farrell, 2B	4
C. Bassett, 2B	3
A. Irwin, SS	3
J. McCormick, SP	2
L. Knight, OF	1
E. Seward, RP	1
E. Smith, SP	1

St. Louis (36-72)	WS
Hitting	**40.6**
Fielding	**23.5**
Pitching	**43.8**
H. Boyle, SP	24
J. Glasscock, SS	17
F. Dunlap, 2B	14
C. Sweeney, OF	12
A. McKinnon, 1B	11
J. Kirby, SP	6
F. Lewis, OF	6
E. Healy, SP	3
J. Quinn, OF	3
O. Shaffer, OF	3
F. Briody, C	2
E. Caskin, 3B	2
O. Daily, SP	2
D. Burns, OF	1
T. McSorley, 3B	1
E. Seery, OF	1

1885 American Assoc.

Baltimore (41-68)	WS
Hitting	**50.5**
Fielding	**23.7**
Pitching	**48.8**
H. Henderson, SP	36
O. Burns, OF	13
J. Macullar, SS	11
M. Muldoon, 3B	11
J. Sommer, OF	10
D. Casey, OF	9
E. Stearns, 1B	6
B. Emslie, SP	4
G. Gardner, 2B	3
J. Henry, SP	3
T. Manning, 2B	3
B. Traffley, C	3
J. Evans, OF	2
J. Field, 1B	2
B. Mountjoy, SP	2
S. Trott, C	2
T. York, OF	2
E. Greer, OF	1

Brooklyn (53-59)	WS
Hitting	**75.9**
Fielding	**27.5**
Pitching	**55.6**
H. Porter, SP	35
B. Phillips, 1B	17
J. Harkins, SP	16
P. Hotaling, OF	15
G. Smith, SS	15
B. McClellan, 3B	14
G. Pinckney, 2B	14
E. Swartwood, OF	13
A. Terry, OF	9
J. McTamany, OF	4
J. Cassidy, OF	2
D. Oldfield, C	2
J. Peoples, C	2
J. Hayes, C	1

Cincinnati (63-49)	WS
Hitting	**85.5**
Fielding	**36.0**
Pitching	**67.5**
C. Jones, OF	24
F. Fennelly, SS	23
L. McKeon, SP	22
W. White, SP	18
J. Reilly, 1B	16
H. Carpenter, 3B	13
P. Corkhill, OF	13
B. McPhee, 2B	13
B. Mountjoy, SP	11
J. Clinton, OF	8
G. Pechiney, SP	8
J. Keenan, C	6
G. Shallix, SP	6
P. Snyder, C	5
K. Baldwin, C	2
P. Powers, C	1

Louisville (53-59)	WS
Hitting	**63.3**
Fielding	**30.5**
Pitching	**65.3**
G. Hecker, SP	42
P. Browning, OF	28
C. Wolf, OF	16
N. Baker, SP	12
J. Kerins, 1B	10
A. Mays, SP	9
L. Maskrey, OF	8
P. Reccius, 3B	8
T. McLaughlin, 2B	7
J. Miller, SS	6
T. Ramsey, SP	6
A. Cross, C	3
J. Connor, SP	1
J. Crotty, C	1
B. Geer, SS	1
R. Mack, 2B	1

New York (44-64)	WS
Hitting	**98.4**
Fielding	**13.4**
Pitching	**20.2**
D. Orr, 1B	27
C. Nelson, SS	21
C. Roseman, OF	19
S. Brady, OF	18
J. Lynch, SP	12
E. Cushman, SP	7
F. Hankinson, 3B	7
C. Reipschlager, C	6
T. Forster, 2B	4
D. Troy, 2B	3
D. Crothers, SP	2
B. Holbert, C	2
E. Kennedy, OF	2
B. Becannon, SP	1
E. Begley, SP	1

Philadelphia (55-57)	WS
Hitting	**97.3**
Fielding	**20.4**
Pitching	**47.2**

B. Mathews, SP	26
H. Larkin, OF	23
H. Stovey, 1B	23
J. Coleman, OF	17
F. Corey, 3B	9
S. Houck, SS	9
B. Purcell, OF	9
J. O'Brien, C	8
J. Milligan, C	7
C. Stricker, 2B	7
T. Lovett, SP	6
E. Knouff, SP	5
G. Strief, 3B	5
E. Cushman, SP	3
B. Vinton, SP	3
L. Knight, OF	2
B. Taylor, SP	2
E. Fusselback, C	1

Pittsburgh (56-55)	WS
Hitting	**54.1**
Fielding	**35.9**
Pitching	**78.0**
E. Morris, SP	56
T. Brown, OF	20
P. Smith, 2B	13
F. Mann, OF	11
P. Meegan, SP	10
F. Carroll, C	9
B. Kuehne, 3B	9
C. Eden, OF	8
H. O'Day, SP	6
A. Whitney, SS	6
J. Field, 1B	5
P. Galvin, SP	4
M. Scott, 1B	3
D. Miller, C	2
F. Mountain, SP	2
J. Richmond, SS	2
J. Hofford, SP	1
R. Kemmler, C	1

St. Louis (79-33)	WS
Hitting	**118.3**
Fielding	**36.3**
Pitching	**82.4**
B. Caruthers, SP	51
D. Foutz, SP	37
C. Welch, OF	22
S. Barkley, 2B	21
B. Gleason, SS	17
Y. Robinson, OF	16
D. Bushong, C	15
T. O'Neill, OF	15
C. Comiskey, 1B	13
H. Nicol, OF	12
A. Latham, 3B	10
J. McGinnis, SP	7
D. Sullivan, C	1

1886
National League

Boston (56-61)	WS
Hitting	**92.0**
Fielding	**24.1**
Pitching	**51.9**
O. Radbourn, SP	32
B. Stemmeyer, SP	23
J. Morrill, SS	17
S. Wise, 1B	17
E. Sutton, OF	16
B. Nash, 3B	15
T. Poorman, OF	12
C. Buffinton, 1B	8
J. Hornung, OF	8
D. Johnston, OF	8
C. Daily, C	4
J. Burdock, 2B	2
P. Dealy, C	2
P. Tate, C	2
T. Gunning, C	1
C. Parsons, SP	1

Chicago (90-34)	WS
Hitting	**128.9**
Fielding	**40.8**
Pitching	**100.3**
J. Clarkson, SP	42
K. Kelly, OF	35
J. McCormick, SP	33
C. Anson, 1B	30
J. Flynn, SP	27
G. Gore, OF	26
F. Pfeffer, 2B	16
T. Burns, 3B	14
J. Ryan, OF	14
N. Williamson, SS	14
A. Dalrymple, OF	10
S. Flint, C	4
B. Sunday, OF	3
L. Hardie, C	1
G. Moolic, C	1

Detroit (87-36)	WS
Hitting	**122.0**
Fielding	**40.8**
Pitching	**98.2**
L. Baldwin, SP	53
C. Getzien, SP	32
H. Richardson, OF	32
D. Brouthers, 1B	31
S. Thompson, OF	21
J. Rowe, SS	18
D. White, 3B	15
C. Bennett, C	13
N. Hanlon, OF	13
F. Dunlap, 2B	8
C. Ganzel, C	7
P. Conway, SP	6
B. Smith, SP	4
S. Crane, 2B	2
P. Smith, SP	2
H. Decker, C	1
J. Manning, OF	1
J. McGeachey, OF	1
B. Shindle, SS	1

Kansas City (30-91)	WS
Hitting	**31.0**
Fielding	**20.6**
Pitching	**38.4**
J. Whitney, SP	21
S. Wiedman, SP	17
A. Myers, 2B	10
C. Bassett, SS	9
P. Radford, OF	7
M. McQuery, 1B	6
D. Rowe, OF	5
P. Conway, OF	4
J. Donnelly, 3B	3
F. Briody, C	2
M. Hackett, C	2
J. Lillie, OF	2
S. King, SP	1
F. Ringo, C	1

New York (75-44)	WS
Hitting	**126.6**
Fielding	**32.1**
Pitching	**66.3**
T. Keefe, SP	38
R. Connor, 1B	36
M. Welch, SP	29
J. O'Rourke, OF	24
M. Ward, SS	21
B. Ewing, C	17
M. Dorgan, OF	16
D. Esterbrook, 3B	16
P. Gillespie, OF	11
J. Gerhardt, 2B	7
P. Deasley, C	5
D. Richardson, OF	5

Philadelphia (71-43)	WS
Hitting	**89.4**
Fielding	**38.5**
Pitching	**85.1**
C. Ferguson, SP	49
D. Casey, SP	29
E. Daily, OF	22
J. Fogarty, OF	18
G. Wood, OF	18
E. Andrews, OF	17
J. Mulvey, 3B	14
C. Bastian, 2B	12
S. Farrar, 1B	12
A. Irwin, SS	12
D. McGuire, C	4
J. Clements, C	3
T. Cusick, C	2
T. McCarthy, OF	1

St. Louis (43-79)	WS
Hitting	**59.0**
Fielding	**24.9**
Pitching	**45.1**
J. Glasscock, SS	22
E. Healy, SP	16
H. Boyle, SP	15
J. Denny, 3B	14
A. McKinnon, 1B	14
J. Kirby, SP	11
E. Seery, OF	11
F. Dunlap, 2B	9
J. Quinn, OF	4
J. Cahill, OF	3
C. Sweeney, SP	3
J. McGeachey, OF	2
G. Myers, C	2
S. Crane, 2B	1
T. Dolan, C	1
F. Graves, C	1

Washington (28-92)	WS
Hitting	**37.7**
Fielding	**18.5**
Pitching	**27.8**
P. Hines, OF	17
D. Shaw, SP	15
C. Carroll, OF	6
J. Knowles, 2B	6
B. Barr, SP	4
J. Farrell, 2B	4
B. Gilligan, C	4
F. Gilmore, SP	4
P. Baker, 1B	3
D. Force, SS	3
H. O'Day, SP	3
B. Krieg, 1B	2
C. Mack, C	2
G. Shoch, OF	2
E. Crane, OF	1
H. Decker, C	1
B. Gladman, 3B	1
J. Hayes, C	1
J. Henry, SP	1
S. Houck, SS	1
G. Keefe, SP	1
T. Madigan, SP	1
J. Start, 1B	1

1886
American Assoc.

Baltimore (48-83)	WS
Hitting	**73.7**
Fielding	**23.5**
Pitching	**46.8**
M. Kilroy, SP	32
C. Fulmer, C	14
J. Manning, OF	14
J. McGinnis, SP	11
M. Muldoon, 2B	10
J. Sommer, OF	9
J. Macullar, SS	8
M. Scott, 1B	8
J. Farrell, 2B	5
H. Henderson, SP	5
J. Davis, 3B	4
B. Hoover, OF	4
B. Purcell, OF	3
L. Sowders, OF	3
B. Traffley, C	3
S. Houck, SS	2
B. Taylor, SP	2
J. Clinton, OF	1
B. Conway, C	1
D. Conway, SP	1
T. Dolan, C	1
E. Knouff, SP	1
P. O'Connell, OF	1
A. Powell, SP	1

Brooklyn (76-61)	WS
Hitting	**117.6**
Fielding	**34.6**
Pitching	**75.9**
H. Porter, SP	27
A. Terry, SP	26
E. Swartwood, OF	21
J. Harkins, SP	19
B. McClellan, 2B	19
G. Pinckney, 3B	19
J. McTamany, OF	18
B. Phillips, 1B	18
E. Burch, OF	14
G. Smith, SS	14
H. Henderson, SP	9
J. Peoples, C	9
S. Toole, SP	6
B. Clark, C	5
J. McCauley, C	2
D. Oldfield, C	1
J. Strauss, OF	1

Cincinnati (65-73)	WS
Hitting	**113.5**
Fielding	**27.8**
Pitching	**53.7**
T. Mullane, SP	34
F. Fennelly, SS	23
B. McPhee, 2B	23
C. Jones, OF	18
G. Pechiney, SP	15
P. Corkhill, OF	13
J. Reilly, 1B	13
F. Lewis, OF	12
K. Baldwin, C	7
H. Carpenter, 3B	7
J. Keenan, C	7
L. McKeon, SP	6
E. Smith, SP	5
P. Snyder, C	3
A. Powell, OF	2
L. Marr, OF	1
L. Maskrey, OF	1
J. Murphy, SP	1
L. Richmond, OF	1
C. Stephens, SP	1
L. Sylvester, OF	1
W. White, SP	1

Louisville (66-70)	WS
Hitting	**89.6**
Fielding	**32.8**
Pitching	**75.5**
T. Ramsey, SP	47
G. Hecker, SP	39
P. Browning, OF	17
J. Kerins, C	17
R. Mack, 2B	14
C. Wolf, OF	14
B. White, SS	13
J. Werrick, 3B	11
A. Cross, C	10

L. Sylvester, OF	4
H. Collins, OF	3
J. Strauss, OF	3
P. Cook, 1B	2
T. Sullivan, SP	2
B. Ely, SP	1
P. Reccius, OF	1

New York (53-82)	WS
Hitting	**51.4**
Fielding	**35.6**
Pitching	**72.0**
E. Cushman, SP	23
D. Orr, 1B	23
J. Lynch, SP	22
A. Mays, SP	19
F. Hankinson, 3B	15
C. Roseman, OF	10
C. Nelson, SS	9
S. Brady, OF	8
J. Shaffer, SP	7
C. Reipschlager, C	4
S. Behel, OF	3
T. Forster, 2B	3
B. Holbert, C	3
T. McLaughlin, SS	3
J. Meister, 2B	3
J. Donahue, OF	2
J. Crotty, C	1
E. Foster, 2B	1

Philadelphia (63-72)	WS
Hitting	**103.2**
Fielding	**27.2**
Pitching	**58.7**
H. Larkin, OF	29
H. Stovey, OF	24
A. Atkinson, SP	21
J. Coleman, OF	15
J. O'Brien, C	13
B. Mathews, SP	11
C. Miller, SP	11
L. Bierbauer, 2B	10
J. Milligan, C	10
B. Hart, SP	9
C. McGarr, SS	9
T. Kennedy, SP	5
W. Robinson, C	5
J. Gleason, 3B	4
J. Quest, SS	4
O. Shaffer, OF	3
E. Greer, OF	2
D. Lyons, 3B	2
J. Aydelott, SP	1
G. Bradley, SS	1

Pittsburgh (80-57)	WS
Hitting	**117.7**
Fielding	**40.3**
Pitching	**82.1**
E. Morris, SP	44
P. Galvin, SP	32
F. Carroll, C	22
S. Barkley, 2B	20
T. Brown, OF	19
A. Whitney, 3B	19
P. Smith, SS	18
F. Mann, OF	16
O. Schomberg, 1B	12
D. Miller, C	11
B. Kuehne, OF	10
J. Handiboe, SP	6
E. Glenn, OF	4
J. Hofford, SP	3
J. Coleman, OF	2
F. Mountain, 1B	1
F. Ringo, 1B	1

St. Louis (93-46)	WS
Hitting	**118.6**
Fielding	**45.0**
Pitching	**115.4**
D. Foutz, SP	62
B. Caruthers, SP	57
T. O'Neill, OF	27
A. Latham, 3B	23
N. Hudson, SP	22
C. Welch, OF	21
Y. Robinson, 2B	20
B. Gleason, SS	15
D. Bushong, C	11
C. Comiskey, 1B	10
J. McGinnis, SP	4
H. Nicol, OF	4
R. Kemmler, C	2
J. Murphy, SP	1

1887 National League

Boston (61-60)	WS
Hitting	**101.5**
Fielding	**27.1**
Pitching	**54.4**
K. Kelly, OF	23
O. Radbourn, SP	22
S. Wise, SS	22
K. Madden, SP	21
B. Nash, 3B	19
D. Johnston, OF	13
J. Morrill, 1B	13
D. Conway, SP	12
E. Sutton, SS	11
J. Hornung, OF	9
P. Tate, C	5
B. Stemmeyer, SP	4
B. Wheelock, OF	4
J. Burdock, 2B	3
C. Daily, C	1
T. O'Rourke, C	1

Chicago (71-50)	WS
Hitting	**77.4**
Fielding	**41.1**
Pitching	**94.5**
J. Clarkson, SP	51
M. Baldwin, SP	27
C. Anson, 1B	19
J. Ryan, OF	18
F. Pfeffer, 2B	16
T. Burns, 3B	13
G. Van Haltren, OF	13
N. Williamson, SS	13
M. Sullivan, OF	12
T. Daly, C	8
D. Darling, C-OF	7
B. Sunday, OF	6
S. Flint, C	5
B. Pettit, OF	2
S. Pyle, SP	1
C. Sprague, SP	1
P. Tebeau, 3B	1

Detroit (79-45)	WS
Hitting	**130.3**
Fielding	**38.6**
Pitching	**68.1**
S. Thompson, OF	29
D. Brouthers, 1B	26
C. Getzien, SP	25
H. Richardson, 2B	23
J. Rowe, SS	20
N. Hanlon, OF	15
L. Twitchell, OF	15
D. White, 3B	15
L. Baldwin, SP	14
P. Conway, SP	10
F. Dunlap, 2B	10
C. Bennett, C	8
S. Wiedman, SP	8
C. Ganzel, C	6
H. Gruber, SP	5
F. Briody, C	4
B. Shindle, 3B	3
E. Beatin, SP	1

Indianapolis (37-89)	WS
Hitting	**59.8**
Fielding	**20.5**
Pitching	**30.7**
J. Denny, 3B	19
J. Glasscock, SS	17
H. Boyle, SP	15
O. Schomberg, 1B	15
E. Seery, OF	10
E. Healy, SP	9
J. McGeachey, OF	6
C. Bassett, 2B	5
L. Shreve, SP	4
G. Myers, C	3
M. Hackett, C	2
T. Arundel, C	1
J. Cahill, OF	1
G. Gardner, OF	1
J. Kirby, SP	1
D. Leitner, SP	1
S. Moffett, SP	1

New York (68-55)	WS
Hitting	**94.1**
Fielding	**36.5**
Pitching	**73.4**
T. Keefe, SP	39
M. Welch, SP	27
M. Ward, SS	25
R. Connor, 1B	21
G. Gore, OF	14
D. Richardson, 2B	14
J. O'Rourke, C	13
M. Tiernan, OF	12
B. Ewing, 3B	11
P. Gillespie, OF	6
M. Dorgan, OF	4
M. Mattimore, SP	4
C. Titcomb, SP	4
P. Deasley, C	3
W. Brown, C	2
B. George, SP	2
P. Murphy, C	1
J. Rainey, 3B	1
S. Wiedman, SP	1

Philadelphia (75-48)	WS
Hitting	**116.6**
Fielding	**34.3**
Pitching	**74.1**
C. Ferguson, SP	36
D. Casey, SP	30
J. Fogarty, OF	25
C. Buffinton, SP	23
E. Andrews, OF	18
G. Wood, OF	18
S. Farrar, 1B	15
J. Mulvey, 3B	14
A. Irwin, SS	12
J. Clements, C	9
D. McGuire, C	7
T. Gunning, C	4
A. Maul, OF	4
C. Bastian, 2B	3
E. Daily, OF	3
B. McLaughlin, 2B	2
T. Cusick, C	1
T. McCarthy, OF	1

Pittsburgh (55-69)	WS
Hitting	**66.4**
Fielding	**32.8**
Pitching	**65.8**
P. Galvin, SP	33
F. Carroll, OF	18
J. McCormick, SP	18
E. Morris, SP	16
A. Whitney, 3B	14
B. Kuehne, SS	13
J. Coleman, OF	12
D. Miller, C	8
P. Smith, 2B	8
A. McKinnon, 1B	7
A. Dalrymple, OF	6
J. Fields, OF	4
S. Barkley, 1B	3
T. Brown, OF	3
E. Beecher, OF	2

Washington (46-76)	WS
Hitting	**57.1**
Fielding	**25.1**
Pitching	**55.8**
J. Whitney, SP	34
P. Hines, OF	18
B. O'Brien, 1B	13
H. O'Day, SP	12
F. Gilmore, SP	11
A. Myers, 2B	7
C. Carroll, OF	6
J. Farrell, SS	6
E. Daily, OF	5
P. Dealy, C	5
J. Donnelly, 3B	5
G. Shoch, OF	4
C. Mack, C	3
D. Shaw, SP	3
J. Irwin, SS	2
B. Krieg, 1B	2
S. Crane, SS	1
B. Gilligan, C	1

1887 American Assoc.

Baltimore (77-58)	WS
Hitting	**118.8**
Fielding	**34.7**
Pitching	**77.5**
M. Kilroy, SP	51
P. Smith, SP	32
O. Burns, SS	28
J. Davis, 3B	20
M. Griffin, OF	20
T. Tucker, 1B	16
B. Greenwood, 2B	15
B. Purcell, OF	13
J. Sommer, OF	13
S. Trott, C	9
C. Fulmer, C	8
L. Daniels, C	3
L. Shreve, SP	2
E. Knouff, SP	1

Brooklyn (60-74)	WS
Hitting	**89.2**
Fielding	**29.7**
Pitching	**61.0**
A. Terry, OF	27
G. Pinckney, 3B	18
H. Porter, SP	18
G. Smith, SS	16
J. McTamany, OF	15
B. McClellan, 2B	14
S. Toole, SP	13
B. Phillips, 1B	12
E. Swartwood, OF	8
E. Greer, OF	7
J. Harkins, SP	7
E. Burch, OF	6
H. Henderson, SP	6
J. Peoples, C	6
B. Clark, C	3
J. O'Brien, C	2
B. Otterson, SS	2

Cincinnati (81-54)	WS
Hitting	**83.8**
Fielding	**44.0**
Pitching	**115.1**
E. Smith, SP	54
T. Mullane, SP	46
F. Fennelly, SS	20
P. Corkhill, OF	19

B. McPhee, 2B	19
J. Reilly, 1B	18
B. Serad, SP	15
W. Tebeau, OF	11
H. Nicol, OF	9
K. Baldwin, C	8
H. Carpenter, 3B	7
C. Jones, OF	6
J. Keenan, C	4
J. McGinnis, SP	3
H. Kappel, 3B	2
J. O'Connor, OF	1
W. Widner, SP	1

Cleveland (39-92)	WS
Hitting	**67.4**
Fielding	**19.8**
Pitching	**29.8**
P. Hotaling, OF	15
E. McKean, SS	15
C. Stricker, 2B	12
M. Allen, OF	11
B. Crowell, SP	11
F. Mann, OF	9
B. Gilks, SP	7
M. Morrison, SP	7
P. Snyder, C	7
O. Daily, SP	5
P. Reccius, 3B	3
C. Reipschlager, C	3
J. Toy, 1B	3
J. McGlone, 3B	2
J. Say, 3B	2
C. Sweeney, 1B	2
J. Herr, 3B	1
J. Munyan, OF	1
C. Zimmer, C	1

Louisville (76-60)	WS
Hitting	**100.1**
Fielding	**40.1**
Pitching	**87.8**
T. Ramsey, SP	46
P. Browning, OF	30
G. Hecker, 1B	30
E. Chamberlin, SP	22
R. Mack, 2B	19
J. Kerins, 1B	15
C. Wolf, OF	15
J. Werrick, 3B	14
H. Collins, OF	13
B. White, SS	13
L. Cross, C	5
P. Cook, C	4
P. Reccius, OF	1
P. Veach, SP	1

New York (44-89)	WS
Hitting	**87.7**
Fielding	**17.7**
Pitching	**26.6**
D. O'Brien, OF	18
P. Radford, SS	18
D. Orr, 1B	16
F. Hankinson, 3B	14
A. Mays, SP	14
C. Nelson, OF	7
J. Donahue, C	6
E. Cushman, SP	5
C. Jones, OF	5
J. Lynch, SP	5
J. Gerhardt, 2B	4
E. Hogan, OF	3
B. Holbert, C	3
J. Meister, OF	3
S. Wiedman, SP	3
C. Roseman, OF	2
B. Fagan, SP	1
J. Knowles, 2B	1
F. O'Neill, OF	1
C. Parsons, SP	1
J. Shaffer, SP	1
P. Sommers, C	1

Philadelphia (64-69)	WS
Hitting	**90.4**
Fielding	**35.4**
Pitching	**66.1**
E. Seward, SP	33
D. Lyons, 3B	27
G. Weyhing, SP	27
H. Larkin, OF	17
H. Stovey, OF	17
C. McGarr, SS	16
T. Poorman, OF	13
J. Milligan, 1B	11
L. Bierbauer, 2B	10
F. Mann, OF	6
A. Atkinson, SP	4
W. Robinson, C	4
C. Roseman, OF	2
E. Flanagan, 1B	1
B. Hart, SP	1
B. Mathews, SP	1
B. Taylor, SP	1
G. Townsend, C	1

St. Louis (95-40)	WS
Hitting	**135.7**
Fielding	**44.7**
Pitching	**104.6**
B. Caruthers, OF	54
D. Foutz, OF	43
S. King, SP	37
T. O'Neill, OF	36
A. Latham, 3B	24
Y. Robinson, 2B	20
C. Welch, OF	18
C. Comiskey, 1B	17
B. Gleason, SS	17
D. Bushong, C	4
N. Hudson, SP	4
E. Knouff, OF	4
J. Boyle, C	3
L. Sylvester, OF	3
J. Murphy, SP	1

1888 National League

Boston (70-64)	WS
Hitting	**95.3**
Fielding	**37.2**
Pitching	**77.5**
J. Clarkson, SP	32
D. Johnston, OF	24
K. Kelly, C	24
B. Nash, 3B	23
B. Sowders, SP	21
S. Wise, SS	14
T. Brown, OF	13
O. Radbourn, SP	11
K. Madden, SP	10
J. Hornung, OF	8
J. Morrill, 1B	8
J. Quinn, 2B	6
I. Ray, SS	4
D. Conway, SP	3
P. Tate, C	3
E. Sutton, 3B	2
E. Glenn, OF	1
B. Higgins, 2B	1
B. Klusman, 2B	1
T. O'Rourke, C	1

Chicago (77-58)	WS
Hitting	**125.2**
Fielding	**36.6**
Pitching	**69.2**
J. Ryan, OF	34
C. Anson, 1B	29
G. Krock, SP	26
G. Van Haltren, OF	24
F. Pfeffer, 2B	20
N. Williamson, SS	20
M. Baldwin, SP	15
T. Burns, 3B	13
H. Duffy, OF	10
M. Sullivan, OF	7
J. Tener, SP	6
T. Daly, C	5
F. Dwyer, SP	4
D. Farrell, C	4
A. Gumbert, SP	4
B. Pettit, OF	4
G. Borchers, SP	2
D. Darling, C	2
D. Clarke, SP	1
S. Flint, C	1

Detroit (68-63)	WS
Hitting	**115.8**
Fielding	**28.7**
Pitching	**59.5**
P. Conway, SP	29
D. Brouthers, 1B	27
C. Getzien, SP	20
D. White, 3B	18
J. Rowe, SS	14
C. Bennett, C	12
H. Gruber, SP	12
N. Hanlon, OF	12
H. Richardson, 2B	11
S. Thompson, OF	10
L. Twitchell, OF	10
C. Ganzel, 2B	9
E. Beatin, SP	6
S. Sutcliffe, SS	5
C. Campau, OF	4
P. Nicholson, 2B	3
T. Scheffler, OF	1
J. Wells, C	1

Indianapolis (50-85)	WS
Hitting	**90.2**
Fielding	**22.3**
Pitching	**37.5**
J. Denny, 3B	19
P. Hines, OF	18
E. Seery, OF	17
J. Glasscock, SS	16
H. Boyle, SP	13
C. Bassett, 2B	12
E. Healy, SP	11
B. Burdick, SP	9
D. Buckley, C	8
G. Myers, C	7
J. McGeachey, OF	5
L. Shreve, SP	5
C. Daily, C	3
J. Schoeneck, 1B	3
O. Schomberg, 1B-OF	2
D. Esterbrook, 1B	1
S. Moffett, SP	1

New York (84-47)	WS
Hitting	**124.2**
Fielding	**41.4**
Pitching	**86.4**
T. Keefe, SP	35
R. Connor, 1B	32
M. Welch, SP	32
B. Ewing, C	27
M. Tiernan, OF	26
J. O'Rourke, OF	17
D. Richardson, 2B	15
M. Ward, SS	15
M. Slattery, OF	12
C. Titcomb, SP	12
G. Gore, OF	7
E. Crane, SP	5
A. Whitney, 3B	5
B. George, OF	4
W. Brown, C	2
E. Cleveland, 3B	2
P. Murphy, C	2
E. Foster, OF	1
G. Hatfield, 3B	1

Philadelphia (69-61)	WS
Hitting	**58.9**
Fielding	**42.7**
Pitching	**105.4**
C. Buffinton, SP	44
B. Sanders, SP	35
J. Fogarty, OF	19
D. Casey, SP	18
K. Gleason, SP	13
G. Wood, OF	13
E. Andrews, OF	12
S. Farrar, 1B	12
A. Irwin, SS	12
J. Clements, C	7
E. Delahanty, 2B	7
C. Bastian, 2B	6
J. Mulvey, 3B	4
D. McGuire, C	3
P. Schriver, C	2

Pittsburgh (66-68)	WS
Hitting	**84.0**
Fielding	**37.7**
Pitching	**76.3**
E. Morris, SP	34
P. Galvin, SP	30
B. Kuehne, 3B	18
D. Miller, C	15
J. Beckley, 1B	14
F. Carroll, C	13
F. Dunlap, 2B	13
B. Sunday, OF	13
P. Smith, SS	12
H. Staley, SP	12
J. Coleman, OF	9
A. Maul, 1B	5
E. Cleveland, 3B	3
A. Dalrymple, OF	3
J. Fields, OF	2
P. McShannic, 3B	2

Washington (48-86)	WS
Hitting	**67.4**
Fielding	**24.8**
Pitching	**51.9**
D. Hoy, OF	28
H. O'Day, SP	20
J. Whitney, SP	17
W. Wilmot, OF	12
E. Daily, OF	8
G. Keefe, SP	8
C. Mack, C	8
A. Myers, 2B	8
J. Donnelly, 3B	7
B. O'Brien, 1B	6
G. Shoch, SS	6
W. Widner, SP	6
J. Irwin, SS	4
P. Deasley, C	2
S. Fuller, SS	2
T. Arundel, C	1
G. Haddock, SP	1

1888 American Assoc.

Baltimore (57-80)	WS
Hitting	**89.0**
Fielding	**28.6**
Pitching	**53.4**
B. Cunningham, SP	24
T. Tucker, 1B	20
M. Griffin, OF	18
P. Smith, SP	18
O. Burns, OF	15
B. Shindle, 3B	15

Ma. Kilroy, SP	13
J. Farrell, SS	10
B. Purcell, OF	8
B. Greenwood, 2B	6
J. O'Brien, C	6
J. Sommer, OF	5
S. Trott, C	4
C. Fulmer, C	3
W. Goldsby, OF	3
S. Shaw, SP	2
B. Cantz, C	1

Brooklyn (88-52)	WS
Hitting	**103.6**
Fielding	**46.3**
Pitching	**114.1**
B. Caruthers, OF	46
D. Foutz, OF	33
M. Hughes, SP	33
G. Pinckney, 3B	23
A. Terry, SP	21
D. O'Brien, OF	19
D. Orr, 1B	13
A. Mays, SP	12
G. Smith, SS	12
P. Radford, OF	10
O. Burns, SS	9
B. McClellan, 2B	7
B. Clark, C	5
P. Corkhill, OF	5
D. Bushong, C	4
J. Peoples, C	4
J. Burdock, 2B	3
H. Collins, 2B	3
B. Holbert, C	1
E. Silch, OF	1

Cincinnati (80-54)	WS
Hitting	**100.2**
Fielding	**44.4**
Pitching	**95.4**
T. Mullane, SP	33
E. Smith, SP	30
L. Viau, SP	30
J. Reilly, 1B	25
B. McPhee, 2B	17
P. Corkhill, OF	16
F. Fennelly, SS	16
H. Nicol, OF	15
W. Tebeau, OF	15
H. Carpenter, 3B	14
J. Keenan, C	10
K. Baldwin, C	6
J. Weyhing, SP	6
H. Kappel, SS	4
J. O'Connor, OF	2
B. Serad, SP	1

Cleveland (50-82)	WS
Hitting	**92.7**
Fielding	**22.1**
Pitching	**35.1**
E. McKean, SS	25
J. Bakely, SP	21
C. Stricker, 2B	15
J. Faatz, 1B	12
G. Alberts, SS	10
E. Hogan, OF	10
P. Hotaling, OF	9
D. O'Brien, SP	9
C. Zimmer, C	8
B. Gilks, OF	6
M. Goodfellow, OF	5
P. Snyder, C	5
D. McGuire, C	4
G. Proeser, SP	3
E. Keas, SP	2
J. McGlone, 3B	2
E. Knouff, SP	1
B. McClellan, OF	1
B. Stemmeyer, SP	1
D. Van Zant, 3B	1

Kansas City (43-89)	WS
Hitting	**56.1**
Fielding	**24.5**
Pitching	**48.4**
H. Porter, SP	22
J. McTamany, OF	16
J. Davis, 3B	15
T. Sullivan, SP	12
B. Phillips, 1B	9
S. Barkley, 2B	8
J. Donahue, C	7
H. Easterday, SS	7
F. Hoffman, SP	6
M. Cline, OF	5
M. Allen, OF	4
L. Daniels, OF	3
R. Ehret, OF	3
B. Hamilton, OF	3
J. Burns, OF	2
B. Fagan, SP	2
J. Brennan, C	1
F. Hankinson, 2B	1
J. Kirby, SP	1
D. Rowe, OF	1
S. Toole, SP	1

Louisville (48-87)	WS
Hitting	**96.5**
Fielding	**19.0**
Pitching	**28.5**
H. Collins, OF	20
P. Browning, OF	17
C. Wolf, OF	17
R. Mack, 2B	12
S. Stratton, OF	11
G. Hecker, 1B	9
J. Kerins, OF	8
E. Chamberlin, SP	7
J. Werrick, 3B	7
J. Ewing, SP	6
S. Smith, 1B	6
B. White, SS	6
T. Ramsey, SP	5
W. Andrews, 1B	2
L. Cross, C	2
P. Tomney, SS	2
F. Vaughn, OF	2
F. Weaver, OF	2
P. Cook, C	1
D. Esterbrook, 1B	1
H. Raymond, 3B	1

Philadelphia (81-52)	WS
Hitting	**121.5**
Fielding	**38.8**
Pitching	**82.6**
E. Seward, SP	42
G. Weyhing, SP	31
H. Stovey, OF	28
C. Welch, OF	25
D. Lyons, 3B	20
L. Bierbauer, 2B	19
H. Larkin, 1B	19
M. Mattimore, SP	15
T. Poorman, OF	10
B. Gleason, SS	9
W. Robinson, C	9
M. Sullivan, OF	4
F. Fennelly, SS	3
B. Blair, SP	2
T. Gunning, C	2
P. Smith, SP	2
G. Townsend, C	2
B. Purcell, OF	1

St. Louis (92-43)	WS
Hitting	**109.4**
Fielding	**44.4**
Pitching	**122.2**
S. King, SP	71
N. Hudson, SP	36
T. O'Neill, OF	28
A. Latham, 3B	21
Y. Robinson, 2B	21
T. McCarthy, OF	19
C. Comiskey, 1B	15
E. Chamberlin, SP	13
J. Boyle, C	9
J. Milligan, C	9
H. Lyons, OF	8
J. Devlin, SP	7
J. Herr, SS	6
E. Knouff, SP	6
B. White, SS	4
C. McGarr, 2B	2
T. Dolan, C	1

1889
National League

Boston (83-45)	WS
Hitting	**111.2**
Fielding	**43.1**
Pitching	**94.7**
J. Clarkson, SP	60
D. Brouthers, 1B	28
H. Richardson, 2B	25
K. Kelly, OF	24
O. Radbourn, SP	21
B. Nash, 3B	20
T. Brown, OF	12
D. Johnston, OF	11
K. Madden, SP	10
J. Quinn, SS	10
C. Bennett, C	8
C. Ganzel, C	8
P. Smith, SS	7
B. Daley, SP	3
I. Ray, SS	1
B. Sowders, SP	1

Chicago (67-65)	WS
Hitting	**101.3**
Fielding	**31.0**
Pitching	**68.7**
J. Ryan, OF	25
C. Anson, 1B	21
G. Van Haltren, OF	21
A. Gumbert, SP	19
J. Tener, SP	18
H. Duffy, OF	17
B. Hutchison, SP	17
F. Dwyer, SP	16
F. Pfeffer, 2B	13
D. Farrell, C	12
T. Burns, 3B	11
N. Williamson, SS	3
C. Bastian, SS	2
D. Darling, C	2
G. Krock, SP	2
S. Flint, C	1
E. Healy, SP	1

Cleveland (61-72)	WS
Hitting	**59.5**
Fielding	**44.0**
Pitching	**79.5**
D. O'Brien, SP	23
J. Bakely, SP	22
E. Beatin, SP	22
E. McKean, SS	20
P. Tebeau, 3B	15
H. Gruber, SP	13
P. Radford, OF	13
C. Stricker, 2B	12
L. Twitchell, OF	11
C. Zimmer, C	11
J. McAleer, OF	9
J. Faatz, 1B	4
S. Sutcliffe, C	4
B. Gilks, OF	3
P. Snyder, C	1

Indianapolis (59-75)	WS
Hitting	**83.7**
Fielding	**30.2**
Pitching	**63.1**
H. Boyle, SP	28
J. Glasscock, SS	27
C. Getzien, SP	20
E. Seery, OF	18
J. Denny, 3B	15
P. Hines, 1B	14
A. Rusie, SP	10
M. Sullivan, OF	9
C. Bassett, 2B	8
J. McGeachey, OF	7
D. Buckley, C	4
C. Daily, C	4
E. Andrews, OF	3
B. Burdick, RP	2
J. Fee, RP	2
J. Whitney, SP	2
G. Krock, SP	1
G. Myers, OF	1
J. Schoeneck, 1B	1
P. Sommers, C	1

New York (83-43)	WS
Hitting	**128.7**
Fielding	**40.6**
Pitching	**79.8**
M. Welch, SP	31
M. Tiernan, OF	28
T. Keefe, SP	27
R. Connor, 1B	26
B. Ewing, C	23
G. Gore, OF	23
J. O'Rourke, OF	19
D. Richardson, 2B	17
M. Ward, SS	17
E. Crane, SP	15
A. Whitney, 3B	9
H. O'Day, SP	5
W. Brown, C	4
G. Hatfield, SS	3
P. Murphy, C	1
M. Slattery, OF	1

Philadelphia (63-64)	WS
Hitting	**78.3**
Fielding	**33.9**
Pitching	**76.8**
C. Buffinton, SP	33
B. Sanders, SP	28
J. Fogarty, OF	18
S. Thompson, OF	17
J. Mulvey, 3B	15
B. Hallman, SS	13
D. Casey, SP	10
S. Farrar, 1B	10
J. Clements, C	9
G. Wood, OF	9
K. Gleason, SP	8
A. Myers, 2B	6
E. Delahanty, OF	5
P. Schriver, C	5
E. Andrews, OF	1
A. Irwin, SS	1
P. Wood, SP	1

Pittsburgh (61-71)	WS
Hitting	**110.4**
Fielding	**25.1**
Pitching	**47.5**
F. Carroll, C	23
H. Staley, SP	22
J. Beckley, 1B	19
P. Galvin, SP	16
N. Hanlon, OF	13
D. Miller, C	13
J. Fields, OF	12
F. Dunlap, 2B	10
A. Maul, OF	9
J. Rowe, SS	9
B. Kuehne, 3B	8
B. Sunday, OF	8
E. Morris, SP	7
P. Smith, SS	7
D. White, 3B	4

Player	WS
P. Conway, SP	1
A. Jones, SP	1
B. Sowders, SP	1

Washington (41-83)	WS
Hitting	**73.6**
Fielding	**19.8**
Pitching	**29.6**
W. Wilmot, OF	17
D. Hoy, OF	13
T. Daly, C	11
A. Ferson, SP	11
G. Haddock, SP	11
S. Wise, 2B	10
C. Mack, C	9
A. Irwin, SS	7
J. Irwin, 3B	6
G. Keefe, SP	6
E. Beecher, OF	3
S. Clark, C	3
A. Myers, 2B	3
H. O'Day, SP	3
G. Shoch, OF	3
H. Ebright, C	2
J. Morrill, 1B	2
P. Sweeney, 3B	2
J. Carney, 1B	1

1889 American Assoc.

Baltimore (70-65)	WS
Hitting	**93.6**
Fielding	**37.1**
Pitching	**79.3**
M. Kilroy, SP	44
T. Tucker, 1B	30
F. Foreman, SP	28
B. Shindle, 3B	27
M. Griffin, OF	23
R. Mack, 2B	13
B. Cunningham, SP	11
J. Hornung, OF	8
J. Sommer, OF	6
I. Ray, SS	4
J. Farrell, SS	3
T. Quinn, C	3
P. Tate, C	3
B. Cantz, C	1
J. Dowie, OF	1
C. Fulmer, OF	1
G. Goetz, SP	1
W. Holland, SS	1
J. Kerins, 1B	1
P. Whitaker, SP	1

Brooklyn (93-44)	WS
Hitting	**150.2**
Fielding	**42.4**
Pitching	**86.3**
B. Caruthers, SP	46
D. O'Brien, OF	30
A. Terry, SP	30
O. Burns, OF	25
H. Collins, 2B	24
D. Foutz, 1B	24
G. Pinckney, 3B	22
P. Corkhill, OF	17
T. Lovett, SP	15
G. Smith, SS	15
J. Visner, C	14
B. Clark, C	9
M. Hughes, SP	6
D. Bushong, C	1
C. Reynolds, C	1

Cincinnati (76-63)	WS
Hitting	**96.9**
Fielding	**45.4**
Pitching	**85.7**
J. Duryea, SP	37
T. Mullane, SP	24
L. Viau, SP	24
O. Beard, SS	21
B. Holliday, OF	21
B. McPhee, 2B	20
J. Keenan, C	14
W. Tebeau, OF	14
H. Nicol, OF	12
J. Reilly, 1B	12
E. Smith, SP	9
H. Carpenter, 3B	7
B. Earle, OF	7
K. Baldwin, C	4
C. Petty, SP	2

Columbus (60-78)	WS
Hitting	**105.8**
Fielding	**24.2**
Pitching	**50.0**
M. Baldwin, SP	27
L. Marr, 3B	24
J. McTamany, OF	20
D. Orr, 1B	17
S. Johnson, OF	13
J. O'Connor, C	12
E. Daily, OF	11
B. Greenwood, 2B	10
W. Widner, SP	9
H. Gastright, SP	8
H. Kappel, 3B-SS	6
H. Easterday, SS	5
A. Mays, SP	5
J. Crooks, 2B	4
C. Reilly, 3B	3
J. Doyle, C	2
J. Peoples, C	2
N. Bligh, C	1
J. Easton, RP	1

Kansas City (55-82)	WS
Hitting	**84.5**
Fielding	**25.6**
Pitching	**54.9**
B. Hamilton, OF	24
H. Long, SS	22
J. Conway, SP	20
P. Swartzel, SP	19
J. Burns, OF	17
E. Stearns, 1B	16
J. Manning, OF	7
J. McCarty, SP	6
J. Sowders, SP	6
J. Davis, 3B	5
C. Hoover, C	5
S. Barkley, 2B	4
B. Alvord, 3B	3
J. Donahue, C	3
C. McGarr, 3B	2
T. Sullivan, SP	2
C. Bell, SP-OF	1
J. Gunson, C	1
F. Pears, SP	1
J. Pickett, OF	1

Louisville (27-111)	WS
Hitting	**35.9**
Fielding	**18.1**
Pitching	**27.1**
R. Ehret, SP	11
D. Shannon, 2B	8
F. Weaver, OF	8
C. Wolf, OF	8
J. Ewing, SP	7
G. Hecker, 1B	7
S. Stratton, OF	7
P. Tomney, SS	6
P. Browning, OF	4
H. Raymond, 3B	4
P. Cook, C	2
M. McDermott, SP	2
T. Ramsey, SP	2
F. Vaughn, C	2
F. Carl, OF	1
D. Esterbrook, 1B	1
E. Flanagan, 1B	1

Philadelphia (75-58)	WS
Hitting	**113.6**
Fielding	**40.0**
Pitching	**71.3**
G. Weyhing, SP	30
H. Stovey, OF	28
D. Lyons, 3B	25
E. Seward, SP	21
C. Welch, OF	20
H. Larkin, 1B	19
L. Bierbauer, 2B	18
B. Purcell, OF	15
S. McMahon, SP	14
F. Fennelly, SS	12
L. Cross, C	5
W. Robinson, C	5
M. Mattimore, OF	3
G. Bausewine, SP	2
J. Coleman, SP	2
E. Knouff, SP	2
P. Smith, SP	2
J. Brennan, C	1
T. Gunning, C	1

St. Louis (90-45)	WS
Hitting	**107.4**
Fielding	**45.6**
Pitching	**117.0**
S. King, SP	44
E. Chamberlin, SP	42
T. O'Neill, OF	27
J. Stivetts, SP	21
C. Duffee, OF	19
T. McCarthy, OF	19
J. Milligan, C	17
C. Comiskey, 1B	15
A. Latham, 3B	15
S. Fuller, SS	13
Y. Robinson, 2B	13
J. Boyle, C	9
J. Devlin, SP	6
N. Hudson, SP	4
T. Ramsey, SP	3
P. Sweeney, 3B	2
T. Gettinger, OF	1

1890 National League

Boston (76-57)	WS
Hitting	**82.6**
Fielding	**43.4**
Pitching	**102.0**
K. Nichols, SP	43
J. Clarkson, SP	33
C. Getzien, SP	29
S. Brodie, OF	17
T. Tucker, 1B	17
M. Sullivan, OF	16
H. Long, SS	14
P. Smith, 2B	12
C. Bennett, C	11
C. McGarr, 3B	11
B. Lowe, SS	8
P. Hines, OF	6
C. Ganzel, C	4
L. Hardie, C	4
P. Donovan, OF	2
J. Taber, SP-RP	1

Brooklyn (86-43)	WS
Hitting	**135.8**
Fielding	**41.3**
Pitching	**80.9**
A. Terry, OF	41
B. Caruthers, OF	30
T. Lovett, SP	29
G. Pinckney, 3B	29
H. Collins, 2B	28
D. Foutz, 1B	27
O. Burns, OF	21
D. O'Brien, OF	19
T. Daly, C	11
G. Smith, SS	10
B. Clark, C	4
P. Corkhill, OF	4
P. Donovan, OF	2
M. Hughes, SP	2
D. Bushong, C	1

Chicago (84-53)	WS
Hitting	**106.8**
Fielding	**45.0**
Pitching	**100.2**
B. Hutchison, SP	54
P. Luby, SP	27
W. Wilmot, OF	26
C. Anson, 1B	24
J. Cooney, SS	22
T. Burns, 3B	20
C. Carroll, OF	20
E. Stein, SP	11
B. Glenalvin, 2B	9
H. Earl, OF	7
R. Coughlin, SP	6
M. Kittridge, C	6
E. Foster, OF	5
P. O'Brien, 2B	4
M. Sullivan, SP	4
J. Andrews, OF	3
T. Nagle, C	3
R. Gibson, SP	1

Cincinnati (77-55)	WS
Hitting	**88.4**
Fielding	**43.4**
Pitching	**99.2**
B. Rhines, SP	41
T. Mullane, OF	28
J. Duryea, SP	23
B. McPhee, 2B	21
B. Holliday, OF	18
O. Beard, SS	17
J. Knight, OF	17
L. Marr, OF	16
J. Reilly, 1B	16
F. Foreman, SP	11
J. Harrington, C	5
A. Latham, 3B	5
L. Viau, SP	4
J. Keenan, C	3
H. Nicol, OF	3
K. Baldwin, C	1
B. Clingman, SS	1
J. Dolan, SP	1

Cleveland (44-88)	WS
Hitting	**63.7**
Fielding	**23.2**
Pitching	**45.1**
E. Beatin, SP	22
E. McKean, SS	21
G. Davis, OF	14
C. Zimmer, C	11
J. Virtue, 1B	10
W. Smalley, 3B	8
C. Young, SP	8
V. Dailey, OF	7
P. Veach, 1B	5
L. Viau, SP	5
B. Gilks, OF	4
J. Ardner, 2B	3
E. Smith, SP	3
J. Wadsworth, SP	3
B. Delaney, 2B	2
E. Lincoln, SP	2
B. West, OF	2
T. Dowse, OF	1
B. Garfield, SP	1

New York (63-68)	WS
Hitting	**90.7**
Fielding	**31.7**
Pitching	**66.6**
A. Rusie, SP	40
M. Tiernan, OF	26
J. Glasscock, SS	25
M. Welch, SP	19
J. Burkett, OF	14
J. Sharrott, SP	11
C. Bassett, 2B	9
A. Clarke, C	8
D. Buckley, C	7
J. Denny, 3B	6
J. Hornung, OF	6
L. Whistler, 1B	6
D. Esterbrook, 1B	5
P. Murphy, C	3
J. Henry, OF	2
E. Daily, OF	1
S. Howe, 2B	1

Philadelphia (78-54)	WS
Hitting	**103.7**
Fielding	**43.1**
Pitching	**87.3**
K. Gleason, SP	45
B. Hamilton, OF	25
T. Vickery, SP	25
B. Allen, SS	21
S. Thompson, OF	19
J. Clements, C	18
A. Myers, 2B	18
E. Burke, OF	14
P. Smith, SP	13
E. Mayer, 3B	8
A. McCauley, 1B	8
P. Schriver, C	6
B. Sunday, OF	5
D. Esper, SP	3
B. Gray, OF	2
J. McFetridge, SP	2
B. Day, SP-RP	1
H. Decker, 1B-OF	1

Pittsburgh (23-113)	WS
Hitting	**53.8**
Fielding	**6.1**
Pitching	**9.1**
D. Miller, 3B	13
T. Berger, OF	7
H. Decker, C	7
S. LaRoque, 2B	7
B. Sunday, OF	7
G. Hecker, 1B	5
J. Kelty, OF	3
B. Gumbert, SP	2
F. Roat, 3B	2
E. Sales, SS	2
B. Sowders, SP	2
P. Veach, 1B	2
D. Anderson, SP	1
K. Baker, SP	1
S. Bowman, SP	1
E. Burke, OF	1
D. Hemp, OF	1
H. Jones, SP	1
F. Osborne, OF	1
B. Phillips, SP	1
P. Smith, SP	1
B. Wilson, C	1

1890 Players League

Boston (81-48)	WS
Hitting	**108.4**
Fielding	**42.1**
Pitching	**92.5**
O. Radbourn, SP	34
A. Gumbert, SP	25
B. Nash, 3B	20
H. Richardson, OF	20
H. Stovey, OF	20
D. Brouthers, 1B	19
T. Brown, OF	18
B. Daley, SP	18
J. Quinn, 2B	17
K. Kelly, C	16
M. Kilroy, SP	15
A. Irwin, SS	11
M. Murphy, C	5
K. Madden, SP	3
P. Swett, C	2

Brooklyn (76-56)	WS
Hitting	**100.2**
Fielding	**42.5**
Pitching	**85.4**
G. Weyhing, SP	32
G. Van Haltren, OF	30
M. Ward, SS	27
J. Sowders, SP	22
L. Bierbauer, 2B	20
D. Orr, 1B	19
B. Joyce, 3B	18
G. Hemming, SP	10
E. Seery, OF	10
E. Andrews, OF	9
T. Kinslow, C	7
C. Murphy, SP	7
J. McGeachey, OF	6
P. Cook, C	4
C. Daily, C	4
A. Sunday, OF	3

Buffalo (36-96)	WS
Hitting	**79.4**
Fielding	**11.5**
Pitching	**17.2**
D. Hoy, OF	17
S. Wise, 2B	14
C. Mack, C	11
E. Beecher, OF	10
D. White, 3B	10
J. Rowe, SS	8
G. Haddock, SP	7
J. Irwin, 3B	5
S. Clark, OF	4
B. Cunningham, SP	4
L. Twitchell, OF	4
J. Halligan, OF	3
J. Rainey, OF	3
G. Keefe, SP	2
G. Stafford, SP	2
L. Baldwin, SP	1
J. Carney, 1B	1
J. Faatz, 1B	1
A. Ferson, SP	1

Chicago (75-62)	WS
Hitting	**80.1**
Fielding	**44.7**
Pitching	**100.2**
S. King, SP	44
M. Baldwin, SP	42
H. Duffy, OF	26
J. Ryan, OF	23
T. O'Neill, OF	19
D. Farrell, C	17
F. Pfeffer, 2B	13
C. Bartson, SP	12
J. Boyle, C	9
D. Darling, 1B	5
A. Latham, 3B	4
C. Bastian, SS	3
C. Comiskey, 1B	3
F. Dwyer, SP-RP	2
N. Williamson, 3B	2
F. Shugart, SS	1

Cleveland (55-75)	WS
Hitting	**99.7**
Fielding	**21.5**
Pitching	**43.8**
P. Browning, OF	23
H. Larkin, 1B	18
P. Radford, OF	17
H. Gruber, SP	16
E. Delahanty, SS	13
P. Tebeau, 3B	13
S. Sutcliffe, C	12
J. Bakely, SP	11
D. O'Brien, SP	9
C. Stricker, 2B	9
W. McGill, SP	8
J. McAleer, OF	7
J. Carney, OF	4
J. Brennan, C	3
C. Dewald, SP	1
L. Twitchell, OF	1

New York (74-57)	WS
Hitting	**99.3**
Fielding	**42.2**
Pitching	**80.4**
R. Connor, 1B	25
H. O'Day, SP	23
E. Crane, SP	22
B. Ewing, C	20
J. O'Rourke, OF	20
J. Ewing, SP	19
T. Keefe, SP	19
G. Gore, OF	18
D. Richardson, SS	13
M. Slattery, OF	12
G. Hatfield, 3B	7
A. Whitney, 3B	6
W. Brown, C	5
D. Johnston, OF	5
D. Shannon, 2B	5
F. Vaughn, C	3

Philadelphia (68-63)	WS
Hitting	**94.5**
Fielding	**35.9**
Pitching	**73.6**
B. Sanders, SP	28
B. Shindle, SS	26
C. Buffinton, SP	21
P. Knell, SP	21
M. Griffin, OF	17
G. Wood, OF	16
J. Mulvey, 3B	12
J. Fogarty, OF	11
J. Pickett, 2B	10
L. Cross, C	8
S. Farrar, 1B	8
B. Hallman, OF	8
J. Milligan, C	8
B. Husted, SP	6
B. Cunningham, SP	3
D. Shannon, 2B	1

Pittsburgh (60-68)	WS
Hitting	**97.1**
Fielding	**24.3**
Pitching	**58.5**
H. Staley, SP	27
J. Beckley, 1B	21
A. Maul, SP	18
N. Hanlon, OF	17
F. Carroll, C	16
J. Fields, OF	16
J. Visner, OF	14
T. Corcoran, SS	11
P. Galvin, SP	10
B. Kuehne, 3B	10
Y. Robinson, 2B	10
E. Morris, SP	7
T. Quinn, C	2
A. Doe, RP	1

1890 American Assoc.

Baltimore (15-19)	WS
Hitting	**15.6**
Fielding	**9.9**
Pitching	**19.5**
S. McMahon, SP	8
L. German, SP	6
I. Ray, SS	6
P. Gilbert, 3B	3
B. Johnson, OF	3
R. Mack, 2B	3
M. O'Rourke, SP	3
J. Sommer, OF	3
N. Baker, SP	1
B. Hill, 3B	1
D. Long, OF	1
J. McGuckin, OF	1
M. Morrison, SP	1
T. Power, 1B	1
W. Robinson, C	1
P. Tate, C	1
G. Townsend, C	1
C. Welch, OF	1

Brooklyn (26-72)	WS
Hitting	**46.4**
Fielding	**12.7**
Pitching	**19.0**
E. Daily, OF	13
B. O'Brien, 1B	10
H. Simon, OF	9
J. Gerhardt, 2B	6
C. Nelson, SS	6
J. Peltz, OF	6
J. Davis, 3B	5
F. Fennelly, SS	5
M. Mattimore, SP	4
C. McCullough, SP	4
F. Bowes, C	2
H. Pitz, C	2
S. Toole, SP	2
J. Lynch, SP	1
C. Murphy, SP	1
P. O'Connell, PH-PR	1
J. Toy, C	1

Columbus (79-55)	WS
Hitting	**107.2**
Fielding	**45.0**
Pitching	**84.8**
H. Gastright, SP	30
S. Johnson, OF	25
F. Knauss, SP	22
J. McTamany, OF	22
J. O'Connor, C	21
C. Reilly, 3B	20
J. Sneed, OF	19
E. Chamberlin, SP	16
J. Easton, SP	15
J. Crooks, 2B	14
J. Doyle, C	9
M. Lehane, 1B	7
B. Wheelock, SS	6
W. Widner, SP	6
H. Easterday, SS	3
N. Bligh, C	1
S. Nicholl, OF	1

Louisville (88-44)	WS
Hitting	**103.4**
Fielding	**44.0**
Pitching	**116.6**
S. Stratton, SP	51
R. Ehret, SP	34
C. Wolf, OF	27
H. Taylor, 1B	19
P. Tomney, SS	18
F. Weaver, OF	18
C. Hamburg, OF	17
G. Meakim, SP	17
T. Shinnick, 2B	15
E. Daily, SP	12
H. Raymond, 3B	12
H. Goodall, SP	11
J. Ryan, C	6

M. Jones, SP	2
D. O'Connor, 1B	2
P. Weckbecker, C	2
N. Bligh, C	1

Philadelphia (54-78)	WS
Hitting	**101.6**
Fielding	**21.6**
Pitching	**38.8**
D. Lyons, 3B	27
S. McMahon, SP	25
J. O'Brien, 1B	17
C. Welch, OF	17
B. Purcell, OF	14
O. Shaffer, OF	14
W. Robinson, C	8
D. Esper, SP	7
E. Seward, SP	6
J. Kappel, OF	5
B. Conroy, SS	4
E. Green, SP	3
K. Baldwin, C	2
J. Daly, OF	2
A. Knox, 1B	2
E. Pabst, OF	2
T. Shaffer, 2B	2
H. Easterday, SS	1
B. Price, SP	1
C. Snyder, C-OF	1
P. Sweeney, 2B	1
J. Whitney, SP	1

Rochester (63-63)	WS
Hitting	**94.4**
Fielding	**32.6**
Pitching	**61.9**
B. Barr, SP	31
J. Knowles, 3B	21
S. Griffin, OF	18
W. Callahan, SP	17
T. Scheffler, OF	16
H. Lyons, OF	15
D. McGuire, C	15
B. Greenwood, 2B	11
J. Grim, SS	7
J. Field, 1B	6
D. McKeough, C	6
C. Titcomb, SP	6
M. Phillips, SS	5
B. Miller, SP	4
J. Fitzgerald, SP	3
T. O'Brien, 1B	3
L. Smith, SS	3
D. Burke, OF	2

St. Louis (77-58)	WS
Hitting	**94.5**
Fielding	**41.7**
Pitching	**94.9**
J. Stivetts, SP	41
T. Ramsey, SP	28
T. McCarthy, OF	24
B. Hart, SP	18
S. Fuller, SS	17
C. Roseman, OF	13
C. Campau, OF	12
C. Duffee, OF	11
J. Munyan, C	11
E. Cartwright, 1B	9
B. Whitrock, SP	8
B. Higgins, 2B	6
J. Neale, SP	6
T. Gettinger, OF	4
J. Gerhardt, 2B	3
J. Wells, C	3
J. Davis, 3B	2
B. Earle, C	2
D. Miller, OF	2
P. Sweeney, 2B	2
M. Trost, C	2
J. Burke, 3B	1
E. Chamberlin, SP	1
J. Donnelly, 3B	1
P. Hartnett, 1B	1
J. Herr, 2B	1
B. Klusman, 2B	1
G. Nicol, SP	1

Syracuse (55-72)	WS
Hitting	**113.3**
Fielding	**20.7**
Pitching	**31.0**
C. Childs, 2B	31
M. McQuery, 1B	19
R. Wright, OF	17
D. Casey, SP	13
B. Ely, OF	13
J. Keefe, SP	12
B. McLaughlin, SS	12
Ti. O'Rourke, 3B	12
P. Friel, OF	6
E. Mars, SP	6
H. Simon, OF	6
M. Morrison, SP	4
To. O'Rourke, C	3
G. Briggs, C	2
M. Dorgan, OF	2
H. Pitz, C	2
G. Proeser, OF	2
J. Battin, 3B	1
J. Leighton, OF	1
J. Peltz, OF	1

Toledo (68-64)	WS
Hitting	**86.8**
Fielding	**37.0**
Pitching	**80.3**
E. Healy, SP	34
E. Swartwood, OF	23
F. Smith, SP	22
P. Werden, 1B	20
E. Cushman, SP	17
P. Nicholson, 2B	14
F. Scheibeck, SS	14
B. Alvord, 3B	13
W. Tebeau, OF	12
C. Sprague, OF	11
B. Van Dyke, OF	10
H. Sage, C	5
T. Welsh, C	4
E. Rogers, C	2
B. Doty, SP	1
J. Peltz, OF	1
J. Sneed, OF	1

1891 National League

Boston (87-51)	WS
Hitting	**105.5**
Fielding	**45.3**
Pitching	**110.1**
J. Clarkson, SP	42
K. Nichols, SP	39
H. Long, SS	29
H. Stovey, OF	26
H. Staley, SP	25
B. Nash, 3B	20
S. Brodie, OF	16
B. Lowe, OF	15
T. Tucker, 1B	12
C. Bennett, C	9
J. Quinn, 2B	9
C. Ganzel, C	8
C. Getzien, SP	6
M. Sullivan, OF	2
J. Kelley, OF	1
K. Kelly, C	1
C. Ryan, RP	1

Brooklyn (61-76)	WS
Hitting	**99.7**
Fielding	**27.3**
Pitching	**56.0**
B. Caruthers, SP	22
M. Griffin, OF	19
T. Lovett, SP	19
G. Pinckney, 3B	17
D. Foutz, 1B	16
O. Burns, OF	15
M. Ward, SS	15
H. Collins, 2B	12
D. O'Brien, OF	11
A. Terry, SP	9
C. Daily, C	8
T. Daly, C	5
G. Hemming, SP	5
B. Inks, SP	4
B. Ely, SS	2
T. Kinslow, C	2
J. O'Brien, 2B	2

Chicago (82-53)	WS
Hitting	**114.0**
Fielding	**44.4**
Pitching	**87.6**
B. Hutchison, SP	49
A. Gumbert, SP	23
J. Ryan, OF	22
C. Anson, 1B	21
B. Dahlen, 3B	21
F. Pfeffer, 2B	21
W. Wilmot, OF	21
C. Carroll, OF	16
J. Cooney, SS	14
P. Luby, SP	12
E. Stein, SP	6
T. Burns, 3B	5
M. Kittridge, C	5
P. Schriver, C	5
T. Vickery, SP	4
B. Bowman, C	1

Cincinnati (56-81)	WS
Hitting	**81.8**
Fielding	**29.5**
Pitching	**56.7**
A. Latham, 3B	25
T. Mullane, SP	24
B. Rhines, SP	21
B. McPhee, 2B	19
B. Holliday, OF	18
P. Browning, OF	9
O. Radbourn, SP	9
J. Halligan, OF	8
J. Reilly, 1B	7
G. Smith, SS	7
L. Marr, OF	6
J. Harrington, C	4
J. Keenan, 1B	4
E. Crane, SP	3
J. Curtis, OF	3
M. Slattery, OF	1

Cleveland (65-74)	WS
Hitting	**101.4**
Fielding	**28.4**
Pitching	**65.1**
C. Young, SP	28
C. Childs, 2B	21
G. Davis, OF	21
L. Viau, SP	19
E. McKean, SS	18
H. Gruber, SP	16
J. Virtue, 1B	15
C. Zimmer, C	14
J. McAleer, OF	12
J. Doyle, C	9
S. Johnson, OF	6
P. Tebeau, 3B	6
J. Burkett, OF	4
B. Alvord, 3B	2
J. Shearon, OF	2
J. Denny, 3B	1
E. Seward, SP-OF	1

New York (71-61)	WS
Hitting	**109.7**
Fielding	**35.0**
Pitching	**68.3**
A. Rusie, SP	36
M. Tiernan, OF	26
R. Connor, 1B	23
J. Ewing, SP	21
G. Gore, OF	18
J. O'Rourke, OF	17
D. Richardson, 2B	17
C. Bassett, 3B	14
J. Glasscock, SS	10
D. Buckley, C	6
J. Sharrott, SP	6
L. Whistler, SS	6
M. Welch, SP	3
A. Clarke, C	2
D. Clarkson, RP	2
R. Coughlin, SP	2
B. Ewing, 2B	2
M. Sullivan, SP	1
J. Taylor, SP	1

Philadelphia (68-69)	WS
Hitting	**105.0**
Fielding	**33.3**
Pitching	**65.7**
B. Hamilton, OF	36
K. Gleason, SP	29
S. Thompson, OF	22
J. Clements, C	19
D. Esper, SP	17
J. Thornton, SP	14
A. Myers, 2B	13
E. Delahanty, OF	12
B. Allen, SS	10
W. Brown, 1B	8
B. Shindle, 3B	7
T. Keefe, SP	4
B. Kling, SP	3
E. Cassian, SP	2
J. Denny, 1B	2
E. Mayer, 3B	2
J. Donohue, OF	1
J. Fields, C	1
B. Gray, C	1
P. Smith, SP	1

Pittsburgh (55-80)	WS
Hitting	**67.2**
Fielding	**30.8**
Pitching	**67.0**
M. Baldwin, SP	25
S. King, SP	20
D. Miller, C	17
J. Beckley, 1B	16
P. Galvin, SP	15
N. Hanlon, OF	14
F. Shugart, SS	10
P. Browning, OF	8
F. Carroll, OF	8
C. Reilly, 3B	6
L. Bierbauer, 2B	4
C. Mack, C	4
A. Maul, OF	4
H. Staley, SP	4
P. Corkhill, OF	3
T. Berger, C	2
D. Lally, OF	2
J. Fields, C	1
S. Stratton, SP	1
P. Ward, OF	1

1891 American Assoc.

Baltimore (71-64)	WS
Hitting	**102.3**
Fielding	**35.5**
Pitching	**75.2**
S. McMahon, SP	39
G. Van Haltren, OF	26
C. Welch, OF	24
P. Werden, 1B	19
B. Johnson, OF	18
P. Gilbert, 3B	13
K. Madden, SP	13
I. Ray, OF	12
S. Wise, 2B	12

B. Cunningham, SP	11
E. Healy, SP	8
J. Bakely, SP	5
W. Robinson, C	5
J. McGraw, SS	3
L. Hardie, OF	2
G. Townsend, C	2
J. Walsh, 2B-SS	1

Boston (93-42)	WS
Hitting	**151.2**
Fielding	**43.2**
Pitching	**84.6**
G. Haddock, SP	34
T. Brown, OF	31
C. Buffinton, SP	31
D. Brouthers, 1B	29
H. Duffy, OF	28
D. Farrell, 3B	24
P. Radford, SS	22
B. Joyce, 3B	17
D. O'Brien, SP	14
C. Stricker, 2B	13
M. Murphy, C	11
H. Richardson, OF	10
B. Daley, SP	8
J. McGeachey, OF	3
C. Griffith, SP	2
J. Irwin, OF	1
K. Kelly, C	1

Cincinnati (43-57)	WS
Hitting	**45.5**
Fielding	**26.4**
Pitching	**57.1**
E. Crane, SP	20
W. Mains, SP	17
F. Dwyer, SP	16
E. Seery, OF	15
K. Kelly, C	13
J. Carney, 1B	8
J. Canavan, SS	7
D. Johnston, OF	6
E. Andrews, OF	5
Y. Robinson, 2B	5
F. Vaughn, C	5
W. McGill, SP	3
A. Whitney, 3B	3
J. Hurley, C	2
M. Kilroy, SP	2
C. Bell, SP	1
K. Keenan, SP	1

Columbus (61-76)	WS
Hitting	**87.1**
Fielding	**36.1**
Pitching	**59.8**
P. Knell, SP	32
J. Crooks, 2B	23
C. Duffee, OF	22
B. Wheelock, SS	17
H. Gastright, SP	14
J. McTamany, OF	13
J. Sneed, OF	11
J. Dolan, SP	9
L. Twitchell, OF	8
J. Donahue, C	5
J. Easton, SP	5
J. O'Connor, OF	5
T. O'Rourke, 3B	5
B. Kuehne, 3B	4
M. Lehane, 1B	4
T. Dowse, C	3
J. Donnelly, 3B	2
E. Cleveland, 3B	1

Louisville (54-83)	WS
Hitting	**87.1**
Fielding	**24.2**
Pitching	**50.7**
J. Fitzgerald, SP	16
P. Donovan, OF	14
F. Weaver, OF	14
T. Cahill, C	13
R. Ehret, SP	13
H. Jennings, SS	12
J. Meekin, SP	12
H. Taylor, 1B	12
T. Shinnick, 2B	9
S. Stratton, SP	9
C. Wolf, OF	9
O. Beard, 3B	6
B. Kuehne, 3B	4
M. Cline, OF	3
J. Ryan, C	3
C. Bell, SP	2
P. Cook, C	2
E. Daily, SP	2
J. Doran, SP	2
S. LaRoque, 2B	2
J. Irwin, 3B	1
J. Long, OF	1
H. Raymond, SS	1

Milwaukee (21-15)	WS
Hitting	**22.7**
Fielding	**11.7**
Pitching	**28.7**
F. Killen, SP	11
G. Davies, SP	10
F. Dwyer, SP	8
G. Shoch, SS	7
J. Carney, 1B	5
A. Dalrymple, OF	5
E. Burke, OF	4
J. Canavan, 2B	4
F. Vaughn, C	3
H. Earl, OF	2
J. Grim, C	2
J. Hughey, SP-RP	1
B. Pettit, 2B	1

Philadelphia (73-66)	WS
Hitting	**94.9**
Fielding	**43.8**
Pitching	**80.3**
G. Weyhing, SP	37
E. Chamberlin, SP	27
J. Milligan, C	21
G. Wood, OF	20
T. Corcoran, SS	19
B. Hallman, 2B	17
H. Larkin, 1B	17
L. Cross, C-OF	16
B. Sanders, OF	13
J. Mulvey, 3B	11
J. McTamany, OF	6
S. Bowman, SP	4
P. Corkhill, OF	4
W. Callahan, SP	2
J. McGeachey, OF	2
E. Beecher, OF	1
D. McKeough, C	1
M. Sullivan, SP	1

St. Louis (85-51)	WS
Hitting	**114.3**
Fielding	**45.0**
Pitching	**95.7**
J. Stivetts, SP	46
D. Hoy, OF	28
D. Lyons, 3B	23
T. O'Neill, OF	23
T. McCarthy, OF	22
W. McGill, SP	22
J. Boyle, C	15
C. Griffith, SP	13
S. Fuller, SS	12
C. Comiskey, 1B	11
B. Eagan, 2B	9
J. Neale, SP	7
G. Rettger, SP	7
J. Munyan, C	6
T. Breitenstein, RP	3
H. Burrell, SP	2
J. Duryea, SP	2
J. Easton, SP	2
D. Darling, C	1
M. McQuaid, 2B	1

Washington (44-91)	WS
Hitting	**86.3**
Fielding	**18.3**
Pitching	**27.4**
F. Foreman, SP	17
D. McGuire, C	17
G. Hatfield, SS	14
L. Murphy, OF	10
K. Carsey, SP	9
S. Sutcliffe, OF	9
T. Dowd, 2B	7
A. McCauley, 1B	7
P. Hines, OF	6
E. Beecher, OF	5
M. McQuery, 1B	4
J. Davis, 3B	3
B. Alvord, 3B	2
J. Burns, OF	2
J. Curtis, OF	2
B. Freeman, SP	2
S. Griffin, OF	2
P. Lohman, C	2
T. McLaughlin, SS	2
J. Visner, OF	2
J. Bakely, SP	1
E. Cassian, SP	1
E. Daily, OF	1
F. Dunlap, 2B	1
G. Keefe, SP	1
D. Shannon, SS	1
M. Slattery, OF	1
P. Smith, 2B	1

1892
National League

Baltimore (46-101)	WS
Hitting	**94.3**
Fielding	**17.5**
Pitching	**26.2**
G. Van Haltren, OF	19
B. Shindle, 3B	15
S. McMahon, SP	11
H. Stovey, OF	9
G. Cobb, SP	7
J. McGraw, 2B-OF	7
T. O'Rourke, SS	7
G. Shoch, SS	7
C. Stricker, 2B	7
J. Halligan, OF	6
W. Robinson, C	6
S. Sutcliffe, 1B	6
P. Ward, OF	6
T. Vickery, SP	5
C. Welch, OF	5
C. Buffinton, SP	3
L. Whistler, 1B	3
J. Gunson, C	2
E. Healy, SP	2
C. Schmit, SP	2
J. Pickett, 2B	1
G. Stephens, RP	1
G. Wood, OF	1

Boston (102-48)	WS
Hitting	**122.4**
Fielding	**49.2**
Pitching	**134.4**
J. Stivetts, SP	49
K. Nichols, SP	48
H. Duffy, OF	29
H. Staley, SP	29
H. Long, SS	28
B. Nash, 3B	22
T. McCarthy, OF	21
T. Tucker, 1B	17
J. Clarkson, SP	16
B. Lowe, OF	16
J. Quinn, 2B	9
C. Ganzel, C	6
K. Kelly, C	6
C. Bennett, C	4
H. Stovey, OF	3
L. Viau, SP	2
D. Clarkson, SP	1

Brooklyn (95-59)	WS
Hitting	**142.4**
Fielding	**49.7**
Pitching	**92.9**
D. Brouthers, 1B	34
E. Stein, SP	30
G. Haddock, SP	27
O. Burns, OF	26
M. Griffin, OF	23
M. Ward, 2B	23
T. Daly, 3B	16
B. Joyce, 3B	16
T. Corcoran, SS	14
D. Foutz, OF	13
B. Hart, SP	12
T. Kinslow, C	12
D. O'Brien, OF	12
C. Daily, C	10
B. Kennedy, SP	10
B. Inks, SP	4
H. Collins, OF	3

Chicago (70-76)	WS
Hitting	**92.8**
Fielding	**38.4**
Pitching	**78.8**
B. Hutchison, SP	45
B. Dahlen, SS	32
J. Ryan, OF	25
A. Gumbert, SP	24
C. Anson, 1B	19
S. Dungan, OF	14
P. Luby, SP	14
P. Schriver, C	9
W. Wilmot, OF	8
J. Canavan, 2B	5
J. Parrott, 3B	5
G. Decker, OF	4
M. Kittridge, C	4
J. Cooney, SS	2

Cincinnati (82-68)	WS
Hitting	**98.3**
Fielding	**50.2**
Pitching	**97.6**
B. McPhee, 2B	27
E. Chamberlin, SP	26
F. Dwyer, SP	26
B. Holliday, OF	26
T. Mullane, SP	26
G. Smith, SS	20
A. Latham, 3B	17
P. Browning, OF	13
T. O'Neill, OF	12
M. Sullivan, SP	12
F. Vaughn, C	8
C. Comiskey, 1B	7
J. Duryea, SP	4
J. Halligan, OF	4
M. Murphy, C	4
D. Daub, SP	2
F. Genins, SS	2
C. Welch, OF	2
J. Harrington, C	1
B. Hoover, OF	1
B. Jones, SP	1
B. Kuehne, 3B	1
W. McGill, SP	1
G. Rettger, SP-OF	1
C. Stephens, SP	1
G. Wood, OF	1

Cleveland (93-56)	WS
Hitting	**122.7**
Fielding	**49.5**
Pitching	**106.7**
C. Young, SP	44
C. Childs, 2B	32
N. Cuppy, SP	31
J. Burkett, OF	23
J. Virtue, 1B	22
J. McAleer, OF	21
G. Davis, 3B	19
C. Zimmer, C	18
J. Clarkson, SP	17
G. Davies, SP	13
E. McKean, SS	12
J. O'Connor, OF	12
P. Tebeau, 3B	10
J. Doyle, OF	3
G. Rettger, SP	1
T. Williams, SP-RP	1

Louisville (63-89)	WS
Hitting	**86.9**
Fielding	**33.5**
Pitching	**68.6**
S. Stratton, SP	29
B. Sanders, SP	22
F. Pfeffer, 2B	20
T. Brown, OF	16
H. Jennings, SS	14
H. Taylor, OF	13
F. Weaver, OF	13
F. Clausen, SP	10
J. Grim, C	8
L. Whistler, 1B	8
A. Jones, SP	7
C. Bassett, 3B	5
J. Meekin, SP	5
L. Viau, SP	5
E. Seery, OF	3
P. Browning, OF	2
E. Healy, SP	2
B. Kuehne, 3B	2
B. Merritt, C	2
T. Dowse, C	1
J. Fitzgerald, SP	1
G. Hemming, SP	1

New York (71-80)	WS
Hitting	**118.0**
Fielding	**28.4**
Pitching	**66.6**
A. Rusie, SP	32
S. King, SP	24
B. Ewing, 1B	20
M. Tiernan, OF	18
J. O'Rourke, OF	15
E. Burke, 2B	14
E. Crane, SP	14
J. Doyle, 2B	14
D. Lyons, 3B	14
S. Fuller, SS	11
G. Gore, OF	10
H. Lyons, OF	8
H. Richardson, 2B	5
J. Boyle, C	4
J. Fields, OF	3
J. McMahon, 1B	3
W. Keeler, 3B	2
C. Bassett, 2B	1
C. Newman, OF	1

Philadelphia (87-66)	WS
Hitting	**113.9**
Fielding	**50.2**
Pitching	**96.9**
G. Weyhing, SP	36
B. Hamilton, OF	25
R. Connor, 1B	24
T. Keefe, SP	24
S. Thompson, OF	22
K. Carsey, SP	21
E. Delahanty, OF	20
B. Allen, SS	18
L. Cross, 3B	17
J. Clements, C	15
B. Hallman, 2B	15
D. Esper, SP	11
C. Reilly, 3B	5
P. Knell, SP	4
J. Taylor, SP	2
T. Dowse, C	1
J. Mulvey, 3B	1

Pittsburgh (80-73)	WS
Hitting	**133.8**
Fielding	**33.2**
Pitching	**73.1**
E. Smith, OF	31
D. Miller, OF	24
F. Shugart, SS	22
M. Baldwin, SP	20
R. Ehret, SP	20
A. Terry, SP	20
J. Beckley, 1B	19
L. Bierbauer, 2B	17
P. Donovan, OF	16
D. Farrell, 3B	13
C. Mack, C	13
P. Galvin, SP	6
J. Kelley, OF	6
B. Gumbert, SP-RP	4
P. Corkhill, OF	2
B. Earle, C	2
E. Swartwood, OF	2
D. Esper, SP	1
G. Van Haltren, OF	1
F. Woodcock, SP	1

St. Louis (56-94)	WS
Hitting	**93.8**
Fielding	**25.4**
Pitching	**48.9**
K. Gleason, SP	25
J. Glasscock, SS	20
B. Caruthers, OF	19
J. Crooks, 2B	18
P. Werden, 1B	17
C. Carroll, OF	13
S. Brodie, OF	12
T. Breitenstein, SP	8
D. Buckley, C	8
P. Hawley, SP	7
P. Galvin, SP	5
B. Hawke, SP	4
L. Camp, 3B	3
C. Getzien, SP	2
G. Gore, OF	2
G. Pinckney, 3B	2
F. Bird, C	1
B. Moran, C	1
C. Stricker, 2B	1

Washington (58-93)	WS
Hitting	**79.6**
Fielding	**30.1**
Pitching	**64.2**
F. Killen, SP	28
D. Hoy, OF	20
P. Radford, OF	13
C. Duffee, OF	12
H. Larkin, 1B	12
D. Richardson, SS	11
D. McGuire, C	10
J. Milligan, C	10
J. Duryea, SP	9
B. Abbey, SP	8
T. Dowd, 2B	8
P. Knell, SP	7
F. Foreman, SP	5
J. Meekin, SP	4
P. Donovan, OF	3
H. Gastright, SP	3
L. Twitchell, OF	3
C. Dolan, SP	2
M. Kilroy, SP	2
Y. Robinson, 3B	2
T. Berger, SS	1
A. Jones, SP	1

1893
National League

Baltimore (60-70)	WS
Hitting	**78.4**
Fielding	**33.7**
Pitching	**67.9**
S. McMahon, SP	26
J. Kelley, OF	20
J. McGraw, SS	20
T. Mullane, SP	17
H. Reitz, 2B	14
B. Shindle, 3B	14
B. Hawke, SP	13
W. Robinson, C	12
E. McNabb, SP	10
G. Treadway, OF	10
H. Taylor, 1B	6
S. Brodie, OF	4
T. O'Rourke, OF	4
B. Clarke, C	2
J. Long, OF	2
K. Baker, SP	1
B. Gilks, OF	1
H. Jennings, SS	1
J. Milligan, 1B	1
C. Schmit, SP	1
P. Ward, OF	1

Boston (86-43)	WS
Hitting	**132.0**
Fielding	**42.4**
Pitching	**83.7**
K. Nichols, SP	40
H. Duffy, OF	28
H. Long, SS	26
B. Nash, 3B	25
J. Stivetts, SP	25
T. McCarthy, OF	24
B. Lowe, 2B	22
H. Staley, SP	15
C. Carroll, OF	11
T. Tucker, 1B	11
H. Gastright, SP	9
C. Ganzel, C	7
B. Merritt, C	7
C. Bennett, C	6
B. Quarles, SP	2

Brooklyn (65-63)	WS
Hitting	**99.9**
Fielding	**32.2**
Pitching	**62.9**
B. Kennedy, SP	29
T. Daly, 2B	20
E. Stein, SP	20
M. Griffin, OF	17
D. Brouthers, 1B	16
T. Corcoran, SS	16
O. Burns, OF	12
D. Foutz, OF	10
G. Shoch, OF	10
H. Stovey, OF	8
D. Daub, SP	7
C. Daily, C	6
G. Haddock, SP	6
T. Kinslow, C	6
G. Hatfield, 3B	4
G. Sharrott, SP	3
W. Keeler, 3B	2
D. Richardson, 2B	2
T. Lovett, SP	1

Chicago (56-71)	WS
Hitting	**77.4**
Fielding	**29.0**
Pitching	**61.6**
B. Hutchison, SP	20
W. McGill, SP	20
B. Dahlen, SS	17
B. Lange, 2B	12
J. Ryan, OF	12
C. Anson, 1B	11
W. Wilmot, OF	11
S. Dungan, OF	9
H. Mauck, SP	8
F. Clausen, SP	6
J. Parrott, 3B	6
P. Schriver, C	6
L. Camp, 3B	5
G. Decker, OF	5
M. Kittridge, C	4
F. Donnelly, SP	3
C. Irwin, SS	3
G. McGinnis, RP	3
B. Abbey, SP	2
B. Glenalvin, 2B	2
C. Griffith, SP-RP	1
J. O'Brien, 2B	1
S. Shaw, SP	1

Cincinnati (65-63)	WS
Hitting	**71.7**
Fielding	**42.4**
Pitching	**80.9**
F. Dwyer, SP	22
B. McPhee, 2B	21
E. Chamberlin, SP	20
B. Holliday, OF	19
A. Latham, 3B	16
G. Smith, SS	14
T. Parrott, SP	12
F. Vaughn, C	12
T. Mullane, SP	10
M. Sullivan, SP	10
J. Canavan, OF	8
S. King, SP	7
P. Ward, OF	6
J. McCarthy, OF	5
F. Motz, 1B	3
M. Murphy, C	3
B. Caruthers, OF	2
G. Henry, OF	2
C. Comiskey, 1B	1
L. Cross, SP	1
J. Smith, OF	1

Cleveland (73-55)	WS
Hitting	**112.6**
Fielding	**33.2**
Pitching	**73.2**
C. Young, SP	35
J. Burkett, OF	24
C. Childs, 2B	23
B. Ewing, OF	19
E. McKean, SS	19
J. Clarkson, SP	16
N. Cuppy, SP	15
P. Tebeau, 1B	15
J. O'Connor, C	11
J. Virtue, 1B	9
C. Zimmer, C	9
C. McGarr, 3B	7
J. McAleer, OF	6
C. Hastings, SP	5
J. Scheible, SP	2
T. Williams, RP	2
J. Gunson, C	1
E. McFarland, OF	1

Louisville (50-75)	WS
Hitting	**86.5**
Fielding	**22.3**
Pitching	**41.2**
G. Hemming, SP	18
S. Stratton, SP	16
W. Brown, 1B	13
T. O'Rourke, SS	13
F. Pfeffer, 2B	13
T. Brown, OF	11
P. Browning, OF	11

Player	WS
F. Weaver, OF	11
J. Grim, C	10
J. Menefee, SP	10
G. Pinckney, 3B	9
L. Twitchell, OF	6
J. Denny, SS	3
F. Clausen, SP	1
H. Jennings, SS	1
M. Kilroy, SP	1
C. Welch, OF	1
L. Whistler, 1B	1
B. Whitrock, SP	1

New York (68-64)	WS
Hitting	**91.8**
Fielding	**35.1**
Pitching	**77.1**
A. Rusie, SP	41
G. Davis, 3B	22
M. Baldwin, SP	20
M. Ward, 2B	17
R. Connor, 1B	16
M. Tiernan, OF	16
E. Burke, OF	15
J. Doyle, C	10
L. German, SP	10
S. Fuller, SS	9
G. Stafford, OF	6
C. Petty, SP	5
E. Crane, SP	4
H. Lyons, OF	3
J. Milligan, C	3
G. Davies, RP	2
P. Wilson, C	2
W. Keeler, OF	1
K. Kelly, C	1
J. McMahon, C	1

Philadelphia (72-57)	WS
Hitting	**114.7**
Fielding	**35.5**
Pitching	**65.8**
E. Delahanty, OF	28
S. Thompson, OF	22
B. Hamilton, OF	20
G. Weyhing, SP	19
B. Allen, SS	17
K. Carsey, SP	17
B. Hallman, 2B	16
J. Clements, C	12
J. Boyle, 1B	11
L. Cross, C	11
J. Taylor, SP	11
T. Keefe, SP	10
C. Reilly, 3B	8
J. Sharrott, OF	4
T. Turner, OF	4
T. Vickery, SP	4
G. McGinnis, SP	2

Pittsburgh (81-48)	WS
Hitting	**110.0**
Fielding	**42.4**
Pitching	**90.6**
F. Killen, SP	42
E. Smith, OF	25
R. Ehret, SP	24
D. Lyons, 3B	21
G. Van Haltren, OF	20
J. Beckley, 1B	17
P. Donovan, OF	14
L. Bierbauer, 2B	13
A. Terry, SP	13
J. Glasscock, SS	12
A. Gumbert, SP	11
J. Stenzel, OF	10
F. Shugart, SS	5
C. Mack, C	4
T. Colcolough, RP	3
B. Earle, C	3
H. Gastright, SP	2
D. Miller, C	2
J. Sugden, C	2

St. Louis (57-75)	WS
Hitting	**59.7**
Fielding	**39.2**
Pitching	**72.0**
T. Breitenstein, SP	30
K. Gleason, SP	22
S. Brodie, OF	15
J. Crooks, 3B	15
D. Clarkson, SP	12
T. Dowd, OF	11
P. Hawley, SP	11
P. Werden, 1B	11
H. Peitz, C	9
J. Glasscock, SS	6
C. Frank, OF	5
F. Shugart, OF	5
B. Ely, SS	4
J. Quinn, 2B	4
J. Bannon, OF	3
D. Cooley, OF	3
J. Gunson, C	3
S. Griffin, OF	1
A. Twineham, C	1

Washington (40-89)	WS
Hitting	**80.0**
Fielding	**16.0**
Pitching	**24.0**
S. Wise, 2B	17
D. Farrell, C	14
D. Esper, SP	11
H. Larkin, 1B	11
A. Maul, SP	11
J. O'Rourke, OF	11
P. Radford, OF	10
D. Hoy, OF	9
J. Meekin, SP	7
J. Sullivan, SS	7
D. McGuire, C	5
C. Abbey, OF	2
J. Duryea, SP	1
J. Mulvey, 3B	1
G. Stephens, SP	1
O. Stocksdale, SP	1
C. Stricker, 2B	1

1894
National League

Baltimore (89-39)	WS
Hitting	**144.7**
Fielding	**41.8**
Pitching	**80.5**
J. Kelley, OF	30
H. Jennings, SS	24
J. McGraw, 3B	24
S. McMahon, SP	24
W. Keeler, OF	23
D. Brouthers, 1B	21
S. Brodie, OF	19
H. Reitz, 2B	17
K. Gleason, SP	16
W. Robinson, C	15
B. Hawke, SP	13
D. Esper, SP	11
B. Inks, SP	9
T. Mullane, SP	7
G. Hemming, SP	5
F. Bonner, 2B	4
S. Brown, SP	3
B. Clarke, C	2

Boston (83-49)	WS
Hitting	**122.5**
Fielding	**40.0**
Pitching	**86.5**
K. Nichols, SP	37
H. Duffy, OF	33
J. Stivetts, SP	33
B. Lowe, 2B	20
T. McCarthy, OF	19
J. Bannon, OF	18
B. Nash, 3B	17
H. Long, SS	16
T. Tucker, 1B	13
H. Staley, SP	12
F. Connaughton, SS	6
T. Lovett, SP	6
C. Ganzel, C	5
G. Hodson, SP	4
J. Ryan, C	4
F. Tenney, C	4
B. Merritt, C	1
G. Stultz, SP	1

Brooklyn (70-61)	WS
Hitting	**117.5**
Fielding	**31.0**
Pitching	**61.5**
E. Stein, SP	27
B. Kennedy, SP	24
T. Daly, 2B	20
M. Griffin, OF	20
G. Treadway, OF	19
O. Burns, OF	18
T. Corcoran, SS	16
B. Shindle, 3B	13
C. LaChance, 1B	8
G. Shoch, OF	8
D. Daub, SP	7
C. Daily, C	6
D. Foutz, 1B	6
T. Kinslow, C	6
H. Gastright, SP-RP	4
C. Lucid, SP	3
J. Anderson, OF	2
B. Earle, C	2
F. Underwood, SP	1

Chicago (57-75)	WS
Hitting	**81.6**
Fielding	**30.1**
Pitching	**59.3**
B. Dahlen, SS	21
C. Griffith, SP	19
B. Hutchison, SP	16
B. Lange, OF	13
J. Ryan, OF	13
W. Wilmot, OF	13
C. Anson, 1B	11
C. Irwin, 3B	11
W. McGill, SP	11
S. Stratton, SP	8
A. Terry, SP	8
G. Decker, 1B	7
P. Schriver, C	6
B. Abbey, SP	5
M. Kittridge, C	4
J. Parrott, 2B	3
K. Camp, SP	1
J. Houseman, SS	1

Cincinnati (55-75)	WS
Hitting	**80.0**
Fielding	**29.7**
Pitching	**55.3**
F. Dwyer, SP	23
T. Parrott, SP	22
B. Holliday, OF	18
B. McPhee, 2B	17
D. Hoy, OF	15
A. Latham, 3B	14
E. Chamberlin, SP	11
J. Canavan, OF	10
G. Smith, SS	10
F. Vaughn, C	7
M. Murphy, C	4
B. Merritt, C	3
C. Fisher, SP	2
J. McCarthy, OF	2
B. Whitrock, SP	2
F. Blank, SP	1
C. Comiskey, 1B	1
H. Fournier, SP	1
B. Massey, 1B	1
J. Tannehill, RP	1

Cleveland (68-61)	WS
Hitting	**74.1**
Fielding	**42.1**
Pitching	**87.8**
C. Young, SP	39
N. Cuppy, SP	28
J. Burkett, OF	21
C. Childs, 2B	20
E. McKean, SS	19
J. Clarkson, SP	13
C. Zimmer, C	10
J. O'Connor, C	9
C. McGarr, 3B	8
P. Tebeau, 1B	8
J. McAleer, OF	6
M. Sullivan, SP	6
H. Blake, OF	4
B. Ewing, OF	4
W. Tebeau, OF	4
B. Wallace, SP	2
F. Knauss, SP	1
T. Mullane, SP	1
J. Virtue, OF	1

Louisville (36-94)	WS
Hitting	**50.2**
Fielding	**21.5**
Pitching	**36.4**
G. Hemming, SP	16
F. Pfeffer, 2B	11
J. Grim, C	10
J. Menefee, SP	10
T. Brown, OF	9
P. Knell, SP	8
D. Richardson, SS	8
F. Clarke, OF	5
O. Smith, OF	4
J. Denny, 3B	3
T. O'Rourke, 1B	3
B. Earle, C	2
P. Flaherty, 3B	2
P. Gilbert, 3B	2
B. Inks, SP	2
F. Lake, 2B	2
G. Nicol, OF	2
L. Twitchell, OF	2
H. Cote, C	1
S. Dungan, OF	1
M. Kilroy, SP	1
L. Lutenberg, 1B	1
S. Stratton, SP	1
J. Wadsworth, SP	1
F. Weaver, OF	1

New York (88-44)	WS
Hitting	**97.5**
Fielding	**45.0**
Pitching	**121.5**
A. Rusie, SP	56
J. Meekin, SP	48
G. Davis, 3B	25
G. Van Haltren, OF	21
J. Doyle, 1B	17
E. Burke, OF	15
D. Farrell, C	14
M. Tiernan, OF	11
S. Fuller, SS	10
M. Ward, 2B	9
H. Westervelt, SP	9
L. German, SP	7
Y. Murphy, SS	7
D. Clarke, RP	6
P. Wilson, C	6
R. Connor, 1B	2
G. Stafford, 3B	1

Philadelphia (71-57)	WS
Hitting	**129.5**
Fielding	**29.5**
Pitching	**54.0**
B. Hamilton, OF	29
J. Taylor, SP	23
L. Cross, 3B	22
E. Delahanty, OF	22
S. Thompson, OF	20
K. Carsey, SP	15
T. Turner, OF	12
G. Weyhing, SP	12
B. Hallman, 2B	10
J. Boyle, 1B	9
J. Sullivan, SS	9
J. Clements, C	7
M. Grady, C	6
B. Allen, SS	3
D. Buckley, C	3
G. Haddock, SP	3
G. Harper, SP	3
C. Reilly, 3B	3
J. Johnson, SP	1
A. Jones, SP	1

Pittsburgh (65-65)	WS
Hitting	**97.7**
Fielding	**32.4**
Pitching	**64.9**
J. Stenzel, OF	24
R. Ehret, SP	21
E. Smith, OF	19
J. Beckley, 1B	17
A. Gumbert, SP	15
F. Killen, SP	15
L. Bierbauer, 2B	12
P. Donovan, OF	10
D. Lyons, 3B	10
J. Glasscock, SS	7
F. Hartman, 3B	6
J. Menefee, SP	6
T. Colcolough, SP	5
C. Mack, C	5
J. Sugden, C	5
F. Weaver, C	4
M. Cross, SS	3
B. Merritt, C	3
G. Nicol, SP	3
F. Scheibeck, SS	3
J. Easton, RP	1
H. Jordan, SP	1

St. Louis (56-76)	WS
Hitting	**51.2**
Fielding	**39.6**
Pitching	**77.2**
T. Breitenstein, SP	36
P. Hawley, SP	29
B. Ely, SS	14
D. Miller, 3B	13
R. Connor, 1B	12
F. Shugart, OF	12
D. Clarkson, SP	9
J. Quinn, 2B	8
T. Dowd, OF	7
H. Peitz, 3B	7
C. Frank, OF	6
A. Twineham, C	4
K. Gleason, SP	3
D. Buckley, C	2
D. Cooley, OF	2
J. Peitz, OF	2
M. Hogan, OF	1
T. O'Rourke, 3B	1

Washington (45-87)	WS
Hitting	**75.4**
Fielding	**21.6**
Pitching	**38.0**
W. Mercer, SP	19
B. Joyce, 3B	18
C. Abbey, OF	13
E. Cartwright, 1B	11
B. Hassamaer, OF	11
D. McGuire, C	9
K. Selbach, OF	9
P. Ward, 2B	9
A. Maul, SP	8
P. Radford, SS	6
O. Stocksdale, SP	5
F. Scheibeck, SS	4
D. Esper, SP	3
C. Petty, SP	3
M. Sullivan, SP	2
W. Tebeau, OF	2
D. Dugdale, C	1
J. Malarkey, SP	1
J. Sullivan, 2B	1

1895
National League

Baltimore (87-43)	WS
Hitting	**113.9**
Fielding	**42.7**
Pitching	**104.3**
B. Hoffer, SP	35
H. Jennings, SS	29
J. Kelley, OF	27
G. Hemming, SP	24
W. Keeler, OF	23
S. Brodie, OF	20
J. McGraw, 3B	20
D. Esper, SP	18
S. McMahon, SP	15
D. Clarkson, SP	12
K. Gleason, 2B	12
B. Clarke, C	7
H. Reitz, 2B	6
W. Robinson, C	6
S. Carey, 1B	4
F. Bonner, 3B	1
B. Kissinger, SP	1
A. Pond, RP	1

Boston (71-60)	WS
Hitting	**92.8**
Fielding	**38.4**
Pitching	**81.7**
K. Nichols, SP	34
H. Duffy, OF	23
J. Bannon, OF	19
H. Long, SS	19
J. Stivetts, SP	18
B. Nash, 3B	17
C. Dolan, SP	14
B. Lowe, 2B	14
T. McCarthy, OF	11
J. Sullivan, SP	11
T. Tucker, 1B	9
C. Ganzel, C	7
J. Ryan, C	4
F. Tenney, OF	4
J. Harrington, 2B	2
F. Sexton, SP	2
Z. Wilson, SP	2
B. Banks, SP	1
C. Nyce, SS	1
O. Stocksdale, SP	1

Brooklyn (71-60)	WS
Hitting	**109.0**
Fielding	**36.3**
Pitching	**67.7**
M. Griffin, OF	29
B. Kennedy, SP	19
C. LaChance, 1B	19
E. Stein, SP	18
A. Gumbert, SP	16
B. Shindle, 3B	16
T. Corcoran, SS	15
T. Daly, 2B	14
J. Anderson, OF	12
D. Daub, SP	11
J. Grim, C	11
G. Treadway, OF	8
C. Lucid, SP	7
G. Shoch, OF	7
B. Abbey, SP	4
C. Daily, C	2
D. Foutz, OF	2
J. Mulvey, 3B	2
O. Burns, OF	1

Chicago (72-58)	WS
Hitting	**95.3**
Fielding	**39.3**
Pitching	**81.4**
C. Griffith, SP	34
B. Lange, OF	29
A. Terry, SP	22
B. Dahlen, SS	20
B. Everitt, 3B	19
B. Hutchison, SP	19
C. Anson, 1B	14
J. Ryan, OF	14
W. Wilmot, OF	10
A. Stewart, 2B	7
G. Decker, OF	5
T. Donahue, C	5
D. Parker, SP	5
H. Truby, 2B	4
D. Friend, SP	3
M. Kittridge, C	3
M. McFarland, SP	1
S. Stratton, SP	1
W. Thornton, RP	1

Cincinnati (66-64)	WS
Hitting	**84.4**
Fielding	**40.0**
Pitching	**73.6**
F. Dwyer, SP	21
F. Foreman, SP	18
D. Miller, OF	18
T. Parrott, SP	18
B. Rhines, SP	18
B. McPhee, 2B	16
G. Smith, SS	14
A. Latham, 3B	12
B. Ewing, 1B	11
D. Hoy, OF	11
F. Vaughn, C	9
G. Hogriever, OF	8
B. Phillips, SP-RP	6
E. Burke, OF	5
B. Gray, 3B	5
B. Holliday, OF	3
M. Murphy, C	2
K. Bailey, SP	1
B. Merritt, C	1
H. Spies, C	1

Cleveland (84-46)	WS
Hitting	**120.6**
Fielding	**42.7**
Pitching	**88.7**
C. Young, SP	37
J. Burkett, OF	35
N. Cuppy, SP	33
E. McKean, SS	25
C. Childs, 2B	18
C. Zimmer, C	17
J. McAleer, OF	14
B. Wallace, SP	14
W. Tebeau, OF	13
C. McGarr, 3B	10
J. O'Connor, C	10
Pa. Tebeau, 1B	9
H. Blake, OF	7
P. Knell, SP	5
Z. Wilson, SP	3
E. Gremminger, 3B	1
Pu. Tebeau, OF	1

Louisville (35-96)	WS
Hitting	**61.0**
Fielding	**17.6**
Pitching	**26.4**
F. Clarke, OF	16
J. Collins, 3B	10
B. Cunningham, SP	10
D. Holmes, OF	6
J. O'Brien, 2B	6
F. Shugart, SS	6
G. Weyhing, SP	5
B. Inks, SP	4
T. McCreery, OF	4
M. McDermott, SP	4
W. Preston, OF	4
H. Spies, 1B	4
D. Brouthers, 1B	3
J. Warner, C	3
J. Wright, OF	3
T. Gettinger, OF	2
J. Glasscock, SS	2
P. Luby, SP	2
A. McGann, SS	2
D. Sweeney, OF	2
H. Burnett, OF	1
H. Cote, C	1
P. Knell, SP	1
G. Meakim, SP	1
D. Minnehan, 3B	1
F. Pfeffer, SS	1
T. Welsh, C	1

New York (66-65)	WS
Hitting	**98.2**
Fielding	**31.4**
Pitching	**68.5**
A. Rusie, SP	28
D. Clarke, SP	22
M. Tiernan, OF	22
G. Van Haltren, OF	22
G. Davis, 3B	21
J. Meekin, SP	14
D. Farrell, C	11
S. Fuller, SS	11
G. Stafford, 2B	11
J. Doyle, 1B	10
L. German, SP	7
O. Burns, OF	4
T. Bannon, OF	3
E. Burke, OF	3
P. Schriver, C	3
P. Wilson, C	3
A. Boswell, SP	1
W. Clark, 1B	1
Y. Murphy, OF	1

Philadelphia (78-53)	WS
Hitting	**143.3**
Fielding	**29.7**
Pitching	**60.9**
E. Delahanty, OF	31
B. Hamilton, OF	30
S. Thompson, OF	28
J. Taylor, SP	25
K. Carsey, SP	21
J. Clements, C	18
L. Cross, 3B	14
B. Hallman, 2B	13
J. Sullivan, SS	10
A. Orth, SP	9
T. Turner, OF	9
W. McGill, SP	7
M. Grady, C	4
C. Lucid, SP	4
J. Boyle, 1B	3
C. Reilly, SS	3
D. Buckley, C	2
T. Smith, SP	2
A. Madison, SS	1

Pittsburgh (71-61)	WS
Hitting	**88.8**
Fielding	**41.0**
Pitching	**83.2**
P. Hawley, SP	44

J. Stenzel, OF	28
J. Beckley, 1B	18
B. Hart, SP	16
E. Smith, OF	16
P. Donovan, OF	15
B. Clingman, 3B	11
B. Foreman, SP	11
M. Cross, SS	9
L. Bierbauer, 2B	8
J. Gardner, SP	8
F. Killen, SP	6
B. Merritt, C	5
J. Sugden, C	5
F. Genins, OF	4
J. Hewitt, SP-RP	2
T. Colcolough, SP	1
H. Jordan, SP	1
T. Kinslow, C	1
C. Mack, C	1
B. Niles, 3B	1
B. Stuart, SS	1
G. Weyhing, SP	1

St. Louis (39-92)	WS
Hitting	**53.1**
Fielding	**22.5**
Pitching	**41.3**
T. Breitenstein, SP	25
D. Cooley, OF	13
R. Connor, 1B	12
T. Dowd, OF	10
J. Quinn, 2B	10
R. Ehret, SP	7
B. Ely, SS	7
D. Miller, C-3B	7
H. Peitz, C	7
H. Staley, SP	6
B. Sheehan, OF	4
T. Brown, OF	3
B. Kissinger, SP	3
D. Lyons, 3B	2
J. Otten, C	1

Washington (43-85)	WS
Hitting	**71.0**
Fielding	**21.8**
Pitching	**36.2**
D. McGuire, C	17
B. Joyce, 3B	16
E. Cartwright, 1B	14
K. Selbach, OF	14
W. Mercer, SP	13
J. Crooks, 2B	11
A. Maul, SP	10
C. Abbey, OF	7
V. Anderson, SP	7
O. Stocksdale, SP	4
J. Boyd, OF	3
B. Hassamaer, OF	3
T. Brown, OF	2
J. Malarkey, RP	2
A. Boswell, SP-RP	1
G. DeMontreville, SS	1
J. Gilroy, SP-RP	1
J. Glasscock, SS	1
D. McJames, SP	1
F. Scheibeck, SS	1

1896 National League

Baltimore (90-39)	WS
Hitting	**136.9**
Fielding	**42.7**
Pitching	**90.4**
H. Jennings, SS	36
B. Hoffer, SP	31
J. Kelley, OF	31
W. Keeler, OF	25
J. Doyle, 1B	17
S. Brodie, OF	16
G. Hemming, SP	16
A. Pond, SP	16
J. Donnelly, 3B	14
D. Esper, SP	13
H. Reitz, 2B	13
S. McMahon, SP	11
W. Robinson, C	9
B. Clarke, C	8
J. Corbett, RP	5
J. McGraw, 3B	3
D. Clarkson, SP	2
J. Quinn, 2B-OF	2
B. Keister, 2B	1
J. Nops, SP	1

Boston (74-57)	WS
Hitting	**97.7**
Fielding	**41.6**
Pitching	**82.7**
K. Nichols, SP	33
B. Hamilton, OF	30
J. Stivetts, SP	29
H. Long, SS	20
H. Duffy, OF	17
J. Sullivan, SP	15
F. Tenney, OF	12
J. Collins, 3B	11
B. Lowe, 2B	10
T. Tucker, 1B	10
F. Klobedanz, SP	8
M. Bergen, C	6
D. McGann, 2B	6
J. Bannon, OF	5
C. Ganzel, C	3
T. Lewis, SP	2
W. Mains, SP	2
C. Dolan, SP	1
J. Harrington, 3B	1
J. Ryan, C	1

Brooklyn (58-73)	WS
Hitting	**88.9**
Fielding	**30.0**
Pitching	**55.2**
M. Griffin, OF	17
H. Payne, SP	17
D. Daub, SP	16
F. Jones, OF	16
T. Corcoran, SS	15
J. Anderson, OF	14
B. Kennedy, SP	13
B. Shindle, 3B	12
C. LaChance, 1B	10
T. Daly, 2B	9
G. Shoch, 2B	8
B. Burrell, C	6
J. Grim, C	6
T. McCarthy, OF	5
B. Abbey, SP	4
A. Gumbert, SP	2
G. Harper, SP	2
E. Stein, SP	2

Chicago (71-57)	WS
Hitting	**89.0**
Fielding	**42.0**
Pitching	**82.0**
B. Dahlen, SS	31
C. Griffith, SP	30
B. Lange, OF	24
D. Friend, SP	21
A. Terry, SP	18
B. Everitt, 3B	16
B. Briggs, SP	14
J. Ryan, OF	14
C. Anson, 1B	12
G. Decker, OF	9
F. Pfeffer, 2B	7
M. Kittridge, C	4
T. Donahue, C	3
G. Flynn, OF	2
D. Parker, SP	2
W. Thornton, SP	2
H. Truby, 2B	2
A. McBride, OF	1
B. McCormick, 3B	1

Cincinnati (77-50)	WS
Hitting	**91.9**
Fielding	**41.4**
Pitching	**97.6**
F. Dwyer, SP	30
R. Ehret, SP	24
E. Burke, OF	20
D. Miller, OF	19
D. Hoy, OF	18
F. Foreman, SP	17
B. McPhee, 2B	17
B. Rhines, SP	16
C. Irwin, 3B	15
G. Smith, SS	14
C. Fisher, SP	11
F. Vaughn, C-1B	10
H. Peitz, C	8
B. Ewing, 1B	7
B. Gray, 2B	2
B. Holliday, OF	2
B. Inks, SP	1

Cleveland (80-48)	WS
Hitting	**86.4**
Fielding	**43.7**
Pitching	**109.9**
C. Young, SP	43
N. Cuppy, SP	38
J. Burkett, OF	29
C. Childs, 2B	27
Z. Wilson, SP	20
E. McKean, SS	17
B. Wallace, OF	15
J. McAleer, OF	13
C. Zimmer, C	10
C. McGarr, 3B	7
P. Tebeau, 1B	7
H. Blake, OF	6
J. O'Connor, C	6
T. Delahanty, 3B	1
D. Gear, SP	1

Louisville (38-93)	WS
Hitting	**56.8**
Fielding	**21.9**
Pitching	**35.2**
F. Clarke, OF	17
T. McCreery, OF	16
B. Hill, SP	13
C. Fraser, SP	12
B. Clingman, 3B	9
B. Cunningham, SP	7
C. Dexter, C	7
D. Miller, C	6
J. O'Brien, 2B	5
O. Pickering, OF	4
J. Crooks, 2B	3
A. Herman, SP	3
J. Rogers, 1B	3
B. Hassamaer, 1B	2
D. Holmes, OF	2
P. Cassidy, 1B	1
J. Dolan, SS	1
T. Smith, RP	1
S. Strang, SS	1
J. Warner, C	1

New York (64-67)	WS
Hitting	**102.7**
Fielding	**28.9**
Pitching	**60.4**
J. Meekin, SP	27
M. Tiernan, OF	25
G. Van Haltren, OF	23
G. Davis, 3B	21
D. Clarke, SP	19
K. Gleason, 2B	15
B. Joyce, 3B	11
M. Sullivan, SP	9
H. Davis, OF	7
F. Connaughton, SS	6
J. Beckley, 1B	5
W. Clark, 1B	5
E. Doheny, SP	5
D. Farrell, C	4
G. Stafford, OF	4
S. Campfield, RP	2
P. Wilson, C	2
S. Fuller, SS	1
J. Warner, C	1

Philadelphia (62-68)	WS
Hitting	**110.1**
Fielding	**25.6**
Pitching	**50.3**
E. Delahanty, OF	31
J. Taylor, SP	17
B. Hallman, 2B	14
A. Orth, SP	14
S. Thompson, OF	13
M. Grady, C	10
D. Brouthers, 1B	9
J. Clements, C	9
B. Hulen, SS	9
K. Carsey, SP	8
L. Cross, 3B	8
D. Cooley, OF	6
B. Nash, 3B	6
A. Gumbert, SP	5
N. Lajoie, 1B	5
H. Keener, SP	4
W. McGill, SP	4
J. Sullivan, OF	4
J. Boyle, C	3
W. Gallagher, SS	2
S. Mertes, OF	2
T. Turner, OF	1
G. Wheeler, SP	1
B. Whitrock, SP-RP	1

Pittsburgh (66-63)	WS
Hitting	**98.1**
Fielding	**34.2**
Pitching	**65.7**
F. Killen, SP	32
P. Hawley, SP	27
E. Smith, OF	26
J. Stenzel, OF	22
P. Donovan, OF	17
D. Lyons, 3B	16
B. Ely, SS	14
J. Sugden, C	9
B. Merritt, C	7
L. Bierbauer, 2B	6
J. Hughey, SP	6
J. Beckley, 1B	5
D. Padden, 2B	4
C. Hastings, SP	2
H. Davis, 1B	1
B. Foreman, SP	1
C. Mack, 1B	1
J. Smith, 3B	1
J. Wright, OF	1

St. Louis (40-90)	WS
Hitting	**53.1**
Fielding	**21.9**
Pitching	**45.1**
T. Breitenstein, SP	22
R. Connor, 1B	14
B. Hart, SP	14
T. Dowd, 2B	10
T. Parrott, OF	10
M. Cross, SS	9
R. Donahue, SP	7
E. McFarland, C	7
K. Douglass, OF	6
B. Myers, 3B	6
J. Sullivan, OF	4
D. Cooley, OF	3
M. Murphy, C	3
B. Kissinger, SP	2
T. Turner, OF	2
J. Quinn, 2B	1

Washington (58-73)	WS
Hitting	**109.5**
Fielding	**21.8**
Pitching	**42.7**
G. DeMontreville, SS	21
B. Joyce, 3B	18
W. Mercer, SP	18
K. Selbach, OF	18
D. McGuire, C	14
T. Brown, OF	12
D. McJames, SP	11
E. Cartwright, 1B	10
B. Lush, OF	9
S. King, SP	8
J. O'Brien, 2B	6
C. Abbey, OF	5
D. Farrell, C	4
J. Crooks, 2B	3
A. Maul, SP	3
E. Norton, SP	3
J. Rogers, 3B	3
H. Smith, 3B	3
L. German, SP	2
P. McCauley, C	2
J. Malarkey, SP	1

1897 National League

Baltimore (90-40)	WS
Hitting	**145.8**
Fielding	**42.5**
Pitching	**81.6**
W. Keeler, OF	32
H. Jennings, SS	29
J. Kelley, OF	26
J. Stenzel, OF	24
J. Corbett, SP	23
J. McGraw, 3B	20
A. Pond, SP	19
J. Doyle, 1B	18
B. Hoffer, SP	18
J. Nops, SP	18
H. Reitz, 2B	17
J. Quinn, 3B	7
D. Amole, SP	5
B. Clarke, C	4
W. Robinson, C	4
F. Bowerman, C	3
T. O'Brien, 1B	3

Boston (93-39)	WS
Hitting	**136.2**
Fielding	**43.7**
Pitching	**99.1**
K. Nichols, SP	41
B. Hamilton, OF	28
J. Collins, 3B	26
H. Duffy, OF	25
F. Klobedanz, SP	25
T. Lewis, SP	22
C. Stahl, OF	20
J. Stivetts, OF	20
H. Long, SS	17
B. Lowe, 2B	16
F. Tenney, 1B	15
M. Bergen, C	6
J. Sullivan, SP	6
B. Allen, SS	5
C. Ganzel, C	3
G. Yeager, C	2
C. Hickman, RP	1
F. Lake, C	1

Brooklyn (61-71)	WS
Hitting	**85.7**
Fielding	**32.9**
Pitching	**64.5**
B. Kennedy, SP	25
M. Griffin, OF	22
F. Jones, OF	18
J. Anderson, OF	16
C. LaChance, 1B	14
H. Payne, SP	14
B. Shindle, 3B	14
J. Dunn, SP	13
C. Fisher, SP	10
G. Shoch, 2B	9
A. Smith, C	6
D. Daub, SP	5
G. Smith, SS	5
J. Canavan, 2B	3
J. Grim, C	3
B. Burrell, C	2
J. Sheckard, SS	2
P. Hannifin, OF	1
S. McMahon, SP	1

Chicago (59-73)	WS
Hitting	**93.5**
Fielding	**27.0**
Pitching	**56.5**
C. Griffith, SP	22
B. Lange, OF	21
N. Callahan, 2B	19
J. Ryan, OF	16
B. Dahlen, SS	14
W. Thornton, OF	14
D. Friend, SP	12
B. Everitt, 3B	11
C. Anson, 1B	10
B. McCormick, 3B	9
J. Connor, 2B	8
G. Decker, OF	8
B. Briggs, SP	4
T. Donahue, C	3
M. Kittridge, C	3
R. Denzer, SP	2
F. Pfeffer, 2B	1

Cincinnati (76-56)	WS
Hitting	**86.1**
Fielding	**43.4**
Pitching	**98.5**
T. Breitenstein, SP	34
B. Rhines, SP	24
F. Dwyer, SP	23
C. Irwin, 3B	17
D. Hoy, OF	16
D. Miller, OF	15
J. Beckley, 1B	14
T. Corcoran, SS	12
R. Ehret, SP	11
B. McPhee, 2B	11
H. Peitz, C	9
C. Ritchey, SS	9
E. Burke, OF	7
B. Dammann, SP	7
B. Holliday, OF	7
P. Schriver, C	7
F. Vaughn, 1B	4
S. Brown, SP-RP	1

Cleveland (69-62)	WS
Hitting	**77.9**
Fielding	**42.7**
Pitching	**86.4**
C. Young, SP	28
J. Burkett, OF	23
J. Powell, SP	21
B. Wallace, 3B	21
Z. Wilson, SP	19
C. Childs, 2B	18
N. Cuppy, SP	13
C. Zimmer, C	10
E. McKean, SS	9
L. Sockalexis, OF	9
J. O'Connor, OF	8
O. Pickering, OF	7
P. Tebeau, 1B	6
M. McDermott, SP	4
H. Blake, OF	3
L. Criger, C	3
S. McAllister, OF	2
I. Belden, OF	1
H. Clarke, SP	1
J. McAleer, OF	1

Louisville (52-78)	WS
Hitting	**76.6**
Fielding	**25.6**
Pitching	**53.8**
F. Clarke, OF	30
B. Cunningham, SP	15
P. Werden, 1B	15
C. Fraser, SP	14
B. Hill, SP	11
B. Clingman, 3B	9
G. Stafford, SS	9
H. Wagner, OF	9
T. McCreery, OF	8
C. Dexter, OF	7
O. Pickering, OF	5
B. Magee, SP	4
D. Nance, OF	4
D. Clarke, SP	3
R. Evans, SP	3
B. Wilson, C	3
G. Hemming, SP	2
A. Herman, SP	1
A. Johnson, 2B	1
J. Rogers, 2B	1
H. Smith, 2B	1
R. Waddell, SP-RP	1

New York (83-48)	WS
Hitting	**123.4**
Fielding	**41.4**
Pitching	**84.2**
G. Davis, SS	31
A. Rusie, SP	31
G. Van Haltren, OF	24
J. Meekin, SP	23
M. Tiernan, OF	23
C. Seymour, SP	21
B. Joyce, 3B	18
K. Gleason, 2B	17
J. Warner, C	13
W. Clark, 1B	12
E. Doheny, SP	7
D. Holmes, OF	7
M. Sullivan, SP	7
T. McCreery, OF	6
P. Wilson, C	6
J. Beckley, 1B	1
W. Wilmot, OF	1
D. Zearfoss, C	1

Philadelphia (55-77)	WS
Hitting	**81.2**
Fielding	**28.7**
Pitching	**55.1**
E. Delahanty, OF	23
N. Lajoie, 1B	21
J. Taylor, SP	18
D. Cooley, OF	16
A. Orth, SP	16
G. Wheeler, SP	12
B. Nash, 3B	9
J. Fifield, SP	7
P. Geier, OF	7
T. Dowd, OF	6
L. Cross, 3B	5
J. Boyle, C	4
J. Clements, C	4
D. Dunkle, SP	4
S. Gillen, SS	4
F. Shugart, SS	3
E. McFarland, C	2
B. Becker, RP	1
K. Carsey, SP	1
B. Hallman, 2B	1
Y. Johnson, RP	1

Pittsburgh (60-71)	WS
Hitting	**78.9**
Fielding	**31.4**
Pitching	**69.7**
F. Killen, SP	22
E. Smith, OF	20
P. Hawley, SP	19
H. Davis, 1B	14
B. Ely, SS	14
D. Padden, 2B	14
J. Tannehill, OF	14
P. Donovan, OF	13
S. Brodie, OF	10
C. Hastings, SP	8
J. Hughey, SP	7
J. Gardner, SP	5
J. Hoffmeister, 3B	5
J. Sugden, C	4
D. Lyons, 1B	3
B. Merritt, C	3
J. Rothfuss, 1B	3
J. Donnelly, 3B	1
T. Leahy, OF	1

St. Louis (29-102)	WS
Hitting	**65.3**
Fielding	**8.7**
Pitching	**13.0**
K. Douglass, C	15
M. Cross, SS	13
F. Hartman, 3B	10
T. Turner, OF	8
D. Harley, OF	7
M. Grady, 1B	6
R. Donahue, SP	4
B. Hart, SP	3
J. Houseman, 2B	3
D. Lally, OF	3
E. McFarland, C	3
K. Carsey, SP	2
W. Sudhoff, SP	2
R. Connor, 1B	1
T. Dowd, OF	1
D. Esper, SP	1
B. Hallman, 2B	1
B. Hutchison, SP	1
B. Kissinger, SP-OF	1
C. Lucid, SP	1
M. Murphy, C	1

Washington (61-71)	WS
Hitting	**86.1**
Fielding	**31.0**
Pitching	**65.9**
W. Mercer, SP	27
D. McJames, SP	19
K. Selbach, OF	19
G. DeMontreville, SS	18
D. McGuire, C	13
T. Brown, OF	11
T. Tucker, 1B	11
C. Reilly, 3B	10
D. Farrell, C	9
C. Swaim, SP	9
S. King, SP	7
Z. Wrigley, OF	7
C. Abbey, OF	5
J. Gettman, OF	4
J. O'Brien, 2B	4
R. Bresnahan, SP	3
L. German, RP	3
T. Leahy, OF	3
E. Norton, SP-RP	1

1898 National League

Baltimore (96-53)	WS
Hitting	**145.3**
Fielding	**48.6**
Pitching	**94.1**
H. Jennings, SS	32
J. McGraw, 3B	31

D. McJames, SP	30
G. DeMontreville, 2B	24
A. Maul, SP	24
W. Keeler, OF	23
J. Hughes, SP	22
J. Kelley, OF	22
D. McGann, 1B	21
J. Nops, SP	14
D. Holmes, OF	13
F. Kitson, SP	9
W. Robinson, C	6
B. Clarke, C	4
S. Brodie, OF	3
A. Pond, SP	3
J. Stenzel, OF	3
A. Ball, 3B	1
F. Bowerman, C	1
T. O'Brien, OF	1
J. Quinn, 3B	1

Boston (102-47)	**WS**
Hitting	**140.4**
Fielding	**49.2**
Pitching	**116.3**
K. Nichols, SP	44
J. Collins, 3B	34
B. Hamilton, OF	33
T. Lewis, SP	31
H. Duffy, OF	25
V. Willis, SP	25
H. Long, SS	19
C. Stahl, OF	19
F. Tenney, 1B	17
F. Klobedanz, SP	15
B. Lowe, 2B	15
M. Bergen, C	12
G. Yeager, C	7
C. Hickman, OF	5
G. Stafford, OF	2
J. Stivetts, OF	2
D. Pickett, OF	1

Brooklyn (54-91)	**WS**
Hitting	**78.2**
Fielding	**30.4**
Pitching	**53.4**
M. Griffin, OF	20
B. Kennedy, SP	20
F. Jones, OF	19
J. Dunn, SP	17
J. Sheckard, OF	13
J. Yeager, SP	13
C. LaChance, 1B	11
B. Hallman, 2B	8
G. Magoon, SS	6
T. Tucker, 1B	6
T. Daly, 2B	5
J. Grim, C	4
J. Ryan, C	4
B. Shindle, 3B	4
A. Smith, OF	3
J. Anderson, OF	2
R. Miller, SP	2
W. Gaston, SP	1
H. Howell, SP	1
K. McKenna, SP	1
H. Payne, SP	1
B. Wagner, 3B	1

Chicago (85-65)	**WS**
Hitting	**116.6**
Fielding	**45.6**
Pitching	**92.7**
C. Griffith, SP	32
J. Ryan, OF	28
B. Dahlen, SS	27
N. Callahan, SP	23
B. Lange, OF	21
W. Thornton, OF	19
B. Everitt, 1B	18
B. McCormick, 3B	13
S. Mertes, OF	12
W. Woods, SP	11
T. Donahue, C	10
J. Connor, 2B	8
D. Green, OF	7
M. Kilroy, SP	5
J. Taylor, SP	5
F. Chance, C	4
F. Isbell, OF	4
A. Nichols, C	2
B. Phyle, SP	2
B. Briggs, SP	1
H. Clarke, SP-OF	1
J. Katoll, SP-RP	1
H. Wolverton, 3B	1

Cincinnati (92-60)	**WS**
Hitting	**118.2**
Fielding	**50.8**
Pitching	**106.9**
P. Hawley, SP	28
E. Smith, OF	27
T. Breitenstein, SP	25
F. Dwyer, SP	21
A. McBride, OF	21
D. Miller, OF	21
T. Corcoran, SS	18
B. Dammann, SP	17
B. Hill, SP	16
B. McPhee, 2B	15
J. Beckley, 1B	14
C. Irwin, 3B	13
H. Peitz, C	13
H. Steinfeldt, 2B	10
F. Vaughn, 1B	9
H. McFarland, OF	3
B. Wood, C	3
B. Holliday, OF	2

Cleveland (81-68)	**WS**
Hitting	**111.8**
Fielding	**44.2**
Pitching	**87.0**
C. Young, SP	34
J. Burkett, OF	29
J. Powell, SP	25
B. Wallace, 3B	25
C. Childs, 2B	18
E. McKean, SS	17
L. Criger, C	15
Z. Wilson, SP	13
H. Blake, OF	12
P. Tebeau, 1B	12
J. O'Connor, 1B	9
N. Cuppy, SP	8
J. McAleer, OF	8
C. Jones, SP	4
S. McAllister, SP	3
F. Bates, SP	2
E. Heidrick, OF	2
O. Schreckengost, C	2
C. Zimmer, C	2
F. Frank, OF	1
C. Fraser, SP	1
P. McBride, SP	1

Louisville (70-81)	**WS**
Hitting	**111.3**
Fielding	**32.9**
Pitching	**65.8**
B. Cunningham, SP	30
F. Clarke, OF	25
D. Hoy, OF	24
H. Wagner, 1B	22
B. Clingman, 3B	16
C. Dexter, OF	16
B. Magee, SP	16
P. Dowling, SP	15
C. Ritchey, SS	13
M. Kittridge, C	5
G. Stafford, 2B	5
G. Decker, 1B	4
D. Nance, OF	4
C. Fraser, SP	3
T. Hartsel, OF	3
M. Powers, C	3
N. Altrock, SP	2
H. Davis, 1B	1
R. Ehret, SP	1
B. Taylor, 3B	1
B. Wilson, C	1

New York (77-73)	**WS**
Hitting	**134.5**
Fielding	**30.1**
Pitching	**66.4**
G. Van Haltren, OF	29
C. Seymour, SP	26
B. Joyce, 1B	25
G. Davis, SS	20
A. Rusie, SP	19
M. Grady, C	17
M. Tiernan, OF	16
J. Meekin, SP	15
F. Hartman, 3B	13
J. Warner, C	13
J. Doyle, OF	8
C. Gettig, OF	8
K. Gleason, 2B	8
E. Doheny, SP	6
W. Wilmot, OF	3
B. Carrick, SP	2
T. McCreery, OF	2
P. Foster, OF	1

Philadelphia (78-71)	**WS**
Hitting	**143.6**
Fielding	**28.9**
Pitching	**61.5**
E. Delahanty, OF	33
E. Flick, OF	26
N. Lajoie, 2B	26
D. Cooley, OF	22
W. Piatt, SP	21
M. Cross, SS	20
A. Orth, SP	18
E. McFarland, C	17
R. Donahue, SP	13
K. Douglass, 1B	11
J. Fifield, SP	9
B. Lauder, 3B	5
S. Thompson, OF	3
B. Duggleby, SP	2
B. Nash, 3B	2
G. Wheeler, SP	2
E. Abbaticchio, 3B	1
K. Elberfeld, 3B	1
E. Murphy, RP	1
M. Murphy, C	1

Pittsburgh (72-76)	**WS**
Hitting	**78.6**
Fielding	**44.5**
Pitching	**92.9**
J. Tannehill, SP	34
P. Donovan, OF	19
J. McCarthy, OF	16
B. Rhines, SP	15
J. Gardner, SP	13
D. Padden, 2B	13
F. Killen, SP	11
B. Ely, SS	10
W. Clark, 1B	9
H. Davis, 1B	9
C. Hastings, SP	9
T. McCreery, OF	9
T. O'Brien, OF	9
P. Schriver, C	7
F. Bowerman, C	6
B. Hart, SP	5
B. Eagan, 2B	4
B. Gray, 3B	4
B. Hoffer, SP	4
S. Leever, SP	4
S. Brodie, OF	3
J. Cronin, SP	2
Z. Rosebraugh, SP-RP	1

St. Louis (39-111)	**WS**
Hitting	**34.6**
Fielding	**26.6**
Pitching	**55.7**
J. Taylor, SP	22
L. Cross, 3B	17
J. Hughey, SP	15
W. Sudhoff, SP	14
J. Stenzel, OF	10
J. Clements, C	6
D. Harley, OF	5
J. Crooks, 2B	4
J. Sugden, C	4
P. Daniels, SP	3
G. Decker, 1B	3
T. Dowd, OF	3
J. Quinn, 2B	3
D. Esper, SP	2
T. Tucker, 1B	2
T. Kinslow, C	1
H. Maupin, SP	1
T. Smith, SP	1
S. Sullivan, SS	1

Washington (51-101)	**WS**
Hitting	**82.9**
Fielding	**25.4**
Pitching	**44.7**
K. Selbach, OF	17
J. Anderson, OF	15
W. Mercer, SP	13
G. Weyhing, SP	13
H. Reitz, 2B	12
D. Farrell, C	11
B. Dinneen, SP	9
J. Gettman, OF	9
D. McGuire, C	8
F. Killen, SP	7
J. Smith, 3B	7
Z. Wrigley, SS	7
J. Doyle, 1B	4
B. Freeman, OF	4
K. Baker, SP	3
R. Evans, SP	3
C. Swaim, SP	3
D. Casey, 3B	2
W. Donovan, OF	2
B. Myers, 3B	2
T. Leahy, 3B	1
B. Wagner, 3B	1

1899 National League

Baltimore (86-62)	**WS**
Hitting	**105.3**
Fielding	**49.2**
Pitching	**103.5**
J. McGinnity, SP	35
J. McGraw, 3B	34
F. Kitson, SP	31
J. Sheckard, OF	21
D. Holmes, OF	20
B. Keister, SS	18
J. Nops, SP	17
S. Brodie, OF	15
H. Howell, SP	14
C. LaChance, 1B	11
G. Magoon, SS	7
G. DeMontreville, 2B	6
W. Robinson, C	6
D. Fultz, OF	5
B. Hill, SP	5
A. Smith, C	5
P. Crisham, 1B	2
R. Miller, SP	2
J. O'Brien, 2B	2
C. Harris, 3B	1
K. McKenna, SP-RP	1

Boston (95-57)	**WS**
Hitting	**115.5**
Fielding	**49.5**
Pitching	**120.0**

V. Willis, SP	39
C. Stahl, OF	32
K. Nichols, SP	31
F. Tenney, 1B	25
J. Collins, 3B	23
T. Lewis, SP	20
H. Duffy, OF	17
H. Long, SS	16
B. Hamilton, OF	15
B. Lowe, 2B	13
J. Meekin, SP	10
C. Hickman, SP	9
H. Bailey, SP	7
M. Bergen, C	5
C. Frisbee, OF	5
F. Killen, SP	5
G. Stafford, OF	5
B. Clarke, C	2
F. Klobedanz, SP	2
B. Sullivan, C	2
B. Ging, SP	1
M. Sullivan, SP	1

Brooklyn (101-47)	WS
Hitting	**144.3**
Fielding	**48.6**
Pitching	**110.1**
J. Hughes, SP	33
J. Kelley, OF	30
W. Keeler, OF	29
T. Daly, 2B	28
B. Kennedy, SP	28
J. Dunn, SP	24
B. Dahlen, SS	23
D. McJames, SP	19
D. Farrell, C	15
F. Jones, OF	14
J. Anderson, OF	12
D. Casey, 3B	11
H. Jennings, 1B	9
D. McGuire, C	8
D. McGann, 1B	7
J. Yeager, SS	3
B. Hill, SP-RP	2
W. Donovan, RP	1
W. Gaston, RP	1
J. Grim, C	1
A. Maul, SP	1
D. McFarlan, RP	1
B. Reidy, SP-RP	1
A. Smith, C	1
Z. Wrigley, SS	1

Chicago (75-73)	WS
Hitting	**110.4**
Fielding	**35.8**
Pitching	**78.9**
C. Griffith, SP	25
N. Callahan, SP	23
J. Taylor, SP	21
B. Lange, OF	19
S. Mertes, OF	18
J. Ryan, OF	17
D. Green, OF	15
B. Everitt, 1B	14
N. Garvin, SP	12
H. Wolverton, 3B	11
G. DeMontreville, SS	9
B. McCormick, 2B	9
T. Donahue, C	8
F. Chance, C	7
B. Bradley, 3B	5
G. Magoon, SS	4
D. Cogan, SP	2
J. Connor, 2B	2
B. Phyle, SP	2
A. Nichols, C	1
S. Roach, SP	1

Cincinnati (83-67)	WS
Hitting	**107.1**
Fielding	**49.3**
Pitching	**92.6**
N. Hahn, SP	29
K. Selbach, OF	23
J. Beckley, 1B	20
T. Breitenstein, SP	19
B. Phillips, SP	17
T. Corcoran, SS	16
P. Hawley, SP	14
B. McPhee, 2B	12
E. Smith, OF	12
A. McBride, OF	11
H. Peitz, C	11
J. Taylor, SP	10
H. Steinfeldt, 3B	9
B. Wood, C	9
C. Irwin, 3B	6
J. Barrett, OF	5
D. Miller, OF	5
S. Crawford, OF	4
K. Elberfeld, SS	4
E. Frisk, SP	4
B. Dammann, SP	2
J. Cronin, SP	1
F. Dwyer, SP	1
L. Houtz, OF	1
M. Kahoe, C	1
S. Seybold, OF	1
J. Stenzel, OF	1
F. Vaughn, 1B	1

Cleveland (20-134)	WS
Hitting	**13.2**
Fielding	**18.7**
Pitching	**28.1**
J. Hughey, SP	9
C. Knepper, SP	6
J. Quinn, 2B	5
T. Dowd, OF	4
S. Sullivan, 3B	4
K. Carsey, SP	3
H. Lochhead, SS	3
C. Schmit, SP	3
J. Sugden, C	3
L. Cross, 3B	2
D. Harley, OF	2
J. Harper, SP	2
B. Hill, SP	2
O. Schreckengost, C	2
W. Sudhoff, SP	2
T. Tucker, 1B	2
F. Bates, SP	1
J. Duncan, 1B	1
C. Hemphill, OF	1
S. McAllister, OF	1
J. Stivetts, SP-OF	1
C. Zimmer, C	1

Louisville (75-77)	WS
Hitting	**96.9**
Fielding	**39.9**
Pitching	**88.2**
H. Wagner, 3B	26
F. Clarke, OF	25
D. Phillippe, SP	23
B. Cunningham, SP	21
P. Dowling, SP	20
D. Hoy, OF	20
C. Ritchey, 2B	15
T. Leach, 3B	13
W. Woods, SP	12
B. Clingman, SS	10
C. Zimmer, C	9
R. Waddell, SP	7
C. Dexter, OF	4
M. Kelley, 1B	4
P. Flaherty, SP	3
M. Kittridge, C	3
G. Decker, 1B	2
M. Powers, C	2
C. Fauver, SP	1
T. Hartsel, OF	1
F. Ketcham, OF	1
T. Latimer, C	1
B. Magee, SP	1
H. Wilhelm, SP	1

New York (60-90)	WS
Hitting	**93.3**
Fielding	**30.2**
Pitching	**56.5**
C. Seymour, SP	21
G. Davis, SS	20
G. Van Haltren, OF	18
T. O'Brien, OF	16
M. Grady, C	14
B. Carrick, SP	13
J. Doyle, 1B	12
E. Doheny, SP	10
K. Gleason, 2B	10
P. Wilson, C	8
P. Foster, OF	7
J. Warner, C	7
J. Meekin, SP	6
T. Colcolough, SP	5
C. Gettig, SP	5
F. Hartman, 3B	2
M. Tiernan, OF	2
P. Woodruff, OF	2
K. Carsey, 3B	1
S. Hardesty, SS	1

Philadelphia (94-58)	WS
Hitting	**151.2**
Fielding	**42.0**
Pitching	**88.8**
E. Delahanty, OF	41
R. Thomas, OF	30
E. Flick, OF	23
W. Piatt, SP	21
E. McFarland, C	20
R. Donahue, SP	19
C. Fraser, SP	19
N. Lajoie, 2B	19
M. Cross, SS	18
A. Orth, SP	14
P. Chiles, OF	12
B. Lauder, 3B	11
B. Bernhard, SP	10
D. Cooley, 1B	9
K. Douglass, C	6
J. Fifield, SP	4
J. Dolan, 2B	3
B. Goeckel, 1B	1
B. Magee, SP	1
G. Wheeler, SP	1

Pittsburgh (76-73)	WS
Hitting	**105.7**
Fielding	**41.4**
Pitching	**80.9**
J. Williams, 3B	32
S. Leever, SP	27
J. Tannehill, SP	27
G. Beaumont, OF	20
J. McCarthy, OF	17
T. McCreery, OF	16
B. Ely, SS	10
P. Schriver, C	10
F. Bowerman, C	9
W. Clark, 1B	9
P. Donovan, OF	9
B. Hoffer, SP	9
T. Sparks, SP	9
J. Chesbro, SP	6
C. Gray, SP	4
A. Madison, 2B	3
J. O'Brien, 2B	3
H. Reitz, 2B	2
B. Rhines, SP	2
P. Dillon, 1B	1
P. Fox, 1B	1
H. Payne, SP	1
H. Smith, 2B	1

St. Louis (84-67)	WS
Hitting	**99.7**
Fielding	**46.6**
Pitching	**105.7**
C. Young, SP	35
J. Burkett, OF	30
J. Powell, SP	29
B. Wallace, SS	25
E. Heidrick, OF	19
L. Cross, 3B	15
N. Cuppy, SP	14
W. Sudhoff, SP	14
C. Childs, 2B	12
M. Donlin, OF	9
H. Blake, OF	7
L. Criger, C	7
C. Jones, SP	6
O. Schreckengost, 1B	5
E. McKean, SS	4
J. O'Connor, C	4
J. Stenzel, OF	4
P. McBride, SP	3
P. Tebeau, 1B	3
T. Thomas, SP-RP	2
F. Bates, RP	1
F. Buelow, C	1
T. Flood, 2B	1
C. Hemphill, OF	1
Z. Wilson, RP	1

Washington (54-98)	WS
Hitting	**100.2**
Fielding	**24.7**
Pitching	**37.1**
B. Freeman, OF	25
W. Mercer, 3B	15
D. Padden, SS	15
B. Dinneen, SP	13
D. McGann, 1B	13
G. Weyhing, SP	12
J. Slagle, OF	11
J. O'Brien, OF	9
F. Bonner, 2B	7
P. Cassidy, 1B	6
S. Barry, OF	5
D. McFarlan, SP	5
D. McGuire, C	5
C. Atherton, 3B	3
F. Scheibeck, SS	3
M. Kittridge, C	2
G. Stafford, 2B	2
D. Butler, C	1
K. Carsey, SP	1
H. Davis, 1B	1
J. Duncan, C	1
R. Evans, SP	1
D. Farrell, C	1
J. Fifield, SP	1
L. Herring, RP	1
B. Hulen, SS	1
F. McManus, C	1
M. Roach, C	1

1900
National League

Boston (66-72)	WS
Hitting	**70.0**
Fielding	**46.0**
Pitching	**82.0**
B. Dinneen, SP	27
B. Hamilton, OF	23
J. Collins, 3B	18
K. Nichols, SP	18
C. Stahl, OF	15
T. Lewis, SP	13
H. Long, SS	13
V. Willis, SP	12
B. Freeman, OF	10
N. Cuppy, SP	9
B. Lowe, 2B	8
F. Tenney, 1B	7
B. Clarke, C	6
B. Sullivan, C	6
H. Duffy, OF	5
S. Barry, OF	4
T. Pittinger, SP	2
H. Bailey, RP	1
J. Clements, C	1

Brooklyn (82-54)	WS
Hitting	**117.3**
Fielding	**44.5**
Pitching	**84.2**
J. McGinnity, SP	30
B. Kennedy, SP	23
W. Keeler, OF	22
J. Kelley, OF	22
B. Dahlen, SS	21
F. Jones, OF	20
F. Kitson, SP	19
L. Cross, 3B	15
T. Daly, 2B	15
J. Sheckard, OF	15
H. Jennings, 1B	10
H. Howell, RP	9
D. McGuire, C	7
D. Farrell, C	6
J. Nops, SP	4
G. DeMontreville, 2B	3
G. Weyhing, SP	3
J. Dunn, SP	2

Chicago (65-75)	WS
Hitting	**86.9**
Fielding	**32.5**
Pitching	**75.6**
C. Griffith, SP	19
S. Mertes, OF	18
N. Garvin, SP	17
B. Bradley, 3B	16
J. Taylor, SP	16
N. Callahan, SP	14
D. Green, OF	14
C. Childs, 2B	12
J. McCarthy, OF	12
J. Ryan, OF	12
F. Chance, C	7
J. Ganzel, 1B	7
B. McCormick, SS	6
J. Menefee, SP	6
T. Donahue, C	4
B. Clingman, SS	2
B. Cunningham, SP	2
F. Killen, SP	2
S. Strang, 3B	2
C. Dexter, C	1
C. Dolan, OF	1
M. Eason, SP	1
B. Everitt, 1B	1
E. Harvey, RP	1
L. Hughes, SP	1
J. Kling, C	1

Cincinnati (62-77)	WS
Hitting	**92.1**
Fielding	**31.9**
Pitching	**62.0**
J. Barrett, OF	23
J. Beckley, 1B	21
N. Hahn, SP	21
E. Scott, SP	14
S. Crawford, OF	12
H. Steinfeldt, 3B	11
T. Breitenstein, SP	10
D. Newton, SP	10
T. Corcoran, SS	9
A. McBride, OF	9
H. Peitz, C	9
C. Irwin, 3B	8
B. Phillips, SP	7
J. Quinn, 2B	5
E. Smith, OF	5
T. Hartsel, OF	3
M. Kahoe, C	3
B. Wood, C	3
P. Geier, OF	2
D. Harley, OF	1

New York (60-78)	WS
Hitting	**100.0**
Fielding	**25.3**
Pitching	**54.7**
K. Selbach, OF	27
G. Van Haltren, OF	21
W. Mercer, SP	20
G. Davis, SS	18
P. Hawley, SP	18
B. Carrick, SP	17
C. Hickman, 3B	16
J. Doyle, 1B	9
E. Smith, OF	6
K. Gleason, 2B	5
M. Grady, C	5
L. Taylor, SP	5
F. Bowerman, C	4
P. Foster, OF	2
D. Murphy, 2B	2
J. Warner, C	2
C. Bernard, OF	1
E. Doheny, SP	1
C. Seymour, SP	1

Philadelphia (75-63)	WS
Hitting	**126.0**
Fielding	**33.7**
Pitching	**65.3**
E. Flick, OF	32
R. Thomas, OF	25
N. Lajoie, 2B	22
E. Delahanty, 1B	19
A. Orth, SP	18
C. Fraser, SP	17
J. Slagle, OF	15
R. Donahue, SP	14
E. McFarland, C	14
B. Bernhard, SP	9
H. Wolverton, 3B	9
M. Cross, SS	8
K. Douglass, C	6
W. Piatt, SP	6
J. Dunn, SP	4
J. Dolan, 3B	3
P. Chiles, 1B	1
A. Maul, SP	1
W. McLaughlin, RP	1
M. Murphy, C	1

Pittsburgh (79-60)	WS
Hitting	**97.2**
Fielding	**45.3**
Pitching	**94.5**
H. Wagner, OF	34
D. Phillippe, SP	23
J. Tannehill, SP	23
S. Leever, SP	20
F. Clarke, OF	18
C. Ritchey, 2B	16
R. Waddell, SP	16
J. Williams, 3B	15
G. Beaumont, OF	14
J. Chesbro, SP	14
B. Ely, SS	11
T. O'Brien, 1B	11
C. Zimmer, C	10
T. Leach, 3B	3
P. Schriver, C	3
T. McCreery, OF	2
E. Poole, RP-OF	2
D. Cooley, 1B	1
J. O'Connor, C	1

St. Louis (65-75)	WS
Hitting	**109.5**
Fielding	**26.7**
Pitching	**58.7**
J. Burkett, OF	25
C. Young, SP	22
J. McGraw, 3B	21
J. Powell, SP	14
P. Donovan, OF	13
C. Jones, SP	13
B. Keister, 2B	13
D. McGann, 1B	13
B. Wallace, SS	13
M. Donlin, OF	10
E. Heidrick, OF	9
W. Sudhoff, SP	9
L. Criger, C	6
O. Krueger, 2B	3
W. Robinson, C	3
P. Dillard, OF	2
J. Hughey, SP	2
J. Quinn, 2B	2
L. Cross, 3B	1
T. Thomas, RP	1

1901
American League

Baltimore (68-65)	WS
Hitting	**97.8**
Fielding	**33.2**
Pitching	**73.1**
J. McGinnity, SP	27
J. Williams, 2B	22
M. Donlin, OF	21
H. Howell, SP	19
B. Keister, SS	18
J. McGraw, 3B	16
F. Foreman, SP	15
C. Seymour, OF	14
J. Nops, SP	10
S. Brodie, OF	9
J. Dunn, 3B	8
R. Bresnahan, C	6
J. Jackson, OF	6
B. Hart, 1B	5
W. Robinson, C	5
F. Foutz, 1B	1
G. Rohe, 1B	1
C. Schmit, SP	1

Boston (79-57)	WS
Hitting	**107.9**
Fielding	**43.4**
Pitching	**85.7**
C. Young, SP	41
J. Collins, 3B	28
B. Freeman, 1B	24
C. Stahl, OF	24
F. Parent, SS	21
T. Lewis, SP	18
G. Winter, SP	16
T. Dowd, OF	15
H. Ferris, 2B	11
C. Hemphill, OF	11
O. Schreckengost, C	11
L. Criger, C	6
F. Mitchell, SP	5
N. Cuppy, SP	4
D. Morrissey, RP	1
G. Prentiss, SP-RP	1

Chicago (83-53)	WS
Hitting	**120.2**
Fielding	**42.8**
Pitching	**86.1**
C. Griffith, SP	27
D. Hoy, OF	25
N. Callahan, SP	23
F. Jones, OF	23
H. McFarland, OF	21
S. Mertes, 2B	21
R. Patterson, SP	20
F. Hartman, 3B	19
F. Isbell, 1B	13
J. Katoll, SP	12
F. Shugart, SS	10
B. Sullivan, C	9
J. Skopec, SP	6
E. Harvey, SP	5
J. Sugden, C	5
J. Burke, SS	4
W. Piatt, SP	3
P. Foster, OF	2
D. Brain, 2B	1

Cleveland (54-82)	WS
Hitting	**87.1**
Fielding	**27.1**
Pitching	**47.8**
O. Pickering, OF	22
B. Bradley, 3B	19
E. Moore, SP	16
E. Beck, 2B	14
C. LaChance, 1B	12
P. Dowling, SP	11
J. McCarthy, OF	11
B. Wood, C	11
E. Harvey, OF	8
J. O'Brien, OF	8
B. Hart, SP	7
E. Scott, SP	6
B. Hoffer, SP	3
H. McNeal, SP	3
B. Cristall, SP	2
F. Scheibeck, SS	2
J. Bracken, SP	1
D. Braggins, SP	1
J. Connor, C	1
F. Genins, OF	1
J. McGuire, SS	1
D. Shay, SS	1
G. Yeager, C	1

Detroit (74-61)	WS
Hitting	**88.7**
Fielding	**42.6**
Pitching	**90.8**
R. Miller, SP	30
J. Barrett, OF	23
K. Elberfeld, SS	22
E. Siever, SP	22
J. Yeager, SP	21
D. Holmes, OF	16
D. Casey, 3B	15
J. Cronin, SP	15
K. Gleason, 2B	15
D. Nance, OF	13
S. McAllister, C	8
P. Dillon, 1B	6
E. Frisk, SP	5
F. Buelow, C	3
A. Shaw, C	3
D. Crockett, 1B	2
F. Owen, SP	2
E. High, RP	1

Milwaukee (48-89)	WS
Hitting	**68.6**
Fielding	**25.4**
Pitching	**50.0**
J. Anderson, 1B	20
B. Reidy, SP	14
W. Conroy, SS	13
N. Garvin, SP	12
B. Gilbert, 2B	9
B. Husting, SP	9
H. Duffy, OF	8
T. Sparks, SP	8
B. Friel, 3B	7
P. Hawley, SP	7
B. Maloney, C	7
B. Hallman, OF	6
I. Waldron, OF	6
J. Donahue, C	4
G. Hogriever, OF	4
T. Leahy, C	3
J. Connor, C	2
G. Bone, SS	1
J. Burke, 3B	1
P. Dowling, RP	1
P. Geier, OF	1
D. Jones, OF	1

Philadelphia (74-62)	WS
Hitting	**118.4**
Fielding	**34.1**
Pitching	**69.5**

N. Lajoie, 2B	42
S. Seybold, OF	21
L. Cross, 3B	19
C. Fraser, SP	19
E. Plank, SP	19
H. Davis, 1B	17
S. Wiltse, SP	15
D. Fultz, OF	14
B. Bernhard, SP	13
M. Powers, C	10
M. McIntyre, OF	8
J. Dolan, SS	6
W. Piatt, SP	5
P. Geier, OF	3
J. Hayden, OF	3
B. Ely, SS	2
B. Milligan, SP-RP	2
F. Steelman, C	2
T. Leahy, OF	1
H. Smith, C	1

Washington (61-72)	WS
Hitting	**89.9**
Fielding	**31.7**
Pitching	**61.4**
B. Carrick, SP	18
S. Dungan, OF	17
J. Farrell, 2B	17
B. Coughlin, 3B	15
M. Grady, 1B	14
W. Lee, SP	14
C. Patten, SP	14
B. Clingman, SS	13
P. Foster, OF	13
W. Mercer, SP	13
B. Clarke, C	12
D. Gear, OF	9
I. Waldron, OF	9
J. Quinn, 2B	4
B. Everitt, 1B	1

1901 National League

Boston (69-69)	WS
Hitting	**49.8**
Fielding	**45.3**
Pitching	**111.9**
V. Willis, SP	33
K. Nichols, SP	32
B. Dinneen, SP	27
T. Pittinger, SP	21
B. Hamilton, OF	16
G. DeMontreville, 2B	15
M. Kittridge, C	10
F. Tenney, 1B	9
H. Long, SS	8
B. Lowe, 3B	8
J. Slagle, OF	7
D. Cooley, OF	5
F. Murphy, OF	4
B. Lawson, SP	3
F. Crolius, OF	2
P. Moran, C	2
P. Carney, OF	1
D. Gammons, OF	1
G. Grosart, OF	1
B. Lush, OF	1
J. Rickert, OF	1

Brooklyn (79-57)	WS
Hitting	**119.1**
Fielding	**40.3**
Pitching	**77.6**
J. Sheckard, OF	33
W. Donovan, SP	27
T. Daly, 2B	25
F. Kitson, SP	21
W. Keeler, OF	20
B. Dahlen, SS	18
J. Kelley, 1B	18
J. Hughes, SP	15
T. McCreery, OF	14
D. McGuire, C	10
D. Farrell, C	9
D. Newton, SP	8
C. Dolan, OF	5
B. Kennedy, SP	5
C. Irwin, 3B	3
F. Gatins, 3B	2
J. Gochnauer, SS	1
G. McCann, SP	1
D. McJames, SP	1
C. Wright, SP	1

Chicago (53-86)	WS
Hitting	**69.9**
Fielding	**28.5**
Pitching	**60.7**
T. Hartsel, OF	27
D. Green, OF	20
R. Waddell, SP	17
L. Hughes, SP	14
J. Taylor, SP	13
J. Menefee, OF	11
F. Chance, OF	9
M. Eason, SP	8
C. Dexter, 1B	7
B. McCormick, SS	7
C. Childs, 2B	6
J. Kling, C	5
P. Childs, 2B	4
M. Kahoe, C	3
F. Raymer, 3B	3
C. Dolan, OF	2
J. Doyle, 1B	1
L. Hoffman, 3B	1
G. Schaefer, 2B-3B	1

Cincinnati (52-87)	WS
Hitting	**87.3**
Fielding	**23.3**
Pitching	**45.4**
N. Hahn, SP	26
S. Crawford, OF	24
J. Beckley, 1B	18
G. Magoon, SS	12
H. Peitz, C	11
H. Steinfeldt, 3B	11
J. Dobbs, OF	10
D. Harley, OF	10
B. Phillips, SP	8
C. Irwin, 3B	5
A. Stimmel, SP	5
B. Bergen, C	4
D. Newton, SP	4
T. Corcoran, SS	2
L. Swormstedt, SP	2
H. Bay, OF	1
B. Fox, 2B	1
M. Kahoe, C	1
A. McBride, OF	1

New York (52-85)	WS
Hitting	**89.0**
Fielding	**23.1**
Pitching	**43.9**
G. Davis, SS	24
G. Van Haltren, OF	23
C. Mathewson, SP	21
S. Strang, 3B	20
K. Selbach, OF	15
L. Taylor, SP	14
C. Hickman, OF	12
A. McBride, OF	5
J. Warner, C	4
J. Ganzel, 1B	3
B. Phyle, SP	3
F. Bowerman, C	2
R. Denzer, SP	2
E. Doheny, SP	2
C. Bernard, OF	1
C. Buelow, 3B	1
J. Jones, OF	1
A. Smith, C	1
H. Smith, 2B	1
J. Wall, C	1

Philadelphia (83-57)	WS
Hitting	**107.1**
Fielding	**45.3**
Pitching	**96.6**
E. Delahanty, OF	33
E. Flick, OF	30
A. Orth, SP	29
R. Donahue, SP	24
R. Thomas, OF	24
B. Duggleby, SP	22
D. White, SP	16
H. Wolverton, 3B	15
E. McFarland, C	10
H. Jennings, 1B	8
J. Townsend, SP	8
M. Cross, SS	7
K. Douglass, C	7
B. Hallman, 2B	5
S. Barry, 2B	4
F. Jacklitsch, C	4
J. Slagle, OF	3

Pittsburgh (90-49)	WS
Hitting	**138.2**
Fielding	**42.4**
Pitching	**89.4**
H. Wagner, SS	37
F. Clarke, OF	28
G. Beaumont, OF	25
D. Phillippe, SP	25
J. Chesbro, SP	23
J. Tannehill, SP	22
L. Davis, OF	19
C. Ritchey, 2B	19
K. Bransfield, 1B	17
T. Leach, 3B	17
S. Leever, SP	11
E. Doheny, SP	6
C. Zimmer, C	5
E. Poole, SP-OF	4
B. Ely, SS	3
J. O'Connor, C	2
G. Yeager, C	2
J. Burke, 3B	1
L. Carr, SS	1
G. Merritt, SP	1
T. Turner, 3B	1
S. Wiltse, SP	1

St. Louis (76-64)	WS
Hitting	**138.6**
Fielding	**30.4**
Pitching	**59.0**
J. Burkett, OF	38
B. Wallace, SS	26
E. Heidrick, OF	23
O. Krueger, 3B	18
P. Donovan, OF	17
J. Powell, SP	17
J. Harper, SP	16
W. Sudhoff, SP	14
D. McGann, 1B	13
D. Padden, 2B	13
E. Murphy, SP	6
A. Nichols, C	6
M. O'Neill, SP	5
P. Schriver, C	5
J. Ryan, C	3
P. Childs, 2B	2
S. Yerkes, SP	2
M. Heydon, C	1
C. Jones, SP	1
B. Magee, SP	1
B. Richardson, 1B	1

1902 American League

Baltimore (50-88)	WS
Hitting	**90.0**
Fielding	**23.1**
Pitching	**36.9**
J. Williams, 2B	19
K. Selbach, OF	16
H. Howell, SP-2B	13
B. Gilbert, SS	11
J. McGinnity, SP	11
H. McFarland, OF	10
J. Kelley, OF	8
D. McGann, 1B	7
W. Robinson, C	7
S. Wiltse, SP	7
R. Bresnahan, 3B	6
H. Arndt, OF	5
L. Hughes, SP	5
J. Cronin, SP	4
C. Seymour, OF	4
C. Shields, SP	4
J. Katoll, SP	3
J. McGraw, 3B	3
T. Jones, 1B	2
E. Courtney, 3B	1
J. Mathison, 3B	1
B. Mellor, 1B	1
A. Oyler, 3B	1
A. Smith, C	1

Boston (77-60)	WS
Hitting	**98.9**
Fielding	**44.0**
Pitching	**88.1**
C. Young, SP	38
B. Dinneen, SP	27
B. Freeman, OF	23
J. Collins, 3B	20
C. Stahl, OF	20
P. Dougherty, OF	17
F. Parent, SS	16
H. Ferris, 2B	12
G. Winter, SP	12
L. Criger, C	10
C. LaChance, 1B	9
T. Sparks, SP	7
J. Warner, C	6
C. Hickman, OF	4
L. Hughes, SP	4
H. Gleason, 3B	3
N. Altrock, SP	1
P. Deininger, SP-RP	1
G. Prentiss, SP	1

Chicago (74-60)	WS
Hitting	**105.9**
Fielding	**41.8**
Pitching	**74.3**
G. Davis, SS	26
F. Jones, OF	25
S. Strang, 3B	25
D. Green, OF	21
S. Mertes, OF	19
R. Patterson, SP	19
N. Callahan, SP	16
N. Garvin, SP	14
W. Piatt, SP	14
T. Daly, 2B	11
C. Griffith, SP	11
F. Isbell, 1B	9
E. McFarland, C	6
B. Sullivan, C	6

Cleveland (69-67)	WS
Hitting	**107.9**
Fielding	**34.0**
Pitching	**65.2**
B. Bradley, 3B	26
N. Lajoie, 2B	22
B. Bernhard, SP	19
C. Hickman, 1B	19
A. Joss, SP	17
E. Moore, SP	17
E. Flick, OF	15
H. Bay, OF	12

H. Bemis, C	11
J. McCarthy, OF	9
B. Wood, C	8
O. Pickering, OF	6
C. Wright, SP	5
G. Dorner, SP	4
J. Gochnauer, SS	4
J. Thoney, 2B	3
F. Bonner, 2B	2
E. Harvey, OF	2
L. Taylor, SP	2
C. Hemphill, OF	1
H. O'Hagen, 1B	1
O. Schreckengost, 1B	1
C. Smith, SP	1

Detroit (52-83)	WS
Hitting	**61.8**
Fielding	**31.1**
Pitching	**63.1**
J. Barrett, OF	22
W. Mercer, SP	19
G. Mullin, SP	16
E. Siever, SP	16
K. Elberfeld, SS	15
D. Casey, 3B	14
D. Harley, OF	11
D. Holmes, OF	7
R. Miller, SP	7
K. Gleason, 2B	6
J. Yeager, SP	6
D. McGuire, C	4
E. Beck, 1B	3
R. Kisinger, SP	3
F. Buelow, C	2
P. Dillon, 1B	1
W. Egan, SP	1
P. LePine, OF	1
S. McAllister, 1B	1
S. McMackin, SP	1

Philadelphia (83-53)	WS
Hitting	**117.4**
Fielding	**43.5**
Pitching	**88.1**
R. Waddell, SP	33
L. Cross, 3B	26
T. Hartsel, OF	25
E. Plank, SP	25
S. Seybold, OF	24
D. Fultz, OF	20
H. Davis, 1B	19
O. Schreckengost, C	13
B. Husting, SP	11
M. Cross, SS	10
D. Murphy, 2B	9
M. Powers, C	8
H. Wilson, SP	8
F. Mitchell, SP	5
S. Wiltse, SP	4
A. Coakley, SP	3
E. Flick, OF	2
B. Bernhard, SP	1
L. Castro, 2B	1
B. Duggleby, SP	1
F. Steelman, C-OF	1

St. Louis (78-58)	WS
Hitting	**87.3**
Fielding	**45.3**
Pitching	**101.4**
J. Powell, SP	31
R. Donahue, SP	30
J. Burkett, OF	25
B. Wallace, SS	22
C. Hemphill, OF	19
W. Sudhoff, SP	19
E. Heidrick, OF	16
J. Harper, SP	13
D. Padden, 2B	13
J. Anderson, 1B	12
B. McCormick, 3B	9
B. Reidy, SP	5
J. Sugden, C	5
M. Kahoe, C	4
B. Friel, OF	3
C. Shields, SP	3
J. Donahue, C	2
D. Jones, OF	2
B. Maloney, OF	1

Washington (61-75)	WS
Hitting	**108.8**
Fielding	**22.6**
Pitching	**51.6**
E. Delahanty, OF	31
A. Orth, SP	19
J. Ryan, OF	19
B. Coughlin, 3B	17
B. Keister, OF	15
C. Patten, SP	14
S. Carey, 1B	13
W. Lee, OF	11
J. Townsend, SP	9
B. Clarke, C	8
B. Carrick, SP	7
L. Drill, C	6
J. Doyle, 2B	5
B. Ely, SS	5
H. Wolverton, 3B	4

1902
National League

Boston (73-64)	WS
Hitting	**107.8**
Fielding	**37.7**
Pitching	**73.5**
V. Willis, SP	29
F. Tenney, 1B	25
T. Pittinger, SP	24
D. Cooley, OF	20
E. Gremminger, 3B	19
P. Carney, OF	17
B. Lush, OF	14
H. Long, SS	13
G. DeMontreville, 2B	10
M. Eason, SP	10
M. Kittridge, C	9
J. Malarkey, SP	9
P. Moran, C	9
C. Dexter, SS	6
E. Courtney, OF	2
S. Curran, RP	1
F. Klobedanz, SP	1
R. Long, SP	1

Brooklyn (75-63)	WS
Hitting	**111.4**
Fielding	**38.3**
Pitching	**75.3**
J. Sheckard, OF	25
W. Keeler, OF	24
B. Dahlen, SS	23
F. Kitson, SP	20
C. Dolan, OF	19
W. Donovan, SP	18
C. Irwin, 3B	18
D. Newton, SP	18
J. Hughes, SP	15
T. McCreery, 1B	10
H. Hearne, C	8
T. Flood, 2B	7
R. Evans, SP	6
D. Farrell, C	5
N. Garvin, SP	2
P. Deisel, C	1
G. Hildebrand, OF	1
G. McCann, SP	1
J. McMakin, SP	1
L. Ritter, C	1
R. Ward, OF	1
E. Wheeler, 3B	1

Chicago (68-69)	WS
Hitting	**87.0**
Fielding	**37.5**
Pitching	**79.6**
J. Taylor, SP	32
J. Slagle, OF	23
J. Kling, C	17
J. Tinker, SS	17
J. Menefee, OF	14
P. Williams, SP	14
F. Chance, 1B	13
D. Jones, OF	12
B. Lowe, 2B	10
C. Lundgren, SP	10
J. Dobbs, OF	8
J. St. Vrain, SP	6
C. Dexter, 3B	4
D. Miller, OF	4
B. Rhoads, SP	3
A. Williams, OF	3
B. Congalton, OF	2
D. Morrissey, SP	2
H. Schlafly, OF	2
M. Eason, SP	1
J. Evers, 2B	1
J. Gardner, SP	1
A. Hardy, SP	1
J. Hendricks, OF	1
H. O'Hagen, 1B	1
G. Schaefer, 3B	1
S. Strang, 2B-3B	1

Cincinnati (70-70)	WS
Hitting	**99.8**
Fielding	**37.4**
Pitching	**72.7**
N. Hahn, SP	29
S. Crawford, OF	23
B. Phillips, SP	20
J. Beckley, 1B	18
H. Peitz, 2B	15
H. Steinfeldt, 3B	14
E. Poole, SP	11
D. Hoy, OF	10
C. Seymour, OF	10
J. Dobbs, OF	8
H. Thielman, SP	8
T. Corcoran, SS	7
J. Kelley, OF	7
E. Beck, 2B	5
B. Bergen, C	5
M. Donlin, OF	4
B. Ewing, SP	4
G. Magoon, 2B	4
C. Currie, SP	2
C. Heismann, SP	2
H. Bay, OF	1
B. Maloney, OF	1
J. Morrissey, 2B	1
A. Stimmel, SP	1

New York (48-88)	WS
Hitting	**43.1**
Fielding	**33.9**
Pitching	**67.0**
C. Mathewson, SP	22
J. McGinnity, SP	12
S. Brodie, OF	11
L. Taylor, SP	11
R. Evans, SP	9
H. Smith, 2B	9
J. Cronin, SP	8
F. Bowerman, C	7
G. Browne, OF	7
D. McGann, 1B	7
R. Bresnahan, OF	6
J. Doyle, 1B	5
B. Lauder, 3B	5
J. McGraw, SS	4
T. Sparks, SP	4
J. Dunn, OF	3
J. Jones, OF	3
G. Van Haltren, OF	3
J. Bean, SS	1
J. Jackson, OF	1
B. Kennedy, SP	1
R. Miller, SP	1
H. O'Hagen, 1B	1
J. Wall, OF	1
L. Washburn, OF	1
G. Yeager, C	1

Philadelphia (56-81)	WS
Hitting	**72.8**
Fielding	**30.6**
Pitching	**64.7**
D. White, SP	27
R. Thomas, OF	25
S. Barry, OF	17
R. Hulswitt, SS	15
B. Duggleby, SP	14
C. Fraser, SP	13
H. Jennings, 1B	9
H. Iburg, SP	8
B. Hallman, 3B	7
G. Browne, OF	6
H. Wolverton, 3B	6
K. Douglass, 1B	5
R. Dooin, C	4
P. Childs, 2B	3
B. Magee, SP	3
C. Vorhees, SP-RP	3
P. Greene, 3B	1
F. Jacklitsch, C	1
H. Krug, OF	1

Pittsburgh (103-36)	WS
Hitting	**163.0**
Fielding	**46.0**
Pitching	**100.1**
H. Wagner, OF	35
G. Beaumont, OF	31
F. Clarke, OF	29
T. Leach, 3B	27
J. Chesbro, SP	25
J. Tannehill, SP	24
D. Phillippe, SP	23
S. Leever, SP	17
C. Ritchey, 2B	17
K. Bransfield, 1B	15
E. Doheny, SP	14
W. Conroy, SS	12
L. Davis, OF	10
J. Burke, 2B	9
J. O'Connor, C	5
C. Zimmer, C	5
J. Sebring, OF	4
W. McLaughlin, SP	2
H. Smith, C	2
F. Crolius, OF	1
M. Hopkins, C	1
E. Phelps, C	1

St. Louis (56-78)	WS
Hitting	**105.7**
Fielding	**22.9**
Pitching	**39.4**
P. Donovan, OF	21
H. Smoot, OF	21
G. Barclay, OF	20
M. O'Neill, SP	18
J. Farrell, 2B	15
O. Krueger, SS	14
R. Brashear, 1B	11
A. Nichols, 1B	9
E. Murphy, SP	7
S. Yerkes, SP	7
C. Currie, SP	6
B. Wicker, SP	5
F. Hartman, 3B	3
J. Ryan, C	3
J. O'Neill, C	2
A. Pearson, SP	2
J. Calhoun, 3B	1
J. Hackett, SP	1

R. Kling, SS	1
J. Murphy, 3B	1

1903 American League

Boston (91-47)	WS
Hitting	**126.0**
Fielding	**45.6**
Pitching	**101.4**
C. Young, SP	38
P. Dougherty, OF	28
B. Dinneen, SP	27
J. Collins, 3B	26
F. Parent, SS	26
B. Freeman, OF	24
L. Hughes, SP	23
H. Ferris, 2B	15
N. Gibson, SP	12
C. Stahl, OF	12
C. LaChance, 1B	10
L. Criger, C	9
G. Winter, SP	9
J. O'Brien, OF	5
D. Farrell, C	4
J. Stahl, C	4
A. Smith, C	1

Chicago (60-77)	WS
Hitting	**94.2**
Fielding	**28.7**
Pitching	**57.1**
D. Green, OF	26
D. White, SP	23
F. Jones, OF	20
R. Patterson, SP	17
N. Callahan, 3B	16
D. Holmes, OF	12
F. Isbell, 1B	9
L. Tannehill, SS	8
P. Flaherty, SP	7
B. Hallman, OF	6
G. Magoon, 2B	6
F. Owen, SP	6
N. Altrock, SP	5
T. Daly, 2B	4
E. McFarland, C	4
P. Clark, 3B	3
C. Dolan, 1B	3
D. Dunkle, SP	2
J. Slattery, C	2
B. Sullivan, C	1

Cleveland (77-63)	WS
Hitting	**129.6**
Fielding	**31.8**
Pitching	**69.6**
N. Lajoie, 2B	31
B. Bradley, 3B	29
E. Flick, OF	25
H. Bay, OF	21
C. Hickman, 1B	21
A. Joss, SP	20
E. Moore, SP	19
B. Bernhard, SP	12
J. McCarthy, OF	10
H. Bemis, C	9
R. Donahue, SP	7
F. Abbott, C	6
J. Stovall, SP	5
J. Gochnauer, SS	4
E. Killian, SP	4
B. Clingman, 2B	3
M. Glendon, SP	2
A. Pearson, SP	1
J. Thoney, OF	1
C. Wright, SP	1

Detroit (65-71)	WS
Hitting	**98.3**
Fielding	**31.5**
Pitching	**65.3**
J. Barrett, OF	26
S. Crawford, OF	25
G. Mullin, SP	23
W. Donovan, SP	22
B. Lush, OF	19
F. Kitson, SP	14
C. Carr, 1B	13
J. Yeager, 3B	9
K. Elberfeld, SS	8
D. McGuire, C	6
R. Kisinger, SP	5
S. McAllister, SS	5
H. Smith, 2B	5
H. Long, SS	4
F. Buelow, C	3
J. Deering, SP	2
D. Gessler, OF	2
J. Burns, 2B	1
E. Courtney, 3B	1
M. Eason, SP	1
J. Skopec, SP	1

New York (72-62)	WS
Hitting	**110.2**
Fielding	**34.4**
Pitching	**71.4**
J. Chesbro, SP	22
J. Williams, 2B	22
W. Conroy, 3B	21
W. Keeler, OF	20
J. Ganzel, 1B	18
K. Elberfeld, SS	17
C. Griffith, SP	16
H. McFarland, OF	16
J. Tannehill, SP	15
H. Howell, SP	9
D. Fultz, OF	8
B. Wolfe, SP	8
L. Davis, OF	7
E. Courtney, SS	4
M. Beville, C	3
J. Deering, SP	2
J. O'Connor, C	2
A. Puttmann, SP	2
E. Bliss, RP	1
P. Greene, 3B	1
H. Long, SS	1
J. Zalusky, C	1

Philadelphia (75-60)	WS
Hitting	**103.9**
Fielding	**40.3**
Pitching	**80.9**
E. Plank, SP	28
R. Waddell, SP	27
S. Seybold, OF	22
T. Hartsel, OF	20
O. Pickering, OF	19
C. Bender, SP	18
M. Cross, SS	18
H. Davis, 1B	17
L. Cross, 3B	16
D. Murphy, 2B	14
O. Schreckengost, C	10
W. Henley, SP	6
M. Powers, C	5
D. Hoffman, OF	4
E. Pinnance, SP-RP	1

St. Louis (65-74)	WS
Hitting	**83.2**
Fielding	**36.1**
Pitching	**75.7**
W. Sudhoff, SP	25
J. Burkett, OF	22
J. Powell, SP	20
B. Wallace, SS	20
J. Anderson, 1B	19
E. Siever, SP	17
E. Heidrick, OF	16
R. Donahue, SP	8
C. Hemphill, OF	8
B. Friel, 2B	7
H. Hill, 3B	5
B. McCormick, 2B-3B	5
J. Sugden, C	5
M. Kahoe, C	4
B. Pelty, SP	3
P. Swander, OF	3
B. Bowcock, 2B	2
D. Padden, 2B	2
C. Wright, SP	2
J. Martin, OF	1
J. Terry, RP	1

Washington (43-94)	WS
Hitting	**42.0**
Fielding	**29.8**
Pitching	**57.2**
A. Orth, SP	15
C. Patten, SP	15
H. Wilson, SP	15
W. Lee, OF	13
K. Selbach, OF	11
B. Coughlin, 3B	9
J. Ryan, OF	9
C. Moran, SS	8
E. Delahanty, OF	6
R. Robinson, 2B	6
B. Clarke, 1B	5
L. Drill, C	4
D. Dunkle, SP	4
D. Holmes, OF	2
M. Kittridge, C	2
B. McCormick, 2B	2
J. Martin, 2B	1
C. Osteen, SS	1
J. Townsend, SP	1

1903 National League

Boston (58-80)	WS
Hitting	**78.5**
Fielding	**31.1**
Pitching	**64.5**
F. Tenney, 1B	21
V. Willis, SP	19
D. Cooley, OF	18
E. Gremminger, 3B	17
P. Moran, C	17
T. Pittinger, SP	17
J. Malarkey, SP	13
E. Abbaticchio, 2B	10
W. Piatt, SP	10
C. Dexter, OF	9
P. Carney, OF	8
J. Stanley, OF	6
P. Williams, SP	3
M. Kittridge, C	2
T. McCreery, OF	2
H. Aubrey, SS	1
F. Bonner, 2B	1

Brooklyn (70-66)	WS
Hitting	**102.1**
Fielding	**36.9**
Pitching	**70.9**
J. Sheckard, OF	33
B. Dahlen, SS	23
O. Jones, SP	23
J. Doyle, 1B	19
S. Strang, 3B	19
H. Schmidt, SP	18
N. Garvin, SP	17
J. Dobbs, OF	10
F. Jacklitsch, C	7
J. McCredie, OF	7
B. Reidy, SP	6
R. Evans, SP	5
T. Flood, 2B	4
D. Gessler, OF	4
L. Ritter, C	4
D. Jordan, 2B	3
T. McCreery, OF	3
H. Hearne, C	2
G. Thatcher, SP	2
H. Thielman, OF	1

Chicago (82-56)	WS
Hitting	**122.9**
Fielding	**38.7**
Pitching	**84.4**
F. Chance, 1B	31
J. Slagle, OF	25
J. Taylor, SP	25
J. Weimer, SP	23
J. Kling, C	22
J. Tinker, SS	21
B. Wicker, SP	19
D. Jones, OF	17
J. Evers, 2B	15
C. Lundgren, SP	11
D. Casey, 3B	9
D. Harley, OF	9
J. Menefee, SP	7
B. Lowe, 2B	3
C. Currie, SP-RP	2
J. Dobbs, OF	2
J. McCarthy, OF	2
O. Williams, SS	2
T. Raub, C	1

Cincinnati (74-65)	WS
Hitting	**106.1**
Fielding	**37.7**
Pitching	**78.2**
M. Donlin, OF	24
N. Hahn, SP	24
C. Seymour, OF	24
H. Steinfeldt, 3B	21
B. Ewing, SP	18
J. Beckley, 1B	17
J. Sutthoff, SP	16
J. Kelley, OF	15
E. Poole, SP	10
H. Peitz, C	9
T. Corcoran, SS	8
T. Daly, 2B	8
C. Dolan, OF	8
J. Harper, SP	6
B. Phillips, SP	6
B. Bergen, C	2
G. Magoon, 2B	2
C. DeArmond, 3B	1
L. Fohl, C	1
D. Kerwin, OF	1
J. Morrissey, 2B	1

New York (84-55)	WS
Hitting	**105.8**
Fielding	**46.0**
Pitching	**100.2**
J. McGinnity, SP	40
C. Mathewson, SP	37
R. Bresnahan, OF	27
S. Mertes, OF	26
G. Browne, OF	19
C. Babb, SS	16
B. Gilbert, 2B	13
D. McGann, 1B	12
L. Taylor, SP	11
J. Warner, C	11
B. Lauder, 3B	9
F. Bowerman, C	7
J. Cronin, SP	6
J. Dunn, SS	6
G. Van Haltren, OF	6
R. Miller, SP	4
R. Ames, SP	2

Philadelphia (49-86)	WS
Hitting	**84.1**
Fielding	**22.8**
Pitching	**40.2**
R. Thomas, OF	23
H. Wolverton, 3B	15

T. Sparks, SP	14
B. Keister, OF	13
S. Barry, OF	12
B. Duggleby, SP	10
K. Gleason, 2B	10
R. Hulswitt, SS	10
C. Fraser, SP	9
J. Titus, OF	7
K. Douglass, 1B	5
F. Mitchell, SP	5
F. Roth, C	5
R. Dooin, C	2
C. Zimmer, C	2
R. Brashear, 2B	1
F. Burchell, SP-RP	1
B. Hallman, 2B	1
J. McFetridge, SP	1
P. Williams, SP	1

Pittsburgh (91-49)	WS
Hitting	**135.5**
Fielding	**45.0**
Pitching	**92.5**
H. Wagner, SS	35
G. Beaumont, OF	28
S. Leever, SP	28
D. Phillippe, SP	27
F. Clarke, OF	25
T. Leach, 3B	21
C. Ritchey, 2B	21
J. Sebring, OF	16
E. Doheny, SP	15
B. Kennedy, SP	11
K. Bransfield, 1B	10
E. Phelps, C	8
O. Krueger, SS	7
K. Wilhelm, SP	5
B. Veil, SP-RP	4
H. Smith, C	3
L. Winham, SP	3
G. Thompson, SP	2
F. Carisch, C	1
G. Curtis, OF	1
C. Falkenberg, SP	1
A. Weaver, C	1

St. Louis (43-94)	WS
Hitting	**56.8**
Fielding	**24.1**
Pitching	**48.2**
J. Farrell, 2B	16
P. Donovan, OF	13
H. Smoot, OF	13
T. Brown, SP	12
J. Burke, 3B	11
C. McFarland, SP	11
D. Brain, SS	7
J. Dunleavy, OF	7
C. Currie, SP	5
J. Hackett, 1B	5
E. Murphy, SP	5
J. O'Neill, C	5
G. Barclay, OF	4
M. O'Neill, SP	4
B. Rhoads, SP	3
L. DeMontreville, SS	2
J. Ryan, C	2
C. Moran, SP	1
A. Weaver, C	1
B. Wicker, RP	1
O. Williams, SS	1

1904 American League

Boston (95-59)	WS
Hitting	**125.7**
Fielding	**50.8**
Pitching	**108.5**
C. Young, SP	35
C. Stahl, OF	31
F. Parent, SS	29
J. Collins, 3B	28
B. Dinneen, SP	26
B. Freeman, OF	25
J. Tannehill, SP	25
K. Selbach, OF	17
N. Gibson, SP	16
H. Ferris, 2B	12
L. Criger, C	11
P. Dougherty, OF	9
G. Winter, SP	9
C. LaChance, 1B	7
D. Farrell, C	5

Chicago (89-65)	WS
Hitting	**130.4**
Fielding	**46.5**
Pitching	**90.0**
G. Davis, SS	28
D. Green, OF	27
F. Owen, SP	26
F. Jones, OF	22
N. Callahan, OF	17
F. Smith, SP	17
L. Tannehill, 3B	17
D. White, SP	17
N. Altrock, SP	16
D. Holmes, OF	16
J. Donahue, 1B	11
G. Dundon, 2B	10
R. Patterson, SP	10
B. Sullivan, C	9
E. McFarland, C	8
E. Walsh, RP	7
F. Isbell, 1B	5
P. Flaherty, SP	3
C. Jones, OF	1

Cleveland (86-65)	WS
Hitting	**133.7**
Fielding	**38.8**
Pitching	**85.5**
N. Lajoie, 2B	41
E. Flick, OF	31
B. Bradley, 3B	28
B. Bernhard, SP	22
R. Donahue, SP	18
H. Bay, OF	17
B. Lush, OF	17
A. Joss, SP	16
C. Hickman, 2B	14
E. Moore, SP	13
O. Hess, SP	9
B. Rhoads, SP	8
T. Turner, SS	8
H. Bemis, C	5
G. Stovall, 1B	5
R. Vinson, OF	3
F. Abbott, C	1
F. Buelow, C	1
C. Carr, 1B	1

Detroit (62-90)	WS
Hitting	**90.9**
Fielding	**33.1**
Pitching	**62.0**
J. Barrett, OF	26
G. Mullin, SP	25
S. Crawford, OF	21
W. Donovan, SP	19
E. Killian, SP	18
M. McIntyre, OF	17
R. Robinson, SS	11
F. Kitson, SP	7
C. O'Leary, SS	7
L. Drill, C	6
C. Hickman, 1B	5
B. Lowe, 2B	5
B. Wood, C	5
E. Gremminger, 3B	4
M. Beville, C	2
F. Buelow, C	2
C. Carr, 1B	2
B. Coughlin, 3B	2
F. Huelsman, OF	1
C. Jaeger, SP	1

New York (92-59)	WS
Hitting	**116.6**
Fielding	**49.6**
Pitching	**109.7**
J. Chesbro, SP	53
J. Powell, SP	29
W. Keeler, OF	25
J. Williams, 2B	20
J. Anderson, OF	19
W. Conroy, 3B	18
K. Elberfeld, SS	18
P. Dougherty, OF	15
J. Ganzel, 1B	15
D. Fultz, OF	14
A. Orth, SP	14
D. McGuire, C	8
C. Griffith, SP	7
L. Hughes, SP	5
R. Kleinow, C	4
A. Puttmann, RP	4
C. Osteen, 3B	2
M. Beville, 1B	1
W. Clarkson, RP	1
O. Collins, OF	1
N. Garvin, SP	1
J. Thoney, 3B	1
B. Wolfe, RP	1

Philadelphia (81-70)	WS
Hitting	**110.9**
Fielding	**42.0**
Pitching	**90.1**
R. Waddell, SP	32
E. Plank, SP	29
D. Murphy, 2B	26
L. Cross, 3B	21
H. Davis, 1B	21
T. Hartsel, OF	21
S. Seybold, OF	21
W. Henley, SP	16
C. Bender, SP	11
M. Cross, SS	10
O. Pickering, OF	10
D. Hoffman, OF	9
A. Coakley, SP	5
O. Schreckengost, C	4
L. Bruce, OF	2
J. Mullin, 1B	2
M. Powers, C	2
P. Noonan, C	1

St. Louis (65-87)	WS
Hitting	**89.9**
Fielding	**34.7**
Pitching	**70.4**
J. Burkett, OF	25
B. Wallace, SS	23
H. Howell, SP	22
F. Glade, SP	21
E. Heidrick, OF	17
D. Padden, 2B	15
B. Pelty, SP	15
J. Sugden, C	13
C. Hemphill, OF	12
T. Jones, 1B	10
E. Siever, SP	8
M. Kahoe, C	4
W. Sudhoff, SP	4
H. Gleason, 3B-SS	1
F. Huelsman, OF	1
P. Hynes, OF	1
C. Moran, 3B	1
C. Morgan, RP	1
J. O'Connor, C	1

Washington (38-113)	WS
Hitting	**78.6**
Fielding	**14.2**
Pitching	**21.3**
J. Stahl, 1B	18
J. Cassidy, SS	11
F. Huelsman, OF	9
K. Selbach, OF	9
B. Coughlin, 3B	8
L. Drill, C	8
C. Patten, SP	8
B. O'Neill, OF	7
B. Jacobson, SP	4
B. McCormick, 2B	4
C. Moran, SS	4
J. Townsend, SP	4
B. Clarke, C	3
P. Donovan, OF	3
L. Hughes, SP	3
M. Kittridge, C	3
B. Wolfe, SP	3
J. Thoney, OF	2
H. Hill, 3B	1
J. Mullin, 2B	1
A. Orth, OF	1

1904 National League

Boston (55-98)	WS
Hitting	**84.4**
Fielding	**26.9**
Pitching	**53.7**
J. Delahanty, 3B	20
T. Pittinger, SP	19
F. Tenney, 1B	19
V. Willis, SP	19
E. Abbaticchio, SS	18
D. Cooley, OF	14
P. Geier, OF	12
K. Wilhelm, SP	11
P. Moran, C	9
T. Needham, C	9
R. Cannell, OF	3
T. Fisher, SP	3
F. Raymer, 2B	3
E. McNichol, SP	2
G. Barclay, OF	1
P. Carney, OF	1
B. Lauterborn, 2B	1
D. Marshall, C	1

Brooklyn (56-97)	WS
Hitting	**70.9**
Fielding	**33.7**
Pitching	**63.4**
H. Lumley, OF	20
C. Babb, SS	18
O. Jones, SP	18
J. Cronin, SP	15
D. Gessler, OF	11
J. Sheckard, OF	11
P. Dillon, 1B	10
N. Garvin, SP	10
L. Ritter, C	7
D. Scanlan, SP	7
J. Dobbs, OF	6
M. McCormick, 3B	6
E. Poole, SP	6
B. Bergen, C	5
D. Reisling, SP	4
S. Strang, 2B	4
E. Batch, 3B	2
F. Jacklitsch, 1B	2
F. Mitchell, SP	2
J. Doscher, RP	1
J. Doyle, 1B	1
B. Durham, SP	1
D. Jordan, 2B	1

Chicago (93-60)	WS
Hitting	**115.9**
Fielding	**50.5**
Pitching	**112.5**
F. Chance, 1B	29

J. Weimer, SP	28
B. Briggs, SP	24
T. Brown, SP	20
J. Evers, 2B	20
J. Tinker, SS	20
C. Lundgren, SP	19
J. Slagle, OF	19
B. Wicker, SP	17
D. Casey, 3B	16
D. Jones, OF	14
J. McCarthy, OF	13
J. Kling, C	10
S. Barry, OF	8
F. Corridon, SP	6
W. Schulte, OF	5
H. McChesney, OF	3
J. O'Neill, C	3
O. Williams, OF	3
S. Hofman, OF	1
A. Smith, OF	1

Cincinnati (88-65)	WS
Hitting	**107.2**
Fielding	**50.8**
Pitching	**106.0**
C. Seymour, OF	26
N. Hahn, SP	25
J. Harper, SP	24
M. Huggins, 2B	20
F. Odwell, OF	19
B. Ewing, SP	17
W. Kellum, SP	17
T. Walker, SP	17
C. Dolan, OF	16
J. Kelley, 1B	16
M. Donlin, OF	13
T. Corcoran, SS	12
A. Schlei, C	9
H. Steinfeldt, 3B	9
H. Peitz, C	7
J. Sutthoff, SP	5
C. Elliott, SP	4
J. Sebring, OF	4
S. Woodruff, 3B	3
G. Street, C	1

New York (106-47)	WS
Hitting	**149.8**
Fielding	**51.2**
Pitching	**117.0**
J. McGinnity, SP	42
C. Mathewson, SP	34
S. Mertes, OF	27
B. Dahlen, SS	25
A. Devlin, 3B	25
R. Bresnahan, OF	23
D. McGann, 1B	22
L. Taylor, SP	22
G. Browne, OF	20
B. Gilbert, 2B	19
H. Wiltse, SP	13
F. Bowerman, C	9
J. Dunn, 3B	9
R. Ames, SP	8
M. McCormick, OF	8
M. Donlin, OF	5
J. Warner, C	5
D. Marshall, C	1
J. McGraw, 2B-SS	1

Philadelphia (52-100)	WS
Hitting	**111.2**
Fielding	**17.9**
Pitching	**26.9**
R. Thomas, OF	28
J. Titus, OF	21
K. Gleason, 2B	15
J. Lush, 1B	12
H. Wolverton, 3B	12
S. Magee, OF	11
R. Dooin, C	8
C. Fraser, SP	7
R. Hulswitt, SS	6
F. Roth, C	6
T. Sparks, SP	5
F. Corridon, SP	4
B. Duggleby, SP	4
J. Doyle, 1B	3
H. Duffy, OF	3
F. Mitchell, SP	3
J. Sutthoff, SP	3
R. Caldwell, SP	2
S. Barry, OF	1
J. McPherson, SP	1
D. Van Buren, OF	1

Pittsburgh (87-66)	WS
Hitting	**141.0**
Fielding	**40.1**
Pitching	**79.9**
H. Wagner, SS	43
T. Leach, 3B	25
G. Beaumont, OF	24
P. Flaherty, SP	22
S. Leever, SP	22
C. Ritchey, 2B	22
M. Lynch, SP	15
F. Clarke, OF	14
J. Sebring, OF	10
C. Case, SP	9
M. McCormick, OF	9
D. Phillippe, SP	7
K. Bransfield, 1B	6
E. Phelps, C	6
R. Miller, SP	5
C. Robitaille, SP	5
H. Smith, C	5
O. Krueger, OF	4
F. Carisch, C	3
J. Gilbert, OF	2
E. Diehl, OF	1
W. Lee, SP	1
J. Pfiester, SP	1

St. Louis (75-79)	WS
Hitting	**105.6**
Fielding	**38.0**
Pitching	**81.3**
K. Nichols, SP	27
J. Taylor, SP	27
J. Beckley, 1B	23
H. Smoot, OF	19
D. Brain, SS	18
M. Grady, C	17
M. O'Neill, SP	17
S. Shannon, OF	17
J. Farrell, 2B	16
D. Shay, SS	14
C. McFarland, SP	9
J. Burke, 3B	6
J. Dunleavy, OF	6
G. Barclay, OF	2
H. Hill, OF	2
J. McGinley, SP	2
J. Corbett, SP	1
S. Murch, 2B-3B	1
D. Zearfoss, C	1

1905
American League

Boston (78-74)	WS
Hitting	**115.9**
Fielding	**36.2**
Pitching	**81.8**
C. Young, SP	28
J. Tannehill, SP	26
J. Collins, 3B	23
J. Burkett, OF	22
K. Selbach, OF	17
C. Stahl, OF	17
G. Winter, SP	17
H. Ferris, 2B	15
F. Parent, SS	15
B. Freeman, 1B	13
L. Criger, C	11
B. Dinneen, SP	8
M. Grimshaw, 1B	6
C. Armbruster, C	3
J. Godwin, OF	3
E. Barry, SP	2
N. Gibson, SP	2
J. Harris, SP	2
B. Unglaub, 3B	2
D. Farrell, C	1
H. Olmsted, SP	1

Chicago (92-60)	WS
Hitting	**124.7**
Fielding	**50.7**
Pitching	**100.6**
F. Jones, OF	29
G. Davis, SS	28
N. Altrock, SP	24
J. Donahue, 1B	22
F. Owen, SP	22
F. Smith, SP	22
D. White, SP	22
F. Isbell, 2B	17
N. Callahan, OF	16
D. Green, OF	14
E. McFarland, C	13
L. Tannehill, 3B	13
E. Walsh, SP	8
B. Sullivan, C	7
G. Dundon, 2B	6
R. Patterson, SP	6
D. Holmes, OF	4
G. Rohe, 3B	3

Cleveland (76-78)	WS
Hitting	**114.6**
Fielding	**38.7**
Pitching	**74.7**
E. Flick, OF	29
A. Joss, SP	25
H. Bay, OF	23
B. Bradley, 3B	22
B. Rhoads, SP	17
T. Turner, SS	16
E. Moore, SP	15
O. Hess, OF	14
N. Lajoie, 2B	14
J. Jackson, OF	12
G. Stovall, 1B	11
H. Bemis, C	9
C. Carr, 1B	5
B. Bernhard, SP	4
R. Donahue, SP	4
F. Buelow, C	2
N. Clarke, C	2
B. Congalton, OF	2
J. Barbeau, 2B	1
N. Kahl, 2B	1

Detroit (79-74)	WS
Hitting	**114.9**
Fielding	**40.8**
Pitching	**81.4**
S. Crawford, OF	36
E. Killian, SP	29
G. Mullin, SP	26
W. Donovan, SP	20
M. McIntyre, OF	20
G. Schaefer, 2B	18
B. Coughlin, 3B	17
D. Cooley, OF	12
L. Drill, C	12
C. Lindsay, 1B	9
F. Kitson, SP	8
C. O'Leary, SS	7
C. Hickman, OF	5
T. Cobb, OF	4
J. Warner, C	3
G. Disch, RP	2
B. Lowe, OF	2
J. Barrett, OF	1
E. Cicotte, RP	1
N. Clarke, C	1
T. Doran, C	1
J. Eubank, SP	1
J. Sullivan, C	1
J. Wiggs, SP	1

New York (71-78)	WS
Hitting	**112.4**
Fielding	**32.9**
Pitching	**67.8**
J. Chesbro, SP	20
W. Keeler, OF	19
W. Conroy, 3B	18
A. Orth, SP	18
J. Williams, 2B	16
K. Elberfeld, SS	15
J. Yeager, 3B	15
P. Dougherty, OF	12
D. Fultz, OF	12
C. Griffith, RP	10
H. Chase, 1B	9
E. Hahn, OF	8
B. Hogg, SP	7
R. Kleinow, C	6
J. Powell, SP	6
D. McGuire, C	5
D. Newton, SP	4
J. Anderson, OF	3
F. LaPorte, 2B	3
R. Oldring, SS	3
A. Puttmann, SP	2
W. Clarkson, RP	1
L. LeRoy, SP	1

Philadelphia (92-56)	WS
Hitting	**115.3**
Fielding	**49.2**
Pitching	**111.4**
R. Waddell, SP	35
E. Plank, SP	31
T. Hartsel, OF	30
H. Davis, 1B	26
D. Murphy, 2B	23
A. Coakley, SP	21
S. Seybold, OF	21
D. Hoffman, OF	16
C. Bender, SP	15
L. Cross, 3B	15
O. Schreckengost, C	14
W. Henley, SP	10
M. Cross, SS	9
B. Lord, OF	5
J. Knight, SS	2
M. Powers, C	2
H. Barton, C	1

St. Louis (54-99)	WS
Hitting	**83.7**
Fielding	**25.5**
Pitching	**52.8**
G. Stone, OF	27
B. Wallace, SS	21
H. Howell, SP	20
E. Frisk, OF	13
B. Koehler, OF	12
B. Pelty, SP	11
F. Glade, SP	9
I. Rockenfield, 2B	8
W. Sudhoff, SP	8
H. Gleason, 3B	7
T. Jones, 1B	7
J. Sugden, C	4
I. Van Zandt, OF	4
J. Buchanan, SP	3
J. Powell, SP	2
F. Roth, C	2
T. Spencer, C	2
C. Moran, 2B	1
A. Weaver, C	1

Washington (64-87)	WS
Hitting	**90.6**
Fielding	**32.1**
Pitching	**69.3**

L. Hughes, SP	22
J. Stahl, 1B	21
F. Huelsman, OF	18
J. Anderson, OF	17
C. Hickman, 2B	16
J. Townsend, SP	14
C. Patten, SP	13
B. Wolfe, SP	11
J. Cassidy, SS	10
C. Jones, OF	9
M. Heydon, C	7
H. Hill, 3B	5
B. Jacobson, SP	5
R. Nill, 3B	5
M. Kittridge, C	4
C. Falkenberg, SP	3
P. Knoll, OF	3
J. Stanley, OF	3
R. Adams, SP	2
H. Hardy, SP	2
J. Mullin, 2B	1
H. Tate, OF	1

1905 National League

Boston (51-103)	WS
Hitting	**55.3**
Fielding	**32.0**
Pitching	**65.7**
I. Young, SP	29
C. Fraser, SP	19
F. Tenney, 1B	17
V. Willis, SP	17
E. Abbaticchio, SS	16
R. Cannell, OF	10
J. Delahanty, OF	10
C. Dolan, OF	10
H. Wolverton, 3B	8
P. Moran, C	7
T. Needham, C	5
F. Raymer, 2B	3
B. Lauterborn, 3B	1
B. Sharpe, OF	1

Brooklyn (48-104)	WS
Hitting	**80.0**
Fielding	**25.4**
Pitching	**38.6**
J. Sheckard, OF	21
H. Lumley, OF	17
D. Gessler, 1B	16
D. Scanlan, SP	12
E. Batch, 3B	11
H. McIntire, SP	10
J. Dobbs, OF	8
E. Stricklett, SP	8
P. Lewis, SS	7
C. Malay, 2B	5
L. Ritter, C	5
M. Eason, SP	4
J. Hummel, 2B	4
C. Babb, SS	3
B. Bergen, C	3
J. Doscher, SP	3
O. Jones, SP	3
B. Hall, OF	2
F. Mitchell, SP	1
R. Owens, 2B	1

Chicago (92-61)	WS
Hitting	**105.2**
Fielding	**50.2**
Pitching	**120.7**
E. Reulbach, SP	29
F. Chance, 1B	25
J. Slagle, OF	25
B. Maloney, OF	21
J. Weimer, SP	21
T. Brown, SP	20
J. Tinker, SS	18
B. Wicker, SP	17
W. Schulte, OF	16
C. Lundgren, SP	15
D. Casey, 3B	13
B. Briggs, SP	12
J. Evers, 2B	11
S. Hofman, 2B	8
J. Kling, C	8
B. Pfeffer, SP	7
J. McCarthy, OF	5
J. O'Neill, C	3
S. Barry, 1B	1
H. Lobert, 3B	1

Cincinnati (79-74)	WS
Hitting	**134.1**
Fielding	**34.2**
Pitching	**68.7**
C. Seymour, OF	42
M. Huggins, 2B	27
B. Ewing, SP	23
S. Barry, 1B	18
O. Overall, SP	17
T. Corcoran, SS	14
C. Chech, SP	13
H. Steinfeldt, 3B	13
F. Odwell, OF	11
J. Kelley, OF	10
A. Schlei, C	7
J. Sebring, OF	7
T. Walker, SP	7
J. Harper, SP	5
A. Bridwell, 3B	4
N. Hahn, SP	4
E. Phelps, C	4
B. Hinchman, OF	3
J. Siegle, OF	3
G. Street, C	3
C. Dolan, 1B	1
R. Vowinkel, SP	1

New York (105-48)	WS
Hitting	**161.4**
Fielding	**47.4**
Pitching	**106.1**
C. Mathewson, SP	39
M. Donlin, OF	36
S. Mertes, OF	25
B. Dahlen, SS	24
D. McGann, 1B	24
A. Devlin, 3B	23
J. McGinnity, SP	22
R. Bresnahan, C	19
H. Wiltse, SP	19
R. Ames, SP	17
G. Browne, OF	16
S. Strang, 2B	14
L. Taylor, SP	14
B. Gilbert, 2B	13
F. Bowerman, C	9
C. Elliott, RP	1

Philadelphia (83-69)	WS
Hitting	**116.9**
Fielding	**45.3**
Pitching	**86.9**
R. Thomas, OF	31
J. Titus, OF	29
S. Magee, OF	28
T. Sparks, SP	21
B. Duggleby, SP	20
T. Pittinger, SP	19
E. Courtney, 3B	17
M. Doolan, SS	17
K. Bransfield, 1B	13
K. Gleason, 2B	12
F. Corridon, SP	11
K. Nichols, SP	11
R. Dooin, C	10
F. Abbott, C	2
J. Lush, SP	2
J. Sutthoff, RP	2
H. Duffy, OF	1
M. Kahoe, C	1
H. Kane, SP	1
O. Krueger, SS	1

Pittsburgh (96-57)	WS
Hitting	**132.9**
Fielding	**50.2**
Pitching	**104.9**
H. Wagner, SS	46
D. Phillippe, SP	26
F. Clarke, OF	24
G. Beaumont, OF	19
S. Leever, SP	19
C. Case, SP	17
T. Leach, OF	17
C. Ritchey, 2B	17
D. Howard, 1B	15
O. Clymer, OF	12
D. Brain, 3B	11
P. Flaherty, SP	11
M. Lynch, SP	11
C. Robitaille, SP	8
H. Hillebrand, 1B	7
L. Leifield, SP	6
H. Peitz, C	5
B. Ganley, OF	4
G. Gibson, C	3
F. Carisch, C	2
B. Clancy, 1B	2
S. Flanagan, OF	1
E. Kinsella, SP	1
O. Knabe, 3B	1
G. McBride, 3B	1
F. Moore, RP	1
J. Wallace, OF	1

St. Louis (58-96)	WS
Hitting	**100.2**
Fielding	**25.2**
Pitching	**48.6**
H. Smoot, OF	23
J. Beckley, 1B	16
M. Grady, C	16
J. Taylor, SP	14
S. Shannon, OF	13
J. Thielman, SP	12
J. Dunleavy, OF	11
H. Arndt, 2B	8
B. Brown, SP	8
J. Burke, 3B	8
J. Clarke, OF	7
C. McFarland, SP	7
D. Shay, 2B-SS	7
W. Egan, SP	5
W. Kellum, SP	4
D. Brain, SS	3
G. McBride, SS	3
J. Warner, C	3
A. Hoelskoetter, 3B	2
R. DeGroff, OF	1
T. Leahy, C	1
S. McDougal, SP	1
D. Zearfoss, C	1

1906 American League

Boston (49-105)	WS
Hitting	**68.2**
Fielding	**25.4**
Pitching	**53.4**
C. Stahl, OF	21
M. Grimshaw, 1B	13
J. Tannehill, SP	13
C. Young, SP	13
B. Dinneen, SP	10
H. Ferris, 2B	10
F. Parent, SS	10
B. Freeman, OF	9
J. Harris, SP	6
R. Glaze, SP	5
J. Hayden, OF	5
G. Winter, SP	5
J. Collins, 3B	4
C. Graham, C	3
J. Hoey, OF	3
K. Selbach, OF	3
C. Armbruster, C	2
R. Morgan, 3B	2
B. Peterson, C	2
L. Swormstedt, SP	2
B. Carrigan, C	1
C. Chadbourne, 2B	1
J. Godwin, 3B	1
R. Kroh, SP	1
F. Oberlin, SP	1
H. Wagner, 2B	1

Chicago (93-58)	WS
Hitting	**135.0**
Fielding	**45.1**
Pitching	**98.9**
G. Davis, SS	29
F. Jones, OF	27
F. Isbell, 2B	26
D. White, SP	25
E. Walsh, SP	22
N. Altrock, SP	21
J. Donahue, 1B	21
E. Hahn, OF	18
F. Owen, SP	18
B. Sullivan, C	11
B. O'Neill, OF	10
R. Patterson, SP	10
L. Tannehill, 3B	10
G. Rohe, 3B	9
P. Dougherty, OF	8
F. Smith, SP	6
B. Towne, C	2
G. Dundon, 2B	1
L. Fiene, RP	1
F. Hemphill, OF	1
E. McFarland, C	1
F. Roth, C	1
R. Vinson, OF	1

Cleveland (89-64)	WS
Hitting	**124.8**
Fielding	**50.8**
Pitching	**91.4**
N. Lajoie, 2B	33
E. Flick, OF	30
T. Turner, SS	28
O. Hess, SP	24
A. Joss, SP	23
B. Rhoads, SP	23
B. Congalton, OF	15
B. Bernhard, SP	14
B. Bradley, 3B	11
N. Clarke, C	11
C. Rossman, 1B	10
H. Bay, OF	9
H. Bemis, C	9
G. Stovall, 1B	8
J. Jackson, OF	7
H. Eells, SP	4
G. Liebhardt, SP	2
J. Townsend, SP	2
J. Barbeau, 3B	1
J. Birmingham, OF	1
F. Buelow, C	1
B. Caffyn, OF	1

Detroit (71-78)	WS
Hitting	**86.4**
Fielding	**42.4**
Pitching	**84.1**
G. Mullin, SP	26
S. Crawford, OF	23
M. McIntyre, OF	19
R. Donahue, SP	17
T. Cobb, OF	16
E. Siever, SP	16
D. Jones, OF	13
B. Coughlin, 3B	12
W. Donovan, SP	11
G. Schaefer, 2B	11
E. Killian, SP	9
F. Payne, C	8

Player	WS
J. Warner, C	7
J. Eubank, SP-RP	6
C. Lindsay, 1B	6
C. O'Leary, SS	6
B. Schmidt, C	5
B. Lowe, SS	2

New York (90-61)	WS
Hitting	**109.9**
Fielding	**50.2**
Pitching	**109.9**
A. Orth, SP	36
J. Chesbro, SP	25
H. Chase, 1B	20
J. Williams, 2B	20
W. Conroy, OF	19
W. Keeler, OF	19
K. Elberfeld, SS	18
B. Hogg, SP	16
F. LaPorte, 3B	14
W. Clarkson, SP-RP	13
D. Hoffman, OF	11
D. Newton, SP	9
F. Delahanty, OF	8
R. Kleinow, C	6
D. McGuire, C	6
G. Moriarty, 3B	6
J. Yeager, SS	6
S. Doyle, SP	4
C. Griffith, RP	4
L. LeRoy, RP	4
N. Hahn, SP	3
P. Dougherty, OF	1
T. Hughes, RP	1
I. Thomas, C	1

Philadelphia (78-67)	WS
Hitting	**127.6**
Fielding	**34.8**
Pitching	**71.6**
H. Davis, 1B	31
T. Hartsel, OF	24
D. Murphy, 2B	21
S. Seybold, OF	19
R. Waddell, SP	18
C. Bender, SP	17
E. Plank, SP	16
O. Schreckengost, C	15
J. Coombs, SP	11
H. Armbruster, OF	10
M. Cross, SS	10
J. Dygert, SP	10
B. Lord, OF	7
J. Knight, 3B	5
A. Coakley, SP	4
R. Oldring, 3B	4
M. Powers, C	4
D. Shean, 2B	2
C. Berry, C	1
A. Brouthers, 3B	1
M. Cunningham, RP	1
J. Hannifin, PH-PR	1
D. Hoffman, OF	1
E. Lennox, 3B	1

St. Louis (76-73)	WS
Hitting	**103.8**
Fielding	**39.5**
Pitching	**84.6**
G. Stone, OF	38
C. Hemphill, OF	24
B. Wallace, SS	23
B. Pelty, SP	21
J. Powell, SP	20
H. Howell, SP	18
F. Glade, SP	16
H. Niles, OF	13
T. Jones, 1B	11
P. O'Brien, 2B	10
B. Rickey, C	8
B. Jacobson, SP	7
R. Hartzell, 3B	5
B. Koehler, OF	4
E. Smith, SP	3
L. Nordyke, 1B	2
J. O'Connor, C	2
T. Spencer, C	2
I. Rockenfield, 2B	1

Washington (55-95)	WS
Hitting	**107.4**
Fielding	**23.0**
Pitching	**34.5**
H. Schlafly, 2B	19
J. Anderson, OF	18
C. Hickman, OF	17
L. Cross, 3B	16
D. Altizer, SS	15
C. Jones, OF	12
R. Nill, SS	11
C. Patten, SP	11
C. Falkenberg, SP	9
F. Kitson, SP	8
J. Stahl, 1B	8
H. Wakefield, C	7
C. Smith, SP	6
L. Hughes, SP	4
J. Warner, C	2
M. Heydon, C	1
M. Kittridge, C	1

1906 National League

Boston (49-102)	WS
Hitting	**54.6**
Fielding	**28.7**
Pitching	**63.7**
V. Lindaman, SP	20
I. Young, SP	20
B. Pfeffer, SP	18
F. Tenney, 1B	17
J. Bates, OF	12
D. Brain, 3B	12
C. Dolan, OF	11
D. Howard, OF	11
A. Bridwell, SS	7
G. Dorner, SP	6
T. Needham, C	4
J. O'Neill, C	3
A. Strobel, 2B	3
S. Brown, C	2
E. Diehl, OF	1

Brooklyn (66-86)	WS
Hitting	**128.0**
Fielding	**25.1**
Pitching	**44.9**
H. Lumley, OF	35
T. Jordan, 1B	25
D. Casey, 3B	16
B. Maloney, OF	14
J. McCarthy, OF	13
E. Stricklett, SP	13
P. Lewis, SS	12
W. Alperman, 2B	11
D. Scanlan, SP	11
H. McIntire, SP	10
E. Batch, OF	7
J. Hummel, 2B	7
M. Eason, SP	6
B. Bergen, C	5
J. Pastorius, SP	4
L. Ritter, C	4
D. Gessler, 1B	2
J. Doscher, SP-RP	1
H. Knolls, RP	1
J. Whiting, SP	1

Chicago (116-36)	WS
Hitting	**162.5**
Fielding	**50.2**
Pitching	**135.3**
T. Brown, SP	35
F. Chance, 1B	35
H. Steinfeldt, 3B	33
J. Sheckard, OF	25
J. Pfiester, SP	24
W. Schulte, OF	24
E. Reulbach, SP	23
J. Kling, C	21
J. Evers, 2B	20
C. Lundgren, SP	19
J. Slagle, OF	19
J. Tinker, SS	17
J. Taylor, SP	14
O. Overall, SP	13
S. Hofman, OF	8
P. Moran, C	7
F. Beebe, RP	5
D. Gessler, OF	4
B. Wicker, SP	2

Cincinnati (64-87)	WS
Hitting	**68.0**
Fielding	**42.0**
Pitching	**82.0**
J. Weimer, SP	27
M. Huggins, 2B	22
B. Ewing, SP	21
C. Fraser, SP	14
J. Delahanty, 3B	13
A. Schlei, C	11
C. Seymour, OF	10
H. Lobert, 3B	9
S. Barry, 1B	8
J. Kelley, OF	8
B. Wicker, SP	8
T. Corcoran, SS	6
H. Smoot, OF	5
C. Chech, RP	4
F. Jude, OF	3
F. Odwell, OF	3
B. Essick, SP	2
L. Hafford, RP	2
S. Hall, SP	2
P. Livingston, C	2
M. Mowrey, 3B	2
E. Phelps, C	2
S. Deal, 1B	1
G. Dorner, SP-RP	1
C. Druhot, SP	1
J. Harper, SP	1
B. Hinchman, OF	1
L. McLean, C	1
O. Overall, SP	1
J. Siegle, OF	1

New York (96-56)	WS
Hitting	**154.7**
Fielding	**40.8**
Pitching	**92.6**
A. Devlin, 3B	36
R. Bresnahan, C	29
J. McGinnity, SP	24
S. Strang, 2B	23
C. Mathewson, SP	20
B. Dahlen, SS	19
H. Wiltse, SP	19
D. McGann, 1B	16
L. Taylor, SP	16
C. Seymour, OF	15
R. Ames, SP	12
B. Gilbert, 2B	12
G. Browne, OF	10
S. Mertes, OF	9
S. Shannon, OF	8
F. Bowerman, C	7
M. Donlin, OF	5
G. Ferguson, RP	5
F. Burke, OF	1
M. Fitzgerald, C	1
D. Marshall, OF	1

Philadelphia (71-82)	WS
Hitting	**115.8**
Fielding	**33.1**
Pitching	**64.1**
S. Magee, OF	31
R. Thomas, OF	26
J. Titus, OF	23
T. Sparks, SP	21
J. Lush, SP	19
B. Duggleby, SP	16
M. Doolan, SS	15
K. Bransfield, 1B	14
E. Courtney, 3B	10
L. Richie, SP	9
K. Gleason, 2B	7
R. Dooin, C	6
J. Ward, 3B	6
P. Sentell, 3B	4
T. Pittinger, SP	3
J. McCloskey, RP	2
J. Donovan, C	1

Pittsburgh (93-60)	WS
Hitting	**131.5**
Fielding	**47.5**
Pitching	**100.0**
H. Wagner, SS	46
V. Willis, SP	29
C. Ritchey, 2B	23
F. Clarke, OF	21
S. Leever, SP	21
T. Leach, 3B	19
L. Leifield, SP	19
J. Nealon, 1B	18
D. Phillippe, SP	16
B. Ganley, OF	12
T. Sheehan, 3B	8
G. Beaumont, OF	7
M. Lynch, SP	7
D. Meier, OF	7
B. Hallman, OF	4
H. Hillebrand, SP	4
H. Peitz, C	4
G. Gibson, C	3
E. Phelps, C	3
E. Karger, RP	2
C. McFarland, SP	2
K. Brady, SP	1
H. Camnitz, SP-RP	1
O. Clymer, OF	1
A. Storke, 3B	1

St. Louis (52-98)	WS
Hitting	**65.0**
Fielding	**30.5**
Pitching	**60.5**
P. Bennett, 2B	15
B. Brown, SP	12
J. Taylor, SP	12
M. Grady, C	11
H. Arndt, 3B	10
E. Karger, SP	10
F. Beebe, SP	9
A. Burch, OF	8
C. Druhot, SP	7
S. Shannon, OF	7
H. Smoot, OF	6
J. Beckley, 1B	5
R. Murray, OF	5
S. Barry, OF	4
J. Himes, OF	4
A. Hoelskoetter, 3B	3
D. Marshall, C	3
G. McBride, SS	3
S. McGlynn, SP	3
S. Mertes, OF	3
T. Raub, C	3
A. Fromme, SP	2
I. Higginbotham, SP	2
C. McFarland, SP	2
C. Rhodes, SP	2
F. Crawford, SS	1
J. McCarthy, C	1
P. Noonan, C	1
T. O'Hara, OF	1
B. Phyle, 3B	1

1907 American League

Boston (59-90)	WS
Hitting	**57.3**
Fielding	**41.5**
Pitching	**78.2**
C. Young, SP	27
G. Winter, SP	17
B. Congalton, OF	12
F. Parent, OF	12
D. Sullivan, OF	12
H. Ferris, 2B	10
R. Glaze, SP	10
B. Unglaub, 1B	10
J. Barrett, OF	9
H. Wagner, SS	9
C. Morgan, SP	8
J. Tannehill, SP	7
T. Pruiett, RP	6
J. Knight, 3B	5
J. Collins, 3B	4
L. Criger, C	4
A. Shaw, C	4
C. Chadbourne, OF	2
M. Grimshaw, OF	2
R. Kroh, SP	2
C. Armbruster, C	1
E. Barry, SP	1
B. Freeman, OF	1
J. Harris, RP	1
D. McGuire, PH-PR	1

Chicago (87-64)	WS
Hitting	**108.6**
Fielding	**50.3**
Pitching	**102.1**
E. Walsh, SP	37
E. Hahn, OF	27
F. Jones, OF	25
D. White, SP	25
F. Smith, SP	24
P. Dougherty, OF	20
G. Davis, SS	17
J. Donahue, 1B	17
F. Isbell, 2B	15
N. Altrock, SP	13
G. Rohe, 3B	10
E. McFarland, C	8
B. Sullivan, C	6
R. Patterson, SP	4
L. Tannehill, 3B	4
L. Quillen, 3B	3
H. Hart, C	2
F. Owen, RP	2
C. Hickman, OF	1
M. Welday, OF	1

Cleveland (85-67)	WS
Hitting	**121.2**
Fielding	**45.6**
Pitching	**88.2**
E. Flick, OF	37
N. Lajoie, 2B	32
A. Joss, SP	28
G. Liebhardt, SP	19
N. Clarke, C	17
T. Turner, SS	17
B. Hinchman, OF	16
B. Rhoads, SP	16
J. Birmingham, OF	13
B. Bradley, 3B	12
J. Thielman, SP	11
G. Stovall, 1B	9
O. Hess, SP	5
H. Berger, SP-RP	4
W. Clarkson, SP	4
H. Bemis, C	3
P. O'Brien, 2B	3
H. Bay, OF	2
H. Hinchman, 2B	2
P. Lister, 1B	2
R. Nill, 3B	2
B. Congalton, OF	1

Detroit (92-58)	WS
Hitting	**152.7**
Fielding	**40.0**
Pitching	**83.3**
T. Cobb, OF	41
S. Crawford, OF	36
E. Killian, SP	29
D. Jones, OF	24
W. Donovan, SP	23
G. Mullin, SP	21
E. Siever, SP	18
C. Rossman, 1B	17
C. O'Leary, SS	16
B. Coughlin, 3B	13
G. Schaefer, 2B	13
B. Schmidt, C	9
R. Downs, 2B	4
M. McIntyre, OF	4
J. Eubank, SP	3
F. Payne, C	3
J. Archer, C	1
B. Lowe, 3B	1

New York (70-78)	WS
Hitting	**113.3**
Fielding	**30.1**
Pitching	**66.6**
K. Elberfeld, SS	21
D. Hoffman, OF	19
J. Williams, 2B	19
H. Chase, 1B	17
F. LaPorte, 3B	16
G. Moriarty, 3B	16
A. Orth, SP	16
W. Conroy, OF	15
J. Chesbro, SP	13
S. Doyle, SP	11
B. Hogg, SP	9
R. Kleinow, C	9
D. Newton, SP	6
B. Keefe, RP	5
T. Neuer, SP	4
F. Kitson, RP	3
I. Thomas, C	3
T. Hughes, SP	2
W. Keeler, OF	2
J. Bell, OF	1
R. Castleton, SP	1
E. Moore, SP	1
B. Rickey, OF	1

Philadelphia (88-57)	WS
Hitting	**115.7**
Fielding	**48.1**
Pitching	**100.2**
T. Hartsel, OF	29
E. Plank, SP	29
C. Bender, SP	22
H. Davis, 1B	21
J. Dygert, SP	20
R. Waddell, SP	20
S. Seybold, OF	19
R. Oldring, OF	17
D. Murphy, 2B	16
O. Schreckengost, C	16
S. Nicholls, SS	14
J. Collins, 3B	12
M. Cross, SS	9
J. Coombs, SP	6
M. Powers, C	5
B. Bartley, RP	3
J. Knight, 3B	2
B. Lord, OF	2
C. Berry, C	1
R. Vickers, RP	1

St. Louis (69-83)	WS
Hitting	**96.2**
Fielding	**37.6**
Pitching	**73.1**
G. Stone, OF	27
H. Howell, SP	23
B. Wallace, SS	20
C. Hemphill, OF	16
H. Niles, 2B	16
B. Pelty, SP	14
O. Pickering, OF	14
J. Yeager, 3B	13
F. Glade, SP	12
J. Powell, SP	12
B. Dinneen, SP	9
T. Jones, 1B	9
T. Spencer, C	6
R. Hartzell, 3B	4
B. Bailey, SP	3
J. Stephens, C	3
F. Buelow, C	1
K. Butler, 2B	1
J. Delahanty, 3B	1
B. Jacobson, SP	1
B. McGill, SP	1
J. O'Connor, C	1

Washington (49-102)	WS
Hitting	**99.7**
Fielding	**18.9**
Pitching	**28.4**
J. Delahanty, 2B	17
B. Ganley, OF	16
D. Altizer, SS	15
J. Anderson, 1B	13
C. Jones, OF	11
O. Clymer, OF	10
C. Smith, SP	7
C. Falkenberg, SP	6
C. Hickman, 1B	6
L. Hughes, SP	6
C. Milan, OF	5
W. Johnson, SP	4
C. Patten, SP	4
J. Warner, C	4
R. Nill, 2B	3
B. Shipke, 3B	3
L. Cross, 3B	2
H. Gehring, SP	2
O. Graham, SP	2
M. Heydon, C	2
B. Kay, OF	2
P. O'Brien, 3B	2
H. Schlafly, 2B	2
C. Blankenship, C	1
N. Perrine, 2B	1
T. Smith, SS	1

1907 National League

Boston (58-90)	WS
Hitting	**110.9**
Fielding	**24.9**
Pitching	**38.2**
G. Beaumont, OF	28
D. Brain, 3B	22
F. Tenney, 1B	22
C. Ritchey, 2B	16
J. Bates, OF	14
A. Bridwell, SS	11
P. Flaherty, SP	10
G. Dorner, SP	9
D. Howard, OF	6
V. Lindaman, SP	6
B. Pfeffer, SP	6
J. Boultes, SP-RP	4
B. Sweeney, 3B	4
I. Young, SP	4
I. Hoffman, OF	3
T. Needham, C	3
N. Randall, OF	3
S. Brown, C	2
S. Frock, SP	1

Brooklyn (65-83)	WS
Hitting	**84.6**
Fielding	**35.9**
Pitching	**74.5**
T. Jordan, 1B	22
H. Lumley, OF	19
N. Rucker, SP	18
J. Pastorius, SP	16
W. Alperman, 2B	15
E. Stricklett, SP	14
G. Bell, SP	13
D. Casey, 3B	12
B. Maloney, OF	12
H. McIntire, SP	11
J. Hummel, 2B	10
P. Lewis, SS	8
E. Batch, OF	7
A. Burch, OF	5
D. Scanlan, SP	5
L. Ritter, C	4
B. Bergen, C	2
J. Butler, C	1
W. Henley, SP	1

Chicago (107-45)	WS
Hitting	**132.4**
Fielding	**50.2**
Pitching	**138.4**
O. Overall, SP	32
T. Brown, SP	29
C. Lundgren, SP	25
F. Chance, 1B	23
J. Sheckard, OF	23
J. Evers, 2B	22
J. Slagle, OF	22
E. Reulbach, SP	21
H. Steinfeldt, 3B	20
J. Kling, C	19
J. Pfiester, SP	19
S. Hofman, OF	18
W. Schulte, OF	14
J. Tinker, SS	11
C. Fraser, SP	9
P. Moran, C	5
J. Taylor, SP	4
D. Howard, 1B	2
N. Randall, OF	2
K. Durbin, RP-OF	1

Cincinnati (66-87)	WS
Hitting	**102.5**
Fielding	**34.0**
Pitching	**61.4**
B. Ewing, SP	21
M. Mitchell, OF	21
M. Huggins, 2B	19
H. Lobert, SS	16
J. Ganzel, 1B	14
A. Coakley, SP	13
L. McLean, C	13
M. Mowrey, 3B	11
J. Weimer, SP	11
J. Kane, OF	9
F. Odwell, OF	9
A. Schlei, C	9
A. Kruger, OF	7
L. Davis, OF	6
S. Hall, SP	4
R. Hitt, SP	3
D. Mason, SP	3
B. Spade, SP	3
B. Campbell, SP	2
D. Paskert, OF	2
F. Leary, SP-RP	1
F. Smith, SP-RP	1

New York (82-71)	WS
Hitting	**114.8**
Fielding	**40.0**
Pitching	**91.1**
C. Mathewson, SP	29
A. Devlin, 3B	22
S. Shannon, OF	21
C. Seymour, OF	20
R. Bresnahan, C	18

J. McGinnity, SP	16
S. Strang, OF	16
R. Ames, SP	15
H. Wiltse, SP	15
B. Dahlen, SS	13
G. Browne, OF	11
D. McGann, 1B	11
L. Taylor, SP	11
F. Bowerman, C	8
T. Corcoran, 2B	4
L. Doyle, 2B	4
J. Hannifin, 1B	4
G. Ferguson, RP	3
M. Lynch, SP	3
D. Shay, 2B	2

Philadelphia (83-64)	WS
Hitting	**111.5**
Fielding	**45.9**
Pitching	**91.6**
S. Magee, OF	38
T. Sparks, SP	24
J. Titus, OF	22
R. Thomas, OF	21
F. Corridon, SP	18
O. Knabe, 2B	18
E. Courtney, 3B	15
L. Moren, SP	13
M. Doolan, SS	12
B. Brown, SP	9
L. Richie, RP	9
R. Dooin, C	8
F. Jacklitsch, C	8
G. McQuillan, SP	8
T. Pittinger, SP	6
E. Grant, 3B	5
K. Bransfield, 1B	4
F. Osborn, OF	4
H. Coveleski, RP	3
J. Lush, SP	3
K. Gleason, 2B	1

Pittsburgh (91-63)	WS
Hitting	**142.9**
Fielding	**40.2**
Pitching	**89.9**
H. Wagner, SS	44
F. Clarke, OF	29
T. Leach, OF	29
E. Abbaticchio, 2B	20
V. Willis, SP	20
L. Leifield, SP	18
S. Leever, SP	17
D. Phillippe, SP	13
G. Anderson, OF	12
H. Camnitz, SP	12
J. Nealon, 1B	9
T. Sheehan, 3B	9
A. Storke, 3B	9
G. Gibson, C	8
B. Hallman, OF	7
N. Maddox, SP	7
B. Duggleby, RP	2
M. Lynch, SP	2
E. Phelps, C	2
H. Smith, C	2
O. Clymer, OF	1
D. Moeller, OF	1

St. Louis (52-101)	WS
Hitting	**68.3**
Fielding	**27.9**
Pitching	**59.9**
E. Karger, SP	21
R. Murray, OF	16
B. Byrne, 3B	15
S. McGlynn, SP	14
E. Holly, SS	11
F. Beebe, SP	10
E. Konetchy, 1B	10
J. Lush, SP	10
A. Hoelskoetter, 2B	8
S. Barry, OF	6
J. Burnett, OF	5
P. Bennett, 2B	4
A. Burch, OF	4
A. Fromme, SP	4
D. Marshall, C	3
P. Noonan, C	3
B. Raymond, SP	3
T. O'Hara, OF	2
H. Wolter, OF	2
B. Brown, SP	1
J. Delahanty, OF	1
B. Hopkins, OF	1
J. Kelly, OF	1
A. Shaw, OF	1

1908 American League

Boston (75-79)	WS
Hitting	**115.0**
Fielding	**34.8**
Pitching	**75.2**
C. Young, SP	27
D. Gessler, OF	26
A. McConnell, 2B	20
H. Wagner, SS	18
H. Lord, 3B	14
E. Cicotte, SP	12
G. Cravath, OF	12
J. Stahl, 1B	11
J. Thoney, OF	11
C. Morgan, SP	10
D. Sullivan, OF	9
F. Burchell, SP	7
E. Steele, SP	7
B. Unglaub, 1B	6
F. Arellanes, SP	5
L. Criger, C	5
B. Carrigan, C	4
P. Donahue, C	3
F. LaPorte, 2B	3
G. Winter, SP	3
J. McHale, OF	2
H. Niles, 2B	2
T. Pruiett, RP	2
T. Speaker, OF	2
K. Brady, SP	1
E. McFarland, C	1
D. McMahon, SP	1
J. Wood, RP	1

Chicago (88-64)	WS
Hitting	**125.5**
Fielding	**44.7**
Pitching	**93.9**
E. Walsh, SP	47
F. Jones, OF	32
P. Dougherty, OF	29
F. Smith, SP	21
D. White, SP	20
E. Hahn, OF	19
J. Anderson, OF	15
G. Davis, 2B	14
L. Tannehill, 3B	13
F. Isbell, 1B	12
F. Parent, SS	11
B. Sullivan, C	7
N. Altrock, SP	6
J. Atz, 2B	6
J. Donahue, 1B	6
M. Manuel, RP	2
B. Purtell, 3B	2
F. Owen, SP	1
A. Shaw, C	1

Cleveland (90-64)	WS
Hitting	**111.1**
Fielding	**50.8**
Pitching	**108.0**
A. Joss, SP	35
N. Lajoie, 2B	32
B. Rhoads, SP	23
G. Stovall, 1B	21
J. Clarke, OF	20
B. Hinchman, OF	17
G. Liebhardt, SP	17
B. Bradley, 3B	15
H. Berger, SP	14
C. Chech, SP	13
J. Birmingham, OF	10
N. Clarke, C	10
W. Good, OF	6
G. Perring, SS	6
T. Turner, OF	6
H. Bemis, C	5
J. Thielman, SP	5
D. Altizer, OF	4
C. Hickman, OF	4
J. Ryan, RP	3
S. Foster, RP	2
E. Flick, OF	1
B. Lattimore, SP	1

Detroit (90-63)	WS
Hitting	**157.4**
Fielding	**34.8**
Pitching	**77.7**
T. Cobb, OF	36
M. McIntyre, OF	33
S. Crawford, OF	32
C. Rossman, 1B	23
G. Schaefer, SS	23
E. Summers, SP	21
W. Donovan, SP	18
B. Schmidt, C	15
G. Mullin, SP	14
E. Willett, SP	13

E. Killian, SP	8
C. O'Leary, SS	7
B. Coughlin, 3B	6
R. Downs, 2B	4
I. Thomas, C	4
G. Winter, SP	4
D. Bush, SS	3
D. Jones, OF	2
G. Suggs, RP	2
R. Killefer, 2B	1
F. Payne, C	1

New York (51-103)	WS
Hitting	**102.3**
Fielding	**20.3**
Pitching	**30.4**
C. Hemphill, OF	28
N. Ball, SS	12
H. Niles, 2B	12
W. Conroy, 3B	11
H. Chase, 1B	10
W. Keeler, OF	10
J. Stahl, OF	10
J. Chesbro, SP	8
R. Manning, SP	7
G. Moriarty, 1B	7
J. Lake, SP	5
F. LaPorte, 2B	5
A. Orth, SP	5
F. Delahanty, OF	4
B. Cree, OF	3
I. McIlveen, OF	3
K. Elberfeld, SS	2
B. Hogg, SP	2
R. Kleinow, C	2
D. Newton, SP	2
W. Blair, C	1
S. Doyle, RP	1
Q. O'Rourke, OF	1
J. Sweeney, C	1
P. Wilson, SP	1

Philadelphia (68-85)	WS
Hitting	**76.2**
Fielding	**42.3**
Pitching	**85.5**
R. Vickers, SP	22
T. Hartsel, OF	19
E. Plank, SP	19
H. Davis, 1B	18
D. Murphy, OF	18
J. Coombs, OF	17
C. Bender, SP	12
J. Dygert, SP	12
E. Collins, 2B	11
S. Nicholls, SS	9
J. Collins, 3B	7
R. Oldring, OF	7
B. Schlitzer, SP	6
O. Schreckengost, C	5
J. Barry, 2B	3
M. Powers, C	3
S. Smith, C	3
H. Baker, 3B	2
N. Carter, RP	2
J. Flater, SP	2
H. Krause, SP-RP	1
J. Lapp, C	1
F. Manush, 3B	1
H. Moran, OF	1
S. Seybold, OF	1
S. Shaughnessy, OF	1
A. Strunk, OF	1

St. Louis (83-69)	WS
Hitting	**108.0**
Fielding	**48.5**
Pitching	**92.6**
G. Stone, OF	26
H. Howell, SP	23
R. Waddell, SP	21
B. Wallace, SS	21
H. Ferris, 3B	20
J. Powell, SP	20
J. Williams, 2B	18
B. Dinneen, SP	13
R. Hartzell, OF	13
D. Hoffman, OF	13
T. Jones, 1B	10
A. Schweitzer, OF	10
B. Pelty, SP	8
C. Jones, OF	7
B. Graham, SP	6
D. Criss, OF	5
T. Spencer, C	5
B. Bailey, SP	2
B. Blue, C	2
E. Heidrick, OF	2
J. Stephens, C	2
S. Smith, C	1
J. Yeager, 2B	1

Washington (67-85)	WS
Hitting	**92.5**
Fielding	**35.5**
Pitching	**72.9**
W. Johnson, SP	20
L. Hughes, SP	19
G. McBride, SS	17
J. Delahanty, 2B	16
C. Milan, OF	15
B. Ganley, OF	14
B. Unglaub, 3B	12
J. Freeman, 1B	11
G. Street, C	11
B. Burns, SP	10
O. Clymer, OF	9
B. Shipke, 3B	8
C. Smith, SP	8
O. Pickering, OF	7
C. Falkenberg, RP	6
E. Cates, SP	5
J. Warner, C	4
D. Altizer, 2B	3
B. Keeley, SP	3
H. Gehring, RP	1
J. Tannehill, SP	1
R. Witherup, SP	1

1908 National League

Boston (63-91)	WS
Hitting	**101.0**
Fielding	**30.3**
Pitching	**57.7**
G. Beaumont, OF	17
C. Ritchey, 2B	17
B. Dahlen, SS	16
J. Bates, OF	13
V. Lindaman, SP	13
B. Sweeney, 3B	13
G. Ferguson, SP	12
D. McGann, 1B	11
G. Browne, OF	8
P. Flaherty, SP	8
P. Graham, C	8
J. Kelley, OF	8
T. McCarthy, SP	8
F. Bowerman, C	5
J. Hannifin, 3B	5
B. Becker, OF	4
B. Chappelle, SP	4
H. Smith, C	4
T. Tuckey, SP	4
G. Dorner, SP	3
J. Boultes, RP	2
A. Mattern, SP	2
I. Young, SP	2
H. Moran, OF	1
F. Stem, 1B	1

Brooklyn (53-101)	WS
Hitting	**54.5**
Fielding	**35.8**
Pitching	**68.7**
N. Rucker, SP	23
K. Wilhelm, SP	23
T. Jordan, 1B	16
J. Hummel, OF	14
H. McIntire, SP	14
A. Burch, OF	11
T. Sheehan, 3B	10
H. Lumley, OF	8
J. Pastorius, SP	8
B. Bergen, C	6
B. Maloney, OF	6
H. Pattee, 2B	6
P. Lewis, SS	5
T. McMillan, SS	2
L. Ritter, C	2
W. Alperman, 2B	1
G. Bell, SP	1
T. Catterson, OF	1
J. Dunn, C	1
A. Farmer, C	1

Chicago (99-55)	WS
Hitting	**142.5**
Fielding	**51.2**
Pitching	**103.3**
T. Brown, SP	34
J. Tinker, SS	32
J. Evers, 2B	28
E. Reulbach, SP	27
J. Kling, C	22
F. Chance, 1B	20
O. Overall, SP	17
J. Pfiester, SP	16
H. Steinfeldt, 3B	16
J. Sheckard, OF	15
S. Hofman, OF	14
D. Howard, OF	13
W. Schulte, OF	11
C. Fraser, SP	8
J. Slagle, OF	8
P. Moran, C	7
H. Zimmerman, 2B	3
A. Coakley, SP	2
K. Durbin, OF	1
R. Kroh, SP-RP	1
B. Mack, RP	1
D. Marshall, C	1

Cincinnati (73-81)	WS
Hitting	**99.5**
Fielding	**39.9**
Pitching	**79.5**
H. Lobert, 3B	32
B. Ewing, SP	20
M. Huggins, 2B	17
A. Coakley, SP	16
J. Kane, OF	14
B. Spade, SP	13
D. Paskert, OF	12
J. Ganzel, 1B	11
R. Hulswitt, SS	11
B. Campbell, SP	10
M. Mitchell, OF	10
J. Weimer, SP	9
A. Schlei, C	7
B. Bescher, OF	6
L. McLean, C	5
M. Mowrey, 3B	5
J. Dubuc, SP	4
D. Hoblitzell, 1B	3
J. Rowan, SP	3
D. Bayless, OF	2
B. Coulson, OF	2
J. Doscher, SP	2
D. Egan, 2B	1
M. O'Toole, SP	1
R. Savidge, RP	1
B. Tozer, RP	1
J. Volz, SP	1

New York (98-56)	WS
Hitting	**152.4**
Fielding	**43.9**
Pitching	**97.8**
C. Mathewson, SP	39
M. Donlin, OF	31
R. Bresnahan, C	27
H. Wiltse, SP	25
A. Bridwell, SS	24
A. Devlin, 3B	24
C. Seymour, OF	19
F. Tenney, 1B	19
L. Doyle, 2B	17
B. Herzog, 2B	12
D. Crandall, SP	11
J. McGinnity, SP	10
R. Ames, SP	8
M. McCormick, OF	8
L. Taylor, SP	7
S. Shannon, OF	6
T. Needham, C	3
F. Merkle, 1B	2
B. Malarkey, RP	1
S. Strang, 2B	1

Philadelphia (83-71)	WS
Hitting	**106.4**
Fielding	**46.5**
Pitching	**96.1**
G. McQuillan, SP	33
S. Magee, OF	26
J. Titus, OF	23
K. Bransfield, 1B	20
F. Osborn, OF	19
R. Dooin, C	16
E. Grant, 3B	15
O. Knabe, 2B	15
F. Corridon, SP	13
T. Sparks, SP	13
L. Richie, SP	12
M. Doolan, SS	11
B. Foxen, SP	10
L. Moren, SP	6
H. Coveleski, SP	5
F. Jacklitsch, C	4
E. Moore, SP	4
H. Hoch, SP	2
E. Courtney, 3B	1
C. Johnson, OF	1

Pittsburgh (98-56)	WS
Hitting	**159.9**
Fielding	**45.3**
Pitching	**88.8**
H. Wagner, SS	59
T. Leach, 3B	31
F. Clarke, OF	28
E. Abbaticchio, 2B	22
N. Maddox, SP	20
V. Willis, SP	20
R. Thomas, OF	19
H. Camnitz, SP	16
L. Leifield, SP	15
S. Leever, SP	13
G. Gibson, C	12
C. Wilson, OF	9
A. Storke, 1B	5
I. Young, RP	5
J. Kane, 1B	4
W. Gill, 1B	3
C. Brandom, RP	2
E. Phelps, C	2
S. Shannon, OF	2
C. Starr, 2B	2
H. Swacina, 1B	2
T. McCarthy, SP-RP	1
D. Moeller, OF	1
H. Young, RP	1

St. Louis (49-105)	WS
Hitting	**68.4**
Fielding	**25.2**
Pitching	**53.4**
R. Murray, OF	27
B. Raymond, SP	19
E. Konetchy, 1B	18
J. Delahanty, OF	14
J. Lush, SP	13
A. Shaw, OF	11
F. Beebe, SP	5
S. Barry, OF	4
B. Byrne, 3B	4
B. Gilbert, 2B	4
E. Karger, SP	4
A. Fromme, SP	3
I. Higginbotham, SP	3
S. Sallee, RP	3
J. Bliss, C	2
C. Charles, 2B	2
A. Hoelskoetter, C	2
B. Ludwig, C	2
W. Murdoch, OF	2
C. Rhodes, SP	2
S. McGlynn, RP	1
P. O'Rourke, SS	1
C. Osteen, SS	1

1909 American League

Boston (88-63)	WS
Hitting	**136.9**
Fielding	**40.0**
Pitching	**87.1**
T. Speaker, OF	34
J. Stahl, 1B	23
H. Lord, 3B	21
F. Arellanes, SP	19
H. Wagner, SS	17
D. Gessler, OF	16
E. Cicotte, SP	14
H. Niles, OF	14
J. Wood, SP	13
B. Carrigan, C	12
A. McConnell, 2B	12
H. Hooper, OF	9
P. Donahue, C	6
C. Chech, SP	5
C. French, 2B	5
L. Pape, RP	5
R. Collins, SP	4
S. Hall, SP	4
C. Morgan, SP	4
E. Steele, SP-RP	4
H. Wolter, 1B	4
F. Burchell, SP-RP	3
E. Karger, SP-RP	3
B. Schlitzer, SP	3
C. Smith, SP	3
L. Gardner, 3B	2
J. Ryan, SP	2
F. Anderson, SP	1
B. Matthews, RP	1
T. Spencer, C	1

Chicago (78-74)	WS
Hitting	**92.4**
Fielding	**46.4**
Pitching	**95.2**
F. Smith, SP	31
P. Dougherty, OF	25
F. Parent, SS	23
E. Walsh, SP	23
D. White, OF	20
D. Altizer, OF	14
L. Tannehill, 3B	14
J. Atz, 2B	13
J. Scott, SP	13
B. Purtell, 3B	11
B. Burns, SP	9
F. Isbell, 1B	9
W. Cole, OF	5
F. Olmstead, SP	4
B. Sullivan, C	4
R. Suter, RP	4
E. Hahn, OF	3
G. Cravath, OF	2
F. Owens, C	2
F. Payne, C	2
B. Messenger, OF	1
B. Reilly, 2B	1
M. Welday, OF	1

Cleveland (71-82)	WS
Hitting	**91.2**
Fielding	**40.2**
Pitching	**81.6**
N. Lajoie, 2B	27
A. Joss, SP	20
C. Young, SP	20
B. Hinchman, OF	17
H. Berger, SP	14
J. Birmingham, OF	13
C. Falkenberg, SP	11
T. Easterly, C	10
G. Stovall, 1B	9
N. Ball, SS	8
G. Perring, 3B	8
E. Flick, OF	7
B. Lord, OF	7
T. Turner, 2B-SS	7
W. Good, OF	6
N. Clarke, C	5
B. Rhoads, SP	5
B. Bradley, 3B	3
C. Sitton, RP	3
W. Mitchell, SP	2
H. Otis, SP	2
J. Upp, SP	2
H. Ables, SP	1
H. Bemis, C	1
R. Booles, RP	1
G. Liebhardt, RP	1
T. Raftery, OF	1
D. Reilley, OF	1
D. Stark, SS	1

Detroit (98-54)	WS
Hitting	**139.4**
Fielding	**49.4**
Pitching	**105.2**
T. Cobb, OF	44
S. Crawford, OF	32
G. Mullin, SP	28
D. Bush, SS	27
E. Summers, SP	21

E. Willett, SP	21
G. Moriarty, 3B	17
E. Killian, SP	15
M. McIntyre, OF	15
W. Donovan, SP	10
D. Jones, OF	8
O. Stanage, C	8
J. Delahanty, 2B	7
G. Schaefer, 2B	7
C. Rossman, 1B	6
R. Works, RP	6
T. Jones, 1B	4
B. Schmidt, C	4
R. Killefer, 2B	3
C. O'Leary, 3B	3
K. Speer, SP	3
G. Suggs, RP	3
H. Beckendorf, C	1
E. Jones, SP	1

New York (74-77)	WS
Hitting	**125.4**
Fielding	**31.1**
Pitching	**65.4**
C. Engle, OF	23
R. Demmitt, OF	18
H. Chase, 1B	17
J. Austin, 3B	13
K. Elberfeld, SS	13
J. Lake, SP	13
J. Warhop, SP	13
B. Cree, OF	12
L. Brockett, SP	11
W. Keeler, OF	11
F. LaPorte, 2B	11
J. Knight, SS	10
R. Kleinow, C	8
S. Doyle, SP	7
C. Hemphill, OF	7
T. Hughes, SP	7
J. Quinn, RP	7
R. Manning, SP	6
J. Sweeney, C	6
E. Gardner, 2B	3
W. Blair, C	2
P. Wilson, SP	2
A. Orth, 2B	1
E. Tiemeyer, 1B	1

Philadelphia (95-58)	WS
Hitting	**135.9**
Fielding	**49.5**
Pitching	**99.6**
E. Collins, 2B	43
H. Baker, 3B	27
D. Murphy, OF	23
C. Bender, SP	22
E. Plank, SP	22
H. Krause, SP	20
H. Davis, 1B	19
C. Morgan, SP	18
J. Coombs, SP	13
J. Barry, SS	11
T. Hartsel, OF	11
H. Heitmuller, OF	10
R. Oldring, OF	9
I. Thomas, C	9
P. Livingston, C	8
J. Dygert, RP	6
B. Ganley, OF	6
J. Lapp, C	3
S. Barr, OF	1
J. Kull, RP	1
S. McInnis, SS	1
S. Nicholls, SS	1
M. Rath, SS	1

St. Louis (61-89)	WS
Hitting	**91.0**
Fielding	**30.6**
Pitching	**61.4**
R. Hartzell, OF	18
D. Hoffman, OF	17
J. Powell, SP	15
A. Griggs, 1B	14
B. Bailey, SP	13
B. Wallace, SS	13
B. Pelty, SP	12
R. Waddell, SP	12
G. Stone, OF	11
H. Ferris, 3B	8
T. Jones, 1B	8
B. Graham, SP	7
J. Stephens, C	7
J. McAleese, OF	6
L. Criger, C	4
B. Dinneen, SP	4
J. Williams, 2B	4
D. Criss, SP	3
W. Devoy, OF	2
A. Schweitzer, OF	2
B. Shotton, OF	2
H. Howell, RP	1

Washington (42-110)	WS
Hitting	**63.8**
Fielding	**24.9**
Pitching	**37.3**
W. Conroy, 3B	12
W. Johnson, SP	12
B. Unglaub, 1B	12
J. Lelivelt, OF	11
G. McBride, SS	11
G. Browne, OF	10
J. Delahanty, 2B	7
B. Groom, SP	7
G. Street, C	6
J. Donahue, 1B	5
L. Hughes, SP	4
D. Gessler, OF	3
D. Gray, SP	3
C. Milan, OF	3
G. Schaefer, 2B	3
C. Smith, SP	3
B. Burns, SP	2
O. Clymer, OF	2
D. Reisling, SP	2
D. Walker, SP	2
C. Blankenship, C	1
T. Crooke, 1B	1
B. Ganley, OF	1
F. Oberlin, RP	1
J. Tannehill, OF	1
B. Yohe, 3B	1

1909 National League

Boston (45-108)	WS
Hitting	**52.0**
Fielding	**27.5**
Pitching	**55.5**
A. Mattern, SP	17
B. Becker, OF	11
B. Sweeney, 3B	10
J. Bates, OF	9
G. Beaumont, OF	9
C. Curtis, SP	8
L. Richie, SP	8
R. Thomas, OF	8
B. Brown, SP	6
B. Dahlen, SS	6
G. Ferguson, SP	6
D. Shean, 2B	6
K. White, SP	6
P. Graham, C	5
C. Starr, 2B	4
F. Beck, OF	2
B. Chappelle, SP	2
J. Coffey, SS	2
G. Dorner, RP	2
C. Autry, 1B	1
F. Bowerman, C	1
B. Cooney, RP	1
G. Getz, 3B	1
T. McCarthy, SP	1
H. Moran, OF	1
H. Smith, C	1
F. Stem, 1B	1

Brooklyn (55-98)	WS
Hitting	**67.7**
Fielding	**34.5**
Pitching	**62.9**
N. Rucker, SP	22
A. Burch, OF	17
G. Bell, SP	15
E. Lennox, 3B	15
J. Hummel, 1B	14
T. Jordan, 1B	14
D. Scanlan, SP	10
W. Alperman, 2B	9
B. Bergen, C	8
G. Hunter, OF	7
W. Clement, OF	6
H. McIntire, SP	6
Z. Wheat, OF	4
K. Wilhelm, SP	4
H. Lumley, OF	3
D. Marshall, C	3
T. McMillan, SS	3
P. McElveen, 3B	2
R. Downey, OF	1
E. Knetzer, SP	1
J. Kustus, OF	1

Chicago (104-49)	WS
Hitting	**140.1**
Fielding	**50.2**
Pitching	**121.7**
T. Brown, SP	36
O. Overall, SP	30
J. Evers, 2B	27
S. Hofman, OF	27
H. Steinfeldt, 3B	25
J. Tinker, SS	24
J. Sheckard, OF	23
E. Reulbach, SP	21
W. Schulte, OF	18
F. Chance, 1B	14
J. Pfiester, SP	14
R. Kroh, SP	11
J. Archer, C	7
P. Moran, C	7
H. Zimmerman, 2B	7
R. Hagerman, SP	5
I. Higginbotham, RP	5
K. Cole, SP	3
D. Howard, 1B	3
F. Luderus, 1B	2
R. Brown, SP	1
G. Browne, OF	1
J. Kane, OF	1

Cincinnati (77-76)	WS
Hitting	**134.1**
Fielding	**32.0**
Pitching	**64.9**
M. Mitchell, OF	28
D. Hoblitzell, 1B	23
D. Egan, 2B	19
A. Fromme, SP	19
B. Bescher, OF	16
H. Gaspar, SP	15
R. Oakes, OF	15
H. Lobert, 3B	12
T. Downey, SS	10
D. Paskert, OF	10
J. Rowan, SP	10
B. Ewing, SP	9
L. McLean, C	9
B. Campbell, SP-RP	6
B. Spade, SP	6
M. Huggins, 2B	5
W. Miller, OF	4
F. Roth, C	4
T. Cantwell, RP	2
T. Clarke, C	2
M. Mowrey, 3B	2
R. Castleton, RP	1
C. Charles, 2B	1
R. Ellam, SS	1
E. Karger, SP	1
S. McCabe, OF	1

New York (92-61)	WS
Hitting	**130.3**
Fielding	**43.8**
Pitching	**101.9**
C. Mathewson, SP	34
L. Doyle, 2B	27
A. Bridwell, SS	24
A. Devlin, 3B	23
H. Wiltse, SP	22
R. Murray, OF	19
B. Raymond, SP	18
M. McCormick, OF	17
C. Seymour, OF	13
R. Ames, SP	12
C. Meyers, C	10
B. O'Hara, OF	10
A. Schlei, C	10
F. Tenney, 1B	9
D. Crandall, RP	7
R. Marquard, SP	7
F. Snodgrass, OF	4
A. Klawitter, SP-RP	3
L. Drucke, SP	2
A. Fletcher, SS	1
B. Herzog, OF	1
F. Merkle, 1B	1
T. Shafer, 3B	1
A. Wilson, C	1

Philadelphia (74-79)	WS
Hitting	**80.6**
Fielding	**48.9**
Pitching	**92.5**
E. Moore, SP	24
S. Magee, OF	20
J. Titus, OF	20
G. McQuillan, SP	18
E. Grant, 3B	17
L. Moren, SP	16
K. Bransfield, 1B	14
F. Corridon, SP	14
M. Doolan, SS	13
J. Bates, OF	10
R. Dooin, C	9
O. Knabe, 2B	9
H. Coveleski, SP	6
T. Sparks, SP	5
P. Deininger, OF	4
B. Foxen, RP	4
L. Richie, RP	4
J. Ward, 2B	4
F. Osborn, OF	3
F. Jacklitsch, C	2
D. Martel, C	2
D. Shean, 2B	2
B. Brown, RP	1
F. Scanlan, RP	1

Pittsburgh (110-42)	WS
Hitting	**159.1**
Fielding	**49.9**
Pitching	**121.1**
H. Wagner, SS	42
F. Clarke, OF	31
Ho. Camnitz, SP	30
T. Leach, OF	26
G. Gibson, C	24
D. Miller, 2B	24
V. Willis, SP	24
C. Wilson, OF	19
B. Adams, RP	16
L. Leifield, SP	16
N. Maddox, SP	16
B. Abstein, 1B	13
D. Phillippe, SP	10
B. Byrne, 3B	9
J. Barbeau, 3B	8
S. Leever, RP	5
E. Abbaticchio, SS	4
C. Brandom, RP	4

H. Hyatt, OF	3
A. Storke, 1B	3
S. Frock, SP-RP	2
P. O'Connor, C	1

St. Louis (54-98)	WS
Hitting	**113.4**
Fielding	**19.4**
Pitching	**29.2**
E. Konetchy, 1B	24
R. Ellis, OF	16
S. Evans, OF	16
A. Shaw, OF	12
B. Byrne, 3B	9
E. Phelps, C	9
F. Beebe, SP	8
R. Bresnahan, C	8
R. Hulswitt, SS	8
J. Lush, SP	7
J. Barbeau, 3B	6
C. Charles, 2B	6
J. Delahanty, OF	6
S. Sallee, SP	6
B. Harmon, SP	4
A. Storke, SS	4
L. Backman, SP	2
J. Bliss, C	2
B. Gilbert, 2B	1
I. Higginbotham, RP	1
E. Higgins, RP	1
B. James, OF	1
S. Melter, RP	1
M. Mowrey, 2B	1
C. Osteen, SS	1
J. Raleigh, SP	1
C. Rhodes, SP	1

1910 American League

Boston (81-72)	WS
Hitting	**125.5**
Fielding	**36.4**
Pitching	**81.0**
T. Speaker, OF	34
H. Hooper, OF	19
D. Lewis, OF	19
J. Stahl, 1B	19
R. Collins, SP	18
H. Wagner, SS	18
L. Gardner, 2B	15
S. Hall, RP	14
J. Wood, RP	14
E. Cicotte, SP	13
C. Engle, 3B	12
E. Karger, SP	11
C. Smith, SP	10
B. Carrigan, C	8
H. Lord, 3B	7
F. Arellanes, SP	4
B. Madden, C	2
B. Purtell, 3B	2
B. Hunt, SP	1
R. Kleinow, C	1
A. McConnell, 2B	1
H. Niles, OF	1

Chicago (68-85)	WS
Hitting	**68.0**
Fielding	**43.2**
Pitching	**92.9**
E. Walsh, SP	36
D. White, SP	15
R. Zeider, 2B	15
P. Dougherty, OF	14
F. Lange, SP	11
F. Olmstead, SP	11
J. Scott, SP	10
H. Lord, 3B	9
P. Meloan, OF	8
F. Smith, SP	8
B. Purtell, 3B	7
S. Collins, OF	6
F. Payne, C	6
C. Gandil, 1B	5
A. McConnell, 2B	5
L. Tannehill, SS	5
I. Young, SP	5
L. Blackburne, SS	4
B. Block, C	4
F. Parent, OF	4
G. Browne, OF	3
F. Chouinard, OF	3
B. Sullivan, C	3
D. Zwilling, OF	2
W. Cole, OF	1
C. French, 2B	1
R. Kelly, OF	1
B. Messenger, OF	1
C. Mullen, 1B	1

Cleveland (71-81)	WS
Hitting	**99.9**
Fielding	**38.8**
Pitching	**74.2**
N. Lajoie, 2B	47
T. Easterly, C	15
C. Falkenberg, SP	14
T. Turner, SS	14
W. Mitchell, SP	11
J. Graney, OF	10
G. Stovall, 1B	10
C. Young, SP	10
J. Birmingham, OF	8
S. Harkness, SP	7
A. Joss, SP	7
G. Kahler, SP	7
J. Jackson, OF	6
E. Koestner, RP	6
F. Link, SP	6
B. Lord, OF	4
H. Berger, SP	3
E. Flick, OF	3
E. Hohnhorst, 1B	3
H. Niles, OF	3
N. Ball, SS	2
H. Bemis, C	2
F. Blanding, SP	2
B. Bradley, 3B	2
C. Knaupp, SS	2
G. Perring, 3B	2
M. Rath, 3B	2
N. Clarke, C	1
H. Fanwell, SP	1

A. Kruger, OF	1
G. Land, C	1
S. Smith, C	1

Detroit (86-68)	WS
Hitting	**142.2**
Fielding	**38.2**
Pitching	**77.6**
T. Cobb, OF	45
D. Bush, SS	24
S. Crawford, OF	23
G. Mullin, SP	19
J. Delahanty, 2B	16
G. Moriarty, 3B	16
W. Donovan, SP	15
E. Willett, SP	15
D. Jones, OF	14
E. Summers, SP	14
T. Jones, 1B	10
M. McIntyre, OF	9
B. Schmidt, C	6
O. Stanage, C	5
S. Stroud, SP	5
F. Browning, SP	4
E. Killian, SP	3
C. O'Leary, 2B	3
H. Pernoll, RP	3
R. Works, SP	3
H. Simmons, 1B	2
H. Beckendorf, C	1
J. Casey, C	1
C. Lathers, 3B	1
B. Lelivelt, SP	1

New York (88-63)	WS
Hitting	**123.2**
Fielding	**44.3**
Pitching	**96.5**
R. Ford, SP	35
J. Knight, SS	23
B. Cree, OF	22
H. Wolter, OF	21
J. Quinn, SP	19
H. Vaughn, SP	18
H. Chase, 1B	17
B. Daniels, OF	17
F. LaPorte, 2B	14
J. Warhop, SP	14
J. Austin, 3B	12
C. Hemphill, OF	12
E. Gardner, 2B	7
R. Roach, SS	7
R. Fisher, RP	5
T. Hughes, SP	5
J. Sweeney, C	5
F. Mitchell, C	4
R. Manning, SP	2
R. Caldwell, RP	1
L. Channell, OF	1
L. Criger, C	1
E. Foster, SS	1
R. Kleinow, C	1

Philadelphia (102-48)	WS
Hitting	**149.2**
Fielding	**50.2**
Pitching	**106.7**
E. Collins, 2B	39
J. Coombs, SP	37
C. Bender, SP	26
H. Baker, 3B	25
R. Oldring, OF	25
D. Murphy, OF	24
C. Morgan, SP	20
J. Barry, SS	19
E. Plank, SP	16
H. Davis, 1B	13
B. Lord, OF	12
T. Hartsel, OF	9
I. Thomas, C	8
J. Lapp, C	7
H. Krause, SP	5
P. Livingston, C	4
S. McInnis, SS	4
J. Dygert, RP	3
H. Heitmuller, OF	3
A. Strunk, OF	3
T. Atkins, RP	1
P. Donahue, C	1
E. Mack, C	1
L. Russell, SP	1

St. Louis (47-107)	WS
Hitting	**86.7**
Fielding	**21.7**
Pitching	**32.6**
B. Wallace, SS	20
G. Stone, OF	17
R. Hartzell, 3B	12
D. Hoffman, OF	10
J. Lake, SP	10
A. Griggs, OF	9
A. Schweitzer, OF	9
F. Truesdale, 2B	9
P. Newnam, 1B	6
J. Powell, SP	5
J. Stephens, C	5
D. Criss, 1B	4
B. Pelty, SP	4
B. Killefer, C	3
R. Nelson, SP	3
F. Ray, SP	3
B. Bailey, SP	2
R. Corriden, SS	2
R. Mitchell, SP	2
J. Gilligan, SP	1
R. Jansen, 3B	1
E. Kinsella, SP-RP	1
A. Malloy, SP	1
B. Spade, SP	1
R. Waddell, RP	1

Washington (66-85)	WS
Hitting	**84.4**
Fielding	**37.7**
Pitching	**75.9**
W. Johnson, SP	36
C. Milan, OF	23
D. Gessler, OF	17
G. McBride, SS	16
K. Elberfeld, 3B	12
D. Reisling, SP	11
D. Gray, SP	10
B. Groom, SP	10
J. Lelivelt, OF	10
W. Conroy, 3B-OF	9
R. Killefer, 2B	8
G. Schaefer, 2B	8
D. Walker, SP	8
B. Unglaub, 1B	5
B. Cunningham, 2B	4
G. Street, C	4
H. Beckendorf, C	2
E. Ainsmith, C	1
J. Henry, C	1
F. Oberlin, SP	1
B. Otey, RP	1
D. Ralston, OF	1

1910 National League

Boston (53-100)	WS
Hitting	**40.3**
Fielding	**40.6**
Pitching	**78.1**
A. Mattern, SP	20
B. Brown, SP	19
S. Frock, SP	14
F. Beck, OF	13
B. Collins, OF	11
B. Sweeney, SS	11
D. Miller, OF	10
D. Shean, 2B	9
C. Curtis, SP	8
B. Herzog, 3B	8
G. Ferguson, SP	7
P. Graham, C	6
W. Good, OF	4
B. Burke, RP	3
K. White, SP	3
B. Rariden, C	2
B. Sharpe, 1B	2
E. Abbaticchio, SS	1
P. Burg, 3B	1
C. Evans, RP	1
G. Getz, 3B	1
R. Good, RP	1
H. Moran, OF	1
J. Parson, RP	1
H. Smith, C	1
L. Tyler, RP	1

Brooklyn (64-90)	WS
Hitting	**68.1**
Fielding	**42.6**
Pitching	**81.4**
N. Rucker, SP	23
Z. Wheat, OF	21
C. Barger, SP	19
G. Bell, SP	17
J. Daubert, 1B	17
J. Hummel, 2B	16
D. Scanlan, SP	16
E. Lennox, 3B	11
T. Smith, SS	10
B. Bergen, C	6
B. Davidson, OF	6
E. Knetzer, SP	6

A. Burch, OF	4
J. Dalton, OF	4
T. Erwin, C	4
P. McElveen, 3B	4
B. Coulson, OF	2
O. Miller, C	2
T. McMillan, SS	1
H. Smith, OF	1
D. Stark, SS	1
K. Wilhelm, RP	1

Chicago (104-50)	WS
Hitting	**152.1**
Fielding	**49.9**
Pitching	**110.1**
S. Hofman, OF	31
T. Brown, SP	29
W. Schulte, OF	26
K. Cole, SP	25
J. Sheckard, OF	23
J. Evers, 2B	22
J. Tinker, SS	22
H. Steinfeldt, 3B	15
F. Chance, 1B	14
J. Kling, C	14
H. McIntire, SP	13
H. Zimmerman, 2B	13
O. Overall, SP	12
L. Richie, RP	12
J. Archer, C	10
J. Pfiester, SP	9
E. Reulbach, SP	9
G. Beaumont, OF	7
J. Kane, OF	2
T. Needham, C	2
R. Kroh, SP	1
O. Weaver, RP	1

Cincinnati (75-79)	WS
Hitting	**119.8**
Fielding	**34.6**
Pitching	**70.5**
D. Paskert, OF	24
M. Mitchell, OF	22
G. Suggs, SP	20
B. Bescher, OF	18
H. Gaspar, SP	18
D. Hoblitzell, 1B	18
L. McLean, C	17
H. Lobert, 3B	14
J. Rowan, SP	14
T. Downey, SS	12
F. Beebe, SP	10
D. Egan, 2B	10
T. Clarke, C	7
B. Burns, SP	6
T. McMillan, SS	3
W. Miller, OF	3
D. Altizer, SS	2
A. Fromme, RP	2
R. Castleton, SP-RP	1
M. Corcoran, 2B	1
S. McCabe, OF	1
A. Phelan, 3B	1
S. Woodruff, 3B	1

New York (91-63)	WS
Hitting	**146.9**
Fielding	**36.8**
Pitching	**89.3**
C. Mathewson, SP	30
L. Doyle, 2B	25
F. Snodgrass, OF	23
A. Bridwell, SS	22
F. Merkle, 1B	20
D. Crandall, RP	19
A. Devlin, 3B	19
J. Devore, OF	17
R. Murray, OF	17
L. Drucke, SP	16
C. Meyers, C	16
H. Wiltse, SP	15
R. Ames, SP	13
C. Seymour, OF	6
B. Becker, OF	5
A. Wilson, C	3
R. Marquard, SP	2
A. Schlei, C	2
A. Fletcher, SS	1
W. Keeler, OF	1
B. Raymond, SP	1

Philadelphia (78-75)	WS
Hitting	**121.1**
Fielding	**38.7**
Pitching	**74.1**
S. Magee, OF	36
J. Bates, OF	24
M. Doolan, SS	22
E. Moore, SP	21
J. Titus, OF	17
O. Knabe, 2B	16
B. Ewing, SP	15
E. Grant, 3B	14
G. McQuillan, SP	13
L. Moren, SP	8
R. Dooin, C	7
J. Walsh, 2B-OF	7
K. Bransfield, 1B	6
A. Brennan, RP	5
B. Foxen, SP	5
P. Moran, C	5
L. Schettler, RP	4
F. Luderus, 1B	3
E. Stack, SP	3
J. Moroney, RP	2
F. Jacklitsch, C	1

Pittsburgh (86-67)	WS
Hitting	**112.9**
Fielding	**46.7**
Pitching	**98.3**
H. Wagner, SS	30
B. Byrne, 3B	27
B. Adams, SP	21
G. Gibson, C	18
L. Leifield, SP	17
T. Leach, OF	16
H. Camnitz, SP	15
F. Clarke, OF	15
C. Wilson, OF	14
D. Phillippe, RP	13
V. Campbell, OF	12
K. White, SP	10
J. Flynn, 1B	8
S. Leever, RP	8
D. Miller, 2B	7
B. Powell, SP	6
N. Maddox, RP	5
H. Hyatt, 1B	4
J. Ferry, SP-RP	3
B. McKechnie, 2B	3
E. Steele, SP	2
M. Carey, OF	1
J. Kading, 1B	1
G. Moore, RP	1
M. Simon, C	1

St. Louis (63-90)	WS
Hitting	**122.9**
Fielding	**25.1**
Pitching	**41.1**
E. Konetchy, 1B	27
M. Huggins, 2B	23
M. Mowrey, 3B	23
S. Evans, OF	17
R. Ellis, OF	15
R. Bresnahan, C	13
J. Lush, SP	10
R. Oakes, OF	9
E. Phelps, C	8
V. Willis, SP	7
B. Harmon, SP	6
A. Hauser, SS	6
S. Sallee, SP	6
L. Backman, RP	5
F. Corridon, SP	4
R. Hulswitt, SS	3
B. Steele, SP	3
J. Barbeau, 3B	1
F. Betcher, SS	1
R. Golden, SP	1
E. Zacher, OF	1

1911 American League

Boston (78-75)	WS
Hitting	**103.2**
Fielding	**40.9**
Pitching	**89.9**
T. Speaker, OF	27
J. Wood, SP	26
H. Hooper, OF	20
L. Gardner, 3B	18
R. Collins, SP	15
D. Lewis, OF	15
L. Pape, SP	13
S. Yerkes, SS	13
E. Cicotte, SP	11
C. Engle, 1B	10
B. Carrigan, C	8
H. Wagner, 2B	8
S. Hall, RP	7
E. Karger, SP	7
B. O'Brien, SP	6
R. Williams, 1B	5
O. Henriksen, OF	4
J. Killilay, SP-RP	4
L. Nunamaker, C	4
J. Lewis, 2B	2
H. Myers, 1B	2
J. Nagle, RP	2
B. Purtell, 3B	2
J. Riggert, OF	2
H. Bradley, 1B	1
C. Hageman, SP	1
B. Thomas, SP	1

Chicago (77-74)	WS
Hitting	**107.6**
Fielding	**40.3**
Pitching	**83.1**
E. Walsh, SP	31
H. Lord, 3B	23
M. McIntyre, OF	23
P. Bodie, OF	20
J. Scott, SP	16
L. Tannehill, SS	15
D. White, SP	14
N. Callahan, OF	11
F. Lange, SP	11
A. McConnell, 2B	11
S. Collins, 1B	9
P. Dougherty, OF	9
R. Zeider, 1B	7
J. Benz, SP-RP	4
B. Block, C	4
R. Corhan, SS	4
B. Sullivan, C	4
J. Baker, RP	3
J. Hovlik, RP	3
F. Olmstead, RP	3
F. Payne, C	2
I. Young, RP	2
C. Barrows, OF	1
F. Parent, 2B	1

Cleveland (80-73)	WS
Hitting	**103.0**
Fielding	**47.0**
Pitching	**90.0**
J. Jackson, OF	39
V. Gregg, SP	28
G. Krapp, SP	16
J. Birmingham, OF	14
J. Graney, OF	14
N. Lajoie, 1B	14
N. Ball, 2B	12
F. Blanding, SP	11
T. Turner, 3B	11
G. Kahler, SP	10
I. Olson, SS	10
T. Easterly, OF	8
C. Falkenberg, SP	7
W. Mitchell, SP	7
G. Stovall, 1B	7
S. Smith, C	6
G. Fisher, C	5
H. Butcher, OF	3
H. West, SP	3
J. Baskette, SP-RP	2
S. Harkness, SP-RP	2
G. Land, C	2
C. Young, SP	2
A. Griggs, 2B	1
B. James, SP	1
B. Lindsay, 3B	1
J. Mills, 3B	1
S. O'Neill, C	1
J. Swindell, RP	1
E. Yingling, SP	1

Detroit (89-65)	WS
Hitting	**138.1**
Fielding	**40.4**
Pitching	**88.5**
T. Cobb, OF	47
S. Crawford, OF	32
J. Delahanty, 1B	24
G. Mullin, SP	23
D. Bush, SS	18
E. Willett, SP	16
W. Donovan, SP	14
E. Summers, SP	11
R. Works, SP-RP	10
E. Lafitte, SP	9
O. Stanage, C	9
D. Gainer, 1B	8
D. Jones, OF	8
G. Moriarty, 3B	8
D. Drake, OF	7
T. Covington, RP	6
J. Lively, SP	6
C. O'Leary, 2B	6
P. Baumann, 2B	2
C. Lathers, 2B	1
B. Schmidt, C	1
W. Taylor, SP	1

New York (76-76)	WS
Hitting	**91.1**
Fielding	**43.2**
Pitching	**93.6**
R. Ford, SP	28
B. Cree, OF	25
R. Caldwell, SP	23
R. Hartzell, 3B	17
H. Wolter, OF	17
B. Daniels, OF	15
H. Chase, 1B	14
R. Fisher, SP	12
J. Knight, SS	12
J. Warhop, SP	11
J. Quinn, RP	9
H. Vaughn, SP	7
E. Gardner, 2B	6
C. Hemphill, OF	6
O. Johnson, SS	6
W. Blair, C	4
L. Brockett, SP-RP	4
J. Sweeney, C	4
C. Dolan, 3B	3
R. Hoff, RP	2
M. Fitzgerald, OF	1
R. Roach, SS	1
B. Williams, C	1

Philadelphia (101-50)	WS
Hitting	**168.3**
Fielding	**46.3**

Pitching	88.4
H. Baker, 3B	35
E. Collins, 2B	35
D. Murphy, OF	25
J. Coombs, SP	23
B. Lord, OF	22
E. Plank, SP	22
C. Bender, SP	18
S. McInnis, 1B	18
J. Barry, SS	16
R. Oldring, OF	16
C. Morgan, SP	15
I. Thomas, C	13
H. Krause, SP	12
J. Lapp, C	12
A. Strunk, OF	7
P. Livingston, C	3
D. Danforth, RP	2
H. Davis, 1B	2
C. Derrick, 2B	2
C. Emerson, OF	1
T. Hartsel, OF	1
E. Leonard, RP	1
D. Martin, RP	1
L. Russell, RP	1

St. Louis (45-107)	WS
Hitting	**66.9**
Fielding	**24.9**
Pitching	**43.2**
J. Austin, 3B	17
F. LaPorte, 2B	17
B. Shotton, OF	11
W. Hogan, OF	10
J. Lake, SP	10
B. Pelty, SP	10
J. Powell, SP	8
B. Wallace, SS	7
E. Hamilton, SP	6
R. Mitchell, RP	5
A. Schweitzer, OF	5
P. Meloan, OF	4
J. Stephens, C	3
M. Allison, SP	2
N. Clarke, C	2
P. Compton, OF	2
D. Criss, 1B	2
L. George, RP	2
D. Hoffman, OF	2
J. Kutina, 1B	2
D. Rowan, 1B	2
C. Brown, SP	1
E. Hallinan, SS	1
E. Hawk, SP	1
P. Krichell, C	1
H. Myers, 1B	1
P. Newnam, 1B	1

Washington (64-90)	WS
Hitting	**93.2**
Fielding	**31.2**
Pitching	**67.6**
W. Johnson, SP	31
C. Milan, OF	27
G. Schaefer, 1B	19
D. Gessler, OF	18
K. Elberfeld, 2B	17
B. Groom, SP	11
G. McBride, SS	11
D. Walker, SP	11
L. Hughes, SP	10
J. Lelivelt, OF	8
T. Walker, OF	6
W. Conroy, 3B	5
G. Street, C	4
C. Becker, RP	3
C. Cashion, SP	3
J. Henry, C	3
E. Ainsmith, C	2
B. Cunningham, 2B	2
D. Gray, SP	1

1911
National League

Boston (44-107)	WS
Hitting	**94.4**
Fielding	**15.0**
Pitching	**22.5**
B. Sweeney, 2B	19
D. Miller, OF	18
B. Herzog, SS	11
M. Donlin, OF	7
S. Ingerton, 3B	7
F. Tenney, 1B	7
B. Brown, SP	6
A. Bridwell, SS	5
G. Jackson, OF	5
J. Clarke, OF	4
W. Good, OF	3
J. Kirke, OF	3
J. Kling, C	3
A. Mattern, SP	3
E. McDonald, 3B	3
L. Tyler, SP	3
C. Curtis, SP	2
E. Donnelly, SP	2
P. Flaherty, OF	2
H. Gowdy, 1B	2
P. Graham, C	2
H. Perdue, SP	2
B. Pfeffer, RP	2
B. Rariden, C	2
H. Spratt, SS	2
C. Young, SP	2
H. Griffin, RP	1
B. Hogg, RP	1
B. Houser, 1B	1
B. Jones, OF	1
H. Steinfeldt, 3B	1

Brooklyn (64-86)	WS
Hitting	**69.4**
Fielding	**41.4**
Pitching	**81.2**
N. Rucker, SP	31
J. Daubert, 1B	20
J. Hummel, 2B	18
Z. Wheat, OF	16
C. Barger, SP	12
T. Erwin, C	11
E. Knetzer, SP	11
P. Ragan, RP	9
B. Schardt, SP	9
B. Coulson, OF	8
B. Tooley, SS	7
D. Stark, SS	6
E. Zimmerman, 3B	6
B. Bergen, C	5
H. Northen, OF	4
D. Scanlan, SP	4
G. Bell, SP	3
B. Davidson, OF	3
A. Burch, OF	2
E. Dent, SP	2
R. Smith, 3B	2
J. Daley, OF	1
O. Miller, C	1
E. Steele, RP	1

Chicago (92-62)	WS
Hitting	**136.1**
Fielding	**44.6**
Pitching	**95.3**
W. Schulte, OF	31
J. Sheckard, OF	30
T. Brown, SP	25
H. Zimmerman, 2B	22
J. Tinker, SS	21
L. Richie, SP	20
J. Doyle, 3B	19
K. Cole, SP	15
E. Reulbach, SP	14
S. Hofman, OF	13
J. Archer, C	11
H. McIntire, SP	7
V. Saier, 1B	6
F. Chance, 1B	5
J. Evers, 2B	5
W. Good, OF	4
C. Smith, SP	4
O. Weaver, SP	4
P. Graham, C	3
F. Toney, RP	3
L. Cheney, RP	2
A. Kaiser, OF	2
T. Needham, C	2
R. Richter, RP	2
D. Shean, 2B	2
K. Bransfield, 1B	1
B. Foxen, RP	1
J. Kling, C	1
C. Slapnicka, SP	1

Cincinnati (70-83)	WS
Hitting	**109.7**
Fielding	**32.2**
Pitching	**68.1**
J. Bates, OF	23
B. Bescher, OF	20
D. Hoblitzell, 1B	18
M. Mitchell, OF	17
G. Suggs, SP	17
B. Keefe, SP	15
H. Gaspar, SP	13
D. Egan, 2B	11
T. Downey, SS	10
L. McLean, C	10
A. Fromme, SP	8
E. Grant, 3B	8
T. Clarke, C	7
J. Esmond, SS	6
F. Smith, SP	5
B. Humphries, SP-RP	4
R. Almeida, 3B	3
R. Benton, SP	3
A. Marsans, OF	3
D. Altizer, SS	2
R. Boyd, SP	2
B. Burns, SP-RP	2
H. Severeid, C	2
J. Compton, RP	1

New York (99-54)	WS
Hitting	**137.5**
Fielding	**45.5**
Pitching	**114.0**
C. Mathewson, SP	32
L. Doyle, 2B	28
R. Marquard, SP	26
F. Snodgrass, OF	23
D. Crandall, RP	20
C. Meyers, C	19
J. Devore, OF	18
F. Merkle, 1B	18
A. Fletcher, SS	17
R. Ames, SP	16
R. Murray, OF	16
H. Wiltse, SP	12
A. Devlin, 3B	11
A. Bridwell, SS	10
B. Herzog, 3B	9
A. Wilson, C	6
B. Becker, OF	5
B. Raymond, SP	5
L. Drucke, SP	3
B. Maxwell, SP	2
G. Hartley, C	1

Philadelphia (79-73)	WS
Hitting	**97.1**
Fielding	**47.3**
Pitching	**92.6**
P. Alexander, SP	34
E. Moore, SP	24
F. Luderus, 1B	20
S. Magee, OF	19
H. Lobert, 3B	18
D. Paskert, OF	18
M. Doolan, SS	15
G. Chalmers, SP	14
O. Knabe, 2B	14
R. Dooin, C	11
J. Titus, OF	9
B. Burns, SP	7
J. Walsh, OF	7
F. Beck, OF	6
C. Curtis, SP	4
F. Beebe, SP	3
B. Humphries, RP	3
E. Stack, SP	3
P. Moran, C	2
A. Brennan, SP	1
D. Cotter, C	1
B. Hall, RP	1
B. Madden, C	1
J. Smith, RP	1
H. Welchonce, OF	1

Pittsburgh (85-69)	WS
Hitting	**116.1**
Fielding	**46.2**
Pitching	**92.7**
H. Wagner, SS	30
B. Adams, SP	25
L. Leifield, SP	24
C. Wilson, OF	22
B. Byrne, 3B	20
F. Clarke, OF	20
H. Camnitz, SP	16
D. Miller, 2B	16
M. Carey, OF	14
E. Steele, SP	11
T. Leach, OF	10
J. Ferry, RP	7
C. Hendrix, SP	7
G. Gibson, C	6
N. Hunter, 1B	5
A. McCarthy, SS	5
B. McKechnie, 1B	5
M. Simon, C	4
V. Campbell, OF	3
M. O'Toole, SP	3
H. Gardner, RP	1
J. Nagle, RP	1

St. Louis (75-74)	WS
Hitting	**111.7**
Fielding	**40.6**
Pitching	**72.6**
E. Konetchy, 1B	26
B. Harmon, SP	23
S. Evans, OF	22
M. Huggins, 2B	18
M. Mowrey, 3B	18
S. Sallee, SP	18
R. Oakes, OF	15
B. Steele, SP	15
R. Bresnahan, C	14
R. Ellis, OF	14
R. Geyer, RP	8
A. Hauser, SS	8
J. Bliss, C	7
W. Smith, 3B	4
R. Golden, SP	2
L. Lowdermilk, RP	2
L. Magee, 2B	2
O. McIvor, OF	2
D. Wilie, OF	2
H. Camnitz, RP	1
R. Radebaugh, SP-RP	1
J. Reis, RP	1
G. Woodburn, SP	1
E. Zmich, RP	1

1912
American League

Boston (105-47)	WS
Hitting	**145.5**
Fielding	**49.9**
Pitching	**119.6**
T. Speaker, OF	51
J. Wood, SP	44

L. Gardner, 3B	29
B. O'Brien, SP	23
H. Bedient, SP	21
D. Lewis, OF	21
H. Wagner, SS	20
R. Collins, SP	19
S. Hall, SP	17
H. Hooper, OF	15
J. Stahl, 1B	13
B. Carrigan, C	10
S. Yerkes, 2B	10
H. Cady, C	6
C. Engle, 1B	5
O. Henriksen, OF	3
L. Nunamaker, C	3
M. Krug, SS	2
H. Bradley, 1B	1
L. Pape, RP	1
P. Thomas, C	1

Chicago (78-76)	WS
Hitting	**97.3**
Fielding	**44.6**
Pitching	**92.2**
E. Walsh, SP	40
M. Rath, 2B	26
S. Collins, OF	18
P. Bodie, OF	17
H. Lord, 3B	17
J. Benz, SP	14
R. Zeider, 1B	13
E. Cicotte, SP	11
F. Lange, SP	10
W. Mattick, OF	9
D. White, SP	9
B. Weaver, SS	8
N. Callahan, OF	7
B. Block, C	5
B. Borton, 1B	5
W. Kuhn, C	5
T. Easterly, C	3
G. Mogridge, RP	3
R. Schalk, C	3
J. Scott, SP	3
R. Peters, RP	2
B. Sullivan, C	2
R. Crabb, SP-RP	1
J. Fournier, 1B	1
E. Johnson, SS	1
H. Smith, SP	1

Cleveland (75-78)	WS
Hitting	**100.7**
Fielding	**43.4**
Pitching	**81.0**
J. Jackson, OF	37
V. Gregg, SP	23
N. Lajoie, 2B	22
F. Blanding, SP	20
T. Turner, 3B	13
G. Kahler, SP	11
A. Griggs, 1B	9
W. Mitchell, SP	9
B. Ryan, OF	9
B. Steen, SP	9
J. Baskette, RP	8
I. Olson, SS	8
J. Birmingham, OF	7
J. Graney, OF	7
T. Easterly, C	5
R. Chapman, SS	4
D. Johnston, 1B	4
S. O'Neill, C	4
R. Peckinpaugh, SS	3
N. Ball, 2B	2
F. Carisch, C	2
T. Hendryx, OF	2
G. Krapp, SP	2
B. Adams, C	1
B. Brenner, SP-RP	1
H. Butcher, OF	1
B. Hunter, OF	1
P. Livingston, C	1

Detroit (69-84)	WS
Hitting	**122.1**
Fielding	**26.7**
Pitching	**58.3**
T. Cobb, OF	40
S. Crawford, OF	24
D. Bush, SS	19
J. Dubuc, SP	19
G. Mullin, SP	14
E. Willett, SP	14
B. Louden, 2B	11
J. Delahanty, 2B	10
D. Jones, OF	9
J. Lake, SP	7
G. Moriarty, 1B	7
O. Stanage, C	6
D. Gainer, 1B	4
O. Vitt, OF	4
T. Covington, SP	3
B. Veach, OF	3
R. Works, SP	3
C. Deal, 3B	2
P. Baumann, 3B	1
B. Burns, SP	1
R. Corriden, 3B	1
H. Dauss, SP	1
W. Donovan, RP	1
E. Irvin, 3B	1
R. McDermott, OF	1
E. Summers, SP	1

New York (50-102)	WS
Hitting	**76.1**
Fielding	**25.1**
Pitching	**48.9**
R. Ford, SP	16
J. Warhop, SP	16
B. Daniels, OF	14
G. McConnell, SP	12
R. Hartzell, 3B	11
H. Chase, 1B	9
G. Zinn, OF	9
B. Cree, OF	8
R. Caldwell, SP	7
J. Lelivelt, OF	7
J. Sweeney, C	7
J. Martin, SS	5
D. Paddock, 3B	5
H. Simmons, 2B	4
D. Sterrett, OF	4
T. McMillan, SS	3
E. Gardner, 2B	2
H. Wolter, OF	2
C. Coleman, 3B	1
R. Keating, SP	1
P. Maloney, OF	1
E. Midkiff, 3B	1
A. Schulz, RP	1
G. Street, C	1
B. Stumpf, SS	1
H. Vaughn, SP	1
H. Wolverton, 3B	1

Philadelphia (90-62)	WS
Hitting	**151.4**
Fielding	**40.9**
Pitching	**77.7**
H. Baker, 3B	39
E. Collins, 2B	36
E. Plank, SP	25
S. McInnis, 1B	24
J. Coombs, SP	18
A. Strunk, OF	18
J. Barry, SS	16
C. Bender, SP	13
R. Oldring, OF	11
B. Houck, SP	10
J. Lapp, C	10
H. Maggert, OF	8
B. Brown, SP	7
B. Lord, OF	7
D. Murphy, OF	6
E. Murphy, OF	5
I. Thomas, C	3
J. Walsh, OF	3
R. Crabb, SP	2
B. Egan, C	2
C. Morgan, SP	2
J. Bush, SP	1
S. Coveleski, RP	1
C. Derrick, SS	1
S. Harrell, RP	1
H. Pennock, RP	1

St. Louis (53-101)	WS
Hitting	**65.1**
Fielding	**31.1**
Pitching	**62.8**
D. Pratt, 2B	19
B. Shotton, OF	19
E. Hamilton, SP	16
G. Baumgardner, SP	13
J. Powell, SP	13
J. Austin, 3B	10
F. LaPorte, 2B	8
B. Wallace, SS	8
G. Williams, OF	8
E. Brown, RP	7
M. Allison, SP	6
P. Compton, OF	6
G. Stovall, 1B	4
C. Weilman, SP	4
W. Hogan, OF	3
R. Mitchell, SP	3
J. Stephens, C	3
P. Krichell, C	2
W. Adams, RP	1
W. Alexander, C	1
B. Brief, OF	1
J. Daley, SS	1
E. Hallinan, SS	1
H. Jantzen, OF	1
J. Kutina, 1B	1

Washington (91-61)	WS
Hitting	**120.5**
Fielding	**49.9**
Pitching	**102.6**
W. Johnson, SP	47
C. Milan, OF	33
E. Foster, 3B	26
B. Groom, SP	23
D. Moeller, OF	22
C. Gandil, 1B	18
G. McBride, SS	13
C. Cashion, SP	12
L. Hughes, SP	12
H. Shanks, OF	9
R. Williams, C	9
J. Henry, C	7
R. Morgan, 2B	7
E. Ainsmith, C	5
F. LaPorte, 2B	5
G. Schaefer, OF	5
H. Vaughn, SP	5
B. Pelty, RP	3
T. Walker, OF	3
J. Engel, SP	2
P. Musser, RP	2
D. Kenworthy, OF	1
J. Knight, 2B	1
R. Moran, OF	1
R. Roach, SS	1
D. Walker, SP	1

1912 National League

Boston (52-101)	WS
Hitting	**67.2**
Fielding	**29.0**
Pitching	**59.8**
B. Sweeney, 2B	20
O. Hess, SP	14
H. Perdue, SP	13
V. Campbell, OF	11
J. Titus, OF	11
L. Tyler, SP	11
E. McDonald, 3B	10
A. Devlin, 1B	9
B. Brown, SP	7
W. Dickson, SP	7
E. Donnelly, RP	7
J. Kling, C	7
B. Houser, 1B	6
G. Jackson, OF	6
J. Kirke, OF	6
H. Gowdy, C	3
B. Rariden, C	2
A. Bridwell, SS	1
R. Maranville, SS	1
B. McTigue, RP	1
D. Miller, OF	1
F. O'Rourke, SS	1
H. Spratt, SS	1

Brooklyn (58-95)	WS
Hitting	**89.8**
Fielding	**28.5**
Pitching	**55.7**
N. Rucker, SP	24
J. Daubert, 1B	17
R. Smith, 3B	16
Z. Wheat, OF	16
H. Moran, OF	13
J. Hummel, 2B	12
H. Northen, OF	10
G. Cutshaw, 2B	8
O. Miller, C	8
P. Ragan, SP	8
E. Yingling, SP	7
E. Stack, SP	6
C. Curtis, RP	4
J. Daley, OF	4
E. Knetzer, RP	4
E. Phelps, C	4
F. Allen, SP	3
C. Stengel, OF	3
T. Erwin, C	2
B. Tooley, SS	2
T. Fisher, SS	1
M. Kent, RP	1
E. Kirkpatrick, 3B	1

Chicago (91-59)	WS
Hitting	**135.8**
Fielding	**45.3**
Pitching	**91.9**
H. Zimmerman, 3B	34
L. Cheney, SP	27
J. Evers, 2B	27
J. Sheckard, OF	21
J. Tinker, SS	19
J. Lavender, SP	18
L. Richie, SP	17
W. Schulte, OF	17
J. Archer, C	13
V. Saier, 1B	13
T. Leach, OF	10
E. Reulbach, RP	10
T. Brown, SP	8
W. Miller, OF	8
L. Leifield, SP	7
S. Hofman, OF	5
C. Smith, RP	5
R. Downs, 2B	3
D. Cotter, C	2
E. Lennox, 3B	2
H. McIntire, SP	2
J. Moroney, RP	2
T. Needham, C	2
C. Williams, OF	1

Cincinnati (75-78)	WS
Hitting	**109.3**
Fielding	**37.4**
Pitching	**78.3**
B. Bescher, OF	23
G. Suggs, SP	22

A. Fromme, SP	20
D. Hoblitzell, 1B	19
R. Benton, SP	18
M. Mitchell, OF	16
A. Marsans, OF	15
D. Egan, 2B	13
A. Phelan, 3B	13
J. Bates, OF	12
B. Humphries, SP-RP	10
T. Clarke, C	8
L. McLean, C	8
E. Grant, SS	5
P. Knisely, OF	4
T. McDonald, SS	4
J. Bagby, RP	2
J. Esmond, SS	2
H. Severeid, C	2
R. Almeida, 3B	1
D. Davis, RP	1
H. Gaspar, SP	1
F. Gregory, SP-RP	1
F. Harter, SP-RP	1
A. Kyle, OF	1
G. Packard, SP	1
C. Tompkins, RP	1
R. Works, RP	1

New York (103-48)	WS
Hitting	**149.6**
Fielding	**46.7**
Pitching	**112.7**
C. Mathewson, SP	31
L. Doyle, 2B	29
R. Marquard, SP	26
C. Meyers, C	23
J. Tesreau, SP	21
B. Herzog, 3B	20
F. Merkle, 1B	19
A. Fletcher, SS	18
F. Snodgrass, OF	18
R. Murray, OF	17
B. Becker, OF	15
R. Ames, SP	14
D. Crandall, RP	12
J. Devore, OF	12
H. Wiltse, SP	11
T. Shafer, SS	7
A. Wilson, C	5
L. Bader, SP-RP	2
G. Burns, OF	2
A. Demaree, SP	2
H. Groh, 2B	2
M. McCormick, OF	2
G. Hartley, C	1

Philadelphia (73-79)	WS
Hitting	**93.9**
Fielding	**40.7**
Pitching	**84.4**
P. Alexander, SP	24
D. Paskert, OF	24
S. Magee, OF	17
T. Seaton, SP	17
G. Cravath, OF	15
E. Rixey, SP	14
M. Doolan, SS	13
F. Luderus, 1B	13
A. Brennan, SP	12
O. Knabe, 2B	12
H. Lobert, 3B	9
E. Moore, SP	9
J. Titus, OF	6
T. Downey, 3B	5
B. Killefer, C	5
D. Miller, OF	4
G. Chalmers, SP	3
R. Dooin, C	3
H. Finneran, RP	3
J. Walsh, 2B	3
C. Curtis, SP	2
P. Graham, C	2
J. Dodge, 3B	1
C. Dolan, 3B	1
R. Nelson, SP-RP	1
T. Shultz, RP	1

Pittsburgh (93-58)	WS
Hitting	**124.6**
Fielding	**49.2**
Pitching	**105.2**
H. Wagner, SS	35
C. Hendrix, SP	29
C. Wilson, OF	24
H. Camnitz, SP	23
M. Carey, OF	22
M. O'Toole, SP	20
B. Byrne, 3B	18
H. Robinson, RP	17
D. Miller, 1B	14
B. Adams, SP	13
A. McCarthy, 2B	11
M. Donlin, OF	9
G. Gibson, C	8
A. Butler, 2B	4
W. Cooper, SP	4
B. Kelly, C	4
T. Leach, OF	4
E. Mensor, OF	4
M. Simon, C	4
J. Ferry, RP	2
S. Hofman, OF	2
H. Hyatt, OF	2
E. Warner, RP	2
S. Edington, OF	1
B. McKechnie, 3B	1
O. Nicholson, OF	1
J. Viox, 3B	1

St. Louis (63-90)	WS
Hitting	**104.1**
Fielding	**28.0**
Pitching	**56.9**
E. Konetchy, 1B	22
S. Sallee, SP	21
M. Huggins, 2B	17
S. Evans, OF	14
B. Harmon, SP	12
L. Magee, OF	11
R. Oakes, OF	11
A. Hauser, SS	10
M. Mowrey, 3B	10
I. Wingo, C	10
R. Ellis, OF	8
R. Geyer, RP	8
R. Bresnahan, C	6
W. Smith, 3B	6
B. Steele, SP	4
J. Willis, SP	4
J. Bliss, C	3
S. Burk, RP	3
D. Griner, SP	2
P. Perritt, SP-RP	2
T. Cather, OF	1
L. Lowdermilk, RP	1
P. Redding, SP	1
P. Whitted, 3B	1
D. Wilie, OF	1

1913
American League

Boston (79-71)	WS
Hitting	**119.4**
Fielding	**35.8**
Pitching	**81.7**
T. Speaker, OF	36
H. Hooper, OF	21
R. Collins, SP	19
H. Bedient, SP	17
D. Leonard, SP	17
D. Lewis, OF	17
C. Engle, 1B	16
L. Gardner, 3B	16
J. Wood, SP	13
S. Yerkes, 2B	13
H. Wagner, SS	11
B. Carrigan, C	9
E. Moseley, SP	6
S. Hall, RP	4
H. Cady, C	3
R. Foster, RP	3
H. Janvrin, SS	3
L. Nunamaker, C	3
B. O'Brien, SP	3
P. Thomas, C	3
O. Henriksen, OF	2
W. Rehg, OF	2

Chicago (78-74)	WS
Hitting	**79.8**
Fielding	**49.3**
Pitching	**104.9**
R. Russell, SP	32
E. Cicotte, SP	27
J. Scott, SP	27
B. Weaver, SS	23
P. Bodie, OF	16
H. Lord, 3B	15
R. Schalk, C	13
H. Chase, 1B	11
S. Collins, OF	11
J. Benz, SP	8
E. Walsh, SP	8
J. Berger, 2B	7
M. Rath, 2B	6
J. Fournier, 1B	5
B. Borton, 1B	4
L. Chappell, OF	4
W. Mattick, OF	3
J. Beall, OF	2
D. Jones, OF	2
B. Schaller, OF	2
D. White, RP	2
J. Breton, SS	1
T. Easterly, C	1
W. Kuhn, C	1
B. Meyer, C	1
P. Smith, RP	1
R. Zeider, 3B	1

Cleveland (86-66)	WS
Hitting	**106.3**
Fielding	**50.2**
Pitching	**101.5**
J. Jackson, OF	36
C. Falkenberg, SP	25
V. Gregg, SP	23
N. Lajoie, 2B	23
W. Mitchell, SP	20
F. Blanding, SP	18
R. Chapman, SS	15
J. Graney, OF	15
T. Turner, 3B	13
D. Johnston, 1B	11
S. O'Neill, C	10
B. Steen, SP	9
I. Olson, 3B	8
F. Carisch, C	6
N. Leibold, OF	6
B. Ryan, OF	6
G. Kahler, SP	5
J. Birmingham, OF	3
G. Land, C	2
R. Bates, 3B	1
N. Cullop, RP	1
L. James, RP	1
J. Lelivelt, OF	1

Detroit (66-87)	WS
Hitting	**115.8**
Fielding	**26.0**
Pitching	**56.3**
T. Cobb, OF	31
S. Crawford, OF	27
D. Bush, SS	18
J. Dubuc, SP	15
H. Dauss, SP	14
B. Veach, OF	13
E. Willett, SP	13
D. Gainer, 1B	9
M. Hall, SP	7
J. Lake, RP	7
P. Baumann, 2B	6
R. McKee, C	6
O. Vitt, 2B	6
B. Louden, 2B	5
G. Moriarty, 3B	5
H. High, OF	4
G. Mullin, SP	3
O. Stanage, C	3
C. Zamloch, RP	3
J. Burns, OF	1
E. Onslow, 1B	1
H. Rondeau, C	1

New York (57-94)	WS
Hitting	**80.0**
Fielding	**28.4**
Pitching	**62.5**
R. Caldwell, SP	14
B. Cree, OF	14
R. Fisher, SP	14
R. Ford, SP	14
H. Wolter, OF	14
R. Hartzell, 2B	13
J. Sweeney, C	12
R. Peckinpaugh, SS	8
B. Daniels, OF	7
F. Maisel, 3B	7
G. McConnell, SP	7
R. Keating, SP	6
A. Schulz, SP	6
J. Knight, 1B	4
E. Midkiff, 3B	4
F. Gilhooley, OF	3
H. Williams, 1B	3
R. Zeider, SS	3
D. Cook, OF	2
C. Derrick, SS	2
B. Holden, OF	2
M. McHale, SP	2
G. Whiteman, OF	2
L. Boone, SS	1
B. Borton, 1B	1
F. Chance, 1B	1
H. Chase, 1B	1
D. Gossett, C	1
B. McKechnie, 2B	1
C. Pieh, RP	1
J. Warhop, RP	1

Philadelphia (96-57)	WS
Hitting	**185.1**
Fielding	**35.6**
Pitching	**67.3**
E. Collins, 2B	39
H. Baker, 3B	38
S. McInnis, 1B	26
E. Murphy, OF	22
J. Barry, SS	20
C. Bender, RP	20
R. Oldring, OF	19
E. Plank, SP	16
A. Strunk, OF	14
W. Schang, C	13
B. Brown, SP	12
J. Walsh, OF	11
J. Bush, RP	8
J. Lapp, C	8
B. Shawkey, SP	6
T. Daley, OF	4
B. Houck, RP	4
I. Thomas, C	3
D. Murphy, OF	2
P. Bohen, SP	1
H. Davis, 1B	1
B. Orr, SS	1

St. Louis (57-96)	WS
Hitting	**77.0**
Fielding	**30.5**
Pitching	**63.5**
B. Shotton, OF	23
D. Pratt, 2B	19
G. Williams, OF	16
J. Austin, 3B	15
E. Hamilton, SP	13
G. Baumgardner, SP	12
R. Mitchell, SP	12
W. Leverenz, SP	11
C. Weilman, SP	9
J. Johnston, OF	6
G. Stovall, 1B	6
S. Agnew, C	5
B. Brief, 1B	3
D. Stone, RP	3
M. Allison, RP	2
M. Balenti, SS	2
T. Walker, OF	2
B. Wallace, SS	2
W. Alexander, C	1
C. Brown, SP	1
P. Compton, OF	1
F. Graff, 3B	1
D. Lavan, SS	1
B. McAllester, C	1
H. Schwenk, SP	1
T. Sloan, OF	1
D. Walsh, SS	1
B. Wares, 2B	1

Washington (90-64)	WS
Hitting	**112.9**
Fielding	**50.2**
Pitching	**106.9**
W. Johnson, SP	54
C. Milan, OF	28
J. Boehling, SP	23
C. Gandil, 1B	23
R. Morgan, 2B	21
D. Moeller, OF	17
B. Groom, SP	15
G. McBride, SS	14
E. Foster, 3B	11
H. Shanks, OF	10
J. Engel, SP	9
J. Henry, C	9
F. LaPorte, 3B	7
E. Ainsmith, C	5
G. Schaefer, 2B	5
R. Williams, C	5
D. Ayers, SP-RP	2
J. Bentley, RP	2
L. Hughes, RP	2
S. Love, RP	2
M. Acosta, OF	1
J. Calvo, OF	1
J. Gedeon, OF	1
C. Griffith, RP-OF	1
J. Shaw, SP-RP	1
B. Spencer, OF	1

1913 National League

Boston (69-82)	WS
Hitting	**118.9**
Fielding	**27.4**
Pitching	**60.7**
J. Connolly, OF	19
R. Maranville, SS	17
L. Tyler, SP	17
D. Rudolph, SP	16
B. Sweeney, 2B	15
H. Myers, 1B	13
J. Titus, OF	13
L. Mann, OF	10
O. Hess, SP	9
H. Perdue, SP	9
T. McDonald, 3B	8
B. Rariden, C	8
A. Devlin, 3B	6
B. James, SP	6
W. Dickson, SP	5
B. Lord, OF	5
B. Whaling, C	5
G. Zinn, OF	5
J. Quinn, SP	4
F. Smith, 3B	4
T. Griffith, OF	3
B. Schmidt, 1B	3
D. Brown, C	2
O. Clymer, OF	2
C. Deal, 2B	1
H. Gowdy, C	1
P. Strand, RP	1

Brooklyn (65-84)	WS
Hitting	**77.7**
Fielding	**40.4**
Pitching	**76.9**
N. Rucker, SP	19
R. Smith, 3B	19
J. Daubert, 1B	17
Z. Wheat, OF	16
G. Cutshaw, 2B	15
C. Stengel, OF	13
E. Yingling, SP-RP	13
P. Ragan, SP	10
E. Reulbach, SP	10
F. Allen, SP	9
H. Moran, OF	9
T. Fisher, SS	8
C. Curtis, SP	7
O. Miller, C	7
E. Stack, RP	7
W. Fischer, C	4
J. Hummel, OF	4
M. Walker, SP	3
E. Brown, RP	1
T. Erwin, C	1
M. Kent, RP	1
E. Kirkpatrick, SS	1
B. Meyer, OF	1

Chicago (88-65)	WS
Hitting	**144.8**
Fielding	**38.1**
Pitching	**81.0**
V. Saier, 1B	26
L. Cheney, SP	25
H. Zimmerman, 3B	25
T. Leach, OF	24
J. Evers, 2B	20
W. Schulte, OF	18
A. Bridwell, SS	15
B. Humphries, SP	14
G. Pearce, SP	13
J. Archer, C	12
M. Mitchell, OF	11
A. Phelan, 2B	9
C. Smith, SP	9
J. Lavender, SP-RP	7
W. Miller, OF	7
H. Vaughn, SP	6
R. Bresnahan, C	5
O. Overall, SP	4
W. Good, OF	3
C. Williams, OF	3
O. Clymer, OF	2
E. Stack, SP	2
R. Corriden, SS	1
T. Needham, C	1
D. Watson, SP	1
Z. Zabel, SP	1

Cincinnati (64-89)	WS
Hitting	**95.4**
Fielding	**32.8**
Pitching	**63.8**
B. Bescher, OF	17
J. Tinker, SS	17
J. Bates, OF	15
H. Groh, 2B	13
C. Johnson, SP	13
D. Hoblitzell, 1B	12
R. Ames, SP	11
T. Brown, RP	11
T. Clarke, C	10
A. Marsans, OF	9
G. Packard, SP	9
R. Benton, SP	7
G. Suggs, SP	7
J. Dodge, 3B	5
D. Egan, 2B	5
J. Kling, C	5
R. Almeida, 3B	4
J. Devore, OF	4
B. Becker, OF	3
J. Rowan, SP	3
M. Berghammer, SS	2
F. Harter, RP	2
J. Sheckard, OF	2
A. Wickland, OF	2
A. Fromme, SP	1
E. Grant, 3B	1
E. Herbert, RP	1
C. Smith, RP	1

New York (101-51)	WS
Hitting	**131.7**
Fielding	**50.5**
Pitching	**120.8**
C. Mathewson, SP	30
R. Marquard, SP	26
J. Tesreau, SP	25
A. Fletcher, SS	24
T. Shafer, 3B	23
G. Burns, OF	22
L. Doyle, 2B	21
F. Snodgrass, OF	21
C. Meyers, C	20
A. Demaree, SP	17
F. Merkle, 1B	14
R. Murray, OF	14
B. Herzog, 3B	13
D. Crandall, RP	8
A. Fromme, SP-RP	5
H. Wiltse, RP	5
R. Ames, SP	4
L. McLean, C	3
M. McCormick, OF	2
F. Schupp, RP	2
C. Cooper, OF	1
G. Hartley, C	1
B. Hearn, SP	1
A. Wilson, C	1

Philadelphia (88-63)	WS
Hitting	**109.0**
Fielding	**51.2**
Pitching	**103.8**
G. Cravath, OF	29
T. Seaton, SP	29
P. Alexander, SP	27
H. Lobert, 3B	20
A. Brennan, SP	19
S. Magee, OF	19
D. Paskert, OF	17
B. Becker, OF	14
O. Knabe, 2B	14
F. Luderus, 1B	14
E. Rixey, SP	12
E. Mayer, RP	11
B. Killefer, C	10
M. Doolan, SS	9
H. Camnitz, SP	3
R. Dooin, C	3
D. Miller, OF	3
E. Burns, C	1
B. Byrne, 3B	1
G. Chalmers, SP	1
J. Devore, OF	1
C. Dolan, OF	1
V. Duncan, OF	1
H. Finneran, RP	1
D. Howley, C	1
R. Marshall, RP	1
R. Nelson, RP	1
J. Walsh, 2B	1

Pittsburgh (78-71)	WS
Hitting	**117.3**
Fielding	**37.6**
Pitching	**79.1**
B. Adams, SP	29
J. Viox, 2B	23
M. Carey, OF	20
C. Hendrix, SP	18
D. Miller, 1B	18
H. Wagner, SS	18
C. Wilson, OF	15
H. Robinson, SP	14
B. Byrne, 3B	12
A. Butler, 2B	8
G. McQuillan, SP	7
M. Simon, C	7
M. Mitchell, OF	6
M. O'Toole, SP	6
G. Gibson, C	5
H. Camnitz, SP	4
H. Hyatt, 1B-OF	4
W. Cooper, RP	3
B. Kelly, C	3
C. Dolan, 3B	2
S. Hofman, OF	2
F. Kommers, OF	2
W. Luhrsen, SP	2
A. McCarthy, 3B-SS	2
E. Booe, OF	1
B. Coleman, C	1
J. Conzelman, SP	1
R. Wood, OF	1

St. Louis (51-99)	WS
Hitting	**80.8**
Fielding	**26.9**
Pitching	**45.2**
S. Sallee, SP	22
E. Konetchy, 1B	19
M. Huggins, 2B	18
M. Mowrey, 3B	14
R. Oakes, OF	14
B. Harmon, SP	12
L. Magee, OF	11
S. Evans, OF	6
I. Wingo, C	6
B. Doak, SP	5
D. Griner, SP	4
P. Whitted, OF	4
L. McLean, C	3
C. O'Leary, SS	3
J. Sheckard, OF	3
A. Hauser, SS	2
S. Burk, RP	1
W. Callahan, SS	1
T. Cather, OF	1
B. Hopper, SP	1
D. Niehaus, SP	1
P. Perritt, SP	1
B. Steele, SP	1

1914 American League

Boston (91-62)	WS
Hitting	**124.6**
Fielding	**48.7**
Pitching	**99.7**
T. Speaker, OF	45
D. Leonard, SP	29

L. Gardner, 3B	20
H. Hooper, OF	20
D. Lewis, OF	20
R. Collins, SP	19
R. Foster, SP	18
E. Scott, SS	13
B. Carrigan, C	11
E. Shore, SP	11
D. Hoblitzell, 1B	10
H. Janvrin, 2B	9
J. Wood, SP	8
H. Cady, C	6
F. Coumbe, RP	5
O. Henriksen, OF	5
S. Yerkes, 2B	5
D. Gainer, 1B	4
R. Johnson, SP	4
H. Bedient, RP	3
P. Thomas, C	3
W. Rehg, OF	2
V. Gregg, SP	1
B. Ruth, SP	1
M. Zeiser, RP	1

Chicago (70-84)	WS
Hitting	**79.7**
Fielding	**39.5**
Pitching	**90.8**
E. Cicotte, SP	21
J. Benz, SP	20
S. Collins, OF	18
J. Fournier, 1B	17
R. Schalk, C	17
R. Demmitt, OF	16
J. Scott, SP	14
L. Blackburne, 2B	12
R. Faber, RP	12
M. Wolfgang, RP	11
R. Russell, SP	9
B. Weaver, SS	8
H. Chase, 1B	7
P. Bodie, OF	6
B. Roth, OF	6
J. Breton, 3B	3
W. Kuhn, C	2
B. Lathrop, RP	2
W. Mayer, C	2
E. Walsh, SP	2
S. Alcock, 3B	1
H. Baker, 3B	1
J. Berger, SS	1
T. Daly, OF	1
C. Manda, 2B	1

Cleveland (51-102)	WS
Hitting	**81.2**
Fielding	**25.7**
Pitching	**46.1**
J. Jackson, OF	20
R. Chapman, SS	13
J. Graney, OF	13
B. Steen, SP	11
T. Turner, 3B	11
N. Leibold, OF	9
W. Mitchell, SP	9
R. Hagerman, SP	7
N. Lajoie, 2B	7
S. O'Neill, C	6
V. Gregg, SP	5
D. Johnston, 1B	5
G. Morton, SP	4
I. Olson, SS	4
A. Collamore, RP	3
J. Kirke, OF	3
W. Barbare, 3B	2
F. Carisch, C	2
F. Coumbe, RP	2
L. James, RP	2
J. Lelivelt, OF	2
E. Smith, OF	2
A. Tedrow, SP	2
R. Wood, OF	2
J. Bassler, C	1
F. Blanding, RP	1
A. Bowman, RP	1
P. Carter, SP	1
B. Egan, C	1
L. Pezold, 3B	1
B. Wambsganss, SS	1

Detroit (80-73)	WS
Hitting	**124.2**
Fielding	**37.0**
Pitching	**78.7**
S. Crawford, OF	31
T. Cobb, OF	26
H. Coveleski, SP	23
D. Bush, SS	22
H. Dauss, SP	19
B. Veach, OF	18
G. Burns, 1B	17
G. Moriarty, 3B	15
M. Kavanagh, 2B	11
P. Cavet, RP	9
J. Dubuc, SP	9
A. Main, RP	8
R. Reynolds, RP	6
H. High, OF	5
O. Vitt, 2B	5
M. Hall, RP	4
H. Heilmann, OF	3
O. Stanage, C	3
R. Oldham, SP	2
D. Baker, C	1
G. Boehler, RP	1
R. McKee, C	1
B. Purtell, 3B	1

New York (70-84)	WS
Hitting	**90.0**
Fielding	**38.5**
Pitching	**81.5**
R. Caldwell, SP	22
F. Maisel, 3B	20
R. Peckinpaugh, SS	16
B. Cree, OF	15
R. Fisher, SP	15
J. Warhop, SP	14
D. Cook, OF	13
R. Hartzell, OF	12
L. Nunamaker, C	11
R. Keating, SP	9
M. McHale, SP	9
J. Sweeney, C	9
T. Daley, OF	8
K. Cole, RP	7
L. Boone, 2B	6
B. Brown, SP	6
C. Mullen, 1B	6
F. Truesdale, 2B	5
J. Walsh, OF	3
F. Gilhooley, OF	1
D. Gossett, C	1
B. Holden, OF	1
H. Williams, 1B	1

Philadelphia (99-53)	WS
Hitting	**174.7**
Fielding	**40.6**
Pitching	**81.7**
E. Collins, 2B	43
H. Baker, 3B	35
E. Murphy, OF	23
S. McInnis, 1B	21
W. Schang, C	19
J. Barry, SS	18
A. Strunk, OF	17
C. Bender, SP	15
R. Bressler, RP	14
B. Shawkey, SP	14
R. Oldring, OF	13
J. Bush, SP	11
E. Plank, SP	11
H. Pennock, SP-RP	10
J. Lapp, C	8
J. Walsh, OF	8
J. Wyckoff, SP	8
T. Daley, OF	3
L. Kopf, SS	3
C. Davies, OF	2
S. Thompson, OF	1

St. Louis (71-82)	WS
Hitting	**103.2**
Fielding	**35.3**
Pitching	**74.5**
T. Walker, OF	28
D. Pratt, 2B	26
C. Weilman, SP	24
E. Hamilton, SP	22
B. Shotton, OF	19
B. James, SP	15
G. Williams, OF	13
G. Baumgardner, RP	12
J. Austin, 3B	10
J. Leary, 1B	10
D. Lavan, SS	7
S. Agnew, C	6
I. Howard, 3B	6
E. Walker, OF	6
B. Wares, SS	4
W. Taylor, SP-RP	2
F. Crossin, C	1
H. Hoch, RP	1
B. Wallace, SS	1

Washington (81-73)	WS
Hitting	**103.3**
Fielding	**48.0**
Pitching	**91.7**
W. Johnson, SP	38
E. Foster, 3B	23
C. Milan, OF	19
R. Morgan, 2B	19
C. Gandil, 1B	17
D. Moeller, OF	17
D. Ayers, SP	14
J. Shaw, SP	14
J. Boehling, SP	12
G. McBride, SS	12
H. Shanks, OF	10
J. Bentley, RP	9
M. Mitchell, OF	8
J. Engel, RP	7
R. Williams, C	7
J. Henry, C	6
E. Ainsmith, C	3
M. Acosta, OF	2
H. Harper, RP	2
C. Pick, OF	2
G. Schaefer, 2B-OF	1
W. Smith, 2B	1

1914 National League

Boston (94-59)	WS
Hitting	**128.6**
Fielding	**51.2**
Pitching	**102.3**
B. James, SP	36
D. Rudolph, SP	29
J. Connolly, OF	25
J. Evers, 2B	25
R. Maranville, SS	24
B. Schmidt, 1B	19
L. Tyler, SP	18
H. Gowdy, C	16
R. Smith, 3B	14
L. Mann, OF	13
L. Gilbert, OF	9
P. Whitted, OF	8
D. Crutcher, RP	6
O. Hess, SP	6
T. Cather, OF	5
P. Strand, RP	5
B. Whaling, C	5
C. Deal, 3B	4
H. Moran, OF	4
I. Davis, SP	3
J. Devore, OF	3
W. Collins, OF	1
O. Dugey, 2B-OF	1
T. Hughes, SP	1
J. Martin, 3B	1
J. Murray, OF	1

Brooklyn (75-79)	WS
Hitting	**115.9**
Fielding	**37.2**
Pitching	**72.0**
J. Pfeffer, SP	26
Z. Wheat, OF	26
C. Stengel, OF	20
J. Dalton, OF	19
J. Daubert, 1B	19
G. Cutshaw, 2B	15
E. Reulbach, SP	14
R. Smith, 3B	12
R. Aitchison, SP	11
P. Ragan, SP	8
F. Allen, SP	7
L. McCarty, C	7
H. Myers, OF	6
O. O'Mara, SS	6
D. Egan, SS	5
J. Hummel, 1B	5
G. Getz, 3B	4
N. Rucker, SP	4
W. Fischer, C	3
O. Miller, C	3
C. Schmutz, RP	2
K. Elberfeld, SS	1
T. Erwin, C	1
J. Riggert, OF	1

Chicago (78-76)	WS
Hitting	**121.9**
Fielding	**36.4**
Pitching	**75.7**
T. Leach, OF	27
V. Saier, 1B	24
H. Zimmerman, 3B	22
H. Vaughn, SP	21
L. Cheney, SP	20
W. Good, OF	20
R. Bresnahan, C	14
W. Schulte, OF	13
B. Sweeney, 2B	11
J. Lavender, SP	10
B. Humphries, SP	9
Z. Zabel, RP	9
J. Archer, C	7
R. Corriden, SS	7
G. Pearce, SP	4
C. Hageman, RP	3
T. Fisher, SS	2
J. Johnston, OF	2
A. Phelan, 3B	2
C. Williams, OF	2
A. Bues, 3B	1
C. Derrick, SS	1
P. Knisely, OF	1
G. McConnell, SP	1
C. Smith, RP	1

Cincinnati (60-94)	WS
Hitting	**77.1**
Fielding	**34.4**
Pitching	**68.5**
B. Herzog, SS	21
H. Groh, 2B	19
R. Ames, SP	17
R. Benton, SP	14
P. Douglas, SP	12
T. Clarke, C	11
B. Niehoff, 3B	11
H. Moran, OF	8
E. Yingling, SP	8
P. Schneider, SP	7
J. Bates, OF	6
B. Daniels, OF	5
R. Killefer, OF	5

Player	WS
D. Davenport, SP	4
A. Marsans, OF	4
D. Miller, OF	4
M. Gonzalez, C	3
D. Hoblitzell, 1B	3
K. Lear, RP	3
G. Twombly, OF	3
M. Berghammer, SS	2
T. Erwin, C	2
P. Fittery, SP-RP	2
P. Fahrer, RP	1
B. Ingersoll, RP	1
J. Rawlings, 3B	1
J. Rowan, RP	1
M. Uhler, OF	1
F. Von Kolnitz, 3B	1

New York (84-70)	WS
Hitting	**140.6**
Fielding	**36.9**
Pitching	**74.6**
G. Burns, OF	31
J. Tesreau, SP	26
A. Fletcher, SS	22
L. Doyle, 2B	19
C. Mathewson, SP	19
B. Bescher, OF	18
F. Merkle, 1B	17
C. Meyers, C	16
M. Stock, 3B	15
F. Snodgrass, OF	12
R. Marquard, SP	11
A. Demaree, SP	9
E. Grant, 3B	9
A. Fromme, RP	8
D. Robertson, OF	7
L. McLean, C	4
R. Murray, OF	2
H. Wiltse, RP	2
M. O'Toole, SP-RP	1
S. Piez, OF	1
H. Ritter, RP	1
R. Schauer, RP	1
H. Smith, C	1

Philadelphia (74-80)	WS
Hitting	**130.0**
Fielding	**25.2**
Pitching	**66.8**
S. Magee, OF	29
G. Cravath, OF	28
P. Alexander, SP	26
B. Becker, OF	22
E. Mayer, SP	21
D. Paskert, OF	15
H. Lobert, 3B	13
B. Byrne, 2B	11
F. Luderus, 1B	11
B. Tincup, SP	8
B. Killefer, C	7
E. Burns, C	6
J. Martin, SS	6
H. Irelan, 2B	4
R. Marshall, SP	4
H. Matteson, RP	3
J. Oeschger, RP	3
S. Baumgartner, RP	2
R. Dooin, C	2
J. Devore, OF	1

Pittsburgh (69-85)	WS
Hitting	**79.1**
Fielding	**43.2**
Pitching	**84.7**
B. Adams, SP	19
W. Cooper, SP	19
H. Wagner, SS	19
M. Carey, OF	17
B. Harmon, SP	16
J. Viox, 2B	16
G. McQuillan, SP	14
E. Konetchy, 1B	13
G. Gibson, C	12
Jo. Kelly, OF	9
M. Mowrey, 3B	9
J. Conzelman, RP	6
A. Mamaux, RP	6
M. Mitchell, OF	6
B. Coleman, C	5
E. Kantlehner, RP	3
A. McCarthy, 3B	3
E. Mensor, OF	3
Z. Collins, OF	2
D. Costello, OF	2
W. Gerber, SS	2
H. Kelly, RP	2
H. Hyatt, 1B	1
Ji. Kelly, OF	1
J. Leonard, 3B	1
F. Scheeren, OF	1

St. Louis (81-72)	WS
Hitting	**91.2**
Fielding	**50.5**
Pitching	**101.3**
S. Sallee, SP	25
B. Doak, SP	24
M. Huggins, 2B	22
D. Miller, 1B	21
P. Perritt, SP	20
C. Wilson, OF	18
L. Magee, OF	16
D. Griner, RP	13
Z. Beck, 3B	12
C. Dolan, OF	11
I. Wingo, C	11
H. Perdue, SP	9
F. Snyder, C	7
A. Butler, SS	6
W. Cruise, OF	6
H. Robinson, SP	6
C. Hageman, SP	3
T. Cather, OF	2
L. Dressen, 1B	2
K. Nash, 3B	2
J. Roche, C	2
B. Steele, RP	2
R. Daringer, SS	1
D. Niehaus, RP	1
J. Riggert, OF	1

1914 Federal League

Baltimore (84-70)	WS
Hitting	**116.9**
Fielding	**40.2**
Pitching	**94.9**
J. Quinn, SP	32
G. Suggs, SP	28
B. Meyer, OF	21
V. Duncan, OF	19
J. Walsh, 3B	19
M. Doolan, SS	18
F. Jacklitsch, C	16
H. Swacina, 1B	12
F. Smith, SP	11
O. Knabe, 2B	10
J. Bates, OF	9
S. Conley, RP	9
H. Simmons, OF	9
K. Wilhelm, SP	9
B. Bailey, SP	8
G. Zinn, OF	7
E. Kirkpatrick, 3B	6
H. Russell, C	3
M. Boucher, C	1
F. Chouinard, OF	1
D. Kerr, C	1
F. Kommers, OF	1
J. McCandless, OF	1
D. Yount, RP	1

Brooklyn (77-77)	WS
Hitting	**118.8**
Fielding	**37.5**
Pitching	**74.7**
S. Evans, OF	30
E. Lafitte, SP	23
T. Seaton, SP	22
S. Hofman, 2B	20
A. Shaw, OF	19
T. Wisterzil, 3B	16
G. Anderson, OF	13
H. Finneran, SP	10
C. Cooper, OF	8
J. Delahanty, 2B	7
G. Land, C	7
H. Myers, 1B	7
D. Murphy, OF	6
B. Houck, SP	5
F. Owens, C	5
E. Gagnier, SS	4
A. Halt, SS	4
B. Maxwell, SP	4
J. Bluejacket, RP	3
B. Chappelle, RP	3
A. Griggs, 1B	3
D. Marion, SP	3
R. Sommers, RP	2
A. Watson, C	2
B. Bradley, PH-PR	1
T. Brown, SP	1
F. Chouinard, OF	1
R. Peters, RP	1
R. Williams, 3B	1

Buffalo (80-71)	WS
Hitting	**98.6**
Fielding	**50.2**
Pitching	**91.3**
R. Ford, SP	29
C. Hanford, OF	29
G. Krapp, SP	21
B. Louden, SS	21
J. Agler, 1B	17
F. Anderson, SP	15
H. Chase, 1B	14
W. Blair, C	13
T. McDonald, OF	11
T. Downey, 2B	10
A. Schulz, SP	10
F. Smith, 3B	10
E. Moore, SP	6
H. Moran, RP	6
E. Booe, OF	4
F. Delahanty, OF	4
H. Schlafly, 2B	4
D. Young, OF	4
C. Engle, 3B	3
B. Smith, RP	3
A. LaVigne, C	2
D. Woodman, RP	2
N. Allen, C	1
L. Bonin, OF	1

Chicago (87-67)	WS
Hitting	**118.3**
Fielding	**47.5**
Pitching	**95.1**
C. Hendrix, SP	37
D. Zwilling, OF	29
A. Wilson, C	27
A. Wickland, OF	22
F. Beck, 1B	17
J. Tinker, SS	16
R. Zeider, 3B	15
E. Lange, SP	14
J. Farrell, 2B	13
M. Flack, OF	13
D. Watson, SP	13
R. Johnson, SP	11
M. Fiske, SP	10
M. Prendergast, SP	7
T. McGuire, SP-RP	4
A. Brennan, SP	3
H. Fritz, 3B	3
B. Block, C	2
J. Stanley, SS	2
A. Walsh, OF	2
J. Smith, SS	1

Indianapolis (88-65)	WS
Hitting	**128.7**
Fielding	**43.8**
Pitching	**91.5**
B. Kauff, OF	38
C. Falkenberg, SP	34
B. McKechnie, 3B	23
V. Campbell, OF	20
J. Esmond, SS	18
F. LaPorte, 2B	18
G. Kaiserling, SP	17
E. Moseley, SP	17
G. Mullin, SP	17
A. Scheer, OF	14
B. Rariden, C	13
C. Carr, 1B	10
H. Billiard, SP-RP	6
E. Roush, OF	6
A. Kaiser, OF	3
B. Dolan, 1B	2
C. Vandagrift, 2B	2
E. Booe, OF	1
F. Harter, RP	1
K. Keifer, SP	1
G. Textor, C	1
B. Warren, C	1
C. Whitehouse, RP	1

Kansas City (67-84)	WS
Hitting	**115.9**
Fielding	**27.1**
Pitching	**58.0**
D. Kenworthy, 2B	30
G. Packard, SP	21
C. Chadbourne, OF	19
N. Cullop, SP	19
T. Easterly, C	19
G. Perring, 3B	17
G. Gilmore, OF	14
G. Stovall, 1B	12
A. Kruger, OF	10
P. Goodwin, SS	7
D. Adams, RP	5
C. Johnson, SP	5
C. Daringer, SS	4
B. Harris, RP	4
J. Potts, OF	4
J. Rawlings, SS	4
D. Stone, SP	3
C. Coles, OF	2
P. Henning, SP-RP	2

Pittsburgh (64-86)	WS
Hitting	**104.5**
Fielding	**29.2**
Pitching	**58.3**
E. Lennox, 3B	24
R. Oakes, OF	21
E. Knetzer, SP	18
J. Savage, OF	15
H. Camnitz, SP	13
H. Bradley, 1B	12
W. Dickson, SP	12
D. Jones, OF	11
T. McDonald, OF	10
C. Berry, C	8
S. Yerkes, SS	8
C. Barger, SP	7
E. Holly, SS	6
J. Lewis, 2B	5
G. LeClair, RP	4
M. Menosky, OF	4
W. Adams, RP	2
F. Delahanty, OF	2
D. Kerr, C	2
M. Walker, SP	2
F. Allen, SP	1
F. Chouinard, 2B	1

R. Mattis, OF	1
C. Rheam, 1B	1
S. Roberts, C	1
J. Scott, SS	1

St. Louis (62-89)	WS
Hitting	**73.6**
Fielding	**35.4**
Pitching	**77.0**
D. Crandall, 2B	26
B. Groom, SP	17
W. Miller, OF	17
J. Tobin, OF	15
T. Brown, SP	14
D. Davenport, SP	13
A. Bridwell, SS	11
A. Boucher, 3B	9
F. Kommers, OF	9
D. Drake, OF	8
H. Keupper, SP	7
G. Hartley, C	6
D. Watson, SP	6
E. Willett, SP	6
L. Kirby, OF	4
M. Simon, C	4
E. Herbert, RP	3
J. Misse, 2B	3
H. Chapman, C	2
A. Marsans, 2B	2
J. Mathes, 2B	2
H. Miller, 1B	2

1915 American League

Boston (101-50)	WS
Hitting	**141.1**
Fielding	**50.2**
Pitching	**111.7**
T. Speaker, OF	36
R. Foster, SP	25
D. Lewis, OF	24
B. Ruth, SP	23
E. Shore, SP	22
J. Wood, SP	20
H. Hooper, OF	19
D. Leonard, SP	18
D. Hoblitzell, 1B	16
L. Gardner, 3B	14
H. Cady, C	11
C. Mays, RP	11
J. Barry, 2B	10
D. Gainer, 1B	10
H. Wagner, 2B	9
H. Janvrin, SS	8
P. Thomas, C	7
E. Scott, SS	6
V. Gregg, SP-RP	5
B. Carrigan, C	4
R. Collins, RP	3
R. Comstock, RP	1
O. Henriksen, OF	1

Chicago (93-61)	WS
Hitting	**140.2**
Fielding	**42.6**
Pitching	**96.3**
E. Collins, 2B	40
J. Fournier, 1B	28
J. Scott, SP	23
R. Faber, SP	21
B. Weaver, SS	21
R. Schalk, C	18
J. Benz, SP	17
R. Russell, SP	16
S. Collins, OF	15
H. Felsch, OF	14
E. Murphy, OF	14
E. Cicotte, SP	13
B. Roth, 3B	9
J. Jackson, OF	7
L. Blackburne, 3B	5
E. Walsh, SP	4
M. Wolfgang, RP	4
B. Brief, 1B	3
P. Johns, 3B	2
N. Leibold, OF	2
E. Klepfer, SP	1
W. Mayer, C	1
F. Quinlan, OF	1

Cleveland (57-95)	WS
Hitting	**68.0**
Fielding	**32.3**
Pitching	**70.6**
G. Morton, SP	21
R. Chapman, SS	17
W. Mitchell, SP	14
J. Jackson, OF	11
J. Graney, OF	10
S. O'Neill, C	9
J. Kirke, 1B	8
E. Smith, OF	8
S. Jones, RP	7
N. Leibold, OF	6
B. Roth, OF	6
A. Collamore, SP	5
F. Coumbe, RP	5
R. Hagerman, SP	5
J. Evans, 3B	4
O. Harstad, RP	4
B. Southworth, OF	4
T. Turner, 2B	4
R. Walker, SP	4
W. Barbare, 3B	3
D. Wilie, OF	3
L. Brenton, RP	2
P. Carter, RP	2
B. Egan, C	2
E. Klepfer, SP	2
B. Wambsganss, 2B	2
J. Eschen, OF	1
C. Garrett, SP	1
B. Rodgers, 2B	1

Detroit (100-54)	WS
Hitting	**156.1**
Fielding	**45.6**
Pitching	**98.3**
T. Cobb, OF	48
B. Veach, OF	30
S. Crawford, OF	28
H. Dauss, SP	25
H. Coveleski, SP	24
O. Vitt, 3B	23
D. Bush, SS	20
J. Dubuc, SP	16
M. Kavanagh, 1B	16
B. Boland, RP	13
G. Burns, 1B	10
R. Young, 2B	10
B. James, SP	6
B. Steen, RP	6
R. Oldham, RP	5
O. Stanage, C	5
D. Baker, C	4
R. McKee, C	4
P. Cavet, RP	3
G. Boehler, RP	1
B. Jacobson, 1B	1
G. Lowdermilk, SP	1
G. Moriarty, 3B	1

New York (69-83)	WS
Hitting	**91.2**
Fielding	**40.1**
Pitching	**75.7**
R. Caldwell, SP	24
R. Fisher, SP	21
F. Maisel, 3B	20
W. Pipp, 1B	16
D. Cook, OF	15
H. High, OF	14
R. Peckinpaugh, SS	14
P. Baumann, 2B	10
R. Hartzell, OF	9
L. Boone, 2B	8
L. Nunamaker, C	6
C. Pieh, RP	5
B. Shawkey, SP	5
W. Alexander, C	4
B. Cree, OF	4
G. Mogridge, SP	4
J. Warhop, SP	4
R. Keating, SP	3
C. Markle, SP	3
J. Sweeney, C	3
B. Brown, SP	2
K. Cole, SP	2
M. McHale, SP	2
C. Mullen, 1B	2
A. Russell, SP	2
D. Tipple, SP	2
D. Vance, RP	2
P. Schwert, C	1

Philadelphia (43-109)	WS
Hitting	**100.6**
Fielding	**11.4**
Pitching	**17.0**
A. Strunk, OF	21
W. Schang, 3B	17
S. McInnis, 1B	13
N. Lajoie, 2B	12
J. Lapp, C	12
R. Oldring, OF	10
L. Kopf, SS	6
J. Walsh, OF	6
E. Murphy, OF	5
J. Wyckoff, SP	5
L. Malone, 2B	3
J. Barry, SS	2
J. Bush, SP	2
B. Davis, RP	2
T. Knowlson, SP-RP	2
B. Shawkey, SP	2
S. Thompson, OF	2
R. Bressler, SP	1
D. Fillingim, SP-RP	1
W. McAvoy, C	1
B. Morrisette, RP	1
H. Pennock, SP	1
T. Sheehan, SP	1
J. Sherman, SP-RP	1

St. Louis (63-91)	WS
Hitting	**87.7**
Fielding	**34.4**
Pitching	**66.9**
B. Shotton, OF	24
D. Pratt, 2B	21
C. Weilman, SP	21
T. Walker, OF	16
J. Austin, 3B	15
I. Howard, 1B	13
G. Sisler, 1B	10
D. Lavan, SS	9
E. Hamilton, SP	8
E. Koob, RP	8
G. Lowdermilk, SP	8
B. James, SP	6
T. McCabe, SP	4
R. Hoff, RP	3
J. Park, SP	3
S. Agnew, C	2
D. Kauffman, 1B	2
J. Leary, 1B	2
H. Severeid, C	2
E. Walker, OF	2
D. Walsh, OF	2
B. Jacobson, OF	1
B. Lee, OF	1
P. Perryman, RP	1
T. Phillips, SP	1
P. Sims, SP	1
J. Tillman, SP-RP	1
B. Wallace, SS	1
G. Williams, OF	1

Washington (85-68)	WS
Hitting	**88.5**
Fielding	**50.2**
Pitching	**116.3**
W. Johnson, SP	42
E. Foster, 3B	22
B. Gallia, SP	22
C. Milan, OF	22
D. Ayers, RP	19
C. Gandil, 1B	16
J. Boehling, SP	12
H. Shanks, OF	12
D. Moeller, OF	11
J. Henry, C	10
J. Shaw, SP	10
G. McBride, SS	9
H. Harper, SP	8
R. Morgan, 2B	6
R. Williams, C	6
M. Acosta, OF	3
E. Ainsmith, C	3
G. Dumont, SP	3
C. Jamieson, OF	3
J. Judge, 1B	3
H. Milan, OF	3
T. Barber, OF	2
S. Rice, SP-RP	2
J. Bentley, SP-RP	1
T. Connolly, 3B	1
J. Engel, RP	1
M. Kopp, OF	1
H. Rondeau, OF	1
C. Sawyer, 2B	1

1915 National League

Boston (83-69)	WS
Hitting	**123.7**
Fielding	**41.7**
Pitching	**83.6**
S. Magee, OF	26
D. Rudolph, SP	24
R. Smith, 3B	24
T. Hughes, SP-RP	22
R. Maranville, SS	20
P. Ragan, SP	16
J. Connolly, OF	15
H. Gowdy, C	15
B. Schmidt, 1B	12
L. Tyler, SP	12
J. Evers, 2B	11
E. Fitzpatrick, 2B	10
H. Moran, OF	8
D. Egan, OF	7
A. Nehf, SP	5
J. Barnes, RP	4
B. Whaling, C	4
P. Compton, OF	3
B. James, SP	3
T. Cather, OF	2
F. Snodgrass, OF	2
E. Blackburn, C	1
Z. Collins, OF	1
I. Davis, SP	1
P. Strand, RP	1

Brooklyn (80-72)	WS
Hitting	**104.2**
Fielding	**45.7**
Pitching	**90.1**
J. Daubert, 1B	27
J. Pfeffer, SP	26
Z. Wheat, OF	24
J. Coombs, SP	16
G. Cutshaw, 2B	16
W. Dell, SP	15
H. Myers, OF	14
O. O'Mara, SS	14

C. Stengel, OF	14
G. Getz, 3B	13
S. Smith, SP	13
N. Rucker, SP	10
P. Douglas, SP	7
L. McCarty, C	7
O. Miller, C	7
J. Schultz, 3B	5
E. Appleton, RP	4
L. Cheney, SP	2
J. Hummel, OF	2
P. Ragan, RP	2
B. Zimmerman, OF	2

Chicago (73-80)	WS
Hitting	**112.4**
Fielding	**33.6**
Pitching	**73.0**
V. Saier, 1B	24
H. Vaughn, SP	19
C. Williams, OF	19
T. Fisher, SS	17
W. Schulte, OF	17
H. Zimmerman, 2B	16
J. Lavender, SP	15
W. Good, OF	12
B. Humphries, SP	12
A. Phelan, 3B	11
G. Pearce, SP	9
J. Archer, C	8
R. Bresnahan, C	7
Z. Zabel, RP	6
R. Murray, OF	5
P. Standridge, RP	5
L. Cheney, SP	4
P. Knisely, OF	4
A. McCarthy, 2B-3B	3
P. Douglas, SP	2
J. Mulligan, SS	2
B. Hogg, SP	1
P. McLarry, 2B	1

Cincinnati (71-83)	WS
Hitting	**85.1**
Fielding	**46.8**
Pitching	**81.2**
H. Groh, 3B	25
F. Toney, SP	23
G. Dale, SP	20
T. Griffith, OF	20
B. Herzog, SS	20
R. Killefer, OF	18
P. Schneider, SP	18
T. Clarke, C	10
R. Benton, SP	7
T. Leach, OF	7
K. Lear, RP	7
F. Mollwitz, 1B	7
L. McKenry, SP	6
B. Rodgers, 2B	6
I. Olson, 2B	4
K. Williams, OF	4
I. Wingo, C	4
L. George, SP	2
J. Wagner, 2B	2
J. Beall, OF	1
C. Brown, RP	1
R. Dooin, C	1

New York (69-83)	WS
Hitting	**130.1**
Fielding	**25.4**
Pitching	**51.5**
L. Doyle, 2B	33
G. Burns, OF	24
F. Merkle, 1B	22
D. Robertson, OF	21
J. Tesreau, SP	21
A. Fletcher, SS	18
H. Lobert, 3B	10
C. Meyers, C	10
P. Perritt, SP	9
S. Stroud, SP	8
C. Mathewson, SP	5
R. Marquard, SP	4
R. Benton, SP	3
F. Brainerd, 1B	3
F. Snodgrass, OF	3
R. Murray, OF	2
R. Schauer, RP	2
C. Babington, OF	1
R. Dooin, C	1
B. Dyer, 3B	1
A. Fromme, RP	1
E. Grant, 3B	1
F. Herbert, SP	1
B. Kocher, C	1
J. Thorpe, OF	1
L. Wendell, C	1

Philadelphia (90-62)	WS
Hitting	**111.2**
Fielding	**49.3**
Pitching	**109.5**
P. Alexander, SP	43
G. Cravath, OF	35
F. Luderus, 1B	26
E. Mayer, SP	24
D. Bancroft, SS	21
P. Whitted, OF	15
G. Chalmers, SP	12
A. Demaree, SP	12
E. Rixey, SP	12
B. Niehoff, 2B	11
D. Paskert, OF	11
B. Becker, OF	10
B. Killefer, C	9
M. Stock, 3B	8
E. Burns, C	6
B. Byrne, 3B	6
G. McQuillan, SP	4
S. Baumgartner, RP	2
B. Tincup, RP	2
J. Oeschger, RP	1

Pittsburgh (73-81)	WS
Hitting	**102.2**
Fielding	**38.7**
Pitching	**78.1**
B. Hinchman, OF	24
H. Wagner, SS	23
A. Mamaux, SP	21
J. Viox, 2B	18
M. Carey, OF	16
B. Harmon, SP	15
D. Johnston, 1B	15
B. Adams, SP	13
D. Baird, 3B	11
Z. Collins, OF	11
G. Gibson, C	11
E. Kantlehner, SP	11
G. McQuillan, SP	7
C. Hill, RP	5
E. Barney, OF	4
W. Cooper, SP-RP	4
J. Conzelman, RP	2
W. Gerber, 3B	2
B. Schang, C	2
D. Costello, OF	1
L. LeJeune, OF	1
A. McCarthy, 2B	1
P. Slattery, RP	1

St. Louis (72-81)	WS
Hitting	**113.7**
Fielding	**33.6**
Pitching	**68.7**
F. Snyder, C	24
T. Long, OF	20
B. Doak, SP	17
D. Miller, 1B	16
B. Bescher, OF	15
M. Huggins, 2B	13
S. Sallee, SP	13
C. Dolan, OF	12
C. Wilson, OF	11
A. Butler, SS	10
H. Hyatt, 1B	10
L. Meadows, SP	10
R. Ames, SP	9
D. Griner, RP	9
H. Robinson, RP	8
B. Betzel, 3B	7
Z. Beck, 3B	4
M. Gonzalez, C	3
C. Boardman, RP	2
H. Glenn, C	1
H. Perdue, RP	1
J. Roche, C	1

1915 Federal League

Baltimore (47-107)	WS
Hitting	**70.2**
Fielding	**25.2**
Pitching	**45.6**
J. Quinn, SP	13
S. Evans, OF	11
J. Walsh, 3B	11
V. Duncan, OF	10
R. Johnson, SP	8
O. Knabe, 2B	8
F. Owens, C	8
G. Suggs, SP	8
G. Zinn, OF	8
M. Doolan, SS	7
C. Bender, SP	6
F. Jacklitsch, C	5
E. Kirkpatrick, 3B	4
G. LeClair, SP-RP	4
J. McCandless, OF	4
B. Meyer, OF	4
J. Agler, 1B	3
B. Bailey, SP	3
S. Conley, RP	3
H. Russell, C	3
F. Smith, SP	2
H. Swacina, 1B	2
D. Black, SP-RP	1
J. Gallagher, 2B	1
J. Hickman, OF	1
K. Kolseth, 1B	1
H. Simmons, 2B-OF	1
J. Smith, SS	1

Brooklyn (70-82)	WS
Hitting	**127.6**
Fielding	**26.0**
Pitching	**56.4**
B. Kauff, OF	34
C. Cooper, OF	23
L. Magee, 2B	17
G. Anderson, OF	14
A. Halt, 3B	13
H. Finneran, SP	11
S. Evans, OF	10
D. Marion, SP	10
H. Myers, 1B	9
Fre. Smith, SS	9
J. Bluejacket, SP	7
B. Upham, RP	6
T. Wisterzil, 3B	6
H. Wiltse, RP	5
C. Falkenberg, SP	4
E. Lafitte, SP	4
G. Land, C	4
T. Seaton, SP	4
Fra. Smith, RP	4
F. Wilson, SP	3
E. Gagnier, SS	2
T. Helfrich, 2B	2
M. Walker, SP	2
H. Bradley, 1B	1
J. Delahanty, 2B	1
A. Griggs, 1B	1
M. Reed, SS	1
M. Simon, C	1
H. Smith, C	1
A. Watson, C	1

Buffalo (74-78)	WS
Hitting	**109.8**
Fielding	**38.4**
Pitching	**73.8**
H. Chase, 1B	23
B. Louden, 2B	23
A. Schulz, SP	21
F. Anderson, SP	20
J. Dalton, OF	18
H. Bedient, SP	15
C. Engle, OF	15
R. Roach, SS	12
G. Krapp, SP	10
H. Lord, 3B	10
T. McDonald, OF	10
W. Blair, C	8
S. Hofman, OF	7
B. Meyer, OF	7
N. Allen, C	4
F. Smith, SS	4
T. Downey, 2B	3
R. Ford, SP	3
R. Marshall, RP	3
J. Agler, OF	2
E. Lafitte, RP	2
A. Watson, C	2

Chicago (86-66)	WS
Hitting	**132.8**
Fielding	**41.0**
Pitching	**84.2**
D. Zwilling, OF	30
M. Flack, OF	26
G. McConnell, SP	25
L. Mann, OF	23
T. Brown, SP	21
A. Wilson, C	19
C. Hendrix, SP	18
W. Fischer, C	16
M. Prendergast, SP	15
R. Zeider, 2B	11
D. Black, RP	7
H. Fritz, 3B	7
J. Smith, SS	6
F. Beck, 1B	5
J. Farrell, 2B	5
C. Hanford, OF	4
T. Wisterzil, 3B	4
B. Bailey, SP	3
J. Tinker, SS	3
A. Wickland, OF	3
A. Brennan, SP	2
M. Doolan, SS	2
A. Hauser, SS	1
C. Pechous, 3B	1
J. Weiss, 1B	1

Kansas City (81-72)	WS
Hitting	**111.2**
Fielding	**40.5**
Pitching	**91.3**
N. Cullop, SP	25
D. Kenworthy, 2B	22
G. Packard, SP	22
G. Perring, 3B	22
G. Gilmore, OF	21
A. Shaw, OF	21
C. Chadbourne, OF	18
C. Johnson, SP	17
A. Main, SP	17
T. Easterly, C	14
P. Henning, SP-RP	10
G. Stovall, 1B	9
D. Brown, C	7
J. Rawlings, SS	6
A. Kruger, OF	5
P. Goodwin, SS	4
B. Bradley, 3B	2
J. Enzenroth, C	1

Newark (80-72)	WS
Hitting	**110.0**
Fielding	**42.3**
Pitching	**87.7**
B. Rariden, C	25
J. Esmond, SS	22
E. Reulbach, SP	22
E. Roush, OF	22
E. Moseley, SP	21
A. Scheer, OF	20
V. Campbell, OF	19
G. Kaiserling, SP	19
F. LaPorte, 2B	17
B. McKechnie, 3B	14
H. Moran, SP	14
C. Falkenberg, SP	7
E. Huhn, 1B	5
T. Seaton, SP	5
G. Schaefer, OF	3
G. Whitehouse, OF	2
C. Brandom, RP	1
L. Pratt, C	1
T. Reed, 3B	1

Pittsburgh (86-67)	WS
Hitting	**109.2**
Fielding	**50.5**
Pitching	**98.3**
E. Konetchy, 1B	27
F. Allen, SP	24
M. Mowrey, 3B	21
J. Kelly, OF	20
E. Knetzer, SP	20
C. Rogge, SP	19
A. Wickland, OF	17
C. Barger, RP	16
M. Berghammer, SS	16
R. Oakes, OF	16
S. Yerkes, 2B	16
B. Hearn, SP	8
C. Berry, C	7
P. O'Connor, C	6
J. Lewis, 2B	5
S. Burk, SP	3
R. Comstock, SP	3
W. Dickson, RP	3
D. Jones, OF	2
G. LeClair, RP	2
E. Lennox, 3B	2
H. Bradley, OF	1
A. Braithwood, RP	1
F. Delahanty, OF	1
E. Holly, SS	1
C. Rheam, OF	1

St. Louis (87-67)	WS
Hitting	**107.2**
Fielding	**48.8**
Pitching	**105.1**
D. Davenport, SP	34
D. Crandall, SP	29
E. Plank, SP	29
J. Tobin, OF	23
W. Miller, OF	22
B. Borton, 1B	20
E. Johnson, SS	18
B. Vaughn, 2B	17
G. Hartley, C	14
B. Groom, SP	11
C. Deal, 3B	10
D. Drake, OF	8
A. Kores, 3B	7
D. Watson, SP	5
A. Bridwell, 2B	4
H. Chapman, C	3
E. Herbert, RP	3
L. Kirby, OF	2
A. Marsans, OF	1
T. Wisterzil, 3B	1

1916 American League

Boston (91-63)	WS
Hitting	**120.8**
Fielding	**49.7**
Pitching	**102.5**
B. Ruth, SP	37
L. Gardner, 3B	27
H. Hooper, OF	26
D. Leonard, SP	22
C. Mays, SP	22
D. Lewis, OF	19
T. Walker, OF	18
E. Shore, SP	14
D. Hoblitzell, 1B	13
E. Scott, SS	11
P. Thomas, C	11
R. Foster, SP	10
H. Janvrin, SS	9
J. Barry, 2B	6
B. Carrigan, C	4
D. Gainer, 1B	4
C. Shorten, OF	4
H. Cady, C	3
V. Gregg, RP	3
O. Henriksen, OF	3
S. Agnew, C	2
M. McNally, 2B	2
S. Jones, RP	1
H. Pennock, RP	1
H. Wagner, 3B	1

Chicago (89-65)	WS
Hitting	**115.6**
Fielding	**49.9**
Pitching	**101.5**
J. Jackson, OF	34
E. Collins, 2B	31
H. Felsch, OF	24
R. Russell, RP	20
E. Cicotte, RP	19
R. Faber, SP	17
R. Schalk, C	16
S. Collins, OF	15
B. Weaver, 3B	14
J. Benz, SP	12
L. Williams, SP	11
M. Wolfgang, SP	10
J. Fournier, 1B	9
J. Scott, SP	9
J. Ness, 1B	6
Z. Terry, SS	6
F. McMullin, 3B	5
D. Danforth, RP	4
J. Lapp, C	2
N. Leibold, OF	1
B. Lynn, C	1
E. Murphy, OF	1

Cleveland (77-77)	WS
Hitting	**118.3**
Fielding	**35.9**
Pitching	**76.8**
T. Speaker, OF	41
J. Graney, OF	22
J. Bagby, SP	17
B. Roth, OF	15
T. Turner, 3B	13
C. Gandil, 1B	12
S. Coveleski, SP	11
R. Chapman, SS	10
S. O'Neill, C	10
B. Wambsganss, SS	10
F. Coumbe, RP	9
E. Klepfer, RP	9
G. Morton, SP	9
A. Gould, RP	7
E. Smith, OF	7
F. Beebe, SP	6
I. Howard, 2B	5
J. Boehling, SP	4
O. Lambeth, SP	4
H. DeBerry, C	2
M. Allison, OF	1
W. Barbare, 3B	1
B. Coleman, C	1
T. Daly, C	1
J. Evans, 3B	1
M. Kavanagh, 2B	1
G. Lowdermilk, SP	1
P. Smith, SP	1

Detroit (87-67)	WS
Hitting	**140.4**
Fielding	**40.8**
Pitching	**79.8**
T. Cobb, OF	40
H. Coveleski, SP	27
B. Veach, OF	27
O. Vitt, 3B	21
H. Dauss, SP	17
H. Heilmann, OF	17
R. Young, 2B	17
G. Burns, 1B	15
S. Crawford, OF	13
D. Bush, SS	12
J. Dubuc, RP	11
G. Cunningham, RP	9
W. Mitchell, SP	7
B. Boland, RP	6
O. Stanage, C	6
B. James, SP	4
T. Spencer, C	4
H. Ehmke, SP	2
E. Hamilton, SP	2
D. Baker, C	1
B. Dyer, SS	1
E. Erickson, RP	1
R. McKee, C	1

New York (80-74)	WS
Hitting	**109.6**
Fielding	**43.6**
Pitching	**86.8**
B. Shawkey, SP	27
R. Peckinpaugh, SS	21
W. Pipp, 1B	20
H. Baker, 3B	17
L. Magee, OF	15
L. Nunamaker, C	15
N. Cullop, SP	13
H. High, OF	12
G. Mogridge, SP	12
R. Fisher, SP	9
F. Gilhooley, OF	9
P. Baumann, OF	8
R. Caldwell, SP	8
R. Walters, C	8
A. Russell, SP	7
U. Shocker, SP	6
J. Gedeon, 2B	5
W. Alexander, C	4
R. Keating, SP	4
C. Mullen, 2B	4
T. Hendryx, OF	3
F. Maisel, OF	3
E. Miller, OF	3
R. Oldring, OF	3
L. Boone, 3B	2
S. Hofman, OF	1
C. Markle, SP	1

Philadelphia (36-117)	WS
Hitting	**74.9**
Fielding	**13.2**
Pitching	**19.8**
A. Strunk, OF	23
S. McInnis, 1B	12
W. Schang, OF	12
W. Witt, SS	10
J. Bush, SP	7
J. Walsh, OF	7
C. Pick, 3B	6
E. Myers, SP	5
N. Lajoie, 2B	4
J. Nabors, SP	3
R. Grover, 2B	2
L. McElwee, 3B	2
B. Meyer, C	2
R. Oldring, OF	2
T. Sheehan, RP	2
J. Brown, OF	1
R. Haley, C	1
T. Healy, 3B	1
J. Johnson, SP	1
R. Lanning, OF	1
R. Parnham, SP	1
V. Picinich, C	1
B. Stellbauer, OF	1
B. Thrasher, OF	1

St. Louis (79-75)	WS
Hitting	**114.3**
Fielding	**38.6**
Pitching	**84.1**
B. Shotton, OF	26
G. Sisler, 1B	25
D. Pratt, 2B	24
C. Weilman, SP	19
E. Plank, SP	17
W. Miller, OF	16
D. Davenport, SP	15
A. Marsans, OF	14
B. Groom, SP	13
J. Austin, 3B	11
E. Koob, SP	11
D. Lavan, SS	11
H. Severeid, C	8
E. Johnson, SS	7
G. Hartley, C	5
J. Park, RP	4
B. Borton, 1B	3
E. Hamilton, SP	2
W. Rumler, C	2
C. Deal, 3B	1
B. Fincher, RP	1
J. Tobin, OF	1
B. Wallace, 3B	1

Washington (76-77)	WS
Hitting	**94.4**
Fielding	**43.3**
Pitching	**90.3**
W. Johnson, SP	36
H. Harper, SP	19
B. Gallia, SP	18
C. Milan, OF	18
E. Foster, 3B	17
R. Morgan, 2B	15
J. Henry, C	13
G. McBride, SS	13
H. Shanks, OF	13
J. Judge, 1B	8
S. Rice, OF	8
J. Boehling, SP	7
D. Moeller, OF	6
J. Shaw, RP	6
R. Williams, 1B	6
J. Leonard, 3B	5
H. Rondeau, OF	4
E. Smith, OF	4
C. Jamieson, OF	3
E. Ainsmith, C	2
D. Ayers, RP	2
G. Dumont, RP	2
P. Gharrity, C-1B	2
C. Sawyer, 2B	1

1916 National League

Boston (89-63)	WS
Hitting	**128.9**
Fielding	**45.8**
Pitching	**92.3**
R. Maranville, SS	27
E. Konetchy, 1B	26
R. Smith, 3B	24
D. Rudolph, SP	21
L. Tyler, SP	20
H. Gowdy, C	17
S. Magee, OF	16

Player	WS
F. Snodgrass, OF	16
T. Hughes, RP	14
P. Ragan, SP	12
F. Allen, SP	10
J. Wilhoit, OF	10
J. Evers, 2B	8
J. Barnes, SP	7
A. Nehf, SP	7
E. Blackburn, C	6
D. Egan, 2B	5
E. Reulbach, SP	5
Z. Collins, OF	4
J. Connolly, OF	4
E. Fitzpatrick, 2B	4
W. Tragesser, C	2
L. Chappell, OF	1
P. Compton, OF	1

Brooklyn (94-60)	WS
Hitting	**126.2**
Fielding	**50.2**
Pitching	**105.6**
J. Pfeffer, SP	32
Z. Wheat, OF	32
J. Daubert, 1B	21
R. Marquard, SP	20
C. Stengel, OF	19
L. Cheney, SP	17
M. Mowrey, 3B	17
S. Smith, SP	17
G. Cutshaw, 2B	16
H. Myers, OF	15
J. Johnston, OF	13
J. Coombs, SP	11
W. Dell, SP-RP	10
C. Meyers, C	10
I. Olson, SS	10
L. McCarty, C	7
O. Miller, C	7
N. Rucker, RP	3
O. O'Mara, SS	2
E. Appleton, RP	1
G. Getz, 3B	1
F. Merkle, 1B	1

Chicago (67-86)	WS
Hitting	**61.7**
Fielding	**43.6**
Pitching	**95.7**
H. Vaughn, SP	24
C. Williams, OF	18
C. Hendrix, SP	15
V. Saier, 1B	13
H. Zimmerman, 3B	13
J. Lavender, SP	12
G. Packard, RP	12
M. Prendergast, RP	11
M. Flack, OF	10
G. McConnell, SP	10
L. Mann, OF	9
W. Schulte, OF	8
T. Seaton, RP	7
R. Zeider, 3B	6
J. Kelly, OF	4
O. Knabe, 2B	3
A. McCarthy, 2B	3
S. Perry, SP	3
S. Yerkes, 2B	3
J. Archer, C	2
P. Carter, SP	2
L. Doyle, 2B	2
W. Fischer, C	2
T. Brown, RP	1
M. Doolan, SS	1
R. Elliott, C	1
S. Hofman, OF	1
F. Mollwitz, 1B	1
J. Mulligan, SS	1
C. Pechous, 3B	1
A. Wilson, C	1
C. Wortman, SS	1

Cincinnati (60-93)	WS
Hitting	**93.3**
Fielding	**31.5**
Pitching	**55.1**
H. Groh, 3B	24
H. Chase, 1B	22
F. Toney, SP	18
T. Griffith, OF	13
P. Schneider, SP	13
B. Louden, 2B	10
E. Roush, OF	10
C. Mitchell, SP	9
G. Neale, OF	9
B. Herzog, SS	8
I. Wingo, C	8
A. Schulz, SP-RP	7
E. Knetzer, RP	6
R. Killefer, OF	5
T. Clarke, C	4
T. Fisher, SS	3
E. Moseley, RP	3
B. McKechnie, 3B	2
J. Beall, OF	1
F. Emmer, SS	1
E. Huhn, C	1
L. Kopf, SS	1
C. Mathewson, SP	1
L. McKenry, RP	1

New York (86-66)	WS
Hitting	**143.7**
Fielding	**37.1**
Pitching	**77.2**
B. Kauff, OF	27
G. Burns, OF	25
A. Fletcher, SS	25
D. Robertson, OF	24
L. Doyle, 2B	18
P. Perritt, SP	15
F. Schupp, RP	15
R. Benton, SP	12
F. Merkle, 1B	12
B. Rariden, C	12
S. Sallee, SP	12
J. Tesreau, SP	12
B. Herzog, 2B	11
W. Holke, 1B	6
L. McCarty, C	6
B. McKechnie, 3B	5
H. Zimmerman, 3B	4
F. Anderson, SP	3
C. Mathewson, SP-RP	3
M. Doolan, SS	2
H. Lobert, 3B	2
G. Smith, RP	2
S. Stroud, RP	2
B. Kocher, C	1
H. Ritter, RP	1
R. Schauer, RP	1

Philadelphia (91-62)	WS
Hitting	**135.8**
Fielding	**42.5**
Pitching	**94.7**
P. Alexander, SP	44
D. Paskert, OF	27
G. Cravath, OF	26
E. Rixey, SP	24
M. Stock, 3B	21
D. Bancroft, SS	20
F. Luderus, 1B	20
P. Whitted, OF	20
A. Demaree, SP	18
B. Niehoff, 2B	18
E. Burns, C	6
B. Killefer, C	6
E. Mayer, SP	6
B. Byrne, 3B	5
W. Good, OF	4
C. Bender, RP	3
O. Dugey, 2B	2
J. Oeschger, RP	2
G. McQuillan, RP	1

Pittsburgh (65-89)	WS
Hitting	**84.3**
Fielding	**37.1**
Pitching	**73.6**
B. Hinchman, OF	26
M. Carey, OF	25
W. Cooper, SP	20
A. Mamaux, SP	19
H. Wagner, SS	17
F. Miller, SP	11
B. Harmon, SP	7
E. Kantlehner, SP	6
W. Fischer, C	5
E. Jacobs, SP-RP	5
A. Wilson, C	5
D. Baird, 3B	4
J. Farmer, 2B	4
D. Johnston, 1B	4
W. Schulte, OF	4
J. Schultz, 2B-3B	4
E. Barney, OF	3
C. Bigbee, 2B	3
W. Schmidt, C	3
J. Viox, 2B	3
D. Costello, OF	2
B. Evans, SP	2
G. Gibson, C	2
B. Grimes, SP	2
A. McCarthy, SS	2
H. Warner, 3B	2
B. Adams, SP	1
J. Altenburg, OF	1
J. Smith, SS	1
F. Smykal, SS	1
B. Wagner, C	1

St. Louis (60-93)	WS
Hitting	**101.3**
Fielding	**25.9**
Pitching	**52.8**
R. Hornsby, 3B	28
B. Bescher, OF	16
L. Meadows, SP	14
R. Ames, SP	12
B. Betzel, 2B	12
T. Long, OF	12
D. Miller, 1B	12
M. Gonzalez, C	11
F. Snyder, C	11
B. Doak, SP	10
J. Smith, OF	8
C. Wilson, OF	6
H. Jasper, RP	4
B. Steele, SP	4
M. Watson, SP	4
Z. Beck, 3B	3
R. Corhan, SS	3
S. Sallee, RP	3
S. Williams, RP	2
S. Bohne, SS	1
A. Butler, OF	1
M. Currie, RP	1
M. Huggins, 2B	1
J. Lotz, RP	1

1917 American League

Boston (90-62)	WS
Hitting	**107.3**
Fielding	**50.8**
Pitching	**111.9**
B. Ruth, SP	36
C. Mays, SP	30
D. Lewis, OF	24
H. Hooper, OF	22
D. Leonard, SP	22
L. Gardner, 3B	18
E. Shore, SP	17
E. Scott, SS	15
D. Hoblitzell, 1B	14
T. Walker, OF	12
J. Barry, 2B	9
R. Foster, SP	9
D. Gainer, 1B	8
J. Walsh, OF	8
P. Thomas, C	7
S. Agnew, C	4
H. Pennock, RP	4
L. Bader, RP	3
J. Cooney, 2B	2
M. McNally, 3B	2
H. Cady, C	1
H. Janvrin, 2B	1
W. Mayer, C	1
C. Shorten, OF	1

Chicago (100-54)	WS
Hitting	**145.4**
Fielding	**50.3**
Pitching	**104.3**
E. Cicotte, SP	35
E. Collins, 2B	32
J. Jackson, OF	31
H. Felsch, OF	30
B. Weaver, 3B	21
R. Schalk, C	20
R. Russell, SP	18
R. Faber, SP	16
C. Gandil, 1B	16
N. Leibold, OF	15
S. Risberg, SS	14
D. Danforth, RP	12
L. Williams, SP	11
J. Scott, SP	9
F. McMullin, 3B	6
J. Benz, SP	5
S. Collins, OF	5
B. Lynn, C	2
E. Murphy, OF	2

Cleveland (88-66)	WS
Hitting	**105.3**
Fielding	**50.5**
Pitching	**108.2**
T. Speaker, OF	37
J. Bagby, SP	34
R. Chapman, SS	30
S. Coveleski, SP	29
B. Roth, OF	19
J. Graney, OF	17
J. Harris, 1B	16
E. Klepfer, SP	16
B. Wambsganss, 2B	13
F. Coumbe, RP	11
G. Morton, SP	9
S. O'Neill, C	7
J. Evans, 3B	5
O. Lambeth, RP	5
A. Gould, RP	4
E. Smith, OF	4
J. Billings, C	2
T. Turner, 3B	2
H. DeBerry, C	1
L. Guisto, 1B	1
R. Miller, 1B	1
J. Wood, RP	1

Detroit (78-75)	WS
Hitting	**129.0**
Fielding	**34.2**
Pitching	**70.8**
T. Cobb, OF	46
B. Veach, OF	31
D. Bush, SS	21
H. Heilmann, OF	18
H. Dauss, SP	15
O. Vitt, 3B	14
B. Boland, SP	13
B. James, SP	13
R. Young, 2B	12
W. Mitchell, SP	11
H. Ehmke, SP	10

T. Spencer, C	6
G. Burns, 1B	5
O. Stanage, C	5
G. Cunningham, RP	4
D. Jones, RP	3
H. Coveleski, SP	2
B. Dyer, SS	1
B. Ellison, 1B	1
G. Harper, OF	1
B. Jones, 2B	1
A. Yelle, C	1

New York (71-82)	WS
Hitting	**84.2**
Fielding	**42.1**
Pitching	**86.7**
H. Baker, 3B	21
R. Peckinpaugh, SS	20
R. Caldwell, SP	18
W. Pipp, 1B	17
B. Shawkey, SP	17
T. Hendryx, OF	13
R. Fisher, SP	11
E. Miller, OF	10
G. Mogridge, SP	10
H. High, OF	9
S. Love, RP	9
L. Nunamaker, C	9
A. Russell, RP	9
U. Shocker, SP-RP	9
N. Cullop, SP	5
F. Gilhooley, OF	5
R. Walters, C	5
F. Maisel, 2B	4
J. Gedeon, 2B	2
A. Marsans, OF	2
W. Alexander, C	1
P. Baumann, 2B	1
N. Brady, SP-RP	1
C. Fewster, 2B	1
L. Magee, OF	1
B. McGraw, SP	1
E. Monroe, RP	1
S. Vick, OF	1

Philadelphia (55-98)	WS
Hitting	**100.2**
Fielding	**25.2**
Pitching	**39.6**
P. Bodie, OF	22
A. Strunk, OF	20
S. McInnis, 1B	17
W. Schang, C	15
W. Witt, SS	13
J. Bush, SP	10
R. Bates, 3B	9
J. Johnson, SP	9
C. Jamieson, OF	8
R. Grover, 2B	7
W. Noyes, SP	6
R. Schauer, SP	5
E. Myers, SP	3
S. Seibold, RP	3
W. Anderson, RP	2
L. Gooch, OF	2
R. Haley, C	2
B. Meyer, C	2
R. Naylor, SP	2
E. Bacon, RP	1
J. Dugan, SS	1
C. Falkenberg, SP	1
W. McAvoy, C	1
E. Palmer, 3B	1
R. Shannon, SS	1
R. Sharman, OF	1
B. Thrasher, OF	1

St. Louis (57-97)	WS
Hitting	**103.9**
Fielding	**25.4**
Pitching	**41.7**
G. Sisler, 1B	29
J. Austin, 3B	14
B. Jacobson, OF	12
D. Pratt, 2B	12
H. Severeid, C	12
A. Sothoron, SP	10
D. Davenport, SP	9
B. Groom, SP	9
D. Lavan, SS	8
B. Shotton, OF	8
E. Plank, SP	7
E. Smith, OF	7
E. Johnson, SS	6
T. Sloan, OF	5
A. Marsans, OF	4
E. Hamilton, RP	3
W. Rumler, OF	3
W. Gerber, SS	2
E. Koob, RP	2
W. Miller, OF	2
T. Rogers, RP	2
R. Demmitt, OF	1
G. Hale, C	1
G. Lowdermilk, SP	1
L. Magee, 3B	1
C. Weilman, SP	1

Washington (74-79)	WS
Hitting	**108.3**
Fielding	**38.1**
Pitching	**75.6**
W. Johnson, SP	29
S. Rice, OF	24
C. Milan, OF	22
J. Judge, 1B	19
D. Ayers, RP	15
M. Menosky, OF	14
E. Foster, 3B	13
R. Morgan, 2B	12
J. Shaw, SP	11
G. Dumont, SP	10
E. Ainsmith, C	9
B. Gallia, SP	9
H. Shanks, SS	8
H. Harper, SP	6
J. Leonard, 3B	6
P. Gharrity, 1B	5
J. Henry, C	4
G. McBride, SS	2
H. Milan, OF	2
S. Crane, SS	1
E. Smith, OF	1

1917 National League

Boston (72-81)	WS
Hitting	**108.1**
Fielding	**35.3**
Pitching	**72.7**
R. Maranville, SS	22
R. Smith, 3B	22
A. Nehf, SP	19
L. Tyler, SP	18
E. Konetchy, 1B	17
J. Barnes, SP	16
J. Rawlings, 2B	14
R. Powell, OF	12
W. Rehg, OF	10
D. Rudolph, SP	9
J. Kelly, OF	7
T. Hughes, SP	6
S. Magee, OF	6
P. Ragan, RP	6
W. Tragesser, C	6
E. Fitzpatrick, 2B	5
J. Wilhoit, OF	5
H. Gowdy, C	4
C. Meyers, C	3
J. Scott, RP	2
F. Allen, RP	1
F. Bailey, OF	1
S. Covington, 1B	1
J. Evers, 2B	1
M. Massey, 2B	1
E. Reulbach, RP	1
G. Twombly, OF	1

Brooklyn (70-81)	WS
Hitting	**88.1**
Fielding	**40.5**
Pitching	**81.5**
L. Cadore, SP	21
C. Stengel, OF	20
J. Pfeffer, SP	18
R. Marquard, SP	17
Z. Wheat, OF	16
L. Cheney, SP	14
I. Olson, SS	14
G. Cutshaw, 2B	12
J. Daubert, 1B	12
H. Myers, OF	12
J. Johnston, OF	9
S. Smith, SP	9
J. Hickman, OF	7
O. Miller, C	6
M. Mowrey, 3B	6
F. O'Rourke, 3B	5
J. Coombs, RP	3
E. Krueger, C	3
C. Meyers, C	2
J. Miljus, RP	2
B. Fabrique, SS	1
M. Wheat, C	1

Chicago (74-80)	WS
Hitting	**104.5**
Fielding	**37.8**
Pitching	**79.7**
H. Vaughn, SP	24
F. Merkle, 1B	19
L. Doyle, 2B	18
C. Williams, OF	16
P. Douglas, SP	15
L. Mann, OF	14
C. Deal, 3B	13
M. Flack, OF	13
C. Hendrix, SP	13
H. Wolter, OF	10
A. Demaree, SP	8
R. Elliott, C	8
A. Wilson, C	8
R. Zeider, SS	8
P. Kilduff, SS	6
P. Carter, SP	5
M. Prendergast, RP	5
D. Ruether, RP	5
T. Seaton, SP	5
V. Aldridge, RP	4
P. Dillhoefer, C	2
B. O'Farrell, C	1
C. Pechous, 3B	1
H. Weaver, SP-RP	1

Cincinnati (78-76)	WS
Hitting	**145.7**
Fielding	**28.5**
Pitching	**59.8**
H. Groh, 3B	37
E. Roush, OF	30
F. Toney, SP	19
P. Schneider, SP	18
H. Chase, 1B	17
G. Neale, OF	16
L. Kopf, SS	15
I. Wingo, C	15
T. Griffith, OF	11
S. Magee, OF	9
H. Eller, RP	8
M. Regan, SP	8
C. Mitchell, SP	7
J. Thorpe, OF	6
T. Clarke, C	5
D. Shean, 2B	5
B. McKechnie, 2B	3
M. Cueto, OF	2
G. Getz, 2B	1
J. Ring, RP	1
D. Ruether, SP	1

New York (98-56)	WS
Hitting	**150.3**
Fielding	**47.3**
Pitching	**96.5**
G. Burns, OF	34
B. Kauff, OF	30
A. Fletcher, SS	27
H. Zimmerman, 3B	26
F. Schupp, SP	23
W. Holke, 1B	17
P. Perritt, SP	17
S. Sallee, SP	17
D. Robertson, OF	16
F. Anderson, RP	14
B. Herzog, 2B	13
R. Benton, SP	12
B. Rariden, C	12
J. Tesreau, SP	9
L. McCarty, C	6
J. Wilhoit, OF	4
A. Demaree, SP	3
J. Smith, 2B	3
R. Youngs, OF	2
A. Baird, 2B	1
G. Gibson, C	1
E. Hemingway, 3B	1
G. Kelly, OF	1
P. Kilduff, 2B	1
H. Lobert, 3B	1
J. Middleton, RP	1
G. Smith, RP	1
J. Thorpe, OF	1

Philadelphia (87-65)	WS
Hitting	**113.2**
Fielding	**46.2**
Pitching	**101.6**
P. Alexander, SP	40
G. Cravath, OF	26
E. Rixey, SP	20
D. Paskert, OF	19
M. Stock, 3B	19
D. Bancroft, SS	18
F. Luderus, 1B	18
P. Whitted, OF	18
B. Killefer, C	15
J. Oeschger, SP	15
C. Bender, SP-RP	13
E. Mayer, SP	11
B. Niehoff, 2B	11
J. Evers, 2B	5
J. Lavender, SP-RP	4
W. Schulte, OF	3
B. Adams, C	2
E. Burns, C	1
O. Dugey, 2B	1
P. McGaffigan, SS	1
H. Pearce, SS	1

Pittsburgh (51-103)	WS
Hitting	**59.1**
Fielding	**31.8**
Pitching	**62.1**
M. Carey, OF	23
W. Cooper, SP	22
E. Jacobs, SP	11
B. Steele, SP	9
W. Fischer, C	8
F. Miller, SP	8
C. Bigbee, OF	7
H. Carlson, SP-RP	7
C, Ward, SS	7
J. Pitler, 2B	6
L. King, OF	5
H. Wagner, 1B	5
D. Baird, 3B	4
T. Boeckel, 3B	4
B. Grimes, RP	4
B. Hinchman, OF	3
W. Schmidt, C	3
B. Brief, 1B	2
A. DeBus, SS	2
C. Jackson, OF	2

A. McCarthy, 3B	2
F. Mollwitz, 1B	2
E. Ponder, SP	2
B. Wagner, C	2
H. Caton, SS	1
D. Flinn, OF	1
W. Schulte, OF	1

St. Louis (82-70)	WS
Hitting	**119.9**
Fielding	**43.9**
Pitching	**82.2**
R. Hornsby, SS	38
W. Cruise, OF	23
J. Smith, OF	21
R. Ames, RP	17
L. Meadows, SP	16
D. Miller, 2B	15
G. Packard, RP	15
D. Baird, 3B	14
B. Doak, SP	13
G. Paulette, 1B	11
M. Gonzalez, C	10
T. Long, OF	10
F. Snyder, C	10
M. Goodwin, SP	7
O. Horstmann, RP	6
M. Watson, RP	6
B. Betzel, 2B	5
B. Steele, SP-RP	3
F. Smith, 3B	2
B. Bescher, OF	1
J. Brock, C	1
J. May, RP	1
R. Smyth, OF	1

1918 American League

Boston (75-51)	WS
Hitting	**111.4**
Fielding	**38.5**
Pitching	**75.1**
B. Ruth, OF	40
H. Hooper, OF	29
C. Mays, SP	25
J. Bush, SP	21
A. Strunk, OF	16
D. Shean, 2B	15
S. Jones, SP	14
S. McInnis, 1B	12
W. Schang, C	10
E. Scott, SS	9
G. Whiteman, OF	8
D. Leonard, SP	7
F. Thomas, 3B	6
S. Agnew, C	3
W. Mayer, C	2
G. Cochran, 3B	1
J. Coffey, 3B	1
E. Gonzalez, SS	1
W. Kinney, RP	1
H. Miller, OF	1
V. Molyneaux, RP	1
J. Stansbury, 3B	1
F. Truesdale, 2B	1

Chicago (57-67)	WS
Hitting	**81.8**
Fielding	**28.8**
Pitching	**60.3**
E. Collins, 2B	16
B. Weaver, SS	15
E. Cicotte, SP	14
N. Leibold, OF	12
S. Collins, OF	11
C. Gandil, 1B	10
J. Benz, SP	9
F. Shellenback, SP	9
F. McMullin, 3B	8
E. Murphy, OF	8
S. Risberg, SS	8
R. Faber, SP	7
R. Russell, SP	7
R. Schalk, C	7
L. Williams, SP	7
J. Quinn, SP	5
H. Felsch, OF	4
W. Good, OF	4
J. Jackson, OF	4
D. Danforth, RP	3
O. Jacobs, C	1
J. Mostil, 2B	1
B. Pinelli, 3B	1

Cleveland (73-54)	WS
Hitting	**99.0**
Fielding	**36.8**
Pitching	**83.3**
S. Coveleski, SP	29
T. Speaker, OF	27
R. Chapman, SS	21
J. Bagby, SP	19
B. Roth, OF	16
J. Wood, OF	16
G. Morton, SP	14
S. O'Neill, C	13
F. Coumbe, SP	10
J. Enzmann, RP	10
B. Wambsganss, 2B	10
J. Evans, 3B	9
T. Turner, 3B	6
J. Graney, OF	5
B. Bescher, OF	4
D. Johnston, 1B	3
E. Miller, 1B	2
P. Thomas, C	2
M. Kavanagh, 1B	1
G. McQuillan, RP	1
R. Williams, 1B	1

Detroit (55-71)	WS
Hitting	**98.8**
Fielding	**21.3**
Pitching	**44.9**
T. Cobb, OF	31
B. Veach, OF	17
D. Bush, SS	13
H. Dauss, SP	13
B. Boland, SP	12
H. Heilmann, OF	12
B. Jones, 3B	8
G. Cunningham, SP	7
O. Vitt, 3B	7
A. Griggs, 1B	6
E. Erickson, SP	5
R. Kallio, SP	5
T. Spencer, C	4
O. Stanage, C	4
R. Young, 2B	4
G. Harper, OF	3
L. Dressen, 1B	2
B. James, SP	2
D. Jones, RP	2
M. Kavanagh, 1B	2
A. Yelle, C	2
J. Coffey, 2B	1
W. Donovan, SP-RP	1
B. Ellison, OF	1
F. Walker, OF	1

New York (60-63)	WS
Hitting	**95.4**
Fielding	**30.8**
Pitching	**53.8**
H. Baker, 3B	23
G. Mogridge, RP	17
D. Pratt, 2B	17
F. Gilhooley, OF	14
R. Peckinpaugh, SS	14
R. Caldwell, SP	13
W. Pipp, 1B	13
S. Love, SP	11
T. Hannah, C	10
P. Bodie, OF	9
H. Thormahlen, SP	7
J. Fournier, 1B	5
E. Miller, OF	5
A. Russell, SP	4
H. Finneran, SP	3
J. Hummel, OF	3
H. Hyatt, OF	2
H. Robinson, RP	2
B. Shawkey, SP	2
R. Walters, C	2
R. Keating, RP	1
B. Lamar, OF	1
A. Marsans, OF	1
A. Ward, SS	1

Philadelphia (52-76)	WS
Hitting	**71.3**
Fielding	**29.4**
Pitching	**55.3**
S. Perry, SP	30
G. Burns, 1B	24
L. Gardner, 3B	17
T. Walker, OF	17
V. Gregg, SP	11
M. Kopp, OF	8
R. Shannon, SS	7
M. Acosta, OF	6
B. Geary, RP	6
W. McAvoy, C	6
M. Watson, SP	5
J. Dugan, SS	4
C. Jamieson, OF	4
C. Perkins, C	4
W. Adams, RP	2
J. Dykes, 2B	1
R. Johnson, SP	1
R. Oldring, OF	1
B. Pierson, RP	1
T. Zachary, SP	1

St. Louis (58-64)	WS
Hitting	**77.8**
Fielding	**31.8**
Pitching	**64.4**
G. Sisler, 1B	22
A. Sothoron, SP	17
J. Tobin, OF	15
R. Demmitt, OF	14
J. Austin, SS	11
U. Shocker, SP	11
T. Hendryx, OF	9
L. Nunamaker, C	9
R. Wright, SP	9
D. Davenport, SP	8
T. Rogers, SP	8
E. Smith, OF	7
J. Gedeon, 2B	6
F. Maisel, 3B	6
B. Houck, RP	5
B. Gallia, SP	4
L. Leifield, RP	4
H. Severeid, C	4
W. Gerber, SS	3
G. Lowdermilk, SP	2

Washington (72-56)	WS
Hitting	**85.6**
Fielding	**42.0**
Pitching	**88.4**
W. Johnson, SP	38
E. Foster, 3B	18
C. Milan, OF	18
H. Harper, SP	16
B. Shotton, OF	16
J. Shaw, SP	15
J. Judge, 1B	13
D. Lavan, SS	13
W. Schulte, OF	13
H. Shanks, OF	12
D. Ayers, SP	10
E. Ainsmith, C	8
H. Matteson, RP	6
R. Morgan, 2B	6
V. Picinich, C	3
E. Yingling, RP	3
E. Hovlik, RP	2
N. Altrock, SP	1
M. Craft, RP	1
R. Hansen, RP	1
G. McBride, SS	1
S. Rees, RP	1
S. Rice, OF	1

1918 National League

Boston (53-71)	WS
Hitting	**82.9**
Fielding	**24.4**
Pitching	**51.7**
R. Smith, 3B	21
A. Nehf, SP	15
A. Wickland, OF	15
B. Herzog, 2B	9
E. Konetchy, 1B	9
D. Fillingim, SP	8
B. Hearn, SP	7
Ji. Kelly, OF	7
R. Massey, OF	7
D. Rudolph, SP	7
A. Wilson, C	7
P. Ragan, SP	6
R. Powell, OF	5
J. Rawlings, SS	5
Z. Terry, SS	5
J. Northrop, SP	4
D. Crandall, SP	3
B. Murphy, OF	3
C. Chadbourne, OF	2
L. George, SP	2
Jo. Kelly, OF	2
R. Maranville, SS	2
W. Rehg, OF	2
J. Smith, 2B	2
J. Henry, C	1
T. Hughes, SP	1
H. McQuillan, SP	1
B. Wagner, C	1

Brooklyn (57-69)	WS
Hitting	**56.0**
Fielding	**38.0**
Pitching	**77.0**
B. Grimes, SP	25
Z. Wheat, OF	16
J. Daubert, 1B	15
J. Johnston, OF	14
R. Marquard, SP	14
L. Cheney, SP	13
H. Myers, OF	12
I. Olson, SS	7
O. O'Mara, 3B	6
D. Robertson, SP	6
J. Coombs, SP	5
R. Schmandt, 2B	5
G. Smith, SP	5
M. Doolan, 2B	4
D. Griner, SP	4
O. Miller, C	4
L. Cadore, SP	3
J. Hickman, OF	3
E. Krueger, C	3
J. Pfeffer, SP	2
M. Wheat, C	2
J. Archer, C	1
A. Nixon, OF	1
N. Plitt, RP	1

Chicago (84-45)	WS
Hitting	**118.0**
Fielding	**42.4**
Pitching	**91.6**
C. Hollocher, SS	28
H. Vaughn, SP	28
L. Tyler, SP	24
D. Paskert, OF	23
F. Merkle, 1B	22
M. Flack, OF	20

L. Mann, OF	20
C. Hendrix, SP	18
P. Douglas, SP	12
C. Deal, 3B	10
B. Killefer, C	10
B. O'Farrell, C	7
C. Pick, 2B	6
S. Martin, SP	5
R. Zeider, 2B	5
P. Carter, RP	4
P. Alexander, SP	2
T. Barber, OF	2
P. Kilduff, 2B	2
H. Weaver, RP	2
V. Aldridge, RP	1
B. McCabe, 2B	1

Cincinnati (68-60)	WS
Hitting	**127.4**
Fielding	**26.8**
Pitching	**49.8**
H. Groh, 3B	28
E. Roush, OF	22
L. Magee, 2B	18
S. Magee, 1B	18
H. Eller, SP	14
T. Griffith, OF	11
G. Neale, OF	11
L. Blackburne, SS	10
I. Wingo, C	10
R. Bressler, SP	9
H. Chase, 1B	9
P. Schneider, SP	8
J. Ring, SP	7
M. Cueto, OF	6
F. Toney, SP	5
D. Luque, SP	4
R. Mitchell, SP	4
M. Regan, RP	4
N. Allen, C	3
J. Archer, C	1
J. Haines, RP	1
H. Smith, C	1

New York (71-53)	WS
Hitting	**110.3**
Fielding	**33.3**
Pitching	**69.4**
G. Burns, OF	23
R. Youngs, OF	22
A. Fletcher, SS	20
B. Kauff, OF	15
H. Zimmerman, 3B	15
P. Perritt, SP	14
L. Doyle, 2B	12
R. Causey, SP	9
L. McCarty, C	9
S. Sallee, SP	9
F. Toney, SP	9
A. Demaree, SP	8
W. Holke, 1B	7
J. Wilhoit, OF	6
J. Barnes, SP	5
J. Tesreau, SP	5
F. Anderson, RP	4
B. Rariden, C	4
B. Steele, SP	4
J. Thorpe, OF	4
E. Sicking, 3B	3
R. Benton, SP	2
P. Compton, OF	1
J. Kirke, 1B	1
J. Rodriguez, 2B	1
G. Smith, RP	1

Philadelphia (55-68)	WS
Hitting	**67.9**
Fielding	**32.4**
Pitching	**64.8**
B. Hogg, SP	19
D. Bancroft, SS	17
F. Luderus, 1B	15
I. Meusel, OF	15
M. Prendergast, SP	15
M. Stock, 3B	13
C. Williams, OF	12
G. Cravath, OF	11
E. Jacobs, SP	11
J. Oeschger, SP	8
E. Mayer, SP	7
M. Watson, RP	5
M. Fitzgerald, OF	4
B. Adams, C	3
E. Burns, C	3
H. Pearce, 2B	2
D. Davis, RP	1
E. Hemingway, 2B	1
A. Main, SP-RP	1
P. McGaffigan, 2B	1
P. Whitted, OF	1

Pittsburgh (65-60)	WS
Hitting	**81.9**
Fielding	**38.8**
Pitching	**74.3**
W. Cooper, SP	23
M. Carey, OF	22
G. Cutshaw, 2B	17
B. Southworth, OF	14
B. McKechnie, 3B	13
F. Miller, SP	11
C. Bigbee, OF	10
E. Mayer, SP	10
W. Schmidt, C	10
F. Mollwitz, 1B	9
R. Sanders, SP-RP	9
H. Caton, SS	8
E. Hamilton, SP	8
R. Comstock, SP	4
B. Harmon, SP	4
C. Hill, SP	4
C. Stengel, OF	4
B. Adams, SP	3
B. Hinchman, OF	3
L. King, OF	2
T. Leach, OF	2
B. Steele, RP	2
J. Archer, C	1
L. Boone, SS	1
R. Ellam, SS	1

St. Louis (51-78)	WS
Hitting	**82.1**
Fielding	**23.7**
Pitching	**47.2**
R. Hornsby, SS	18
B. Doak, SP	12
M. Gonzalez, C	12
R. Ames, SP	11
T. Fisher, 2B	11
G. Paulette, 1B	11
D. Baird, 3B	9
W. Cruise, OF	9
B. Sherdel, RP	9
C. Heathcote, OF	8
A. McHenry, OF	7
G. Packard, SP	7
G. Anderson, OF	6
O. Tuero, RP	4
B. Betzel, 3B	3
L. Meadows, SP	3
F. Snyder, C	3
J. May, SP	2
R. Smyth, OF	2
H. Bronkie, 3B	1
C. Grimm, 1B	1
R. Johnson, RP	1
B. Niehoff, 2B	1
J. Smith, OF	1
B. Wallace, 2B	1

1919
American League

Boston (66-71)	WS
Hitting	**106.3**
Fielding	**31.8**
Pitching	**59.9**
B. Ruth, OF	43
W. Schang, C	19
H. Hooper, OF	17
H. Pennock, SP	16
E. Scott, SS	14
S. McInnis, 1B	12
A. Russell, SP	11
C. Mays, SP	9
O. Vitt, 3B	9
S. Jones, SP	8
R. Shannon, 2B	7
B. Roth, OF	6
W. Hoyt, SP	5
A. Strunk, OF	5
R. Caldwell, SP	3
B. Lamar, OF	3
J. Barry, 2B	2
D. Gainer, 1B	2
R. Walters, C	2
F. Gilhooley, OF	1
B. James, SP	1
M. McNally, 3B-SS	1
D. Shean, 2B	1
J. Wilhoit, OF	1

Chicago (88-52)	WS
Hitting	**136.2**
Fielding	**42.0**
Pitching	**85.7**
E. Cicotte, SP	32
J. Jackson, OF	32
E. Collins, 2B	27
L. Williams, SP	23
H. Felsch, OF	21
B. Weaver, 3B	20
N. Leibold, OF	18
R. Schalk, C	17
D. Kerr, RP	16
C. Gandil, 1B	13
S. Risberg, SS	12
F. McMullin, 3B	7
R. Faber, SP	6
S. Collins, OF	5
G. Lowdermilk, SP	5
B. James, SP	3
E. Murphy, OF	3
R. Wilkinson, RP	2
B. Lynn, C	1
H. McClellan, 3B	1

Cleveland (84-55)	WS
Hitting	**119.9**
Fielding	**41.9**
Pitching	**90.2**
S. Coveleski, SP	27
T. Speaker, OF	27
J. Bagby, SP	21
L. Gardner, 3B	20
R. Chapman, SS	18
S. O'Neill, C	18
J. Graney, OF	15
E. Smith, OF	15
B. Wambsganss, 2B	14
J. Harris, 1B	12
G. Uhle, RP	10
D. Johnston, 1B	9
G. Morton, SP	9
R. Caldwell, SP	7
E. Myers, SP	7
J. Wood, OF	6
J. Enzmann, RP	4
H. Jasper, SP	4
T. Phillips, RP	4
T. Faeth, RP	2
F. Coumbe, RP	1
C. Jamieson, RP	1
H. Lunte, SS	1

Detroit (80-60)	WS
Hitting	**132.6**
Fielding	**35.2**
Pitching	**72.1**
T. Cobb, OF	32
B. Veach, OF	32
H. Heilmann, 1B	23
B. Boland, SP	16
H. Ehmke, SP	16
I. Flagstead, OF	16
E. Ainsmith, C	15
D. Bush, SS	15
D. Leonard, SP	14
H. Dauss, SP	13
B. Jones, 3B	11
C. Shorten, OF	9
R. Young, 2B	8
D. Ayers, RP	7
S. Love, RP	6
O. Stanage, C	3
B. Dyer, 3B	2
G. Cunningham, RP	1
B. Ellison, 2B	1

New York (80-59)	WS
Hitting	**96.3**
Fielding	**45.6**
Pitching	**98.1**
R. Peckinpaugh, SS	24
B. Shawkey, SP	24
J. Quinn, SP	22
H. Baker, 3B	20
D. Pratt, 2B	20
P. Bodie, OF	18
H. Thormahlen, SP	16
C. Mays, SP	14
W. Pipp, 1B	14
D. Lewis, OF	13
G. Mogridge, SP	12
C. Fewster, OF	10
S. Vick, OF	9
T. Hannah, C	6
M. Ruel, C	6
A. Russell, RP	4
E. Shore, SP	3
L. Nelson, RP	2
B. McGraw, RP	1
P. Schneider, SP	1
A. Ward, 1B	1

Philadelphia (36-104)	WS
Hitting	**49.6**
Fielding	**22.9**
Pitching	**35.5**
G. Burns, 1B	11
W. Kinney, RP	10
T. Walker, OF	10
C. Perkins, C	9
J. Johnson, SP	8
R. Naylor, SP	7
S. Perry, SP	7
B. Roth, OF	7
W. Witt, OF	7
J. Dugan, SS	6
T. Rogers, SP	4
M. Kopp, OF	3
W. McAvoy, C	3
R. Shannon, 2B	3
F. Thomas, 3B	3
D. Burrus, 1B	2
W. Anderson, RP	1
C. Galloway, SS	1
B. Geary, RP	1
I. Griffin, 1B	1
A. Strunk, OF	1
L. Styles, C	1
T. Turner, SS	1
A. Wingo, OF	1

St. Louis (67-72)	WS
Hitting	**86.5**
Fielding	**37.3**
Pitching	**77.1**
G. Sisler, 1B	24

A. Sothoron, SP	24
B. Jacobson, OF	18
J. Tobin, OF	18
U. Shocker, SP	17
C. Weilman, SP	14
B. Gallia, SP	11
J. Gedeon, 2B	10
K. Williams, OF	10
W. Gerber, SS	9
J. Austin, 3B	8
H. Severeid, C	8
L. Leifield, RP	6
H. Bronkie, 3B	5
E. Smith, OF	5
D. Davenport, SP	2
R. Demmitt, OF	2
G. Lowdermilk, RP	2
W. Mayer, C	2
T. Sloan, OF	2
E. Vangilder, RP	2
J. Billings, C	1
E. Koob, RP	1

Washington (56-84)	WS
Hitting	**75.6**
Fielding	**30.2**
Pitching	**62.2**
W. Johnson, SP	27
S. Rice, OF	18
J. Shaw, SP	18
J. Judge, 1B	17
E. Foster, 3B	11
M. Menosky, OF	11
P. Gharrity, C	9
C. Milan, OF	9
V. Picinich, C	7
H. Shanks, SS	7
J. Leonard, 2B	5
B. Murphy, OF	5
H. Harper, SP	4
S. Agnew, C	3
E. Erickson, SP	3
T. Zachary, RP	3
H. Courtney, SP	2
F. Ellerbe, SS	2
H. Thompson, RP	2
D. Ayers, RP	1
M. Craft, RP	1
G. McBride, SS	1
D. Robertson, SP	1
A. Schacht, SP	1

1919 National League

Boston (57-82)	WS
Hitting	**86.5**
Fielding	**28.6**
Pitching	**55.9**
D. Rudolph, SP	20
R. Maranville, SS	18
W. Holke, 1B	13
T. Boeckel, 3B	9
A. Nehf, SP	9
J. Riggert, OF	9
D. Fillingim, SP	8
H. Gowdy, C	8
R. Powell, OF	8
B. Herzog, 2B	7
R. Smith, OF	7
A. Wilson, C	7
R. Keating, SP	6
J. Thorpe, OF	6
L. Mann, OF	5
J. Rawlings, 2B	5
J. Scott, SP	5
J. Oeschger, SP	4
A. Demaree, SP	3
L. Blackburne, 3B	2
D. Carroll, OF	2
H. McQuillan, RP	2
C. Pick, 2B	2
R. Causey, SP	1
L. Christenbury, OF	1
W. Cruise, OF	1
H. Ford, SS	1
J. Northrop, RP	1
M. O'Neil, C	1

Brooklyn (69-71)	WS
Hitting	**100.9**
Fielding	**32.3**
Pitching	**73.8**
H. Myers, OF	23
Z. Wheat, OF	21
I. Olson, SS	19
L. Cadore, SP	18
E. Konetchy, 1B	18
J. Pfeffer, SP	18
T. Griffith, OF	14
J. Johnston, 2B	13
A. Mamaux, SP	11
S. Smith, SP	11
E. Krueger, C	8
C. Mitchell, RP	8
B. Grimes, SP	6
R. Marquard, SP	5
P. Kilduff, 3B	3
L. Magee, 2B	3
O. Miller, C	2
C. Ward, 3B	2
D. Baird, 3B	1
L. Malone, 3B	1
R. Schmandt, 2B	1
M. Wheat, C	1

Chicago (75-65)	WS
Hitting	**75.3**
Fielding	**45.3**
Pitching	**104.4**
H. Vaughn, SP	30
P. Alexander, SP	26
M. Flack, OF	17
C. Deal, 3B	15
C. Hollocher, SS	15
P. Douglas, SP	13
B. Killefer, C	13
C. Hendrix, SP	12
F. Merkle, 1B	12
S. Martin, RP	11
L. Magee, OF	9
T. Barber, OF	8
P. Carter, RP	6
B. Herzog, 2B	6
C. Pick, 2B	6
L. Mann, OF	5
S. Bailey, RP	4
D. Paskert, OF	4
P. Kilduff, 3B	3
L. Tyler, SP	3
F. Lear, 1B-2B	2
B. O'Farrell, C	2
T. Daly, C	1
B. McCabe, OF	1
D. Robertson, OF	1

Cincinnati (96-44)	WS
Hitting	**134.9**
Fielding	**45.3**
Pitching	**107.7**
E. Roush, OF	33
H. Groh, 3B	30
D. Ruether, SP	26
H. Eller, SP	23
S. Sallee, SP	22
M. Rath, 2B	21
J. Daubert, 1B	17
R. Fisher, SP	17
L. Kopf, SS	16
G. Neale, OF	15
J. Ring, SP	14
I. Wingo, C	13
D. Luque, RP	9
R. Bressler, OF	6
B. Rariden, C	6
S. Magee, OF	5
P. Duncan, OF	4
M. Cueto, OF	3
J. Smith, 3B	3
N. Allen, C	2
R. Mitchell, RP	1
H. Schreiber, 3B	1
C. See, OF	1

New York (87-53)	WS
Hitting	**144.8**
Fielding	**37.1**
Pitching	**79.1**
G. Burns, OF	32
R. Youngs, OF	27
J. Barnes, SP	24
B. Kauff, OF	24
L. Doyle, 2B	20
A. Fletcher, SS	20
F. Toney, SP	16
R. Benton, SP	14
H. Chase, 1B	14
H. Zimmerman, 3B	14
A. Nehf, SP	11
L. McCarty, C	9
J. Dubuc, RP	7
G. Kelly, 1B	4
R. Causey, SP	3
F. Frisch, 2B	3
M. Gonzalez, C	3
P. Ragan, RP	3
J. Statz, OF	3
A. Baird, 2B	2
P. Douglas, SP	2
F. Snyder, C	2
B. Hubbell, SP	1
R. Ryan, SP	1
E. Sicking, SS	1
E. Smith, C	1

Philadelphia (47-90)	WS
Hitting	**85.1**
Fielding	**22.4**
Pitching	**33.6**
F. Luderus, 1B	18
G. Cravath, OF	16
I. Meusel, OF	14
C. Williams, OF	12
D. Bancroft, SS	11
L. Meadows, SP	9
D. Baird, 3B	7
G. Smith, SP	6
L. Callahan, OF	5
G. Paulette, 2B	5
B. Hogg, SP	4
E. Jacobs, SP	4
G. Packard, SP	4
E. Rixey, SP	4
P. Whitted, OF	4
B. Adams, C	3
L. Blackburne, 3B	2
H. Pearce, 2B	2
E. Sicking, SS	2
W. Tragesser, C	2
F. Woodward, SP	2
H. Cady, C	1
L. Cheney, SP	1
N. Clarke, C	1
B. LeBourveau, OF	1
L. Weinert, RP	1

Pittsburgh (71-68)	WS
Hitting	**83.3**
Fielding	**44.9**
Pitching	**84.9**
B. Adams, SP	27
W. Cooper, SP	25
C. Bigbee, OF	18
B. Southworth, OF	17
C. Stengel, OF	15
G. Cutshaw, 2B	13
H. Carlson, SP	12
F. Miller, SP	12
M. Carey, OF	11
Z. Terry, SS	10
W. Barbare, 3B	9
P. Whitted, 1B	9
W. Schmidt, C	8
E. Hamilton, SP	6
T. Boeckel, 3B	5
V. Saier, 1B	4
C. Grimm, 1B	2
E. Mayer, SP	2
F. Nicholson, OF	2
J. Wisner, RP	2
F. Blackwell, C	1
H. Caton, SS	1
C. Lee, C	1
F. Mollwitz, 1B	1

St. Louis (54-83)	WS
Hitting	**88.7**
Fielding	**25.7**
Pitching	**47.6**
R. Hornsby, 3B	26
M. Stock, 2B	20
A. McHenry, OF	13
M. Goodwin, SP	11
C. Heathcote, OF	11
V. Clemons, C	10
B. Doak, SP	9
B. Shotton, OF	9
E. Jacobs, RP	6
O. Tuero, RP	6
D. Lavan, SS	5
B. Sherdel, RP	5
D. Miller, 1B	4
J. Schultz, OF	4
J. Smith, OF	4
F. Woodward, RP	4
J. May, SP	3
L. Meadows, SP	3
P. Dillhoefer, C	2
F. Schupp, SP	2
F. Snyder, C	2
O. Horstmann, RP	1
F. Mollwitz, 1B	1
G. Paulette, 1B	1

1920 American League

Boston (72-81)	WS
Hitting	**92.7**
Fielding	**42.7**
Pitching	**80.6**
H. Hooper, OF	24
W. Schang, C	20
H. Pennock, SP	19
M. Menosky, OF	17
S. Jones, SP	15
E. Scott, SS	15
T. Hendryx, OF	13
J. Bush, SP	12
E. Myers, SP	12
E. Foster, 3B	11
H. Harper, SP	10
S. McInnis, 1B	10
A. Russell, SP	8
O. Vitt, 3B	6
R. Walters, C	5
W. Hoyt, SP-RP	4
B. Karr, RP	4
M. McNally, 2B	4
C. Brady, 2B	2
G. Bailey, OF	1
E. Chaplin, C	1
H. Deviney, RP	1
G. Orme, OF	1
B. Paschal, OF	1

Chicago (96-58)	WS
Hitting	**143.5**
Fielding	**49.1**
Pitching	**95.4**
E. Collins, 2B	38

J. Jackson, OF	37
H. Felsch, OF	30
R. Faber, SP	25
E. Cicotte, SP	24
B. Weaver, 3B	22
R. Schalk, C	21
D. Kerr, SP	20
L. Williams, SP	19
S. Risberg, SS	15
S. Collins, 1B	12
R. Wilkinson, RP	7
N. Leibold, OF	4
E. Murphy, OF	4
A. Strunk, OF	4
T. Jourdan, 1B	2
S. Hodge, SP-RP	1
B. Lynn, C	1
H. McClellan, SS	1
F. McMullin, 3B	1

Cleveland (98-56)	WS
Hitting	**144.1**
Fielding	**48.3**
Pitching	**101.6**
T. Speaker, OF	39
J. Bagby, SP	34
S. Coveleski, SP	32
S. O'Neill, C	25
L. Gardner, 3B	23
E. Smith, OF	21
R. Chapman, SS	20
R. Caldwell, SP	14
C. Jamieson, OF	12
D. Johnston, 1B	11
B. Wambsganss, 2B	9
J. Evans, OF	8
D. Mails, SP	8
J. Graney, OF	6
G. Morton, SP	6
J. Wood, OF	5
J. Sewell, SS	4
G. Uhle, RP	4
B. Clark, RP	3
D. Niehaus, RP	3
L. Nunamaker, C	2
G. Burns, 1B	1
H. Lunte, SS	1
T. Murchison, RP	1
E. Myers, RP	1
P. Thomas, C	1

Detroit (61-93)	WS
Hitting	**84.6**
Fielding	**33.2**
Pitching	**65.2**
B. Veach, OF	25
T. Cobb, OF	20
H. Ehmke, SP	18
H. Heilmann, 1B	16
R. Young, 2B	16
H. Dauss, SP	14
D. Ayers, SP-RP	10
D. Bush, SS	9
D. Leonard, SP	9
R. Oldham, SP	9
C. Shorten, OF	9
I. Flagstead, OF	6
B. Jones, 3B	4
S. Hale, 3B	3
B. Pinelli, 3B	3
J. Bogart, SP-RP	2
O. Stanage, C	2
E. Ainsmith, C	1
H. Baumgartner, RP	1
R. Crumpler, SP	1
B. Ellison, 1B	1
C. Huber, 3B	1
C. Manion, C	1
B. Morrisette, RP	1
F. Okrie, RP	1

New York (95-59)	WS
Hitting	**141.4**
Fielding	**46.1**
Pitching	**97.5**
B. Ruth, OF	51
C. Mays, SP	27
B. Shawkey, SP	27
D. Pratt, 2B	25
R. Peckinpaugh, SS	21
B. Meusel, OF	19
J. Quinn, SP	19
W. Pipp, 1B	18
P. Bodie, OF	16
A. Ward, 3B	16
R. Collins, SP-RP	13
D. Lewis, OF	7
H. Thormahlen, SP	7
M. Ruel, C	6
T. Hannah, C	5
G. Mogridge, SP	4
S. Vick, OF	2
C. Fewster, SS	1
E. Shore, RP	1

Philadelphia (48-106)	WS
Hitting	**51.6**
Fielding	**27.6**
Pitching	**64.8**
J. Dugan, 3B	14
E. Rommel, RP	14
C. Perkins, C	13
S. Perry, SP	13
J. Dykes, 2B	12
R. Naylor, SP	12
T. Walker, OF	11
D. Keefe, RP	10
S. Harriss, SP	8
W. Witt, OF	6
W. Kinney, SP	4
F. Thomas, 3B	4
F. Welch, OF	4
R. Moore, SP	3
A. Strunk, OF	3
C. Galloway, SS	2
I. Griffin, 1B	2
B. Hasty, RP	2
G. Myatt, OF	2
G. Burns, OF	1
C. High, OF	1
E. McCann, SS	1
R. Shannon, SS	1
L. Styles, C	1

St. Louis (76-77)	WS
Hitting	**108.9**
Fielding	**40.6**
Pitching	**78.6**
G. Sisler, 1B	33
B. Jacobson, OF	25
U. Shocker, SP	24
D. Davis, SP	22
J. Tobin, OF	18
K. Williams, OF	17
W. Gerber, SS	14
J. Gedeon, 2B	11
H. Severeid, C	11
C. Weilman, SP	9
B. Burwell, RP	8
E. Smith, 3B	8
A. Sothoron, SP	7
B. Bayne, SP	6
J. Austin, 3B	5
J. Billings, C	3
J. DeBerry, SP	2
L. Lamb, OF	1
A. Lynch, SP	1
R. Sanders, RP	1
E. Vangilder, SP	1
D. Wetzel, OF	1

Washington (68-84)	WS
Hitting	**117.3**
Fielding	**30.7**
Pitching	**56.1**
S. Rice, OF	23
J. Judge, 1B	22
B. Roth, OF	18
B. Harris, 2B	15
C. Milan, OF	14
T. Zachary, SP	14
E. Erickson, SP	11
P. Gharrity, C	10
W. Johnson, SP	10
H. Shanks, 3B	9
J. Shaw, SP	9
J. O'Neill, SS	8
F. Ellerbe, 3B	7
R. Shannon, SS	6
J. Acosta, RP	5
H. Courtney, SP	5
F. Brower, OF	4
A. Schacht, SP-RP	4
V. Picinich, C	3
F. O'Rourke, SS	2
B. Snyder, RP	2
L. Carlson, RP	1
D. Prothro, 3B-SS	1
R. Torres, 1B	1

1920
National League

Boston (62-90)	WS
Hitting	**92.0**
Fielding	**32.8**
Pitching	**61.2**
J. Oeschger, SP	16
D. Fillingim, SP	14
R. Maranville, SS	14
T. Boeckel, 3B	13
W. Holke, 1B	13
H. McQuillan, SP	13
L. Mann, OF	12
M. O'Neil, C	12
E. Eayrs, OF	11
J. Scott, SP	11
J. Sullivan, OF	10
W. Cruise, OF	8
H. Gowdy, C	8
C. Pick, 2B	8
R. Powell, OF	7
H. Ford, 2B	5
M. Watson, SP	4
L. Townsend, RP	3
A. Pierotti, RP	2
L. Christenbury, OF	1
D. Rudolph, SP	1

Brooklyn (93-61)	WS
Hitting	**114.5**
Fielding	**50.2**
Pitching	**114.3**
B. Grimes, SP	32
Z. Wheat, OF	28
H. Myers, OF	27
L. Cadore, SP	21
J. Johnston, 3B	20
P. Kilduff, 2B	18
E. Konetchy, 1B	18
A. Mamaux, RP	16
J. Pfeffer, SP	16
S. Smith, RP	15
I. Olson, SS	12
R. Marquard, SP	11
O. Miller, C	9
T. Griffith, OF	6
E. Krueger, C	6
C. Mitchell, RP	6
B. Neis, OF	6
R. Elliott, C	2
J. Miljus, RP	2
G. Mohart, RP	2
D. Baird, 3B	1
W. Hood, OF	1
B. Lamar, OF	1
B. McCabe, SS	1
R. Schmandt, 1B	1
C. Ward, SS	1

Chicago (75-79)	WS
Hitting	**117.3**
Fielding	**34.6**
Pitching	**73.1**
P. Alexander, SP	36
H. Vaughn, SP	22
M. Flack, OF	20
D. Paskert, OF	20
D. Robertson, OF	20
Z. Terry, SS	17
C. Hollocher, SS	16
L. Tyler, SP	12
F. Merkle, 1B	11
B. O'Farrell, C	11
C. Deal, 3B	10
C. Hendrix, SP	7
T. Barber, 1B	5
B. Killefer, C	5
T. Daly, C	4
B. Herzog, 2B	2
W. Marriott, 2B	2
B. Twombly, OF	2
V. Cheeves, RP	1
B. Friberg, 2B-OF	1
H. Leathers, SS	1

Cincinnati (82-71)	WS
Hitting	**136.2**
Fielding	**38.3**
Pitching	**71.4**
E. Roush, OF	33
H. Groh, 3B	28
J. Daubert, 1B	24
P. Duncan, OF	21
D. Ruether, SP	18
D. Luque, SP	16
G. Neale, OF	16
M. Rath, 2B	14
H. Eller, SP	12
I. Wingo, C	11
R. Fisher, SP	10
L. Kopf, SS	10
J. Ring, SP	8
B. Napier, SP	5
N. Allen, C	4
S. Sallee, SP	4
E. Sicking, 2B	4
B. Rariden, C	3
R. Bressler, RP	2
C. See, OF	2
S. Crane, SS	1

New York (86-68)	WS
Hitting	**128.9**
Fielding	**42.3**
Pitching	**86.8**
R. Youngs, OF	33
G. Burns, OF	24
D. Bancroft, SS	21
F. Toney, SP	21
J. Barnes, SP	19
A. Nehf, SP	19
L. Doyle, 2B	16
G. Kelly, 1B	16
F. Frisch, 3B	15
P. Douglas, RP	14
E. Smith, C	10
R. Benton, SP	9
L. King, OF	9
F. Snyder, C	8
B. Kauff, OF	7
A. Fletcher, SS	4
B. Hubbell, RP	2
F. Lear, 3B	2
P. Perritt, RP	2
S. Sallee, RP	2
J. Winters, RP	2
R. Ryan, RP	1
E. Sicking, 3B	1
V. Spencer, OF	1

Philadelphia (62-91)	WS
Hitting	**76.5**
Fielding	**36.3**
Pitching	**73.2**
C. Williams, OF	24
L. Meadows, SP	19
E. Rixey, SP	18
I. Meusel, OF	17
G. Smith, SP	15
A. Fletcher, SS	14
C. Stengel, OF	13
G. Paulette, 1B	11
B. Hubbell, SP	8
R. Causey, SP	6
D. Bancroft, SS	5
H. Betts, RP	4
D. Miller, 2B	4
J. Rawlings, 2B	4
M. Wheat, C	4
R. Wrightstone, 3B	4
B. LeBourveau, OF	3
R. Miller, 3B	3
W. Tragesser, C	3
G. Cravath, OF	2
J. Enzmann, RP	2
F. Withrow, C	2
B. Gallia, RP	1

Pittsburgh (79-75)	WS
Hitting	**81.8**
Fielding	**50.2**
Pitching	**105.0**
W. Cooper, SP	31
B. Adams, SP	25
M. Carey, OF	20
C. Bigbee, OF	18
H. Carlson, SP	17
B. Southworth, OF	17
F. Nicholson, OF	14
E. Ponder, SP	14
P. Whitted, 3B	14
E. Hamilton, SP	13
W. Schmidt, C	11
G. Cutshaw, 2B	9
H. Caton, SS	7
C. Grimm, 1B	7
W. Barbare, SS	4
C. Barnhart, 3B	2
B. Haeffner, C	2
B. McKechnie, 3B	2
J. Wisner, RP	2
J. Zinn, SP-RP	2
W. Glazner, RP	1
C. Lee, C	1
J. Meador, RP	1
J. Morrison, SP-RP	1
H. Summa, OF	1
C. Tierney, 2B	1

St. Louis (75-79)	WS
Hitting	**130.6**
Fielding	**31.4**
Pitching	**62.9**
R. Hornsby, 2B	38
M. Stock, 3B	20
J. Fournier, 1B	19
B. Doak, SP	18
D. Lavan, SS	15
J. Haines, SP	14
A. McHenry, OF	14
F. Schupp, SP	13
J. Smith, OF	13
C. Heathcote, OF	12
V. Clemons, C	11
B. Sherdel, RP	10
P. Dillhoefer, C	5
H. Janvrin, SS	5
L. North, RP	4
J. Schultz, OF	4
J. May, RP	3
B. Shotton, OF	3
G. Lyons, RP	2
L. McCarty, C	1
H. Mueller, OF	1

1921 American League

Boston (75-79)	WS
Hitting	**83.6**
Fielding	**49.9**
Pitching	**91.5**
S. Jones, SP	29
J. Bush, SP	24
D. Pratt, 2B	20
M. Menosky, OF	16
E. Scott, SS	16
N. Leibold, OF	14
S. McInnis, 1B	14
H. Pennock, SP	14
E. Foster, 3B	13
S. Collins, OF	12
M. Ruel, C	11
B. Karr, RP	10
A. Russell, RP	9
E. Myers, SP	6
H. Thormahlen, RP	4
O. Vitt, 3B	4
R. Walters, C	4
T. Hendryx, OF	3
E. Neitzke, OF	1
P. Pittenger, OF	1

Chicago (62-92)	WS
Hitting	**84.8**
Fielding	**35.9**
Pitching	**65.3**
R. Faber, SP	37
E. Collins, 2B	21
D. Kerr, SP	19
H. Hooper, OF	15
E. Sheely, 1B	15
E. Johnson, SS	13
A. Strunk, OF	12
B. Falk, OF	11
R. Schalk, C	11
J. Mostil, OF	9
R. Wilkinson, SP	6
J. Russell, SP	4
J. Mulligan, 3B	3
Y. Yaryan, C	3
S. Hodge, RP	2
H. McClellan, 2B	2
S. Connally, RP	1
L. Davenport, RP	1
D. McWeeny, RP	1

Cleveland (94-60)	WS
Hitting	**145.8**
Fielding	**43.1**
Pitching	**93.1**
T. Speaker, OF	27
J. Sewell, SS	26
S. Coveleski, SP	25
L. Gardner, 3B	23
C. Jamieson, OF	17
S. O'Neill, C	16
E. Smith, OF	16
G. Uhle, SP	16
A. Sothoron, SP	13
D. Mails, SP	12
J. Bagby, SP	10
B. Wambsganss, 2B	10
J. Wood, OF	10
G. Burns, 1B	9
G. Morton, RP	9
D. Johnston, 1B	8
R. Stephenson, 2B	8
R. Caldwell, RP	7
L. Nunamaker, C	6
J. Evans, OF	5
J. Graney, OF	3
T. Odenwald, RP	2
G. Shinault, C	2
J. Petty, RP	1
P. Thomas, C	1

Detroit (71-82)	WS
Hitting	**125.6**
Fielding	**29.1**
Pitching	**58.3**
H. Heilmann, OF	28
T. Cobb, OF	26
B. Veach, OF	22
L. Blue, 1B	17
J. Bassler, C	13
D. Leonard, SP	13
B. Jones, 3B	12
R. Oldham, SP	11
H. Dauss, SP	10
R. Young, 2B	9
H. Ehmke, SP	8
D. Bush, SS	6
B. Cole, SP	6
I. Flagstead, SS	6
C. Holling, RP	5
J. Middleton, RP	4
J. Sargent, 2B	4
C. Shorten, OF	3
S. Sutherland, SP	3
E. Ainsmith, C	2
L. Woodall, C	2
H. Merritt, SS	1
S. Parks, RP	1
P. Perritt, SP-RP	1

New York (98-55)	WS
Hitting	**155.3**
Fielding	**43.2**
Pitching	**95.6**
B. Ruth, OF	53
C. Mays, SP	35
W. Hoyt, SP	24
B. Meusel, OF	24
R. Peckinpaugh, SS	20
W. Schang, C	20
A. Ward, 2B	20
B. Shawkey, SP	17
W. Pipp, 1B	15
H. Baker, 3B	12
E. Miller, OF	8
J. Quinn, RP	8
B. Piercy, SP	7
C. Fewster, OF	6
M. McNally, 3B	5
R. Collins, SP	4
H. Harper, SP	4
B. Roth, OF	4
A. DeVormer, C	2
C. Hawks, OF	2
T. Sheehan, RP	2
A. Ferguson, RP	1
J. Mitchell, SS	1

Philadelphia (53-100)	WS
Hitting	**57.8**
Fielding	**32.3**
Pitching	**68.8**
E. Rommel, SP	19
J. Dykes, 2B	16
T. Walker, OF	16
W. Witt, OF	13
S. Harriss, SP	12
R. Moore, SP	12
C. Perkins, C	12
J. Dugan, 3B	9
B. Hasty, SP	8
F. Welch, OF	7
C. Galloway, SS	6
D. Keefe, RP	6
R. Naylor, SP	6
S. Perry, SP	4
F. Brazill, 1B	2
F. Heimach, SP	2
P. Johnson, OF	2
Z. Collins, OF	1
I. Griffin, 1B	1
E. McCann, SS	1
G. Myatt, C	1
J. Sullivan, SP	1
F. Walker, OF	1
J. Walker, 1B	1

St. Louis (81-73)	WS
Hitting	**125.4**
Fielding	**39.0**
Pitching	**78.6**
U. Shocker, SP	30
G. Sisler, 1B	27
K. Williams, OF	27
B. Jacobson, OF	25
J. Tobin, OF	25
H. Severeid, C	18
D. Davis, SP	15
E. Vangilder, SP	12
B. Bayne, RP	11
F. Ellerbe, 3B	10
W. Gerber, SS	10
R. Kolp, RP	6
M. McManus, 2B	6
E. Palmero, RP	4
B. Burwell, RP	3
E. Smith, 3B	3
P. Collins, C	2
L. Lamb, 3B	2
D. Lee, SS	2
J. Austin, SS	1
J. Billings, C	1
B. Gleason, 2B	1
A. Sothoron, SP	1
D. Wetzel, OF	1

Washington (80-73)	WS
Hitting	**101.4**
Fielding	**46.3**
Pitching	**92.3**
G. Mogridge, SP	26
W. Johnson, SP	23
S. Rice, OF	23
H. Shanks, 3B	21
B. Harris, 2B	20
P. Gharrity, C	19
J. Judge, 1B	19
T. Zachary, SP	19
E. Erickson, SP	12
B. Miller, OF	12
C. Milan, OF	10
F. O'Rourke, SS	8
J. Acosta, RP	7
F. Brower, OF	4
V. Picinich, C	4
A. Schacht, RP	3
H. Courtney, SP-RP	2
D. Bush, SS	1
N. Gaines, RP	1
G. Goslin, OF	1
B. LaMotte, SS	1
D. Lewis, OF	1
T. Phillips, SP	1
J. Shaw, RP	1
E. Smith, OF	1

1921 National League

Boston (79-74)	WS
Hitting	**124.2**
Fielding	**39.7**
Pitching	**73.1**
R. Powell, OF	24
T. Boeckel, 3B	23
J. Oeschger, SP	20
W. Cruise, OF	19
B. Southworth, OF	19
J. Scott, SP	17
D. Fillingim, SP	16
W. Barbare, SS	15
H. Ford, 2B	14

M. Watson, SP	12
H. McQuillan, SP	11
F. Nicholson, OF	10
M. O'Neil, C	9
H. Gowdy, C	8
L. Christenbury, 2B	7
W. Holke, 1B	6
F. Gibson, C	4
A. Nixon, OF	2
J. Cooney, RP	1

Brooklyn (77-75)	WS
Hitting	**95.4**
Fielding	**42.2**
Pitching	**93.4**
B. Grimes, SP	29
J. Johnston, 3B	24
Z. Wheat, OF	23
T. Griffith, OF	17
C. Mitchell, RP	17
D. Ruether, SP	15
L. Cadore, SP	12
P. Kilduff, 2B	12
H. Myers, OF	12
I. Olson, SS	12
S. Smith, RP	11
R. Schmandt, 1B	7
E. Krueger, C	6
E. Konetchy, 1B	5
J. Miljus, RP	5
O. Miller, C	5
B. Neis, OF	5
A. Mamaux, RP	4
F. Schupp, RP	3
Z. Taylor, C	2
S. Bailey, RP	1
R. Gordinier, SP	1
W. Hood, OF	1
H. Janvrin, SS	1
J. Pfeffer, SP	1

Chicago (64-89)	WS
Hitting	**90.1**
Fielding	**35.4**
Pitching	**66.5**
P. Alexander, SP	22
R. Grimes, 1B	21
C. Hollocher, SS	14
M. Flack, OF	13
T. Barber, OF	12
S. Martin, SP	12
C. Deal, 3B	11
B. Freeman, SP	10
J. Kelleher, 3B	9
J. Sullivan, OF	8
V. Cheeves, SP	7
G. Maisel, OF	7
B. O'Farrell, C	7
Z. Terry, 2B	7
B. Twombly, OF	6
L. York, RP	5
P. Jones, RP	4
B. Killefer, C	4
L. Tyler, SP	4
T. Daly, C	2
T. Kaufmann, SP-RP	2
E. Ponder, SP	2
C. Elliott, SS	1
W. Marriott, 2B	1
R. Thomas, OF	1

Cincinnati (70-83)	WS
Hitting	**84.2**
Fielding	**42.3**
Pitching	**83.6**
D. Luque, SP	23
E. Rixey, SP	22
S. Bohne, 2B	20
E. Roush, OF	18
R. Marquard, SP	17
P. Duncan, OF	15
H. Groh, 3B	15
J. Daubert, 1B	12
R. Bressler, OF	10
P. Donohue, SP	9
B. Hargrave, C	8
I. Wingo, C	7
F. Coumbe, RP	6
L. Fonseca, 2B	5
L. Kopf, SS	4
S. Crane, SS	3
C. Markle, SP	3
G. Neale, OF	3
L. Brenton, RP	2
C. Rogge, RP	2
C. See, OF	2
H. Eller, RP	1
B. Geary, RP	1
B. Napier, RP	1
D. Paskert, OF	1

New York (94-59)	WS
Hitting	**153.6**
Fielding	**43.3**
Pitching	**85.1**
D. Bancroft, SS	31
F. Frisch, 3B	31
G. Kelly, 1B	24
R. Youngs, OF	23
G. Burns, OF	22
J. Barnes, SP	18
A. Nehf, SP	17
F. Snyder, C	16
F. Toney, SP	16
E. Smith, C	14
P. Douglas, SP	10
I. Meusel, OF	9
R. Ryan, RP	8
C. Walker, OF	7
J. Rawlings, 2B	6
S. Sallee, RP	6
R. Benton, SP-RP	5
E. Brown, OF	3
G. Rapp, 3B	3
R. Shea, RP	3
B. Cunningham, OF	2
P. Patterson, 3B	2
J. Berry, 2B	1
R. Causey, RP	1
M. Gonzalez, 1B	1
C. Jonnard, RP	1
L. King, OF	1
P. Perritt, RP	1

Philadelphia (51-103)	WS
Hitting	**71.8**
Fielding	**25.2**
Pitching	**56.0**
C. Williams, OF	17
I. Meusel, OF	12
L. Meadows, SP	11
J. Ring, SP	11
B. Hubbell, SP	10
F. Bruggy, C	8
E. Konetchy, 1B	8
R. Wrightstone, 3B	8
B. LeBourveau, OF	6
J. Winters, SP	6
H. Betts, RP	5
C. Lee, 1B	5
G. Smith, SP	5
R. Causey, SP	4
D. Miller, 3B	4
J. Rawlings, 2B	4
L. King, OF	3
R. Miller, SS	3
J. Monroe, 2B	3
F. Parkinson, SS	3
B. Henline, C	2
J. Peters, C	2
G. Rapp, 3B	2
D. Sedgwick, RP	2
J. Smith, 2B	2
C. Walker, OF	2
L. Weinert, RP	2
D. Rader, SS	1
C. Stengel, OF	1
K. Wilhelm, RP	1

Pittsburgh (90-63)	WS
Hitting	**103.5**
Fielding	**49.9**
Pitching	**116.6**
W. Cooper, SP	27
M. Carey, OF	24
R. Maranville, SS	23
C. Bigbee, OF	21
W. Glazner, SP	21
B. Adams, SP	18
E. Hamilton, SP	16
C. Grimm, 1B	14
J. Morrison, SP	13
C. Tierney, 2B	12
G. Cutshaw, 2B	11
P. Whitted, OF	11
C. Barnhart, 3B	10
W. Schmidt, C	10
D. Robertson, OF	9
J. Zinn, RP	9
H. Carlson, RP	6
C. Yellowhorse, RP	5
E. Ponder, RP	3
L. Bigbee, RP	1
T. Brottem, C	1
J. Gooch, C	1
J. Mokan, OF	1
R. Rohwer, OF	1
B. Skiff, C	1
P. Traynor, 3B	1

St. Louis (87-66)	WS
Hitting	**150.0**
Fielding	**37.3**
Pitching	**73.7**
R. Hornsby, 2B	41
A. McHenry, OF	25
J. Fournier, 1B	24
M. Stock, 3B	17
B. Doak, SP	16
J. Smith, OF	15
V. Clemons, C	14
J. Haines, SP	14
D. Lavan, SS	14
L. Mann, OF	12
B. Pertica, SP	11
J. Schultz, OF	9
B. Sherdel, RP	9
H. Mueller, OF	8
R. Walker, SP	7
L. North, RP	6
J. Pfeffer, SP	5
P. Dillhoefer, C	3
E. Ainsmith, C	2
B. Bailey, RP	2
M. Goodwin, RP	1
C. Heathcote, OF	1
J. May, SP	1
T. Riviere, RP	1
F. Schupp, RP	1
B. Shotton, OF	1
S. Toporcer, 2B	1

1922
American League

Boston (61-93)	WS
Hitting	**74.0**
Fielding	**36.6**
Pitching	**72.4**
D. Pratt, 2B	19
J. Quinn, SP	19
R. Collins, SP	16
G. Burns, 1B	15
J. Harris, OF	14
M. Menosky, OF	11
H. Pennock, SP	11
A. Ferguson, SP	10
M. Ruel, C	9
E. Smith, OF	8
J. Dugan, 3B	7
B. Karr, RP	7
N. Leibold, OF	7
S. Collins, OF	5
F. O'Rourke, SS	4
B. Piercy, RP	4
A. Russell, RP	4
C. Fewster, 3B	3
J. Mitchell, SS	3
C. Fullerton, RP	2
R. Walters, C	2
E. Chaplin, C	1
E. Miller, OF	1
P. Pittenger, 3B	1

Chicago (77-77)	WS
Hitting	**96.5**
Fielding	**47.6**
Pitching	**86.9**
R. Faber, SP	31
E. Collins, 2B	23
R. Schalk, C	22
H. Hooper, OF	21
J. Mostil, OF	19
E. Sheely, 1B	19
D. Leverett, SP	18
C. Robertson, SP	17
B. Falk, OF	13
E. Johnson, SS	9
T. Blankenship, SP	8
A. Strunk, OF	8
S. Hodge, RP	7
H. Courtney, SP	4
H. McClellan, 3B	4
J. Mulligan, 3B	4
F. Mack, SP-RP	2
L. Duff, RP	1
Y. Yaryan, C	1

Cleveland (78-76)	WS
Hitting	**128.5**
Fielding	**34.4**
Pitching	**71.1**
T. Speaker, OF	30
S. Coveleski, SP	22
G. Uhle, SP	22
J. Sewell, SS	21
C. Jamieson, OF	19
S. O'Neill, C	16
J. Wood, OF	16
L. Gardner, 3B	14
G. Morton, SP	12
R. Stephenson, 3B	12
S. McInnis, 1B	11
B. Wambsganss, 2B	10
D. Boone, SP	4
J. Edwards, RP	4
D. Mails, SP-RP	3
J. Evans, OF	2
S. Smith, SP	2
H. Summa, OF	2
G. Winn, RP	2
J. Bagby, RP	1
P. Bedgood, SP	1
J. Connolly, OF	1
L. Guisto, 1B	1
J. Lindsey, RP	1
P. McNulty, OF	1
D. Metivier, SP	1
L. Nunamaker, C	1
L. Sewell, C	1
A. Sothoron, SP	1

Detroit (79-75)	WS
Hitting	**137.7**
Fielding	**32.8**
Pitching	**66.6**
T. Cobb, OF	29
H. Heilmann, OF	24
H. Pillette, SP	22
B. Veach, OF	22

L. Blue, 1B	20
J. Bassler, C	15
T. Rigney, SS	15
H. Ehmke, SP	14
H. Dauss, SP	12
F. Haney, 3B	9
B. Jones, 3B	9
R. Oldham, SP	9
G. Cutshaw, 2B	7
S. Johnson, RP	6
D. Clark, 2B	5
O. Olsen, RP	5
I. Flagstead, OF	4
B. Fothergill, OF	4
L. Woodall, C	4
B. Cole, RP	1
C. Manion, C	1

New York (94-60)	WS
Hitting	**122.0**
Fielding	**49.9**
Pitching	**110.1**
B. Ruth, OF	29
B. Shawkey, SP	27
J. Bush, SP	26
W. Pipp, 1B	22
W. Hoyt, SP	21
B. Meusel, OF	21
S. Jones, SP	20
W. Witt, OF	19
W. Schang, C	18
C. Mays, SP	17
E. Scott, SS	16
A. Ward, 2B	14
H. Baker, 3B	7
J. Dugan, 3B	7
M. McNally, 3B	4
E. Miller, OF	4
G. Murray, RP	4
F. Hofmann, C	3
C. Fewster, OF	2
N. McMillan, OF	1

Philadelphia (65-89)	WS
Hitting	**98.6**
Fielding	**30.3**
Pitching	**66.1**
E. Rommel, SP	27
B. Miller, OF	22
T. Walker, OF	22
C. Galloway, SS	19
J. Dykes, 3B	17
J. Hauser, 1B	12
C. Perkins, C	12
B. Hasty, SP	10
F. Welch, OF	9
S. Harriss, SP	8
F. Heimach, SP	7
R. Naylor, SP	7
C. Ogden, RP	6
B. McGowan, OF	4
R. Young, 2B	4
D. Johnston, 1B	3
F. Bruggy, C	2
C. Eckert, RP	2
O. Rettig, SP	1
H. Scheer, 2B	1

St. Louis (93-61)	WS
Hitting	**130.6**
Fielding	**47.7**
Pitching	**100.7**
K. Williams, OF	30
U. Shocker, SP	29
G. Sisler, 1B	29
E. Vangilder, SP	22
B. Jacobson, OF	20
M. McManus, 2B	20
J. Tobin, OF	19
H. Severeid, C	18
W. Gerber, SS	15
R. Wright, SP	13
H. Pruett, RP	12
R. Kolp, SP	11
D. Davis, SP	9
P. Collins, C	6
F. Ellerbe, 3B	6
D. Danforth, SP-RP	5
B. Bayne, RP	4
E. Foster, 3B	4
C. Shorten, OF	4
J. Austin, 3B	1
H. Bronkie, 3B	1
G. Robertson, 3B	1

Washington (69-85)	WS
Hitting	**98.5**
Fielding	**38.3**
Pitching	**70.2**
W. Johnson, SP	21
S. Rice, OF	20
J. Judge, 1B	18
B. Harris, 2B	17
G. Mogridge, SP	17
F. Brower, OF	16
T. Zachary, SP	16
R. Peckinpaugh, SS	14
G. Goslin, OF	12
P. Gharrity, C	11
H. Shanks, 3B	9
J. Brillheart, RP	6
R. Francis, SP	6
V. Picinich, C	5
B. LaMotte, 3B	4
D. Bush, 3B	3
E. Smith, OF	3
P. Lapan, C	2
C. Warmoth, RP	2
O. Bluege, 3B	1
E. Erickson, SP	1
J. Gleason, SP	1
E. Goebel, OF	1
T. Phillips, RP	1

1922 National League

Boston (53-100)	WS
Hitting	**67.7**
Fielding	**32.2**
Pitching	**59.1**
R. Powell, OF	17
F. Miller, SP	13
H. Ford, SS	12
T. Boeckel, 3B	11
W. Cruise, OF	10
H. Gowdy, C	9
L. Kopf, 2B	7
R. Marquard, SP	7
T. McNamara, RP	7
H. McQuillan, SP	7
B. Southworth, OF	7
M. Watson, SP	6
D. Fillingim, RP	5
F. Gibson, C	5
W. Holke, 1B	5
G. Braxton, RP	4
F. Nicholson, OF	4
A. Nixon, OF	4
J. Oeschger, SP-RP	4
M. O'Neil, C	3
W. Barbare, 2B	2
L. Christenbury, OF	2
J. Cooney, SP	2
H. Hulihan, SP	2
B. Roser, OF	2
D. Rudolph, SP	1
J. Yeargin, SP	1

Brooklyn (76-78)	WS
Hitting	**110.3**
Fielding	**40.8**
Pitching	**76.9**
Z. Wheat, OF	27
A. High, 3B	20
J. Johnston, 2B	20
D. Ruether, SP	20
H. Myers, OF	17
D. Vance, SP	16
T. Griffith, OF	12
I. Olson, 2B	12
B. Grimes, SP	11
H. DeBerry, C	9
L. Cadore, SP	8
B. Griffith, OF	8
A. Decatur, RP	7
H. Shriver, SP	7
A. Mamaux, RP	6
C. Mitchell, 1B	6
R. Schmandt, 1B	6
O. Miller, C	4
S. Smith, RP	4
B. Hungling, C	2
H. Janvrin, 2B	2
B. Neis, OF	2
C. Ward, SS	2

Chicago (80-74)	WS
Hitting	**119.8**
Fielding	**41.8**
Pitching	**78.4**
R. Grimes, 1B	29
B. O'Farrell, C	26
C. Hollocher, SS	24
V. Aldridge, SP	19
H. Miller, OF	19
P. Alexander, SP	18
V. Cheeves, SP	12
J. Statz, OF	12
M. Krug, 3B	11
T. Kaufmann, RP	10
Z. Terry, 2B	10
B. Friberg, OF	8
T. Osborne, RP	8
T. Barber, OF	7
P. Jones, SP	6
C. Heathcote, OF	5
M. Callaghan, OF	3
J. Kelleher, 3B	3
G. Hartnett, C	2
V. Keen, RP	2
G. Stueland, RP	2
H. Fitzgerald, OF	1
F. Fussell, SP	1
G. Maisel, OF	1
K. Wirts, C	1

Cincinnati (86-68)	WS
Hitting	**118.7**
Fielding	**46.3**
Pitching	**93.0**
J. Daubert, 1B	24
E. Rixey, SP	23
P. Duncan, OF	21
G. Burns, OF	19
P. Donohue, SP	19
D. Luque, SP	18
B. Pinelli, 3B	18
G. Harper, OF	17
J. Couch, SP	16
B. Hargrave, C	14
L. Fonseca, 2B	13
S. Bohne, 2B	12
E. Roush, OF	9
I. Caveney, SS	8
C. Keck, SP	8
I. Wingo, C	8
C. Markle, RP	4
J. Gillespie, RP	3
R. Bressler, 1B	1
W. Kimmick, SS	1
G. Neale, OF	1
K. Schnell, RP	1

New York (93-61)	WS
Hitting	**131.3**
Fielding	**49.0**
Pitching	**98.7**
D. Bancroft, SS	27
I. Meusel, OF	23
R. Youngs, OF	22
A. Nehf, SP	21
F. Frisch, 2B	20
G. Kelly, 1B	20
R. Ryan, RP	16
P. Douglas, SP	15
C. Stengel, OF	14
J. Barnes, SP	13
F. Snyder, C	13
H. Groh, 3B	12
E. Smith, C	10
J. Rawlings, 2B	8
B. Cunningham, OF	7
C. Jonnard, RP	7
H. McQuillan, SP	6
R. Causey, RP	5
J. Scott, SP	5
V. Barnes, RP	4
F. Toney, SP	4
C. Blume, SP	2
C. Hill, SP-RP	1
F. Johnson, SP	1
L. King, 1B-OF	1
D. Robertson, OF	1
R. Shinners, OF	1

Philadelphia (57-96)	WS
Hitting	**67.1**
Fielding	**33.8**
Pitching	**70.1**
L. Meadows, SP	17
C. Williams, OF	17
C. Walker, OF	16
J. Ring, SP	13
B. Henline, C	12
F. Parkinson, 2B	12
L. Weinert, SP	12
C. Lee, OF	11
G. Smith, RP	9
B. Hubbell, SP	8
R. Wrightstone, 3B	8
A. Fletcher, SS	7
J. Winters, RP	6
P. Behan, SP	4
R. Leslie, 1B	4
G. Rapp, 3B	4
B. LeBourveau, OF	2
J. Mokan, OF	2
J. Peters, C	2
L. King, OF	1
L. Pinto, RP	1
J. Singleton, RP	1
J. Smith, SS	1
F. Withrow, C	1

Pittsburgh (85-69)	WS
Hitting	**127.0**
Fielding	**41.1**
Pitching	**86.9**
M. Carey, OF	29
W. Cooper, SP	27
C. Bigbee, OF	23
R. Maranville, SS	22
J. Morrison, SP	21
C. Tierney, 2B	15
J. Gooch, C	14
B. Adams, SP	13
C. Grimm, 1B	13
P. Traynor, 3B	13
R. Russell, OF	12
W. Glazner, SP	10
E. Hamilton, RP	10
C. Barnhart, 3B	7
W. Schmidt, C	5
H. Carlson, RP	4
R. Rohwer, OF	4
C. Yellowhorse, RP	4
J. Ens, 2B	3
W. Mueller, OF	2
M. Brown, SP	1
J. Mattox, C	1
J. Mokan, OF	1
J. Zinn, RP	1

St. Louis (85-69)	WS
Hitting	**148.3**
Fielding	**33.0**
Pitching	**73.7**
R. Hornsby, 2B	47
J. Pfeffer, SP	21
J. Smith, OF	17
M. Stock, 3B	17
E. Ainsmith, C	16
B. Sherdel, SP	16
S. Toporcer, SS	14
J. Fournier, 1B	13
J. Haines, SP	11
L. North, RP	10
J. Schultz, OF	9
C. Barfoot, RP	7
L. Mann, OF	7
A. McHenry, OF	7
J. Bottomley, 1B	6
M. Flack, OF	6
R. Blades, OF	5
B. Doak, SP	5
V. Clemons, C	4
D. Gainer, 1B	3
D. Lavan, SS	3
H. Mueller, OF	3
B. Pertica, RP	2
B. Bailey, RP	1
E. Dyer, RP	1
C. Heathcote, OF	1
H. McCurdy, C	1
E. Sell, SP	1
R. Walker, RP	1

1923
American League

Boston (61-91)	WS
Hitting	**69.6**
Fielding	**37.4**
Pitching	**76.1**
H. Ehmke, SP	25
J. Harris, OF	23
G. Burns, 1B	21
J. Quinn, SP	18
I. Flagstead, OF	14
B. Piercy, SP	11
A. Ferguson, SP	10
V. Picinich, C	10
N. McMillan, 3B	9
G. Murray, RP	6
H. Shanks, 3B	6
J. Mitchell, SS	5
D. Reichle, OF	5
A. DeVormer, C	3
C. Fewster, 2B	3
C. Fullerton, RP	3
L. Howe, RP	3
S. Collins, OF	2
M. Menosky, OF	2
R. Walters, C	2
J. Donahue, OF	1
P. Pittenger, 2B	1

Chicago (69-85)	WS
Hitting	**92.7**
Fielding	**39.3**
Pitching	**75.1**
E. Collins, 2B	24
W. Kamm, 3B	20
J. Mostil, OF	20
S. Thurston, RP	17
R. Faber, SP	16
E. Sheely, 1B	16
H. Hooper, OF	15
C. Robertson, SP	14
M. Cvengros, SP	11
D. Leverett, SP	11
T. Blankenship, SP	9
B. Falk, OF	9
R. Schalk, C	7
H. McClellan, SS	5
M. Archdeacon, OF	3
B. Barrett, OF	3
R. Elsh, OF	2
B. Crouse, C	1
R. Graham, C	1
J. Happenny, 2B	1
F. Mack, RP	1
A. Strunk, OF	1

Cleveland (82-71)	WS
Hitting	**138.8**
Fielding	**32.9**
Pitching	**74.3**
T. Speaker, OF	35
J. Sewell, SS	29
G. Uhle, SP	29
C. Jamieson, OF	25
S. Coveleski, SP	16
F. Brower, 1B	15
H. Summa, OF	14
R. Lutzke, 3B	12
R. Stephenson, 2B	11
B. Wambsganss, 2B	10
J. Edwards, SP	9
J. Shaute, RP	9
S. Smith, SP	9
G. Morton, RP	6
S. O'Neill, C	5
G. Myatt, C	4
J. Connolly, OF	3
L. Gardner, 3B	2
D. Boone, RP	1
R. Knode, 1B	1
D. Levsen, RP	1

Detroit (83-71)	WS
Hitting	**140.8**
Fielding	**33.6**
Pitching	**74.7**
H. Heilmann, OF	35
H. Dauss, SP	25
T. Cobb, OF	24
J. Bassler, C	19
L. Blue, 1B	16
T. Rigney, SS	16
H. Pillette, SP	15
F. Haney, 2B	12
H. Manush, OF	12
S. Johnson, RP	11
B. Cole, RP	10
D. Pratt, 2B	9
B. Veach, OF	9
B. Fothergill, OF	7
K. Holloway, SP	7
B. Jones, 3B	6
L. Woodall, C	6
R. Francis, RP	3
E. Whitehill, RP	3
R. Collins, SP	2
G. Cutshaw, 2B	1
R. Moore, RP	1

New York (98-54)	WS
Hitting	**139.0**
Fielding	**49.2**
Pitching	**105.8**
B. Ruth, OF	55
J. Bush, SP	24
H. Pennock, SP	23
A. Ward, 2B	22
W. Witt, OF	22
W. Hoyt, SP	21
S. Jones, SP	20
B. Shawkey, SP	19
J. Dugan, 3B	17
B. Meusel, OF	16
W. Pipp, 1B	14
E. Scott, SS	9
F. Hofmann, C	8
W. Schang, C	8
E. Smith, OF	7
E. Johnson, SS	3
L. Gehrig, 1B	2
H. Hendrick, OF	2
B. Bengough, C	1
C. Mays, RP	1

Philadelphia (69-83)	WS
Hitting	**87.5**
Fielding	**39.6**
Pitching	**79.9**
E. Rommel, SP	25
J. Hauser, 1B	22
B. Miller, OF	15
C. Perkins, C	15
F. Welch, OF	14
C. Galloway, SS	13
S. Harriss, SP	12
R. Naylor, SP	12
B. Hasty, SP	11
F. Heimach, RP	11
S. Hale, 3B	10
J. Dykes, 2B	9
W. Matthews, OF	9
B. McGowan, OF	6
H. Riconda, 3B	4
R. Walberg, RP	4
D. Burns, SP	3
H. Scheer, 2B	3
T. Walker, OF	3
R. Meeker, RP	2
F. Bruggy, C	1
W. French, OF	1
R. Kelly, RP	1
C. Wolfe, RP	1

St. Louis (74-78)	WS
Hitting	**86.9**
Fielding	**46.2**
Pitching	**88.9**
K. Williams, OF	29
U. Shocker, SP	25
E. Vangilder, SP	23
M. McManus, 2B	19
J. Tobin, OF	18
W. Gerber, SS	17
D. Danforth, SP	16
H. Severeid, C	16
B. Jacobson, OF	15
R. Kolp, SP-RP	9
D. Schliebner, 1B	8
D. Davis, SP	7
H. Pruett, RP	6
H. Ezzell, 3B	3
G. Robertson, 3B	3
B. Bayne, RP	2
P. Collins, C	2
C. Durst, OF	1
E. Foster, 2B	1
B. Whaley, OF	1
R. Wright, RP	1

Washington (75-78)	WS
Hitting	**119.8**
Fielding	**38.0**
Pitching	**67.2**
S. Rice, OF	24
M. Ruel, C	23
G. Goslin, OF	21
B. Harris, 2B	18
W. Johnson, SP	17
J. Judge, 1B	17
R. Peckinpaugh, SS	17
G. Mogridge, SP	14
N. Leibold, OF	13
A. Russell, RP	13
O. Bluege, 3B	10
P. Zahniser, SP	7
J. Evans, OF	6
T. Zachary, SP	6
P. Gharrity, C	4
F. Marberry, RP	4
C. Warmoth, SP	4
B. Hollingsworth, RP	2
D. Bush, 3B	1
P. Hargrave, 3B	1
J. O'Neill, 2B	1
F. Schemanske, RP	1
R. Wade, OF	1

1923
National League

Boston (54-100)	WS
Hitting	**70.5**
Fielding	**31.2**
Pitching	**60.2**
B. Southworth, OF	17
J. Barnes, SP	15
T. Boeckel, 3B	15
J. Genewich, SP	15
R. Marquard, SP	12
S. McInnis, 1B	12
J. Cooney, RP	9
R. Powell, OF	9
G. Felix, OF	8
H. Ford, 2B	8
A. Nixon, OF	6
B. Smith, SS	6
E. Smith, C	6
L. Benton, RP	4
M. O'Neil, C	4
L. Kopf, SS	3
T. McNamara, SP-RP	3
B. Bagwell, OF	2
J. Oeschger, RP	2
J. Conlon, 2B	1
D. Fillingim, RP	1
F. Gibson, C	1
H. Gowdy, C	1
F. Miller, SP	1
D. Rudolph, SP	1

Brooklyn (76-78)	WS
Hitting	**113.9**
Fielding	**33.9**
Pitching	**80.2**
J. Fournier, 1B	27
J. Johnston, 2B	22
B. Grimes, SP	21
D. Vance, SP	18
D. Ruether, SP	15
Z. Wheat, OF	15
T. Griffith, OF	14
A. High, 3B	13
B. Neis, OF	10
G. Bailey, OF	9
H. DeBerry, C	8
A. Decatur, RP	8
L. Dickerman, SP	8
Z. Taylor, C	8
B. Griffith, OF	5
D. Henry, SP	5
I. Olson, 2B	5
B. McCarren, 3B	4
G. Smith, RP	4
L. Cadore, SP-RP	3
M. Berg, SS	1
R. French, SS	1
C. Hargreaves, C	1
D. Schliebner, 1B	1
P. Schreiber, RP	1
S. Stewart, 2B	1

Chicago (83-71)	WS
Hitting	**113.8**
Fielding	**45.7**
Pitching	**89.5**
P. Alexander, SP	27
J. Statz, OF	26
B. O'Farrell, C	25
B. Friberg, 3B	23
V. Aldridge, SP	18
T. Kaufmann, SP	18
G. Grantham, 2B	17
H. Miller, OF	17
V. Keen, RP	15
C. Hollocher, SS	10
G. Hartnett, C	9

R. Grimes, 1B	8
S. Adams, SS	7
J. Kelleher, 1B	6
T. Osborne, SP	6
C. Heathcote, OF	5
N. Dumovich, RP	4
F. Fussell, RP	2
D. Grigsby, OF	2
M. Callaghan, OF	1
P. Collins, SP	1
A. Elliott, 1B	1
R. Wheeler, SP	1

Cincinnati (91-63)	WS
Hitting	**114.7**
Fielding	**48.6**
Pitching	**109.7**
D. Luque, SP	39
E. Roush, OF	28
E. Rixey, SP	26
B. Hargrave, C	25
P. Donohue, SP	21
G. Burns, OF	20
P. Duncan, OF	20
R. Benton, SP	16
I. Caveney, SS	13
J. Daubert, 1B	13
S. Bohne, 2B	12
B. Pinelli, 3B	9
L. Fonseca, 2B	7
I. Wingo, C	5
R. Bressler, 1B	4
C. Keck, RP	4
G. Harper, OF	3
H. McQuaid, RP	3
B. Harris, RP	2
B. Fowler, SS	1
W. Kimmick, 2B	1
E. Pick, OF	1

New York (95-58)	WS
Hitting	**150.3**
Fielding	**45.9**
Pitching	**88.7**
F. Frisch, 2B	31
R. Youngs, OF	25
D. Bancroft, SS	20
G. Kelly, 1B	20
I. Meusel, OF	20
H. Groh, 3B	18
H. McQuillan, SP	17
J. Scott, SP	17
J. Bentley, SP	15
R. Ryan, RP	15
F. Snyder, C	12
C. Stengel, OF	11
T. Jackson, SS	10
A. Nehf, SP	9
J. O'Connell, OF	8
M. Watson, SP	8
H. Gowdy, C	7
C. Jonnard, RP	7
B. Cunningham, OF	5
V. Barnes, RP	2
C. Blume, RP	2
D. Gearin, RP	2
J. Barnes, RP	1
A. Gaston, C	1
F. Johnson, SP	1
E. Smith, C	1

Philadelphia (50-104)	WS
Hitting	**72.1**
Fielding	**27.3**
Pitching	**50.5**
J. Ring, SP	20
C. Williams, OF	17
C. Tierney, 2B	13
B. Henline, C	10
J. Mokan, OF	10
W. Holke, 1B	9
H. Sand, SS	9
W. Glazner, SP	8
C. Lee, OF	8
C. Mitchell, SP	8
R. Wrightstone, 3B	7
H. Betts, RP	6
C. Walker, OF	6
L. Weinert, SP	4
P. Behan, SP	3
J. Couch, SP	3
F. Parkinson, 2B	2
G. Rapp, 3B	2
R. Head, RP	1
L. Meadows, SP	1
M. O'Brien, C	1
J. Wilson, C	1
A. Woehr, 3B	1

Pittsburgh (87-67)	WS
Hitting	**129.2**
Fielding	**45.2**
Pitching	**86.5**
M. Carey, OF	29
P. Traynor, 3B	28
C. Grimm, 1B	23
J. Morrison, SP	23
W. Cooper, SP	21
L. Meadows, SP	20
C. Barnhart, OF	18
R. Maranville, SS	16
C. Bigbee, OF	13
B. Adams, SP	11
J. Rawlings, 2B	11
R. Russell, OF	10
E. Hamilton, SP	9
J. Gooch, C	7
W. Schmidt, C	6
W. Glazner, SP	3
W. Mueller, OF	3
R. Steineder, RP	3
C. Tierney, 2B	3
S. Adams, 2B	1
J. Bagby, RP	1
F. Luce, OF	1
E. Moore, SS	1

St. Louis (79-74)	WS
Hitting	**120.2**
Fielding	**39.3**
Pitching	**77.5**
R. Hornsby, 2B	26
J. Bottomley, 1B	24
J. Haines, SP	20
M. Stock, 3B	15
B. Sherdel, SP	14
H. Mueller, OF	12
J. Smith, OF	12
B. Doak, SP	11
M. Flack, OF	11
F. Toney, SP	10
H. Myers, OF	9
R. Blades, OF	8
H. Freigau, SS	8
J. Stuart, RP	8
J. Pfeffer, SP	7
S. Toporcer, 2B	7
C. Barfoot, RP	6
L. Mann, OF	6
E. Ainsmith, C	4
V. Clemons, C	4
H. McCurdy, C	4
L. Bell, SS	3
E. Dyer, OF	3
D. Lavan, SS	2
J. Flowers, SS	1
L. North, RP	1
F. Wigington, RP	1

1924 American League

Boston (67-87)	WS
Hitting	**88.3**
Fielding	**37.3**
Pitching	**75.4**
H. Ehmke, SP	25
I. Flagstead, OF	19
I. Boone, OF	18
J. Quinn, SP	18
J. Harris, 1B	16
A. Ferguson, SP	15
B. Veach, OF	13
B. Wambsganss, 2B	11
D. Clark, 3B	10
C. Fullerton, SP	7
S. O'Neill, C	6
B. Ross, RP	6
S. Collins, OF	5
H. Ezzell, 3B	5
D. Lee, SS	5
V. Picinich, C	5
H. Shanks, SS	5
D. Williams, OF	3
J. Heving, C	2
B. Piercy, SP	2
P. Todt, 1B	2
T. Wingfield, SP	2
C. Geygan, SS	1

Chicago (66-87)	WS
Hitting	**115.9**
Fielding	**26.6**
Pitching	**55.4**
E. Collins, 2B	25
B. Falk, OF	21
S. Thurston, SP	20
H. Hooper, OF	19
E. Sheely, 1B	19
W. Kamm, 3B	14
J. Mostil, OF	13
M. Archdeacon, OF	9
R. Faber, SP	9
S. Connally, RP	8
T. Lyons, SP	8
T. Blankenship, RP	7
B. Barrett, SS	6
B. Crouse, C	6
R. Elsh, OF	3
D. McWeeny, RP	2
C. Robertson, SP	2
R. Schalk, C	2
M. Cvengros, SP	1
J. Grabowski, C	1
D. Leverett, SP	1
H. McClellan, SS	1
R. Morehart, SS	1

Cleveland (67-86)	WS
Hitting	**103.9**
Fielding	**31.4**
Pitching	**65.7**
J. Sewell, SS	22
J. Shaute, SP	22
T. Speaker, OF	21
C. Jamieson, OF	19
S. Smith, SP	18
G. Myatt, C	15
G. Burns, 1B	12
S. Coveleski, SP	12
R. Stephenson, 2B	10
G. Uhle, SP	8
R. Lutzke, 3B	7
F. Brower, 1B	5
L. Sewell, C	5
H. Summa, OF	5
J. Edwards, SP	4
P. McNulty, OF	4
C. Fewster, 2B	3
D. Metivier, RP	2
R. Walters, C	2
F. Ellerbe, 3B	1
D. Levsen, RP	1
B. Messenger, RP	1
J. Miller, SP	1
E. Yoter, 3B	1

Detroit (86-68)	WS
Hitting	**139.1**
Fielding	**38.3**
Pitching	**80.5**
H. Heilmann, OF	30
T. Cobb, OF	27
T. Rigney, SS	22
J. Bassler, C	21
R. Collins, SP	16
E. Whitehill, SP	16
L. Blue, 1B	15
H. Manush, OF	13
K. Holloway, RP	11
D. Pratt, 2B	11
L. Stoner, SP	10
F. Haney, 3B	9
H. Dauss, RP	8
B. Jones, 3B	7
L. Woodall, C	7
E. Wells, SP	6
B. Cole, RP	5
S. Johnson, RP	5
L. Burke, 2B	4
F. O'Rourke, 2B	4
A. Wingo, OF	4
B. Fothergill, OF	3
D. Leonard, SP	2
C. Gehringer, 2B	1
H. Pillette, RP	1

New York (89-63)	WS
Hitting	**125.8**
Fielding	**46.5**
Pitching	**94.7**
B. Ruth, OF	45
H. Pennock, SP	27
J. Bush, SP	23
B. Meusel, OF	19
W. Pipp, 1B	18
J. Dugan, 3B	17
W. Hoyt, SP	17
W. Schang, C	16
B. Shawkey, SP	15
S. Jones, SP	13
W. Witt, OF	13
A. Ward, 2B	12
E. Scott, SS	11
E. Johnson, 2B	6
M. Gaston, RP	4
F. Hofmann, C	3
W. Beall, SP-RP	2
E. Combs, OF	2
B. Bengough, C	1
L. Gehrig, 1B	1
H. Hendrick, OF	1
M. McNally, 2B	1

Philadelphia (71-81)	WS
Hitting	**88.6**
Fielding	**42.4**
Pitching	**82.0**
J. Hauser, 1B	21
E. Rommel, SP	21
S. Baumgartner, RP	20
A. Simmons, OF	17
J. Dykes, 2B	16
F. Heimach, SP	13
B. Miller, OF	13
B. Lamar, OF	12
M. Bishop, 2B	10
S. Gray, SP	9
C. Galloway, SS	8
S. Hale, 3B	8
F. Welch, OF	8
R. Meeker, RP	7
C. Perkins, C	7
D. Burns, RP	6
S. Harriss, RP	6
H. Riconda, 3B	5
F. Bruggy, C	2
J. Chapman, SS	2
B. Hasty, RP	1
P. Strand, OF	1

St. Louis (74-78)	WS
Hitting	**100.7**
Fielding	**41.3**
Pitching	**80.0**
B. Jacobson, OF	23
U. Shocker, SP	20
E. Wingard, SP	19
K. Williams, OF	18
M. McManus, 2B	17
H. Severeid, C	16
D. Danforth, SP	15
G. Robertson, 3B	14
W. Gerber, SS	12
J. Tobin, OF	12
D. Davis, SP	11
G. Sisler, 1B	11
B. Bayne, RP	4
N. McMillan, 2B	4
E. Vangilder, RP	4
H. Bennett, OF	3
R. Kolp, RP	3
G. Lyons, RP	3
H. Pruett, RP	3
P. Collins, C	2
J. Evans, OF	2
H. Rice, 3B	2
F. Ellerbe, 3B	1
T. Rego, C	1
S. Simon, 3B	1
O. Voigt, RP	1

Washington (92-62)	WS
Hitting	**117.2**
Fielding	**50.5**
Pitching	**108.3**
G. Goslin, OF	29
W. Johnson, SP	29
S. Rice, OF	24
R. Peckinpaugh, SS	22
T. Zachary, SP	21
J. Judge, 1B	19
F. Marberry, RP	17
M. Ruel, C	17
G. Mogridge, SP	14
B. Harris, 2B	13
C. Ogden, SP	12
O. Bluege, 3B	9
N. Leibold, OF	8
J. Martina, SP	6
E. McNeely, OF	6
D. Prothro, 3B	6
A. Russell, RP	6
W. Matthews, OF	5
B. Speece, RP	4
P. Zahniser, SP	3
N. Altrock, RP	1
W. Lefler, OF	1
L. Richbourg, OF	1
B. Tate, C	1
T. Taylor, 3B	1
T. Wingfield, RP	1

1924 National League

Boston (53-100)	WS
Hitting	**69.8**
Fielding	**30.7**
Pitching	**58.5**
J. Barnes, SP	21
J. Cooney, SP	16
S. McInnis, 1B	12
E. Padgett, 3B	12
C. Stengel, OF	12
D. Bancroft, SS	10
B. Cunningham, OF	9
F. Gibson, C	9
C. Tierney, 2B	8
L. Benton, RP	7
J. Genewich, SP	4
T. McNamara, SP	4
M. O'Neil, C	4
R. Powell, OF	4
B. Smith, SS	4
L. Mann, OF	3
R. Marquard, SP	3
F. Wilson, OF	3
S. Graham, SP	2
R. Lucas, RP	2
E. Sperber, OF	2
H. Thomas, OF	2
J. Yeargin, RP	2
W. Cruise, PH-PR	1
G. Felix, OF	1
M. Shay, 2B	1
E. Smith, C	1

Brooklyn (92-62)	WS
Hitting	**140.0**
Fielding	**42.6**
Pitching	**93.4**
D. Vance, SP	36
Z. Wheat, OF	35
J. Fournier, 1B	34
A. High, 2B	28
B. Grimes, SP	21
E. Brown, OF	16
B. Doak, SP	13
Z. Taylor, C	13
H. DeBerry, C	10
J. Johnston, SS	10
B. Neis, OF	9
D. Ruether, SP	9
R. Ehrhardt, SP	8
J. Mitchell, SS	8
T. Griffith, OF	7
A. Decatur, RP	6
M. Stock, 3B	4
T. Osborne, SP	3
C. Hargreaves, C	2
D. Loftus, OF	2
G. Bailey, OF	1
J. Klugmann, 2B	1

Chicago (81-72)	WS
Hitting	**115.7**
Fielding	**42.7**
Pitching	**84.6**
G. Grantham, 2B	21
G. Hartnett, C	19
B. Friberg, 3B	18
V. Aldridge, SP	17
T. Kaufmann, SP	16
J. Statz, OF	16
V. Keen, SP	15
P. Alexander, SP	14
S. Adams, SS	12
D. Grigsby, OF	12
C. Heathcote, OF	12
E. Jacobs, SP	12
R. Grimes, 1B	9
H. Cotter, 1B	8
C. Hollocher, SS	6
H. Miller, OF	6
B. O'Farrell, C	6
S. Blake, RP	5
R. Wheeler, RP	5
O. Vogel, OF	4
B. Weis, OF	4
B. Barrett, 2B	3
G. Bush, SP-RP	2
R. Michaels, SS	1

Cincinnati (83-70)	WS
Hitting	**101.0**
Fielding	**44.4**
Pitching	**103.6**
E. Rixey, SP	21
C. Mays, SP	20
E. Roush, OF	20
R. Bressler, 1B	15
P. Donohue, SP	15
B. Pinelli, 3B	15
C. Walker, OF	15
H. Critz, 2B	14
B. Hargrave, C	14
D. Luque, SP	14
R. Benton, SP	13
T. Sheehan, RP	13
J. Daubert, 1B	8
J. May, RP	8
S. Bohne, 2B	7
I. Caveney, SS	7
G. Burns, OF	6
I. Wingo, C	6
P. Dibut, RP	5
P. Duncan, OF	5
B. Fowler, SS	3
G. Harper, OF	2
L. Fonseca, 2B	1
G. Sandberg, C	1
C. Shorten, OF	1

New York (93-60)	WS
Hitting	**163.7**
Fielding	**38.7**
Pitching	**76.5**
F. Frisch, 2B	30
R. Youngs, OF	29
G. Kelly, 1B	26
T. Jackson, SS	20
H. Groh, 3B	19
I. Meusel, OF	17
V. Barnes, SP	16
H. Wilson, OF	16
H. McQuillan, SP	14
F. Snyder, C	14
J. Bentley, SP	12
A. Nehf, SP	12
H. Gowdy, C	11
C. Jonnard, RP	7
M. Watson, SP	6
R. Ryan, RP	5
B. Southworth, OF	5
J. O'Connell, OF	4
B. Terry, 1B	4
H. Baldwin, RP	2
W. Dean, SP	2
D. Gearin, SP-RP	2
F. Lindstrom, 2B	2
J. Oeschger, RP	2
L. Cadore, RP	1
W. Huntzinger, RP	1

Philadelphia (55-96)	WS
Hitting	**72.1**
Fielding	**32.0**
Pitching	**60.9**
C. Williams, OF	21
J. Ring, SP	13
G. Harper, OF	11
R. Wrightstone, 3B	11
H. Carlson, SP	10
B. Hubbell, SP	10
H. Sand, SS	10
H. Betts, RP	9
B. Henline, C	9
W. Holke, 1B	9
H. Ford, 2B	8
J. Wilson, C	8
J. Couch, RP	5
C. Mitchell, SP	5
J. Mokan, OF	5
J. Schultz, OF	5
W. Glazner, SP	3
J. Oeschger, RP	3
F. Leach, OF	2
R. Steineder, RP	2
C. Walker, OF	2
C. Lee, OF	1
F. Parkinson, 3B	1
L. Weinert, RP	1
A. Woehr, 3B	1

Pittsburgh (90-63)	WS
Hitting	**112.6**
Fielding	**49.5**
Pitching	**107.9**
M. Carey, OF	25
W. Cooper, SP	24
K. Cuyler, OF	24
G. Wright, SS	22
R. Kremer, SP	21
E. Yde, SP	19
L. Meadows, SP	17
P. Traynor, 3B	17
R. Maranville, 2B	15
J. Morrison, SP	14
C. Grimm, 1B	13
E. Moore, OF	10
C. Barnhart, OF	9
E. Smith, C	8
J. Gooch, C	7
B. Adams, RP	5
C. Bigbee, OF	5
J. Pfeffer, RP	5
A. Stone, RP	5
W. Schmidt, C	4
W. Mueller, OF	1

St. Louis (65-89)	WS
Hitting	**105.5**
Fielding	**32.4**
Pitching	**57.2**
R. Hornsby, 2B	38
J. Bottomley, 1B	16
R. Blades, OF	15
J. Cooney, SS	11
M. Gonzalez, C	11
B. Sherdel, RP	11
L. Dickerman, SP	10
A. Sothoron, SP	9
J. Smith, OF	8
H. Freigau, 3B	7
J. Haines, SP	7
E. Dyer, SP	5
W. Holm, OF	5
S. Toporcer, 3B	5
T. Douthit, OF	4
M. Flack, OF	4
H. Mueller, OF	4
J. Stuart, SP	4
H. Bell, RP	3
A. Delaney, RP	2
B. Doak, RP	2
C. Hafey, OF	2
C. Niebergall, C	2
T. Thevenow, SS	2
L. Bell, SS	1
V. Clemons, C	1
J. Fowler, RP	1
H. Myers, OF	1
J. Pfeffer, SP	1
F. Rhem, SP-RP	1
V. Shields, SP-RP	1
E. Vick, C	1

1925 American League

Boston (47-105)	WS
Hitting	**67.4**
Fielding	**24.9**
Pitching	**48.7**
I. Boone, OF	15
T. Wingfield, SP	15
H. Ehmke, SP	14
I. Flagstead, OF	14
D. Prothro, 3B	11
P. Todt, 1B	11
R. Ruffing, SP	9
R. Carlyle, OF	7
T. Vache, OF	7
J. Quinn, SP	5
P. Zahniser, SP	5
V. Picinich, C	4
B. Wambsganss, 2B	4
H. Ezzell, 3B	3

D. Lee, SS	3
J. Bischoff, C	2
B. Connolly, SS	2
J. Rothrock, SS	2
C. Fullerton, SP-RP	1
M. Herrera, 2B	1
J. Heving, C	1
T. Jenkins, OF	1
B. Rogell, 2B	1
S. Rosenthal, OF	1
H. Welch, SS	1
D. Williams, OF	1

Chicago (79-75)	WS
Hitting	**117.9**
Fielding	**40.1**
Pitching	**79.0**
T. Lyons, SP	23
J. Mostil, OF	23
T. Blankenship, SP	22
E. Collins, 2B	22
E. Sheely, 1B	20
W. Kamm, 3B	19
R. Faber, SP	15
B. Falk, OF	15
I. Davis, SS	13
R. Schalk, C	12
B. Barrett, 2B	11
H. Hooper, OF	10
S. Connally, RP	6
B. Crouse, C	6
M. Cvengros, SP-RP	5
C. Robertson, SP	4
S. Thurston, SP	4
J. Edwards, RP	2
S. Harris, OF	2
J. Grabowski, C	1
J. Kane, SS	1
D. Kerr, RP	1

Cleveland (70-84)	WS
Hitting	**94.8**
Fielding	**36.1**
Pitching	**79.1**
T. Speaker, OF	25
J. Sewell, SS	24
J. Miller, SP	15
G. Uhle, SP	15
G. Burns, 1B	14
G. Buckeye, SP	13
S. Smith, SP	13
C. Jamieson, OF	12
B. Karr, SP	10
P. McNulty, OF	10
G. Myatt, C	9
C. Lee, OF	7
J. Shaute, SP	6
B. Speece, RP	5
H. Summa, OF	5
L. Sewell, C	4
F. Spurgeon, 3B	4
C. Fewster, 2B	3
J. Klugmann, 2B	3
R. Benge, SP	2
R. Lutzke, 3B	2
R. Stephenson, OF	2
C. Yowell, RP	2
B. Cole, RP	1
H. Hendrick, 1B	1
J. Hodapp, 3B	1
R. Knode, 1B	1
D. Levsen, SP	1

Detroit (81-73)	WS
Hitting	**133.2**
Fielding	**37.4**
Pitching	**72.4**
H. Heilmann, OF	30
T. Cobb, OF	25
A. Wingo, OF	22
H. Dauss, SP	18
L. Blue, 1B	17
F. O'Rourke, 2B	14
J. Bassler, C	13
E. Whitehill, SP	13
F. Haney, 3B	12
L. Stoner, SP	11
K. Holloway, RP	10
H. Manush, OF	8
J. Tavener, SS	8
D. Leonard, SP	7
R. Collins, SP	6
B. Fothergill, OF	6
L. Burke, 2B	4
J. Doyle, RP	4
T. Rigney, SS	3
O. Carroll, RP	2
B. Jones, 3B	2
E. Wells, RP	2
L. Woodall, C	2
B. Cole, RP	1
S. Johnson, RP	1
J. Neun, 1B	1
J. Warner, 3B	1

New York (69-85)	WS
Hitting	**85.7**
Fielding	**41.0**
Pitching	**80.3**
H. Pennock, SP	23
E. Combs, OF	20
U. Shocker, SP	19
B. Meusel, OF	18
W. Hoyt, SP	17
L. Gehrig, 1B	15
B. Ruth, OF	13
S. Jones, SP	11
B. Paschal, OF	10
J. Dugan, 3B	9
B. Shawkey, SP	9
A. Ward, 2B	8
B. Bengough, C	7
P. Wanninger, SS	5
W. Schang, C	4
E. Johnson, 2B	3
S. O'Neill, C	3
H. Shanks, 3B	3
B. Veach, OF	3
W. Pipp, 1B	2
B. Shields, SP-RP	2
M. Koenig, SS	1
F. Merkle, 1B	1
E. Scott, SS	1

Philadelphia (88-64)	WS
Hitting	**115.2**
Fielding	**47.6**
Pitching	**101.2**
A. Simmons, OF	34
S. Harriss, SP	21
E. Rommel, SP	21
S. Gray, SP	19
J. Dykes, 3B	18
B. Lamar, OF	17
M. Cochrane, C	16
M. Bishop, 2B	14
S. Hale, 3B	14
B. Miller, OF	13
R. Walberg, RP	13
S. Baumgartner, RP	10
C. Galloway, SS	9
L. Grove, RP	9
J. Poole, 1B	9
C. Perkins, C	6
J. Quinn, SP	6
F. Welch, OF	5
W. French, OF	3
R. Holt, 1B	2
B. Bagwell, OF	1
J. Foxx, C	1
F. Heimach, RP	1
C. Husta, SS	1
A. Stokes, RP	1

St. Louis (82-71)	WS
Hitting	**128.6**
Fielding	**39.9**
Pitching	**77.5**
B. Jacobson, OF	23
M. McManus, 2B	20
K. Williams, OF	20
H. Rice, OF	19
G. Sisler, 1B	19
G. Robertson, 3B	17
M. Gaston, SP	16
J. Bush, SP	14
E. Vangilder, RP	12
D. Danforth, RP	10
D. Davis, SP	10
J. Giard, SP	9
P. Hargrave, C	8
B. LaMotte, SS	8
W. Gerber, SS	6
H. Severeid, C	6
E. Wingard, SP	6
L. Dixon, C	5
J. Evans, OF	5
H. Bennett, OF	4
J. Tobin, OF	4
T. Rego, C	2
C. Falk, RP	1
G. Mogridge, SP	1
E. Stauffer, RP	1

Washington (96-55)	WS
Hitting	**137.4**
Fielding	**49.2**
Pitching	**101.4**
G. Goslin, OF	31
W. Johnson, SP	26
S. Rice, OF	24
S. Coveleski, SP	23
D. Ruether, SP	20
M. Ruel, C	18
J. Harris, 1B	17
O. Bluege, 3B	16
B. Harris, 2B	16
J. Judge, 1B	15
R. Peckinpaugh, SS	15
T. Zachary, SP	13
F. Marberry, RP	11
E. McNeely, OF	11
H. Severeid, C	6
A. Ferguson, SP	5
V. Gregg, RP	4
G. Mogridge, SP	3
N. Leibold, OF	2
C. Ogden, RP	2
E. Scott, SS	2
B. Tate, C	2
S. Adams, 2B	1
W. Ballou, RP	1
P. Hargrave, C	1
T. Jeanes, OF	1
S. Stewart, 3B	1
L. Thomas, SP	1

1925 National League

Boston (70-83)	WS
Hitting	**105.6**
Fielding	**36.1**
Pitching	**68.4**
D. Bancroft, SS	22
D. Burrus, 1B	21
J. Cooney, SP	19
L. Benton, SP	17
J. Welsh, OF	15
G. Felix, OF	13
J. Genewich, SP	11
B. Neis, OF	10
J. Barnes, SP	9
B. Smith, SS	8
F. Gibson, C	7
S. Graham, SP	7
D. Harris, OF	7
L. Mann, OF	7
A. High, 3B	6
E. Padgett, 2B	6
D. Gautreau, 2B	5
W. Marriott, 3B	5
M. O'Neil, C	5
B. Vargus, RP	2
F. Wilson, OF	2
S. Hogan, OF	1
A. Hood, 2B	1
I. Kamp, RP	1
H. Kibbie, 2B	1
R. Ryan, RP	1
O. Siemer, C	1

Brooklyn (68-85)	WS
Hitting	**122.4**
Fielding	**26.2**
Pitching	**55.4**
J. Fournier, 1B	29
Z. Wheat, OF	27
D. Vance, SP	20
M. Stock, 2B	19
E. Brown, OF	15
D. Cox, OF	15
Z. Taylor, C	12
B. Grimes, SP	9
J. Johnston, 3B	9
R. Ehrhardt, SP	8
T. Osborne, SP	7
H. DeBerry, C	6
H. Ford, SS	5
J. Mitchell, SS	5
J. Petty, SP	5
C. Tierney, 3B	3
L. Brown, RP	2
G. Cantrell, RP	2
C. Hargreaves, C	2
B. Hubbell, RP	2
R. Hutson, OF	1
B. McGraw, SP	1

Chicago (68-86)	WS
Hitting	**89.0**
Fielding	**39.7**
Pitching	**75.3**
P. Alexander, SP	20
G. Hartnett, C	19
S. Adams, 2B	17
H. Freigau, 3B	14
C. Grimm, 1B	14
W. Cooper, SP	13
M. Brooks, OF	12
T. Kaufmann, SP	12
G. Bush, RP	10
S. Blake, SP	9
C. Heathcote, OF	8
T. Griffith, OF	6
P. Jones, RP	6
M. Gonzalez, C	5
A. Jahn, OF	5
P. Pittenger, 3B-SS	5
R. Maranville, SS	4
B. Friberg, 3B	3
I. McAuley, SS	3
J. Statz, OF	3
B. Weis, OF	3
D. Grigsby, OF	2
E. Jacobs, RP	2
J. Munson, OF	2
H. Brett, RP	1
V. Keen, RP	1
R. Michaels, 3B	1
H. Miller, OF	1
G. Milstead, SP	1
G. Staley, 2B	1
G. Stueland, RP	1

Cincinnati (80-73)	WS
Hitting	**90.7**
Fielding	**46.5**
Pitching	**102.8**
P. Donohue, SP	28
D. Luque, SP	27
E. Rixey, SP	26
E. Roush, OF	23

C. Walker, OF	21
R. Bressler, 1B	14
H. Critz, 2B	13
B. Pinelli, 3B	12
I. Caveney, SS	8
B. Hargrave, C	8
J. May, RP	8
E. Smith, OF	8
R. Benton, RP	7
C. Dressen, 3B	6
C. Mays, RP	5
B. Zitzmann, OF	5
S. Bohne, SS	4
W. Holke, 1B	4
A. Niehaus, 1B	3
H. Biemiller, RP	2
N. Brady, RP	2
E. Krueger, C	2
J. Schultz, OF	2
J. Hudgens, 1B	1
I. Wingo, C	1

New York (86-66)	WS
Hitting	**114.5**
Fielding	**43.8**
Pitching	**99.6**
J. Scott, SP	25
G. Kelly, 2B	22
F. Frisch, 3B	20
I. Meusel, OF	20
B. Terry, 1B	18
V. Barnes, SP	17
J. Bentley, SP	12
K. Greenfield, SP	12
T. Jackson, SS	12
A. Nehf, SP	12
B. Southworth, OF	12
F. Snyder, C	11
R. Youngs, OF	11
F. Lindstrom, 3B	10
F. Fitzsimmons, SP	9
W. Dean, RP	8
H. Gowdy, C	7
W. Huntzinger, RP	6
G. Hartley, C	4
H. Wilson, OF	4
J. Wisner, RP	3
M. Devine, C	1
H. Groh, 3B	1
H. McQuillan, SP	1

Philadelphia (68-85)	WS
Hitting	**94.1**
Fielding	**36.7**
Pitching	**73.2**
G. Harper, OF	18
H. Carlson, SP	17
J. Ring, SP	17
H. Sand, SS	13
C. Williams, OF	12
L. Fonseca, 2B	11
C. Mitchell, SP	10
J. Wilson, C	10
R. Wrightstone, OF	10
B. Henline, C	9
C. Huber, 3B	9
C. Hawks, 1B	8
B. Friberg, 2B	7
J. Mokan, OF	7
G. Burns, OF	6
A. Decatur, SP	6
D. Ulrich, RP	6
F. Leach, OF	5
J. Couch, RP	4
W. Kimmick, SS	4
R. Pierce, RP	4
H. Betts, RP	3
C. Willoughby, SP	3
J. Knight, RP	2
J. Schultz, OF	2
G. Durning, OF	1

Pittsburgh (95-58)	WS
Hitting	**146.1**
Fielding	**48.1**
Pitching	**90.8**
K. Cuyler, OF	34
M. Carey, OF	26
P. Traynor, 3B	26
G. Wright, SS	24
C. Barnhart, OF	19
L. Meadows, SP	18
E. Moore, 2B	18
V. Aldridge, SP	16
R. Kremer, SP	16
G. Grantham, 1B	15
E. Smith, C	15
J. Morrison, SP	13
E. Yde, SP	12
J. Gooch, C	7
S. McInnis, 1B	6
T. Sheehan, RP	5
B. Adams, RP	4
R. Oldham, RP	4
J. Rawlings, 2B	3
B. Culloton, RP	2
C. Bigbee, OF	1
D. Songer, RP	1

St. Louis (77-76)	WS
Hitting	**118.8**
Fielding	**39.4**
Pitching	**72.8**
R. Hornsby, 2B	36
J. Bottomley, 1B	27
R. Blades, OF	20
B. Sherdel, SP	19
L. Bell, 3B	15
A. Reinhart, SP	14
J. Haines, SP	11
B. O'Farrell, C	10
A. Sothoron, SP	9
S. Toporcer, SS	9
C. Hafey, OF	7
D. Mails, SP	6
H. Mueller, OF	6
F. Rhem, SP	6
R. Shinners, OF	6
J. Smith, OF	5
E. Dyer, RP	4
T. Thevenow, SS	4
J. Cooney, SS	3
M. Flack, OF	3
L. Dickerman, SP	2
M. Gonzalez, C	2
W. Schmidt, C	2
T. Douthit, OF	1
H. Freigau, SS	1
W. Hallahan, RP	1
W. Holm, OF	1
B. Warwick, C	1

1926
American League

Boston (46-107)	WS
Hitting	**51.9**
Fielding	**29.8**
Pitching	**56.2**
T. Rigney, SS	17
I. Flagstead, OF	12
H. Wiltse, SP	10
T. Wingfield, RP	10
B. Jacobson, OF	9
R. Ruffing, SP	8
P. Todt, 1B	8
F. Haney, 3B	7
J. Russell, RP	7
S. Harriss, SP	6
B. Regan, 2B	6
T. Welzer, RP	6
P. Zahniser, SP	6
S. Rosenthal, OF	4
W. Shaner, OF	4
J. Bischoff, C	2
F. Bratschi, OF	2
R. Carlyle, OF	2
A. Gaston, C	2
F. Heimach, SP	2
M. Herrera, 2B	2
J. Tobin, OF	2
H. Ehmke, SP	1
H. Foreman, RP	1
J. Kiefer, RP	1
A. Stokes, C	1

Chicago (81-72)	WS
Hitting	**118.2**
Fielding	**41.3**
Pitching	**83.5**
J. Mostil, OF	28
B. Falk, OF	24
T. Lyons, SP	24
W. Kamm, 3B	22
E. Sheely, 1B	18
E. Collins, 2B	17
T. Thomas, SP	16
T. Blankenship, SP	13
R. Faber, SP	13
B. Hunnefield, SS	12
B. Barrett, OF	11
S. Connally, RP	8
J. Edwards, SP-RP	6
R. Schalk, C	5
S. Thurston, RP	5
S. Harris, OF	4
R. Morehart, 2B	4
H. McCurdy, C	3
E. Scott, SS	3
B. Crouse, C	2
M. Berg, SS	1
B. Clancy, 1B	1
J. Grabowski, C	1
T. Gulley, OF	1
M. Steengrafe, RP	1

Cleveland (88-66)	WS
Hitting	**111.6**
Fielding	**49.9**
Pitching	**102.6**
G. Uhle, SP	32
J. Sewell, SS	29
T. Speaker, OF	29
G. Burns, 1B	24
H. Summa, OF	20
C. Jamieson, OF	17
D. Levsen, SP	17
J. Shaute, SP	16
F. Spurgeon, 2B	15
S. Smith, SP	14
G. Buckeye, SP	11
R. Lutzke, 3B	11
L. Sewell, C	8
J. Miller, SP	7
B. Karr, RP	3
G. Myatt, C	3
I. Eichrodt, OF	2
W. Hudlin, RP	2
R. Benge, RP	1
R. Knode, 1B	1
N. Lehr, RP	1
E. Padgett, 3B	1

Detroit (79-75)	WS
Hitting	**135.8**
Fielding	**33.8**
Pitching	**67.4**
H. Heilmann, OF	27
H. Manush, OF	26
L. Blue, 1B	17
B. Fothergill, OF	17
J. Tavener, SS	16
E. Whitehill, SP	15
S. Gibson, SP	14
H. Dauss, RP	11
C. Gehringer, 2B	11
J. Bassler, C	10
T. Cobb, OF	10
R. Collins, RP	9
E. Wells, SP	9
A. Wingo, OF	8
J. Warner, 3B	7
J. Neun, 1B	6
F. O'Rourke, 3B	6
K. Holloway, RP	4
A. Johns, RP	3
C. Manion, C	3
L. Woodall, C	3
L. Stoner, SP	2
L. Burke, 2B	1
J. Doyle, RP	1
R. Kneisch, SP	1

New York (91-63)	WS
Hitting	**155.8**
Fielding	**35.8**
Pitching	**81.3**
B. Ruth, OF	45
L. Gehrig, 1B	30
E. Combs, OF	19
T. Lazzeri, 2B	19
U. Shocker, SP	19
H. Pennock, SP	18
P. Collins, C	17
M. Koenig, SS	16
W. Hoyt, SP	13
B. Meusel, OF	13
J. Dugan, 3B	10
B. Shawkey, RP	8
G. Braxton, RP	7
B. Paschal, OF	7
M. Thomas, RP	6
B. Bengough, C	5
S. Jones, SP	5
W. Beall, RP	4
H. Severeid, C	4
R. Carlyle, OF	3
M. Gazella, 3B	2
D. Ruether, SP	2
A. Ward, 2B	1

Philadelphia (83-67)	WS
Hitting	**82.0**
Fielding	**48.6**
Pitching	**118.4**
A. Simmons, OF	27
L. Grove, SP	25
E. Rommel, SP	18
M. Bishop, 2B	16
J. Dykes, 3B	15
H. Ehmke, SP	15
M. Cochrane, C	14
J. Pate, RP	14
J. Quinn, SP	13
R. Walberg, RP	13
S. Gray, RP	10
W. French, OF	9
J. Poole, 1B	9
S. Hale, 3B	8
B. Lamar, OF	7
C. Galloway, SS	5
F. Welch, OF	5
C. Perkins, C	4
L. Willis, RP	4
J. Hauser, 1B	3
F. Heimach, RP	3
B. Miller, OF	3
S. Baumgartner, RP	2
S. Harriss, SP	2
B. Wambsganss, SS	2
C. Engle, SS	1
J. Foxx, C	1
A. Metzler, OF	1

St. Louis (62-92)	WS
Hitting	**86.5**
Fielding	**34.4**
Pitching	**65.1**
H. Rice, OF	19

Player	WS
T. Zachary, SP	19
M. McManus, 3B	16
W. Schang, C	14
K. Williams, OF	12
E. Wingard, RP	12
M. Gaston, SP	11
B. Miller, OF	11
G. Sisler, 1B	11
W. Ballou, RP	7
W. Gerber, SS	7
P. Hargrave, C	7
E. Vangilder, RP	7
S. Melillo, 2B	6
H. Bennett, OF	4
B. Jacobson, OF	4
E. Nevers, SP	4
G. Robertson, 3B	4
D. Davis, RP	3
C. Durst, OF	3
L. Dixon, C	2
C. Falk, RP	2
B. LaMotte, SS	1

Washington (81-69)	WS
Hitting	**142.9**
Fielding	**34.3**
Pitching	**65.8**
G. Goslin, OF	33
S. Rice, OF	23
M. Ruel, C	18
B. Harris, 2B	17
S. Coveleski, SP	16
J. Judge, 1B	16
F. Marberry, RP	16
O. Bluege, 3B	15
W. Johnson, SP	15
E. McNeely, OF	15
B. Myer, SS	14
J. Harris, 1B	12
D. Ruether, SP	7
G. Crowder, SP	5
B. Tate, C	5
C. Ogden, RP	4
R. Peckinpaugh, SS	4
B. Morrell, RP	2
D. Jones, SP	1
G. Murray, SP	1
B. Reeves, 3B	1
H. Severeid, C	1
S. Stewart, 2B	1
D. Taylor, OF	1

1926 National League

Boston (66-86)	WS
Hitting	**104.5**
Fielding	**31.2**
Pitching	**62.2**
D. Bancroft, SS	20
E. Brown, OF	19
A. High, 3B	15
B. Smith, SP	14
J. Werts, SP	14
Z. Taylor, C	12
J. Welsh, OF	12
L. Benton, SP	11
J. Smith, OF	11
D. Burrus, 1B	10
J. Genewich, SP	9
E. Taylor, 3B	8
J. Cooney, 1B	6
D. Gautreau, 2B	6
B. Hearn, RP	4
L. Mann, OF	4
G. Mogridge, RP	4
F. Edwards, SP	3
F. Gibson, C	3
H. Goldsmith, SP	3
E. Moore, 2B	3
F. Wilson, OF	3
S. Hogan, C	1
J. Johnston, 3B	1
B. Neis, OF	1
O. Siemer, C	1

Brooklyn (71-82)	WS
Hitting	**92.1**
Fielding	**36.0**
Pitching	**85.0**
J. Petty, SP	24
B. Herman, 1B	20
D. McWeeny, SP	17
J. Butler, SS	15
B. Grimes, SP	15
G. Felix, OF	13
D. Cox, OF	12
D. Vance, SP	11
Z. Wheat, OF	10
J. Fournier, 1B	9
C. Hargreaves, C	7
W. Marriott, 3B	7
B. McGraw, SP	7
R. Ehrhardt, RP	6
C. Fewster, 2B	6
H. DeBerry, C	5
M. Jacobson, OF	5
R. Maranville, SS	5
J. Barnes, SP	4
M. O'Neil, C	4
J. Standaert, 2B	4
S. Bohne, 2B	2
M. Carey, OF	2
W. Witt, OF	2
G. Boehler, RP	1

Chicago (82-72)	WS
Hitting	**98.5**
Fielding	**50.2**
Pitching	**97.3**
H. Wilson, OF	26
C. Root, SP	22
S. Adams, 2B	21
C. Heathcote, OF	16
G. Bush, RP	14
P. Jones, SP	14
T. Kaufmann, SP	14
S. Blake, SP	12
J. Cooney, SS	12
H. Freigau, 3B	12
G. Hartnett, C	12
C. Grimm, 1B	11
R. Stephenson, OF	11
B. Osborn, RP	7
M. Gonzalez, C	6
P. Scott, OF	6
J. Kelly, OF	5
P. Alexander, SP	4
W. Huntzinger, RP	4
B. Piercy, RP	4
W. Cooper, SP	3
G. Milstead, RP	2
J. Munson, OF	2
R. Shannon, SS	2
C. Tolson, 1B	2
C. Beck, 2B	1
J. Welch, RP	1

Cincinnati (87-67)	WS
Hitting	**130.8**
Fielding	**42.8**
Pitching	**87.4**
C. Walker, OF	22
P. Donohue, SP	21
E. Roush, OF	21
C. Mays, SP	20
H. Critz, 2B	19
W. Pipp, 1B	19
C. Dressen, 3B	18
B. Hargrave, C	18
C. Christensen, OF	16
R. Bressler, OF	15
D. Luque, SP	14
E. Rixey, SP	14
R. Lucas, RP	12
J. May, RP	12
V. Picinich, C	8
H. Ford, SS	4
B. Pinelli, 3B	4
F. Emmer, SS	1
M. Holland, RP	1
E. Scott, SS	1
B. Zitzmann, OF	1

New York (74-77)	WS
Hitting	**106.2**
Fielding	**39.8**
Pitching	**76.0**
F. Frisch, 2B	20
F. Lindstrom, 3B	20
T. Jackson, SS	18
F. Fitzsimmons, SP	17
G. Kelly, 1B	17
J. Scott, RP	15
V. Barnes, SP	14
K. Greenfield, SP	12
I. Meusel, OF	12
R. Youngs, OF	12
H. McQuillan, SP	11
T. Tyson, OF	9
B. Terry, 1B	8
D. Farrell, SS	5
H. Mueller, OF	5
J. Ring, SP	5
B. Southworth, OF	5
C. Davies, RP	4
P. Florence, C	3
M. Ott, OF	2
F. Snyder, C	2
J. Wisner, SP	2
J. Cummings, C	1
H. McMullen, C	1
A. Moore, OF	1
F. Thompson, 2B	1

Philadelphia (58-93)	WS
Hitting	**97.3**
Fielding	**24.9**
Pitching	**51.8**
H. Carlson, SP	23
C. Williams, OF	17
F. Leach, OF	16
H. Sand, SS	13
J. Mokan, OF	12
B. Friberg, 2B	11
R. Wrightstone, 1B	11
W. Dean, SP	9
C. Mitchell, SP	9
D. Ulrich, RP	9
J. Wilson, C	9
C. Huber, 3B	8
G. Harper, OF	7
B. Henline, C	6
A. Nixon, OF	6
C. Willoughby, RP	3
R. Grimes, 1B	2
E. Baecht, RP	1
J. Bentley, 1B	1
D. Sothern, OF	1

Pittsburgh (84-69)	WS
Hitting	**113.4**
Fielding	**48.3**
Pitching	**90.3**
P. Waner, OF	28
K. Cuyler, OF	26
R. Kremer, SP	25
P. Traynor, 3B	22
G. Grantham, 1B	19
G. Wright, SS	17
E. Smith, C	14
L. Meadows, SP	13
E. Yde, SP	11
V. Aldridge, SP	10
J. Bush, SP	10
H. Rhyne, 2B	9
D. Songer, RP	9
J. Morrison, SP-RP	8
J. Gooch, C	7
M. Carey, OF	5
C. Hill, SP	3
C. Barnhart, OF	2
G. Brickell, OF	2
J. Cronin, 2B	2
S. McInnis, 1B	2
J. Rawlings, 2B	2
R. Spencer, C	2
C. Bigbee, OF	1
L. Koupal, RP	1
E. Moore, 2B	1
R. Oldham, RP	1

St. Louis (89-65)	WS
Hitting	**135.2**
Fielding	**45.1**
Pitching	**86.7**
L. Bell, 3B	25
J. Bottomley, 1B	23
B. O'Farrell, C	23
R. Hornsby, 2B	21
R. Blades, OF	19
T. Douthit, OF	19
F. Rhem, SP	18
B. Sherdel, SP	17
B. Southworth, OF	15
T. Thevenow, SS	15
J. Haines, SP	14
P. Alexander, SP	12
A. Reinhart, RP	9
H. Bell, RP	6
C. Hafey, OF	5
V. Keen, SP	5
H. Mueller, OF	5
W. Hallahan, RP	3
W. Holm, OF	3
J. Flowers, 2B	2
S. Johnson, RP	2
A. Sothoron, RP	2
W. Huntzinger, RP	1
S. Toporcer, 2B	1
E. Vick, C	1
B. Warwick, C	1

1927 American League

Boston (51-103)	WS
Hitting	**64.2**
Fielding	**31.5**
Pitching	**57.3**
I. Flagstead, OF	14
B. Myer, SS	14
S. Harriss, SP	12
D. MacFayden, RP	11
B. Regan, 2B	10
J. Tobin, OF	9
J. Rothrock, SS	8
R. Ruffing, SP	8
J. Russell, RP	8
W. Shaner, OF	7
T. Welzer, SP	7
H. Wiltse, SP	7
B. Rogell, 3B	6
P. Todt, 1B	5
C. Carlyle, OF	4
F. Haney, 3B	4
F. Hofmann, C	4
G. Hartley, C	3
R. Rollings, 3B	3
H. Bradley, RP	2
F. Bennett, RP	1
B. Jacobson, OF	1
D. Lundgren, SP	1
B. Moore, C	1
P. Wanninger, SS	1
J. Wilson, RP	1
T. Wingfield, RP	1

Chicago (70-83)	WS
Hitting	**83.2**
Fielding	**43.7**
Pitching	**83.1**

T. Lyons, SP	30
T. Thomas, SP	27
B. Falk, OF	21
A. Metzler, OF	21
W. Kamm, 3B	15
B. Barrett, OF	13
S. Connally, RP	13
A. Ward, 2B	12
H. McCurdy, C	9
B. Clancy, 1B	8
T. Blankenship, SP	7
B. Hunnefield, SS	7
R. Peckinpaugh, SS	6
R. Faber, SP	5
B. Crouse, C	4
B. Cole, RP	2
E. Jacobs, RP	2
B. Neis, OF	2
J. Battle, 3B	1
M. Berg, C-2B	1
I. Boone, OF	1
R. Flaskamper, SS	1
C. Reynolds, OF	1
E. Sheely, 1B	1

Cleveland (66-87)	WS
Hitting	**84.1**
Fielding	**37.6**
Pitching	**76.4**
J. Sewell, SS	21
W. Hudlin, SP	19
G. Burns, 1B	17
C. Jamieson, OF	15
J. Miller, SP	15
G. Buckeye, SP	13
J. Shaute, SP	13
H. Summa, OF	12
L. Fonseca, 2B	11
L. Sewell, C	11
G. Uhle, SP	9
J. Hodapp, 3B	8
R. Lutzke, 3B	5
B. Neis, OF	5
G. Grant, RP	3
B. Karr, RP	3
F. Spurgeon, 2B	3
I. Eichrodt, OF	2
S. Langford, OF	2
D. Levsen, SP	2
G. Myatt, C	2
C. Autry, C	1
J. Brown, RP	1
N. Cullop, OF	1
J. Gill, OF	1
B. Jacobson, OF	1
P. McNulty, OF	1
S. Smith, RP	1

Detroit (82-71)	WS
Hitting	**126.1**
Fielding	**41.8**
Pitching	**78.1**
H. Heilmann, OF	32
B. Fothergill, OF	22
C. Gehringer, 2B	20
E. Whitehill, SP	19
H. Manush, OF	18
J. Tavener, SS	13
L. Stoner, SP	12
J. Warner, 3B	12
K. Holloway, SP	11
M. McManus, SS	11
O. Carroll, RP	10
S. Gibson, SP	10
L. Woodall, C	10
L. Blue, 1B	9
J. Bassler, C	8
R. Collins, SP	8
J. Neun, 1B	7
G. Smith, RP	5
J. Billings, SP	4
A. Wingo, OF	2
A. Ruble, OF	1
M. Shea, C	1
R. Smith, SP	1

New York (110-44)	WS
Hitting	**175.7**
Fielding	**45.9**
Pitching	**108.3**
B. Ruth, OF	45
L. Gehrig, 1B	44
E. Combs, OF	31
T. Lazzeri, 2B	24
W. Moore, RP	24
W. Hoyt, SP	23
B. Meusel, OF	21
H. Pennock, SP	17
U. Shocker, SP	16
M. Koenig, SS	15
D. Ruether, SP	13
P. Collins, C	12
G. Pipgras, SP	9
J. Grabowski, C	7
J. Dugan, 3B	6
R. Morehart, 2B	5
M. Gazella, 3B	4
B. Shawkey, RP	4
B. Paschal, OF	3
M. Thomas, RP	3
B. Bengough, C	2
C. Durst, OF	1
J. Wera, 3B	1

Philadelphia (91-63)	WS
Hitting	**138.1**
Fielding	**43.0**
Pitching	**91.9**
A. Simmons, OF	26
L. Grove, SP	24
M. Cochrane, C	23
T. Cobb, OF	22
S. Hale, 3B	18
J. Quinn, SP	17
R. Walberg, SP	17
J. Dykes, 1B	16
M. Bishop, 2B	15
J. Boley, SS	12
E. Collins, 2B	11
H. Ehmke, SP	11
E. Rommel, SP	8
W. French, OF	7
S. Gray, RP	7
B. Lamar, OF	7
Z. Wheat, OF	7
J. Foxx, 1B	6
C. Galloway, SS	5
J. Johnson, RP	4
C. Perkins, C	3
J. Pate, RP	2
C. Bates, OF	1
G. Cantrell, SP	1
J. Poole, 1B	1
I. Powers, RP	1
L. Willis, RP	1

St. Louis (59-94)	WS
Hitting	**87.9**
Fielding	**29.8**
Pitching	**59.4**
K. Williams, OF	18
G. Sisler, 1B	16
B. Miller, OF	15
H. Rice, OF	13
M. Gaston, SP	12
F. O'Rourke, 3B	12
W. Schang, C	12
L. Stewart, SP	11
E. Vangilder, SP	10
S. Jones, SP	9
F. Schulte, OF	7
W. Gerber, SS	6
S. Adams, 2B	4
W. Ballou, SP	4
H. Bennett, OF	4
G. Crowder, RP	4
E. Nevers, RP	4
T. Zachary, SP	4
S. Melillo, 2B	2
S. O'Neill, C	2
B. Beck, RP	1
G. Blaeholder, SP	1
L. Dixon, C	1
R. Kress, SS	1
O. Miller, SS	1
G. Sturdy, 1B	1
E. Wingard, RP	1
J. Wright, SP-RP	1

Washington (85-69)	WS
Hitting	**123.4**
Fielding	**45.0**
Pitching	**86.6**
G. Goslin, OF	28
T. Speaker, OF	21
M. Ruel, C	20
B. Hadley, SP	19
O. Bluege, 3B	18
G. Braxton, RP	17
S. Rice, OF	17
J. Judge, 1B	16
H. Lisenbee, SP	16
B. Harris, 2B	13
S. Thurston, SP	12
F. Marberry, RP	8
B. Reeves, SS	6
B. Burke, RP	5
W. Johnson, SP	5
T. Rigney, SS	5
B. Tate, C	5
T. Zachary, SP	5
B. Ganzel, OF	4
E. McNeely, OF	4
G. Crowder, SP	2
S. Stewart, 2B	2
J. Berger, C	1
D. Coffman, RP	1
S. Coveleski, SP	1
G. Gillis, SS	1
P. Hopkins, SP-RP	1
B. Myer, SS	1
S. West, OF	1

1927
National League

Boston (60-94)	WS
Hitting	**96.1**
Fielding	**26.3**
Pitching	**57.6**
E. Brown, OF	14
B. Smith, SP	14
J. Welsh, OF	13
J. Fournier, 1B	11
A. High, 3B	11
E. Moore, 3B	11
L. Richbourg, OF	11
J. Genewich, RP	10
K. Greenfield, SP	10
D. Bancroft, SS	9
D. Farrell, SS	8
S. Hogan, C	8
D. Burrus, 1B	6
J. Smith, OF	6
G. Mogridge, RP	5
J. Werts, RP	5
D. Gautreau, 2B	4
H. Goldsmith, RP	4
C. Robertson, SP	4
L. Benton, SP	3
Z. Taylor, C	3
F. Gibson, C	2
A. Mills, RP	2
L. Urban, C	2
F. Edwards, RP	1
L. Mann, OF	1
G. Morrison, RP	1
H. Thomas, 2B	1

Brooklyn (65-88)	WS
Hitting	**54.5**
Fielding	**44.7**
Pitching	**95.8**
D. Vance, SP	25
J. Petty, SP	21
M. Carey, OF	13
J. Elliott, SP	13
H. Hendrick, OF	12
B. Herman, 1B	12
J. Statz, OF	12
W. Clark, RP	9
B. Doak, SP	9
D. McWeeny, SP	9
J. Butler, SS	8
G. Felix, OF	8
J. Partridge, 2B	7
H. DeBerry, C	6
R. Ehrhardt, RP	6
B. Henline, C	6
B. Barrett, 3B	5
J. Flowers, SS	4
C. Hargreaves, C	4
I. Meusel, OF	2
G. Cantrell, RP	1
C. Corgan, 2B	1
R. Moss, SP	1
N. Plitt, RP	1

Chicago (85-68)	WS
Hitting	**124.8**
Fielding	**44.0**
Pitching	**86.2**
H. Wilson, OF	31
R. Stephenson, OF	27
G. Hartnett, C	21
C. Root, SP	21
S. Adams, 2B	16
S. Blake, SP	15
G. Bush, SP	15
C. Grimm, 1B	15
E. Webb, OF	15
H. Carlson, SP	14
C. Beck, 2B	10
W. English, SS	8
C. Heathcote, OF	8
P. Jones, RP	6
P. Scott, OF	6
J. Brillheart, RP	5
B. Osborn, SP-RP	5
A. Nehf, RP	4
M. Gonzalez, C	3
J. Cooney, SS	2
L. Roy, RP	2
C. Tolson, 1B	2
H. Freigau, 3B	1
T. Kaufmann, SP	1
E. Pick, 3B	1
E. Yoter, 3B	1

Cincinnati (75-78)	WS
Hitting	**96.9**
Fielding	**42.1**
Pitching	**86.0**
C. Dressen, 3B	23
R. Lucas, SP	23
D. Luque, SP	16
C. Walker, OF	16
J. May, SP	15
E. Rixey, SP	15
B. Hargrave, C	13
R. Bressler, OF	12
H. Ford, SS	11
E. Allen, OF	10
H. Critz, 2B	10
W. Pipp, 1B	8
P. Donohue, SP	7
G. Kelly, 1B	6
R. Kolp, RP	6
C. Mays, SP	6
V. Picinich, C	6
B. Zitzmann, OF	6
P. Appleton, RP	4
C. Christensen, OF	3
P. Purdy, OF	3

	WS
P. Pittenger, 2B	2
P. Wanninger, SS	2
B. Pinelli, 3B	1
C. Sukeforth, C	1

New York (92-62)	WS
Hitting	**156.7**
Fielding	**39.2**
Pitching	**80.0**
R. Hornsby, 2B	40
B. Terry, 1B	27
G. Harper, OF	26
T. Jackson, SS	24
F. Lindstrom, 3B	20
B. Grimes, SP	19
E. Roush, OF	16
F. Fitzsimmons, SP	15
V. Barnes, SP	12
L. Benton, SP	11
D. Farrell, SS	9
D. Henry, RP	9
H. Mueller, OF	6
R. Reese, 3B	6
J. Cummings, C	4
M. Ott, OF	4
D. Songer, RP	4
B. Clarkson, RP	3
A. DeVormer, C	3
L. Mann, OF	3
H. McQuillan, SP	3
Z. Taylor, C	3
T. Tyson, OF	2
J. Bentley, RP	1
B. Cantwell, RP	1
J. Faulkner, RP	1
M. Holland, RP	1
M. O'Neil, C	1
N. Plitt, RP	1
F. Thomas, RP	1

Philadelphia (51-103)	WS
Hitting	**85.6**
Fielding	**25.4**
Pitching	**42.0**
C. Williams, OF	16
H. Sand, SS	15
F. Leach, OF	14
F. Thompson, 2B	14
D. Ulrich, SP	14
R. Wrightstone, 1B	13
J. Scott, SP	9
A. Ferguson, SP	8
J. Wilson, C	8
C. Mitchell, SP	7
D. Spalding, OF	7
B. Friberg, 3B	6
J. Cooney, SS	4
J. Mokan, OF	4
A. Nixon, OF	3
H. Carlson, SP	2
B. Jonnard, C	2
H. Pruett, SP	2
L. Sweetland, SP	2
D. Attreau, 1B	1
W. Dean, RP	1
R. Miller, SP	1

Pittsburgh (94-60)	WS
Hitting	**139.9**
Fielding	**48.4**
Pitching	**93.6**
P. Waner, OF	36
P. Traynor, 3B	26
L. Waner, OF	25
C. Hill, SP	22
R. Kremer, SP	22
G. Grantham, 2B	21
L. Meadows, SP	20
G. Wright, SS	17
J. Harris, 1B	16
C. Barnhart, OF	14
V. Aldridge, SP	12
K. Cuyler, OF	12
J. Miljus, RP	8
J. Gooch, C	7
E. Smith, C	6
M. Cvengros, RP	4
J. Dawson, RP	3
J. Morrison, RP	3
H. Rhyne, 2B	3
R. Spencer, C	2
J. Bush, SP	1
A. Comorosky, OF	1
H. Groh, 3B	1

St. Louis (92-61)	WS
Hitting	**130.6**
Fielding	**48.0**
Pitching	**97.4**
F. Frisch, 2B	34
P. Alexander, SP	28
J. Haines, SP	28
J. Bottomley, 1B	26
C. Hafey, OF	21
B. Sherdel, SP	18
T. Douthit, OF	16
J. Schulte, C	12
L. Bell, 3B	11
W. Holm, OF	11
B. Southworth, OF	9
R. Blades, OF	8
B. O'Farrell, C	6
F. Rhem, SP	6
S. Toporcer, 3B	6
F. Frankhouse, SP	5
A. Reinhart, RP	5
H. Schuble, SS	5
E. Orsatti, OF	4
F. Snyder, C	4
C. Littlejohn, RP	3
T. Thevenow, SS	3
H. Bell, RP	2
B. McGraw, SP	2
D. Clark, OF	1
V. Keen, RP	1
R. Maranville, SS	1

1928 American League

Boston (57-96)	WS
Hitting	**68.1**
Fielding	**34.6**
Pitching	**68.3**
E. Morris, SP	21
R. Ruffing, SP	21
B. Myer, 3B	18
I. Flagstead, OF	15
J. Russell, SP	13
D. Taitt, OF	13
K. Williams, OF	12
B. Regan, 2B	9
P. Todt, 1B	9
D. MacFayden, SP	7
S. Harriss, SP	6
J. Rothrock, OF	6
W. Gerber, SS	5
C. Berry, C	4
B. Rogell, SS	3
P. Simmons, RP	3
J. Heving, C	2
F. Hofmann, C	2
M. Griffin, RP	1
C. Sumner, OF	1

Chicago (72-82)	WS
Hitting	**91.8**
Fielding	**43.5**
Pitching	**80.6**
T. Thomas, SP	26
W. Kamm, 3B	24
A. Metzler, OF	19
T. Lyons, SP	15
J. Mostil, OF	14
G. Adkins, SP	13
R. Faber, SP	13
C. Reynolds, OF	12
B. Cissell, SS	11
B. Clancy, 1B	9
B. Hunnefield, 2B	9
B. Falk, OF	8
B. Barrett, OF	6
T. Blankenship, SP	6
M. Berg, C	5
B. Crouse, C	5
A. Shires, 1B	5
H. McCurdy, C	3
B. Redfern, 2B	3
S. Connally, RP	2
E. Walsh, SP	2
B. Weiland, SP	2
C. Barnabe, RP	1
G. Cox, RP	1
K. Swanson, 2B	1
R. Wilson, RP	1

Cleveland (62-92)	WS
Hitting	**83.6**
Fielding	**34.8**
Pitching	**67.7**
J. Sewell, SS	23
W. Hudlin, SP	16
J. Shaute, SP	15
G. Uhle, SP	14
C. Lind, 2B	13
J. Hodapp, 3B	12
C. Jamieson, OF	12
L. Sewell, C	10
E. Morgan, 1B	8
L. Fonseca, 1B	7
J. Miller, SP	7
H. Summa, OF	7
G. Grant, SP	6
S. Langford, OF	6
B. Bayne, RP	5
J. Miljus, RP	4
G. Burns, 1B	3
R. Dorman, OF	3
G. Myatt, C	3
C. Autry, C	2
W. Ferrell, SP	2
J. Brown, RP	1
J. Burnett, SS	1
H. Collard, RP	1
G. Gerken, OF	1
L. Harvel, OF	1
E. Montague, SS	1
J. Moore, SP	1
W. Underhill, RP	1

Detroit (68-86)	WS
Hitting	**104.8**
Fielding	**33.2**
Pitching	**66.1**
C. Gehringer, 2B	23
H. Heilmann, OF	22
O. Carroll, SP	18
M. McManus, 3B	15
H. Rice, OF	15
J. Tavener, SS	13
B. Fothergill, OF	12
E. Vangilder, RP	11
P. Hargrave, C	10
E. Whitehill, SP	7
A. Wingo, OF	7
V. Sorrell, SP	6
L. Stoner, RP	6
K. Holloway, RP	5
G. Smith, RP	5
J. Stone, OF	5
P. Easterling, OF	4
J. Billings, SP	3
C. Galloway, SS	3
S. Gibson, SP	3
L. Woodall, C	3
P. Page, SP	2
M. Shea, C	2
B. Sweeney, 1B	2
J. Warner, 3B	2

New York (101-53)	WS
Hitting	**181.5**
Fielding	**37.8**
Pitching	**83.7**
B. Ruth, OF	45
L. Gehrig, 1B	42
E. Combs, OF	28
W. Hoyt, SP	22
T. Lazzeri, 2B	22
G. Pipgras, SP	21
M. Koenig, SS	20
H. Pennock, SP	20
B. Meusel, OF	18
H. Johnson, SP	9
P. Collins, C	7
J. Dugan, 3B	7
L. Durocher, 2B	7
B. Bengough, C	5
J. Grabowski, C	5
G. Robertson, 3B	5
F. Heimach, SP	4
B. Paschal, OF	3
A. Shealy, SP	3
C. Durst, OF	2
W. Moore, RP	2
M. Thomas, RP	2
T. Zachary, SP	2
S. Coveleski, SP	1
M. Gazella, 3B	1

Philadelphia (98-55)	WS
Hitting	**138.4**
Fielding	**49.2**
Pitching	**106.4**
L. Grove, SP	27
M. Bishop, 2B	24
A. Simmons, OF	23
M. Cochrane, C	22
J. Foxx, 3B	22
B. Miller, OF	20
J. Quinn, SP	18
E. Rommel, RP	17
R. Walberg, SP	17
S. Hale, 3B	13
T. Cobb, OF	12
J. Hauser, 1B	11
J. Boley, SS	10
H. Ehmke, SP	10
O. Orwoll, 1B	10
G. Earnshaw, SP	9
M. Haas, OF	9
J. Dykes, 2B	8
T. Speaker, OF	6
J. Bush, RP	1
E. Collins, 2B	1
W. French, OF	1
I. Powers, RP	1
B. Shores, SP	1
C. Yerkes, SP-RP	1

St. Louis (82-72)	WS
Hitting	**115.5**
Fielding	**43.4**
Pitching	**87.1**
H. Manush, OF	35
L. Blue, 1B	23
S. Gray, SP	23
G. Crowder, SP	20
F. Schulte, OF	19
R. Kress, SS	16
J. Ogden, SP	16
W. Schang, C	14
G. Blaeholder, SP	12
O. Brannan, 2B	12
B. McGowan, OF	9
L. Stewart, SP	9
F. O'Rourke, 3B	7

L. Bettencourt, 3B	6
E. McNeely, OF	6
C. Manion, C	5
B. Beck, RP	3
E. Strelecki, RP	3
H. Wiltse, RP	2
I. Danning, C	1
S. Melillo, 2B	1
B. Mullen, 3B	1
E. Nevers, RP	1
S. O'Neill, C	1
G. Sturdy, 1B	1

Washington (75-79)	WS
Hitting	**100.8**
Fielding	**41.0**
Pitching	**83.2**
G. Goslin, OF	26
S. Jones, SP	22
G. Braxton, SP	21
S. Rice, OF	19
R. Barnes, OF	17
O. Bluege, 3B	17
J. Judge, 1B	17
B. Hadley, SP	16
F. Marberry, RP	11
S. West, OF	10
B. Reeves, SS	9
M. Ruel, C	8
L. Brown, RP	5
B. Burke, RP	5
J. Cronin, SS	4
B. Harris, 2B	4
J. Hayes, 2B	3
E. Kenna, C	3
B. Tate, C	2
T. Zachary, SP	2
M. Gaston, SP	1
G. Gillis, SS	1
C. Van Alstyne, RP	1
J. Weaver, RP	1

1928 National League

Boston (50-103)	WS
Hitting	**90.8**
Fielding	**23.7**
Pitching	**35.5**
R. Hornsby, 2B	33
L. Richbourg, OF	20
L. Bell, 3B	16
G. Sisler, 1B	15
B. Smith, SP	10
A. Delaney, SP	8
E. Brandt, SP	6
E. Brown, OF	6
Z. Taylor, C	6
J. Smith, OF	4
D. Burrus, 1B	3
Jo. Cooney, RP	3
J. Genewich, SP	3
B. Cantwell, RP	2
E. Clark, OF	2
D. Farrell, SS	2
H. Freigau, SS	2
K. Greenfield, SP	2
E. Moore, OF	2
F. Edwards, RP	1
D. Gautreau, 2B	1
H. Mueller, OF	1
C. Robertson, SP	1
A. Spohrer, C	1

Brooklyn (77-76)	WS
Hitting	**91.4**
Fielding	**41.3**
Pitching	**98.3**
D. Vance, SP	32
D. Bissonette, 1B	25
B. Herman, OF	19
R. Bressler, OF	18
H. Hendrick, 3B	18
W. Clark, RP	17
D. McWeeny, SP	17
J. Petty, SP	12
D. Bancroft, SS	11
J. Elliott, SP	9
J. Flowers, 2B	9
M. Carey, OF	7
B. Doak, RP	6
H. DeBerry, C	5
H. Riconda, 2B	4
T. Tyson, OF	4
J. Gooch, C	3
W. Gilbert, 3B	2
J. Harris, OF	2
B. Henline, C	2
L. Koupal, RP	2
J. Statz, OF	2
R. Ehrhardt, RP	1
C. Hargreaves, C	1
R. Moss, RP	1
J. Partridge, 2B	1
M. West, OF	1

Chicago (91-63)	WS
Hitting	**119.7**
Fielding	**49.9**
Pitching	**103.4**
H. Wilson, OF	28
G. Hartnett, C	26
S. Blake, SP	24
P. Malone, SP	23
R. Stephenson, OF	23
K. Cuyler, OF	18
A. Nehf, SP	18
C. Root, SP	16
W. English, SS	14
F. Maguire, 2B	14
C. Grimm, 1B	13
C. Beck, 3B	12
G. Bush, SP	12
P. Jones, RP	9
M. Gonzalez, C	6
J. Butler, 3B	5
C. Heathcote, OF	4
E. Webb, OF	3
E. Holley, RP	2
N. McMillan, 2B	2
L. Weinert, RP	1

Cincinnati (78-74)	WS
Hitting	**106.3**
Fielding	**44.1**
Pitching	**83.5**
E. Rixey, SP	22
H. Critz, 2B	20
R. Kolp, SP	18
C. Dressen, 3B	16
E. Allen, OF	15
H. Ford, SS	15
R. Lucas, SP	15
D. Luque, SP	15
G. Kelly, 1B	14
C. Walker, OF	14
V. Picinich, C	13
B. Hargrave, C	8
M. Callaghan, OF	7
W. Pipp, 1B	7
P. Purdy, OF	7
B. Zitzmann, OF	7
P. Donohue, SP	5
C. Mays, SP-RP	5
J. Stripp, OF	4
P. Appleton, RP	3
J. May, SP	3
C. Sukeforth, C	1

New York (93-61)	WS
Hitting	**138.6**
Fielding	**44.2**
Pitching	**96.2**
F. Lindstrom, 3B	32
L. Benton, SP	30
B. Terry, 1B	24
T. Jackson, SS	22
M. Ott, OF	20
S. Hogan, C	19
F. Fitzsimmons, SP	18
J. Welsh, OF	15
A. Cohen, 2B	14
J. Genewich, SP	14
L. O'Doul, OF	12
C. Hubbell, SP	11
R. Reese, OF	10
J. Faulkner, RP	8
V. Aldridge, SP	5
J. Scott, RP	4
D. Henry, RP	3
L. Mann, OF	3
B. O'Farrell, C	3
E. Roush, OF	3
V. Barnes, SP	2
G. Harper, OF	2
B. Walker, RP	2
B. Cantwell, RP	1
J. Cummings, C	1
A. Jahn, OF	1

Philadelphia (43-109)	WS
Hitting	**68.6**
Fielding	**24.2**
Pitching	**36.3**
F. Leach, OF	13
P. Whitney, 3B	13
D. Hurst, 1B	12
R. Benge, SP	10
F. Thompson, 2B	10
C. Klein, OF	9
D. Sothern, OF	8
W. Lerian, C	7
C. Williams, OF	7
B. McGraw, RP	6
C. Willoughby, RP	4
S. Davis, C	3
A. Ferguson, SP	3
J. Milligan, SP	3
H. Pruett, SP	3
H. Sand, SS	3
A. Walsh, RP	3
R. Miller, RP	2
J. Schulte, C	2
J. Wilson, C	2
E. Baecht, RP	1
E. Caldwell, SP	1
B. Friberg, SS	1
J. Ring, SP	1
L. Sweetland, RP	1
R. Wrightstone, OF	1

Pittsburgh (85-67)	WS
Hitting	**132.7**
Fielding	**39.9**
Pitching	**82.4**
P. Waner, OF	34
B. Grimes, SP	30
L. Waner, OF	26
P. Traynor, 3B	22
G. Grantham, 1B	18
C. Hill, SP	17
S. Adams, 2B	12
G. Wright, SS	12
J. Dawson, RP	11
R. Kremer, SP	10
F. Fussell, SP	9
D. Bartell, 2B	7
G. Brickell, OF	7
P. Scott, OF	7
C. Barnhart, OF	5
E. Brame, RP	5
A. Comorosky, OF	5
C. Hargreaves, C	5
J. Harris, 1B	2
R. Hemsley, C	2
J. Miljus, RP	2
E. Smith, C	2
B. Burwell, RP	1
J. Gooch, C	1
M. Hillis, 2B	1
G. Spencer, RP	1
W. Tauscher, RP	1

St. Louis (95-59)	WS
Hitting	**132.9**
Fielding	**49.0**
Pitching	**103.1**
J. Bottomley, 1B	30
C. Hafey, OF	25
T. Douthit, OF	24
B. Sherdel, SP	24
F. Frisch, 2B	22
P. Alexander, SP	19
J. Haines, SP	19
G. Harper, OF	14
J. Wilson, C	13
R. Maranville, SS	11
A. High, 3B	10
C. Mitchell, SP	10
W. Roettger, OF	10
W. Holm, 3B	9
S. Johnson, RP	8
F. Rhem, SP	8
H. Haid, RP	5
A. Reinhart, RP	5
F. Frankhouse, RP	4
R. Blades, OF	3
E. Orsatti, OF	3
T. Thevenow, SS	3
C. Littlejohn, RP	2
B. O'Farrell, C	2
G. Mancuso, C	1
E. Smith, C	1

1929 American League

Boston (58-96)	WS
Hitting	**63.9**
Fielding	**37.8**
Pitching	**72.3**
M. Gaston, SP	18
D. MacFayden, SP	15
E. Morris, SP	13
J. Rothrock, OF	13
R. Ruffing, SP	11
J. Russell, SP	11
R. Scarritt, OF	11
Bi. Barrett, OF	9
B. Reeves, 3B	9
B. Regan, 2B	8
P. Todt, 1B	8
H. Rhyne, SS	7
J. Heving, C	6
C. Berry, C	5
B. Narleski, SS	5
K. Williams, OF	5
E. Bigelow, OF	4
Bo. Barrett, 3B	3
R. Dobens, RP	2
A. Gaston, C	2
P. Simmons, RP	2
B. Bayne, RP	1
E. Carroll, RP	1
J. Cicero, OF	1
I. Flagstead, OF	1
W. Gerber, SS	1
G. Gillis, 2B	1
D. Taitt, OF	1

Chicago (59-93)	WS
Hitting	**72.2**
Fielding	**37.3**
Pitching	**67.6**
T. Thomas, SP	20
W. Kamm, 3B	16
T. Lyons, SP	16
R. Faber, SP	15
A. Metzler, OF	15
C. Reynolds, OF	15
B. Cissell, SS	12

H. McKain, RP	11
A. Shires, 1B	9
M. Berg, C	7
D. Hoffman, OF	7
J. Kerr, 2B	7
C. Watwood, OF	7
B. Clancy, 1B	5
G. Adkins, RP	3
B. Crouse, C	3
E. Walsh, SP	3
C. Autry, C	1
S. Connally, RP	1
B. Hunnefield, 2B	1
J. Mostil, OF	1
D. Taitt, OF	1
B. Weiland, SP	1

Cleveland (81-71)	WS
Hitting	**100.9**
Fielding	**44.3**
Pitching	**97.8**
E. Averill, OF	26
W. Ferrell, SP	25
L. Fonseca, 1B	25
W. Hudlin, SP	25
J. Sewell, 3B	21
J. Miller, SP	17
B. Falk, OF	15
K. Holloway, RP	11
J. Hodapp, 2B	10
E. Morgan, OF	10
J. Shaute, SP	10
C. Jamieson, OF	7
D. Porter, OF	6
J. Zinn, SP	6
R. Gardner, SS	5
J. Miljus, RP	5
L. Sewell, C	5
J. Tavener, SS	5
C. Lind, 2B	3
M. Shoffner, RP	2
C. Brown, RP	1
J. Burnett, SS	1
J. Hauser, 1B	1
G. Myatt, C	1

Detroit (70-84)	WS
Hitting	**134.3**
Fielding	**25.4**
Pitching	**50.3**
C. Gehringer, 2B	27
D. Alexander, 1B	24
H. Heilmann, OF	19
R. Johnson, OF	19
M. McManus, 3B	18
G. Uhle, SP	16
H. Rice, OF	15
E. Whitehill, SP	12
B. Fothergill, OF	10
O. Carroll, SP	8
P. Hargrave, C	7
V. Sorrell, SP	7
M. Shea, C	4
E. Yde, RP	4
E. Phillips, C	3
H. Schuble, SS	3
B. Akers, SS	2
A. Herring, SP	2
C. Hogsett, SP	2
J. Stone, OF	2
L. Stoner, RP	2
S. Graham, RP	1
A. Prudhomme, RP	1
G. Smith, RP	1
Y. Wuestling, SS	1

New York (88-66)	WS
Hitting	**157.4**
Fielding	**35.3**
Pitching	**71.2**
L. Gehrig, 1B	32
B. Ruth, OF	32
T. Lazzeri, 2B	30
E. Combs, OF	25
B. Dickey, C	18
T. Zachary, RP	12
M. Koenig, SS	11
G. Pipgras, SP	10
E. Wells, SP	10
L. Durocher, SS	9
F. Heimach, RP	9
W. Hoyt, SP	9
L. Lary, 3B	9
G. Robertson, 3B	8
R. Sherid, RP	8
S. Byrd, OF	7
B. Meusel, OF	6
W. Moore, RP	5
H. Pennock, SP	5
C. Durst, OF	3
B. Bengough, C	1
J. Grabowski, C	1
H. Johnson, SP	1
A. Jorgens, C	1
B. Nekola, RP	1
G. Rhodes, RP	1

Philadelphia (104-46)	WS
Hitting	**147.6**
Fielding	**48.9**
Pitching	**115.5**
J. Foxx, 1B	34
A. Simmons, OF	34
L. Grove, SP	28
M. Cochrane, C	27
G. Earnshaw, SP	23
B. Miller, OF	23
M. Haas, OF	22
R. Walberg, SP	22
J. Dykes, SS	21
M. Bishop, 2B	15
B. Shores, RP	13
E. Rommel, RP	12
J. Quinn, SP	10
J. Boley, SS	8
S. Hale, 3B	6
H. Ehmke, SP	5
C. Yerkes, RP	2
G. Burns, 1B	1
J. Cronin, 2B	1
B. LeBourveau, OF	1
E. McNair, SS	1
O. Orwoll, RP	1
C. Perkins, C	1
H. Summa, OF	1

St. Louis (79-73)	WS
Hitting	**94.4**
Fielding	**49.3**
Pitching	**93.4**
S. Gray, SP	24
H. Manush, OF	23
L. Blue, 1B	22
R. Kress, SS	21
G. Crowder, SP	20
F. Schulte, OF	18
G. Blaeholder, SP	15
S. Melillo, 2B	15
R. Collins, SP	13
L. Stewart, SP	12
W. Schang, C	11
B. McGowan, OF	10
F. O'Rourke, 3B	9
J. Ogden, RP	5
R. Ferrell, C	4
R. Badgro, OF	3
C. Kimsey, RP	3
C. Manion, C	3
F. Stiely, SP	2
O. Brannan, 2B	1
D. Coffman, RP	1
E. McNeely, OF	1
E. Roetz, SS	1

Washington (71-81)	WS
Hitting	**101.4**
Fielding	**36.6**
Pitching	**75.0**
F. Marberry, SP	26
J. Judge, 1B	20
S. Rice, OF	20
J. Cronin, SS	19
G. Goslin, OF	19
B. Myer, 2B	18
S. West, OF	11
L. Brown, RP	10
S. Jones, SP	10
M. Thomas, SP	9
G. Braxton, SP	8
J. Hayes, 3B	8
O. Bluege, 3B	7
B. Tate, C	7
B. Burke, RP	5
M. Ruel, C	5
A. Liska, RP	4
B. Hadley, SP	2
H. Boss, 1B	1
I. Flagstead, OF	1
C. Gooch, 1B-3B	1
P. Hopkins, RP	1
R. Spencer, C	1

1929 National League

Boston (56-98)	WS
Hitting	**72.0**
Fielding	**34.2**
Pitching	**61.8**
R. Maranville, SS	17
G. Harper, OF	14
L. Richbourg, OF	13
S. Seibold, SP	13
G. Sisler, 1B	13
B. Smith, SP	13
L. Bell, 3B	11
P. Jones, SP	9
B. Cantwell, SP	8
E. Brandt, SP	7
E. Clark, OF	7
A. Spohrer, C	7
B. Cunningham, RP	6
J. Welsh, OF	6
F. Maguire, 2B	5
J. Cooney, OF	4
J. Dugan, 3B	2
B. Dunlap, OF	2
B. James, 2B	2
R. Peery, RP	2
B. Boyle, OF	1
A. Delaney, RP	1
H. Gowdy, C	1
B. Hearn, RP	1
D. Leverett, SP-RP	1
H. Mueller, OF	1
Z. Taylor, C	1

Brooklyn (70-83)	WS
Hitting	**106.4**
Fielding	**32.7**
Pitching	**70.9**
B. Herman, OF	26
W. Clark, SP	23
J. Frederick, OF	22
D. Vance, SP	19
H. Hendrick, OF	15
R. Bressler, OF	14
W. Gilbert, 3B	14
D. Bissonette, 1B	11
J. Morrison, RP	11
E. Moore, 2B	9
R. Moss, SP	9
V. Picinich, C	8
D. Bancroft, SS	6
H. DeBerry, C	5
B. Rhiel, 2B	4
C. Moore, RP	3
C. Dudley, SP	2
B. Henline, C	2
D. McWeeny, SP	2
N. Cullop, OF	1
J. Flowers, 2B	1
L. Koupal, RP	1
J. Pattison, RP	1
J. Warner, SS	1

Chicago (98-54)	WS
Hitting	**152.7**
Fielding	**45.8**
Pitching	**95.4**
R. Hornsby, 2B	42
H. Wilson, OF	32
R. Stephenson, OF	26
K. Cuyler, OF	25
P. Malone, SP	23
C. Root, SP	23
G. Bush, SP	21
W. English, SS	17
S. Blake, SP	13
C. Grimm, 1B	13
N. McMillan, 3B	12
C. Heathcote, OF	7
Z. Taylor, C	7
H. Carlson, RP	6
A. Nehf, RP	5
M. Cvengros, RP	4
M. Gonzalez, C	4
E. Grace, C	3
C. Beck, 3B	2
F. Blair, 3B	2
J. Schulte, C	2
G. Hartnett, C	1
T. Horne, RP	1
J. Moore, OF	1
B. Osborn, RP	1
C. Tolson, 1B	1

Cincinnati (66-88)	WS
Hitting	**73.2**
Fielding	**40.9**
Pitching	**83.9**
R. Lucas, SP	26
C. Walker, OF	19
E. Rixey, SP	14
E. Swanson, OF	14
E. Allen, OF	13
G. Kelly, 1B	12
J. May, SP	12
H. Ford, SS	11
J. Gooch, C	9
R. Kolp, SP	9
D. Luque, SP	9
C. Sukeforth, C	9
P. Donohue, SP	7
C. Dressen, 3B	6
H. Critz, 2B	5
P. Pittenger, SS	4
P. Purdy, OF	4
K. Ash, RP	3
J. Stripp, 3B	3
R. Ehrhardt, RP	2
B. Frey, SP	2
M. Gudat, RP	2
L. Dixon, C	1
W. Shaner, 1B	1
B. Zitzmann, OF	1

New York (84-67)	WS
Hitting	**120.7**
Fielding	**41.8**
Pitching	**89.5**
M. Ott, OF	31
B. Terry, 1B	24
T. Jackson, SS	23
C. Hubbell, SP	19
F. Lindstrom, 3B	17
E. Roush, OF	15
B. Walker, SP	15
L. Benton, SP	13
F. Fitzsimmons, SP	13
A. Cohen, 2B	9
C. Mays, RP	9
S. Hogan, C	8

F. Leach, OF	8
B. O'Farrell, C	8
J. Scott, RP	8
D. Henry, RP	7
C. Fullis, OF	6
R. Judd, RP	5
R. Reese, 2B	4
P. Crawford, 1B	2
D. Farrell, 3B	2
R. Lucas, RP	2
J. Welsh, OF	2
J. Genewich, RP	1
E. Marshall, 2B	1

Philadelphia (71-82)	WS
Hitting	**118.4**
Fielding	**33.3**
Pitching	**61.3**
L. O'Doul, OF	31
C. Klein, OF	26
P. Whitney, 3B	21
D. Hurst, 1B	17
F. Thompson, 2B	16
C. Willoughby, SP	15
L. Sweetland, SP	13
S. Davis, C	9
B. Friberg, SS	9
R. Benge, SP	8
P. Collins, RP	8
W. Lerian, C	7
D. Sothern, OF	7
L. Koupal, SP	5
H. Elliott, RP	4
B. McGraw, RP	4
H. Smythe, RP	4
C. Williams, OF	3
H. Peel, OF	2
T. Sigman, OF	2
G. Susce, C	1
T. Thevenow, SS	1

Pittsburgh (88-65)	WS
Hitting	**126.5**
Fielding	**46.9**
Pitching	**90.6**
P. Waner, OF	30
L. Waner, OF	27
B. Grimes, SP	23
P. Traynor, 3B	21
G. Grantham, 2B	19
E. Brame, SP	18
D. Bartell, SS	16
A. Comorosky, OF	15
R. Kremer, SP	15
E. Sheely, 1B	13
J. Petty, SP	12
S. Swetonic, RP	9
C. Hargreaves, C	7
R. Hemsley, C	7
L. French, RP	6
H. Meine, SP	6
S. Clarke, SS	5
C. Hill, RP	5
S. Adams, SS	3
G. Brickell, OF	3
I. Flagstead, OF	1
C. Jones, SS	1
J. Mosolf, OF	1
H. Riconda, SS	1

St. Louis (78-74)	WS
Hitting	**111.2**
Fielding	**41.1**
Pitching	**81.6**
T. Douthit, OF	22
C. Hafey, OF	22
J. Bottomley, 1B	21
F. Frisch, 2B	20
S. Johnson, RP	16
J. Wilson, C	16
C. Gelbert, SS	15
A. High, 3B	14
C. Mitchell, SP	12
F. Frankhouse, RP	11
P. Alexander, SP	10
H. Haid, RP	10
E. Orsatti, OF	10
A. Grabowski, SP	6
J. Haines, SP	6
W. Hallahan, SP	6
B. Sherdel, SP	5
E. Smith, C	5
W. Roettger, OF	2
J. Butler, 3B	1
W. Holm, OF	1
B. Jonnard, C	1
J. Lindsey, SP	1
C. Selph, 2B	1

1930

American League

Boston (52-102)	WS
Hitting	**50.6**
Fielding	**37.3**
Pitching	**68.1**
M. Gaston, SP	20
D. MacFayden, SP	17
H. Lisenbee, SP	15
E. Webb, OF	14
T. Oliver, OF	13
C. Berry, C	8
O. Miller, 3B	8
B. Regan, 2B	8
P. Todt, 1B	7
E. Durham, RP	6
J. Russell, SP	6
R. Scarritt, OF	6
B. Reeves, 3B	5
J. Heving, C	4
E. Morris, SP-RP	4
H. Rhyne, SS	4
B. Sweeney, 1B	4
C. Durst, OF	3
R. Warstler, SS	2
E. Connolly, C	1
B. Narleski, SS	1

Chicago (62-92)	WS
Hitting	**82.8**
Fielding	**30.6**
Pitching	**72.6**
T. Lyons, SP	26
C. Reynolds, OF	25
S. Jolley, OF	18
P. Caraway, SP	15
C. Watwood, 1B	11
R. Faber, SP	10
W. Kamm, 3B	10
B. Cissell, 2B	8
J. Kerr, 2B	7
B. Tate, C	7
H. McKain, RP	6
D. Henry, RP	5
T. Thomas, SP	5
R. Barnes, OF	4
Jim Moore, SP-OF	4
E. Walsh, RP	4
B. Crouse, C	3
G. Mulleavy, SS	3
B. Clancy, 1B	2
B. Fothergill, OF	2
D. Harris, OF	2
C. Autry, C	1
M. Berg, C	1
G. Braxton, SP	1
B. Campbell, OF	1
B. Hunnefield, SS	1
I. Jeffries, 3B	1
J. Riddle, C	1
B. Ryan, 3B	1
A. Shires, 1B	1

Cleveland (81-73)	WS
Hitting	**123.7**
Fielding	**38.0**
Pitching	**81.3**
W. Ferrell, SP	32
E. Morgan, 1B	28
J. Hodapp, 2B	25
E. Averill, OF	24
D. Porter, OF	20
W. Hudlin, SP	14
C. Brown, SP	13
M. Harder, SP	12
P. Appleton, RP	9
J. Sewell, 3B	9
C. Jamieson, OF	8
B. Falk, OF	7
G. Myatt, C	7
J. Burnett, 3B	5
J. Goldman, SS	5
E. Montague, SS	5
L. Sewell, C	5
B. Bean, RP	4
B. Seeds, OF	4
L. Fonseca, 1B	2
G. Hartley, C	1
R. Lawson, SP	1
C. Lind, SS	1
J. Sprinz, C	1
R. Winegarner, 3B	1

Detroit (75-79)	WS
Hitting	**95.0**
Fielding	**45.0**
Pitching	**84.9**
C. Gehringer, 2B	29
G. Uhle, SP	23
M. McManus, 3B	21
D. Alexander, 1B	19
V. Sorrell, SP	19
E. Whitehill, SP	14
L. Funk, OF	11
J. Stone, OF	11
B. Akers, SS	10
R. Johnson, OF	9
W. Wyatt, RP	9
W. Hoyt, SP	8
C. Hogsett, SP	7
P. Hargrave, C	5
R. Hayworth, C	4
M. Koenig, SS	4
T. Bridges, SP	3
A. Herring, RP	3
H. Rice, OF	3
C. Sullivan, RP	3
G. Desautels, C	2
B. Fothergill, OF	2
T. Hughes, OF	2
B. Rogell, SS	2
F. Doljack, OF	1
T. Rensa, C	1

New York (86-68)	WS
Hitting	**179.7**
Fielding	**25.2**
Pitching	**53.1**
L. Gehrig, 1B	39
B. Ruth, OF	38
E. Combs, OF	23
T. Lazzeri, 2B	19
B. Chapman, 3B	17
R. Ruffing, SP	16
B. Dickey, C	15
L. Lary, SS	14
G. Pipgras, SP	11
H. Rice, OF	10
H. Johnson, RP	9
H. Pennock, SP	7
J. Reese, 2B	7
S. Byrd, OF	6
R. Sherid, SP	6
E. Wells, SP	6
D. Cooke, OF	5
B. Hargrave, C	2
W. Hoyt, SP	2
B. Bengough, C	1
L. Gomez, RP	1
K. Holloway, RP	1
A. Jorgens, C	1
M. Koenig, SS	1
Y. Wuestling, SS	1

Philadelphia (102-52)	WS
Hitting	**151.2**
Fielding	**48.9**
Pitching	**105.9**
L. Grove, SP	37
A. Simmons, OF	36
J. Foxx, 1B	34
M. Cochrane, C	31
M. Bishop, 2B	21
G. Earnshaw, SP	21
J. Dykes, 3B	18
B. Miller, OF	17
M. Haas, OF	16
J. Boley, SS	12
E. Rommel, RP	12
R. Walberg, SP	12
B. Shores, SP	11
J. Quinn, RP	8
R. Mahaffey, SP	6
D. Williams, 2B	5
E. McNair, SS	3
J. Moore, OF	2
W. Schang, C	2
Cy Perkins, C	1
H. Summa, OF	1

St. Louis (64-90)	WS
Hitting	**73.9**
Fielding	**41.3**
Pitching	**76.7**
L. Stewart, SP	28
G. Goslin, OF	20
R. Kress, SS	20
G. Blaeholder, SP	13
R. Collins, SP	13
S. Melillo, 2B	11
R. Ferrell, C	9
F. Schulte, OF	9
L. Blue, 1B	8
D. Coffman, SP	8
C. Kimsey, RP	6
H. Manush, OF	6
F. O'Rourke, 3B	6
G. Crowder, SP	5
T. Gullic, OF	4
E. McNeely, OF	4
R. Stiles, RP	4
S. Gray, SP	3
S. Hale, 3B	3
C. Manion, C	3
A. Metzler, OF	3
R. Badgro, OF	2
J. Burns, 1B	1
B. Hungling, C	1
J. Levey, SS	1
L. Storti, 2B	1

Washington (94-60)	WS
Hitting	**127.8**
Fielding	**49.9**
Pitching	**104.4**
J. Cronin, SS	33
S. Rice, OF	23
B. Hadley, SP	21
J. Judge, 1B	18
S. West, OF	18
G. Crowder, SP	17
H. Manush, OF	17
F. Marberry, SP	16
L. Brown, SP	15
O. Bluege, 3B	14
B. Myer, 2B	14
S. Jones, SP	13
A. Liska, SP-RP	12
D. Harris, OF	10
R. Spencer, C	7
B. Burke, RP	6
G. Goslin, OF	5
M. Ruel, C	5

G. Braxton, RP	4
J. Hayes, 2B	3
G. Loepp, OF	3
A. Shires, 1B	3
J. Kuhel, 1B	2
C. Fischer, SP-RP	1
P. Hargrave, C	1
C. Moore, RP	1

1930 National League

Boston (70-84)	WS
Hitting	**75.9**
Fielding	**48.0**
Pitching	**86.1**
W. Berger, OF	26
S. Seibold, SP	20
R. Maranville, SS	17
B. Smith, SP	17
B. Cantwell, SP	12
L. Richbourg, OF	11
A. Spohrer, C	11
J. Welsh, OF	11
T. Zachary, SP	11
B. Chatham, 3B	10
F. Maguire, 2B	9
E. Brandt, RP	8
G. Sisler, 1B	8
F. Frankhouse, RP	7
B. Sherdel, SP	7
J. Neun, 1B	6
E. Clark, OF	5
B. Cunningham, RP	5
R. Moore, OF	4
B. Cronin, C	2
R. Rollings, 3B	2
G. Robertson, 3B	1

Brooklyn (86-68)	WS
Hitting	**108.8**
Fielding	**49.1**
Pitching	**100.1**
B. Herman, OF	32
D. Vance, SP	26
J. Frederick, OF	24
G. Wright, SS	21
D. Bissonette, 1B	17
W. Clark, SP	16
J. Elliott, SP	15
D. Luque, SP	15
W. Gilbert, 3B	14
A. Lopez, C	13
R. Phelps, SP	13
R. Bressler, OF	10
S. Thurston, RP	10
J. Flowers, 2B	7
R. Moss, RP	6
N. Finn, 2B	5
E. Moore, 2B-OF	4
I. Boone, OF	3
H. Hendrick, OF	3
H. DeBerry, C	2
J. Morrison, RP	1
G. Slade, SS	1

Chicago (90-64)	WS
Hitting	**136.5**
Fielding	**44.3**
Pitching	**89.2**
H. Wilson, OF	35
K. Cuyler, OF	29
G. Hartnett, C	29
W. English, 3B	28
P. Malone, SP	24
C. Root, SP	17
B. Teachout, RP	13
R. Stephenson, OF	11
F. Blair, 2B	9
S. Blake, SP	9
C. Grimm, 1B	9
G. Bush, SP	8
B. Osborn, RP	8
L. Bell, 3B	6
D. Taylor, OF	5
C. Heathcote, OF	4
G. Kelly, 1B	4
L. Nelson, RP	4
C. Beck, SS	3
H. Carlson, SP	3
R. Hornsby, 2B	3
J. Petty, RP	3
D. Farrell, SS	2
Z. Taylor, C	2
M. Moss, RP	1
C. Tolson, 1B	1

Cincinnati (59-95)	WS
Hitting	**71.5**
Fielding	**35.2**
Pitching	**70.3**
H. Heilmann, OF	20
B. Frey, SP	16
R. Kolp, SP	14
R. Lucas, SP	14
J. Stripp, 1B	13
C. Walker, OF	13
T. Cuccinello, 3B	12
B. Meusel, OF	9
E. Rixey, SP	8
L. Benton, SP	7
L. Durocher, SS	6
H. Ford, SS	6
P. Crawford, 2B	5
E. Swanson, OF	5
S. Johnson, RP	4
C. Sukeforth, C	4
K. Ash, RP	3
M. Callaghan, OF	3
A. Campbell, RP	3
J. Gooch, C	3
G. Kelly, 1B	3
J. May, SP	2
E. Allen, OF	1
O. Carroll, SP	1
H. Critz, 2B	1
P. Donohue, SP	1

New York (87-67)	WS
Hitting	**137.4**
Fielding	**38.3**
Pitching	**85.3**
B. Terry, 1B	32
F. Lindstrom, 3B	28
M. Ott, OF	28
F. Fitzsimmons, SP	18
C. Hubbell, SP	18
B. Walker, SP	18
T. Jackson, SS	17
S. Hogan, C	15
F. Leach, OF	15
C. Mitchell, SP	10
B. O'Farrell, C	9
H. Critz, 2B	8
W. Roettger, OF	8
H. Pruett, RP	7
E. Allen, OF	6
J. Heving, RP	6
E. Marshall, SS	5
T. Chaplin, RP	3
P. Donohue, SP	3
P. Crawford, 2B	2
J. Genewich, SP-RP	2
R. Reese, OF	2
B. Morrell, RP	1

Philadelphia (52-102)	WS
Hitting	**91.7**
Fielding	**25.5**
Pitching	**38.7**
C. Klein, OF	28
L. O'Doul, OF	20
P. Collins, SP	16
P. Whitney, 3B	16
D. Hurst, 1B	10
R. Benge, SP	9
S. Davis, C	8
B. Friberg, 2B	8
M. Sherlock, 1B	5
F. Thompson, 2B	5
H. Collard, SP-RP	4
D. Sothern, OF	4
H. McCurdy, C	3
T. Rensa, C	3
L. Sweetland, SP	3
T. Thevenow, SS	3
J. Milligan, RP	2
C. Nichols, RP	2
G. Brickell, OF	1
H. Elliott, RP	1
S. Hansen, RP	1
B. Phillips, RP	1
T. Sigman, OF	1
C. Williams, OF	1
C. Willoughby, SP	1

Pittsburgh (80-74)	WS
Hitting	**126.1**
Fielding	**40.8**
Pitching	**73.0**
P. Waner, OF	26
G. Grantham, 2B	24
P. Traynor, 3B	22
A. Comorosky, OF	21
L. French, SP	19
D. Bartell, SS	18
E. Brame, SP	18
G. Suhr, 1B	17
R. Kremer, SP	15
R. Hemsley, C	8
S. Swetonic, RP	8
L. Waner, OF	8
A. Bool, C	7
G. Spencer, RP	7
G. Brickell, OF	4
C. Engle, 3B	4
S. Wood, SP	4
H. Meine, SP	3
I. Flagstead, OF	2
L. Chagnon, RP	1
S. Clarke, 2B	1
G. Dugas, OF	1
C. Hargreaves, C	1
J. Mosolf, OF	1

St. Louis (92-62)	WS
Hitting	**132.8**
Fielding	**44.8**
Pitching	**98.4**
F. Frisch, 2B	25
C. Hafey, OF	20
C. Gelbert, SS	18
T. Douthit, OF	17
G. Watkins, OF	17
B. Grimes, SP	16
S. Adams, 3B	15
W. Hallahan, SP	15
J. Bottomley, 1B	13
J. Haines, SP	13
S. Johnson, SP	13
J. Wilson, C	13
S. Fisher, OF	11
G. Mancuso, C	11
H. Bell, RP	10
F. Rhem, SP	9
J. Lindsey, RP	8
A. Grabowski, RP	7
R. Blades, OF	6
A. High, 3B	4
E. Orsatti, 1B	4
B. Sherdel, SP	4
H. Haid, RP	3
G. Puccinelli, OF	2
D. Dean, SP	1
D. Farrell, SS	1

1931 American League

Boston (62-90)	WS
Hitting	**72.4**
Fielding	**35.6**
Pitching	**78.0**
E. Webb, OF	25
W. Moore, RP	18
D. MacFayden, SP	17
H. Rhyne, SS	14
T. Oliver, OF	12
C. Berry, C	11
E. Durham, RP	10
J. Rothrock, OF	10
J. Russell, SP	10
U. Pickering, 3B	8
B. Sweeney, 1B	8
B. Kline, RP	7
H. Lisenbee, RP	6
E. Morris, RP	6
O. Miller, 3B	5
A. Van Camp, OF	5
M. Gaston, SP	4
M. Ruel, C	3
M. McManus, 3B	2
R. Warstler, 2B	2
J. Brillheart, RP	1
E. Connolly, C	1
B. Reeves, 2B	1

Chicago (56-97)	WS
Hitting	**94.0**
Fielding	**25.5**
Pitching	**48.5**
L. Blue, 1B	27
C. Reynolds, OF	14
V. Frasier, SP	13
L. Fonseca, OF	12
C. Watwood, OF	12
R. Faber, RP	11
T. Thomas, SP	10
J. Kerr, 2B	9
B. Tate, C	8
B. Sullivan, 3B	7
B. Fothergill, OF	6
T. Lyons, SP	6
L. Appling, SS	5
F. Grube, C	4
S. Jolley, OF	4
B. Cissell, SS	3
J. Moore, RP	3
M. Simons, OF	3
P. Caraway, SP	2
I. Jeffries, 3B	2
H. McKain, RP	2
B. Weiland, SP	2
G. Bowler, RP	1
B. Campbell, OF	1
W. Kamm, 3B	1

Cleveland (78-76)	WS
Hitting	**121.6**
Fielding	**35.1**
Pitching	**77.3**
E. Averill, OF	30
W. Ferrell, SP	28
E. Morgan, 1B	21
J. Vosmik, OF	18
W. Hudlin, SP	15
W. Kamm, 3B	13
C. Brown, SP	12
J. Burnett, SS	12
M. Harder, SP	12
D. Porter, OF	11
J. Hodapp, 2B	10
L. Sewell, C	10
S. Connally, SP	5
E. Montague, SS	5
P. Appleton, RP	4
B. Falk, OF	4
L. Fonseca, 1B	4
G. Myatt, C	4
B. Seeds, OF	3
O. Hale, 3B	2

O. Hildebrand, RP	2
J. Miller, SP-RP	2
F. Thomas, RP	2
B. Connatser, 1B	1
G. Detore, 3B	1
J. Goldman, SS	1
B. Hunnefield, SS	1
C. Jamieson, OF	1

Detroit (61-93)	WS
Hitting	**61.1**
Fielding	**42.2**
Pitching	**79.7**
G. Uhle, SP	19
E. Whitehill, SP	18
V. Sorrell, SP	17
J. Stone, OF	17
R. Johnson, OF	15
D. Alexander, 1B	13
C. Gehringer, 2B	10
A. Herring, RP	10
M. McManus, 3B	9
T. Bridges, SP	7
B. Rogell, SS	6
F. Doljack, OF	5
C. Sullivan, RP	5
H. Walker, OF	5
R. Hayworth, C	4
M. Koenig, 2B	4
G. Walker, OF	4
C. Hogsett, SP	3
M. Owen, 3B-SS	3
J. Grabowski, C	2
N. Richardson, 3B	2
B. Akers, SS	1
W. Hoyt, SP	1
G. Quellich, OF	1
M. Ruel, C	1
W. Schang, C	1

New York (94-59)	WS
Hitting	**172.8**
Fielding	**35.3**
Pitching	**73.9**
B. Ruth, OF	38
L. Gehrig, 1B	36
L. Lary, SS	24
B. Chapman, OF	22
E. Combs, OF	20
B. Dickey, C	20
L. Gomez, SP	20
T. Lazzeri, 2B	15
R. Ruffing, SP	15
J. Sewell, 3B	15
H. Pennock, SP	10
H. Johnson, SP	9
G. Pipgras, RP	7
S. Byrd, OF	6
E. Wells, RP	6
G. Rhodes, SP	5
J. Reese, 2B	4
I. Andrews, RP	2
D. Cooke, OF	2
A. Jorgens, C	2
R. Sherid, RP	2
C. Perkins, C	1
J. Weaver, RP	1

Philadelphia (107-45)	WS
Hitting	**139.8**
Fielding	**49.5**
Pitching	**131.7**
L. Grove, SP	42
A. Simmons, OF	34
G. Earnshaw, SP	29
M. Cochrane, C	28
M. Bishop, 2B	25
J. Foxx, 1B	24
R. Walberg, SP	24
M. Haas, OF	17
B. Miller, OF	15
J. Dykes, 3B	13
R. Mahaffey, SP	13
E. Rommel, RP	12
W. Hoyt, SP	9
D. Williams, SS	9
E. McNair, 3B	6
D. Cramer, OF	4
H. McDonald, SP	4
J. Boley, SS	3
P. Todt, 1B	3
L. Finney, OF	2
J. Heving, C	2
L. Krausse, RP	1
J. Moore, OF	1
J. Palmisano, C	1

St. Louis (63-91)	WS
Hitting	**81.3**
Fielding	**34.1**
Pitching	**73.5**
G. Goslin, OF	25
R. Kress, 3B	17
S. Melillo, 2B	17
L. Stewart, SP	17
F. Schulte, OF	16
R. Ferrell, C	15
G. Blaeholder, SP	13
D. Coffman, SP	13
S. Gray, SP	10
R. Collins, SP	8
C. Kimsey, RP	8
J. Burns, 1B	7
L. Bettencourt, OF	4
W. Hebert, SP	4
B. Cooney, SP	3
T. Jenkins, OF	3
J. Levey, SS	3
B. Bengough, C	2
L. Storti, 3B	2
E. Grimes, 3B	1
R. Young, C	1

Washington (92-62)	WS
Hitting	**128.5**
Fielding	**50.5**
Pitching	**97.0**
J. Cronin, SS	35
S. West, OF	24
F. Marberry, SP	20
B. Myer, 2B	20
L. Brown, SP	19
H. Manush, OF	19
O. Bluege, 3B	17
G. Crowder, SP	16
B. Hadley, RP	16
J. Kuhel, 1B	14
S. Rice, OF	13
D. Harris, OF	12
R. Spencer, C	12
C. Fischer, SP-RP	10
B. Burke, RP	8
S. Jones, SP	8
P. Hargrave, C	4
H. Rice, OF	3
J. Judge, 1B	2
J. Gill, OF	1
J. Hayes, 2B	1
W. Masters, RP	1
M. Weaver, RP	1

1931 National League

Boston (64-90)	WS
Hitting	**66.2**
Fielding	**43.0**
Pitching	**82.7**
W. Berger, OF	31
E. Brandt, SP	27
T. Zachary, SP	20
R. Worthington, OF	13
B. Cantwell, RP	11
W. Schulmerich, OF	11
R. Maranville, SS	9
F. Frankhouse, SP	8
E. Sheely, 1B	8
B. Sherdel, SP	8
F. Maguire, 2B	7
L. Richbourg, OF	7
A. Spohrer, C	6
S. Seibold, SP	5
B. Cunningham, RP	4
R. Moore, OF	4
B. Urbanski, 3B	4
B. Dreesen, 3B	3
A. Bool, C	1
B. Chatham, 3B-SS	1
E. Clark, OF	1
B. Cronin, C	1
H. Haid, RP	1
J. Neun, 1B	1

Brooklyn (79-73)	WS
Hitting	**113.2**
Fielding	**37.2**
Pitching	**86.6**
B. Herman, OF	26
W. Clark, SP	22
L. O'Doul, OF	22
D. Bissonette, 1B	19
J. Frederick, OF	16
D. Vance, SP	15
W. Gilbert, 3B	13
G. Wright, SS	11
F. Heimach, RP	10
J. Quinn, RP	10
N. Finn, 2B	9
A. Lopez, C	9
S. Thurston, SP	9
G. Slade, SS	8
E. Lombardi, C	6
F. Thompson, 2B	5
D. Luque, SP	4
V. Mungo, SP	4
R. Phelps, SP	4
J. Shaute, SP	4
R. Bressler, OF	3
C. Moore, RP	3
P. Day, RP	2
J. Flowers, 2B	1
E. Mattingly, RP	1
V. Picinich, C	1

Chicago (84-70)	WS
Hitting	**147.0**
Fielding	**34.4**
Pitching	**70.6**
K. Cuyler, OF	26
W. English, SS	24
C. Grimm, 1B	21
R. Hornsby, 2B	20
C. Root, SP	17
B. Smith, SP	17
G. Hartnett, C	16
P. Malone, SP	13
H. Wilson, OF	13
R. Stephenson, OF	10
D. Taylor, OF	10
R. Hemsley, C	9
L. Bell, 3B	8
V. Barton, OF	7
G. Bush, SP	7
F. Blair, 2B	5
J. May, RP	5
B. Herman, 2B	4
L. Sweetland, SP	4
L. Warneke, RP	4
E. Baecht, RP	3
B. Jurges, 3B	3
J. Welch, RP	3
J. Adair, SS	1
S. Blake, RP	1
J. Moore, OF	1

Cincinnati (58-96)	WS
Hitting	**86.3**
Fielding	**32.0**
Pitching	**55.7**
T. Cuccinello, 2B	23
R. Lucas, SP	17
H. Hendrick, 1B	16
J. Stripp, 3B	15
L. Benton, SP	12
S. Johnson, SP	12
E. Crabtree, OF	9
N. Cullop, OF	8
T. Douthit, OF	7
W. Roettger, OF	7
C. Heathcote, OF	6
C. Sukeforth, C	6
L. Durocher, SS	5
B. Frey, SP-RP	5
J. Ogden, RP	5
E. Rixey, SP	5
E. Roush, OF	5
A. Asbjornson, C	3
H. Ford, SS	3
R. Kolp, RP	2
C. Beck, 3B	1
W. Hilcher, SP-RP	1
L. Styles, C	1

New York (87-65)	WS
Hitting	**134.3**
Fielding	**39.7**
Pitching	**87.0**
B. Terry, 1B	29
M. Ott, OF	26
T. Jackson, SS	22
B. Walker, SP	21
C. Hubbell, SP	20
F. Fitzsimmons, SP	18
S. Hogan, C	18
F. Leach, OF	15
J. Vergez, 3B	14
C. Fullis, OF	11
E. Allen, OF	10
F. Lindstrom, OF	10
C. Mitchell, SP	8
J. Mooney, SP	7
H. Critz, 2B	6
J. Berly, RP	5
B. O'Farrell, C	5
T. Chaplin, RP	3
B. Hunnefield, 2B	3
B. Morrell, RP	3
R. Parmelee, RP	3
S. Leslie, 1B	2
E. Marshall, 2B	2

Philadelphia (66-88)	WS
Hitting	**88.9**
Fielding	**35.9**
Pitching	**73.3**
C. Klein, OF	25
R. Benge, SP	21
B. Arlett, OF	16
P. Collins, SP	16
S. Davis, C	16
J. Elliott, SP	16
D. Hurst, 1B	15
C. Dudley, SP	12
P. Whitney, 3B	12
D. Bartell, SS	11
L. Mallon, 2B	8
G. Brickell, OF	7
B. Friberg, 2B	6
H. McCurdy, C	5
F. Watt, RP	5
S. Blake, SP	2
F. Koster, OF	1
H. Lee, OF	1
T. Rensa, C	1
B. Stevens, SS	1
D. Taitt, OF	1

Pittsburgh (75-79)	WS
Hitting	**95.5**
Fielding	**44.4**
Pitching	**85.1**
P. Waner, OF	26
L. Waner, OF	24

H. Meine, SP	22
P. Traynor, 3B	20
L. French, SP	19
G. Grantham, 1B	19
R. Kremer, SP	15
G. Spencer, RP	13
E. Phillips, C	10
E. Brame, SP	9
T. Thevenow, SS	8
T. Piet, 2B	6
A. Comorosky, OF	5
E. Grace, C	4
B. Harris, SP	4
G. Suhr, 1B	4
H. Grosklos, 2B	3
W. Jensen, OF	3
B. Sankey, SS	3
F. Bennett, OF	2
B. Osborn, RP	2
H. Finney, C	1
J. Mosolf, OF	1
B. Regan, 2B	1
S. Swetonic, RP	1

St. Louis (101-53)	WS
Hitting	**147.2**
Fielding	**49.9**
Pitching	**105.9**
C. Hafey, OF	25
F. Frisch, 2B	21
W. Hallahan, SP	21
S. Adams, 3B	20
C. Gelbert, SS	20
J. Bottomley, 1B	19
P. Derringer, SP	17
S. Johnson, SP	17
G. Watkins, OF	17
P. Martin, OF	16
B. Grimes, SP	15
J. Wilson, C	14
F. Rhem, SP	13
J. Haines, SP	11
R. Collins, 1B	10
J. Lindsey, RP	8
G. Mancuso, C	7
T. Douthit, OF	6
E. Orsatti, OF	6
A. High, 3B	5
A. Stout, RP	5
J. Flowers, SS	4
W. Roettger, OF	4
R. Blades, OF	2

1932 American League

Boston (43-111)	WS
Hitting	**46.1**
Fielding	**28.5**
Pitching	**54.4**
D. Alexander, 1B	14
E. Durham, SP	11
S. Jolley, OF	11
I. Andrews, SP	10
R. Johnson, OF	9
B. Weiland, SP	9
B. Kline, RP	7
T. Oliver, OF	6
U. Pickering, 3B	6
M. Olson, 2B	5
R. Warstler, SS	5
M. McManus, 2B	4
H. Rhyne, SS	4
E. Webb, OF	4
W. Moore, RP	3
G. Rhodes, SP	3
B. Tate, C	3
J. Welch, RP	3
L. Boerner, RP	2
D. MacFayden, SP	2
J. Michaels, RP	2
P. Appleton, RP	1
E. Connolly, C	1
H. Lisenbee, RP	1
A. Spognardi, 2B	1
G. Stumpf, OF	1
C. Watwood, OF	1

Chicago (49-102)	WS
Hitting	**79.7**
Fielding	**24.9**
Pitching	**42.4**
R. Kress, OF	15
T. Lyons, SP	14
L. Appling, SS	12
C. Berry, C	8
B. Fothergill, OF	8
S. Jones, SP	8
B. Seeds, OF	8
C. Selph, 3B	8
L. Blue, 1B	7
L. Funk, OF	7
F. Grube, C	7
J. Hayes, 2B	7
B. Sullivan, 1B	7
R. Faber, RP	6
M. Gaston, SP	6
P. Gregory, RP	4
C. English, 3B	2
E. Swanson, OF	2
B. Chamberlain, RP	1
B. Cissell, SS	1
P. Daglia, RP	1
A. Evans, RP	1
C. Fieber, RP	1
B. Hadley, SP	1
J. Hodapp, OF	1
S. Jolley, OF	1
C. Kimsey, RP	1
F. Kowalik, SP-RP-3B	1
C. Watwood, OF	1

Cleveland (87-65)	WS
Hitting	**108.5**
Fielding	**46.1**
Pitching	**106.3**
E. Averill, OF	30
W. Ferrell, SP	26
J. Vosmik, OF	24
C. Brown, SP	21
M. Harder, SP	21
W. Kamm, 3B	21
D. Porter, OF	18
B. Cissell, 2B	15
E. Morgan, 1B	15
J. Burnett, SS	12
W. Hudlin, SP	12
O. Hildebrand, SP	10
S. Connally, RP	9
L. Sewell, C	8
G. Myatt, C	7
J. Russell, SP	7
E. Montague, SS	2
R. Winegarner, RP	2
F. Pytlak, C	1

Detroit (76-75)	WS
Hitting	**105.1**
Fielding	**43.3**
Pitching	**79.6**
C. Gehringer, 2B	25
J. Stone, OF	22
B. Rogell, SS	17
G. Walker, OF	17
T. Bridges, SP	16
C. Hogsett, RP	14
V. Sorrell, SP	14
E. Whitehill, SP	14
H. Davis, 1B	12
R. Hayworth, C	12
E. Webb, OF	10
H. Schuble, 3B	9
G. Uhle, RP	9
W. Wyatt, SP	8
B. Rhiel, 3B	6
R. Johnson, OF	4
B. Marrow, RP	3
M. Ruel, C	3
J. White, OF	3
G. Desautels, C	2
I. Goldstein, RP	2
N. Richardson, 3B	2
D. Alexander, 1B	1
F. Doljack, OF	1
A. Herring, RP	1
B. Lawrence, OF	1

New York (107-47)	WS
Hitting	**185.4**
Fielding	**41.8**
Pitching	**93.9**
L. Gehrig, 1B	38
B. Ruth, OF	36
T. Lazzeri, 2B	27
R. Ruffing, SP	26
E. Combs, OF	25
B. Chapman, OF	22
B. Dickey, C	18
L. Gomez, SP	17
J. Sewell, 3B	17
J. Allen, SP	15
F. Crosetti, SS	13
G. Pipgras, SP	13
L. Lary, SS	10
S. Byrd, OF	8
D. MacFayden, SP	6
H. Pennock, SP	6
W. Moore, RP	4
I. Andrews, RP	3
J. Brown, RP	3
M. Hoag, OF	3
A. Jorgens, C	3
E. Phillips, C	2
E. Wells, RP	2
C. Devens, SP	1
D. Farrell, 2B	1
H. Johnson, SP	1
J. Saltzgaver, 2B	1

Philadelphia (94-60)	WS
Hitting	**141.9**
Fielding	**46.7**
Pitching	**93.4**
J. Foxx, 1B	40
L. Grove, SP	33
M. Cochrane, C	30
A. Simmons, OF	24
M. Haas, OF	17
E. McNair, SS	17
M. Bishop, 2B	15
G. Earnshaw, SP	15
R. Walberg, SP	15
J. Dykes, 3B	14
D. Cramer, OF	13
T. Freitas, SP	12
R. Mahaffey, SP	10
B. Miller, OF	8
D. Williams, 2B	5
L. Krausse, RP	4
E. Rommel, RP	3
S. Cain, SP	2
E. Coleman, OF	2
J. Heving, C	2
E. Madjeski, C	1

St. Louis (63-91)	WS
Hitting	**81.7**
Fielding	**35.5**
Pitching	**71.8**
G. Goslin, OF	19
R. Ferrell, C	17
L. Stewart, SP	17
J. Burns, 1B	15
F. Schulte, OF	15
G. Blaeholder, SP	14
B. Campbell, OF	13
S. Gray, RP	13
B. Hadley, SP	11
J. Levey, SS	10
A. Scharein, 3B	8
C. Kimsey, RP	7
S. Melillo, 2B	7
D. Coffman, SP	6
C. Fischer, RP	4
B. Bengough, C	3
D. Garms, OF	3
L. Storti, 3B	3
E. Grimes, 3B	1
W. Hebert, RP	1
T. Jenkins, OF	1
R. Kress, 3B	1

Washington (93-61)	WS
Hitting	**131.5**
Fielding	**49.9**
Pitching	**97.7**
J. Cronin, SS	31
G. Crowder, SP	30
H. Manush, OF	28
B. Myer, 2B	20
M. Weaver, SP	19
S. West, OF	19
O. Bluege, 3B	18
F. Marberry, RP	16
C. Reynolds, OF	13
L. Brown, SP	12
S. Rice, OF	11
J. Kuhel, 1B	10
T. Thomas, SP	10
D. Harris, OF	7
J. Judge, 1B	7
R. Spencer, C	6
M. Berg, C	4
B. Burke, RP	3
C. Fischer, SP	3
J. Kerr, 2B	3
B. McAfee, SP	3
D. Coffman, RP	2
W. Kingdon, 3B	2
H. Maple, C	1
B. Thomas, RP	1

1932 National League

Boston (77-77)	WS
Hitting	**104.2**
Fielding	**42.4**
Pitching	**84.4**
W. Berger, OF	26
H. Betts, SP	18
B. Urbanski, SS	17
T. Zachary, SP	17
R. Worthington, OF	16
B. Brown, SP	15
B. Cantwell, RP	14
E. Brandt, SP	13
W. Schulmerich, OF	12
R. Maranville, 2B	11
R. Moore, OF	10
P. Hargrave, C	9
A. Spohrer, C	9
B. Jordan, 1B	7
F. Knothe, 3B	7
F. Frankhouse, RP	5
D. Holland, OF	5
A. Shires, 1B	5
F. Leach, OF	4
B. Cunningham, RP	3
H. Ford, 2B	3
B. Akers, 3B	2
E. Clark, OF	1
J. Schulte, C	1
B. Walters, 3B	1

Brooklyn (81-73)	WS
Hitting	**138.0**
Fielding	**33.6**
Pitching	**71.4**
L. O'Doul, OF	33
H. Wilson, OF	21
W. Clark, SP	20

T. Cuccinello, 2B	20
J. Stripp, 3B	19
D. Taylor, OF	18
J. Frederick, OF	15
A. Lopez, C	12
G. Wright, SS	12
V. Mungo, SP	11
S. Thurston, SP	10
F. Heimach, RP	9
D. Vance, SP	9
J. Quinn, RP	7
J. Shaute, RP	6
B. Clancy, 1B	4
G. Kelly, 1B	4
G. Slade, SS	4
N. Finn, 3B	2
V. Picinich, C	2
M. Rosenfeld, OF	2
C. Sukeforth, C	2
C. Moore, RP	1

Chicago (90-64)	WS
Hitting	**117.4**
Fielding	**48.9**
Pitching	**103.8**
L. Warneke, SP	31
B. Herman, 2B	23
R. Stephenson, OF	23
G. Bush, SP	19
G. Hartnett, C	19
J. Moore, OF	18
C. Grimm, 1B	17
W. English, 3B	16
P. Malone, SP	16
C. Root, SP	16
K. Cuyler, OF	15
B. Jurges, SS	12
B. Tinning, RP	8
M. Koenig, SS	6
B. Smith, RP	6
B. Grimes, SP	4
S. Hack, 3B	4
R. Hemsley, C	4
M. Gudat, OF	3
V. Barton, OF	2
J. May, RP	2
L. Richbourg, OF	2
F. Demaree, OF	1
R. Hornsby, OF	1
Z. Taylor, C	1
C. Yerkes, RP	1

Cincinnati (60-94)	WS
Hitting	**70.2**
Fielding	**37.2**
Pitching	**72.7**
B. Herman, OF	24
R. Lucas, SP	23
S. Johnson, SP	16
E. Lombardi, C	14
G. Grantham, 2B	13
E. Crabtree, OF	9
C. Hafey, OF	9
H. Hendrick, 1B	9
E. Rixey, RP	9
R. Kolp, SP	8
O. Carroll, SP	7
W. Roettger, OF	7
L. Benton, SP	6
L. Durocher, SS	6
T. Douthit, OF	4
B. Frey, SP	4
W. Gilbert, 3B	4
J. Morrissey, SS	3
M. Heath, 1B	1
A. High, 3B	1
C. Manion, C	1
J. Ogden, RP	1
B. Wysong, RP	1

New York (72-82)	WS
Hitting	**118.0**
Fielding	**31.3**
Pitching	**66.7**
M. Ott, OF	33
B. Terry, 1B	32
C. Hubbell, SP	25
H. Critz, 2B	15
S. Hogan, C	15
F. Lindstrom, OF	13
F. Fitzsimmons, SP	9
J. Vergez, 3B	9
J. Moore, OF	8
H. Bell, RP	7
D. Luque, RP	6
C. Fullis, OF	5
W. Hoyt, SP	5
T. Jackson, SS	5
B. Walker, SP	5
H. Schumacher, RP	4
L. Koenecke, OF	3
G. English, 3B	2
S. Gibson, RP	2
S. Leslie, 1B	2
E. Marshall, SS	2
J. Mooney, SP	2
E. Moore, SS	2
B. O'Farrell, C	2
F. Healy, C	1
C. Mitchell, RP	1
R. Parmelee, RP	1

Philadelphia (78-76)	WS
Hitting	**117.1**
Fielding	**38.9**
Pitching	**78.0**
C. Klein, OF	31
D. Hurst, 1B	23
D. Bartell, SS	21
K. Davis, OF	17
S. Davis, C	17
H. Lee, OF	17
P. Whitney, 3B	17
R. Benge, SP	15
E. Holley, SP	14
S. Hansen, SP	13
F. Rhem, SP	13
P. Collins, RP	9
J. Elliott, SP	5
A. Liska, RP	4
L. Mallon, 2B	4
G. Brickell, OF	2
B. Friberg, 2B	2
R. Grabowski, RP	2
H. McCurdy, C	2
B. Adams, RP	1
S. Bolen, RP	1
R. Bressler, OF	1
C. Dudley, RP	1
H. Elliott, RP	1
C. Heathcote, 1B	1

Pittsburgh (86-68)	WS
Hitting	**126.9**
Fielding	**45.3**
Pitching	**85.8**
P. Waner, OF	32
L. Waner, OF	23
L. French, SP	22
P. Traynor, 3B	21
A. Vaughan, SS	21
T. Piet, 2B	17
B. Swift, SP	16
G. Suhr, 1B	15
S. Swetonic, SP	15
E. Grace, C	14
A. Comorosky, OF	11
B. Harris, RP	11
H. Meine, SP	9
L. Chagnon, RP	8
D. Barbee, OF	7
T. Padden, C	4
B. Brubaker, 3B	2
G. Dugas, OF	2
R. Kremer, SP	2
H. Smith, SP-RP	2
T. Thevenow, SS	2
H. Finney, C	1
G. Spencer, RP	1

St. Louis (72-82)	WS
Hitting	**93.7**
Fielding	**41.0**
Pitching	**81.4**
D. Dean, SP	24
G. Watkins, OF	16
R. Collins, 1B	15
W. Hallahan, SP	15
F. Frisch, 2B	14
C. Gelbert, SS	14
E. Orsatti, OF	12
T. Carleton, SP-RP	11
P. Derringer, SP	11
G. Mancuso, C	11
J. Bottomley, 1B	9
J. Reese, 2B	7
J. Flowers, 3B	6
P. Martin, OF	6
J. Wilson, C	6
F. Rhem, SP	5
R. Blades, OF	4
S. Johnson, SP	4
J. Medwick, OF	4
S. Adams, 3B	3
J. Haines, SP-RP	3
J. Lindsey, RP	3
G. Puccinelli, OF	3
A. Stout, RP	3
R. Starr, SP	2
E. Delker, 2B	1
H. Hendrick, 3B	1
R. Pepper, OF	1
B. Sherdel, RP	1
C. Wilson, SS	1

1933 American League

Boston (63-86)	WS
Hitting	**86.7**
Fielding	**34.6**
Pitching	**67.7**
R. Johnson, OF	16
D. Cooke, OF	15
R. Ferrell, C	15
G. Rhodes, SP	14
J. Hodapp, 2B	12
B. Weiland, SP	12
M. McManus, 3B	11
L. Brown, SP	10
H. Johnson, SP	10
S. Jolley, OF	10
G. Pipgras, SP	8
B. Werber, SS	8
B. Kline, RP	7
D. Alexander, 1B	6
J. Welch, RP	5
I. Andrews, SP-RP	4
T. Oliver, OF	4
B. Walters, 3B	4
R. Warstler, SS	4
J. Judge, 1B	3
B. Seeds, 1B	3
M. Almada, OF	2
G. Stumpf, OF	2
B. Fothergill, OF	1
B. Friberg, 2B	1
J. Gooch, C	1
M. Shea, C	1

Chicago (67-83)	WS
Hitting	**93.6**
Fielding	**36.0**
Pitching	**71.4**
L. Appling, SS	25
A. Simmons, OF	25
E. Swanson, OF	18
J. Dykes, 3B	15
M. Haas, OF	14
J. Hayes, 2B	13
J. Heving, RP	13
S. Jones, SP	13
T. Lyons, SP	12
E. Durham, SP	8
R. Faber, RP	7
R. Kress, 1B	7
M. Gaston, SP	6
W. Wyatt, RP	4
C. Berry, C	3
F. Grube, C	3
E. Webb, OF	3
P. Gregory, SP	2
C. Kimsey, RP	2
J. Miller, SP	2
L. Tietje, SP	2
M. Bocek, OF	1
C. English, 2B	1
L. Fonseca, 1B	1
H. Rhyne, 2B	1

Cleveland (75-76)	WS
Hitting	**74.9**
Fielding	**48.5**
Pitching	**101.6**
E. Averill, OF	26
M. Harder, SP	24
W. Ferrell, SP	18
O. Hildebrand, SP	17
M. Pearson, SP	16
C. Brown, SP	15
W. Kamm, 3B	13
J. Vosmik, OF	12
O. Hale, 2B	11
F. Pytlak, C	11
D. Porter, OF	10
W. Hudlin, SP-RP	8
H. Boss, 1B	6
J. Burnett, SS	6
B. Cissell, 2B	6
S. Connally, RP	5
R. Spencer, C	5
B. Knickerbocker, SS	3
B. Bean, RP	2
M. Galatzer, OF	2
T. Lee, SP	2
E. Morgan, 1B	2
G. Myatt, C	2
J. Oulliber, OF	1
M. Powers, OF	1
H. Trosky, 1B	1

Detroit (75-79)	WS
Hitting	**88.4**
Fielding	**48.7**
Pitching	**87.9**
C. Gehringer, 2B	28
B. Rogell, SS	25
T. Bridges, SP	20
F. Marberry, SP	20
J. Stone, OF	16
V. Sorrell, SP	15
P. Fox, OF	14
H. Greenberg, 1B	14
C. Fischer, SP	13
G. Walker, OF	10
M. Owen, 3B	9
S. Rowe, SP	9
R. Hayworth, C	8
C. Hogsett, RP	5
J. White, OF	5
A. Herring, RP	3
E. Auker, RP	2
F. Doljack, OF	2
H. Davis, 1B	1
G. Desautels, C	1
L. Hamlin, SP	1
J. Pasek, C	1
F. Reiber, C	1
H. Schuble, 3B	1
W. Wyatt, RP	1

New York (91-59)	WS
Hitting	**178.9**
Fielding	**28.8**
Pitching	**65.3**
L. Gehrig, 1B	36
B. Ruth, OF	29
B. Dickey, C	25
T. Lazzeri, 2B	24
B. Chapman, OF	21
E. Combs, OF	16
L. Gomez, SP	16
J. Sewell, 3B	16
F. Crosetti, SS	15
R. Ruffing, SP	15
D. Walker, OF	11
J. Allen, SP	10
R. Van Atta, SP	10
D. Brennan, SP	4
L. Lary, 3B	4
S. Byrd, OF	3
G. Uhle, SP-RP	3
J. Brown, RP	2
C. Devens, SP	2
D. Farrell, SS	2
A. Jorgens, C	2
H. Pennock, RP	2
G. Pipgras, SP	2
D. MacFayden, RP	1
W. Moore, RP	1
T. Rensa, C	1

Philadelphia (79-72)	WS
Hitting	**153.3**
Fielding	**25.8**
Pitching	**57.9**
J. Foxx, 1B	41
M. Cochrane, C	26
L. Grove, SP	23
M. Higgins, 3B	23
B. Johnson, OF	21
M. Bishop, 2B	17
D. Cramer, OF	14
D. Williams, SS	13
S. Cain, SP	11
E. Coleman, OF	8
R. Mahaffey, SP	7
R. Walberg, SP-RP	7
E. McNair, SS	6
J. Marcum, SP	4
L. Finney, OF	3
B. Miller, OF	3
D. Barrett, RP	2
E. Madjeski, C	2
J. Peterson, RP	2
E. Cihocki, SS	1
B. Dietrich, RP	1
G. Earnshaw, SP	1
T. McKeithan, RP	1

St. Louis (55-96)	WS
Hitting	**55.6**
Fielding	**37.8**
Pitching	**71.6**
B. Hadley, SP	23
G. Blaeholder, SP	14
S. West, OF	14
B. Campbell, OF	13
E. Wells, SP	12
S. Melillo, 2B	11
J. Burns, 1B	10
S. Gray, RP	10
C. Reynolds, OF	10
M. Shea, C	8
D. Garms, OF	5
J. Levey, SS	5
A. Scharein, 3B	5
T. Gullic, OF	4
W. Hebert, RP	4
R. Stiles, RP	4
J. Knott, RP	3
D. Coffman, SP	2
R. Ferrell, C	2
R. Hemsley, C	2
M. Ruel, C	2
L. Storti, 2B	2

Washington (99-53)	WS
Hitting	**149.2**
Fielding	**49.5**
Pitching	**98.3**
J. Cronin, SS	34
H. Manush, OF	27
J. Kuhel, 1B	26
B. Myer, 2B	23
E. Whitehill, SP	23
G. Crowder, SP	21
F. Schulte, OF	21
G. Goslin, OF	20
L. Sewell, C	16
J. Russell, RP	15
L. Stewart, SP	14
O. Bluege, 3B	12
M. Weaver, SP	12
D. Harris, OF	6
B. Burke, RP	5
T. Thomas, RP	5
B. Boken, 2B	4
C. Bolton, C	3
S. Rice, OF	3
A. McColl, RP	2
M. Berg, C	1
E. Linke, SP	1
B. McAfee, RP	1
R. Prim, SP-RP	1
C. Travis, 3B	1

1933 National League

Boston (83-71)	WS
Hitting	**101.2**
Fielding	**50.2**
Pitching	**97.6**
W. Berger, OF	36
E. Brandt, SP	29
R. Moore, OF	22
B. Cantwell, SP	21
H. Betts, SP	19
B. Jordan, 1B	19
F. Frankhouse, SP	16
B. Urbanski, SS	15
P. Whitney, 3B	12
S. Hogan, C	9
H. Lee, OF	6
R. Maranville, 2B	6
L. Mangum, RP	5
A. Spohrer, C	5
F. Knothe, 3B	4
J. Mowry, OF	4
B. Smith, RP	4
T. Zachary, SP	4
D. Gyselman, 3B	3
W. Schulmerich, OF	3
E. Clark, OF	1
E. Fallenstein, RP	1
H. Ford, SS	1
P. Hargrave, C	1
D. Holland, OF	1
S. Seibold, RP	1
T. Thompson, OF	1

Brooklyn (65-88)	WS
Hitting	**111.4**
Fielding	**26.5**
Pitching	**57.1**
J. Frederick, OF	19
V. Mungo, SP	17
A. Lopez, C	16
D. Taylor, OF	16
J. Stripp, 3B	14
T. Cuccinello, 2B	12
H. Wilson, OF	12
B. Beck, SP	10
R. Benge, SP	10
B. Boyle, OF	9
S. Leslie, 1B	9
O. Carroll, SP	8
C. Outen, C	6
J. Flowers, SS	5
L. Frey, SS	5
J. Jordan, SS	4
L. O'Doul, OF	4
J. Shaute, RP	4
J. Hutcheson, OF	3
S. Thurston, RP	3
G. Wright, SS	3
D. Leonard, RP	2
D. Bissonette, 1B	1
W. Clark, SP	1
R. Ryan, RP	1
C. Sukeforth, C	1

Chicago (86-68)	WS
Hitting	**127.0**
Fielding	**44.2**
Pitching	**86.8**
L. Warneke, SP	29
Ba. Herman, OF	23
G. Hartnett, C	21
G. Bush, SP	18
Bi. Herman, 2B	18
B. Jurges, SS	18
C. Root, SP	17
R. Stephenson, OF	16
F. Demaree, OF	14
W. English, 3B	14
K. Cuyler, OF	11
B. Tinning, SP	11
H. Hendrick, 1B	8
M. Koenig, 3B	8
C. Grimm, 1B	5
S. Hack, 3B	5
P. Malone, SP	5
L. Nelson, RP	5
G. Campbell, C	3
B. Grimes, RP	3
J. Mosolf, OF	3
D. Camilli, 1B	1
T. Douthit, OF	1
R. Henshaw, RP	1

Cincinnati (58-94)	WS
Hitting	**72.4**
Fielding	**33.5**
Pitching	**68.1**
C. Hafey, OF	23
J. Bottomley, 1B	15
R. Lucas, SP	15
S. Adams, 3B	14
P. Derringer, SP	11
J. Moore, OF	11
H. Rice, OF	11
S. Johnson, SP	9
L. Benton, SP	8
R. Kolp, RP	8
E. Lombardi, C	8
B. Frey, RP	7
G. Grantham, 2B	6
E. Rixey, SP	6
B. Smith, RP	6
J. Morrissey, 2B	4
O. Bluege, SS	3
A. Stout, RP	3
L. Durocher, SS	1
R. Hemsley, C	1
A. High, 3B	1
C. Manion, C	1
T. Robello, 2B	1
W. Roettger, OF	1

New York (91-61)	WS
Hitting	**122.2**
Fielding	**47.7**
Pitching	**103.1**
C. Hubbell, SP	33
M. Ott, OF	31
H. Schumacher, SP	23
B. Terry, 1B	21
J. Moore, OF	17
J. Vergez, 3B	17
H. Critz, 2B	16
G. Mancuso, C	16
F. Fitzsimmons, SP	15
K. Davis, OF	13
L. O'Doul, OF	13
R. Parmelee, SP	12
H. Bell, RP	10
S. Leslie, 1B	8
D. Luque, RP	8
B. Ryan, SS	8
B. James, 2B	3
H. Peel, OF	3
T. Jackson, 3B-SS	2
B. Shores, RP	2
W. Clark, RP	1
P. Richards, C	1

Philadelphia (60-92)	WS
Hitting	**79.1**
Fielding	**35.6**
Pitching	**65.3**
C. Klein, OF	30
S. Davis, C	18
C. Fullis, OF	15
E. Holley, SP	15
D. Bartell, SS	13
W. Schulmerich, OF	12
C. Moore, SP-RP	11
P. Collins, RP	9
J. Elliott, SP	9
D. Hurst, 1B	9
S. Hansen, SP	6
R. Grabowski, SP-RP	5
F. Pearce, RP	5
H. Lee, OF	4
A. Liska, RP	3
J. Warner, 2B	3
J. Berly, RP	2
F. Knothe, 3B	2
H. McCurdy, C	2
J. McLeod, 3B	2
N. Finn, 2B	1
M. Haslin, 2B	1
C. Pickrel, RP	1
A. Todd, C	1
P. Whitney, 3B	1

Pittsburgh (87-67)	WS
Hitting	**141.3**
Fielding	**39.7**
Pitching	**80.0**
A. Vaughan, SS	34
P. Waner, OF	28
F. Lindstrom, OF	23
L. French, SP	21
G. Suhr, 1B	20
P. Traynor, 3B	20
T. Piet, 2B	15
B. Swift, SP	13
E. Grace, C	12
L. Waner, OF	10
H. Meine, SP	9
W. Hoyt, RP	8
H. Smith, SP	8
S. Swetonic, SP	8
L. Chagnon, RP	5
W. Jensen, OF	5
T. Thevenow, 2B	5
R. Birkofer, SP	4
B. Harris, RP	4
A. Comorosky, OF	2
H. Finney, C	2
T. Padden, C	2
V. Picinich, C	2
P. Young, 2B-SS	1

St. Louis (82-71)	WS
Hitting	**123.0**
Fielding	**40.9**
Pitching	**82.1**
P. Martin, 3B	29
J. Medwick, OF	24
D. Dean, SP	22

F. Frisch, 2B	22
R. Collins, 1B	19
T. Carleton, SP	18
G. Watkins, OF	15
E. Orsatti, OF	14
W. Hallahan, SP	13
L. Durocher, SS	11
J. Haines, RP	9
B. Walker, SP	8
J. Wilson, C	8
D. Vance, RP	6
E. Allen, OF	4
P. Crawford, 1B	4
R. Hornsby, 2B	4
S. Johnson, RP	3
J. Mooney, RP	3
G. Moore, OF	3
B. O'Farrell, C	3
B. Lewis, C	2
E. Crabtree, OF	1
G. Slade, SS	1

1934 American League

Boston (76-76)	WS
Hitting	**101.2**
Fielding	**40.3**
Pitching	**86.5**
B. Werber, 3B	26
R. Johnson, OF	19
R. Ferrell, C	18
W. Ferrell, SP	18
F. Ostermueller, SP	17
C. Reynolds, OF	13
J. Welch, SP	13
G. Rhodes, SP	12
E. Morgan, 1B	11
M. Bishop, 2B	10
M. Solters, OF	10
L. Lary, SS	9
B. Cissell, 2B	7
R. Walberg, RP	7
D. Porter, OF	6
D. Cooke, OF	5
H. Pennock, RP	5
G. Hockette, SP	4
H. Johnson, RP	4
J. Mulligan, RP	3
L. Grove, SP	2
S. Merena, SP	2
B. Walters, 3B	2
M. Almada, OF	1
G. Hinkle, C	1
J. Judge, 1B	1
L. Legett, C	1
B. Weiland, SP	1

Chicago (53-99)	WS
Hitting	**79.4**
Fielding	**27.3**
Pitching	**52.3**
A. Simmons, OF	23
Z. Bonura, 1B	20
G. Earnshaw, SP	15
L. Appling, SS	14
J. Dykes, 3B	11
T. Lyons, SP	10
E. Swanson, OF	10
S. Jones, SP	9
L. Tietje, SP	8
M. Haas, OF	7
P. Gallivan, RP	4
M. Gaston, SP	4
M. Hopkins, 3B	4
E. Madjeski, C	3
J. Conlan, OF	2
J. Hayes, 2B	2
V. Kennedy, SP	2
M. Shea, C	2
F. Uhalt, OF	2
B. Boken, 2B	1
F. Bordagaray, OF	1
G. Caithamer, C	1
J. Chamberlain, SS	1
H. Kinzy, RP	1
M. Mauldin, 3B	1
M. Ruel, C	1

Cleveland (85-69)	WS
Hitting	**123.0**
Fielding	**42.8**
Pitching	**89.2**
E. Averill, OF	33
H. Trosky, 1B	28
M. Harder, SP	27
O. Hale, 2B	20
M. Pearson, SP	17
B. Knickerbocker, SS	16
J. Vosmik, OF	15
W. Hudlin, SP	13
W. Kamm, 3B	13
O. Hildebrand, SP	11
F. Pytlak, C	9
L. Brown, RP	8
S. Rice, OF	7
J. Burnett, 3B	6
B. Bean, RP	4
M. Galatzer, OF	4
G. Myatt, C	4
T. Lee, RP	3
B. Weiland, RP	3
R. Winegarner, RP	3
M. Berg, C	2
D. Holland, OF	2
B. Seeds, OF	2
B. Brenzel, C	1
C. Brown, RP	1
K. Carson, OF	1
E. Moore, 2B	1
D. Porter, OF	1

Detroit (101-53)	WS
Hitting	**165.4**
Fielding	**44.3**
Pitching	**93.2**
C. Gehringer, 2B	37
H. Greenberg, 1B	31
S. Rowe, SP	28
B. Rogell, SS	24
M. Cochrane, C	23
M. Owen, 3B	23
T. Bridges, SP	22
G. Goslin, OF	22
J. White, OF	16
E. Auker, RP	15
P. Fox, OF	13
F. Marberry, SP-RP	10
G. Walker, OF	10
R. Hayworth, C	6
V. Sorrell, SP	6
C. Fischer, SP	5
G. Crowder, SP	4
C. Hogsett, RP	3
F. Doljack, OF	2
L. Hamlin, RP	2
R. Phillips, RP	1

New York (94-60)	WS
Hitting	**141.7**
Fielding	**44.7**
Pitching	**95.6**
L. Gehrig, 1B	41
L. Gomez, SP	31
B. Dickey, C	20
B. Ruth, OF	20
B. Chapman, OF	19
F. Crosetti, SS	18
J. Murphy, SP-RP	18
T. Lazzeri, 2B	17
R. Ruffing, SP	17
E. Combs, OF	10
J. Broaca, SP	9
J. Saltzgaver, 3B	9
J. DeShong, RP	8
R. Rolfe, SS	8
J. Allen, SP	6
G. Selkirk, OF	6
D. Heffner, 2B	5
S. Byrd, OF	4
M. Hoag, OF	4
A. Jorgens, C	4
D. MacFayden, SP-RP	3
C. Devens, SP	2
V. Tamulis, SP	2
G. Uhle, RP	1

Philadelphia (68-82)	WS
Hitting	**103.9**
Fielding	**33.8**
Pitching	**66.3**
J. Foxx, 1B	32
B. Johnson, OF	22
M. Higgins, 3B	20
D. Cramer, OF	17
J. Marcum, SP	15
E. McNair, SS	14
S. Cain, SP	12
B. Dietrich, SP	12
J. Cascarella, SP	10
E. Coleman, OF	9
A. Benton, SP	7
R. Warstler, 2B	6
C. Berry, C	5
R. Mahaffey, RP	5
L. Finney, OF	4
D. Williams, 2B	4
G. Caster, SP	3
F. Hayes, C	2
B. Miller, OF	2
M. Flohr, RP	1
B. Kline, RP	1
H. Matuzak, RP	1

St. Louis (67-85)	WS
Hitting	**69.1**
Fielding	**44.1**
Pitching	**87.9**
B. Newsom, SP	21
S. West, OF	18
G. Blaeholder, SP	16
H. Clift, 3B	15
R. Hemsley, C	15
B. Hadley, SP	14
D. Coffman, SP	11
R. Pepper, OF	11
B. Campbell, OF	10
I. Andrews, RP	9
J. Burns, 1B	9
J. Knott, RP	9
A. Strange, SS	8
O. Bejma, SS	7
S. Melillo, 2B	7
D. Garms, OF	5
F. Grube, C	5
E. Wells, RP	4
B. McAfee, RP	2
R. Hornsby, 3B-OF	1
L. Mills, RP	1
G. Puccinelli, OF	1
J. Walkup, RP	1
J. Weaver, SP	1

Washington (66-86)	WS
Hitting	**89.0**
Fielding	**36.6**
Pitching	**72.4**
H. Manush, OF	20
B. Myer, 2B	19
J. Cronin, SS	17
B. Burke, RP	15
J. Stone, OF	14
E. Whitehill, SP	14
F. Schulte, OF	13
J. Russell, RP	11
C. Travis, 3B	10
L. Stewart, SP	9
M. Weaver, SP	8
A. McColl, RP	7
J. Kuhel, 1B	5
T. Thomas, SP	5
O. Bluege, 3B	4
D. Harris, OF	4
P. Susko, 1B	4
C. Bolton, C	3
L. Sewell, C	3
O. Armbrust, SP	2
J. Kerr, 3B	2
R. Kress, 1B	2
E. Linke, SP	2
E. Phillips, C	2
M. Berg, C	1
J. Gill, OF	1
J. Powell, OF	1

1934 National League

Boston (78-73)	WS
Hitting	**131.4**
Fielding	**33.1**
Pitching	**69.5**
W. Berger, OF	33
B. Urbanski, SS	25
H. Lee, OF	20
E. Brandt, SP	19
F. Frankhouse, SP	18
B. Jordan, 1B	18
P. Whitney, 3B	15
R. Moore, OF	14
H. Betts, SP	13
M. McManus, 2B	13
F. Rhem, SP	8
S. Hogan, C	7
B. Cantwell, SP	6
T. Thompson, OF	6
L. Mallon, 2B	5
B. Smith, RP	5
A. Spohrer, C	4
T. Zachary, SP	2
L. Mangum, RP	1
J. Mowry, OF	1
R. Worthington, OF	1

Brooklyn (71-81)	WS
Hitting	**128.7**
Fielding	**27.7**
Pitching	**56.6**
L. Koenecke, OF	23
S. Leslie, 1B	22
V. Mungo, SP	22
B. Boyle, OF	17
L. Frey, SS	16
T. Cuccinello, 2B	15
D. Taylor, OF	15
D. Leonard, RP	12
A. Lopez, C	12
J. Stripp, 3B	11
R. Benge, SP	10
J. Frederick, OF	9
H. Wilson, OF	6
J. Babich, SP	5
T. Zachary, SP	5
J. Jordan, SS	4
L. Munns, RP	3
G. Chapman, OF	2
R. Berres, C	1
J. Bucher, 2B	1
W. Clark, RP	1
H. Smythe, RP	1

Chicago (86-65)	WS
Hitting	**115.8**
Fielding	**47.0**
Pitching	**95.1**
L. Warneke, SP	26
G. Hartnett, C	24
K. Cuyler, OF	23
C. Klein, OF	19
Ba. Herman, OF	17
G. Bush, SP	16

Bi. Herman, 2B	16
B. Lee, SP	16
W. English, SS	15
P. Malone, SP	14
S. Hack, 3B	13
B. Tinning, RP	9
J. Weaver, SP	9
T. Stainback, OF	8
B. Jurges, SS	7
C. Grimm, 1B	6
C. Root, RP	6
A. Galan, 2B	5
D. Camilli, 1B	3
B. O'Farrell, C	2
B. Phelps, C	2
P. Cavarretta, 1B	1
D. Hurst, 1B	1

Cincinnati (52-99)	WS
Hitting	**68.3**
Fielding	**28.6**
Pitching	**59.1**
P. Derringer, SP	17
C. Hafey, OF	17
B. Frey, SP	16
J. Bottomley, 1B	13
G. Slade, SS	12
E. Lombardi, C	11
H. Pool, OF	10
T. Freitas, SP	8
M. Koenig, 3B	8
T. Piet, 3B	6
A. Stout, RP	5
S. Adams, 3B	4
D. Brennan, RP	4
A. Comorosky, OF	4
W. Schulmerich, OF	4
Si Johnson, SP	3
R. Kolp, RP	3
B. O'Farrell, C	3
L. Blakely, OF	1
J. Flowers, PH-PR	1
Sy. Johnson, RP	1
C. Manion, C	1
B. Richmond, RP	1
J. Shaute, RP	1
J. Shevlin, 1B	1
W. Wistert, SP-RP	1

New York (93-60)	WS
Hitting	**128.7**
Fielding	**45.0**
Pitching	**105.2**
M. Ott, OF	38
C. Hubbell, SP	32
B. Terry, 1B	29
J. Moore, OF	26
H. Schumacher, SP	24
F. Fitzsimmons, SP	20
T. Jackson, SS	17
H. Critz, 2B	11
R. Parmelee, SP	11
G. Mancuso, C	10
L. O'Doul, OF	9
G. Watkins, OF	8
J. Bowman, RP	7
J. Vergez, 3B	6
B. Ryan, 3B	5
H. Bell, RP	4
P. Weintraub, OF	4
H. Danning, C	3
D. Luque, RP	3
J. Salveson, RP	3
A. Smith, RP	3
H. Leiber, OF	2
P. Richards, C	2
S. Castleman, RP	1
G. Grantham, 1B	1

Philadelphia (56-93)	WS
Hitting	**68.3**
Fielding	**36.6**
Pitching	**63.1**
C. Davis, SP	24
D. Bartell, SS	18
J. Moore, OF	17
E. Allen, OF	16
P. Collins, SP	14
K. Davis, OF	11
S. Johnson, RP	11
L. Chiozza, 2B	9
D. Camilli, 1B	7
E. Moore, SP	7
A. Todd, C	7
B. Walters, 3B	5
J. Wilson, C	5
S. Hansen, RP	4
M. Haslin, 3B	2
H. Hendrick, OF	2
D. Hurst, 1B	2
I. Jeffries, 2B	2
B. Clancy, 1B	1
G. Darrow, RP	1
C. Fullis, OF	1
C. Moore, RP	1
A. Ruble, OF	1

Pittsburgh (74-76)	WS
Hitting	**109.2**
Fielding	**38.3**
Pitching	**74.5**
A. Vaughan, SS	36
P. Waner, OF	30
G. Suhr, 1B	19
W. Hoyt, RP	18
L. French, SP	15
L. Waner, OF	14
B. Swift, SP	12
R. Birkofer, SP	11
P. Traynor, 3B	11
F. Lindstrom, OF	9
R. Lucas, SP	9
T. Padden, C	7
E. Grace, C	6
T. Thevenow, 2B	6
C. Lavagetto, 2B	5
H. Meine, SP	5
W. Jensen, OF	4
L. Chagnon, RP	3
E. Holley, SP	1
W. Roettger, OF	1

St. Louis (95-58)	WS
Hitting	**125.7**
Fielding	**49.9**
Pitching	**109.5**
D. Dean, SP	37
R. Collins, 1B	32
J. Medwick, OF	24
P. Dean, SP	22
F. Frisch, 2B	19
J. Rothrock, OF	18
B. DeLancey, C	16
T. Carleton, SP	15
S. Davis, C	15
P. Martin, 3B	15
B. Walker, SP	14
L. Durocher, SS	13
E. Orsatti, OF	10
W. Hallahan, SP	8
B. Whitehead, 2B	8
J. Haines, RP	7
D. Vance, RP	4
C. Fullis, OF	3
P. Crawford, 3B	1
K. Davis, OF	1
B. Grimes, RP	1
B. Mills, OF	1
J. Mooney, RP	1

1935 American League

Boston (78-75)	WS
Hitting	**83.2**
Fielding	**46.8**
Pitching	**104.0**
W. Ferrell, SP	35
L. Grove, SP	29
R. Ferrell, C	17
R. Johnson, OF	17
J. Cronin, SS	16
M. Almada, OF	14
B. Werber, 3B	14
F. Ostermueller, SP	11
R. Walberg, RP	11
D. Cooke, OF	10
J. Welch, SP	10
B. Dahlgren, 1B	8
S. Melillo, 2B	8
C. Reynolds, OF	7
J. Wilson, RP	5
G. Rhodes, SP	4
D. Williams, 3B	4
M. Berg, C	3
B. Miller, OF	3
M. Bishop, 2B	2
S. Bowers, RP	2
G. Hockette, RP	2
H. Johnson, RP	1
M. Solters, OF	1

Chicago (74-78)	WS
Hitting	**87.6**
Fielding	**46.2**
Pitching	**88.2**
L. Appling, SS	24
T. Lyons, SP	20
Z. Bonura, 1B	17
J. Whitehead, SP	17
V. Kennedy, SP	16
R. Radcliff, OF	13
A. Simmons, OF	13
L. Sewell, C	12
J. Dykes, 3B	11
L. Tietje, SP	11
S. Jones, SP	10
T. Piet, 2B	9
M. Haas, OF	8
G. Washington, OF	7
J. Hayes, 2B	6
R. Phelps, SP	5
J. Salveson, RP	4
M. Shea, C	4
J. Conlan, OF	3
M. Hopkins, 3B	3
M. Stratton, SP	3
C. Fischer, RP	2
W. Wyatt, RP	2
F. Grube, C	1
M. Kreevich, 3B	1

Cleveland (82-71)	WS
Hitting	**111.6**
Fielding	**40.0**
Pitching	**94.4**
J. Vosmik, OF	28
M. Harder, SP	27
E. Averill, OF	22
W. Hudlin, SP	21
O. Hale, 3B	20
H. Trosky, 1B	15
B. Knickerbocker, SS	14
O. Hildebrand, SP	13
B. Campbell, OF	12
T. Lee, SP	12
L. Brown, RP	11
B. Berger, 2B	10
R. Hughes, 2B	8
M. Pearson, SP	7
M. Galatzer, OF	6
E. Phillips, C	4
F. Pytlak, C	4
R. Winegarner, RP	4
C. Brown, RP	2
L. Stewart, RP	2
A. Wright, OF	2
B. Brenzel, C	1
B. Garbark, C	1

Detroit (93-58)	WS
Hitting	**147.8**
Fielding	**44.4**
Pitching	**86.8**
H. Greenberg, 1B	34
C. Gehringer, 2B	31
M. Cochrane, C	24
B. Rogell, SS	23
S. Rowe, SP	23
P. Fox, OF	21
T. Bridges, SP	19
G. Goslin, OF	17
E. Auker, SP	14
G. Crowder, SP	12
M. Owen, 3B	10
G. Walker, OF	10
J. White, OF	9
R. Hayworth, C	7
C. Hogsett, RP	7
J. Sullivan, RP	7
R. Lawson, SP	5
V. Sorrell, SP-RP	3
F. Clifton, 3B	1
F. Marberry, RP	1
F. Reiber, C	1

New York (89-60)	WS
Hitting	**136.9**
Fielding	**42.6**
Pitching	**87.5**
L. Gehrig, 1B	34
R. Rolfe, 3B	22
R. Ruffing, SP	22
B. Chapman, OF	21
B. Dickey, C	20
G. Selkirk, OF	19
L. Gomez, SP	16
T. Lazzeri, 2B	15
J. Allen, SP	12
J. Broaca, SP	12
F. Crosetti, SS	12
J. Hill, OF	12
V. Tamulis, SP	10
E. Combs, OF	8
J. Murphy, RP	8
J. Brown, RP	6
J. DeShong, RP	6
J. Saltzgaver, 2B	4
A. Jorgens, C	3
M. Hoag, OF	2
J. Glenn, C	1
D. Heffner, 2B	1
B. Ryan, SS	1

Philadelphia (58-91)	WS
Hitting	**90.2**
Fielding	**28.2**
Pitching	**55.6**
J. Foxx, 1B	30
J. Marcum, SP	19
B. Johnson, OF	18
D. Cramer, OF	16
M. Higgins, 3B	15
R. Mahaffey, SP	9
W. Moses, OF	9
W. Wilshere, SP	9
G. Blaeholder, SP	8
E. McNair, SS	7
R. Warstler, 2B	7
B. Dietrich, RP	5
L. Finney, OF	4
D. Lieber, RP	4
P. Richards, C	4
C. Berry, C	3
J. Cascarella, RP	1
C. Doyle, SP	1
V. Eaves, SP	1
S. Newsome, SS	1
B. Patton, C	1
B. Snyder, 2B	1
W. Upchurch, SP	1

St. Louis (65-87)	**WS**
Hitting	**83.7**
Fielding	**36.5**
Pitching	**74.8**
I. Andrews, RP	21
M. Solters, OF	19
S. West, OF	18
H. Clift, 3B	17
R. Hemsley, C	15
J. Knott, RP	14
L. Lary, SS	14
E. Coleman, OF	12
J. Burns, 1B	9
S. Cain, SP	9
R. Van Atta, RP	9
F. Thomas, RP	8
E. Caldwell, SP	4
T. Carey, 2B	4
J. Walkup, RP	4
D. Coffman, RP	3
R. Pepper, OF	3
B. Bell, OF	2
J. Burnett, 3B	2
T. Heath, C	2
B. Newsom, SP	2
A. Strange, SS	2
O. Bejma, 2B	1
M. Mazzera, OF	1

Washington (67-86)	**WS**
Hitting	**129.7**
Fielding	**26.7**
Pitching	**44.6**
B. Myer, 2B	33
C. Travis, 3B	20
J. Powell, OF	17
J. Stone, OF	15
C. Bolton, C	13
E. Whitehill, SP	13
J. Kuhel, 1B	12
H. Manush, OF	11
B. Newsom, SP	10
R. Kress, SS	9
O. Bluege, SS	8
E. Linke, SP	8
B. Hadley, SP	7
L. Pettit, RP	5
S. Holbrook, C	4
F. Schulte, OF	4
B. Estalella, 3B	3
J. Russell, RP	3
B. Bean, RP	1
H. Coppola, RP	1
L. Lary, SS	1
J. Mihalic, SS	1
D. Miles, OF	1
A. Strange, SS	1

1935
National League

Boston (38-115)	**WS**
Hitting	**63.3**
Fielding	**20.3**
Pitching	**30.4**
W. Berger, OF	21
B. Smith, RP	9
P. Whitney, 3B	9
F. Frankhouse, SP	7
B. Jordan, 1B	7
H. Lee, OF	7
L. Mallon, 2B	7
B. Cantwell, SP	6
S. Hogan, C	6
R. Moore, OF	6
T. Thompson, OF	5
E. Brandt, SP	4
D. MacFayden, SP	3
J. Coscarart, 3B	2
J. Mowry, OF	2
R. Mueller, C	2
B. Ruth, OF	2
A. Spohrer, C	2
J. Tyler, OF	2
H. Betts, RP	1
A. Blanche, RP	1
E. Fletcher, 1B	1
E. Moriarty, 2B	1
B. Urbanski, SS	1

Brooklyn (70-83)	**WS**
Hitting	**116.5**
Fielding	**31.7**
Pitching	**61.8**
L. Frey, SS	19
S. Leslie, 1B	18
V. Mungo, SP	15
W. Clark, SP	14
T. Cuccinello, 2B	14
D. Taylor, OF	13
B. Boyle, OF	12
J. Bucher, 2B	12
J. Stripp, 3B	11
L. Koenecke, OF	10
F. Bordagaray, OF	9
A. Lopez, C	9
T. Zachary, SP	9
G. Earnshaw, SP	7
D. Leonard, RP	7
B. Phelps, C	7
J. Jordan, 2B	5
R. Benge, SP	4
B. Reis, OF	4
T. Baker, RP	3
V. Sherlock, 2B	2
D. Vance, RP	2
J. Cooney, OF	1
B. Mills, OF	1
F. Skaff, 3B	1
Z. Taylor, C	1

Chicago (100-54)	**WS**
Hitting	**147.1**
Fielding	**49.9**
Pitching	**103.0**
A. Galan, OF	32
B. Herman, 2B	32
G. Hartnett, C	26
S. Hack, 3B	22
L. Warneke, SP	22
B. Lee, SP	21
L. French, SP	19
C. Klein, OF	17
C. Root, RP	16
P. Cavarretta, 1B	14
B. Jurges, SS	14
F. Demaree, OF	13
R. Henshaw, SP	12
T. Carleton, SP	9
F. Lindstrom, OF	8
K. O'Dea, C	8
K. Cuyler, OF	5
W. English, 3B	3
F. Kowalik, RP	2
C. Bryant, RP	1
H. Casey, RP	1
C. Shoun, RP	1
T. Stainback, OF	1
W. Stephenson, C	1

Cincinnati (68-85)	**WS**
Hitting	**103.8**
Fielding	**34.0**
Pitching	**66.2**
P. Derringer, SP	20
B. Herman, OF	17
E. Lombardi, C	17
I. Goodman, OF	16
L. Riggs, 3B	16
D. Brennan, RP	11
S. Byrd, OF	11
B. Myers, SS	11
A. Kampouris, 2B	9
G. Schott, SP	9
G. Campbell, C	8
A. Hollingsworth, SP	8
L. Herrmann, RP	7
K. Cuyler, OF	6
G. Slade, SS	5
B. Sullivan, 1B	5
J. Bottomley, 1B	4
T. Freitas, SP	4
H. Erickson, C	3
C. Hafey, OF	3
E. Nelson, RP	3
C. Chapman, SS	2
A. Comorosky, OF	2
W. Hilcher, SP-RP	2
B. Frey, RP	1
L. Gamble, OF	1
L. Grissom, SP	1
D. MacFayden, SP	1
L. Scarsella, 1B	1

New York (91-62)	**WS**
Hitting	**135.7**
Fielding	**44.5**
Pitching	**92.8**
M. Ott, OF	35
H. Leiber, OF	28
C. Hubbell, SP	26
J. Moore, OF	24
H. Schumacher, SP	23
B. Terry, 1B	23
D. Bartell, SS	18
T. Jackson, 3B	16
G. Mancuso, C	14
R. Parmelee, SP	12
A. Smith, RP	11
S. Castleman, SP	10
M. Koenig, 2B	7
F. Fitzsimmons, SP	6
H. Danning, C	4
H. Critz, 2B	3
A. Cuccinello, 2B	3
K. Davis, OF	3
L. Chagnon, RP	2
A. Stout, RP	2
P. Weintraub, 1B	2
D. Luque, RP	1

Philadelphia (64-89)	**WS**
Hitting	**72.2**
Fielding	**41.1**
Pitching	**78.7**
C. Davis, SP	21
E. Allen, OF	20
J. Moore, OF	20
S. Johnson, RP	18
D. Camilli, 1B	14
G. Watkins, OF	12
L. Chiozza, 2B	11
B. Walters, SP	11
J. Bowman, SP	10
J. Vergez, 3B	10
O. Jorgens, RP	8
A. Todd, C	7
J. Wilson, C	7
M. Haslin, SS	6
H. Kelleher, SP	4
J. Bivin, RP	3
C. Gomez, SS	3
H. Mulcahy, RP	2
R. Prim, RP	2
B. Ryan, SS	2
P. Pezzullo, RP	1

Pittsburgh (86-67)	**WS**
Hitting	**111.3**
Fielding	**44.8**
Pitching	**101.9**
A. Vaughan, SS	39
C. Blanton, SP	24
P. Waner, OF	22
B. Swift, SP	20
W. Jensen, OF	17
G. Suhr, 1B	16
L. Waner, OF	16
W. Hoyt, RP	13
J. Weaver, SP	12
R. Lucas, SP	11
G. Bush, SP	10
T. Padden, C	10
P. Young, 2B	9
R. Birkofer, RP	8
E. Grace, C	7
C. Lavagetto, 2B	5
T. Thevenow, 3B	5
M. Brown, RP	4
B. Hafey, OF	4
P. Traynor, 3B	4
A. Epps, C	1
B. Herman, OF	1

St. Louis (96-58)	**WS**
Hitting	**134.6**
Fielding	**49.9**
Pitching	**103.6**
J. Medwick, OF	33
D. Dean, SP	31
R. Collins, 1B	28
P. Dean, SP	22
P. Martin, 3B	19
L. Durocher, SS	18
T. Moore, OF	15
S. Davis, C	14
B. DeLancey, C	13
W. Hallahan, SP	13
J. Rothrock, OF	13
F. Frisch, 2B	12
B. Walker, SP	12
E. Heusser, RP	10
J. Haines, RP	9
C. Gelbert, 3B	7
B. Whitehead, 2B	6
P. Collins, RP	4
E. Orsatti, OF	3
L. King, OF	1
B. McGee, SP	1
M. Ryba, SP-RP	1
C. Wilson, 3B	1
J. Winford, SP-RP	1
T. Winsett, OF	1

1936
American League

Boston (74-80)	**WS**
Hitting	**71.9**
Fielding	**48.5**
Pitching	**101.6**
L. Grove, SP	29
W. Ferrell, SP	27
J. Foxx, 1B	26
R. Ferrell, C	16
D. Cramer, OF	15
B. Werber, 3B	13
J. Marcum, SP	11
E. McNair, SS	11
F. Ostermueller, SP	11
D. Cooke, OF	9
J. Wilson, RP	9
J. Cronin, SS	7
J. Kroner, 2B	7
R. Walberg, RP	7
J. Henry, RP	5
H. Manush, OF	4
M. Almada, OF	3
S. Melillo, 2B	3
M. Berg, C	2
J. Russell, RP	2
J. Welch, RP	2
B. Dahlgren, 1B	1
M. Meola, SP-RP	1
B. Miller, OF	1

Chicago (81-70)	**WS**
Hitting	**120.5**
Fielding	**40.7**
Pitching	**81.8**

L. Appling, SS	29
Z. Bonura, 1B	24
V. Kennedy, SP	20
R. Radcliff, OF	17
M. Kreevich, OF	16
J. Whitehead, SP	16
J. Hayes, 2B	14
L. Sewell, C	14
S. Cain, SP	13
T. Piet, 2B	12
L. Rosenthal, OF	11
M. Haas, OF	10
J. Dykes, 3B	9
T. Lyons, SP	9
C. Brown, RP	6
I. Chelini, RP	5
B. Dietrich, SP	5
M. Stratton, SP	5
F. Grube, C	2
R. Phelps, RP	2
D. Walker, OF	2
M. Shea, C	1
W. Wyatt, RP	1

Cleveland (80-74)	WS
Hitting	**105.4**
Fielding	**41.1**
Pitching	**93.5**
E. Averill, OF	27
J. Allen, SP	25
H. Trosky, 1B	21
O. Hale, 3B	20
R. Hughes, 2B	13
B. Knickerbocker, SS	13
M. Harder, SP	12
O. Hildebrand, SP	12
L. Brown, SP	11
B. Sullivan, C	11
J. Vosmik, OF	11
D. Galehouse, RP	10
R. Weatherly, OF	9
G. Blaeholder, RP	8
B. Campbell, OF	7
T. Lee, RP	7
F. Pytlak, C	7
B. Feller, SP	6
J. Gleeson, OF	3
G. George, C	2
B. Berger, 1B-2B	1
M. Galatzer, OF	1
J. Heath, OF	1
G. Uhle, RP	1
R. Winegarner, RP	1

Detroit (83-71)	WS
Hitting	**131.1**
Fielding	**38.0**
Pitching	**79.9**
C. Gehringer, 2B	34
T. Bridges, SP	26
G. Goslin, OF	23
S. Rowe, SP	21
A. Simmons, OF	20
G. Walker, OF	20
M. Owen, 3B	16
B. Rogell, SS	16
E. Auker, SP	13
J. Burns, 1B	12
R. Lawson, RP	7
V. Sorrell, RP	7
M. Cochrane, C	6
P. Fox, OF	6
R. Hayworth, C	5
C. Kimsey, RP	4
H. Greenberg, 1B	3
J. Wade, SP	3
R. Phillips, RP	2
B. Tebbetts, C	2
G. Myatt, C	1
F. Reiber, C	1
J. White, OF	1

New York (102-51)	WS
Hitting	**163.4**
Fielding	**45.7**
Pitching	**96.9**
L. Gehrig, 1B	38
B. Dickey, C	25
J. DiMaggio, OF	25
F. Crosetti, SS	24
R. Rolfe, 3B	24
R. Ruffing, SP	23
G. Selkirk, OF	21
M. Pearson, SP	20
T. Lazzeri, 2B	18
P. Malone, RP	13
J. Broaca, SP	12
L. Gomez, SP	11
B. Hadley, SP	11
J. Murphy, RP	10
J. Powell, OF	9
B. Chapman, OF	4
J. Glenn, C	4
M. Hoag, OF	4
R. Johnson, OF	3
B. Seeds, OF	2
J. Brown, RP	1
D. Heffner, 3B	1
A. Jorgens, C	1
J. Saltzgaver, 3B	1
D. Walker, OF	1

Philadelphia (53-100)	WS
Hitting	**70.6**
Fielding	**31.5**
Pitching	**56.9**
W. Moses, OF	21
H. Kelley, SP	20
B. Johnson, OF	19
M. Higgins, 3B	14
L. Finney, 1B	10
G. Puccinelli, OF	10
H. Fink, SP	9
F. Hayes, C	8
G. Rhodes, SP	8
B. Ross, SP	8
S. Newsome, SS	6
C. Dean, 1B	5
R. Warstler, 2B	5
R. Gumpert, RP	4
B. Dietrich, RP	2
H. Lisenbee, RP	2
A. Niemiec, 2B	2
E. Smith, SP	2
F. Archer, SP	1
J. Peerson, SS	1
R. Peters, SS	1
G. Turbeville, SP-RP	1

St. Louis (57-95)	WS
Hitting	**85.2**
Fielding	**28.7**
Pitching	**57.1**
H. Clift, 3B	23
B. Bell, OF	18
L. Lary, SS	17
I. Andrews, SP	15
C. Hogsett, SP	13
M. Solters, OF	12
S. West, OF	12
J. Bottomley, 1B	11
T. Thomas, SP	10
E. Caldwell, SP	8
R. Hemsley, C	7
T. Carey, 2B	5
J. Knott, RP	4
R. Van Atta, RP	4
O. Bejma, 2B	3
E. Coleman, OF	3
T. Giuliani, C	2
S. Cain, SP	1
H. Kimberlin, RP	1
R. Pepper, OF	1
L. Tietje, SP-RP	1

Washington (82-71)	WS
Hitting	**122.0**
Fielding	**41.5**
Pitching	**82.5**
J. Kuhel, 1B	21
J. Stone, OF	21
B. Chapman, OF	19
B. Newsom, SP	19
P. Appleton, SP	18
B. Lewis, 3B	16
C. Travis, SS	15
J. DeShong, SP	14
R. Kress, SS	12
E. Whitehill, SP	12
J. Cascarella, SP	10
O. Bluege, 2B	9
C. Bolton, C	9
J. Hill, OF	8
W. Millies, C	6
B. Myer, 2B	6
C. Reynolds, OF	6
M. Weaver, RP	6
J. Powell, OF	5
S. Hogan, C	3
F. Sington, OF	3
J. Mihalic, 2B	2
S. Cohen, RP	1
H. Coppola, RP	1
B. Estalella, PH-PR	1
E. Linke, RP	1
F. Marberry, RP	1
J. Russell, RP	1

1936 National League

Boston (71-83)	WS
Hitting	**93.5**
Fielding	**40.9**
Pitching	**78.6**
W. Berger, OF	23
T. Cuccinello, 2B	23
D. MacFayden, SP	22
G. Moore, OF	22
B. Jordan, 1B	16
A. Lopez, C	12
B. Cantwell, RP	11
B. Smith, RP	10
T. Chaplin, SP	9
H. Lee, OF	9
J. Lanning, SP	8
B. Urbanski, SS	8
T. Thompson, OF	7
G. Bush, SP	6
B. Reis, RP	6
R. Weir, SP	6
J. Coscarart, 3B	5
B. Lewis, C	3
R. Warstler, SS	3
M. Haslin, 3B	2
R. Mueller, C	1
P. Whitney, 3B	1

Brooklyn (67-87)	WS
Hitting	**78.0**
Fielding	**40.9**
Pitching	**82.1**
V. Mungo, SP	24
E. Brandt, SP	17
F. Frankhouse, SP	16
B. Hassett, 1B	16
B. Phelps, C	16
L. Frey, SS	13
J. Stripp, 3B	13
F. Bordagaray, OF	11
J. Cooney, OF	11
G. Watkins, OF	9
M. Butcher, RP	8
J. Bucher, 3B	6
W. Clark, RP	6
E. Wilson, OF	6
R. Berres, C	5
G. Jeffcoat, RP	5
T. Baker, RP	3
D. Taylor, OF	3
G. Earnshaw, SP	2
J. Jordan, 2B	2
D. Leonard, RP	2
T. Winsett, OF	2
O. Eckhardt, OF	1
S. Gautreaux, C	1
B. Geraghty, SS	1
F. Lindstrom, OF	1
N. Tremark, OF	1

Chicago (87-67)	WS
Hitting	**111.6**
Fielding	**49.9**
Pitching	**99.6**
B. Herman, 2B	29
F. Demaree, OF	24
L. French, SP	21
B. Lee, SP	20
S. Hack, 3B	19
G. Hartnett, C	18
L. Warneke, SP	17
T. Carleton, SP	16
A. Galan, OF	16
B. Jurges, SS	13
C. Davis, SP	12
K. O'Dea, C	9
E. Allen, OF	8
P. Cavarretta, 1B	7
W. English, SS	7
R. Henshaw, RP	6
C. Root, RP	5
C. Bryant, RP	4
J. Gill, OF	4
C. Klein, OF	4
C. Grimm, 1B	1
T. Stainback, OF	1

Cincinnati (74-80)	WS
Hitting	**121.3**
Fielding	**32.1**
Pitching	**68.6**
K. Cuyler, OF	24
I. Goodman, OF	18
P. Derringer, SP	17
E. Lombardi, C	17
L. Riggs, 3B	15
B. Herman, OF	13
L. Scarsella, 1B	13
G. Schott, SP	13
A. Hollingsworth, SP	11
B. Myers, SS	10
G. Campbell, C	9
H. Walker, OF	9
P. Davis, SP	8
B. Frey, RP	7
A. Kampouris, 2B	7
D. Brennan, RP	5
W. Hallahan, SP	5
L. Stine, RP	4
C. Chapman, OF	3
L. Handley, 2B	3
T. Thevenow, SS	3
S. Byrd, OF	2
D. Moore, SP-RP	2
T. Freitas, RP	1
G. McQuinn, 1B	1
J. Mooty, RP	1
E. Nelson, RP	1

New York (92-62)	WS
Hitting	**124.2**
Fielding	**46.6**
Pitching	**105.2**
C. Hubbell, SP	37
M. Ott, OF	36
D. Bartell, SS	24
J. Moore, OF	23
G. Mancuso, C	20
B. Whitehead, 2B	17
F. Gabler, RP	15
H. Schumacher, SP	15

Player	WS
H. Leiber, OF	12
J. Ripple, OF	12
F. Fitzsimmons, SP	11
A. Smith, SP	11
S. Leslie, 1B	10
H. Gumbert, RP	9
D. Coffman, RP	7
B. Terry, 1B	7
T. Jackson, 3B	3
M. Koenig, SS	2
H. Danning, C	1
K. Davis, OF	1
E. Mayo, 3B	1
J. McCarthy, 1B	1
R. Spencer, C	1

Philadelphia (54-100)	WS
Hitting	**74.5**
Fielding	**28.1**
Pitching	**59.3**
D. Camilli, 1B	22
C. Passeau, RP	15
B. Walters, SP	14
C. Klein, OF	13
L. Chiozza, OF	11
J. Moore, OF	11
P. Whitney, 3B	10
L. Norris, SS	9
J. Bowman, SP	7
S. Johnson, RP	7
O. Jorgens, SP	7
E. Sulik, OF	7
E. Grace, C	4
B. Atwood, C	3
C. Gomez, 2B	3
P. Sivess, RP	3
E. Allen, OF	2
C. Davis, SP	2
H. Mulcahy, SP	2
J. Wilson, C	2
M. Arnovich, OF	1
R. Benge, RP	1
E. Burkart, SP	1
M. Haslin, 2B	1
F. Kowalik, RP	1
C. Sheerin, 2B	1
J. Vergez, 3B	1
G. Watkins, OF	1

Pittsburgh (84-70)	WS
Hitting	**131.1**
Fielding	**39.2**
Pitching	**81.7**
A. Vaughan, SS	35
P. Waner, OF	32
G. Suhr, 1B	25
B. Swift, SP	18
C. Blanton, SP	15
B. Brubaker, 3B	15
W. Jensen, OF	15
R. Lucas, SP	15
L. Waner, OF	14
W. Hoyt, RP	10
J. Weaver, SP	10
M. Brown, RP	9
P. Young, 2B	9
A. Todd, C	7
T. Padden, C	5
R. Birkofer, RP	4
C. Lavagetto, 2B	4
F. Schulte, OF	4
B. Hafey, OF	2
J. Tising, SP	2
E. Browne, OF	1
J. Welch, RP	1

St. Louis (87-67)	WS
Hitting	**145.7**
Fielding	**39.2**
Pitching	**76.1**
J. Medwick, OF	36
D. Dean, SP	31
J. Mize, 1B	26
P. Martin, OF	24
R. Collins, 1B	15
T. Moore, OF	15
L. Durocher, SS	14
S. Davis, C	13
S. Martin, 2B	13
J. Winford, SP	13
R. Parmelee, SP	10
F. Frisch, 2B	7
J. Haines, RP	7
A. Garibaldi, 3B	5
C. Gelbert, 3B	5
D. Gutteridge, 3B	4
E. Heusser, RP	4
S. Johnson, SP	4
P. Dean, SP	3
C. Fullis, OF	3
B. Ogrodowski, C	3
W. Hallahan, SP	1
E. Morgan, OF	1
L. Munns, RP	1
M. Ryba, RP	1
L. Scoffic, OF	1
B. Walker, SP	1

1937 American League

Boston (80-72)	WS
Hitting	**104.3**
Fielding	**42.5**
Pitching	**93.2**
L. Grove, SP	27
J. Cronin, SS	24
J. Foxx, 1B	23
J. Wilson, RP	20
M. Higgins, 3B	16
B. Chapman, OF	15
B. Newsom, SP	15
D. Cramer, OF	14
J. Marcum, SP	14
E. McNair, 2B	13
B. Mills, OF	12
A. McKain, SP-RP	9
G. Desautels, C	8
F. Gaffke, OF	5
F. Ostermueller, RP	4
R. Walberg, RP	4
R. Ferrell, C	3
M. Almada, OF	2
M. Berg, C	2
D. Dallessandro, OF	2
B. Doerr, 2B	2
J. Gonzales, RP	2
W. Ferrell, SP	1
J. Henry, SP	1
J. Peacock, C	1
T. Thomas, RP	1

Chicago (86-68)	WS
Hitting	**106.8**
Fielding	**49.9**
Pitching	**101.4**
L. Appling, SS	28
M. Kreevich, OF	23
Z. Bonura, 1B	21
R. Radcliff, OF	21
D. Walker, OF	20
M. Stratton, SP	19
T. Lee, SP	18
C. Brown, RP	14
T. Lyons, SP	13
L. Sewell, C	13
J. Whitehead, SP	12
V. Kennedy, SP	10
J. Hayes, 2B	8
B. Dietrich, SP	7
T. Piet, 3B	6
B. Berger, 3B	3
T. Rensa, C	3
J. Rigney, RP	3
L. Rosenthal, OF	3
S. Cain, RP	2
M. Connors, 3B	2
B. Cox, SP	2
J. Dykes, 1B	2
M. Shea, C	2
G. Gick, RP	1
M. Haas, 1B	1
H. Steinbacher, OF	1

Cleveland (83-71)	WS
Hitting	**123.2**
Fielding	**36.9**
Pitching	**88.9**
E. Averill, OF	24
H. Trosky, 1B	24
L. Lary, SS	23
M. Solters, OF	21
J. Allen, SP	20
F. Pytlak, C	17
B. Campbell, OF	16
M. Harder, SP	16
O. Hale, 3B	15
B. Feller, SP	13
D. Galehouse, SP	12
W. Hudlin, SP	11
R. Hughes, 3B	9
W. Wyatt, RP	6
J. Heving, RP	5
B. Sullivan, C	5
I. Andrews, RP	4
J. Kroner, 2B	4
E. Whitehill, SP	3
J. Becker, C	1

Detroit (89-65)	WS
Hitting	**135.8**
Fielding	**42.8**
Pitching	**88.3**
H. Greenberg, 1B	33
C. Gehringer, 2B	30
E. Auker, SP	22
G. Walker, OF	22
T. Bridges, SP	19
P. Fox, OF	19
B. Rogell, SS	18
R. York, C	18
R. Lawson, SP	13
M. Owen, 3B	10
B. Poffenberger, SP	10
G. Gill, RP	9
S. Coffman, RP	7
J. Wade, SP	7
J. White, OF	6
M. Cochrane, C	5
C. Laabs, OF	5
G. Goslin, OF	4
R. Hayworth, C	3
C. Bolton, C	2
B. Tebbetts, C	2
G. English, 2B	1
B. Herman, OF	1
P. McLaughlin, RP	1

New York (102-52)	WS
Hitting	**158.0**
Fielding	**44.2**
Pitching	**103.8**
J. DiMaggio, OF	39
L. Gehrig, 1B	36
B. Dickey, C	33
L. Gomez, SP	29
R. Ruffing, SP	24
R. Rolfe, 3B	19
F. Crosetti, SS	16
G. Selkirk, OF	14
T. Lazzeri, 2B	13
M. Pearson, SP	12
T. Henrich, OF	10
M. Hoag, OF	10
J. Murphy, RP	10
S. Chandler, SP	7
B. Hadley, SP	6
J. Powell, OF	6
I. Andrews, RP	4
K. Wicker, SP	4
D. Heffner, 2B	3
F. Makosky, RP	3
P. Malone, RP	3
J. Glenn, C	2
J. Broaca, SP	1
R. Johnson, OF	1
J. Vance, SP	1

Philadelphia (54-97)	WS
Hitting	**76.6**
Fielding	**29.1**
Pitching	**56.3**
W. Moses, OF	20
B. Johnson, OF	19
B. Werber, 3B	14
E. Smith, SP	13
G. Caster, SP	11
S. Newsome, SS	8
E. Brucker, C	7
L. Nelson, RP	7
H. Kelley, SP	6
R. Peters, 2B	6
B. Thomas, SP	6
C. Dean, 1B	5
H. Fink, RP	5
F. Hayes, C	5
J. Hill, OF	5
B. Ross, SP	5
G. Hasson, 1B	3
J. Rothrock, OF	3
G. Turbeville, RP	3
A. Williams, SP-RP	3
B. Cissell, 2B	2
L. Finney, 1B	2
W. Ambler, 2B	1
B. Barna, OF	1
B. Kalfass, RP	1
A. Parker, SS	1

St. Louis (46-108)	WS
Hitting	**69.7**
Fielding	**25.5**
Pitching	**42.8**
H. Clift, 3B	23
B. Bell, OF	16
J. Vosmik, OF	12
S. West, OF	12
J. Knott, SP	11
O. Hildebrand, SP	10
H. Davis, 1B	6
J. Bonetti, SP	5
B. Knickerbocker, SS	5
E. Allen, OF	4
T. Carey, 2B	4
C. Hogsett, SP	4
B. Trotter, RP	4
R. Hemsley, C	3
R. Van Atta, RP	3
B. Huffman, C	2
N. Lipscomb, 2B	2
L. Tietje, SP	2
J. Walkup, SP	2
R. Barkley, 2B	1
J. Bottomley, 1B	1
E. Caldwell, RP	1
T. Giuliani, C	1
T. Heath, C	1
R. Hornsby, 2B	1
H. Kimberlin, SP	1
L. Koupal, SP-RP	1

Washington (73-80)	WS
Hitting	**108.7**
Fielding	**41.2**
Pitching	**69.1**
J. Stone, OF	22
C. Travis, SS	22
B. Lewis, 3B	20
B. Myer, 2B	15
M. Almada, OF	14
J. Kuhel, 1B	14
W. Ferrell, SP	13

Player	WS
J. DeShong, SP	11
A. Simmons, OF	11
M. Weaver, SP	11
P. Appleton, SP	7
R. Ferrell, C	6
B. Phebus, SP	5
F. Sington, OF	5
O. Bluege, SS	4
B. Chapman, OF	4
K. Chase, SP	4
S. Cohen, RP	4
C. Fischer, SP	4
J. Krakauskas, SP	4
E. Linke, RP	4
J. Mihalic, 2B	3
G. Case, OF	2
J. Hill, OF	2
W. Millies, C	2
J. Wasdell, 1B	2
S. Hogan, C	1
B. Jacobs, RP	1
J. Kohlman, SP	1
B. Newsom, SP	1

1937 National League

Boston (79-73)	WS
Hitting	**97.7**
Fielding	**45.8**
Pitching	**93.6**
G. Moore, OF	27
J. Turner, SP	27
T. Cuccinello, 2B	23
L. Fette, SP	23
V. DiMaggio, OF	17
D. MacFayden, SP	17
D. Garms, OF	13
E. Fletcher, 1B	11
R. Johnson, OF	10
R. Warstler, SS	10
G. Bush, SP	9
G. English, 3B	8
A. Lopez, C	7
R. Mueller, C	7
W. Berger, OF	6
J. Lanning, RP	5
I. Hutchinson, RP	4
M. Shoffner, SP	4
B. Reis, OF	3
E. Mayo, 3B	2
B. Smith, RP	2
F. Gabler, RP	1
R. Weir, RP	1

Brooklyn (62-91)	WS
Hitting	**78.0**
Fielding	**33.9**
Pitching	**74.1**
H. Manush, OF	17
C. Lavagetto, 2B	16
V. Mungo, SP	16
B. Phelps, C	15
L. Hamlin, SP	13
G. Brack, OF	11
B. Hassett, 1B	11
W. Hoyt, SP	11
M. Butcher, SP	10
J. Cooney, OF	9
F. Frankhouse, SP	9
W. English, SS	8
T. Winsett, OF	7
J. Bucher, 2B	5
F. Fitzsimmons, SP	5
H. Eisenstat, RP	3
R. Henshaw, RP	3
G. Rosen, OF	3
G. Jeffcoat, RP	2
J. Lindsey, RP	2
R. Spencer, C	2
J. Stripp, 3B	2
E. Wilson, OF	2
L. Brown, SS	1
B. Cantwell, RP	1
B. Haas, OF	1
A. Parks, OF	1

Chicago (93-61)	WS
Hitting	**147.7**
Fielding	**46.0**
Pitching	**85.3**
B. Herman, 2B	29
F. Demaree, OF	26
G. Hartnett, C	25
S. Hack, 3B	23
A. Galan, OF	20
T. Carleton, SP	18
B. Lee, SP	18
B. Jurges, SS	16
C. Root, RP	16
R. Collins, 1B	12
L. French, SP	12
P. Cavarretta, OF	11
K. O'Dea, C	11
C. Bryant, RP	10
J. Marty, OF	9
C. Davis, SP-RP	8
L. Frey, SS	7
R. Parmelee, SP	3
J. Bottarini, C	2
B. Logan, RP	1
C. Shoun, RP	1
T. Stainback, OF	1

Cincinnati (56-98)	WS
Hitting	**83.8**
Fielding	**26.2**
Pitching	**58.1**
I. Goodman, OF	16
L. Grissom, SP	14
A. Kampouris, 2B	14
E. Lombardi, C	12
B. Myers, SS	11
P. Davis, SP	10
P. Derringer, SP	9
A. Hollingsworth, SP	9
L. Riggs, 3B	8
G. Schott, RP	8
C. Hafey, OF	7
K. Cuyler, OF	6
B. Jordan, 1B	6
S. Davis, C	5
H. Walker, OF	5
J. Vander Meer, SP	4
P. Weintraub, OF	4
K. Davis, OF	3
J. Outlaw, 3B	3
L. Scarsella, 1B	3
C. Gelbert, SS	2
T. Kleinhans, RP	2
R. Barrett, RP	1
G. Campbell, C	1
J. Cascarella, RP	1
H. Craft, OF	1
C. English, 3B	1
F. McCormick, 1B	1
E. Miller, SS	1

New York (95-57)	WS
Hitting	**134.3**
Fielding	**45.9**
Pitching	**104.8**
M. Ott, OF	32
D. Bartell, SS	28
C. Melton, SP	25
C. Hubbell, SP	23
J. Moore, OF	21
B. Whitehead, 2B	19
H. Schumacher, SP	15
J. Ripple, OF	14
S. Castleman, SP	12
H. Danning, C	12
H. Gumbert, SP	12
G. Mancuso, C	11
J. McCarthy, 1B	11
W. Berger, OF	10
D. Coffman, RP	8
S. Leslie, 1B	6
H. Leiber, OF	5
L. Chiozza, 3B	4
A. Smith, RP	4
T. Baker, RP	2
K. Davis, OF	2
F. Fitzsimmons, SP	2
B. Lohrman, SP-RP	2
B. Ryan, SS	2
J. Brown, RP	1
M. Haslin, SS	1
P. Weintraub, OF	1

Philadelphia (61-92)	WS
Hitting	**88.8**
Fielding	**32.7**
Pitching	**61.5**
D. Camilli, 1B	25
C. Passeau, SP	18
P. Whitney, 3B	16
H. Martin, OF	15
B. Walters, SP	14
C. Klein, OF	13
M. Arnovich, OF	10
W. LaMaster, SP	10
O. Jorgens, RP	8
J. Moore, OF	8
E. Browne, OF	7
H. Mulcahy, RP	7
L. Norris, 2B	7
S. Johnson, RP	6
G. Scharein, SS	6
B. Atwood, C	5
E. Grace, C	4
D. Young, 2B	3
J. Wilson, C	1

Pittsburgh (86-68)	WS
Hitting	**116.6**
Fielding	**46.7**
Pitching	**94.7**
P. Waner, OF	28
A. Vaughan, SS	25
G. Suhr, 1B	19
L. Waner, OF	19
R. Bauers, SP	17
A. Todd, C	17
C. Blanton, SP	16
E. Brandt, SP	14
B. Brubaker, 3B	12
P. Young, SS	12
L. Handley, 2B	11
W. Jensen, OF	10
B. Swift, RP	10
J. Tobin, RP	10
M. Brown, RP	8
J. Weaver, RP	8
R. Lucas, SP	7
J. Bowman, SP	5
J. Dickshot, OF	4
T. Padden, C	3
K. Heintzelman, SP	1
W. Hoyt, RP	1
B. Schuster, SS	1

St. Louis (81-73)	WS
Hitting	**129.9**
Fielding	**37.7**
Pitching	**75.4**
J. Medwick, OF	40
J. Mize, 1B	34
D. Dean, SP	17
D. Padgett, OF	16
B. Weiland, SP	16
D. Gutteridge, 3B	14
P. Martin, OF	14
S. Johnson, SP	12
L. Warneke, SP	12
J. Brown, 2B	11
T. Moore, OF	10
F. Bordagaray, 3B	8
M. Ryba, RP	8
L. Durocher, SS	6
S. Martin, 2B	5
B. Ogrodowski, C	4
J. Haines, RP	3
M. Owen, C	3
T. Sunkel, RP	3
S. Blake, RP	2
H. Krist, SP	2
N. Andrews, RP	1
H. Bremer, C	1
B. McGee, RP	1

1938 American League

Boston (88-61)	WS
Hitting	**128.0**
Fielding	**42.0**
Pitching	**94.0**
J. Foxx, 1B	34
J. Cronin, SS	30
B. Chapman, OF	19
J. Vosmik, OF	19
D. Cramer, OF	17
L. Grove, SP	17
J. Bagby Jr., SP	15
B. Doerr, 2B	14
M. Higgins, 3B	14
J. Wilson, SP	14
F. Ostermueller, SP	13
G. Desautels, C	12
J. Heving, SP	8
B. Harris, SP	7
J. Marcum, SP	7
A. McKain, RP	7
E. Dickman, RP	5
J. Peacock, C	5
R. Nonnenkamp, OF	3
B. LeFebvre, RP	1
E. McNair, SS	1
D. Midkiff, RP	1
J. Tabor, 3B	1

Chicago (65-83)	WS
Hitting	**79.1**
Fielding	**38.4**
Pitching	**77.5**
T. Lee, SP	19
M. Kreevich, OF	16
M. Stratton, SP	15
T. Lyons, SP	14
R. Radcliff, OF	13
J. Rigney, RP	13
M. Owen, 3B	12
H. Steinbacher, OF	12
G. Walker, OF	12
J. Kuhel, 1B	10
L. Appling, SS	9
J. Whitehead, SP	9
J. Hayes, 2B	7
J. Knott, SP	7
B. Berger, SS	5
T. Rensa, C	4
M. Connors, 1B	3
J. Dykes, 2B	3
L. Sewell, C	3
G. Meyer, 2B	2
L. Rosenthal, OF	2
C. Brown, RP	1
B. Dietrich, SP	1
J. Gerlach, SS	1
N. Schlueter, C	1
M. Tresh, C	1

Cleveland (86-66)	WS
Hitting	**125.8**
Fielding	**44.5**
Pitching	**87.7**

E. Averill, OF	26
H. Trosky, 1B	25
J. Heath, OF	23
B. Feller, SP	22
M. Harder, SP	20
K. Keltner, 3B	18
L. Lary, SS	18
J. Allen, SP	16
B. Campbell, OF	15
O. Hale, 2B	13
F. Pytlak, C	13
D. Galehouse, RP	8
R. Hemsley, C	8
W. Hudlin, SP	6
J. Humphries, RP	6
E. Whitehill, SP	6
J. Kroner, 2B	4
R. Weatherly, OF	4
A. Milnar, RP	3
S. Webb, SS	2
M. Solters, OF	1
B. Zuber, RP	1

Detroit (84-70)	WS
Hitting	**117.1**
Fielding	**43.8**
Pitching	**91.2**
H. Greenberg, 1B	34
C. Gehringer, 2B	27
R. York, C	27
B. Rogell, SS	16
G. Gill, SP	14
D. Walker, OF	14
H. Eisenstat, RP	13
P. Fox, OF	13
V. Kennedy, SP	13
T. Bridges, SP	12
A. Benton, SP	10
E. Auker, SP	9
B. Poffenberger, SP	8
R. Lawson, SP	6
M. Christman, 3B	5
D. Ross, 3B	5
S. Coffman, RP	4
C. Morgan, OF	4
B. Tebbetts, C	4
C. Laabs, OF	3
J. White, OF	3
R. Cullenbine, OF	2
S. Rowe, SP	2
W. Davis, RP	1
T. Piet, 3B	1
J. Rogalski, RP	1
J. Wade, RP	1

New York (99-53)	WS
Hitting	**147.7**
Fielding	**44.3**
Pitching	**105.0**
J. DiMaggio, OF	30
B. Dickey, C	27
L. Gehrig, 1B	25
R. Ruffing, SP	25
F. Crosetti, SS	23
R. Rolfe, 3B	22
L. Gomez, SP	19
J. Gordon, 2B	19
T. Henrich, OF	19
M. Pearson, SP	15
S. Chandler, SP	13
B. Hadley, SP	13
G. Selkirk, OF	11
J. Murphy, RP	9
M. Hoag, OF	5
S. Sundra, RP	5
I. Andrews, RP	4
J. Glenn, C	3
B. Knickerbocker, 2B	3
J. Powell, OF	3
J. Beggs, SP	2
L. Stine, RP	1
J. Vance, RP	1

Philadelphia (53-99)	WS
Hitting	**78.9**
Fielding	**27.1**
Pitching	**52.9**
B. Johnson, OF	23
G. Caster, SP	19
W. Moses, OF	14
B. Werber, 3B	13
B. Thomas, SP	10
S. Chapman, OF	9
L. Finney, 1B	9
F. Hayes, C	9
L. Nelson, SP	8
E. Brucker, C	7
D. Lodigiani, 2B	7
B. Ross, SP	7
W. Ambler, SS	4
E. Smith, RP	4
C. Dean, RP	3
G. Hasson, 1B	2
N. Potter, RP	2
D. Siebert, 1B	2
D. Smith, RP	2
S. Sperry, 2B	2
N. Etten, 1B	1
A. Parker, SS	1
H. Wagner, C	1

St. Louis (55-97)	WS
Hitting	**77.5**
Fielding	**32.5**
Pitching	**55.0**
H. Clift, 3B	25
B. Newsom, SP	21
G. McQuinn, 1B	16
R. Kress, SS	15
L. Mills, SP	11
M. Almada, OF	10
B. Bell, OF	9
O. Hildebrand, SP	9
B. Sullivan, C	8
D. Heffner, 2B	6
B. Mills, OF	6
T. Heath, C	4
E. Cole, RP	3
F. Johnson, RP	3
M. Mazzera, OF	3
R. Van Atta, RP	3
S. West, OF	3
R. Hughes, 2B	2
J. Knott, SP	2
E. Allen, OF	1
J. Bonetti, RP	1
J. Grace, OF	1
S. Gryska, SS	1
H. Kimberlin, SP	1
G. McQuillen, OF	1

Washington (75-76)	WS
Hitting	**123.3**
Fielding	**35.7**
Pitching	**65.9**
B. Myer, 2B	24
B. Lewis, 3B	20
C. Travis, SS	20
D. Leonard, SP	17
Z. Bonura, 1B	16
R. Ferrell, C	16
A. Simmons, OF	16
P. Appleton, RP	10
G. Case, OF	10
J. Krakauskas, RP	10
S. West, OF	10
T. Wright, OF	10
H. Kelley, RP	8
K. Chase, SP	6
W. Ferrell, SP	6
M. Weaver, SP	6
O. Bluege, 2B	4
J. Stone, OF	4
M. Almada, OF	3
C. Hogsett, RP	3
J. DeShong, RP	2
T. Giuliani, C	1
M. Livingston, C	1
R. Monteagudo, SP	1
J. Wasdell, 1B	1

1938
National League

Boston (77-75)	WS
Hitting	**106.1**
Fielding	**42.4**
Pitching	**82.6**
V. DiMaggio, OF	20
E. Fletcher, 1B	20
D. Garms, OF	18
T. Cuccinello, 2B	17
L. Fette, SP	16
D. MacFayden, SP	16
J. Turner, SP	15
I. Hutchinson, RP	12
J. Cooney, OF	11
M. West, OF	11
D. Errickson, RP	9
R. Mueller, C	9
M. Shoffner, SP	9
R. Warstler, SS	9
A. Lopez, C	7
G. Moore, OF	7
J. Stripp, 3B	7
J. Lanning, SP	5
G. English, 3B	4
H. Maggert, OF	4
J. Riddle, C	2
A. Doll, RP	1
J. Hitchcock, SS	1
H. Moran, RP	1

Brooklyn (69-80)	WS
Hitting	**112.4**
Fielding	**32.4**
Pitching	**62.2**
D. Camilli, 1B	25
E. Koy, OF	18
C. Lavagetto, 3B	18
G. Rosen, OF	16
F. Fitzsimmons, SP	14
L. Hamlin, SP	14
T. Pressnell, RP	12
L. Durocher, SS	9
J. Hudson, 2B	9
V. Tamulis, RP	9
K. Cuyler, OF	8
B. Hassett, OF	8
B. Phelps, C	8
V. Mungo, SP	5
F. Frankhouse, RP	4
F. Sington, OF	4
T. Stainback, OF	4
G. Campbell, C	3
O. Hockett, OF	3
J. Gaddy, SP	2
B. Posedel, SP	2
M. Shea, C	2
W. Williams, SS	2
G. Brack, OF	1
P. Coscarart, 2B	1
W. English, 3B	1
H. Manush, OF	1
B. Marrow, RP	1
S. Nahem, SP	1
R. Spencer, C	1
T. Winsett, OF	1

Chicago (89-63)	WS
Hitting	**114.6**
Fielding	**49.9**
Pitching	**102.5**
S. Hack, 3B	33
B. Lee, SP	28
C. Bryant, SP	23
B. Herman, 2B	20
C. Reynolds, OF	18
A. Galan, OF	16
G. Hartnett, C	16
R. Collins, 1B	15
C. Root, RP	15
F. Demaree, OF	13
L. French, SP	11
B. Jurges, SS	11
D. Dean, SP	9
J. Russell, RP	8
J. Marty, OF	6
K. O'Dea, C	6
T. Lazzeri, SS	5
V. Page, SP	4
P. Cavarretta, OF	3
T. Carleton, SP	2
A. Epperly, RP	2
B. Logan, RP	2
B. Garbark, C	1

Cincinnati (82-68)	WS
Hitting	**126.4**
Fielding	**39.7**
Pitching	**79.9**
I. Goodman, OF	28
P. Derringer, SP	25
E. Lombardi, C	24
H. Craft, OF	19
F. McCormick, 1B	19
W. Berger, OF	17
J. Vander Meer, SP	16
B. Myers, SS	15
L. Frey, 2B	14
L. Riggs, 3B	13
B. Walters, SP	9
J. Weaver, SP-RP	9
D. Cooke, OF	7
P. Davis, SP	7
W. Moore, SP	5
J. Cascarella, RP	3
N. Richardson, SS	3
G. Schott, RP	3
R. Barrett, RP	2
L. Gamble, OF	2
W. Hershberger, C	2
A. Kampouris, 2B	2
R. Benge, RP	1
D. Lang, 3B	1

New York (83-67)	WS
Hitting	**120.8**
Fielding	**38.6**
Pitching	**89.6**
M. Ott, 3B	36
D. Bartell, SS	17
H. Danning, C	17
J. Moore, OF	16
C. Hubbell, SP	15
H. Schumacher, SP	15
J. Brown, RP	12
H. Gumbert, SP	12
C. Melton, SP	12
D. Coffman, RP	11
J. McCarthy, 1B	11
H. Leiber, OF	10
B. Lohrman, RP	10
J. Ripple, OF	10
G. Mancuso, C	8
B. Seeds, OF	8
A. Kampouris, 2B	7
G. Myatt, SS	6
M. Haslin, 3B	4
S. Castleman, SP	3
L. Chiozza, 2B	3
B. Cissell, 2B	3
S. Leslie, 1B	2
J. Wittig, RP	1

Philadelphia (45-105)	WS
Hitting	**69.3**
Fielding	**24.7**
Pitching	**40.9**
P. Weintraub, 1B	15
H. Martin, OF	13
M. Arnovich, OF	10
H. Mueller, 2B	10

H. Mulcahy, SP	9
G. Brack, OF	8
A. Hollingsworth, SP	8
C. Passeau, SP	8
M. Butcher, SP	7
B. Jordan, 3B	7
C. Klein, OF	7
P. Whitney, 3B	6
G. Scharein, SS	4
D. Young, SS	4
S. Johnson, RP	3
B. Walters, SP	3
B. Atwood, C	2
S. Davis, C	2
P. Sivess, RP	2
E. Browne, 1B	1
C. Clark, C	1
W. Hallahan, RP	1
W. LaMaster, SP	1
A. Pitko, OF	1
T. Stainback, OF	1
J. Stein, 3B	1

Pittsburgh (86-64)	WS
Hitting	**123.1**
Fielding	**46.0**
Pitching	**88.9**
A. Vaughan, SS	34
J. Rizzo, OF	23
G. Suhr, 1B	21
R. Bauers, SP	19
L. Waner, OF	19
P. Young, 2B	18
L. Handley, 3B	17
J. Tobin, SP	17
P. Waner, OF	15
A. Todd, C	13
B. Klinger, SP	12
B. Swift, RP	11
C. Blanton, SP	9
M. Brown, RP	9
E. Brandt, SP	7
R. Lucas, SP	5
J. Bowman, RP	3
B. Brubaker, 3B	3
R. Berres, C	2
J. Dickshot, OF	1

St. Louis (71-80)	WS
Hitting	**102.2**
Fielding	**34.9**
Pitching	**75.8**
J. Mize, 1B	28
J. Medwick, OF	22
B. McGee, SP	15
C. Davis, SP	13
B. Weiland, SP	13
L. Warneke, SP	12
D. Gutteridge, 3B	11
J. Brown, 2B	10
T. Moore, OF	10
S. Martin, 2B	9
M. Owen, C	9
E. Slaughter, OF	9
P. Martin, OF	7
D. Padgett, OF	7
C. Shoun, RP	7
R. Henshaw, SP	6
M. Macon, RP	5
J. Stripp, 3B	4
P. Dean, SP	3
L. Myers, SS	3
F. Bordagaray, OF	2
H. Bremer, C	2
M. Cooper, SP	2
R. Harrell, RP	2
H. Epps, OF	1
M. Lanier, RP	1

1939 American League

Boston (89-62)	WS
Hitting	**129.5**
Fielding	**41.2**
Pitching	**96.4**
T. Williams, OF	32
J. Foxx, 1B	30
L. Grove, SP	23
J. Cronin, SS	22
B. Doerr, 2B	17
J. Tabor, 3B	16
D. Cramer, OF	14
F. Ostermueller, SP	13
J. Heving, RP	11
J. Vosmik, OF	11
J. Wilson, SP	11
E. Dickman, RP	9
D. Galehouse, SP	9
G. Desautels, C	8
J. Peacock, C	8
E. Auker, SP	7
L. Finney, 1B	7
W. Rich, SP	5
C. Wagner, SP	3
J. Bagby Jr., SP	2
T. Carey, 2B	2
B. LeFebvre, SP	2
M. Berg, C	1
B. Berger, SS	1
R. Nonnenkamp, OF	1
J. Wade, RP	1
M. Weaver, RP	1

Chicago (85-69)	WS
Hitting	**94.1**
Fielding	**50.2**
Pitching	**110.7**
L. Appling, SS	24
M. Kreevich, OF	22
T. Lyons, SP	20
J. Rigney, SP	20
J. Kuhel, 1B	19
T. Lee, SP	18
C. Brown, RP	16
E. McNair, 3B	16
G. Walker, OF	16
E. Smith, SP	15
J. Knott, SP	12
L. Rosenthal, OF	11
M. Tresh, C	10
O. Bejma, 2B	8
B. Dietrich, SP	7
R. Radcliff, OF	6
J. Hayes, 2B	5
J. Marcum, RP	3
M. Owen, 3B	2
V. Eaves, SP-RP	1
A. Herring, RP	1
N. Schlueter, C	1
K. Silvestri, C	1
H. Steinbacher, OF	1

Cleveland (87-67)	WS
Hitting	**119.9**
Fielding	**45.7**
Pitching	**95.4**
B. Feller, SP	32
K. Keltner, 3B	26
H. Trosky, 1B	23
B. Chapman, OF	19
A. Milnar, SP	18
M. Harder, SP	17
B. Campbell, OF	16
J. Heath, OF	16
O. Grimes, 2B	11
J. Allen, SP	10
R. Hemsley, C	10
H. Eisenstat, RP	9
R. Weatherly, OF	9
O. Hale, 2B	8
L. Boudreau, SS	7
W. Hudlin, SP	7
F. Pytlak, C	6
S. Webb, SS	6
M. Solters, OF	3
E. Averill, OF	2
J. Shilling, 2B	2
J. Broaca, RP	1
J. Dobson, RP	1
R. Mack, 2B	1
B. Zuber, RP	1

Detroit (81-73)	WS
Hitting	**101.1**
Fielding	**45.4**
Pitching	**96.5**
H. Greenberg, 1B	24
B. McCosky, OF	23
B. Newsom, SP	23
T. Bridges, SP	19
C. Gehringer, 2B	19
D. Trout, SP	13
R. York, C	13
A. McKain, RP	12
P. Fox, OF	11
M. Higgins, 3B	10
E. Averill, OF	9
A. Benton, RP	8
S. Rowe, SP	8
B. McCoy, 2B	7
B. Tebbetts, C	7
F. Croucher, SS	5
D. Walker, OF	5
R. Cullenbine, OF	4
F. Hutchinson, SP	4
B. Rogell, SS	4
B. Thomas, RP	4
B. Bell, OF	2
B. Harris, RP	2
R. Kress, SS	2
S. Coffman, RP	1
H. Eisenstat, RP	1
F. Giebell, RP	1
C. Laabs, OF	1
R. Lawson, SP-RP	1

New York (106-45)	WS
Hitting	**163.1**
Fielding	**49.2**
Pitching	**105.7**
J. DiMaggio, OF	34
R. Rolfe, 3B	30
B. Dickey, C	27
J. Gordon, 2B	25
G. Selkirk, OF	25
C. Keller, OF	22
R. Ruffing, SP	22
F. Crosetti, SS	17
L. Gomez, SP	13
T. Henrich, OF	13
B. Hadley, SP	12
M. Russo, SP	12
S. Sundra, RP	12
A. Donald, SP	11
O. Hildebrand, SP	11
M. Pearson, SP	9
B. Dahlgren, 1B	8
J. Murphy, RP	7
B. Rosar, C	3
S. Chandler, RP	2
W. Ferrell, SP	1
J. Gallagher, OF	1
J. Powell, OF	1

Philadelphia (55-97)	WS
Hitting	**99.4**
Fielding	**25.1**
Pitching	**40.5**
B. Johnson, OF	29
F. Hayes, C	17
S. Chapman, OF	12
W. Moses, OF	12
L. Nelson, SP	10
D. Lodigiani, 3B	9
D. Siebert, 1B	9
G. Caster, SP	7
C. Dean, RP	7
J. Gantenbein, 2B	7
B. Beckmann, SP	6
E. Brucker, C	6
D. Miles, OF	6
B. Nagel, 2B	5
N. Etten, 1B	3
S. Newsome, SS	3
N. Potter, SP	3
B. Ross, SP	3
W. Ambler, SS	2
L. McCrabb, SP	2
C. Pippen, SP	2
A. Brancato, 3B	1
F. Chapman, SS	1
B. Joyce, RP	1
B. Lillard, SS	1
E. Tipton, OF	1

St. Louis (43-111)	WS
Hitting	**69.1**
Fielding	**24.0**
Pitching	**36.0**
H. Clift, 3B	18
G. McQuinn, 1B	18
C. Laabs, OF	8
M. Hoag, OF	7
V. Kennedy, SP	6
J. Kramer, SP	6
R. Lawson, RP	6
B. Sullivan, OF	6
J. Berardino, 2B	5
J. Gallagher, OF	5
J. Glenn, C	5
J. Grace, OF	4
D. Heffner, SS	4
B. Trotter, RP	4
B. Harris, SP	3
M. Mazzera, OF	3
L. Mills, RP	3
B. Newsom, SP	3
T. Thompson, OF	3
M. Christman, SS	2
J. Whitehead, RP	2
M. Almada, OF	1
E. Bildilli, SP	1
S. Gryska, SS	1
L. Hanning, RP	1
S. Harshaney, C	1
H. Kimberlin, RP	1
J. Marcum, SP-RP	1
H. Spindel, C	1

Washington (65-87)	WS
Hitting	**94.1**
Fielding	**34.2**
Pitching	**66.7**
B. Lewis, 3B	22
D. Leonard, SP	21
G. Case, OF	15
K. Chase, SP	13
C. Travis, SS	13
S. West, OF	13
T. Wright, OF	13
J. Krakauskas, SP	11
B. Myer, 2B	9
A. Carrasquel, RP	8
B. Estalella, OF	8
J. Bloodworth, 2B	7
R. Ferrell, C	7
P. Appleton, RP	5
C. Gelbert, SS	5
J. Haynes, SP	4
J. Welaj, OF	4
H. Kelley, RP	3
M. Vernon, 1B	3
J. Early, C	2
B. Prichard, 1B	2
J. Wasdell, 1B	2
A. Evans, C	1
T. Giuliani, C	1
B. Jacobs, RP	1
E. Leip, 2B	1
W. Masterson, RP	1

1939 National League

Boston (63-88)	WS
Hitting	**90.2**
Fielding	**34.5**
Pitching	**64.3**
M. West, OF	20
D. Garms, OF	17
B. Hassett, 1B	13
A. Lopez, C	12
T. Cuccinello, 2B	10
L. Fette, SP	10
H. Majeski, 3B	10
B. Posedel, SP	10
A. Simmons, OF	9
J. Lanning, RP	8
E. Miller, SS	8
M. Shoffner, RP	8
J. Cooney, OF	7
D. MacFayden, SP	7
J. Sullivan, RP	7
D. Errickson, RP	6
R. Warstler, SS	6
J. Turner, SP	5
F. Frankhouse, RP	3
P. Masi, C	3
E. Fletcher, 1B	2
J. Outlaw, OF	2
S. Sisti, 2B	2
J. Callahan, RP	1
H. Moran, RP	1
C. Ross, OF	1
W. Wietelmann, SS	1

Brooklyn (84-69)	WS
Hitting	**104.2**
Fielding	**49.1**
Pitching	**98.8**
D. Camilli, 1B	28
C. Lavagetto, 3B	23
H. Casey, SP	21
L. Hamlin, SP	19
P. Coscarart, 2B	13
E. Koy, OF	13
W. Wyatt, SP	12
L. Durocher, SS	11
B. Phelps, C	11
F. Fitzsimmons, SP	10
T. Pressnell, SP	10
V. Tamulis, RP	9
J. Hudson, SS	7
V. Mungo, SP	7
A. Todd, C	7
G. Moore, OF	6
A. Parks, OF	6
D. Walker, OF	6
I. Hutchinson, RP	5
G. Rosen, OF	5
B. Crouch, SP-RP	4
J. Ripple, OF	4
C. Doyle, RP	3
T. Lazzeri, 2B	3
T. Stainback, OF	3
M. Almada, OF	2
F. Sington, OF	2
R. Evans, RP	1
L. Lary, SS	1

Chicago (84-70)	WS
Hitting	**123.6**
Fielding	**38.3**
Pitching	**90.1**
B. Herman, 2B	25
S. Hack, 3B	23
A. Galan, OF	22
H. Leiber, OF	21
B. Lee, SP	20
C. Passeau, SP	19
L. French, SP	16
G. Hartnett, C	15
R. Russell, 1B	12
D. Bartell, SS	10
C. Root, RP	10
B. Nicholson, OF	9
V. Page, SP	8
D. Dean, SP	7
J. Gleeson, OF	6
G. Mancuso, C	6
B. Mattick, SS	5
C. Reynolds, OF	5
J. Russell, RP	5
K. Higbe, RP	2
S. Mesner, SS	2
V. Olsen, RP	2
P. Cavarretta, 1B	1
E. Whitehill, RP	1

Cincinnati (97-57)	WS
Hitting	**137.3**
Fielding	**50.5**
Pitching	**103.2**
B. Walters, SP	38
P. Derringer, SP	26
L. Frey, 2B	25
I. Goodman, OF	25
F. McCormick, 1B	25
B. Werber, 3B	25
B. Myers, SS	23
E. Lombardi, C	17
J. Thompson, RP	16
H. Craft, OF	14
W. Moore, SP	12
W. Berger, OF	11
L. Grissom, SP	7
W. Hershberger, C	7
L. Gamble, OF	4
N. Bongiovanni, OF	3
H. Johnson, RP	3
E. Joost, 2B	3
J. Vander Meer, SP	3
M. Shoffner, RP	2
R. Barrett, RP	1
F. Bordagaray, OF	1

New York (77-74)	WS
Hitting	**122.5**
Fielding	**32.9**
Pitching	**75.6**
M. Ott, OF	28
H. Danning, C	27
Z. Bonura, 1B	19
F. Demaree, OF	19
B. Jurges, SS	17
C. Melton, SP	15
C. Hubbell, SP	14
H. Gumbert, SP	13
J. Moore, OF	13
B. Lohrman, SP	12
A. Kampouris, 2B	7
H. Schumacher, SP	7
J. Brown, RP	5
B. Seeds, OF	5
B. Whitehead, 2B	5
T. Hafey, 3B	4
R. Lynn, RP	4
L. Chiozza, 3B	3
D. Coffman, RP	3
M. Salvo, SP	3
B. Young, 1B	3
S. Castleman, RP	2
T. Lazzeri, 3B	1
J. McCarthy, 1B	1
K. O'Dea, C	1

Philadelphia (45-106)	WS
Hitting	**78.1**
Fielding	**22.8**
Pitching	**34.2**
M. Arnovich, OF	17
P. May, 3B	12
H. Martin, OF	11
H. Mueller, 2B	9
G. Suhr, 1B	9
G. Brack, OF	8
S. Johnson, SP	7
H. Mulcahy, SP	7
B. Beck, RP	6
S. Davis, C	6
K. Higbe, SP	6
J. Marty, OF	6
L. Scott, OF	5
J. Bolling, 1B	4
G. Scharein, SS	3
D. Young, SS	3
C. Passeau, SP	2
L. Powers, 1B	2
B. Bates, OF	1
E. Burkart, RP	1
M. Butcher, SP	1
R. Harrell, RP	1
J. Henry, RP	1
R. Hughes, 2B	1
C. Klein, OF	1
W. Millies, C	1
I. Pearson, SP-RP	1
J. Poindexter, RP	1
J. Shilling, 2B	1
B. Warren, C	1

Pittsburgh (68-85)	WS
Hitting	**102.2**
Fielding	**33.1**
Pitching	**68.7**
A. Vaughan, SS	25
M. Brown, RP	14
E. Fletcher, 1B	14
P. Waner, OF	14
J. Bowman, SP	11
C. Klein, OF	10
B. Klinger, SP	10
R. Sewell, RP	10
F. Bell, OF	9
L. Handley, 3B	8
J. Rizzo, OF	8
B. Swift, RP	8
J. Tobin, SP	7
L. Waner, OF	7
P. Young, 2B	7
B. Brubaker, 2B	6
M. Butcher, SP	5
B. Elliott, OF	5
G. Suhr, 1B	5
R. Mueller, C	4
R. Bauers, SP	3
R. Berres, C	3
M. Van Robays, OF	3
C. Blanton, SP	2
G. Susce, C	2
F. Gustine, 3B	1
K. Heintzelman, RP	1
J. Schultz, C	1
O. Swigart, SP	1

St. Louis (92-61)	WS
Hitting	**128.7**
Fielding	**46.1**
Pitching	**101.1**
J. Mize, 1B	33
J. Medwick, OF	24
E. Slaughter, OF	23
C. Davis, SP	22
B. Bowman, RP	19
J. Brown, SS	18
M. Cooper, SP	17
T. Moore, OF	17
D. Padgett, C	12
L. Warneke, SP	12
S. Martin, 2B	10
B. McGee, RP	10
D. Gutteridge, 3B	9
P. Martin, OF	9
M. Owen, C	9
B. Weiland, SP	9
C. Shoun, RP	8
T. Sunkel, SP	5
M. Lanier, SP	4
L. King, OF	2
L. Myers, SS	2
M. Dickson, RP	1
L. Lary, SS	1

1940 American League

Boston (82-72)	WS
Hitting	**135.6**
Fielding	**37.1**
Pitching	**73.4**
T. Williams, OF	30
J. Cronin, SS	24
J. Foxx, 1B	24
B. Doerr, 2B	21
J. Tabor, 3B	16
L. Finney, OF	15
D. DiMaggio, OF	14
D. Cramer, OF	12
L. Grove, SP	11
J. Bagby Jr., SP	10
J. Heving, RP	10
J. Wilson, RP	9
F. Ostermueller, SP	8
H. Hash, RP	7
E. Johnson, SP	5
G. Desautels, C	4
D. Galehouse, SP	4
M. Harris, SP	4
E. Dickman, RP	3
J. Peacock, C	3
T. Carey, SS	2
B. Fleming, SP	2
T. Lupien, 1B	2
W. Rich, RP	2
B. Butland, SP	1
C. Gelbert, 3B	1
S. Spence, OF	1
C. Wagner, RP	1

Chicago (82-72)	WS
Hitting	**92.6**
Fielding	**48.5**
Pitching	**104.9**
L. Appling, SS	28
J. Rigney, SP	24
J. Kuhel, 1B	21
T. Wright, OF	21
T. Lee, SP	19
E. Smith, SP	18
M. Kreevich, OF	15
T. Lyons, SP	15
L. Rosenthal, OF	14
M. Solters, OF	14
M. Tresh, C	12
B. Dietrich, SP	11
B. Kennedy, 3B	8
J. Knott, SP	8
C. Brown, RP	7
S. Webb, 2B	4
P. Appleton, RP	3
E. McNair, 2B	2
K. Silvestri, C	1
T. Turner, C	1

Cleveland (89-65)	WS
Hitting	**120.3**
Fielding	**49.6**
Pitching	**97.1**
B. Feller, SP	34
L. Boudreau, SS	30
H. Trosky, 1B	27
R. Weatherly, OF	20
B. Chapman, OF	18
R. Mack, 2B	18
A. Milnar, SP	17
K. Keltner, 3B	16
A. Smith, SP	16
R. Hemsley, C	14
J. Allen, SP	11
B. Bell, OF	10
M. Harder, SP	10
J. Heath, OF	8

H. Eisenstat, RP	6
F. Pytlak, C	4
J. Dobson, RP	2
S. Campbell, OF	1
O. Hale, 3B	1
D. Howell, RP	1
W. Hudlin, SP	1
M. Naymick, RP	1
R. Peters, 2B	1

Detroit (90-64)	WS
Hitting	**122.7**
Fielding	**42.2**
Pitching	**105.1**
H. Greenberg, OF	31
B. Newsom, SP	26
R. York, 1B	26
B. McCosky, OF	24
C. Gehringer, 2B	20
S. Rowe, SP	18
T. Bridges, SP	16
B. Tebbetts, C	13
D. Bartell, SS	11
M. Higgins, 3B	11
J. Gorsica, SP	10
B. Sullivan, C	9
A. Benton, RP	8
B. Campbell, OF	8
P. Fox, OF	7
A. McKain, RP	7
H. Newhouser, SP	7
D. Trout, RP	5
F. Giebell, SP	3
F. Hutchinson, SP	2
T. Seats, RP	2
E. Averill, OF	1
R. Kress, 3B	1
D. Meyer, 2B	1
L. Nelson, RP	1
C. Smith, RP	1
T. Stainback, OF	1

New York (88-66)	WS
Hitting	**129.8**
Fielding	**44.7**
Pitching	**89.5**
J. DiMaggio, OF	31
J. Gordon, 2B	26
C. Keller, OF	24
G. Selkirk, OF	17
R. Ruffing, SP	16
M. Russo, SP	16
T. Henrich, OF	14
R. Rolfe, 3B	14
T. Bonham, SP	13
B. Dickey, C	13
B. Dahlgren, 1B	11
A. Donald, RP	10
B. Rosar, C	10
F. Crosetti, SS	8
J. Murphy, RP	8
M. Pearson, SP	8
M. Breuer, SP	7
S. Chandler, SP	7
B. Knickerbocker, SS	3
B. Mills, OF	3
O. Hildebrand, RP	2
S. Sundra, RP	2
L. Grissom, RP	1

Philadelphia (54-100)	WS
Hitting	**93.4**
Fielding	**25.2**
Pitching	**43.4**
W. Moses, OF	21
B. Johnson, OF	19
F. Hayes, C	17
J. Babich, SP	14
S. Chapman, OF	14
B. McCoy, 2B	10
N. Potter, SP	10
D. Siebert, 1B	10
B. Beckmann, RP	7
B. Ross, SP	7
A. Rubeling, 3B	7
D. Miles, OF	5
E. Heusser, RP	4
B. Lillard, SS	3
A. Brancato, SS	2
C. Dean, SP	2
J. Gantenbein, 3B	2
A. Simmons, OF	2
P. Vaughan, SP	2
H. Wagner, C	2
C. Davis, 2B	1
E. Valo, OF	1

St. Louis (67-87)	WS
Hitting	**97.1**
Fielding	**35.6**
Pitching	**68.3**
H. Clift, 3B	23
E. Auker, SP	22
W. Judnich, OF	20
R. Radcliff, OF	20
G. McQuinn, 1B	16
J. Berardino, SS	12
B. Harris, SP	11
V. Kennedy, SP	11
J. Niggeling, SP	9
C. Laabs, OF	8
B. Trotter, RP	7
R. Cullenbine, OF	6
D. Heffner, 2B	6
J. Grace, OF	5
B. Swift, C	5
R. Lawson, RP	4
E. Bildilli, RP	3
J. Lucadello, 2B	3
M. Hoag, OF	2
A. Strange, SS	2
G. Susce, C	2
S. Coffman, RP	1
J. Gallagher, OF	1
J. Kramer, SP	1
J. Whitehead, RP	1

Washington (64-90)	WS
Hitting	**96.2**
Fielding	**32.9**
Pitching	**62.8**
B. Lewis, OF	22
C. Travis, 3B	22
K. Chase, SP	20
D. Leonard, SP	20
G. Case, OF	17
G. Walker, OF	14
S. Hudson, SP	13
R. Ferrell, C	9
J. Bloodworth, 2B	8
Z. Bonura, 1B	8
B. Myer, 2B	8
J. Early, C	6
J. Pofahl, SS	6
A. Carrasquel, RP	3
C. Gelbert, SS	3
W. Masterson, SP	3
J. Welaj, OF	3
S. West, 1B	2
R. Anderson, SP	1
A. Evans, C	1
A. Hollingsworth, SP	1
R. Monteagudo, RP	1
S. Robertson, SS	1

1940 National League

Boston (65-87)	WS
Hitting	**101.9**
Fielding	**33.7**
Pitching	**59.4**
C. Ross, OF	24
E. Miller, SS	21
D. Errickson, SP	18
M. West, OF	17
B. Rowell, 2B	15
J. Cooney, OF	12
M. Salvo, SP	12
S. Sisti, 3B	12
G. Moore, OF	11
B. Posedel, SP	11
J. Sullivan, SP	10
J. Tobin, SP	7
A. Glossop, 2B-3B	4
A. Lopez, C	4
R. Berres, C	3
T. Cuccinello, 3B	3
T. Earley, RP	2
B. Hassett, 1B	2
P. Masi, C	2
L. Scarsella, 1B	2
S. Broskie, C	1
B. Loane, OF	1
D. Manno, OF	1

Brooklyn (88-65)	WS
Hitting	**107.1**
Fielding	**50.5**
Pitching	**106.4**
D. Camilli, 1B	25
D. Walker, OF	22
J. Medwick, OF	16
W. Wyatt, SP	16
F. Fitzsimmons, SP	15
B. Phelps, C	14
H. Casey, RP	13
L. Hamlin, SP	13
C. Lavagetto, 3B	13
P. Reese, SS	13
V. Tamulis, RP	13
P. Coscarart, 2B	10
T. Carleton, SP-RP	9
C. Davis, SP	9
J. Vosmik, OF	9
P. Reiser, 3B	7
L. Grissom, SP	6
J. Wasdell, OF	6
T. Pressnell, RP	5
L. Durocher, SS	4
C. Gilbert, OF	3
N. Kimball, RP	3
G. Mancuso, C	3
R. Cullenbine, OF	2
H. Franks, C	2
J. Gallagher, OF	2
E. Head, RP	2
J. Hudson, SS	2
V. Mungo, RP	2
L. Fette, RP	1
W. Flowers, RP	1
E. Koy, OF	1
G. Moore, OF	1
D. Ross, 3B	1

Chicago (75-79)	WS
Hitting	**104.0**
Fielding	**37.5**
Pitching	**83.4**
C. Passeau, SP	28
S. Hack, 3B	25
J. Gleeson, OF	20
B. Nicholson, OF	20
L. French, SP	18
B. Herman, 2B	17
H. Leiber, OF	17
V. Olsen, SP	15
J. Mooty, SP	9
P. Cavarretta, 1B	7
D. Dallessandro, OF	7
K. Raffensberger, RP	7
A. Galan, OF	6
A. Todd, C	6
B. Mattick, SS	5
C. Root, RP	4
B. Lee, SP	3
Z. Bonura, 1B	2
V. Page, RP	2
R. Russell, 1B	2
R. Warstler, SS	2
R. Collins, C	1
D. Dean, SP	1
G. Hartnett, C	1

Cincinnati (100-53)	WS
Hitting	**126.7**
Fielding	**50.2**
Pitching	**123.1**
B. Walters, SP	32
F. McCormick, 1B	27
B. Werber, 3B	27
P. Derringer, SP	24
L. Frey, 2B	24
E. Lombardi, C	19
J. Thompson, SP	18
J. Turner, SP	18
I. Goodman, OF	17
J. Beggs, RP	13
M. McCormick, OF	12
H. Craft, OF	10
W. Moore, SP	7
B. Myers, SS	7
E. Joost, SS	6
J. Ripple, OF	6
M. Arnovich, OF	5
J. Rizzo, OF	5
W. Hershberger, C	4
J. Hutchings, RP	4
E. Riddle, RP	4
J. Vander Meer, SP	4
L. Riggs, 3B	2
D. West, C	2
B. Baker, C	1
W. Guise, RP	1
J. Wilson, C	1

New York (72-80)	WS
Hitting	**100.1**
Fielding	**36.6**
Pitching	**79.3**
M. Ott, OF	24
H. Danning, C	21
B. Young, 1B	20
H. Schumacher, SP	17
F. Demaree, OF	14
H. Gumbert, SP	14
J. Moore, OF	13
C. Hubbell, SP	12
B. Whitehead, 3B	12
B. Lohrman, SP	10
M. Witek, SS	7
J. Rucker, OF	6
J. Brown, RP	5
P. Dean, RP	5
B. Jurges, SS	5
C. Melton, SP	5
B. Seeds, OF	5
R. Joiner, RP	4
B. Carpenter, SP	3
T. Cuccinello, 2B	3
R. Lynn, RP	3
K. O'Dea, C	3
A. Glossop, 2B	2
H. Vandenberg, RP	2
B. Maynard, OF	1

Philadelphia (50-103)	WS
Hitting	**54.4**
Fielding	**32.9**
Pitching	**62.7**
K. Higbe, SP	21
H. Mulcahy, SP	19
P. May, 3B	16
J. Rizzo, OF	14
J. Marty, OF	10
B. Warren, C	8
B. Beck, SP	6
H. Mueller, 2B	6
C. Klein, OF	5
D. Litwhiler, OF	5
A. Mahan, 1B	5
H. Schulte, 2B	5

C. Blanton, SP	4
B. Bragan, SS	4
Si Johnson, RP	4
Sy. Johnson, RP	3
J. Podgajny, SP	3
B. Atwood, C	2
H. Martin, OF	2
M. Mazzera, OF	2
I. Pearson, SP	2
M. Arnovich, OF	1
W. Berger, OF	1
C. Frye, RP	1
F. Hoerst, RP	1

Pittsburgh (78-76)	WS
Hitting	**154.2**
Fielding	**25.5**
Pitching	**54.3**
A. Vaughan, SS	31
E. Fletcher, 1B	26
D. Garms, 3B	19
B. Elliott, OF	18
V. DiMaggio, OF	17
R. Sewell, SP	15
S. Davis, C	14
M. Van Robays, OF	13
F. Gustine, 2B	12
M. Brown, RP	11
J. Bowman, SP	8
L. Handley, 3B	8
P. Waner, OF	7
K. Heintzelman, RP	6
J. Lanning, RP	6
D. MacFayden, RP	5
D. Lanahan, RP	4
A. Lopez, C	4
P. Young, 2B	4
M. Butcher, SP	2
L. Waner, OF	2
B. Brubaker, 3B	1
B. Klinger, SP	1

St. Louis (84-69)	WS
Hitting	**125.2**
Fielding	**40.3**
Pitching	**86.5**
J. Mize, 1B	33
T. Moore, OF	22
E. Slaughter, OF	22
L. Warneke, SP	18
J. Orengo, 2B	17
M. Cooper, SP	15
E. Koy, OF	13
B. McGee, SP	13
C. Shoun, RP	13
M. Marion, SS	11
J. Brown, 2B	9
P. Martin, OF	9
M. Lanier, RP	8
M. Owen, C	8
S. Martin, 3B	6
D. Padgett, C	6
B. Bowman, SP	5
I. Hutchinson, RP	5
J. Russell, RP	5
J. Hopp, OF	3
J. Medwick, OF	3
D. Gutteridge, 3B	2
N. Kimball, SP-RP	2
W. Cooper, C	1
C. Doyle, RP	1
E. Lake, 2B	1
E. White, RP	1

1941 American League

Boston (84-70)	WS
Hitting	**138.0**
Fielding	**35.7**
Pitching	**78.3**
T. Williams, OF	42
J. Cronin, SS	23
D. DiMaggio, OF	21
J. Foxx, 1B	20
B. Doerr, 2B	15
C. Wagner, SP	15
M. Harris, SP	14
D. Newsome, SP	14
J. Tabor, 3B	12
L. Finney, OF	10
F. Pytlak, C	9
J. Dobson, SP	8
J. Peacock, C	8
P. Fox, OF	7
M. Ryba, RP	7
L. Grove, SP	5
T. Hughson, SP	4
E. Johnson, SP	4
B. Fleming, RP	3
S. Newsome, SS	3
S. Spence, OF	3
J. Wilson, RP	2
H. Hash, RP	1
O. Judd, RP	1
N. Potter, RP	1

Chicago (77-77)	WS
Hitting	**88.9**
Fielding	**46.3**
Pitching	**95.8**
T. Lee, SP	32
L. Appling, SS	29
T. Wright, OF	25
E. Smith, SP	20
J. Kuhel, 1B	17
T. Lyons, SP	13
J. Rigney, SP	13
B. Knickerbocker, 2B	10
J. Humphries, RP	9
M. Tresh, C	9
M. Kreevich, OF	8
D. Lodigiani, 3B	7
B. Ross, SP	7
M. Solters, OF	6
M. Hoag, OF	5
D. Kolloway, 2B	5
B. Chapman, OF	4
B. Kennedy, 3B	3
J. Haynes, RP	2
T. Turner, C	2
G. Dickey, C	1
B. Dietrich, SP	1
S. Goletz, PH-PR	1
L. Rosenthal, OF	1
S. Webb, 2B	1

Cleveland (75-79)	WS
Hitting	**91.2**
Fielding	**44.9**
Pitching	**88.9**
B. Feller, SP	30
J. Heath, OF	28
K. Keltner, 3B	23
L. Boudreau, SS	22
A. Smith, SP	13
J. Bagby Jr., SP	11
H. Trosky, 1B	11
A. Milnar, SP	10
G. Walker, OF	10
J. Heving, RP	9
R. Mack, 2B	9
R. Weatherly, OF	9
C. Brown, RP	7
O. Grimes, 1B	6
R. Hemsley, C	6
S. Campbell, OF	4
G. Desautels, C	4
C. Dean, SP	2
H. Eisenstat, RP	2
S. Gromek, RP	2
M. Harder, SP	2
J. Hegan, C	2
J. Krakauskas, RP	1
R. Peters, SS	1
L. Rosenthal, OF	1

Detroit (75-79)	WS
Hitting	**84.1**
Fielding	**42.6**
Pitching	**98.3**
A. Benton, RP	20
B. McCosky, OF	19
M. Higgins, 3B	16
R. York, 1B	16
B. Campbell, OF	15
B. Newsom, SP	14
T. Bridges, SP	13
D. Trout, RP	13
J. Gorsica, SP	12
S. Rowe, SP	12
B. Tebbetts, C	11
C. Gehringer, 2B	10
P. Mullin, OF	9
H. Newhouser, SP	8
R. Radcliff, OF	8
B. Sullivan, C	8
F. Croucher, SS	6
B. Thomas, RP	4
H. Greenberg, OF	2
H. Manders, RP	2
A. McKain, RP	2
D. Meyer, 2B	2
N. Harris, OF	1
B. Perry, SS	1
T. Stainback, OF	1

New York (101-53)	WS
Hitting	**157.3**
Fielding	**48.3**
Pitching	**97.4**
J. DiMaggio, OF	41
C. Keller, OF	32
T. Henrich, OF	26
J. Gordon, 2B	24
P. Rizzuto, SS	21
B. Dickey, C	17
R. Rolfe, 3B	16
M. Russo, SP	16
R. Ruffing, SP	15
S. Chandler, SP	13
J. Murphy, RP	12
T. Bonham, SP	11
A. Donald, SP	10
L. Gomez, SP	10
B. Rosar, C	9
M. Breuer, SP	7
N. Branch, RP	5
G. Selkirk, OF	4
J. Sturm, 1B	4
F. Crosetti, SS	3
S. Peek, RP	2
J. Priddy, 2B	2
K. Silvestri, C	2
F. Bordagaray, OF	1

Philadelphia (64-90)	WS
Hitting	**101.7**
Fielding	**32.3**
Pitching	**58.0**
S. Chapman, OF	25
B. Johnson, OF	21
F. Hayes, C	15
B. McCoy, 2B	15
W. Moses, OF	15
D. Siebert, 1B	15
P. Marchildon, SP	13
T. Ferrick, RP	9
J. Knott, SP	9
A. Brancato, SS	8
B. Beckmann, SP	6
L. Harris, RP	6
P. Suder, 3B	5
L. McCrabb, SP	4
F. Caligiuri, SP	3
B. Hadley, RP	3
D. Miles, OF	3
E. Valo, OF	3
H. Wagner, C	3
J. Babich, SP	2
E. Collins, OF	2
D. Fowler, SP	2
F. Chapman, SS	1
C. Davis, 2B	1
C. Dean, RP	1
T. Shirley, RP	1
R. Wolff, SP	1

St. Louis (70-84)	WS
Hitting	**109.6**
Fielding	**34.3**
Pitching	**66.1**
R. Cullenbine, OF	23
H. Clift, 3B	21
B. Muncrief, SP	18
W. Judnich, OF	17
G. McQuinn, 1B	17
D. Galehouse, SP	14
J. Grace, OF	12
C. Laabs, OF	12
J. Niggeling, SP	11
J. Lucadello, 2B	10
R. Ferrell, C	9
J. Berardino, SS	8
B. Harris, SP	7
E. Auker, SP	5
G. Caster, RP	4
D. Heffner, 2B	4
B. Swift, C	4
V. Kennedy, SP	3
J. Kramer, RP	2
F. Ostermueller, RP	2
R. Radcliff, OF	2
G. Archie, 1B	1
B. Estalella, OF	1
F. Grube, C	1
A. Strange, SS	1
B. Trotter, RP	1

Washington (70-84)	WS
Hitting	**112.8**
Fielding	**31.8**
Pitching	**65.4**
C. Travis, SS	34
B. Lewis, OF	22
D. Leonard, SP	19
S. Hudson, SP	17
M. Vernon, 1B	16
G. Case, OF	15
J. Bloodworth, 2B	12
D. Cramer, OF	11
J. Early, C	11
G. Archie, 3B	8
A. Carrasquel, RP	8
R. Anderson, RP	5
S. Sundra, SP	5
K. Chase, SP	4
E. Wynn, SP	4
A. Evans, C	3
B. Zuber, RP	3
R. Ferrell, C	2
B. Myer, 2B	2
R. Ortiz, OF	2
S. West, OF	2
B. Chapman, OF	1
H. Layne, 3B	1
W. Masterson, RP	1
J. Pofahl, SS	1
J. Sanford, 1B	1

1941 National League

Boston (62-92)	WS
Hitting	**94.7**
Fielding	**32.1**
Pitching	**59.2**
M. West, OF	20
J. Tobin, SP	17

J. Cooney, OF	14
B. Rowell, 2B	14
E. Miller, SS	13
G. Moore, OF	13
T. Earley, RP	12
B. Hassett, 1B	11
S. Sisti, 3B	9
P. Waner, OF	9
A. Johnson, RP	8
M. Salvo, SP	7
A. Javery, SP	6
R. Berres, C	5
B. Dahlgren, 1B	4
P. Masi, C	4
D. Errickson, SP	3
L. Waner, OF	3
F. Demaree, OF	2
J. Dudra, 2B-3B	2
J. Hutchings, RP	2
B. Posedel, SP-RP	2
J. Sullivan, RP	2
W. Ferrell, SP	1
H. LaManna, RP	1
A. Montgomery, C	1
S. Roberge, 2B	1

Brooklyn (100-54)	WS
Hitting	**147.8**
Fielding	**50.5**
Pitching	**101.8**
P. Reiser, OF	34
D. Camilli, 1B	29
W. Wyatt, SP	28
D. Walker, OF	26
J. Medwick, OF	24
K. Higbe, SP	21
B. Herman, 2B	17
C. Lavagetto, 3B	16
P. Reese, SS	15
C. Davis, SP	12
M. Owen, C	10
H. Casey, RP	9
J. Wasdell, OF	9
L. Riggs, 3B	8
F. Fitzsimmons, SP	7
J. Allen, RP	5
M. Brown, RP	4
L. Hamlin, SP	4
A. Kampouris, 2B	4
H. Franks, C	3
N. Kimball, RP	3
B. Swift, RP	2
K. Wicker, RP	2
B. Chipman, RP	1
T. Drake, RP	1
L. Durocher, SS	1
L. French, RP	1
A. Galan, OF	1
L. Grissom, RP	1
B. Phelps, C	1
V. Tamulis, RP	1

Chicago (70-84)	WS
Hitting	**115.1**
Fielding	**29.6**
Pitching	**65.3**
S. Hack, 3B	30
B. Nicholson, OF	21
D. Dallessandro, OF	16
L. Stringer, 2B	16
B. Dahlgren, 1B	15
C. Passeau, SP	15
P. Cavarretta, OF	14
V. Olsen, SP	12
J. Mooty, RP	9
B. Lee, SP	7
C. McCullough, C	7
P. Erickson, RP	6
T. Pressnell, RP	6
B. Sturgeon, SS	6
V. Eaves, SP	3
H. Leiber, OF	3
L. Novikoff, OF	3
J. Schmitz, SP	3
A. Galan, OF	2
C. Gilbert, OF	2
B. Myers, SS	2
B. Olsen, OF	2
V. Page, RP	2
C. Root, SP	2
L. French, SP	1
B. Herman, 2B	1
J. Hudson, SS	1
R. Meers, SP	1
L. Merullo, SS	1
B. Scheffing, C	1

Cincinnati (88-66)	WS
Hitting	**107.8**
Fielding	**49.9**
Pitching	**106.3**
B. Walters, SP	27
E. Riddle, SP	26
L. Frey, 2B	24
E. Joost, SS	21
F. McCormick, 1B	20
J. Vander Meer, SP	19
P. Derringer, SP	15
M. McCormick, OF	15
B. Werber, 3B	15
H. Craft, OF	14
E. Lombardi, C	13
J. Gleeson, OF	8
J. Turner, RP	8
C. Aleno, 3B	5
I. Goodman, OF	5
E. Koy, OF	5
J. Beggs, RP	4
R. Starr, SP	3
J. Thompson, SP	3
L. Waner, OF	3
E. Lukon, OF	2
W. Moore, RP	2
J. Ripple, OF	2
D. West, C	2
B. Mattick, SS	1
H. Sauer, OF	1
B. Zientara, 2B	1

New York (74-79)	WS
Hitting	**110.8**
Fielding	**34.2**
Pitching	**77.0**
M. Ott, OF	26
B. Young, 1B	20
B. Jurges, SS	18
H. Schumacher, SP	16
D. Bartell, 3B	15
C. Melton, SP	14
J. Rucker, OF	13
H. Danning, C	12
C. Hubbell, SP	11
B. Lohrman, SP	9
J. Moore, OF	9
B. Carpenter, SP	8
J. Brown, RP	6
G. Hartnett, C	6
J. Orengo, 3B	6
M. Arnovich, OF	5
M. Witek, 2B	4
A. Adams, RP	3
B. Whitehead, 2B	3
O. Hale, 2B	2
D. Koslo, SP	2
K. O'Dea, C	2
T. Sunkel, SP	2
B. Bowman, RP	1
J. Davis, 3B	1
H. East, SP	1
H. Feldman, SP	1
R. Fischer, SP-RP	1
S. Gordon, OF	1
H. Gumbert, SP	1
J. McCarthy, 1B	1
B. McGee, SP	1
J. Wittig, RP	1

Philadelphia (43-111)	WS
Hitting	**59.1**
Fielding	**25.4**
Pitching	**44.5**
N. Etten, 1B	20
D. Litwhiler, OF	17
P. May, 3B	12
J. Marty, OF	10
I. Pearson, RP	7
J. Podgajny, SP	7
B. Bragan, SS	6
B. Warren, C	6
C. Blanton, SP	5
L. Grissom, SP	5
T. Hughes, SP	5
S. Johnson, SP	5
B. Crouch, RP	3
H. Mueller, 2B	3
D. Murtaugh, 2B	3
B. Beck, RP	2
S. Benjamin, OF	2
H. Marnie, 2B	2
R. Melton, RP	2
J. Rizzo, OF	2
F. Hoerst, RP	1
G. Jumonville, 2B-SS	1
G. Lambert, SP-RP	1
M. Livingston, C	1
P. Masterson, SP-RP	1

Pittsburgh (81-73)	WS
Hitting	**119.4**
Fielding	**39.8**
Pitching	**83.8**
E. Fletcher, 1B	28
V. DiMaggio, OF	24
A. Vaughan, SS	19
M. Butcher, SP	17
B. Elliott, OF	16
M. Van Robays, OF	13
J. Lanning, SP	12
R. Sewell, SP	12
F. Gustine, 2B	11
L. Handley, 3B	11
K. Heintzelman, SP	11
D. Dietz, RP	10
A. Lopez, C	10
B. Klinger, RP	8
S. Martin, 2B	7
J. Bowman, RP	6
D. Garms, 3B	6
S. Davis, C	3
B. Stewart, OF	3
J. Sullivan, RP	3
L. Wilkie, RP	3
A. Anderson, SS	2
B. Baker, C	2
R. Bauers, SP	1
B. Clemensen, SP-RP	1
R. Collins, 1B	1
D. Conger, SP-RP	1
B. Cox, SS	1
V. Smith, C	1

St. Louis (97-56)	WS
Hitting	**126.7**
Fielding	**50.2**
Pitching	**114.1**
J. Mize, 1B	26
E. White, SP	22
J. Brown, 3B	21
T. Moore, OF	20
E. Slaughter, OF	20
J. Hopp, OF	19
L. Warneke, SP	19
C. Crespi, 2B	18
H. Gumbert, SP	16
M. Lanier, SP	14
M. Marion, SS	14
M. Cooper, SP	11
E. Crabtree, OF	10
H. Krist, RP	8
H. Pollet, SP	8
G. Mancuso, C	7
S. Nahem, RP	6
B. Crouch, RP	5
D. Padgett, OF	5
C. Triplett, OF	5
W. Cooper, C	4
I. Hutchinson, RP	4
S. Musial, OF	3
J. Beazley, SP	1
H. Gornicki, RP	1
J. Grodzicki, RP	1
W. Kurowski, 3B	1
E. Lake, 3B-SS	1
S. Mesner, 3B	1

1942 American League

Boston (93-59)	WS
Hitting	**141.5**
Fielding	**46.1**
Pitching	**91.3**
T. Williams, OF	46
D. DiMaggio, OF	28
T. Hughson, SP	28
J. Pesky, SS	28
B. Doerr, 2B	24
C. Wagner, SP	13
J. Dobson, SP	12
T. Lupien, 1B	12
B. Butland, RP	11
L. Finney, OF	11
O. Judd, SP	10
J. Tabor, 3B	8
J. Peacock, C	7
M. Brown, RP	6
B. Conroy, C	6
K. Chase, SP	5
P. Fox, OF	5
J. Foxx, 1B	4
Y. Terry, SP	4
J. Cronin, 3B	3
D. Newsome, SP	3
M. Ryba, RP	3
S. Newsome, 3B	2

Chicago (66-82)	WS
Hitting	**79.4**
Fielding	**40.9**
Pitching	**77.7**
T. Lyons, SP	21
L. Appling, SS	20
J. Humphries, SP	20
W. Moses, OF	20
D. Kolloway, 2B	15
T. Wright, OF	15
J. Kuhel, 1B	12
J. Haynes, RP	11
M. Hoag, OF	7
E. Smith, SP	7
B. Kennedy, 3B	6
D. Lodigiani, 3B	5
T. Turner, C	5
S. West, OF	5
T. Lee, SP	4
J. Rigney, SP	4
M. Tresh, C	4
J. Wade, SP	4
B. Dietrich, SP	2
B. Mueller, OF	2
L. Perme, RP	2
B. Ross, SP	2
G. Dickey, C	1
J. Grant, 3B	1
V. Heim, OF	1
S. Webb, 2B	1
L. Wells, SS	1

Cleveland (75-79)	WS
Hitting	**112.0**
Fielding	**39.4**
Pitching	**73.7**
L. Fleming, 1B	29
J. Heath, OF	24
L. Boudreau, SS	23
J. Bagby Jr., SP	20
K. Keltner, 3B	20
O. Hockett, OF	13
R. Weatherly, OF	13
M. Harder, SP	11
C. Dean, SP	10
T. Ferrick, RP	9
R. Mack, 2B	8
B. Mills, OF	6
A. Smith, SP	6
A. Milnar, SP	5
O. Denning, C	4
H. Eisenstat, RP	4
V. Kennedy, RP	4
G. Desautels, C	3
S. Gromek, RP	3
J. Hegan, C	3
R. Embree, RP	2
H. Edwards, OF	1
O. Grimes, 2B	1
J. Heving, RP	1
R. Peters, SS	1
A. Reynolds, RP	1

Detroit (73-81)	WS
Hitting	**64.2**
Fielding	**48.3**
Pitching	**106.4**
B. McCosky, OF	19
H. White, SP	18
A. Benton, SP	17
H. Newhouser, SP	17
D. Trout, SP	16
T. Bridges, SP	15
V. Trucks, SP	15
R. York, 1B	15
D. Cramer, OF	12
M. Higgins, 3B	12
J. Bloodworth, 2B	11
N. Harris, OF	11
B. Tebbetts, C	9
D. Ross, OF	6
D. Parsons, C	4
M. Franklin, SS	3
R. Henshaw, RP	3
D. Meyer, 2B	3
J. Gorsica, RP	2
B. Hitchcock, SS	2
H. Manders, RP	2
R. Radcliff, OF	2
S. Rowe, SP-RP	2
C. Gehringer, 2B	1
J. Lipon, SS	1
H. Riebe, C	1

New York (103-51)	WS
Hitting	**157.8**
Fielding	**49.9**
Pitching	**101.3**
C. Keller, OF	34
J. DiMaggio, OF	32
J. Gordon, 2B	31
P. Rizzuto, SS	25
T. Bonham, SP	21
S. Chandler, SP	19
T. Henrich, OF	19
H. Borowy, SP	15
R. Ruffing, SP	15
B. Hassett, 1B	13
B. Dickey, C	11
M. Breuer, SP	9
F. Crosetti, 3B	9
A. Donald, SP	9
J. Priddy, 3B	9
R. Rolfe, 3B	7
R. Cullenbine, OF	6
B. Rosar, C	5
J. Murphy, RP	4
M. Russo, SP	4
R. Hemsley, C	3
J. Lindell, RP	3
L. Gomez, SP	2
E. Kearse, C	1
M. Queen, RP	1
G. Selkirk, OF	1
J. Turner, RP	1

Philadelphia (55-99)	WS
Hitting	**82.8**
Fielding	**29.1**
Pitching	**53.1**
B. Johnson, OF	26
B. Blair, 3B	15
R. Wolff, SP	14
P. Marchildon, SP	13
E. Valo, OF	12
M. Kreevich, OF	10
D. Siebert, 1B	10
L. Harris, SP	9
R. Christopher, SP	8
P. Suder, SS	8
D. Miles, OF	7
H. Wagner, C	6
B. Harris, SP-RP	5
B. Knickerbocker, 2B	5
D. Fowler, SP	3
J. Wallaesa, SS	3
C. Davis, 2B	2
E. McNair, SS	2
B. Swift, C	2
B. Beckmann, RP	1
J. Castiglia, C	1
E. Collins, OF	1
F. Hayes, C	1
B. Savage, RP	1

St. Louis (82-69)	WS
Hitting	**122.2**
Fielding	**38.7**
Pitching	**85.1**
W. Judnich, OF	25
H. Clift, 3B	24
C. Laabs, OF	23
V. Stephens, SS	19
J. Niggeling, SP	17
G. McQuinn, 1B	16
D. Gutteridge, 2B	15
A. Hollingsworth, SP	12
E. Auker, SP	11
D. Galehouse, SP	11
G. Caster, RP	9
M. Chartak, OF	9
B. Muncrief, SP	7
S. Sundra, SP	7
R. Ferrell, C	6
F. Hayes, C	6
G. McQuillen, OF	6
T. Criscola, OF	4
S. Ferens, RP	4
P. Appleton, RP	3
F. Biscan, RP	3
R. Cullenbine, OF	3
J. Berardino, 3B-SS	2
F. Ostermueller, RP	2
A. Strange, 3B	1
B. Swift, C	1

Washington (62-89)	WS
Hitting	**129.1**
Fielding	**22.8**
Pitching	**34.2**
S. Spence, OF	29
G. Case, OF	22
B. Estalella, 3B	20
M. Vernon, 1B	20
B. Campbell, OF	11
R. Cullenbine, OF	11
E. Clary, 2B	9
A. Carrasquel, RP	7
J. Early, C	7
S. Hudson, SP	7
B. Repass, 2B	7
W. Masterson, SP	5
J. Sullivan, SS	5
B. Zuber, RP	5
A. Evans, C	4
B. Newsom, SP	4
E. Wynn, SP	3
M. Chartak, OF	2
J. Pofahl, SS	2
R. Scarborough, RP	2
F. Croucher, 2B	1
C. Gomez, 2B	1
D. Leonard, SP	1
R. Ortiz, OF	1

1942
National League

Boston (59-89)	WS
Hitting	**89.6**
Fielding	**31.1**
Pitching	**56.3**
T. Holmes, OF	21
M. West, 1B	19
A. Javery, SP	16
E. Lombardi, C	16
J. Tobin, SP	15
N. Fernandez, 3B	13
E. Miller, SS	11
P. Waner, OF	11
M. Salvo, SP	8
L. Tost, SP	8
S. Sisti, 2B	7
C. Kluttz, C	5
B. Donovan, RP	4
J. Sain, RP	3
F. Demaree, OF	2
D. Detweiler, 3B	2
B. Gremp, 1B	2
J. Hutchings, RP	2
P. Masi, C	2
S. Roberge, 2B	2
C. Ross, OF	2
L. Wallace, RP	2
J. Cooney, OF	1
T. Cuccinello, 3B	1
T. Earley, SP	1
A. Johnson, RP	1

Brooklyn (104-50)	WS
Hitting	**157.9**
Fielding	**50.2**
Pitching	**103.9**
D. Camilli, 1B	28
P. Reiser, OF	28
P. Reese, SS	27
J. Medwick, OF	21
B. Herman, 2B	20
A. Vaughan, 3B	19
D. Walker, OF	19
C. Davis, SP	18
L. French, RP	17
W. Wyatt, SP	16
M. Owen, C	15
H. Casey, RP	13
K. Higbe, SP	12
E. Head, RP	9
M. Macon, SP	9
J. Allen, SP	7
A. Galan, OF	7
L. Riggs, 3B	6
J. Rizzo, OF	5
B. Sullivan, C	4
L. Webber, RP	4
C. Dapper, C	2
B. Newsom, SP	2
F. Bordagaray, OF	1
A. Kampouris, 2B	1
C. Kehn, RP	1
N. Kimball, RP	1

Chicago (68-86)	WS
Hitting	**109.4**
Fielding	**30.6**
Pitching	**64.0**
B. Nicholson, OF	28
S. Hack, 3B	26
C. Passeau, SP	19
P. Cavarretta, OF	16
L. Novikoff, OF	14
C. McCullough, C	13
L. Merullo, SS	11
B. Lee, SP	10
B. Fleming, RP	9
L. Stringer, 2B	8
L. Warneke, SP	8
D. Dallessandro, OF	7
H. Bithorn, RP	5
V. Olsen, SP	4
R. Russell, 1B	4
J. Schmitz, RP	4
B. Sturgeon, 2B	3
C. Block, 3B	2
C. Hernandez, C	2
B. Scheffing, C	2
H. Wyse, SP	2
D. Errickson, RP	1
J. Foxx, 1B	1
C. Gilbert, OF	1
P. Gillespie, C	1
E. Hanyzewski, RP	1
J. Mooty, SP	1
T. Pressnell, RP	1

Cincinnati (76-76)	WS
Hitting	**83.8**
Fielding	**46.8**
Pitching	**97.4**
L. Frey, 2B	23
R. Starr, SP	21
J. Vander Meer, SP	21
B. Walters, SP	20
F. McCormick, 1B	17
E. Joost, SS	15
B. Haas, 3B	14
R. Lamanno, C	13
P. Derringer, SP	12
M. Marshall, OF	12
J. Beggs, RP	10
G. Walker, OF	10
E. Riddle, SP	7
C. Shoun, RP	6
I. Goodman, OF	5
E. Tipton, OF	5
M. McCormick, OF	3
J. Thompson, RP	3
R. Hemsley, C	2
F. Kelleher, OF	2
J. Abreu, 3B	1
H. Craft, OF	1
A. Lakeman, C	1
D. Phillips, SS	1
H. Sauer, 1B	1
C. Vollmer, OF	1
D. West, C	1

New York (85-67)	WS
Hitting	**134.1**
Fielding	**38.1**
Pitching	**82.8**
M. Ott, OF	35
J. Mize, 1B	32
H. Danning, C	14
H. Schumacher, SP	14
M. Witek, 2B	14
B. Young, OF	14
B. Lohrman, SP	13
A. Adams, RP	12
D. Bartell, 3B	12
C. Melton, SP	12
B. Barna, OF	11
B. Carpenter, SP	11
B. Jurges, SS	11
W. Marshall, OF	11
H. Feldman, RP	8

C. Hubbell, SP	7
B. Werber, 3B	7
B. McGee, RP	6
B. Maynard, OF	4
H. Leiber, OF	3
H. East, RP	1
C. Fox, C	1
S. Gordon, 3B	1
G. Mancuso, C	1

Philadelphia (42-109)	WS
Hitting	**44.5**
Fielding	**28.0**
Pitching	**53.5**
T. Hughes, SP	18
R. Melton, SP	13
N. Etten, 1B	12
D. Litwhiler, OF	12
S. Johnson, SP	9
P. May, 3B	9
D. Murtaugh, SS	8
J. Podgajny, SP	8
R. Northey, OF	6
A. Glossop, 2B	5
E. Koy, OF	4
L. Waner, OF	4
B. Warren, C	4
B. Bragan, SS	3
M. Livingston, C	3
G. Hennessey, RP	2
I. Pearson, RP	2
B. Beck, RP	1
S. Benjamin, OF	1
B. Burich, SS	1
E. Freed, OF	1

Pittsburgh (66-81)	WS
Hitting	**98.4**
Fielding	**32.2**
Pitching	**67.4**
E. Fletcher, 1B	26
B. Elliott, 3B	22
V. DiMaggio, OF	15
R. Sewell, SP	13
B. Phelps, C	11
J. Barrett, OF	10
M. Butcher, SP	10
A. Lopez, C	10
J. Wasdell, OF	10
B. Klinger, SP	9
H. Gornicki, SP	8
P. Coscarart, SS	7
J. Lanning, RP	7
D. Dietz, RP	6
M. Van Robays, OF	5
L. Wilkie, RP	5
A. Anderson, SS	4
F. Gustine, 2B	4
L. Hamlin, SP	4
K. Heintzelman, SP	3
B. Stewart, OF	3
S. Martin, 2B	2
N. Strincevich, RP	2
D. Conger, SP-RP	1
J. Hallett, SP	1

St. Louis (106-48)	WS
Hitting	**149.2**
Fielding	**50.5**
Pitching	**118.3**
E. Slaughter, OF	37
M. Cooper, SP	29
S. Musial, OF	28
J. Beazley, SP	22
M. Marion, SS	22
T. Moore, OF	20
J. Brown, 2B	16
W. Cooper, C	16
W. Kurowski, 3B	13
M. Lanier, SP	13
H. Krist, RP	12
H. Gumbert, SP-RP	10
J. Hopp, 1B	10
M. Dickson, RP	9
R. Sanders, 1B	9
E. White, SP	9
H. Pollet, RP	8
H. Walker, OF	8
K. O'Dea, C	6
L. Warneke, SP	6
C. Crespi, 2B	5
C. Triplett, OF	5
B. Lohrman, RP	2
B. Beckmann, RP	1
E. Crabtree, PH-PR	1
S. Narron, C	1

1943 American League

Boston (68-84)	WS
Hitting	**84.7**
Fielding	**41.6**
Pitching	**77.7**
B. Doerr, 2B	24
T. Hughson, SP	20
T. Lupien, 1B	14
P. Fox, OF	13
O. Judd, SP	13
J. Tabor, 3B	12
M. Brown, RP	11
L. Culberson, OF	11
S. Newsome, SS	11
R. Partee, C	10
J. Dobson, SP	9
M. Ryba, RP	9
Y. Terry, SP	8
E. Lake, SS	7
C. Metkovich, OF	6
J. Cronin, 3B	4
F. Garrison, OF	3
J. Lazor, OF	3
L. Lucier, SP	3
D. Newsome, SP	3
B. Conroy, C	2
A. Karl, RP	2
B. Barna, OF	1
T. McBride, OF	1
D. Miles, OF	1
E. O'Neill, RP	1
J. Peacock, C	1
A. Simmons, OF	1

Chicago (82-72)	WS
Hitting	**115.7**
Fielding	**42.1**
Pitching	**88.2**
L. Appling, SS	40
G. Curtright, OF	21
O. Grove, SP	18
R. Hodgin, 3B	18
W. Moses, OF	18
T. Tucker, OF	16
B. Dietrich, SP	14
J. Humphries, SP	13
G. Maltzberger, RP	13
J. Kuhel, 1B	12
B. Ross, SP	9
J. Haynes, RP	8
E. Smith, SP	8
J. Grant, 3B	6
M. Tresh, C	6
T. Cuccinello, 3B	5
J. Wade, RP	5
T. Turner, C	4
D. Kolloway, 2B	3
V. Castino, C	2
D. Culler, 3B	2
T. Lee, SP	2
S. Webb, 2B	2
B. Swift, RP	1

Cleveland (82-71)	WS
Hitting	**138.9**
Fielding	**37.5**
Pitching	**69.6**
L. Boudreau, SS	32
R. Cullenbine, OF	27
J. Heath, OF	24
O. Hockett, OF	18
K. Keltner, 3B	15
B. Rosar, C	15
A. Smith, SP	15
J. Bagby Jr., SP	14
H. Edwards, OF	11
R. Mack, 2B	11
M. Rocco, 1B	11
V. Kennedy, SP	10
A. Reynolds, SP	10
M. Harder, SP	6
J. Heving, RP	5
J. Salveson, RP	5
M. Naymick, RP	4
R. Peters, 3B	3
P. Center, RP	2
G. Desautels, C	2
G. Woodling, OF	2
O. Denning, 1B	1
S. Gromek, RP	1
E. Klieman, SP	1
P. Seerey, OF	1

Detroit (78-76)	WS
Hitting	**100.0**
Fielding	**41.2**
Pitching	**92.8**
R. York, 1B	26
D. Wakefield, OF	24
D. Trout, SP	23
D. Cramer, OF	18
T. Bridges, SP	17
V. Trucks, SP	16
M. Higgins, 3B	15
P. Richards, C	11
N. Harris, OF	10
H. Newhouser, SP	10
J. Hoover, SS	9
S. Overmire, SP	9
H. White, SP	8
J. Bloodworth, 2B	7
J. Gorsica, RP	6
D. Ross, OF	5
J. Wood, 2B	5
A. Unser, C	3
R. Henshaw, RP	2
P. Oana, RP	2
J. Outlaw, OF	2
D. Parsons, C	2
R. Radcliff, OF	2
R. Gentry, SP	1
J. Orrell, RP	1

New York (98-56)	WS
Hitting	**149.1**
Fielding	**46.0**
Pitching	**98.9**
C. Keller, OF	36
S. Chandler, SP	29
J. Gordon, 2B	28
N. Etten, 1B	22
B. Johnson, 3B	22
T. Bonham, SP	20
B. Dickey, C	20
B. Wensloff, SP	16
H. Borowy, SP	15
J. Lindell, OF	13
B. Metheny, OF	12
F. Crosetti, SS	9
J. Murphy, RP	9
R. Weatherly, OF	9
K. Sears, C	7
S. Stirnweiss, SS	7
R. Hemsley, C	5
B. Zuber, SP	5
T. Stainback, OF	4
M. Russo, SP	3
J. Turner, RP	2
A. Donald, SP	1

Philadelphia (49-105)	WS
Hitting	**67.8**
Fielding	**27.4**
Pitching	**51.7**
J. Flores, SP	15
B. Estalella, OF	13
J. White, OF	13
R. Wolff, SP	12
I. Hall, SS	11
D. Siebert, 1B	9
R. Christopher, SP	7
H. Wagner, C	7
D. Black, SP	6
E. Mayo, 3B	6
B. Burgo, OF	5
L. Harris, SP	5
O. Arntzen, SP	4
P. Suder, 2B	4
J. Tyack, OF	4
E. Valo, OF	4
J. Welaj, OF	4
G. Staller, OF	3
B. Swift, C	3
D. Heffner, 2B	2
J. Rullo, 2B	2
F. Skaff, 1B	2
H. Besse, RP	1
C. Bowles, SP	1
N. Brown, SP	1
L. Flick, OF	1
J. Ripple, OF	1
W. Wheaton, OF	1

St. Louis (72-80)	WS
Hitting	**103.3**
Fielding	**35.3**
Pitching	**77.4**
V. Stephens, SS	23
C. Laabs, OF	17
M. Byrnes, OF	15
D. Galehouse, SP	15
D. Gutteridge, 2B	14
G. McQuinn, 1B	13
B. Muncrief, SP	13
N. Potter, RP	13
S. Sundra, SP	13
H. Clift, 3B	12
M. Chartak, OF	10
M. Christman, 3B	9
G. Caster, RP	8
J. Niggeling, SP	8
R. Ferrell, C	7
F. Hayes, C	5
M. Kreevich, OF	5
A. Hollingsworth, SP	4
A. Zarilla, OF	4
E. Clary, 3B	2
P. Dean, RP	1
H. Epps, OF	1
A. McKain, RP	1
S. Peterson, RP	1
F. Sanford, RP	1
J. Schultz, C	1

Washington (84-69)	WS
Hitting	**137.5**
Fielding	**37.6**
Pitching	**76.9**
S. Spence, OF	28
G. Case, OF	25
M. Vernon, 1B	21
J. Priddy, 2B	20
B. Johnson, OF	19
E. Wynn, SP	19
J. Early, C	17
M. Haefner, RP	14
M. Candini, SP	12
D. Leonard, SP	10
J. Sullivan, SS	10
E. Clary, 3B	8
G. Moore, OF	7
J. Niggeling, SP	7
A. Carrasquel, RP	6

A. Kampouris, 3B	5
R. Scarborough, RP	5
J. Powell, OF	3
S. Robertson, 3B	3
T. Giuliani, C	2
J. Mertz, RP	2
G. Myatt, 2B	2
E. Pyle, SP	2
D. Adkins, RP	1
H. Clift, 3B	1
B. LeFebvre, SP-RP	1
B. Newsom, SP	1
R. Roberts, SS	1

1943 National League

Boston (68-85)	WS
Hitting	**62.8**
Fielding	**46.1**
Pitching	**95.1**
N. Andrews, SP	25
J. Tobin, SP	24
T. Holmes, OF	23
A. Javery, SP	20
R. Barrett, SP	16
C. Workman, OF	15
B. Nieman, OF	12
J. McCarthy, 1B	9
W. Wietelmann, SS	9
P. Masi, C	8
E. Joost, 3B	7
M. Salvo, SP	6
K. Farrell, 1B	5
C. Ross, OF	5
C. Ryan, 2B	5
C. Kluttz, C	4
B. Brubaker, 3B	2
J. Dagenhard, SP-RP	2
B. Donovan, RP	2
J. Burns, 3B	1
B. Etchison, 1B	1
H. Heltzel, 3B	1
G. Jeffcoat, RP	1
H. Poland, C	1

Brooklyn (81-72)	WS
Hitting	**151.1**
Fielding	**31.7**
Pitching	**60.2**
A. Galan, OF	29
A. Vaughan, SS	28
B. Herman, 2B	27
D. Walker, OF	22
W. Wyatt, SP	16
D. Camilli, 1B	13
F. Bordagaray, OF	11
P. Waner, OF	10
K. Higbe, SP	9
M. Owen, C	9
E. Head, RP	8
B. Newsom, SP	8
L. Olmo, OF	7
B. Bragan, C	6
C. Davis, SP	6
L. Webber, RP	5
H. Schultz, 1B	4
G. Hermanski, OF	3
A. Kampouris, 2B	3
J. Medwick, OF	3
R. Melton, SP	3
D. Moore, C	3
J. Allen, RP	2
R. Barkley, SS	2
A. Glossop, SS	2
N. Kimball, RP	1
B. Lohrman, RP	1
J. Orengo, 3B	1
F. Ostermueller, RP	1

Chicago (74-79)	WS
Hitting	**114.1**
Fielding	**34.0**
Pitching	**73.9**
B. Nicholson, OF	31
S. Hack, 3B	21
H. Bithorn, SP	19
P. Cavarretta, 1B	18
P. Lowrey, OF	16
C. Passeau, SP	16
E. Stanky, 2B	14
I. Goodman, OF	10
H. Wyse, RP	10
L. Merullo, SS	9
E. Hanyzewski, RP	8
P. Derringer, SP	7
D. Dallessandro, OF	5
C. McCullough, C	4
L. Novikoff, OF	4
R. Prim, RP	4
L. Warneke, RP	4
C. Hernandez, C	3
B. Lee, SP	3
M. Livingston, C	3
J. Burrows, RP	2
S. Martin, 2B	2
A. Pafko, OF	2
B. Schuster, SS	2
W. Signer, SP-RP	2
D. Johnson, 2B	1
E. Sauer, OF	1
A. Todd, C	1

Cincinnati (87-67)	WS
Hitting	**118.5**
Fielding	**50.2**
Pitching	**92.3**
E. Tipton, OF	27
L. Frey, 2B	25
R. Mueller, C	24
E. Riddle, SP	23
F. McCormick, 1B	19
J. Vander Meer, SP	19
C. Shoun, RP	15
B. Walters, SP	15
E. Miller, SS	14
S. Mesner, 3B	12
J. Beggs, RP	11
B. Haas, 1B	10
M. Marshall, OF	10
R. Starr, SP	9
E. Crabtree, OF	7
G. Walker, OF	6
E. Heusser, RP	4
W. Williams, 2B	4
D. Clay, OF	3
A. Lakeman, C	2
C. Aleno, OF	1
T. DePhillips, C	1

New York (55-98)	WS
Hitting	**83.9**
Fielding	**26.1**
Pitching	**55.0**
M. Witek, 2B	19
M. Ott, OF	16
A. Adams, RP	13
D. Bartell, 3B	13
S. Gordon, 3B	10
C. Melton, SP	10
J. Rucker, OF	9
B. Jurges, SS	8
E. Lombardi, C	8
V. Mungo, RP	7
J. Medwick, OF	6
J. Orengo, 1B	5
J. Wittig, SP	5
K. Chase, SP	4
R. Fischer, SP	4
J. Allen, RP	3
H. Feldman, RP	3
B. Kerr, SS	3
C. Mead, OF	3
C. Hubbell, SP	2
G. Mancuso, C	2
B. Maynard, OF	2
N. Reyes, 1B	2
B. Sayles, RP	2
K. Trinkle, SP	2
B. Voiselle, SP	2
B. Barna, OF	1
B. Lohrman, SP	1

Philadelphia (64-90)	WS
Hitting	**101.9**
Fielding	**29.5**
Pitching	**60.5**
R. Northey, OF	22
S. Rowe, SP	19
D. Murtaugh, 2B	16
P. May, 3B	15
D. Barrett, SP	14
B. Dahlgren, 1B	14
C. Triplett, OF	13
J. Wasdell, 1B	12
B. Adams, OF	11
J. Kraus, SP	10
A. Gerheauser, SP	7
S. Johnson, SP	7
M. Livingston, C	7
D. Litwhiler, OF	4
D. Moore, C	3
G. Stewart, SS	3
B. Finley, C	2
C. Fuchs, SP	2
N. Kimball, RP	2
J. Podgajny, RP	2
G. Eyrich, RP	1
R. Hamrick, 2B	1
B. Lee, SP	1
E. Naylor, OF	1
T. Padden, C	1
K. Raffensberger, SP	1
A. Seminick, C	1

Pittsburgh (80-74)	WS
Hitting	**116.0**
Fielding	**39.9**
Pitching	**84.1**
B. Elliott, 3B	25
R. Sewell, SP	23
E. Fletcher, 1B	22
V. DiMaggio, OF	20
J. Russell, OF	16
M. Butcher, SP	14
A. Lopez, C	14
B. Klinger, SP	13
F. Gustine, SS	12
W. Hebert, SP	11
P. Coscarart, 2B	10
T. O'Brien, OF	8
X. Rescigno, RP	8
B. Baker, C	7
M. Van Robays, OF	7
J. Barrett, OF	6
J. Hallett, RP	5
H. Gornicki, RP	4
B. Brandt, RP	3
J. Lanning, RP	3
A. Rubeling, 2B	3
F. Colman, OF	2
H. Geary, SS	2
J. Gee, SP	2

St. Louis (105-49)	WS
Hitting	**130.8**
Fielding	**50.8**
Pitching	**133.4**
S. Musial, OF	39
M. Cooper, SP	28
L. Klein, 2B	25
M. Lanier, SP	23
W. Cooper, C	18
W. Kurowski, 3B	18
R. Sanders, 1B	18
M. Marion, SS	17
H. Walker, OF	17
H. Brecheen, RP	15
H. Krist, SP-RP	14
H. Pollet, SP	14
A. Brazle, SP	12
H. Gumbert, SP	11
D. Litwhiler, OF	9
M. Dickson, RP	8
K. O'Dea, C	8
G. Munger, RP	5
D. Garms, OF	4
J. Hopp, OF	4
E. White, SP	3
J. Brown, 2B	2
B. Byerly, SP	1
F. Demaree, OF	1
G. Fallon, 2B	1

1944 American League

Boston (77-77)	WS
Hitting	**133.9**
Fielding	**33.1**
Pitching	**64.0**
B. Johnson, OF	31
B. Doerr, 2B	27
T. Hughson, SP	20
P. Fox, OF	17
C. Metkovich, OF	17
J. Tabor, 3B	16
H. Wagner, C	13
S. Newsome, SS	9
M. Ryba, RP	9
P. Woods, SP	8
J. Bucher, 3B	7
C. Hausmann, RP	7
R. Partee, C	7
L. Finney, 1B	6
F. Barrett, RP	5
J. Bowman, SP	5
L. Culberson, OF	5
J. Cronin, 1B	4
Y. Terry, SP	4
E. Lake, SS	3
E. O'Neill, SP	3
B. Conroy, C	2
C. Dreisewerd, SP	2
T. McBride, OF	2
F. Garrison, OF	1
O. Judd, SP	1

Chicago (71-83)	WS
Hitting	**91.7**
Fielding	**40.6**
Pitching	**80.7**
W. Moses, OF	21
T. Tucker, OF	20
R. Hodgin, 3B	17
E. Lopat, SP	16
J. Haynes, RP	14
H. Trosky, 1B	14
E. Carnett, OF	13
G. Maltzberger, RP	13
O. Grove, SP	12
B. Dietrich, SP	11
J. Humphries, SP	9
M. Tresh, C	9
S. Webb, SS	7
T. Lee, SP	6
G. Clarke, 3B	5
G. Curtright, OF	5
J. Dickshot, OF	5
R. Schalk, 2B	5
T. Cuccinello, 3B	3
V. Castino, C	2
J. Wade, RP	2
M. Hoag, OF	1
T. Jordan, C	1
C. Michaels, SS	1
T. Turner, C	1

Cleveland (72-82)	WS
Hitting	**106.7**
Fielding	**38.2**
Pitching	**71.1**
L. Boudreau, SS	28
K. Keltner, 3B	22
R. Cullenbine, OF	21
S. Gromek, SP	17
M. Rocco, 1B	15
J. Heving, RP	13
O. Hockett, OF	11
E. Klieman, RP	11
A. Reynolds, SP	10
M. Harder, SP	9
B. Rosar, C	9
A. Smith, SP	8
J. Heath, OF	7
M. Hoag, OF	7
P. Seerey, OF	6
P. O'Dea, OF	5
R. Mack, 2B	4
J. Grant, 2B	3
R. Peters, 2B	3
J. Bagby Jr., SP	2
P. Calvert, RP	1
E. Henry, SP	1
R. Poat, RP	1
N. Schlueter, C	1
G. Susce, C	1

Detroit (88-66)	WS
Hitting	**111.7**
Fielding	**46.2**
Pitching	**106.1**
D. Trout, SP	42
H. Newhouser, SP	35
M. Higgins, 3B	22
D. Wakefield, OF	22
R. York, 1B	22
D. Cramer, OF	19
E. Mayo, 2B	16
S. Overmire, SP	14
J. Outlaw, OF	12
P. Richards, C	10
J. Hoover, SS	9
B. Swift, C	9
R. Gentry, SP	8
C. Hostetler, OF	7
J. Gorsica, SP	5
B. Beck, RP	4
J. Orengo, SS	2
J. Orrell, RP	2
B. Floyd, SS	1
D. Heffner, 2B	1
C. Metro, OF	1
D. Ross, OF	1

New York (83-71)	WS
Hitting	**120.8**
Fielding	**46.1**
Pitching	**82.0**
S. Stirnweiss, 2B	35
J. Lindell, OF	26
N. Etten, 1B	25
H. Borowy, SP	20
O. Grimes, 3B	16
T. Bonham, SP	15
M. Dubiel, SP	14
H. Martin, OF	13
A. Donald, SP	10
B. Metheny, OF	9
M. Garbark, C	8
M. Milosevich, SS	8
R. Hemsley, C	6
M. Queen, SP	6
F. Crosetti, SS	5
D. Savage, 3B	5
B. Bevens, SP	4
R. Derry, OF	4
S. Roser, RP	4
E. Levy, OF	3
J. Turner, RP	3
B. Zuber, SP	3
J. Johnson, RP	2
A. Lyons, RP	2
L. Rosenthal, OF	2
J. Page, SP	1

Philadelphia (72-82)	WS
Hitting	**73.7**
Fielding	**45.4**
Pitching	**96.9**
B. Estalella, OF	20
B. Newsom, SP	20
D. Siebert, 1B	20
J. Berry, RP	18
R. Christopher, SP	18
F. Hayes, C	18
J. Flores, SP	12
I. Hall, 2B	12
L. Harris, SP	12
F. Garrison, OF	9
L. Hamlin, SP	9
E. Busch, SS	8
G. Kell, 3B	8
D. Black, SP	7
H. Epps, OF	6
B. McGhee, 1B	6
J. White, OF	5
C. Scheib, RP	2
W. Wheaton, RP	2
B. Burgo, OF	1
J. Burns, 3B	1
L. Rosenthal, OF	1
J. Rullo, 2B	1

St. Louis (89-65)	WS
Hitting	**124.1**
Fielding	**45.2**
Pitching	**97.7**
V. Stephens, SS	34
J. Kramer, SP	22
M. Christman, 3B	21
G. McQuinn, 1B	20
N. Potter, SP	20
M. Byrnes, OF	19
B. Muncrief, SP	17
D. Gutteridge, 2B	16
M. Kreevich, OF	16
A. Zarilla, OF	15
S. Jakucki, SP	12
D. Galehouse, SP	10
G. Caster, RP	8
C. Laabs, OF	7
G. Moore, OF	7
E. Clary, 3B	3
T. Shirley, RP	3
S. Sundra, SP	3
M. Chartak, 1B	2
R. Hayworth, C	2
A. Hollingsworth, RP	2
F. Baker, 2B	1
F. Demaree, OF	1
H. Epps, OF	1
T. Hafey, OF	1
F. Mancuso, C	1
B. Martin, OF	1
T. Turner, C	1
S. Zoldak, RP	1

Washington (64-90)	WS
Hitting	**105.8**
Fielding	**27.8**
Pitching	**58.4**
S. Spence, OF	33
J. Kuhel, 1B	17
G. Myatt, 2B	17
J. Niggeling, SP	15
D. Leonard, SP	13
R. Ferrell, C	12
M. Haefner, SP	12
G. Case, OF	10
J. Sullivan, SS	10
G. Torres, 3B	10
R. Ortiz, OF	8
E. Wynn, SP	8
A. Carrasquel, RP	6
M. Guerra, C	6
M. Candini, RP	4
J. Powell, OF	3
B. LeFebvre, RP	2
F. Vaughn, 2B	2
E. Boland, OF	1
V. Curtis, RP	1
H. Layne, 3B	1
R. Monteagudo, OF	1

1944 National League

Boston (65-89)	WS
Hitting	**91.2**
Fielding	**34.6**
Pitching	**69.2**
T. Holmes, OF	27
J. Tobin, SP	23
N. Andrews, SP	17
B. Nieman, OF	15
C. Ryan, 2B	13
A. Javery, SP	12
P. Masi, C	10
D. Phillips, 3B	10
R. Barrett, SP	8
W. Wietelmann, SS	8
C. Kluttz, C	7
C. Workman, OF	7
I. Hutchinson, RP	6
M. Macon, 1B	6
A. Wright, OF	5
F. Drews, 2B	4
B. Etchison, 1B	4
C. Ross, OF	3
B. Cardoni, RP	2
S. Hofferth, C	2
J. Hutchings, SP-RP	2
R. Gladu, 3B	1
W. Huston, 3B	1
M. Sandlock, 3B	1
S. Shemo, 2B	1

Brooklyn (63-91)	WS
Hitting	**126.8**
Fielding	**24.9**
Pitching	**37.3**
D. Walker, OF	33
A. Galan, OF	32
F. Bordagaray, 3B	14
M. Owen, C	11
H. Schultz, 1B	10
C. Davis, SP	9
L. Olmo, OF	9
E. Stanky, 2B	9
J. Bolling, 1B	7
R. Melton, SP	7
B. Chapman, SP	6
G. Rosen, OF	6
B. Bragan, SS	5
P. Waner, OF	5
E. Head, SP	4
L. Webber, RP	3
M. Aderholt, OF	2
E. Basinski, 2B	2
H. Gregg, SP	2
A. Herring, SP-RP	2
C. King, RP	2
F. Ostermueller, RP	2
T. Brown, SS	1
B. Chipman, RP	1
J. Cooney, OF	1
G. English, SS	1
W. Flowers, RP	1
B. Hart, SS	1
T. Warren, RP	1

Chicago (75-79)	WS
Hitting	**117.8**
Fielding	**34.0**
Pitching	**73.2**
B. Nicholson, OF	31
P. Cavarretta, 1B	25
C. Passeau, SP	18
D. Dallessandro, OF	16
H. Wyse, SP	16
R. Hughes, 3B	15
D. Johnson, 2B	14
S. Hack, 3B	13
A. Pafko, OF	10
B. Fleming, RP	9
B. Chipman, SP	7
P. Derringer, RP	6
P. Erickson, RP	6
H. Vandenberg, RP	6
D. Williams, C	5
I. Goodman, OF	4
R. Lynn, RP	4
L. Novikoff, OF	4
L. Merullo, SS	3
F. Secory, OF	3
B. Holm, C	2
B. Schuster, SS	2
C. Brewster, SS	1
P. Gillespie, C	1
E. Hanyzewski, SP-RP	1
M. Kreitner, C	1
M. Stewart, RP	1
T. York, SS	1

Cincinnati (89-65)	WS
Hitting	**100.0**
Fielding	**50.2**
Pitching	**116.8**
B. Walters, SP	32
F. McCormick, 1B	29
R. Mueller, C	26
E. Tipton, OF	21
E. Heusser, SP	20
A. Carter, SP	16
C. Shoun, SP	15
W. Williams, 2B	15
T. de la Cruz, SP	13
G. Walker, OF	13
E. Miller, SS	12
H. Gumbert, SP	11
J. Konstanty, SP	9
S. Mesner, 3B	8
D. Clay, OF	7
M. Marshall, OF	7
E. Crabtree, OF	3
T. Criscola, OF	2
J. White, OF	2
C. Aleno, 3B	1
J. Beggs, SP	1
B. Katz, RP	1
B. Malloy, RP	1
C. Ramos, OF	1
E. Riddle, SP	1

New York (67-87)	WS
Hitting	**114.9**
Fielding	**28.4**
Pitching	**57.6**
M. Ott, OF	25
B. Voiselle, SP	24
P. Weintraub, 1B	20
J. Medwick, OF	19
B. Kerr, SS	16
N. Reyes, 1B	11
H. Luby, 3B	10
H. Feldman, SP	9
G. Hausmann, 2B	9
A. Adams, RP	8
E. Lombardi, C	7
E. Pyle, SP	7
J. Rucker, OF	7
G. Mancuso, C	5
R. Treadway, OF	4
J. Allen, SP	3
D. Gardella, OF	3
R. Berres, C	2
R. Fischer, RP	2
B. Jurges, 3B	2
C. Melton, SP	2

B. Sloan, OF	2
J. Gee, RP	1
K. Miller, RP	1
L. Polli, RP	1
F. Seward, RP	1

Philadelphia (61-92)	WS
Hitting	**66.8**
Fielding	**36.5**
Pitching	**79.7**
B. Adams, OF	22
R. Northey, OF	22
K. Raffensberger, SP	18
C. Schanz, SP	16
B. Lee, SP	15
T. Lupien, 1B	15
D. Barrett, SP	11
A. Karl, RP	9
J. Wasdell, OF	9
M. Mullen, 2B	8
A. Gerheauser, SP	6
B. Finley, C	4
R. Hamrick, SS	4
C. Letchas, 2B	4
J. Peacock, C	4
T. Cieslak, 3B	3
G. Stewart, 3B	3
V. Kennedy, SP	2
D. Matthewson, RP	2
C. Covington, RP	1
G. Hamner, SS	1
A. Seminick, C	1
M. Shea, C	1
H. Shuman, RP	1
C. Triplett, OF	1

Pittsburgh (90-63)	WS
Hitting	**132.4**
Fielding	**42.5**
Pitching	**95.1**
J. Russell, OF	31
B. Elliott, 3B	27
J. Barrett, OF	25
R. Sewell, SP	24
B. Dahlgren, 1B	19
F. Ostermueller, SP	17
M. Butcher, SP	15
P. Coscarart, 2B	14
N. Strincevich, SP	14
P. Roe, SP	13
V. DiMaggio, OF	10
F. Colman, OF	8
A. Lopez, C	8
C. Cuccurullo, RP	6
X. Rescigno, RP	6
F. Zak, SS	6
H. Camelli, C	5
S. Davis, C	5
A. Rubeling, OF	5
F. Gustine, SS	4
T. O'Brien, OF	4
R. Starr, RP	2
L. Handley, 2B	1
L. Waner, OF	1

St. Louis (105-49)	WS
Hitting	**146.5**
Fielding	**50.8**
Pitching	**117.6**
S. Musial, OF	38
J. Hopp, OF	28
M. Cooper, SP	24
W. Kurowski, 3B	22
R. Sanders, 1B	22
M. Marion, SS	20
W. Cooper, C	18
T. Wilks, SP	18
M. Lanier, SP	17
H. Brecheen, SP	15
D. Litwhiler, OF	15
G. Munger, SP	15
K. O'Dea, C	11
E. Verban, 2B	9
A. Bergamo, OF	8
F. Schmidt, RP	8
A. Jurisich, RP	7
B. Donnelly, RP	6
H. Gumbert, SP	5
G. Fallon, 2B	3
P. Martin, OF	3
B. Byerly, RP	2
D. Garms, OF	1

1945 American League

Boston (71-83)	WS
Hitting	**111.0**
Fielding	**36.5**
Pitching	**65.5**
E. Lake, SS	27
B. Ferriss, SP	24
B. Johnson, OF	20
C. Metkovich, 1B	14
S. Newsome, 2B	13
J. Lazor, OF	12
T. McBride, OF	11
M. Ryba, RP	11
L. Culberson, OF	10
J. Wilson, SP	9
F. Barrett, RP	8
B. Steiner, 2B	7
O. Clark, SP	5
B. Garbark, C	5
J. Tobin, 3B	5
D. Camilli, 1B	4
V. Johnson, RP	4
P. Fox, OF	3
R. Heflin, SP	3
T. LaForest, 3B	3
P. Woods, SP-RP	3
B. Holm, C	2
E. O'Neill, SP	2
R. Steiner, C	2
F. Walters, C	2
J. Bucher, 3B	1
J. Cronin, 3B	1
C. Hausmann, RP	1
Y. Terry, RP	1

Chicago (71-78)	WS
Hitting	**121.2**
Fielding	**28.6**
Pitching	**63.2**
W. Moses, OF	28
J. Dickshot, OF	20
T. Cuccinello, 3B	19
T. Lee, SP	18
M. Tresh, C	15
G. Curtright, OF	13
O. Hockett, OF	13
O. Grove, SP	11
C. Michaels, SS	10
E. Lopat, SP	9
R. Schalk, 2B	9
L. Appling, SS	6
F. Baker, 3B	6
E. Caldwell, RP	6
K. Farrell, 1B	6
J. Haynes, SP	6
F. Papish, RP	5
B. Dietrich, SP	4
J. Humphries, SP	3
J. Johnson, RP	3
B. Nagel, 1B	2
D. Reynolds, SS	1

Cleveland (73-72)	WS
Hitting	**104.1**
Fielding	**39.0**
Pitching	**76.0**
S. Gromek, SP	24
J. Heath, OF	20
D. Meyer, 2B	19
L. Boudreau, SS	17
F. Hayes, C	15
A. Reynolds, SP	15
M. Rocco, 1B	15
P. Seerey, OF	13
F. Mackiewicz, OF	11
J. Bagby Jr., SP	9
D. Ross, 3B	9
R. Embree, SP	7
B. Feller, SP	7
L. Fleming, OF	6
E. Klieman, RP	5
A. Smith, SP	5
P. Center, RP	4
A. Cihocki, SS	4
M. Harder, SP	2
M. Hoag, OF	2
P. O'Dea, OF	2
J. Salveson, RP	2
S. Benjamin, OF	1
E. Carnett, OF	1
R. Cullenbine, OF	1
J. McDonnell, C	1
H. Ruszkowski, C	1
E. Weingartner, SS	1

Detroit (88-65)	WS
Hitting	**114.1**
Fielding	**48.7**
Pitching	**101.2**
H. Newhouser, SP	38
R. Cullenbine, OF	30
E. Mayo, 2B	22
D. Trout, SP	18
A. Benton, SP	17
R. York, 1B	17
D. Cramer, OF	16
H. Greenberg, OF	16
J. Outlaw, OF	12
P. Richards, C	11
B. Maier, 3B	9
J. Hoover, SS	8
S. Overmire, SP	8
L. Mueller, SP	7
B. Swift, C	7
S. Webb, SS	6
R. Borom, 2B	3
G. Caster, RP	3
Z. Eaton, RP	3
J. Orrell, RP	3
J. Tobin, RP	3
P. Oana, RP	2
D. Ross, 3B	2
T. Bridges, RP	1
B. Pierce, RP	1
W. Wilson, RP	1

New York (81-71)	WS
Hitting	**129.8**
Fielding	**37.7**
Pitching	**75.5**
S. Stirnweiss, 2B	34
N. Etten, 1B	22
O. Grimes, 3B	21
H. Martin, OF	16
F. Crosetti, SS	14
T. Bonham, SP	11
C. Keller, OF	11
B. Metheny, OF	11
B. Bevens, SP	9
A. Gettel, SP	9
H. Borowy, SP	8
A. Robinson, C	8
R. Derry, OF	7
J. Page, RP	7
R. Ruffing, SP	7
T. Stainback, OF	7
B. Zuber, SP	7
M. Dubiel, SP	5
K. Holcombe, RP	5
J. Lindell, OF	5
A. Donald, SP	4
M. Garbark, C	4
J. Turner, RP	4
B. Drescher, C	2
J. Buzas, SS	1
S. Chandler, SP	1
H. Crompton, C	1
M. Milosevich, SS	1
S. Roser, RP	1

Philadelphia (52-98)	WS
Hitting	**63.0**
Fielding	**31.7**
Pitching	**61.2**
B. Estalella, OF	18
R. Christopher, SP	15
G. Kell, 3B	15
J. Berry, RP	14
I. Hall, 2B	12
B. Newsom, SP	12
D. Siebert, 1B	12
H. Peck, OF	11
J. Flores, SP	10
E. Busch, SS	7
C. Gassaway, RP	4
F. Hayes, C	3
B. McGhee, OF	3
M. Smith, OF	3
D. Fowler, RP	2
S. Gerkin, SP	2
L. Knerr, SP	2
C. Metro, OF	2
B. Rosar, C	2
B. Wilkins, SS	2
F. Garrison, OF	1
G. George, C	1
E. Kish, OF	1
L. Rosenthal, OF	1
C. Scheib, RP	1

St. Louis (81-70)	WS
Hitting	**85.3**
Fielding	**49.9**
Pitching	**107.9**
N. Potter, SP	27
V. Stephens, SS	27
M. Byrnes, OF	18
G. McQuinn, 1B	17
A. Hollingsworth, SP	16
B. Muncrief, SP	14
S. Jakucki, SP	13
J. Kramer, SP	12
F. Mancuso, C	12
T. Shirley, SP	12
G. Moore, OF	11
M. Christman, 3B	9
D. Gutteridge, 2B	8
M. Kreevich, OF	8
L. Finney, OF	6
L. Schulte, 3B	6
O. Miller, SP	4
S. Zoldak, RP	4
R. Hayworth, C	3
E. Jones, RP	3
C. Laabs, OF	3
L. West, RP	3
P. Gray, OF	2
B. Martin, OF	2
C. Fannin, RP	1
A. LaMacchia, RP	1
J. Schultz, C	1

Washington (87-67)	WS
Hitting	**130.9**
Fielding	**39.8**
Pitching	**90.3**
J. Kuhel, 1B	25
R. Wolff, SP	24
G. Myatt, 2B	23
G. Case, OF	21
G. Binks, OF	20
D. Leonard, SP	19
B. Lewis, OF	17
H. Clift, 3B	14
M. Haefner, SP	14

R. Ferrell, C	11
M. Pieretti, SP	10
A. Carrasquel, RP	8
J. Niggeling, SP	7
G. Torres, SS	7
A. Evans, C	6
M. Kreevich, OF	6
H. Layne, 3B	6
F. Vaughn, 2B	5
J. Zardon, OF	4
M. Guerra, C	2
W. Holborow, RP	2
W. Masterson, SP-RP	2
S. Ullrich, RP	2
P. Appleton, RP	1
W. Chipple, OF	1
D. Kimble, SS	1
J. Powell, OF	1
D. Stone, RP	1
C. Travis, 3B	1

1945 National League

Boston (67-85)	WS
Hitting	**79.1**
Fielding	**41.8**
Pitching	**80.2**
T. Holmes, OF	29
C. Gillenwater, OF	17
J. Hutchings, RP	13
B. Logan, SP	13
C. Workman, 3B	13
J. Tobin, SP	12
P. Masi, C	11
D. Culler, SS	10
W. Wietelmann, 2B	10
E. Wright, SP	10
B. Lee, SP	9
B. Nieman, OF	7
N. Andrews, SP	6
M. Cooper, SP	6
M. Aderholt, OF	3
D. Hendrickson, RP	3
S. Hofferth, C	3
J. Mack, 1B	3
J. Medwick, OF	3
R. Barrett, SP	2
T. Earley, RP	2
E. Joost, 2B	2
C. Kluttz, C	2
B. Ramsey, OF	2
V. Shupe, 1B	2
F. Drews, 2B	1
J. Heving, RP	1
I. Hutchinson, RP	1
T. Nelson, 3B	1
E. Singleton, SP	1
M. Ulisney, C	1
L. Wallace, SP	1
B. Whitcher, SP-RP	1

Brooklyn (87-67)	WS
Hitting	**149.8**
Fielding	**36.8**
Pitching	**74.4**
G. Rosen, OF	31
A. Galan, 1B	30
D. Walker, OF	28
E. Stanky, 2B	27
L. Olmo, OF	22
H. Gregg, SP	17
V. Lombardi, SP	12
C. Davis, SP	9
E. Stevens, 1B	8
F. Bordagaray, 3B	7
R. Branca, SP	7
C. Buker, RP	7
A. Herring, SP	7
M. Sandlock, C	7
E. Basinski, SS	6
T. Seats, SP	5
L. Webber, RP	5
T. Brown, SS	4
C. King, RP	4
J. Peacock, C	4
B. Hart, 3B	3
M. Owen, C	3
F. Dantonio, C	2
H. Schultz, 1B	2
S. Andrews, C	1
B. Chapman, SP	1
B. Herman, OF	1
C. Sukeforth, C	1

Chicago (98-56)	WS
Hitting	**134.2**
Fielding	**50.2**
Pitching	**109.7**
S. Hack, 3B	34
P. Cavarretta, 1B	30
A. Pafko, OF	25
H. Wyse, SP	24
C. Passeau, SP	22
B. Nicholson, OF	19
D. Johnson, 2B	18
P. Lowrey, OF	17
R. Prim, SP	17
H. Borowy, SP	14
P. Derringer, SP	14
P. Erickson, RP	9
P. Gillespie, C	7
M. Livingston, C	7
L. Merullo, SS	6
H. Vandenberg, RP	6
H. Becker, 1B	5
R. Hughes, SS	5
B. Chipman, RP	4
D. Williams, C	4
E. Sauer, OF	3
J. Ostrowski, 3B	1
R. Otero, 1B	1
L. Rice, C	1
B. Schuster, SS	1

Cincinnati (61-93)	WS
Hitting	**74.2**
Fielding	**38.9**
Pitching	**69.9**
F. McCormick, 1B	17
D. Clay, OF	16
B. Walters, SP	16
E. Heusser, SP	14
S. Mesner, 3B	14
A. Libke, OF	13
E. Miller, SS	12
J. Bowman, SP	10
V. Kennedy, SP	8
E. Tipton, OF	7
W. Williams, 2B	7
A. Lakeman, C	6
A. Unser, C	6
F. Dasso, SP	5
H. Fox, RP	4
H. Sauer, OF	4
G. Walker, OF	4
B. Beck, RP	3
A. Carter, RP	3
E. Harrist, RP	3
K. Wahl, 2B	3
M. Bosser, RP	2
J. Hetki, RP	2
D. Sipek, OF	2
W. Flager, SS	1
J. Riddle, C	1

New York (78-74)	WS
Hitting	**108.6**
Fielding	**38.8**
Pitching	**86.6**
M. Ott, OF	22
E. Lombardi, C	18
G. Hausmann, 2B	17
V. Mungo, SP	17
H. Feldman, SP	16
A. Adams, RP	13
D. Gardella, OF	12
B. Kerr, SS	12
N. Reyes, 3B	11
J. Rucker, OF	11
B. Voiselle, SP	10
P. Weintraub, 1B	10
J. Brewer, SP	9
S. Maglie, SP	9
B. Jurges, 3B	8
C. Kluttz, C	7
W. Lockman, OF	6
S. Emmerich, RP	4
A. Hansen, SP	4
M. Schemer, 1B	3
R. Treadway, OF	3
D. Fisher, SP-RP	2
J. Mallory, OF	2
J. Medwick, OF	2
A. Zabala, RP	2
R. Zimmerman, 1B	2
R. Fischer, RP	1
C. Mead, OF	1

Philadelphia (46-108)	WS
Hitting	**76.2**
Fielding	**24.7**
Pitching	**37.1**
V. DiMaggio, OF	15
J. Wasdell, OF	15
A. Karl, RP	12
G. Crawford, OF	11
V. Dinges, OF	10
J. Foxx, 1B	8
J. Antonelli, 3B	7
D. Mauney, SP	6
C. Triplett, OF	6
R. Monteagudo, OF	5
A. Seminick, C	5
W. Flager, SS	4
O. Judd, RP	4
C. Schanz, SP	4
D. Barrett, SP	3
B. Mott, SS	3
S. Andrews, C	2
B. Lee, SP	2
T. Lupien, 1B	2
G. Mancuso, C	2
B. Adams, OF	1
B. Chapman, OF	1
D. Coffman, RP	1
T. Daniels, 2B	1
Ga. Hamner, 2B	1
J. Kraus, SP	1
L. Lucier, RP	1
H. Mulcahy, SP	1
J. Peacock, C	1
J. Powell, OF	1
L. Scott, RP	1
H. Spindel, C	1

Pittsburgh (82-72)	WS
Hitting	**119.2**
Fielding	**39.8**
Pitching	**87.0**
J. Russell, OF	21
B. Elliott, 3B	20
P. Roe, SP	20
J. Barrett, OF	18
B. Salkeld, C	18
N. Strincevich, SP	18
A. Gionfriddo, OF	15
M. Butcher, SP	13
P. Coscarart, 2B	13
F. Gustine, SS	12
L. Handley, 3B	10
R. Sewell, SP	10
B. Dahlgren, 1B	9
K. Gables, SP	8
A. Gerheauser, RP	8
B. Beck, RP	7
A. Lopez, C	6
T. O'Brien, OF	6
F. Ostermueller, SP	4
J. Saltzgaver, 2B	4
V. Barnhart, SS	2
F. Colman, 1B	1
C. Cuccurullo, RP	1
S. Davis, C	1
X. Rescigno, RP	1

St. Louis (95-59)	WS
Hitting	**133.5**
Fielding	**50.2**
Pitching	**101.3**
W. Kurowski, 3B	27
B. Adams, OF	23
R. Barrett, SP	22
K. Burkhart, SP	20
R. Sanders, 1B	19
H. Brecheen, SP	17
M. Marion, SS	17
J. Hopp, OF	16
K. O'Dea, C	15
A. Bergamo, OF	14
E. Verban, 2B	14
R. Schoendienst, OF	11
G. Dockins, RP	9
B. Donnelly, SP	9
D. Rice, C	9
D. Garms, 3B	8
T. Wilks, SP	6
G. Gardner, RP	5
J. Creel, RP	4
M. Cooper, SP	3
L. Klein, SS-OF	3
A. Rebel, OF	3
B. Byerly, RP	2
G. Fallon, SS	2
M. Lanier, SP	2
D. Bartosch, OF	1
W. Cooper, C	1
B. Crouch, RP	1
A. Lopatka, RP	1
P. Young, SS	1

1946 American League

Boston (104-50)	WS
Hitting	**158.3**
Fielding	**49.7**
Pitching	**103.9**
T. Williams, OF	49
J. Pesky, SS	34
B. Doerr, 2B	27
D. DiMaggio, OF	26
T. Hughson, SP	25
B. Ferriss, SP	23
R. York, 1B	22
M. Harris, SP	14
H. Wagner, C	12
J. Dobson, SP	11
B. Klinger, RP	8
C. Metkovich, OF	8
L. Culberson, OF	7
M. Higgins, 3B	6
J. Bagby Jr., SP	5
E. Johnson, RP	5
B. Zuber, RP	5
T. McBride, OF	4
R. Partee, C	4
M. Brown, RP	3
C. Dreisewerd, RP	3
W. Moses, OF	3
R. Russell, 3B	2
E. Andres, 3B	1
D. Gutteridge, 2B	1
R. Heflin, RP	1
E. McGah, C	1
E. Pellagrini, 3B	1
M. Ryba, RP	1

Chicago (74-80)	WS
Hitting	**92.4**
Fielding	**42.1**
Pitching	**87.5**

L. Appling, SS	26
E. Lopat, SP	19
T. Tucker, OF	16
E. Caldwell, RP	14
T. Wright, OF	13
D. Kolloway, 2B	12
O. Grove, SP	10
F. Papish, RP	10
J. Haynes, SP	9
C. Michaels, 2B	8
E. Smith, SP	8
M. Tresh, C	8
B. Kennedy, OF	7
J. Kuhel, 1B	6
W. Moses, OF	6
H. Trosky, 1B	6
B. Dietrich, SP	5
G. Maltzberger, RP	5
F. Hayes, C	4
D. Philley, OF	4
W. Platt, OF	4
R. Hodgin, OF	3
D. Lodigiani, 3B	3
T. Lyons, SP	3
J. Rigney, SP	3
G. Dickey, C	2
J. Jones, 1B	2
T. Lee, SP	2
G. Curtright, OF	1
E. Fernandes, C	1
A. Hollingsworth, RP	1
L. Wells, 3B	1

Cleveland (68-86)	WS
Hitting	**107.1**
Fielding	**34.5**
Pitching	**62.4**
B. Feller, SP	32
L. Boudreau, SS	24
H. Edwards, OF	23
P. Seerey, OF	15
L. Fleming, 1B	14
K. Keltner, 3B	9
R. Embree, SP	8
H. Becker, 1B	6
B. Lemon, RP	6
F. Mackiewicz, OF	6
A. Reynolds, SP	6
G. Case, OF	5
F. Hayes, C	5
J. Hegan, C	5
D. Ross, 3B	5
M. Harder, SP	4
D. Meyer, 2B	4
J. Conway, 2B	3
S. Gromek, SP	3
R. Mack, 2B	3
D. Mitchell, OF	3
E. Robinson, 1B	3
M. Rocco, 1B	3
J. Berry, RP	2
S. Lollar, C	2
C. Gassaway, RP	1
B. Kuzava, SP	1
R. Peters, SS	1
T. Sepkowski, 3B	1
G. Woodling, OF	1

Detroit (92-62)	WS
Hitting	**124.6**
Fielding	**45.5**
Pitching	**106.0**
H. Newhouser, SP	33
H. Greenberg, 1B	31
D. Trout, SP	27
R. Cullenbine, OF	25
F. Hutchinson, SP	19
E. Lake, SS	19
G. Kell, 3B	18
V. Trucks, SP	16
D. Wakefield, OF	15
H. Evers, OF	10
A. Benton, SP	8
B. Tebbetts, C	7
P. Mullin, OF	6
J. Outlaw, OF	6
J. Bloodworth, 2B	5
D. Cramer, OF	5
P. Richards, C	5
E. Mayo, 2B	4
S. Overmire, SP	3
B. Swift, C	3
S. Webb, 2B	3
B. McCosky, OF	2
G. Caster, RP	1
J. Gorsica, RP	1
M. Higgins, 3B	1
L. Kretlow, SP	1
J. Lipon, SS	1
A. Moore, OF	1

New York (87-67)	WS
Hitting	**125.7**
Fielding	**43.9**
Pitching	**91.4**
C. Keller, OF	31
S. Chandler, SP	25
J. DiMaggio, OF	24
B. Bevens, SP	21
T. Henrich, OF	21
A. Robinson, C	19
S. Stirnweiss, 3B	13
R. Gumpert, RP	12
P. Rizzuto, SS	12
J. Gordon, 2B	9
B. Johnson, 3B	9
J. Lindell, OF	9
J. Page, SP	7
R. Ruffing, SP	7
N. Etten, 1B	6
A. Gettel, RP	6
T. Bonham, SP	5
B. Dickey, C	5
J. Murphy, RP	4
S. Souchock, 1B	3
J. Wade, RP	3
Y. Berra, C	2
F. Crosetti, SS	2
G. Niarhos, C	2
B. Brown, SS	1
V. Raschi, SP	1
K. Silvestri, C	1
B. Wight, RP	1

Philadelphia (49-105)	WS
Hitting	**61.9**
Fielding	**29.3**
Pitching	**55.8**
J. Flores, SP	15
S. Chapman, OF	12
P. Marchildon, SP	12
B. McCosky, OF	12
E. Valo, OF	12
D. Fowler, SP	11
B. Rosar, C	11
G. McQuinn, 1B	7
P. Suder, SS	7
B. Savage, RP	6
H. Majeski, 3B	5
G. Kell, 3B	4
R. Christopher, RP	3
R. Derry, OF	3
O. Grimes, 2B	3
G. Handley, 2B	3
B. McCahan, SP-RP	3
B. Newsom, SP	3
H. Peck, OF	3
G. Desautels, C	2
T. Stainback, OF	2
J. Berry, RP	1
J. Caulfield, SS	1
E. Fagan, RP	1
L. Griffeth, RP	1
I. Hall, 2B	1
L. Harris, RP	1
D. Richmond, 3B	1
J. Wallaesa, SS	1

St. Louis (66-88)	WS
Hitting	**101.9**
Fielding	**30.6**
Pitching	**65.5**
V. Stephens, SS	20
W. Judnich, OF	18
J. Berardino, 2B	13
J. Heath, OF	13
J. Kramer, SP	13
S. Zoldak, SP	11
D. Galehouse, SP	9
C. Laabs, OF	9
A. Zarilla, OF	9
M. Christman, 3B	8
N. Potter, SP	8
C. Stevens, 1B	8
C. Fannin, RP	7
B. Dillinger, 3B	6
E. Kinder, RP	6
J. Lucadello, 3B	6
F. Mancuso, C	6
T. Ferrick, RP	5
J. Schultz, C	4
F. Sanford, SP	3
J. Grace, OF	2
H. Helf, C	2
G. McQuillen, OF	2
A. Milnar, SP-RP	2
L. Moss, C	2
T. Shirley, SP	2
F. Biscan, RP	1
S. Ferens, RP	1
L. Finney, OF	1
P. Lehner, OF	1

Washington (76-78)	WS
Hitting	**131.9**
Fielding	**31.6**
Pitching	**64.5**
M. Vernon, 1B	33
S. Spence, OF	30
B. Lewis, OF	24
M. Haefner, SP	17
J. Priddy, 2B	17
B. Newsom, SP	13
J. Grace, OF	11
C. Travis, SS	10
J. Heath, OF	9
E. Wynn, SP	9
A. Evans, C	7
S. Hudson, RP	7
D. Leonard, SP	7
R. Wolff, SP	7
S. Robertson, 3B	5
R. Scarborough, SP	4
M. Candini, RP	3
J. Early, C	3
B. Hitchcock, SS	3
G. Torres, SS	3
G. Coan, OF	2
G. Binks, OF	1
M. Guerra, C	1
G. Myatt, 3B	1
J. Niggeling, SP	1

1946 National League

Boston (81-72)	WS
Hitting	**129.6**
Fielding	**37.7**
Pitching	**75.7**
J. Sain, SP	26
T. Holmes, OF	25
J. Hopp, 1B	21
P. Masi, C	15
D. Culler, SS	14
C. Ryan, 2B	14
M. Cooper, SP	13
B. Herman, 2B	13
D. Litwhiler, OF	11
B. Rowell, OF	11
E. Wright, SP	11
N. Fernandez, 3B	9
R. Sanders, 1B	9
W. Spahn, SP	9
S. Johnson, RP	8
C. Gillenwater, OF	6
B. Lee, SP	4
M. McCormick, OF	4
S. Roberge, 3B	4
J. Niggeling, SP	3
J. Barrett, OF	2
D. Padgett, C	2
S. Roser, RP	2
D. Mulligan, RP	1
T. Neill, OF	1
K. O'Dea, C	1
E. Singleton, RP	1
L. Wallace, RP	1
E. White, RP	1
W. Wietelmann, SS	1

Brooklyn (96-60)	WS
Hitting	**139.5**
Fielding	**49.6**
Pitching	**98.9**
E. Stanky, 2B	28
D. Walker, OF	27
P. Reese, SS	26
P. Reiser, OF	19
A. Galan, OF	18
J. Hatten, SP	15
C. Furillo, OF	14
K. Higbe, SP	14
V. Lombardi, SP	14
H. Behrman, RP	11
H. Casey, RP	11
B. Edwards, C	11
R. Melton, SP-RP	9
H. Gregg, SP	8
E. Stevens, 1B	8
D. Whitman, OF	8
B. Herman, 3B	7
F. Anderson, C	6
A. Herring, RP	6
C. Lavagetto, 3B	6
E. Head, SP	4
H. Schultz, 1B	4
L. Webber, RP	4
R. Branca, RP	3
J. Medwick, OF	3
G. Hermanski, OF	1
B. Ramazzotti, 3B	1
S. Rojek, SS	1
M. Sandlock, C	1

Chicago (82-71)	WS
Hitting	**123.6**
Fielding	**37.2**
Pitching	**85.3**
P. Cavarretta, OF	25
S. Hack, 3B	17
J. Schmitz, SP	16
H. Wyse, SP	16
P. Lowrey, OF	15
E. Waitkus, 1B	15
C. McCullough, C	14
P. Erickson, RP	11
E. Kush, RP	10
M. Rickert, OF	10
H. Borowy, SP	9
A. Pafko, OF	9
C. Passeau, SP	9
B. Nicholson, OF	8
B. Sturgeon, SS	8
B. Chipman, RP	7
M. Livingston, C	7
D. Johnson, 2B	6
B. Jurges, SS	6
L. Stringer, 2B	5
B. Scheffing, C	4
R. Bauers, RP	3
H. Bithorn, RP	3
D. Dallessandro, OF	3

J. Ostrowski, 3B	3
F. Secory, OF	2
C. Block, 3B	1
R. Meers, RP	1
L. Merullo, SS	1
R. Meyer, RP	1
V. Olsen, RP	1

Cincinnati (67-87)	WS
Hitting	**66.2**
Fielding	**45.2**
Pitching	**89.5**
J. Beggs, SP	17
G. Hatton, 3B	16
E. Blackwell, SP	14
J. Vander Meer, SP	13
R. Mueller, C	12
L. Frey, 2B	11
B. Walters, SP	11
B. Haas, 1B	10
J. Hetki, RP	10
E. Heusser, SP	10
E. Lukon, OF	9
B. Adams, 2B	8
D. Clay, OF	8
H. Gumbert, RP	8
A. Libke, OF	8
B. Zientara, 2B	7
C. Corbitt, SS	6
B. Malloy, RP	5
E. Miller, SS	5
R. Lamanno, C	4
M. West, OF	4
C. Lambert, RP	2
M. McCormick, OF	1
C. Shoun, RP	1
B. Usher, OF	1

New York (61-93)	WS
Hitting	**97.4**
Fielding	**30.2**
Pitching	**55.4**
J. Mize, 1B	22
B. Blattner, 2B	13
S. Gordon, OF	13
B. Kerr, SS	12
D. Koslo, SP	12
W. Marshall, OF	12
M. Kennedy, SP	10
G. Rosen, OF	10
E. Lombardi, C	8
J. Thompson, RP	7
B. Voiselle, SP	7
B. Young, 1B	7
M. Budnick, RP	6
W. Cooper, C	6
M. Witek, 2B	6
J. Graham, OF	5
B. Rigney, 3B	5
K. Trinkle, RP	5
J. Rucker, OF	3
H. Schumacher, SP	3
W. Abernathy, RP	2
S. Jones, SP	2
B. Thomson, 3B	2
B. Warren, C	2
B. Carpenter, SP-RP	1
J. Gee, RP	1
J. Pike, OF	1

Philadelphia (69-85)	WS
Hitting	**114.9**
Fielding	**31.1**
Pitching	**61.0**
D. Ennis, OF	26
J. Wyrostek, OF	22
F. McCormick, 1B	17
A. Seminick, C	15
R. Northey, OF	14
S. Rowe, SP	14
J. Tabor, 3B	13
O. Judd, SP	12
E. Verban, 2B	11
K. Raffensberger, SP	10
D. Mauney, RP	7
B. Donnelly, SP	6
S. Newsome, SS	6
C. Gilbert, OF	5
V. Dinges, 1B	4
A. Jurisich, SP	4
R. Hemsley, C	3
R. Hughes, SS	3
T. Hughes, RP	3
H. Mulcahy, RP	2
J. O'Neil, SS	2
C. Stanceu, SP	2
D. Grate, RP	1
A. Karl, RP	1
D. Mulligan, RP	1
D. Murtaugh, 2B	1
I. Pearson, RP	1
J. Wasdell, OF	1

Pittsburgh (63-91)	WS
Hitting	**80.4**
Fielding	**33.6**
Pitching	**75.0**
F. Ostermueller, SP	19
E. Fletcher, 1B	17
J. Russell, OF	16
R. Kiner, OF	15
B. Elliott, OF	12
E. Bahr, SP	11
B. Cox, SS	11
F. Gustine, 2B	11
N. Strincevich, SP	11
J. Hallett, RP	8
B. Salkeld, C	8
R. Sewell, SP	8
K. Heintzelman, SP	7
J. Lanning, RP	7
L. Handley, 3B	6
A. Lopez, C	5
A. Gerheauser, RP	4
B. Baker, C	2
J. Brown, SS	2
A. Gionfriddo, OF	2
C. Workman, OF	2
H. Camelli, C	1
K. Gables, RP	1
L. Howard, SP	1
M. Van Robays, OF	1
B. Whitehead, 2B	1

St. Louis (98-58)	WS
Hitting	**139.0**
Fielding	**50.5**
Pitching	**104.5**
S. Musial, 1B	44
E. Slaughter, OF	29
H. Pollet, SP	27
W. Kurowski, 3B	26
H. Brecheen, SP	20
M. Marion, SS	19
R. Schoendienst, 2B	19
M. Dickson, RP	16
A. Brazle, RP	8
K. Burkhart, SP	8
E. Dusak, OF	8
H. Walker, OF	8
M. Lanier, SP	7
T. Moore, OF	7
T. Wilks, RP	7
J. Garagiola, C	6
D. Sisler, 1B	5
C. Kluttz, C	4
G. Munger, SP	4
D. Rice, C	4
B. Adams, OF	3
J. Beazley, SP	3
R. Barrett, RP	2
J. Cross, SS	2
L. Klein, 2B	2
F. Martin, SP-RP	2
F. Schmidt, RP	2
B. Donnelly, RP	1
K. O'Dea, C	1

1947 American League

Boston (83-71)	WS
Hitting	**123.7**
Fielding	**40.4**
Pitching	**84.9**
T. Williams, OF	44
J. Pesky, SS	25
D. DiMaggio, OF	20
J. Dobson, SP	20
B. Doerr, 2B	19
S. Mele, OF	15
B. Ferriss, SP	13
E. Johnson, RP	13
T. Hughson, SP	12
D. Galehouse, SP	10
J. Jones, 1B	9
W. Moses, OF	7
B. Tebbetts, C	7
M. Harris, RP	6
J. Murphy, RP	5
H. Dorish, RP	4
B. Klinger, RP	3
E. Pellagrini, 3B	3
M. Batts, C	2
S. Dente, 3B	2
R. Partee, C	2
R. York, 1B	2
M. Combs, 3B	1
L. Culberson, OF	1
T. Fine, SP	1
D. Gutteridge, 2B	1
H. Wagner, C	1
B. Zuber, RP	1

Chicago (70-84)	WS
Hitting	**90.3**
Fielding	**39.2**
Pitching	**80.6**
L. Appling, SS	22
E. Lopat, SP	21
J. Haynes, SP	18
T. Wright, OF	15
F. Baker, 3B	14
F. Papish, SP	14
C. Michaels, 2B	11
D. Philley, OF	11
D. Kolloway, 2B	10
R. York, 1B	10
B. Kennedy, OF	7
T. Tucker, OF	7
R. Hodgin, OF	6
E. Harrist, RP	5
G. Maltzberger, RP	5
J. Rigney, SP	5
E. Caldwell, RP	4
G. Dickey, C	4
M. Tresh, C	4
J. Wallaesa, SS	4
O. Grove, SP	3
J. Jones, 1B	3
P. Gebrian, RP	2
B. Gillespie, SP	2
T. Lee, SP	2
H. Bithorn, RP	1

Cleveland (80-74)	WS
Hitting	**121.8**
Fielding	**42.1**
Pitching	**76.1**
L. Boudreau, SS	28
J. Gordon, 2B	25
B. Feller, SP	23
K. Keltner, 3B	17
D. Mitchell, OF	16
J. Hegan, C	13
B. Lemon, RP	13
C. Metkovich, OF	12
H. Peck, OF	12
H. Edwards, OF	11
A. Gettel, SP	10
E. Klieman, RP	9
R. Embree, SP	8
L. Fleming, 1B	8
E. Robinson, 1B	8
D. Black, SP	6
S. Gromek, RP	4
A. Lopez, C	3
P. Seerey, OF	3
B. Stephens, RP	3
E. Bockman, 3B	2
M. Harder, SP	2
H. Ruszkowski, C	2
B. Kuzava, SP	1
L. Willis, RP	1

Detroit (85-69)	WS
Hitting	**124.8**
Fielding	**36.9**
Pitching	**93.3**
G. Kell, 3B	24
H. Newhouser, SP	24
F. Hutchinson, SP	22
R. Cullenbine, 1B	21
H. Evers, OF	17
E. Mayo, 2B	16
D. Wakefield, OF	16
P. Mullin, OF	15
D. Trout, SP	13
V. Wertz, OF	12
E. Lake, SS	11
H. Wagner, C	10
S. Overmire, SP	9
A. Houtteman, RP	8
B. Swift, C	8
V. Trucks, SP	7
A. Benton, RP	5
H. White, RP	5
J. Gorsica, RP	4
D. Cramer, OF	2
J. Outlaw, OF	2
B. Tebbetts, C	2
J. McHale, 1B	1
S. Webb, 2B	1

New York (97-57)	WS
Hitting	**161.3**
Fielding	**44.2**
Pitching	**85.6**
J. DiMaggio, OF	30
T. Henrich, OF	27
P. Rizzuto, SS	26
G. McQuinn, 1B	24
S. Stirnweiss, 2B	20
J. Page, RP	17
B. Johnson, 3B	16
A. Reynolds, SP	16
J. Lindell, OF	15
S. Shea, SP	14
A. Robinson, C	12
Y. Berra, C	11
S. Chandler, SP	11
C. Keller, OF	10
B. Newsom, SP	8
V. Raschi, SP	6
B. Bevens, SP	5
B. Brown, 3B	5
B. Wensloff, RP	4
A. Clark, OF	3
R. Houk, C	3
D. Johnson, SP	2
K. Drews, RP	1
L. Frey, 2B	1
A. Lyons, RP	1
J. Phillips, 1B	1
D. Starr, RP	1
B. Wight, SP	1

Philadelphia (78-76)	WS
Hitting	**104.1**
Fielding	**43.3**
Pitching	**86.6**

B. McCosky, OF	22
P. Marchildon, SP	21
F. Fain, 1B	19
D. Fowler, SP	18
E. Joost, SS	18
H. Majeski, 3B	18
S. Chapman, OF	17
E. Valo, OF	17
B. Rosar, C	12
R. Christopher, RP	11
B. McCahan, SP	11
P. Suder, 2B	9
J. Flores, SP	8
G. Binks, OF	7
B. Savage, RP	7
J. Coleman, SP	5
B. Dietrich, SP	5
M. Guerra, C	3
G. Handley, 2B	2
D. Adams, 1B	1
A. Knickerbocker, OF	1
C. Laabs, OF	1
C. Scheib, SP	1

St. Louis (59-95)	WS
Hitting	**79.1**
Fielding	**33.4**
Pitching	**64.5**
V. Stephens, SS	23
J. Heath, OF	18
B. Dillinger, 3B	16
W. Judnich, 1B	13
S. Zoldak, SP	13
F. Sanford, SP	12
C. Fannin, SP	9
J. Berardino, 2B	8
J. Early, C	8
E. Kinder, SP	8
N. Potter, RP	8
P. Lehner, OF	7
J. Kramer, SP	5
G. Moulder, RP	5
R. Coleman, OF	4
B. Muncrief, SP	4
A. Zarilla, OF	4
B. Hitchcock, 2B	3
L. Moss, C	3
R. Peters, 2B	2
H. Thompson, 2B	2
Wa. Brown, RP	1
D. Dean, SP	1

Washington (64-90)	WS
Hitting	**76.5**
Fielding	**37.2**
Pitching	**78.3**
S. Spence, OF	25
W. Masterson, SP	21
E. Wynn, SP	20
M. Vernon, 1B	15
M. Haefner, SP	13
B. Lewis, OF	10
R. Scarborough, SP	10
J. Priddy, 2B	9
A. Evans, C	7
T. Ferrick, RP	7
J. Grace, OF	7
E. Yost, 3B	7
M. Christman, SS	6
G. Coan, OF	5
R. Ferrell, C	5
B. Newsom, SP	4
S. Robertson, OF	4
J. Sullivan, SS	4
T. McBride, OF	3
S. Hudson, SP	2
M. Pieretti, RP	2
M. Candini, RP	1
B. Dozier, RP	1
L. Harris, RP	1
E. Lyons, 2B	1
F. Mancuso, C	1
C. Travis, 3B	1

1947
National League

Boston (86-68)	WS
Hitting	**120.4**
Fielding	**42.9**
Pitching	**94.7**
W. Spahn, SP	32
B. Elliott, 3B	29
J. Sain, SP	24
T. Holmes, OF	21
P. Masi, C	19
E. Torgeson, 1B	18
C. Ryan, 2B	17
J. Hopp, OF	14
R. Barrett, SP	12
B. Rowell, OF	9
F. McCormick, 1B	8
M. McCormick, OF	7
S. Johnson, RP	6
W. Lanfranconi, RP	6
D. Litwhiler, OF	6
B. Voiselle, SP	6
S. Sisti, SS	5
H. Camelli, C	3
D. Culler, SS	3
C. Shoun, RP	3
M. Cooper, SP	2
N. Fernandez, SS	2
A. Karl, RP	2
J. Beazley, RP	1
G. Elliott, RP	1
R. Martin, SP	1
E. White, SP	1

Brooklyn (94-60)	WS
Hitting	**136.4**
Fielding	**50.2**
Pitching	**95.4**
R. Branca, SP	26
P. Reese, SS	26
D. Walker, OF	23
J. Robinson, 1B	21
B. Edwards, C	20
E. Stanky, 2B	20
P. Reiser, OF	18
J. Hatten, SP	17
S. Jorgensen, 3B	16
V. Lombardi, SP	15
C. Furillo, OF	14
H. Taylor, SP	13
H. Casey, RP	10
G. Hermanski, OF	8
C. King, RP	7
A. Vaughan, OF	7
H. Behrman, RP	3
C. Lavagetto, 3B	3
E. Miksis, 2B	3
R. Barney, RP	2
S. Rojek, SS	2
B. Bragan, C	1
A. Gionfriddo, OF	1
P. Haugstad, RP	1
K. Higbe, SP	1
G. Hodges, C	1
D. Lund, OF	1
D. Snider, OF	1
D. Whitman, OF	1

Chicago (69-85)	WS
Hitting	**80.2**
Fielding	**42.9**
Pitching	**83.9**
B. Nicholson, OF	18
J. Schmitz, SP	18
P. Cavarretta, OF	16
A. Pafko, OF	16
P. Lowrey, 3B	12
E. Waitkus, 1B	12
D. Lade, SP	11
B. Chipman, SP	10
P. Erickson, SP-RP	10
E. Kush, RP	10
H. Borowy, SP	9
S. Hack, 3B	8
D. Johnson, 2B	8
B. Scheffing, C	8
C. McCullough, C	6
H. Wyse, SP	6
R. Meyer, RP	5
C. Aberson, OF	4
L. Merullo, SS	4
D. Dallessandro, OF	3
R. Meers, RP	3
B. Sturgeon, SS	3
R. Hamner, SP	2
R. Mack, 2B	2
B. Jurges, SS	1
O. Miller, SP	1
M. Rickert, OF	1

Cincinnati (73-81)	WS
Hitting	**119.9**
Fielding	**31.2**
Pitching	**67.9**
E. Blackwell, SP	28
G. Hatton, 3B	22
E. Miller, SS	22
A. Galan, OF	21
F. Baumholtz, OF	17
B. Haas, OF	13
B. Young, 1B	13
R. Lamanno, C	12
H. Gumbert, RP	9
B. Adams, 2B	8
K. Peterson, RP	8
J. Vander Meer, SP	7
K. Raffensberger, SP	6
B. Zientara, 2B	6
E. Lukon, OF	5
R. Mueller, C	5
B. Lively, RP	4
T. Tatum, OF	4
B. Walters, SP	3
E. Erautt, RP	2
H. Perkowski, RP	1
H. Poland, C	1
C. Vollmer, OF	1
K. Wahl, 3B	1

New York (81-73)	WS
Hitting	**142.1**
Fielding	**31.1**
Pitching	**69.8**
J. Mize, 1B	32
W. Marshall, OF	24
W. Cooper, C	23
L. Jansen, SP	20
B. Thomson, OF	20
B. Kerr, SS	16
B. Rigney, 2B	16
S. Gordon, OF	13
D. Koslo, SP	11
C. Hartung, SP	10
J. Lohrke, 3B	8
K. Trinkle, RP	8
R. Poat, SP	6
M. Kennedy, SP	5
B. Blattner, 2B	4
G. Gearhart, OF	4
J. Beggs, RP	3
A. Hansen, RP	3
S. Jones, RP	3
E. Lombardi, C	3
R. Rhawn, 2B	2
J. Thompson, RP	2
M. Witek, 2B	2
M. Cooper, SP	1
H. Iott, RP	1
J. Lafata, OF	1
B. Voiselle, RP	1
W. Westrum, C	1

Philadelphia (62-92)	WS
Hitting	**69.8**
Fielding	**37.5**
Pitching	**78.7**
H. Walker, OF	24
D. Leonard, SP	23
S. Rowe, SP	13
E. Verban, 2B	13
J. Wyrostek, OF	12
B. Donnelly, RP	11
D. Ennis, OF	11
A. Seminick, C	11
T. Hughes, SP	9
K. Heintzelman, SP	7
R. Lapointe, SS	6
O. Judd, SP	5
S. Newsome, SS	5
D. Padgett, C	4
C. Schanz, RP	4
B. Adams, OF	3
L. Handley, 3B	3
A. Jurisich, RP	3
F. Schmidt, RP	3
J. Tabor, 3B	3
J. Albright, SS	2
C. Gilbert, OF	2
H. Schultz, 1B	2
C. Simmons, SP	2
N. Etten, 1B	1
P. Jones, 3B	1
A. Lakeman, 1B	1
D. Mauney, RP	1
R. Northey, OF	1

Pittsburgh (62-92)	WS
Hitting	**101.5**
Fielding	**29.7**
Pitching	**54.8**
R. Kiner, OF	30
F. Gustine, 3B	19
B. Cox, SS	14
H. Greenberg, 1B	14
K. Higbe, SP	13
T. Bonham, SP	10
F. Ostermueller, SP	10
J. Russell, OF	10
C. Rikard, OF	9
W. Westlake, OF	9
C. Kluttz, C	8
R. Sewell, SP-RP	7
D. Howell, C	6
J. Bagby Jr., RP	4
E. Bahr, SP	3
J. Bloodworth, 2B	3
E. Fletcher, 1B	3
M. Queen, SP	3
P. Roe, SP	3
E. Basinski, 2B	1
P. Castiglione, SS	1
G. Mauch, 2B	1
E. Singleton, RP	1
N. Strincevich, RP	1
B. Sullivan, C	1
W. Wietelmann, SS	1
G. Woodling, OF	1

St. Louis (89-65)	WS
Hitting	**116.6**
Fielding	**50.0**
Pitching	**100.4**
W. Kurowski, 3B	26
S. Musial, 1B	25
E. Slaughter, OF	20
H. Brecheen, SP	19
M. Dickson, SP	18
M. Marion, SS	18
G. Munger, SP	18
A. Brazle, RP	16
J. Hearn, SP	13
R. Northey, OF	13
R. Schoendienst, 2B	13
T. Moore, OF	12
E. Dusak, OF	11
J. Garagiola, C	9
H. Pollet, SP	8
D. Rice, C	8
J. Medwick, OF	5

C. Diering, OF	3
T. Wilks, RP	3
K. Burkhart, RP	2
K. Johnson, SP-RP	2
G. Staley, RP	2
J. Cross, 3B	1
N. Jones, 2B	1
D. Wilber, C	1

1948 American League

Boston (96-59)	WS
Hitting	**153.9**
Fielding	**42.1**
Pitching	**92.1**
T. Williams, OF	39
B. Doerr, 2B	27
D. DiMaggio, OF	26
V. Stephens, SS	25
J. Dobson, SP	20
J. Pesky, 3B	20
M. Parnell, SP	18
B. Goodman, 1B	15
J. Kramer, SP	14
B. Tebbetts, C	14
E. Kinder, SP	12
S. Spence, OF	12
D. Galehouse, SP	10
E. Johnson, RP	7
B. Ferriss, RP	6
M. Batts, C	5
W. Moses, OF	5
M. Harris, SP	4
B. Hitchcock, 2B-3B	4
S. Mele, OF	2
C. Deal, RP	1
T. Hughson, RP	1
M. McDermott, RP	1

Chicago (51-101)	WS
Hitting	**66.9**
Fielding	**29.3**
Pitching	**56.8**
L. Appling, 3B	17
D. Philley, OF	13
C. Michaels, SS	11
A. Gettel, SP	10
J. Haynes, SP	10
T. Lupien, 1B	9
P. Seerey, OF	9
B. Wight, SP	9
T. Wright, OF	9
A. Robinson, C	8
R. Gumpert, SP	7
H. Judson, RP	7
D. Kolloway, 2B	7
F. Baker, 3B	6
M. Pieretti, SP	6
R. Hodgin, OF	4
F. Papish, RP	3
B. Gillespie, RP	2
I. Pearson, RP	2
E. Caldwell, RP	1
B. Kennedy, OF	1
M. Tresh, C	1
R. Weigel, C	1

Cleveland (97-58)	WS
Hitting	**139.4**
Fielding	**50.0**
Pitching	**101.5**
L. Boudreau, SS	34
B. Lemon, SP	26
K. Keltner, 3B	25
J. Gordon, 2B	24
G. Bearden, SP	22
D. Mitchell, OF	20
L. Doby, OF	18
J. Hegan, C	17
B. Feller, SP	15
S. Gromek, RP	10
E. Robinson, 1B	9
R. Christopher, RP	8
A. Clark, OF	8
W. Judnich, OF	8
T. Tucker, OF	8
S. Zoldak, SP	8
E. Klieman, RP	7
S. Paige, RP	7
H. Edwards, OF	5
B. Muncrief, RP	3
J. Tipton, C	3
J. Berardino, 2B	2
Bo. Kennedy, OF	2
H. Peck, OF	1
P. Seerey, OF	1

Detroit (78-76)	WS
Hitting	**107.7**
Fielding	**37.5**
Pitching	**88.9**
H. Newhouser, SP	27
P. Mullin, OF	22
H. Evers, OF	20
J. Lipon, SS	18
V. Trucks, SP	16
D. Trout, SP	15
F. Hutchinson, SP	14
D. Wakefield, OF	14
G. Kell, 3B	11
S. Vico, 1B	9
V. Wertz, OF	9
E. Lake, 2B	8
B. Swift, C	8
A. Houtteman, RP	7
N. Berry, SS	6
T. Gray, RP	6
E. Mayo, 2B	5
J. Outlaw, 3B	5
J. Groth, OF	2
L. Kretlow, RP	2
H. Wagner, C	2
A. Benton, RP	1
P. Campbell, 1B	1
R. Gentry, RP	1
J. Ginsberg, C	1
S. Overmire, RP	1
B. Pierce, RP	1
H. Riebe, C	1
H. White, RP	1

New York (94-60)	WS
Hitting	**148.0**
Fielding	**45.0**
Pitching	**89.1**
J. DiMaggio, OF	34
T. Henrich, OF	29
Y. Berra, C	18
S. Stirnweiss, 2B	17
A. Reynolds, SP	16
B. Johnson, 3B	15
V. Raschi, SP	15
P. Rizzuto, SS	15
B. Brown, 3B	14
J. Lindell, OF	14
E. Lopat, SP	14
T. Byrne, RP	12
S. Shea, SP	11
G. Niarhos, C	10
C. Keller, OF	8
G. McQuinn, 1B	8
J. Page, RP	8
F. Hiller, RP	5
R. Embree, RP	4
B. Porterfield, SP	4
K. Drews, RP	2
R. Gumpert, RP	2
C. Mapes, OF	2
H. Bauer, OF	1
F. Crosetti, 2B	1
R. Houk, C	1
C. Silvera, C	1
S. Souchock, 1B	1

Philadelphia (84-70)	WS
Hitting	**122.6**
Fielding	**43.0**
Pitching	**86.3**
E. Joost, SS	26
H. Majeski, 3B	25
F. Fain, 1B	21
C. Scheib, SP	20
B. McCosky, OF	19
D. Fowler, SP	17
E. Valo, OF	17
L. Brissie, SP	15
J. Coleman, SP	15
P. Suder, 2B	15
S. Chapman, OF	14
B. Rosar, C	11
P. Marchildon, SP	9
C. Harris, RP	8
D. White, OF	4
R. Coleman, OF	3
H. Franks, C	3
M. Guerra, C	2
B. McCahan, SP	2
N. Potter, RP	2
W. Holborow, RP	1
B. Savage, RP	1
S. Webb, 2B	1
B. Wellman, 1B	1

St. Louis (59-94)	WS
Hitting	**77.5**
Fielding	**34.1**
Pitching	**65.4**
J. Priddy, 2B	20
N. Garver, SP	18
B. Dillinger, 3B	17
A. Zarilla, OF	17
C. Fannin, SP	14
F. Sanford, SP	13
L. Moss, C	8
B. Kennedy, SP	7
D. Kokos, OF	7
E. Pellagrini, SS	7
W. Platt, OF	7
S. Dente, SS	6
P. Lehner, OF	5
C. Stevens, 1B	5
A. Widmar, RP	5
H. Arft, 1B	4
J. Ostrowski, RP	3
R. Partee, C	3
S. Zoldak, SP	3
F. Biscan, RP	2
D. Lund, OF	2
B. Stephens, RP	2
A. Anderson, 2B	1
N. Potter, SP	1

Washington (56-97)	WS
Hitting	**65.3**
Fielding	**36.5**
Pitching	**66.3**
R. Scarborough, SP	18
B. Stewart, OF	15
E. Yost, 3B	14
W. Masterson, SP	13
G. Coan, OF	10
D. Thompson, RP	10
A. Kozar, 2B	9
A. Evans, C	8
J. Early, C	7
C. Gillenwater, OF	7
M. Haefner, SP	7
M. Vernon, 1B	7
T. Ferrick, RP	6
J. Wooten, OF	6
M. Candini, RP	5
S. Robertson, OF	5
M. Christman, SS	4
T. McBride, OF	4
E. Harrist, RP	3
E. Wynn, SP	3
S. Hudson, SP	2
D. Welteroth, RP	2
L. Okrie, C	1
J. Sullivan, SS	1
D. Weik, SP	1

1948 National League

Boston (91-62)	WS
Hitting	**130.7**
Fielding	**45.2**
Pitching	**97.1**
J. Sain, SP	28
B. Elliott, 3B	27
A. Dark, SS	20
J. Heath, OF	20
T. Holmes, OF	19
W. Spahn, SP	14
E. Stanky, 2B	14
E. Torgeson, 1B	14
B. Voiselle, SP	12
V. Bickford, SP	11
M. McCormick, OF	11
J. Russell, OF	11
P. Masi, C	10
B. Salkeld, C	10
N. Potter, RP	9
R. Barrett, RP	7
C. Conatser, OF	7
B. Hogue, RP	7
C. Shoun, RP	5
S. Sisti, 2B	5
F. McCormick, 1B	3
C. Ryan, 2B	3
E. White, RP	3
J. Antonelli, RP	1
D. Litwhiler, OF	1
B. Sturgeon, 2B	1

Brooklyn (84-70)	WS
Hitting	**117.5**
Fielding	**46.9**
Pitching	**87.7**
J. Robinson, 2B	25
P. Reese, SS	23
G. Hermanski, OF	19
R. Barney, SP	18
P. Roe, SP	16
R. Branca, SP	15
C. Furillo, OF	15
J. Hatten, SP	14
R. Campanella, C	12
G. Hodges, 1B	10
M. Rackley, OF	10
B. Edwards, C	9
B. Cox, 3B	6
P. Minner, RP	6
E. Palica, RP	6
G. Shuba, OF	6
H. Behrman, RP	5
C. Erskine, SP	5
D. Snider, OF	5
D. Whitman, OF	5
S. Jorgensen, 3B	4
E. Miksis, 2B	4
P. Reiser, OF	4
A. Vaughan, OF	3
P. Ward, 1B	3
T. Brown, 3B	1
D. Lund, OF	1
W. Ramsdell, RP	1
H. Taylor, SP	1

Chicago (64-90)	WS
Hitting	**89.8**
Fielding	**33.6**
Pitching	**68.6**
A. Pafko, 3B	23
J. Schmitz, SP	22
B. Nicholson, OF	17
E. Waitkus, 1B	15
H. Jeffcoat, OF	10
R. Meyer, SP	10

Player	WS
B. Scheffing, C	10
P. Cavarretta, 1B	9
P. Lowrey, OF	9
J. Dobernic, RP	8
B. Rush, RP	6
H. Schenz, 2B	5
E. Verban, 2B	5
R. Walker, C	5
B. Chipman, RP	4
D. Lade, SP	4
C. Maddern, OF	4
R. Smalley, SS	4
H. Borowy, RP	3
C. Chambers, RP	3
R. Hamner, SP	3
E. Kush, RP	3
D. McCall, SP	3
G. Mauch, 2B	2
C. McCullough, C	2
D. Culler, SS	1
D. Lynch, 2B	1
C. Mauro, OF	1

Cincinnati (64-89)	WS
Hitting	**85.0**
Fielding	**34.5**
Pitching	**72.5**
J. Vander Meer, SP	20
H. Sauer, OF	19
J. Wyrostek, OF	18
H. Gumbert, RP	13
G. Hatton, 3B	13
D. Litwhiler, OF	12
K. Raffensberger, SP	12
F. Baumholtz, OF	11
B. Adams, 2B	9
T. Kluszewski, 1B	9
E. Blackwell, SP	8
H. Fox, SP	7
R. Lamanno, C	6
V. Stallcup, SS	6
C. Corbitt, 2B	4
A. Galan, OF	4
K. Peterson, RP	4
W. Cress, RP	3
B. Young, 1B	3
B. Lively, RP	2
H. Wehmeier, SP	2
B. Zientara, 2B	2
J. Blackburn, RP	1
K. Burkhart, RP	1
S. Filipowicz, OF	1
B. Walters, SP	1
D. Williams, C	1

New York (78-76)	WS
Hitting	**128.2**
Fielding	**33.8**
Pitching	**72.0**
J. Mize, 1B	30
S. Gordon, 3B	25
W. Lockman, OF	23
L. Jansen, SP	17
W. Marshall, OF	16
S. Jones, RP	15
B. Rigney, 2B	13
B. Kerr, SS	12
W. Cooper, C	10
B. Thomson, OF	9
A. Hansen, RP	8
D. Koslo, SP	8
J. Lohrke, 3B	7
K. Trinkle, RP	6
C. Hartung, SP	5
R. Poat, SP	5
M. Kennedy, SP	4
M. Livingston, C	3
D. Mueller, OF	3
W. Westrum, C	3
L. Layton, OF	2
R. Rhawn, SS	2
R. Webb, SP	2
J. Conway, 2B	1
L. Frey, 2B	1
T. Lee, RP	1
J. McCarthy, 1B	1
B. Newsom, RP	1
S. Yvars, C	1

Philadelphia (66-88)	WS
Hitting	**94.1**
Fielding	**32.2**
Pitching	**71.8**
D. Ennis, OF	24
R. Ashburn, OF	21
D. Leonard, SP	19
D. Sisler, 1B	13
R. Roberts, SP	12
A. Seminick, C	11
E. Miller, SS	10
J. Blatnik, OF	9
S. Rowe, SP	9
H. Walker, OF	9
B. Donnelly, SP	8
M. Dubiel, RP	8
B. Haas, 3B	8
G. Hamner, 2B	8
K. Heintzelman, SP	6
P. Caballero, 3B	4
P. Jones, 3B	3
C. Simmons, SP	3
E. Heusser, RP	2
J. Konstanty, RP	2
B. Rowell, 3B	2
P. Erickson, SP-RP	1
A. Lakeman, C	1
J. Mayo, OF	1
A. Porto, RP	1
L. Possehl, SP	1
J. Thompson, SP	1
E. Verban, 2B	1

Pittsburgh (83-71)	WS
Hitting	**115.7**
Fielding	**45.2**
Pitching	**88.1**
R. Kiner, OF	30
S. Rojek, SS	21
D. Murtaugh, 2B	19
W. Westlake, OF	17
B. Chesnes, SP	16
E. Riddle, SP	15
D. Walker, OF	15
K. Higbe, RP	14
F. Gustine, 3B	13
V. Lombardi, RP	13
J. Hopp, OF	12
R. Sewell, SP	11
E. Stevens, 1B	10
E. Fitz Gerald, C	8
T. Bonham, SP	6
F. Ostermueller, SP	6
C. Kluttz, C	5
E. Bockman, 3B	4
H. Gregg, RP	4
E. Singleton, RP	4
M. West, 1B	3
T. Beard, OF	2
M. Basgall, 2B	1

St. Louis (85-69)	WS
Hitting	**122.0**
Fielding	**44.0**
Pitching	**89.0**
S. Musial, OF	46
H. Brecheen, SP	27
E. Slaughter, OF	26
T. Wilks, RP	17
M. Dickson, SP	15
M. Marion, SS	13
R. Northey, OF	13
R. Schoendienst, 2B	12
D. Lang, 3B	10
A. Brazle, SP	9
H. Pollet, SP	8
D. Rice, C	8
E. Dusak, OF	7
N. Jones, 1B	7
G. Munger, SP	7
B. Baker, C	5
J. Hearn, RP	5
W. Kurowski, 3B	5
T. Moore, OF	4
R. Lapointe, 2B	3
K. Johnson, RP	2
Ba. Young, 1B	2
K. Burkhart, RP	1
J. Garagiola, C	1
H. Rice, OF	1
D. Wilber, C	1

1949 American League

Boston (96-58)	WS
Hitting	**142.5**
Fielding	**45.7**
Pitching	**99.8**
T. Williams, OF	40
V. Stephens, SS	32
M. Parnell, SP	31
B. Doerr, 2B	25
D. DiMaggio, OF	24
J. Pesky, 3B	23
E. Kinder, SP	22
J. Dobson, SP	15
A. Zarilla, OF	12
B. Goodman, 1B	11
C. Stobbs, SP	11
B. Tebbetts, C	11
M. McDermott, SP	6
J. Kramer, SP	5
M. Batts, C	4
T. Hughson, RP	3
W. Masterson, RP	3
T. O'Brien, OF	2
F. Quinn, RP	2
M. Combs, 3B	1
H. Dorish, RP	1
B. Ferriss, RP	1
M. Harris, SP	1
B. Hitchcock, 1B	1
L. Stringer, 2B	1

Chicago (63-91)	WS
Hitting	**86.5**
Fielding	**35.4**
Pitching	**67.0**
C. Michaels, 2B	22
L. Appling, SS	19
B. Wight, SP	18
R. Gumpert, SP	14
F. Baker, 3B	13
D. Philley, OF	12
B. Kuzava, SP	9
B. Pierce, SP	9
C. Kress, 1B	7
G. Zernial, OF	7
M. Haefner, SP	5
E. Malone, C	5
S. Souchock, OF	5
D. Wheeler, C	5
H. Adams, OF	4
E. Klieman, RP	4
C. Metkovich, OF	4
J. Ostrowski, OF	4
M. Pieretti, RP	3
J. Scala, OF	3
M. Surkont, RP	3
J. Tipton, C	3
G. Goldsberry, 1B	2
H. Judson, RP	2
J. Baumer, SS	1
B. Bowers, OF	1
B. Cain, RP	1
B. Higdon, OF	1
R. Krsnich, 3B	1
E. Rapp, OF	1
R. Rhawn, 3B	1

Cleveland (89-65)	WS
Hitting	**107.9**
Fielding	**49.8**
Pitching	**109.3**
B. Lemon, SP	31
L. Doby, OF	24
D. Mitchell, OF	23
M. Garcia, RP	21
M. Vernon, 1B	21
J. Gordon, 2B	19
A. Benton, RP	18
L. Boudreau, SS	17
J. Hegan, C	15
B. Feller, SP	14
B. Kennedy, OF	12
R. Boone, SS	8
S. Paige, RP	8
E. Wynn, SP	8
K. Keltner, 3B	7
S. Gromek, RP	6
F. Papish, RP	5
T. Tucker, OF	3
G. Bearden, SP	2
S. Zoldak, RP	2
J. Berardino, 3B	1
H. Peck, OF	1
M. Tresh, C	1

Detroit (87-67)	WS
Hitting	**110.2**
Fielding	**46.5**
Pitching	**104.3**
V. Trucks, SP	27
H. Newhouser, SP	25
G. Kell, 3B	24
V. Wertz, OF	23
F. Hutchinson, SP	19
H. Evers, OF	18
J. Groth, OF	15
A. Robinson, C	15
T. Gray, SP	14
A. Houtteman, SP	14
J. Lipon, SS	13
D. Kolloway, 2B	11
P. Mullin, OF	11
P. Campbell, 1B	7
E. Lake, SS	5
B. Swift, C	5
D. Wakefield, OF	4
N. Berry, 2B	3
D. Trout, RP	3
H. White, RP	3
S. Vico, 1B	2

New York (97-57)	WS
Hitting	**152.6**
Fielding	**47.3**
Pitching	**91.1**
T. Henrich, OF	24
P. Rizzuto, SS	22
Y. Berra, C	21
J. DiMaggio, OF	21
J. Page, RP	19
V. Raschi, SP	19
J. Coleman, 2B	17
E. Lopat, SP	17
A. Reynolds, SP	14
T. Byrne, SP	13
B. Brown, 3B	12
C. Mapes, OF	12
G. Woodling, OF	12
H. Bauer, OF	11
B. Johnson, 3B	9
J. Lindell, OF	6
C. Silvera, C	6
S. Stirnweiss, 2B	6
C. Keller, OF	5
D. Kryhoski, 1B	4
J. Phillips, 1B	4
F. Sanford, RP	4
G. Niarhos, C	3
B. Porterfield, SP	3
R. Buxton, RP	1
J. Delsing, OF	1

Player	WS
R. Houk, C	1
C. Marshall, RP	1
J. Mize, 1B	1
D. Pillette, RP	1
S. Shea, RP	1

Philadelphia (81-73)	WS
Hitting	**120.4**
Fielding	**43.8**
Pitching	**78.8**
E. Joost, SS	35
S. Chapman, OF	24
E. Valo, OF	24
F. Fain, 1B	19
A. Kellner, SP	17
L. Brissie, SP	15
J. Coleman, SP	14
D. Fowler, SP	14
H. Majeski, 3B	13
P. Suder, 2B	12
B. Shantz, RP	11
W. Moses, OF	10
M. Guerra, C	9
N. Fox, 2B	6
C. Scheib, SP	5
J. Astroth, C	4
T. Davis, SS	2
A. Galan, OF	2
B. McCahan, SP	2
T. Wright, OF	2
C. Harris, RP	1
B. Rosar, C	1
D. White, OF	1

St. Louis (53-101)	WS
Hitting	**86.6**
Fielding	**25.4**
Pitching	**47.0**
J. Priddy, 2B	17
R. Sievers, OF	16
D. Kokos, OF	15
B. Dillinger, 3B	14
N. Garver, SP	13
J. Graham, 1B	10
L. Moss, C	10
T. Ferrick, RP	8
S. Spence, OF	8
S. Lollar, C	7
J. Ostrowski, RP	7
B. Kennedy, RP	6
A. Papai, RP	4
D. Starr, RP	4
J. Sullivan, SS	4
R. Embree, SP	3
E. Pellagrini, SS	3
W. Platt, OF	3
C. Fannin, SP	2
A. Anderson, SS	1
G. Elder, OF	1
P. Lehner, OF	1
B. Malloy, RP	1
A. Zarilla, OF	1

Washington (50-104)	WS
Hitting	**81.9**
Fielding	**25.2**
Pitching	**42.8**
E. Robinson, 1B	18
E. Yost, 3B	15
B. Stewart, OF	13
C. Vollmer, OF	11
S. Hudson, SP	10
A. Evans, C	9
S. Robertson, 2B	9
R. Scarborough, SP	9
S. Dente, SS	8
A. Kozar, 2B	6
B. Lewis, OF	6
M. Haefner, SP	5
L. Hittle, RP	5
W. Masterson, SP	4
P. Calvert, SP	3
J. Early, C	3
M. Harris, SP	3
G. Coan, OF	2
S. Mele, OF	2
R. Ortiz, OF	2
D. Weik, SP	2
M. Candini, RP	1
M. Christman, 3B	1
J. Gonzales, RP	1
D. Thompson, RP	1
R. Weigel, C	1

1949 National League

Boston (75-79)	WS
Hitting	**118.4**
Fielding	**34.9**
Pitching	**71.7**
W. Spahn, SP	24
B. Elliott, 3B	23
E. Stanky, 2B	21
E. Fletcher, 1B	15
A. Dark, SS	12
V. Bickford, SP	10
T. Holmes, OF	10
M. Rickert, OF	9
J. Russell, OF	9
P. Reiser, OF	8
B. Salkeld, C	8
B. Voiselle, SP	8
D. Crandall, C	6
J. Heath, OF	6
B. Hogue, RP	6
N. Potter, RP	6
C. Ryan, 3B	6
J. Sain, SP	6
S. Sisti, OF	6
J. Antonelli, RP	5
B. Hall, RP	5
E. Sauer, OF	5
C. Conatser, OF	3
G. Elliott, RP	3
E. Torgeson, 1B	3
M. Livingston, C	1
P. Masi, C	1

Brooklyn (97-57)	WS
Hitting	**153.7**
Fielding	**46.9**
Pitching	**90.4**
J. Robinson, 2B	36
P. Reese, SS	32
R. Campanella, C	24
D. Snider, OF	24
C. Furillo, OF	23
G. Hodges, 1B	21
D. Newcombe, SP	21
P. Roe, SP	19
G. Hermanski, OF	12
J. Banta, RP	11
J. Hatten, SP	9
R. Branca, SP	8
B. Cox, 3B	8
E. Palica, RP	8
R. Barney, SP	7
S. Jorgensen, 3B	5
B. Edwards, C	4
C. Erskine, RP	4
M. Rackley, OF	4
T. Brown, OF	3
P. Minner, RP	3
L. Olmo, OF	2
M. McCormick, OF	1
P. McGlothin, RP	1
E. Miksis, 3B	1

Chicago (61-93)	WS
Hitting	**88.2**
Fielding	**29.3**
Pitching	**65.5**
A. Pafko, OF	19
H. Sauer, OF	17
P. Cavarretta, 1B	14
B. Rush, SP	11
M. Dubiel, SP	10
J. Schmitz, SP	10
R. Smalley, SS	10
D. Leonard, SP	9
H. Edwards, OF	7
B. Chipman, RP	6
W. Hacker, RP	6
H. Jeffcoat, OF	6
H. Reich, 1B	6
E. Verban, 2B	6
D. Lade, RP	5
B. Muncrief, RP	5
M. Owen, C	5
E. Kush, RP	4
F. Gustine, 3B	3
G. Mauch, 2B	3
B. Scheffing, C	3
W. Terwilliger, 2B	3
H. Walker, OF	3
P. Lowrey, OF	2
R. Walker, C	2
D. Adkins, RP	1
F. Baumholtz, OF	1
S. Burgess, C	1
C. Maddern, 1B	1
R. Novotney, C	1
B. Ramazzotti, 3B	1
H. Schenz, 3B	1
B. Serena, 3B	1

Cincinnati (62-92)	WS
Hitting	**86.3**
Fielding	**34.9**
Pitching	**64.8**
K. Raffensberger, SP	20
G. Hatton, 3B	17
T. Kluszewski, 1B	13
D. Litwhiler, OF	12
W. Cooper, C	11
J. Wyrostek, OF	11
J. Bloodworth, 2B	10
H. Walker, OF	10
H. Fox, SP	9
H. Wehmeier, SP	9
V. Stallcup, SS	8
E. Erautt, RP	7
P. Lowrey, OF	7
B. Lively, RP	6
B. Adams, 2B	5
E. Blackwell, RP	5
L. Merriman, OF	4
J. Vander Meer, SP	4
K. Burkhart, RP	3
D. (Homer) Howell, C	3
R. Mueller, C	3
S. Meeks, 2B	2
H. Sauer, OF	2
F. Baumholtz, OF	1
C. Corbitt, SS	1
H. Gumbert, RP	1
H. Perkowski, SP	1
J. Pramesa, C	1

New York (73-81)	WS
Hitting	**108.5**
Fielding	**35.5**
Pitching	**75.1**
B. Thomson, OF	26
S. Gordon, 3B	19
D. Koslo, SP	19
W. Lockman, OF	19
W. Marshall, OF	18
L. Jansen, SP	14
S. Jones, SP	14
M. Kennedy, SP	13
J. Mize, 1B	11
B. Rigney, SS	11
H. Thompson, 2B	10
W. Westrum, C	7
C. Hartung, SP	5
K. Higbe, RP	5
J. Lohrke, 2B	5
B. Kerr, SS	3
R. Mueller, C	3
H. Behrman, RP	2
W. Cooper, C	2
A. Hansen, RP	2
M. Irvin, OF	2
J. Lafata, 1B	2
M. Livingston, C	2
R. Webb, RP	2
B. Haas, 1B	1
D. Williams, 2B	1
A. Zabala, RP	1

Philadelphia (81-73)	WS
Hitting	**106.4**
Fielding	**43.5**
Pitching	**93.1**
D. Ennis, OF	27
K. Heintzelman, SP	23
R. Meyer, SP	20
R. Ashburn, OF	19
A. Seminick, C	18
G. Hamner, SS	16
R. Roberts, SP	16
P. Jones, 3B	15
H. Borowy, SP	12
J. Konstanty, RP	11
D. Sisler, 1B	11
B. Nicholson, OF	9
E. Waitkus, 1B	8
S. Lopata, C	7
E. Miller, 2B	5
C. Simmons, RP	5
B. Blattner, 2B	4
S. Hollmig, OF	4
K. Trinkle, RP	4
M. Goliat, 2B	3
S. Rowe, RP	2
P. Caballero, 2B	1
B. Donnelly, RP	1
B. Miller, RP	1
E. Sanicki, OF	1

Pittsburgh (71-83)	WS
Hitting	**102.3**
Fielding	**38.6**
Pitching	**72.1**
R. Kiner, OF	37
M. Dickson, RP	19
W. Westlake, OF	17
C. Chambers, SP	14
J. Hopp, 1B	12
B. Werle, SP	12
P. Castiglione, 3B	9
V. Lombardi, RP	9
S. Rojek, SS	9
C. McCullough, C	8
D. Restelli, OF	8
T. Saffell, OF	7
T. Bonham, SP	6
R. Sewell, RP	6
P. Masi, C	5
E. Stevens, 1B	5
E. Bockman, 3B	4
D. Walker, OF	4
M. Basgall, 2B	3
H. Casey, RP	3
B. Chesnes, SP	3
E. Fitz Gerald, C	3
D. Murtaugh, 2B	3
E. Riddle, SP	2
L. Fleming, 1B	1
H. Gregg, RP	1
J. Phillips, 1B	1
M. Rackley, OF	1
J. Walsh, SP	1

St. Louis (96-58)	WS
Hitting	**121.7**
Fielding	**50.8**
Pitching	**115.5**
S. Musial, OF	40
E. Slaughter, OF	29
H. Pollet, SP	24
R. Schoendienst, 2B	20
H. Brecheen, SP	18
G. Staley, RP	17
A. Brazle, SP	16
G. Munger, SP	15
M. Marion, SS	13
T. Wilks, RP	12
C. Diering, OF	11
E. Kazak, 3B	10
T. Glaviano, 3B	9
J. Garagiola, C	8
N. Jones, 1B	8
F. Martin, RP	8
D. Rice, C	8
R. Northey, OF	7
M. Lanier, SP	6
L. Klein, SS	3
S. Hemus, 2B	2
S. Bilko, 1B	1
J. Hearn, RP	1
R. Nelson, 1B	1
B. Reeder, RP	1

1950 American League

Boston (94-60)	WS
Hitting	**152.7**
Fielding	**42.2**
Pitching	**87.1**
D. DiMaggio, OF	24
B. Doerr, 2B	23
M. Parnell, SP	22
V. Stephens, SS	22
W. Dropo, 1B	21
A. Zarilla, OF	20
J. Pesky, 3B	19
T. Williams, OF	19
J. Dobson, SP	17
E. Kinder, RP	17
B. Goodman, OF	16
M. McDermott, RP	10
C. Stobbs, SP	10
B. Tebbetts, C	10
M. Batts, C	7
W. Masterson, RP	5
C. Vollmer, OF	5
W. Nixon, SP	3
H. Taylor, SP	3
J. McDonald, RP	2
B. Rosar, C	2
T. Wright, OF	2
K. Keltner, 3B	1
A. Papai, RP	1
J. Piersall, OF	1

Chicago (60-94)	WS
Hitting	**65.4**
Fielding	**38.3**
Pitching	**76.3**
B. Pierce, SP	16
E. Robinson, 1B	15
B. Wight, SP	15
C. Carrasquel, SS	14
B. Cain, SP	13
G. Zernial, OF	13
H. Majeski, 3B	11
P. Masi, C	11
L. Aloma, RP	8
H. Judson, RP	8
D. Philley, OF	8
R. Gumpert, RP	7
F. Baker, 3B	6
N. Fox, 2B	5
R. Scarborough, SP	5
C. Michaels, 2B	4
G. Niarhos, C	4
G. Goldsberry, 1B	3
K. Holcombe, SP	2
M. Rickert, OF	2
H. Adams, OF	1
L. Appling, SS	1
J. Bruner, RP	1
M. Haefner, RP	1
L. Kretlow, RP	1
B. Kuzava, SP	1
E. Malone, C	1
M. McCormick, OF	1
J. Ostrowski, OF	1
J. Scala, OF	1

Cleveland (92-62)	WS
Hitting	**131.3**
Fielding	**45.5**
Pitching	**99.2**
L. Doby, OF	30
A. Rosen, 3B	29
B. Lemon, SP	25
E. Wynn, SP	21
L. Easter, 1B	20
B. Feller, SP	19
R. Boone, SS	16
D. Mitchell, OF	16
B. Kennedy, OF	15
J. Hegan, C	14
M. Garcia, SP	12
J. Gordon, 2B	12
S. Gromek, RP	8
B. Avila, 2B	7
L. Boudreau, SS	7
A. Benton, RP	5
S. Zoldak, RP	5
J. Flores, RP	4
R. Murray, C	3
M. Pieretti, RP	3
A. Aber, SP	1
A. Clark, OF	1
D. Rozek, RP	1
T. Tucker, OF	1
D. Weik, RP	1

Detroit (95-59)	WS
Hitting	**134.2**
Fielding	**48.3**
Pitching	**102.6**
H. Evers, OF	26
G. Kell, 3B	26
V. Wertz, OF	26
A. Houtteman, SP	25
J. Priddy, 2B	24
J. Groth, OF	22
F. Hutchinson, SP	21
J. Lipon, SS	19
D. Trout, SP	17
H. Newhouser, SP	15
A. Robinson, C	13
T. Gray, SP	9
D. Kolloway, 1B	8
H. White, RP	7
B. Swift, C	4
V. Trucks, SP	4
H. Borowy, RP	3
C. Keller, OF	3
P. Mullin, OF	3
S. Rogovin, RP	3
J. Ginsberg, C	2
R. Herbert, RP	2
N. Berry, SS	1
D. Kryhoski, 1B	1
M. Stuart, RP	1

New York (98-56)	WS
Hitting	**157.5**
Fielding	**46.0**
Pitching	**90.5**
P. Rizzuto, SS	35
Y. Berra, C	32
J. DiMaggio, OF	29
E. Lopat, SP	20
J. Coleman, 2B	19
V. Raschi, SP	18
A. Reynolds, SP	17
H. Bauer, OF	16
G. Woodling, OF	16
T. Byrne, SP	12
J. Mize, 1B	12
W. Ford, SP	11
B. Johnson, 3B	9
C. Mapes, OF	8
B. Brown, 3B	7
T. Ferrick, RP	7
J. Collins, 1B	6
T. Henrich, 1B	6
F. Sanford, RP	5
J. Page, RP	3
J. Hopp, 1B	2
J. Ostrowski, RP	2
B. Martin, 2B	1
D. Pillette, RP	1

Philadelphia (52-102)	WS
Hitting	**84.3**
Fielding	**26.1**
Pitching	**45.6**
F. Fain, 1B	17
L. Brissie, SP	15
E. Joost, SS	14
S. Chapman, OF	13
E. Valo, OF	13
P. Lehner, OF	10
B. Shantz, SP	10
B. Dillinger, 3B	9
B. Hooper, RP	9
B. Hitchcock, 2B	6
A. Kellner, SP	6
W. Moses, OF	6
M. Guerra, C	5
J. Tipton, C	5
J. Astroth, C	4
P. Suder, 2B	4
K. Wahl, 3B	4
H. Wyse, SP	3
J. Kucab, SP-RP	2
B. McCosky, OF	1

St. Louis (58-96)	WS
Hitting	**70.5**
Fielding	**31.2**
Pitching	**72.3**
N. Garver, SP	25
D. Lenhardt, 1B	17
D. Kokos, OF	15
S. Lollar, C	14
S. Overmire, SP	12
A. Widmar, SP	12
R. Coleman, OF	8
H. Arft, 1B	7
J. Ostrowski, SP	7
D. Starr, SP-RP	7
R. Sievers, OF	6
T. Upton, SS	6
O. Friend, 2B	5
L. Moss, C	5
S. Stirnweiss, 2B	4
K. Wood, OF	4
J. Delsing, OF	3
D. Johnson, RP	3
J. Bruner, RP	2
B. DeMars, SS	2
H. Dorish, RP	2
C. Fannin, SP	2
T. Ferrick, RP	2
B. Sommers, 3B	2
D. Pillette, RP	1
L. Thomas, 3B	1

Washington (67-87)	WS
Hitting	**88.8**
Fielding	**37.4**
Pitching	**74.7**
E. Yost, 3B	24
I. Noren, OF	22
S. Hudson, SP	15
M. Vernon, 1B	13
G. Coan, OF	11
S. Mele, OF	11
B. Kuzava, SP	10
M. Harris, RP	9
C. Michaels, 2B	9
B. Stewart, OF	9
S. Consuegra, SP	8
C. Marrero, SP	8
S. Dente, SS	7
G. Bearden, SP	5
M. Grasso, C	4
R. Scarborough, SP	4
A. Evans, C	3
J. Haynes, RP	3
J. Ostrowski, OF	3
S. Robertson, OF	3
E. Robinson, 1B	3
A. Sima, SP	3
M. Combs, SS	2
L. Hittle, RP	2
C. Pascual, SP	2
E. Singleton, RP	2
D. Weik, RP	2
A. Kozar, 2B	1
J. Moreno, SP	1
L. Okrie, C	1
J. Pearce, RP	1

1950 National League

Boston (83-71)	WS
Hitting	**153.7**
Fielding	**30.1**
Pitching	**65.2**
E. Torgeson, 1B	32
S. Gordon, OF	29
B. Elliott, 3B	27
S. Jethroe, OF	22
W. Spahn, SP	21
W. Cooper, C	19
V. Bickford, SP	18
J. Sain, SP	15
T. Holmes, OF	13
R. Hartsfield, 2B	11
B. Kerr, SS	10
W. Marshall, OF	5
M. Surkont, SP	5
B. Chipman, RP	4
D. Crandall, C	3
L. Olmo, OF	3
B. Hogue, RP	2
G. Mauch, 2B	2
P. Reiser, OF	2
C. Ryan, 2B	2
D. Cole, RP	1
W. Linden, C	1
N. Roy, RP	1
S. Sisti, SS	1

Brooklyn (89-65)	WS
Hitting	**140.2**
Fielding	**42.9**
Pitching	**83.8**
J. Robinson, 2B	29
D. Snider, OF	29
R. Campanella, C	22
D. Newcombe, SP	22
G. Hodges, 1B	21
P. Roe, SP	21
P. Reese, SS	20
C. Furillo, OF	18
E. Palica, RP	16
B. Cox, 3B	10
G. Hermanski, OF	10
R. Branca, RP	7

B. Morgan, 3B	7
C. Erskine, SP	6
J. Russell, OF	6
D. Bankhead, RP	4
T. Brown, OF	4
J. Banta, RP	3
B. Edwards, C	2
J. Hatten, RP	2
E. Miksis, 2B-SS	2
B. Podbielan, SP-RP	2
G. Shuba, OF	2
W. Ramsdell, RP	1
C. Van Cuyk, RP	1

Chicago (64-89)	WS
Hitting	**83.4**
Fielding	**33.9**
Pitching	**74.7**
A. Pafko, OF	27
H. Sauer, OF	18
B. Rush, SP	17
F. Hiller, RP	13
R. Smalley, SS	12
P. Minner, SP	11
B. Serena, 3B	10
W. Terwilliger, 2B	9
P. Cavarretta, 1B	8
M. Dubiel, RP	8
D. Leonard, RP	7
D. Lade, RP	6
J. Schmitz, SP	6
B. Borkowski, OF	5
H. Edwards, OF	5
P. Ward, 1B	5
M. Owen, C	4
J. Vander Meer, RP	4
R. Walker, C	4
J. Klippstein, RP	3
R. Northey, OF	3
B. Ramazzotti, 2B	2
C. Sawatski, C	2
R. Jackson, 3B	1
H. Jeffcoat, OF	1
C. Mauro, OF	1

Cincinnati (66-87)	WS
Hitting	**81.4**
Fielding	**38.3**
Pitching	**78.3**
E. Blackwell, SP	26
T. Kluszewski, 1B	16
G. Hatton, 3B	14
J. Wyrostek, OF	14
K. Raffensberger, SP	13
B. Adams, 2B	12
H. Fox, SP	12
W. Ramsdell, SP	11
C. Ryan, 2B	10
J. Adcock, OF	9
V. Stallcup, SS	9
J. Pramesa, C	7
L. Merriman, OF	6
F. Smith, RP	6
B. Usher, OF	6
D. Howell, C	4
H. Wehmeier, SP	4
D. Litwhiler, OF	3
P. Lowrey, OF	3
R. Northey, OF	3
E. Erautt, RP	2
J. Hetki, RP	2
S. Meeks, SS	2
H. Perkowski, RP	2
B. Byerly, RP	1
B. Scheffing, C	1

New York (86-68)	WS
Hitting	**117.9**
Fielding	**45.4**
Pitching	**94.7**
E. Stanky, 2B	30
L. Jansen, SP	25
H. Thompson, 3B	23
W. Westrum, C	22
S. Maglie, RP	21
A. Dark, SS	19
B. Thomson, OF	18
M. Irvin, 1B	16
W. Lockman, OF	16
J. Hearn, SP	15
D. Koslo, SP	12
D. Mueller, OF	10
S. Jones, SP	8
J. Kramer, RP	5
M. Kennedy, RP	4
T. Gilbert, 1B	3
G. Spencer, RP	3
C. Hartung, RP	2
R. Weatherly, OF	2
S. Calderone, C	1
A. Hansen, RP	1
K. Higbe, RP	1
B. Rigney, 2B	1

Philadelphia (91-63)	WS
Hitting	**120.8**
Fielding	**48.1**
Pitching	**104.1**
D. Ennis, OF	26
R. Roberts, SP	26
R. Ashburn, OF	23
J. Konstanty, RP	23
P. Jones, 3B	22
A. Seminick, C	22
D. Sisler, OF	20
G. Hamner, SS	19
C. Simmons, SP	16
E. Waitkus, 1B	15
B. Church, SP	13
M. Goliat, 2B	13
B. Miller, SP	12
K. Heintzelman, SP	5
M. Candini, RP	3
K. Johnson, SP	3
S. Lopata, C	2
R. Meyer, SP	2
D. Whitman, OF	2
J. Bloodworth, 2B	1
B. Donnelly, RP	1
B. Nicholson, OF	1
K. Silvestri, C	1
P. Stuffel, RP	1
J. Thompson, RP	1

Pittsburgh (57-96)	WS
Hitting	**84.5**
Fielding	**29.9**
Pitching	**56.6**
R. Kiner, OF	23
M. Dickson, RP	16
C. Chambers, SP	14
W. Westlake, OF	14
J. Hopp, 1B	12
B. Werle, RP	11
D. Murtaugh, 2B	10
G. Bell, OF	9
C. McCullough, C	8
D. O'Connell, SS	8
B. MacDonald, SP	7
J. Phillips, 1B	5
V. Law, SP	4
R. Mueller, C	4
T. Beard, OF	3
P. Castiglione, 3B	3
B. Dillinger, 3B	3
N. Fernandez, 3B	3
S. Rojek, SS	3
J. Walsh, RP	3
T. Saffell, OF	2
J. Berardino, 2B	1
B. Chesnes, SP	1
D. Coogan, 1B	1
W. Main, RP	1
H. Schenz, 2B	1
E. Turner, C	1

St. Louis (78-75)	WS
Hitting	**100.3**
Fielding	**43.7**
Pitching	**90.0**
S. Musial, OF	32
H. Pollet, SP	19
T. Glaviano, 3B	18
R. Schoendienst, 2B	18
M. Lanier, SP	16
E. Slaughter, OF	16
H. Brecheen, SP	12
B. Howerton, OF	12
D. Rice, C	12
A. Brazle, RP	11
C. Boyer, RP	10
G. Munger, SP	10
M. Marion, SS	9
G. Staley, SP	7
C. Diering, OF	6
J. Garagiola, C	4
E. Miller, SS	4
R. Nelson, 1B	4
E. Kazak, 3B	3
E. Dusak, RP	2
J. Lindell, OF	2
F. Martin, RP	2
P. Lowrey, 2B	1
A. Papai, RP	1
T. Poholsky, RP	1
H. Rice, OF	1
H. Walker, OF	1

1951
American League

Boston (87-67)	WS
Hitting	**120.3**
Fielding	**43.1**
Pitching	**97.6**
T. Williams, OF	34
M. Parnell, SP	22
D. DiMaggio, OF	21
J. Pesky, SS	21
E. Kinder, RP	18
B. Goodman, 1B	17
B. Doerr, 2B	16
M. McDermott, SP	16
V. Stephens, 3B	14
C. Vollmer, OF	10
L. Kiely, SP	9
L. Boudreau, SS	8
R. Scarborough, SP	8
C. Stobbs, SP	8
W. Nixon, RP	7
W. Masterson, RP	6
W. Dropo, 1B	5
B. Rosar, C	4
B. Wight, SP-RP	4
L. Moss, C	3
F. Hatfield, 3B	2
A. Robinson, C	2
B. Evans, RP	1
B. Flowers, RP	1
M. Guerra, C	1
M. Hoderlein, 2B-3B	1
H. Taylor, RP	1
T. Wright, OF	1

Chicago (81-73)	WS
Hitting	**107.1**
Fielding	**45.6**
Pitching	**90.3**
M. Minoso, OF	24
N. Fox, 2B	22
B. Pierce, SP	19
E. Robinson, 1B	19
C. Carrasquel, SS	17
S. Rogovin, SP	17
J. Busby, OF	12
L. Aloma, RP	10
K. Holcombe, SP	10
A. Zarilla, OF	10
J. Dobson, SP	8
R. Gumpert, RP	8
P. Masi, C	8
D. Lenhardt, OF	7
G. Niarhos, C	7
B. Stewart, OF	7
R. Coleman, OF	5
B. Dillinger, 3B	5
H. Dorish, RP	5
H. Judson, SP	5
L. Kretlow, SP	4
M. Rotblatt, RP	4
F. Baker, 3B	3
B. Cain, SP	1
J. DeMaestri, SS	1
J. Erautt, C	1
R. Grimsley, RP	1
S. Hairston, C	1
P. Lehner, OF	1
B. Sheely, C	1

Cleveland (93-61)	WS
Hitting	**127.5**
Fielding	**45.5**
Pitching	**106.0**
L. Doby, OF	29
A. Rosen, 3B	25
B. Avila, 2B	24
E. Wynn, SP	24
M. Garcia, SP	22
B. Lemon, SP	19
D. Mitchell, OF	19
B. Feller, SP	18
L. Easter, 1B	17
R. Boone, SS	14
J. Hegan, C	14
L. Brissie, RP	11
S. Gromek, RP	11
B. Kennedy, OF	7
H. Simpson, OF	6
S. Chapman, OF	5
B. Tebbetts, C	4
S. Stirnweiss, 2B	3
B. Chakales, SP	2
A. Clark, OF	1
M. Combs, SS	1
S. Jones, SP-RP	1
B. McCosky, OF	1
M. Minoso, 1B	1

Detroit (73-81)	WS
Hitting	**96.0**
Fielding	**38.0**
Pitching	**85.0**
G. Kell, 3B	22
V. Wertz, OF	22
J. Priddy, 2B	16
D. Trout, SP	15
F. Hutchinson, SP	14
J. Groth, OF	12
T. Gray, SP	11
D. Kryhoski, 1B	11
P. Mullin, OF	11
J. Ginsberg, C	10
V. Trucks, RP	10
M. Stuart, SP	9
B. Cain, SP	8
J. Lipon, SS	8
H. Newhouser, SP	7
G. Bearden, RP	6
H. Evers, OF	5
S. Souchock, OF	5
H. White, RP	4
R. Herbert, RP	3
C. Keller, OF	2
D. Kolloway, 1B	2
A. Robinson, C	2
N. Berry, SS	1
F. House, C	1
S. Rogovin, SP	1
B. Swift, C	1

New York (98-56)	WS
Hitting	**162.6**
Fielding	**41.7**
Pitching	**89.6**
Y. Berra, C	31
G. McDougald, 3B	23
P. Rizzuto, SS	23
E. Lopat, SP	19
A. Reynolds, SP	19
G. Woodling, OF	19
J. DiMaggio, OF	17
V. Raschi, SP	17
H. Bauer, OF	15
B. Brown, 3B	13
M. Mantle, OF	13
J. Collins, 1B	11
J. Mize, 1B	11
J. Coleman, 2B	10
J. Jensen, OF	9
B. Kuzava, RP	9
T. Morgan, SP	9
J. Ostrowski, RP	6
A. Schallock, SP	3
S. Shea, RP	3
J. Hopp, 1B	2
B. Johnson, 3B	2
J. Sain, SP	2
C. Silvera, C	2
B. Hogue, RP	1
C. Mapes, OF	1
B. Martin, 2B	1
E. Nevel, RP	1
S. Overmire, RP	1
F. Sanford, RP	1

Philadelphia (70-84)	WS
Hitting	**103.8**
Fielding	**36.4**
Pitching	**69.8**
E. Joost, SS	25
F. Fain, 1B	19
G. Zernial, OF	19
E. Valo, OF	17
B. Shantz, SP	15
D. Philley, OF	13
B. Hooper, SP	11
A. Kellner, SP	10
H. Majeski, 3B	10
C. Scheib, RP	10
M. Martin, RP	9
S. Zoldak, SP	9
J. Tipton, C	8
B. Hitchcock, 3B	7
J. Kucab, RP	5
P. Suder, 2B	5
J. Astroth, C	4
A. Clark, OF	3
D. Fowler, SP	2
L. Klein, 2B	2
R. Murray, C	2
J. Coleman, RP	1
L. Limmer, 1B	1
B. McCosky, OF	1
W. Moses, OF	1
K. Wahl, 3B	1

St. Louis (52-102)	WS
Hitting	**68.5**
Fielding	**33.0**
Pitching	**54.6**
N. Garver, SP	22
J. Delsing, OF	10
T. Byrne, SP	9
S. Lollar, C	9
B. Young, 2B	9
H. Arft, 1B	8
M. Batts, C	8
R. Coleman, OF	8
F. Marsh, 3B	7
C. Mapes, OF	6
D. Pillette, SP	6
K. Wood, OF	6
J. McDonald, SP	5
B. Mahoney, RP	4
E. Rapp, OF	4
J. Bero, SS	3
D. Lenhardt, OF	3
B. Nieman, OF	3
S. Overmire, SP	3
S. Paige, RP	3
J. Berardino, 3B	2
B. Hogue, RP	2
B. Jennings, SS	2
D. Long, 1B	2
L. Sleater, RP	2
B. Taylor, 1B	2
B. Kennedy, RP	1
C. Kluttz, C	1
J. Maguire, OF	1
R. Sievers, OF	1
J. Suchecki, RP	1
B. Thomas, SS	1
T. Upton, SS	1
K. Wahl, 3B	1

Washington (62-92)	WS
Hitting	**98.9**
Fielding	**32.0**
Pitching	**55.1**
E. Yost, 3B	27
G. Coan, OF	19
I. Noren, OF	18
M. Vernon, 1B	18
S. Mele, OF	12
C. Marrero, SP	11
C. Michaels, 2B	10
B. Porterfield, SP	10
S. Consuegra, RP	8
P. Runnels, SS	8
D. Johnson, SP	7
M. Harris, RP	5
C. Kluttz, C	5
M. McCormick, OF	5
S. Dente, SS	4
T. Ferrick, RP	4
S. Hudson, SP	3
J. Moreno, SP	3
J. Haynes, RP	2
A. Sima, RP	2
F. Campos, OF	1
M. Grasso, C	1
M. Guerra, C	1
B. Kuzava, SP	1
G. Verble, SS	1

1951 National League

Boston (76-78)	WS
Hitting	**120.2**
Fielding	**34.2**
Pitching	**73.6**
W. Spahn, SP	26
S. Jethroe, OF	23
S. Gordon, OF	22
E. Torgeson, 1B	20
B. Elliott, 3B	18
W. Cooper, C	17
W. Marshall, OF	13
C. Nichols, SP	12
V. Bickford, SP	11
R. Hartsfield, 2B	11
S. Sisti, SS	10
M. Surkont, SP	10
E. St. Claire, C	7
J. Sain, SP	5
B. Addis, OF	3
D. Cole, RP	3
B. Kerr, SS	3
J. Logan, SS	3
P. Paine, RP	3
B. Chipman, RP	2
G. Estock, RP	2
J. Wilson, SP	2
L. Marquez, OF	1
R. Mueller, C	1

Brooklyn (97-60)	WS
Hitting	**160.4**
Fielding	**44.5**
Pitching	**86.1**
J. Robinson, 2B	38
R. Campanella, C	33
G. Hodges, 1B	26
P. Reese, SS	22
D. Snider, OF	22
C. Furillo, OF	21
D. Newcombe, SP	21
P. Roe, SP	21
R. Branca, SP	14
B. Cox, 3B	14
A. Pafko, OF	10
C. Erskine, RP	8
C. King, RP	8
C. Labine, RP	7
C. Abrams, OF	6
B. Podbielan, RP	5
J. Hatten, SP	2
G. Hermanski, OF	2
E. Palica, RP	2
W. Terwilliger, 2B	2
R. Walker, C	2
R. Bridges, 3B	1
B. Edwards, C	1
J. Schmitz, RP	1
D. Thompson, OF	1
D. Williams, OF	1

Chicago (62-92)	WS
Hitting	**83.9**
Fielding	**33.3**
Pitching	**68.8**
H. Sauer, OF	18
R. Jackson, 3B	15
F. Baumholtz, OF	14
P. Minner, SP	13
B. Rush, SP	13
D. Leonard, RP	10
E. Miksis, 2B	9
P. Cavarretta, 1B	8
G. Hermanski, OF	8
H. Jeffcoat, OF	7
A. Pafko, OF	7
M. Dubiel, RP	6
B. Kelly, RP	6
J. Klippstein, RP	6
C. McLish, SP	6
R. Smalley, SS	6
S. Burgess, C	4
F. Hiller, SP	4
B. Edwards, C	3
D. Fondy, 1B	3
B. Ramazzotti, SS	3
C. Connors, 1B	2
J. Cusick, SS	2
T. Lown, SP	2
B. Serena, 3B	2
W. Terwilliger, 2B	2
R. Walker, C	2
H. Chiti, C	1
J. Hatten, RP	1
M. Owen, C	1
F. Richards, 1B	1
B. Schultz, SP	1

Cincinnati (68-86)	WS
Hitting	**69.0**
Fielding	**44.7**
Pitching	**90.4**
E. Blackwell, SP	19
K. Raffensberger, SP	18
J. Wyrostek, OF	18
C. Ryan, 2B	15
H. Fox, SP	13
T. Kluszewski, 1B	13
H. Wehmeier, SP	13
B. Adams, 3B	10
L. Merriman, OF	10
G. Hatton, 3B	9
F. Smith, RP	9
H. Perkowski, RP	8
W. Ramsdell, SP	8
V. Stallcup, SS	8
J. Adcock, OF	5
H. Edwards, OF	5
B. Byerly, RP	4
D. Howell, C	3
R. McMillan, SS	3
B. Scheffing, C	3
B. Usher, OF	3
B. McCosky, OF	2
J. Pramesa, C	2
H. Landrith, C	1
D. Litwhiler, OF	1
W. Post, OF	1

New York (98-59)	WS
Hitting	**146.1**
Fielding	**45.0**
Pitching	**102.9**
M. Irvin, OF	29
S. Maglie, SP	28
A. Dark, SS	27
B. Thomson, OF	26
L. Jansen, SP	24
E. Stanky, 2B	24
W. Westrum, C	20
W. Mays, OF	19
W. Lockman, 1B	15
J. Hearn, SP	14
D. Mueller, OF	12
D. Koslo, RP	11
G. Spencer, RP	10
H. Thompson, 3B	7
M. Kennedy, RP	6
A. Corwin, SP	4
S. Jones, RP	4
J. Maguire, OF	2
R. Noble, C	2
B. Rigney, 3B	2
D. Williams, 2B	2
S. Yvars, C	2
A. Gettel, RP	1
S. Jorgensen, OF	1
A. Konikowski, RP	1
J. Lohrke, 3B	1

Philadelphia (73-81)	WS
Hitting	**97.8**
Fielding	**38.6**
Pitching	**82.6**
R. Ashburn, OF	28
R. Roberts, SP	28
P. Jones, 3B	22
B. Church, SP	18
D. Ennis, OF	14
G. Hamner, SS	14
D. Sisler, OF	12
A. Seminick, C	11
R. Meyer, SP	10
E. Waitkus, 1B	9
D. Wilber, C	8
J. Konstanty, RP	6
J. Thompson, RP	6
K. Heintzelman, RP	5
B. Nicholson, OF	5
E. Pellagrini, 2B	5
A. Hansen, RP	4
K. Johnson, SP	3
T. Brown, OF	2
P. Caballero, 2B	2
M. Goliat, 2B	2
N. Jordan, SP	2
M. Clark, OF	1
L. Cristante, RP	1
E. Sanicki, OF	1

Pittsburgh (64-90)	WS
Hitting	**100.7**
Fielding	**32.0**
Pitching	**59.2**
R. Kiner, OF	35

M. Dickson, SP	18
G. Bell, OF	16
C. McCullough, C	10
T. Wilks, RP	10
P. Castiglione, 3B	9
C. Metkovich, OF	9
G. Strickland, SS	9
J. Garagiola, C	8
B. Howerton, OF	7
V. Law, SP-RP	7
M. Queen, SP	7
W. Westlake, 3B	7
B. Friend, SP	5
P. Reiser, OF	5
B. Werle, RP	5
H. Pollet, SP	4
R. Nelson, 1B	3
F. Thomas, OF	3
M. Basgall, 2B	2
D. Carlsen, SP	2
C. Chambers, SP	2
D. Cole, 2B	2
J. Merson, 2B	2
E. Dusak, OF	1
E. Fitz Gerald, C	1
J. Muir, RP	1
D. Murtaugh, 2B	1
J. Phillips, 1B	1

St. Louis (81-73)	WS
Hitting	**109.7**
Fielding	**45.3**
Pitching	**88.0**
S. Musial, OF	39
S. Hemus, SS	17
R. Schoendienst, 2B	17
G. Staley, SP	15
A. Brazle, RP	14
B. Johnson, 3B	14
E. Slaughter, OF	14
M. Lanier, SP	13
H. Brecheen, SP	12
P. Lowrey, OF	12
D. Rice, C	12
C. Chambers, SP	9
T. Poholsky, SP	7
J. Presko, SP	7
W. Westlake, OF	6
H. Rice, OF	4
S. Rojek, SS	4
D. Bokelmann, RP	3
J. Collum, SP	3
V. Benson, 3B	2
C. Diering, OF	2
T. Glaviano, OF	2
B. Howerton, OF	2
N. Jones, 1B	2
G. Munger, RP	2
T. Wilks, RP	2
S. Bilko, 1B	1
C. Boyer, RP	1
D. Cole, 2B	1
J. Garagiola, C	1
D. Richmond, 3B	1
B. Sarni, C	1
H. Walker, OF	1

1952 American League

Boston (76-78)	WS
Hitting	**101.6**
Fielding	**42.3**
Pitching	**84.0**
B. Goodman, 2B	20
D. DiMaggio, OF	16
M. Parnell, SP	13
M. McDermott, SP	12
S. White, C	12
H. Evers, OF	11
D. Gernert, 1B	11
G. Kell, 3B	10
E. Kinder, RP	9
V. Stephens, SS	9
C. Vollmer, OF	9
S. Hudson, SP	8
T. Lepcio, 2B	8
F. Throneberry, OF	8
D. Trout, SP	8
A. Benton, RP	5
I. Delock, RP	5
B. Henry, SP	5
D. Lenhardt, OF	5
J. Piersall, SS	5
D. Wilber, C	5
R. Brickner, RP	4
D. Brodowski, SP	4
J. Lipon, SS	4
W. Dropo, 1B	3
W. Nixon, SP	3
H. Freeman, RP	2
R. Scarborough, RP	2
B. Wight, RP	2
J. Atkins, RP	1
M. Bolling, SS	1
R. Gumpert, RP	1
F. Hatfield, 3B	1
P. Lehner, OF	1
G. Niarhos, C	1
G. Schmees, OF	1
H. Taylor, SP-RP	1
T. Williams, OF	1
A. Zarilla, OF	1

Chicago (81-73)	WS
Hitting	**97.0**
Fielding	**47.4**
Pitching	**98.6**
E. Robinson, 1B	25
B. Pierce, SP	23
N. Fox, 2B	22
M. Minoso, OF	21
J. Dobson, SP	18
S. Lollar, C	13
S. Rogovin, SP	13
H. Dorish, RP	12
H. Rodriguez, 3B	11
S. Mele, OF	10
C. Carrasquel, SS	8
M. Grissom, SP	8
C. Stobbs, RP	8
J. Rivera, OF	7
B. Stewart, OF	7
B. Kennedy, RP	6
L. Kretlow, SP	5
T. Wright, OF	4
L. Aloma, RP	3
R. Krsnich, 3B	3
W. Miranda, SS	3
H. Brown, RP	2
R. Coleman, OF	2
S. Dente, SS	2
P. Masi, C	2
A. Zarilla, OF	2
J. Busby, OF	1
H. Judson, RP	1
B. Sheely, C	1

Cleveland (93-61)	WS
Hitting	**164.2**
Fielding	**34.6**
Pitching	**80.2**
L. Doby, OF	34
A. Rosen, 3B	31
B. Lemon, SP	25
B. Avila, 2B	24
M. Garcia, SP	23
D. Mitchell, OF	21
E. Wynn, SP	21
L. Easter, 1B	20
H. Simpson, OF	18
R. Boone, SS	13
J. Hegan, C	9
J. Tipton, C	6
S. Gromek, RP	5
L. Brissie, RP	4
J. Fridley, OF	4
B. Kennedy, OF	3
G. Strickland, SS	3
B. Tebbetts, C	3
M. Combs, SS	2
B. Glynn, 1B	2
W. Westlake, OF	2
B. Feller, SP	1
M. Harris, RP	1
H. Majeski, 3B	1
B. McCosky, OF	1
D. Pope, OF	1
T. Wilks, RP	1

Detroit (50-104)	WS
Hitting	**68.3**
Fielding	**25.8**
Pitching	**55.9**
W. Dropo, 1B	11
J. Groth, OF	11
H. Newhouser, SP	10
V. Wertz, OF	10
T. Gray, SP	9
J. Priddy, 2B	9
V. Trucks, SP	8
A. Houtteman, SP	7
B. Wight, SP	7
J. Ginsberg, C	6
P. Mullin, OF	6
F. Hatfield, 3B	5
J. Pesky, SS	5
S. Souchock, OF	5
B. Hoeft, RP	4
G. Kell, 3B	4
H. White, RP	4
M. Batts, C	3
J. Delsing, OF	3
C. Mapes, OF	3
N. Berry, SS	2
A. Federoff, 2B	2
F. Hutchinson, RP	2
H. Kuenn, SS	2
J. Lipon, SS	2
D. Littlefield, RP	2
R. Sullivan, OF	2
N. Garver, SP	1
D. Kolloway, 1B	1
D. Lenhardt, OF	1
D. Lund, OF	1
M. Stuart, RP	1
B. Swift, C	1

New York (95-59)	WS
Hitting	**151.6**
Fielding	**44.8**
Pitching	**88.5**
M. Mantle, OF	32
Y. Berra, C	29
A. Reynolds, SP	24
H. Bauer, OF	21
P. Rizzuto, SS	21
G. Woodling, OF	21
J. Collins, 1B	18
G. McDougald, 3B	18
V. Raschi, SP	17
E. Lopat, SP	12
B. Martin, 2B	11
J. Sain, RP	10
B. Kuzava, RP	7
I. Noren, OF	7
T. Morgan, SP	6
J. McDonald, RP	4
B. Miller, SP	4
J. Mize, 1B	4
R. Scarborough, RP	4
J. Coleman, 2B	3
E. Blackwell, RP	2
B. Brown, 3B	2
B. Cerv, OF	2
T. Gorman, SP-RP	2
C. Silvera, C	2
J. Brideweser, SS	1
J. Schmitz, RP	1

Philadelphia (79-75)	WS
Hitting	**117.2**
Fielding	**38.3**
Pitching	**81.5**
B. Shantz, SP	33
F. Fain, 1B	28
E. Joost, SS	26
G. Zernial, OF	21
E. Valo, OF	19
H. Byrd, SP	18
D. Philley, OF	15
A. Kellner, SP	11
C. Scheib, SP	9
B. Hitchcock, 3B	7
J. Astroth, C	6
A. Clark, OF	5
C. Michaels, 2B	5
K. Thomas, OF	5
H. Majeski, 3B	4
B. Newsom, RP	4
B. Hooper, RP	3
R. Murray, C	3
P. Suder, 2B	3
J. Tipton, C	3
S. Zoldak, SP	3
S. Kell, 2B	2
S. Robertson, 2B	2
H. Bevan, 3B	1
M. Fricano, RP	1

St. Louis (64-90)	WS
Hitting	**89.6**
Fielding	**35.4**
Pitching	**67.0**
J. Dyck, 3B	15
B. Nieman, OF	15
C. Courtney, C	14
S. Paige, RP	13
B. Young, 2B	12
D. Pillette, SP	11
B. Cain, SP	9
N. Garver, SP	8
J. Rivera, OF	8
G. Bearden, RP	7
F. Marsh, SS	7
V. Wertz, OF	7
T. Byrne, SP	6
D. Kryhoski, 1B	6
C. Michaels, 3B	6
J. Delsing, OF	5
E. Harrist, RP	5
G. Goldsberry, 1B	4
M. Marion, SS	4
A. Zarilla, OF	4
D. Johnson, C	3
D. Littlefield, SP	3
D. Madison, RP	3
L. Thomas, 3B	3
J. DeMaestri, SS	2
D. Lenhardt, OF	2
L. Moss, C	2
J. Porter, OF	2
R. Coleman, OF	1
B. Hogue, RP	1
K. Holcombe, RP	1
S. Overmire, RP	1
M. Stuart, RP	1
T. Wright, OF	1

Washington (78-76)	WS
Hitting	**94.8**
Fielding	**46.2**
Pitching	**93.0**
E. Yost, 3B	23
P. Runnels, SS	22
J. Jensen, OF	21
B. Porterfield, SP	20
M. Vernon, 1B	20
S. Shea, SP	15
C. Marrero, SP	14
J. Busby, OF	10
W. Masterson, SP	9
F. Baker, 2B	8
K. Wood, OF	8

S. Consuegra, RP 7
J. Moreno, SP 6
G. Coan, OF 5
T. Ferrick, RP 5
M. Hoderlein, 2B 5
S. Hudson, SP 5
M. Grasso, C 4
M. Fornieles, SP-RP 3
R. Gumpert, SP 3
S. Mele, OF 3
L. Sleater, SP 3
F. Campos, OF 2
C. Kluttz, C 2
C. Michaels, 2B 2
I. Noren, OF 2
E. Rapp, OF 2
J. Haynes, RP 1
R. Sanchez, SP 1
J. Snyder, 2B 1
F. Taylor, 1B 1
A. Wilson, OF 1

1952 National League

Boston (64-89)	WS
Hitting	**89.5**
Fielding	**32.7**
Pitching	**69.8**
S. Gordon, OF	25
W. Spahn, SP	22
E. Mathews, 3B	19
J. Logan, SS	17
S. Jethroe, OF	16
M. Surkont, SP	11
E. Torgeson, 1B	11
W. Cooper, C	9
J. Wilson, SP	9
L. Burdette, RP	8
V. Bickford, SP	7
G. Crowe, 1B	6
V. Jester, RP	5
J. Dittmer, 2B	4
B. Thorpe, OF	4
B. Chipman, RP	3
E. Johnson, RP	3
P. Burris, C	2
D. Cole, RP	2
J. Daniels, OF	2
R. Hartsfield, 2B	2
S. Sisti, 2B	2
J. Cusick, SS	1
W. Marshall, OF	1
E. St. Claire, C	1

Brooklyn (96-57)	WS
Hitting	**150.0**
Fielding	**46.3**
Pitching	**91.7**
J. Robinson, 2B	34
G. Hodges, 1B	26
D. Snider, OF	25
P. Reese, SS	23
R. Campanella, C	22
A. Pafko, OF	21
J. Black, RP	20
C. Erskine, SP	17
B. Loes, SP	16
P. Roe, SP	12
G. Shuba, OF	11
B. Wade, SP	10
B. Cox, 3B	9
B. Morgan, 3B	9
C. Furillo, OF	7
J. Rutherford, SP-RP	5
R. Walker, C	4
R. Branca, RP	3
J. Hughes, RP	2
C. Labine, RP	2
C. Van Cuyk, SP	2
D. Williams, OF	2
S. Amoros, OF	1
R. Bridges, 2B	1
C. King, RP	1
R. Negray, RP	1
R. Nelson, 1B	1
J. Schmitz, RP	1

Chicago (77-77)	WS
Hitting	**97.8**
Fielding	**42.6**
Pitching	**90.5**
H. Sauer, OF	28
B. Rush, SP	23
W. Hacker, SP	18
F. Baumholtz, OF	16
D. Fondy, 1B	15
B. Serena, 3B	15
P. Minner, SP	13
T. Atwell, C	11
D. Leonard, RP	10
B. Addis, OF	9
G. Hermanski, OF	7
J. Klippstein, SP	7
T. Brown, SS	6
R. Jackson, 3B	6
B. Kelly, RP	6
W. Ramsdell, RP	6
H. Jeffcoat, OF	5
B. Ramazzotti, 2B	5
B. Schultz, RP	5
R. Smalley, SS	5
T. Lown, SP	4
E. Miksis, 2B	4
H. Chiti, C	3
P. Cavarretta, 1B	2
B. Edwards, C	1
J. Pramesa, C	1

Cincinnati (69-85)	WS
Hitting	**98.5**
Fielding	**38.0**
Pitching	**70.5**
T. Kluszewski, 1B	23
K. Raffensberger, SP	22
B. Adams, 3B	17
R. McMillan, SS	16
J. Adcock, OF	12
A. Seminick, C	12
G. Hatton, 2B	11
W. Marshall, OF	11
H. Perkowski, SP	11
F. Smith, RP	10
B. Podbielan, RP	8
B. Borkowski, OF	7
H. Edwards, OF	7
J. Nuxhall, RP	6
C. Abrams, OF	5
B. Church, SP	5
J. Greengrass, OF	4
F. Hiller, SP	4
J. Rossi, C	3
H. Wehmeier, SP	3
W. Westlake, OF	2
J. Wyrostek, OF	2
E. Blake, RP	1
D. Howell, C	1
H. Landrith, C	1
E. Pellagrini, 2B	1
J. Schmitz, RP	1
J. Temple, 2B	1

New York (92-62)	WS
Hitting	**147.5**
Fielding	**39.8**
Pitching	**88.7**
A. Dark, SS	28
B. Thomson, 3B	25
W. Lockman, 1B	23
D. Williams, 2B	19
H. Thompson, OF	18
W. Westrum, C	18
H. Wilhelm, RP	18
S. Maglie, SP	17
D. Mueller, OF	15
J. Hearn, SP	12
D. Koslo, RP	12
L. Jansen, SP	8
M. Lanier, RP	8
B. Elliott, OF	7
D. Rhodes, OF	7
A. Corwin, RP	6
M. Irvin, OF	5
M. Kennedy, RP	5
W. Mays, OF	5
B. Rigney, 3B	4
S. Yvars, C	4
B. Connelly, RP	3
B. Hofman, 2B	3
C. Hartung, OF	2
G. Wilson, OF	2
D. Spencer, 3B-SS	1
G. Spencer, RP	1

Philadelphia (87-67)	WS
Hitting	**116.7**
Fielding	**43.1**
Pitching	**101.2**
R. Roberts, SP	32
R. Ashburn, OF	21
D. Ennis, OF	21
G. Hamner, SS	20
K. Drews, SP	18
S. Burgess, C	17
C. Ryan, 2B	17
C. Simmons, SP	17
P. Jones, 3B	16
E. Waitkus, 1B	16
R. Meyer, SP	14
S. Lopata, C	9
J. Wyrostek, OF	9
M. Clark, OF	6
S. Ridzik, RP	6
A. Hansen, RP	5
B. Nicholson, OF	5
J. Konstanty, RP	4
K. Heintzelman, RP	3
J. Mayo, OF	2
K. Peterson, RP	2
P. Stuffel, SP-RP	1

Pittsburgh (42-112)	WS
Hitting	**51.8**
Fielding	**26.4**
Pitching	**47.8**
R. Kiner, OF	19
M. Dickson, SP	17
J. Garagiola, C	11
H. Pollet, SP	9
G. Bell, OF	8
B. Friend, SP	7
C. Metkovich, 1B	7
W. Main, RP	6
T. Wilks, RP	6
D. Groat, SS	5
C. Koshorek, SS	5
J. Merson, 2B	5
P. Castiglione, 3B	4
B. Del Greco, OF	3
T. Bartirome, 1B	2
P. LaPalme, RP	2
C. McCullough, C	2
G. Strickland, 2B	2
J. Berardino, 2B	1
C. Hogue, SP	1
B. Howerton, OF	1
S. Senerchia, 3B	1
D. Smith, 3B	1
L. Walls, OF	1

St. Louis (88-66)	WS
Hitting	**135.3**
Fielding	**42.6**
Pitching	**86.1**
S. Musial, OF	37
S. Hemus, SS	27
R. Schoendienst, 2B	25
E. Slaughter, OF	23
D. Rice, C	18
A. Brazle, RP	15
G. Staley, SP	15
E. Yuhas, RP	11
P. Lowrey, OF	10
D. Sisler, 1B	10
S. Miller, SP	9
V. Mizell, SP	9
H. Brecheen, SP	8
H. Rice, OF	8
B. Johnson, 3B	6
C. Boyer, SP	5
C. Chambers, SP-RP	5
J. Presko, SP	5
T. Glaviano, 3B	4
H. Haddix, SP	3
E. Stanky, 2B	3
W. Westlake, OF	2
V. Benson, 3B	1
S. Bilko, 1B	1
L. Fusselman, C	1
L. Miggins, OF	1
W. Schmidt, RP	1
B. Werle, RP	1

1953 American League

Boston (84-69)	WS
Hitting	**89.5**
Fielding	**49.5**
Pitching	**113.0**
E. Kinder, RP	23
M. Parnell, SP	23
M. McDermott, SP	22
B. Goodman, 2B	20
G. Kell, 3B	18
S. White, C	16
D. Gernert, 1B	14
T. Umphlett, OF	14
J. Piersall, OF	12
S. Hudson, SP	11
H. Brown, SP	10
M. Bolling, SS	9
T. Williams, OF	9
B. Henry, SP	7
W. Nixon, SP	7
H. Evers, OF	5
B. Flowers, RP	5
F. Baker, 3B	4
T. Lepcio, 2B	4
I. Delock, RP	3
J. Lipon, SS	3
D. Wilber, C	3
M. Grissom, SP	2
B. Kennedy, RP	2
G. Stephens, OF	2
B. Consolo, 3B	1
G. Niarhos, C	1
F. Sullivan, RP	1
B. Werle, RP	1

Chicago (89-65)	WS
Hitting	**114.1**
Fielding	**50.5**
Pitching	**102.4**
M. Minoso, OF	26
B. Pierce, SP	24
N. Fox, 2B	21
J. Rivera, OF	20
S. Lollar, C	18
S. Mele, OF	18
V. Trucks, SP	17
C. Carrasquel, SS	16
F. Fain, 1B	16
H. Dorish, RP	14
S. Consuegra, RP	12
B. Keegan, SP-RP	10
M. Fornieles, RP	9
B. Elliott, 3B	7
J. Dobson, SP	6
B. Boyd, 1B	5
R. Wilson, C	5
G. Bearden, RP	4
C. Johnson, SP	3

B. Stewart, OF	3
T. Wright, OF	3
L. Aloma, RP	2
S. Rogovin, SP	2
L. Kretlow, RP	1
R. Krsnich, 3B	1
F. Marsh, 3B	1
C. Ryan, 3B	1
B. Sheely, C	1
V. Stephens, 3B	1

Cleveland (92-62)	WS
Hitting	**151.1**
Fielding	**39.3**
Pitching	**85.7**
A. Rosen, 3B	42
L. Doby, OF	26
B. Avila, 2B	22
B. Lemon, SP	22
M. Garcia, SP	21
G. Strickland, SS	20
D. Mitchell, OF	18
E. Wynn, SP	16
W. Westlake, OF	12
B. Feller, SP	10
B. Glynn, 1B	7
D. Hoskins, RP	7
L. Easter, 1B	6
A. Houtteman, SP	6
R. Boone, SS	5
J. Hegan, C	5
B. Hooper, RP	5
A. Smith, OF	4
J. Tipton, C	4
J. Ginsberg, C	3
H. Simpson, OF	3
B. Chakales, RP	2
O. Friend, 2B	2
B. Kennedy, OF	2
H. Majeski, 2B	2
B. Wight, RP	2
S. Gromek, RP	1
D. Tomanek, SP	1

Detroit (60-94)	WS
Hitting	**117.8**
Fielding	**24.9**
Pitching	**37.3**
R. Boone, 3B	22
H. Kuenn, SS	19
J. Delsing, OF	18
B. Nieman, OF	16
M. Batts, C	11
J. Pesky, 2B	9
W. Dropo, 1B	8
D. Lund, OF	8
S. Souchock, OF	8
N. Garver, SP	7
F. Hatfield, 3B	7
T. Gray, SP	6
B. Hoeft, SP	6
R. Branca, SP	4
S. Gromek, SP	4
A. Aber, SP	3
J. Bucha, C	3
J. Ginsberg, C	3
D. Marlowe, RP	3
P. Mullin, OF	3
R. Herbert, RP	2
J. Priddy, 2B	2
R. Sullivan, OF	2
H. Erickson, RP	1
O. Friend, 2B	1
A. Houtteman, SP	1
F. Hutchinson, RP	1
A. Kaline, OF	1
H. Newhouser, SP	1

New York (99-52)	WS
Hitting	**161.9**
Fielding	**42.6**
Pitching	**92.5**
Y. Berra, C	28
M. Mantle, OF	26
G. McDougald, 3B	21
H. Bauer, OF	20
G. Woodling, OF	20
P. Rizzuto, SS	18
W. Ford, SP	17
B. Martin, 2B	17
E. Lopat, SP	16
J. Sain, RP	16
J. Collins, 1B	14
I. Noren, OF	11
V. Raschi, SP	11
A. Reynolds, RP	11
D. Bollweg, 1B	8
B. Kuzava, RP	6
A. Carey, 3B	5
T. Gorman, RP	5
J. McDonald, SP	5
B. Renna, OF	5
C. Silvera, C	4
J. Mize, 1B	3
R. Scarborough, RP	3
L. Babe, 3B	1
E. Blackwell, SP-RP	1
J. Brideweser, SS	1
S. Kraly, SP	1
B. Miller, RP	1
W. Miranda, SS	1
A. Schallock, RP	1

Philadelphia (59-95)	WS
Hitting	**75.0**
Fielding	**34.7**
Pitching	**67.3**
G. Zernial, OF	21
A. Kellner, SP	15
D. Philley, OF	15
M. Fricano, SP	14
E. Robinson, 1B	12
J. Astroth, C	10
M. Martin, RP	10
C. Michaels, 2B	9
R. Murray, C	9
P. Suder, 3B	8
B. Shantz, SP	7
J. Coleman, RP	6
E. Joost, SS	6
E. McGhee, OF	6
H. Byrd, SP	5
J. DeMaestri, SS	5
C. Scheib, RP	4
L. Babe, 3B	3
C. Bishop, SP	2
C. Mauro, OF	2
B. Newsom, RP	2
F. Fanovich, RP	1
T. Giordano, 2B	1
R. Monahan, RP	1
B. Trice, SP	1
E. Valo, OF	1
N. Watlington, C	1

St. Louis (54-100)	WS
Hitting	**52.6**
Fielding	**35.0**
Pitching	**74.4**
D. Larsen, SP	14
V. Wertz, OF	12
B. Hunter, SS	11
S. Paige, RP	11
H. Brecheen, SP	10
J. Groth, OF	10
D. Lenhardt, OF	9
M. Stuart, RP	9
D. Kryhoski, 1B	8
D. Pillette, SP	8
V. Trucks, SP	8
D. Kokos, OF	7
B. Young, 2B	6
D. Littlefield, SP	5
R. Sievers, 1B	5
V. Stephens, 3B	5
B. Turley, SP	5
B. Elliott, 3B	4
C. Courtney, C	3
J. Dyck, OF	3
L. Moss, C	3
B. Holloman, RP	2
L. Kretlow, SP-RP	2
N. Berry, 3B	1
H. White, RP	1

Washington (76-76)	WS
Hitting	**113.9**
Fielding	**42.7**
Pitching	**71.5**
M. Vernon, 1B	29
J. Busby, OF	25
E. Yost, 3B	24
B. Porterfield, SP	21
J. Jensen, OF	17
W. Terwilliger, 2B	15
P. Runnels, SS	12
C. Vollmer, OF	12
C. Marrero, SP	10
C. Stobbs, SP	10
W. Masterson, SP	8
S. Shea, SP	7
S. Dixon, RP	6
E. Fitz Gerald, C	6
J. Schmitz, SP	4
G. Coan, OF	3
M. Grasso, C	3
J. Moreno, RP	3
A. Sima, RP	3
J. Snyder, SS	3
K. Thomas, OF	2
Y. Davalillo, SS	1
M. Hoderlein, 2B	1
J. Lane, RP	1
L. Peden, C	1
F. Sacka, C	1

1953
National League

Brooklyn (105-49)	WS
Hitting	**174.6**
Fielding	**47.0**
Pitching	**93.4**
D. Snider, OF	37
R. Campanella, C	33
J. Gilliam, 2B	25
G. Hodges, 1B	25
J. Robinson, OF	25
C. Furillo, OF	23
P. Reese, SS	21
C. Erskine, SP	20
C. Labine, RP	13
B. Cox, 3B	12
J. Hughes, RP	9
R. Meyer, SP	9
B. Milliken, RP	9
P. Roe, SP	9
B. Loes, SP	8
B. Morgan, 3B	7
J. Podres, SP	7
B. Wade, RP	7
W. Belardi, 1B	4
J. Black, RP	4
G. Shuba, OF	4
R. Walker, C	3
D. Thompson, OF	1

Chicago (65-89)	WS
Hitting	**84.6**
Fielding	**35.2**
Pitching	**75.2**
D. Fondy, 1B	18
R. Kiner, OF	18
R. Jackson, 3B	16
F. Baumholtz, OF	15
W. Hacker, SP	14
P. Minner, SP	14
H. Sauer, OF	12
B. Rush, SP	9
J. Klippstein, RP	8
T. Lown, RP	7
H. Pollet, SP	7
B. Serena, 2B	7
J. Garagiola, C	6
B. Church, RP	5
D. Leonard, RP	5
C. McCullough, C	5
E. Miksis, 2B	5
R. Smalley, SS	5
J. Willis, RP	4
H. Jeffcoat, OF	3
T. Atwell, C	2
E. Banks, SS	2
C. Metkovich, OF	2
P. Ward, OF	2
T. Brown, SS	1
P. Cavarretta, PH-PR	1
S. Jones, RP	1
D. Talbot, OF	1

Cincinnati (68-86)	WS
Hitting	**97.6**
Fielding	**37.0**
Pitching	**69.3**
G. Bell, OF	24
T. Kluszewski, 1B	24
J. Greengrass, OF	15
B. Adams, 3B	14
F. Baczewski, SP	13
W. Marshall, OF	11
R. McMillan, SS	11
J. Nuxhall, SP	11
H. Perkowski, SP	11
J. Collum, RP	10
K. Raffensberger, SP	10
A. Seminick, C	10
B. Podbielan, SP	7
B. Borkowski, OF	5
R. Bridges, 2B	5
G. Hatton, 2B	4
B. Kelly, RP	3
C. King, RP	3
H. Landrith, C	3
F. Smith, RP	3
J. Temple, 2B	2
B. Church, SP	1
H. Judson, SP	1
G. Lerchen, OF	1
B. Marquis, OF	1
W. Post, OF	1

Milwaukee (92-62)	WS
Hitting	**127.7**
Fielding	**47.1**
Pitching	**101.2**
E. Mathews, 3B	39
W. Spahn, SP	31
J. Logan, SS	24
S. Gordon, OF	19
A. Pafko, OF	18
J. Adcock, 1B	17
D. Crandall, C	16
L. Burdette, RP	15
B. Bruton, OF	14
B. Buhl, SP	12
J. Antonelli, SP	11
J. Dittmer, 2B	11
M. Surkont, SP	11
D. Liddle, RP	9
J. Pendleton, OF	9
E. Johnson, RP	6
J. Wilson, SP	4
W. Cooper, C	2
H. Hanebrink, 2B	2
J. Jay, RP	2
D. Jolly, RP	2
G. Crowe, 1B	1
E. St. Claire, C	1

New York (70-84)	WS
Hitting	**107.9**
Fielding	**31.2**
Pitching	**70.9**

A. Dark, SS	21
M. Irvin, OF	18
H. Thompson, 3B	18
B. Thomson, OF	17
R. Gomez, SP	14
W. Lockman, 1B	14
H. Wilhelm, RP	14
D. Mueller, OF	11
D. Williams, 2B	10
L. Jansen, SP	9
W. Westrum, C	9
J. Hearn, SP	8
S. Maglie, SP	7
D. Spencer, SS	7
A. Corwin, RP	5
M. Grissom, RP	5
B. Hofman, 3B	5
A. Worthington, SP	5
D. Koslo, RP	4
R. Noble, C	3
D. Rhodes, OF	3
S. Calderone, C	1
T. Gilbert, 1B	1
S. Yvars, C	1

Philadelphia (83-71)	WS
Hitting	**110.5**
Fielding	**43.2**
Pitching	**95.3**
R. Roberts, SP	35
R. Ashburn, OF	26
D. Ennis, OF	19
G. Hamner, 2B	19
C. Simmons, SP	19
P. Jones, 3B	15
E. Torgeson, 1B	14
S. Burgess, C	12
J. Konstanty, RP	11
C. Ryan, 2B	11
B. Miller, SP	10
S. Lopata, C	9
S. Ridzik, RP	9
J. Wyrostek, OF	8
K. Drews, SP	7
T. Kazanski, SS	5
E. Waitkus, 1B	5
M. Clark, OF	4
T. Glaviano, 3B	3
A. Hansen, RP	3
T. Kipper, RP	2
J. Lindell, SP	2
B. Nicholson, OF	1

Pittsburgh (50-104)	WS
Hitting	**63.2**
Fielding	**28.7**
Pitching	**58.1**
D. O'Connell, 3B	16
F. Thomas, OF	14
C. Abrams, OF	13
J. Lindell, SP	12
M. Dickson, SP	11
J. Hetki, RP	10
P. LaPalme, SP	9
B. Friend, SP	8
H. Rice, OF	7
P. Smith, 1B	6
D. Cole, SS	5
B. Hall, RP	5
R. Kiner, OF	5
C. Bernier, OF	4
J. O'Brien, 2B	4
R. Bowman, RP	3
E. Pellagrini, 2B	3
P. Ward, 1B	3
T. Atwell, C	2
J. Garagiola, C	2
M. Sandlock, C	2
P. Castiglione, 3B	1
R. Face, RP	1
C. Hogue, SP	1
V. Janowicz, C	1
E. O'Brien, SS	1
J. Waugh, RP	1

St. Louis (83-71)	WS
Hitting	**116.7**
Fielding	**42.6**
Pitching	**89.7**
S. Musial, OF	33
H. Haddix, SP	27
R. Schoendienst, 2B	27
S. Hemus, SS	23
V. Mizell, SP	17
E. Slaughter, OF	17
G. Staley, SP	15
R. Repulski, OF	13
S. Bilko, 1B	12
R. Jablonski, 3B	11
D. Rice, C	11
A. Brazle, RP	9
H. White, RP	9
J. Presko, SP	6
P. Lowrey, OF	4
S. Miller, RP	4
C. Chambers, RP	2
F. Anderson, C	1
P. Castiglione, 3B	1
M. Clark, RP	1
G. Dunlap, OF	1
H. Elliott, OF	1
E. Erautt, RP	1
D. Rand, C	1
E. Stanky, 2B	1
S. Yvars, C	1

1954
American League

Baltimore (54-100)	WS
Hitting	**61.8**
Fielding	**34.3**
Pitching	**65.9**
C. Abrams, OF	16
B. Turley, SP	16
J. Coleman, SP	13
D. Pillette, SP	12
C. Courtney, C	10
C. Diering, OF	9
V. Stephens, 3B	9
B. Young, 2B	9
E. Waitkus, 1B	7
B. Chakales, RP	6
L. Kretlow, SP	6
D. Larsen, SP	6
G. Coan, OF	5
B. Hunter, SS	5
B. Kennedy, 3B	5
J. Brideweser, SS	4
H. Fox, RP	4
J. Fridley, OF	3
D. Kryhoski, 1B	3
S. Mele, OF	3
M. Blyzka, RP	2
L. Moss, C	2
C. Garcia, 2B	1
D. Koslo, RP	1
B. Kuzava, SP	1
R. Murray, C	1
B. O'Dell, RP	1
M. Stuart, RP	1
V. Wertz, OF	1

Boston (69-85)	WS
Hitting	**103.3**
Fielding	**32.5**
Pitching	**71.1**
T. Williams, OF	29
J. Jensen, OF	17
F. Sullivan, SP	15
B. Goodman, 2B	13
W. Nixon, SP	11
S. White, C	11
M. Bolling, SS	10
G. Hatton, 3B	10
E. Kinder, RP	10
T. Lepcio, 2B	10
J. Piersall, OF	10
H. Agganis, 1B	9
T. Brewer, SP	7
L. Kiely, SP	6
S. Mele, 1B	5
H. Brown, RP	4
B. Consolo, SS	4
R. Kemmerer, RP	4
M. Parnell, SP	4
S. Hudson, RP	3
T. Hurd, RP	3
T. Clevenger, RP	2
B. Henry, SP	2
G. Kell, 3B	2
K. Olson, OF	2
D. Lenhardt, OF	1
C. Maxwell, OF	1
M. Owen, C	1
B. Werle, RP	1

Chicago (94-60)	WS
Hitting	**126.3**
Fielding	**50.2**
Pitching	**105.6**
M. Minoso, OF	32
N. Fox, 2B	26
C. Carrasquel, SS	24
V. Trucks, SP	22
J. Rivera, OF	17
S. Consuegra, RP	15
J. Harshman, SP	15
B. Keegan, SP	14
C. Michaels, 3B	13
S. Lollar, C	12
J. Groth, OF	11
D. Johnson, RP	11
H. Dorish, RP	10
F. Fain, 1B	10
B. Pierce, SP	10
M. Martin, RP	8
P. Cavarretta, 1B	7
G. Kell, 1B	6
M. Batts, C	4
F. Marsh, 3B	4
R. Jackson, 1B	3
W. Marshall, OF	2
C. Sawatski, C	2
M. Fornieles, RP	1
J. Kirrene, 3B	1
E. McGhee, OF	1
R. Wilson, C	1

Cleveland (111-43)	WS
Hitting	**152.3**
Fielding	**50.5**
Pitching	**130.2**
B. Avila, 2B	34
L. Doby, OF	33
A. Rosen, 3B	27
A. Smith, OF	25
M. Garcia, SP	24
B. Lemon, SP	24
E. Wynn, SP	24
J. Hegan, C	15
A. Houtteman, SP	14
D. Mossi, RP	13
R. Narleski, RP	12
V. Wertz, 1B	12
B. Feller, SP	11
G. Strickland, SS	10
D. Philley, OF	9
W. Westlake, OF	9
H. Newhouser, RP	7
S. Dente, SS	5
B. Glynn, 1B	4
H. Majeski, 2B	4
D. Pope, OF	4
R. Regalado, 3B	4
H. Naragon, C	3
B. Chakales, RP	2
D. Mitchell, OF	2
M. Grasso, C	1
D. Hoskins, RP	1

Detroit (68-86)	WS
Hitting	**89.1**
Fielding	**38.2**
Pitching	**76.7**
S. Gromek, SP	24
R. Boone, 3B	22
N. Garver, SP	20
H. Kuenn, SS	19
B. Tuttle, OF	15
F. House, C	11
G. Zuverink, SP	11
J. Delsing, OF	10
F. Hatfield, 2B	8
R. Wilson, C	8
W. Belardi, 1B	7
A. Kaline, OF	7
A. Aber, SP	6
F. Bolling, 2B	6
W. Dropo, 1B	6
B. Hoeft, SP	6
B. Miller, RP	6
B. Nieman, OF	6
D. Marlowe, RP	4
M. Batts, C	1
R. Bertoia, 2B	1

New York (103-51)	WS
Hitting	**174.7**
Fielding	**43.2**
Pitching	**91.1**
M. Mantle, OF	36
Y. Berra, C	34
I. Noren, OF	21
G. McDougald, 2B	20
A. Carey, 3B	18
H. Bauer, OF	16
W. Ford, SP	16
J. Collins, 1B	15
B. Grim, SP	13
B. Skowron, 1B	13
A. Reynolds, SP-RP	11
J. Sain, RP	11
G. Woodling, OF	10
H. Byrd, SP	8
E. Lopat, SP	8
T. Morgan, SP	8
J. Coleman, 2B	6
P. Rizzuto, SS	6
T. Byrne, SP	5
J. McDonald, SP	5
E. Robinson, 1B	5
E. Slaughter, OF	5
W. Miranda, SS	4
B. Cerv, OF	3
T. Gorman, RP	3
J. Konstanty, RP	3
B. Wiesler, SP	2
R. Branca, SP	1
B. Brown, 3B	1
C. Silvera, C	1
M. Stuart, RP	1

Philadelphia (51-103)	WS
Hitting	**84.4**
Fielding	**25.5**
Pitching	**43.1**
J. Finigan, 3B	21
A. Portocarrero, SP	12
S. Jacobs, 2B	11
B. Wilson, OF	11
G. Zernial, OF	9
B. Renna, OF	8
M. Burtschy, RP	7
L. Limmer, 1B	7
V. Power, OF	7
E. Valo, OF	7
D. Bollweg, 1B	6
C. Bishop, SP	5
J. DeMaestri, SS	5
S. Dixon, RP	5
J. Astroth, C	4
M. Fricano, SP	4

Bi. Shantz, C	4
B. Trice, SP	4
E. Joost, SS	3
A. Kellner, SP	3
J. Littrell, SS	2
A. Sima, RP	2
P. Suder, 2B	2
M. Martin, RP	1
E. McGhee, OF	1
J. Robertson, C	1
B. Upton, RP	1

Washington (66-88)	WS
Hitting	**102.5**
Fielding	**32.1**
Pitching	**63.4**
M. Vernon, 1B	24
E. Yost, 3B	23
J. Busby, OF	22
P. Runnels, SS	18
R. Sievers, OF	16
J. Schmitz, SP	14
B. Porterfield, SP	13
D. Stone, SP	11
E. Fitz Gerald, C	9
M. McDermott, SP	9
C. Stobbs, SP	8
C. Pascual, RP	4
W. Terwilliger, 2B	4
J. Pesky, 2B	3
J. Snyder, SS	3
J. Tipton, C	3
T. Wright, OF	3
S. Dixon, RP	2
G. Keriazakos, RP	2
T. Umphlett, OF	2
C. Vollmer, OF	2
J. Lemon, OF	1
C. Marrero, RP	1
B. Oldis, C	1

1954 National League

Brooklyn (92-62)	WS
Hitting	**146.5**
Fielding	**41.6**
Pitching	**87.9**
D. Snider, OF	39
G. Hodges, 1B	29
P. Reese, SS	26
J. Gilliam, 2B	20
J. Robinson, OF	20
C. Furillo, OF	17
C. Erskine, SP	16
J. Hughes, RP	14
R. Meyer, SP	11
S. Amoros, OF	10
R. Campanella, C	10
J. Podres, SP	10
B. Loes, SP	9
D. Newcombe, SP	8
C. Labine, RP	7
D. Hoak, 3B	6
B. Milliken, RP	5
K. Spooner, SP	4
B. Cox, 3B	3
R. Walker, C	3
W. Moryn, OF	2
E. Palica, RP	2
P. Roe, SP	2
P. Wojey, RP	2
B. Darnell, RP	1

Chicago (64-90)	WS
Hitting	**96.5**
Fielding	**31.9**
Pitching	**63.6**
H. Sauer, OF	22
R. Kiner, OF	19
B. Rush, SP	16
E. Banks, SS	15
G. Baker, 2B	14
D. Fondy, 1B	13
R. Jackson, 3B	13
P. Minner, SP	12
J. Davis, RP	10
F. Baumholtz, OF	8
H. Pollet, SP	8
W. Cooper, C	7
W. Hacker, RP	7
J. Garagiola, C	6
H. Jeffcoat, RP	4
D. Talbot, OF	3
B. Tremel, RP	3
S. Bilko, 1B	2
J. Klippstein, SP	2
C. McCullough, C	2
D. Cole, SP	1
A. Lary, SP	1
E. Miksis, 2B	1
B. Serena, 3B	1
E. Tappe, C	1
J. Willis, RP	1

Cincinnati (74-80)	WS
Hitting	**111.1**
Fielding	**37.9**
Pitching	**73.0**
T. Kluszewski, 1B	33
G. Bell, OF	20
J. Temple, 2B	19
J. Greengrass, OF	15
A. Fowler, SP	14
R. McMillan, SS	14
J. Nuxhall, RP	13
F. Smith, RP	13
B. Adams, 3B	12
A. Seminick, C	10
C. Valentine, SP	10
W. Post, OF	8
J. Collum, RP	6
H. Judson, RP	6
E. Bailey, C	5
L. Merriman, OF	4
F. Baczewski, SP	3
C. Harmon, 3B	3
H. Landrith, C	3
B. Podbielan, SP	3
J. Pearce, SP-RP	2
B. Borkowski, OF	1
R. Bridges, SS	1
K. Drews, RP	1
J. Lane, RP	1
C. Ross, RP	1
M. Savransky, RP	1

Milwaukee (89-65)	WS
Hitting	**115.7**
Fielding	**49.8**
Pitching	**101.6**
E. Mathews, 3B	33
W. Spahn, SP	23
J. Adcock, 1B	21
J. Logan, SS	20
L. Burdette, SP	18
B. Bruton, OF	17
D. Crandall, C	17
D. O'Connell, 2B	15
G. Conley, SP	14
D. Jolly, RP	14
A. Pafko, OF	14
H. Aaron, OF	13
E. Johnson, RP	9
J. Wilson, SP	8
J. Dittmer, 2B	6
R. Crone, RP	5
B. Buhl, RP	4
C. Metkovich, 1B	3
C. Nichols, SP	3
S. Calderone, C	2
D. Koslo, RP	2
C. Gorin, RP	1
P. Paine, RP	1
J. Pendleton, OF	1
R. Smalley, SS	1
B. Thomson, OF	1
C. White, C	1

New York (97-57)	WS
Hitting	**119.5**
Fielding	**49.9**
Pitching	**121.6**
W. Mays, OF	40
J. Antonelli, SP	28
A. Dark, SS	23
H. Thompson, 3B	21
R. Gomez, SP	19
D. Mueller, OF	19
S. Maglie, SP	18
M. Grissom, RP	17
H. Wilhelm, RP	15
M. Irvin, OF	14
D. Liddle, SP	11
W. Lockman, 1B	11
D. Rhodes, OF	11
D. Williams, 2B	10
J. Hearn, SP	6
R. Katt, C	6
W. Westrum, C	6
W. McCall, RP	4
B. Hofman, 1B	3
E. St. Claire, C	3
B. Gardner, 3B	2
A. Corwin, RP	1
J. Garagiola, C	1
G. Spencer, RP	1
A. Worthington, RP	1

Philadelphia (75-79)	WS
Hitting	**94.9**
Fielding	**41.4**
Pitching	**88.8**
R. Roberts, SP	31
R. Ashburn, OF	26
C. Simmons, SP	21
G. Hamner, 2B	20
P. Jones, 3B	16
S. Burgess, C	15
B. Morgan, SS	15
M. Dickson, SP	13
D. Ennis, OF	11
S. Lopata, C	10
E. Torgeson, 1B	10
H. Wehmeier, SP	9
B. Miller, SP	5
D. Schell, OF	5
S. Ridzik, RP	4
J. Wyrostek, OF	4
J. Konstanty, RP	3
M. Clark, OF	2
B. Greenwood, RP	2
R. Mrozinski, RP	2
T. Kazanski, SS	1

Pittsburgh (53-101)	WS
Hitting	**78.7**
Fielding	**26.8**
Pitching	**53.4**
F. Thomas, OF	26
S. Gordon, OF	16
T. Atwell, C	11
D. Littlefield, SP	11
M. Surkont, SP	9
P. Ward, 1B	9
C. Roberts, 2B	8
J. Shepard, C	8
B. Skinner, 1B	8
D. Cole, SS	7
B. Friend, SP	7
J. Thies, SP	7
V. Law, RP	5
J. Hetki, RP	4
J. Lynch, OF	4
G. O'Donnell, RP	4
B. Purkey, RP	4
D. Hall, OF	3
P. LaPalme, RP	3
G. Allie, SS	2
G. Henley, OF	1
E. Pellagrini, 3B	1
H. Rice, OF	1

St. Louis (72-82)	WS
Hitting	**126.1**
Fielding	**31.2**
Pitching	**58.7**
S. Musial, OF	30
R. Schoendienst, 2B	21
W. Moon, OF	20
H. Haddix, SP	17
R. Jablonski, 3B	14
R. Repulski, OF	14
B. Sarni, C	13
A. Grammas, SS	11
S. Hemus, SS	11
B. Lawrence, SP	11
J. Cunningham, 1B	10
G. Jones, SP	7
T. Poholsky, SP	7
V. Raschi, SP	6
A. Brazle, RP	5
D. Rice, C	4
T. Alston, 1B	3
J. Frazier, OF	3
R. Beard, SP	2
R. Lint, RP	2
G. Staley, RP	2
S. Yvars, C	2
S. Miller, RP	1

1955 American League

Baltimore (57-97)	WS
Hitting	**82.3**
Fielding	**28.9**
Pitching	**59.8**
W. Miranda, SS	14
G. Triandos, 1B	14
C. Abrams, OF	13
J. Wilson, SP	13
D. Philley, OF	11
C. Diering, OF	10
H. Smith, C	10
B. Wight, SP	9
R. Moore, RP	8
G. Zuverink, RP	8
J. Dyck, OF	7
H. Dorish, RP	6
E. Palica, SP	6
B. Hale, 1B	5
H. Evers, OF	4
F. Marsh, 2B	4
D. Pope, OF	4
L. Moss, C	3
G. Woodling, OF	3
H. Brown, RP	2
H. Byrd, SP	2
G. Coan, OF	2
B. Cox, 3B	2
E. Lopat, SP	2
A. Schallock, RP	2
E. Waitkus, 1B	2
B. Young, 2B	2
W. Causey, 3B	1
D. Ferrarese, RP	1
S. Rogovin, SP	1

Boston (84-70)	WS
Hitting	**99.1**
Fielding	**48.2**
Pitching	**104.7**
T. Williams, OF	23
F. Sullivan, SP	22
J. Piersall, OF	20
J. Jensen, OF	19
B. Goodman, 2B	15
B. Klaus, SS	15
W. Nixon, SP	14
E. Kinder, RP	13

G. Susce, SP	12
S. White, C	12
N. Zauchin, 1B	11
T. Brewer, SP	10
I. Delock, SP	10
G. Hatton, 3B	10
T. Hurd, RP	9
L. Kiely, RP	9
G. Stephens, OF	6
B. Henry, RP	4
F. Throneberry, OF	4
H. Agganis, 1B	3
T. Lepcio, 3B	3
E. Joost, SS	2
D. Brodowski, RP	1
H. Brown, RP	1
P. Daley, C	1
O. Friend, SS	1
F. Malzone, 3B	1
K. Olson, OF	1

Chicago (91-63)	WS
Hitting	**120.1**
Fielding	**47.8**
Pitching	**105.1**
N. Fox, 2B	25
B. Pierce, SP	23
S. Lollar, C	21
M. Minoso, OF	21
G. Kell, 3B	16
C. Carrasquel, SS	15
D. Donovan, SP	15
J. Rivera, OF	15
S. Consuegra, RP	13
W. Dropo, 1B	13
J. Harshman, SP	13
D. Howell, RP	10
B. Nieman, OF	10
V. Trucks, SP	10
C. Johnson, SP	7
B. Kennedy, 3B	7
J. Busby, OF	6
M. Fornieles, RP	6
J. Groth, OF	4
H. Byrd, RP	3
C. Courtney, C	3
M. Martin, RP	3
H. Dorish, RP	2
L. Moss, C	2
V. Stephens, 3B	2
J. Brideweser, SS	1
B. Chakales, RP	1
R. Jackson, 1B	1
S. Jok, 3B	1
W. Marshall, OF	1
R. Northey, OF	1
A. Papai, RP	1
B. Peterson, SS	1

Cleveland (93-61)	WS
Hitting	**120.3**
Fielding	**48.7**
Pitching	**110.0**
A. Smith, OF	29
L. Doby, OF	22
E. Wynn, SP	21
B. Avila, 2B	20
H. Score, SP	19
A. Rosen, 3B	16
B. Lemon, SP	15
R. Narleski, RP	14
M. Garcia, SP	12
R. Kiner, OF	11
D. Mossi, RP	10
G. Strickland, SS	10
J. Hegan, C	9
V. Wertz, 1B	8
A. Houtteman, RP	7
H. Naragon, C	7
G. Woodling, OF	7
F. Fain, 1B	5
H. Foiles, C	5
D. Pope, OF	5
B. Feller, RP	4
J. Santiago, RP	4
S. Dente, SS	3
D. Philley, OF	3
H. Aguirre, RP	2
H. Evers, OF	2
B. Wight, RP	2
J. Altobelli, 1B	1
R. Colavito, OF	1
B. Harrell, SS	1
S. Maglie, RP	1
H. Majeski, 3B	1
R. Regalado, 3B	1
B. Young, 2B	1

Detroit (79-75)	WS
Hitting	**125.8**
Fielding	**34.5**
Pitching	**76.7**
A. Kaline, OF	31
H. Kuenn, SS	22
R. Boone, 3B	19
B. Hoeft, SP	18
B. Tuttle, OF	18
F. Lary, SP	15
F. Hatfield, 2B	12
E. Torgeson, 1B	12
N. Garver, SP	11
F. House, C	11
S. Gromek, SP	10
J. Delsing, OF	9
F. Fain, 1B	7
A. Aber, RP	6
B. Birrer, RP	5
H. Malmberg, 2B	4
C. Maxwell, OF	4
J. Phillips, 1B	4
J. Coleman, RP	3
L. Cristante, RP	2
D. Maas, SP	2
D. Marlowe, RP	2
B. Miller, RP	2
B. Phillips, OF	2
R. Wilson, C	2
R. Bertoia, 3B	1
B. Black, SP	1
P. Foytack, RP	1
J. Porter, 1B	1

Kansas City (63-91)	WS
Hitting	**110.6**
Fielding	**28.5**
Pitching	**49.9**
V. Power, 1B	26
E. Valo, OF	18
H. Lopez, 3B	15
J. Finigan, 2B	14
G. Zernial, OF	13
T. Gorman, RP	12
H. Simpson, OF	12
E. Slaughter, OF	12
A. Kellner, SP	10
J. Astroth, C	9
A. Ditmar, SP	7
B. Wilson, OF	6
Bo. Shantz, SP	5
J. DeMaestri, SS	4
B. Harrington, RP	4
A. Portocarrero, SP	4
B. Renna, OF	4
A. Ceccarelli, SP	3
V. Raschi, SP	3
Bi. Shantz, C	3
M. Fricano, RP	2
Cle. Boyer, SS	1
J. Sain, RP	1
P. Suder, 2B	1

New York (96-58)	WS
Hitting	**147.1**
Fielding	**48.6**
Pitching	**92.3**
M. Mantle, OF	41
Y. Berra, C	24
G. McDougald, 2B	24
W. Ford, SP	22
H. Bauer, OF	21
B. Turley, SP	16
A. Carey, 3B	14
T. Byrne, SP	12
B. Skowron, 1B	12
E. Howard, OF	11
I. Noren, OF	11
J. Collins, 1B	9
J. Konstanty, RP	9
D. Larsen, SP	8
J. Kucks, RP	7
T. Morgan, RP	7
E. Robinson, 1B	7
P. Rizzuto, SS	6
B. Cerv, OF	5
B. Grim, RP	4
B. Hunter, SS	4
T. Sturdivant, RP	4
E. Lopat, SP	3
J. Coleman, SS	2
B. Martin, 2B	2
C. Silvera, C	1
M. Throneberry, 1B	1
B. Wiesler, RP	1

Washington (53-101)	WS
Hitting	**93.9**
Fielding	**25.2**
Pitching	**39.9**
M. Vernon, 1B	21
R. Sievers, OF	20
E. Yost, 3B	16
P. Runnels, 2B	14
M. McDermott, SP	10
C. Paula, OF	10
J. Schmitz, SP	8
C. Courtney, C	7
P. Ramos, RP	6
D. Stone, SP	6
J. Valdivielso, SS	6
B. Porterfield, SP	5
E. Fitz Gerald, C	4
E. Oravetz, OF	4
J. Busby, OF	3
S. Shea, RP	3
C. Stobbs, RP	3
J. Groth, OF	2
B. Kline, SS	2
B. Chakales, RP	1
W. Clarke, RP	1
B. Edwards, C	1
H. Killebrew, 3B	1
S. Korcheck, C	1
T. Roig, SS	1
J. Snyder, 2B	1
B. Stewart, RP	1
T. Umphlett, OF	1

1955 National League

Brooklyn (98-55)	WS
Hitting	**152.3**
Fielding	**44.7**
Pitching	**97.0**
D. Snider, OF	36
R. Campanella, C	28
D. Newcombe, SP	25
G. Hodges, 1B	23
C. Furillo, OF	22
P. Reese, SS	18
C. Labine, RP	15
J. Gilliam, 2B	14
S. Amoros, OF	12
C. Erskine, SP	12
J. Robinson, 3B	12
D. Hoak, 3B	9
B. Loes, SP	8
J. Podres, SP	8
K. Spooner, RP	8
D. Bessent, RP	7
R. Craig, RP	7
D. Zimmer, 2B	7
F. Kellert, 1B	4
E. Roebuck, RP	4
S. Koufax, RP	3
R. Walker, C	3
J. Hughes, RP	2
R. Meyer, SP	2
G. Shuba, OF	2
J. Black, RP	1
D. Howell, C	1
W. Moryn, OF	1

Chicago (72-81)	WS
Hitting	**90.8**
Fielding	**41.9**
Pitching	**83.3**
E. Banks, SS	32
B. Rush, SP	18
G. Baker, 2B	16
R. Jackson, 3B	16
S. Jones, SP	14
P. Minner, SP	14
D. Fondy, 1B	13
W. Hacker, SP	13
H. Jeffcoat, RP	10
J. King, OF	10
H. Chiti, C	7
E. Miksis, OF	7
F. Baumholtz, OF	6
J. Davis, RP	6
B. Speake, OF	6
W. Cooper, C	5
H. Sauer, OF	5
B. Tremel, RP	4
L. Merriman, OF	3
H. Pollet, RP	3
T. Tappe, OF	3
J. Bolger, OF	2
D. Hillman, RP	1
C. McCullough, C	1
H. Perkowski, RP	1

Cincinnati (75-79)	WS
Hitting	**106.6**
Fielding	**37.3**
Pitching	**81.1**
T. Kluszewski, 1B	25
W. Post, OF	23
G. Bell, OF	21
J. Nuxhall, SP	20
S. Burgess, C	16
R. McMillan, SS	16
J. Temple, 2B	16
A. Fowler, SP	13
H. Freeman, RP	12
J. Collum, SP	9
J. Klippstein, RP	9
B. Adams, 3B	5
J. Black, RP	5
C. Harmon, 3B	5
G. Staley, SP	4
R. Bridges, 3B	3
D. Gross, SP	3
R. Jablonski, 3B-OF	3
R. Minarcin, RP	3
B. Podbielan, RP	3
H. Landrith, C	2
S. Palys, OF	2
B. Thurman, OF	2
E. Bailey, C	1
M. Batts, C	1
G. Gorbous, OF	1
S. Ridzik, RP	1
M. Smith, 3B	1

Milwaukee (85-69)	WS
Hitting	**143.6**
Fielding	**36.3**
Pitching	**75.1**
E. Mathews, 3B	34
H. Aaron, OF	29
J. Logan, SS	26
B. Bruton, OF	22
W. Spahn, SP	19
D. Crandall, C	16
G. Crowe, 1B	14
B. Buhl, SP	13
L. Burdette, SP	11
J. Adcock, 1B	9
D. O'Connell, 2B	9
B. Thomson, OF	9
R. Crone, RP	8
G. Conley, SP	7
E. Johnson, RP	6
C. Nichols, SP	5
C. Tanner, OF	5
A. Pafko, OF	4
H. Robinson, RP	3
P. Paine, RP	2
J. Dittmer, 2B	1
J. Jay, RP	1
D. Rice, C	1
C. White, C	1

New York (80-74)	WS
Hitting	**112.5**
Fielding	**38.7**
Pitching	**88.7**
W. Mays, OF	40
J. Antonelli, SP	18
H. Thompson, 3B	18
J. Hearn, SP	14
A. Dark, SS	13
W. Lockman, OF	13
D. Mueller, OF	13
R. Gomez, SP	9
M. Grissom, RP	9
S. Maglie, SP	8
D. Rhodes, OF	8
W. Terwilliger, 2B	8
D. Liddle, RP	7
W. McCall, RP	7
P. Giel, RP	6
S. Gordon, 3B	6
B. Hofman, 1B	6
H. Wilhelm, RP	6
G. Harris, 1B	5
R. Monzant, RP	5
D. Williams, 2B	5
R. Katt, C	4
M. Irvin, OF	3
W. Westrum, C	3
B. Gardner, SS	2
P. Burnside, SP	1
F. Castleman, 2B	1
A. Corwin, RP	1
B. Taylor, OF	1

Philadelphia (77-77)	WS
Hitting	**107.0**
Fielding	**40.8**
Pitching	**83.2**
R. Ashburn, OF	29
R. Roberts, SP	27
D. Ennis, OF	21
S. Lopata, C	17
P. Jones, 3B	16
M. Dickson, SP	14
J. Meyer, RP	11
A. Seminick, C	11
B. Miller, RP	10
B. Morgan, 2B	10
H. Wehmeier, SP	10
J. Greengrass, OF	9
G. Hamner, 2B	8
S. Rogovin, SP	7
R. Negray, SP	5
M. Blaylock, 1B	4
C. Simmons, SP	4
R. Smalley, SS	4
E. Torgeson, 1B	4
G. Gorbous, OF	3
E. Waitkus, 1B	3
S. Palys, OF	2
T. Kipper, RP	1
L. Lovenguth, RP	1

Pittsburgh (60-94)	WS
Hitting	**76.8**
Fielding	**34.9**
Pitching	**68.3**
B. Friend, RP	19
D. Long, 1B	17
F. Thomas, OF	15
V. Law, SP	14
Gen. Freese, 3B	13
D. Groat, SS	13
R. Face, RP	9
J. O'Brien, 2B	9
J. Lynch, OF	8
R. Clemente, OF	7
D. Hall, SP	7
R. Kline, SP	6
T. Atwell, C	5
J. Shepard, C	5
Geo. Freese, 3B	4
N. King, RP	4
D. Cole, 3B	3
P. Ward, 1B	3
L. Donoso, RP	2
D. Littlefield, RP	2
F. Montemayor, OF	2
E. O'Brien, OF	2
H. Peterson, C	2
B. Purkey, SP	2
M. Surkont, SP	2
B. Wade, RP	2
A. Grunwald, RP	1
R. Mejias, OF	1
T. Saffell, OF	1

St. Louis (68-86)	WS
Hitting	**95.9**
Fielding	**37.7**
Pitching	**70.5**
S. Musial, 1B	29
W. Moon, OF	18
R. Schoendienst, 2B	16
K. Boyer, 3B	14
R. Repulski, OF	14
B. Virdon, OF	14
W. Schmidt, SP	13
L. Arroyo, SP	10
H. Haddix, SP	10
T. Poholsky, SP	10
L. Jackson, SP	9
P. LaPalme, RP	9
A. Grammas, SS	8
S. Hemus, 3B	6
B. Sarni, C	5
F. Smith, RP	4
N. Burbrink, C	3
B. Flowers, SP	2
F. Wooldridge, RP	2
D. Blasingame, 2B	1
J. Frazier, OF	1
A. Gettel, RP	1
L. McDaniel, SP-RP	1
B. Stephenson, SS	1
B. Tiefenauer, RP	1
H. Walker, OF	1
P. Whisenant, OF	1

1956
American League

Baltimore (69-85)	WS
Hitting	**87.8**
Fielding	**35.7**
Pitching	**83.5**
B. Nieman, OF	23
G. Triandos, C	19
C. Johnson, SP	16
R. Moore, SP	15
H. Brown, RP	12
T. Francona, OF	12
D. Williams, OF	12
B. Wight, SP	10
G. Kell, 3B	9
G. Zuverink, RP	9
B. Boyd, 1B	8
B. Gardner, 2B	7
W. Miranda, SS	7
M. Fornieles, RP	6
H. Smith, C	6
H. Evers, OF	4
E. Palica, RP	4
B. Adams, 3B	3
D. Ferrarese, RP	3
J. Wilson, SP	3
C. Beamon, SP-RP	2
J. Frazier, OF	2
B. Loes, RP	2
W. Causey, 3B	1
S. Consuegra, RP	1
C. Diering, OF	1
H. Dorish, RP	1
J. Dyck, OF	1
T. Gastall, C	1
B. Hale, 1B	1
G. Hatton, 2B	1
B. O'Dell, RP	1
D. Philley, OF	1
J. Pyburn, OF	1
B. Robinson, 3B	1
J. Schmitz, RP	1

Boston (84-70)	WS
Hitting	**118.8**
Fielding	**42.2**
Pitching	**91.0**
T. Williams, OF	25
T. Brewer, SP	24
J. Jensen, OF	23
J. Piersall, OF	21
F. Sullivan, SP	19
B. Klaus, 3B	16
M. Vernon, 1B	15
D. Gernert, OF	12
I. Delock, RP	11
B. Goodman, 2B	11
D. Buddin, SS	9
W. Nixon, SP	9
T. Lepcio, 2B	8
M. Parnell, SP	8
D. Sisler, RP	8
S. White, C	6
P. Daley, C	4
T. Hurd, RP	4
B. Porterfield, SP	4
F. Baumann, RP	3
M. Bolling, SS	2
H. Dorish, RP	2
G. Stephens, OF	2
L. Kiely, RP	1
F. Malzone, 3B	1
G. Mauch, 2B	1
R. Minarcin, RP	1
G. Susce, RP	1
N. Zauchin, 1B	1

Chicago (85-69)	WS
Hitting	**117.3**
Fielding	**43.2**
Pitching	**94.5**
M. Minoso, OF	29
L. Doby, OF	23
B. Pierce, SP	21
J. Harshman, SP	20
N. Fox, 2B	19
D. Donovan, SP	18
S. Lollar, C	18
L. Aparicio, SS	14
J. Rivera, OF	12
F. Hatfield, 3B	9
G. Staley, RP	9
J. Wilson, SP	9
W. Dropo, 1B	7
S. Esposito, 3B	6
B. Keegan, SP	5
P. LaPalme, RP	5
D. Philley, 1B	5
E. Kinder, RP	4
L. Moss, C	4
D. Howell, RP	3
R. Northey, OF	3
B. Phillips, OF	3
G. Kell, 3B	2
H. Pollet, RP	2
S. Consuegra, RP	1
R. Jackson, 1B	1
C. Johnson, RP	1
M. Martin, RP	1
B. Nieman, OF	1

Cleveland (88-66)	WS
Hitting	**106.5**
Fielding	**47.8**
Pitching	**109.7**
E. Wynn, SP	28
H. Score, SP	25
B. Lemon, SP	23
A. Smith, OF	21
V. Wertz, 1B	21
R. Colavito, OF	16
A. Rosen, 3B	15
B. Avila, 2B	14
J. Busby, OF	12
C. Carrasquel, SS	12
G. Woodling, OF	12
M. Garcia, SP	11
D. Mossi, RP	9
R. Narleski, RP	9
J. Hegan, C	8
P. Ward, 1B	5
H. Naragon, C	4
G. Strickland, 2B-SS	4
H. Aguirre, SP	3
E. Averill, C	3
S. Mele, OF	3
J. Caffie, OF	2
C. McLish, RP	2
B. Feller, RP	1
D. Pope, OF	1

Detroit (82-72)	WS
Hitting	**129.6**
Fielding	**36.8**
Pitching	**79.6**
A. Kaline, OF	26
H. Kuenn, SS	26
C. Maxwell, OF	25
R. Boone, 3B	22
F. Lary, SP	22
P. Foytack, SP	15
B. Hoeft, SP	15
F. Bolling, 2B	13
E. Torgeson, 1B	12
R. Wilson, C	11
S. Gromek, RP	8
V. Trucks, SP	7
B. Tuttle, OF	7
A. Aber, RP	6
W. Belardi, 1B	5
F. House, C	5
J. Bunning, RP	4
J. Phillips, 1B	4
J. Brideweser, SS	2
B. Kennedy, OF	2
W. Masterson, RP	2
J. Small, OF	2

R. Bertoia, 2B	1
B. Black, RP	1
N. Garver, SP-RP	1
F. Hatfield, 2B	1
B. Hicks, SS	1

Kansas City (52-102)	WS
Hitting	**67.2**
Fielding	**31.9**
Pitching	**56.9**
H. Lopez, 3B	15
V. Power, 1B	14
H. Simpson, OF	14
A. Ditmar, SP	11
T. Gorman, RP	11
W. Burnette, SP	10
L. Skizas, OF	8
B. Shantz, RP	7
J. DeMaestri, SS	6
G. Zernial, OF	6
J. Groth, OF	5
A. Kellner, SP	5
A. Pilarcik, OF	5
E. Slaughter, OF	5
T. Thompson, C	5
J. Crimian, RP	4
M. Burtschy, RP	3
J. Ginsberg, C	3
L. Kretlow, SP	3
H. Smith, C	3
M. Baxes, SS	2
J. Finigan, 2B	2
C. Boyer, 2B	1
G. Cox, SP	1
B. Harrington, RP	1
S. Jacobs, 2B	1
J. McMahan, RP	1
J. Pisoni, OF	1
R. Pless, 1B	1
B. Renna, OF	1
E. Robinson, 1B	1

New York (97-57)	WS
Hitting	**157.3**
Fielding	**44.4**
Pitching	**89.3**
M. Mantle, OF	49
Y. Berra, C	31
G. McDougald, SS	24
W. Ford, SP	22
B. Skowron, 1B	21
H. Bauer, OF	16
D. Larsen, SP	14
B. Martin, 2B	14
T. Sturdivant, SP	14
J. Kucks, SP	11
T. Byrne, RP	9
A. Carey, 3B	8
B. Grim, RP	7
B. Cerv, OF	6
J. Collins, OF	6
E. Howard, OF	6
T. Morgan, RP	5
J. Coleman, 2B	4
R. Coleman, RP	4
B. Turley, SP	4
B. Hunter, SS	3
M. McDermott, RP	3
E. Robinson, 1B	2
N. Siebern, OF	2
E. Slaughter, OF	2
T. Carroll, 3B	1
J. Lumpe, SS	1
I. Noren, OF	1
P. Rizzuto, SS	1

Washington (59-95)	WS
Hitting	**98.4**
Fielding	**27.1**
Pitching	**51.5**
R. Sievers, OF	20
J. Lemon, OF	19
C. Stobbs, SP	19
E. Yost, 3B	19
P. Runnels, 1B	18
C. Courtney, C	9
L. Berberet, C	8
B. Chakales, RP	7
P. Ramos, RP	7
B. Byerly, RP	6
E. Fitz Gerald, C	6
W. Herzog, OF	5
H. Plews, 2B	5
C. Pascual, SP	4
J. Valdivielso, SS	4
K. Olson, OF	3
E. Oravetz, OF	3
B. Stewart, RP	3
T. Abernathy, SP	2
H. Killebrew, 3B	2
J. Snyder, SS	2
T. Clevenger, RP	1
E. Hernandez, SP	1
L. Luttrell, SS	1
T. Roig, 2B	1
D. Stone, SP	1
D. Tettelbach, OF	1

1956 National League

Brooklyn (93-61)	WS
Hitting	**131.3**
Fielding	**48.3**
Pitching	**99.3**
D. Snider, OF	34
J. Gilliam, 2B	28
D. Newcombe, SP	27
G. Hodges, 1B	21
C. Furillo, OF	17
J. Robinson, 3B	17
S. Maglie, SP	16
S. Amoros, OF	14
P. Reese, SS	14
C. Labine, RP	13
R. Campanella, C	12
R. Jackson, 3B	12
R. Craig, SP	11
D. Bessent, RP	10
D. Drysdale, RP	9
C. Erskine, SP	9
C. Neal, 2B	5
E. Roebuck, RP	5
R. Walker, C	2
C. Fernandez, SS	1
S. Koufax, SP	1
R. Nelson, 1B	1

Chicago (60-94)	WS
Hitting	**81.2**
Fielding	**34.3**
Pitching	**64.5**
E. Banks, SS	22
W. Moryn, OF	19
B. Rush, SP	15
G. Baker, 2B	11
M. Irvin, OF	11
T. Lown, RP	10
D. Fondy, 1B	9
S. Jones, SP	9
J. King, OF	9
P. Whisenant, OF	8
J. Davis, RP	7
D. Kaiser, SP	7
H. Landrith, C	6
E. Miksis, 3B	6
J. Brosnan, RP	5
S. Drake, OF	5
D. Hoak, 3B	5
V. Valentinetti, RP	5
M. Drabowsky, SP	4
H. Chiti, C	3
W. Hacker, SP	2
J. Briggs, RP	1
J. Kindall, SS	1

Cincinnati (91-63)	WS
Hitting	**135.2**
Fielding	**40.9**
Pitching	**97.0**
F. Robinson, OF	26
E. Bailey, C	23
G. Bell, OF	22
T. Kluszewski, 1B	20
R. McMillan, SS	20
W. Post, OF	16
J. Temple, 2B	16
H. Freeman, RP	15
B. Lawrence, SP	14
J. Nuxhall, SP	14
H. Jeffcoat, RP	11
J. Klippstein, SP	11
S. Burgess, C	10
A. Fowler, SP	10
T. Acker, RP	9
R. Jablonski, 3B	9
D. Gross, RP	7
B. Thurman, OF	5
G. Crowe, 1B	4
J. Black, RP	3
A. Grammas, 3B	3
P. LaPalme, RP	2
L. Jansen, SP	1
S. Palys, OF	1
A. Schult, OF	1

Milwaukee (92-62)	WS
Hitting	**141.5**
Fielding	**43.7**
Pitching	**90.8**
H. Aaron, OF	30
E. Mathews, 3B	29
J. Logan, SS	24
W. Spahn, SP	24
J. Adcock, 1B	22
L. Burdette, SP	20
B. Bruton, OF	17
D. O'Connell, 2B	16
D. Crandall, C	15
B. Buhl, SP	12
B. Thomson, OF	12
G. Conley, SP	8
T. Phillips, RP	8
R. Crone, SP	6
W. Covington, OF	4
D. Rice, C	4
L. Sleater, RP	4
B. Trowbridge, RP	4
J. Dittmer, 2B	3
E. Johnson, RP	3
A. Pafko, OF	3
D. Jolly, RP	2
F. Torre, 1B	2
T. Atwell, C	1
F. Mantilla, SS	1
B. Roselli, C	1
C. Tanner, OF	1

New York (67-87)	WS
Hitting	**75.0**
Fielding	**37.3**
Pitching	**88.7**
W. Mays, OF	27
J. Antonelli, SP	25
B. White, 1B	16
M. Grissom, RP	13
J. Brandt, OF	11
R. Schoendienst, 2B	10
D. Spencer, 2B	8
A. Worthington, SP	8
F. Castleman, 3B	6
D. Littlefield, RP	6
W. McCall, RP	6
S. Ridzik, RP	6
B. Sarni, C	6
H. Thompson, 3B	6
H. Wilhelm, RP	6
R. Gomez, SP	5
J. Hearn, SP	5
J. Margoneri, SP	5
W. Westrum, C	5
A. Dark, SS	3
R. Katt, C	3
W. Lockman, OF	3
D. Mueller, OF	3
D. Rhodes, OF	3
D. Liddle, RP	2
E. Bressoud, SS	1
R. Monzant, RP	1
M. Surkont, SP-RP	1
O. Virgil, 3B	1

Philadelphia (71-83)	WS
Hitting	**124.6**
Fielding	**29.6**
Pitching	**58.9**
R. Ashburn, OF	28
S. Lopata, C	26
P. Jones, 3B	25
D. Ennis, OF	15
M. Blaylock, 1B	13
H. Haddix, SP	13
C. Simmons, SP	13
R. Roberts, SP	12
E. Valo, OF	12
S. Hemus, 2B	9
G. Hamner, SS	8
B. Miller, RP	7
R. Smalley, SS	5
J. Meyer, RP	4
A. Seminick, C	4
T. Kazanski, 2B	3
S. Miller, SP	3
R. Negray, RP	3
J. Greengrass, OF	2
S. Rogovin, SP	2
J. Sanford, RP	2
F. Baumholtz, OF	1
E. Bouchee, 1B	1
A. LiPetri, RP	1
H. Wehmeier, SP	1

Pittsburgh (66-88)	WS
Hitting	**84.2**
Fielding	**37.8**
Pitching	**76.0**
B. Friend, SP	20
B. Virdon, OF	20
R. Kline, SP	17
F. Thomas, 3B	16
D. Long, 1B	15
R. Clemente, OF	14
L. Walls, OF	14
D. Groat, SS	12
R. Face, RP	11
J. Shepard, C	7
N. King, RP	6
V. Law, SP	6
B. Mazeroski, 2B	5
H. Foiles, C	4
G. Munger, RP	4
F. Waters, RP	4
G. Freese, 3B	3
D. Hall, RP	2
D. Kravitz, C	2
E. O'Brien, SS	2
L. Pepper, SP	2
H. Pollet, RP	2
B. Skinner, OF	2
P. Ward, 3B-OF	2
L. Arroyo, RP	1
D. Cole, 3B	1
B. Del Greco, OF	1
C. Naranjo, RP	1
J. O'Brien, 2B	1
C. Roberts, 2B	1

St. Louis (76-78)	WS
Hitting	115.5
Fielding	38.3
Pitching	74.3
S. Musial, 1B	26
K. Boyer, 3B	23
W. Moon, OF	22
D. Blasingame, 2B	17
M. Dickson, SP	15
V. Mizell, SP	11
H. Wehmeier, SP	11
A. Dark, SS	10
T. Poholsky, SP	9
R. Repulski, OF	9
W. Schmidt, SP	8
H. Smith, C	7
B. Del Greco, OF	6
L. McDaniel, RP	6
B. Sarni, C	6
H. Sauer, OF	6
L. Jackson, RP	5
R. Schoendienst, 2B	5
J. Collum, RP	4
R. Katt, C	4
E. Kinder, RP	3
W. Cooper, C	2
G. Hatton, 2B	2
J. Konstanty, RP	2
W. Lockman, OF	2
J. Brandt, OF	1
J. Frazier, OF	1
H. Haddix, SP	1
B. Morgan, 2B	1
R. Nelson, 1B	1
C. Peete, OF	1
B. Virdon, OF	1
D. Williams, OF	2
W. Causey, 2B	1
S. Consuegra, RP	1
J. Durham, OF	1
M. Fornieles, RP	1
T. Nelson, OF	1
M. Pappas, RP	1
C. Powis, OF	1
J. Pyburn, OF	1

Boston (82-72)	WS
Hitting	114.9
Fielding	39.6
Pitching	91.5
T. Williams, OF	38
F. Sullivan, SP	23
J. Piersall, OF	19
J. Jensen, OF	18
F. Malzone, 3B	18
T. Brewer, SP	16
W. Nixon, SP	15
B. Klaus, SS	13
I. Delock, RP	10
M. Fornieles, SP	9
D. Gernert, 1B	7
T. Lepcio, 2B	6
B. Porterfield, RP	6
M. Vernon, 1B	6
B. Consolo, SS	5
G. Mauch, 2B	5
D. Sisler, SP	5
G. Stephens, OF	5
G. Susce, RP	5
S. White, C	5
P. Daley, C	3
M. Wall, RP	3
K. Aspromonte, 2B	2
N. Zauchin, 1B	2
F. Baumann, RP	1
R. Minarcin, RP	1

Chicago (90-64)	WS
Hitting	129.9
Fielding	45.9
Pitching	94.2
N. Fox, 2B	32
M. Minoso, OF	26
L. Doby, OF	18
D. Donovan, SP	18
B. Pierce, SP	18
L. Aparicio, SS	16
S. Lollar, C	14
B. Phillips, 3B	13
J. Rivera, OF	13
G. Staley, RP	12
J. Wilson, SP	12
E. Torgeson, 1B	11
B. Keegan, SP	8
B. Fischer, RP	7
J. Harshman, SP	7
D. Howell, RP	7
J. Landis, OF	7
W. Dropo, 1B	5
S. Esposito, 3B	5
P. LaPalme, RP	4
L. Moss, C	4
E. Battey, C	2
F. Hatfield, 3B	2
R. Jackson, 1B	2
J. McDonald, RP	2
D. Philley, OF	2
T. Beard, OF	1
R. Northey, PH-PR	1
D. Rudolph, RP	1

Cleveland (76-77)	WS
Hitting	129.1
Fielding	31.4
Pitching	67.6
G. Woodling, OF	25
V. Wertz, 1B	24
R. Colavito, OF	18
A. Smith, 3B	17
R. Narleski, RP	15
C. Carrasquel, SS	14
B. Avila, 2B	13
R. Maris, OF	13
C. McLish, RP	13
M. Garcia, SP	12
E. Wynn, SP	10
D. Mossi, SP	9
L. Raines, 3B	6
R. Nixon, C	5
G. Strickland, 2B	5
D. Williams, OF	5
J. Hegan, C	4
H. Score, SP	4
D. Brown, C	3
B. Lemon, SP	3
J. Caffie, OF	2
B. Harrell, SS	2
H. Naragon, C	2
B. Daley, RP	1
S. Pitula, RP	1
V. Valentinetti, RP	1
H. Wilhelm, RP	1

Detroit (78-76)	WS
Hitting	87.3
Fielding	47.7
Pitching	99.0
J. Bunning, SP	26
C. Maxwell, OF	22
A. Kaline, OF	20
P. Foytack, SP	18
F. Bolling, 2B	17
H. Kuenn, SS	15
D. Maas, SP	15
B. Hoeft, SP	14
R. Boone, 1B	12
F. Lary, SP	12
F. House, C	10
B. Tuttle, OF	8
R. Bertoia, 3B	6
H. Byrd, RP	6
R. Wilson, C	6
L. Sleater, RP	5
J. Finigan, 3B	4
J. Groth, OF	3
D. Philley, 1B	3
J. Porter, OF	3
R. Samford, SS	2
J. Stump, RP	2
E. Torgeson, 1B	2
D. Lee, SP	1
J. Presko, RP	1
B. Taylor, OF	1

Kansas City (59-94)	WS
Hitting	75.9
Fielding	34.7
Pitching	66.4
W. Held, OF	13
H. Lopez, 3B	13
H. Smith, C	12
V. Trucks, RP	11
J. Urban, RP	10
G. Zernial, OF	10
J. DeMaestri, SS	9
L. Skizas, OF	9
V. Power, 1B	8
B. Cerv, OF	7
N. Garver, SP	7
T. Gorman, RP	7
A. Kellner, SP	7
R. Terry, SP	7
B. Martin, 2B	6
T. Morgan, RP	6
H. Simpson, 1B	6
W. Burnette, RP	5
A. Portocarrero, SP	5
B. Hunter, 2B	4
J. Pisoni, OF	3
T. Thompson, C	3
M. Graff, 2B	2
B. Martyn, OF	2
M. McDermott, RP	2
J. Groth, OF	1
I. Noren, 1B	1
H. Taylor, RP	1

New York (98-56)	WS
Hitting	149.2
Fielding	47.2
Pitching	97.6
M. Mantle, OF	51
G. McDougald, SS	27
Y. Berra, C	23
H. Bauer, OF	17
B. Skowron, 1B	17
T. Sturdivant, SP	16
B. Shantz, SP	15
T. Kubek, OF	14
B. Turley, SP	13
B. Grim, RP	11
W. Ford, SP	10
A. Ditmar, RP	8
A. Carey, 3B	7
J. Kucks, SP	7
D. Larsen, SP	7
E. Slaughter, OF	7
E. Howard, OF	6
H. Simpson, OF	6
J. Coleman, 2B	5
J. Lumpe, 3B	5
A. Cicotte, RP	4
B. Richardson, 2B	4
T. Byrne, RP	3
S. Maglie, SP-RP	3
J. Collins, 1B	2
B. Martin, 2B	2
R. Terry, RP	2
B. Del Greco, OF	1
D. Johnson, C	1

Washington (55-99)	WS
Hitting	94.6
Fielding	25.2
Pitching	45.1
R. Sievers, OF	32
J. Lemon, OF	16
E. Yost, 3B	13
L. Berberet, C	10
T. Clevenger, RP	9
B. Byerly, RP	8
C. Courtney, C	8
R. Bridges, SS	7
C. Pascual, SP	7
H. Plews, 2B	7
P. Ramos, SP	7
P. Runnels, 1B	7
B. Usher, OF	6
D. Hyde, RP	5
R. Kemmerer, SP	4
A. Schult, 1B	4
M. Bolling, 2B	3
C. Stobbs, SP	3
E. Fitz Gerald, C	2
H. Killebrew, 3B	2
H. Griggs, SP	1
E. Hernandez, RP	1
J. Snyder, SS	1
F. Throneberry, OF	1
B. Wiesler, SP	1

1957 American League

Baltimore (76-76)	WS
Hitting	102.6
Fielding	39.2
Pitching	86.1
B. Gardner, 2B	20
B. Boyd, 1B	19
B. Nieman, OF	16
C. Johnson, SP	15
A. Pilarcik, OF	15
G. Triandos, C	14
R. Moore, SP	12
G. Zuverink, RP	12
B. Loes, SP	11
B. O'Dell, RP	11
G. Kell, 3B	10
K. Lehman, RP	9
B. Goodman, 3B	8
H. Brown, SP	7
J. Busby, OF	7
J. Brideweser, SS	6
T. Francona, OF	6
B. Wight, SP	6
J. Ginsberg, C	5
W. Miranda, SS	5
B. Robinson, 3B	2
J. Walker, RP	2

1957 National League

Brooklyn (84-70)	WS
Hitting	91.8
Fielding	49.5
Pitching	110.7
D. Snider, OF	25
D. Drysdale, SP	21
G. Hodges, 1B	21
J. Podres, SP	19
G. Cimoli, OF	15
J. Gilliam, 2B	15
C. Neal, SS	15
D. Newcombe, SP	15
C. Furillo, OF	12
E. Roebuck, RP	12
R. Campanella, C	11
C. Labine, RP	11
S. Amoros, OF	9
S. Maglie, SP	8
D. McDevitt, SP	8
S. Koufax, RP	6
R. Craig, RP	5
C. Erskine, RP	5
E. Valo, OF	5
P. Reese, 3B	4
R. Walker, C	3
D. Zimmer, 3B	3
D. Bessent, RP	1
R. Jackson, 3B	1
K. Lehman, RP	1
J. Roseboro, C	1

Chicago (62-92)	WS
Hitting	**89.7**
Fielding	**31.4**
Pitching	**64.9**
E. Banks, SS	28
D. Long, 1B	17
W. Moryn, OF	17
M. Drabowsky, SP	15
D. Drott, SP	13
C. Neeman, C	11
D. Elston, RP	10
B. Speake, OF	9
J. Brosnan, RP	8
T. Lown, RP	8
C. Tanner, OF	8
B. Morgan, 2B	7
B. Rush, SP	7
J. Bolger, OF	4
D. Hillman, RP	4
L. Walls, OF	4
B. Adams, 3B	3
F. Ernaga, OF	3
G. Baker, 3B	1
B. Del Greco, OF	1
J. Fanning, C	1
D. Fondy, 1B	1
J. Kindall, 2B	1
J. Littrell, SS	1
G. Massa, C	1
C. Silvera, C	1
V. Valentinetti, RP	1
C. Wise, 2B	1

Cincinnati (80-74)	WS
Hitting	**130.0**
Fielding	**36.4**
Pitching	**73.6**
F. Robinson, OF	27
D. Hoak, 3B	22
B. Lawrence, SP	21
J. Temple, 2B	19
E. Bailey, C	17
R. McMillan, SS	17
G. Crowe, 1B	14
G. Bell, OF	13
H. Jeffcoat, SP	11
S. Burgess, C	9
W. Post, OF	9
D. Gross, RP	8
J. Nuxhall, SP	8
H. Freeman, RP	7
T. Acker, RP	6
J. Klippstein, RP	6
B. Thurman, OF	6
R. Sanchez, RP	4
A. Grammas, SS	3
T. Kluszewski, 1B	3
W. Hacker, RP	2
J. Lynch, OF	2
J. Taylor, OF	2
P. Whisenant, OF	2
C. Rabe, SP-RP	1
D. Skaugstad, RP	1

Milwaukee (95-59)	WS
Hitting	**164.9**
Fielding	**39.9**
Pitching	**80.2**
H. Aaron, OF	35
E. Mathews, 3B	33
W. Spahn, SP	22
J. Logan, SS	18
B. Buhl, SP	16
R. Schoendienst, 2B	16
W. Covington, OF	15
D. Crandall, C	13
L. Burdette, SP	12
B. Bruton, OF	11
B. Hazle, OF	10
F. Torre, 1B	10
J. Adcock, 1B	9
G. Conley, SP	9
D. McMahon, RP	7
A. Pafko, OF	6
D. Rice, C	6
B. Trowbridge, SP-RP	6
E. Johnson, RP	5
F. Mantilla, SS	5
D. O'Connell, 2B	5
C. Sawatski, C	4
B. Thomson, OF	3
N. Jones, 1B	2
J. Pizarro, RP	2
C. Tanner, OF	2
R. Crone, RP	1
D. Jolly, RP	1
R. Murff, RP	1

New York (69-85)	WS
Hitting	**94.6**
Fielding	**34.2**
Pitching	**78.2**
W. Mays, OF	34
R. Gomez, SP	14
D. Spencer, SS	14
J. Antonelli, SP	13
H. Sauer, OF	13
C. Barclay, SP	11
D. O'Connell, 2B	11
M. Grissom, RP	10
R. Schoendienst, 2B	10
R. Jablonski, 3B	9
S. Miller, RP	8
A. Worthington, RP	8
W. Lockman, 1B	7
V. Thomas, C	6
G. Harris, 1B	5
B. Thomson, OF	5
R. Crone, SP	4
M. McCormick, RP	4
D. Mueller, OF	4
E. Bressoud, SS	3
R. Monzant, RP	3
A. Rodgers, SS	3
J. Constable, RP	2
R. Katt, C	2
O. Virgil, 3B	2
S. Ridzik, RP	1
W. Westrum, C	1

Philadelphia (77-77)	WS
Hitting	**100.2**
Fielding	**40.3**
Pitching	**90.6**
E. Bouchee, 1B	27
R. Ashburn, OF	26
J. Sanford, SP	20
S. Lopata, C	15
C. Simmons, SP	15
H. Anderson, OF	14
R. Repulski, OF	13
T. Farrell, RP	12
R. Roberts, SP	12
C. Fernandez, SS	11
H. Haddix, SP	10
P. Jones, 3B	10
B. Miller, RP	8
B. Bowman, OF	7
G. Hamner, 2B	5
J. Hearn, RP	5
D. Cardwell, SP	4
T. Kazanski, 3B	4
S. Morehead, RP	4
W. Hacker, SP-RP	3
J. Lonnett, C	3
M. Blaylock, 1B	1
C. Harmon, OF	1
R. Northey, PH-PR	1

Pittsburgh (62-92)	WS
Hitting	**83.7**
Fielding	**36.3**
Pitching	**66.0**
B. Friend, SP	16
D. Groat, SS	16
F. Thomas, 1B	16
B. Mazeroski, 2B	14
B. Skinner, OF	14
V. Law, SP	12
B. Virdon, OF	12
H. Foiles, C	9
B. Purkey, RP	9
G. Freese, 3B	8
G. Baker, 3B	7
R. Face, RP	7
D. Fondy, 1B	7
R. Kline, SP	7
R. Clemente, OF	5
R. Mejias, OF	3
B. Smith, RP	3
R. Swanson, RP	3
L. Arroyo, RP	2
W. Douglas, SP	2
N. King, RP	2
H. Peterson, C	2
J. Powers, OF	2
D. Rand, C	2
P. Smith, OF	2
B. Daniels, SP	1
E. O'Brien, RP	1
J. O'Brien, RP	1
J. Pendleton, OF	1

St. Louis (87-67)	WS
Hitting	**128.1**
Fielding	**42.7**
Pitching	**90.2**
S. Musial, 1B	30
D. Blasingame, 2B	24
W. Moon, OF	21
A. Dark, SS	18
K. Boyer, OF	16
L. Jackson, SP	16
J. Cunningham, 1B	14
D. Ennis, OF	14
L. McDaniel, SP	14
S. Jones, SP	12
E. Kasko, 3B	11
H. Smith, C	9
V. Mizell, SP	8
B. Muffett, RP	7
H. Wehmeier, SP-RP	7
H. Landrith, C	6
V. McDaniel, SP	6
L. Merritt, RP	5
W. Schmidt, RP	5
H. Wilhelm, RP	4
M. Dickson, SP	3
W. Cooper, C	2
I. Noren, OF	2
Bobb. Smith, OF	2
J. King, OF	1
L. Lovenguth, SP-RP	1
M. Martin, RP	1
E. Miksis, OF	1
D. Schofield, SS	1

1958
American League

Baltimore (74-79)	WS
Hitting	**83.8**
Fielding	**43.9**
Pitching	**94.3**
J. Harshman, SP	22
B. O'Dell, SP	20
G. Triandos, C	18
B. Nieman, OF	17
A. Portocarrero, SP	16
G. Woodling, OF	16
B. Boyd, 1B	15
B. Gardner, 2B	9
D. Williams, OF	9
H. Brown, SP	8
A. Pilarcik, OF	7
B. Robinson, 3B	7
J. Busby, OF	6
C. Johnson, SP	6
B. Loes, RP	6
M. Pappas, SP	6
G. Zuverink, RP	6
K. Lehman, RP	4
W. Miranda, SS	4
H. Wilhelm, RP	4
F. Castleman, SS	3
J. Ginsberg, C	3
J. Marshall, 1B	3
J. Taylor, OF	2
C. Beamon, RP	1
L. Burke, OF	1
L. Green, OF	1
B. Hale, 1B	1
W. Tasby, OF	1

Boston (79-75)	WS
Hitting	**117.1**
Fielding	**36.7**
Pitching	**83.1**
J. Jensen, OF	27
P. Runnels, 2B	26
T. Williams, OF	25
F. Malzone, 3B	18
D. Buddin, SS	14
F. Sullivan, SP	14
I. Delock, SP	13
T. Brewer, SP	12
D. Gernert, 1B	11
L. Kiely, RP	10
M. Wall, RP	10
J. Piersall, OF	9
S. White, C	7
T. Bowsfield, SP	4
D. Sisler, SP	4
R. Smith, RP	4
G. Stephens, OF	4
F. Baumann, SP	3
L. Berberet, C	3
B. Byerly, RP	3
P. Daley, C	3
M. Fornieles, RP	3
B. Monbouquette, SP	3
T. Lepcio, 2B	2
B. Renna, OF	2
B. Consolo, 2B	1
M. Keough, OF	1
A. Schroll, RP	1

Chicago (82-72)	WS
Hitting	**114.0**
Fielding	**46.2**
Pitching	**85.9**
N. Fox, 2B	22
J. Landis, OF	22
B. Pierce, SP	22
S. Lollar, C	21
L. Aparicio, SS	19
D. Donovan, SP	18
B. Goodman, 3B	14
A. Smith, OF	13
E. Wynn, SP	11
E. Torgeson, 1B	10
R. Moore, SP	8
E. Battey, C	7
B. Latman, RP	7
J. Rivera, OF	7
G. Staley, RP	7
B. Phillips, 3B	6
J. Wilson, SP	6
R. Boone, 1B	4
R. Jackson, 1B	4
J. Callison, OF	3
S. Esposito, 3B	3
T. Francona, OF	3
T. Lown, RP	2
D. Mueller, OF	2
B. Shaw, RP	2

C. Lindstrom, C	1
T. Qualters, RP	1
D. Rudolph, RP	1

Cleveland (77-76)	WS
Hitting	**125.7**
Fielding	**34.2**
Pitching	**71.1**
R. Colavito, OF	32
M. Minoso, OF	25
V. Power, 3B	16
C. McLish, SP	15
M. Vernon, 1B	13
B. Avila, 2B	12
G. Bell, SP	12
R. Nixon, C	11
L. Doby, OF	10
M. Grant, SP	9
R. Narleski, SP	9
H. Wilhelm, RP	7
P. Ward, 3B	6
D. Brown, C	5
R. Maris, OF	5
D. Mossi, RP	5
D. Ferrarese, RP	4
G. Geiger, OF	4
B. Harrell, 3B	4
H. Woodeshick, SP	4
C. Carrasquel, SS	3
B. Moran, 2B	3
D. Brodowski, RP	2
W. Held, OF	2
B. Hunter, SS	2
R. Jackson, 3B	2
M. Martin, RP	2
H. Score, RP	2
V. Wertz, 1B	2
C. Hardy, OF	1
H. Naragon, PH-PR	1
J. Porter, C	1

Detroit (77-77)	WS
Hitting	**103.7**
Fielding	**39.1**
Pitching	**88.2**
A. Kaline, OF	23
F. Bolling, 2B	21
H. Kuenn, OF	21
F. Lary, SP	21
P. Foytack, SP	16
C. Maxwell, OF	15
J. Bunning, SP	14
G. Harris, 1B	13
R. Wilson, C	13
B. Hoeft, SP	9
B. Martin, SS	6
H. Moford, RP	6
H. Aguirre, RP	5
G. Susce, RP	5
R. Bertoia, 3B	4
J. Groth, OF	4
T. Morgan, RP	4
G. Zernial, OF	4
R. Boone, 1B	3
A. Cicotte, RP	3
C. Veal, SS	3
O. Virgil, 3B	3
T. Francona, OF	2
J. Hegan, C	2
V. Valentinetti, RP	2
H. Wehmeier, RP	2
B. Hazle, OF	1
C. Lau, C	1
J. Presko, RP	1
B. Shaw, RP	1
L. Skizas, OF	1
L. Sleater, RP	1
G. Spencer, RP	1

Kansas City (73-81)	WS
Hitting	**100.6**
Fielding	**35.9**
Pitching	**82.6**
B. Cerv, OF	29
H. Lopez, 2B	17
R. Herbert, RP	13
N. Garver, SP	12
R. Maris, OF	12
B. Tuttle, OF	12
R. Terry, SP	11
H. Chiti, C	10
H. Smith, 3B	10
M. Dickson, RP	9
T. Gorman, RP	8
B. Grim, SP	8
B. Martyn, OF	7
H. Simpson, 1B	7
D. Tomanek, RP	7
J. DeMaestri, SS	6
V. Power, 1B	6
P. Ward, 1B	6
B. Daley, RP	5
F. House, C	4
D. Maas, SP	4
C. Carrasquel, 3B	3
V. Trucks, RP	3
M. Baxes, 2B	2
W. Burnette, RP	2
W. Herzog, OF	2
H. Reed, RP	2
W. Held, OF	1
B. Hunter, SS	1

New York (92-62)	WS
Hitting	**148.6**
Fielding	**41.9**
Pitching	**85.5**
M. Mantle, OF	39
Y. Berra, C	21
N. Siebern, OF	21
W. Ford, SP	20
E. Howard, C	18
B. Turley, SP	18
A. Carey, 3B	15
G. McDougald, 2B	15
H. Bauer, OF	13
T. Kubek, SS	13
R. Duren, RP	12
B. Skowron, 1B	12
D. Larsen, SP	10
A. Ditmar, RP	7
B. Shantz, RP	7
J. Lumpe, 3B	6
E. Slaughter, OF	6
J. Kucks, RP	4
D. Maas, SP	4
M. Throneberry, 1B	4
Z. Monroe, RP	3
B. Richardson, 2B	3
T. Sturdivant, SP	2
S. Maglie, RP	1
H. Simpson, OF	1
V. Trucks, RP	1

Washington (61-93)	WS
Hitting	**85.4**
Fielding	**33.7**
Pitching	**63.9**
R. Sievers, OF	26
D. Hyde, RP	19
J. Lemon, OF	15
A. Pearson, OF	15
C. Courtney, C	13
C. Pascual, SP	13
P. Ramos, SP	13
R. Bridges, SS	11
E. Yost, 3B	11
N. Zauchin, 1B	8
T. Clevenger, RP	7
R. Kemmerer, SP	6
H. Plews, 2B	6
K. Aspromonte, 2B	4
O. Alvarez, SS	3
V. Valentinetti, RP	3
N. Chrisley, OF	2
J. Becquer, 1B	1
J. Constable, RP	1
B. Fischer, SP	1
E. Fitz Gerald, C	1
S. Korcheck, C	1
B. Malkmus, 2B	1
J. Romonosky, RP	1
F. Throneberry, OF	1

1958
National League

Chicago (72-82)	WS
Hitting	**118.3**
Fielding	**32.0**
Pitching	**65.7**
E. Banks, SS	31
L. Walls, OF	20
W. Moryn, OF	19
B. Thomson, OF	19
D. Long, 1B	15
D. Elston, RP	12
A. Dark, 3B	10
G. Hobbie, RP	10
B. Henry, RP	9
T. Taylor, 2B	8
D. Hillman, SP	7
C. Neeman, C	7
S. Taylor, C	7
B. Anderson, RP	4
J. Briggs, SP	4
J. Brosnan, SP	4
M. Drabowsky, SP	4
J. Goryl, 3B	4
T. Phillips, SP	4
J. Buzhardt, RP	3
J. Marshall, 1B	3
B. Adams, 1B	2
D. Drott, SP	2
E. Mayer, RP	2
C. Tanner, OF	2
J. Bolger, OF	1
G. Fodge, RP	1
E. Singleton, RP	1
M. Thacker, C	1

Cincinnati (76-78)	WS
Hitting	**92.6**
Fielding	**41.7**
Pitching	**93.7**
J. Temple, 2B	21
F. Robinson, OF	20
B. Purkey, SP	17
H. Haddix, SP	13
J. Lynch, OF	12
J. Nuxhall, SP	12
E. Bailey, C	11
D. Newcombe, SP	11
A. Kellner, RP	10
B. Lawrence, SP-RP	10
R. McMillan, SS	10
G. Crowe, 1B	9
D. Hoak, 3B	9
H. Jeffcoat, RP	8
G. Bell, OF	7
S. Burgess, C	7
T. Acker, RP	5
W. Schmidt, RP	5
P. Whisenant, OF	5
W. Dropo, 1B	4
A. Grammas, SS	4
O. Pena, RP	4
V. Pinson, OF	3
B. Thurman, OF	3
S. Bilko, 1B	2
D. Dotterer, C	1
D. Fondy, 1B	1
H. Freeman, RP	1
J. Klippstein, RP	1
E. Miksis, OF	1
J. O'Toole, SP	1

Los Angeles (71-83)	WS
Hitting	**101.0**
Fielding	**39.4**
Pitching	**72.6**
C. Neal, 2B	18
J. Gilliam, OF	15
D. Drysdale, SP	14
J. Podres, SP	14
J. Roseboro, C	14
D. Zimmer, SS	14
C. Furillo, OF	13
D. Snider, OF	13
G. Hodges, 1B	12
C. Labine, RP	9
D. Gray, 3B	7
J. Klippstein, RP	7
S. Koufax, SP	7
N. Larker, OF	7
S. Williams, SP	7
J. Pignatano, C	5
G. Cimoli, OF	4
F. Kipp, RP	4
B. Lillis, SS	4
P. Reese, SS	4
E. Roebuck, RP	4
C. Erskine, RP	3
S. Bilko, 1B	2
B. Birrer, RP	2
R. Fairly, OF	2
D. Bessent, RP	1
R. Craig, RP	1
D. Demeter, OF	1
B. Giallombardo, SP	1
R. Jackson, 3B	1
R. Mauriello, SP	1
D. Newcombe, SP	1
E. Valo, OF	1

Milwaukee (92-62)	WS
Hitting	**134.4**
Fielding	**43.2**
Pitching	**98.4**
H. Aaron, OF	32
W. Spahn, SP	28
E. Mathews, 3B	24
L. Burdette, SP	23
D. Crandall, C	22
W. Covington, OF	17
F. Torre, 1B	16
J. Adcock, 1B	11
J. Logan, SS	11
R. Schoendienst, 2B	11
C. Willey, SP	11
B. Bruton, OF	10
J. Jay, SP	9
B. Rush, SP	9
J. Pizarro, SP	8
D. McMahon, RP	6
M. Roach, 2B	5
B. Buhl, SP	4
F. Mantilla, OF	4
A. Pafko, OF	4
H. Robinson, RP	3
D. Rice, C	2
B. Trowbridge, RP	2
H. Hanebrink, OF	1
B. Hazle, OF	1
J. Koppe, SS	1
C. Wise, 2B	1

Philadelphia (69-85)	WS
Hitting	**107.0**
Fielding	**31.0**
Pitching	**69.0**
R. Ashburn, OF	28
R. Roberts, SP	20
H. Anderson, OF	19
S. Hemus, 2B	13
P. Jones, 3B	12
T. Farrell, RP	10
W. Post, OF	10
R. Semproch, SP	10
E. Bouchee, 1B	9
C. Fernandez, SS	9
S. Lopata, C	9
J. Sanford, SP	7
J. Meyer, RP	6

C. Simmons, SP	6
B. Bowman, OF	5
D. Philley, OF	5
D. Cardwell, SP	4
G. Hamner, 3B	4
R. Repulski, OF	4
C. Essegian, OF	3
J. Hearn, RP	3
T. Kazanski, 2B	3
C. Sawatski, C	3
J. Gray, RP	1
J. Hegan, C	1
P. Herrera, 3B	1
J. Lonnett, C	1
J. Owens, SP	1

Pittsburgh (84-70)	WS
Hitting	**117.3**
Fielding	**44.6**
Pitching	**90.1**
B. Skinner, OF	25
B. Mazeroski, 2B	20
F. Thomas, 3B	20
B. Virdon, OF	20
D. Groat, SS	19
R. Clemente, OF	16
B. Friend, SP	16
R. Kline, SP	14
G. Witt, SP	13
R. Face, RP	12
V. Law, SP	11
H. Foiles, C	9
T. Kluszewski, 1B	8
D. Stuart, 1B	8
B. Porterfield, RP	7
C. Raydon, SP	7
D. Gross, RP	5
B. Hall, C	5
R. Blackburn, RP	4
R. Mejias, OF	4
R. Stevens, 1B	4
D. Kravitz, C	2
G. Baker, 3B	1
H. Bright, 3B	1
B. Smith, RP	1

San Francisco (80-74)	WS
Hitting	**127.3**
Fielding	**36.8**
Pitching	**75.9**
W. Mays, OF	40
O. Cepeda, 1B	20
J. Antonelli, SP	18
D. Spencer, SS	18
S. Miller, RP	15
W. Kirkland, OF	13
J. Davenport, 3B	11
B. Schmidt, C	10
L. Wagner, OF	10
A. Worthington, RP	10
R. Gomez, SP	9
D. O'Connell, 2B	8
H. Sauer, OF	8
M. McCormick, SP	7
F. Alou, OF	5
M. Grissom, RP	5

R. Jablonski, 3B	4
R. Monzant, RP	4
V. Thomas, C	4
E. Bressoud, 2B	3
G. Jones, RP	3
C. Barclay, RP	2
P. Giel, RP	2
J. King, OF	2
W. Lockman, OF	2
B. Speake, OF	2
J. Brandt, OF	1
J. Constable, RP	1
A. Rodgers, SS	1
B. White, 1B	1
D. Zanni, RP	1

St. Louis (72-82)	WS
Hitting	**85.6**
Fielding	**42.7**
Pitching	**87.7**
K. Boyer, 3B	24
S. Jones, SP	23
S. Musial, 1B	21
J. Cunningham, 1B	17
L. Jackson, RP	16
V. Mizell, SP	14
D. Blasingame, 2B	13
J. Brosnan, RP	12
G. Green, OF	11
C. Flood, OF	10
P. Paine, RP	7
W. Moon, OF	6
B. Mabe, RP	4
I. Noren, OF	4
D. Ennis, OF	3
G. Freese, SS	3
H. Landrith, C	3
B. Muffett, RP	3
H. Smith, C	3
C. Stobbs, RP	3
S. Maglie, SP	2
M. Martin, RP	2
D. Schofield, SS	2
Bo. Smith, OF	2
B. Wight, RP	2
E. Burton, OF	1
A. Dark, 3B-SS	1
E. Kasko, SS	1
R. Katt, C	1
L. McDaniel, SP	1
J. Taylor, OF	1

1959 American League

Baltimore (74-80)	WS
Hitting	**81.0**
Fielding	**43.8**
Pitching	**97.2**
H. Wilhelm, SP	23
G. Woodling, OF	20
M. Pappas, SP	17
J. Walker, SP	16
B. Nieman, OF	15
B. O'Dell, SP	15
G. Triandos, C	13
W. Tasby, OF	12
H. Brown, SP	10
B. Gardner, 2B	9
B. Klaus, SS	9
B. Robinson, 3B	9
A. Pilarcik, OF	8
B. Boyd, 1B	6
C. Carrasquel, SS	6
J. Fisher, RP	6
B. Loes, RP	6
W. Dropo, 1B	4
J. Finigan, 3B	2
J. Ginsberg, C	2
E. Johnson, RP	2
W. Miranda, SS	2
A. Pearson, OF	2
J. Adair, 2B	1
R. Coleman, RP	1
L. Green, OF	1
J. Harshman, SP	1
W. Lockman, 1B	1
W. Stock, RP	1
J. Taylor, OF	1
G. Zuverink, RP	1

Boston (75-79)	WS
Hitting	**109.7**
Fielding	**38.6**
Pitching	**76.7**
P. Runnels, 2B	24
J. Jensen, OF	22
F. Malzone, 3B	19
D. Buddin, SS	16
T. Brewer, SP	13
J. Casale, SP	11
I. Delock, SP	11
F. Sullivan, SP	10
S. White, C	10
M. Fornieles, RP	9
D. Gernert, 1B	9
T. Williams, OF	9
G. Stephens, OF	8
G. Geiger, OF	7
M. Keough, OF	7
F. Baumann, RP	6
B. Monbouquette, SP-RP	6
V. Wertz, 1B	6
P. Green, 2B	5
N. Chittum, RP	4
L. Kiely, RP	4
P. Daley, C	3
B. Avila, 2B	1
J. Busby, OF	1
A. Schroll, RP	1
M. Wall, RP	1
T. Wills, SP	1
E. Wilson, RP	1

Chicago (94-60)	WS
Hitting	**121.3**
Fielding	**50.5**
Pitching	**110.2**
N. Fox, 2B	30
J. Landis, OF	25
S. Lollar, C	23
E. Wynn, SP	23
B. Shaw, SP	22
L. Aparicio, SS	19
G. Staley, RP	16
B. Pierce, SP	14
A. Smith, OF	14
T. Lown, RP	13
B. Phillips, 3B	11
D. Donovan, SP	9
B. Latman, SP	8
J. Romano, C	8
E. Torgeson, 1B	8
B. Goodman, 3B	6
J. McAnany, OF	6
N. Cash, 1B	4
J. Rivera, OF	4
E. Battey, C	3
T. Kluszewski, 1B	3
R. Moore, RP	3
R. Arias, RP	2
R. Boone, 1B	1
J. Callison, OF	1
D. Ennis, OF	1
S. Esposito, 3B	1
K. McBride, RP	1
D. Rudolph, RP	1
H. Simpson, OF	1
J. Stanka, RP	1

Cleveland (89-65)	WS
Hitting	**143.5**
Fielding	**43.0**
Pitching	**80.6**
R. Colavito, OF	29
M. Minoso, OF	29
T. Francona, OF	27
W. Held, SS	22
V. Power, 1B	19
J. Perry, RP	15
G. Bell, SP	14
C. McLish, SP	14
G. Strickland, 3B	11
J. Piersall, OF	9
M. Grant, SP-RP	8
J. Baxes, 2B	7
J. Harshman, RP	7
B. Martin, 2B	7
D. Ferrarese, SP	6
B. Locke, RP	6
D. Brown, C	5
E. Fitz Gerald, C	5
R. Nixon, C	5
D. Brodowski, RP	4
H. Score, SP	3
G. Coleman, 1B	2
M. Garcia, RP	2
H. Naragon, C	2
J. Briggs, RP	1
A. Cicotte, RP	1
C. Hardy, OF	1
G. Leek, 3B	1
H. Robinson, RP	1
J. Striker, SP	1
C. Tanner, OF	1
E. Valo, OF	1
R. Webster, 2B	1

Detroit (76-78)	WS
Hitting	**115.0**
Fielding	**37.3**
Pitching	**75.7**
A. Kaline, OF	27
E. Yost, 3B	27
H. Kuenn, OF	25
C. Maxwell, OF	18
D. Mossi, SP	18
J. Bunning, SP	17
F. Bolling, 2B	15
F. Lary, SP	15
R. Bridges, SS	9
P. Foytack, SP	9
T. Morgan, RP	8
L. Berberet, C	6
T. Lepcio, SS	6
R. Wilson, C	5
D. Sisler, RP	4
P. Burnside, RP	3
G. Harris, 1B	3
J. Davie, RP	2
J. Groth, OF	2
J. Stump, RP	2
C. Veal, SS	2
G. Zernial, 1B	2
L. Doby, OF	1
B. Osborne, 1B	1
B. Schultz, RP	1

Kansas City (66-88)	WS
Hitting	**106.5**
Fielding	**29.4**
Pitching	**62.2**
B. Daley, SP	18
R. Maris, OF	17
B. Tuttle, OF	16
B. Cerv, OF	15
N. Garver, SP	14
D. Williams, 3B	12
H. Smith, 3B	9
J. DeMaestri, SS	8
J. Kucks, SP	8
J. Lumpe, 2B	8
R. Snyder, OF	8
R. Herbert, SP	7
B. Grim, RP	6
K. Hadley, 1B	6
W. Herzog, OF	6
H. Lopez, 2B	6
H. Chiti, C	5
W. Terwilliger, 2B	5
R. Boone, 1B	4
F. House, C	3
R. Coleman, RP	2
M. Dickson, RP	2
L. Klimchock, 2B	2
T. Sturdivant, RP	2
J. Tsitouris, RP	2
R. Jablonski, 3B	1
K. Johnson, SP	1
M. Kutyna, RP	1
R. Meyer, RP	1
H. Simpson, 1B	1
R. Terry, SP	1
P. Ward, 1B	1

New York (79-75)	WS
Hitting	**124.1**
Fielding	**37.1**
Pitching	**75.8**
M. Mantle, OF	30
Y. Berra, C	23
W. Ford, SP	16
A. Ditmar, SP	14
E. Howard, 1B	14
T. Kubek, SS	14
H. Lopez, 3B	14
B. Richardson, 2B	14
N. Siebern, OF	12
B. Skowron, 1B	11
R. Duren, RP	10
G. McDougald, 2B	10
B. Shantz, RP	9
H. Bauer, OF	7
J. Coates, RP	7
R. Terry, SP	6
D. Larsen, SP	5
D. Maas, SP	5
M. Throneberry, 1B	4
B. Turley, SP	4
A. Carey, 3B	2
G. Blaylock, RP	1
C. Boyer, SS	1
F. Brickell, SS	1
J. Gabler, RP	1
J. Lumpe, 3B	1
E. Slaughter, OF	1

Washington (63-91)	WS
Hitting	**86.5**
Fielding	**30.3**
Pitching	**72.2**
C. Pascual, SP	24
H. Killebrew, 3B	23
J. Lemon, OF	19
B. Allison, OF	18
R. Sievers, 1B	12
P. Ramos, SP	10
T. Clevenger, RP	9
B. Fischer, SP	8
F. Throneberry, OF	8
R. Kemmerer, SP	7
C. Stobbs, RP	7
R. Bertoia, 2B	5
B. Consolo, SS	5
K. Aspromonte, 2B	4
J. Becquer, 1B	3
C. Courtney, C	3
L. Green, OF	3
J. Romonosky, RP	3
R. Samford, SS	3
D. Hyde, RP	2
H. Naragon, C	2
J. Porter, C	2
H. Woodeshick, RP	2
D. Dobbek, OF	1
E. Fitz Gerald, C	1
H. Griggs, RP	1
S. Korcheck, C	1
J. Schaive, 2B	1
Z. Versalles, SS	1
N. Zauchin, 1B	1

1959 National League

Chicago (74-80)	WS
Hitting	**104.8**
Fielding	**38.4**
Pitching	**78.7**
E. Banks, SS	33
T. Taylor, 2B	19
B. Henry, RP	16
A. Dark, 3B	14
G. Hobbie, SP	14
D. Hillman, SP	12
G. Altman, OF	11
B. Anderson, SP	11
D. Elston, RP	11
B. Thomson, OF	10
L. Walls, OF	10
W. Moryn, OF	9
S. Taylor, C	8
D. Long, 1B	7
J. Marshall, 1B	7
I. Noren, OF	7
M. Drabowsky, SP	5
E. Averill, C	4
E. Singleton, RP	4
A. Ceccarelli, SP	3
J. Buzhardt, RP	2
A. Schult, 1B	2
E. Donnelly, RP	1
R. Jackson, 3B	1
B. Johnson, SP-RP	1

Cincinnati (74-80)	WS
Hitting	**122.2**
Fielding	**32.9**
Pitching	**66.9**
V. Pinson, OF	27
F. Robinson, 1B	25
J. Temple, 2B	22
D. Newcombe, SP	21
E. Bailey, C	15
G. Bell, OF	15
B. Purkey, SP	11
J. Lynch, OF	10
R. McMillan, SS	9
E. Kasko, SS	8
J. Brosnan, RP	7
J. Nuxhall, SP	6
D. Dotterer, C	5
P. Jones, 3B	5
B. Lawrence, RP	5
O. Pena, RP	5
W. Schmidt, RP	4
F. Thomas, 3B	4
T. Acker, RP	3
J. O'Toole, SP	3
J. Hook, SP	2
H. Jeffcoat, RP	2
J. Pendleton, OF	2
P. Whisenant, OF	2
C. Cook, 3B	1
B. Gilbert, OF	1
W. Lockman, 1B	1
J. Powers, OF	1

Los Angeles (88-68)	WS
Hitting	**116.7**
Fielding	**48.0**
Pitching	**99.3**
W. Moon, OF	25
C. Neal, 2B	25
D. Drysdale, SP	22
J. Gilliam, 3B	20
D. Snider, OF	18
R. Craig, SP	17
G. Hodges, 1B	17
J. Roseboro, C	15
J. Podres, SP	14
L. Sherry, RP	12
D. Demeter, OF	9
S. Koufax, SP	9
N. Larker, 1B	8
D. McDevitt, SP	8
C. Labine, RP	7
S. Williams, RP	7
R. Fairly, OF	5
J. Pignatano, C	5
M. Wills, SS	5
D. Zimmer, SS	4
J. Baxes, 3B	2
C. Churn, RP	2
C. Essegian, OF	2
R. Repulski, OF	2
A. Fowler, RP	1
C. Furillo, OF	1
J. Klippstein, RP	1
B. Lillis, SS	1

Milwaukee (86-70)	WS
Hitting	**138.3**
Fielding	**35.7**
Pitching	**83.9**
H. Aaron, OF	38
E. Mathews, 3B	37
W. Spahn, SP	23
D. Crandall, C	20
J. Logan, SS	19
J. Adcock, 1B	17
B. Buhl, SP	15
B. Bruton, OF	14
L. Burdette, SP	14
D. McMahon, RP	10
W. Covington, OF	8
B. Rush, RP	7
J. Pizarro, RP	6
F. Torre, 1B	5
B. Avila, 2B	4
J. Jay, SP	4
L. Maye, OF	4
C. Willey, SP	4
F. Mantilla, 2B	2
A. Pafko, OF	2
B. Giggie, RP	1
J. O'Brien, 2B	1
A. Spangler, OF	1
M. Vernon, 1B	1
C. Wise, 2B	1

Philadelphia (64-90)	WS
Hitting	**87.2**
Fielding	**34.8**
Pitching	**70.1**
E. Bouchee, 1B	17
G. Conley, SP	17
J. Owens, SP	16
G. Freese, 3B	15
R. Ashburn, OF	14
W. Post, OF	14
J. Koppe, SS	13
R. Roberts, SP	13
H. Anderson, OF	12
C. Sawatski, C	9
D. Cardwell, SP	8
D. Philley, OF	8
S. Anderson, 2B	7
J. Meyer, RP	7
P. Jones, 3B	6
H. Robinson, RP	5
T. Farrell, RP	3
G. Hamner, SS	2
T. Phillips, RP	2
C. Fernandez, SS	1
H. Hanebrink, 2B	1
R. Semproch, SP	1
V. Thomas, C	1

Pittsburgh (78-76)	WS
Hitting	**105.3**
Fielding	**42.2**
Pitching	**86.5**
V. Law, SP	24
D. Hoak, 3B	22
B. Skinner, OF	18
H. Haddix, SP	17
D. Stuart, 1B	17
S. Burgess, C	16
R. Face, RP	15
D. Groat, SS	15
B. Virdon, OF	15
R. Clemente, OF	10
B. Friend, SP	9
B. Mazeroski, 2B	9
R. Kline, SP	8
R. Nelson, 1B	7
R. Mejias, OF	5
D. Schofield, 2B	4
R. Blackburn, RP	3
B. Daniels, RP	3
F. Green, RP	3
D. Gross, RP	3
D. Kravitz, C	3
H. Foiles, C	2
T. Kluszewski, 1B	2
B. Porterfield, RP	2
H. Bright, OF	1
B. Smith, RP	1

San Francisco (83-71)	WS
Hitting	**123.8**
Fielding	**39.0**
Pitching	**86.3**
W. Mays, OF	32
O. Cepeda, 1B	23
S. Jones, SP	22
J. Antonelli, SP	20
W. Kirkland, OF	16
J. Sanford, SP	15
D. Spencer, 2B	15
S. Miller, RP	13
J. Brandt, OF	12
W. McCovey, 1B	12
H. Landrith, C	10
J. Davenport, 3B	9
M. McCormick, SP	9
E. Bressoud, SS	8
F. Alou, OF	7
A. Rodgers, SS	7
B. Schmidt, C	5
L. Wagner, OF	4
A. Worthington, RP	4
B. Byerly, RP	2
G. Jones, RP	2
J. Hegan, C	1
D. O'Connell, 3B	1

St. Louis (71-83)	WS
Hitting	**90.9**
Fielding	**39.1**
Pitching	**83.0**
K. Boyer, 3B	24
L. Jackson, SP	21
J. Cunningham, OF	20
D. Blasingame, 2B	18
L. McDaniel, RP	14
B. White, OF	14
V. Mizell, SP	12
G. Cimoli, OF	11
H. Smith, C	10
A. Grammas, SS	8
S. Musial, 1B	8
E. Broglio, SP	7
M. Bridges, RP	6
B. Miller, SP	6
B. Gibson, SP	5
C. Flood, OF	4
G. Blaylock, RP	3
G. Crowe, 1B	3
A. Kellner, RP	3
J. Brosnan, RP	2
B. Duliba, RP	2
G. Oliver, OF	2
D. Stone, RP	2
D. Gray, SS	1
G. Green, OF	1
S. Hemus, 2B-3B	1
R. Jablonski, 3B	1
J. Porter, C	1
W. Shannon, SS	1
Bi. Smith, RP	1
L. Tate, SS	1

1960 American League

Baltimore (89-65)	WS
Hitting	**127.3**
Fielding	**46.6**
Pitching	**93.1**
R. Hansen, SS	24
G. Woodling, OF	22

J. Gentile, 1B	21
B. Robinson, 3B	21
J. Brandt, OF	17
M. Breeding, 2B	16
C. Estrada, SP	15
H. Brown, SP	14
M. Pappas, SP	14
J. Fisher, SP-RP	13
G. Triandos, C	13
S. Barber, SP	12
H. Wilhelm, RP	11
J. Walker, SP	9
G. Stephens, OF	7
J. Busby, OF	4
C. Courtney, C	4
W. Dropo, 1B	4
A. Pilarcik, OF	4
B. Boyd, 1B	3
G. Jones, RP	3
A. Pearson, OF	3
W. Stock, RP	3
B. Klaus, 2B	2
D. Nicholson, OF	2
D. Philley, OF	2
J. Ginsberg, C	1
B. Hoeft, RP	1
A. Portocarrero, RP	1
W. Tasby, OF	1

Boston (65-89)	WS
Hitting	**98.6**
Fielding	**29.9**
Pitching	**66.5**
T. Williams, OF	21
P. Runnels, 2B	20
M. Fornieles, RP	16
B. Monbouquette, SP	16
F. Malzone, 3B	13
B. Muffett, SP	11
W. Tasby, OF	11
V. Wertz, 1B	11
D. Buddin, SS	9
G. Geiger, OF	9
R. Nixon, C	7
T. Brewer, SP	6
P. Green, 2B	6
I. Delock, SP	5
J. Pagliaroni, C	4
T. Sturdivant, RP	4
F. Sullivan, SP	4
L. Clinton, OF	3
B. Thomson, OF	3
E. Wilson, SP	3
C. Hardy, OF	2
M. Keough, OF	2
G. Stephens, OF	2
H. Sullivan, C	2
T. Bowsfield, RP	1
J. Casale, RP	1
R. Repulski, OF	1
E. Sadowski, C	1
T. Stallard, RP	1

Chicago (87-67)	WS
Hitting	**132.5**
Fielding	**41.7**
Pitching	**86.8**
M. Minoso, OF	24
R. Sievers, 1B	22
N. Fox, 2B	21
L. Aparicio, SS	20
A. Smith, OF	20
J. Landis, OF	19
F. Baumann, RP	16
E. Wynn, SP	16
G. Freese, 3B	14
G. Staley, RP	14
S. Lollar, C	13
B. Pierce, SP	13
R. Kemmerer, RP	9
B. Shaw, SP	9
T. Kluszewski, 1B	6
H. Score, SP	5
T. Lown, RP	4
J. Ginsberg, C	3
E. Torgeson, 1B	3
D. Donovan, RP	2
B. Goodman, 3B	2
E. Averill, C	1
D. Brown, C	1
S. Esposito, 3B	1
J. Rivera, OF	1
F. Robinson, OF	1
A. Worthington, RP	1

Cleveland (76-78)	WS
Hitting	**117.3**
Fielding	**39.6**
Pitching	**71.1**
T. Francona, OF	24
W. Held, SS	19
H. Kuenn, OF	18
K. Aspromonte, 2B	16
J. Perry, SP	16
J. Piersall, OF	15
V. Power, 1B	15
J. Romano, C	15
J. Klippstein, RP	9
B. Locke, RP	8
J. Temple, 2B	8
G. Bell, SP	7
M. Grant, SP	6
B. Latman, SP	6
M. de la Hoz, SS	5
D. Stigman, RP	5
F. Funk, RP	4
W. Bond, OF	3
H. Foiles, C	3
W. Hawkins, SP	3
J. Briggs, RP	2
B. Hale, 1B	2
M. Keough, OF	2
J. Morgan, 3B	2
D. Newcombe, RP	2
R. Nixon, C	2
B. Phillips, 3B	2
R. Wilson, C	2
R. Bridges, SS	1
T. Cline, OF	1
J. Harshman, SP	1
M. Lee, RP	1
C. Mathias, RP	1
C. Tanner, OF	1
B. Tiefenauer, RP	1

Detroit (71-83)	WS
Hitting	**81.3**
Fielding	**40.0**
Pitching	**91.7**
J. Bunning, SP	20
F. Lary, SP	19
A. Kaline, OF	17
E. Yost, 3B	17
N. Cash, 1B	16
R. Colavito, OF	13
C. Maxwell, OF	13
F. Bolling, 2B	12
H. Aguirre, RP	11
D. Mossi, SP	11
D. Sisler, RP	10
C. Fernandez, SS	8
B. Bruce, RP	6
P. Burnside, RP	6
L. Berberet, C	5
B. Fischer, RP	5
N. Chrisley, OF	4
S. Bilko, 1B	3
C. Veal, SS	3
P. Regan, RP	2
R. Semproch, RP	2
O. Virgil, 3B	2
R. Wilson, C	2
H. Chiti, C	1
H. Foiles, C	1
D. Gernert, 1B	1
J. Groth, OF	1
T. Morgan, RP	1
C. Wise, 2B	1

Kansas City (58-96)	WS
Hitting	**83.6**
Fielding	**31.0**
Pitching	**59.4**
N. Siebern, OF	21
R. Herbert, SP	18
J. Lumpe, 2B	15
D. Williams, 3B	14
B. Tuttle, OF	12
B. Daley, SP	10
D. Hall, SP	8
W. Herzog, OF	8
A. Carey, 3B	7
N. Garver, SP	6
R. Snyder, OF	6
M. Throneberry, 1B	6
P. Daley, C	5
K. Johnson, RP	5
H. Bauer, OF	4
M. Kutyna, RP	4
B. Cerv, OF	3
K. Hamlin, SS	3
L. Kiely, RP	3
H. Chiti, C	2
B. Davis, RP	2
B. Johnson, SS	2
D. Kravitz, C	2
L. Posada, OF	2
B. Trowbridge, RP	2
D. Wickersham, RP	2
J. Delsing, OF	1
H. Foiles, C	1

New York (97-57)	WS
Hitting	**158.2**
Fielding	**43.1**
Pitching	**89.7**
M. Mantle, OF	36
R. Maris, OF	31
B. Skowron, 1B	24
T. Kubek, SS	19
Y. Berra, C	16
H. Lopez, OF	16
A. Ditmar, SP	14
W. Ford, SP	14
G. McDougald, 3B	12
B. Turley, SP	12
C. Boyer, 3B	11
E. Howard, C	10
R. Terry, SP	9
B. Cerv, OF	8
J. Coates, SP	8
B. Richardson, 2B	8
Bo. Shantz, RP	8
L. Arroyo, RP	6
B. Stafford, SP	5
E. Grba, RP	4
J. Blanchard, C	3
J. James, RP	3
D. Long, 1B	3
D. Maas, RP	3
R. Duren, RP	2
J. Gabler, RP	2
J. Gonder, C	1
K. Hadley, 1B	1
K. Hunt, OF	1
B. Short, SP	1

Washington (73-81)	WS
Hitting	**100.5**
Fielding	**35.2**
Pitching	**83.3**
J. Lemon, OF	21
H. Killebrew, 1B	20
B. Allison, OF	16
E. Battey, C	16
P. Ramos, SP	16
B. Gardner, 2B	13
L. Green, OF	13
C. Pascual, SP	13
J. Kralick, SP	12
D. Lee, RP	11
R. Bertoia, 3B	9
R. Moore, RP	9
C. Stobbs, RP	9
D. Dobbek, OF	6
T. Clevenger, RP	5
B. Consolo, SS	4
J. Valdivielso, SS	4
H. Woodeshick, RP	4
J. Becquer, 1B	3
P. Whisenant, OF	3
B. Fischer, RP	2
F. Throneberry, OF	2
E. Valo, OF	2
R. Hernandez, RP	1
D. Mincher, 1B	1
T. Morgan, RP	1
H. Naragon, C	1
T. Sadowski, RP	1
Z. Versalles, SS	1

1960
National League

Chicago (60-94)	WS
Hitting	**95.5**
Fielding	**29.2**
Pitching	**55.3**
E. Banks, SS	29
R. Ashburn, OF	22
G. Hobbie, SP	12
G. Altman, OF	11
B. Will, OF	10
D. Elston, RP	9
B. Anderson, SP	8
D. Ellsworth, SP	8
F. Thomas, 1B	8
D. Zimmer, 2B	8
E. Bouchee, 1B	7
D. Cardwell, SP	6
R. Santo, 3B	6
S. Morehead, RP	5
J. Schaffernoth, RP	5
A. Heist, OF	3
J. Kindall, 2B	3
W. Moryn, OF	3
T. Taylor, 2B	3
E. Averill, C	2
E. Tappe, C	2
B. Williams, OF	2
M. Freeman, RP	1
D. Gernert, 1B	1
G. Hatton, 2B	1
B. Johnson, RP	1
L. Johnson, OF	1
S. Taylor, C	1
M. Thacker, C	1
M. Wright, RP	1

Cincinnati (67-87)	WS
Hitting	**95.9**
Fielding	**34.4**
Pitching	**70.7**
F. Robinson, 1B	23
V. Pinson, OF	21
B. Purkey, SP	15
E. Bailey, C	14
J. Brosnan, RP	14
E. Kasko, 3B	14
J. O'Toole, SP	10
G. Bell, OF	9
R. McMillan, SS	9
B. Henry, RP	8
W. Post, OF	8
J. Hook, SP	7
M. Bridges, RP	5
G. Coleman, 1B	5
P. Jones, 3B	5
J. Lynch, OF	5
B. Martin, 2B	5
C. McLish, SP	4
J. Nuxhall, RP	3
L. Cardenas, SS	2
C. Cook, 3B	2
D. Dotterer, C	2
D. Newcombe, SP	2
L. Walls, OF	2

J. Azcue, C	1
E. Chacon, 2B	1
T. Gonzalez, OF	1
B. Grim, RP	1
J. Maloney, SP	1
C. Osteen, RP	1
O. Pena, RP	1

Los Angeles (82-72)	WS
Hitting	**90.4**
Fielding	**49.9**
Pitching	**105.7**
D. Drysdale, SP	25
J. Podres, SP	18
S. Williams, SP	17
J. Gilliam, 3B	16
W. Moon, OF	16
M. Wills, SS	16
N. Larker, 1B	14
F. Howard, OF	13
E. Roebuck, RP	13
L. Sherry, RP	11
J. Roseboro, C	10
R. Craig, SP	9
T. Davis, OF	9
S. Koufax, SP	9
C. Neal, 2B	9
D. Snider, OF	9
N. Sherry, C	7
D. Demeter, OF	5
J. Pignatano, C	4
W. Davis, OF	3
G. Hodges, 1B	3
E. Palmquist, RP	3
B. Lillis, SS	2
D. McDevitt, RP	2
D. Camilli, C	1
C. Essegian, OF	1
C. Smith, 3B	1

Milwaukee (88-66)	WS
Hitting	**165.5**
Fielding	**31.6**
Pitching	**66.9**
E. Mathews, 3B	38
H. Aaron, OF	35
J. Adcock, 1B	25
B. Bruton, OF	24
D. Crandall, C	23
L. Burdette, SP	18
B. Buhl, SP	16
W. Spahn, SP	16
J. Logan, SS	14
J. Jay, RP	7
W. Covington, OF	6
R. Schoendienst, 2B	5
C. Cottier, 2B	4
A. Dark, OF	4
F. Mantilla, 2B	4
M. Roach, OF	4
A. Spangler, OF	4
C. Willey, SP	4
L. Maye, OF	3
R. Piche, RP	3
J. Pizarro, SP	3
R. Boone, 1B	1
E. Haas, OF	1

C. Lau, C	1
B. Rush, RP	1

Philadelphia (59-95)	WS
Hitting	**66.9**
Fielding	**34.7**
Pitching	**75.4**
T. Farrell, RP	15
P. Herrera, 1B	15
R. Roberts, SP	13
T. Taylor, 2B	13
J. Callison, OF	10
G. Conley, SP	10
B. Del Greco, OF	10
A. Mahaffey, SP	10
J. Buzhardt, SP	9
T. Gonzalez, OF	8
C. Short, RP	6
T. Curry, OF	5
C. Dalrymple, C	5
D. Green, RP	5
R. Amaro, SS	4
J. Coker, C	4
B. Smith, OF	4
A. Dark, 3B	3
W. Post, OF	3
H. Robinson, RP	3
K. Walters, OF	3
H. Anderson, OF	2
D. Cardwell, SP	2
J. Koppe, SS	2
T. Lepcio, 3B	2
B. Malkmus, SS	2
J. Meyer, SP	2
C. Neeman, C	2
E. Bouchee, 1B	1
J. Morgan, 3B	1
J. Owens, SP	1
D. Philley, OF	1
L. Walls, 3B	1

Pittsburgh (95-59)	WS
Hitting	**143.8**
Fielding	**43.5**
Pitching	**97.7**
D. Groat, SS	25
D. Hoak, 3B	23
B. Mazeroski, 2B	21
R. Clemente, OF	20
B. Friend, SP	20
V. Law, SP	20
B. Skinner, OF	18
R. Face, RP	17
S. Burgess, C	15
B. Virdon, OF	14
H. Smith, C	13
D. Stuart, 1B	13
V. Mizell, SP	11
H. Haddix, SP	9
R. Nelson, 1B	9
G. Cimoli, OF	7
F. Green, RP	7
D. Schofield, SS	6
C. Labine, RP	5
J. Gibbon, RP	4
T. Cheney, SP	2
E. Francis, RP	2

J. Christopher, OF	1
D. Olivo, RP	1
J. Umbricht, RP	1
G. Witt, SP	1

San Francisco (79-75)	WS
Hitting	**137.1**
Fielding	**30.9**
Pitching	**68.9**
W. Mays, OF	38
O. Cepeda, OF	26
W. Kirkland, OF	19
M. McCormick, SP	18
D. Blasingame, 2B	13
Sa. Jones, SP	12
W. McCovey, 1B	12
E. Bressoud, SS	11
B. O'Dell, SP	11
J. Amalfitano, 3B	10
F. Alou, OF	9
J. Davenport, 3B	9
J. Sanford, SP	8
B. Schmidt, C	8
J. Antonelli, RP	7
J. Marichal, SP	6
A. Rodgers, SS	6
H. Landrith, C	4
S. Miller, RP	4
J. Marshall, 1B	2
E. Fisher, RP	1
Sh. Jones, RP	1
B. Loes, RP	1
J. Pagan, SS	1

St. Louis (86-68)	WS
Hitting	**100.4**
Fielding	**50.2**
Pitching	**107.4**
K. Boyer, 3B	31
L. McDaniel, RP	25
E. Broglio, RP	24
L. Jackson, SP	21
D. Spencer, SS	19
B. White, 1B	18
C. Simmons, SP	15
J. Cunningham, OF	14
S. Musial, OF	13
R. Sadecki, SP	10
J. Javier, 2B	9
H. Smith, C	9
C. Flood, OF	8
B. Nieman, OF	7
C. Sawatski, C	6
W. Moryn, OF	5
A. Grammas, SS	4
B. Miller, RP	4
B. Duliba, RP	3
M. Bridges, RP	2
B. Grim, RP	2
D. Landrum, OF	2
V. Mizell, SP	2
L. Wagner, OF	2
C. Cannizzaro, C	1
G. Crowe, 1B	1
M. Nelson, SP-RP	1

1961 American League

Baltimore (95-67)	WS
Hitting	**114.1**
Fielding	**52.8**
Pitching	**118.1**
J. Gentile, 1B	32
J. Brandt, OF	21
S. Barber, SP	19
B. Robinson, 3B	18
R. Hansen, SS	16
B. Hoeft, RP	16
H. Wilhelm, RP	16
M. Pappas, SP	15
J. Adair, 2B	14
G. Triandos, C	14
H. Brown, SP	13
C. Estrada, SP	13
W. Herzog, OF	12
D. Hall, RP	10
E. Robinson, OF	9
J. Fisher, SP	8
R. Snyder, OF	8
W. Stock, RP	8
H. Foiles, C	5
M. Breeding, 2B	4
J. Busby, OF	3
C. Courtney, C	2
M. Throneberry, OF	2
D. Williams, OF	2
W. Dropo, 1B	1
C. Lau, C	1
D. Philley, OF	1
G. Stephens, OF	1
F. Zupo, C	1

Boston (76-86)	WS
Hitting	**107.8**
Fielding	**40.6**
Pitching	**79.6**
C. Schilling, 2B	19
G. Geiger, OF	18
B. Monbouquette, SP	17
D. Buddin, SS	15
D. Schwall, SP	15
J. Jensen, OF	14
F. Malzone, 3B	14
P. Runnels, 1B	14
C. Yastrzemski, OF	12
J. Pagliaroni, C	11
G. Conley, SP	9
M. Fornieles, RP	9
P. Green, SS	9
V. Wertz, 1B	9
C. Hardy, OF	7
D. Hillman, RP	7
C. Nichols, RP	7
T. Brewer, SP	4
A. Earley, RP	4
R. Nixon, C	4
T. Stallard, RP	4
I. Delock, SP	3
L. Clinton, OF	1
D. Gile, 1B	1
B. Muffett, RP	1

Chicago (86-76)	WS
Hitting	**131.9**
Fielding	**39.3**
Pitching	**86.8**
J. Landis, OF	23
R. Sievers, 1B	23
A. Smith, 3B	20
M. Minoso, OF	19
F. Robinson, OF	19
J. Pizarro, SP	18
L. Aparicio, SS	17
S. Lollar, C	14
T. Lown, RP	12
N. Fox, 2B	11
B. Pierce, SP	11
R. Herbert, SP	9
E. Wynn, SP	9
C. Carreon, C	8
C. McLish, SP	7
D. Larsen, RP	6
W. Hacker, RP	5
R. Kemmerer, RP	5
F. Baumann, RP	4
A. Carey, 3B	4
J. Martin, 1B	4
B. Shaw, SP	3
W. Covington, OF	2
S. Esposito, 3B	1
B. Goodman, 3B	1
M. Hershberger, OF	1
G. Peters, RP	1
B. Roselli, C	1

Cleveland (78-83)	WS
Hitting	**122.5**
Fielding	**37.5**
Pitching	**74.0**
J. Romano, C	25
T. Francona, OF	21
W. Held, SS	21
W. Kirkland, OF	18
J. Piersall, OF	18
M. Grant, SP	14
B. Phillips, 3B	12
J. Temple, 2B	12
F. Funk, RP	11
B. Latman, RP	11
G. Bell, SP	10
V. Power, 1B	10
C. Essegian, OF	6
W. Hawkins, SP	6
J. Perry, SP	6
B. Allen, RP	5
D. Dillard, OF	5
M. de la Hoz, 2B-SS	4
B. Locke, RP	4
B. Nieman, OF	3
B. Dailey, RP	2
D. Stigman, RP	2
V. Thomas, C	2
K. Aspromonte, 2B	1
W. Bond, OF	1
T. Cline, OF	1
S. Hamilton, RP	1
R. Heman, RP	1
S. McDowell, SP	1

Detroit (101-61)	WS
Hitting	**151.3**
Fielding	**46.7**
Pitching	**105.0**
N. Cash, 1B	42
R. Colavito, OF	33
A. Kaline, OF	29
F. Lary, SP	22
D. Mossi, SP	20
J. Bunning, SP	19
J. Wood, 2B	18
B. Bruton, OF	17
S. Boros, 3B	13
D. Brown, C	11
T. Fox, RP	11
C. Fernandez, SS	10
P. Foytack, SP	10
D. McAuliffe, SS	8
H. Aguirre, RP	6
R. Kline, SP	5
C. Maxwell, OF	4
P. Regan, SP-RP	4
M. Roarke, C	4
B. Morton, OF	3
B. Osborne, 1B	3
B. Fischer, RP	2
R. Bertoia, 3B	1
B. Bruce, RP	1
J. Donohue, RP	1
B. Freehan, C	1
F. Gladding, RP	1
F. House, C	1
H. Koplitz, RP	1
M. Montejo, RP	1
G. Staley, RP	1

Kansas City (61-100)	WS
Hitting	**92.9**
Fielding	**30.3**
Pitching	**59.8**
N. Siebern, 1B	23
D. Howser, SS	20
J. Lumpe, 2B	18
J. Archer, SP	15
W. Causey, 3B	11
H. Sullivan, C	8
N. Bass, SP	7
J. Pignatano, C	7
L. Posada, OF	7
B. Shaw, SP	7
J. Walker, SP	7
J. Nuxhall, RP	6
B. Del Greco, OF	5
A. Carey, 3B	4
E. Rakow, RP	4
B. Kunkel, RP	3
J. Rivera, OF	3
M. Throneberry, 1B	3
H. Bauer, OF	2
B. Fischer, RP	2
R. Herbert, SP	2
D. Johnson, OF	2
L. Krausse, SP	2
G. Staley, RP	2
G. Stephens, OF	2
B. Tuttle, OF	2
D. Wickersham, RP	2
R. Bertoia, 3B	1
B. Daley, SP	1
A. Ditmar, RP	1
J. Hankins, OF	1
D. Larsen, RP	1
C. Shoemaker, 2B	1
J. Wyatt, RP	1

Los Angeles (70-91)	WS
Hitting	**84.1**
Fielding	**37.5**
Pitching	**88.4**
K. McBride, SP	17
A. Pearson, OF	15
T. Morgan, RP	14
L. Wagner, OF	14
E. Averill, C	13
E. Grba, SP	13
L. Thomas, OF	12
T. Bowsfield, SP	11
K. Hunt, OF	11
S. Bilko, 1B	10
A. Fowler, RP	10
J. Donohue, RP	7
J. Koppe, SS	7
G. Thomas, OF	6
T. Kluszewski, 1B	5
K. Aspromonte, 2B	4
R. Bridges, 2B	4
R. Kline, RP	4
R. Duren, RP	3
R. Moeller, SP	3
B. Moran, 2B	3
D. Rice, C	3
E. Sadowski, C	3
J. Spring, RP	3
E. Yost, 3B	3
T. Clevenger, RP	2
J. James, RP	2
G. Leek, 3B	2
J. Casale, SP	1
N. Garver, RP	1
K. Hamlin, SS	1
R. Heman, RP	1
B. Rodgers, C	1
T. Satriano, 3B	1

Minnesota (70-90)	WS
Hitting	**92.1**
Fielding	**37.0**
Pitching	**80.9**
H. Killebrew, 1B	27
E. Battey, C	20
L. Green, OF	19
B. Allison, OF	17
J. Kralick, SP	17
C. Pascual, SP	17
P. Ramos, SP	15
Z. Versalles, SS	13
J. Kaat, SP	11
J. Lemon, OF	9
D. Lee, RP	8
R. Moore, RP	6
B. Tuttle, 3B	5
B. Martin, 2B	4
H. Naragon, C	3
B. Pleis, RP	3
D. McDevitt, RP	2
D. Mincher, 1B	2
A. Schroll, SP	2
J. Valdivielso, SS	2
J. Altobelli, OF	1
J. Becquer, 1B	1
R. Bertoia, 3B	1
D. Dobbek, OF	1
B. Gardner, 2B	1
T. Lepcio, 3B	1
R. Rollins, 2B	1
L. Stange, RP	1

New York (109-53)	WS
Hitting	**169.2**
Fielding	**50.9**
Pitching	**106.9**
M. Mantle, OF	48
R. Maris, OF	36
E. Howard, C	29
L. Arroyo, RP	23
W. Ford, SP	22
T. Kubek, SS	21
J. Blanchard, C	17
B. Skowron, 1B	17
B. Stafford, SP	17
Y. Berra, OF	16
C. Boyer, 3B	15
R. Terry, SP	15
B. Richardson, 2B	12
J. Coates, RP	10
R. Sheldon, SP	9
B. Daley, SP	5
B. Cerv, OF	4
H. Reniff, RP	4
H. Lopez, OF	3
T. Clevenger, RP	1
J. DeMaestri, SS	1
A. Ditmar, SP	1
B. Gardner, 3B	1

Washington (61-100)	WS
Hitting	**85.3**
Fielding	**33.5**
Pitching	**64.2**
D. Donovan, SP	15
B. Daniels, SP	14
D. O'Connell, 3B	14
G. Woodling, OF	14
W. Tasby, OF	11
G. Green, C	10
J. King, OF	10
J. McClain, SP	10
C. Hinton, OF	9
M. Keough, OF	9
D. Long, 1B	9
C. Cottier, 2B	7
B. Johnson, SS	7
M. Kutyna, RP	7
E. Hobaugh, SP	5
B. Klaus, 3B	5
H. Bright, 3B	3
P. Burnside, RP	3
D. Sisler, RP	3
P. Daley, C	2
J. Gabler, RP	2
K. Retzer, C	2
T. Sturdivant, SP	2
C. Veal, SS	2
H. Woodeshick, SP	2
B. Zipfel, 1B	2
T. Cheney, SP	1
D. Dotterer, C	1
J. Mahoney, SS	1
C. Osteen, SP	1

1961
National League

Chicago (64-90)	WS
Hitting	**98.5**
Fielding	**29.2**
Pitching	**64.3**
G. Altman, OF	20
E. Banks, SS	19
R. Santo, 3B	18
D. Cardwell, SP	16
B. Williams, OF	15
D. Ellsworth, SP	11
E. Bouchee, 1B	9
G. Hobbie, SP	9
B. Anderson, RP	8
D. Zimmer, 2B	8
A. Heist, OF	7
B. Schultz, RP	7
R. Ashburn, OF	6
J. Curtis, SP	6
J. Kindall, 2B	6
D. Bertell, C	5
D. Drott, RP	5
A. Rodgers, 1B	5
S. Taylor, C	5
D. Elston, RP	3
B. Will, OF	2
D. Murphy, OF	1
F. Thomas, OF	1

Cincinnati (93-61)	WS
Hitting	**124.5**
Fielding	**49.0**
Pitching	**105.5**
F. Robinson, OF	34
V. Pinson, OF	32
J. O'Toole, SP	22
J. Jay, SP	20
G. Coleman, 1B	19
G. Freese, 3B	17
B. Purkey, SP	16
J. Brosnan, RP	13
W. Post, OF	13
E. Kasko, SS	11
B. Henry, RP	10
J. Lynch, OF	10
L. Cardenas, SS	8
K. Hunt, SP	8
K. Johnson, SP	8
D. Blasingame, 2B	6
J. Maloney, RP	6
E. Chacon, 2B	5
G. Bell, OF	4
H. Nunn, RP	3
J. Zimmerman, C	3
E. Bailey, C	2
J. Edwards, C	2
D. Gernert, 1B	2
D. Johnson, C	2
S. Jones, RP	2
B. Schmidt, C	1

Los Angeles (89-65)	WS
Hitting	**126.6**
Fielding	**43.7**
Pitching	**96.7**
W. Moon, OF	25
M. Wills, SS	21
S. Koufax, SP	20
J. Roseboro, C	20
D. Drysdale, SP	19
J. Podres, SP	16
S. Williams, SP	16
R. Fairly, OF	15
J. Gilliam, 3B	15
T. Davis, OF	11
R. Perranoski, RP	11
D. Snider, OF	11
W. Davis, OF	10
L. Sherry, RP	10
F. Howard, OF	9
C. Neal, 2B	8
N. Larker, 1B	6
D. Spencer, 3B	6
G. Hodges, 1B	5
T. Farrell, RP	4
N. Sherry, C	4
D. Camilli, C	1
T. Harkness, 1B	1
E. Roebuck, RP	1
C. Smith, 3B	1
G. Windhorn, OF	1

Milwaukee (83-71)	WS
Hitting	**132.7**
Fielding	**39.1**
Pitching	**77.2**
H. Aaron, OF	35
E. Mathews, 3B	33
W. Spahn, SP	25
J. Adcock, 1B	22
F. Bolling, 2B	17
L. Burdette, SP	15
F. Thomas, OF	15
L. Maye, OF	14
J. Torre, C	13
R. McMillan, SS	10
D. McMahon, RP	9
B. Buhl, SP	7
C. Willey, SP	7
D. Nottebart, RP	6
B. Hendley, SP	4
A. Spangler, OF	4
T. Cloninger, SP	2
M. Jones, OF	2
C. Lau, C	2
G. Cimoli, OF	1
J. DeMerit, OF	1
M. Drabowsky, RP	1
F. Mantilla, SS	1
R. Piche, RP	1
C. Raymond, RP	1
S. White, C	1

Philadelphia (47-107)	WS
Hitting	**64.5**
Fielding	**26.3**
Pitching	**50.2**
J. Callison, OF	13
T. Gonzalez, OF	12
A. Mahaffey, SP	11
R. Amaro, SS	10
D. Demeter, OF	9
P. Herrera, 1B	9
D. Ferrarese, RP	8
J. Buzhardt, SP	7
J. Baldschun, RP	6
C. Smith, 3B	6
F. Sullivan, RP	6
W. Covington, OF	5
T. Taylor, 2B	5
L. Walls, 1B	5
C. Dalrymple, C	4
D. Green, RP	4
B. Malkmus, 2B	4
J. Owens, SP	4
K. Lehman, RP	3
J. Coker, C	2
B. Del Greco, OF	2
B. Smith, OF	2
D. Johnson, C	1
E. Valo, OF	1
K. Walters, OF	1
J. Woods, 3B	1

Pittsburgh (75-79)	WS
Hitting	**107.2**
Fielding	**36.3**
Pitching	**81.5**
R. Clemente, OF	26
D. Hoak, 3B	20
D. Stuart, 1B	19
B. Mazeroski, 2B	16
D. Groat, SS	15
B. Virdon, OF	14
S. Burgess, C	13
J. Gibbon, SP	13
B. Friend, SP	12
R. Face, RP	10
H. Haddix, SP	9
B. Skinner, OF	9
B. Shantz, RP	8
T. Sturdivant, SP	8
C. Labine, RP	7
A. McBean, RP	5
J. Christopher, OF	3
E. Francis, SP	3
V. Mizell, SP	3
A. Jackson, SP	2
V. Law, SP	2
R. Nelson, 1B	2
H. Smith, C	2
G. Cimoli, OF	1
D. Clendenon, OF	1
D. Leppert, C	1
D. Schofield, 3B	1

San Francisco (85-69)	WS
Hitting	**131.6**
Fielding	**39.0**
Pitching	**84.4**
W. Mays, OF	34
O. Cepeda, 1B	29
J. Davenport, 3B	18
S. Miller, RP	18
M. McCormick, SP	17
F. Alou, OF	14
W. McCovey, 1B	13
E. Bailey, C	11
J. Sanford, SP	11
H. Kuenn, OF	10
J. Marichal, SP	10
J. Pagan, SS	10
J. Amalfitano, 2B	9
M. Alou, OF	7
B. O'Dell, RP	7
C. Hiller, 2B	5
S. Jones, RP	5
D. LeMay, RP	5
B. Bolin, RP	4
J. Duffalo, RP	4
B. Loes, SP	4
J. Orsino, C	4
H. Landrith, C	3
E. Bressoud, SS	1
T. Haller, C	1
D. Zanni, RP	1

St. Louis (80-74)	WS
Hitting	**93.1**
Fielding	**46.4**
Pitching	**100.4**
K. Boyer, 3B	27
B. Gibson, SP	18
R. Sadecki, SP	18
C. Simmons, SP	17
B. White, 1B	16
L. Jackson, SP	15
S. Musial, OF	14
C. Flood, OF	13
J. Cunningham, OF	12
E. Broglio, SP	9
J. Javier, 2B	9
C. Sawatski, C	8
L. McDaniel, RP	6
D. Taussig, OF	6
E. Bauta, RP	5
B. Miller, RP	5
C. Anderson, RP	4
C. James, OF	4
J. Schaffer, C	4
H. Smith, C	4
C. Warwick, OF	4
G. Oliver, C	3
R. Schoendienst, 2B	3
D. Spencer, SS	3
A. Cicotte, RP	2
A. Grammas, SS	2
B. Lillis, SS	2
M. McDermott, RP	2
R. Washburn, SP	2
D. Landrum, OF	1
T. McCarver, C	1
B. Nieman, OF	1

1962 American League

Baltimore (77-85)	WS
Hitting	**106.9**
Fielding	**40.7**
Pitching	**83.4**
B. Robinson, 3B	27
J. Gentile, 1B	20
J. Brandt, OF	18
J. Adair, SS	16
R. Roberts, SP	16
H. Wilhelm, RP	14
D. Hall, RP	13
R. Snyder, OF	13
W. Herzog, OF	9
S. Barber, SP	8
C. Estrada, SP	8
M. Pappas, SP	8
B. Powell, OF	8
J. Temple, 2B	8
C. Lau, C	7
M. Breeding, 2B	5
H. Brown, SP-RP	5
B. Hoeft, RP	5
H. Landrith, C	4
D. Nicholson, OF	3
W. Stock, RP	3
R. Hansen, SS	2
D. McNally, SP	2
E. Robinson, OF	2
G. Triandos, C	2
D. Williams, OF	2
J. Lehew, RP	1
D. Luebke, RP	1
J. Miller, SP-RP	1

Boston (76-84)	WS
Hitting	**106.4**
Fielding	**40.5**
Pitching	**81.0**
P. Runnels, 1B	24
E. Bressoud, SS	21
D. Radatz, RP	21
C. Yastrzemski, OF	21
F. Malzone, 3B	17
B. Monbouquette, SP	17
L. Clinton, OF	16
G. Conley, SP	15
G. Geiger, OF	14
E. Wilson, SP	13
J. Pagliaroni, C	9
C. Hardy, OF	6
C. Schilling, 2B	6
I. Delock, SP	5
B. Tillman, C	5
C. Nichols, RP	4
D. Schwall, SP	4
B. Gardner, 2B	3
R. Nixon, C	3
P. Green, 2B	2
A. Earley, RP	1
M. Fornieles, RP	1

Chicago (85-77)	WS
Hitting	**120.3**
Fielding	**41.7**
Pitching	**93.0**
F. Robinson, OF	27
J. Cunningham, 1B	24
R. Herbert, SP	20
A. Smith, 3B	18
J. Landis, OF	17
N. Fox, 2B	16
E. Fisher, RP	14
L. Aparicio, SS	13
F. Baumann, RP	11
J. Pizarro, SP	11
C. Carreon, C	10
C. Maxwell, OF	10
S. Lollar, C	8
M. Hershberger, OF	7
D. Zanni, RP	7
J. Buzhardt, SP	6
T. Lown, RP	6
E. Wynn, SP	5
M. Joyce, RP	4
D. Stone, RP	4
J. Horlen, SP	3
B. Sadowski, 3B	3
S. Esposito, 3B	2
R. Kemmerer, RP	2
B. Roselli, C	2
D. DeBusschere, RP	1
B. Farley, 1B	1
D. Jones, 1B	1
B. McCall, OF	1
C. Smith, 3B	1

Cleveland (80-82)	WS
Hitting	**118.9**
Fielding	**41.0**
Pitching	**80.1**
J. Romano, C	26
W. Held, SS	21
D. Donovan, SP	20
T. Francona, 1B	18
C. Essegian, OF	16
A. Luplow, OF	15
J. Kindall, 2B	14
P. Ramos, SP	11
J. Perry, SP	10
B. Phillips, 3B	10
B. Latman, RP	9
G. Bell, RP	8
T. Cline, OF	8
F. Funk, RP	7
M. Grant, SP	7
W. Kirkland, OF	7
D. Edwards, C	6
W. Bond, OF	5
G. Green, OF	5
W. Tasby, OF	4
B. Dailey, RP	3
D. Dillard, OF	2
R. Gomez, RP	2
J. Mahoney, SS	2
B. Hartman, RP	1
H. Jones, 1B	1
J. Kubiszyn, SS	1
F. Weaver, SP	1

Detroit (85-76)	WS
Hitting	**116.5**
Fielding	**41.8**
Pitching	**96.7**
R. Colavito, OF	26
N. Cash, 1B	23
H. Aguirre, SP	22
J. Bunning, SP	21
B. Bruton, OF	19
A. Kaline, OF	19
C. Fernandez, SS	14
D. McAuliffe, 2B	13
T. Fox, RP	12
D. Brown, C	10
D. Mossi, SP	10
S. Boros, 3B	9
P. Regan, SP	9
P. Foytack, SP	6
B. Morton, OF	6
J. Wood, 2B	6
R. Nischwitz, RP	5
S. Jones, RP	4
R. Kline, RP	4
V. Wertz, 1B	4
D. Buddin, SS	3
M. Roarke, C	3
J. Casale, RP	1
B. Farley, OF	1
F. Gladding, RP	1
P. Goldy, OF	1
H. Koplitz, SP	1
F. Kostro, 3B	1
B. Osborne, 3B	1

Kansas City (72-90)	WS
Hitting	**112.2**
Fielding	**35.4**
Pitching	**68.4**
N. Siebern, 1B	27
E. Charles, 3B	21
J. Lumpe, 2B	19
G. Cimoli, OF	13
M. Jimenez, OF	13
B. Del Greco, OF	12
E. Rakow, SP	12
D. Segui, RP	11
J. Wyatt, RP	9
O. Pena, SP	8
D. Pfister, SP	8
D. Wickersham, RP	8
W. Causey, SS	7
B. Fischer, RP	7
D. Howser, SS	7
J. Tartabull, OF	7
G. Alusik, OF	6
H. Sullivan, C	5
J. Walker, SP	4
J. Azcue, C	3
J. Wojcik, OF	3
B. Consolo, SS	2
M. Drabowsky, RP	1
B. Grim, RP	1
G. Jones, RP	1
F. Norman, RP	1

Los Angeles (86-76)	WS
Hitting	**125.0**
Fielding	**40.6**
Pitching	**92.3**
B. Moran, 2B	24
L. Wagner, OF	24
L. Thomas, 1B	22
A. Pearson, OF	21
D. Chance, RP	17
B. Rodgers, C	15
J. Koppe, SS	12
B. Belinsky, SP	11
D. Lee, SP	11
K. McBride, SP	10
F. Torres, 3B	9
S. Bilko, 1B	8
A. Fowler, RP	8
J. Fregosi, SS	7
T. Morgan, RP	7
E. Averill, OF	6
E. Grba, SP	6
T. Bowsfield, SP	5
D. Osinski, RP	5
G. Thomas, OF	5
B. Botz, RP	4
J. Spring, RP	4
E. Yost, 3B	4
T. Burgess, 1B	3
R. Duren, RP	3
L. Burke, OF	2
J. Donohue, RP	1
J. Navarro, RP	1
E. Sadowski, C	1
T. Satriano, 3B	1
G. Windhorn, OF	1

Minnesota (91-71)	WS
Hitting	**133.8**
Fielding	**44.4**
Pitching	**94.8**
H. Killebrew, OF	24
B. Allison, OF	23
L. Green, OF	23
C. Pascual, SP	23
R. Rollins, 3B	23
J. Kaat, SP	22
B. Allen, 2B	19
E. Battey, C	19
Z. Versalles, SS	16
V. Power, 1B	15
J. Kralick, SP	13
D. Stigman, RP	11
J. Bonikowski, RP	6
D. Mincher, 1B	6
R. Moore, RP	6
L. Stange, RP	4
F. Sullivan, RP	4
G. Banks, OF	3
D. Lee, SP	2
G. Maranda, RP	2
B. Pleis, RP	2
B. Tuttle, OF	2
J. Zimmerman, C	2
R. Gomez, RP	1
T. Oliva, OF	1
T. Sadowski, RP	1

New York (96-66)	WS
Hitting	**161.0**
Fielding	**39.5**
Pitching	**87.5**
M. Mantle, OF	33
R. Maris, OF	25
T. Tresh, SS	25
B. Richardson, 2B	22
C. Boyer, 3B	21
R. Terry, SP	21
W. Ford, SP	20
E. Howard, C	20
B. Skowron, 1B	14
B. Stafford, SP	12
M. Bridges, RP	10
H. Lopez, OF	8
J. Blanchard, OF	7
B. Daley, RP	7
T. Kubek, SS	7
Y. Berra, C	6
J. Bouton, RP	6
J. Coates, RP	5
D. Long, 1B	5
T. Clevenger, RP	3
P. Linz, SS	3
L. Arroyo, RP	2
J. Pepitone, OF	2
J. Reed, OF	2
J. Cullen, RP	1
B. Turley, RP	1

Washington (60-101)	WS
Hitting	**65.0**
Fielding	**38.0**
Pitching	**77.0**
C. Hinton, OF	17
T. Cheney, SP	13
D. Stenhouse, SP	13
D. Rudolph, SP	11
B. Johnson, 3B	10
C. Osteen, SP	10
C. Cottier, 2B	9
K. Retzer, C	9
H. Bright, 1B	8
J. King, OF	8
J. Piersall, OF	7
S. Hamilton, RP	6
J. Hannan, RP	6
B. Schmidt, C	6
P. Burnside, SP-RP	5
D. Lock, OF	5
B. Daniels, RP	4
E. Hobaugh, RP	4
M. Kutyna, RP	4
D. O'Connell, 3B	4
G. Woodling, OF	4
K. Hamlin, SS	3
J. Schaive, 3B	3
B. Zipfel, 1B	3
J. Hicks, OF	2
D. Long, 1B	2
E. Brinkman, SS	1
J. Jenkins, RP	1
J. Kennedy, SS	1
R. Rippelmeyer, RP	1

1962 National League

Chicago (59-103)	WS
Hitting	**72.1**
Fielding	**35.6**
Pitching	**69.3**
G. Altman, OF	20
B. Williams, OF	18
E. Banks, 1B	14
B. Buhl, SP	13
C. Koonce, SP	12
A. Rodgers, SS	10
L. Brock, OF	9
D. Elston, RP	9
K. Hubbs, 2B	9
R. Santo, 3B	9
D. Cardwell, SP	7
D. Ellsworth, SP	7
B. Schultz, RP	7
D. Bertell, C	5
D. Landrum, OF	5
B. Anderson, RP	3
G. Hobbie, SP	3
D. Gerard, RP	2
M. Steevens, RP	2
M. Thacker, C	2
P. Toth, SP	2
C. Barragan, C	1
F. Burdette, RP	1
J. Curtis, SP	1
G. Gerberman, SP	1
A. Grammas, SS	1
N. Mathews, OF	1
E. Tappe, C	1
E. White, SS	1
B. Will, OF	1

Cincinnati (98-64)	WS
Hitting	**143.2**
Fielding	**49.0**
Pitching	**101.7**
F. Robinson, OF	41
V. Pinson, OF	26
B. Purkey, SP	26
L. Cardenas, SS	21
J. Jay, SP	19
J. Edwards, C	18
D. Blasingame, 2B	17
G. Coleman, 1B	16
J. O'Toole, SP	16
E. Kasko, 3B	12
J. Lynch, OF	10
W. Post, OF	10
M. Keough, OF	8
J. Maloney, SP	8
J. Nuxhall, SP	8
J. Brosnan, RP	7
H. Foiles, C	6
J. Klippstein, RP	5
D. Zimmer, 3B	4
B. Henry, RP	3
D. Sisler, RP	3
J. Tsitouris, SP-RP	3
M. Drabowsky, RP	2
T. Wills, RP	2
J. Gaines, OF	1
D. Pavletich, 1B	1
C. Rojas, 2B	1

Houston (64-96)	WS
Hitting	**80.6**
Fielding	**32.8**
Pitching	**78.6**
T. Farrell, SP	19
N. Larker, 1B	15
R. Mejias, OF	15
A. Spangler, OF	15
B. Aspromonte, 3B	14
D. McMahon, RP	12
C. Warwick, OF	11
B. Bruce, SP	9
K. Johnson, SP	8
B. Lillis, SS	8
J. Umbricht, RP	8
J. Golden, RP	7
H. Smith, C	7
J. Amalfitano, 2B	6
R. Kemmerer, RP	5
M. Ranew, C	5
J. Pendleton, OF	4
B. Tiefenauer, RP	4
H. Woodeshick, SP	3
D. Buddin, SS	2
J. Campbell, C	2
J. Hartman, SS	2
B. Shantz, SP	2
D. Stone, RP	2
P. Browne, 1B	1
G. Brunet, SP	1
D. Giusti, RP	1
B. Goodman, 2B	1
D. Roberts, OF	1
J. Temple, 2B	1
J. Weekly, OF	1

Los Angeles (102-63)	WS
Hitting	**178.4**
Fielding	**38.1**
Pitching	**89.5**
T. Davis, OF	36
M. Wills, SS	32
W. Davis, OF	26
F. Howard, OF	25
D. Drysdale, SP	24
J. Gilliam, 2B	23
R. Fairly, 1B	21
J. Roseboro, C	16
S. Koufax, SP	15
R. Perranoski, RP	12
J. Podres, SP	12
E. Roebuck, RP	9
D. Snider, OF	9
L. Sherry, RP	7
W. Moon, OF	6
D. Camilli, C	5
D. Spencer, 3B	5
S. Williams, SP	5
L. Burright, 2B	4
P. Richert, SP	4
A. Carey, 3B	3
T. Harkness, 1B	3
L. Walls, OF	2
J. Moeller, SP	1
N. Sherry, C	1

Milwaukee (86-76)	WS
Hitting	**120.5**
Fielding	**43.9**
Pitching	**93.5**
H. Aaron, OF	34
E. Mathews, 3B	26
W. Spahn, SP	23
B. Shaw, SP	20
F. Bolling, 2B	14
R. McMillan, SS	14
J. Adcock, 1B	13
D. Crandall, C	13
B. Hendley, SP	13
M. Jones, OF	10
J. Torre, C	9
T. Aaron, 1B	7
L. Maye, OF	7
G. Bell, OF	6
D. Lemaster, SP	6
C. Raymond, RP	6
T. Cloninger, SP	5
L. Johnson, OF	5
D. Nottebart, RP	5
L. Burdette, SP	4
J. Curtis, RP	4
C. Butler, RP	3
J. Constable, SP	2
D. Menke, 2B	2
A. Samuel, SS	2
B. Uecker, C	2
K. Aspromonte, 2B	1
R. Piche, SP	1
C. Willey, RP	1

New York (40-120)	WS
Hitting	**57.3**
Fielding	**25.1**
Pitching	**37.6**
R. Ashburn, OF	12
F. Thomas, OF	12
R. Craig, SP	9
A. Jackson, SP	9
F. Mantilla, 3B	8
J. Hickman, OF	7
J. Hook, SP	7
C. Neal, 2B	7
E. Chacon, SS	5
M. Throneberry, 1B	5
J. Christopher, OF	4
C. Coleman, C	3
R. Kanehl, 2B	3
K. MacKenzie, RP	3
B.L. Miller, SP	3
B. Moorhead, RP	3
G. Woodling, OF	3
C. Cannizzaro, C	2
G. Hodges, 1B	2
S. Taylor, C	2
C. Anderson, RP	1
G. Bell, OF	1
G. Cisco, SP-RP	1
C. Cook, 3B	1
L. Foss, RP	1

R. Herrscher, 1B	1
W. Hunter, RP	1
H. Landrith, C	1
J. Marshall, 1B	1
J. Pignatano, C	1
D. Zimmer, 3B	1

Philadelphia (81-80)	WS
Hitting	**127.9**
Fielding	**40.1**
Pitching	**74.9**
J. Callison, OF	27
D. Demeter, 3B	25
T. Gonzalez, OF	20
C. Dalrymple, C	19
A. Mahaffey, SP	17
R. Sievers, 1B	17
T. Taylor, 2B	16
J. Baldschun, RP	14
D. Bennett, SP	11
C. Short, RP	11
T. Savage, OF	10
D. Green, RP	8
C. McLish, SP	8
R. Amaro, SS	7
W. Covington, OF	7
F. Torre, 1B	6
B. Wine, SS	5
J. Hamilton, SP	4
B. Klaus, 3B	4
B. Oldis, C	3
E. Keegan, RP	1
M. Roach, 3B	1
B. Smith, RP	1
S. White, C	1

Pittsburgh (93-68)	WS
Hitting	**117.4**
Fielding	**49.5**
Pitching	**112.2**
B. Skinner, OF	26
B. Mazeroski, 2B	23
B. Friend, SP	21
D. Groat, SS	21
R. Clemente, OF	20
R. Face, RP	20
S. Burgess, C	19
E. Francis, SP	13
A. McBean, SP	12
B. Virdon, OF	12
D. Clendenon, 1B	10
V. Law, SP	10
D. Hoak, 3B	9
D. Olivo, RP	9
H. Haddix, SP	8
T. Sturdivant, RP	8
J. Lamabe, RP	6
D. Stuart, 1B	6
D. Leppert, C	5
D. Schofield, 3B	4
J. Gibbon, RP	3
B. Veale, SP	3
H. Goss, OF	2
J. Logan, 3B	2
J. Marshall, 1B	2
T. Butters, RP	1
L. Elliot, OF	1
C. Neeman, C	1
T. Sisk, SP	1
W. Stargell, OF	1

San Francisco (103-62)	WS
Hitting	**170.1**
Fielding	**44.3**
Pitching	**94.6**
W. Mays, OF	41
O. Cepeda, 1B	26
F. Alou, OF	25
J. Davenport, 3B	20
J. Sanford, SP	20
J. Marichal, SP	19
H. Kuenn, OF	18
C. Hiller, 2B	17
B. O'Dell, SP	17
T. Haller, C	16
J. Pagan, SS	16
B. Pierce, SP	13
E. Bailey, C	12
W. McCovey, OF	12
B. Bolin, RP	8
S. Miller, RP	8
M. Alou, OF	6
D. Larsen, RP	6
C. Boles, OF	1
E. Bowman, 2B	1
J. Duffalo, RP	1
M. McCormick, SP	1
M. Mota, OF	1
B. Nieman, OF	1
J. Orsino, C	1
G. Perry, SP	1
J. Pignatano, C	1

St. Louis (84-78)	WS
Hitting	**100.1**
Fielding	**50.5**
Pitching	**101.4**
K. Boyer, 3B	22
C. Flood, OF	22
B. White, 1B	22
B. Gibson, SP	21
S. Musial, OF	19
E. Broglio, SP	17
L. Jackson, SP	16
J. Javier, 2B	14
G. Oliver, C	12
R. Washburn, SP	10
C. Sawatski, C	9
C. Simmons, SP	9
L. McDaniel, RP	8
J. Gotay, SS	7
C. James, OF	7
B. Shantz, RP	7
B. Duliba, RP	5
D. Ferrarese, RP	5
D. Maxvill, SS	3
R. Schoendienst, 2B	3
F. Whitfield, 1B	3
D. Clemens, OF	2
J. Anderson, RP	1
E. Bauta, RP	1
D. Landrum, OF	1
M. Minoso, OF	1
R. Sadecki, SP	1
J. Schaffer, C	1
B. Smith, OF	1
P. Toth, RP	1
C. Warwick, OF	1

1963 American League

Baltimore (86-76)	WS
Hitting	**128.1**
Fielding	**42.7**
Pitching	**87.2**
J. Gentile, 1B	20
J. Orsino, C	20
B. Robinson, 3B	19
L. Aparicio, SS	18
S. Barber, SP	18
B. Powell, OF	18
S. Miller, RP	16
M. Pappas, SP	15
R. Roberts, SP	15
D. Hall, RP	13
R. Snyder, OF	13
J. Brandt, OF	12
B. Johnson, 2B	12
A. Smith, OF	11
J. Adair, 2B	6
J. Gaines, OF	6
D. Brown, C	5
B. Saverine, OF	5
S. Bowens, OF	3
M. McCormick, SP	3
W. Stock, RP	3
D. McNally, SP	2
C. Estrada, SP	1
J. Miller, SP	1
B. Narum, RP	1
H. Starrette, RP	1
F. Valentine, OF	1

Boston (76-85)	WS
Hitting	**105.2**
Fielding	**38.8**
Pitching	**84.0**
C. Yastrzemski, OF	29
D. Radatz, RP	24
E. Bressoud, SS	17
F. Malzone, 3B	16
B. Monbouquette, SP	16
D. Stuart, 1B	16
G. Geiger, OF	14
L. Clinton, OF	12
J. Lamabe, RP	12
E. Wilson, SP	12
D. Morehead, SP	9
C. Schilling, 2B	9
R. Nixon, C	8
F. Mantilla, SS	7
B. Tillman, C	7
B. Heffner, SP	4
R. Mejias, OF	4
A. Earley, RP	3
D. Williams, 3B	3
W. Wood, RP	2
I. Delock, SP	1
B. Gardner, 2B	1
C. Nichols, RP	1
P. Smith, RP	1

Chicago (94-68)	WS
Hitting	**123.6**
Fielding	**45.9**
Pitching	**112.5**
G. Peters, SP	25
P. Ward, 3B	25
F. Robinson, OF	20
R. Hansen, SS	19
J. Pizarro, SP	19
R. Herbert, SP	15
M. Hershberger, OF	15
D. Nicholson, OF	15
H. Wilhelm, RP	15
N. Fox, 2B	12
J. Landis, OF	12
J. Buzhardt, SP	11
J. Brosnan, RP	8
C. Carreon, C	8
J. Cunningham, 1B	8
J. Horlen, SP	8
A. Weis, 2B	8
T. McCraw, 1B	7
J. Martin, C	6
E. Fisher, RP	5
C. Maxwell, OF	5
D. DeBusschere, RP	4
F. Baumann, RP	3
B. Howard, RP	2
S. Lollar, C	2
F. Ackley, SP	1
D. Buford, 3B	1
F. Kreutzer, SP	1
J. Lemon, 1B	1
G. Stephens, OF	1

Cleveland (79-83)	WS
Hitting	**118.9**
Fielding	**38.0**
Pitching	**80.1**
M. Alvis, 3B	25
W. Held, 2B	19
J. Kralick, SP	16
J. Azcue, C	14
V. Davalillo, OF	14
M. Grant, SP	13
P. Ramos, SP	13
F. Whitfield, 1B	13
W. Kirkland, OF	11
G. Bell, RP	10
T. Francona, OF	10
J. Romano, C	10
T. Abernathy, RP	8
J. Adcock, 1B	8
D. Donovan, SP	7
A. Luplow, OF	7
L. Brown, SS	6
M. de la Hoz, 2B	6
E. Wynn, RP	6
D. Howser, SS	4
J. Kindall, SS	3
B. Chance, OF	2
B. Latman, SP	2
W. Tasby, OF	2
J. Walker, RP	2
B. Allen, RP	1
D. Edwards, C	1
T. John, SP-RP	1
T. Martinez, SS	1
S. McDowell, SP	1
G. Seyfried, RP	1

Detroit (79-83)	WS
Hitting	**122.1**
Fielding	**38.3**
Pitching	**76.7**
A. Kaline, OF	25
N. Cash, 1B	23
R. Colavito, OF	21
D. McAuliffe, SS	17
B. Bruton, OF	15
H. Aguirre, SP	12
J. Bunning, SP	11
G. Triandos, C	11
J. Wood, 2B	11
B. Freehan, C	10
P. Regan, SP	9
D. Mossi, SP	8
T. Fox, RP	7
F. Lary, SP	7
M. Lolich, SP	7
D. Wert, 3B	7
B. Phillips, 3B	6
F. Gladding, RP	5
B. Anderson, RP	4
B. Faul, RP	3
G. Smith, 2B	3
T. Sturdivant, RP	3
G. Brown, OF	2
W. Horton, OF	2
G. Thomas, OF	2
C. Fernandez, SS	1
F. Kostro, 3B	1
D. McLain, SP	1
M. Roarke, C	1
W. Smith, RP	1
C. Veal, SS	1

Kansas City (73-89)	WS
Hitting	**84.9**
Fielding	**42.1**
Pitching	**92.0**
W. Causey, SS	20
J. Lumpe, 2B	18
N. Siebern, 1B	18
E. Charles, 3B	16
M. Drabowsky, SP	14
O. Pena, SP	14
D. Wickersham, SP	12
J. Wyatt, RP	12
G. Cimoli, OF	11
D. Segui, SP	10
E. Rakow, SP	9
B. Fischer, RP	8
G. Alusik, OF	7
B. Del Greco, OF	6
T. Bowsfield, RP	5
D. Edwards, C	5
C. Lau, C	5
J. Tartabull, OF	5
M. Jimenez, OF	4

C. Essegian, OF	3
K. Harrelson, 1B	3
T. Sturdivant, RP	3
H. Sullivan, C	2
B. Bryan, C	1
D. Green, SS	1
T. La Russa, SS	1
A. Monteagudo, RP	1
J. O'Donoghue, SP	1
D. Pfister, RP	1
D. Thies, RP	1
D. Willis, RP	1
J. Wojcik, OF	1

Los Angeles (70-91)	WS
Hitting	**104.6**
Fielding	**34.9**
Pitching	**70.5**
A. Pearson, OF	28
L. Wagner, OF	22
J. Fregosi, SS	20
B. Moran, 2B	17
K. McBride, SP	13
D. Chance, SP	12
A. Fowler, RP	11
F. Torres, 3B	10
L. Thomas, 1B	9
J. Navarro, RP	8
D. Osinski, RP	8
C. Dees, 1B	7
B. Rodgers, C	6
D. Lee, SP	5
P. Foytack, RP	3
B. Perry, OF	3
B. Sadowski, OF	3
E. Sadowski, C	3
J. Spring, RP	3
B. Turley, SP	3
H. Foiles, C	2
A. Gatewood, SP	2
K. Hunt, OF	2
E. Kirkpatrick, C	2
G. Thomas, OF	2
B. Duliba, RP	1
J. Koppe, SS	1
F. Kostro, 3B	1
M. Lee, SP	1
J. Piersall, OF	1
T. Satriano, 3B	1

Minnesota (91-70)	WS
Hitting	**139.3**
Fielding	**42.3**
Pitching	**91.4**
B. Allison, OF	28
E. Battey, C	26
H. Killebrew, OF	23
C. Pascual, SP	22
J. Hall, OF	21
R. Rollins, 3B	19
Z. Versalles, SS	19
B. Dailey, RP	17
D. Stigman, SP	14
L. Stange, SP	12
D. Mincher, 1B	10
V. Power, 1B	10
B. Allen, 2B	8
J. Perry, SP	8
J. Goryl, 2B	6
L. Green, OF	6
J. Kaat, SP	5
J. Roland, SP	4
B. Pleis, RP	3
G. Roggenburk, RP	3
D. Siebler, SP	3
G. Arrigo, RP	1
G. Banks, 3B	1
M. Fornieles, RP	1
J. Kralick, SP	1
P. Ratliff, C	1
J. Zimmerman, C	1

New York (104-57)	WS
Hitting	**148.6**
Fielding	**50.5**
Pitching	**112.9**
T. Tresh, OF	29
E. Howard, C	28
W. Ford, SP	23
J. Bouton, SP	22
T. Kubek, SS	18
J. Pepitone, 1B	18
B. Richardson, 2B	18
C. Boyer, 3B	17
R. Maris, OF	17
R. Terry, SP	17
A. Downing, SP	16
M. Mantle, OF	14
H. Reniff, RP	12
H. Lopez, OF	11
Y. Berra, C	9
S. Williams, SP	9
J. Blanchard, OF	8
S. Hamilton, RP	8
P. Linz, SS	5
H. Bright, 1B	4
B. Kunkel, RP	4
J. Reed, OF	2
M. Bridges, RP	1
T. Metcalf, RP	1
B. Stafford, SP-RP	1

Washington (56-106)	WS
Hitting	**89.9**
Fielding	**27.1**
Pitching	**50.9**
D. Lock, OF	21
C. Hinton, OF	20
J. King, OF	13
C. Osteen, SP	11
R. Kline, RP	10
E. Brinkman, SS	9
T. Cheney, SP	9
B. Osborne, 1B	8
D. Blasingame, 2B	7
D. Phillips, 1B	7
D. Zimmer, 3B	7
B. Daniels, SP	6
K. Retzer, C	5
D. Rudolph, SP	5
M. Breeding, 3B	4
C. Cottier, 2B	4
D. Leppert, C	4
M. Minoso, OF	4
E. Roebuck, RP	4
S. Ridzik, SP-RP	2
D. Stenhouse, SP	2
J. Coates, RP	1
J. Hannan, RP	1
E. Hobaugh, RP	1
H. Landrith, C	1
J. Piersall, OF	1
A. Quirk, RP	1

1963 National League

Chicago (82-80)	WS
Hitting	**89.9**
Fielding	**48.8**
Pitching	**107.3**
D. Ellsworth, SP	32
B. Williams, OF	28
R. Santo, 3B	26
L. Jackson, SP	22
L. Brock, OF	15
L. McDaniel, RP	14
B. Buhl, SP	13
K. Hubbs, 2B	12
A. Rodgers, SS	11
E. Banks, 1B	9
E. Burton, OF	9
D. Bertell, C	8
P. Toth, SP	8
D. Elston, RP	7
M. Ranew, C	7
G. Hobbie, SP	6
J. Schaffer, C	5
D. Landrum, OF	3
S. Boros, 1B	2
B. Schultz, RP	2
J. Warner, RP	2
J. Boccabella, 1B	1
J. Brewer, RP	1
L. Burke, 2B	1
N. Mathews, OF	1
J. Stewart, SS	1

Cincinnati (86-76)	WS
Hitting	**121.6**
Fielding	**43.6**
Pitching	**92.8**
V. Pinson, OF	31
F. Robinson, OF	23
J. Maloney, SP	22
J. Edwards, C	21
J. Nuxhall, SP	19
P. Rose, 2B	19
J. O'Toole, SP	17
T. Harper, OF	13
J. Tsitouris, SP	13
L. Cardenas, SS	12
G. Coleman, 1B	11
A. Worthington, RP	7
G. Freese, 3B	6
B. Purkey, SP	6
D. Spencer, 3B	6
E. Kasko, 3B	5
M. Keough, 1B	5
B. Skinner, OF	5
B. Henry, RP	4
D. Pavletich, 1B	4
J. Jay, SP	3
J. Gonder, C	2
D. Zanni, RP	2
D. Blasingame, 2B	1
J. Lynch, OF	1

Houston (66-96)	WS
Hitting	**80.6**
Fielding	**34.8**
Pitching	**82.6**
A. Spangler, OF	18
H. Woodeshick, RP	17
T. Farrell, SP	15
K. Johnson, SP	15
C. Warwick, OF	15
D. Nottebart, SP	12
R. Staub, 1B	12
J. Temple, 2B	12
P. Runnels, 1B	9
J. Wynn, OF	9
B. Bruce, SP	8
H. Goss, OF	8
B. Aspromonte, 3B	7
H. Brown, SP	7
B. Lillis, SS	7
J. Umbricht, RP	7
J. Bateman, C	6
E. Fazio, 2B	3
D. McMahon, RP	3
J. Campbell, C	2
J. Weekly, OF	2
C. Hardy, OF	1
J. Hartman, SS	1
J. Morgan, 2B	1
J. Paciorek, OF	1

Los Angeles (99-63)	WS
Hitting	**152.7**
Fielding	**44.1**
Pitching	**100.3**
S. Koufax, SP	32
T. Davis, OF	29
J. Gilliam, 2B	28
M. Wills, SS	27
F. Howard, OF	23
D. Drysdale, SP	21
R. Fairly, 1B	21
R. Perranoski, RP	20
W. Davis, OF	17
J. Roseboro, C	16
W. Moon, OF	13
B. Miller, SP	11
J. Podres, SP	8
K. McMullen, 3B	6
D. Tracewski, SS	5
N. Oliver, 2B	4
D. Calmus, RP	3
D. Camilli, C	2
P. Richert, SP	2
L. Sherry, RP	2
L. Walls, OF	2
R. Gleason, PH-PR	1
K. Rowe, RP	1
B. Skowron, 1B	1
N. Willhite, SP	1
D. Zimmer, 3B	1

Milwaukee (84-78)	WS
Hitting	**126.4**
Fielding	**44.5**
Pitching	**81.0**
H. Aaron, OF	41
E. Mathews, 3B	31
W. Spahn, SP	22
J. Torre, C	20
L. Maye, OF	17
D. Lemaster, SP	14
D. Menke, SS	13
B. Shaw, RP	13
F. Bolling, 2B	12
R. McMillan, SS	9
G. Oliver, 1B	8
B. Sadowski, SP	8
B. Hendley, SP	6
M. Jones, OF	6
T. Cloninger, RP	5
B. Tiefenauer, RP	4
L. Burdette, SP	3
T. Cline, OF	3
D. Crandall, C	3
F. Funk, RP	3
D. Dillard, OF	2
L. Gabrielson, OF	2
D. Schneider, RP	2
T. Aaron, 1B	1
N. Larker, 1B	1
R. Piche, RP	1
C. Raymond, RP	1
B. Uecker, C	1

New York (51-111)	WS
Hitting	**72.4**
Fielding	**26.5**
Pitching	**54.1**
R. Hunt, 2B	19
J. Hickman, OF	13
D. Snider, OF	13
C. Willey, SP	12
F. Thomas, OF	10
R. Craig, SP	9
A. Jackson, SP	9
L. Bearnarth, RP	8
T. Harkness, 1B	7
C. Neal, 3B	6
G. Cisco, RP	5
D. Carmel, OF	4
J. Gonder, C	4
P. Green, 3B	3
J. Hicks, OF	3
A. Moran, SS	3
G. Powell, RP	3
T. Stallard, SP	3
L. Burright, SS	2
J. Christopher, OF	2
C. Coleman, C	2
K. MacKenzie, RP	2
D. Rowe, RP	2
C. Cook, OF	1
C. Fernandez, SS	1
R. Kanehl, OF	1
E. Kranepool, OF	1
J. Piersall, OF	1
T. Schreiber, 3B	1
N. Sherry, C	1

D. Smith, OF	1
S. Taylor, C	1

Philadelphia (87-75)	WS
Hitting	**125.6**
Fielding	**44.3**
Pitching	**91.1**
J. Callison, OF	32
T. Gonzalez, OF	26
T. Taylor, 2B	23
W. Covington, OF	17
D. Demeter, OF	17
C. Dalrymple, C	16
J. Baldschun, RP	13
R. Culp, SP	13
R. Sievers, 1B	13
J. Klippstein, RP	12
C. McLish, SP	12
C. Short, SP	11
D. Bennett, SP	9
D. Hoak, 3B	7
R. Duren, RP	6
D. Green, RP	6
J. Boozer, RP	5
B. Wine, SS	5
R. Amaro, SS	4
A. Mahaffey, SP	4
E. Averill, C	3
F. Torre, 1B	3
J. Lemon, OF	2
B. Oldis, C	1
C. Rojas, 2B	1

Pittsburgh (74-88)	WS
Hitting	**95.4**
Fielding	**41.1**
Pitching	**85.5**
R. Clemente, OF	22
B. Friend, SP	21
B. Virdon, OF	16
D. Clendenon, 1B	15
B. Mazeroski, 2B	15
A. McBean, RP	14
D. Schofield, SS	14
B. Bailey, 3B	12
D. Cardwell, SP	11
B. Veale, RP	10
S. Burgess, C	8
J. Pagliaroni, C	8
J. Lynch, OF	7
D. Schwall, SP	7
W. Stargell, OF	7
J. Gibbon, SP	6
T. Sisk, RP	6
R. Face, RP	5
H. Haddix, RP	4
R. Brand, C	3
J. Logan, SS	3
B. Skinner, OF	3
M. Mota, OF	2
G. Alley, 3B	1
E. Francis, RP	1
T. Savage, OF	1

San Francisco (88-74)	WS
Hitting	**153.6**
Fielding	**34.0**
Pitching	**76.4**
W. Mays, OF	38
O. Cepeda, 1B	30
W. McCovey, OF	29
J. Marichal, SP	26
F. Alou, OF	21
E. Bailey, C	17
H. Kuenn, OF	14
T. Haller, C	13
B. O'Dell, SP	13
J. Sanford, SP	13
J. Pagan, SS	10
J. Davenport, 3B	9
B. Bolin, RP	7
J. Duffalo, RP	5
D. Larsen, RP	5
C. Hiller, 2B	4
B. Pierce, RP	3
B. Hoeft, RP	2
J. Amalfitano, 2B	1
E. Bowman, SS	1
B. Garibaldi, RP	1
G. Perry, RP	1
C. Peterson, 2B	1

St. Louis (93-69)	WS
Hitting	**140.1**
Fielding	**43.9**
Pitching	**95.0**
D. Groat, SS	31
B. White, 1B	27
C. Flood, OF	24
K. Boyer, 3B	23
C. Simmons, SP	18
E. Broglio, SP	17
B. Gibson, SP	17
G. Altman, OF	15
J. Javier, 2B	15
T. McCarver, C	15
R. Taylor, RP	13
B. Shantz, RP	11
S. Musial, OF	10
C. James, OF	7
R. Sadecki, SP	6
G. Kolb, OF	5
C. Sawatski, C	4
R. Washburn, SP	4
E. Bauta, RP	3
L. Burdette, SP	3
G. Oliver, C	3
D. Carmel, OF	2
B. Schultz, RP	2
L. Burke, OF	1
H. Fanok, RP	1
D. Maxvill, SS	1
M. Shannon, OF	1

1964 American League

Baltimore (97-65)	WS
Hitting	**130.3**
Fielding	**49.7**
Pitching	**110.9**
B. Robinson, 3B	33
B. Powell, OF	29
L. Aparicio, SS	21
N. Siebern, 1B	20
W. Bunker, SP	19
S. Bowens, OF	18
M. Pappas, SP	18
J. Brandt, OF	16
R. Roberts, SP	15
J. Adair, 2B	14
D. Hall, RP	13
S. Miller, RP	13
H. Haddix, RP	11
D. McNally, SP	8
S. Barber, SP	7
D. Brown, C	6
J. Orsino, C	6
C. Lau, C	5
E. Robinson, OF	4
B. Johnson, SS	3
W. Kirkland, OF	3
R. Snyder, OF	3
F. Bertaina, SP	2
L. Green, OF	1
S. Jones, RP	1
H. Starrette, RP	1
W. Stock, RP	1

Boston (72-90)	WS
Hitting	**124.7**
Fielding	**29.2**
Pitching	**62.1**
E. Bressoud, SS	25
D. Radatz, RP	24
C. Yastrzemski, OF	20
F. Mantilla, OF	19
D. Stuart, 1B	18
T. Conigliaro, OF	16
B. Tillman, C	16
F. Malzone, 3B	14
B. Monbouquette, SP	11
L. Thomas, OF	9
B. Heffner, RP	8
E. Wilson, SP	8
D. Jones, 2B	5
A. Earley, RP	4
L. Clinton, OF	3
D. Morehead, SP	3
J. Ritchie, RP	3
E. Connolly, SP	2
A. Smith, 3B	2
P. Charton, RP	1
G. Geiger, OF	1
R. Mejias, OF	1
R. Nixon, C	1
C. Schilling, 2B	1
D. Williams, 1B	1

Chicago (98-64)	WS
Hitting	**124.0**
Fielding	**52.4**
Pitching	**117.5**
R. Hansen, SS	30
P. Ward, 3B	27
F. Robinson, OF	25
G. Peters, SP	22
H. Wilhelm, RP	21
J. Horlen, SP	19
J. Pizarro, SP	19
D. Buford, 2B	15
T. McCraw, 1B	11
J. Buzhardt, SP	10
E. Fisher, RP	10
M. Hershberger, OF	10
D. Nicholson, OF	9
B. Skowron, 1B	9
A. Weis, 2B	8
J. Landis, OF	7
J. McNertney, C	5
G. Stephens, OF	5
R. Herbert, SP	4
J. Martin, C	4
D. Mossi, RP	4
F. Talbot, SP	4
C. Carreon, C	3
J. Cunningham, 1B	3
B. Howard, SP	3
F. Kreutzer, RP	3
K. Berry, OF	2
S. Burgess, PH-PR	1
M. Minoso, OF	1

Cleveland (79-83)	WS
Hitting	**118.1**
Fielding	**36.4**
Pitching	**82.5**
D. Howser, SS	20
L. Wagner, OF	18
J. Romano, C	15
S. McDowell, SP	14
D. McMahon, RP	14
M. Alvis, 3B	13
B. Chance, 1B	13
V. Davalillo, OF	13
W. Held, 2B	13
J. Kralick, SP	12
S. Siebert, RP	12
L. Tiant, SP	11
C. Salmon, OF	10
T. Francona, OF	9
J. Azcue, C	8
L. Brown, 2B	8
F. Whitfield, 1B	7
G. Bell, RP	5
D. Donovan, SP	5
T. Abernathy, RP	3
L. Stange, SP	3
G. Banks, OF	2
T. John, SP	2
J. Kindall, 1B	2
B. Moran, 3B	2
P. Ramos, SP	2
M. Grant, SP	1

Detroit (85-77)	WS
Hitting	**133.1**
Fielding	**38.8**
Pitching	**83.0**
B. Freehan, C	25
A. Kaline, OF	24
D. McAuliffe, SS	21
N. Cash, 1B	18
M. Lolich, SP	18
D. Wickersham, SP	16
G. Brown, OF	15
D. Wert, 3B	15
J. Lumpe, 2B	13
D. Demeter, OF	12
G. Thomas, OF	11
B. Bruton, OF	10
E. Rakow, RP	8
H. Aguirre, SP	7
F. Gladding, RP	7
L. Sherry, RP	7
J. Sparma, SP	6
T. Fox, RP	5
D. McLain, SP	4
P. Regan, SP	3
J. Navarro, RP	2
B. Phillips, 3B	2
M. Roarke, C	2
D. Egan, RP	1
B. Roman, 1B	1
J. Seale, RP	1
J. Wood, 1B	1

Kansas City (57-105)	WS
Hitting	**85.9**
Fielding	**29.2**
Pitching	**55.9**
R. Colavito, OF	22
W. Causey, SS	20
J. Gentile, 1B	15
D. Green, 2B	12
W. Stock, RP	12
J. Wyatt, RP	12
E. Charles, 3B	10
N. Mathews, OF	8
O. Pena, SP	8
D. Segui, SP	7
B. Bryan, C	6
B. Campaneris, SS	6
T. Bowsfield, RP	5
J. O'Donoghue, SP	5
G. Alusik, OF	4
M. Drabowsky, RP	3
D. Edwards, C	3
C. Lau, C	3
M. Jimenez, OF	2
K. Sanders, RP	2
D. Duncan, C	1
K. Harrelson, OF	1
B. Meyer, SP	1
J. Santiago, RP	1
L. Stahl, OF	1
G. Williams, 2B	1

Los Angeles (82-80)	WS
Hitting	**96.5**
Fielding	**45.7**
Pitching	**103.8**
D. Chance, SP	32
J. Fregosi, SS	28
B. Lee, RP	20
J. Adcock, 1B	15
F. Newman, SP	14
B. Rodgers, C	14
W. Smith, OF	14
L. Clinton, OF	11
B. Knoop, 2B	11
B. Belinsky, SP	9
J. Piersall, OF	9
D. Lee, RP	6
B. Perry, OF	6
L. Thomas, OF	6
A. Gatewood, RP	5
E. Kirkpatrick, OF	5
A. Pearson, OF	5
B. Duliba, RP	4
J. Koppe, SS	4
F. Torres, 3B	4
B. Latman, RP	3
B. Moran, 3B	3
D. Osinski, RP	3
V. Power, 1B	3
G. Brunet, SP	2
L. Green, OF	2
B. Kelso, RP	2
T. Satriano, 3B	2
J. Hiatt, C	1
J. Navarro, RP	1
R. Reichardt, OF	1
J. Spring, RP	1

Minnesota (79-83)	WS
Hitting	**122.0**
Fielding	**37.3**
Pitching	**77.7**
T. Oliva, OF	27
B. Allison, 1B	25
H. Killebrew, OF	24
J. Hall, OF	19
Z. Versalles, SS	18
J. Kaat, SP	15
C. Pascual, SP	14
R. Rollins, 3B	14
E. Battey, C	12
A. Worthington, RP	11
M. Grant, SP	10
D. Mincher, 1B	8
G. Arrigo, RP	5
J. Perry, RP	5
D. Stigman, SP	5
B. Allen, 2B	4
J. Klippstein, RP	4
B. Pleis, RP	3
J. Roland, RP	3
F. Kostro, 3B	2
J. Zimmerman, C	2
D. Boswell, SP	1
J. Goryl, 2B	1
R. Henry, C	1
J. Kindall, 2B	1
J. Snyder, 2B	1
L. Stange, SP	1
J. Ward, 2B	1

New York (99-63)	WS
Hitting	**138.3**
Fielding	**49.0**
Pitching	**109.7**
M. Mantle, OF	34
E. Howard, C	32
R. Maris, OF	25
W. Ford, SP	24
T. Tresh, OF	20
J. Bouton, SP	18
B. Richardson, 2B	15
A. Downing, SP	13
J. Pepitone, 1B	13
P. Linz, SS	12
T. Kubek, SS	10
M. Stottlemyre, SP	10
H. Lopez, OF	9
C. Boyer, 3B	8
H. Reniff, RP	8
J. Blanchard, C	7
P. Mikkelsen, RP	7
S. Hamilton, RP	6
P. Ramos, RP	6
B. Stafford, RP	6
R. Sheldon, SP	5
P. Gonzalez, 1B	3
R. Terry, SP	3
S. Williams, RP	2
B. Daley, RP	1

Washington (62-100)	WS
Hitting	**86.9**
Fielding	**32.7**
Pitching	**66.4**
D. Lock, OF	22
C. Osteen, SP	17
C. Hinton, OF	16
J. King, OF	14
D. Blasingame, 2B	12
R. Kline, RP	12
E. Brinkman, SS	9
S. Ridzik, RP	9
M. Brumley, C	8
B. Daniels, SP	8
B. Skowron, 1B	8
D. Zimmer, 3B	8
J. Kennedy, 3B	6
B. Narum, SP	6
J. Hannan, RP	4
D. Phillips, 1B	4
F. Valentine, OF	3
T. Cheney, RP	2
C. Cottier, 2B	2
J. Cunningham, 1B	2
W. Kirkland, OF	2
A. Koch, RP	2
D. Rudolph, RP	2
D. Stenhouse, SP	2
J. Duckworth, RP	1
K. Hunt, OF	1
F. Kreutzer, SP	1
D. Leppert, C	1
D. Loun, SP	1
R. Sievers, 1B	1

1964
National League

Chicago (76-86)	WS
Hitting	**109.3**
Fielding	**37.0**
Pitching	**81.7**
R. Santo, 3B	36
B. Williams, OF	28
L. Jackson, SP	25
E. Banks, 1B	15
B. Buhl, SP	14
D. Ellsworth, SP	13
A. Rodgers, SS	11
B. Cowan, OF	10
J. Stewart, 2B	9
J. Amalfitano, 2B	8
L. McDaniel, RP	8
L. Burdette, SP	6
D. Bertell, C	5
E. Broglio, SP	5
D. Clemens, OF	5
L. Gabrielson, OF	5
L. Brock, OF	4
C. Koonce, RP	4
W. Schurr, RP	3
F. Burdette, RP	2
L. Burke, OF	2
R. Campbell, 2B	2
P. Jaeckel, RP	2
J. Boccabella, 1B	1
E. Burton, OF	1
L. Gregory, RP	1
V. Roznovsky, C	1
J. Schaffer, C	1
J. Warner, RP	1

Cincinnati (92-70)	WS
Hitting	**109.4**
Fielding	**52.8**
Pitching	**113.8**
F. Robinson, OF	33
V. Pinson, OF	22
J. Edwards, C	19
J. O'Toole, SP	19
J. Maloney, SP	18
L. Cardenas, SS	17
S. Ellis, RP	16
D. Johnson, 1B	16
B. Purkey, SP	13
P. Rose, 2B	12
J. Jay, SP	11
S. Boros, 3B	10
B. McCool, RP	10
B. Henry, RP	9
T. Harper, OF	8
M. Keough, OF	8
J. Nuxhall, SP	7
J. Tsitouris, SP	7
C. Ruiz, 3B	5
D. Pavletich, C	4
G. Coleman, 1B	3
R. Duren, RP	3
J. Coker, C	2
B. Klaus, 2B	1
M. Queen, OF	1
B. Skinner, OF	1
H. Smith, C	1

Houston (66-96)	WS
Hitting	**73.3**
Fielding	**38.8**
Pitching	**85.9**
B. Aspromonte, 3B	19
B. Bruce, SP	18
W. Bond, 1B	16
N. Fox, 2B	13
T. Farrell, SP	12
E. Kasko, SS	11
K. Johnson, SP	10
A. Spangler, OF	10
H. Woodeshick, RP	10
J. Gaines, OF	9
D. Larsen, RP	9
J. Owens, RP	9
B. Lillis, 2B	7
M. White, OF	7
C. Raymond, RP	6
D. Nottebart, SP	5
R. Staub, 1B	5
J. Grote, C	4
J. Wynn, OF	4
J. Bateman, C	3
H. Brown, SP	3
D. Giusti, RP	2
G. Jones, RP	2
L. Dierker, RP	1
C. Hardy, OF	1
S. Jackson, SS	1
D. Roberts, 1B	1

Los Angeles (80-82)	WS
Hitting	**109.5**
Fielding	**40.0**
Pitching	**90.5**
W. Davis, OF	26
D. Drysdale, SP	26
S. Koufax, SP	24
M. Wills, SS	20
J. Roseboro, C	19
T. Davis, OF	17
R. Fairly, 1B	17
F. Howard, OF	13
B. Miller, RP	12
D. Tracewski, 2B	8
D. Griffith, 3B	7
R. Perranoski, RP	7
J. Brewer, RP	6
J. Gilliam, 3B	6
N. Oliver, 2B	5
W. Parker, OF	5
H. Reed, RP	5
P. Ortega, SP	4
J. Purdin, SP	3
D. Camilli, C	2
L. Miller, SP	1
W. Moon, OF	1
P. Richert, SP	1
B. Shirley, 3B	1
B. Singer, SP	1
J. Torborg, C	1
J. Werhas, 3B	1
N. Willhite, SP	1

Milwaukee (88-74)	WS
Hitting	**177.9**
Fielding	**30.0**
Pitching	**56.1**
H. Aaron, OF	33
D. Menke, SS	29
J. Torre, C	28
R. Carty, OF	27
L. Maye, OF	23
E. Mathews, 3B	20
F. Alou, OF	12
T. Cloninger, SP	12
E. Bailey, C	10
G. Oliver, 1B	9
D. Lemaster, SP	8
M. de la Hoz, 2B-3B	7
W. Blasingame, RP	6
B. Sadowski, RP	6
B. Tiefenauer, RP	6
T. Cline, OF	5
H. Fischer, SP	5
B. Hoeft, RP	4
C. Olivo, RP	4
F. Bolling, 2B	2
C. Carroll, RP	2
S. Alomar, SS	1
L. Klimchock, 3B	1
J. Smith, RP	1
B. Southworth, 3B	1
W. Spahn, SP	1
W. Woodward, 2B	1

New York (53-109)	WS
Hitting	**87.8**
Fielding	**26.7**
Pitching	**44.5**
J. Christopher, OF	21
R. Hunt, 2B	17
J. Hickman, OF	10
E. Kranepool, 1B	10
J. Gonder, C	9
C. Smith, 3B	9
T. Stallard, SP	8
G. Cisco, SP	7
A. Jackson, SP	7
C. Cannizzaro, C	6
L. Elliot, OF	6
J. Fisher, SP	6
G. Altman, OF	5
B. Klaus, 3B	5
B. Wakefield, RP	5
L. Bearnarth, RP	3
T. Harkness, 1B	3
W. Hunter, RP	3
R. Kanehl, 2B	3
R. McMillan, SS	3
H. Taylor, C	3
F. Thomas, OF	3
G. Kroll, RP	1
F. Lary, SP	1
R. Locke, RP	1
T. Parsons, SP-RP	1
A. Samuel, SS	1
D. Smith, 1B	1
C. Willey, RP	1

Philadelphia (92-70)	WS
Hitting	**140.9**
Fielding	**44.7**
Pitching	**90.3**
D. Allen, 3B	41
J. Callison, OF	29
J. Bunning, SP	22
C. Short, SP	21
T. Gonzalez, OF	15
T. Taylor, 2B	15
W. Covington, OF	14
C. Dalrymple, C	13
J. Baldschun, RP	12
E. Roebuck, RP	11
C. Rojas, OF	11
De. Bennett, SP	10
R. Amaro, SS	9
G. Triandos, C	8
B. Wine, SS	7
J. Herrnstein, OF	6
A. Johnson, OF	5
F. Thomas, 1B	5
D. Cater, OF	4
A. Mahaffey, SP	4
R. Culp, SP	3
B. Shantz, RP	3
J. Briggs, OF	2
R. Wise, RP	2
J. Klippstein, RP	1
B. Locke, RP	1
A. Phillips, OF	1
R. Sievers, 1B	1

Pittsburgh (80-82)	WS
Hitting	**115.9**
Fielding	**39.1**
Pitching	**85.0**
R. Clemente, OF	30
B. Veale, SP	21
B. Mazeroski, 2B	17
A. McBean, RP	16
B. Bailey, 3B	15
J. Pagliaroni, C	15
D. Schofield, SS	14
D. Clendenon, 1B	13
B. Friend, SP	13
W. Stargell, OF	13
V. Law, SP	12
J. Lynch, OF	10
J. Gibbon, SP	9
M. Mota, OF	6
G. Alley, SS	5
T. Butters, RP	5
B. Virdon, OF	5
G. Freese, 3B	4
S. Blass, SP	3
F. Bork, RP	2
S. Burgess, C	2
B. Priddy, RP	2
D. Schwall, SP	2
D. Cardwell, SP	1
R. Face, RP	1
F. Green, RP	1
J. May, C	1
O. McFarlane, C	1
W. Wood, SP	1

San Francisco (90-72)	WS
Hitting	**116.8**
Fielding	**48.3**
Pitching	**104.9**
W. Mays, OF	38
J. Hart, 3B	25
J. Marichal, SP	25
O. Cepeda, 1B	23
G. Perry, RP	19
T. Haller, C	18
W. McCovey, OF	11
B. Bolin, SP	10
R. Herbel, SP	10
H. Lanier, 2B	9
B. Hendley, SP	8
H. Kuenn, OF	8
J. Davenport, SS	7
J. Duffalo, RP	7
B. Pierce, RP	7
J. Sanford, SP	7
B. Shaw, RP	7
J. Alou, OF	6
D. Crandall, C	6
M. Alou, OF	4
J. Pagan, SS	4
D. Estelle, SP	3
C. Hiller, 2B	3
M. Murakami, RP	2
D. Snider, OF	2
B. O'Dell, RP	1

St. Louis (93-69)	WS
Hitting	**124.8**
Fielding	**48.2**
Pitching	**106.0**
K. Boyer, 3B	28
B. White, 1B	26
C. Flood, OF	25
B. Gibson, SP	24
L. Brock, OF	22
D. Groat, SS	20
T. McCarver, C	17
C. Simmons, SP	16
R. Sadecki, SP	15
R. Craig, RP	12
J. Javier, 2B	11
B. Schultz, RP	10
M. Shannon, OF	7
R. Taylor, RP	6
B. Humphreys, RP	5
G. Richardson, RP	5
E. Broglio, SP	4
M. Cuellar, RP	3
B. Skinner, OF	3
C. Warwick, OF	3
R. Washburn, SP	3
G. Hobbie, RP	2
C. James, OF	2
J. Lewis, OF	2
B. Uecker, C	2
J. Buchek, SS	1
L. Burdette, RP	1
D. Clemens, OF	1
P. Gagliano, 2B	1
J. Long, OF	1
B. Shantz, RP	1

1965 American League

Baltimore (94-68)	WS
Hitting	**125.5**
Fielding	**48.0**
Pitching	**108.6**
C. Blefary, OF	26
B. Robinson, 3B	26
S. Miller, RP	22
B. Powell, 1B	19
J. Adair, 2B	18
L. Aparicio, SS	17
S. Barber, SP	16
M. Pappas, SP	15
D. McNally, SP	14
N. Siebern, 1B	13
D. Hall, RP	12
P. Blair, OF	10
W. Bunker, SP	10
R. Snyder, OF	9
J. Brandt, OF	8
J. Orsino, C	7
B. Johnson, 1B	6
C. Lau, C	6
D. Brown, C	5
J. Miller, SP	5
R. Roberts, SP	5
D. Larsen, RP	4
J. Palmer, RP	4
S. Bowens, OF	2
H. Haddix, RP	1
K. Rowe, RP	1
H. Starrette, RP	1

Boston (62-100)	WS
Hitting	**99.3**
Fielding	**27.1**
Pitching	**59.6**
C. Yastrzemski, OF	21
T. Conigliaro, OF	17
F. Mantilla, 2B	15
L. Thomas, 1B	15
E. Wilson, SP	12
L. Green, OF	11
D. Radatz, RP	11
B. Monbouquette, SP	10
R. Petrocelli, SS	9
J. Gosger, OF	8
D. Jones, 3B	8
D. Morehead, SP	7
E. Bressoud, SS	6
D. Bennett, SP	5
T. Horton, 1B	5
J. Lonborg, SP	5
B. Duliba, RP	4
J. Ritchie, RP	4
A. Earley, RP	3
F. Malzone, 3B	3
B. Tillman, C	3
G. Geiger, OF	1
R. Nixon, C	1
M. Ryan, C	1
C. Schilling, 2B	1

California (75-87)	WS
Hitting	**87.9**
Fielding	**43.0**
Pitching	**94.0**
J. Fregosi, SS	24
B. Lee, RP	20
B. Knoop, 2B	16
F. Newman, SP	16
G. Brunet, SP	15
M. Lopez, SP	15
A. Pearson, OF	15
J. Cardenal, OF	14
D. Chance, SP	14
W. Smith, OF	14
J. Adcock, 1B	9
P. Schaal, 3B	9
B. Rodgers, C	6
L. Clinton, OF	5
A. Gatewood, RP	4
R. May, SP	4
J. Piersall, OF	3
V. Power, 1B	3
J. Coates, RP	2
E. Kirkpatrick, OF	2
B. Latman, RP	2
R. Reichardt, OF	2
A. Spangler, OF	2
T. Egan, C	1
J. Gotay, 2B	1
J. Koppe, 2B	1
M. Ranew, C	1
P. Roof, C	1
T. Satriano, 3B	1
C. Shockley, 1B	1
B. Smith, OF	1
E. Sukla, RP	1

Chicago (95-67)	WS
Hitting	**137.9**
Fielding	**46.1**
Pitching	**101.0**
D. Buford, 2B	30
F. Robinson, OF	24
E. Fisher, RP	20
J. Romano, C	20
H. Wilhelm, RP	19
R. Hansen, SS	18
B. Skowron, 1B	17
P. Ward, 3B	17
D. Cater, OF	16
K. Berry, OF	12
T. John, SP	12
J. Buzhardt, SP	11
J. Horlen, SP	11
J. Martin, C	9
A. Weis, 2B	8
B. Howard, SP	7
G. Peters, SP	7
T. McCraw, 1B	6
B. Locker, RP	5
J. Pizarro, SP	5
S. Burgess, C	3
G. Freese, 3B	2
F. Lary, RP	2
G. Bollo, RP	1
J. Schaffer, C	1
B. Voss, OF	1
T. Wills, RP	1

Cleveland (87-75)	WS
Hitting	**127.2**
Fielding	**40.7**
Pitching	**93.0**
R. Colavito, OF	28
S. McDowell, SP	25
L. Wagner, OF	24
V. Davalillo, OF	18
C. Hinton, OF	17
S. Siebert, SP	17
F. Whitfield, 1B	17
M. Alvis, 3B	15
L. Brown, SS	14
D. Howser, SS	11
G. Bell, RP	10
P. Gonzalez, 2B	9
L. Stange, RP	9
R. Terry, SP	9
L. Tiant, SP	9
J. Azcue, C	6
D. McMahon, RP	6
S. Hargan, RP	4
T. Kelley, SP	3
D. Sims, C	3
C. Carreon, C	2
P. Roof, C	2
C. Salmon, 1B	2
J. Spring, RP	1

Detroit (89-73)	WS
Hitting	**124.0**
Fielding	**43.3**
Pitching	**99.7**
N. Cash, 1B	24
D. Wert, 3B	21
W. Horton, OF	20
A. Kaline, OF	20
D. McLain, SP	20
D. McAuliffe, SS	17
M. Lolich, SP	15
J. Lumpe, 2B	15
B. Freehan, C	14
D. Demeter, OF	13
H. Aguirre, SP	12
J. Sparma, SP	11
T. Fox, RP	9
G. Brown, OF	8
F. Gladding, RP	8
D. Wickersham, SP	8
L. Sherry, RP	7
O. Pena, RP	6
J. Sullivan, C	4
R. Oyler, SS	3
R. Nischwitz, RP	2
M. Stanley, OF	2
J. Wood, 2B	2
J. Hiller, RP	1
J. Moore, C	1
J. Navarro, RP	1
J. Northrup, OF	1
G. Smith, 2B	1
G. Thomas, OF	1

Kansas City (59-103)	WS
Hitting	**101.2**
Fielding	**29.2**
Pitching	**46.7**
B. Campaneris, SS	18
E. Charles, 3B	16
W. Causey, SS	15
K. Harrelson, 1B	13
B. Bryan, C	12
D. Green, 2B	11
J. Landis, OF	9
J. Tartabull, OF	9
R. Sheldon, SP	7
F. Talbot, SP	7
J. Wyatt, RP	7
M. Hershberger, OF	6
J. O'Donoghue, SP	6
T. Reynolds, OF	5
J. Aker, RP	4
J. Dickson, RP	4
J. Gentile, 1B	4
C. Hunter, SP	4
R. Lachemann, C	4
N. Mathews, OF	3
D. Mossi, RP	3
D. Segui, SP	2
L. Stahl, OF	2
J. Blanchard, OF	1
D. Buschhorn, RP	1
M. Drabowsky, RP	1
S. Rosario, 1B	1
W. Stock, RP	1
R. Tompkins, RP	1

Minnesota (102-60)	WS
Hitting	**161.9**
Fielding	**47.0**
Pitching	**97.1**
T. Oliva, OF	33
Z. Versalles, SS	32
J. Hall, OF	26
B. Allison, OF	22
E. Battey, C	22
H. Killebrew, 1B	22
M. Grant, SP	17
J. Kaat, SP	17
D. Mincher, 1B	17
J. Perry, SP	13
A. Worthington, RP	12
R. Rollins, 3B	10
C. Pascual, SP	9
J. Klippstein, RP	8
D. Boswell, RP	7
J. Kindall, 2B	6
S. Valdespino, OF	6
J. Merritt, SP	5
B. Pleis, RP	4
J. Zimmerman, C	4
D. Stigman, RP	3
J. Nossek, OF	2
F. Quilici, 2B	2
B. Allen, 2B	1
J. Fosnow, RP	1
A. Kosco, OF	1
M. Nelson, RP	1
R. Reese, 1B	1
G. Roggenburk, RP	1
J. Sevcik, C	1

New York (77-85)	WS
Hitting	**101.7**
Fielding	**40.4**
Pitching	**88.9**
T. Tresh, OF	25
M. Stottlemyre, SP	23
C. Boyer, 3B	18
W. Ford, SP	16
M. Mantle, OF	16
B. Richardson, 2B	14
J. Pepitone, 1B	13
P. Ramos, RP	11
A. Downing, SP	10
S. Hamilton, RP	8
E. Howard, C	8
H. Lopez, OF	7
R. Repoz, OF	7
R. Barker, 1B	6
R. Maris, OF	6
P. Linz, SS	5
B. Stafford, SP	5
J. Cullen, SP	4
T. Kubek, SS	4
P. Mikkelsen, RP	4
H. Reniff, RP	4
R. Beck, SP	2
H. Clarke, 3B	2
D. Edwards, C	2
B. Murcer, SS	2
R. White, OF	2
J. Blanchard, C	1
G. Blanco, RP	1
J. Gibbs, C	1
A. Moore, OF	1
B. Schmidt, C	1
R. Sheldon, RP	1
B. Tiefenauer, RP	1

Washington (70-92)	WS
Hitting	**106.9**
Fielding	**36.6**
Pitching	**66.5**
F. Howard, OF	25
K. McMullen, 3B	21
P. Richert, SP	16
W. Held, OF	14
R. Kline, RP	14
K. Hamlin, 2B	13
D. Lock, OF	11
J. King, OF	10
M. McCormick, RP	10
D. Blasingame, 2B	7
J. Cunningham, 1B	7
W. Kirkland, OF	7
D. Nen, 1B	7
E. Brinkman, SS	6
B. Chance, 1B	5
S. Ridzik, RP	5
H. Koplitz, RP	4
P. Ortega, SP	4
M. Bridges, RP	3
B. Narum, SP	3
M. Brumley, C	2
D. Camilli, C	2
J. Coleman, SP	2
J. Duckworth, RP	2
J. French, C	2
F. Kreutzer, RP	2
D. Zimmer, C	2
B. Daniels, SP	1
D. Green, RP	1
J. McCabe, C	1
F. Valentine, OF	1

1965 National League

Chicago (72-90)	WS
Hitting	**101.5**
Fielding	**35.8**
Pitching	**78.7**
B. Williams, OF	33
R. Santo, 3B	32
T. Abernathy, RP	18
E. Banks, 1B	18
L. Jackson, SP	11
L. McDaniel, RP	11
D. Ellsworth, SP	10
D. Landrum, OF	9
G. Beckert, 2B	8
C. Koonce, SP	8
E. Bailey, C	6
B. Buhl, SP	6
B. Faul, SP	5
B. Humphreys, RP	5
D. Clemens, OF	4
B. Hoeft, RP	4
V. Roznovsky, C	4
J. Stewart, OF	4
G. Altman, OF	3
J. Amalfitano, 2B	3
D. Bertell, C	2
B. Hendley, SP	2
D. Kessinger, SS	2
C. Krug, C	2
H. Kuenn, OF	2
R. Pena, SS	2
J. Boccabella, 1B	1
L. Gabrielson, OF	1

Cincinnati (89-73)	WS
Hitting	**154.1**
Fielding	**37.9**
Pitching	**74.9**
P. Rose, 2B	27
F. Robinson, OF	26
V. Pinson, OF	24
D. Johnson, 3B	23
J. Maloney, SP	23
L. Cardenas, SS	22
T. Harper, OF	18
J. Edwards, C	17
S. Ellis, SP	14
G. Coleman, 1B	11
J. Nuxhall, SP-RP	10
D. Pavletich, C	10
B. McCool, RP	8
T. Davidson, RP	6
T. Perez, 1B	6
J. Jay, SP	5
R. Craig, RP	3
T. Helms, SS	3
A. Shamsky, OF	3
J. Coker, C	2
J. Duffalo, RP	2
B. Henry, RP	1
D. Osteen, RP	1
J. Tsitouris, SP	1
D. Zanni, RP	1

Houston (65-97)	WS
Hitting	**106.1**
Fielding	**28.8**
Pitching	**60.1**
J. Wynn, OF	31
J. Morgan, 2B	30
B. Aspromonte, 3B	14
R. Staub, OF	13
W. Bond, 1B	12
T. Farrell, SP	10
B. Bruce, SP	8
J. Gentile, 1B	8
C. Raymond, RP	8
R. Roberts, SP	8
L. Maye, OF	7
J. Owens, RP	7
L. Dierker, SP	6
D. Giusti, RP	5
R. Brand, C	4
J. Gaines, OF	4
M. Cuellar, RP	3
E. Kasko, SS	3
B. Lillis, SS	3
H. Woodeshick, RP	3
J. Bateman, C	2
K. Johnson, SP	2
N. Fox, 3B	1
C. Harrison, 1B	1
K. MacKenzie, RP	1
A. Spangler, OF	1

Los Angeles (97-65)	WS
Hitting	**127.4**
Fielding	**52.4**
Pitching	**111.1**
S. Koufax, SP	33
M. Wills, SS	28
D. Drysdale, SP	27
R. Fairly, OF	26
J. Lefebvre, 2B	23
W. Parker, 1B	20
J. Gilliam, 3B	18
C. Osteen, SP	18
L. Johnson, OF	17
W. Davis, OF	15
R. Perranoski, RP	13
J. Roseboro, C	13
B. Miller, RP	8
J. Podres, SP	6
J. Brewer, RP	5
H. Reed, RP	5
J. Torborg, C	5
D. Tracewski, 3B	3
A. Ferrara, OF	2
W. Moon, OF	2
J. Kennedy, 3B	1
D. LeJohn, 3B	1
H. Valle, C	1
N. Willhite, RP	1

Milwaukee (86-76)	WS
Hitting	**127.4**
Fielding	**41.2**
Pitching	**89.3**
H. Aaron, OF	31
J. Torre, C	23
E. Mathews, 3B	22
F. Alou, OF	21
T. Cloninger, SP	19
M. Jones, OF	19
B. O'Dell, RP	16
G. Oliver, C	14
W. Blasingame, SP	12
K. Johnson, SP	12
F. Bolling, 2B	11
R. Carty, OF	10
D. Osinski, RP	6
H. Fischer, SP	5
D. Menke, SS	5
P. Niekro, RP	5
D. Lemaster, SP	4
B. Sadowski, RP	4
W. Woodward, SS	4
M. de la Hoz, SS	3
D. Kelley, RP	3
S. Alomar, SS	2
T. Cline, OF	2
L. Maye, OF	2
C. Carroll, RP	1
J. Gonder, C	1
C. Olivo, RP	1

New York (50-112)	WS
Hitting	**57.0**
Fielding	**30.9**
Pitching	**62.1**
J. Lewis, OF	13
J. Fisher, SP	11
E. Kranepool, 1B	10
C. Smith, 3B	10
R. Swoboda, OF	9
J. Christopher, OF	8
J. Hickman, OF	8
R. McMillan, SS	8
A. Jackson, SP	6
F. Lary, SP-RP	5
T. McGraw, RP	5
D. Sutherland, RP	5
G. Cisco, RP	4
C. Hiller, 2B	4
B. Klaus, 2B	4
W. Spahn, SP	4
C. Cannizzaro, C	3
R. Hunt, 2B	3
G. Kroll, RP	3
D. Musgraves, RP	3
D. Ribant, RP	3
G. Richardson, RP	3
J. Bethke, RP	2
J. Gonder, C	2
D. Selma, SP	2
L. Bearnarth, RP	1
B. Cowan, OF	1
D. Eilers, RP	1
R. Gardner, SP	1
G. Goossen, C	1
C. Jones, OF	1

G. Kolb, OF	1
L. Miller, RP	1
B. Moorhead, RP	1
T. Parsons, RP	1
J. Stephenson, C	1
C. Willey, RP	1

Philadelphia (85-76)	WS
Hitting	**129.6**
Fielding	**37.1**
Pitching	**88.3**
D. Allen, 3B	33
J. Callison, OF	28
J. Bunning, SP	27
C. Short, SP	24
C. Rojas, 2B	19
R. Culp, SP	13
T. Gonzalez, OF	13
D. Stuart, 1B	13
W. Covington, OF	9
A. Johnson, OF	9
G. Wagner, RP	9
J. Briggs, OF	8
C. Dalrymple, C	8
B. Wine, SS	7
R. Herbert, SP	6
T. Taylor, 2B	6
J. Baldschun, RP	5
P. Corrales, C	5
E. Roebuck, RP	4
R. Amaro, 1B-SS	3
F. Jenkins, RP	2
A. Phillips, OF	1
B. Sorrell, 3B	1
F. Thomas, OF	1
G. Triandos, C	1

Pittsburgh (90-72)	WS
Hitting	**120.2**
Fielding	**47.4**
Pitching	**102.4**
R. Clemente, OF	27
D. Clendenon, 1B	22
V. Law, SP	21
W. Stargell, OF	21
B. Veale, SP	18
J. Pagliaroni, C	17
G. Alley, SS	15
B. Bailey, 3B	14
D. Cardwell, SP	14
A. McBean, RP	14
B. Virdon, OF	14
B. Mazeroski, 2B	13
B. Friend, SP	11
M. Mota, OF	9
A. Rodgers, SS	6
D. Schwall, RP	6
T. Sisk, RP	6
F. Carpin, RP	3
D. Crandall, C	3
R. Face, RP	3
D. Schofield, SS	3
W. Wood, RP	3
J. Gibbon, RP	2
J. Lynch, OF	2
G. Freese, 3B	1
O. Virgil, C	1
L. Walker, RP	1

San Francisco (95-67)	WS
Hitting	**124.0**
Fielding	**48.7**
Pitching	**112.3**
W. Mays, OF	43
J. Marichal, SP	30
W. McCovey, 1B	29
J. Hart, 3B	25
B. Shaw, SP	19
T. Haller, C	18
F. Linzy, RP	16
B. Bolin, RP	15
J. Alou, OF	14
L. Gabrielson, OF	11
R. Herbel, RP	8
H. Lanier, 2B	7
M. Murakami, RP	7
J. Davenport, 3B	6
G. Perry, SP	6
M. Alou, OF	4
D. Schofield, SS	4
B. Henry, RP	3
J. Hiatt, C	3
J. Sanford, SP	3
W. Spahn, SP	3
C. Peterson, OF	2
E. Bailey, C	1
B. Barton, C	1
D. Bertell, C	1
T. Fuentes, SS	1
K. Henderson, OF	1
R. Hundley, C	1
H. Kuenn, OF	1
J. Pagan, SS	1
B. Priddy, RP	1

St. Louis (80-81)	WS
Hitting	**110.7**
Fielding	**42.5**
Pitching	**86.8**
B. Gibson, SP	26
C. Flood, OF	24
L. Brock, OF	22
B. White, 1B	22
D. Groat, SS	16
T. McCarver, C	15
K. Boyer, 3B	13
T. Stallard, SP	12
H. Woodeshick, RP	11
P. Gagliano, 2B	9
D. Dennis, RP	7
C. Simmons, SP	7
R. Washburn, SP	7
N. Briles, RP	6
J. Buchek, 2B	5
M. Shannon, OF	5
B. Skinner, OF	5
B. Uecker, C	5
T. Francona, OF	4
L. Jaster, SP	4
J. Javier, 2B	3
S. Carlton, RP	2
R. Sadecki, SP	2
B. Schultz, RP	2
R. Taylor, RP	2
D. Aust, RP	1
G. Kernek, 1B	1
D. Maxvill, 2B	1
B. Purkey, SP	1

1966 American League

Baltimore (97-63)	WS
Hitting	**158.0**
Fielding	**41.5**
Pitching	**91.5**
F. Robinson, OF	41
B. Powell, 1B	26
B. Robinson, 3B	24
L. Aparicio, SS	22
C. Blefary, OF	20
R. Snyder, OF	15
S. Miller, RP	14
D. Johnson, 2B	13
A. Etchebarren, C	12
D. McNally, SP	12
S. Barber, SP	11
J. Palmer, SP	11
M. Drabowsky, RP	10
P. Blair, OF	9
E. Fisher, RP	8
E. Watt, RP	8
D. Hall, RP	5
G. Brabender, RP	4
W. Bunker, SP	4
S. Bowens, OF	3
T. Phoebus, SP	3
V. Roznovsky, C	3
J. Adair, 2B	2
F. Bertaina, SP	2
W. Held, OF	2
C. Lau, PH-PR	2
B. Short, SP	2
C. Carreon, C	1
L. Haney, C	1
B. Johnson, 2B	1

Boston (72-90)	WS
Hitting	**102.5**
Fielding	**37.9**
Pitching	**75.7**
J. Foy, 3B	22
C. Yastrzemski, OF	21
T. Conigliaro, OF	20
G. Scott, 1B	16
R. Petrocelli, SS	15
B. Brandon, RP	10
J. Lonborg, SP	9
D. McMahon, RP	9
J. Santiago, SP	9
L. Stange, SP	9
D. Demeter, OF	7
G. Smith, 2B	7
E. Wilson, SP	7
J. Wyatt, RP	7
D. Bennett, SP	5
D. Jones, 2B	5
M. Ryan, C	5
B. Tillman, C	5
J. Gosger, OF	4
D. Osinski, RP	4
J. Tartabull, OF	4
G. Thomas, OF	4
H. Fischer, SP	3
K. Sanders, RP	3
E. Kasko, SS	2
L. Green, OF	1
D. Morehead, RP	1
R. Sheldon, RP	1
D. Stigman, RP	1

California (80-82)	WS
Hitting	**116.8**
Fielding	**41.2**
Pitching	**82.0**
J. Fregosi, SS	26
J. Cardenal, OF	20
B. Knoop, 2B	18
R. Reichardt, OF	16
P. Schaal, 3B	15
D. Chance, SP	14
J. Adcock, 1B	12
G. Brunet, SP	12
B. Rodgers, C	12
N. Siebern, 1B	12
B. Lee, RP	11
M. Rojas, RP	9
E. Kirkpatrick, OF	8
J. Sanford, RP	8
L. Burdette, RP	7
M. Lopez, SP	7
J. Johnstone, OF	6
T. Satriano, C	5
C. Wright, SP	4
H. Reed, RP	3
J. Warner, OF	3
F. Newman, SP	2
J. Rubio, SP	2
J. Coates, RP	1
B. Kelso, RP	1
F. Malzone, 3B	1
J. McGlothlin, SP	1
J. Piersall, OF	1
W. Smith, OF	1
A. Spangler, OF	1
C. Vinson, 1B	1

Chicago (83-79)	WS
Hitting	**101.8**
Fielding	**43.6**
Pitching	**103.5**
T. Agee, OF	28
D. Buford, 3B	21
G. Peters, SP	20
J. Romano, C	16
J. Horlen, SP	15
T. John, SP	15
K. Berry, OF	14
B. Locker, RP	12
B. Howard, SP	11
F. Robinson, OF	11
H. Wilhelm, RP	10
J. Adair, SS	8
D. Higgins, RP	8
T. McCraw, 1B	8
B. Skowron, 1B	7
W. Causey, 2B	6
J. Martin, C	5
P. Ward, OF	5
E. Fisher, RP	4
S. Burgess, C	3
J. Buzhardt, SP	3
L. Elia, SS	3
J. Lamabe, SP-RP	3
J. Pizarro, RP	3
A. Weis, 2B	3
G. Freese, 3B	2
F. Klages, SP	2
R. Hansen, SS	1
D. Josephson, C	1
J. McNertney, C	1

Cleveland (81-81)	WS
Hitting	**94.0**
Fielding	**45.3**
Pitching	**103.7**
S. Siebert, SP	20
L. Wagner, OF	19
R. Colavito, OF	18
S. Hargan, SP	18
S. McDowell, SP	17
M. Alvis, 3B	16
G. Bell, SP	16
L. Tiant, RP	16
F. Whitfield, 1B	13
C. Salmon, SS	12
C. Hinton, OF	11
J. Azcue, C	10
L. Brown, SS	8
V. Davalillo, OF	7
P. Gonzalez, 2B	7
J. O'Donoghue, RP	5
D. Sims, C	5
J. Landis, OF	4
B. Allen, RP	3
D. Crandall, C	3
V. Fuller, 2B	3
D. Howser, 2B-SS	3
J. Kralick, RP	3
D. Radatz, RP	2
T. Kelley, RP	1
D. McMahon, RP	1
L. Stange, RP	1
J. Vidal, OF	1

Detroit (88-74)	WS
Hitting	**153.3**
Fielding	**38.4**
Pitching	**72.3**
A. Kaline, OF	31
N. Cash, 1B	27
D. McAuliffe, SS	26
W. Horton, OF	21
D. Wert, 3B	17
E. Wilson, SP	17
B. Freehan, C	16
J. Northrup, OF	14
D. McLain, SP	13
L. Sherry, RP	9
M. Stanley, OF	9
D. Wickersham, RP	8
G. Brown, OF	7
O. Pena, RP	7
J. Podres, RP	6
J. Wood, 2B	6

F. Gladding, RP	5
J. Lumpe, 2B	5
O. McFarlane, C	5
H. Aguirre, RP	4
M. Lolich, SP	4
R. Oyler, SS	3
B. Monbouquette, RP	2
D. Demeter, OF	1
D. Tracewski, 2B	1

Kansas City (74-86)	WS
Hitting	**108.1**
Fielding	**40.2**
Pitching	**73.8**
B. Campaneris, SS	22
J. Aker, RP	20
E. Charles, 3B	18
D. Green, 2B	16
D. Cater, 1B	15
M. Hershberger, OF	15
L. Krausse, SP	12
J. Nash, SP	12
R. Repoz, OF	10
J. Gosger, OF	9
L. Stahl, OF	9
P. Roof, C	7
B. Odom, SP	6
K. Harrelson, 1B	5
C. Hunter, SP	5
J. Nossek, OF	5
O. Chavarria, OF	4
W. Stock, RP	4
J. Tartabull, OF	4
K. Sanders, RP	3
R. Sheldon, SP	3
T. Talton, C	3
C. Dobson, SP	2
P. Lindblad, RP	2
R. Terry, SP	2
S. Bando, 3B	1
B. Bryan, C	1
W. Causey, 3B	1
E. Fazio, 2B	1
J. Grzenda, RP	1
V. Handrahan, RP	1
A. Monteagudo, RP	1
K. Suarez, C	1
F. Talbot, SP	1

Minnesota (89-73)	WS
Hitting	**114.4**
Fielding	**45.5**
Pitching	**107.2**
H. Killebrew, 3B	33
T. Oliva, OF	28
J. Kaat, SP	26
J. Perry, SP	17
M. Grant, SP	16
A. Worthington, RP	15
D. Mincher, 1B	14
C. Tovar, 2B	14
E. Battey, C	13
D. Boswell, SP	12
Z. Versalles, SS	12
J. Hall, OF	10
J. Merritt, SP	9
B. Allen, 2B	7
B. Allison, OF	7
T. Uhlaender, OF	7
P. Cimino, RP	5
R. Rollins, 3B	5
J. Zimmerman, C	5
J. Klippstein, RP	3
R. Nixon, C	2
C. Pascual, SP	2
D. Siebler, RP	2
A. Kosco, OF	1
J. Ollom, RP	1
B. Pleis, RP	1

New York (70-89)	WS
Hitting	**107.7**
Fielding	**31.2**
Pitching	**71.1**
T. Tresh, OF	22
M. Mantle, OF	18
J. Pepitone, 1B	17
C. Boyer, 3B	16
F. Peterson, SP	12
E. Howard, C	11
B. Richardson, 2B	10
H. Clarke, SS	9
M. Stottlemyre, SP	9
A. Downing, SP	8
R. Maris, OF	8
S. Hamilton, RP	7
H. Reniff, RP	7
R. White, OF	7
D. Womack, RP	7
J. Bouton, SP	6
J. Gibbs, C	5
P. Ramos, RP	5
L. Clinton, OF	4
W. Ford, RP	4
F. Talbot, SP	4
S. Whitaker, OF	4
R. Repoz, OF	3
B. Bryan, C	2
H. Lopez, OF	2
S. Bahnsen, SP	1
R. Barker, 1B	1
J. Cullen, RP	1

Washington (71-88)	WS
Hitting	**103.5**
Fielding	**35.9**
Pitching	**73.6**
F. Valentine, OF	24
F. Howard, OF	21
D. Lock, OF	14
R. Kline, RP	13
P. Richert, SP	13
P. Casanova, C	12
K. McMullen, 3B	12
E. Brinkman, SS	11
J. King, OF	11
M. McCormick, SP	11
B. Humphreys, RP	10
B. Saverine, 2B	10
D. Lines, RP	8
P. Ortega, SP	8
K. Harrelson, 1B	7
C. Cox, RP	6
D. Blasingame, 2B	4
D. Nen, 1B	4
B. Moore, SP	3
H. Allen, OF	2
K. Hamlin, 2B	2
J. Hannan, SP	2
W. Kirkland, OF	2
D. Camilli, C	1
J. Coleman, SP	1
T. Cullen, 3B	1

1966
National League

Atlanta (85-77)	WS
Hitting	**146.6**
Fielding	**31.9**
Pitching	**76.5**
J. Torre, C	29
F. Alou, 1B	28
H. Aaron, OF	27
R. Carty, OF	21
E. Mathews, 3B	16
D. Menke, SS	16
C. Carroll, RP	14
M. Jones, OF	14
K. Johnson, SP	12
T. Cloninger, SP	11
W. Woodward, 2B	10
D. Lemaster, SP	8
P. Jarvis, SP	6
G. Geiger, OF	5
D. Kelley, SP	4
B. O'Dell, RP	4
G. Oliver, C	4
C. Olivo, RP	4
T. Abernathy, RP	3
H. Fischer, SP	2
P. Niekro, RP	2
J. Ritchie, RP	2
D. Schneider, RP	2
L. Thomas, 1B	2
A. Umbach, RP	2
F. Bolling, 2B	1
M. de la Hoz, 3B	1
F. Millan, 2B	1
R. Reed, SP	1
D. Schwall, SP	1
C. Upshaw, RP	1
C. Vaughan, SP	1

Chicago (59-103)	WS
Hitting	**94.3**
Fielding	**27.1**
Pitching	**55.6**
R. Santo, 3B	30
B. Williams, OF	21
A. Phillips, OF	14
F. Jenkins, RP	12
E. Banks, 1B	11
G. Beckert, 2B	11
R. Hundley, C	11
B. Browne, OF	10
K. Holtzman, SP	10
D. Ellsworth, SP	9
D. Kessinger, SS	6
B. Hands, SP	5
B. Hendley, RP	5
C. Koonce, RP	5
C. Simmons, SP	3
J. Boccabella, OF	2
L. Thomas, 1B	2
G. Altman, OF	1
E. Broglio, SP	1
D. Bryant, C	1
D. Dowling, SP	1
A. Earley, RP	1
B. Faul, RP	1
C. Hartenstein, RP	1
B. Hoeft, RP	1
M. Keough, OF	1
R. Nye, SP	1

Cincinnati (76-84)	WS
Hitting	**100.6**
Fielding	**42.4**
Pitching	**85.0**
P. Rose, 2B	25
J. Maloney, SP	21
L. Cardenas, SS	19
V. Pinson, OF	19
B. McCool, RP	16
T. Harper, OF	15
D. Johnson, OF	14
T. Helms, 3B	12
D. Nottebart, RP	11
D. Pavletich, C	10
M. Pappas, SP	9
J. O'Toole, SP	8
A. Shamsky, OF	8
T. Davidson, RP	6
J. Jay, SP	5
G. Coleman, 1B	4
J. Edwards, C	4
S. Ellis, SP	4
J. Nuxhall, RP	4
T. Perez, 1B	4
J. Coker, C	3
L. May, 1B	2
D. Simpson, OF	2
J. Baldschun, RP	1
C. Ruiz, 3B	1
D. Zanni, RP	1

Houston (72-90)	WS
Hitting	**109.4**
Fielding	**34.0**
Pitching	**72.6**
M. Cuellar, SP	19
S. Jackson, SS	19
J. Morgan, 2B	19
R. Staub, OF	18
J. Bateman, C	15
J. Wynn, OF	14
L. Dierker, SP	12
D. Nicholson, OF	11
C. Harrison, 1B	10
L. Maye, OF	10
C. Raymond, RP	10
D. Giusti, SP	9
B. Aspromonte, 3B	8
B. Latman, RP	6
J. Gentile, 1B	5
R. Davis, OF	4
B. Heath, C	4
T. Farrell, SP	3
R. Roberts, SP	3
C. Zachary, SP	3
D. Lee, RP	2
F. Mantilla, 1B-3B	2
A. Pointer, OF	2
C. Sembera, RP	2
R. Brand, C	1
G. Kroll, RP	1
B. Lillis, 2B	1
A. Monteagudo, RP	1
J. Owens, RP	1
D. Wilson, RP	1

Los Angeles (95-67)	WS
Hitting	**115.0**
Fielding	**48.0**
Pitching	**122.0**
S. Koufax, SP	35
J. Lefebvre, 2B	25
P. Regan, RP	23
J. Roseboro, C	21
W. Davis, OF	20
R. Fairly, OF	17
C. Osteen, SP	17
W. Parker, 1B	17
M. Wills, SS	16
L. Johnson, OF	15
D. Sutton, SP	14
D. Drysdale, SP	13
T. Davis, OF	9
B. Miller, RP	7
R. Perranoski, RP	7
J. Moeller, RP	5
A. Ferrara, OF	4
J. Gilliam, 3B	4
J. Barbieri, OF	3
J. Kennedy, 3B	3
D. Stuart, 1B	3
N. Oliver, 2B	2
J. Torborg, C	2
J. Brewer, RP	1
D. Schofield, 3B	1
B. Singer, RP	1

New York (66-95)	WS
Hitting	**108.8**
Fielding	**30.8**
Pitching	**58.5**
R. Hunt, 2B	18
K. Boyer, 3B	17
E. Kranepool, 1B	16
C. Jones, OF	15
D. Ribant, SP	14
E. Bressoud, SS	11
J. Fisher, SP	11
J. Grote, C	9
C. Hiller, 2B	9
B. Shaw, SP	9
A. Luplow, OF	8
R. Swoboda, OF	7
L. Elliot, OF	6
J. Hamilton, RP	6
G. Arrigo, RP	4
B. Hepler, RP	4
J. Hickman, OF	4

	WS
J. Lewis, OF	4
B. Harrelson, SS	3
R. McMillan, SS	3
D. Selma, RP	3
L. Bearnarth, RP	2
B. Friend, SP	2
R. Gardner, RP	2
B. Murphy, OF	2
D. Rusteck, RP	2
D. Sutherland, RP	2
D. Eilers, RP	1
J. Stephenson, C	1
D. Stuart, 1B	1
H. Taylor, C	1
R. Terry, RP	1

Philadelphia (87-75)	WS
Hitting	**128.0**
Fielding	**43.5**
Pitching	**89.6**
D. Allen, 3B	35
J. Bunning, SP	30
B. White, 1B	24
J. Callison, OF	20
L. Jackson, SP	19
C. Short, SP	17
D. Groat, SS	15
C. Dalrymple, C	14
J. Briggs, OF	13
C. Rojas, 2B	13
T. Gonzalez, OF	12
D. Knowles, RP	10
T. Taylor, 2B	9
B. Uecker, C	5
R. Wise, SP	4
J. Brandt, OF	3
D. Clemens, OF	3
H. Kuenn, OF	3
B. Buhl, SP	2
R. Culp, RP	2
T. Fox, RP	2
R. Herbert, RP	2
B. Wine, SS	2
B. Belinsky, RP	1
P. Linz, 3B	1

Pittsburgh (92-70)	WS
Hitting	**145.3**
Fielding	**46.1**
Pitching	**84.6**
R. Clemente, OF	29
W. Stargell, OF	25
D. Clendenon, 1B	23
G. Alley, SS	22
M. Alou, OF	20
B. Mazeroski, 2B	20
B. Veale, SP	17
B. Bailey, 3B	14
M. Mota, OF	14
P. Mikkelsen, RP	12
J. Pagliaroni, C	12
R. Face, RP	8
W. Fryman, SP	8
V. Law, SP	8
S. Blass, SP	7
J. Pagan, 3B	7
B. O'Dell, RP	6
T. Sisk, SP	6
A. McBean, RP	5
D. Schwall, RP	4
J. Gonder, C	3
D. Cardwell, RP	2
J. May, C	2
B. Purkey, RP	2

San Francisco (93-68)	WS
Hitting	**129.9**
Fielding	**44.1**
Pitching	**104.9**
W. Mays, OF	37
W. McCovey, 1B	34
J. Marichal, SP	33
J. Hart, 3B	27
T. Haller, C	22
G. Perry, SP	21
B. Bolin, SP	17
T. Fuentes, SS	14
L. McDaniel, RP	11
F. Linzy, RP	10
J. Davenport, SS	8
H. Lanier, 2B	7
O. Brown, OF	6
J. Gibbon, RP	4
B. Priddy, RP	4
J. Alou, OF	3
L. Gabrielson, OF	3
R. Herbel, SP	3
B. Barton, C	2
O. Cepeda, OF	2
K. Henderson, OF	2
B. Henry, RP	2
C. Peterson, OF	2
R. Sadecki, SP	2
J. Hiatt, 1B	1
D. Landrum, OF	1
O. Virgil, C-3B	1

St. Louis (83-79)	WS
Hitting	**90.6**
Fielding	**52.4**
Pitching	**106.0**
B. Gibson, SP	26
L. Brock, OF	21
T. McCarver, C	21
A. Jackson, SP	19
C. Flood, OF	18
M. Shannon, OF	18
O. Cepeda, 1B	17
J. Hoerner, RP	13
D. Maxvill, SS	12
L. Jaster, SP	11
J. Javier, 2B	10
C. Smith, 3B	10
N. Briles, RP	8
R. Washburn, SP	8
H. Woodeshick, RP	8
J. Buchek, 2B	6
P. Gagliano, 3B	5
S. Carlton, SP	3
D. Hughes, RP	3
R. Sadecki, SP	3
J. Cosman, SP	2
P. Corrales, C	1
D. Dennis, RP	1
T. Francona, 1B	1
R. Piche, RP	1
C. Simmons, SP-RP	1
E. Spiezio, 3B	1
R. Willis, RP	1

1967 American League

Baltimore (76-85)	WS
Hitting	**124.0**
Fielding	**34.6**
Pitching	**69.4**
F. Robinson, OF	30
P. Blair, OF	24
B. Robinson, 3B	24
C. Blefary, OF	19
D. Johnson, 2B	16
M. Drabowsky, RP	13
B. Powell, 1B	10
E. Watt, RP	10
T. Phoebus, SP	9
L. Aparicio, SS	8
A. Etchebarren, C	8
J. Hardin, SP	8
R. Snyder, OF	7
S. Miller, RP	6
P. Richert, SP	6
L. Haney, C	5
G. Brabender, SP	4
E. Fisher, RP	4
J. Palmer, SP	3
B. Dillman, RP	2
S. Barber, SP	1
M. Belanger, SS	1
F. Bertaina, RP	1
S. Bowens, OF	1
W. Bunker, RP	1
W. Held, 2B	1
D. Leonhard, SP	1
M. Lopez, SP	1
D. May, OF	1
D. McNally, SP	1
C. Motton, OF	1
V. Roznovsky, C	1

Boston (92-70)	WS
Hitting	**135.3**
Fielding	**45.3**
Pitching	**95.4**
C. Yastrzemski, OF	42
R. Petrocelli, SS	23
G. Scott, 1B	23
J. Lonborg, SP	19
R. Smith, OF	19
M. Andrews, 2B	16
T. Conigliaro, OF	16
J. Wyatt, RP	14
J. Foy, 3B	13
L. Stange, SP	13
G. Bell, SP	11
J. Santiago, RP	11
J. Adair, 3B	8
D. Osinski, RP	6
D. Jones, 3B	5
S. Lyle, RP	5
B. Brandon, RP	4
M. Ryan, C	4
D. Bennett, SP	3
D. Demeter, OF	2
R. Gibson, C	2
E. Howard, C	2
D. Morehead, SP	2
J. Stephenson, SP	2
G. Waslewski, SP	2
G. Cisco, RP	1
H. Fischer, RP	1
K. Harrelson, OF	1
T. Horton, 1B	1
D. McMahon, RP	1
N. Siebern, 1B	1
J. Tartabull, OF	1
G. Thomas, OF	1
B. Tillman, C	1

California (84-77)	WS
Hitting	**125.7**
Fielding	**41.6**
Pitching	**84.7**
J. Fregosi, SS	28
D. Mincher, 1B	28
B. Knoop, 2B	18
R. Reichardt, OF	18
M. Rojas, RP	16
J. Hall, OF	15
J. McGlothlin, SP	12
G. Brunet, SP	11
R. Clark, SP	11
B. Rodgers, C	10
B. Kelso, RP	9
B. Morton, OF	9
J. Cardenal, OF	8
J. Hamilton, SP	7
R. Repoz, OF	7
T. Satriano, 3B	6
P. Schaal, 3B	6
P. Cimino, RP	5
W. Held, 3B	4
C. Wright, SP	4
B. Locke, RP	3
C. Simmons, RP	3
H. Taylor, C	3
J. Weaver, RP	3
J. Johnstone, OF	2
A. Rodriguez, 3B	2
J. Coates, RP	1
J. Rubio, SP	1
J. Sanford, SP	1
J. Werhas, 3B	1

Chicago (89-73)	WS
Hitting	**104.4**
Fielding	**49.3**
Pitching	**113.2**
J. Horlen, SP	23
G. Peters, SP	21
T. Agee, OF	20
P. Ward, OF	20
D. Buford, 3B	17
R. Hansen, SS	17
B. Locker, RP	16
K. Berry, OF	14
H. Wilhelm, RP	13
T. McCraw, 1B	12
T. John, SP	11
J. Martin, C	10
D. McMahon, RP	10
W. Causey, 2B	8
W. Williams, OF	7
W. Wood, RP	7
C. Carlos, SP	5
R. Colavito, OF	5
J. McNertney, C	5
K. Boyer, 3B	4
D. Josephson, C	4
J. O'Toole, SP	3
B. Howard, SP	2
D. Kenworthy, 3B	2
J. Adair, 2B	1
S. Burgess, PH-PR	1
J. Buzhardt, RP	1
E. Herrmann, C	1
S. Jones, RP	1
F. Klages, SP	1
J. Lamabe, RP	1
R. Nelson, RP	1
M. Staehle, 2B	1
E. Stroud, OF	1
A. Weis, 2B	1

Cleveland (75-87)	WS
Hitting	**98.9**
Fielding	**39.9**
Pitching	**86.1**
M. Alvis, 3B	17
L. Tiant, SP	17
S. Hargan, SP	16
S. Siebert, SP	15
L. Brown, SS	14
J. Azcue, C	13
T. Horton, 1B	12
L. Wagner, OF	12
C. Hinton, OF	11
L. Maye, OF	10
D. Sims, C	10
V. Davalillo, OF	9
S. McDowell, SP	8
V. Fuller, 2B	7
J. O'Donoghue, SP	7
O. Pena, RP	6
S. Williams, SP-RP	6
R. Colavito, OF	5
C. Salmon, OF	5
F. Whitfield, 1B	5
G. Culver, RP	4
B. Allen, RP	3
R. Scheinblum, OF	3
S. Bailey, RP	2
D. Demeter, OF	2
G. Gil, 2B	2
P. Gonzalez, 2B	2
G. Bell, SP	1
B. Tiefenauer, RP	1

Detroit (91-71)	WS
Hitting	**145.9**
Fielding	**41.1**
Pitching	**85.9**
B. Freehan, C	30

Player	WS
A. Kaline, OF	30
D. McAuliffe, 2B	27
N. Cash, 1B	21
E. Wilson, SP	18
W. Horton, OF	17
J. Northrup, OF	16
D. Wert, 3B	14
M. Lolich, SP	13
F. Gladding, RP	10
D. McLain, SP	8
J. Sparma, SP	8
M. Marshall, RP	7
R. Oyler, SS	7
J. Hiller, RP	6
M. Stanley, OF	6
D. Wickersham, RP	6
L. Green, OF	4
E. Mathews, 3B	4
D. Tracewski, SS	4
H. Aguirre, RP	3
P. Dobson, RP	3
F. Lasher, RP	3
J. Lumpe, 2B	3
J. Podres, RP	2
G. Brown, OF	1
J. Landis, OF	1
J. Price, C	1

Kansas City (62-99)	WS
Hitting	**92.4**
Fielding	**34.8**
Pitching	**58.8**
C. Hunter, SP	17
B. Campaneris, SS	16
R. Monday, OF	16
J. Donaldson, 2B	13
D. Cater, 3B	11
J. Gosger, OF	11
M. Hershberger, OF	11
R. Webster, 1B	11
C. Dobson, SP	8
K. Harrelson, 1B	8
J. Nash, SP	7
P. Roof, C	7
T. Pierce, RP	6
D. Green, 3B	5
P. Lindblad, RP	5
L. Krausse, RP	4
D. Segui, RP	4
K. Suarez, C	4
J. Aker, RP	3
R. Repoz, OF	3
S. Bando, 3B	2
E. Charles, 3B	2
R. Jackson, OF	2
R. Rodriguez, RP	2
O. Chavarria, 2B	1
D. Duncan, C	1
B. Edgerton, RP	1
T. Kubiak, SS	1
G. Lauzerique, SP	1
J. Nossek, OF	1
B. Stafford, RP	1
T. Talton, C	1

Minnesota (91-71)	WS
Hitting	**132.4**
Fielding	**40.6**
Pitching	**100.0**
H. Killebrew, 1B	38
T. Oliva, OF	25
B. Allison, OF	24
C. Tovar, OF	21
D. Chance, SP	20
R. Carew, 2B	19
J. Merritt, SP	19
J. Kaat, SP	17
D. Boswell, SP	15
T. Uhlaender, OF	11
A. Worthington, RP	11
J. Perry, RP	9
Z. Versalles, SS	9
R. Rollins, 3B	7
R. Kline, RP	5
R. Nixon, C	5
J. Zimmerman, C	5
R. Reese, 1B	3
J. Roland, RP	3
E. Battey, C	2
W. Bond, OF	1
M. Grant, SP	1
C. Hardy, OF	1
H. Izquierdo, C	1
F. Kostro, OF	1

New York (72-90)	WS
Hitting	**97.2**
Fielding	**35.0**
Pitching	**83.8**
M. Mantle, 1B	25
H. Clarke, 2B	22
A. Downing, SP	16
M. Stottlemyre, SP	16
J. Pepitone, OF	14
T. Tresh, OF	13
D. Womack, RP	13
B. Monbouquette, RP	12
S. Whitaker, OF	10
C. Smith, 3B	8
R. Amaro, SS	7
J. Gibbs, C	7
D. Howser, 2B	6
F. Peterson, SP	6
J. Verbanic, RP	6
W. Ford, SP	4
J. Kenney, SS	4
R. White, OF	4
S. Barber, SP	3
S. Hamilton, RP	3
E. Howard, C	2
J. Kennedy, SS	2
B. Robinson, OF	2
F. Talbot, SP	2
B. Tillman, C	2
T. Tillotson, RP	2
B. Bryan, C	1
L. Clinton, OF	1
F. Fernandez, C	1
M. Hegan, 1B	1
T. Shopay, OF	1

Washington (76-85)	WS
Hitting	**104.0**
Fielding	**39.5**
Pitching	**84.6**
F. Howard, OF	28
K. McMullen, 3B	20
F. Valentine, OF	18
P. Ortega, SP	14
P. Casanova, C	12
D. Knowles, RP	12
T. Cullen, SS	11
D. Baldwin, RP	10
M. Epstein, 1B	10
C. Pascual, SP	10
C. Peterson, OF	10
F. Bertaina, SP	6
D. Bosman, SP	6
E. Brinkman, SS	6
B. Priddy, RP	6
C. Cox, RP	5
B. Humphreys, RP	5
B. Moore, SP	5
B. Saverine, 2B	5
D. Lines, RP	4
D. Nen, 1B	4
B. Allen, 2B	3
H. Allen, OF	3
F. Coggins, 2B	3
J. King, OF	3
E. Stroud, OF	3
B. Chance, 1B	2
D. Camilli, C	1
J. Coleman, SP	1
K. Harrelson, 1B	1
B. Narum, SP	1

1967
National League

Atlanta (77-85)	WS
Hitting	**111.9**
Fielding	**37.4**
Pitching	**81.7**
H. Aaron, OF	34
P. Niekro, RP	21
M. Jones, OF	18
J. Torre, C	18
C. Boyer, 3B	17
F. Alou, 1B	15
K. Johnson, SP	15
R. Carty, OF	12
D. Lemaster, SP	12
D. Menke, SS	12
P. Jarvis, SP	10
W. Woodward, 2B	7
J. Ritchie, RP	6
C. Upshaw, RP	6
T. Francona, 1B	5
D. Kelley, RP	4
C. Raymond, RP	4
M. Martinez, SS	3
F. Millan, 2B	3
R. Hernandez, RP	2
W. Blasingame, RP	1
M. de la Hoz, 2B	1
G. Geiger, OF	1

Player	WS
R. Hermoso, SS	1
G. Oliver, C	1
R. Reed, SP	1
B. Uecker, C	1

Chicago (87-74)	WS
Hitting	**133.2**
Fielding	**42.7**
Pitching	**85.1**
R. Santo, 3B	38
B. Williams, OF	28
A. Phillips, OF	26
R. Hundley, C	22
F. Jenkins, SP	21
G. Beckert, 2B	18
E. Banks, 1B	17
B. Hands, RP	13
R. Nye, SP	13
J. Niekro, SP	10
C. Hartenstein, RP	8
K. Holtzman, SP	8
D. Kessinger, SS	8
T. Savage, OF	7
R. Culp, SP	6
A. Spangler, OF	4
B. Stoneman, RP	4
C. Jones, OF	3
L. Thomas, OF	2
J. Ellis, RP	1
R. Gardner, RP	1
C. Koonce, RP	1
P. Popovich, SS	1
J. Stephenson, C	1

Cincinnati (87-75)	WS
Hitting	**93.0**
Fielding	**52.3**
Pitching	**115.7**
T. Abernathy, RP	24
V. Pinson, OF	24
P. Rose, OF	24
T. Perez, 3B	23
G. Nolan, SP	19
M. Queen, SP	17
M. Pappas, SP	14
J. Maloney, SP	13
T. Helms, 2B	12
L. May, 1B	12
L. Cardenas, SS	11
T. Harper, OF	10
D. Nottebart, RP	8
S. Ellis, SP	7
D. Pavletich, C	7
D. Johnson, 1B	6
G. Arrigo, RP	5
J. Edwards, C	4
B. McCool, RP	4
F. Robinson, OF	3
C. Ruiz, 2B	3
J. Bench, C	2
B. Lee, RP	2
A. Shamsky, OF	2
D. Simpson, OF	2
J. Coker, C	1
T. Davidson, RP	1
J. Tsitouris, SP-RP	1

Houston (69-93)	WS
Hitting	**136.2**
Fielding	**26.5**
Pitching	**44.3**
R. Staub, OF	28
J. Wynn, OF	28
J. Morgan, 2B	26
B. Aspromonte, 3B	18
M. Cuellar, SP	13
E. Mathews, 1B	10
D. Wilson, SP	10
R. Davis, OF	8
J. Gotay, 2B	7
S. Jackson, SS	7
D. Rader, 1B	7
R. Brand, C	6
D. Giusti, SP	6
L. Dierker, SP	5
J. Landis, OF	5
J. Bateman, C	3
C. Harrison, 1B	3
J. Brandt, 1B	2
D. Coombs, RP	2
D. Eilers, RP	2
C. Raymond, RP	2
D. Adlesh, C	1
H. King, C	1
B. Latman, RP	1
B. Lillis, SS	1
N. Miller, OF	1
I. Murrell, OF	1
A. Pointer, OF	1
H. Reed, SP-RP	1
C. Sembera, RP	1

Los Angeles (73-89)	WS
Hitting	**99.7**
Fielding	**35.1**
Pitching	**84.2**
D. Drysdale, SP	18
J. Lefebvre, 3B	16
C. Osteen, SP	16
W. Davis, OF	15
A. Ferrara, OF	15
W. Parker, 1B	15
B. Singer, SP	15
R. Hunt, 2B	14
J. Roseboro, C	13
R. Perranoski, RP	12
L. Johnson, OF	11
R. Fairly, OF	9
J. Brewer, RP	8
L. Gabrielson, OF	7
P. Regan, RP	7
D. Sutton, SP	7
B. Bailey, 3B	6
D. Schofield, SS	5
N. Oliver, 2B	3
G. Michael, SS	2
J. Torborg, C	2
L. Alcaraz, 2B	1
J. Campanis, C	1
A. Foster, SP-RP	1

New York (61-101)	WS
Hitting	**74.8**
Fielding	**36.2**
Pitching	**72.0**
T. Seaver, SP	21
T. Davis, OF	19
R. Swoboda, OF	15
B. Harrelson, SS	13
B. Johnson, 2B	10
J. Buchek, 2B	9
E. Kranepool, 1B	9
R. Taylor, RP	9
E. Charles, 3B	8
C. Jones, OF	7
D. Cardwell, SP	6
D. Selma, RP	6
K. Boyer, 3B	5
D. Shaw, RP	5
J. Fisher, SP	3
D. Frisella, SP	3
J. Grote, C	3
B. Hendley, SP	3
C. Koonce, SP	3
H. Reniff, RP	3
B. Graham, SP	2
J. Grzenda, RP	2
J. Hamilton, RP	2
B. Heise, 2B	2
L. Rohr, SP	2
B. Shaw, SP	2
L. Stahl, OF	2
D. Bosch, OF	1
K. Boswell, 2B	1
J. Lamabe, RP	1
P. Linz, 2B	1
A. Luplow, OF	1
T. Reynolds, OF	1
J. Sullivan, C	1
H. Taylor, C	1
R. Terry, RP	1

Philadelphia (82-80)	WS
Hitting	**107.5**
Fielding	**42.6**
Pitching	**95.9**
D. Allen, 3B	29
T. Gonzalez, OF	26
J. Bunning, SP	25
J. Callison, OF	17
C. Short, SP	16
L. Jackson, SP	14
T. Farrell, RP	13
D. Lock, OF	13
C. Rojas, 2B	12
B. White, 1B	11
R. Wise, SP	11
D. Hall, RP	10
J. Briggs, OF	9
G. Oliver, C	7
T. Taylor, 1B	7
B. Wine, SS	7
C. Dalrymple, C	5
G. Sutherland, SS	4
J. Boozer, RP	3
G. Jackson, RP	3
D. Ellsworth, SP	1
D. Groat, SS	1
C. Hiller, 2B	1
R. Joseph, 1B	1

Pittsburgh (81-81)	WS
Hitting	**142.9**
Fielding	**35.1**
Pitching	**65.1**
R. Clemente, OF	35
M. Alou, OF	23
W. Stargell, OF	20
M. Wills, 3B	20
G. Alley, SS	19
B. Mazeroski, 2B	14
M. Mota, OF	14
J. May, C	11
A. McBean, RP	11
R. Face, RP	10
T. Sisk, SP	10
D. Clendenon, 1B	9
B. Veale, SP	9
D. Ribant, SP	8
J. Pagan, 3B	6
J. Pizarro, RP	5
S. Blass, SP-RP	4
B. Dal Canton, RP	3
J. Pagliaroni, C	2
M. Sanguillen, C	2
W. Fryman, SP	1
M. Jimenez, OF	1
V. Law, RP	1
A. Luplow, OF	1
P. Mikkelsen, RP	1
B. Moose, SP	1
A. Rodgers, 1B	1
J. Shellenback, RP	1

San Francisco (91-71)	WS
Hitting	**122.2**
Fielding	**48.7**
Pitching	**102.1**
J. Hart, 3B	29
W. McCovey, 1B	24
T. Haller, C	21
W. Mays, OF	21
M. McCormick, SP	20
G. Perry, SP	20
F. Linzy, RP	15
R. Sadecki, SP	15
J. Marichal, SP	14
J. Alou, OF	12
O. Brown, OF	11
J. Davenport, 3B	11
H. Lanier, SS	9
T. Fuentes, 2B	7
J. Hiatt, 1B	7
R. Herbel, RP	6
D. Dietz, C	5
J. Gibbon, RP	5
T. Cline, OF	4
B. Henry, RP	3
L. McDaniel, RP	3
B. Schroder, 2B	3
B. Etheridge, 3B	2
K. Henderson, OF	2
B. Bolin, RP	1
N. Chavez, RP	1
D. Groat, SS	1
N. Siebern, 1B	1

St. Louis (101-60)	WS
Hitting	**152.2**
Fielding	**45.7**
Pitching	**105.1**
O. Cepeda, 1B	34
L. Brock, OF	30
T. McCarver, C	30
C. Flood, OF	26
D. Hughes, SP	18
J. Javier, 2B	17
R. Maris, OF	17
N. Briles, RP	16
S. Carlton, SP	13
B. Gibson, SP	12
D. Maxvill, SS	12
M. Shannon, 3B	12
L. Jaster, SP	10
J. Hoerner, RP	9
R. Washburn, SP	9
B. Tolan, OF	8
R. Willis, RP	8
A. Jackson, RP	4
J. Lamabe, RP	4
P. Gagliano, 2B	3
A. Johnson, OF	3
D. Ricketts, C	3
J. Cosman, SP-RP	2
E. Bressoud, SS	1
J. Romano, C	1
E. Spiezio, 3B	1

1968 American League

Baltimore (91-71)	WS
Hitting	**128.6**
Fielding	**46.6**
Pitching	**97.8**
D. McNally, SP	26
D. Buford, OF	25
B. Robinson, 3B	25
F. Robinson, OF	24
B. Powell, 1B	22
J. Hardin, SP	16
D. Johnson, 2B	16
T. Phoebus, SP	15
C. Blefary, OF	13
P. Blair, OF	11
M. Belanger, SS	10
A. Etchebarren, C	8
E. Watt, RP	8
M. Drabowsky, RP	7
D. Leonhard, SP	6
E. Hendricks, C	5
C. Motton, OF	5
R. Nelson, RP	5
M. Rettenmund, OF	5
P. Richert, RP	5
G. Brabender, RP	4
W. Bunker, SP	4
L. Haney, C	2
D. May, OF	2
J. Morris, RP	2
B. Howard, SP-RP	1
F. Valentine, OF	1

Boston (86-76)	WS
Hitting	**136.6**
Fielding	**39.4**
Pitching	**82.1**
C. Yastrzemski, OF	39
K. Harrelson, OF	28
R. Smith, OF	25
M. Andrews, 2B	24
J. Foy, 3B	19
R. Culp, SP	15
R. Petrocelli, SS	15
D. Ellsworth, SP	13
G. Bell, SP	11
J. Santiago, SP	11
S. Lyle, RP	7
E. Howard, C	6
L. Stange, RP	6
J. Pizarro, SP	5
D. Jones, 1B	4
B. Landis, RP	4
J. Lonborg, SP	4
D. Morehead, SP	4
R. Gibson, C	3
J. Tartabull, OF	3
G. Waslewski, RP	3
J. Adair, SS	2
L. Alvarado, SS	1
J. Lahoud, OF	1
J. Moses, C	1
R. Nixon, C	1
G. Roggenburk, RP	1
G. Scott, 1B	1
G. Thomas, OF	1

California (67-95)	WS
Hitting	**110.9**
Fielding	**31.8**
Pitching	**58.3**
J. Fregosi, SS	22
R. Reichardt, OF	21
B. Knoop, 2B	15
G. Brunet, SP	13
V. Davalillo, OF	13
D. Mincher, 1B	13
R. Repoz, OF	13
T. Satriano, C	12
J. McGlothlin, SP	8
A. Messersmith, RP	7
T. Murphy, SP	7
M. Pattin, RP	6
B. Morton, OF	5
P. Schaal, 3B	5
C. Wright, RP	5
S. Ellis, SP	4
C. Hinton, 1B	4
E. Kirkpatrick, OF	4
A. Rodriguez, 3B	4
J. Johnstone, OF	3
B. Rodgers, C	3
J. Hall, OF	2
J. Hamilton, RP	2
M. Rojas, RP	2
D. Bennett, RP	1
T. Burgmeier, RP	1
R. Clark, SP	1
C. Cottier, 3B	1
B. Heffner, RP	1
S. Kealey, RP	1
O. McFarlane, C	1
J. Weaver, RP	1

Chicago (67-95)	WS
Hitting	**75.0**
Fielding	**39.8**
Pitching	**86.3**
L. Aparicio, SS	19
W. Wood, RP	19
T. John, SP	15
P. Ward, 3B	15
D. Josephson, C	14
J. Horlen, SP	13
T. McCraw, 1B	12
H. Wilhelm, RP	12
K. Berry, OF	11
B. Locker, RP	9
T. Davis, OF	8
J. Fisher, SP	7
S. Alomar, 2B	6
J. McNertney, C	6
L. Wagner, OF	5
B. Bradford, OF	4
D. McMahon, RP	4
B. Melton, 3B	4
J. Nyman, SP	3
G. Peters, SP	3
T. Cullen, 2B	2
R. Hansen, 3B	2
B. Priddy, SP	2
W. Causey, 2B	1
G. Hopkins, 1B	1
D. Kenworthy, 3B	1
F. Rath, RP	1
B. Voss, OF	1
W. Williams, OF	1

Cleveland (86-75)	WS
Hitting	**103.1**
Fielding	**49.6**
Pitching	**105.2**
L. Tiant, SP	28
S. McDowell, SP	23
J. Cardenal, OF	21
D. Sims, C	18
L. Brown, SS	17
T. Horton, 1B	16
S. Williams, SP	16
J. Azcue, C	15
V. Romo, RP	14
S. Siebert, SP	11
M. Alvis, 3B	10
L. Maye, OF	10
R. Snyder, OF	9
V. Fuller, 2B	7
T. Harper, OF	7
L. Johnson, OF	7
D. Nelson, 2B	7
E. Fisher, RP	6
V. Davalillo, OF	3
H. Pina, RP	3
C. Salmon, 2B	3
B. Harris, 2B	2

M. Paul, RP	2
J. Hall, OF	1
S. Hargan, SP	1
R. Scheinblum, OF	1

Detroit (103-59)	WS
Hitting	**149.5**
Fielding	**51.6**
Pitching	**107.9**
B. Freehan, C	35
D. McLain, SP	33
W. Horton, OF	28
D. McAuliffe, 2B	28
J. Northrup, OF	24
N. Cash, 1B	18
A. Kaline, OF	18
M. Stanley, OF	18
E. Wilson, SP	17
M. Lolich, SP	12
J. Hiller, RP	11
P. Dobson, RP	9
G. Brown, OF	8
D. Patterson, RP	7
D. Wert, 3B	7
J. Sparma, SP	5
F. Lasher, RP	4
D. McMahon, RP	4
R. Oyler, SS	4
T. Matchick, SS	3
D. Tracewski, SS	3
J. Warden, RP	3
J. Wyatt, RP	3
E. Mathews, 1B-3B	2
J. Price, C	2
D. Ribant, RP	2
L. Cain, SP-RP	1

Minnesota (79-83)	WS
Hitting	**107.8**
Fielding	**36.7**
Pitching	**92.6**
C. Tovar, OF	22
D. Chance, SP	21
T. Oliva, OF	21
T. Uhlaender, OF	18
B. Allison, OF	16
R. Carew, 2B	13
J. Kaat, SP	13
J. Perry, SP	13
H. Killebrew, 1B	12
J. Merritt, SP	11
D. Boswell, SP	10
J. Roseboro, C	10
A. Worthington, RP	10
F. Quilici, 2B	7
R. Reese, 1B	7
R. Perranoski, RP	6
B. Look, C	4
B. Miller, RP	4
R. Rollins, 3B	4
G. Nettles, OF	3
R. Clark, 3B	2
T. Hall, SP-RP	2
R. Renick, SS	2
J. Roland, RP	2
J. Hernandez, SS	1
R. Keller, RP	1
F. Kostro, OF	1
J. Zimmerman, C	1

New York (83-79)	WS
Hitting	**117.0**
Fielding	**39.1**
Pitching	**92.8**
R. White, OF	29
M. Mantle, 1B	24
S. Bahnsen, SP	23
M. Stottlemyre, SP	22
J. Pepitone, OF	15
T. Tresh, SS	15
F. Peterson, SP	13
B. Cox, 3B	12
H. Clarke, 2B	11
A. Kosco, OF	11
B. Robinson, OF	10
J. Gibbs, C	9
L. McDaniel, RP	9
F. Fernandez, C	8
S. Hamilton, RP	8
R. Colavito, OF	5
J. Verbanic, RP	5
S. Barber, SP	4
D. Howser, 2B	3
D. Womack, RP	3
A. Downing, SP	2
C. Smith, 3B	2
F. Talbot, RP	2
J. Bouton, RP	1
M. Ferraro, 3B	1
G. Michael, SS	1
E. Rodriguez, C	1

Oakland (82-80)	WS
Hitting	**128.6**
Fielding	**39.6**
Pitching	**77.8**
B. Campaneris, SS	29
R. Monday, OF	26
R. Jackson, OF	25
S. Bando, 3B	21
D. Cater, 1B	17
B. Odom, SP	17
J. Nash, SP	16
M. Hershberger, OF	10
C. Hunter, SP	10
L. Krausse, SP	10
C. Dobson, SP	9
J. Donaldson, 2B	9
D. Green, 2B	8
D. Segui, RP	8
J. Pagliaroni, C	7
P. Lindblad, RP	4
D. Duncan, C	3
T. Kubiak, 2B	3
E. Sprague, RP	3
R. Webster, 1B	3
J. Aker, RP	2
J. Keough, OF	2
F. Robinson, OF	2
J. Gosger, OF	1
J. Rudi, OF	1

Washington (65-96)	WS
Hitting	**126.6**
Fielding	**26.4**
Pitching	**42.1**
F. Howard, OF	38
K. McMullen, 3B	24
M. Epstein, 1B	14
B. Allen, 2B	13
D. Unser, OF	12
C. Pascual, SP	9
E. Stroud, OF	8
B. Alyea, OF	7
J. Coleman, SP	7
J. Hannan, SP	6
R. Hansen, SS	6
T. Cullen, SS	5
D. Higgins, RP	5
G. Holman, 1B	5
D. Bosman, RP	4
B. Bryan, C	3
J. French, C	3
B. Humphreys, RP	3
D. Knowles, RP	3
B. Moore, SP	3
C. Peterson, OF	3
H. Allen, OF	2
S. Bowens, OF	2
E. Brinkman, SS	2
P. Casanova, C	2
F. Valentine, OF	2
D. Baldwin, RP	1
D. Billings, OF	1
F. Coggins, 2B	1
G. Martin, OF	1

1968 National League

Atlanta (81-81)	WS
Hitting	**107.4**
Fielding	**42.1**
Pitching	**93.5**
H. Aaron, OF	32
F. Alou, OF	31
P. Jarvis, SP	19
P. Niekro, SP	18
F. Millan, 2B	17
J. Torre, C	15
T. Francona, OF	12
C. Upshaw, RP	12
M. Pappas, SP	11
R. Reed, SP	8
G. Stone, SP	7
S. Jackson, SS	6
M. Martinez, SS	6
C. Raymond, RP	6
C. Boyer, 3B	5
J. Britton, RP	5
D. Johnson, 1B	5
D. Kelley, RP	5
T. Aaron, OF	4
B. Johnson, 3B	4
K. Johnson, SP	4
B. Tillman, C	4
M. Lum, OF	3
S. Valdespino, OF	2
G. Garrido, SS	1
W. Hriniak, C	1

Chicago (84-78)	WS
Hitting	**123.1**
Fielding	**43.9**
Pitching	**85.0**
B. Williams, OF	30
R. Santo, 3B	28
F. Jenkins, SP	25
G. Beckert, 2B	23
P. Regan, RP	19
E. Banks, 1B	18
B. Hands, SP	18
A. Phillips, OF	16
D. Kessinger, SS	14
R. Hundley, C	13
K. Holtzman, SP	10
W. Smith, OF	7
A. Spangler, OF	6
J. Hickman, OF	5
J. Niekro, SP	5
L. Johnson, OF	4
R. Nye, SP	4
J. Lamabe, RP	2
J. Arcia, OF	1
C. Hartenstein, RP	1
G. Oliver, 1B	1
G. Ross, RP	1
J. Upham, RP-OF	1

Cincinnati (83-79)	WS
Hitting	**141.0**
Fielding	**37.1**
Pitching	**70.9**
P. Rose, OF	32
T. Perez, 3B	25
J. Bench, C	24
L. May, 1B	20
A. Johnson, OF	19
V. Pinson, OF	15
C. Carroll, RP	14
T. Abernathy, RP	13
T. Helms, 2B	13
G. Nolan, SP	11
G. Culver, SP	10
J. Maloney, SP	10
G. Arrigo, SP	9
M. Jones, OF	8
L. Cardenas, SS	5
F. Whitfield, 1B	4
T. Cloninger, SP	3
D. Pavletich, 1B	3
C. Ruiz, 2B	3
J. Beauchamp, OF	2
P. Corrales, C	2
B. Kelso, RP	2
J. Ritchie, RP	1
W. Woodward, SS	1

Houston (72-90)	WS
Hitting	**106.4**
Fielding	**33.8**
Pitching	**75.8**
J. Wynn, OF	32
R. Staub, 1B	28
D. Menke, 2B	21
D. Giusti, SP	13
D. Lemaster, SP	13
D. Rader, 3B	13
M. Cuellar, SP	12
D. Wilson, SP	11
L. Dierker, SP	10
J. Bateman, C	8
N. Miller, OF	8
J. Buzhardt, RP	6
B. Aspromonte, 3B	5
J. Ray, RP	5
H. Torres, SS	5
S. Shea, RP	4
D. Coombs, RP	3
R. Davis, OF	3
D. Simpson, OF	3
J. Gotay, 2B	2
L. McFadden, SS	2
J. Morgan, 2B	2
B. Watson, OF	2
D. Adlesh, C	1
R. Brand, C	1
B. Browne, OF	1
J. Herrera, OF	1
L. Thomas, OF	1

Los Angeles (76-86)	WS
Hitting	**103.2**
Fielding	**38.0**
Pitching	**86.9**
T. Haller, C	27
W. Davis, OF	19
D. Drysdale, SP	18
L. Gabrielson, OF	13
D. Sutton, SP	13
W. Parker, 1B	12
B. Singer, SP	12
J. Brewer, RP	10
B. Bailey, 3B	9
R. Fairly, OF	9
J. Lefebvre, 2B	9
P. Popovich, 2B	9
J. Billingham, RP	8
K. Boyer, 3B	8
M. Grant, RP	8
C. Osteen, SP	8
W. Crawford, OF	7
B. Sudakis, 3B	6
H. Aguirre, RP	5
Z. Versalles, SS	5
J. Purdin, RP	3
A. Foster, SP	2
J. Torborg, C	2
L. Alcaraz, 2B	1
R. Colavito, OF	1
J. Fairey, OF	1
P. Regan, RP	1
T. Savage, OF	1
B. Shirley, SS	1

New York (73-89)	WS
Hitting	**73.0**
Fielding	**47.2**
Pitching	**98.7**
J. Koosman, SP	23
T. Seaver, SP	23

C. Jones, OF	20
J. Grote, C	16
E. Charles, 3B	14
R. Swoboda, OF	14
C. Koonce, RP	11
D. Selma, SP	10
A. Shamsky, OF	10
D. Cardwell, SP	8
R. Taylor, RP	8
K. Boswell, 2B	7
B. Harrelson, SS	6
J. Martin, C	6
J. McAndrew, SP	6
N. Ryan, SP	6
L. Stahl, OF	6
T. Agee, OF	5
E. Kranepool, 1B	4
A. Jackson, RP	3
A. Weis, SS	3
J. Buchek, 3B	2
P. Linz, 2B	2
D. Shaw, RP	2
D. Bosch, OF	1
K. Collins, 3B	1
D. Frisella, RP	1
G. Goossen, 1B	1

Philadelphia (76-86)	WS
Hitting	**123.9**
Fielding	**33.6**
Pitching	**70.5**
D. Allen, OF	32
C. Short, SP	18
T. Taylor, 3B	17
J. Briggs, OF	16
J. Callison, OF	16
L. Jackson, SP	15
R. Pena, SS	14
W. Fryman, SP	13
T. Gonzalez, OF	13
B. White, 1B	12
C. Rojas, 2B	10
G. Wagner, RP	7
C. Dalrymple, C	5
D. Lock, OF	5
G. Sutherland, 2B	5
T. Farrell, RP	4
J. Johnson, SP	4
M. Ryan, C	4
J. Boozer, RP	3
G. Jackson, RP	3
R. Joseph, 1B	3
R. Wise, SP	3
D. Clemens, OF	2
D. Hall, RP	1
L. Hisle, OF	1
J. James, RP	1
B. Wine, SS	1

Pittsburgh (80-82)	WS
Hitting	**113.6**
Fielding	**41.8**
Pitching	**84.6**
R. Clemente, OF	25
M. Alou, OF	23
S. Blass, SP	17
D. Clendenon, 1B	17
B. Veale, SP	17
W. Stargell, OF	16
M. Wills, 3B	16
G. Alley, SS	13
R. Kline, RP	13
B. Mazeroski, 2B	13
B. Moose, SP	9
M. Mota, OF	9
J. May, C	8
D. Ellis, RP	6
R. Face, RP	6
F. Patek, SS	6
A. McBean, SP	5
L. Walker, RP	4
M. Jimenez, OF	3
J. Pagan, 3B	3
T. Sisk, RP	3
C. Cannizzaro, C	2
B. Dal Canton, RP	2
G. Kolb, OF	2
J. Bunning, SP	1
C. Hiller, 2B	1

San Francisco (88-74)	WS
Hitting	**135.6**
Fielding	**37.9**
Pitching	**90.5**
W. McCovey, 1B	34
W. Mays, OF	30
J. Marichal, SP	24
R. Hunt, 2B	21
J. Hart, 3B	19
G. Perry, SP	19
B. Bolin, SP	15
B. Bonds, OF	15
D. Dietz, C	14
R. Sadecki, SP	12
F. Linzy, RP	11
J. Hiatt, C	9
H. Lanier, SS	8
J. Alou, OF	6
D. Marshall, OF	6
M. McCormick, SP	6
J. Gibbon, RP	4
B. Barton, C	3
T. Cline, OF	3
J. Davenport, 3B	3
O. Brown, OF	1
F. Johnson, 3B	1

St. Louis (97-65)	WS
Hitting	**133.1**
Fielding	**49.5**
Pitching	**108.4**
B. Gibson, SP	36
L. Brock, OF	31
C. Flood, OF	27
M. Shannon, 3B	23
D. Maxvill, SS	20
O. Cepeda, 1B	17
J. Javier, 2B	16
R. Washburn, SP	15
N. Briles, SP	14
T. McCarver, C	14
J. Hoerner, RP	12
S. Carlton, SP	11
R. Maris, OF	11
J. Edwards, C	6
L. Jaster, SP	5
D. Schofield, SS	5
B. Tolan, OF	5
W. Granger, RP	4
P. Gagliano, 2B	3
D. Hughes, RP	3
M. Nelson, RP	3
R. Willis, RP	3
D. Simpson, OF	2
M. Torrez, RP	2
R. Davis, OF	1
J. Hague, OF	1
P. Mikkelsen, RP	1

1969
American League

Baltimore (109-53)	WS
Hitting	**154.1**
Fielding	**52.4**
Pitching	**120.5**
F. Robinson, OF	32
P. Blair, OF	28
B. Powell, 1B	27
D. Buford, OF	24
M. Cuellar, SP	24
D. Johnson, 2B	19
M. Belanger, SS	18
J. Palmer, SP	18
D. McNally, SP	17
B. Robinson, 3B	17
E. Watt, RP	13
E. Hendricks, C	12
T. Phoebus, SP	11
D. Hall, RP	9
P. Richert, RP	9
A. Etchebarren, C	8
D. Leonhard, RP	8
J. Hardin, SP	6
M. Rettenmund, OF	6
C. Motton, OF	5
C. Salmon, 1B	4
C. Dalrymple, C	3
M. Lopez, RP	3
D. May, OF	2
A. Severinsen, RP	2
F. Bertaina, RP	1
B. Floyd, 2B-SS	1

Boston (87-75)	WS
Hitting	**134.9**
Fielding	**42.4**
Pitching	**83.7**
R. Petrocelli, SS	37
C. Yastrzemski, OF	26
M. Andrews, 2B	24
R. Smith, OF	24
G. Scott, 3B	15
R. Culp, SP	14
S. Lyle, RP	14
M. Nagy, SP	14
T. Conigliaro, OF	13
V. Romo, RP	11
S. Siebert, SP	9
D. Schofield, 2B	7
L. Stange, RP	7
S. O'Brien, 3B	6
D. Jones, 1B	5
J. Lonborg, SP	5
B. Conigliaro, OF	4
J. Lahoud, OF	4
J. Moses, C	4
R. Gibson, C	3
R. Jarvis, RP	3
B. Landis, RP	2
B. Lee, RP	2
G. Thomas, OF	2
K. Brett, SP	1
D. Ellsworth, SP	1
M. Garman, SP	1
K. Harrelson, 1B	1
D. Lock, OF	1
T. Satriano, C	1

California (71-91)	WS
Hitting	**82.1**
Fielding	**41.5**
Pitching	**89.4**
J. Fregosi, SS	26
A. Messersmith, SP	22
K. Tatum, RP	20
J. Johnstone, OF	17
R. Reichardt, OF	12
S. Alomar, 2B	11
R. May, SP	10
J. McGlothlin, SP	10
J. Spencer, 1B	10
A. Rodriguez, 3B	9
B. Voss, OF	9
H. Wilhelm, RP	9
B. Morton, OF	8
T. Murphy, SP	6
J. Azcue, C	5
E. Fisher, RP	5
G. Brunet, SP	4
T. Satriano, C	4
B. Cowan, OF	3
T. Egan, C	2
S. Kealey, RP	2
R. Repoz, OF	2
R. Amaro, 1B	1
R. Brown, C	1
V. Geishert, RP	1
L. Johnson, OF	1
B. Knoop, 2B	1
B. Rodgers, C	1
C. Wright, RP	1

Chicago (68-94)	WS
Hitting	**87.1**
Fielding	**36.8**
Pitching	**80.1**
L. Aparicio, SS	20
T. John, SP	17
J. Horlen, SP	15
C. May, OF	14
B. Melton, 3B	14
W. Wood, RP	14
W. Williams, OF	12
G. Hopkins, 1B	9
G. Peters, SP	9
B. Bradford, OF	8
B. Knoop, 2B	8
B. Wynne, SP	7
E. Herrmann, C	6
D. Pavletich, C	6
P. Ward, 1B	6
P. Edmondson, SP	5
D. Murphy, RP	5
D. Osinski, RP	5
K. Berry, OF	4
T. McCraw, 1B	4
R. Hansen, 2B	3
A. Bravo, OF	2
B. Johnson, SP	2
D. Josephson, C	2
R. Morales, 2B	2
S. Alomar, 2B	1
C. Carlos, RP	1
B. Christian, OF	1
W. Held, OF	1
J. Nyman, SP-RP	1

Cleveland (62-99)	WS
Hitting	**95.0**
Fielding	**31.1**
Pitching	**60.0**
S. McDowell, SP	20
T. Horton, 1B	19
K. Harrelson, OF	17
D. Sims, C	17
J. Cardenal, OF	14
L. Tiant, SP	11
L. Brown, SS	10
L. Klimchock, 3B	9
S. Williams, RP	8
V. Fuller, 2B	6
M. Paul, RP	6
J. Pizarro, RP	6
E. Leon, SS	5
F. Baker, OF	4
D. Ellsworth, SP	4
R. Snyder, OF	4
K. Suarez, C	4
Z. Versalles, 2B	4
C. Hinton, OF	3
L. Maye, OF	2
C. Peterson, OF	2
M. Alvis, 3B	1
J. Azcue, C	1
R. Fosse, C	1
P. Hennigan, RP	1
G. Kroll, RP	1
R. Nagelson, OF	1
D. Nelson, 2B	1
H. Pina, RP	1
V. Romo, RP	1
R. Scheinblum, OF	1
S. Siebert, SP	1

Detroit (90-72)	WS
Hitting	**123.7**
Fielding	**44.3**
Pitching	**102.0**
D. McLain, SP	29
J. Northrup, OF	27
N. Cash, 1B	21
B. Freehan, C	20

M. Lolich, SP	20
W. Horton, OF	19
A. Kaline, OF	17
D. McAuliffe, 2B	13
M. Stanley, OF	13
E. Wilson, SP	13
D. Wert, 3B	10
M. Kilkenny, RP	9
T. Tresh, SS	9
P. Dobson, RP	7
J. Price, C	7
I. Brown, 2B	5
J. Hiller, RP	5
D. McMahon, RP	5
T. Timmermann, RP	5
T. Matchick, 2B	4
F. Lasher, RP	3
B. Reed, RP	2
J. Sparma, SP	2
C. Gutierrez, SS	1
D. Patterson, RP	1
D. Radatz, RP	1
D. Tracewski, SS	1
R. Woods, OF	1

Kansas City (69-93)	WS
Hitting	**83.6**
Fielding	**39.7**
Pitching	**83.7**
W. Bunker, SP	16
M. Fiore, 1B	16
J. Foy, 3B	16
P. Kelly, OF	16
L. Piniella, OF	16
M. Drabowsky, RP	13
E. Kirkpatrick, OF	13
R. Nelson, SP	12
D. Drago, SP	10
B. Butler, SP	9
M. Hedlund, RP	8
B. Oliver, OF	8
J. Rooker, SP	8
J. Hernandez, SS	7
E. Rodriguez, C	5
P. Schaal, 3B	5
J. Adair, 2B	3
B. Martinez, C	3
D. Wickersham, RP	3
L. Alcaraz, 2B	2
T. Burgmeier, RP	2
C. Harrison, 1B	2
S. Northey, OF	2
F. Rico, OF	2
H. Taylor, OF	2
J. Campanis, C	1
G. Cisco, RP	1
G. Cram, RP	1
A. Fitzmorris, RP	1
F. Healy, C	1
S. Jones, RP	1
J. Keough, OF	1
J. Rios, 2B	1

Minnesota (97-65)	WS
Hitting	**144.4**
Fielding	**43.8**
Pitching	**102.8**
H. Killebrew, 3B	34
T. Oliva, OF	25
L. Cardenas, SS	23
R. Carew, 2B	21
R. Perranoski, RP	20
J. Perry, SP	20
C. Tovar, OF	19
R. Reese, 1B	17
D. Boswell, SP	16
T. Uhlaender, OF	14
J. Kaat, SP	13
J. Roseboro, C	10
T. Hall, SP	8
B. Miller, RP	8
G. Mitterwald, C	6
D. Woodson, RP	6
B. Allison, OF	5
D. Chance, SP	5
G. Nettles, OF	5
J. Grzenda, RP	3
A. Worthington, RP	3
C. Manuel, OF	2
F. Quilici, 3B	2
R. Renick, 3B	2
J. Crider, RP	1
R. Dempsey, C	1
J. Holt, OF	1
T. Tischinski, C	1

New York (80-81)	WS
Hitting	**95.8**
Fielding	**45.6**
Pitching	**98.6**
M. Stottlemyre, SP	26
H. Clarke, 2B	23
F. Peterson, SP	23
R. White, OF	22
B. Murcer, OF	20
G. Michael, SS	14
J. Aker, RP	12
F. Fernandez, C	12
J. Kenney, 3B	12
J. Pepitone, 1B	12
S. Bahnsen, SP	9
A. Downing, SP-RP	7
B. Burbach, SP	6
L. McDaniel, RP	6
J. Gibbs, C	5
J. Hall, OF	5
B. Cox, 3B	4
S. Hamilton, RP	4
J. Ellis, C	2
M. Kekich, RP	2
R. Klimkowski, RP	2
T. Munson, C	2
T. Tresh, SS	2
R. Woods, OF	2
R. Blomberg, OF	1
L. Boehmer, 1B	1
K. Johnson, RP	1
J. Lyttle, OF	1
B. Robinson, OF	1
D. Simpson, OF	1

Oakland (88-74)	WS
Hitting	**155.4**
Fielding	**37.5**
Pitching	**71.0**
R. Jackson, OF	41
S. Bando, 3B	36
D. Green, 2B	22
R. Monday, OF	20
B. Odom, SP	18
B. Campaneris, SS	16
C. Hunter, SP	13
D. Cater, 1B	10
C. Dobson, SP	9
J. Roland, RP	8
T. Kubiak, SS	7
T. Reynolds, OF	7
P. Roof, C	7
R. Fingers, RP	6
T. Francona, 1B	6
P. Lindblad, RP	6
L. Krausse, RP	5
J. Nash, SP	5
B. Brooks, OF	4
J. Tartabull, OF	4
B. Johnson, 1B	3
M. Lachemann, RP	2
R. Webster, 1B	2
D. Duncan, C	1
L. Haney, C	1
G. Lauzerique, RP	1
J. Pagliaroni, C	1
J. Pizarro, RP	1
J. Rudi, OF	1
E. Sprague, RP	1

Seattle (64-98)	WS
Hitting	**108.9**
Fielding	**26.7**
Pitching	**56.4**
D. Mincher, 1B	18
T. Harper, 2B-3B	17
W. Comer, OF	16
M. Hegan, OF	15
D. Segui, RP	12
T. Davis, OF	10
S. Hovley, OF	10
J. McNertney, C	9
G. Goossen, 1B	8
G. Brabender, SP	7
B. Locker, RP	7
J. Gelnar, RP	6
J. Donaldson, 2B	5
J. O'Donoghue, RP	5
J. Pagliaroni, C	5
F. Talbot, SP	5
J. Bouton, RP	4
J. Kennedy, SS	4
S. Whitaker, OF	4
R. Rollins, 3B	3
S. Barber, SP	2
G. Gil, 3B	2
L. Haney, C	2
M. Marshall, SP	2
R. Oyler, SS	2
D. Baney, RP	1
G. Bell, SP	1
R. Clark, SS	1
M. Fuentes, SP-RP	1
S. Lockwood, SP-RP	1
G. Lund, SS	1
B. Meyer, SP	1
M. Ranew, C	1
G. Roggenburk, SP	1
F. Stanley, SS	1
D. Walton, OF	1
D. Womack, RP	1

Washington (86-76)	WS
Hitting	**136.8**
Fielding	**40.3**
Pitching	**80.9**
F. Howard, OF	34
M. Epstein, 1B	24
K. McMullen, 3B	24
D. Unser, OF	20
D. Bosman, SP	17
E. Brinkman, SS	16
B. Allen, 2B	13
J. Coleman, SP	13
C. Cox, RP	12
D. Knowles, RP	11
J. French, C	8
L. Maye, OF	8
B. Alyea, OF	7
E. Stroud, OF	7
P. Casanova, C	6
J. Hannan, SP	6
D. Higgins, RP	6
H. Allen, OF	5
B. Humphreys, RP	5
B. Moore, SP	4
D. Baldwin, RP	3
T. Cullen, 2B	3
J. Shellenback, RP	2
Z. Versalles, SS	2
C. Carlos, SP	1
J. Dukes, RP	1

1969 National League

Atlanta (93-69)	WS
Hitting	**129.1**
Fielding	**46.9**
Pitching	**103.0**
H. Aaron, OF	38
P. Niekro, SP	28
O. Cepeda, 1B	19
F. Millan, 2B	19
R. Carty, OF	17
R. Reed, SP	16
C. Upshaw, RP	16
C. Boyer, 3B	15
T. Gonzalez, OF	15
F. Alou, OF	13
B. Didier, C	10
G. Stone, SP	10
S. Jackson, SS	8
P. Jarvis, SP	8
M. Pappas, SP	8
J. Britton, SP	6
P. Doyle, RP	5
M. Lum, OF	5
B. Tillman, C	5
B. Aspromonte, OF	4
T. Francona, OF	4
H. Wilhelm, RP	4
G. Garrido, SS	3
G. Neibauer, RP	2
T. Aaron, 1B	1

Chicago (92-70)	WS
Hitting	**117.6**
Fielding	**46.9**
Pitching	**111.5**
B. Hands, SP	28
R. Santo, 3B	26
F. Jenkins, SP	25
B. Williams, OF	24
D. Kessinger, SS	23
R. Hundley, C	21
K. Holtzman, SP	17
E. Banks, 1B	14
G. Beckert, 2B	14
J. Hickman, OF	12
P. Regan, RP	12
D. Selma, SP	11
D. Young, OF	8
T. Abernathy, RP	7
P. Popovich, 2B	6
W. Smith, OF	6
H. Aguirre, RP	5
K. Johnson, RP	2
A. Phillips, OF	2
J. Qualls, OF	2
A. Spangler, OF	2
J. Colborn, RP	1
J. Decker, RP	1
O. Gamble, OF	1
B. Heath, C	1
J. Niekro, SP	1
R. Nye, RP	1
N. Oliver, 2B	1
A. Reynolds, SP	1
K. Rudolph, C	1

Cincinnati (89-73)	WS
Hitting	**165.2**
Fielding	**34.4**
Pitching	**67.4**
P. Rose, OF	37
T. Perez, 3B	31
J. Bench, C	28
B. Tolan, OF	27
L. May, 1B	26
A. Johnson, OF	19
W. Granger, RP	15
J. Maloney, SP	15
C. Carroll, RP	10
J. Merritt, SP	10
G. Nolan, SP	7
T. Helms, 2B	6
W. Woodward, SS	6
J. Stewart, OF	5
T. Savage, OF	4
G. Arrigo, SP	3
P. Corrales, C	3
G. Culver, RP	3
C. Ruiz, 2B	3
D. Chaney, SS	2

Player	WS
T. Cloninger, SP	2
J. Beauchamp, OF	1
A. Jackson, RP	1
M. Queen, SP	1
P. Ramos, RP	1
D. Ribant, RP	1

Houston (81-81)	WS
Hitting	**128.3**
Fielding	**36.2**
Pitching	**78.5**
J. Wynn, OF	36
L. Dierker, SP	25
J. Morgan, 2B	24
D. Menke, SS	21
C. Blefary, 1B	17
D. Rader, 3B	16
D. Lemaster, SP	15
J. Edwards, C	14
N. Miller, OF	13
T. Griffin, SP	11
D. Wilson, SP	8
F. Gladding, RP	6
M. Martinez, OF	6
J. Ray, RP	6
J. Alou, OF	5
J. Billingham, RP	3
G. Geiger, OF	3
D. Womack, RP	3
J. Gotay, 2B	2
S. Valdespino, OF	2
B. Watson, OF	2
J. Bouton, RP	1
D. Bryant, C	1
T. Davis, OF	1
B. Henry, RP	1
K. Lampard, OF	1

Los Angeles (85-77)	WS
Hitting	**116.4**
Fielding	**43.6**
Pitching	**95.0**
C. Osteen, SP	26
B. Singer, SP	26
W. Davis, OF	22
W. Parker, 1B	18
T. Sizemore, 2B	17
M. Wills, SS	17
T. Haller, C	16
D. Sutton, SP	14
B. Sudakis, 3B	13
J. Brewer, RP	12
W. Crawford, OF	12
M. Mota, OF	11
J. Lefebvre, 3B	10
A. Kosco, OF	9
P. Mikkelsen, RP	7
B. Russell, OF	5
J. Bunning, SP	3
L. Gabrielson, OF	3
R. Lamb, RP	2
A. McBean, RP	2
J. Moeller, RP	2
J. Torborg, C	2
D. Drysdale, SP	1
R. Fairly, 1B	1
A. Foster, SP	1

Player	WS
B. Grabarkewitz, SS	1
T. Hutton, 1B	1
P. Popovich, 2B	1

Montreal (52-110)	WS
Hitting	**80.7**
Fielding	**26.5**
Pitching	**48.7**
R. Staub, OF	27
M. Jones, OF	16
C. Laboy, 3B	13
R. Fairly, 1B	9
B. Bailey, 1B	8
D. McGinn, RP	7
J. Robertson, SP	7
B. Stoneman, SP	7
G. Sutherland, 2B	6
G. Waslewski, RP	5
M. Wegener, SP	5
R. Brand, C	4
T. Cline, OF	4
R. Face, RP	4
S. Renko, SP	4
B. Wine, SS	4
H. Reed, RP	3
J. Bateman, C	2
K. Collins, 2B	2
J. Herrera, OF	2
A. Phillips, OF	2
C. Sembera, RP	2
M. Wills, SS	2
J. Boccabella, C	1
D. Clendenon, 1B	1
R. Hermoso, 2B	1
L. Jaster, RP	1
C. Morton, SP	1
M. Mota, OF	1
D. Radatz, RP	1
C. Raymond, RP	1
D. Shaw, RP	1
S. Shea, RP	1
M. Staehle, 2B	1

New York (100-62)	WS
Hitting	**116.8**
Fielding	**52.4**
Pitching	**130.8**
T. Seaver, SP	32
C. Jones, OF	30
T. Agee, OF	28
J. Koosman, SP	25
A. Shamsky, OF	17
G. Gentry, SP	14
J. Grote, C	14
B. Harrelson, SS	14
T. McGraw, RP	14
K. Boswell, 2B	13
R. Taylor, RP	13
D. Cardwell, SP	10
R. Swoboda, OF	10
E. Kranepool, 1B	8
D. Clendenon, 1B	7
W. Garrett, 3B	7
J. McAndrew, SP	7
J. DiLauro, RP	6
N. Ryan, RP	6
R. Gaspar, OF	5

Player	WS
A. Weis, SS	4
E. Charles, 3B	3
D. Dyer, C	3
J. Martin, C	3
C. Koonce, RP	2
B. Pfeil, 3B	2
B. Heise, SS	1
B. Johnson, RP	1
A. Otis, OF	1

Philadelphia (63-99)	WS
Hitting	**105.2**
Fielding	**28.0**
Pitching	**55.9**
D. Allen, 1B	22
L. Hisle, OF	18
J. Callison, OF	17
R. Wise, SP	15
G. Jackson, SP	14
D. Johnson, OF	14
J. Briggs, OF	13
T. Taylor, 3B	12
D. Money, SS	10
R. Joseph, 3B	7
M. Ryan, C	7
W. Fryman, SP	6
T. Harmon, SS	5
J. Johnson, SP	5
T. Farrell, RP	4
B. Wilson, RP	4
J. Boozer, RP	3
A. Raffo, RP	3
R. Stone, OF	3
B. Champion, SP	2
C. Rojas, 2B	2
D. Watkins, C	2
L. Palmer, RP	1

Pittsburgh (88-74)	WS
Hitting	**148.1**
Fielding	**36.2**
Pitching	**79.7**
R. Clemente, OF	28
M. Alou, OF	27
W. Stargell, OF	27
R. Hebner, 3B	20
B. Moose, RP	14
M. Sanguillen, C	14
A. Oliver, 1B	13
B. Veale, SP	12
C. Taylor, OF	11
J. Pagan, 3B	10
D. Ellis, SP	9
B. Dal Canton, RP	8
J. Gibbon, RP	8
F. Patek, SS	8
G. Alley, 2B	7
S. Blass, SP	7
C. Hartenstein, RP	7
J. Bunning, SP	6
B. Mazeroski, 2B	6
L. Walker, RP	5
J. Martinez, 2B	4
J. May, C	4
D. Cash, 2B	3
L. Marone, RP	3
R. Davis, OF	1

Player	WS
J. Jeter, OF	1
J. Shellenback, RP	1

San Diego (52-110)	WS
Hitting	**59.9**
Fielding	**32.0**
Pitching	**64.1**
O. Brown, OF	16
N. Colbert, 1B	16
A. Ferrara, OF	13
J. Niekro, SP	12
C. Kirby, SP	10
D. Kelley, SP	8
A. Santorini, SP	8
E. Spiezio, 3B	8
F. Reberger, RP	7
C. Cannizzaro, C	6
R. Pena, SS	6
J. Baldschun, RP	4
C. Gaston, OF	4
I. Murrell, OF	4
G. Ross, RP	4
T. Sisk, RP	4
T. Gonzalez, OF	3
V. Kelly, 3B	3
B. McCool, RP	3
J. Podres, SP	3
J. Sipin, 2B	3
J. Arcia, 2B	2
T. Dean, SS	2
D. Selma, SP	2
W. Hriniak, C	1
D. Roberts, RP	1
R. Slocum, 2B-3B	1
L. Stahl, OF	1
J. Williams, OF	1

San Francisco (90-72)	WS
Hitting	**134.3**
Fielding	**40.7**
Pitching	**95.1**
W. McCovey, 1B	39
B. Bonds, OF	31
J. Marichal, SP	29
G. Perry, SP	26
R. Hunt, 2B	19
W. Mays, OF	17
M. McCormick, SP	12
F. Linzy, RP	10
D. Dietz, C	9
H. Lanier, SS	9
K. Henderson, OF	8
T. Fuentes, 3B	6
J. Hiatt, C	6
J. Hart, OF	5
D. Marshall, OF	5
D. Mason, 2B	5
B. Bolin, SP	4
B. Burda, 1B	4
J. Davenport, 3B	4
R. Herbel, RP	4
R. Sadecki, SP	4
R. Bryant, SP-RP	3
B. Etheridge, 3B	3
D. McMahon, RP	3
B. Barton, C	1

Player	WS
J. Gibbon, RP	1
C. Gutierrez, 3B	1
J. Harrell, C	1
L. Wagner, OF	1

St. Louis (87-75)	WS
Hitting	**92.9**
Fielding	**52.4**
Pitching	**115.6**
B. Gibson, SP	33
S. Carlton, SP	24
L. Brock, OF	23
J. Torre, 1B	23
C. Flood, OF	20
J. Javier, 2B	17
T. McCarver, C	14
M. Shannon, 3B	12
N. Briles, SP	11
V. Pinson, OF	11
C. Taylor, RP	11
D. Maxvill, SS	10
J. Hoerner, RP	8
M. Torrez, SP	6
R. Washburn, SP	6
M. Grant, RP	5
D. Giusti, SP	4
S. Huntz, SS	4
B. Browne, OF	2
S. Campisi, RP	2
V. Davalillo, OF	2
J. DaVanon, SS	2
T. Hilgendorf, RP	2
C. Coulter, 2B	1
J. Ellis, SP-RP	1
P. Gagliano, 2B	1
J. Hague, OF	1
J. Hicks, OF	1
J. Reuss, SP	1
D. Ricketts, C	1
G. Waslewski, RP	1
R. Willis, RP	1

1970
American League

Baltimore (108-54)	WS
Hitting	**164.1**
Fielding	**49.6**
Pitching	**110.3**
B. Powell, 1B	31
D. Buford, OF	26
F. Robinson, OF	26
J. Palmer, SP	25
D. Johnson, 2B	23
P. Blair, OF	22
D. McNally, SP	22
B. Robinson, 3B	21
M. Rettenmund, OF	19
M. Cuellar, SP	18
M. Belanger, SS	12
E. Hendricks, C	10
P. Richert, RP	10
J. Hardin, SP	8
T. Phoebus, SP	7
E. Watt, RP	7
T. Crowley, OF	6

A. Etchebarren, C	6
D. Hall, RP	6
M. Lopez, RP	5
C. Salmon, SS	4
C. Motton, OF	3
C. Dalrymple, C	2
M. Drabowsky, RP	2
B. Grich, SS	2
J. Oates, C	1

Boston (87-75)	WS
Hitting	**134.7**
Fielding	**39.7**
Pitching	**86.7**
C. Yastrzemski, 1B	36
R. Smith, OF	25
R. Petrocelli, SS	23
T. Conigliaro, OF	18
R. Culp, SP	17
M. Andrews, 2B	16
G. Scott, 3B	15
S. Siebert, SP	14
G. Peters, SP	13
B. Conigliaro, OF	12
K. Brett, RP	9
J. Moses, C	9
V. Romo, RP	7
S. Lyle, RP	6
C. Koonce, RP	5
M. Nagy, SP	5
J. Lonborg, RP	4
T. Satriano, C	4
G. Thomas, OF	4
G. Wagner, RP	4
B. Bolin, RP	3
J. Kennedy, 3B	3
L. Alvarado, 3B	2
J. Lahoud, OF	2
B. Lee, RP	1
B. Montgomery, C	1
R. Moret, RP	1
D. Pavletich, 1B	1
D. Schofield, 2B-3B	1

California (86-76)	WS
Hitting	**123.6**
Fielding	**47.5**
Pitching	**86.9**
J. Fregosi, SS	33
A. Johnson, OF	28
C. Wright, SP	20
S. Alomar, 2B	17
R. Repoz, OF	17
K. McMullen, 3B	15
J. Spencer, 1B	15
A. Messersmith, SP	14
K. Tatum, RP	11
E. Fisher, RP	10
J. Johnstone, OF	10
T. Murphy, SP	8
J. Azcue, C	7
G. Garrett, RP	6
B. Voss, OF	6
B. Cowan, OF	5
T. Egan, C	5
R. May, SP	5
D. LaRoche, RP	4
M. Queen, RP	3
J. Tatum, OF	3
L. Allen, RP	2
T. Gonzalez, OF	2
T. Reynolds, OF	2
M. Rivers, OF	2
A. Rodriguez, 3B	2
C. Ruiz, 3B	2
T. Bradley, SP	1
P. Doyle, RP	1
D. Griffin, 2B	1
S. Kealey, RP	1

Chicago (56-106)	WS
Hitting	**84.2**
Fielding	**26.5**
Pitching	**57.2**
L. Aparicio, SS	18
T. John, SP	17
B. Melton, OF	17
C. May, OF	15
W. Wood, RP	14
E. Herrmann, C	12
K. Berry, OF	10
D. Josephson, C	9
G. Hopkins, 1B	7
B. Knoop, 2B	6
J. Janeski, SP	5
S. O'Brien, 3B	5
J. Crider, RP	4
J. Horlen, SP	4
W. Williams, OF	4
B. Johnson, SP	3
T. McCraw, 1B	3
B. Miller, SP	2
D. Murphy, RP	2
B. Spence, 1B	2
F. Weaver, RP	2
C. Brinkman, C	1
D. Eddy, RP	1
J. Magnuson, RP	1
R. McKinney, 3B	1
R. Morales, SS	1
J. Ortiz, OF	1
L. Stange, RP	1

Cleveland (76-86)	WS
Hitting	**78.5**
Fielding	**46.6**
Pitching	**102.9**
S. McDowell, SP	30
G. Nettles, 3B	18
R. Fosse, C	17
S. Hargan, SP	15
V. Pinson, OF	14
R. Foster, OF	13
E. Leon, 2B	13
D. Sims, C	12
R. Hand, SP	11
D. Chance, RP	9
T. Horton, 1B	9
T. Uhlaender, OF	9
D. Higgins, RP	8
C. Hinton, 1B	7
P. Hennigan, RP	6
J. Heidemann, SS	4
B. Moore, SP	4
R. Austin, RP	3
L. Brown, SS	3
S. Dunning, SP	3
D. Ellsworth, RP	3
F. Lasher, RP	3
B. Bradford, OF	2
B. Miller, RP	2
S. Mingori, RP	2
M. Paul, SP-RP	2
J. Rittwage, RP	2
V. Fuller, 2B	1
K. Harrelson, 1B	1
J. Lowenstein, 2B	1
R. Rollins, 3B	1

Detroit (79-83)	WS
Hitting	**114.2**
Fielding	**37.3**
Pitching	**85.5**
A. Kaline, OF	19
D. McAuliffe, 2B	19
M. Lolich, SP	17
J. Northrup, OF	17
N. Cash, 1B	16
B. Freehan, C	16
W. Horton, OF	15
M. Stanley, OF	13
J. Niekro, SP	12
L. Cain, SP	11
T. Timmermann, RP	11
J. Hiller, RP	10
E. Maddox, 3B	7
C. Gutierrez, SS	6
F. Scherman, RP	6
D. Jones, 2B	5
D. Wert, 3B	5
I. Brown, 2B	4
D. Patterson, RP	4
E. Wilson, SP	4
M. Kilkenny, SP	3
D. McLain, SP	3
J. Price, C	3
G. Brown, OF	2
G. Lamont, C	2
N. McRae, RP	2
B. Reed, RP	2
J. Robertson, RP	1
D. Saunders, RP	1
K. Szotkiewicz, SS	1

Kansas City (65-97)	WS
Hitting	**85.4**
Fielding	**38.6**
Pitching	**71.0**
A. Otis, OF	25
B. Oliver, 1B	16
L. Piniella, OF	15
B. Johnson, SP	14
E. Kirkpatrick, C	12
P. Kelly, OF	11
D. Drago, SP	10
J. Rooker, SP	10
P. Schaal, 3B	9
T. Abernathy, RP	8
J. Keough, OF	7
C. Rojas, 2B	7
A. Fitzmorris, RP	6
T. Burgmeier, RP	5
B. Butler, SP	5
D. Morehead, SP	5
R. Severson, SS	5
E. Rodriguez, C	4
W. Bunker, SP	3
M. Drabowsky, RP	3
J. Hernandez, SS	3
B. Floyd, SS	2
T. Matchick, SS	2
A. Monteagudo, RP	2
B. Sorrell, 3B	2
L. Alcaraz, 2B	1
G. Spriggs, OF	1
K. Wright, RP	1
J. York, RP	1

Milwaukee (65-97)	WS
Hitting	**96.4**
Fielding	**32.2**
Pitching	**66.5**
T. Harper, 3B	33
M. Pattin, SP	15
K. Sanders, RP	15
T. Savage, OF	13
D. Walton, OF	13
M. Hegan, 1B	12
T. Kubiak, 2B	10
P. Roof, C	9
D. May, OF	8
S. Lockwood, SP	6
J. Gelnar, RP	5
L. Krausse, SP	5
J. McNertney, C	5
B. Burda, OF	4
A. Downing, SP	4
S. Hovley, OF	4
B. Humphreys, RP	4
J. Morris, RP	4
R. Pena, SS	4
D. Baldwin, RP	3
B. Bolin, SP	2
D. Ellsworth, RP	2
G. Gil, 2B	2
G. Goossen, 1B	2
B. Smith, OF	2
R. Snyder, OF	2
H. Allen, OF	1
M. Alvis, 3B	1
T. Francona, 1B	1
M. Hershberger, OF	1
J. Kennedy, 2B	1
B. Locker, RP	1
J. O'Donoghue, RP	1

Minnesota (98-64)	WS
Hitting	**142.3**
Fielding	**46.2**
Pitching	**105.6**
H. Killebrew, 3B	30
T. Oliva, OF	30
C. Tovar, OF	28
J. Perry, SP	21
L. Cardenas, SS	19
S. Williams, RP	16
R. Perranoski, RP	15
T. Hall, RP	14
R. Reese, 1B	14
G. Mitterwald, C	13
B. Alyea, OF	12
J. Kaat, SP	12
R. Carew, 2B	11
B. Blyleven, SP	10
B. Zepp, RP	9
P. Ratliff, C	8
L. Tiant, SP	8
J. Holt, OF	7
R. Renick, 3B	4
D. Thompson, 2B	3
B. Allison, OF	2
H. Haydel, RP	2
F. Quilici, 2B	2
T. Tischinski, C	2
S. Barber, RP	1
D. Woodson, RP	1

New York (93-69)	WS
Hitting	**137.7**
Fielding	**42.1**
Pitching	**99.3**
R. White, OF	34
B. Murcer, OF	27
T. Munson, C	26
D. Cater, 1B	19
L. McDaniel, RP	19
F. Peterson, SP	19
M. Stottlemyre, SP	18
H. Clarke, 2B	14
S. Bahnsen, SP	12
J. Aker, RP	10
J. Gibbs, C	9
J. Kenney, 3B	7
R. Klimkowski, RP	7
G. Michael, SS	7
C. Blefary, OF	6
J. Ellis, 1B	6
R. Hansen, SS	6
R. Woods, OF	6
S. Kline, SP	5
J. Lyttle, OF	5
S. Hamilton, RP	4
F. Baker, SS	3
G. Waslewski, RP	3
J. Cumberland, SP	2
P. Ward, 1B	2
R. Gardner, SP	1
M. Kekich, SP	1
B. Mitchell, OF	1

Oakland (89-73)	WS
Hitting	**126.9**
Fielding	**45.3**
Pitching	**94.8**
B. Campaneris, SS	26
S. Bando, 3B	24
M. Grant, RP	20
R. Monday, OF	19
R. Jackson, OF	17
D. Mincher, 1B	15
F. Alou, OF	13
J. Rudi, OF	13
D. Segui, RP	13
C. Hunter, SP	12
C. Dobson, SP	11

F. Fernandez, C	10
D. Duncan, C	9
B. Odom, SP	8
G. Tenace, C	8
R. Fingers, RP	7
P. Lindblad, RP	6
D. Green, 2B	5
M. Lachemann, RP	5
B. Locker, RP	5
T. Davis, OF	4
J. Roland, RP	4
V. Blue, SP	3
J. Donaldson, 2B	2
A. Downing, SP	2
T. La Russa, 2B	2
B. Brooks, OF	1
S. Hovley, OF	1
R. Pena, SS	1
R. Rodriguez, RP	1

Washington (70-92)	WS
Hitting	**102.7**
Fielding	**36.1**
Pitching	**71.2**
F. Howard, OF	30
D. Bosman, SP	16
E. Brinkman, SS	16
M. Epstein, 1B	16
D. Knowles, RP	15
A. Rodriguez, 3B	15
E. Stroud, OF	11
J. Coleman, SP	10
B. Allen, 2B	8
R. Reichardt, OF	8
H. Pina, RP	7
L. Maye, OF	6
D. Unser, OF	6
P. Casanova, C	5
J. Hannan, RP	5
J. Shellenback, RP	5
G. Brunet, SP	4
C. Cox, SP	4
T. Cullen, 2B	4
J. French, C	3
J. Roseboro, C	3
J. Brown, RP	2
W. Comer, OF	2
D. Billings, C	1
C. Carlos, RP	1
B. Gogolewski, SP	1
T. Grieve, OF	1
J. Grzenda, RP	1
B. Humphreys, RP	1
K. McMullen, 3B	1
D. Nelson, 2B	1
D. Riddleberger, RP	1

1970 National League

Atlanta (76-86)	WS
Hitting	**109.8**
Fielding	**36.3**
Pitching	**81.8**
R. Carty, OF	27
H. Aaron, OF	25
O. Cepeda, 1B	21
P. Jarvis, SP	19
F. Millan, 2B	15
J. Nash, SP	13
G. Stone, SP	13
C. Boyer, 3B	11
P. Niekro, SP	11
H. Wilhelm, RP	11
T. Gonzalez, OF	10
S. Jackson, SS	7
H. King, C	7
R. Reed, SP	7
M. Lum, OF	6
B. Tillman, C	5
B. Priddy, RP	4
O. Brown, OF	3
G. Garrido, SS	3
D. Evans, 3B	2
J. Navarro, RP	2
B. Aspromonte, 3B	1
B. Didier, C	1
R. Garr, OF	1
J. Hall, OF	1
M. McQueen, RP	1
E. Williams, 1B	1

Chicago (84-78)	WS
Hitting	**98.3**
Fielding	**45.3**
Pitching	**108.4**
B. Williams, OF	29
F. Jenkins, SP	26
J. Hickman, OF	24
K. Holtzman, SP	23
B. Hands, SP	21
R. Santo, 3B	19
M. Pappas, SP	15
J. Callison, OF	14
D. Kessinger, SS	14
G. Beckert, 2B	11
J. Pepitone, OF	7
J. Colborn, RP	6
P. Regan, RP	6
E. Banks, 1B	5
J. Decker, SP	5
J. Hiatt, C	5
R. Hundley, C	4
C. James, OF	3
P. Popovich, 2B	3
L. Gura, RP	2
T. Abernathy, RP	1
H. Aguirre, RP	1
T. Davis, OF	1
J. Dunegan, RP	1
J. Martin, C	1
B. Miller, RP	1
J. Pizarro, RP	1
R. Rodriguez, RP	1
K. Rudolph, C	1
W. Smith, 1B	1

Cincinnati (102-60)	WS
Hitting	**141.3**
Fielding	**51.0**
Pitching	**113.7**
J. Bench, C	34
T. Perez, 3B	33
P. Rose, OF	29
B. Tolan, OF	29
B. Carbo, OF	25
G. Nolan, SP	19
W. Granger, RP	15
J. McGlothlin, SP	15
J. Merritt, SP	15
C. Carroll, RP	14
L. May, 1B	14
W. Simpson, SP	14
T. Cloninger, SP	10
D. Gullett, RP	10
T. Helms, 2B	7
D. Concepcion, SS	5
H. McRae, OF	4
M. Wilcox, RP	3
W. Woodward, SS	3
T. Cline, OF	2
P. Corrales, C	2
J. Stewart, OF	2
A. Bravo, OF	1
D. Chaney, SS	1

Houston (79-83)	WS
Hitting	**132.3**
Fielding	**33.2**
Pitching	**71.5**
J. Wynn, OF	27
D. Menke, SS	24
J. Morgan, 2B	24
D. Rader, 3B	19
L. Dierker, SP	15
C. Cedeno, OF	12
J. Edwards, C	12
J. Alou, OF	10
J. Billingham, SP	9
J. Ray, RP	9
B. Watson, 1B	9
D. Wilson, SP	9
F. Gladding, RP	7
J. Pepitone, 1B	7
R. Cook, RP	6
D. Lemaster, SP	6
N. Miller, OF	6
W. Blasingame, SP	5
T. Davis, OF	5
G. Culver, RP	4
L. Howard, C	4
J. Mayberry, 1B	3
J. Bouton, RP	1
J. DiLauro, RP	1
K. Lampard, OF	1
M. Martinez, SS	1
H. Torres, SS	1

Los Angeles (87-74)	WS
Hitting	**141.4**
Fielding	**39.9**
Pitching	**79.7**
B. Grabarkewitz, 3B	29
W. Parker, 1B	29
W. Davis, OF	24
T. Haller, C	15
M. Mota, OF	14
J. Brewer, RP	13
C. Osteen, SP	13
M. Wills, SS	13
B. Sudakis, C	12
T. Sizemore, 2B	11
D. Sutton, SP	11
W. Crawford, OF	8
J. Lefebvre, 2B	8
P. Mikkelsen, RP	7
B. Russell, OF	7
B. Singer, SP	7
S. Vance, SP	7
A. Foster, SP	6
J. Moeller, SP	6
R. Lamb, RP	4
J. Pena, RP	3
J. Torborg, C	3
S. Garvey, 3B	2
V. Joshua, OF	2
A. Kosco, OF	2
M. Strahler, RP	2
B. Buckner, OF	1
F. Norman, RP	1
C. Pascual, RP	1

Montreal (73-89)	WS
Hitting	**107.9**
Fielding	**39.6**
Pitching	**71.5**
R. Staub, OF	30
B. Bailey, 3B	21
C. Morton, SP	21
R. Fairly, 1B	19
M. Jones, OF	14
J. Bateman, C	11
S. Renko, SP	11
B. Wine, SS	11
C. Raymond, RP	9
H. Reed, RP	9
J. Gosger, OF	8
A. Phillips, OF	7
B. Stoneman, SP	7
D. Hahn, OF	5
J. Boccabella, 1B	4
M. Marshall, RP	4
J. Fairey, OF	3
J. Hiatt, C	3
R. Nye, SP	3
M. Staehle, 2B	3
G. Sutherland, 2B	3
R. Brand, SS	2
B. Day, OF	2
C. Laboy, 3B	2
D. McGinn, RP	2
J. Strohmayer, RP	2
B. Dillman, RP	1
J. O'Donoghue, RP	1
M. Wegener, SP	1

New York (83-79)	WS
Hitting	**97.5**
Fielding	**49.6**
Pitching	**101.9**
T. Seaver, SP	25
T. Agee, OF	23
B. Harrelson, SS	17
W. Garrett, 3B	16
C. Jones, OF	14
J. Koosman, SP	14
D. Clendenon, 1B	13
A. Shamsky, OF	13
J. McAndrew, SP	12
J. Foy, 3B	10
G. Gentry, SP	10
J. Grote, C	10
K. Boswell, 2B	9
T. McGraw, RP	9
N. Ryan, SP	8
R. Sadecki, SP	8
D. Frisella, RP	7
R. Taylor, RP	7
R. Swoboda, OF	6
K. Singleton, OF	5
D. Marshall, OF	4
D. Dyer, C	3
R. Herbel, RP	2
M. Jorgensen, 1B	2
C. Koonce, RP	1
A. Weis, 2B	1

Philadelphia (73-88)	WS
Hitting	**83.2**
Fielding	**41.9**
Pitching	**93.9**
D. Money, 3B	21
D. Selma, RP	21
D. Johnson, 1B	19
T. Taylor, 2B	19
B. Lersch, RP	13
R. Wise, SP	13
J. Bunning, SP	11
L. Bowa, SS	10
J. Hoerner, RP	10
J. Briggs, OF	9
C. Short, SP	9
W. Fryman, SP	8
B. Browne, OF	7
T. McCarver, C	7
R. Stone, OF	7
L. Hisle, OF	6
O. Gamble, OF	5
D. Doyle, 2B	4
T. Harmon, SS	4
M. Compton, C	2
D. Edwards, C	2
G. Jackson, SP	2
M. Ryan, C	2
F. Wenz, RP	2
B. Wilson, RP	2
D. Bates, C	1
M. Jackson, RP	1
J. Lis, OF	1
L. Palmer, RP	1

Pittsburgh (89-73)	WS
Hitting	**127.4**
Fielding	**45.5**
Pitching	**94.2**
R. Clemente, OF	23
M. Sanguillen, C	19
B. Robertson, 1B	18
W. Stargell, OF	17
M. Alou, OF	16
R. Hebner, 3B	16
D. Giusti, RP	15
A. Oliver, OF	15
L. Walker, RP	15

D. Ellis, SP	14
G. Alley, SS	12
S. Blass, SP	10
B. Moose, SP	10
B. Veale, SP	9
D. Cash, 2B	8
B. Mazeroski, 2B	8
F. Patek, SS	8
J. Pagan, 3B	6
B. Dal Canton, RP	4
J. May, C	4
J. Nelson, SP	4
J. Lamb, RP	3
F. Cambria, SP	2
M. Grant, RP	2
J. Jeter, OF	2
O. Pena, RP	2
G. Brunet, RP	1
G. Clines, OF	1
J. Gibbon, RP	1
C. Hartenstein, RP	1
M. May, PH-PR	1

San Diego (63-99)	WS
Hitting	**102.0**
Fielding	**30.7**
Pitching	**56.3**
C. Gaston, OF	24
N. Colbert, 1B	18
O. Brown, OF	16
E. Spiezio, 3B	13
P. Dobson, SP	12
A. Ferrara, OF	12
D. Coombs, SP	11
D. Campbell, 2B	10
C. Cannizzaro, C	10
S. Huntz, SS	9
D. Roberts, RP	9
C. Kirby, SP	6
I. Murrell, OF	5
M. Corkins, SP	4
T. Dukes, RP	4
R. Herbel, RP	4
J. Arcia, SS	3
B. Barton, C	3
R. Willis, RP	3
T. Dean, SS	2
D. Robinson, OF	2
G. Ross, RP	2
R. Webster, 1B	2
S. Arlin, SP	1
V. Kelly, 3B	1
R. Robles, SS	1
R. Slocum, C	1
E. Wilson, SP	1

San Francisco (86-76)	WS
Hitting	**162.7**
Fielding	**29.8**
Pitching	**65.5**
W. McCovey, 1B	33
B. Bonds, OF	32
D. Dietz, C	29
K. Henderson, OF	24
W. Mays, OF	24
G. Perry, SP	24
D. McMahon, RP	14
R. Hunt, 2B	13
J. Marichal, SP	11
T. Fuentes, 2B	9
J. Hart, 3B	7
A. Gallagher, 3B	6
H. Lanier, SS	6
R. Robertson, SP	5
R. Bryant, RP	3
F. Johnson, OF	3
Je. Johnson, RP	3
S. Pitlock, SP	3
J. Cumberland, RP	2
F. Reberger, RP	2
J. Davenport, 3B	1
G. Foster, OF	1
R. Gibson, C	1
B. Heise, SS	1
B. Taylor, OF	1

St. Louis (76-86)	WS
Hitting	**102.7**
Fielding	**37.7**
Pitching	**87.5**
B. Gibson, SP	28
J. Torre, C	25
L. Brock, OF	20
D. Allen, 1B	19
J. Cardenal, OF	16
S. Carlton, SP	14
J. Hague, 1B	13
Ch. Taylor, RP	12
D. Maxvill, SS	9
M. Torrez, SP	9
J. Javier, 2B	8
J. Reuss, SP	6
T. Simmons, C	6
Ca. Taylor, OF	6
V. Davalillo, OF	5
S. Campisi, RP	4
L. Lee, OF	4
F. Linzy, RP	4
T. Abernathy, RP	2
F. Bertaina, SP	2
E. Crosby, SS	2
G. Culver, SP	2
J. Johnson, RP	2
M. Ramirez, SS	2
J. Beauchamp, OF	1
J. Cruz, OF	1
T. Hilgendorf, RP	1
A. Hrabosky, RP	1
L. Melendez, OF	1
R. Nye, RP	1
H. Parker, SP	1
C. Rojas, 2B	1

1971
American League

Baltimore (101-57)	WS
Hitting	**156.5**
Fielding	**46.2**
Pitching	**100.3**
M. Rettenmund, OF	27
D. Buford, OF	26
D. Johnson, 2B	23
B. Robinson, 3B	23
F. Robinson, OF	23
J. Palmer, SP	22
M. Belanger, SS	21
P. Dobson, SP	19
D. McNally, SP	19
B. Powell, 1B	19
M. Cuellar, SP	18
P. Blair, OF	15
E. Hendricks, C	10
A. Etchebarren, C	8
E. Watt, RP	7
G. Jackson, RP	4
D. Leonhard, SP-RP	4
P. Richert, RP	3
C. Dalrymple, C	2
J. DaVanon, 2B	2
T. Dukes, RP	2
B. Grich, SS	2
C. Motton, OF	2
D. Hall, RP	1
T. Shopay, OF	1

Boston (85-77)	WS
Hitting	**128.0**
Fielding	**40.8**
Pitching	**86.2**
R. Smith, OF	29
R. Petrocelli, 3B	27
S. Siebert, SP	22
C. Yastrzemski, OF	21
G. Scott, 1B	15
R. Culp, SP	13
B. Conigliaro, OF	11
G. Peters, SP	11
D. Griffin, 2B	10
B. Lee, RP	10
S. Lyle, RP	10
J. Kennedy, 2B	9
J. Lahoud, OF	9
L. Aparicio, SS	8
D. Josephson, C	7
J. Lonborg, SP	7
R. Moret, SP	6
B. Bolin, RP	5
B. Montgomery, C	5
K. Tatum, RP	4
P. Gagliano, OF	3
C. Cooper, 1B	2
J. Curtis, SP	2
C. Fisk, C	2
R. Miller, OF	2
J. Beniquez, SS	1
M. Garman, SP	1
B. Oglivie, OF	1
D. Pavletich, C	1
L. Tiant, RP	1

California (76-86)	WS
Hitting	**80.2**
Fielding	**47.1**
Pitching	**100.7**
S. Alomar, 2B	21
A. Messersmith, SP	19
K. McMullen, 3B	18
C. Wright, SP	18
J. Spencer, 1B	14
R. May, SP	13
L. Allen, RP	12
R. Repoz, OF	12
E. Fisher, RP	10
D. LaRoche, RP	10
J. Fregosi, SS	9
M. Rivers, OF	9
T. Murphy, SP	8
T. Gonzalez, OF	7
M. Queen, RP	7
K. Berry, OF	6
J. Stephenson, C	6
T. Conigliaro, OF	5
B. Cowan, OF	5
R. Clark, SP	4
A. Johnson, OF	4
J. Moses, C	4
S. O'Brien, SS	2
J. Torborg, C	2
B. Christensen, SS	1
B. Parker, 2B	1
T. Reynolds, OF	1

Chicago (79-83)	WS
Hitting	**102.4**
Fielding	**36.1**
Pitching	**98.6**
W. Wood, SP	33
B. Melton, 3B	23
T. Bradley, SP	20
B. Johnson, RP	16
C. May, 1B	15
M. Andrews, 2B	13
R. Reichardt, OF	13
J. Johnstone, OF	12
W. Williams, OF	11
T. John, SP	10
T. Egan, C	9
E. Herrmann, C	9
R. McKinney, 2B	8
P. Kelly, OF	7
V. Romo, RP	6
M. Hershberger, OF	5
J. Horlen, SP	5
S. Kealey, RP	4
R. Morales, SS	4
T. Forster, RP	3
L. Richard, SS	3
L. Alvarado, SS	2
D. Eddy, RP	2
R. Hinton, RP	1
S. Huntz, 2B	1
J. Magnuson, RP	1
E. Stroud, OF	1

Cleveland (60-102)	WS
Hitting	**74.9**
Fielding	**37.5**
Pitching	**67.6**
G. Nettles, 3B	27
R. Fosse, C	16
S. McDowell, SP	15
C. Chambliss, 1B	11
V. Pinson, OF	11
T. Uhlaender, OF	11
R. Foster, OF	10
R. Lamb, RP	10
S. Mingori, RP	9
V. Colbert, RP	8
S. Dunning, SP	7
A. Foster, SP	7
E. Leon, 2B	7
E. Farmer, RP	4
P. Hennigan, RP	4
F. Stanley, SS	4
C. Hinton, 1B-OF	3
C. Pascual, RP	3
K. Suarez, C	3
K. Harrelson, 1B	2
J. Heidemann, SS	2
F. Baker, OF	1
M. Ballinger, RP	1
K. Bevacqua, 2B	1
L. Camilli, SS	1
T. Ford, OF	1
J. Lowenstein, 2B	1

Detroit (91-71)	WS
Hitting	**147.9**
Fielding	**39.8**
Pitching	**85.3**
M. Lolich, SP	29
B. Freehan, C	25
N. Cash, 1B	24
A. Kaline, OF	22
J. Coleman, SP	20
J. Northrup, OF	18
W. Horton, OF	17
F. Scherman, RP	15
D. McAuliffe, 2B	14
A. Rodriguez, 3B	14
M. Stanley, OF	13
G. Brown, OF	12
E. Brinkman, SS	11
T. Taylor, 2B	7
I. Brown, 1B	5
T. Timmermann, RP	5
L. Cain, SP	4
D. Chance, RP	4
D. Jones, OF	3
J. Niekro, RP	3
K. Collins, 3B	1
B. Denehy, RP	1
B. Gilbreth, SP	1
J. Hannan, RP	1
T. Hosley, C	1
M. Kilkenny, RP	1
R. Perranoski, RP	1
J. Price, C	1

Kansas City (85-76)	WS
Hitting	**113.6**
Fielding	**44.2**
Pitching	**97.2**
A. Otis, OF	27
P. Schaal, 3B	26
F. Patek, SS	24
D. Drago, SP	18
C. Rojas, 2B	18
M. Hedlund, SP	16
T. Burgmeier, RP	15
T. Abernathy, RP	11
G. Hopkins, 1B	11

L. Piniella, OF	11
P. Splittorff, SP	10
E. Kirkpatrick, OF	9
J. York, RP	8
B. Dal Canton, SP	7
J. May, C	7
J. Keough, OF	6
A. Fitzmorris, RP	5
B. Oliver, 1B	5
M. Montgomery, SP	3
S. Valdespino, OF	3
K. Wright, SP	3
B. Butler, RP	2
B. Knoop, 2B	2
D. Paepke, C	2
R. Severson, 2B-SS	2
L. Clemons, RP	1
B. Floyd, SS	1
C. Harrison, 1B	1
B. Martinez, C	1

Milwaukee (69-92)	WS
Hitting	**81.7**
Fielding	**43.0**
Pitching	**82.3**
K. Sanders, RP	21
T. Harper, OF	20
J. Briggs, OF	18
D. May, OF	18
M. Pattin, SP	16
B. Parsons, SP	15
L. Krausse, SP	11
R. Theobald, 2B	11
S. Lockwood, SP	9
E. Rodriguez, C	8
T. Kubiak, 2B	7
J. Slaton, SP	7
B. Voss, OF	7
J. Cardenal, OF	5
A. Kosco, OF	5
M. Hegan, 1B	4
R. Pena, 1B	4
R. Auerbach, SS	3
B. Heise, SS	3
J. Morris, RP	3
D. Porter, C	2
P. Roof, C	2
J. Bell, RP	1
R. Ellis, 3B	1
G. Gil, 2B	1
T. Matchick, 3B	1
B. Mitchell, OF	1
P. Ratliff, C	1
D. Walton, OF	1
A. Yates, OF	1

Minnesota (74-86)	WS
Hitting	**116.5**
Fielding	**34.9**
Pitching	**70.5**
H. Killebrew, 1B	23
T. Oliva, OF	23
L. Cardenas, SS	22
C. Tovar, OF	21
B. Blyleven, SP	20
R. Carew, 2B	17
J. Kaat, SP	15

G. Mitterwald, C	13
S. Braun, 3B	10
T. Hall, RP	10
J. Perry, SP	10
R. Corbin, RP	5
J. Holt, OF	5
J. Nettles, OF	5
R. Reese, 1B	5
J. Strickland, RP	3
S. Williams, RP	3
H. Haydel, RP	2
P. Roof, C	2
B. Alyea, OF	1
S. Brye, OF	1
R. Dempsey, C	1
B. Gebhard, RP	1
P. Ratliff, C	1
R. Renick, 3B-OF	1
G. Thomas, OF	1
T. Tischinski, C	1

New York (82-80)	WS
Hitting	**135.7**
Fielding	**34.7**
Pitching	**75.5**
B. Murcer, OF	38
R. White, OF	29
M. Stottlemyre, SP	19
T. Munson, C	18
H. Clarke, 2B	16
F. Peterson, SP	16
F. Alou, OF	14
S. Bahnsen, SP	13
S. Kline, SP	13
J. Kenney, 3B	10
R. Blomberg, OF	9
G. Michael, SS	9
D. Cater, 1B	8
J. Aker, RP	5
J. Ellis, 1B	5
M. Kekich, SP	5
R. Swoboda, OF	5
J. Gibbs, C	4
R. Hambright, RP	2
R. Torres, OF	2
G. Waslewski, RP	2
F. Baker, SS	1
C. Blefary, OF	1
R. Hansen, 3B	1
R. Woods, OF	1

Oakland (101-60)	WS
Hitting	**156.5**
Fielding	**47.4**
Pitching	**99.0**
R. Jackson, OF	32
V. Blue, SP	30
S. Bando, 3B	29
C. Hunter, SP	22
D. Green, 2B	20
M. Epstein, 1B	17
B. Campaneris, SS	15
R. Monday, OF	15
J. Rudi, OF	15
D. Duncan, C	14
R. Fingers, RP	12
G. Tenace, C	10

T. Davis, 1B	9
C. Dobson, SP	9
A. Mangual, OF	8
D. Segui, SP	8
B. Locker, RP	7
D. Knowles, RP	5
D. Mincher, 1B	4
C. Blefary, C-OF	3
L. Brown, SS	3
M. Grant, RP	3
R. Klimkowski, RP	3
D. Anderson, SS	2
B. Odom, SP	2
J. Roland, RP	2
M. Hegan, 1B	1
G. Hendrick, OF	1
S. Hovley, OF	1
P. Lindblad, RP	1

Washington (63-96)	WS
Hitting	**96.7**
Fielding	**31.9**
Pitching	**60.4**
F. Howard, OF	23
D. Unser, OF	17
D. Mincher, 1B	15
B. Allen, 2B	9
D. Bosman, SP	9
B. Gogolewski, SP	9
J. Grzenda, RP	9
P. Lindblad, RP	9
D. Nelson, 3B	9
D. Billings, C	8
T. Harrah, SS	7
E. Maddox, OF	7
P. Broberg, SP	5
J. Burroughs, OF	5
T. Cullen, 2B	5
L. Randle, 2B	5
C. Cox, RP	4
J. Foy, 3B	4
T. McCraw, OF	4
D. McLain, SP	4
D. Riddleberger, RP	4
J. Shellenback, RP	4
L. Biittner, OF	3
P. Casanova, C	3
M. Epstein, 1B	3
H. Pina, RP	3
J. French, C	1
D. Knowles, RP	1

1971 National League

Atlanta (82-80)	WS
Hitting	**107.1**
Fielding	**45.2**
Pitching	**93.7**
H. Aaron, 1B	33
R. Garr, OF	25
P. Niekro, SP	22
E. Williams, C	19
F. Millan, 2B	18
M. Lum, OF	14
R. Reed, SP	13

T. Kelley, SP	12
C. Upshaw, RP	11
G. Stone, SP	10
D. Evans, 3B	9
S. Jackson, OF	9
O. Cepeda, 1B	7
P. Jarvis, SP	7
M. McQueen, RP	5
H. King, C	4
M. Perez, SS	4
S. Barber, RP	3
C. Boyer, 3B	3
J. Nash, SP	3
G. Neibauer, RP	3
B. Didier, C	2
G. Garrido, SS	2
T. House, RP	2
B. Priddy, RP	2
Z. Versalles, 3B	2
R. Herbel, RP	1
M. Staehle, 2B	1

Chicago (83-79)	WS
Hitting	**100.4**
Fielding	**45.5**
Pitching	**103.1**
F. Jenkins, SP	37
B. Williams, OF	26
G. Beckert, 2B	20
M. Pappas, SP	20
R. Santo, 3B	19
B. Hands, SP	15
D. Kessinger, SS	14
J. Pepitone, 1B	14
J. Hickman, OF	12
J. Pizarro, SP	8
B. Davis, OF	7
K. Holtzman, SP	7
J. Callison, OF	5
C. James, OF	5
P. Regan, RP	5
C. Cannizzaro, C	4
J. Martin, C	4
F. Fernandez, C	3
B. Hooton, SP	3
R. Newman, RP	3
J. Ortiz, OF	3
R. Tompkins, RP	3
J. Decker, RP	2
P. Popovich, 2B	2
K. Rudolph, C	2
B. Bonham, RP	1
D. Breeden, C	1
R. Hundley, C	1
B. North, OF	1
E. Stephenson, RP	1
H. Torres, SS	1

Cincinnati (79-83)	WS
Hitting	**110.0**
Fielding	**44.0**
Pitching	**82.9**
P. Rose, OF	28
L. May, 1B	24
T. Perez, 3B	23
J. Bench, C	19
D. Gullett, SP	17

T. Helms, 2B	14
C. Carroll, RP	13
G. Nolan, SP	13
G. Foster, OF	10
B. Carbo, OF	9
W. Granger, RP	9
J. McGlothlin, SP	9
H. McRae, OF	9
R. Grimsley, SP	8
J. Gibbon, RP	7
W. Woodward, SS	6
T. Cloninger, RP	4
D. Concepcion, SS	4
B. Bradford, OF	2
T. Cline, OF	2
E. Sprague, RP	2
M. Wilcox, RP	2
P. Corrales, C	1
G. Garrett, SP-RP	1
J. Stewart, OF	1

Houston (79-83)	WS
Hitting	**104.3**
Fielding	**42.0**
Pitching	**90.8**
J. Morgan, 2B	29
D. Wilson, SP	22
C. Cedeno, OF	17
D. Rader, 3B	15
B. Watson, OF	15
K. Forsch, SP	14
R. Metzger, SS	14
L. Dierker, SP	12
D. Menke, 1B	11
J. Ray, RP	11
J. Edwards, C	10
J. Hiatt, C	10
J. Alou, OF	9
J. Billingham, SP	9
G. Culver, RP	8
J. Wynn, OF	7
F. Gladding, RP	6
W. Blasingame, SP	3
D. Lemaster, RP	3
L. Howard, C	2
J. Mayberry, 1B	2
N. Miller, OF	2
R. Chiles, OF	1
C. Geronimo, OF	1
S. Guinn, RP	1
M. Martinez, 2B	1
J. Richard, SP	1
S. Spinks, SP	1

Los Angeles (89-73)	WS
Hitting	**137.0**
Fielding	**40.0**
Pitching	**90.0**
D. Allen, 3B	29
W. Davis, OF	25
D. Sutton, SP	21
A. Downing, SP	19
M. Wills, SS	19
W. Parker, 1B	18
J. Brewer, RP	15
W. Crawford, OF	13
J. Lefebvre, 2B	12

C. Osteen, SP	12
D. Sims, C	11
B. Buckner, OF	9
M. Mota, OF	9
T. Haller, C	8
S. Garvey, 3B	6
P. Mikkelsen, RP	5
B. Valentine, SS	5
D. Alexander, SP	4
B. Russell, 2B	4
B. Singer, SP	4
B. Grabarkewitz, 2B	3
J. Pena, RP	3
H. Wilhelm, RP	3
J. Ferguson, C	2
J. Moeller, RP	2
B. O'Brien, RP	2
B. Sudakis, C	2
B. Darwin, OF	1
M. Strahler, RP	1

Montreal (71-90)	WS
Hitting	**117.9**
Fielding	**32.4**
Pitching	**62.6**
R. Staub, OF	32
R. Hunt, 2B	26
B. Bailey, 3B	21
B. Stoneman, SP	20
R. Fairly, 1B	19
S. Renko, SP	15
B. Day, OF	13
J. Bateman, C	9
M. Marshall, RP	9
E. McAnally, SP	8
R. Woods, OF	6
G. Sutherland, 2B	5
C. Morton, SP	4
J. Strohmayer, SP	4
J. Boccabella, C-1B	3
J. Fairey, OF	3
R. Swoboda, OF	3
B. Wine, SS	3
M. Jones, OF	2
C. Laboy, 3B	2
H. Reed, RP	2
S. Swanson, OF	2
C. Mashore, OF	1
M. Torrez, RP	1

New York (83-79)	WS
Hitting	**101.1**
Fielding	**47.1**
Pitching	**100.8**
T. Seaver, SP	32
C. Jones, OF	24
T. Agee, OF	19
B. Harrelson, SS	19
T. McGraw, RP	17
E. Kranepool, 1B	15
D. Frisella, RP	12
J. Grote, C	12
K. Boswell, 2B	11
G. Gentry, SP	11
R. Sadecki, SP	11
K. Singleton, OF	11
J. Koosman, SP	9
D. Clendenon, 1B	5
D. Marshall, OF	5
T. Martinez, SS	5
B. Aspromonte, 3B	4
D. Dyer, C	4
T. Foli, 2B	4
N. Ryan, SP	4
R. Taylor, RP	4
D. Hahn, OF	3
A. Shamsky, OF	3
W. Garrett, 3B	2
M. Jorgensen, OF	2
J. Matlack, SP	1

Philadelphia (67-95)	WS
Hitting	**79.4**
Fielding	**39.7**
Pitching	**81.9**
R. Wise, SP	23
D. Johnson, 1B	21
W. Montanez, OF	20
T. McCarver, C	16
L. Bowa, SS	12
W. Fryman, RP	11
J. Hoerner, RP	11
B. Lersch, SP	10
D. Money, 3B	8
C. Short, SP	7
B. Wilson, RP	7
R. Freed, OF	6
B. Brandon, RP	5
D. Doyle, 2B	5
O. Gamble, OF	4
G. Luzinski, 1B	4
K. Reynolds, SP	4
M. Anderson, OF	3
T. Harmon, 2B	3
J. Lis, OF	3
R. Stone, OF	3
B. Browne, OF	2
B. Champion, RP	2
B. Pfeil, 3B	2
M. Ryan, C	2
D. Selma, RP	2
W. Twitchell, RP	2
J. Vukovich, 3B	2
T. Taylor, 2B	1

Pittsburgh (97-65)	WS
Hitting	**168.0**
Fielding	**38.8**
Pitching	**84.2**
W. Stargell, OF	35
R. Clemente, OF	24
M. Sanguillen, C	24
B. Robertson, 1B	20
A. Oliver, OF	18
D. Cash, 2B	16
R. Hebner, 3B	16
S. Blass, SP	15
D. Ellis, SP	14
G. Clines, OF	11
D. Giusti, RP	10
N. Briles, RP	9
G. Alley, SS	8
V. Davalillo, OF	8
B. Johnson, SP	7
R. Stennett, 2B	7
L. Walker, SP	7
M. Grant, RP	5
M. May, C	5
B. Kison, SP	4
B. Mazeroski, 2B	4
B. Moose, SP	4
J. Nelson, RP	4
J. Pagan, 3B	4
J. Hernandez, SS	3
R. Hernandez, RP	3
B. Miller, RP	3
J. Lamb, RP	1
C. Sands, C	1
R. Zisk, OF	1

San Diego (61-100)	WS
Hitting	**66.2**
Fielding	**36.3**
Pitching	**80.5**
D. Roberts, SP	24
N. Colbert, 1B	19
C. Kirby, SP	17
O. Brown, OF	13
B. Barton, C	10
B. Miller, RP	10
C. Gaston, OF	9
L. Stahl, OF	8
S. Arlin, SP	7
D. Campbell, 2B	7
E. Hernandez, SS	7
F. Norman, SP	7
L. Lee, OF	6
E. Spiezio, 3B	5
G. Jestadt, 3B	4
A. Severinsen, RP	4
E. Acosta, SP	3
J. Jeter, OF	3
D. Kelley, RP	3
I. Murrell, OF	3
M. Caldwell, RP	2
F. Kendall, C	2
D. Mason, 2B	2
T. Phoebus, SP	2
C. Cannizzaro, C	1
M. Corkins, RP	1
T. Dean, SS	1
M. Ivie, C	1
G. Ross, RP	1
A. Santorini, RP	1

San Francisco (90-72)	WS
Hitting	**146.6**
Fielding	**39.3**
Pitching	**84.1**
B. Bonds, OF	32
W. Mays, OF	27
K. Henderson, OF	23
D. Dietz, C	19
J. Marichal, SP	18
T. Fuentes, 2B	17
G. Perry, SP	17
W. McCovey, 1B	16
C. Speier, SS	16
J. Cumberland, RP	13
A. Gallagher, 3B	13
J. Johnson, RP	12
D. Kingman, 1B	6
R. Bryant, SP	5
S. Hamilton, RP	5
D. McMahon, RP	5
J. Rosario, OF	5
D. Carrithers, SP	3
F. Healy, C	3
H. Lanier, 3B	3
S. Stone, SP	3
J. Barr, RP	2
G. Foster, OF	2
F. Reberger, SP	2
C. Arnold, 2B	1
J. Hart, 3B-OF	1
J. Howarth, OF	1

St. Louis (90-72)	WS
Hitting	**156.5**
Fielding	**35.7**
Pitching	**77.8**
J. Torre, 3B	41
L. Brock, OF	30
M. Alou, OF	23
T. Simmons, C	20
B. Gibson, SP	17
S. Carlton, SP	16
J. Cruz, OF	14
T. Sizemore, 2B	13
J. Hague, 1B	12
R. Cleveland, SP	9
D. Maxvill, SS	9
J. Cardenal, OF	8
F. Linzy, RP	8
M. Drabowsky, RP	7
J. Javier, 2B	5
J. McNertney, C	5
D. Shaw, RP	5
C. Taylor, RP	5
J. Reuss, SP	4
T. Kubiak, SS	3
A. Santorini, RP	3
J. Beauchamp, 1B	2
B. Burda, 1B	2
L. Melendez, OF	2
D. Schofield, SS	2
S. Williams, RP	2
S. Guzman, SP-RP	1
D. Higgins, RP	1
D. Patterson, RP	1

1972
American League

Baltimore (80-74)	WS
Hitting	**100.2**
Fielding	**45.6**
Pitching	**94.3**
J. Palmer, SP	25
B. Grich, SS	23
B. Powell, 1B	18
M. Cuellar, SP	16
B. Robinson, 3B	16
P. Dobson, SP	15
D. Johnson, 2B	14
D. Baylor, OF	13
D. McNally, SP	12
P. Blair, OF	11
J. Oates, C	10
D. Buford, OF	9
M. Rettenmund, OF	9
T. Crowley, OF	8
R. Harrison, RP	8
D. Alexander, RP	7
M. Belanger, SS	5
E. Watt, RP	5
A. Etchebarren, C	4
G. Jackson, RP	4
R. Coggins, OF	2
M. Scott, RP	2
A. Bumbry, OF	1
T. Davis, OF	1
E. Hendricks, C	1
B. Reynolds, RP	1

Boston (85-70)	WS
Hitting	**148.1**
Fielding	**33.3**
Pitching	**73.6**
C. Fisk, C	33
R. Smith, OF	26
T. Harper, OF	24
R. Petrocelli, 3B	21
L. Tiant, RP	19
C. Yastrzemski, OF	19
D. Griffin, 2B	14
M. Pattin, SP	14
L. Aparicio, SS	11
J. Curtis, SP	7
B. Lee, RP	7
L. McGlothen, SP	7
B. Oglivie, OF	7
S. Siebert, SP	7
J. Kennedy, 2B	6
D. Cater, 1B	4
D. Newhauser, RP	4
B. Bolin, RP	3
P. Gagliano, OF	3
R. Miller, OF	3
B. Montgomery, C	3
B. Veale, RP	3
J. Beniquez, SS	2
D. Evans, OF	2
C. Cooper, 1B	1
R. Culp, SP	1
D. Josephson, 1B	1
A. Kosco, OF	1
G. Peters, RP	1
K. Tatum, RP	1

California (75-80)	WS
Hitting	**110.5**
Fielding	**39.4**
Pitching	**75.0**
N. Ryan, SP	24
K. Berry, OF	22
K. McMullen, 3B	21
B. Oliver, 1B	21
V. Pinson, OF	20
C. Wright, SP	16
S. Alomar, 2B	15
A. Messersmith, SP	12
L. Stanton, OF	12

L. Cardenas, SS	11
R. May, SP	11
S. Barber, RP	6
J. Stephenson, C	6
A. Kosco, OF	4
A. Kusnyer, C	4
E. Fisher, RP	3
J. Torborg, C	3
L. Allen, RP	2
J. Hiatt, C	2
B. Parker, 3B	2
C. Coletta, OF	1
T. Dukes, RP	1
D. Howard, OF	1
W. Llenas, 3B	1
S. O'Brien, 3B	1
M. Rivers, OF	1
D. Sells, RP	1
J. Spencer, 1B	1

Chicago (87-67)	WS
Hitting	**123.4**
Fielding	**40.5**
Pitching	**97.2**
D. Allen, 1B	40
C. May, OF	29
W. Wood, SP	29
T. Forster, RP	19
P. Kelly, OF	17
T. Bradley, SP	16
M. Andrews, 2B	15
E. Herrmann, C	15
S. Bahnsen, SP	12
R. Reichardt, OF	10
B. Melton, 3B	8
C. Acosta, RP	6
S. Kealey, RP	5
D. Lemonds, SP	5
E. Spiezio, 3B	5
W. Williams, OF	5
L. Alvarado, SS	3
G. Gossage, RP	3
J. Johnstone, OF	3
R. Morales, SS	3
V. Romo, RP	3
B. Bradford, OF	2
T. Egan, C	2
T. Muser, 1B	2
C. Brinkman, C	1
M. Drabowsky, RP	1
J. Lyttle, OF	1
J. Orta, SS	1

Cleveland (72-84)	WS
Hitting	**69.3**
Fielding	**48.5**
Pitching	**98.2**
G. Perry, SP	39
G. Nettles, 3B	21
D. Tidrow, SP	17
R. Fosse, C	14
B. Bell, OF	13
C. Chambliss, 1B	13
T. McCraw, OF	11
J. Brohamer, 2B	10
F. Duffy, SS	9
S. Dunning, SP	9
P. Hennigan, RP	8
M. Wilcox, SP	7
R. Lamb, RP	6
D. Unser, OF	6
T. Hilgendorf, RP	4
A. Johnson, OF	4
M. Kilkenny, RP	4
J. Lowenstein, OF	4
J. Moses, C	4
R. Foster, OF	3
E. Leon, 2B	3
D. Riddleberger, RP	3
E. Farmer, RP	2
B. Butler, RP	1
R. Lolich, OF	1

Detroit (86-70)	WS
Hitting	**110.3**
Fielding	**46.9**
Pitching	**100.7**
M. Lolich, SP	26
B. Freehan, C	20
J. Coleman, SP	19
N. Cash, 1B	18
D. McAuliffe, 2B	16
A. Kaline, OF	14
A. Rodriguez, 3B	14
C. Seelbach, RP	12
M. Stanley, OF	12
W. Fryman, SP	11
J. Northrup, OF	11
E. Brinkman, SS	10
W. Horton, OF	9
T. Taylor, 2B	9
T. Timmermann, SP	9
D. Sims, C	8
G. Brown, OF	7
F. Scherman, RP	5
C. Zachary, RP	5
T. Haller, C	4
J. Hiller, RP	4
L. LaGrow, RP	4
B. Slayback, SP	4
I. Brown, OF	3
J. Niekro, RP	2
F. Howard, 1B	1
P. Jata, 1B	1

Kansas City (76-78)	WS
Hitting	**121.5**
Fielding	**34.4**
Pitching	**72.1**
J. Mayberry, 1B	27
A. Otis, OF	22
L. Piniella, OF	21
R. Scheinblum, OF	18
E. Kirkpatrick, C	16
R. Nelson, SP	16
F. Patek, SS	13
D. Drago, SP	12
C. Rojas, 2B	12
P. Splittorff, SP	12
P. Schaal, 3B	9
T. Abernathy, RP	7
B. Dal Canton, RP	6
S. Hovley, OF	6
S. Busby, SP	5
T. Murphy, SP-RP	4
A. Fitzmorris, RP	3
M. Montgomery, SP	3
C. Taylor, C	3
N. Angelini, RP	2
T. Burgmeier, RP	2
B. Knoop, 2B	2
J. May, C	2
B. Oliver, OF	2
B. Floyd, 3B	1
J. Keough, OF	1
J. Rooker, SP	1

Milwaukee (65-91)	WS
Hitting	**98.7**
Fielding	**33.7**
Pitching	**62.6**
G. Scott, 1B	21
J. Briggs, OF	20
E. Rodriguez, C	17
J. Lonborg, SP	14
D. May, OF	13
J. Lahoud, OF	11
R. Theobald, 2B	10
R. Auerbach, SS	9
J. Colborn, RP	8
J. Bell, RP	7
O. Brown, OF	6
B. Heise, 2B	6
F. Linzy, RP	6
B. Parsons, SP	6
K. Sanders, RP	6
B. Davis, OF	5
M. Ferraro, 3B	5
S. Lockwood, SP	5
B. Conigliaro, OF	4
E. Stephenson, RP	4
G. Ryerson, SP	3
R. Newman, RP	2
C. Taylor, RP	2
K. Brett, SP	1
R. Clark, 2B	1
J. Felske, C	1
D. Porter, C	1
T. Reynolds, OF	1

Minnesota (77-77)	WS
Hitting	**99.6**
Fielding	**41.3**
Pitching	**90.2**
R. Carew, 2B	22
B. Blyleven, SP	19
B. Darwin, OF	18
H. Killebrew, 1B	18
C. Tovar, OF	17
D. Thompson, SS	15
D. Woodson, SP	15
S. Braun, 3B	14
J. Kaat, SP	12
R. Corbin, SP	10
J. Perry, SP	9
W. Granger, RP	8
D. LaRoche, RP	8
S. Brye, OF	6
D. Goltz, SP	6
G. Borgmann, C	5
J. Nettles, OF	5
E. Soderholm, 3B	5
R. Reese, 1B	4
J. Strickland, RP	3
J. Holt, OF	2
G. Mitterwald, C	2
D. Monzon, 2B	2
P. Roof, C	2
C. Manuel, OF	1
T. Norton, RP	1
T. Oliva, OF	1
R. Renick, OF	1

New York (79-76)	WS
Hitting	**133.2**
Fielding	**32.6**
Pitching	**71.2**
B. Murcer, OF	36
R. White, OF	26
T. Munson, C	19
S. Lyle, RP	18
H. Clarke, 2B	17
R. Blomberg, 1B	15
S. Kline, SP	14
F. Peterson, SP	11
M. Stottlemyre, SP	11
F. Alou, 1B	10
G. Michael, SS	9
J. Callison, OF	8
B. Allen, 3B	7
J. Ellis, C	5
L. McDaniel, RP	5
R. Gardner, SP	4
M. Kekich, SP	4
C. Sanchez, 3B	4
R. Swoboda, OF	4
F. Beene, RP	3
J. Kenney, SS	2
R. Torres, OF	2
L. Gowell, SP-RP	1
H. Lanier, 3B	1
R. McKinney, 3B	1

Oakland (93-62)	WS
Hitting	**140.4**
Fielding	**42.6**
Pitching	**96.0**
J. Rudi, OF	29
M. Epstein, 1B	27
R. Jackson, OF	26
C. Hunter, SP	24
S. Bando, 3B	23
B. Campaneris, SS	21
K. Holtzman, SP	16
D. Duncan, C	14
R. Fingers, RP	13
B. Odom, SP	12
D. Knowles, RP	9
B. Locker, RP	7
G. Tenace, C	7
V. Blue, SP	6
A. Mangual, OF	6
M. Alou, OF	5
D. Hamilton, SP	5
M. Hegan, 1B	4
T. Cullen, 2B	3
J. Horlen, RP	3
B. Voss, OF	3
L. Brown, 2B	2
O. Brown, OF	2
D. Green, 2B	2
B. Alyea, OF	1
C. Blefary, 1B-2B-OF	1
B. Brooks, OF	1
R. Clark, 2B	1
G. Hendrick, OF	1
T. Kubiak, 2B	1
G. Marquez, 1B	1
M. Martinez, 2B	1
D. Maxvill, 2B	1
G. Waslewski, RP	1

Texas (54-100)	WS
Hitting	**89.9**
Fielding	**25.2**
Pitching	**46.9**
D. Nelson, 3B	15
T. Ford, OF	14
T. Harrah, SS	13
D. Billings, C	12
D. Mincher, 1B	11
M. Paul, RP	11
L. Biittner, 1B-OF	10
E. Maddox, OF	10
F. Howard, 1B	9
R. Hand, SP	8
P. Lindblad, RP	7
J. Lovitto, OF	6
H. King, C	5
H. Pina, RP	5
D. Bosman, SP	4
B. Gogolewski, SP	3
P. Broberg, SP	2
B. Fahey, C	2
T. Grieve, OF	2
J. Shellenback, RP	2
D. Stanhouse, SP	2
C. Cox, RP	1
V. Harris, 2B	1
J. Janeski, RP	1
D. Jones, 3B	1
T. Kubiak, 2B	1
S. Lawson, RP	1
J. Mason, SS	1
J. Panther, RP	1
L. Randle, 2B	1

1972 National League

Atlanta (70-84)	WS
Hitting	**113.0**
Fielding	**31.9**
Pitching	**65.2**
D. Baker, OF	23
P. Niekro, SP	22
H. Aaron, 1B	21
D. Evans, 3B	20
R. Garr, OF	19
E. Williams, C	18
R. Carty, OF	10
R. Reed, SP	10
F. Millan, 2B	9
M. Lum, OF	8

R. Schueler, RP	8
C. Upshaw, RP	7
P. Jarvis, RP	6
L. Blanks, 2B	4
J. Hardin, RP	4
T. Kelley, SP	4
O. Cepeda, 1B	3
M. Perez, SS	3
J. Breazeale, 1B	2
G. Garrido, 2B	2
O. Brown, OF	1
P. Casanova, C	1
B. Didier, C	1
T. House, RP	1
S. Jackson, SS	1
M. McQueen, RP	1
G. Stone, SP	1

Chicago (85-70)	WS
Hitting	**108.2**
Fielding	**43.9**
Pitching	**102.9**
B. Williams, OF	32
F. Jenkins, SP	22
R. Santo, 3B	21
J. Cardenal, OF	18
M. Pappas, SP	17
B. Hooton, SP	16
R. Monday, OF	16
D. Kessinger, SS	15
B. Hands, SP	13
J. Hickman, 1B	13
G. Beckert, 2B	11
R. Reuschel, SP	10
J. Aker, RP	8
C. Fanzone, 3B	6
R. Hundley, C	6
B. Bonham, RP	5
J. Pepitone, 1B	5
T. Phoebus, RP	5
J. Pizarro, RP	3
P. Popovich, 2B	2
K. Rudolph, C	2
P. Bourque, 1B	1
J. Decker, RP	1
L. Gura, RP	1
S. Hamilton, RP	1
E. Hendricks, C	1
P. LaCock, OF	1
J. Martin, C	1
B. North, OF	1
D. Rosello, SS	1

Cincinnati (95-59)	WS
Hitting	**162.7**
Fielding	**40.6**
Pitching	**81.7**
J. Morgan, 2B	39
J. Bench, C	37
P. Rose, OF	32
T. Perez, 1B	25
B. Tolan, OF	22
G. Nolan, SP	15
D. Menke, 3B	14
C. Carroll, RP	13
R. Grimsley, SP	11
T. Hall, RP	11
J. Billingham, SP	10
P. Borbon, RP	9
C. Geronimo, OF	9
D. Chaney, SS	8
D. Concepcion, SS	6
D. Gullett, SP	5
J. Hague, 1B	5
J. McGlothlin, SP	4
H. McRae, OF	3
W. Simpson, SP	3
G. Foster, OF	1
J. Javier, 3B	1
B. Plummer, C	1
E. Sprague, RP	1

Houston (84-69)	WS
Hitting	**142.1**
Fielding	**36.2**
Pitching	**73.7**
C. Cedeno, OF	33
J. Wynn, OF	28
B. Watson, OF	26
L. May, 1B	24
D. Rader, 3B	19
D. Wilson, SP	17
T. Helms, 2B	14
L. Dierker, SP	13
J. Edwards, C	12
R. Metzger, SS	11
G. Culver, RP	8
F. Gladding, RP	8
T. Griffin, RP	7
D. Roberts, SP	7
K. Forsch, SP	5
J. Ray, RP	5
J. Reuss, SP	5
L. Howard, C	3
N. Miller, OF	3
J. Alou, OF	2
J. Hiatt, C	1
J. Stewart, OF	1

Los Angeles (85-70)	WS
Hitting	**118.8**
Fielding	**39.8**
Pitching	**96.4**
W. Davis, OF	25
D. Sutton, SP	24
C. Osteen, SP	22
J. Brewer, RP	16
B. Russell, SS	16
M. Mota, OF	15
W. Parker, 1B	14
F. Robinson, OF	14
B. Buckner, OF	13
T. John, SP	11
A. Downing, SP	10
W. Crawford, OF	9
B. Valentine, 2B	9
S. Garvey, 3B	8
C. Cannizzaro, C	6
L. Lacy, 2B	6
P. Richert, RP	6
S. Yeager, C	5
J. Lefebvre, 2B	3
D. Rau, RP	3
B. Singer, SP	3
R. Cey, 3B	2
D. Dietz, C	2
B. Grabarkewitz, 3B	2
P. Mikkelsen, RP	2
D. Sims, C	2
M. Strahler, RP	2
J. Ferguson, C	1
D. Lopes, 2B	1
T. Paciorek, 1B-OF	1
R. Perranoski, RP	1
M. Wills, SS	1

Montreal (70-86)	WS
Hitting	**75.5**
Fielding	**42.2**
Pitching	**92.3**
M. Marshall, RP	22
K. Singleton, OF	18
B. Stoneman, SP	18
M. Torrez, SP	18
R. Fairly, OF	17
R. Hunt, 2B	15
B. Bailey, 3B	12
M. Jorgensen, 1B	10
T. Foli, SS	9
B. Moore, SP	9
E. McAnally, SP	7
C. Morton, SP	7
T. Walker, RP	7
R. Woods, OF	7
T. McCarver, C	6
B. Day, OF	5
J. Strohmayer, RP	5
J. Boccabella, C	4
T. Humphrey, C	3
C. Laboy, 3B	3
C. Mashore, OF	3
H. Breeden, 1B	2
H. Torres, 2B	2
J. Fairey, OF	1

New York (83-73)	WS
Hitting	**101.0**
Fielding	**47.9**
Pitching	**100.1**
J. Matlack, SP	22
T. McGraw, RP	22
T. Seaver, SP	22
D. Dyer, C	16
J. Milner, OF	15
W. Garrett, 3B	13
B. Harrelson, SS	13
J. McAndrew, SP	13
R. Staub, OF	12
T. Agee, OF	11
E. Kranepool, 1B	11
W. Mays, OF	11
J. Fregosi, 3B	10
J. Grote, C	8
C. Jones, OF	7
D. Frisella, RP	6
K. Boswell, 2B	5
J. Koosman, SP	5
D. Marshall, OF	5
G. Gentry, SP	4
T. Martinez, 2B	4
R. Sadecki, RP	4
J. Beauchamp, 1B	3
L. Barnes, 2B	2
B. Capra, RP	2
T. Moore, RP	1
D. Schneck, OF	1
B. Sudakis, 1B	1

Philadelphia (59-97)	WS
Hitting	**67.0**
Fielding	**36.3**
Pitching	**73.6**
S. Carlton, SP	40
G. Luzinski, OF	16
W. Montanez, OF	16
L. Bowa, SS	12
D. Money, 3B	10
T. Hutton, 1B	9
T. Harmon, 2B	8
B. Lersch, RP	7
B. Brandon, RP	6
D. Doyle, 2B	6
J. Lis, 1B	5
R. Freed, OF	4
W. Twitchell, RP	4
W. Fryman, SP	3
O. Gamble, OF	3
J. Hoerner, RP	3
D. Johnson, 1B	3
T. McCarver, C	3
K. Reynolds, SP	3
M. Scarce, RP	3
M. Anderson, OF	2
D. Downs, SP	2
B. Robinson, OF	2
B. Wilson, RP	2
J. Bateman, C	1
B. Boone, C	1
M. Ryan, C	1
M. Schmidt, 3B	1
C. Short, RP	1

Pittsburgh (96-59)	WS
Hitting	**140.2**
Fielding	**46.3**
Pitching	**101.5**
W. Stargell, 1B	26
A. Oliver, OF	23
R. Hebner, 3B	22
S. Blass, SP	19
M. Sanguillen, C	18
R. Clemente, OF	16
V. Davalillo, OF	16
D. Cash, 2B	15
B. Moose, SP	14
D. Giusti, RP	13
G. Clines, OF	12
G. Alley, SS	11
D. Ellis, SP	11
R. Hernandez, RP	11
N. Briles, SP	10
R. Stennett, 2B	10
B. Kison, SP	8
B. Johnson, RP	7
M. May, C	5
B. Robertson, 1B	5
B. Miller, RP	4
L. Walker, RP	4
J. Hernandez, SS	3
J. Pagan, 3B	3
B. Mazeroski, 2B	1
J. McKee, RP	1

San Diego (58-95)	WS
Hitting	**86.2**
Fielding	**30.8**
Pitching	**57.0**
N. Colbert, 1B	28
L. Lee, OF	18
C. Kirby, SP	14
F. Norman, SP	11
S. Arlin, SP	10
J. Morales, OF	9
D. Thomas, 2B	9
M. Corkins, RP	8
C. Gaston, OF	8
D. Roberts, 3B	8
G. Ross, RP	7
L. Stahl, OF	7
F. Kendall, C	6
G. Jestadt, 2B	5
E. Hernandez, SS	4
J. Jeter, OF	4
M. Caldwell, RP	3
C. Blefary, C	2
D. Campbell, 3B	2
P. Corrales, C	2
A. Severinsen, RP	2
F. Stanley, 2B	2
E. Acosta, RP	1
B. Barton, C	1
J. Grubb, OF	1
D. Hilton, 3B	1
M. Schaeffer, RP	1

San Francisco (69-86)	WS
Hitting	**114.8**
Fielding	**30.0**
Pitching	**62.1**
C. Speier, SS	25
B. Bonds, OF	23
D. Kingman, 3B	15
T. Fuentes, 2B	14
K. Henderson, OF	14
R. Bryant, SP	13
G. Maddox, OF	13
J. Barr, RP	11
D. Rader, C	10
W. McCovey, 1B	7
S. Stone, SP	7
J. Willoughby, SP	7
J. Marichal, SP	5
A. Gallagher, 3B	4
J. Hart, 3B	4
J. Johnson, RP	4
S. McDowell, SP	4
D. McMahon, RP	4
F. Reberger, SP	4
E. Goodson, 1B	3
G. Matthews, OF	3
R. Moffitt, RP	3
J. Howarth, OF	2
E. Sosa, RP	2
C. Arnold, 3B	1

D. Blanco, 3B	1
F. Healy, C	1
W. Mays, OF	1
G. Thomasson, 1B	1
B. Williams, OF	1

St. Louis (75-81)	WS
Hitting	**89.3**
Fielding	**42.7**
Pitching	**93.1**
B. Gibson, SP	29
T. Simmons, C	23
L. Brock, OF	21
R. Wise, SP	20
J. Torre, 3B	18
B. Carbo, OF	12
M. Alou, 1B	11
T. Sizemore, 2B	11
R. Cleveland, SP	10
S. Spinks, SP	10
J. Cruz, OF	8
D. Segui, RP	7
A. Santorini, SP	6
L. Melendez, OF	5
D. Maxvill, SS	4
D. Anderson, SS	3
R. Bare, RP	3
E. Crosby, SS	3
J. Hague, 1B	3
J. Bibby, SP	2
M. Drabowsky, RP	2
D. Durham, SP	2
K. Reitz, 3B	2
R. Folkers, RP	1
D. Higgins, RP	1
A. Hrabosky, RP	1
S. Jutze, C	1
M. Kelleher, SS	1
J. McNertney, C	1
L. Palmer, RP	1
J. Roque, OF	1
B. Stein, 3B-OF	1
M. Tyson, 2B	1

1973 American League

Baltimore (97-65)	WS
Hitting	**129.2**
Fielding	**52.4**
Pitching	**109.3**
B. Grich, 2B	28
J. Palmer, SP	28
P. Blair, OF	18
D. McNally, SP	18
A. Bumbry, OF	17
D. Baylor, OF	16
R. Coggins, OF	16
M. Cuellar, SP	16
E. Williams, C	15
M. Rettenmund, OF	14
B. Reynolds, RP	14
B. Powell, 1B	13
T. Davis, DH	12
G. Jackson, RP	12
B. Robinson, 3B	12
M. Belanger, SS	10
D. Alexander, SP	8
E. Watt, RP	5
A. Etchebarren, C	4
J. Jefferson, SP	4
F. Baker, SS	2
E. Hendricks, C	2
D. Hood, SP-RP	2
O. Pena, RP	2
L. Brown, 3B	1
T. Crowley, DH	1
C. Motton, DH-OF	1

Boston (89-73)	WS
Hitting	**117.1**
Fielding	**50.6**
Pitching	**99.3**
B. Lee, SP	24
C. Yastrzemski, 1B	24
R. Smith, OF	23
T. Harper, OF	21
L. Tiant, SP	21
C. Fisk, C	17
R. Moret, SP-RP	14
L. Aparicio, SS	13
O. Cepeda, DH	13
J. Curtis, SP	13
R. Miller, OF	12
R. Petrocelli, 3B	11
M. Pattin, SP	10
B. Bolin, RP	9
D. Evans, OF	7
D. Griffin, 2B	7
B. Montgomery, C	6
D. Cater, 1B	5
B. Veale, RP	5
M. Guerrero, SS	3
J. Kennedy, 2B	2
D. Newhauser, RP	2
C. Cooper, 1B	1
R. Culp, SP	1
B. Hunter, 3B	1
B. Oglivie, OF	1
D. Pole, SP	1

California (79-83)	WS
Hitting	**107.7**
Fielding	**40.1**
Pitching	**89.2**
N. Ryan, SP	28
F. Robinson, DH	26
B. Singer, SP	23
B. Oliver, 3B	16
C. Wright, SP	13
R. Scheinblum, OF	12
K. Berry, OF	10
S. Alomar, 2B	9
A. Gallagher, 3B	9
V. Pinson, OF	9
T. McCraw, OF	8
M. Rivers, OF	7
S. Barber, RP	6
M. Epstein, 1B	6
R. Meoli, SS	6
D. Sells, RP	6
L. Stanton, OF	6
R. May, SP	5
B. Valentine, SS	5
R. Hand, RP	3
J. Spencer, 1B	3
J. Torborg, C	3
D. Chalk, SS	2
B. Grabarkewitz, 2B	2
W. Llenas, 2B	2
A. Monteagudo, RP	2
C. Sands, C	2
J. Stephenson, C	2
F. Tanana, SP	2
J. DaVanon, SS	1
A. Kusnyer, C	1
D. Lange, RP	1
B. Parker, 2B	1

Chicago (77-85)	WS
Hitting	**98.5**
Fielding	**39.9**
Pitching	**92.6**
W. Wood, SP	23
B. Melton, 3B	22
S. Bahnsen, SP	18
C. Acosta, RP	15
D. Allen, 1B	15
T. Forster, RP	15
C. May, DH	15
P. Kelly, OF	13
E. Herrmann, C	10
T. Muser, 1B	10
J. Orta, 2B	10
S. Stone, SP	8
B. Sharp, OF	7
J. Hairston, OF	6
E. Leon, SS	6
B. Bradford, OF	5
K. Henderson, OF	5
E. Fisher, SP	4
J. Jeter, OF	4
B. Johnson, RP	4
C. Brinkman, C	3
R. Reichardt, OF	3
B. Dent, SS	2
K. Frailing, RP	2
J. Kaat, SP	2
L. Alvarado, 2B	1
B. Downing, OF	1
J. Geddes, RP	1
J. McGlothlin, RP	1

Cleveland (71-91)	WS
Hitting	**117.6**
Fielding	**31.5**
Pitching	**63.9**
G. Perry, SP	24
B. Bell, 3B	21
C. Chambliss, 1B	16
J. Ellis, C	14
O. Gamble, DH	14
G. Hendrick, OF	13
C. Spikes, OF	12
D. Tidrow, SP	12
F. Duffy, SS	11
D. Duncan, C	11
J. Lowenstein, OF	10
T. Hilgendorf, RP	9
W. Williams, OF	9
J. Brohamer, 2B	6
K. Sanders, RP	6
T. Timmermann, SP	5
R. Torres, OF	5
R. Lamb, RP	4
T. Ragland, 2B	3
B. Strom, SP	3
L. Cardenas, SS	2
M. Wilcox, SP	2
T. Smith, OF	1

Detroit (85-77)	WS
Hitting	**103.2**
Fielding	**49.3**
Pitching	**102.4**
J. Hiller, RP	31
J. Coleman, SP	21
M. Lolich, SP	19
D. McAuliffe, 2B	16
J. Northrup, OF	16
N. Cash, 1B	15
W. Horton, OF	15
M. Stanley, OF	15
B. Freehan, C	12
J. Perry, SP	12
A. Rodriguez, 3B	9
D. Sims, C	9
A. Kaline, OF	8
E. Brinkman, SS	7
G. Brown, DH	6
F. Howard, DH	5
B. Miller, RP	4
D. Sharon, OF	4
T. Taylor, 2B	4
I. Brown, 1B	3
L. LaGrow, RP	3
F. Scherman, RP	3
M. Strahler, SP-RP	3
T. Timmermann, RP	3
R. Cash, OF	2
B. Didier, C	2
E. Farmer, RP	2
W. Fryman, SP	2
J. Knox, 2B	1
M. Lane, OF	1
C. Seelbach, RP	1
T. Veryzer, SS	1

Kansas City (88-74)	WS
Hitting	**129.7**
Fielding	**42.2**
Pitching	**92.0**
J. Mayberry, 1B	31
A. Otis, OF	29
P. Splittorff, SP	17
F. Patek, SS	16
C. Rojas, 2B	16
D. Bird, RP	15
P. Schaal, 3B	15
S. Busby, SP	14
D. Drago, SP	11
G. Garber, RP	11
F. Healy, C	11
E. Kirkpatrick, OF	11
A. Fitzmorris, SP	9
H. McRae, OF	8
S. Hovley, OF	6
L. Piniella, OF	6
K. Bevacqua, 3B	5
S. Mingori, RP	5
B. Dal Canton, RP	4
C. Taylor, C	4
B. Floyd, 2B	3
G. Hopkins, DH	3
J. Wohlford, DH	3
K. Wright, RP	3
F. White, SS	2
J. Hoerner, RP	1
M. Littell, SP	1
B. Martinez, C	1
F. Ortenzio, 1B	1
R. Reichardt, DH	1
W. Simpson, SP	1

Milwaukee (74-88)	WS
Hitting	**117.7**
Fielding	**34.6**
Pitching	**69.7**
D. May, OF	24
G. Scott, 1B	24
J. Colborn, SP	20
J. Briggs, OF	18
D. Money, 3B	18
D. Porter, C	16
J. Slaton, SP	13
B. Coluccio, OF	12
P. Garcia, 2B	12
El. Rodriguez, C	9
J. Bell, SP	8
O. Brown, DH	7
B. Champion, RP	7
S. Lockwood, RP	6
Ed Rodriguez, RP	6
T. Johnson, SS	4
F. Linzy, RP	4
C. Velazquez, RP	3
J. Lahoud, DH	2
B. Mitchell, OF	2
R. Newman, RP	2
B. Heise, SS	1
C. Moore, C	1
C. Short, RP	1
G. Thomas, OF	1
J. Vukovich, 3B	1

Minnesota (81-81)	WS
Hitting	**114.4**
Fielding	**38.6**
Pitching	**90.0**
B. Blyleven, SP	29
R. Carew, 2B	28
L. Hisle, OF	17
S. Braun, 3B	16
R. Corbin, RP	15
G. Mitterwald, C	15
T. Oliva, DH	13
J. Holt, OF	12
B. Darwin, OF	10
S. Brye, OF	8
J. Decker, SP	8
B. Hands, RP	8
D. Woodson, SP	8
J. Kaat, SP	7
J. Terrell, SS	7

B. Campbell, RP	6
H. Killebrew, 1B	5
J. Lis, 1B	5
E. Soderholm, 3B	4
D. Fife, SP	3
D. Thompson, SS	3
M. Adams, OF	2
V. Albury, RP	2
D. Goltz, RP	2
D. Monzon, 2B	2
P. Roof, C	2
E. Bane, RP	1
G. Borgmann, C	1
C. Kusick, 1B	1
R. Reese, 1B	1
K. Sanders, RP	1
D. Walton, OF	1

New York (80-82)	WS
Hitting	**100.6**
Fielding	**42.4**
Pitching	**97.0**
T. Munson, C	25
B. Murcer, OF	25
G. Nettles, 3B	19
D. Medich, SP	18
M. Stottlemyre, SP	18
L. McDaniel, RP	15
R. White, OF	15
S. Lyle, RP	14
R. Blomberg, DH	13
H. Clarke, 2B	12
M. Alou, OF	10
F. Beene, RP	10
F. Peterson, SP	7
P. Dobson, SP	6
J. Hart, DH	6
G. Michael, SS	5
S. McDowell, SP	4
M. Hegan, 1B	3
S. Kline, SP	3
F. Alou, 1B	2
O. Velez, OF	2
B. Allen, 2B	1
J. Callison, OF	1
W. Granger, RP	1
H. Lanier, SS	1
J. Moses, C	1
D. Pagan, RP	1
D. Sims, DH	1
F. Stanley, SS	1

Oakland (94-68)	WS
Hitting	**157.0**
Fielding	**41.9**
Pitching	**83.1**
R. Jackson, OF	32
S. Bando, 3B	31
G. Tenace, 1B	26
B. North, OF	25
B. Campaneris, SS	20
K. Holtzman, SP	19
V. Blue, SP	15
C. Hunter, SP	15
R. Fingers, RP	14
R. Fosse, C	14
D. Johnson, DH	13
J. Rudi, OF	13
D. Green, 2B	10
H. Pina, RP	8
D. Knowles, RP	6
T. Kubiak, 2B	4
J. Alou, OF	3
P. Bourque, DH	2
D. Hamilton, SP	2
P. Lindblad, RP	2
A. Mangual, OF	2
B. Odom, SP	2
G. Abbott, SP	1
R. Carty, DH	1
B. Conigliaro, OF	1
R. McKinney, 3B	1

Texas (57-105)	WS
Hitting	**99.6**
Fielding	**26.5**
Pitching	**44.8**
J. Burroughs, OF	23
D. Nelson, 2B	15
T. Harrah, SS	13
A. Johnson, DH	12
J. Bibby, SP	10
V. Harris, OF	10
J. Spencer, 1B	8
B. Sudakis, 3B	8
J. Merritt, SP	6
K. Suarez, C	6
J. Fregosi, 3B	5
B. Gogolewski, RP	5
T. Grieve, OF	5
S. Siebert, SP	5
R. Carty, OF	4
B. Madlock, 3B	4
L. Biittner, OF	3
J. Brown, RP	3
S. Foucault, RP	3
E. Maddox, OF	3
J. Mason, SS	3
D. Billings, C	2
P. Broberg, SP	2
R. Henninger, RP	2
C. Hudson, RP	2
M. Paul, RP	2
D. Bosman, SP	1
D. Clyde, SP	1
S. Dunning, SP	1
M. Epstein, 1B	1
R. Hand, SP	1
P. Mackanin, SS	1
D. Stanhouse, RP	1

1973
National League

Atlanta (76-85)	WS
Hitting	**116.7**
Fielding	**34.8**
Pitching	**76.5**
D. Evans, 3B	31
D. Johnson, 2B	21
H. Aaron, OF	20
D. Baker, OF	20
C. Morton, SP	18
P. Niekro, SP	17
R. Garr, OF	14
M. Lum, 1B	14
R. Harrison, SP	10
R. Schueler, SP	10
M. Perez, SS	8
D. Dietz, 1B	6
G. Gentry, SP	6
T. House, RP	4
J. Oates, C	4
R. Reed, SP	4
P. Casanova, C	3
D. Frisella, RP	3
F. Tepedino, 1B	3
S. Jackson, OF	2
J. Niekro, RP	2
P. Dobson, SP	1
W. Ford, SP-RP	1
R. Gilbreath, 3B	1
C. Goggin, 2B	1
T. Kelley, RP	1
M. Leon, RP	1
N. Miller, OF	1
F. Velazquez, C	1

Chicago (77-84)	WS
Hitting	**82.8**
Fielding	**42.9**
Pitching	**105.3**
R. Monday, OF	22
R. Reuschel, SP	20
B. Williams, OF	20
J. Cardenal, OF	18
B. Locker, RP	17
B. Hooton, SP	16
B. Bonham, RP	15
F. Jenkins, SP	15
R. Santo, 3B	13
D. Kessinger, SS	12
R. Hundley, C	9
M. Pappas, SP	7
G. Beckert, 2B	6
R. Burris, RP	6
J. Aker, RP	5
P. Popovich, 2B	5
C. Fanzone, 3B	4
J. Hickman, 1B	4
P. Bourque, 1B	3
K. Rudolph, C	3
L. Gura, RP	2
D. LaRoche, RP	2
J. Pepitone, 1B	2
A. Garrett, OF	1
G. Hiser, OF	1
M. Paul, RP	1
D. Rosello, 2B	1
A. Thornton, 1B	1

Cincinnati (99-63)	WS
Hitting	**159.6**
Fielding	**46.5**
Pitching	**90.9**
J. Morgan, 2B	40
P. Rose, OF	34
T. Perez, 1B	32
J. Bench, C	26
J. Billingham, SP	19
D. Concepcion, SS	16
P. Borbon, RP	15
D. Gullett, SP	15
R. Grimsley, SP	14
D. Driessen, 3B	12
F. Norman, SP	10
T. Hall, RP	8
D. Menke, 3B	8
K. Griffey Sr., OF	6
A. Kosco, OF	6
C. Carroll, RP	5
D. Chaney, SS	4
C. Geronimo, OF	4
D. Baney, RP	3
B. Tolan, OF	3
E. Crosby, SS	2
G. Foster, OF	2
P. Gagliano, 3B	2
H. King, C	2
R. Nelson, SP	2
B. Plummer, C	2
R. Scheinblum, OF	2
L. Stahl, OF	2
E. Armbrister, OF	1

Houston (82-80)	WS
Hitting	**127.1**
Fielding	**38.4**
Pitching	**80.4**
C. Cedeno, OF	30
B. Watson, OF	28
D. Roberts, SP	20
L. May, 1B	19
D. Rader, 3B	18
T. Helms, 2B	17
D. Wilson, SP	17
J. Wynn, OF	16
R. Metzger, SS	15
J. Reuss, SP	15
K. Forsch, SP	8
J. Edwards, C	7
T. Agee, OF	4
T. Griffin, RP	4
J. Ray, RP	4
J. Richard, SP	4
J. Crawford, RP	3
B. Gallagher, OF	3
J. York, RP	3
S. Jutze, C	2
D. Campbell, 3B	1
M. Cosgrove, RP	1
L. Dierker, RP	1
F. Gladding, RP	1
G. Gross, OF	1
C. Johnson, 1B	1
G. Sutherland, 2B	1
H. Torres, SS	1
C. Upshaw, RP	1

Los Angeles (95-66)	WS
Hitting	**123.7**
Fielding	**51.9**
Pitching	**109.4**
J. Ferguson, C	29
W. Crawford, OF	24
W. Davis, OF	23
D. Sutton, SP	22
D. Lopes, 2B	19
A. Messersmith, SP	18
R. Cey, 3B	17
B. Russell, SS	17
T. John, SP	15
C. Osteen, SP	14
J. Brewer, RP	11
B. Buckner, 1B	11
S. Garvey, 1B	11
A. Downing, SP	9
M. Mota, OF	8
C. Hough, RP	7
P. Richert, RP	5
S. Yeager, C	5
T. Paciorek, OF	4
G. Culver, RP	3
V. Joshua, OF	3
K. McMullen, 3B	3
D. Rau, RP	3
G. Zahn, RP	2
L. Lacy, 2B	1
G. Shanahan, RP	1

Montreal (79-83)	WS
Hitting	**109.0**
Fielding	**42.2**
Pitching	**85.7**
K. Singleton, OF	28
M. Marshall, RP	23
S. Renko, SP	22
B. Bailey, 3B	21
R. Fairly, OF	20
R. Hunt, 2B	15
S. Rogers, SP	15
H. Breeden, 1B	11
M. Jorgensen, 1B	10
R. Woods, OF	9
J. Boccabella, C	6
T. Foli, SS	6
M. Torrez, SP	6
B. Day, OF	5
E. McAnally, SP	5
T. Walker, RP	5
B. Moore, SP	4
B. Stinson, C	4
P. Frias, SS	3
L. Lintz, 2B	3
J. Lyttle, OF	3
C. Taylor, RP	3
P. Jarvis, RP	2
C. Mashore, OF	2
B. Allen, 2B	1
F. Alou, OF	1
B. Foote, PH-PR	1
J. Gilbert, RP	1
T. Humphrey, C	1
J. Montague, RP	1

New York (82-79)	WS
Hitting	**96.2**
Fielding	**48.0**
Pitching	**101.8**
T. Seaver, SP	29
R. Staub, OF	23
W. Garrett, 3B	21
F. Millan, 2B	20
J. Koosman, SP	18

J. Matlack, SP	16
J. Milner, 1B	15
B. Harrelson, SS	13
G. Stone, SP	13
T. McGraw, RP	10
C. Jones, OF	9
J. Grote, C	7
H. Parker, RP	7
R. Sadecki, RP	7
E. Kranepool, 1B	5
T. Martinez, SS	5
W. Mays, OF	5
D. Hahn, OF	4
R. Hodges, C	4
D. Dyer, C	3
J. Fregosi, 3B-SS	3
J. Beauchamp, 1B	2
K. Boswell, 3B	2
B. Capra, RP	2
G. Theodore, OF	2
J. Gosger, OF	1

Philadelphia (71-91)	WS
Hitting	**93.5**
Fielding	**39.8**
Pitching	**79.6**
G. Luzinski, OF	21
W. Twitchell, SP	21
K. Brett, SP	17
B. Boone, C	16
B. Robinson, OF	16
D. Unser, OF	16
S. Carlton, SP	14
W. Montanez, 1B	11
M. Schmidt, 3B	10
D. Doyle, 2B	9
M. Scarce, RP	9
C. Tovar, 3B	8
T. Hutton, 1B	6
M. Anderson, OF	5
L. Bowa, SS	5
J. Lonborg, SP	5
D. Ruthven, SP	5
B. Lersch, RP	4
B. Grabarkewitz, 2B	3
R. Diorio, RP	2
C. Robinson, SS	2
M. Rogodzinski, OF	2
M. Wallace, RP	2
B. Brandon, RP	1
G. Culver, RP	1
T. Harmon, 2B	1
M. Ryan, C	1

Pittsburgh (80-82)	WS
Hitting	**138.0**
Fielding	**32.2**
Pitching	**69.9**
W. Stargell, OF	36
A. Oliver, OF	22
R. Hebner, 3B	21
R. Zisk, OF	16
M. Sanguillen, C	15
N. Briles, SP	12
D. Cash, 2B	12
D. Giusti, RP	12
J. Rooker, RP	12
B. Robertson, 1B	10
R. Hernandez, RP	9
M. May, C	9
R. Stennett, 2B	9
D. Ellis, SP	8
B. Moose, SP	8
G. Clines, OF	5
B. Johnson, RP	4
D. Parker, OF	4
B. Kison, SP	3
D. Maxvill, SS	3
G. Alley, SS	2
J. Hernandez, SS	2
J. Morlan, SP	2
S. Blass, SP	1
F. Gonzalez, 3B	1
L. Walker, RP	1
C. Zachary, RP	1

San Diego (60-102)	WS
Hitting	**95.8**
Fielding	**29.3**
Pitching	**54.9**
N. Colbert, 1B	20
D. Roberts, 3B	19
J. Grubb, OF	18
F. Kendall, C	14
B. Greif, SP	12
J. Morales, OF	11
C. Gaston, OF	10
R. Jones, SP	9
M. Caldwell, RP	8
D. Thomas, SS	6
R. Troedson, RP	6
L. Lee, OF	5
V. Romo, RP	5
S. Arlin, SP	4
M. Corkins, RP	4
G. Locklear, OF	4
I. Murrell, OF	4
R. Morales, 2B	3
D. Winfield, OF	3
E. Hernandez, SS	2
D. Hilton, 3B	2
C. Kirby, SP	2
F. Norman, SP	2
D. Anderson, SS	1
D. Campbell, 2B	1
P. Corrales, C	1
D. Marshall, OF	1
B. Miller, RP	1
G. Ross, RP	1
F. Snook, RP	1

San Francisco (88-74)	WS
Hitting	**136.4**
Fielding	**40.3**
Pitching	**87.3**
B. Bonds, OF	31
G. Maddox, OF	23
W. McCovey, 1B	22
G. Matthews, OF	21
T. Fuentes, 2B	19
R. Bryant, SP	17
C. Speier, SS	15
E. Sosa, RP	13
J. Barr, SP	12
R. Moffitt, RP	12
D. Rader, C	12
T. Bradley, SP	11
E. Goodson, 3B	11
J. Marichal, SP	10
D. Kingman, 3B	8
G. Thomasson, 1B	8
D. McMahon, RP	7
J. Willoughby, RP	3
C. Arnold, C	2
D. Carrithers, RP	1
J. D'Acquisto, RP	1
J. Howarth, OF	1
S. McDowell, RP	1
S. Ontiveros, 1B	1
M. Phillips, 3B	1
M. Sadek, C	1

St. Louis (81-81)	WS
Hitting	**123.5**
Fielding	**38.1**
Pitching	**81.3**
T. Simmons, C	28
L. Brock, OF	26
T. Sizemore, 2B	22
J. Torre, 1B	19
B. Carbo, OF	16
R. Cleveland, SP	13
R. Wise, SP	13
J. Cruz, OF	12
B. Gibson, SP	12
A. Foster, SP	11
T. McCarver, 1B	10
D. Segui, RP	10
M. Tyson, SS	8
L. Melendez, OF	7
A. Hrabosky, RP	6
O. Pena, RP	6
K. Reitz, 3B	5
R. Folkers, RP	4
T. Murphy, SP	3
E. Fisher, RP	2
B. McBride, OF	2
T. Agee, OF	1
R. Busse, SS	1
W. Granger, RP	1
T. Heintzelman, 2B	1
M. Kelleher, SS	1
E. Sprague, RP	1
B. Stein, OF	1
M. Thompson, SP	1

1974 American League

Baltimore (91-71)	WS
Hitting	**132.6**
Fielding	**45.2**
Pitching	**95.2**
B. Grich, 2B	32
B. Robinson, 3B	23
P. Blair, OF	21
R. Grimsley, SP	21
M. Cuellar, SP	19
D. Baylor, OF	16
M. Belanger, SS	16
T. Davis, DH	15
D. McNally, SP	14
E. Williams, C	14
B. Powell, 1B	13
G. Jackson, RP	10
R. Coggins, OF	9
J. Palmer, SP	9
B. Reynolds, RP	7
W. Garland, RP	6
A. Bumbry, OF	4
J. Fuller, OF	4
E. Hendricks, C	4
D. Alexander, RP	3
A. Etchebarren, C	3
D. Hood, RP	3
E. Cabell, 1B	2
D. Johnson, RP	2
J. Jefferson, RP	1
T. Nordbrook, SS	1
J. Northrup, OF	1

Boston (84-78)	WS
Hitting	**110.0**
Fielding	**45.9**
Pitching	**96.1**
L. Tiant, SP	29
C. Yastrzemski, 1B	24
B. Lee, SP	19
D. Evans, OF	15
R. Petrocelli, 3B	15
D. Drago, SP	13
B. Carbo, OF	12
R. Burleson, SS	11
C. Fisk, C	11
R. Moret, SP	11
C. Cooper, 1B	10
R. Miller, OF	10
R. Cleveland, SP	9
J. Beniquez, OF	8
D. Griffin, 2B	7
D. Segui, RP	7
T. Harper, OF	6
D. McAuliffe, 2B	6
M. Guerrero, SS	5
B. Montgomery, C	5
F. Lynn, OF	4
J. Marichal, SP	3
R. Wise, SP	3
T. Blackwell, C	2
D. Cater, 1B	2
S. Barr, SP	1
T. Hughes, 3B	1
T. McCarver, C	1
D. Pole, RP	1
J. Rice, DH	1

California (68-94)	WS
Hitting	**106.7**
Fielding	**32.2**
Pitching	**65.0**
N. Ryan, SP	21
E. Rodriguez, C	18
F. Robinson, DH	17
M. Rivers, OF	16
F. Tanana, SP	15
J. Lahoud, OF	14
L. Stanton, OF	12
D. Doyle, 2B	11
A. Hassler, SP	9
D. Chalk, SS	7
B. Valentine, OF	7
B. Singer, SP	6
B. Bochte, OF	5
J. Doherty, 1B	4
E. Figueroa, RP	4
T. McCraw, 1B	4
W. Llenas, OF	3
M. Nettles, OF	3
B. Oliver, 1B	3
C. Sands, DH	3
P. Schaal, 3B	3
T. Egan, C	2
M. Epstein, 1B	2
B. Heise, 2B	2
D. Lange, SP	2
S. Lockwood, RP	2
O. Pena, RP	2
J. Balaz, OF	1
J. Cumberland, RP	1
R. Meoli, 3B	1
H. Pina, RP	1
L. Quintana, RP	1
O. Ramirez, SS	1
D. Sells, RP	1

Chicago (80-80)	WS
Hitting	**120.1**
Fielding	**39.6**
Pitching	**80.2**
K. Henderson, OF	26
D. Allen, 1B	24
J. Orta, 2B	22
J. Kaat, SP	21
W. Wood, SP	19
B. Dent, SS	16
T. Forster, RP	13
B. Melton, 3B	13
B. Johnson, SP	11
B. Downing, C	10
E. Herrmann, C	10
P. Kelly, DH	10
C. May, OF	8
S. Bahnsen, SP	6
B. Bradford, OF	5
B. Sharp, OF	5
G. Gossage, RP	4
T. Muser, 1B	3
S. Pitlock, RP	3
R. Santo, DH	3
C. Acosta, RP	2
N. Nyman, OF	2
J. Hairston, OF	1
E. Leon, SS	1
C. Moran, RP	1
B. Stein, 3B	1

Cleveland (77-85)	WS
Hitting	**113.6**
Fielding	**37.6**
Pitching	**79.8**
G. Perry, SP	30
O. Gamble, DH	20
J. Perry, SP	20

G. Hendrick, OF	19
C. Spikes, OF	19
J. Ellis, 1B	16
B. Bell, 3B	13
J. Lowenstein, OF	13
J. Brohamer, 2B	11
T. Buskey, RP	9
F. Duffy, SS	9
D. Duncan, C	7
D. Bosman, SP	5
F. Peterson, SP	5
R. Carty, DH	4
L. Lee, OF	4
T. McCraw, 1B	4
F. Beene, RP	2
C. Chambliss, 1B	2
B. Ellingsen, RP	2
R. Hermoso, 2B	2
T. Hilgendorf, RP	2
B. Johnson, SP	2
D. Kuiper, 2B	2
J. Lis, 1B	2
M. Wilcox, RP	2
L. Alvarado, 2B	1
E. Crosby, 3B	1
S. Kline, SP	1
F. Robinson, DH	1
R. Torres, OF	1

Detroit (72-90)	WS
Hitting	**96.6**
Fielding	**41.3**
Pitching	**78.1**
B. Freehan, 1B	23
J. Hiller, RP	20
M. Lolich, SP	17
A. Kaline, DH	15
J. Coleman, SP	13
W. Horton, OF	12
E. Brinkman, SS	11
J. Northrup, OF	9
B. Oglivie, OF	9
A. Rodriguez, 3B	8
G. Sutherland, 2B	8
W. Fryman, SP	7
L. LaGrow, SP	6
N. Cash, 1B	5
R. LeFlore, OF	5
J. Moses, C	5
M. Stanley, OF	5
M. Lane, OF	4
D. Lemanczyk, RP	4
J. Nettles, OF	4
J. Ray, RP	3
V. Ruhle, SP	3
R. Sanders, 1B	3
L. Walker, RP	3
G. Brown, DH	2
J. Knox, 2B	2
G. Lamont, C	2
D. Sharon, OF	2
T. Veryzer, SS	2
F. Holdsworth, SP	1
D. Meyer, OF	1
L. Roberts, OF	1
B. Slayback, RP	1

Kansas City (77-85)	WS
Hitting	**97.2**
Fielding	**41.4**
Pitching	**92.4**
S. Busby, SP	22
A. Otis, OF	22
H. McRae, DH	20
A. Fitzmorris, SP	16
F. Patek, SS	15
J. Mayberry, 1B	14
B. Dal Canton, SP	12
F. Healy, C	12
D. Bird, RP	10
V. Pinson, OF	10
C. Rojas, 2B	10
J. Wohlford, OF	10
G. Brett, 3B	9
P. Splittorff, SP	9
T. Solaita, 1B	7
L. McDaniel, RP	6
N. Briles, SP	5
S. Mingori, RP	5
M. Pattin, RP	5
A. Cowens, OF	4
J. Hoerner, RP	3
F. White, 2B	3
B. Martinez, C	2

Milwaukee (76-86)	WS
Hitting	**103.5**
Fielding	**42.8**
Pitching	**81.7**
D. Money, 3B	26
J. Briggs, OF	20
T. Murphy, RP	19
G. Scott, 1B	19
D. Porter, C	15
J. Slaton, SP	12
B. Champion, SP	10
J. Colborn, SP	10
B. Coluccio, OF	9
E. Sprague, SP-RP	9
R. Yount, SS	8
P. Garcia, 2B	7
E. Rodriguez, RP	7
C. Wright, SP	7
M. Hegan, DH	6
T. Johnson, SS	6
K. Kobel, SP	6
D. May, OF	6
C. Moore, C	6
K. Berry, OF	5
B. Mitchell, DH	4
B. Hansen, DH	3
G. Thomas, OF	2
J. Bell, RP	1
R. Ellis, OF	1
S. Lezcano, OF	1
J. Lind, SS	1
B. Travers, RP	1
J. Vukovich, 3B-SS	1

Minnesota (82-80)	WS
Hitting	**114.6**
Fielding	**41.1**
Pitching	**90.3**
R. Carew, 2B	32
B. Blyleven, SP	23
L. Hisle, OF	18
J. Decker, SP	17
B. Darwin, OF	16
B. Campbell, RP	15
E. Soderholm, 3B	15
S. Braun, OF	13
G. Borgmann, C	12
S. Brye, OF	11
D. Goltz, SP	11
T. Oliva, DH	9
V. Albury, SP	7
C. Kusick, 1B	7
T. Burgmeier, RP	5
B. Hands, RP	5
H. Killebrew, DH	5
B. Butler, RP	4
P. Roof, C	3
J. Terrell, SS	3
D. Thompson, SS	3
S. Ferrer, SS	2
L. Gomez, SS	2
J. Holt, 1B	2
T. Johnson, RP	2
P. Bourque, 1B	1
R. Corbin, SP	1
R. Hundley, C	1
D. Woodson, SP	1

New York (89-73)	WS
Hitting	**132.4**
Fielding	**42.7**
Pitching	**91.9**
E. Maddox, OF	23
G. Nettles, 3B	22
B. Murcer, OF	20
P. Dobson, SP	19
R. White, OF	19
T. Munson, C	17
L. Piniella, OF	17
S. Lyle, RP	16
D. Medich, SP	16
R. Blomberg, DH	13
J. Mason, SS	13
R. May, SP	10
D. Tidrow, SP	8
C. Chambliss, 1B	7
S. Alomar, 2B	6
L. Gura, SP	6
M. Stottlemyre, SP	5
B. Sudakis, DH	5
M. Wallace, RP	5
G. Michael, 2B	4
C. Upshaw, RP	4
R. Dempsey, C	2
F. Gonzalez, 2B	2
S. Kline, SP	2
O. Velez, 1B	2
F. Beene, RP	1
H. Clarke, 2B	1
M. Hegan, 1B	1
F. Stanley, SS	1

Oakland (90-72)	WS
Hitting	**128.2**
Fielding	**42.8**
Pitching	**99.0**
R. Jackson, OF	30
C. Hunter, SP	27
J. Rudi, OF	24
B. Campaneris, SS	22
G. Tenace, 1B	22
S. Bando, 3B	21
B. North, OF	19
V. Blue, SP	16
K. Holtzman, SP	15
R. Fingers, RP	14
P. Lindblad, RP	10
D. Hamilton, SP	7
G. Abbott, SP	6
A. Mangual, OF	6
D. Green, 2B	5
C. Washington, DH	5
R. Fosse, C	3
T. Kubiak, 2B	3
B. Odom, RP	3
J. Alou, DH	2
P. Bourque, 1B	2
L. Haney, C	2
D. Maxvill, 2B	2
D. Johnson, DH	1
D. Knowles, RP	1
G. Pitts, 3B	1
M. Trillo, 2B	1

Texas (84-76)	WS
Hitting	**141.3**
Fielding	**36.1**
Pitching	**74.7**
J. Burroughs, OF	33
F. Jenkins, SP	26
C. Tovar, OF	22
M. Hargrove, 1B	20
T. Harrah, SS	20
L. Randle, 3B	16
S. Foucault, RP	15
J. Sundberg, C	15
J. Brown, SP	12
A. Johnson, OF	11
J. Spencer, 1B	10
J. Bibby, SP	8
J. Fregosi, 1B	7
T. Grieve, DH	7
S. Hargan, SP	7
D. Nelson, 2B	7
D. Clyde, SP	3
L. Cardenas, 3B	2
B. Hands, SP	2
J. Lovitto, OF	2
D. Sims, C	2
D. Billings, C	1
L. Brown, 3B	1
R. Howell, 3B	1
J. Merritt, RP	1
J. Terpko, RP	1

1974 National League

Atlanta (88-74)	WS
Hitting	**101.6**
Fielding	**51.6**
Pitching	**110.7**
D. Evans, 3B	28
P. Niekro, SP	28
R. Garr, OF	27
B. Capra, SP	21
D. Baker, OF	20
C. Morton, SP	17
T. House, RP	15
D. Johnson, 1B	15
H. Aaron, OF	13
M. Perez, 2B	12
R. Reed, SP	11
V. Correll, C	7
M. Leon, RP	7
M. Lum, 1B	7
J. Oates, C	6
C. Robinson, SS	6
L. Krausse, RP	4
R. Office, OF	4
R. Harrison, SP	3
J. Niekro, RP	3
P. Casanova, C	2
I. Murrell, OF	2
M. Beard, RP	1
L. Foster, SS	1
D. Frisella, RP	1
G. Gentry, RP	1
N. Miller, OF	1
M. Thompson, SP	1

Chicago (66-96)	WS
Hitting	**104.9**
Fielding	**26.6**
Pitching	**66.5**
R. Monday, OF	22
J. Cardenal, OF	17
B. Madlock, 3B	16
B. Williams, 1B	16
D. Kessinger, SS	13
J. Morales, OF	12
R. Reuschel, SP	12
A. Thornton, 1B	12
B. Bonham, SP	11
O. Zamora, RP	9
S. Stone, SP	8
K. Frailing, RP	7
D. LaRoche, RP	5
G. Mitterwald, C	5
S. Swisher, C	5
J. Todd, RP	5
B. Hooton, RP	4
T. Dettore, SP	3
R. Dunn, 2B	3
B. Grabarkewitz, 2B	3
H. Pina, RP	3
V. Harris, 2B	2
M. Alexander, 3B	1
C. Fanzone, 3B	1
H. Hutson, RP	1
D. Rosello, 2B	1
R. Stelmaszek, C	1

Cincinnati (98-64)	WS
Hitting	**159.8**
Fielding	**45.2**
Pitching	**89.0**
J. Morgan, 2B	37
J. Bench, C	34
P. Rose, OF	27
D. Concepcion, SS	25
T. Perez, 1B	20
D. Gullett, SP	18
C. Geronimo, OF	17
D. Driessen, 3B	14
P. Borbon, RP	12
C. Carroll, RP	12
C. Kirby, SP	12
F. Norman, SP	12
J. Billingham, SP	9
G. Foster, OF	9
K. Griffey Sr., OF	7
R. Nelson, SP	5
M. Rettenmund, OF	5
D. Chaney, 3B	4
T. Carroll, SP	3
T. Hall, RP	3
T. Crowley, OF	2
R. Eastwick, RP	2
B. Plummer, C	2
P. Darcy, RP	1
R. Freed, 1B	1
W. McEnaney, RP	1

Houston (81-81)	WS
Hitting	**112.2**
Fielding	**43.1**
Pitching	**87.7**
C. Cedeno, OF	27
G. Gross, OF	20
D. Rader, 3B	18
B. Watson, OF	18
L. Dierker, SP	17
M. May, C	17
T. Griffin, SP	14
L. May, 1B	14
D. Roberts, SP	13
D. Wilson, SP	13
T. Helms, 2B	11
K. Forsch, RP	10
R. Metzger, SS	10
C. Osteen, SP	8
M. Cosgrove, RP	7
C. Johnson, C	7
L. Milbourne, 2B	4
J. Edwards, C	3
J. Richard, SP	2
F. Scherman, RP	2
J. York, RP	2
O. Brown, OF	1
R. de los Santos, RP	1
W. Howard, OF	1
J. Johnson, RP	1
M. Kelleher, SS	1
P. Siebert, SP	1

Los Angeles (102-60)	WS
Hitting	**168.7**
Fielding	**41.5**
Pitching	**95.7**
J. Wynn, OF	32
S. Garvey, 1B	27
A. Messersmith, SP	25
R. Cey, 3B	23
B. Buckner, OF	21
D. Lopes, 2B	21
M. Marshall, RP	21
W. Crawford, OF	20
J. Ferguson, C	19
B. Russell, SS	16
D. Sutton, SP	15
S. Yeager, C	15
T. John, SP	11
D. Rau, SP	8
C. Hough, RP	5
G. Zahn, RP	5
R. Auerbach, SS	3
J. Brewer, RP	3
A. Downing, SP	3
T. Paciorek, OF	3
L. Lacy, 2B	2
K. McMullen, 3B	2
J. Hale, OF	1
G. Hopkins, C-1B	1
V. Joshua, OF	1
M. Mota, OF	1
R. Rhoden, RP	1
E. Solomon, RP	1

Montreal (79-82)	WS
Hitting	**104.0**
Fielding	**42.0**
Pitching	**91.0**
B. Bailey, OF	20
W. Davis, OF	20
M. Jorgensen, 1B	17
K. Singleton, OF	16
B. Foote, C	15
C. Taylor, RP	15
D. Murray, RP	12
R. Hunt, 3B	11
S. Renko, SP	11
M. Torrez, SP	11
D. Blair, SP	10
R. Fairly, 1B	10
L. Lintz, 2B	9
T. Foli, SS	8
S. Rogers, SP	8
D. Carrithers, RP	6
J. Montague, RP	6
T. Walker, RP	5
D. DeMola, RP	4
H. Breeden, 1B	3
J. Cox, 2B	3
E. McAnally, SP	3
G. Carter, C	2
P. Frias, SS	2
P. Mangual, OF	2
B. Stinson, C	2
T. Humphrey, C	1
J. Morales, C	1
J. Northrup, OF	1
L. Parrish, 3B	1
J. White, OF	1
R. Woods, OF	1

New York (71-91)	WS
Hitting	**83.6**
Fielding	**40.0**
Pitching	**89.4**
J. Matlack, SP	24
J. Koosman, SP	17
R. Staub, OF	17
W. Garrett, 3B	16
T. Seaver, SP	16
J. Milner, 1B	15
B. Harrelson, SS	14
C. Jones, OF	14
F. Millan, 2B	13
B. Apodaca, RP	7
D. Hahn, OF	7
E. Kranepool, OF	7
R. Sadecki, RP	7
J. Grote, C	5
T. Martinez, SS	5
H. Parker, RP	5
J. Aker, RP	4
T. McGraw, RP	4
B. Miller, RP	4
G. Cram, RP	3
D. Schneck, OF	3
K. Boswell, 2B	2
R. Hodges, C	2
B. Ayala, OF	1
C. Swan, SP	1

Philadelphia (80-82)	WS
Hitting	**114.0**
Fielding	**42.9**
Pitching	**83.1**
M. Schmidt, 3B	39
D. Cash, 2B	26
S. Carlton, SP	22
J. Lonborg, SP	21
W. Montanez, 1B	16
L. Bowa, SS	15
D. Unser, OF	15
R. Schueler, SP	12
D. Ruthven, SP	10
J. Johnstone, OF	9
G. Luzinski, OF	9
M. Anderson, OF	8
B. Boone, C	8
G. Garber, RP	7
T. Hutton, 1B	5
B. Robinson, OF	3
T. Taylor, 1B	3
O. Brown, OF	2
F. Linzy, RP	2
P. Richert, RP	2
M. Scarce, RP	2
E. Watt, RP	2
L. Christenson, RP	1
W. Twitchell, SP	1

Pittsburgh (88-74)	WS
Hitting	**143.6**
Fielding	**38.2**
Pitching	**82.2**
W. Stargell, OF	29
A. Oliver, OF	26
R. Zisk, OF	25
R. Hebner, 3B	22
J. Rooker, SP	21
R. Stennett, 2B	20
M. Sanguillen, C	16
K. Brett, SP	14
J. Reuss, SP	13
D. Ellis, SP	12
D. Giusti, RP	9
E. Kirkpatrick, 1B	8
B. Robertson, 1B	8
R. Hernandez, RP	6
B. Kison, RP	6
D. Parker, OF	6
F. Taveras, SS	6
G. Clines, OF	4
L. Demery, SP	3
A. Howe, 3B	2
M. Mendoza, SS	2
J. Pizarro, RP	2
K. Macha, C	1
J. Morlan, RP	1
P. Popovich, 2B	1
M. Ryan, C	1

San Diego (60-102)	WS
Hitting	**110.4**
Fielding	**26.5**
Pitching	**43.1**
W. McCovey, 1B	25
J. Grubb, OF	21
D. Winfield, OF	17
F. Kendall, C	12
D. Thomas, 2B	12
N. Colbert, 1B	11
D. Freisleben, SP	10
B. Tolan, OF	10
E. Hernandez, SS	9
B. Greif, SP	6
R. Jones, SP	6
D. Spillner, SP	6
L. Hardy, RP	4
V. Romo, RP	3
D. Tomlin, RP	3
B. Almon, SS	2
B. Barton, C	2
G. Beckert, 2B	2
M. Corkins, RP	2
C. Gaston, OF	2
D. Hilton, 3B	2
B. Laxton, RP	2
G. Locklear, OF	2
D. Roberts, 3B	2
C. Cannizzaro, C	1
R. Elliott, OF	1
R. Gaspar, OF	1
J. McIntosh, SP-RP	1
R. Morales, SS	1
G. Ross, RP	1
J. Turner, OF	1

San Francisco (72-90)	WS
Hitting	**94.4**
Fielding	**40.0**
Pitching	**81.6**
J. Barr, SP	23
B. Bonds, OF	23
G. Matthews, OF	20
C. Speier, SS	17
G. Maddox, OF	16
M. Caldwell, SP	15
J. D'Acquisto, SP	12
R. Moffitt, RP	9
S. Ontiveros, 3B	9
D. Rader, C	9
D. Kingman, 1B	7
E. Sosa, RP	7
C. Williams, RP	7
E. Goodson, 1B	6
G. Thomasson, OF	6
T. Fuentes, 2B	5
B. Miller, 3B	4
K. Rudolph, C	4
C. Arnold, 2B	3
M. Phillips, 3B	3
T. Bradley, SP	2
J. Montefusco, SP	2
J. Morris, RP	2
J. Boccabella, C	1
E. Halicki, SP	1
G. Lavelle, RP	1
D. McMahon, RP	1
B. Metzger, RP	1

St. Louis (86-75)	WS
Hitting	**109.7**
Fielding	**50.5**
Pitching	**97.9**
R. Smith, OF	25
L. Brock, OF	22
B. McBride, OF	22
L. McGlothen, SP	21
T. Simmons, C	21
J. Torre, 1B	16
T. Sizemore, 2B	15
B. Gibson, SP	12
A. Hrabosky, RP	11
J. Curtis, SP	10
M. Garman, RP	10
B. Forsch, SP	9
K. Reitz, 3B	9
R. Folkers, RP	8
M. Tyson, SS	8
A. Foster, SP	7
S. Siebert, SP	6
J. Cruz, OF	5
O. Pena, RP	5
J. Dwyer, OF	3
T. Heintzelman, 2B	2
T. McCarver, C	2
L. Melendez, OF	2
L. Alvarado, SS	1
J. DaVanon, SS	1
J. Heidemann, SS	1
K. Hernandez, 1B	1
J. Hickman, 1B	1
M. Hill, C	1
P. Richert, RP	1

1975 American League

Baltimore (90-69)	WS
Hitting	**121.8**
Fielding	**49.9**
Pitching	**98.3**
K. Singleton, OF	33
J. Palmer, SP	31
B. Grich, 2B	29
D. Baylor, OF	24
M. Torrez, SP	19
M. Belanger, SS	14
L. May, 1B	13
M. Cuellar, SP	12
A. Bumbry, DH	10
D. Alexander, RP	9
T. Davis, DH	8
E. Hendricks, C	8
R. Grimsley, SP	7
D. Miller, RP	7
P. Blair, OF	6
J. Northrup, OF	6
B. Robinson, 3B	6
D. DeCinces, 3B	5
D. Duncan, C	5
G. Jackson, RP	5
W. Garland, RP	4
P. Mitchell, RP	3
T. Muser, 1B	3
M. Flanagan, SP-RP	1
T. Nordbrook, SS	1
R. Stillman, OF	1

Boston (95-65)	WS
Hitting	**138.6**
Fielding	**47.3**
Pitching	**99.2**
F. Lynn, OF	33
J. Rice, OF	20
C. Yastrzemski, 1B	20
B. Lee, SP	18
B. Carbo, OF	17
D. Evans, OF	17
L. Tiant, SP	17
R. Wise, SP	17
C. Fisk, C	15
R. Burleson, SS	14
C. Cooper, DH	13
R. Moret, RP	13
R. Cleveland, SP	10
D. Doyle, 2B	9
D. Drago, RP	8
J. Beniquez, OF	7
R. Petrocelli, 3B	6
J. Willoughby, RP	6
D. Pole, SP	5
T. Blackwell, C	3
J. Burton, RP	3
B. Montgomery, C	3
D. Segui, RP	3
D. Griffin, 2B	2
D. Johnson, 1B	2
T. McCarver, C	2
B. Heise, 3B	1
R. Miller, OF	1

California (72-89)	WS
Hitting	**109.0**
Fielding	**35.6**
Pitching	**71.4**
M. Rivers, OF	22
F. Tanana, SP	22
D. Chalk, 3B	18
E. Figueroa, SP	18
L. Stanton, OF	17
J. Remy, 2B	15
B. Bochte, 1B	13
N. Ryan, SP	12
D. Collins, OF	10
E. Rodriguez, C	9
J. Lahoud, DH	8
D. Kirkwood, RP	7
T. Harper, DH	6
A. Garrett, DH	5
J. Brewer, RP	4
A. Etchebarren, C	4
M. Scott, RP	4
M. Nettles, OF	3
B. Singer, SP	3
J. Balaz, OF	2
R. Meoli, SS	2
M. Miley, SS	2
O. Ramirez, SS	2
P. Dade, DH	1
T. Egan, C	1
W. Llenas, 2B	1
S. Monge, SP-RP	1
J. Pactwa, SP	1
O. Pena, RP	1
B. Smith, SS	1
B. Valentine, 1B	1

Chicago (75-86)	WS
Hitting	**95.9**
Fielding	**41.9**
Pitching	**87.2**
G. Gossage, RP	23
J. Kaat, SP	22
J. Orta, 2B	21
B. Dent, SS	16
B. Downing, C	16
K. Henderson, OF	15
P. Kelly, OF	14
C. May, 1B	14
W. Wood, SP	13
B. Melton, 3B	12
J. Hairston, OF	8
D. Hamilton, RP	7
D. Johnson, DH	7
C. Osteen, SP	7
T. Forster, RP	4
B. Stein, 2B	4
P. Varney, C	4
D. Osborn, RP	3
C. Upshaw, RP	3
B. Coluccio, OF	2
J. Jefferson, SP	2
N. Nyman, OF	2
B. Bradford, OF	1
B. Gogolewski, RP	1
R. Hinton, RP	1
C. Lemon, 3B	1
T. Muser, 1B	1
M. Squires, 1B	1

Cleveland (79-80)	WS
Hitting	**116.5**
Fielding	**39.9**
Pitching	**80.6**
B. Powell, 1B	23
D. Eckersley, SP	17
B. Bell, 3B	16
R. Carty, DH	16
R. Manning, OF	15
O. Gamble, OF	14
G. Hendrick, OF	13
F. Duffy, SS	12
D. LaRoche, RP	11
D. Kuiper, 2B	9
T. Buskey, RP	8
F. Peterson, SP	8
J. Bibby, SP-RP	7
A. Ashby, C	6
J. Lowenstein, OF	6
G. Perry, SP	6
F. Robinson, DH	6
C. Spikes, OF	6
R. Waits, RP	6
J. Brohamer, 2B	4
J. Ellis, C	4
R. Harrison, SP	4
D. Hood, SP	4
J. Kern, SP	4
J. Brown, RP	2
E. Crosby, SS	2
J. Lis, 1B	2
T. McCraw, 1B	2
D. Bosman, SP-RP	1
B. Odom, RP	1
E. Raich, SP	1
J. Strickland, RP	1

Detroit (57-102)	WS
Hitting	**70.7**
Fielding	**31.5**
Pitching	**68.8**
M. Lolich, SP	15
B. Freehan, C	13
W. Horton, DH	13
A. Rodriguez, 3B	13
J. Hiller, RP	12
V. Ruhle, SP	11
G. Sutherland, 2B	10
R. LeFlore, OF	9
L. Roberts, OF	9
R. Bare, SP	7
B. Oglivie, OF	7
L. LaGrow, SP	6
T. Veryzer, SS	6
J. Pierce, 1B	5
D. Lemanczyk, RP	4
D. Meyer, OF	4
M. Stanley, OF	4
T. Walker, RP	4
J. Wockenfuss, C	4
F. Arroyo, RP	3
J. Coleman, SP	3
B. Baldwin, OF	2
S. Grilli, RP	1
T. Humphrey, C	1
J. Knox, 2B	1
G. Lamont, C	1
G. Michael, SS	1
G. Pentz, RP	1
B. Reynolds, RP	1

Kansas City (91-71)	WS
Hitting	**120.1**
Fielding	**47.6**
Pitching	**105.3**
J. Mayberry, 1B	33
G. Brett, 3B	25
S. Busby, SP	22
H. McRae, OF	17
A. Otis, OF	17
A. Fitzmorris, SP	16
D. Leonard, SP	14
M. Pattin, RP	13
D. Bird, RP	11
F. Patek, SS	11
P. Splittorff, SP	11
A. Cowens, OF	10
T. Solaita, DH	10
F. White, 2B	9
C. Rojas, 2B	8
B. Stinson, C	6
J. Wohlford, OF	6
N. Briles, SP	5
H. Killebrew, DH	5
B. Martinez, C	5
F. Healy, C	4
L. McDaniel, RP	4
S. Mingori, RP	4
B. McClure, RP	3
V. Pinson, OF	2
M. Littell, RP	1
G. Throop, RP	1

Milwaukee (68-94)	WS
Hitting	**113.3**
Fielding	**31.6**
Pitching	**59.1**
G. Scott, 1B	23
D. Porter, C	19
D. Money, 3B	14
R. Yount, SS	14
P. Broberg, SP	10
S. Lezcano, OF	10
H. Aaron, DH	9
J. Colborn, SP	9
E. Rodriguez, RP	8
B. Mitchell, OF	7
C. Moore, C	7
B. Sharp, OF	7
B. Castro, RP	6
P. Garcia, 2B	6
M. Hegan, OF	6
J. Slaton, SP	6
B. Darwin, OF	5
T. Hausman, RP	5
B. Travers, SP	5
K. Bevacqua, 3B	4
J. Briggs, OF	4
B. Sheldon, 2B	4
G. Thomas, OF	4
T. Murphy, RP	3
J. Augustine, SP	2
R. Austin, RP	2
L. Anderson, RP	1
B. Champion, RP	1
B. Coluccio, OF	1
T. Johnson, 2B-3B	1
E. Sprague, SP	1

Minnesota (76-83)	WS
Hitting	**116.8**
Fielding	**35.8**
Pitching	**75.4**
R. Carew, 2B	30
B. Blyleven, SP	21
S. Braun, OF	17
D. Goltz, SP	15
J. Hughes, SP	14
E. Soderholm, 3B	14
D. Ford, OF	12
L. Hisle, OF	11
J. Briggs, 1B	9
T. Oliva, DH	9
G. Borgmann, C	8
L. Bostock, OF	8
T. Burgmeier, RP	7
B. Campbell, RP	7
P. Roof, C	7
J. Terrell, SS	7
S. Brye, OF	6
D. Thompson, SS	5
V. Albury, RP	4
C. Kusick, 1B	4
E. Bane, SP	3
R. Corbin, SP	2
B. Darwin, OF	2
T. Johnson, RP	2
D. McKay, 3B	2
L. Gomez, SS	1
T. Kelly, 1B	1

New York (83-77)	WS
Hitting	**108.0**
Fielding	**44.1**
Pitching	**96.9**
C. Hunter, SP	29
B. Bonds, OF	24
T. Munson, C	23
G. Nettles, 3B	21
R. White, OF	21
D. Medich, SP	16
C. Chambliss, 1B	15
R. May, SP	15
S. Alomar, 2B	10
P. Dobson, SP	9
L. Gura, SP	9
E. Maddox, OF	8
S. Lyle, RP	7
D. Tidrow, RP	6
E. Herrmann, DH	5
T. Martinez, RP	4
F. Stanley, SS	4
W. Williams, OF	4
R. Blomberg, DH	3
R. Dempsey, C	3
J. Mason, SS	3
R. Bladt, OF	2
E. Brinkman, SS	1
R. Coggins, OF	1
K. Dineen, OF	1
R. Guidry, RP	1

A. Johnson, DH	1
D. Pagan, RP	1
L. Piniella, OF	1
T. Whitfield, OF	1

Oakland (98-64)	WS
Hitting	**156.4**
Fielding	**43.0**
Pitching	**94.6**
G. Tenace, C	32
R. Jackson, OF	27
B. North, OF	22
C. Washington, OF	22
J. Rudi, 1B	20
S. Bando, 3B	19
V. Blue, SP	19
B. Campaneris, SS	17
B. Williams, DH	17
R. Fingers, RP	15
K. Holtzman, SP	15
J. Todd, RP	13
P. Garner, 2B	12
P. Lindblad, RP	11
D. Bosman, SP	7
S. Bahnsen, SP	5
T. Harper, 1B	4
G. Abbott, SP-RP	3
S. Siebert, SP	3
R. Fosse, C	2
M. Norris, SP	2
D. Hamilton, RP	1
L. Haney, C	1
J. Holt, 1B	1
T. Kubiak, 3B-SS	1
T. Martinez, SS	1
J. Perry, SP	1
C. Tovar, DH-2B	1

Texas (79-83)	WS
Hitting	**120.3**
Fielding	**36.6**
Pitching	**80.1**
T. Harrah, SS	32
M. Hargrove, OF	22
L. Randle, 2B	17
J. Burroughs, OF	15
F. Jenkins, SP	15
G. Perry, SP	15
R. Howell, 3B	11
J. Spencer, 1B	11
T. Grieve, OF	10
S. Hargan, SP	9
S. Foucault, RP	7
J. Sundberg, C	7
J. Umbarger, RP	7
S. Thomas, RP	6
J. Fregosi, 1B	5
B. Hands, SP	5
S. Perzanowski, SP	5
R. Smalley, SS	5
C. Tovar, DH	5
M. Cubbage, 2B	4
W. Davis, OF	4
D. Moates, OF	4
J. Brown, RP	3
L. Cardenas, 3B	3
C. Wright, SP	3
M. Kekich, RP	2
M. Bacsik, RP	1
J. Bibby, SP	1
B. Fahey, C	1
J. Lovitto, OF	1
D. Nelson, 2B	1

1975 National League

Atlanta (67-94)	WS
Hitting	**102.9**
Fielding	**28.6**
Pitching	**69.5**
D. Evans, 3B	28
P. Niekro, SP	19
D. Baker, OF	17
C. Morton, SP	17
R. Garr, OF	16
M. Perez, 2B	11
D. May, OF	9
R. Office, OF	9
T. House, RP	8
L. Blanks, SS	7
V. Correll, C	6
E. Williams, 1B	6
M. Beard, RP	5
R. Gilbreath, 2B	5
M. Lum, 1B	5
B. Dal Canton, RP	4
C. Gaston, OF	4
M. Leon, RP	4
B. Pocoroba, C	4
B. Capra, SP	3
R. Reed, SP	3
R. Harrison, RP	2
R. Sadecki, RP	2
E. Sosa, RP	2
B. Beall, 1B	1
B. Belloir, SS	1
A. Devine, RP	1
P. Hanna, RP	1
P. Torrealba, RP	1

Chicago (75-87)	WS
Hitting	**128.4**
Fielding	**29.4**
Pitching	**67.2**
J. Cardenal, OF	26
B. Madlock, 3B	26
A. Thornton, 1B	23
R. Monday, OF	22
R. Burris, SP	14
R. Reuschel, SP	14
D. Kessinger, SS	13
J. Morales, OF	13
S. Stone, SP	13
M. Trillo, 2B	11
B. Bonham, SP	9
T. Hosley, C	6
P. LaCock, 1B	4
G. Mitterwald, C	4
O. Zamora, RP	4
D. Knowles, RP	3
P. Reuschel, RP	3
S. Swisher, C	3
T. Dettore, RP	2
J. Wallis, OF	2
G. Zahn, SP	2
K. Crosby, RP	1
R. Dunn, 3B	1
K. Frailing, RP	1
G. Hiser, OF	1
B. Locker, RP	1
D. Rosello, SS	1
R. Sperring, 3B	1
C. Summers, OF	1

Cincinnati (108-54)	WS
Hitting	**173.2**
Fielding	**51.8**
Pitching	**99.0**
J. Morgan, 2B	44
P. Rose, 3B	31
J. Bench, C	30
G. Foster, OF	21
D. Concepcion, SS	19
T. Perez, 1B	19
K. Griffey Sr., OF	18
C. Geronimo, OF	16
D. Gullett, SP	15
G. Nolan, SP	15
R. Eastwick, RP	13
P. Borbon, RP	10
W. McEnaney, RP	10
C. Carroll, RP	9
F. Norman, SP	9
J. Billingham, SP	8
D. Driessen, 1B	8
P. Darcy, SP	7
M. Rettenmund, OF	5
D. Chaney, SS	4
D. Flynn, 3B	4
B. Plummer, C	4
C. Kirby, SP	3
T. Carroll, SP	1
T. Crowley, 1B-OF	1

Houston (64-97)	WS
Hitting	**106.5**
Fielding	**30.5**
Pitching	**55.0**
C. Cedeno, OF	20
B. Watson, 1B	20
C. Johnson, 1B	15
G. Gross, OF	14
J. Cruz, OF	11
W. Howard, OF	10
L. Dierker, SP	9
D. Rader, 3B	9
R. Metzger, SS	8
E. Cabell, OF	7
M. May, C	7
J. Niekro, RP	7
J. Richard, SP	7
K. Forsch, RP	6
D. Roberts, SP	6
R. Andrews, 2B	5
M. Cosgrove, RP	5
J. Crawford, RP	5
J. DaVanon, SS	4
K. Boswell, 2B	3
W. Granger, RP	3
D. Konieczny, SP	3
J. Sosa, RP	2
J. York, RP	2
T. Helms, 2B	1
S. Jutze, C	1
L. Milbourne, 2B	1
P. Siebert, RP	1

Los Angeles (88-74)	WS
Hitting	**114.0**
Fielding	**47.2**
Pitching	**102.8**
A. Messersmith, SP	28
R. Cey, 3B	27
S. Garvey, 1B	25
D. Lopes, 2B	25
J. Wynn, OF	21
B. Hooton, SP	17
D. Sutton, SP	17
D. Rau, SP	16
W. Crawford, OF	12
S. Yeager, C	12
L. Lacy, 2B-OF	11
M. Marshall, RP	8
B. Buckner, OF	5
J. Ferguson, C	5
J. Hale, OF	5
R. Rhoden, RP	5
A. Downing, RP	4
C. Hough, RP	4
B. Russell, SS	3
R. Auerbach, SS	2
H. Cruz, OF	2
I. DeJesus, SS	2
K. McMullen, 3B	2
L. Lee, OF	1
D. Lewallyn, RP	1
M. Mota, OF	1
T. Paciorek, OF	1
J. Royster, OF	1
S. Wall, RP	1

Montreal (75-87)	WS
Hitting	**79.5**
Fielding	**47.9**
Pitching	**97.6**
S. Rogers, SP	19
G. Carter, OF	18
M. Jorgensen, 1B	16
D. Warthen, RP	14
P. Mangual, OF	13
W. Fryman, SP	12
L. Parrish, 3B	12
L. Biittner, OF	11
D. Murray, RP	10
D. Blair, SP	9
T. Foli, SS	9
P. Mackanin, 2B	9
S. Renko, SP	9
D. Carrithers, SP	8
B. Bailey, OF	7
C. Taylor, RP	7
J. Dwyer, OF	6
B. Foote, C	6
D. DeMola, RP	5
F. Scherman, RP	5
J. White, OF	4
J. Morales, 1B	3
L. Lintz, 2B	2
J. Lyttle, OF	2
E. Valentine, OF	2
R. Coggins, OF	1
N. Colbert, 1B	1
J. Cox, 2B	1
P. Frias, SS	1
D. McNally, SP	1
P. Scanlon, 3B	1
T. Scott, OF	1

New York (82-80)	WS
Hitting	**116.1**
Fielding	**41.5**
Pitching	**88.4**
T. Seaver, SP	26
R. Staub, OF	25
D. Unser, OF	19
J. Grote, C	18
F. Millan, 2B	17
D. Kingman, OF	15
B. Apodaca, RP	13
W. Garrett, 3B	13
J. Koosman, SP	13
E. Kranepool, 1B	12
J. Matlack, SP	12
M. Phillips, SS	8
J. Torre, 3B	8
R. Baldwin, RP	6
M. Vail, OF	6
S. Lockwood, RP	5
K. Sanders, RP	5
H. Webb, SP	5
J. Milner, OF	4
J. Stearns, C	4
G. Clines, OF	2
J. Heidemann, SS	2
H. Parker, RP	2
R. Tate, SP	2
J. Alou, OF	1
T. Hall, RP	1
B. Harrelson, SS	1
R. Hodges, C	1

Philadelphia (86-76)	WS
Hitting	**134.1**
Fielding	**40.6**
Pitching	**83.2**
G. Luzinski, OF	28
M. Schmidt, 3B	28
D. Cash, 2B	24
G. Maddox, OF	17
L. Bowa, SS	15
S. Carlton, SP	14
J. Johnstone, OF	14
L. Christenson, SP	13
T. McGraw, RP	12
G. Garber, RP	10
T. Hilgendorf, RP	10
J. Oates, C	10
T. Underwood, SP	9
D. Allen, 1B	8
B. Boone, C	7
O. Brown, OF	6
J. Lonborg, SP	6
M. Anderson, OF	5

W. Twitchell, SP	3
J. Hoerner, RP	2
T. Hutton, 1B	2
J. Martin, OF	2
T. McCarver, C	2
W. Montanez, 1B	2
R. Schueler, RP	2
W. Simpson, SP	2
T. Taylor, 3B	2
A. Bannister, OF	1
T. Harmon, SS	1
D. Ruthven, SP	1

Pittsburgh (92-69)	WS
Hitting	**131.8**
Fielding	**45.0**
Pitching	**99.3**
D. Parker, OF	26
M. Sanguillen, C	23
W. Stargell, 1B	22
R. Zisk, OF	22
A. Oliver, OF	21
R. Stennett, 2B	21
J. Reuss, SP	20
R. Hebner, 3B	12
J. Rooker, SP	12
D. Giusti, RP	10
L. Demery, RP	9
B. Kison, SP	9
K. Brett, SP	8
J. Candelaria, SP	8
R. Hernandez, RP	7
F. Taveras, SS	7
B. Robertson, 1B	6
B. Robinson, OF	6
D. Ellis, SP	5
K. Tekulve, RP	5
D. Dyer, C	3
E. Kirkpatrick, 1B	3
S. McDowell, RP	3
B. Moose, RP	3
A. Howe, 3B	1
M. Mendoza, SS	1
P. Popovich, 2B-SS	1
W. Randolph, 2B	1
C. Reynolds, SS	1

San Diego (71-91)	WS
Hitting	**89.4**
Fielding	**39.1**
Pitching	**84.5**
R. Jones, SP	28
D. Winfield, OF	20
J. Grubb, OF	17
W. McCovey, 1B	16
T. Fuentes, 2B	15
B. Strom, SP	11
G. Locklear, OF	10
H. Torres, SS	10
J. McIntosh, SP	9
D. Frisella, RP	8
B. Tolan, OF	8
E. Hernandez, SS	7
R. Folkers, RP	6
M. Ivie, 1B	6
D. Tomlin, RP	6
A. Foster, RP	5
D. Roberts, 3B	4
D. Spillner, SP	4
B. Davis, C	3
D. Freisleben, SP	3
B. Greif, RP	3
D. Hahn, OF	2
R. Hundley, C	2
F. Kendall, C	2
T. Kubiak, 3B	2
D. Sharon, OF	2
S. Siebert, SP	2
B. Almon, SS	1
G. Beckert, 3B	1

San Francisco (80-81)	WS
Hitting	**109.3**
Fielding	**43.7**
Pitching	**87.0**
B. Murcer, OF	21
J. Montefusco, SP	20
C. Speier, SS	20
V. Joshua, OF	19
J. Barr, SP	17
D. Thomas, 2B	17
G. Matthews, OF	16
W. Montanez, 1B	13
S. Ontiveros, 3B	12
D. Rader, C	11
G. Lavelle, RP	9
P. Falcone, SP	8
E. Halicki, SP	8
G. Thomasson, OF	8
D. Heaverlo, RP	7
C. Williams, RP	7
R. Moffitt, RP	6
G. Adams, OF	4
M. Hill, C	4
B. Miller, 3B	3
M. Sadek, C	3
M. Caldwell, SP	2
R. Dressler, SP	2
E. Goodson, 1B	1
J. LeMaster, SS	1
G. Maddox, OF	1

St. Louis (82-80)	WS
Hitting	**112.2**
Fielding	**42.0**
Pitching	**91.8**
T. Simmons, C	28
B. Forsch, SP	21
R. Smith, OF	20
A. Hrabosky, RP	19
L. Brock, OF	18
B. McBride, OF	16
L. McGlothen, SP	12
W. Davis, OF	11
R. Fairly, 1B	11
M. Tyson, SS	11
R. Reed, SP	10
J. Curtis, RP	9
K. Reitz, 3B	9
M. Garman, RP	8
T. Sizemore, 2B	8
J. Denny, SP	6
L. Melendez, OF	5
M. Guerrero, SS	3
K. Hernandez, 1B	3
E. Rasmussen, SP	3
B. Bradford, OF	2
E. Brinkman, SS	2
K. Reynolds, RP	2
B. Gibson, SP	1
L. Lintz, 2B-SS	1
T. Moore, RP	1
J. Mumphrey, OF	1
K. Rudolph, C	1
R. Sadecki, RP	1
E. Sosa, RP	1
G. Terlecky, RP	1
M. Wallace, RP	1

1976 American League

Baltimore (88-74)	WS
Hitting	**126.4**
Fielding	**44.3**
Pitching	**93.3**
B. Grich, 2B	31
J. Palmer, SP	27
R. Jackson, OF	25
K. Singleton, OF	24
M. Belanger, SS	23
W. Garland, SP	20
L. May, 1B	19
A. Bumbry, OF	16
D. DeCinces, 3B	10
K. Holtzman, SP	7
R. May, SP	7
D. Miller, RP	7
D. Duncan, C	5
R. Grimsley, SP	5
F. Holdsworth, RP	5
T. Martinez, RP	5
D. Alexander, SP	3
P. Blair, OF	3
R. Dempsey, C	3
A. Mora, DH	3
M. Flanagan, SP-RP	2
T. Harper, DH	2
D. Martinez, SP-RP	2
T. Muser, 1B	2
B. Robinson, 3B	2
T. Crowley, DH	1
K. Garcia, SS	1
E. Hendricks, C	1
G. Jackson, RP	1
T. Nordbrook, 2B	1
T. Shopay, OF	1

Boston (83-79)	WS
Hitting	**112.2**
Fielding	**43.8**
Pitching	**93.0**
F. Lynn, OF	22
L. Tiant, SP	22
R. Burleson, SS	21
C. Fisk, C	19
C. Yastrzemski, 1B	18
J. Rice, OF	17
D. Evans, OF	15
F. Jenkins, SP	14
R. Wise, SP	14
R. Cleveland, RP	12
C. Cooper, 1B	12
J. Willoughby, RP	9
R. Miller, OF	8
D. Doyle, 2B	6
R. Jones, SP	6
T. Murphy, RP	6
D. Pole, RP	5
S. Dillard, 3B	4
B. Hobson, 3B	4
B. Montgomery, C	3
R. Petrocelli, 3B	3
B. Carbo, DH	2
T. House, RP	2
R. Kreuger, SP-RP	2
D. Griffin, 2B	1
B. Heise, 3B	1
E. Whitt, C	1

California (76-86)	WS
Hitting	**97.5**
Fielding	**42.6**
Pitching	**87.8**
F. Tanana, SP	27
J. Remy, 2B	17
N. Ryan, SP	17
B. Bonds, OF	16
B. Bochte, OF	15
G. Ross, SP	13
D. Collins, OF	12
P. Hartzell, RP	12
R. Jackson, 3B	11
T. Solaita, 1B	11
D. Chalk, SS	8
M. Guerrero, 2B-SS	8
B. Melton, DH	8
R. Torres, OF	8
S. Monge, RP	6
A. Etchebarren, C	5
T. Humphrey, C	5
B. Jones, OF	4
J. Brewer, RP	3
T. Davis, DH	3
D. Drago, RP	3
M. Scott, RP	3
J. Verhoeven, RP	3
D. Briggs, 1B	2
E. Herrmann, C	2
D. Kirkwood, SP	2
L. Stanton, OF	2
J. Lahoud, OF	1
O. Ramirez, SS	1

Chicago (64-97)	WS
Hitting	**95.5**
Fielding	**33.0**
Pitching	**63.4**
J. Orta, OF	17
R. Garr, OF	14
K. Brett, SP	13
J. Spencer, 1B	12
J. Brohamer, 2B	11
B. Downing, C	10
G. Gossage, SP	10
B. Dent, SS	9
P. Kelly, DH	9
C. Carroll, RP	8
D. Hamilton, RP	8
C. Lemon, OF	8
B. Stein, 2B-3B	8
L. Johnson, DH	7
F. Barrios, RP	6
K. Bell, 3B	6
J. Essian, C	5
B. Johnson, SP	5
W. Wood, SP	5
B. Bradford, OF	4
P. Vuckovich, RP	4
A. Bannister, OF	3
T. Forster, SP	3
J. Hairston, OF	3
C. Knapp, SP	1
K. Kravec, SP	1
L. Monroe, RP	1
P. Varney, C	1

Cleveland (81-78)	WS
Hitting	**113.5**
Fielding	**41.7**
Pitching	**87.8**
R. Carty, DH	24
B. Bell, 3B	20
G. Hendrick, OF	20
R. Manning, OF	19
J. Kern, RP	14
D. LaRoche, RP	14
L. Blanks, SS	12
P. Dobson, SP	12
R. Fosse, C	12
J. Bibby, SP	11
D. Eckersley, SP	11
D. Kuiper, 2B	11
S. Thomas, RP	10
A. Ashby, C	8
F. Duffy, SS	6
C. Spikes, OF	6
J. Brown, SP	5
T. Buskey, RP	5
B. Powell, 1B	5
R. Waits, SP	4
J. Lis, 1B	3
R. Pruitt, OF	3
T. Smith, OF	3
J. Lowenstein, OF	2
D. Hood, RP	1
H. Parker, RP	1
F. Robinson, DH	1

Detroit (74-87)	WS
Hitting	**101.3**
Fielding	**38.5**
Pitching	**82.2**
M. Fidrych, SP	27
R. LeFlore, OF	26
R. Staub, OF	26
J. Hiller, RP	17
D. Roberts, SP	14
J. Thompson, 1B	12
W. Horton, DH	11
B. Oglivie, OF	11
V. Ruhle, SP	10
B. Freehan, C	7

A. Johnson, OF	7
M. Stanley, OF	6
A. Rodriguez, 3B	5
B. Kimm, C	4
B. Laxton, RP	4
D. Meyer, OF	4
C. Scrivener, 2B	4
T. Veryzer, SS	4
R. Bare, SP	3
J. Crawford, RP	3
M. Wagner, SS	3
J. Wockenfuss, C	3
P. Garcia, 2B	2
S. Grilli, RP	2
D. Lemanczyk, SP-RP	2
P. Mankowski, 3B	2
J. Coleman, SP	1
J. Manuel, 2B	1
G. Sutherland, 2B	1

Kansas City (90-72)	WS
Hitting	**132.8**
Fielding	**44.1**
Pitching	**93.1**
G. Brett, 3B	33
H. McRae, DH	26
A. Otis, OF	25
J. Mayberry, 1B	15
A. Fitzmorris, SP	14
D. Leonard, SP	14
M. Littell, RP	14
F. Patek, SS	14
T. Poquette, OF	14
A. Cowens, OF	12
M. Pattin, RP	11
D. Bird, SP	10
S. Mingori, RP	10
F. White, 2B	9
B. Martinez, C	8
B. Stinson, C	8
L. Gura, RP	6
A. Hassler, SP	6
P. Splittorff, SP	6
J. Wohlford, OF	5
D. Nelson, 2B	3
S. Busby, SP	1
R. Jones, OF	1
R. Nelson, RP	1
C. Rojas, 2B	1
R. Sadecki, RP	1
T. Solaita, DH	1
J. Wathan, C	1

Milwaukee (66-95)	WS
Hitting	**84.2**
Fielding	**40.1**
Pitching	**73.7**
G. Scott, 1B	19
S. Lezcano, OF	17
B. Travers, SP	16
J. Slaton, SP	15
D. Money, 3B	14
R. Yount, SS	14
J. Augustine, SP	10
J. Colborn, SP	10
V. Joshua, OF	9
T. Johnson, 2B	7
D. Porter, C	7
D. Frisella, RP	6
E. Rodriguez, RP	6
H. Aaron, DH	5
B. Carbo, OF	5
B. Castro, RP	5
M. Hegan, DH	5
C. Moore, C	5
D. Thomas, OF	5
G. Thomas, OF	5
G. Beare, SP	2
B. Darwin, OF	2
P. Garcia, 2B	2
B. Sharp, OF	2
S. Bowling, OF	1
J. Gantner, 3B	1
J. Heidemann, 3B	1
R. Sadecki, RP	1
G. Sutherland, 2B	1

Minnesota (85-77)	WS
Hitting	**150.8**
Fielding	**34.2**
Pitching	**70.0**
R. Carew, 1B	30
B. Wynegar, C	20
L. Bostock, OF	19
L. Hisle, OF	19
D. Ford, OF	18
B. Campbell, RP	17
S. Braun, DH	16
R. Smalley, SS	14
D. Goltz, SP	13
M. Cubbage, 3B	12
B. Randall, 2B	12
T. Burgmeier, RP	10
C. Kusick, DH	10
B. Singer, SP	7
B. Blyleven, SP	5
S. Luebber, RP	5
P. Redfern, SP	5
S. Brye, OF	4
T. Johnson, RP	4
V. Albury, RP	3
G. Borgmann, C	3
J. Terrell, 2B	3
D. Thompson, SS	2
L. Gomez, SS	1
J. Hughes, SP	1
D. McKay, 3B	1
P. Roof, C	1

New York (97-62)	WS
Hitting	**149.3**
Fielding	**45.5**
Pitching	**96.1**
G. Nettles, 3B	28
M. Rivers, OF	26
R. White, OF	26
T. Munson, C	24
C. Chambliss, 1B	21
W. Randolph, 2B	17
E. Figueroa, SP	16
C. Hunter, SP	15
S. Lyle, RP	14
D. Ellis, SP	13
O. Gamble, OF	12
L. Piniella, OF	9
D. Tidrow, RP	9
D. Alexander, SP	8
C. May, DH	8
G. Jackson, RP	7
F. Stanley, SS	7
K. Holtzman, SP	5
O. Velez, OF	5
S. Alomar, 2B	3
F. Healy, C	3
T. Martinez, RP	3
J. Mason, SS	3
R. May, SP	3
E. Hendricks, C	2
D. Pagan, RP	2
K. Brett, RP	1
R. Dempsey, C	1

Oakland (87-74)	WS
Hitting	**129.7**
Fielding	**40.1**
Pitching	**91.2**
V. Blue, SP	25
S. Bando, 3B	24
G. Tenace, 1B	22
B. North, OF	21
M. Torrez, SP	20
D. Baylor, OF	19
B. Campaneris, SS	19
P. Garner, 2B	19
R. Fingers, RP	17
J. Rudi, OF	16
C. Washington, OF	10
S. Bahnsen, RP	8
P. Lindblad, RP	8
B. Williams, DH	7
D. Bosman, SP	4
K. McMullen, 3B	4
P. Mitchell, SP	4
J. Todd, RP	4
L. Haney, C	3
R. Fairly, 1B	2
J. Holt, DH	1
T. Hosley, C	1
J. Newman, C	1
M. Norris, SP	1
T. Sandt, SS	1

Texas (76-86)	WS
Hitting	**100.9**
Fielding	**40.7**
Pitching	**86.4**
M. Hargrove, 1B	24
T. Harrah, SS	24
G. Perry, SP	17
B. Blyleven, SP	15
J. Burroughs, OF	14
N. Briles, SP	13
T. Grieve, DH	13
J. Beniquez, OF	12
J. Sundberg, C	12
J. Umbarger, SP	12
R. Howell, 3B	10
L. Randle, 2B	8
G. Clines, OF	6
S. Foucault, RP	6
S. Hargan, RP	6
J. Terpko, RP	5
T. Boggs, SP	4
B. Fahey, C	4
B. Singer, SP	4
R. Smalley, 2B	4
J. Fregosi, 1B	3
D. Moates, OF	3
M. Bacsik, RP	2
J. Ellis, C	2
L. Barker, SP	1
J. Lahoud, DH	1
K. Pape, SS	1
F. Peterson, SP-RP	1
D. Thompson, 3B	1

1976 National League

Atlanta (70-92)	WS
Hitting	**79.4**
Fielding	**39.8**
Pitching	**90.8**
P. Niekro, SP	21
J. Wynn, OF	18
A. Messersmith, SP	17
D. Ruthven, SP	14
K. Henderson, OF	13
J. Royster, 3B	13
D. Chaney, SS	12
W. Montanez, 1B	11
R. Office, OF	10
R. Gilbreath, 2B	9
A. Devine, RP	8
T. Paciorek, OF	8
C. Morton, SP	6
V. Correll, C	4
B. Dal Canton, RP	4
C. Gaston, OF	4
M. Leon, RP	4
M. Marshall, RP	4
F. LaCorte, SP	3
L. Lacy, 2B	3
D. May, OF	3
B. Pocoroba, C	3
P. Torrealba, RP	3
E. Williams, C	3
R. Moret, RP	2
D. Murphy, C	2
M. Beard, RP	1
B. Belloir, SS	1
J. Easterly, SP	1
D. Evans, 1B	1
J. Moore, 3B	1
M. Perez, 2B	1
C. Robinson, 2B	1
E. Sosa, RP	1

Chicago (75-87)	WS
Hitting	**90.1**
Fielding	**42.1**
Pitching	**92.8**
B. Madlock, 3B	25
R. Monday, OF	23
R. Burris, SP	19
R. Reuschel, SP	19
J. Cardenal, OF	16
M. Trillo, 2B	14
J. Morales, OF	12
B. Sutter, RP	12
B. Bonham, SP	9
D. Knowles, RP	9
S. Renko, SP	8
J. Wallis, OF	8
D. Rosello, SS	7
P. LaCock, 1B	6
M. Kelleher, SS	5
S. Swisher, C	5
J. Coleman, RP	4
P. Reuschel, RP	4
G. Mitterwald, C	3
S. Stone, SP	3
A. Thornton, 1B	3
L. Biittner, 1B	2
K. Frailing, SP-RP	2
M. Garman, RP	2
O. Zamora, RP	2
R. Sperring, 3B	1
C. Summers, OF	1
J. Tabb, 1B	1

Cincinnati (102-60)	WS
Hitting	**178.1**
Fielding	**42.9**
Pitching	**85.0**
J. Morgan, 2B	37
P. Rose, 3B	30
G. Foster, OF	25
K. Griffey Sr., OF	25
D. Concepcion, SS	23
J. Bench, C	19
C. Geronimo, OF	19
R. Eastwick, RP	17
T. Perez, 1B	16
P. Zachry, SP	14
G. Nolan, SP	12
F. Norman, SP	11
P. Borbon, RP	8
D. Gullett, SP	8
D. Driessen, 1B	7
B. Bailey, OF	5
J. Billingham, SP	5
D. Flynn, 2B	5
B. Plummer, C	4
M. Sarmiento, RP	4
S. Alcala, SP	3
E. Armbrister, OF	3
M. Lum, OF	3
J. Henderson, RP	2
W. McEnaney, RP	1

Houston (80-82)	WS
Hitting	**146.9**
Fielding	**32.3**
Pitching	**60.7**
B. Watson, 1B	31
C. Cedeno, OF	30
J. Cruz, OF	22
J. Richard, SP	17
E. Cabell, 3B	16
G. Gross, OF	16
C. Johnson, C	14
K. Forsch, RP	11

L. Roberts, OF	11
R. Andrews, 2B	10
R. Metzger, SS	9
J. Andujar, SP	6
J. DaVanon, 2B-SS	6
L. Dierker, SP	6
D. Larson, SP	5
E. Herrmann, C	4
B. McLaughlin, SP	4
L. Milbourne, 2B	4
J. Niekro, RP	4
G. Pentz, RP	4
J. Sambito, RP	3
K. Boswell, 3B	2
M. Lemongello, SP	2
W. Howard, OF	1
S. Jutze, C	1
P. Siebert, RP	1

Los Angeles (92-70)	WS
Hitting	**109.3**
Fielding	**52.4**
Pitching	**114.3**
R. Cey, 3B	27
S. Garvey, 1B	26
D. Rau, SP	21
B. Buckner, OF	20
C. Hough, RP	20
D. Sutton, SP	20
R. Rhoden, SP	17
D. Lopes, 2B	16
B. Russell, SS	15
T. John, SP	13
S. Yeager, C	13
B. Hooton, SP	12
R. Smith, OF	10
D. Baker, OF	6
J. Ferguson, OF	6
M. Marshall, RP	4
T. Sizemore, 2B	4
L. Lacy, OF	3
E. Rodriguez, C	3
S. Wall, RP	3
A. Downing, RP	2
D. Lewallyn, SP-RP	2
M. Mota, OF	2
E. Sosa, RP	2
R. Auerbach, SS	1
G. Burke, OF	1
H. Cruz, OF	1
I. DeJesus, SS	1
E. Goodson, 3B	1
J. Hale, OF	1
J. Lyttle, OF	1
K. Pasley, C	1
R. Sutcliffe, SP	1

Montreal (55-107)	WS
Hitting	**65.9**
Fielding	**34.7**
Pitching	**64.4**
W. Fryman, SP	14
S. Rogers, SP	14
D. Stanhouse, SP	11
T. Foli, SS	10
D. Murray, RP	10
E. Valentine, OF	10
M. Jorgensen, 1B	9
P. Mangual, OF	9
L. Parrish, 3B	8
B. Foote, C	7
G. Carter, C	6
W. Garrett, 2B	5
B. Rivera, OF	5
J. White, OF	5
P. Mackanin, 2B	4
J. Morales, 1B	4
A. Thornton, 1B	4
E. Williams, 1B	4
D. Carrithers, SP	3
S. Dunning, RP	3
J. Kerrigan, RP	3
D. Unser, OF	3
W. Granger, RP	2
C. Lang, RP	2
J. Lyttle, OF	2
B. Atkinson, RP	1
N. Colbert, OF	1
A. Dawson, OF	1
P. Frias, 2B-SS	1
G. Roenicke, OF	1
F. Scherman, RP	1
R. Scott, 2B	1
C. Taylor, RP	1

New York (86-76)	WS
Hitting	**115.2**
Fielding	**45.0**
Pitching	**97.8**
J. Koosman, SP	20
T. Seaver, SP	20
J. Milner, OF	19
J. Matlack, SP	18
D. Kingman, OF	17
F. Millan, 2B	16
E. Kranepool, 1B	15
S. Lockwood, RP	15
B. Harrelson, SS	13
J. Grote, C	12
B. Boisclair, OF	10
J. Torre, 1B	10
W. Garrett, 3B	9
M. Lolich, SP	8
M. Phillips, SS	8
B. Apodaca, RP	6
R. Staiger, 3B	6
D. Unser, OF	6
R. Hodges, C	5
J. Stearns, C	4
C. Swan, SP	4
K. Sanders, RP	3
R. Baldwin, RP	2
N. Espinosa, RP	2
L. Foster, 3B	2
P. Mangual, OF	2
L. Mazzilli, OF	2
B. Baldwin, OF	1
L. Brown, OF	1
B. Myrick, RP	1
M. Vail, OF	1

Philadelphia (101-61)	WS
Hitting	**145.3**
Fielding	**49.5**
Pitching	**108.2**
M. Schmidt, 3B	35
G. Maddox, OF	26
G. Luzinski, OF	23
D. Cash, 2B	21
J. Johnstone, OF	19
S. Carlton, SP	18
J. Lonborg, SP	15
R. Reed, RP	15
B. Boone, C	14
L. Bowa, SS	14
J. Kaat, SP	12
D. Allen, 1B	11
G. Garber, RP	11
T. McCarver, C	10
T. McGraw, RP	10
L. Christenson, SP	9
T. Underwood, SP	9
O. Brown, OF	7
W. Twitchell, RP	6
R. Schueler, RP	4
T. Harmon, SS	3
B. Tolan, 1B	3
T. Hutton, 1B	2
J. Martin, OF	2
J. Oates, C	2
F. Andrews, 2B	1
R. Lerch, RP	1

Pittsburgh (92-70)	WS
Hitting	**140.5**
Fielding	**41.8**
Pitching	**93.6**
R. Zisk, OF	24
D. Parker, OF	23
A. Oliver, OF	22
B. Robinson, OF	17
W. Stargell, 1B	17
R. Stennett, 2B	16
F. Taveras, SS	16
J. Candelaria, SP	15
B. Kison, SP	13
J. Reuss, SP	13
J. Rooker, SP	13
M. Sanguillen, C	13
R. Hebner, 3B	12
K. Tekulve, RP	11
L. Demery, RP	10
D. Medich, SP	8
D. Dyer, C	7
B. Moose, RP	5
O. Moreno, OF	5
D. Giusti, RP	3
T. Helms, 3B	3
R. Hernandez, RP	3
E. Kirkpatrick, 1B	2
M. Mendoza, SS	2
B. Robertson, 1B	2
E. Ott, C	1

San Diego (73-89)	WS
Hitting	**119.2**
Fielding	**33.2**
Pitching	**66.6**
D. Winfield, OF	25
R. Jones, SP	21
J. Grubb, OF	18
D. Rader, 3B	17
W. Davis, OF	16
M. Ivie, 1B	15
B. Metzger, RP	12
J. Turner, OF	11
T. Fuentes, 2B	9
E. Hernandez, SS	9
F. Kendall, C	9
D. Freisleben, SP	8
B. Strom, SP	8
R. Sawyer, SP	7
M. Rettenmund, OF	5
A. Foster, RP	4
T. Griffin, SP	4
W. McCovey, 1B	4
D. Tomlin, RP	4
T. Kubiak, 3B	3
B. Valentine, OF	3
B. Almon, SS	2
T. Ashford, 3B	1
B. Davis, C	1
G. Locklear, OF	1
L. Melendez, OF	1
H. Torres, SS	1

San Francisco (74-88)	WS
Hitting	**92.2**
Fielding	**38.1**
Pitching	**91.7**
G. Matthews, OF	24
J. Montefusco, SP	21
B. Murcer, OF	21
J. Barr, SP	20
G. Lavelle, RP	14
R. Moffitt, RP	14
E. Halicki, SP	11
C. Speier, SS	11
G. Thomasson, OF	10
L. Herndon, OF	9
M. Perez, 2B	9
K. Reitz, 3B	9
D. Evans, 1B	8
W. Montanez, 1B	7
C. Williams, RP	7
D. Rader, C	6
D. Thomas, 2B	5
J. Clark, OF	3
D. Heaverlo, RP	3
M. Hill, C	2
B. Knepper, SP	2
G. Alexander, C	1
R. Dressler, SP	1
V. Joshua, OF	1
J. LeMaster, SS	1
C. Robinson, 2B	1
M. Sadek, C	1

St. Louis (72-90)	WS
Hitting	**95.9**
Fielding	**40.5**
Pitching	**79.6**
T. Simmons, C	20
J. Denny, SP	18
W. Crawford, OF	14
L. Brock, OF	13
P. Falcone, SP	13
K. Hernandez, 1B	13
B. McBride, OF	13
D. Kessinger, SS	11
L. McGlothen, SP	10
J. Mumphrey, OF	10
A. Hrabosky, RP	9
M. Tyson, 2B	8
E. Rasmussen, RP	7
M. Anderson, OF	6
H. Cruz, 3B	6
B. Forsch, SP	6
J. Curtis, RP	5
J. Ferguson, C	5
G. Templeton, SS	5
R. Smith, 1B	4
R. Fairly, 1B	3
L. LaGrow, RP	3
M. Wallace, RP	3
B. Greif, RP	2
V. Harris, 2B	2
T. Walker, RP	2
L. Alvarado, 2B	1
D. Frisella, RP	1
M. Proly, RP	1
L. Richard, 2B	1
E. Solomon, RP	1

1977 American League

Baltimore (97-64)	WS
Hitting	**143.9**
Fielding	**48.1**
Pitching	**99.0**
K. Singleton, OF	36
J. Palmer, SP	29
A. Bumbry, OF	24
D. DeCinces, 3B	21
E. Murray, DH	21
M. Flanagan, SP	16
R. May, SP	16
L. May, 1B	14
P. Kelly, OF	13
R. Grimsley, SP	12
M. Belanger, SS	11
D. Martinez, RP	10
D. Skaggs, C	9
B. Smith, 2B	9
R. Dauer, 2B	8
R. Dempsey, C	8
T. Martinez, RP	7
A. Mora, OF	6
S. McGregor, RP	5
D. Drago, RP	4
E. Maddox, OF	4
K. Garcia, SS	3
D. Criscione, C	1

T. Crowley, DH 1
L. Harlow, OF 1
T. Muser, 1B 1
K. Rudolph, C 1

Boston (97-64)	WS
Hitting	**133.0**
Fielding	**48.4**
Pitching	**109.6**
C. Fisk, C	30
J. Rice, DH	26
C. Yastrzemski, OF	24
B. Campbell, RP	23
R. Burleson, SS	21
F. Lynn, OF	15
G. Scott, 1B	15
F. Jenkins, SP	14
R. Cleveland, SP	13
B. Hobson, 3B	13
L. Tiant, SP	12
B. Carbo, OF	11
B. Stanley, RP	11
D. Aase, SP	9
D. Evans, OF	9
B. Lee, SP	8
M. Paxton, RP	8
R. Wise, SP	8
D. Doyle, 2B	6
R. Miller, OF	4
J. Willoughby, RP	4
T. Cox, DH	2
S. Dillard, 2B	2
B. Montgomery, C	2
T. Helms, DH	1

California (74-88)	WS
Hitting	**104.4**
Fielding	**38.2**
Pitching	**79.4**
B. Bonds, OF	24
N. Ryan, SP	22
F. Tanana, SP	20
D. Baylor, OF	16
D. Chalk, 3B	14
J. Remy, 2B	14
P. Hartzell, SP	10
J. Rudi, OF	10
T. Solaita, 1B	10
D. LaRoche, RP	9
R. Mulliniks, SS	9
B. Grich, SS	7
D. Miller, RP	7
G. Flores, OF	6
R. Jackson, 1B	6
T. Bosley, OF	5
K. Brett, SP	5
T. Humphrey, C	5
M. Guerrero, SS	4
B. Bochte, OF	3
A. Etchebarren, C	3
M. Barlow, RP	2
D. Drago, RP	2
I. Hampton, C	2
K. Landreaux, OF	2
J. Caneira, SP	1
D. Kingman, 1B	1
C. May, 1B	1
S. Monge, RP	1
R. Torres, OF	1

Chicago (90-72)	WS
Hitting	**153.6**
Fielding	**35.8**
Pitching	**80.6**
C. Lemon, OF	23
O. Gamble, DH	22
E. Soderholm, 3B	20
R. Zisk, OF	20
J. Essian, C	16
L. LaGrow, RP	16
R. Garr, OF	15
J. Orta, 2B	14
F. Barrios, SP	13
L. Johnson, DH	12
A. Bannister, SS	11
B. Downing, C	9
K. Kravec, SP	9
J. Spencer, 1B	9
S. Stone, SP	9
J. Brohamer, 3B	6
C. Knapp, SP	6
D. Hamilton, RP	5
B. Johnson, RP	5
W. Nordhagen, OF	4
S. Renko, SP	4
W. Wood, SP	4
K. Brett, SP	3
B. Dal Canton, RP	2
D. Frost, SP	2
R. Stillman, OF	2
B. Coluccio, OF	1
H. Cruz, OF	1
J. Hairston, OF	1
D. Kessinger, SS	1
D. Kirkwood, RP	1
J. Kucek, RP	1
B. Nahorodny, C	1
T. Nordbrook, SS	1
J. Verhoeven, RP	1

Cleveland (71-90)	WS
Hitting	**95.2**
Fielding	**38.1**
Pitching	**79.7**
A. Thornton, 1B	20
D. Eckersley, SP	18
W. Garland, SP	17
B. Bell, 3B	15
J. Bibby, SP	13
D. Kuiper, 2B	13
R. Carty, DH	12
J. Norris, OF	12
B. Bochte, OF	11
P. Dade, OF	10
J. Kern, RP	10
L. Blanks, SS	9
D. Hood, RP	8
R. Waits, RP	8
R. Fosse, C	5
F. Kendall, C	5
R. Pruitt, OF	5
F. Duffy, SS	4
J. Grubb, OF	4
R. Manning, OF	4
A. Fitzmorris, SP	2
J. Lowenstein, OF	2
L. Andersen, RP	1
C. Camper, RP	1
D. LaRoche, RP	1
B. Melton, 1B	1
D. Oliver, 2B	1
C. Spikes, OF	1

Detroit (74-88)	WS
Hitting	**95.3**
Fielding	**40.0**
Pitching	**86.8**
R. LeFlore, OF	23
D. Rozema, SP	18
J. Thompson, 1B	18
T. Fuentes, 2B	16
S. Kemp, OF	14
R. Staub, DH	12
F. Arroyo, SP	11
B. Oglivie, OF	11
S. Foucault, RP	10
J. Hiller, RP	9
M. May, C	9
M. Wilcox, SP	8
M. Fidrych, SP	7
P. Mankowski, 3B	7
B. Sykes, SP	6
J. Wockenfuss, C	6
A. Rodriguez, 3B	5
T. Veryzer, SS	5
J. Crawford, RP	4
S. Grilli, RP	3
J. Morris, SP	3
D. Roberts, SP	3
M. Stanley, OF	3
B. Taylor, RP	3
T. Corcoran, OF	2
B. Adams, 1B	1
E. Glynn, RP	1
L. Parrish, C	1
V. Ruhle, SP	1
C. Scrivener, SS	1
M. Wagner, SS	1

Kansas City (102-60)	WS
Hitting	**146.8**
Fielding	**49.0**
Pitching	**110.2**
G. Brett, 3B	29
A. Cowens, OF	27
H. McRae, DH	26
D. Leonard, SP	24
A. Otis, OF	18
D. Porter, C	18
J. Colborn, SP	16
F. Patek, SS	15
P. Splittorff, SP	15
J. Mayberry, 1B	14
F. White, 2B	13
D. Bird, RP	11
L. Gura, RP	11
T. Poquette, OF	11
M. Littell, RP	10
M. Pattin, RP	9
A. Hassler, SP	7
P. LaCock, 1B	6
S. Mingori, RP	5
J. Wathan, C	5
J. Zdeb, OF	5
B. Heise, 2B-SS	2
J. Lahoud, OF	2
C. Rojas, 3B	2
C. Hurdle, OF	1
B. Martinez, C	1
G. Throop, RP	1
U. Washington, SS	1
W. Wilson, OF	1

Milwaukee (67-95)	WS
Hitting	**90.6**
Fielding	**38.0**
Pitching	**72.4**
D. Money, 2B	22
C. Cooper, 1B	18
S. Bando, 3B	17
S. Lezcano, OF	17
R. Yount, SS	16
J. Slaton, SP	14
M. Haas, SP	10
J. Augustine, SP	9
V. Joshua, OF	8
B. McClure, RP	8
C. Moore, C	8
E. Rodriguez, RP	8
B. Castro, RP	7
L. Sorensen, SP	7
S. Brye, OF	6
M. Caldwell, SP	3
J. Wohlford, OF	3
B. Cort, RP	2
L. Haney, C	2
S. Hinds, RP	2
E. Kirkpatrick, OF	2
K. McMullen, DH	2
L. Sakata, 2B	2
D. Thomas, DH-OF	2
B. Travers, SP	2
J. Gantner, 3B	1
M. Hegan, OF	1
E. Romero, SS	1
J. Wynn, OF	1

Minnesota (84-77)	WS
Hitting	**143.2**
Fielding	**35.4**
Pitching	**73.3**
R. Carew, 1B	37
L. Bostock, OF	27
L. Hisle, OF	24
D. Goltz, SP	22
B. Wynegar, C	18
T. Johnson, RP	16
R. Smalley, SS	13
D. Ford, OF	12
M. Cubbage, 3B	11
G. Adams, DH	9
P. Thormodsgard, SP	9
G. Zahn, SP	8
C. Kusick, DH	7
R. Schueler, RP	7
B. Randall, 2B	5
T. Burgmeier, RP	4
R. Chiles, DH	4
P. Redfern, SP	3
R. Wilfong, 2B	3
G. Borgmann, C	2
D. Johnson, RP	2
W. Norwood, OF	2
M. Pazik, SP	2
J. Terrell, 3B	2
L. Gomez, 2B	1
S. Perlozzo, 2B	1
G. Serum, RP	1

New York (100-62)	WS
Hitting	**156.0**
Fielding	**46.4**
Pitching	**97.6**
R. Jackson, OF	27
G. Nettles, 3B	25
T. Munson, C	22
M. Rivers, OF	22
S. Lyle, RP	20
W. Randolph, 2B	20
R. Guidry, SP	18
C. Chambliss, 1B	17
R. White, OF	17
E. Figueroa, SP	15
B. Dent, SS	14
L. Piniella, OF	13
D. Tidrow, RP	13
M. Torrez, SP	12
D. Gullett, SP	11
C. Johnson, DH	9
C. Hunter, SP	4
G. Zeber, 2B	4
P. Blair, OF	3
K. Clay, RP	2
D. Ellis, SP	2
D. Kingman, DH	2
F. Stanley, SS	2
W. Alston, DH	1
F. Healy, C	1
E. Hendricks, C	1
M. Klutts, 3B	1
C. May, DH	1
J. Wynn, DH	1

Oakland (63-98)	WS
Hitting	**83.0**
Fielding	**33.4**
Pitching	**72.6**
M. Page, OF	30
W. Gross, 3B	16
V. Blue, SP	14
B. Lacey, RP	10
J. Coleman, RP	9
R. Langford, SP	9
M. Sanguillen, C	9
R. Scott, 2B	9
P. Torrealba, RP	9
T. Armas, OF	8
D. Bair, RP	6
D. Giusti, RP	6
M. Perez, 2B	6
M. Jorgensen, 1B	5
D. Medich, SP	5
B. North, OF	5
R. Picciolo, SS	5
J. Tyrone, OF	5

E. Williams, DH	5
D. Allen, 1B	4
J. Newman, C	3
M. Norris, SP	2
W. Crawford, OF	1
S. Dunning, RP	1
T. Hosley, C	1
M. Keough, SP	1
L. Lintz, 2B	1
S. Mallory, OF	1
L. Murray, OF	1
J. Tabb, 1B	1
M. Torrez, SP	1

Seattle (64-98)	WS
Hitting	**96.4**
Fielding	**34.5**
Pitching	**61.1**
Ru. Jones, OF	22
L. Stanton, OF	19
D. Meyer, 1B	16
E. Romo, RP	15
B. Stein, 3B	11
G. Abbott, SP	10
S. Braun, OF	10
C. Lopez, OF	10
J. Montague, RP	10
B. Stinson, C	10
J. Baez, 2B	6
D. Collins, OF	6
T. House, RP	6
C. Reynolds, SS	6
J. Cruz, 2B	5
D. Pole, SP	4
L. Cox, C	3
M. Kekich, RP	3
B. Laxton, RP	3
L. Milbourne, 2B	3
G. Wheelock, SP	3
D. Medich, SP	2
J. Bernhardt, DH	1
S. Burke, RP	1
R. Fosse, C	1
R. Honeycutt, RP	1
Ri. Jones, SP	1
S. Jutze, C	1
P. Mitchell, SP	1
T. Moore, RP	1
D. Segui, RP	1

Texas (94-68)	WS
Hitting	**122.6**
Fielding	**50.5**
Pitching	**108.9**
M. Hargrove, 1B	25
T. Harrah, 3B	25
J. Sundberg, C	22
B. Wills, 2B	22
B. Blyleven, SP	21
D. Alexander, SP	17
G. Perry, SP	16
B. Campaneris, SS	15
D. Ellis, SP	15
J. Beniquez, OF	13
C. Washington, OF	13
A. Devine, RP	12
W. Horton, DH	12
N. Briles, SP	6
D. May, OF	6
L. Barker, RP	5
D. Knowles, RP	5
P. Lindblad, RP	5
K. Bevacqua, OF	4
K. Henderson, OF	4
R. Moret, RP	4
T. Grieve, OF	3
S. Alomar, DH	2
J. Ellis, C	2
M. Marshall, RP	2
K. Smith, OF	2
B. Cuellar, RP	1
B. Fahey, C	1
J. Fregosi, 1B	1
J. Mason, SS	1

Toronto (54-107)	WS
Hitting	**63.1**
Fielding	**32.1**
Pitching	**66.8**
J. Garvin, SP	13
D. Lemanczyk, SP	13
P. Vuckovich, RP	13
B. Bailor, OF	12
R. Fairly, DH	12
R. Howell, 3B	12
O. Velez, OF	11
J. Jefferson, SP	10
A. Woods, OF	8
D. Rader, 3B	7
M. Willis, RP	7
A. Ashby, C	6
D. Ault, 1B	6
S. Staggs, 2B	5
S. Ewing, OF	4
J. Johnson, RP	4
T. Murphy, RP	4
H. Torres, SS	3
S. Bowling, OF	2
J. Clancy, SP	2
D. McKay, 2B	2
G. Woods, OF	2
R. Cerone, C	1
S. Hargan, SP	1
T. Nordbrook, SS	1
J. Scott, OF	1

1977 National League

Atlanta (61-101)	WS
Hitting	**78.7**
Fielding	**32.5**
Pitching	**71.8**
J. Burroughs, OF	22
P. Niekro, SP	20
G. Matthews, OF	16
B. Pocoroba, C	14
W. Montanez, 1B	13
D. Campbell, RP	11
B. Bonnell, OF	9
D. Ruthven, SP	9
R. Gilbreath, 2B	7
R. Camp, RP	6
M. Leon, RP	6
A. Messersmith, SP	6
J. Moore, 3B	6
B. Capra, RP	4
V. Correll, C	4
D. Collins, RP	3
J. Nolan, C	3
R. Office, OF	3
P. Rockett, SS	3
J. Royster, 3B	3
E. Solomon, SP	3
D. Chaney, SS	2
P. Hanna, SP	2
D. Murphy, C	2
B. Asselstine, OF	1
M. Davey, RP	1
J. Easterly, RP	1
C. Gaston, OF	1
M. Mahler, SP	1
T. Paciorek, 1B	1

Chicago (81-81)	WS
Hitting	**87.8**
Fielding	**43.6**
Pitching	**111.6**
B. Sutter, RP	27
R. Reuschel, SP	26
B. Murcer, OF	19
S. Ontiveros, 3B	18
I. DeJesus, SS	15
J. Morales, OF	15
M. Trillo, 2B	14
B. Bonham, SP	12
L. Biittner, 1B	11
W. Hernandez, RP	11
R. Burris, SP	10
G. Gross, OF	9
M. Krukow, SP	8
B. Buckner, 1B	7
G. Mitterwald, C	7
P. Reuschel, RP	7
G. Clines, OF	5
D. Moore, RP	4
D. Roberts, RP	4
J. Cardenal, OF	3
S. Swisher, C	3
M. Kelleher, 2B	2
S. Renko, SP	2
J. Wallis, OF	2
P. Broberg, RP	1
D. Rosello, 3B	1

Cincinnati (88-74)	WS
Hitting	**147.0**
Fielding	**41.8**
Pitching	**75.2**
G. Foster, OF	32
J. Morgan, 2B	30
K. Griffey Sr., OF	23
P. Rose, 3B	23
J. Bench, C	22
D. Concepcion, SS	19
D. Driessen, 1B	19
T. Seaver, SP	17
P. Borbon, RP	14
F. Norman, SP	13
C. Geronimo, OF	11
P. Moskau, SP	6
R. Eastwick, RP	5
D. Capilla, SP	4
M. Sarmiento, RP	4
D. Murray, RP	3
B. Bailey, 1B	2
J. Billingham, SP	2
M. Caldwell, RP	2
W. Fryman, SP	2
R. Knight, 3B	2
G. Nolan, SP	2
E. Armbrister, OF	1
R. Auerbach, 2B	1
D. Flynn, 3B	1
B. Plummer, C	1
A. Torres, RP	1
D. Werner, C	1
P. Zachry, SP	1

Houston (81-81)	WS
Hitting	**121.3**
Fielding	**39.3**
Pitching	**82.4**
J. Cruz, OF	24
C. Cedeno, OF	23
B. Watson, 1B	23
J. Richard, SP	21
J. Ferguson, C	20
E. Cabell, 3B	17
A. Howe, 2B	14
J. Niekro, RP	14
M. Lemongello, SP	10
T. Puhl, OF	9
J. Sambito, RP	9
K. Forsch, RP	8
C. Johnson, OF	8
J. Andujar, SP	7
E. Herrmann, C	6
F. Bannister, SP	5
J. Gonzalez, SS	5
G. Pentz, RP	4
W. Crawford, OF	3
W. Howard, OF	3
B. McLaughlin, RP	3
T. Dixon, RP	2
K. Boswell, 2B	1
J. Fuller, OF	1
R. Metzger, SS	1
R. Sperring, SS	1
D. Walling, OF	1

Los Angeles (98-64)	WS
Hitting	**132.6**
Fielding	**48.8**
Pitching	**112.7**
R. Smith, OF	29
D. Lopes, 2B	24
D. Baker, OF	21
R. Cey, 3B	21
S. Garvey, 1B	21
B. Hooton, SP	19
T. John, SP	19
D. Sutton, SP	17
S. Yeager, C	16
B. Russell, SS	15
D. Rau, SP	13
R. Rhoden, SP	13
C. Hough, RP	12
R. Monday, OF	10
M. Garman, RP	7
E. Sosa, RP	7
L. Lacy, OF	5
J. Oates, C	5
T. Martinez, 2B	4
J. Hale, OF	3
G. Burke, OF	2
M. Mota, OF	2
L. Rautzhan, RP	2
B. Castillo, RP	1
V. Davalillo, OF	1
J. Grote, C	1
R. Landestoy, 2B	1
D. Lewallyn, RP	1
B. Powell, 1B	1
H. Webb, RP	1

Montreal (75-87)	WS
Hitting	**102.9**
Fielding	**40.9**
Pitching	**81.3**
G. Carter, C	25
S. Rogers, SP	21
A. Dawson, OF	18
D. Cash, 2B	17
T. Perez, 1B	17
E. Valentine, OF	15
W. Cromartie, OF	14
D. Stanhouse, RP	12
C. Speier, SS	11
B. Atkinson, RP	9
J. Kerrigan, RP	9
D. Unser, OF	8
L. Parrish, 3B	7
W. Twitchell, SP	7
J. Brown, SP	6
W. Garrett, 3B	5
W. McEnaney, RP	5
S. Alcala, RP	3
S. Bahnsen, SP	3
F. Holdsworth, RP	3
D. Schatzeder, SP-RP	3
H. Dues, SP	1
T. Foli, SS	1
B. Foote, C	1
P. Frias, 2B	1
P. Mackanin, 2B	1
S. Mejias, OF	1
T. Walker, RP	1

New York (64-98)	WS
Hitting	**76.9**
Fielding	**36.4**
Pitching	**78.7**
L. Randle, 3B	18
J. Stearns, C	15
S. Lockwood, RP	13
L. Mazzilli, OF	13
N. Espinosa, SP	12
S. Henderson, OF	12
J. Koosman, SP	11
J. Milner, 1B	11
B. Boisclair, OF	8
T. Seaver, SP	8

E. Kranepool, OF	7
B. Apodaca, RP	6
J. Matlack, SP	6
C. Swan, SP	6
P. Zachry, SP	6
B. Myrick, RP	5
B. Harrelson, SS	4
F. Millan, 2B	4
M. Vail, OF	4
R. Baldwin, RP	3
D. Flynn, SS	3
J. Youngblood, 2B	3
J. Grote, C	2
R. Hodges, C	2
D. Kingman, OF	2
P. Siebert, RP	2
R. Staiger, 3B	2
L. Foster, 2B	1
M. Phillips, SS	1
J. Todd, SP	1
B. Valentine, 1B	1

Philadelphia (101-61)	**WS**
Hitting	**161.9**
Fielding	**44.7**
Pitching	**96.5**
M. Schmidt, 3B	33
G. Luzinski, OF	30
S. Carlton, SP	26
G. Maddox, OF	20
B. Boone, C	18
L. Bowa, SS	16
R. Hebner, 1B	16
B. McBride, OF	16
G. Garber, RP	15
R. Reed, RP	14
T. Sizemore, 2B	14
J. Johnstone, OF	13
L. Christenson, SP	11
T. McCarver, C	10
T. McGraw, RP	10
D. Johnson, 1B	8
W. Brusstar, RP	7
J. Lonborg, SP	7
J. Martin, OF	6
R. Lerch, SP	4
T. Hutton, 1B	3
J. Kaat, SP	2
O. Brown, OF	1
T. Harmon, 2B	1
J. Morrison, 3B	1
T. Underwood, RP	1

Pittsburgh (96-66)	**WS**
Hitting	**126.6**
Fielding	**52.0**
Pitching	**109.4**
D. Parker, OF	33
J. Candelaria, SP	26
G. Gossage, RP	26
A. Oliver, OF	21
P. Garner, 3B	20
B. Robinson, 1B	18
R. Stennett, 2B	18
J. Rooker, SP	15
F. Taveras, SS	14
O. Moreno, OF	12
D. Dyer, C	11
K. Tekulve, RP	11
E. Ott, C	10
J. Reuss, SP	9
W. Stargell, 1B	8
G. Jackson, RP	6
B. Kison, SP	6
T. Forster, RP	5
F. Gonzalez, 3B	4
J. Fregosi, 1B	3
L. Demery, RP	2
M. Easler, OF	2
O. Jones, RP	2
T. Jones, RP	2
J. Hairston, OF	1
K. Macha, 3B	1
M. Mendoza, SS	1
E. Whitson, RP	1

San Diego (69-93)	**WS**
Hitting	**140.3**
Fielding	**26.5**
Pitching	**40.2**
G. Hendrick, OF	28
G. Tenace, C	25
D. Winfield, OF	24
G. Richards, OF	21
B. Almon, SS	15
M. Ivie, 1B	15
R. Fingers, RP	12
J. Turner, OF	9
D. Rader, 3B	8
M. Rettenmund, OF	7
B. Shirley, SP	6
D. Kingman, OF	5
D. Spillner, RP	5
D. Tomlin, RP	5
B. Owchinko, SP	4
T. Ashford, 3B	3
T. Griffin, SP	3
R. Jones, SP	3
M. Champion, 2B	2
D. Freisleben, SP	2
D. Roberts, C	2
B. Davis, C	1
R. Sawyer, RP	1
G. Sutherland, 2B	1

San Francisco (75-87)	**WS**
Hitting	**92.0**
Fielding	**39.7**
Pitching	**93.3**
E. Halicki, SP	20
G. Lavelle, RP	18
W. McCovey, 1B	16
G. Thomasson, OF	16
B. Madlock, 3B	14
D. Evans, OF	13
D. Thomas, OF	13
B. Knepper, SP	12
J. Clark, OF	11
D. Heaverlo, RP	9
T. Whitfield, OF	9
R. Andrews, 2B	8
J. Barr, SP	8
M. Hill, C	8
J. Montefusco, SP	8
R. Moffitt, RP	7
C. Williams, RP	7
T. Foli, SS	6
G. Alexander, C	5
V. Harris, 2B	4
M. Sadek, C	3
T. Cornutt, RP	2
J. Curtis, RP	2
R. Elliott, OF	2
J. LeMaster, SS	2
L. Herndon, OF	1
G. Minton, SP	1

St. Louis (83-79)	**WS**
Hitting	**132.9**
Fielding	**42.1**
Pitching	**74.0**
T. Simmons, C	28
K. Hernandez, 1B	24
G. Templeton, SS	24
J. Mumphrey, OF	16
K. Reitz, 3B	15
B. Forsch, SP	14
E. Rasmussen, SP	12
T. Scott, OF	12
M. Tyson, 2B	12
J. Urrea, RP	10
L. Brock, OF	9
H. Cruz, OF	9
C. Carroll, RP	8
B. Metzger, RP	8
B. Schultz, RP	8
R. Freed, 1B	6
A. Hrabosky, RP	5
B. McBride, OF	4
M. Anderson, OF	3
J. Denny, SP	3
D. Kessinger, SS	3
M. Phillips, 2B	3
D. Rader, C	3
J. Sutton, RP	2
R. Bosetti, OF	1
L. Dierker, SP	1
T. Duncan, 3B	1
J. Dwyer, OF	1
R. Eastwick, RP	1
P. Falcone, SP	1
D. Iorg, OF	1
T. Underwood, SP	1

1978 American League

Baltimore (90-71)	**WS**
Hitting	**138.4**
Fielding	**42.8**
Pitching	**88.8**
E. Murray, 1B	28
K. Singleton, OF	28
D. DeCinces, 3B	27
J. Palmer, SP	27
R. Dempsey, C	17
D. Martinez, SP	16
S. McGregor, SP	15
M. Flanagan, SP	14
L. Harlow, OF	12
R. Dauer, 2B	10
P. Kelly, OF	10
L. May, DH	10
B. Smith, 2B	10
D. Stanhouse, RP	10
M. Belanger, SS	9
K. Garcia, SS	5
A. Bumbry, OF	3
A. Mora, OF	3
D. Ford, SP-RP	2
E. Hendricks, C	2
C. Lopez, OF	2
G. Roenicke, OF	2
D. Skaggs, C	2
N. Briles, SP-RP	1
T. Crowley, DH	1
J. Kerrigan, RP	1
T. Martinez, RP	1
E. Stephenson, RP	1
S. Stewart, SP	1

Boston (99-64)	**WS**
Hitting	**137.2**
Fielding	**50.8**
Pitching	**109.0**
J. Rice, OF	36
C. Fisk, C	31
F. Lynn, OF	27
D. Eckersley, SP	24
C. Yastrzemski, OF	19
D. Evans, OF	17
B. Stanley, RP	17
L. Tiant, SP	17
R. Burleson, SS	16
J. Remy, 2B	16
M. Torrez, SP	14
B. Hobson, 3B	11
B. Lee, SP	11
D. Drago, RP	8
J. Wright, SP	8
G. Scott, 1B	6
B. Campbell, RP	4
J. Brohamer, 3B	3
T. Burgmeier, RP	3
F. Duffy, 3B	3
B. Bailey, DH	2
A. Hassler, RP	2
B. Carbo, OF	1
B. Montgomery, C	1

California (87-75)	**WS**
Hitting	**129.4**
Fielding	**44.3**
Pitching	**87.3**
D. Baylor, DH	23
B. Grich, 2B	20
L. Bostock, OF	19
B. Downing, C	18
C. Lansford, 3B	17
R. Jackson, 1B	14
D. LaRoche, RP	14
J. Rudi, OF	14
F. Tanana, SP	14
R. Miller, OF	13
N. Ryan, SP	12
D. Chalk, SS	10
P. Hartzell, RP	10
C. Knapp, SP	9
D. Aase, SP	8
D. Frost, SP	7
D. Miller, RP	7
K. Landreaux, OF	5
M. Rettenmund, OF	5
R. Fairly, 1B	4
A. Fitzmorris, RP	3
D. Goodwin, DH	3
T. Humphrey, C	3
J. Anderson, SS	2
T. Solaita, DH	2
K. Brett, RP	1
T. Griffin, RP	1
I. Hampton, C	1
D. Machemer, 2B	1
R. Mulliniks, SS	1

Chicago (71-90)	**WS**
Hitting	**105.6**
Fielding	**37.6**
Pitching	**69.9**
C. Lemon, OF	20
E. Soderholm, 3B	16
J. Orta, 2B	15
Lam. Johnson, 1B	12
F. Barrios, SP	10
R. Garr, OF	10
D. Kessinger, SS	9
K. Kravec, SP	9
S. Stone, SP	9
L. LaGrow, RP	7
B. Molinaro, OF	7
B. Nahorodny, C	7
C. Washington, OF	7
J. Willoughby, RP	7
W. Nordhagen, OF	6
M. Proly, RP	6
G. Pryor, 2B	5
M. Squires, 1B	5
T. Bosley, OF	4
R. Hinton, RP	4
W. Wood, SP	4
R. Wortham, SP	4
B. Bonds, OF	3
M. Colbern, C	3
J. Kucek, SP-RP	3
R. Torres, OF	3
R. Blomberg, DH	2
H. Chappas, SS	2
H. Cruz, OF	2
R. Schueler, RP	2
S. Trout, SP	2
A. Bannister, DH	1
K. Bell, 3B	1
J. Breazeale, 1B	1
M. Foley, C	1
J. Gates, 2B	1
J. Moore, DH	1
T. Spencer, OF	1
P. Torrealba, RP	1

Cleveland (69-90)	WS
Hitting	**104.5**
Fielding	**32.8**
Pitching	**69.7**
A. Thornton, 1B	25
B. Bell, 3B	16
J. Grubb, OF	16
R. Waits, SP	14
R. Manning, OF	11
G. Alexander, C	10
J. Kern, RP	10
D. Kuiper, 2B	10
J. Norris, OF	10
M. Paxton, SP	10
T. Veryzer, SS	8
P. Dade, OF	7
S. Monge, RP	7
D. Clyde, SP	6
P. Reuschel, RP	6
R. Wise, SP	6
B. Carbo, DH	5
D. Hood, SP	5
R. Pruitt, C	4
D. Spillner, RP	4
L. Blanks, SS	3
W. Cage, DH	3
W. Horton, DH	3
T. Cox, OF	2
D. Kinney, RP	2
B. Diaz, C	1
A. Griffin, SS	1
R. Hassey, C	1
H. Speed, OF	1

Detroit (86-76)	WS
Hitting	**112.6**
Fielding	**48.9**
Pitching	**96.5**
R. LeFlore, OF	24
J. Thompson, 1B	22
S. Kemp, OF	20
L. Whitaker, 2B	17
R. Staub, DH	16
J. Hiller, RP	15
D. Rozema, SP	15
A. Trammell, SS	14
J. Slaton, SP	13
M. Wilcox, SP	13
J. Billingham, SP	12
A. Rodriguez, 3B	10
K. Young, SP	9
M. May, C	8
L. Parrish, C	7
P. Mankowski, 3B	6
B. Sykes, RP	6
T. Corcoran, OF	5
J. Wockenfuss, OF	5
J. Morris, RP	4
M. Stanley, OF	3
S. Baker, SP	2
S. Dillard, 2B	2
M. Fidrych, SP	2
S. Foucault, RP	2
M. Wagner, SS	2
J. Crawford, RP	1
E. Glynn, RP	1
D. Stegman, OF	1
D. Tobik, RP	1

Kansas City (92-70)	WS
Hitting	**135.1**
Fielding	**46.5**
Pitching	**94.4**
A. Otis, OF	29
G. Brett, 3B	23
D. Porter, C	23
L. Gura, SP	19
D. Leonard, SP	19
H. McRae, DH	16
P. Splittorff, SP	16
F. White, 2B	16
A. Cowens, OF	15
C. Hurdle, OF	14
R. Gale, SP	13
A. Hrabosky, RP	12
F. Patek, SS	11
P. LaCock, 1B	10
S. Mingori, RP	6
S. Braun, OF	5
J. Wathan, 1B	5
M. Pattin, RP	4
W. Wilson, OF	4
T. Poquette, OF	3
J. Terrell, 2B	2
U. Washington, SS	2
J. Zdeb, OF	2
D. Bird, RP	1
A. Hassler, SP	1
A. Kusnyer, C	1
B. Paschall, RP	1
J. Quirk, 3B	1
L. Silverio, OF	1
G. Throop, RP	1

Milwaukee (93-69)	WS
Hitting	**150.0**
Fielding	**38.6**
Pitching	**90.4**
M. Caldwell, SP	28
S. Bando, 3B	23
L. Hisle, OF	23
G. Thomas, OF	21
S. Lezcano, OF	20
L. Sorensen, SP	20
D. Money, 1B	19
B. Oglivie, OF	19
R. Yount, SS	19
C. Cooper, 1B	15
P. Molitor, 2B	12
J. Augustine, SP	7
B. Castro, RP	7
C. Moore, C	7
A. Replogle, SP	7
B. Travers, SP	7
E. Rodriguez, RP	6
B. McClure, RP	5
B. Martinez, C	3
J. Wohlford, OF	3
D. Davis, DH	2
E. Farmer, RP	2
J. Gantner, 2B	1
D. May, OF	1
L. Sakata, 2B	1
R. Stein, RP	1

Minnesota (73-89)	WS
Hitting	**100.3**
Fielding	**37.2**
Pitching	**81.4**
R. Carew, 1B	22
R. Smalley, SS	22
D. Goltz, SP	19
G. Zahn, SP	17
D. Ford, OF	15
M. Marshall, RP	14
M. Cubbage, 3B	12
R. Erickson, SP	12
B. Wynegar, C	10
B. Randall, 2B	9
G. Serum, SP	8
H. Powell, OF	7
B. Rivera, OF	7
W. Norwood, OF	6
J. Morales, DH	5
R. Wilfong, 2B	5
L. Wolfe, 3B	5
G. Adams, DH	4
G. Borgmann, C	4
R. Chiles, OF	3
D. Edwards, OF	2
J. Holly, RP	2
D. Jackson, SP	2
J. Sutton, RP	2
G. Thayer, RP	2
C. Kusick, DH	1
M. Scarce, RP	1
P. Thormodsgard, SP	1

New York (100-63)	WS
Hitting	**142.4**
Fielding	**49.2**
Pitching	**108.5**
R. Guidry, SP	31
G. Nettles, 3B	26
R. Jackson, OF	23
W. Randolph, 2B	23
G. Gossage, RP	20
C. Chambliss, 1B	19
E. Figueroa, SP	19
T. Munson, C	19
L. Piniella, OF	19
M. Rivers, OF	19
R. White, OF	11
B. Dent, SS	9
S. Lyle, RP	9
C. Hunter, SP	8
D. Tidrow, SP	8
J. Beattie, SP	6
G. Thomasson, OF	5
J. Spencer, DH	4
F. Stanley, SS	4
D. Gullett, SP	3
C. Johnson, DH	3
K. Clay, RP	2
R. Eastwick, RP	2
M. Heath, C	2
P. Blair, OF	1
B. Doyle, 2B	1
D. Garcia, 2B	1
K. Holtzman, SP	1
J. Johnstone, OF	1
M. Klutts, 3B	1

Oakland (69-93)	WS
Hitting	**77.4**
Fielding	**41.2**
Pitching	**88.5**
M. Page, OF	20
E. Sosa, RP	14
J. Johnson, SP	13
M. Keough, SP	12
D. Revering, 1B	12
M. Guerrero, SS	11
R. Langford, SP	11
J. Essian, C	10
D. Heaverlo, RP	10
B. Lacey, RP	10
J. Wallis, OF	7
R. Carty, DH	6
T. Duncan, 3B	6
M. Edwards, 2B	6
W. Gross, 3B	6
J. Newman, C	6
S. Renko, SP	6
P. Broberg, SP	5
A. Wirth, SP	5
M. Dilone, OF	4
W. Horton, DH	4
G. Alexander, DH	3
J. Coleman, RP	3
S. Staggs, 2B	3
T. Armas, OF	2
G. Burke, OF	2
B. Robinson, C	2
G. Thomasson, OF	2
M. Adams, 2B	1
W. Alston, OF	1
T. Hosley, C	1
D. Murphy, OF	1
B. North, OF	1
R. Picciolo, SS	1

Seattle (56-104)	WS
Hitting	**90.7**
Fielding	**26.7**
Pitching	**50.6**
L. Roberts, OF	21
C. Reynolds, SS	17
B. Stinson, C	13
B. Bochte, OF	12
J. Cruz, 2B	12
E. Romo, RP	10
Ru. Jones, OF	9
B. Stein, 3B	9
P. Mitchell, SP	8
T. Paciorek, OF	8
S. Rawley, RP	6
J. Todd, RP	6
R. Honeycutt, SP	4
T. House, RP	4
B. McLaughlin, SP	4
B. Robertson, DH	4
G. Abbott, SP	3
S. Burke, RP	3
D. Meyer, 1B	3
L. Milbourne, 3B	2
B. Plummer, C	2
J. Baez, 2B	1
J. Bernhardt, 1B	1
S. Braun, DH	1
T. Brown, RP	1
J. Colborn, SP	1
J. Hale, OF	1
M. Parrott, RP	1
K. Pasley, C	1

Texas (87-75)	WS
Hitting	**121.1**
Fielding	**40.5**
Pitching	**99.3**
J. Matlack, SP	25
J. Sundberg, C	23
A. Oliver, OF	22
F. Jenkins, SP	21
B. Bonds, OF	20
B. Wills, 2B	19
M. Hargrove, 1B	16
T. Harrah, 3B	15
R. Zisk, OF	15
S. Comer, RP	13
D. Alexander, SP	10
D. Medich, SP	10
J. Beniquez, OF	9
R. Cleveland, RP	8
J. Lowenstein, 3B	6
D. Ellis, SP	5
B. Campaneris, SS	3
J. Grubb, OF	3
P. Lindblad, RP	3
B. Thompson, OF	3
K. Bevacqua, 3B	2
J. Ellis, C	2
J. Umbarger, RP	2
L. Barker, RP	1
D. Darwin, RP	1
G. Gray, DH	1
M. Jorgensen, 1B	1
J. Mason, SS	1
B. Sample, DH	1

Toronto (59-102)	WS
Hitting	**79.7**
Fielding	**35.6**
Pitching	**61.7**
R. Howell, 3B	15
J. Mayberry, 1B	14
R. Carty, DH	13
B. Bailor, OF	12
R. Bosetti, OF	12
J. Clancy, SP	10
V. Cruz, RP	10
O. Velez, OF	10
A. Ashby, C	9
J. Jefferson, SP	9
D. McKay, 2B	8
T. Underwood, SP	8
T. Murphy, RP	7
L. Gomez, SS	5
M. Willis, RP	5
R. Cerone, C	4
B. Moore, RP	4
T. Hutton, OF	3
D. Kirkwood, SP	3
A. Woods, OF	3
D. Ault, 1B	2
J. Coleman, RP	2
T. Johnson, SS	2

W. Upshaw, OF 2
T. Buskey, RP 1
J. Garvin, SP 1
G. Iorg, 2B 1
B. Milner, C 1
D. Wallace, RP 1

1978
National League

Atlanta (69-93)	WS
Hitting	**81.3**
Fielding	**40.4**
Pitching	**85.3**
P. Niekro, SP	30
J. Burroughs, OF	27
G. Matthews, OF	17
G. Garber, RP	16
B. Horner, 3B	14
J. Royster, 2B	11
L. McWilliams, SP	10
R. Office, OF	8
D. Murphy, 1B	7
R. Gilbreath, 3B	6
E. Solomon, RP	6
J. Nolan, C	5
B. Pocoroba, C	5
B. Asselstine, OF	4
R. Camp, RP	4
D. Chaney, SS	4
B. Beall, 1B	3
B. Bonnell, OF	3
D. Campbell, RP	3
P. Hanna, SP	3
G. Hubbard, 2B	3
M. Mahler, SP	3
D. Ruthven, SP	3
C. Skok, RP	3
B. Benedict, C	1
J. Bouton, SP	1
A. Devine, RP	1
J. Easterly, RP	1
C. Gaston, OF	1
F. LaCorte, SP	1
P. Rockett, SS	1
C. Ruiz, 2B	1
D. Theiss, RP	1

Chicago (79-83)	WS
Hitting	**102.5**
Fielding	**42.9**
Pitching	**91.6**
I. DeJesus, SS	19
B. Murcer, OF	18
R. Reuschel, SP	18
D. Kingman, OF	17
B. Sutter, RP	16
D. Lamp, SP	15
M. Trillo, 2B	15
B. Buckner, 1B	12
M. Krukow, SP	11
G. Gross, OF	8
D. Moore, RP	8
R. Scott, 3B	8
L. McGlothen, RP	7
S. Ontiveros, 3B	7
R. Burris, SP	6
W. Hernandez, RP	6
L. Biittner, 1B	5
D. Roberts, SP	5
M. Vail, OF	5
J. White, OF	5
G. Clines, OF	4
L. Cox, C	4
T. Blackwell, C	3
D. Rader, C	3
D. Johnson, 3B	2
M. Kelleher, 3B	2
S. Thompson, OF	2
J. Wallis, OF	2
H. Cruz, OF	1
W. Fryman, SP	1
D. Geisel, RP	1
P. Reuschel, RP	1

Cincinnati (92-69)	WS
Hitting	**150.3**
Fielding	**40.1**
Pitching	**85.6**
G. Foster, OF	30
P. Rose, 3B	27
D. Concepcion, SS	25
K. Griffey Sr., OF	22
J. Bench, C	20
T. Seaver, SP	19
D. Bair, RP	18
D. Driessen, 1B	18
J. Morgan, 2B	17
B. Bonham, SP	10
F. Norman, SP	9
C. Geronimo, OF	8
P. Moskau, SP	8
T. Hume, SP	6
J. Kennedy, 2B	6
M. Lum, OF	6
M. Sarmiento, RP	6
R. Auerbach, SS	4
P. Borbon, RP	4
V. Correll, C	2
M. LaCoss, SP	2
M. Soto, RP	2
D. Werner, C	2
D. Dumoulin, RP	1
K. Henderson, OF	1
R. Knight, 3B	1
D. Murray, RP	1
C. Summers, OF	1

Houston (74-88)	WS
Hitting	**115.0**
Fielding	**34.6**
Pitching	**72.4**
J. Cruz, OF	26
E. Cabell, 3B	20
T. Puhl, OF	19
J. Richard, SP	19
B. Watson, 1B	17
A. Howe, 2B	16
K. Forsch, RP	13
C. Cedeno, OF	9
J. Niekro, SP	8
J. Sambito, RP	8
D. Walling, OF	8
J. Ferguson, C	7
M. Lemongello, SP	7
J. Andujar, RP	6
V. Ruhle, SP	6
J. Alou, OF	4
D. Bergman, 1B	4
B. Bochy, C	4
T. Dixon, SP	4
R. Landestoy, SS	3
J. Sexton, SS	3
J. Gonzalez, 2B	2
L. Pujols, C	2
R. Baldwin, C	1
F. Bannister, SP	1
M. Fischlin, SS	1
W. Howard, OF	1
J. Leonard, OF	1
R. Metzger, SS	1
F. Riccelli, RP	1

Los Angeles (95-67)	WS
Hitting	**146.1**
Fielding	**42.1**
Pitching	**96.8**
D. Lopes, 2B	26
R. Cey, 3B	25
S. Garvey, 1B	25
R. Smith, OF	24
B. Hooton, SP	19
B. Russell, SS	18
D. Baker, OF	13
R. Monday, OF	13
T. Forster, RP	12
T. John, SP	12
D. Rau, SP	12
B. Welch, SP	12
D. Sutton, SP	11
L. Lacy, OF	10
B. North, OF	9
C. Hough, RP	8
J. Ferguson, C	7
R. Rhoden, SP	7
S. Yeager, C	6
L. Rautzhan, RP	5
J. Grote, C	3
V. Davalillo, OF	2
T. Martinez, SS	2
J. Oates, C	2
P. Guerrero, 1B	1
M. Mota, PH-PR	1

Montreal (76-86)	WS
Hitting	**107.4**
Fielding	**43.9**
Pitching	**76.7**
G. Carter, C	22
E. Valentine, OF	22
A. Dawson, OF	21
W. Cromartie, OF	20
T. Perez, 1B	18
S. Rogers, SP	17
R. Grimsley, SP	16
L. Parrish, 3B	15
C. Speier, SS	15
D. Cash, 2B	11
D. Schatzeder, SP	9
H. Dues, RP	8
D. Knowles, RP	7
W. Fryman, SP	4
M. Garman, RP	4
R. May, SP	4
S. Sanderson, SP	4
S. Bahnsen, RP	3
B. Atkinson, RP	2
S. Papi, SS	2
D. Unser, 1B	2
P. Frias, 2B	1
T. Hutton, 1B	1

New York (66-96)	WS
Hitting	**100.5**
Fielding	**33.2**
Pitching	**64.3**
J. Stearns, C	22
L. Mazzilli, OF	21
C. Swan, SP	17
S. Henderson, OF	16
W. Montanez, 1B	15
E. Maddox, OF	11
L. Randle, 3B	10
J. Youngblood, OF	9
J. Koosman, SP	8
S. Lockwood, RP	8
P. Zachry, SP	8
D. Flynn, 2B	7
T. Foli, SS	7
K. Kobel, RP	7
D. Murray, RP	6
M. Cornejo, RP	4
B. Valentine, 2B	4
B. Boisclair, OF	3
N. Espinosa, SP	3
R. Hodges, C	2
D. Norman, OF	2
D. Bernard, RP	1
S. Ferrer, SS	1
G. Flores, OF	1
T. Grieve, OF	1
T. Hausman, SP	1
K. Henderson, OF	1
E. Kranepool, OF	1
B. Myrick, RP	1

Philadelphia (90-72)	WS
Hitting	**126.1**
Fielding	**46.9**
Pitching	**97.0**
G. Luzinski, OF	27
M. Schmidt, 3B	23
L. Bowa, SS	22
G. Maddox, OF	21
S. Carlton, SP	20
B. Boone, C	17
R. Hebner, 1B	16
R. Reed, RP	14
L. Christenson, SP	13
B. McBride, OF	13
D. Ruthven, SP	13
R. Lerch, SP	10
J. Martin, OF	9
W. Brusstar, RP	8
T. McGraw, RP	8
G. Garber, RP	6
J. Kaat, SP	5
T. McCarver, C	5
T. Sizemore, 2B	5
J. Cardenal, 1B	4
B. Harrelson, 2B	3
R. Eastwick, RP	2
J. Morrison, 2B	2
B. Foote, C	1
D. Johnson, 2B	1
J. Lonborg, SP	1
L. Smith, OF	1

Pittsburgh (88-73)	WS
Hitting	**124.6**
Fielding	**42.7**
Pitching	**96.7**
D. Parker, OF	37
W. Stargell, 1B	22
K. Tekulve, RP	20
P. Garner, 2B-3B	19
O. Moreno, OF	18
B. Blyleven, SP	16
F. Taveras, SS	16
D. Robinson, SP	15
J. Candelaria, SP	14
B. Robinson, OF	14
E. Ott, C	12
J. Milner, OF	10
J. Bibby, RP	6
G. Jackson, RP	6
B. Kison, RP	6
R. Stennett, 2B	5
E. Whitson, RP	5
J. Rooker, SP	4
M. Sanguillen, 1B	4
D. Berra, 3B	3
D. Dyer, C	3
S. Brye, OF	2
J. Reuss, SP	2
J. Fregosi, 3B	1
D. Hamilton, RP	1
O. Jones, RP	1
K. Macha, 3B	1
M. Mendoza, 2B	1

San Diego (84-78)	WS
Hitting	**123.5**
Fielding	**38.7**
Pitching	**89.8**
D. Winfield, OF	28
G. Richards, OF	24
G. Tenace, 1B	22
O. Smith, SS	20
G. Perry, SP	18
R. Fingers, RP	17
O. Gamble, OF	15
R. Jones, SP	14
J. D'Acquisto, RP	11
B. Owchinko, SP	9
B. Almon, 3B	8
J. Turner, OF	8
F. Gonzalez, 2B	7
B. Shirley, RP	7
D. Thomas, OF	7
M. Lee, RP	5
E. Rasmussen, SP	5
T. Ashford, 3B	4
M. Lolich, RP	4

R. Sweet, C	4
G. Hendrick, OF	3
B. Perkins, 1B	3
B. Evans, 3B	2
D. Reynolds, OF	2
D. Roberts, C	2
C. Baker, 2B	1
M. Champion, 2B	1
J. Wilhelm, OF	1

San Francisco (89-73)	WS
Hitting	**131.0**
Fielding	**40.4**
Pitching	**95.6**
J. Clark, OF	30
D. Evans, 3B	26
B. Madlock, 2B	25
V. Blue, SP	22
B. Knepper, SP	22
M. Ivie, 1B	14
T. Whitfield, OF	14
E. Halicki, SP	13
L. Herndon, OF	10
M. Hill, C	10
G. Lavelle, RP	10
J. Montefusco, SP	9
J. Barr, SP	8
W. McCovey, 1B	8
R. Moffitt, RP	8
J. LeMaster, SS	7
J. Dwyer, OF	6
R. Metzger, SS	5
R. Andrews, 2B	4
H. Cruz, OF	4
J. Tamargo, C	4
J. Curtis, RP	3
M. Sadek, C	3
V. Harris, SS	1
T. Heintzelman, 2B	1

St. Louis (69-93)	WS
Hitting	**104.0**
Fielding	**36.4**
Pitching	**66.7**
T. Simmons, C	30
G. Templeton, SS	21
K. Hernandez, 1B	19
G. Hendrick, OF	18
J. Denny, SP	15
P. Vuckovich, SP	14
K. Reitz, 3B	12
M. Littell, RP	9
B. Forsch, SP	8
J. Morales, OF	7
J. Mumphrey, OF	7
S. Martinez, SP	6
T. Bruno, RP	5
M. Phillips, 2B	5
B. Schultz, RP	5
M. Tyson, 2B	5
S. Swisher, C	4
W. Garrett, 3B	3
L. Brock, OF	2
R. Freed, 1B	2
D. Iorg, OF	2
A. Lopez, RP	2
R. Thomas, RP	2
R. Dressler, SP	1
J. Dwyer, OF	1
E. Rasmussen, SP	1
T. Scott, OF	1

1979 American League

Baltimore (102-57)	WS
Hitting	**133.7**
Fielding	**51.5**
Pitching	**120.8**
K. Singleton, OF	32
E. Murray, 1B	25
M. Flanagan, SP	23
A. Bumbry, OF	19
G. Roenicke, OF	19
D. Martinez, SP	18
R. Dempsey, C	14
S. McGregor, SP	14
D. DeCinces, 3B	13
D. Stanhouse, RP	13
J. Palmer, SP	12
R. Dauer, 2B	11
S. Stone, SP	11
K. Garcia, SS	9
J. Lowenstein, OF	9
T. Martinez, RP	9
S. Stewart, RP	9
T. Stoddard, RP	8
P. Kelly, OF	7
B. Smith, 2B	7
L. May, DH	6
D. Ford, RP	4
D. Skaggs, C	4
B. Ayala, OF	3
M. Belanger, SS	3
T. Crowley, DH	3
L. Harlow, OF	1

Boston (91-69)	WS
Hitting	**123.7**
Fielding	**44.6**
Pitching	**104.7**
F. Lynn, OF	34
J. Rice, OF	28
D. Eckersley, SP	24
R. Burleson, SS	19
D. Evans, OF	16
B. Stanley, SP	15
M. Torrez, SP	14
D. Drago, RP	13
B. Watson, 1B	13
C. Yastrzemski, DH	13
B. Hobson, 3B	11
S. Renko, SP	11
T. Burgmeier, RP	9
C. Rainey, SP	8
J. Remy, 2B	7
C. Fisk, DH	6
B. Campbell, RP	5
T. Poquette, OF	4
B. Montgomery, C	3
A. Ripley, RP	3
L. Wolfe, 2B	3
G. Allenson, C	2
J. Brohamer, 2B	2
J. Dwyer, 1B	2
J. Finch, RP	2
S. Papi, 2B	2
T. Sizemore, 2B	2
G. Scott, 1B	1
J. Wright, RP	1

California (88-74)	WS
Hitting	**162.7**
Fielding	**33.6**
Pitching	**67.6**
D. Baylor, OF	29
B. Grich, 2B	28
B. Downing, C	25
C. Lansford, 3B	21
D. Ford, OF	18
R. Carew, 1B	16
W. Aikens, 1B	15
D. Frost, SP	15
R. Miller, OF	14
N. Ryan, SP	13
M. Clear, RP	10
J. Barr, SP	9
D. Aase, SP	6
J. Anderson, SS	6
J. Rudi, OF	6
B. Campaneris, SS	5
F. Tanana, SP	5
L. Harlow, OF	3
M. Barlow, RP	2
B. Clark, OF	2
T. Donohue, C	2
D. LaRoche, RP	2
D. Miller, RP	2
M. Rettenmund, DH	2
D. Thon, 2B	2
W. Davis, OF	1
S. Eddy, SP	1
B. Ferris, RP	1
C. Knapp, SP	1
J. Montague, RP	1
R. Mulliniks, SS	1

Chicago (73-87)	WS
Hitting	**102.0**
Fielding	**36.7**
Pitching	**80.3**
C. Lemon, OF	26
K. Kravec, SP	16
L. Johnson, 1B	14
A. Bannister, 2B	13
R. Baumgarten, SP	13
C. Washington, OF	13
E. Farmer, RP	10
S. Trout, SP	10
J. Morrison, 2B	9
G. Pryor, SS	9
J. Orta, DH	8
R. Wortham, SP	7
F. Barrios, SP	6
R. Garr, OF	6
M. Proly, RP	6
M. May, C	5
B. Nahorodny, C	5
E. Soderholm, 3B	5
R. Torres, OF	5
K. Bell, 3B	4
W. Nordhagen, DH	4
R. Scarbery, RP	4
M. Squires, 1B	4
T. Bosley, OF	3
F. Howard, RP	3
R. Dotson, SP	2
J. Moore, OF	2
H. Chappas, SS	1
M. Colbern, C	1
M. Foley, C	1
G. Hoffman, RP	1
D. Kessinger, SS	1
G. Rondon, RP	1
P. Torrealba, RP	1

Cleveland (81-80)	WS
Hitting	**121.4**
Fielding	**38.1**
Pitching	**83.5**
T. Harrah, 3B	24
B. Bonds, OF	21
S. Monge, RP	21
M. Hargrove, OF	19
A. Thornton, 1B	19
R. Wise, SP	17
R. Waits, SP	14
R. Manning, OF	11
C. Johnson, DH	10
G. Alexander, C	9
D. Kuiper, 2B	9
D. Spillner, RP	9
T. Veryzer, SS	9
R. Hassey, C	7
L. Barker, SP	6
V. Cruz, RP	6
J. Norris, OF	6
P. Dade, OF	4
R. Pruitt, OF	4
D. Rosello, 2B	4
E. Wilkins, SP	3
W. Alston, OF	2
W. Garland, SP	2
D. Hood, RP	2
M. Paxton, SP	2
D. Clyde, SP	1
T. Cox, 3B	1
S. Wihtol, RP	1

Detroit (85-76)	WS
Hitting	**124.2**
Fielding	**45.5**
Pitching	**85.3**
S. Kemp, OF	25
R. LeFlore, OF	21
L. Parrish, C	21
L. Whitaker, 2B	20
A. Lopez, RP	19
J. Morris, SP	17
C. Summers, OF	15
J. Thompson, 1B	13
A. Trammell, SS	13
J. Billingham, SP	12
M. Wilcox, SP	10
J. Wockenfuss, 1B	7
T. Brookens, 3B	6
L. Jones, OF	6
D. Petry, SP	6
A. Rodriguez, 3B	6
P. Underwood, SP	6
D. Rozema, SP	5
R. Staub, DH	5
J. Morales, OF	4
D. Tobik, RP	4
M. Wagner, SS	4
J. Hiller, RP	3
B. Robbins, SP	3
P. Mankowski, 3B	1
R. Peters, DH-3B	1
E. Putman, C	1
D. Stegman, OF	1

Kansas City (85-77)	WS
Hitting	**138.7**
Fielding	**41.9**
Pitching	**74.5**
G. Brett, 3B	33
D. Porter, C	31
W. Wilson, OF	24
A. Otis, OF	23
A. Cowens, OF	14
D. Leonard, SP	14
H. McRae, DH	12
P. Splittorff, SP	12
F. White, 2B	11
L. Gura, SP	10
P. LaCock, 1B	8
A. Hrabosky, RP	7
S. Busby, SP	6
C. Chamberlain, SP	5
M. Pattin, RP	5
U. Washington, SS	5
S. Braun, OF	4
C. Hurdle, OF	4
D. Quisenberry, RP	4
E. Rodriguez, RP	4
R. Gale, SP	3
F. Patek, SS	3
J. Quirk, DH-C	3
R. Martin, RP	2
G. Barranca, DH-2B-3B	1
G. Christenson, RP	1
T. Cruz, SS	1
C. Eaton, RP	1
S. Mingori, RP	1
G. Scott, 1B	1
J. Terrell, 3B	1
J. Wathan, 1B	1

Milwaukee (95-66)	WS
Hitting	**144.8**
Fielding	**44.7**
Pitching	**95.5**
S. Lezcano, OF	27
P. Molitor, 2B	26
G. Thomas, OF	26
C. Cooper, 1B	24
M. Caldwell, SP	20
B. Oglivie, OF	20
J. Slaton, SP	16
L. Sorensen, SP	15
C. Moore, C	14

R. Yount, SS	14
B. Travers, SP	13
S. Bando, 3B	9
J. Augustine, RP	8
B. Castro, RP	7
M. Haas, SP	7
J. Gantner, 3B	6
D. Money, DH	6
D. Davis, DH	5
B. Martinez, C	5
B. McClure, RP	4
B. Galasso, RP	3
L. Hisle, DH	3
J. Wohlford, OF	3
D. Boitano, RP	1
R. Fosse, C	1
P. Mitchell, RP	1
L. Sakata, 2B	1

Minnesota (82-80)	WS
Hitting	**102.4**
Fielding	**43.7**
Pitching	**100.0**
R. Smalley, SS	24
J. Koosman, SP	23
M. Marshall, RP	23
R. Wilfong, 2B	18
B. Wynegar, C	17
D. Goltz, SP	16
K. Landreaux, OF	16
R. Jackson, 1B	14
G. Zahn, SP	14
J. Castino, 3B	9
P. Redfern, RP	9
G. Adams, DH	8
H. Powell, OF	8
M. Cubbage, 3B	5
D. Edwards, OF	5
P. Hartzell, SP	5
B. Rivera, OF	5
D. Goodwin, DH	4
D. Jackson, RP	4
W. Norwood, OF	4
M. Bacsik, RP	3
B. Randall, 2B	3
G. Borgmann, C	2
R. Erickson, SP	2
R. Sofield, OF	2
K. Brett, RP	1
C. Kusick, DH	1
J. Morales, DH	1

New York (89-71)	WS
Hitting	**122.6**
Fielding	**44.3**
Pitching	**100.1**
R. Jackson, OF	23
T. John, SP	23
W. Randolph, 2B	23
R. Guidry, SP	22
C. Chambliss, 1B	16
G. Nettles, 3B	15
J. Spencer, DH	14
R. Davis, RP	12
B. Dent, SS	12
L. Piniella, OF	12
L. Tiant, SP	12
G. Gossage, RP	11
T. Munson, C	11
O. Gamble, DH-OF	10
B. Murcer, OF	8
M. Rivers, OF	7
D. Hood, RP	6
E. Figueroa, SP	5
J. Beniquez, OF	3
J. Kaat, RP	3
J. Beattie, SP	2
B. Gulden, C	2
C. Johnson, DH	2
G. Scott, DH	2
F. Stanley, SS	2
B. Brown, OF	1
K. Clay, RP	1
D. Garcia, SS	1
C. Hunter, SP	1
J. Johnstone, OF	1
D. Jones, DH	1
J. Narron, C	1
D. Righetti, SP	1
R. White, DH	1

Oakland (54-108)	WS
Hitting	**81.7**
Fielding	**26.5**
Pitching	**53.8**
D. Revering, 1B	19
D. Murphy, OF	16
W. Gross, 3B	13
R. Langford, SP	12
J. Newman, C	12
R. Henderson, OF	10
S. McCatty, SP	10
J. Essian, C	9
M. Page, DH	8
T. Armas, OF	7
B. Kingman, SP	7
D. Hamilton, RP	6
D. Heaverlo, RP	6
M. Norris, SP	5
M. Heath, OF	4
J. Johnson, SP	4
R. Picciolo, SS	4
D. Chalk, 2B	3
M. Keough, SP	3
M. Edwards, 2B	1
M. Guerrero, SS	1
C. Minetto, RP	1
L. Murray, OF	1

Seattle (67-95)	WS
Hitting	**95.0**
Fielding	**33.3**
Pitching	**72.7**
B. Bochte, 1B	19
R. Jones, OF	18
M. Parrott, SP	17
J. Cruz, 2B	13
L. Roberts, OF	13
W. Horton, DH	12
D. Meyer, 3B	12
F. Bannister, SP	11
R. Honeycutt, SP	11
B. McLaughlin, RP	11
T. Paciorek, OF	8
S. Rawley, RP	8
L. Milbourne, SS	7
M. Mendoza, SS	5
B. Stinson, C	5
R. Dressler, SP	4
J. Montague, RP	4
B. Stein, 3B	4
G. Abbott, SP	3
L. Cox, C	3
J. Simpson, OF	3
B. Valentine, SS	3
R. Craig, OF	2
J. Decker, RP	1
J. Hale, OF	1
P. Mitchell, SP	1
R. Stein, RP	1
R. Vasquez, RP	1

Texas (83-79)	WS
Hitting	**111.9**
Fielding	**44.5**
Pitching	**92.6**
J. Kern, RP	25
B. Bell, 3B	22
A. Oliver, OF	18
J. Sundberg, C	18
S. Comer, SP	15
B. Wills, 2B	15
F. Jenkins, SP	14
R. Zisk, OF	13
B. Sample, OF	11
S. Lyle, RP	10
P. Putnam, 1B	10
O. Gamble, DH	9
J. Grubb, OF	9
D. Medich, SP	8
M. Rivers, OF	8
J. Ellis, DH	7
W. Montanez, 1B	5
D. Alexander, SP	4
D. Darwin, RP	4
J. Matlack, SP	4
M. Jorgensen, 1B	3
D. Rajsich, RP	3
D. Roberts, C	3
E. Soderholm, 3B	3
J. Johnson, SP	2
B. Allard, SP	1
L. Blanks, SS	1
E. Farmer, RP	1
L. McCall, SP-RP	1
N. Norman, SS	1
L. Washington, OF	1

Toronto (53-109)	WS
Hitting	**61.3**
Fielding	**36.0**
Pitching	**61.7**
T. Underwood, SP	15
A. Griffin, SS	14
J. Mayberry, 1B	14
O. Velez, OF	11
R. Howell, 3B	10
D. Lemanczyk, SP	10
R. Bosetti, OF	9
A. Woods, OF	9
T. Buskey, RP	8
R. Cerone, C	8
D. Stieb, SP	8
B. Moore, RP	6
R. Carty, DH	5
B. Bailor, OF	4
D. Freisleben, RP	4
D. Ainge, 2B	3
J. Jefferson, RP	3
T. Solaita, DH	3
B. Edge, SP	2
J. Garvin, RP	2
P. Huffman, SP	2
D. McKay, 2B	2
J. Cannon, OF	1
J. Clancy, SP	1
B. Davis, C	1
L. Gomez, 3B	1
T. Johnson, 2B	1
C. Kusick, 1B	1
T. Murphy, RP	1

1979 National League

Atlanta (66-94)	WS
Hitting	**90.6**
Fielding	**31.6**
Pitching	**75.8**
G. Matthews, OF	25
P. Niekro, SP	24
B. Horner, 3B	19
J. Royster, 3B	17
D. Murphy, 1B	11
G. Garber, RP	9
E. Solomon, SP	9
B. Bonnell, OF	8
J. Burroughs, OF	8
R. Matula, SP	8
J. McLaughlin, RP	8
P. Frias, SS	7
A. Devine, RP	5
J. Nolan, C	5
R. Office, OF	5
G. Hubbard, 2B	4
B. Benedict, C	3
L. Bradford, RP	3
E. Miller, OF	3
C. Skok, RP	3
T. Brizzolara, SP	2
P. Hanna, SP	2
M. Lum, 1B	2
L. McWilliams, SP	2
C. Spikes, OF	2
D. Chaney, SS	1
B. McLaughlin, RP	1
B. Pocoroba, C	1
L. Whisenton, OF	1

Chicago (80-82)	WS
Hitting	**99.0**
Fielding	**43.3**
Pitching	**97.7**
D. Kingman, OF	24
B. Sutter, RP	22
R. Reuschel, SP	17
I. DeJesus, SS	16
J. Martin, OF	15
B. Buckner, 1B	14
S. Ontiveros, 3B	13
D. Lamp, SP	12
L. McGlothen, SP	12
D. Tidrow, RP	12
B. Foote, C	11
M. Krukow, SP	10
T. Sizemore, 2B	8
S. Dillard, 2B	7
B. Murcer, OF	7
S. Thompson, OF	7
M. Vail, OF	7
L. Biittner, OF	5
K. Holtzman, SP	4
M. Kelleher, 3B	3
T. Blackwell, C	2
B. Caudill, RP	2
D. Geisel, RP	2
K. Henderson, OF	2
W. Hernandez, RP	2
D. Capilla, RP	1
M. Dilone, OF	1
S. Macko, 2B	1
D. Moore, RP	1

Cincinnati (90-71)	WS
Hitting	**137.0**
Fielding	**41.1**
Pitching	**91.9**
D. Concepcion, SS	24
J. Bench, C	22
G. Foster, OF	22
R. Knight, 3B	20
T. Hume, RP	18
J. Morgan, 2B	18
K. Griffey Sr., OF	16
T. Seaver, SP	16
D. Driessen, 1B	15
D. Collins, OF	12
M. LaCoss, SP	12
F. Norman, SP	11
B. Bonham, SP	9
D. Bair, RP	8
C. Geronimo, OF	8
J. Kennedy, 2B	6
H. Cruz, OF	5
F. Pastore, RP	5
P. Borbon, RP	4
V. Correll, C	4
P. Moskau, SP	4
D. Tomlin, RP	4
R. Auerbach, 3B	2
P. Blair, OF	1
M. Sarmiento, RP	1
M. Soto, RP	1
H. Spilman, 1B	1
C. Summers, OF	1

Houston (89-73)	WS
Hitting	**113.1**
Fielding	**50.1**
Pitching	**103.7**
J. Cruz, OF	27
T. Puhl, OF	23
J. Richard, SP	23
J. Niekro, SP	19

J. Sambito, RP	18
C. Cedeno, 1B	17
C. Reynolds, SS	17
J. Leonard, OF	14
E. Cabell, 3B	12
K. Forsch, SP	12
A. Howe, 2B	12
R. Landestoy, 2B	12
J. Andujar, SP-RP	11
D. Walling, OF	9
R. Williams, SP	8
B. Roberge, RP	6
A. Ashby, C	5
J. Gonzalez, 2B	4
R. Niemann, RP	3
B. Watson, 1B	3
B. Bochy, C	2
J. Alou, OF	1
D. Bergman, 1B	1
P. Ladd, RP	1
L. Pujols, C	1
F. Riccelli, RP	1
V. Ruhle, SP	1
J. Sexton, SS	1
B. Sprowl, RP	1
G. Throop, RP	1
T. Wiedenbauer, OF	1

Los Angeles (79-83)	WS
Hitting	**133.9**
Fielding	**31.5**
Pitching	**71.6**
D. Lopes, 2B	27
R. Cey, 3B	25
S. Garvey, 1B	22
D. Baker, OF	18
J. Ferguson, C	17
R. Sutcliffe, SP	16
B. Hooton, SP	14
B. Russell, SS	10
D. Sutton, SP	10
D. Thomas, OF	10
G. Thomasson, OF	10
R. Smith, OF	9
J. Reuss, SP	7
S. Yeager, C	7
B. Castillo, RP	4
C. Hough, RP	4
L. LaGrow, RP	4
B. Welch, RP	4
K. Brett, RP	3
V. Joshua, OF	3
J. Beckwith, RP	2
T. Martinez, 3B	2
D. Patterson, RP	2
P. Guerrero, OF	1
G. Hannahs, SP-RP	1
M. Hatcher, OF	1
A. Messersmith, SP	1
R. Monday, OF	1
M. Mota, OF	1
J. Oates, C	1

Montreal (95-65)	WS
Hitting	**126.5**
Fielding	**50.4**
Pitching	**108.1**
L. Parrish, 3B	28
G. Carter, C	27
A. Dawson, OF	24
W. Cromartie, OF	17
B. Lee, SP	16
S. Rogers, SP	16
E. Sosa, RP	16
T. Perez, 1B	14
D. Schatzeder, SP	14
R. Scott, 2B	14
E. Valentine, OF	14
D. Palmer, RP	11
S. Sanderson, SP	10
R. May, RP	9
C. Speier, SS	9
S. Bahnsen, RP	7
D. Cash, 2B	7
W. Fryman, RP	6
J. White, OF	6
T. Bernazard, 2B	3
D. Dyer, C	3
R. Staub, 1B	3
B. Atkinson, RP	2
T. Hutton, 1B	2
T. Solaita, 1B	2
J. Tamargo, C	2
K. Macha, 3B	1
J. Mason, SS	1
D. Murray, RP	1

New York (63-99)	WS
Hitting	**80.9**
Fielding	**37.3**
Pitching	**70.8**
L. Mazzilli, OF	25
J. Youngblood, OF	18
C. Swan, SP	15
R. Hebner, 3B	14
S. Henderson, OF	12
F. Taveras, SS	12
J. Stearns, C	11
K. Kobel, SP	8
S. Lockwood, RP	7
N. Allen, RP	6
P. Falcone, SP	6
D. Flynn, 2B	6
T. Hausman, SP	6
E. Glynn, RP	5
A. Hassler, RP	5
E. Maddox, OF	5
A. Trevino, C	5
J. Reardon, RP	3
P. Zachry, SP	3
J. Berenguer, SP	2
J. Cardenal, OF	2
R. Jackson, RP	2
W. Montanez, 1B	2
D. Murray, RP	2
D. Norman, OF	2
R. Burris, SP	1
K. Chapman, 2B	1
R. Hodges, C	1
E. Kranepool, 1B	1
W. Twitchell, RP	1

Philadelphia (84-78)	WS
Hitting	**128.0**
Fielding	**41.7**
Pitching	**82.4**
M. Schmidt, 3B	33
P. Rose, 1B	27
S. Carlton, SP	18
B. McBride, OF	17
B. Boone, C	16
G. Maddox, OF	16
N. Espinosa, SP	14
G. Luzinski, OF	13
L. Bowa, SS	12
R. Lerch, SP	12
G. Gross, OF	8
R. Reed, RP	8
M. Trillo, 2B	8
D. Ruthven, SP	6
L. Christenson, SP	5
T. McGraw, RP	5
D. Noles, SP	5
D. Unser, OF	5
R. Eastwick, RP	3
B. Harrelson, 2B	3
T. McCarver, C	3
K. Moreland, C	3
K. Saucier, RP	3
M. Anderson, OF	2
R. Aviles, 2B	2
D. Bird, RP	2
J. Kaat, RP	1
D. Larson, SP	1
R. Meoli, SS	1

Pittsburgh (98-64)	WS
Hitting	**137.5**
Fielding	**50.6**
Pitching	**105.9**
D. Parker, OF	31
P. Garner, 2B	23
O. Moreno, OF	23
K. Tekulve, RP	20
W. Stargell, 1B	18
T. Foli, SS	17
J. Candelaria, SP	14
B. Blyleven, SP	13
B. Madlock, 3B	13
J. Milner, OF	13
E. Ott, C	13
J. Bibby, SP-RP	12
B. Kison, SP	12
B. Robinson, OF	12
E. Romo, RP	11
G. Jackson, RP	10
S. Nicosia, C	8
D. Robinson, SP	8
L. Lacy, OF	5
R. Stennett, 2B	5
D. Roberts, RP	3
M. Alexander, OF	2
D. Berra, 3B-SS	2
M. Easler, OF	2
J. Rooker, SP	2
D. Ellis, RP	1
E. Whitson, RP	1

San Diego (68-93)	WS
Hitting	**96.1**
Fielding	**35.4**
Pitching	**72.5**
D. Winfield, OF	33
G. Tenace, C	24
G. Perry, SP	16
G. Richards, OF	16
R. Jones, SP	13
E. Rasmussen, RP	11
B. Shirley, SP	11
J. Turner, OF	9
B. Fahey, C	8
P. Dade, 3B	7
O. Smith, SS	7
K. Bevacqua, 3B	6
B. Owchinko, RP	6
R. Fingers, RP	5
J. Johnstone, OF	5
S. Mura, RP	5
F. Gonzalez, 2B	4
B. Almon, 2B	3
D. Briggs, 1B	3
J. D'Acquisto, RP	2
M. Lee, RP	2
J. Eichelberger, SP	1
B. Evans, 3B	1
T. Flannery, 2B	1
M. Hargrove, 1B	1
F. Kendall, C	1
D. Kinney, RP	1
B. Perkins, 1B	1
J. Wilhelm, OF	1

San Francisco (71-91)	WS
Hitting	**129.5**
Fielding	**29.3**
Pitching	**54.1**
J. Clark, OF	23
D. Evans, 3B	23
M. Ivie, 1B	22
B. North, OF	20
T. Whitfield, OF	12
G. Lavelle, RP	11
L. Herndon, OF	10
W. McCovey, 1B	10
B. Madlock, 2B	8
G. Minton, RP	8
J. LeMaster, SS	7
R. Metzger, SS	6
J. Curtis, SP	5
B. Knepper, SP	5
J. Montefusco, SP	5
T. Griffin, RP	4
M. Hill, C	4
J. Strain, 2B	4
E. Whitson, SP	4
V. Blue, SP	3
D. Littlejohn, C	3
P. Nastu, SP	3
D. Roberts, RP	3
M. Sadek, C	3
R. Andrews, 2B	2
E. Halicki, SP	2
P. Borbon, RP	1
A. Holland, RP	1
J. Tamargo, C	1

St. Louis (86-76)	WS
Hitting	**119.1**
Fielding	**46.7**
Pitching	**92.2**
K. Hernandez, 1B	29
G. Templeton, SS	25
T. Simmons, C	20
G. Hendrick, OF	17
K. Oberkfell, 2B	15
J. Fulgham, SP	14
M. Littell, RP	14
S. Martinez, SP	14
P. Vuckovich, SP	14
T. Scott, OF	13
B. Forsch, SP	12
K. Reitz, 3B	11
L. Brock, OF	10
J. Mumphrey, OF	7
R. Thomas, RP	6
J. Denny, SP	5
W. McEnaney, RP	5
D. Iorg, OF	4
M. Tyson, 2B	4
T. Kennedy, C	3
D. Knowles, RP	3
B. Schultz, RP	3
T. Bruno, RP	2
B. Carbo, OF	2
M. Phillips, SS	2
G. Frazier, RP	1
R. Freed, 1B	1
J. Lentine, OF	1
S. Swisher, C	1

1980
American League

Baltimore (100-62)	WS
Hitting	**149.0**
Fielding	**50.2**
Pitching	**100.9**
A. Bumbry, OF	33
K. Singleton, OF	27
E. Murray, 1B	26
S. Stone, SP	20
S. McGregor, SP	18
R. Dauer, 2B	17
D. DeCinces, 3B	16
R. Dempsey, C	15
T. Stoddard, RP	14
M. Flanagan, SP	12
J. Palmer, SP	12
D. Graham, C	11
J. Lowenstein, OF	9
G. Roenicke, OF	9
T. Crowley, DH	8
T. Martinez, RP	8
S. Stewart, RP	8
P. Kelly, OF	7
B. Ayala, DH	6
D. Martinez, RP	6
M. Belanger, SS	5
K. Garcia, SS	5
D. Ford, RP	3
L. May, DH	3
M. Corey, OF	1
L. Sakata, 2B	1

Boston (83-77)	WS
Hitting	**121.3**
Fielding	**40.6**
Pitching	**87.0**
F. Lynn, OF	19
R. Burleson, SS	18
C. Fisk, C	18
T. Burgmeier, RP	17
D. Evans, OF	17
J. Rice, OF	16
B. Stanley, RP	15
D. Stapleton, 2B	15
T. Perez, 1B	13
D. Eckersley, SP	10
C. Yastrzemski, DH	10
S. Renko, SP	9
D. Drago, RP	8
J. Dwyer, OF	8
J. Tudor, SP	8
G. Hoffman, 3B	6
D. Rader, C	6
J. Remy, 2B	6
M. Torrez, SP	6
G. Allenson, C	4
C. Rainey, SP	4
B. Campbell, RP	2
S. Crawford, SP	2
G. Hancock, OF	2
B. Hobson, 3B	2
S. Lockwood, RP	2
W. Remmerswaal, RP	2
L. Aponte, RP	1
J. Brohamer, 3B	1
K. MacWhorter, RP	1
J. Valdez, SS	1

California (65-95)	WS
Hitting	**106.3**
Fielding	**29.6**
Pitching	**59.1**
R. Carew, 1B	20
B. Grich, 2B	20
J. Thompson, 1B	18
C. Lansford, 3B	15
R. Miller, OF	11
L. Harlow, OF	10
A. Hassler, RP	10
D. Aase, SP	9
M. Clear, RP	9
F. Tanana, SP	9
D. LaRoche, RP	7
J. Rudi, OF	7
F. Martinez, SP	6
D. Baylor, OF	5
F. Patek, SS	5
B. Campaneris, SS	4
D. Ford, OF	4
D. Thon, SS	3
B. Clark, OF	2
T. Donohue, C	2
B. Downing, C	2
J. Harris, 1B	2
B. Kison, SP	2
D. Lemanczyk, RP	2
J. Montague, RP	2
J. Barr, RP	1
S. Cliburn, C	1
A. Cowens, OF	1
T. Cruz, SS	1
D. Frost, SP	1
E. Halicki, SP	1
G. Kubski, OF	1
D. Schuler, RP	1
D. Whitmer, C	1

Chicago (70-90)	WS
Hitting	**79.2**
Fielding	**41.6**
Pitching	**89.2**
C. Lemon, OF	24
B. Burns, SP	21
J. Morrison, 2B	18
E. Farmer, RP	14
L. Johnson, 1B	13
M. Proly, RP	12
S. Trout, SP	11
R. Dotson, SP	10
B. Molinaro, OF	10
W. Nordhagen, OF	9
H. Baines, OF	8
R. Baumgarten, SP	8
M. Squires, 1B	8
G. Pryor, SS	6
L. Hoyt, SP	5
T. Cruz, SS	4
G. Hoffman, RP	4
G. Borgmann, C	3
B. Kimm, C	3
D. Robinson, RP	3
M. Foley, C	2
R. Pruitt, OF	2
R. Scarbery, RP	2
C. Washington, OF	2
A. Bannister, OF	1
F. Barrios, SP	1
K. Bell, 3B	1
T. Bosley, OF	1
H. Chappas, SS	1
R. Kuntz, OF	1
J. Moore, 3B	1
R. Seilheimer, C	1

Cleveland (79-81)	WS
Hitting	**130.2**
Fielding	**34.8**
Pitching	**72.1**
M. Hargrove, 1B	25
T. Harrah, 3B	23
M. Dilone, OF	21
R. Hassey, C	20
J. Orta, OF	18
L. Barker, SP	15
J. Charboneau, OF	15
R. Waits, SP	12
A. Bannister, 2B	11
V. Cruz, RP	10
S. Monge, RP	10
R. Manning, OF	8
D. Spillner, SP	7
T. Veryzer, SS	7
J. Denny, SP	6
W. Garland, SP	6
J. Dybzinski, SS	4
B. Diaz, C	3
D. Kuiper, 2B	3
C. Johnson, DH	2
B. Owchinko, RP	2
D. Rosello, 2B	2
M. Stanton, RP	2
S. Wihtol, RP	2
G. Alexander, DH	1
J. Brohamer, 2B	1
R. Pruitt, OF	1

Detroit (84-78)	WS
Hitting	**130.7**
Fielding	**39.8**
Pitching	**81.4**
A. Trammell, SS	21
L. Parrish, C	20
S. Kemp, OF	19
C. Summers, DH	15
J. Wockenfuss, 1B	15
T. Brookens, 3B	14
J. Morris, SP	14
A. Lopez, RP	13
R. Peters, OF	13
R. Hebner, 1B	12
D. Schatzeder, SP	11
L. Whitaker, 2B	11
A. Cowens, OF	9
D. Petry, SP	9
D. Rozema, RP	9
M. Wilcox, SP	9
P. Underwood, RP	8
T. Corcoran, 1B	5
J. Lentine, OF	5
K. Gibson, OF	4
D. Tobik, RP	4
R. Weaver, RP	3
J. Hiller, RP	2
S. Papi, 2B	2
D. Dyer, C	1
L. Jones, OF	1
D. Stegman, OF	1
J. Thompson, 1B	1
M. Wagner, SS	1

Kansas City (97-65)	WS
Hitting	**148.6**
Fielding	**46.2**
Pitching	**96.2**
G. Brett, 3B	36
W. Wilson, OF	31
L. Gura, SP	22
D. Quisenberry, RP	19
D. Leonard, SP	18
J. Wathan, C	17
W. Aikens, 1B	16
H. McRae, DH	16
U. Washington, SS	16
C. Hurdle, OF	14
F. White, 2B	13
A. Otis, OF	12
D. Porter, C	12
R. Gale, SP	11
P. Splittorff, SP	11
M. Pattin, RP	6
R. Martin, SP	5
D. Chalk, 3B	4
J. Quirk, 3B	3
K. Brett, RP	2
J. Cardenal, OF	2
G. Christenson, RP	1
B. Detherage, OF	1
P. LaCock, 1B	1
R. Mulliniks, SS	1
R. Torres, OF	1

Milwaukee (86-76)	WS
Hitting	**139.6**
Fielding	**39.1**
Pitching	**79.3**
C. Cooper, 1B	27
B. Oglivie, OF	27
R. Yount, SS	25
P. Molitor, 2B	19
G. Thomas, OF	19
M. Haas, SP	17
D. Money, 3B	11
M. Caldwell, SP	10
J. Gantner, 3B	10
L. Sorensen, SP	10
R. Cleveland, RP	9
S. Lezcano, OF	9
C. Moore, C	9
B. McClure, RP	8
B. Travers, SP	8
B. Castro, RP	7
D. Davis, DH	5
P. Mitchell, SP	5
B. Martinez, C	4
J. Augustine, RP	3
L. Hisle, DH	3
E. Romero, SS	3
S. Bando, 3B	2
M. Brouhard, DH	2
J. Flinn, RP	2
V. Harris, OF	1
B. Keeton, SP	1
J. Poff, DH-OF	1
N. Yost, C	1

Minnesota (77-84)	WS
Hitting	**86.4**
Fielding	**45.2**
Pitching	**99.5**
D. Corbett, RP	24
R. Smalley, SS	19
J. Castino, 3B	18
J. Koosman, SP	16
R. Erickson, SP	14
K. Landreaux, OF	13
B. Wynegar, C	13
D. Jackson, SP	12
R. Wilfong, 2B	11
G. Zahn, SP	11
H. Powell, OF	9
R. Sofield, OF	8
R. Jackson, 1B	7
P. Mackanin, 2B	7
J. Morales, DH	7
A. Williams, SP-RP	7
M. Cubbage, 1B	6
P. Redfern, SP	6
J. Verhoeven, RP	5
G. Adams, DH	4
F. Arroyo, SP	4
G. Ward, OF	4
D. Edwards, OF	3
M. Bacsik, RP	1
W. Norwood, OF	1
B. Rivera, OF	1

New York (103-59)	WS
Hitting	**159.7**
Fielding	**43.2**
Pitching	**106.1**
R. Jackson, OF	31
W. Randolph, 2B	31
R. Cerone, C	21
B. Dent, SS	19
T. John, SP	19
G. Gossage, RP	18
R. May, RP	17
B. Watson, 1B	17
R. Guidry, SP	15
R. Davis, RP	12
T. Underwood, SP	12
B. Brown, OF	11
O. Gamble, OF	11
G. Nettles, 3B	10
B. Murcer, OF	9
E. Soderholm, DH	9
R. Jones, OF	8
L. Piniella, OF	7
J. Spencer, 1B	7
D. Bird, RP	5
J. Lefebvre, OF	4
L. Tiant, SP	4
D. Werth, 1B	3
T. Lollar, RP	2
G. Perry, SP	2
B. Doyle, 2B	1
M. Griffin, SP	1
J. Oates, C	1
A. Rodriguez, 3B	1
F. Stanley, SS	1

Oakland (83-79)	WS
Hitting	**108.7**
Fielding	**48.0**
Pitching	**92.3**
R. Henderson, OF	34
D. Murphy, OF	27
M. Norris, SP	25
T. Armas, OF	22
R. Langford, SP	19
M. Keough, SP	18
W. Gross, 3B	16
D. Revering, 1B	14
S. McCatty, SP	11
B. Kingman, SP	8
M. Page, DH	8
B. Lacey, RP	7
J. Newman, 1B	7
J. Essian, C	6
M. Klutts, 3B	5
D. McKay, 2B	5
M. Heath, C	4
M. Guerrero, SS	3
J. Jones, RP	3
R. Picciolo, SS	3
D. Beard, RP	1
J. Cox, 2B	1

M. Davis, OF 1
O. Gonzalez, 1B 1

Seattle (59-103)	WS
Hitting	**64.2**
Fielding	**36.2**
Pitching	**76.7**
B. Bochte, 1B	19
F. Bannister, SP	15
G. Abbott, SP	12
R. Honeycutt, SP	12
S. Rawley, RP	12
D. Meyer, OF	11
J. Cruz, 2B	8
R. Dressler, RP	8
T. Paciorek, OF	8
L. Roberts, OF	8
J. Beattie, SP	6
D. Heaverlo, RP	6
J. Anderson, SS	5
M. Mendoza, SS	5
J. Simpson, OF	5
B. Stein, 3B	5
L. Cox, C	4
L. Milbourne, 2B	4
D. Roberts, RP	4
T. Cox, 3B	3
W. Horton, DH	3
J. Beniquez, OF	2
R. Craig, OF	2
J. Narron, C	2
R. Walton, OF	2
K. Allen, 2B	1
R. Anderson, RP	1
D. Edler, 3B	1
M. Hill, C	1
M. Sarmiento, RP	1
B. Stinson, C	1

Texas (76-85)	WS
Hitting	**118.4**
Fielding	**33.4**
Pitching	**76.2**
B. Bell, 3B	21
A. Oliver, OF	21
M. Rivers, OF	20
J. Sundberg, C	18
B. Wills, 2B	16
J. Matlack, SP	13
D. Darwin, RP	12
F. Jenkins, SP	12
D. Medich, SP	11
R. Zisk, DH	11
R. Staub, DH	10
G. Perry, SP	9
J. Grubb, OF	8
P. Putnam, 1B	8
B. Harrelson, SS	5
J. Johnson, RP	5
D. Roberts, 3B	4
B. Sample, OF	4
C. Hough, RP	3
S. Lyle, RP	3
J. Butcher, SP	2
P. Frias, SS	2
D. Kainer, SP	2
J. Kern, RP	2
B. Babcock, RP	1
K. Clay, SP	1
J. Ellis, 1B	1
J. Gleaton, RP	1
J. Norris, OF	1
M. Richardt, 2B	1

Toronto (67-95)	WS
Hitting	**73.6**
Fielding	**45.6**
Pitching	**81.7**
J. Clancy, SP	19
J. Mayberry, 1B	17
D. Stieb, SP	16
A. Woods, OF	15
R. Howell, 3B	14
B. Bonnell, OF	12
D. Garcia, 2B	12
O. Velez, DH	12
J. Garvin, RP	11
A. Griffin, SS	9
B. Bailor, OF	6
J. McLaughlin, RP	6
J. Todd, SP	6
E. Whitt, C	6
P. Mirabella, SP	5
L. Moseby, OF	5
M. Barlow, RP	4
G. Iorg, 2B	4
M. Willis, RP	4
T. Buskey, RP	3
B. Davis, C	3
R. Bosetti, OF	2
J. Jefferson, SP	2
L. Leal, SP	2
D. Ainge, OF	1
S. Braun, DH	1
D. Lemanczyk, SP	1
B. Moore, RP	1
K. Schrom, RP	1
W. Upshaw, 1B	1

1980
National League

Atlanta (81-80)	WS
Hitting	**106.9**
Fielding	**43.7**
Pitching	**92.4**
D. Murphy, OF	28
C. Chambliss, 1B	21
R. Camp, RP	20
B. Horner, 3B	19
G. Matthews, OF	17
P. Niekro, SP	17
G. Hubbard, 2B	14
T. Boggs, SP	13
J. Burroughs, OF	11
D. Alexander, SP	10
B. Benedict, C	9
J. Royster, 2B	8
L. Bradford, RP	6
G. Garber, RP	6
P. Hanna, RP	6
A. Hrabosky, RP	5
R. Matula, SP	5
B. Asselstine, OF	4
L. Gomez, SS	4
B. Nahorodny, C	4
R. Ramirez, SS	4
L. Blanks, SS	3
L. McWilliams, SP	3
B. Pocoroba, C	2
M. Lum, OF	1
J. Nolan, C	1
C. Ruiz, 3B	1
C. Spikes, OF	1

Chicago (64-98)	WS
Hitting	**76.1**
Fielding	**36.3**
Pitching	**79.5**
B. Buckner, 1B	17
B. Sutter, RP	16
R. Reuschel, SP	15
T. Blackwell, C	14
I. DeJesus, SS	14
B. Caudill, RP	12
D. Tidrow, RP	11
L. Randle, 3B	10
J. Martin, OF	9
D. Kingman, OF	8
M. Krukow, SP	7
M. Vail, OF	7
L. McGlothen, SP	6
B. Foote, C	5
C. Johnson, 1B	5
M. Tyson, 2B	5
L. Biittner, 1B	3
D. Capilla, RP	3
S. Dillard, 3B	3
W. Hernandez, RP	3
D. Lamp, SP	3
J. Tracy, OF	3
J. Figueroa, OF	2
R. Martz, SP	2
L. Smith, RP	2
S. Thompson, OF	2
K. Henderson, OF	1
M. Kelleher, 2B	1
C. Lezcano, OF	1
M. O'Berry, C	1
S. Ontiveros, 3B	1

Cincinnati (89-73)	WS
Hitting	**139.1**
Fielding	**42.6**
Pitching	**85.3**
K. Griffey Sr., OF	25
G. Foster, OF	23
D. Collins, OF	22
D. Driessen, 1B	21
T. Hume, RP	19
D. Concepcion, SS	17
R. Knight, 3B	16
J. Bench, C	15
M. Soto, RP	14
F. Pastore, SP	12
J. Kennedy, 2B	11
R. Oester, 2B	10
T. Seaver, SP	9
P. Moskau, SP	8
C. Leibrandt, SP	7
J. Nolan, C	7
J. Price, SP	7
D. Bair, RP	4
C. Geronimo, OF	4
M. LaCoss, SP	3
S. Mejias, OF	3
H. Spilman, 1B	3
R. Auerbach, 3B-SS	1
B. Bonham, SP	1
S. Burnside, RP	1
V. Correll, C	1
H. Cruz, OF	1
P. Householder, OF	1
D. Tomlin, RP	1

Houston (93-70)	WS
Hitting	**128.5**
Fielding	**46.0**
Pitching	**104.5**
C. Cedeno, OF	26
J. Cruz, OF	25
T. Puhl, OF	23
J. Morgan, 2B	21
V. Ruhle, SP	15
J. Niekro, SP	14
J. Sambito, RP	14
K. Forsch, SP	13
D. Smith, RP	13
A. Howe, 1B	12
J. Richard, SP	12
A. Ashby, C	11
E. Cabell, 3B	11
R. Landestoy, 2B	11
N. Ryan, SP	11
D. Walling, 1B	11
F. LaCorte, RP	9
C. Reynolds, SS	8
J. Andujar, RP	4
D. Heep, 1B	3
J. Leonard, OF	3
L. Pujols, C	3
G. Woods, OF	3
D. Bergman, 1B	2
J. Gonzalez, SS	1

Los Angeles (92-71)	WS
Hitting	**130.3**
Fielding	**47.1**
Pitching	**98.6**
D. Baker, OF	24
R. Cey, 3B	23
S. Garvey, 1B	22
J. Reuss, SP	21
D. Sutton, SP	20
R. Smith, OF	17
D. Lopes, 2B	16
B. Welch, SP	14
B. Russell, SS	12
S. Howe, RP	11
B. Castillo, RP	10
B. Hooton, SP	10
J. Johnstone, OF	10
P. Guerrero, OF	9
J. Ferguson, C	8
R. Law, OF	8
R. Monday, OF	8
D. Thomas, OF	8
J. Beckwith, RP	6
M. Scioscia, C	5
S. Yeager, C	4
D. Goltz, SP	3
F. Valenzuela, RP	3
T. Forster, RP	1
M. Hatcher, OF	1
J. Perconte, 2B	1
G. Thomasson, OF	1

Montreal (90-72)	WS
Hitting	**136.1**
Fielding	**42.1**
Pitching	**91.9**
G. Carter, C	30
A. Dawson, OF	29
S. Rogers, SP	20
R. LeFlore, OF	18
W. Cromartie, 1B	17
E. Valentine, OF	15
S. Sanderson, SP	14
W. Fryman, RP	13
L. Parrish, 3B	13
R. Scott, 2B	13
C. Speier, SS	12
B. Gullickson, SP	10
R. Office, OF	9
E. Sosa, RP	9
D. Palmer, SP	8
J. White, OF	8
S. Bahnsen, RP	7
T. Bernazard, 2B	4
C. Lea, SP	4
F. Norman, RP	4
K. Macha, 3B	3
J. D'Acquisto, RP	2
B. Mills, 3B	2
J. Tamargo, C	2
B. Almon, SS	1
B. Lee, SP	1
B. Pate, OF	1
B. Ramos, C	1

New York (67-95)	WS
Hitting	**102.9**
Fielding	**33.6**
Pitching	**64.5**
L. Mazzilli, 1B	24
S. Henderson, OF	17
J. Youngblood, OF	16
J. Stearns, C	12
J. Reardon, RP	11
N. Allen, RP	10
E. Maddox, 3B	10
F. Taveras, SS	10
C. Washington, OF	10
P. Zachry, SP	9
M. Bomback, SP	8
D. Flynn, 2B	8
M. Jorgensen, 1B	8
C. Swan, SP	6
R. Burris, SP	5
T. Hausman, RP	5
A. Trevino, C	5
D. Miller, RP	4
J. Morales, OF	4
W. Backman, 2B	3

H. Brooks, 3B	3
P. Falcone, SP	3
E. Glynn, RP	2
M. Wilson, OF	2
B. Almon, SS	1
R. Hodges, C	1
S. Holman, RP	1
R. Jackson, RP	1
J. Moreno, 2B-3B	1
M. Scott, SP	1

Philadelphia (91-71)	WS
Hitting	**130.4**
Fielding	**43.3**
Pitching	**99.3**
M. Schmidt, 3B	37
S. Carlton, SP	29
M. Trillo, 2B	19
B. McBride, OF	18
T. McGraw, RP	18
P. Rose, 1B	17
G. Maddox, OF	14
D. Ruthven, SP	14
G. Luzinski, OF	13
L. Smith, OF	13
B. Boone, C	11
L. Bowa, SS	9
R. Reed, RP	7
K. Moreland, C	6
M. Bystrom, SP	5
L. Christenson, SP	5
B. Walk, SP	5
D. Noles, RP	4
K. Saucier, RP	4
R. Aviles, SS	3
N. Espinosa, SP	3
G. Gross, OF	3
D. Unser, 1B	3
L. Aguayo, 2B	2
W. Brusstar, RP	2
D. Larson, SP	2
S. Lyle, RP	2
B. Dernier, OF	1
O. Isales, OF	1
L. LaGrow, RP	1
R. Lerch, SP	1
J. Vukovich, 3B	1

Pittsburgh (83-79)	WS
Hitting	**111.7**
Fielding	**44.7**
Pitching	**92.6**
M. Easler, OF	22
J. Bibby, SP	17
O. Moreno, OF	17
D. Parker, OF	17
P. Garner, 2B	16
L. Lacy, OF	15
B. Madlock, 3B	13
T. Foli, SS	12
E. Romo, RP	12
J. Candelaria, SP	10
E. Ott, C	10
K. Tekulve, RP	10
B. Blyleven, SP	9
R. Rhoden, SP	9
D. Robinson, SP	9
G. Jackson, RP	8
J. Milner, 1B	7
B. Robinson, 1B	7
E. Solomon, RP	7
W. Stargell, 1B	7
D. Berra, 3B	4
S. Nicosia, C	3
R. Scurry, RP	3
J. Rooker, SP	2
J. Jefferson, SP	1
V. Law, 2B	1
T. Pena, C	1

San Diego (73-89)	WS
Hitting	**107.7**
Fielding	**37.5**
Pitching	**73.7**
G. Richards, OF	22
D. Winfield, OF	22
J. Mumphrey, OF	19
O. Smith, SS	17
R. Fingers, RP	15
G. Tenace, C	15
W. Montanez, 1B	10
J. Curtis, SP	9
G. Lucas, RP	9
S. Mura, SP	8
B. Shirley, RP	8
L. Salazar, 3B	7
B. Perkins, 1B	6
R. Wise, SP	6
D. Cash, 2B	5
J. Eichelberger, SP	4
B. Fahey, C	4
T. Flannery, 2B	4
R. Jones, SP	4
J. Turner, OF	4
R. Bass, 1B	3
J. D'Acquisto, RP	3
B. Evans, 3B	3
T. Tellmann, RP	3
K. Bevacqua, 3B	2
D. Kinney, RP	2
E. Rasmussen, RP	2
V. Joshua, OF	1
A. Rodriguez, 3B	1
G. Stablein, SP-RP	1

San Francisco (75-86)	WS
Hitting	**101.8**
Fielding	**38.5**
Pitching	**84.7**
D. Evans, 3B	27
J. Clark, OF	24
V. Blue, SP	16
B. North, OF	15
G. Minton, RP	13
E. Whitson, SP	12
A. Holland, RP	11
M. May, C	11
T. Whitfield, OF	11
L. Herndon, OF	10
T. Griffin, RP	9
G. Lavelle, RP	7
B. Knepper, SP	6
M. Sadek, C	6
R. Stennett, 2B	6
M. Ivie, 1B	5
J. Wohlford, OF	5
J. LeMaster, SS	4
A. Ripley, SP	4
J. Pettini, SS	3
J. Strain, 2B	3
M. Venable, OF	3
A. Hargesheimer, SP	2
W. McCovey, 1B	2
J. Montefusco, SP	2
R. Murray, 1B	2
M. Rowland, RP	2
G. Sularz, 2B	2
M. Hill, C	1
D. Littlejohn, C	1

St. Louis (74-88)	WS
Hitting	**123.3**
Fielding	**33.5**
Pitching	**65.1**
K. Hernandez, 1B	28
T. Simmons, C	22
G. Hendrick, OF	21
G. Templeton, SS	17
K. Oberkfell, 2B	15
B. Forsch, SP	12
P. Vuckovich, SP	12
K. Reitz, 3B	10
L. Durham, OF	8
D. Iorg, OF	8
J. Kaat, RP	7
T. Scott, OF	7
T. Kennedy, C	6
J. Littlefield, RP	5
B. Bonds, OF	4
J. Fulgham, SP	4
T. Herr, 2B	4
D. Hood, RP	4
J. Urrea, RP	4
A. Rincon, SP	3
K. Seaman, RP	3
B. Sykes, SP	3
G. Frazier, RP	2
J. Martin, SP	2
A. Olmsted, SP	2
M. Phillips, SS	2
M. Ramsey, 2B	2
P. Borbon, RP	1
T. Landrum, OF	1
J. Little, RP	1
S. Martinez, SP	1
R. Thomas, RP	1

1981 American League

Baltimore (59-46)	WS
Hitting	**91.1**
Fielding	**28.4**
Pitching	**57.5**
E. Murray, 1B	21
D. DeCinces, 3B	15
K. Singleton, OF	15
A. Bumbry, OF	13
R. Dauer, 2B	12
D. Martinez, SP	12
S. McGregor, SP	12
S. Stewart, RP	11
R. Dempsey, C	9
T. Martinez, RP	7
M. Flanagan, SP	6
J. Palmer, SP	6
G. Roenicke, OF	6
T. Crowley, DH	5
J. Lowenstein, OF	5
L. Sakata, SS	5
B. Ayala, DH	3
M. Belanger, SS	3
J. Dwyer, OF	3
T. Stoddard, RP	3
D. Graham, C	2
B. Bonner, SS	1
W. Krenchicki, SS	1
S. Stone, SP	1

Boston (59-49)	WS
Hitting	**94.4**
Fielding	**26.8**
Pitching	**55.8**
D. Evans, OF	26
C. Lansford, 3B	18
J. Rice, OF	15
J. Remy, 2B	12
R. Miller, OF	10
D. Stapleton, SS	10
M. Torrez, SP	8
T. Perez, 1B	7
C. Yastrzemski, DH	7
T. Burgmeier, RP	6
M. Clear, RP	6
D. Eckersley, SP	6
R. Gedman, C	6
B. Stanley, RP	6
F. Tanana, SP	6
B. Ojeda, SP	5
G. Allenson, C	4
B. Campbell, RP	4
L. Aponte, RP	3
G. Hoffman, SS	3
J. Tudor, SP	3
C. Rainey, RP	2
B. Hurst, SP	1
R. Nichols, OF	1
J. Rudi, DH	1
D. Schmidt, C	1

California (51-59)	WS
Hitting	**80.2**
Fielding	**23.8**
Pitching	**49.0**
B. Grich, 2B	21
R. Burleson, SS	17
R. Carew, 1B	12
B. Downing, OF	10
D. Ford, OF	10
K. Forsch, SP	10
D. Baylor, DH	9
D. Aase, RP	8
B. Hobson, 3B	6
S. Renko, SP	6
M. Witt, SP	6
A. Hassler, RP	5
F. Lynn, OF	5
G. Zahn, SP	4
B. Clark, OF	3
J. Jefferson, RP	3
E. Ott, C	3
B. Campaneris, 3B	2
B. Kison, RP	2
A. Moreno, SP-RP	2
J. Beniquez, OF	1
T. Brunansky, OF	1
J. Ferguson, C	1
L. Harlow, OF	1
J. Harris, 1B	1
M. Mahler, RP	1
F. Patek, 2B	1
L. Sanchez, RP	1
D. Sconiers, 1B	1

Chicago (54-52)	WS
Hitting	**86.8**
Fielding	**24.8**
Pitching	**50.4**
T. Bernazard, 2B	16
C. Lemon, OF	16
G. Luzinski, DH	15
B. Almon, SS	13
C. Fisk, C	13
B. Burns, SP	12
H. Baines, OF	10
D. Lamp, RP	10
L. Hoyt, RP	7
S. Trout, SP	7
R. Dotson, SP	6
W. Nordhagen, OF	6
R. LeFlore, OF	5
M. Squires, 1B	5
J. Morrison, 3B	4
R. Baumgarten, SP	3
J. Essian, C	2
K. Hickey, RP	2
L. Johnson, 1B	2
F. Barrios, SP	1
E. Farmer, RP	1
J. Hairston, OF	1
J. Koosman, RP	1
R. Kuntz, OF	1
L. McGlothen, RP	1
B. Molinaro, DH	1
G. Pryor, 3B	1

Cleveland (52-51)	WS
Hitting	**80.3**
Fielding	**21.9**
Pitching	**53.8**
T. Harrah, 3B	18
M. Hargrove, 1B	16
B. Blyleven, SP	14
J. Denny, SP	11
R. Manning, OF	11
B. Diaz, C	10
L. Barker, SP	8
D. Spillner, RP	8
A. Bannister, OF	7
M. Dilone, OF	7
J. Orta, OF	7
R. Hassey, C	4
V. Hayes, DH	4

D. Kuiper, 2B	4
T. Brennan, SP	3
S. Monge, RP	3
A. Thornton, DH	3
T. Veryzer, SS	3
R. Waits, SP	3
J. Dybzinski, SS	2
K. Pagel, 1B	2
D. Rosello, 2B	2
M. Stanton, RP	2
J. Charboneau, OF	1
M. Fischlin, SS	1
E. Glynn, RP	1
P. Kelly, DH	1

Detroit (60-49)	WS
Hitting	**76.1**
Fielding	**35.2**
Pitching	**68.7**
S. Kemp, OF	17
J. Morris, SP	16
A. Trammell, SS	14
K. Gibson, OF	13
L. Whitaker, 2B	13
M. Wilcox, SP	13
L. Parrish, C	11
D. Petry, SP	10
K. Saucier, RP	10
A. Cowens, OF	7
A. Lopez, RP	6
D. Rozema, RP	6
T. Brookens, 3B	5
R. Peters, OF	5
C. Summers, DH	5
D. Tobik, RP	5
J. Wockenfuss, DH	5
R. Hebner, 1B	4
R. Jackson, 1B	4
L. Jones, OF	4
G. Cappuzzello, RP	2
B. Fahey, C	1
M. Kelleher, 3B	1
R. Leach, 1B	1
S. Papi, 3B	1
L. Rothschild, RP	1

Kansas City (50-53)	WS
Hitting	**64.1**
Fielding	**29.0**
Pitching	**57.0**
G. Brett, 3B	14
D. Leonard, SP	14
W. Wilson, OF	14
W. Aikens, 1B	13
L. Gura, SP	13
A. Otis, OF	12
D. Quisenberry, RP	10
H. McRae, DH	8
U. Washington, SS	8
F. White, 2B	7
C. Hurdle, OF	5
M. Jones, SP	5
R. Martin, RP	5
P. Splittorff, SP	4
J. Wathan, C	4
J. Grote, C	3
J. Wright, RP	3
C. Geronimo, OF	2
K. Brett, RP	1
R. Gale, SP	1
L. May, 1B	1
D. Motley, OF	1
R. Mulliniks, 2B	1
J. Quirk, C	1

Milwaukee (62-47)	WS
Hitting	**109.7**
Fielding	**24.9**
Pitching	**51.4**
C. Cooper, 1B	22
G. Thomas, OF	20
R. Yount, SS	20
R. Fingers, RP	17
J. Gantner, 2B	13
B. Oglivie, OF	13
P. Vuckovich, SP	9
P. Molitor, OF	8
T. Simmons, C	8
R. Howell, 3B	7
C. Moore, C	7
M. Caldwell, SP	6
M. Brouhard, OF	5
J. Easterly, RP	5
M. Haas, SP	5
D. Money, 3B	4
L. Hisle, DH	3
R. Lerch, SP	3
J. Slaton, SP	3
J. Augustine, RP	2
E. Romero, SS	2
N. Yost, C	2
S. Bando, 3B	1
M. Edwards, OF	1

Minnesota (41-68)	WS
Hitting	**43.5**
Fielding	**25.7**
Pitching	**53.8**
J. Castino, 3B	12
D. Corbett, RP	12
P. Redfern, SP	8
R. Wilfong, 2B	8
M. Hatcher, OF	7
G. Ward, OF	7
A. Williams, SP	7
F. Arroyo, SP	6
R. Smalley, SS	6
D. Engle, OF	5
B. Havens, SP	5
J. Koosman, SP	5
S. Butera, C	4
R. Erickson, SP	4
R. Jackson, 1B	4
H. Powell, OF	3
B. Wynegar, C	3
D. Cooper, RP	2
D. Goodwin, 1B	2
D. Jackson, RP	2
P. Mackanin, 2B	2
J. Verhoeven, RP	2
B. Veselic, RP	2
C. Baker, SS	1
K. Hrbek, 1B	1
T. Laudner, C	1
R. Sofield, OF	1
R. Washington, SS	1

New York (59-48)	WS
Hitting	**72.2**
Fielding	**33.1**
Pitching	**71.7**
D. Winfield, OF	16
G. Gossage, RP	12
J. Mumphrey, OF	12
G. Nettles, 3B	12
R. Guidry, SP	10
R. Jackson, OF	10
T. John, SP	10
D. Righetti, SP	10
W. Randolph, 2B	9
B. Dent, SS	8
R. Davis, RP	7
O. Gamble, OF	7
L. Milbourne, SS	6
R. Reuschel, SP	5
D. Bird, RP	4
R. Cerone, C	4
D. LaRoche, RP	4
R. May, SP	4
B. Murcer, DH	4
L. Piniella, OF	4
B. Foote, C	3
G. Frazier, RP	3
B. Watson, 1B	3
D. Revering, 1B	2
A. Rodriguez, 3B	2
S. Balboni, 1B	1
B. Brown, OF	1
G. Nelson, SP	1
J. Spencer, 1B	1
T. Underwood, SP	1
D. Werth, 1B	1

Oakland (64-45)	WS
Hitting	**95.0**
Fielding	**31.7**
Pitching	**65.3**
R. Henderson, OF	27
D. Murphy, OF	20
T. Armas, OF	18
S. McCatty, SP	18
C. Johnson, DH	12
R. Langford, SP	12
M. Keough, SP	9
M. Norris, SP	9
W. Gross, 3B	8
M. Heath, C	8
D. McKay, 3B	8
R. Picciolo, SS	6
J. Jones, RP	4
M. Klutts, 3B	4
S. Babitt, 2B	3
B. Kingman, SP	3
J. Newman, C	3
B. Owchinko, RP	3
F. Stanley, SS	3
T. Underwood, RP	3
D. Beard, RP	2
K. Drumright, 2B	2
D. Revering, 1B	2
D. Heaverlo, RP	1
C. Minetto, RP	1
K. Moore, 1B	1
M. Patterson, OF	1
J. Spencer, 1B	1

Seattle (44-65)	WS
Hitting	**65.4**
Fielding	**20.6**
Pitching	**46.0**
T. Paciorek, OF	17
J. Cruz, 2B	12
R. Zisk, DH	12
B. Bochte, 1B	9
J. Burroughs, OF	8
L. Andersen, RP	7
G. Abbott, SP	6
F. Bannister, SP	6
J. Beattie, SP	6
S. Rawley, RP	5
T. Bulling, C	4
D. Meyer, 3B	4
L. Randle, 3B	4
B. Allard, SP	3
B. Clark, RP	3
G. Gray, 1B	3
B. Stoddard, SP	3
J. Anderson, SS	2
K. Clay, SP	2
J. Gleaton, SP	2
J. Narron, C	2
M. Parrott, SP-RP	2
P. Serna, SS	2
J. Simpson, OF	2
R. Auerbach, SS	1
D. Drago, RP	1
B. Galasso, RP	1
D. Henderson, OF	1
J. Maler, 1B	1
C. Parsons, OF	1

Texas (57-48)	WS
Hitting	**91.5**
Fielding	**26.1**
Pitching	**53.4**
B. Bell, 3B	18
J. Sundberg, C	17
M. Rivers, OF	14
A. Oliver, DH	13
D. Medich, SP	10
B. Sample, OF	10
P. Putnam, 1B	9
L. Roberts, OF	9
B. Wills, 2B	9
S. Comer, RP	8
R. Honeycutt, SP	8
D. Darwin, SP	6
C. Hough, RP	6
J. Grubb, OF	4
B. Stein, 1B	4
J. Butcher, SP	3
J. Johnson, RP	3
J. Kern, RP	3
M. Wagner, SS	3
B. Babcock, RP	2
F. Jenkins, SP	2
B. Jones, OF	2
J. Matlack, SP	2
M. Mendoza, SS	2
D. Schmidt, RP	2
B. Johnson, C	1
R. Lisi, OF	1

Toronto (37-69)	WS
Hitting	**28.0**
Fielding	**27.9**
Pitching	**55.1**
D. Stieb, SP	15
J. Mayberry, 1B	9
L. Leal, SP	7
J. McLaughlin, RP	7
L. Moseby, OF	7
R. Jackson, RP	6
O. Velez, DH	6
E. Whitt, C	6
M. Bomback, SP	5
J. Garvin, RP	4
B. Martinez, C	4
J. Todd, SP	4
D. Ainge, 3B	3
J. Clancy, SP	3
D. Garcia, 2B	3
A. Griffin, SS	3
A. Woods, OF	3
J. Barfield, OF	2
G. Bell, OF	2
J. Berenguer, SP	2
B. Bonnell, OF	2
T. Cox, 3B	2
G. Iorg, 2B	2
D. Murray, RP	2
R. Bosetti, OF	1
W. Upshaw, DH	1

1981
National League

Atlanta (50-56)	WS
Hitting	**60.9**
Fielding	**27.8**
Pitching	**61.3**
R. Camp, RP	14
B. Benedict, C	12
C. Chambliss, 1B	12
B. Horner, 3B	11
D. Murphy, OF	11
G. Hubbard, 2B	10
C. Washington, OF	10
R. Mahler, RP	9
P. Niekro, SP	8
G. Perry, SP	7
G. Garber, RP	5
A. Hrabosky, RP	5
R. Ramirez, SS	5
B. Butler, OF	4
R. Linares, OF	4
J. Montefusco, RP	4
T. Boggs, SP	3
L. McWilliams, SP	3
L. Bradford, RP	2
T. Harper, OF	2
E. Miller, OF	2
M. Sinatro, C	2
B. Asselstine, OF	1

S. Bedrosian, RP	1
B. Pocoroba, 3B	1
J. Royster, 3B	1
P. Runge, SS	1

Chicago (38-65)	WS
Hitting	**49.0**
Fielding	**20.8**
Pitching	**44.1**
B. Buckner, 1B	13
L. Durham, OF	10
S. Henderson, OF	9
M. Krukow, SP	8
R. Martz, RP	7
T. Blackwell, C	5
J. Davis, C	5
J. Morales, OF	5
D. Bird, SP	4
D. Capilla, RP	4
I. DeJesus, SS	4
R. Eastwick, RP	4
R. Reuschel, SP	4
L. Smith, RP	4
B. Bonds, OF	3
H. Cruz, 3B	3
D. Tidrow, RP	3
S. Dillard, 2B	2
D. Geisel, RP	2
M. Griffin, SP	2
K. Reitz, 3B	2
T. Waller, 3B	2
S. Fletcher, 2B	1
W. Hernandez, RP	1
J. Howell, RP	1
M. Lum, OF	1
L. McGlothen, RP	1
J. Strain, 2B	1
P. Tabler, 2B	1
J. Tracy, OF	1
M. Tyson, 2B	1

Cincinnati (66-42)	WS
Hitting	**109.2**
Fielding	**30.0**
Pitching	**58.8**
G. Foster, OF	24
D. Concepcion, SS	20
K. Griffey Sr., OF	19
T. Seaver, SP	17
R. Oester, 2B	15
D. Collins, OF	14
J. Nolan, C	12
M. Soto, SP	11
R. Knight, 3B	10
J. Bench, 1B	9
B. Berenyi, SP	8
D. Driessen, 1B	8
T. Hume, RP	8
J. Price, RP	7
P. Householder, OF	3
F. Pastore, SP	3
J. Edelen, RP	2
C. Leibrandt, SP	2
M. O'Berry, C	2
S. Brown, RP	1
J. Kennedy, 2B	1
S. Mejias, OF	1
P. Moskau, RP	1

Houston (61-49)	WS
Hitting	**77.9**
Fielding	**32.5**
Pitching	**72.5**
A. Howe, 3B	16
N. Ryan, SP	15
J. Cruz, OF	14
B. Knepper, SP	13
A. Ashby, C	11
T. Puhl, OF	11
D. Sutton, SP	11
C. Reynolds, SS	10
C. Cedeno, 1B	9
J. Niekro, SP	9
T. Scott, OF	9
J. Sambito, RP	8
V. Ruhle, SP	7
D. Smith, RP	7
D. Walling, 1B-OF	5
K. Garcia, SS	4
P. Garner, 2B	3
F. LaCorte, RP	3
J. Pittman, 2B	3
L. Pujols, C	3
D. Thon, 2B	3
A. Knicely, C	2
D. Heep, 1B	1
R. Landestoy, 2B	1
S. Loucks, OF	1
D. Roberts, 1B	1
B. Smith, RP	1
H. Spilman, 1B	1
G. Woods, OF	1

Los Angeles (63-47)	WS
Hitting	**86.6**
Fielding	**31.7**
Pitching	**70.7**
F. Valenzuela, SP	17
D. Baker, OF	16
R. Cey, 3B	16
P. Guerrero, OF	14
S. Garvey, 1B	13
B. Hooton, SP	13
J. Reuss, SP	13
M. Scioscia, C	11
K. Landreaux, OF	10
R. Monday, OF	9
B. Welch, SP	8
S. Howe, RP	7
D. Thomas, 2B	7
D. Stewart, RP	6
D. Lopes, 2B	5
B. Russell, SS	5
S. Sax, 2B	3
D. Goltz, RP	2
T. Niedenfuer, RP	2
A. Pena, RP	2
S. Yeager, C	2
B. Castillo, RP	1
T. Forster, RP	1
P. Frias, SS	1
J. Johnstone, OF	1
J. Perconte, 2B	1
T. Power, RP	1
R. Roenicke, OF	1
R. Sutcliffe, RP	1

Montreal (60-48)	WS
Hitting	**86.0**
Fielding	**30.4**
Pitching	**63.6**
A. Dawson, OF	25
T. Raines, OF	18
G. Carter, C	17
W. Cromartie, 1B	14
B. Gullickson, SP	10
S. Sanderson, SP	10
S. Rogers, SP	9
R. Burris, SP	8
B. Lee, RP	8
L. Parrish, 3B	8
C. Speier, SS	8
J. Reardon, RP	7
R. Scott, 2B	7
W. Fryman, RP	6
T. Wallach, OF	4
T. Francona, OF	3
J. Milner, 1B	3
J. White, OF	3
C. Lea, SP	2
J. Manuel, 2B	2
E. Sosa, RP	2
S. Bahnsen, RP	1
D. Hostetler, 1B	1
M. Phillips, SS	1
B. Ramos, C	1
B. Smith, RP	1
E. Valentine, OF	1

New York (41-62)	WS
Hitting	**54.8**
Fielding	**22.3**
Pitching	**45.9**
H. Brooks, 3B	11
D. Kingman, 1B	10
M. Wilson, OF	9
N. Allen, RP	8
L. Mazzilli, OF	8
P. Falcone, RP	7
J. Youngblood, OF	7
R. Staub, 1B	6
J. Stearns, C	6
D. Flynn, 2B	5
E. Lynch, SP	5
M. Scott, SP	4
T. Hausman, RP	3
T. Leach, RP	3
M. Marshall, RP	3
F. Taveras, SS	3
P. Zachry, SP	3
B. Bailor, SS	2
M. Jorgensen, 1B	2
D. Miller, RP	2
J. Orosco, RP	2
C. Puleo, RP	2
J. Reardon, RP	2
R. Searage, RP	2
A. Trevino, C	2
W. Backman, 2B	1
M. Cubbage, 3B	1
R. Gardenhire, SS	1
G. Harris, SP	1
R. Hodges, C	1
E. Valentine, OF	1

Philadelphia (59-48)	WS
Hitting	**103.6**
Fielding	**23.4**
Pitching	**49.9**
M. Schmidt, 3B	30
G. Matthews, OF	19
P. Rose, 1B	17
S. Carlton, SP	16
M. Trillo, 2B	12
L. Bowa, SS	9
L. Smith, OF	9
G. Maddox, OF	7
R. Reed, RP	7
T. McGraw, RP	6
L. Christenson, SP	5
D. Davis, OF	5
B. McBride, OF	5
S. Lyle, RP	4
K. Moreland, C	4
B. Boone, C	3
M. Bystrom, SP	3
M. Proly, RP	3
L. Aguayo, 2B-SS	2
D. Larson, SP	2
D. Noles, SP	2
D. Ruthven, SP	2
G. Vukovich, OF	2
B. Dernier, OF	1
G. Gross, OF	1
L. Matuszek, 1B-3B	1

Pittsburgh (46-56)	WS
Hitting	**66.3**
Fielding	**23.6**
Pitching	**48.1**
B. Madlock, 3B	15
O. Moreno, OF	11
J. Thompson, 1B	11
M. Easler, OF	9
J. Bibby, SP	8
E. Solomon, SP	8
T. Pena, C	7
L. Lacy, OF	6
D. Parker, OF	6
R. Rhoden, SP	6
K. Tekulve, RP	6
D. Berra, 3B	5
T. Foli, SS	5
P. Garner, 2B	4
R. Scurry, RP	4
V. Cruz, RP	3
G. Jackson, RP	3
O. Jones, SP	3
S. Nicosia, C	3
J. Candelaria, SP	2
M. Lee, RP	2
J. Ray, 2B	2
L. Tiant, SP	2
G. Alexander, 1B	1
K. Bevacqua, 2B	1
V. Law, 2B	1
J. Milner, 1B-OF	1
P. Perez, SP	1
E. Romo, RP	1
W. Stargell, 1B	1

San Diego (41-69)	WS
Hitting	**60.6**
Fielding	**21.3**
Pitching	**41.1**
G. Richards, OF	14
G. Lucas, RP	11
L. Salazar, 3B	11
R. Jones, OF	10
T. Kennedy, C	10
J. Bonilla, 2B	8
O. Smith, SS	8
J. Lefebvre, OF	7
J. Eichelberger, SP	6
B. Perkins, 1B	6
D. Boone, RP	4
J. Urrea, RP	4
C. Welsh, SP	4
B. Evans, 3B	3
J. Littlefield, RP	3
R. Wise, SP	3
R. Bass, 1B	2
F. Kuhaulua, SP	2
S. Mura, SP	2
E. Show, RP	2
D. Edwards, OF	1
S. Fireovid, SP	1
T. Flannery, 3B	1

San Francisco (56-55)	WS
Hitting	**75.8**
Fielding	**30.1**
Pitching	**62.1**
J. Clark, OF	15
D. Evans, 3B	14
M. May, C	14
J. Morgan, 2B	14
D. Alexander, SP	11
L. Herndon, OF	11
V. Blue, SP	10
A. Holland, RP	10
G. Minton, RP	10
J. Leonard, OF	7
F. Breining, RP	6
T. Griffin, SP	6
J. LeMaster, SS	5
J. Martin, OF	5
D. Bergman, 1B	4
E. Cabell, 1B	4
B. North, OF	4
B. Brenly, C	3
G. Lavelle, RP	3
E. Whitson, SP	3
A. Ripley, SP	2
M. Sadek, C	2
M. Ivie, 1B	1
M. Rowland, RP	1
B. Smith, SS	1
R. Stennett, 2B	1
M. Venable, OF	1

St. Louis (59-43)	WS
Hitting	**94.8**
Fielding	**26.8**
Pitching	**55.4**
K. Hernandez, 1B	20
G. Hendrick, OF	18

T. Herr, 2B	14
K. Oberkfell, 3B	13
B. Sutter, RP	13
G. Templeton, SS	10
B. Forsch, SP	8
S. Lezcano, OF	8
D. Porter, C	8
G. Tenace, C	8
D. Iorg, OF	7
L. Sorensen, SP	7
J. Martin, SP	6
J. Kaat, RP	4
A. Rincon, SP	4
J. Andujar, SP	3
T. Landrum, OF	3
S. Martinez, SP	3
G. Roof, OF	3
B. Shirley, RP	3
D. Bair, RP	2
S. Braun, OF	2
M. Ramsey, SS	2
T. Scott, OF	2
L. DeLeon, RP	1
J. Gonzalez, SS	1
D. LaPoint, SP	1
M. Littell, RP	1
O. Sanchez, C	1
B. Sykes, RP	1

1982
American League

Baltimore (94-68)	WS
Hitting	**140.8**
Fielding	**44.9**
Pitching	**96.4**
E. Murray, 1B	29
C. Ripken Jr., SS	23
J. Lowenstein, OF	21
J. Palmer, SP	20
G. Roenicke, OF	20
R. Dauer, 2B	15
M. Flanagan, SP	14
D. Martinez, SP	14
A. Bumbry, OF	12
T. Martinez, RP	12
K. Singleton, DH	12
R. Dempsey, C	11
L. Sakata, 2B	10
S. McGregor, SP	9
S. Stewart, RP	9
S. Davis, RP	8
J. Dwyer, OF	8
D. Ford, OF	7
J. Nolan, C	5
T. Stoddard, RP	5
B. Ayala, OF	4
G. Gulliver, 3B	4
M. Boddicker, RP	2
T. Crowley, DH	2
J. Flinn, RP	2
B. Bonner, SS	1
R. Grimsley, RP	1
F. Rayford, 3B	1
J. Shelby, OF	1

Boston (89-73)	WS
Hitting	**113.3**
Fielding	**48.8**
Pitching	**104.9**
D. Evans, OF	31
J. Rice, OF	21
B. Stanley, RP	20
D. Eckersley, SP	17
C. Lansford, 3B	16
W. Boggs, 1B	15
J. Tudor, SP	15
M. Clear, RP	14
J. Remy, 2B	14
T. Burgmeier, RP	13
C. Yastrzemski, DH	13
D. Stapleton, 1B	10
G. Hoffman, SS	9
R. Nichols, OF	9
L. Aponte, RP	8
R. Miller, OF	7
G. Allenson, C	6
M. Torrez, SP	6
C. Rainey, SP	5
R. Gedman, C	4
T. Perez, DH	4
B. Denman, SP	2
B. Ojeda, SP	2
M. Brown, RP	1
S. Crawford, RP	1
B. Hurst, SP	1
E. Jurak, 3B	1
R. LaFrancois, C	1
J. Valdez, SS	1

California (93-69)	WS
Hitting	**140.4**
Fielding	**41.6**
Pitching	**97.0**
D. DeCinces, 3B	28
B. Downing, OF	25
Re. Jackson, OF	22
B. Grich, 2B	21
F. Lynn, OF	21
R. Carew, 1B	17
G. Zahn, SP	16
D. Baylor, DH	13
B. Boone, C	13
K. Forsch, SP	13
B. Kison, RP	12
M. Witt, SP	12
L. Sanchez, RP	9
S. Renko, SP	8
A. Hassler, RP	7
T. Foli, SS	6
D. Goltz, RP	6
D. Aase, RP	5
Ro. Jackson, 1B	5
J. Beniquez, OF	4
D. Corbett, RP	3
J. Ferguson, C	3
T. John, SP	2
R. Wilfong, 2B	2
R. Burleson, SS	1
B. Clark, OF	1
M. Kelleher, SS	1
M. Mahler, RP	1
A. Moreno, SP	1
R. Steirer, RP	1

Chicago (87-75)	WS
Hitting	**142.1**
Fielding	**33.6**
Pitching	**85.3**
S. Kemp, OF	22
G. Luzinski, DH	22
T. Bernazard, 2B	20
H. Baines, OF	19
C. Fisk, C	19
L. Hoyt, SP	16
T. Paciorek, 1B	15
R. Law, OF	13
S. Barojas, RP	11
R. Dotson, SP	10
J. Koosman, RP	10
D. Lamp, SP	10
V. Law, SS	10
B. Burns, SP	9
B. Almon, SS	8
R. LeFlore, OF	8
K. Hickey, RP	7
C. Escarrega, RP	4
S. Trout, SP	4
M. Hill, C	3
J. Morrison, 3B	3
A. Rodriguez, 3B	3
M. Squires, 1B	3
W. Brusstar, RP	2
J. Hairston, OF	2
J. Kern, RP	2
G. Walker, DH	2
S. Dillard, 2B	1
L. Gray, 3B	1
R. Kittle, OF	1
S. Lyle, RP	1

Cleveland (78-84)	WS
Hitting	**101.0**
Fielding	**40.1**
Pitching	**92.9**
T. Harrah, 3B	28
D. Spillner, RP	21
R. Sutcliffe, SP	20
A. Thornton, DH	20
L. Barker, SP	16
M. Hargrove, 1B	15
R. Hassey, C	12
R. Manning, OF	12
V. Hayes, OF	11
A. Bannister, OF	9
E. Whitson, RP	9
M. Fischlin, SS	8
B. Anderson, RP	6
T. Brennan, RP	5
J. Denny, SP	5
C. Bando, C	4
E. Glynn, RP	4
L. Milbourne, 2B	4
J. Perconte, 2B	4
M. Dilone, OF	3
J. Dybzinski, SS	3
B. McBride, OF	3
L. Sorensen, SP	3
B. Nahorodny, C	2
B. Blyleven, SP	1
C. Castillo, OF	1
J. Charboneau, OF	1

J. Reed, RP	1
K. Rhomberg, OF	1
R. Waits, SP	1
S. Wihtol, RP	1

Detroit (83-79)	WS
Hitting	**115.1**
Fielding	**45.3**
Pitching	**88.6**
L. Parrish, C	24
L. Whitaker, 2B	22
L. Herndon, OF	19
D. Petry, SP	18
A. Trammell, SS	16
C. Lemon, OF	15
J. Morris, SP	14
M. Wilcox, SP	12
J. Ujdur, SP	11
G. Wilson, OF	10
K. Gibson, OF	9
J. Wockenfuss, C	9
D. Tobik, RP	8
R. Hebner, 1B	6
T. Brookens, 3B	5
M. Ivie, DH	5
H. Johnson, 3B	5
L. Pashnick, RP	5
D. Rucker, RP	5
E. Cabell, 1B	4
D. Rozema, RP	4
K. Saucier, RP	4
R. Leach, 1B	3
E. Sosa, RP	3
J. Turner, DH	3
H. Bailey, RP	2
M. Laga, 1B	2
P. Underwood, RP	2
M. DeJohn, SS	1
B. Fahey, C	1
L. Jones, OF	1
A. Lopez, RP	1

Kansas City (90-72)	WS
Hitting	**143.6**
Fielding	**44.1**
Pitching	**82.3**
G. Brett, 3B	27
H. McRae, DH	26
W. Wilson, OF	25
D. Quisenberry, RP	22
U. Washington, SS	18
F. White, 2B	18
A. Otis, OF	15
W. Aikens, 1B	14
J. Martin, OF	14
L. Gura, SP	13
V. Blue, SP	11
M. Armstrong, RP	9
J. Wathan, C	9
P. Splittorff, SP	7
B. Castro, RP	5
C. Geronimo, OF	4
D. Hood, RP	4
D. Leonard, SP	4
L. May, 1B	4
G. Pryor, 3B	4
D. Slaught, C	4

B. Black, SP	3
O. Concepcion, SS	2
D. Botelho, SP-RP	1
D. Frost, SP	1
S. Hammond, OF	1
G. Jackson, RP	1
R. Johnson, 1B	1
T. Poquette, OF	1
J. Quirk, C	1
B. Tufts, RP	1

Milwaukee (95-67)	WS
Hitting	**177.6**
Fielding	**36.4**
Pitching	**71.0**
R. Yount, SS	39
P. Molitor, 3B	30
C. Cooper, 1B	29
G. Thomas, OF	25
B. Oglivie, OF	21
T. Simmons, C	19
J. Gantner, 2B	15
D. Money, DH	13
P. Vuckovich, SP	13
M. Caldwell, SP	12
R. Fingers, RP	12
C. Moore, OF	8
J. Slaton, RP	8
B. McClure, SP	7
M. Haas, SP	6
R. Howell, DH	5
D. Bernard, RP	4
N. Yost, C	4
M. Brouhard, OF	3
E. Romero, 2B	3
D. Sutton, SP	3
R. Lerch, SP	2
D. Medich, SP	2
M. Edwards, OF	1
P. Ladd, RP	1

Minnesota (60-102)	WS
Hitting	**84.4**
Fielding	**38.2**
Pitching	**57.4**
G. Ward, OF	20
T. Brunansky, OF	18
K. Hrbek, 1B	18
B. Castillo, SP	14
G. Gaetti, 3B	11
B. Havens, SP	9
B. Mitchell, OF	9
J. Castino, 2B	8
R. Davis, RP	8
R. Washington, SS	8
A. Williams, SP	8
T. Laudner, C	7
J. O'Connor, SP	6
R. Johnson, DH	5
J. Eisenreich, OF	4
L. Faedo, SS	4
P. Boris, RP	3
F. Viola, SP	3
R. Bush, DH	2
S. Butera, C	2
T. Felton, RP	2
J. Little, RP	2

J. Vega, DH	2
D. Corbett, RP	1
D. Engle, OF	1
R. Erickson, SP	1
M. Hatcher, OF	1
L. Milbourne, 2B	1
R. Wilfong, 2B	1
B. Wynegar, C	1

New York (79-83)	WS
Hitting	**116.2**
Fielding	**35.5**
Pitching	**85.2**
D. Winfield, OF	20
W. Randolph, 2B	19
R. Smalley, SS	19
G. Gossage, RP	17
J. Mumphrey, OF	17
O. Gamble, DH	15
K. Griffey Sr., OF	13
R. Guidry, SP	12
T. John, SP	10
G. Nettles, 3B	10
D. Righetti, SP	10
S. Rawley, RP	9
R. May, RP	8
B. Wynegar, C	8
L. Piniella, DH	7
G. Frazier, RP	6
M. Morgan, SP	6
D. Collins, OF	5
D. LaRoche, RP	4
J. Mayberry, 1B	4
L. Mazzilli, 1B	4
B. Dent, SS	3
R. Erickson, SP	3
R. Cerone, C	2
B. Murcer, DH	2
A. Robertson, SS	2
B. Evans, 2B	1
R. Scott, SS	1

Oakland (68-94)	WS
Hitting	**118.2**
Fielding	**31.5**
Pitching	**54.3**
R. Henderson, OF	28
D. Murphy, OF	24
J. Burroughs, DH	14
W. Gross, 3B	14
T. Armas, OF	13
T. Underwood, RP	12
R. Langford, SP	10
D. Lopes, 2B	10
D. Beard, RP	9
M. Heath, C	9
S. McCatty, SP	7
C. Johnson, DH	5
D. Meyer, 1B	5
J. Sexton, SS	5
M. Davis, OF	4
B. Kingman, SP	4
M. Norris, SP	4
J. Newman, C	3
J. Rudi, 1B	3
F. Stanley, SS	3
M. Keough, SP	2
B. Owchinko, RP	2
M. Page, DH	2
T. Phillips, SS	2
S. Baker, SP	1
D. Brown, OF	1
C. Codiroli, SP	1
T. Conroy, SP	1
J. Jones, RP	1
B. Kearney, C	1
M. Klutts, 3B	1
D. McKay, 2B	1
B. McLaughlin, RP	1
R. Picciolo, SS	1

Seattle (76-86)	WS
Hitting	**77.3**
Fielding	**47.3**
Pitching	**103.4**
B. Caudill, RP	20
F. Bannister, SP	17
A. Cowens, OF	17
J. Cruz, 2B	16
B. Bochte, OF	15
R. Zisk, DH	14
J. Beattie, SP	13
D. Henderson, OF	11
E. Vande Berg, RP	11
B. Clark, RP	10
G. Perry, SP	10
T. Cruz, SS	8
B. Stoddard, SP	7
R. Sweet, C	7
J. Essian, C	5
G. Gray, 1B	5
G. Nelson, SP	5
J. Simpson, OF	5
M. Stanton, RP	5
B. Brown, OF	4
M. Castillo, 3B	4
T. Bulling, C	3
D. Edler, 3B	3
M. Moore, SP	3
J. Maler, 1B	2
J. Moses, OF	2
E. Nunez, SP	2
P. Serna, SS	2
R. Musselman, RP	1
D. Revering, 1B	1

Texas (64-98)	WS
Hitting	**86.3**
Fielding	**33.3**
Pitching	**72.4**
B. Bell, 3B	25
C. Hough, SP	15
J. Sundberg, C	15
J. Matlack, RP	11
G. Wright, OF	11
D. Hostetler, 1B	10
L. Parrish, OF	10
D. Schmidt, RP	10
D. Darwin, RP	9
J. Grubb, OF	9
B. Sample, OF	9
F. Tanana, SP	9
L. Johnson, DH	5
M. Richardt, 2B	5
L. Mazzilli, OF	4
D. Medich, SP	4
J. Butcher, SP	3
D. Flynn, 2B	3
B. Stein, 2B	3
B. Dent, SS	2
T. Henke, RP	2
R. Honeycutt, SP	2
P. Mirabella, RP	2
P. O'Brien, OF	2
M. Smithson, SP	2
M. Wagner, SS	2
N. Capra, OF	1
S. Comer, RP	1
J. Farr, RP	1
B. Johnson, C	1
M. Mason, SP	1
P. Putnam, 1B	1
W. Tolleson, SS	1
D. Werner, C	1

Toronto (78-84)	WS
Hitting	**81.9**
Fielding	**48.0**
Pitching	**104.1**
D. Stieb, SP	25
D. Garcia, 2B	21
J. Clancy, SP	20
L. Leal, SP	17
B. Bonnell, OF	14
W. Upshaw, 1B	14
D. Murray, RP	13
J. Barfield, OF	11
R. Jackson, RP	11
L. Moseby, OF	11
A. Griffin, SS	10
J. McLaughlin, RP	10
G. Iorg, 3B	9
E. Whitt, C	9
B. Martinez, C	7
J. Gott, SP	6
R. Mulliniks, 3B	6
H. Powell, OF	5
A. Woods, OF	3
D. Geisel, RP	2
J. Mayberry, DH	2
G. Petralli, C	2
D. Revering, DH	2
D. Baker, 3B	1
T. Johnson, DH-OF	1
W. Nordhagen, DH	1
O. Velez, DH	1

1982 National League

Atlanta (89-73)	WS
Hitting	**135.4**
Fielding	**42.7**
Pitching	**88.9**
D. Murphy, OF	32
B. Horner, 3B	21
R. Ramirez, SS	21
C. Chambliss, 1B	19
G. Garber, RP	19
G. Hubbard, 2B	19
C. Washington, OF	18
S. Bedrosian, RP	15
P. Niekro, SP	14
B. Benedict, C	12
R. Camp, RP	10
J. Royster, 3B	9
R. Mahler, SP	8
P. Perez, SP	5
B. Pocoroba, C	5
T. Harper, OF	4
R. Linares, OF	4
B. Walk, SP	4
L. Whisenton, OF	4
T. Boggs, SP	3
K. Dayley, SP	3
P. Hanna, RP	3
B. Watson, 1B	3
B. Butler, OF	2
R. Johnson, 2B	2
D. Moore, RP	2
M. Sinatro, C	2
J. Cowley, RP	1
C. Diaz, RP	1
A. Hrabosky, RP	1
K. Smith, 1B	1

Chicago (73-89)	WS
Hitting	**105.7**
Fielding	**35.5**
Pitching	**77.8**
L. Durham, OF	25
B. Buckner, 1B	21
R. Sandberg, 3B	17
J. Davis, C	15
F. Jenkins, SP	14
K. Moreland, OF	13
L. Smith, RP	13
B. Wills, 2B	13
J. Johnstone, OF	9
M. Proly, RP	9
D. Tidrow, RP	9
W. Hernandez, RP	8
B. Campbell, RP	7
G. Woods, OF	7
R. Martz, SP	6
L. Bowa, SS	5
D. Noles, SP	5
A. Ripley, SP	5
S. Henderson, OF	3
J. Morales, OF	3
S. Thompson, OF	3
D. Bird, SP	2
M. Hall, OF	2
J. Kennedy, 2B	2
P. Tabler, 3B	2
R. Stein, RP	1

Cincinnati (61-101)	WS
Hitting	**60.4**
Fielding	**42.2**
Pitching	**80.4**
M. Soto, SP	20
D. Concepcion, SS	17
D. Driessen, 1B	15
B. Berenyi, SP	13
C. Cedeno, OF	13
R. Oester, 2B	11
E. Milner, OF	9
T. Hume, RP	8
F. Pastore, SP	8
J. Bench, 3B	7
B. Shirley, RP	7
J. Kern, RP	6
J. Price, RP	6
L. Biittner, OF	5
B. Hayes, RP	5
A. Trevino, C	5
P. Householder, OF	4
W. Krenchicki, 3B	4
B. Lesley, RP	4
D. Walker, OF	4
T. Lawless, 2B	2
M. Vail, OF	2
G. Barranca, 2B	1
G. Harris, RP	1
R. Landestoy, 3B	1
C. Leibrandt, RP	1
M. O'Berry, C	1
G. Redus, OF	1
B. Scherrer, RP	1
D. Van Gorder, C	1

Houston (77-85)	WS
Hitting	**98.8**
Fielding	**44.2**
Pitching	**88.0**
J. Niekro, SP	25
P. Garner, 2B	22
D. Thon, SS	22
R. Knight, 1B	20
J. Cruz, OF	18
N. Ryan, SP	16
T. Puhl, OF	15
D. Sutton, SP	14
A. Ashby, C	11
A. Howe, 3B	9
M. LaCoss, RP	9
D. Heep, OF	5
T. Scott, OF	5
R. Moffitt, RP	4
C. Reynolds, SS	4
V. Ruhle, SP	4
D. Smith, RP	4
B. Doran, 2B	3
J. Sambito, RP	3
B. Knepper, SP	2
F. LaCorte, RP	2
L. Pujols, C	2
H. Spilman, 1B	2
D. Walling, OF	2
D. Boone, RP	1
G. Cappuzzello, RP	1
K. Garcia, SS	1
A. Knicely, C	1
S. Loucks, OF	1
B. Roberge, RP	1
M. Ross, RP	1
T. Tolman, OF	1

Los Angeles (88-74)	WS
Hitting	**129.4**
Fielding	**39.9**
Pitching	**94.7**
P. Guerrero, OF	30

D. Baker, OF	22
F. Valenzuela, SP	20
S. Sax, 2B	18
R. Cey, 3B	17
K. Landreaux, OF	17
J. Reuss, SP	17
B. Russell, SS	16
S. Garvey, 1B	15
S. Howe, RP	14
B. Welch, SP	13
R. Monday, OF	9
M. Scioscia, C	8
T. Niedenfuer, RP	7
T. Forster, RP	6
D. Stewart, RP	6
S. Yeager, C	5
B. Hooton, SP	4
R. Roenicke, OF	4
J. Beckwith, RP	3
M. Marshall, OF	3
V. Romo, RP	2
D. Thomas, OF	2
R. Wright, RP	2
M. Belanger, SS	1
J. Morales, PH-PR	1
J. Orta, OF	1
S. Shirley, RP	1

Montreal (86-76)	WS
Hitting	**121.0**
Fielding	**44.4**
Pitching	**92.6**
G. Carter, C	31
A. Dawson, OF	26
A. Oliver, 1B	26
S. Rogers, SP	24
T. Raines, OF	21
T. Wallach, 3B	20
J. Reardon, RP	18
W. Cromartie, OF	14
C. Speier, SS	14
S. Sanderson, SP	12
B. Gullickson, SP	11
C. Lea, SP	11
W. Fryman, RP	6
D. Palmer, SP	4
T. Francona, OF	3
B. Smith, RP	3
D. Flynn, 2B	2
M. Gates, 2B	2
D. Schatzeder, RP	2
J. White, OF	2
T. Blackwell, C	1
R. Burris, RP	1
R. Lerch, SP	1
D. Norman, OF	1
F. Taveras, SS	1
J. Youngblood, OF	1

New York (65-97)	WS
Hitting	**97.2**
Fielding	**31.8**
Pitching	**66.0**
M. Wilson, OF	19
J. Stearns, C	14
G. Foster, OF	12
D. Kingman, 1B	12
C. Swan, SP	12
W. Backman, 2B	10
B. Bailor, SS	10
R. Hodges, C	9
J. Orosco, RP	9
N. Allen, RP	8
P. Falcone, SP	8
E. Lynch, RP	8
R. Gardenhire, SS	7
E. Valentine, OF	7
H. Brooks, 3B	6
P. Zachry, RP	5
M. Jorgensen, 1B	4
C. Puleo, SP	4
G. Rajsich, OF	4
B. Bochy, C	3
B. Giles, 2B	3
T. Leach, RP	3
R. Staub, OF	3
J. Youngblood, OF	3
S. Holman, SP	2
R. Jones, SP	2
R. Ownbey, SP	2
T. Veryzer, 2B	2
T. Gorman, RP	1
M. Howard, OF	1
D. Sisk, RP	1
W. Terrell, SP	1

Philadelphia (89-73)	WS
Hitting	**131.8**
Fielding	**40.3**
Pitching	**94.9**
M. Schmidt, 3B	37
S. Carlton, SP	25
G. Matthews, OF	23
B. Diaz, C	21
P. Rose, 1B	17
M. Krukow, SP	15
I. DeJesus, SS	14
R. Reed, RP	14
M. Trillo, 2B	14
L. Christenson, SP	13
G. Maddox, OF	12
D. Ruthven, SP	10
B. Dernier, OF	9
G. Vukovich, OF	9
S. Monge, RP	5
G. Gross, OF	4
L. Aguayo, 2B	3
P. Altamirano, RP	3
T. McGraw, RP	3
O. Virgil, C	3
S. Bahnsen, RP	2
D. Davis, OF	2
E. Farmer, RP	2
B. Robinson, OF	2
W. Brusstar, RP	1
M. Bystrom, SP	1
J. Denny, SP	1
S. Lyle, RP	1
A. Sanchez, OF	1

Pittsburgh (84-78)	WS
Hitting	**125.2**
Fielding	**40.5**
Pitching	**86.3**
J. Thompson, 1B	27
B. Madlock, 3B	25
J. Ray, 2B	19
T. Pena, C	16
K. Tekulve, RP	15
D. Berra, SS	14
J. Candelaria, SP	14
M. Easler, OF	14
L. Lacy, OF	13
R. Scurry, RP	13
O. Moreno, OF	11
R. Rhoden, SP	11
D. Robinson, SP	10
M. Sarmiento, RP	10
L. McWilliams, SP	8
D. Parker, OF	7
E. Romo, RP	5
J. Morrison, 3B	3
S. Nicosia, C	3
R. Hebner, OF	2
J. Milner, 1B	2
B. Robinson, OF	2
W. Stargell, 1B	2
C. Guante, RP	1
B. Harper, OF	1
P. Moskau, RP	1
R. Niemann, RP	1
J. Smith, SS	1
L. Tunnell, SP	1

San Diego (81-81)	WS
Hitting	**131.3**
Fielding	**39.8**
Pitching	**72.0**
T. Kennedy, C	28
S. Lezcano, OF	28
R. Jones, OF	22
T. Lollar, SP	17
G. Richards, OF	16
L. DeLeon, RP	14
L. Salazar, 3B	12
T. Flannery, 2B	11
E. Show, RP	11
G. Templeton, SS	11
B. Perkins, 1B	9
D. Dravecky, RP	7
T. Gwynn, OF	7
G. Lucas, RP	7
J. Lefebvre, 3B	6
A. Wiggins, OF	6
J. Bonilla, 2B	5
F. Chiffer, RP	5
J. Montefusco, SP	5
J. Curtis, SP	4
K. Bevacqua, 1B	3
J. Eichelberger, SP	2
J. Pittman, 2B	2
R. Bass, 1B	1
A. Hawkins, SP	1
G. Hinshaw, OF	1
S. Swisher, C	1
C. Welsh, SP	1

San Francisco (87-75)	WS
Hitting	**141.8**
Fielding	**35.6**
Pitching	**83.6**
J. Morgan, 2B	29
J. Clark, OF	26
G. Minton, RP	21
D. Evans, 3B	20
C. Davis, OF	19
R. Smith, 1B	16
M. May, C	14
B. Laskey, SP	12
G. Lavelle, RP	11
F. Breining, RP	10
J. Barr, RP	8
B. Brenly, C	8
A. Holland, RP	8
T. O'Malley, 3B	8
A. Hammaker, SP	7
D. Kuiper, 2B	7
J. Leonard, OF	7
J. Wohlford, OF	6
D. Bergman, 1B	5
R. Gale, SP	4
J. LeMaster, SS	4
C. Summers, OF	4
R. Martin, SP	2
G. Sularz, SS	2
A. McGaffigan, RP	1
J. Ransom, C	1
M. Venable, OF	1

St. Louis (92-70)	WS
Hitting	**123.8**
Fielding	**50.3**
Pitching	**101.9**
L. Smith, OF	26
K. Hernandez, 1B	24
J. Andujar, SP	22
O. Smith, SS	19
G. Hendrick, OF	17
B. Sutter, RP	17
B. Forsch, SP	16
D. Porter, C	16
T. Herr, 2B	15
K. Oberkfell, 3B	15
D. Bair, RP	11
W. McGee, OF	11
D. LaPoint, SP-RP	9
G. Tenace, C	9
J. Stuper, SP	8
S. Mura, SP	7
D. Iorg, OF	6
D. Green, OF	5
M. Ramsey, 2B	4
J. Kaat, RP	3
J. Lahti, RP	3
T. Landrum, OF	3
S. Braun, OF	2
J. Keener, RP	2
J. Martin, RP	2
G. Brummer, C	1
J. Gonzalez, 3B	1
A. Rincon, SP	1
O. Sanchez, C	1

1983
American League

Baltimore (98-64)	WS
Hitting	**146.0**
Fielding	**45.9**
Pitching	**102.0**
C. Ripken Jr., SS	35
E. Murray, 1B	31
S. McGregor, SP	21
T. Martinez, RP	17
K. Singleton, DH	17
M. Boddicker, SP	16
J. Lowenstein, OF	15
S. Davis, SP	13
R. Dempsey, C	13
D. Ford, OF	13
G. Roenicke, OF	11
S. Stewart, RP	11
A. Bumbry, OF	10
M. Flanagan, SP	10
J. Dwyer, OF	9
R. Dauer, 2B	8
J. Shelby, OF	8
J. Nolan, C	7
D. Morogiello, RP	4
A. Ramirez, SP	4
L. Sakata, 2B	4
L. Hernandez, 3B	3
J. Palmer, SP	3
B. Ayala, OF	2
T. Cruz, 3B	2
B. Swaggerty, RP	2
G. Gulliver, 3B	1
T. Landrum, OF	1
A. Rodriguez, 3B	1
J. Stefero, C	1
T. Stoddard, RP	1

Boston (78-84)	WS
Hitting	**108.5**
Fielding	**42.9**
Pitching	**82.6**
W. Boggs, 3B	34
J. Rice, OF	24
B. Stanley, RP	21
J. Tudor, SP	14
D. Evans, OF	13
B. Hurst, SP	13
G. Hoffman, SS	12
B. Ojeda, SP	11
J. Remy, 2B	11
C. Yastrzemski, DH	9
R. Nichols, OF	8
T. Armas, OF	7
R. Gedman, C	7
D. Stapleton, 1B	7
O. Boyd, SP	6
R. Miller, OF	6
G. Allenson, C	5
L. Aponte, RP	5
E. Jurak, SS	5
M. Brown, SP	4
D. Eckersley, SP	3
J. Johnson, RP	3
J. Newman, C	2

A. Nipper, SP	2
M. Clear, RP	1
C. Walker, OF	1

California (70-92)	WS
Hitting	**106.7**
Fielding	**30.7**
Pitching	**72.6**
B. Grich, 2B	20
R. Carew, 1B	16
F. Lynn, OF	16
G. Zahn, SP	14
D. DeCinces, 3B	13
B. Downing, OF	13
K. Forsch, SP	12
T. John, SP	10
B. Boone, C	9
B. Kison, SP	9
L. Sanchez, RP	9
J. Beniquez, OF	7
D. Sconiers, 1B	7
J. Curtis, RP	6
E. Valentine, OF	5
M. Witt, RP	5
T. Foli, SS	4
Re. Jackson, DH	4
Ro. Jackson, 3B	4
S. Brown, RP	3
R. Burleson, SS	3
G. Pettis, OF	3
R. Wilfong, 2B	3
R. Adams, SS	2
B. Clark, OF	2
S. Lubratich, SS	2
B. McLaughlin, RP	2
R. Steirer, RP	2
M. Brown, OF	1
D. Corbett, RP	1
A. Hassler, RP	1
M. O'Berry, C	1
D. Schofield, SS	1

Chicago (99-63)	WS
Hitting	**137.8**
Fielding	**49.2**
Pitching	**110.0**
C. Fisk, C	26
R. Dotson, SP	21
H. Baines, OF	20
L. Hoyt, SP	20
R. Law, OF	20
G. Luzinski, DH	20
R. Kittle, OF	19
F. Bannister, SP	17
T. Paciorek, 1B	16
S. Barojas, RP	12
V. Law, 3B	12
B. Burns, SP	11
D. Lamp, RP	11
G. Walker, 1B	10
J. Cruz, 2B	9
S. Fletcher, SS	9
J. Hairston, OF	7
J. Koosman, SP	7
T. Bernazard, 2B	6
J. Dybzinski, SS	5
D. Tidrow, RP	5
J. Agosto, RP	4
M. Squires, 1B	3
M. Hill, C	2
C. Nyman, DH-1B	2
L. Gray, 3B	1
K. Hickey, RP	1
R. Kuntz, OF	1

Cleveland (70-92)	WS
Hitting	**99.9**
Fielding	**34.5**
Pitching	**75.5**
A. Thornton, DH	18
T. Harrah, 3B	16
M. Hargrove, 1B	14
R. Sutcliffe, SP	14
L. Sorensen, SP	13
J. Franco, SS	12
R. Hassey, C	12
P. Tabler, OF	12
N. Heaton, RP	11
B. Blyleven, SP	10
G. Thomas, OF	10
A. Bannister, OF	9
M. Trillo, 2B	6
B. Anderson, RP	5
L. Barker, SP	5
J. Easterly, RP	5
C. Bando, C	4
J. Eichelberger, SP	4
M. Fischlin, 2B	4
J. Essian, C	3
R. Manning, OF	3
B. McBride, OF	3
D. Spillner, RP	3
G. Vukovich, OF	3
T. Brennan, RP	2
M. Jeffcoat, RP	2
R. Behenna, SP	1
C. Castillo, OF	1
M. Dilone, OF	1
J. Perconte, 2B	1
B. Perkins, 1B	1
K. Rhomberg, OF	1
R. Waits, RP	1

Detroit (92-70)	WS
Hitting	**142.0**
Fielding	**46.0**
Pitching	**88.0**
L. Whitaker, 2B	29
A. Trammell, SS	26
L. Parrish, C	24
L. Herndon, OF	22
C. Lemon, OF	21
J. Morris, SP	20
A. Lopez, RP	14
D. Petry, SP	14
G. Wilson, OF	12
J. Berenguer, SP	11
K. Gibson, DH	11
E. Cabell, 1B	10
M. Wilcox, SP	9
J. Wockenfuss, DH	9
D. Rozema, SP	7
T. Brookens, 3B	6
J. Grubb, OF	5
G. Abbott, SP	4
D. Bair, RP	4
W. Krenchicki, 3B	4
R. Leach, 1B	4
D. Gumpert, RP	3
H. Bailey, RP	2
M. Castillo, 3B	2
B. Fahey, C	1
H. Johnson, 3B	1
L. Jones, OF	1

Kansas City (79-83)	WS
Hitting	**114.7**
Fielding	**40.2**
Pitching	**82.0**
D. Quisenberry, RP	28
G. Brett, 3B	24
H. McRae, DH	20
W. Aikens, 1B	17
F. White, 2B	15
W. Wilson, OF	15
U. Washington, SS	13
B. Black, SP	10
P. Splittorff, SP	10
P. Sheridan, OF	9
A. Otis, OF	8
M. Armstrong, RP	7
D. Slaught, C	7
L. Gura, SP	6
J. Wathan, C	6
B. Davis, OF	5
S. Renko, SP	5
L. Roberts, OF	5
O. Concepcion, 3B	4
D. Hood, RP	4
D. Leonard, SP	4
G. Perry, SP	3
J. Martin, OF	2
E. Rasmussen, SP	2
F. Wills, SP	2
C. Geronimo, OF	1
M. Huismann, RP	1
R. Johnson, 1B	1
D. Motley, OF	1
G. Pryor, 3B	1
J. Simpson, 1B	1

Milwaukee (87-75)	WS
Hitting	**143.7**
Fielding	**38.6**
Pitching	**78.7**
R. Yount, SS	33
C. Cooper, 1B	25
P. Molitor, 3B	23
J. Gantner, 2B	21
T. Simmons, C	20
B. Oglivie, OF	16
C. Moore, OF	15
M. Haas, SP	14
P. Ladd, RP	10
T. Tellmann, RP	10
D. Sutton, SP	9
M. Caldwell, SP	8
J. Slaton, RP	7
M. Brouhard, OF	5
R. Howell, DH	5
R. Manning, OF	5
B. McClure, SP	5
C. Porter, SP	5
E. Romero, SS	5
T. Candiotti, SP	4
B. Gibson, RP	4
J. Cocanower, SP	3
R. Ready, DH	3
G. Thomas, OF	2
N. Yost, C	2
M. Edwards, OF	1
D. Money, DH	1

Minnesota (70-92)	WS
Hitting	**101.7**
Fielding	**39.9**
Pitching	**68.4**
J. Castino, 2B	21
K. Hrbek, 1B	19
G. Gaetti, 3B	17
G. Ward, OF	17
T. Brunansky, OF	15
K. Schrom, SP	13
R. Davis, RP	12
D. Engle, C	12
M. Hatcher, OF	11
A. Williams, SP	10
R. Bush, DH	8
R. Lysander, RP	8
P. Filson, RP	7
B. Castillo, SP	6
L. Whitehouse, RP	5
F. Viola, SP	4
R. Washington, SS	4
D. Brown, OF	3
B. Mitchell, OF	3
T. Teufel, 2B	3
M. Walters, RP	3
L. Faedo, SS	2
T. Laudner, C	2
R. Smith, C	2
H. Jimenez, SS	1
R. Kuntz, OF	1
J. O'Connor, RP	1

New York (91-71)	WS
Hitting	**141.0**
Fielding	**39.9**
Pitching	**92.1**
D. Winfield, OF	22
D. Baylor, DH	21
R. Smalley, SS	20
R. Guidry, SP	19
K. Griffey Sr., 1B	17
G. Gossage, RP	16
G. Nettles, 3B	16
W. Randolph, 2B	15
D. Righetti, SP	15
S. Rawley, SP	14
B. Wynegar, C	14
G. Frazier, RP	10
S. Kemp, OF	8
J. Mumphrey, OF	8
R. Fontenot, SP	7
O. Gamble, OF	7
D. Mattingly, OF	7
A. Robertson, SS	7
B. Campaneris, 2B	4
J. Montefusco, SP	4
L. Piniella, OF	4
D. Murray, RP	3
S. Balboni, 1B	2
R. Cerone, C	2
B. Meacham, SS	2
O. Moreno, OF	2
B. Shirley, SP	2
R. Erickson, RP	1
J. Espino, C	1
J. Howell, SP	1
C. Kaufman, RP	1
L. Milbourne, 2B	1

Oakland (74-88)	WS
Hitting	**123.3**
Fielding	**34.2**
Pitching	**64.6**
R. Henderson, OF	30
D. Lopes, 2B	18
M. Davis, OF	13
C. Lansford, 3B	12
T. Phillips, SS	12
D. Murphy, OF	11
B. Almon, SS	10
J. Burroughs, DH	9
W. Gross, 1B	9
M. Heath, C	9
T. Burgmeier, RP	8
S. McCatty, SP	8
T. Underwood, RP	8
C. Codiroli, SP	7
B. Kearney, C	7
K. Atherton, RP	6
T. Conroy, RP	6
G. Hancock, OF	6
B. Krueger, SP	6
D. Hill, SS	4
M. Norris, SP	4
G. Heimueller, SP	3
R. Peters, OF	3
M. Warren, SP	3
S. Baker, RP	2
D. Beard, RP	2
D. Cias, C	1
E. Farmer, RP	1
M. Keough, RP	1
D. Meyer, 1B	1
K. Moore, 1B	1
M. Page, DH	1

Seattle (60-102)	WS
Hitting	**60.4**
Fielding	**37.8**
Pitching	**81.8**
M. Young, SP	16
J. Beattie, SP	13
D. Henderson, OF	13
S. Henderson, OF	12
P. Putnam, 1B	12
T. Bernazard, 2B	9
B. Clark, RP	9
B. Stoddard, SP	8
R. Roenicke, OF	7
B. Caudill, RP	6
J. Cruz, 2B	6
M. Stanton, RP	6

R. Thomas, RP	6
M. Moore, SP	5
E. Vande Berg, RP	5
R. Zisk, DH	5
G. Abbott, SP	4
R. Nelson, OF	4
J. Allen, 3B	3
T. Cruz, SS	3
O. Mercado, C	3
S. Owen, SS	3
G. Perry, SP	3
K. Phelps, 1B	3
D. Ramos, SS	3
R. Sweet, C	3
J. Nelson, C	2
P. Bradley, OF	1
M. Castillo, 3B	1
A. Chambers, DH	1
D. Coles, 3B	1
A. Cowens, OF	1
J. Moses, OF	1
E. Nunez, RP	1
H. Reynolds, 2B	1

Texas (77-85)	WS
Hitting	**81.0**
Fielding	**46.2**
Pitching	**103.8**
G. Wright, OF	20
C. Hough, SP	18
B. Bell, 3B	17
B. Sample, OF	17
R. Honeycutt, SP	16
L. Parrish, OF	16
M. Smithson, SP	11
D. Darwin, SP	10
P. O'Brien, 1B	10
F. Tanana, SP	10
W. Tolleson, 2B	10
J. Butcher, RP	9
O. Jones, RP	7
J. Sundberg, C	7
B. Dent, SS	6
B. Stein, 2B	6
D. Stewart, SP	6
M. Rivers, DH	5
D. Tobik, RP	5
V. Cruz, RP	4
D. Hostetler, DH	4
B. Johnson, C	4
D. Schmidt, RP	3
L. Biittner, 1B	2
T. Henke, RP	2
J. Matlack, RP	2
J. Anderson, SS	1
B. Jones, DH-OF	1
A. Lachowicz, SP-RP	1
M. Richardt, 2B	1

Toronto (89-73)	WS
Hitting	**125.9**
Fielding	**46.0**
Pitching	**95.1**
L. Moseby, OF	25
D. Stieb, SP	24
W. Upshaw, 1B	22
E. Whitt, C	15
B. Bonnell, OF	14
J. Clancy, SP	14
R. Mulliniks, 3B	14
D. Garcia, 2B	13
C. Johnson, DH	13
L. Leal, SP	12
J. Barfield, OF	11
A. Griffin, SS	11
D. Collins, OF	10
B. Martinez, C	9
D. Alexander, SP	8
J. Gott, SP	7
G. Iorg, 3B	7
R. Jackson, RP	7
R. Moffitt, RP	7
J. Acker, RP	6
J. McLaughlin, RP	5
D. Geisel, RP	3
J. Orta, DH	3
G. Bell, OF	2
S. Clarke, RP	1
T. Fernandez, SS	1
M. Klutts, 3B	1
M. Morgan, RP	1
H. Powell, OF	1

1983 National League

Atlanta (88-74)	WS
Hitting	**125.8**
Fielding	**45.7**
Pitching	**92.5**
D. Murphy, OF	32
G. Hubbard, 2B	19
B. Benedict, C	18
R. Ramirez, SS	18
B. Horner, 3B	17
B. Butler, OF	16
C. Chambliss, 1B	16
C. McMurtry, SP	16
P. Perez, SP	14
C. Washington, OF	13
S. Bedrosian, RP	12
T. Forster, RP	12
P. Niekro, SP	9
R. Camp, RP	7
P. Falcone, RP	7
D. Moore, RP	5
B. Watson, 1B	5
K. Dayley, SP	4
T. Harper, OF	4
J. Royster, 3B	4
R. Johnson, 3B	3
B. Pocoroba, C	3
R. Behenna, RP	2
T. Brizzolara, RP	2
G. Garber, RP	2
G. Perry, 1B	2
L. Barker, SP	1
M. Jorgensen, 1B	1

Chicago (71-91)	WS
Hitting	**108.5**
Fielding	**32.5**
Pitching	**72.0**
L. Smith, RP	19
K. Moreland, OF	18
R. Sandberg, 2B	18
B. Buckner, 1B	16
R. Cey, 3B	16
J. Davis, C	16
M. Hall, OF	15
L. Bowa, SS	13
L. Durham, OF	13
W. Brusstar, RP	7
D. Ruthven, SP	7
B. Campbell, RP	6
F. Jenkins, SP	6
C. Lefferts, RP	6
C. Rainey, SP	6
S. Trout, SP	5
J. Johnstone, OF	4
M. Proly, RP	4
T. Bosley, OF	3
D. Noles, SP	3
W. Hernandez, RP	2
C. Martinez, 1B	2
D. Rohn, 2B	2
G. Woods, OF	2
B. Johnson, RP	1
S. Lake, C	1
R. Reuschel, SP	1
T. Veryzer, SS	1

Cincinnati (74-88)	WS
Hitting	**98.7**
Fielding	**43.9**
Pitching	**79.4**
M. Soto, SP	25
E. Milner, OF	20
G. Redus, OF	18
D. Driessen, 1B	16
R. Oester, 2B	14
J. Price, SP	14
N. Esasky, 3B	11
P. Householder, OF	11
B. Scherrer, RP	11
B. Berenyi, SP	10
D. Bilardello, C	9
J. Bench, 3B	8
D. Concepcion, SS	8
C. Cedeno, OF	7
F. Pastore, SP	5
J. Russell, SP	5
T. Power, RP	4
A. Trevino, C	4
D. Walker, OF	4
K. Paris, 3B	3
T. Foley, SS	2
T. Hume, RP	2
J. Jones, OF	2
A. Knicely, C	2
W. Krenchicki, 3B	2
C. Puleo, SP	2
S. Barnes, 1B-3B	1
K. Cato, RP	1
B. Lesley, RP	1

Houston (85-77)	WS
Hitting	**134.1**
Fielding	**41.0**
Pitching	**79.9**
J. Cruz, OF	30
D. Thon, SS	30
B. Doran, 2B	22
R. Knight, 1B	18
T. Puhl, OF	18
P. Garner, 3B	16
F. DiPino, RP	12
N. Ryan, SP	12
J. Niekro, SP	11
B. Dawley, RP	10
O. Moreno, OF	9
J. Mumphrey, OF	9
B. Knepper, SP	8
A. Ashby, C	6
M. Madden, RP	6
V. Ruhle, RP	6
M. Scott, SP	6
D. Walling, 1B	6
D. Smith, RP	5
G. Bjorkman, C	3
K. Bass, OF	2
J. Heathcock, SP-RP	2
T. Scott, OF	2
F. LaCorte, RP	1
M. LaCoss, RP	1
J. Mizerock, C	1
L. Pujols, C	1
C. Reynolds, 2B	1
T. Tolman, 1B	1

Los Angeles (91-71)	WS
Hitting	**123.6**
Fielding	**43.0**
Pitching	**106.4**
P. Guerrero, 3B	32
D. Baker, OF	19
K. Landreaux, OF	19
M. Marshall, OF	17
S. Sax, 2B	17
B. Welch, SP	16
G. Brock, 1B	15
T. Niedenfuer, RP	15
J. Reuss, SP	15
S. Howe, RP	14
A. Pena, SP	13
F. Valenzuela, SP	12
B. Russell, SS	11
D. Stewart, RP	8
D. Thomas, OF	7
S. Yeager, C	7
R. Monday, OF	6
P. Zachry, RP	6
J. Fimple, C	5
B. Hooton, SP	5
J. Beckwith, RP	3
D. Anderson, SS	2
J. Morales, 1B	2
R. Roenicke, OF	2
M. Scioscia, C	2
R. Reynolds, OF	1
G. Rivera, 3B	1
L. White, RP	1

Montreal (82-80)	WS
Hitting	**116.8**
Fielding	**42.7**
Pitching	**86.5**
T. Raines, OF	29
A. Dawson, OF	28
G. Carter, C	24
T. Wallach, 3B	19
S. Rogers, SP	17
C. Lea, SP	15
A. Oliver, 1B	14
B. Gullickson, SP	13
B. Smith, RP	13
W. Cromartie, OF	10
J. Reardon, RP	10
B. Little, SS	9
R. Burris, RP	8
C. Speier, SS	7
D. Schatzeder, RP	6
D. Flynn, 2B	5
B. James, RP	5
M. Trillo, 2B	4
T. Francona, OF	2
B. Ramos, C	2
M. Vail, OF	2
J. Wohlford, OF	2
S. Sanderson, SP	1
J. White, OF	1

New York (68-94)	WS
Hitting	**85.5**
Fielding	**38.7**
Pitching	**79.9**
J. Orosco, RP	20
D. Strawberry, OF	18
M. Wilson, OF	17
K. Hernandez, 1B	16
G. Foster, OF	14
T. Seaver, SP	12
D. Sisk, RP	12
H. Brooks, 3B	10
C. Diaz, RP	9
B. Giles, 2B	9
W. Terrell, SP	8
D. Heep, OF	7
B. Bailor, SS	6
R. Hodges, C	6
M. Torrez, SP	6
E. Lynch, SP	5
J. Oquendo, SS	5
S. Holman, RP	4
D. Kingman, 1B	4
R. Staub, 1B-OF	4
R. Darling, SP	3
J. Ortiz, C	2
G. Rajsich, 1B	2
N. Allen, RP	1
T. Ashford, 3B	1
M. Bradley, OF	1
M. Jorgensen, 1B	1
R. Ownbey, RP	1

Philadelphia (90-72)	WS
Hitting	**126.9**
Fielding	**39.9**
Pitching	**103.2**
M. Schmidt, 3B	35
J. Denny, SP	23
J. Morgan, 2B	19
S. Carlton, SP	18
A. Holland, RP	18

B. Diaz, C	15
J. Lefebvre, OF	14
G. Matthews, OF	14
I. DeJesus, SS	12
G. Gross, OF	9
V. Hayes, OF	9
W. Hernandez, RP	9
C. Hudson, SP	9
R. Reed, RP	9
G. Maddox, OF	7
P. Rose, 1B	7
T. Perez, 1B	6
B. Dernier, OF	5
K. Garcia, 2B	4
K. Gross, SP	4
L. Andersen, RP	3
L. Matuszek, 1B	3
T. McGraw, RP	3
O. Virgil, C	3
P. Altamirano, RP	2
M. Bystrom, SP	2
L. Christenson, SP	2
J. Samuel, 2B	2
T. Ghelfi, SP	1
S. Lezcano, OF	1
L. Milbourne, 2B	1
J. Stone, OF	1

Pittsburgh (84-78)	WS
Hitting	**110.4**
Fielding	**46.0**
Pitching	**95.6**
T. Pena, C	21
J. Ray, 2B	20
D. Berra, SS	19
B. Madlock, 3B	17
K. Tekulve, RP	17
J. Thompson, 1B	17
R. Rhoden, SP	16
J. Candelaria, SP	15
L. McWilliams, SP	15
D. Parker, OF	12
M. Easler, OF	11
L. Tunnell, SP	10
J. DeLeon, SP	9
L. Lacy, OF	9
M. Wynne, OF	8
C. Guante, RP	7
L. Mazzilli, OF	7
J. Morrison, 2B	6
M. Sarmiento, RP	6
R. Hebner, 3B	4
D. Frobel, OF	2
B. Harper, OF	1
S. Nicosia, C	1
D. Robinson, SP	1
G. Tenace, 1B	1

San Diego (81-81)	WS
Hitting	**115.5**
Fielding	**42.8**
Pitching	**84.7**
T. Kennedy, C	24
A. Wiggins, OF	20
L. Salazar, 3B	15
S. Garvey, 1B	14
L. DeLeon, RP	13
J. Bonilla, 2B	12
D. Dravecky, SP	10
T. Gwynn, OF	10
G. Templeton, SS	10
R. Jones, OF	9
S. Lezcano, OF	9
G. Lucas, RP	9
M. Thurmond, SP	9
B. Brown, OF	8
J. Montefusco, RP	8
E. Show, SP	8
T. Flannery, 3B	7
A. Hawkins, SP	7
S. Monge, RP	7
G. Richards, OF	7
T. Lollar, SP	5
E. Whitson, SP	4
K. Bevacqua, 1B	3
K. McReynolds, OF	3
M. Ramirez, SS	3
F. Chiffer, RP	1
G. Davis, OF	1
M. Decker, RP	1
D. Gwosdz, C	1
G. Hinshaw, 3B	1
J. Lefebvre, OF	1
D. Rasmussen, RP	1
E. Sosa, RP	1
C. Welsh, RP	1

San Francisco (79-83)	WS
Hitting	**126.4**
Fielding	**33.5**
Pitching	**77.1**
D. Evans, 1B	28
J. Clark, OF	20
J. Leonard, OF	19
J. Youngblood, 2B	16
A. Hammaker, SP	13
G. Lavelle, RP	13
C. Davis, OF	11
J. LeMaster, SS	11
T. O'Malley, 3B	11
G. Minton, RP	10
F. Breining, SP	8
B. Brenly, C	8
M. Krukow, SP	8
D. Bergman, 1B	7
M. Davis, SP	6
B. Laskey, SP	6
M. May, C	6
M. Venable, OF	6
J. Barr, RP	4
R. Martin, RP	4
A. McGaffigan, RP	4
C. Smith, 1B	4
S. Garrelts, SP	3
D. Kuiper, 2B	3
J. Rabb, C	3
D. Gladden, OF	1
R. Lerch, RP	1
S. Nicosia, C	1
J. Pettini, SS	1
B. Wellman, 2B	1

St. Louis (79-83)	WS
Hitting	**126.5**
Fielding	**36.5**
Pitching	**74.1**
G. Hendrick, 1B	21
L. Smith, OF	19
O. Smith, SS	18
K. Oberkfell, 3B	17
D. Porter, C	17
W. McGee, OF	15
T. Herr, 2B	12
A. Van Slyke, OF	11
D. Green, OF	10
J. Stuper, SP	10
D. LaPoint, SP	9
B. Sutter, RP	9
N. Allen, SP	7
J. Andujar, SP	7
B. Forsch, SP	7
K. Hernandez, 1B	7
J. Lahti, RP	5
D. Von Ohlen, RP	5
S. Braun, OF	4
D. Cox, SP	4
J. Martin, RP	4
M. Ramsey, 2B	4
D. Rucker, RP	4
D. Bair, RP	2
G. Brummer, C	2
D. Iorg, OF	2
S. Baker, RP	1
R. Citarella, RP	1
J. Doyle, 2B	1
J. Kaat, RP	1
F. Rayford, 3B	1

1984 American League

Baltimore (85-77)	WS
Hitting	**118.2**
Fielding	**44.7**
Pitching	**92.1**
C. Ripken Jr., SS	37
E. Murray, 1B	33
M. Boddicker, SP	23
S. Davis, SP	18
M. Young, OF	16
M. Flanagan, SP	14
W. Gross, 3B	13
S. McGregor, SP	11
R. Dempsey, C	10
G. Roenicke, OF	10
S. Stewart, RP	9
A. Bumbry, OF	7
R. Dauer, 2B	7
T. Martinez, RP	7
F. Rayford, C	7
J. Lowenstein, OF	6
J. Dwyer, OF	4
J. Shelby, OF	4
T. Underwood, RP	4
D. Martinez, SP	3
J. Nolan, DH	2
L. Sakata, 2B	2
B. Ayala, DH	1
M. Brown, RP	1
T. Cruz, 3B	1
K. Dixon, SP	1
D. Ford, OF	1
V. Rodriguez, 2B	1
L. Sheets, OF	1
N. Snell, RP	1

Boston (86-76)	WS
Hitting	**127.4**
Fielding	**38.8**
Pitching	**91.8**
D. Evans, OF	29
W. Boggs, 3B	28
M. Easler, DH	23
T. Armas, OF	20
J. Rice, OF	17
M. Barrett, 2B	16
R. Gedman, C	15
B. Hurst, SP	14
B. Ojeda, SP	14
A. Nipper, SP	12
B. Stanley, RP	12
O. Boyd, SP	10
B. Buckner, 1B	9
R. Clemens, SP	8
M. Clear, RP	6
S. Crawford, RP	5
J. Johnson, RP	5
D. Eckersley, SP	3
E. Jurak, 1B	2
R. Miller, OF	2
R. Nichols, OF	2
G. Allenson, C	1
R. Gale, RP	1
C. Mitchell, RP	1
J. Newman, C	1
J. Remy, 2B	1
M. Sullivan, C	1

California (81-81)	WS
Hitting	**109.8**
Fielding	**41.6**
Pitching	**91.6**
F. Lynn, OF	22
B. Downing, OF	20
D. DeCinces, 3B	17
M. Witt, SP	17
B. Grich, 2B	16
G. Zahn, SP	16
R. Romanick, SP	14
J. Beniquez, OF	13
D. Corbett, RP	10
Re. Jackson, DH	10
G. Pettis, OF	10
R. Carew, 1B	9
L. Sanchez, RP	9
R. Wilfong, 2B	9
D. Schofield, SS	8
D. Aase, RP	7
B. Boone, C	7
T. John, SP	7
M. Brown, OF	5
J. Slaton, SP	4
C. Kaufman, RP	3
K. Forsch, SP	2
J. Narron, C	2
R. Picciolo, SS	2
D. Sconiers, 1B	2
J. Curtis, RP	1
B. Kison, RP	1

Chicago (74-88)	WS
Hitting	**88.0**
Fielding	**45.3**
Pitching	**88.7**
H. Baines, OF	24
R. Dotson, SP	18
T. Seaver, SP	16
G. Walker, 1B	15
S. Fletcher, SS	13
L. Hoyt, SP	11
R. Kittle, OF	11
C. Fisk, C	10
V. Law, 3B	10
F. Bannister, SP	9
J. Cruz, 2B	9
R. Law, OF	9
R. Reed, RP	9
J. Hairston, OF	7
J. Agosto, RP	6
G. Luzinski, DH	6
T. Paciorek, 1B	6
J. Dybzinski, SS	4
G. Nelson, RP	4
B. Burns, RP	3
B. Roberge, RP	3
D. Spillner, RP	3
S. Barojas, RP	2
M. Hill, C	2
D. Stegman, OF	2
D. Boston, OF	1
S. Christmas, C	1
B. Fallon, SP	1
J. Gleaton, RP	1
A. Jones, RP	1
R. Niemann, RP	1
J. Siwy, RP	1
J. Skinner, C	1
R. Smalley, 3B	1
M. Squires, 1B	1

Cleveland (75-87)	WS
Hitting	**112.1**
Fielding	**36.5**
Pitching	**76.3**
A. Thornton, DH	21
B. Blyleven, SP	20
B. Butler, OF	19
J. Franco, SS	17
G. Vukovich, OF	15
E. Camacho, RP	14
P. Tabler, 1B	13
C. Bando, C	10
T. Waddell, RP	9
M. Hall, OF	8
B. Jacoby, 3B	8
J. Carter, OF	7
M. Hargrove, 1B	7
T. Bernazard, 2B	6
C. Castillo, OF	6
M. Jeffcoat, RP	6
J. Willard, C	6
J. Easterly, RP	5

S. Farr, SP	4
N. Heaton, SP	4
G. Frazier, RP	3
R. Hassey, C	3
R. Smith, SP	3
L. Aponte, RP	2
M. Fischlin, 2B	2
D. Schulze, SP	2
R. Sutcliffe, SP	2
S. Comer, SP	1
O. Nixon, OF	1
J. Quirk, C	1

Detroit (104-58)	WS
Hitting	**165.0**
Fielding	**45.8**
Pitching	**101.2**
A. Trammell, SS	29
K. Gibson, OF	26
W. Hernandez, RP	24
C. Lemon, OF	24
L. Whitaker, 2B	22
L. Parrish, C	19
D. Petry, SP	16
J. Morris, SP	14
A. Lopez, RP	13
D. Evans, DH	12
L. Herndon, OF	12
H. Johnson, 3B	10
J. Berenguer, SP	9
D. Bergman, 1B	9
R. Jones, OF	9
M. Wilcox, SP	9
J. Grubb, OF	8
T. Brookens, 3B	7
B. Garbey, 1B	7
D. Bair, RP	6
R. Kuntz, OF	6
D. Rozema, SP	5
M. Castillo, C	3
D. Baker, SS	2
D. Lowry, C	2
B. Scherrer, RP	2
N. Simmons, OF	2
R. Allen, DH	1
M. Laga, DH-1B	1
R. Mason, RP	1
S. Monge, RP	1
R. O'Neal, SP	1

Kansas City (84-78)	WS
Hitting	**109.7**
Fielding	**46.8**
Pitching	**95.5**
D. Quisenberry, RP	24
W. Wilson, OF	23
B. Black, SP	20
F. White, 2B	18
P. Sheridan, OF	16
S. Balboni, 1B	14
G. Brett, 3B	14
D. Motley, OF	13
J. Orta, DH	13
M. Gubicza, SP	10
B. Saberhagen, RP	10
D. Slaught, C	10
C. Leibrandt, SP	9
J. Beckwith, RP	8
O. Concepcion, SS	8
H. McRae, DH	8
L. Gura, SP	5
G. Pryor, 3B	5
M. Huismann, RP	4
D. Iorg, 1B	4
D. Jackson, SP	3
B. Biancalana, SS	2
L. Jones, OF	2
M. Jones, SP	2
U. Washington, SS	2
J. Wathan, C	2
B. Davis, OF	1
L. Roberts, OF	1
F. Wills, SP-RP	1

Milwaukee (67-94)	WS
Hitting	**100.0**
Fielding	**31.9**
Pitching	**69.0**
R. Yount, SS	27
J. Gantner, 2B	16
J. Sundberg, C	15
C. Cooper, 1B	14
D. James, OF	11
B. Oglivie, OF	11
D. Sutton, SP	11
M. Haas, SP	9
R. Fingers, RP	8
R. Manning, OF	7
B. Schroeder, C	7
R. Searage, RP	7
T. Tellmann, RP	7
J. Cocanower, SP	6
E. Romero, 3B	6
C. Porter, SP	5
D. Loman, OF	4
W. Lozado, 3B	4
B. McClure, RP	4
R. Waits, RP	4
M. Brouhard, OF	3
M. Caldwell, SP	3
B. Clark, OF	2
R. Ready, 3B	2
J. Augustine, RP	1
B. Gibson, SP-RP	1
R. Howell, 3B	1
J. Kern, RP	1
P. Ladd, RP	1
J. Lazorko, RP	1
C. Moore, OF	1
T. Simmons, DH	1

Minnesota (81-81)	WS
Hitting	**92.4**
Fielding	**50.6**
Pitching	**99.9**
K. Hrbek, 1B	24
F. Viola, SP	22
T. Teufel, 2B	19
M. Smithson, SP	18
T. Brunansky, OF	17
J. Butcher, SP	17
G. Gaetti, 3B	16
M. Hatcher, OF	16
K. Puckett, OF	16
R. Davis, RP	9
P. Filson, RP	7
D. Engle, C	6
K. Schrom, SP	6
R. Washington, SS	6
D. Brown, OF	5
R. Bush, DH	5
T. Laudner, C	5
R. Lysander, RP	5
E. Hodge, SP	4
B. Castillo, RP	3
H. Jimenez, SS	3
L. Pashnick, RP	3
L. Whitehouse, RP	3
J. Castino, 3B	2
M. Walters, RP	2
A. David, OF	1
L. Faedo, SS	1
D. Meier, OF	1
A. Williams, SP	1

New York (87-75)	WS
Hitting	**137.0**
Fielding	**37.7**
Pitching	**86.2**
D. Mattingly, 1B	29
D. Winfield, OF	26
W. Randolph, 2B	21
D. Baylor, DH	16
D. Righetti, RP	16
P. Niekro, SP	15
B. Wynegar, C	15
J. Howell, RP	11
S. Kemp, OF	10
R. Fontenot, SP	9
K. Griffey Sr., OF	9
B. Meacham, SS	9
R. Guidry, SP	7
J. Cowley, SP	6
O. Moreno, OF	6
M. Pagliarulo, 3B	6
B. Shirley, RP	6
T. Harrah, 3B	5
D. Rasmussen, SP	5
M. Armstrong, RP	4
O. Gamble, DH	4
R. Smalley, 3B	4
M. Bystrom, SP	3
B. Dayett, OF	3
J. Montefusco, SP	3
R. Cerone, C	2
T. Foli, SS	2
V. Mata, OF	2
L. Piniella, OF	2
A. Robertson, SS	2
C. Brown, RP	1
M. O'Berry, C	1
J. Rijo, RP	1

Oakland (77-85)	WS
Hitting	**149.9**
Fielding	**28.8**
Pitching	**52.3**
R. Henderson, OF	28
C. Lansford, 3B	25
D. Murphy, OF	22
D. Kingman, DH	21
T. Phillips, SS	15
B. Caudill, RP	14
R. Burris, SP	12
M. Heath, C	12
J. Morgan, 2B	12
B. Bochte, 1B	10
D. Lopes, OF	9
M. Davis, OF	7
J. Essian, C	6
C. Young, SP	5
K. Atherton, RP	4
S. McCatty, SP	4
T. Burgmeier, RP	3
B. Krueger, SP	3
L. Sorensen, RP	3
M. Tettleton, C	3
B. Almon, OF	2
J. Burroughs, DH	2
D. Hill, SS	2
M. Wagner, SS	2
M. Warren, SP-RP	2
T. Conroy, RP	1
J. Jones, RP	1
D. Meyer, 1B	1

Seattle (74-88)	WS
Hitting	**103.9**
Fielding	**36.2**
Pitching	**81.9**
A. Davis, 1B	27
J. Perconte, 2B	20
M. Langston, SP	19
J. Beattie, SP	17
S. Owen, SS	14
K. Phelps, DH	13
A. Cowens, OF	11
D. Henderson, OF	11
P. Bradley, OF	9
E. Nunez, RP	8
S. Barojas, SP	7
B. Bonnell, OF	7
S. Henderson, OF	7
B. Kearney, C	7
M. Moore, SP	7
M. Stanton, RP	7
E. Vande Berg, RP	6
D. Geisel, RP	3
P. Mirabella, RP	3
J. Presley, 3B	3
L. Milbourne, 3B	2
J. Moses, OF	2
B. Stoddard, RP	2
D. Tartabull, SS	2
D. Beard, RP	1
K. Best, RP	1
O. Mercado, C	1
B. Nahorodny, C	1
D. Ramos, 3B	1
R. Thomas, RP	1
D. Valle, C	1
M. Young, SP	1

Texas (69-92)	WS
Hitting	**92.0**
Fielding	**38.6**
Pitching	**76.4**
B. Bell, 3B	26
G. Ward, OF	20
P. O'Brien, 1B	18
L. Parrish, OF	18
C. Hough, SP	15
F. Tanana, SP	15
D. Darwin, SP	11
M. Mason, SP	11
D. Schmidt, RP	9
M. Rivers, DH	7
B. Sample, OF	7
D. Stewart, SP	6
G. Wright, OF	6
A. Bannister, 2B	5
C. Wilkerson, SS	5
M. Foley, C	3
B. Jones, OF	3
O. Jones, RP	3
D. Scott, C	3
D. Tobik, RP	3
W. Tolleson, 2B	3
N. Yost, C	2
J. Anderson, SS	1
J. Bibby, RP	1
T. Dunbar, OF	1
D. Hostetler, 1B	1
J. Kunkel, SS	1
J. McLaughlin, RP	1
D. Noles, RP	1
B. Stein, 2B	1

Toronto (89-73)	WS
Hitting	**121.6**
Fielding	**48.0**
Pitching	**97.4**
L. Moseby, OF	26
D. Stieb, SP	25
D. Alexander, SP	23
G. Bell, OF	19
D. Collins, OF	17
W. Upshaw, 1B	17
D. Garcia, 2B	16
L. Leal, SP	14
C. Johnson, DH	13
R. Mulliniks, 3B	13
E. Whitt, C	12
J. Barfield, OF	11
R. Jackson, RP	9
J. Clancy, SP	7
J. Gott, RP	7
B. Martinez, C	7
T. Fernandez, SS	6
A. Griffin, SS	6
D. Lamp, RP	5
J. Acker, RP	3
J. Key, RP	3
W. Aikens, DH	2
G. Iorg, 3B	2
R. Musselman, RP	2
R. Leach, OF	1
J. McLaughlin, RP	1

1984 National League

Atlanta (80-82)	WS
Hitting	**93.2**
Fielding	**48.3**
Pitching	**98.5**
D. Murphy, OF	33
R. Mahler, SP	18
C. Washington, OF	17
G. Hubbard, 2B	15
S. Bedrosian, RP	12
P. Perez, SP	12
R. Camp, SP	10
C. Chambliss, 1B	10
G. Garber, RP	10
G. Perry, 1B	10
D. Moore, RP	9
R. Ramirez, SS	8
A. Trevino, C	8
B. Benedict, C	7
R. Johnson, 3B	7
L. Barker, SP	6
P. Falcone, RP	6
C. McMurtry, SP	6
J. Dedmon, RP	5
T. Forster, RP	4
B. Horner, 3B	4
M. Thompson, OF	4
A. Hall, OF	3
B. Komminsk, OF	3
J. Royster, 2B	3
P. Runge, 2B	3
K. Oberkfell, 3B	2
Z. Smith, SP	2
T. Harper, OF	1
R. Linares, OF	1
B. Watson, 1B	1

Chicago (96-65)	WS
Hitting	**141.0**
Fielding	**42.3**
Pitching	**104.6**
R. Sandberg, 2B	38
G. Matthews, OF	23
L. Durham, 1B	22
J. Davis, C	18
B. Dernier, OF	18
R. Cey, 3B	17
R. Sutcliffe, SP	16
L. Smith, RP	15
S. Trout, SP	14
D. Eckersley, SP	13
K. Moreland, OF	13
S. Sanderson, SP	11
T. Stoddard, RP	8
R. Bordi, RP	7
L. Bowa, SS	6
W. Brusstar, RP	6
G. Frazier, RP	5
M. Hall, OF	5
T. Bosley, OF	4
R. Hebner, 3B	4
H. Cotto, OF	3
C. Rainey, SP	3
R. Reuschel, SP	3
D. Ruthven, SP	3
G. Woods, OF	3
R. Hassey, C	2
J. Johnstone, OF	2
B. Johnson, RP	1
S. Lake, C	1
D. Lopes, OF	1
D. Noles, RP	1
D. Owen, SS	1
T. Veryzer, SS	1

Cincinnati (70-92)	WS
Hitting	**95.1**
Fielding	**38.7**
Pitching	**76.3**
M. Soto, SP	18
D. Parker, OF	17
T. Power, RP	14
G. Redus, OF	13
C. Cedeno, OF	11
D. Concepcion, SS	11
D. Walker, OF	11
E. Milner, OF	10
J. Franco, RP	9
J. Tibbs, SP	9
D. Driessen, 1B	8
R. Oester, 2B	8
E. Davis, OF	7
T. Foley, SS	7
W. Krenchicki, 3B	7
J. Price, SP	7
N. Esasky, 3B	6
B. Gulden, C	6
J. Russell, SP	6
B. Owchinko, RP	5
P. Rose, 1B	4
D. Bilardello, C	3
T. Browning, SP	3
R. Robinson, RP	3
D. Van Gorder, C	2
T. Lawless, 2B	1
T. Perez, 1B	1
B. Scherrer, RP	1
F. Toliver, RP	1
C. Willis, RP	1

Houston (80-82)	WS
Hitting	**130.8**
Fielding	**36.3**
Pitching	**72.9**
J. Cruz, OF	29
J. Mumphrey, OF	19
T. Puhl, OF	19
B. Doran, 2B	18
C. Reynolds, SS	16
P. Garner, 3B	14
B. Knepper, SP	13
J. Niekro, SP	13
E. Cabell, 1B	12
B. Dawley, RP	12
M. Bailey, C	9
N. Ryan, SP	9
D. Smith, RP	8
D. Walling, 3B	8
A. Ashby, C	6
K. Bass, OF	6
F. DiPino, RP	5
M. LaCoss, RP	5
J. Solano, RP	4
J. Sambito, RP	3
H. Spilman, 1B	3
R. Knight, 3B	2
J. Pankovits, 2B	2
J. Calhoun, RP	1
G. Davis, 1B	1
B. Pena, SS	1
M. Ross, RP	1
D. Thon, SS	1

Los Angeles (79-83)	WS
Hitting	**90.6**
Fielding	**41.9**
Pitching	**104.5**
P. Guerrero, 3B	23
O. Hershiser, RP	18
A. Pena, SP	18
F. Valenzuela, SP	18
M. Marshall, OF	15
M. Scioscia, C	15
R. Honeycutt, SP	13
D. Anderson, SS	12
S. Sax, 2B	11
K. Landreaux, OF	10
B. Welch, SP	9
G. Brock, 1B	8
B. Hooton, RP	7
T. Niedenfuer, RP	7
B. Russell, SS	7
K. Howell, RP	6
C. Maldonado, OF	6
G. Rivera, 3B	5
S. Yeager, C	5
P. Zachry, RP	5
J. Reuss, SP-RP	4
R. Reynolds, OF	4
B. Bailor, 2B	3
F. Stubbs, 1B	3
T. Whitfield, OF	3
R. Monday, 1B	1
L. White, RP	1

Montreal (78-83)	WS
Hitting	**102.4**
Fielding	**44.9**
Pitching	**86.8**
T. Raines, OF	32
G. Carter, C	30
T. Wallach, 3B	18
C. Lea, SP	15
A. Dawson, OF	12
J. Reardon, RP	12
D. Schatzeder, RP	12
B. Gullickson, SP	10
B. Smith, SP	10
T. Francona, 1B	8
J. Wohlford, OF	8
M. Dilone, OF	6
B. Little, 2B	6
D. Driessen, 1B	5
B. James, RP	5
D. Palmer, SP	5
D. Flynn, 2B	4
J. Hesketh, RP	4
G. Lucas, RP	4
A. McGaffigan, RP	4
P. Rose, 1B	4
D. Thomas, SS	4
D. Grapenthin, RP	2
G. Harris, RP	2
B. Ramos, C	2
S. Rogers, SP	2
A. Salazar, SS	2
M. Stenhouse, OF	2
F. Breining, RP	1
M. Ramsey, SS	1
T. Scott, OF	1
M. Venable, OF	1

New York (90-72)	WS
Hitting	**139.1**
Fielding	**43.2**
Pitching	**87.7**
K. Hernandez, 1B	33
D. Strawberry, OF	24
M. Wilson, OF	23
H. Brooks, 3B	21
G. Foster, OF	18
D. Gooden, SP	18
W. Backman, 2B	17
J. Orosco, RP	17
W. Terrell, SP	10
R. Darling, SP	9
D. Sisk, RP	9
K. Chapman, 2B	8
M. Fitzgerald, C	8
B. Berenyi, SP	6
S. Fernandez, SP	5
T. Gorman, RP	5
R. Santana, SS	5
B. Gaff, RP	4
R. Gardenhire, SS	4
D. Heep, OF	4
R. Hodges, C	4
J. Oquendo, SS	4
R. Knight, 3B	3
T. Leary, RP	3
E. Lynch, RP	3
H. Winningham, OF	2
J. Ortiz, C	1
R. Staub, 1B	1
J. Stearns, C	1

Philadelphia (81-81)	WS
Hitting	**129.5**
Fielding	**33.4**
Pitching	**80.1**
M. Schmidt, 3B	26
V. Hayes, OF	21
J. Samuel, 2B	19
O. Virgil, C	14
S. Carlton, SP	12
J. Denny, SP	12
A. Holland, RP	12
J. Koosman, SP	12
T. Corcoran, 1B	10
S. Lezcano, OF	9
L. Matuszek, 1B	9
L. Andersen, RP	8
I. DeJesus, SS	8
J. Stone, OF	8
G. Gross, OF	7
G. Maddox, OF	6
S. Rawley, SP	6
J. Wockenfuss, 1B	6
K. Gross, RP	5
C. Hudson, SP	5
B. Campbell, RP	4
G. Wilson, OF	4
L. Aguayo, 3B	3
J. Lefebvre, OF	3
J. Russell, OF	3
T. McGraw, RP	2
A. Oliver, 1B	2
R. Schu, 3B	2
M. Bystrom, SP	1
B. Diaz, C	1
S. Fireovid, RP	1
K. Garcia, SS	1
S. Jeltz, SS	1

Pittsburgh (75-87)	WS
Hitting	**86.4**
Fielding	**44.7**
Pitching	**93.9**
T. Pena, C	21
J. Ray, 2B	20
R. Rhoden, SP	20
L. Lacy, OF	18
L. McWilliams, SP	14
J. Thompson, 1B	14
J. Tudor, SP	13
J. Candelaria, SP	12
M. Wynne, OF	12
D. Robinson, RP	11
J. Morrison, 3B	9
D. Berra, SS	8
K. Tekulve, RP	8
J. DeLeon, SP	7
B. Madlock, 3B	6
L. Mazzilli, OF	6
D. Frobel, OF	5
R. Scurry, RP	5
C. Guante, RP	4
B. Harper, OF	2
M. Bielecki, RP	1
D. Gonzalez, 3B	1
M. May, C	1
J. Orsulak, OF	1
A. Otis, OF	1
M. Page, PH-PR	1
B. Walk, SP	1
J. Winn, RP	1
R. Wotus, SS	1
J. Zaske, RP	1

San Diego (92-70)	WS
Hitting	**139.8**
Fielding	**46.7**
Pitching	**89.5**
T. Gwynn, OF	35
K. McReynolds, OF	25
A. Wiggins, 2B	23
C. Martinez, OF	21
G. Nettles, 3B	16
G. Templeton, SS	16
S. Garvey, 1B	15
G. Gossage, RP	15
D. Dravecky, RP	12

T. Kennedy, C	12
C. Lefferts, RP	12
E. Show, SP	12
M. Thurmond, SP	12
E. Whitson, SP	11
T. Lollar, SP	10
T. Flannery, 2B	6
B. Brown, OF	5
L. Salazar, 3B	4
B. Bochy, C	3
G. Booker, RP	3
G. Harris, RP	3
K. Bevacqua, 1B	1
A. Hawkins, SP	1
E. Miller, OF	1
M. Ramirez, SS	1
R. Roenicke, OF	1

San Francisco (66-96)	WS
Hitting	**131.7**
Fielding	**26.5**
Pitching	**39.8**
C. Davis, OF	21
B. Brenly, C	20
J. Leonard, OF	20
D. Gladden, OF	17
J. Clark, OF	12
D. Baker, OF	9
M. Trillo, 2B	9
J. Youngblood, 3B	9
G. Lavelle, RP	8
J. LeMaster, SS	8
S. Thompson, 1B	7
G. Minton, RP	6
A. Oliver, 1B	6
F. Williams, RP	6
B. Laskey, SP	5
S. Nicosia, C	5
M. Krukow, SP	4
B. Wellman, 2B	4
R. Lerch, RP	3
J. Robinson, SP	3
C. Brown, 3B	2
A. Hammaker, SP	2
B. Lacey, RP	2
F. Mullins, 3B-SS	2
G. Richards, OF	2
M. Davis, SP	1
R. Deer, OF	1
D. Kuiper, 2B	1
R. Martin, RP	1
J. Rabb, 1B	1
G. Riley, SP	1

St. Louis (84-78)	WS
Hitting	**121.3**
Fielding	**43.5**
Pitching	**87.2**
B. Sutter, RP	23
T. Herr, 2B	20
W. McGee, OF	20
O. Smith, SS	19
J. Andujar, SP	17
L. Smith, OF	16
D. Porter, C	14
A. Van Slyke, OF	14
G. Hendrick, OF	12
D. Green, 1B	11
T. Pendleton, 3B	11
N. Allen, RP	8
R. Horton, RP	7
D. LaPoint, SP	7
K. Oberkfell, 3B	7
K. Kepshire, SP	6
D. Rucker, RP	6
D. Cox, SP	5
J. Lahti, RP	5
S. Braun, OF	4
T. Landrum, OF	3
T. Nieto, C	3
D. Von Ohlen, RP	3
A. Howe, 3B	2
M. Jorgensen, 1B	2
B. Lyons, 2B	2
C. Speier, SS	2
G. Brummer, C	1
R. Citarella, RP	1
K. Hagen, RP	1

1985
American League

Baltimore (83-78)	WS
Hitting	**143.3**
Fielding	**34.5**
Pitching	**71.2**
E. Murray, 1B	28
C. Ripken Jr., SS	25
M. Young, OF	17
F. Lynn, OF	16
R. Dempsey, C	14
L. Lacy, OF	14
F. Rayford, 3B	14
M. Boddicker, SP	10
K. Dixon, SP	10
D. Aase, RP	9
W. Gross, 3B	9
S. Stewart, RP	9
S. Davis, SP	8
G. Roenicke, OF	8
N. Snell, RP	8
A. Wiggins, 2B	8
J. Dwyer, OF	7
S. McGregor, SP	7
L. Sheets, DH	7
D. Martinez, SP	5
J. Shelby, OF	5
F. Connally, 3B	3
M. Flanagan, SP	3
T. Martinez, RP	2
R. Dauer, 2B	1
A. Pardo, C	1
L. Sakata, 2B	1

Boston (81-81)	WS
Hitting	**118.6**
Fielding	**36.8**
Pitching	**87.6**
W. Boggs, 3B	31
D. Evans, OF	21
R. Gedman, C	20
O. Boyd, SP	17
B. Buckner, 1B	16
J. Rice, OF	14
M. Barrett, 2B	13
B. Hurst, SP	10
B. Stanley, RP	10
T. Armas, OF	9
M. Easler, DH	9
B. Ojeda, SP	9
R. Clemens, SP	8
G. Hoffman, SS	8
A. Nipper, SP	8
S. Crawford, RP	7
S. Lyons, OF	7
B. Kison, RP	5
M. Clear, RP	3
T. Lollar, SP	3
R. Woodward, RP	3
M. Greenwell, OF	2
J. Gutierrez, SS	2
J. Sellers, SP	2
M. Trujillo, RP	2
R. Miller, OF	1
D. Sax, C	1
D. Stapleton, 2B	1
M. Sullivan, C	1

California (90-72)	WS
Hitting	**122.8**
Fielding	**49.8**
Pitching	**97.4**
B. Downing, OF	21
D. Moore, RP	20
B. Grich, 2B	18
R. Jackson, OF	18
G. Pettis, OF	16
M. Witt, SP	16
R. Jones, OF	14
J. Beniquez, OF	13
S. Cliburn, RP	13
B. Boone, C	12
R. Carew, 1B	12
D. DeCinces, 3B	12
D. Schofield, SS	12
R. Romanick, SP	10
K. McCaskill, SP	7
P. Clements, RP	6
J. Slaton, SP	6
J. Candelaria, SP	5
U. Lugo, SP-RP	5
J. Narron, C	4
D. Sconiers, DH	4
R. Wilfong, 2B	4
M. Brown, OF	3
A. Holland, RP	3
D. Miller, OF	3
C. Gerber, SS	2
J. Howell, 3B	2
D. Sutton, SP	2
G. Zahn, SP	2
D. Corbett, RP	1
T. John, SP-RP	1
P. Keedy, 3B	1
R. Linares, DH	1
L. Sanchez, RP	1

Chicago (85-77)	WS
Hitting	**112.5**
Fielding	**47.0**
Pitching	**95.5**
H. Baines, OF	25
C. Fisk, C	24
B. James, RP	22
T. Seaver, SP	18
G. Walker, 1B	17
B. Burns, SP	15
O. Guillen, SS	15
T. Hulett, 3B	11
R. Law, OF	11
R. Kittle, DH-OF	9
G. Nelson, RP	8
F. Bannister, SP	7
S. Fletcher, 3B	7
B. Little, 2B	7
L. Salazar, OF	7
D. Spillner, RP	7
J. Agosto, RP	4
D. Boston, OF	4
J. Cruz, 2B	4
J. Davis, SP	4
O. Gamble, DH	4
J. Hairston, DH	4
R. Nichols, OF	4
T. Lollar, SP	3
J. Skinner, C	3
D. Wehrmeister, RP	3
R. Dotson, SP	2
M. Gilbert, OF	1
J. Gleaton, RP	1
M. Hill, C	1
A. Jones, RP	1
T. Paciorek, OF	1
B. Tanner, RP	1

Cleveland (60-102)	WS
Hitting	**106.3**
Fielding	**26.5**
Pitching	**47.2**
B. Butler, OF	23
T. Bernazard, 2B	17
J. Franco, SS	16
B. Jacoby, 3B	16
B. Blyleven, SP	12
J. Carter, OF	11
J. Willard, C	10
M. Hargrove, 1B	8
A. Thornton, DH	8
N. Heaton, SP	7
P. Tabler, 1B	6
G. Vukovich, OF	6
T. Waddell, RP	6
J. Easterly, RP	5
J. Reed, RP	5
V. Ruhle, RP	5
C. Castillo, OF	4
D. Von Ohlen, RP	3
C. Bando, C	2
K. Creel, SP	2
M. Hall, OF	2
B. Ayala, OF	1
J. Barkley, RP	1
M. Fischlin, 2B	1
M. Jeffcoat, RP	1
O. Nixon, OF	1
R. Smith, SP	1

Detroit (84-77)	WS
Hitting	**110.0**
Fielding	**43.5**
Pitching	**98.5**
K. Gibson, OF	24
L. Whitaker, 2B	24
L. Parrish, C	20
W. Hernandez, RP	19
J. Morris, SP	19
D. Evans, 1B	18
C. Lemon, OF	18
D. Petry, SP	17
A. Trammell, SS	16
W. Terrell, SP	14
F. Tanana, SP	10
T. Brookens, 3B	9
L. Herndon, OF	8
R. O'Neal, RP	7
N. Simmons, OF	4
B. Garbey, 1B	3
J. Grubb, DH	3
A. Lopez, RP	3
B. Scherrer, RP	3
C. Cary, RP	2
M. Castillo, C	2
M. Mahler, SP	2
B. Melvin, C	2
J. Berenguer, RP	1
D. Flynn, 2B	1
C. Pittaro, 3B	1
A. Sanchez, OF	1
M. Wilcox, SP	1

Kansas City (91-71)	WS
Hitting	**102.0**
Fielding	**48.6**
Pitching	**122.4**
G. Brett, 3B	37
C. Leibrandt, SP	24
B. Saberhagen, SP	24
D. Quisenberry, RP	23
W. Wilson, OF	19
S. Balboni, 1B	16
D. Jackson, SP	16
F. White, 2B	16
M. Gubicza, SP	12
L. Smith, OF	12
J. Sundberg, C	11
B. Black, SP	10
H. McRae, DH	8
J. Beckwith, RP	5
O. Concepcion, SS	5
J. Orta, DH	5
J. Wathan, C	5
D. Motley, OF	4
P. Sheridan, OF	4
B. Biancalana, SS	3
S. Farr, RP	3
M. Huismann, RP	2
M. Jones, RP	2
J. Quirk, C	2
D. Iorg, OF	1
L. Jones, OF	1
M. LaCoss, RP	1

O. Moreno, OF	1
G. Pryor, 3B	1

Milwaukee (71-90)	WS
Hitting	**102.1**
Fielding	**37.3**
Pitching	**73.5**
P. Molitor, 3B	21
C. Cooper, 1B	17
R. Yount, OF	16
T. Higuera, SP	14
E. Riles, SS	13
T. Simmons, DH	13
D. Darwin, SP	12
B. Oglivie, OF	12
J. Gantner, 2B	11
M. Haas, SP	9
P. Householder, OF	9
B. Gibson, RP	8
R. Burris, SP	7
E. Romero, SS	7
J. Cocanower, SP	5
B. McClure, RP	5
C. Moore, C	5
R. Fingers, RP	4
R. Ready, OF	4
B. Schroeder, C	4
M. Brouhard, OF	2
P. Ladd, RP	2
R. Manning, OF	2
B. Robidoux, OF	2
P. Vuckovich, SP	2
B. Wegman, SP	2
B. Clark, OF	1
B. Giles, SS	1
T. Leary, SP	1
D. Loman, OF	1
C. Porter, RP	1

Minnesota (77-85)	WS
Hitting	**105.7**
Fielding	**40.3**
Pitching	**85.0**
K. Hrbek, 1B	19
K. Puckett, OF	19
T. Brunansky, OF	16
F. Viola, SP	16
G. Gaetti, 3B	15
M. Smithson, SP	15
M. Salas, C	13
R. Smalley, DH	12
B. Blyleven, SP	11
T. Teufel, 2B	11
R. Davis, RP	10
J. Butcher, SP	8
P. Filson, RP	8
M. Hatcher, OF	7
K. Schrom, SP	7
R. Bush, OF	6
F. Eufemia, RP	6
D. Engle, DH	5
G. Gagne, SS	4
T. Laudner, C	4
S. Lombardozzi, 2B	3
M. Stenhouse, DH	3
R. Washington, SS	3
D. Burtt, RP	2
M. Funderburk, DH	2
D. Meier, OF	2
A. Espinoza, SS	1
R. Lysander, RP	1
M. Portugal, SP	1
C. Wardle, RP	1

New York (97-64)	WS
Hitting	**154.7**
Fielding	**44.5**
Pitching	**91.9**
R. Henderson, OF	38
D. Mattingly, 1B	32
D. Winfield, OF	21
W. Randolph, 2B	20
R. Guidry, SP	18
D. Righetti, RP	15
K. Griffey Sr., OF	14
R. Hassey, C	13
M. Pagliarulo, 3B	13
D. Baylor, DH	12
B. Fisher, RP	12
B. Meacham, SS	11
P. Niekro, SP	10
B. Wynegar, C	10
J. Cowley, SP	9
B. Shirley, RP	9
R. Bordi, RP	6
D. Pasqua, OF	4
D. Rasmussen, SP	4
A. Robertson, 3B	4
E. Whitson, SP	4
B. Sample, OF	3
N. Allen, RP	2
H. Cotto, OF	2
M. Armstrong, RP	1
D. Berra, 3B	1
R. Hudler, 2B	1
O. Moreno, OF	1
R. Scurry, RP	1

Oakland (77-85)	WS
Hitting	**137.4**
Fielding	**33.0**
Pitching	**60.6**
M. Davis, OF	23
D. Murphy, OF	18
B. Bochte, 1B	17
A. Griffin, SS	16
D. Baker, 1B	13
M. Heath, C	13
D. Kingman, DH	13
J. Howell, RP	12
C. Lansford, 3B	12
D. Hill, 2B	9
S. Ontiveros, RP	9
D. Sutton, SP	9
D. Collins, OF	8
C. Codiroli, SP	7
T. Phillips, 3B	7
M. Tettleton, C	7
T. Birtsas, SP	6
S. Henderson, OF	6
K. Atherton, RP	4
J. Canseco, OF	4
B. Krueger, SP	4
J. Rijo, SP	4
R. Langford, RP	3
M. Gallego, 2B	2
S. Mura, RP	2
S. McCatty, RP	1
C. O'Brien, C	1
R. Picciolo, 3B	1

Seattle (74-88)	WS
Hitting	**120.7**
Fielding	**31.9**
Pitching	**69.4**
P. Bradley, OF	26
A. Davis, 1B	22
M. Moore, SP	19
J. Presley, 3B	17
J. Perconte, 2B	13
G. Thomas, DH	13
E. Nunez, RP	12
D. Henderson, OF	11
S. Owen, SS	11
A. Cowens, OF	10
R. Thomas, RP	8
I. Calderon, OF	7
B. Kearney, C	7
M. Young, SP	7
K. Best, RP	5
E. Vande Berg, RP	5
K. Phelps, DH	4
D. Scott, C	4
B. Swift, SP	4
D. Tartabull, SS	3
D. Coles, SS	2
M. Langston, SP	2
B. Long, RP	2
B. Bonnell, OF	1
J. Lazorko, RP	1
P. Mirabella, RP	1
D. Ramos, SS	1
H. Reynolds, 2B	1
M. Stanton, RP	1
D. Valle, C	1
F. Wills, SP	1

Texas (62-99)	WS
Hitting	**60.5**
Fielding	**39.2**
Pitching	**86.3**
C. Hough, SP	21
T. Harrah, 2B	17
G. Harris, RP	16
P. O'Brien, 1B	13
G. Ward, OF	12
O. McDowell, OF	10
D. Schmidt, RP	9
D. Slaught, C	8
W. Tolleson, SS	8
M. Mason, SP	7
D. Rozema, RP	7
B. Bell, 3B	5
B. Hooton, SP	5
C. Johnson, DH	5
L. Parrish, OF	5
D. Noles, RP	4
C. Welsh, RP	4
C. Wilkerson, SS	4
S. Buechele, 3B	3
J. Guzman, SP	3
D. Henry, RP	3
M. Williams, SP-RP	3
A. Bannister, DH	2
G. Brummer, C	2
G. Petralli, C	2
D. Stewart, RP	2
G. Wright, OF	2
B. Jones, OF	1
B. Stein, 3B	1
F. Tanana, SP	1
D. Walker, OF	1

Toronto (99-62)	WS
Hitting	**120.5**
Fielding	**52.1**
Pitching	**124.3**
J. Barfield, OF	26
D. Stieb, SP	24
G. Bell, OF	21
T. Fernandez, SS	21
L. Moseby, OF	21
D. Alexander, SP	20
J. Key, SP	19
R. Mulliniks, 3B	15
E. Whitt, C	15
W. Upshaw, 1B	14
D. Garcia, 2B	13
G. Iorg, 3B	11
D. Lamp, RP	10
J. Acker, RP	9
B. Caudill, RP	9
J. Clancy, SP	9
T. Henke, RP	9
G. Lavelle, RP	8
J. Burroughs, DH	5
T. Filer, SP	4
C. Fielder, 1B	3
R. Musselman, RP	3
S. Davis, SP-RP	2
B. Martinez, C	2
C. Johnson, DH	1
M. Lee, 2B	1
A. Oliver, DH	1
L. Thornton, OF	1

1985 National League

Atlanta (66-96)	WS
Hitting	**92.3**
Fielding	**36.3**
Pitching	**69.4**
D. Murphy, OF	31
R. Mahler, SP	17
B. Horner, 1B	16
G. Hubbard, 2B	14
K. Oberkfell, 3B	12
C. Washington, OF	12
T. Harper, OF	11
S. Bedrosian, SP	10
Z. Smith, RP	8
B. Sutter, RP	8
G. Garber, RP	7
R. Camp, RP	6
R. Ramirez, SS	6
T. Forster, RP	5
B. Komminsk, OF	5
P. Zuvella, 2B	5
J. Dedmon, RP	4
J. Johnson, SP	4
M. Thompson, OF	4
R. Cerone, C	3
B. Benedict, C	2
C. Chambliss, 1B	2
L. Owen, C	2
P. Runge, 3B	2
G. Perry, 1B	1
S. Shields, RP	1

Chicago (77-84)	WS
Hitting	**105.0**
Fielding	**40.0**
Pitching	**86.0**
R. Sandberg, 2B	28
K. Moreland, OF	19
L. Durham, 1B	18
L. Smith, RP	17
D. Eckersley, SP	15
J. Davis, C	13
D. Lopes, OF	11
R. Sutcliffe, SP	11
R. Cey, 3B	10
S. Trout, SP	10
B. Dernier, OF	9
S. Sanderson, SP	9
T. Bosley, OF	8
S. Dunston, SS	8
G. Matthews, OF	8
R. Fontenot, SP	6
J. Baller, RP	4
L. Bowa, SS	4
R. Patterson, SP	4
R. Meridith, RP	3
D. Ruthven, SP	3
L. Sorensen, RP	3
C. Speier, SS	3
S. Lake, C	2
D. Botelho, SP	1
D. Gumpert, RP	1
B. Hatcher, OF	1
D. Owen, 3B-SS	1
G. Woods, OF	1

Cincinnati (89-72)	WS
Hitting	**122.6**
Fielding	**48.7**
Pitching	**95.7**
D. Parker, OF	29
R. Oester, 2B	21
T. Browning, SP	18
E. Milner, OF	17
J. Franco, RP	16
N. Esasky, 3B	15
T. Power, RP	14
P. Rose, 1B	14
M. Soto, SP	14
D. Concepcion, SS	12
G. Redus, OF	12
J. Tibbs, SP	9
T. Perez, 1B	8
W. Krenchicki, 3B	7
T. Hume, RP	6
B. Bell, 3B	5

E. Davis, OF 5
B. Diaz, C 5
A. Knicely, C 5
A. McGaffigan, SP 5
R. Robinson, RP 5
M. Venable, OF 5
C. Cedeno, OF 4
F. Pastore, RP 3
J. Price, RP 3
J. Stuper, RP 3
D. Bilardello, C 2
D. Van Gorder, C 2
T. Foley, 2B 1
P. O'Neill, OF 1
D. Walker, OF 1

Houston (83-79)	WS
Hitting	**147.6**
Fielding	**34.3**
Pitching	**67.1**
B. Doran, 2B	28
J. Cruz, OF	21
K. Bass, OF	19
M. Bailey, C	14
P. Garner, 3B	14
J. Mumphrey, OF	14
C. Reynolds, SS	14
G. Davis, 1B	13
D. Smith, RP	13
M. Scott, SP	12
D. Walling, 3B	10
B. Knepper, SP	9
D. Thon, SS	9
A. Ashby, C	8
J. Niekro, SP	8
T. Puhl, OF	8
N. Ryan, SP	7
J. Calhoun, RP	5
B. Dawley, RP	4
J. Pankovits, OF	4
E. Cabell, 1B	3
J. Heathcock, SP-RP	3
F. DiPino, RP	2
C. Kerfeld, SP	2
J. Solano, RP	2
E. Bullock, OF	1
B. Pena, 3B	1
G. Rivera, 3B	1

Los Angeles (95-67)	WS
Hitting	**141.1**
Fielding	**41.7**
Pitching	**102.2**
P. Guerrero, OF	35
M. Scioscia, C	26
O. Hershiser, SP	23
M. Marshall, OF	23
F. Valenzuela, SP	21
G. Brock, 1B	15
K. Landreaux, OF	15
B. Welch, SP	15
M. Duncan, SS	13
T. Niedenfuer, RP	13
J. Reuss, SP	13
S. Sax, 2B	12
E. Cabell, 3B	7
B. Madlock, 3B	7
C. Diaz, RP	6
K. Howell, RP	6
D. Anderson, 3B	5
R. Honeycutt, SP	5
C. Maldonado, OF	5
R. Reynolds, OF	5
B. Russell, SS	4
T. Whitfield, OF	3
B. Bailor, 3B	2
L. Matuszek, OF	2
S. Yeager, C	2
A. Oliver, OF	1
G. Reyes, C	1

Montreal (84-77)	WS
Hitting	**121.7**
Fielding	**41.4**
Pitching	**88.9**
T. Raines, OF	36
V. Law, 2B	24
T. Wallach, 3B	23
A. Dawson, OF	16
B. Smith, SP	16
H. Brooks, SS	15
T. Burke, RP	13
J. Reardon, RP	13
J. Hesketh, SP	11
B. Gullickson, SP	9
M. Webster, OF	9
D. Driessen, 1B	8
H. Winningham, OF	7
M. Fitzgerald, C	6
T. Francona, 1B	6
D. Palmer, SP	5
U. Washington, 2B	5
F. Youmans, SP	5
G. Lucas, RP	4
B. Roberge, RP	4
D. Schatzeder, SP	4
S. Butera, C	3
R. St. Claire, RP	3
M. Mahler, SP	2
F. Manrique, 2B-SS	1
S. Nicosia, C	1
M. O'Berry, C	1
S. Thompson, 1B-OF	1
J. Wohlford, OF	1

New York (98-64)	WS
Hitting	**136.2**
Fielding	**49.6**
Pitching	**108.2**
G. Carter, C	33
D. Gooden, SP	33
K. Hernandez, 1B	27
D. Strawberry, OF	24
W. Backman, 2B	17
R. Darling, SP	17
G. Foster, OF	17
R. McDowell, RP	13
S. Fernandez, SP	12
M. Wilson, OF	12
H. Johnson, 3B	11
R. Santana, SS	11
E. Lynch, SP	10
J. Orosco, RP	10
D. Heep, OF	9
R. Aguilera, SP	8
L. Dykstra, OF	8
T. Leach, RP	4
T. Paciorek, OF	3
K. Chapman, 2B	2
J. Christensen, OF	2
C. Hurdle, C	2
R. Knight, 3B	2
R. Staub, OF	2
B. Berenyi, SP	1
R. Gardenhire, SS	1
B. Latham, RP	1
R. Niemann, RP	1
R. Reynolds, C	1

Philadelphia (75-87)	WS
Hitting	**107.1**
Fielding	**37.9**
Pitching	**80.0**
M. Schmidt, 1B	26
J. Samuel, 2B	21
V. Hayes, OF	19
O. Virgil, C	16
G. Wilson, OF	15
K. Gross, SP	13
S. Rawley, SP	13
D. Carman, RP	12
J. Denny, SP	10
R. Schu, 3B	9
L. Aguayo, SS	8
C. Hudson, SP	8
K. Tekulve, RP	8
G. Gross, OF	5
S. Carlton, SP	4
D. Daulton, C	4
T. Foley, SS	4
J. Russell, OF	4
J. Stone, OF	4
L. Andersen, RP	3
J. Koosman, SP	3
G. Maddox, OF	3
D. Rucker, RP	3
D. Shipanoff, RP	3
T. Corcoran, 1B	2
S. Jeltz, SS	2
D. Thomas, SS	2
B. Diaz, C	1

Pittsburgh (57-104)	WS
Hitting	**70.6**
Fielding	**31.5**
Pitching	**69.0**
R. Reuschel, SP	20
T. Pena, C	11
J. Ray, 2B	11
J. Thompson, 1B	11
C. Guante, RP	10
J. Orsulak, OF	9
M. Brown, OF	8
B. Madlock, 3B	7
B. Almon, SS	6
S. Khalifa, SS	6
R. Rhoden, SP	6
J. Candelaria, RP	5
A. Holland, RP	5
D. Robinson, RP	5
S. Kemp, OF	4
L. Mazzilli, 1B	4
R. Reynolds, OF	4
L. Tunnell, SP	4
S. Lezcano, OF	3
L. McWilliams, SP	3
J. Morrison, 3B	3
R. Scurry, RP	3
B. Walk, SP	3
M. Wynne, OF	3
S. Bream, 1B	2
P. Clements, RP	2
J. DeLeon, SP	2
G. Hendrick, OF	2
J. Ortiz, C	2
M. Bielecki, SP	1
T. Foli, SS	1
D. Frobel, OF	1
D. Gonzalez, 3B	1
J. LeMaster, SS	1
S. Loucks, OF	1
J. Winn, RP	1

San Diego (83-79)	WS
Hitting	**114.3**
Fielding	**43.0**
Pitching	**91.7**
G. Templeton, SS	21
T. Gwynn, OF	20
C. Martinez, OF	19
S. Garvey, 1B	17
G. Nettles, 3B	17
T. Flannery, 2B	15
G. Gossage, RP	15
A. Hawkins, SP	15
D. Dravecky, SP	14
T. Kennedy, C	14
E. Show, SP	13
L. Hoyt, SP	12
K. McReynolds, OF	12
J. Royster, 2B	10
C. Lefferts, RP	6
M. Thurmond, SP	5
K. Bevacqua, 3B	4
B. Bochy, C	4
R. Jackson, RP	4
L. McCullers, RP	3
G. Walter, RP	3
M. Ramirez, SS	2
G. Davis, OF	1
L. DeLeon, RP	1
M. Dilone, OF	1
T. Stoddard, RP	1

San Francisco (62-100)	WS
Hitting	**83.0**
Fielding	**33.1**
Pitching	**69.9**
C. Brown, 3B	16
C. Davis, OF	16
S. Garrelts, RP	13
B. Brenly, C	12
M. Krukow, SP	11
D. Gladden, OF	10
J. Uribe, SS	10
D. LaPoint, SP	8
J. Leonard, OF	8
M. Trillo, 2B	8
M. Davis, RP	7
R. Roenicke, OF	7
J. Gott, SP	6
A. Hammaker, SP	6
G. Minton, RP	6
J. Youngblood, OF	6
B. Laskey, SP	5
V. Blue, SP	4
D. Green, 1B	4
A. Trevino, C	4
R. Deer, OF	3
D. Driessen, 1B	3
B. Wellman, 2B	3
R. Mason, SP	2
F. Williams, RP	2
M. Woodard, 2B	2
R. Adams, SS	1
D. Kuiper, PH-PR	1
B. Moore, RP	1
G. Rajsich, 1B	1

St. Louis (101-61)	WS
Hitting	**155.4**
Fielding	**47.0**
Pitching	**100.6**
W. McGee, OF	36
T. Herr, 2B	30
J. Tudor, SP	27
O. Smith, SS	25
J. Clark, 1B	22
V. Coleman, OF	20
A. Van Slyke, OF	18
D. Cox, SP	16
J. Andujar, SP	14
J. Lahti, RP	11
D. Porter, C	11
T. Pendleton, 3B	10
C. Cedeno, 1B	7
K. Dayley, RP	7
B. Forsch, SP	7
R. Horton, RP	6
T. Landrum, OF	6
T. Nieto, C	5
B. Campbell, RP	4
M. Jorgensen, 1B	3
L. Smith, OF	3
T. Worrell, RP	3
S. Braun, OF	2
C. Ford, OF	2
K. Kepshire, SP	2
P. Perry, RP	2
I. DeJesus, 3B	1
B. Harper, OF	1
M. LaValliere, C	1
T. Lawless, 3B	1

1986
American League

Baltimore (73-89)	WS
Hitting	**105.5**
Fielding	**36.3**
Pitching	**77.1**
C. Ripken Jr., SS	28
E. Murray, 1B	20

D. Aase, RP	14
F. Lynn, OF	14
L. Lacy, OF	11
J. Beniquez, OF	10
S. Davis, SP	10
M. Boddicker, SP	9
R. Dempsey, C	9
K. Dixon, SP	9
S. McGregor, SP	9
M. Flanagan, SP	8
L. Sheets, DH	8
M. Young, OF	8
R. Bordi, RP	6
J. Traber, 1B	6
J. Dwyer, DH-OF	5
J. Shelby, OF	5
N. Snell, RP	4
A. Wiggins, 2B	4
J. Bonilla, 2B	3
B. Havens, RP	3
O. Jones, RP	3
T. O'Malley, 3B	3
J. Stefero, C	3
F. Rayford, 3B	2
T. Arnold, RP	1
E. Bell, SP	1
J. Gutierrez, 2B	1
J. Habyan, SP	1
R. Jones, 2B	1

Boston (95-66)	WS
Hitting	**138.6**
Fielding	**45.5**
Pitching	**100.9**
W. Boggs, 3B	37
R. Clemens, SP	29
J. Rice, OF	28
D. Evans, OF	24
M. Barrett, 2B	22
R. Gedman, C	18
D. Baylor, DH	16
B. Hurst, SP	16
O. Boyd, SP	15
B. Buckner, 1B	13
C. Schiraldi, RP	10
T. Armas, OF	9
T. Seaver, SP	7
B. Stanley, RP	6
R. Quinones, SS	4
S. Stewart, RP	4
S. Crawford, RP	3
A. Nipper, SP	3
J. Sambito, RP	3
M. Brown, SP	2
P. Dodson, 1B	2
S. Lyons, OF	2
E. Romero, SS	2
J. Sellers, SP	2
M. Sullivan, C	2
M. Greenwell, OF	1
D. Henderson, OF	1
S. Owen, SS	1
K. Romine, OF	1
D. Sax, C	1
R. Woodward, SP	1

California (92-70)	WS
Hitting	**134.8**
Fielding	**42.9**
Pitching	**98.2**
B. Downing, OF	23
M. Witt, SP	23
W. Joyner, 1B	21
K. McCaskill, SP	18
G. Pettis, OF	18
D. Schofield, SS	18
D. DeCinces, 3B	16
R. Jackson, DH	13
R. Jones, OF	13
D. Sutton, SP	13
B. Grich, 2B	11
D. Moore, RP	11
B. Boone, C	10
R. Burleson, DH	9
J. Candelaria, SP	9
G. Hendrick, OF	9
D. Corbett, RP	7
J. Howell, 3B	6
C. Finley, RP	4
T. Forster, RP	4
G. Lucas, RP	4
R. Wilfong, 2B	4
J. Narron, C	2
R. Romanick, SP	2
V. Ruhle, RP	2
M. Ryal, OF	2
D. White, OF	2
T. Fischer, RP	1
U. Lugo, SP-RP	1

Chicago (72-90)	WS
Hitting	**74.9**
Fielding	**46.0**
Pitching	**95.2**
H. Baines, OF	20
F. Bannister, SP	11
J. Cangelosi, OF	11
J. Cowley, SP	10
G. Walker, 1B	10
O. Guillen, SS	9
G. Nelson, RP	9
N. Allen, SP	8
T. Hulett, 3B	8
D. Schmidt, RP	8
B. Bonilla, OF	7
D. Boston, OF	7
B. Dawley, RP	7
J. DeLeon, SP	7
R. Hassey, DH	7
B. Thigpen, RP	7
C. Fisk, C	6
W. Tolleson, 3B	6
J. Hairston, DH	5
R. Kittle, DH	5
S. Carlton, SP	4
J. Cruz, 2B	4
J. Davis, SP	4
R. Dotson, SP	4
B. James, RP	4
R. Karkovice, C	4
J. McKeon, RP	4
R. Searage, RP	4
R. Morman, 1B	3

T. Seaver, SP	3
J. Skinner, C	3
R. Nichols, OF	2
I. Calderon, DH	1
M. Hill, C	1
B. Little, 2B	1
S. Lyons, OF	1
J. Perconte, 2B	1

Cleveland (84-78)	WS
Hitting	**150.0**
Fielding	**32.6**
Pitching	**69.4**
J. Carter, OF	28
T. Bernazard, 2B	25
B. Jacoby, 3B	21
B. Butler, OF	20
J. Franco, SS	18
M. Hall, OF	18
T. Candiotti, SP	17
P. Tabler, 1B	16
C. Snyder, OF	13
K. Schrom, SP	10
P. Niekro, SP	9
A. Thornton, DH	9
E. Camacho, RP	7
S. Bailes, RP	6
C. Castillo, OF	4
C. Bando, C	3
N. Heaton, SP	3
O. Nixon, OF	3
B. Oelkers, RP	3
D. Schulze, SP	3
G. Swindell, SP	3
F. Wills, RP	3
R. Yett, RP	3
D. Clark, OF	2
D. Jones, RP	2
D. Noles, RP	2
J. Bell, DH-2B	1

Detroit (87-75)	WS
Hitting	**138.5**
Fielding	**42.6**
Pitching	**79.9**
A. Trammell, SS	26
K. Gibson, OF	20
J. Morris, SP	20
L. Whitaker, 2B	19
D. Coles, 3B	17
D. Evans, 1B	17
L. Parrish, C	15
J. Grubb, DH	12
C. Lemon, OF	12
W. Hernandez, RP	11
E. King, RP	11
D. Collins, OF	9
F. Tanana, SP	9
W. Terrell, SP	9
L. Herndon, OF	7
T. Brookens, 3B	6
D. Lowry, C	6
M. Thurmond, RP	6
P. Sheridan, OF	5
R. O'Neal, RP	4
B. Campbell, RP	3
M. Heath, C	3

D. Bergman, 1B	2
D. Petry, SP	2
J. Slaton, RP	2
C. Cary, RP	1
D. Engle, 1B	1
B. Fields, OF	1
B. Kelly, SP	1
M. Laga, 1B	1
M. Nokes, C	1
J. Pacella, RP	1
H. Spilman, DH	1

Kansas City (76-86)	WS
Hitting	**83.0**
Fielding	**43.8**
Pitching	**101.3**
F. White, 2B	20
G. Brett, 3B	19
W. Wilson, OF	15
M. Gubicza, SP	14
D. Jackson, SP	14
C. Leibrandt, SP	14
L. Smith, OF	14
B. Black, RP	12
S. Farr, RP	12
S. Balboni, 1B	10
D. Quisenberry, RP	10
J. Sundberg, C	10
D. Leonard, SP	8
B. Saberhagen, SP	8
R. Law, OF	7
S. Bankhead, SP	6
J. Orta, DH	5
K. Seitzer, 1B	5
B. Biancalana, SS	4
M. Kingery, OF	4
J. Quirk, C	4
A. Salazar, SS	4
H. McRae, DH	2
M. Huismann, RP	1
B. Jackson, OF	1
R. Johnson, 2B	1
D. Motley, OF	1
B. Pecota, 3B	1
G. Pryor, 3B	1
S. Shields, RP	1

Milwaukee (77-84)	WS
Hitting	**93.3**
Fielding	**42.2**
Pitching	**95.5**
T. Higuera, SP	25
R. Yount, OF	23
R. Deer, OF	17
P. Molitor, 3B	14
M. Clear, RP	13
J. Gantner, 2B	13
D. Plesac, RP	13
T. Leary, SP	11
E. Riles, SS	11
D. Darwin, SP	9
C. Cooper, 1B	8
C. Moore, C	8
B. Oglivie, OF	8
R. Cerone, C	7
D. Sveum, 3B	7
J. Nieves, SP	6

B. Wegman, SP	6
R. Manning, OF	5
J. Johnson, RP	4
B. Schroeder, C	4
M. Felder, OF	3
G. Braggs, OF	2
B. Clutterbuck, RP	2
B. Robidoux, 1B	2
G. Thomas, DH	2
P. Vuckovich, SP	2
M. Birkbeck, SP	1
J. Castillo, 2B	1
J. Cocanower, RP	1
B. Gibson, RP	1
P. Householder, OF	1
B. McClure, RP	1

Minnesota (71-91)	WS
Hitting	**102.8**
Fielding	**37.5**
Pitching	**72.7**
K. Puckett, OF	26
G. Gaetti, 3B	23
B. Blyleven, SP	18
K. Hrbek, 1B	17
F. Viola, SP	13
T. Brunansky, OF	12
S. Lombardozzi, 2B	11
G. Gagne, SS	10
R. Smalley, DH	10
R. Bush, OF	9
M. Smithson, SP	9
K. Atherton, RP	8
N. Heaton, SP	7
M. Portugal, SP	7
T. Laudner, C	6
M. Hatcher, OF	5
R. Jackson, RP	4
G. Frazier, RP	3
F. Pastore, RP	3
J. Reed, C	3
M. Salas, C	3
A. Anderson, RP	2
B. Beane, OF	1
A. Espinoza, 2B	1
R. Washington, 2B	1
A. Woods, DH	1

New York (90-72)	WS
Hitting	**138.1**
Fielding	**41.7**
Pitching	**90.2**
D. Mattingly, 1B	34
R. Henderson, OF	26
D. Righetti, RP	20
W. Randolph, 2B	18
D. Winfield, OF	17
M. Pagliarulo, 3B	15
D. Pasqua, OF	14
D. Rasmussen, SP	14
M. Easler, DH	13
R. Guidry, SP	10
B. Tewksbury, SP	9
D. Drabek, SP	7
R. Hassey, C	7
K. Griffey Sr., OF	6
T. John, SP	6

Player	WS
W. Tolleson, SS	6
B. Fisher, RP	4
J. Niekro, SP	4
G. Roenicke, OF	4
B. Meacham, SS	3
S. Nielsen, SP	3
R. Scurry, RP	3
B. Shirley, RP	3
T. Stoddard, RP	3
B. Wynegar, C	3
D. Berra, SS	2
M. Fischlin, SS	2
J. Skinner, C	2
C. Washington, OF	2
B. Arnsberg, SP-RP	1
H. Cotto, OF	1
L. Hernandez, 3B	1
A. Holland, RP	1
R. Kittle, DH	1
B. Little, 2B	1
P. Lombardi, OF	1
J. Montefusco, RP	1
A. Pulido, RP	1
P. Zuvella, SS	1

Oakland (76-86)	WS
Hitting	**127.7**
Fielding	**34.3**
Pitching	**66.0**
J. Canseco, OF	21
C. Lansford, 3B	19
M. Davis, OF	18
A. Griffin, SS	17
T. Phillips, 2B	17
D. Murphy, OF	15
C. Young, SP	12
B. Bochte, 1B	11
D. Hill, 2B	10
J. Andujar, SP	9
D. Kingman, DH	8
D. Stewart, SP	8
M. Tettleton, C	8
M. Haas, SP	6
J. Howell, RP	6
J. Willard, C	6
J. Rijo, SP	5
D. Bair, RP	4
D. Baker, OF	4
B. Mooneyham, RP	4
S. Ontiveros, RP	4
C. Codiroli, SP	3
S. Javier, OF	3
E. Plunk, SP	2
B. Bathe, C	1
M. Gallego, 2B	1
D. Leiper, RP	1
M. McGwire, 3B	1
L. Sakata, 2B	1
T. Steinbach, C	1
R. Tillman, OF	1
D. Von Ohlen, RP	1

Seattle (67-95)	WS
Hitting	**95.2**
Fielding	**31.5**
Pitching	**74.3**
P. Bradley, OF	19
M. Moore, SP	15
K. Phelps, 1B	15
D. Tartabull, OF	15
J. Presley, 3B	14
A. Davis, 1B	13
M. Langston, SP	11
M. Morgan, SP	11
D. Henderson, OF	10
M. Young, RP	10
S. Owen, SS	8
P. Ladd, RP	7
S. Bradley, C	6
M. Huismann, RP	6
B. Kearney, C	5
H. Reynolds, 2B	5
M. Trujillo, RP	5
J. Moses, OF	4
J. Reed, RP	4
D. Valle, C	3
K. Best, RP	2
S. Fireovid, RP	2
B. Swift, SP	2
G. Thomas, DH	2
S. Yeager, C	2
M. Brantley, OF	1
I. Calderon, OF	1
R. Quinones, SS	1
D. Ramos, SS	1
M. Wilcox, SP	1

Texas (87-75)	WS
Hitting	**133.7**
Fielding	**42.5**
Pitching	**84.8**
P. O'Brien, 1B	24
S. Fletcher, SS	20
O. McDowell, OF	20
L. Parrish, DH	17
P. Incaviglia, OF	16
G. Harris, RP	14
C. Hough, SP	14
G. Ward, OF	14
S. Buechele, 3B	12
D. Slaught, C	12
R. Sierra, OF	11
E. Correa, SP	10
M. Williams, RP	9
D. Mohorcic, RP	8
D. Porter, C	8
T. Harrah, 2B	7
M. Mason, SP	7
J. Guzman, SP	6
J. Russell, RP	6
T. Paciorek, OF	4
M. Mahler, RP	3
O. Mercado, C	3
G. Petralli, C	3
C. Wilkerson, 2B	3
B. Witt, SP	3
M. Stanley, 3B	2
J. Browne, 2B	1
D. Henry, RP	1
M. Loynd, SP	1
G. Wright, OF	1
R. Wright, RP	1

Toronto (86-76)	WS
Hitting	**121.8**
Fielding	**43.0**
Pitching	**93.2**
J. Barfield, OF	28
T. Fernandez, SS	24
G. Bell, OF	23
M. Eichhorn, RP	21
L. Moseby, OF	17
T. Henke, RP	15
J. Key, SP	15
W. Upshaw, 1B	15
J. Clancy, SP	13
E. Whitt, C	13
R. Mulliniks, 3B	10
D. Garcia, 2B	9
C. Johnson, DH	9
J. Cerutti, SP	8
G. Iorg, 3B	6
J. Johnson, SP	6
R. Leach, DH	6
D. Stieb, SP	6
D. Alexander, SP	5
J. Acker, RP	2
D. Lamp, RP	2
B. Martinez, C	2
B. Caudill, RP	1
K. Gruber, 3B	1
M. Lee, 2B	1

1986 National League

Atlanta (72-89)	WS
Hitting	**91.1**
Fielding	**38.6**
Pitching	**86.3**
D. Murphy, OF	22
K. Oberkfell, 3B	17
G. Garber, RP	15
B. Horner, 1B	15
O. Virgil, C	14
D. Palmer, SP	13
G. Hubbard, 2B	12
K. Griffey Sr., OF	11
P. Assenmacher, RP	9
J. Dedmon, RP	9
Z. Smith, SP	9
D. Alexander, SP	7
R. Mahler, SP	7
R. Ramirez, SS	6
B. Sample, OF	6
J. Acker, SP	5
C. Chambliss, 1B	4
T. Harper, OF	4
E. Olwine, RP	4
A. Thomas, SS	4
O. Moreno, OF	3
T. Simmons, 1B	3
C. Washington, OF	3
B. Benedict, C	2
J. Johnson, SP	2
C. McMurtry, RP	2
C. Puleo, SP	2
C. Speck, RP	2
B. Sutter, RP	2
A. Hall, OF	1
G. Perry, OF	1

Chicago (70-90)	WS
Hitting	**101.4**
Fielding	**33.8**
Pitching	**74.8**
R. Sandberg, 2B	20
L. Smith, RP	17
J. Davis, C	16
L. Durham, 1B	15
S. Dunston, SS	14
R. Cey, 3B	11
G. Matthews, OF	11
K. Moreland, OF	11
S. Sanderson, SP	9
D. Eckersley, SP	8
J. Mumphrey, OF	8
D. Lopes, 3B	7
R. Sutcliffe, SP	7
G. Hoffman, RP	6
E. Lynch, SP	6
S. Trout, SP	6
C. Speier, 3B	5
R. Fontenot, RP	4
M. Trillo, 3B	4
T. Bosley, OF	3
B. Dernier, OF	3
D. Gumpert, RP	3
J. Moyer, SP	3
B. Dayett, OF	2
C. Walker, OF	2
J. Baller, RP	1
F. DiPino, RP	1
T. Francona, OF	1
G. Frazier, RP	1
D. Hall, SP	1
M. Keough, RP	1
S. Lake, C	1
G. Maddux, SP	1
R. Palmeiro, OF	1

Cincinnati (86-76)	WS
Hitting	**128.1**
Fielding	**40.9**
Pitching	**89.0**
E. Davis, OF	25
B. Bell, 3B	23
D. Parker, OF	20
B. Gullickson, SP	16
B. Diaz, C	15
J. Franco, RP	15
R. Oester, 2B	15
E. Milner, OF	14
R. Robinson, RP	13
T. Browning, SP	12
K. Daniels, OF	10
R. Murphy, RP	9
T. Power, RP	9
D. Concepcion, SS	8
J. Denny, SP	8
N. Esasky, 1B	8
B. Larkin, SS	6
K. Stillwell, SS	5
S. Butera, C	4
T. Jones, OF	4
T. Perez, 1B	4
C. Welsh, SP	4
P. Rose, 1B	3
W. Rowdon, 3B	2
M. Soto, SP	2
M. Venable, OF	2
C. Willis, RP	2

Houston (96-66)	WS
Hitting	**123.2**
Fielding	**52.4**
Pitching	**112.4**
K. Bass, OF	27
M. Scott, SP	27
G. Davis, 1B	24
B. Doran, 2B	19
D. Walling, 3B	18
J. Cruz, OF	17
B. Knepper, SP	17
B. Hatcher, OF	12
C. Kerfeld, RP	12
A. Ashby, C	11
N. Ryan, SP	11
D. Smith, RP	11
J. Deshaies, SP	10
P. Garner, 3B	9
D. Thon, SS	8
C. Reynolds, SS	7
A. Lopez, RP	6
L. Andersen, RP	5
D. Darwin, SP	5
M. Bailey, C	3
F. DiPino, RP	3
T. Gainey, OF	3
M. Keough, SP-RP	3
D. Lopes, OF	3
J. Mizerock, C	3
J. Pankovits, 2B	3
T. Puhl, OF	3
T. Walker, OF	3
J. Calhoun, RP	1
D. Driessen, 1B	1
M. Hernandez, RP	1
M. Knudson, SP	1
M. Madden, RP	1

Los Angeles (73-89)	WS
Hitting	**109.5**
Fielding	**31.1**
Pitching	**78.3**
S. Sax, 2B	31
F. Valenzuela, SP	21
M. Scioscia, C	13
B. Welch, SP	13
O. Hershiser, SP	12
B. Madlock, 3B	12
R. Honeycutt, SP	11
F. Stubbs, OF	11
G. Brock, 1B	9
M. Marshall, OF	9
R. Williams, OF	8
M. Duncan, SS	7
T. Niedenfuer, RP	7
A. Trevino, C	7
K. Howell, RP	6
K. Landreaux, OF	6
L. Matuszek, OF	6
D. Anderson, 3B	4

E. Cabell, 1B	4
B. Russell, OF	4
R. Bryant, OF	3
E. Vande Berg, RP	3
P. Guerrero, OF	2
J. Hamilton, 3B	2
D. Powell, RP	2
C. Cedeno, OF	1
C. Diaz, RP	1
B. Galvez, RP	1
J. Gonzalez, OF	1
B. Holton, RP	1
A. Pena, RP	1

Montreal (78-83)	WS
Hitting	**110.0**
Fielding	**39.7**
Pitching	**84.3**
T. Raines, OF	32
M. Webster, OF	22
A. Dawson, OF	16
H. Brooks, SS	15
T. Wallach, 3B	14
A. McGaffigan, RP	13
F. Youmans, SP	13
J. Reardon, RP	11
T. Burke, RP	9
M. Fitzgerald, C	9
A. Galarraga, 1B	8
V. Law, 2B	8
B. Smith, SP	7
J. Tibbs, SP	7
B. McClure, RP	6
D. Schatzeder, RP	6
T. Foley, SS	5
B. Sebra, SP	5
W. Krenchicki, 1B	3
R. St. Claire, RP	3
D. Bilardello, C	2
J. Hesketh, SP	2
W. Johnson, 1B	2
D. Martinez, SP	2
A. Newman, 2B	2
H. Winningham, OF	2
J. Wohlford, OF	2
C. Brown, RP	1
C. Candaele, 2B	1
R. Hunt, C	1
T. Nieto, C	1
B. Owchinko, SP	1
L. Rivera, SS	1
J. Thompson, 1B	1
G. Wright, OF	1

New York (108-54)	WS
Hitting	**169.6**
Fielding	**45.5**
Pitching	**109.0**
K. Hernandez, 1B	29
D. Strawberry, OF	25
G. Carter, C	23
L. Dykstra, OF	23
B. Ojeda, SP	18
R. Darling, SP	17
D. Gooden, SP	17
R. Knight, 3B	17
W. Backman, 2B	16
R. McDowell, RP	16
M. Wilson, OF	16
K. Mitchell, OF	14
J. Orosco, RP	13
S. Fernandez, SP	12
H. Johnson, 3B	10
D. Heep, OF	8
R. Santana, SS	8
T. Teufel, 2B	8
R. Aguilera, SP	6
G. Foster, OF	6
R. Anderson, RP	4
E. Hearn, C	4
D. Sisk, RP	4
J. Gibbons, C	3
L. Mazzilli, OF	3
R. Niemann, RP	2
K. Elster, SS	1
D. Magadan, 1B	1

Philadelphia (86-75)	WS
Hitting	**133.9**
Fielding	**40.4**
Pitching	**83.7**
M. Schmidt, 3B	31
V. Hayes, 1B	26
J. Samuel, 2B	18
G. Wilson, OF	17
S. Bedrosian, RP	13
G. Redus, OF	13
K. Gross, SP	12
B. Ruffin, SP	12
K. Tekulve, RP	12
D. Carman, RP	10
S. Rawley, SP	10
R. Roenicke, OF	10
S. Jeltz, SS	9
J. Russell, C	9
T. Hume, RP	8
J. Stone, OF	8
D. Daulton, C	7
R. Schu, 3B	7
M. Thompson, OF	7
T. Foley, SS	3
L. Aguayo, 2B	2
M. Freeman, SP	2
G. Gross, OF	2
C. Hudson, SP	2
D. Schatzeder, RP	2
M. Jackson, RP	1
C. James, OF	1
G. Legg, 2B	1
G. Maddox, OF	1
R. Reynolds, C	1
F. Toliver, SP	1

Pittsburgh (64-98)	WS
Hitting	**93.3**
Fielding	**32.7**
Pitching	**66.0**
R. Rhoden, SP	20
J. Ray, 2B	18
J. Morrison, 3B	16
B. Bonds, OF	15
S. Bream, 1B	15
T. Pena, C	15
R. Reynolds, OF	10
R. Reuschel, SP	8
D. Robinson, RP	8
J. Orsulak, OF	7
M. Diaz, OF	6
C. Guante, RP	6
B. Walk, RP	6
B. Almon, OF	4
R. Belliard, SS	4
P. Clements, RP	4
B. Kipper, SP	4
J. Winn, RP	4
B. Bonilla, OF	3
B. Jones, RP	3
J. Ortiz, C	3
M. Bielecki, SP	2
M. Brown, OF	2
S. Khalifa, SS	2
L. Mazzilli, OF	2
S. Fansler, SP	1
L. McWilliams, RP	1
B. Patterson, RP	1
J. Smiley, RP	1
U. Washington, SS	1

San Diego (74-88)	WS
Hitting	**121.1**
Fielding	**33.6**
Pitching	**67.3**
T. Gwynn, OF	29
K. McReynolds, OF	26
T. Kennedy, C	14
T. Flannery, 2B	13
L. McCullers, RP	12
J. Kruk, OF	11
D. Dravecky, SP	10
S. Garvey, 1B	10
E. Show, SP	10
C. Lefferts, RP	9
G. Nettles, 3B	9
G. Templeton, SS	8
J. Royster, 3B	7
M. Wynne, OF	7
B. Bochy, C	6
A. Hawkins, SP	6
C. Martinez, OF	6
G. Gossage, RP	5
B. Roberts, 2B	4
G. Walter, RP	4
R. Asadoor, 3B	2
J. Jones, SP	2
B. Santiago, C	2
B. Stoddard, RP	2
T. Stoddard, RP	2
E. Wojna, SP	2
G. Booker, RP	1
G. Green, SS	1
L. Hoyt, SP	1
D. LaPoint, RP	1

San Francisco (83-79)	WS
Hitting	**124.7**
Fielding	**40.7**
Pitching	**83.6**
C. Davis, OF	21
B. Brenly, C	20
C. Brown, 3B	16
M. Krukow, SP	16
R. Thompson, 2B	15
W. Clark, 1B	14
S. Garrelts, RP	13
D. Gladden, OF	13
J. Uribe, SS	13
C. Maldonado, OF	12
J. Leonard, OF	10
M. LaCoss, SP	9
V. Blue, SP	8
M. Aldrete, 1B	7
J. Robinson, RP	7
F. Williams, RP	7
J. Berenguer, RP	6
M. Davis, RP	6
K. Downs, SP	6
B. Melvin, C	6
J. Youngblood, OF	5
R. Kutcher, OF	4
G. Minton, RP	4
H. Spilman, 1B	4
M. Woodard, 2B	3
C. Hensley, RP	1
B. Laskey, RP	1
R. Mason, SP	1
L. Quinones, SS	1

St. Louis (79-82)	WS
Hitting	**87.4**
Fielding	**52.1**
Pitching	**97.5**
O. Smith, SS	23
T. Worrell, RP	19
T. Herr, 2B	18
A. Van Slyke, OF	17
B. Forsch, SP	16
J. Tudor, SP	16
D. Cox, SP	15
V. Coleman, OF	14
T. Pendleton, 3B	13
W. McGee, OF	12
R. Horton, RP	11
J. Clark, 1B	9
G. Mathews, SP	8
M. LaValliere, C	7
C. Ford, OF	6
J. Oquendo, SS	4
P. Perry, RP	4
M. Heath, C	3
C. Hurdle, 1B	3
T. Landrum, OF	3
R. Soff, RP	3
J. Boever, RP	2
K. Dayley, RP	2
A. Knicely, 1B	2
M. Laga, 1B	2
R. Ownbey, RP	2
S. Lake, C	1
T. Lawless, 3B	1
J. Morris, OF	1

1987 American League

Baltimore (67-95)	WS
Hitting	**101.8**
Fielding	**34.9**
Pitching	**64.3**
E. Murray, 1B	20
C. Ripken Jr., SS	20
L. Sheets, OF	18
M. Boddicker, SP	14
T. Kennedy, C	11
R. Knight, 3B	11
F. Lynn, OF	11
D. Schmidt, RP	10
M. Williamson, RP	10
J. Dwyer, DH	9
B. Ripken, 2B	7
M. Young, OF	7
J. Habyan, RP	6
L. Lacy, OF	6
E. Bell, SP	5
K. Gerhart, OF	5
M. Flanagan, SP	4
M. Griffin, RP	4
T. Niedenfuer, RP	4
J. O'Connor, RP	3
R. Burleson, 2B	2
P. Stanicek, 2B	2
A. Wiggins, DH	2
D. Aase, RP	1
T. Arnold, RP	1
L. DeLeon, RP	1
K. Dixon, RP	1
R. Gonzales, 3B	1
M. Hart, OF	1
C. Nichols, C	1
F. Rayford, C	1
D. Van Gorder, C	1
R. Washington, 3B	1

Boston (78-84)	WS
Hitting	**121.6**
Fielding	**35.9**
Pitching	**76.4**
W. Boggs, 3B	32
R. Clemens, SP	28
D. Evans, 1B	25
M. Greenwell, OF	17
M. Barrett, 2B	16
E. Burks, OF	15
B. Hurst, SP	15
S. Owen, SS	9
J. Rice, OF	8
D. Baylor, DH	7
C. Schiraldi, RP	7
T. Benzinger, OF	6
A. Nipper, SP	6
J. Sellers, SP	6
S. Horn, DH	5
B. Stanley, SP	5
W. Gardner, RP	4
J. Marzano, C	4
T. Bolton, RP	3
S. Crawford, RP	3
D. Henderson, OF	3

E. Romero, 2B	3
M. Sullivan, C	2
B. Buckner, 1B	1
R. Gedman, C	1
G. Hoffman, SS	1
J. Reed, SS	1
D. Sheaffer, C	1

California (75-87)	WS
Hitting	**107.2**
Fielding	**38.9**
Pitching	**78.9**
B. Downing, DH	23
W. Joyner, 1B	22
D. White, OF	17
J. Howell, OF	14
M. Witt, SP	14
D. Buice, RP	13
D. Schofield, SS	13
D. DeCinces, 3B	12
W. Fraser, SP	11
B. Boone, C	10
G. Minton, RP	9
D. Sutton, SP	9
M. McLemore, 2B	8
J. Candelaria, SP	5
J. Lazorko, RP	5
G. Pettis, OF	5
B. Buckner, DH	4
R. Jones, OF	4
G. Lucas, RP	4
J. Ray, 2B	4
C. Finley, RP	3
D. Moore, RP	3
G. Hendrick, OF	2
D. Miller, C	2
G. Polidor, SS	2
J. Reuss, SP	2
B. Wynegar, C	2
M. Cook, RP	1
B. Harvey, RP	1
K. McCaskill, SP	1

Chicago (77-85)	WS
Hitting	**90.2**
Fielding	**49.8**
Pitching	**91.0**
I. Calderon, OF	20
F. Bannister, SP	17
C. Fisk, C	16
G. Walker, 1B	15
O. Guillen, SS	14
H. Baines, DH	13
G. Redus, OF	13
J. DeLeon, SP	12
R. Dotson, SP	12
B. Thigpen, RP	12
K. Williams, OF	11
B. Long, SP	10
D. Boston, OF	8
D. LaPoint, SP	8
F. Manrique, 2B	7
D. Hill, 2B	6
S. Lyons, 3B	5
B. James, RP	4
J. Royster, 3B	4
R. Searage, RP	4
J. Winn, RP	4
J. Hairston, DH-OF	3
J. McDowell, SP	3
B. Clark, RP	2
T. Hulett, 3B	2
J. Davis, SP	1
R. Hassey, C	1
R. Karkovice, C	1
P. Keedy, 3B	1
B. Lindsey, C	1
S. Nielsen, RP	1

Cleveland (61-101)	WS
Hitting	**100.8**
Fielding	**28.5**
Pitching	**53.7**
B. Jacoby, 3B	22
B. Butler, OF	20
P. Tabler, 1B	15
J. Carter, 1B	14
J. Franco, SS	14
C. Snyder, OF	11
M. Hall, OF	10
D. Jones, RP	9
T. Candiotti, SP	8
S. Bailes, RP	6
J. Farrell, SP	6
T. Bernazard, 2B	5
C. Castillo, DH	5
A. Allanson, C	4
P. Niekro, SP	4
G. Swindell, SP	4
C. Bando, C	3
S. Carlton, SP	3
T. Hinzo, 2B	3
E. Vande Berg, RP	3
R. Yett, RP	3
R. Dempsey, C	2
J. Easterly, RP	2
M. Huismann, RP	2
J. Bell, SS	1
D. Gordon, RP	1
K. Schrom, SP	1
S. Stewart, RP	1
E. Williams, 3B	1

Detroit (98-64)	WS
Hitting	**154.7**
Fielding	**41.1**
Pitching	**98.2**
A. Trammell, SS	35
D. Evans, 1B	22
J. Morris, SP	21
K. Gibson, OF	20
M. Nokes, C	20
L. Whitaker, 2B	20
C. Lemon, OF	19
W. Terrell, SP	16
F. Tanana, SP	15
D. Alexander, SP	12
M. Henneman, RP	12
M. Heath, C	10
T. Brookens, 3B	9
L. Herndon, OF	9
B. Madlock, DH	9
P. Sheridan, OF	8
D. Bergman, 1B	7
E. King, RP	6
W. Hernandez, RP	4
J. Robinson, SP	4
M. Thurmond, RP	3
S. Lusader, OF	2
D. Petry, SP	2
N. Snell, RP	2
J. Walewander, 2B	2
B. Bean, OF	1
D. Coles, 3B	1
J. Grubb, OF	1
T. Harper, DH	1
J. Morrison, 3B	1

Kansas City (83-79)	WS
Hitting	**92.8**
Fielding	**45.0**
Pitching	**111.3**
D. Tartabull, OF	24
B. Saberhagen, SP	23
K. Seitzer, 3B	23
C. Leibrandt, SP	20
M. Gubicza, SP	16
G. Brett, 1B	15
W. Wilson, OF	15
F. White, 2B	14
D. Jackson, SP	13
B. Black, SP	9
B. Jackson, OF	8
D. Quisenberry, RP	7
J. Davis, RP	6
S. Farr, RP	6
J. Quirk, C	6
J. Gleaton, RP	5
B. Pecota, SS	5
A. Salazar, SS	5
S. Balboni, 1B	4
L. Owen, C	4
G. Garber, RP	3
L. Smith, OF	3
G. Thurman, OF	3
T. Bosley, OF	2
R. Jones, SS	2
B. Stoddard, RP	2
J. Beniquez, OF	1
B. Biancalana, SS	1
J. Eisenreich, DH	1
E. Hearn, C	1
M. Macfarlane, C	1
H. McRae, DH	1

Milwaukee (91-71)	WS
Hitting	**137.5**
Fielding	**39.9**
Pitching	**95.6**
P. Molitor, DH	29
R. Yount, OF	26
T. Higuera, SP	20
G. Brock, 1B	17
R. Deer, OF	17
B. Surhoff, C	15
D. Sveum, SS	15
D. Plesac, RP	14
B. Wegman, SP	14
B. Schroeder, C	13
G. Braggs, OF	12
C. Crim, RP	12
J. Nieves, SP	10
C. Bosio, RP	8
M. Felder, OF	7
J. Gantner, 2B	7
J. Castillo, 2B	6
M. Clear, RP	6
E. Riles, 3B	6
J. Aldrich, RP	3
C. Cooper, DH	3
L. Barker, SP	2
M. Knudson, SP	2
P. Mirabella, RP	2
D. Stapleton, RP	2
R. Burris, RP	1
S. Kiefer, 3B	1
R. Manning, OF	1
C. O'Brien, C	1
J. Paciorek, 1B	1

Minnesota (85-77)	WS
Hitting	**124.1**
Fielding	**45.1**
Pitching	**85.8**
K. Puckett, OF	29
K. Hrbek, 1B	25
F. Viola, SP	24
T. Brunansky, OF	20
B. Blyleven, SP	18
G. Gagne, SS	18
G. Gaetti, 3B	17
J. Reardon, RP	12
J. Berenguer, RP	10
S. Lombardozzi, 2B	10
R. Bush, OF	9
D. Gladden, OF	9
L. Straker, SP	9
R. Smalley, DH	8
A. Newman, SS	6
K. Atherton, RP	5
G. Larkin, DH	5
G. Frazier, RP	4
T. Laudner, C	4
M. Davidson, OF	3
M. Salas, C	3
M. Smithson, SP	2
D. Baylor, DH	1
S. Butera, C	1
T. Nieto, C	1
C. Pittaro, 2B	1
R. Smith, RP	1

New York (89-73)	WS
Hitting	**125.8**
Fielding	**44.6**
Pitching	**96.6**
D. Mattingly, 1B	27
W. Randolph, 2B	22
R. Henderson, OF	20
D. Winfield, OF	18
M. Pagliarulo, 3B	17
R. Rhoden, SP	14
C. Hudson, RP	13
T. John, SP	13
D. Righetti, RP	13
T. Stoddard, RP	10
C. Washington, OF	10
R. Cerone, C	9
R. Guidry, SP	9
D. Rasmussen, SP	8
B. Meacham, SS	7
D. Pasqua, OF	7
G. Ward, OF	7
W. Tolleson, SS	6
P. Clements, RP	5
R. Kittle, DH	5
M. Easler, DH	3
J. Niekro, SP	3
J. Skinner, C	3
H. Cotto, OF	2
P. Filson, RP	2
B. Gullickson, SP	2
R. Kelly, OF	2
M. Salas, C	2
B. Shirley, RP	2
N. Allen, RP	1
J. Bonilla, 2B	1
O. Destrade, 1B	1
C. Guante, RP	1
J. Royster, 3B	1
L. Sakata, 3B	1

Oakland (81-81)	WS
Hitting	**135.0**
Fielding	**32.5**
Pitching	**75.5**
M. McGwire, 1B	30
C. Lansford, 3B	23
J. Canseco, OF	17
D. Stewart, SP	17
T. Steinbach, C	15
M. Davis, OF	14
D. Eckersley, RP	13
L. Polonia, OF	13
A. Griffin, SS	11
C. Young, SP	11
T. Phillips, 2B	9
D. Murphy, OF	8
G. Nelson, RP	8
S. Ontiveros, SP	8
T. Bernazard, 2B	6
R. Jackson, DH	6
D. Leiper, RP	4
E. Plunk, RP	4
M. Tettleton, C	4
R. Cey, DH	3
M. Gallego, 2B	3
S. Henderson, OF	3
G. Cadaret, RP	2
S. Davis, SP	2
J. Howell, RP	2
R. Rodriguez, RP	2
W. Weiss, SS	2
M. Haas, SP	1
S. Javier, OF	1
D. Lamp, RP	1

Seattle (78-84)	WS
Hitting	**102.8**
Fielding	**38.8**
Pitching	**92.4**
P. Bradley, OF	21
M. Langston, SP	21
A. Davis, 1B	20
K. Phelps, DH	15

H. Reynolds, 2B	15
J. Presley, 3B	12
M. Brantley, OF	11
M. Morgan, SP	11
M. Moore, SP	10
R. Quinones, SS	10
B. Wilkinson, RP	10
L. Guetterman, SP	9
M. Kingery, OF	9
J. Reed, RP	9
D. Valle, C	8
E. Nunez, RP	7
S. Bankhead, SP	6
S. Bradley, C	6
J. Moses, OF	4
D. Powell, RP	3
D. Ramos, SS	3
M. Campbell, SP	2
J. Christensen, OF	2
E. Martinez, 3B	2
D. Nixon, OF	2
M. Trujillo, RP	2
S. Clarke, RP	1
M. Diaz, SS	1
B. Kearney, C	1
R. Thomas, RP	1

Texas (75-87)	WS
Hitting	**113.9**
Fielding	**37.5**
Pitching	**73.6**
P. O'Brien, 1B	19
S. Fletcher, SS	17
C. Hough, SP	17
P. Incaviglia, OF	16
R. Sierra, OF	15
O. McDowell, OF	14
L. Parrish, DH	14
J. Browne, 2B	13
D. Mohorcic, RP	13
B. Brower, OF	10
J. Guzman, SP	10
M. Williams, RP	10
S. Buechele, 3B	7
G. Petralli, C	7
B. Witt, SP	6
G. Harris, RP	5
P. Kilgus, RP	5
J. Russell, RP	5
M. Stanley, C	5
D. Porter, DH	4
C. Wilkerson, SS	4
D. Slaught, C	3
S. Howe, RP	2
T. O'Malley, 3B	2
M. Loynd, RP	1
T. Paciorek, 1B-OF	1

Toronto (96-66)	WS
Hitting	**125.6**
Fielding	**49.5**
Pitching	**112.9**
G. Bell, OF	26
T. Fernandez, SS	24
J. Key, SP	23
L. Moseby, OF	22
J. Barfield, OF	19
T. Henke, RP	18
J. Clancy, SP	17
E. Whitt, C	16
M. Eichhorn, RP	12
R. Mulliniks, 3B	12
F. McGriff, DH	11
D. Stieb, SP	11
W. Upshaw, 1B	11
J. Cerutti, RP	9
J. Musselman, RP	8
C. Fielder, DH	6
K. Gruber, 3B	6
M. Flanagan, SP	5
R. Leach, OF	5
N. Liriano, 2B	4
J. Nunez, RP	4
G. Iorg, 2B	3
M. Lee, 2B	3
J. Beniquez, DH	2
J. Johnson, SP	2
C. Moore, C	2
D. Wells, RP	2
J. DeWillis, C	1
R. Ducey, OF	1
D. Gordon, RP	1
G. Lavelle, RP	1
M. Sharperson, 2B	1

1987 National League

Atlanta (69-92)	WS
Hitting	**101.5**
Fielding	**35.7**
Pitching	**69.9**
D. Murphy, OF	29
D. James, OF	19
G. Hubbard, 2B	15
Z. Smith, SP	14
O. Virgil, C	13
J. Acker, RP	10
K. Griffey Sr., OF	10
K. Oberkfell, 3B	10
G. Perry, 1B	10
A. Hall, OF	9
J. Dedmon, RP	7
R. Mahler, SP	7
C. Puleo, RP	7
D. Alexander, SP	6
G. Garber, RP	5
D. Palmer, SP	5
J. Blauser, SS	4
G. Roenicke, OF	4
T. Simmons, 1B	4
R. Ramirez, SS	3
A. Thomas, SS	3
P. Assenmacher, RP	2
R. O'Neal, SP	2
B. Benedict, C	1
C. Cary, RP	1
K. Coffman, SP	1
R. Gant, 2B	1
T. Glavine, SP	1
G. Nettles, 3B	1
E. Olwine, RP	1
P. Runge, 3B	1
P. Smith, SP	1

Chicago (76-85)	WS
Hitting	**107.9**
Fielding	**37.5**
Pitching	**82.6**
A. Dawson, OF	20
R. Sandberg, 2B	20
R. Sutcliffe, SP	19
L. Smith, RP	15
L. Durham, 1B	14
D. Martinez, OF	14
J. Davis, C	13
K. Moreland, 3B	13
J. Mumphrey, OF	13
F. DiPino, RP	9
S. Sanderson, SP	9
B. Dernier, OF	7
J. Moyer, SP	7
R. Palmeiro, OF	7
S. Trout, SP	7
L. Lancaster, SP	6
D. Noles, RP	6
B. Dayett, OF	5
S. Dunston, SS	5
M. Trillo, 1B	5
P. Noce, 2B	3
J. Sundberg, C	3
E. Lynch, RP	2
M. Mason, RP	2
M. Brumley, SS	1
D. Jackson, OF	1
G. Maddux, SP	1
L. Quinones, SS	1

Cincinnati (84-78)	WS
Hitting	**122.8**
Fielding	**41.1**
Pitching	**88.1**
E. Davis, OF	30
K. Daniels, OF	22
B. Bell, 3B	17
B. Diaz, C	15
J. Franco, RP	15
D. Parker, OF	13
N. Esasky, 1B	11
B. Larkin, SS	11
R. Murphy, RP	11
R. Robinson, RP	11
F. Williams, RP	11
T. Jones, OF	10
D. Concepcion, 2B	8
T. Power, SP	8
K. Stillwell, SS	8
G. Hoffman, SP	7
T. Browning, SP	6
B. Gullickson, SP	6
R. Oester, 2B	5
P. O'Neill, OF	5
D. Collins, OF	3
B. Landrum, RP	3
P. Perry, RP	3
D. Rasmussen, SP	3
J. Treadway, 2B	3
T. McGriff, C	2
B. Scherrer, RP	2
T. Francona, 1B	1
T. Hume, RP	1
M. Soto, SP	1

Houston (76-86)	WS
Hitting	**99.0**
Fielding	**41.9**
Pitching	**87.1**
B. Doran, 2B	24
B. Hatcher, OF	19
K. Bass, OF	18
M. Scott, SP	18
N. Ryan, SP	15
D. Smith, RP	15
G. Davis, 1B	14
A. Ashby, C	13
D. Darwin, SP	12
D. Walling, 3B	11
G. Young, OF	10
L. Andersen, RP	9
J. Cruz, OF	9
C. Reynolds, SS	8
J. Deshaies, SP	6
R. Childress, RP	4
J. Heathcock, RP	4
J. Agosto, RP	3
K. Caminiti, 3B	3
P. Garner, 3B	2
A. Lopez, RP	2
D. Thon, SS	2
D. Berra, SS	1
C. Jackson, 3B	1
D. Lopes, OF	1
D. Meads, RP	1
J. Pankovits, 2B	1
T. Puhl, OF	1
R. Reynolds, C	1

Los Angeles (73-89)	WS
Hitting	**94.6**
Fielding	**37.7**
Pitching	**86.8**
P. Guerrero, OF	28
O. Hershiser, SP	21
B. Welch, SP	19
S. Sax, 2B	18
M. Scioscia, C	18
J. Shelby, OF	15
F. Valenzuela, SP	12
M. Marshall, OF	11
F. Stubbs, 1B	9
M. Hatcher, 3B	8
A. Pena, RP	6
D. Anderson, SS	5
B. Holton, RP	5
T. Belcher, SP	4
M. Duncan, SS	4
S. Hillegas, SP	4
M. Young, RP	4
T. Crews, RP	3
T. Leary, RP	3
R. Bryant, OF	2
P. Garner, 3B	2
K. Howell, RP	2
T. Niedenfuer, RP	2
A. Trevino, C	2
T. Woodson, 3B	2
J. Gonzalez, OF	1
J. Hamilton, 3B	1
B. Havens, RP	1
G. Hoffman, SS	1
R. Honeycutt, SP	1
K. Landreaux, OF	1
T. Landrum, OF	1
O. Mercado, C	1
M. Ramsey, OF	1
M. Sharperson, 3B	1

Montreal (91-71)	WS
Hitting	**124.7**
Fielding	**43.8**
Pitching	**104.5**
T. Raines, OF	34
T. Wallach, 3B	28
M. Webster, OF	23
T. Burke, RP	20
A. Galarraga, 1B	19
V. Law, 2B	16
A. McGaffigan, RP	16
C. Candaele, 2B	12
H. Brooks, SS	11
D. Martinez, SP	11
N. Heaton, SP	10
T. Foley, SS	8
P. Perez, SP	8
B. Smith, SP	7
H. Winningham, OF	7
B. Sebra, SP	6
R. St. Claire, RP	6
B. McClure, RP	5
R. Nichols, OF	5
J. Parrett, RP	5
F. Youmans, SP	5
M. Fitzgerald, C	3
J. Hesketh, RP	2
W. Johnson, 1B	2
J. Tibbs, SP	2
D. Engle, OF	1
L. Sorensen, RP	1

New York (92-70)	WS
Hitting	**153.0**
Fielding	**36.4**
Pitching	**86.6**
D. Strawberry, OF	30
H. Johnson, 3B	24
K. Hernandez, 1B	21
K. McReynolds, OF	19
L. Dykstra, OF	17
T. Teufel, 2B	15
M. Wilson, OF	15
D. Gooden, SP	14
G. Carter, C	13
R. Santana, SS	11
T. Leach, RP	10
R. McDowell, RP	9
R. Aguilera, SP	8
R. Darling, SP	8
S. Fernandez, SP	8
D. Magadan, 3B	8
R. Myers, RP	6
D. Cone, SP	5
L. Mazzilli, OF	5
J. Orosco, RP	5
D. Sisk, RP	5
W. Backman, 2B	4
B. Lyons, C	3
J. Mitchell, SP	3

J. Innis, RP	2
K. Miller, 2B	2
B. Ojeda, SP	2
B. Almon, SS	1
K. Elster, SS	1
G. Jefferies, PH-PR	1
G. Walter, RP	1

Philadelphia (80-82)	WS
Hitting	**103.7**
Fielding	**47.1**
Pitching	**89.2**
M. Schmidt, 3B	26
V. Hayes, 1B	23
J. Samuel, 2B	22
M. Thompson, OF	19
S. Bedrosian, RP	16
C. James, OF	14
S. Rawley, SP	12
K. Tekulve, RP	11
D. Carman, SP	10
L. Parrish, C	10
G. Wilson, OF	10
K. Gross, SP	9
B. Ruffin, SP	8
J. Calhoun, RP	6
S. Jeltz, SS	6
L. Aguayo, SS	5
M. Jackson, RP	5
W. Ritchie, RP	5
G. Gross, OF	4
R. Schu, 3B	4
D. Daulton, C	3
M. Easler, OF	2
T. Frohwirth, RP	2
M. Maddux, RP	2
D. Schatzeder, RP	2
J. Stone, OF	2
K. Dowell, SS	1
K. Hughes, OF	1

Pittsburgh (80-82)	WS
Hitting	**112.0**
Fielding	**43.2**
Pitching	**84.8**
A. Van Slyke, OF	25
B. Bonds, OF	22
M. LaValliere, C	17
B. Bonilla, 3B	16
R. Reuschel, SP	15
M. Dunne, SP	13
S. Bream, 1B	10
D. Drabek, SP	10
J. Ray, 2B	10
B. Fisher, SP	9
R. Reynolds, OF	9
B. Walk, RP	9
J. Cangelosi, OF	8
J. Morrison, 3B	8
M. Diaz, OF	7
D. Robinson, RP	7
J. Gott, RP	6
A. Pedrique, SS	6
J. Lind, 2B	5
J. Robinson, RP	5
J. Ortiz, C	4
D. Coles, OF	3
R. Belliard, SS	2
M. Bielecki, SP	2
B. Gideon, RP	2
V. Palacios, SP	2
J. Smiley, RP	2
L. Easley, RP	1
F. Fermin, SS	1
T. Harper, OF	1
B. Kipper, SP	1
H. Pena, RP	1
D. Taylor, SP	1

San Diego (65-97)	WS
Hitting	**94.6**
Fielding	**33.0**
Pitching	**67.5**
T. Gwynn, OF	29
J. Kruk, 1B	18
R. Ready, 3B	18
B. Santiago, C	15
C. Martinez, OF	13
L. McCullers, RP	10
E. Show, SP	9
G. Gossage, RP	7
M. Davis, RP	6
S. Jefferson, OF	6
J. Jones, SP	6
G. Templeton, SS	6
E. Whitson, SP	6
G. Booker, RP	5
D. Dravecky, RP	4
T. Flannery, 2B	4
K. Mitchell, 3B	4
E. Nolte, SP	4
J. Cora, 2B	3
M. Grant, SP	3
S. Mack, OF	3
L. Salazar, 3B	3
M. Wynne, OF	3
C. Brown, 3B	2
A. Hawkins, SP	2
C. Lefferts, RP	2
S. Abner, OF	1
K. Comstock, RP	1
T. Gorman, RP	1
D. Leiper, RP	1

San Francisco (90-72)	WS
Hitting	**137.5**
Fielding	**41.7**
Pitching	**90.8**
W. Clark, 1B	25
B. Brenly, C	18
M. Aldrete, OF	16
C. Davis, OF	16
C. Maldonado, OF	16
R. Thompson, 2B	14
J. Uribe, SS	14
S. Garrelts, RP	12
J. Leonard, OF	12
K. Mitchell, 3B	12
K. Downs, SP	11
C. Speier, 2B	11
M. LaCoss, SP	10
J. Robinson, RP	10
A. Hammaker, SP	9
D. Dravecky, SP	8
D. Robinson, RP	7
C. Lefferts, RP	5
B. Melvin, C	5
E. Milner, OF	5
M. Williams, SS	5
M. Grant, SP-RP	3
M. Krukow, SP	3
J. Price, RP	3
C. Brown, 3B	2
K. Comstock, RP	2
M. Davis, SP	2
G. Minton, RP	2
R. Reuschel, SP	2
M. Wasinger, 3B	2
J. Youngblood, OF	2
R. Bockus, RP	1
J. Gott, RP	1
D. Henderson, OF	1
R. Kutcher, OF	1
R. Mason, SP	1
H. Spilman, 3B	1

St. Louis (95-67)	WS
Hitting	**143.6**
Fielding	**44.8**
Pitching	**96.6**
J. Clark, 1B	33
O. Smith, SS	33
V. Coleman, OF	24
T. Pendleton, 3B	21
W. McGee, OF	17
T. Worrell, RP	17
T. Herr, 2B	16
G. Mathews, SP	12
B. Forsch, SP	11
J. Magrane, SP	11
J. Oquendo, OF	11
D. Cox, SP	10
R. Horton, RP	9
K. Dayley, RP	8
C. Ford, OF	7
J. Tudor, SP	7
T. Pena, C	6
B. Dawley, RP	5
S. Lake, C	5
J. Morris, OF	4
J. Lindeman, OF	3
P. Perry, RP	3
R. Booker, 2B	2
S. Peters, RP	2
L. Tunnell, RP	2
D. Driessen, 1B	1
D. Green, OF	1
T. Landrum, OF	1
R. O'Neal, SP	1
T. Pagnozzi, C	1
S. Terry, RP	1

1988
American League

Baltimore (54-107)	WS
Hitting	**72.5**
Fielding	**30.7**
Pitching	**58.7**
C. Ripken Jr., SS	25
E. Murray, 1B	21
J. Orsulak, OF	9
D. Schmidt, RP	9
M. Tettleton, C	9
J. Bautista, SP	7
M. Boddicker, SP	7
T. Niedenfuer, RP	7
J. Ballard, SP	6
F. Lynn, OF	6
L. Sheets, OF	6
D. Sisk, RP	6
R. Schu, 3B	5
B. Milacki, SP	4
B. Ripken, 2B	4
M. Williamson, RP	4
R. Gonzales, 3B	3
P. Stanicek, OF	3
J. Traber, 1B	3
D. Aase, RP	2
K. Gerhart, OF	2
T. Kennedy, C	2
M. Thurmond, RP	2
B. Anderson, OF	1
J. Dwyer, DH	1
J. Habyan, RP	1
K. Hughes, OF	1
M. Morgan, RP	1
C. Nichols, C	1
G. Olson, RP	1
O. Peraza, SP	1
J. Tibbs, SP	1
C. Worthington, 3B	1

Boston (89-73)	WS
Hitting	**135.2**
Fielding	**41.7**
Pitching	**90.1**
W. Boggs, 3B	31
M. Greenwell, OF	30
E. Burks, OF	24
D. Evans, OF	23
R. Clemens, SP	22
B. Hurst, SP	15
M. Barrett, 2B	14
L. Smith, RP	12
W. Gardner, SP-RP	11
J. Reed, SS	11
J. Rice, DH	9
B. Stanley, RP	9
M. Boddicker, SP	8
R. Gedman, C	8
R. Cerone, C	7
T. Benzinger, 1B	6
D. Lamp, RP	6
S. Owen, SS	4
L. Parrish, 1B	4
O. Boyd, SP	3
B. Anderson, OF	2
J. Sellers, SP	2
M. Smithson, SP	2
T. Bolton, RP	1
J. Marzano, C	1
C. Quintana, OF	1
E. Romero, 3B	1

California (75-87)	WS
Hitting	**127.0**
Fielding	**30.8**
Pitching	**67.2**
W. Joyner, 1B	22
J. Ray, 2B	21
B. Boone, C	17
C. Davis, OF	16
J. Howell, 3B	16
B. Downing, DH	15
D. Schofield, SS	14
B. Harvey, RP	13
D. White, OF	11
M. Witt, SP	11
T. Armas, OF	9
C. Finley, SP	8
G. Minton, RP	7
K. McCaskill, SP	6
D. Petry, SP	5
S. Cliburn, RP	4
M. McLemore, 2B	4
T. Clark, SP	3
W. Fraser, SP	3
D. Miller, C	3
S. Corbett, RP	2
J. Eppard, OF	2
G. Hendrick, OF	2
J. Lazorko, RP	2
D. Moore, RP	2
B. Wynegar, C	2
D. Bichette, OF	1
T. Bosley, OF	1
R. Krawczyk, RP	1
R. Monteleone, RP	1
G. Polidor, SS	1

Chicago (71-90)	WS
Hitting	**99.0**
Fielding	**38.5**
Pitching	**75.5**
H. Baines, DH	18
O. Guillen, SS	17
C. Fisk, C	15
D. Gallagher, OF	13
S. Lyons, 3B	13
J. Reuss, SP	12
B. Thigpen, RP	11
D. LaPoint, SP	10
M. Perez, SP	10
G. Redus, OF	10
D. Pasqua, OF	9
B. Long, RP	8
F. Manrique, 2B	8
G. Walker, 1B	8
D. Boston, OF	7
I. Calderon, OF	7
J. McDowell, SP	6
R. Horton, RP	4
D. Hill, 2B	3
S. Hillegas, SP	3
B. Jones, RP	3
M. Salas, C	3
J. Bittiger, RP	2
R. Karkovice, C	2
T. McCarthy, RP	2
D. Pall, RP	2
S. Rosenberg, RP	2

M. Diaz, 1B	1
K. Paris, 1B	1
K. Patterson, RP	1
K. Williams, OF	1
M. Woodard, 2B	1

Cleveland (78-84)	WS
Hitting	**106.7**
Fielding	**37.6**
Pitching	**89.6**
J. Carter, OF	26
J. Franco, 2B	22
G. Swindell, SP	19
D. Jones, RP	18
C. Snyder, OF	18
T. Candiotti, SP	17
A. Allanson, C	14
M. Hall, OF	13
J. Farrell, SP	12
B. Jacoby, 3B	10
W. Upshaw, 1B	10
R. Kittle, DH	8
R. Yett, SP	6
T. Francona, DH	5
B. Havens, RP	5
S. Bailes, SP	4
R. Washington, SS	4
C. Castillo, OF	3
D. Gordon, RP	3
P. Tabler, DH	3
J. Bell, SS	2
B. Black, RP	2
D. Clark, DH	2
L. Medina, 1B	2
C. Bando, C	1
J. Dedmon, RP	1
B. Laskey, RP	1
R. Nichols, SP	1
D. Ramos, 2B	1
P. Zuvella, SS	1

Detroit (88-74)	WS
Hitting	**128.5**
Fielding	**43.3**
Pitching	**92.2**
. Trammell, SS	23
L. Whitaker, 2B	20
C. Lemon, OF	19
M. Henneman, RP	17
M. Nokes, C	17
L. Salazar, OF	15
J. Robinson, SP	14
J. Morris, SP	12
G. Pettis, OF	12
P. Sheridan, OF	12
D. Bergman, 1B	11
T. Brookens, 3B	11
D. Evans, DH	11
D. Alexander, SP	9
F. Tanana, SP	9
W. Hernandez, RP	8
W. Terrell, SP	8
P. Gibson, RP	7
D. Murphy, OF	7
M. Heath, C	6
E. King, RP	5
D. Heinkel, RP	2
L. Herndon, DH	2
T. Lovullo, 2B	2
F. Lynn, OF	2
J. Walewander, 2B	2
R. Knight, 1B	1

Kansas City (84-77)	WS
Hitting	**112.5**
Fielding	**41.7**
Pitching	**97.8**
G. Brett, 1B	26
M. Gubicza, SP	24
D. Tartabull, OF	22
K. Seitzer, 3B	21
C. Leibrandt, SP	17
K. Stillwell, SS	16
B. Saberhagen, SP	15
S. Farr, RP	13
B. Jackson, OF	12
W. Wilson, OF	12
P. Tabler, DH	10
F. White, 2B	9
F. Bannister, SP	8
M. Macfarlane, C	7
J. Montgomery, RP	6
J. Quirk, C	6
B. Pecota, SS	4
B. Buckner, DH	3
G. Garber, RP	3
J. Gleaton, RP	3
R. Anderson, RP	2
L. Aquino, SP	2
L. Owen, C	2
D. Quisenberry, RP	2
Z. Sanchez, RP	2
B. Wellman, 2B	2
B. Black, RP	1
J. Eisenreich, OF	1
T. Power, SP	1

Milwaukee (87-75)	WS
Hitting	**104.3**
Fielding	**48.3**
Pitching	**108.4**
R. Yount, OF	31
P. Molitor, 3B	27
T. Higuera, SP	22
R. Deer, OF	19
J. Gantner, 2B	14
D. August, SP	12
C. Bosio, SP	12
C. Crim, RP	11
B. Surhoff, C	11
D. Plesac, RP	10
D. Sveum, SS	10
G. Braggs, OF	9
B. Wegman, SP	9
P. Mirabella, RP	8
G. Brock, 1B	7
J. Meyer, DH	7
J. Nieves, SP	6
M. Birkbeck, SP	5
T. Filer, SP	4
O. Jones, RP	4
J. Leonard, OF	4
C. O'Brien, C	3
J. Adduci, OF	2
M. Clear, RP	2
M. Knudson, RP	2
E. Riles, 3B	2
B. Schroeder, C	2
G. Sheffield, SS	2
J. Castillo, 2B	1
D. Hamilton, OF	1
S. Kiefer, 2B-3B	1
B. Robidoux, 1B	1

Minnesota (91-71)	WS
Hitting	**125.7**
Fielding	**48.8**
Pitching	**98.5**
K. Puckett, OF	32
F. Viola, SP	25
G. Gaetti, 3B	22
A. Anderson, SP	19
K. Hrbek, 1B	19
D. Gladden, OF	18
R. Bush, OF	14
G. Larkin, DH	14
J. Reardon, RP	13
G. Gagne, SS	12
T. Laudner, C	9
J. Berenguer, RP	8
K. Atherton, RP	7
T. Herr, 2B	7
S. Lombardozzi, 2B	6
J. Moses, OF	6
F. Toliver, SP	6
B. Blyleven, SP	4
C. Lea, SP	4
A. Newman, 3B	4
R. Smith, RP	4
L. Straker, SP	4
J. Dwyer, DH	3
B. Harper, C	3
M. Portugal, RP	3
J. Christensen, OF	2
G. Gonzalez, RP	2
M. Davidson, OF	1
T. Nieto, C	1
D. Schatzeder, RP	1

New York (85-76)	WS
Hitting	**144.2**
Fielding	**36.1**
Pitching	**74.8**
D. Winfield, OF	31
R. Henderson, OF	28
D. Mattingly, 1B	24
J. Clark, DH	21
C. Washington, OF	15
M. Pagliarulo, 3B	13
W. Randolph, 2B	13
J. Candelaria, SP	11
D. Righetti, RP	11
C. Guante, RP	9
D. Slaught, C	9
R. Rhoden, SP	8
N. Allen, RP	7
T. John, SP	7
R. Santana, SS	7
R. Dotson, SP	5
C. Hudson, RP	5
K. Phelps, DH	4
A. Leiter, SP	3
S. Shields, RP	3
J. Skinner, C	3
G. Ward, OF	3
R. Guidry, SP	2
B. Meacham, SS	2
D. Mohorcic, RP	2
W. Tolleson, 2B	2
R. Velarde, 2B	2
L. Aguayo, 3B	1
J. Buhner, OF	1
L. Guetterman, RP	1
R. Kelly, OF	1
H. Pena, RP	1

Oakland (104-58)	WS
Hitting	**162.8**
Fielding	**47.0**
Pitching	**102.2**
J. Canseco, OF	39
M. McGwire, 1B	28
D. Henderson, OF	26
C. Lansford, 3B	18
D. Stewart, SP	18
D. Eckersley, RP	15
W. Weiss, SS	15
T. Steinbach, C	13
B. Welch, SP	13
R. Hassey, C	12
S. Davis, SP	11
G. Hubbard, 2B	11
D. Parker, DH	10
L. Polonia, OF	10
G. Nelson, RP	9
S. Javier, OF	8
T. Burns, SP	7
G. Cadaret, RP	7
E. Plunk, RP	7
D. Baylor, DH	6
M. Gallego, 2B	6
R. Honeycutt, RP	6
C. Young, SP	6
T. Phillips, 3B	4
D. Jennings, OF	3
J. Corsi, RP	1
S. Ontiveros, SP	1
D. Otto, SP	1
M. Sinatro, C	1

Seattle (68-93)	WS
Hitting	**86.8**
Fielding	**38.1**
Pitching	**79.1**
M. Langston, SP	19
A. Davis, 1B	18
H. Reynolds, 2B	17
M. Moore, SP	13
R. Quinones, SS	12
S. Bankhead, SP	10
M. Brantley, OF	10
M. Jackson, RP	10
K. Phelps, DH	10
D. Valle, C	9
S. Balboni, DH	8
S. Bradley, C	7
H. Cotto, OF	7
B. Swift, SP	7
J. Buhner, OF	6
D. Coles, OF	6
J. Presley, 3B	6
M. Schooler, RP	6
J. Reed, RP	5
E. Hanson, SP	3
B. Wilkinson, RP	3
M. Diaz, SS	2
M. Kingery, OF	2
M. Campbell, SP	1
E. Martinez, 3B	1
J. Rabb, DH	1
R. Renteria, SS	1
R. Scurry, RP	1
J. Solano, RP	1
G. Walter, RP	1
G. Wilson, OF	1

Texas (70-91)	WS
Hitting	**90.9**
Fielding	**39.5**
Pitching	**79.6**
S. Fletcher, SS	17
C. Hough, SP	17
P. O'Brien, 1B	17
R. Sierra, OF	16
S. Buechele, 3B	15
J. Guzman, SP	12
P. Incaviglia, OF	12
O. McDowell, OF	12
J. Russell, SP	12
C. Espy, OF	11
P. Kilgus, SP	10
B. Witt, SP	10
C. Wilkerson, 2B	9
G. Petralli, C	8
C. McMurtry, RP	7
M. Williams, RP	6
M. Stanley, C	5
J. Browne, 2B	2
C. Kreuter, C	2
J. Sundberg, C	2
E. Vande Berg, RP	2
B. Brower, OF	1
K. Brown, SP	1
J. Cecena, RP	1
R. Hayward, SP	1
J. Kunkel, 2B	1
D. Mohorcic, RP	1

Toronto (87-75)	WS
Hitting	**130.4**
Fielding	**43.8**
Pitching	**86.8**
T. Fernandez, SS	25
F. McGriff, 1B	24
K. Gruber, 3B	23
G. Bell, OF	16
D. Stieb, SP	16
E. Whitt, C	16
L. Moseby, OF	13
J. Barfield, OF	12
R. Mulliniks, DH	12
M. Lee, 2B	11
D. Ward, RP	11
M. Flanagan, SP	10
T. Henke, RP	10

J. Key, SP	10
J. Cerutti, RP	8
J. Clancy, SP	7
J. Musselman, SP	6
R. Leach, OF	5
N. Liriano, 2B	5
P. Borders, C	3
S. Campusano, OF	3
C. Fielder, DH	3
R. Ducey, OF	2
M. Eichhorn, RP	2
J. Nunez, RP	2
D. Wells, RP	2
D. Bair, RP	1
J. Beniquez, DH	1
S. Butera, C	1
T. Castillo, RP	1

1988 National League

Atlanta (54-106)	WS
Hitting	**71.3**
Fielding	**29.2**
Pitching	**61.5**
R. Gant, 2B	16
G. Perry, 1B	15
D. Murphy, OF	12
R. Mahler, SP	10
J. Alvarez, RP	9
P. Assenmacher, RP	9
D. James, OF	9
K. Oberkfell, 3B	9
P. Smith, SP	9
A. Thomas, SS	9
O. Virgil, C	8
C. Puleo, RP	7
B. Benedict, C	5
Z. Smith, SP	5
T. Glavine, SP	4
A. Hall, OF	4
B. Sutter, RP	3
T. Blocker, OF	2
J. Boever, RP	2
J. Eichelberger, RP	2
K. Griffey Sr., OF	2
L. Smith, OF	2
J. Acker, RP	1
K. Blankenship, SP	1
J. Blauser, 2B	1
J. Davis, C	1
T. Gregg, OF	1
J. Morrison, 3B	1
J. Royster, OF	1
P. Runge, 3B	1
T. Simmons, 1B	1

Chicago (77-85)	WS
Hitting	**113.3**
Fielding	**36.3**
Pitching	**81.4**
R. Sandberg, 2B	22
V. Law, 3B	20
G. Maddux, SP	20
A. Dawson, OF	19
R. Palmeiro, OF	17
M. Grace, 1B	16
R. Sutcliffe, SP	14
S. Dunston, SS	13
J. Moyer, SP	12
M. Webster, OF	10
D. Berryhill, C	7
D. Martinez, OF	7
J. Davis, C	6
L. Lancaster, RP	5
A. Nipper, SP	5
J. Pico, RP	5
C. Schiraldi, SP	5
G. Gossage, RP	4
P. Perry, RP	4
M. Bielecki, RP	3
D. Jackson, OF	3
F. DiPino, RP	2
M. Harkey, SP	2
J. Sundberg, C	2
M. Trillo, 1B	2
G. Varsho, OF	2
M. Capel, RP	1
D. Dascenzo, OF	1
L. Durham, 1B	1
A. Salazar, SS	1

Cincinnati (87-74)	WS
Hitting	**113.9**
Fielding	**48.0**
Pitching	**99.1**
B. Larkin, SS	28
E. Davis, OF	27
K. Daniels, OF	26
D. Jackson, SP	22
J. Franco, RP	20
C. Sabo, 3B	17
T. Browning, SP	16
J. Rijo, RP	15
P. O'Neill, OF	13
N. Esasky, 1B	10
J. Treadway, 2B	10
R. Dibble, RP	7
R. Murphy, RP	6
B. Diaz, C	5
F. Williams, RP	5
J. Reed, C	4
N. Charlton, SP	3
D. Collins, OF	3
L. Harris, 3B	3
R. Oester, 2B	3
K. Brown, SP	2
D. Concepcion, 2B	2
L. McClendon, C	2
L. Quinones, SS	2
H. Winningham, OF	2
T. Birtsas, RP	1
K. Griffey Sr., 1B	1
T. Jones, OF	1
T. McGriff, C	1
R. Robinson, SP	1
V. Snider, OF	1
M. Soto, SP	1
R. St. Claire, RP	1

Houston (82-80)	WS
Hitting	**126.2**
Fielding	**41.2**
Pitching	**78.6**
G. Davis, 1B	23
G. Young, OF	21
K. Bass, OF	19
B. Doran, 2B	19
R. Ramirez, SS	18
B. Hatcher, OF	17
M. Scott, SP	14
T. Puhl, OF	12
J. Agosto, RP	11
J. Deshaies, SP	11
B. Knepper, SP	10
N. Ryan, SP	9
B. Bell, 3B	8
A. Ashby, C	7
D. Smith, RP	7
L. Andersen, RP	6
D. Darwin, RP	6
D. Walling, 3B	6
A. Trevino, C	5
C. Reynolds, SS	4
J. Andujar, RP	2
C. Jackson, 3B	2
D. Meads, RP	2
J. Pankovits, 2B	2
C. Biggio, C	1
K. Caminiti, 3B	1
J. Fishel, OF	1
L. Meadows, OF	1
B. Meyer, RP	1

Los Angeles (94-67)	WS
Hitting	**123.4**
Fielding	**47.3**
Pitching	**111.2**
K. Gibson, OF	31
O. Hershiser, SP	25
S. Sax, 2B	24
M. Marshall, OF	19
J. Shelby, OF	19
T. Leary, SP	17
M. Scioscia, C	14
T. Belcher, SP	13
J. Howell, RP	13
A. Pena, RP	12
R. Dempsey, C	11
P. Guerrero, 3B	10
B. Holton, RP	10
D. Anderson, SS	8
J. Hamilton, 3B	7
A. Griffin, SS	6
M. Hatcher, OF	6
J. Orosco, RP	6
F. Stubbs, 1B	6
T. Crews, RP	5
J. Tudor, SP	4
D. Heep, OF	3
F. Valenzuela, SP	3
M. Davis, OF	2
S. Hillegas, SP	2
D. Sutton, SP	2
T. Woodson, 3B	2
R. Martinez, SP	1
M. Sharperson, 2B	1

Montreal (81-81)	WS
Hitting	**101.7**
Fielding	**48.2**
Pitching	**93.1**
A. Galarraga, 1B	25
H. Brooks, OF	19
T. Raines, OF	19
T. Wallach, 3B	16
De. Martinez, SP	15
P. Perez, SP	14
T. Foley, 2B	11
B. Smith, SP	11
J. Parrett, RP	10
A. McGaffigan, RP	9
N. Santovenia, C	8
T. Burke, RP	7
J. Dopson, SP	7
J. Hesketh, RP	7
O. Nixon, OF	7
M. Webster, OF	7
R. Hudler, 2B	6
T. Jones, OF	6
M. Fitzgerald, C	5
B. Holman, SP	5
Da. Martinez, OF	5
L. Rivera, SS	5
F. Youmans, SP	4
C. Candaele, 2B	2
R. Johnson, SP	2
J. Paredes, 2B	2
J. Reed, C	2
H. Winningham, OF	2
J. Huson, SS	1
W. Johnson, 1B	1
T. O'Malley, 3B	1
M. Smith, RP	1
W. Tejada, C	1

New York (100-60)	WS
Hitting	**163.8**
Fielding	**39.6**
Pitching	**96.6**
K. McReynolds, OF	31
D. Strawberry, OF	30
H. Johnson, 3B	21
D. Cone, SP	19
M. Wilson, OF	17
L. Dykstra, OF	15
D. Magadan, 1B	14
R. Myers, RP	14
R. Darling, SP	13
D. Gooden, SP	13
K. Hernandez, 1B	13
W. Backman, 2B	12
G. Carter, C	12
K. Elster, SS	12
S. Fernandez, SP	11
R. McDowell, RP	10
B. Ojeda, SP	9
T. Teufel, 2B	8
G. Jefferies, 3B	7
T. Leach, RP	7
M. Sasser, C	4
M. Carreon, OF	2
J. Innis, RP	2
B. Lyons, C	2
B. McClure, RP	1
D. West, SP-RP	1

Philadelphia (65-96)	WS
Hitting	**104.1**
Fielding	**31.4**
Pitching	**59.5**
J. Samuel, 2B	18
P. Bradley, OF	17
V. Hayes, 1B	14
M. Schmidt, 3B	14
R. Jordan, 1B	12
L. Parrish, C	12
M. Thompson, OF	12
K. Gross, SP	11
G. Harris, RP	10
S. Bedrosian, RP	8
C. James, OF	8
S. Jeltz, SS	8
D. Carman, SP	6
R. Jones, OF	5
D. Palmer, SP	5
K. Tekulve, RP	5
B. Dernier, OF	4
M. Maddux, RP	4
S. Rawley, SP	4
M. Young, OF	4
L. Aguayo, SS	3
B. Ruffin, RP	3
T. Barrett, 2B	1
D. Daulton, C	1
J. Gutierrez, SS	1
A. Madrid, RP	1
K. Miller, OF	1
B. Moore, RP	1
W. Ritchie, RP	1
S. Service, RP	1

Pittsburgh (85-75)	WS
Hitting	**132.4**
Fielding	**40.0**
Pitching	**82.7**
B. Bonilla, 3B	31
A. Van Slyke, OF	28
B. Bonds, OF	26
M. LaValliere, C	17
S. Bream, 1B	16
D. Drabek, SP	15
J. Lind, 2B	15
B. Walk, SP	14
J. Robinson, RP	12
J. Smiley, SP	12
J. Gott, RP	11
R. Reynolds, OF	8
D. Coles, OF	6
R. Belliard, SS	4
J. Cangelosi, OF	4
M. Dunne, SP	4
B. Jones, RP	4
D. LaPoint, SP	4
R. Milligan, 1B	3
M. Diaz, OF	2
B. Distefano, 1B	2
F. Fermin, SS	2
B. Fisher, SP	2
B. Kipper, RP	2
J. Ortiz, C	2
G. Wilson, OF	2
M. Madden, RP	1
S. Medvin, RP	1

K. Oberkfell, 2B	1
A. Pedrique, SS	1
T. Prince, C	1
G. Redus, OF	1
R. Reed, SP	1

San Diego (83-78)	WS
Hitting	**111.1**
Fielding	**44.1**
Pitching	**93.8**
T. Gwynn, OF	23
R. Alomar, 2B	22
M. Davis, RP	19
M. Wynne, OF	15
E. Show, SP	14
J. Kruk, 1B	13
D. Rasmussen, SP	13
R. Ready, 3B	13
A. Hawkins, SP	12
G. Templeton, SS	12
C. Martinez, OF	11
L. McCullers, RP	10
B. Santiago, C	10
K. Moreland, 1B	9
D. Thon, SS	9
E. Whitson, SP	9
T. Flannery, 3B	6
D. Leiper, RP	5
J. Jones, SP	4
S. Mack, OF	4
G. Booker, RP	3
C. Brown, 3B	3
M. Grant, RP	3
M. Parent, C	3
G. Harris, RP	2
J. Clark, OF	1
S. Jefferson, OF	1

San Francisco (83-79)	WS
Hitting	**138.3**
Fielding	**34.8**
Pitching	**75.8**
W. Clark, 1B	37
B. Butler, OF	27
K. Mitchell, 3B	20
R. Thompson, 2B	16
R. Reuschel, SP	15
D. Robinson, RP	14
M. Aldrete, OF	13
C. Maldonado, OF	12
J. Uribe, SS	12
K. Downs, SP	9
C. Lefferts, RP	8
S. Garrelts, RP	7
E. Riles, 3B	7
A. Hammaker, RP	6
M. Krukow, SP	6
M. LaCoss, SP	5
B. Melvin, C	5
J. Leonard, OF	4
D. Nixon, OF	4
C. Speier, 2B	4
B. Brenly, C	3
K. Manwaring, C	3
D. Cook, SP	2
T. Mulholland, SP	2
M. Williams, 3B	2
J. Youngblood, OF	2
D. Dravecky, SP	1
J. Price, RP	1
R. Samuels, RP	1
R. Tillman, OF	1

St. Louis (76-86)	WS
Hitting	**92.1**
Fielding	**43.1**
Pitching	**92.7**
O. Smith, SS	22
T. Pena, C	17
T. Brunansky, OF	16
W. McGee, OF	16
T. Worrell, RP	15
V. Coleman, OF	14
J. Oquendo, 2B	14
J. Magrane, SP	13
J. DeLeon, SP	12
J. Tudor, SP	12
S. Terry, RP	11
T. Pendleton, 3B	9
P. Guerrero, 1B	8
B. Forsch, RP	7
J. Costello, RP	6
K. Dayley, RP	6
L. McWilliams, RP	6
B. Horner, 1B	4
T. Pagnozzi, C-1B	4
L. Alicea, 2B	3
D. Cox, SP	3
T. Jones, SS	2
G. Mathews, SP	2
R. Booker, 3B	1
C. Carpenter, SP	1
C. Ford, OF	1
T. Herr, 2B	1
S. Lake, C	1
R. O'Neal, SP	1

1989 American League

Baltimore (87-75)	WS
Hitting	**130.4**
Fielding	**43.8**
Pitching	**86.8**
C. Ripken Jr., SS	26
P. Bradley, OF	20
M. Tettleton, C	20
C. Worthington, 3B	20
R. Milligan, 1B	19
G. Olson, RP	18
J. Ballard, SP	15
B. Milacki, SP	14
J. Orsulak, OF	14
M. Devereaux, OF	12
M. Williamson, RP	12
B. Anderson, OF	7
B. Ripken, 2B	6
S. Finley, OF	5
K. Hickey, RP	5
T. Hulett, 2B	5
B. Melvin, C	5
L. Sheets, DH	5
M. Thurmond, RP	5
J. Tibbs, SP	5
B. Holton, RP	4
S. Jefferson, OF	4
D. Johnson, SP	4
P. Harnisch, SP	3
R. Gonzales, 2B	2
J. Quirk, C	2
J. Traber, 1B	2
J. Bautista, SP	1
D. Schmidt, SP	1

Boston (83-79)	WS
Hitting	**126.0**
Fielding	**40.0**
Pitching	**83.0**
W. Boggs, 3B	29
N. Esasky, 1B	24
D. Evans, OF	21
R. Clemens, SP	18
J. Reed, SS	17
E. Burks, OF	16
M. Greenwell, OF	15
M. Boddicker, SP	11
L. Smith, RP	11
D. Lamp, RP	10
R. Murphy, RP	10
J. Dopson, SP	9
D. Heep, OF	9
R. Cerone, C	8
M. Barrett, 2B	6
L. Rivera, SS	6
K. Romine, OF	4
M. Smithson, RP	4
O. Boyd, SP	3
R. Gedman, C	3
R. Kutcher, OF	3
J. Price, RP	3
G. Harris, RP	2
J. Rice, DH	2
E. Romero, 2B	2
B. Stanley, RP	2
J. Marzano, C	1

California (91-71)	WS
Hitting	**111.8**
Fielding	**49.6**
Pitching	**111.6**
B. Blyleven, SP	22
C. Davis, OF	22
C. Finley, SP	19
W. Joyner, 1B	19
K. McCaskill, SP	18
J. Ray, 2B	18
B. Downing, DH	17
J. Howell, 3B	16
D. White, OF	14
G. Minton, RP	12
L. Parrish, C	12
C. Washington, OF	12
J. Abbott, SP	8
B. Harvey, RP	8
B. McClure, RP	8
D. Schofield, SS	8
T. Armas, OF	7
W. Fraser, RP	7
M. Witt, SP	6
K. Anderson, SS	5
M. McLemore, 2B	3
R. Monteleone, RP	3
D. Bichette, OF	2
B. Schroeder, C	2
M. Venable, OF	2
G. Hoffman, SS	1
J. Orton, C	1
D. Petry, RP	1

Chicago (69-92)	WS
Hitting	**116.8**
Fielding	**33.0**
Pitching	**57.2**
I. Calderon, OF	18
C. Fisk, C	18
H. Baines, DH	16
O. Guillen, SS	12
S. Lyons, 2B	11
D. Gallagher, OF	10
E. King, SP	9
R. Kittle, 1B	9
D. Pasqua, OF	9
G. Hibbard, SP	8
B. Thigpen, RP	8
R. Karkovice, C	7
F. Manrique, 2B	7
D. Boston, OF	6
S. Fletcher, 2B	6
L. Johnson, OF	6
C. Martinez, 3B	6
D. Pall, RP	6
B. Long, RP	4
M. Perez, SP	4
R. Dotson, SP	3
S. Hillegas, RP	3
B. Jones, RP	3
T. McCarthy, RP	3
K. Patterson, RP	3
E. Williams, 3B	3
J. Reuss, SP	2
S. Sosa, OF	2
G. Walker, 1B	2
M. Merullo, C	1
S. Rosenberg, SP	1
R. Ventura, 3B	1

Cleveland (73-89)	WS
Hitting	**74.3**
Fielding	**44.0**
Pitching	**100.7**
J. Carter, OF	20
J. Browne, 2B	17
T. Candiotti, SP	16
D. Jones, RP	16
B. Black, SP	15
B. Jacoby, 3B	14
P. O'Brien, 1B	14
G. Swindell, SP	14
J. Farrell, SP	12
J. Orosco, RP	10
F. Fermin, SS	9
B. Komminsk, OF	9
C. Snyder, OF	8
A. Belle, OF	6
D. James, OF	6
S. Bailes, RP	5
A. Allanson, C	4
D. Clark, DH	3
O. McDowell, OF	3
R. Yett, RP	3
R. Nichols, SP	2
S. Olin, RP	2
J. Skinner, C	2
T. Stoddard, RP	2
L. Aguayo, 3B	1
B. Allred, OF	1
K. Atherton, RP	1
B. Havens, RP	1
M. Salas, DH	1
E. Wojna, RP	1
P. Zuvella, SS	1

Detroit (59-103)	WS
Hitting	**95.2**
Fielding	**28.2**
Pitching	**53.6**
L. Whitaker, 2B	25
A. Trammell, SS	13
F. Tanana, SP	12
M. Heath, C	11
D. Bergman, 1B	10
C. Lemon, OF	10
G. Pettis, OF	10
F. Lynn, OF	9
D. Alexander, SP	8
M. Henneman, RP	8
M. Nokes, C	8
K. Moreland, DH	6
P. Gibson, RP	5
T. Jones, OF	5
J. Morris, SP	4
F. Williams, RP	4
B. DuBois, SP	3
K. Ritz, SP	3
P. Sheridan, OF	3
K. Williams, OF	3
M. Brumley, SS	2
S. Lusader, OF	2
E. Nunez, RP	2
R. Richie, OF	2
J. Robinson, SP	2
G. Ward, OF	2
W. Hernandez, RP	1
S. Holman, RP	1
A. Pedrique, 3B-SS	1
R. Schu, 3B	1
D. Strange, 3B	1

Kansas City (92-70)	WS
Hitting	**124.7**
Fielding	**44.0**
Pitching	**107.2**
B. Saberhagen, SP	28
K. Seitzer, 3B	22
J. Eisenreich, OF	21
B. Boone, C	20
M. Gubicza, SP	19
B. Jackson, OF	19
J. Montgomery, RP	19
G. Brett, 1B	17
K. Stillwell, SS	15
F. White, 2B	14
F. Gordon, RP	13

Player	WS
D. Tartabull, OF	13
W. Wilson, OF	10
L. Aquino, RP	8
S. Crawford, RP	5
P. Tabler, OF	5
S. Farr, RP	4
M. Macfarlane, C	4
F. Bannister, SP	3
B. Wellman, 2B	3
T. Leach, RP	2
C. Leibrandt, SP	2
R. Luecken, RP	2
L. McWilliams, SP	2
G. Thurman, OF	2
L. de los Santos, 1B	1
R. Palacios, 3B	1
B. Pecota, SS	1
M. Winters, OF	1

Milwaukee (81-81)	WS
Hitting	**119.8**
Fielding	**38.5**
Pitching	**84.7**
R. Yount, OF	34
P. Molitor, 3B	27
C. Bosio, SP	17
R. Deer, OF	12
J. Gantner, 2B	12
C. Crim, RP	11
D. Plesac, RP	11
G. Braggs, OF	10
G. Brock, 1B	10
T. Higuera, SP	9
C. O'Brien, C	9
B. Spiers, SS	9
M. Knudson, RP	8
B. Surhoff, C	8
J. Navarro, SP	7
M. Felder, OF	6
G. Sheffield, SS	6
G. Vaughn, OF	6
T. Filer, SP	5
B. Krueger, RP	5
T. Fossas, RP	4
T. Francona, 1B	3
J. Meyer, DH	3
J. Aldrich, RP	2
D. August, SP	2
B. Clutterbuck, SP	2
G. Polidor, 3B	2
G. Canale, 1B	1
D. Engle, 1B	1
J. Peterek, SP	1

Minnesota (80-82)	WS
Hitting	**120.3**
Fielding	**40.3**
Pitching	**79.4**
K. Puckett, OF	27
K. Hrbek, 1B	18
B. Harper, C	14
R. Bush, OF	13
A. Anderson, SP	12
G. Gaetti, 3B	12
G. Gagne, SS	12
D. Gladden, OF	12
G. Larkin, 1B	11
A. Newman, 2B	11
J. Reardon, RP	11
R. Smith, SP	10
F. Viola, SP	10
J. Berenguer, RP	9
J. Moses, OF	8
J. Dwyer, DH	6
G. Wayne, RP	6
R. Aguilera, SP	5
C. Castillo, OF	5
W. Backman, 2B	4
D. Baker, 2B	3
T. Laudner, C	3
F. Oliveras, SP	3
S. Rawley, SP	3
M. Dyer, SP	2
M. Guthrie, SP	2
K. Tapani, SP	2
M. Cook, RP	1
T. Drummond, RP	1
G. Gonzalez, RP	1
O. Mercado, C	1
R. St. Claire, RP	1
L. Webster, C	1

New York (74-87)	WS
Hitting	**124.8**
Fielding	**33.7**
Pitching	**63.6**
D. Mattingly, 1B	26
S. Sax, 2B	21
R. Kelly, OF	16
J. Barfield, OF	15
L. Guetterman, RP	13
A. Espinoza, SS	12
D. Slaught, C	11
R. Henderson, OF	10
B. Geren, C	8
M. Hall, OF	8
D. Righetti, RP	8
S. Balboni, DH	7
A. Hawkins, SP	7
C. Parker, SP	7
L. Polonia, OF	7
C. Cary, SP-RP	6
K. Phelps, DH	5
E. Plunk, RP	5
R. Velarde, 3B	5
L. McCullers, RP	4
G. Cadaret, SP	3
J. Candelaria, SP	2
B. Dorsett, C	2
D. LaPoint, SP	2
W. Terrell, SP	2
M. Blowers, 3B	1
T. Brookens, 3B	1
R. Dotson, SP	1
G. Gossage, RP	1
J. Jones, SP	1
D. Mohorcic, RP	1
M. Pagliarulo, 3B	1
D. Sanders, OF	1
D. Schulze, SP	1
W. Tolleson, 3B-SS	1

Oakland (99-63)	WS
Hitting	**134.5**
Fielding	**51.4**
Pitching	**111.1**
C. Lansford, 3B	21
M. McGwire, 1B	21
R. Henderson, OF	20
D. Henderson, OF	19
M. Moore, SP	19
D. Stewart, SP	16
D. Parker, DH	15
J. Canseco, OF	14
D. Eckersley, RP	14
T. Phillips, 2B	14
B. Welch, SP	14
T. Steinbach, C	13
M. Gallego, SS	12
T. Burns, RP	11
R. Honeycutt, RP	10
S. Javier, OF	9
S. Davis, SP	7
L. Polonia, OF	7
W. Weiss, SS	7
R. Hassey, C	6
G. Nelson, RP	6
J. Corsi, RP	4
G. Hubbard, 2B	4
C. Young, SP	4
E. Plunk, RP	3
B. Beane, OF	2
L. Blankenship, OF	2
G. Cadaret, RP	2
F. Jose, OF	1

Seattle (73-89)	WS
Hitting	**102.3**
Fielding	**36.4**
Pitching	**80.3**
A. Davis, 1B	26
H. Reynolds, 2B	20
S. Bankhead, SP	15
K. Griffey Jr., OF	14
G. Briley, OF	11
M. Schooler, RP	11
B. Holman, SP	10
J. Leonard, DH	10
E. Hanson, SP	9
D. Valle, C	9
S. Bradley, C	8
J. Buhner, OF	8
D. Coles, OF	8
H. Cotto, OF	8
M. Jackson, RP	8
J. Reed, RP	7
B. Swift, RP	6
R. Johnson, SP	5
M. Langston, SP	5
E. Martinez, 3B	4
J. Presley, 3B	4
O. Vizquel, SS	3
K. Comstock, RP	2
M. Kingery, OF	2
D. Powell, RP	2
M. Brantley, OF	1
D. Cochrane, SS	1
B. McGuire, C	1
C. Zavaras, SP	1

Texas (83-79)	WS
Hitting	**117.9**
Fielding	**41.6**
Pitching	**89.5**
R. Sierra, OF	34
J. Franco, 2B	30
N. Ryan, SP	18
R. Palmeiro, 1B	17
J. Russell, RP	16
P. Incaviglia, OF	14
K. Brown, SP	13
S. Buechele, 3B	11
C. Espy, OF	10
J. Kunkel, SS	9
C. Hough, SP	8
M. Jeffcoat, SP	8
K. Rogers, RP	7
F. Manrique, SS	6
G. Petralli, C	5
B. Witt, SP	5
S. Fletcher, SS	4
C. Guante, RP	4
D. Hall, RP	4
R. Leach, DH	4
G. Mielke, RP	4
J. Daugherty, 1B	3
J. Sundberg, C	3
B. Arnsberg, RP	2
H. Baines, DH	2
S. Coolbaugh, 3B	2
C. Kreuter, C	2
T. Bosley, OF	1
J. Gonzalez, OF	1
J. Moyer, SP	1
M. Stanley, C	1

Toronto (89-73)	WS
Hitting	**139.9**
Fielding	**38.1**
Pitching	**89.0**
F. McGriff, 1B	30
G. Bell, OF	22
T. Fernandez, SS	20
K. Gruber, 3B	20
E. Whitt, C	16
T. Henke, RP	15
N. Liriano, 2B	15
D. Stieb, SP	13
J. Cerutti, SP	12
L. Moseby, OF	12
J. Felix, OF	11
J. Key, SP	10
D. Wells, RP	9
M. Lee, 2B	8
D. Ward, RP	8
M. Flanagan, SP	7
T. Stottlemyre, SP	6
P. Borders, C	5
F. Wills, RP	4
M. Wilson, OF	4
J. Acker, RP	3
L. Mazzilli, DH	3
R. Mulliniks, DH	3
S. Cummings, RP	2
R. Ducey, OF	2
G. Hill, OF	2
J. Barfield, OF	1
M. Gozzo, RP	1
T. Lawless, OF	1
J. Nunez, RP	1
O. Virgil, DH	1

1989 National League

Atlanta (63-97)	WS
Hitting	**76.2**
Fielding	**34.9**
Pitching	**77.9**
L. Smith, OF	27
J. Smoltz, SP	15
D. Murphy, OF	14
J. Blauser, 3B	12
O. McDowell, OF	11
J. Treadway, 2B	11
T. Glavine, SP	10
J. Acker, RP	8
J. Boever, RP	8
M. Clary, SP	7
D. Lilliquist, SP	6
D. Evans, 1B	5
M. Stanton, RP	5
A. Thomas, SS	5
J. Alvarez, RP	4
B. Benedict, C	4
G. Perry, 1B	4
P. Assenmacher, RP	3
J. Davis, C	3
G. Eave, SP	3
M. Eichhorn, RP	3
T. Gregg, OF	3
D. James, OF	3
G. Berroa, OF	2
J. Russell, C	2
P. Smith, SP	2
J. Aldrich, RP	1
D. Denson, 1B	1
R. Gant, 3B	1
T. Greene, SP	1
D. Henry, RP	1
M. Lemke, 2B	1
C. Puleo, RP	1
E. Romero, 2B	1
J. Wetherby, OF	1

Chicago (93-69)	WS
Hitting	**127.9**
Fielding	**46.6**
Pitching	**104.5**
R. Sandberg, 2B	28
M. Grace, 1B	25
G. Maddux, SP	20
S. Dunston, SS	18
J. Walton, OF	17
M. Bielecki, SP	16
D. Smith, OF	16
R. Sutcliffe, SP	14
A. Dawson, OF	13
L. Lancaster, RP	13
D. Berryhill, C	12
M. Williams, RP	12
L. McClendon, OF	11
S. Sanderson, SP	7

M. Webster, OF	7
D. Ramos, SS	6
J. Pico, RP	5
C. Schiraldi, RP	5
S. Wilson, RP	5
J. Girardi, C	4
P. Perry, RP	4
L. Salazar, 3B	4
R. Wrona, C	4
P. Kilgus, SP	3
V. Law, 3B	3
D. Jackson, OF	2
P. Assenmacher, RP	1
K. Blankenship, RP	1
D. Dascenzo, OF	1
G. Smith, 2B	1
C. Wilkerson, 3B	1

Cincinnati (75-87)	**WS**
Hitting	**105.3**
Fielding	**38.3**
Pitching	**81.4**
E. Davis, OF	26
P. O'Neill, OF	18
B. Larkin, SS	15
T. Browning, SP	14
R. Dibble, RP	14
T. Benzinger, 1B	10
J. Franco, RP	10
L. Quinones, 2B	10
R. Mahler, SP	9
J. Rijo, SP	9
C. Sabo, 3B	9
N. Charlton, RP	8
K. Griffey Sr., OF	8
R. Roomes, OF	8
R. Oester, 2B	7
J. Reed, C	7
M. Duncan, SS	5
R. Robinson, SP	5
T. Birtsas, RP	4
K. Daniels, OF	4
T. Leary, SP	4
J. Oliver, C	4
H. Winningham, OF	4
B. Diaz, C	2
L. Harris, 2B	2
S. Scudder, SP	2
J. Armstrong, SP	1
D. Collins, OF	1
S. Madison, 3B	1
T. McGriff, C	1
J. Richardson, SS	1
M. Roesler, RP	1
J. Youngblood, OF	1

Houston (86-76)	**WS**
Hitting	**133.7**
Fielding	**40.1**
Pitching	**84.2**
G. Davis, 1B	30
K. Caminiti, 3B	25
C. Biggio, C	18
G. Young, OF	18
K. Bass, OF	17
B. Doran, 2B	17
J. Deshaies, SP	15
M. Scott, SP	15
D. Darwin, RP	14
T. Puhl, OF	13
L. Andersen, RP	11
D. Smith, RP	10
B. Hatcher, OF	9
M. Portugal, SP	9
R. Ramirez, SS	9
J. Agosto, RP	6
A. Trevino, C	4
E. Yelding, SS	3
G. Gross, OF	2
C. Reynolds, 2B	2
R. Rhoden, SP	2
D. Schatzeder, RP	2
G. Wilson, OF	2
E. Anthony, OF	1
M. Davidson, OF	1
B. Knepper, SP	1
S. Lombardozzi, 2B	1
H. Spilman, 1B	1

Los Angeles (77-83)	**WS**
Hitting	**88.0**
Fielding	**46.2**
Pitching	**96.8**
O. Hershiser, SP	21
E. Murray, 1B	21
W. Randolph, 2B	20
J. Howell, RP	16
M. Scioscia, C	16
T. Belcher, SP	15
A. Griffin, SS	11
M. Marshall, OF	11
M. Morgan, RP	10
J. Hamilton, 3B	9
A. Pena, RP	9
F. Valenzuela, SP	8
J. Gonzalez, OF	7
R. Dempsey, C	6
K. Gibson, OF	5
T. Leary, SP	5
R. Martinez, SP	5
F. Stubbs, OF	5
D. Anderson, SS	4
M. Hatcher, OF	4
K. Daniels, OF	3
M. Davis, OF	3
J. Wetteland, RP	3
T. Crews, RP	2
M. Duncan, SS	2
L. Harris, OF	2
R. Searage, RP	2
J. Shelby, OF	2
D. Fletcher, C	1
C. Gwynn, OF	1
M. Sharperson, 2B	1
J. Tudor, SP-RP	1

Montreal (81-81)	**WS**
Hitting	**107.7**
Fielding	**42.7**
Pitching	**92.6**
T. Raines, OF	25
T. Wallach, 3B	20
T. Burke, RP	17
A. Galarraga, 1B	16
De. Martinez, SP	16
M. Langston, SP	15
S. Owen, SS	15
B. Smith, SP	15
H. Brooks, OF	13
T. Foley, 2B	13
Da. Martinez, OF	12
P. Perez, SP	11
M. Fitzgerald, C	9
N. Santovenia, C	7
K. Gross, SP	6
O. Nixon, OF	6
Z. Smith, RP	6
D. Garcia, 2B	5
R. Hudler, 2B	3
M. Grissom, OF	2
A. McGaffigan, RP	2
R. Thompson, RP	2
M. Aldrete, OF	1
J. Candelaria, RP	1
J. Dwyer, PH-PR	1
J. Huson, SS	1
W. Johnson, 1B	1
J. Noboa, 2B	1
M. Pevey, C	1

New York (87-75)	**WS**
Hitting	**135.8**
Fielding	**39.6**
Pitching	**85.6**
H. Johnson, 3B	38
K. McReynolds, OF	21
K. Elster, SS	18
D. Strawberry, OF	18
S. Fernandez, SP	16
D. Magadan, 1B	16
G. Jefferies, 2B	14
R. Myers, RP	13
D. Cone, SP	11
R. Darling, SP	9
L. Dykstra, OF	8
D. Gooden, SP	8
B. Ojeda, SP	8
R. Aguilera, RP	7
J. Samuel, OF	7
M. Sasser, C	6
T. Teufel, 2B	6
M. Carreon, OF	5
B. Lyons, C	5
F. Viola, SP	4
K. Hernandez, 1B	3
L. Mazzilli, OF	3
D. Aase, RP	2
G. Carter, C	2
J. Innis, RP	2
J. Musselman, RP	2
T. O'Malley, 3B	2
M. Wilson, OF	2
B. Beatty, SP-RP	1
P. Lombardi, C	1
J. Machado, RP	1
R. McDowell, RP	1
K. Miller, 2B	1

Philadelphia (67-95)	**WS**
Hitting	**110.6**
Fielding	**31.2**
Pitching	**59.1**
V. Hayes, OF	25
D. Thon, SS	20
T. Herr, 2B	17
R. Jordan, 1B	12
D. Daulton, C	11
K. Howell, SP	11
J. Kruk, OF	11
R. McDowell, RP	10
J. Parrett, RP	10
S. Jeltz, SS	9
L. Dykstra, OF	6
C. Hayes, 3B	6
R. Ready, OF	6
J. Samuel, OF	5
P. Combs, SP	4
D. Cook, SP	4
G. Harris, RP	4
D. Murphy, OF	4
S. Bedrosian, RP	3
T. Frohwirth, RP	3
S. Lake, C	3
B. Ruffin, SP	3
M. Schmidt, 3B	3
L. McWilliams, RP	2
B. Dernier, OF	1
C. Ford, OF	1
C. James, OF	1
R. Jones, OF	1
C. McElroy, RP	1
T. Mulholland, SP	1
T. Nieto, C	1
S. Ontiveros, SP	1
B. Sebra, SP	1

Pittsburgh (74-88)	**WS**
Hitting	**117.0**
Fielding	**34.0**
Pitching	**71.1**
B. Bonilla, 3B	29
B. Bonds, OF	23
D. Drabek, SP	14
B. Landrum, RP	14
A. Van Slyke, OF	14
G. Wilson, OF	14
G. Redus, 1B	13
J. Smiley, SP	12
R. Reynolds, OF	11
J. Lind, 2B	10
J. Bell, SS	8
N. Heaton, RP	8
M. LaValliere, C	8
D. Bair, RP	6
B. Kipper, RP	6
J. Cangelosi, OF	4
R. Quinones, SS	4
B. Walk, SP	4
J. King, 1B	3
R. Kramer, RP	3
R. Belliard, SS	2
D. Bilardello, C	2
B. Distefano, 1B	2
J. Ortiz, C	2
S. Bream, 1B	1
L. Easley, RP	1
B. Hatcher, OF	1
B. Patterson, RP	1
J. Robinson, RP	1
M. Smith, RP	1

San Diego (89-73)	**WS**
Hitting	**128.2**
Fielding	**43.3**
Pitching	**95.4**
Ja. Clark, 1B	31
T. Gwynn, OF	30
R. Alomar, 2B	23
M. Davis, RP	19
B. Hurst, SP	18
B. Roberts, OF	18
E. Whitson, SP	18
G. Harris, RP	13
B. Santiago, C	13
G. Templeton, SS	11
M. Grant, RP	8
M. Wynne, OF	8
C. James, OF	7
L. Salazar, 3B	6
A. Benes, SP	5
D. Rasmussen, SP	5
C. Martinez, OF	4
E. Show, SP	4
R. Nelson, 1B	3
M. Pagliarulo, 3B	3
W. Terrell, SP	3
P. Clements, RP	2
T. Flannery, 3B	2
M. Parent, C	2
R. Ready, 3B	2
C. Schiraldi, SP	2
S. Abner, OF	1
S. Alomar Jr., C	1
J. Cora, SS	1
G. Green, SS	1
D. Jackson, OF	1
J. Kruk, OF	1
P. Stephenson, 1B	1

San Francisco (92-70)	**WS**
Hitting	**148.3**
Fielding	**42.2**
Pitching	**85.5**
W. Clark, 1B	44
K. Mitchell, OF	38
B. Butler, OF	20
R. Thompson, 2B	19
S. Garrelts, SP	15
R. Reuschel, SP	13
T. Kennedy, C	12
C. Lefferts, RP	11
E. Riles, 3B	11
J. Uribe, SS	11
D. Robinson, SP	10
M. LaCoss, RP	8
S. Bedrosian, RP	7
C. Maldonado, OF	7
M. Williams, 3B	7
G. Gossage, RP	4
A. Hammaker, RP	4
G. Litton, 3B	4

K. Manwaring, C	4
K. Oberkfell, 3B	4
J. Brantley, RP	3
B. Knepper, RP	3
D. Nixon, OF	3
E. Camacho, RP	2
D. Cook, SP	2
M. Krukow, SP	2
P. Sheridan, OF	2
B. Brenly, C	1
D. Dravecky, SP	1
E. Jurak, SS	1
M. Laga, 1B	1
C. Speier, 3B-SS	1
T. Wilson, RP	1

St. Louis (86-76)	WS
Hitting	**116.5**
Fielding	**44.2**
Pitching	**97.3**
P. Guerrero, 1B	30
J. Oquendo, 2B	22
O. Smith, SS	20
M. Thompson, OF	19
J. Magrane, SP	18
T. Pendleton, 3B	18
T. Brunansky, OF	16
J. DeLeon, SP	15
V. Coleman, OF	11
K. Dayley, RP	10
T. Pena, C	10
F. DiPino, RP	9
D. Quisenberry, RP	8
S. Terry, SP	8
K. Hill, SP	7
T. Worrell, RP	7
J. Costello, RP	6
C. Carpenter, RP	4
W. McGee, OF	4
T. Power, SP	4
D. Walling, 1B	3
T. Jones, 2B-SS	2
J. Morris, OF	2
B. Tewksbury, SP	2
T. Zeile, C	2
R. Horton, SP	1

1990
American League

Baltimore (76-85)	WS
Hitting	**112.5**
Fielding	**40.6**
Pitching	**75.0**
C. Ripken Jr., SS	20
R. Milligan, 1B	17
B. Ripken, 2B	16
M. Tettleton, C	16
G. Olson, RP	14
J. Orsulak, OF	14
B. McDonald, SP	10
P. Bradley, OF	9
D. Johnson, SP	9
M. Williamson, RP	9
M. Devereaux, OF	8
S. Finley, OF	8
S. Horn, DH	8
C. Worthington, 3B	8
B. Anderson, OF	7
P. Harnisch, SP	7
B. Melvin, C	7
T. Hulett, 3B	6
C. Schilling, RP	5
B. Milacki, SP	4
J. Price, RP	4
J. Mesa, SP	3
J. Mitchell, SP	3
J. Ballard, RP	2
R. Gonzales, 2B	2
B. Holton, RP	2
B. Komminsk, OF	2
D. Segui, 1B	2
J. Bautista, RP	1
D. Boone, RP	1
D. Gallagher, OF	1
L. Gomez, 3B	1
D. Nixon, OF	1
A. Telford, SP	1

Boston (88-74)	WS
Hitting	**110.1**
Fielding	**43.5**
Pitching	**110.4**
R. Clemens, SP	28
W. Boggs, 3B	24
Jo. Reed, 2B	22
E. Burks, OF	21
M. Boddicker, SP	19
M. Greenwell, OF	16
T. Pena, C	15
C. Quintana, 1B	13
T. Brunansky, OF	12
G. Harris, SP	12
T. Bolton, SP	10
J. Reardon, RP	10
D. Evans, DH	9
D. Kiecker, SP	9
L. Rivera, SS	6
M. Barrett, 2B	4
J. Gray, RP	4
D. Lamp, RP	4
L. Andersen, RP	3
W. Gardner, RP	3
M. Marshall, DH	3
T. Naehring, SS	3
L. Smith, RP	3
J. Dopson, SP	2
J. Marzano, C	2
Je. Reed, RP	2
K. Romine, OF	2
J. Hesketh, RP	1
D. Irvine, RP	1
R. Kutcher, OF	1

California (80-82)	WS
Hitting	**114.8**
Fielding	**35.7**
Pitching	**89.5**
L. Parrish, C	24
C. Finley, SP	23
B. Downing, DH	13
D. Winfield, OF	13
K. McCaskill, SP	12
L. Polonia, OF	12
B. Harvey, RP	11
C. Davis, DH	10
J. Ray, 2B	10
W. Joyner, 1B	9
D. Schofield, SS	9
J. Abbott, SP	8
M. Eichhorn, RP	8
D. Hill, 2B	8
M. Langston, SP	8
D. Bichette, OF	7
W. Fraser, RP	7
J. Howell, 3B	7
D. White, OF	7
M. Venable, OF	5
K. Anderson, SS	3
B. Blyleven, SP	3
M. Fetters, RP	3
L. Stevens, 1B	3
P. Coachman, 3B	2
S. Lewis, SP	2
G. Minton, RP	2
B. Schroeder, C	2
R. Schu, 3B	2
M. Witt, RP	2
C. Young, RP	2
J. Grahe, SP	1
J. Orton, C	1
B. Rose, 2B	1

Chicago (94-68)	WS
Hitting	**121.7**
Fielding	**51.5**
Pitching	**108.9**
I. Calderon, OF	22
C. Fisk, C	22
B. Thigpen, RP	21
O. Guillen, SS	18
L. Johnson, OF	18
G. Hibbard, SP	16
D. Pasqua, DH	15
R. Ventura, 3B	15
S. Fletcher, 2B	13
S. Sosa, OF	13
F. Thomas, 1B	13
E. King, SP	12
J. McDowell, SP	12
B. Jones, RP	11
R. Karkovice, C	8
R. Kittle, DH	8
W. Edwards, RP	7
M. Perez, SP	7
D. Pall, RP	6
A. Fernandez, SP	5
K. Patterson, RP	5
S. Radinsky, RP	4
P. Bradley, OF	2
C. Grebeck, 3B	2
S. Hillegas, RP	2
A. Peterson, SP	2
D. Gallagher, OF	1
S. Lyons, 1B	1
C. Martinez, 1B	1

Cleveland (77-85)	WS
Hitting	**123.7**
Fielding	**37.1**
Pitching	**70.2**
B. Jacoby, 3B	19
C. Maldonado, OF	18
J. Browne, 2B	17
C. James, DH	16
S. Alomar Jr., C	15
D. Jones, RP	15
M. Webster, OF	13
T. Candiotti, SP	12
B. Black, SP	11
A. Cole, OF	10
F. Fermin, SS	9
G. Swindell, SP	9
C. Baerga, 3B	8
C. Snyder, OF	7
D. James, 1B	6
S. Olin, RP	6
T. Brookens, 3B	5
J. Manto, 1B	5
J. Farrell, SP	4
J. Skinner, C	4
S. Jefferson, OF	3
J. Orosco, RP	3
S. Valdez, SP	3
T. Ward, OF	3
C. Ward, RP	2
C. Guante, RP	1
K. Hernandez, 1B	1
J. Kaiser, RP	1
R. Santana, SS	1
R. Seanez, RP	1
E. Valdez, RP	1
M. Walker, SP	1
K. Wickander, RP	1

Detroit (79-83)	WS
Hitting	**132.5**
Fielding	**37.2**
Pitching	**67.3**
C. Fielder, 1B	29
A. Trammell, SS	29
T. Phillips, 3B	22
L. Whitaker, 2B	19
M. Henneman, RP	12
L. Moseby, OF	11
J. Gleaton, RP	9
C. Lemon, OF	9
T. Fryman, 3B	8
J. Morris, SP	8
E. Nunez, RP	8
G. Ward, OF	8
P. Gibson, RP	7
L. Sheets, OF	7
D. Petry, SP	6
D. Bergman, DH	5
M. Heath, C	5
M. Salas, C	5
F. Tanana, SP	4
S. Lusader, OF	3
C. Parker, RP	3
J. Shelby, OF	3
W. Terrell, SP	3
M. Cuyler, OF	2
L. McCullers, RP	2
S. Searcy, SP	2
S. Aldred, SP	1
D. Coles, DH	1
B. DuBois, SP	1
J. Lindeman, DH	1
M. Nokes, DH	1
J. Robinson, SP	1
E. Romero, 3B	1
K. Williams, OF	1

Kansas City (75-86)	WS
Hitting	**115.6**
Fielding	**36.3**
Pitching	**73.2**
G. Brett, 1B	26
K. Seitzer, 3B	21
B. Jackson, OF	16
K. Appier, SP	13
S. Farr, RP	13
J. Eisenreich, OF	12
J. Montgomery, RP	12
K. Stillwell, SS	12
W. Wilson, OF	11
D. Tartabull, OF	10
F. Gordon, SP	9
M. Macfarlane, C	8
B. Pecota, 2B	8
G. Perry, DH	7
B. Saberhagen, SP	7
B. McRae, OF	5
L. Aquino, RP	4
S. Crawford, RP	4
A. McGaffigan, RP	4
P. Tabler, OF	4
F. White, 2B	4
S. Davis, SP	3
M. Gubicza, SP	3
S. Jeltz, 2B	2
T. Shumpert, 2B	2
S. Berry, 3B	1
B. Boone, C	1
M. Davis, RP	1
R. Morman, OF	1
R. Palacios, C	1

Milwaukee (74-88)	WS
Hitting	**127.0**
Fielding	**28.0**
Pitching	**67.1**
G. Sheffield, 3B	20
P. Molitor, 2B	19
R. Yount, OF	18
R. Deer, OF	15
D. Parker, DH	15
B. Surhoff, C	15
R. Robinson, SP	10
G. Vaughn, OF	10
G. Brock, 1B	9
T. Higuera, SP	8
C. Crim, RP	7
M. Felder, OF	7
J. Gantner, 2B	7
M. Knudson, SP	7
D. Plesac, RP	6
C. Bosio, SP	5
D. Hamilton, OF	5
B. Krueger, SP	5

J. Navarro, SP	5
B. Spiers, SS	5
E. Diaz, SS	3
T. Edens, RP	3
P. Mirabella, RP	3
G. Braggs, OF	2
K. Brown, SP	2
M. Lee, RP	2
J. Machado, RP	2
C. O'Brien, C	2
D. Sveum, 3B	2
R. Veres, RP	2
B. Bates, 2B	1

Minnesota (74-88)	WS
Hitting	**93.4**
Fielding	**41.8**
Pitching	**86.8**
K. Puckett, OF	22
K. Hrbek, 1B	19
B. Harper, C	14
S. Mack, OF	14
G. Gaetti, 3B	13
R. Aguilera, RP	12
D. Gladden, OF	11
K. Tapani, SP	10
S. Erickson, SP	9
M. Guthrie, SP	9
G. Larkin, OF	9
J. Berenguer, RP	8
J. Ortiz, C	8
A. Anderson, SP	7
J. Candelaria, RP	7
G. Gagne, SS	7
T. Leach, RP	7
N. Liriano, 2B	5
A. Newman, 2B	5
R. Smith, SP	5
T. Drummond, RP	4
D. West, SP	4
R. Bush, OF	3
L. Casian, SP	2
F. Manrique, 2B	2
G. Wayne, RP	2
R. Garces, RP	1
J. Moses, OF	1
P. Munoz, OF	1
P. Sorrento, DH	1

New York (67-95)	WS
Hitting	**87.7**
Fielding	**38.3**
Pitching	**75.0**
J. Barfield, OF	22
R. Kelly, OF	19
S. Sax, 2B	14
K. Maas, 1B	11
L. Guetterman, RP	10
T. Leary, SP	10
G. Cadaret, RP	7
C. Cary, SP	7
A. Espinoza, SS	7
B. Geren, C	7
M. Hall, DH	7
D. LaPoint, SP	7
D. Mattingly, 1B	7
E. Plunk, RP	7
D. Righetti, RP	7
M. Nokes, C	6
J. Robinson, RP	6
S. Balboni, DH	4
R. Cerone, C	4
J. Leyritz, 3B	4
M. Witt, SP	4
O. Azocar, OF	3
H. Meulens, OF	3
M. Blowers, 3B	2
D. Eiland, SP	2
A. Hawkins, SP	2
A. Mills, RP	2
P. Perez, SP	2
W. Tolleson, SS	2
R. Velarde, 3B	2
J. Habyan, RP	1
L. McCullers, RP	1
C. Parker, RP	1
D. Sanders, OF	1

Oakland (103-59)	WS
Hitting	**150.5**
Fielding	**52.4**
Pitching	**106.1**
R. Henderson, OF	39
M. McGwire, 1B	27
J. Canseco, OF	26
D. Stewart, SP	21
D. Henderson, OF	20
D. Eckersley, RP	19
B. Welch, SP	18
W. Weiss, SS	15
F. Jose, OF	12
C. Lansford, 3B	12
T. Steinbach, C	11
G. Nelson, RP	10
S. Sanderson, SP	9
R. Honeycutt, RP	8
J. Quirk, C	8
W. Randolph, 2B	8
M. Gallego, 2B	7
R. Hassey, C	6
T. Burns, RP	5
J. Klink, RP	4
M. Moore, SP	4
H. Baines, DH	3
W. McGee, OF	3
C. Young, SP	3
L. Blankenship, 3B-OF	2
S. Chitren, RP	2
R. Harris, RP	2
M. Norris, RP	2
S. Javier, OF	1
D. Jennings, OF	1
K. Phelps, DH	1

Seattle (77-85)	WS
Hitting	**94.7**
Fielding	**43.1**
Pitching	**93.2**
K. Griffey Jr., OF	24
H. Reynolds, 2B	19
E. Hanson, SP	18
E. Martinez, 3B	17
A. Davis, DH	16
R. Johnson, SP	13
B. Swift, RP	12
M. Young, SP	12
B. Holman, SP	10
M. Schooler, RP	10
G. Briley, OF	8
J. Leonard, OF	8
D. Valle, C	8
J. Buhner, OF	6
K. Comstock, RP	6
H. Cotto, OF	5
S. Bradley, C	4
K. Griffey Sr., OF	4
M. Jackson, RP	4
R. DeLucia, SP	3
B. Giles, SS	3
T. Jones, DH-OF	3
R. Swan, SP	3
O. Vizquel, SS	3
M. Brumley, SS	2
P. O'Brien, 1B	2
J. Schaefer, 3B	2
M. Sinatro, C	2
B. Clark, RP	1
D. Coles, OF	1
G. Eave, SP	1
G. Harris, RP	1

Texas (83-79)	WS
Hitting	**111.8**
Fielding	**42.0**
Pitching	**95.3**
J. Franco, 2B	27
R. Palmeiro, 1B	22
R. Sierra, OF	21
B. Witt, SP	17
N. Ryan, SP	15
K. Brown, SP	12
C. Hough, SP	12
P. Incaviglia, OF	12
K. Rogers, RP	12
G. Pettis, OF	11
J. Daugherty, OF	10
B. Arnsberg, RP	9
J. Huson, SS	9
H. Baines, DH	8
S. Buechele, 3B	7
M. Jeffcoat, RP	6
G. Petralli, C	6
M. Stanley, C	5
S. Chiamparino, SP	3
J. Kunkel, SS	3
J. Moyer, RP	3
K. Reimer, DH	3
J. Barfield, RP	2
S. Coolbaugh, 3B	2
J. Gonzalez, OF	2
G. Green, SS	2
G. Mielke, RP	2
Je. Russell, RP	2
J. Bitker, RP	1
C. Espy, OF	1
C. McMurtry, RP	1
Jo. Russell, C	1

Toronto (86-76)	WS
Hitting	**124.0**
Fielding	**41.9**
Pitching	**92.1**
F. McGriff, 1B	26
T. Fernandez, SS	25
K. Gruber, 3B	25
D. Stieb, SP	18
J. Felix, OF	15
D. Wells, SP	15
T. Henke, RP	14
G. Bell, OF	12
P. Borders, C	12
J. Olerud, DH	11
D. Ward, RP	11
M. Wilson, OF	11
T. Stottlemyre, SP	9
J. Key, SP	8
M. Lee, 2B	7
J. Cerutti, SP	5
G. Hill, OF	5
J. Acker, RP	4
R. Mulliniks, 3B	4
G. Myers, C	4
F. Wills, RP	4
W. Blair, RP	3
R. Ducey, OF	3
M. Whiten, OF	2
B. Black, SP	1
A. Leiter, RP	1
N. Liriano, 2B	1
L. Sojo, 2B	1
K. Williams, OF	1

1990 National League

Atlanta (65-97)	WS
Hitting	**107.2**
Fielding	**27.0**
Pitching	**60.8**
R. Gant, OF	21
D. Justice, 1B	20
L. Smith, OF	15
J. Treadway, 2B	15
J. Smoltz, SP	14
C. Leibrandt, SP	11
D. Murphy, OF	11
J. Blauser, SS	10
T. Glavine, SP	10
G. Olson, C	8
O. McDowell, OF	7
J. Presley, 3B	7
T. Gregg, 1B	5
K. Mercker, RP	5
F. Cabrera, 1B	4
T. Castillo, RP	4
M. Lemke, 3B	4
M. Grant, RP	3
J. Parrett, RP	3
P. Smith, SP	3
J. Boever, RP	2
M. Freeman, RP	2
P. Marak, SP	2
A. Thomas, SS	2
M. Bell, 1B	1
D. Henry, RP	1
J. Hesketh, RP	1
C. Kerfeld, RP	1
J. Kremers, C	1
D. Lilliquist, SP	1
E. Whitt, C	1

Chicago (77-85)	WS
Hitting	**110.3**
Fielding	**37.5**
Pitching	**83.2**
R. Sandberg, 2B	34
A. Dawson, OF	22
M. Grace, 1B	22
S. Dunston, SS	15
M. Harkey, SP	15
G. Maddux, SP	15
P. Assenmacher, RP	13
J. Girardi, C	9
J. Walton, OF	9
S. Boskie, SP	7
D. Dascenzo, OF	7
L. Lancaster, RP	7
L. Salazar, 3B	7
D. Smith, OF	6
M. Bielecki, SP	5
H. Villanueva, C	5
M. Williams, RP	5
S. Wilson, RP	5
B. Long, RP	4
J. Pico, RP	4
D. Clark, OF	3
D. Ramos, 3B	3
D. Pavlas, RP	2
M. Wynne, OF	2
R. Kramer, RP	1
D. May, OF	1
L. McClendon, OF	1
G. Smith, 2B-SS	1
C. Wilkerson, 3B	1

Cincinnati (91-71)	WS
Hitting	**113.1**
Fielding	**49.7**
Pitching	**110.2**
B. Larkin, SS	25
C. Sabo, 3B	20
E. Davis, OF	17
R. Dibble, RP	17
R. Myers, RP	17
J. Rijo, SP	17
P. O'Neill, OF	16
M. Duncan, 2B	15
N. Charlton, RP	14
T. Browning, SP	13
B. Hatcher, OF	12
J. Oliver, C	12
H. Morris, 1B	11
J. Armstrong, SP	10
G. Braggs, OF	9
D. Jackson, SP	6
T. Layana, RP	6
R. Mahler, RP	6
T. Benzinger, 1B	5
J. Reed, C	5
H. Winningham, OF	5
B. Doran, 2B	3

R. Oester, 2B	3
L. Quinones, 3B	3
T. Birtsas, RP	2
S. Scudder, RP	2
R. Robinson, SP	1
A. Trevino, C	1

Houston (75-87)	WS
Hitting	**93.1**
Fielding	**45.8**
Pitching	**86.1**
C. Biggio, C	18
B. Doran, 2B	18
D. Darwin, RP	17
F. Stubbs, 1B	16
G. Davis, 1B	15
D. Smith, RP	12
K. Caminiti, 3B	11
C. Candaele, OF	11
R. Ramirez, SS	11
L. Andersen, RP	10
M. Portugal, SP	9
J. Deshaies, SP	8
M. Scott, SP	8
E. Yelding, OF	8
B. Gullickson, SP	7
G. Wilson, OF	7
J. Agosto, RP	5
D. Schatzeder, RP	5
M. Davidson, OF	4
R. Gedman, C	4
E. Anthony, OF	3
X. Hernandez, RP	2
B. Meyer, RP	2
C. Nichols, C	2
J. Ortiz, OF	2
T. Puhl, OF	2
K. Rhodes, OF	2
R. Hennis, RP	1
K. Oberkfell, 3B	1
A. Osuna, RP	1
D. Rohde, 2B	1
A. Trevino, C	1
G. Young, OF	1

Los Angeles (86-76)	WS
Hitting	**142.7**
Fielding	**37.4**
Pitching	**77.8**
E. Murray, 1B	31
K. Daniels, OF	26
M. Scioscia, C	20
R. Martinez, SP	17
H. Brooks, OF	14
K. Gibson, OF	14
L. Harris, 3B	14
M. Sharperson, 3B	14
S. Javier, OF	12
J. Samuel, 2B	12
J. Howell, RP	10
T. Crews, RP	9
M. Morgan, SP	9
F. Valenzuela, SP	8
T. Belcher, SP	6
A. Griffin, SS	6
M. Hartley, RP	6
J. Neidlinger, SP	5
J. Gott, RP	4
C. Gwynn, OF	4
R. Dempsey, C	3
W. Randolph, 2B	3
J. Gonzalez, OF	2
R. Searage, RP	2
D. Aase, RP	1
O. Hershiser, SP	1
B. Lyons, C	1
J. Offerman, SS	1
J. Vizcaino, SS	1
D. Walsh, RP	1
J. Wetteland, RP	1

Montreal (85-77)	WS
Hitting	**106.6**
Fielding	**49.2**
Pitching	**99.2**
T. Wallach, 3B	26
D. DeShields, 2B	19
T. Raines, OF	19
A. Galarraga, 1B	15
De. Martinez, SP	15
O. Boyd, SP	13
M. Fitzgerald, C	13
S. Owen, SS	13
L. Walker, OF	12
Da. Martinez, OF	11
T. Burke, RP	10
S. Frey, RP	9
M. Gardner, SP	8
M. Grissom, OF	8
O. Nixon, OF	8
B. Sampen, RP	8
Z. Smith, SP	8
C. Nabholz, SP	6
K. Gross, SP	5
M. Aldrete, OF	3
T. Foley, SS	3
D. Mohorcic, RP	3
J. Noboa, 2B	3
M. Rojas, RP	3
S. Ruskin, RP	3
D. Schmidt, RP	3
B. Barnes, SP	2
S. Anderson, SP	1
J. Goff, C	1
D. Hall, RP	1
J. Hesketh, RP	1
J. Paredes, 2B	1
N. Santovenia, C	1

New York (91-71)	WS
Hitting	**145.4**
Fielding	**37.0**
Pitching	**90.7**
D. Strawberry, OF	26
D. Magadan, 1B	25
H. Johnson, 3B	24
K. McReynolds, OF	21
G. Jefferies, 2B	20
F. Viola, SP	20
D. Cone, SP	13
D. Gooden, SP	13
D. Boston, OF	12
J. Franco, RP	11
K. Elster, SS	10
S. Fernandez, SP	9
M. Sasser, C	9
M. Carreon, OF	7
K. Miller, OF	6
B. Ojeda, RP	6
A. Pena, RP	6
W. Whitehurst, RP	5
T. Teufel, 1B-2B	4
T. Herr, 2B	3
J. Machado, RP	3
T. O'Malley, 3B	3
R. Darling, SP	2
J. Innis, RP	2
B. Lyons, C	2
M. Marshall, 1B	2
P. Tabler, OF	2
K. Torve, 1B	2
T. Hundley, C	1
O. Mercado, C	1
C. O'Brien, C	1
D. Reed, OF	1
D. Schatzeder, RP	1

Philadelphia (77-85)	WS
Hitting	**112.2**
Fielding	**41.4**
Pitching	**77.4**
L. Dykstra, OF	35
D. Daulton, C	23
J. Kruk, OF	17
V. Hayes, OF	16
D. Cook, RP	11
T. Mulholland, SP	11
D. Thon, SS	10
P. Combs, SP	9
C. Hayes, 3B	9
R. McDowell, RP	9
T. Herr, 2B	8
D. Akerfelds, RP	7
J. Boever, RP	7
J. DeJesus, SP	7
R. Ready, OF	7
D. Carman, RP	6
C. Martinez, 1B	6
J. Grimsley, SP	4
D. Murphy, OF	4
K. Howell, SP	3
R. Jordan, 1B	3
S. Lake, C	3
W. Chamberlain, OF	2
T. Greene, SP	2
D. Hollins, 3B	2
R. Jones, OF	2
J. Vatcher, OF	2
R. Booker, SS	1
C. Malone, RP	1
M. Morandini, 2B	1
T. Nieto, C	1
S. Ontiveros, RP	1
J. Parrett, RP	1

Pittsburgh (95-67)	WS
Hitting	**144.7**
Fielding	**44.7**
Pitching	**95.6**
B. Bonds, OF	37
B. Bonilla, OF	23
A. Van Slyke, OF	23
D. Drabek, SP	20
J. Bell, SS	17
S. Bream, 1B	15
J. Lind, 2B	15
W. Backman, 3B	12
M. LaValliere, C	12
D. Slaught, C	12
B. Landrum, RP	10
B. Patterson, RP	9
N. Heaton, SP	8
Z. Smith, SP	8
J. King, 3B	7
G. Redus, 1B	7
B. Kipper, RP	6
R. Tomlin, SP	6
B. Walk, SP	6
S. Belinda, RP	5
V. Palacios, RP	4
T. Power, RP	4
R. Reynolds, OF	4
S. Ruskin, RP	3
J. Smiley, SP	3
R. Belliard, 2B	1
D. Bilardello, C	1
J. Cangelosi, OF	1
C. Martinez, 1B	1
R. Reed, SP	1
M. Roesler, RP	1
M. Ross, RP	1
J. Tibbs, RP	1
M. York, RP	1

San Diego (75-87)	WS
Hitting	**99.6**
Fielding	**40.9**
Pitching	**84.4**
B. Roberts, OF	22
R. Alomar, 2B	19
E. Whitson, SP	19
Ja. Clark, 1B	17
T. Gwynn, OF	17
J. Carter, OF	16
G. Harris, RP	14
B. Hurst, SP	14
C. Lefferts, RP	13
B. Santiago, C	12
A. Benes, SP	10
G. Templeton, SS	10
M. Pagliarulo, 3B	8
D. Rasmussen, SP	6
F. Lynn, OF	4
M. Parent, C	4
R. Rodriguez, RP	4
S. Abner, OF	3
C. Schiraldi, RP	3
D. Lilliquist, RP	2
P. Stephenson, 1B	2
Je. Clark, 1B	1
J. Cora, SS	1
M. Grant, RP	1
D. Jackson, OF	1
T. Lampkin, C	1
E. Williams, 3B	1

San Francisco (85-77)	WS
Hitting	**140.7**
Fielding	**37.8**
Pitching	**76.5**
M. Williams, 3B	28
B. Butler, OF	27
W. Clark, 1B	25
K. Mitchell, OF	20
J. Brantley, RP	15
R. Thompson, 2B	15
J. Burkett, SP	11
T. Kennedy, C	10
G. Carter, C	8
K. Bass, OF	7
S. Bedrosian, RP	7
S. Garrelts, SP	7
M. Kingery, OF	7
R. Leach, OF	6
J. Uribe, SS	6
D. Robinson, SP	5
T. Wilson, SP	5
K. Downs, SP	4
M. LaCoss, SP	4
F. Oliveras, RP	4
E. Riles, SS	4
M. Thurmond, RP	4
D. Anderson, SS	3
A. Hammaker, RP	3
G. Litton, OF	3
R. Reuschel, SP	3
B. Bathe, C	2
S. Decker, C	2
M. Dewey, RP	2
R. O'Neal, RP	2
R. Parker, OF	2
M. Bailey, C	1
M. Benjamin, SS	1
E. Camacho, RP	1
B. Knepper, SP	1

St. Louis (70-92)	WS
Hitting	**82.1**
Fielding	**38.2**
Pitching	**89.7**
W. McGee, OF	18
J. Tudor, SP	15
V. Coleman, OF	14
L. Smith, RP	14
J. Oquendo, 2B	13
J. Magrane, SP	12
T. Zeile, C	12
O. Smith, SS	11
P. Guerrero, 1B	10
B. Tewksbury, SP	10
T. Pagnozzi, C	8
B. Smith, SP	7
K. Dayley, RP	6
J. DeLeon, SP	6
M. Thompson, OF	6
R. Hudler, OF	5
R. Lankford, OF	5
T. Niedenfuer, RP	5
T. Pendleton, 3B	5
F. DiPino, RP	4
O. Olivares, SP	4
B. Gilkey, OF	3

F. Jose, OF	3
K. Hill, SP	2
T. Jones, SS	2
M. Perez, RP	2
S. Terry, RP	2
D. Collins, 1B	1
H. Hilton, RP	1
R. Horton, RP	1
G. Pena, 2B	1
D. Walling, 1B	1
C. Wilson, 3B-OF	1

1991 American League

Baltimore (67-95)	WS
Hitting	**106.5**
Fielding	**31.2**
Pitching	**63.3**
C. Ripken Jr., SS	34
M. Devereaux, OF	15
R. Milligan, 1B	13
T. Frohwirth, RP	11
S. Horn, DH	11
D. Evans, OF	10
G. Olson, RP	10
M. Flanagan, RP	9
B. Milacki, SP	9
J. Orsulak, OF	9
L. Gomez, 3B	7
C. Hoiles, C	7
C. Martinez, OF	7
B. Anderson, OF	6
M. Mussina, SP	6
B. Melvin, C	5
G. Davis, 1B	4
B. McDonald, SP	4
J. Poole, RP	4
M. Williamson, RP	4
B. Ripken, 2B	3
D. Segui, 1B	3
J. Bell, 2B	2
J. Robinson, SP	2
C. Worthington, 3B	2
T. Hulett, 3B	1
P. Kilgus, RP	1
R. Smith, SP	1
A. Telford, RP	1

Boston (84-78)	WS
Hitting	**110.5**
Fielding	**45.8**
Pitching	**95.7**
R. Clemens, SP	26
W. Boggs, 3B	25
J. Reed, 2B	20
M. Greenwell, OF	17
J. Clark, DH	15
C. Quintana, 1B	14
J. Hesketh, RP	13
G. Harris, RP	12
T. Brunansky, OF	11
E. Burks, OF	10
J. Reardon, RP	10
T. Pena, C	9
P. Plantier, OF	9
L. Rivera, SS	9
J. Gray, RP	8
M. Vaughn, 1B	6
T. Fossas, RP	5
M. Gardiner, SP	5
D. Lamp, RP	4
K. Morton, SP	4
T. Bolton, SP	3
S. Cooper, 3B	3
S. Lyons, OF	3
M. Brumley, SS	2
D. Darwin, SP	2
J. Marzano, C	2
M. Young, SP	2
T. Naehring, SS	1
D. Petry, RP	1
J. Plympton, RP	1

California (81-81)	WS
Hitting	**100.3**
Fielding	**44.7**
Pitching	**98.0**
W. Joyner, 1B	25
J. Abbott, SP	20
M. Langston, SP	20
B. Harvey, RP	18
L. Polonia, OF	18
D. Winfield, OF	17
L. Parrish, C	15
C. Finley, SP	14
G. Gaetti, 3B	14
M. Eichhorn, RP	10
D. Gallagher, OF	9
D. Schofield, SS	8
D. Hill, 2B	7
K. McCaskill, SP	7
D. Parker, DH	5
L. Sojo, 2B	5
J. Felix, OF	4
B. Rose, 2B	3
M. Venable, OF	3
S. Abner, OF	2
S. Bailes, RP	2
J. Grahe, SP	2
J. Howell, 2B	2
J. Orton, C	2
R. Tingley, C	2
K. Abbott, SP	1
R. Amaro, OF	1
F. Bannister, RP	1
C. Beasley, RP	1
G. DiSarcina, SS	1
M. Fetters, RP	1
J. Robinson, RP	1
L. Stevens, 1B	1
C. Young, RP	1

Chicago (87-75)	WS
Hitting	**123.3**
Fielding	**46.6**
Pitching	**91.1**
F. Thomas, DH	34
R. Ventura, 3B	25
T. Raines, OF	19
J. McDowell, SP	18
D. Pasqua, 1B	14
C. Fisk, C	13
L. Johnson, OF	13
C. Grebeck, 3B	11
M. Perez, RP	11
S. Radinsky, RP	11
O. Guillen, SS	9
C. Hough, SP	9
D. Pall, RP	8
B. Thigpen, RP	8
A. Fernandez, SP	7
G. Hibbard, SP	7
R. Karkovice, C	7
W. Newson, OF	6
K. Patterson, RP	5
M. Huff, OF	4
S. Sosa, OF	4
W. Alvarez, SP	3
J. Cora, 2B	3
S. Fletcher, 2B	3
B. Drahman, RP	2
B. Jackson, DH	2
W. Edwards, RP	1
R. Garcia, SP	1
M. Merullo, C	1
C. Snyder, OF	1
D. Wakamatsu, C	1

Cleveland (57-105)	WS
Hitting	**71.2**
Fielding	**30.1**
Pitching	**69.7**
C. Baerga, 3B	18
A. Belle, OF	15
G. Swindell, SP	13
T. Candiotti, SP	10
A. Cole, OF	10
C. Nagy, SP	10
F. Fermin, SS	8
R. Nichols, SP	7
M. Aldrete, 1B	6
S. Olin, RP	6
S. Hillegas, RP	5
E. King, SP	5
M. Lewis, 2B	5
M. Whiten, OF	5
C. Martinez, DH	4
J. Shaw, RP	4
J. Skinner, C	4
E. Bell, RP	3
J. Browne, 2B	3
G. Hill, OF	3
M. Huff, OF	3
B. Jacoby, 1B	3
J. Orosco, RP	3
D. Otto, SP	3
B. Allred, OF	2
S. Alomar Jr., C	2
C. James, DH	2
J. Manto, 3B	2
J. Gonzalez, OF	1
D. Jones, RP	1
T. Perezchica, SS	1
E. Taubensee, C	1
J. Thome, 3B	1
E. Valdez, RP	1
T. Ward, OF	1

Detroit (84-78)	WS
Hitting	**142.9**
Fielding	**35.2**
Pitching	**73.9**
M. Tettleton, C	27
C. Fielder, 1B	26
L. Whitaker, 2B	26
T. Phillips, OF	23
T. Fryman, 3B	17
B. Gullickson, SP	14
M. Henneman, RP	13
F. Tanana, SP	13
A. Trammell, SS	12
R. Deer, OF	11
W. Terrell, SP	10
M. Cuyler, OF	9
D. Bergman, 1B	7
M. Leiter, RP	7
L. Moseby, OF	7
S. Barnes, OF	5
P. Gibson, RP	5
J. Gleaton, RP	4
A. Allanson, C	3
J. Cerutti, RP	3
S. Livingstone, 3B	3
P. Incaviglia, OF	2
S. Aldred, SP	1
D. Gakeler, RP	1
R. Meacham, RP	1
D. Petry, RP	1
J. Shelby, OF	1

Kansas City (82-80)	WS
Hitting	**115.7**
Fielding	**38.7**
Pitching	**91.5**
D. Tartabull, OF	28
B. Saberhagen, SP	16
J. Montgomery, RP	15
K. Appier, SP	14
B. Pecota, 3B	14
L. Aquino, RP	12
K. Gibson, OF	12
M. Macfarlane, C	11
B. McRae, OF	11
M. Boddicker, SP	10
K. Stillwell, SS	10
J. Eisenreich, OF	9
F. Gordon, RP	9
T. Benzinger, 1B	8
G. Brett, DH	8
B. Mayne, C	8
K. Seitzer, 3B	7
T. Shumpert, 2B	6
W. Cromartie, 1B	5
J. Johnston, RP	4
M. Magnante, RP	4
G. Thurman, OF	4
M. Davis, RP	3
S. Davis, RP	3
D. Howard, SS	3
C. Martinez, 1B	3
M. Gubicza, SP	2
T. Spehr, C	2
S. Berry, 3B	1
S. Crawford, RP	1
N. Liriano, 2B	1
J. Pedre, C	1
H. Pulliam, OF	1

Milwaukee (83-79)	WS
Hitting	**132.9**
Fielding	**38.4**
Pitching	**77.7**
P. Molitor, DH	30
W. Randolph, 2B	22
G. Vaughn, OF	20
B. Spiers, SS	16
R. Yount, OF	16
D. Hamilton, OF	15
B. Wegman, SP	15
C. Bosio, SP	14
B. Surhoff, C	13
J. Navarro, SP	12
J. Gantner, 3B	10
D. Henry, RP	9
D. Bichette, OF	7
D. Sveum, SS	7
J. Machado, RP	6
R. Dempsey, C	5
C. Crim, RP	4
D. Plesac, RP	4
F. Stubbs, 1B	4
D. August, SP	3
G. Brock, 1B	3
M. Lee, RP	3
C. Maldonado, OF	3
T. Higuera, SP	2
D. Holmes, RP	2
K. Brown, SP	1
G. Canale, 1B	1
C. Eldred, SP	1
G. Sheffield, 3B	1

Minnesota (95-67)	WS
Hitting	**124.7**
Fielding	**52.1**
Pitching	**108.2**
C. Davis, DH	22
K. Puckett, OF	21
K. Tapani, SP	21
C. Knoblauch, 2B	20
S. Mack, OF	20
K. Hrbek, 1B	19
S. Erickson, SP	18
J. Morris, SP	18
R. Aguilera, RP	15
B. Harper, C	15
G. Gagne, SS	12
C. Willis, RP	10
M. Pagliarulo, 3B	9
S. Leius, 3B	8
D. Gladden, OF	7
R. Bush, OF	6
P. Munoz, OF	6
S. Bedrosian, RP	5
M. Guthrie, RP	5
G. Larkin, OF	4
T. Leach, RP	4
A. Newman, SS	4
A. Anderson, SP	3
D. West, SP	3
P. Abbott, RP	2
T. Edens, SP	2

Player	WS
L. Webster, C	2
D. Neagle, RP	1
J. Ortiz, C	1
P. Sorrento, 1B	1
G. Wayne, RP	1

New York (71-91)	WS
Hitting	**101.2**
Fielding	**35.5**
Pitching	**76.2**
S. Sax, 2B	24
R. Kelly, OF	16
M. Nokes, C	16
M. Hall, OF	14
D. Mattingly, 1B	14
S. Farr, RP	13
S. Sanderson, SP	13
A. Espinoza, SS	11
J. Habyan, RP	10
K. Maas, DH	10
B. Williams, OF	10
G. Cadaret, RP	9
J. Barfield, OF	8
S. Howe, RP	7
L. Guetterman, RP	6
P. Kelly, 3B	5
P. Perez, SP	5
S. Kamieniecki, SP	3
H. Meulens, OF	3
R. Monteleone, RP	3
E. Plunk, RP	3
R. Velarde, 3B	3
B. Geren, C	2
D. Eiland, SP	1
M. Humphreys, OF	1
J. Johnson, SP	1
A. Mills, RP	1
C. Rodriguez, SS	1

Oakland (84-78)	WS
Hitting	**154.8**
Fielding	**34.7**
Pitching	**62.5**
J. Canseco, OF	31
D. Henderson, OF	25
R. Henderson, OF	25
H. Baines, DH	22
M. Gallego, 2B	18
M. McGwire, 1B	18
M. Moore, SP	16
D. Eckersley, RP	14
T. Steinbach, C	13
L. Blankenship, 2B	7
E. Riles, 3B	7
B. Welch, SP	7
M. Bordick, SS	6
J. Klink, RP	5
D. Stewart, SP	5
W. Wilson, OF	5
J. Quirk, C	4
R. Darling, SP	3
A. Hawkins, SP	3
V. Law, 3B	3
K. Campbell, RP	2
S. Chitren, RP	2
R. Honeycutt, RP	2
J. Slusarski, SP	2
W. Weiss, SS	2
C. Young, RP	2
S. Brosius, 2B	1
T. Burns, RP	1
B. Jacoby, 3B	1

Seattle (83-79)	WS
Hitting	**104.2**
Fielding	**48.1**
Pitching	**96.7**
K. Griffey Jr., OF	30
H. Reynolds, 2B	21
E. Martinez, 3B	20
B. Swift, RP	14
O. Vizquel, SS	14
J. Buhner, OF	13
P. O'Brien, 1B	13
B. Holman, SP	12
M. Jackson, RP	11
R. Johnson, SP	11
B. Krueger, SP	10
E. Hanson, SP	9
H. Cotto, OF	7
A. Davis, DH	7
G. Briley, OF	6
R. Swan, RP	6
D. Valle, C	6
R. DeLucia, SP	5
M. Schooler, RP	5
D. Cochrane, OF	4
C. Jones, RP	4
R. Murphy, RP	4
K. Griffey Sr., OF	3
S. Bankhead, SP	2
S. Bradley, C	2
D. Burba, RP	2
T. Jones, DH	2
J. Schaefer, SS	2
T. Martinez, 1B	1
A. Powell, OF	1
P. Rice, RP	1
M. Sinatro, C	1

Texas (85-77)	WS
Hitting	**157.9**
Fielding	**31.4**
Pitching	**65.7**
J. Franco, 2B	28
R. Sierra, OF	28
R. Palmeiro, 1B	26
J. Gonzalez, OF	19
S. Buechele, 3B	18
B. Downing, DH	14
K. Reimer, OF	13
N. Ryan, SP	13
J. Guzman, SP	12
Je. Russell, RP	10
K. Brown, SP	7
J. Huson, SS	7
D. Palmer, 3B	7
G. Pettis, OF	6
I. Rodriguez, C	6
M. Stanley, C	6
G. Petralli, C	5
M. Diaz, SS	4
T. Mathews, RP	4
J. Barfield, RP	3
G. Gossage, RP	3
M. Jeffcoat, RP	3
G. Alexander, RP	2
B. Bohanon, SP	2
B. Manuel, RP	2
K. Rogers, RP	2
S. Chiamparino, SP	1
M. Fariss, OF	1
D. Harris, OF	1
J. Hernandez, SS	1
W. Rosenthal, RP	1

Toronto (91-71)	WS
Hitting	**95.2**
Fielding	**51.4**
Pitching	**126.5**
R. Alomar, 2B	25
D. White, OF	24
J. Carter, OF	23
D. Ward, RP	19
J. Key, SP	17
T. Stottlemyre, SP	15
D. Wells, SP	14
J. Olerud, 1B	13
K. Gruber, 3B	12
J. Guzman, SP	12
T. Henke, RP	12
T. Candiotti, SP	11
M. Timlin, RP	11
C. Maldonado, OF	8
R. Mulliniks, DH	6
P. Borders, C	5
B. MacDonald, RP	5
G. Myers, C	5
E. Sprague, 3B	5
D. Stieb, SP	5
M. Lee, SS	4
M. Wilson, OF	4
J. Acker, RP	3
R. Gonzales, SS	2
G. Hill, DH	2
P. Tabler, DH	2
M. Whiten, OF	2
D. Boucher, SP	1
R. Ducey, OF	1
P. Hentgen, RP	1
V. Horsman, RP	1
D. Parker, DH	1
D. Weathers, RP	1
K. Williams, OF	1

1991 National League

Atlanta (94-68)	WS
Hitting	**125.3**
Fielding	**47.4**
Pitching	**109.4**
T. Pendleton, 3B	27
R. Gant, OF	25
T. Glavine, SP	23
D. Justice, OF	22
S. Avery, SP	16
O. Nixon, OF	15
J. Blauser, SS	13
C. Leibrandt, SP	13
L. Smith, OF	13
J. Smoltz, SP	13
G. Olson, C	12
J. Berenguer, RP	11
J. Treadway, 2B	11
M. Stanton, RP	10
K. Mercker, RP	9
B. Hunter, 1B	8
R. Belliard, SS	7
S. Bream, 1B	6
A. Pena, RP	5
M. Freeman, RP	4
M. Lemke, 2B	4
K. Mitchell, OF	3
D. Sanders, OF	3
F. Cabrera, C	2
M. Wohlers, RP	2
J. Clancy, RP	1
T. Gregg, OF	1
M. Heath, C	1
D. Heep, 1B-OF	1
R. St. Claire, RP	1

Chicago (77-83)	WS
Hitting	**114.6**
Fielding	**35.8**
Pitching	**80.6**
R. Sandberg, 2B	37
A. Dawson, OF	20
M. Grace, 1B	17
G. Maddux, SP	17
G. Bell, OF	14
S. Dunston, SS	14
P. Assenmacher, RP	13
C. McElroy, RP	12
L. Lancaster, RP	11
H. Villanueva, C	9
C. Walker, 3B	9
M. Bielecki, SP	7
L. Salazar, 3B	6
B. Scanlan, RP	5
R. Wilkins, C	5
F. Castillo, SP	4
H. Slocumb, RP	4
Dw. Smith, OF	4
R. Sutcliffe, SP	4
D. Dascenzo, OF	3
C. Landrum, OF	3
S. Boskie, SP	2
J. Vizcaino, 3B	2
J. Walton, OF	2
D. Berryhill, C	1
J. Girardi, C	1
D. May, OF	1
Y. Perez, RP	1
R. Sanchez, SS	1
G. Scott, 3B	1
D. Strange, 3B	1

Cincinnati (74-88)	WS
Hitting	**106.4**
Fielding	**36.9**
Pitching	**78.7**
B. Larkin, SS	26
C. Sabo, 3B	22
P. O'Neill, OF	19
J. Rijo, SP	17
H. Morris, 1B	15
R. Dibble, RP	13
M. Duncan, 2B	10
T. Browning, SP	9
B. Doran, 2B	9
B. Hatcher, OF	9
N. Charlton, RP	8
E. Davis, OF	8
R. Myers, RP	8
G. Braggs, OF	7
C. Hammond, SP	6
T. Power, RP	6
K. Gross, RP	5
J. Reed, C	5
J. Oliver, C	4
S. Scudder, SP	4
M. Hill, RP	2
C. Martinez, 1B	2
L. Quinones, 2B	2
F. Benavides, SS	1
K. Brown, RP	1
S. Foster, RP	1
C. Jones, OF	1
M. Sanford, SP	1
H. Winningham, OF	1

Houston (65-97)	WS
Hitting	**98.6**
Fielding	**35.4**
Pitching	**61.0**
J. Bagwell, 1B	23
C. Biggio, C	20
S. Finley, OF	18
K. Caminiti, 3B	17
P. Harnisch, SP	16
L. Gonzalez, OF	15
C. Candaele, 2B	14
A. Osuna, RP	8
A. Cedeno, SS	5
J. Clancy, RP	5
D. Henry, RP	5
D. Kile, SP	5
M. Portugal, SP	5
C. Schilling, RP	5
J. Corsi, RP	3
J. Jones, SP	3
G. Young, OF	3
M. Capel, RP	2
K. Oberkfell, 1B	2
J. Ortiz, OF	2
M. Simms, OF	2
J. Tolentino, 1B	2
E. Anthony, OF	1
R. Bowen, SP	1
G. Cooper, 3B	1
M. Davidson, OF	1
J. Deshaies, SP	1
C. Gardner, SP	1
X. Hernandez, RP	1
R. Mallicoat, RP	1
M. McLemore, 2B	1
A. Mota, 2B	1
C. Nichols, C	1
R. Ramirez, SS	1
K. Rhodes, OF	1
S. Servais, C	1
E. Yelding, SS	1

Los Angeles (93-69)	WS
Hitting	**121.0**
Fielding	**47.2**
Pitching	**110.7**
B. Butler, OF	26
D. Strawberry, OF	24
J. Samuel, 2B	20
K. Daniels, OF	18
M. Morgan, SP	17
E. Murray, 1B	16
T. Belcher, SP	15
R. Martinez, SP	14
M. Scioscia, C	14
L. Harris, 3B	13
B. Ojeda, SP	12
A. Griffin, SS	9
J. Howell, RP	9
O. Hershiser, SP	8
G. Carter, C	7
K. Gross, RP	7
T. Crews, RP	6
J. Gott, RP	6
R. McDowell, RP	6
M. Sharperson, 3B	6
C. Gwynn, OF	4
J. Candelaria, RP	3
D. Cook, RP	3
M. Webster, OF	3
S. Wilson, RP	3
J. Hamilton, 3B	2
M. Hartley, RP	2
J. Offerman, SS	2
M. Christopher, RP	1
D. Hansen, 3B	1
S. Javier, OF	1
J. Wetteland, RP	1

Montreal (71-90)	WS
Hitting	**99.0**
Fielding	**37.8**
Pitching	**76.1**
I. Calderon, OF	21
L. Walker, OF	20
M. Grissom, OF	19
De. Martinez, SP	18
D. DeShields, 2B	15
Da. Martinez, OF	13
S. Owen, SS	11
T. Wallach, 3B	11
B. Barberie, SS	8
B. Jones, RP	8
J. Fassero, RP	7
C. Nabholz, SP	7
O. Boyd, SP	6
M. Gardner, SP	6
M. Fitzgerald, C	5
B. Barnes, SP	4
G. Reyes, C	4
M. Rojas, RP	4
S. Ruskin, RP	4
B. Sampen, RP	4
T. Burke, RP	3
D. Piatt, RP	3
T. Foley, SS	2
A. Galarraga, 1B	2
R. Hassey, C	2
N. Santovenia, C	2
E. Bullock, OF	1
C. Haney, SP	1
R. Mahler, SP	1
K. Williams, OF	1

New York (77-84)	WS
Hitting	**105.4**
Fielding	**35.8**
Pitching	**89.8**
H. Johnson, 3B	25
K. McReynolds, OF	17
D. Cone, SP	15
G. Jefferies, 2B	15
D. Magadan, 1B	14
D. Gooden, SP	13
K. Miller, 2B	11
K. Elster, SS	10
F. Viola, SP	10
D. Boston, OF	9
J. Franco, RP	8
A. Pena, RP	8
H. Brooks, OF	7
R. Cerone, C	7
V. Coleman, OF	7
J. Innis, RP	7
M. Sasser, C	7
T. Burke, RP	5
W. Whitehurst, SP	5
R. Darling, SP	4
C. O'Brien, C	4
P. Schourek, RP	4
S. Fernandez, SP	3
T. Herr, 2B	3
A. Young, SP	3
T. Castillo, RP	2
G. Templeton, SS	2
B. Beatty, RP	1
T. Bross, RP	1
M. Carreon, OF	1
C. Donnels, 1B	1
T. Hundley, C	1
D. Simons, RP	1

Philadelphia (78-84)	WS
Hitting	**105.2**
Fielding	**42.9**
Pitching	**85.9**
J. Kruk, 1B	25
M. Williams, RP	18
T. Greene, SP	17
T. Mulholland, SP	14
L. Dykstra, OF	13
D. Murphy, OF	13
W. Chamberlain, OF	12
D. Thon, SS	12
J. DeJesus, SP	11
D. Daulton, C	9
R. Jordan, 1B	9
M. Morandini, 2B	9
C. Hayes, 3B	8
D. Hollins, 3B	8
R. Ready, 2B	8
B. Ruffin, RP	6
W. Backman, 2B	5
J. Boever, RP	5
V. Hayes, OF	5
J. Lindeman, OF	4
R. McDowell, RP	4
W. Ritchie, RP	4
C. Brantley, SP	2
D. Cox, SP	2
D. Fletcher, C	2
M. Hartley, RP	2
S. Lake, C	2
D. Akerfelds, RP	1
R. Booker, SS	1
B. Castillo, OF	1
J. Morris, OF	1
S. Searcy, RP	1

Pittsburgh (98-64)	WS
Hitting	**162.9**
Fielding	**39.7**
Pitching	**91.4**
B. Bonds, OF	37
B. Bonilla, OF	31
J. Bell, SS	22
A. Van Slyke, OF	22
O. Merced, 1B	17
D. Drabek, SP	14
J. Smiley, SP	14
Z. Smith, SP	14
J. Lind, 2B	13
M. LaValliere, C	12
D. Slaught, C	10
R. Tomlin, SP	10
S. Belinda, RP	9
B. Landrum, RP	8
G. Varsho, OF	7
L. McClendon, OF	6
G. Redus, 1B	6
B. Walk, SP	6
V. Palacios, RP	5
J. Wehner, 3B	5
S. Buechele, 3B	4
J. King, 3B	4
B. Patterson, RP	4
R. Mason, RP	3
C. Espy, OF	2
N. Heaton, RP	2
B. Kipper, RP	2
C. Wilkerson, 2B	2
T. Prince, C	1
R. Rodriguez, RP	1
M. Webster, OF	1

San Diego (84-78)	WS
Hitting	**110.4**
Fielding	**45.5**
Pitching	**96.1**
F. McGriff, 1B	25
T. Gwynn, OF	22
T. Fernandez, SS	21
A. Benes, SP	16
B. Santiago, C	16
B. Hurst, SP	15
B. Roberts, 2B	14
D. Jackson, OF	13
G. Harris, SP	12
M. Maddux, RP	11
T. Teufel, 2B	11
L. Andersen, RP	9
J. Melendez, RP	8
J. Clark, OF	7
T. Howard, OF	7
C. Lefferts, RP	7
R. Rodriguez, RP	6
J. Howell, 3B	5
D. Rasmussen, SP	5
J. Hernandez, RP	3
D. Bilardello, C	2
S. Coolbaugh, 3B	2
J. Costello, RP	2
P. Faries, 2B	2
C. Shipley, SS	2
S. Abner, OF	1
O. Azocar, OF	1
M. Barrett, 2B-3B	1
R. Bones, SP	1
P. Clements, RP	1
A. Peterson, SP	1
J. Vatcher, OF	1
K. Ward, OF	1
E. Whitson, SP	1

San Francisco (75-87)	WS
Hitting	**125.7**
Fielding	**35.6**
Pitching	**63.7**
W. Clark, 1B	34
R. Thompson, 2B	22
M. Williams, 3B	22
W. McGee, OF	18
K. Mitchell, OF	16
J. Brantley, RP	11
T. Wilson, SP	11
M. Felder, OF	9
B. Black, SP	8
D. Righetti, RP	8
D. Lewis, OF	7
J. Burkett, SP	6
K. Bass, OF	5
F. Oliveras, RP	5
J. Uribe, SS	5
K. Downs, RP	4
T. Kennedy, C	4
K. Manwaring, C	4
R. Beck, RP	3
S. Decker, C	3
M. Leonard, OF	3
D. Robinson, RP	3
D. Anderson, SS	2
M. Benjamin, SS	2
G. Heredia, SP	2
T. Herr, 2B	2
B. Hickerson, RP	2
M. Kingery, OF	1
G. Litton, 1B-2B	1
P. McClellan, SP	1
M. Remlinger, SP	1

St. Louis (84-78)	WS
Hitting	**124.7**
Fielding	**42.8**
Pitching	**84.5**
F. Jose, OF	25
O. Smith, SS	25
T. Zeile, 3B	22
R. Lankford, OF	18
T. Pagnozzi, C	17
L. Smith, RP	15
J. Oquendo, 2B	14
P. Guerrero, 1B	13
J. DeLeon, SP	11
M. Thompson, OF	11
K. Hill, SP	10
O. Olivares, SP	10
B. Tewksbury, SP	10
B. Smith, SP	9
G. Perry, 1B	7
S. Terry, RP	7
G. Pena, 2B	6
C. Carpenter, RP	5
B. Gilkey, OF	3
R. Hudler, OF	3
J. Agosto, RP	2
R. Cormier, SP	2
R. Gedman, C	2
B. McClure, RP	2
M. Clark, RP	1
W. Fraser, RP	1
M. Grater, RP	1

1992 American League

Baltimore (89-73)	WS
Hitting	**117.9**
Fielding	**47.9**
Pitching	**101.2**
B. Anderson, OF	29
M. Mussina, SP	24
M. Devereaux, OF	22
C. Ripken Jr., SS	21
L. Gomez, 3B	15
R. Milligan, 1B	13
G. Olson, RP	13
C. Hoiles, C	12
J. Orsulak, OF	12
T. Frohwirth, RP	11
B. McDonald, SP	11
A. Mills, RP	11
R. Sutcliffe, SP	10
G. Davis, DH	8
S. Davis, RP	8
A. Rhodes, SP	7
B. Ripken, 2B	7
T. Hulett, 3B	6
C. Martinez, OF	6
M. McLemore, 2B	6
J. Tackett, C	4
P. Clements, RP	2
D. Segui, 1B	2
M. Williamson, RP	2
S. Horn, DH	1
C. Lefferts, SP	1
L. Mercedes, OF	1
J. Mesa, SP	1
M. Parent, C	1

Boston (73-89)	WS
Hitting	**70.2**
Fielding	**45.6**
Pitching	**103.2**
R. Clemens, SP	26
F. Viola, SP	18

W. Boggs, 3B	15
T. Brunansky, OF	15
G. Harris, RP	12
J. Reed, 2B	12
D. Darwin, RP	11
B. Zupcic, OF	10
S. Cooper, 1B	9
J. Dopson, SP	7
J. Hesketh, SP	7
J. Valentin, SS	7
M. Vaughn, 1B	7
T. Naehring, SS	6
T. Pena, C	6
E. Burks, OF	5
P. Plantier, OF	5
P. Quantrill, RP	5
J. Reardon, RP	5
L. Rivera, SS	5
J. Clark, DH	4
T. Fossas, RP	4
M. Gardiner, SP	4
E. Wedge, DH	4
T. Bolton, RP	2
B. Hatcher, OF	2
H. Winningham, OF	2
M. Young, RP	2
M. Greenwell, OF	1
S. Taylor, RP	1

California (72-90)	WS
Hitting	**71.9**
Fielding	**45.7**
Pitching	**98.4**
J. Abbott, SP	18
R. Gonzales, 3B	15
M. Langston, SP	15
C. Curtis, OF	13
L. Polonia, OF	13
J. Felix, OF	12
J. Grahe, RP	12
J. Valera, SP	12
C. Finley, SP	11
L. Sojo, 2B	11
G. DiSarcina, SS	9
G. Gaetti, 3B	9
M. Eichhorn, RP	6
L. Stevens, 1B	6
B. Blyleven, SP	5
S. Frey, RP	5
B. Harvey, RP	5
A. Davis, 1B	4
D. Easley, 3B	4
M. Fitzgerald, C	4
V. Hayes, OF	4
S. Lewis, RP	3
J. Orton, C	3
B. Rose, 2B	3
R. Tingley, C	3
M. Butcher, RP	2
C. Crim, RP	2
L. Parrish, C	2
D. Robinson, SP	2
H. Brooks, DH	1
T. Fortugno, RP	1
K. Oberkfell, 2B	1

Chicago (86-76)	WS
Hitting	**137.0**
Fielding	**37.1**
Pitching	**83.9**
F. Thomas, 1B	33
R. Ventura, 3B	30
T. Raines, OF	28
J. McDowell, SP	20
L. Johnson, OF	15
G. Bell, DH	13
R. Hernandez, RP	13
R. Karkovice, C	13
C. Grebeck, SS	10
T. Leach, RP	8
K. McCaskill, SP	8
G. Hibbard, SP	7
C. Hough, SP	7
S. Radinsky, RP	7
A. Fernandez, SP	6
S. Abner, OF	5
D. Pasqua, OF	5
S. Sax, 2B	5
J. Cora, 2B	4
C. Fisk, C	4
W. Newson, OF	3
B. Thigpen, RP	3
D. Pall, RP	2
D. Sveum, SS	2
W. Alvarez, RP	1
E. Beltre, SS	1
B. Drahman, RP	1
M. Dunne, RP	1
O. Guillen, SS	1
M. Huff, OF	1
N. Santovenia, C	1

Cleveland (76-86)	WS
Hitting	**99.6**
Fielding	**43.6**
Pitching	**84.8**
C. Baerga, 2B	28
K. Lofton, OF	24
C. Nagy, SP	20
A. Belle, DH	16
S. Olin, RP	14
P. Sorrento, 1B	11
M. Whiten, OF	11
D. Lilliquist, RP	10
T. Power, RP	10
S. Alomar Jr., C	9
D. Cook, SP	7
T. Howard, OF	7
M. Lewis, SS	7
G. Hill, OF	6
B. Jacoby, 3B	6
E. Plunk, RP	6
F. Fermin, SS	5
J. Ortiz, C	5
J. Armstrong, SP	4
J. Mesa, SP	4
R. Nichols, RP	4
K. Wickander, RP	4
R. Jefferson, 1B	3
C. Martinez, 1B	3
M. Christopher, RP	1
J. Levis, C	1
S. Scudder, SP	1
J. Thome, 3B	1

Detroit (75-87)	WS
Hitting	**137.5**
Fielding	**29.7**
Pitching	**57.8**
M. Tettleton, C	24
L. Whitaker, 2B	24
T. Phillips, OF	23
C. Fielder, 1B	19
T. Fryman, SS	19
R. Deer, OF	14
B. Gullickson, SP	10
D. Gladden, OF	8
M. Henneman, RP	8
S. Livingstone, 3B	8
F. Tanana, SP	7
S. Barnes, 3B	6
J. Doherty, RP	6
J. Kiely, RP	5
C. Kreuter, C	5
M. Leiter, RP	5
P. Clark, OF	4
M. Cuyler, OF	4
M. Munoz, RP	4
A. Trammell, SS	4
M. Carreon, OF	3
D. Haas, SP	3
K. Knudsen, RP	3
G. Pettis, OF	3
W. Terrell, RP	3
E. King, SP	2
K. Ritz, RP	1

Kansas City (72-90)	WS
Hitting	**77.9**
Fielding	**45.0**
Pitching	**93.0**
K. Appier, SP	20
J. Montgomery, RP	16
K. Miller, 2B	15
G. Jefferies, 3B	14
W. Joyner, 1B	14
K. McReynolds, OF	13
G. Brett, DH	11
B. McRae, OF	11
R. Meacham, RP	11
M. Macfarlane, C	10
H. Pichardo, SP	8
M. Gubicza, SP	7
D. Rasmussen, SP	5
R. Reed, SP	5
C. Wilkerson, SS	5
J. Eisenreich, OF	4
F. Gordon, RP	4
D. Howard, SS	4
B. Mayne, C	4
S. Shifflett, RP	4
G. Thurman, OF	4
J. Conine, OF	3
K. Koslofski, OF	3
R. Rossy, SS	3
J. Samuel, OF	3
L. Aquino, SP	2
M. Boddicker, RP	2
C. Haney, SP	2
N. Heaton, RP	2
M. Magnante, RP	2
C. Gwynn, OF	1

B. Melvin, C	1
B. Sampen, RP	1
T. Shumpert, 2B	1
C. Young, RP	1

Milwaukee (92-70)	WS
Hitting	**134.0**
Fielding	**46.7**
Pitching	**95.3**
P. Molitor, DH	28
P. Listach, SS	21
R. Yount, OF	20
D. Hamilton, OF	18
S. Fletcher, 2B	17
K. Seitzer, 3B	16
B. Surhoff, C	16
G. Vaughn, OF	16
B. Wegman, SP	16
J. Navarro, SP	15
C. Bosio, SP	13
C. Eldred, SP	11
D. Bichette, OF	8
M. Fetters, RP	8
J. Austin, RP	7
F. Stubbs, 1B	7
D. Henry, RP	6
D. Holmes, RP	6
D. Plesac, RP	6
J. Gantner, 2B	5
D. Nilsson, C	5
R. Bones, SP	4
J. Orosco, RP	3
J. Jaha, 1B	2
T. McIntosh, C	1
E. Nunez, RP	1

Minnesota (90-72)	WS
Hitting	**125.0**
Fielding	**45.7**
Pitching	**99.3**
K. Puckett, OF	31
S. Mack, OF	27
C. Knoblauch, 2B	23
J. Smiley, SP	18
C. Davis, DH	14
S. Erickson, SP	14
G. Gagne, SS	13
B. Harper, C	12
K. Tapani, SP	12
R. Aguilera, RP	11
P. Munoz, OF	11
K. Hrbek, 1B	10
T. Edens, RP	8
M. Guthrie, RP	8
B. Krueger, SP	8
G. Larkin, 1B	8
C. Willis, RP	8
S. Leius, 3B	7
J. Reboulet, SS	6
G. Wayne, RP	4
M. Trombley, SP	3
D. Hill, SS	2
P. Mahomes, SP	2
L. Webster, C	2
P. Abbott, RP	1
W. Banks, SP	1
J. Bruett, OF	1

R. Bush, DH-OF	1
L. Casian, RP	1
T. Jorgensen, 1B	1
B. Kipper, RP	1
M. Pagliarulo, 3B	1

New York (76-86)	WS
Hitting	**121.9**
Fielding	**34.7**
Pitching	**71.4**
D. Tartabull, OF	23
D. Mattingly, 1B	20
M. Perez, SP	17
M. Hall, OF	15
R. Kelly, OF	13
R. Velarde, SS	13
A. Stankiewicz, SS	12
C. Hayes, 3B	11
S. Farr, RP	10
M. Nokes, C	9
P. Kelly, 2B	7
R. Monteleone, RP	7
B. Williams, OF	7
S. Kamieniecki, SP	6
M. Stanley, C	6
M. Gallego, 2B	5
J. Habyan, RP	5
S. Howe, RP	5
J. Leyritz, DH	5
K. Maas, DH	5
S. Sanderson, SP	5
G. Cadaret, RP	4
D. James, OF	4
S. Militello, SP	3
B. Wickman, SP	3
T. Burke, RP	2
C. Young, RP	2
T. Leary, SP	1
H. Meulens, 3B	1
J. Nielsen, RP	1
G. Williams, OF	1

Oakland (96-66)	WS
Hitting	**157.9**
Fielding	**42.7**
Pitching	**87.5**
M. McGwire, 1B	29
R. Henderson, OF	25
M. Bordick, 2B	22
T. Steinbach, C	20
D. Eckersley, RP	18
H. Baines, DH	15
L. Blankenship, 2B	15
C. Lansford, 3B	15
J. Browne, 3B	13
J. Canseco, OF	12
R. Darling, SP	10
W. Wilson, OF	10
M. Moore, SP	9
J. Parrett, RP	9
D. Stewart, SP	9
B. Welch, SP	9
R. Sierra, OF	6
J. Corsi, RP	5
K. Downs, SP	5
W. Weiss, SS	5
V. Horsman, RP	4

R. Honeycutt, RP	3
R. Ready, DH-OF	3
J. Russell, RP	3
S. Brosius, OF	2
E. Fox, OF	2
G. Gossage, RP	2
T. Neel, DH-OF	2
J. Quirk, C	2
B. Witt, SP	2
K. Campbell, RP	1
H. Mercedes, C	1

Seattle (64-98)	WS
Hitting	**101.4**
Fielding	**31.4**
Pitching	**59.2**
K. Griffey Jr., OF	25
E. Martinez, 3B	24
J. Buhner, OF	16
D. Fleming, SP	16
O. Vizquel, SS	12
R. Johnson, SP	11
K. Mitchell, OF	11
H. Reynolds, 2B	8
T. Martinez, 1B	7
H. Cotto, OF	6
P. O'Brien, 1B	6
E. Hanson, SP	5
J. Nelson, RP	5
D. Valle, C	5
B. Fisher, SP	4
M. Grant, RP	4
R. Swan, RP	4
L. Parrish, C	3
D. Powell, RP	3
M. Schooler, RP	3
G. Briley, OF	2
R. Amaral, 3B-SS	1
S. Barton, RP	1
M. Blowers, 3B	1
B. Boone, 2B	1
D. Cochrane, OF	1
R. DeLucia, RP	1
D. Howitt, OF	1
C. Jones, RP	1
T. Leary, SP	1
J. Schaefer, SS	1
S. Turner, 3B	1
K. Woodson, RP	1

Texas (77-85)	WS
Hitting	**123.3**
Fielding	**31.5**
Pitching	**76.2**
R. Palmeiro, 1B	24
J. Gonzalez, OF	19
K. Brown, SP	18
D. Palmer, 3B	16
R. Sierra, OF	15
J. Guzman, SP	14
B. Downing, DH	13
I. Rodriguez, C	13
K. Reimer, OF	12
Je. Russell, RP	10
J. Huson, SS	9
D. Thon, SS	9
N. Ryan, SP	8
K. Rogers, RP	7
B. Witt, SP	6
T. Burns, RP	5
J. Canseco, OF	4
J. Frye, 2B	4
A. Newman, 2B	4
G. Petralli, C	4
M. Whiteside, RP	4
R. Pavlik, SP	3
M. Fariss, OF	2
J. Franco, DH	2
J. Cangelosi, OF	1
S. Chiamparino, SP	1
J. Daugherty, OF	1
D. Hulse, OF	1
E. Nunez, RP	1
J. Robinson, RP	1

Toronto (96-66)	WS
Hitting	**150.7**
Fielding	**42.2**
Pitching	**95.1**
R. Alomar, 2B	34
D. Winfield, DH	27
J. Carter, OF	24
C. Maldonado, OF	19
D. White, OF	19
J. Guzman, SP	17
J. Olerud, 1B	16
D. Ward, RP	16
J. Morris, SP	15
J. Key, SP	14
M. Lee, SS	14
P. Borders, C	12
T. Henke, RP	11
J. Kent, 3B	7
T. Stottlemyre, SP	7
K. Gruber, 3B	6
D. Cone, SP	5
D. Bell, OF	4
A. Griffin, SS	3
M. Eichhorn, RP	2
P. Hentgen, RP	2
B. MacDonald, RP	2
E. Sprague, C	2
D. Stieb, SP	2
P. Tabler, 1B	2
M. Timlin, RP	2
D. Martinez, 1B	1
G. Myers, C	1
T. Ward, OF	1
D. Wells, RP	1

1992 National League

Atlanta (98-64)	WS
Hitting	**141.1**
Fielding	**46.4**
Pitching	**106.5**
T. Pendleton, 3B	35
D. Justice, OF	23
T. Glavine, SP	19
J. Blauser, SS	18
J. Smoltz, SP	18
R. Gant, OF	17
O. Nixon, OF	16
S. Bream, 1B	15
S. Avery, SP	13
D. Sanders, OF	13
C. Leibrandt, SP	12
D. Berryhill, C	10
P. Smith, SP	9
G. Olson, C	8
L. Smith, OF	8
B. Hunter, 1B	7
M. Lemke, 2B	7
M. Freeman, RP	6
K. Mercker, RP	6
R. Belliard, SS	5
M. Bielecki, SP	5
M. Stanton, RP	5
J. Reardon, RP	4
M. Wohlers, RP	4
D. Nied, RP	3
A. Pena, RP	3
F. Cabrera, C	1
V. Castilla, 3B-SS	1
J. Lopez, C	1
J. Treadway, 2B	1
J. Willard, C	1

Chicago (78-84)	WS
Hitting	**97.8**
Fielding	**45.1**
Pitching	**91.1**
R. Sandberg, 2B	33
G. Maddux, SP	27
M. Grace, 1B	25
M. Morgan, SP	19
A. Dawson, OF	16
F. Castillo, SP	10
B. Scanlan, RP	10
R. Wilkins, C	10
D. May, OF	7
S. Sosa, OF	7
D. Dascenzo, OF	6
J. Girardi, C	6
C. McElroy, RP	6
J. Robinson, RP	6
Dw. Smith, OF	6
S. Buechele, 3B	5
R. Sanchez, SS	5
P. Assenmacher, RP	4
M. Harkey, SP	4
J. Vizcaino, SS	4
A. Arias, SS	3
K. Daniels, OF	3
J. Bullinger, RP	2
D. Jackson, SP	2
L. Salazar, 3B	2
H. Villanueva, C	2
S. Dunston, SS	1
K. Patterson, RP	1
Da. Smith, RP	1
D. Strange, 3B	1

Cincinnati (90-72)	WS
Hitting	**130.4**
Fielding	**43.0**
Pitching	**96.6**
B. Larkin, SS	32
B. Roberts, OF	28
J. Rijo, SP	19
G. Swindell, SP	16
R. Sanders, OF	14
H. Morris, 1B	13
J. Oliver, C	13
P. O'Neill, OF	13
R. Dibble, RP	12
B. Doran, 2B	12
T. Belcher, SP	10
N. Charlton, RP	9
D. Martinez, OF	9
S. Bankhead, RP	8
C. Sabo, 3B	8
G. Braggs, OF	7
D. Coles, 3B	7
D. Henry, RP	6
C. Hammond, SP	5
F. Benavides, 2B	4
S. Foster, RP	4
W. Greene, 3B	4
T. Pugh, SP	4
J. Branson, 2B	3
T. Afenir, C	1
B. Ayala, SP	1
T. Browning, SP	1
G. Green, SS	1
B. Hatcher, OF	1
C. Hernandez, OF	1
M. Hill, RP	1
T. Menendez, RP	1
S. Ruskin, RP	1
D. Wilson, C	1

Houston (81-81)	WS
Hitting	**135.3**
Fielding	**36.5**
Pitching	**71.2**
C. Biggio, 2B	32
J. Bagwell, 1B	29
S. Finley, OF	28
K. Caminiti, 3B	21
D. Jones, RP	18
E. Anthony, OF	15
L. Gonzalez, OF	11
X. Hernandez, RP	11
P. Incaviglia, OF	11
E. Taubensee, C	8
J. Boever, RP	7
P. Harnisch, SP	7
M. Portugal, SP	6
J. Jones, SP	5
C. Candaele, SS	4
B. Henry, SP	4
A. Cedeno, SS	3
D. Kile, SP	3
A. Osuna, RP	3
R. Ramirez, SS	3
S. Servais, C	3
B. Williams, SP	3
R. Murphy, RP	2
W. Blair, RP	1
B. Distefano, OF	1
J. Guerrero, SS	1
C. Jones, OF	1
E. Riles, SS	1
G. Young, OF	1

Los Angeles (63-99)	WS
Hitting	**89.2**
Fielding	**29.3**
Pitching	**70.5**
B. Butler, OF	24
E. Karros, 1B	13
M. Sharperson, 2B	13
T. Candiotti, SP	12
Ke. Gross, SP	10
J. Offerman, SS	10
J. Gott, RP	9
L. Harris, 2B	9
O. Hershiser, SP	8
P. Astacio, SP	7
M. Webster, OF	7
E. Davis, OF	6
J. Howell, RP	6
B. Ojeda, SP	6
M. Scioscia, C	6
D. Strawberry, OF	6
T. Benzinger, OF	4
J. Candelaria, RP	4
D. Hansen, 3B	4
C. Hernandez, C	4
E. Young, 2B	4
R. Martinez, SP	3
R. McDowell, RP	3
J. Samuel, 2B	2
D. Anderson, 3B	1
B. Ashley, OF	1
T. Goodwin, OF	1
Ki. Gross, RP	1
S. Javier, OF	1
P. Martinez, SP-RP	1
M. Piazza, C	1
H. Rodriguez, OF	1
S. Wilson, RP	1

Montreal (87-75)	WS
Hitting	**113.3**
Fielding	**45.9**
Pitching	**101.8**
M. Grissom, OF	27
L. Walker, OF	26
D. DeShields, 2B	19
K. Hill, SP	17
D. Martinez, SP	17
M. Rojas, RP	16
M. Alou, OF	15
S. Owen, SS	14
T. Wallach, 3B	12
J. Wetteland, RP	12
C. Nabholz, SP	10
B. Barberie, 3B	8
B. Barnes, SP	7
G. Carter, C	7
J. Fassero, RP	7
I. Calderon, OF	5
M. Gardner, SP	5
J. Vander Wal, OF	5
A. Cianfrocco, 1B	4
W. Cordero, SS	4
D. Fletcher, C	4
K. Bottenfield, RP	3
B. Sampen, RP	3
R. Cerone, C	2
G. Colbrunn, 1B	2

S. Valdez, RP	2
S. Berry, 3B	1
T. Foley, SS	1
G. Heredia, RP	1
T. Laker, C	1
D. Reed, OF	1
B. Risley, SP	1
M. Stairs, OF	1
P. Young, RP	1

New York (72-90)	WS
Hitting	**109.1**
Fielding	**33.1**
Pitching	**73.8**
E. Murray, 1B	20
B. Bonilla, OF	18
S. Fernandez, SP	16
D. Cone, SP	13
D. Magadan, 3B	13
D. Schofield, SS	13
D. Boston, OF	12
D. Gooden, SP	11
H. Johnson, OF	10
C. Walker, 3B	10
V. Coleman, OF	9
J. Franco, RP	8
J. Innis, RP	7
W. Randolph, 2B	7
T. Hundley, C	6
P. Schourek, SP	6
B. Pecota, 3B	5
B. Saberhagen, SP	5
W. Whitehurst, RP	4
A. Young, RP	4
K. Bass, OF	3
J. Kent, 2B	3
D. Gallagher, OF	2
J. McKnight, 2B	2
C. O'Brien, C	2
R. Thompson, OF	2
M. Dewey, RP	1
C. Donnels, 3B	1
D. Dozier, OF	1
T. Filer, RP	1
P. Howell, OF	1

Philadelphia (70-92)	WS
Hitting	**132.5**
Fielding	**26.5**
Pitching	**51.0**
D. Daulton, C	31
D. Hollins, 3B	27
J. Kruk, 1B	24
L. Dykstra, OF	17
C. Schilling, SP	17
M. Duncan, OF	12
S. Javier, OF	9
M. Morandini, 2B	9
T. Mulholland, SP	9
B. Rivera, SP	7
R. Jordan, 1B	6
Mit. Williams, RP	6
W. Chamberlain, OF	5
R. Amaro, OF	4
M. Hartley, RP	4
B. Ayrault, RP	3
J. Bell, SS	2
T. Pratt, C	2
W. Ritchie, RP	2
K. Shepherd, RP	2
D. Sveum, SS	2
W. Backman, 2B	1
K. Batiste, SS	1
C. Brantley, RP	1
J. DeLeon, SP	1
J. Grotewold, C-OF	1
B. Jones, RP	1
J. Lindeman, OF	1
J. Millette, SS	1
D. Robinson, SP	1
Mik. Williams, SP	1

Pittsburgh (96-66)	WS
Hitting	**145.0**
Fielding	**45.6**
Pitching	**97.4**
B. Bonds, OF	41
A. Van Slyke, OF	35
J. Bell, SS	24
D. Drabek, SP	20
O. Merced, 1B	14
D. Slaught, C	12
R. Tomlin, SP	12
M. LaValliere, C	11
S. Belinda, RP	10
S. Buechele, 3B	10
T. Wakefield, SP	9
B. Walk, SP	9
J. Lind, 2B	8
B. Patterson, RP	8
Z. Smith, SP	8
J. King, 3B	7
A. Cole, OF	5
R. Mason, RP	5
L. McClendon, OF	5
G. Redus, 1B	5
C. Espy, OF	4
D. Jackson, SP	4
D. Cox, RP	3
G. Varsho, OF	3
S. Cooke, RP	2
D. Neagle, RP	2
V. Palacios, RP	2
P. Wagner, RP	2
D. Clark, OF	1
C. Garcia, 2B	1
J. Gleaton, RP	1
P. Miller, RP	1
T. Prince, C	1
J. Robinson, SP	1
J. Wehner, 3B	1
K. Young, 3B	1

San Diego (82-80)	WS
Hitting	**108.1**
Fielding	**41.1**
Pitching	**96.8**
G. Sheffield, 3B	32
F. McGriff, 1B	27
T. Fernandez, SS	18
T. Gwynn, OF	18
A. Benes, SP	16
D. Jackson, OF	15
B. Hurst, SP	12
J. Clark, OF	11
C. Lefferts, SP	9
M. Maddux, RP	9
R. Rodriguez, RP	9
J. Melendez, RP	8
R. Myers, RP	7
B. Santiago, C	7
J. Deshaies, SP	6
F. Seminara, SP	6
T. Teufel, 2B	5
L. Andersen, RP	4
Gr. Harris, SP	4
K. Stillwell, 2B	4
D. Walters, C	4
P. Clements, RP	2
J. Hernandez, RP	2
C. Shipley, SS	2
D. Bilardello, C	1
P. Faries, 2B	1
Ge. Harris, RP	1
T. Lampkin, C	1
T. Scott, RP	1
P. Stephenson, OF	1
J. Vatcher, OF	1
G. Velasquez, 1B	1
K. Ward, OF	1

San Francisco (72-90)	WS
Hitting	**100.7**
Fielding	**41.0**
Pitching	**74.3**
W. Clark, 1B	28
R. Beck, RP	16
B. Swift, SP	16
R. Thompson, 2B	16
W. McGee, OF	15
C. Snyder, OF	11
M. Williams, 3B	11
M. Felder, OF	10
K. Manwaring, C	10
J. Brantley, RP	8
J. Burkett, SP	7
B. Hickerson, RP	7
D. Lewis, OF	7
J. Uribe, SS	6
K. Bass, OF	5
B. Black, SP	5
R. Clayton, SS	5
M. Jackson, RP	5
C. James, OF	5
M. Leonard, OF	4
G. Litton, 2B	3
J. McNamara, C	3
T. Wilson, SP	3
K. Downs, RP	2
J. Pena, RP	2
M. Benjamin, SS	1
C. Colbert, C	1
S. Decker, C	1
F. Oliveras, RP	1
J. Patterson, 2B	1
S. Reed, RP	1

St. Louis (83-79)	WS
Hitting	**113.8**
Fielding	**45.1**
Pitching	**90.1**
R. Lankford, OF	31
B. Tewksbury, SP	21
O. Smith, SS	20
B. Gilkey, OF	17
F. Jose, OF	15
G. Pena, 2B	12
L. Smith, RP	12
T. Pagnozzi, C	11
M. Perez, RP	11
T. Zeile, 3B	11
O. Olivares, SP	9
T. Worrell, RP	9
L. Alicea, 2B	8
C. Carpenter, RP	7
R. Cormier, SP	7
D. Osborne, SP	6
M. Thompson, OF	6
T. Woodson, 3B	5
R. Brewer, 1B	3
A. Galarraga, 1B	3
B. McClure, RP	3
C. Wilson, 3B	3
R. Gedman, C	2
T. Jones, SS	2
B. Jordan, OF	2
J. Oquendo, 2B	2
S. Royer, 3B	2
O. Canseco, OF	1
C. Carr, OF	1
M. Clark, SP	1
J. DeLeon, SP	1
F. DiPino, RP	1
R. Hudler, 2B	1
J. Magrane, SP	1
G. Perry, 1B	1
B. Smith, RP	1

1993
American League

Baltimore (85-77)	WS
Hitting	**115.4**
Fielding	**45.7**
Pitching	**93.9**
C. Hoiles, C	26
B. Anderson, OF	18
B. McDonald, SP	17
C. Ripken Jr., SS	17
H. Baines, DH	15
M. McLemore, OF	14
H. Reynolds, 2B	14
M. Devereaux, OF	13
J. Moyer, SP	13
M. Mussina, SP	11
G. Olson, RP	10
D. Segui, 1B	10
A. Mills, RP	9
T. Frohwirth, RP	8
T. Hulett, 3B	8
J. Poole, RP	7
F. Valenzuela, SP	7
J. Voigt, OF	6
M. Pagliarulo, 3B	5
L. Gomez, 3B	4
J. Hammonds, OF	4
R. Sutcliffe, SP	4
M. Williamson, RP	4
D. Buford, OF	2
S. Obando, DH	2
M. Cook, RP	1
J. O'Donoghue, RP	1
M. Oquist, RP	1
M. Parent, C	1
A. Rhodes, SP	1
L. Smith, DH	1
J. Tackett, C	1

Boston (80-82)	WS
Hitting	**78.2**
Fielding	**51.4**
Pitching	**110.5**
D. Darwin, SP	20
M. Greenwell, OF	19
M. Vaughn, 1B	19
J. Valentin, SS	16
F. Viola, SP	16
S. Fletcher, 2B	14
B. Hatcher, OF	13
S. Cooper, 3B	12
R. Clemens, SP	11
A. Sele, SP	11
G. Harris, RP	10
J. Russell, RP	10
P. Quantrill, RP	8
A. Dawson, DH	7
T. Pena, C	7
J. Dopson, SP	6
S. Bankhead, RP	5
K. Ryan, RP	5
B. Zupcic, OF	5
T. Naehring, 2B	4
I. Calderon, OF	2
R. Deer, OF	2
T. Fossas, RP	2
J. Hesketh, RP	2
J. Melendez, RP	2
B. Melvin, C	2
N. Minchey, SP	2
C. Quintana, 1B	2
L. Rivera, 2B-SS	2
C. Bailey, RP	1
J. McNeely, OF	1
J. Richardson, 2B	1
E. Riles, 2B	1

California (71-91)	WS
Hitting	**88.0**
Fielding	**40.2**
Pitching	**84.8**
T. Salmon, OF	24
M. Langston, SP	20
C. Finley, SP	19
C. Davis, DH	16
C. Curtis, OF	14
L. Polonia, OF	11
J. Snow, 1B	9
R. Gonzales, 3B	8
D. Easley, 2B	7
S. Frey, RP	7

Player	WS
J. Grahe, RP	7
T. Lovullo, 2B	7
G. DiSarcina, SS	6
S. Javier, OF	6
S. Sanderson, SP	6
M. Butcher, RP	5
P. Leftwich, SP	5
G. Nelson, RP	4
E. Perez, 3B	4
R. Correia, SS	3
J. Magrane, SP	3
G. Myers, C	3
K. Patterson, RP	3
C. Turner, C	3
K. Gruber, 3B	2
H. Hathaway, SP	2
S. Lewis, RP	2
B. Anderson, RP	1
J. Edmonds, OF	1
J. Orton, C	1
D. Scott, RP	1
K. Stillwell, 2B	1
R. Tingley, C	1
J. Walewander, SS	1

Chicago (94-68)	WS
Hitting	**126.0**
Fielding	**46.9**
Pitching	**109.1**
F. Thomas, 1B	32
L. Johnson, OF	21
J. McDowell, SP	21
R. Ventura, 3B	21
A. Fernandez, SP	20
T. Raines, OF	19
W. Alvarez, SP	18
J. Cora, 2B	16
R. Hernandez, RP	16
R. Karkovice, C	15
E. Burks, OF	14
O. Guillen, SS	12
J. Bere, SP	11
B. Jackson, OF	7
D. Pall, RP	5
S. Radinsky, RP	5
J. Schwarz, RP	4
T. Belcher, SP	3
C. Grebeck, SS	3
M. LaValliere, C	3
K. McCaskill, RP	3
T. Leach, RP	2
W. Newson, DH	2
D. Pasqua, OF	2
G. Bell, DH	1
C. Cary, RP	1
J. DeLeon, RP	1
B. Drahman, RP	1
C. Howard, RP	1
M. Huff, OF	1
N. Martin, 2B	1

Cleveland (76-86)	WS
Hitting	**132.6**
Fielding	**32.7**
Pitching	**62.7**
C. Baerga, 2B	28
A. Belle, OF	27
K. Lofton, OF	25
W. Kirby, OF	13
P. Sorrento, 1B	12
E. Plunk, RP	9
F. Fermin, SS	8
D. Lilliquist, RP	8
J. Hernandez, RP	7
J. Treadway, 3B	7
S. Alomar Jr., C	6
J. Dipoto, RP	6
T. Kramer, RP	6
J. Mesa, SP	6
J. Thome, 3B	6
M. Clark, SP	5
A. Espinoza, 3B	5
J. Ortiz, C	5
R. Jefferson, DH	4
C. Maldonado, OF	4
R. Milligan, 1B	4
C. Martinez, 3B	3
B. Wertz, RP	3
G. Hill, OF	2
S. Horn, DH	2
T. Howard, OF	2
B. Ojeda, SP	2
C. Young, RP	2
M. Bielecki, SP	1
D. Cook, RP	1
J. Grimsley, SP	1
J. Levis, C	1
A. Lopez, SP	1
B. Milacki, RP	1
D. Mlicki, SP	1
J. Mutis, SP	1
L. Parrish, C	1
H. Slocumb, RP	1
M. Young, RP	1

Detroit (85-77)	WS
Hitting	**154.5**
Fielding	**32.4**
Pitching	**68.1**
T. Fryman, SS	28
T. Phillips, OF	25
M. Tettleton, 1B	24
L. Whitaker, 2B	19
C. Fielder, 1B	17
A. Trammell, SS	17
C. Kreuter, C	16
M. Henneman, RP	11
D. Wells, SP	10
J. Doherty, SP	9
K. Gibson, DH	9
D. Gladden, OF	8
M. Moore, SP	7
T. Bolton, RP	5
R. Deer, OF	5
B. Gullickson, SP	5
B. Krueger, RP	5
S. Davis, RP	4
M. Leiter, RP	4
S. Livingstone, 3B	4
S. Barnes, 1B	3
J. Boever, RP	3
E. Davis, OF	3
B. MacDonald, RP	3
M. Cuyler, OF	2
C. Gomez, SS	2
K. Knudsen, RP	2
G. Thurman, OF	2
D. Bautista, OF	1
M. Gardiner, RP	1
R. Rowland, C	1

Kansas City (84-78)	WS
Hitting	**84.7**
Fielding	**52.0**
Pitching	**115.3**
K. Appier, SP	27
J. Montgomery, RP	22
D. Cone, SP	21
G. Gagne, SS	18
M. Macfarlane, C	18
B. McRae, OF	18
W. Joyner, 1B	17
F. Gordon, RP	14
H. Pichardo, SP	10
G. Gaetti, 3B	9
K. McReynolds, OF	9
F. Jose, OF	8
J. Lind, 2B	7
G. Brett, DH	6
C. Gwynn, OF	6
M. Gubicza, RP	5
B. Mayne, C	5
B. Brewer, RP	4
H. Brooks, OF	3
C. Haney, SP	3
P. Hiatt, 3B	3
S. Belinda, RP	2
G. Cadaret, RP	2
M. Magnante, SP	2
H. Pulliam, OF	2
R. Rossy, 2B	2
C. Wilson, 3B	2
M. Gardner, SP	1
J. Habyan, RP	1
B. Hamelin, 1B	1
D. Howard, 2B	1
K. Koslofski, OF	1
R. Meacham, RP	1
B. Sampen, RP	1

Milwaukee (69-93)	WS
Hitting	**97.4**
Fielding	**36.6**
Pitching	**73.0**
G. Vaughn, OF	22
C. Eldred, SP	16
D. Hamilton, OF	16
B. Surhoff, 3B	16
J. Jaha, 1B	15
R. Yount, OF	10
R. Bones, SP	8
P. Listach, SS	8
A. Miranda, SP	8
J. Orosco, RP	7
K. Seitzer, 3B	7
D. Thon, SS	7
J. Bell, 2B	6
J. Navarro, SP	6
D. Nilsson, C	6
G. Lloyd, RP	5
K. Reimer, DH	5
M. Fetters, RP	4
T. Lampkin, C	4
B. Wegman, SP	4
D. Henry, RP	3
J. Kmak, C	3
B. Spiers, 2B	3
J. Austin, RP	2
M. Ignasiak, RP	2
M. Kiefer, RP	2
C. Maldonado, RP	2
R. Novoa, RP	2
J. Valentin, SS	2
M. Boddicker, SP	1
T. Brunansky, OF	1
B. Doran, 2B	1
M. Maysey, RP	1
M. Mieske, OF	1
T. O'Leary, OF	1

Minnesota (71-91)	WS
Hitting	**92.0**
Fielding	**38.5**
Pitching	**82.5**
K. Puckett, OF	18
B. Harper, C	17
C. Knoblauch, 2B	16
S. Mack, OF	16
R. Aguilera, RP	14
K. Hrbek, 1B	12
K. Tapani, SP	12
W. Banks, SP	11
J. Deshaies, SP	10
D. Winfield, DH	10
M. Pagliarulo, 3B	9
C. Willis, RP	8
L. Casian, RP	7
S. Erickson, SP	7
C. Hale, 2B	7
J. Reboulet, SS	6
M. Hartley, RP	5
P. Munoz, OF	5
M. Trombley, RP	5
P. Meares, SS	4
G. Larkin, OF	3
T. Jorgensen, 3B	2
D. McCarty, OF	2
B. Brito, OF	1
G. Brummett, SP	1
E. Guardado, SP	1
M. Guthrie, RP	1
S. Stahoviak, 3B	1
G. Tsamis, RP	1
L. Webster, C	1

New York (88-74)	WS
Hitting	**147.1**
Fielding	**38.3**
Pitching	**78.6**
M. Stanley, C	24
J. Key, SP	21
D. Tartabull, DH	21
W. Boggs, 3B	20
D. Mattingly, 1B	20
P. O'Neill, OF	15
B. Williams, OF	15
J. Leyritz, 1B	14
M. Gallego, SS	13
D. James, OF	11
J. Abbott, SP	10
P. Kelly, 2B	10
S. Kamieniecki, SP	9
R. Velarde, OF	7
B. Wickman, RP	7
S. Farr, RP	5
K. Maas, DH	5
M. Nokes, C	5
S. Owen, SS	5
P. Gibson, RP	3
J. Habyan, RP	3
R. Monteleone, RP	3
M. Perez, SP	3
P. Assenmacher, RP	2
S. Howe, RP	2
D. Jean, SP	2
B. Munoz, RP	2
L. Smith, RP	2
S. Hitchcock, SP	1
M. Humphreys, OF	1
D. Silvestri, SS	1
F. Tanana, SP	1
M. Witt, SP	1

Oakland (68-94)	WS
Hitting	**118.7**
Fielding	**29.3**
Pitching	**56.0**
R. Henderson, OF	22
B. Gates, 2B	18
M. Bordick, SS	14
T. Neel, DH	13
R. Sierra, OF	13
M. Aldrete, 1B	11
B. Witt, SP	11
S. Hemond, C	10
D. Eckersley, RP	9
T. Steinbach, C	9
L. Blankenship, OF	7
M. McGwire, 1B	6
S. Brosius, OF	5
C. Paquette, 3B	5
J. Boever, RP	4
R. Darling, SP	4
D. Henderson, OF	4
R. Honeycutt, RP	4
E. Nunez, RP	4
B. Welch, SP	4
G. Gossage, RP	3
S. Karsay, SP	3
K. Seitzer, 3B	3
T. Van Poppel, SP	3
K. Abbott, OF	2
J. Browne, OF	2
M. Jimenez, SP	2
R. Smithberg, RP	2
K. Downs, RP	1
E. Helfand, C	1
V. Horsman, RP	1
S. Lydy, OF	1
H. Mercedes, C	1
D. Sveum, 1B	1
C. Young, SP	1

Seattle (82-80)	WS
Hitting	**106.8**
Fielding	**45.7**
Pitching	**93.5**
K. Griffey Jr., OF	29
J. Buhner, OF	22
R. Johnson, SP	22
D. Valle, C	17
E. Hanson, SP	15
M. Blowers, 3B	14
R. Amaral, 2B	12
C. Bosio, SP	12
T. Martinez, 1B	12
O. Vizquel, SS	12
D. Fleming, SP	10
B. Boone, 2B	8
N. Charlton, RP	7
T. Leary, SP	6
G. Litton, OF	6
D. Magadan, 1B	4
E. Martinez, DH	4
J. Nelson, RP	4
T. Power, RP	4
B. Holman, RP	3
P. O'Brien, DH	3
D. Powell, RP	3
B. Turang, OF	3
B. Ayrault, RP	2
R. DeLucia, RP	2
M. Felder, OF	2
B. Haselman, C	2
S. Ontiveros, RP	2
H. Cotto, OF	1
D. Howitt, OF	1
R. Salkeld, SP	1
F. Vina, 2B	1

Texas (86-76)	WS
Hitting	**144.0**
Fielding	**33.9**
Pitching	**80.1**
J. Gonzalez, OF	31
R. Palmeiro, 1B	31
J. Franco, DH	18
D. Palmer, 3B	16
K. Brown, SP	15
I. Rodriguez, C	15
T. Henke, RP	14
R. Pavlik, SP	12
D. Strange, 2B	12
D. Hulse, OF	11
K. Rogers, SP	11
J. Canseco, OF	8
G. Redus, OF	8
C. Leibrandt, SP	6
B. Davis, OF	5
M. Diaz, SS	5
M. Whiteside, RP	4
B. Bohanon, RP	3
C. Carpenter, RP	3
R. Ducey, OF	3
M. Lee, SS	3
J. Bronkey, RP	2
T. Burns, RP	2
C. James, OF	2
B. Patterson, RP	2
D. Peltier, OF	2
G. Petralli, C	2
B. Ripken, 2B	2
N. Ryan, SP	2
S. Balboni, DH	1
D. Dascenzo, OF	1
S. Dreyer, SP	1
B. Gil, SS	1
G. Nelson, RP	1
R. Reed, RP	1
M. Schooler, RP	1
J. Shave, SS	1

Toronto (95-67)	WS
Hitting	**142.8**
Fielding	**42.7**
Pitching	**99.5**
J. Olerud, 1B	37
R. Alomar, 2B	30
P. Molitor, DH	29
D. White, OF	20
J. Carter, OF	17
T. Fernandez, SS	17
D. Ward, RP	17
P. Hentgen, SP	16
J. Guzman, SP	15
D. Cox, RP	9
D. Stewart, SP	9
P. Borders, C	8
A. Leiter, RP	8
M. Eichhorn, RP	7
E. Sprague, 3B	7
T. Stottlemyre, SP	7
T. Castillo, RP	5
D. Coles, OF	4
R. Knorr, C	4
R. Henderson, OF	3
D. Schofield, SS	3
M. Timlin, RP	3
T. Ward, OF	2
W. Williams, RP	2
R. Butler, OF	1
D. Cedeno, SS	1
A. Griffin, SS	1
D. Jackson, OF	1
J. Morris, SP	1
L. Sojo, 2B-SS	1

1993
National League

Atlanta (104-58)	WS
Hitting	**130.2**
Fielding	**52.4**
Pitching	**129.4**
J. Blauser, SS	29
D. Justice, OF	29
R. Gant, OF	25
G. Maddux, SP	25
T. Glavine, SP	20
S. Avery, SP	19
G. McMichael, RP	17
F. McGriff, 1B	16
T. Pendleton, 3B	16
J. Smoltz, SP	16
M. Lemke, 2B	15
O. Nixon, OF	13
D. Sanders, OF	11
D. Berryhill, C	8
S. Bream, 1B	8
S. Bedrosian, RP	7
J. Howell, RP	6
K. Mercker, RP	6
G. Olson, C	5
M. Stanton, RP	5
P. Smith, SP	4
M. Wohlers, RP	4
R. Belliard, SS	2
R. Klesko, 1B	2
B. Pecota, 3B	2
F. Cabrera, 1B	1
J. Lopez, C	1

Chicago (84-78)	WS
Hitting	**120.9**
Fielding	**42.1**
Pitching	**89.0**
R. Wilkins, C	28
M. Grace, 1B	23
R. Myers, RP	15
S. Sosa, OF	15
J. Vizcaino, SS	15
S. Buechele, 3B	14
R. Sandberg, 2B	14
J. Bautista, RP	13
D. May, OF	13
G. Hibbard, SP	11
M. Morgan, SP	11
D. Smith, OF	10
J. Guzman, SP	9
R. Sanchez, SS	9
G. Hill, OF	6
S. Boskie, RP	5
B. Scanlan, RP	5
F. Castillo, SP	4
K. Rhodes, OF	4
P. Assenmacher, RP	3
M. Harkey, SP	3
D. Plesac, RP	3
W. Wilson, OF	3
D. Jennings, 1B	2
S. Lake, C	2
C. McElroy, RP	2
K. Roberson, OF	2
B. Brennan, RP	1
J. Bullinger, RP	1
S. Dunston, SS	1
H. Slocumb, RP	1
S. Trachsel, SP	1
M. Walbeck, C	1
T. Wendell, SP	1
E. Yelding, 2B	1

Cincinnati (73-89)	WS
Hitting	**114.7**
Fielding	**34.1**
Pitching	**70.2**
J. Rijo, SP	26
B. Larkin, SS	18
R. Sanders, OF	17
C. Sabo, 3B	16
K. Mitchell, OF	15
J. Oliver, C	14
H. Morris, 1B	11
R. Kelly, OF	10
R. Milligan, 1B	9
J. Brumfield, OF	8
T. Belcher, SP	7
J. Samuel, 2B	6
T. Browning, SP	5
J. Reardon, RP	5
B. Roberts, 2B	5
J. Branson, SS	4
T. Howard, OF	4
T. Pugh, SP	4
J. Spradlin, RP	4
S. Foster, RP	3
J. Ruffin, RP	3
S. Service, RP	3
J. Daugherty, OF	2
B. Dorsett, C	2
L. Luebbers, SP	2
J. Smiley, SP	2
G. Varsho, OF	2
B. Ayala, RP	1
G. Cadaret, RP	1
T. Costo, OF	1
C. Espy, OF	1
W. Greene, SS	1
M. Hill, RP	1
K. Kessinger, SS	1
B. Landrum, RP	1
R. Powell, RP	1
J. Roper, SP	1
G. Tubbs, OF	1
D. Wilson, C	1

Colorado (67-95)	WS
Hitting	**89.2**
Fielding	**38.6**
Pitching	**73.2**
A. Galarraga, 1B	23
C. Hayes, 3B	20
D. Bichette, OF	19
A. Reynoso, SP	13
D. Holmes, RP	12
J. Clark, OF	11
B. Ruffin, RP	11
E. Young, 2B	10
J. Girardi, C	9
S. Reed, RP	8
W. Blair, RP	7
A. Cole, OF	7
F. Benavides, SS	5
C. Jones, OF	5
D. Nied, SP	5
D. Sheaffer, C	5
D. Boston, OF	4
J. Parrett, RP	4
G. Wayne, RP	4
K. Bottenfield, SP	3
V. Castilla, SS	3
N. Liriano, SS	3
C. Leskanic, RP	2
L. Painter, SP	2
B. Henry, SP	1
R. Mejia, 2B	1
M. Moore, RP	1
M. Munoz, RP	1
J. Owens, C	1
M. Sanford, SP	1

Florida (64-98)	WS
Hitting	**62.2**
Fielding	**43.0**
Pitching	**86.9**
B. Harvey, RP	18
J. Conine, OF	15
W. Weiss, SS	13
C. Carr, OF	12
O. Destrade, 1B	12
B. Barberie, 2B	10
L. Aquino, RP	8
C. Hammond, SP	8
C. Hough, SP	8
D. Magadan, 3B	8
B. Santiago, C	8
G. Sheffield, 3B	8
J. Armstrong, SP	7
M. Turner, RP	7
R. Bowen, SP	6
R. Lewis, RP	6
R. Renteria, 2B	6
P. Rapp, SP	5
A. Arias, 2B	4
H. Cotto, OF	4
T. Hoffman, RP	4
C. Carpenter, RP	3
J. Felix, OF	3
B. Natal, C	2
R. Rodriguez, RP	2
D. Whitmore, OF	2
G. Briley, OF	1
J. Klink, RP	1
D. Weathers, RP	1

Houston (85-77)	WS
Hitting	**115.5**
Fielding	**43.5**
Pitching	**96.1**
C. Biggio, 2B	26
J. Bagwell, 1B	22
L. Gonzalez, OF	20
M. Portugal, SP	19
P. Harnisch, SP	16
K. Caminiti, 3B	14
S. Finley, OF	14
A. Cedeno, SS	13
X. Hernandez, RP	12
E. Anthony, OF	11
D. Kile, SP	11
D. Drabek, SP	10
K. Bass, OF	9
S. Servais, C	9
G. Swindell, SP	8
E. Taubensee, C	7
D. Jones, RP	6
C. James, OF	5
C. Donnels, 3B	4
T. Edens, RP	4
T. Jones, RP	3
A. Osuna, RP	3
B. Williams, RP	3
C. Candaele, 2B	2
M. Grant, RP	1
R. Parker, OF	1
S. Reynolds, RP	1
J. Uribe, SS	1

Los Angeles (81-81)	WS
Hitting	**103.2**
Fielding	**41.4**
Pitching	**98.5**
M. Piazza, C	31
B. Butler, OF	23
T. Candiotti, SP	14
J. Gott, RP	14
J. Offerman, SS	14
J. Reed, 2B	14
O. Hershiser, SP	13
R. Martinez, SP	13
P. Astacio, SP	12
P. Martinez, RP	12
C. Snyder, OF	12
E. Karros, 1B	10
E. Davis, OF	9
Ke. Gross, SP	9
D. Hansen, 3B	8
R. McDowell, RP	6
T. Wallach, 3B	6
L. Harris, 2B	4
R. Mondesi, OF	3
H. Rodriguez, OF	3
R. Trlicek, RP	3
Ki. Gross, RP	2
M. Sharperson, 2B	2
M. Webster, OF	2
R. Bournigal, 2B-SS	1
O. Daal, RP	1
C. Hernandez, C	1
S. Wilson, RP	1

Montreal (94-68)	WS
Hitting	**131.4**
Fielding	**46.4**
Pitching	**104.2**
M. Grissom, OF	30
L. Walker, OF	24
M. Alou, OF	21
D. DeShields, 2B	21
J. Wetteland, RP	21
M. Lansing, 3B	17
J. Fassero, RP	15
W. Cordero, SS	13
S. Berry, 3B	12
D. Martinez, SP	12
K. Hill, SP	11
M. Rojas, RP	9
D. Fletcher, C	8
K. Rueter, SP	8
L. Frazier, OF	6
C. Nabholz, SP	6
J. Vander Wal, 1B	6
B. Barnes, RP	4
R. Ready, 2B	4
J. Shaw, RP	4
F. Bolick, 1B	3
D. Boucher, SP	3
G. Colbrunn, 1B	3
G. Heredia, RP	3
T. Scott, RP	3
R. White, OF	3
K. Bottenfield, RP	2
C. Pride, OF	2
T. Spehr, C	2
C. Floyd, 1B	1
B. Henry, RP	1
O. Marrero, 1B	1
C. Montoyo, 2B	1
T. Wood, OF	1
P. Young, RP	1

New York (59-103)	WS
Hitting	**82.7**
Fielding	**29.6**
Pitching	**64.7**
B. Bonilla, OF	16
E. Murray, 1B	15
D. Gooden, SP	14
J. Kent, 2B	13
S. Fernandez, SP	9
B. Saberhagen, SP	9
J. Burnitz, OF	8
J. Orsulak, OF	8
T. Hundley, C	7
T. Bogar, SS	6
V. Coleman, OF	6
D. Gallagher, OF	6
H. Johnson, 3B	6
M. Maddux, RP	6
C. O'Brien, C	6
F. Tanana, SP	6
R. Thompson, OF	5
E. Hillman, SP	4
J. Innis, RP	4
T. Fernandez, SS	3
D. Telgheder, RP	3
A. Young, RP	3
K. Baez, SS	2
M. Draper, RP	2
B. Jones, SP	2
J. McKnight, SS	2
C. Walker, 2B	2
J. Franco, RP	1
M. Gozzo, RP	1
D. Jackson, OF	1
J. Manzanillo, RP	1

Philadelphia (97-65)	WS
Hitting	**161.8**
Fielding	**39.9**
Pitching	**89.3**
L. Dykstra, OF	32
D. Daulton, C	29
J. Kruk, 1B	25
D. Hollins, 3B	20
T. Greene, SP	16
P. Incaviglia, OF	14
M. Duncan, 2B	13
J. Eisenreich, OF	13
T. Mulholland, SP	13
C. Schilling, SP	13
D. Jackson, SP	11
M. Morandini, 2B	10
K. Stocker, SS	10
W. Chamberlain, OF	9
D. West, RP	9
Mit. Williams, RP	9
M. Thompson, OF	8
L. Andersen, RP	7
K. Batiste, 3B	5
B. Rivera, SP	5
T. Pratt, C	4
R. Amaro, OF	3
J. DeLeon, RP	3
R. Jordan, 1B	3
R. Mason, RP	2
D. Pall, RP	2
J. Bell, SS	1
B. Thigpen, RP	1
Mik. Williams, RP	1

Pittsburgh (75-87)	WS
Hitting	**116.8**
Fielding	**37.0**
Pitching	**71.2**
J. Bell, SS	26
J. King, 3B	20
O. Merced, OF	20
A. Martin, OF	16
D. Slaught, C	14
S. Cooke, SP	12
A. Van Slyke, OF	12
C. Garcia, 2B	10
D. Clark, OF	9
S. Belinda, RP	8
B. Minor, RP	8
L. Smith, OF	8
P. Wagner, RP	8
M. Dewey, RP	6
J. Johnston, RP	6
K. Young, 1B	5
J. Ballard, RP	3
T. Foley, 2B	3
J. Goff, C	3
D. Otto, RP	3
T. Prince, C	3
Z. Smith, SP	3
R. Tomlin, SP	3
B. Walk, SP	3
J. Hope, SP	2
T. Menendez, RP	2
D. Neagle, RP	2
F. Toliver, RP	2
T. Wakefield, SP	2
L. McClendon, OF	1
B. Shelton, OF	1
A. Tomberlin, OF	1

San Diego (61-101)	WS
Hitting	**88.6**
Fielding	**29.6**
Pitching	**64.8**
T. Gwynn, OF	18
P. Plantier, OF	16
D. Bell, OF	12
A. Benes, SP	12
J. Gardner, 2B	10
Gr. Harris, SP	9
R. Gutierrez, SS	8
Ge. Harris, RP	8
G. Sheffield, 3B	8
F. McGriff, 1B	7
A. Cianfrocco, 3B	6
P. Clark, OF	6
T. Teufel, 2B	6
W. Whitehurst, SP	5
B. Bean, OF	4
D. Brocail, SP	4
P. Martinez, RP	4
B. Ausmus, C	3
T. Hoffman, RP	3
R. Mason, RP	3
T. Scott, RP	3
C. Shipley, SS	3
J. Brown, OF	2
M. Davis, RP	2
B. Geren, C	2
K. Higgins, C	2
T. Mauser, RP	2
R. Rodriguez, RP	2
S. Sanders, SP	2
D. Staton, 1B	2
T. Worrell, SP	2
A. Ashby, SP	1
P. Gomez, RP	1
J. Hernandez, RP	1
F. Seminara, RP	1
K. Stillwell, SS	1
G. Velasquez, 1B	1
D. Walters, C	1

San Francisco (103-59)	WS
Hitting	**164.6**
Fielding	**50.4**
Pitching	**93.9**
B. Bonds, OF	47
M. Williams, 3B	28
R. Thompson, 2B	26
B. Swift, SP	19
K. Manwaring, C	18
R. Beck, RP	16
W. Clark, 1B	15
R. Clayton, SS	15
D. Lewis, OF	15
J. Burkett, SP	14
W. McGee, OF	13
M. Jackson, RP	9
M. Carreon, OF	8
K. Rogers, RP	7
B. Black, SP	6
D. Martinez, OF	6
T. Wilson, SP	6
M. Benjamin, 2B-SS	5
T. Benzinger, 1B	5
D. Burba, RP	5
B. Hickerson, RP	5
J. Reed, C	4
J. Brantley, RP	3
S. Sanderson, SP	3
S. Scarsone, 2B	3
C. Colbert, C	2
S. Torres, SP	2
G. Brummett, SP	1
J. Deshaies, SP	1
P. Faries, 2B	1
J. Phillips, 1B	1

St. Louis (87-75)	WS
Hitting	**143.0**
Fielding	**37.1**
Pitching	**80.9**
G. Jefferies, 1B	28
B. Gilkey, OF	21
O. Smith, SS	19
T. Zeile, 3B	19
M. Whiten, OF	17
L. Alicea, 2B	15
R. Lankford, OF	12
B. Tewksbury, SP	12
R. Arocha, SP	10
B. Jordan, OF	10
M. Perez, RP	10
D. Osborne, SP	9
G. Pena, 2B	8
T. Pagnozzi, C	7
E. Pappas, C	7
L. Smith, RP	7
R. Cormier, SP	6
O. Olivares, RP	6
P. Kilgus, RP	5
L. Lancaster, RP	5
G. Perry, 1B	5
R. Brewer, OF	4
L. Guetterman, RP	4
J. Magrane, SP	3
R. Murphy, RP	3
A. Watson, SP	3
T. Jones, SS	2
S. Royer, 3B	2
J. Oquendo, SS	1
H. Villanueva, C	1

1994 American League

Baltimore (63-49)	WS
Hitting	**76.8**
Fielding	**36.1**
Pitching	**76.1**
M. Mussina, SP	18
C. Ripken Jr., SS	18
R. Palmeiro, 1B	17
C. Hoiles, C	14
B. Anderson, OF	12
L. Gomez, 3B	12
B. McDonald, SP	12
M. Eichhorn, RP	10
M. McLemore, 2B	9
J. Moyer, SP	8
Le. Smith, RP	8
C. Sabo, 3B	7
H. Baines, DH	6
S. Fernandez, SP	6
J. Hammonds, OF	6
M. Williamson, RP	5
M. Devereaux, OF	3
T. Hulett, 2B	3
A. Mills, RP	3
J. Voigt, OF	3
A. Rhodes, SP	2
D. Smith, OF	2
A. Benitez, RP	1
T. Bolton, RP	1
S. Klingenbeck, SP	1
M. Oquist, SP	1
J. Tackett, C	1

Boston (54-61)	WS
Hitting	**65.0**
Fielding	**31.3**
Pitching	**65.7**
M. Vaughn, 1B	17
R. Clemens, SP	16
J. Valentin, SS	14
A. Sele, SP	11
S. Cooper, 3B	10
O. Nixon, OF	10
K. Ryan, RP	9
M. Greenwell, OF	8
T. Naehring, 2B	8
J. Hesketh, SP	7
C. Rodriguez, SS	6
D. Berryhill, C	5
T. Brunansky, OF	5
C. Howard, RP	4
S. Bankhead, RP	3
D. Darwin, SP	3
S. Fletcher, 2B	3
T. Fossas, RP	3
R. Rowland, C	3
J. Russell, RP	3
L. Tinsley, OF	3
P. Quantrill, RP	2
F. Viola, SP	2
W. Chamberlain, OF	1
A. Dawson, DH	1
G. Finnvold, SP	1
B. Hatcher, OF	1
C. Nabholz, SP	1
D. Valle, C	1
T. VanEgmond, SP	1

California (47-68)	WS
Hitting	**63.8**
Fielding	**25.4**
Pitching	**51.8**
C. Davis, DH	15
C. Finley, SP	14
T. Salmon, OF	13
S. Owen, 3B	11
C. Curtis, OF	8
M. Langston, SP	8
J. Edmonds, OF	7
B. Jackson, OF	7
B. Anderson, SP	6
G. DiSarcina, SS	6
M. Leiter, RP	6
P. Leftwich, SP	5
R. Hudler, 2B	4
B. Patterson, RP	4
D. Easley, 3B	3
J. Snow, 1B	3
R. Springer, RP	3
J. Dopson, RP	2
J. Fabregas, C	2
C. Lefferts, RP	2
G. Myers, C	2
H. Reynolds, 2B	2
D. Smith, OF	2
C. Turner, C	2
M. Butcher, RP	1
S. Lewis, RP	1
E. Perez, 1B	1
J. Schwarz, RP	1

Chicago (67-46)	WS
Hitting	**97.5**
Fielding	**32.0**
Pitching	**71.4**
F. Thomas, 1B	25
R. Ventura, 3B	16
J. Franco, DH	15
T. Raines, OF	14
W. Alvarez, SP	12
L. Johnson, OF	12
J. McDowell, SP	12
A. Fernandez, SP	11
D. Jackson, OF	11
J. Bere, SP	10
J. Cora, 2B	8
O. Guillen, SS	8
J. DeLeon, RP	6
R. Hernandez, RP	5
R. Karkovice, C	5
P. Assenmacher, RP	4
M. LaValliere, C	4
N. Martin, 2B	4
K. McCaskill, RP	4
S. Sanderson, SP	4
D. Cook, RP	3
C. Grebeck, 2B-SS	3
J. Hall, OF	2
D. Howitt, OF	1
W. Newson, OF	1
B. Zupcic, OF	1

Cleveland (66-47)	WS
Hitting	**100.3**
Fielding	**28.0**
Pitching	**69.6**
A. Belle, OF	24
K. Lofton, OF	21
D. Martinez, SP	14
C. Baerga, 2B	13
C. Nagy, SP	13
S. Alomar Jr., C	12
M. Ramirez, OF	11
M. Clark, SP	10
J. Thome, 3B	10
E. Murray, DH	9
E. Plunk, RP	9
P. Sorrento, 1B	9
J. Mesa, RP	7
O. Vizquel, SS	7
J. Grimsley, SP	5
J. Morris, SP	5
W. Kirby, OF	4
A. Espinoza, 3B	3
T. Pena, C	3
D. Lilliquist, RP	2
C. Maldonado, DH	2
J. Russell, RP	2
R. Gonzales, 3B	1
A. Lopez, SP	1
M. Turner, RP	1

Detroit (53-62)	WS
Hitting	**92.8**
Fielding	**21.7**
Pitching	**44.6**
T. Phillips, OF	16
T. Fryman, 3B	15
K. Gibson, DH	14
M. Tettleton, C	14
C. Fielder, 1B	12
J. Felix, OF	10
L. Whitaker, 2B	10
C. Gomez, SS	8
J. Boever, RP	7
D. Wells, SP	7
M. Moore, SP	6
J. Samuel, OF	5
M. Gardiner, RP	4
T. Belcher, SP	3
S. Davis, RP	3
B. Groom, RP	3
B. Gullickson, SP	3
C. Kreuter, C	3
A. Trammell, SS	3
G. Cadaret, RP	2
J. Doherty, SP	2
G. Gohr, SP	2
M. Henneman, RP	2
D. Bautista, OF	1
S. Bergman, SP	1
M. Cuyler, OF	1
E. Davis, OF	1
J. Flaherty, C	1

Kansas City (64-51)	WS
Hitting	**67.6**
Fielding	**37.2**
Pitching	**87.2**
D. Cone, SP	20
K. Appier, SP	13
F. Gordon, SP	12
B. Hamelin, DH	12
G. Gagne, SS	11
F. Jose, OF	11
W. Joyner, 1B	11
M. Macfarlane, C	11
B. McRae, OF	11
G. Gaetti, 3B	10
V. Coleman, OF	8
M. Gubicza, SP	8
B. Brewer, RP	7
J. Montgomery, RP	7
J. Lind, 2B	6
R. Meacham, RP	6
H. Pichardo, RP	5
T. Shumpert, 2B	5
D. Henderson, OF	4
B. Mayne, C	4
M. Magnante, RP	3
S. Belinda, RP	2
J. DeJesus, SP	2
D. Howard, 3B	2
B. Milacki, SP	1

Milwaukee (53-62)	WS
Hitting	**60.9**
Fielding	**33.2**
Pitching	**64.9**
R. Bones, SP	14
J. Reed, 2B	12
J. Valentin, SS	12
C. Eldred, SP	11
K. Seitzer, 3B	11
D. Nilsson, C	9
G. Vaughn, OF	9
T. Ward, OF	9
M. Fetters, RP	8
B. Scanlan, RP	7
B. Wegman, SP	7
M. Mieske, OF	6
J. Jaha, 1B	4
J. Mercedes, RP	4
B. Surhoff, 3B	4
B. Harper, DH	3
M. Ignasiak, RP	3
G. Lloyd, RP	3
B. Spiers, 3B-SS	3
J. Bronkey, RP	2
J. Cirillo, 3B	2
A. Diaz, OF	2
D. Hamilton, OF	2
D. Henry, RP	2
A. Miranda, SP	2
J. Orosco, RP	2
D. Valle, C	2
P. Listach, SS	1
J. Navarro, RP	1
T. O'Leary, OF	1
R. Wrona, C	1

Minnesota (53-60)	WS
Hitting	**92.1**
Fielding	**21.8**
Pitching	**45.1**
C. Knoblauch, 2B	20
K. Puckett, OF	20
S. Mack, OF	15
K. Tapani, SP	11
K. Hrbek, 1B	10
A. Cole, OF	9
P. Mahomes, SP	8
P. Munoz, OF	7
R. Aguilera, RP	6
S. Erickson, SP	6
S. Leius, 3B	6
P. Meares, SS	6
J. Reboulet, SS	5
M. Walbeck, C	5
D. Winfield, DH	5
K. Campbell, RP	3
C. Pulido, SP	3
M. Guthrie, RP	2
C. Hale, 3B	2
D. McCarty, 1B	2
C. Willis, RP	2
R. Becker, OF	1
D. Hocking, SS	1
D. Parks, C	1
E. Schullstrom, RP	1
D. Stevens, RP	1
M. Trombley, RP	1

New York (70-43)	WS
Hitting	**110.5**
Fielding	**30.7**
Pitching	**68.8**
P. O'Neill, OF	23
W. Boggs, 3B	18
J. Key, SP	15
D. Mattingly, 1B	15
M. Stanley, C	14
B. Williams, OF	14
L. Polonia, OF	12
S. Howe, RP	10
J. Leyritz, C	10
D. Tartabull, DH	10
M. Perez, SP	9
B. Wickman, RP	9
J. Abbott, SP	8
S. Kamieniecki, SP	8
R. Velarde, SS	8
M. Gallego, SS	7
P. Kelly, 2B	6
S. Hitchcock, RP	4
M. Nokes, C	2
D. Pall, RP	2
J. Ausanio, RP	1
D. Boston, OF	1
P. Gibson, RP	1
X. Hernandez, RP	1
B. Melvin, C-1B	1
T. Mulholland, SP	1

Oakland (51-63)	WS
Hitting	**80.0**
Fielding	**24.8**
Pitching	**48.2**
T. Steinbach, C	15
G. Berroa, DH	14
R. Sierra, OF	13
R. Henderson, OF	11
S. Javier, OF	11
S. Ontiveros, RP	10
M. Bordick, SS	8
T. Neel, 1B	8
R. Darling, SP	7
S. Brosius, 3B	6
M. McGwire, 1B	6
D. Eckersley, RP	5
J. Briscoe, RP	4
C. Reyes, RP	4
B. Witt, SP	4
M. Acre, RP	3
M. Aldrete, OF	3
B. Gates, 2B	3
S. Hemond, C	3
S. Karsay, SP	3
B. Taylor, RP	3
D. Leiper, RP	2
J. Noboa, 2B	2
T. Van Poppel, SP	2
F. Cruz, SS	1
V. Horsman, RP	1
E. Vosberg, RP	1

Seattle (49-63)	WS
Hitting	**67.0**
Fielding	**24.4**
Pitching	**55.7**
K. Griffey Jr., OF	20
R. Johnson, SP	15
J. Buhner, OF	13
E. Martinez, 3B	11
B. Ayala, RP	10
M. Blowers, 3B	7
C. Bosio, SP	7
R. Jefferson, DH	7

T. Martinez, 1B 7
F. Fermin, SS 6
B. Risley, RP 6
R. Amaral, 2B 4
T. Davis, RP 4
G. Gossage, RP 4
L. Sojo, 2B 4
D. Wilson, C 4
E. Anthony, OF 3
J. Nelson, RP 3
J. Cummings, RP 2
D. Fleming, SP 2
B. Haselman, C 1
M. Hill, RP 1
T. Lovullo, 2B 1
K. Mitchell, OF 1
G. Pirkl, DH 1
E. Plantenberg, RP 1
B. Turang, OF 1
B. Wells, RP 1

Texas (52-62)	WS
Hitting	**93.1**
Fielding	**21.2**
Pitching	**41.8**
W. Clark, 1B	19
J. Canseco, DH	16
I. Rodriguez, C	15
R. Greer, OF	12
J. Gonzalez, OF	11
K. Rogers, SP	9
J. Frye, 2B	8
M. Lee, SS	8
K. Brown, SP	7
D. Palmer, 3B	7
T. Henke, RP	6
O. McDowell, OF	5
D. Oliver, RP	5
D. Hulse, OF	4
C. Carpenter, RP	3
C. James, OF	3
M. Whiteside, RP	3
E. Beltre, SS	2
R. Helling, SP	2
J. Howell, RP	2
J. Ortiz, C	2
B. Ripken, 3B	2
J. Armstrong, SP	1
J. Dettmer, SP	1
H. Fajardo, SP	1
D. Smith, RP	1
D. Strange, 2B	1

Toronto (55-60)	WS
Hitting	**72.5**
Fielding	**29.4**
Pitching	**63.1**
P. Molitor, DH	19
P. Hentgen, SP	15
J. Carter, OF	14
J. Olerud, 1B	14
R. Alomar, 2B	13
D. White, OF	11
T. Stottlemyre, SP	10
T. Castillo, RP	8
D. Schofield, SS	8
D. Hall, RP	6
M. Huff, OF	6
J. Guzman, SP	5
A. Leiter, SP	5
W. Williams, RP	5
P. Borders, C	4
D. Cox, RP	4
E. Sprague, 3B	4
D. Stewart, SP	4
C. Delgado, OF	3
R. Knorr, C	2
M. Timlin, RP	2
D. Cedeno, 2B	1
D. Coles, OF	1
A. Gonzalez, SS	1

1994 National League

Atlanta (68-46)	WS
Hitting	**88.0**
Fielding	**33.2**
Pitching	**82.8**
G. Maddux, SP	26
F. McGriff, 1B	22
D. Justice, OF	19
T. Glavine, SP	12
M. Lemke, 2B	12
J. Blauser, SS	10
R. Kelly, OF	10
S. Avery, SP	9
K. Mercker, SP	9
R. Klesko, OF	8
G. McMichael, RP	8
D. Sanders, OF	7
C. O'Brien, C	6
T. Pendleton, 3B	6
J. Smoltz, SP	6
J. Lopez, C	5
M. Stanton, RP	5
T. Tarasco, OF	4
S. Bedrosian, RP	3
D. Gallagher, OF	3
J. Oliva, 3B	3
M. Wohlers, RP	3
R. Belliard, SS	2
M. Bielecki, RP	2
B. Pecota, 3B	2
M. Kelly, OF	1
M. Mordecai, SS	1

Chicago (49-64)	WS
Hitting	**72.6**
Fielding	**24.4**
Pitching	**50.0**
S. Sosa, OF	15
M. Grace, 1B	12
S. Trachsel, SP	10
S. Buechele, 3B	9
D. May, OF	9
R. Wilkins, C	9
S. Dunston, SS	8
G. Hill, OF	8
J. Bullinger, RP	7
R. Sanchez, 2B	7
R. Sandberg, 2B	7
K. Foster, SP	6
A. Young, SP	6
J. Bautista, RP	5
R. Myers, RP	5
E. Zambrano, OF	4
C. Crim, RP	3
M. Parent, C	3
K. Rhodes, OF	3
W. Banks, SP	2
D. Otto, RP	2
D. Plesac, RP	2
S. Boskie, RP	1
F. Castillo, SP	1
J. Hernandez, 3B	1
M. Maksudian, 1B	1
K. Roberson, OF	1

Cincinnati (66-48)	WS
Hitting	**101.0**
Fielding	**30.3**
Pitching	**66.7**
B. Larkin, SS	19
K. Mitchell, OF	18
B. Boone, 2B	15
H. Morris, 1B	15
T. Fernandez, 3B	14
R. Sanders, OF	13
J. Rijo, SP	11
J. Brantley, RP	10
J. Smiley, SP	8
H. Carrasco, RP	7
C. McElroy, RP	7
J. Ruffin, RP	7
E. Taubensee, C	6
J. Brumfield, OF	5
E. Hanson, SP	5
R. Kelly, OF	5
J. Branson, 2B	4
B. Dorsett, C	4
T. Howard, OF	4
J. Roper, SP	4
D. Sanders, OF	4
P. Schourek, RP	4
L. Harris, 3B	3
T. Browning, SP	2
T. Fortugno, RP	1
B. Hunter, OF	1
T. Pugh, SP	1
J. Walton, OF	1

Colorado (53-64)	WS
Hitting	**70.6**
Fielding	**30.0**
Pitching	**58.4**
D. Bichette, OF	13
M. Freeman, SP	13
A. Galarraga, 1B	13
M. Kingery, OF	12
C. Hayes, 3B	10
B. Ruffin, RP	9
J. Girardi, C	8
D. Nied, SP	7
W. Weiss, SS	7
H. Johnson, OF	6
N. Liriano, 2B	6
S. Reed, RP	6
E. Young, OF	6
E. Burks, OF	5
V. Castilla, SS	5
M. Munoz, RP	5
M. Harkey, SP	3
A. Reynoso, SP	3
K. Ritz, SP	3
J. Vander Wal, 1B	3
W. Blair, RP	2
K. Bottenfield, RP	2
R. Mejia, 2B	2
L. Painter, SP	2
D. Sheaffer, C	2
J. Czajkowski, RP	1
G. Harris, SP	1
T. Hubbard, OF	1
C. Leskanic, RP	1
M. Moore, RP	1
J. Owens, C	1

Florida (51-64)	WS
Hitting	**64.5**
Fielding	**30.4**
Pitching	**58.1**
J. Conine, OF	15
G. Sheffield, OF	15
B. Santiago, C	12
R. Nen, RP	11
J. Browne, 3B	10
B. Barberie, 2B	9
C. Carr, OF	8
P. Rapp, SP	8
K. Abbott, SS	6
C. Hammond, SP	6
G. Colbrunn, 1B	5
J. Hernandez, RP	5
Y. Perez, RP	5
L. Aquino, RP	4
M. Gardner, SP	4
T. Mathews, RP	4
M. Diaz, 3B	3
C. Hough, SP	3
D. Magadan, 3B	3
D. Weathers, SP	3
R. Bowen, SP	2
R. Scheid, SP	2
A. Arias, SS	1
M. Carrillo, OF	1
O. Destrade, 1B	1
W. Fraser, RP	1
B. Harvey, RP	1
C. Johnson, C	1
J. Mutis, RP	1
B. Natal, C	1
J. Tavarez, OF	1
R. Tingley, C	1

Houston (66-49)	WS
Hitting	**112.2**
Fielding	**26.7**
Pitching	**59.1**
J. Bagwell, 1B	30
C. Biggio, 2B	26
K. Caminiti, 3B	16
D. Drabek, SP	13
L. Gonzalez, OF	13
A. Cedeno, SS	12
K. Bass, OF	9
S. Finley, OF	9
T. Jones, RP	9
S. Reynolds, RP	9
T. Eusebio, C	6
J. Hudek, RP	6
D. Kile, SP	5
G. Swindell, SP	5
S. Servais, C	4
D. Veres, RP	4
T. Edens, RP	3
M. Hampton, RP	3
O. Miller, SS	3
J. Mouton, OF	3
S. Bream, 1B	2
C. Donnels, 3B	2
P. Harnisch, SP	2
A. Stankiewicz, SS	2
M. Felder, OF	1
R. Powell, RP	1

Los Angeles (58-56)	WS
Hitting	**97.4**
Fielding	**22.9**
Pitching	**53.8**
M. Piazza, C	21
B. Butler, OF	19
T. Wallach, 3B	18
R. Mondesi, OF	15
K. Gross, SP	11
D. DeShields, 2B	10
R. Martinez, SP	10
H. Rodriguez, OF	9
T. Candiotti, SP	7
O. Hershiser, SP	7
E. Karros, 1B	7
P. Astacio, SP	6
J. Offerman, SS	6
T. Worrell, RP	6
C. Snyder, OF	4
I. Valdes, RP	3
R. Bournigal, SS	2
C. Gwynn, OF	2
G. Ingram, 2B	2
R. Seanez, RP	2
O. Daal, RP	1
J. Gott, RP	1
D. Hansen, 3B	1
C. Hernandez, C	1
T. Prince, C	1
J. Treadway, 2B	1
M. Webster, OF	1

Montreal (74-40)	WS
Hitting	**98.3**
Fielding	**36.9**
Pitching	**86.8**
M. Alou, OF	22
L. Walker, OF	21
W. Cordero, SS	17
M. Grissom, OF	17
B. Henry, SP	12
K. Hill, SP	12
J. Wetteland, RP	12
P. Martinez, SP	11
M. Rojas, RP	11
S. Berry, 3B	10
J. Fassero, SP	10
M. Lansing, 2B	10

C. Floyd, 1B	9
D. Fletcher, C	7
G. Heredia, RP	6
T. Scott, RP	6
L. Frazier, OF	5
J. Shaw, RP	5
L. Webster, C	5
J. Bell, 2B	4
R. White, OF	4
K. Rueter, SP	2
T. Spehr, C	2
F. Benavides, 2B	1
R. Milligan, 1B	1

New York (55-58)	WS
Hitting	**77.1**
Fielding	**28.3**
Pitching	**59.5**
B. Bonilla, 3B	19
J. Kent, 2B	18
B. Saberhagen, SP	16
B. Jones, SP	11
R. Thompson, OF	10
J. Franco, RP	8
T. Hundley, C	8
R. Brogna, 1B	7
J. Vizcaino, SS	7
J. Manzanillo, RP	6
J. Jacome, SP	5
J. Lindeman, OF	5
K. McReynolds, OF	5
J. Orsulak, OF	5
D. Segui, 1B	5
R. Mason, RP	4
K. Stinnett, C	4
J. Cangelosi, OF	3
D. Linton, RP	3
F. Vina, 2B	3
J. Burnitz, OF	2
M. Gozzo, RP	2
E. Gunderson, RP	2
M. Maddux, RP	2
L. Rivera, SS	2
T. Bogar, 3B	1
M. Remlinger, SP	1
P. Smith, SP	1

Philadelphia (54-61)	WS
Hitting	**73.2**
Fielding	**28.0**
Pitching	**60.7**
L. Dykstra, OF	14
D. Jackson, SP	14
D. Daulton, C	13
M. Duncan, 2B	10
J. Eisenreich, OF	10
D. Jones, RP	10
M. Morandini, 2B	10
K. Stocker, SS	10
B. Munoz, SP	9
J. Kruk, 1B	7
H. Slocumb, RP	7
M. Thompson, OF	7
R. Jordan, 1B	5
D. West, RP	5
T. Borland, RP	3
D. Hollins, 3B	3
P. Incaviglia, OF	3
F. Valenzuela, SP	3
T. Longmire, OF	2
T. Pratt, C	2
R. Ready, 2B	2
C. Schilling, SP	2
L. Andersen, RP	1
K. Batiste, 3B	1
S. Boskie, SP	1
A. Carter, RP	1
W. Chamberlain, OF	1
T. Edens, RP	1
T. Greene, SP	1
B. Hatcher, OF	1
T. Marsh, OF	1
B. Wells, RP	1
M. Williams, SP	1

Pittsburgh (53-61)	WS
Hitting	**74.0**
Fielding	**28.1**
Pitching	**56.8**
J. Bell, SS	19
Z. Smith, SP	13
A. Martin, OF	11
O. Merced, OF	10
D. Clark, OF	9
C. Garcia, 2B	9
J. King, 3B	8
A. Van Slyke, OF	8
D. Slaught, C	7
R. White, RP	7
B. Hunter, 1B	6
J. Lieber, SP	6
D. Neagle, SP	6
P. Wagner, SP	6
M. Dewey, RP	5
S. Cooke, SP	4
R. Manzanillo, RP	4
L. Parrish, C	4
A. Pena, RP	4
T. Foley, 2B	3
M. Cummings, OF	2
M. Dyer, RP	1
L. McClendon, OF	1
D. Miceli, RP	1
S. Pegues, OF	1
R. Tomlin, RP	1
G. Varsho, OF	1
T. Womack, 2B	1
K. Young, 1B	1

San Diego (47-70)	WS
Hitting	**57.0**
Fielding	**24.2**
Pitching	**59.7**
T. Gwynn, OF	17
B. Roberts, 2B	13
D. Bell, OF	11
T. Hoffman, RP	11
A. Ashby, SP	9
A. Benes, SP	8
J. Hamilton, SP	8
C. Shipley, 3B	7
E. Williams, 1B	7
P. Martinez, RP	6
B. Ausmus, C	5
L. Lopez, SS	5
P. Plantier, OF	5
T. Mauser, RP	4
S. Sanders, SP	4
R. Gutierrez, SS	3
J. Tabaka, RP	3
D. Elliott, RP	2
B. Krueger, SP	2
W. Whitehurst, SP	2
B. Bean, OF	1
A. Cianfrocco, 3B	1
P. Clark, 1B	1
B. Florie, RP	1
T. Hyers, 1B	1
B. Johnson, C	1
S. Livingstone, 3B	1
M. Nieves, OF	1
T. Worrell, SP	1

San Francisco (55-60)	WS
Hitting	**75.3**
Fielding	**30.7**
Pitching	**58.9**
B. Bonds, OF	25
M. Williams, 3B	18
D. Lewis, OF	11
R. Clayton, SS	9
M. Portugal, SP	9
J. Burkett, SP	8
M. Jackson, RP	8
K. Manwaring, C	8
R. Beck, RP	7
J. Patterson, 2B	7
B. Swift, SP	7
W. VanLandingham, SP	6
T. Benzinger, 1B	4
M. Carreon, OF	4
R. Monteleone, RP	4
S. Scarsone, 2B	4
M. Benjamin, SS	3
D. Burba, RP	3
D. Martinez, OF	3
W. McGee, OF	3
D. Strawberry, OF	3
B. Black, SP	2
P. Gomez, RP	2
B. Brink, RP	1
S. Frey, RP	1
B. Hickerson, SP-RP	1
M. Leonard, OF	1
J. Reed, C	1
K. Rogers, RP	1
R. Thompson, 2B	1

St. Louis (53-61)	WS
Hitting	**96.0**
Fielding	**21.7**
Pitching	**41.3**
G. Jefferies, 1B	17
R. Lankford, OF	16
T. Zeile, 3B	15
M. Whiten, OF	12
G. Pena, 2B	10
B. Gilkey, OF	9
T. Pagnozzi, C	9
O. Smith, SS	9
L. Alicea, 2B	8
R. Arocha, RP	7
J. Habyan, RP	5
V. Palacios, SP	5
B. Tewksbury, SP	5
R. Murphy, RP	4
R. Rodriguez, RP	4
B. Eversgerd, RP	3
J. Oquendo, SS	3
G. Perry, 1B	3
A. Watson, SP	3
R. Cormier, SP	2
T. McGriff, C	2
T. Urbani, SP-RP	2
G. Young, OF	2
G. Buckels, RP	1
B. Jordan, OF	1
J. Mabry, OF	1
O. Olivares, SP	1

1995
American League

Baltimore (71-73)	WS
Hitting	**87.7**
Fielding	**41.1**
Pitching	**84.2**
R. Palmeiro, 1B	21
M. Mussina, SP	20
B. Anderson, OF	19
C. Ripken Jr., SS	16
C. Hoiles, C	14
K. Brown, SP	13
H. Baines, DH	11
B. Bonilla, OF	9
S. Erickson, SP	9
J. Manto, 3B	6
J. Orosco, RP	6
B. Barberie, 2B	5
C. Goodwin, OF	5
B. McDonald, SP	5
J. Moyer, SP	5
T. Clark, RP	4
J. Hammonds, OF	4
D. Jones, RP	4
R. Krivda, SP	4
M. Alexander, 2B	3
L. Gomez, 3B	3
J. Haynes, SP	3
M. Oquist, RP	3
M. Smith, OF	3
G. Zaun, C	3
K. Bass, OF	2
J. Huson, 3B	2
S. Klingenbeck, SP	2
M. Lee, RP	2
A. Benitez, RP	1
J. Borowski, RP	1
D. Buford, OF	1
J. Dedrick, RP	1
M. Hartley, RP	1
A. Rhodes, RP	1
A. Van Slyke, OF	1

Boston (86-58)	WS
Hitting	**122.8**
Fielding	**39.2**
Pitching	**96.0**
J. Valentin, SS	29
M. Vaughn, 1B	24
T. Wakefield, SP	18
T. Naehring, 3B	17
J. Canseco, DH	15
L. Alicea, 2B	13
M. Greenwell, OF	13
E. Hanson, SP	13
S. Belinda, RP	12
T. O'Leary, OF	12
R. Clemens, SP	10
L. Tinsley, OF	10
R. Cormier, RP	8
M. Macfarlane, C	8
M. Maddux, RP	8
R. Aguilera, RP	6
V. Eshelman, SP	5
B. Haselman, C	4
D. Hosey, OF	4
R. Jefferson, DH	4
Z. Smith, SP	4
J. Hudson, RP	3
W. McGee, OF	3
A. Sele, SP	3
K. Ryan, RP	2
M. Stanton, RP	2
C. Donnels, 3B	1
E. Gunderson, RP	1
D. Lilliquist, RP	1
C. Rodriguez, 2B	1
T. Shumpert, 2B	1
M. Stairs, OF	1
J. Suppan, RP	1
M. Whiten, OF	1

California (78-67)	WS
Hitting	**118.1**
Fielding	**35.6**
Pitching	**80.3**
T. Salmon, OF	29
J. Edmonds, OF	21
T. Phillips, 3B	19
C. Davis, DH	18
J. Snow, 1B	15
G. DiSarcina, SS	12
C. Finley, SP	12
T. Percival, RP	12
G. Anderson, OF	11
M. Langston, SP	11
L. Smith, RP	8
R. Hudler, 2B	7
G. Myers, C	6
B. Patterson, RP	6
J. Abbott, SP	5
S. Boskie, SP	4
D. Easley, 2B	4
M. Harkey, SP	4
M. James, RP	4
B. Anderson, SP	3
M. Butcher, RP	3
S. Owen, 3B	3
A. Allanson, C	2
J. Fabregas, C	2

J. Habyan, RP	2
S. Sanderson, SP	2
M. Bielecki, SP-RP	1
R. Correia, SS	1
K. Edenfield, RP	1
R. Gonzales, 3B	1
J. Lind, 2B	1
R. Monteleone, RP	1
O. Palmeiro, OF	1
D. Schofield, SS	1
R. Springer, RP	1

Chicago (68-76)	**WS**
Hitting	**113.4**
Fielding	**30.6**
Pitching	**60.1**
F. Thomas, 1B	28
L. Johnson, OF	18
R. Ventura, 3B	17
T. Raines, OF	14
A. Fernandez, SP	12
R. Karkovice, C	10
D. Martinez, OF	10
W. Alvarez, SP	8
M. Devereaux, OF	8
R. Durham, 2B	8
J. Abbott, SP	7
R. Hernandez, RP	6
C. Grebeck, SS	5
O. Guillen, SS	5
L. Mouton, OF	5
M. Karchner, RP	4
J. Kruk, DH	4
J. DeLeon, RP	3
B. Keyser, RP	3
M. LaValliere, C	3
B. Lyons, C	3
K. McCaskill, RP	3
D. Righetti, SP	3
L. Andujar, SP	2
N. Martin, 2B	2
W. Newson, OF	2
M. Sirotka, SP	2
C. Snopek, 3B	2
L. Thomas, RP	2
T. Fortugno, RP	1
A. Lorraine, RP	1
S. Radinsky, RP	1
C. Sabo, DH	1
B. Simas, RP	1

Cleveland (100-44)	**WS**
Hitting	**148.7**
Fielding	**44.2**
Pitching	**107.1**
A. Belle, OF	30
M. Ramirez, OF	25
J. Thome, 3B	24
C. Baerga, 2B	23
K. Lofton, OF	21
J. Mesa, RP	17
O. Vizquel, SS	17
D. Martinez, SP	16
E. Murray, DH	16
O. Hershiser, SP	13
C. Nagy, SP	11
P. Sorrento, 1B	11
C. Ogea, SP	10
J. Tavarez, RP	10
E. Plunk, RP	8
S. Alomar Jr., C	7
T. Pena, C	6
P. Assenmacher, RP	5
M. Clark, SP	5
K. Hill, SP	5
H. Perry, 1B	5
J. Poole, RP	4
R. Amaro, OF	2
A. Espinoza, 2B-3B	2
A. Lopez, RP	2
J. Burnitz, OF	1
A. Embree, RP	1
B. Giles, OF	1
W. Kirby, OF	1
J. Levis, C	1

Detroit (60-84)	**WS**
Hitting	**87.6**
Fielding	**28.8**
Pitching	**63.6**
T. Fryman, 3B	19
C. Curtis, OF	15
C. Fielder, 1B	13
D. Wells, SP	13
L. Whitaker, 2B	11
F. Lira, SP	10
B. Higginson, OF	8
J. Samuel, 1B	8
J. Doherty, RP	7
J. Flaherty, C	7
M. Henneman, RP	7
M. Christopher, RP	6
K. Gibson, DH	6
C. Gomez, SS	6
A. Trammell, SS	6
S. Bergman, SP	5
B. Bohanon, RP	5
S. Fletcher, 2B	4
F. Stubbs, 1B-OF	4
R. Tingley, C	3
J. Boever, RP	2
T. Clark, 1B	2
G. Gohr, RP	2
J. Lima, SP	2
P. Nevin, OF	2
K. Wickander, RP	2
D. Bautista, OF	1
D. Henry, RP	1
R. Pemberton, OF	1
C. Sodowsky, SP	1
T. Steverson, OF	1

Kansas City (70-74)	**WS**
Hitting	**81.8**
Fielding	**41.6**
Pitching	**86.6**
W. Joyner, 1B	18
G. Gaetti, 3B	17
K. Appier, SP	16
M. Gubicza, SP	16
F. Gordon, SP	11
K. Lockhart, 2B	11
J. Montgomery, RP	11
J. Nunnally, OF	11
G. Gagne, SS	10
T. Goodwin, OF	10
V. Coleman, OF	8
B. Mayne, C	7
J. Damon, OF	6
C. Haney, SP	6
D. Howard, 2B	5
H. Pichardo, RP	5
R. Meacham, RP	4
G. Olson, RP	4
J. Jacome, SP	3
M. Magnante, RP	3
M. Tucker, OF	3
P. Borders, C	2
E. Caceres, 2B	2
D. Fleming, SP	2
C. James, DH	2
J. Lind, 2B	2
J. Vitiello, DH	2
S. Anderson, SP	1
B. Brewer, RP	1
M. Bunch, RP	1
J. Converse, RP	1
J. Grotewold, DH	1
P. Hiatt, OF	1
H. Mercedes, C	1
K. Miller, DH-OF	1
L. Norman, OF	1
J. Randa, 3B	1
J. Samuel, DH	1
C. Stynes, 2B	1
D. Torres, RP	1

Milwaukee (65-79)	**WS**
Hitting	**86.2**
Fielding	**37.3**
Pitching	**71.5**
K. Seitzer, 3B	17
B. Surhoff, OF	16
J. Jaha, 1B	13
R. Bones, SP	11
S. Sparks, SP	11
J. Cirillo, 3B	10
D. Hamilton, OF	10
S. Karl, SP	8
J. Oliver, C	8
J. Valentin, SS	8
F. Vina, 2B	8
M. Mieske, OF	6
D. Nilsson, OF	6
M. Fetters, RP	5
D. Hulse, OF	5
M. Kiefer, RP	5
G. Vaughn, DH	5
B. Givens, SP	4
P. Listach, 2B	4
A. Reyes, RP	4
G. Lloyd, RP	3
M. Matheny, C	3
A. Miranda, RP	3
S. Roberson, SP-RP	3
T. Ward, OF	3
B. Wegman, RP	3
C. Eldred, SP	2
M. Ignasiak, RP	2
J. McAndrew, RP	2
R. Rightnowar, RP	2
J. Bronkey, RP	1
M. Loretta, SS	1
D. May, OF	1
B. Scanlan, SP	1
K. Wickander, RP	1

Minnesota (56-88)	**WS**
Hitting	**96.3**
Fielding	**25.9**
Pitching	**45.9**
C. Knoblauch, 2B	27
K. Puckett, OF	20
M. Cordova, OF	17
P. Meares, SS	7
P. Munoz, DH	7
B. Radke, SP	7
J. Reboulet, SS	7
S. Leius, 3B	6
S. Stahoviak, 1B	6
K. Tapani, SP	6
R. Aguilera, RP	5
M. Walbeck, C	5
A. Cole, OF	4
E. Guardado, RP	4
M. Lawton, OF	4
D. Stevens, RP	4
R. Becker, OF	3
M. Guthrie, RP	3
R. Robertson, RP	3
F. Rodriguez, SP	3
M. Trombley, SP	3
J. Clark, OF	2
R. Coomer, 1B	2
S. Erickson, SP	2
C. Hale, DH	2
P. Mahomes, RP	2
M. Merullo, C	2
K. Campbell, RP	1
D. Masteller, 1B	1
O. Munoz, RP	1
M. Sanford, RP	1
S. Watkins, RP	1

New York (79-65)	**WS**
Hitting	**114.8**
Fielding	**39.2**
Pitching	**83.0**
B. Williams, OF	27
W. Boggs, 3B	18
P. O'Neill, OF	18
M. Stanley, C	16
J. McDowell, SP	15
R. Velarde, 2B	13
J. Wetteland, RP	13
A. Pettitte, SP	11
T. Fernandez, SS	9
S. Hitchcock, SP	9
D. Cone, SP	8
J. Leyritz, C	8
D. Mattingly, 1B	8
R. Sierra, DH	7
G. Williams, OF	7
S. Kamieniecki, SP	6
B. Wickman, RP	6
P. Kelly, 2B	5
D. James, OF	4
D. Strawberry, DH	4
R. Davis, 3B	3
S. Howe, RP	3
L. Polonia, OF	3
D. Tartabull, DH	3
B. MacDonald, RP	2
J. Manzanillo, RP	2
M. Perez, SP	2
M. Rivera, SP	2
J. Ausanio, RP	1
S. Bankhead, RP	1
D. Jeter, SS	1
J. Key, SP	1
D. Silvestri, 2B	1

Oakland (67-77)	**WS**
Hitting	**121.0**
Fielding	**26.1**
Pitching	**53.9**
M. McGwire, 1B	23
R. Henderson, OF	19
G. Berroa, DH	16
T. Steinbach, C	16
S. Javier, OF	13
M. Bordick, SS	10
S. Brosius, 3B	10
B. Gates, 2B	10
T. Stottlemyre, SP	10
D. Eckersley, RP	6
R. Honeycutt, RP	6
S. Ontiveros, SP	6
R. Sierra, OF	6
J. Corsi, RP	5
J. Giambi, 3B	5
T. Van Poppel, RP	5
M. Aldrete, 1B	4
C. Paquette, 3B	4
G. Williams, C	4
D. Johns, SP	3
E. Helfand, C	2
M. Mohler, RP	2
A. Prieto, SP	2
C. Reyes, RP	2
D. Wengert, RP	2
S. Wojciechowski, SP-RP	2
M. Acre, RP	1
F. Cruz, SS	1
M. Gallego, 2B	1
M. Harkey, SP	1
D. Leiper, RP	1
D. Tartabull, DH	1
J. Wasdin, RP	1
E. Young, OF	1

Seattle (79-66)	**WS**
Hitting	**119.0**
Fielding	**34.7**
Pitching	**83.4**
E. Martinez, DH	32
R. Johnson, SP	22
T. Martinez, 1B	20
J. Buhner, OF	16
D. Wilson, C	16
M. Blowers, 3B	14
N. Charlton, RP	11
J. Cora, 2B	10
J. Nelson, RP	10

T. Belcher, SP	9
K. Griffey Jr., OF	9
L. Sojo, SS	9
C. Bosio, SP	8
B. Ayala, RP	7
R. Amaral, OF	6
B. Risley, RP	6
A. Benes, SP	3
V. Coleman, OF	3
A. Diaz, OF	3
D. Strange, 3B	3
D. Bragg, OF	2
F. Fermin, SS	2
C. Kreuter, C	2
W. Newson, OF	2
A. Rodriguez, SS	2
B. Wells, RP	2
B. Wolcott, SP	2
R. Carmona, RP	1
B. Krueger, SP	1
J. Mecir, RP	1
M. Newfield, OF	1
G. Thurman, OF	1
S. Torres, SP	1

Texas (74-70)	WS
Hitting	**90.0**
Fielding	**41.4**
Pitching	**90.6**
K. Rogers, SP	21
W. Clark, 1B	18
M. Tettleton, OF	17
I. Rodriguez, C	16
R. Pavlik, SP	14
O. Nixon, OF	13
R. Greer, OF	12
J. Gonzalez, DH	11
M. McLemore, OF	11
R. McDowell, RP	9
J. Frye, 2B	8
B. Gil, SS	8
B. Tewksbury, SP	8
K. Gross, SP	7
D. Palmer, 3B	7
J. Russell, RP	7
M. Whiteside, RP	6
E. Vosberg, RP	5
D. Cook, RP	4
D. Oliver, RP	4
B. Witt, SP	4
M. Pagliarulo, 3B	2
D. Valle, C	2
E. Beltre, SS	1
M. Brandenburg, RP	1
L. Frazier, OF	1
W. Heredia, RP	1
C. Howard, RP	1
C. Maldonado, OF	1
L. Ortiz, 3B	1
C. Worthington, 3B	1

Toronto (56-88)	WS
Hitting	**71.8**
Fielding	**31.0**
Pitching	**65.2**
R. Alomar, 2B	16
A. Leiter, SP	14
P. Molitor, DH	12
D. White, OF	12
D. Cone, SP	11
J. Olerud, 1B	11
S. Green, OF	10
T. Castillo, RP	9
E. Sprague, 3B	9
J. Carter, OF	8
A. Gonzalez, SS	7
P. Hentgen, SP	7
M. Timlin, RP	6
C. Maldonado, OF	5
S. Martinez, C	5
W. Williams, RP	4
E. Hurtado, SP	3
P. Menhart, RP	3
L. Parrish, C	3
D. Cedeno, SS	2
T. Crabtree, RP	2
K. Robinson, RP	2
J. Guzman, SP	1
D. Hall, RP	1
M. Huff, OF	1
R. Knorr, C	1
T. Perez, SS	1
J. Rogers, RP	1
J. Ware, SP	1

1995
National League

Atlanta (90-54)	WS
Hitting	**100.7**
Fielding	**46.6**
Pitching	**122.7**
G. Maddux, SP	30
T. Glavine, SP	20
C. Jones, 3B	20
F. McGriff, 1B	20
D. Justice, OF	19
M. Grissom, OF	18
R. Klesko, OF	17
J. Smoltz, SP	17
M. Wohlers, RP	16
J. Lopez, C	12
M. Lemke, 2B	11
G. McMichael, RP	11
J. Blauser, SS	10
S. Avery, SP	8
B. Clontz, RP	8
K. Mercker, SP	7
R. Belliard, SS	4
P. Borbon, RP	4
M. Mordecai, 2B	4
C. O'Brien, C	3
D. Smith, OF	3
M. Devereaux, OF	2
M. Kelly, OF	2
J. Oliva, 3B	1
A. Pena, RP	1
E. Perez, C	1
L. Polonia, OF	1

Chicago (73-71)	WS
Hitting	**106.2**
Fielding	**36.5**
Pitching	**76.2**
S. Sosa, OF	25
M. Grace, 1B	23
B. McRae, OF	18
S. Dunston, SS	16
J. Navarro, SP	15
F. Castillo, SP	13
L. Gonzalez, OF	10
K. Foster, SP	9
J. Bullinger, SP	8
R. Myers, RP	8
S. Servais, C	8
R. Sanchez, 2B	7
J. Hernandez, SS	6
T. Haney, 2B	5
M. Perez, RP	5
O. Timmons, OF	5
S. Bullett, OF	4
S. Trachsel, SP	4
T. Zeile, 3B	4
L. Casian, RP	3
H. Johnson, 3B	3
M. Walker, RP	3
R. Wilkins, C	3
A. Young, RP	3
M. Morgan, SP	2
T. Wendell, RP	2
S. Buechele, 3B	1
R. Garces, RP	1
J. Kmak, C	1
C. Nabholz, RP	1
M. Parent, C	1
T. Pratt, C	1
D. Swartzbaugh, RP	1

Cincinnati (85-59)	WS
Hitting	**132.2**
Fielding	**39.6**
Pitching	**83.3**
B. Larkin, SS	30
R. Sanders, OF	27
R. Gant, OF	21
P. Schourek, SP	16
B. Boone, 2B	15
J. Brantley, RP	13
J. Smiley, SP	13
J. Branson, 3B	12
B. Santiago, C	12
M. Lewis, 3B	10
E. Taubensee, C	9
T. Howard, OF	8
M. Jackson, RP	7
H. Morris, 1B	7
J. Walton, OF	7
D. Burba, SP	5
H. Carrasco, RP	5
X. Hernandez, RP	5
M. Portugal, SP	5
T. Pugh, RP	5
J. Rijo, SP	4
D. Wells, SP	4
E. Anthony, OF	3
D. Sanders, OF	3
M. Duncan, 2B	2
L. Harris, 3B	2
D. Lewis, OF	2
J. Ruffin, RP	2
D. Berryhill, C	1

Colorado (77-67)	WS
Hitting	**93.7**
Fielding	**42.6**
Pitching	**94.7**
D. Bichette, OF	23
L. Walker, OF	18
A. Galarraga, 1B	14
C. Leskanic, RP	14
V. Castilla, 3B	13
K. Ritz, SP	13
D. Holmes, RP	12
S. Reed, RP	12
W. Weiss, SS	12
E. Young, 2B	12
J. Bates, 2B	10
J. Girardi, C	10
E. Burks, OF	8
B. Ruffin, RP	8
M. Kingery, OF	7
B. Swift, SP	7
R. Bailey, RP	5
A. Reynoso, SP	5
M. Freeman, SP	4
L. Painter, RP	4
B. Rekar, SP	4
J. Vander Wal, 1B-OF	4
J. Grahe, SP	3
J. Owens, C	2
J. Acevedo, SP	1
J. Brito, C	1
T. Hubbard, OF	1
M. Munoz, RP	1
H. Pulliam, OF	1
B. Saberhagen, SP	1
M. Thompson, RP	1

Florida (67-76)	WS
Hitting	**102.4**
Fielding	**33.4**
Pitching	**65.2**
J. Conine, OF	20
T. Pendleton, 3B	17
Q. Veras, 2B	15
G. Colbrunn, 1B	14
G. Sheffield, OF	13
C. Johnson, C	12
K. Abbott, SS	11
P. Rapp, SP	11
C. Hammond, SP	10
J. Burkett, SP	8
R. Nen, RP	8
T. Mathews, RP	7
C. Carr, OF	6
J. Tavarez, OF	6
A. Arias, SS	5
B. Witt, SP	5
A. Dawson, OF	4
S. Decker, C	4
M. Gardner, RP	3
T. Gregg, OF	3
A. Pena, RP	3
R. Veres, RP	3
W. Banks, SP	2
J. Browne, OF	2
R. Lewis, RP	2
Y. Perez, RP	2
R. Bowen, SP	1
R. Morman, OF	1
B. Natal, C	1
J. Powell, RP	1
A. Small, RP	1

Houston (76-68)	WS
Hitting	**138.6**
Fielding	**25.5**
Pitching	**64.0**
C. Biggio, 2B	29
J. Bagwell, 1B	20
D. Bell, OF	16
D. Magadan, 3B	15
T. Eusebio, C	14
J. Cangelosi, OF	10
B. Hunter, OF	10
D. Veres, RP	10
T. Jones, RP	9
D. May, OF	9
S. Reynolds, SP	9
M. Hampton, SP	8
O. Miller, SS	8
D. Drabek, SP	6
J. Mouton, OF	6
G. Swindell, SP	6
L. Gonzalez, OF	5
M. Simms, 1B	4
D. Brocail, RP	3
J. Dougherty, RP	3
R. Gutierrez, SS	3
D. Hartgraves, RP	3
M. Henneman, RP	3
P. Plantier, OF	3
M. Thompson, OF	3
J. Hudek, RP	2
S. Servais, C	2
C. Shipley, 3B	2
J. Tabaka, RP	2
R. Wilkins, C	2
J. Goff, C	1
D. Kile, SP	1
A. Stankiewicz, SS	1

Los Angeles (78-66)	WS
Hitting	**115.4**
Fielding	**36.3**
Pitching	**82.3**
M. Piazza, C	27
E. Karros, 1B	25
R. Mondesi, OF	22
H. Nomo, SP	17
D. DeShields, 2B	16
I. Valdes, SP	15
J. Offerman, SS	14
T. Worrell, RP	14
R. Martinez, SP	13
T. Candiotti, SP	9
T. Wallach, 3B	9
R. Kelly, OF	8
C. Fonville, SS	7
P. Astacio, RP	5
D. Hansen, 3B	5

B. Butler, OF	4
J. Cummings, RP	4
B. Ashley, OF	3
C. Hernandez, C	2
T. Hollandsworth, OF	2
A. Osuna, RP	2
M. Busch, 3B	1
R. Cedeno, OF	1
J. Eischen, RP	1
M. Guthrie, RP	1
G. Ingram, 3B	1
R. Parker, OF	1
T. Prince, C	1
F. Rodriguez, RP	1
H. Rodriguez, OF	1
K. Tapani, SP	1
T. Williams, RP	1

Montreal (66-78)	WS
Hitting	**83.8**
Fielding	**36.2**
Pitching	**78.0**
M. Lansing, 2B	15
P. Martinez, SP	14
R. White, OF	14
S. Berry, 3B	12
W. Cordero, SS	12
D. Segui, 1B	12
T. Tarasco, OF	12
M. Alou, OF	11
B. Henry, SP	10
C. Perez, SP	10
J. Fassero, SP	8
D. Fletcher, C	8
M. Rojas, RP	8
G. Heredia, RP	6
T. Scott, RP	5
S. Andrews, 3B	4
G. Harris, RP	4
K. Rueter, SP	4
M. Grudzielanek, SS	3
T. Laker, C	3
D. Leiper, RP	3
F. Santangelo, OF	3
J. Shaw, RP	3
L. Aquino, RP	2
Y. Benitez, OF	2
D. Silvestri, SS	2
B. Eversgerd, RP	1
C. Floyd, 1B	1
W. Fraser, RP	1
L. Frazier, OF	1
R. Kelly, OF	1
J. Siddall, C	1
T. Spehr, C	1
J. Treadway, 2B	1

New York (69-75)	WS
Hitting	**98.0**
Fielding	**33.0**
Pitching	**76.0**
J. Vizcaino, SS	16
R. Brogna, 1B	15
B. Bonilla, 3B	13
T. Hundley, C	13
B. Butler, OF	12
J. Kent, 2B	11
J. Franco, RP	10
E. Alfonzo, 3B	8
C. Everett, OF	8
J. Isringhausen, SP	8
D. Henry, RP	7
B. Jones, SP	7
D. Mlicki, SP	7
J. Orsulak, OF	7
B. Saberhagen, SP	7
C. Jones, OF	6
B. Pulsipher, SP	6
J. Dipoto, RP	5
R. Thompson, OF	5
T. Bogar, SS	4
P. Harnisch, SP	4
K. Stinnett, C	4
M. Birkbeck, SP	3
D. Buford, OF	3
P. Byrd, RP	3
B. Minor, RP	3
D. Florence, RP	2
E. Gunderson, RP	2
R. Person, RP	2
R. Cornelius, SP	1
B. Huskey, 3B	1
A. Ledesma, 3B	1
D. Segui, OF	1
B. Spiers, 3B	1
P. Walker, RP	1

Philadelphia (69-75)	WS
Hitting	**82.3**
Fielding	**41.4**
Pitching	**83.3**
M. Morandini, 2B	17
J. Eisenreich, OF	13
C. Hayes, 3B	13
D. Daulton, C	12
R. Bottalico, RP	11
H. Slocumb, RP	11
G. Jefferies, 1B	10
M. Whiten, OF	9
L. Dykstra, OF	8
M. Mimbs, SP	8
C. Schilling, SP	8
K. Stocker, SS	8
P. Quantrill, SP	7
S. Fernandez, SP	6
D. Hollins, 1B	6
T. Longmire, OF	6
M. Williams, RP	6
T. Borland, RP	5
M. Duncan, 2B	5
T. Green, SP	5
D. Gallagher, OF	3
J. Juden, SP	3
A. Van Slyke, OF	3
L. Webster, C	3
D. West, SP	3
K. Abbott, RP	2
S. Frey, RP	2
G. Harris, RP	2
T. Marsh, OF	2
R. Springer, RP	2
K. Elster, SS	1
P. Fletcher, RP	1
K. Flora, OF	1
M. Grace, SP	1
K. Jordan, 2B	1
M. Lieberthal, C	1
C. Ricci, RP	1
G. Varsho, OF	1

Pittsburgh (58-86)	WS
Hitting	**82.1**
Fielding	**28.2**
Pitching	**63.6**
O. Merced, OF	18
D. Neagle, SP	16
J. King, 3B	14
J. Bell, SS	13
A. Martin, OF	11
C. Garcia, 2B	10
J. Brumfield, OF	9
N. Liriano, 2B	9
P. Wagner, SP	7
D. Miceli, RP	6
M. Parent, C	6
D. Plesac, RP	6
M. Dyer, RP	5
E. Loaiza, SP	5
J. Christiansen, RP	4
J. Ericks, SP	4
S. Parris, SP	4
D. Clark, OF	3
A. Encarnacion, C	3
M. Johnson, 1B	3
D. Slaught, C	3
M. Cummings, OF	2
L. Hancock, RP	2
J. McCurry, RP	2
J. Wehner, OF	2
R. White, SP	2
K. Young, 3B	2
R. Aude, 1B	1
J. Gott, RP	1
R. Morel, RP	1

San Diego (70-74)	WS
Hitting	**113.6**
Fielding	**30.8**
Pitching	**65.6**
K. Caminiti, 3B	24
T. Gwynn, OF	23
S. Finley, OF	19
A. Ashby, SP	14
J. Reed, 2B	14
B. Ausmus, C	13
J. Hamilton, SP	12
B. Roberts, OF	11
T. Hoffman, RP	9
S. Livingstone, 1B	8
B. Johnson, C	6
W. Blair, RP	5
A. Cedeno, SS	5
A. Cianfrocco, 1B	5
B. Florie, RP	5
S. Sanders, SP	5
A. Benes, SP	4
D. Bochtler, RP	4
P. Plantier, OF	4
F. Valenzuela, SP	4
R. Petagine, 1B	3
E. Williams, 1B	3
G. Dishman, SP	2
M. Newfield, OF	2
M. Nieves, OF	2
R. Villone, RP	2
A. Berumen, RP	1
T. Worrell, RP	1

San Francisco (67-77)	WS
Hitting	**124.4**
Fielding	**27.8**
Pitching	**48.8**
B. Bonds, OF	36
M. Williams, 3B	20
M. Carreon, 1B	15
G. Hill, OF	15
R. Clayton, SS	12
M. Leiter, SP	10
K. Manwaring, C	8
R. Thompson, 2B	8
R. Beck, RP	7
D. Sanders, OF	7
S. Scarsone, 3B	7
W. VanLandingham, SP	6
T. Wilson, SP	5
J. Brewington, SP	4
D. Lewis, OF	4
M. Portugal, SP	4
J. Reed, C	4
S. Barton, RP	3
T. Lampkin, C	3
S. Service, RP	3
R. Aurilia, SS	2
M. Benard, OF	2
M. Benjamin, 3B	2
D. Burba, RP	2
M. Dewey, RP	2
C. Hook, RP	2
J. Patterson, 2B	2
J. Phillips, 1B	2
S. Valdez, SP	2
M. Leonard, OF	1
D. McCarty, OF	1

St. Louis (62-81)	WS
Hitting	**74.1**
Fielding	**37.5**
Pitching	**74.4**
R. Lankford, OF	22
B. Jordan, OF	18
B. Gilkey, OF	16
T. Henke, RP	12
J. Mabry, 1B	9
T. Fossas, RP	7
M. Petkovsek, SP	7
R. DeLucia, RP	6
M. Morgan, SP	6
J. Oquendo, 2B	6
D. Osborne, SP	6
D. Sheaffer, C	6
T. Urbani, SP	6
S. Cooper, 3B	5
T. Mathews, RP	5
J. Parrett, RP	5
A. Watson, SP	5
T. Cromer, SS	4
T. Zeile, 1B	4
R. Arocha, RP	3
A. Battle, OF	3
J. Habyan, RP	3
K. Hill, SP	3
T. Pagnozzi, C	3
G. Pena, 2B	3
D. Bell, 2B	2
D. Coles, 3B	2
S. Hemond, C	2
O. Smith, SS	2
B. Barber, RP	1
R. Caraballo, 2B	1
D. Creek, RP	1
J. Frascatore, RP	1
M. Sweeney, 1B	1

1996 American League

Baltimore (88-74)	WS
Hitting	**147.1**
Fielding	**37.1**
Pitching	**79.8**
R. Alomar, 2B	31
R. Palmeiro, 1B	30
B. Anderson, OF	28
C. Ripken Jr., SS	22
B. Bonilla, OF	19
B. Surhoff, 3B	17
C. Hoiles, C	14
M. Mussina, SP	13
S. Erickson, SP	10
D. Wells, SP	10
R. Myers, RP	9
R. Coppinger, SP	6
J. Orosco, RP	6
A. Mills, RP	5
A. Rhodes, RP	5
R. Krivda, SP-RP	4
R. McDowell, RP	4
E. Murray, DH	4
A. Benitez, RP	3
A. Corbin, RP	3
M. Devereaux, OF	3
J. Hammonds, OF	3
T. Zeile, 3B	3
T. Mathews, RP	2
B. Ripken, 2B	2
G. Zaun, C	2
M. Alexander, SS	1
J. Huson, 2B	1
P. Incaviglia, OF	1
M. Parent, C	1
N. Rodriguez, RP	1
M. Smith, OF	1

Boston (85-77)	WS
Hitting	**127.2**
Fielding	**37.9**
Pitching	**89.9**
M. Vaughn, 1B	29
R. Clemens, SP	20
J. Valentin, SS	17
H. Slocumb, RP	15
J. Frye, 2B	14

R. Jefferson, DH	14
J. Canseco, DH	13
T. Naehring, 3B	13
T. O'Leary, OF	12
M. Stanley, C	12
F. Gordon, SP	10
T. Wakefield, SP	10
M. Greenwell, OF	7
J. Moyer, RP	6
A. Sele, SP	6
M. Stanton, RP	6
D. Bragg, OF	5
W. Cordero, 2B	5
B. Haselman, C	4
M. Maddux, RP	4
R. Pemberton, OF	4
M. Brandenburg, RP	3
R. Garces, RP	3
M. Cuyler, OF	2
N. Garciaparra, SS	2
J. Hudson, RP	2
J. Manto, 3B	2
K. Mitchell, OF	2
L. Tinsley, OF	2
S. Belinda, RP	1
E. Beltre, 3B	1
V. Eshelman, RP	1
D. Hosey, OF	1
K. Lacy, RP	1
P. Mahomes, RP	1
J. Malave, OF	1
B. Pennington, RP	1
A. Pozo, 2B-3B	1
T. Rodriguez, SS	1
B. Selby, 2B-3B	1

California (70-91)	WS
Hitting	**96.5**
Fielding	**36.6**
Pitching	**76.9**
T. Salmon, OF	22
C. Davis, DH	18
J. Edmonds, OF	18
R. Velarde, 2B	17
C. Finley, SP	16
T. Percival, RP	16
R. Hudler, 2B	10
M. James, RP	9
S. Boskie, SP	8
M. Langston, SP	7
D. Slaught, C	7
J. Snow, 1B	7
G. Anderson, OF	6
G. DiSarcina, SS	6
J. Fabregas, C	6
G. Arias, 3B	4
C. McElroy, RP	4
D. Erstad, OF	3
M. Holtz, RP	3
J. Howell, 3B	3
D. Springer, SP	3
J. Dickson, SP	2
M. Eichhorn, RP	2
P. Harris, RP	2
O. Palmeiro, OF	2
T. Wallach, 3B	2
P. Borders, C	1
D. Easley, SS	1
R. Ellis, RP	1
T. Greene, C	1
J. Grimsley, SP	1
R. Hancock, RP	1
L. Smith, RP	1

Chicago (85-77)	WS
Hitting	**126.9**
Fielding	**39.1**
Pitching	**88.9**
F. Thomas, 1B	28
T. Phillips, OF	21
R. Ventura, 3B	20
A. Fernandez, SP	19
R. Durham, 2B	17
R. Hernandez, RP	17
D. Martinez, OF	16
W. Alvarez, SP	13
H. Baines, DH	13
D. Tartabull, OF	13
K. Tapani, SP	11
J. Baldwin, SP	10
O. Guillen, SS	7
D. Lewis, OF	7
R. Karkovice, C	6
L. Mouton, OF	6
N. Martin, SS	4
B. Simas, RP	4
T. Castillo, RP	3
J. Darwin, RP	3
C. Kreuter, C	3
C. Snopek, 3B	3
L. Thomas, RP	3
M. Karchner, RP	2
B. Keyser, RP	2
M. Bertotti, RP	1
P. Borders, C	1
R. Machado, C	1
D. Slaught, C	1

Cleveland (99-62)	WS
Hitting	**136.8**
Fielding	**45.7**
Pitching	**114.5**
A. Belle, OF	31
J. Thome, 3B	28
K. Lofton, OF	23
M. Ramirez, OF	23
C. Nagy, SP	21
O. Vizquel, SS	16
O. Hershiser, SP	14
J. Franco, 1B	13
J. Mesa, RP	12
E. Plunk, RP	11
J. McDowell, SP	10
C. Ogea, SP	9
S. Alomar Jr., C	8
D. Martinez, SP	7
P. Shuey, RP	7
P. Assenmacher, RP	6
C. Baerga, 2B	6
B. Giles, DH	6
J. Burnitz, OF	5
M. Carreon, 1B	4
K. Seitzer, DH	4
J. Tavarez, RP	4
J. Vizcaino, 2B	4
B. Anderson, SP	3
J. Kent, 1B	3
T. Pena, C	3
J. Poole, RP	3
D. Graves, RP	2
A. Lopez, SP	2
E. Murray, DH	2
C. Candaele, 2B	1
A. Espinoza, 3B	1
D. Jackson, SS	1
K. Mercker, RP	1
G. Swindell, RP	1
R. Thompson, OF	1
N. Wilson, DH	1

Detroit (53-109)	WS
Hitting	**97.7**
Fielding	**24.5**
Pitching	**36.8**
B. Higginson, OF	21
T. Fryman, 3B	17
C. Fielder, 1B	14
M. Lewis, 2B	11
M. Nieves, OF	9
C. Pride, OF	9
T. Clark, 1B	8
B. Ausmus, C	7
O. Olivares, SP	7
C. Curtis, OF	6
F. Lira, SP	6
R. Lewis, RP	5
P. Nevin, 3B	5
J. Flaherty, C	3
J. Lima, RP	3
M. Myers, RP	3
G. Olson, RP	3
A. Sager, RP	3
D. Easley, 2B-SS	2
J. Eischen, RP	2
C. Gomez, SS	2
M. Parent, C	2
J. Thompson, SP	2
K. Bartee, OF	1
D. Bautista, OF	1
A. Cedeno, SS	1
J. Cummings, RP	1
G. Gohr, SP	1
G. Keagle, RP	1
R. Sierra, OF	1
A. Trammell, SS	1
B. Williams, RP	1

Kansas City (75-86)	WS
Hitting	**79.4**
Fielding	**44.4**
Pitching	**101.3**
K. Appier, SP	19
T. Belcher, SP	19
J. Offerman, 1B	18
M. Macfarlane, C	13
C. Haney, SP	12
J. Rosado, SP	11
K. Lockhart, 2B	10
J. Damon, OF	9
T. Goodwin, OF	9
D. Howard, SS	9
J. Montgomery, RP	9
J. Randa, 3B	9
M. Tucker, OF	9
B. Roberts, 2B	8
B. Hamelin, DH	7
M. Gubicza, SP	5
D. Linton, SP	5
C. Paquette, 3B	5
S. Fasano, C	4
H. Pichardo, RP	4
M. Sweeney, C	4
J. Vitiello, DH	4
J. Bluma, RP	3
K. Young, 1B	3
R. Huisman, RP	2
J. Jacome, RP	2
M. Magnante, RP	2
R. Myers, OF	2
J. Nunnally, OF	2
J. Valera, RP	2
B. Bevil, RP	1
L. Norman, OF	1
T. Pugh, RP	1
B. Scanlan, RP	1
C. Stynes, OF	1

Milwaukee (80-82)	WS
Hitting	**115.6**
Fielding	**43.8**
Pitching	**80.6**
J. Cirillo, 3B	20
J. Valentin, SS	20
J. Jaha, 1B	19
D. Nilsson, OF	17
B. McDonald, SP	16
K. Seitzer, 1B	14
G. Vaughn, OF	14
F. Vina, 2B	13
S. Karl, SP	11
M. Fetters, RP	10
M. Mieske, OF	9
P. Listach, OF	6
G. Lloyd, RP	6
A. Miranda, RP	6
M. Newfield, OF	6
C. Eldred, SP	5
J. Levis, C	5
R. Bones, SP	4
C. Carr, OF	4
J. D'Amico, SP	4
D. Jones, RP	4
M. Matheny, C	4
R. Villone, RP	3
T. Burrows, RP	2
R. Garcia, RP	2
M. Loretta, 2B	2
S. Sparks, SP	2
T. VanEgmond, SP	2
K. Wickander, RP	2
B. Wickman, RP	2
B. Banks, OF	1
J. Burnitz, OF	1
D. Hulse, OF	1
K. Koslofski, OF	1
T. Ward, OF	1
G. Williams, OF	1

Minnesota (78-84)	WS
Hitting	**112.3**
Fielding	**42.5**
Pitching	**79.3**
C. Knoblauch, 2B	32
R. Becker, OF	20
M. Cordova, OF	18
P. Molitor, DH	18
B. Radke, SP	14
S. Stahoviak, 1B	12
D. Hollins, 3B	11
F. Rodriguez, SP	11
R. Kelly, OF	9
M. Trombley, RP	9
P. Meares, SS	8
R. Robertson, SP	8
M. Lawton, OF	7
R. Aguilera, SP	6
S. Aldred, SP	6
E. Guardado, RP	6
G. Myers, C	6
D. Naulty, RP	6
D. Stevens, RP	6
R. Coomer, 1B	5
G. Hansell, RP	4
M. Walbeck, C	3
C. Hale, 2B	2
J. Parra, RP	2
J. Reboulet, SS	2
M. Durant, C	1
D. Hocking, OF	1
T. Walker, 3B	1

New York (92-70)	WS
Hitting	**126.1**
Fielding	**42.0**
Pitching	**107.8**
B. Williams, OF	26
P. O'Neill, OF	22
T. Martinez, 1B	21
D. Jeter, SS	18
A. Pettitte, SP	18
M. Rivera, RP	18
W. Boggs, 3B	15
J. Wetteland, RP	13
M. Duncan, 2B	12
J. Girardi, C	11
K. Rogers, SP	11
J. Key, SP	10
D. Gooden, SP	9
D. Cone, SP	8
J. Leyritz, C	7
T. Raines, OF	7
J. Nelson, RP	6
D. Strawberry, OF	6
R. Sierra, DH	5
B. Wickman, RP	5
R. Rivera, OF	4
G. Williams, OF	4
C. Fielder, DH	3
D. Pavlas, RP	3
M. Aldrete, DH-OF	2
B. Boehringer, RP	2
A. Fox, 2B	2
C. Hayes, 3B	2
J. Mecir, RP	2
S. Howe, RP	1

M. Hutton, RP	1
R. Mendoza, SP	1
L. Sojo, 2B	1

Oakland (78-84)	WS
Hitting	**112.4**
Fielding	**42.0**
Pitching	**79.6**
M. McGwire, 1B	29
S. Brosius, 3B	19
T. Steinbach, C	18
G. Berroa, DH	16
J. Giambi, 1B-OF	15
M. Bordick, SS	10
B. Taylor, RP	10
E. Young, OF	10
T. Batista, 2B	9
M. Mohler, RP	9
A. Prieto, SP	8
J. Corsi, RP	7
B. Groom, RP	7
C. Reyes, RP	7
D. Wengert, SP	6
W. Adams, SP	5
J. Herrera, OF	5
D. Telgheder, SP	5
D. Johns, SP	4
M. Stairs, OF	4
J. Wasdin, SP	4
R. Bournigal, 2B	3
B. Gates, 2B	3
P. Munoz, DH	3
S. Wojciechowski, SP	3
J. Briscoe, RP	2
B. Chouinard, SP	2
D. Mashore, OF	2
P. Plantier, OF	2
S. Spiezio, 3B	2
M. Acre, RP	1
A. Battle, OF	1
B. Lesher, OF	1
T. Lovullo, 1B	1
G. Williams, C	1

Seattle (85-76)	WS
Hitting	**148.3**
Fielding	**35.2**
Pitching	**71.5**
A. Rodriguez, SS	34
K. Griffey Jr., OF	28
E. Martinez, DH	23
J. Buhner, OF	22
P. Sorrento, 1B	15
D. Wilson, C	15
J. Cora, 2B	11
N. Charlton, RP	9
S. Hitchcock, SP	8
R. Amaral, OF	7
M. Jackson, RP	7
M. Whiten, OF	7
R. Carmona, RP	6
B. Wells, RP	6
D. Bragg, OF	5
R. Johnson, SP	5
J. Moyer, SP	5
B. Wolcott, SP	5
B. Ayala, RP	4
D. Hollins, 3B	4
T. Mulholland, SP	4
T. Davis, RP	3
B. Hunter, 1B	3
S. Torres, SP	3
C. Bosio, SP-RP	2
R. Davis, 3B	2
J. Marzano, C	2
L. Sojo, 3B	2
A. Diaz, OF	1
M. Martinez, OF	1
G. McCarthy, RP	1
R. Meacham, RP	1
B. Minor, RP	1
A. Sheets, 3B	1
D. Strange, 3B	1
M. Wagner, SP	1

Texas (90-72)	WS
Hitting	**117.5**
Fielding	**45.4**
Pitching	**107.1**
I. Rodriguez, C	23
K. Hill, SP	22
J. Gonzalez, OF	21
R. Greer, OF	21
M. McLemore, 2B	16
D. Palmer, 3B	15
K. Elster, SS	14
D. Oliver, SP	12
R. Pavlik, SP	12
W. Clark, 1B	11
D. Hamilton, OF	11
M. Tettleton, DH	11
B. Witt, SP	10
K. Gross, SP	8
D. Cook, RP	7
J. Russell, RP	7
J. Burkett, SP	6
D. Valle, C	6
E. Vosberg, RP	6
M. Henneman, RP	5
W. Newson, OF	5
M. Brandenburg, RP	4
D. Buford, OF	4
G. Heredia, RP	3
M. Stanton, RP	3
L. Stevens, 1B	2
L. Frazier, OF	1
R. Gonzales, 1B	1
D. Patterson, RP	1
K. Stillwell, 2B	1
M. Whiteside, RP	1

Toronto (74-88)	WS
Hitting	**83.5**
Fielding	**45.3**
Pitching	**93.3**
P. Hentgen, SP	24
J. Guzman, SP	17
E. Sprague, 3B	17
A. Gonzalez, SS	14
J. Carter, OF	13
C. Delgado, DH	12
O. Nixon, OF	12
C. O'Brien, C	11
J. Olerud, 1B	10
M. Timlin, RP	10
J. Brumfield, OF	8
T. Crabtree, RP	8
S. Green, OF	8
E. Hanson, SP	8
T. Castillo, RP	5
R. Perez, OF	5
D. Cedeno, 2B	4
H. Flener, SP	4
S. Martinez, C	4
P. Quantrill, SP	4
J. Samuel, DH-OF	4
P. Spoljaric, RP	4
T. Perez, 2B	3
B. Risley, RP	3
W. Williams, SP	3
T. Brito, 2B	2
F. Crespo, 2B	2
L. Andujar, SP	1
S. Brow, RP	1
D. Johnson, RP	1

1996 National League

Atlanta (96-66)	WS
Hitting	**115.4**
Fielding	**46.6**
Pitching	**126.1**
J. Smoltz, SP	27
C. Jones, 3B	26
M. Grissom, OF	24
G. Maddux, SP	23
T. Glavine, SP	22
R. Klesko, OF	20
F. McGriff, 1B	19
J. Lopez, C	15
M. Wohlers, RP	14
M. Lemke, 2B	12
J. Blauser, SS	9
G. McMichael, RP	9
M. Bielecki, RP	8
S. Avery, SP	7
D. Justice, OF	7
T. Wade, RP	7
P. Borbon, RP	5
J. Dye, OF	5
E. Perez, C	5
M. Whiten, OF	4
B. Clontz, RP	3
A. Jones, OF	3
R. Belliard, SS	2
J. Walton, OF	2
J. Borowski, RP	1
E. Giovanola, SS	1
T. Graffanino, 2B	1
D. Hartgraves, RP	1
T. Houston, 1B	1
M. Mordecai, 2B	1
D. Neagle, SP	1
L. Polonia, OF	1
D. Smith, OF	1
T. Thobe, RP	1

Chicago (76-86)	WS
Hitting	**109.7**
Fielding	**40.4**
Pitching	**78.0**
B. McRae, OF	21
M. Grace, 1B	20
R. Sandberg, 2B	19
S. Sosa, OF	18
L. Gonzalez, OF	17
S. Trachsel, SP	15
J. Navarro, SP	13
S. Servais, C	13
T. Wendell, RP	12
L. Gomez, 3B	10
T. Adams, RP	9
B. Patterson, RP	7
K. Bottenfield, RP	6
J. Hernandez, SS	6
T. Houston, C	5
R. Sanchez, SS	5
L. Casian, RP	3
F. Castillo, SP	3
K. Foster, SP	3
D. Magadan, 3B	3
R. Myers, RP	3
M. Campbell, RP	2
D. Glanville, OF	2
O. Timmons, OF	2
B. Brown, 1B	1
S. Bullett, OF	1
J. Bullinger, SP	1
B. Dorsett, C	1
T. Haney, 2B	1
R. Jennings, OF	1
D. Jones, RP	1
B. Kieschnick, OF	1
M. Perez, RP	1
T. Shumpert, 3B	1
A. Telemaco, SP	1

Cincinnati (81-81)	WS
Hitting	**122.7**
Fielding	**40.2**
Pitching	**80.0**
B. Larkin, SS	31
E. Davis, OF	22
H. Morris, 1B	18
J. Brantley, RP	14
J. Smiley, SP	14
J. Shaw, RP	12
W. Greene, 3B	11
E. Taubensee, C	11
B. Boone, 2B	10
D. Burba, SP	10
L. Harris, OF	10
T. Howard, OF	9
J. Oliver, C	8
M. Portugal, SP	8
J. Branson, 3B	7
R. Sanders, OF	7
Kev. Mitchell, OF	6
H. Carrasco, RP	5
C. Sabo, 3B	4
R. Salkeld, SP	4
E. Anthony, OF	3
S. Service, RP	3
L. Smith, RP	3
M. Morgan, SP	2
B. Fordyce, C	1
C. Goodwin, OF	1
M. Kelly, OF	1
C. Lyons, SP	1
M. Moore, RP	1
C. Mottola, OF	1
E. Owens, OF	1
E. Perez, 1B	1
J. Ruffin, RP	1
P. Schourek, SP	1
S. Sullivan, RP	1

Colorado (83-79)	WS
Hitting	**119.9**
Fielding	**41.8**
Pitching	**87.3**
E. Burks, OF	28
A. Galarraga, 1B	25
V. Castilla, 3B	23
D. Bichette, OF	20
E. Young, 2B	17
K. Ritz, SP	14
B. Ruffin, RP	14
A. Reynoso, SP	10
L. Walker, OF	10
J. Reed, C	9
Ma. Thompson, SP	9
S. Reed, RP	8
W. Weiss, SS	8
D. Holmes, RP	7
Q. McCracken, OF	7
C. Leskanic, RP	5
J. Wright, SP	5
R. Bailey, RP	4
M. Freeman, SP	4
J. Vander Wal, OF	4
L. Painter, RP	3
S. Decker, C	2
T. Hubbard, OF	2
M. Munoz, RP	2
J. Owens, C	2
B. Swift, RP	2
E. Anthony, OF	1
J. Bates, 2B	1
J. Burke, RP	1
M. Farmer, SP	1
J. Habyan, RP	1

Florida (80-82)	WS
Hitting	**104.0**
Fielding	**43.0**
Pitching	**93.0**
G. Sheffield, OF	34
K. Brown, SP	26
A. Leiter, SP	19
R. Nen, RP	19
D. White, OF	18
J. Conine, OF	17
E. Renteria, SS	15
G. Colbrunn, 1B	10
C. Johnson, C	10
T. Pendleton, 3B	9
K. Abbott, SS	8
Q. Veras, 2B	7
A. Arias, 3B	6
J. Burkett, SP	6

M. Hutton, SP 4
J. Powell, RP 4
L. Castillo, 2B 3
R. Helling, SP 3
P. Rapp, SP 3
D. Weathers, RP 3
A. Dawson, OF 2
T. Mathews, RP 2
Y. Perez, RP 2
J. Brooks, OF 1
C. Grebeck, 2B 1
F. Heredia, RP 1
L. Hernandez, RP 1
R. Milliard, 2B 1
B. Natal, C 1
J. Orsulak, OF 1
J. Tavarez, OF 1
M. Valdes, SP 1
G. Zaun, C 1

Houston (82-80)	WS
Hitting	**140.4**
Fielding	**31.8**
Pitching	**73.7**
J. Bagwell, 1B	41
C. Biggio, 2B	32
S. Berry, 3B	19
S. Reynolds, SP	15
D. Bell, OF	14
M. Hampton, SP	11
D. Kile, SP	10
O. Miller, SS	8
J. Mouton, OF	8
B. Wagner, RP	8
J. Cangelosi, OF	7
B. Hunter, OF	7
B. Spiers, 3B	7
R. Wilkins, C	7
D. Drabek, SP	6
D. May, OF	6
D. Wall, SP	6
T. Eusebio, C	5
X. Hernandez, RP	5
T. Jones, RP	5
R. Gutierrez, SS	4
J. Hudek, RP	2
R. Knorr, C	2
K. Manwaring, C	2
A. Morman, RP	2
A. Young, RP	2
D. Brocail, RP	1
J. Goff, C	1
R. Montgomery, OF	1
G. Olson, RP	1
M. Simms, OF	1

Los Angeles (90-72)	WS
Hitting	**123.6**
Fielding	**43.3**
Pitching	**103.1**
M. Piazza, C	33
R. Mondesi, OF	25
G. Gagne, SS	20
E. Karros, 1B	20
T. Hollandsworth, OF	19
H. Nomo, SP	16
I. Valdes, SP	16
P. Astacio, SP	13
R. Martinez, SP	12
D. DeShields, 2B	11
T. Worrell, RP	11
A. Osuna, RP	10
M. Guthrie, RP	8
R. Cedeno, OF	7
C. Park, RP	7
M. Blowers, 3B	6
S. Radinsky, RP	6
B. Ashley, OF	4
T. Candiotti, SP	4
W. Kirby, OF	4
C. Fonville, OF	3
T. Prince, C	3
B. Butler, OF	2
J. Castro, SS	2
C. Curtis, OF	2
T. Wallach, 3B	2
M. Busch, 3B	1
D. Clark, OF	1
J. Eischen, RP	1
O. Marrero, 1B	1

Montreal (88-74)	WS
Hitting	**108.0**
Fielding	**47.6**
Pitching	**108.5**
M. Alou, OF	20
M. Lansing, 2B	19
H. Rodriguez, OF	19
J. Fassero, SP	18
M. Rojas, RP	18
F. Santangelo, OF	18
M. Grudzielanek, SS	17
D. Segui, 1B	15
P. Martinez, SP	14
S. Andrews, 3B	11
R. White, OF	10
R. Cormier, SP	8
D. Fletcher, C	8
U. Urbina, SP	8
B. Manuel, RP	7
O. Daal, RP	6
C. Floyd, OF	6
D. Veres, RP	6
M. Dyer, RP	5
T. Scott, RP	5
M. Leiter, SP	4
S. Obando, OF	4
J. Juden, RP	3
J. Paniagua, SP	3
K. Rueter, SP	3
T. Alvarez, RP	2
D. Silvestri, 3B	2
A. Stankiewicz, 2B	2
L. Webster, C	2
T. Spehr, C	1

New York (71-91)	WS
Hitting	**117.1**
Fielding	**30.7**
Pitching	**65.2**
B. Gilkey, OF	30
L. Johnson, OF	26
T. Hundley, C	24
M. Clark, SP	13
J. Franco, RP	10
J. Vizcaino, 2B	10
B. Huskey, 1B	8
B. Jones, SP	8
J. Kent, 3B	8
A. Ochoa, OF	8
P. Harnisch, SP	7
R. Ordonez, SS	7
E. Alfonzo, 2B	6
J. Isringhausen, SP	6
D. Mlicki, RP	6
R. Brogna, 1B	4
J. Dipoto, RP	4
A. Espinoza, 3B	3
D. Henry, RP	3
C. Jones, OF	3
R. Person, RP	3
P. Byrd, RP	2
C. Everett, OF	2
D. Wallace, RP	2
T. Bogar, 1B	1
A. Castillo, C	1
J. Hardtke, 2B	1
B. MacDonald, RP	1
B. Mayne, C	1
B. Minor, RP	1
R. Petagine, 1B	1
K. Roberson, OF	1
A. Tomberlin, OF	1
P. Wilson, SP	1

Philadelphia (67-95)	WS
Hitting	**87.7**
Fielding	**37.3**
Pitching	**76.0**
B. Santiago, C	19
J. Eisenreich, OF	14
C. Schilling, SP	14
R. Bottalico, RP	13
T. Zeile, 3B	13
K. Stocker, SS	12
K. Ryan, RP	11
G. Jefferies, 1B	10
M. Morandini, 2B	10
R. Otero, OF	8
T. Borland, RP	6
M. Grace, SP	6
L. Dykstra, OF	5
P. Incaviglia, OF	5
T. Mulholland, SP	5
R. Amaro, OF	4
S. Fernandez, SP	4
M. Benjamin, SS	3
R. Jordan, RP	3
M. Lieberthal, C	3
J. Parrett, RP	3
G. Schall, 1B	3
R. Springer, RP	3
M. Whiten, OF	3
M. Williams, SP	3
D. Doster, 2B	2
K. Jordan, 1B	2
S. Rolen, 3B	2
K. Sefcik, SS	2
R. Blazier, RP	1
B. Estalella, C	1
S. Frey, RP	1
C. Maduro, SP-RP	1
W. Magee, OF	1
M. Mimbs, SP	1
L. Mitchell, RP	1
J. Phillips, OF	1
D. West, SP	1
J. Zuber, 1B	1

Pittsburgh (73-89)	WS
Hitting	**112.3**
Fielding	**33.8**
Pitching	**73.0**
J. King, 1B	22
A. Martin, OF	17
O. Merced, OF	16
D. Neagle, SP	16
J. Bell, SS	15
M. Johnson, 1B	12
J. Kendall, C	12
C. Garcia, 2B	11
D. Darwin, SP	10
J. Lieber, RP	9
F. Cordova, RP	8
C. Hayes, 3B	8
D. Plesac, RP	8
D. Clark, OF	7
J. Allensworth, OF	6
M. Wilkins, RP	5
N. Liriano, 2B	4
K. Osik, C	4
M. Kingery, OF	3
Z. Smith, SP	3
E. Loaiza, SP	2
R. Loiselle, SP	2
M. Ruebel, RP	2
J. Schmidt, SP	2
D. Sveum, 3B	2
P. Wagner, SP	2
T. Womack, OF	2
T. Beamon, OF	1
J. Brumfield, OF	1
M. Cummings, OF	1
E. Dessens, RP	1
J. Ericks, RP	1
R. Morel, RP	1
C. Peters, SP	1
D. Wainhouse, RP	1
J. Wehner, OF	1

San Diego (91-71)	WS
Hitting	**129.5**
Fielding	**41.4**
Pitching	**102.1**
K. Caminiti, 3B	38
S. Finley, OF	27
T. Hoffman, RP	20
T. Gwynn, OF	17
R. Henderson, OF	16
W. Joyner, 1B	16
A. Ashby, SP	11
J. Hamilton, SP	11
J. Reed, 2B	11
S. Sanders, RP	10
F. Valenzuela, SP	10
T. Worrell, RP	10
C. Gomez, SS	9
D. Bochtler, RP	7
J. Flaherty, C	7
B. Tewksbury, SP	7
A. Cianfrocco, 1B	5
B. Johnson, C	5
S. Bergman, RP	4
S. Livingstone, 1B	4
W. Blair, RP	3
A. Cedeno, SS	3
B. Florie, RP	3
C. Shipley, 2B	3
G. Vaughn, OF	3
D. Veras, RP	3
R. Deer, OF	2
M. Newfield, OF	2
R. Villone, RP	2
B. Ausmus, C	1
L. Lopez, SS	1
M. Oquist, RP	1
J. Thompson, 1B	1

San Francisco (68-94)	WS
Hitting	**117.7**
Fielding	**31.1**
Pitching	**55.2**
B. Bonds, OF	39
M. Williams, 3B	18
G. Hill, OF	13
R. Beck, RP	10
B. Mueller, 3B	9
M. Benard, OF	8
S. Dunston, SS	8
M. Carreon, 1B	7
M. Gardner, SP	7
A. Watson, SP	7
R. Wilkins, C	7
O. Fernandez, SP	6
T. Lampkin, C	6
R. Aurilia, SS	5
M. Dewey, RP	5
S. Javier, OF	5
J. Bautista, RP	4
S. Estes, SP	4
K. Manwaring, C	3
J. Poole, RP	3
R. Thompson, 2B	3
J. Cruz, OF	2
S. Decker, C	2
J. Juden, RP	2
M. Leiter, SP	2
D. McCarty, 1B	2
K. Rueter, SP	2
S. Scarsone, 2B	2
W. VanLandingham, SP	2
D. Wilson, 1B	2
J. Canizaro, 2B	1
D. Carlson, RP	1
W. Delgado, SS	1
R. DeLucia, RP	1
M. Jensen, C	1
D. Jones, OF	1
D. Mirabelli, C	1
D. Peltier, 1B	1
J. Phillips, 1B	1

St. Louis (88-74)	WS
Hitting	**122.2**
Fielding	**47.4**
Pitching	**94.4**
B. Jordan, OF	27
R. Lankford, OF	25
R. Gant, OF	18
G. Gaetti, 3B	16
An. Benes, SP	14
D. Osborne, SP	14
T. Pagnozzi, C	14
T. Stottlemyre, SP	14
J. Mabry, 1B	13
R. Clayton, SS	12
L. Alicea, 2B	11
W. McGee, OF	9
D. Eckersley, RP	8
T. Mathews, RP	8
M. Petkovsek, RP	8
O. Smith, SS	8
R. Honeycutt, RP	7
M. Sweeney, OF	7
C. Bailey, RP	6
Al. Benes, SP	5
T. Fossas, RP	4
D. Sheaffer, C	3
R. Batchelor, RP	2
P. Borders, C	2
D. Jackson, RP	2
M. Morgan, SP	2
J. Parrett, RP	2
D. Bell, 3B	1
T. Bradshaw, OF	1
M. Gallego, 2B	1
D. May, RP	2
G. Cadaret, RP	1
T. Chavez, RP	1
R. Eenhoorn, 3B	1
A. Encarnacion, C	1
J. Fabregas, C	1
R. Henderson, DH	1
M. Langston, SP	1
C. McElroy, RP	1
O. Palmeiro, OF	1
C. Turner, C	1

1997 American League

Anaheim (84-78)	WS
Hitting	**117.6**
Fielding	**42.6**
Pitching	**91.8**
T. Salmon, OF	29
J. Edmonds, OF	19
D. Erstad, 1B	19
G. Anderson, OF	16
D. Hollins, 3B	15
L. Alicea, 2B	14
J. Dickson, SP	12
T. Phillips, 2B	12
C. Finley, SP	11
J. Leyritz, C	10
T. Percival, RP	10
A. Watson, SP	9
D. Springer, SP	8
P. Harris, RP	7
S. Hasegawa, RP	7
G. DiSarcina, SS	6
K. Hill, SP	6
M. James, RP	6
R. DeLucia, RP	5
M. Holtz, RP	5
T. Greene, C	4
C. Kreuter, C	4
C. Grebeck, 2B	3
J. Howell, 3B	3
J. Wasdin, RP	7
J. Corsi, RP	6
S. Hatteberg, C	6
J. Suppan, SP	4
J. Hudson, RP	3
R. Mahay, RP	3
C. Hammond, RP	2
S. Mack, OF	2
R. Pemberton, OF	2
S. Avery, SP	1
M. Benjamin, 3B	1
M. Brandenburg, RP	1
R. Checo, RP	1
V. Eshelman, RP	1
B. Haselman, C	1
K. Lacy, RP	1
D. Lowe, RP	1
H. Slocumb, RP	1
J. Tavarez, OF	1
R. Trlicek, RP	1

Baltimore (98-64)	WS
Hitting	**127.9**
Fielding	**49.9**
Pitching	**116.1**
B. Anderson, OF	26
R. Alomar, 2B	21
M. Mussina, SP	19
B. Surhoff, OF	19
R. Palmeiro, 1B	18
C. Ripken Jr., 3B	18
J. Key, SP	17
S. Erickson, SP	16
R. Myers, RP	15
J. Hammonds, OF	14
C. Hoiles, C	14
S. Kamieniecki, SP	12
A. Benitez, RP	11
A. Rhodes, RP	10
G. Berroa, DH	7
M. Bordick, SS	7
J. Orosco, RP	7
L. Webster, C	7
E. Davis, OF	6
J. Reboulet, 2B	5
T. Tarasco, OF	5
A. Ledesma, 2B	4
T. Mathews, RP	4
H. Baines, DH	2
J. Walton, OF	2
B. Williams, RP	2
S. Boskie, RP	1
D. Dellucci, OF	1
P. Incaviglia, DH	1
R. Krivda, SP	1
A. Mills, RP	1
N. Rodriguez, RP	1

Boston (78-84)	WS
Hitting	**124.7**
Fielding	**33.6**
Pitching	**75.7**
N. Garciaparra, SS	26
M. Vaughn, 1B	22
J. Valentin, 2B	21
F. Gordon, SP	15
T. O'Leary, OF	15
J. Frye, 2B	12
T. Wakefield, SP	12
D. Bragg, OF	11
W. Cordero, OF	11
R. Jefferson, DH	10
M. Stanley, DH	10
B. Henry, RP	9
T. Naehring, 3B	7
A. Sele, SP	7

Chicago (80-81)	WS
Hitting	**130.8**
Fielding	**35.4**
Pitching	**73.8**
F. Thomas, 1B	39
A. Belle, OF	18
M. Cameron, OF	17
D. Martinez, OF	15
R. Durham, 2B	13
W. Alvarez, SP	12
H. Baines, DH	10
O. Guillen, SS	10
R. Hernandez, RP	10
J. Fabregas, C	8
M. Karchner, RP	8
R. Ventura, 3B	8
J. Baldwin, SP	6
D. Darwin, SP	6
N. Martin, SS	6
T. Phillips, OF	6
D. Drabek, SP	5
C. Castillo, RP	4
K. Foulke, RP	4
C. McElroy, RP	4
M. Sirotka, SP	4
T. Castillo, RP	3
L. Mouton, OF	3
J. Navarro, SP	3
M. Ordonez, OF	3
J. Bere, SP	2
S. Eyre, SP	2
R. Karkovice, C	2
B. Simas, RP	2
C. Snopek, 3B	2
C. Kreuter, C	1
D. Lewis, OF	1
G. Norton, 3B	1
T. Pena, C	1
M. Valdez, 1B	1

Cleveland (86-75)	WS
Hitting	**140.7**
Fielding	**38.3**
Pitching	**79.0**
D. Justice, OF	26
J. Thome, 1B	26
M. Ramirez, OF	21
S. Alomar Jr., C	18
M. Williams, 3B	18
M. Grissom, OF	14
O. Vizquel, SS	14
B. Giles, OF	13
C. Nagy, SP	13
T. Fernandez, 2B	11
O. Hershiser, SP	11
M. Jackson, RP	11
J. Mesa, RP	11
P. Assenmacher, RP	7
J. Wright, SP	6
J. Franco, DH	5
C. Ogea, SP	5
P. Borders, C	3
E. Plunk, RP	3
K. Seitzer, DH	3
B. Anderson, SP	2
B. Colon, SP	2
J. Jacome, RP	2
J. McDowell, SP	2
B. Roberts, 2B	2
J. Branson, 2B	1
C. Candaele, 2B	1
C. Curtis, OF	1
J. Juden, SP	1
S. Kline, RP	1
J. Manto, 3B	1
P. Shuey, RP	1
J. Smiley, SP	1
E. Wilson, SS	1

Detroit (79-83)	WS
Hitting	**107.9**
Fielding	**40.2**
Pitching	**88.9**
B. Higginson, OF	25
T. Clark, 1B	24
J. Thompson, SP	21
D. Easley, 2B	18
T. Fryman, 3B	17
B. Hunter, OF	17
W. Blair, SP	13
T. Jones, RP	13
M. Nieves, OF	10
B. Hamelin, DH	9
B. Moehler, SP	9
D. Brocail, RP	7
D. Cruz, SS	7
P. Nevin, OF	6
O. Olivares, SP	6
A. Sager, RP	6
D. Miceli, RP	5
S. Sanders, SP	3
R. Casanova, C	2
F. Lira, SP	2
C. Pride, OF	2
J. Reed, 2B	2
B. Trammell, OF	2
M. Walbeck, C	2
F. Catalanotto, 2B	1
G. Dishman, SP	1
J. Encarnacion, OF	1
E. Gaillard, RP	1
J. Hall, OF	1
K. Jarvis, RP	1
B. Johnson, C	1
O. Miller, SS	1
M. Myers, RP	1

Kansas City (67-94)	WS
Hitting	**86.1**
Fielding	**38.9**
Pitching	**76.0**
J. Bell, SS	21
K. Appier, SP	18
J. King, 1B	17
C. Davis, DH	15
J. Damon, OF	11
T. Belcher, SP	9
J. Offerman, 2B	9
J. Rosado, SP	9
J. Montgomery, RP	8
M. Macfarlane, C	7
B. Roberts, OF	6
T. Goodwin, OF	5
D. Palmer, 3B	5
H. Pichardo, RP	5
G. Rusch, SP	5
M. Sweeney, C	5
J. Hansen, 2B	4
G. Olson, RP	4
J. Pittsley, SP	4
Y. Benitez, OF	3
R. Veres, RP	3
J. Dye, OF	2
D. Howard, 2B	2
R. Myers, OF	2
C. Paquette, 3B	2
M. Perez, RP	2
L. Sutton, 1B	2
J. Vitiello, OF	2
J. Walker, RP	2
M. Whisenant, RP	2
R. Bones, SP	1
H. Carrasco, RP	1
L. Casian, RP	1
S. Cooper, 3B	1
S. Fasano, C	1
S. Halter, OF	1
C. Haney, RP	1
F. Martinez, SS	1
J. Nunnally, OF	1
S. Service, RP	1

Milwaukee (78-83)	WS
Hitting	**83.6**
Fielding	**50.6**
Pitching	**99.7**
J. Cirillo, 3B	24
J. Burnitz, OF	20
D. Jones, RP	19
J. Valentin, SS	13
M. Loretta, 2B	12
D. Nilsson, 1B	12
B. Wickman, RP	11
S. Karl, SP	10
J. Mercedes, SP	10
C. Eldred, SP	9
G. Williams, OF	9
M. Matheny, C	8
B. McDonald, SP	8
M. Fetters, RP	7

J. Levis, C	7
F. Vina, 2B	7
J. Adamson, RP	6
J. D'Amico, SP	6
J. Voigt, OF	5
B. Florie, RP	4
J. Franco, DH	4
D. Jackson, OF	4
R. Villone, RP	4
J. Jaha, 1B	3
M. Mieske, OF	2
E. Diaz, 2B	1
T. Dunn, OF	1
P. Harnisch, SP	1
J. Huson, 2B	1
A. Miranda, RP	1
M. Newfield, OF	1
A. Reyes, RP	1
K. Stinnett, C	1
T. Unroe, 1B	1
S. Woodard, SP	1

Minnesota (68-94)	WS
Hitting	**98.6**
Fielding	**35.0**
Pitching	**70.4**
C. Knoblauch, 2B	23
B. Radke, SP	16
R. Coomer, 3B	14
M. Lawton, OF	14
P. Meares, SS	13
P. Molitor, DH	13
R. Becker, OF	12
G. Swindell, RP	10
R. Aguilera, RP	9
B. Tewksbury, SP	9
T. Steinbach, C	7
M. Cordova, OF	6
D. Hocking, SS	6
R. Kelly, OF	6
F. Rodriguez, RP	6
M. Trombley, RP	5
S. Stahoviak, 1B	4
B. Brede, OF	3
G. Colbrunn, 1B	3
E. Guardado, RP	3
G. Myers, C	3
T. Ritchie, RP	3
R. Robertson, SP	3
L. Hawkins, SP	2
D. Jackson, OF	2
D. Miller, C	2
D. Ortiz, 1B	2
D. Serafini, SP	2
T. Walker, 3B	2
D. Naulty, RP	1

New York (96-66)	WS
Hitting	**143.0**
Fielding	**41.6**
Pitching	**103.4**
P. O'Neill, OF	28
T. Martinez, 1B	27
B. Williams, OF	24
A. Pettitte, SP	20
D. Jeter, SS	19
D. Cone, SP	16
M. Rivera, RP	15
D. Wells, SP	12
C. Curtis, OF	11
W. Boggs, 3B	10
J. Girardi, C	9
T. Raines, OF	9
M. Stanton, RP	9
J. Nelson, RP	8
C. Fielder, DH	7
R. Mendoza, RP	7
L. Sojo, 2B	7
C. Hayes, 3B	6
J. Posada, C	6
D. Gooden, SP	5
R. Sanchez, 2B	5
M. Whiten, OF	5
B. Boehringer, RP	4
M. Stanley, DH	4
M. Duncan, 2B	3
G. Lloyd, RP	3
W. Banks, RP	2
P. Kelly, 2B	2
K. Rogers, SP	2
H. Bush, 2B	1
A. Fox, 3B	1
S. Pose, OF	1

Oakland (65-97)	WS
Hitting	**107.0**
Fielding	**29.5**
Pitching	**58.5**
J. Giambi, OF	18
M. McGwire, 1B	15
M. Stairs, OF	15
S. Spiezio, 2B	10
B. Taylor, RP	10
D. Magadan, 3B	9
J. Canseco, DH	8
G. Berroa, OF	7
A. Small, RP	7
G. Williams, C	7
D. Mashore, OF	6
B. Mayne, C	6
J. McDonald, OF	6
M. Bellhorn, 3B	5
S. Brosius, 3B	5
M. Oquist, SP	5
R. Bournigal, SS	4
B. Grieve, OF	4
J. Haynes, SP	4
A. Prieto, SP	4
B. Groom, RP	3
D. Johnson, RP	3
S. Karsay, SP	3
P. Lennon, OF	3
T. Mathews, RP	3
M. Mohler, RP	3
B. Rigby, SP	3
D. Wengert, RP	3
T. Batista, SS	2
T. Brito, 3B	2
C. Reyes, RP	2
D. Telgheder, SP	2
M. Acre, RP	1
J. Johnstone, RP	1
B. Lesher, OF	1
A. Lorraine, SP-RP	1
I. Molina, C	1
S. Sheldon, SS	1
M. Tejada, SS	1
E. Young, OF	1

Seattle (90-72)	WS
Hitting	**153.8**
Fielding	**36.8**
Pitching	**79.4**
K. Griffey Jr., OF	36
E. Martinez, DH	27
R. Johnson, SP	23
A. Rodriguez, SS	22
D. Wilson, C	21
J. Buhner, OF	19
J. Cora, 2B	18
J. Fassero, SP	17
J. Moyer, SP	14
R. Davis, 3B	11
P. Sorrento, 1B	11
B. Ayala, RP	9
J. Cruz, OF	6
R. Kelly, OF	6
M. Blowers, 1B	4
H. Slocumb, RP	3
K. Cloude, SP	2
R. Ducey, OF	2
B. Gates, 3B	2
J. Marzano, C	2
O. Olivares, SP	2
M. Timlin, RP	2
B. Wolcott, SP	2
R. Amaral, OF	1
A. Espinoza, SS	1
G. McCarthy, RP	1
D. Rohrmeier, DH	1
S. Sanders, RP	1
A. Sheets, 3B	1
P. Spoljaric, RP	1
L. Tinsley, OF	1
B. Wells, RP	1

Texas (77-85)	WS
Hitting	**108.8**
Fielding	**37.1**
Pitching	**85.1**
I. Rodriguez, C	26
R. Greer, OF	23
J. Gonzalez, DH	19
J. Wetteland, RP	16
W. Clark, 1B	14
D. Oliver, SP	12
L. Stevens, 1B	11
B. Witt, SP	11
J. Burkett, SP	10
D. Cedeno, 2B	9
D. Patterson, RP	8
D. Palmer, 3B	6
E. Gunderson, RP	5
J. Leyritz, C	5
M. McLemore, 2B	5
D. Buford, OF	4
B. Gil, SS	4
T. Goodwin, OF	4
K. Hill, SP	4
W. Newson, OF	4
R. Helling, SP	3
X. Hernandez, RP	3
R. Pavlik, SP	3
B. Ripken, SS	3
M. Simms, DH	3
F. Tatis, 3B	3
M. Whiteside, RP	3
S. Bailes, RP	2
W. Heredia, RP	2
E. Vosberg, RP	2
T. Clark, SP	1
M. Devereaux, OF	1
H. Mercedes, C	1
E. Moody, RP	1

Toronto (76-86)	WS
Hitting	**73.7**
Fielding	**49.0**
Pitching	**105.3**
R. Clemens, SP	32
P. Hentgen, SP	19
C. Delgado, 1B	18
S. Green, OF	14
P. Quantrill, RP	12
W. Williams, SP	11
J. Carter, DH	10
A. Gonzalez, SS	10
C. O'Brien, C	9
B. Santiago, C	9
O. Merced, OF	8
O. Nixon, OF	8
S. Stewart, OF	7
M. Timlin, RP	7
K. Escobar, RP	6
E. Sprague, 3B	6
J. Cruz, OF	5
D. Plesac, RP	5
P. Spoljaric, RP	5
C. Garcia, 2B	4
J. Samuel, DH	3
T. Brito, 2B	2
J. Brumfield, OF	2
C. Carpenter, SP	2
O. Daal, RP	2
M. Duncan, 2B	2
M. Janzen, RP	2
T. Perez, SS	2
R. Person, SP	2
R. Butler, OF	1
F. Crespo, 3B	1
T. Evans, 3B	1
J. Guzman, SP	1

1997
National League

Atlanta (101-61)	WS
Hitting	**129.4**
Fielding	**48.8**
Pitching	**124.9**
J. Blauser, SS	27
G. Maddux, SP	26
C. Jones, 3B	23
T. Glavine, SP	21
K. Lofton, OF	21
D. Neagle, SP	21
J. Smoltz, SP	21
J. Lopez, C	19
R. Klesko, OF	16
M. Tucker, OF	15
F. McGriff, 1B	14
A. Jones, OF	13
M. Wohlers, RP	11
M. Lemke, 2B	9
A. Embree, RP	6
T. Graffanino, 2B	6
K. Lockhart, 2B	5
M. Cather, RP	4
B. Clontz, RP	4
M. Bielecki, RP	3
K. Millwood, SP	3
D. Bautista, OF	2
J. Borowski, RP	2
C. Fox, RP	2
K. Ligtenberg, RP	2
E. Perez, C	2
R. Belliard, SS	1
P. Byrd, RP	1
G. Colbrunn, 1B	1
R. Simon, 1B	1
T. Spehr, C	1

Chicago (68-94)	WS
Hitting	**84.3**
Fielding	**39.2**
Pitching	**80.5**
M. Grace, 1B	20
S. Sosa, OF	14
K. Orie, 3B	12
R. Sandberg, 2B	11
S. Servais, C	10
D. Glanville, OF	9
J. Gonzalez, SP	9
S. Trachsel, SP	9
B. McRae, OF	8
T. Mulholland, SP	8
K. Tapani, SP	8
S. Dunston, SS	7
K. Foster, SP	7
K. Bottenfield, RP	6
M. Clark, SP	6
D. Hansen, 3B	6
B. Patterson, RP	6
T. Adams, RP	5
D. Clark, OF	5
M. Rojas, RP	5
J. Hernandez, 3B	4
T. Houston, C	4
L. Johnson, OF	4
M. Pisciotta, RP	4
T. Wendell, RP	4
M. Alexander, SS	2
B. Brown, OF	2
F. Castillo, SP	2
B. Kieschnick, OF	2
R. Sanchez, SS	2
M. Hubbard, C	1
T. Lowery, OF	1
R. Tatis, RP	1

Cincinnati (76-86)	WS
Hitting	**91.4**
Fielding	**45.9**
Pitching	**90.7**

Player	WS
J. Shaw, RP	21
W. Greene, 3B	17
R. Sanders, OF	13
B. Larkin, SS	12
J. Nunnally, OF	12
D. Sanders, OF	10
C. Stynes, OF	10
B. Tomko, SP	10
K. Mercker, SP	9
J. Oliver, C	9
M. Remlinger, RP	9
S. Sullivan, RP	9
S. Belinda, RP	8
B. Boone, 2B	8
E. Perez, 1B	8
D. Burba, SP	7
P. Reese, SS	7
E. Taubensee, C	7
M. Morgan, SP	6
M. Kelly, OF	5
C. Goodwin, OF	4
H. Morris, 1B	4
H. Carrasco, RP	3
L. Harris, OF	3
T. Pendleton, 3B	3
J. Smiley, SP	3
G. White, SP-RP	3
F. Rodriguez, RP	2
J. Branson, 3B	1
J. Brantley, RP	1
B. Fordyce, C	1
D. Jackson, SS	1
P. Schourek, SP	1
R. Sierra, OF	1

Colorado (83-79)	WS
Hitting	**123.7**
Fielding	**42.3**
Pitching	**83.0**
L. Walker, OF	32
V. Castilla, 3B	21
A. Galarraga, 1B	20
D. Bichette, OF	15
E. Burks, OF	15
R. Bailey, SP	13
W. Weiss, SS	13
E. Young, 2B	13
J. Reed, C	11
J. Dipoto, RP	10
J. Thomson, SP	10
N. Perez, SS	9
Q. McCracken, OF	8
M. DeJean, RP	7
S. Reed, RP	7
D. Holmes, RP	5
M. Munoz, RP	5
P. Astacio, SP	4
F. Castillo, SP	4
C. Leskanic, RP	4
K. Manwaring, C	4
K. Ritz, SP	4
J. McCurry, RP	3
J. Wright, SP	3
J. Bates, 2B	2
T. Helton, OF	2
B. Ruffin, RP	2
J. Burke, SP	1
H. Pulliam, OF	1
B. Swift, SP	1

Florida (92-70)	WS
Hitting	**129.0**
Fielding	**47.2**
Pitching	**99.8**
M. Alou, OF	23
K. Brown, SP	23
G. Sheffield, OF	22
B. Bonilla, 3B	21
C. Johnson, C	21
A. Fernandez, SP	16
E. Renteria, SS	15
R. Nen, RP	11
J. Conine, 1B	9
J. Powell, RP	9
D. White, OF	9
G. Zaun, C	9
K. Abbott, 2B	8
C. Counsell, 2B	8
L. Hernandez, SP	8
A. Leiter, SP	7
J. Eisenreich, OF	6
D. Cook, RP	5
D. Daulton, 1B	5
C. Floyd, OF	5
P. Rapp, SP	4
J. Cangelosi, OF	3
L. Castillo, 2B	3
R. Helling, RP	3
F. Heredia, RP	3
M. Hutton, RP	3
T. Saunders, SP	3
R. Stanifer, RP	3
T. Dunwoody, OF	2
K. Ojala, SP	2
A. Arias, 3B	1
J. Booty, 3B	1
M. Kotsay, OF	1
R. Milliard, 2B	1
R. Morman, OF	1
B. Natal, C	1
E. Vosberg, RP	1

Houston (84-78)	WS
Hitting	**125.3**
Fielding	**39.2**
Pitching	**87.5**
C. Biggio, 2B	38
J. Bagwell, 1B	32
D. Kile, SP	21
B. Spiers, 3B	18
B. Ausmus, C	13
L. Gonzalez, OF	12
D. Bell, OF	11
M. Hampton, SP	11
B. Wagner, RP	11
C. Holt, SP	10
R. Garcia, RP	9
T. Bogar, SS	7
T. Martin, RP	7
S. Reynolds, SP	7
B. Abreu, OF	6
S. Berry, 3B	5
C. Carr, OF	5
M. Magnante, RP	5
T. Eusebio, C	4
R. Gutierrez, SS	4
T. Howard, OF	3
R. Springer, RP	3
J. Cabrera, RP	2
R. Hidalgo, OF	2
R. Johnson, 3B	2
J. Lima, RP	1
P. Listach, SS	1
B. Minor, RP	1
J. Mouton, OF	1

Los Angeles (88-74)	WS
Hitting	**127.6**
Fielding	**42.8**
Pitching	**93.6**
M. Piazza, C	39
R. Mondesi, OF	24
E. Karros, 1B	18
T. Zeile, 3B	18
I. Valdes, SP	15
C. Park, SP	13
G. Gagne, SS	10
R. Cedeno, OF	9
H. Nomo, SP	9
T. Candiotti, RP	8
W. Guerrero, 2B	8
R. Martinez, SP	8
S. Radinsky, RP	8
B. Butler, OF	7
D. Dreifort, RP	7
T. Hollandsworth, OF	7
A. Osuna, RP	7
P. Astacio, SP	6
D. Hall, RP	6
T. Cromer, 2B	5
O. Nixon, OF	5
T. Worrell, RP	4
E. Young, 2B	4
D. Lewis, OF	3
T. Prince, C	3
E. Anthony, OF	2
B. Ashley, OF	2
D. Reyes, RP	2
J. Castro, SS	1
K. Garcia, OF	1
M. Guthrie, RP	1
M. Harkey, RP	1
G. Ingram, OF	1
W. Kirby, OF	1
N. Liriano, 2B	1

Montreal (78-84)	WS
Hitting	**99.8**
Fielding	**43.6**
Pitching	**90.5**
P. Martinez, SP	26
M. Lansing, 2B	21
R. White, OF	17
H. Rodriguez, OF	16
D. Segui, 1B	16
M. Grudzielanek, SS	14
C. Perez, SP	11
D. Strange, 3B	11
D. Fletcher, C	10
V. Guerrero, OF	10
D. Hermanson, SP	10
F. Santangelo, OF	10
U. Urbina, RP	10
J. Juden, SP	8
A. Telford, RP	8
M. Valdes, RP	8
D. Veres, RP	5
C. Widger, C	5
R. McGuire, OF	4
J. Vidro, 3B	3
S. Bennett, RP	2
J. Bullinger, SP	2
B. Fullmer, 1B	2
S. Andrews, 3B	1
R. DeHart, RP	1
H. Meulens, OF	1
J. Orsulak, OF	1
A. Stankiewicz, 2B	1

New York (88-74)	WS
Hitting	**131.8**
Fielding	**42.7**
Pitching	**89.4**
E. Alfonzo, 3B	28
J. Olerud, 1B	27
T. Hundley, C	22
R. Reed, SP	17
B. Gilkey, OF	16
C. Everett, OF	13
J. Franco, RP	12
B. Huskey, OF	12
C. Baerga, 2B	11
B. Jones, SP	11
L. Johnson, OF	10
G. McMichael, RP	10
D. Mlicki, SP	10
M. Clark, SP	6
C. Lidle, RP	6
R. Ordonez, SS	6
B. Bohanon, SP	5
L. Lopez, SS	5
T. Pratt, C	5
A. Reynoso, SP	5
M. Alexander, 2B	4
M. Franco, 3B	4
B. McRae, OF	4
J. Acevedo, RP	3
J. Crawford, RP	3
T. Kashiwada, RP	2
A. Ochoa, OF	2
S. Bieser, OF	1
A. Castillo, C	1
J. Hardtke, 2B	1
C. Mendoza, OF	1
M. Rojas, RP	1

Philadelphia (68-94)	WS
Hitting	**101.3**
Fielding	**34.8**
Pitching	**67.9**
S. Rolen, 3B	29
C. Schilling, SP	22
M. Morandini, 2B	16
M. Lieberthal, C	15
K. Stocker, SS	12
R. Brogna, 1B	11
D. Daulton, OF	11
R. Bottalico, RP	10
G. Jefferies, OF	10
G. Stephenson, SP	10
M. Cummings, OF	9
T. Barron, OF	4
M. Beech, SP	4
J. Spradlin, RP	4
R. Butler, OF	3
M. Grace, SP	3
T. Green, SP	3
R. Blazier, RP	2
B. Brewer, RP	2
B. Estalella, C	2
W. Gomes, RP	2
R. Harris, RP	2
K. Jordan, 1B	2
M. Leiter, SP	2
B. McMillon, OF	2
R. Otero, OF	2
R. Amaro, OF	1
R. Hudler, OF	1
W. Magee, OF	1
D. May, OF	1
M. Parent, C	1
E. Plantenberg, RP	1
D. Relaford, SS	1
M. Robertson, 1B-OF	1
K. Sefcik, 2B	1
D. Winston, RP	1

Pittsburgh (79-83)	WS
Hitting	**108.7**
Fielding	**37.9**
Pitching	**90.3**
J. Kendall, C	22
T. Womack, 2B	18
J. Randa, 3B	16
F. Cordova, SP	13
A. Martin, OF	13
K. Young, 1B	12
E. Loaiza, SP	11
R. Loiselle, RP	11
J. Lieber, SP	9
M. Smith, OF	9
T. Ward, OF	9
J. Schmidt, SP	8
M. Wilkins, RP	8
J. Allensworth, OF	7
S. Cooke, SP	7
J. Guillen, OF	7
R. Rincon, RP	7
K. Polcovich, SS	6
D. Sveum, 3B	6
K. Elster, SS	5
J. Christiansen, RP	4
S. Dunston, SS	4
M. Johnson, 1B	4
C. Sodowsky, RP	4
K. Osik, C	3
J. Ericks, RP	2
C. Peters, RP	2
J. Wallace, RP	2
A. Brown, OF	1
E. Brown, OF	1
L. Collier, SS	1
E. Dessens, RP	1
A. Nunez, SS	1
J. Silva, RP	1

P. Wagner, RP	1
E. Williams, 1B	1

San Diego (76-86)	WS
Hitting	**162.5**
Fielding	**26.2**
Pitching	**39.3**
T. Gwynn, OF	39
K. Caminiti, 3B	26
W. Joyner, 1B	21
S. Finley, OF	19
Q. Veras, 2B	15
R. Henderson, OF	14
J. Flaherty, C	11
T. Hoffman, RP	11
C. Gomez, SS	7
G. Vaughn, OF	7
A. Ashby, SP	6
J. Hamilton, SP	6
A. Cianfrocco, 1B	5
C. Jones, OF	5
M. Sweeney, OF	5
C. Hernandez, C	4
C. Shipley, SS	4
S. Hitchcock, SP	3
P. Smith, RP	3
T. Worrell, RP	3
D. Bochtler, RP	2
J. Bruske, RP	2
W. Cunnane, RP	2
D. Lee, 1B	2
T. Beamon, OF	1
P. Menhart, SP	1
R. Rivera, OF	1
M. Romero, C	1
T. Shumpert, 2B	1
F. Valenzuela, SP	1

San Francisco (90-72)	WS
Hitting	**157.8**
Fielding	**35.3**
Pitching	**77.0**
B. Bonds, OF	36
J. Snow, 1B	28
J. Kent, 2B	22
S. Javier, OF	17
J. Vizcaino, SS	17
S. Estes, SP	16
D. Hamilton, OF	15
B. Mueller, 3B	14
R. Beck, RP	12
K. Rueter, SP	12
G. Hill, OF	11
M. Lewis, 3B	9
M. Gardner, SP	8
R. Rodriguez, RP	6
J. Tavarez, RP	6
R. Aurilia, SS	5
D. Berryhill, C	5
R. Hernandez, RP	5
B. Johnson, C	5
R. Wilkins, C	4
W. Alvarez, SP	3
D. Henry, RP	3
M. Benard, OF	2
D. Powell, OF	2
W. VanLandingham, SP	2
D. Darwin, SP	1
O. Fernandez, SP	1
M. Jensen, C	1
J. Johnstone, RP	1
J. Roa, RP	1

St. Louis (73-89)	WS
Hitting	**93.6**
Fielding	**37.1**
Pitching	**88.3**
R. Lankford, OF	24
D. DeShields, 2B	21
M. Morris, SP	16
An. Benes, SP	14
R. Clayton, SS	13
Al. Benes, SP	12
R. Gant, OF	11
T. Stottlemyre, SP	11
M. McGwire, 1B	10
G. Gaetti, 3B	9
D. Eckersley, RP	8
J. Frascatore, RP	8
J. Mabry, OF	8
W. McGee, OF	7
M. DiFelice, C	6
T. Lampkin, C	5
T. Mathews, RP	5
D. Young, 1B	5
M. Aybar, SP	3
R. Beltran, RP	3
C. King, RP	3
D. Bell, 3B	2
T. Fossas, RP	2
D. Osborne, SP	2
M. Petkovsek, RP	2
P. Plantier, OF	2
M. Franklin, OF	1
M. Gallego, 2B	1
B. Jordan, OF	1
E. Marrero, C	1
L. Ordaz, SS	1
L. Painter, RP	1
D. Sheaffer, 3B	1

1998 American League

Anaheim (85-77)	WS
Hitting	**119.0**
Fielding	**43.0**
Pitching	**93.0**
J. Edmonds, OF	24
T. Salmon, DH	22
D. Erstad, OF	21
G. Anderson, OF	18
C. Finley, SP	17
G. DiSarcina, SS	15
T. Percival, RP	12
S. Hasegawa, RP	11
O. Olivares, SP	11
D. Hollins, 3B	9
M. Walbeck, C	9
C. Fielder, 1B	8
S. Sparks, SP	8
R. Velarde, 2B	8
R. DeLucia, RP	5
K. Hill, SP	5
O. Palmeiro, OF	5
P. Harris, RP	4
J. Washburn, SP	4
J. Baughman, 2B	3
G. Cadaret, RP	3
T. Glaus, 3B	3
G. Jefferies, OF	3
N. Martin, 2B	3
J. McDowell, SP	3
C. Shipley, 3B	3
J. Dickson, SP	2
M. Holtz, RP	2
M. James, RP	2
D. Mashore, OF	2
P. Nevin, C	2
A. Watson, SP-RP	2
R. Williams, OF	2
C. Garcia, 2B	1
T. Greene, OF	1
C. Pritchett, 1B	1
T. Wilson, RP	1

Baltimore (79-83)	WS
Hitting	**121.9**
Fielding	**35.5**
Pitching	**79.6**
R. Palmeiro, 1B	24
R. Alomar, 2B	19
E. Davis, OF	18
S. Erickson, SP	15
M. Mussina, SP	15
B. Anderson, OF	13
M. Bordick, SS	13
C. Ripken Jr., 3B	13
B. Surhoff, OF	13
C. Hoiles, C	12
A. Benitez, RP	10
H. Baines, DH	8
A. Mills, RP	7
J. Orosco, RP	7
A. Rhodes, RP	7
L. Webster, C	7
J. Hammonds, OF	6
J. Key, RP	5
S. Ponson, SP	5
J. Guzman, SP	4
D. Johns, RP	4
J. Carter, OF	3
R. Becker, OF	2
L. Mouton, OF	2
J. Reboulet, 2B-SS	2
R. Coppinger, RP	1
W. Greene, OF	1
P. Smith, RP	1

Boston (92-70)	WS
Hitting	**129.0**
Fielding	**46.2**
Pitching	**100.8**
N. Garciaparra, SS	27
M. Vaughn, 1B	25
P. Martinez, SP	21
J. Valentin, 3B	19
F. Gordon, RP	17
D. Lewis, OF	17
T. O'Leary, OF	14
B. Saberhagen, SP	12
D. Bragg, OF	11
S. Hatteberg, C	11
T. Wakefield, SP	11
D. Buford, OF	9
M. Benjamin, 2B	8
J. Corsi, RP	7
D. Lowe, RP	7
M. Stanley, DH	7
R. Jefferson, DH	6
S. Avery, SP	5
J. Varitek, C	5
R. Garces, RP	4
L. Merloni, 2B	4
J. Wasdin, RP	4
M. Cummings, DH	3
D. Eckersley, RP	3
J. Leyritz, DH	3
C. Reyes, RP	3
D. Sadler, 2B	3
R. Mahay, RP	2
P. Schourek, SP	2
G. Swindell, RP	2
B. Ashley, DH	1
M. Lemke, 2B	1
K. Mitchell, DH	1
C. Valdez, RP	1

Chicago (80-82)	WS
Hitting	**146.5**
Fielding	**32.7**
Pitching	**60.8**
A. Belle, OF	37
R. Durham, 2B	25
F. Thomas, DH	25
R. Ventura, 3B	21
M. Caruso, SS	13
M. Ordonez, OF	13
B. Simas, RP	10
W. Cordero, 1B	8
Je. Abbott, OF	7
B. Howry, RP	7
C. Kreuter, C	7
M. Sirotka, SP	7
J. Baldwin, SP	6
M. Cameron, OF	6
K. Foulke, RP	5
C. Wilson, SS	5
C. Castillo, RP	4
G. Norton, 1B	4
C. O'Brien, C	4
J. Parque, SP	4
J. Snyder, SP	4
C. Bradford, RP	3
M. Karchner, RP	3
Ji. Abbott, SP	2
S. Eyre, SP	2
B. Simmons, OF	2
B. Ward, RP	2
R. Machado, C	1
J. Navarro, SP	1
R. Sierra, OF	1
C. Snopek, SS	1

Cleveland (89-73)	WS
Hitting	**116.6**
Fielding	**46.6**
Pitching	**103.8**
M. Ramirez, OF	25
K. Lofton, OF	21
J. Thome, 1B	19
T. Fryman, 3B	18
O. Vizquel, SS	18
B. Colon, SP	16
M. Jackson, RP	16
D. Burba, SP	15
B. Giles, OF	14
D. Justice, DH	13
J. Wright, SP	11
D. Gooden, SP	10
C. Nagy, SP	9
D. Bell, 2B	8
S. Alomar Jr., C	6
P. Shuey, RP	6
M. Whiten, OF	6
P. Assenmacher, RP	5
R. Sexson, 1B	5
D. Jones, RP	3
C. Ogea, RP	3
E. Plunk, RP	3
E. Wilson, 2B	3
S. Dunston, 2B	2
R. Krivda, RP	2
J. Mesa, RP	2
G. Berroa, OF	1
P. Borders, C	1
J. Branson, 2B	1
J. Cora, 2B	1
E. Diaz, C	1
A. Morman, RP	1
S. Reed, RP	1
R. Villone, RP	1

Detroit (65-97)	WS
Hitting	**82.9**
Fielding	**35.0**
Pitching	**77.1**
D. Easley, 2B	23
B. Moehler, SP	17
B. Higginson, OF	16
T. Clark, 1B	15
J. Thompson, SP	14
L. Gonzalez, OF	12
B. Hunter, OF	9
J. Randa, 3B	9
D. Brocail, RP	8
D. Cruz, SS	7
B. Florie, RP	7
T. Jones, RP	7
S. Greisinger, SP	6
M. Anderson, RP	5
P. Bako, C	5
F. Catalanotto, 2B	4
J. Encarnacion, OF	4
S. Runyan, RP	4
G. Alvarez, 3B	3
D. Crow, RP	3
R. Fick, C	2
B. Roberts, DH	2
K. Bartee, OF	1
G. Berroa, DH	1

D. Bochtler, RP	1
W. Brunson, RP	1
G. Keagle, SP	1
J. Oliver, C	1
B. Powell, SP	1
B. Ripken, SS	1
A. Sager, RP	1
M. Santana, RP	1
J. Siddall, C	1
A. Tomberlin, DH	1
T. Worrell, SP	1

Kansas City (72-89)	WS
Hitting	**92.0**
Fielding	**40.9**
Pitching	**83.0**
J. Offerman, 2B	29
T. Belcher, SP	17
J. Damon, OF	17
J. King, 1B	12
D. Palmer, 3B	12
S. Service, RP	11
J. Rosado, SP	10
P. Rapp, SP	9
J. Montgomery, RP	8
M. Sweeney, C	8
S. Fasano, C	7
R. Bones, RP	6
J. Conine, OF	6
S. Mack, OF	6
H. Pichardo, SP	6
L. Sutton, OF	6
M. Lopez, SS	5
H. Morris, 1B	5
G. Rusch, SP	5
M. Whisenant, RP	5
S. Halter, SS	3
L. Rivera, SS	3
C. Beltran, OF	2
J. Dye, OF	2
C. Febles, 2B	2
F. Martinez, SS	2
T. Pendleton, DH	2
T. Spehr, C	2
J. Suppan, RP	2
J. Allensworth, OF	1
B. Barber, SP	1
B. Bevil, RP	1
B. Evans, RP	1
C. Haney, RP	1
E. Young, OF	1

Minnesota (70-92)	WS
Hitting	**84.0**
Fielding	**39.3**
Pitching	**86.7**
M. Lawton, OF	21
T. Walker, 2B	19
B. Radke, SP	14
R. Aguilera, RP	12
P. Meares, SS	11
P. Molitor, DH	10
T. Steinbach, C	10
D. Ortiz, 1B	9
M. Trombley, RP	9
M. Cordova, OF	8
B. Gates, 3B	8
M. Morgan, SP	8
O. Nixon, OF	8
B. Tewksbury, SP	8
G. Swindell, RP	7
R. Coomer, 3B	6
L. Hawkins, SP	6
E. Milton, SP	6
H. Carrasco, RP	5
E. Guardado, RP	5
O. Merced, 1B	4
A. Ochoa, OF	3
D. Hocking, 2B	2
B. Sampson, RP	2
D. Serafini, RP	2
J. Valentin, C	2
T. Baptist, RP	1
T. Miller, RP	1
D. Naulty, RP	1
A. Pierzynski, C	1
J. Shave, 3B	1

New York (114-48)	WS
Hitting	**171.5**
Fielding	**51.6**
Pitching	**118.9**
S. Brosius, 3B	27
D. Jeter, SS	27
B. Williams, OF	27
P. O'Neill, OF	26
C. Knoblauch, 2B	22
T. Martinez, 1B	21
D. Wells, SP	18
D. Cone, SP	17
J. Posada, C	15
C. Curtis, OF	14
M. Rivera, RP	14
O. Hernandez, SP	13
A. Pettitte, SP	13
H. Irabu, SP	12
R. Mendoza, RP	12
T. Raines, DH	11
D. Strawberry, DH	11
J. Girardi, C	7
S. Spencer, OF	6
G. Lloyd, RP	5
D. Holmes, RP	4
J. Nelson, RP	4
M. Stanton, RP	4
H. Bush, 2B	3
C. Davis, DH	2
R. Ledee, OF	2
R. Bradley, RP	1
J. Bruske, RP	1
M. Buddie, RP	1
L. Sojo, SS	1
J. Tessmer, RP	1

Oakland (74-88)	WS
Hitting	**123.5**
Fielding	**31.5**
Pitching	**67.0**
J. Giambi, 1B	23
B. Grieve, OF	22
R. Henderson, OF	20
M. Stairs, DH	20
K. Rogers, SP	19
M. Blowers, 3B	10
S. Spiezio, 2B	10
B. Taylor, RP	10
R. Christenson, OF	9
T. Candiotti, SP	8
J. Haynes, SP	7
M. Tejada, SS	7
A. Hinch, C	5
M. Macfarlane, C	5
D. Magadan, 3B	5
T. Mathews, RP	5
B. Roberts, 2B	5
M. Fetters, RP	4
B. Groom, RP	4
G. Heredia, SP	4
J. McDonald, OF	4
K. Abbott, SS	2
R. Bournigal, 2B	2
E. Chavez, 3B	2
K. Mitchell, DH	2
M. Mohler, RP	2
M. Oquist, SP	2
T. Worrell, RP	2
E. Sprague, 3B	1
D. Telgheder, RP	1

Seattle (76-85)	WS
Hitting	**126.1**
Fielding	**32.5**
Pitching	**69.4**
A. Rodriguez, SS	30
K. Griffey Jr., OF	29
E. Martinez, DH	24
J. Moyer, SP	18
D. Segui, 1B	15
J. Fassero, SP	14
M. Timlin, RP	12
R. Davis, 3B	11
J. Cora, 2B	10
J. Buhner, OF	8
R. Johnson, SP	8
D. Wilson, C	7
R. Ducey, OF	4
G. Hill, OF	4
B. Swift, SP	4
J. Marzano, C	3
J. Paniagua, RP	3
H. Slocumb, RP	3
P. Abbott, SP	2
R. Amaral, OF	2
D. Bell, 2B	2
K. Cloude, SP	2
C. Guillen, 2B	2
S. Monahan, OF	2
C. Gipson, OF	1
R. Ibanez, OF	1
F. Lira, RP	1
G. McCarthy, RP	1
D. McCarty, OF	1
J. Oliver, C	1
R. Rossy, 3B	1
P. Spoljaric, RP	1
B. Wells, RP	1

Tampa Bay (63-99)	WS
Hitting	**46.6**
Fielding	**47.3**
Pitching	**95.2**
R. Arrojo, SP	17
F. McGriff, 1B	13
Q. McCracken, OF	12
T. Saunders, SP	12
M. Cairo, 2B	10
R. Hernandez, RP	10
A. Lopez, RP	9
J. Mecir, RP	9
J. Santana, SP	8
B. Smith, 3B	8
W. Alvarez, SP	7
A. Ledesma, SS	7
E. Yan, RP	7
W. Boggs, 3B	6
M. DiFelice, C	5
J. Flaherty, C	5
K. Stocker, SS	5
R. White, RP	5
R. Winn, OF	5
P. Sorrento, DH	4
B. Trammell, OF	4
S. Aldred, RP	3
M. Kelly, OF	3
D. Martinez, OF	3
B. Rekar, SP	3
D. Springer, SP	3
R. Butler, OF	2
J. Johnson, SP	2
R. Gorecki, SP	1
T. Wade, SP	1

Texas (88-74)	WS
Hitting	**143.1**
Fielding	**35.5**
Pitching	**85.4**
I. Rodriguez, C	27
J. Gonzalez, OF	25
W. Clark, 1B	19
R. Greer, OF	19
R. Helling, SP	15
J. Wetteland, RP	15
A. Sele, SP	14
T. Goodwin, OF	13
M. McLemore, 2B	12
L. Alicea, 2B	9
R. Kelly, OF	8
M. Simms, OF	8
L. Stevens, DH	8
J. Burkett, SP	7
T. Crabtree, RP	7
K. Elster, SS	7
X. Hernandez, RP	6
T. Zeile, 3B	6
R. Clayton, SS	5
B. Haselman, C	5
D. Patterson, RP	5
T. Stottlemyre, SP	4
F. Tatis, 3B	4
E. Gunderson, RP	3
A. Levine, RP	3
D. Cedeno, SS	2
E. Loaiza, SP	2
D. Oliver, SP	2
S. Bailes, RP	1
M. Cuyler, DH-OF	1
T. Fossas, RP	1
R. Pavlik, RP	1

Toronto (88-74)	WS
Hitting	**115.7**
Fielding	**46.1**
Pitching	**102.2**
R. Clemens, SP	25
C. Delgado, 1B	24
S. Green, OF	21
T. Fernandez, 2B	19
S. Stewart, OF	18
J. Canseco, DH	15
J. Cruz, OF	12
W. Williams, SP	12
C. Carpenter, SP	11
D. Fletcher, C	11
P. Quantrill, RP	11
A. Gonzalez, SS	9
P. Hentgen, SP	8
M. Stanley, DH	8
K. Escobar, RP	7
C. Grebeck, 2B	7
J. Guzman, SP	7
D. Plesac, RP	7
R. Myers, RP	6
E. Sprague, 3B	5
F. Crespo, OF	4
K. Brown, C	3
T. Phillips, OF	3
M. Dalesandro, C	2
R. Halladay, SP	2
B. Risley, RP	2
D. Stieb, RP	2
C. Almanzar, RP	1
B. Santiago, C	1
S. Sinclair, RP	1

1998 National League

Arizona (65-97)	WS
Hitting	**91.0**
Fielding	**35.6**
Pitching	**68.4**
J. Bell, SS	20
D. White, OF	18
A. Fox, 2B	15
A. Benes, SP	14
T. Lee, 1B	13
O. Daal, SP	12
G. Olson, RP	12
M. Williams, 3B	12
T. Batista, 2B	10
D. Dellucci, OF	10
K. Stinnett, C	10
B. Anderson, SP	9
D. Miller, C	6
A. Telemaco, SP	6
K. Garcia, OF	4
W. Banks, RP	3
B. Brede, OF	3
A. Embree, RP	3
W. Blair, SP	2
B. Chouinard, RP	2
J. Fabregas, C	2
A. Small, RP	2
R. Springer, RP	2
Y. Benitez, OF	1

B. Gilkey, OF	1
F. Rodriguez, RP	1
C. Sodowsky, RP	1
A. Stankiewicz, 2B	1

Atlanta (106-56)	WS
Hitting	**146.2**
Fielding	**48.9**
Pitching	**122.9**
C. Jones, 3B	29
A. Galarraga, 1B	27
A. Jones, OF	26
J. Lopez, C	25
G. Maddux, SP	25
T. Glavine, SP	23
J. Smoltz, SP	16
K. Ligtenberg, RP	15
D. Neagle, SP	14
R. Klesko, OF	13
W. Weiss, SS	12
G. Williams, OF	12
M. Tucker, OF	11
K. Lockhart, 2B	10
K. Millwood, SP	10
E. Perez, C	10
O. Guillen, SS	7
J. Rocker, RP	5
R. Seanez, RP	5
T. Graffanino, 2B	4
D. Martinez, RP	4
D. Bautista, OF	2
M. Cather, RP	2
N. Charlton, RP	2
G. Colbrunn, 1B	2
C. Pride, OF	2
B. Chen, SP	1
W. Helms, 3B	1
M. Malloy, 2B	1
O. Perez, RP	1
R. Springer, RP	1

Chicago (90-73)	WS
Hitting	**146.9**
Fielding	**37.7**
Pitching	**85.4**
S. Sosa, OF	35
M. Grace, 1B	27
M. Morandini, 2B	23
J. Hernandez, 3B	16
H. Rodriguez, OF	16
K. Wood, SP	14
R. Beck, RP	13
B. Brown, OF	13
S. Trachsel, SP	13
T. Mulholland, RP	12
K. Tapani, SP	11
G. Gaetti, 3B	8
M. Clark, SP	7
G. Hill, OF	7
T. Houston, C	7
J. Blauser, SS	6
L. Johnson, OF	6
T. Adams, RP	5
S. Servais, C	4
M. Alexander, SS	3
M. Mieske, OF	3
J. Gonzalez, SP	2
F. Heredia, RP	2
S. Martinez, C	2
K. Orie, 3B	2
M. Pisciotta, RP	2
D. Stevens, RP	2
A. Telemaco, RP	2
J. Hardtke, 3B	1
M. Karchner, RP	1
J. Maxwell, 2B	1
K. Miller, RP	1
M. Morgan, SP	1
B. VanRyn, RP	1
D. Wengert, RP	1

Cincinnati (77-85)	WS
Hitting	**112.0**
Fielding	**39.6**
Pitching	**79.4**
B. Larkin, SS	25
B. Boone, 2B	18
P. Harnisch, SP	16
E. Taubensee, C	16
D. Young, OF	16
R. Sanders, OF	14
W. Greene, 3B	13
S. Casey, 1B	10
J. Shaw, RP	10
B. Tomko, SP	9
D. Graves, RP	8
G. White, RP	8
A. Boone, 3B	6
S. Parris, SP	6
S. Belinda, RP	5
M. Remlinger, SP	5
C. Stynes, OF	5
J. Hudek, RP	4
J. Nunnally, OF	4
E. Perez, 1B	4
J. Hammonds, OF	3
P. Reese, 3B	3
S. Sullivan, RP	3
J. Bere, SP	2
B. Fordyce, C	2
M. Frank, OF	2
D. Jackson, SS	2
M. Nieves, OF	2
R. Petagine, 1B-OF	2
D. Reyes, SP	2
P. Watkins, OF	2
S. Cooke, SP	1
K. Glauber, RP	1
L. Harris, OF	1
P. Konerko, 3B	1

Colorado (77-85)	WS
Hitting	**86.3**
Fielding	**47.4**
Pitching	**97.3**
V. Castilla, 3B	21
D. Bichette, OF	17
T. Helton, 1B	17
L. Walker, OF	17
J. Dipoto, RP	13
D. Kile, SP	13
N. Perez, SS	12
M. Lansing, 2B	11
D. Veres, RP	11
C. McElroy, RP	10
M. DeJean, RP	9
J. Thomson, SP	9
E. Burks, OF	8
J. Reed, C	8
J. Wright, SP	8
D. Hamilton, OF	7
B. Jones, SP	7
C. Leskanic, RP	7
P. Astacio, SP	6
K. Manwaring, C	4
J. Vander Wal, OF	3
G. Colbrunn, 1B	2
C. Goodwin, OF	2
M. Munoz, RP	2
K. Abbott, OF	1
M. Brownson, SP	1
A. Echevarria, 1B-OF	1
D. Gibson, OF	1
F. Rath, RP	1
J. Stoops, RP	1
D. Wainhouse, RP	1

Florida (54-108)	WS
Hitting	**104.8**
Fielding	**22.9**
Pitching	**34.3**
C. Floyd, OF	18
C. Counsell, 2B	13
M. Kotsay, OF	13
E. Renteria, SS	11
D. Lee, 1B	10
T. Zeile, 3B	10
D. Berg, 2B	9
G. Sheffield, OF	8
T. Dunwoody, OF	6
L. Hernandez, SP	6
M. Mantei, RP	5
K. Orie, 3B	5
R. Jackson, 1B	4
B. Meadows, SP	4
M. Redmond, C	4
J. Sanchez, SP	4
A. Alfonseca, RP	3
L. Castillo, 2B	3
V. Darensbourg, RP	3
B. Edmondson, RP	3
C. Johnson, C	3
K. Ojala, RP	3
G. Zaun, C	3
B. Bonilla, 3B	2
J. Cangelosi, OF	2
J. Powell, RP	2
A. Gonzalez, SS	1
F. Heredia, RP	1
R. Knorr, C	1
D. Pall, RP	1
R. Stanifer, RP	1

Houston (102-60)	WS
Hitting	**154.7**
Fielding	**44.2**
Pitching	**107.1**
C. Biggio, 2B	35
M. Alou, OF	29
J. Bagwell, 1B	29
D. Bell, OF	22
C. Everett, OF	16
S. Reynolds, SP	16
M. Hampton, SP	15
B. Ausmus, C	14
J. Lima, SP	14
B. Spiers, 3B	13
S. Berry, 3B	12
R. Gutierrez, SS	12
Ra. Johnson, SP	11
B. Wagner, RP	11
S. Bergman, SP	9
D. Henry, RP	7
R. Hidalgo, OF	6
S. Elarton, RP	5
T. Eusebio, C	5
J. Powell, RP	5
T. Miller, RP	4
C. Nitkowski, RP	4
T. Bogar, SS	3
P. Schourek, SP	3
M. Magnante, RP	2
B. Scanlan, RP	2
J. Howell, 1B	1
J. Phillips, 1B	1

Los Angeles (83-79)	WS
Hitting	**115.0**
Fielding	**40.2**
Pitching	**93.8**
E. Karros, 1B	22
G. Sheffield, OF	22
R. Mondesi, OF	20
E. Young, 2B	17
C. Park, SP	13
C. Johnson, C	12
D. Dreifort, SP	9
M. Piazza, C	9
I. Valdes, SP	9
B. Bohanon, SP	8
R. Martinez, SP	8
A. Osuna, RP	8
S. Radinsky, RP	8
J. Vizcaino, SS	8
T. Hollandsworth, OF	6
T. Hubbard, OF	6
D. Mlicki, SP	6
J. Shaw, RP	6
M. Luke, OF	5
C. Perez, SP	5
T. Zeile, 3B	5
A. Beltre, 3B	4
J. Bruske, RP	4
M. Grudzielanek, SS	4
B. Bonilla, 3B	3
J. Castro, SS	3
R. Cedeno, OF	3
M. Guthrie, RP	3
J. Kubenka, RP	2
T. Prince, C	2
E. Weaver, RP	2
B. Clontz, RP	1
A. Cora, SS	1
W. Guerrero, 2B	1
T. Howard, OF	1
P. Konerko, 1B	1
G. McMichael, RP	1
H. Nomo, SP	1

Milwaukee (74-88)	WS
Hitting	**109.2**
Fielding	**40.7**
Pitching	**72.0**
F. Vina, 2B	30
J. Cirillo, 3B	26
J. Burnitz, OF	19
M. Loretta, 1B	16
J. Valentin, SS	15
M. Grissom, OF	11
B. Wickman, RP	11
D. Nilsson, 1B	10
S. Woodard, SP	9
S. Karl, SP	8
M. Myers, RP	6
J. Jaha, 1B	5
B. Woodall, SP	5
C. Fox, RP	4
M. Matheny, C	4
M. Newfield, OF	4
B. Patrick, RP	4
A. Reyes, RP	4
D. Weathers, RP	4
C. Eldred, SP	3
B. Hughes, C	3
D. Jackson, OF	3
D. Jones, RP	3
B. Pulsipher, SP	3
V. de los Santos, RP	2
J. Juden, SP	2
E. Plunk, RP	2
R. Roque, SP	2
B. Banks, C	1
B. Hamelin, 1B	1
G. Jenkins, OF	1
J. Levis, C	1

Montreal (65-97)	WS
Hitting	**94.0**
Fielding	**30.8**
Pitching	**70.2**
V. Guerrero, OF	29
U. Urbina, RP	17
R. White, OF	16
B. Fullmer, 1B	15
S. Andrews, 3B	13
D. Hermanson, SP	13
C. Widger, C	10
M. Grudzielanek, SS	9
C. Perez, SP	8
M. Batista, RP	6
O. Cabrera, SS	6
W. Guerrero, 2B	6
S. Kline, RP	6
C. Pavano, SP	6
F. Santangelo, OF	6
B. Henley, C	5
A. Telford, RP	5
M. Maddux, RP	4
T. Jones, OF	3
S. Bennett, RP	2
T. Moore, SP	2
M. Thurman, SP	2
J. Vidro, 2B	2
M. Barrett, C-3B	1
D. May, OF	1
R. McGuire, 1B	1
M. Mordecai, SS	1

New York (88-74)	WS
Hitting	**112.8**
Fielding	**48.7**
Pitching	**102.6**
J. Olerud, 1B	34
M. Piazza, C	24
E. Alfonzo, 3B	22
A. Leiter, SP	21
B. McRae, OF	20
R. Reed, SP	16
B. Jones, SP	11
C. Baerga, 2B	10
T. Wendell, RP	10
D. Cook, RP	9
R. Ordonez, SS	9
M. Yoshii, SP	9
J. Franco, RP	8
B. Huskey, OF	7
B. Bohanon, RP	5
B. Gilkey, OF	5
L. Lopez, 2B	5
A. Reynoso, SP	5
T. Phillips, OF	4
R. Becker, OF	3
W. Blair, RP	3
A. Castillo, C	3
M. Franco, 3B-OF	3
G. McMichael, RP	3
H. Nomo, SP	3
L. Harris, OF	2
T. Pratt, C	2
T. Spehr, C	2
R. Beltran, RP	1
J. Hudek, RP	1
T. Hundley, OF	1
M. Rojas, RP	1
J. Tatum, 1B	1
P. Wilson, OF	1
G. Bennett, C	1
B. Estalella, C	1
C. Loewer, SP	1
M. Parent, C	1
K. Ryan, RP	1
J. Zuber, OF	1

Philadelphia (75-87)	WS
Hitting	**102.7**
Fielding	**40.5**
Pitching	**81.8**
S. Rolen, 3B	30
B. Abreu, OF	26
C. Schilling, SP	22
D. Glanville, OF	17
R. Brogna, 1B	15
M. Leiter, RP	14
G. Jefferies, OF	11
M. Portugal, SP	10
M. Lewis, 2B	8
M. Lieberthal, C	8
J. Spradlin, RP	8
P. Byrd, SP	7
W. Gomes, RP	7
K. Sefcik, OF	7
T. Green, SP	5
D. Relaford, SS	5
Y. Perez, RP	4
A. Arias, SS	3
K. Jordan, 1B	3
M. Anderson, 2B	2
M. Beech, SP	2
M. Grace, SP	2
W. Magee, OF	2
R. Amaro, OF	1

Pittsburgh (69-93)	WS
Hitting	**77.8**
Fielding	**39.4**
Pitching	**89.8**
J. Kendall, C	26
T. Womack, 2B	17
F. Cordova, SP	15
K. Young, 1B	13
J. Guillen, OF	11
J. Schmidt, SP	11
C. Peters, SP	10
J. Christiansen, RP	9
R. Rincon, RP	9
T. Ward, OF	9
J. Allensworth, OF	8
L. Collier, SS	8
J. Lieber, SP	8
M. Williams, RP	7
R. Loiselle, RP	6
F. Garcia, 3B	5
A. Martin, OF	5
E. Loaiza, SP	4
J. Silva, SP	4
J. Tabaka, RP	4
M. Martinez, OF	3
K. Polcovich, SS	3
A. Brown, OF	2
A. Ramirez, 3B	2
E. Dessens, RP	1
T. Laker, 1B	1
A. Nunez, SS	1
K. Osik, C	1
M. Smith, OF	1
D. Strange, 3B	1
T. Van Poppel, RP	1
M. Wilkins, RP	1

San Diego (98-64)	WS
Hitting	**147.4**
Fielding	**42.8**
Pitching	**103.8**
G. Vaughn, OF	30
K. Brown, SP	26
Q. Veras, 2B	23
W. Joyner, 1B	22
K. Caminiti, 3B	20
T. Hoffman, RP	20
T. Gwynn, OF	19
A. Ashby, SP	15
S. Finley, OF	15
C. Gomez, SS	15
C. Hernandez, C	10
A. Sheets, SS	10
S. Hitchcock, SP	9
J. Hamilton, SP	8
D. Miceli, RP	8
D. Wall, RP	8
J. Leyritz, C	6
R. Rivera, OF	6
B. Boehringer, RP	4
E. Giovanola, 3B	4
G. Myers, C	4
M. Sweeney, OF	3
C. Reyes, RP	2
P. Smith, SP	2
G. Arias, 3B	1
M. Clement, SP-RP	1
S. Sanders, RP	1
S. Spencer, SP	1
J. Vander Wal, OF	1

San Francisco (89-74)	WS
Hitting	**150.6**
Fielding	**37.4**
Pitching	**79.0**
B. Bonds, OF	34
J. Kent, 2B	25
R. Nen, RP	19
B. Mueller, 3B	18
R. Aurilia, SS	13
J. Snow, 1B	13
D. Hamilton, OF	12
S. Javier, OF	12
C. Hayes, 3B	11
M. Benard, OF	10
M. Gardner, SP	9
B. Mayne, C	9
K. Rueter, SP	8
R. Sanchez, SS	8
O. Hershiser, SP	7
B. Johnson, C	7
J. Johnstone, RP	7
S. Reed, RP	7
E. Burks, OF	6
J. Carter, OF	6
R. Rodriguez, RP	5
J. Tavarez, RP	5
S. Estes, SP	3
J. Mesa, RP	3
R. Ortiz, SP	3
A. Rios, OF	2
C. Brock, RP	1
D. Darwin, SP	1
S. Dunston, SS	1
D. Mirabelli, C	1
D. Powell, OF	1

St. Louis (83-79)	WS
Hitting	**132.9**
Fielding	**35.0**
Pitching	**81.1**
M. McGwire, 1B	41
R. Lankford, OF	27
B. Jordan, OF	21
D. DeShields, 2B	15
J. Acevedo, RP	13
R. Gant, OF	11
M. Morris, SP	10
T. Stottlemyre, SP	10
G. Gaetti, 3B	8
R. Clayton, SS	7
K. Bottenfield, RP	6
E. Marrero, C	6
J. Brantley, RP	5
J. Frascatore, RP	5
T. Lampkin, C	5
J. Mabry, OF	5
K. Mercker, SP	5
M. Petkovsek, RP	5
F. Tatis, 3B	5
C. King, RP	4
D. Osborne, SP	4
L. Painter, RP	4
M. Busby, RP	3
R. Croushore, RP	3
J. Drew, OF	3
W. McGee, OF	3
D. Howard, 2B	2
J. Jimenez, SP	2
P. Kelly, 2B	2
D. Oliver, SP	2
L. Ordaz, SS	2
P. Polanco, SS	2
M. Aybar, SP	1
T. Pagnozzi, C	1
B. Witt, RP	1

1999
American League

Anaheim (70-92)	WS
Hitting	**79.0**
Fielding	**41.9**
Pitching	**89.1**
M. Vaughn, 1B	19
G. Anderson, OF	16
T. Glaus, 3B	16
C. Finley, SP	14
T. Salmon, OF	14
R. Velarde, 2B	14
T. Percival, RP	11
O. Olivares, SP	10
D. Erstad, 1B	9
M. Petkovsek, RP	9
K. Hill, SP	7
A. Levine, RP	7
M. Magnante, RP	7
O. Palmeiro, OF	6
J. Edmonds, OF	5
S. Hasegawa, RP	5
L. Pote, RP	5
S. Sparks, SP	5
M. Walbeck, C	4
T. Greene, DH	3
B. Molina, C	3
J. Washburn, SP	3
B. Cooper, SP	2
G. DiSarcina, SS	2
M. Fyhrie, RP	2
J. Huson, 2B	2
T. Belcher, SP	1
S. Decker, C	1
T. Durrington, 2B	1
M. Luke, OF	1
C. O'Brien, C	1
R. Ortiz, SP	1
S. Schoeneweis, RP	1
A. Sheets, SS	1
T. Unroe, OF	1
R. Williams, OF	1

Baltimore (78-84)	WS
Hitting	**115.7**
Fielding	**41.4**
Pitching	**76.9**
A. Belle, OF	24
B. Anderson, OF	23
M. Bordick, SS	17
M. Mussina, SP	17
B. Surhoff, OF	17
H. Baines, DH	13
S. Erickson, SP	12
C. Johnson, C	12
C. Ripken Jr., 3B	12
J. Conine, 1B	10
S. Ponson, SP	10
M. Timlin, RP	9
W. Clark, 1B	8
D. DeShields, 2B	7
J. Guzman, SP	7
J. Hairston Jr., 2B	5
D. Johns, RP	5
J. Johnson, SP	4
S. Kamieniecki, RP	3
R. Amaral, OF	2
J. Reboulet, 3B	2
A. Reyes, RP	2
A. Rhodes, RP	2
B. Ryan, RP	2
R. Bones, RP	1
J. Corsi, RP	1
M. Fetters, RP	1
M. Figga, C	1
G. Kingsale, OF	1
D. Linton, SP	1
D. May, DH	1
R. Minor, 3B	1
J. Orosco, RP	1

Boston (94-68)	WS
Hitting	**113.2**
Fielding	**48.9**
Pitching	**119.9**
N. Garciaparra, SS	32
P. Martinez, SP	27
D. Lowe, RP	19
J. Offerman, 2B	19
T. O'Leary, OF	19
B. Daubach, 1B	14
M. Stanley, 1B	14
B. Saberhagen, SP	12
J. Valentin, 3B	12
J. Varitek, C	12
T. Nixon, OF	10
P. Rapp, SP	9
T. Wakefield, RP	8
R. Garces, RP	7
D. Lewis, OF	7
J. Wasdin, RP	7
D. Buford, OF	6
R. Cormier, RP	5
M. Portugal, SP	5
B. Rose, SP	5
S. Hatteberg, C	4
R. Beck, RP	3
J. Frye, 2B	3
B. Huskey, DH	3
B. Florie, RP	2

F. Gordon, RP	2
M. Guthrie, RP	2
R. Martinez, SP	2
K. Mercker, SP	2
L. Merloni, SS	2
J. Pena, SP	2
J. Cho, SP	1
J. Corsi, RP	1
C. Gubanich, C	1
R. Jefferson, DH	1
D. Sadler, SS	1
W. Veras, 3B	1

Chicago (75-86)	**WS**
Hitting	**105.7**
Fielding	**39.1**
Pitching	**80.2**
R. Durham, 2B	20
M. Ordonez, OF	20
C. Singleton, OF	18
K. Foulke, RP	16
F. Thomas, DH	16
P. Konerko, 1B	14
M. Sirotka, SP	13
B. Fordyce, C	12
G. Norton, 3B	11
B. Howry, RP	10
C. Lee, OF	10
J. Baldwin, SP	9
S. Lowe, RP	8
J. Parque, SP	7
B. Simas, RP	6
C. Wilson, 3B	6
M. Caruso, SS	5
M. Johnson, C	5
L. Rodriguez, 2B	3
K. Wells, SP	3
C. Castillo, RP	2
D. Jackson, OF	2
J. Navarro, SP	2
B. Simmons, OF	2
M. Christensen, OF	1
P. Daneker, SP	1
J. Liefer, OF	1
J. Snyder, SP	1
T. Sturtze, SP	1

Cleveland (97-65)	**WS**
Hitting	**160.2**
Fielding	**40.8**
Pitching	**90.0**
R. Alomar, 2B	35
M. Ramirez, OF	35
J. Thome, 1B	26
O. Vizquel, SS	22
B. Colon, SP	16
D. Justice, OF	16
K. Lofton, OF	16
D. Burba, SP	15
M. Jackson, RP	11
C. Nagy, SP	11
R. Sexson, 1B	10
P. Shuey, RP	10
S. Karsay, RP	9
E. Diaz, C	8
T. Fryman, 3B	7
W. Cordero, OF	5
S. Alomar Jr., C	4
S. Reed, RP	4
J. Cruz, OF	3
D. Gooden, SP	3
R. Rincon, RP	3
E. Wilson, 3B	3
J. Wright, SP	3
H. Baines, DH	2
J. Brower, RP	2
C. Haney, RP	2
M. Langston, RP	2
A. Ramirez, OF	2
D. Roberts, OF	2
C. Baerga, 3B	1
R. Branyan, 3B	1
S. DePaula, RP	1
J. Manto, 3B	1

Detroit (69-92)	**WS**
Hitting	**90.8**
Fielding	**37.7**
Pitching	**78.4**
T. Clark, 1B	19
B. Ausmus, C	17
D. Palmer, 3B	17
D. Cruz, SS	13
D. Easley, 2B	13
D. Brocail, RP	12
D. Mlicki, SP	12
T. Jones, RP	10
B. Moehler, SP	10
L. Polonia, DH	10
B. Higginson, OF	9
J. Encarnacion, OF	8
G. Kapler, OF	8
J. Thompson, SP	7
J. Weaver, SP	7
C. Nitkowski, RP	6
F. Catalanotto, 1B-2B	5
K. Garcia, OF	4
B. Florie, RP	3
B. Haselman, C	3
F. Cordero, RP	2
N. Cruz, RP	2
R. Fick, DH	2
M. Kida, RP	2
M. Anderson, RP	1
K. Bartee, OF	1
W. Blair, RP	1
D. Borkowski, SP	1
B. Hunter, OF	1
S. Runyan, RP	1

Kansas City (64-97)	**WS**
Hitting	**99.3**
Fielding	**32.4**
Pitching	**60.3**
C. Beltran, OF	18
J. Damon, OF	18
J. Randa, 3B	17
J. Dye, OF	16
M. Sweeney, 1B	16
J. Rosado, SP	13
R. Sanchez, SS	12
J. Suppan, SP	12
C. Febles, 2B	10
K. Appier, SP	7
J. Witasick, SP	5
J. Giambi, DH	4
J. Santiago, RP	4
T. Spehr, C	4
B. Stein, SP	4
S. Fasano, C	3
C. Kreuter, C	3
T. Mathews, RP	3
A. Morman, RP	3
M. Quinn, OF	3
S. Service, RP	3
M. Suzuki, RP	3
S. Pose, OF	2
J. Hansen, 2B	1
R. Holbert, SS	1
J. King, 1B	1
M. Lopez, 2B	1
J. Montgomery, RP	1
S. Scarsone, SS	1
L. Sutton, 1B	1
D. Wallace, RP	1
M. Whisenant, RP	1

Minnesota (63-97)	**WS**
Hitting	**63.3**
Fielding	**42.3**
Pitching	**83.4**
B. Radke, SP	17
C. Koskie, 3B	13
E. Milton, SP	12
T. Steinbach, C	12
J. Mays, RP	10
M. Trombley, RP	10
M. Cordova, DH	9
J. Jones, OF	9
T. Walker, 2B	9
B. Wells, RP	9
R. Coomer, 1B	8
D. Hocking, SS	8
M. Lawton, OF	8
C. Allen, OF	7
R. Aguilera, RP	6
C. Guzman, SS	5
T. Hunter, OF	5
T. Miller, RP	5
J. Valentin, C	5
B. Gates, 3B	4
E. Guardado, RP	4
H. Carrasco, RP	3
L. Hawkins, SP	3
D. Mientkiewicz, 1B	3
J. Ryan, SP	2
M. Cummings, OF	1
M. Lincoln, SP	1
J. Romero, RP	1

New York (98-64)	**WS**
Hitting	**147.9**
Fielding	**42.4**
Pitching	**103.6**
D. Jeter, SS	35
B. Williams, OF	33
C. Knoblauch, 2B	25
T. Martinez, 1B	19
M. Rivera, RP	17
P. O'Neill, OF	16
D. Cone, SP	15
O. Hernandez, SP	14
S. Brosius, 3B	13
C. Davis, DH	13
R. Clemens, SP	10
A. Pettitte, SP	10
J. Posada, C	10
R. Ledee, OF	9
H. Irabu, SP	8
R. Mendoza, RP	8
J. Grimsley, RP	6
C. Curtis, OF	5
M. Stanton, RP	4
A. Watson, RP	4
J. Girardi, C	3
D. Naulty, RP	3
S. Spencer, OF	3
D. Strawberry, DH	3
J. Nelson, RP	2
L. Sojo, 3B	2
C. Bellinger, 3B	1
D. Jimenez, 3B	1
J. Leyritz, DH	1
E. Yarnall, RP	1

Oakland (87-75)	**WS**
Hitting	**140.0**
Fielding	**35.7**
Pitching	**85.2**
J. Giambi, 1B	30
J. Jaha, DH	22
M. Stairs, OF	20
M. Tejada, SS	20
B. Grieve, OF	16
T. Phillips, 2B	14
T. Hudson, SP	12
D. Jones, RP	11
G. Heredia, SP	10
R. Velarde, 2B	10
E. Chavez, 3B	9
T. Mathews, RP	7
K. Rogers, SP	7
O. Saenz, 3B	7
R. Hernandez, C	6
M. Oquist, SP	6
S. Spiezio, 2B	6
O. Olivares, SP	5
B. Taylor, RP	5
J. Isringhausen, RP	4
B. Rigby, RP	4
T. Worrell, RP	4
R. Becker, OF	3
R. Christenson, OF	3
B. Groom, RP	3
A. Hinch, C	3
M. Macfarlane, C	3
R. Mahay, RP	3
K. Appier, SP	2
J. McDonald, OF	2
T. Candiotti, SP	1
J. Haynes, SP	1
T. Raines, OF	1
J. Velandia, 2B	1

Seattle (79-83)	**WS**
Hitting	**119.6**
Fielding	**38.6**
Pitching	**78.8**
K. Griffey Jr., OF	31
A. Rodriguez, SS	23
E. Martinez, DH	22
J. Moyer, SP	18
D. Bell, 2B	16
F. Garcia, SP	16
J. Halama, SP	13
B. Huskey, OF	9
D. Wilson, C	9
J. Buhner, OF	8
P. Abbott, RP	7
T. Lampkin, C	7
J. Paniagua, RP	7
D. Segui, 1B	7
R. Davis, 3B	6
G. Meche, SP	6
J. Mesa, RP	5
R. Ibanez, OF	4
R. Bournigal, SS	3
B. Hunter, OF	3
J. Mabry, OF	3
F. Rodriguez, RP	3
D. Cedeno, SS	2
M. Mieske, OF	2
M. Blowers, 1B	1
T. Davey, RP	1
R. Franklin, RP	1
C. Gipson, OF	1
B. Henry, SP	1
S. Sinclair, RP	1
T. Williams, RP	1

Tampa Bay (69-93)	**WS**
Hitting	**98.7**
Fielding	**34.4**
Pitching	**74.0**
F. McGriff, 1B	24
R. Hernandez, RP	14
J. Canseco, DH	13
D. Martinez, OF	13
J. Flaherty, C	12
W. Alvarez, SP	10
M. Cairo, 2B	10
B. Trammell, OF	9
M. DiFelice, C	8
R. Rupe, SP	8
T. Graffanino, 2B-SS	7
P. Sorrento, OF	7
K. Stocker, SS	7
R. White, RP	7
R. Arrojo, SP	6
W. Boggs, 3B	6
B. Witt, SP	5
A. Lopez, RP	4
R. Winn, OF	4
N. Charlton, RP	3
M. Duvall, RP	3
A. Ledesma, SS	3
T. Lowery, OF	3
H. Perry, 3B	3
B. Rekar, RP	3
D. Eiland, SP	2
Q. McCracken, OF	2
J. Mecir, RP	2
B. Smith, 3B	2
E. Yan, RP	2
S. Aldred, RP	1

J. Guillen, OF	1
D. Lamb, SS	1
J. Sparks, RP	1
D. Wheeler, SP	1

Texas (95-67)	WS
Hitting	**148.3**
Fielding	**40.4**
Pitching	**96.3**
R. Palmeiro, DH	31
I. Rodriguez, C	28
J. Gonzalez, OF	24
R. Greer, OF	24
T. Zeile, 3B	19
R. Clayton, SS	15
M. McLemore, 2B	15
J. Zimmerman, RP	14
A. Sele, SP	13
R. Helling, SP	12
J. Wetteland, RP	12
L. Stevens, 1B	11
E. Loaiza, SP-RP	8
T. Crabtree, RP	7
R. Kelly, OF	7
M. Venafro, RP	7
J. Burkett, SP	6
T. Goodwin, OF	5
M. Munoz, RP	5
M. Morgan, SP	4
R. Mateo, OF	3
D. Patterson, RP	3
J. Shave, SS	3
G. Zaun, C	3
D. Kolb, RP	2
L. Alicea, 2B	1
K. Dransfeldt, SS	1
J. Fassero, RP	1
M. Perisho, RP	1

Toronto (84-78)	WS
Hitting	**126.9**
Fielding	**40.6**
Pitching	**84.5**
S. Green, OF	24
C. Delgado, 1B	21
T. Fernandez, 3B	20
S. Stewart, OF	17
T. Batista, SS	15
H. Bush, 2B	15
D. Fletcher, C	13
D. Wells, SP	13
J. Cruz, OF	11
R. Halladay, SP-RP	10
P. Hentgen, SP	10
B. Koch, RP	10
C. Carpenter, SP	9
K. Escobar, SP	7
G. Lloyd, RP	7
A. Gonzalez, SS	6
J. Frascatore, RP	5
P. Quantrill, RP	5
C. Grebeck, 2B	4
J. Brumfield, OF	3
P. Kelly, 2B	3
M. Matheny, C	3
D. Segui, DH	3
P. Spoljaric, RP	3
T. Davey, RP	2
W. Greene, DH	2
J. Hamilton, SP	2
B. McRae, DH	2
C. Blake, 3B	1
P. Borders, DH-C	1
K. Brown, C	1
P. Lennon, OF	1
P. Munro, RP	1
W. Otanez, 3B	1
V. Wells, OF	1

1999 National League

Arizona (100-62)	WS
Hitting	**138.6**
Fielding	**49.2**
Pitching	**112.2**
L. Gonzalez, OF	26
R. Johnson, SP	26
M. Williams, 3B	26
S. Finley, OF	24
J. Bell, 2B	23
O. Daal, SP	16
T. Womack, OF	14
D. Miller, C	10
E. Durazo, 1B	9
G. Olson, RP	9
A. Benes, SP	8
B. Gilkey, OF	8
T. Lee, 1B	8
A. Reynoso, SP	8
G. Swindell, RP	8
B. Anderson, SP	7
A. Fox, SS	7
T. Batista, SS	6
M. Mantei, RP	6
K. Stinnett, C	6
T. Stottlemyre, SP	6
B. Chouinard, RP	5
G. Colbrunn, 1B	5
D. Dellucci, OF	5
H. Frias, SS	4
D. Holmes, RP	4
V. Nunez, RP	3
J. Frascatore, RP	2
L. Harris, 3B	2
B. Kim, RP	2
D. Plesac, RP	2
T. Ward, OF	2
R. Barajas, C	1
E. Diaz, 2B-SS	1
R. Ryan, OF	1

Atlanta (103-59)	WS
Hitting	**134.9**
Fielding	**47.6**
Pitching	**126.5**
C. Jones, 3B	32
A. Jones, OF	28
B. Jordan, OF	22
K. Millwood, SP	22
R. Klesko, 1B	18
J. Smoltz, SP	18
B. Boone, 2B	17
G. Maddux, SP	17
J. Rocker, RP	16
T. Glavine, SP	14
G. Williams, OF	13
M. Remlinger, RP	12
J. Lopez, C	11
K. McGlinchy, RP	8
E. Perez, C	8
R. Seanez, RP	7
W. Weiss, SS	7
B. Hunter, 1B	6
T. Mulholland, SP-RP	6
R. Springer, RP	5
R. Simon, 1B	4
O. Guillen, SS	3
J. Hernandez, SS	3
K. Lockhart, 2B	3
G. Myers, C	3
H. Battle, 3B	1
S. Bergman, RP	1
B. Chen, RP	1
O. Nixon, OF	1
O. Perez, SP	1
J. Speier, RP	1

Chicago (67-95)	WS
Hitting	**99.4**
Fielding	**32.7**
Pitching	**68.9**
S. Sosa, OF	26
M. Grace, 1B	21
H. Rodriguez, OF	17
J. Hernandez, SS	13
J. Lieber, SP	13
T. Adams, RP	9
R. Aguilera, RP	7
G. Hill, OF	7
M. Morandini, 2B	7
B. Santiago, C	7
K. Tapani, SP	6
S. Trachsel, SP	6
J. Blauser, 2B	5
K. Farnsworth, SP	5
L. Johnson, OF	5
T. Mulholland, SP	5
R. Myers, RP	5
S. Sanders, RP	5
M. Alexander, SS	4
J. Reed, C	4
G. Gaetti, 3B	3
F. Heredia, RP	3
T. Houston, 3B	3
J. Nieves, SS	3
S. Andrews, 3B	2
B. Ayala, RP	2
M. Karchner, RP	2
A. Lorraine, SP	2
C. Goodwin, OF	1
M. Guthrie, RP	1
C. Meyers, 2B	1
B. Woodall, SP-RP	1

Cincinnati (96-67)	WS
Hitting	**128.9**
Fielding	**52.8**
Pitching	**106.4**
B. Larkin, SS	24
G. Vaughn, OF	24
S. Casey, 1B	23
M. Cameron, OF	19
P. Reese, 2B	18
S. Williamson, RP	17
D. Graves, RP	16
A. Boone, 3B	15
E. Taubensee, C	15
P. Harnisch, SP	14
S. Sullivan, RP	11
M. Tucker, OF	10
D. Young, OF	10
S. Parris, SP	9
J. Hammonds, OF	8
R. Villone, SP	8
D. Neagle, SP	7
J. Guzman, SP	6
B. Tomko, SP	6
D. Reyes, RP	5
M. Lewis, 3B	4
S. Avery, SP	3
H. Morris, 1B	3
G. White, RP	3
S. Belinda, RP	2
B. Johnson, C	2
J. LaRue, C	2
C. Stynes, 2B	2
M. Sweeney, 1B-OF	2

Colorado (72-90)	WS
Hitting	**91.6**
Fielding	**42.9**
Pitching	**81.5**
L. Walker, OF	24
P. Astacio, SP	19
T. Helton, 1B	19
D. Bichette, OF	15
N. Perez, SS	14
V. Castilla, 3B	11
D. Veres, RP	11
T. Shumpert, 2B	10
B. Bohanon, SP	9
J. Dipoto, RP	9
C. Leskanic, RP	8
K. Abbott, 2B	7
J. Wright, SP	7
H. Blanco, C	6
D. Kile, SP	6
D. Hamilton, OF	5
D. Lee, RP	5
A. Echevarria, OF	4
B. Jones, SP	4
J. Barry, OF	3
M. Lansing, 2B	3
K. Manwaring, C	3
C. McElroy, RP	3
E. Clemente, OF	2
L. Harris, 2B	2
B. Petrick, C	2
J. Reed, C	2
D. Gibson, OF	1
C. Sexton, OF	1
D. Wainhouse, RP	1

Florida (64-98)	WS
Hitting	**92.3**
Fielding	**32.5**
Pitching	**67.2**
B. Aven, OF	14
L. Castillo, 2B	14
P. Wilson, OF	13
K. Millar, 1B	12
M. Redmond, C	12
A. Alfonseca, RP	11
A. Gonzalez, SS	11
A. Fernandez, SP	10
C. Floyd, OF	9
M. Lowell, 3B	8
D. Berg, SS	6
R. Dempster, SP	6
L. Hernandez, SP	6
M. Kotsay, OF	6
M. Mantei, RP	6
K. Orie, 3B	6
D. Springer, SP	6
J. Fabregas, C	5
B. Looper, RP	5
B. Meadows, SP	4
D. Bautista, OF	3
A. Burnett, SP	3
B. Edmondson, RP	3
A. Almanza, RP	2
R. Cornelius, RP	2
V. Nunez, SP	2
H. Almonte, RP	1
R. Castro, C	1
C. Clapinski, 3B	1
T. Dunwoody, OF	1
A. Garcia, 2B	1
D. Lee, 1B	1
J. Sanchez, RP	1

Houston (97-65)	WS
Hitting	**131.9**
Fielding	**44.5**
Pitching	**114.5**
J. Bagwell, 1B	37
C. Biggio, 2B	31
M. Hampton, SP	26
C. Everett, OF	25
B. Wagner, RP	20
J. Lima, SP	18
S. Reynolds, SP	16
B. Spiers, 3B	12
K. Caminiti, 3B	10
S. Elarton, RP	10
T. Eusebio, C	10
R. Hidalgo, OF	9
T. Bogar, SS	7
R. Gutierrez, SS	6
C. Holt, SP	6
J. Powell, RP	6
P. Bako, C	5
J. Cabrera, RP	5
R. Johnson, 3B	5
D. Bell, OF	4
B. Williams, RP	4
G. Barker, OF	3
M. Mieske, OF	3
D. Ward, OF	3
S. Bergman, SP	2

D. Henry, RP	2
S. Javier, OF	2
T. Miller, RP	2
L. Berkman, OF	1
J. Slusarski, RP	1

Los Angeles (77-85)	WS
Hitting	**117.4**
Fielding	**35.6**
Pitching	**78.0**
G. Sheffield, OF	24
R. Mondesi, OF	21
E. Karros, 1B	20
K. Brown, SP	19
A. Beltre, 3B	15
E. Young, 2B	14
M. Grudzielanek, SS	13
J. Shaw, RP	12
D. White, OF	12
I. Valdes, SP	10
D. Dreifort, SP	8
T. Hollandsworth, OF	7
T. Hundley, C	6
C. Park, SP	6
A. Mills, RP	5
P. Borbon, RP	4
T. Hubbard, OF	4
M. Maddux, RP	4
O. Masaoka, RP	4
J. Vizcaino, SS	4
E. Gagne, SP	3
D. Hansen, 1B	3
C. Counsell, 2B	2
P. Lo Duca, C	2
A. Pena, C	2
J. Arnold, RP	1
J. Brumfield, OF	1
T. Cromer, 2B-SS	1
M. Herges, RP	1
M. Judd, SP	1
C. Perez, SP	1
J. Williams, SP	1

Milwaukee (74-87)	WS
Hitting	**119.1**
Fielding	**35.1**
Pitching	**67.8**
J. Cirillo, 3B	22
J. Burnitz, OF	19
G. Jenkins, OF	18
R. Belliard, 2B	15
D. Nilsson, C	15
M. Loretta, SS	14
M. Grissom, OF	13
B. Wickman, RP	11
H. Nomo, SP	10
A. Ochoa, OF	10
S. Karl, SP	9
S. Woodard, SP	9
J. Valentin, SS	8
D. Weathers, RP	6
K. Barker, 1B	4
R. Becker, OF	4
R. Coppinger, RP	4
E. Plunk, RP	4
F. Vina, 2B	4
B. Banks, 1B	3
K. Peterson, SP	3
A. Reyes, RP	3
L. Collier, SS	2
M. Myers, RP	2
H. Ramirez, RP	2
R. Roque, RP	2
J. Bere, SP	1
S. Berry, 1B	1
C. Greene, C	1
R. Harris, RP	1
J. Pittsley, RP	1
B. Pulsipher, SP	1

Montreal (68-94)	WS
Hitting	**87.1**
Fielding	**32.9**
Pitching	**84.1**
V. Guerrero, OF	28
R. White, OF	15
U. Urbina, RP	14
D. Hermanson, SP	12
M. Barrett, 3B	11
J. Vidro, 2B	11
O. Cabrera, SS	8
M. Thurman, SP	8
J. Vazquez, SP	8
C. Widger, C	8
W. Guerrero, 2B	7
S. Kline, RP	7
A. Telford, RP	7
M. Batista, RP	6
B. Fullmer, 1B	5
M. Martinez, OF	5
O. Merced, OF	5
G. Mota, RP	5
B. Ayala, RP	4
M. Mordecai, 2B-SS	4
J. Powell, SP	4
G. Blum, SS	3
C. Pavano, SP	3
S. Andrews, 3B	2
R. McGuire, 1B	2
J. Mouton, OF	2
F. Seguignol, 1B	2
J. Smart, RP	2
D. Smith, SP	2
P. Bergeron, OF	1
T. Coquillette, 3B	1
T. Jones, OF	1
S. Strickland, RP	1

New York (97-66)	WS
Hitting	**140.8**
Fielding	**49.1**
Pitching	**101.1**
R. Ventura, 3B	30
E. Alfonzo, 2B	29
J. Olerud, 1B	26
M. Piazza, C	21
A. Benitez, RP	19
R. Cedeno, OF	17
R. Henderson, OF	16
R. Ordonez, SS	13
A. Leiter, SP	11
B. Agbayani, OF	9
T. Wendell, RP	9
M. Yoshii, SP	9
D. Hamilton, OF	8
O. Hershiser, SP	8
R. Reed, SP	8
D. Cook, RP	7
P. Mahomes, RP	7
J. Franco, RP	6
T. Pratt, C	5
K. Rogers, SP	5
S. Dunston, OF	4
O. Dotel, SP	3
M. Franco, 1B-OF	3
L. Lopez, SS	3
B. McRae, OF	3
A. Watson, RP	3
R. Beltran, RP	2
B. Jones, SP	2
J. Allensworth, OF	1
J. Manzanillo, RP	1
C. McElroy, RP	1
G. McMichael, RP	1
J. Tam, RP	1

Philadelphia (77-85)	WS
Hitting	**118.1**
Fielding	**40.4**
Pitching	**72.4**
B. Abreu, OF	26
D. Glanville, OF	23
M. Lieberthal, C	20
R. Gant, OF	16
S. Rolen, 3B	15
C. Schilling, SP	15
R. Brogna, 1B	13
A. Arias, SS	10
P. Byrd, SP	10
M. Anderson, 2B	8
W. Gomes, RP	8
R. Person, SP	8
R. Ducey, OF	7
K. Jordan, 3B	7
S. Montgomery, RP	6
C. Ogea, SP	4
D. Relaford, SS	4
R. Wolf, SP	4
S. Aldred, RP	3
C. Loewer, SP	3
Y. Perez, RP	3
S. Schrenk, RP	3
K. Sefcik, OF	3
G. Bennett, C	2
J. Grahe, RP	2
J. Poole, RP	2
A. Telemaco, RP	2
J. Brantley, RP	1
D. Cedeno, SS	1
D. Doster, 2B	1
W. Magee, OF	1

Pittsburgh (78-83)	WS
Hitting	**104.4**
Fielding	**39.4**
Pitching	**90.2**
B. Giles, OF	27
K. Young, 1B	21
W. Morris, 2B	16
E. Sprague, 3B	15
A. Martin, OF	14
T. Ritchie, SP	14
J. Kendall, C	13
J. Schmidt, SP	13
K. Benson, SP	12
M. Benjamin, SS	10
F. Cordova, SP	9
S. Sauerbeck, RP	9
B. Brown, OF	7
B. Clontz, RP	5
M. Williams, RP	5
J. Christiansen, RP	4
A. Nunez, SS	4
J. Anderson, RP	3
A. Brown, OF	3
G. Hansell, RP	3
P. Meares, SS	3
J. Oliver, C	3
K. Osik, C	3
P. Schourek, SP	3
J. Wallace, RP	3
M. Wilkins, RP	3
J. Guillen, OF	2
J. Silva, RP	2
F. Garcia, OF	1
M. Garcia, RP	1
R. Loiselle, RP	1
C. Peters, SP	1
D. Sveum, 3B	1

San Diego (74-88)	WS
Hitting	**106.1**
Fielding	**37.6**
Pitching	**78.4**
P. Nevin, 3B	19
R. Sanders, OF	19
T. Gwynn, OF	18
Q. Veras, 2B	16
T. Hoffman, RP	14
A. Ashby, SP	13
D. Jackson, SS	11
E. Owens, OF	11
S. Hitchcock, SP	10
W. Williams, SP	10
J. Vander Wal, OF	8
B. Boehringer, RP	7
W. Joyner, 1B	7
D. Wall, RP	7
M. Clement, SP	6
C. Gomez, SS	6
Ru. Rivera, OF	6
C. Reyes, RP	5
J. Leyritz, C	4
D. Magadan, 3B	4
D. Miceli, RP	4
G. Arias, 3B	3
B. Davis, C	3
G. Myers, C	3
C. Baerga, 2B-3B	1
W. Cunnane, RP	1
M. Darr, OF	1
E. Giovanola, 3B	1
W. Gonzalez, C	1
G. Matthews Jr., OF	1
D. Newhan, 2B	1
M. Whisenant, RP	1

San Francisco (86-76)	WS
Hitting	**157.8**
Fielding	**33.6**
Pitching	**66.7**
E. Burks, OF	24
J. Kent, 2B	23
M. Benard, OF	20
B. Bonds, OF	19
R. Aurilia, SS	18
J. Snow, 1B	18
B. Mayne, C	13
B. Mueller, 3B	12
R. Ortiz, SP	12
F. Santangelo, OF	10
J. Johnstone, RP	8
R. Nen, RP	8
A. Rios, OF	7
A. Embree, RP	6
S. Estes, SP	6
S. Javier, OF	6
R. Martinez, 2B	5
J. Nathan, SP	5
K. Rueter, SP	5
S. Servais, C	5
C. Hayes, 3B	4
F. Rodriguez, RP	4
L. Hernandez, SP	3
D. Mirabelli, C	3
R. Rodriguez, RP	3
J. Spradlin, RP	3
C. Brock, SP	2
J. Canizaro, 2B	2
W. Delgado, SS	1
M. del Toro, RP	1
C. Murray, OF	1
J. Tavarez, RP	1

St. Louis (75-86)	WS
Hitting	**112.6**
Fielding	**34.6**
Pitching	**77.8**
M. McGwire, 1B	30
F. Tatis, 3B	23
K. Bottenfield, SP	14
R. Lankford, OF	13
D. Oliver, SP	13
E. Renteria, SS	13
J. McEwing, 2B	11
J. Drew, OF	10
D. Bragg, OF	7
A. Castillo, C	7
H. Slocumb, RP	7
R. Croushore, RP	5
E. Davis, OF	5
E. Marrero, C	5
C. Paquette, OF	5
G. Stephenson, SP	5
M. Aybar, RP	4
R. Bottalico, RP	4
S. Dunston, OF	4
T. Howard, OF	4
K. Mercker, SP	4
L. Painter, RP	4
J. Acevedo, RP	3
R. Ankiel, SP	3
M. Mohler, RP	3

P. Polanco, 2B	3
J. Jimenez, SP	2
A. Kennedy, 2B	2
L. Luebbers, SP	2
E. Perez, OF	2
S. Radinsky, RP	2
M. Thompson, SP	2
D. Howard, SS	1
M. Jensen, C	1
W. McGee, OF	1
D. Osborne, SP	1

2000 American League

Anaheim (82-80)	WS
Hitting	**116.4**
Fielding	**45.7**
Pitching	**83.8**
D. Erstad, OF	30
T. Glaus, 3B	25
T. Salmon, OF	23
M. Vaughn, 1B	17
G. Anderson, OF	15
B. Molina, C	13
S. Hasegawa, RP	11
A. Kennedy, 2B	11
T. Percival, RP	8
A. Levine, RP	7
O. Palmeiro, OF	7
M. Petkovsek, RP	7
J. Washburn, SP	7
M. Fyhrie, RP	6
R. Ortiz, SP	6
S. Schoeneweis, SP	6
S. Spiezio, DH	6
K. Bottenfield, SP	5
B. Gil, SS	4
L. Pote, RP	4
S. Etherton, SP	3
M. Holtz, RP	3
K. Stocker, SS	3
B. Cooper, SP	2
G. DiSarcina, SS	2
R. Gant, OF	2
D. Turnbow, RP	2
M. Walbeck, C	2
B. Weber, RP	2
M. Wise, SP	2
T. Belcher, SP	1
J. Dickson, SP	1
K. Hill, SP	1
K. Johnson, 1B	1
K. Mercker, RP	1

Baltimore (74-88)	WS
Hitting	**116.8**
Fielding	**34.3**
Pitching	**70.9**
D. DeShields, 2B	21
M. Mussina, SP	18
B. Anderson, OF	15
A. Belle, OF	15
M. Bordick, SS	13
C. Johnson, C	11
J. Mercedes, SP	11
S. Ponson, SP	11
B. Surhoff, OF	11
W. Clark, 1B	10
J. Conine, 3B	9
C. Ripken Jr., 3B	8
B. Fordyce, C	7
B. Groom, RP	6
M. Mora, SS	6
C. Richard, 1B	6
M. Trombley, RP	6
J. Hairston Jr., 2B	4
R. Kohlmeier, RP	4
M. Lewis, 3B	4
C. McElroy, RP	4
P. Rapp, SP	4
H. Baines, DH	3
M. Timlin, RP	3
L. Matos, OF	2
B. Ryan, RP	2
R. Amaral, OF	1
I. Coffie, 3B	1
G. Kingsale, OF	1
M. Kinkade, DH	1
A. Mills, RP	1
R. Minor, 3B	1
G. Myers, C	1
J. Spurgeon, SP	1

Boston (85-77)	WS
Hitting	**93.5**
Fielding	**48.1**
Pitching	**113.4**
N. Garciaparra, SS	29
P. Martinez, SP	29
C. Everett, OF	24
D. Lowe, RP	19
T. Nixon, OF	14
T. O'Leary, OF	11
B. Daubach, 1B	10
R. Garces, RP	10
J. Offerman, 2B	9
J. Fassero, SP	8
J. Varitek, C	7
J. Frye, 2B	6
T. Ohka, SP	6
H. Pichardo, RP	6
R. Beck, RP	5
S. Hatteberg, C	5
T. Wakefield, RP	5
R. Arrojo, SP	4
R. Cormier, RP	4
D. Lewis, OF	4
R. Martinez, SP	4
P. Schourek, SP	4
M. Alexander, 3B	3
L. Merloni, 3B	3
M. Stanley, 1B	3
I. Alcantara, DH	2
D. Bichette, DH	2
M. Burkhart, DH	2
P. Crawford, SP	2
B. Florie, RP	2
M. Lansing, 2B	2
D. Sadler, SS	2
W. Veras, 3B	2
J. Wasdin, RP	2
R. Brogna, 1B	1
B. Gilkey, OF	1
S. Lee, RP	1
B. Rose, SP	1
E. Sprague, 3B	1

Chicago (95-67)	WS
Hitting	**144.1**
Fielding	**44.1**
Pitching	**96.8**
F. Thomas, DH	34
J. Valentin, SS	24
M. Ordonez, OF	22
R. Durham, 2B	19
K. Foulke, RP	16
P. Konerko, 1B	15
C. Lee, OF	14
M. Sirotka, SP	14
H. Perry, 3B	13
J. Baldwin, SP	11
J. Parque, SP	11
C. Singleton, OF	11
B. Howry, RP	9
C. Johnson, C	9
K. Wunsch, RP	8
C. Eldred, SP	7
B. Simas, RP	6
T. Graffanino, SS	5
M. Johnson, C	5
J. Abbott, OF	4
M. Buehrle, RP	4
B. Fordyce, C	4
L. Barcelo, RP	3
S. Lowe, RP	3
G. Norton, 3B	3
J. Paul, C	3
C. Bradford, RP	2
K. Wells, SP	2
H. Baines, DH	1
J. Garland, SP	1
J. Pena, RP	1
C. Wilson, 3B	1

Cleveland (90-72)	WS
Hitting	**131.4**
Fielding	**41.2**
Pitching	**97.5**
M. Ramirez, OF	27
T. Fryman, 3B	22
R. Alomar, 2B	20
J. Thome, 1B	20
K. Lofton, OF	17
C. Finley, SP	16
O. Vizquel, SS	16
B. Colon, SP	15
D. Burba, SP	13
S. Karsay, RP	11
D. Justice, OF	9
S. Alomar Jr., C	8
P. Shuey, RP	8
D. Segui, 1B	7
J. Speier, RP	7
E. Diaz, C	6
R. Branyan, OF	5
R. Sexson, OF	5
S. Reed, RP	4
B. Wickman, RP	4
R. Rincon, RP	3
E. Wilson, 3B	3
J. Wright, SP	3
J. Bere, SP	2
J. Brewington, RP	2
J. Cabrera, OF	2
W. Cordero, OF	2
T. Martin, RP	2
S. Woodard, SP	2
J. Brower, SP	1
C. Cairncross, RP	1
J. Cruz, OF	1
S. DePaula, RP	1
S. Kamieniecki, RP	1
R. Ledee, OF	1
A. Lorraine, RP	1
A. Ramirez, OF	1
B. Williams, RP	1

Detroit (79-83)	WS
Hitting	**111.5**
Fielding	**40.6**
Pitching	**84.9**
B. Higginson, OF	26
B. Ausmus, C	16
D. Cruz, SS	15
D. Palmer, 3B	15
D. Easley, 2B	14
J. Encarnacion, OF	14
J. Weaver, SP	12
T. Jones, RP	10
B. Moehler, SP	10
H. Nomo, SP	10
J. Gonzalez, OF	9
W. Blair, RP	8
R. Becker, OF	7
S. Sparks, SP	7
T. Clark, 1B	6
D. Brocail, RP	5
J. Macias, 2B	5
B. McMillon, DH	5
D. Patterson, RP	5
L. Polonia, DH	5
M. Anderson, RP	4
N. Cruz, RP	4
R. Fick, 1B	4
W. Magee, OF	4
D. Mlicki, SP	4
S. Halter, 3B	3
C. Nitkowski, RP	3
A. Bernero, RP	2
G. Jefferies, 1B	2
H. Morris, 1B	2
J. Cardona, C	1

Kansas City (77-85)	WS
Hitting	**113.7**
Fielding	**43.9**
Pitching	**73.5**
J. Damon, OF	26
M. Sweeney, 1B	26
J. Dye, OF	21
J. Randa, 3B	18
M. Quinn, OF	13
J. Suppan, SP	12
M. Suzuki, SP	12
D. Reichert, RP	9
R. Sanchez, SS	9
G. Zaun, C	9
R. Bottalico, RP	8
C. Febles, 2B	7
D. McCarty, 1B	7
J. Santiago, RP	7
B. Stein, SP	7
C. Beltran, OF	5
B. Meadows, SP	5
H. Ortiz, C	5
J. Spradlin, RP	5
J. Fabregas, C	3
J. Reboulet, 2B	3
W. Delgado, 2B	2
C. Fussell, RP	2
K. Wilson, RP	2
J. Witasick, SP	2
T. Dunwoody, OF	1
B. Johnson, C	1
S. Mullen, RP	1
D. Murray, RP	1
L. Ordaz, SS	1
J. Rosado, SP	1

Minnesota (69-93)	WS
Hitting	**76.0**
Fielding	**43.5**
Pitching	**87.5**
M. Lawton, OF	20
C. Koskie, 3B	17
B. Radke, SP	15
C. Guzman, SS	12
L. Hawkins, RP	12
D. Hocking, OF	11
J. Jones, OF	11
E. Milton, SP	11
M. Redman, SP	10
B. Wells, RP	10
R. Coomer, 1B	9
E. Guardado, RP	8
T. Hunter, OF	8
D. Ortiz, DH	8
J. Canizaro, 2B	7
H. Carrasco, RP	6
J. Mays, SP	6
T. Miller, RP	5
A. Pierzynski, C	3
M. Jensen, C	2
M. Kinney, SP	2
M. LeCroy, C	2
J. Maxwell, 2B	2
C. Moeller, C	2
J. Santana, RP	2
C. Allen, OF	1
J. Barnes, OF	1
J. Cressend, RP	1
M. Cummings, OF	1
B. Huskey, DH	1
L. Rivas, 2B	1

New York (87-74)	WS
Hitting	**123.9**
Fielding	**41.0**
Pitching	**96.1**
J. Posada, C	29
B. Williams, OF	26
D. Jeter, SS	23
R. Clemens, SP	16

M. Rivera, RP	16
A. Pettitte, SP	14
P. O'Neill, OF	13
O. Hernandez, SP	12
T. Martinez, 1B	12
D. Justice, OF	11
C. Knoblauch, 2B	10
J. Nelson, RP	9
S. Brosius, 3B	8
D. Gooden, RP	6
G. Hill, DH	6
S. Spencer, OF	6
M. Stanton, RP	6
J. Grimsley, RP	5
R. Ledee, OF	5
R. Mendoza, SP	5
C. Bellinger, OF	3
J. Canseco, DH	3
D. Neagle, SP	3
L. Sojo, 2B	3
R. Thompson, OF	2
J. Vizcaino, 2B	2
R. Choate, RP	1
W. Delgado, 2B	1
D. Einertson, RP	1
T. Erdos, RP	1
L. Johnson, OF	1
L. Polonia, OF	1
C. Turner, C	1

Oakland (91-70)	WS
Hitting	**149.4**
Fielding	**35.2**
Pitching	**88.4**
Ja. Giambi, 1B	38
M. Tejada, SS	23
T. Long, OF	18
B. Grieve, OF	17
E. Chavez, 3B	16
T. Hudson, SP	15
R. Velarde, 2B	14
G. Heredia, SP	13
K. Appier, SP	11
R. Hernandez, C	10
J. Isringhausen, RP	10
M. Stairs, OF	10
J. Tam, RP	10
B. Zito, SP	9
O. Saenz, DH	8
Je. Giambi, OF	6
D. Jones, RP	6
F. Menechino, 2B	6
A. Piatt, OF	6
J. Mecir, RP	5
M. Mulder, SP	5
R. Christenson, OF	3
M. Stanley, 1B	3
R. Becker, OF	2
S. Fasano, C	2
M. Magnante, RP	2
T. Mathews, RP	2
O. Olivares, SP	1
A. Prieto, SP	1
R. Sauveur, RP	1

Seattle (91-71)	WS
Hitting	**147.5**
Fielding	**40.5**
Pitching	**85.0**
A. Rodriguez, SS	37
E. Martinez, DH	28
J. Olerud, 1B	22
M. Cameron, OF	19
J. Buhner, OF	16
M. McLemore, 2B	13
A. Sele, SP	12
P. Abbott, SP	11
K. Sasaki, RP	11
S. Javier, OF	9
D. Bell, 3B	8
F. Garcia, SP	8
C. Guillen, 3B	8
J. Oliver, C	8
J. Paniagua, RP	8
R. Henderson, OF	7
J. Halama, SP	6
G. Meche, SP	6
A. Rhodes, RP	6
J. Moyer, SP	5
B. Tomko, RP	5
R. Ramsay, RP	4
D. Wilson, C	4
T. Lampkin, C	3
J. Mesa, RP	3
C. Gipson, OF	1
K. Hodges, RP	1
R. Ibanez, OF	1
B. Lesher, 1B	1
A. Martin, OF	1
F. Rodriguez, RP	1

Tampa Bay (69-92)	WS
Hitting	**80.3**
Fielding	**39.9**
Pitching	**86.8**
F. McGriff, 1B	16
G. Vaughn, OF	16
G. Williams, OF	14
A. Lopez, SP	13
R. Hernandez, RP	12
B. Rekar, SP	11
M. Cairo, 2B	10
S. Cox, OF	8
J. Flaherty, C	8
S. Trachsel, SP	8
J. Mecir, RP	7
R. White, RP	7
J. Guillen, OF	6
T. Sturtze, RP	6
B. Trammell, OF	6
J. Canseco, DH	5
F. Martinez, SS	5
D. Creek, RP	4
R. Johnson, 3B	4
C. Lidle, RP	4
P. Wilson, SP	4
E. Yan, RP	4
V. Castilla, 3B	3
A. Huff, 3B	3
B. Smith, 2B	3
K. Stocker, SS	3
M. DiFelice, C	2
M. Guthrie, RP	2
T. Harper, SP	2
J. Sparks, RP	2
R. Winn, OF	2
T. Graffanino, 2B	1
O. Guillen, SS	1
D. Martinez, OF	1
R. Rupe, SP	1
O. Timmons, OF	1
J. Tyner, OF	1
D. Wheeler, RP	1

Texas (71-91)	WS
Hitting	**108.5**
Fielding	**33.2**
Pitching	**71.3**
R. Palmeiro, 1B	23
I. Rodriguez, C	19
R. Helling, SP	15
K. Rogers, SP	15
L. Alicea, 2B	12
R. Greer, OF	12
D. Segui, DH	11
G. Kapler, OF	10
F. Catalanotto, 2B	8
R. Clayton, SS	8
J. Wetteland, RP	8
B. Haselman, C	7
C. Curtis, OF	6
M. Lamb, 3B	6
M. Venafro, RP	6
T. Crabtree, RP	5
D. Davis, RP	5
E. Loaiza, SP	5
R. Ledee, OF	4
J. Zimmerman, RP	4
F. Cordero, RP	3
R. Glynn, SP	3
R. Mateo, OF	3
J. McDonald, OF	3
S. Sheldon, SS	3
K. Dransfeldt, SS	1
T. Evans, 3B	1
S. Green, OF	1
J. Johnson, RP	1
R. Knorr, C	1
D. Martinez, OF	1
R. Sierra, DH	1
B. Sikorski, SP-RP	1
P. Valdes, OF	1

Toronto (83-79)	WS
Hitting	**122.5**
Fielding	**40.5**
Pitching	**86.0**
C. Delgado, 1B	36
T. Batista, 3B	18
D. Wells, SP	18
S. Stewart, OF	17
B. Koch, RP	16
J. Cruz, OF	15
B. Fullmer, DH	15
D. Fletcher, C	14
F. Castillo, SP	12
A. Gonzalez, SS	11
R. Mondesi, OF	11
K. Escobar, SP	8
C. Grebeck, 2B	8
E. Loaiza, SP	7
P. Quantrill, RP	6
C. Carpenter, SP	5
D. Martinez, OF	5
H. Bush, 2B	4
A. Castillo, C	4
L. Painter, RP	4
J. Frascatore, RP	3
J. Hamilton, SP	3
S. Trachsel, SP	3
M. Morandini, 2B	2
C. Woodward, SS	2
M. Cordova, OF	1
M. Guthrie, RP	1

2000 National League

Arizona (85-77)	WS
Hitting	**108.2**
Fielding	**45.1**
Pitching	**101.7**
L. Gonzalez, OF	27
R. Johnson, SP	26
S. Finley, OF	21
J. Bell, 2B	19
T. Womack, SS	16
B. Anderson, SP	14
G. Colbrunn, 1B	12
D. Miller, C	11
D. Bautista, OF	9
B. Kim, RP	8
C. Schilling, SP	8
M. Morgan, RP	7
A. Reynoso, SP	7
G. Swindell, RP	7
M. Williams, 3B	7
M. Mantei, RP	6
T. Stottlemyre, SP	6
C. Counsell, 2B	5
E. Durazo, 1B	5
V. Padilla, RP	5
K. Stinnett, C	5
D. Plesac, RP	4
J. Conti, OF	3
T. Lee, OF	3
R. Springer, RP	3
G. Guzman, SP	2
D. Klassen, 3B	2
A. Cabrera, 1B	1
O. Daal, SP	1
D. Dellucci, OF	1
A. Fox, 3B	1
H. Frias, SS	1
R. Ryan, OF	1
T. Ward, OF	1

Atlanta (95-67)	WS
Hitting	**125.2**
Fielding	**44.7**
Pitching	**115.1**
A. Jones, OF	30
C. Jones, 3B	27
G. Maddux, SP	24
T. Glavine, SP	21
R. Furcal, SS	17
A. Galarraga, 1B	16
J. Lopez, C	16
B. Jordan, OF	14
Q. Veras, 2B	13
M. Remlinger, RP	12
K. Millwood, SP	10
K. Ligtenberg, RP	8
J. Rocker, RP	8
J. Burkett, SP	7
W. Joyner, 1B	7
K. Lockhart, 2B	7
T. Mulholland, RP	7
A. Ashby, SP	6
B. Bonilla, OF	6
R. Sanders, OF	6
W. Weiss, SS	5
B. Chen, RP	4
B. Surhoff, OF	3
R. Seanez, RP	2
P. Bako, C	1
M. DeRosa, SS	1
T. Hubbard, OF	1
S. Kamieniecki, RP	1
F. Lunar, C	1
J. Marquis, RP	1
K. McGlinchy, RP	1
G. McMichael, RP	1
L. Rivera, RP	1

Chicago (65-97)	WS
Hitting	**109.9**
Fielding	**31.4**
Pitching	**53.7**
S. Sosa, OF	30
M. Grace, 1B	18
E. Young, 2B	18
R. Gutierrez, SS	15
J. Lieber, SP	12
D. Buford, OF	9
J. Girardi, C	9
H. Rodriguez, OF	8
W. Greene, 3B	7
K. Wood, SP	7
T. Worrell, RP	7
K. Tapani, SP	6
T. Van Poppel, RP	6
S. Andrews, 3B	5
J. Reed, C	5
R. Aguilera, RP	4
F. Heredia, RP	4
R. Brown, OF	3
S. Downs, SP	3
S. Rain, RP	3
G. Hill, OF	2
J. Nieves, 3B	2
A. Ojeda, SS	2
I. Valdes, SP	2
R. White, OF	2
J. Zuleta, 1B	2
B. Brown, OF	1
M. Guthrie, RP	1
J. Huson, 3B	1
G. Matthews Jr., OF	1

Cincinnati (85-77)	WS
Hitting	**106.3**
Fielding	**48.8**
Pitching	**99.9**
K. Griffey Jr., OF	24
D. Graves, RP	18
S. Casey, 1B	17
D. Young, OF	14
B. Larkin, SS	13
C. Stynes, 3B	13
D. Bichette, OF	12
A. Ochoa, OF	11
P. Reese, 2B	11
S. Williamson, RP	11
A. Boone, 3B	10
E. Dessens, RP	10
D. Neagle, SP	10
S. Sullivan, RP	10
S. Parris, SP	9
P. Harnisch, SP	7
M. Tucker, OF	7
O. Fernandez, SP	6
B. Santiago, C	6
R. Bell, SP	5
R. Villone, SP	5
E. Taubensee, C	4
J. Castro, SS	3
J. LaRue, C	3
M. Aybar, RP	2
D. Cromer, 1B	2
D. Reyes, RP	2
J. Riedling, RP	2
M. Wohlers, RP	2
M. Bell, 3B	1
G. Dawkins, SS	1
K. Glauber, RP	1
B. Hunter, OF	1
H. Mercado, RP	1
C. Sexton, SS	1

Colorado (82-80)	WS
Hitting	**95.9**
Fielding	**48.4**
Pitching	**101.7**
T. Helton, 1B	29
J. Cirillo, 3B	19
J. Jimenez, RP	15
N. Perez, SS	15
G. White, RP	15
J. Hammonds, OF	14
B. Bohanon, SP	13
P. Astacio, SP	11
T. Goodwin, OF	11
L. Walker, OF	11
J. Tavarez, RP	10
B. Mayne, C	8
M. Myers, RP	7
M. Yoshii, SP	7
M. Lansing, 2B	5
T. Shumpert, OF	5
T. Walker, 2B	5
R. Arrojo, SP	4
M. DeJean, RP	4
T. Hollandsworth, OF	4
K. Jarvis, SP	4
B. Chouinard, RP	3
B. Hunter, OF	3
B. Huskey, OF	3
B. Petrick, C	3
J. Pierre, OF	3
B. Rose, SP	3
D. Bragg, OF	2
J. Frye, 2B	2
S. Belinda, RP	1
B. Carpenter, OF	1
R. Croushore, RP	1
J. Dipoto, RP	1
S. Karl, SP	1
J. Manto, 1B-3B	1
S. Servais, C	1
J. Wasdin, RP	1

Florida (79-82)	WS
Hitting	**111.6**
Fielding	**38.2**
Pitching	**87.2**
M. Lowell, 3B	20
P. Wilson, OF	20
C. Floyd, OF	19
L. Castillo, 2B	18
R. Dempster, SP	17
D. Lee, 1B	16
M. Kotsay, OF	12
A. Alfonseca, RP	10
K. Millar, 1B	10
C. Smith, SP	10
J. Sanchez, SP	6
D. Berg, SS	5
A. Burnett, SP	5
V. Darensbourg, RP	5
B. Looper, RP	5
D. Miceli, RP	5
B. Penny, SP	5
M. Redmond, C	5
P. Bako, C	4
R. Bones, RP	4
R. Cornelius, SP	4
A. Fernandez, SP	4
M. Smith, OF	4
A. Almanza, RP	3
M. Aybar, RP	3
R. Castro, C	3
A. Fox, SS	3
A. Gonzalez, SS	3
H. Rodriguez, OF	3
C. Clapinski, 2B	2
D. Bautista, OF	1
R. Mahay, RP	1
S. Martinez, C	1
P. Ozuna, 2B	1

Houston (72-90)	WS
Hitting	**124.0**
Fielding	**30.6**
Pitching	**61.4**
J. Bagwell, 1B	25
R. Hidalgo, OF	21
M. Alou, OF	17
M. Meluskey, C	13
C. Biggio, 2B	11
S. Elarton, SP	11
B. Spiers, 3B	11
L. Berkman, OF	10
K. Caminiti, 3B	9
J. Lugo, SS	9
C. Holt, SP	8
O. Dotel, RP	7
C. Truby, 3B	7
S. Reynolds, SP	6
J. Slusarski, RP	6
T. Bogar, SS	5
R. Cedeno, OF	5
T. Eusebio, C	5
D. Henry, RP	4
W. Miller, SP	4
T. McKnight, SP	3
M. Valdes, RP	3
D. Ward, OF	3
J. Cabrera, RP	2
J. Lima, SP	2
G. Barker, OF	1
F. Charles, C	1
W. Franklin, RP	1
S. Linebrink, RP	1
M. Maddux, RP	1
Y. Perez, RP	1
B. Powell, SP	1
J. Powell, RP	1
B. Wagner, RP	1

Los Angeles (86-76)	WS
Hitting	**127.7**
Fielding	**39.0**
Pitching	**91.3**
G. Sheffield, OF	31
A. Beltre, 3B	22
S. Green, OF	22
K. Brown, SP	20
C. Park, SP	18
T. Hundley, C	17
M. Grudzielanek, 2B	15
E. Karros, 1B	14
M. Herges, RP	10
D. Dreifort, SP	9
C. Kreuter, C	9
K. Elster, SS	7
M. Fetters, RP	7
J. Shaw, RP	7
T. Adams, RP	6
A. Cora, SS	6
D. Hansen, 1B-3B	6
T. Hollandsworth, OF	4
A. Osuna, RP	4
T. Goodwin, OF	3
C. Donnels, OF	2
E. Gagne, SP	2
P. Lo Duca, C	2
O. Masaoka, RP	2
A. Mills, RP	2
C. Perez, SP	2
D. White, OF	2
B. Aven, OF	1
G. Berroa, OF	1
J. Leyritz, 1B	1
L. Prokopec, SP	1
A. Reyes, RP	1
F. Santangelo, OF	1
J. Vizcaino, SS	1

Milwaukee (73-89)	WS
Hitting	**97.2**
Fielding	**42.0**
Pitching	**79.8**
G. Jenkins, OF	20
R. Belliard, 2B	17
J. Burnitz, OF	16
J. D'Amico, SP	15
C. Leskanic, RP	12
M. Loretta, SS	12
R. Sexson, 1B	11
H. Blanco, C	9
J. Hernandez, 3B	9
J. Wright, SP	9
R. Casanova, C	8
M. Grissom, OF	8
B. Wickman, RP	8
C. Hayes, 3B	7
D. Weathers, RP	7
J. Acevedo, RP	6
J. Haynes, SP	6
J. Bere, SP	5
T. Houston, 1B	5
R. King, RP	4
L. Lopez, SS	4
J. Mouton, OF	4
L. Mouton, OF	4
V. de los Santos, RP	3
P. Rigdon, SP	3
K. Barker, 1B	2
A. Echevarria, 1B	1
H. Estrada, SP	1
S. Perez, SS	1
E. Stull, RP	1
M. Sweeney, DH	1

Montreal (67-95)	WS
Hitting	**101.6**
Fielding	**29.4**
Pitching	**70.0**
V. Guerrero, OF	29
J. Vidro, 2B	25
J. Vazquez, SP	14
R. White, OF	12
L. Stevens, 1B	11
G. Blum, 3B	10
O. Cabrera, SS	9
D. Hermanson, SP	9
S. Kline, RP	9
C. Pavano, SP	8
S. Strickland, RP	8
A. Telford, RP	7
P. Bergeron, OF	6
T. Armas Jr., SP	5
A. Tracy, 3B	5
C. Widger, C	4
M. Bradley, OF	3
T. de la Rosa, SS	3
T. Jones, OF	3
F. Lira, RP	3
M. Mordecai, 3B	3
W. Guerrero, OF	2
M. Johnson, RP	2
F. Seguignol, 1B-OF	2
U. Urbina, RP	2
M. Barrett, 3B	1
M. Blank, RP	1
G. Mota, RP	1
J. Powell, RP	1
J. Santana, RP	1
B. Schneider, C	1
L. Webster, C	1

New York (94-68)	WS
Hitting	**137.0**
Fielding	**42.2**
Pitching	**102.8**
E. Alfonzo, 2B	36
M. Piazza, C	28
M. Hampton, SP	19
T. Zeile, 1B	18
A. Benitez, RP	17
A. Leiter, SP	17
D. Bell, OF	16
R. Ventura, 3B	15
B. Agbayani, OF	14
J. Payton, OF	14
R. Reed, SP	11
G. Rusch, SP	11
T. Wendell, RP	8
J. Franco, RP	7
B.J. Jones, SP	6
M. Mora, SS	6
L. Harris, 3B	5
T. Pratt, C	5
M. Bordick, SS	3
D. Cook, RP	3
M. Franco, 1B	3
D. Hamilton, OF	3
K. Abbott, SS	2
P. Mahomes, RP	2
J. McEwing, OF	2
J. Nunnally, OF	2
T. Perez, OF	2
B. Trammell, OF	2
R. White, RP	2
R. Henderson, OF	1
B.M. Jones, RP	1
R. Ordonez, SS	1

Philadelphia (65-97)	WS
Hitting	**76.4**
Fielding	**41.4**
Pitching	**77.2**
B. Abreu, OF	23
S. Rolen, 3B	18
M. Lieberthal, C	14
R. Person, SP	13
R. Wolf, SP	13
P. Burrell, 1B	12
D. Glanville, OF	10
C. Schilling, SP	8
C. Brock, RP	7
B. Chen, SP	7
D. Relaford, SS	7
W. Gomes, RP	6
R. Gant, OF	5
M. Morandini, 2B	5
C. Politte, SP	5
O. Daal, SP	4
G. Bennett, C	3
J. Brantley, RP	3
R. Ducey, OF	3
B. Hunter, 1B	3

Player	WS
K. Jordan, 2B	3
T. Lee, 1B	3
M. Anderson, 2B	2
A. Arias, SS	2
A. Ashby, SP	2
K. Bottenfield, SP	2
T. Prince, C	2
E. Vosberg, RP	2
B. Ward, RP	2
R. Brogna, 1B	1
D. Coggin, SP	1
V. Padilla, RP	1
T. Perez, SS	1
J. Rollins, SS	1
K. Sefcik, OF	1

Pittsburgh (69-93)	WS
Hitting	**108.1**
Fielding	**29.1**
Pitching	**69.8**
B. Giles, OF	27
J. Kendall, C	24
J. Vander Wal, OF	19
K. Benson, SP	14
M. Williams, RP	11
W. Morris, 2B	10
A. Brown, OF	9
P. Meares, SS	9
W. Cordero, OF	8
T. Ritchie, SP	8
K. Young, 1B	7
S. Sauerbeck, RP	6
M. Benjamin, 3B	5
J. Manzanillo, RP	5
K. Osik, C	5
J. Anderson, SP	4
J. Silva, RP	4
J. Christiansen, RP	3
F. Cordova, SP	3
C. Peters, RP	3
Ar. Ramirez, 3B	3
L. Sojo, 3B	3
M. Wilkins, RP	3
R. Loiselle, RP	2
D. Serafini, SP	2
E. Wilson, 3B	2
B. Aven, OF	1
E. Brown, OF	1
A. Hyzdu, OF	1
A. Nunez, SS	1
Al. Ramirez, OF	1
T. Redman, OF	1
J. Schmidt, SP	1
J. Wehner, 3B	1

San Diego (76-86)	WS
Hitting	**119.3**
Fielding	**35.5**
Pitching	**73.2**
R. Klesko, 1B	23
P. Nevin, 3B	22
B. Boone, 2B	15
D. Jackson, SS	15
E. Owens, OF	15
T. Hoffman, RP	13
W. Williams, SP	12
R. Rivera, OF	10
A. Eaton, SP	9
A. Martin, OF	9
M. Darr, OF	6
W. Gonzalez, C	6
B. Tollberg, SP	6
D. Wall, RP	6
M. Clement, SP	5
C. Hernandez, C	5
D. Relaford, SS	5
E. Sprague, 1B	5
K. Walker, RP	5
D. Magadan, 3B	4
C. Almanzar, RP	3
B. Davis, C	3
T. Gwynn, OF	3
J. Mabry, OF	3
S. Spencer, SP	3
W. Cunnane, RP	2
T. Davey, RP	2
B. Meadows, SP	2
M. Whiteside, RP	2
K. DeHaan, OF	1
C. Gomez, SS	1
S. Hitchcock, SP	1
D. Maurer, RP	1
K. Nicholson, SS	1
H. Slocumb, RP	1
J. Vitiello, 1B	1
M. Whisenant, RP	1
J. Witasick, SP	1

San Francisco (97-65)	WS
Hitting	**169.8**
Fielding	**36.8**
Pitching	**84.4**
J. Kent, 2B	37
B. Bonds, OF	32
E. Burks, OF	21
R. Aurilia, SS	20
J. Snow, 1B	16
B. Estalella, C	15
R. Nen, RP	15
M. Benard, OF	14
L. Hernandez, SP	14
A. Rios, OF	11
S. Estes, SP	10
B. Mueller, 3B	10
F. Rodriguez, RP	9
K. Rueter, SP	9
M. Gardner, SP	8
R. Martinez, SS	7
R. Ortiz, SP	7
D. Mirabelli, C	6
C. Murray, OF	6
R. Davis, 3B	4
F. Crespo, OF	3
A. Embree, RP	3
A. Fultz, RP	3
T. Lowery, OF	3
D. Henry, RP	2
D. Minor, 1B	2
J. Nathan, SP	2
M. del Toro, RP	1
R. Vogelsong, RP	1

St. Louis (95-67)	WS
Hitting	**145.3**
Fielding	**44.8**
Pitching	**94.9**
J. Edmonds, OF	29
M. McGwire, 1B	20
J. Drew, OF	18
F. Vina, 2B	18
D. Kile, SP	17
E. Renteria, SS	15
R. Ankiel, SP	14
M. Matheny, C	14
D. Veres, RP	14
P. Polanco, 2B	11
G. Stephenson, SP	11
F. Tatis, 3B	11
W. Clark, 1B	10
P. Hentgen, SP	10
R. Lankford, OF	10
An. Benes, SP	8
E. Davis, OF	8
C. Paquette, 3B	8
M. Morris, RP	6
M. James, RP	5
E. Marrero, C	5
S. Dunston, OF	4
T. Howard, OF	3
B. Reames, SP	3
M. Timlin, RP	3
C. Hernandez, C	2
H. Slocumb, RP	2
Al. Benes, RP	1
J. Christiansen, RP	1
K. McDonald, C	1
E. Perez, 1B	1
J. Rodriguez, RP	1
L. Sutton, 1B	1

2001
American League

Anaheim (75-87)	WS
Hitting	**76.4**
Fielding	**46.7**
Pitching	**101.9**
T. Glaus, 3B	21
G. Anderson, OF	17
J. Washburn, SP	15
D. Erstad, OF	14
T. Percival, RP	14
D. Eckstein, SS	12
R. Ortiz, SP	12
T. Salmon, OF	11
A. Levine, RP	10
I. Valdes, SP	10
S. Schoeneweis, SP	9
S. Spiezio, 1B	9
A. Kennedy, 2B	8
B. Molina, C	7
P. Rapp, SP	7
B. Weber, RP	7
B. Gil, SS	6
L. Pote, RP	6
S. Wooten, DH	6
S. Hasegawa, RP	5
O. Palmeiro, OF	4
J. Fabregas, C	3
M. Holtz, RP	2
W. Joyner, 1B	2
S. Shields, RP	2
M. Wise, SP	2
B. Cooper, RP	1
J. DaVanon, OF	1
J. Molina, C	1
J. Nieves, 2B	1

Baltimore (63-98)	WS
Hitting	**99.1**
Fielding	**30.6**
Pitching	**59.3**
J. Conine, 1B	24
D. Segui, 1B	14
C. Richard, OF	12
M. Mora, OF	11
J. Hairston Jr., 2B	10
J. Johnson, SP	9
C. Ripken Jr., 3B	9
B. Anderson, OF	8
T. Batista, DH	8
B. Groom, RP	8
M. Bordick, SS	6
W. Roberts, RP	6
J. Towers, SP	6
M. Trombley, RP	6
C. Maduro, SP	5
J. Gibbons, DH-OF	4
P. Hentgen, SP	4
S. Ponson, SP	4
D. DeShields, OF	3
L. Matos, OF	3
G. Myers, DH	3
B. Roberts, SS	3
B. Ryan, RP	3
J. Bale, RP	2
L. Bigbie, OF	2
B. Fordyce, C	2
G. Gil, C	2
M. Kinkade, OF	2
F. Lunar, C	2
J. Mercedes, SP	2
J. Wasdin, RP	2
S. Douglass, SP	1
K. Foster, RP	1
J. Julio, RP	1
C. McElroy, RP	1

Boston (82-79)	WS
Hitting	**106.1**
Fielding	**41.3**
Pitching	**98.6**
M. Ramirez, DH	25
T. Nixon, OF	20
J. Offerman, 2B	14
B. Daubach, 1B	13
P. Martinez, SP	12
C. Everett, OF	11
D. Lowe, RP	11
H. Nomo, SP	11
T. Wakefield, RP	11
R. Arrojo, RP	9
F. Castillo, SP	8
D. Cone, SP	8
C. Stynes, 3B	8
J. Varitek, C	8
R. Beck, RP	7
D. Bichette, OF	7
R. Garces, RP	6
M. Lansing, SS	6
D. Mirabelli, C	6
T. O'Leary, OF	6
S. Hatteberg, C	5
S. Hillenbrand, 3B	5
U. Urbina, RP	5
D. Lewis, OF	4
N. Garciaparra, SS	3
P. Crawford, SP	2
C. Fossum, SP	2
L. Merloni, SS	2
I. Alcantara, OF	1
W. Banks, RP	1
T. Erdos, RP	1
C. Grebeck, SS	1
S. Kim, RP	1
J. Oliver, C	1
H. Pichardo, RP	1
C. Pickering, 1B	1
B. Pulsipher, RP	1
P. Schourek, RP	1
J. Valentin, SS	1

Chicago (83-79)	WS
Hitting	**118.0**
Fielding	**40.5**
Pitching	**90.5**
M. Ordonez, OF	25
R. Durham, 2B	21
M. Buehrle, SP	18
K. Foulke, RP	17
P. Konerko, 1B	17
C. Lee, OF	15
J. Valentin, 3B	15
C. Singleton, OF	12
R. Clayton, SS	10
S. Lowe, RP	10
J. Canseco, DH	8
J. Garland, RP	8
J. Liefer, OF	6
K. Wells, SP-RP	6
J. Baldwin, SP	5
B. Howry, RP	5
M. Johnson, C	5
H. Perry, 3B	5
A. Rowand, OF	5
D. Wells, SP	5
S. Alomar Jr., C	4
R. Biddle, SP	4
G. Glover, RP	4
J. Paul, C	4
T. Graffanino, 3B	3
A. Embree, RP	2
J. Fogg, RP	2
M. Ginter, RP	2
D. Wright, SP	2
L. Barcelo, RP	1
J. Crede, 3B	1
J. Ramirez, OF	1
F. Thomas, DH	1

Cleveland (91-71)	WS
Hitting	**150.3**
Fielding	**33.4**
Pitching	**89.2**
R. Alomar, 2B	37
J. Thome, 1B	31
J. Gonzalez, OF	23
E. Diaz, C	15
E. Burks, DH	14
B. Colon, SP	14
B. Wickman, RP	14
K. Lofton, OF	13
C. Sabathia, SP	12
O. Vizquel, SS	12
M. Cordova, OF	11
R. Branyan, 3B	10
D. Baez, RP	6
J. Cabrera, OF	6
S. Karsay, RP	6
R. Rincon, RP	6
P. Shuey, RP	6
T. Fryman, 3B	5
S. Woodard, RP	4
D. Burba, SP	3
R. Drese, RP	3
C. Finley, SP	3
K. Garcia, OF	3
D. Riske, RP	3
S. Reed, RP	2
J. Rocker, RP	2
R. Rodriguez, RP	2
J. Westbrook, RP	2
W. Cordero, OF	1
J. Cruz, OF	1
T. Laker, C	1
C. Nagy, SP	1
E. Taubensee, C	1

Detroit (66-96)	WS
Hitting	**102.8**
Fielding	**33.0**
Pitching	**62.2**
B. Higginson, OF	18
T. Clark, 1B	16
S. Halter, 3B	16
S. Sparks, SP	16
D. Easley, 2B	15
R. Cedeno, OF	14
J. Weaver, SP	13
J. Macias, 3B	12
R. Fick, C	10
M. Anderson, RP	8
D. Cruz, SS	8
D. Patterson, RP	7
R. Simon, 1B	7
D. Palmer, DH	6
J. Encarnacion, OF	5
V. Santos, RP	5
J. Lima, SP	4
C. Holt, SP	3
B. Inge, C	3
T. Jones, RP	3
W. Magee, OF	2
J. Cardona, C	1
R. Jackson, 1B	1
B. Moehler, SP	1
C. Nitkowski, RP	1
M. Perisho, RP	1
L. Pineda, RP	1
C. Wakeland, OF	1

Kansas City (65-97)	WS
Hitting	**80.1**
Fielding	**42.7**
Pitching	**72.1**
C. Beltran, OF	27
M. Sweeney, 1B	18
J. Suppan, SP	12
J. Randa, 3B	11
R. Sanchez, SS	10
R. Hernandez, RP	9
R. Ibanez, OF	9
C. Durbin, SP	8
J. Grimsley, RP	8
J. Dye, OF	7
B. Stein, RP	7
C. Bailey, RP	6
P. Byrd, SP	6
M. Quinn, OF	6
L. Alicea, 2B	5
C. Febles, 2B	5
D. Brown, OF	4
D. Reichert, SP	4
K. Wilson, SP	4
G. Zaun, C	4
N. Perez, SS	3
C. George, SP	2
D. Henry, RP	2
A. Hinch, C	2
B. Mayne, C	2
D. McCarty, 1B	2
H. Ortiz, C	2
D. Sadler, OF	2
M. Suzuki, SP	2
J. Austin, RP	1
B. Berger, OF	1
A. Berroa, SS	1
M. MacDougal, SP	1
L. Ordaz, 2B	1
B. Voyles, RP	1

Minnesota (85-77)	WS
Hitting	**111.0**
Fielding	**47.1**
Pitching	**96.9**
C. Koskie, 3B	24
J. Mays, SP	22
T. Hunter, OF	19
C. Guzman, SS	18
D. Mientkiewicz, 1B	18
B. Radke, SP	17
E. Milton, SP	15
A. Pierzynski, C	15
M. Lawton, OF	13
E. Guardado, RP	12
J. Jones, OF	10
L. Rivas, 2B	8
D. Ortiz, DH	7
T. Prince, C	6
B. Buchanan, OF	5
J. Cressend, RP	5
D. Hocking, SS	5
B. Wells, RP	5
H. Carrasco, RP	4
L. Hawkins, RP	3
M. LeCroy, DH	3
K. Lohse, SP	3
M. Redman, SP	3
C. Allen, OF	2
T. Jones, RP	2
T. Miller, RP	2
R. Reed, SP	2
J. Santana, RP	2
C. Blake, 3B	1
B. Kielty, OF	1
J. Maxwell, SS	1
D. Mohr, OF	1
J. Romero, SP	1

New York (95-65)	WS
Hitting	**130.2**
Fielding	**42.9**
Pitching	**111.9**
D. Jeter, SS	28
B. Williams, OF	24
J. Posada, C	23
T. Martinez, 1B	21
M. Mussina, SP	20
R. Clemens, SP	19
M. Rivera, RP	19
A. Soriano, 2B	16
S. Brosius, 3B	15
P. O'Neill, OF	13
A. Pettitte, SP	13
C. Knoblauch, OF	11
R. Mendoza, RP	10
M. Stanton, RP	10
D. Justice, DH	8
S. Spencer, OF	8
R. Choate, RP	4
O. Hernandez, SP	4
B. Boehringer, RP	3
T. Lilly, SP	3
E. Wilson, SS	2
J. Witasick, RP	2
M. Wohlers, RP	2
C. Almanzar, RP	1
E. Almonte, SS	1
C. Bellinger, OF	1
A. Hernandez, SP-RP	1
S. Hitchcock, SP	1
L. Sojo, 3B	1
T. Williams, RP	1

Oakland (102-60)	WS
Hitting	**147.4**
Fielding	**45.4**
Pitching	**113.3**
Ja. Giambi, 1B	38
E. Chavez, 3B	26
M. Tejada, SS	25
F. Menechino, 2B	18
M. Mulder, SP	18
J. Damon, OF	17
T. Hudson, SP	17
T. Long, OF	17
B. Zito, SP	15
J. Isringhausen, RP	14
R. Hernandez, C	13
C. Lidle, SP	13
Je. Giambi, DH	12
J. Dye, OF	11
J. Tam, RP	8
J. Mecir, RP	6
E. Hiljus, SP	5
M. Magnante, RP	5
C. Bradford, RP	3
M. Guthrie, RP	3
G. Myers, C	3
R. Gant, DH	2
G. Heredia, SP	2
B. McMillon, OF	2
F. Santangelo, 2B	2
M. Valdez, DH	2
L. Vizcaino, RP	2
M. Bellhorn, 2B	1
E. Byrnes, OF	1
M. Fyhrie, RP	1
C. Harville, RP	1
T. Mathews, RP	1
A. Piatt, OF	1
O. Saenz, DH	1

Seattle (116-46)	WS
Hitting	**181.0**
Fielding	**52.4**
Pitching	**114.5**
I. Suzuki, OF	36
B. Boone, 2B	32
M. Cameron, OF	29
E. Martinez, DH	25
J. Olerud, 1B	21
F. Garcia, SP	18
M. McLemore, OF	18
J. Moyer, SP	15
D. Bell, 3B	14
C. Guillen, SS	14
A. Sele, SP	14
D. Wilson, C	14
A. Rhodes, RP	12
K. Sasaki, RP	12
S. Javier, OF	11
P. Abbott, SP	9
A. Martin, OF	8
J. Nelson, RP	8
J. Pineiro, SP	7
T. Lampkin, C	6
N. Charlton, RP	5
R. Franklin, RP	5
J. Halama, SP	4
J. Paniagua, RP	4
E. Sprague, 1B	3
B. Fuentes, RP	1
C. Gipson, OF	1
G. Kingsale, OF	1
B. Tomko, RP	1

Tampa Bay (62-100)	WS
Hitting	**88.8**
Fielding	**34.4**
Pitching	**62.8**
B. Grieve, OF	17
G. Vaughn, DH	15
F. McGriff, 1B	13
R. Johnson, 3B	11
T. Sturtze, SP	11
B. Abernathy, 2B	10
R. Winn, OF	10
E. Yan, RP	8
C. Gomez, SS	7
T. Hall, C	6
J. Kennedy, SP	6
T. Phelps, RP	6
J. Tyner, OF	6
P. Wilson, SP	6
V. Zambrano, RP	6
S. Cox, 1B	5
A. Huff, 3B	5
J. Colome, RP	4
J. Flaherty, C	4
N. Bierbrodt, SP	3
D. Creek, RP	3
A. Lopez, SP	3
J. Wallace, RP	3
J. Guillen, OF	2
F. Martinez, SS	2
D. Rolls, 2B	2
A. Sheets, SS	2
G. Williams, OF	2
V. Castilla, 3B	1
M. DiFelice, C	1
M. Judd, RP	1
R. Meacham, RP	1
B. Rekar, SP	1
R. Rupe, SP	1
J. Sandberg, 3B	1
J. Standridge, RP	1

Texas (73-89)	WS
Hitting	**146.2**
Fielding	**26.6**
Pitching	**46.3**
A. Rodriguez, SS	37
R. Palmeiro, 1B	25
I. Rodriguez, C	18
F. Catalanotto, OF	17
G. Kapler, OF	13
J. Zimmerman, RP	12
D. Davis, SP	8
M. Lamb, 3B	8
R. Greer, OF	7
R. Helling, SP	7
R. Velarde, 2B	7
M. Young, 2B	7
R. Sierra, DH	6
B. Haselman, C	5
K. Caminiti, 3B	4
A. Galarraga, DH	4
R. Ledee, OF	4
M. Venafro, RP	4
C. Curtis, OF	3
P. Mahomes, RP	3
J. Moreno, RP	3
D. Oliver, SP	3
C. Pena, 1B	3
C. Michalak, RP	2
K. Rogers, SP	2
J. Brantley, RP	1
D. Kolb, RP	1
R. Mateo, OF	1
D. Mirabelli, C	1
C. Monroe, OF	1
B. Porter, OF	1
S. Sheldon, 3B	1

Toronto (80-82)	WS
Hitting	**93.9**
Fielding	**46.4**
Pitching	**99.7**
C. Delgado, 1B	23
S. Stewart, OF	18
J. Cruz, OF	16
A. Gonzalez, SS	16
R. Mondesi, OF	15
C. Carpenter, SP	13
K. Escobar, RP	11
P. Quantrill, RP	11
H. Bush, 2B	9
B. Fullmer, DH	9
R. Halladay, SP	9
B. Koch, RP	8
E. Loaiza, SP	8
B. File, RP	7
C. Michalak, SP	6
D. Fletcher, C	5
F. Lopez, 3B	5
S. Parris, SP	5
D. Plesac, RP	5
T. Batista, 3B	4
P. Borbon, RP	4
C. Izturis, 2B	4
B. Lyon, SP	4
A. Castillo, C	3
J. Frye, 2B	3
C. Latham, OF	3
V. Wells, OF	3
S. Eyre, RP	2
J. Frascatore, RP	2
J. Hamilton, SP	2
B. Bowles, RP	1
P. Coco, RP	1
M. DeWitt, RP	1
T. Fernandez, DH	1
L. Lopez, 3B	1
B. Simmons, OF	1
C. Woodward, 2B	1

2001 National League

Arizona (92-70)	WS
Hitting	**119.2**
Fielding	**49.3**
Pitching	**107.6**
L. Gonzalez, OF	37
R. Johnson, SP	26
C. Schilling, SP	24
M. Grace, 1B	16
B. Kim, RP	16
S. Finley, OF	15
C. Counsell, SS	14
R. Sanders, OF	14
J. Bell, 2B	12
M. Batista, RP	11
D. Miller, C	10
M. Williams, 3B	10
T. Womack, SS	10
D. Dellucci, OF	7
E. Durazo, 1B	7
B. Prinz, RP	7
D. Bautista, OF	6
J. Spivey, 2B	6
A. Lopez, SP	5
G. Swindell, RP	4
G. Colbrunn, 1B	3
E. Sabel, RP	3
B. Anderson, SP	2
T. Brohawn, RP	2
R. Ellis, SP	2
M. Morgan, RP	2
B. Witt, SP-RP	2
R. Barajas, C	1
G. Guzman, RP	1
M. Mantei, RP	1

Atlanta (88-74)	WS
Hitting	**104.1**
Fielding	**46.4**
Pitching	**113.5**
C. Jones, 3B	29
A. Jones, OF	22
G. Maddux, SP	20
B. Jordan, OF	19
J. Burkett, SP	17
T. Glavine, SP	16
J. Lopez, C	13
B. Surhoff, OF	12
R. Furcal, SS	9
M. Giles, 2B	9
M. Remlinger, RP	9
J. Marquis, RP	8
J. Smoltz, RP	8
J. Cabrera, RP	7
M. DeRosa, SS	6
J. Rocker, RP	6
Q. Veras, 2B	6
W. Helms, 1B	5
S. Karsay, RP	5
K. Ligtenberg, RP	5
K. Millwood, SP	5
P. Bako, C	3
K. Caminiti, 1B	3
J. Franco, 1B	3
D. Martinez, OF	3
O. Perez, SP	3
S. Reed, RP	3
R. Sanchez, SS	3
R. Brogna, 1B	2
K. Lockhart, 2B	2
B. Gilkey, OF	1
D. Moss, RP	1
R. Seanez, RP	1

Chicago (88-74)	WS
Hitting	**128.0**
Fielding	**39.3**
Pitching	**96.7**
S. Sosa, OF	42
R. Gutierrez, SS	16
J. Lieber, SP	16
E. Young, 2B	16
K. Wood, SP	13
R. White, OF	12
M. Stairs, 1B	11
J. Fassero, RP	10
J. Bere, SP	9
K. Farnsworth, RP	9
F. McGriff, 1B	9
J. Girardi, C	8
F. Gordon, RP	8
B. Mueller, 3B	8
T. Van Poppel, RP	8
K. Tapani, SP	7
R. Coomer, 3B	6
G. Matthews Jr., OF	6
J. Tavarez, SP	6
M. Tucker, OF	6
D. DeShields, OF	5
R. Brown, OF	4
J. Cruz, SP	4
T. Hundley, C	4
R. Machado, C	3
C. Patterson, OF	3
M. Cairo, 3B	2
C. Duncan, RP	2
R. Mahay, RP	2
A. Ojeda, 3B	2
D. Weathers, RP	2
M. Aybar, RP	1
D. Buford, OF	1
S. Chiasson, RP	1
M. Fyhrie, RP	1
J. Zuleta, 1B	1

Cincinnati (66-96)	WS
Hitting	**105.3**
Fielding	**28.1**
Pitching	**64.6**
S. Casey, 1B	18
K. Griffey Jr., OF	14
A. Boone, 3B	13
D. Young, OF	13
D. Graves, RP	11
E. Dessens, SP	10
A. Dunn, OF	10
J. LaRue, C	9
S. Sullivan, RP	9
J. Brower, RP	8
A. Ochoa, OF	7
P. Reese, SS	7
T. Walker, 2B	6
L. Davis, SP	5
B. Larkin, SS	5
R. Rivera, OF	5
K. Stinnett, C	5
B. Clark, OF	4
W. Guerrero, SS	4
J. Riedling, RP	4
M. Tucker, OF	4
R. Jennings, OF	3
H. Mercado, RP	3
C. Reitsma, SP	3
J. Acevedo, SP	2
D. Cromer, 1B	2
S. MacRae, RP	2
C. Miller, C	2
J. Rijo, RP	2
M. Wohlers, RP	2
R. Bell, SP	1
J. Castro, SS	1
C. Nichting, RP	1
C. Piersoll, RP	1
D. Reyes, RP	1
B. Selby, 2B	1

Colorado (73-89)	WS
Hitting	**99.5**
Fielding	**41.3**
Pitching	**78.2**
T. Helton, 1B	26
L. Walker, OF	25
J. Pierre, OF	17
J. Cirillo, 3B	14
M. Hampton, SP	11
J. Jimenez, RP	8
D. Neagle, SP	8
N. Perez, SS	8
S. Chacon, SP	7
J. Thomson, SP	7
J. Uribe, SS	7
J. Powell, RP	6
T. Walker, 2B	6
P. Astacio, SP	5
K. Davis, RP	5
T. Shumpert, 2B	5
J. Speier, RP	5
T. Hollandsworth, OF	4
B. Mayne, C	4
M. Myers, RP	4
J. Ortiz, 2B	4
B. Petrick, C	4
J. Jennings, SP	3
M. Little, OF	3
D. Miceli, RP	3
G. Norton, OF	3
B. Bohanon, SP	2
S. Fasano, C	2
R. Gant, OF	2
A. Ochoa, OF	2
G. White, RP	2
J. Acevedo, RP	1
B. Butler, 2B	1
J. Davenport, RP	1
M. Encarnacion, OF	1
B. Kieschnick, OF	1
R. Villone, RP	1
J. Wasdin, RP	1

Florida (76-86)	WS
Hitting	**113.8**
Fielding	**36.2**
Pitching	**78.0**
C. Floyd, OF	26
M. Lowell, 3B	20
K. Millar, OF	20
C. Johnson, C	17
D. Lee, 1B	16
L. Castillo, 2B	14
B. Penny, SP	12
A. Gonzalez, SS	10
P. Wilson, OF	10
A. Alfonseca, RP	9
A. Burnett, SP	9
V. Nunez, RP	8
R. Dempster, SP	7
B. Looper, RP	7
M. Redmond, C	6
M. Clement, SP	4
C. Smith, SP	4
J. Acevedo, RP	3
J. Beckett, SP	3
D. Berg, 2B	3
V. Darensbourg, RP	3
E. Owens, OF	3
A. Almanza, RP	2
R. Bones, RP	2
K. Olsen, SP-RP	2
J. Sanchez, SP	2
J. Abbott, OF	1
A. Fox, SS	1
J. Grilli, SP	1
J. Mabry, OF	1
R. McGuire, OF	1
J. Strong, RP	1

Houston (93-69)	WS
Hitting	**135.2**
Fielding	**45.4**
Pitching	**98.4**
L. Berkman, OF	32
J. Bagwell, 1B	30
C. Biggio, 2B	25
M. Alou, OF	21
R. Hidalgo, OF	17
W. Miller, SP	17
R. Oswalt, SP	15
B. Wagner, RP	13
V. Castilla, 3B	12
O. Dotel, RP	12
B. Ausmus, C	10
S. Reynolds, SP	10
J. Lugo, SS	9
N. Cruz, RP	6
M. Jackson, RP	6
T. Eusebio, C	5
D. Ward, OF	5
O. Merced, OF	4
D. Mlicki, SP	4
J. Vizcaino, SS	4
J. Powell, RP	3
C. Truby, 3B	3
P. Astacio, SP	2
C. Hernandez, SP	2
T. Redding, SP	2
R. Villone, RP	2
M. Williams, RP	2
G. Barker, OF	1
C. Hayes, 3B	1
S. Linebrink, RP	1
M. Lopez, 2B	1
T. McKnight, SP	1
R. Stone, RP	1

Los Angeles (86-76)	WS
Hitting	**139.9**
Fielding	**36.5**
Pitching	**81.6**
S. Green, OF	34
G. Sheffield, OF	30
P. Lo Duca, C	28
M. Grudzielanek, 2B	17
C. Park, SP	16
J. Shaw, RP	13
A. Beltre, 3B	12
K. Brown, SP	11
J. Reboulet, SS	10
M. Herges, RP	9
T. Adams, SP	8
G. Carrara, RP	8

E. Karros, 1B	8
C. Kreuter, C	8
A. Cora, SS	6
M. Grissom, OF	6
T. Goodwin, OF	5
E. Gagne, SP	4
D. Hansen, 1B	4
L. Prokopec, SP	4
J. Baldwin, SP	3
H. Bocachica, 2B	3
M. Christensen, OF	2
A. Reyes, RP	2
A. Ashby, SP	1
B. Aven, OF	1
D. Dreifort, SP	1
P. Hiatt, 3B	1
J. Orosco, RP	1
A. Pena, C	1
D. Springer, SP	1

Milwaukee (68-94)	WS
Hitting	**99.6**
Fielding	**34.9**
Pitching	**69.5**
R. Sexson, 1B	19
J. Burnitz, OF	18
R. Belliard, 2B	13
J. Hernandez, SS	13
G. Jenkins, OF	11
D. White, OF	11
C. Fox, RP	9
M. Loretta, 2B	9
M. DeJean, RP	8
T. Houston, 3B	8
D. Weathers, RP	8
C. Leskanic, RP	7
J. Wright, SP	7
H. Blanco, C	6
R. Casanova, C	6
J. Haynes, SP	6
B. Sheets, SP	6
J. Hammonds, OF	5
R. King, RP	5
L. Collier, OF	4
L. Lopez, 3B	4
M. Buddie, RP	3
J. Mouton, OF	3
R. Quevedo, SP	3
M. Leiter, RP	2
K. Brown, C	1
W. Cunnane, RP	1
A. Echevarria, OF	1
T. Fernandez, 3B	1
A. Levrault, SP	1
L. Painter, RP	1
E. Pena, 2B	1
P. Rigdon, SP	1
M. Suzuki, SP	1
M. Sweeney, OF	1

Montreal (68-94)	WS
Hitting	**80.4**
Fielding	**38.6**
Pitching	**85.1**
O. Cabrera, SS	26
V. Guerrero, OF	23
J. Vazquez, SP	21
J. Vidro, 2B	18
L. Stevens, 1B	13
T. Armas Jr., SP	12
S. Strickland, RP	10
G. Blum, 3B	8
G. Lloyd, RP	6
M. Mordecai, 3B	6
S. Stewart, RP	6
U. Urbina, RP	6
M. Thurman, SP	5
M. Yoshii, RP	5
P. Bergeron, OF	3
M. Bradley, OF	3
T. Raines, OF	3
M. Smith, OF	3
M. Barrett, C	2
M. Blank, SP	2
D. Cubillan, RP	2
R. Ducey, OF	2
G. Mota, RP	2
T. Ohka, SP	2
B. Reames, RP	2
B. Schneider, C	2
F. Tatis, 3B	2
J. Eischen, RP	1
H. Irabu, SP	1
M. Johnson, RP	1
T. Jones, OF	1
R. Knorr, C	1
T. Mattes, SP	1
B. Munoz, RP	1
C. Pride, OF	1
B. Wilkerson, OF	1

New York (82-80)	WS
Hitting	**101.2**
Fielding	**44.6**
Pitching	**100.2**
M. Piazza, C	21
T. Zeile, 1B	18
R. Ventura, 3B	17
E. Alfonzo, 2B	15
K. Appier, SP	15
A. Benitez, RP	14
A. Leiter, SP	14
D. Relaford, 2B	13
R. Ordonez, SS	12
R. Reed, SP	11
T. Shinjo, OF	11
B. Agbayani, OF	8
J. McEwing, OF	8
S. Trachsel, SP	8
M. Lawton, OF	7
G. Rusch, SP	6
J. Franco, RP	5
T. Wendell, RP	5
R. White, RP	5
M. Johnson, 1B	4
T. Perez, OF	4
J. Riggan, RP	4
D. Cook, RP	3
J. Payton, OF	3
D. Bragg, OF	2
B. Chen, SP	2
D. Gonzalez, RP	2
D. Hamilton, OF	2
G. Roberts, RP	2
A. Escobar, OF	1
C. Nitkowski, RP	1
P. Walker, RP	1
D. Wall, RP	1
V. Wilson, C	1

Philadelphia (86-76)	WS
Hitting	**116.1**
Fielding	**44.8**
Pitching	**97.2**
S. Rolen, 3B	29
B. Abreu, OF	26
J. Rollins, SS	20
P. Burrell, OF	17
M. Anderson, 2B	16
T. Lee, 1B	15
J. Mesa, RP	14
R. Person, SP	12
O. Daal, SP	11
D. Glanville, OF	11
R. Wolf, SP	11
R. Bottalico, RP	6
N. Figueroa, SP	6
D. Coggin, SP	5
B. Duckworth, SP	5
J. Estrada, C	5
B. Hunter, OF	5
T. Perez, 2B	5
J. Santiago, RP	5
R. Cormier, RP	4
W. Gomes, RP	4
C. Brock, RP	3
K. Jordan, 1B-2B-3B	3
M. Lieberthal, C	3
V. Padilla, RP	3
C. Politte, RP	3
B. Chen, SP	2
T. Pratt, C	2
A. Telemaco, SP	2
G. Bennett, C	1
R. Ducey, OF	1
E. Oropesa, RP	1
E. Valent, OF	1
E. Vosberg, RP	1

Pittsburgh (62-100)	WS
Hitting	**90.7**
Fielding	**30.8**
Pitching	**64.5**
B. Giles, OF	29
A. Ramirez, 3B	27
T. Ritchie, SP	10
J. Vander Wal, OF	10
J. Kendall, C	9
J. Manzanillo, RP	8
C. Wilson, 1B	8
J. Anderson, SP	7
D. Williams, SP	7
K. Young, 1B	7
A. Nunez, 2B-SS	6
M. Williams, RP	6
J. Wilson, SS	5
J. Beimel, RP	4
M. Lincoln, RP	4
R. Mackowiak, OF	4
G. Matthews Jr., OF	4
J. Schmidt, SP	4
B. Arroyo, SP	3
T. Mulholland, RP	3
S. Sauerbeck, RP	3
E. Brown, OF	2
M. Fetters, RP	2
T. McKnight, SP	2
P. Meares, 2B	2
A. Barkett, OF	1
D. Bell, OF	1
A. Hyzdu, OF	1
M. Lopez, 2B	1
D. Marte, RP	1
W. Morris, 2B	1
O. Olivares, RP	1
K. Osik, C	1
T. Redman, OF	1
E. Wilson, SS	1

San Diego (79-83)	WS
Hitting	**147.9**
Fielding	**28.3**
Pitching	**60.8**
P. Nevin, 3B	31
R. Klesko, 1B	29
B. Trammell, OF	17
M. Kotsay, OF	16
B. Davis, C	15
R. Henderson, OF	12
D. Jackson, 2B	11
T. Hoffman, RP	9
D. Jimenez, SS	8
M. Darr, OF	7
W. Gonzalez, C	7
K. Jarvis, SP	7
R. Lankford, OF	7
B. Lawrence, SP	6
B. Tollberg, SP	6
A. Eaton, SP	5
T. Gwynn, OF	4
J. Nunez, RP	4
J. Witasick, RP	4
A. Arias, 3B	3
C. Crespo, 2B	3
J. Fikac, RP	3
D. Lee, RP	3
W. Williams, SP	3
T. Davey, RP	2
B. Jones, SP	2
R. Seanez, RP	2
M. Colangelo, OF	1
C. Gomez, SS	1
S. Hitchcock, SP	1
B. Jodie, RP	1
D. Magadan, 3B	1
J. Middlebrook, SP	1
R. Myers, RP	1
S. Perez, OF	1
K. Walker, RP	1
R. Wilkins, C	1
K. Witt, 1B	1

San Francisco (90-72)	WS
Hitting	**153.9**
Fielding	**36.1**
Pitching	**79.9**
B. Bonds, OF	54
R. Aurilia, SS	33
J. Kent, 2B	27
R. Ortiz, SP	15
R. Nen, RP	14
F. Rodriguez, RP	12
M. Benard, OF	11
A. Rios, OF	10
B. Santiago, C	10
R. Martinez, 3B	9
S. Estes, SP	7
A. Galarraga, 1B	7
C. Murray, OF	7
K. Rueter, SP	7
J. Snow, 1B	6
L. Hernandez, SP	5
J. Schmidt, SP	5
T. Worrell, RP	5
S. Dunston, OF	4
B. Estalella, C	3
A. Fultz, RP	3
J. Vander Wal, OF	3
J. Christiansen, RP	2
R. Davis, 3B	2
R. Jensen, SP	2
C. Zerbe, RP	2
B. Boehringer, RP	1
E. Davis, OF	1
M. Gardner, SP	1
E. Guzman, C	1
Y. Torrealba, C	1

St. Louis (93-69)	WS
Hitting	**134.0**
Fielding	**47.5**
Pitching	**97.5**
J. Edmonds, OF	30
A. Pujols, OF	29
J. Drew, OF	22
F. Vina, 2B	22
D. Kile, SP	18
M. Morris, SP	17
P. Polanco, 3B	14
E. Renteria, SS	13
S. Kline, RP	12
C. Paquette, OF	12
D. Hermanson, SP	8
R. Lankford, OF	8
M. Matheny, C	8
M. McGwire, 1B	8
W. Williams, SP	8
E. Marrero, C	7
M. Matthews, RP	7
D. Veres, RP	7
B. Smith, SP	5
G. Stechschulte, RP	5
M. Timlin, RP	5
K. Robinson, OF	4
M. Cairo, OF	2
J. Christiansen, RP	2
L. Hackman, RP	2
B. Bonilla, 1B	1
M. James, RP	1
J. Karnuth, RP	1
T. Mathews, RP	1

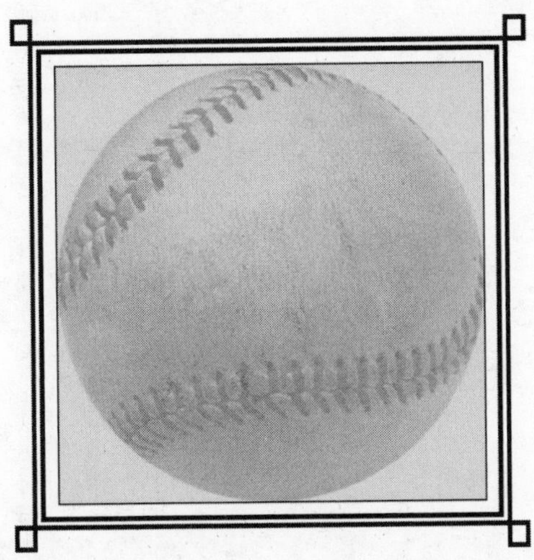

Win Shares by Decade

This section details Win Shares totals for each decade since 1876. Players are listed if they accumulated at least 250 Win Shares in their career or a minimum number in the given decade. That minimum is 25 for the 1870s, 10 for the 2000s, and 75 for every other 10-year span. Players are sorted in descending order of Win Shares each decade (Dec), which is the column of the chart that is bolded. A year-by-year breakdown is included, with blanks listed in seasons the player did not play.

The last four columns in each record are based upon career totals (Car). The percentage of total Win Shares generated by batting (B), fielding (F) and pitching (P) are presented in integer form. If a player never made a plate appearance during his career, a dash is listed in his batting percentage column. Likewise, if he never played a "Win Shares" position in the field (C, 1B, 2B, 3B, SS or OF), a dash is listed in his fielding percentage column. And if he never pitched in his career, a dash shows up in his pitching percentage column. The sum of the three percentages may not always equal 100, due to rounding.

Player	1876	77	78	79	Dec	B	F	P	Car
Tommy Bond	47	47	60	50	**204**	7	0	93	243
Jim Devlin	53	60			**113**	7	0	93	113
Terry Larkin	0	31	34	39	**104**	12	1	88	106
George Bradley	57	19		14	**90**	14	5	81	176
Monte Ward			24	51	**75**	39	19	42	409
Will White		2	30	33	**65**	3	0	97	239
Al Spalding	57	5	0		**62**	16	2	82	62
Pud Galvin				61	**61**	3	0	97	403
Jim O'Rourke	17	15	12	17	**61**	85	15	0	305
Deacon White	13	16	11	17	**57**	78	21	0	190
Paul Hines	12	6	15	22	**55**	83	17	0	249
Cal McVey	16	14	11	13	**54**	75	9	16	54
Charley Jones	9	9	12	21	**51**	87	13	0	161
George Wright	17	8	8	16	**49**	63	37	0	51
Tom York	10	10	13	14	**47**	80	20	–	107
Cap Anson	14	11	9	9	**43**	89	11	0	381
John Clapp	14	10	10	9	**43**	74	26	–	64
Joe Start	9	11	10	12	**42**	89	11	–	124
Jim McCormick			6	33	**39**	6	0	94	334
Lew Brown	5	9	12	9	**35**	69	31	0	50
Jack Manning	19	8	7		**34**	81	7	12	91
Bobby Mathews	18	1		14	**33**	2	0	98	158
Jack Burdock	8	6	11	8	**33**	65	35	–	98
John Peters	12	9	5	7	**33**	62	37	0	53
Orator Shaffer		7	13	12	**32**	80	20	–	120
Ross Barnes	20	2		10	**32**	80	20	0	41
Lip Pike	17	7	7		**31**	90	10	–	31
John Morrill	8	6	5	11	**30**	80	18	1	151
Bob Ferguson	9	7	11	3	**30**	73	25	1	64
Ezra Sutton	5	9	7	8	**29**	74	26	–	158
King Kelly			8	20	**28**	81	18	1	278
Pop Snyder	4	6	6	12	**28**	41	59	–	88
Joe Gerhardt	6	6	10	4	**26**	50	50	–	81
Tricky Nichols	1	24	1		**26**	0	1	99	27
Tom Carey	8	6	5	7	**26**	56	44	–	26
Andy Leonard	10	8	7		**25**	79	21	–	27
Dick Higham	13		12		**25**	88	12	–	25
Players with at least 250 career Win Shares									
George Gore				8	**8**	80	20	–	250
Dan Brouthers				5	**5**	93	7	0	355
Jack Glasscock				4	**4**	65	35	0	261

Player	1880	81	82	83	84	85	86	87	88	89	Dec	B	F	P	Car
Tim Keefe	11	23	24	70	47	42	38	39	35	27	**356**	5	0	95	413
Old Hoss Radbourn	0	24	50	60	89	39	32	22	11	21	**348**	8	1	91	391
Mickey Welch	42	25	12	31	46	57	29	27	32	31	**332**	6	0	93	354
Pud Galvin	14	36	29	47	57	12	32	33	30	16	**306**	3	0	97	403
Jim McCormick	54	34	42	40	53	21	33	18			**295**	6	0	94	334
Tony Mullane		0	36	55	58		34	46	33	24	**286**	12	1	87	399
Jim Whitney		42	40	57	37	24	21	34	17	2	**274**	19	1	81	275
Bob Caruthers					10	51	57	54	46	46	**264**	27	2	71	337
John Clarkson			1		11	62	42	51	32	60	**259**	3	0	97	396
Guy Hecker			17	36	74	42	39	30	9	7	**254**	26	1	73	259
Monte Ward	51	27	31	28	16	12	21	25	15	17	**243**	39	19	42	409
Roger Connor	17	11	19	19	23	30	36	21	32	26	**234**	89	11	–	363
Charlie Buffinton			2	28	62	28	8	23	44	33	**228**	9	1	90	283
Dan Brouthers	0	15	20	24	22	26	31	26	27	28	**219**	93	7	0	355
Dave Foutz					19	37	62	43	33	24	**218**	37	7	56	292
Cap Anson	20	22	18	15	19	23	30	19	29	21	**216**	89	11	0	381
King Kelly	16	16	16	13	21	24	35	23	24	24	**212**	81	18	1	278
Ed Morris					44	56	44	16	34	7	**201**	1	0	99	208
Harry Stovey	13	9	10	25	22	23	24	17	28	28	**199**	87	13	0	265
George Gore	24	15	17	22	16	30	26	14	7	23	**194**	80	20	–	250
Larry Corcoran	52	30	28	38	37	8	0	0			**193**	6	0	93	193
Hardy Richardson	11	15	11	17	19	19	32	23	11	25	**183**	78	21	1	230
Paul Hines	19	16	18	17	28	17	17	18	18	14	**182**	83	17	0	249
Jim O'Rourke	17	14	11	17	25	24	24	13	17	19	**181**	85	15	0	305
Jack Glasscock	10	10	19	14	22	17	22	17	16	27	**174**	65	35	0	261
Will White	17	0	54	51	33	18	1				**174**	3	0	97	239
Fred Dunlap	17	15	14	16	38	14	17	10	13	10	**164**	76	24	0	165
Pete Browning			20	20	23	28	17	30	17	4	**159**	87	13	0	225
Tip O'Neill				5	21	15	27	36	28	27	**159**	78	16	7	213
Buck Ewing	0	10	13	17	21	19	17	11	27	23	**158**	76	23	1	241
Silver King							1	37	71	44	**153**	4	0	96	263
Ned Williamson	12	14	16	16	19	21	14	13	20	3	**148**	70	28	2	173
Adonis Terry					29	9	26	27	21	30	**142**	15	2	83	273
Charlie Ferguson					16	41	49	36			**142**	23	2	75	142
Matt Kilroy							32	51	13	44	**140**	9	0	91	166
Jack Rowe	8	12	9	11	19	15	18	20	14	9	**135**	78	22	–	144
Bid McPhee			8	11	18	13	23	19	17	20	**129**	68	32	–	305
Ezra Sutton	8	12	9	21	28	22	16	11	2		**129**	74	26	–	158
Tom Burns	15	12	10	16	7	18	14	13	13	11	**129**	67	33	0	154
Arlie Latham	0			12	23	10	23	24	21	15	**128**	66	34	–	221
George Wood	8	11	13	17	10	11	18	18	13	9	**128**	82	18	0	166
John Reilly	1			18	25	16	13	18	25	12	**128**	88	12	–	151
Abner Dalrymple	23	15	16	13	17	25	10	6	3		**128**	80	20	–	150
Dave Orr				3	27	27	23	16	13	17	**126**	91	9	0	145
Bobby Mathews		5	21	30	31	26	11	1			**125**	2	0	98	158
Charlie Bennett	6	15	19	18	11	15	13	8	12	8	**125**	63	37	–	157
Jerry Denny		8	10	15	16	9	14	19	19	15	**125**	66	34	0	140
Deacon White	4	12	10	12	21	12	15	15	18	4	**123**	78	21	0	190
John Morrill	10	11	12	20	14	14	17	13	8	2	**121**	80	18	1	151
Jumbo McGinnis			26	42	28	7	15	3			**121**	5	0	95	121

Player	1880	81	82	83	84	85	86	87	88	89	Dec	B	F	P	Car
Henry Boyle					25	24	15	15	13	28	**120**	8	2	89	120
Henry Larkin					12	23	29	17	19	19	**119**	90	10	–	177
Frank Fennelly					21	23	23	20	19	12	**118**	69	31	–	123
Charlie Getzien					7	13	32	25	20	20	**117**	3	0	97	154
Fred Pfeffer			5	8	19	18	16	16	20	13	**115**	64	34	2	202
Curt Welch					9	22	21	18	25	20	**115**	70	30	0	165
Chicken Wolf			12	13	20	16	14	15	17	8	**115**	79	21	0	151
Ned Hanlon	8	10	11	8	11	14	13	15	12	13	**115**	78	22	–	146
Sam Wise		0	6	14	12	19	17	22	14	10	**114**	77	23	–	157
Yank Robinson			0		24	16	20	20	21	13	**114**	75	21	3	131
Fred Goldsmith	24	25	29	27	9						**114**	8	1	91	116
Stump Wiedman	2	10	35	17	5	14	17	12	0		**112**	1	1	98	112
Charley Jones	12			18	27	24	18	11	0		**110**	87	13	0	161
Toad Ramsey						6	47	46	5	5	**109**	2	0	98	137
Bill Gleason			16	16	19	17	15	17	9	0	**109**	75	25	–	109
Henry Porter					6	35	27	18	22	0	**108**	1	0	99	108
Pop Corkhill				8	16	13	13	19	21	17	**107**	61	37	3	120
Tom Brown			8	12	18	20	19	3	13	12	**105**	81	19	0	218
Hick Carpenter	5	4	18	16	12	13	7	7	14	7	**103**	66	34	–	105
Charlie Comiskey			9	14	9	13	10	17	15	15	**102**	79	21	1	125
Pop Smith	3	0	1	15	18	13	18	8	12	14	**102**	58	42	0	115
Jim Fogarty					7	15	18	25	19	18	**102**	70	30	0	113
Blondie Purcell	12	8	11	7	13	10	3	13	9	15	**101**	79	10	10	125
George Pinckney					4	14	19	18	23	22	**100**	74	26	0	157
Joe Hornung	10	8	14	16	18	1	8	9	8	8	**100**	72	28	0	115
Hardie Henderson				12	32	36	14	6	0		**100**	7	0	93	100
Oyster Burns					9	13		28	24	25	**99**	83	13	4	196
Fred Carroll					14	9	22	18	13	23	**99**	82	18	–	123
Bill Phillips	10	8	10	7	8	17	18	12	9		**99**	86	14	–	106
Elmer Smith							5	54	30	9	**98**	56	10	34	285
Jack Lynch		8		15	36	12	22	5			**98**	2	0	98	99
Ed Seward						1		33	42	21	**97**	3	1	96	104
Arthur Irwin	13	5	4	13	14	3	12	12	12	8	**96**	55	45	0	107
Ed Swartwood		0	16	19	16	13	21	8			**93**	89	11	0	118
Jack Farrell	13	13	11	18	11	4	4	6	10	3	**93**	71	29	–	103
One Arm Daily			14	34	38	2	0	5			**93**	3	0	97	93
Dupee Shaw				12	40	23	15	3	0		**93**	3	0	97	93
Charlie Sweeney			0	9	67	12	3	2			**93**	18	2	80	93
Billy Taylor		2	12	9	65	2	2	1			**93**	33	4	63	93
Jimmy Ryan						1	14	18	34	25	**92**	80	18	2	316
Dan Casey					1	4	29	30	18	10	**92**	0	0	100	105
Lee Richmond	42	26	13	9			1				**91**	20	0	80	92
Joe Sommer	0		16	13	17	10	9	13	5	6	**89**	71	29	0	92
Gus Weyhing								27	31	30	**88**	1	0	99	258
Hugh Nicol		2	3	14	17	12	4	9	15	12	**88**	63	37	–	91
Sam Thompson						10	21	29	10	17	**87**	88	12	–	236
George Bradley	24	5	5	23	28		1		0		**86**	14	5	81	176
Pete Gillespie	10	9	8	15	11	15	11	6			**85**	81	19	–	85
Billy Nash					5	2	15	19	23	20	**84**	67	33	0	222
Elton Chamberlin							0	22	20	42	**84**	3	0	97	185

Player	1880	81	82	83	84	85	86	87	88	89	Dec	B	F	P	Car
Ed Daily						35	22	8	8	11	**84**	33	6	61	113
Pete Hotaling	9	10	9	10	7	15		15	9		**84**	81	19	–	98
Lady Baldwin					3	14	53	14	0		**84**	6	0	94	85
Joe Start	12	16	14	10	14	15	1				**82**	89	11	–	124
Germany Smith					9	15	14	16	12	15	**81**	42	58	0	175
Bill Kuehne				7	15	9	10	13	18	8	**80**	54	46	–	101
Emmett Seery					22	1	11	10	17	18	**79**	83	17	0	107
Candy Nelson		3		15	23	21	9	7			**78**	80	20	–	87
Bill McClellan		2		5	15	14	19	14	8		**77**	77	23	–	79
Sam Barkley					21	21	20	3	8	4	**77**	74	26	–	77
Fred Mann			4	10	20	11	16	15			**76**	83	17	–	76
Players with at least 250 career Win Shares															
Mike Tiernan								12	26	28	**66**	88	12	0	251
George Van Haltren								13	24	21	**58**	74	14	12	344
Dummy Hoy									28	13	**41**	81	19	–	254
Jake Beckley									14	19	**33**	88	12	0	318
Billy Hamilton									3	24	**27**	85	15	–	337
Hugh Duffy									10	17	**27**	80	20	–	295
Herman Long										22	**22**	61	39	–	265
Kid Gleason									13	8	**21**	32	17	51	294
Jack Stivetts										21	**21**	16	1	82	285
Ed Delahanty									7	5	**12**	88	12	–	355
Lave Cross								5	2	5	**12**	59	41	–	278
Amos Rusie										10	**10**	3	0	97	293

Player	1890	91	92	93	94	95	96	97	98	99	Dec	B	F	P	Car
Kid Nichols	43	39	48	40	37	34	33	41	44	31	**390**	2	0	98	478
Cy Young	8	28	44	35	39	37	43	28	34	35	**331**	1	0	99	634
Amos Rusie	40	36	32	41	56	28		31	19		**283**	3	0	97	293
Billy Hamilton	25	36	25	20	29	30	30	28	33	15	**271**	85	15	–	337
Jack Stivetts	41	46	49	25	33	18	29	20	2	1	**264**	16	1	82	285
Ed Delahanty	13	12	20	28	22	31	31	23	33	41	**254**	88	12	–	355
Hugh Duffy	26	28	29	28	33	23	17	25	25	17	**251**	80	20	–	295
George Van Haltren	30	26	20	20	21	22	23	24	29	18	**233**	74	14	12	344
Jesse Burkett	14	4	23	24	21	35	29	23	29	30	**232**	86	14	0	389
Cupid Childs	31	21	32	23	20	18	27	18	18	12	**220**	76	24	–	238
George Davis	14	21	19	22	25	21	21	31	20	20	**214**	75	25	0	398
Bill Dahlen		21	32	17	21	20	31	14	27	23	**206**	63	37	–	394
Herman Long	14	29	28	26	16	19	20	17	19	16	**204**	61	39	–	265
Bill Hutchison	54	49	45	20	16	19		1			**204**	2	0	98	221
Kid Gleason	45	29	25	22	19	12	15	17	8	10	**202**	32	17	51	294
Ted Breitenstein		3	8	30	36	25	22	34	25	19	**202**	3	0	96	212
Joe Kelley		1	6	20	30	27	31	26	22	30	**193**	83	17	–	305
Frank Dwyer	2	24	26	22	23	21	30	23	21	1	**193**	3	0	97	213
Hughie Jennings		12	14	2	24	29	36	29	32	9	**187**	69	31	–	214
Mike Tiernan	26	26	18	16	11	22	25	23	16	2	**185**	88	12	0	251
Jimmy Ryan	23	22	25	12	13	14	14	16	28	17	**184**	80	18	2	316
Mike Griffin	17	19	23	17	20	29	17	22	20		**184**	80	20	–	245
Nig Cuppy			31	15	28	33	38	13	8	14	**180**	4	0	96	193
Pink Hawley			7	11	29	44	27	19	28	14	**179**	3	0	97	204
Frank Killen		11	28	42	15	6	32	22	18	5	**179**	7	0	93	181
Clark Griffith		15		1	19	34	30	22	32	25	**178**	6	0	94	273
Dummy Hoy	17	28	20	9	15	11	18	16	24	20	**178**	81	19	–	254
Bid McPhee	21	19	27	21	17	16	17	11	15	12	**176**	68	32	–	305
Elmer Smith			31	25	19	16	26	20	27	12	**176**	56	10	34	285
Jouett Meekin		12	9	7	48	14	27	23	15	16	**171**	7	0	93	171
Brickyard Kennedy			10	29	24	19	13	25	20	28	**168**	6	0	94	208
Jake Beckley	21	16	19	17	17	18	10	15	14	20	**167**	88	12	0	318
Gus Weyhing	32	37	36	19	12	6	0		13	12	**167**	1	0	99	258
John McGraw		3	7	20	24	20	3	20	31	34	**162**	81	19	–	207
Ed McKean	21	18	12	19	19	25	17	9	17	4	**161**	80	20	–	221
Willie Keeler			2	3	23	23	25	32	23	29	**160**	85	15	–	333
Sadie McMahon	33	39	11	26	24	15	11	1			**160**	2	0	98	174
Bill Joyce	18	17	16		18	16	29	18	25		**157**	89	11	–	157
Red Ehret	34	13	20	24	21	7	24	11	1		**155**	2	0	98	169
Tommy Corcoran	11	19	14	16	16	15	15	12	18	16	**152**	44	56	–	214
Steve Brodie	17	16	12	19	19	20	16	10	6	15	**150**	70	30	–	170
Sam Thompson	19	22	22	22	20	28	13	0	3		**149**	88	12	–	236
Bobby Lowe	8	15	16	22	20	14	10	16	15	13	**149**	61	39	0	188
Bill Lange				12	13	29	24	21	21	19	**139**	78	22	–	139
Billy Nash	20	20	22	25	17	17	6	9	2		**138**	67	33	0	222
John Clarkson	33	42	33	16	13						**137**	3	0	97	396
Duke Farrell	17	24	13	14	14	11	8	9	11	16	**137**	63	37	–	183
Billy Rhines	41	21	0	0		18	16	24	15	2	**137**	1	0	99	137
Lave Cross	8	16	17	11	22	14	8	5	17	17	**135**	59	41	–	278
Patsy Donovan	4	14	19	14	10	15	17	13	19	9	**134**	84	16	–	201

Player	1890	91	92	93	94	95	96	97	98	99	Dec	B	F	P	Car
Dan Brouthers	19	29	34	16	21	3	9				**131**	93	7	0	355
Adonis Terry	41	9	20	13	8	22	18	0			**131**	15	2	83	273
Jack Doyle	9	9	17	10	17	10	17	18	12	12	**131**	84	16	–	176
Roger Connor	25	23	24	16	14	12	14	1			**129**	89	11	–	363
Jack Taylor		1	2	11	23	25	17	18	22	10	**129**	5	0	95	129
Tom Daly	11	5	16	20	20	14	9		5	28	**128**	74	26	–	215
Tommy McCarthy	24	22	21	24	19	11	5				**126**	77	22	1	170
Jake Stenzel	0		0	10	24	28	22	24	13	5	**126**	84	16	–	126
Cap Anson	24	21	19	11	11	14	12	10			**122**	89	11	0	381
Deacon McGuire	15	17	10	5	9	17	14	13	8	13	**121**	63	37	0	189
Billy Shindle	26	7	15	14	13	16	12	14	4		**121**	59	41	–	167
Ad Gumbert	25	23	24	11	15	16	7				**121**	13	0	87	144
Fred Clarke					5	16	17	30	25	25	**118**	84	16	–	400
Harry Staley	27	29	29	15	12	6					**118**	2	0	98	152
Denny Lyons	27	23	14	21	10	2	16	3			**116**	82	18	–	190
Scott Stratton	51	10	29	16	9	1					**116**	20	1	79	134
Ed Stein	11	6	30	20	27	18	2		0		**114**	3	–	97	114
Tony Mullane	28	24	26	27	8						**113**	12	1	87	399
Tom Brown	18	31	16	11	9	5	12	11	0		**113**	81	19	0	218
Bug Holliday	18	18	26	19	18	3	2	7	2		**113**	81	19	0	134
Chief Zimmer	11	14	18	9	10	17	10	10	2	10	**111**	56	44	–	153
Silver King	44	20	24	7			8	7			**110**	4	0	96	263
Tommy Tucker	17	12	17	11	13	9	10	11	8	2	**110**	86	14	0	176
Jack Clements	18	19	15	12	7	18	9	4	6	0	**108**	68	32	–	146
Mark Baldwin	42	25	20	20							**107**	0	0	100	176
Win Mercer					19	13	18	27	13	15	**105**	19	1	80	157
Jimmy Collins						10	11	26	34	23	**104**	67	33	–	274
Bill Hallman	8	17	15	16	10	13	14	2	8		**103**	63	37	0	129
Bobby Wallace					2	14	15	21	25	25	**102**	58	33	9	345
Elton Chamberlin	17	27	26	20	11		0				**101**	3	0	97	185
Bert Cunningham	7	11				10	7	15	30	21	**101**	3	0	97	138
Kip Selbach					9	14	18	19	17	23	**100**	86	14	–	215
Kid Carsey		9	21	17	15	21	8	3	0	5	**99**	5	0	95	99
Eddie Burke	15	4	14	15	15	8	20	7			**98**	72	28	–	98
Duke Esper	10	17	12	11	14	18	13	1	2		**98**	6	0	94	98
Oyster Burns	21	15	26	12	18	5					**97**	83	13	4	196
Bill Hoffer						35	31	18	4	9	**97**	4	0	95	100
George Hemming	10	5	1	18	21	24	16	2			**97**	4	0	96	97
Jack O'Connor	21	5	12	11	9	10	6	8	9	4	**95**	57	43	–	124
Germany Smith	10	7	20	14	10	14	14	5	0		**94**	42	58	0	175
Arlie Latham	9	25	17	16	14	12	0			0	**93**	66	34	–	221
Walt Wilmot	26	21	8	11	13	10		1	3		**93**	79	21	–	122
Monte Ward	27	15	23	17	9						**91**	39	19	42	409
Jack Crooks	14	23	18	15		11	6		4		**91**	70	30	–	95
Patsy Tebeau	13	6	10	15	8	9	7	6	12	3	**89**	65	35	0	105
Bones Ely	13	2		4	14	7	14	14	10	10	**88**	36	63	1	110
Jimmy McAleer	7	12	21	6	6	14	13	1	8		**88**	53	47	0	97
Fred Pfeffer	13	21	20	13	11	1	7	1			**87**	64	34	2	202
Jack Glasscock	25	10	20	18	7	3					**83**	65	35	0	261
Buck Ewing	20	2	20	19	4	11	7	0			**83**	76	23	1	241

Player	1890	91	92	93	94	95	96	97	98	99	Dec	B	F	P	Car
Doggie Miller	13	17	24	2	13	7	6				**82**	76	24	–	135
Perry Werden	20	19	17	11				15			**82**	72	13	15	97
Heinie Reitz				14	17	6	13	17	12	2	**81**	64	36	–	81
Lou Bierbauer	20	4	17	13	12	8	6	0	0		**80**	58	41	1	137
Doc McJames						1	11	19	30	19	**80**	0	–	100	81
Dusty Miller	2					18	19	15	21	5	**80**	77	23	–	80
Gene DeMontreville					0	1	21	18	24	15	**79**	66	34	–	107
Al Maul	18	4		11	8	10	3	0	24	1	**79**	25	4	71	98
Wilbert Robinson	9	5	6	12	15	6	9	4	6	6	**78**	56	44	–	116
Bill Everitt						19	16	11	18	14	**78**	85	15	–	80
Phil Knell	21	32	11		8	6					**78**	1	0	99	78
Fred Tenney					4	4	12	15	17	25	**77**	85	15	0	249
George Haddock	7	34	27	6	3						**77**	9	0	90	89
Jesse Tannehill					1			14	34	27	**76**	10	1	89	233
Joe Quinn	17	9	9	4	8	10	3	7	4	5	**76**	56	44	–	120
Willie McGill	8	25	1	20	11	7	4				**76**	4	0	96	76
Jack Powell								21	25	29	**75**	1	0	99	287
Ted Lewis							2	22	31	20	**75**	2	0	98	106
Players with at least 250 career Win Shares															
Dave Foutz	27	16	13	10	6	2	0				**74**	37	7	56	292
Bob Caruthers	30	22	19	2							**73**	27	2	71	337
Nap Lajoie							5	21	26	19	**71**	81	19	–	496
Cy Seymour							0	21	26	21	**68**	62	16	22	272
Fielder Jones							16	18	19	14	**67**	77	23	–	290
Harry Stovey	20	26	12	8							**66**	87	13	0	265
Vic Willis									25	39	**64**	0	0	100	293
Jim O'Rourke	20	17	15	11							**63**	85	15	0	305
Honus Wagner								9	22	26	**57**	78	22	0	655
Tim Keefe	19	4	24	10							**57**	5	0	95	413
Charlie Buffinton	21	31	3								**55**	9	1	90	283
Elmer Flick									26	23	**49**	89	11	–	291
George Gore	18	18	12								**48**	80	20	–	250
Old Hoss Radbourn	34	9									**43**	8	1	91	391
King Kelly	16	15	6	1							**38**	81	18	1	278
Pud Galvin	10	15	11								**36**	3	0	97	403
Jimmy Sheckard								2	13	21	**36**	80	20	–	339
Joe McGinnity										35	**35**	1	0	99	269
Roy Thomas										30	**30**	83	17	0	260
Mickey Welch	19	3	0								**22**	6	0	93	354
Tommy Leach									0	13	**13**	71	29	–	328
Guy Hecker	5										**5**	26	1	73	259
Sam Crawford										4	**4**	89	11	–	446
Jim Whitney	1										**1**	19	1	81	275

Player	1900	01	02	03	04	05	06	07	08	09	Dec	B	F	P	Car
Honus Wagner	34	37	35	35	43	46	46	44	59	42	**421**	78	22	0	655
Nap Lajoie	22	42	22	31	41	14	33	32	32	27	**296**	81	19	–	496
Cy Young	22	41	38	38	35	28	13	27	27	20	**289**	1	0	99	634
Christy Mathewson	0	21	22	37	34	39	20	29	39	34	**275**	3	0	97	426
Sam Crawford	12	24	23	25	21	36	23	36	32	32	**264**	89	11	–	446
Fred Clarke	18	28	29	25	14	24	21	29	28	31	**247**	84	16	–	400
Elmer Flick	32	30	17	25	31	29	30	37	1	7	**239**	89	11	–	291
Joe McGinnity	30	27	23	40	42	22	24	16	10		**234**	1	0	99	269
Rube Waddell	16	17	33	27	32	35	18	20	21	12	**231**	1	0	99	240
Roy Thomas	25	24	25	23	28	31	26	21	19	8	**230**	83	17	0	260
Jimmy Sheckard	15	33	25	33	11	21	25	23	15	23	**224**	80	20	–	339
Fielder Jones	20	23	25	20	22	29	27	25	32		**223**	77	23	–	290
Vic Willis	12	33	29	19	19	17	29	20	20	24	**222**	0	0	100	293
Eddie Plank		19	25	28	29	31	16	29	19	22	**218**	1	–	99	361
Tommy Leach	3	17	27	21	25	17	19	29	31	26	**215**	71	29	–	328
Topsy Hartsel	3	27	25	20	21	30	24	29	19	11	**209**	87	13	–	223
Frank Chance	7	9	13	31	29	25	35	23	20	14	**206**	91	9	–	237
Jack Chesbro	14	23	25	22	53	20	25	13	8	0	**203**	1	0	99	209
Bobby Wallace	13	26	22	20	23	21	23	20	21	13	**202**	58	33	9	345
Ginger Beaumont	14	25	31	28	24	19	7	28	17	9	**202**	83	17	–	229
Cy Seymour	1	14	14	24	26	42	25	20	19	13	**198**	62	16	22	272
Doc White		16	27	23	17	22	25	25	20	20	**195**	7	1	92	235
Harry Davis		17	19	17	21	26	31	21	18	19	**189**	88	12	–	238
Bill Dahlen	21	18	23	23	25	24	19	13	16	6	**188**	63	37	–	394
Three Finger Brown				12	20	20	35	29	34	36	**186**	1	0	99	296
Jack Powell	14	17	31	20	29	8	20	12	20	15	**186**	1	0	99	287
George Davis	18	24	26	0	28	28	29	17	14	0	**184**	75	25	0	398
Addie Joss			17	20	16	25	23	28	35	20	**184**	0	0	100	191
Bill Bradley	16	19	26	29	28	22	11	12	15	3	**181**	67	33	0	191
George Mullin			16	23	25	26	26	21	14	28	**179**	13	0	87	255
Bill Dinneen	27	27	27	27	26	8	10	9	13	4	**178**	2	0	98	200
Jimmy Williams	15	22	19	22	20	16	20	19	18	4	**175**	73	27	–	207
Sam Leever	20	11	17	28	22	19	21	17	13	5	**173**	1	0	99	212
Harry Steinfeldt	11	11	14	21	9	13	33	20	16	25	**173**	70	30	–	208
Willie Keeler	22	20	24	20	25	19	19	2	10	11	**172**	85	15	–	333
Al Orth	18	29	19	15	15	18	36	16	5	1	**172**	11	0	89	243
Jimmy Collins	18	28	20	26	28	23	4	16	7		**170**	67	33	–	274
Deacon Phillippe	23	25	23	27	7	26	16	13	0	10	**170**	1	0	99	206
Roger Bresnahan	0	6	12	27	23	19	29	18	27	8	**169**	76	23	1	231
Claude Ritchey	16	19	17	21	22	17	23	16	17	0	**168**	69	31	–	205
Wild Bill Donovan	0	27	18	22	19	20	11	23	18	10	**168**	4	0	96	202
Jimmy Slagle	15	10	23	25	19	25	19	22	8		**166**	76	24	–	177
Fred Tenney	7	9	25	21	19	17	17	22	19	9	**165**	85	15	0	249
Patsy Dougherty			17	28	24	12	9	20	29	25	**164**	87	13	–	187
Freddy Parent		21	16	26	29	15	10	12	11	23	**163**	64	36	–	168
Joe Tinker			17	21	20	18	17	11	32	24	**160**	56	44	–	258
Jesse Burkett	25	38	25	22	25	22					**157**	86	14	0	389
Jesse Tannehill	23	22	24	15	25	26	13	7	1	1	**157**	10	1	89	233
Jack Taylor	16	13	32	25	27	14	26	4			**157**	4	0	96	183
Harry Howell	9	19	13	9	22	20	18	23	23	1	**157**	6	2	93	172

Player	1900	01	02	03	04	05	06	07	08	09	Dec	B	F	P	Car
Sherry Magee					11	28	31	38	26	20	**154**	87	13	–	354
Art Devlin					25	23	36	22	24	23	**153**	69	31	–	198
Danny Murphy	2	0	9	14	26	23	21	16	18	23	**152**	80	20	–	215
Kid Elberfeld		22	15	25	18	15	18	21	2	13	**149**	69	31	–	184
Mike Donlin	10	21	4	24	18	36	5		31		**149**	89	11	0	174
Sam Mertes	18	21	19	26	27	25	12				**148**	81	19	1	180
Socks Seybold		21	24	22	21	21	19	19	1		**148**	84	16	–	149
John Titus				7	21	29	23	22	23	20	**145**	87	13	–	201
Johnny Evers			1	15	20	11	20	22	28	27	**144**	74	26	–	268
Ed Walsh					7	8	22	37	47	23	**144**	2	0	98	265
Ty Cobb						4	16	41	36	44	**141**	88	11	0	722
Chick Stahl	15	24	20	12	31	17	21				**140**	81	19	0	211
Charlie Hickman	16	12	23	21	19	21	17	7	4		**140**	84	9	7	155
Wid Conroy		13	12	21	18	18	19	15	11	12	**139**	66	34	–	153
John Anderson		20	12	19	19	20	18	13	15		**136**	86	14	–	209
Dan McGann	13	13	14	12	22	24	16	11	11		**136**	87	13	–	183
Bob Ewing			4	18	17	23	21	21	20	9	**133**	3	0	97	148
Noodles Hahn	21	26	29	24	25	4	3				**132**	1	0	99	161
Lave Cross	16	19	26	16	21	15	16	2			**131**	59	41	–	278
Jimmy Barrett	23	23	22	26	26	1	0	9	0		**130**	79	21	–	135
Buck Freeman	10	24	23	24	25	13	9	1			**129**	89	10	1	160
George Stone				0		27	38	27	26	11	**129**	89	11	–	146
Charlie Hemphill		11	20	8	12		24	16	28	7	**126**	82	18	–	146
Johnny Kling	1	5	17	22	10	8	21	19	22		**125**	63	37	–	155
Sammy Strang	2	20	26	19	4	14	23	16	1		**125**	82	18	–	126
Red Donahue	14	24	30	15	18	4	17				**122**	0	0	100	165
Danny Green	14	20	21	26	27	14					**122**	85	15	–	144
Tully Sparks		8	11	14	5	21	21	24	13	5	**122**	0	–	100	131
Ed Reulbach						29	23	21	27	21	**121**	1	0	99	206
Frank Smith					17	22	6	24	21	31	**121**	7	0	93	151
Jake Weimer				23	28	21	27	11	9	0	**119**	2	–	98	119
Jake Beckley	21	18	18	17	23	16	5	0			**118**	88	12	0	318
Chief Bender				18	11	15	17	22	12	22	**117**	5	0	95	231
Matty McIntyre		8			17	20	19	4	33	15	**116**	81	19	–	148
Kip Selbach	27	15	16	11	26	17	3				**115**	86	14	–	215
Chick Fraser	17	19	13	9	7	19	14	9	8	0	**115**	2	0	98	164
Frank Isbell		13	9	9	5	17	26	15	12	9	**115**	74	23	3	119
Hooks Wiltse					13	19	19	15	25	22	**113**	4	0	96	163
Kitty Bransfield		17	15	10	6	13	14	4	20	14	**113**	84	16	–	120
Hobe Ferris		11	12	15	12	15	10	10	20	8	**113**	53	47	–	113
Luther Taylor	5	14	13	11	22	14	16	11	7		**113**	0	0	100	113
Joe Kelley	22	18	15	15	16	10	8		8		**112**	83	17	–	305
Ed Killian				4	18	29	9	29	8	15	**112**	7	0	93	115
Togie Pittinger	2	21	24	17	19	19	3	6			**111**	0	–	100	111
Miller Huggins					20	27	22	19	17	5	**110**	77	23	–	222
Long Tom Hughes	1	14	9	23	8	22	4	6	19	4	**110**	6	0	94	134
Orval Overall						17	14	32	17	30	**110**	2	0	98	126
Earl Moore		16	17	19	13	15	0	1	4	24	**109**	0	–	100	169
George Browne		0	13	19	20	16	10	11	8	11	**108**	84	16	–	111
Nixey Callahan	14	23	16	16	17	16					**102**	38	7	54	185

Player	1900	01	02	03	04	05	06	07	08	09	Dec	B	F	P	Car
Harry Lumley					20	17	35	19	8	3	**102**	91	9	–	102
Frank Kitson	19	21	20	14	7	8	8	3			**100**	9	0	91	140
Bill Coughlin		15	17	9	10	17	12	13	6		**99**	64	36	–	99
Carl Lundgren			10	11	19	15	19	25	0	0	**99**	1	0	98	99
Bob Rhoads			3	3	8	17	23	16	23	5	**98**	2	0	97	98
Ed Siever		22	16	17	8		16	18	0		**97**	0	0	100	97
Jake Stahl				4	18	21	8		21	23	**95**	90	10	–	127
Doc Casey	0	15	14	9	16	13	16	12			**95**	67	33	–	108
Clark Griffith	19	27	11	16	7	10	4	0		0	**94**	6	0	94	273
Bill Bernhard	9	13	20	12	22	4	14	0			**94**	0	–	100	104
Davy Jones		1	14	17	14		13	24	2	8	**93**	80	20	–	139
George Winter		16	12	9	9	17	5	17	7		**92**	2	–	98	92
Jim Delahanty		0	0		20	10	13	18	16	14	**91**	85	15	0	149
Danny Hoffman				4	9	16	12	19	13	17	**90**	78	21	0	102
Ed Abbaticchio				10	18	16		20	22	4	**90**	77	23	–	92
Ed Delahanty	19	33	31	6							**89**	88	12	–	355
O. Schreckengost		11	14	10	4	14	15	16	5		**89**	47	53	–	98
Bill Duggleby		22	15	10	4	20	16	2			**89**	1	–	99	91
Kid Nichols	18	32			27	11	0				**88**	2	0	98	478
Wildfire Schulte					5	16	24	14	11	18	**88**	82	18	–	239
Jiggs Donahue	0	4	2		11	22	21	17	6	5	**88**	85	15	–	88
Shad Barry	4	4	17	12	9	19	12	6	4		**87**	82	18	–	92
Homer Smoot			21	13	19	23	11				**87**	84	16	–	87
Nick Altrock			1	5	16	24	21	13	6	0	**86**	3	0	97	90
Harry Bay		1	13	21	17	23	9	2	0		**86**	73	27	–	86
Roy Patterson		20	19	17	10	6	10	4			**86**	1	–	99	86
Doc Gessler				6	11	16	6		26	19	**84**	90	10	–	119
Barney Pelty				3	15	11	21	14	8	12	**84**	0	0	100	101
Terry Turner		1			8	16	28	17	6	7	**83**	56	44	–	171
Emmett Heidrick	9	23	16	16	17				2		**83**	78	22	0	104
Billy Gilbert		9	11	13	19	13	12		4	1	**82**	57	43	–	82
Monte Cross	8	7	10	18	10	9	10	9			**81**	57	43	–	153
Willie Sudhoff	9	14	19	25	4	8	0				**79**	1	0	99	111
Lee Tannehill				8	17	13	10	4	13	14	**79**	36	64	–	99
Casey Patten		14	14	15	8	13	11	4	0		**79**	0	0	100	79
Ollie Pickering		22	6	19	10			14	7		**78**	76	24	–	94
Germany Schaefer		1	1			18	11	13	23	10	**77**	75	25	0	118
Tim Jordan		0		0			25	22	16	14	**77**	93	7	–	77
Frank Owen		2		6	26	22	18	2	1	0	**77**	3	0	97	77
Solly Hofman				0	1	8	8	18	14	27	**76**	74	26	–	158
Cozy Dolan	1	7	19	11	16	11	11				**76**	67	16	18	93
Jack McCarthy	12	11	9	12	13	5	13	0			**75**	77	23	–	115
Ed Hahn						8	18	27	19	3	**75**	84	16	–	75

Players with at least 250 career Win Shares

Player	1900	01	02	03	04	05	06	07	08	09	Dec	B	F	P	Car
Kid Gleason	5	15	6	10	15	12	7	1	0		**71**	32	17	51	294
Eddie Collins							0	0	11	43	**54**	81	19	–	574
George Van Haltren	21	23	3	6							**53**	74	14	12	344
Ed Konetchy								10	18	24	**52**	86	14	0	287
Larry Doyle								4	17	27	**48**	83	17	–	289

Player	1900	01	02	03	04	05	06	07	08	09	Dec	B	F	P	Car
Jimmy Ryan	12		19	9							**40**	80	18	2	316
Billy Hamilton	23	16									**39**	85	15	–	337
Herman Long	13	8	13	5	0						**39**	61	39	–	265
Tris Speaker								0	2	34	**36**	81	19	0	630
Walter Johnson								4	20	12	**36**	5	0	95	560
Dummy Hoy		25	10								**35**	81	19	–	254
Home Run Baker									2	27	**29**	78	22	–	301
Clyde Milan								5	15	3	**23**	79	21	–	266
Hugh Duffy	5	8			3	1	0				**17**	80	20	–	295
Elmer Smith	11	0									**11**	56	10	34	285
Harry Hooper										9	**9**	83	17	0	321
Jack Quinn										7	**7**	2	0	98	287
Zack Wheat										4	**4**	85	15	–	380
Gus Weyhing	3	0									**3**	1	0	99	258
Larry Gardner									0	2	**2**	69	31	–	258
Joe Jackson									0	0	**0**	90	10	–	294

Player	1910	11	12	13	14	15	16	17	18	19	Dec	B	F	P	Car
Ty Cobb	45	47	40	31	26	48	40	46	31	32	**386**	88	11	0	722
Walter Johnson	36	31	47	54	38	42	36	29	38	27	**378**	5	0	95	560
Tris Speaker	34	27	51	36	45	36	41	37	27	27	**361**	81	19	0	630
Eddie Collins	39	35	36	39	43	40	31	32	16	27	**338**	81	19	–	574
Pete Alexander		34	24	27	26	43	44	40	2	26	**266**	2	–	98	476
Joe Jackson	6	39	37	36	20	18	34	31	4	32	**257**	90	10	–	294
Home Run Baker	25	35	39	38	35		17	21	23	20	**253**	78	22	–	301
Larry Doyle	25	28	29	21	19	33	20	18	12	20	**225**	83	17	–	289
Clyde Milan	23	27	33	28	19	22	18	22	18	9	**219**	79	21	–	266
Harry Hooper	19	20	15	21	20	19	26	22	29	17	**208**	83	17	0	321
Zack Wheat	21	16	16	16	26	24	32	16	16	21	**204**	85	15	–	380
Ed Konetchy	27	26	22	19	13	27	26	17	9	18	**204**	86	14	0	287
Heinie Zimmerman	13	22	34	25	22	16	17	26	15	14	**204**	79	21	–	214
Sherry Magee	36	19	17	19	29	26	16	15	18	5	**200**	87	13	–	354
Eddie Cicotte	13	11	11	27	21	13	19	35	14	32	**196**	1	–	99	247
Larry Gardner	15	18	29	16	20	14	27	18	17	20	**194**	69	31	–	258
George Burns		0	2	22	31	24	25	34	23	32	**193**	84	16	–	290
Art Fletcher	1	17	18	24	22	18	25	27	20	20	**192**	58	42	–	218
Gavy Cravath			15	29	28	35	26	26	11	16	**186**	91	9	–	202
Hippo Vaughn	18	7	6	6	21	19	24	24	28	30	**183**	1	–	99	205
Jake Daubert	17	20	17	17	19	27	21	12	15	17	**182**	87	13	–	263
Donie Bush	24	18	19	18	22	20	12	21	13	15	**182**	67	33	–	232
Dode Paskert	24	18	24	17	15	11	27	19	23	4	**182**	77	23	–	227
Babe Ruth					1	23	37	36	40	43	**180**	81	6	14	756
Sam Crawford	23	32	24	27	31	28	13	0			**178**	89	11	–	446
Heine Groh			2	13	19	25	24	37	28	30	**178**	74	26	–	272
Honus Wagner	30	30	35	18	19	23	17	5			**177**	78	22	0	655
Fred Merkle	20	18	19	14	17	22	13	19	22	12	**176**	87	13	–	191
Duffy Lewis	19	15	21	17	20	24	19	24		13	**172**	77	23	0	180
Max Carey	1	14	22	20	17	16	25	23	22	11	**171**	73	27	–	351
Bobby Veach			3	13	18	30	27	31	17	32	**171**	82	18	0	265
Slim Sallee	6	18	21	22	25	13	15	17	9	22	**168**	1	–	99	189
Benny Kauff			0		38	34	27	30	15	24	**168**	85	15	–	175
Claude Hendrix		7	29	18	37	18	15	13	18	12	**167**	9	0	91	174
Red Smith		2	16	19	26	24	24	22	21	7	**161**	77	23	–	161
Stuffy McInnis	4	18	24	26	21	13	12	17	12	12	**159**	84	16	–	227
Del Pratt			19	19	26	21	24	12	17	20	**158**	74	26	–	242
Hal Chase	17	14	9	12	21	23	22	17	9	14	**158**	89	11	0	231
Fred Luderus	3	20	13	14	11	26	20	18	15	18	**158**	87	13	–	160
Buck Herzog	8	20	20	13	21	20	19	13	9	13	**156**	64	36	–	171
Burt Shotton		11	19	23	19	24	26	8	16	9	**155**	83	17	–	161
Christy Mathewson	30	32	31	30	19	5	4				**151**	3	0	97	426
Babe Adams	21	25	13	29	19	13	1		3	27	**151**	3	–	97	243
Wildfire Schulte	26	31	17	18	13	17	12	4	13		**151**	82	18	–	239
Rube Marquard	2	26	26	26	11	4	20	17	14	5	**151**	0	–	100	208
Joe Wood	14	26	44	13	8	20		1	16	6	**148**	28	4	68	193
Amos Strunk	3	7	18	14	17	21	23	20	16	6	**145**	83	17	–	174
Eddie Plank	16	22	25	16	11	29	17	7			**143**	1	–	99	361
Eddie Foster	1		26	11	23	22	17	13	18	11	**142**	67	33	–	171
Ray Caldwell	1	23	7	14	22	24	8	18	13	10	**140**	9	1	90	161

Player	1910	11	12	13	14	15	16	17	18	19	Dec	B	F	P	Car
Bob Bescher	18	20	23	17	18	15	16	1	4		**132**	85	15	–	154
Rabbit Maranville			1	17	24	20	27	22	2	18	**131**	53	47	–	302
Buck Weaver			8	23	8	21	14	21	15	20	**130**	58	42	–	152
Chick Gandil	5		18	23	17	16	12	16	10	13	**130**	85	15	–	130
Nap Lajoie	47	14	22	23	7	12	4				**129**	81	19	–	496
Dutch Leonard				17	29	18	22	22	7	14	**129**	2	–	98	160
Ray Chapman			4	15	13	17	10	30	21	18	**128**	67	33	–	148
Jack Graney	10	14	7	15	13	10	22	17	5	15	**128**	80	20	0	137
Lefty Tyler	1	3	11	17	18	12	20	18	24	3	**127**	7	0	93	143
Dick Rudolph	0	0		16	29	24	21	9	7	20	**126**	2	–	98	129
Larry Cheney		2	27	25	20	6	17	14	13	1	**125**	1	0	99	125
Russ Ford	35	28	16	14	29	3					**125**	3	0	97	125
Johnny Evers	22	5	27	20	25	11	8	6			**124**	74	26	–	268
Red Ames	13	16	14	15	17	9	12	17	11	0	**124**	0	–	100	198
Edd Roush				0	6	22	10	30	22	33	**123**	81	19	–	314
Dots Miller	7	16	14	18	21	16	12	15		4	**123**	73	27	–	155
Doc Hoblitzell	18	18	19	12	13	16	13	14	0		**123**	88	12	–	149
Jimmy Austin	12	17	10	15	10	15	11	14	11	8	**123**	63	37	–	143
Jeff Pfeffer		0		0	26	26	32	18	2	18	**122**	2	0	98	178
Ed Walsh	36	31	40	8	2	4	0	0			**121**	2	0	98	265
Wilbur Cooper			4	3	19	4	20	22	23	25	**120**	4	–	96	266
Roger Peckinpaugh	0		3	8	16	14	21	20	14	24	**120**	55	45	–	239
Chief Meyers	16	19	23	20	16	10	10	5			**119**	71	29	–	129
Jeff Tesreau			21	25	26	21	12	9	5		**119**	3	–	97	119
Mike Mowrey	23	18	10	14	9	21	17	6			**118**	66	34	–	139
Jack Barry	19	16	16	20	18	12	6	9		2	**118**	61	39	–	132
Fred Snodgrass	23	23	18	21	12	5	16				**118**	79	21	–	122
Hooks Dauss			1	14	19	25	17	15	13	13	**117**	4	0	96	215
Doc Crandall	19	20	12	8	26	29	0		3		**117**	21	1	78	135
Chief Bender	26	18	13	20	15	6	3	13			**114**	5	0	95	231
Nap Rucker	23	31	24	19	4	10	3				**114**	0	–	100	177
Jack Coombs	37	23	18	0	0	16	11	3	5		**113**	9	1	90	160
Shano Collins	6	9	18	11	18	15	15	5	11	5	**113**	74	26	–	149
Miller Huggins	23	18	17	18	22	13	1				**112**	77	23	–	222
Tilly Walker		6	3	2	28	16	18	12	17	10	**112**	81	19	–	164
George Cutshaw			8	15	15	16	16	12	17	13	**112**	61	39	–	140
Carl Mays						11	22	30	25	23	**111**	7	–	93	256
Ray Schalk			3	13	17	18	16	20	7	17	**111**	49	51	–	191
Jim Scott	10	16	3	27	14	23	9	9			**111**	0	–	100	124
Rogers Hornsby						0	28	38	18	26	**110**	88	12	–	502
Three Finger Brown	29	25	8	11	15	21	1				**110**	1	0	99	296
George Sisler						10	25	29	22	24	**110**	89	8	3	292
Chief Wilson	14	22	24	15	18	11	6				**110**	76	24	–	138
Steve Evans	17	22	14	6	30	21					**110**	90	10	–	126
Vic Saier		6	13	26	24	24	13	0		4	**110**	90	10	–	110
Bob Groom	10	11	23	15	17	11	13	9	0		**109**	0	0	100	116
Casey Stengel			3	13	20	14	19	20	4	15	**108**	83	17	–	159
Ping Bodie		20	17	16	6			22	9	18	**108**	78	22	–	124
Wally Schang				13	19	17	12	15	10	19	**105**	75	25	–	245
Jack Quinn	19	9	0	4	32	13			5	22	**104**	2	0	98	287

Player	1910	11	12	13	14	15	16	17	18	19	Dec	B	F	P	Car
Ray Fisher	5	12	0	14	15	21	9	11		17	**104**	2	–	98	114
Lee Magee		2	11	11	16	17	15	2	18	12	**104**	75	25	–	104
Reb Russell				32	9	16	20	18	7	0	**102**	20	2	78	124
George Suggs	20	17	22	7	28	8					**102**	2	–	98	107
Tommy Leach	16	10	14	24	27	7			2		**100**	71	29	–	328
Rube Oldring	25	16	11	19	13	10	5		1		**100**	79	21	–	140
Bobby Byrne	27	20	18	13	11	6	5	0			**100**	68	32	–	137
Les Mann				10	13	23	9	14	20	10	**99**	80	20	–	157
Max Flack					13	26	10	13	20	17	**99**	80	20	–	156
Vean Gregg		28	23	23	6	5	3		11		**99**	1	–	99	103
Joe Tinker	22	21	19	17	16	3	0				**98**	56	44	–	258
Stan Coveleski			1				11	29	29	27	**97**	1	–	99	245
Bob Shawkey				6	14	7	27	17	2	24	**97**	2	–	98	223
Milt Stock				0	15	8	21	19	13	20	**96**	72	28	–	188
Bob Harmon	6	23	12	12	16	15	7		4		**95**	2	–	98	99
Mickey Doolan	22	15	13	9	18	9	3		4		**93**	36	64	–	161
Fred Toney		3	0	0		23	18	19	14	16	**93**	1	–	99	144
Jim Bagby			2				17	34	19	21	**93**	3	–	97	139
Happy Felsch						14	24	30	4	21	**93**	76	24	–	123
Ray Collins	18	15	19	19	19	3					**93**	2	–	98	97
Rube Benton	0	3	18	7	14	10	12	12	2	14	**92**	1	–	99	142
Cy Falkenberg	14	7		25	34	11		1			**92**	0	–	100	128
George McBride	16	11	13	14	12	9	13	2	1	1	**92**	31	69	–	127
Carl Weilman			4	9	24	21	19	1		14	**92**	0	–	100	101
Erskine Mayer			0	11	21	24	6	11	17	2	**92**	2	–	98	92
Gene Packard			1	9	21	22	12	15	7	4	**91**	2	0	98	91
Bill Doak			0	5	24	17	10	13	12	9	**90**	0	–	100	170
Johnny Bates	24	23	12	15	15						**89**	86	14	–	147
Ossie Vitt			4	6	5	23	21	14	7	9	**89**	55	45	–	99
Art Wilson	3	6	5	1	27	19	6	8	7	7	**89**	70	30	–	90
Joe Benz		4	14	8	20	17	12	5	9	0	**89**	0	–	100	89
Tom Seaton			17	29	22	9	7	5			**89**	2	–	98	89
Terry Turner	14	11	13	13	11	4	13	2	6	1	**88**	56	44	–	171
Birdie Cree	22	25	8	14	15	4					**88**	85	15	–	103
Willie Mitchell	11	7	9	20	9	14	7	11	0	0	**88**	1	0	99	90
Dave Bancroft						21	20	18	17	11	**87**	61	39	–	269
Hans Lobert	14	18	9	20	13	10	2	1			**87**	79	21	–	157
Eppa Rixey			14	12	0	12	24	20		4	**86**	0	–	100	315
Mike Mitchell	22	17	16	17	14						**86**	84	16	–	145
Frank LaPorte	14	17	13	7	18	17					**86**	78	22	–	138
Earl Hamilton		6	16	13	22	8	4	3	8	6	**86**	2	–	98	134
Rebel Oakes	9	15	11	14	21	16					**86**	76	24	–	101
Bill Rariden	2	2	2	8	13	25	12	12	4	6	**86**	55	45	–	89
Ray Morgan		0	7	21	19	6	15	12	6		**86**	75	25	–	86
Ed Reulbach	9	14	10	10	14	22	5	1			**85**	1	0	99	206
Dave Davenport					17	34	15	9	8	2	**85**	0	–	100	85
Ivy Olson		10	8	8	4	4	10	14	7	19	**84**	52	48	–	125
Braggo Roth					6	15	15	19	16	13	**84**	88	12	–	106
Rollie Zeider	15	7	13	4	15	11	6	8	5		**84**	65	35	–	84
Cy Williams			1	3	2	19	18	16	12	12	**83**	80	20	–	235

Player	1910	11	12	13	14	15	16	17	18	19	Dec	B	F	P	Car
Eddie Murphy			5	22	23	19	1	2	8	3	**83**	92	8	–	87
George Burns					17	10	15	5	24	11	**82**	87	13	–	200
Solly Hofman	31	13	7	2	20	7	2				**82**	74	26	–	158
Hi Myers		0			6	14	15	12	12	23	**82**	67	33	–	148
Howard Shanks			9	10	10	12	13	8	12	7	**81**	59	41	–	134
Harry Lord	16	23	17	15	0	10					**81**	83	17	–	116
Wally Pipp				0		16	20	17	13	14	**80**	83	17	–	203
Possum Whitted			1	4	8	15	20	18	1	13	**80**	72	28	–	105
Al Demaree			2	17	9	12	18	11	8	3	**80**	0	–	100	80
Pat Ragan		9	8	10	8	18	12	6	6	3	**80**	1	–	99	80
Jimmy Sheckard	23	30	21	5							**79**	80	20	–	339
Red Faber					12	21	17	16	7	6	**79**	1	–	99	292
Steve O'Neill		1	4	10	6	9	10	7	13	18	**78**	59	41	–	152
Bill Killefer	3	0	5	10	7	9	6	15	10	13	**78**	29	71	–	87
Pol Perritt			2	1	20	9	15	17	14	0	**78**	0	–	100	82
Otto Knabe	16	14	12	14	10	8	3				**77**	60	40	–	120
Ivy Wingo		0	10	6	11	4	8	15	10	13	**77**	62	38	–	115
Jean Dubuc			19	15	9	16	11		0	7	**77**	8	0	92	81
George Mullin	19	23	14	3	17	0					**76**	13	0	87	255
Bill Sweeney	11	19	20	15	11						**76**	74	26	–	103
Harry Coveleski	0				23	24	27	2	0		**76**	0	–	100	90
Jim Shaw				1	14	10	6	11	15	18	**75**	1	–	99	85
Ward Miller	3		8	7	17	22	16	2			**75**	83	17	–	79
Players with at least 250 career Win Shares															
Harry Heilmann					3		17	18	12	23	**73**	91	9	–	356
Joe Judge						3	8	19	13	17	**60**	88	12	–	270
Sam Rice						2	8	24	1	18	**53**	83	17	1	327
Bobby Wallace	20	7	8	2	1	1	1	0	1		**41**	58	33	9	345
Burleigh Grimes							2	4	25	6	**37**	4	–	96	286
Fred Clarke	15	20		0	0	0					**35**	84	16	–	400
Jack Powell	5	8	13								**26**	1	0	99	287
Cy Young	10	4									**14**	1	0	99	634
Vic Willis	7										**7**	0	0	100	293
Cy Seymour	6			0							**6**	62	16	22	272
Waite Hoyt									0	5	**5**	1	–	99	262
Frankie Frisch										3	**3**	71	29	–	366
Elmer Flick	3										**3**	89	11	–	291
Willie Keeler	1										**1**	85	15	–	333
Clark Griffith	0		0	1	0						**1**	6	0	94	273
Bill Dahlen	0	0									**0**	63	37	–	394
Kid Gleason			0								**0**	32	17	51	294
Fielder Jones					0	0					**0**	77	23	–	290
Roy Thomas	0	0									**0**	83	17	0	260

Player	1920	21	22	23	24	25	26	27	28	29	Dec	B	F	P	Car
Babe Ruth	51	53	29	55	45	13	45	45	45	32	**413**	81	6	14	756
Rogers Hornsby	38	41	47	26	38	36	21	40	33	42	**362**	88	12	–	502
Harry Heilmann	16	28	24	35	30	30	27	32	22	19	**263**	91	9	–	356
Frankie Frisch	15	31	20	31	30	20	20	34	22	20	**243**	71	29	–	366
Tris Speaker	39	27	30	35	21	25	29	21	6		**233**	81	19	0	630
Joe Sewell	4	26	21	29	22	24	29	21	23	21	**220**	68	32	–	277
Sam Rice	23	23	20	24	24	24	23	17	19	20	**217**	83	17	1	327
Pete Alexander	36	22	18	27	14	20	16	28	19	10	**210**	2	–	98	476
Burleigh Grimes	32	29	11	21	21	9	15	19	30	23	**210**	4	–	96	286
Eppa Rixey	18	22	23	26	21	26	14	15	22	14	**201**	0	–	100	315
Goose Goslin		1	12	21	29	31	33	28	26	19	**200**	86	14	–	355
Ty Cobb	20	26	29	24	27	25	10	22	12		**195**	88	11	0	722
Dolf Luque	16	23	18	39	14	27	14	16	15	9	**191**	4	0	96	241
Ken Williams	17	27	30	29	18	20	12	18	12	5	**188**	84	16	–	202
Edd Roush	33	18	9	28	20	23	21	16	3	15	**186**	81	19	–	314
Eddie Collins	38	21	23	24	25	22	17	11	1	0	**182**	81	19	–	574
Dave Bancroft	26	31	27	20	10	22	20	9	11	6	**182**	61	39	–	269
Urban Shocker	24	30	29	25	20	19	19	16	0		**182**	2	–	98	225
Eddie Rommel	14	19	27	25	21	21	18	8	17	12	**182**	1	–	99	209
Max Carey	20	24	29	29	25	26	7	13	7	0	**180**	73	27	–	351
Red Faber	25	37	31	16	9	15	13	5	13	15	**179**	1	–	99	292
Joe Judge	22	19	18	17	19	15	16	16	17	20	**179**	88	12	–	270
Dazzy Vance			16	18	36	20	11	25	32	19	**177**	0	–	100	241
Herb Pennock	19	14	11	23	27	23	18	17	20	5	**177**	1	–	99	240
George Kelly	16	24	20	20	26	22	17	6	14	12	**177**	83	17	0	193
Pie Traynor	0	1	13	28	17	26	22	26	22	21	**176**	71	29	–	274
Bob Meusel	19	24	21	16	19	18	13	21	18	6	**175**	85	15	–	184
George Sisler	33	27	29		11	19	11	16	15	13	**174**	89	8	3	292
Jim Bottomley			6	24	16	27	23	26	30	21	**173**	90	10	–	258
Zack Wheat	28	23	27	15	35	27	10	7			**172**	85	15	–	380
Waite Hoyt	4	24	21	21	17	17	13	23	22	9	**171**	1	–	99	262
Lou Gehrig				2	1	15	30	44	42	32	**166**	93	7	–	489
Jack Fournier	19	24	13	27	34	29	9	11			**166**	92	8	0	231
George Uhle	4	16	22	29	8	15	32	9	14	16	**165**	9	0	91	231
Al Simmons					17	34	27	26	23	34	**161**	82	18	–	375
Lu Blue		17	20	16	15	17	17	9	23	22	**156**	88	12	–	198
Ross Youngs	33	23	22	25	29	11	12				**155**	88	12	–	206
Charlie Jamieson	12	17	19	25	19	12	17	15	12	7	**155**	80	19	0	183
Sad Sam Jones	15	29	20	20	13	11	5	9	22	10	**154**	3	0	97	245
Jack Quinn	19	8	19	18	18	11	13	17	18	10	**151**	2	0	98	287
Cy Williams	24	17	17	17	21	12	17	16	7	3	**151**	80	20	–	235
Stan Coveleski	32	25	22	16	12	23	16	1	1		**148**	1	–	99	245
Jimmy Dykes	12	16	17	9	16	18	15	16	8	21	**148**	68	32	0	245
Bing Miller		12	22	15	13	13	14	15	20	23	**147**	80	20	–	196
Walter Johnson	10	23	21	17	29	26	15	5			**146**	5	0	95	560
Wilbur Cooper	31	27	27	21	24	13	3				**146**	4	–	96	266
Baby Doll Jacobson	25	25	20	15	23	23	13	2			**146**	76	24	–	178
Howard Ehmke	18	8	14	25	25	14	16	11	10	5	**146**	1	–	99	174
Carl Mays	27	35	17	1	20	5	20	6	5	9	**145**	7	–	93	256
Jesse Haines	14	14	11	20	7	11	14	28	19	6	**144**	0	0	100	207

Player	1920	21	22	23	24	25	26	27	28	29	Dec	B	F	P	Car
Bill Sherdel	10	9	16	14	11	19	17	18	24	5	**143**	3	0	97	177
Marty McManus	0	6	20	19	17	20	16	11	15	18	**142**	69	31	–	202
Curt Walker	0	9	16	6	17	21	22	16	14	19	**140**	81	19	–	153
Kiki Cuyler		0	0	0	24	34	26	12	18	25	**139**	84	16	–	292
Wally Schang	20	20	18	8	16	4	14	12	14	11	**137**	75	25	–	245
Hack Wilson				0	16	4	26	31	28	32	**137**	87	13	–	224
Bibb Falk	0	11	13	9	21	15	24	21	8	15	**137**	83	17	–	148
Charlie Grimm	7	14	13	23	13	14	11	15	13	13	**136**	80	20	–	198
Lee Meadows	19	11	17	21	17	18	13	20	0	0	**136**	1	–	99	191
Heinie Manush				12	13	8	26	18	35	23	**135**	86	14	–	285
Joe Bush	12	24	26	24	23	14	10	1	1		**135**	9	0	91	195
Muddy Ruel	6	11	9	23	17	18	18	20	8	5	**135**	53	47	–	156
Tom Zachary	14	19	16	6	21	13	19	9	4	12	**133**	4	–	96	205
Bucky Harris	15	20	17	18	13	16	17	13	4	0	**133**	66	34	–	133
Irish Meusel	17	21	23	20	17	20	12	2			**132**	86	14	–	161
Pete Donohue		9	19	21	15	28	21	7	5	7	**132**	3	–	97	136
Willie Kamm				20	14	19	22	15	24	16	**130**	62	38	–	201
George Grantham			0	17	21	15	19	21	18	19	**130**	84	16	–	193
Riggs Stephenson		8	12	11	10	2	11	27	23	26	**130**	86	14	–	190
Travis Jackson			0	10	20	12	18	24	22	23	**129**	65	35	–	211
Paul Waner							28	36	34	30	**128**	85	15	–	423
Rabbit Maranville	14	23	22	16	15	4	5	1	11	17	**128**	53	47	–	302
Bob O'Farrell	11	7	26	25	6	10	23	6	5	8	**127**	62	38	–	161
Johnny Mostil		9	19	20	13	23	28	0	14	1	**127**	75	25	–	128
Bob Shawkey	27	17	27	19	15	9	8	4			**126**	2	–	98	223
Earle Combs					2	20	19	31	28	25	**125**	86	14	–	227
Wally Pipp	18	15	22	14	18	2	19	8	7		**123**	83	17	–	203
Earl Sheely		15	19	16	19	20	18	1		13	**121**	86	14	–	129
Roger Peckinpaugh	21	20	14	17	22	15	4	6			**119**	55	45	–	239
Dutch Ruether	18	15	20	15	9	20	9	13			**119**	10	0	90	151
George Burns	2	9	15	21	12	14	24	17	3	1	**118**	87	13	–	200
Art Nehf	19	17	21	9	12	12	0	4	18	5	**117**	4	0	96	183
Andy High			20	13	28	6	15	11	10	14	**117**	74	26	–	128
Ted Lyons				0	8	23	24	30	15	16	**116**	2	0	98	312
George Harper			17	3	13	18	7	26	16	14	**114**	84	16	–	118
Lefty Grove						9	25	24	27	28	**113**	0	–	100	391
Jack Scott	11	17	5	17		25	15	9	4	8	**111**	10	0	90	118
Gabby Hartnett			2	9	19	19	12	21	26	1	**109**	66	34	–	325
Ray Kremer					21	16	25	22	10	15	**109**	0	–	100	141
Bubbles Hargrave		8	14	25	14	8	18	13	8		**108**	73	27	–	110
Jack Tobin	18	25	19	18	12	4	2	9			**107**	83	17	–	179
Ira Flagstead	6	6	4	14	19	14	12	14	15	3	**107**	74	26	–	125
Johnny Morrison	1	13	21	23	14	13	8	3		11	**107**	0	–	100	108
Jimmy Johnston	20	24	20	22	10	9	1				**106**	74	26	–	157
Billy Southworth	17	19	7	17	5	12	20	9		0	**106**	80	20	–	141
Bill Terry				0	4	18	8	27	24	24	**105**	88	12	–	278
Rube Bressler	2	10	1	4	15	14	15	12	18	14	**105**	69	14	16	149
Joe Dugan	14	9	14	17	17	9	10	6	7	2	**105**	62	38	–	116
Aaron Ward	16	20	14	22	12	8	1	12	0		**105**	57	43	–	107
Harry Hooper	24	15	21	15	19	10					**104**	83	17	0	321

Player	1920	21	22	23	24	25	26	27	28	29	Dec	B	F	P	Car
Mickey Cochrane						16	14	23	22	27	**102**	70	30	–	275
Joe Harris			14	23	16	17	12	16	4		**102**	89	11	–	130
Elam Vangilder	1	12	22	23	4	12	7	10	11	0	**102**	5	–	95	104
Freddy Lindstrom					2	10	20	20	32	17	**101**	75	25	–	193
Jesse Barnes	19	18	13	16	21	9	4	0			**100**	2	–	98	156
Hal Carlson	17	6	4	0	10	17	23	16	0	6	**99**	2	–	98	121
Johnny Bassler		13	15	19	21	13	10	8			**99**	66	34	–	100
Hooks Dauss	14	10	12	25	8	18	11				**98**	4	0	96	215
George Burns	24	22	19	20	6	6					**97**	84	16	–	290
Vic Aldridge			19	18	17	16	10	12	5		**97**	2	–	98	102
Hank Severeid	11	18	18	16	16	12	5				**96**	59	41	–	134
Larry Benton				4	7	17	11	14	30	13	**96**	0	–	100	129
Tony Lazzeri							19	24	22	30	**95**	79	21	–	252
Heine Groh	28	15	12	18	19	1	0	1			**94**	74	26	–	272
Bobby Veach	25	22	22	9	13	3					**94**	82	18	0	265
Max Bishop					10	14	16	15	24	15	**94**	71	29	–	184
Ossie Bluege			1	10	9	16	15	18	17	7	**93**	62	38	–	183
Firpo Marberry				4	17	11	16	8	11	26	**93**	1	–	99	177
Wally Gerber	14	10	15	17	12	6	7	6	5	1	**93**	37	63	–	111
Hod Ford	5	14	12	8	8	5	4	11	15	11	**93**	49	51	–	107
Earl Smith	10	14	10	7	9	15	14	6	3	5	**93**	71	29	–	94
Slim Harriss	8	12	8	12	6	21	8	12	6		**93**	0	–	100	93
Milt Stock	20	17	17	15	4	19	0				**92**	72	28	–	188
Glenn Wright					22	24	17	17	12	0	**92**	62	38	–	139
Sam Gray					9	19	10	7	23	24	**92**	0	–	100	128
Jack Smith	13	15	17	12	8	5	11	6	4	0	**91**	84	16	–	125
Joe Shaute			0	9	22	6	16	13	15	10	**91**	6	–	94	106
Clarence Mitchell	6	17	6	8	5	10	9	7	10	12	**90**	10	1	89	133
Tommy Thomas							16	27	26	20	**89**	0	–	100	135
George Mogridge	4	26	17	14	14	4	4	5			**88**	1	–	99	146
Sparky Adams			0	7	12	17	21	16	12	3	**88**	63	37	–	144
Jimmy Ring	8	11	13	20	13	17	5	0	1		**88**	0	–	100	110
Sherry Smith	15	11	6	9	18	13	14	1			**87**	4	–	96	137
Rip Collins	13	4	16	2	16	6	9	8		13	**87**	1	–	99	108
Bernie Friberg	1		8	23	18	10	11	6	1	9	**87**	63	36	0	104
Rube Walberg				4	0	13	13	17	17	22	**86**	1	–	99	173
Taylor Douthit				0	4	1	19	16	24	22	**86**	68	32	–	121
Clyde Barnhart	2	10	7	18	9	19	2	14	5		**86**	77	23	–	86
Earl Whitehill				3	16	13	15	19	7	12	**85**	1	–	99	203
Del Pratt	25	20	19	9	11						**84**	74	26	–	242
Harry Rice				0	2	19	19	13	15	15	**83**	81	19	–	110
Hugh McQuillan	13	11	13	17	14	1	11	3			**83**	2	–	98	86
Charlie Gehringer					1	0	11	20	23	27	**82**	77	23	–	383
Charlie Root				0			22	21	16	23	**82**	0	–	100	223
Chick Hafey					2	7	5	21	25	22	**82**	87	13	–	186
Carson Bigbee	18	21	23	13	5	1	1				**82**	74	26	–	120
Les Bell				3	1	15	25	11	16	11	**82**	74	26	–	96
Pat Duncan	21	15	21	20	5						**82**	79	21	–	86
Jake Daubert	24	12	24	13	8						**81**	87	13	–	263
Hughie Critz					14	13	19	10	20	5	**81**	50	50	–	141

Player	1920	21	22	23	24	25	26	27	28	29	Dec	B	F	P	Car
Bob Fothergill			4	7	3	6	17	22	12	10	**81**	88	12	–	100
Ray Schalk	21	11	22	7	2	12	5	0	0	0	**80**	49	51	–	191
Bill Doak	18	16	5	11	15			9	6	0	**80**	0	–	100	170
Frank Snyder	8	16	13	12	14	11	2	4			**80**	56	44	–	139
Lew Fonseca		5	13	7	1	11		11	7	25	**80**	78	22	0	99
Sammy Hale	3	0		10	8	14	8	18	13	6	**80**	67	33	–	83
Cliff Heathcote	12	1	6	5	12	8	16	8	4	7	**79**	73	27	–	109
Lloyd Waner								25	26	27	**78**	72	28	–	245
Red Lucas				0	2	0	12	23	15	26	**78**	12	0	88	194
Sheriff Blake	0				5	9	12	15	24	13	**78**	1	–	99	92
Ray Blades			5	8	15	20	19	8	3		**78**	86	14	–	90
Topper Rigney			15	16	22	3	17	5			**78**	72	28	–	78
Babe Herman							20	12	19	26	**77**	89	11	–	232
Dixie Davis	22	15	9	7	11	10	3				**77**	0	–	100	79
Babe Adams	25	18	13	11	5	4	0				**76**	3	–	97	243
Whitey Witt	6	13	19	22	13	0	2				**75**	78	22	–	105
Jesse Petty		1				5	24	21	12	12	**75**	0	–	100	78

Players with at least 250 career Win Shares

Player	1920	21	22	23	24	25	26	27	28	29	Dec	B	F	P	Car
Buddy Myer						0	14	15	18	18	**65**	75	25	–	258
Jimmie Foxx						1	1	6	22	34	**64**	89	11	0	435
Larry Gardner	23	23	14	2	0						**62**	69	31	–	258
Mel Ott							2	4	20	31	**57**	90	10	–	528
Red Ruffing					0	9	8	8	21	11	**57**	10	0	90	322
Joe Jackson	37										**37**	90	10	–	294
Ed Konetchy	18	13									**31**	86	14	0	287
Carl Hubbell									11	19	**30**	0	–	100	305
Earl Averill										26	**26**	80	20	–	280
Joe Cronin							2	0	4	19	**25**	71	29	–	333
Clyde Milan	14	10	0								**24**	79	21	–	266
Dick Bartell								0	7	16	**23**	62	38	–	252
Home Run Baker		12	7								**19**	78	22	–	301
Bill Dickey									0	18	**18**	70	30	–	314
Larry Doyle	16										**16**	83	17	–	289
Johnny Evers			0							0	**0**	74	26	–	268

Player	1930	31	32	33	34	35	36	37	38	39	Dec	B	F	P	Car
Mel Ott	28	26	33	31	38	35	36	32	36	28	**323**	90	10	–	528
Lou Gehrig	39	36	38	36	41	34	38	36	25	0	**323**	93	7	–	489
Jimmie Foxx	34	24	40	41	32	30	26	23	34	30	**314**	89	11	0	435
Charlie Gehringer	29	10	25	28	37	31	34	30	27	19	**270**	77	23	–	383
Lefty Grove	37	42	33	23	2	29	29	27	17	23	**262**	0	–	100	391
Paul Waner	26	26	32	28	30	22	32	28	15	14	**253**	85	15	–	423
Earl Averill	24	30	30	26	33	22	27	24	26	11	**253**	80	20	–	280
Arky Vaughan			21	34	36	39	35	25	34	25	**249**	77	23	–	356
Joe Cronin	33	35	31	34	17	16	7	24	30	22	**249**	71	29	–	333
Carl Hubbell	18	20	25	33	32	26	37	23	15	14	**243**	0	–	100	305
Wally Berger	26	31	26	36	33	21	23	16	17	11	**240**	84	16	–	241
Bill Dickey	15	20	18	25	20	20	25	33	27	27	**230**	70	30	–	314
Al Simmons	36	34	24	25	23	13	20	11	16	9	**211**	82	18	–	375
Gabby Hartnett	29	16	19	21	24	26	18	25	16	15	**209**	66	34	–	325
Joe Medwick			4	24	24	33	36	40	22	24	**207**	86	14	–	312
Red Ruffing	16	15	26	15	17	22	23	24	25	22	**205**	10	0	90	322
Wes Ferrell	32	28	26	18	18	35	27	14	6	1	**205**	11	0	89	233
Ben Chapman	17	22	22	21	19	21	23	19	19	19	**202**	80	18	2	233
Chuck Klein	28	25	31	30	19	17	17	13	7	11	**198**	88	12	–	238
Billy Herman		4	23	18	16	32	29	29	20	25	**196**	74	26	–	298
Mel Harder	12	12	21	24	27	27	12	16	20	17	**188**	0	–	100	234
Buddy Myer	14	20	20	23	19	33	6	15	24	9	**183**	75	25	–	258
Dizzy Dean	1		24	22	37	31	31	17	9	7	**179**	0	–	100	181
Dick Bartell	18	11	21	13	18	18	24	28	17	10	**178**	62	38	–	252
Larry French	19	19	22	21	15	19	21	12	11	16	**175**	1	–	99	218
Bill Terry	32	29	32	21	29	23	7				**173**	88	12	–	278
Mickey Cochrane	31	28	30	26	23	24	6	5			**173**	70	30	–	275
Hank Greenberg	0			14	31	34	3	33	34	24	**173**	90	10	–	267
Lefty Gomez	1	20	17	16	31	16	11	29	19	13	**173**	0	–	100	185
Luke Appling	0	5	12	25	14	24	29	28	9	24	**170**	71	29	–	378
Gus Suhr	17	4	15	20	19	16	25	19	21	14	**170**	87	13	–	170
Tony Cuccinello	12	23	20	12	15	14	23	23	17	10	**169**	74	26	–	203
Lon Warneke	0	4	31	29	26	22	17	12	12	12	**165**	2	–	98	220
Babe Ruth	38	38	36	29	20	2					**163**	81	6	14	756
Tommy Bridges	3	7	16	20	22	19	26	19	12	19	**163**	0	–	100	225
Sammy West	18	24	19	14	18	18	12	12	13	13	**161**	71	29	–	192
Tony Lazzeri	19	15	27	24	17	15	18	13	5	4	**157**	79	21	–	252
Goose Goslin	25	25	19	20	22	17	23	4	0		**155**	86	14	–	355
Lloyd Waner	8	24	23	10	14	16	14	19	19	7	**154**	72	28	–	245
Babe Herman	32	26	24	23	17	18	13	1			**154**	89	11	–	232
Kiki Cuyler	29	26	15	11	23	11	24	6	8		**153**	84	16	–	292
Paul Derringer		17	11	11	17	20	17	9	25	26	**153**	0	–	100	231
Bob Johnson				21	22	18	19	19	23	29	**151**	87	13	–	287
Billy Rogell	2	6	17	25	24	23	16	18	16	4	**151**	55	45	–	161
Heinie Manush	23	19	28	27	20	11	4	17	1	0	**150**	86	14	–	285
Joe Vosmik	0	18	24	12	15	28	11	12	19	11	**150**	77	23	–	159
Jo-Jo Moore	0	0	8	17	26	24	23	21	16	13	**148**	86	14	–	170
Ripper Collins		10	15	19	32	28	15	12	15		**146**	89	11	–	147
Ted Lyons	26	6	14	12	10	20	9	13	14	20	**144**	2	0	98	312
Stan Hack			4	5	13	22	19	23	33	23	**142**	79	21	–	316

Player	1930	31	32	33	34	35	36	37	38	39	Dec	B	F	P	Car
John Stone	11	17	22	16	14	15	21	22	4		**142**	83	17	–	149
Rick Ferrell	9	15	17	17	18	17	16	9	16	7	**141**	60	40	–	206
Pepper Martin	0	16	6	29	15	19	24	14	7	9	**139**	82	17	0	151
Frankie Crosetti			13	15	18	12	24	16	23	17	**138**	56	44	–	189
Ed Brandt	8	27	13	29	19	4	17	14	7		**138**	3	–	97	151
Hal Trosky				1	28	15	21	24	25	23	**137**	90	10	–	195
Lyn Lary	14	24	10	4	9	15	17	23	18	2	**136**	64	36	–	145
Charlie Root	17	17	16	17	6	16	5	16	15	10	**135**	0	–	100	223
Bump Hadley	21	16	12	23	14	7	11	6	13	12	**135**	1	–	99	175
Joe Kuhel	2	14	10	26	5	12	21	14	10	19	**133**	86	14	–	243
Joe DiMaggio							25	39	30	34	**128**	84	16	–	387
Freddie Fitzsimmons	18	18	9	15	20	6	11	7	14	10	**128**	2	–	98	222
Ernie Lombardi		6	14	8	11	17	17	12	24	17	**126**	76	24	–	218
Hal Schumacher		0	4	23	24	23	15	15	15	7	**126**	2	0	98	176
Dolph Camilli				1	10	14	22	25	25	28	**125**	90	10	–	224
Red Rolfe		0			8	22	24	19	22	30	**125**	73	27	–	162
Doc Cramer	0	4	13	14	17	16	15	14	17	14	**124**	67	33	0	219
Bill Lee					16	21	20	18	28	20	**123**	0	–	100	177
Johnny Mize							26	34	28	33	**121**	92	8	–	338
Harlond Clift					15	17	23	23	25	18	**121**	71	29	–	216
Gee Walker		4	17	10	10	10	20	22	12	16	**121**	77	23	–	178
Van Lingle Mungo		4	11	17	22	15	24	16	5	7	**121**	2	–	98	147
Frankie Frisch	25	21	14	22	19	12	7	0			**120**	71	29	–	366
Earl Whitehill	14	18	14	23	14	13	12	3	6	1	**118**	1	–	99	203
Zeke Bonura					20	17	24	21	16	19	**117**	88	12	–	127
Red Lucas	14	17	23	15	9	11	15	7	5		**116**	12	0	88	194
Woody English	28	24	16	14	15	3	7	8	1		**116**	66	34	–	155
Bobo Newsom	0		0		21	12	19	16	21	26	**115**	1	–	99	237
Pinky Whitney	16	12	17	13	15	9	11	16	6	0	**115**	64	36	–	149
Spud Davis	8	16	17	18	15	14	13	5	2	6	**114**	67	33	–	149
Johnny Allen			15	10	6	12	25	20	16	10	**114**	1	–	99	145
Gus Mancuso	11	7	11	16	10	14	20	11	8	6	**114**	52	48	–	135
Bill Werber	0			8	26	14	13	14	13	25	**113**	67	33	–	162
Mike Higgins	0			23	20	15	14	16	14	10	**112**	79	21	–	195
Danny MacFayden	17	17	8	1	3	4	22	17	16	7	**112**	1	0	99	150
Augie Galan					5	32	16	20	16	22	**111**	85	15	–	263
Billy Jurges		3	12	18	7	14	13	16	11	17	**111**	50	50	–	170
Carl Reynolds	25	14	13	10	13	7	6	0	18	5	**111**	79	21	–	139
Frank Demaree			1	14		13	24	26	13	19	**110**	82	18	–	130
Al Lopez	13	9	12	16	12	9	12	7	7	12	**109**	49	51	–	173
Joe Stripp	13	15	19	14	11	11	13	2	11		**109**	69	31	–	116
Odell Hale		2		11	20	20	20	15	13	8	**109**	69	31	–	112
Bill Swift			16	13	12	20	18	10	11	8	**108**	2	–	98	111
Willis Hudlin	14	15	12	8	13	21	0	11	6	7	**107**	1	–	99	170
General Crowder	22	16	30	21	4	12	0				**105**	0	–	100	156
Chick Hafey	20	25	9	23	17	3		7			**104**	87	13	–	186
Bruce Campbell	1	1	13	13	10	12	7	16	15	16	**104**	85	15	–	138
Ival Goodman						16	18	16	28	25	**103**	85	15	–	144
Roy Johnson	9	15	13	16	19	17	3	11	0		**103**	81	19	–	122
Earle Combs	23	20	25	16	10	8					**102**	86	14	–	227

Player	1930	31	32	33	34	35	36	37	38	39	Dec	B	F	P	Car
Curt Davis					24	21	14	8	13	22	**102**	2	–	98	165
Bucky Walters		0	1	4	7	11	14	14	12	38	**101**	7	2	91	258
Cecil Travis				1	10	20	15	22	20	13	**101**	73	27	–	169
Lefty O'Doul	20	22	33	17	9						**101**	92	8	0	144
Clint Brown	13	12	21	15	1	2	6	14	1	16	**101**	2	–	98	116
Red Kress	20	17	16	7	2	9	12		15	2	**100**	67	33	0	139
Leo Durocher	6	5	6	12	13	18	14	6	9	11	**100**	33	67	–	121
Lonny Frey				5	16	19	13	7	14	25	**99**	72	28	–	208
Pie Traynor	22	20	21	20	11	4		0			**98**	71	29	–	274
Pete Fox				14	13	21	6	19	13	11	**97**	79	21	–	149
Jimmy Dykes	18	13	14	15	11	11	9	2	3	0	**96**	68	32	0	245
George Selkirk					6	19	21	14	11	25	**96**	85	15	–	118
Monte Pearson			0	16	17	7	20	12	15	9	**96**	3	–	97	104
Oral Hildebrand		2	10	17	11	13	12	10	9	11	**95**	0	–	100	97
George Watkins	17	17	16	15	8	12	10				**95**	83	17	–	95
Eric McNair	3	6	17	6	14	7	11	13	1	16	**94**	58	42	–	99
Guy Bush	8	7	19	18	16	10	6	9	0		**93**	0	–	100	167
Fred Frankhouse	7	8	5	16	18	7	16	9	4	3	**93**	2	–	98	113
Freddy Lindstrom	28	10	13	23	9	8	1				**92**	75	25	–	193
Wild Bill Hallahan	15	21	15	13	8	13	6	0	1		**92**	1	–	99	102
Schoolboy Rowe				9	28	23	21	0	2	8	**91**	9	–	91	180
Max Bishop	21	25	15	17	10	2					**90**	71	29	–	184
Ossie Bluege	14	17	18	12	4	8	9	4	4	0	**90**	62	38	–	183
Syl Johnson	13	17	4	3	12	18	7	6	3	7	**90**	0	–	100	142
George Earnshaw	21	29	15	1	15	7	2				**90**	1	–	99	122
Mule Haas	16	17	17	14	7	8	10	1	0		**90**	72	28	–	121
Tex Carleton			11	18	15	9	16	18	2		**89**	1	–	99	98
Pat Malone	24	13	16	5	14	0	13	3			**88**	0	–	100	134
Hack Wilson	35	13	21	12	6						**87**	87	13	–	224
Rube Walberg	12	24	15	7	7	11	7	4			**87**	1	–	99	173
Lefty Stewart	28	17	17	14	9	2					**87**	3	–	97	119
Waite Hoyt	10	10	5	8	18	13	10	12	0		**86**	1	–	99	262
George Blaeholder	13	13	14	14	16	8	8				**86**	0	–	100	114
Lloyd Brown	15	19	12	10	8	11	11	0			**86**	2	–	98	103
Johnny Moore		1	18	11	17	20	11	8			**86**	80	20	–	87
Jim Bottomley	13	19	9	15	13	4	11	1			**85**	90	10	–	258
Marv Owen		3		9	23	10	16	10	12	2	**85**	62	38	–	85
Firpo Marberry	16	20	16	20	10	1	1				**84**	1	–	99	177
Luke Sewell	5	10	8	16	3	12	14	13	3	0	**84**	43	57	–	128
Johnny Frederick	24	16	15	19	9						**83**	84	16	–	105
Travis Jackson	17	22	5	2	17	16	3				**82**	65	35	–	211
Rollie Hemsley	8	9	4	3	15	15	7	3	8	10	**82**	42	58	–	130
Fred Schulte	9	16	15	21	13	4	4	0			**82**	71	29	–	126
Eldon Auker				2	15	14	13	22	9	7	**82**	1	–	99	120
Ben Cantwell	12	11	14	21	6	6	11	1			**82**	2	–	98	94
Watty Clark	16	22	20	2	1	14	6	0			**81**	1	–	99	130
Vic Sorrell	19	17	14	15	6	3	7	0			**81**	0	–	100	94
Danny Taylor	5	10	18	16	15	13	3				**80**	88	12	–	81
Buck Jordan		0	7	19	18	7	16	6	7		**80**	86	14	–	80
Thornton Lee				2	3	12	7	18	19	18	**79**	1	–	99	165

Player	1930	31	32	33	34	35	36	37	38	39	Dec	B	F	P	Car
Bill Walker	18	21	5	8	14	12	1				**79**	0	–	100	96
Sam Leslie	0	2	2	17	22	18	10	6	2		**79**	91	9	–	79
Buddy Lewis						0	16	20	20	22	**78**	81	19	–	179
Mike Kreevich		0				1	16	23	16	22	**78**	64	36	–	146
Hank Leiber				0	2	28	12	5	10	21	**78**	85	15	0	101
Eddie Morgan	28	21	15	2	11						**77**	91	9	–	95
Wally Moses						9	21	20	14	12	**76**	85	15	–	237
Bob Smith	17	17	6	10	5	9	10	2			**76**	4	7	89	145
Ivy Andrews		2	13	4	9	21	15	8	4		**76**	1	–	99	76
Players with at least 250 career Win Shares															
Bob Feller							6	13	22	32	**73**	0	–	100	292
Dixie Walker		0		11	0	0	3	20	14	11	**59**	84	16	–	278
Sam Rice	23	13	11	3	7						**57**	83	17	1	327
Joe Sewell	9	15	17	16							**57**	68	32	–	277
Rabbit Maranville	17	9	11	6		0					**43**	53	47	–	302
Burleigh Grimes	16	15	4	3	1						**39**	4	–	96	286
Red Faber	10	11	6	7							**34**	1	–	99	292
Bobby Doerr								2	14	17	**33**	70	30	–	281
Ted Williams										32	**32**	92	8	0	555
Enos Slaughter									9	23	**32**	85	15	–	323
Joe Judge	18	2	7	3	1						**31**	88	12	–	270
Rogers Hornsby	3	20	1	4	1	0	0	1			**30**	88	12	–	502
Eppa Rixey	8	5	9	6							**28**	0	–	100	315
Jack Quinn	8	10	7	0							**25**	2	0	98	287
Harry Heilmann	20		0								**20**	91	9	–	356
George Sisler	8										**8**	89	8	3	292
Lou Boudreau									0	7	**7**	68	32	–	277
Edd Roush		5									**5**	81	19	–	314
Bob Elliott										5	**5**	82	18	–	287
Mickey Vernon										3	**3**	88	12	–	296
Eddie Collins	0										**0**	81	19	–	574
Pete Alexander	0										**0**	2	–	98	476
Early Wynn										0	**0**	5	–	95	309
Dave Bancroft	0										**0**	61	39	–	269
Hal Newhouser										0	**0**	1	–	99	264

Player	1940	41	42	43	44	45	46	47	48	49	Dec	B	F	P	Car
Ted Williams	30	42	46				49	44	39	40	**290**	92	8	0	555
Stan Musial		3	28	39	38		44	25	46	40	**263**	89	11	0	604
Lou Boudreau	30	22	23	32	28	17	24	28	34	17	**255**	68	32	–	277
Hal Newhouser	7	8	17	10	35	38	33	24	27	25	**224**	1	–	99	264
Bob Elliott	18	16	22	25	27	20	12	29	27	23	**219**	82	18	–	287
Dixie Walker	22	26	19	22	33	28	27	23	15	4	**219**	84	16	–	278
Joe DiMaggio	31	41	32				24	30	34	21	**213**	84	16	–	387
Bobby Doerr	21	15	24	24	27		27	19	27	25	**209**	70	30	–	281
Luke Appling	28	29	20	40		6	26	22	17	19	**207**	71	29	–	378
Vern Stephens		0	19	23	34	27	20	23	25	32	**203**	72	28	–	265
Bill Nicholson	20	21	28	31	31	19	8	18	17	9	**202**	88	12	–	223
Charlie Keller	24	32	34	36		11	31	10	8	5	**191**	89	11	–	218
Johnny Mize	33	26	32				22	32	30	12	**187**	92	8	–	338
Joe Gordon	26	24	31	28			9	25	24	19	**186**	71	29	–	242
Enos Slaughter	22	20	37				29	20	26	29	**183**	85	15	–	323
Jeff Heath	8	28	24	24	7	20	22	18	20	6	**177**	89	11	–	217
Roy Cullenbine	8	23	20	27	21	31	25	21			**176**	88	12	–	182
Dizzy Trout	5	13	16	23	42	18	27	13	15	3	**175**	3	–	97	228
Tommy Holmes			21	23	27	29	25	21	19	10	**175**	82	18	–	188
Stan Hack	25	30	26	21	13	34	17	8			**174**	79	21	–	316
Phil Cavarretta	7	14	16	18	25	30	25	16	9	14	**174**	89	11	–	237
Stan Spence	1	3	29	28	33		30	25	12	8	**169**	86	14	–	169
Marty Marion	11	14	22	17	20	17	19	18	13	13	**164**	45	55	–	177
Pee Wee Reese	13	15	27				26	26	23	32	**162**	65	35	–	314
Tommy Henrich	14	26	19				21	27	29	24	**160**	88	12	–	208
Dom DiMaggio	14	21	28				26	20	26	24	**159**	74	26	–	220
Bucky Walters	32	27	20	15	32	16	11	3	1		**157**	7	2	91	258
Frank McCormick	27	20	17	19	29	17	17	8	3		**157**	86	14	–	202
Rudy York	26	16	15	26	22	17	22	12	0		**156**	83	17	–	214
Bob Feller	34	30				7	32	23	15	14	**155**	0	–	100	292
Wally Moses	21	15	20	18	21	28	9	7	5	10	**154**	85	15	–	237
Ken Keltner	16	23	20	15	22		9	17	25	7	**154**	71	29	–	199
Augie Galan	6	3	7	29	32	30	18	21	4	2	**152**	85	15	–	263
Mel Ott	24	26	35	16	25	22	0	0			**148**	90	10	–	528
Dutch Leonard	20	19	1	10	13	19	7	23	19	9	**140**	0	–	100	233
Johnny Hopp	3	19	10	4	28	16	21	14	12	12	**139**	84	16	–	155
George McQuinn	16	17	16	13	20	17	7	24	8		**138**	84	16	–	173
Whitey Kurowski		1	13	18	22	27	26	26	5	0	**138**	79	21	–	138
Elbie Fletcher	26	28	26	22			17	3		15	**137**	88	12	–	185
Bob Johnson	19	21	26	19	31	20					**136**	87	13	–	287
Mickey Vernon	0	16	20	21			33	15	7	21	**133**	88	12	–	296
Eddie Stanky				14	9	27	28	20	14	21	**133**	73	27	–	191
Mort Cooper	15	11	29	28	24	9	13	3		0	**132**	1	–	99	151
Snuffy Stirnweiss				7	35	34	13	20	17	6	**132**	69	31	–	139
Harry Brecheen	0			15	15	17	20	19	27	18	**131**	1	–	99	173
Eddie Joost	6	21	15	7		2		18	26	35	**130**	68	32	–	209
Johnny Pesky			28				34	25	20	23	**130**	72	28	–	187
Rip Sewell	15	12	13	23	24	10	8	7	11	6	**129**	2	–	98	139
Claude Passeau	28	15	19	16	18	22	9	0			**127**	1	–	99	189
Eddie Miller	21	13	11	14	12	12	5	22	10	5	**125**	48	52	–	138

Player	1940	41	42	43	44	45	46	47	48	49	Dec	B	F	P	Car
Phil Rizzuto		21	25				12	26	15	22	**121**	58	42	–	231
Pete Reiser	7	34	28				19	18	4	8	**118**	81	19	–	125
Tiny Bonham	13	11	21	20	15	11	5	10	6	6	**118**	0	–	100	118
Barney McCosky	24	19	19				14	22	19		**117**	77	23	–	146
Bobo Newsom	26	14	6	9	20	12	16	12	1		**116**	1	–	99	237
George Case	17	15	22	25	10	21	5	0			**115**	83	17	–	142
Jim Russell			0	16	31	21	16	10	11	9	**114**	80	20	–	120
Tex Hughson		4	28	20	20		25	12	1	3	**113**	0	–	100	113
Ralph Kiner							15	30	30	37	**112**	89	11	–	242
Joe Kuhel	21	17	12	12	17	25	6	0			**110**	86	14	–	243
Walker Cooper	1	4	16	18	18	1	6	23	10	13	**110**	72	28	–	173
Kirby Higbe	21	21	12	9			14	14	14	5	**110**	0	–	100	119
Lonny Frey	24	24	23	25			11	1	1		**109**	72	28	–	208
Nick Etten		20	12	22	25	22	6	1			**108**	93	7	–	112
Arky Vaughan	31	19	19	28				7	3		**107**	77	23	–	356
Johnny Vander Meer	4	19	21	19			13	7	20	4	**107**	1	–	99	134
Sam Chapman	14	25				0	12	17	14	24	**106**	76	24	–	145
Joe Medwick	19	24	21	9	19	5	3	5	0		**105**	86	14	–	312
Spud Chandler	7	13	19	29	0	1	25	11			**105**	2	–	98	127
Nels Potter	10	1		13	20	27	8	8	12	6	**105**	3	–	97	110
Hank Borowy			15	15	20	22	9	9	3	12	**105**	1	–	99	108
George Kell				0	8	15	22	24	11	24	**104**	76	24	–	229
Andy Pafko				2	10	25	9	16	23	19	**104**	80	20	–	220
Danny Litwhiler	5	17	12	13	15		11	6	13	12	**104**	83	17	–	108
Billy Herman	17	18	20	27			20	0			**102**	74	26	–	298
Buddy Lewis	22	22				17	24	10		6	**101**	81	19	–	179
Vince DiMaggio	17	24	15	20	10	15	0				**101**	74	26	–	138
Jim Tobin	7	17	15	24	23	15					**101**	8	0	92	135
Frankie Gustine	12	11	4	12	4	12	11	19	13	3	**101**	67	33	–	102
Wally Judnich	20	17	25				18	13	8	0	**101**	83	17	–	101
Taffy Wright	21	25	15				13	15	9	2	**100**	84	16	–	123
Dolph Camilli	25	29	28	13		4					**99**	90	10	–	224
Harry Gumbert	14	17	10	11	16		8	9	13	1	**99**	2	–	98	145
Ron Northey			6	22	22		14	14	13	7	**98**	88	12	–	110
Virgil Trucks		0	15	16		0	16	7	16	27	**97**	0	–	100	198
Howie Pollet		8	8	14			27	8	8	24	**97**	1	–	99	151
Joe Dobson	2	8	12	9			11	20	20	15	**97**	0	–	100	147
Ed Lopat					16	9	19	21	14	17	**96**	4	–	96	176
Doc Cramer	12	11	12	18	19	16	5	2	0		**95**	67	33	0	219
Harlond Clift	23	21	24	13	0	14					**95**	71	29	–	216
Dick Wakefield		0		24	22		15	16	14	4	**95**	88	12	–	95
Hank Greenberg	31	2				16	31	14			**94**	90	10	–	267
Jerry Priddy		2	9	20			17	9	20	17	**94**	64	36	–	145
Al Benton	8	20	17			17	8	5	1	18	**94**	0	–	100	129
Ernie Lombardi	19	13	16	8	7	18	8	3			**92**	76	24	–	218
Johnny Lindell		0	3	13	26	5	9	15	14	6	**91**	69	19	12	107
Elmer Valo	1	3	12	4			12	17	17	24	**90**	89	11	–	187
Max Lanier	8	14	13	23	17	2	7			6	**90**	1	–	99	132
Schoolboy Rowe	18	12	2	19			14	13	9	2	**89**	9	–	91	180
Frankie Hayes	17	15	7	5	18	18	9	0			**89**	66	34	–	130

Player	1940	41	42	43	44	45	46	47	48	49	Dec	B	F	P	Car
Del Ennis							26	11	24	27	**88**	86	14	–	233
Allie Reynolds			1	10	10	15	6	16	16	14	**88**	1	–	99	170
Johnny Sain			3				26	24	28	6	**87**	4	–	96	147
Phil Masi	2	4	2	8	10	11	15	19	10	6	**87**	59	41	–	111
Mickey Haefner				14	12	14	17	13	7	10	**87**	1	–	99	88
Thornton Lee	19	32	4	2	6	18	2	2	1		**86**	1	–	99	165
Murry Dickson	0		9	8			16	18	15	19	**85**	2	–	98	204
Terry Moore	22	20	20				7	12	4		**85**	70	30	0	152
Buddy Rosar	10	9	5	15	9	2	11	12	11	1	**85**	48	52	–	94
Mike Higgins	11	16	12	15	22		7				**83**	79	21	–	195
Denny Galehouse	4	14	11	15	10		9	10	10	0	**83**	0	–	100	122
Jackie Robinson								21	25	36	**82**	79	21	–	257
Sid Gordon		1	1	10			13	13	25	19	**82**	87	13	–	199
Eddie Lake	1	1		7	3	27	19	11	8	5	**82**	72	28	0	82
Willard Marshall			11				12	24	16	18	**81**	85	15	–	125
Bob Muncrief		18	7	13	17	14	0	4	3	5	**81**	0	–	100	81
Chet Laabs	8	12	23	17	7	3	9	1			**80**	84	16	–	97
Jim Tabor	16	12	8	12	16		13	3			**80**	73	27	–	97
Warren Spahn			0				9	32	14	24	**79**	2	–	98	412
Harry Walker	0	0	8	17			8	24	9	13	**79**	77	23	–	82
Babe Young	20	20	14				7	13	5		**79**	88	12	–	82
Paul Derringer	24	15	12	7	6	14					**78**	0	–	100	231
Peanuts Lowrey			0	16		17	15	12	9	9	**78**	72	28	–	108
Joe Haynes	0	2	11	8	14	6	9	18	10	0	**78**	2	–	98	88
Johnny Niggeling	9	11	17	15	15	7	4				**78**	0	–	100	78
Elmer Riddle	4	26	7	23	1	0		0	15	2	**78**	1	–	99	78
Ray Sanders			9	18	22	19	9		0	0	**77**	90	10	–	77
Bob Lemon		0	0				6	13	26	31	**76**	9	0	91	232
Whit Wyatt	16	28	16	16	0	0					**76**	3	–	97	119
Fred Hutchinson	2	0					19	22	14	19	**76**	8	0	92	118
Dick Siebert	10	15	10	9	20	12					**76**	84	16	–	87
Red Schoendienst						11	19	13	12	20	**75**	63	37	–	262
Jim Bagby Jr.	10	11	20	14	2	9	5	4			**75**	3	0	97	92

Players with at least 250 career Win Shares

Player	1940	41	42	43	44	45	46	47	48	49	Dec	B	F	P	Car
Early Wynn		4	3	19	8		9	20	3	8	**74**	5	–	95	309
Bill Dickey	13	17	11	20			5				**66**	70	30	–	314
Red Ruffing	16	15	15			7	7	0			**60**	10	0	90	322
Joe Cronin	24	23	3	4	4	1					**59**	71	29	–	333
Jimmie Foxx	24	20	5		0	8					**57**	89	11	0	435
Yogi Berra							2	11	18	21	**52**	72	28	–	375
Ted Lyons	15	13	21				3				**52**	2	0	98	312
Dick Bartell	11	15	12	13			0				**51**	62	38	–	252
Paul Waner	7	9	11	10	5	0					**42**	85	15	–	423
Larry Doby								0	18	24	**42**	83	17	–	268
Richie Ashburn									21	19	**40**	78	22	–	329
Eddie Yost					0		0	7	14	15	**36**	83	17	–	267
Carl Hubbell	12	11	7	2							**32**	0	–	100	305
Gil Hodges				0				1	10	21	**32**	87	13	–	263
Charlie Gehringer	20	10	1								**31**	77	23	–	383

Player	1940	41	42	43	44	45	46	47	48	49	Dec	B	F	P	Car
Duke Snider								1	5	24	**30**	84	16	–	352
Robin Roberts									12	16	**28**	2	–	98	339
Lefty Grove	11	5									**16**	0	–	100	391
Buddy Myer	8	2									**10**	75	25	–	258
Gabby Hartnett	1	6									**7**	66	34	–	325
Nellie Fox								0	0	6	**6**	63	37	–	304
Al Simmons	2	0		1	0						**3**	82	18	–	375
Earl Averill	1	0									**1**	80	20	–	280
Minnie Minoso										0	**0**	85	15	–	283

Player	1950	51	52	53	54	55	56	57	58	59	Dec	B	F	P	Car
Mickey Mantle		13	32	26	36	41	49	51	39	30	**317**	90	10	–	565
Stan Musial	32	39	37	33	30	29	26	30	21	8	**285**	89	11	0	604
Duke Snider	29	22	25	37	39	36	34	25	13	18	**278**	84	16	–	352
Yogi Berra	32	31	29	28	34	24	31	23	21	23	**276**	72	28	–	375
Richie Ashburn	23	28	21	26	26	29	28	26	28	14	**249**	78	22	–	329
Eddie Mathews			19	39	33	34	29	33	24	37	**248**	87	13	–	450
Warren Spahn	21	26	22	31	23	19	24	22	28	23	**239**	2	–	98	412
Willie Mays		19	5		40	40	27	34	40	32	**237**	84	16	–	642
Robin Roberts	26	28	32	35	31	27	12	12	20	13	**236**	2	–	98	339
Minnie Minoso		25	21	26	32	21	29	26	25	29	**234**	85	15	–	283
Larry Doby	30	29	34	26	33	22	23	18	10	1	**226**	83	17	–	268
Nellie Fox	5	22	22	21	26	25	19	32	22	30	**224**	63	37	–	304
Gil Hodges	21	26	26	25	29	23	21	21	12	17	**221**	87	13	–	263
Ted Williams	19	34	1	9	29	23	25	38	25	9	**212**	92	8	0	555
Eddie Yost	24	27	23	24	23	16	19	13	11	27	**207**	83	17	–	267
Early Wynn	21	24	21	16	24	21	28	10	11	23	**199**	5	–	95	309
Billy Pierce	16	19	23	24	10	23	21	18	22	14	**190**	1	0	99	248
Al Dark	19	27	28	21	23	13	13	18	11	14	**187**	68	32	0	226
Al Rosen	29	25	31	42	27	16	15				**185**	83	17	–	185
Gil McDougald		23	18	21	20	24	24	27	15	10	**182**	71	29	–	194
Hank Aaron					13	29	30	35	32	38	**177**	89	11	–	643
Red Schoendienst	18	17	25	27	21	16	15	26	11	0	**176**	63	37	–	262
Jackie Robinson	29	38	34	25	20	12	17				**175**	79	21	–	257
Bobby Avila	7	24	24	22	34	20	14	13	12	5	**175**	70	30	–	175
Jackie Jensen	0	9	21	17	17	19	23	18	27	22	**173**	83	17	–	187
Roy Campanella	22	33	22	33	10	28	12	11			**171**	67	33	–	207
Ted Kluszewski	16	13	23	24	33	25	20	3	8	5	**170**	90	10	–	203
Gene Woodling	16	19	21	20	10	10	12	25	16	20	**169**	87	13	–	228
Puddin' Head Jones	22	22	16	15	16	16	25	10	12	11	**165**	71	29	–	189
Ernie Banks				2	15	32	22	28	31	33	**163**	80	20	–	332
Sherm Lollar	14	9	13	18	12	21	18	14	21	23	**163**	63	37	–	209
Johnny Logan		3	17	24	20	26	24	18	11	19	**162**	61	39	–	181
Hank Bauer	16	15	21	20	16	21	16	17	13	7	**162**	86	14	–	180
Mickey Vernon	13	18	20	29	24	21	15	6	13	1	**160**	88	12	–	296
Ray Boone	16	14	13	27	22	19	22	12	7	5	**157**	76	24	–	166
Bob Lemon	25	19	25	22	24	15	23	3	0		**156**	9	0	91	232
Gus Bell	9	16	8	24	20	21	22	13	7	15	**155**	82	18	–	175
Pee Wee Reese	20	22	23	21	26	18	14	4	4		**152**	65	35	–	314
Vic Wertz	26	22	17	12	13	8	21	24	2	6	**151**	88	12	–	219
Carl Furillo	18	21	7	23	17	22	17	12	13	1	**151**	80	20	–	217
Don Newcombe	22	21			8	25	27	15	12	21	**151**	9	–	91	176
Harvey Kuenn			2	19	19	22	26	15	21	25	**149**	80	20	–	223
Pete Runnels		8	22	12	18	14	18	7	26	24	**149**	76	24	–	216
Earl Torgeson	32	20	11	14	10	16	12	13	10	8	**146**	90	10	–	184
Del Ennis	26	14	21	19	11	21	15	14	3	1	**145**	86	14	–	233
Bobby Thomson	18	26	25	17	1	9	12	8	19	10	**145**	78	22	–	205
Billy Goodman	16	17	20	20	13	15	11	8	14	6	**140**	77	23	–	170
Mike Garcia	12	22	23	21	24	12	11	12	0	2	**139**	0	–	100	160
Roy Sievers	6	1	0	5	16	20	20	32	26	12	**138**	89	11	–	231
Jim Gilliam				25	20	14	28	15	15	20	**137**	72	28	–	247

Player	1950	51	52	53	54	55	56	57	58	59	Dec	B	F	P	Car
Al Kaline				1	7	31	26	20	23	27	**135**	87	13	–	443
Whitey Ford	11			17	16	22	22	10	20	16	**134**	1	–	99	261
Bob Rush	17	13	23	9	16	18	15	7	9	7	**134**	2	–	98	152
Johnny Antonelli	0			11	28	18	25	13	18	20	**133**	0	–	100	146
Joe Adcock	9	5	12	17	21	9	22	9	11	17	**132**	87	13	–	236
Chico Carrasquel	14	17	8	16	24	15	12	14	6	6	**132**	53	47	–	132
Ralph Kiner	23	35	19	23	19	11					**130**	89	11	–	242
Hank Sauer	18	18	28	12	22	5	6	13	8	0	**130**	84	16	–	174
Sal Maglie	21	28	17	7	18	9	16	11	3		**130**	0	–	100	139
Ned Garver	25	22	9	7	20	11	1	7	12	14	**128**	3	0	97	166
George Kell	26	22	14	18	8	16	11	10			**125**	76	24	–	229
Al Smith				4	25	29	21	17	13	14	**123**	85	15	–	194
Del Crandall	3			16	17	16	15	13	22	20	**122**	54	46	–	179
Bob Nieman		3	15	16	6	10	24	16	17	15	**122**	89	11	–	134
Lew Burdette	0	0	8	15	18	11	20	12	23	14	**121**	2	–	98	178
Granny Hamner	19	14	20	19	20	8	8	5	4	2	**119**	53	47	0	144
Murry Dickson	16	18	17	11	13	14	15	3	9	2	**118**	2	–	98	204
Gus Zernial	13	19	21	21	9	13	6	10	4	2	**118**	86	14	–	125
Sid Gordon	29	22	25	19	16	6					**117**	87	13	–	199
Andy Pafko	27	17	21	18	14	4	3	6	4	2	**116**	80	20	–	220
Roy McMillan		3	16	11	14	16	20	17	10	9	**116**	41	59	–	172
Johnny Temple			1	2	19	16	16	19	21	22	**116**	72	28	–	157
Frank Thomas		3	0	14	26	15	16	16	20	4	**114**	82	18	–	169
Wally Moon					20	18	22	21	6	25	**112**	86	14	–	175
Curt Simmons	16		17	19	21	4	13	15	6	0	**111**	1	–	99	210
Harvey Haddix			3	27	17	10	14	10	13	17	**111**	3	0	97	153
Hank Thompson	23	7	18	18	21	18	6				**111**	79	21	–	123
Phil Rizzuto	35	23	21	18	6	6	1				**110**	58	42	–	231
Enos Slaughter	16	14	23	17	5	12	7	7	6	1	**108**	85	15	–	323
Bobby Shantz	10	15	33	7	0	5	7	15	7	9	**108**	1	0	99	159
Whitey Lockman	16	15	23	14	11	13	5	7	2	2	**108**	83	17	–	156
Bob Friend		5	7	8	7	19	20	16	16	9	**107**	0	–	100	207
Solly Hemus	0	17	27	23	11	6	9	0	13	1	**107**	77	23	–	109
Irv Noren	22	18	9	11	21	11	1	3	4	7	**107**	76	24	–	107
Smoky Burgess		4	17	12	15	16	10	9	7	16	**106**	74	26	–	172
Jimmy Piersall	1		5	12	10	20	21	19	9	9	**106**	63	37	–	162
Bill Bruton				14	17	22	17	11	10	14	**105**	74	26	–	190
Jim Busby	0	12	11	25	22	9	12	7	6	1	**105**	59	41	–	112
Frank Sullivan				1	15	22	19	23	14	10	**104**	0	–	100	118
Jim Rivera			15	20	17	15	12	13	7	4	**103**	73	27	–	107
Ferris Fain	17	19	28	16	10	12					**102**	90	10	–	161
Gerry Staley	7	15	15	15	2	4	9	12	7	16	**102**	0	–	100	138
Ken Boyer						14	23	16	24	24	**101**	75	25	–	279
Virgil Trucks	4	10	8	25	22	10	7	11	4		**101**	0	–	100	198
Frank Robinson							26	27	20	25	**98**	90	10	–	519
Hoyt Wilhelm			18	14	15	6	6	5	11	23	**98**	0	–	100	256
Dave Philley	8	13	15	15	9	14	6	5	5	8	**98**	74	26	–	142
Ellis Kinder	17	18	9	23	10	13	7	0			**97**	0	–	100	145
Stan Lopata	2	0	9	9	10	17	26	15	9	0	**97**	72	28	–	104
Rocky Colavito						1	16	18	32	29	**96**	86	14	0	273

Player	1950	51	52	53	54	55	56	57	58	59	Dec	B	F	P	Car
Vic Power					7	26	14	8	22	19	**96**	79	21	–	152
Carl Erskine	6	8	17	20	16	12	9	5	3	0	**96**	0	–	100	105
Monte Irvin	16	29	5	18	14	3	11				**96**	86	14	–	98
Elmer Valo	13	17	19	1	7	18	12	5	1	1	**94**	89	11	–	187
Mel Parnell	22	22	13	23	4	0	8				**92**	1	–	99	141
Joe Nuxhall			6	11	13	20	14	8	12	6	**90**	3	–	97	147
Eddie Robinson	18	19	25	12	5	7	3	0			**89**	88	12	–	127
Danny O'Connell	8			16	15	9	16	16	8	1	**89**	60	40	–	107
Don Mueller	10	12	15	11	19	13	3	4	2	0	**89**	82	18	–	92
Bob Porterfield	0	10	20	21	13	5	4	6	7	2	**88**	3	–	97	95
Johnny Groth	22	12	11	10	11	6	5	4	4	2	**87**	71	29	–	105
Walt Dropo	21	5	14	8	6	13	7	5	4	4	**87**	83	17	–	92
Bill Skowron					13	12	21	17	12	11	**86**	89	11	–	183
Frank Lary					0	15	22	12	21	15	**85**	0	–	100	141
Charlie Maxwell	0	0	0		1	4	25	22	15	18	**85**	84	16	–	117
Jack Harshman	0		0		15	13	20	7	22	8	**85**	7	0	93	86
Clem Labine	0	7	2	13	7	15	13	11	9	7	**84**	0	–	100	96
Wes Westrum	22	20	18	9	6	3	5	1			**84**	55	45	–	95
Mickey McDermott	10	16	12	22	9	10	3	2	0		**84**	9	0	91	93
Randy Jackson	1	15	6	16	13	16	12	1	3	1	**84**	69	31	–	84
Vern Law	4	7			5	14	6	12	11	24	**83**	4	0	96	157
Allie Reynolds	17	19	24	11	11						**82**	1	–	99	170
Bill Virdon						14	21	12	20	15	**82**	66	34	–	157
Jim Hegan	14	14	9	5	15	9	8	4	3	1	**82**	37	63	–	137
Wally Post		1	0	1	8	23	16	9	10	14	**82**	84	16	–	116
Jim Hearn	15	14	12	8	6	14	5	5	3	0	**82**	0	–	100	101
Tom Brewer					7	10	24	16	12	13	**82**	1	–	99	92
Sam Jones		1	0			14	9	12	23	22	**81**	0	–	100	103
Joe Collins	6	11	18	14	15	9	6	2			**81**	87	13	–	81
Dick Groat			5			13	12	16	19	15	**80**	57	43	–	225
Ed Lopat	20	19	12	16	8	5					**80**	4	–	96	176
Andy Seminick	22	11	12	10	10	11	4	0			**80**	67	33	–	142
Hector Lopez						15	15	13	17	20	**80**	78	22	–	136
Alex Kellner	6	10	11	15	3	10	5	7	10	3	**80**	1	–	99	97
Dee Fondy		3	15	18	13	13	9	8	1		**80**	84	16	–	80
Chuck Stobbs	10	8	8	10	8	3	19	3	3	7	**79**	1	–	99	99
Sammy White		0	12	16	11	12	6	5	7	10	**79**	44	56	–	81
Dick Donovan	0	0	0		0	15	18	18	18	9	**78**	2	–	98	127
Gus Triandos				0	0	14	19	14	18	13	**78**	68	32	–	127
Bobby Adams	12	10	17	14	12	5	3	3	2	0	**78**	69	31	–	108
Paul Minner	11	13	13	14	12	14	0				**77**	3	–	97	86
Eddie Joost	14	25	26	6	3	2					**76**	68	32	–	209
Bob Buhl				12	4	13	12	16	4	15	**76**	0	–	100	147
Dale Mitchell	16	19	21	18	2	0	0				**76**	86	14	–	138
Bill Tuttle			0		15	18	7	8	12	16	**76**	68	32	–	97
Bob Turley		0		5	16	16	4	13	18	4	**76**	0	–	100	92
Harry Simpson		6	18	3		12	14	12	8	2	**75**	85	15	–	75

Player	1950	51	52	53	54	55	56	57	58	59	Dec	B	F	P	Car
Players with at least 250 career Win Shares															
Luis Aparicio							14	16	19	19	**68**	58	42	–	293
Don Drysdale							9	21	14	22	**66**	3	–	97	258
Bob Feller	19	18	1	10	11	4	1				**64**	0	–	100	292
Bob Elliott	27	18	7	11							**63**	82	18	–	287
Vern Stephens	22	14	9	6	9	2					**62**	72	28	–	265
Jim Bunning						0	4	26	14	17	**61**	0	–	100	257
Roberto Clemente						7	14	5	16	10	**52**	84	16	–	377
Joe DiMaggio	29	17									**46**	84	16	–	387
Orlando Cepeda									20	23	**43**	91	9	–	310
Hal Newhouser	15	7	10	1	7	0					**40**	1	–	99	264
Bobby Doerr	23	16									**39**	70	30	–	281
Johnny Mize	12	11	4	3							**30**	92	8	–	338
Vada Pinson									3	27	**30**	78	22	–	321
Harmon Killebrew					0	1	2	2	0	23	**28**	91	9	–	371
Brooks Robinson						0	1	2	7	9	**19**	70	30	–	356
Lou Boudreau	7	8	0								**15**	68	32	–	277
Willie McCovey										12	**12**	93	7	–	408
Ron Fairly									2	5	**7**	86	14	–	269
Bob Gibson										5	**5**	2	–	98	317
Maury Wills										5	**5**	67	33	–	253
Norm Cash									0	4	**4**	89	11	–	315
Luke Appling	1										**1**	71	29	–	378
Bucky Walters	0										**0**	7	2	91	258

Player	1960	61	62	63	64	65	66	67	68	69	Dec	B	F	P	Car
Hank Aaron	35	35	34	41	33	31	27	34	32	38	**340**	89	11	–	643
Willie Mays	38	34	41	38	38	43	37	21	30	17	**337**	84	16	–	642
Frank Robinson	23	34	41	23	33	26	41	30	24	32	**307**	90	10	–	519
Roberto Clemente	20	26	20	22	30	27	29	35	25	28	**262**	84	16	–	377
Harmon Killebrew	20	27	24	23	24	22	33	38	12	34	**257**	91	9	–	371
Ron Santo	6	18	9	26	36	32	30	38	28	26	**249**	79	21	–	324
Mickey Mantle	36	48	33	14	34	16	18	25	24		**248**	90	10	–	565
Willie McCovey	12	13	12	29	11	29	34	24	34	39	**237**	93	7	–	408
Brooks Robinson	21	18	27	19	33	26	24	24	25	17	**234**	70	30	–	356
Norm Cash	16	42	23	23	18	24	27	21	18	21	**233**	89	11	–	315
Carl Yastrzemski		12	21	29	20	21	21	42	39	26	**231**	87	13	–	488
Al Kaline	17	29	19	25	24	20	31	30	18	17	**230**	87	13	–	443
Frank Howard	13	9	25	23	13	25	21	28	38	34	**229**	92	8	–	297
Billy Williams	2	15	18	28	28	33	21	28	30	24	**227**	88	12	–	374
Vada Pinson	21	32	26	31	22	24	19	24	15	11	**225**	78	22	–	321
Orlando Cepeda	26	29	26	30	23	0	19	34	17	19	**223**	91	9	–	310
Juan Marichal	6	10	19	26	25	30	33	14	24	29	**216**	0	–	100	263
Maury Wills	16	21	32	27	20	28	16	20	16	19	**215**	67	33	–	253
Bob Gibson	0	18	21	17	24	26	26	12	36	33	**213**	2	–	98	317
Johnny Callison	10	13	27	32	29	28	20	17	16	17	**209**	83	17	–	241
Curt Flood	8	13	22	24	25	24	18	26	27	20	**207**	66	34	–	221
Eddie Mathews	38	33	26	31	20	22	16	14	2		**202**	87	13	–	450
Dick Allen				0	41	33	35	29	32	22	**192**	91	9	–	342
Don Drysdale	25	19	24	21	26	27	13	18	18	1	**192**	3	–	97	258
Felipe Alou	9	14	25	21	12	21	28	15	31	13	**189**	85	15	–	241
Jim Bunning	20	19	21	11	22	27	30	25	1	9	**185**	0	–	100	257
Bob Allison	16	17	23	28	25	22	7	24	16	5	**183**	85	15	–	203
Jim Fregosi		0	7	20	28	24	26	28	22	26	**181**	76	24	–	261
Joe Torre	0	13	9	20	28	23	29	18	15	23	**178**	82	18	–	315
Ken Boyer	31	27	22	23	28	13	17	9	8	0	**178**	75	25	–	279
Bill White	18	16	22	27	26	22	24	11	12	0	**178**	86	14	–	209
Lou Brock		0	9	15	26	22	21	30	31	23	**177**	86	14	–	348
Rocky Colavito	13	33	26	21	22	28	18	10	6		**177**	86	14	0	273
Pete Rose				19	12	27	25	24	32	37	**176**	84	16	–	547
Roger Maris	31	36	25	17	25	6	8	17	11		**176**	87	13	–	223
Luis Aparicio	20	17	13	18	21	17	22	8	19	20	**175**	58	42	–	293
Willie Davis	3	10	26	17	26	15	20	15	19	22	**173**	76	24	–	322
Dick McAuliffe	0	8	13	17	21	17	26	27	28	13	**170**	75	25	–	241
Sandy Koufax	9	20	15	32	24	33	35				**168**	0	–	100	194
Ernie Banks	29	19	14	9	15	18	11	17	18	14	**164**	80	20	–	332
Tony Gonzalez	9	12	20	26	15	13	12	26	13	18	**164**	82	18	–	183
Tony Oliva			1	0	27	33	28	25	21	25	**160**	89	11	–	245
Tom Tresh		0	25	29	20	25	22	13	15	11	**160**	81	19	–	160
Boog Powell		0	8	18	29	19	26	10	22	27	**159**	91	9	–	282
Larry Jackson	21	15	16	22	25	11	19	14	15		**158**	0	–	100	225
Bill Mazeroski	21	16	23	15	17	13	20	14	13	6	**158**	48	52	–	219
Jimmy Wynn				9	4	31	14	28	32	36	**154**	85	15	–	305
Tom Haller		1	16	13	18	18	22	21	27	16	**152**	67	33	–	179
Bill Freehan		1		10	25	14	16	30	35	20	**151**	66	34	–	267
Tommy Davis	9	11	36	29	17	0	9	19	8	11	**149**	88	12	–	207

Player	1960	61	62	63	64	65	66	67	68	69	Dec	B	F	P	Car
Elston Howard	10	29	20	28	32	8	11	4	6		**148**	67	33	–	203
John Roseboro	10	20	16	16	19	13	21	13	10	10	**148**	59	41	–	181
Ron Fairly	0	15	21	21	17	26	17	9	9	10	**145**	86	14	–	269
Dick Groat	25	15	21	31	20	16	15	2			**145**	57	43	–	225
Hoyt Wilhelm	11	16	14	15	21	19	10	13	12	13	**144**	0	–	100	256
Clete Boyer	11	15	21	17	8	18	16	17	5	15	**143**	58	42	–	160
Leon Wagner	2	14	24	22	18	24	19	12	5	1	**141**	90	10	–	155
Leo Cardenas	2	8	21	12	17	22	19	11	5	23	**140**	53	47	–	199
Jim Kaat	0	11	22	5	15	17	26	17	13	13	**139**	2	–	98	268
Ron Hansen	24	16	2	19	30	18	1	17	8	3	**138**	57	43	–	145
Jim Maloney	1	6	8	22	18	23	21	13	10	15	**137**	3	0	97	137
Norm Siebern	21	23	27	18	20	13	12	2	0		**136**	88	12	–	171
Dean Chance		0	17	12	32	14	14	20	21	5	**135**	0	–	100	148
Don Buford				1	15	30	21	17	25	24	**133**	81	19	–	194
Floyd Robinson	1	19	27	20	25	24	11	3	2		**132**	86	14	–	132
Rusty Staub				12	5	13	18	28	28	27	**131**	90	10	–	358
Zoilo Versalles	1	13	16	19	18	32	12	9	5	6	**131**	55	45	–	134
Willie Stargell			1	7	13	21	25	20	16	27	**130**	92	8	–	370
Jim Ray Hart				0	25	25	27	29	19	5	**130**	86	14	–	148
Earl Battey	16	20	19	26	12	22	13	2			**130**	60	40	–	142
John Romano	15	25	26	10	15	20	16	1			**128**	70	30	–	136
Whitey Ford	14	22	20	23	24	16	4	4			**127**	1	–	99	261
Milt Pappas	14	15	8	15	18	15	9	14	11	8	**127**	0	0	100	210
Tim McCarver	0	1		15	17	15	21	30	14	14	**127**	67	33	–	204
Tony Taylor	16	5	16	23	15	6	9	7	17	12	**126**	67	33	–	198
Claude Osteen	1	1	10	11	17	18	17	16	8	26	**125**	2	0	98	201
Jim Gentile	21	32	20	20	15	12	5				**125**	91	9	–	125
Chris Short	6	0	11	11	21	24	17	16	18	0	**124**	0	0	100	142
Julian Javier	9	9	14	15	11	3	10	17	16	17	**121**	55	45	–	135
Earl Wilson	3		13	12	8	12	24	18	17	13	**120**	8	–	92	126
Denis Menke			2	13	29	5	16	12	21	21	**119**	74	26	–	176
Camilo Pascual	13	17	23	22	14	9	2	10	9	0	**119**	2	–	98	175
Donn Clendenon		1	10	15	13	22	23	9	17	8	**118**	89	11	–	136
Jim Perry	16	6	10	8	5	13	17	9	13	20	**117**	1	0	99	205
Don Mincher	1	2	6	10	8	17	14	28	13	18	**117**	90	10	–	162
Woodie Held	19	21	21	19	13	14	2	5	0	1	**115**	72	28	–	153
Pete Ward			0	25	27	17	5	20	15	6	**115**	84	16	–	117
Matty Alou	0	7	6	0	4	4	20	23	23	27	**114**	82	18	0	179
Tito Francona	24	21	18	10	9	4	1	5	12	10	**114**	87	13	–	165
Gaylord Perry			1	1	19	6	21	20	19	26	**113**	0	–	100	369
Lee Maye	3	14	7	17	23	9	10	10	10	10	**113**	86	14	–	123
Ron Hunt				19	17	3	18	14	21	19	**111**	79	21	–	191
Jim Gilliam	16	15	23	28	6	18	4				**110**	72	28	–	247
Sam McDowell		1	0	1	14	25	17	8	23	20	**109**	0	0	100	166
Dick Ellsworth	8	11	7	32	13	10	9	1	13	5	**109**	0	–	100	114
Gary Peters	0	1	0	25	22	7	20	21	3	9	**108**	5	–	95	133
Ron Perranoski		11	12	20	7	13	7	12	6	20	**108**	0	–	100	125
Chuck Hinton		9	17	20	16	17	11	11	4	3	**108**	84	16	–	118
Denny McLain				1	4	20	13	8	33	29	**108**	0	–	100	115
Ed Charles			21	16	10	16	18	10	14	3	**108**	73	27	–	108

Player	1960	61	62	63	64	65	66	67	68	69	Dec	B	F	P	Car
Bert Campaneris					6	18	22	16	29	16	**107**	64	36	0	280
Willie Horton				2	0	20	21	17	28	19	**107**	92	8	–	233
Ken McMullen			0	6	0	21	12	20	24	24	**107**	76	24	–	175
Bob Veale			3	10	21	18	17	9	17	12	**107**	0	–	100	124
Joe Horlen		0	3	8	19	11	15	23	13	15	**107**	0	–	100	119
Mel Stottlemyre					10	23	9	16	22	26	**106**	1	–	99	177
Jerry Lumpe	15	18	19	18	13	15	5	3			**106**	66	34	–	127
Johnny Edwards		2	18	21	19	17	4	4	6	14	**105**	50	50	–	149
Joe Adcock	25	22	13	8	15	9	12				**104**	87	13	–	236
Joe Pepitone			2	18	13	13	17	14	15	12	**104**	83	17	–	139
Joe Morgan				1	0	30	19	26	2	24	**102**	82	18	–	512
Lindy McDaniel	25	6	8	14	8	11	11	3	9	6	**101**	0	–	100	186
Stu Miller	4	18	8	16	13	22	14	6	0		**101**	1	–	99	154
Steve Barber	12	19	8	18	7	16	11	4	4	2	**101**	0	–	100	116
Bill Monbouquette	16	17	17	16	11	10	2	12	0		**101**	0	–	100	110
Bob Friend	20	12	21	21	13	11	2				**100**	0	–	100	207
Rico Petrocelli				0		9	15	23	15	37	**99**	67	33	–	205
Turk Farrell	15	4	19	15	12	10	3	13	4	4	**99**	0	–	100	124
Bobby Richardson	8	12	22	18	15	14	10				**99**	58	42	–	120
Jimmie Hall				21	19	26	10	15	3	5	**99**	78	22	–	100
Mudcat Grant	6	14	7	13	11	17	16	1	8	5	**98**	2	–	98	145
Mike McCormick	18	17	1	3	0	10	11	20	6	12	**98**	0	–	100	118
Bill Skowron	24	17	14	1	17	17	7	0			**97**	89	11	–	183
Jim Landis	19	23	17	12	7	9	4	6			**97**	73	27	–	151
Jackie Brandt	17	21	18	12	16	8	3	2			**97**	75	25	–	122
Max Alvis			0	25	13	15	16	17	10	1	**97**	75	25	–	98
Juan Pizarro	3	18	11	19	19	5	3	5	5	7	**95**	2	–	98	125
Jim Davenport	9	18	20	9	7	6	8	11	3	4	**95**	69	31	–	116
Curt Blefary						26	20	19	13	17	**95**	86	14	–	108
Jim O'Toole	10	22	16	17	19	0	8	3			**95**	0	–	100	99
Warren Spahn	16	25	23	22	1	7					**94**	2	–	98	412
Dick Hall	8	10	13	13	13	12	5	10	1	9	**94**	5	2	93	113
Ken Johnson	5	8	8	15	10	14	12	15	4	3	**94**	0	–	100	95
Mack Jones		2	10	6		19	14	18	8	16	**93**	87	13	–	109
Eddie Bressoud	11	1	21	17	25	6	11	1			**93**	66	34	–	108
Don Demeter	5	9	25	17	12	13	8	4			**93**	80	20	–	103
Luis Tiant					11	9	16	17	28	11	**92**	1	–	99	256
Clay Dalrymple	5	4	19	16	13	8	14	5	5	3	**92**	54	46	–	96
Jerry Adair	0	14	16	6	14	18	10	9	2	3	**92**	46	54	–	93
Don Lock			5	21	22	11	14	13	5	1	**92**	80	20	–	92
Don Wert				7	15	21	17	14	7	10	**91**	64	36	–	96
Jim Pagliaroni	4	11	9	8	15	17	12	2	7	6	**91**	71	29	–	91
Gary Bell	7	10	8	10	5	10	16	12	11	1	**90**	1	–	99	116
Tony Perez					0	6	4	23	25	31	**89**	86	14	–	349
Mickey Lolich				7	18	15	4	13	12	20	**89**	0	–	100	224
Curt Simmons	15	17	9	18	16	7	4	3			**89**	1	–	99	210
Bob Shaw	9	10	20	13	7	19	9	2			**89**	1	–	99	114
Dick Stuart	13	19	6	16	18	13	4			0	**89**	94	6	–	114
Phil Regan	2	4	9	9	3	0	23	7	20	12	**89**	2	–	98	100
Bob Aspromonte	0	0	14	7	19	14	8	18	5	4	**89**	66	34	–	94

Player	1960	61	62	63	64	65	66	67	68	69	Dec	B	F	P	Car
Wayne Causey		11	7	20	20	15	7	8	1		**89**	68	32	–	92
Tommy Harper			0	13	8	18	15	10	7	17	**88**	82	18	–	204
Ray Sadecki	10	18	1	6	15	2	5	15	12	4	**88**	2	–	98	130
Rico Carty				0	27	10	21	12		17	**87**	93	7	–	209
Wes Parker					5	20	17	15	12	18	**87**	84	16	–	148
Albie Pearson	3	15	21	28	5	15	0				**87**	79	21	–	104
Hank Aguirre	11	6	22	12	7	12	4	3	5	5	**87**	1	–	99	98
Bobby Knoop					11	16	18	18	15	9	**87**	49	51	–	97
Russ Snyder	6	8	13	13	3	9	15	7	9	4	**87**	80	20	–	97
Rich Rollins		1	23	19	14	10	5	7	4	3	**86**	79	21	–	87
Fergie Jenkins						2	12	21	25	25	**85**	1	–	99	323
Bill Bruton	24	17	19	15	10						**85**	74	26	–	190
Sonny Siebert					12	17	20	15	11	10	**85**	3	–	97	144
Ken Harrelson				3	1	13	12	10	28	18	**85**	87	13	–	88
Roy Face	17	10	20	5	1	3	8	10	6	4	**84**	1	–	99	139
Al McBean		5	12	14	16	14	5	11	5	2	**84**	1	0	99	84
Dick Radatz			21	24	24	11	2	0		2	**84**	0	–	100	84
Jim Lefebvre						23	25	16	9	10	**83**	71	29	–	106
Don Cardwell	8	16	7	11	1	14	2	6	8	10	**83**	1	–	99	99
Paul Blair					0	10	9	24	11	28	**82**	65	35	–	183
Dave McNally			2	2	8	14	12	1	26	17	**82**	0	–	100	168
Jim Northrup					0	1	14	16	24	27	**82**	83	17	–	161
Gene Alley				1	5	15	22	19	13	7	**82**	55	45	–	115
Tony Conigliaro					16	17	20	16		13	**82**	85	15	–	105
Tommie Agee			0	0	0	0	28	20	5	28	**81**	71	29	–	139
Don McMahon	0	9	12	3	14	6	10	11	8	8	**81**	1	–	99	135
Bobby Bolin		4	8	7	10	15	17	1	15	4	**81**	1	–	99	103
Deron Johnson	0	2	0		16	23	14	6	5	14	**80**	84	16	–	146
Ron Kline	0	9	4	10	12	14	13	5	13	0	**80**	0	0	100	132
Pedro Ramos	16	15	11	13	8	11	5	0		1	**80**	0	–	100	123
Denny Lemaster			6	14	8	4	8	12	13	15	**80**	0	–	100	89
Lenny Green	13	19	23	6	3	11	1	4	0		**80**	78	22	–	85
Lee Thomas		12	22	9	15	15	4	2	1		**80**	84	16	–	80
Bob Purkey	15	16	26	6	13	1	2				**79**	0	–	100	122
Tony Kubek	19	21	7	18	10	4					**79**	58	42	–	120
Stan Williams	17	16	5	9	2	0		6	16	8	**79**	0	–	100	114
Vic Davalillo				14	13	18	7	9	16	2	**79**	78	22	0	111
Bob Bailey			0	12	15	14	14	6	9	8	**78**	80	20	–	189
Frank Malzone	13	14	17	16	14	3	1				**78**	64	36	–	135
Ralph Terry	9	15	21	17	3	9	3	1			**78**	1	–	99	105
Mike Shannon			0	1	7	5	18	12	23	12	**78**	73	27	–	78
Roy Sievers	22	23	17	13	2	0					**77**	89	11	–	231
Jose Cardenal				0	0	14	20	8	21	14	**77**	80	20	–	212
Eddie Fisher	1	0	14	5	10	20	12	4	6	5	**77**	1	–	99	106
Larry Brown				6	8	14	8	14	17	10	**77**	47	53	–	87
Ernie Broglio	24	9	17	17	9	0	1				**77**	1	–	99	84
Tom Seaver								21	23	32	**76**	0	–	100	388
Cesar Tovar						0	14	21	22	19	**76**	79	21	0	178
Ted Abernathy	0			8	3	18	3	24	13	7	**76**	1	–	99	107
Ray Herbert	18	11	20	15	4	6	2				**76**	2	–	98	103

Player	1960	61	62	63	64	65	66	67	68	69	Dec	B	F	P	Car
Joe Azcue	1		3	14	8	6	10	13	15	6	**76**	51	49	–	83
Robin Roberts	13	0	16	15	15	13	3				**75**	2	–	98	339
Bill Virdon	14	14	12	16	5	14			0		**75**	66	34	–	157
Billy O'Dell	11	7	17	13	1	16	10	0			**75**	0	0	100	123
Dick Green				1	12	11	16	5	8	22	**75**	56	44	–	117
George Altman	11	20	20	15	5	3	1	0			**75**	81	19	–	86
Mike Hershberger		1	7	15	10	6	15	11	10	0	**75**	71	29	–	81

Players with at least 250 career Win Shares

Player	1960	61	62	63	64	65	66	67	68	69	Dec	B	F	P	Car
Phil Niekro					0	5	2	21	18	28	**74**	0	–	100	374
Nellie Fox	21	11	16	12	13	1					**74**	63	37	–	304
Tommy John				1	2	12	15	11	15	17	**73**	0	–	100	289
Reggie Jackson								2	25	41	**68**	91	9	–	444
Reggie Smith							0	19	25	24	**68**	84	16	–	325
Roy White						2	7	4	29	22	**64**	87	13	–	263
Rick Monday							0	16	26	20	**62**	83	17	–	258
Sal Bando							1	2	21	36	**60**	81	19	0	283
Stan Musial	13	14	19	10							**56**	89	11	0	604
Johnny Bench								2	24	28	**54**	72	28	–	356
Rod Carew								19	13	21	**53**	86	14	–	384
Steve Carlton						2	3	13	11	24	**53**	1	–	99	366
Minnie Minoso	24	19	1	4	1						**49**	85	15	–	283
Don Sutton							14	7	13	14	**48**	0	–	100	319
Yogi Berra	16	16	6	9		0					**47**	72	28	–	375
Bobby Bonds									15	31	**46**	86	14	–	302
Duke Snider	9	11	9	13	2						**44**	84	16	–	352
Richie Ashburn	22	6	12								**40**	78	22	–	329
Jim Palmer						4	11	3		18	**36**	0	–	100	312
Early Wynn	16	9	5	6							**36**	5	–	95	309
Eddie Yost	17	3	4								**24**	83	17	–	267
Bobby Murcer						2	0			20	**22**	85	15	–	277
Ted Williams	21										**21**	92	8	0	555
Al Oliver									0	13	**13**	85	15	–	305
Nolan Ryan							0		6	6	**12**	0	–	100	334
Red Schoendienst	5	3	3	0							**11**	63	37	–	262
Gil Hodges	3	5	2	0							**10**	87	13	–	263
Graig Nettles								0	3	5	**8**	71	29	–	321
Amos Otis								0		1	**1**	75	25	–	286
Carlton Fisk										0	**0**	69	31	–	368
Darrell Evans										0	**0**	81	19	–	363
Ted Simmons									0	0	**0**	77	23	–	315
Toby Harrah										0	**0**	80	20	–	287
Steve Garvey										0	**0**	85	15	–	279
George Foster										0	**0**	85	15	–	269

Player	1970	71	72	73	74	75	76	77	78	79	Dec	B	F	P	Car
Joe Morgan	24	29	39	40	37	44	37	30	17	18	**315**	82	18	–	512
Pete Rose	29	28	32	34	27	31	30	23	27	27	**288**	84	16	–	547
Johnny Bench	34	19	37	26	34	30	19	22	20	22	**263**	72	28	–	356
Reggie Jackson	17	32	26	32	30	27	25	27	23	23	**262**	91	9	–	444
Bobby Bonds	32	32	23	31	23	24	16	24	23	21	**249**	86	14	–	302
Rod Carew	11	17	22	28	32	30	30	37	22	16	**245**	86	14	–	384
Bobby Murcer	27	38	36	25	20	21	21	19	18	15	**240**	85	15	–	277
Amos Otis	25	27	22	29	22	17	25	18	29	23	**237**	75	25	–	286
Jim Palmer	25	22	25	28	9	31	27	29	27	12	**235**	0	–	100	312
Ken Singleton	5	11	18	28	16	33	24	36	28	32	**231**	90	10	–	302
Tom Seaver	25	32	22	29	16	26	20	25	19	16	**230**	0	–	100	388
Willie Stargell	17	35	26	36	29	22	17	8	22	18	**230**	92	8	–	370
Reggie Smith	25	29	26	23	25	20	14	29	24	9	**224**	84	16	–	325
Ted Simmons	6	20	23	28	21	28	20	28	30	20	**224**	77	23	–	315
Gaylord Perry	24	17	39	24	30	21	17	16	18	16	**222**	0	–	100	369
Graig Nettles	18	27	21	19	22	21	28	25	26	15	**222**	71	29	–	321
Sal Bando	24	29	23	31	21	19	24	17	23	9	**220**	81	19	0	283
Carl Yastrzemski	36	21	19	24	24	20	18	24	19	13	**218**	87	13	–	488
Cesar Cedeno	12	17	33	30	27	20	30	23	9	17	**218**	82	18	–	296
Tony Perez	33	23	25	32	20	19	16	17	18	14	**217**	86	14	–	349
Phil Niekro	11	22	22	17	28	19	21	20	30	24	**214**	0	–	100	374
Al Oliver	15	18	23	22	26	21	22	21	22	18	**208**	85	15	–	305
Fergie Jenkins	26	37	22	15	26	15	14	14	21	14	**204**	1	–	99	323
Thurman Munson	26	18	19	25	17	23	24	22	19	11	**204**	70	30	–	206
Bob Watson	9	15	26	28	18	20	31	23	17	16	**203**	91	9	–	236
Mike Schmidt			1	10	39	28	35	33	23	33	**202**	81	19	–	467
Steve Carlton	14	16	40	14	22	14	18	26	20	18	**202**	1	–	99	366
Bobby Grich	2	2	23	28	32	29	31	7	20	28	**202**	72	28	–	329
Rusty Staub	30	32	12	23	17	25	26	12	16	8	**201**	90	10	–	358
Roy White	34	29	26	15	19	21	26	17	11	1	**199**	87	13	–	263
Gene Tenace	8	10	7	26	22	32	22	25	22	24	**198**	82	18	–	231
Bert Blyleven	10	20	19	29	23	21	20	21	16	13	**192**	0	–	100	339
Darrell Evans	2	9	20	31	28	28	9	13	26	23	**189**	81	19	–	363
Toby Harrah		7	13	13	20	32	24	25	15	24	**173**	80	20	–	287
Steve Garvey	2	6	8	11	27	25	26	21	25	22	**173**	85	15	–	279
Lou Brock	20	30	21	26	22	18	13	9	2	10	**171**	86	14	–	348
Greg Luzinski	0	4	16	21	9	28	23	30	27	13	**171**	93	7	–	247
Don Sutton	11	21	24	22	15	17	20	17	11	10	**168**	0	–	100	319
Ron Cey		0	2	17	23	27	27	21	25	25	**167**	79	21	–	280
Richie Hebner	16	16	22	21	22	12	12	16	16	14	**167**	86	14	–	219
John Mayberry	3	2	27	31	14	33	15	14	14	14	**167**	90	10	–	199
Dave Concepcion	5	4	6	16	25	19	23	19	25	24	**166**	54	46	0	269
Carlton Fisk		2	33	17	11	15	19	30	31	6	**164**	69	31	–	368
Bert Campaneris	26	15	21	20	22	17	19	15	3	5	**163**	64	36	0	280
Rick Monday	19	15	16	22	22	22	23	10	13	1	**163**	83	17	–	258
Nolan Ryan	8	4	24	28	21	12	17	22	12	13	**161**	0	–	100	334
George Scott	15	15	21	24	19	23	19	15	6	4	**161**	86	14	–	216
Dave Parker				4	6	26	23	33	37	31	**160**	87	13	–	327
Joe Rudi	13	15	29	13	24	20	16	10	14	6	**160**	85	15	–	173
Davey Lopes			1	19	21	25	16	24	26	27	**159**	77	23	–	240

Player	1970	71	72	73	74	75	76	77	78	79	Dec	B	F	P	Car
Luis Tiant	8	1	19	21	29	17	22	12	17	12	**158**	1	–	99	256
Don Money	21	8	10	18	26	14	14	22	19	6	**158**	74	26	–	197
Willie McCovey	33	16	7	22	25	16	4	16	8	10	**157**	93	7	–	408
Lee May	14	24	24	19	14	13	19	14	10	6	**157**	90	10	–	225
Catfish Hunter	12	22	24	15	27	29	15	4	8	1	**157**	2	0	98	206
Dave Cash	8	16	15	12	26	24	21	17	11	7	**157**	64	36	–	165
Don Baylor	0	0	13	16	16	24	19	16	23	29	**156**	93	7	–	262
George Foster	1	12	1	2	9	21	25	32	30	22	**155**	85	15	–	269
Garry Maddox			13	23	16	18	26	20	21	16	**153**	72	28	–	203
Vida Blue	3	30	6	15	16	19	25	14	22	3	**153**	0	–	100	202
George Brett				0	9	25	33	29	23	33	**152**	86	14	–	432
Jimmy Wynn	27	7	28	16	32	21	18	2			**151**	85	15	–	305
Dave Winfield				3	17	20	25	24	28	33	**150**	90	10	–	415
Dick Allen	19	29	40	15	24	8	11	4			**150**	91	9	–	342
Jose Cruz	1	14	8	12	5	11	22	24	26	27	**150**	84	16	–	313
Willie Davis	24	25	25	23	20	15	16			1	**149**	76	24	–	322
Billy Williams	29	26	32	20	16	17	7				**147**	88	12	–	374
Jeff Burroughs	0	5	0	23	33	15	14	22	27	8	**147**	91	9	–	196
Ralph Garr	1	25	19	14	27	16	14	15	10	6	**147**	86	14	–	147
Wilbur Wood	14	33	29	23	19	13	5	4	4		**144**	0	–	100	190
Gary Matthews			3	21	20	16	24	16	17	25	**142**	87	13	–	257
Hal McRae	4	9	3	8	20	17	26	26	16	12	**141**	95	5	–	230
Manny Sanguillen	19	24	18	15	16	23	13	9	4	0	**141**	67	33	–	157
Andy Messersmith	14	19	12	18	25	28	17	6	0	1	**140**	1	–	99	169
Chris Speier		16	25	15	17	20	11	11	15	9	**139**	55	45	–	206
Mickey Rivers	2	9	1	7	16	22	26	22	19	15	**139**	79	21	–	185
Dusty Baker	0	0	23	20	20	17	6	21	13	18	**138**	83	17	–	245
Jerry Koosman	14	9	5	18	17	13	20	11	8	23	**138**	0	–	100	240
Joe Torre	25	41	18	19	16	8	10	0			**137**	82	18	–	315
Chris Chambliss		11	13	16	9	15	21	17	19	16	**137**	87	13	–	221
Buddy Bell			13	21	13	16	20	15	16	22	**136**	71	29	–	301
Rick Reuschel			10	20	12	14	19	26	18	17	**136**	0	–	100	240
Richie Zisk		1	0	16	25	22	24	20	15	13	**136**	90	10	–	178
Fred Lynn					4	33	22	15	27	34	**135**	81	19	–	280
Mickey Lolich	17	29	26	19	17	15	8		4	0	**135**	0	–	100	224
Rick Wise	13	23	20	13	3	17	14	8	6	17	**134**	3	–	97	178
Mike Marshall	4	9	22	23	21	8	8	2	14	23	**134**	1	–	99	146
George Hendrick		1	1	13	19	13	20	28	21	17	**133**	84	16	–	237
Jose Cardenal	16	13	18	18	17	26	16	3	4	2	**133**	80	20	–	212
Larry Bowa	10	12	12	5	15	15	14	16	22	12	**133**	51	49	–	179
Darrell Porter		2	1	16	15	19	7	18	23	31	**132**	73	27	–	222
Tommy John	17	10	11	15	11		13	19	12	23	**131**	0	–	100	289
Bill Madlock				4	16	26	25	14	25	21	**131**	84	16	–	242
Willie Montanez	0	20	16	11	16	15	18	13	15	7	**131**	82	18	–	141
Doug Rader	19	15	19	18	18	9	17	15			**130**	73	27	–	166
Freddie Patek	8	24	13	16	15	11	14	15	11	3	**130**	52	48	–	150
Jim Rice					1	20	17	26	36	28	**128**	87	13	–	282
Oscar Gamble	5	4	3	14	20	14	12	22	15	19	**128**	92	8	–	177
Jon Matlack		1	22	16	24	12	18	6	25	4	**128**	0	–	100	156
Ken Henderson	24	23	14	5	26	15	13	4	2	2	**128**	79	21	–	142

Player	1970	71	72	73	74	75	76	77	78	79	Dec	B	F	P	Car
Mike Hargrove					20	22	24	25	16	20	**127**	90	10	–	212
Hank Aaron	25	33	21	20	13	9	5				**126**	89	11	–	643
Rollie Fingers	7	12	13	14	14	15	17	12	17	5	**126**	1	–	99	188
Mike Torrez	9	1	18	6	11	19	20	13	14	14	**125**	0	–	100	159
Lou Piniella	15	11	21	6	17	1	9	13	19	12	**124**	82	18	–	164
Mark Belanger	12	21	5	10	16	14	23	11	9	3	**124**	36	64	–	162
Sparky Lyle	6	10	18	14	16	7	14	20	9	10	**124**	1	–	99	161
Bill North		1	1	25	19	22	21	5	10	20	**124**	77	23	–	143
Boog Powell	31	19	18	13	13	23	5	1			**123**	91	9	–	282
Willie Horton	15	17	9	15	12	13	11	12	7	12	**123**	92	8	–	233
Rico Carty	27		10	5	4	16	24	12	19	5	**122**	93	7	–	209
Bill Russell	7	4	16	17	16	3	15	15	18	10	**121**	55	45	–	185
John Hiller	10		4	31	20	12	17	9	15	3	**121**	0	–	100	146
Larry Hisle	6	0		17	18	11	19	24	23	3	**121**	88	12	–	146
Burt Hooton		3	16	16	4	17	12	19	19	14	**120**	0	–	100	164
Dave Kingman		6	15	8	7	15	17	10	17	24	**119**	90	10	0	195
Joe Ferguson	0	2	1	29	19	5	11	20	14	17	**118**	69	31	–	130
Ron Fairly	19	19	17	20	10	11	5	12	4		**117**	86	14	–	269
Ken Griffey Sr.				6	7	18	25	23	22	16	**117**	87	13	–	259
Bernie Carbo	25	9	12	16	12	17	7	11	6	2	**117**	85	15	–	117
Bill Freehan	16	25	20	12	23	13	7				**116**	66	34	–	267
Tommy Harper	33	20	24	21	6	10	2				**116**	82	18	–	204
Frank Robinson	26	23	14	26	18	6	1				**114**	90	10	–	519
Jim Kaat	12	15	12	9	21	22	12	2	5	4	**114**	2	–	98	268
Bill Lee	1	10	7	24	19	18	0	8	11	16	**114**	1	–	99	125
Bill Buckner	1	9	13	11	21	5	20	7	12	14	**113**	83	17	–	226
Ted Sizemore	11	13	11	22	15	8	4	14	5	10	**113**	52	48	–	130
Ken Holtzman	23	7	16	19	15	15	12	0	1	4	**112**	0	–	100	157
Felix Millan	15	18	9	20	13	17	16	4			**112**	61	39	–	152
Bob Bailey	21	21	12	21	20	7	5	2	2		**111**	80	20	–	189
Pat Kelly	11	7	17	13	10	14	9	13	10	7	**111**	86	14	–	135
Rennie Stennett		7	10	9	20	21	16	18	5	5	**111**	56	44	–	118
Dave Roberts	9	24	7	20	13	6	14	7	5	6	**111**	2	–	98	116
Steve Rogers				15	8	19	14	21	17	16	**110**	0	–	100	182
Jim Barr		2	11	12	23	17	20	8	8	9	**110**	1	–	99	123
Ron Reed	7	13	10	4	11	13	15	14	14	8	**109**	1	–	99	181
Jorge Orta			1	10	22	21	17	14	15	8	**108**	86	14	–	160
Paul Splittorff	0	10	12	17	9	11	6	15	16	12	**108**	0	–	100	140
Ron LeFlore					5	9	26	23	24	21	**108**	81	19	–	139
Andre Thornton				1	12	23	7	20	25	19	**107**	94	6	–	186
Dave Johnson	23	23	14	21	15	0		8	3		**107**	71	29	–	171
Tug McGraw	9	17	22	10	4	12	10	10	8	5	**107**	1	–	99	158
Johnny Grubb			1	18	21	17	18	4	19	9	**107**	89	11	–	157
Rico Petrocelli	23	27	21	11	15	6	3				**106**	67	33	–	205
Don Kessinger	14	14	15	12	13	13	11	4	9	1	**106**	52	48	–	159
Steve Braun		10	14	16	13	17	16	10	6	4	**106**	86	14	–	121
Carlos May	15	15	29	15	8	14	8	2			**106**	89	11	–	120
Frank Tanana				2	15	22	27	20	14	5	**105**	0	–	100	241
Joe Coleman	10	20	19	21	13	3	5	9	5	0	**105**	0	–	100	129
Tito Fuentes	9	17	14	19	5	15	9	16	0		**104**	61	39	–	132

Player	1970	71	72	73	74	75	76	77	78	79	Dec	B	F	P	Car
Willie Crawford	8	13	9	24	20	12	14	4			**104**	84	16	–	123
Bill Melton	17	23	8	22	13	12	8	1			**104**	81	19	–	122
Dave Goltz			6	2	11	15	13	22	19	16	**104**	0	–	100	115
Brooks Robinson	21	23	16	12	23	6	2	0			**103**	70	30	–	356
Del Unser	6	17	6	16	15	19	9	8	2	5	**103**	74	26	–	138
Bake McBride				2	22	16	13	20	13	17	**103**	80	20	–	132
Wayne Garrett	16	2	13	21	16	13	14	5	3		**103**	69	31	–	110
Cesar Tovar	28	21	17	8	22	6	0				**102**	79	21	0	178
Rick Burleson					11	14	21	21	16	19	**102**	49	51	–	152
Dick Drago	10	18	12	11	13	8	3	6	8	13	**102**	0	–	100	121
John Milner		0	15	15	15	4	19	11	10	13	**102**	86	14	–	115
Marty Pattin	15	16	14	10	5	13	11	9	4	5	**102**	0	–	100	114
Don Gullett	10	17	5	15	18	15	8	11	3		**102**	0	–	100	102
Paul Blair	22	15	11	18	21	6	3	3	1	1	**101**	65	35	–	183
Aurelio Rodriguez	17	14	14	9	8	13	5	5	10	6	**101**	47	53	–	124
Jim Spencer	15	14	1	11	10	11	12	9	4	14	**101**	83	17	–	120
Gary Carter					2	18	6	25	22	27	**100**	63	37	–	337
Bud Harrelson	17	19	13	13	14	1	13	4	3	3	**100**	52	48	–	141
Dock Ellis	14	14	11	8	12	5	13	17	5	1	**100**	0	–	100	115
Bob Gibson	28	17	29	12	12	1					**99**	2	–	98	317
Mike Cuellar	18	18	16	16	19	12	0	0			**99**	0	–	100	173
Steve Renko	11	15	0	22	11	9	8	6	6	11	**99**	2	0	98	131
Dwight Evans			2	7	15	17	15	9	17	16	**98**	85	15	–	347
John Briggs	9	18	20	18	20	13					**98**	88	12	–	159
Rudy May	5	13	11	5	10	15	10	16	4	9	**98**	0	–	100	141
Nate Colbert	18	19	28	20	11	1	1				**98**	87	13	–	114
Merv Rettenmund	19	27	9	14	5	5	5	7	5	2	**98**	85	15	–	109
Goose Gossage			3	0	4	23	10	26	20	11	**97**	0	–	100	223
Bob Boone			1	16	8	7	14	18	17	16	**97**	49	51	–	210
Jim Sundberg					15	7	12	22	23	18	**97**	47	53	–	200
Cecil Cooper		2	1	1	10	13	12	18	15	24	**96**	92	8	–	241
Jim Slaton		7	0	13	12	6	15	14	13	16	**96**	0	–	100	126
Fred Norman	1	7	11	12	12	9	11	13	9	11	**96**	0	–	100	101
Jack Billingham	9	9	10	19	9	8	5	2	12	12	**95**	0	–	100	106
Dennis Eckersley						17	11	18	24	24	**94**	0	–	100	301
Jerry Reuss	6	4	5	15	13	20	13	9	2	7	**94**	1	–	99	194
Al Bumbry			1	17	4	10	16	24	3	19	**94**	80	20	–	169
J.R. Richard		1	0	4	2	7	17	21	19	23	**94**	0	–	100	106
Randy Jones				9	6	28	21	3	14	13	**94**	0	–	100	100
Ross Grimsley		8	11	14	21	7	5	12	16	0	**94**	0	–	100	95
Phil Garner				0	0	12	19	20	19	23	**93**	68	32	–	195
Dan Driessen				12	14	8	7	19	18	15	**93**	87	13	–	179
Pat Dobson	12	19	15	7	19	9	12	0			**93**	0	–	100	112
Cesar Geronimo	0	1	9	4	17	16	19	11	8	8	**93**	70	30	–	104
Sixto Lezcano					1	10	17	17	20	27	**92**	84	16	–	159
Jim Rooker	10	0	1	12	21	12	13	15	4	2	**90**	5	0	95	100
Carl Morton	21	4	7	18	17	17	6				**90**	0	–	100	91
Keith Hernandez					1	3	13	24	19	29	**89**	89	11	–	311
Brian Downing				1	10	16	10	9	18	25	**89**	85	15	–	298
Bill Robinson			2	16	3	6	17	18	14	12	**88**	79	21	–	112

Player	1970	71	72	73	74	75	76	77	78	79	Dec	B	F	P	Car
Dave May	8	18	13	24	6	9	3	6	1		**88**	74	26	–	93
Jay Johnstone	10	12	3	0	9	14	19	13	1	6	**87**	80	20	–	141
Ken Forsch	0	14	5	8	10	6	11	8	13	12	**87**	0	–	100	137
Stan Bahnsen	12	13	12	18	6	5	8	3	3	7	**87**	0	–	100	130
Harmon Killebrew	30	23	18	5	5	5					**86**	91	9	–	371
Ben Oglivie		1	7	1	9	7	11	11	19	20	**86**	87	13	–	194
Dave McNally	22	19	12	18	14	1					**86**	0	–	100	168
Robin Yount					8	14	14	16	19	14	**85**	75	25	–	423
Tony Oliva	30	23	1	13	9	9	0				**85**	89	11	–	245
Gene Garber	0		0	11	7	10	11	15	22	9	**85**	0	–	100	160
Dennis Leonard					0	14	14	24	19	14	**85**	–	–	100	133
Dick Tidrow			17	12	8	6	9	13	8	12	**85**	0	–	100	113
Ray Fosse	17	16	14	14	3	2	12	6		1	**85**	53	47	–	86
Earl Williams	1	19	18	15	14	6	7	5			**85**	77	23	–	85
Willie Randolph						1	17	20	23	23	**84**	69	31	–	312
Reggie Cleveland	0	9	10	13	9	10	12	13	8	0	**84**	0	–	100	93
Mike Caldwell		2	3	8	15	2	0	5	28	20	**83**	1	–	99	122
Doc Medich			0	18	16	16	8	7	10	8	**83**	0	–	100	110
Sandy Alomar	17	21	15	9	6	10	3	2	0		**83**	52	48	–	104
Jerry Morales	0	0	9	11	12	13	12	15	7	4	**83**	77	23	–	95
Roy Smalley						5	18	13	22	24	**82**	70	30	–	181
Al Cowens					4	10	12	27	15	14	**82**	75	25	–	138
Clay Carroll	14	13	13	5	12	9	8	8	0		**82**	0	–	100	123
Eric Soderholm		0	5	4	15	14		20	16	8	**82**	72	28	–	91
Woodie Fryman	8	11	14	2	7	12	14	2	5	6	**81**	1	–	99	134
Bill Bonham		1	5	15	11	9	9	12	10	9	**81**	0	–	100	82
Jim Fregosi	33	9	10	8	7	5	3	4	1		**80**	76	24	–	261
Ron Hunt	13	26	15	15	11						**80**	79	21	–	191
Jim Lonborg	4	7	14	5	21	6	15	7	1	0	**80**	2	–	98	122
Dave LaRoche	4	10	8	2	5	11	14	10	14	2	**80**	1	–	99	95
Jim Colborn	6	0	8	20	10	9	10	16	1		**80**	0	–	100	81
Roger Metzger	0	14	11	15	10	8	9	1	6	6	**80**	47	53	–	80
Jim Northrup	17	18	11	16	11	6					**79**	83	17	–	161
Derrel Thomas		0	9	6	12	17	5	13	7	10	**79**	65	35	–	109
Steve Yeager			5	5	15	12	13	16	6	7	**79**	43	57	–	106
Al Kaline	19	22	14	8	15						**78**	87	13	–	443
Norm Cash	16	24	18	15	5						**78**	89	11	–	315
Chet Lemon						1	8	23	20	26	**78**	76	24	–	265
Bruce Bochte					5	13	15	14	12	19	**78**	86	14	–	159
Jerry Grote	10	12	8	7	5	18	12	3	3		**78**	49	51	–	127
Dave Giusti	15	10	13	12	9	10	3	6			**78**	2	–	98	118
Bucky Dent				2	16	16	9	14	9	12	**78**	40	60	–	116
Don Wilson	9	22	17	17	13						**78**	0	–	100	108
Elliott Maddox	7	7	10	3	23	8	0	4	11	5	**78**	77	23	–	88
Tim McCarver	7	16	9	10	3	4	10	10	5	3	**77**	67	33	–	204
John Candelaria						8	15	26	14	14	**77**	0	–	100	182
Bruce Sutter							12	27	16	22	**77**	0	–	100	168
Bill Campbell				6	15	7	17	23	4	5	**77**	0	–	100	107
Tim Foli	0	4	9	6	8	9	10	7	7	17	**77**	33	67	–	107
Clyde Wright	20	18	16	13	7	3					**77**	1	–	99	91

Player	1970	71	72	73	74	75	76	77	78	79	Dec	B	F	P	Car
Pedro Borbon	0	0	9	15	12	10	8	14	4	5	**77**	1	–	99	78
Ed Figueroa					4	18	16	15	19	5	**77**	–	–	100	77
Doug DeCinces				0	0	5	10	21	27	13	**76**	77	23	–	205
Claude Osteen	13	12	22	14	8	7					**76**	2	0	98	201
Greg Gross				1	20	14	16	9	8	8	**76**	84	16	0	113
Gary Nolan	19	13	15	0		15	12	2			**76**	0	–	100	113
Ken Brett	9	0	1	17	14	8	14	8	1	4	**76**	8	–	92	80
Skip Lockwood	6	9	5	6	2	5	15	13	8	7	**76**	1	0	99	79
Doug Rau			3	3	8	16	21	13	12	0	**76**	0	–	100	76
Ron Santo	19	19	21	13	3						**75**	79	21	–	324
Garry Templeton							5	24	21	25	**75**	58	42	–	209
Cookie Rojas	8	18	12	16	10	8	1	2			**75**	57	42	0	144
Bobby Tolan	29		22	3	10	8	3	0		0	**75**	77	23	–	115
Dan Ford						12	18	12	15	18	**75**	85	15	–	110
Mike Jorgensen	2	2	10	10	17	16	9	5	1	3	**75**	82	18	–	96
Lenny Randle		5	1	0	16	17	8	18	10	0	**75**	67	33	–	89
Players with at least 250 career Win Shares															
Eddie Murray								21	28	25	**74**	91	9	–	437
Willie Mays	24	27	12	5							**68**	84	16	–	642
Frank Howard	30	23	10	5							**68**	92	8	–	297
Jack Clark						0	3	11	30	23	**67**	92	8	–	316
Vada Pinson	14	11	20	9	10	2					**66**	78	22	–	321
Andre Dawson							1	18	21	24	**64**	82	18	–	340
Roberto Clemente	23	24	16								**63**	84	16	–	377
Luis Aparicio	18	8	11	13							**50**	58	42	–	293
Juan Marichal	11	18	5	10	3	0					**47**	0	–	100	263
Orlando Cepeda	21	7	3	13	0						**44**	91	9	–	310
Paul Molitor									12	26	**38**	89	11	–	414
Lou Whitaker								0	17	20	**37**	75	25	–	351
Maury Wills	13	19	1								**33**	67	33	–	253
Ozzie Smith									20	7	**27**	57	43	–	325
Alan Trammell								0	14	13	**27**	71	29	–	318
Dale Murphy							2	2	7	11	**22**	83	17	–	294
Hoyt Wilhelm	11	3	0								**14**	0	–	100	256
Jim Bunning	11	0									**11**	0	–	100	257
Rickey Henderson										10	**10**	89	11	–	530
Ernie Banks	5	0									**5**	80	20	–	332
Tim Raines										0	**0**	86	14	–	390
Minnie Minoso							0				**0**	85	15	–	283

Player	1980	81	82	83	84	85	86	87	88	89	Dec	B	F	P	Car
Rickey Henderson	34	27	28	30	28	38	26	20	28	30	**289**	89	11	–	530
Robin Yount	25	20	39	33	27	16	23	26	31	34	**274**	75	25	–	423
Mike Schmidt	37	30	37	35	26	26	31	26	14	3	**265**	81	19	–	467
Eddie Murray	26	21	29	31	33	28	20	20	21	21	**250**	91	9	–	437
Tim Raines	0	18	21	29	32	36	32	34	19	25	**246**	86	14	–	390
Dale Murphy	28	11	32	32	33	31	22	29	12	14	**244**	83	17	–	294
Wade Boggs			15	34	28	31	37	32	31	29	**237**	81	19	0	394
Dwight Evans	17	26	31	13	29	21	24	25	23	21	**230**	85	15	–	347
George Brett	36	14	27	24	14	37	19	15	26	17	**229**	86	14	–	432
Keith Hernandez	28	20	24	23	33	27	29	21	13	3	**221**	89	11	–	311
Pedro Guerrero	9	14	30	32	23	35	2	28	18	30	**221**	90	10	–	246
Cal Ripken Jr.		0	23	35	37	25	28	20	25	26	**219**	68	32	–	427
Alan Trammell	21	14	16	26	29	16	26	35	23	13	**219**	71	29	–	318
Gary Carter	30	17	31	24	30	33	23	13	12	2	**215**	63	37	–	337
Jack Clark	24	15	26	20	12	22	9	33	21	31	**213**	92	8	–	316
Lou Whitaker	11	13	22	29	22	24	19	20	20	25	**205**	75	25	–	351
Andre Dawson	29	25	26	28	12	16	16	20	19	13	**204**	82	18	–	340
Ozzie Smith	17	8	19	18	19	25	23	33	22	20	**204**	57	43	–	325
Paul Molitor	19	8	30	23	0	21	14	29	27	27	**198**	89	11	–	414
Dave Winfield	22	16	20	22	26	21	17	18	31		**193**	90	10	–	415
Ryne Sandberg		0	17	18	38	28	20	20	22	28	**191**	73	27	–	346
Willie Randolph	31	9	19	15	21	20	18	22	13	20	**188**	69	31	–	312
Tony Gwynn			7	10	35	20	29	29	23	30	**183**	89	11	–	398
Don Mattingly			0	7	29	32	34	27	24	26	**179**	89	11	–	263
Carney Lansford	15	18	16	12	25	12	19	23	18	21	**179**	82	18	–	244
Willie Wilson	31	14	25	15	23	19	15	15	12	10	**179**	71	29	–	237
Chet Lemon	24	16	15	21	24	18	12	19	19	10	**178**	76	24	–	265
Harold Baines	8	10	19	20	24	25	20	13	18	18	**175**	92	8	–	307
Dave Stieb	16	15	25	24	25	24	6	11	16	13	**175**	0	0	100	210
Darrell Evans	27	14	20	28	12	18	17	22	11	5	**174**	81	19	–	363
Brian Downing	2	10	25	13	20	21	23	23	15	17	**169**	85	15	–	298
Darryl Strawberry				18	24	24	25	30	30	18	**169**	90	10	–	252
Lance Parrish	20	11	24	24	19	20	15	10	12	12	**167**	59	41	–	248
Carlton Fisk	18	13	19	26	10	24	6	16	15	18	**165**	69	31	–	368
Buddy Bell	21	18	25	17	26	10	23	17	8	0	**165**	71	29	–	301
Jose Cruz	25	14	18	30	29	21	17	9	0		**163**	84	16	–	313
Kirk Gibson	4	13	9	11	26	24	20	20	31	5	**163**	89	11	–	218
Tim Wallach	0	4	20	19	18	23	14	28	16	20	**162**	67	33	0	248
Kent Hrbek		1	18	19	24	19	17	25	19	18	**160**	87	13	–	230
Lloyd Moseby	5	7	11	25	26	21	17	22	13	12	**159**	72	28	–	177
Dwayne Murphy	27	20	24	11	22	18	15	8	7	4	**156**	78	22	–	173
Steve Sax		3	18	17	11	12	31	18	24	21	**155**	72	28	–	198
Jim Rice	16	15	21	24	17	14	28	8	9	2	**154**	87	13	–	282
Jack Morris	14	16	14	20	14	19	20	21	12	4	**154**	0	–	100	225
Tom Herr	4	14	15	12	20	30	18	16	8	17	**154**	69	31	–	170
Dan Quisenberry	19	10	22	28	24	23	10	7	2	8	**153**	0	–	100	157
Von Hayes		4	11	9	21	19	26	23	14	25	**152**	83	17	–	177
Brett Butler		4	2	16	19	23	20	20	27	20	**151**	81	19	–	295
Bill Doran			3	22	18	28	19	24	19	17	**150**	74	26	–	193
Kirby Puckett					16	19	26	29	32	27	**149**	79	21	–	281

Player	1980	81	82	83	84	85	86	87	88	89	Dec	B	F	P	Car
Dave Parker	17	6	7	12	17	29	20	13	10	15	**146**	87	13	–	327
Cecil Cooper	27	22	29	25	14	17	8	3			**145**	92	8	–	241
Frank White	13	7	18	15	18	16	20	14	9	14	**144**	49	51	–	211
Lonnie Smith	13	9	26	19	16	15	14	3	2	27	**144**	88	12	–	190
Johnny Ray		2	19	20	20	11	18	14	21	18	**143**	68	32	–	153
Chili Davis		0	19	11	21	16	21	16	16	22	**142**	92	8	0	285
Fred Lynn	19	5	21	16	22	16	14	11	8	9	**141**	81	19	–	280
Bert Blyleven	9	14	1	10	20	23	18	18	4	22	**139**	0	–	100	339
Kevin McReynolds				3	25	12	26	19	31	21	**137**	82	18	–	202
Jesse Barfield		2	11	11	11	26	28	19	12	16	**136**	77	23	–	166
Mookie Wilson	2	9	19	17	23	12	16	15	17	6	**136**	76	24	–	151
Ken Griffey Sr.	25	19	13	17	9	14	17	10	3	8	**135**	87	13	–	259
F. Valenzuela	3	17	20	12	18	21	21	12	3	8	**135**	2	0	98	168
Charlie Hough	3	6	15	18	15	21	14	17	17	8	**134**	0	–	100	233
Bob Welch	14	8	13	16	9	15	13	19	13	14	**134**	0	0	100	188
Gary Gaetti		0	11	17	16	15	23	17	22	12	**133**	65	35	0	249
Terry Kennedy	6	10	28	24	12	14	14	11	2	12	**133**	67	33	–	150
Glenn Hubbard	14	10	19	19	15	14	12	15	11	4	**133**	53	47	–	140
Jim Gantner	10	13	15	21	16	11	13	7	14	12	**132**	57	42	0	163
Willie McGee			11	15	20	36	12	17	16	4	**131**	79	21	–	224
Tom Brunansky		1	18	15	17	16	12	20	16	16	**131**	78	22	–	175
George Bell		2		2	19	21	23	26	16	22	**131**	86	14	–	171
Julio Franco			0	12	17	16	18	14	22	30	**129**	81	19	–	244
Doug DeCinces	16	15	28	13	17	12	16	12			**129**	77	23	–	205
Mike Scioscia	5	11	8	2	15	26	13	18	14	16	**128**	57	43	–	168
Bobby Grich	20	21	21	20	16	18	11				**127**	72	28	–	329
Andy Van Slyke				11	14	18	17	25	28	14	**127**	81	19	–	231
Alvin Davis					27	22	13	20	18	26	**126**	92	8	–	153
Leon Durham	8	10	25	13	22	18	15	14	1	0	**126**	88	12	–	126
Lee Smith	2	4	13	19	15	17	17	15	12	11	**125**	0	–	100	198
Tony Pena	1	7	16	21	21	11	15	6	17	10	**125**	42	58	–	175
Claudell Washington	12	10	18	13	17	12	5	10	15	12	**124**	84	16	–	194
Hubie Brooks	3	11	6	10	21	15	15	11	19	13	**124**	78	22	–	149
Ernie Whitt	6	6	9	15	12	15	13	16	16	16	**124**	58	42	–	126
Nolan Ryan	11	15	16	12	9	7	11	15	9	18	**123**	0	–	100	334
Terry Puhl	23	11	15	18	19	8	3	1	12	13	**123**	81	19	–	176
Garry Templeton	17	10	11	10	16	21	8	6	12	11	**122**	58	42	–	209
Ken Oberkfell	15	13	15	17	9	12	17	10	10	4	**122**	72	28	–	141
Tony Fernandez				1	6	21	24	24	25	20	**121**	64	36	–	280
Frank Viola			3	4	22	16	13	24	25	14	**121**	0	–	100	187
Will Clark							14	25	37	44	**120**	92	8	–	331
Eric Davis					7	5	25	30	27	26	**120**	85	15	–	224
Orel Hershiser				0	18	23	12	21	25	21	**120**	1	0	99	210
Howard Johnson			5	1	10	11	10	24	21	38	**120**	83	17	–	194
Jeff Reardon	11	9	18	10	12	13	11	12	13	11	**120**	0	–	100	157
John Tudor	8	3	15	14	13	27	16	7	16	1	**120**	0	–	100	135
Doyle Alexander	10	11	0	8	23	20	12	18	9	8	**119**	0	–	100	192
Jerry Mumphrey	19	12	17	17	19	14	8	13	0		**119**	80	20	–	160
Rick Sutcliffe	0	1	20	14	18	11	7	19	14	14	**118**	0	–	100	153
Dave Righetti		10	10	15	16	15	20	13	11	8	**118**	0	–	100	137

Player	1980	81	82	83	84	85	86	87	88	89	Dec	B	F	P	Car
Dennis Eckersley	10	6	17	3	16	15	8	13	15	14	**117**	0	–	100	301
Pete O'Brien			2	10	18	13	24	19	17	14	**117**	78	22	–	141
Gary Matthews	17	19	23	14	23	8	11	0			**115**	87	13	–	257
Reggie Jackson	31	10	22	4	10	18	13	6			**114**	91	9	–	444
Toby Harrah	23	18	28	16	5	17	7				**114**	80	20	–	287
George Foster	23	24	12	14	18	17	6				**114**	85	15	–	269
Goose Gossage	18	12	17	16	15	15	5	7	4	5	**114**	0	–	100	223
Tony Armas	22	18	13	7	20	9	9	0	9	7	**114**	75	25	–	131
Tony Bernazard	4	16	20	15	6	17	25	11			**114**	71	29	–	117
Roger Clemens					8	8	29	28	22	18	**113**	0	–	100	352
Ron Cey	23	16	17	16	17	10	11	3			**113**	79	21	–	280
Bill Buckner	17	13	21	16	9	16	13	5	3	0	**113**	83	17	–	226
Phil Bradley				1	9	26	19	21	17	20	**113**	88	12	–	124
Bob Boone	11	3	13	9	7	12	10	10	17	20	**112**	49	51	–	210
Juan Samuel				2	19	21	18	22	18	12	**112**	78	22	–	176
Rick Rhoden	9	6	11	16	20	6	20	14	8	2	**112**	5	–	95	155
Keith Moreland	6	4	13	18	13	19	11	13	9	6	**112**	81	19	–	115
Steve Carlton	29	16	25	18	12	4	4	3	0		**111**	1	–	99	366
Bill Madlock	13	15	25	17	6	14	12	9			**111**	84	16	–	242
Floyd Bannister	15	6	17	17	9	7	11	17	8	3	**110**	0	–	100	128
Mike Witt		6	12	5	17	16	23	14	11	6	**110**	–	–	100	117
Jim Clancy	19	3	20	14	7	9	13	17	7	0	**109**	0	–	100	128
Ron Oester	10	15	11	14	8	21	15	5	3	7	**109**	58	42	–	112
Ben Oglivie	27	13	21	16	11	12	8				**108**	87	13	–	194
Bret Saberhagen					10	24	8	23	15	28	**108**	0	–	100	193
Kevin Bass			0	2	6	19	27	18	19	17	**108**	82	18	–	148
Mike Marshall		0	3	17	15	23	9	11	19	11	**108**	86	14	–	113
Dusty Baker	24	16	22	19	9	13	4				**107**	83	17	–	245
Dave Henderson		1	11	13	11	11	11	4	26	19	**107**	77	23	–	160
Dickie Thon	3	3	22	30	1	9	8	2	9	20	**107**	64	36	–	147
Bob Horner	19	11	21	17	4	16	15		4		**107**	84	16	–	140
Steve Garvey	22	13	15	14	15	17	10	0			**106**	85	15	–	279
Don Baylor	5	9	13	21	16	12	16	8	6		**106**	93	7	–	262
Joe Carter				0	7	11	28	14	26	20	**106**	83	17	–	240
Danny Darwin	12	6	9	10	11	12	14	12	6	14	**106**	0	–	100	182
Bob Stanley	15	6	20	21	12	10	6	5	9	2	**106**	–	–	100	149
Gary Ward	4	7	20	17	20	12	14	7	3	2	**106**	77	23	–	114
Mike Easler	22	9	14	11	23	9	13	5			**106**	91	9	–	110
Mario Soto	14	11	20	25	18	14	2	1	1		**106**	1	–	99	109
Jody Davis		5	15	16	18	13	16	13	7	3	**106**	52	48	–	106
Frank Tanana	9	6	9	10	15	11	9	15	9	12	**105**	0	–	100	241
Larry Parrish	13	8	10	16	18	5	17	14	4		**105**	83	17	–	176
Glenn Davis					1	13	24	14	23	30	**105**	88	12	–	132
Vance Law	1	1	10	12	10	24	8	16	20	3	**105**	69	31	0	108
Willie Upshaw	1	1	14	22	17	14	15	11	10		**105**	85	15	–	107
George Hendrick	21	18	17	21	12	2	9	2	2		**104**	84	16	–	237
Jeffrey Leonard	3	7	7	19	20	8	10	12	8	10	**104**	84	16	–	127
Don Sutton	20	11	17	9	11	11	13	9	2		**103**	0	–	100	319
Dave Concepcion	17	20	17	8	11	12	8	8	2		**103**	54	46	0	269
Jim Sundberg	18	17	15	7	15	11	10	3	4	3	**103**	47	53	–	200

Player	1980	81	82	83	84	85	86	87	88	89	Dec	B	F	P	Car
Dwight Gooden					18	33	17	14	13	8	**103**	2	–	98	187
Bruce Hurst	0	1	1	13	14	10	16	15	15	18	**103**	0	–	100	144
Phil Garner	16	7	22	16	14	14	9	4	0		**102**	68	32	–	195
Ron Guidry	15	10	12	19	7	18	10	9	2		**102**	–	0	100	174
Rick Reuschel	15	9		1	3	20	8	17	15	13	**101**	0	–	100	240
Jason Thompson	19	11	27	17	14	11	1				**100**	89	11	–	165
Rick Dempsey	15	9	11	13	10	14	9	2	11	6	**100**	49	51	0	158
Alfredo Griffin	9	3	10	11	6	16	17	11	6	11	**100**	38	62	–	134
Mike Boddicker	0	0	2	16	23	10	9	14	15	11	**100**	–	–	100	132
Larry Herndon	10	11	19	22	12	8	7	9	2		**100**	80	20	–	130
Ray Knight	16	10	20	18	5	2	17	11	1		**100**	74	26	–	123
Greg Minton	13	10	21	10	6	6	4	11	7	12	**100**	2	–	98	111
Jerry Reuss	21	13	17	15	4	13	0	2	12	2	**99**	1	–	99	194
Roy Smalley	19	6	19	20	5	12	10	8			**99**	70	30	–	181
Ron Hassey	20	4	12	12	5	13	14	1	12	6	**99**	62	38	–	115
Rafael Ramirez	4	5	21	18	8	6	6	3	18	9	**98**	55	45	–	113
Steve Bedrosian		1	15	12	12	10	13	16	8	10	**97**	0	–	100	119
Mike Scott	1	4	0	6	0	12	27	18	14	15	**97**	0	–	100	105
Charlie Leibrandt	7	2	1		9	24	14	20	17	2	**96**	0	–	100	138
Joe Morgan	21	14	29	19	12						**95**	82	18	–	512
Jose Canseco						4	21	17	39	14	**95**	93	7	0	272
Mark Gubicza					10	12	14	16	24	19	**95**	–	–	100	141
Scott Fletcher		1	0	9	13	7	20	17	17	10	**94**	57	43	–	148
Gary Redus			1	18	13	12	13	13	11	13	**94**	85	15	–	120
Dan Petry	9	10	18	14	16	17	2	2	5	1	**94**	0	–	100	108
Mike Flanagan	12	6	14	10	14	3	8	9	10	7	**93**	–	–	100	158
Gorman Thomas	19	20	25	12	0	13	4				**93**	83	17	–	152
Dave Stewart		6	6	14	6	2	8	17	18	16	**93**	0	–	100	141
Dave Smith	13	7	4	5	8	13	11	15	7	10	**93**	0	–	100	106
Bo Diaz	3	10	21	15	1	6	15	15	5	2	**93**	53	47	–	94
Bob Brenly		3	8	8	20	12	20	18	3	1	**93**	71	29	–	93
Mark Langston					19	2	11	21	19	20	**92**	0	–	100	184
Kent Tekulve	10	6	15	17	8	8	12	11	5	0	**92**	0	0	100	159
Lee Lacy	15	6	13	9	18	14	11	6			**92**	80	20	–	138
Jesse Orosco		2	9	20	17	10	13	5	6	10	**92**	1	0	99	138
Dave Collins	22	14	5	10	17	8	9	3	3	1	**92**	82	18	–	133
Rich Dotson	10	6	10	21	18	2	4	12	5	4	**92**	–	–	100	94
Damaso Garcia	12	3	21	13	16	13	9		0	5	**92**	57	43	–	94
Graig Nettles	10	12	10	16	16	17	9	1	0		**91**	71	29	–	321
Ted Simmons	22	8	19	20	1	13	3	4	1		**91**	77	23	–	315
John Candelaria	10	2	14	15	12	10	9	5	11	3	**91**	0	–	100	182
Bruce Sutter	16	13	17	9	23	8	2		3		**91**	0	–	100	168
Mike Moore			3	5	7	19	15	10	13	19	**91**	0	–	100	133
Brook Jacoby		0		0	8	16	21	22	10	14	**91**	76	24	–	120
Ken Landreaux	13	10	17	19	10	15	6	1			**91**	77	23	–	114
Darrell Porter	12	8	16	17	14	11	8	4			**90**	73	27	–	222
Willie Hernandez	3	1	8	11	24	19	11	4	8	1	**90**	1	–	99	109
Teddy Higuera						14	25	20	22	9	**90**	–	–	100	100
Hal McRae	16	8	26	20	8	8	2	1			**89**	95	5	–	230
Ruppert Jones	8	10	22	9	9	14	13	4			**89**	77	23	–	139

Player	1980	81	82	83	84	85	86	87	88	89	Dec	B	F	P	Car
Kevin Mitchell					0		14	16	20	38	**88**	89	11	–	178
Shane Rawley	12	5	9	14	6	13	10	12	4	3	**88**	0	–	100	102
Mike Heath	4	8	9	9	12	13	6	10	6	11	**88**	56	44	–	100
Joe Niekro	14	9	25	11	13	8	4	3	0		**87**	1	–	99	189
Bill Gullickson	10	10	11	13	10	9	16	8			**87**	0	–	100	126
Scott McGregor	18	12	9	21	11	7	9	0	0		**87**	–	–	100	121
Rance Mulliniks	1	1	6	14	13	15	10	12	12	3	**87**	77	23	–	108
Glenn Wilson			10	12	4	15	17	10	3	16	**87**	71	28	0	94
Marty Barrett			0	0	16	13	22	16	14	6	**87**	55	45	–	92
Barry Bonds							15	22	26	23	**86**	92	8	–	523
Rod Carew	20	12	17	16	9	12					**86**	86	14	–	384
Phil Niekro	17	8	14	9	15	10	9	4			**86**	0	–	100	374
Bobby Bonilla							10	16	31	29	**86**	86	14	0	267
Dan Driessen	21	8	15	16	13	11	1	1			**86**	87	13	–	179
Tommy John	19	10	12	10	7	1	6	13	7	0	**85**	0	–	100	289
Mike Hargrove	25	16	15	14	7	8					**85**	90	10	–	212
John Franco					9	16	15	15	20	10	**85**	0	–	100	179
Rick Mahler	0	9	8	0	18	17	7	7	10	9	**85**	1	–	99	92
Mike Davis	1	0	4	13	7	23	18	14	2	3	**85**	84	16	–	85
Nick Esasky				11	6	15	8	11	10	24	**85**	83	17	–	85
Al Oliver	21	13	26	14	8	2					**84**	85	15	–	305
Wally Joyner							21	22	22	19	**84**	89	11	–	253
Dennis Martinez	6	12	14	0	3	5	2	11	15	16	**84**	0	–	100	233
Chris Chambliss	21	12	19	16	10	2	4		0		**84**	87	13	–	221
Bob Forsch	12	8	16	7	0	7	16	11	7	0	**84**	5	–	95	154
Rick Honeycutt	12	8	2	16	13	5	11	1	6	10	**84**	0	–	100	130
Alan Ashby	11	11	11	6	6	8	11	13	7	0	**84**	59	41	–	118
Wally Backman	3	1	10	0	17	17	16	4	12	4	**84**	73	27	–	102
Luis Salazar	7	11	12	15	4	7	0	3	15	10	**84**	70	30	0	99
Pete Rose	17	17	17	7	8	14	3				**83**	84	16	–	547
Manny Trillo	19	12	14	10	9	8	4	5	2	0	**83**	52	48	–	146
Vince Coleman						20	14	24	14	11	**83**	81	19	–	138
Bryn Smith		1	3	13	10	16	7	7	11	15	**83**	0	–	100	100
Pat Tabler		1	2	12	13	6	16	15	13	5	**83**	86	14	–	93
Eric Show		2	11	8	12	13	10	9	14	4	**83**	1	–	99	83
Tom Seaver	9	17	0	12	16	18	10				**82**	0	–	100	388
Terry Pendleton					11	10	13	21	9	18	**82**	67	33	–	202
Scott Sanderson	14	10	12	1	11	9	9	9	0	7	**82**	0	–	100	138
Bob Knepper	6	13	2	8	13	9	17	0	10	4	**82**	1	–	99	124
Don Robinson	9	0	10	1	11	5	8	14	14	10	**82**	6	0	94	116
Bud Black		0	3	10	20	10	12	9	3	15	**82**	0	–	100	115
Rich Gedman	0	6	4	7	15	20	18	1	8	3	**82**	53	47	–	90
Davey Lopes	16	5	10	18	10	11	10	1			**81**	77	23	–	240
Bruce Bochte	19	9	15		10	17	11				**81**	86	14	–	159
Mel Hall		0	2	15	13	2	18	10	13	8	**81**	86	14	–	117
Greg Brock			0	15	8	15	9	17	7	10	**81**	87	13	–	93
Mark McGwire							1	30	28	21	**80**	94	6	–	342
Tony Phillips			2	12	15	7	17	9	4	14	**80**	79	21	–	268
Jimmy Key					3	19	15	23	10	10	**80**	0	–	100	188
Steve Kemp	19	17	22	8	10	4	0		0		**80**	87	13	–	139

Player	1980	81	82	83	84	85	86	87	88	89	Dec	B	F	P	Car
Dan Gladden				1	17	10	13	9	18	12	**80**	77	23	0	114
Mike Krukow	7	8	15	8	4	11	16	3	6	2	**80**	2	–	98	109
Denny Walling	11	5	2	6	8	10	18	11	6	3	**80**	81	19	–	99
Danny Tartabull					2	3	15	24	22	13	**79**	92	8	–	188
Andre Thornton		3	20	18	21	8	9	0			**79**	94	6	–	186
Greg Walker			2	10	15	17	10	15	8	2	**79**	90	10	–	79
Cesar Cedeno	26	9	13	7	11	11	1				**78**	82	18	–	296
Joaquin Andujar	4	3	22	7	17	14	9	0	2		**78**	0	–	100	108
Mitch Webster				0	0	9	22	23	17	7	**78**	78	22	–	105
Bobby Ojeda	0	5	2	11	14	9	18	2	9	8	**78**	0	–	100	104
Lenny Dykstra						8	23	17	15	14	**77**	81	19	–	201
Storm Davis			8	13	18	8	10	2	11	7	**77**	0	–	100	98
Greg Luzinski	13	15	22	20	6						**76**	93	7	–	247
Ruben Sierra							11	15	16	34	**76**	87	13	–	200
Dave Kingman	8	10	12	4	21	13	8				**76**	90	10	0	195
John Denny	6	11	6	23	12	10	8				**76**	0	–	100	123
Ed Whitson	12	3	9	4	11	4	0	6	9	18	**76**	0	–	100	107
Ron Darling				3	9	17	17	8	13	9	**76**	1	–	99	106
Carmelo Martinez				2	21	19	6	13	11	4	**76**	82	18	–	88
Al Bumbry	33	13	12	10	7	0					**75**	80	20	–	169
Gene Garber	6	5	19	2	10	7	15	8	3		**75**	0	–	100	160
Eddie Milner	0	0	9	20	10	17	14	5	0		**75**	70	30	–	75

Players with at least 250 career Win Shares

Player	1980	81	82	83	84	85	86	87	88	89	Dec	B	F	P	Car
Ken Singleton	27	15	12	17	0						**71**	90	10	–	302
Fred McGriff							0	11	24	30	**65**	91	9	–	316
Barry Larkin							6	11	28	15	**60**	71	29	–	320
Amos Otis	12	12	15	8	1						**48**	75	25	–	286
Roberto Alomar									22	23	**45**	75	25	–	345
Tony Perez	13	7	4	6	1	8	4				**43**	86	14	–	349
Rafael Palmeiro							1	7	17	17	**42**	90	10	–	334
Greg Maddux							1	1	20	20	**42**	0	–	100	317
Jim Palmer	12	6	20	3	0						**41**	0	–	100	312
Mark Grace									16	25	**41**	87	13	–	285
Carl Yastrzemski	10	7	13	9							**39**	87	13	–	488
Johnny Bench	15	9	7	8							**39**	72	28	–	356
Paul O'Neill						1	0	5	13	18	**37**	84	16	0	259
Gaylord Perry	11	7	10	6							**34**	0	–	100	369
Fergie Jenkins	12	2	14	6							**34**	1	–	99	323
Reggie Smith	17	0	16								**33**	84	16	–	325
Rick Monday	8	9	9	6	1						**33**	83	17	–	258
Rusty Staub	10	6	3	4	1	2					**26**	90	10	–	358
Craig Biggio									1	18	**19**	78	22	–	342
Bobby Murcer	9	4	2	0							**15**	85	15	–	277
Jim Kaat	7	4	3	1							**15**	2	–	98	268
Ken Griffey Jr.										14	**14**	84	16	–	313
Willie Stargell	7	1	2								**10**	92	8	–	370
Bert Campaneris	4	2		4							**10**	64	36	0	280
Gary Sheffield									2	6	**8**	89	11	–	276
Bobby Bonds	4	3									**7**	86	14	–	302

Player	1980	81	82	83	84	85	86	87	88	89	Dec	B	F	P	Car
Edgar Martinez								2	1	4	**7**	95	5	–	264
Luis Tiant	4	2	0								**6**	1	–	99	256
Sal Bando	2	1									**3**	81	19	0	283
Willie McCovey	2										**2**	93	7	–	408
Minnie Minoso	0										**0**	85	15	–	283

Player	1990	91	92	93	94	95	96	97	98	99	Dec	B	F	P	Car
Barry Bonds	37	37	41	47	25	36	39	36	34	19	**351**	92	8	–	523
Craig Biggio	18	20	32	26	26	29	32	38	35	31	**287**	78	22	–	342
Frank Thomas	13	34	33	32	25	28	28	39	25	16	**273**	98	2	–	308
Jeff Bagwell		23	29	22	30	20	41	32	29	37	**263**	92	8	–	318
Ken Griffey Jr.	24	30	25	29	20	9	28	36	29	31	**261**	84	16	–	313
Rafael Palmeiro	22	26	24	31	17	21	30	18	24	31	**244**	90	10	–	334
Roberto Alomar	19	25	34	30	13	16	31	21	19	35	**243**	75	25	–	345
Barry Larkin	25	26	32	18	19	30	31	12	25	24	**242**	71	29	–	320
Mark McGwire	27	18	29	6	6	23	29	25	41	30	**234**	94	6	–	342
Greg Maddux	15	17	27	25	26	30	23	26	25	17	**231**	0	–	100	317
Albert Belle	0	15	16	27	24	30	31	18	37	24	**222**	90	10	–	243
Fred McGriff	26	25	27	23	22	20	19	14	13	24	**213**	91	9	–	316
Rickey Henderson	39	25	25	25	11	19	16	15	20	16	**211**	89	11	–	530
Mark Grace	22	17	25	23	12	23	20	20	27	21	**210**	87	13	–	285
Tony Gwynn	17	22	18	18	17	23	17	39	19	18	**208**	89	11	–	398
Chuck Knoblauch		20	23	16	20	27	32	23	22	25	**208**	77	23	–	229
Gary Sheffield	20	1	32	16	15	13	34	22	30	24	**207**	89	11	–	276
Mike Piazza			1	31	21	27	33	39	33	21	**206**	81	19	–	255
Roger Clemens	28	26	26	11	16	10	20	32	25	10	**204**	0	–	100	352
Edgar Martinez	17	20	24	4	11	32	23	27	24	22	**204**	95	5	–	264
Larry Walker	12	20	26	24	21	18	10	32	17	24	**204**	82	18	–	240
Robin Ventura	15	25	30	21	16	17	20	8	21	30	**203**	74	26	–	236
Matt Williams	28	22	11	28	18	20	18	18	12	26	**201**	75	25	–	232
Jay Bell	17	22	24	26	19	13	15	21	20	23	**200**	68	32	–	243
John Olerud	11	13	16	37	14	11	10	27	34	26	**199**	88	12	–	242
Ken Caminiti	11	17	21	14	16	24	38	26	20	10	**197**	78	22	–	242
Paul O'Neill	16	19	13	15	23	18	22	28	26	16	**196**	84	16	0	259
David Justice	20	22	23	29	19	19	7	26	13	16	**194**	87	13	–	222
Ray Lankford	5	18	31	12	16	22	25	24	27	13	**193**	83	17	–	218
Cal Ripken Jr.	20	34	21	17	18	16	22	18	13	12	**191**	68	32	–	427
Will Clark	25	34	28	15	19	18	11	14	19	8	**191**	92	8	–	331
Tony Phillips	22	23	23	25	16	19	21	18	7	14	**188**	79	21	–	268
Tom Glavine	10	23	19	20	12	20	22	21	23	14	**184**	0	–	100	236
Bernie Williams		10	7	15	14	27	26	24	27	33	**183**	80	20	–	233
Juan Gonzalez	2	19	19	31	11	11	21	19	25	24	**182**	93	7	–	215
Steve Finley	8	18	28	14	9	19	27	19	15	24	**181**	77	22	0	222
Brady Anderson	7	6	29	18	12	19	28	26	13	23	**181**	82	18	–	214
Marquis Grissom	8	19	27	30	17	18	24	14	11	13	**181**	66	34	–	197
Paul Molitor	19	30	28	29	19	12	18	13	10		**178**	89	11	–	414
Bobby Bonilla	23	31	18	16	19	22	19	21	5	0	**174**	86	14	0	267
Sammy Sosa	13	4	7	15	15	25	18	14	35	26	**172**	86	14	–	246
Kenny Lofton		0	24	25	21	21	23	21	21	16	**172**	78	22	–	202
Ivan Rodriguez		6	13	15	15	16	23	26	27	28	**169**	55	45	–	206
Mo Vaughn		6	7	19	17	24	29	22	25	19	**168**	94	6	–	185
Randy Johnson	13	11	11	22	15	22	5	23	19	26	**167**	0	0	100	226
Kevin Brown	12	7	18	15	7	13	26	23	26	19	**166**	0	–	100	211
John Smoltz	14	13	18	16	6	17	27	21	16	18	**166**	2	–	98	189
Ron Gant	21	25	17	25		21	18	11	11	16	**165**	82	18	–	194
Travis Fryman	8	17	19	28	15	19	17	17	18	7	**165**	74	26	–	192
David Cone	13	15	18	21	20	19	8	16	17	15	**162**	0	–	100	205

Player	1990	91	92	93	94	95	96	97	98	99	Dec	B	F	P	Car
Jose Canseco	26	31	16	8	16	15	13	8	15	13	**161**	93	7	0	272
Todd Zeile	12	22	11	19	15	8	16	18	21	19	**161**	78	22	–	199
Wally Joyner	9	25	14	17	11	18	16	21	22	7	**160**	89	11	–	253
Greg Vaughn	10	20	16	22	9	5	17	7	30	24	**160**	87	13	–	197
Wade Boggs	24	25	15	20	18	18	15	10	6	6	**157**	81	19	0	394
Tony Fernandez	25	21	18	20	14	9		11	19	20	**157**	64	36	–	280
Ryne Sandberg	34	37	33	14	7		19	11			**155**	73	27	–	346
Delino DeShields	19	15	19	21	10	16	11	21	15	7	**154**	75	25	–	183
Tim Salmon			0	24	13	29	22	29	22	14	**153**	86	14	–	187
Chuck Finley	23	14	11	19	14	12	16	11	17	14	**151**	0	–	100	204
Devon White	7	24	19	20	11	12	18	9	18	12	**150**	72	28	–	207
Kevin Appier	13	14	20	27	13	16	19	18	0	9	**149**	0	–	100	175
Cecil Fielder	29	26	19	17	12	13	17	7	8		**148**	94	6	–	160
Lance Johnson	18	13	15	21	12	18	26	14	6	5	**148**	72	28	–	155
Carlos Baerga	8	18	28	28	13	23	6	11	10	2	**147**	69	31	–	147
B.J. Surhoff	15	13	16	16	4	16	17	19	13	17	**146**	71	29	–	206
Brett Butler	27	26	24	23	19	16	2	7			**144**	81	19	–	295
Ellis Burks	21	10	5	14	5	8	28	15	14	24	**144**	83	17	–	234
Dante Bichette	7	7	8	19	13	23	20	15	17	15	**144**	80	20	–	168
Chili Davis	10	22	14	16	15	18	18	15	2	13	**143**	92	8	0	285
Mike Mussina		6	24	11	18	20	13	19	15	17	**143**	0	–	100	181
Jay Buhner	6	13	16	22	13	16	22	19	8	8	**143**	86	14	–	174
Andres Galarraga	15	2	3	23	13	14	25	20	27		**142**	89	11	–	237
Tim Raines	19	19	28	19	14	14	7	9	11	1	**141**	86	14	–	390
Luis Gonzalez	0	15	11	20	13	15	17	12	12	26	**141**	83	17	–	205
Jim Thome		1	1	6	10	24	28	26	19	26	**141**	89	11	–	192
Moises Alou	0		15	21	22	11	20	23	29		**141**	85	15	–	179
Manny Ramirez				0	11	25	23	21	25	35	**140**	89	11	–	192
Gregg Jefferies	20	15	14	28	17	10	10	10	14	0	**138**	83	17	–	162
Jeff Blauser	10	13	18	29	10	10	9	27	6	5	**137**	73	27	–	154
Tino Martinez	0	1	7	12	7	20	21	27	21	19	**135**	82	18	–	168
Omar Vizquel	3	14	12	12	7	17	16	14	18	22	**135**	53	47	–	166
Eric Karros		0	13	10	7	25	20	18	22	20	**135**	85	15	–	157
John Valentin			7	16	14	29	17	21	19	12	**135**	65	35	–	136
Joe Carter	16	23	24	17	14	8	13	10	9		**134**	83	17	–	240
Jeff Kent			10	13	18	11	11	22	25	23	**133**	79	21	–	197
Mickey Tettleton	16	27	24	24	14	17	11	0			**133**	81	19	–	184
Darren Daulton	23	9	31	29	13	12	0	16			**133**	75	25	–	159
Kirby Puckett	22	21	31	18	20	20					**132**	79	21	–	281
Brian McRae	5	11	11	18	11	18	21	12	20	5	**132**	68	32	–	132
Terry Steinbach	11	13	20	9	15	16	18	7	10	12	**131**	64	36	–	173
Chipper Jones				0		20	26	23	29	32	**130**	90	10	–	186
Raul Mondesi				3	15	22	25	24	20	21	**130**	83	17	–	156
Bernard Gilkey	3	3	17	21	9	16	30	16	6	8	**129**	84	16	–	131
Harold Baines	11	22	15	15	6	11	13	12	8	15	**128**	92	8	–	307
Pedro Martinez			1	12	11	14	14	26	21	27	**126**	0	0	100	167
Mike Stanley	5	6	6	24	14	16	12	14	15	14	**126**	87	13	–	145
Lenny Dykstra	35	13	17	32	14	8	5				**124**	81	19	–	201
Reggie Sanders		0	14	17	13	27	7	13	14	19	**124**	83	17	–	144
Darryl Hamilton	5	15	18	16	2	10	11	15	19	13	**124**	76	24	–	130

Player	1990	91	92	93	94	95	96	97	98	99	Dec	B	F	P	Car
Curt Schilling	5	5	17	13	2	8	14	22	22	15	**123**	0	–	100	163
Jose Offerman	1	2	10	14	6	14	18	9	29	19	**122**	72	28	–	145
Terry Pendleton	5	27	35	16	6	17	9	3	2		**120**	67	33	–	202
Andy Benes	10	16	16	12	8	7	14	14	14	8	**119**	0	–	100	132
Roberto Kelly	19	16	13	10	15	9	9	12	8	7	**118**	80	20	–	137
Scott Erickson	9	18	14	7	6	11	10	16	15	12	**118**	0	–	100	118
Ruben Sierra	21	28	21	13	13	13	6	1	1		**117**	87	13	–	200
David Wells	15	14	1	10	7	17	10	12	18	13	**117**	0	–	100	153
Gary Gaetti	13	14	9	9	10	17	16	9	16	3	**116**	65	35	0	249
Bip Roberts	22	14	28	5	13	11	8	8	7		**116**	79	21	–	138
John Wetteland	1	1	12	21	12	13	13	16	15	12	**116**	0	–	100	127
Eddie Murray	31	16	20	15	9	16	6	0			**113**	91	9	–	437
Jack McDowell	12	18	20	21	12	15	10	2	3	0	**113**	–	–	100	122
Chris Hoiles	0	7	12	26	14	14	14	14	12		**113**	69	31	–	113
Julio Franco	27	28	2	18	15		13	9		0	**112**	81	19	–	244
Mickey Morandini	1	9	9	10	10	17	10	16	23	7	**112**	66	34	–	119
Orlando Merced	0	17	14	20	10	18	16	8	4	5	**112**	88	12	–	116
Jeff King	7	4	7	20	8	14	22	17	12	1	**112**	75	25	–	115
Alex Rodriguez					0	2	34	22	30	23	**111**	79	21	–	185
Rusty Greer					12	12	21	23	19	24	**111**	90	10	–	130
Lou Whitaker	19	26	24	19	10	11					**109**	75	25	–	351
Danny Tartabull	10	28	23	21	10	4	13	0			**109**	92	8	–	188
Rick Aguilera	12	15	11	14	6	11	6	9	12	13	**109**	0	–	100	147
Jeff Montgomery	12	15	16	22	7	11	9	8	8	1	**109**	0	–	100	134
Otis Nixon	8	15	16	13	10	13	12	13	8	1	**109**	62	38	–	127
Kevin Tapani	10	21	12	12	11	7	11	8	11	6	**109**	0	–	100	124
Jimmy Key	8	17	14	21	15	1	10	17	5		**108**	0	–	100	188
Dean Palmer		7	16	16	7	7	15	11	12	17	**108**	85	15	–	129
Charles Nagy	0	10	20	0	13	11	21	13	9	11	**108**	0	–	100	109
Jody Reed	22	20	12	14	12	14	11	2			**107**	55	45	–	136
Mike Bordick	0	6	22	14	8	10	10	7	13	17	**107**	50	50	–	129
Kenny Rogers	12	2	7	11	9	21	11	2	19	12	**106**	0	–	100	130
Alex Fernandez	5	7	6	20	11	12	19	16		10	**106**	0	–	100	110
Dave Hollins	2	8	27	20	3	6	15	15	9	0	**105**	85	15	–	105
Andy Van Slyke	23	22	35	12	8	4					**104**	81	19	–	231
Jeff Cirillo					2	10	20	24	26	22	**104**	72	28	–	137
Ken Hill	2	10	17	11	12	8	22	10	5	7	**104**	0	–	100	112
Dennis Martinez	15	18	17	12	14	16	7	0	4		**103**	0	–	100	233
Kevin Seitzer	21	7	16	10	11	17	18	3			**103**	80	20	0	174
Benito Santiago	12	16	7	8	12	12	19	9	1	7	**103**	52	48	–	159
Dave Magadan	25	14	13	12	3	15	3	9	5	4	**103**	85	15	–	147
Flash Gordon	9	9	4	14	12	11	10	15	17	2	**103**	–	–	100	124
Todd Stottlemyre	9	15	7	7	10	10	14	11	14	6	**103**	1	–	99	115
John Kruk	17	25	24	25	7	4					**102**	90	10	–	156
Brian Jordan			2	10	1	18	27	1	21	22	**102**	79	21	–	135
Charlie Hayes	9	8	11	20	10	13	10	6	11	4	**102**	65	35	–	116
Pat Hentgen		1	2	16	15	7	24	19	8	10	**102**	0	–	100	116
Hal Morris	11	15	13	11	15	7	18	4	5	3	**102**	86	14	–	104
Greg Gagne	7	12	13	18	11	10	20	10			**101**	42	58	–	157
Derek Jeter						1	18	19	27	35	**100**	78	22	–	151

Player	1990	91	92	93	94	95	96	97	98	99	Dec	B	F	P	Car
Ramon Martinez	17	14	3	13	10	13	12	8	8	2	**100**	0	–	100	110
Shane Mack	14	20	27	16	15			2	6		**100**	81	19	–	107
Dave Martinez	11	13	9	6	3	10	16	15	3	13	**99**	76	23	0	147
Tim Belcher	6	15	10	10	3	9	19	9	17	1	**99**	0	–	100	132
Vinny Castilla		0	1	3	5	13	23	21	21	11	**98**	66	34	–	114
Eric Young			4	10	6	12	17	17	17	14	**97**	71	29	–	131
Jeff Fassero		7	7	15	10	8	18	17	14	1	**97**	0	–	100	115
Tom Candiotti	12	21	12	14	7	9	4	8	8	1	**96**	0	–	100	158
Stan Javier	13	1	10	6	11	13	5	17	12	8	**96**	79	21	–	137
Roberto Hernandez		0	13	16	5	6	17	15	10	14	**96**	0	–	100	117
Mike Lansing				17	10	15	19	21	11	3	**96**	56	44	–	109
Eric Davis	17	8	6	12	1		22	6	18	5	**95**	85	15	–	224
Jim Edmonds				1	7	21	18	19	24	5	**95**	79	21	–	154
Doug Jones	15	1	18	6	10	4	5	19	6	11	**95**	0	–	100	146
Jeff Conine	0		3	15	15	20	17	9	6	10	**95**	86	14	–	128
Randy Velarde	2	3	13	7	8	13	17	0	8	24	**95**	70	30	–	123
Ozzie Smith	11	25	20	19	9	2	8				**94**	57	43	–	325
Ryan Klesko			0	2	8	17	20	16	13	18	**94**	91	9	–	146
Doug Drabek	20	14	20	10	13	6	6	5	0		**94**	1	–	99	140
Jose Rijo	17	17	19	26	11	4					**94**	0	–	100	130
Walt Weiss	15	2	5	13	7	12	8	13	12	7	**94**	51	49	–	123
Derek Bell		0	4	12	11	16	14	11	22	4	**94**	82	18	0	111
Mike Macfarlane	8	11	10	18	11	8	13	7	5	3	**94**	59	41	–	106
Willie McGee	21	18	15	13	3	3	9	7	3	1	**93**	79	21	–	224
Edgardo Alfonzo						8	6	28	22	29	**93**	76	24	–	144
J.T. Snow			0	9	3	15	7	28	13	18	**93**	85	15	–	115
Royce Clayton		0	5	15	9	12	12	13	12	15	**93**	45	55	–	111
Mark Langston	8	20	15	20	8	11	7	1	0	2	**92**	0	–	100	184
Bret Boone			1	8	15	15	10	8	18	17	**92**	64	36	–	139
Trevor Hoffman				7	11	9	20	11	20	14	**92**	1	–	99	114
Juan Guzman		12	17	15	5	1	17	1	11	13	**92**	0	–	100	92
Jason Giambi						5	15	18	23	30	**91**	93	7	–	167
Robby Thompson	15	22	16	26	1	8	3				**91**	70	30	–	155
David Segui	2	3	2	10	5	13	15	16	15	10	**91**	86	14	–	123
Dennis Eckersley	19	14	18	9	5	6	8	8	3		**90**	0	–	100	301
Orel Hershiser	1	8	8	13	7	13	14	11	7	8	**90**	1	0	99	210
Kevin Mitchell	20	16	11	15	18		8	0	2		**90**	89	11	–	178
Jamie Moyer	3	0		13	8	5	11	14	18	18	**90**	0	–	100	133
Randy Myers	17	8	7	15	5	8	9	15	6		**90**	1	–	99	123
Bob Tewksbury	10	10	21	12	5	8	7	9	8		**90**	0	–	100	101
Pete Harnisch	7	16	7	16	2	4	7	1	16	14	**90**	0	–	100	100
Mark McLemore	0	1	6	14	9	11	16	5	12	15	**89**	60	40	–	135
Mike Jackson	4	11	5	9	8	7	7	11	16	11	**89**	1	–	99	119
Javy Lopez			1	1	5	12	15	19	25	11	**89**	66	34	–	118
John Burkett	11	6	7	14	8	8	12	10	7	6	**89**	0	–	100	113
Todd Hundley	1	1	6	7	8	13	24	22	1	6	**89**	71	29	–	110
Glenallen Hill	5	5	6	8	8	15	13	11	11	7	**89**	90	10	–	99
Chad Curtis			13	14	8	15	8	12	14	5	**89**	76	24	–	98
Scott Brosius		1	2	5	6	10	19	5	27	13	**88**	67	33	–	111
Terry Mulholland	11	14	9	13	1	0	9	8	12	11	**88**	1	–	99	101

Player	1990	91	92	93	94	95	96	97	98	99	Dec	B	F	P	Car
Jose Vizcaino	1	2	4	15	7	16	14	17	8	4	**88**	56	44	–	95
Mike Morgan	9	17	19	11	0	8	4	6	9	4	**87**	1	–	99	136
Nomar Garciaparra							2	26	27	32	**87**	77	23	–	119
Al Martin			0	16	11	11	17	13	5	14	**87**	87	13	–	105
Sandy Alomar Jr.	15	2	9	6	12	7	8	18	6	4	**87**	55	45	–	100
Rod Beck		3	16	16	7	7	10	12	13	3	**87**	0	–	100	99
Wilson Alvarez		3	1	18	12	8	13	15	7	10	**87**	0	–	100	87
Tim Wallach	26	11	12	6	18	9	4				**86**	67	33	0	248
Al Leiter	1	0	0	8	5	14	19	7	21	11	**86**	0	–	100	120
Denny Neagle		1	2	2	6	16	17	21	14	7	**86**	0	–	100	107
Bret Saberhagen	7	16	5	9	16	8		0	12	12	**85**	0	–	100	193
Shawon Dunston	15	14	1	1	8	16	8	11	3	8	**85**	64	36	–	151
Greg Swindell	9	13	16	8	5	6	1	10	9	8	**85**	1	–	99	136
Don Mattingly	7	14	20	20	15	8					**84**	89	11	–	263
Mariano Duncan	15	10	12	13	10	7	12	5			**84**	67	33	–	115
Mark Whiten	2	7	11	17	12	10	14	5	6	0	**84**	79	21	0	84
Darryl Strawberry	26	24	6	0	3	4	6	0	11	3	**83**	90	10	–	252
Ray Durham						8	17	13	25	20	**83**	74	26	–	123
John Jaha			2	15	4	13	19	3	5	22	**83**	93	7	–	83
Ben McDonald	10	4	11	17	12	5	16	8			**83**	0	–	100	83
John Franco	11	8	8	1	8	10	10	12	8	6	**82**	0	–	100	179
Bill Swift	12	14	16	19	7	7	2	1	4		**82**	0	–	100	101
Henry Rodriguez			1	3	9	1	19	16	16	17	**82**	86	14	–	93
Joey Cora	1	3	4	16	8	10	11	18	11		**82**	71	29	–	86
Paul Sorrento	1	1	11	12	9	11	15	11	4	7	**82**	87	13	–	82
Mike Greenwell	16	17	1	19	8	13	7				**81**	84	16	–	146
Luis Polonia	12	18	13	11	12	4	1			10	**81**	84	16	–	124
Jim Eisenreich	12	9	4	13	10	13	14	6	0		**81**	81	19	–	108
Darren Lewis	0	7	7	15	11	6	7	4	17	7	**81**	57	43	–	89
Jeff Brantley	15	11	8	3	10	13	14	1	5	1	**81**	0	–	100	88
Steve Avery	0	16	13	19	9	8	7	1	5	3	**81**	1	–	99	81
Ozzie Guillen	18	9	1	12	8	5	7	10	7	3	**80**	40	60	–	148
Mark Portugal	9	5	6	19	9	9	8	0	10	5	**80**	1	–	99	100
Gregg Olson	14	10	13	10	0	4	4	4	12	9	**80**	1	–	99	99
Eddie Taubensee		1	8	7	6	9	11	7	16	15	**80**	71	29	–	85
Dave Nilsson			5	6	9	6	17	12	10	15	**80**	85	15	–	80
Bobby Higginson						8	21	25	16	9	**79**	88	12	–	123
Rondell White				3	4	14	10	17	16	15	**79**	74	26	–	105
Luis Alicea		0	8	15	8	13	11	14	9	1	**79**	69	31	–	99
Dwight Gooden	13	13	11	14	0		9	5	10	3	**78**	2	–	98	187
Carlos Delgado				0	3	0	12	18	24	21	**78**	92	8	–	137
Jose Valentin			0	2	12	8	20	13	15	8	**78**	63	37	–	117
Chris Sabo	20	22	8	16	7	1	4				**78**	76	24	–	104
Bill Spiers	5	16	0	3	3	1	7	18	13	12	**78**	71	29	–	98
Pedro Astacio			7	12	6	5	13	10	6	19	**78**	0	–	100	96
Jim Abbott	8	20	18	10	8	12	0		2	0	**78**	0	–	100	86
Shawn Green				0	0	10	8	14	21	24	**77**	86	14	–	133
Jeff Shaw	0	4	0	4	5	3	12	21	16	12	**77**	0	–	100	97
Jim Leyritz	4	0	5	14	10	8	7	15	9	5	**77**	79	21	–	78
Scott Rolen							2	29	30	15	**76**	78	22	–	123

Player	1990	91	92	93	94	95	96	97	98	99	Dec	B	F	P	Car
Robb Nen				0	11	8	19	11	19	8	**76**	0	–	100	105
John Smiley	3	14	18	2	8	13	14	4			**76**	0	–	100	103
Bobby Witt	17	0	8	11	4	9	10	11	1	5	**76**	1	–	99	102
Quilvio Veras						15	7	15	23	16	**76**	66	34	–	95
Mel Rojas	3	4	16	9	11	8	18	6	1	0	**76**	1	–	99	76
Darryl Kile		5	3	11	5	1	10	21	13	6	**75**	0	–	100	110
Jeromy Burnitz				8	2	1	6	20	19	19	**75**	84	16	–	109
Damion Easley			4	7	3	4	3	18	23	13	**75**	61	39	–	104
Mike Devereaux	8	15	22	13	3	10	3	1	0		**75**	70	30	–	87
Wil Cordero			4	13	17	12	5	11	8	5	**75**	76	24	–	86
Mark Lemke	4	4	7	15	12	11	12	9	1		**75**	38	62	–	76
Rick Wilkins		5	10	28	9	5	14	4	0	0	**75**	54	46	–	76
Players with at least 250 career Win Shares															
Dave Winfield	13	17	27	10	5	0					**72**	90	10	–	415
Andre Dawson	22	20	16	7	1	4	2				**72**	82	18	–	340
Alan Trammell	29	12	4	17	3	6	1				**72**	71	29	–	318
Robin Yount	18	16	20	10							**64**	75	25	–	423
George Brett	26	8	11	6							**51**	86	14	–	432
Willie Randolph	11	22	7								**40**	69	31	–	312
Brian Downing	13	14	13								**40**	85	15	–	298
Carlton Fisk	22	13	4	0							**39**	69	31	–	368
Nolan Ryan	15	13	8	2							**38**	0	–	100	334
Jack Clark	17	15	4								**36**	92	8	–	316
Dale Murphy	15	13	0	0							**28**	83	17	–	294
Gary Carter	8	7	7								**22**	63	37	–	337
Dave Parker	15	6									**21**	87	13	–	327
Dwight Evans	9	10									**19**	85	15	–	347
Chet Lemon	9										**9**	76	24	–	265
Bert Blyleven	3		5								**8**	0	–	100	339
Ken Griffey Sr.	4	3									**7**	87	13	–	259
Fred Lynn	4										**4**	81	19	–	280
Keith Hernandez	1										**1**	89	11	–	311

Player	00	01	Dec	B	F	P	Car
Barry Bonds	32	54	**86**	92	8	–	523
Jason Giambi	38	38	**76**	93	7	–	167
Alex Rodriguez	37	37	**74**	79	21	–	185
Sammy Sosa	30	42	**72**	86	14	–	246
Luis Gonzalez	27	37	**64**	83	17	–	205
Jeff Kent	37	27	**64**	79	21	–	197
Gary Sheffield	31	30	**61**	89	11	–	276
Jim Edmonds	29	30	**59**	79	21	–	154
Carlos Delgado	36	23	**59**	92	8	–	137
Roberto Alomar	20	37	**57**	75	25	–	345
Chipper Jones	27	29	**56**	90	10	–	186
Shawn Green	22	34	**56**	86	14	–	133
Brian Giles	27	29	**56**	89	11	–	117
Jeff Bagwell	25	30	**55**	92	8	–	318
Todd Helton	29	26	**55**	86	14	–	93
Edgar Martinez	28	25	**53**	95	5	–	264
Rich Aurilia	20	33	**53**	69	31	–	96
Phil Nevin	22	31	**53**	84	16	–	87
Randy Johnson	26	26	**52**	0	0	100	226
Manny Ramirez	27	25	**52**	89	11	–	192
Ryan Klesko	23	29	**52**	91	9	–	146
Andruw Jones	30	22	**52**	63	37	–	122
Vladimir Guerrero	29	23	**52**	89	11	–	119
Jorge Posada	29	23	**52**	72	28	–	83
Jim Thome	20	31	**51**	89	11	–	192
Derek Jeter	23	28	**51**	78	22	–	151
Edgardo Alfonzo	36	15	**51**	76	24	–	144
Bernie Williams	26	24	**50**	80	20	–	233
Mike Piazza	28	21	**49**	81	19	–	255
Bobby Abreu	23	26	**49**	87	13	–	107
Rafael Palmeiro	23	25	**48**	90	10	–	334
Mike Cameron	19	29	**48**	70	30	–	90
Miguel Tejada	23	25	**48**	65	35	–	76
Bret Boone	15	32	**47**	64	36	–	139
Scott Rolen	18	29	**47**	78	22	–	123
Magglio Ordonez	22	25	**47**	85	15	–	83
Troy Glaus	25	21	**46**	78	22	–	65
Cliff Floyd	19	26	**45**	91	9	–	94
Greg Maddux	24	20	**44**	0	–	100	317
Bobby Higginson	26	18	**44**	88	12	–	123
Darin Erstad	30	14	**44**	76	24	–	96
Mike Sweeney	26	18	**44**	85	15	–	77
John Olerud	22	21	**43**	88	12	–	242
Johnny Damon	26	17	**43**	77	23	–	104
Jose Vidro	25	18	**43**	80	20	–	59
Eric Chavez	16	26	**42**	78	22	–	53
Lance Berkman	10	32	**42**	89	11	–	43
Pedro Martinez	29	12	**41**	0	0	100	167
Corey Koskie	17	24	**41**	74	26	–	54
Curt Schilling	16	24	**40**	0	–	100	163

Player	00	01	Dec	B	F	P	Car
Ray Durham	19	21	**40**	74	26	–	123
Fernando Vina	18	22	**40**	65	35	–	106
Matt Lawton	20	20	**40**	82	18	–	94
J.D. Drew	18	22	**40**	88	12	–	53
Mike Lowell	20	20	**40**	77	23	–	48
Jose Valentin	24	15	**39**	63	37	–	117
Jermaine Dye	21	18	**39**	78	22	–	64
Fred McGriff	16	22	**38**	91	9	–	316
Ken Griffey Jr.	24	14	**38**	84	16	–	313
Mike Mussina	18	20	**38**	0	–	100	181
Moises Alou	17	21	**38**	85	15	–	179
Richard Hidalgo	21	17	**38**	76	24	–	55
Tom Glavine	21	16	**37**	0	–	100	236
Ivan Rodriguez	19	18	**37**	55	45	–	206
Charles Johnson	20	17	**37**	52	48	–	108
Craig Biggio	11	25	**36**	78	22	–	342
Larry Walker	11	25	**36**	82	18	–	240
Steve Finley	21	15	**36**	77	22	0	222
Todd Zeile	18	18	**36**	78	22	–	199
Ichiro Suzuki		36	**36**	86	14	–	36
Roger Clemens	16	19	**35**	0	–	100	352
Frank Thomas	34	1	**35**	98	2	–	308
Ellis Burks	21	14	**35**	83	17	–	234
Darryl Kile	17	18	**35**	0	–	100	110
Mariano Rivera	16	19	**35**	–	–	100	101
Carl Everett	24	11	**35**	79	21	–	99
Shannon Stewart	17	18	**35**	84	16	–	77
Sean Casey	17	18	**35**	91	9	–	68
Richie Sexson	16	19	**35**	87	13	–	50
Orlando Cabrera	9	26	**35**	49	51	–	49
Javier Vazquez	14	21	**35**	1	–	99	43
Terrence Long	18	17	**35**	81	19	–	35
Mark Grace	18	16	**34**	87	13	–	285
Tim Salmon	23	11	**34**	86	14	–	187
Eric Young	18	16	**34**	71	29	–	131
Jeromy Burnitz	16	18	**34**	84	16	–	109
Ben Grieve	17	17	**34**	90	10	–	76
Chan Ho Park	18	16	**34**	0	–	100	73
Adrian Beltre	22	12	**34**	75	25	–	53
Trot Nixon	14	20	**34**	75	25	–	44
Tino Martinez	12	21	**33**	82	18	–	168
Jeff Cirillo	19	14	**33**	72	28	–	137
Brian Jordan	14	19	**33**	79	21	–	135
Jeff Conine	9	24	**33**	86	14	–	128
Jason Kendall	24	9	**33**	72	28	–	106
Keith Foulke	16	17	**33**	0	–	100	58
Robin Ventura	15	17	**32**	74	26	–	236
Juan Gonzalez	9	23	**32**	93	7	–	215
David Segui	18	14	**32**	86	14	–	123
Nomar Garciaparra	29	3	**32**	77	23	–	119

Player	00	01	Dec	B	F	P	Car
Brad Radke	15	17	**32**	0	–	100	100
Garret Anderson	15	17	**32**	72	28	–	99
Mark Grudzielanek	15	17	**32**	63	37	–	92
John Vander Wal	19	13	**32**	88	12	–	66
Luis Castillo	18	14	**32**	68	32	–	55
Carlos Beltran	5	27	**32**	75	25	–	52
Paul Konerko	15	17	**32**	87	13	–	48
Derrek Lee	16	16	**32**	85	15	–	45
Tim Hudson	15	17	**32**	0	–	100	44
Jay Bell	19	12	**31**	68	32	–	243
Kevin Brown	20	11	**31**	0	–	100	211
Greg Vaughn	16	15	**31**	87	13	–	197
Mark McLemore	13	18	**31**	60	40	–	135
Al Leiter	17	14	**31**	0	–	100	120
Armando Benitez	17	14	**31**	0	–	100	76
Ricky Gutierrez	15	16	**31**	58	42	–	71
Jose Cruz	15	16	**31**	75	25	–	65
Geoff Jenkins	20	11	**31**	83	17	–	50
Kenny Lofton	17	13	**30**	78	22	–	202
Mike Hampton	19	11	**30**	5	–	95	104
Tony Batista	18	12	**30**	66	34	–	72
Derek Lowe	19	11	**30**	0	–	100	57
Ronnie Belliard	17	13	**30**	71	29	–	45
Preston Wilson	20	10	**30**	77	23	–	44
Kevin Millar	10	20	**30**	91	9	–	42
Cristian Guzman	12	18	**30**	52	48	–	35
Paul Lo Duca	2	28	**30**	75	25	–	32
Aramis Ramirez	3	27	**30**	80	20	–	32
Delino DeShields	21	8	**29**	75	25	–	183
Javy Lopez	16	13	**29**	66	34	–	118
Robb Nen	15	14	**29**	0	–	100	105
Damion Easley	14	15	**29**	61	39	–	104
Joe Randa	18	11	**29**	73	27	–	81
Bartolo Colon	15	14	**29**	0	–	100	63
Danny Graves	18	11	**29**	2	–	98	55
Carlos Lee	14	15	**29**	82	18	–	39
Pat Burrell	12	17	**29**	85	15	–	29
Albert Pujols		29	**29**	87	13	–	29
Mark McGwire	20	8	**28**	94	6	–	342
David Justice	20	8	**28**	87	13	–	222
Omar Vizquel	16	12	**28**	53	47	–	166
Edgar Renteria	15	13	**28**	59	41	–	82
Jon Lieber	12	16	**28**	0	–	100	73
Mark Kotsay	12	16	**28**	79	21	–	48
Joe Mays	6	22	**28**	0	–	100	38
Andres Galarraga	16	11	**27**	89	11	–	237
Travis Fryman	22	5	**27**	74	26	–	192
Andy Pettitte	14	13	**27**	0	–	100	99
Alex S. Gonzalez	11	16	**27**	35	65	–	74
Dmitri Young	14	13	**27**	84	16	–	58

Player	00	01	Dec	B	F	P	Car
Torii Hunter	8	19	**27**	53	47	–	32
Paul O'Neill	13	13	**26**	84	16	0	259
B.J. Surhoff	14	12	**26**	71	29	–	206
Kevin Appier	11	15	**26**	0	–	100	175
Raul Mondesi	11	15	**26**	83	17	–	156
Rondell White	14	12	**26**	74	26	–	105
Brad Ausmus	16	10	**26**	43	57	–	99
Aaron Sele	12	14	**26**	0	–	100	91
Bob Wickman	12	14	**26**	0	–	100	91
Tony Womack	16	10	**26**	63	37	–	78
Neifi Perez	15	11	**26**	32	68	–	61
Eric Milton	11	15	**26**	1	–	99	44
Freddy Garcia	8	18	**26**	1	–	99	42
Damian Jackson	15	11	**26**	63	37	–	41
Rafael Furcal	17	9	**26**	64	36	–	26
Ray Lankford	10	15	**25**	83	17	–	218
Marvin Benard	14	11	**25**	85	15	–	67
Robert Person	13	12	**25**	1	–	99	40
Bubba Trammell	8	17	**25**	88	12	–	40
Frank Catalanotto	8	17	**25**	89	11	–	35
Desi Relaford	12	13	**25**	60	40	1	35
Jeff Weaver	12	13	**25**	1	–	99	32
Placido Polanco	11	14	**25**	53	47	–	30
John Burkett	7	17	**24**	0	–	100	113
Rick Reed	11	13	**24**	1	0	99	73
Lee Stevens	11	13	**24**	86	14	–	66
Brad Fullmer	15	9	**24**	98	2	–	46
Jeff Suppan	12	12	**24**	1	–	99	43
J. Isringhausen	10	14	**24**	4	–	96	42
Billy Koch	16	8	**24**	0	–	100	34
Ryan Dempster	17	7	**24**	0	–	100	30
Randy Wolf	13	11	**24**	0	–	100	28
Byung-Hyun Kim	8	16	**24**	0	–	100	26
Frank Menechino	6	18	**24**	60	40	0	24
Barry Zito	9	15	**24**	0	–	100	24
Brady Anderson	15	8	**23**	82	18	–	214
David Wells	18	5	**23**	0	–	100	153
Jose Offerman	9	14	**23**	72	28	–	145
Scott Brosius	8	15	**23**	67	33	–	111
Woody Williams	12	11	**23**	2	–	98	70
Deivi Cruz	15	8	**23**	44	56	–	50
Matt Morris	6	17	**23**	0	–	100	49
Steve W. Sparks	7	16	**23**	0	–	100	49
Aaron Boone	10	13	**23**	71	29	–	44
Chris Singleton	11	12	**23**	64	36	–	41
Brian Daubach	10	13	**23**	87	13	–	37
Gabe Kapler	10	13	**23**	83	17	–	31
Ramon Hernandez	10	13	**23**	61	39	–	29
Jose Jimenez	15	8	**23**	0	–	100	27
Melvin Mora	12	11	**23**	65	35	–	23

Player	00	01	Dec	B	F	P	Car
Mark Mulder	5	18	**23**	0	–	100	23
Kazuhiro Sasaki	11	12	**23**	–	–	100	23
Eric Karros	14	8	**22**	85	15	–	157
Mike Bordick	16	6	**22**	50	50	–	129
J.T. Snow	16	6	**22**	85	15	–	115
Trevor Hoffman	13	9	**22**	1	–	99	114
Tony Clark	6	16	**22**	90	10	–	90
Troy Percival	8	14	**22**	0	–	100	83
Rey Sanchez	9	13	**22**	37	63	–	83
Jose Hernandez	9	13	**22**	60	40	–	72
Rick Helling	15	7	**22**	0	–	100	60
David Bell	8	14	**22**	58	42	–	53
Mike Matheny	14	8	**22**	21	79	–	44
Steve Karsay	11	11	**22**	0	–	100	40
Russ Ortiz	7	15	**22**	2	–	98	37
Benny Agbayani	14	8	**22**	87	13	–	31
Jarrod Washburn	7	15	**22**	2	–	98	29
Carlos Guillen	8	14	**22**	66	34	–	24
Mark Buehrle	4	18	**22**	0	–	100	22
Chuck Knoblauch	10	11	**21**	77	23	–	229
Dante Bichette	14	7	**21**	80	20	–	168
Dean Palmer	15	6	**21**	85	15	–	129
Randy Velarde	14	7	**21**	70	30	–	123
R. Hernandez	12	9	**21**	0	–	100	117
Todd Hundley	17	4	**21**	71	29	–	110
Denny Neagle	13	8	**21**	0	–	100	107
Matt Stairs	10	11	**21**	92	8	–	82
Hideo Nomo	10	11	**21**	1	–	99	77
Doug Glanville	10	11	**21**	64	36	–	72
Dave Veres	14	7	**21**	1	–	99	68
Mark Loretta	12	9	**21**	66	34	0	66
Mike Remlinger	12	9	**21**	0	–	100	49
Travis Lee	6	15	**21**	75	25	–	42
Albie Lopez	13	8	**21**	0	–	100	40
Chris Stynes	13	8	**21**	69	31	–	40
Damian Miller	11	10	**21**	50	50	–	39
Steve Kline	9	12	**21**	0	–	100	35
Einar Diaz	6	15	**21**	48	52	–	30
Jacque Jones	11	10	**21**	66	34	–	30
Armando Rios	11	10	**21**	90	10	–	30
Felix Rodriguez	9	12	**21**	1	–	99	29
Wade Miller	4	17	**21**	0	–	100	21
Jimmy Rollins	1	20	**21**	68	32	–	21
Rickey Henderson	8	12	**20**	89	11	–	530
Will Clark	20		**20**	92	8	–	331
Reggie Sanders	6	14	**20**	83	17	–	144
Stan Javier	9	11	**20**	79	21	–	137
Jamie Moyer	5	15	**20**	0	–	100	133
Jeff Shaw	7	13	**20**	0	–	100	97
Frank Castillo	12	8	**20**	0	–	100	61

Player	00	01	Dec	B	F	P	Car
Esteban Loaiza	12	8	**20**	0	–	100	52
Eddie Guardado	8	12	**20**	–	–	100	43
Alex Ochoa	11	9	**20**	78	22	–	43
Craig Paquette	8	12	**20**	72	28	–	41
Kerry Wood	7	13	**20**	3	–	97	34
Paul Abbott	11	9	**20**	1	–	99	32
Elmer Dessens	10	10	**20**	2	–	98	23
Ben Molina	13	7	**20**	32	68	–	23
Juan Pierre	3	17	**20**	58	42	–	20
Chuck Finley	16	3	**19**	0	–	100	204
Rusty Greer	12	7	**19**	90	10	–	130
Quilvio Veras	13	6	**19**	66	34	–	95
Darrin Fletcher	14	5	**19**	63	37	–	91
Steve Trachsel	11	8	**19**	2	–	98	77
Jeffrey Hammonds	14	5	**19**	73	27	–	67
Tom Goodwin	14	5	**19**	64	36	–	66
Curtis Leskanic	12	7	**19**	1	–	99	60
Roger Cedeno	5	14	**19**	79	21	–	56
James Baldwin	11	8	**19**	1	–	99	50
Livan Hernandez	14	5	**19**	4	–	96	43
Scott Sullivan	10	9	**19**	0	–	100	43
Mike Williams	11	8	**19**	2	–	98	43
Craig Counsell	5	14	**19**	61	39	–	42
Kelvim Escobar	8	11	**19**	0	–	100	39
Antonio Alfonseca	10	9	**19**	0	–	100	33
Juan Encarnacion	14	5	**19**	75	25	–	32
Shane Halter	3	16	**19**	57	43	0	23
Octavio Dotel	7	12	**19**	0	–	100	22
Mark Quinn	13	6	**19**	80	20	–	22
Adam Kennedy	11	8	**19**	50	50	–	21
Matt Herges	10	9	**19**	2	–	98	20
Barry Larkin	13	5	**18**	71	29	–	320
Jeff Fassero	8	10	**18**	0	–	100	115
Royce Clayton	8	10	**18**	45	55	–	111
Al Martin	10	8	**18**	87	13	–	105
Pedro Astacio	11	7	**18**	0	–	100	96
Dan Wilson	4	14	**18**	47	53	–	92
Bill Mueller	10	8	**18**	80	20	–	71
Arthur Rhodes	6	12	**18**	0	–	100	53
Pokey Reese	11	7	**18**	44	56	–	46
Chris Carpenter	5	13	**18**	0	–	100	40
Todd Ritchie	8	10	**18**	0	–	100	35
Jim Mecir	12	6	**18**	0	–	100	32
Eric Owens	15	3	**18**	76	24	–	30
Marlon Anderson	2	16	**18**	60	40	–	28
Herbert Perry	13	5	**18**	79	21	–	26
Bobby Estalella	15	3	**18**	69	31	–	22
Jeremy Giambi	6	12	**18**	94	6	–	22
Geoff Blum	10	8	**18**	65	35	–	21
Ben Davis	3	15	**18**	53	47	–	21

Player	00	01	Dec	B	F	P	Car
Doug Mientkiewicz	0	18	**18**	77	23	–	21
Ramon Ortiz	6	12	**18**	0	–	100	19
A.J. Pierzynski	3	15	**18**	52	48	–	19
Scott Strickland	8	10	**18**	0	–	100	19
Jeff Tam	10	8	**18**	0	–	100	19
Julio Lugo	9	9	**18**	50	50	–	18
Chris Richard	6	12	**18**	83	17	–	18
Cal Ripken Jr.	8	9	**17**	68	32	–	427
Matt Williams	7	10	**17**	75	25	–	232
Mo Vaughn	17		**17**	94	6	–	185
Kenny Rogers	15	2	**17**	0	–	100	130
Derek Bell	16	1	**17**	82	18	0	111
Luis Alicea	12	5	**17**	69	31	–	99
Joe Girardi	9	8	**17**	44	56	–	94
Troy O'Leary	11	6	**17**	74	26	–	91
Jose Mesa	3	14	**17**	0	–	100	88
Paul Quantrill	6	11	**17**	0	–	100	71
Chad Kreuter	9	8	**17**	50	50	–	65
Michael Tucker	7	10	**17**	75	25	–	65
Mike Lieberthal	14	3	**17**	61	39	–	64
Jeff Nelson	9	8	**17**	0	0	100	59
Dustin Hermanson	9	8	**17**	0	–	100	52
Todd Walker	5	12	**17**	68	32	–	48
Shawn Estes	10	7	**17**	0	–	100	46
Rolando Arrojo	8	9	**17**	0	–	100	40
Dave Weathers	7	10	**17**	0	–	100	35
Gabe White	15	2	**17**	1	–	99	31
Al Levine	7	10	**17**	–	–	100	27
Glendon Rusch	11	6	**17**	0	–	100	27
Cory Lidle	4	13	**17**	0	–	100	23
Tanyon Sturtze	6	11	**17**	0	–	100	18
Tony Armas Jr.	5	12	**17**	0	–	100	17
Jose Macias	5	12	**17**	66	34	–	17
Jay Payton	14	3	**17**	53	47	–	17
Brad Penny	5	12	**17**	0	–	100	17
Jose Canseco	8	8	**16**	93	7	0	272
Ken Caminiti	9	7	**16**	78	22	–	242
Jay Buhner	16	0	**16**	86	14	–	174
Benito Santiago	6	10	**16**	52	48	–	159
Vinny Castilla	3	13	**16**	66	34	–	114
Shane Reynolds	6	10	**16**	1	–	99	89
Tim Wakefield	5	11	**16**	0	–	100	86
Dave Burba	13	3	**16**	1	–	99	80
Mike Stanton	6	10	**16**	2	–	98	74
Gerald Williams	14	2	**16**	63	37	–	63
Kirk Rueter	9	7	**16**	0	–	100	60
Omar Daal	5	11	**16**	3	–	97	54
Brian Anderson	14	2	**16**	0	–	100	47
O. Hernandez	12	4	**16**	0	–	100	43
Jason Bere	7	9	**16**	1	–	99	42

Player	00	01	Dec	B	F	P	Car
Julian Tavarez	10	6	**16**	0	–	100	42
S. Hasegawa	11	5	**16**	0	–	100	39
Jamey Wright	9	7	**16**	0	–	100	39
John Rocker	8	8	**16**	–	–	100	37
Denny Hocking	11	5	**16**	54	46	–	34
Rich Garces	10	6	**16**	0	–	100	32
Jeff Zimmerman	4	12	**16**	–	–	100	30
Danny Bautista	10	6	**16**	69	31	–	27
Ramon E. Martinez	7	9	**16**	69	31	–	21
Alfonso Soriano	0	16	**16**	60	40	–	16
Albert Belle	15		**15**	90	10	–	243
Todd Jones	10	5	**15**	0	–	100	71
Greg Colbrunn	12	3	**15**	85	15	–	62
Brian Bohanon	13	2	**15**	3	–	97	52
Ron Coomer	9	6	**15**	69	31	–	50
Gil Heredia	13	2	**15**	2	–	98	50
Kevin Millwood	10	5	**15**	0	–	100	50
Ramiro Mendoza	5	10	**15**	0	–	100	43
Scott Spiezio	6	9	**15**	68	32	–	43
Bob Wells	10	5	**15**	0	–	100	36
Ruben Rivera	10	5	**15**	65	35	–	32
Jason Varitek	7	8	**15**	60	40	–	32
Sidney Ponson	11	4	**15**	1	–	99	30
LaTroy Hawkins	12	3	**15**	0	–	100	26
David Ortiz	8	7	**15**	93	7	–	26
Jeff D'Amico	15	0	**15**	0	–	100	25
Russ Johnson	4	11	**15**	73	27	–	22
Henry Blanco	9	6	**15**	16	84	–	21
Mac Suzuki	12	3	**15**	0	–	100	18
Bruce Chen	11	4	**15**	0	–	100	17
Russell Branyan	5	10	**15**	85	15	–	16
Scott Schoeneweis	6	9	**15**	3	–	97	16
Roy Oswalt		15	**15**	0	–	100	15
Marquis Grissom	8	6	**14**	66	34	–	197
Pat Hentgen	10	4	**14**	0	–	100	116
Kevin Young	7	7	**14**	82	18	–	72
Brent Mayne	8	6	**14**	52	48	0	71
Billy Wagner	1	13	**14**	0	–	100	64
Ricky Bottalico	8	6	**14**	0	–	100	52
Terry Adams	6	8	**14**	0	–	100	42
Mike Sirotka	14		**14**	0	–	100	40
Paul Shuey	8	6	**14**	0	–	100	38
Rick White	9	5	**14**	1	–	99	35
Miguel Cairo	10	4	**14**	50	50	–	34
Buddy Groom	6	8	**14**	–	–	100	34
Steve Parris	9	5	**14**	1	–	99	33
Bob Howry	9	5	**14**	–	–	100	31
Kris Benson	14		**14**	0	–	100	26
Ricky Ledee	10	4	**14**	81	19	–	25
Todd Van Poppel	6	8	**14**	1	–	99	25

Player	00	01	Dec	B	F	P	Car
Shane Spencer	6	8	**14**	78	22	–	23
Jerry Hairston Jr.	4	10	**14**	56	44	–	19
Robert Fick	4	10	**14**	83	17	–	18
Blake Stein	7	7	**14**	0	–	100	18
Rick Ankiel	14	0	**14**	3	–	97	17
A.J. Burnett	5	9	**14**	8	–	92	17
Raul Casanova	8	6	**14**	51	49	–	16
Adam Eaton	9	5	**14**	8	–	92	14
Mike Lamb	6	8	**14**	77	23	–	14
Chuck Smith	10	4	**14**	0	–	100	14
Devon White	2	11	**13**	72	28	–	207
Kevin Tapani	6	7	**13**	0	–	100	124
Mike Lansing	7	6	**13**	56	44	–	109
Ugueth Urbina	2	11	**13**	0	–	100	62
Turk Wendell	8	5	**13**	0	–	100	51
Rey Ordonez	1	12	**13**	16	84	–	48
Jeff Reboulet	3	10	**13**	50	50	–	48
Fernando Tatis	11	2	**13**	78	22	–	48
Gregg Zaun	9	4	**13**	59	41	–	34
Tyler Houston	5	8	**13**	75	25	–	33
Homer Bush	4	9	**13**	53	47	–	32
Jason Grimsley	5	8	**13**	1	–	99	30
Kerry Ligtenberg	8	5	**13**	–	–	100	30
Brook Fordyce	11	2	**13**	60	40	–	29
Jose Mercedes	11	2	**13**	0	–	100	27
Alex Gonzalez	3	10	**13**	59	41	–	25
Josias Manzanillo	5	8	**13**	1	–	99	23
Sean Lowe	3	10	**13**	0	–	100	21
Doug Mirabelli	6	7	**13**	57	43	–	18
Mike Darr	6	7	**13**	79	21	–	14
Wiki Gonzalez	6	7	**13**	50	50	–	14
Calvin Murray	6	7	**13**	77	23	–	14
Steve Cox	8	5	**13**	84	16	–	13
Doug Davis	5	8	**13**	0	–	100	13
Mitch Meluskey	13		**13**	88	12	–	13
Mark Redman	10	3	**13**	0	–	100	13
Dan Reichert	9	4	**13**	0	–	100	13
John Franco	7	5	**12**	0	–	100	179
Sandy Alomar Jr.	8	4	**12**	55	45	–	100
Rod Beck	5	7	**12**	0	–	100	99
Ismael Valdes	2	10	**12**	0	–	100	80
Marty Cordova	1	11	**12**	82	18	–	70
John Flaherty	8	4	**12**	46	54	–	58
Mike Trombley	6	6	**12**	0	–	100	57
T. Hollandsworth	8	4	**12**	75	25	–	53
Tim Worrell	7	5	**12**	2	–	98	36
Bill Haselman	7	5	**12**	56	44	–	32
Masato Yoshii	7	5	**12**	0	–	100	30
Danny Patterson	5	7	**12**	0	–	100	29
Mike DeJean	4	8	**12**	0	–	100	28

Player	00	01	Dec	B	F	P	Car
Jimmy Haynes	6	6	**12**	0	–	100	27
Jose Paniagua	8	4	**12**	0	–	100	25
Carlos Febles	7	5	**12**	60	40	–	24
Eli Marrero	5	7	**12**	36	64	–	24
Bryan Rekar	11	1	**12**	1	–	99	22
Erubiel Durazo	5	7	**12**	89	11	–	21
Randy Winn	2	10	**12**	62	38	–	21
Esteban Yan	4	8	**12**	2	–	98	21
Matt Anderson	4	8	**12**	–	–	100	18
Braden Looper	5	7	**12**	0	–	100	17
Jose Santiago	7	5	**12**	0	–	100	16
Jason LaRue	3	9	**12**	41	59	–	14
Alex Cora	6	6	**12**	32	68	–	13
Justin Speier	7	5	**12**	0	–	100	13
David Eckstein		12	**12**	67	33	–	12
C.C. Sabathia		12	**12**	0	–	100	12
Brian Tollberg	6	6	**12**	0	–	100	12
Ron Gant	7	4	**11**	82	18	–	194
Greg Swindell	7	4	**11**	1	–	99	136
Bill Spiers	11	0	**11**	71	29	–	98
Henry Rodriguez	11	0	**11**	86	14	–	93
Wil Cordero	10	1	**11**	76	24	–	86
Mike Timlin	6	5	**11**	0	–	100	75
Pat Meares	9	2	**11**	46	54	–	63
Jeff Frye	8	3	**11**	60	40	–	60
Pat Rapp	4	7	**11**	0	–	100	60
Brian Moehler	10	1	**11**	0	–	100	47
Scott Williamson	11	0	**11**	0	–	100	28
Chris Holt	8	3	**11**	0	–	100	27
Warren Morris	10	1	**11**	59	41	–	27
Mike Redmond	5	6	**11**	47	53	–	27
Scott Elarton	11	0	**11**	0	–	100	26
Orlando Palmeiro	7	4	**11**	72	28	–	26
G. Stephenson	11		**11**	0	–	100	26
Miguel Batista	0	11	**11**	0	–	100	23
Mike Myers	7	4	**11**	0	–	100	23
Jim Parque	11	0	**11**	1	–	99	22
Jimmy Anderson	4	7	**11**	3	–	97	14
Kevin Jarvis	4	7	**11**	1	–	99	12
Gary Matthews Jr.	1	10	**11**	71	29	–	12
Tsuyoshi Shinjo		11	**11**	66	34	–	11
Dave Martinez	7	3	**10**	76	23	0	147
Terry Mulholland	7	3	**10**	1	–	99	101
Tony Eusebio	5	5	**10**	61	39	–	54
Jason Schmidt	1	9	**10**	0	–	100	44
Damon Buford	9	1	**10**	59	41	–	39
Hector Carrasco	6	4	**10**	0	–	100	39
Dave Hansen	6	4	**10**	80	20	–	38
Jay Powell	1	9	**10**	0	–	100	37
Terry Shumpert	5	5	**10**	57	43	–	37

Player	00	01	Dec	B	F	P	Car
Kelly Stinnett	5	5	**10**	55	45	–	35
Darren Dreifort	9	1	**10**	2	–	98	34
Scott Hatteberg	5	5	**10**	73	27	–	31
Juan Acevedo	6	4	**10**	1	–	99	30
Wayne Gomes	6	4	**10**	1	–	99	27
Benji Gil	4	6	**10**	25	75	–	23
John Halama	6	4	**10**	1	–	99	23
Joe McEwing	2	8	**10**	65	35	–	21
Mike Venafro	6	4	**10**	–	–	100	17
Raul Ibanez	1	9	**10**	81	19	–	15
Mark L. Johnson	5	5	**10**	35	65	–	15
Lou Pote	4	6	**10**	–	–	100	15
Chris Brock	7	3	**10**	1	–	99	13
Nelson Cruz	4	6	**10**	0	–	100	12
Paul Wilson	4	6	**10**	0	–	100	11
Brent Abernathy		10	**10**	74	26	–	10
Adam Dunn		10	**10**	92	8	–	10
Chris Truby	7	3	**10**	73	27	–	10

Players with at least 250 career Win Shares

Player	00	01	Dec	B	F	P	Car
Wally Joyner	7	2	**9**	89	11	–	253
Tony Gwynn	3	4	**7**	89	11	–	398
Bobby Bonilla	6	1	**7**	86	14	0	267
Harold Baines	4	0	**4**	92	8	–	307
Tim Raines		3	**3**	86	14	–	390
Tony Fernandez		2	**2**	64	36	–	280

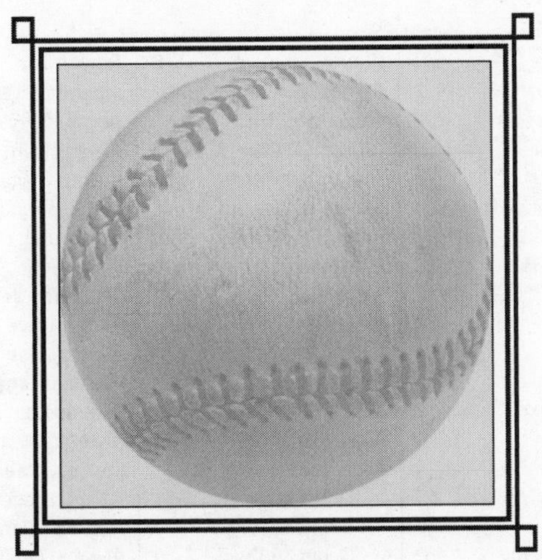

Supplementary Register

The Supplementary Register provides career Win Shares totals for every major league player dating back to 1876 who *didn't* reach the minimums to appear in the Win Shares by Decade section. Players who appear in the Win Shares by Decade section are not duplicated here.

Those major leaguers who have identical first and last names are distinguished by the year they debuted in the majors. For instance, there are three players listed as Bob Adams. The Supplementary Register shows the one who debuted in 1925 with zero Win Shares. One Win Share each goes to the ones who debuted in 1931 and 1977.

All players not listed in Decade Summary

A

Player	WS
Aaron, Tommie	13
Aase, Don	81
Abad, Andy	0
Abbey, Bert	23
Abbey, Charlie	32
Abbott, Dan	0
Abbott, Fred	9
Abbott, Glenn	52
Abbott, Jeff	12
Abbott, Kurt	47
Abbott, Kyle	3
Abbott, Ody	0
Aber, Al	22
Abernathie, Bill	0
Abernathy, Ted	0
Abernathy, Woody	2
Aberson, Cliff	4
Ables, Harry	1
Abner, Shawn	13
Abrams, Cal	53
Abrams, George	0
Abrego, Johnny	0
Abreu, Joe	1
Abstein, Bill	13
Acevedo, Jose	2
Acker, Jim	54
Acker, Tom	23
Ackley, Fritz	1
Acosta, Cy	23
Acosta, Ed	4
Acosta, Jose	12
Acosta, Merito	12
Acre, Mark	6
Adair, Jimmy	1
Adams, Ace	49
Adams, Bert	9
Adams, Bob	
Debut 1925	0
Debut 1931	1
Debut 1977	1
Adams, Buster	63
Adams, Dan	5
Adams, Dick	1
Adams, Doug	0
Adams, George	0
Adams, Glenn	29
Adams, Herb	5
Adams, Joe	0
Adams, John	0
Adams, Karl	0
Adams, Mike	3
Adams, Red	0
Adams, Rick	2

Player	WS
Adams, Ricky	3
Adams, Spencer	6
Adams, Willie	
Debut 1912	5
Debut 1996	5
Adamson, Joel	6
Adamson, Mike	0
Addis, Bob	12
Adduci, Jim	2
Addy, Bob	7
Aderholt, Morrie	5
Adkins, Dewey	2
Adkins, Dick	0
Adkins, Doc	0
Adkins, Grady	16
Adkins, Steve	0
Adkinson, Henry	0
Adlesh, Dave	2
Afenir, Troy	1
Agganis, Harry	12
Agler, Joe	22
Agnew, Sam	25
Agosto, Juan	41
Aguayo, Luis	30
Ahearn, Charlie	0
Ahearne, Pat	0
Aikens, Willie	77
Ainge, Danny	7
Ainsmith, Eddie	78
Ainsworth, Kurt	0
Aitchison, Raleigh	11
Aiton, George	0
Ake, John	0
Aker, Jack	73
Akerfelds, Darrel	8
Akers, Bill	15
Akers, Jerry	0
Alba, Gibson	0
Albanese, Joe	0
Alberro, Jose	0
Alberts, Butch	0
Alberts, Cy	0
Alberts, Gus	11
Albosta, Ed	0
Albrecht, Ed	0
Albright, Jack	2
Albury, Vic	16
Alcala, Santo	6
Alcantara, Israel	3
Alcaraz, Luis	5
Alcock, Scotty	1
Alderson, Dale	0
Aldred, Scott	15
Aldrete, Mike	66
Aldrich, Jay	6
Aldridge, Cory	0

Player	WS
Aleno, Chuck	7
Alexander, Bob	0
Alexander, Dale	77
Alexander, Gary	30
Alexander, Gerald	2
Alexander, Hugh	0
Alexander, Manny	20
Alexander, Matt	3
Alexander, Nin	0
Alexander, Walt	11
Allanson, Andy	27
Allard, Brian	4
Allen, Bernie	94
Allen, Bob	
Debut 1890	74
Debut 1919	0
Debut 1937	0
Debut 1961	12
Allen, Chad	10
Allen, Dusty	0
Allen, Ethan	110
Allen, Frank	55
Allen, Hank	13
Allen, Hezekiah	0
Allen, Horace	0
Allen, Jack	1
Allen, Jamie	3
Allen, John	0
Allen, Kim	1
Allen, Lloyd	16
Allen, Myron	16
Allen, Neil	66
Allen, Nick	14
Allen, Pete	0
Allen, Rod	1
Allen, Ron	0
Allen, Sled	0
Allenson, Gary	22
Allensworth, J.	23
Allie, Gair	2
Allietta, Bob	0
Allison, Art	1
Allison, Dana	0
Allison, Doug	9
Allison, Mack	10
Allison, Milo	1
Allred, Beau	3
Almada, Mel	52
Almanza, Armando	7
Almanzar, Carlos	5
Almeida, Rafael	8
Almon, Bill	77
Almonte, Erick	1
Almonte, Hector	1
Aloma, Luis	23
Alou, Jesus	78

Player	WS
Alperman, Whitey	36
Alston, Garvin	0
Alston, Tom	3
Alston, Walter	0
Alston, Wendell	4
Altamirano, Porfi	5
Alten, Ernie	0
Altenburg, Jesse	1
Altizer, Dave	55
Altobelli, Joe	2
Alusik, George	17
Alvarado, Luis	12
Alvarez, Clemente	0
Alvarez, Gabe	3
Alvarez, Jose	13
Alvarez, Juan	0
Alvarez, Orlando	0
Alvarez, Ossie	3
Alvarez, Rogelio	0
Alvarez, Tavo	2
Alvord, Billy	20
Alyea, Brant	28
Amalfitano, Joey	37
Amaral, Rich	36
Amaro, Ruben	
Debut 1958	45
Debut 1991	16
Ambler, Wayne	7
Amelung, Ed	0
Amole, Doc	5
Amor, Vincente	0
Amoros, Sandy	46
Ancker, Walter	0
Andersen, Larry	87
Anderson, Alf	6
Anderson, Allan	43
Anderson, Andy	2
Anderson, Bill	0
Anderson, Bob	38
Anderson, Bud	11
Anderson, Craig	5
Anderson, Dave	
Debut 1889	1
Debut 1983	46
Anderson, Dwain	6
Anderson, Ferrell	7
Anderson, Fred	57
Anderson, George	33
Anderson, Goat	12
Anderson, Hal	0
Anderson, Harry	47
Anderson, Jim	17
Anderson, John	1
Anderson, Kent	8
Anderson, Larry	1

Player	WS
Anderson, Mike	
Debut 1971	34
Debut 1993	0
Anderson, Red	6
Anderson, Rick	
Debut 1979	1
Debut 1986	6
Anderson, Scott	2
Anderson, Sparky	7
Anderson, Varney	7
Anderson, Walter	3
Anderson, Wingo	0
Andre, John	0
Andres, Ernie	1
Andrew, Kim	0
Andrews, Clayton	0
Andrews, Ed	85
Andrews, Elbert	0
Andrews, Fred	1
Andrews, Hub	0
Andrews, Jim	3
Andrews, John	0
Andrews, Mike	108
Andrews, Nate	49
Andrews, Rob	29
Andrews, Shane	38
Andrews, Stan	3
Andrews, Wally	3
Andrus, Bill	0
Andrus, Fred	2
Andrus, Wiman	0
Andujar, Luis	3
Angelini, Norm	2
Angley, Tom	0
Ankenman, Pat	0
Annis, Bill	0
Anthony, Eric	43
Antolick, Joe	0
Antonelli, John	7
Antonello, Bill	0
Apodaca, Bob	32
Aponte, Luis	19
Applegate, Fred	0
Appleton, Ed	5
Appleton, Pete	68
Aquino, Luis	42
Aragon, Angel	0
Aragon, Jack	0
Archdeacon, M.	12
Archer, Fred	1
Archer, Jim	15
Archer, Jimmy	74
Archie, George	9
Arcia, Jose	6
Ardell, Dan	0
Ardizoia, Rugger	0

Player	WS
Ardner, Joe	3
Ardoin, Danny	0
Arellanes, Frank	28
Arft, Hank	19
Arias, Alex	38
Arias, George	8
Arias, Rudy	2
Arlett, Buzz	16
Arlich, Don	0
Arlin, Steve	22
Armas, Marcos	0
Armbrister, Ed	5
Armbrust, Orville	2
Armbruster, Charlie	6
Armbruster, Harry	10
Armstrong, George	0
Armstrong, Howard	0
Armstrong, Jack	23
Armstrong, Mike	21
Arndt, Harry	23
Arndt, Larry	0
Arnold, Chris	7
Arnold, Jamie	1
Arnold, Scott	0
Arnold, Tony	2
Arnovich, Morrie	49
Arnsberg, Brad	12
Arntzen, Orie	4
Arocha, Rene	20
Arrigo, Gerry	27
Arroyo, Bronson	3
Arroyo, Fredie	24
Arroyo, Luis	44
Arroyo, Rudy	0
Arundel, Harry	3
Arundel, Tug	3
Asadoor, Randy	2
Asbell, Jim	0
Asbjornson, Asby	3
Ash, Ken	6
Ashby, Andy	78
Ashford, Tucker	9
Ashley, Billy	11
Asmussen, Tom	0
Aspromonte, Ken	32
Asselstine, Brian	10
Assenmacher, Paul	86
Astroth, Joe	41
Atchley, Justin	0
Atherton, Charlie	3
Atherton, Keith	35
Atkins, James	1
Atkins, Tommy	1
Atkinson, Al	50
Atkinson, Bill	14
Atkinson, Lefty	0
Attreau, Dick	1
Atwell, Toby	32
Atwood, Bill	12
Atz, Jake	19

Player	WS
Aubrey, Harry	1
Aucoin, Derek	0
Aude, Rich	1
Auerbach, Rick	27
August, Don	17
Augustine, Dave	0
Augustine, Jerry	42
Aulds, Tex	0
Ault, Doug	8
Ausanio, Joe	2
Aust, Dennis	1
Austin, James	9
Austin, Jeff	1
Austin, Rick	5
Autry, Al	0
Autry, Chick	
Debut 1907	1
Debut 1924	5
Aven, Bruce	17
Averill, Earl	32
Aviles, Ramon	5
Avrea, Jim	0
Ayala, Bennie	21
Ayala, Bobby	38
Aybar, Manny	14
Aydelott, Jake	3
Ayers, Bill	0
Ayers, Doc	80
Aylward, Dick	0
Ayrault, Bob	5
Ayrault, Joe	0
Azocar, Oscar	4

B

Player	WS
Babb, Charlie	37
Babcock, Bob	3
Babe, Loren	4
Babich, Johnny	21
Babington, Charlie	1
Babitt, Shooty	3
Backman, Les	7
Bacon, Eddie	1
Bacsik, Mike	
Debut 1975	7
Debut 2001	0
Baczewski, Fred	16
Bader, Art	0
Bader, Lore	5
Badgro, Red	5
Baecht, Ed	5
Baez, Benito	0
Baez, Danys	6
Baez, Jose	7
Baez, Kevin	2
Bagwell, Bill	3
Bahr, Ed	14
Bahret, Frank	0

Player	WS
Baichley, Grover	0
Bailes, Scott	26
Bailey, Bill	
Debut 1907	37
Debut 1911	0
Bailey, Cory	13
Bailey, Ed	145
Bailey, Fred	1
Bailey, Gene	11
Bailey, Harvey	8
Bailey, Howard	4
Bailey, James	0
Bailey, King	1
Bailey, Mark	27
Bailey, Roger	22
Bailey, Steve	2
Bailey, Sweetbreads	5
Bailor, Bob	57
Bain, Loren	0
Bair, Doug	72
Baird, Al	3
Baird, Bob	0
Baird, Doug	51
Bakely, Jersey	70
Bakenhaster, Dave	0
Baker, Al	0
Baker, Bill	17
Baker, Bock	0
Baker, Charlie	0
Baker, Chuck	2
Baker, Dave	1
Baker, Del	6
Baker, Doug	5
Baker, Ernie	0
Baker, Floyd	61
Baker, Frank	
Debut 1969	5
Debut 1970	6
Baker, Gene	50
Baker, George	6
Baker, Howard	1
Baker, Jack	0
Baker, Jesse	
Debut 1911	3
Debut 1919	0
Baker, Kirtley	5
Baker, Neal	0
Baker, Norm	13
Baker, Phil	18
Baker, Scott	0
Baker, Steve	6
Baker, Tom	
Debut 1935	8
Debut 1963	0
Baker, Tracy	0
Bako, Paul	18
Balas, Mike	0
Balaz, John	3
Balboni, Steve	67
Balcena, Bobby	0

Player	WS
Baldschun, Jack	55
Baldwin, Billy	3
Baldwin, Dave	17
Baldwin, Frank	0
Baldwin, Harry	2
Baldwin, Henry	0
Baldwin, Jeff	0
Baldwin, Kid	32
Baldwin, O.F.	0
Baldwin, Reggie	1
Baldwin, Rick	11
Bale, John	2
Balenti, Mike	2
Bales, Lee	0
Balfour, Grant	0
Ball, Art	1
Ball, Jeff	0
Ball, Jim	0
Ball, Neal	36
Ballard, Jeff	26
Ballenger, Pelham	0
Baller, Jay	5
Ballinger, Mark	1
Ballou, Win	12
Balsamo, Tony	0
Bamberger, George	0
Bamberger, Hal	0
Bando, Chris	27
Bane, Eddie	4
Baney, Dick	4
Banister, Jeff	0
Bankhead, Dan	4
Bankhead, Scott	56
Banks, Bill	1
Banks, Brian	5
Banks, George	6
Banks, Willie	22
Bankston, Bill	0
Banning, Jim	0
Bannister, Alan	73
Bannon, Jimmy	45
Bannon, Tom	3
Banta, Jack	14
Baptist, Travis	1
Barajas, Rod	2
Barbare, Walter	36
Barbary, Red	0
Barbeau, Jap	17
Barbee, Dave	7
Barber, Brian	2
Barber, Charlie	5
Barber, Steve	1
Barber, Turner	36
Barberich, Frank	0
Barberie, Bret	40
Barbieri, Jim	3
Barcelo, Lorenzo	4
Barclay, Curt	13
Barclay, George	27
Bare, Ray	13

Player	WS
Barfield, John	5
Barfoot, Clyde	13
Bargar, Greg	0
Barger, Cy	54
Bark, Brian	0
Barker, Glen	5
Barker, Kevin	6
Barker, Len	66
Barker, Ray	7
Barker, Richie	0
Barkett, Andy	1
Barkley, Brian	0
Barkley, Jeff	1
Barkley, Red	3
Barlow, Mike	8
Barmes, Bruce	0
Barna, Babe	14
Barnabe, Charlie	1
Barnes, Bill	0
Barnes, Bob	0
Barnes, Brian	17
Barnes, Eppie	0
Barnes, Frank	
Debut 1929	0
Debut 1957	0
Barnes, Honey	0
Barnes, John	1
Barnes, Junie	0
Barnes, Larry	0
Barnes, Lute	2
Barnes, Red	21
Barnes, Rich	0
Barnes, Sam	0
Barnes, Skeeter	15
Barnes, Virgil	67
Barney, Ed	7
Barney, Rex	27
Barnhart, Edgar	0
Barnhart, Les	0
Barnhart, Vic	2
Barnicle, George	0
Barnie, Billy	0
Barnowski, Ed	0
Barojas, Salome	32
Barone, Dick	0
Barr, Bob	
Debut 1883	48
Debut 1935	0
Barr, Scotty	1
Barr, Steve	1
Barragan, Cuno	1
Barranca, German	2
Barrett, Bill	59
Barrett, Bob	11
Barrett, Dick	30
Barrett, Frank	13
Barrett, Johnny	61
Barrett, Marty	0
Barrett, Michael	15
Barrett, Red	73

Player	WS
Barrett, Tim	0
Barrett, Tom	1
Barrios, Francisco	37
Barrios, Jose	0
Barrios, Manny	0
Barron, Frank	0
Barron, Red	0
Barron, Tony	4
Barrows, Cuke	1
Barry, Ed	3
Barry, Hardin	0
Barry, Jeff	3
Barry, Rich	0
Barry, Tom	0
Bartee, Kimera	3
Barthelson, Bob	0
Barthold, John	0
Bartholomew, Les	0
Bartirome, Tony	2
Bartley, Bill	3
Bartley, Boyd	0
Bartling, Irv	0
Barton, Bob	23
Barton, Harry	1
Barton, Shawn	4
Barton, Vince	9
Bartosch, Dave	1
Bartson, Charlie	12
Basgall, Monty	6
Bashang, Al	0
Bashore, Walt	0
Basinski, Eddie	9
Baskette, Jim	10
Bass, Dick	0
Bass, Doc	0
Bass, John	0
Bass, Norm	7
Bass, Randy	6
Bassett, Charley	67
Bastian, Charlie	36
Batch, Emil	27
Batchelder, Joe	0
Batchelor, Richard	2
Bateman, John	60
Bates, Billy	1
Bates, Bud	1
Bates, Charlie	1
Bates, Del	1
Bates, Dick	0
Bates, Frank	4
Bates, Jason	13
Bates, John	0
Bates, Ray	10
Bathe, Bill	3
Batista, Rafael	0
Batiste, Kevin	0
Batiste, Kim	7
Batsch, Bill	0
Battam, Larry	0
Batten, George	0
Battin, Joe	34
Battle, Allen	4
Battle, Howard	1
Battle, Jim	1
Batton, Chris	0
Batts, Matt	46
Bauer, Albert	1
Bauer, Lou	0
Bauer, Rick	0
Bauers, Russ	43
Baughman, Justin	3
Baumann, Frank	47
Baumann, Paddy	28
Baumer, Jim	1
Baumgardner, G.	37
Baumgarten, Ross	24
Baumgartner, Harry	1
Baumgartner, John	0
Baumgartner, Stan	36
Baumholtz, Frankie	90
Bausewine, George	2
Bauta, Ed	9
Bautista, Jose	31
Baxes, Jim	9
Baxes, Mike	4
Baxter, John	0
Bayless, Dick	2
Bayne, Bill	33
Beach, Jack	0
Beall, Bob	4
Beall, Johnny	4
Beall, Walter	6
Beals, Tommy	0
Beam, Alex	0
Beam, Ernie	0
Beamon, Charlie	
Debut 1956	3
Debut 1978	0
Beamon, Trey	2
Bean, Belve	11
Bean, Billy	6
Bean, Joe	1
Beane, Billy	3
Beard, Dave	15
Beard, Mike	7
Beard, Ollie	44
Beard, Ralph	2
Beard, Ted	6
Bearden, Gene	46
Beare, Gary	2
Bearnarth, Larry	14
Bearse, Kevin	0
Beasley, Chris	1
Beasley, Lew	0
Beatin, Ed	51
Beatle, Dave	0
Beattie, Jim	63
Beatty, Blaine	2
Beatty, Des	0
Beauchamp, Jim	11
Beazley, Johnny	27
Becannon, Buck	2
Bechtel, George	0
Beck, Boom-Boom	43
Beck, Clyde	29
Beck, Erve	22
Beck, Frank	0
Beck, Fred	43
Beck, George	0
Beck, Rich	2
Beck, Zinn	19
Beckendorf, Hennie	4
Becker, Beals	89
Becker, Bob	1
Becker, Charlie	3
Becker, Heinz	11
Becker, Joe	1
Becker, Marty	0
Becker, Rich	57
Beckert, Glenn	125
Beckett, Josh	3
Beckett, Robbie	0
Beckman, Jim	0
Beckmann, Bill	21
Beckwith, Joe	27
Becquer, Julio	8
Bedell, Howie	0
Bedford, Gene	0
Bedgood, Phil	1
Bedient, Hugh	56
Bednar, Andy	0
Beebe, Fred	56
Beech, Matt	6
Beecher, Ed	21
Beecher, Roy	0
Beeler, Jodie	0
Beene, Andy	0
Beene, Fred	16
Beers, Clarence	0
Beggs, Joe	61
Begley, Ed	10
Begley, Gene	0
Begley, Jim	0
Behan, Petie	7
Behel, Steve	4
Behenna, Rick	3
Behney, Mel	0
Behrman, Hank	21
Beimel, Joe	4
Beirne, Kevin	0
Bejma, Ollie	19
Belardi, Wayne	16
Belcher, Kevin	0
Belden, Ira	1
Belinda, Stan	65
Belinsky, Bo	21
Belitz, Todd	0
Belk, Tim	0
Bell, Beau	57
Bell, Bill	0
Bell, Charlie	4
Bell, Eric	9
Bell, Fern	9
Bell, Frank	0
Bell, George	49
Bell, Hi	42
Bell, Jerry	17
Bell, John	1
Bell, Juan	15
Bell, Kevin	12
Bell, Mike	1
Bell, Mike A.	1
Bell, Ralph	0
Bell, Rob	6
Bell, Terry	0
Bella, Zeke	0
Bellhorn, Mark	6
Belliard, Rafael	36
Bellinger, Clay	5
Bellman, John	0
Belloir, Bob	2
Beltran, Rigo	6
Beltre, Esteban	5
Bemis, Harry	54
Benavides, Freddie	11
Benedict, Art	0
Benedict, Bruce	76
Benes, Alan	18
Benes, Joe	0
Benge, Ray	92
Bengough, Benny	28
Beniquez, Juan	109
Benitez, Yamil	6
Benjamin, Mike	41
Benjamin, Stan	4
Benn, Henry	0
Benners, Ike	3
Bennett, Bugs	0
Bennett, Dave	0
Bennett, Dennis	44
Bennett, Erik	0
Bennett, Frank	1
Bennett, Fred	2
Bennett, Gary	7
Bennett, Herschel	15
Bennett, Joe	0
Bennett, Joel	0
Bennett, Pug	19
Bennett, Shayne	4
Benoit, Joaquin	0
Benson, Allen	0
Benson, Vern	3
Bentley, Jack	53
Benton, Butch	0
Benton, Rabbit	0
Benton, Sid	0
Benzinger, Todd	48
Berardino, Johnny	55
Berberet, Lou	32
Berblinger, Jeff	0
Berenguer, Juan	77
Berenyi, Bruce	38
Berg, Dave	23
Berg, Moe	32
Bergamo, Augie	22
Bergen, Bill	51
Bergen, Marty	29
Berger, Boze	20
Berger, Brandon	1
Berger, Clarence	0
Berger, Heinie	35
Berger, Joe	8
Berger, Johnny	1
Berger, Tun	10
Bergeron, Peter	10
Bergh, John	1
Berghammer, Marty	20
Bergman, Al	0
Bergman, Dave	74
Bergman, Sean	22
Berkelbach, Frank	1
Berly, Jack	7
Berman, Bob	0
Bernal, Vic	0
Bernard, Curt	2
Bernard, Dwight	5
Bernard, Joe	0
Bernero, Adam	2
Bernhardt, Juan	2
Bernhardt, Walter	0
Bernier, Carlos	4
Bero, Johnny	3
Berra, Dale	59
Berran, Dennis	0
Berres, Ray	21
Berroa, Angel	1
Berroa, Geronimo	65
Berry, Charlie	
Debut 1884	3
Debut 1925	47
Berry, Claude	17
Berry, Joe	
Debut 1902	0
Debut 1921	1
Debut 1942	35
Berry, Ken	110
Berry, Neil	14
Berry, Sean	74
Berryhill, Damon	49
Bertaina, Frank	14
Berte, Harry	0
Bertell, Dick	26
Bertoia, Reno	30
Bertotti, Mike	1
Bertrand, Lefty	0
Berumen, Andres	1
Besana, Fred	0
Besse, Herman	1
Bessent, Don	19
Best, Karl	8

Player	WS
Beswick, Jim	0
Betcher, Frank	1
Betemit, Wilson	0
Bethea, Bill	0
Bethke, Jim	2
Bettencourt, Larry	10
Bettendorf, Jeff	0
Betts, Harry	0
Betts, Huck	78
Betzel, Bruno	27
Bevacqua, Kurt	36
Bevan, Hal	1
Bevens, Bill	39
Bevil, Brian	2
Bevil, Lou	0
Beville, Ben	0
Beville, Monte	6
Biancalana, Buddy	10
Bianco, Tommy	0
Biasatti, Hank	0
Bibby, Jim	96
Bickford, Vern	57
Bickham, Dan	0
Bicknell, Charlie	0
Biddle, Rocky	4
Biecher, Ed	0
Bielaski, Oscar	0
Bielecki, Mike	57
Biemiller, Harry	2
Bierbrodt, Nick	3
Bieser, Steve	1
Bigbee, Lyle	1
Bigbie, Larry	2
Bigelow, Elliott	4
Biggs, Charlie	0
Bigler, Ivan	0
Bignell, George	0
Biittner, Larry	60
Bilardello, Dann	22
Bilbrey, Jim	0
Bildilli, Emil	4
Bilko, Steve	42
Billiard, Harry	6
Billings, Dick	25
Billings, Josh	
Debut 1913	7
Debut 1927	7
Billingsley, Brent	0
Binks, George	28
Biras, Steve	0
Birchall, Jud	25
Bird, Doug	75
Bird, Frank	1
Bird, Red	0
Birkbeck, Mike	9
Birkofer, Ralph	27
Birmingham, Joe	69
Birrer, Babe	7
Birtsas, Tim	13
Biscan, Frank	6

Player	WS
Bischoff, John	4
Bishop, Bill	
Debut 1886	0
Debut 1921	0
Bishop, Charlie	7
Bishop, Frank	0
Bishop, Jim	0
Bishop, Lloyd	0
Bishop, Mike	0
Bisland, Rivington	0
Bissonette, Del	73
Bithorn, Hi	28
Bitker, Joe	1
Bittiger, Jeff	2
Bittmann, Red	0
Bivin, Jim	3
Bjorkman, George	3
Black, Bill	0
Black, Bob	7
Black, Bud	2
Black, Dave	8
Black, Don	19
Black, Joe	33
Black, John	0
Blackaby, Ethan	0
Blackburn, Charlie	0
Blackburn, Earl	7
Blackburn, George	0
Blackburn, Jim	1
Blackburn, Ron	7
Blackburne, Lena	35
Blackerby, George	0
Blackwell, Ewell	103
Blackwell, Fred	1
Blackwell, Tim	30
Bladt, Rick	2
Blaemire, Rae	0
Blair, Bill	2
Blair, Buddy	15
Blair, Dennis	19
Blair, Footsie	16
Blair, Walter	28
Blair, Willie	48
Blaisdell, Dick	1
Blake, Casey	2
Blake, Ed	1
Blake, Harry	39
Blakely, Link	1
Blakiston, Bob	14
Blanchard, Johnny	44
Blanche, Al	1
Blanco, Damaso	1
Blanco, Gil	1
Blanco, Ossie	0
Blanding, Fred	52
Blank, Coonie	0
Blank, Fred	1
Blank, Matt	3
Blankenship, Cliff	2
Blankenship, Homer	0

Player	WS
Blankenship, Kevin	2
Blankenship, Lance	33
Blankenship, Ted	72
Blanks, Larvell	39
Blanton, Cy	75
Blasingame, Don	140
Blasingame, Wade	27
Blass, Steve	83
Blateric, Steve	0
Blatnik, Johnny	9
Blattner, Buddy	21
Blauvelt, Henry	0
Blaylock, Bob	0
Blaylock, Gary	4
Blaylock, Marv	18
Blazier, Ron	3
Blemker, Ray	0
Blessitt, Ike	0
Blethen, Clarence	0
Blewett, Bob	0
Bligh, Ned	3
Bliss, Elmer	1
Bliss, Frank	0
Bliss, Jack	14
Block, Bruno	15
Block, Cy	3
Blocker, Terry	2
Blogg, Wes	0
Blomberg, Ron	56
Blomdahl, Ben	0
Blong, Joe	21
Bloodworth, Jimmy	64
Bloomfield, Clyde	0
Blosser, Greg	0
Blott, Jack	0
Blowers, Mike	60
Blue, Bert	2
Bluege, Otto	3
Bluejacket, Jim	10
Bluhm, Red	0
Bluma, Jaime	3
Blume, Clint	4
Blyzka, Mike	2
Boak, Chet	0
Boardman, Charlie	2
Bobb, Randy	0
Bocachica, Hiram	3
Boccabella, John	24
Bocek, Milt	1
Bochtler, Doug	14
Bochy, Bruce	22
Bockman, Eddie	10
Bockus, Randy	1
Boeckel, Tony	80
Boehler, George	3
Boehling, Joe	58
Boehmer, Len	1
Boehringer, Brian	21
Boerner, Larry	2
Boever, Joe	49

Player	WS
Bogar, Tim	34
Bogart, John	2
Bogener, Terry	0
Boggs, Ray	0
Boggs, Tommy	23
Bogle, Warren	0
Bohen, Pat	1
Bohn, Charlie	1
Bohne, Sammy	58
Bohnet, John	0
Boisclair, Bruce	21
Boitano, Dan	1
Bokelmann, Dick	3
Boken, Bob	5
Bokina, Joe	0
Boland, Bernie	60
Boland, Ed	1
Bold, Charlie	0
Bolden, Bill	0
Bolen, Stew	1
Boles, Carl	1
Boley, Joe	45
Bolger, Jim	7
Bolick, Frank	3
Bolling, Frank	141
Bolling, Jack	11
Bolling, Milt	25
Bollo, Greg	1
Bollweg, Don	14
Bolton, Cecil	0
Bolton, Cliff	30
Bolton, Rod	0
Bolton, Tom	25
Bomback, Mark	13
Bond, Walt	38
Bone, George	1
Bones, Ricky	56
Bonetti, Julio	6
Boney, Hank	0
Bongiovanni, Nino	3
Bonikowski, Joe	6
Bonilla, Juan	29
Bonin, Luther	1
Bonnell, Barry	70
Bonner, Bobby	2
Bonner, Frank	15
Bonness, Bill	0
Bono, Gus	0
Booe, Everitt	6
Booker, Buddy	0
Booker, Greg	12
Booker, Rod	5
Bool, Al	8
Booles, Red	1
Boone, Dan	6
Boone, Danny	5
Boone, George	0
Boone, Ike	37
Boone, Luke	18
Booth, Amos	6

Player	WS
Booth, Eddie	2
Booty, Josh	1
Boozer, John	14
Borbon, Pedro	17
Borchers, George	2
Bordagaray, F.	66
Borden, Joe	10
Borders, Pat	60
Bordi, Rich	19
Bordley, Bill	0
Borgmann, Glenn	40
Boris, Paul	3
Bork, Frank	2
Borkowski, Bob	18
Borkowski, Dave	1
Borland, Toby	14
Borland, Tom	0
Borom, Red	3
Boros, Steve	34
Borowski, Joe	4
Borton, Babe	33
Bosch, Don	2
Bosetti, Rick	25
Bosio, Chris	98
Boskie, Shawn	29
Bosley, Thad	35
Bosman, Dick	74
Boss, Harley	7
Bosser, Mel	2
Bostick, Henry	0
Bostock, Lyman	73
Boston, Daryl	71
Boswell, Andy	2
Boswell, Dave	61
Boswell, Ken	56
Botelho, Derek	2
Bottarini, John	2
Bottenfield, Kent	49
Botting, Ralph	0
Botz, Bob	4
Bouchee, Ed	71
Boucher, Al	9
Boucher, Denis	4
Boucher, Medric	1
Bouldin, Carl	0
Boultes, Jake	6
Bourgeois, Steve	0
Bourjos, Chris	0
Bournigal, Rafael	15
Bourque, Pat	9
Bouton, Jim	60
Bovee, Mike	0
Bowcock, Benny	2
Bowden, Tim	0
Bowen, Chick	0
Bowen, Cy	0
Bowen, Ryan	10
Bowen, Sam	0
Bowens, Sam	29
Bowerman, Frank	78

Player	WS
Bowers, Billy	1
Bowers, Brent	0
Bowers, Shane	0
Bowers, Stew	2
Bowes, Frank	2
Bowie, Jim	0
Bowie, Micah	0
Bowler, Grant	1
Bowles, Brian	1
Bowles, Charlie	1
Bowles, Emmett	0
Bowlin, Hoss	0
Bowling, Steve	3
Bowman, Abe	1
Bowman, Bill	1
Bowman, Bob	
Debut 1939	25
Debut 1955	12
Bowman, Elmer	0
Bowman, Ernie	2
Bowman, Joe	72
Bowman, Roger	3
Bowman, Sumner	5
Bowser, Red	0
Bowsfield, Ted	31
Boyd, Bob	56
Boyd, Frank	0
Boyd, Gary	0
Boyd, Jake	3
Boyd, Jason	0
Boyd, Oil Can	73
Boyd, Ray	2
Boyer, Cloyd	16
Boyland, Doe	0
Boyle, Buzz	39
Boyle, Eddie	0
Boyle, Jack	
Debut 1886	79
Debut 1912	0
Boyle, Jim	0
Boyles, Harry	0
Boze, Marshall	0
Brabender, Gene	19
Brack, Gibby	28
Bracken, Jack	1
Brackenridge, John	0
Bradey, Don	0
Bradford, Bill	0
Bradford, Buddy	35
Bradford, Chad	8
Bradford, Larry	11
Bradford, Vic	0
Bradley, Al	0
Bradley, Bert	0
Bradley, Foghorn	9
Bradley, Fred	0
Bradley, George	0
Bradley, Herb	2
Bradley, Hugh	16
Bradley, Jack	0

Player	WS
Bradley, Mark	1
Bradley, Milton	6
Bradley, Ryan	1
Bradley, Scott	33
Bradley, Tom	50
Bradshaw, Dallas	0
Bradshaw, George	0
Bradshaw, Joe	0
Bradshaw, Terry	1
Brady, Bill	0
Brady, Bob	0
Brady, Brian	0
Brady, Cliff	2
Brady, Doug	0
Brady, Jim	0
Brady, King	2
Brady, Neal	3
Brady, Steve	48
Bragan, Bobby	25
Bragg, Darren	45
Braggins, Dick	1
Braggs, Glenn	58
Brain, Dave	74
Brainerd, Fred	3
Braithwood, Al	1
Brame, Erv	50
Bramhall, Art	0
Branca, Ralph	88
Brancato, Al	11
Branch, Harvey	0
Branch, Norm	5
Branch, Roy	0
Brand, Ron	21
Brandenburg, Mark	9
Brandom, Chick	7
Brandon, Bucky	26
Brandt, Bill	3
Brannan, Otis	13
Branom, Dud	0
Branson, Jeff	33
Brant, Marshall	0
Brantley, Cliff	3
Brantley, Mickey	23
Brashear, Kitty	0
Brashear, Roy	12
Bratcher, Joe	0
Bratschi, Fred	2
Braun, John	0
Bravo, Angel	3
Braxton, Garland	62
Bray, Buster	0
Brazill, Frank	2
Brazle, Al	115
Brea, Leslie	0
Bream, Sid	90
Breazeale, Jim	3
Breckinridge, Bill	0
Brede, Brent	6
Breeden, Danny	1
Breeden, Hal	16

Player	WS
Breeding, Marv	29
Breining, Fred	25
Breitenstein, Alonzo	0
Bremer, Herb	3
Brenegan, Sam	0
Brennan, Ad	42
Brennan, Bill	1
Brennan, Don	24
Brennan, Jack	10
Brennan, Tom	10
Brenneman, Jim	0
Brenner, Bert	1
Brenton, Lynn	4
Brenzel, Bill	2
Breton, Jim	4
Brett, Herb	1
Breuer, Marv	23
Brewer, Billy	14
Brewer, Jack	9
Brewer, Jim	108
Brewer, Mike	0
Brewer, Rod	7
Brewer, Tony	0
Brewington, Jamie	6
Brewster, Charlie	1
Brice, Alan	0
Brickell, Fritz	1
Brickell, George	26
Brickley, George	0
Brickner, Ralph	4
Brideweser, Jim	15
Bridges, Marshall	27
Bridges, Rocky	43
Bridwell, Al	138
Brief, Bunny	9
Briggs, Buttons	55
Briggs, Charlie	1
Briggs, Dan	5
Briggs, Grant	2
Briggs, John	8
Bright, Harry	17
Briles, Nelson	116
Briley, Greg	28
Brill, Frank	1
Brillheart, Jim	12
Brink, Brad	1
Brinker, Bill	0
Brinkman, Chuck	5
Brinkman, Ed	118
Brinkopf, Leon	0
Briody, Fatty	24
Briscoe, John	6
Brissie, Lou	60
Bristow, George	0
Brito, Bernardo	1
Brito, Jorge	1
Brito, Tilson	6
Brittain, Gus	0
Brittin, Jack	0
Britton, Gil	0

Player	WS
Britton, Jim	11
Brizzolara, Tony	4
Broaca, Johnny	35
Broberg, Pete	25
Brocail, Doug	40
Brock, John	1
Brock, Tarrik	0
Brockett, Lew	15
Broderick, Matt	0
Brodowski, Dick	11
Brogna, Rico	69
Brohamer, Jack	55
Brohawn, Troy	2
Brondell, Ken	0
Bronkey, Jeff	5
Bronkie, Herman	7
Bronstad, Jim	0
Brookens, Ike	0
Brookens, Tom	84
Brooks, Bobby	6
Brooks, Harry	0
Brooks, Jerry	1
Brooks, Mandy	12
Broskie, Sig	1
Brosnan, Jim	80
Bross, Terry	1
Brosseau, Frank	0
Brottem, Tony	1
Broughton, Cal	2
Brouhard, Mark	20
Brouthers, Art	1
Brovia, Joe	0
Brow, Scott	1
Brower, Bob	11
Brower, Frank	44
Brower, Jim	11
Brower, Louis	0
Brown, Adrian	15
Brown, Alton	0
Brown, Bill	0
Brown, Boardwalk	27
Brown, Bob	15
Brown, Bobby	
Debut 1946	55
Debut 1979	30
Brown, Brant	24
Brown, Buster	69
Brown, Charlie	0
Brown, Chris	41
Brown, Curly	3
Brown, Curt	2
Brown, Curtis	0
Brown, Darrell	9
Brown, Dee	4
Brown, Delos	0
Brown, Dick	51
Brown, Drummond	9
Brown, Ed	0
Brown, Eddie	73
Brown, Elmer	8

Player	WS
Brown, Emil	4
Brown, Fred	0
Brown, Gates	70
Brown, Hal	98
Brown, Ike	20
Brown, Jackie	33
Brown, Jake	0
Brown, Jarvis	2
Brown, Jim	
Debut 1884	4
Debut 1915	1
Brown, Jimmy	89
Brown, Joe	
Debut 1884	2
Debut 1927	0
Brown, John	0
Brown, Jophrey	0
Brown, Jumbo	43
Brown, Keith	3
Brown, Kevin	3
Brown, Kevin L.	5
Brown, Leon	1
Brown, Lindsay	1
Brown, Mace	79
Brown, Mark	1
Brown, Marty	0
Brown, Mike	
Debut 1982	7
Debut 1983	19
Brown, Myrl	1
Brown, Norm	1
Brown, Ollie	95
Brown, Oscar	4
Brown, Paul	0
Brown, Randy	1
Brown, Ray	1
Brown, Roosevelt	7
Brown, Sam	4
Brown, Scott	1
Brown, Steve	3
Brown, Stub	4
Brown, Tom	
Debut 1963	0
Debut 1978	1
Brown, Tommy	22
Brown, Walter	1
Brown, Willard	
Debut 1887	34
Debut 1947	0
Browne, Byron	22
Browne, Earl	9
Browne, Jerry	80
Browne, Pidge	1
Browning, Cal	0
Browning, Frank	4
Browning, Tom	99
Brownson, Mark	1
Brubaker, Bill	41
Brubaker, Bruce	0
Bruce, Bob	50

Player	WS
Bruce, Lou	2
Bruckbauer, Fred	0
Brucker, Earle	
Debut 1937	20
Debut 1948	0
Bruckmiller, Andy	0
Bruett, J.T.	1
Bruggy, Frank	13
Bruhert, Mike	0
Brumbaugh, Cliff	0
Brumfield, Jacob	37
Brumley, Duff	0
Brumley, Mike	
Debut 1964	10
Debut 1987	7
Brummer, Glenn	6
Brummett, Greg	2
Bruner, Jack	3
Bruner, Roy	0
Brunet, George	63
Brunette, Justin	0
Bruno, Tom	7
Brunsberg, Arlo	0
Brunson, Will	1
Brush, Bob	0
Bruske, Jim	7
Brusstar, Warren	33
Bruyette, Ed	0
Bryan, Billy	26
Bryant, Clay	38
Bryant, Derek	0
Bryant, Don	2
Bryant, George	0
Bryant, Ralph	5
Bryant, Ron	41
Bryden, T.R.	0
Brye, Steve	44
Brynan, Tod	0
Bubser, Hal	0
Bucha, Johnny	3
Buchanan, Bob	0
Buchanan, Brian	5
Buchanan, Jim	3
Buchek, Jerry	23
Bucher, Jim	32
Buckels, Gary	1
Buckeye, Garland	37
Buckingham, Ed	0
Buckles, Jess	0
Buckley, Dick	40
Buckley, John	0
Buckley, Kevin	0
Budaska, Mark	0
Budd	0
Buddie, Mike	4
Buddin, Don	68
Budnick, Mike	6
Buechele, Steve	116
Buelow, Charlie	1
Buelow, Fritz	16

Player	WS
Bues, Art	1
Buice, DeWayne	13
Buker, Cy	7
Buker, Harry	1
Bullard, George	0
Bullas, Sim	0
Bullett, Scott	5
Bulling, Terry	7
Bullinger, Jim	21
Bullinger, Kirk	0
Bullock, Eric	2
Bullock, Red	0
Bunce, Josh	0
Bunch, Mel	1
Bunker, Wally	57
Burbach, Bill	6
Burbrink, Nels	3
Burch, Al	51
Burch, Ernie	21
Burchart, Larry	0
Burchell, Fred	11
Burda, Bob	10
Burdette, Freddie	3
Burdick, Bill	11
Burg, Pete	1
Burgess, Tom	3
Burgmeier, Tom	110
Burgo, Bill	6
Burgos, Enrique	0
Burich, Bill	1
Burk, Mack	0
Burk, Sandy	7
Burkam, Bob	0
Burkart, Elmer	2
Burke, Billy	3
Burke, Bobby	52
Burke, Dan	2
Burke, Frank	1
Burke, Glenn	5
Burke, Jamie	0
Burke, Jimmy	40
Burke, Joe	1
Burke, John	
Debut 1902	0
Debut 1996	2
Burke, Leo	7
Burke, Les	9
Burke, Mike	1
Burke, Pat	0
Burke, Steve	4
Burke, Tim	86
Burke, Walter	24
Burkhart, Ken	35
Burkhart, Morgan	2
Burnett, Hercules	1
Burnett, Jack	5
Burnett, Johnny	45
Burnette, Wally	17
Burns, Bill	37
Burns, Britt	71

Player	WS
Burns, C.B.	0
Burns, Dennis	9
Burns, Dick	44
Burns, Ed	23
Burns, Farmer	0
Burns, Jack	
Debut 1903	1
Debut 1930	63
Burns, Jim	21
Burns, Joe	
Debut 1910	1
Debut 1924	0
Debut 1943	2
Burns, Pat	1
Burns, Todd	31
Burnside, Pete	18
Burnside, Sheldon	1
Burpo, George	0
Burr, Alex	0
Burrell, Buster	8
Burrell, Harry	2
Burright, Larry	6
Burris, Al	0
Burris, Paul	2
Burris, Ray	98
Burrows, John	2
Burrows, Terry	2
Burrus, Dick	42
Burt, Frank	0
Burton, Ellis	11
Burton, Jim	3
Burtschy, Moe	10
Burtt, Dennis	2
Burwell, Bill	12
Burwell, Dick	0
Busby, Mike	3
Busby, Paul	0
Busby, Steve	70
Busch, Ed	15
Busch, Mike	2
Buschhorn, Don	1
Bush, Randy	76
Bushelman, Jack	0
Bushey, Frank	0
Bushing, Chris	0
Bushong, Doc	56
Buskey, Joe	0
Buskey, Mike	0
Buskey, Tom	34
Busse, Ray	1
Butcher, Hank	4
Butcher, John	42
Butcher, Max	102
Butcher, Mike	11
Butera, Sal	15
Butka, Ed	0
Butland, Bill	12
Butler, Adam	0
Butler, Art	29

Player	WS
Butler, Bill	
Debut 1884	1
Debut 1969	21
Butler, Brent	1
Butler, Cecil	3
Butler, Charlie	0
Butler, Dick	1
Butler, Frank	0
Butler, Ike	0
Butler, John	1
Butler, Johnny	29
Butler, Kid	
Debut 1884	3
Debut 1907	1
Butler, Rich	3
Butler, Rob	4
Butters, Tom	6
Buxton, Ralph	1
Buzas, Joe	1
Buzhardt, John	69
Byerly, Bud	29
Byers, Bill	0
Byers, Burley	0
Byers, Randy	0
Byrd, Harry	42
Byrd, Jeff	0
Byrd, Jim	0
Byrd, Paul	29
Byrd, Sammy	47
Byrdak, Tim	0
Byrne, Jerry	0
Byrne, Tommy	81
Byrnes, Eric	1
Byrnes, Jim	0
Byrnes, Milt	52
Bystrom, Marty	15

C

Player	WS
Caballero, Putsy	7
Cabell, Enos	129
Cabrera, Al	0
Cabrera, Alex	1
Cabrera, Francisco	8
Cabrera, Jolbert	8
Cabrera, Jose	16
Cacek, Craig	0
Caceres, Edgar	2
Cadaret, Greg	43
Cadore, Leon	87
Cady, Charlie	2
Cady, Hick	31
Cafego, Tom	0
Caffie, Joe	4
Caffyn, Ben	1
Cage, Wayne	3
Cahill, John	7
Cahill, Tom	13

Player	WS
Cain, Bob	32
Cain, Les	16
Cain, Sugar	50
Cairncross, Cam	1
Caithamer, George	1
Calderon, Ivan	104
Calderone, Sam	4
Caldwell, Bruce	0
Caldwell, Charlie	0
Caldwell, Earl	39
Caldwell, Ralph	2
Calhoun, Bill	0
Calhoun, Jack	1
Calhoun, Jeff	13
Caligiuri, Fred	3
Callaghan, Marty	14
Callahan, Ben	0
Callahan, Dave	0
Callahan, Ed	2
Callahan, Jim	
Debut 1898	0
Debut 1902	0
Callahan, Joe	1
Callahan, Leo	5
Callahan, Pat	5
Callahan, Ray	0
Callahan, Wesley	1
Callahan, Will	19
Callaway, Frank	0
Callaway, Mickey	0
Calmus, Dick	3
Calvert, Mark	0
Calvert, Paul	4
Calvo, Jack	1
Camacho, Ernie	24
Cambria, Fred	2
Camelli, Hank	9
Cameron, Jack	0
Camilli, Doug	15
Camilli, Lou	1
Cammack, Eric	0
Camnitz, Harry	1
Camnitz, Howie	133
Camp, Howie	0
Camp, Kid	1
Camp, Lew	8
Camp, Rick	77
Campanis, Al	0
Campanis, Jim	2
Campau, Count	16
Campbell, Archie	3
Campbell, Billy	18
Campbell, Dave	
Debut 1967	21
Debut 1977	14
Campbell, Gilly	24
Campbell, Jim	
Debut 1962	4
Debut 1970	0
Debut 1990	0

Player	WS
Campbell, Joe	0
Campbell, John	0
Campbell, Kevin	7
Campbell, Marc	0
Campbell, Mike	5
Campbell, Paul	8
Campbell, Ron	2
Campbell, Sam	0
Campbell, Soup	5
Campbell, Vin	65
Camper, Cardell	1
Campfield, Sal	2
Campisi, Sal	6
Campos, Frank	3
Campusano, Sil	3
Canale, George	2
Canate, Willie	0
Canavan, Hugh	0
Canavan, Jim	37
Cancel, Robinson	0
Candaele, Casey	48
Candini, Milo	29
Caneira, John	1
Cangelosi, John	54
Canizaro, Jay	10
Cannell, Rip	13
Cannizzaro, Chris	42
Cannon, Joe	1
Cano, Jose	0
Canseco, Ozzie	1
Cantrell, Guy	4
Cantwell, Mike	0
Cantwell, Tom	2
Cantz, Bart	2
Capel, Mike	3
Capilla, Doug	12
Cappuzzello, G.	3
Capra, Buzz	32
Capra, Nick	1
Capri, Pat	0
Capron, Ralph	0
Caraballo, Ramon	1
Caraway, Pat	17
Carbine, John	0
Carden, John	0
Cardinal, Conrad	0
Cardona, Javier	2
Cardoni, Ben	2
Carey, Andy	87
Carey, Paul	0
Carey, Roger	0
Carey, Scoops	17
Carey, Tom	17
Cargo, Bobby	0
Carisch, Fred	16
Carl, Fred	1
Carlin, Jim	0
Carlisle, Walter	0
Carlos, Cisco	8
Carlsen, Don	2
Carlson, Dan	1
Carlson, Leon	1
Carlstrom, Swede	0
Carlyle, Buddy	0
Carlyle, Cleo	4
Carlyle, Roy	12
Carman, Don	44
Carman, George	0
Carmel, Duke	6
Carmichael, Chet	0
Carmona, Rafael	7
Carnett, Eddie	14
Carney, Bill	0
Carney, John	19
Carney, Pat	27
Carpenter, Bob	23
Carpenter, Bubba	1
Carpenter, Cris	26
Carpenter, Lew	0
Carpenter, Paul	0
Carpin, Frank	3
Carr, Charlie	31
Carr, Chuck	36
Carr, Lew	1
Carrara, Giovanni	8
Carrasquel, Alex	46
Carreno, Amalio	0
Carreon, Cam	32
Carreon, Mark	56
Carrick, Bill	57
Carrigan, Bill	71
Carrillo, Matias	1
Carrithers, Don	21
Carroll, Chick	0
Carroll, Cliff	109
Carroll, Dick	0
Carroll, Dixie	2
Carroll, Doc	0
Carroll, Ed	1
Carroll, Ownie	54
Carroll, Pat	0
Carroll, Scrappy	0
Carroll, Tom	
Debut 1955	1
Debut 1974	4
Carson, Al	0
Carson, Kit	1
Carswell, Frank	0
Carter, Andy	1
Carter, Arnold	19
Carter, Blackie	0
Carter, Howie	0
Carter, Jeff	0
Carter, Lance	0
Carter, Larry	0
Carter, Nick	2
Carter, Paul	20
Carter, Sol	0
Carter, Steve	0
Cartwright, Ed	44
Caruso, Mike	18
Cary, Chuck	18
Cary, Scott	0
Casale, Jerry	14
Casanova, Paul	46
Cascarella, Joe	25
Case, Charlie	26
Casey, Bill	0
Casey, Bob	1
Casey, Dennis	14
Casey, Hugh	81
Casey, Joe	1
Cash, Ron	2
Cashion, Carl	15
Casian, Larry	17
Casimiro, Carlos	0
Caskey, Craig	0
Caskin, Ed	37
Cassady, Harry	0
Cassian, Ed	3
Cassidy, Joe	21
Cassidy, John	51
Cassidy, Pete	7
Cassini, Jack	0
Castellano, Pedro	0
Caster, George	73
Castiglia, Jim	1
Castiglione, Pete	28
Castillo, Alberto	19
Castillo, Bobby	39
Castillo, Braulio	1
Castillo, Carlos	10
Castillo, Carmen	29
Castillo, Juan	
Debut 1986	8
Debut 1994	0
Castillo, Manny	5
Castillo, Marty	7
Castillo, Tony	
Debut 1978	0
Debut 1988	40
Castino, John	70
Castino, Vince	4
Castle, Don	0
Castle, John	0
Castleman, Foster	10
Castleman, Slick	28
Castleton, Roy	3
Castner, Paul	0
Castro, Bill	44
Castro, Juan	10
Castro, Louis	1
Castro, Ramon	4
Cater, Danny	111
Cates, Eli	5
Cather, Mike	6
Cather, Ted	11
Cathey, Hardin	0
Cato, Keefe	1
Caton, Howdy	17
Cattanach, John	1
Catterson, Tom	1
Caudill, Bill	64
Caulfield, Jake	1
Causey, Red	29
Cavanaugh, John	0
Caveney, Ike	36
Cavet, Pug	12
Ceccarelli, Art	6
Cecena, Jose	1
Cecil, Rex	0
Cedeno, Andujar	42
Cedeno, Domingo	22
Center, Pete	6
Cermak, Ed	0
Cerone, Rick	91
Cerutti, John	45
Cerv, Bob	82
Chacon, Elio	11
Chacon, Shawn	7
Chadbourne, Chet	42
Chadwick, Ray	0
Chagnon, Leon	19
Chakales, Bob	21
Chalk, Dave	66
Chalmers, George	30
Chamberlain, Bill	1
Chamberlain, Craig	5
Chamberlain, Joe	1
Chamberlain, Wes	30
Chambers, Al	1
Chambers, Bill	0
Chambers, Cliff	49
Chambers, John	0
Chambers, Rome	0
Champion, Billy	22
Champion, Mike	3
Chance, Bob	22
Chandler, Ed	0
Chaney, Darrel	42
Chaney, Esty	0
Channell, Les	1
Chant, Charlie	0
Chapin, Darrin	0
Chaplin, Ed	2
Chaplin, Tiny	15
Chapman, Calvin	5
Chapman, Ed	0
Chapman, Fred	
Debut 1887	0
Debut 1939	2
Chapman, Glenn	2
Chapman, Harry	5
Chapman, Jack	0
Chapman, John	2
Chapman, Kelvin	11
Chappas, Harry	4
Chappell, Larry	5
Chappelle, Bill	9
Charboneau, Joe	17
Charles, Chappy	9
Charles, Frank	1
Charlton, Norm	79
Chartak, Mike	23
Charton, Pete	1
Chase, Ken	56
Chatham, Buster	11
Chatterton, Jim	0
Chavarria, Ossie	5
Chavez, Endy	0
Chavez, Nestor	1
Chavez, Raul	0
Chavez, Tony	1
Cheadle, Dave	0
Chech, Charlie	35
Checo, Robinson	1
Cheek, Harry	0
Cheeves, Virgil	20
Chelini, Italo	5
Cheney, Tom	27
Chervinko, Paul	0
Chesnes, Bob	20
Chetkovich, Mitch	0
Chevez, Tony	0
Chiamparino, Scott	5
Chiasson, Scott	1
Chiffer, Floyd	6
Child, Harry	0
Childers	0
Childress, Rocky	4
Childs, Pete	9
Chiles, Pearce	13
Chiles, Rich	8
Chiozza, Dino	0
Chiozza, Lou	41
Chipman, Bob	49
Chipple, Walt	1
Chism, Tom	0
Chiti, Harry	32
Chitren, Steve	4
Chittum, Nels	4
Chlupsa, Bob	0
Cho, Jin Ho	1
Choate, Don	0
Choate, Randy	5
Chouinard, Bobby	12
Chouinard, Felix	6
Chouneau, Chief	0
Chozen, Harry	0
Chris, Mike	0
Chrisley, Neil	6
Christenbury, Lloyd	11
Christensen, Bruce	1
Christensen, Cuckoo	19
Christensen, John	6
Christensen, McKay	3
Christenson, Gary	2
Christenson, Larry	77
Christenson, Ryan	15

Player	WS
Christian, Bob	1
Christiansen, Clay	0
Christiansen, Jason	29
Christman, Mark	65
Christman, Tim	0
Christmas, Steve	1
Christopher, Joe	39
Christopher, Loyd	0
Christopher, Mike	8
Christopher, Russ	70
Church, Bubba	42
Church, Hi	0
Church, Len	0
Churn, Chuck	2
Churry, John	0
Ciaffone, Larry	0
Cianfrocco, Archi	26
Ciardi, Mark	0
Cias, Darryl	1
Cicero, Joe	1
Cicotte, Al	10
Cieslak, Ted	3
Cihocki, Al	4
Cihocki, Ed	1
Cimino, Pete	10
Cimoli, Gino	63
Cimorelli, Frank	0
Cintron, Alex	0
Ciola, Lou	0
Cipriani, Frank	0
Cisar, George	0
Cisco, Galen	19
Cissell, Bill	68
Citarella, Ralph	2
Clabaugh, Moose	0
Clack, Bobby	0
Claire, Danny	0
Clancy, Al	0
Clancy, Bill	2
Clancy, Bud	30
Clanton, Uke	0
Clapinski, Chris	3
Clapp, Aaron	4
Clapp, Stubby	0
Clarey, Doug	0
Clark, Allie	21
Clark, Bill	0
Clark, Bob	
Debut 1886	26
Debut 1920	3
Clark, Bobby	13
Clark, Brady	4
Clark, Bryan	25
Clark, Cap	1
Clark, Dad	0
Clark, Danny	16
Clark, Dave	45
Clark, Earl	17
Clark, Ed	0
Clark, George	0
Clark, Ginger	0
Clark, Glen	0
Clark, Jerald	33
Clark, Jermaine	0
Clark, Jim	
Debut 1911	0
Debut 1948	0
Debut 1971	0
Clark, Mark	54
Clark, Mel	13
Clark, Mike	1
Clark, Otie	5
Clark, Pep	3
Clark, Phil	
Debut 1958	0
Debut 1992	11
Clark, Rickey	16
Clark, Ron	5
Clark, Roy	0
Clark, Spider	7
Clark, Terry	8
Clark, Willie	36
Clarke, Artie	10
Clarke, Boileryard	63
Clarke, Dad	51
Clarke, Grey	5
Clarke, Harry	0
Clarke, Henry	2
Clarke, Horace	127
Clarke, Josh	31
Clarke, Lefty	0
Clarke, Nig	50
Clarke, Rufe	0
Clarke, Stan	2
Clarke, Stu	6
Clarke, Sumpter	0
Clarke, Tommy	64
Clarke, Webbo	1
Clarkson, Bill	3
Clarkson, Buzz	0
Clarkson, Dad	38
Clarkson, Walter	19
Clary, Ellis	22
Clary, Marty	7
Claset, Gowell	0
Clausen, Fritz	17
Clauss, Al	0
Clay, Bill	0
Clay, Dain	34
Clay, Danny	0
Clay, Ken	8
Clear, Mark	70
Cleary, Joe	0
Clemens, Bob	0
Clemens, Chet	0
Clemens, Clem	0
Clemens, Doug	17
Clemensen, Bill	1
Clement, Matt	16
Clement, Wally	6
Clemente, Edgard	2
Clements, Ed	0
Clements, Pat	24
Clemons, Chris	0
Clemons, Lance	1
Clemons, Verne	44
Cleveland, Elmer	12
Clevenger, Tex	39
Cliburn, Stan	1
Cliburn, Stew	17
Clifton, Flea	1
Cline, Monk	29
Cline, Ty	35
Clines, Gene	50
Clingman, Billy	74
Clinton, Jim	41
Clinton, Lu	56
Cloninger, Tony	73
Clontz, Brad	21
Closter, Al	0
Cloude, Ken	4
Clough, Ed	0
Clowers, Bill	0
Clutterbuck, Bryan	4
Clyburn, Danny	0
Clyde, David	11
Clyde, Tom	0
Clymer, Bill	0
Clymer, Otis	39
Coachman, Pete	2
Coakley, Andy	64
Coan, Gil	64
Coates, Jim	35
Cobb, George	7
Cobb, Herb	0
Cobb, Joe	0
Coble, Dave	0
Cocanower, Jamie	15
Cochran, George	1
Cochran, Goat	0
Cochrane, Dave	6
Cockman, Jim	0
Cockrell, Alan	0
Coco, Pasqual	1
Cocreham, Gene	0
Codiroli, Chris	18
Coffey, Jack	4
Coffie, Ivanon	1
Coffman, Dick	77
Coffman, Kevin	1
Coffman, Slick	13
Cogan, Dick	2
Cogan, Tony	0
Coggin, Dave	6
Coggins, Frank	4
Coggins, Rich	29
Cogswell, Ed	16
Cohen, Alta	0
Cohen, Andy	23
Cohen, Hy	0
Cohen, Syd	5
Coker, Jimmie	14
Colangelo, Mike	1
Colbern, Mike	4
Colbert, Craig	3
Colbert, Vince	8
Colcolough, Tom	14
Cole, Alex	45
Cole, Bert	26
Cole, Dave	7
Cole, Dick	19
Cole, Ed	3
Cole, King	52
Cole, Stu	0
Cole, Victor	0
Cole, Willis	6
Coleman, Bob	7
Coleman, Choo Choo	5
Coleman, Curt	1
Coleman, Dave	0
Coleman, Ed	34
Coleman, Gordy	71
Coleman, Jerry	66
Coleman, Joe	57
Coleman, John	
Debut 1883	73
Debut 1890	0
Debut 1895	0
Coleman, Michael	0
Coleman, Percy	0
Coleman, Ray	31
Coleman, Rip	7
Coles, Cad	2
Coles, Chuck	0
Coles, Darnell	60
Coletta, Chris	1
Colgan, Ed	2
Collamore, Allan	8
Collard, Hap	5
Collier, Lou	15
Collier, Orlin	0
Colliflower, Harry	0
Collins, Bill	
Debut 1889	0
Debut 1910	11
Collins, Chub	4
Collins, Dan	0
Collins, Don	3
Collins, Eddie	3
Collins, Hub	106
Collins, Hugh	0
Collins, Kevin	4
Collins, Orth	1
Collins, Pat	48
Collins, Phil	77
Collins, Rip	1
Collins, Wilson	1
Collins, Zip	19
Collins	0
Collum, Jackie	32
Collver, Bill	0
Colman, Frank	11
Colome, Jesus	4
Colon, Cris	0
Colpaert, Dick	0
Colson, Loyd	0
Colton, Larry	0
Coluccio, Bob	25
Combe, Geoff	0
Combs, Merrill	7
Combs, Pat	13
Comellas, Jorge	0
Comer, Steve	38
Comer, Wayne	18
Command, Jim	0
Comorosky, Adam	66
Compton, Clint	0
Compton, Jack	1
Compton, Mike	2
Compton, Pete	14
Comstock, Keith	11
Comstock, Ralph	8
Conatser, Clint	10
Concepcion, Onix	19
Conde, Ramon	0
Cone, Bob	0
Congalton, Bunk	32
Conger, Dick	2
Conigliaro, Billy	32
Conkwright, Allen	0
Conlan, Jocko	5
Conley, Bob	0
Conley, Ed	4
Conley, Gene	89
Conley, Snipe	12
Conlon, Jocko	1
Conn, Bert	0
Connally, Fritz	3
Connally, Red	0
Connally, Sarge	58
Connatser, Bruce	1
Connaughton, F.	12
Connell, Gene	0
Connell, Joe	0
Connell, Pete	0
Connelly, Bill	3
Connelly, Steve	0
Connelly, Tom	0
Connolly, Bud	2
Connolly, Ed	
Debut 1929	3
Debut 1964	2
Connolly, Joe	
Debut 1913	63
Debut 1921	4
Connolly, Tom	1
Connor, Jim	18
Connor, Joe	3
Connor, John	3

Player	WS
Connors, Billy	0
Connors, Chuck	2
Connors, Jerry	0
Connors, Joe	0
Connors, Merv	5
Conover, Ted	0
Conroy, Ben	4
Conroy, Bill	
Debut 1923	0
Debut 1935	10
Conroy, Tim	8
Consolo, Billy	22
Constable, Jim	6
Consuegra, Sandy	66
Conti, Jason	3
Contreras, Nardi	0
Converse, Jim	1
Conway, Bill	1
Conway, Charlie	0
Conway, Dick	16
Conway, Jack	4
Conway, Jerry	0
Conway, Jim	22
Conway, Owen	0
Conway, Pete	54
Conway, Rip	0
Conwell, Ed	0
Conyers, Herb	0
Conzelman, Joe	9
Coogan, Dale	1
Coogan, Dan	0
Cook, Andy	0
Cook, Cliff	5
Cook, Dennis	71
Cook, Doc	30
Cook, Earl	0
Cook, Glen	0
Cook, Jim	0
Cook, Mike	3
Cook, Paul	15
Cook, Rollin	0
Cook, Ron	6
Cooke, Dusty	53
Cooke, Fred	0
Cooke, Steve	26
Cookson, Brent	0
Coolbaugh, Mike	0
Coolbaugh, Scott	6
Cooley, Duff	144
Coombs, Bobby	0
Coombs, Cecil	0
Coombs, Danny	16
Coon, William	1
Cooney, Bill	1
Cooney, Bob	3
Cooney, Jimmy	
Debut 1890	38
Debut 1917	34
Cooney, Johnny	127
Cooney, Phil	0
Cooper, Brian	5
Cooper, Cal	0
Cooper, Claude	32
Cooper, Don	2
Cooper, Gary	
Debut 1980	0
Debut 1991	1
Cooper, Guy	0
Cooper, Pat	0
Cooper, Scott	40
Copeland, Mays	0
Coppinger, Rocky	11
Coppola, Henry	2
Coquillette, Trace	1
Corbett, Doug	59
Corbett, Gene	0
Corbett, Joe	29
Corbett, Sherman	2
Corbin, Archie	3
Corbin, Ray	33
Corbitt, Claude	11
Corcoran, Art	0
Corcoran, Jack	3
Corcoran, John	0
Corcoran, Mickey	1
Corcoran, Mike	0
Corcoran, Tim	24
Cordero, Francisco	5
Cordova, Francisco	48
Corey, Bryan	0
Corey, Ed	0
Corey, Fred	70
Corey, Mark	0
Corey, Mark M.	1
Corgan, Chuck	1
Corhan, Roy	7
Corkins, Mike	19
Cormier, Rheal	46
Cornejo, Mardie	4
Cornejo, Nate	0
Cornelius, Reid	7
Cornell, Jeff	0
Cornett, Brad	0
Cornutt, Terry	2
Corrales, Pat	17
Correa, Edwin	10
Correia, Rod	4
Correll, Vic	28
Corridan, Phil	0
Corriden, John	0
Corriden, Red	11
Corridon, Frank	70
Corsi, Jim	40
Cort, Barry	2
Cortazzo, Jess	0
Cortes, David	0
Corwin, Al	17
Coscarart, Joe	7
Coscarart, Pete	68
Cosey, Ray	0
Cosgrove, Mike	13
Cosman, Jim	4
Costello, Dan	5
Costello, John	14
Costo, Tim	1
Cota, Humberto	0
Cote, Henry	2
Cote, Pete	0
Cotter, Dan	0
Cotter, Dick	3
Cotter, Ed	0
Cotter, Hooks	8
Cotter, Tom	0
Cottier, Chuck	27
Cotto, Henry	46
Cottrell, Ensign	0
Couch, Johnny	28
Couchee, Mike	0
Coughlin, Ed	0
Coughlin, Roscoe	8
Coughtry, Marlan	0
Coulson, Bob	12
Coulter, Chip	1
Coumbe, Fritz	49
Courtney, Clint	76
Courtney, Ernie	51
Courtney, Henry	13
Courtright, John	0
Cousineau, Dee	0
Coveney, Jack	0
Covington, Chet	1
Covington, Sam	1
Covington, Tex	9
Covington, Wes	104
Cowan, Billy	24
Cowley, Joe	26
Cox, Bill	2
Cox, Billy	90
Cox, Bobby	16
Cox, Casey	32
Cox, Danny	71
Cox, Darron	0
Cox, Dick	27
Cox, Ernie	0
Cox, Frank	1
Cox, George	1
Cox, Glenn	1
Cox, Jeff	1
Cox, Jim	4
Cox, Larry	14
Cox, Les	0
Cox, Red	0
Cox, Ted	10
Cox, Terry	0
Coyle, Bill	0
Coyne, Toots	0
Cozart, Charlie	0
Crabb, Roy	3
Crable, George	0
Crabtree, Estel	40
Crabtree, Tim	29
Craddock, Walt	0
Cradle, Rickey	0
Craft, Harry	59
Craft, Molly	2
Craghead, Howard	0
Craig, George	0
Craig, Pete	0
Craig, Rodney	4
Craig, Roger	83
Cram, Gerald	4
Cramer, Bill	0
Cramer, Dick	0
Crane, Ed	108
Crane, Sam	
Debut 1880	19
Debut 1914	5
Craver, Bill	8
Crawford, Carlos	0
Crawford, Forrest	1
Crawford, George	0
Crawford, Glenn	11
Crawford, Jake	0
Crawford, Jim	16
Crawford, Joe	3
Crawford, Ken	0
Crawford, Larry	0
Crawford, Pat	14
Crawford, Paxton	4
Crawford, Steve	31
Creamer, George	23
Crede, Joe	1
Creeden, Connie	0
Creeden, Pat	0
Creegan, Marty	0
Creek, Doug	8
Creel, Jack	4
Creel, Keith	2
Creely, Gus	0
Cregan, Pete	0
Creger, Bernie	0
Cremins, Bob	0
Crespi, Creepy	23
Crespo, Cesar	3
Crespo, Felipe	10
Cress, Walker	3
Cressend, Jack	6
Crews, Tim	25
Crider, Jerry	5
Criger, Lou	92
Crim, Chuck	50
Crimian, Jack	4
Cripe, Dave	0
Criscione, Dave	1
Criscola, Tony	6
Crisham, Pat	2
Crisp, Joe	0
Criss, Dode	14
Crist, Ches	0
Cristall, Bill	2
Cristante, Leo	3
Critchley, Morrie	2
Crocker, Claude	0
Crockett, Davey	2
Croft, Art	4
Croft, Harry	0
Crolius, Fred	3
Cromartie, Warren	111
Cromer, D.T.	4
Cromer, Tripp	10
Crompton, Herb	1
Crompton, Ned	0
Cron, Chris	0
Crone, Ray	24
Cronin, Bill	3
Cronin, Dan	0
Cronin, Jack	51
Cronin, Jim	1
Crooke, Tom	1
Crosby, Ed	10
Crosby, George	2
Crosby, Ken	1
Cross, Amos	13
Cross, Clarence	2
Cross, Frank	0
Cross, Jeff	3
Cross, Lem	1
Crossin, Frank	1
Crothers, Doug	2
Crotty, Joe	5
Crouch, Bill	
Debut 1910	0
Debut 1939	13
Crouch, Jack	0
Crouch, Zach	0
Croucher, Frank	12
Crouse, Buck	30
Croushore, Rick	9
Crow, Dean	3
Crow, Don	0
Crowe, George	52
Crowell, Billy	11
Crowell, Cap	0
Crowell, Jim	0
Crowley, Bill	53
Crowley, Ed	0
Crowley, John	5
Crowley, Terry	39
Crowson, Woody	0
Cruise, Walton	77
Crum, Cal	0
Crumling, Gene	0
Crump, Buddy	0
Crumpler, Roy	1
Crutcher, Dick	6
Cruthers, Press	0
Cruz, Fausto	2
Cruz, Heity	29
Cruz, Henry	6
Cruz, Ivan	0

Player	WS
Cruz, Jacob	7
Cruz, Juan	4
Cruz, Julio	98
Cruz, Todd	20
Cruz, Tommy	0
Cruz, Victor	33
Cubbage, Mike	51
Cubillan, Darwin	2
Cuccinello, Al	3
Cuccurullo, Cookie	7
Cuddyer, Mike	0
Cudworth, Jim	0
Cuellar, Bobby	1
Cuellar, Charlie	0
Cueto, Bert	0
Cueto, Manuel	11
Cuff, John	0
Culberson, Leon	34
Cullen, Jack	6
Cullen, John	0
Cullen, Tim	34
Culler, Dick	30
Cullop, Nick	
Debut 1913	63
Debut 1926	10
Culloton, Bud	2
Culmer, Wil	0
Culp, Benny	0
Culp, Bill	0
Culp, Ray	98
Culver, George	43
Cumberland, John	18
Cummings, Candy	24
Cummings, Jack	6
Cummings, John	7
Cummings, Midre	19
Cummings, Steve	2
Cunnane, Will	6
Cunningham, Bill	
Debut 1910	6
Debut 1921	23
Cunningham, Bruce	18
Cunningham, G.	21
Cunningham, Joe	131
Cunningham, Mike	1
Cunningham, Ray	0
Curley, Doc	0
Curran, Sammy	1
Curren, Pete	0
Currence, Lafayette	0
Currie, Bill	0
Currie, Clarence	15
Currie, Murphy	1
Currin, Perry	0
Curry, George	0
Curry, Jim	0
Curry, Steve	0
Curry, Tony	5
Curry, Wes	0
Curtis, Cliff	35

Player	WS
Curtis, Fred	0
Curtis, Gene	1
Curtis, Harry	0
Curtis, Jack	11
Curtis, Jim	5
Curtis, John	76
Curtis, Vern	1
Curtright, Guy	40
Cushman, Ed	64
Cushman, Harvey	0
Cusick, Jack	3
Cusick, Tony	4
Cust, Jack	0
Cuthbert, Ned	18
Cuyler, Milt	21
Cvengros, Mike	25
Cypert, Al	0
Czajkowski, Jim	1

D

Player	WS
D'Acquisto, John	31
Dade, Paul	29
Dagenhard, John	2
Daglia, Pete	1
Dagres, Angelo	0
Dahl, Jay	0
Dahlgren, Babe	89
Dahlke, Jerry	0
Dailey, Bill	22
Dailey, Sam	0
Dailey, Vince	7
Daily, Con	56
Daisey, George	0
Dal Canton, Bruce	56
Dale, Carl	0
Dale, Gene	20
Dalena, Pete	0
Dalesandro, Mark	2
Daley, Bill	29
Daley, Bud	48
Daley, John	1
Daley, Jud	5
Daley, Pete	21
Daley, Tom	15
Dallessandro, Dom	59
Dalrymple, Bill	0
Dalton, Jack	41
Dalton, Mike	0
Daly, Bert	0
Daly, George	0
Daly, Joe	2
Daly, Sun	0
Daly, Tom	9
Dam, Bill	0
Damaska, Jack	0
D'Amico, Jeff M.	0
Dammann, Bill	26

Player	WS
Damrau, Harry	0
Daneker, Pat	1
Daney, Art	0
Danforth, Dave	67
Daniel, Chuck	0
Daniel, Jake	0
Daniels, Bennie	37
Daniels, Bert	58
Daniels, Charlie	1
Daniels, Jack	2
Daniels, Kal	112
Daniels, Law	6
Daniels, Pete	3
Daniels, Tony	1
Danner, Buck	0
Danning, Harry	111
Danning, Ike	1
Dantonio, Fats	2
Danzig, Babe	0
Dapper, Cliff	2
Darby, George	0
Darcy, Pat	8
Darensbourg, Vic	11
Daringer, Cliff	4
Daringer, Rolla	1
Darling, Dell	17
Darnell, Bob	1
Darr, Mike	0
Darragh, Jack	0
Darrow, George	1
Darwin, Bobby	54
Darwin, Jeff	3
Dascenzo, Doug	19
Dashiell, Wally	0
Dashner, Lee	0
Dasso, Frank	5
Datz, Jeff	0
Daub, Dan	48
Daubert, Harry	0
Dauer, Rich	89
Daugherty, Doc	0
Daugherty, Jack	16
Daughters, Bob	0
Davalillo, Yo-Yo	1
DaVanon, Jeff	1
DaVanon, Jerry	16
Davenport, Claude	0
Davenport, Joe	1
Davenport, Lum	1
Davey, Mike	1
Davey, Tom	7
Daviault, Ray	0
David, Andre	1
Davidson, Bill	9
Davidson, Bob	0
Davidson, Claude	0
Davidson, Cleatus	0
Davidson, Homer	0
Davidson, Mark	10
Davidson, Ted	13

Player	WS
Davie, Jerry	2
Davies, Chick	6
Davies, George	25
Davis, Bill	0
Davis, Bob	
Debut 1958	2
Debut 1973	9
Davis, Brandy	0
Davis, Brock	12
Davis, Bud	2
Davis, Butch	11
Davis, Crash	4
Davis, Daisy	17
Davis, Dick	19
Davis, Doug	0
Davis, Gerry	2
Davis, Harry	19
Davis, Ike	13
Davis, Ira	0
Davis, Iron	4
Davis, Jacke	0
Davis, Jim	23
Davis, Joel	9
Davis, John	
Debut 1941	1
Debut 1987	6
Davis, Jumbo	54
Davis, Kane	5
Davis, Kiddo	51
Davis, Lance	5
Davis, Lefty	42
Davis, Mark	
Debut 1980	72
Debut 1991	0
Davis, Odie	0
Davis, Otis	0
Davis, Peaches	25
Davis, Ron	
Debut 1962	17
Debut 1978	70
Davis, Russ	39
Davis, Steve	
Debut 1979	0
Debut 1985	2
Davis, Tim	7
Davis, Tod	2
Davis, Tommy	0
Davis, Trench	0
Davis, Wiley	0
Davis, Woody	1
Davison, Mike	0
Davison, Scott	0
Dawkins, Gookie	1
Dawley, Bill	38
Dawson, Joe	14
Dawson, Rex	0
Day, Bill	1
Day, Boots	25
Day, Pea Ridge	2
Dayett, Brian	10

Player	WS
Dayley, Ken	46
Deagle, Ren	16
Deal, Charlie	77
Deal, Cot	1
Deal, Lindsay	0
Deal, Snake	1
Dealy, Pat	10
Dean, Chubby	35
Dean, Dory	3
Dean, Harry	0
Dean, Paul	56
Dean, Tommy	5
Dean, Wayland	20
Dear, Buddy	0
DeArmond, Charlie	1
Deasley, John	3
Deasley, Pat	39
DeBarr, Denny	0
DeBerry, Hank	59
DeBerry, Joe	2
DeBus, Adam	2
DeBusschere, Dave	5
Decatur, Art	27
Decker, Frank	0
Decker, George	47
Decker, Harry	10
Decker, Joe	35
Decker, Marty	1
Decker, Steve	15
Dede, Artie	0
Dedeaux, Rod	0
Dedmon, Jeff	26
Dedrick, Jim	1
Dee, Jim	0
Dee, Shorty	0
Deegan, Dummy	0
Deer, Rob	118
Deering, John	4
Dees, Charlie	7
DeFate, Tony	0
DeFreites, Arturo	0
DeGerick, Mike	0
DeGroff, Rube	1
DeHaan, Kory	1
DeHart, Rick	1
Dehlman, Herman	3
Deidel, Jim	0
Deininger, Pep	5
Deisel, Pat	1
Deitrick, Bill	0
Dejan, Mike	0
DeJesus, Ivan	106
DeJesus, Jose	20
DeJohn, Mark	1
DeKoning, Bill	0
de la Cruz, Tommy	13
Delahanty, Frank	19
Delahanty, Joe	21
Delahanty, Tom	1
de la Hoz, Mike	27

Player	WS
de la Maza, Roland	0
DeLancey, Bill	29
Delaney, Art	11
Delaney, Bill	2
de la Rosa, F.	0
de la Rosa, Jesus	0
de la Rosa, Tomas	3
DeLeon, Jose	96
DeLeon, Luis	30
Delgado, Alex	0
Delgado, Puchy	0
Delgado, Wilson	5
Del Greco, Bobby	47
Delhi, Flame	0
Delis, Juan	0
Delker, Eddie	1
Dell, Wheezer	25
Dellaero, Jason	0
Dellucci, David	24
Delmas, Bert	0
Delock, Ike	77
de los Santos, Luis	1
de los Santos, R.	1
de los Santos, V.	5
Del Savio, Garton	0
Delsing, Jim	60
del Toro, Miguel	2
DeLucia, Rich	28
DeMaestri, Joe	47
Demarais, Fred	0
DeMars, Billy	2
DeMerit, John	1
Demery, Larry	24
Demeter, Steve	0
DeMiller, Harry	0
Demmitt, Ray	51
DeMola, Don	9
DeMontreville, Lee	2
DeMott, Ben	0
Dempsey, Con	0
Dempsey, Mark	0
Denehy, Bill	1
Denman, Brian	2
Dennehey, Tod	0
Denning, Otto	5
Dennis, Don	8
Denson, Drew	1
Dent, Eddie	2
Dente, Sam	37
Denzer, Roger	4
DePangher, Mike	0
DePaula, Sean	2
DePhillips, Tony	1
Derby, Gene	0
Derby, George	53
Dernier, Bob	58
DeRosa, Mark	7
Derrick, Claud	6
Derrick, Mike	0
Derrington, Jim	0
Derry, Russ	14
DeSa, Joe	0
Desautels, Gene	48
Deshaies, Jim	68
DeShong, Jimmie	41
DeSilva, John	0
Desjardien, Shorty	0
Dessau, Rube	0
Destrade, Orestes	14
Detherage, Bob	1
Detore, George	1
Dettmer, John	1
Dettore, Tom	5
Detweiler, Ducky	2
Deutsch, Mel	0
Devarez, Cesar	0
Devens, Charlie	5
Devine, Adrian	27
Devine, Jim	0
Devine, Mickey	1
Deviney, Hal	1
DeViveiros, Bernie	0
Devlin, Jim	
Debut 1886	13
Debut 1944	0
DeVogt, Rex	0
Devore, Josh	56
DeVormer, Al	8
Devoy, Walt	2
Dewald, Charlie	1
Dewey, Mark	21
DeWillis, Jeff	1
DeWitt, Matt	1
Dexter, Charlie	61
Diaz, Alex	6
Diaz, Carlos	
Debut 1982	17
Debut 1990	0
Diaz, Eddy	1
Diaz, Edgar	3
Diaz, Edwin	1
Diaz, Mario	15
Diaz, Mike	16
Dibble, Rob	63
Dibut, Pedro	5
Dicken, Paul	0
Dickerman, Leo	20
Dickerson, Buttercup	59
Dickerson, George	0
Dickey, George	8
Dickey, R.A.	0
Dickman, Emerson	17
Dickshot, Johnny	30
Dickson, Jason	17
Dickson, Jim	4
Dickson, Lance	0
Dickson, Walt	27
Didier, Bob	16
Diehl, Ernie	2
Diehl, George	0
Diering, Chuck	42
Dierker, Larry	133
Dietrich, Bill	93
Dietz, Dick	84
Dietz, Dutch	16
Dietzel, Roy	0
Difani, Jay	0
DiFelice, Mike	22
Diggs, Reese	0
Dignan, Steve	2
DiLauro, Jack	7
Dillard, Don	9
Dillard, Gordon	0
Dillard, Pat	2
Dillard, Steve	21
Dillhoefer, Pickles	12
Dillinger, Bob	70
Dillinger, Harley	0
Dillman, Bill	3
Dillon, Pop	18
Dillon, Steve	0
Dilone, Miguel	44
DiMichele, Frank	0
Dimmel, Mike	0
Dineen, Kerry	1
Dinges, Vance	14
Dingman, Craig	0
Diorio, Ron	2
DiPietro, Bob	0
DiPino, Frank	48
Dipoto, Jerry	48
DiSarcina, Gary	65
Disch, George	2
Dishman, Glenn	3
Distaso, Alec	0
Distefano, Benny	5
Distel, Dutch	0
Ditmar, Art	63
Dittmer, Jack	25
Divis, Moxie	0
Dixon, Ken	21
Dixon, Leo	9
Dixon, Sonny	13
Dixon, Steve	0
Dixon, Tom	6
Doane, Walt	0
Dobb, John	0
Dobbek, Dan	8
Dobbs, John	52
Dobens, Ray	2
Dobernic, Jess	8
Dobson, Chuck	48
Dockins, George	9
Dodd, Oran	0
Dodd, Robert	0
Dodd, Tom	0
Dodge, John	6
Dodge, Sam	0
Dodson, Pat	2
Doe, Al	1
Doheny, Ed	66
Doherty, John	
Debut 1974	4
Debut 1992	24
Dolan, Biddy	2
Dolan, Cozy	30
Dolan, Joe	13
Dolan, John	10
Dolan, Tom	17
Doljack, Frank	11
Doll, Art	1
Donahue, Deacon	0
Donahue, Jim	23
Donahue, John	1
Donahue, Pat	10
Donahue, She	0
Donahue, Tim	33
Donald, Atley	55
Donalds, Ed	0
Donaldson, John	29
Dondero, Len	0
Donnelly, Blix	43
Donnelly, Ed	
Debut 1911	9
Debut 1959	1
Donnelly, Frank	3
Donnelly, James	0
Donnelly, Jim	39
Donnels, Chris	11
Donohue, Jim	9
Donohue, Joe	1
Donohue, Tom	4
Donoso, Lino	2
Donovan, Bill	6
Donovan, Fred	0
Donovan, Jerry	1
Donovan, Mike	0
Donovan, Tom	0
Dooin, Red	91
Dooms, Harry	0
Dopson, John	33
Doran, Bill	0
Doran, John	2
Doran, Tom	1
Dorgan, Jerry	15
Dorgan, Mike	90
Dorish, Harry	59
Dorman, Charlie	0
Dorman, Red	3
Dorner, Gus	25
Dorr, Bert	3
Dorsett, Brian	9
Dorsett, Cal	0
Dorsey, Jerry	
Debut 1884	0
Debut 1911	0
Dorsey, Jim	0
Doscher, Herm	4
Doscher, Jack	7
Doster, David	3
Dotter, Gary	0
Dotterer, Dutch	9
Doty, Babe	1
Dougherty, Charlie	1
Dougherty, Jim	3
Dougherty, Tom	0
Douglas, John	0
Douglas, Larry	0
Douglas, Phil	102
Douglas, Whammy	2
Douglass, Astyanax	0
Douglass, Klondike	61
Douglass, Sean	1
Dow, Clarence	0
Dowd, John	0
Dowd, Skip	0
Dowd, Snooks	0
Dowd, Tommy	82
Dowell, Ken	1
Dowie, Joe	1
Dowling, Dave	1
Dowling, Pete	47
Downey, Red	1
Downey, Tom	50
Downing, Al	125
Downs, Dave	2
Downs, Kelly	42
Downs, Red	11
Downs, Scott	3
Dowse, Tom	6
Doyle, Brian	2
Doyle, Carl	5
Doyle, Conny	2
Doyle, Danny	0
Doyle, Denny	56
Doyle, Jeff	1
Doyle, Jess	5
Doyle, Jim	19
Doyle, John	0
Doyle, Paul	6
Doyle, Slow Joe	23
Dozier, Buzz	1
Dozier, D.J.	1
Dozier, Tom	0
Drabowsky, Moe	108
Drahman, Brian	4
Drake, Delos	23
Drake, Larry	0
Drake, Logan	0
Drake, Lyman	0
Drake, Sammy	0
Drake, Solly	5
Drake, Tom	1
Dransfeldt, Kelly	2
Draper, Mike	2
Drauby, Jake	0
Dravecky, Dave	67
Drees, Tom	0
Dreesen, Bill	3

Player	WS
Dreisewerd, Clem	5
Drescher, Bill	2
Drese, Ryan	3
Dressen, Chuck	69
Dressen, Lee	4
Dressendorfer, Kirk	0
Dresser, Bob	0
Dressler, Rob	16
Drew, Cameron	0
Drew, Dave	3
Drew, Tim	0
Drews, Frank	5
Drews, Karl	29
Dreyer, Steve	1
Drill, Lew	36
Driscoll, Dennis	0
Driscoll, Denny	31
Driscoll, Jim	0
Driscoll, Mike	0
Driscoll, Paddy	0
Drissel, Mike	0
Drohan, Tom	0
Drott, Dick	20
Drucke, Louis	21
Druhot, Carl	8
Drummond, Tim	5
Drumright, Keith	2
Dubiel, Monk	51
DuBois, Brian	4
Ducey, Rob	31
Duchscherer, Justin	0
Duckworth, Brandon	5
Duckworth, Jim	3
Dudley, Clise	15
Dudra, John	2
Dues, Hal	9
Duff, Larry	1
Duff, Pat	0
Duffalo, Jim	19
Duffee, Charlie	64
Duffie, John	0
Duffy, Bernie	0
Duffy, Frank	54
Dugan, Bill	0
Dugan, Dan	0
Dugan, Ed	3
Dugas, Gus	3
Dugdale, Dan	1
Dugey, Oscar	4
Duggan, Jim	0
Duke, Martin	0
Dukes, Jan	1
Dukes, Tom	7
Duliba, Bob	19
Dumont, George	15
Dumoulin, Dan	1
Dumovich, Nick	4
Dunbar, Matt	0
Dunbar, Tommy	1
Duncan, Courtney	2

Player	WS
Duncan, Dave	71
Duncan, Jim	2
Duncan, Taylor	7
Duncan, Vern	30
Dundon, Ed	7
Dundon, Gus	17
Dunegan, Jim	1
Dungan, Sam	41
Dunham, Lee	0
Dunham, Wiley	0
Dunkle, Davey	10
Dunlap, Bill	2
Dunlap, Grant	1
Dunleavy, Jack	24
Dunlop, George	0
Dunn, Jack	86
Dunn, Jim	0
Dunn, Joe	1
Dunn, Ron	4
Dunn, Steve	
Debut 1884	1
Debut 1994	0
Dunn, Todd	1
Dunne, Mike	18
Dunning, Andy	0
Dunning, Steve	24
Dunwoody, Todd	10
Dupee, Frank	0
Dupree, Mike	0
Duran, Dan	0
Duran, Roberto	0
Durant, Mike	1
Durbin, Chad	8
Durbin, Kid	2
Duren, Ryne	39
Durham, Bull	1
Durham, Don	2
Durham, Ed	35
Durham, Joe	1
Durham, John	0
Durnbaugh, Bobby	0
Durning, George	1
Durning, Rich	0
Durrett, Red	0
Durrington, Trent	1
Durst, Cedric	13
Duryea, Jesse	76
Dusak, Erv	29
Duser, Carl	0
Dustal, Bob	0
Duvall, Mike	3
Duzen, Bill	0
Dwight, Al	1
Dwyer, Double Joe	0
Dwyer, Jim	83
Dwyer, John	0
Dybzinski, Jerry	18
Dyck, Jim	26
Dyer, Ben	5
Dyer, Duffy	57

Player	WS
Dyer, Eddie	13
Dyer, Mike	13
Dygert, Jimmy	51
Dykhoff, Radhames	0
Dyler, John	0

E

Player	WS
Eaddy, Don	0
Eagan, Bill	13
Eagan, Truck	0
Eagle, Bill	0
Eakle, Charlie	0
Earl, Howard	9
Earl, Scott	0
Earle, Billy	18
Earley, Arnold	16
Earley, Bill	0
Earley, Tom	17
Early, Jake	64
Easley, Logan	2
Eason, Mal	31
East, Carl	0
East, Harry	0
East, Hugh	2
Easter, Luke	63
Easterday, Henry	19
Easterling, Paul	4
Easterly, Jamie	25
Easterly, Ted	75
Easterwood, Roy	0
Easton, Jack	24
Easton, John	0
Eastwick, Rawly	49
Eaton, Craig	1
Eaton, Zeb	3
Eave, Gary	4
Eaves, Vallie	5
Eayrs, Eddie	11
Ebert, Derrin	0
Ebright, Hi	2
Eccles, Harry	0
Echevarria, Angel	7
Echols, Johnny	0
Eckert, Al	0
Eckert, Charlie	2
Eckhardt, Ox	1
Eddy, Chris	0
Eddy, Don	3
Eddy, Steve	1
Edelen, Ed	0
Edelen, Joe	2
Edelman, John	0
Eden, Charlie	22
Eden, Mike	0
Edenfield, Ken	1
Edens, Tom	21
Edge, Butch	2

Player	WS
Edgerton, Bill	1
Edington, Stump	1
Edler, Dave	4
Edmondson, Bob	0
Edmondson, Brian	6
Edmondson, G.	0
Edmondson, Paul	5
Edmondston, Sam	0
Edmonson, Eddie	0
Edwards, Bruce	52
Edwards, Dave	11
Edwards, Doc	19
Edwards, Foster	5
Edwards, Hank	75
Edwards, Jim Joe	25
Edwards, Marshall	3
Edwards, Mike	7
Edwards, Ralph	0
Edwards, Sherman	0
Edwards, Wayne	8
Eells, Harry	4
Eenhoorn, Robert	1
Egan, Ben	5
Egan, Dick	
Debut 1908	76
Debut 1963	1
Egan, Jim	3
Egan, Rip	0
Egan, Tom	22
Egan, Wish	6
Eggert, Elmer	0
Eggler, Dave	15
Egloff, Bruce	0
Ehrhardt, Rube	31
Eibel, Hack	0
Eichelberger, Juan	19
Eichhorn, Mark	83
Eichrodt, Ike	4
Eiland, Dave	5
Eilers, Dave	4
Einertson, Darrell	1
Eischen, Joey	5
Eisenhart, Jake	0
Eisenstat, Harry	38
Eiteljorge, Ed	0
Elder, George	1
Elder, Heinie	0
Eldred, Cal	65
Elia, Lee	3
Elko, Pete	0
Ellam, Roy	2
Eller, Hod	58
Ellerbe, Frank	27
Ellick, Joe	8
Ellingsen, Bruce	2
Elliot, Larry	13
Elliott, Allen	1
Elliott, Carter	1
Elliott, Claud	5
Elliott, Donnie	2

Player	WS
Elliott, Gene	0
Elliott, Glenn	4
Elliott, Hal	6
Elliott, Harry	1
Elliott, Jumbo	67
Elliott, Randy	3
Elliott, Rowdy	11
Ellis, Ben	0
Ellis, Jim	2
Ellis, John	66
Ellis, Rob	2
Ellis, Robert	3
Ellis, Rube	53
Ellis, Sammy	45
Ellison, Babe	4
Ellison, George	0
Ellsworth, Steve	0
Elmore, Verdo	0
Elsh, Roy	5
Elster, Kevin	86
Elston, Don	61
Elvira, Narciso	0
Ely, Harry	0
Embree, Alan	21
Embree, Red	32
Embrey, Slim	0
Emerson, Chester	1
Emery, Cal	0
Emery, Spoke	0
Emig, Charlie	0
Emmer, Frank	2
Emmerich, Bob	0
Emmerich, Slim	4
Emslie, Bob	45
Encarnacion, A.	4
Encarnacion, Luis	0
Encarnacion, Mario	1
Enders, Trevor	0
Endicott, Bill	0
Engel, Joe	19
Engel, Steve	0
Engle, Charlie	5
Engle, Clyde	84
Engle, Dave	32
Engle, Rick	0
English, Charlie	4
English, Gil	16
Ennis, Russ	0
Enright, George	0
Enright, Jack	0
Ens, Jewel	3
Ens, Mutz	0
Ensberg, Morgan	0
Enwright, Charlie	0
Enyart, Terry	0
Enzenroth, Jack	1
Enzmann, Johnny	16
Eppard, Jim	2
Epperly, Al	2
Epps, Aubrey	1

Player	WS
Epps, Hal	9
Epstein, Mike	120
Erardi, Greg	0
Erautt, Eddie	12
Erautt, Joe	1
Erdos, Todd	2
Ericks, John	7
Erickson, Don	0
Erickson, Eric	33
Erickson, Hal	1
Erickson, Hank	3
Erickson, Paul	43
Erickson, Ralph	0
Erickson, Roger	37
Ermer, Cal	0
Ernaga, Frank	3
Errickson, Dick	37
Erwin, Tex	21
Escalera, Nino	0
Escarrega, Chico	4
Eschen, Jim	1
Eschen, Larry	0
Escobar, Alex	1
Escobar, Angel	0
Escobar, Jose	0
Eshelman, Vaughn	7
Esmond, Jimmy	48
Espino, Juan	1
Espinosa, Nino	34
Espinoza, Alvaro	47
Esposito, Sammy	19
Espy, Cecil	29
Essegian, Chuck	31
Esser, Mark	0
Essian, Jim	62
Essick, Bill	2
Estalella, Bobby	84
Estelle, Dick	3
Esterbrook, Dude	79
Estock, George	2
Estrada, Chuck	37
Estrada, Frank	0
Estrada, Horacio	1
Estrada, Johnny	5
Estrada, Oscar	0
Estrella, Leo	0
Etchebarren, Andy	73
Etchison, Buck	5
Etheridge, Bobby	5
Etherton, Seth	3
Ettles, Mark	0
Eubank, John	10
Eubanks, Uel	0
Eufemia, Frank	6
Eunick, Fred	0
Eustace, Frank	0
Evans, Al	49
Evans, Art	1
Evans, Barry	10
Evans, Bart	1

Player	WS
Evans, Bill	
Debut 1916	2
Debut 1949	1
Evans, Chick	1
Evans, Jake	32
Evans, Joe	47
Evans, Red	1
Evans, Roy	27
Evans, Tom	2
Everett, Adam	0
Everitt, Leon	0
Evers, Hoot	122
Evers, Joe	0
Evers, Tom	9
Eversgerd, Bryan	4
Ewing, John	53
Ewing, Reuben	0
Ewing, Sam	4
Ewoldt, Art	0
Eyre, Scott	6
Eyrich, George	1
Ezzell, Homer	11

F

Player	WS
Faatz, Jay	19
Fabregas, Jorge	32
Fabrique, Bunny	1
Faedo, Lenny	7
Faeth, Tony	2
Fagan, Bill	3
Fagan, Everett	1
Fagin, Fred	0
Fahey, Bill	23
Fahey, Frank	0
Fahey, Howard	0
Fahr, Red	0
Fahrer, Pete	1
Fair, George	0
Fairbank, Jim	0
Faircloth, Rags	0
Fairey, Jim	8
Fajardo, Hector	1
Falch, Anton	0
Falcone, Pete	59
Falk, Chet	3
Falkenborg, Brian	0
Fallenstein, Ed	1
Fallon, Bob	1
Fallon, Charlie	0
Fallon, George	6
Falsey, Pete	0
Falteisek, Steve	0
Faneyte, Rikkert	0
Fannin, Cliff	35
Fanning, Jack	0
Fanning, Jim	1
Fanok, Harry	1

Player	WS
Fanovich, Frank	1
Fansler, Stan	1
Fanwell, Harry	1
Fanzone, Carmen	11
Faries, Paul	4
Fariss, Monty	3
Farley, Bob	2
Farley, Tom	1
Farmer, Alex	1
Farmer, Bill	0
Farmer, Ed	39
Farmer, Howard	0
Farmer, Jack	4
Farmer, Mike	1
Farnsworth, Kyle	14
Farr, Jim	1
Farr, Steve	83
Farrar, Sid	81
Farrell, Bill	0
Farrell, Doc	32
Farrell, Jack	18
Farrell, Joe	26
Farrell, John	
Debut 1901	64
Debut 1987	34
Farrell, Kerby	11
Farrow, John	1
Fasano, Sal	19
Fast, Darcy	0
Fast	0
Faszholz, Jack	0
Faul, Bill	9
Faulkner, Jim	9
Fausett, Buck	0
Faust, Charlie	0
Fautsch, Joe	0
Fauver, Clay	1
Fazio, Ernie	4
Fear, Vern	0
Federoff, Al	2
Fee, Jack	2
Fehring, Bill	0
Feinberg, Eddie	0
Felder, Mike	45
Felderman, Marv	0
Feldman, Harry	37
Felix, Gus	43
Felix, Harry	0
Felix, Junior	55
Feliz, Pedro	0
Feller, Jack	0
Felske, John	1
Felton, Terry	2
Fenner, Hod	0
Fenwick, Bobby	0
Ferens, Stan	5
Ferguson, Alex	52
Ferguson, Bob	0
Ferguson, Charlie	0
Ferguson, George	33

Player	WS
Fermin, Felix	50
Fermin, Ramon	0
Fernandes, Ed	1
Fernandez, Chico	
Debut 1956	56
Debut 1968	0
Fernandez, Frank	34
Fernandez, Jared	0
Fernandez, Jose	0
Fernandez, Nanny	27
Fernandez, Osvaldo	13
Fernandez, Sid	117
Ferrara, Al	46
Ferrarese, Don	27
Ferraro, Mike	6
Ferrazzi, Bill	0
Ferreira, Tony	0
Ferrer, Sergio	3
Ferrick, Tom	62
Ferris, Bob	1
Ferriss, Boo	67
Ferry, Cy	0
Ferry, Jack	12
Ferson, Alex	12
Fette, Lou	50
Fetters, Mike	60
Fetzer, Willy	0
Fewster, Chick	38
Fiala, Neil	0
Fick, John	0
Fidrych, Mark	36
Fieber, Clarence	1
Field, Jim	30
Field, Sam	0
Fields, Bruce	1
Fields, Jocko	39
Fiene, Lou	1
Fife, Danny	3
Fifield, Jack	21
Figga, Mike	1
Figgemeier, Frank	0
Figueroa, Bien	0
Figueroa, Jesus	2
Figueroa, Luis	0
Figueroa, Nelson	6
Fikac, Jeremy	3
File, Bob	7
File, Sam	0
Filer, Tom	14
Files, Eddie	0
Filipowicz, Steve	1
Filley, Marc	0
Fillingim, Dana	53
Filson, Pete	24
Fimple, Jack	5
Finch, Joel	2
Fincher, Bill	1
Fine, Tommy	1
Finigan, Jim	43
Fink, Herman	14

Player	WS
Finlayson, P.	0
Finley, Bill	0
Finley, Bob	6
Finn, Neal	17
Finneran, Happy	28
Finney, Hal	4
Finney, Lou	90
Finnvold, Gar	1
Fiore, Mike	16
Fiore, Tony	0
Fireovid, Steve	4
Firova, Dan	0
Firth, Ted	0
Fischer, Bill	42
Fischer, Carl	42
Fischer, Hank	16
Fischer, Jeff	0
Fischer, Rube	8
Fischer, Todd	1
Fischer, William	38
Fischlin, Mike	19
Fishburn, Sam	0
Fishel, John	1
Fishel, Leo	0
Fisher, Brian	31
Fisher, Charles	0
Fisher, Charlie	1
Fisher, Chauncey	23
Fisher, Cherokee	2
Fisher, Clarence	0
Fisher, Don	2
Fisher, Ed	0
Fisher, Fritz	0
Fisher, George	2
Fisher, Gus	5
Fisher, Harry	0
Fisher, Jack	65
Fisher, Maurice	0
Fisher, Newt	0
Fisher, Red	0
Fisher, Showboat	11
Fisher, Tom	
Debut 1904	3
Debut 1912	42
Debut 1967	0
Fisher, Wilbur	0
Fiske, Max	10
Fisler, Wes	5
Fittery, Paul	2
Fitzberger, Charlie	0
Fitzgerald, Dennis	0
Fitz Gerald, Ed	46
Fitzgerald, Howie	1
Fitzgerald, John	
Debut 1890	3
Debut 1891	0
Debut 1891	17
Debut 1958	0
Fitzgerald, Matty	1

Player	WS
Fitzgerald, Mike	
Debut 1911	5
Debut 1983	62
Debut 1988	0
Fitzgerald, Ray	0
Fitzke, Robert Paul	0
Fitzmaurice, Shaun	0
Fitzmorris, Al	75
Fitzpatrick, Ed	19
Fitzsimmons, Tom	0
Flager, Wally	5
Flaherty, Martin	0
Flaherty, Pat	2
Flaherty, Patsy	66
Flair, Al	0
Flanagan, Charlie	0
Flanagan, Ed	2
Flanagan, Steamer	1
Flanigan, Ray	0
Flanigan, Tom	0
Flannery, John	0
Flannery, Tim	70
Flaskamper, Roy	1
Flater, Jack	2
Flavin, John	0
Fleitas, Angel	0
Fleming, Bill	23
Fleming, Dave	30
Fleming, Les	58
Fleming, Tom	0
Flener, Huck	4
Fletcher, Frank	0
Fletcher, Paul	1
Fletcher, Sam	0
Fletcher, Tom	0
Fletcher, Van	0
Flick, Lew	1
Flinn, Don	1
Flinn, John	4
Flint, Silver	73
Flitcraft, Hilly	0
Flohr, Mort	1
Flood, Tim	12
Flora, Kevin	1
Florence, Don	2
Florence, Paul	3
Flores, Gil	7
Flores, Jesse	64
Florie, Bryce	27
Flowers, Ben	8
Flowers, Jake	41
Flowers, Wes	2
Floyd, Bobby	8
Floyd, Bubba	1
Fluhrer, John	0
Flynn, Carney	0
Flynn, Doug	54
Flynn, Ed	0
Flynn, George	2
Flynn, Jocko	27

Player	WS
Flynn, Joe	6
Flynn, John	8
Flynn, Mike	0
Flythe, Stu	0
Fodge, Gene	1
Fogarty, Joe	0
Fogg, Josh	2
Fohl, Lee	1
Foiles, Hank	47
Foley, Curry	52
Foley, John	0
Foley, Marv	7
Foley, Ray	0
Foley, Tom	66
Foley, Will	11
Folkers, Rich	19
Fontenot, Joe	0
Fontenot, Ray	26
Fonville, Chad	10
Foor, Jim	0
Foote, Barry	50
Forbes, P.J.	0
Force, Davy	50
Ford, Ben	0
Ford, Curt	17
Ford, Dave	9
Ford, Ed	0
Ford, Gene	
Debut 1905	0
Debut 1936	0
Ford, Ted	15
Ford, Tom	0
Ford, Wenty	1
Fordham, Tom	0
Foreman, Brownie	12
Foreman, Frank	111
Foreman, Happy	1
Forman, Bill	0
Fornieles, Mike	74
Forster, Scott	0
Forster, Terry	107
Forster, Tom	10
Forsyth, Ed	0
Fortugno, Tim	3
Fortune, Gary	0
Fosnow, Jerry	1
Foss, George	0
Foss, Larry	1
Fossas, Tony	32
Fossum, Casey	2
Foster, Alan	44
Foster, Elmer	7
Foster, Kevin	25
Foster, Kris	1
Foster, Larry	0
Foster, Leo	4
Foster, Pop	25
Foster, Reddy	0
Foster, Roy	26
Foster, Rube	65

Player	WS
Foster, Slim	2
Foster, Steve	8
Foucault, Steve	43
Fournier, Henry	1
Fouser, Bill	0
Foutz, Frank	1
Fowler, Art	67
Fowler, Boob	4
Fowler, Dick	69
Fowler, Jesse	1
Fowlkes, Alan	0
Fox, Andy	30
Fox, Bill	1
Fox, Chad	15
Fox, Charlie	1
Fox, Eric	2
Fox, Henry	0
Fox, Howie	49
Fox, Jack	0
Fox, John	11
Fox, Paddy	1
Fox, Terry	46
Foxen, Bill	20
Foy, Joe	84
Foytack, Paul	78
Frailing, Ken	12
France, Ossie	0
Francis, Earl	19
Francis, Ray	9
Franco, Matt	13
Francona, Terry	32
Frank, Charlie	11
Frank, Fred	1
Frank, Mike	2
Franklin, Jack	0
Franklin, Jay	0
Franklin, Micah	1
Franklin, Murray	3
Franklin, Ryan	6
Franklin, Wayne	1
Franklin	0
Franks, Herman	8
Frascatore, John	26
Fraser, Willie	31
Frasier, Vic	13
Frazier, George	38
Frazier, Joe	7
Frazier, Lou	14
Fredrickson, Scott	0
Freed, Ed	1
Freed, Roger	20
Freel, Ryan	0
Freeman, Buck	10
Freeman, Harvey	0
Freeman, Hersh	37
Freeman, Jerry	11
Freeman, Jimmy	0
Freeman, John	0
Freeman, Julie	0
Freeman, LaVel	0

Player	WS
Freeman, Mark	1
Freeman, Marvin	35
Freese, Gene	88
Freese, George	4
Freeze, Jake	0
Freiburger, Vern	0
Freigau, Howard	45
Freisleben, Dave	27
Freitas, Tony	25
French, Charlie	6
French, Jim	17
French, Pat	0
French, Ray	1
French, Walt	21
Frey, Benny	58
Frey, Steve	25
Frias, Hanley	5
Frias, Pepe	19
Fricano, Marion	21
Friday, Skipper	0
Fridley, Jim	7
Fried, Cy	0
Friedrichs, Bob	0
Friel, Bill	17
Friel, Pat	6
Friend, Danny	36
Friend, Frank	0
Friend, Owen	9
Frierson, Buck	0
Fries, Pete	0
Frill, John	0
Frink, Fred	0
Frisbee, Charlie	5
Frisella, Danny	48
Frisk, Emil	22
Fritz, Charlie	0
Fritz, Harry	10
Fritz, Larry	0
Froats, Bill	0
Frobel, Doug	8
Frock, Sam	17
Froelich, Ben	0
Frohwirth, Todd	35
Fromme, Art	73
Frost, Dave	26
Fry, Jay	0
Fry, Jerry	0
Frye, Charlie	1
Fuchs, Charlie	2
Fuentes, Brian	1
Fuentes, Miguel	1
Fuentes, Mike	0
Fuhr, Oscar	0
Fuhrman, Ollie	0
Fulgham, John	18
Fulghum, Dot	0
Fuller, Ed	0
Fuller, Frank	0
Fuller, Harry	0
Fuller, Jim	5

Player	WS
Fuller, John	0
Fuller, Nig	0
Fuller, Shorty	86
Fuller, Vern	24
Fullerton, Curt	13
Fullis, Chick	44
Fulmer, Chris	33
Fulmer, Chuck	40
Fulton, Bill	0
Fultz, Aaron	6
Fultz, Dave	73
Funderburk, Mark	2
Funk, Frank	25
Funk, Liz	18
Funk, Tom	0
Fusselback, Eddie	17
Fussell, Chris	2
Fussell, Fred	12
Fusselman, Les	1
Fyhrie, Mike	10

G

Player	WS
Gabler, Frank	16
Gabler, Gabe	0
Gabler, John	5
Gables, Ken	9
Gabrielson, Len	
Debut 1939	0
Debut 1960	45
Gaddy, John	2
Gaedel, Eddie	0
Gaff, Brent	4
Gaffke, Fabian	5
Gagliano, Phil	30
Gagliano, Ralph	0
Gagne, Eric	9
Gagnier, Ed	6
Gagnon, Chick	0
Gaillard, Eddie	1
Gainer, Del	52
Gainer, Jay	0
Gaines, Joe	20
Gaines, Nemo	1
Gainey, Ty	3
Gaiser, Fred	0
Gajkowski, Steve	0
Gakeler, Dan	1
Galasso, Bob	4
Galatzer, Milt	13
Gale, Rich	33
Gallagher, Al	32
Gallagher, Bill	1
Gallagher, Bob	3
Gallagher, Dave	48
Gallagher, Doug	0
Gallagher, Ed	0
Gallagher, Gil	0

Player	WS
Gallagher, Jackie	0
Gallagher, Jim	0
Gallagher, Joe	9
Gallagher, John	1
Gallagher, Shorty	0
Gallagher, William	2
Galle, Stan	0
Gallego, Mike	77
Gallia, Bert	65
Galligan, Jim	0
Gallivan, Phil	4
Galloway, Chick	71
Galloway, Jim	0
Galvez, Balvino	1
Galvin, Jim	0
Galvin, Lou	1
Gamble, Bob	0
Gamble, John	0
Gamble, Lee	7
Gammons, Daff	1
Gandarillas, Gus	0
Gandy, Bob	0
Ganley, Bob	53
Gannon, Bill	0
Gannon, Gussie	0
Gannon, Joseph	0
Gantenbein, Joe	9
Ganzel, Babe	4
Ganzel, Charlie	74
Ganzel, John	68
Garagiola, Joe	63
Garagozzo, Keith	0
Garbark, Bob	7
Garbark, Mike	12
Garber, Bob	0
Garbey, Barbaro	10
Garbowski, Alex	0
Garcia, Amaury	1
Garcia, Carlos	46
Garcia, Chico	1
Garcia, Dan	0
Garcia, Freddy	6
Garcia, Guillermo	0
Garcia, Jesse	0
Garcia, Karim	12
Garcia, Kiko	33
Garcia, Leo	0
Garcia, Luis	0
Garcia, Miguel	0
Garcia, Mike	1
Garcia, Pedro	29
Garcia, Ralph	0
Garcia, Ramon	
Debut 1948	0
Debut 1991	12
Gardella, Al	0
Gardella, Danny	15
Gardenhire, Ron	13
Gardiner, Art	0
Gardiner, Mike	14
Gardner, Alex	0
Gardner, Art	0
Gardner, Billy	68
Gardner, Chris	1
Gardner, Earle	18
Gardner, Fred	0
Gardner, Gid	23
Gardner, Glenn	5
Gardner, Harry	1
Gardner, Jeff	10
Gardner, Jim	27
Gardner, Mark	60
Gardner, Ray	5
Gardner, Rob	9
Gardner, Wes	18
Garfield, Bill	1
Garibaldi, Art	5
Garibaldi, Bob	1
Garibay, Daniel	0
Garland, Jon	9
Garland, Lou	0
Garland, Wayne	55
Garman, Mike	33
Garms, Debs	99
Garoni, Willie	0
Garrelts, Scott	70
Garrett, Adrian	6
Garrett, Clarence	1
Garrett, Greg	7
Garrido, Gil	11
Garriott, Cecil	0
Garrison, Cliff	0
Garrison, Ford	14
Garrison, Webster	0
Garrity, Hank	0
Garry, Jim	0
Garvin, Jerry	31
Garvin, Ned	85
Gaspar, Harry	47
Gaspar, Rod	6
Gassaway, Charlie	5
Gastall, Tom	1
Gastfield, Ed	1
Gaston, Alex	5
Gaston, Cito	67
Gaston, Milt	102
Gaston, Welcome	2
Gastright, Hank	70
Gates, Brent	48
Gates, Joe	1
Gates, Mike	2
Gatewood, Aubrey	11
Gatins, Frank	2
Gaudet, Jim	0
Gaule, Mike	0
Gautreau, Doc	16
Gautreaux, Sid	1
Gaw, Chippy	0
Gazella, Mike	7
Gear, Dale	10
Gearhart, Gary	4
Gearin, Dinty	4
Geary, Bob	8
Geary, Huck	2
Gebhard, Bob	1
Gebrian, Pete	2
Geddes, Jim	1
Gedeon, Elmer	0
Gedeon, Joe	35
Gee, Johnny	4
Geer, Billy	22
Geggus, Charlie	15
Gehring, Henry	3
Gehrman, Paul	0
Geier, Phil	25
Geiger, Gary	77
Geis, Emil	2
Geisel, Dave	13
Geishert, Vern	1
Geiss, Bill	1
Geiss, Emil	0
Gelbert, Charlie	90
Gelnar, John	11
Genewich, Joe	69
Genins, Frank	7
Genovese, George	0
Gentile, Sam	0
Gentry, Gary	46
Gentry, Harvey	0
Gentry, Rufe	10
George, Alex	0
George, Bill	6
George, Chris	2
George, Chris S.	0
George, Greek	3
George, Lefty	6
Georgy, Oscar	0
Geraghty, Ben	1
Gerard, Dave	2
Gerber, Craig	2
Gerberman, George	1
Geren, Bob	19
Gerhardt, Allen	0
Gerhart, Ken	7
Gerheauser, Al	25
Gerken, George	1
Gerkin, Steve	2
Gerlach, Johnny	1
German, Les	35
Gerner, Ed	0
Gernert, Dick	68
Gertenrich, Lou	0
Gervais, Lefty	0
Gessner, Charlie	0
Gettel, Al	37
Gettig, Charlie	13
Gettinger, Tom	7
Gettman, Jake	13
Getz, Gus	21
Geyer, Rube	16
Geygan, Chappie	1
Gharrity, Patsy	60
Ghelfi, Tony	1
Giallombardo, Bob	1
Giannelli, Ray	0
Giannini, Joe	0
Giard, Joe	9
Gibbon, Joe	67
Gibbons, Jay	4
Gibbons, John	3
Gibbs, Jake	40
Gibralter, Steve	0
Gibson, Bob	14
Gibson, Charlie	
Debut 1905	0
Debut 1924	0
Gibson, Derrick	2
Gibson, Frank	31
Gibson, George	113
Gibson, Norwood	30
Gibson, Paul	28
Gibson, Robert	1
Gibson, Russ	9
Gibson, Sam	29
Gibson, Whitey	0
Gick, George	1
Gideon, Brett	2
Gideon, Jim	0
Giebel, Joe	0
Giebell, Floyd	4
Giel, Paul	8
Giggie, Bob	1
Gigon, Norm	0
Gil, Geronimo	2
Gil, Gus	7
Gilbert, Andy	0
Gilbert, Bill	0
Gilbert, Buddy	1
Gilbert, Charlie	13
Gilbert, Harry	0
Gilbert, Jack	2
Gilbert, Joe	1
Gilbert, John	0
Gilbert, Larry	9
Gilbert, Mark	1
Gilbert, Pete	18
Gilbert, Shawn	0
Gilbert, Tookie	4
Gilbert, Wally	47
Gilbreath, Rod	28
Gilbreth, Bill	1
Gile, Don	1
Giles, Brian J.	16
Giles, Marcus	9
Gilham, George	0
Gilhooley, Frank	33
Gilks, Bob	21
Gill, Ed	0
Gill, George	23
Gill, Haddie	0
Gill, Jim	0
Gill, Johnny	7
Gill, Warren	3
Gillen, Sam	4
Gillen, Tom	1
Gillenwater, Carden	30
Gillenwater, Claral	0
Gilles, Tom	0
Gillespie, Bob	4
Gillespie, Jim	0
Gillespie, John	3
Gillespie, Paul	9
Gilliford, Paul	0
Gilligan, Barney	46
Gilligan, Jack	1
Gillis, Grant	3
Gillpatrick, George	0
Gilman, Jim	0
Gilman, Pit	0
Gilmore, Frank	15
Gilmore, Grover	35
Gilmore, Len	0
Gilroy, John	1
Gilson, Hal	0
Ging, Billy	1
Gingras, Joe	0
Ginn, Tinsley	0
Ginsberg, Joe	42
Ginter, Keith	0
Ginter, Matt	2
Gionfriddo, Al	18
Giordano, Tommy	1
Giovanola, Ed	6
Gipson, Charles	4
Girard, Charlie	0
Giuliani, Tony	7
Givens, Brian	4
Gladd, Jim	0
Gladding, Fred	65
Glade, Fred	58
Gladman, Buck	1
Gladu, Roland	1
Glaiser, John	0
Glass, Tom	0
Glauber, Keith	2
Glavenich, Luke	0
Glaviano, Tommy	36
Glaze, Ralph	15
Glazner, Whitey	46
Gleason, Bill	0
Gleason, Billy	1
Gleason, Harry	11
Gleason, Jack	50
Gleason, Joe	1
Gleason, Roy	1
Gleaton, Jerry Don	27
Gleeson, Jim	37
Gleich, Frank	0
Glenalvin, Bob	11
Glendon, Martin	2

Player	WS
Glenn, Bob	0
Glenn, Ed	
Debut 1884	8
Debut 1898	0
Glenn, Harry	1
Glenn, Joe	15
Glenn, John	
Debut 1876	11
Debut 1960	0
Gliatto, Sal	0
Glinatsis, George	0
Gload, Ross	0
Glockson, Norm	0
Glossop, Al	13
Glover, Gary	4
Glynn, Bill	13
Glynn, Ed	14
Glynn, Ryan	3
Goar, Jot	0
Gochnauer, John	9
Godar, John	0
Godby, Danny	0
Goddard, Joe	0
Godwin, John	4
Goebel, Ed	1
Goeckel, Billy	1
Goetz, George	1
Goetz, John	0
Goff, Jerry	6
Goggin, Chuck	1
Gogolewski, Bill	19
Gohr, Greg	5
Golden, Jim	7
Golden, Mike	2
Golden, Roy	3
Goldman, Jonah	6
Goldsberry, Gordon	9
Goldsby, Walt	4
Goldsmith, Hal	7
Goldstein, Izzy	2
Goldstein, Lonnie	0
Goldy, Purnal	1
Goletz, Stan	1
Goliat, Mike	18
Golvin, Walt	0
Gomez, Chile	7
Gomez, Chris	64
Gomez, Leo	52
Gomez, Luis	15
Gomez, Pat	3
Gomez, Preston	0
Gomez, Randy	0
Gomez, Ruben	73
Gonder, Jesse	22
Gonzales, Dan	0
Gonzales, Joe	2
Gonzales, Julio	1
Gonzales, Larry	0
Gonzales, Rene	36
Gonzales, Vince	0
Gonzalez, Denny	2
Gonzalez, Dicky	2
Gonzalez, Eusebio	1
Gonzalez, Fernando	18
Gonzalez, Gabe	0
Gonzalez, German	3
Gonzalez, Jeremi	11
Gonzalez, Jose	12
Gonzalez, Julio	14
Gonzalez, Lariel	0
Gonzalez, Mike	80
Gonzalez, Orlando	1
Gonzalez, Pedro	21
Gonzalez, Raul	0
Gooch, Charlie	1
Gooch, Johnny	67
Gooch, Lee	2
Good, Gene	0
Good, Ralph	1
Good, Wilbur	66
Goodall, Herb	11
Goodell, John	0
Goodenough, Bill	0
Goodfellow, Mike	5
Goodman, Jake	4
Goodson, Ed	22
Goodwin, Art	0
Goodwin, Clyde	0
Goodwin, Curtis	13
Goodwin, Danny	9
Goodwin, Jim	0
Goodwin, Marv	19
Goodwin, Pep	11
Goolsby, Ray	0
Goossen, Greg	12
Gorbous, Glen	4
Gordinier, Ray	1
Gordon, Don	5
Gordon, Keith	0
Gordon, Mike	0
Gorecki, Rick	1
Gorin, Charlie	1
Gorinski, Bob	0
Gorman, Herb	0
Gorman, Howie	0
Gorman, Jack	6
Gorman, Tom	
Debut 1939	0
Debut 1952	48
Debut 1981	7
Gormley, Joe	0
Gornicki, Hank	13
Gorsica, Johnny	40
Goryl, Johnny	11
Gosger, Jim	42
Goss, Howie	10
Gossett, Dick	2
Gotay, Julio	19
Gott, Jim	79
Goulait, Ted	0
Gould, Al	11
Gould, Charlie	5
Goulish, Nick	0
Gouzzie, Claude	0
Gowdy, Hank	118
Gowell, Larry	1
Gozzo, Mauro	4
Grabarkewitz, Billy	43
Graber, Rod	0
Grabowski, Al	13
Grabowski, Johnny	18
Grabowski, Reggie	7
Grace, Earl	54
Grace, Joe	42
Grace, Mike	
Debut 1978	0
Debut 1995	12
Grady, John	1
Grady, Mike	120
Graff, Fred	1
Graff, John	0
Graff, Louis	0
Graff, Milt	2
Graffanino, Tony	27
Graham, Barney	0
Graham, Bernie	5
Graham, Bert	0
Graham, Bill	
Debut 1908	13
Debut 1966	2
Graham, Charlie	3
Graham, Dan	13
Graham, Jack	15
Graham, Lee	0
Graham, Moonlight	0
Graham, Oscar	2
Graham, Peaches	26
Graham, Roy	1
Graham, Skinny	
Debut 1924	10
Debut 1934	0
Graham, Tiny	0
Graham, Wayne	0
Grahe, Joe	27
Gramly, Tommy	0
Grammas, Alex	44
Grampp, Hank	0
Granger, Jeff	0
Granger, Wayne	58
Grant, Eddie	75
Grant, George	9
Grant, Jim	0
Grant, Jimmy	10
Grant, Mark	26
Grant, Tom	0
Grapenthin, Dick	2
Grasmick, Lou	0
Grasso, Mickey	13
Grate, Don	1
Grater, Mark	1
Graterol, Beiker	0
Graulich, Lew	0
Graves, Frank	1
Graves, Joe	0
Graves, Sid	0
Gray, Bill	14
Gray, Charlie	0
Gray, Chummy	4
Gray, Dave	0
Gray, Dick	8
Gray, Dolly	14
Gray, Gary	9
Gray, Jeff	12
Gray, Jim	0
Gray, Johnny	1
Gray, Lorenzo	2
Gray, Milt	0
Gray, Pete	2
Gray, Reddy	0
Gray, Stan	0
Gray, Ted	55
Grba, Eli	23
Greason, Bill	0
Grebeck, Craig	58
Green, Chris	0
Green, Dallas	24
Green, David	31
Green, Ed	3
Green, Fred	11
Green, Gary	5
Green, Gene	27
Green, Harvey	0
Green, Jason	0
Green, Jim	0
Green, Joe	0
Green, Pumpsie	25
Green, Scarborough	1
Green, Steve	0
Green, Tyler	13
Greene, Al	0
Greene, Charlie	1
Greene, June	0
Greene, Nelson	0
Greene, Paddy	2
Greene, Rick	0
Greene, Todd	9
Greene, Tommy	37
Greene, Willie	56
Greenfield, Kent	36
Greengrass, Jim	45
Greening, John	0
Greenwood, Bill	48
Greenwood, Bob	2
Greer, Brian	0
Greer, Ed	10
Greer, Kenny	0
Gregg, Dave	0
Gregg, Hal	32
Gregg, Tommy	13
Gregory, Frank	1
Gregory, Howie	0
Gregory, Lee	1
Gregory, Paul	6
Greif, Bill	23
Greisinger, Seth	6
Gremminger, Ed	41
Gremp, Buddy	2
Grevell, Bill	0
Grey, Reddy	0
Griesenbeck, Tim	0
Grieve, Tom	42
Griffeth, Lee	1
Griffin, Doug	42
Griffin, Hank	1
Griffin, Ivy	4
Griffin, Marty	1
Griffin, Mike	7
Griffin, Pat	0
Griffin, Pug	0
Griffin, Sandy	21
Griffin, Thomas	1
Griffin, Tom	63
Griffith, Bert	13
Griffith, Derrell	7
Griffith, Frank	0
Griffith, Tommy	134
Griggs, Art	43
Griggs, Hal	2
Grigsby, Denver	16
Grilli, Guido	0
Grilli, Jason	1
Grilli, Steve	6
Grim, Bob	53
Grim, John	62
Grimes, Ed	2
Grimes, John	0
Grimes, Oscar	58
Grimes, Ray	69
Grimes, Roy	0
Grimshaw, Moose	21
Grimsley, Ross	1
Griner, Dan	32
Grissom, Lee	35
Grissom, Marv	69
Grob, Connie	0
Grodzicki, Johnny	1
Groh, Lew	0
Gromek, Steve	141
Grosart, George	1
Grosklos, Howdie	3
Gross, Don	26
Gross, Emil	44
Gross, Kevin	117
Gross, Kip	8
Gross, Turkey	0
Gross, Wayne	104
Grossman, Harley	0
Grotewold, Jeff	2
Groth, Ernest	0
Groth, Ernie	0

Player	WS
Grott, Matt	0
Grove, Orval	54
Grover, Charlie	0
Grover, Roy	9
Grubb, Harvey	0
Grubbs, Tom	0
Grube, Frank	23
Gruber, Henry	62
Gruber, Kelly	95
Grundt, Ken	0
Grunwald, Al	1
Gryska, Sig	2
Grzanich, Mike	0
Grzenda, Joe	16
Guante, Cecilio	43
Gubanich, C.	1
Gudat, Marv	5
Guerra, Mike	30
Guerrero, Juan	1
Guerrero, Mario	38
Guerrero, Wilton	28
Guese, Whitey	0
Guetterman, Lee	43
Guevara, Giomar	0
Guillen, Jose	29
Guindon, Bobby	0
Guiney, Ben	0
Guinn, Skip	1
Guintini, Ben	0
Guise, Witt	1
Guisto, Lou	2
Gulan, Mike	0
Gulden, Brad	8
Gulley, Tom	1
Gullic, Ted	8
Gulliver, Glenn	5
Gumbert, Billy	6
Gumpert, Dave	7
Gumpert, Randy	58
Gunderson, Eric	13
Gunkel, Red	0
Gunkle, Fred	0
Gunning, Hy	0
Gunning, Tom	11
Gunson, Joe	9
Gura, Larry	125
Gust, Ernie	0
Guth, Bucky	0
Guth, Charlie	0
Guthrie, Mark	53
Gutierrez, Cesar	8
Gutierrez, Jackie	4
Gutteridge, Don	95
Guzman, Domingo	0
Guzman, Edwards	1
Guzman, Geraldo	3
Guzman, Johnny	0
Guzman, Jose	66
Guzman, Santiago	1
Gwosdz, Doug	1

Player	WS
Gwynn, Chris	18
Gyselman, Dick	3

H

Player	WS
Haad, Yamid	0
Haas, Bert	57
Haas, Bruno	0
Haas, Dave	3
Haas, Eddie	1
Haas, Moose	84
Habenicht, Bob	0
Haberer, Emil	0
Habyan, John	39
Hach, Irv	0
Hacker, Rich	0
Hacker, Warren	70
Hackett, Jim	6
Hackett, Mert	16
Hackett, Walter	13
Hackman, Luther	2
Hadley, Kent	7
Haeffner, Bill	2
Hafey, Bud	6
Hafey, Tom	5
Hafford, Leo	2
Hafner, Frank	0
Hagan, Art	1
Hageman, Casey	7
Hagen, Kevin	1
Hagerman, Rip	17
Hague, Bill	13
Hague, Joe	35
Hahn, Dick	0
Hahn, Don	21
Hahn, Fred	0
Haid, Hal	19
Haigh, Ed	0
Haines, Hinkey	0
Hairston, Jerry	49
Hairston, Johnny	0
Hairston, Sammy	1
Haislip, Jim	0
Hajduk, Chet	0
Hajek, Dave	0
Halas, George	0
Halbriter, Ed	0
Haldeman, John	0
Hale, Bob	9
Hale, Chip	13
Hale, Dad	0
Hale, George	1
Hale, John	12
Haley, Fred	0
Haley, Ray	3
Halicki, Ed	56
Hall, Al	5
Hall, Albert	17

Player	WS
Hall, Bert	1
Hall, Bill	
Debut 1913	0
Debut 1954	5
Hall, Bob	
Debut 1904	2
Debut 1949	10
Hall, Charlie	0
Hall, Darren	13
Hall, Drew	6
Hall, George	18
Hall, Herb	0
Hall, Irv	36
Hall, Joe	3
Hall, John	0
Hall, Marc	11
Hall, Russ	0
Hall, Sea Lion	52
Hall, Toby	6
Hall, Tom	57
Halla, John	0
Halladay, Roy	21
Hallett, Jack	14
Halliday, Newt	0
Halligan, Jocko	21
Hallinan, Ed	2
Hallinan, Jimmy	19
Hallman, Bill	23
Hallstrom, Charlie	0
Halpin, Jim	1
Halt, Al	17
Hamann, Doc	0
Hambright, Roger	2
Hamburg, Charlie	17
Hamby, Jim	0
Hamelin, Bob	30
Hamill, John	1
Hamilton, Dave	42
Hamilton, Jack	21
Hamilton, Jeff	21
Hamilton, Joey	52
Hamilton, Steve	61
Hamilton, Tom	0
Hamlin, Ken	22
Hamlin, Luke	79
Hamm, Pete	0
Hammaker, Atlee	50
Hammond, Chris	37
Hammond, Jack	0
Hammond, Steve	1
Hamner, Garvin	1
Hamner, Ralph	5
Hampton, Ike	3
Hamric, Bert	0
Hamrick, Ray	5
Hancken, Buddy	0
Hancock, Fred	0
Hancock, Gary	8
Hancock, Lee	2
Hancock, Ryan	1

Player	WS
Hand, Rich	23
Handiboe, Jim	6
Handiboe, Mike	0
Handley, Gene	5
Handley, Lee	78
Handrahan, Vern	1
Hands, Bill	133
Hanebrink, Harry	4
Haney, Chris	28
Haney, Fred	53
Haney, Larry	19
Haney, Todd	6
Hanford, Charlie	33
Hankins, Don	0
Hankins, Jay	1
Hankinson, Frank	87
Hanley, Jim	0
Hanlon, Bill	0
Hanna, John	1
Hanna, Preston	17
Hannah, Truck	21
Hannahs, Gerry	1
Hannan, Jim	31
Hannifin, Jack	10
Hannifin, Pat	1
Hanning, Loy	1
Hansell, Greg	7
Hansen, Andy	30
Hansen, Bob	3
Hansen, Doug	0
Hansen, Jed	5
Hansen, Roy	1
Hansen, Snipe	24
Hansford, F.C.	0
Hanski, Don	0
Hanson, Erik	85
Hanson, Joe	0
Hanson, Ollie	0
Hanyzewski, Ed	10
Happenny, John	1
Harbridge, Bill	29
Hardesty, Scott	1
Hardgrove, Pat	0
Hardie, Lou	7
Hardin, Bud	0
Hardin, Jim	42
Harding, Charlie	0
Harding, Lou	0
Hardtke, Jason	3
Hardy, Alex	1
Hardy, Carroll	20
Hardy, Harry	2
Hardy, Jack	
Debut 1903	0
Debut 1989	0
Hardy, Larry	4
Hardy, Red	0
Hare, Shawn	0
Hargan, Steve	77
Hargesheimer, Alan	2

Player	WS
Hargis, Gary	0
Hargrave, Pinky	54
Hargreaves, Charlie	30
Harikkala, Tim	0
Harkey, Mike	33
Harkins, John	59
Harkness, Specs	9
Harkness, Tim	14
Harley, Dick	
Debut 1897	45
Debut 1905	0
Harlow, Larry	28
Harman, Bill	0
Harmon, Chuck	9
Harmon, Terry	26
Harper, Bill	0
Harper, Brian	83
Harper, George	5
Harper, Harry	69
Harper, Jack	
Debut 1899	67
Debut 1915	0
Harper, Terry	28
Harper, Travis	2
Harrell, Billy	7
Harrell, John	1
Harrell, Ray	3
Harrell, Slim	1
Harrelson, Bill	0
Harriger, Denny	0
Harrington, Andy	
Debut 1913	0
Debut 1925	0
Harrington, Bill	5
Harrington, Jerry	10
Harrington, Joe	3
Harrington, Mickey	0
Harris, Ben	4
Harris, Bill	
Debut 1923	28
Debut 1957	0
Harris, Billy	2
Harris, Bob	28
Harris, Buddy	0
Harris, Candy	0
Harris, Charlie	
Debut 1899	1
Debut 1948	9
Harris, Dave	48
Harris, Donald	1
Harris, Frank	1
Harris, Gail	26
Harris, Gene	12
Harris, Greg	
Debut 1981	108
Debut 1988	55
Harris, Herb	0
Harris, Joe	9
Harris, John	3
Harris, Lenny	77

Player	WS
Harris, Lum	34
Harris, Mickey	61
Harris, Ned	22
Harris, Pep	13
Harris, Reggie	5
Harris, Spencer	6
Harris, Vic	21
Harris, Willie	0
Harrison, Ben	0
Harrison, Chuck	17
Harrison, Rob	0
Harrison, Roric	27
Harrison, Tom	0
Harrist, Earl	16
Harshaney, Sam	1
Harstad, Oscar	4
Hart, Bill	
Debut 1886	67
Debut 1943	4
Hart, Billy	18
Hart, Burt	5
Hart, Hub	2
Hart, Mike	
Debut 1980	0
Debut 1984	1
Hart, Tom	0
Hartenstein, Chuck	18
Harter, Frank	4
Hartford, Bruce	0
Hartgraves, Dean	4
Hartje, Chris	0
Hartley, Chick	0
Hartley, Grover	36
Hartley, Mike	20
Hartman, Bob	1
Hartman, Charlie	0
Hartman, Fred	53
Hartman, J.C.	3
Hartnett, Pat	1
Hartranft, Ray	0
Harts, Greg	0
Hartsfield, Roy	24
Hartsock, Jeff	0
Hartung, Clint	24
Hartzell, Paul	37
Hartzell, Roy	114
Harvel, Luther	1
Harvey, Bryan	75
Harvey, Erwin	16
Harvey, Ken	0
Harville, Chad	1
Hasbrook, Ziggy	0
Hasenmayer, Don	0
Hash, Herb	8
Haslin, Mickey	17
Hasney, Pete	0
Hassamaer, Bill	16
Hassett, Buddy	74
Hassler, Andy	53
Hassler, Joe	0

Player	WS
Hasson, Gene	5
Hastings, Charlie	24
Hastings, Scott	5
Hasty, Bob	32
Hatcher, Billy	98
Hatcher, Chris	0
Hatcher, Mickey	67
Hatfield, Fred	47
Hatfield, Gil	29
Hatfield, John	0
Hathaway, Hilly	2
Hathaway, Ray	0
Hatten, Joe	60
Hatter, Clyde	0
Hatton, Grady	130
Hauger, Arthur	0
Haughey, Chris	0
Haught, Gary	0
Haugstad, Phil	1
Hauser, Arnold	27
Hauser, Joe	70
Hausman, Tom	20
Hausmann, Clem	8
Hausmann, George	26
Hautz, Charlie	0
Havens, Brad	24
Hawblitzel, Ryan	0
Hawes, Bill	11
Hawes, Roy	0
Hawk, Ed	1
Hawke, Bill	30
Hawkes, Thorny	6
Hawkins, Andy	56
Hawkins, Wynn	9
Hawks, Chicken	10
Hawley, Scott	0
Haworth, Howie	0
Haydel, Hal	4
Hayden, Gene	0
Hayden, Jack	8
Hayes, Ben	5
Hayes, Bill	0
Hayes, Jackie	
Debut 1882	22
Debut 1927	77
Hayes, Jim	0
Hayes, Mike	0
Hayner, Fred	0
Haynes, Heath	0
Hayward, Ray	1
Haywood, Bill	0
Hayworth, Ray	49
Hayworth, Red	5
Hazewood, Drungo	0
Hazle, Bob	12
Hazleton, Doc	0
Head, Ed	27
Head, Ralph	1
Healey, Tom	5
Healy, Egyptian	86

Player	WS
Healy, Fran	36
Healy, Francis	1
Healy, Thomas	1
Heard, Charlie	0
Heard, Jay	0
Hearn, Bunny	
Debut 1910	16
Debut 1926	5
Hearn, Ed	5
Hearne, Ed	0
Hearne, Hughie	10
Hearron, Jeff	0
Heath, Bill	5
Heath, Kelly	0
Heath, Mickey	1
Heath, Spencer	0
Heath, Tommy	7
Heathcock, Jeff	9
Heathcott, Mike	0
Heaton, Neal	62
Heaverlo, Dave	42
Hebert, Wally	20
Hechinger, Mike	0
Hedgpeth, Harry	0
Hedlund, Mike	24
Heep, Danny	50
Heffernan, Bert	0
Heffner, Bob	13
Heffner, Don	33
Heflin, Bronson	0
Heflin, Randy	4
Hegan, Mike	59
Hegman, Bob	0
Hehl, Jake	0
Heidemann, Jack	10
Heileman, Chink	0
Heim, Val	1
Heimach, Fred	71
Heimueller, Gorman	3
Heine, Bud	0
Heinkel, Don	2
Heintzelman, Ken	78
Heintzelman, Tom	4
Heinzman, Jack	0
Heise, Bob	20
Heise, Clarence	0
Heise, Jim	0
Heiser, Roy	0
Heiserman, Rick	0
Heismann, Crese	2
Heist, Al	10
Heitmann, Harry	0
Heitmuller, Heine	13
Held, Mel	0
Helf, Hank	2
Helfand, Eric	3
Helfrich, Ty	2
Hellman, Tony	0
Helmbold, Horace	0
Helms, Tommy	114

Player	WS
Helms, Wes	6
Heltzel, Heinie	1
Heman, Russ	2
Hemingway, Ed	2
Hemond, Scott	15
Hemp, Ducky	1
Hemphill, Bret	0
Hemphill, Frank	1
Henderson, Bernie	0
Henderson, Bill	0
Henderson, Ed	0
Henderson, Joe	2
Henderson, Rod	0
Henderson, Steve	97
Hendley, Bob	41
Hendrick, Harvey	88
Hendricks, Ed	0
Hendricks, Ellie	59
Hendricks, Jack	1
Hendrickson, Don	3
Hendryx, Tim	43
Hengel, Dave	0
Hengle, Moxie	1
Henion, Lafayette	0
Henke, Tom	140
Henley, Bob	5
Henley, Gail	1
Henley, Weldon	33
Henline, Butch	58
Henneman, Mike	98
Hennessey, George	2
Hennessy, Les	0
Hennigan, Phil	19
Henning, Pete	12
Henninger, Rick	2
Hennis, Randy	1
Henrich, Bobby	0
Henrich, Fritz	0
Henriksen, Olaf	18
Henriquez, Oscar	0
Henry, Bill	
Debut 1952	87
Debut 1966	0
Henry, Butch	38
Henry, Doug	50
Henry, Dutch	29
Henry, Dwayne	18
Henry, Earl	1
Henry, George	2
Henry, Jim	7
Henry, John	
Debut 1884	7
Debut 1910	54
Henry, Ron	1
Henry, Snake	0
Henshaw, Roy	33
Hensiek, Phil	0
Hensley, Chuck	1
Hepler, Bill	4
Herbel, Ron	38

Player	WS
Herbert, Ernie	7
Herbert, Fred	1
Heredia, Felix	14
Heredia, Ubaldo	0
Heredia, Wilson	3
Herman, Art	4
Hermann, Al	0
Hermansen, Chad	0
Hermanski, Gene	70
Hermoso, Remy	4
Hernaiz, Jesus	0
Hernandez, Adrian	1
Hernandez, Alex	0
Hernandez, Carlos	
Debut 1990	29
Debut 1999	0
Debut 2001	2
Hernandez, Cesar	1
Hernandez, Chico	5
Hernandez, Enzo	38
Hernandez, Evelio	2
Hernandez, F.	0
Hernandez, Jackie	19
Hernandez, Jeremy	18
Hernandez, Leo	4
Hernandez, Manny	1
Hernandez, Pedro	0
Hernandez, Ramon	41
Hernandez, Rudy	
Debut 1960	1
Debut 1972	0
Hernandez, Toby	0
Hernandez, Xavier	46
Herndon, Junior	0
Hernon, Tom	0
Herr, Joseph	8
Herrell, Walt	0
Herrera, Jose	
Debut 1967	3
Debut 1995	5
Herrera, Mike	3
Herrera, Pancho	25
Herrera, Tito	0
Herriage, Troy	0
Herrin, Tom	0
Herring, Art	35
Herring, Bill	0
Herring, Herb	0
Herring, Lefty	1
Herrmann, Ed	80
Herrmann, LeRoy	7
Herrmann, Marty	0
Herrnstein, John	6
Herrscher, Rick	1
Hersh, Earl	0
Hershberger, W.	13
Hershey, Frank	0
Hertweck, Neal	0
Hertz, Steve	0
Herzog, Whitey	42

Player	WS
Hesketh, Joe	58
Hess, Otto	81
Hess, Tom	0
Hesselbacher, Geo.	0
Hesterfer, Larry	0
Hetki, Johnny	28
Hetling, Gus	0
Hetzel, Eric	0
Heubel, George	0
Heusser, Ed	68
Heving, Joe	82
Heving, Johnny	19
Hewitt, Jake	2
Heydeman, Greg	0
Heydon, Mike	11
Hiatt, Jack	48
Hiatt, Phil	5
Hibbard, Greg	49
Hibbard, John	1
Hibbs, Jim	0
Hickerson, Bryan	15
Hickey, Eddie	0
Hickey, Jim	0
Hickey, John	0
Hickey, Kevin	15
Hickey, Mike	0
Hickman, Ernie	1
Hickman, Jesse	0
Hickman, Jim	
Debut 1915	11
Debut 1962	113
Hicks, Buddy	1
Hicks, Jim	1
Hicks, Joe	5
Hicks, Nat	5
Higbee, Mahlon	0
Higdon, Bill	1
Higginbotham, Irv	11
Higgins, Bill	7
Higgins, Bob	0
Higgins, Dennis	29
Higgins, Eddie	1
Higgins, Kevin	2
Higgins, Mark	0
High, Charlie	1
High, Ed	1
High, Hugh	44
Hiland, John	0
Hilcher, Whitey	3
Hildebrand, George	1
Hildebrand, Palmer	0
Hildebrand, R.E.	0
Hilgendorf, Tom	28
Hiljus, Erik	5
Hill, Belden	1
Hill, Bill	49
Hill, Carmen	57
Hill, Dave	0
Hill, Donnie	51
Hill, Garry	0
Hill, Herbert	0
Hill, Herman	0
Hill, Hugh	2
Hill, Hunter	11
Hill, Jesse	27
Hill, Marc	40
Hill, Milt	5
Hill, Oliver	0
Hill, Red	0
Hillebrand, Homer	11
Hillegas, Shawn	19
Hillenbrand, Shea	5
Hiller, Chuck	44
Hiller, Frank	26
Hiller, Hob	0
Hilley, Ed	0
Hillis, Mack	1
Hillman, Dave	31
Hillman, Eric	4
Hilly, Pat	0
Hilsey, Charlie	1
Hilton, Dave	5
Hilton, Howard	1
Himes, Jack	4
Hinch, A.J.	10
Hinchliffe, Brett	0
Hinchman, Bill	110
Hinchman, Harry	2
Hinds, Sam	2
Hines, Hunkey	0
Hines, Mike	9
Hinkle, Gordie	1
Hinrichs, Dutch	0
Hinrichs, Paul	0
Hinshaw, George	2
Hinsley, Jerry	0
Hinson, Paul	0
Hinton, John	0
Hinton, Rich	6
Hinzo, Tommy	3
Hippauf, Herb	0
Hiser, Gene	2
Hisner, Harley	0
Hitchcock, Billy	33
Hitchcock, Jim	1
Hitchcock, Sterling	47
Hitt, Bruce	0
Hitt, Roy	3
Hittle, Lloyd	7
Hoag, Myril	59
Hoak, Don	132
Hobaugh, Ed	10
Hobbie, Glen	56
Hobbs, Bill	0
Hobbs, Jack	0
Hobson, Butch	47
Hoch, Harry	3
Hock, Ed	0
Hockenbery, Chuck	0
Hockett, Oris	58
Hockette, George	6
Hodapp, Johnny	79
Hoderlein, Mel	7
Hodge, Ed	4
Hodge, Gomer	0
Hodge, Shovel	10
Hodges, Bert	0
Hodges, Kevin	1
Hodges, Ron	38
Hodgin, Ralph	48
Hodgson, Paul	0
Hodkey, Eli	0
Hodnett, Charlie	17
Hodson, George	4
Hoeft, Billy	105
Hoelskoetter, Art	15
Hoerner, Joe	72
Hoerst, Frank	2
Hoey, Jack	3
Hoff, Red	5
Hofferth, Stew	5
Hoffman, Bill	0
Hoffman, Dutch	7
Hoffman, Frank	6
Hoffman, Glenn	41
Hoffman, Guy	18
Hoffman, Hickey	0
Hoffman, Izzy	3
Hoffman, John	0
Hoffman, Larry	1
Hoffman, Ray	0
Hoffman, Tex	0
Hoffmeister, Jesse	5
Hofford, John	4
Hofman, Bobby	17
Hofmann, Fred	20
Hogan, Eddie	15
Hogan, George	0
Hogan, Harry	0
Hogan, Kenny	0
Hogan, Marty	1
Hogan, Shanty	111
Hogan, Willie	13
Hogg, Bert	0
Hogg, Bill	34
Hogg, Brad	25
Hogriever, George	12
Hogsett, Chief	61
Hogue, Bobby	19
Hogue, Cal	2
Hohman, Bill	0
Hohnhorst, Eddie	3
Holbert, Aaron	0
Holbert, Bill	42
Holbert, Ray	1
Holborow, Wally	3
Holbrook, Sammy	4
Holcombe, Ken	18
Holden, Bill	3
Holden, Joe	0
Holdridge, David	0
Holdsworth, Fred	9
Holdsworth, Jim	12
Holke, Walter	89
Hollahan, Bill	0
Holland, Al	69
Holland, Bill	0
Holland, Dutch	8
Holland, Mul	2
Holland, Will	1
Holle, Gary	0
Holley, Ed	32
Holling, Carl	5
Hollingsworth, Al	72
Hollingsworth, B.	2
Hollins, Damon	0
Hollins, Jessie	0
Hollison, John	0
Hollmig, Stan	4
Hollocher, Charlie	113
Holloman, Bobo	2
Holloway, Jim	0
Holloway, Ken	60
Holly, Ed	18
Holly, Jeff	2
Holm, Billy	4
Holm, Wattie	30
Holman, Brad	3
Holman, Brian	37
Holman, Gary	5
Holman, Scott	7
Holman, Shawn	1
Holmes, Chuck	0
Holmes, Darren	52
Holmes, Ducky	
Debut 1895	105
Debut 1906	0
Holmes, Fred	0
Holmes, Jim	0
Holshouser, Herm	0
Holt, Jim	31
Holt, Red	2
Holt, Roger	0
Holtgrave, Vern	0
Holton, Brian	22
Holtz, Mike	15
Holzemer, Mark	0
Honan, Marty	0
Hood, Abie	1
Hood, Don	43
Hood, Wally	
Debut 1920	2
Debut 1949	0
Hook, Chris	2
Hook, Jay	16
Hooker, Buck	0
Hooks, Alex	0
Hooper, Bob	28
Hooten, Leon	0
Hoover, Buster	19
Hoover, Charlie	5
Hoover, Dick	0
Hoover, Joe	26
Hoover, John	0
Hoover, Paul	0
Hope, John	2
Hope, Sam	0
Hopkins, Buck	1
Hopkins, Don	0
Hopkins, Gail	32
Hopkins, Marty	7
Hopkins, Mike	1
Hopkins, Paul	2
Hopper, Bill	1
Hopper, Jim	0
Hopper, Lefty	0
Horan, P.J.	3
Horan, Shags	0
Horn, Sam	27
Horne, Trader	1
Horner, Jack	0
Horsey, Hanson	0
Horsman, Vince	7
Horstmann, Oscar	7
Horton, Elmer	0
Horton, Ricky	39
Horton, Tony	62
Hosey, Dwayne	5
Hosey, Steve	0
Hoskins, Dave	8
Hosley, Tim	10
Host, Gene	0
Hostetler, Chuck	7
Hostetler, Dave	16
Hottman, Ken	0
Houck, Byron	24
Houck, Sadie	67
Houk, Ralph	5
House, Craig	0
House, Frank	46
House, Fred	0
House, Pat	0
House, Tom	42
Householder, C.	
Debut 1882	17
Debut 1884	7
Householder, Ed	0
Householder, Paul	29
Houseman, Frank	0
Houseman, John	4
Houser, Ben	7
Houser, Joe	0
Housie, Wayne	0
Houtteman, Art	89
Houtz, Lefty	1
Hovley, Steve	28
Hovlik, Ed	2
Hovlik, Joe	3
Howard, Bruce	26

Player	WS
Howard, Chris	
Debut 1991	0
Debut 1993	6
Howard, Dave	0
Howard, David	29
Howard, Del	50
Howard, Doug	1
Howard, Earl	0
Howard, Fred	3
Howard, Ivan	24
Howard, Larry	9
Howard, Lee	1
Howard, Matt	0
Howard, Mike	1
Howard, Paul	0
Howard, Steve	0
Howard, Thomas	52
Howard, Wilbur	16
Howarth, Jim	4
Howe, Art	84
Howe, Cal	0
Howe, Les	3
Howe, Shorty	1
Howe, Steve	76
Howell, Dixie	
Debut 1940	21
Debut 1947	18
Howell, Jack	75
Howell, Jay	95
Howell, Ken	34
Howell, Pat	1
Howell, Red	0
Howell, Roland	0
Howell, Roy	91
Howerton, Bill	22
Howitt, Dann	3
Howley, Dan	1
Howser, Dick	74
Hoy, Peter	0
Hoyle, Tex	0
Hoyt, LaMarr	72
Hrabosky, Al	82
Hriniak, Walt	2
Hubbard, Al	1
Hubbard, Mike	1
Hubbard, Trenidad	15
Hubbell, Bill	41
Hubbs, Ken	21
Huber, Clarence	18
Huber, Otto	0
Huckaby, Ken	0
Huckleberry, Earl	0
Hudek, John	15
Hudgens, Dave	0
Hudgens, Jimmy	1
Hudler, Rex	41
Hudson, Charles	42
Hudson, Charlie	2
Hudson, Hal	0
Hudson, Jesse	0

Player	WS
Hudson, Joe	8
Hudson, Johnny	19
Hudson, Nat	66
Hudson, Rex	0
Hudson, Sid	103
Huelsman, Frank	29
Huenke, Al	0
Huff, Aubrey	8
Huff, Mike	16
Huffman, Ben	2
Huffman, Phil	2
Hug, Ed	0
Hughes, Bill	
Debut 1884	0
Debut 1921	0
Hughes, Bobby	3
Hughes, Dick	24
Hughes, Ed	0
Hughes, Jim	
Debut 1898	85
Debut 1952	27
Debut 1974	15
Hughes, Joe	0
Hughes, Keith	2
Hughes, Mickey	41
Hughes, Roy	56
Hughes, Terry	1
Hughes, Tom	
Debut 1906	59
Debut 1930	2
Debut 1959	0
Hughes, Tommy	35
Hughes, Vern	0
Hughey, Jim	40
Huhn, Emil	6
Huisman, Rick	2
Huismann, Mark	16
Hulen, Billy	10
Hulett, Tim	50
Hulihan, Harry	2
Hulse, David	22
Hulswitt, Rudy	53
Hulvey, Hank	0
Hume, Tom	76
Hummel, John	109
Humphrey, Al	0
Humphrey, Bill	0
Humphrey, Terry	19
Humphreys, Bob	38
Humphreys, Mike	2
Humphries, Bert	52
Humphries, John	3
Humphries, Johnny	60
Hundley, Randy	91
Hungling, Bernie	3
Hunnefield, Bill	34
Hunt, Ben	1
Hunt, Joel	0

Player	WS
Hunt, Ken	
Debut 1959	15
Debut 1961	8
Hunt, Randy	1
Hunter, Bill	
Debut 1884	0
Debut 1912	1
Hunter, Billy	30
Hunter, Brian	34
Hunter, Brian L.	56
Hunter, Buddy	1
Hunter, Eddie	0
Hunter, George	7
Hunter, Herb	0
Hunter, Jim	0
Hunter, Lem	0
Hunter, Newt	5
Hunter, Rich	0
Hunter, Willard	4
Huntz, Steve	14
Huntzinger, Walter	12
Huppert, Dave	0
Hurd, Tom	16
Hurdle, Clint	43
Hurley, Jerry	
Debut 1889	2
Debut 1901	0
Hurst, Bill	0
Hurst, Don	89
Hurst, James	0
Hurst, Jimmy	0
Hurst, Jon	0
Hurtado, Edwin	3
Huskey, Butch	44
Huson, Jeff	34
Husta, Carl	1
Husted, Bill	6
Husting, Bert	20
Huston, Harry	0
Huston, Warren	1
Hutcheson, Joe	3
Hutchings, Johnny	23
Hutchinson, Chad	0
Hutchinson, Ed	0
Hutchinson, Ira	37
Hutson, Herb	1
Hutson, Roy	1
Hutto, Jim	0
Hutton, Mark	8
Hutton, Tom	34
Hyatt, Ham	26
Hyde, Dick	26
Hyers, Tim	1
Hyndman, Jim	0
Hynes, Pat	1
Hyzdu, Adam	2

I

Player	WS
Iburg, Ham	8
Ignasiak, Gary	0
Ignasiak, Mike	7
Ilsley, Blaise	0
Imlay, Doc	0
Incaviglia, Pete	107
Infante, Alexis	0
Inge, Brandon	3
Ingersoll, Bob	1
Ingerton, Scotty	7
Ingraham, Charlie	0
Ingram, Garey	4
Ingram, Mel	0
Ingram, Riccardo	0
Inks, Bert	24
Innis, Jeff	26
Iorg, Dane	35
Iorg, Garth	45
Iott, Happy	0
Iott, Hooks	1
Irabu, Hideki	21
Irelan, Hal	4
Ireland, Tim	0
Irvin, Ed	1
Irvine, Daryl	1
Irwin, Bill	0
Irwin, Charlie	99
Irwin, John	32
Irwin, Tommy	0
Irwin, Walt	0
Isales, Orlando	1
Ivie, Mike	84
Izquierdo, Hank	1
Izturis, Cesar	4

J

Player	WS
Jablonski, Ray	52
Jacklitsch, Fred	50
Jackson, Al	60
Jackson, Bill	0
Jackson, Bo	72
Jackson, Charlie	
Debut 1905	0
Debut 1915	2
Jackson, Chuck	3
Jackson, Danny	107
Jackson, Darrell	20
Jackson, Darrin	60
Jackson, George	11
Jackson, Grant	99
Jackson, Henry	0
Jackson, Jim	26
Jackson, John	0
Jackson, Ken	0

Player	WS
Jackson, Lou	0
Jackson, Mike	1
Jackson, Ron	
Debut 1954	11
Debut 1975	69
Jackson, Roy Lee	44
Jackson, Ryan	5
Jackson, Sonny	60
Jacobs, Art	0
Jacobs, Bucky	2
Jacobs, Elmer	53
Jacobs, Jake	0
Jacobs, Mike	0
Jacobs, Otto	1
Jacobs, Ray	0
Jacobs, Spook	12
Jacobs, Tony	0
Jacobson, Beany	17
Jacobson, Merwin	5
Jacobus, Larry	0
Jacoby, Harry	1
Jacome, Jason	12
Jacquez, Pat	0
Jacquez, Tom	0
Jaeckel, Paul	2
Jaeger, Charlie	1
Jaeger, Joe	0
Jahn, Art	6
Jakucki, Sig	25
Jamerson, Charlie	0
James, Art	0
James, Bernie	5
James, Bert	1
James, Bill	
Debut 1911	51
Debut 1913	45
James, Bob	40
James, Charlie	20
James, Chris	66
James, Cleo	8
James, Dion	73
James, Jeff	1
James, Johnny	5
James, Lefty	3
James, Mike	27
James, Rick	0
James, Skip	0
Janeski, Jerry	6
Janowicz, Vic	1
Jansen, Larry	118
Jansen, Ray	1
Jantzen, Heinie	1
Janvrin, Hal	38
Janzen, Marty	2
Jarvis, Pat	77
Jarvis, Ray	3
Jarvis, Roy	0
Jasper, Hi	8
Jaster, Larry	31
Jata, Paul	1

Player	WS
Javery, Al	54
Javier, Al	0
Jay, Joey	86
Jean, Domingo	2
Jeanes, Tex	1
Jeffcoat, George	8
Jeffcoat, Hal	78
Jeffcoat, Mike	26
Jefferson, Jesse	35
Jefferson, Reggie	49
Jefferson, Stan	14
Jeffries, Irv	5
Jelic, Chris	0
Jelinich, Frank	0
Jelks, Greg	0
Jeltz, Steve	37
Jenkins, Jack	1
Jenkins, Joe	0
Jenkins, John	0
Jenkins, Tom	5
Jennings, Alamazoo	0
Jennings, Bill	2
Jennings, Doug	6
Jennings, Jason	3
Jennings, Robin	4
Jensen, Marcus	5
Jensen, Ryan	2
Jensen, Willie	0
Jensen, Woody	54
Jerzembeck, Mike	0
Jessee, Dan	0
Jestadt, Garry	9
Jester, Virgil	5
Jeter, Johnny	14
Jeter, Shawn	0
Jethroe, Sam	61
Jimenez, D'Angelo	9
Jimenez, Elvio	0
Jimenez, German	0
Jimenez, Houston	4
Jimenez, Juan	0
Jimenez, Manny	23
Jimenez, Miguel	2
Jodie, Brett	1
Johns, Augie	3
Johns, Doug	16
Johns, Keith	0
Johns, Ollie	0
Johns, Pete	2
Johnson, Abbie	1
Johnson, Abe	0
Johnson, Adam	0
Johnson, Alex	122
Johnson, Art	
Debut 1927	0
Debut 1940	9
Johnson, Bart	46
Johnson, Ben	2

Player	WS
Johnson, Bill	
Debut 1884	21
Debut 1916	0
Debut 1943	102
Debut 1983	2
Johnson, Bob	
Debut 1960	58
Debut 1969	35
Johnson, Bobby	6
Johnson, Brian	28
Johnson, Charlie	1
Johnson, Chet	0
Johnson, Chief	35
Johnson, Cliff	134
Johnson, Connie	48
Johnson, Dane	4
Johnson, Darrell	7
Johnson, Dave	
Debut 1974	4
Debut 1987	13
Johnson, Don	
Debut 1943	47
Debut 1947	23
Johnson, Earl	34
Johnson, Ed	0
Johnson, Elmer	0
Johnson, Erik	0
Johnson, Ernie	
Debut 1912	66
Debut 1950	34
Johnson, Footer	0
Johnson, Frank	4
Johnson, Fred	5
Johnson, Hank	47
Johnson, Jason	15
Johnson, Jeff	1
Johnson, Jerry	35
Johnson, Jim	0
Johnson, Jing	22
Johnson, Joe	14
Johnson, John	1
Johnson, John H.	39
Johnson, Johnny	5
Johnson, Jonathan	1
Johnson, Keith	1
Johnson, Ken	10
Johnson, Lamar	65
Johnson, Larry	0
Johnson, Lloyd	0
Johnson, Lou	61
Johnson, Mark	0
Johnson, Mark P.	23
Johnson, Mike	
Debut 1974	0
Debut 1997	3
Johnson, Nick	0
Johnson, Otis	6
Johnson, Paul	2

Player	WS
Johnson, Randy	
Debut 1980	5
Debut 1982	12
Johnson, Rankin	
Debut 1914	24
Debut 1941	0
Johnson, Ron	2
Johnson, Rondin	1
Johnson, Roy	
Debut 1918	1
Debut 1982	0
Johnson, Si	99
Johnson, Spud	44
Johnson, Stan	0
Johnson, Tim	21
Johnson, Tom	24
Johnson, Tony	1
Johnson, Vic	4
Johnson, Wallace	6
Johnson, Walt	0
Johnson, Youngy	1
Johnston, Dick	74
Johnston, Doc	73
Johnston, Fred	0
Johnston, Greg	0
Johnston, Joel	10
Johnston, Johnny	6
Johnston, Rex	0
Johnstone, John	17
Joiner, Roy	4
Jok, Stan	1
Jolley, Smead	44
Jolly, Dave	19
Jones, Al	2
Jones, Alex	10
Jones, Art	0
Jones, Barry	33
Jones, Bill	
Debut 1882	0
Debut 1911	1
Jones, Binky	0
Jones, Bob	60
Jones, Bobby	11
Jones, Bobby J.	60
Jones, Bobby M.	12
Jones, Broadway	0
Jones, Bumpus	1
Jones, Calvin	5
Jones, Charlie	
Debut 1884	0
Debut 1901	40
Jones, Chris	
Debut 1985	0
Debut 1991	21
Jones, Clarence	3
Jones, Cleon	141
Jones, Cobe	1
Jones, Cowboy	24
Jones, Dale	0
Jones, Dalton	41

Player	WS
Jones, Darryl	1
Jones, Dax	1
Jones, Deacon	
Debut 1916	5
Debut 1962	1
Jones, Dick	1
Jones, Earl	3
Jones, Elijah	1
Jones, Frank	0
Jones, Gary	0
Jones, Gordon	18
Jones, Hal	1
Jones, Henry	3
Jones, Howie	0
Jones, Jack	
Debut 1883	9
Debut 1883	9
Jones, Jake	14
Jones, Jeff	
Debut 1980	9
Debut 1983	2
Jones, Jim	4
Jones, Jimmy	21
Jones, John	0
Jones, Johnny	0
Jones, Ken	0
Jones, Lynn	16
Jones, Marcus	0
Jones, Mike	
Debut 1890	2
Debut 1980	9
Jones, Nippy	20
Jones, Odell	23
Jones, Oscar	44
Jones, Percy	54
Jones, Red	0
Jones, Rick	7
Jones, Ricky	1
Jones, Ron	8
Jones, Ross	2
Jones, Sheldon	47
Jones, Sherman	3
Jones, Stacy	0
Jones, Steve	2
Jones, Terry	8
Jones, Tex	0
Jones, Tim	
Debut 1977	2
Debut 1988	10
Jones, Tom	71
Jones, Tracy	31
Jones	
Debut 1884	1
Debut 1885	0
Jonnard, Bubber	3
Jonnard, Claude	22
Jordan, Charlie	0
Jordan, Dutch	4
Jordan, Harry	2
Jordan, Jimmy	15

Player	WS
Jordan, Kevin	21
Jordan, Mike	0
Jordan, Milt	0
Jordan, Niles	2
Jordan, Ricardo	3
Jordan, Ricky	50
Jordan, Rip	0
Jordan, Scott	0
Jordan, Slats	0
Jordan, Tom	1
Jorgens, Art	17
Jorgens, Orville	23
Jorgensen, Pinky	0
Jorgensen, Spider	26
Jorgensen, Terry	3
Jose, Felix	75
Joseph, Rick	11
Josephson, Duane	38
Joshua, Von	47
Jourdan, Ted	2
Joy, Pop	1
Joyce, Bob	1
Joyce, Dick	0
Joyce, Mike	4
Joyce	0
Judd, Mike	2
Judd, Oscar	46
Judd, Ralph	5
Jude, Frank	3
Juden, Jeff	19
Judson, Howie	30
Judy, Lyle	0
Juelich, Red	0
Julio, Jorge	1
Jumonville, George	1
Jungels, Ken	0
Jurak, Ed	9
Jurewicz, Mike	0
Jurisich, Al	14
Just, Joe	0
Justis, Walt	0
Jutze, Skip	6
Juul, Herb	0
Juul, Herold	0

K

Player	WS
Kading, Jack	1
Kafora, Jake	0
Kahdot, Ike	0
Kahl, Nick	1
Kahle, Bob	0
Kahler, George	33
Kahn, Owen	0
Kahoe, Mike	21
Kainer, Don	2
Kaiser, Al	5
Kaiser, Bob	0
Kaiser, Don	7

Player	WS
Kaiser, Jeff	1
Kaiserling, George	36
Kalahan, John	0
Kalbfus, Charlie	0
Kalfass, Bill	1
Kalin, Frank	0
Kallio, Rudy	5
Kamieniecki, Scott	49
Kammeyer, Bob	0
Kamp, Ike	1
Kampouris, Alex	59
Kane, Frank	0
Kane, Harry	1
Kane, Jerry	0
Kane, Jim	4
Kane, John	
Debut 1907	26
Debut 1925	1
Kane, Tom	0
Kanehl, Rod	7
Kantlehner, Erv	20
Kappel, Heinie	12
Kappel, Joe	5
Karchner, Matt	20
Kardow, Paul	0
Karger, Ed	59
Karkovice, Ron	80
Karl, Andy	26
Karl, Scott	47
Karlon, Bill	0
Karns, Bill	0
Karnuth, Jason	1
Karow, Marty	0
Karp, Ryan	0
Karpel, Herb	0
Karr, Benn	37
Karst, Jack	0
Kashiwada, Takashi	2
Kasko, Eddie	78
Katoll, John	16
Katt, Ray	20
Katz, Bob	1
Kauffman, Dick	2
Kaufman, Curt	4
Kaufmann, Tony	73
Kavanagh, Charlie	0
Kavanagh, Leo	0
Kavanagh, Marty	31
Kay, Bill	2
Kazak, Eddie	13
Kazanski, Ted	16
Keagle, Greg	2
Kealey, Steve	13
Kearney, Bob	28
Kearns, Teddy	0
Kearns, Tom	0
Kearse, Eddie	1
Keas, Ed	2
Keating, Chick	0
Keating, Ed	0

Player	WS
Keating, Ray	30
Keatley, Greg	0
Keck, Cactus	12
Keedy, Pat	2
Keefe, Bobby	20
Keefe, Dave	16
Keefe, George	18
Keefe, John	12
Keegan, Bob	37
Keegan, Ed	1
Keeley, Burt	3
Keely, Bob	0
Keen, Bill	0
Keen, Vic	39
Keenan, Jim	
Debut 1880	60
Debut 1920	0
Keenan, Kid	1
Keener, Harry	4
Keener, Jeff	2
Keener, Joe	0
Keesey, Jim	0
Keeton, Buster	1
Keffer, Frank	0
Kehn, Chet	1
Keifer, Katsy	1
Keisler, Randy	0
Keister, Bill	78
Kekich, Mike	17
Kelb, George	0
Keliher, Mickey	0
Kell, Skeeter	2
Kelleher, Duke	0
Kelleher, Frankie	2
Kelleher, Hal	4
Kelleher, John	18
Kelleher, Mick	18
Keller, Hal	0
Keller, Ron	1
Kellert, Frank	4
Kellett, Al	0
Kellett, Red	0
Kelley, Dick	27
Kelley, Harry	37
Kelley, Mike	4
Kelley, Tom	21
Kelliher, Frank	0
Kellner, Walt	0
Kellogg, Al	0
Kellogg, Bill	0
Kellogg, Nate	0
Kellum, Win	21
Kelly, Bill	0
Kelly, Billy	7
Kelly, Bob	15
Kelly, Bryan	1
Kelly, Charlie	0
Kelly, Ed	0
Kelly, Herb	2
Kelly, Jim	28

Player	WS
Kelly, Joe	
Debut 1914	22
Debut 1926	5
Kelly, John	
Debut 1882	9
Debut 1907	1
Kelly, Kenny	0
Kelly, Kick	0
Kelly, Mike	
Debut 1926	0
Debut 1994	12
Kelly, Pat	
Debut 1980	0
Debut 1991	40
Kelly, Red	1
Kelly, Ren	1
Kelly, Speed	0
Kelly, Tom	1
Kelly, Van	4
Kelsey, Billy	0
Kelso, Bill	14
Kelty, John	3
Kemmer, Bill	0
Kemmerer, Russ	42
Kemmler, Rudy	13
Kemner, Dutch	0
Kendall, Fred	51
Kenders, Al	0
Kenna, Ed	0
Kenna, Eddie	3
Kennedy, Bill	
Debut 1942	0
Debut 1948	22
Kennedy, Bob	87
Kennedy, Doc	16
Kennedy, Ed	
Debut 1883	12
Debut 1884	1
Kennedy, Jim	0
Kennedy, Joe	6
Kennedy, John	
Debut 1957	0
Debut 1962	38
Kennedy, Junior	26
Kennedy, Monte	47
Kennedy, Ray	0
Kennedy, Snapper	0
Kennedy, Ted	9
Kennedy, Vern	105
Kenney, Art	0
Kenney, Jerry	35
Kent, Ed	0
Kent, Maury	2
Kenworthy, Dick	3
Kenworthy, Duke	53
Keough, Joe	17
Keough, Marty	43
Keough, Matt	50
Kepshire, Kurt	8
Kerfeld, Charlie	15

Player	WS
Keriazakos, Gus	2
Kerins, John	54
Kerksieck, Bill	0
Kerlin, Orie	0
Kern, Bill	0
Kern, Jim	77
Kernek, George	1
Kerns, Russ	0
Kerr, Buddy	87
Kerr, Dickie	56
Kerr, Doc	3
Kerr, John	28
Kerr, Mel	0
Kerrigan, Joe	13
Kerwin, Dan	1
Kessinger, Keith	1
Kessler, Henry	3
Kester, Rick	0
Ketcham, Fred	1
Ketchum, Gus	0
Ketter, Phil	0
Keupper, Henry	7
Keyser, Brian	5
Khalifa, Sammy	8
Kibbie, Hod	1
Kibble, Jack	0
Kida, Masao	2
Kiecker, Dana	9
Kiefer, Joe	1
Kiefer, Mark	7
Kiefer, Steve	2
Kielty, Bobby	1
Kiely, John	5
Kiely, Leo	42
Kienzle, Bill	10
Kieschnick, Brooks	4
Kilduff, Pete	45
Kiley, John	1
Kilgus, Paul	24
Kilhullen, Pat	0
Kilkenny, Mike	17
Killeen, Evans	0
Killeen, Henry	0
Killefer, Red	40
Killilay, Jack	4
Kilroy, Mike	0
Kim, Sun-Woo	1
Kimball, Newt	12
Kimber, Sam	16
Kimberlin, Harry	4
Kimble, Dick	1
Kime, Hal	0
Kimm, Bruce	7
Kimmick, Wally	6
Kimsey, Chad	31
Kindall, Jerry	37
King, Chick	0
King, Clyde	25
King, Curtis	7
King, Eric	50

Player	WS
King, Hal	19
King, Jim	91
King, Kevin	0
King, Lee	
Debut 1916	22
Debut 1916	0
King, Lynn	3
King, Nellie	12
King, Ray	9
King, Sam	0
Kingdon, Wes	2
Kingery, Mike	47
Kingman, Brian	22
Kingman, Harry	0
Kingsale, Gene	3
Kinkade, Mike	3
Kinlock, Walt	0
Kinney, Dennis	5
Kinney, Matt	2
Kinney, Walt	15
Kinnunen, Mike	0
Kinsella, Bob	0
Kinsella, Ed	2
Kinsler, William	0
Kinslow, Tom	35
Kinzer, Matt	0
Kinzie, Walt	2
Kinzy, Harry	1
Kipp, Fred	4
Kipper, Bob	22
Kipper, Thornton	3
Kippert, Ed	0
Kirby, Clay	64
Kirby, Jim	0
Kirby, John	19
Kirby, LaRue	6
Kirby, Wayne	23
Kircher, Mike	0
Kirk, Bill	0
Kirk, Tom	0
Kirke, Jay	21
Kirkland, Willie	98
Kirkpatrick, Ed	97
Kirkpatrick, Enos	12
Kirkwood, Don	13
Kirrene, Joe	1
Kirsch, Harry	0
Kiser, Garland	0
Kish, Ernie	1
Kisinger, Rube	8
Kison, Bruce	98
Kissinger, Bill	7
Kitsos, Chris	0
Kittle, Ron	76
Kittridge, Malachi	74
Klaerner, Hugo	0
Klages, Fred	3
Klassen, Danny	2
Klaus, Billy	64
Klaus, Bobby	10

Player	WS
Klawitter, Al	3
Klawitter, Tom	0
Klee, Ollie	0
Klein, Lou	35
Kleine, Hal	0
Kleinhans, Ted	2
Kleinke, Nub	0
Kleinow, Red	37
Klepfer, Ed	28
Kleven, Jay	0
Klieman, Ed	37
Klimchock, Lou	12
Klimkowski, Ron	12
Kline, Bob	22
Kline, Bobby	2
Kline, Steve	38
Kling, Bill	3
Kling, Rudy	1
Klingenbeck, Scott	3
Klinger, Bob	64
Klinger, Joe	0
Klink, Joe	10
Klippstein, Johnny	103
Klobedanz, Fred	51
Klopp, Stan	0
Kloza, Nap	0
Klugmann, Joe	4
Klumpp, Elmer	0
Klusman, Billy	2
Klutts, Mickey	13
Kluttz, Clyde	50
Kmak, Joe	4
Knackert, Brent	0
Knapp, Chris	17
Knaupp, Cotton	2
Knauss, Frank	23
Kneisch, Rudy	1
Knepper, Charlie	6
Knerr, Lou	2
Knetzer, Elmer	66
Knicely, Alan	12
Knickerbocker, A.	1
Knickerbocker, Bill	72
Knight, Brandon	0
Knight, Jack	2
Knight, Joe	18
Knight, John	64
Knight, Lon	54
Knisely, Pete	9
Knode, Mike	0
Knode, Ray	3
Knoll, Punch	3
Knolls, Hub	1
Knorr, Randy	12
Knothe, Fritz	13
Knothe, George	0
Knott, Eric	0
Knott, Jack	79
Knotts, Gary	0
Knotts, Joe	0

Player	WS
Knouff, Ed	20
Knowdell, Jake	0
Knowles, Darold	100
Knowles, Jimmy	33
Knowlson, Tom	2
Knowlton, Bill	0
Knox, Andy	2
Knox, Cliff	0
Knox, John	4
Knudsen, Kurt	5
Knudson, Mark	20
Koback, Nick	0
Kobel, Kevin	21
Koch, Alan	2
Koch, Barney	0
Kocher, Brad	2
Koecher, Dick	0
Koegel, Pete	0
Koehler, Ben	16
Koehler, Pip	0
Koelling, Brian	0
Koenecke, Len	36
Koenig, Mark	103
Koenigsmark, Will	0
Koestner, Elmer	6
Kohlman, Joe	1
Kohlmeier, Ryan	4
Kokos, Dick	44
Kolb, Brandon	0
Kolb, Danny	3
Kolb, Eddie	0
Kolb, Gary	8
Kolloway, Don	74
Kolp, Ray	97
Kolseth, Karl	1
Kolstad, Hal	0
Kommers, Fred	12
Komminsk, Brad	19
Konieczny, Doug	3
Konikowski, Alex	1
Konnick, Mike	0
Konopka, Bruce	0
Konstanty, Jim	83
Konuszewski, D.	0
Koob, Ernie	22
Koonce, Cal	52
Koons, Harry	1
Kopacz, George	0
Kopf, Larry	65
Kopf, Wally	0
Koplitz, Howie	6
Koplove, Mike	0
Kopp, Merlin	12
Koppe, Joe	41
Kopshaw, George	0
Korcheck, Steve	3
Kores, Art	7
Korince, George	0
Korwan, Jim	0
Kosco, Andy	40

Player	WS
Koshorek, Clem	5
Koski, Bill	0
Koslo, Dave	94
Koslofski, Kevin	5
Kosman, Mike	0
Kostal, Joe	0
Koster, Fred	1
Kostro, Frank	7
Koukalik, Joe	0
Koupal, Lou	10
Kowalik, Fabian	4
Kowitz, Brian	0
Koy, Ernie	54
Kozar, Al	16
Kracher, Joe	0
Kraemer, Joe	0
Kraft, Clarence	0
Krakauskas, Joe	26
Kralick, Jack	74
Kraly, Steve	1
Kramer, Jack	85
Kramer, Randy	4
Kramer, Tom	6
Kranepool, Ed	132
Krapp, Gene	49
Kraus, Jack	11
Krause, Charlie	0
Krause, Harry	38
Krausse, Lew	
Debut 1931	5
Debut 1961	53
Kravec, Ken	35
Kravitz, Danny	9
Krawczyk, Ray	1
Kreeger, Frank	0
Krehmeyer, Charlie	1
Kreitner, Mickey	1
Kreitz, Ralph	0
Kremers, Jimmy	1
Kremmel, Jim	0
Krenchicki, Wayne	28
Kress, Chuck	7
Kretlow, Lou	25
Kreuger, Rick	2
Kreutzer, Frank	7
Krichell, Paul	3
Krieg, Bill	13
Krieger, Kurt	0
Krist, Howie	36
Krivda, Rick	11
Krock, Gus	29
Kroh, Rube	16
Kroll, Gary	6
Kroner, John	15
Kroon, Marc	0
Krsnich, Mike	0
Krsnich, Rocky	5
Krueger, Bill	49
Krueger, Ernie	28
Krueger, Otto	47

Player	WS
Krug, Chris	2
Krug, Gary	0
Krug, Henry	1
Krug, Marty	13
Kruger, Abe	0
Kruger, Art	23
Krumm, Al	0
Kryhoski, Dick	33
Kubenka, Jeff	2
Kubiak, Ted	46
Kubinski, Tim	0
Kubiszyn, Jack	1
Kubski, Gil	1
Kucab, Johnny	7
Kucek, Jack	4
Kucks, Johnny	37
Kuczek, Steve	0
Kuczynski, Bert	0
Kuhaulua, Fred	2
Kuhn, Bub	0
Kuhn, Kenny	0
Kuhn, Walt	8
Kuhns, Charlie	0
Kuiper, Duane	73
Kull, John	1
Kume, Mike	0
Kunkel, Bill	7
Kunkel, Jeff	14
Kuntz, Rusty	10
Kunz, Earl	0
Kurosaki, Ryan	0
Kurtz, Hal	0
Kusel, Ed	0
Kush, Emil	27
Kusick, Craig	32
Kusnyer, Art	6
Kustus, Jul	1
Kutcher, Randy	9
Kutina, Joe	3
Kutyna, Marty	16
Kutzler, Jerry	0
Kuzava, Bob	46
Kvasnak, Al	0
Kyle, Andy	1

L

Player	WS
Laboy, Coco	20
Lacey, Bob	29
LaChance, Candy	111
Lachemann, Marcel	7
Lachemann, Rene	4
Lachowicz, Al	1
Lackey, William	0
LaCock, Pete	36
LaCorte, Frank	19
LaCoss, Mike	69
Lacy, Kerry	2

Player	WS
Lacy, Lee	0
Ladd, Hi	0
Ladd, Pete	22
Lade, Doyle	26
Ladew, Steve	0
Lafata, Joe	3
Lafferty, Flip	0
Lafitte, Ed	38
LaForest, Ty	3
LaFrancois, Roger	1
Laga, Mike	7
Lagger, Ed	0
LaGrow, Lerrin	50
Lahoud, Joe	55
Lahti, Jeff	24
Lajeskie, Dick	0
Lake, Fred	3
Lake, Joe	52
Lake, Steve	22
Lakeman, Al	11
Laker, Tim	6
Lally, Dan	5
Lamabe, Jack	29
LaMacchia, Al	1
LaManna, Hank	1
Lamanno, Ray	35
Lamanske, Frank	0
Lamar, Bill	48
LaMaster, Wayne	11
Lamb, David	1
Lamb, John	4
Lamb, Laymon	3
Lamb, Ray	26
Lambert, Clayton	2
Lambert, Gene	1
Lambeth, Otis	9
Lamers, Pete	0
Lamline, Fred	0
Lamont, Gene	5
LaMotte, Bobby	14
Lamp, Dennis	103
Lampard, Keith	2
Lampe, Henry	0
Lampkin, Tom	41
Lanahan, Dick	4
Lancaster, Les	47
Lance, Gary	0
Lancellotti, Rick	0
Land, Doc	0
Land, Grover	16
Landenberger, Ken	0
Landestoy, Rafael	29
Landis, Bill	6
Landis, Doc	11
Landreth, Larry	0
Landrith, Hobie	48
Landrum, Bill	36
Landrum, Ced	3
Landrum, Don	22
Landrum, Jesse	0

Player	WS
Landrum, Joe	0
Landrum, Tito	22
Lane, Chappy	5
Lane, Dick	0
Lane, Hunter	0
Lane, Jerry	2
Lane, Marvin	5
Lanford, Sam	0
Lanfranconi, Walt	6
Lang, Chip	2
Lang, Don	11
Lang, Marty	0
Lange, Dick	3
Lange, Erv	14
Lange, Frank	32
Langford, Rick	76
Langford, Sam	8
Langsford, Bob	0
Lanier, Hal	60
Lanier, Rimp	0
Lankford, Frank	0
Lanning, Johnny	61
Lanning, Red	1
Lanning, Tom	0
Lansford, Jody	0
Lansing, Gene	0
LaPalme, Paul	34
Lapan, Pete	2
Lapihuska, Andy	0
LaPoint, Dave	66
Lapointe, Ralph	9
Lapp, Jack	63
Lara, Yovanny	0
Larker, Norm	51
Larkin, Andy	0
Larkin, Ed	0
Larkin, Gene	54
Larkin, Pat	0
Larkin, Stephen	0
Larkin, Steve	0
Larkin	1
Larmore, Bob	0
LaRocca, Greg	0
LaRoque, Sam	9
LaRose, John	0
LaRose, Vic	0
LaRoss, Harry	0
Larsen, Don	95
Larsen, Swede	0
Larson, Brandon	0
Larson, Dan	10
La Russa, Tony	3
Lary, Al	1
Lasher, Fred	13
Laskey, Bill	30
Lasley, Bill	0
Lasorda, Tom	0
Lassetter, Don	0
Latham, Bill	1
Latham, Chris	3
Latham, Jumbo	25
Lathers, Chick	2
Lathrop, Bill	2
Latimer, Tacks	1
Latman, Barry	55
Lattimore, Bill	1
Lau, Charlie	33
Lauder, Billy	30
Laudner, Tim	41
Lauer, Chuck	0
Lauterborn, Bill	2
Lauzerique, George	2
Lavagetto, Cookie	109
LaValliere, Mike	95
Lavan, Doc	88
Lavelle, Gary	114
Lavender, Jimmy	66
LaVigne, Art	2
Lavin, Johnny	1
Law, Ron	0
Law, Rudy	68
Lawing, Garland	0
Lawless, Tom	6
Lawlor, Mike	0
Lawrence, Bill	1
Lawrence, Bob	0
Lawrence, Brian	6
Lawrence, Brooks	61
Lawrence, Jim	0
Lawrence, Sean	0
Lawry, Otis	0
Lawson, Al	0
Lawson, Bob	3
Lawson, Roxie	43
Lawson, Steve	1
Lawton, Marcus	0
Laxton, Bill	9
Laxton, Brett	0
Layana, Tim	6
Layden, Gene	0
Layden, Pete	0
Layne, Herman	0
Layne, Hillis	8
Layton, Les	2
Lazar, Danny	0
Lazor, Johnny	15
Lazorko, Jack	9
Lea, Charlie	51
Leach, Freddy	92
Leach, Jalal	0
Leach, Rick	35
Leach, Terry	50
Leahy, Dan	0
Leahy, Tom	10
Leal, Luis	52
Lear, Fred	4
Lear, King	10
Leard, Bill	0
Leary, Frank	1
Leary, Jack	13
Leary, John	12
Leary, Tim	62
Leathers, Hal	1
Leber, Emil	0
LeBourveau, Bevo	13
LeClair, George	10
LeCroy, Matt	5
Ledbetter, Razor	0
Ledesma, Aaron	15
Lee, Billy	1
Lee, Bob	53
Lee, Cliff	34
Lee, Corey	0
Lee, David	8
Lee, Derek	0
Lee, Don	46
Lee, Dud	10
Lee, Hal	64
Lee, Leonidas	0
Lee, Leron	38
Lee, Manuel	60
Lee, Mark	
Debut 1978	9
Debut 1988	7
Lee, Mike	2
Lee, Roy	0
Lee, Sang-Hoon	1
Lee, Terry	0
Lee, Tom	10
Lee, Watty	39
Leek, Gene	3
Leeper, Dave	0
Lees, George	0
LeFebvre, Bill	6
Lefebvre, Joe	35
LeFevre, Al	0
Lefferts, Craig	91
Lefler, Wade	1
Leftwich, Phil	10
Legett, Lou	1
Legg, Greg	1
Lehane, Mike	12
Leheny, Regis	0
Lehew, Jim	1
Lehman, Ken	17
Lehner, Paul	26
Lehr, Clarence	0
Lehr, Norm	1
Leibold, Nemo	117
Leifer, Elmer	0
Leifield, Lefty	132
Leighton, John	1
Leinhauser, Bill	0
Leip, Ed	1
Leiper, Dave	17
Leiper, Jack	0
Leister, John	0
Leiter, Mark	56
Leith, Bill	0
Leitner, Doc	1
Leitner, Dummy	0
Leius, Scott	27
Leja, Frank	0
LeJeune, Larry	1
LeJohn, Don	1
Lelivelt, Bill	1
Lelivelt, Jack	39
Lemanczyk, Dave	36
LeMaster, Johnnie	51
LeMay, Dick	5
Lembo, Steve	0
Lemon, Jim	103
Lemonds, Dave	5
Lemongello, Mark	19
Lenhardt, Don	45
Lennon, Bob	0
Lennon, Ed	0
Lennon, Patrick	4
Lennox, Ed	55
Lentine, Jim	6
Leon, Danilo	0
Leon, Eddie	35
Leon, Izzy	0
Leon, Max	22
Leonard, Elmer	1
Leonard, Joe	17
Leonard, Mark	9
Leonard	0
Leonhard, Dave	19
Leopold, Rudy	0
Leovich, John	0
Lepcio, Ted	50
LePine, Pete	1
Leppert, Don	
Debut 1955	0
Debut 1961	11
Lerch, Randy	38
Lerchen, Dutch	0
Lerchen, George	1
Lerian, Walt	14
LeRoy, John	0
LeRoy, Louis	5
Lersch, Barry	34
Lesher, Brian	3
Leshnock, Don	0
Lesley, Brad	5
Leslie, Roy	4
Letchas, Charlie	4
Letcher, Tom	0
Levan, Jesse	0
Leverenz, Walt	11
Leverett, Dixie	31
Leverette, Hod	0
Levey, Jim	19
Levis, Charlie	7
Levis, Jesse	16
Levrault, Allen	1
Levsen, Dutch	22
Levy, Ed	3
Lewallyn, Dennis	4
Lewandowski, Dan	0
Lewis, Allan	0
Lewis, Bill	5
Lewis, Burt	0
Lewis, Fred	48
Lewis, Jack	12
Lewis, Jim	
Debut 1979	0
Debut 1991	0
Lewis, Johnny	19
Lewis, Mark	58
Lewis, Phil	32
Lewis, Richie	13
Lewis, Scott	8
Lewis	0
Ley, Terry	0
Lezcano, Carlos	1
Libby, Steve	0
Libke, Al	21
Libran, Frankie	0
Lickert, John	0
Liddell, Dave	0
Liddle, Don	29
Lieber, Dutch	4
Liebhardt, Glenn	
Debut 1906	39
Debut 1930	0
Liefer, Jeff	7
Liese, Fred	0
Lillard, Bill	4
Lillard, Gene	0
Lillie, Jim	16
Lilliquist, Derek	30
Lillis, Bob	36
Lilly, Ted	3
Lima, Jose	44
Limmer, Lou	8
Linares, Rufino	10
Lincoln, Ezra	2
Lincoln, Mike	5
Lind, Carl	17
Lind, Jack	1
Lind, Jose	82
Lindaman, Vive	39
Lindbeck, Em	0
Lindblad, Paul	79
Linde, Lymie	0
Lindeman, Jim	14
Lindemann, Bob	0
Lindemann, Ernie	0
Linden, Walt	1
Lindquist, Carl	0
Lindsay, Bill	1
Lindsay, Chris	15
Lindsey, Bill	1
Lindsey, Doug	0
Lindsey, Jim	23
Lindsey, Rod	0
Lindstrom, Axel	0
Lindstrom, Chuck	1

Player	WS
Linebrink, Scott	2
Lines, Dick	12
Linhart, Carl	0
Liniak, Cole	0
Link, Fred	6
Linke, Ed	16
Lint, Royce	2
Linton, Bob	0
Linton, Doug	9
Lintz, Larry	16
Linz, Phil	29
Linzy, Frank	86
LiPetri, Angelo	1
Lipon, Johnny	69
Lipp, Tom	0
Lipscomb, Nig	2
Lipski, Bob	0
Lira, Felipe	22
Liriano, Nelson	54
Lis, Joe	21
Lisenbee, Hod	40
Lisi, Rick	1
Liska, Ad	23
Listach, Pat	41
Lister, Pete	2
Littell, Mark	50
Little, Bryan	24
Little, Harry	0
Little, Jack	0
Little, Jeff	3
Little, Mark	3
Little, Scott	0
Littlefield, Dick	29
Littlefield, John	8
Littlejohn, Carlisle	5
Littlejohn, Dennis	4
Littleton, Larry	0
Litton, Greg	17
Littrell, Jack	3
Lively, Buddy	12
Lively, Jack	6
Livengood, Wes	0
Livingston, Mickey	35
Livingston, Paddy	18
Livingstone, Jake	0
Livingstone, Scott	28
Lizotte, Abel	0
Llenas, Winston	7
Llewellyn, Clem	0
Lloyd, Graeme	38
Loan, Mike	0
Loane, Bob	1
Lobert, Frank	0
Lochhead, Harry	3
Locke, Bobby	22
Locke, Chuck	0
Locke, Marshall	0
Locke, Ron	1
Locker, Bob	87
Lockhart, Keith	48

Player	WS
Locklear, Gene	17
Locklin, Stu	0
Lockwood, Milo	1
Lodigiani, Dario	31
Loepp, George	3
Loes, Billy	71
Loewer, Carlton	4
Lofton, James	0
Loftus, Dick	2
Loftus, Frank	0
Loftus, Tom	0
Logan, Bob	16
Lohman, Pete	2
Lohr, Howard	0
Lohrke, Jack	21
Lohrman, Bill	60
Lohse, Kyle	3
Lois, Alberto	0
Loiselle, Rich	22
Lolich, Ron	1
Lollar, Tim	40
Loman, Doug	5
Lomasney, Steve	0
Lombard, George	0
Lombardi, Phil	2
Lombardi, Vic	63
Lombardo, Lou	0
Lombardozzi, Steve	31
Lomon, Kevin	0
Lonergan, Walter	0
Long, Bill	26
Long, Bob	2
Long, Dale	92
Long, Dan	1
Long, Jeoff	1
Long, Jim	3
Long, Jimmie	0
Long, Joey	0
Long, Lep	0
Long, Red	1
Long, Ryan	0
Long, Tom	
Debut 1911	42
Debut 1924	0
Longmire, Tony	8
Lonnett, Joe	4
Look, Bruce	4
Look, Dean	0
Looney, Brian	0
Loos, Pete	0
Lopatka, Art	1
Lopez, Art	0
Lopez, Aurelio	79
Lopez, Carlos	12
Lopez, Felipe	5
Lopez, Luis	
Debut 1990	0
Debut 1993	27
Debut 2001	1
Lopez, Marcelino	31

Player	WS
Lopez, Mendy	8
Lopez, Ramon	0
Lopez, Rodrigo	0
Lord, Bris	71
Lord, Carlton	0
Lorenzen, Lefty	0
Lorraine, Andrew	5
Lotz, Joe	1
Loucks, Scott	3
Loudell, Art	0
Louden, Baldy	70
Loudenslager, C.	0
Loughlin, Bill	0
Loughlin, Larry	0
Loughran	0
Loun, Don	1
Love, Slim	28
Lovelace, Tom	0
Lovelace, Vance	0
Lovenguth, Lynn	2
Lovett, John	0
Lovett, Mem	0
Lovett, Tom	76
Loviglio, Jay	0
Lovitto, Joe	9
Lovrich, Pete	0
Lovullo, Torey	11
Low, Fletcher	0
Lowdermilk, Grover	20
Lowdermilk, Lou	3
Lowe, Dick	0
Lowe, George	0
Lowenstein, John	110
Lowery, Terrell	7
Lown, Turk	68
Lowry, Dwight	8
Lowry, Sam	0
Loynd, Mike	2
Lozado, Willie	4
Lubratich, Steve	2
Luby, Hal	10
Luby, Pat	55
Lucadello, Johnny	19
Lucas, Fred	0
Lucas, Gary	52
Lucas, Johnny	0
Lucas, Ray	2
Luce, Frank	1
Lucey, Joe	0
Lucid, Con	15
Lucier, Lou	4
Ludolph, Willie	0
Ludwick, Eric	0
Ludwig, Bill	2
Luebbe, Roy	0
Luebber, Steve	5
Luebbers, Larry	4
Luebke, Dick	1
Luecken, Rick	2
Luff, Henry	5

Player	WS
Lugo, Urbano	6
Luhrsen, Wild Bill	2
Lukachyk, Rob	0
Lukasiewicz, Mark	0
Luke, Matt	6
Lukens, Al	0
Lukon, Eddie	16
Lum, Mike	75
Lumenti, Ralph	0
Luna, Memo	0
Lunar, Fernando	3
Lund, Don	13
Lund, Gordy	1
Lundbom, Jack	0
Lundgren, Del	1
Lundquist, David	0
Lundstedt, Tom	0
Lunte, Harry	2
Lupien, Tony	54
Luplow, Al	32
Lusader, Scott	7
Lush, Billy	60
Lush, Ernie	0
Lush, Johnny	76
Luskey, Charlie	0
Lutenberg, Luke	1
Luttrell, Lyle	1
Lutz, Joe	0
Lutz, Red	0
Lutzke, Rube	37
Luuloa, Keith	0
Lyden, Mitch	0
Lydy, Scott	1
Lyle, Jim	0
Lynch, Adrian	1
Lynch, Danny	1
Lynch, Dummy	0
Lynch, Ed	39
Lynch, Henry	0
Lynch, Jerry	81
Lynch, Mike	
Debut 1902	0
Debut 1904	38
Lynch, Tom	6
Lynch, Walt	0
Lynn, Byrd	5
Lynn, Jerry	0
Lynn, Red	11
Lyon, Brandon	4
Lyon, Russ	0
Lyons, Al	3
Lyons, Barry	16
Lyons, Bill	2
Lyons, Curt	1
Lyons, Ed	1
Lyons, George	5
Lyons, Harry	34
Lyons, Hersh	0
Lyons, Pat	0
Lyons, Steve	43

Player	WS
Lyons, Terry	0
Lyons, Toby	0
Lysander, Rick	14
Lyston, Bill	0
Lytle, Dad	0
Lyttle, Jim	15

M

Player	WS
Maas, Duke	33
Maas, Kevin	31
Mabe, Bob	4
Mabry, John	43
MacArthur, Mac	1
MacCormack, Frank	0
MacDonald, Bill	7
MacDonald, Bob	13
MacDonald, Harvey	0
MacDougal, Mike	1
Mace, Jimmy	0
Macey	0
MacGamwell, Ed	0
Macha, Ken	7
Macha, Mike	0
Machado, Julio	12
Machado, Robert	5
Machemehl, Chuck	0
Machemer, Dave	1
Mack, Bill	1
Mack, Connie	61
Mack, Denny	11
Mack, Earle	1
Mack, Frank	3
Mack, Joe	3
Mack, Quinn	0
Mack, Ray	56
Mack, Reddy	62
Mack, Tony	0
Mackanin, Pete	24
MacKenzie, Eric	0
MacKenzie, Gordon	0
MacKenzie, Ken	6
Mackiewicz, Felix	17
Mackinson, Johnny	0
Macko, Steve	1
Mackowiak, Rob	4
MacLeod, Bill	0
Maclin, Lonnie	0
Macon, Max	20
MacPhee, Waddy	0
MacPherson, Harry	0
MacRae, Scott	2
Macullar, Jimmy	47
MacWhorter, Keith	1
Madden, Bunny	3
Madden, Frank	0
Madden, Gene	0
Madden, Kid	57

Player	WS
Madden, Len	0
Madden, Mike	7
Madden, Morris	1
Madden, Tommy	0
Maddern, Clarence	5
Maddox, Jerry	0
Maddox, Nick	48
Maddux, Mike	55
Madigan, Tony	1
Madison, Art	4
Madison, Dave	3
Madison, Scotti	1
Madjeski, Ed	6
Madrid, Alex	1
Madrid, Sal	0
Maduro, Calvin	6
Maestri, Hector	0
Magallanes, Ever	0
Magee, Bill	26
Magee, Wendell	11
Maggert, Harl	
Debut 1907	8
Debut 1938	4
Magnante, Mike	37
Magner, John	0
Magner, Stubby	0
Magnuson, Jim	2
Magoon, George	41
Magrane, Joe	61
Magrann, Tom	0
Magrini, Pete	0
Magruder, Chris	0
Maguire, Freddie	35
Maguire, Jack	3
Mahady, Jim	0
Mahaffey, Art	46
Mahaffey, Lou	0
Mahaffey, Roy	50
Mahan, Art	5
Mahar, Frank	0
Maharg, Billy	0
Mahay, Ron	11
Maher, Tom	0
Mahlberg, Greg	0
Mahler, Mickey	13
Mahomes, Pat	25
Mahon, Al	0
Mahoney, Bob	4
Mahoney, Chris	0
Mahoney, Dan	0
Mahoney, Danny	0
Mahoney, Jim	3
Mahoney, Mike	
Debut 1897	0
Debut 2000	0
Maier, Bob	9
Mailho, Emil	0
Mails, Duster	29
Main, Alex	26
Main, Woody	7
Mains, Jim	0
Mains, Willard	19
Mairena, Oswaldo	0
Maisel, Charlie	0
Maisel, Fritz	60
Maisel, George	8
Majeski, Hank	104
Makosky, Frank	3
Makowski, Tom	0
Maksudian, Mike	1
Malarkey, Bill	1
Malarkey, John	26
Malave, Jose	1
Malay, Charlie	5
Malay, Joe	0
Maldonado, Candy	118
Maldonado, Carlos	2
Maler, Jim	3
Malinosky, Tony	0
Malis, Cy	0
Malkmus, Bobby	7
Mallett, Jerry	0
Mallette, Mal	0
Mallicoat, Rob	1
Mallon, Les	24
Mallonee, Ben	0
Mallonee, Jule	0
Mallory, Jim	2
Mallory, Sheldon	1
Malloy, Alex	1
Malloy, Bob	
Debut 1943	7
Debut 1987	0
Malloy, Herm	0
Malloy, Marty	1
Malmberg, Harry	4
Malone, Chuck	1
Malone, Eddie	6
Malone, Fergy	1
Malone, Lew	4
Maloney, Billy	62
Maloney, Charlie	0
Maloney, John	1
Maloney, Pat	1
Maloney, Sean	0
Maloy, Paul	0
Maltzberger, G.	36
Mamaux, Al	83
Mancuso, Frank	20
Manda, Carl	1
Manders, Hal	4
Mangan, Jim	0
Mangual, Angel	22
Mangual, Pepe	26
Mangum, Leo	6
Mangus, George	0
Manion, Clyde	19
Mankowski, Phil	16
Manlove, Charlie	0
Mann, Garth	0
Mann, Jim	0
Mann, Johnny	0
Mann, Kelly	0
Manning, Ernie	0
Manning, Jim	
Debut 1884	25
Debut 1962	0
Manning, Rick	114
Manning, Rube	15
Manning, Tim	15
Manno, Don	1
Manon, Ramon	0
Manrique, Fred	31
Mansell, John	2
Mansell, Mike	34
Mansell, Tom	17
Manske, Lou	0
Mantei, Matt	24
Mantilla, Felix	68
Manto, Jeff	18
Manuel, Barry	9
Manuel, Charlie	3
Manuel, Jerry	3
Manuel, Moxie	2
Manush, Frank	1
Manville, Dick	0
Manwaring, Kirt	71
Manzanillo, Ravelo	4
Mapel, Rolla	0
Mapes, Cliff	32
Maple, Howard	1
Mappes, George	0
Marak, Paul	2
Maranda, Georges	2
Marbet, Walt	0
Marchildon, Phil	68
Marcum, Johnny	74
Marentette, Leo	0
Margoneri, Joe	5
Marion, Dan	13
Marion, Red	0
Markell, Duke	0
Markland, Gene	0
Markle, Cliff	11
Marlowe, Dick	9
Marnie, Hal	2
Marolewski, Fred	0
Marone, Lou	3
Marquardt, Ollie	0
Marquez, Gonzalo	1
Marquez, Isidro	0
Marquez, Luis	1
Marquis, Bob	1
Marquis, Jason	9
Marquis, Jim	0
Marquis, Roger	0
Marr, Lefty	47
Marrero, Connie	44
Marrero, Oreste	2
Marriott, William	15
Marrow, Buck	4
Mars, Ed	6
Marsans, Armando	55
Marsh, Fred	23
Marsh, Tom	3
Marshall, Bill	0
Marshall, Charlie	0
Marshall, Cuddles	1
Marshall, Dave	26
Marshall, Doc	13
Marshall, Ed	10
Marshall, Jim	18
Marshall, Joe	0
Marshall, Keith	0
Marshall, Max	29
Marshall, Rube	8
Marte, Damaso	1
Martel, Doc	2
Martin, Babe	3
Martin, Barney	0
Martin, Billy	
Debut 1914	0
Debut 1950	76
Martin, Doc	1
Martin, Frank	0
Martin, Freddie	12
Martin, Gene	1
Martin, Hersh	70
Martin, J.C.	53
Martin, Jack	12
Martin, Jerry	64
Martin, Joe	
Debut 1903	2
Debut 1936	0
Martin, John	14
Martin, Mike	0
Martin, Morrie	37
Martin, Norberto	20
Martin, Pat	0
Martin, Paul	0
Martin, Ray	1
Martin, Renie	19
Martin, Speed	28
Martin, Stu	54
Martin, Tom	9
Martina, Joe	6
Martinez, Buck	64
Martinez, Carlos	17
Martinez, Chito	13
Martinez, Domingo	1
Martinez, Felix	10
Martinez, Fred	6
Martinez, Greg	0
Martinez, Hector	0
Martinez, Javier	0
Martinez, Jose	
Debut 1969	4
Debut 1994	0
Martinez, Manny	9
Martinez, Marty	18
Martinez, Pablo	0
Martinez, Pedro A.	10
Martinez, Rogelio	0
Martinez, Sandy	12
Martinez, Silvio	24
Martinez, Ted	28
Martinez, Tippy	82
Martinez, Tony	1
Martinez, Willie	0
Martini, Wedo	0
Marty, Joe	41
Martyn, Bob	9
Martz, Gary	0
Martz, Randy	15
Marzano, John	17
Masaoka, Onan	6
Mashore, Clyde	6
Mashore, Damon	10
Maskrey, Harry	0
Maskrey, Leech	32
Mason, Charlie	0
Mason, Del	3
Mason, Don	7
Mason, Ernie	0
Mason, Hank	0
Mason, Jim	26
Mason, Mike	28
Mason, Roger	22
Massa, Gordon	1
Massey, Bill	1
Massey, Mike	1
Massey, Red	7
Masteller, Dan	1
Masters, Walt	1
Masterson, Paul	1
Masterson, Walt	83
Mata, Victor	2
Matarazzo, Len	0
Matchick, Tommy	10
Mateo, Henry	0
Mateo, Ruben	7
Mathes, Joe	2
Mathews, Greg	22
Mathews, Nelson	13
Mathews, T.J.	37
Mathews, Terry	26
Mathewson, Henry	0
Mathias, Carl	1
Mathis, Ron	0
Mathison, Jimmy	1
Matias, John	0
Matos, Francisco	0
Matos, Luis	5
Matos, Pascual	0
Mattern, Al	42
Mattes, Troy	1
Matteson, C.V.	0
Matteson, Henry	9
Matthews, Bill	1
Matthews, Bob	0

Player	WS
Matthews, Joe	0
Matthews, Mike	7
Matthews, Wid	14
Matthewson, Dale	2
Matthias, Steve	6
Mattick, Bobby	11
Mattick, Wally	12
Mattimore, Mike	26
Mattingly, Earl	1
Mattis, Ralph	1
Mattox, Cloy	0
Mattox, Jim	1
Matula, Rick	13
Matuszek, Len	21
Matuzak, Harry	1
Mauch, Gene	14
Mauck, Hal	8
Mauldin, Mark	1
Maun, Ernie	0
Mauney, Dick	14
Maupin, Harry	1
Maurer, Dave	1
Maurer, Rob	0
Mauriello, Ralph	1
Mauro, Carmen	4
Mauser, Tim	6
Mavis, Bob	0
Maxcy, Brian	0
Maxie, Larry	0
Maxvill, Dal	87
Maxwell, Bert	6
Maxwell, Jason	4
May, Buckshot	0
May, Darrell	2
May, Derrick	50
May, Jakie	77
May, Jerry	39
May, Milt	112
May, Pinky	64
May, Scott	0
Mayer, Ed	
Debut 1890	10
Debut 1957	2
Mayer, Sam	0
Mayer, Wally	8
Mayes, Paddy	0
Maynard, Buster	7
Maynard, Chick	0
Mayo, Eddie	72
Mayo, Jackie	3
Mays, Al	59
Maysey, Matt	1
Mazzera, Mel	9
Mazzilli, Lee	134
McAdams, Jack	0
McAfee, Bill	6
McAleese, John	6
McAllester, Bill	1
McAllister, Sport	20
McAnally, Ernie	23

Player	WS
McAnany, Jim	6
McAndrew, Jamie	2
McAndrew, Jim	38
McArthur, Dixie	0
McAuley, Ike	3
McAuliffe, Gene	0
McAvoy, George	0
McAvoy, Tom	0
McAvoy, Wickey	11
McBee, Pryor	0
McBride, Algie	48
McBride, Dick	0
McBride, John	0
McBride, Ken	41
McBride, Pete	4
McBride, Tom	25
McCabe, Bill	3
McCabe, Dick	0
McCabe, Joe	1
McCabe, Ralph	0
McCabe, Swat	2
McCabe, Tim	4
McCaffery, Harry	7
McCaffrey, Sparrow	0
McCahan, Bill	18
McCall, Brian	1
McCall, Dutch	3
McCall, Larry	1
McCall, Windy	17
McCament, Randy	0
McCandless, Jack	5
McCann, Emmett	2
McCann, Gene	2
McCardell, Roger	0
McCarren, Bill	4
McCarthy, Alex	32
McCarthy, Arch	0
McCarthy, Bill	
Debut 1905	0
Debut 1906	0
McCarthy, Greg	3
McCarthy, Jerry	0
McCarthy, Joe	1
McCarthy, Johnny	35
McCarthy, Tom	
Debut 1908	10
Debut 1985	5
McCarty, Dave	17
McCarty, John	6
McCarty, Lew	52
McCaskill, Kirk	87
McCatty, Steve	59
McCauley, Al	18
McCauley, Bill	0
McCauley, Jim	3
McCauley, Pat	2
McChesney, Harry	3
McClain, Joe	10
McClain, Scott	0
McClanahan, Pete	0

Player	WS
McClellan, Harvey	14
McClellan, Paul	1
McClendon, Lloyd	27
McCleskey, Jeff	0
McCloskey, Bill	0
McCloskey, Jim	0
McCloskey, John	2
McClure, Bob	75
McClure, Hal	0
McClure, Larry	0
McCluskey, Harry	0
McColl, Alex	9
McConnaughey, R.	0
McConnell, Amby	49
McConnell, George	55
McConnell, Sam	0
McCool, Billy	41
McCormack, Don	0
McCormick, Barry	65
McCormick, Harry	52
McCormick, Jerry	17
McCormick, Jim	0
McCormick, Mike	
Debut 1904	6
Debut 1940	60
McCormick, Moose	46
McCorry, Bill	0
McCoy, Art	0
McCoy, Benny	32
McCrabb, Les	6
McCracken, Q.	29
McCraw, Tom	96
McCray, Rodney	0
McCrea, Frank	0
McCredie, Judge	7
McCreery, Ed	0
McCreery, Tom	92
McCue, Frank	0
McCullers, Lance	42
McCullough, Charlie	4
McCullough, Clyde	82
McCullough, Paul	0
McCullough, Phil	0
McCurdy, Harry	32
McCurry, Jeff	5
McDaniel, Terry	0
McDaniel, Von	6
McDavid, Ray	0
McDermott, Mike	10
McDermott, Red	1
McDermott, Sandy	0
McDermott, Terry	0
McDevitt, Danny	20
McDill, Allen	0
McDonald, Dave	0
McDonald, Donzell	0
McDonald, Ed	13
McDonald, Hank	4
McDonald, Jason	15

Player	WS
McDonald, Jim	
Debut 1884	1
Debut 1902	0
Debut 1950	23
McDonald, Joe	0
McDonald, John	
Debut 1907	0
Debut 1999	0
McDonald, Keith	1
McDonald, Tex	43
McDonnell, Jim	1
McDonough, Ed	0
McDougal, John	0
McDougal, Sandy	1
McDowell, Oddibe	82
McDowell, Roger	100
McElroy, Chuck	56
McElroy, Jim	1
McElveen, Pryor	6
McElwee, Lee	2
McElyea, Frank	0
McEnaney, Will	22
McEvoy, Lou	0
McFadden, Barney	0
McFadden, Guy	0
McFadden, Leon	2
McFarlan, Alex	0
McFarlan, Dan	6
McFarland, Chappie	31
McFarland, Chris	0
McFarland, Ed	115
McFarland, Herm	50
McFarland, Howie	0
McFarland, Monte	1
McFarlane, Orlando	7
McFetridge, Jack	3
McGaffigan, Andy	58
McGaffigan, Patsy	2
McGah, Eddie	1
McGann, Ambrose	2
McGarr, Chippy	72
McGarr, Jim	0
McGarvey, Dan	0
McGeachey, Jack	32
McGeary, Mike	31
McGee, Bill	47
McGee, Dan	0
McGee, Frank	0
McGeehan, Connie	0
McGeehan, Dan	0
McGehee, Kevin	0
McGehee, Pat	0
McGhee, Bill	9
McGhee, Ed	8
McGilberry, Randy	0
McGill, Bill	1
McGillen, John	0
McGilvray, Bill	0
McGinley, Jim	2
McGinley, Tim	0

Player	WS
McGinn, Dan	9
McGinn, Frank	0
McGinnis, Gus	5
McGinnis, Russ	0
McGlinchy, Kevin	9
McGlone, John	4
McGlothen, Lynn	77
McGlothin, Pat	1
McGlothlin, Jim	60
McGlynn, Stoney	18
McGovern, Art	0
McGowan, Beauty	29
McGowan, Mickey	0
McGraner, Howard	0
McGraw, Bob	22
McGraw, John	0
McGraw, Tom	0
McGrew, Slim	0
McGriff, Terry	6
McGrillis, Mark	0
McGuckin, Joe	1
McGuinness, John	5
McGuire, Bill	1
McGuire, Jim	1
McGuire, Mickey	0
McGuire, Murray	0
McGuire, Ryan	8
McGuire, Tom	4
McGunnigle, Bill	13
McHale, Bob	0
McHale, Jim	2
McHale, John	1
McHale, Marty	13
McHenry, Austin	66
McHenry, Vance	0
McIlree, Vance	0
McIlveen, Irish	3
McIlwain, Stover	0
McIntire, Harry	73
McIntosh, Joe	10
McIntosh, Tim	1
McIntyre, Frank	1
McIvor, Otto	2
McKain, Archie	38
McKain, Hal	19
McKay, Dave	29
McKay, Reeve	0
McKechnie, Bill	72
McKee, Frank	0
McKee, Jim	1
McKee, Red	12
McKee, Rogers	0
McKeel, Walt	0
McKeever, Jim	0
McKeithan, Tim	1
McKelvy, Russ	4
McKenna, Ed	1
McKenna, Kit	2
McKenry, Limb	7
McKeon, Joel	4

Player	WS
McKeon, Larry	45
McKeough, Dave	7
McKinney, Bob	0
McKinney, Rich	11
McKinnon, Alex	46
McKnight, Jeff	4
McKnight, Jim	0
McKnight, Tony	6
McLane, Ed	0
McLarney, Art	0
McLarry, Polly	1
McLaughlin, Barney	18
McLaughlin, Bo	9
McLaughlin, Byron	17
McLaughlin, Frank	9
McLaughlin, Jim	
Debut 1884	1
Debut 1884	0
Debut 1932	0
McLaughlin, Joey	38
McLaughlin, Jud	0
McLaughlin, Kid	0
McLaughlin, Pat	1
McLaughlin, Tom	28
McLaughlin, Warren	3
McLaurin, Ralph	0
McLean, Larry	73
McLean, Mac	0
McLeland, Wayne	0
McLeod, Jim	2
McLeod, Ralph	0
McLish, Cal	81
McMackin, Samuel	1
McMahan, Jack	1
McMahon, Doc	1
McMahon, Jack	4
McMakin, John	1
McManus, Frank	1
McManus, Jim	0
McManus, Joe	0
McManus, Pat	0
McMath, Jimmy	0
McMichael, Greg	61
McMillan, George	0
McMillan, Norm	28
McMillan, Tom	0
McMillan, Tommy	12
McMillon, Billy	9
McMullen, George	0
McMullen, Hugh	1
McMullin, Fred	27
McMurtry, Craig	32
McNabb, Carl	0
McNabb, Edgar	10
McNally, Mike	19
McNamara, Bob	0
McNamara, Dinny	0
McNamara, George	0
McNamara, Jim	3
McNamara, Tim	14
McNamara, Tom	0
McNaughton, G.	0
McNeal, Harry	3
McNealy, Rusty	0
McNeely, Earl	47
McNeely, Jeff	1
McNeil, Norm	0
McNertney, Jerry	37
McNichol, Brian	0
McNichol, Ed	2
McNulty, Bill	0
McNulty, Pat	16
McPartlin, Frank	0
McPherson, John	1
McQuaid, Herb	3
McQuaid, Mart	1
McQuaig, Jerry	0
McQueen, Mike	7
McQuery, Mox	40
McQuillan, George	106
McQuillen, Glenn	9
McRae, Norm	2
McRemer	0
McShannic, Pete	2
McSorley, Trick	2
McSweeney, Paul	0
McTamany, Jim	114
McTigue, Bill	1
McVey, George	0
McWeeny, Doug	48
McWilliams, Bill	0
McWilliams, Larry	69
Meacham, Bobby	34
Meacham, Rusty	25
Mead, Charlie	4
Meador, Johnny	1
Meadows, Brian	15
Meadows, Louie	1
Meadows, Rufe	0
Meads, Dave	3
Meakim, George	18
Meaney, Pat	0
Meara, Charlie	0
Meche, Gil	12
Medeiros, Ray	0
Medina, Luis	2
Medina, Rafael	0
Medlinger, Irv	0
Medvin, Scott	1
Mee, Tommy	0
Meegan, Pete	15
Meehan, Bill	0
Meek, Dad	0
Meeker, Roy	9
Meeks, Sammy	4
Meeler, Phil	0
Meers, Russ	5
Meier, Dave	3
Meier, Dutch	7
Meine, Heinie	54
Meinert, Walt	0
Meinke, Bob	0
Meinke, Frank	11
Meister, George	1
Meister, John	6
Meister, Karl	0
Meixell, Moxie	0
Mejia, Miguel	0
Mejia, Roberto	3
Mejias, Roman	33
Mejias, Sam	5
Mele, Dutch	0
Mele, Sam	84
Melendez, F.	0
Melendez, Jose	18
Melendez, Luis	23
Melhuse, Adam	0
Melillo, Ski	88
Mellana, Joe	0
Mellor, Bill	1
Melo, Juan	0
Meloan, Paul	12
Melter, Steve	1
Melton, Cliff	95
Melton, Dave	0
Melton, Rube	34
Melvin, Bob	39
Mendez, Donaldo	0
Mendoza, Carlos	1
Mendoza, Mario	19
Mendoza, Mike	0
Mendoza, Minnie	0
Menefee, Jock	64
Menendez, Tony	3
Menhart, Paul	4
Menosky, Mike	75
Mensor, Ed	7
Menze, Ted	0
Meola, Mike	1
Meoli, Rudy	10
Mercado, Hector	4
Mercado, Orlando	10
Mercedes, Henry	4
Mercedes, Luis	1
Mercer, Jack	0
Mercer, John	0
Mercer, Mark	0
Merchant, Andy	0
Mercker, Kent	64
Merena, Spike	2
Merewether, Art	0
Meridith, Ron	3
Merloni, Lou	11
Merrill, Ed	1
Merriman, Brett	0
Merriman, Lloyd	27
Merritt, Bill	32
Merritt, George	1
Merritt, Herm	1
Merritt, Jim	76
Merritt, John	0
Merritt, Lloyd	5
Merson, Jack	7
Mertz, Jim	2
Merullo, Lennie	35
Merullo, Matt	4
Mesner, Steve	37
Messenger, Bobby	2
Messenger, Bud	1
Messitt, Tom	0
Metcalf, Tom	1
Metcalfe, Mike	0
Metha, Scat	0
Metheny, Bud	32
Metivier, Dewey	3
Metkovich, Catfish	82
Metro, Charlie	3
Metz, Lenny	0
Metzger, Butch	21
Metzig, William	0
Metzler, Alex	59
Meulens, Hensley	8
Meyer, Benny	33
Meyer, Billy	5
Meyer, Bob	2
Meyer, Brian	3
Meyer, Dan	62
Meyer, Dutch	29
Meyer, George	2
Meyer, Jack	30
Meyer, Joey	10
Meyer, Lee	0
Meyer, Russ	85
Meyer, Scott	0
Meyerle, Levi	11
Meyers, Chad	1
Meyers, Henry	0
Meyers, Lou	0
Miadich, Bart	0
Miceli, Dan	32
Micelotta, Mickey	0
Michael, Gene	52
Michaels, Cass	121
Michaels, Jason	0
Michaels, John	2
Michaels, Ralph	2
Michaelson, John	0
Michalak, Chris	8
Mickelson, Ed	0
Mickens, Glenn	0
Middlebrook, Jason	1
Middleton, Jim	5
Middleton, John	0
Midkiff, Dick	1
Midkiff, Ezra	5
Mielke, Gary	6
Mierkowicz, Ed	0
Mieske, Matt	32
Miggins, Larry	1
Mihalic, John	6
Mikkelsen, Pete	46
Miklos, John	0
Miksis, Eddie	44
Milacki, Bob	33
Milan, Horace	5
Milbourne, Larry	40
Milchin, Mike	0
Miles, Carl	0
Miles, Dee	23
Miles, Don	0
Miles, Jim	0
Miley, Mike	2
Militello, Sam	3
Miljus, Johnny	28
Millard, Frank	0
Miller, Bill	
Debut 1902	0
Debut 1937	0
Debut 1952	5
Miller, Bob	
Debut 1890	4
Debut 1949	53
Debut 1953	8
Debut 1957	99
Miller, Bruce	7
Miller, Burt	0
Miller, Charlie	
Debut 1912	0
Debut 1915	0
Miller, Chuck	0
Miller, Corky	2
Miller, Cyclone	14
Miller, Darrell	8
Miller, Doc	40
Miller, Dusty	4
Miller, Dyar	36
Miller, Ed	
Debut 1884	0
Debut 1912	2
Miller, Eddie	6
Miller, Elmer	
Debut 1912	31
Debut 1929	0
Miller, Frank	56
Miller, Fred	0
Miller, George	1
Miller, Hack	
Debut 1916	44
Debut 1944	0
Miller, Hughie	2
Miller, Jake	
Debut 1922	0
Debut 1924	66
Miller, Jim	0
Miller, Joe	17
Miller, John	
Debut 1962	7
Debut 1966	0

Player	WS
Miller, Keith	
Debut 1987	36
Debut 1988	1
Miller, Ken	1
Miller, Kohly	0
Miller, Kurt	1
Miller, Larry	2
Miller, Lemmie	0
Miller, Matt	0
Miller, Norm	35
Miller, Orlando	20
Miller, Otto	
Debut 1910	65
Debut 1927	14
Miller, Ox	5
Miller, Paul	1
Miller, Ralph	
Debut 1898	4
Debut 1920	6
Debut 1921	0
Miller, Randy	0
Miller, Ray	1
Miller, Red	0
Miller, Rick	104
Miller, Rod	0
Miller, Roger	0
Miller, Ronnie	0
Miller, Roscoe	47
Miller, Rudy	0
Miller, Russ	3
Miller, Tom	0
Miller, Travis	13
Miller, Trever	6
Miller, Walt	0
Miller, Warren	0
Millette, Joe	1
Milliard, Ralph	2
Millies, Wally	9
Milligan, Billy	2
Milligan, Jocko	108
Milligan, John	5
Milligan, Randy	79
Milliken, Bob	14
Mills, Alan	47
Mills, Art	2
Mills, Bill	0
Mills, Brad	2
Mills, Buster	29
Mills, Dick	0
Mills, Everett	5
Mills, Frank	0
Mills, Jack	1
Mills, Lefty	15
Mills, Rupert	0
Mills, Willie	0
Milnar, Al	55
Milne, Pete	0
Milner, Brian	1
Milosevich, Mike	9
Milstead, George	3

Player	WS
Milton, Larry	0
Mimbs, Michael	9
Minahan, Cotton	0
Minarcin, Rudy	5
Minchey, Nate	2
Miner, Ray	0
Minetto, Craig	2
Mingori, Steve	47
Minnehan, Dan	1
Minnick, Don	0
Minor, Blas	14
Minor, Damon	2
Minor, Ryan	2
Minshall, Jim	0
Mintz, Steve	0
Minutelli, Gino	0
Mirabella, Paul	24
Miranda, Angel	20
Miranda, Willie	40
Misse, John	3
Misuraca, Mike	0
Mitchell, Bobby	
Debut 1877	15
Debut 1970	15
Debut 1980	12
Mitchell, Charlie	1
Mitchell, Craig	0
Mitchell, Fred	25
Mitchell, John	6
Mitchell, Johnny	22
Mitchell, Keith	5
Mitchell, Larry	1
Mitchell, Monroe	0
Mitchell, Paul	23
Mitchell, Roy	27
Mitterling, Ralph	0
Mitterwald, George	68
Mizell, Vinegar Bend	87
Mizerock, John	4
Mizeur, Bill	0
Mlicki, Dave	50
Mmahat, Kevin	0
Moates, Dave	7
Modak, Mike	0
Moeller, Chad	2
Moeller, Danny	75
Moeller, Dennis	0
Moeller, Joe	16
Moeller, Ron	3
Moffett, Joe	1
Moffett, Sam	9
Moffitt, Randy	70
Moford, Herb	6
Mohardt, John	0
Mohart, George	2
Mohler, Kid	0
Mohler, Mike	19
Mohorcic, Dale	28
Mohr, Dustan	1
Moisan, Bill	0

Player	WS
Mokan, Johnny	42
Mole, Fenton	0
Molesworth, Carlton	0
Molina, Gabe	0
Molina, Izzy	1
Molina, Jose	1
Molinaro, Bob	18
Mollenkamp, Fred	0
Mollwitz, Fritz	21
Moloney, Rich	0
Molyneaux, Vince	1
Monaco, Blas	0
Monahan, Rinty	1
Monahan, Shane	2
Moncewicz, Freddie	0
Monchak, Alex	0
Monge, Sid	62
Monroe, Craig	1
Monroe, Ed	1
Monroe, Frank	0
Monroe, John	3
Monroe, Larry	1
Monroe, Zack	3
Montague, Ed	13
Montague, John	24
Montalvo, Rafael	0
Monteagudo, A.	7
Monteagudo, Rene	8
Montefusco, John	92
Montejo, Manny	1
Monteleone, Rich	22
Montemayor, Felipe	2
Montgomery, Al	1
Montgomery, Bob	32
Montgomery, Monty	6
Montgomery, Ray	1
Montgomery, Steve	6
Montoyo, Charlie	1
Montreuil, Al	0
Monzant, Ray	13
Monzon, Dan	4
Moock, Joe	0
Moody, Eric	1
Moolic, George	1
Moon, Leo	0
Mooney, Jim	13
Mooneyham, Bill	4
Moore, Al	1
Moore, Anse	1
Moore, Archie	1
Moore, Balor	24
Moore, Barry	19
Moore, Bill	
Debut 1925	0
Debut 1926	1
Debut 1986	0
Moore, Bob	1
Moore, Bobby	0
Moore, Brad	1
Moore, Carlos	1

Player	WS
Moore, Charley	0
Moore, Charlie	103
Moore, Cy	19
Moore, Dee	8
Moore, Donnie	65
Moore, Eddie	62
Moore, Euel	7
Moore, Ferdie	0
Moore, Frank	1
Moore, Gary	0
Moore, Gene	
Debut 1909	1
Debut 1931	115
Moore, Harry	22
Moore, Jackie	1
Moore, Jerrie	2
Moore, Jim	8
Moore, Jimmy	3
Moore, Junior	11
Moore, Kelvin	2
Moore, Kerwin	0
Moore, Marcus	3
Moore, Randy	60
Moore, Ray	67
Moore, Roy	16
Moore, Scrappy	0
Moore, Tommy	3
Moore, Trey	2
Moore, Whitey	26
Moore, Wilcy	57
Moorhead, Bob	4
Moose, Bob	68
Mooty, Jake	20
Mora, Andres	12
Moraga, David	0
Morales, Jose	24
Morales, Rich	14
Morales, Willie	0
Moran, Al	3
Moran, Bill	1
Moran, Billy	52
Moran, Carl	1
Moran, Charles	14
Moran, Charlie	1
Moran, Harry	20
Moran, Herbie	46
Moran, Hiker	2
Moran, Pat	77
Moran, Roy	1
Moran, Sam	0
Mordecai, Mike	20
More, Forrest	0
Morehart, Ray	10
Morehead, Dave	31
Morehead, Seth	9
Morejon, Danny	0
Morel, Ramon	2
Morelock, Harry	0
Moren, Lew	43
Moreno, Angel	3

Player	WS
Moreno, Jose	1
Moreno, Juan	3
Moreno, Julio	13
Moreno, Omar	119
Moreno, Orber	0
Moret, Roger	51
Morey, Dave	0
Morgan, Bill	
Debut 1878	2
Debut 1883	1
Morgan, Bobby	56
Morgan, Chet	4
Morgan, Cy	
Debut 1903	78
Debut 1921	0
Morgan, Eddie	1
Morgan, Joe	3
Morgan, Kevin	0
Morgan, Red	2
Morgan, Tom	76
Morgan, Vern	0
Morhardt, Moe	0
Moriarity, Gene	0
Moriarty, Bill	0
Moriarty, Ed	1
Moriarty, George	98
Morlan, John	3
Morley, Bill	0
Morman, Alvin	6
Morman, Russ	6
Morogiello, Dan	4
Moroney, Jim	4
Moronko, Jeff	0
Morrell, Bill	6
Morris, Danny	0
Morris, Doyt	0
Morris, E.	0
Morris, Ed	44
Morris, Jim	0
Morris, John	
Debut 1966	11
Debut 1986	8
Morris, P.	0
Morris, Walter	0
Morrisette, Bill	2
Morrison, Guy	1
Morrison, Hank	0
Morrison, Jim	84
Morrison, Jon	6
Morrison, Mike	12
Morrison, Phil	0
Morrison, Tom	0
Morrissey, Deacon	3
Morrissey, Jack	2
Morrissey, Jo-Jo	7
Morrissey, John	0
Morrissey, Tom	0
Morse, Bud	0
Morse, Hap	0
Morton, Bubba	31

Player	WS
Morton, Charlie	6
Morton, Guy	99
Morton, Kevin	4
Morton, Moose	0
Morton, Sparrow	0
Moryn, Walt	75
Moschitto, Ross	0
Moseley, Earl	47
Moser, Arnie	0
Moser, Walter	0
Moses, Jerry	28
Moses, John	28
Moskau, Paul	28
Moskiman, Doc	0
Mosolf, Jim	6
Mosquera, Julio	0
Moss, Charlie	0
Moss, Damian	1
Moss, Howie	0
Moss, Les	51
Moss, Mal	1
Moss, Ray	17
Mossi, Don	120
Mossor, Earl	0
Mota, Andy	1
Mota, Danny	0
Mota, Guillermo	8
Mota, Jose	0
Mota, Manny	121
Motley, Darryl	20
Mott, Bitsy	3
Mottola, Chad	1
Motton, Curt	17
Motz, Frank	3
Moulder, Glen	5
Moulton, Allie	0
Mountain, Frank	65
Mountjoy, Billy	34
Mouton, James	27
Mouton, Lyle	20
Mowe, Ray	0
Mowry, Joe	7
Moyer, Charlie	0
Moynahan, Mike	32
Mrozinski, Ron	2
Mudrock, Phil	0
Mueller, Bill	2
Mueller, Gordy	0
Mueller, Heinie	
Debut 1920	52
Debut 1938	28
Mueller, Les	7
Mueller, Ray	101
Mueller, Walter	6
Mueller, Willie	0
Muffett, Billy	22
Muich, Joe	0
Muir, Joe	1
Mulcahy, Hugh	49
Muldoon, Mike	44

Player	WS
Mulleavy, Greg	3
Mullen, Billy	1
Mullen, Charlie	13
Mullen, John	0
Mullen, Moon	8
Mullen, Scott	1
Muller, Freddie	0
Mulligan, Dick	2
Mulligan, Joe	
Debut 1915	10
Debut 1934	3
Mulligan, John	0
Mulligan, Sean	0
Mullin, Henry	0
Mullin, Jim	4
Mullin, Pat	86
Mullins, Fran	2
Mullins, Greg	0
Mulrenan, Dominic	0
Mulroney, Frank	0
Mulvey, Joe	97
Munce, Big John	0
Munch, Jake	0
Mundinger, George	0
Mundy, Bill	0
Munger, George	80
Muniz, Manny	0
Munninghoff, Scott	0
Munns, Les	4
Munoz, Bobby	12
Munoz, Jose	0
Munoz, Mike	25
Munoz, Noe	0
Munoz, Oscar	1
Munoz, Pedro	40
Munro, Peter	1
Munson, Eric	0
Munson, Joe	4
Munson, Red	0
Munyan, John	18
Mura, Steve	24
Murakami, Masanori	9
Murch, Simmy	1
Murchison, Tim	1
Murdoch, Wilbur	2
Murff, Red	1
Murnane, Tim	25
Murphy, Billy	2
Murphy, Bob	0
Murphy, Buzz	8
Murphy, Clarence	0
Murphy, Con	8
Murphy, Connie	0
Murphy, Dan	0
Murphy, Danny	
Debut 1892	0
Debut 1960	8
Murphy, Dave	0
Murphy, Dick	0
Murphy, Dummy	0

Player	WS
Murphy, Ed	
Debut 1898	19
Debut 1942	0
Murphy, Frank	4
Murphy, Howard	0
Murphy, Joe	3
Murphy, John	
Debut 1884	6
Debut 1902	1
Murphy, Johnny	104
Murphy, Larry	10
Murphy, Leo	0
Murphy, Mike	0
Murphy, Morgan	35
Murphy, Pat	7
Murphy, Rob	49
Murphy, Tom	76
Murphy, Tony	0
Murphy, Walter	0
Murphy, Willie	3
Murphy, Yale	8
Murphy	0
Murray, Amby	0
Murray, Bill	0
Murray, Bobby	0
Murray, Dale	63
Murray, Dan	1
Murray, Ed	0
Murray, George	11
Murray, Glenn	0
Murray, Heath	0
Murray, Jim	
Debut 1902	1
Debut 1922	0
Murray, Joe	0
Murray, Larry	2
Murray, Matt	0
Murray, Miah	0
Murray, Pat	0
Murray, Ray	18
Murray, Red	140
Murray, Rich	2
Murray, Tom	0
Murray, Tony	0
Murrell, Ivan	19
Murtaugh, Danny	61
Muser, Tony	22
Musgraves, Dennis	3
Musselman, Jeff	16
Musselman, Ron	6
Musser, Danny	0
Musser, Paul	2
Mussill, Barney	0
Mustaikis, Alex	0
Mutis, Jeff	2
Myatt, George	49
Myatt, Glenn	65
Myers, Al	72
Myers, Bert	8
Myers, Billy	79

Player	WS
Myers, Elmer	34
Myers, George	19
Myers, Greg	47
Myers, Hap	32
Myers, Henry	2
Myers, Jimmy	0
Myers, Joe	0
Myers, Lynn	5
Myers, Richie	0
Myers, Rod	4
Myers, Rodney	9
Myette, Aaron	0
Myrick, Bob	7

N

Player	WS
Nabholz, Chris	31
Nabors, Jack	3
Nady, Xavier	0
Naehring, Tim	59
Nagel, Bill	7
Nagelsen, Lou	0
Nagelson, Russ	1
Nagle, Judge	3
Nagle, Tom	3
Nagy, Mike	19
Nagy, Steve	0
Nahem, Sam	7
Nahorodny, Bill	20
Naktenis, Pete	0
Naleway, Frank	0
Nance, Doc	21
Napier, Buddy	6
Naples, Al	0
Napoleon, Danny	0
Naragon, Hal	25
Naranjo, Cholly	1
Narleski, Bill	6
Narleski, Ray	59
Narron, Jerry	13
Narron, Sam	1
Narum, Buster	11
Nash, Cotton	0
Nash, Jim	56
Nash, Ken	2
Nastu, Phil	3
Natal, Bob	6
Nathan, Joe	7
Nation, Joey	0
Naton, Pete	0
Naulty, Dan	11
Nava, Sandy	5
Navarro, Jaime	80
Navarro, Julio	15
Navarro, Tito	0
Naylor, Earl	1
Naylor, Rollie	46
Naymick, Mike	5

Player	WS
Neagle, Jack	17
Neal, Blaine	0
Neal, Charlie	93
Neal, Offa	0
Neale, Greasy	71
Neale, Joe	13
Nealon, Jim	27
Necciai, Ron	0
Needham, Tom	31
Neel, Troy	23
Neeman, Cal	21
Neff, Doug	0
Negray, Ron	9
Neher, Jim	0
Neibauer, Gary	5
Neidlinger, Jim	5
Neiger, Al	0
Neighbors, Bob	0
Neighbors, Cy	0
Neill, Mike	0
Neill, Tommy	1
Neis, Bernie	50
Neitzke, Ernie	1
Nekola, Bots	1
Nelson, Andy	0
Nelson, Bill	1
Nelson, Dave	59
Nelson, Emmett	4
Nelson, Gene	65
Nelson, Jamie	2
Nelson, Jim	8
Nelson, Joe	0
Nelson, Luke	2
Nelson, Lynn	35
Nelson, Mel	5
Nelson, Ray	0
Nelson, Red	5
Nelson, Ricky	4
Nelson, Rob	3
Nelson, Rocky	29
Nelson, Roger	42
Nelson, Tex	1
Nelson, Tommy	1
Nen, Dick	15
Ness, Jack	6
Nettles, Jim	14
Nettles, Morris	6
Netzel, Milo	0
Neu, Otto	0
Neubauer, Hal	0
Neuer, Tex	4
Neugebauer, Nick	0
Neumeier, Dan	0
Neun, Johnny	21
Nevel, Ernie	1
Nevers, Ernie	9
Newell, John	0
Newell, T.E.	0
Newell, Tom	0
Newfield, Marc	16

Player	WS
Newhan, David	1
Newhauser, Don	6
Newkirk, Floyd	0
Newkirk, Joel	0
Newlin, Maury	0
Newman, Al	36
Newman, Alan	0
Newman, Charlie	1
Newman, Fred	32
Newman, Jeff	38
Newman, Ray	7
Newnam, Patrick	7
Newsome, Dick	20
Newsome, Skeeter	67
Newson, Warren	25
Newton, Doc	61
Niarhos, Gus	28
Nicholas, Don	0
Nicholl, Sam	1
Nicholls, Simon	24
Nichols, Al	2
Nichols, Art	18
Nichols, Carl	5
Nichols, Chet	
Debut 1926	2
Debut 1951	32
Nichols, Dolan	0
Nichols, Reid	31
Nichols, Rod	14
Nichols, Roy	0
Nicholson, Dave	40
Nicholson, Frank	0
Nicholson, Fred	30
Nicholson, Kevin	1
Nicholson, Ovid	1
Nicholson, Parson	17
Nichting, Chris	1
Nickle, Doug	0
Nicol, George	6
Nicosia, Steve	25
Niebergall, Charlie	2
Nied, David	15
Niedenfuer, Tom	69
Niehaus, Al	3
Niehaus, Dick	5
Niehoff, Bert	52
Nielsen, Jerry	1
Nielsen, Milt	0
Nielsen, Scott	4
Nieman, Butch	34
Niemann, Randy	8
Niemes, Jack	0
Niemiec, Al	2
Nieson, Chuck	0
Nieto, Tom	13
Nieves, Jose	6
Nieves, Juan	22
Nieves, Melvin	24
Niland, Tom	0
Niles, Bill	1

Player	WS
Niles, Harry	61
Nill, Rabbitt	21
Nipper, Al	36
Nippert, Merlin	0
Nischwitz, Ron	7
Nitcholas, Otho	0
Nitkowski, C.J.	15
Nixon, Al	22
Nixon, Donell	10
Nixon, Russ	55
Nixon, Willard	69
Noble, Ray	5
Noboa, Junior	6
Noce, Paul	3
Noftsker, George	0
Nokes, Matt	85
Nolan, Joe	47
Nolan, The Only	29
Nold, Dick	0
Noles, Dickie	33
Nolte, Eric	4
Nonnenkamp, Red	4
Noonan, Pete	5
Nops, Jerry	64
Nordbrook, Tim	5
Nordhagen, Wayne	30
Nordyke, Lou	2
Noriega, John	0
Norman, Bill	0
Norman, Dan	5
Norman, Les	2
Norman, Nelson	1
Norris, Jim	29
Norris, Leo	16
Norris, Mike	54
North, Lou	21
Northen, Hub	14
Northey, Scott	2
Northrop, Jake	5
Norton, Elisha	4
Norton, Greg	22
Norton, Phil	0
Norton, Tom	1
Norwood, Willie	13
Nosek, Randy	0
Nossek, Joe	8
Nottebart, Don	47
Nourse, Chet	0
Novikoff, Lou	25
Novoa, Rafael	2
Novotney, Rube	1
Noyes, Wynn	6
Nunamaker, Les	69
Nunez, Abraham	13
Nunez, Edwin	46
Nunez, Jose	
Debut 1987	7
Debut 2001	4
Nunez, Vladimir	13
Nunn, Howie	3

Player	WS
Nunnally, Jon	32
Nunnari, Talmadge	0
Nusz, Emory	0
Nutter, Dizzy	0
Nyce, Charlie	1
Nye, Rich	23
Nye, Ryan	0
Nyman, Chris	2
Nyman, Jerry	4
Nyman, Nyls	4

O

Player	WS
Oana, Prince	4
Oates, Johnny	42
Obando, Sherman	6
Oberbeck, Henry	2
Oberlander, Doc	0
Oberlin, Frank	3
O'Berry, Mike	7
O'Bradovich, Jim	0
O'Brien, Billy	31
O'Brien, Bob	2
O'Brien, Buck	32
O'Brien, Charlie	63
O'Brien, Dan	0
O'Brien, Darby	
Debut 1887	109
Debut 1888	55
O'Brien, Eddie	6
O'Brien, George	0
O'Brien, Jack	
Debut 1882	85
Debut 1899	22
O'Brien, Jerry	0
O'Brien, John	
Debut 1884	2
Debut 1891	29
O'Brien, Johnny	16
O'Brien, Mickey	1
O'Brien, Pete	
Debut 1890	4
Debut 1901	15
O'Brien, Ray	0
O'Brien, Syd	14
O'Brien, Tom	
Debut 1882	24
Debut 1897	40
O'Brien, Tommy	20
Ock, Whitey	0
Ockey, Walter	0
O'Connell, Jimmy	12
O'Connell, John	
Debut 1891	0
Debut 1928	0
O'Connell, Pat	
Debut 1886	1
Debut 1890	1

Player	WS
O'Connor, Andy	0
O'Connor, Brian	0
O'Connor, Dan	2
O'Connor, Frank	0
O'Connor, Jack	10
O'Connor, Johnny	0
O'Connor, Paddy	7
O'Day, Hank	88
O'Dea, Ken	82
O'Dea, Paul	7
Odenwald, Ted	2
Odom, Blue Moon	69
Odom, Dave	0
Odom, Heinie	0
O'Donnell, George	4
O'Donnell, Harry	0
O'Donnell, John	0
O'Donoghue, John	
Debut 1963	31
Debut 1993	1
Odwell, Fred	42
Oelkers, Bryan	3
Oertel, Chuck	0
Oeschger, Joe	80
Office, Rowland	48
Ogden, Curly	24
Ogden, Jack	27
Ogea, Chad	31
Oglesby, Jim	0
Ogrodowski, Bruce	7
Ogrodowski, Joe	0
O'Hagen, Hal	3
O'Halloran, Greg	0
O'Hara, Bill	10
O'Hara, Kid	0
O'Hara, Tom	3
Ohka, Tomokazu	8
Ohl, Joe	0
Ohman, Will	0
Ojala, Kirt	5
Ojeda, Augie	4
Okrie, Frank	1
Okrie, Len	2
Olander, Jim	0
Oldfield, Dave	3
Oldham, John	0
Oldham, Red	41
Oldis, Bob	5
O'Leary, Charley	58
O'Leary, Dan	5
Olin, Frank	7
Olin, Steve	28
Oliva, Jose	4
Olivares, Ed	0
Olivares, Omar	73
Oliver, Bob	71
Oliver, Darren	53
Oliver, Dave	1
Oliver, Gene	64
Oliver, Joe	86

Player	WS
Oliver, Nate	15
Oliver, Tom	35
Oliveras, Francisco	13
Olivo, Chi Chi	9
Olivo, Diomedes	10
Ollom, Jim	1
Olmo, Luis	43
Olmstead, Fred	18
Olmsted, Al	2
Olmsted, Hank	1
Olsen, Barney	2
Olsen, Kevin	2
Olsen, Ole	5
Olsen, Vern	34
Olson, Greg	33
Olson, Karl	6
Olson, Marv	5
Olson, Ted	0
Olwine, Ed	5
O'Malley, Tom	30
O'Mara, Ollie	28
O'Meara, Tom	0
O'Neal, Randy	18
O'Neal, Skinny	0
O'Neil, Ed	0
O'Neil, John	2
O'Neil, Mickey	43
O'Neill, Bill	17
O'Neill, Denny	0
O'Neill, Emmett	6
O'Neill, Fred	1
O'Neill, Harry	
Debut 1922	0
Debut 1939	0
O'Neill, Jack	16
O'Neill, Jim	9
O'Neill, John	0
O'Neill, Mike	44
O'Neill, Peaches	0
Onis, Ralph	0
Onslow, Eddie	1
Onslow, Jack	0
Ontiveros, Steve	
Debut 1973	61
Debut 1985	42
Oquendo, Jose	99
Oquist, Mike	19
Oravetz, Ernie	7
Ordaz, Luis	5
Ordenana, Tony	0
Orengo, Joe	31
Orie, Kevin	25
O'Riley, Don	0
Orme, George	1
Orndorff, Jess	0
Oropesa, Eddie	1
O'Rourke, Charlie	0
O'Rourke, Frank	78
O'Rourke, Joe	0
O'Rourke, John	40

Player	WS
O'Rourke, Mike	3
O'Rourke, Patsy	1
O'Rourke, Queenie	1
O'Rourke, Tim	45
O'Rourke, Tom	5
Orr, Billy	1
Orrell, Joe	6
Orsatti, Ernie	66
Orsino, John	38
Orsulak, Joe	97
Ortega, Bill	0
Ortega, Phil	30
Ortenzio, Frank	1
Ortiz, Baby	0
Ortiz, Hector	7
Ortiz, Javier	4
Ortiz, Jose	
Debut 1969	4
Debut 2000	4
Ortiz, Junior	37
Ortiz, Luis	1
Ortiz, Roberto	13
Orton, John	8
Orwoll, Ossie	11
Osborn, Bob	23
Osborn, Danny	3
Osborn, Fred	26
Osborne, Bobo	13
Osborne, Donovan	42
Osborne, Fred	1
Osborne, Tiny	24
Osborne, Wayne	0
Osburn, Pat	0
Osgood, Charlie	0
Osik, Keith	17
Osinski, Dan	37
Ostdiek, Harry	0
Osteen, Champ	5
Osteen, Darrell	1
Ostendorf, Fred	0
Oster, Bill	0
Ostergard, Red	0
Osterhout, Charlie	0
Ostermueller, Fritz	140
Osting, Jimmy	0
Ostrosser, Brian	0
Ostrowski, Joe	25
Ostrowski, Johnny	12
Osuna, Al	15
Osuna, Antonio	31
Otanez, Willis	1
Otero, Reggie	1
Otero, Ricky	10
Otey, Bill	1
Otis, Bill	0
Otis, Harry	2
O'Toole, Denny	0
O'Toole, Marty	31
Ott, Billy	0
Ott, Ed	49

Player	WS
Otten, Jim	0
Otten, Joe	1
Otterson, Billy	2
Otto, Dave	9
Ouellette, Phil	0
Oulliber, Johnny	1
Outen, Chink	6
Outlaw, Jimmy	44
Overbay, Lyle	0
Overmire, Stubby	61
Overy, Mike	0
Ovitz, Ernie	0
Owchinko, Bob	32
Owen, Dave	2
Owen, Larry	8
Owen, Mickey	88
Owen, Spike	122
Owens, Frank	15
Owens, Jack	0
Owens, Jayhawk	6
Owens, Jim	39
Owens, Red	1
Ownbey, Rick	5
Oxley, Henry	0
Oyler, Andy	1
Oyler, Ray	19
Ozmer, Doc	0
Ozuna, Pablo	1

P

Player	WS
Pabst, Ed	2
Pacella, John	1
Pacheco, Alex	0
Pacillo, Pat	0
Paciorek, Jim	1
Paciorek, John	1
Paciorek, Tom	105
Pack, Frankie	0
Pactwa, Joe	1
Padden, Dick	89
Padden, Tom	32
Paddock, Del	5
Padgett, Don	52
Padgett, Ernie	19
Padilla, Vicente	9
Paepke, Dennis	2
Pagan, Dave	4
Pagan, Jose	81
Page, Joe	62
Page, Mike	0
Page, Mitchell	70
Page, Phil	2
Page, Sam	0
Page, Vance	16
Pagel, Karl	2
Pagliarulo, Mike	102
Pagnozzi, Tom	75

Player	WS
Paige, Pat	0
Paige, Satchel	42
Paine, Phil	13
Painter, Lance	25
Palacios, Rey	2
Palacios, Vicente	18
Palagyi, Mike	0
Palica, Erv	44
Pall, Donn	34
Palm, Mike	0
Palmer, Billy	0
Palmer, David	56
Palmer, Eddie	1
Palmer, Lowell	3
Palmero, Emilio	4
Palmisano, Joe	1
Palmquist, Ed	3
Palys, Stan	5
Pankovits, Jim	12
Panther, Jim	1
Papa, John	0
Papai, Al	7
Pape, Ken	1
Pape, Larry	19
Papi, Stan	7
Papish, Frank	37
Pappalau, John	0
Pappas, Erik	7
Pardo, Al	1
Paredes, Johnny	3
Parent, Mark	26
Paris, Kelly	4
Parisse, Tony	0
Park, Jim	7
Parker, Ace	2
Parker, Billy	4
Parker, Christian	0
Parker, Clay	11
Parker, Dixie	0
Parker, Doc	7
Parker, Harry	16
Parker, Jay	0
Parker, Pat	0
Parker, Rick	4
Parker, Roy	0
Parker, Salty	0
Parkinson, Frank	18
Parks, Art	7
Parks, Bill	0
Parks, Derek	1
Parks, Slicker	1
Parmelee, Roy	52
Parnham, Rube	1
Paronto, Chad	0
Parra, Jose	2
Parrett, Jeff	52
Parrilla, Sam	0
Parrish, John	0
Parrott, Jiggs	14
Parrott, Mike	20

Player	WS
Parrott, Tom	62
Parson, Jiggs	1
Parsons, Bill	21
Parsons, Casey	1
Parsons, Charlie	2
Parsons, Dixie	6
Parsons, John	0
Parsons, Tom	2
Partee, Roy	26
Partenheimer, Stan	0
Partenheimer, Steve	0
Partridge, Jay	8
Paschal, Ben	24
Paschall, Bill	1
Pascual, Carlos	2
Pasek, Johnny	1
Pashnick, Larry	8
Pasley, Kevin	2
Pasqua, Dan	79
Pasquariello, Mike	0
Pastore, Frank	39
Pastorius, Jim	28
Pastornicky, Cliff	0
Pate, Bob	1
Pate, Joe	16
Patrick, Bob	0
Patrick, Bronswell	4
Pattee, Harry	6
Patterson, Bob	48
Patterson, Claire	0
Patterson, Corey	3
Patterson, Daryl	13
Patterson, Dave	2
Patterson, George	0
Patterson, Gil	0
Patterson, Ham	0
Patterson, Hank	0
Patterson, Jarrod	0
Patterson, Jeff	0
Patterson, John A.	10
Patterson, Ken	18
Patterson, Mike	1
Patterson, Pat	2
Patterson, Reggie	4
Pattison, Jimmy	1
Patton, Bill	1
Patton, Gene	0
Patton, Harry	0
Patton, Tom	0
Paul, Josh	7
Paul, Lou	0
Paul, Mike	24
Paula, Carlos	10
Paulette, Gene	39
Paulsen, Gil	0
Pauxtis, Si	0
Pavano, Carl	17
Pavlas, Dave	5
Pavletich, Don	47
Pavlik, Roger	45

Player	WS
Pawelek, Ted	0
Pawloski, Stan	0
Pawlowski, John	0
Paxton, Mike	20
Payne, Fred	22
Payne, George	0
Payne, Harley	33
Payne, Mike	0
Paynter, George	0
Pazik, Mike	2
Peacock, Johnny	42
Peak, Elias	3
Pearce, Dickey	3
Pearce, Ducky	0
Pearce, Frank	
Debut 1876	0
Debut 1933	5
Pearce, George	26
Pearce, Harry	5
Pearce, Jim	3
Pears, Frank	1
Pearson, Alex	3
Pearson, Ike	15
Peasley, Marv	0
Pechiney, George	23
Pechous, Charlie	3
Peck, Hal	28
Pecota, Bill	42
Peden, Les	1
Pederson, Stuart	0
Pedre, Jorge	1
Pedrique, Al	8
Pedroes, Chick	0
Peek, Steve	2
Peel, Homer	5
Peerson, Jack	1
Peery, Red	2
Peete, Charlie	1
Peffer, Monte	0
Peguero, Julio	0
Pegues, Steve	1
Peitz, Heinie	124
Peitz, Joe	2
Pellagrini, Eddie	24
Pelouze, Louis	0
Peltier, Dan	3
Peltz, John	13
Pemberton, Brock	0
Pemberton, Rudy	7
Pena, Alejandro	91
Pena, Angel	3
Pena, Bert	2
Pena, Carlos	3
Pena, Elvis	1
Pena, Geronimo	40
Pena, Hipolito	2
Pena, Jesus	1
Pena, Jim	2
Pena, Jose	6
Pena, Juan	2

Player	WS
Pena, Orlando	77
Pena, Ramon	0
Pena, Roberto	31
Pence, Elmer	0
Pence, Russ	0
Pendleton, Jim	17
Penn, Shannon	0
Penner, Ken	0
Pennington, Brad	1
Pennington, Kewpie	0
Pennyfeather, W.	0
Penson, Paul	0
Pentz, Gene	9
Peoples, Jimmy	27
Peploski, Henry	0
Peploski, Pepper	0
Pepper, Bob	0
Pepper, Don	0
Pepper, Laurin	2
Pepper, Roy	16
Peppers, Bill	0
Peraza, Luis	0
Peraza, Oswaldo	1
Perconte, Jack	41
Perdue, Hub	34
Perez, Carlos	37
Perez, Danny	0
Perez, Eddie	26
Perez, Eduardo	21
Perez, George	0
Perez, Marty	54
Perez, Melido	63
Perez, Mike	31
Perez, Odalis	5
Perez, Pascual	72
Perez, Robert	5
Perez, Santiago	2
Perez, Timo	6
Perez, Tomas	12
Perez, Yorkis	18
Perezchica, Tony	1
Perisho, Matt	2
Perkins, Broderick	26
Perkins, Cecil	0
Perkins, Charlie	0
Perkins, Cy	88
Perkins, Dan	0
Perkovich, John	0
Perkowski, Harry	35
Perlman, Jon	0
Perlozzo, Sam	1
Perme, Len	2
Pernoll, Hub	3
Perrin, Bill	0
Perrin, John	0
Perrine, Nig	1
Perring, George	55
Perry, Bob	9
Perry, Boyd	1
Perry, Chan	0

Player	WS
Perry, Clay	0
Perry, Gerald	66
Perry, Hank	0
Perry, Pat	20
Perry, Scott	57
Perryman, Parson	1
Pertica, Bill	13
Perzanowski, Stan	5
Petagine, Roberto	6
Peterek, Jeff	1
Peterman, Bill	0
Peters, Chris	17
Peters, John	4
Peters, Ray	0
Peters, Ricky	22
Peters, Rube	3
Peters, Rusty	19
Peters, Steve	2
Petersen, Chris	0
Peterson, Adam	3
Peterson, Bob	2
Peterson, Buddy	1
Peterson, Cap	20
Peterson, Fritz	121
Peterson, Hardy	4
Peterson, Jim	2
Peterson, Kent	14
Peterson, Kyle	3
Peterson, Sid	1
Petkovsek, Mark	38
Petoskey, Ted	0
Petralli, Geno	44
Petrick, Ben	9
Pettee, Pat	0
Pettibone, Jay	0
Pettigrew, Ned	0
Pettini, Joe	4
Pettis, Gary	94
Pettit, Bob	7
Pettit, Leon	5
Pettit, Paul	0
Petty, Charlie	10
Pettyjohn, Adam	0
Pevey, Marty	1
Pezold, Larry	1
Pezzullo, Pretzels	1
Pfann, Bill	0
Pfeffer, Big Jeff	33
Pfeil, Bobby	4
Pfiester, Jack	83
Pfister, Dan	9
Pfister, George	0
Pfund, Lee	0
Pfyl, Monte	0
Phebus, Bill	5
Phelan, Art	36
Phelan, Dan	0
Phelan, Dick	10
Phelps, Babe	85
Phelps, Ed	49

Player	WS
Phelps, Josh	0
Phelps, Ken	70
Phelps, Nealy	0
Phelps, Ray	24
Phelps, Travis	6
Phillips, Adolfo	69
Phillips, Bill	65
Phillips, Bubba	67
Phillips, Buz	1
Phillips, Damon	11
Phillips, Dick	11
Phillips, Ed	0
Phillips, Eddie	
Debut 1924	21
Debut 1953	0
Phillips, J.R.	6
Phillips, Jack	20
Phillips, Jason	0
Phillips, Jason C.	0
Phillips, John	0
Phillips, Marr	17
Phillips, Mike	34
Phillips, Red	3
Phillips, Taylor	14
Phillips, Tom	7
Phoebus, Tom	52
Phoenix, Steve	0
Phyle, Bill	8
Piatt, Adam	7
Piatt, Doug	3
Piatt, Wiley	80
Picciolo, Rob	23
Picciuto, Nick	0
Pichardo, Hipolito	50
Piche, Ron	7
Picinich, Val	82
Pick, Charlie	30
Pick, Eddie	2
Pickering, Calvin	1
Pickering, Urbane	14
Pickett, Charlie	0
Pickett, Dave	1
Pickett, John	12
Pickett, Ricky	0
Pickrel, Clarence	1
Pickup, Ty	0
Pico, Jeff	14
Picone, Mario	0
Piechota, Al	0
Pieh, Cy	6
Pierce, Eddie	0
Pierce, Gracie	2
Pierce, Jack	5
Pierce, Jeff	0
Pierce, Maury	0
Pierce, Ray	4
Pierce, Tony	6
Piercy, Andy	0
Piercy, Bill	28
Pieretti, Marino	24

Player	WS
Pierotti, Al	2
Pierro, Bill	0
Piersoll, Chris	1
Pierson, Bill	1
Pierson, Dave	1
Pierson, Dick	0
Piet, Tony	72
Piez, Sandy	1
Pignatano, Joe	23
Pike, Jay	0
Pike, Jess	1
Piktuzis, George	0
Pilarcik, Al	39
Pillette, Duane	40
Pillette, Herman	38
Pillion, Squiz	0
Pilney, Andy	0
Pina, Horacio	31
Pineda, Luis	1
Pineiro, Joel	7
Pinelli, Babe	63
Pinnance, Ed	1
Pinto, Lerton	1
Pipgras, Ed	0
Pipgras, George	81
Pippen, Cotton	2
Pirie, Dick	0
Pirkl, Greg	1
Pirtle, Gerry	0
Pisciotta, Marc	6
Pisoni, Jim	4
Pitko, Alex	1
Pitler, Jake	6
Pitlock, Skip	6
Pittaro, Chris	2
Pittenger, Pinky	14
Pittman, Joe	5
Pitts, Gaylen	1
Pittsley, Jim	5
Pitula, Stan	1
Pitz, Herman	4
Pladson, Gordy	0
Planeta, Emil	0
Plank, Eddie	0
Plantenberg, Erik	2
Plantier, Phil	46
Plarski, Don	0
Plaskett, Elmo	0
Platt, Whitey	14
Platte, Al	0
Pleis, Bill	16
Plesac, Dan	106
Pless, Rance	1
Plews, Herb	18
Plitt, Norman	3
Plock, Walter	0
Plodinec, Tim	0
Plummer, Bill	16
Plunk, Eric	86
Plympton, Jeff	1

Player	WS
Poat, Ray	12
Pocoroba, Biff	38
Podbielan, Bud	28
Podgajny, Johnny	20
Podres, Johnny	143
Podsednik, Scott	0
Poepping, Mike	0
Poetz, Joe	0
Pofahl, Jimmy	9
Poff, John	1
Poffenberger, Boots	18
Poholsky, Tom	34
Poindexter, J.	1
Pointer, Aaron	3
Poland, Hugh	2
Polchow, Lou	0
Polcovich, Kevin	9
Pole, Dick	16
Polhemus, Mark	0
Polidor, Gus	5
Politte, Cliff	8
Polivka, Ken	0
Polley, Dale	0
Polli, Lou	1
Polly, Nick	0
Poloni, John	0
Pomorski, John	0
Ponce, Carlos	0
Pond, Arlie	39
Pond, Ralph	0
Ponder, Elmer	21
Pool, Harlin	10
Poole, Ed	33
Poole, Jim	
Debut 1925	19
Debut 1990	23
Poole, Ray	0
Poorman, Tom	47
Pope, Dave	15
Popovich, Paul	31
Popp, Bill	0
Poquette, Tom	33
Porray, Ed	0
Porter, Bo	1
Porter, Bob	0
Porter, Chuck	11
Porter, Dan	0
Porter, Dick	72
Porter, Irv	0
Porter, J.W.	10
Porter, Jim	0
Porter, Matthew	0
Porter, Ned	0
Porto, Al	1
Portocarrero, Arnie	38
Porzio, Mike	0
Posada, Leo	9
Pose, Scott	3
Posedel, Bill	25
Poser, Bob	0

Player	WS
Possehl, Lou	1
Post, Lew	0
Post, Sam	0
Pott, Nellie	0
Potter, Dykes	0
Potter, Mike	0
Potter, Squire	0
Potts, Dan	0
Potts, John	4
Potts, Mike	0
Poulsen, Ken	0
Pounds, Bill	0
Powell, Abner	15
Powell, Alonzo	1
Powell, Bill	6
Powell, Brian	2
Powell, Dante	3
Powell, Dennis	13
Powell, Grover	3
Powell, Hosken	33
Powell, Jack	0
Powell, Jake	50
Powell, Jeremy	5
Powell, Jim	4
Powell, Leroy	0
Powell, Martin	31
Powell, Paul	0
Powell, Ray	86
Powell, Ross	2
Power, Ted	79
Power, Tom	1
Powers, Ike	2
Powers, Jim	0
Powers, John	3
Powers, Les	2
Powers, Mike	
Debut 1898	44
Debut 1932	1
Powers, Phil	9
Powis, Carl	1
Pozo, Arquimedez	1
Prall, Willie	0
Pramesa, Johnny	11
Pratt, Frank	0
Pratt, Larry	1
Pratt, Todd	28
Pregenzer, John	0
Preibisch, Mel	0
Prendergast, Jim	0
Prendergast, Mike	53
Prentiss, George	2
Prescott, Bobby	0
Presko, Joe	20
Presley, Jim	63
Pressnell, Tot	34
Preston, Walt	4
Price, Bill	1
Price, Jackie	0
Price, Jim	14

Player	WS
Price, Joe	
Debut 1928	0
Debut 1980	55
Prichard, Bob	2
Priddy, Bob	21
Pride, Curtis	16
Priest, Eddie	0
Priest, Johnny	0
Prieto, Ariel	15
Prim, Ray	24
Prince, Don	0
Prince, Tom	24
Prince, Walter	3
Prinz, Bret	7
Pritchard, Buddy	0
Pritchett, Chris	1
Proctor, Jim	0
Proctor, Red	0
Proeser, George	5
Prokopec, Luke	5
Proly, Mike	41
Propst, Jake	0
Prothro, Doc	18
Prough, Bill	0
Prudhomme, Augie	1
Pruess, Earl	0
Pruett, Hub	33
Pruett, Jim	0
Pruiett, Tex	8
Pruitt, Ron	19
Pryor, Greg	33
Puccinelli, George	16
Puckett, Troy	0
Puente, Miguel	0
Pugh, Tim	15
Puhl, John	0
Puig, Rich	0
Pujols, Luis	12
Puleo, Charlie	25
Pulido, Alfonso	1
Pulido, Carlos	3
Pulliam, Harvey	5
Pulsipher, Bill	11
Pumpelly, Spence	0
Punto, Nick	0
Purdin, John	6
Purdy, Pid	14
Purnell, Jesse	0
Purner, Oscar	0
Purtell, Billy	25
Putman, Ed	1
Putnam, Pat	40
Puttmann, Ambrose	8
Pyburn, Jim	2
Pye, Eddie	0
Pyecha, John	0
Pyle, Ewald	9
Pyle, Harlan	0
Pyle, Shadow	1
Pytlak, Frankie	81
Pyznarski, Tim	0

Q

Player	WS
Qualls, Jim	2
Qualters, Tom	1
Quarles, Bill	2
Queen, Billy	0
Queen, Mel	
Debut 1942	17
Debut 1964	29
Quellich, George	1
Quest, Joe	43
Quevedo, Ruben	3
Quick, Ed	0
Quick, Hal	0
Quilici, Frank	13
Quillen, Lee	3
Quinlan, Finners	1
Quinlan, Frank	0
Quinlan, Tom	0
Quinn, Frank	
Debut 1899	0
Debut 1949	2
Quinn, Joe	0
Quinn, John	0
Quinn, Patrick	0
Quinn, Tad	0
Quinn, Tom	5
Quinn, Wimpy	0
Quinones, Luis	19
Quinones, Rey	31
Quintana, Carlos	30
Quintana, Luis	1
Quinton, Marshall	1
Quirico, Rafael	0
Quirk, Art	1
Quirk, Jamie	44

R

Player	WS
Raabe, Brian	0
Rabb, John	5
Rabbitt, Joe	0
Rabe, Charlie	1
Rachunok, Steve	0
Rackley, Marv	15
Raczka, Mike	0
Radbourn, George	0
Radcliff, Rip	104
Radebaugh, Roy	1
Rader, Dave	60
Rader, Don	1
Rader, Drew	0
Radford, Paul	138
Radinsky, Scott	52
Radlosky, Rob	0
Radmanovich, Ryan	0
Radtke, Jack	0

Player	WS
Raether, Hal	0
Raffensberger, Ken	137
Raffo, Al	3
Rafter, Jack	0
Raftery, Tom	1
Raggio, Brady	0
Ragland, Frank	0
Ragland, Tom	3
Raich, Eric	1
Rain, Steve	3
Raines, Larry	6
Raines Jr., Tim	0
Rainey, Chuck	28
Rainey, John	4
Rajsich, Dave	3
Rajsich, Gary	7
Rakers, Jason	0
Rakow, Ed	33
Raleigh, John	1
Ralston, Doc	1
Ramazzotti, Bob	12
Rambert, Pep	0
Rambo, Pete	0
Ramirez, Alex	4
Ramirez, Allan	4
Ramirez, Hector	2
Ramirez, Julio	1
Ramirez, Mario	6
Ramirez, Milt	2
Ramirez, Orlando	4
Ramirez, Roberto	0
Ramos, Bobby	6
Ramos, Chucho	1
Ramos, Domingo	19
Ramos, Edgar	0
Ramos, John	0
Ramos, Ken	0
Ramsay, Rob	4
Ramsdell, Willie	27
Ramsey, Bill	2
Ramsey, Fernando	0
Ramsey, Mike	
Debut 1978	13
Debut 1987	1
Rand, Dick	3
Randall, Bob	29
Randall, James	0
Randall, Newt	5
Ranew, Merritt	14
Raney, Ribs	0
Ransom, Cody	0
Ransom, Jeff	1
Rapp, Earl	7
Rapp, Goldie	11
Raschi, Vic	113
Rasmussen, Dennis	69
Rasmussen, Eric	43
Rasmussen, Hans	0

Player	WS
Rath, Fred	
Debut 1968	1
Debut 1998	1
Rath, Gary	0
Rath, Morrie	70
Ratliff, Gene	0
Ratliff, Jon	0
Ratliff, Paul	11
Ratzer, Steve	0
Raub, Tommy	4
Rauch, Bob	0
Raudman, Bob	0
Rautzhan, Lance	7
Rawlings, Johnny	73
Ray, Carl	0
Ray, Farmer	3
Ray, Irv	27
Ray, Jim	43
Ray, Ken	0
Ray, Larry	0
Raydon, Curt	7
Rayford, Floyd	26
Raymer, Fred	9
Raymond, Bugs	46
Raymond, Claude	54
Raymond, Harry	18
Raymond, Lou	0
Raziano, Barry	0
Ready, Randy	72
Reagan, Rip	0
Reames, Britt	5
Reams, Leroy	0
Reardon, Jeremiah	0
Reardon, Phil	0
Rebel, Art	3
Reberger, Frank	15
Reccius, John	10
Reccius, Phil	26
Redding, Phil	1
Redding, Tim	2
Reder, Johnny	0
Redfern, Buck	3
Redfern, Pete	31
Redfield, Joe	0
Redman, Tike	2
Redmon, Glenn	0
Redmond, Billy	2
Redmond, Harry	0
Redmond, Jack	0
Redmond, Wayne	0
Reece, Bob	0
Reed, Billy	0
Reed, Bob	4
Reed, Darren	2
Reed, Howie	30
Reed, Jack	4
Reed, Jeff	74
Reed, Jerry	33
Reed, Milt	1
Reed, Steve	63

Player	WS
Reed, Ted	1
Reeder, Bill	1
Reeder, Icicle	0
Reeder, Nick	0
Rees, Stan	1
Reese, Jimmie	18
Reese, Randy	22
Reese, Rich	52
Reeves, Bobby	31
Regalado, Rudy	5
Regan, Bill	42
Regan, Joe	0
Regan, Mike	12
Rego, Tony	3
Rehg, Wally	16
Reiber, Frank	3
Reich, Herman	6
Reichardt, Rick	105
Reichle, Dick	5
Reid, Billy	3
Reid, Earl	0
Reid, Jessie	0
Reid, Scott	0
Reidy, Bill	26
Reilley, Charlie	4
Reilley, Duke	1
Reilly, Arch	0
Reilly, Barney	1
Reilly, Charlie	58
Reilly, Hal	0
Reilly, Joe	0
Reilly, Josh	0
Reilly, Tom	0
Reimer, Kevin	33
Reinbach, Mike	0
Reinecker, Wally	0
Reinhart, Art	33
Reinholz, Art	0
Reipschlager, C.	23
Reis, Bobby	13
Reis, Jack	1
Reis, Laurie	4
Reis, Tommy	0
Reisgl, Bugs	0
Reising, Charlie	0
Reisling, Doc	17
Reiss, Al	0
Reith, Brian	0
Reitsma, Chris	3
Reitz, Ken	84
Rementer, Butch	0
Remmerswaal, Win	2
Remneas, Alex	0
Remsen, Jack	33
Remy, Jerry	113
Renfer, Erwin	0
Renfroe, Laddie	0
Renfroe, Marshall	0
Renick, Rick	10
Reniff, Hal	38

Player	WS
Reninger, Jim	0
Renna, Bill	20
Rensa, Tony	13
Renteria, Rich	7
Repass, Bob	7
Replogle, Andy	7
Repoz, Roger	74
Repulski, Rip	70
Rescigno, Xavier	15
Restelli, Dino	8
Rettger, George	9
Rettig, Otto	1
Retzer, Ken	16
Reuschel, Paul	21
Revenig, Todd	0
Revering, Dave	52
Reyes, Al	17
Reyes, Carlos	25
Reyes, Dennys	12
Reyes, Gil	5
Reyes, Nap	24
Reynolds, Archie	1
Reynolds, Bill	0
Reynolds, Bob	23
Reynolds, Charlie	
Debut 1882	0
Debut 1889	1
Reynolds, Craig	115
Reynolds, Danny	1
Reynolds, Don	2
Reynolds, Harold	123
Reynolds, Ken	9
Reynolds, R.J.	56
Reynolds, Ronn	3
Reynolds, Ross	6
Reynolds, Tommie	17
Reynoso, Armando	56
Rhawn, Rocky	5
Rheam, Cy	2
Rhem, Flint	87
Rhiel, Billy	10
Rhodes, Bill	0
Rhodes, Charlie	5
Rhodes, Dusty	32
Rhodes, Gordon	47
Rhodes, Tuffy	10
Rhomberg, Kevin	2
Rhyne, Hal	42
Ribant, Dennis	28
Riccelli, Frank	2
Ricci, Chuck	1
Rice, Bob	0
Rice, Del	110
Rice, Hal	22
Rice, Len	1
Rice, Pat	1
Rich, Woody	7
Richard, Lee	4
Richards, Duane	0
Richards, Fred	1

Player	WS
Richards, Gene	122
Richards, Paul	44
Richards, Rusty	0
Richardson, Art	0
Richardson, Bill	1
Richardson, Danny	123
Richardson, Gordie	8
Richardson, Jack	0
Richardson, Jeff	
Debut 1989	2
Debut 1990	0
Richardson, Ken	0
Richardson, Nolen	7
Richardson, Tom	0
Richardt, Mike	7
Richbourg, Lance	65
Richert, Pete	83
Richie, Lew	91
Richie, Rob	2
Richmond, Beryl	1
Richmond, Don	2
Richmond, John	46
Richmond, Ray	0
Richter, Al	0
Richter, John	0
Richter, Reggie	2
Rickert, Joe	1
Rickert, Marv	22
Ricketts, Dave	4
Ricketts, Dick	0
Rickey, Branch	9
Rickley, Chris	1
Ricks, John	0
Rico, Art	0
Rico, Fred	2
Riconda, Harry	14
Riddle, John	0
Riddle, Johnny	4
Riddleberger, D.	8
Riddlemoser, D.	0
Ridgway, Jack	0
Ridzik, Steve	43
Riebe, Hank	2
Riedling, John	6
Rieger, Elmer	0
Riesgo, Nikco	0
Rigby, Brad	7
Rigdon, Paul	4
Riggan, Jerrod	4
Riggert, Joe	13
Riggs, Adam	0
Riggs, Lew	68
Rightnowar, Ron	2
Rigney, Bill	52
Rigney, Johnny	85
Rikard, Culley	9
Riles, Ernest	63
Riley, Billy	1
Riley, George	1

Player	WS
Riley, Jim	
Debut 1910	0
Debut 1921	0
Riley, Lee	0
Riley, Matt	0
Rincon, Andy	8
Rincon, Juan	0
Rincon, Ricardo	28
Rineer, Jeff	0
Ringo, Frank	4
Rinker, Bob	0
Rios, Danny	0
Rios, Juan	1
Ripken, Billy	53
Ripley, Allen	14
Ripley, Walt	0
Rippelmeyer, Ray	1
Ripple, Charlie	0
Ripple, Jimmy	49
Risberg, Swede	49
Rising, Pop	0
Riske, David	3
Risley, Bill	18
Ritchie, Jay	16
Ritchie, Wally	12
Ritter, Charlie	0
Ritter, Floyd	0
Ritter, Hank	2
Ritter, Lew	27
Ritter, Reggie	0
Ritterson, Whitey	1
Rittwage, Jim	2
Ritz, Jim	0
Ritz, Kevin	38
Rivas, Luis	9
Rivera, Ben	12
Rivera, Bombo	18
Rivera, German	7
Rivera, Juan	0
Rivera, Luis	1
Rivera, Luis A.	39
Rivera, Mike	0
Rivera, Roberto	0
Riviere, Tink	1
Rizzo, Johnny	57
Rizzo, Todd	0
Roa, Joe	1
Roach, John	0
Roach, Mel	10
Roach, Mike	1
Roach, Roxey	21
Roach, Skel	1
Roarke, Mike	10
Roat, Fred	2
Robbins, Bruce	3
Robello, Tommy	1
Roberge, Bert	14
Roberge, Skippy	7
Roberson, Kevin	4
Roberson, Sid	3

Player	WS
Roberts, Brian	3
Roberts, Curt	9
Roberts, Dale	0
Roberts, Dave	
Debut 1962	2
Debut 1972	45
Debut 1999	2
Roberts, Grant	2
Roberts, Jim	0
Roberts, Leon	78
Roberts, Ray	0
Roberts, Red	1
Roberts, Skipper	1
Roberts, Willis	6
Robertson, Andre	15
Robertson, Bob	73
Robertson, Charlie	42
Robertson, Daryl	0
Robertson, Dave	99
Robertson, Dick	7
Robertson, Don	0
Robertson, Gene	53
Robertson, Jerry	8
Robertson, Jim	1
Robertson, Mike	1
Robertson, Rich	
Debut 1966	5
Debut 1993	14
Robertson, Sherry	32
Robidoux, Billy Joe	5
Robinson, Aaron	79
Robinson, Bill	0
Robinson, Bruce	2
Robinson, Charlie	2
Robinson, Craig	10
Robinson, Dave	2
Robinson, Dewey	3
Robinson, Earl	15
Robinson, Fred	0
Robinson, Hank	47
Robinson, Hum.	15
Robinson, Jack	
Debut 1902	0
Debut 1949	0
Robinson, Jeff	
Debut 1984	51
Debut 1987	25
Robinson, Ken	2
Robinson, Kerry	4
Robinson, Rabbit	17
Robinson, Ron	49
Robitaille, Chick	13
Robles, Rafael	1
Robles, Sergio	0
Robson, Tom	0
Rocco, Mike	44
Roche, Armando	0
Roche, Jack	3
Rochefort, Ben	0
Rochelli, Lou	0

Player	WS
Rochford, Mike	0
Rock, Les	0
Rockenfield, Ike	9
Rockett, Pat	4
Rodas, Rich	0
Rodgers, Andre	61
Rodgers, Bill	
Debut 1915	7
Debut 1944	0
Rodgers, Bob	68
Rodin, Eric	0
Rodriguez, Carlos	8
Rodriguez, Ed	45
Rodriguez, Edwin	0
Rodriguez, Ellie	74
Rodriguez, Frank	24
Rodriguez, Freddy	0
Rodriguez, Hector	11
Rodriguez, Jose	
Debut 1916	1
Debut 2000	1
Rodriguez, Liu	3
Rodriguez, Nerio	2
Rodriguez, Rich	43
Rodriguez, Rick	2
Rodriguez, Roberto	4
Rodriguez, Rosario	1
Rodriguez, Ruben	0
Rodriguez, Steve	0
Rodriguez, Tony	1
Rodriguez, Vic	1
Rodriguez, Wilfredo	0
Roe, Clay	0
Roe, Preacher	136
Roebuck, Ed	67
Roenicke, Gary	94
Roenicke, Ron	32
Roesler, Mike	2
Roettger, Oscar	0
Roettger, Wally	40
Roetz, Ed	1
Rogalski, Joe	1
Rogers, Buck	0
Rogers, Emmett	2
Rogers, Jay	0
Rogers, Jim	7
Rogers, Jimmy	1
Rogers, Kevin	8
Rogers, Lee	0
Rogers, Packy	0
Rogers, Tom	14
Rogge, Clint	21
Roggenburk, Garry	6
Rogodzinski, Mike	2
Rogovin, Saul	46
Rohde, Dave	1
Rohe, George	23
Rohn, Dan	2
Rohr, Billy	0
Rohr, Les	2

Player	WS
Rohrmeier, Dan	1
Rohwer, Ray	5
Roig, Tony	2
Rojas, Minnie	27
Rojek, Stan	40
Roland, Jim	26
Rolison, Nate	0
Rolling, Ray	0
Rollings, Red	5
Rollinson, William	0
Rolls, Damian	2
Roman, Bill	1
Roman, Jose	0
Romanick, Ron	26
Romano, Jim	0
Romano, Mike	0
Romano, Tom	0
Romberger, Dutch	0
Romero, Ed	37
Romero, J.C.	2
Romero, Mandy	1
Romero, Ramon	0
Romine, Kevin	7
Romo, Enrique	54
Romo, Vicente	52
Romonosky, John	4
Ronan, Marc	0
Rondeau, Henri	6
Rondon, Gil	1
Roof, Gene	3
Roof, Phil	52
Rooks, George	0
Roomes, Rolando	8
Rooney, Frank	0
Rooney, Pat	0
Roper, John	5
Roque, Jorge	1
Roque, Rafael	4
Rosado, Jose	44
Rosado, Luis	0
Rosario, Jimmy	5
Rosario, Mel	0
Rosario, Santiago	1
Rosario, Victor	0
Rose, Bobby	7
Rose, Brian	9
Rose, Chuck	0
Rose, Don	0
Rosebraugh, Zeke	1
Rose Jr., Pete	0
Roselli, Bob	4
Rosello, Dave	20
Roseman, Chief	81
Rosen, Goody	71
Rosenberg, Harry	0
Rosenberg, Lou	0
Rosenberg, Steve	3
Rosenfeld, Max	2
Rosenthal, Larry	47
Rosenthal, Si	5

Player	WS
Rosenthal, Wayne	1
Roser, Bunny	2
Roser, Steve	7
Roskos, John	0
Ross, Bob	0
Ross, Buck	48
Ross, Buster	6
Ross, Chet	35
Ross, Cliff	1
Ross, Don	34
Ross, Ernie	0
Ross, Gary	30
Ross, George	0
Ross, Mark	3
Rosselli, Joe	0
Rossi, Joe	3
Rossman, Claude	56
Rosso, Frank	0
Rossy, Rico	6
Rotblatt, Marv	4
Roth, Frank	18
Rothel, Bob	0
Rothermel, Bobby	0
Rothfuss, Jack	3
Rothgeb, Claude	0
Rothrock, Jack	73
Rothschild, Larry	1
Rounsaville, Virle	0
Routcliffe, Phil	0
Rowan, Dave	2
Rowan, Jack	31
Rowand, Aaron	5
Rowdon, Wade	2
Rowe, Dave	37
Rowe, Don	2
Rowe, Harland	0
Rowe, Ken	2
Rowell, Bama	51
Rowen, Ed	14
Rowland, Chuck	0
Rowland, Mike	3
Rowland, Rich	4
Roxburgh, Jim	1
Roy, Charlie	0
Roy, Emil	0
Roy, Jean-Pierre	0
Roy, Luther	2
Roy, Norm	1
Royer, Stan	4
Royster, Jerry	93
Royster, Willie	0
Rozek, Dick	1
Rozema, Dave	76
Roznovsky, Vic	9
Rubeling, Al	15
Ruberto, Sonny	0
Rubio, Jorge	3
Ruble, Art	2
Rucker, Dave	18
Rucker, Johnny	49

Player	WS
Rudderham, John	0
Rudolph, Don	21
Rudolph, Dutch	0
Rudolph, Ernie	0
Rudolph, Ken	15
Ruebel, Matt	2
Rufer, Rudy	0
Ruffcorn, Scott	0
Ruffin, Bruce	76
Ruffin, Johnny	13
Ruhle, Vern	71
Ruiz, Chico	
Debut 1964	17
Debut 1978	2
Rullo, Joe	3
Rumler, William	5
Runge, Paul	8
Runnells, Tom	0
Runyan, Sean	5
Rupe, Ryan	10
Rush, Andy	0
Ruskin, Scott	11
Russ, John	0
Russell, Allan	77
Russell, Harvey	6
Russell, Jack	112
Russell, Jeff	104
Russell, John	
Debut 1917	4
Debut 1984	19
Russell, Lefty	2
Russell, Lloyd	0
Russell, Paul	0
Russell, Rip	20
Russo, Marius	51
Rusteck, Dick	2
Ruszkowski, Hank	3
Rutherford, Jim	0
Rutherford, Johnny	5
Ruthven, Dick	100
Rutner, Mickey	0
Ryal, Mark	2
Ryan, B.J.	7
Ryan, Blondy	19
Ryan, Buddy	15
Ryan, Connie	114
Ryan, Cyclone	1
Ryan, Jack	
Debut 1889	30
Debut 1908	5
Debut 1929	0
Ryan, Jason	2
Ryan, John	
Debut 1884	3
Debut 1884	0
Debut 1895	0
Ryan, Johnny	5
Ryan, Ken	28
Ryan, Mike	28
Ryan, Rob	2

Player	WS
Ryan, Rosy	48
Ryba, Mike	50
Ryder, Tom	0
Rye, Gene	0
Ryerson, Gary	3

S

Player	WS
Sabel, Erik	3
Sabo, Alex	0
Sacka, Frank	1
Sackinsky, Brian	0
Sadek, Mike	22
Sadler, Donnie	8
Sadowski, Bob	
Debut 1960	6
Debut 1963	18
Sadowski, Ed	8
Sadowski, Jim	0
Sadowski, Ted	2
Saenz, Olmedo	16
Saffell, Tom	10
Sage, Harry	5
Sager, A.J.	10
Sagmoen, Marc	0
Saipe, Mike	0
Sakata, Lenn	29
Salas, Mark	30
Salazar, Angel	12
Sale, Freddy	0
Sales, Ed	2
Salisbury, Harry	21
Salisbury, Solly	0
Salkeld, Bill	44
Salkeld, Roger	5
Salmon, Chico	40
Salmon, Roger	0
Saltzgaver, Jack	19
Salve, Gus	0
Salveson, Jack	14
Salvo, Manny	36
Sambito, Joe	69
Samcoff, Ed	0
Samford, Ron	5
Sampen, Bill	17
Sample, Billy	68
Sampson, Benj	2
Samuel, Amado	3
Samuels, Ike	0
Samuels, Joe	0
Samuels, Roger	1
Sanchez, Alejandro	2
Sanchez, Alex	
Debut 1987	0
Debut 2001	0
Sanchez, Celerino	4
Sanchez, Jesus	13
Sanchez, Luis	29

Player	WS
Sanchez, Orlando	2
Sanchez, Raul	5
Sanchez, Zip	2
Sand, Heinie	63
Sandberg, Gus	1
Sandberg, Jared	1
Sanders, Anthony	0
Sanders, Ben	126
Sanders, Dee	0
Sanders, Deion	60
Sanders, John	0
Sanders, Ken	65
Sanders, Reggie	3
Sanders, Roy	
Debut 1917	9
Debut 1918	1
Sanders, Scott	31
Sanders, War	0
Sandlock, Mike	11
Sands, Charlie	6
Sandt, Tommy	1
Sanford, Chance	0
Sanford, Fred	39
Sanford, Jack	
Debut 1940	1
Debut 1956	115
Sanford, Mo	3
Sanicki, Ed	2
Sankey, Ben	3
Santana, Andres	0
Santana, Johan	4
Santana, Julio	9
Santana, Marino	1
Santana, Pedro	0
Santana, Rafael	43
Santangelo, F.P.	50
Santiago, Jose	
Debut 1954	4
Debut 1963	32
Santo Domingo, R.	0
Santorini, Al	18
Santos, Angel	0
Santos, Victor	5
Santovenia, Nelson	19
Santry, Edward	0
Sargent, Joe	4
Sarmiento, Manny	32
Sarni, Bill	31
Sasser, Mackey	26
Sasser, Rob	0
Satriano, Tom	38
Saturria, Luis	0
Saucier, Frank	0
Saucier, Kevin	21
Sauer, Eddie	9
Sauerbeck, Scott	18
Saunders, Dennis	1
Saunders, Doug	0
Saunders, Rusty	0
Saunders, Tony	15
Sauters, Al	0
Sauveur, Rich	1
Savage, Bob	15
Savage, Don	5
Savage, Jack	0
Savage, Jimmie	15
Savage, Ted	36
Saverine, Bob	20
Savidge, Don	0
Savidge, Ralph	1
Savransky, Moe	1
Sawatski, Carl	47
Sawyer, Carl	2
Sawyer, Rick	8
Sawyer, Will	11
Sax, Dave	2
Sax, Ollie	0
Say, Jimmy	4
Say, Lou	24
Sayles, Bill	2
Saylor, Phil	0
Scala, Jerry	4
Scalzi, Johnny	0
Scalzi, Skeeter	0
Scanlan, Bob	31
Scanlan, Doc	65
Scanlan, Frank	1
Scanlan, Mort	0
Scanlon, Pat	1
Scannell, Patrick	1
Scantlebury, Pat	0
Scarbery, Randy	6
Scarborough, Ray	74
Scarce, Mac	15
Scarritt, Russ	17
Scarsella, Les	19
Scarsone, Steve	17
Schaal, Paul	102
Schacht, Al	8
Schacht, Sid	0
Schacker, Hal	0
Schaefer, Jeff	5
Schaeffer, Harry	0
Schaeffer, Mark	1
Schafer, Harry	10
Schaffer, Jimmie	12
Schaffernoth, Joe	5
Schaive, Johnny	4
Schalk, Roy	14
Schall, Gene	3
Schaller, Biff	2
Schallock, Art	6
Schang, Bobby	2
Schanz, Charley	24
Schappert, Jack	6
Schardt, Bill	9
Scharein, Art	13
Scharein, George	13
Scharf, Nick	1
Schattinger, Jeff	0
Schatzeder, Dan	80
Schauer, Rube	9
Scheer, Al	34
Scheer, Heinie	4
Scheeren, Fritz	1
Scheetz, Owen	0
Scheffer, Aaron	0
Scheffing, Bob	32
Scheffler, Ted	17
Schegg, Lefty	0
Scheib, Carl	52
Scheibeck, Frank	27
Scheible, John	2
Scheid, Rich	2
Scheinblum, Richie	37
Schell, Danny	5
Schelle, Jim	0
Schellhase, Al	0
Schemanske, Fred	1
Schemer, Mike	3
Schenck, Bill	9
Scheneberg, John	0
Schenz, Hank	7
Schepner, Joe	0
Scherbarth, Bob	0
Scherer, Harry	0
Scherman, Fred	37
Scherrer, Bill	20
Schesler, Dutch	0
Schettler, Lou	4
Schiappacasse, Lou	0
Schick, Morrie	0
Schilling, Chuck	36
Schillings, Red	0
Schindler, Bill	0
Schiraldi, Calvin	32
Schirick, Dutch	0
Schlafly, Harry	27
Schlei, Admiral	55
Schlesinger, Rudy	0
Schliebner, Dutch	9
Schlitzer, Biff	9
Schlueter, Jay	0
Schlueter, Norm	3
Schmandt, Ray	20
Schmees, George	1
Schmelz, Al	0
Schmidt, Bob	31
Schmidt, Boss	40
Schmidt, Butch	34
Schmidt, Curt	0
Schmidt, Dave	
Debut 1981	1
Debut 1981	64
Schmidt, Freddy	13
Schmidt, Henry	18
Schmidt, Jeff	0
Schmidt, Pete	0
Schmidt, Walter	62
Schmidt, Willard	36
Schmit, Crazy	7
Schmitz, Johnny	110
Schmulbach, Hank	0
Schmutz, Charlie	2
Schneck, Dave	4
Schneiberg, Frank	0
Schneider, Brian	3
Schneider, Dan	4
Schneider, Jeff	0
Schneider, Pete	65
Schnell, Karl	1
Schoen, Gerry	0
Schoeneck, Jumbo	19
Schofield, Dick	
Debut 1953	74
Debut 1983	116
Schomberg, Otto	29
Schooler, Mike	36
Schoonmaker, Jerry	0
Schorr, Ed	0
Schott, Gene	33
Schourek, Pete	45
Schramka, Paul	0
Schreiber, Barney	0
Schreiber, Hank	1
Schreiber, Paul	1
Schreiber, Ted	1
Schrenk, Steve	3
Schriver, Pop	74
Schroder, Bob	3
Schroeder, Bill	34
Schroll, Al	4
Schrom, Ken	38
Schu, Rick	30
Schuble, Heinie	18
Schueler, Ron	45
Schuler, Dave	1
Schullstrom, Erik	1
Schulmerich, Wes	42
Schult, Art	7
Schulte, Ham	5
Schulte, Jack	0
Schulte, Johnny	17
Schulte, Len	6
Schultz, Barney	31
Schultz, Bob	6
Schultz, Buddy	16
Schultz, Howie	22
Schultz, Joe	
Debut 1912	44
Debut 1939	7
Schultz, John	0
Schultz, Mike	0
Schultz, Webb	0
Schultze, John	0
Schulz, Al	45
Schulz, Jeff	0
Schulz, Walt	0
Schulze, Don	6
Schumann, Hack	0
Schupp, Ferdie	59
Schurr, Wayne	3
Schuster, Bill	6
Schutz, Carl	0
Schwabe, Mike	0
Schwall, Don	39
Schwamb, Blackie	0
Schwartz, Bill	
Debut 1883	3
Debut 1904	0
Schwartz, Randy	0
Schwarz, Jeff	5
Schweitzer, Al	26
Schwenck, Rudy	0
Schwenk, Hal	1
Schwert, Pi	1
Schwind, Art	0
Schypinski, Jerry	0
Scoffic, Lou	1
Scoggins, Jim	0
Sconiers, Daryl	14
Score, Herb	58
Scott, Darryl	1
Scott, Dick	
Debut 1901	0
Debut 1963	0
Debut 1989	0
Scott, Donnie	7
Scott, Ed	20
Scott, Everett	142
Scott, Gary	1
Scott, George	0
Scott, Jim	1
Scott, John	1
Scott, Lefty	1
Scott, LeGrant	5
Scott, Mickey	9
Scott, Milt	20
Scott, Pete	19
Scott, Rodney	53
Scott, Tim	23
Scott, Tony	53
Scott	1
Scranton, Jim	0
Scrivener, Chuck	5
Scruggs, Tony	0
Scudder, Scott	9
Scurry, Rod	33
Seabol, Scott	0
Seale, Johnny	1
Seaman, Kim	3
Seanez, Rudy	20
Searage, Ray	21
Searcy, Steve	3
Sears, Ken	7
Seats, Tom	7
Seay, Bobby	0
Sebra, Bob	12
Sebring, Jimmy	41
Sechrist, Doc	0

Player	WS
Secory, Frank	5
Secrist, Don	0
Sedgwick, Duke	2
See, Charlie	5
See, Larry	0
Seeds, Bob	40
Seelbach, Chris	0
Seelbach, Chuck	13
Seerey, Pat	48
Sefcik, Kevin	14
Segelke, Herman	0
Segrist, Kal	0
Segui, Diego	103
Seguignol, F.	4
Segura, Jose	0
Seibert, Kurt	0
Seibold, Socks	42
Seilheimer, Ricky	1
Selby, Bill	2
Sell, Epp	1
Sellers, Jeff	12
Sellers, Rube	0
Sells, Dave	8
Selma, Dick	57
Selph, Carey	9
Sember, Mike	0
Sembera, Carroll	5
Seminara, Frank	7
Semproch, Ray	13
Senerchia, Sonny	1
Sentell, Paul	4
Senteney, Steve	0
Seoane, Manny	0
Sepkowski, Ted	1
Serad, Billy	30
Serafini, Dan	6
Serena, Bill	36
Serna, Paul	4
Serrano, Wascar	0
Serum, Gary	9
Servais, Scott	60
Service, Scott	25
Sessi, Walter	0
Settlemire, Merle	0
Sevcik, John	1
Severinsen, Al	8
Severson, Rich	7
Seward, Frank	1
Seward, George	3
Sewell, Tommy	0
Sexauer, Elmer	0
Sexton, Chris	2
Sexton, Frank	2
Sexton, Jimmy	9
Sexton, Tom	1
Seyfried, Gordon	1
Seymour, Jake	0
Shafer, Ralph	0
Shafer, Tillie	31
Shaffer, John	8
Shaffer, Taylor	4
Shallix, Gus	16
Shamsky, Art	56
Shanahan, Greg	1
Shaner, Wally	12
Shank, Harvey	0
Shanley, Doc	0
Shanley, Jim	0
Shannabrook, W.	0
Shanner, Bill	0
Shannon, Dan	15
Shannon, Frank	0
Shannon, Joe	0
Shannon, Owen	0
Shannon, Red	27
Shannon, Spike	74
Shannon, Wally	1
Shantz, Billy	7
Sharman, Ralph	1
Sharon, Dick	8
Sharp, Bill	21
Sharpe, Bud	3
Sharperson, Mike	39
Sharrott, George	3
Sharrott, John	21
Shaughnessy, Shag	1
Shave, Jon	5
Shaver, Jeff	0
Shaw, Al	
Debut 1901	8
Debut 1907	64
Shaw, Ben	0
Shaw, Don	13
Shaw, Hunky	0
Shaw, Sam	3
Shay, Danny	24
Shay, Marty	1
Shea, Gerry	0
Shea, John	0
Shea, Merv	28
Shea, Mike	0
Shea, Nap	0
Shea, Red	3
Shea, Spec	54
Shea, Steve	5
Sheaffer, Danny	18
Shealy, Al	3
Shean, Dave	42
Shearer, Ray	0
Shearon, John	2
Shears, George	0
Sheehan, Biff	4
Sheehan, Jack	0
Sheehan, Jim	0
Sheehan, Tom	23
Sheehan, Tommy	27
Sheely, Bud	3
Sheerin, Chuck	1
Sheets, Andy	15
Sheets, Ben	6
Sheets, Larry	52
Shelby, John	63
Sheldon, Bob	4
Sheldon, Rollie	26
Sheldon, Scott	5
Shellenback, Frank	9
Shellenback, Jim	15
Shelley, Hugh	0
Shelton, Ben	1
Shelton, Skeeter	0
Shemo, Steve	1
Shepard, Bert	0
Shepard, Jack	20
Shepardson, Ray	0
Shepherd, Keith	2
Shepherd, Ron	0
Sherid, Roy	16
Sheridan, Neill	0
Sheridan, Pat	59
Sheridan, Red	0
Sherling, Ed	0
Sherlock, Monk	5
Sherlock, Vince	2
Sherman, Babe	0
Sherman, Darrell	0
Sherman, Joe	1
Sherrill, Dennis	0
Sherrill, Tim	0
Sherry, Fred	0
Sherry, Larry	65
Sherry, Norm	13
Shetrone, Barry	0
Shetzline, John	6
Shevlin, Jimmy	1
Shields, Ben	2
Shields, Charlie	7
Shields, Pete	0
Shields, Scot	2
Shields, Steve	5
Shields, Tommy	0
Shields, Vince	1
Shifflett, Garland	0
Shifflett, Steve	4
Shilling, Jim	3
Shinall, Zak	0
Shinault, Ginger	2
Shines, Razor	0
Shinners, Ralph	7
Shinnick, Tim	24
Shipanoff, Dave	3
Shipke, Bill	11
Shipley, Craig	26
Shipley, Joe	0
Shires, Art	23
Shirey, Duke	0
Shirley, Bart	2
Shirley, Bob	64
Shirley, Mule	0
Shirley, Steve	1
Shirley, Tex	18
Shiver, Ivey	0
Shoch, George	71
Shockley, Costen	1
Shoemaker, Charlie	1
Shoffner, Milt	25
Shofner, Strick	0
Shokes, Eddie	0
Shook, Ray	0
Shoop, Ron	0
Shopay, Tom	3
Shore, Ernie	68
Shore, Ray	0
Shores, Bill	27
Short, Bill	3
Short, Dave	0
Shorten, Chick	31
Shoun, Clyde	75
Shoupe, John	1
Shouse, Brian	0
Shovlin, John	0
Shreve, Lev	11
Shriver, Harry	7
Shuba, George	25
Shugart, Frank	74
Shultz, Toots	1
Shumaker, Anthony	0
Shuman, Harry	1
Shupe, Vince	2
Sicking, Ed	11
Siddall, Joe	2
Siebert, Paul	5
Siebler, Dwight	5
Siefke, Fred	0
Siegel, John	0
Siegle, Johnny	4
Siemer, Oscar	2
Sierra, Candy	0
Siffell, Frank	0
Sigafoos, Frank	0
Siglin, Paddy	0
Sigman, Tripp	3
Signer, Walter	2
Sigsby, Seth	0
Sikorski, Brian	1
Silber, Eddie	0
Silch, Ed	1
Silva, Danny	0
Silva, Jose	11
Silvera, Al	0
Silvera, Charlie	18
Silverio, Luis	1
Silverio, Tom	0
Silvestri, Dave	6
Silvestri, Ken	6
Sima, Al	10
Simas, Bill	29
Simmons, Brian	5
Simmons, Hack	16
Simmons, John	0
Simmons, Nelson	6
Simmons, Pat	5
Simms, Mike	18
Simon, Hank	15
Simon, Mike	21
Simon, Randall	12
Simon, Syl	1
Simons, Doug	1
Simons, Mel	3
Simpson, Dick	10
Simpson, Duke	0
Simpson, Joe	16
Simpson, Steve	0
Simpson, Wayne	20
Sims, Duke	98
Sims, Greg	0
Sims, Pete	1
Sinatro, Matt	8
Sinclair, Steve	2
Sincock, Bert	0
Siner, Hosea	0
Singer, Bill	112
Singleton, Duane	0
Singleton, Elmer	14
Singleton, John	1
Sington, Fred	14
Sipek, Dick	2
Sipin, John	3
Sisco, Steve	0
Sisk, Doug	37
Sisk, Tommie	36
Sisler, Dave	37
Sisler, Dick	71
Sisti, Sibby	59
Sitton, Carl	3
Sivess, Pete	5
Siwy, Jim	1
Sixsmith, Ed	0
Skaff, Frank	3
Skaggs, Dave	15
Skalski, Joe	0
Skaugstad, Dave	1
Skeels, Dave	0
Sketchley, Bud	0
Skidmore, Roe	0
Skiff, Bill	1
Skinner, Bob	137
Skinner, Camp	0
Skinner, Charles	0
Skinner, Joel	25
Skizas, Lou	18
Skok, Craig	6
Skopec, John	7
Skrmetta, Matt	0
Skube, Bob	0
Slade, Gordon	31
Sladen, Art	0
Slagle, John	0
Slagle, Roger	0
Slagle, Walt	0
Slapnicka, Cy	1

Player	WS
Slappey, John	0
Slattery, Jack	2
Slattery, Mike	33
Slattery, Phil	1
Slaught, Don	130
Slaughter, Barney	0
Slaughter, Sterling	0
Slayback, Bill	5
Slayback, Scottie	0
Slayton, Steve	0
Sleater, Lou	15
Sloan, Bruce	2
Sloan, Tod	8
Sloat, Dwain	0
Slocum, Ron	2
Slocumb, Heathcliff	56
Slusarski, Joe	9
Smajstrla, Craig	0
Small, Aaron	10
Small, Charlie	0
Small, Hank	0
Small, Jim	2
Small, Mark	0
Smalley, Roy	52
Smalley, Will	8
Smallwood, Walt	0
Smart, J.D.	2
Smaza, Joe	0
Smiley, Bill	4
Smith, Al	
Debut 1926	0
Debut 1934	92
Smith, Aleck	19
Smith, Art	0
Smith, Bernie	2
Smith, Bill	
Debut 1884	0
Debut 1886	4
Debut 1958	2
Smith, Billy	
Debut 1975	28
Debut 1981	1
Smith, Bob	
Debut 1913	3
Debut 1955	5
Smith, Bobby	13
Smith, Bobby Gene	12
Smith, Brian	0
Smith, Brick	0
Smith, Bud	5
Smith, Bull	0
Smith, Carr	0
Smith, Charley	48
Smith, Charlie	57
Smith, Chick	1
Smith, Chris	4
Smith, Clay	1
Smith, D.W.	0
Smith, Dan	2
Smith, Danny	1

Player	WS
Smith, Daryl	0
Smith, Dave	2
Smith, Dick	
Debut 1951	1
Debut 1963	2
Debut 1969	0
Smith, Doug	0
Smith, Dwight	50
Smith, Earl	
Debut 1916	34
Debut 1955	0
Smith, Ed	
Debut 1884	2
Debut 1906	3
Smith, Eddie	95
Smith, Edgar	
Debut 1883	2
Debut 1883	5
Smith, Elmer	101
Smith, Ernie	0
Smith, Frank	
Debut 1884	1
Debut 1950	45
Smith, Fred	
Debut 1890	22
Debut 1907	1
Debut 1913	29
Smith, George	
Debut 1916	48
Debut 1926	11
Debut 1963	11
Smith, Greg	2
Smith, Hal	
Debut 1932	10
Debut 1955	73
Debut 1956	42
Smith, Happy	1
Smith, Harry	
Debut 1877	1
Debut 1901	19
Debut 1912	1
Debut 1914	3
Smith, Harvey	3
Smith, Heinie	17
Smith, Jack	
Debut 1912	0
Debut 1962	1
Smith, Jake	1
Smith, Jason	0
Smith, Jim	1
Smith, Jimmy	20
Smith, Joe	0
Smith, John	
Debut 1882	3
Debut 1931	0
Smith, Jud	9
Smith, Keith	
Debut 1977	2
Debut 1984	0
Smith, Ken	1

Player	WS
Smith, Klondike	0
Smith, L.	0
Smith, Leo	3
Smith, Mark	
Debut 1983	0
Debut 1994	21
Smith, Mayo	3
Smith, Michael	0
Smith, Mike	
Debut 1926	0
Debut 1984	2
Smith, Milt	1
Smith, Nate	0
Smith, Ollie	4
Smith, Paddy	0
Smith, Paul	
Debut 1916	0
Debut 1953	8
Smith, Pete	
Debut 1962	1
Debut 1987	35
Smith, Phenomenal	71
Smith, Pop Boy	2
Smith, Ray	2
Smith, Red	
Debut 1917	0
Debut 1925	0
Debut 1927	0
Smith, Rex	0
Smith, Riverboat	4
Smith, Roy	0
Smith, Roy P.	25
Smith, Rufus	1
Smith, Skyrocket	6
Smith, Stub	0
Smith, Syd	11
Smith, Tom	4
Smith, Tommy	4
Smith, Tony	11
Smith, Travis	0
Smith, Vinnie	1
Smith, Wally	11
Smith, Wib	0
Smith, Willie	
Debut 1963	44
Debut 1994	0
Smith, Zane	105
Smith	0
Smithberg, Roger	2
Smithson, Mike	63
Smoll, Lefty	0
Smoyer, Henry	0
Smykal, Frank	1
Smyres, Clancy	0
Smyth, Red	3
Smythe, Harry	5
Sneed, Jon	32
Snell, Charlie	0
Snell, Nate	15
Snell, Wally	0

Player	WS
Snider, Van	1
Snipes, Roxy	0
Snodgrass, Chappie	0
Snook, Frank	1
Snopek, Chris	8
Snover, Colonel	0
Snyder, Bernie	1
Snyder, Bill	2
Snyder, Brian	0
Snyder, Charles	1
Snyder, Cooney	0
Snyder, Cory	85
Snyder, Gene	0
Snyder, George	1
Snyder, Jack	0
Snyder, Jerry	11
Snyder, Jim	1
Snyder, John	5
Snyder, Redleg	0
Sobkowiak, Scott	0
Sockalexis, Louis	9
Sodd, Bill	0
Soderstrom, Steve	0
Sodowsky, Clint	6
Soff, Ray	3
Sofield, Rick	11
Sojo, Luis	51
Solaita, Tony	46
Solano, Julio	7
Solis, Marcelino	0
Solomon, Eddie	35
Solomon, Mose	0
Solters, Moose	87
Somerlott, Jock	0
Somerville, Ed	4
Sommers, Bill	2
Sommers, Pete	2
Sommers, Rudy	2
Sommerville, Andy	0
Songer, Don	14
Sorensen, Lary	82
Sorrell, Bill	3
Sorrells, Chick	0
Sosa, Elias	80
Sosa, Jose	2
Sosa, Juan	0
Sothern, Denny	20
Sothoron, Allen	93
Souchock, Steve	27
Southwick, Clyde	0
Southworth, Bill	1
Souza, Mark	0
Sowders, Bill	25
Sowders, John	28
Sowders, Len	3
Spade, Bob	23
Spalding, Dick	7
Spangler, Al	68
Spanswick, Bill	0
Sparks, Jeff	3

Player	WS
Sparks, Steve	0
Sparma, Joe	32
Speake, Bob	17
Speck, Cliff	2
Speece, Byron	9
Speed, Horace	1
Speer, Floyd	0
Speer, Kid	3
Spehr, Tim	17
Spence, Bob	2
Spencer, Ben	1
Spencer, Chet	0
Spencer, Daryl	102
Spencer, George	16
Spencer, Glenn	22
Spencer, Hack	0
Spencer, Roy	39
Spencer, Sean	0
Spencer, Stan	4
Spencer, Tom	1
Spencer, Tubby	30
Spencer, Vern	1
Speraw, Paul	0
Sperber, Ed	2
Sperring, Rob	3
Sperry, Stan	2
Spicer, Bob	0
Spies, Harry	5
Spiezio, Ed	33
Spikes, Charlie	47
Spillner, Dan	77
Spilman, Harry	17
Spindel, Hal	2
Spinks, Scipio	11
Spivey, Junior	6
Spognardi, Andy	1
Spohrer, Al	45
Spoljaric, Paul	14
Spongberg, Carl	0
Spooner, Karl	12
Spooneybarger, Tim	0
Spotts, Jim	0
Spradlin, Jerry	24
Spragins, Homer	0
Sprague, Charlie	12
Sprague, Ed	
Debut 1968	18
Debut 1991	80
Spratt, Harry	3
Spriggs, George	1
Spring, Jack	12
Springer, Brad	0
Springer, Dennis	21
Springer, Ed	0
Springer, Russ	23
Springer, Steve	0
Sprinz, Joe	1
Sproull, Charlie	0
Sprout, Bob	0
Sprowl, Bobby	1

Player	WS
Spurgeon, Freddy	22
Spurgeon, Jay	1
Spurney, Ed	0
Squires, Mike	30
St. Claire, Ebba	12
St. Claire, Randy	15
St. Vrain, Jim	6
Stablein, George	1
Stack, Eddie	21
Staehle, Marv	6
Stafford, Bill	47
Stafford, Bob	0
Stafford, General	47
Stafford, Heinie	0
Stafford, John	0
Staggs, Steve	8
Stahl, Larry	38
Stahoviak, Scott	23
Staiger, Roy	8
Stainback, Tuck	34
Staley, Gale	1
Stallard, Tracy	28
Stallcup, Virgil	31
Staller, George	3
Stallings, George	0
Stanage, Oscar	59
Stanceu, Charley	2
Standaert, Jerry	4
Standridge, Jason	1
Standridge, Pete	5
Stanek, Al	0
Stanfield, Kevin	0
Stange, Lee	67
Stanhouse, Don	49
Stanicek, Pete	5
Stanicek, Steve	0
Stanifer, Rob	4
Stanka, Joe	1
Stankard, Tom	0
Stankiewicz, Andy	19
Stanley, Buck	0
Stanley, Fred	35
Stanley, Jim	2
Stanley, Joe	
Debut 1884	0
Debut 1897	9
Stanley, Mickey	122
Stansbury, Jack	1
Stanton, Buck	0
Stanton, Harry	0
Stanton, Lee	68
Stanton, Mike	23
Stanton, Tom	0
Staples, Joe	0
Stapleton, Dave	
Debut 1980	43
Debut 1987	2
Stark, Denny	0
Stark, Dolly	8
Stark, Matt	0

Player	WS
Starkel, Con	0
Starnagle, George	0
Starr, Charlie	6
Starr, Chick	0
Starr, Dick	12
Starr, Ray	37
Starrette, Herm	3
Staton, Dave	2
Staton, Joe	0
Statz, Jigger	74
Stauffer, Ed	1
Stearns, Ecky	45
Stearns, John	89
Stecher, Charlie	0
Stechschulte, Gene	5
Stedronsky, John	0
Steele, Bill	25
Steele, Bob	22
Steele, Elmer	25
Steelman, Farmer	3
Steels, Jim	0
Steen, Bill	35
Steengrafe, Milt	1
Steenstra, Kennie	0
Steere, Gene	0
Steevens, Morrie	2
Stefero, John	4
Stegman, Dave	5
Stein, Bill	59
Stein, Irv	0
Stein, Justin	1
Stein, Randy	3
Steinbacher, Hank	14
Steinbrenner, Gene	0
Steinecke, Bill	0
Steineder, Ray	5
Steiner, Ben	7
Steiner, Red	2
Steirer, Rick	3
Stellbauer, Bill	1
Stellberger, Bill	0
Stelmaszek, Rick	1
Stem, Fred	2
Stember, Jeff	0
Stemmeyer, Bill	29
Stenhouse, Dave	17
Stenhouse, Mike	5
Stephen, Buzz	0
Stephens, Bryan	5
Stephens, Clarence	2
Stephens, Gene	45
Stephens, George	2
Stephens, Jim	23
Stephens, Ray	0
Stephenson, Bob	1
Stephenson, D.	0
Stephenson, Earl	6
Stephenson, Jerry	2
Stephenson, Joe	0
Stephenson, John	17

Player	WS
Stephenson, Phil	4
Stephenson, Walter	1
Sterling, John	0
Sterling, Randy	0
Sterrett, Dutch	4
Stevens, Bobby	1
Stevens, Chuck	13
Stevens, Dave	13
Stevens, Ed	31
Stevens, Jim	0
Stevens, R C	4
Steverson, Todd	1
Stewart, Ace	7
Stewart, Andy	0
Stewart, Bill	0
Stewart, Bud	60
Stewart, Bunky	4
Stewart, Frank	0
Stewart, Glen	6
Stewart, Jimmy	23
Stewart, Joe	0
Stewart, Mack	1
Stewart, Mark	0
Stewart, Neb	0
Stewart, Sammy	72
Stewart, Scott	6
Stewart, Stuffy	5
Stewart, Tuffy	0
Stidham, Phil	0
Stiely, Fred	2
Stigman, Dick	41
Stiles, Rollie	8
Stillman, Royle	3
Stillwell, Kurt	73
Stillwell, Ron	0
Stimac, Craig	0
Stimmel, Archie	6
Stimson, Carl	0
Stine, Harry	0
Stine, Lee	5
Stinson, Bob	49
Stock, Wes	36
Stocker, Kevin	70
Stocksdale, Otis	11
Stockwell, Len	0
Stoddard, Bob	24
Stoddard, Tim	57
Stokes, Al	1
Stokes, Art	1
Stone, Arnie	5
Stone, Dean	26
Stone, Dick	1
Stone, Dwight	6
Stone, Gene	0
Stone, George	54
Stone, Jeff	23
Stone, Ricky	1
Stone, Rocky	0
Stone, Ron	13
Stone, Steve	92

Player	WS
Stone, Tige	0
Stoneham, John	0
Stoneman, Bill	56
Stoner, Lil	43
Stoops, Jim	1
Storie, Howie	0
Storke, Alan	22
Storti, Lin	8
Stottlemyre, Mel	0
Stouch, Tom	0
Stout, Allyn	18
Stovall, DaRond	0
Stovall, George	111
Stovall, Jesse	5
Stoviak, Ray	0
Stowe, Hal	0
Stowers, Chris	0
Strahler, Mike	8
Strahs, Dick	0
Strain, Joe	8
Straker, Les	13
Strampe, Bob	0
Strand, Paul	8
Strands, Larry	0
Strange, Alan	15
Strange, Doug	32
Stratton, Asa	0
Stratton, Monty	42
Straub, Joe	0
Strauss, Joe	4
Street, Gabby	30
Streit, Oscar	0
Strelecki, Ed	3
Stremmel, Phil	0
Streuli, Walt	0
Strick, John	2
Stricker, Cub	102
Strickland, Bill	0
Strickland, George	74
Strickland, Jim	7
Stricklett, Elmer	35
Strief, George	22
Strike, John	0
Striker, Jake	1
Strincevich, Nick	46
Stringer, Lou	30
Strittmatter, Mark	0
Strobel, Allie	3
Strohmayer, John	11
Strom, Brent	22
Stromme, Floyd	0
Stroner, Jim	0
Strong, Joe	1
Stroud, Ed	31
Stroud, Sailor	15
Stroughter, Steve	0
Struss, Steamboat	0
Struve, Al	0
Stryker, Dutch	0
Stuart, Bill	1

Player	WS
Stuart, Johnny	12
Stuart, Luke	0
Stuart, Marlin	23
Stubbs, Franklin	65
Stubing, Moose	0
Stueland, George	3
Stuffel, Paul	2
Stull, Everett	1
Stultz, George	1
Stump, Jim	4
Stumpf, Bill	1
Stumpf, George	3
Stuper, John	21
Sturdivant, Tom	66
Sturdy, Guy	2
Sturgeon, Bobby	21
Sturgis, Dean	0
Sturm, Johnny	4
Stutz, George	0
Styles, Lena	3
Stynes, Neil	0
Suarez, Ken	18
Suarez, Luis	0
Such, Dick	0
Suche, Charley	0
Suchecki, Jim	1
Suck, Tony	3
Sudakis, Bill	47
Suder, Pete	83
Suero, William	0
Sugden, Joe	64
Sukeforth, Clyde	25
Sukla, Ed	1
Sularz, Guy	4
Sulik, Ernie	7
Sullivan, Andy	0
Sullivan, Bill	
Debut 1878	0
Debut 1890	0
Sullivan, Billy	
Debut 1899	77
Debut 1931	71
Sullivan, Charlie	8
Sullivan, Chub	9
Sullivan, Dan	19
Sullivan, Denny	
Debut 1879	0
Debut 1905	21
Sullivan, Fleury	16
Sullivan, Harry	0
Sullivan, Haywood	17
Sullivan, Jack	0
Sullivan, Jim	
Debut 1891	32
Debut 1921	1
Sullivan, Joe	
Debut 1893	35
Debut 1935	29

Player	WS
Sullivan, John	
Debut 1905	1
Debut 1919	0
Debut 1920	18
Debut 1942	34
Debut 1963	5
Sullivan, Lefty	0
Sullivan, Marc	6
Sullivan, Marty	46
Sullivan, Mike	
Debut 1888	4
Debut 1889	53
Sullivan, Pat	1
Sullivan, Russ	4
Sullivan, Sleeper	2
Sullivan, Suter	5
Sullivan, Ted	1
Sullivan, Tom	
Debut 1884	17
Debut 1922	0
Debut 1925	0
Summa, Homer	68
Summers, Champ	43
Summers, Ed	68
Summers, Kid	0
Sumner, Carl	1
Sunday, Art	3
Sunday, Billy	48
Sundin, Gordie	0
Sundra, Steve	47
Sunkel, Tom	10
Surhoff, Rich	0
Surkont, Max	52
Susce, George	
Debut 1929	6
Debut 1955	23
Susko, Pete	4
Sutcliffe, Butch	0
Sutcliffe, Sy	37
Suter, Rube	4
Sutherland, Darrell	7
Sutherland, Dizzy	0
Sutherland, Gary	45
Sutherland, Leo	0
Sutherland, Suds	3
Sutko, Glenn	0
Sutthoff, Jack	26
Sutton, Johnny	4
Sutton, Larry	10
Sveum, Dale	55
Swacina, Harry	16
Swaggerty, Bill	2
Swaim, Cy	12
Swan, Andy	1
Swan, Craig	61
Swan, Ducky	0
Swan, Russ	13
Swander, Pinky	3
Swann, Pedro	0
Swanson, Bill	0
Swanson, Evar	49
Swanson, Karl	1
Swanson, Red	3
Swanson, Stan	2
Swarbach, Bill	0
Swartz, Bud	0
Swartz, Dazzy	0
Swartzbaugh, Dave	1
Swartzel, Park	19
Sweasy, Charlie	1
Sweeney, Bill	
Debut 1882	59
Debut 1928	14
Sweeney, Buck	0
Sweeney, Dan	2
Sweeney, Hank	0
Sweeney, Jeff	47
Sweeney, Jerry	3
Sweeney, Mark	20
Sweeney, Pete	7
Sweeney, Rooney	6
Sweet, Rick	14
Sweetland, Leo	23
Sweigert, Ham	0
Swentor, Augie	0
Swetonic, Steve	41
Swett, Pop	2
Swift, Bob	61
Swigart, Oad	1
Swigler, Ad	0
Swindell, Josh	1
Swindells, Charlie	0
Swingle, Paul	0
Swisher, Steve	22
Swoboda, Ron	73
Swormstedt, Len	4
Sykes, Bob	16
Sylvester, Lou	21
Szekely, Joe	0
Szotkiewicz, Ken	1

T

Player	WS
Tabaka, Jeff	9
Tabb, Jerry	2
Taber, John	1
Taber, Lefty	0
Tabor, Greg	0
Tackett, Jeff	6
Taff, John	0
Taitt, Doug	16
Talbot, Dale	4
Talbot, Fred	25
Talcott, Roy	0
Talton, Tim	4
Tamargo, John	9
Tamulis, Vito	44
Tankersley, Leo	0
Tanner, Bruce	1
Tanner, Chuck	20
Tappan, Walter	0
Tappe, El	4
Tappe, Ted	3
Tarasco, Tony	21
Tarbert, Arlie	0
Tartabull, Jose	37
Tarver, LaSchelle	0
Tasby, Willie	42
Tate, Al	0
Tate, Bennie	40
Tate, Hughie	1
Tate, Lee	1
Tate, Pop	14
Tate, Randy	2
Tate, Stu	0
Tatis, Ramon	1
Tatum, Jarvis	3
Tatum, Jimmy	1
Tatum, Ken	36
Tatum, Tommy	4
Tauby, Fred	0
Tauscher, Walt	1
Taussig, Don	6
Tavarez, Jesus	9
Tavener, Jackie	55
Taveras, Alex	0
Taveras, Frank	85
Taylor, Arlas	0
Taylor, Ben	
Debut 1912	0
Debut 1951	2
Taylor, Bill	2
Taylor, Billy	
Debut 1898	1
Debut 1994	38
Taylor, Bob	1
Taylor, Bruce	3
Taylor, Carl	24
Taylor, Chink	0
Taylor, Chuck	56
Taylor, Dorn	1
Taylor, Dwight	0
Taylor, Ed	8
Taylor, Fred	1
Taylor, Gary	0
Taylor, Harry	
Debut 1890	50
Debut 1932	0
Debut 1946	19
Debut 1957	1
Taylor, Hawk	10
Taylor, Joe	6
Taylor, Kerry	0
Taylor, Leo	0
Taylor, Live Oak	1
Taylor, Pete	0
Taylor, Reggie	0
Taylor, Ron	62
Taylor, Rube	0
Taylor, Sammy	24
Taylor, Sandy	0
Taylor, Scott	
Debut 1992	1
Debut 1995	0
Taylor, Terry	0
Taylor, Tommy	1
Taylor, Wade	0
Taylor, Wiley	3
Taylor, Zack	71
Teachout, Bud	13
Tebbetts, Birdie	106
Tebeau, Pussy	1
Tebeau, White Wings	71
Tedrow, Al	2
Teed, Dick	0
Tejada, Wilfredo	1
Tejera, Michael	0
Telemaco, Amaury	13
Telford, Anthony	29
Telgheder, Dave	11
Tellmann, Tom	20
Templeton, Chuck	0
Tener, John	24
Tennant, Jim	0
Tennant, Tom	0
Tenney, Fred	5
Tepedino, Frank	3
Tepsic, Joe	0
Terlecki, Bob	0
Terlecky, Greg	1
Terpko, Jeff	6
Terrell, Jerry	25
Terrell, Tom	0
Terrell, Walt	87
Terry, John	1
Terry, Scott	29
Terry, Yank	17
Terry, Zeb	55
Terwilliger, Dick	0
Terwilliger, Wayne	48
Tesch, Al	0
Tessmer, Jay	1
Testa, Nick	0
Tettelbach, Dick	1
Teufel, Tim	96
Textor, George	1
Thacker, Moe	4
Thatcher, Grant	2
Thayer, Greg	2
Theis, Jack	0
Theiss, Duane	1
Theobald, Ron	21
Theodore, George	2
Thesenga, Jug	0
Thevenow, Tommy	60
Thiel, Bert	0
Thielman, Henry	9
Thielman, Jake	28
Thies, Dave	1
Thies, Jake	7
Thigpen, Bobby	71
Thobe, J.J.	0
Thobe, Tom	1
Thoenen, Dick	0
Thomas, Andres	23
Thomas, Bill	0
Thomas, Blaine	1
Thomas, Brad	0
Thomas, Bud	
Debut 1932	25
Debut 1951	1
Thomas, Carl	0
Thomas, Claude	0
Thomas, Danny	7
Thomas, Fay	11
Thomas, Fred	13
Thomas, Frosty	0
Thomas, George	40
Thomas, Herb	3
Thomas, Ira	44
Thomas, Kite	7
Thomas, Larry	5
Thomas, Lefty	1
Thomas, Leo	4
Thomas, Mike	0
Thomas, Myles	20
Thomas, Pinch	36
Thomas, Ray	0
Thomas, Red	1
Thomas, Roy	25
Thomas, Stan	16
Thomas, Tom	3
Thomas, Valmy	13
Thomas, Walt	0
Thomason, Art	0
Thomason, Erskine	0
Thomasson, Gary	67
Thompson, Andy	0
Thompson, Art	0
Thompson, Bill	0
Thompson, Bobby	3
Thompson, Danny	32
Thompson, Dave	11
Thompson, Don	2
Thompson, Frank	0
Thompson, Fresco	51
Thompson, Fuller	0
Thompson, Gus	2
Thompson, Harry	2
Thompson, Homer	0
Thompson, Jason	1
Thompson, Jocko	8
Thompson, Junior	49
Thompson, Justin	44
Thompson, Lee	0
Thompson, Mark	12
Thompson, Mike	2

Player	WS
Thompson, Milt	106
Thompson, Rich	2
Thompson, Ryan	25
Thompson, Scot	22
Thompson, Shag	3
Thompson, Tim	8
Thompson, Tommy	
Debut 1912	0
Debut 1933	22
Thompson, Tug	0
Thomson, John	26
Thoney, Jack	18
Thormahlen, Hank	34
Thormodsgard, Paul	10
Thornton, John	14
Thornton, Lou	1
Thornton, Otis	0
Thornton, Walter	36
Thorpe, Bob	
Debut 1951	4
Debut 1955	0
Thorpe, Jim	18
Thrasher, Buck	2
Throneberry, Faye	24
Throneberry, Marv	25
Throop, George	4
Thuman, Lou	0
Thurman, Bob	16
Thurman, Gary	16
Thurman, Mike	15
Thurmond, Mark	46
Thurston, Sloppy	90
Tibbs, Jay	34
Tiefenauer, Bobby	18
Tiefenthaler, Verle	0
Tiemeyer, Eddie	1
Tierney, Bill	0
Tierney, Cotton	55
Tietje, Les	24
Tift, Ray	0
Tilley, John	0
Tillman, Bob	53
Tillman, Johnny	1
Tillman, Rusty	2
Tillotson, Thad	2
Timberlake, Gary	0
Timmermann, Tom	38
Timmons, Ozzie	8
Tincup, Ben	10
Tingley, Ron	10
Tinning, Bud	28
Tinsley, Lee	16
Tipple, Dan	2
Tipton, Eric	61
Tipton, Joe	35
Tischinski, Tom	4
Tising, Jack	2
Titcomb, Cannonball	22
Tobik, Dave	30

Player	WS
Tobin, Bill	0
Tobin, Johnny	5
Tobin, Pat	0
Tobin, Tip	0
Toca, Jorge	0
Todd, Al	66
Todd, Frank	0
Todd, Jackson	11
Todd, Jim	28
Todt, Phil	53
Toenes, Hal	0
Tolar, Kevin	0
Tolentino, Jose	2
Toliver, Fred	10
Tolleson, Wayne	45
Tolman, Tim	2
Tolson, Chick	6
Tomanek, Dick	8
Tomasic, Andy	0
Tomberlin, Andy	3
Tomer, George	0
Tomko, Brett	31
Tomlin, Dave	23
Tomlin, Randy	32
Tomney, Phil	26
Tompkins, Chuck	1
Tompkins, Ron	4
Toms, Tommy	0
Tonkin, Doc	0
Tonneman, Tony	0
Toole, Steve	22
Tooley, Bert	9
Toporcer, Specs	43
Toppin, Rupe	0
Torborg, Jeff	25
Torkelson, Red	0
Torphy, Red	0
Torre, Frank	42
Torrealba, Pablo	15
Torrealba, Steve	0
Torrealba, Yorvit	1
Torres, Angel	1
Torres, Dilson	1
Torres, Felix	23
Torres, Gil	20
Torres, Hector	24
Torres, Ricardo	1
Torres, Rusty	28
Torres, Salomon	6
Torve, Kelvin	2
Tost, Lou	8
Toth, Paul	11
Touchstone, Clay	0
Towers, Josh	6
Towne, Babe	2
Townsend, George	6
Townsend, Ira	0
Townsend, Jack	38
Townsend, Leo	3
Toy, Jim	4

Player	WS
Tozer, Bill	1
Traber, Jim	11
Tracewski, Dick	25
Tracy, Andy	5
Tracy, Jim	4
Traffley, Bill	11
Traffley, John	0
Tragesser, Walt	13
Tramback, Red	0
Trautman, Fred	0
Trautwein, John	0
Travers, Al	0
Travers, Bill	52
Traxler, Brian	0
Tray, Jim	1
Treacey, Fred	3
Treacey, Pete	0
Treadaway, Ray	0
Treadway, George	37
Treadway, Jeff	60
Treadway, Red	7
Trechock, Frank	0
Trekell, Harry	0
Tremark, Nick	1
Tremel, Bill	7
Tremie, Chris	0
Tremper, Overton	0
Tresh, Mike	80
Trevino, Alex	53
Trevino, Bobby	0
Trice, Bob	5
Trimble, Joe	0
Trinkle, Ken	25
Triplett, Coaker	30
Trlicek, Ricky	4
Troedson, Rich	6
Trosky, Hal	0
Trost, Mike	2
Trott, Sam	39
Trotter, Bill	16
Trouppe, Quincy	0
Trout, Steve	76
Trowbridge, Bob	14
Troy, Bun	0
Troy, Dasher	25
Truax, Fred	0
Truby, Harry	6
Truesdale, Frank	15
Trujillo, Mike	9
Trumbull, Ed	0
Tsamis, George	1
Tsitouris, John	27
Tubbs, Greg	1
Tucker, Ollie	0
Tucker, Scooter	0
Tucker, T.J.	0
Tucker, Thurman	71
Tuckey, Tom	4
Tuero, Oscar	10
Tufts, Bob	1

Player	WS
Tunnell, Lee	17
Turang, Brian	4
Turbeville, George	4
Turbidy, Jerry	1
Turchin, Eddie	0
Turgeon, Pete	0
Turk, Lucas	0
Turnbow, Derrick	2
Turner, Chris	7
Turner, Earl	1
Turner, Jerry	45
Turner, Jim	83
Turner, Ken	0
Turner, Matt	8
Turner, Shane	1
Turner, Ted	0
Turner, Tink	0
Turner, Tom	14
Turner, Tuck	36
Tutwiler, Elmer	0
Tutwiler, Guy	0
Twineham, Art	5
Twining, Twink	0
Twitchell, Larry	60
Twitchell, Wayne	45
Twitty, Jeff	0
Twombly, Babe	8
Twombly, Cy	0
Twombly, George	4
Tyack, Jim	4
Tyler, Fred	0
Tyler, Johnnie	2
Tyner, Jason	7
Tyng, Jim	1
Tyree, Earl	0
Tyriver, Dave	0
Tyrone, Jim	5
Tyrone, Wayne	0
Tyson, Mike	63
Tyson, Turkey	0
Tyson, Ty	15

U

Player	WS
Uchrinscko, Jimmy	0
Uecker, Bob	16
Uhalt, Frenchy	2
Uhl, Bob	0
Uhlaender, Ted	70
Uhler, Maury	1
Uhlir, Charlie	0
Ujdur, Jerry	11
Ulisney, Mike	1
Ullger, Scott	0
Ullrich, Sandy	2
Ulrich, Dutch	29
Ulrich, George	0
Umbach, Arnie	2
Umbarger, Jim	21
Umbricht, Jim	16
Umphlett, Tom	17
Underhill, Willie	1
Underwood, Fred	1
Underwood, Pat	16
Underwood, Tom	83
Unglaub, Bob	47
Unroe, Tim	2
Unser, Al	9
Upchurch, Woody	1
Upham, Bill	6
Upham, John	1
Upp, Jerry	2
Upright, Dixie	0
Upshaw, Cecil	61
Upton, Bill	1
Upton, Tom	7
Urban, Jack	10
Urban, Luke	2
Urbani, Tom	8
Urbanski, Billy	70
Uribe, Jose	78
Uribe, Juan	7
Urrea, John	18
Ury, Lon	0
Usher, Bob	16
Ussat, Dutch	0

V

Player	WS
Vache, Tex	7
Vadeboncoeur, G.	0
Vahrenhorst, Harry	0
Vail, Bob	0
Vail, Mike	34
Valdes, Marc	12
Valdes, Pedro	1
Valdes, Roy	0
Valdespino, Sandy	13
Valdez, Carlos	1
Valdez, Efrain	2
Valdez, Julio	2
Valdez, Mario	3
Valdez, Rafael	0
Valdez, Rene	0
Valdez, Sergio	7
Valdivielso, Jose	16
Valent, Eric	1
Valentin, Javier	7
Valentine, Bob	0
Valentine, Bobby	38
Valentine, Corky	10
Valentine, Ellis	92
Valentine, Fred	50
Valentine, John	4
Valentinetti, Vito	12
Valenzuela, Benny	0

Player	WS
Valera, Julio	14
Valera, Yohanny	0
Valle, Dave	78
Valle, Hector	1
Van Alstyne, Clay	1
Van Atta, Russ	29
Van Brabant, Ozzie	0
Van Buren, Deacon	1
Van Burkleo, Ty	0
Van Camp, Al	5
Vance, Joe	2
Vance, Sandy	7
Van Cuyk, Chris	3
Van Cuyk, Johnny	0
Vandagrift, Carl	2
Vande Berg, Ed	35
Vandenberg, Hy	14
Van Dusen, Fred	0
Van Dyke, Ben	0
Van Dyke, Bill	10
VanEgmond, Tim	3
Van Gorder, Dave	6
VanLandingham, W.	16
Vann, John	0
Van Noy, Jay	0
Van Robays, M.	42
VanRyn, Ben	1
Van Zandt, Ike	4
Van Zant, Dick	1
Varga, Andy	0
Vargas, Hedi	0
Vargas, Roberto	0
Vargus, Bill	2
Varner, Buck	0
Varney, Dike	0
Varney, Pete	5
Varsho, Gary	16
Vasbinder, Moses	0
Vasquez, Rafael	1
Vatcher, Jim	4
Vaughan, Charlie	1
Vaughan, Glenn	0
Vaughan, Porter	2
Vaughn, Bobby	17
Vaughn, Clarence	0
Vaughn, DeWayne	0
Vaughn, Farmer	75
Vaughn, Fred	7
Vazquez, Ramon	0
Veach, Al	0
Veach, Peek-A-Boo	10
Veal, Coot	11
Vedder, Lou	0
Vega, Jesus	2
Veigel, Al	0
Veil, Bucky	4
Velandia, Jorge	1
Velasquez, G.	2
Velazquez, Carlos	3
Velazquez, Freddie	1

Player	WS
Velez, Otto	60
Veltman, Pat	0
Venable, Max	29
Ventura, Vince	0
Veras, Dario	3
Veras, Wilton	3
Verban, Emil	59
Verbanic, Joe	11
Verble, Gene	1
Verdel, Al	0
Verdi, Frank	0
Vereker, Tommy	0
Veres, Randy	8
Vergez, Johnny	57
Verhoeven, John	11
Vernon, Joe	0
Veryzer, Tom	49
Veselic, Bob	2
Viau, Lee	89
Vick, Ernie	2
Vick, Sammy	12
Vickers, Rube	23
Vickery, Tom	38
Vico, Sam	11
Vidal, Jose	1
Villafuerte, Brandon	0
Villanueva, Hector	17
Villegas, Ismael	0
Villone, Ron	28
Vines, Bob	0
Vineyard, Dave	0
Vining, Ken	0
Vinson, Charlie	1
Vinson, Rube	4
Vinton, Bill	10
Viox, Jim	61
Virgil, Ozzie	
Debut 1956	10
Debut 1980	72
Virtue, Jake	57
Visner, Joe	30
Vitelli, Joe	0
Vitiello, Joe	9
Vitko, Joe	0
Vizcaino, Luis	2
Vogel, Otto	4
Vogelsong, Ryan	1
Voigt, Jack	14
Voigt, Ollie	1
Voiselle, Bill	70
Vollmer, Clyde	51
Volz, Jake	1
Von Fricken, Hon	0
Von Hoff, Bruce	0
Von Kolnitz, Fritz	1
Von Ohlen, Dave	12
Vorhees, Cy	3
Vosberg, Ed	18
Voss, Alex	10
Voss, Bill	27

Player	WS
Vowinkel, Rip	1
Voyles, Brad	1
Voyles, Phil	0
Vuckovich, Pete	83
Vukovich, George	35
Vukovich, John	5

W

Player	WS
Wachtel, Paul	0
Wacker, Charlie	0
Waddell, Tom	15
Waddey, Frank	0
Wade, Ben	19
Wade, Gale	0
Wade, Ham	0
Wade, Jake	26
Wade, Rip	1
Wade, Terrell	8
Wadsworth, Jack	4
Wagenhorst, W.	0
Wagner, Bill	4
Wagner, Bull	0
Wagner, Butts	2
Wagner, Charlie	32
Wagner, Gary	20
Wagner, Hal	57
Wagner, Hector	0
Wagner, Heinie	112
Wagner, Joe	2
Wagner, Mark	18
Wagner, Matt	1
Wagner, Paul	26
Wahl, Kermit	10
Wainhouse, Dave	3
Waitkus, Eddie	107
Waits, Rick	67
Waitt, Charlie	1
Wakamatsu, Don	1
Wakefield, Bill	5
Wakefield, Howard	7
Wakeland, Chris	1
Walbeck, Matt	31
Walczak, Ed	0
Waldbauer, Doc	0
Walden, Fred	0
Waldron, Irv	15
Walewander, Jim	5
Walk, Bob	70
Walker, Chico	24
Walker, Dixie	22
Walker, Duane	21
Walker, Ed	0
Walker, Ernie	8
Walker, Fleet	4
Walker, Frank	2
Walker, George	0
Walker, Hub	19

Player	WS
Walker, Jamie	2
Walker, Jerry	40
Walker, Johnny	1
Walker, Kevin	6
Walker, Luke	40
Walker, Marty	0
Walker, Mike	
Debut 1988	4
Debut 1992	0
Walker, Mysterious	7
Walker, Oscar	33
Walker, Pete	2
Walker, Roy	12
Walker, Rube	33
Walker, Speed	0
Walker, Tom	
Debut 1902	24
Debut 1972	24
Walker, Tony	3
Walker, Walt	0
Walker, Welday	1
Walkup, Jim	
Debut 1927	0
Debut 1934	7
Wall, Donne	28
Wall, Joe	2
Wall, Murray	14
Wall, Stan	4
Wallace, Dave	1
Wallace, Derek	3
Wallace, Doc	0
Wallace, Don	0
Wallace, Huck	0
Wallace, Jack	0
Wallace, Jeff	8
Wallace, Jim	1
Wallace, Lefty	4
Wallace, Mike	11
Wallaesa, Jack	8
Wallen, Norm	0
Waller, Red	0
Waller, Ty	2
Wallis, Joe	21
Walls, Lee	61
Walsh, Augie	3
Walsh, Austin	2
Walsh, Connie	0
Walsh, David	1
Walsh, Dee	3
Walsh, Ed	9
Walsh, Jim	0
Walsh, Jimmy	
Debut 1910	48
Debut 1912	46
Walsh, Joe	
Debut 1891	1
Debut 1910	0
Debut 1938	0
Walsh, John	0
Walsh, Junior	4

Player	WS
Walsh, Tom	0
Walsh, Walt	0
Walter, Bernie	0
Walter, Gene	9
Walters, Charley	0
Walters, Dan	5
Walters, Fred	2
Walters, Ken	4
Walters, Mike	5
Walters, Roxy	32
Walton, Bruce	0
Walton, Danny	16
Walton, Jerome	40
Walton, Reggie	2
Wambsganss, Bill	106
Wanner, Jack	0
Wanninger, Pee Wee	8
Wantz, Dick	0
Wapnick, Steve	0
Ward, Bryan	4
Ward, Chris	0
Ward, Chuck	12
Ward, Colby	2
Ward, Colin	0
Ward, Daryle	11
Ward, Dick	0
Ward, Duane	82
Ward, Hap	0
Ward, Jay	1
Ward, Jim	0
Ward, Joe	10
Ward, John	
Debut 1884	0
Debut 1885	0
Ward, Kevin	2
Ward, Piggy	23
Ward, Preston	45
Ward, Rube	1
Ward, Turner	41
Warden, John	3
Wardle, Curt	1
Ware, Jeff	1
Wares, Buzzy	5
Warhop, Jack	73
Warmoth, Cy	6
Warner, Ed	2
Warner, Fred	15
Warner, Hooks	2
Warner, Jack	
Debut 1925	26
Debut 1962	3
Warner, Jackie	3
Warner, John	89
Warnock, Hal	0
Warren, Bennie	21
Warren, Bill	1
Warren, Mike	5
Warren, Tommy	1
Warstler, Rabbit	61

Player	WS
Warthen, Dan	14
Warwick, Bill	2
Warwick, Carl	34
Wasdell, Jimmy	67
Wasdin, John	29
Wasem, Link	0
Washburn, George	0
Washburn, Greg	0
Washburn, Libe	1
Washburn, Ray	64
Washer, Buck	0
Washington, G.	7
Washington, Herb	0
Washington, LaRue	1
Washington, Ron	28
Washington, U.L.	71
Wasinger, Mark	2
Waslewski, Gary	17
Waszgis, B.J.	0
Waterbury, Steve	0
Waters, Fred	4
Wathan, John	55
Watkins, Bill	1
Watkins, Bob	0
Watkins, Dave	2
Watkins, Ed	0
Watkins, Pat	2
Watkins, Scott	1
Watlington, Neal	1
Watson, Allen	36
Watson, Art	5
Watson, Doc	25
Watson, Johnny	0
Watson, Mark	0
Watson, Milt	15
Watson, Mother	0
Watson, Mule	41
Watt, Allie	0
Watt, Eddie	65
Watt, Frank	5
Watwood, Cliff	32
Waugh, Jim	1
Way, Bob	0
Wayenberg, Frank	0
Wayne, Gary	17
Weafer, Hal	0
Weatherly, Roy	75
Weaver, Art	3
Weaver, Eric	2
Weaver, Farmer	71
Weaver, Floyd	3
Weaver, Harry	3
Weaver, Jim	
Debut 1928	51
Debut 1967	4
Debut 1985	0
Weaver, Montie	64
Weaver, Orlie	5
Weaver, Roger	3
Weaver, Sam	77
Webb, Bill	
Debut 1917	0
Debut 1943	0
Webb, Earl	74
Webb, Hank	6
Webb, Lefty	0
Webb, Red	4
Webb, Skeeter	34
Webber, Joe	0
Webber, Les	21
Weber, Ben	9
Weber, Charlie	0
Weber, Joe	0
Weber, Neil	0
Webster, Lenny	31
Webster, Ray	
Debut 1959	1
Debut 1967	18
Weckbecker, Pete	2
Wedge, Eric	4
Weeden, Bert	0
Weekly, Johnny	3
Wegener, Mike	6
Wegman, Bill	76
Wehde, Biggs	0
Wehmeier, Herm	71
Wehner, John	10
Wehrmeister, Dave	3
Weigel, Ralph	2
Weihe, Podge	6
Weik, Dick	6
Weiland, Bob	68
Weiland, Ed	0
Weinert, Lefty	21
Weingartner, Elmer	1
Weintraub, Phil	56
Weir, Roy	7
Weis, Al	36
Weis, Butch	7
Weiser, Bud	0
Weiss, Gary	0
Weiss, Joe	1
Welaj, Johnny	11
Welch, Frank	52
Welch, Herb	1
Welch, Johnny	38
Welch, Mike	0
Welch, Milt	0
Welch, Ted	0
Welchel, Don	0
Welchonce, Harry	1
Welday, Mike	2
Welf, Ollie	0
Wellman, Bob	1
Wellman, Brad	13
Wells, Ed	57
Wells, Greg	0
Wells, Jake	4
Wells, John	0
Wells, Kip	11
Wells, Leo	2
Wells, Terry	0
Wells, Vernon	4
Welsh, Chris	14
Welsh, Jimmy	74
Welsh, Tub	5
Welteroth, Dick	2
Welzer, Tony	13
Wendell, Lew	1
Wengert, Don	12
Wensloff, Butch	20
Wentz, Jack	0
Wentzel, Stan	0
Wenz, Fred	2
Wera, Julie	1
Werhas, Johnny	2
Werle, Bill	31
Werley, George	0
Werner, Don	4
Werrick, Joe	32
Werth, Dennis	4
Werts, Johnny	19
Wertz, Bill	3
Wertz, Del	0
Wessinger, Jim	0
West, Billy	0
West, Buck	5
West, David	26
West, Dick	5
West, Frank	0
West, Hi	3
West, Lefty	3
West, Max	
Debut 1928	1
Debut 1938	94
Westbrook, Jake	2
Westerberg, Oscar	0
Westervelt, Huyler	9
Westlake, Jim	0
Westlake, Wally	97
Weston, Al	0
Weston, Mickey	0
Wetherby, Jeff	1
Wetzel, Buzz	0
Wetzel, Dutch	2
Wetzel, Shorty	0
Wever, Stefan	0
Weyhing, John	6
Whaley, Bill	1
Whaling, Bert	14
Wheat, Lee	0
Wheat, Mack	8
Wheatley, Charlie	0
Wheaton, Woody	3
Wheeler, Dan	2
Wheeler, Dick	0
Wheeler, Don	5
Wheeler, Ed	
Debut 1902	1
Debut 1945	0
Wheeler, George	
Debut 1896	16
Debut 1910	0
Wheeler, Harry	24
Wheeler, Rip	6
Wheelock, Bobby	27
Wheelock, Gary	3
Whelan, Jimmy	0
Whelan, Tom	0
Whillock, Jack	0
Whisenant, Matt	10
Whisenant, Pete	21
Whisenton, Larry	5
Whistler, Lew	24
Whitaker, Pat	1
Whitaker, Steve	18
Whitby, Bill	0
Whitcher, Bob	1
White, Ade	0
White, Barney	0
White, Bill	
Debut 1879	0
Debut 1884	41
White, C.B.	0
White, Charlie	2
White, Deke	0
White, Derrick	0
White, Don	5
White, Ed	0
White, Elder	1
White, Ernie	40
White, Fuzz	0
White, Hal	60
White, Jack	
Debut 1904	0
Debut 1927	0
White, Jerry	35
White, Jo-Jo	63
White, Kirby	19
White, Larry	2
White, Mike	7
White, Myron	0
White, Sam	0
White, Steve	0
White, Warren	0
Whited, Ed	0
Whitehead, Burgess	71
Whitehead, John	57
Whitehead, Milt	8
Whitehouse, Charlie	1
Whitehouse, Gil	2
Whitehouse, Len	8
Whitehurst, Wally	21
Whiteley, Gurdon	0
Whiteman, George	10
Whiteside, Matt	23
Whiteside, Sean	0
Whitfield, Fred	62
Whitfield, Terry	53
Whiting, Ed	26
Whiting, Jesse	1
Whitman, Dick	16
Whitman, Frank	0
Whitmer, Dan	1
Whitmore, Darrell	2
Whitney, Art	77
Whitney, Frank	3
Whitrock, Bill	12
Whittaker, Walt	0
Wickander, Kevin	10
Wicker, Bob	69
Wicker, Floyd	0
Wicker, Kemp	6
Wickersham, Dave	65
Wickland, Al	59
Widger, Chris	27
Widmar, Al	17
Widner, Wild Bill	22
Wieand, Ted	0
Wiedemeyer, C.	0
Wiedenbauer, Tom	1
Wieghaus, Tom	0
Wieneke, Jack	0
Wiesler, Bob	4
Wietelmann, Whitey	30
Wiggins, Alan	63
Wiggs, Jimmy	1
Wight, Bill	88
Wigington, Fred	1
Wihtol, Sandy	4
Wilber, Del	18
Wilborn, Claude	0
Wilborn, Thad	0
Wilcox, Milt	101
Wiles, Randy	0
Wiley, John	0
Wiley, Mark	0
Wilfong, Rob	68
Wilhelm, Harry	1
Wilhelm, Jim	2
Wilhelm, Kaiser	54
Wilhelm, Spider	0
Wilhoit, Joe	26
Wilie, Denney	6
Wilke, Harry	0
Wilkerson, Brad	1
Wilkerson, Curt	34
Wilkie, Lefty	8
Wilkins, Bobby	2
Wilkins, Dean	0
Wilkins, Eric	3
Wilkins, Marc	20
Wilkinson, Bill	13
Wilkinson, Ed	0
Wilkinson, Roy	15
Wilks, Ted	82
Will, Bob	13
Willard, Jerry	23
Willett, Ed	98
Willey, Carl	41

Player	WS
Willhite, Nick	3
Williams, Ace	0
Williams, Al	
Debut 1937	3
Debut 1980	33
Williams, Art	3
Williams, Bernie	1
Williams, Billy	0
Williams, Bob	1
Williams, Brian	14
Williams, Charlie	28
Williams, Dale	1
Williams, Dallas	0
Williams, Dana	0
Williams, Dave	
Debut 1902	0
Debut 2001	7
Williams, Davey	47
Williams, Denny	4
Williams, Dewey	10
Williams, Dib	40
Williams, Dick	65
Williams, Don	
Debut 1958	0
Debut 1963	0
Williams, Earl	0
Williams, Eddie	16
Williams, Frank	35
Williams, George	
Debut 1961	1
Debut 1995	12
Williams, Gus	
Debut 1890	0
Debut 1911	38
Williams, Harry	4
Williams, Jeff	1
Williams, Jim	1
Williams, Jimy	0
Williams, John	0
Williams, Keith	0
Williams, Ken	19
Williams, Lefty	71
Williams, Leon	0
Williams, Mark	0
Williams, Marsh	0
Williams, Matt E.	3
Williams, Matt T.	0
Williams, Mitch	75
Williams, Mutt	0
Williams, Otto	6
Williams, Papa	0
Williams, Pop	18
Williams, Reggie	
Debut 1985	8
Debut 1992	3
Williams, Rick	8
Williams, Rinaldo	1
Williams, Rip	39
Williams, Shad	0
Williams, Steamboat	2
Williams, Todd	3
Williams, Tom	3
Williams, Walt	53
Williams, Wash	0
Williams, Woody	28
Williamson, Al	0
Williamson, Antone	0
Williamson, Howie	0
Williamson, Mark	50
Willigrod, Julius	0
Willingham, Hugh	0
Willis, Carl	31
Willis, Dale	1
Willis, Jim	5
Willis, Joe	4
Willis, Lefty	5
Willis, Les	1
Willis, Mike	16
Willis, Ron	16
Willoughby, Claude	26
Willoughby, Jim	36
Wills, Bump	94
Wills, Dave	0
Wills, Frank	15
Wills, Ted	4
Wills	0
Willson, Kid	0
Wilmet, Paul	0
Wilshere, Whitey	9
Wilshusen, Terry	0
Wilson, Archie	1
Wilson, Artie	0
Wilson, Bill	
Debut 1890	5
Debut 1950	17
Wilson, Billy	15
Wilson, Bob	0
Wilson, Charlie	2
Wilson, Chink	0
Wilson, Craig	
Debut 1989	6
Debut 1998	12
Wilson, Craig A.	8
Wilson, Desi	2
Wilson, Duane	0
Wilson, Eddie	8
Wilson, Enrique	15
Wilson, Fin	3
Wilson, Frank	8
Wilson, Gary	
Debut 1902	0
Debut 1979	0
Debut 1995	0
Wilson, George	2
Wilson, Grady	0
Wilson, Henry	0
Wilson, Highball	23
Wilson, Icehouse	0
Wilson, Jack	
Debut 1934	70
Debut 2001	5
Wilson, Jim	
Debut 1945	75
Debut 1985	0
Wilson, Jimmie	124
Wilson, John	
Debut 1913	0
Debut 1927	1
Wilson, Kris	6
Wilson, Les	0
Wilson, Max	0
Wilson, Mike	0
Wilson, Mutt	0
Wilson, Neil	0
Wilson, Nigel	1
Wilson, Parke	27
Wilson, Pete	3
Wilson, Red	55
Wilson, Roy	1
Wilson, Squanto	0
Wilson, Steve	15
Wilson, Tack	0
Wilson, Tex	0
Wilson, Tom	
Debut 1914	0
Debut 2001	0
Wilson, Trevor	32
Wilson, Tug	2
Wilson, Vance	1
Wilson, Walter	1
Wilson, Zeke	58
Wiltse, Hal	19
Wiltse, Snake	27
Winceniak, Ed	0
Winchell, Fred	0
Winchester, Scott	0
Windhorn, Gordie	2
Windle, Bill	0
Wine, Bobby	52
Wine, Robbie	0
Wineapple, Ed	0
Winegarner, Ralph	11
Winford, Jim	14
Wingard, Ernie	38
Wingfield, Ted	29
Wingo, Al	44
Wingo, Ed	0
Winham, Lave	3
Winkelman, George	0
Winkelsas, Joe	0
Winn, George	2
Winn, Jim	10
Winningham, Herm	34
Winsett, Tom	11
Winston, Darrin	1
Winston, Hank	0
Winters, Clarence	0
Winters, Jesse	14
Winters, Matt	1
Wirth, Alan	5
Wirts, Kettle	1
Wise, Archie	0
Wise, Bill	31
Wise, Casey	4
Wise, Dewayne	0
Wise, Hughie	0
Wise, Matt	4
Wise, Nick	0
Wise, Roy	0
Wisner, John	9
Wisner, Phil	0
Wissman, Dave	0
Wistert, Whitey	1
Wisterzil, Tex	27
Witasick, Jay	14
Witek, Mickey	52
Withem, Shannon	0
Witherup, Roy	1
Withrow, Corky	0
Withrow, Frank	3
Witmeyer, Ron	0
Witt, George	14
Witt, Kevin	1
Witte, Jerry	0
Wittig, Johnnie	7
Wockenfuss, John	69
Woehr, Andy	2
Woerlin, Joe	0
Wohlers, Mark	60
Wohlford, Jim	57
Wojciechowski, S.	5
Wojcik, John	4
Wojey, Pete	2
Wojna, Ed	3
Wolcott, Bob	9
Wolf, Ernie	0
Wolf, Lefty	0
Wolf, Ray	0
Wolf, Wally	0
Wolfe, Bill	
Debut 1902	0
Debut 1903	23
Wolfe, Chuck	1
Wolfe, Ed	0
Wolfe, Harry	0
Wolfe, Larry	8
Wolfe, Polly	0
Wolff, Roger	58
Wolfgang, Mellie	25
Wolstenholme, Abe	0
Wolter, Harry	70
Wolverton, Harry	82
Womack, Dooley	27
Womack, Sid	0
Wood, Bob	39
Wood, Doc	0
Wood, Fred	0
Wood, Harry	0
Wood, Jake	44
Wood, Jason	0
Wood, Joe	
Debut 1943	5
Debut 1944	0
Wood, John	0
Wood, Ken	18
Wood, Pete	5
Wood, Roy	3
Wood, Spades	4
Wood, Ted	1
Woodall, Brad	6
Woodall, Larry	37
Woodard, Darrell	0
Woodard, Mike	6
Woodard, Steve	25
Woodburn, Gene	1
Woodcock, Fred	1
Woodend, George	0
Woodeshick, Hal	64
Woodhead, Red	1
Woodman, Dan	2
Woodruff, Pete	2
Woodruff, Sam	4
Woods, Al	42
Woods, Clarence	0
Woods, Gary	19
Woods, Jim	1
Woods, John	0
Woods, Pinky	11
Woods, Ron	33
Woods, Walt	23
Woodson, Dick	31
Woodson, Kerry	1
Woodson, Tracy	9
Woodward, Chris	3
Woodward, Frank	6
Woodward, Rob	4
Woodward, Woody	38
Wooldridge, Floyd	2
Wooten, Junior	6
Wooten, Shawn	6
Worden, Fred	0
Workman, Chuck	37
Workman, Hank	0
Workman, Hoge	0
Works, Ralph	23
Worrell, Todd	105
Wortham, Rich	11
Worthington, Al	106
Worthington, Craig	32
Worthington, Red	30
Wortman, Chuck	1
Wotus, Ron	1
Woulfe, Jimmy	0
Wright, Ab	7
Wright, Al	0
Wright, Bill	0
Wright, Bob	0
Wright, Clarence	9

Player	WS
Wright, Cy	0
Wright, Dan	2
Wright, Dave	0
Wright, Dick	0
Wright, Ed	21
Wright, George	41
Wright, Harry	0
Wright, Jaret	23
Wright, Jim	
Debut 1927	1
Debut 1978	9
Debut 1981	3
Wright, Joe	4
Wright, Ken	7
Wright, Lucky	0
Wright, Mel	1
Wright, Pat	0
Wright, Rasty	
Debut 1890	17
Debut 1917	23
Wright, Ricky	3
Wright, Roy	0
Wright, Sam	0
Wright, Tom	14
Wrightstone, Russ	73
Wrigley, Zeke	15
Wrona, Rick	5
Wuestling, Yats	2
Wunsch, Kelly	8
Wurm, Frank	0
Wyatt, Joe	0
Wyatt, John	65
Wyckoff, John	13
Wylie, Ren	0
Wyman, Frank	2
Wynegar, Butch	136
Wynne, Bill	0
Wynne, Billy	7
Wynne, Marvell	58
Wyrostek, Johnny	118
Wyse, Hank	77
Wysong, Biff	1

Y

Player	WS
Yaik, Henry	0
Yale, Ad	0
Yancy, Hugh	0
Yankowski, George	0
Yantz, George	0
Yarnall, Ed	1
Yarnall, Rusty	0
Yarrison, Rube	0
Yaryan, Yam	4
Yates, Al	1
Yde, Emil	46
Yeabsley, Bert	0
Yeager, George	13
Yeager, Joe	87
Yeargin, Jim	3
Yelding, Eric	13
Yelle, Archie	3
Yellen, Larry	0
Yellowhorse, Chief	9
Yerkes, Carroll	4
Yerkes, Stan	9
Yerkes, Steve	68
Yett, Richard	15
Yewcic, Tom	0
Yewell, Ed	1
Yingling, Earl	32
Yingling, Joe	0
Yochim, Len	0
Yochim, Ray	0
Yohe, Bill	1
York, Jim	16
York, Lefty	5
York, Mike	1
York, Tony	1
Yost, Gus	0
Yost, Ned	11
Yoter, Elmer	2
Youmans, Floyd	27
Young, Anthony	21
Young, Bobby	39
Young, Charlie	0
Young, Cliff	5
Young, Curt	47
Young, Danny	0
Young, Del	
Debut 1909	4
Debut 1937	10
Young, Dick	0
Young, Don	8
Young, Ernie	13
Young, George	0
Young, Gerald	56
Young, Harley	1
Young, Herman	0
Young, Irv	67
Young, Joe	0
Young, John	0
Young, Kip	9
Young, Matt	55
Young, Michael	7
Young, Mike	52
Young, Pep	61
Young, Pete	2
Young, Ralph	80
Young, Russ	1
Young, Tim	0
Youngblood, Chief	0
Youngblood, Joel	98
Youngman, Henry	0
Yount, Ducky	1
Yount, Eddie	0
Yount, Larry	0
Yowell, Carl	2
Yuhas, Eddie	11
Yurak, Jeff	0
Yvars, Sal	11

Z

Player	WS
Zabala, Adrian	3
Zabel, Zip	16
Zachary, Chink	0
Zachary, Chris	9
Zacher, Elmer	1
Zachry, Pat	60
Zackert, George	0
Zahn, Geoff	111
Zahner, Fred	0
Zahniser, Paul	21
Zak, Frankie	6
Zalusky, Jack	1
Zambrano, Carlos	0
Zambrano, Eddie	4
Zambrano, Victor	6
Zamloch, Carl	3
Zamora, Oscar	15
Zanni, Dom	13
Zapustas, Joe	0
Zardon, Jose	4
Zarilla, Al	99
Zaske, Jeff	1
Zauchin, Norm	23
Zavaras, Clint	1
Zay	0
Zdeb, Joe	7
Zearfoss, Dave	3
Zeber, George	4
Zeiser, Matt	1
Zeller, Bart	0
Zepp, Bill	9
Zerbe, Chad	2
Zettlein, George	2
Zick, Bob	0
Ziegler, Charlie	0
Ziegler, George	0
Ziem, Steve	0
Zientara, Benny	16
Zies, Bill	0
Zimmer, Don	67
Zimmerman, Bill	2
Zimmerman, Eddie	6
Zimmerman, Jerry	23
Zimmerman, Jordan	0
Zimmerman, Roy	2
Zink, Walt	0
Zinn, Frank	0
Zinn, Guy	29
Zinn, Jimmy	18
Zinser, Bill	0
Zipfel, Bud	5
Zitzmann, Billy	20
Zmich, Ed	1
Zoldak, Sam	59
Zosky, Eddie	0
Zuber, Bill	31
Zuber, Jon	2
Zuleta, Julio	3
Zupcic, Bob	16
Zupo, Frank	1
Zuvella, Paul	8
Zuverink, George	47
Zwilling, Dutch	61

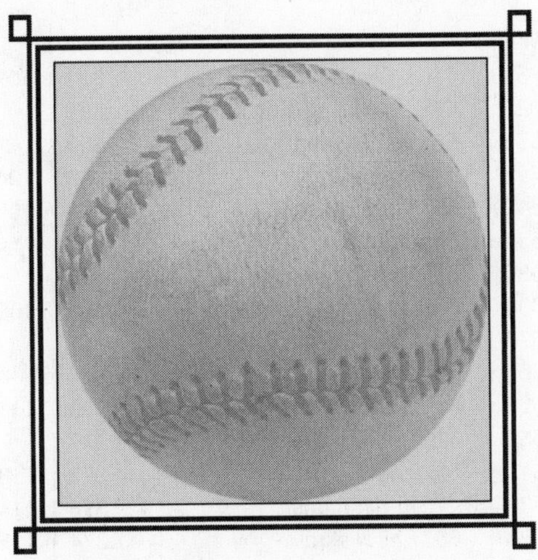

Leader Boards

Who produced the most total Win Shares in their careers? Is Ozzie Smith the defensive Win Shares leader among shortstops? How did Barry Bonds' 2001 campaign compare to other offensive seasons in history?

You'll find answers to these and other questions in the following pages. We begin with the best career totals going back to 1876, presenting leaders for total, batting and pitching Win Shares. While those lists are sorted in descending order of Win Shares, the defensive charts are sorted in descending order of estimated innings at each position. In the years since 1987, when STATS has been tracking actual innings, those figures are used in the estimated totals. The Win Shares generated per 1,000 innings provides insight into each player's defensive ability. And at the bottom of each position, the combined Win Shares per 1,000 innings are broken down by career estimated inning spans.

We also provide charts with the best single-season performances in history. We break it down between years prior to 1900 and those thereafter for the total, batting and pitching lists, while the fielding lists are based on all seasons in history. The teams for whom each player competed during any given season are included in the charts, as well as the leagues. A dash is listed if a player played in more than one league.

Finally, we include charts containing the career and single-season total Win Shares leaders for each of the existing 30 franchises. The single-season leaders are since 1900 only.

While the total Win Shares leaders always are based on integer values, the batting, pitching and fielding values use real numbers. The sum of the batting, pitching and fielding totals may not always round to the total Win Shares, due to particular rounding circumstances.

Total Win Shares

	Player	WS
1.	Babe Ruth	756
2.	Ty Cobb	722
3.	Honus Wagner	655
4.	Hank Aaron	643
5.	Willie Mays	642
6.	Cy Young	634
7.	Tris Speaker	630
8.	Stan Musial	604
9.	Eddie Collins	574
10.	Mickey Mantle	565
11.	Walter Johnson	560
12.	Ted Williams	555
13.	Pete Rose	547
14.	Rickey Henderson	530
15.	Mel Ott	528
16.	Barry Bonds	523
17.	Frank Robinson	519
18.	Joe Morgan	512
19.	Rogers Hornsby	502
20.	Nap Lajoie	496
21.	Lou Gehrig	489
22.	Carl Yastrzemski	488
23.	Kid Nichols	478
24.	Pete Alexander	476
25.	Mike Schmidt	467
26.	Eddie Mathews	450
27.	Sam Crawford	446
28.	Reggie Jackson	444
29.	Al Kaline	443
30.	Eddie Murray	437
31.	Jimmie Foxx	435
32.	George Brett	432
33.	Cal Ripken Jr.	427
34.	Christy Mathewson	426
35.	Paul Waner	423
	Robin Yount	423
37.	Dave Winfield	415
38.	Paul Molitor	414
39.	Tim Keefe	413
40.	Warren Spahn	412
41.	Monte Ward	409
42.	Willie McCovey	408
43.	Pud Galvin	403
44.	Fred Clarke	400
45.	Tony Mullane	399
46.	George Davis	398
	Tony Gwynn	398
48.	John Clarkson	396
49.	Wade Boggs	394
	Bill Dahlen	394
51.	Lefty Grove	391
	Old Hoss Radbourn	391
53.	Tim Raines	390
54.	Jesse Burkett	389
55.	Tom Seaver	388
56.	Joe DiMaggio	387
57.	Rod Carew	384
58.	Charlie Gehringer	383
59.	Cap Anson	381
60.	Zack Wheat	380
61.	Luke Appling	378
62.	Roberto Clemente	377
63.	Yogi Berra	375
	Al Simmons	375
65.	Phil Niekro	374
	Billy Williams	374
67.	Harmon Killebrew	371
68.	Willie Stargell	370
69.	Gaylord Perry	369
70.	Carlton Fisk	368
71.	Steve Carlton	366
	Frankie Frisch	366
73.	Roger Connor	363
	Darrell Evans	363
75.	Eddie Plank	361
76.	Rusty Staub	358
77.	Johnny Bench	356
	Harry Heilmann	356
	Brooks Robinson	356
	Arky Vaughan	356
81.	Dan Brouthers	355
	Ed Delahanty	355
	Goose Goslin	355
84.	Sherry Magee	354
	Mickey Welch	354
86.	Roger Clemens	352
	Duke Snider	352
88.	Max Carey	351
	Lou Whitaker	351
90.	Tony Perez	349
91.	Lou Brock	348
92.	Dwight Evans	347
93.	Ryne Sandberg	346
94.	Roberto Alomar	345
	Bobby Wallace	345
96.	George Van Haltren	344
97.	Dick Allen	342
	Craig Biggio	342
	Mark McGwire	342
100.	Andre Dawson	340
101.	Bert Blyleven	339
	Robin Roberts	339
	Jimmy Sheckard	339
104.	Johnny Mize	338
105.	Gary Carter	337
	Bob Caruthers	337
	Billy Hamilton	337
108.	Jim McCormick	334
	Rafael Palmeiro	334
	Nolan Ryan	334
111.	Joe Cronin	333
	Willie Keeler	333
113.	Ernie Banks	332
114.	Will Clark	331
115.	Richie Ashburn	329
	Bobby Grich	329
117.	Tommy Leach	328
118.	Dave Parker	327
	Sam Rice	327
120.	Gabby Hartnett	325
	Ozzie Smith	325
	Reggie Smith	325
123.	Ron Santo	324
124.	Fergie Jenkins	323
	Enos Slaughter	323
126.	Willie Davis	322
	Red Ruffing	322
128.	Harry Hooper	321
	Graig Nettles	321
	Vada Pinson	321
131.	Barry Larkin	320
132.	Don Sutton	319
133.	Jeff Bagwell	318
	Jake Beckley	318
	Alan Trammell	318
136.	Bob Gibson	317
	Greg Maddux	317
138.	Jack Clark	316
	Stan Hack	316
	Fred McGriff	316
	Jimmy Ryan	316
142.	Norm Cash	315
	Eppa Rixey	315
	Ted Simmons	315
	Joe Torre	315
146.	Bill Dickey	314
	Pee Wee Reese	314
	Edd Roush	314
149.	Jose Cruz	313
	Ken Griffey Jr.	313

	Player	WS
151.	Ted Lyons	312
	Joe Medwick	312
	Jim Palmer	312
	Willie Randolph	312
155.	Keith Hernandez	311
156.	Orlando Cepeda	310
157.	Early Wynn	309
158.	Frank Thomas	308
159.	Harold Baines	307
160.	Carl Hubbell	305
	Joe Kelley	305
	Bid McPhee	305
	Al Oliver	305
	Jim O'Rourke	305
	Jimmy Wynn	305
166.	Nellie Fox	304
167.	Bobby Bonds	302
	Rabbit Maranville	302
	Ken Singleton	302
170.	Home Run Baker	301
	Buddy Bell	301
	Dennis Eckersley	301
173.	Brian Downing	298
	Billy Herman	298
175.	Frank Howard	297
176.	Three Finger Brown	296
	Cesar Cedeno	296
	Mickey Vernon	296
179.	Brett Butler	295
	Hugh Duffy	295
181.	Kid Gleason	294
	Joe Jackson	294
	Dale Murphy	294
184.	Luis Aparicio	293
	Amos Rusie	293
	Vic Willis	293
187.	Kiki Cuyler	292
	Red Faber	292
	Bob Feller	292
	Dave Foutz	292
	George Sisler	292
192.	Elmer Flick	291
193.	George Burns	290
	Fielder Jones	290
195.	Larry Doyle	289
	Tommy John	289
197.	Bob Elliott	287
	Toby Harrah	287
	Bob Johnson	287
	Ed Konetchy	287
	Jack Powell	287
	Jack Quinn	287
203.	Burleigh Grimes	286
	Amos Otis	286
205.	Chili Davis	285
	Mark Grace	285
	Heinie Manush	285
	Elmer Smith	285
	Jack Stivetts	285
210.	Sal Bando	283
	Charlie Buffinton	283
	Minnie Minoso	283
213.	Boog Powell	282
	Jim Rice	282
215.	Bobby Doerr	281
	Kirby Puckett	281
217.	Earl Averill	280
	Bert Campaneris	280
	Ron Cey	280
	Tony Fernandez	280
	Fred Lynn	280
222.	Ken Boyer	279
	Steve Garvey	279
224.	Lave Cross	278
	King Kelly	278
	Bill Terry	278
	Dixie Walker	278
228.	Lou Boudreau	277
	Bobby Murcer	277
	Joe Sewell	277
231.	Gary Sheffield	276
232.	Mickey Cochrane	275
	Jim Whitney	275
234.	Jimmy Collins	274
	Pie Traynor	274
236.	Rocky Colavito	273
	Clark Griffith	273
	Adonis Terry	273
239.	Jose Canseco	272
	Heine Groh	272
	Cy Seymour	272
242.	Joe Judge	270
243.	Dave Bancroft	269
	Dave Concepcion	269
	Ron Fairly	269
	George Foster	269
	Joe McGinnity	269
248.	Larry Doby	268
	Johnny Evers	268
	Jim Kaat	268
	Tony Phillips	268
252.	Bobby Bonilla	267
	Bill Freehan	267
	Hank Greenberg	267
	Eddie Yost	267
256.	Wilbur Cooper	266
	Clyde Milan	266
258.	Chet Lemon	265
	Herman Long	265
	Vern Stephens	265
	Harry Stovey	265
	Bobby Veach	265
	Ed Walsh	265
264.	Edgar Martinez	264
	Hal Newhouser	264
266.	Jake Daubert	263
	Augie Galan	263
	Gil Hodges	263
	Silver King	263
	Juan Marichal	263
	Don Mattingly	263
	Roy White	263
273.	Don Baylor	262
	Waite Hoyt	262
	Red Schoendienst	262
276.	Whitey Ford	261
	Jim Fregosi	261
	Jack Glasscock	261
279.	Roy Thomas	260
280.	Ken Griffey Sr.	259
	Guy Hecker	259
	Paul O'Neill	259
283.	Jim Bottomley	258
	Don Drysdale	258
	Larry Gardner	258
	Rick Monday	258
	Buddy Myer	258
	Joe Tinker	258
	Bucky Walters	258
	Gus Weyhing	258
291.	Jim Bunning	257
	Gary Matthews	257
	Jackie Robinson	257
294.	Carl Mays	256
	Luis Tiant	256
	Hoyt Wilhelm	256
297.	George Mullin	255
	Mike Piazza	255
299.	Dummy Hoy	254
300.	Wally Joyner	253

	Player	WS
	Maury Wills	253
302.	Dick Bartell	252
	Tony Lazzeri	252
	Darryl Strawberry	252
305.	Mike Tiernan	251
306.	George Gore	250
307.	Gary Gaetti	249
	Paul Hines	249
	Fred Tenney	249
310.	Lance Parrish	248
	Billy Pierce	248
	Tim Wallach	248
313.	Eddie Cicotte	247
	Jim Gilliam	247
	Greg Luzinski	247
316.	Pedro Guerrero	246
	Sammy Sosa	246
318.	Dusty Baker	245
	Stan Coveleski	245
	Jimmy Dykes	245
	Mike Griffin	245
	Sad Sam Jones	245
	Tony Oliva	245
	Wally Schang	245
	Lloyd Waner	245
326.	Julio Franco	244
	Carney Lansford	244
328.	Babe Adams	243
	Jay Bell	243
	Albert Belle	243
	Tommy Bond	243
	Joe Kuhel	243
	Al Orth	243
334.	Ken Caminiti	242
	Joe Gordon	242
	Ralph Kiner	242
	Bill Madlock	242
	John Olerud	242
	Del Pratt	242
340.	Felipe Alou	241
	Wally Berger	241
	Johnny Callison	241
	Cecil Cooper	241
	Buck Ewing	241
	Dolf Luque	241
	Dick McAuliffe	241
	Frank Tanana	241
	Dazzy Vance	241
349.	Joe Carter	240
	Jerry Koosman	240

	Player	WS
	Davey Lopes	240
	Herb Pennock	240
	Rick Reuschel	240
	Rube Waddell	240
	Larry Walker	240
356.	Roger Peckinpaugh	239
	Wildfire Schulte	239
	Will White	239
359.	Cupid Childs	238
	Harry Davis	238
	Chuck Klein	238
362.	Phil Cavarretta	237
	Frank Chance	237
	Andres Galarraga	237
	George Hendrick	237
	Wally Moses	237
	Bobo Newsom	237
	Willie Wilson	237
369.	Joe Adcock	236
	Tom Glavine	236
	Sam Thompson	236
	Robin Ventura	236
	Bob Watson	236
374.	Doc White	235
	Cy Williams	235
376.	Ellis Burks	234
	Mel Harder	234
378.	Ben Chapman	233
	Del Ennis	233
	Wes Ferrell	233
	Willie Horton	233
	Charlie Hough	233
	Dutch Leonard	233
	Dennis Martinez	233
	Jesse Tannehill	233
	Bernie Williams	233
387.	Donie Bush	232
	Babe Herman	232
	Bob Lemon	232
	Matt Williams	232
391.	Chief Bender	231
	Roger Bresnahan	231
	Hal Chase	231
	Paul Derringer	231
	Jack Fournier	231
	Phil Rizzuto	231
	Roy Sievers	231
	Gene Tenace	231
	George Uhle	231
	Andy Van Slyke	231

	Player	WS
401.	Kent Hrbek	230
	Hal McRae	230
	Hardy Richardson	230
404.	Ginger Beaumont	229
	George Kell	229
	Chuck Knoblauch	229
407.	Dizzy Trout	228
	Gene Woodling	228
409.	Earle Combs	227
	Stuffy McInnis	227
	Dode Paskert	227
412.	Bill Buckner	226
	Al Dark	226
	Randy Johnson	226
415.	Tommy Bridges	225
	Pete Browning	225
	Dick Groat	225
	Larry Jackson	225
	Lee May	225
	Jack Morris	225
	Urban Shocker	225
422.	Dolph Camilli	224
	Eric Davis	224
	Mickey Lolich	224
	Willie McGee	224
	Hack Wilson	224
427.	Goose Gossage	223
	Topsy Hartsel	223
	Harvey Kuenn	223
	Roger Maris	223
	Bill Nicholson	223
	Charlie Root	223
	Bob Shawkey	223
434.	Steve Finley	222
	Freddie Fitzsimmons	222
	Miller Huggins	222
	David Justice	222
	Billy Nash	222
	Darrell Porter	222
440.	Chris Chambliss	221
	Curt Flood	221
	Bill Hutchison	221
	Arlie Latham	221
	Ed McKean	221
445.	Dom DiMaggio	220
	Andy Pafko	220
	Lon Warneke	220
448.	Doc Cramer	219
	Richie Hebner	219
	Bill Mazeroski	219

	Player	WS
	Vic Wertz	219
452.	Tom Brown	218
	Art Fletcher	218
	Larry French	218
	Kirk Gibson	218
	Charlie Keller	218
	Ray Lankford	218
	Ernie Lombardi	218
459.	Carl Furillo	217
	Jeff Heath	217
461.	Harlond Clift	216
	Pete Runnels	216
	George Scott	216
464.	Tom Daly	215
	Hooks Dauss	215
	Juan Gonzalez	215
	Danny Murphy	215
	Kip Selbach	215
469.	Brady Anderson	214
	Tommy Corcoran	214
	Hughie Jennings	214
	Rudy York	214
	Heinie Zimmerman	214
474.	Frank Dwyer	213
	Tip O'Neill	213
476.	Ted Breitenstein	212
	Jose Cardenal	212
	Mike Hargrove	212
	Sam Leever	212
480.	Kevin Brown	211
	Travis Jackson	211
	Chick Stahl	211
	Frank White	211
484.	Bob Boone	210
	Orel Hershiser	210
	Milt Pappas	210
	Curt Simmons	210
	Dave Stieb	210
489.	John Anderson	209
	Rico Carty	209
	Jack Chesbro	209
	Eddie Joost	209
	Sherm Lollar	209
	Eddie Rommel	209
	Garry Templeton	209
	Bill White	209
497.	Lonny Frey	208
	Tommy Henrich	208
	Brickyard Kennedy	208
	Rube Marquard	208

	Player	WS
	Ed Morris	208
	Harry Steinfeldt	208
503.	Roy Campanella	207
	Tommy Davis	207
	Bob Friend	207
	Jesse Haines	207
	John McGraw	207
	Devon White	207
	Jimmy Williams	207
510.	Rick Ferrell	206
	Catfish Hunter	206
	Thurman Munson	206
	Deacon Phillippe	206
	Ed Reulbach	206
	Ivan Rodriguez	206
	Chris Speier	206
	B.J. Surhoff	206
	Ross Youngs	206
519.	David Cone	205
	Doug DeCinces	205
	Luis Gonzalez	205
	Jim Perry	205
	Rico Petrocelli	205
	Claude Ritchey	205
	Bobby Thomson	205
	Hippo Vaughn	205
	Tom Zachary	205
528.	Murry Dickson	204
	Chuck Finley	204
	Tommy Harper	204
	Pink Hawley	204
	Tim McCarver	204
533.	Bob Allison	203
	Tony Cuccinello	203
	Elston Howard	203
	Ted Kluszewski	203
	Garry Maddox	203
	Wally Pipp	203
	Earl Whitehill	203
540.	Vida Blue	202
	Gavy Cravath	202
	Wild Bill Donovan	202
	Kenny Lofton	202
	Frank McCormick	202
	Marty McManus	202
	Kevin McReynolds	202
	Terry Pendleton	202
	Fred Pfeffer	202
	Ken Williams	202
550.	Patsy Donovan	201

	Player	WS
	Lenny Dykstra	201
	Willie Kamm	201
	Claude Osteen	201
	John Titus	201
555.	George Burns	200
	Bill Dinneen	200
	Ruben Sierra	200
	Jim Sundberg	200
559.	Leo Cardenas	199
	Sid Gordon	199
	Ken Keltner	199
	John Mayberry	199
	Todd Zeile	199
564.	Red Ames	198
	Lu Blue	198
	Art Devlin	198
	Charlie Grimm	198
	Steve Sax	198
	Lee Smith	198
	Tony Taylor	198
	Virgil Trucks	198
572.	Marquis Grissom	197
	Jeff Kent	197
	Don Money	197
	Greg Vaughn	197
576.	Oyster Burns	196
	Jeff Burroughs	196
	Bing Miller	196
579.	Joe Bush	195
	Phil Garner	195
	Mike Higgins	195
	Dave Kingman	195
	Hal Trosky	195
584.	Don Buford	194
	Ron Gant	194
	Howard Johnson	194
	Sandy Koufax	194
	Red Lucas	194
	Gil McDougald	194
	Ben Oglivie	194
	Jerry Reuss	194
	Al Smith	194
	Claudell Washington	194
594.	Larry Corcoran	193
	Nig Cuppy	193
	Bill Doran	193
	George Grantham	193
	George Kelly	193
	Freddy Lindstrom	193
	Bret Saberhagen	193

	Player	WS
	Joe Wood	193
602.	Doyle Alexander	192
	Travis Fryman	192
	Manny Ramirez	192
	Jim Thome	192
	Sammy West	192
607.	Bill Bradley	191
	Ron Hunt	191
	Addie Joss	191
	Lee Meadows	191
	Fred Merkle	191
	Ray Schalk	191
	Eddie Stanky	191
614.	Bill Bruton	190
	Denny Lyons	190
	Lonnie Smith	190
	Riggs Stephenson	190
	Deacon White	190
	Wilbur Wood	190
620.	Bob Bailey	189
	Frankie Crosetti	189
	Puddin' Head Jones	189
	Deacon McGuire	189
	Joe Niekro	189
	Claude Passeau	189
	Slim Sallee	189
	John Smoltz	189
628.	Rollie Fingers	188
	Tommy Holmes	188
	Jimmy Key	188
	Bobby Lowe	188
	Milt Stock	188
	Danny Tartabull	188
	Bob Welch	188
635.	Patsy Dougherty	187
	Dwight Gooden	187
	Jackie Jensen	187
	Johnny Pesky	187
	Tim Salmon	187
	Elmer Valo	187
	Frank Viola	187
642.	Chick Hafey	186
	Chipper Jones	186
	Lindy McDaniel	186
	Andre Thornton	186
646.	Nixey Callahan	185
	Elton Chamberlin	185
	Elbie Fletcher	185
	Lefty Gomez	185
	Mickey Rivers	185

	Player	WS
	Alex Rodriguez	185
	Al Rosen	185
	Bill Russell	185
	Mo Vaughn	185
655.	Max Bishop	184
	Kid Elberfeld	184
	Mark Langston	184
	Bob Meusel	184
	Mickey Tettleton	184
	Earl Torgeson	184
661.	Paul Blair	183
	Ossie Bluege	183
	Delino DeShields	183
	Duke Farrell	183
	Tony Gonzalez	183
	Charlie Jamieson	183
	Dan McGann	183
	Art Nehf	183
	Bill Skowron	183
	Jack Taylor	183
671.	John Candelaria	182
	Roy Cullenbine	182
	Danny Darwin	182
	Steve Rogers	182
675.	Dizzy Dean	181
	Frank Killen	181
	Johnny Logan	181
	Mike Mussina	181
	Ron Reed	181
	John Roseboro	181
	Roy Smalley	181
682.	Hank Bauer	180
	Duffy Lewis	180
	Sam Mertes	180
	Schoolboy Rowe	180
686.	Matty Alou	179
	Moises Alou	179
	Larry Bowa	179
	Del Crandall	179
	Dan Driessen	179
	John Franco	179
	Tom Haller	179
	Buddy Lewis	179
	Jack Tobin	179
695.	Lew Burdette	178
	Baby Doll Jacobson	178
	Kevin Mitchell	178
	Jeff Pfeffer	178
	Cesar Tovar	178
	Gee Walker	178

	Player	WS
	Rick Wise	178
	Richie Zisk	178
703.	Oscar Gamble	177
	Von Hayes	177
	Henry Larkin	177
	Bill Lee	177
	Firpo Marberry	177
	Marty Marion	177
	Lloyd Moseby	177
	Nap Rucker	177
	Bill Sherdel	177
	Jimmy Slagle	177
	Mel Stottlemyre	177
714.	Mark Baldwin	176
	George Bradley	176
	Jack Doyle	176
	Ed Lopat	176
	Denis Menke	176
	Don Newcombe	176
	Larry Parrish	176
	Terry Puhl	176
	Juan Samuel	176
	Hal Schumacher	176
	Tommy Tucker	176
725.	Kevin Appier	175
	Bobby Avila	175
	Gus Bell	175
	Tom Brunansky	175
	Bump Hadley	175
	Benny Kauff	175
	Ken McMullen	175
	Wally Moon	175
	Camilo Pascual	175
	Tony Pena	175
	Germany Smith	175
736.	Jay Buhner	174
	Mike Donlin	174
	Howard Ehmke	174
	Ron Guidry	174
	Claude Hendrix	174
	Sadie McMahon	174
	Hank Sauer	174
	Kevin Seitzer	174
	Amos Strunk	174
745.	Harry Brecheen	173
	Walker Cooper	173
	Mike Cuellar	173
	Al Lopez	173
	George McQuinn	173
	Dwayne Murphy	173

	Player	WS
	Joe Rudi	173
	Terry Steinbach	173
	Rube Walberg	173
	Ned Williamson	173
755.	Smoky Burgess	172
	Harry Howell	172
	Roy McMillan	172
758.	George Bell	171
	Eddie Foster	171
	Buck Herzog	171
	Dave Johnson	171
	Jouett Meekin	171
	Norm Siebern	171
	Terry Turner	171
765.	Steve Brodie	170
	Bill Doak	170
	Billy Goodman	170
	Tom Herr	170
	Willis Hudlin	170
	Billy Jurges	170
	Tommy McCarthy	170
	Jo-Jo Moore	170
	Allie Reynolds	170
	Gus Suhr	170
775.	Al Bumbry	169
	Red Ehret	169
	Andy Messersmith	169
	Earl Moore	169
	Stan Spence	169
	Frank Thomas	169
	Cecil Travis	169
782.	Dante Bichette	168
	Tino Martinez	168
	Dave McNally	168
	Freddy Parent	168
	Mike Scioscia	168
	Bruce Sutter	168
	Fernando Valenzuela	168
789.	Guy Bush	167
	Jason Giambi	167
	Pedro Martinez	167
	Billy Shindle	167
793.	Jesse Barfield	166
	Ray Boone	166
	Ned Garver	166
	Matt Kilroy	166
	Sam McDowell	166
	Doug Rader	166
	Omar Vizquel	166
	George Wood	166
801.	Dave Cash	165
	Curt Davis	165
	Red Donahue	165
	Fred Dunlap	165
	Tito Francona	165
	Thornton Lee	165
	Jason Thompson	165
	Curt Welch	165
809.	Chick Fraser	164
	Burt Hooton	164
	Lou Piniella	164
	Tilly Walker	164
813.	Jim Gantner	163
	Curt Schilling	163
	Hooks Wiltse	163
816.	Mark Belanger	162
	Gregg Jefferies	162
	Don Mincher	162
	Jimmy Piersall	162
	Red Rolfe	162
	Bill Werber	162
822.	Ray Caldwell	161
	Mickey Doolan	161
	Ferris Fain	161
	Noodles Hahn	161
	Charley Jones	161
	Sparky Lyle	161
	Irish Meusel	161
	Jim Northrup	161
	Bob O'Farrell	161
	Billy Rogell	161
	Burt Shotton	161
	Red Smith	161
834.	Clete Boyer	160
	Jack Coombs	160
	Cecil Fielder	160
	Buck Freeman	160
	Gene Garber	160
	Mike Garcia	160
	Dave Henderson	160
	Dutch Leonard	160
	Fred Luderus	160
	Jerry Mumphrey	160
	Jorge Orta	160
	Tom Tresh	160
846.	Bruce Bochte	159
	John Briggs	159
	Darren Daulton	159
	Don Kessinger	159
	Sixto Lezcano	159
	Benito Santiago	159
	Bobby Shantz	159
	Casey Stengel	159
	Kent Tekulve	159
	Mike Torrez	159
	Joe Vosmik	159
857.	Tom Candiotti	158
	Rick Dempsey	158
	Mike Flanagan	158
	Solly Hofman	158
	Bobby Mathews	158
	Tug McGraw	158
	Ezra Sutton	158
864.	Charlie Bennett	157
	Greg Gagne	157
	Johnny Grubb	157
	Ken Holtzman	157
	Jimmy Johnston	157
	Bill Joyce	157
	Eric Karros	157
	Vern Law	157
	Hans Lobert	157
	Les Mann	157
	Win Mercer	157
	George Pinckney	157
	Dan Quisenberry	157
	Jeff Reardon	157
	Manny Sanguillen	157
	Johnny Temple	157
	Bill Virdon	157
	Sam Wise	157
882.	Jesse Barnes	156
	General Crowder	156
	Max Flack	156
	John Kruk	156
	Whitey Lockman	156
	Jon Matlack	156
	Raul Mondesi	156
	Muddy Ruel	156
890.	Woody English	155
	Charlie Hickman	155
	Johnny Hopp	155
	Lance Johnson	155
	Johnny Kling	155
	Dots Miller	155
	Rick Rhoden	155
	Robby Thompson	155
	Leon Wagner	155
899.	Bob Bescher	154
	Jeff Blauser	154

	Player	WS
	Tom Burns	154
	Jim Edmonds	154
	Bob Forsch	154
	Charlie Getzien	154
	Stu Miller	154
906.	Wid Conroy	153
	Monte Cross	153
	Alvin Davis	153
	Harvey Haddix	153
	Woodie Held	153
	Johnny Ray	153
	Rick Sutcliffe	153
	Curt Walker	153
	David Wells	153
	Chief Zimmer	153
916.	Rick Burleson	152
	Felix Millan	152
	Terry Moore	152
	Steve O'Neill	152
	Vic Power	152
	Bob Rush	152
	Harry Staley	152
	Gorman Thomas	152
	Buck Weaver	152
925.	Ed Brandt	151
	Mort Cooper	151
	Shawon Dunston	151
	Derek Jeter	151
	Jim Landis	151
	Pepper Martin	151
	John Morrill	151
	Howie Pollet	151
	John Reilly	151
	Dutch Ruether	151
	Frank Smith	151
	Mookie Wilson	151
	Chicken Wolf	151
938.	Abner Dalrymple	150
	Terry Kennedy	150
	Danny MacFayden	150
	Freddie Patek	150
942.	Rube Bressler	149
	Hubie Brooks	149
	Shano Collins	149
	Spud Davis	149
	Jim Delahanty	149
	Johnny Edwards	149
	Pete Fox	149
	Doc Hoblitzell	149
	Socks Seybold	149
	Bob Stanley	149
	John Stone	149
	Pinky Whitney	149
954.	Kevin Bass	148
	Dean Chance	148
	Ray Chapman	148
	Bob Ewing	148
	Bibb Falk	148
	Scott Fletcher	148
	Ozzie Guillen	148
	Jim Ray Hart	148
	Matty McIntyre	148
	Hi Myers	148
	Wes Parker	148
965.	Rick Aguilera	147
	Carlos Baerga	147
	Johnny Bates	147
	Bob Buhl	147
	Ripper Collins	147
	Joe Dobson	147
	Ralph Garr	147
	Dave Magadan	147
	Dave Martinez	147
	Van Lingle Mungo	147
	Joe Nuxhall	147
	Johnny Sain	147
	Dickie Thon	147
978.	Johnny Antonelli	146
	Jack Clements	146
	Mike Greenwell	146
	Ned Hanlon	146
	Charlie Hemphill	146
	John Hiller	146
	Larry Hisle	146
	Deron Johnson	146
	Doug Jones	146
	Ryan Klesko	146
	Mike Kreevich	146
	Mike Marshall	146
	Barney McCosky	146
	George Mogridge	146
	George Stone	146
	Manny Trillo	146
994.	Johnny Allen	145
	Ed Bailey	145
	Sam Chapman	145
	Mudcat Grant	145
	Harry Gumbert	145
	Ron Hansen	145
	Ellis Kinder	145
	Lyn Lary	145
	Mike Mitchell	145
	Jose Offerman	145
	Dave Orr	145
	Jerry Priddy	145
	Bob Smith	145
	Mike Stanley	145
1008.	Sparky Adams	144
	Edgardo Alfonzo	144
	Duff Cooley	144
	Ival Goodman	144
	Danny Green	144
	Ad Gumbert	144
	Granny Hamner	144
	Bruce Hurst	144
	Lefty O'Doul	144
	Cookie Rojas	144
	Jack Rowe	144
	Reggie Sanders	144
	Sonny Siebert	144
	Fred Toney	144
1022.	Jimmy Austin	143
	Bill North	143
	Johnny Podres	143
	Lefty Tyler	143
1026.	Earl Battey	142
	Rube Benton	142
	George Case	142
	Charlie Ferguson	142
	Ken Henderson	142
	Syl Johnson	142
	Dave Philley	142
	Everett Scott	142
	Andy Seminick	142
	Chris Short	142
1036.	Frank Bolling	141
	Hughie Critz	141
	Steve Gromek	141
	Mark Gubicza	141
	Bud Harrelson	141
	Jay Johnstone	141
	Cleon Jones	141
	Ray Kremer	141
	Frank Lary	141
	Rudy May	141
	Willie Montanez	141
	Ken Oberkfell	141
	Pete O'Brien	141
	Mel Parnell	141
	Billy Southworth	141
	Dave Stewart	141

Batting

	Player	WS
1.	Ty Cobb	639.4
2.	Babe Ruth	608.8
3.	Hank Aaron	573.3
4.	Stan Musial	538.7
5.	Willie Mays	538.0
6.	Honus Wagner	513.8
7.	Ted Williams	512.4
8.	Tris Speaker	511.7
9.	Mickey Mantle	507.0
10.	Barry Bonds	477.9
11.	Mel Ott	474.0
12.	Rickey Henderson	473.7
13.	Frank Robinson	467.8
14.	Eddie Collins	463.6
15.	Pete Rose	461.8
16.	Lou Gehrig	456.5
17.	Rogers Hornsby	443.7
18.	Carl Yastrzemski	426.0
19.	Joe Morgan	423.9
20.	Reggie Jackson	403.8
21.	Sam Crawford	398.8
22.	Nap Lajoie	398.8
23.	Eddie Murray	397.6
24.	Eddie Mathews	387.4
25.	Jimmie Foxx	386.5
26.	Al Kaline	382.9
27.	Willie McCovey	379.4
28.	Mike Schmidt	378.3
29.	Dave Winfield	373.4
30.	George Brett	371.5
31.	Paul Molitor	367.5
32.	Paul Waner	359.8
33.	Tony Gwynn	353.4
34.	Willie Stargell	339.1
35.	Cap Anson	338.1
36.	Harmon Killebrew	337.1
37.	Tim Raines	336.1
38.	Fred Clarke	335.7
39.	Jesse Burkett	335.2
40.	Rod Carew	332.0
41.	Dan Brouthers	329.3
42.	Billy Williams	329.1
43.	Joe DiMaggio	325.8
44.	Harry Heilmann	325.1
45.	Mark McGwire	323.1
46.	Rusty Staub	322.8
47.	Roger Connor	322.3
48.	Zack Wheat	322.1
49.	Wade Boggs	319.3
50.	Robin Yount	317.3
51.	Roberto Clemente	316.4
52.	Dick Allen	312.4
53.	Ed Delahanty	311.1
54.	Johnny Mize	310.0
55.	Sherry Magee	305.8
56.	Goose Goslin	305.4
57.	Al Simmons	305.4
58.	Will Clark	303.6
59.	Frank Thomas	302.0
60.	Rafael Palmeiro	300.3
61.	Lou Brock	300.3
62.	Tony Perez	299.1
63.	Duke Snider	296.8
64.	George Davis	296.7
65.	Charlie Gehringer	295.3
66.	Darrell Evans	294.9
67.	Dwight Evans	293.6
68.	Jeff Bagwell	290.9
69.	Cal Ripken Jr.	290.7
70.	Jack Clark	289.1
71.	Fred McGriff	288.4
72.	Billy Hamilton	287.5
73.	Willie Keeler	284.5
74.	Harold Baines	283.9
75.	Orlando Cepeda	283.2
76.	Dave Parker	281.7
77.	Norm Cash	279.3
78.	Andre Dawson	278.9
79.	Jake Beckley	278.9
80.	Keith Hernandez	277.3
81.	Arky Vaughan	275.6
82.	Enos Slaughter	275.4
83.	Reggie Smith	274.4
84.	Jimmy Sheckard	272.4
85.	Frank Howard	272.1
86.	Ken Singleton	271.4
87.	Sam Rice	268.7
88.	Craig Biggio	268.5
89.	Harry Hooper	268.3
90.	Luke Appling	268.0
91.	Yogi Berra	267.5
92.	Joe Medwick	267.4
93.	Lou Whitaker	265.6
94.	Ernie Banks	264.9
95.	Chili Davis	262.9
96.	Joe Jackson	262.8
97.	Ken Griffey Jr.	262.6
98.	Mickey Vernon	262.5
99.	Jose Cruz	261.7
100.	Jimmy Wynn	260.6
101.	George Sisler	260.2
102.	Al Oliver	259.9
103.	Bobby Bonds	259.3
104.	Jim O'Rourke	258.7
105.	Joe Torre	258.3
106.	Roberto Alomar	258.2
107.	Frankie Frisch	258.0
108.	Boog Powell	257.5
109.	Elmer Flick	257.4
110.	George Van Haltren	256.4
111.	Richie Ashburn	255.9
112.	Edd Roush	255.7
113.	Ron Santo	255.5
114.	Johnny Bench	255.3
115.	Carlton Fisk	254.7
116.	Max Carey	254.0
117.	Jose Canseco	253.7
118.	Brian Downing	253.2
119.	Joe Kelley	252.2
120.	Jimmy Ryan	252.2
121.	Vada Pinson	251.2
122.	Bob Johnson	250.8
123.	Edgar Martinez	250.7
124.	Stan Hack	250.5
125.	Ryne Sandberg	249.7
126.	Bill Dahlen	248.9
127.	Brooks Robinson	248.1
128.	Ed Konetchy	247.1
129.	Mark Grace	246.7
130.	Gary Sheffield	245.7
131.	Bill Terry	245.6
132.	Heinie Manush	245.0
133.	Don Baylor	244.8
134.	Jim Rice	244.2
135.	Willie Davis	243.1
136.	Kiki Cuyler	243.0
137.	Cesar Cedeno	242.9
138.	Dale Murphy	242.7
139.	Ted Simmons	242.3
140.	George Burns	241.3
141.	Hank Greenberg	240.6
142.	Minnie Minoso	239.7
143.	Brett Butler	239.4
144.	Larry Doyle	237.5
145.	Bob Elliott	237.5
146.	Steve Garvey	237.1
147.	Bobby Grich	236.4
148.	Joe Cronin	235.3
149.	Home Run Baker	235.0
150.	Dixie Walker	234.9

Pitching

	Player	WS
1.	Cy Young	625.1
2.	Walter Johnson	529.9
3.	Pete Alexander	468.6
4.	Kid Nichols	467.7
5.	Christy Mathewson	413.0
6.	Warren Spahn	402.6
7.	Tim Keefe	392.6
8.	Lefty Grove	391.9
9.	Pud Galvin	389.9
10.	Tom Seaver	389.4
11.	John Clarkson	384.3
12.	Phil Niekro	375.3
13.	Gaylord Perry	368.4
14.	Steve Carlton	366.9
15.	Eddie Plank	354.8
16.	Old Hoss Radbourn	354.2
17.	Roger Clemens	349.4
18.	Tony Mullane	348.1
19.	Bert Blyleven	338.6
20.	Robin Roberts	332.9
21.	Nolan Ryan	332.3
22.	Mickey Welch	330.1
23.	Fergie Jenkins	319.2
24.	Don Sutton	318.8
25.	Greg Maddux	315.8
26.	Jim McCormick	314.7
27.	Bob Gibson	313.3
28.	Eppa Rixey	310.5
29.	Jim Palmer	310.4
30.	Ted Lyons	305.3
31.	Carl Hubbell	303.3
32.	Dennis Eckersley	298.2
33.	Early Wynn	293.5
34.	Three Finger Brown	292.7
35.	Vic Willis	292.5
36.	Bob Feller	291.7
37.	Red Ruffing	289.8
38.	Tommy John	289.5
39.	Red Faber	289.1
40.	Amos Rusie	284.7
41.	Jack Powell	282.6
42.	Jack Quinn	281.6
43.	Burleigh Grimes	275.6
44.	Jim Kaat	268.2
45.	Joe McGinnity	268.0
46.	Waite Hoyt	263.1
47.	Hal Newhouser	260.8
48.	Juan Marichal	260.5
49.	Ed Walsh	259.4
50.	Clark Griffith	257.5
51.	Wilbur Cooper	257.2
52.	Jim Bunning	256.5
53.	Whitey Ford	255.6
54.	Hoyt Wilhelm	255.6
55.	Gus Weyhing	255.0
56.	Charlie Buffinton	253.2
57.	Silver King	253.1
58.	Don Drysdale	250.9
59.	Luis Tiant	250.3
60.	Eddie Cicotte	244.9
61.	Billy Pierce	243.8
62.	Stan Coveleski	242.6
63.	Frank Tanana	241.4
64.	Jerry Koosman	241.0
65.	Dazzy Vance	240.6
66.	Bob Caruthers	240.2
67.	Rick Reuschel	239.8
68.	Sad Sam Jones	237.4
69.	Carl Mays	237.1
70.	Herb Pennock	236.8
71.	Tom Glavine	236.7
72.	Rube Waddell	235.3
73.	Bucky Walters	234.4
74.	Jack Stivetts	234.2
75.	Dennis Martinez	234.1
76.	Babe Adams	234.1
77.	Mel Harder	234.1
78.	Bobo Newsom	234.0
79.	Dolf Luque	232.6
80.	Will White	232.0
81.	Dutch Leonard	232.0
82.	Charlie Hough	231.2
83.	Paul Derringer	229.7
84.	Randy Johnson	226.4
85.	Tommy Bond	226.2
86.	Adonis Terry	224.8
87.	Tommy Bridges	224.8
88.	Mickey Lolich	224.2
89.	Larry Jackson	224.0
90.	Jack Morris	222.8
91.	Goose Gossage	222.4
92.	George Mullin	222.3
93.	Jim Whitney	222.2
94.	Dizzy Trout	221.0
95.	Charlie Root	220.9
96.	Urban Shocker	219.9
97.	Chief Bender	219.3
98.	Freddie Fitzsimmons	217.3
99.	Bill Hutchison	217.0
100.	Bob Shawkey	216.9
101.	Larry French	216.5
102.	Al Orth	215.7
103.	Doc White	215.6
104.	Lon Warneke	214.6
105.	Bob Lemon	211.8
106.	Kevin Brown	211.1
107.	Dave Stieb	211.1
108.	Milt Pappas	209.8
109.	George Uhle	209.1
110.	Sam Leever	209.1
111.	Jack Chesbro	208.1
112.	Wes Ferrell	208.0
113.	Frank Dwyer	207.8
114.	Curt Simmons	207.5
115.	Bob Friend	207.4
116.	Orel Hershiser	207.1
117.	Jesse Tannehill	206.6
118.	Rube Marquard	206.5
119.	Jesse Haines	206.3
120.	Hooks Dauss	205.9
121.	David Cone	205.9
122.	Ed Morris	205.9
123.	Eddie Rommel	205.7
124.	Ted Breitenstein	205.7
125.	Ed Reulbach	205.2
126.	Chuck Finley	202.9
127.	Jim Perry	202.5
128.	Deacon Phillippe	201.9
129.	Vida Blue	201.9
130.	Hippo Vaughn	201.6
131.	Catfish Hunter	200.6
132.	Earl Whitehill	199.9
133.	Murry Dickson	198.1
134.	Lee Smith	198.1
135.	Bill Dinneen	197.7
136.	Tom Zachary	197.3
137.	Claude Osteen	197.1
138.	Virgil Trucks	196.6
139.	Pink Hawley	196.5
140.	Red Ames	196.0
141.	Brickyard Kennedy	195.1
142.	Jerry Reuss	194.9
143.	Bret Saberhagen	193.8
144.	Sandy Koufax	193.5
145.	Wild Bill Donovan	192.8
146.	Doyle Alexander	192.0
147.	Addie Joss	190.7
148.	Wilbur Wood	190.0
149.	Lee Meadows	188.8
150.	Guy Hecker	188.0

Fielding Win Shares—Catcher (ordered by Innings)

	Player	Innings	WS	WS/ 1000
1.	Carlton Fisk	18554.2	112.2	6.05
2.	Bob Boone	18224.0	107.4	5.90
3.	Gary Carter	17372.2	120.3	6.92
4.	Tony Pena	15990.1	102.4	6.40
5.	Jim Sundberg	15878.0	105.4	6.64
6.	Rick Ferrell	15175.0	83.5	5.50
7.	Lance Parrish	15173.1	101.5	6.69
8.	Al Lopez	15072.0	88.6	5.88
9.	Gabby Hartnett	15036.0	109.4	7.28
10.	Ted Simmons	14953.1	70.0	4.68
11.	Johnny Bench	14584.0	93.3	6.40
12.	Ray Schalk	14443.0	97.5	6.75
13.	Yogi Berra	14409.0	99.4	6.90
14.	Bill Dickey	14312.0	94.9	6.63
15.	Benito Santiago	13474.0	76.2	5.65
16.	Bill Freehan	13462.0	86.8	6.45
17.	Deacon McGuire	13460.0	69.3	5.15
18.	Luke Sewell	13121.0	74.4	5.67
19.	Jim Hegan	12853.0	86.3	6.71
20.	Darrell Porter	12592.0	60.8	4.83
21.	Steve O'Neill	12439.0	62.5	5.02
22.	Sherm Lollar	12406.0	76.7	6.19
23.	Ernie Lombardi	12367.0	51.9	4.20
24.	Rick Dempsey	12343.2	80.3	6.50
25.	Del Crandall	12174.0	82.3	6.76
26.	Rollie Hemsley	11966.0	74.9	6.26
27.	Mickey Cochrane	11918.0	81.3	6.82
28.	John Roseboro	11874.0	73.0	6.15
29.	Tim McCarver	11800.0	65.2	5.52
30.	Muddy Ruel	11518.0	73.1	6.35
31.	Johnny Edwards	11495.0	74.0	6.44
32.	Wally Schang	11407.0	58.0	5.08
33.	Terry Steinbach	11357.0	62.1	5.47
34.	Mike Scioscia	11253.1	70.8	6.29
35.	Gus Mancuso	11197.0	66.0	5.90
36.	Wilbert Robinson	11136.0	52.2	4.68
37.	Ivan Rodriguez	11107.1	92.1	8.29
38.	Terry Kennedy	11097.1	48.9	4.41
39.	Jerry Grote	11096.0	63.9	5.75
40.	Jimmie Wilson	11092.0	57.8	5.21
41.	Thurman Munson	11072.0	61.8	5.58
42.	Chief Zimmer	10704.0	67.2	6.27
43.	Frankie Hayes	10561.0	43.9	4.16
44.	Alan Ashby	10526.1	48.5	4.60
45.	Butch Wynegar	10505.0	53.1	5.06
46.	Roy Campanella	10295.0	68.3	6.63
47.	Malachi Kittridge	10267.0	56.2	5.48
48.	Mike Piazza	10097.2	48.0	4.76
49.	Rick Cerone	10092.1	52.5	5.20
50.	Johnny Kling	10072.0	57.0	5.65
51.	George Gibson	10046.0	54.8	5.45
52.	Andy Seminick	10013.0	46.3	4.62
53.	Bob O'Farrell	9978.0	60.4	6.06
54.	Red Dooin	9943.0	52.1	5.24
55.	Hank Severeid	9928.0	55.5	5.59
56.	Frank Snyder	9902.0	61.1	6.17
57.	Walker Cooper	9889.0	48.3	4.89
58.	Ivy Wingo	9870.0	44.8	4.53
59.	Del Rice	9712.0	64.0	6.59
60.	Don Slaught	9657.2	40.0	4.14
61.	Tom Haller	9633.0	59.4	6.17
62.	Spud Davis	9608.0	48.3	5.02
63.	Ernie Whitt	9527.2	54.2	5.69
64.	Elston Howard	9499.0	61.2	6.45
65.	Manny Sanguillen	9467.0	49.9	5.27
66.	Joe Girardi	9392.2	52.7	5.61
67.	Steve Yeager	9314.0	60.1	6.45
68.	Billy Sullivan	9264.0	54.7	5.90
69.	Jack Clements	9129.0	45.8	5.02
70.	Smoky Burgess	9107.0	44.3	4.86
71.	Mickey Owen	8902.0	48.2	5.42
72.	Birdie Tebbetts	8864.0	51.9	5.85
73.	Oscar Stanage	8838.0	29.9	3.39
74.	Earl Battey	8801.0	56.0	6.36
75.	Cy Perkins	8651.0	50.1	5.79
76.	Darrin Fletcher	8607.0	34.4	4.00
77.	Ed Bailey	8593.0	44.8	5.22
78.	Duke Farrell	8586.0	55.4	6.46
79.	Bill Killefer	8559.0	61.9	7.24
80.	Randy Hundley	8540.0	50.8	5.94
81.	Jody Davis	8538.2	51.2	6.00
82.	Brad Ausmus	8506.1	57.1	6.71
83.	Milt May	8498.0	48.7	5.72
84.	John Warner	8490.0	52.1	6.14
85.	Sandy Alomar Jr.	8476.1	45.3	5.35
86.	Lou Criger	8437.0	58.3	6.91
87.	Sammy White	8428.0	45.2	5.36
88.	Mike Tresh	8407.0	42.1	5.01
89.	Mike Heath	8328.0	40.9	4.92
90.	Mike Macfarlane	8313.2	42.2	5.08
91.	Joe Oliver	8203.0	38.1	4.64
92.	Heinie Peitz	8147.0	48.2	5.91
93.	Charlie Bennett	8131.0	56.0	6.89
94.	Phil Masi	8095.0	44.9	5.55
95.	John Bateman	7991.0	32.1	4.02
96.	Bill Bergen	7968.0	51.7	6.49
97.	Darren Daulton	7944.0	38.0	4.78
98.	Todd Hundley	7938.0	31.9	4.02
99.	Gus Triandos	7925.0	39.3	4.96
100.	Roger Bresnahan	7919.0	41.4	5.23

	Player	Innings	WS	WS/ 1000		Player	Innings	WS	WS/ 1000
101.	Eddie Ainsmith	7889.0	44.1	5.59	151.	John Romano	6511.0	40.1	6.15
102.	Clay Dalrymple	7863.0	42.8	5.45	152.	Paul Casanova	6509.0	28.2	4.33
103.	Bo Diaz	7755.0	43.7	5.63	153.	Ed Herrmann	6474.0	37.2	5.75
104.	Dan Wilson	7742.1	48.0	6.20	154.	George Mitterwald	6385.0	36.0	5.65
105.	Clyde McCullough	7734.0	39.3	5.08	155.	Clint Courtney	6331.0	26.6	4.21
106.	Jeff Reed	7724.1	36.7	4.76	156.	Silver Flint	6222.0	35.3	5.67
107.	Bill Rariden	7720.0	39.7	5.15	157.	Scott Servais	6210.2	33.1	5.33
108.	Buddy Rosar	7708.0	49.1	6.38	158.	Boileryard Clarke	6210.0	29.6	4.76
109.	Kirt Manwaring	7684.2	47.0	6.12	159.	Chad Kreuter	6172.2	32.8	5.31
110.	Rich Gedman	7650.0	42.3	5.53	160.	Johnny Bassler	6153.0	33.5	5.44
111.	Bruce Benedict	7641.2	48.2	6.31	161.	Walter Schmidt	6146.0	36.3	5.90
112.	Ron Hassey	7517.2	43.3	5.76	162.	Al Todd	6139.0	32.0	5.22
113.	Joe Torre	7405.0	34.9	4.72	163.	Joe Ferguson	6100.0	36.3	5.95
114.	Otto Miller	7353.0	41.9	5.69		Jim Pagliaroni	6100.0	26.2	4.29
115.	Shanty Hogan	7312.0	41.3	5.65	165.	Fred Kendall	6097.0	25.4	4.17
116.	Val Picinich	7306.0	36.6	5.01	166.	Jimmy Archer	6094.0	34.2	5.61
117.	Charles Johnson	7302.0	52.8	7.23	167.	Joe Sugden	6054.0	35.3	5.83
118.	Chief Meyers	7280.0	37.9	5.20	168.	Phil Roof	6019.0	29.4	4.89
119.	Bob Rodgers	7269.0	42.4	5.83	169.	Charlie O'Brien	5978.0	36.6	6.13
120.	Javy Lopez	7240.1	40.7	5.62	170.	Bubbles Hargrave	5972.0	29.8	4.99
121.	Dave Duncan	7236.0	30.7	4.24	171.	Larry McLean	5940.0	29.8	5.02
122.	Bob Swift	7198.0	43.1	5.98	172.	Pat Moran	5933.0	37.9	6.39
123.	Buck Martinez	7191.0	40.5	5.64	173.	Doc Bushong	5923.0	36.8	6.21
124.	Ray Fosse	7173.0	40.2	5.61	174.	B.J. Surhoff	5836.1	32.7	5.59
125.	Ed McFarland	7100.0	43.2	6.09	175.	John Stearns	5831.0	31.0	5.32
126.	Andy Etchebarren	7082.0	35.2	4.97	176.	Johnny Gooch	5818.0	30.1	5.18
127.	Ray Mueller	7077.0	47.9	6.77	177.	Stan Lopata	5779.0	28.3	4.90
128.	Pat Borders	7066.1	36.1	5.10	178.	Bob Tillman	5765.0	22.5	3.90
129.	Jack O'Connor	7010.0	39.1	5.58	179.	Mike Fitzgerald	5757.0	23.7	4.11
130.	Ron Karkovice	7003.2	50.0	7.13	180.	Dave Rader	5748.0	25.8	4.49
131.	Dave Valle	7000.2	42.5	6.08	181.	Ellie Rodriguez	5747.0	29.3	5.10
132.	Joe Azcue	6961.0	40.5	5.82	182.	Frankie Pytlak	5684.0	39.1	6.88
133.	Charlie Moore	6958.2	35.3	5.07	183.	Mike Matheny	5634.2	34.6	6.14
134.	Frank Bowerman	6945.0	42.0	6.04	184.	Mike Stanley	5623.2	14.4	2.56
135.	Mickey Tettleton	6933.0	32.4	4.68	185.	Alex Trevino	5622.1	24.7	4.39
136.	Chris Hoiles	6767.0	35.0	5.17	186.	Brian Harper	5581.0	18.5	3.31
137.	Wes Westrum	6733.0	42.6	6.32	187.	Jake Early	5558.0	22.3	4.00
138.	Gene Tenace	6719.0	33.1	4.92	188.	Brian Downing	5491.0	32.0	5.82
139.	Hank Gowdy	6698.0	43.7	6.52	189.	Pop Schriver	5480.0	32.0	5.84
140.	Tom Pagnozzi	6672.1	42.1	6.31	190.	Ozzie Virgil	5463.0	28.4	5.20
141.	Zack Taylor	6664.0	40.8	6.13	191.	Greg Myers	5446.2	24.7	4.53
142.	Mike Gonzalez	6617.0	38.5	5.82	192.	Earl Smith	5440.0	27.7	5.08
143.	Pop Snyder	6594.0	50.3	7.63	193.	Buck Ewing	5413.0	39.7	7.33
144.	John Flaherty	6588.1	31.6	4.79	194.	Al Spohrer	5403.0	23.7	4.38
145.	Brent Mayne	6577.0	33.6	5.11	195.	Gene Desautels	5400.0	33.4	6.19
146.	Eddie Taubensee	6566.0	24.5	3.73	196.	Bob Brenly	5385.0	25.4	4.71
147.	Jason Kendall	6554.1	28.7	4.37	197.	Russ Nixon	5373.0	22.1	4.12
148.	Mike LaValliere	6549.1	42.7	6.52	198.	Art Wilson	5364.0	27.0	5.03
149.	Ossee Schreckengost	6538.0	51.9	7.93	199.	Les Moss	5308.0	21.5	4.05
150.	Harry Danning	6524.0	43.2	6.63	200.	Matt Nokes	5258.2	23.9	4.54

	Player	Innings	WS	WS/ 1000
201.	Connie Mack	5233.0	27.4	5.24
202.	Glenn Myatt	5220.0	23.4	4.48
203.	Doggie Miller	5203.0	23.3	4.48
204.	Ray Hayworth	5182.0	29.4	5.67
	Jocko Milligan	5182.0	29.9	5.77
206.	Hal Smith	5140.0	23.1	4.49
207.	Bill Carrigan	5127.0	28.9	5.64
208.	Chris Cannizzaro	5123.0	20.9	4.09
209.	Mickey O'Neil	5110.0	28.6	5.59
210.	Hobie Landrith	5047.0	23.3	4.62
211.	Barry Foote	5046.0	29.6	5.87
212.	Rick Wilkins	5041.0	34.4	6.83
213.	Duffy Dyer	5031.0	34.3	6.82
214.	Charlie Berry	5015.0	19.9	3.98
215.	Jeff Sweeney	5012.0	24.4	4.86
216.	Duke Sims	4996.0	30.1	6.03
217.	Al Evans	4994.0	18.8	3.76
218.	Mike Ryan	4929.0	24.3	4.92
219.	Hank DeBerry	4928.0	34.2	6.94
220.	Charlie Ganzel	4913.0	34.2	6.97
221.	Harry Bemis	4910.0	19.5	3.96
222.	Tim Laudner	4902.2	17.4	3.55
223.	John Grim	4900.0	24.8	5.06
224.	Junior Ortiz	4885.1	22.3	4.57
225.	Les Nunamaker	4862.0	29.0	5.96
226.	Ken O'Dea	4832.0	33.6	6.96
227.	John Henry	4820.0	31.9	6.62
228.	Mike Lieberthal	4804.0	25.0	5.19
229.	Jim Essian	4783.0	32.9	6.89
230.	Butch Henline	4778.0	20.7	4.33
231.	Dick Brown	4751.0	26.6	5.59
232.	Admiral Schlei	4747.0	26.7	5.63
233.	Hal Wagner	4745.0	19.6	4.12
234.	Ed Fitz Gerald	4729.0	17.3	3.66
235.	Marc Hill	4723.0	26.5	5.61
236.	Bill Holbert	4714.0	31.5	6.67
237.	Red Wilson	4685.0	26.3	5.62
238.	Mike Powers	4675.0	34.2	7.31
239.	Farmer Vaughn	4657.0	24.5	5.25
240.	Con Daily	4651.0	22.9	4.92
241.	Bob Melvin	4626.1	26.8	5.80
242.	Frank House	4622.0	24.4	5.28
243.	Damon Berryhill	4581.2	24.9	5.43
244.	J.C. Martin	4565.0	25.5	5.59
245.	Aaron Robinson	4563.0	25.3	5.54
246.	Joe Garagiola	4558.0	24.5	5.37
247.	Ellie Hendricks	4537.0	23.9	5.28
248.	Matt Walbeck	4515.2	20.5	4.54
249.	Jorge Posada	4476.0	23.3	5.21
250.	Jack Boyle	4463.0	25.0	5.60

	Player	Innings	WS	WS/ 1000
251.	Earl Grace	4458.0	24.1	5.41
252.	Morgan Murphy	4452.0	24.8	5.58
253.	John Wathan	4439.0	19.3	4.35
254.	Roy Spencer	4420.0	25.6	5.78
255.	Jack Ryan	4387.0	22.1	5.05
256.	Babe Phelps	4373.0	22.8	5.21
257.	King Kelly	4365.0	24.5	5.61
258.	Clyde Kluttz	4348.0	23.0	5.29
259.	Bob Stinson	4313.0	18.0	4.17
260.	Dick Dietz	4308.0	12.6	2.94
261.	Red Kleinow	4301.0	18.3	4.25
262.	Sam Agnew	4267.0	18.0	4.22
263.	Hal Smith	4215.0	29.6	7.01
264.	Joe Astroth	4209.0	21.8	5.17
265.	Tommy Clarke	4190.0	18.6	4.45
266.	Ed Phelps	4182.0	17.7	4.23
267.	Joe Ginsberg	4100.0	17.4	4.24
268.	Ed Ott	4093.0	21.9	5.35
269.	Gabby Street	4071.0	21.1	5.18
270.	Jorge Fabregas	4063.2	22.9	5.64
271.	Jeff Torborg	4050.0	20.6	5.08
272.	Tony Eusebio	4031.1	20.8	5.16
273.	Andy Allanson	3998.1	18.1	4.52
274.	Jerry May	3994.0	19.1	4.78
275.	Mike Grady	3983.0	16.1	4.04
276.	Barney Gilligan	3981.0	22.7	5.71
277.	Joel Skinner	3952.2	17.2	4.34
278.	Johnny Oates	3938.0	24.7	6.27
279.	Tim Donahue	3930.0	19.1	4.87
280.	Roxy Walters	3914.0	23.6	6.03
281.	Dick Buckley	3909.0	18.5	4.73
282.	Moe Berg	3895.0	24.1	6.18
283.	Hank Foiles	3874.0	21.5	5.55
284.	Johnny Peacock	3864.0	20.3	5.25
285.	Jake Gibbs	3848.0	19.7	5.12
286.	Paul Richards	3847.0	29.8	7.76
287.	Geno Petralli	3829.0	12.2	3.18
288.	Harry Chiti	3773.0	16.1	4.27
289.	Matt Batts	3765.0	17.8	4.72
290.	Nig Clarke	3757.0	12.8	3.40

Norms for players with:			
10,000 innings	–	–	**5.90**
7,500 - 9,999 innings	–	–	**5.55**
5,000 - 7,499 innings	–	–	**5.39**
2,500 - 4,999 innings	–	–	**5.11**
1,000 - 2,499 innings	–	–	**4.87**
0 - 999 innings	–	–	**4.40**

Fielding Win Shares—First Base (ordered by Innings)

	Player	Innings	WS	WS/ 1000
1.	Eddie Murray	21203.2	36.9	1.74
2.	Jake Beckley	20802.0	37.9	1.82
3.	Mickey Vernon	19621.0	34.2	1.74
4.	Lou Gehrig	18817.0	33.0	1.75
5.	Charlie Grimm	18776.0	38.6	2.06
6.	Ed Konetchy	18463.0	38.8	2.10
7.	Joe Kuhel	18238.0	35.4	1.94
8.	Joe Judge	18188.0	30.8	1.69
9.	Cap Anson	18082.0	31.9	1.76
10.	Steve Garvey	17886.2	37.9	2.12
11.	Jake Daubert	17855.0	34.0	1.90
12.	Mark Grace	17637.0	37.9	2.15
13.	George Sisler	17575.0	23.8	1.35
14.	Stuffy McInnis	17539.0	33.2	1.89
15.	Fred McGriff	17527.1	27.8	1.58
16.	Keith Hernandez	17292.1	34.9	2.02
17.	Chris Chambliss	16863.0	29.1	1.72
18.	Jimmie Foxx	16791.0	35.6	2.12
19.	Jim Bottomley	16666.0	26.1	1.57
20.	Willie McCovey	16553.0	23.6	1.42
21.	Andres Galarraga	16530.1	25.7	1.56
22.	Will Clark	16249.1	25.7	1.58
23.	Norm Cash	16231.0	34.3	2.11
24.	Wally Joyner	16071.0	28.9	1.80
25.	Wally Pipp	16063.0	34.8	2.17
26.	Fred Tenney	15986.0	31.7	1.98
27.	Hal Chase	15971.0	24.6	1.54
28.	Gil Hodges	15772.0	29.7	1.88
29.	Roger Connor	15527.0	34.1	2.20
30.	Rafael Palmeiro	15320.0	31.8	2.08
31.	George Scott	15225.0	24.9	1.64
32.	Mark McGwire	14907.1	19.8	1.33
33.	Tommy Tucker	14586.0	24.3	1.66
34.	Orlando Cepeda	14518.0	23.5	1.62
35.	George Burns	14497.0	24.7	1.71
36.	Harry Davis	14425.0	27.4	1.90
37.	Johnny Mize	14401.0	26.7	1.86
38.	Dan Brouthers	14373.0	24.9	1.73
39.	Jeff Bagwell	14267.1	25.1	1.76
40.	Tony Perez	14215.0	24.2	1.70
41.	Don Mattingly	14099.1	29.0	2.06
42.	Bill Terry	13932.0	31.8	2.28
43.	Lu Blue	13899.0	23.9	1.72
44.	Kent Hrbek	13730.0	28.8	2.10
45.	Fred Merkle	13598.0	24.7	1.81
46.	George McQuinn	13258.0	27.2	2.05
47.	Bill Buckner	13243.1	24.4	1.84
48.	John Olerud	13149.2	29.7	2.26
49.	Dolph Camilli	13017.0	22.4	1.72
50.	Cecil Cooper	12843.0	20.2	1.57
51.	Frank McCormick	12754.0	28.0	2.20
52.	Ted Kluszewski	12680.0	20.6	1.62
53.	John Mayberry	12481.0	19.4	1.55
54.	Eric Karros	12467.0	24.0	1.92
55.	Bill White	12454.0	25.8	2.07
56.	Lee May	12405.0	20.7	1.67
57.	Boog Powell	12393.0	16.8	1.36
58.	Gus Suhr	12370.0	21.7	1.75
59.	Joe Adcock	12275.0	24.1	1.97
60.	Elbie Fletcher	12005.0	21.7	1.80
61.	George Kelly	12000.0	24.7	2.05
62.	Charlie Comiskey	11973.0	24.2	2.02
63.	Dan McGann	11941.0	22.8	1.91
64.	Bill Skowron	11893.0	19.3	1.62
65.	Fred Luderus	11822.0	20.7	1.75
66.	Earl Torgeson	11681.0	18.8	1.61
67.	Tino Martinez	11624.0	30.2	2.60
68.	Hal Trosky	11599.0	20.3	1.75
69.	Pete O'Brien	11468.0	29.6	2.58
70.	Kitty Bransfield	11462.0	18.8	1.64
71.	Jack Fournier	11394.0	15.3	1.34
72.	Jason Thompson	11303.0	19.0	1.68
73.	Mike Hargrove	11280.0	17.8	1.58
74.	Doc Hoblitzell	11207.0	17.5	1.56
75.	Rudy York	11158.0	23.3	2.09
76.	Dan Driessen	10955.2	19.1	1.74
77.	Phil Cavarretta	10789.0	15.3	1.42
78.	Ernie Banks	10776.0	20.3	1.88
79.	Earl Sheely	10765.0	18.4	1.71
80.	George Stovall	10754.0	22.0	2.05
81.	Walter Holke	10548.0	18.1	1.72
82.	Vic Power	10492.0	23.9	2.28
83.	Ed Kranepool	10437.0	16.7	1.60
84.	Candy LaChance	10306.0	21.4	2.08
85.	Rod Carew	10255.0	14.1	1.37
86.	Donn Clendenon	10211.0	14.8	1.44
87.	Chick Gandil	10182.0	20.0	1.96
88.	Hank Greenberg	10002.0	20.5	2.05
89.	Jim Spencer	9944.0	18.9	1.91
90.	Willie Montanez	9921.0	15.4	1.55
91.	J.T. Snow	9909.1	17.4	1.75
92.	Mo Vaughn	9901.1	11.0	1.11
93.	Eddie Robinson	9674.0	15.3	1.58
94.	Ferris Fain	9613.0	16.2	1.68
95.	John Reilly	9517.0	16.5	1.73
96.	Don Mincher	9272.0	15.9	1.71
97.	Ron Fairly	9254.0	17.8	1.92
98.	Wes Parker	9231.0	21.8	2.36
99.	Walt Dropo	9230.0	15.3	1.65
100.	Willie Upshaw	9165.2	14.6	1.60

	Player	Innings	WS	WS/ 1000
101.	Tom Jones	9144.0	16.0	1.75
102.	Bill Phillips	9141.0	14.7	1.61
103.	Eddie Waitkus	9065.0	18.3	2.02
104.	Babe Dahlgren	8992.0	15.1	1.68
105.	Jack Doyle	8981.0	14.1	1.57
106.	Doc Johnston	8805.0	12.8	1.45
107.	David Segui	8722.2	15.9	1.82
108.	Frank Chance	8655.0	15.4	1.78
109.	Dick Stuart	8631.0	6.9	0.80
110.	Bob Watson	8628.0	14.2	1.65
111.	Stan Musial	8477.0	17.0	2.01
112.	Sid Farrar	8309.0	15.6	1.88
113.	Dick Siebert	8253.0	12.5	1.52
114.	Bruce Bochte	8249.0	14.1	1.71
115.	John Morrill	8115.0	15.2	1.87
116.	Frank Thomas	8111.0	6.0	0.74
117.	Zeke Bonura	7930.0	15.1	1.91
118.	Hal Morris	7928.2	14.4	1.82
119.	Nick Etten	7921.0	7.3	0.92
120.	Ripper Collins	7839.0	14.7	1.88
121.	Joe Pepitone	7823.0	13.6	1.74
122.	Pete Rose	7792.0	14.5	1.86
123.	Phil Todt	7767.0	14.7	1.90
124.	Jack Burns	7716.0	10.9	1.42
125.	Harmon Killebrew	7684.0	14.0	1.83
126.	Alvin Davis	7659.2	11.6	1.51
127.	Greg Brock	7646.2	12.1	1.58
128.	Nate Colbert	7602.0	13.8	1.82
129.	Glenn Davis	7528.1	15.5	2.06
130.	Cecil Fielder	7486.0	10.1	1.36
	Dee Fondy	7486.0	12.5	1.67
132.	Don Hurst	7476.0	11.0	1.48
133.	Jake Stahl	7419.0	10.6	1.43
134.	Vic Saier	7405.0	11.4	1.54
135.	Sid Bream	7323.1	13.1	1.79
136.	Joe Start	7179.0	13.2	1.83
137.	Roy Sievers	7161.0	12.2	1.70
138.	Willie Stargell	6984.0	9.7	1.38
139.	Jim Gentile	6953.0	11.2	1.60
140.	Norm Siebern	6932.0	12.4	1.79
141.	Dale Long	6926.0	9.2	1.33
142.	Dave Orr	6875.0	12.8	1.87
143.	Kevin Young	6868.1	10.4	1.51
144.	Mike Epstein	6787.0	9.6	1.42
145.	Darrell Evans	6719.0	11.3	1.68
146.	Carlos Delgado	6713.0	10.1	1.50
147.	Dick Allen	6651.0	10.0	1.50
148.	Deron Johnson	6638.0	12.3	1.85
149.	Rico Brogna	6619.1	13.1	1.97
150.	Jiggs Donahue	6538.0	11.7	1.80

	Player	Innings	WS	WS/ 1000
151.	Dots Miller	6505.0	13.2	2.03
152.	Whitey Lockman	6483.0	10.9	1.68
153.	Buddy Hassett	6481.0	9.6	1.47
154.	Carl Yastrzemski	6434.0	13.2	2.05
155.	Paul Sorrento	6412.0	9.8	1.52
156.	Mike Jorgensen	6348.0	11.9	1.87
157.	John Ganzel	6335.0	14.5	2.29
158.	Joe Torre	6329.0	11.0	1.74
159.	Tom McCraw	6298.0	11.3	1.79
160.	Henry Larkin	6203.0	6.6	1.07
161.	Andre Thornton	6083.0	11.7	1.92
162.	Al Oliver	5991.0	6.4	1.08
163.	Tony Clark	5840.1	9.2	1.58
164.	Perry Werden	5798.0	12.5	2.15
165.	Lee Stevens	5699.0	9.2	1.62
166.	Jason Giambi	5673.1	9.3	1.63
167.	Buck Jordan	5649.0	9.1	1.62
168.	Greg Walker	5639.1	8.0	1.41
169.	Danny Cater	5612.0	9.3	1.66
170.	Frank Isbell	5488.0	12.3	2.24
171.	John Kruk	5432.0	9.4	1.74
172.	Jim Thome	5397.2	9.2	1.71
173.	Dale Alexander	5389.0	7.7	1.42
174.	Vic Wertz	5371.0	8.6	1.60
175.	Tony Lupien	5341.0	8.0	1.49
176.	Del Bissonette	5307.0	8.6	1.62
177.	Todd Helton	5294.0	12.7	2.39
178.	Steve Balboni	5292.2	8.3	1.58
179.	John Anderson	5226.0	10.2	1.95
180.	Ray Sanders	5224.0	7.9	1.52
181.	Gordy Coleman	5218.0	10.9	2.10
182.	Dave Foutz	5215.0	11.7	2.25
183.	Gerald Perry	5203.0	6.7	1.30
184.	Dave Bergman	5191.2	7.9	1.52
185.	Eddie Morgan	5190.0	6.3	1.21
186.	Greg Colbrunn	5185.2	9.4	1.82
187.	Ed Bouchee	5144.0	7.8	1.52
188.	Patsy Tebeau	5094.0	12.0	2.36
189.	Sam Leslie	5025.0	7.3	1.46
190.	Dick Gernert	5022.0	8.3	1.66
191.	Leon Durham	4978.1	8.7	1.74
192.	Pete Runnels	4951.0	9.1	1.83
193.	Jack Clark	4900.0	6.7	1.37
194.	Harry Stovey	4881.0	7.6	1.56
195.	Bob Robertson	4853.0	6.4	1.32
196.	Joe Hauser	4780.0	9.4	1.97
197.	Todd Benzinger	4747.1	7.5	1.58
198.	Fred Whitfield	4736.0	8.1	1.72
199.	Tony Horton	4718.0	7.4	1.57
200.	Babe Young	4695.0	8.3	1.77

	Player	Innings	WS	WS/ 1000
201.	Randy Milligan	4692.0	7.0	1.50
202.	Joe Collins	4681.0	8.1	1.74
203.	Pedro Guerrero	4604.0	4.4	0.96
204.	Gene Tenace	4558.0	7.1	1.56
205.	Tim Jordan	4546.0	5.3	1.16
206.	Joe Cunningham	4518.0	7.1	1.56
207.	Dave Kingman	4488.0	4.4	0.98
208.	Charlie Carr	4457.0	7.5	1.68
209.	Enos Cabell	4453.0	7.0	1.57
210.	Joe Harris	4424.0	6.9	1.56
211.	Ron Jackson	4394.0	8.2	1.86
212.	Mike Ivie	4375.0	8.1	1.85
213.	Willie Aikens	4333.0	5.8	1.35
214.	John Jaha	4279.1	6.1	1.43
215.	John Milner	4243.0	7.0	1.66
216.	Fritz Mollwitz	4228.0	6.8	1.62
217.	Dave Magadan	4218.2	7.4	1.77
218.	George Grantham	4208.0	6.6	1.56
219.	Ed Cartwright	4193.0	6.6	1.58
220.	Sean Casey	4189.1	6.1	1.46
221.	Claude Rossman	4183.0	5.9	1.42
222.	Ricky Jordan	4169.1	7.1	1.70
223.	Rich Reese	4135.0	8.0	1.95
224.	Derrek Lee	4117.2	6.7	1.63
225.	Bud Clancy	4013.0	6.1	1.53
226.	Jeff King	4011.1	8.4	2.09
227.	Travis Lee	3991.1	8.6	2.14
228.	Mike Squires	3947.0	8.9	2.26
229.	George Brett	3923.2	6.3	1.61
230.	Nick Esasky	3883.2	6.8	1.76
231.	Jack Boyle	3880.0	5.1	1.32
232.	Harry Heilmann	3868.0	5.8	1.50
233.	Ecky Stearns	3858.0	5.5	1.42
234.	Steve Bilko	3857.0	7.5	1.94
235.	Mike Rocco	3853.0	7.4	1.93
236.	Dick Kryhoski	3843.0	6.8	1.78
237.	Ken Harrelson	3824.0	5.9	1.54
238.	Dan Meyer	3793.0	5.0	1.31
239.	Franklin Stubbs	3786.1	6.4	1.68
240.	Dick Burrus	3764.0	5.4	1.43
241.	Pat Putnam	3760.0	6.4	1.69
242.	Jeff Conine	3753.2	5.5	1.46
243.	Norm Larker	3738.0	8.1	2.18
244.	Jake Virtue	3722.0	6.8	1.82
245.	Ray Grimes	3721.0	6.0	1.61
246.	Bob Boyd	3690.0	6.5	1.77
247.	Tito Francona	3688.0	6.2	1.68
248.	Mox McQuery	3621.0	5.2	1.45
249.	Johnny Hopp	3615.0	5.4	1.49
250.	Dave Revering	3608.0	4.6	1.26
251.	Howie Schultz	3605.0	6.0	1.65
252.	Lou Finney	3534.0	5.5	1.56
253.	Bob Unglaub	3531.0	5.2	1.48
254.	Lee Thomas	3513.0	4.1	1.18
255.	Luke Easter	3493.0	5.6	1.59
256.	Felipe Alou	3486.0	4.3	1.23
257.	Del Gainer	3475.0	5.9	1.70
258.	Charlie Hickman	3471.0	4.1	1.17
259.	Rusty Staub	3468.0	6.3	1.81
260.	Frank Torre	3466.0	6.9	1.99
261.	Pat Tabler	3463.0	5.6	1.62
262.	Billy Goodman	3434.0	6.3	1.84
263.	Bob Oliver	3413.0	6.4	1.86
264.	Mike Hegan	3357.0	5.8	1.74
265.	Preston Ward	3344.0	5.3	1.57
266.	Alex McKinnon	3334.0	4.5	1.36
267.	Paul Konerko	3326.0	5.5	1.66
268.	Gene Paulette	3310.0	5.8	1.76
269.	Von Hayes	3295.1	5.7	1.73
270.	George Crowe	3295.0	4.9	1.50
271.	Dick Sisler	3281.0	4.2	1.28
272.	Harvey Hendrick	3252.0	4.7	1.44
273.	Johnny McCarthy	3251.0	6.4	1.96
274.	Gregg Jefferies	3219.0	3.6	1.11
275.	Lamar Johnson	3218.0	7.7	2.38
276.	Lew Fonseca	3199.0	6.0	1.89
277.	Todd Zeile	3189.1	8.0	2.52
278.	Shano Collins	3172.0	5.7	1.81
279.	Richie Hebner	3161.0	4.7	1.48
280.	Ryan Klesko	3103.0	2.5	0.82
281.	Milt Scott	2988.0	7.5	2.51
282.	Bill Everitt	2975.0	4.1	1.38
283.	Harry Taylor	2968.0	5.9	2.00
284.	Richie Sexson	2953.1	4.8	1.61
285.	Gail Harris	2953.0	4.3	1.46
286.	Hap Myers	2951.0	4.4	1.48
287.	Billy O'Brien	2938.0	3.9	1.32
288.	Pete LaCock	2931.0	4.9	1.67
289.	Klondike Douglass	2911.0	3.6	1.22
290.	Jim Field	2900.0	4.7	1.61

Norms for players with:			
10,000 innings	–	–	**1.83**
7,500 - 9,999 innings	–	–	**1.67**
5,000 - 7,499 innings	–	–	**1.68**
2,500 - 4,999 innings	–	–	**1.62**
1,000 - 2,499 innings	–	–	**1.52**
0 - 999 innings	–	–	**1.49**

Fielding Win Shares—Second Base (ordered by Innings)

Player	Innings	WS	WS/1000
1. Eddie Collins	23637.0	107.5	4.55
2. Joe Morgan	21521.0	90.8	4.22
3. Nellie Fox	20127.0	111.5	5.54
4. Charlie Gehringer	19343.0	86.8	4.49
5. Lou Whitaker	19061.0	87.2	4.57
6. Bid McPhee	18789.0	98.7	5.25
7. Willie Randolph	18648.0	97.4	5.23
8. Bill Mazeroski	18301.0	112.2	6.13
9. Nap Lajoie	18263.0	85.7	4.69
10. Frank White	17852.2	99.7	5.58
11. Ryne Sandberg	17241.0	89.0	5.16
12. Roberto Alomar	17162.1	86.8	5.06
13. Bobby Doerr	16377.0	85.7	5.23
14. Billy Herman	16029.0	74.9	4.67
15. Red Schoendienst	15782.0	88.6	5.61
16. Frankie Frisch	15483.0	83.9	5.42
17. Bobby Grich	15098.0	85.8	5.68
18. Johnny Evers	15061.0	68.6	4.55
19. Larry Doyle	14978.0	50.3	3.35
20. Del Pratt	14842.0	60.1	4.05
21. Steve Sax	14667.2	54.4	3.71
22. Kid Gleason	13862.0	47.7	3.44
23. Rogers Hornsby	13596.0	41.5	3.06
24. Fred Pfeffer	13585.0	64.1	4.72
25. Joe Gordon	13396.0	69.5	5.19
26. Miller Huggins	13390.0	50.0	3.73
27. George Cutshaw	13354.0	55.7	4.17
28. Claude Ritchey	13092.0	55.8	4.26
29. Hughie Critz	12847.0	69.6	5.41
30. Julian Javier	12803.0	59.9	4.68
31. Frank Bolling	12799.0	59.1	4.62
32. Manny Trillo	12796.2	67.8	5.30
33. Craig Biggio	12748.2	58.5	4.59
34. Cupid Childs	12742.0	57.0	4.48
35. Tony Lazzeri	12720.0	44.6	3.51
36. Felix Millan	12699.0	59.3	4.67
37. Tony Taylor	12261.0	50.7	4.13
38. Jim Gantner	12220.1	61.5	5.03
39. Lou Bierbauer	12045.0	55.9	4.64
40. Davey Lopes	11930.0	49.1	4.12
41. Cookie Rojas	11913.0	55.4	4.65
42. Tom Herr	11886.0	51.8	4.36
43. Chuck Knoblauch	11800.1	50.7	4.30
44. Bobby Lowe	11694.0	53.1	4.54
45. Buddy Myer	11654.0	48.2	4.14
46. Bobby Richardson	11492.0	49.3	4.29
47. Delino DeShields	11438.1	44.4	3.89
48. Bill Doran	11353.2	49.2	4.33
49. Ski Melillo	11340.0	56.7	5.00
50. Dave Cash	11285.0	58.4	5.18
51. Harold Reynolds	11284.0	51.7	4.58
52. Joe Quinn	11199.0	41.4	3.69
53. Glenn Hubbard	11195.0	66.3	5.92
54. Bucky Harris	11121.0	44.5	4.00
55. Don Blasingame	11110.0	51.8	4.66
56. Johnny Temple	11103.0	42.4	3.82
57. Johnny Ray	10950.2	49.1	4.49
58. Ted Sizemore	10902.0	57.7	5.30
59. Otto Knabe	10874.0	47.0	4.32
60. Tito Fuentes	10864.0	45.2	4.16
61. Robby Thompson	10719.2	46.7	4.36
62. Glenn Beckert	10706.0	46.5	4.34
63. Bill Wambsganss	10559.0	37.6	3.56
64. Jimmy Williams	10481.0	43.7	4.17
65. Bret Boone	10449.2	49.3	4.72
66. Tony Cuccinello	10417.0	39.9	3.83
67. Ron Hunt	10395.0	36.8	3.54
68. Max Bishop	10366.0	53.8	5.19
69. Jerry Priddy	10270.0	49.8	4.84
70. Dave Johnson	10268.0	46.6	4.54
71. Mickey Morandini	10172.2	40.8	4.01
72. Juan Samuel	10089.0	32.5	3.22
73. Cub Stricker	10005.0	32.2	3.22
74. Bill Hallman	9914.0	32.3	3.26
75. Bobby Avila	9866.0	52.7	5.34
76. Eddie Stanky	9794.0	50.8	5.19
77. Ron Oester	9747.1	44.3	4.54
78. Dick Green	9579.0	48.9	5.11
79. Horace Clarke	9574.0	48.0	5.01
80. Jerry Remy	9547.0	47.7	5.00
81. Tommy Helms	9536.0	45.4	4.77
82. Mark McLemore	9514.0	43.5	4.57
83. Sandy Alomar	9500.0	44.1	4.64
84. Jeff Kent	9427.1	36.7	3.90
85. Julio Cruz	9405.0	47.8	5.09
86. Rod Carew	9392.0	39.3	4.19
87. Bobby Knoop	9291.0	48.8	5.25
88. Tom Daly	9283.0	32.4	3.49
89. Jerry Lumpe	9181.0	37.3	4.06
90. Hobe Ferris	9109.0	41.1	4.51
91. Rennie Stennett	8980.0	48.3	5.37
92. Ray Durham	8921.0	32.1	3.59
93. Jose Lind	8902.0	48.6	5.46
94. Ralph Young	8885.0	26.7	3.00
95. Jody Reed	8878.1	53.3	6.01
96. Carlos Baerga	8699.2	39.8	4.58
97. Jim Gilliam	8682.0	43.5	5.01
98. Eric Young	8549.0	35.7	4.18
99. Jack Burdock	8458.0	35.0	4.14
100. Lonny Frey	8442.0	45.0	5.33

	Player	Innings	WS	WS/ 1000
101.	Connie Ryan	8430.0	35.5	4.21
102.	Fred Dunlap	8420.0	38.7	4.60
103.	Tony Bernazard	8300.1	32.5	3.92
104.	Phil Garner	8248.0	38.1	4.62
105.	Marty McManus	8208.0	31.1	3.79
106.	Dick McAuliffe	8028.0	33.0	4.11
107.	Damaso Garcia	8024.0	38.8	4.84
108.	Joe Gerhardt	7874.0	36.9	4.68
109.	Joey Cora	7824.2	23.9	3.05
110.	Luis Alicea	7807.2	28.9	3.71
111.	Jackie Hayes	7782.0	33.9	4.36
112.	Marty Barrett	7730.1	41.3	5.34
113.	Mark Lemke	7674.2	46.3	6.04
114.	Rich Dauer	7633.0	33.8	4.43
115.	Duane Kuiper	7607.0	32.1	4.21
116.	Damion Easley	7577.0	33.7	4.45
117.	Jimmy Bloodworth	7530.0	35.1	4.67
	Danny Murphy	7530.0	28.5	3.79
119.	Mike Lansing	7420.2	39.1	5.27
120.	Denny Doyle	7373.0	31.8	4.32
121.	Doug Flynn	7266.0	32.6	4.49
122.	Al Myers	7217.0	22.3	3.09
123.	George Grantham	7204.0	22.5	3.12
124.	Bernie Allen	7184.0	29.4	4.09
125.	Aaron Ward	7056.0	32.9	4.67
126.	Cass Michaels	6952.0	25.5	3.67
127.	Bump Wills	6913.0	33.6	4.86
128.	Billy Gardner	6910.0	35.3	5.10
129.	Ray Mack	6878.0	25.6	3.72
130.	Dick Padden	6870.0	26.6	3.87
131.	Pete Suder	6841.0	26.9	3.93
132.	Mike Andrews	6781.0	25.7	3.79
133.	Emil Verban	6746.0	29.7	4.40
134.	Jerry Adair	6715.0	37.1	5.53
135.	Snuffy Stirnweiss	6687.0	36.3	5.42
136.	Fernando Vina	6641.2	36.5	5.49
137.	Jack Farrell	6600.0	25.0	3.79
138.	Frank LaPorte	6451.0	18.8	2.91
139.	Jimmy Dykes	6389.0	28.5	4.47
140.	Billy Gilbert	6352.0	27.9	4.40
141.	Jackie Robinson	6351.0	37.7	5.94
142.	Pop Smith	6280.0	26.5	4.21
143.	Rob Wilfong	6223.0	33.1	5.32
144.	Billy Ripken	6169.1	26.6	4.30
145.	Wally Backman	6164.0	25.3	4.10
146.	Quilvio Veras	6138.0	32.6	5.31
147.	Yank Robinson	6103.0	16.6	2.72
148.	Burgess Whitehead	6094.0	34.9	5.73
149.	Tim Teufel	6084.2	24.6	4.04
150.	Johnny Rawlings	6036.0	21.2	3.51

	Player	Innings	WS	WS/ 1000
151.	Billy Martin	6035.0	28.2	4.67
152.	Dick Egan	6022.0	21.4	3.56
153.	Danny O'Connell	6021.0	29.7	4.93
154.	Ray Morgan	6002.0	20.5	3.41
155.	Heinie Reitz	5969.0	27.2	4.55
156.	Dots Miller	5899.0	22.7	3.84
157.	Tony Phillips	5883.1	23.7	4.03
158.	Jorge Orta	5796.0	15.3	2.64
159.	Scott Fletcher	5742.1	30.5	5.32
160.	Gary Sutherland	5674.0	18.0	3.18
161.	Julio Franco	5663.0	21.5	3.79
162.	Danny Richardson	5653.0	28.6	5.06
163.	Bobby Young	5616.0	18.5	3.30
164.	Pete Coscarart	5559.0	21.7	3.90
165.	Charlie Neal	5469.0	27.9	5.10
166.	Pete Rose	5450.0	23.3	4.28
167.	Jack Crooks	5444.0	20.4	3.74
168.	Fresco Thompson	5373.0	12.0	2.23
169.	Don Kolloway	5368.0	22.2	4.13
170.	Pete Runnels	5314.0	21.0	3.96
171.	Bill Regan	5285.0	15.4	2.91
172.	Billy Goodman	5183.0	21.5	4.14
173.	Alex Kampouris	5181.0	18.9	3.66
174.	Danny Murtaugh	5175.0	21.5	4.15
175.	Hardy Richardson	5172.0	24.9	4.81
176.	Doug Griffin	5147.0	21.7	4.21
177.	Germany Schaefer	5128.0	18.0	3.50
178.	Jack Brohamer	5109.0	23.1	4.51
179.	Jim Lefebvre	5087.0	24.1	4.74
180.	Wayne Terwilliger	5075.0	23.5	4.63
181.	Hod Ford	5059.0	17.7	3.50
	Freddie Maguire	5059.0	27.3	5.40
183.	Don Gutteridge	5057.0	15.6	3.08
184.	Bill Sweeney	4994.0	15.6	3.13
185.	Jose Oquendo	4975.1	24.8	4.99
186.	Don Heffner	4968.0	17.7	3.56
187.	Randy Velarde	4953.1	22.0	4.43
188.	Jose Offerman	4951.0	22.3	4.50
189.	Joe Gedeon	4944.0	16.4	3.31
190.	Derrel Thomas	4900.0	16.6	3.39
191.	Jerry Browne	4892.2	15.3	3.13
192.	Dave Shean	4872.0	19.1	3.92
193.	Charley Bassett	4858.0	17.0	3.50
194.	Jim Delahanty	4857.0	12.7	2.61
195.	Reddy Mack	4811.0	17.8	3.69
196.	Gil McDougald	4802.0	25.8	5.37
197.	John Hummel	4740.0	17.0	3.60
198.	Joe Quest	4733.0	16.6	3.51
199.	Granny Hamner	4720.0	17.4	3.68
200.	Luis Castillo	4707.1	17.3	3.68

	Player	Innings	WS	WS/ 1000
201.	Sparky Adams	4689.0	22.5	4.80
202.	Frankie Gustine	4688.0	12.7	2.71
203.	Eddie Mayo	4670.0	27.5	5.89
204.	Mike Tyson	4661.0	21.0	4.50
205.	Pep Young	4627.0	17.4	3.77
206.	Pedro Garcia	4623.0	15.5	3.35
207.	Bill Greenwood	4607.0	16.2	3.52
208.	Mariano Duncan	4566.2	18.8	4.12
209.	Steve Yerkes	4562.0	15.6	3.42
210.	Morrie Rath	4535.0	25.5	5.63
211.	Jerry Coleman	4514.0	25.0	5.55
212.	Pat Kelly	4493.0	19.5	4.34
213.	Gene DeMontreville	4490.0	18.0	4.02
214.	Mike Gallego	4466.2	21.6	4.83
215.	Nelson Liriano	4437.1	14.4	3.25
216.	Ken Boswell	4429.0	18.1	4.08
217.	Sam Barkley	4421.0	18.7	4.22
218.	Rabbit Maranville	4408.0	19.4	4.41
219.	Chuck Schilling	4398.0	19.4	4.41
220.	Jeff Frye	4374.1	21.8	4.98
221.	Edgardo Alfonzo	4372.0	21.7	4.95
222.	Monte Ward	4365.0	19.2	4.39
223.	Carlos Garcia	4359.0	16.9	3.87
224.	Odell Hale	4352.0	18.3	4.21
225.	John O'Brien	4290.0	13.1	3.06
226.	Chuck Hiller	4273.0	15.1	3.53
227.	Tony Piet	4259.0	14.6	3.44
228.	Don Johnson	4246.0	18.6	4.37
229.	Bill Cissell	4220.0	14.2	3.38
230.	Buck Herzog	4190.0	14.2	3.38
231.	George Creamer	4183.0	10.8	2.57
232.	Jeff Treadway	4103.0	16.8	4.09
233.	Jerry Kindall	3996.0	17.9	4.48
234.	John Farrell	3988.0	15.2	3.80
235.	Gene Baker	3978.0	14.7	3.69
236.	Johnny Hodapp	3956.0	14.9	3.77
237.	Tim Flannery	3954.2	14.8	3.74
238.	Sam Wise	3892.0	9.0	2.31
239.	Brent Gates	3889.0	15.0	3.85
240.	Cotton Tierney	3869.0	10.3	2.65
241.	Chuck Cottier	3859.0	15.3	3.96
242.	Bill McClellan	3830.0	9.9	2.59
	Davey Williams	3830.0	19.9	5.20
244.	Johnny Berardino	3806.0	12.3	3.24
245.	Stu Martin	3797.0	14.2	3.75
246.	Mickey Witek	3787.0	14.8	3.92
247.	Todd Walker	3780.2	13.8	3.64
248.	Billy Moran	3780.0	17.5	4.62
249.	Bip Roberts	3735.1	15.5	4.15
250.	Jose Vidro	3722.1	10.9	2.92

	Player	Innings	WS	WS/ 1000
251.	Bert Niehoff	3722.0	15.1	4.05
252.	Lenny Randle	3710.0	14.0	3.78
253.	Rabbit Warstler	3699.0	12.5	3.37
254.	Jim Viox	3697.0	8.6	2.32
255.	Ed Abbaticchio	3681.0	11.1	3.01
256.	Dave Nelson	3637.0	14.8	4.07
257.	Rodney Scott	3617.0	15.6	4.32
258.	Bernie Friberg	3564.0	10.3	2.90
259.	Paul Molitor	3517.1	14.7	4.17
260.	Jake Wood	3477.0	11.6	3.34
261.	Marty Perez	3469.0	16.9	4.86
262.	Bob Randall	3417.0	14.7	4.29
263.	Hal Lanier	3411.0	20.9	6.11
264.	Amby McConnell	3401.0	12.1	3.56
265.	Rob Andrews	3393.0	11.6	3.42
266.	Jimmy Brown	3382.0	14.1	4.18
267.	Jay Bell	3349.0	13.5	4.02
268.	Hub Collins	3347.0	13.5	4.03
269.	Donnie Hill	3330.2	11.8	3.56
270.	Luis Sojo	3316.0	15.3	4.62
271.	Miguel Cairo	3287.2	16.4	5.00
272.	Ted Kubiak	3278.0	12.7	3.88
273.	Steve Lombardozzi	3276.0	16.6	5.06
274.	Mark Lewis	3265.0	10.2	3.12
275.	Tim Cullen	3260.0	13.3	4.07
276.	Juan Bonilla	3237.0	12.2	3.78
277.	Larry Milbourne	3227.0	13.7	4.24
278.	Ted Lepcio	3222.0	13.1	4.07
279.	Whitey Alperman	3214.0	12.1	3.77
280.	Jerry Royster	3195.1	13.7	4.30
281.	Jack Perconte	3193.0	12.6	3.93
282.	David Bell	3167.0	13.2	4.17
283.	Ronnie Belliard	3154.0	12.8	4.06
284.	Bobby Adams	3128.0	14.5	4.64
285.	Joey Amalfitano	3122.0	10.4	3.33
286.	Sammy Bohne	3120.0	16.2	5.20
287.	Dave McKay	3089.0	10.1	3.26
288.	Frank Isbell	3082.0	11.8	3.81
	Eddie Miksis	3082.0	10.4	3.38
290.	Bob Ferguson	3078.0	7.5	2.43

Norms for players with:			
10,000 innings	–	–	**4.57**
7,500 - 9,999 innings	–	–	**4.53**
5,000 - 7,499 innings	–	–	**4.21**
2,500 - 4,999 innings	–	–	**3.93**
1,000 - 2,499 innings	–	–	**3.77**
0 - 999 innings	–	–	**3.53**

Fielding Win Shares—Third Base (ordered by Innings)

Player	Innings	WS	WS/ 1000
1. Brooks Robinson	25031.0	106.2	4.24
2. Graig Nettles	20597.1	90.6	4.40
3. Gary Gaetti	19181.0	84.3	4.40
4. Buddy Bell	19137.1	83.3	4.35
5. Mike Schmidt	19028.0	85.9	4.51
6. Eddie Mathews	18990.0	57.3	3.02
7. Wade Boggs	18980.1	72.6	3.82
8. Ron Santo	18756.0	67.0	3.57
9. Tim Wallach	17758.1	80.1	4.51
10. Eddie Yost	17231.0	45.4	2.63
11. Ron Cey	16819.0	60.2	3.58
12. Pie Traynor	16613.0	77.3	4.65
13. Sal Bando	16280.0	52.0	3.20
14. Stan Hack	16243.0	65.2	4.01
15. Aurelio Rodriguez	15916.0	66.2	4.16
16. Mike Higgins	15571.0	40.8	2.62
17. Terry Pendleton	15374.0	66.5	4.32
18. Ken Boyer	15356.0	64.2	4.18
19. Jimmy Collins	15017.0	89.0	5.93
20. Lave Cross	14977.0	90.4	6.03
21. Willie Kamm	14659.0	77.7	5.30
22. George Brett	14513.1	54.1	3.73
23. Larry Gardner	14500.0	72.4	5.00
24. Carney Lansford	14467.2	42.3	2.92
25. George Kell	14393.0	53.3	3.70
26. Ken Caminiti	14252.2	54.0	3.79
27. Robin Ventura	14053.2	60.6	4.31
28. Puddin' Head Jones	14043.0	54.1	3.85
29. Matt Williams	13967.2	51.7	3.70
30. Arlie Latham	13915.0	73.5	5.28
31. Home Run Baker	13877.0	65.3	4.71
32. Harlond Clift	13585.0	61.0	4.49
33. Ken Keltner	13222.0	57.2	4.33
34. Doug DeCinces	13149.0	45.4	3.45
35. Ossie Bluege	12944.0	57.2	4.42
36. Billy Nash	12862.0	70.9	5.51
37. Jimmy Austin	12552.0	49.7	3.96
38. Darrell Evans	12427.0	54.3	4.37
39. Clete Boyer	12342.0	61.3	4.97
40. Harry Steinfeldt	12281.0	54.9	4.47
41. Bill Bradley	12185.0	61.4	5.04
42. Milt Stock	11982.0	45.1	3.77
43. Pinky Whitney	11940.0	51.8	4.34
44. Doug Rader	11918.0	44.0	3.69
45. Bill Madlock	11906.0	31.6	2.65
46. Frank Malzone	11889.0	48.8	4.10
47. Bob Elliott	11777.0	40.9	3.47
48. Heine Groh	11326.0	59.9	5.29
49. Ken Reitz	11173.0	34.8	3.11
50. Billy Shindle	11119.0	58.9	5.30
51. Ken McMullen	11111.0	40.4	3.63
52. Charlie Hayes	10986.2	39.0	3.55
53. Jimmy Dykes	10961.0	44.1	4.02
54. Todd Zeile	10844.1	28.7	2.65
55. Travis Fryman	10770.2	37.8	3.51
56. Art Devlin	10523.0	59.7	5.67
57. Richie Hebner	10459.0	25.4	2.43
58. Mike Mowrey	10399.0	46.0	4.43
59. Don Hoak	10337.0	38.1	3.69
60. Eddie Foster	10336.0	47.9	4.64
61. Bobby Byrne	10238.0	41.2	4.03
62. Steve Buechele	10192.0	39.6	3.89
63. Bill Werber	10021.0	48.4	4.83
64. Dean Palmer	9845.1	18.7	1.90
65. Jerry Denny	9815.0	41.4	4.22
66. Bob Bailey	9775.0	29.1	2.98
67. Brook Jacoby	9681.0	27.2	2.81
68. Red Rolfe	9671.0	40.3	4.17
69. Doc Casey	9663.0	35.9	3.72
70. Denny Lyons	9539.0	34.4	3.60
71. Red Smith	9433.0	35.5	3.77
72. Hick Carpenter	9418.0	35.3	3.75
73. George Pinckney	9337.0	38.2	4.09
74. Bob Aspromonte	9226.0	30.2	3.27
75. Mike Pagliarulo	9201.2	34.5	3.75
76. Toby Harrah	9084.0	22.3	2.45
77. Don Wert	8968.0	33.2	3.71
78. Joe Dugan	8948.0	34.0	3.80
79. Chipper Jones	8781.2	17.4	1.99
80. Vinny Castilla	8773.2	34.0	3.87
81. Don Money	8773.0	34.0	3.88
82. Kevin Seitzer	8733.0	31.4	3.59
83. Ed Sprague	8722.0	24.3	2.78
84. Joe Mulvey	8713.0	34.6	3.98
85. Hans Lobert	8673.0	25.3	2.91
86. Paul Schaal	8659.0	16.7	1.93
87. Larry Parrish	8643.0	22.6	2.61
88. Bill Coughlin	8638.0	34.1	3.95
89. Jeff Cirillo	8592.0	36.5	4.24
90. Jim Tabor	8577.0	25.9	3.02
91. Tommy Leach	8502.0	48.9	5.76
92. Max Alvis	8438.0	24.7	2.92
93. Heinie Zimmerman	8393.0	33.7	4.01
94. Jim Davenport	8262.0	27.2	3.29
95. Ed Charles	8153.0	29.2	3.58
96. Ken Oberkfell	8137.1	27.1	3.32
97. Al Rosen	8137.0	30.0	3.69
98. Marv Owen	8101.0	30.6	3.77
99. Tom Brookens	8078.1	26.5	3.28
100. Howard Johnson	8077.1	19.8	2.45

Player	Innings	WS	WS/1000
101. Bobby Bonilla	8018.1	22.0	2.74
102. Ray Knight	7991.1	26.7	3.34
103. Grady Hatton	7951.0	28.0	3.52
104. Scott Brosius	7873.0	34.6	4.40
105. Harry Lord	7812.0	19.3	2.48
106. Jim Presley	7762.1	20.7	2.67
107. Joe Stripp	7692.0	32.9	4.27
108. Bill Melton	7603.0	21.0	2.76
109. Bill Johnson	7568.0	28.9	3.82
110. Charlie Irwin	7562.0	38.1	5.04
111. Whitey Kurowski	7432.0	28.3	3.81
112. Ossie Vitt	7365.0	40.2	5.45
113. Enos Cabell	7316.0	20.2	2.76
114. Randy Jackson	7308.0	26.5	3.63
115. Hank Majeski	7268.0	29.9	4.12
116. Deacon White	7243.0	25.5	3.53
117. Charlie Deal	7240.0	38.1	5.26
118. Art Whitney	7218.0	38.0	5.27
119. Les Bell	7078.0	23.5	3.32
120. Chris Sabo	7056.2	23.7	3.35
121. Roy Howell	7037.0	19.9	2.82
122. Bill Kuehne	6985.0	34.5	4.93
George Moriarty	6985.0	32.1	4.60
124. Freddy Lindstrom	6958.0	32.2	4.63
125. Paul Molitor	6912.1	25.2	3.65
126. Rich Rollins	6871.0	18.0	2.62
127. Andy Carey	6847.0	25.2	3.68
128. Wayne Gross	6837.0	18.4	2.69
129. Kelly Gruber	6828.1	26.7	3.91
130. Harry Wolverton	6723.0	27.4	4.07
131. Frank Hankinson	6704.0	31.2	4.66
132. Eddie Grant	6689.0	27.7	4.15
133. Joe Randa	6668.2	19.9	2.99
134. Phil Garner	6637.1	24.0	3.61
135. Andy High	6624.0	24.1	3.64
136. Tony Boeckel	6620.0	19.9	3.00
137. Luis Salazar	6616.1	21.0	3.18
138. Tony Perez	6538.0	23.2	3.55
139. John McGraw	6530.0	32.8	5.02
140. Dave Hollins	6516.0	14.9	2.29
141. Scott Rolen	6450.0	27.3	4.23
142. Bob Jones	6415.0	26.8	4.18
143. Bubba Phillips	6400.0	21.1	3.30
144. Bill Joyce	6368.0	15.4	2.42
145. Ned Williamson	6342.0	34.8	5.49
146. Wayne Garrett	6338.0	26.8	4.23
147. Marty McManus	6300.0	28.5	4.53
148. Tom Burns	6271.0	33.2	5.30
149. Gene Freese	6251.0	17.6	2.81
150. Eric Soderholm	6224.0	25.5	4.09

Player	Innings	WS	WS/1000
151. Harmon Killebrew	6203.0	13.2	2.12
152. Rico Petrocelli	6131.0	25.0	4.07
153. Babe Pinelli	6027.0	32.4	5.37
154. Lee Handley	6021.0	23.4	3.88
155. Lee Tannehill	5980.0	39.3	6.58
156. Ezra Sutton	5959.0	29.0	4.87
157. Buddy Lewis	5930.0	22.8	3.84
158. Bob Dillinger	5883.0	13.7	2.32
159. Sammy Hale	5874.0	26.9	4.58
160. Cookie Lavagetto	5862.0	21.8	3.72
161. Cal Ripken Jr.	5731.1	21.2	3.70
162. Wid Conroy	5706.0	22.7	3.98
163. Joe Foy	5701.0	18.4	3.23
164. Joe Sewell	5667.0	26.1	4.61
165. Dick Allen	5653.0	16.8	2.96
166. Butch Hobson	5632.0	12.0	2.13
167. Jim Ray Hart	5610.0	17.1	3.04
168. Billy Cox	5605.0	23.8	4.25
169. Jim Gilliam	5587.0	19.7	3.52
170. Pinky May	5538.0	26.3	4.74
171. Hank Thompson	5503.0	19.9	3.62
172. Johnny Vergez	5476.0	17.7	3.23
173. Lew Riggs	5439.0	22.0	4.04
174. Bobby Adams	5436.0	19.3	3.55
175. Bob Horner	5390.0	18.0	3.35
176. Jim Donnelly	5387.0	18.3	3.40
177. Vance Law	5293.1	13.5	2.54
178. Frank O'Rourke	5241.0	18.6	3.55
179. Charley Smith	5205.0	14.9	2.86
180. Terry Turner	5146.0	27.2	5.29
181. Wally Gilbert	5138.0	23.6	4.60
182. Jack Howell	5124.2	17.6	3.44
183. Pete Rose	5058.0	15.4	3.04
184. Bill Mueller	4994.1	14.0	2.80
185. Fred Hartman	4988.0	11.8	2.37
186. Chuck Dressen	4875.0	25.1	5.15
187. Dave Magadan	4845.1	14.7	3.03
188. Jim Morrison	4833.1	11.0	2.27
189. Mike Blowers	4822.0	11.4	2.36
190. Charlie Reilly	4790.0	27.3	5.69
191. Rance Mulliniks	4775.2	16.5	3.46
192. Bill McKechnie	4766.0	22.4	4.69
193. Ray Jablonski	4755.0	9.2	1.93
194. Sean Berry	4735.0	15.3	3.24
195. Steve Ontiveros	4723.0	14.5	3.07
Gene Robertson	4723.0	14.7	3.11
197. Pete Ward	4710.0	13.4	2.85
198. Jeff King	4707.1	16.8	3.57
199. Chippy McGarr	4677.0	23.1	4.94
200. Leo Gomez	4664.2	14.7	3.15

	Player	Innings	WS	WS/ 1000
201.	Rube Lutzke	4659.0	20.1	4.31
202.	Doug Baird	4651.0	17.3	3.72
203.	George Davis	4642.0	22.8	4.91
204.	Edgar Martinez	4605.1	12.7	2.77
205.	Sparky Adams	4567.0	18.9	4.15
206.	Russ Davis	4531.2	10.2	2.24
207.	Troy Glaus	4510.2	14.2	3.14
208.	Bob Kennedy	4493.0	17.4	3.87
209.	Hubie Brooks	4488.0	13.5	3.01
210.	Ray Boone	4358.0	15.3	3.51
211.	Joe Torre	4321.0	9.2	2.12
212.	Jerry Royster	4311.1	17.5	4.06
213.	Billy Lauder	4216.0	12.5	2.97
214.	Howard Shanks	4201.0	18.1	4.31
215.	Bernie Friberg	4190.0	22.3	5.32
216.	Patsy Tebeau	4167.0	19.7	4.73
217.	Lenny Randle	4160.0	12.5	3.00
218.	Fernando Tatis	4154.2	10.7	2.58
219.	Mike Shannon	4151.0	11.9	2.86
220.	Adrian Beltre	4117.2	13.3	3.23
221.	Jim Thome	4107.0	12.4	3.02
222.	Bill Stein	4081.0	9.4	2.30
223.	Buck Herzog	4041.0	23.7	5.86
224.	Johnny Pesky	4009.0	17.1	4.25
225.	Gary Sheffield	3992.1	12.3	3.09
226.	Frankie Frisch	3976.0	20.3	5.10
227.	Roy Hartzell	3963.0	12.7	3.20
228.	Cecil Travis	3952.0	16.7	4.22
229.	Jimmy Johnston	3948.0	14.5	3.67
230.	Buck Weaver	3905.0	16.8	4.31
231.	Floyd Baker	3898.0	15.3	3.92
232.	Jimmy Burke	3860.0	14.9	3.87
233.	Hector Lopez	3857.0	11.7	3.02
234.	Odell Hale	3851.0	16.7	4.34
235.	Fred Haney	3834.0	16.6	4.34
236.	Dave Chalk	3819.0	13.7	3.58
237.	Dave Brain	3817.0	16.9	4.43
238.	Scott Cooper	3814.0	12.1	3.18
239.	Gil McDougald	3797.0	14.9	3.92
240.	Shane Andrews	3791.2	16.4	4.33
241.	Tony Cuccinello	3789.0	12.4	3.27
242.	Fritz Maisel	3775.0	12.7	3.36
243.	Sid Gordon	3763.0	11.4	3.02
244.	Dude Esterbrook	3699.0	19.2	5.19
245.	Mark Christman	3697.0	20.9	5.64
246.	Steve Mesner	3694.0	17.5	4.73
247.	Bobby Wallace	3661.0	24.7	6.73
248.	Billy Clingman	3636.0	24.0	6.59
249.	Mike Muldoon	3624.0	13.3	3.66
250.	Pepper Martin	3605.0	13.1	3.63

	Player	Innings	WS	WS/ 1000
251.	Barry McCormick	3570.0	13.5	3.79
252.	Tim Hulett	3564.1	12.8	3.59
253.	Chris Brown	3545.2	9.2	2.59
254.	Jumbo Davis	3527.0	11.8	3.35
255.	Woody English	3475.0	17.4	5.02
256.	Mike Cubbage	3454.0	11.7	3.37
257.	Eric Chavez	3449.1	11.9	3.46
258.	Eddie Kasko	3426.0	11.9	3.48
259.	John Castino	3416.0	14.9	4.36
260.	Don Gutteridge	3408.0	12.1	3.56
261.	Phil Nevin	3405.2	10.2	2.99
262.	Scott Leius	3394.2	11.4	3.35
263.	Tony Taylor	3359.0	12.8	3.82
264.	Ed Gremminger	3353.0	15.9	4.74
265.	Sammy Strang	3338.0	14.2	4.26
	Pete Suder	3338.0	13.1	3.91
267.	Garth Iorg	3328.2	11.5	3.44
268.	Ed Spiezio	3297.0	10.6	3.21
269.	Frankie Gustine	3288.0	13.6	4.15
270.	Frank Thomas	3264.0	5.5	1.68
271.	Ed Lennox	3263.0	11.4	3.49
272.	Craig Paquette	3249.2	7.6	2.35
273.	Howard Freigau	3236.0	11.9	3.68
274.	Fred Hatfield	3225.0	12.9	4.01
275.	Aaron Boone	3220.1	13.0	4.04
276.	Mike Lowell	3194.1	10.8	3.38
277.	Joe Werrick	3191.0	8.1	2.53
278.	Rick Schu	3169.0	7.9	2.49
279.	Corey Koskie	3156.0	13.7	4.34
280.	Willie Greene	3140.2	11.3	3.60
281.	Craig Worthington	3132.0	9.8	3.12
282.	Ernie Courtney	3126.0	9.5	3.03
283.	Dave Roberts	3088.0	9.3	3.01
284.	Tony Phillips	3072.2	9.2	2.98
285.	George Perring	3061.0	12.4	4.06
286.	Denis Menke	3054.0	10.3	3.37
287.	Edgardo Alfonzo	3052.0	11.5	3.75
288.	Art Howe	3043.0	12.1	3.97
289.	Bill Brubaker	3033.0	12.5	4.12
	Pedro Guerrero	3033.0	9.7	3.19

Norms for players with:			
10,000 innings	–	–	**4.13**
7,500 - 9,999 innings	–	–	**3.44**
5,000 - 7,499 innings	–	–	**3.83**
2,500 - 4,999 innings	–	–	**3.58**
1,000 - 2,499 innings	–	–	**3.55**
0 - 999 innings	–	–	**3.16**

Fielding Win Shares—Shortstop (ordered by Innings)

Player	Innings	WS	WS/ 1000
1. Luis Aparicio	22439.0	122.8	5.47
2. Ozzie Smith	21778.0	139.8	6.42
3. Cal Ripken Jr.	20244.0	115.2	5.69
4. Luke Appling	19498.0	105.3	5.40
5. Rabbit Maranville	19191.0	123.2	6.42
6. Larry Bowa	18928.0	88.1	4.65
7. Bill Dahlen	18754.0	128.0	6.82
8. Dave Concepcion	18354.2	116.9	6.37
9. Tommy Corcoran	18274.0	114.6	6.27
10. Alan Trammell	18169.0	91.6	5.04
11. Bert Campaneris	17878.0	98.6	5.51
12. Pee Wee Reese	17754.0	107.3	6.04
13. Roger Peckinpaugh	17515.0	106.6	6.09
14. Honus Wagner	16971.0	116.9	6.89
15. Roy McMillan	16916.0	100.1	5.92
16. Garry Templeton	16818.2	88.2	5.24
17. Donie Bush	16637.0	76.6	4.60
18. Dave Bancroft	16591.0	102.9	6.20
19. Don Kessinger	16503.0	73.2	4.44
20. Dick Groat	16211.0	95.7	5.90
21. Joe Cronin	16069.0	94.8	5.90
22. Bobby Wallace	16046.0	87.5	5.46
23. Leo Cardenas	15951.0	91.9	5.76
24. Herman Long	15916.0	101.9	6.40
25. Chris Speier	15812.0	85.7	5.42
26. Ozzie Guillen	15782.1	87.7	5.56
27. Alfredo Griffin	15729.1	81.6	5.19
28. Joe Tinker	15406.0	112.2	7.28
29. Barry Larkin	15315.0	92.0	6.01
30. Mark Belanger	15302.0	102.8	6.72
31. Ed Brinkman	15058.0	80.7	5.36
32. Omar Vizquel	15021.0	76.6	5.10
33. Bill Russell	14833.0	76.7	5.17
34. Dick Bartell	14783.0	84.9	5.74
35. Germany Smith	14658.0	100.5	6.86
36. Monte Cross	14634.0	66.0	4.51
37. Mickey Doolan	14468.0	99.2	6.86
38. Greg Gagne	14437.1	90.3	6.26
39. George McBride	14378.0	87.8	6.11
40. Jack Glasscock	14288.0	86.0	6.02
41. Everett Scott	14189.0	99.0	6.98
42. Phil Rizzuto	13614.0	97.2	7.14
43. Ed McKean	13569.0	44.5	3.28
44. Tony Fernandez	13498.2	83.9	6.22
45. Lou Boudreau	13431.0	87.2	6.49
46. Billy Jurges	13402.0	77.6	5.79
47. Maury Wills	13335.0	74.7	5.60
48. Marty Marion	13320.0	97.5	7.32
49. Frankie Crosetti	13228.0	77.8	5.88
50. Freddie Patek	13180.0	70.3	5.34

Player	Innings	WS	WS/ 1000
51. Arky Vaughan	13064.0	72.4	5.55
52. Robin Yount	13011.0	66.3	5.09
53. Tim Foli	12884.0	68.0	5.28
54. Jay Bell	12858.0	63.0	4.90
55. Art Fletcher	12694.0	89.4	7.04
56. Leo Durocher	12607.0	78.5	6.23
57. Wally Gerber	12400.0	68.5	5.52
58. Al Dark	12284.0	62.1	5.06
59. Eddie Miller	12205.0	68.3	5.60
60. Jim Fregosi	12129.0	55.7	4.59
61. Johnny Logan	12076.0	68.4	5.66
62. George Davis	12058.0	64.7	5.36
63. Walt Weiss	11933.2	59.8	5.01
64. Mike Bordick	11786.1	59.1	5.01
65. Vern Stephens	11761.0	62.9	5.35
66. Bucky Dent	11699.0	69.5	5.94
67. Bud Harrelson	11619.0	66.4	5.71
68. Travis Jackson	11544.0	65.8	5.70
69. Rafael Ramirez	11534.2	48.7	4.22
70. Spike Owen	11393.0	55.9	4.91
71. Dick Schofield	11378.1	61.7	5.42
72. Shawon Dunston	11301.2	50.9	4.50
73. Royce Clayton	11289.2	61.0	5.40
74. Eddie Joost	11272.0	56.6	5.02
75. Zoilo Versalles	10904.0	56.4	5.17
76. Bones Ely	10848.0	66.7	6.15
77. Joe Sewell	10794.0	63.4	5.87
78. Ivan DeJesus	10786.0	42.6	3.95
79. Billy Rogell	10516.0	67.2	6.39
80. Chico Carrasquel	10383.0	61.1	5.89
81. Rick Burleson	10311.0	73.9	7.17
82. Freddy Parent	10003.0	53.5	5.35
83. Ernie Banks	9946.0	44.8	4.51
84. Roger Metzger	9930.0	43.4	4.37
85. Ron Hansen	9850.0	59.7	6.06
86. Doc Lavan	9795.0	49.3	5.04
87. Lyn Lary	9758.0	49.2	5.05
88. Craig Reynolds	9643.0	55.0	5.71
89. Al Bridwell	9505.0	47.3	4.98
90. Ivy Olson	9383.0	40.6	4.33
91. Gary DiSarcina	9304.0	44.5	4.78
92. Dickie Thon	9199.0	49.4	5.37
93. Glenn Wright	8970.0	52.0	5.80
94. Frank Taveras	8899.0	37.9	4.26
95. Dal Maxvill	8872.0	64.3	7.24
96. Buddy Kerr	8836.0	44.9	5.09
97. Roy Smalley	8712.2	48.1	5.53
98. Jeff Blauser	8583.1	37.0	4.31
99. Chick Galloway	8559.0	36.9	4.31
100. Ray Chapman	8552.0	46.1	5.40

	Player	Innings	WS	WS/ 1000
101.	Arthur Irwin	8452.0	46.9	5.55
102.	Kid Elberfeld	8220.0	48.4	5.89
103.	Derek Jeter	8199.0	33.7	4.11
104.	Bobby Wine	8196.0	46.1	5.62
105.	Joe DeMaestri	8177.0	33.7	4.12
106.	Gene Alley	8170.0	44.4	5.43
107.	Alex Rodriguez	8169.2	39.0	4.77
108.	Eddie Bressoud	8121.0	34.7	4.27
109.	Shorty Fuller	8104.0	43.0	5.31
110.	Jose Uribe	8036.2	43.2	5.37
111.	Granny Hamner	8016.0	49.0	6.11
112.	Johnnie LeMaster	7890.0	30.1	3.81
113.	Hughie Jennings	7845.0	60.2	7.68
114.	Alex S. Gonzalez	7713.0	46.5	6.03
115.	Jack Barry	7693.0	37.3	4.85
116.	Tony Kubek	7551.0	46.1	6.11
117.	Jose Valentin	7423.0	40.2	5.42
118.	Pat Meares	7388.0	31.1	4.21
119.	Heinie Wagner	7372.0	36.9	5.00
120.	Skeeter Newsome	7371.0	37.6	5.10
121.	Buck Weaver	7345.0	45.4	6.18
122.	Monte Ward	7253.0	48.9	6.74
123.	Tom Veryzer	7245.0	33.8	4.67
124.	Kevin Elster	7231.1	42.0	5.81
125.	Kevin Stocker	7155.2	38.0	5.31
126.	Red Kress	7115.0	35.6	5.01
127.	Tommy Thevenow	7087.0	37.5	5.29
128.	Bill Gleason	7066.0	28.0	3.97
129.	Edgar Renteria	7049.1	33.7	4.78
130.	Hod Ford	6981.0	36.1	5.18
131.	Ricky Gutierrez	6935.2	28.7	4.14
132.	Woody English	6922.0	35.4	5.12
133.	Frank Duffy	6912.0	35.1	5.08
134.	Frank Fennelly	6823.0	37.2	5.45
135.	Rey Sanchez	6774.1	41.9	6.18
136.	Gene Michael	6762.0	30.1	4.45
137.	Rico Petrocelli	6719.0	40.8	6.07
138.	Denis Menke	6709.0	26.6	3.96
139.	Chico Fernandez	6690.0	37.9	5.66
140.	Toby Harrah	6684.0	29.3	4.38
141.	Charlie Hollocher	6664.0	33.2	4.99
142.	Felix Fermin	6593.0	30.1	4.57
143.	Scott Fletcher	6591.0	32.5	4.92
144.	Chris Gomez	6571.1	24.8	3.78
145.	Roy Smalley	6538.0	24.6	3.76
146.	Terry Turner	6518.0	38.4	5.89
147.	Harvey Kuenn	6499.0	25.5	3.92
148.	Heinie Sand	6460.0	24.8	3.84
149.	Rey Ordonez	6405.1	40.5	6.32
150.	Charley O'Leary	6374.0	29.2	4.58

	Player	Innings	WS	WS/ 1000
151.	Mark Koenig	6312.0	35.5	5.62
152.	Cecil Travis	6175.0	27.7	4.49
153.	Johnny Lipon	6172.0	31.0	5.02
154.	Julio Franco	6138.0	23.2	3.79
155.	Larry Brown	6046.0	34.0	5.63
156.	Billy Myers	6042.0	29.9	4.94
157.	Rabbit Warstler	5987.0	27.5	4.60
158.	Jose Vizcaino	5982.1	31.0	5.18
159.	Larry Kopf	5942.0	19.2	3.23
160.	Deivi Cruz	5923.2	27.8	4.69
161.	U.L. Washington	5877.0	28.2	4.79
162.	Charlie Gelbert	5788.0	38.3	6.61
163.	Billy Urbanski	5771.0	22.2	3.85
164.	Don Buddin	5768.0	22.5	3.91
165.	Neifi Perez	5744.1	38.4	6.69
166.	Rich Aurilia	5641.2	29.3	5.20
167.	Topper Rigney	5618.0	21.2	3.77
168.	George Strickland	5614.0	32.3	5.75
169.	Jack Rowe	5608.0	19.0	3.38
170.	Eric McNair	5601.0	24.6	4.39
171.	Enzo Hernandez	5587.0	22.5	4.03
172.	Bill Knickerbocker	5559.0	25.4	4.57
173.	Rafael Belliard	5540.2	24.0	4.32
174.	Kurt Stillwell	5510.0	20.0	3.64
175.	Jose Pagan	5441.0	25.5	4.69
176.	Luis A. Rivera	5415.1	23.8	4.40
177.	Bob Allen	5396.0	41.7	7.73
178.	Willie Miranda	5386.0	30.3	5.62
179.	Hal Lanier	5364.0	32.4	6.04
180.	Mark Grudzielanek	5352.1	21.8	4.08
181.	Miguel Tejada	5351.2	27.0	5.05
182.	Dick McAuliffe	5350.0	24.7	4.62
183.	Nomar Garciaparra	5331.0	27.5	5.16
184.	Jackie Tavener	5307.0	30.0	5.66
185.	Sonny Jackson	5287.0	21.0	3.97
186.	Ruben Amaro	5246.0	23.5	4.48
187.	Rudy Hulswitt	5207.0	18.6	3.57
188.	Andre Rodgers	5196.0	19.6	3.77
189.	Johnny Pesky	5190.0	31.2	6.02
190.	Ernie Johnson	5158.0	29.7	5.76
191.	Rafael Santana	5134.2	28.4	5.54
192.	Dick Schofield	5113.0	24.1	4.71
193.	Jose Offerman	5065.0	14.4	2.85
194.	Davy Force	5047.0	28.6	5.66
195.	Eddie Lake	5040.0	18.2	3.61
196.	Lennie Merullo	5017.0	21.1	4.20
197.	Sam Wise	4983.0	25.1	5.04
198.	Andujar Cedeno	4961.1	15.9	3.21
199.	Frank Shugart	4871.0	17.0	3.50
200.	Dale Berra	4849.1	27.9	5.76

Player	Innings	WS	WS/ 1000
201. John Valentin	4807.0	28.6	5.95
202. Candy Nelson	4750.0	16.4	3.45
203. Virgil Stallcup	4729.0	24.1	5.10
204. Alvaro Espinoza	4689.0	26.2	5.60
205. Sadie Houck	4656.0	21.9	4.70
206. Glenn Hoffman	4655.2	24.3	5.23
207. Dick Howser	4643.0	18.8	4.06
208. Daryl Spencer	4632.0	19.3	4.16
209. Andres Thomas	4619.2	17.5	3.79
210. Mario Guerrero	4577.0	21.7	4.74
211. Steve Jeltz	4520.2	22.2	4.90
212. John Sullivan	4512.0	17.2	3.80
213. Darrel Chaney	4494.0	20.3	4.51
214. Woodie Held	4489.0	24.0	5.34
215. Bill Almon	4448.1	20.4	4.59
216. Alex Grammas	4442.0	21.0	4.73
217. Jose Hernandez	4369.2	19.3	4.42
218. Phil Lewis	4362.0	12.1	2.77
219. Sam Dente	4361.0	20.2	4.63
220. Eddie Kasko	4317.0	21.4	4.95
221. Joe Boley	4244.0	22.3	5.26
222. Mariano Duncan	4222.2	18.2	4.32
223. Tom Burns	4193.0	15.5	3.69
224. Bob Lillis	4145.0	19.4	4.69
225. Billy Hunter	4140.0	22.8	5.51
226. Jim Mason	4131.0	18.0	4.37
227. John Peters	4125.0	19.3	4.69
228. Fred Stanley	4106.0	18.5	4.51
229. Manuel Lee	4069.1	17.6	4.33
230. Buck Herzog	4013.0	23.2	5.77
231. Ike Caveney	3943.0	17.6	4.46
232. Ned Williamson	3925.0	12.2	3.12
233. Bill White	3904.0	18.5	4.75
234. Jackie Hernandez	3870.0	14.9	3.86
235. Danny Thompson	3856.0	13.5	3.50
236. Ray Boone	3850.0	21.0	5.46
237. Pete Runnels	3849.0	20.4	5.31
238. Jim Levey	3818.0	12.7	3.31
239. Mario Mendoza	3785.0	17.1	4.52
240. Stan Rojek	3762.0	17.9	4.75
241. Solly Hemus	3760.0	18.1	4.82
242. Rey Quinones	3753.0	15.2	4.06
243. Hal Rhyne	3719.0	18.1	4.87
244. Jimmy Esmond	3706.0	17.7	4.77
245. Marty Perez	3705.0	12.6	3.40
246. Bill Cissell	3700.0	16.8	4.54
247. Orlando Cabrera	3687.2	24.3	6.59
248. Woody Woodward	3671.0	15.9	4.34
249. Lonny Frey	3648.0	12.0	3.30
250. Joe Koppe	3626.0	16.9	4.65

Player	Innings	WS	WS/ 1000
251. Rob Picciolo	3598.0	15.0	4.18
252. Ray Oyler	3582.0	18.4	5.15
253. Dale Sveum	3541.1	14.3	4.02
254. Swede Risberg	3539.0	19.6	5.55
255. Dave Anderson	3519.0	18.5	5.26
256. Wayne Causey	3516.0	14.3	4.08
257. Arnold Hauser	3503.0	10.6	3.04
258. Bobby Bragan	3433.0	10.9	3.17
259. Alex Gonzalez	3429.2	10.4	3.04
260. Bill Spiers	3420.0	14.5	4.25
261. Ed Abbaticchio	3411.0	10.2	2.98
262. Cristian Guzman	3391.0	16.7	4.91
263. Jimmy Cooney	3381.0	20.9	6.17
264. Tom Fisher	3380.0	9.3	2.76
265. Wil Cordero	3266.2	11.8	3.60
266. Billy Clingman	3261.0	17.3	5.30
267. Ed Caskin	3249.0	17.1	5.25
268. Gene DeMontreville	3245.0	17.2	5.29
269. Benji Gil	3241.1	15.9	4.91
270. Hector Torres	3227.0	15.1	4.67
271. Hubie Brooks	3223.1	8.2	2.53
272. Lee Tannehill	3223.0	21.6	6.71
273. Rocky Bridges	3221.0	18.2	5.66
274. Bobby Meacham	3196.1	16.8	5.26
275. Luis Gomez	3177.0	13.6	4.29
276. Billy Klaus	3171.0	15.9	5.00
277. Dick Culler	3166.0	15.4	4.86
278. Rogers Hornsby	3147.0	12.4	3.95
279. Rick Auerbach	3143.0	14.4	4.58
280. Roberto Pena	3102.0	11.3	3.64
281. Tim Bogar	3090.2	18.0	5.82
282. Desi Relaford	3069.0	11.7	3.83
283. Frank Scheibeck	3056.0	12.0	3.94
284. Tom Foley	3050.1	14.6	4.79
285. Mark Christman	3048.0	12.0	3.95
286. Paul Radford	3046.0	14.9	4.88
Whitey Wietelmann	3046.0	14.7	4.83
288. Tom Tresh	3026.0	11.5	3.80
289. Kiko Garcia	3015.0	17.8	5.90
290. Skeeter Webb	3003.0	17.0	5.68

Norms for players with:			
10,000 innings	–	–	**5.72**
7,500 - 9,999 innings	–	–	**5.20**
5,000 - 7,499 innings	–	–	**4.88**
2,500 - 4,999 innings	–	–	**4.56**
1,000 - 2,499 innings	–	–	**4.35**
0 - 999 innings	–	–	**4.09**

Fielding Win Shares—Outfield (ordered by Innings)

Player	Innings	WS	WS/ 1000
1. Ty Cobb	25834.0	82.6	3.20
2. Willie Mays	25205.0	103.6	4.11
3. Hank Aaron	23951.0	63.0	2.63
4. Tris Speaker	23880.0	117.8	4.93
5. Rickey Henderson	23290.1	56.3	2.42
6. Lou Brock	21854.0	49.0	2.24
7. Max Carey	21683.0	94.8	4.37
8. Dave Winfield	21333.0	41.0	1.92
9. Vada Pinson	20858.0	69.3	3.32
10. Al Kaline	20851.0	56.4	2.70
11. Roberto Clemente	20764.0	59.5	2.87
12. Zack Wheat	20589.0	58.1	2.82
13. Harry Hooper	20314.0	53.1	2.61
14. Willie Davis	20202.0	78.3	3.88
15. Andre Dawson	20115.1	62.2	3.09
16. Mel Ott	20044.0	44.9	2.24
17. Sam Crawford	19934.0	47.2	2.37
18. Paul Waner	19899.0	60.2	3.03
19. Tony Gwynn	19894.2	45.1	2.26
20. Sam Rice	19416.0	54.2	2.79
21. Babe Ruth	19374.0	44.3	2.29
22. Fred Clarke	19334.0	64.1	3.32
23. Barry Bonds	19203.0	43.3	2.26
24. Goose Goslin	19105.0	49.3	2.58
25. Ted Williams	18854.0	44.0	2.34
26. Doc Cramer	18806.0	72.5	3.85
27. Richie Ashburn	18683.0	73.8	3.95
28. Al Simmons	18638.0	69.0	3.70
29. Brett Butler	18540.2	57.5	3.10
30. Frank Robinson	18371.0	47.3	2.58
31. Billy Williams	18329.0	43.4	2.37
32. Jimmy Sheckard	18160.0	66.3	3.65
33. Tim Raines	18158.0	51.2	2.82
34. Jesse Burkett	18130.0	52.9	2.92
35. Jose Cruz	18083.0	48.8	2.70
36. Dwight Evans	18010.0	50.8	2.82
37. Carl Yastrzemski	17852.0	47.2	2.65
38. Willie Keeler	17851.0	47.8	2.68
39. Reggie Jackson	17736.0	40.4	2.28
40. Mickey Mantle	17462.0	55.1	3.15
41. Enos Slaughter	17317.0	49.6	2.86
42. Jimmy Ryan	17175.0	54.1	3.15
43. Clyde Milan	17133.0	55.0	3.21
44. Amos Otis	17060.0	72.5	4.25
45. Edd Roush	16519.0	58.1	3.52
46. Chet Lemon	16510.0	63.2	3.83
47. Willie Wilson	16429.0	67.8	4.13
48. Sherry Magee	16390.0	44.4	2.71
49. George Burns	16303.0	46.9	2.88
50. Duke Snider	16272.0	54.8	3.37

Player	Innings	WS	WS/ 1000
51. Paul O'Neill	16271.2	41.4	2.54
52. Stan Musial	16208.0	49.7	3.07
53. Dave Parker	16143.2	42.4	2.63
54. Dale Murphy	16141.0	45.2	2.80
55. Del Ennis	16139.0	32.4	2.01
56. Jimmy Wynn	16064.0	44.1	2.75
57. Heinie Manush	16007.0	38.9	2.43
58. Willie McGee	15895.1	47.6	3.00
59. Patsy Donovan	15878.0	31.6	1.99
60. George Van Haltren	15863.0	46.0	2.90
61. Kiki Cuyler	15849.0	47.7	3.01
Lloyd Waner	15849.0	68.6	4.33
63. Joe Medwick	15829.0	44.2	2.79
64. Fred Lynn	15826.1	51.9	3.28
65. George Foster	15732.0	39.3	2.50
66. Fielder Jones	15700.0	67.4	4.29
67. Devon White	15689.2	58.5	3.73
68. Tom Brown	15647.0	40.1	2.56
69. Gary Matthews	15622.0	32.1	2.06
70. Wally Moses	15554.0	36.1	2.32
71. Dummy Hoy	15505.0	48.9	3.15
72. Cy Williams	15439.0	45.9	2.97
73. Bobby Veach	15343.0	47.0	3.06
74. Bob Johnson	15307.0	35.4	2.31
75. Bobby Bonds	15212.0	42.7	2.81
76. Dusty Baker	15176.0	41.0	2.70
77. Joe DiMaggio	15093.0	60.5	4.01
78. George Hendrick	15066.0	36.5	2.42
79. Jose Cardenal	15001.0	42.3	2.82
80. Johnny Callison	14997.0	40.8	2.72
81. Steve Finley	14969.1	49.7	3.32
82. Dixie Walker	14792.0	44.2	2.99
83. Rocky Colavito	14788.0	36.7	2.48
84. Cesar Cedeno	14785.0	49.6	3.35
Wildfire Schulte	14785.0	42.3	2.86
86. Kirby Puckett	14692.2	58.4	3.97
87. Ken Griffey Jr.	14677.1	51.1	3.48
Sammy Sosa	14677.1	35.6	2.43
89. Hugh Duffy	14638.0	58.3	3.99
90. Dode Paskert	14634.0	51.7	3.54
91. Joe Carter	14597.0	37.9	2.59
92. Rusty Staub	14588.0	29.1	1.99
93. Reggie Smith	14474.0	48.5	3.35
94. Minnie Minoso	14370.0	39.6	2.76
95. Ken Griffey Sr.	14359.0	30.3	2.11
96. Roy White	14284.0	34.9	2.44
97. Tom Brunansky	14279.2	38.6	2.71
98. Gee Walker	14273.0	39.9	2.80
99. Rick Monday	14253.0	43.1	3.02
100. Charlie Jamieson	14186.0	35.7	2.51

Player	Innings	WS	WS/ 1000
101. Carl Furillo	14171.0	42.4	2.99
102. Marquis Grissom	14155.2	66.6	4.70
103. Claudell Washington	14137.1	31.8	2.25
104. Curt Flood	14107.0	75.1	5.32
105. Bobby Murcer	14050.0	39.2	2.79
106. Paul Blair	14049.0	64.0	4.55
107. Brady Anderson	13959.1	37.7	2.70
108. Gus Bell	13892.0	31.6	2.28
109. Garry Maddox	13878.0	58.0	4.18
110. Harry Heilmann	13846.0	24.8	1.79
111. Billy Hamilton	13814.0	49.0	3.55
112. Chuck Klein	13739.0	29.4	2.14
113. Bill Bruton	13712.0	48.6	3.55
114. Earl Averill	13661.0	54.5	3.99
115. Kip Selbach	13518.0	30.0	2.22
116. Jim Rice	13511.2	35.6	2.63
117. Bing Miller	13417.0	38.2	2.85
118. Bill Virdon	13400.0	53.6	4.00
119. Ellis Burks	13358.1	40.4	3.02
120. Jimmy Piersall	13254.0	59.6	4.50
121. Sammy West	13224.0	55.6	4.20
122. Lloyd Moseby	13222.0	50.0	3.78
123. Jack Tobin	13099.0	31.0	2.36
124. Ben Chapman	12944.0	38.7	2.99
125. Ken Singleton	12939.0	30.1	2.32
126. Luis Gonzalez	12918.1	33.7	2.61
127. Mike Tiernan	12911.0	31.0	2.40
128. Dante Bichette	12893.0	34.1	2.64
129. Mike Griffin	12854.0	48.0	3.74
130. Bobby Thomson	12843.0	39.3	3.06
131. Elmer Flick	12758.0	31.8	2.49
132. Gene Woodling	12716.0	30.7	2.42
133. Roy Thomas	12709.0	44.5	3.50
134. Kevin McReynolds	12683.0	35.4	2.79
135. Larry Doby	12620.0	45.8	3.63
136. Ruben Sierra	12616.1	26.0	2.06
137. Bill Nicholson	12557.0	26.3	2.09
138. Joe Kelley	12537.0	44.7	3.57
139. Andy Pafko	12536.0	37.7	3.01
140. Duffy Lewis	12512.0	40.1	3.21
141. Ginger Beaumont	12498.0	39.0	3.12
142. Sam Thompson	12468.0	28.4	2.28
143. Steve Brodie	12401.0	51.1	4.12
144. Rick Manning	12386.2	34.6	2.79
145. Felipe Alou	12320.0	32.6	2.65
146. Dave Philley	12254.0	36.1	2.94
147. Ray Lankford	12249.0	36.2	2.95
148. Ben Oglivie	12216.0	24.8	2.03
149. Andy Van Slyke	12141.0	42.4	3.49
150. Jim O'Rourke	12111.0	32.3	2.66

Player	Innings	WS	WS/ 1000
151. Dom DiMaggio	12092.0	56.3	4.66
152. Al Oliver	12041.0	37.9	3.15
153. Jackie Jensen	11999.0	32.7	2.72
154. Bernie Williams	11985.1	46.6	3.89
155. Baby Doll Jacobson	11932.0	42.9	3.59
156. Tilly Walker	11906.0	30.6	2.57
157. John Titus	11842.0	25.3	2.14
158. Joe Vosmik	11832.0	36.3	3.06
159. Ralph Kiner	11795.0	25.1	2.13
160. Earle Combs	11793.0	31.1	2.63
161. Tony Gonzalez	11791.0	33.1	2.81
162. Al Cowens	11765.0	34.1	2.90
163. Cy Seymour	11748.0	43.9	3.73
164. Jay Buhner	11730.0	23.9	2.04
165. Eric Davis	11715.1	33.5	2.86
166. Pete Fox	11685.0	31.9	2.73
167. Dave Martinez	11662.1	33.6	2.88
168. Roger Maris	11656.0	29.9	2.56
169. Ed Delahanty	11645.0	33.1	2.84
170. Darryl Strawberry	11635.2	25.4	2.18
171. Topsy Hartsel	11632.0	29.2	2.51
172. Max Flack	11604.0	30.4	2.62
173. Larry Walker	11587.0	42.0	3.63
174. George Gore	11571.0	50.4	4.35
175. Jimmy Slagle	11557.0	42.5	3.68
176. Ron Gant	11543.0	30.5	2.64
177. Jesse Barfield	11535.0	38.5	3.34
178. Kenny Lofton	11524.1	44.5	3.86
179. Lance Johnson	11523.1	43.4	3.76
180. Augie Galan	11516.0	33.7	2.92
181. Amos Strunk	11511.0	30.0	2.61
182. Chick Stahl	11478.0	40.7	3.55
183. Pete Rose	11450.0	32.6	2.85
184. Ken Williams	11414.0	32.0	2.81
185. Jo-Jo Moore	11394.0	23.6	2.07
186. Albert Belle	11392.0	25.4	2.23
187. Del Unser	11388.0	34.3	3.01
188. Burt Shotton	11366.0	27.2	2.40
189. Joe Jackson	11360.0	29.7	2.61
190. Jack Graney	11359.0	27.8	2.44
191. Frank Howard	11348.0	21.6	1.91
192. Shano Collins	11346.0	32.5	2.87
193. Wally Berger	11341.0	38.7	3.42
194. Curt Walker	11328.0	28.6	2.52
195. Dave Henderson	11291.2	36.5	3.23
196. Bob Meusel	11285.0	24.8	2.20
197. Jerry Mumphrey	11265.0	31.9	2.83
198. Omar Moreno	11259.0	45.6	4.05
199. Vince Coleman	11243.0	25.9	2.30
Brian McRae	11243.0	42.5	3.78

	Player	Innings	WS	WS/ 1000
201.	Paul Hines	11234.0	38.7	3.44
202.	Ned Hanlon	11179.0	32.1	2.87
203.	Mickey Rivers	11138.0	39.1	3.51
204.	Hank Bauer	11131.0	25.6	2.30
205.	Elmer Valo	11118.0	21.5	1.93
206.	Otis Nixon	11117.0	47.7	4.29
207.	Sam Chapman	11092.0	34.6	3.12
208.	Jeff Heath	11030.0	24.3	2.21
209.	Lou Piniella	11015.0	29.0	2.63
210.	Lonnie Smith	10991.2	23.3	2.12
211.	Les Mann	10974.0	31.3	2.85
212.	George Wood	10964.0	28.9	2.64
213.	Tommy Griffith	10942.0	21.7	1.98
214.	Stan Javier	10877.2	28.1	2.59
215.	Dwayne Murphy	10865.1	37.9	3.49
216.	Hack Wilson	10836.0	27.9	2.58
217.	Matty Alou	10810.0	30.2	2.79
218.	Tony Armas	10772.2	33.4	3.10
219.	Jeff Burroughs	10760.0	18.2	1.69
220.	Bob Allison	10733.0	28.6	2.66
221.	Chief Wilson	10667.0	33.1	3.11
222.	Jim Northrup	10663.0	27.1	2.54
223.	Jim Landis	10653.0	40.0	3.76
224.	Mookie Wilson	10645.1	36.2	3.40
225.	Roberto Kelly	10626.0	27.4	2.58
226.	Bob Bescher	10593.0	22.8	2.16
227.	Terry Puhl	10587.1	32.7	3.08
228.	Robin Yount	10574.1	36.7	3.48
229.	Hi Myers	10560.0	45.9	4.35
230.	Irish Meusel	10558.0	22.8	2.16
231.	Kirk Gibson	10553.0	25.2	2.39
232.	Tommy Holmes	10519.0	34.1	3.25
233.	Larry Herndon	10461.2	26.3	2.51
234.	Ross Youngs	10454.0	25.4	2.43
235.	George Bell	10450.0	23.1	2.21
236.	Al Bumbry	10434.0	34.4	3.30
237.	Patsy Dougherty	10418.0	24.8	2.38
238.	George Case	10412.0	24.4	2.34
239.	Kevin Bass	10380.2	27.4	2.64
240.	Tommy McCarthy	10380.0	34.8	3.36
241.	Willie Stargell	10342.0	21.7	2.10
242.	Chili Davis	10332.1	22.2	2.14
243.	Bibb Falk	10323.0	24.8	2.41
244.	Greg Vaughn	10322.2	24.7	2.40
245.	Bruce Campbell	10322.0	19.9	1.93
246.	Charlie Hemphill	10318.0	25.6	2.48
247.	Hank Sauer	10310.0	27.2	2.64
248.	Mike Kreevich	10293.0	52.1	5.06
249.	Ken Henderson	10259.0	29.6	2.88
250.	Greg Luzinski	10256.0	17.7	1.73

	Player	Innings	WS	WS/ 1000
251.	Terry Moore	10250.0	45.2	4.41
252.	Tony Oliva	10191.0	28.2	2.76
253.	Chick Hafey	10172.0	23.7	2.33
254.	Tommy Harper	10136.0	25.8	2.54
255.	Jerry Morales	10134.0	21.7	2.14
256.	Lenny Dykstra	10125.1	38.4	3.79
257.	Babe Herman	10116.0	21.6	2.14
258.	Mickey Stanley	10040.0	35.0	3.48
259.	Ralph Garr	10024.0	20.5	2.05
260.	Rube Oldring	10013.0	26.2	2.62
261.	Raul Mondesi	9986.1	26.6	2.66
262.	Cliff Heathcote	9972.0	29.6	2.97
263.	Jack Smith	9954.0	20.3	2.04
264.	Ruppert Jones	9952.1	31.2	3.13
265.	Ken Berry	9945.0	39.4	3.96
266.	Derek Bell	9923.0	19.4	1.95
267.	Tommy Davis	9901.0	20.6	2.08
268.	Juan Gonzalez	9863.2	15.7	1.59
269.	Mike Greenwell	9858.1	23.7	2.41
270.	Jay Johnstone	9855.0	26.9	2.72
271.	Darryl Hamilton	9850.2	31.2	3.16
272.	John Stone	9822.0	25.5	2.60
273.	Casey Stengel	9805.0	27.8	2.83
274.	Billy Southworth	9797.0	27.7	2.82
275.	Jim Busby	9750.0	46.0	4.71
276.	Willie Horton	9749.0	19.7	2.02
277.	Red Murray	9741.0	23.1	2.37
278.	Sixto Lezcano	9733.0	25.5	2.62
279.	Tommy Leach	9613.0	44.6	4.64
280.	Nemo Leibold	9608.0	28.9	3.00
281.	Gorman Thomas	9601.0	26.1	2.72
282.	Joe Rudi	9582.0	23.1	2.41
283.	Duff Cooley	9557.0	22.1	2.31
284.	Moises Alou	9555.1	27.0	2.83
285.	Reggie Sanders	9542.1	24.6	2.58
286.	Dan Gladden	9540.1	26.2	2.74
287.	Mike Mitchell	9515.0	23.4	2.46
288.	Johnny Bates	9512.0	20.4	2.14
289.	Carl Reynolds	9493.0	28.8	3.04
290.	Wally Moon	9480.0	22.4	2.37
291.	Joe Hornung	9475.0	31.4	3.31
292.	Curt Welch	9451.0	48.3	5.11
293.	Ethan Allen	9444.0	33.3	3.52
294.	Elmer Smith	9429.0	28.9	3.06
295.	Billy Hatcher	9388.1	31.6	3.36
296.	Willard Marshall	9378.0	19.0	2.02
297.	Roy Johnson	9367.0	23.2	2.48
298.	Tim Salmon	9359.1	25.4	2.71
299.	Leon Wagner	9351.0	16.4	1.75
300.	Frank Demaree	9335.0	23.1	2.48

Player	Innings	WS	WS/ 1000	Player	Innings	WS	WS/ 1000
301. Matty McIntyre	9334.0	27.5	2.95	351. Jack Clark	8723.0	19.6	2.25
302. Darren Lewis	9314.1	37.9	4.07	352. Hoot Evers	8721.0	29.8	3.41
303. George Browne	9312.0	18.0	1.93	353. Von Hayes	8701.1	22.9	2.63
304. Ron LeFlore	9307.0	26.9	2.89	354. Ival Goodman	8692.0	21.4	2.46
305. Rick Miller	9303.0	29.9	3.21	355. Brian Jordan	8664.1	27.8	3.21
306. Bill Tuttle	9294.0	29.3	3.15	356. Dan Ford	8630.0	16.8	1.94
307. Cleon Jones	9292.0	24.9	2.68	357. Steve Kemp	8623.2	17.6	2.04
308. Joe Orsulak	9274.0	21.0	2.27	358. John Anderson	8574.0	18.5	2.16
309. Gavy Cravath	9270.0	19.0	2.05	359. Rebel Oakes	8572.0	23.6	2.76
310. Fred Schulte	9268.0	36.5	3.94	360. Gus Zernial	8566.0	17.0	1.99
311. Jeffrey Leonard	9266.0	20.0	2.16	361. Harold Baines	8562.1	23.6	2.76
312. Al Smith	9256.0	22.3	2.41	362. Stan Spence	8562.0	24.1	2.82
313. Chicken Wolf	9239.0	27.6	2.99	363. Wally Post	8543.0	18.6	2.17
314. Johnny Groth	9219.0	30.0	3.25	364. Jose Canseco	8530.2	17.7	2.08
315. Vince DiMaggio	9206.0	36.0	3.91	365. Sam Mertes	8528.0	26.7	3.13
316. Johnny Wyrostek	9203.0	22.8	2.48	366. Walt Wilmot	8500.0	26.0	3.06
317. Cesar Geronimo	9200.0	31.6	3.43	367. Jesus Alou	8477.0	20.3	2.39
318. Jack McCarthy	9193.0	26.5	2.89	368. Abner Dalrymple	8475.0	30.8	3.63
319. Bill North	9167.0	32.9	3.59	369. Luis Polonia	8459.0	19.7	2.33
320. Ken Landreaux	9164.1	26.1	2.85	370. Al Martin	8448.0	13.6	1.61
321. Chad Curtis	9154.1	24.2	2.64	371. Frank Thomas	8416.0	21.5	2.56
322. David Justice	9135.2	28.5	3.12	372. Bobby Tolan	8407.0	25.2	2.99
323. Pop Corkhill	9131.0	41.7	4.56	373. John Briggs	8392.0	17.2	2.04
324. Taylor Douthit	9097.0	38.7	4.25	374. Gary Sheffield	8387.1	14.5	1.73
325. Glenn Wilson	9089.1	26.5	2.92	375. Phil Bradley	8348.1	14.6	1.74
326. Dave Collins	9080.2	23.2	2.56	376. Harry Stovey	8318.0	26.5	3.19
327. Gary Ward	9065.0	25.8	2.84	377. Tommy Dowd	8308.0	16.8	2.03
328. Tommie Agee	9061.0	39.6	4.37	378. Lee Maye	8201.0	17.3	2.11
329. Don Mueller	9016.0	17.2	1.91	379. Manny Ramirez	8198.0	20.5	2.50
330. Mule Haas	9002.0	33.8	3.76	380. Shawn Green	8193.2	19.1	2.33
331. Gary Pettis	8989.1	32.4	3.61	381. Russ Snyder	8178.0	19.5	2.39
332. Tommy Henrich	8974.0	23.6	2.63	382. Vic Davalillo	8170.0	24.1	2.95
333. Carson Bigbee	8965.0	31.1	3.46	383. Mike Devereaux	8162.0	26.6	3.26
334. Ira Flagstead	8950.0	31.6	3.53	384. Dave May	8138.0	23.9	2.94
335. Tip O'Neill	8933.0	33.6	3.76	385. Cesar Tovar	8119.0	25.1	3.09
336. Juan Beniquez	8926.0	27.2	3.05	386. Jim Russell	8115.0	23.5	2.90
337. Charlie Keller	8891.0	23.3	2.62	387. Mel Hall	8111.2	16.4	2.02
338. Barney McCosky	8886.0	34.4	3.87	388. Dale Mitchell	8101.0	19.4	2.39
339. Pete Browning	8868.0	22.8	2.57	389. Mike Hershberger	8097.0	22.9	2.83
340. Davy Jones	8867.0	27.3	3.07	390. Pete Incaviglia	8088.0	18.6	2.30
341. Candy Maldonado	8852.1	18.9	2.14	Emmett Seery	8088.0	18.6	2.29
342. Ping Bodie	8805.0	27.4	3.11	392. Johnny Grubb	8062.0	17.6	2.19
Rob Deer	8805.0	20.0	2.28	393. Alex Johnson	8054.0	16.2	2.01
344. Garret Anderson	8799.1	27.8	3.15	394. Peanuts Lowrey	8051.0	23.7	2.94
345. Cliff Carroll	8778.0	24.6	2.81	395. Troy O'Leary	8043.2	23.9	2.98
346. Larry Hisle	8772.0	18.1	2.06	396. Milt Thompson	8036.0	24.9	3.10
347. Bernard Gilkey	8743.0	21.1	2.41	397. Rusty Greer	8035.1	12.7	1.58
348. Jimmy McAleer	8728.0	45.4	5.20	398. Johnny Mostil	8024.0	31.7	3.95
349. Jackie Brandt	8727.0	29.4	3.37	399. Al Zarilla	7995.0	16.6	2.07
350. Blondie Purcell	8725.0	12.6	1.45	400. Jim Rivera	7985.0	29.2	3.66

Player	Innings	WS	WS/ 1000
401. Socks Seybold	7975.0	22.7	2.85
402. Bake McBride	7956.0	26.1	3.29
403. Danny Green	7925.0	21.0	2.65
404. Bug Holliday	7902.0	25.3	3.20
405. Pat Kelly	7899.0	19.1	2.42
406. Riggs Stephenson	7875.0	19.1	2.43
407. Bob Skinner	7862.0	18.2	2.32
408. Bobby Higginson	7842.2	14.7	1.87
409. Jim Edmonds	7837.2	31.5	4.02
410. Oyster Burns	7825.0	15.3	1.95
411. Willie Kirkland	7820.0	18.3	2.33
412. Paul Radford	7814.0	21.0	2.69
413. Harry Rice	7807.0	20.1	2.57
414. Lee Lacy	7797.1	19.6	2.52
415. George Harper	7788.0	18.8	2.41
416. Jeromy Burnitz	7778.1	17.9	2.30
417. Charley Jones	7771.0	20.7	2.67
418. Jim Eisenreich	7767.0	20.2	2.60
419. Ducky Holmes	7764.0	25.5	3.29
420. Rip Radcliff	7760.0	17.2	2.22
421. Johnny Damon	7758.1	23.8	3.07
422. Bill Robinson	7709.0	20.2	2.62
423. Taffy Wright	7704.0	19.1	2.48
424. Danny Tartabull	7676.0	13.0	1.70
425. Greg Gross	7606.2	16.9	2.22
426. Benny Kauff	7602.0	26.3	3.46
427. Gene Moore	7592.0	23.5	3.10
428. Sid Gordon	7579.0	14.5	1.92
429. Tom Goodwin	7568.1	23.1	3.06
430. Vic Wertz	7560.0	17.0	2.25
431. Manny Mota	7555.0	18.3	2.42
432. Jimmy Barrett	7548.0	29.0	3.84
433. Mike Donlin	7531.0	17.8	2.37
434. Willie Crawford	7511.0	19.5	2.60
435. Ron Fairly	7490.0	18.6	2.48
436. Freddy Leach	7484.0	14.6	1.95
437. Jim Lemon	7473.0	11.4	1.53
438. Ollie Brown	7465.0	18.3	2.45
439. Orator Shaffer	7452.0	23.6	3.16
440. George Stone	7436.0	15.8	2.13
441. Floyd Robinson	7377.0	18.2	2.47
442. Ollie Pickering	7373.0	22.3	3.02
443. Mitch Webster	7368.0	22.6	3.07
444. Pete Hotaling	7361.0	18.1	2.46
445. Steve Evans	7347.0	11.5	1.57
446. Bob Nieman	7337.0	14.4	1.97
447. Ray Powell	7327.0	19.2	2.62
448. Hugh Nicol	7309.0	32.0	4.38
449. Roy Cullenbine	7270.0	17.1	2.35
450. Richie Zisk	7262.0	18.8	2.58

Player	Innings	WS	WS/ 1000
451. Danny Litwhiler	7261.0	17.4	2.40
452. Fred Snodgrass	7247.0	24.9	3.43
453. Mark Whiten	7228.1	17.0	2.35
454. Danny Hoffman	7221.0	21.4	2.97
455. Frankie Baumholtz	7206.0	19.4	2.69
456. Chuck Hinton	7197.0	15.2	2.11
457. Lee Mazzilli	7194.1	17.6	2.45
458. Moose Solters	7134.0	18.2	2.55
459. Steve Henderson	7092.0	12.9	1.82
460. Tony Conigliaro	7090.0	16.1	2.27
461. John Shelby	7077.2	21.3	3.01
462. Tito Francona	7075.0	15.2	2.15
463. Jim McTamany	7073.0	22.2	3.13
464. Cory Snyder	7067.0	18.5	2.62
465. Bobby Bonilla	7053.2	14.0	1.99
466. Roy Sievers	7043.0	12.4	1.76
467. Albie Pearson	7023.0	21.6	3.07
468. Rube Bressler	7016.0	19.0	2.71
469. Elmer Smith	7006.0	16.6	2.37
470. Mack Jones	6987.0	14.5	2.08
471. George Watkins	6970.0	16.4	2.35
472. Gino Cimoli	6953.0	18.7	2.69
473. Gene Richards	6934.0	13.7	1.97
474. Rick Reichardt	6931.0	15.8	2.28
475. Buck Freeman	6930.0	13.4	1.93
Harvey Kuenn	6930.0	15.3	2.21
477. Eddie Burke	6919.0	26.3	3.80
478. Andruw Jones	6882.1	44.6	6.47
479. Rondell White	6874.2	26.8	3.90
480. Chet Laabs	6864.0	15.1	2.20
481. Myril Hoag	6863.0	16.9	2.46
482. B.J. Surhoff	6854.0	16.8	2.46
483. Charlie Maxwell	6839.0	17.7	2.59
484. Ellis Valentine	6819.0	16.9	2.48
485. Wally Westlake	6809.0	17.9	2.63
486. Lefty O'Doul	6736.0	11.5	1.71
487. Rip Repulski	6717.0	14.5	2.15
488. Bob Fothergill	6710.0	11.5	1.72
489. Glenallen Hill	6700.1	9.9	1.48
490. Sam Mele	6695.0	17.9	2.67

Norms for players with:			
10,000 innings	–	–	**2.95**
7,500 - 9,999 innings	–	–	**2.78**
5,000 - 7,499 innings	–	–	**2.69**
2,500 - 4,999 innings	–	–	**2.59**
1,000 - 2,499 innings	–	–	**2.44**
0 - 999 innings	–	–	**2.28**

Single-Season Total Win Shares—1900-2001

	Player, Team(s)	League	Year	Pos	Batting	Fielding	Pitching	WS
1.	Honus Wagner, Pit	NL	1908	SS	49.2	9.7	–	59
2.	Babe Ruth, NYY	AL	1923	OF	48.5	6.2	–	55
3.	Walter Johnson, Was	AL	1913	SP	3.8	0.0	50.3	54
	Barry Bonds, SF	NL	2001	OF	52.2	1.6	–	54
5.	Jack Chesbro, NYA	AL	1904	SP	1.4	–	51.8	53
	Babe Ruth, NYY	AL	1921	OF	47.7	5.0	0.0	53
7.	Tris Speaker, Bos	AL	1912	OF	41.6	9.9	–	51
	Babe Ruth, NYY	AL	1920	OF	47.9	3.3	0.2	51
	Mickey Mantle, NYY	AL	1957	OF	46.1	5.0	–	51
10.	Ted Williams, Bos	AL	1946	OF	45.1	4.0	–	49
	Mickey Mantle, NYY	AL	1956	OF	43.8	4.8	–	49
12.	Ty Cobb, Det	AL	1915	OF	41.6	6.4	–	48
	Mickey Mantle, NYY	AL	1961	OF	43.0	4.9	–	48
14.	Ed Walsh, CWS	AL	1908	SP	0.1	–	46.6	47
	Nap Lajoie, Cle	AL	1910	2B	40.4	6.2	–	47
	Ty Cobb, Det	AL	1911	OF	41.3	6.0	–	47
	Walter Johnson, Was	AL	1912	SP	3.0	–	44.1	47
	Rogers Hornsby, StL	NL	1922	2B	42.9	4.0	–	47
	Barry Bonds, SF	NL	1993	OF	44.0	2.7	–	47
20.	Honus Wagner, Pit	NL	1905	SS	36.8	9.6	–	46
	Honus Wagner, Pit	NL	1906	SS	34.2	11.3	–	46
	Ty Cobb, Det	AL	1917	OF	40.4	5.5	–	46
	Ted Williams, Bos	AL	1942	OF	41.5	4.6	–	46
	Stan Musial, StL	NL	1948	OF	42.4	3.9	–	46

Single-Season Total Win Shares—1876-1899

	Player, Team(s)	League	Year	Pos	Batting	Fielding	Pitching	WS
1.	Old Hoss Radbourn, Prv	NL	1884	SP	5.6	0.4	83.1	89
2.	Guy Hecker, Lou	AA	1884	SP	11.5	0.0	62.2	74
3.	Silver King, StL	AA	1888	SP	5.2	0.0	66.3	71
4.	Tim Keefe, NY	AA	1883	SP	2.8	0.2	66.5	70
5.	Charlie Sweeney, Prv-STL	–	1884	SP	13.0	0.8	53.8	67
6.	Billy Taylor, STL-Phi	–	1884	SP	12.1	0.7	52.7	65
7.	Charlie Buffinton, Bos	NL	1884	SP	8.5	0.4	53.4	62
	John Clarkson, ChN	NL	1885	SP	3.6	0.1	58.4	62
	Dave Foutz, StL	AA	1886	SP	8.6	1.3	52.3	62
10.	Pud Galvin, Buf	NL	1879	SP	3.2	0.0	57.5	61
11.	Jim Devlin, Lou	NL	1877	SP	2.1	–	58.3	60
	Tommy Bond, Bos	NL	1878	SP	1.2	0.0	58.6	60
	Old Hoss Radbourn, Prv	NL	1883	SP	8.2	0.4	51.1	60
	John Clarkson, Bos	NL	1889	SP	0.0	0.0	60.4	60
15.	Tony Mullane, Tol	AA	1884	SP	10.5	0.7	46.7	58
16.	George Bradley, StL	NL	1876	SP	6.0	–	51.2	57
	Al Spalding, ChN	NL	1876	SP	6.2	0.1	50.3	57
	Jim Whitney, Bos	NL	1883	SP	12.2	0.8	43.5	57
	Pud Galvin, Buf	NL	1884	SP	0.0	0.0	56.6	57
	Mickey Welch, NYG	NL	1885	SP	2.0	–	54.9	57
	Bob Caruthers, StL	AA	1886	SP	16.9	0.9	38.9	57

Batting—1876-1899

	Player, Team(s)	Lg	Year	WS
1.	Ed Delahanty, Phi	NL	1899	36.5
2.	Roger Connor, NYG	NL	1886	33.1
3.	Fred Dunlap, STL	UA	1884	32.8
4.	Billy Hamilton, Phi	NL	1891	32.6
5.	Tip O'Neill, StL	AA	1887	31.7
6.	Jesse Burkett, Cle	NL	1895	30.4
7.	Ed Delahanty, Phi	NL	1898	30.4
8.	King Kelly, ChN	NL	1886	30.1
9.	Billy Hamilton, Bos	NL	1898	29.6
10.	Dan Brouthers, Bro	NL	1892	29.5
11.	Dan Brouthers, Det	NL	1886	29.2
12.	Jimmy Ryan, ChN	NL	1888	29.0
13.	Ed Delahanty, Phi	NL	1895	28.8
14.	Ed Delahanty, Phi	NL	1896	28.7
15.	Tommy Tucker, Bal	AA	1889	28.5
16.	Roger Connor, NYG	NL	1888	28.4
17.	Roger Connor, NYG	NL	1885	28.3
18.	Willie Keeler, Bal	NL	1897	28.3
19.	Hugh Duffy, Bos	NL	1894	28.0
20.	Cap Anson, ChN	NL	1886	28.0

Pitching—1876-1899

	Player, Team(s)	Lg	Year	WS
1.	Old Hoss Radbourn, Prv	NL	1884	83.1
2.	Tim Keefe, NY	AA	1883	66.5
3.	Silver King, StL	AA	1888	66.3
4.	Guy Hecker, Lou	AA	1884	62.2
5.	John Clarkson, Bos	NL	1889	60.4
6.	Tommy Bond, Bos	NL	1878	58.6
7.	John Clarkson, ChN	NL	1885	58.4
8.	Jim Devlin, Lou	NL	1877	58.3
9.	Pud Galvin, Buf	NL	1879	57.5
10.	Pud Galvin, Buf	NL	1884	56.6
11.	Ed Morris, Pit	AA	1885	56.0
12.	Mickey Welch, NYG	NL	1885	54.9
13.	Amos Rusie, NYG	NL	1894	54.8
14.	Bill Hutchison, ChN	NL	1890	54.2
15.	Charlie Sweeney, Prv-STL	–	1884	53.8
16.	Charlie Buffinton, Bos	NL	1884	53.4
17.	Billy Taylor, STL-Phi	–	1884	52.7
18.	Dave Foutz, StL	AA	1886	52.3
19.	Lady Baldwin, Det	NL	1886	52.0
20.	Elmer Smith, Cin	AA	1887	51.5

Batting—1900-2001

	Player, Team(s)	Lg	Year	WS
1.	Barry Bonds, SF	NL	2001	52.2
2.	Honus Wagner, Pit	NL	1908	49.2
3.	Babe Ruth, NYY	AL	1923	48.5
4.	Babe Ruth, NYY	AL	1920	47.9
5.	Babe Ruth, NYY	AL	1921	47.7
6.	Mickey Mantle, NYY	AL	1957	46.1
7.	Ted Williams, Bos	AL	1946	45.1
8.	Barry Bonds, SF	NL	1993	44.0
9.	Mickey Mantle, NYY	AL	1956	43.8
10.	Mickey Mantle, NYY	AL	1961	43.0
11.	Rogers Hornsby, StL	NL	1922	42.9
12.	Babe Ruth, NYY	AL	1928	42.7
13.	Babe Ruth, NYY	AL	1926	42.6
14.	Stan Musial, StL	NL	1948	42.4
15.	Babe Ruth, NYY	AL	1924	41.7
16.	Tris Speaker, Bos	AL	1912	41.6
17.	Ty Cobb, Det	AL	1915	41.6
18.	Ted Williams, Bos	AL	1942	41.5
19.	Lou Gehrig, NYY	AL	1927	41.5
20.	Ty Cobb, Det	AL	1911	41.3

Pitching—1900-2001

	Player, Team(s)	Lg	Year	WS
1.	Jack Chesbro, NYA	AL	1904	51.8
2.	Walter Johnson, Was	AL	1913	50.3
3.	Ed Walsh, CWS	AL	1908	46.6
4.	Walter Johnson, Was	AL	1912	44.1
5.	Pete Alexander, Phi	NL	1915	43.3
6.	Joe McGinnity, NYG	NL	1904	42.3
7.	Pete Alexander, Phi	NL	1916	42.0
8.	Lefty Grove, Phi	AL	1931	41.8
9.	Joe McGinnity, NYG	NL	1903	40.4
10.	Cy Young, Bos	AL	1901	40.4
11.	Joe Wood, Bos	AL	1912	40.4
12.	Steve Carlton, Phi	NL	1972	40.4
13.	Walter Johnson, Was	AL	1915	39.3
14.	Pete Alexander, Phi	NL	1917	39.1
15.	Gaylord Perry, Cle	AL	1972	39.0
16.	Dolf Luque, Cin	NL	1923	39.0
17.	Ed Walsh, CWS	AL	1912	38.9
18.	Christy Mathewson, NYG	NL	1908	38.6
19.	Cy Young, Bos	AL	1902	38.5
20.	Dizzy Trout, Det	AL	1944	38.1

Fielding Win Shares

Catcher

	Player, Team(s)	Lg	Year	WS
1.	Ivan Rodriguez, Tex	AL	1999	12.0
2.	Ron Karkovice, CWS	AL	1993	11.6
3.	Ivan Rodriguez, Tex	AL	1996	11.6
4.	Ivan Rodriguez, Tex	AL	1997	11.4
5.	Ray Schalk, CWS	AL	1922	11.2
6.	Mickey Cochrane, Phi	AL	1932	11.2
7.	Gary Carter, Mon	NL	1980	11.1
8.	Charles Johnson, Fla	NL	1997	11.1
9.	Gary Carter, NYM	NL	1985	11.0
10.	Ivan Rodriguez, Tex	AL	1998	11.0

First Base

	Player, Team(s)	Lg	Year	WS
1.	Tino Martinez, NYY	AL	1999	5.2
2.	Charlie Grimm, Pit	NL	1920	4.6
3.	Ed Konetchy, Pit	FL	1915	4.4
4.	Jimmie Foxx, Bos	AL	1937	4.2
5.	Roger Connor, NY	PL	1890	4.2
6.	Mark Grace, ChC	NL	1991	4.1
7.	Dan Brouthers, Bro	NL	1892	4.1
8.	Jiggs Donahue, CWS	AL	1907	4.1
9.	Pete O'Brien, Tex	AL	1987	4.1
10.	Pete O'Brien, Tex	AL	1988	4.1

Second Base

	Player, Team(s)	Lg	Year	WS
1.	Bill Mazeroski, Pit	NL	1962	11.6
2.	Frankie Frisch, StL	NL	1927	11.1
3.	Jerry Priddy, Det	AL	1950	11.0
4.	Bobby Grich, Bal	AL	1973	10.9
5.	Bill Mazeroski, Pit	NL	1966	10.8
6.	Hughie Critz, NYG	NL	1933	10.7
7.	Bobby Doerr, Bos	AL	1946	10.4
8.	Nap Lajoie, Cle	AL	1908	10.3
9.	Bill Mazeroski, Pit	NL	1963	10.0
10.	Dick Green, Oak	AL	1971	9.7

Third Base

	Player, Team(s)	Lg	Year	WS
1.	Ossie Vitt, Det	AL	1916	11.4
2.	Jimmy Collins, Bos	NL	1899	10.9
3.	Lave Cross, Cle-StL	NL	1899	10.5
4.	Billy Shindle, Bal	AA	1888	9.9
5.	Graig Nettles, Cle	AL	1971	9.8
6.	Pie Traynor, Pit	NL	1925	9.5
7.	Ossie Vitt, Det	AL	1915	9.5
8.	Lee Tannehill, CWS	AL	1904	9.4
9.	Bobby Wallace, Cle	NL	1898	9.3
10.	Tommy Leach, Pit	NL	1904	9.3

Shortstop

	Player, Team(s)	Lg	Year	WS
1.	Orlando Cabrera, Mon	NL	2001	13.5
2.	Rabbit Maranville, Bos	NL	1914	13.3
3.	Roger Peckinpaugh, Was	AL	1924	13.1
4.	Bob Allen, Phi	NL	1890	12.8
5.	Joe Tinker, ChC	NL	1908	12.7
6.	Terry Turner, Cle	AL	1906	12.7
7.	Everett Scott, Bos	AL	1921	12.7
8.	Art Fletcher, NYG	NL	1917	12.7
9.	Buck Weaver, CWS	AL	1913	12.4
10.	Germany Smith, Cin	NL	1892	12.3

Outfield

	Player, Team(s)	Lg	Year	WS
1.	Devon White, Tor	AL	1991	11.5
2.	Dwayne Murphy, Oak	AL	1980	10.0
3.	Marquis Grissom, Mon	NL	1993	10.0
4.	Tris Speaker, Bos	AL	1912	9.9
5.	Andruw Jones, Atl	NL	1999	9.8
6.	Jimmy Piersall, Bos	AL	1955	9.5
7.	Andruw Jones, Atl	NL	1998	9.5
8.	Jimmy Piersall, Bos	AL	1956	9.3
9.	Jimmy McAleer, Cle	NL	1892	9.3
10.	Kirby Puckett, Min	AL	1984	9.2
11.	Curt Flood, StL	NL	1962	9.2
12.	Doc Cramer, Bos	AL	1936	9.0
13.	Vada Pinson, Cin	NL	1961	9.0
14.	Charlie Hanford, Buf	FL	1914	8.9
15.	Andruw Jones, Atl	NL	2000	8.9
16.	Tris Speaker, Bos	AL	1914	8.9
17.	Willie Mays, NYG	NL	1954	8.9
18.	Fielder Jones, CWS	AL	1905	8.8
19.	Taylor Douthit, StL	NL	1928	8.7
20.	Curt Flood, StL	NL	1964	8.7
21.	Mike Kreevich, CWS	AL	1940	8.7
22.	Dom DiMaggio, Bos	AL	1942	8.6
23.	Al Simmons, Phi	AL	1925	8.6
24.	Fielder Jones, CWS	AL	1907	8.6
25.	Curt Welch, StL	AA	1887	8.4

Anaheim Angels

(includes Los Angeles Angels, 1961-64 and California Angels, 1965-96)

Total Win Shares

	Player	Bat	Fld	Pit	WS
1.	Brian Downing	199.2	25.9	–	225
2.	Jim Fregosi	167.4	55.3	–	223
3.	Tim Salmon	160.4	25.4	–	187
4.	Chuck Finley	0.0	–	184.0	185
5.	Bobby Grich	132.6	51.1	–	182
6.	Nolan Ryan	0.0	–	147.5	149
7.	Wally Joyner	107.7	13.3	–	120
8.	Chili Davis	110.3	4.0	0.3	115
9.	Frank Tanana	–	–	113.9	114
10.	Mike Witt	–	–	111.6	112
11.	Rod Carew	94.3	8.5	–	102
12.	Garret Anderson	72.0	27.8	–	99
13.	Doug DeCinces	77.0	20.4	–	98
14.	Darin Erstad	73.3	22.9	–	96
15.	Don Baylor	89.9	4.2	–	95
	Jim Edmonds	70.9	23.7	–	95
17.	Dick Schofield	44.8	47.0	–	92
18.	Mark Langston	0.0	–	90.8	90
19.	Dean Chance	0.0	–	87.7	89
20.	Albie Pearson	67.5	17.2	–	84
21.	Troy Percival	0.0	–	82.4	83
22.	Clyde Wright	1.1	–	79.6	81
23.	Bobby Knoop	42.2	36.7	–	79
24.	Bob Boone	28.1	50.4	–	78
25.	Andy Messersmith	0.1	–	74.1	74

Single-Season Win Shares

	Player	Year	WS
1.	Jim Fregosi	1970	33
2.	Dean Chance	1964	32
3.	Darin Erstad	2000	30
4.	Don Baylor	1979	29
	Tim Salmon	1995	29
	Tim Salmon	1997	29
7.	Albie Pearson	1963	28
	Jim Fregosi	1964	28
	Jim Fregosi	1967	28
	Don Mincher	1967	28
	Alex Johnson	1970	28
	Nolan Ryan	1973	28
	Bobby Grich	1979	28
	Doug DeCinces	1982	28

Baltimore Orioles

(includes Milwaukee Brewers, 1901 and St. Louis Browns, 1902-53)

Total Win Shares

	Player	Bat	Fld	Pit	WS
1.	Cal Ripken Jr.	290.7	136.4	–	427
2.	Brooks Robinson	248.1	106.5	–	356
3.	Jim Palmer	0.4	–	310.4	312
4.	Eddie Murray	279.2	26.5	–	307
5.	George Sisler	227.7	21.2	8.2	256
6.	Boog Powell	230.7	22.2	–	253
7.	Ken Singleton	206.1	17.3	–	224
8.	Brady Anderson	173.5	36.8	–	212
9.	Bobby Wallace	129.7	73.9	0.1	203
10.	Harlond Clift	141.6	57.1	–	201
11.	Ken Williams	153.2	27.6	–	181
12.	Paul Blair	115.9	60.5	–	178
13.	Frank Robinson	158.9	16.0	–	176
14.	Al Bumbry	133.5	34.2	–	169
15.	Dave McNally	0.0	–	165.2	167
16.	Baby Doll Jacobson	125.1	40.0	–	166
17.	Mark Belanger	58.0	102.8	–	161
	Mike Mussina	0.3	–	161.3	161
19.	Vern Stephens	117.7	41.8	–	160
20.	Urban Shocker	4.6	–	150.4	156
21.	Bobby Grich	103.8	43.0	–	147
22.	Jack Powell	1.4	0.0	144.2	146
	George Stone	131.1	15.8	–	146
24.	Mike Flanagan	–	–	134.6	136
25.	George McQuinn	111.5	20.8	–	133

Single-Season Win Shares

	Player	Year	WS
1.	Frank Robinson	1966	41
2.	George Stone	1906	38
3.	Cal Ripken Jr.	1984	37
4.	Ken Singleton	1977	36
5.	Heinie Manush	1928	35
	Cal Ripken Jr.	1983	35
7.	Vern Stephens	1944	34
	Cal Ripken Jr.	1991	34
9.	George Sisler	1920	33
	Brooks Robinson	1964	33
	Ken Singleton	1975	33
	Al Bumbry	1980	33
	Eddie Murray	1984	33

Boston Red Sox

Total Win Shares

	Player	Bat	Fld	Pit	WS
1.	Ted Williams	512.4	44.0	0.1	555
2.	Carl Yastrzemski	426.0	61.5	–	488
3.	Dwight Evans	284.1	51.1	–	337
4.	Wade Boggs	248.2	52.9	–	301
5.	Jim Rice	244.2	35.6	–	282
6.	Bobby Doerr	196.4	85.7	–	281
7.	Tris Speaker	212.9	52.9	0.0	265
8.	Roger Clemens	0.3	–	247.8	250
9.	Cy Young	4.7	–	242.1	247
10.	Harry Hooper	199.2	41.4	0.3	241
11.	Dom DiMaggio	162.5	56.3	–	220
12.	Rico Petrocelli	136.4	65.9	–	205
13.	Carlton Fisk	131.3	50.3	–	182
14.	Babe Ruth	75.4	4.5	100.6	180
15.	Reggie Smith	137.8	33.1	–	171
16.	Johnny Pesky	123.6	47.5	–	170
17.	Jimmie Foxx	145.4	16.1	0.2	161
18.	Larry Gardner	115.0	44.3	–	159
	Duffy Lewis	125.1	32.4	0.0	159
20.	Joe Cronin	119.3	38.9	–	158
21.	Fred Lynn	122.1	32.8	–	154
22.	Bob Stanley	–	–	149.9	149
	Mo Vaughn	138.9	9.2	–	149
24.	Mike Greenwell	121.7	23.7	–	146
25.	Lefty Grove	0.0	–	142.8	143

Single-Season Win Shares

	Player	Year	WS
1.	Tris Speaker	1912	51
2.	Ted Williams	1946	49
3.	Ted Williams	1942	46
4.	Tris Speaker	1914	45
5.	Joe Wood	1912	44
	Ted Williams	1947	44
7.	Babe Ruth	1919	43
8.	Ted Williams	1941	42
	Carl Yastrzemski	1967	42
10.	Cy Young	1901	41

Chicago White Sox

Total Win Shares

	Player	Bat	Fld	Pit	WS
1.	Luke Appling	268.0	108.6	–	378
2.	Eddie Collins	250.1	63.4	–	316
3.	Ted Lyons	5.8	0.0	305.3	312
4.	Frank Thomas	302.0	6.0	–	308
5.	Red Faber	2.1	–	289.1	292
6.	Nellie Fox	181.7	103.1	–	284
7.	Ed Walsh	5.3	0.0	259.1	265
8.	Minnie Minoso	189.1	32.2	–	223
	Billy Pierce	0.5	0.0	219.9	223
10.	Fielder Jones	149.2	53.0	–	203
11.	Harold Baines	172.9	23.3	–	197
12.	Eddie Cicotte	0.7	–	195.1	196
13.	Doc White	13.9	1.5	176.4	192
14.	Ray Schalk	94.5	97.5	–	191
15.	Carlton Fisk	123.4	63.1	–	186
16.	Wilbur Wood	0.0	–	184.0	184
17.	Sherm Lollar	110.3	65.8	–	177
18.	Luis Aparicio	100.9	73.8	–	175
19.	Robin Ventura	132.3	42.1	–	174
20.	Buck Weaver	87.5	62.3	–	152
21.	Joe Jackson	127.2	15.5	–	145
22.	George Davis	102.5	39.2	–	142
23.	Willie Kamm	89.1	53.5	–	141
24.	Thornton Lee	1.5	–	139.0	140
25.	Ozzie Guillen	53.3	82.8	–	137

Single-Season Win Shares

	Player	Year	WS
1.	Ed Walsh	1908	47
2.	Ed Walsh	1912	40
	Eddie Collins	1915	40
	Luke Appling	1943	40
	Dick Allen	1972	40
6.	Frank Thomas	1997	39
7.	Eddie Collins	1920	38
8.	Ed Walsh	1907	37
	Joe Jackson	1920	37
	Red Faber	1921	37
	Albert Belle	1998	37

Cleveland Indians

Total Win Shares

	Player	Bat	Fld	Pit	WS
1.	Nap Lajoie	271.6	72.2	–	345
2.	Tris Speaker	277.6	59.1	–	338
3.	Bob Feller	0.7	–	291.7	292
4.	Earl Averill	216.4	52.0	–	270
5.	Lou Boudreau	182.1	86.8	–	269
6.	Mel Harder	0.1	–	234.1	234
7.	Bob Lemon	20.4	0.4	211.8	232
8.	Joe Sewell	153.5	76.2	–	229
9.	Larry Doby	188.6	37.2	–	226
10.	Stan Coveleski	1.4	–	200.4	203
11.	Ken Keltner	139.3	57.1	–	198
12.	Jim Thome	169.6	21.6	–	192
13.	Addie Joss	0.4	0.1	190.7	191
14.	Al Rosen	154.6	31.2	–	185
15.	Kenny Lofton	142.0	39.0	–	181
16.	Early Wynn	4.8	–	172.9	179
17.	Elmer Flick	156.7	19.7	–	178
18.	Hal Trosky	157.6	16.9	–	175
19.	Bobby Avila	119.3	52.1	–	170
	Willis Hudlin	1.4	–	169.1	170
21.	Terry Turner	94.8	74.1	–	169
22.	Bill Bradley	112.0	55.6	0.0	167
	Manny Ramirez	146.9	19.2	–	167
24.	Charlie Jamieson	133.4	31.9	0.4	165
25.	2 tied with				160

Single-Season Win Shares

	Player	Year	WS
1.	Nap Lajoie	1910	47
2.	Al Rosen	1953	42
3.	Nap Lajoie	1904	41
	Tris Speaker	1916	41
5.	Joe Jackson	1911	39
	Tris Speaker	1920	39
	Gaylord Perry	1972	39
8.	Elmer Flick	1907	37
	Joe Jackson	1912	37
	Tris Speaker	1917	37
	Roberto Alomar	2001	37

Detroit Tigers

Total Win Shares

	Player	Bat	Fld	Pit	WS
1.	Ty Cobb	609.6	78.1	0.4	688
2.	Al Kaline	382.9	58.6	–	443
3.	Sam Crawford	342.7	41.1	–	383
	Charlie Gehringer	295.3	87.3	–	383
5.	Lou Whitaker	265.6	87.2	–	351
6.	Harry Heilmann	308.5	27.8	–	336
7.	Alan Trammell	225.1	92.6	–	318
8.	Norm Cash	275.6	34.3	–	311
9.	Bill Freehan	175.4	89.6	–	267
10.	Hal Newhouser	2.7	–	253.4	257
11.	Hank Greenberg	227.5	24.9	–	253
12.	Bobby Veach	206.2	43.7	0.1	249
13.	George Mullin	30.6	0.0	207.8	238
14.	Dick McAuliffe	176.7	58.1	–	235
15.	Donie Bush	152.3	75.8	–	227
16.	Tommy Bridges	0.1	–	224.8	225
17.	Dizzy Trout	6.8	–	212.6	220
18.	Hooks Dauss	7.6	0.0	205.9	215
19.	Mickey Lolich	0.0	–	212.2	212
20.	Willie Horton	179.1	19.6	–	199
21.	Jack Morris	0.0	–	184.2	186
22.	Rudy York	147.5	31.2	–	180
23.	Lance Parrish	100.0	61.5	–	162
24.	Kirk Gibson	140.9	16.8	–	156
25.	Wild Bill Donovan	7.2	0.5	145.7	154

Single-Season Win Shares

	Player	Year	WS
1.	Ty Cobb	1915	48
2.	Ty Cobb	1911	47
3.	Ty Cobb	1917	46
4.	Ty Cobb	1910	45
5.	Ty Cobb	1909	44
6.	Dizzy Trout	1944	42
	Norm Cash	1961	42
8.	Ty Cobb	1907	41
9.	Ty Cobb	1912	40
	Ty Cobb	1916	40

Kansas City Royals

Total Win Shares

	Player	Bat	Fld	Pit	WS
1.	George Brett	371.5	61.5	–	432
2.	Amos Otis	215.3	70.5	–	284
3.	Willie Wilson	155.4	62.0	–	219
4.	Hal McRae	204.8	7.6	–	214
5.	Frank White	102.5	105.6	–	211
6.	Dan Quisenberry	–	–	148.6	149
7.	Kevin Appier	0.0	–	147.5	147
8.	Mark Gubicza	–	–	142.2	141
9.	Paul Splittorff	0.0	–	140.3	140
10.	John Mayberry	121.3	12.8	–	134
	Jeff Montgomery	–	–	133.9	134
12.	Dennis Leonard	–	–	131.3	133
13.	Bret Saberhagen	–	–	132.6	131
14.	Freddie Patek	61.8	59.0	–	122
15.	Larry Gura	–	–	104.7	105
16.	Kevin Seitzer	75.4	22.9	–	99
17.	Danny Tartabull	89.9	7.8	–	97
18.	Mike Macfarlane	55.8	32.9	–	90
19.	Johnny Damon	68.9	18.5	–	87
20.	Charlie Leibrandt	–	–	87.1	86
21.	Darrell Porter	61.8	21.5	–	84
22.	Al Cowens	59.9	21.2	–	82
23.	Mike Sweeney	65.1	11.9	–	77
24.	Cookie Rojas	41.1	33.0	–	74
25.	Flash Gordon	–	–	70.7	72

Single-Season Win Shares

	Player	Year	WS
1.	George Brett	1985	37
2.	George Brett	1980	36
3.	John Mayberry	1975	33
	George Brett	1976	33
	George Brett	1979	33
6.	John Mayberry	1973	31
	Darrell Porter	1979	31
	Willie Wilson	1980	31
9.	Amos Otis	1973	29
	George Brett	1977	29
	Amos Otis	1978	29
	Jose Offerman	1998	29

Minnesota Twins

(includes Washington Senators, 1901-60)

Total Win Shares

	Player	Bat	Fld	Pit	WS
1.	Walter Johnson	30.3	0.2	529.9	560
2.	Harmon Killebrew	331.7	35.0	–	366
3.	Sam Rice	262.9	53.0	2.1	320
4.	Rod Carew	237.6	45.0	–	282
5.	Kirby Puckett	223.8	58.4	–	281
6.	Joe Judge	232.1	30.1	–	266
	Clyde Milan	209.9	55.0	–	266
8.	Tony Oliva	217.4	28.2	–	245
9.	Mickey Vernon	213.1	26.8	–	240
10.	Kent Hrbek	202.3	28.9	–	230
11.	Buddy Myer	170.9	54.2	–	226
12.	Goose Goslin	193.0	32.5	–	225
13.	Eddie Yost	178.4	38.5	–	216
14.	Bob Allison	171.7	30.5	–	203
15.	Jim Kaat	3.5	–	183.9	185
16.	Ossie Bluege	114.1	69.7	–	183
17.	Buddy Lewis	144.5	34.2	–	179
18.	Bert Blyleven	0.0	–	178.1	178
19.	Joe Cronin	115.1	57.9	–	173
20.	Cecil Travis	123.4	45.8	–	169
21.	Chuck Knoblauch	123.4	36.9	–	161
22.	Camilo Pascual	2.9	–	148.3	152
23.	Gary Gaetti	90.4	55.8	–	146
	Joe Kuhel	128.4	19.0	–	146
	Firpo Marberry	1.6	–	142.6	146

Single-Season Win Shares

	Player	Year	WS
1.	Walter Johnson	1913	54
2.	Walter Johnson	1912	47
3.	Walter Johnson	1915	42
4.	Walter Johnson	1914	38
	Walter Johnson	1918	38
	Harmon Killebrew	1967	38
7.	Rod Carew	1977	37
8.	Walter Johnson	1910	36
	Walter Johnson	1916	36
10.	Joe Cronin	1931	35

New York Yankees

(includes Baltimore Orioles, 1901-02)

Total Win Shares

	Player	Bat	Fld	Pit	WS
1.	Babe Ruth	531.5	40.1	1.4	574
2.	Mickey Mantle	507.0	58.1	–	565
3.	Lou Gehrig	456.5	33.0	–	489
4.	Joe DiMaggio	325.8	60.5	–	387
5.	Yogi Berra	267.5	104.7	–	375
6.	Bill Dickey	217.9	94.9	–	314
7.	Red Ruffing	25.6	0.0	238.0	265
8.	Don Mattingly	233.1	30.2	–	263
	Roy White	227.5	35.3	–	263
10.	Whitey Ford	3.0	–	255.6	261
11.	Willie Randolph	172.1	78.4	–	251
12.	Tony Lazzeri	192.9	50.4	–	243
13.	Bernie Williams	186.4	46.6	–	233
14.	Phil Rizzuto	132.9	97.2	–	231
15.	Earle Combs	194.9	31.1	–	227
16.	Charlie Keller	188.8	22.8	–	213
17.	Tommy Henrich	182.9	26.0	–	208
18.	Thurman Munson	145.3	62.3	–	206
19.	Graig Nettles	149.1	55.1	–	204
20.	Bob Shawkey	4.3	–	195.0	201
21.	Elston Howard	129.9	62.9	–	195
22.	Gil McDougald	138.7	56.1	–	194
23.	Bobby Murcer	161.6	27.5	–	191
24.	Frankie Crosetti	104.4	82.1	–	189
25.	Lefty Gomez	0.0	–	185.4	185

Single-Season Win Shares

	Player	Year	WS
1.	Babe Ruth	1923	55
2.	Jack Chesbro	1904	53
	Babe Ruth	1921	53
4.	Babe Ruth	1920	51
	Mickey Mantle	1957	51
6.	Mickey Mantle	1956	49
7.	Mickey Mantle	1961	48
8.	Babe Ruth	1924	45
	Babe Ruth	1926	45
	Babe Ruth	1927	45
	Babe Ruth	1928	45

Oakland Athletics

(includes Philadelphia Athletics, 1901-54 and Kansas City Athletics, 1955-67)

Total Win Shares

	Player	Bat	Fld	Pit	WS
1.	Rickey Henderson	303.8	33.0	–	338
2.	Eddie Plank	4.0	–	303.1	308
3.	Jimmie Foxx	234.7	28.9	–	265
4.	Eddie Collins	213.5	45.3	–	258
5.	Al Simmons	212.8	44.2	–	257
6.	Lefty Grove	0.0	–	249.1	248
7.	Bert Campaneris	166.5	81.1	0.0	247
8.	Reggie Jackson	212.8	24.8	–	238
9.	Mark McGwire	218.1	15.3	–	233
10.	Sal Bando	191.0	39.3	–	231
11.	Mickey Cochrane	151.4	64.8	–	217
	Bob Johnson	189.4	28.1	–	217
13.	Chief Bender	10.0	0.1	198.9	209
	Eddie Rommel	2.4	–	205.7	209
15.	Danny Murphy	167.2	40.8	–	207
16.	Harry Davis	182.1	23.8	–	205
17.	Home Run Baker	162.0	39.1	–	201
18.	Jimmy Dykes	131.7	63.0	0.3	194
19.	Topsy Hartsel	162.6	25.6	–	189
20.	Max Bishop	121.1	50.6	–	172
	Jose Canseco	156.6	15.2	–	172
22.	Jason Giambi	156.0	12.2	–	167
23.	Elmer Valo	146.1	19.4	–	165
	Rube Waddell	2.1	–	161.2	165
25.	Dwayne Murphy	126.8	35.8	–	162

Single-Season Win Shares

	Player	Year	WS
1.	Eddie Collins	1909	43
	Eddie Collins	1914	43
3.	Nap Lajoie	1901	42
	Lefty Grove	1931	42
5.	Jimmie Foxx	1933	41
	Reggie Jackson	1969	41
7.	Jimmie Foxx	1932	40
8.	Eddie Collins	1910	39
	Home Run Baker	1912	39
	Eddie Collins	1913	39
	Jose Canseco	1988	39
	Rickey Henderson	1990	39

Seattle Mariners

Total Win Shares

	Player	Bat	Fld	Pit	WS
1.	Ken Griffey Jr.	232.5	43.2	–	275
2.	Edgar Martinez	250.7	13.2	–	264
3.	Jay Buhner	149.7	23.3	–	173
4.	Alvin Davis	138.8	11.1	–	149
5.	Alex Rodriguez	114.3	33.7	–	148
6.	Randy Johnson	0.0	0.0	135.0	135
7.	Harold Reynolds	62.5	44.4	–	107
8.	Dan Wilson	42.1	46.9	–	90
9.	Mark Langston	–	–	75.6	77
10.	Phil Bradley	68.2	7.7	–	76
11.	Jamie Moyer	0.2	–	75.3	75
12.	Bruce Bochte	65.0	9.8	–	74
13.	Julio Cruz	41.3	30.8	–	72
	Mike Moore	0.0	–	72.2	72
15.	Dave Valle	29.1	37.7	–	67
16.	Ken Phelps	58.8	1.0	–	60
17.	Erik Hanson	–	–	59.0	59
18.	Dave Henderson	42.6	14.5	–	57
19.	Jim Presley	38.3	18.1	–	56
20.	Jim Beattie	–	–	53.0	55
21.	Floyd Bannister	–	–	48.6	49
	Joey Cora	39.0	10.3	–	49
	Ruppert Jones	37.9	11.8	–	49
	Bill Swift	0.0	–	48.5	49
25.	Mike Cameron	36.1	11.8	–	48

Single-Season Win Shares

	Player	Year	WS
1.	Alex Rodriguez	2000	37
2.	Ken Griffey Jr.	1997	36
	Ichiro Suzuki	2001	36
4.	Alex Rodriguez	1996	34
5.	Edgar Martinez	1995	32
	Bret Boone	2001	32
7.	Ken Griffey Jr.	1999	31
8.	Ken Griffey Jr.	1991	30
	Alex Rodriguez	1998	30
10.	Ken Griffey Jr.	1993	29
	Ken Griffey Jr.	1998	29
	Mike Cameron	2001	29

Tampa Bay Devil Rays

Total Win Shares

	Player	Bat	Fld	Pit	WS
1.	Fred McGriff	60.8	4.3	–	66
2.	Roberto Hernandez	–	–	35.9	36
3.	Greg Vaughn	28.1	2.7	–	31
4.	Miguel Cairo	14.4	15.6	–	30
5.	John Flaherty	9.7	19.2	–	29
	Albie Lopez	0.0	–	28.5	29
7.	Rolando Arrojo	0.0	–	23.2	23
8.	Randy Winn	12.4	7.5	–	21
	Esteban Yan	0.5	–	20.8	21
10.	Bubba Trammell	16.6	2.3	–	19
	Rick White	0.0	–	18.6	19
12.	Jose Canseco	17.8	0.1	–	18
	Jim Mecir	0.0	–	18.8	18
	Bryan Rekar	0.2	–	17.7	18
15.	Wilson Alvarez	0.0	–	16.7	17
	Ben Grieve	14.6	2.0	–	17
	Dave Martinez	12.7	4.4	–	17
	Tanyon Sturtze	0.0	–	17.1	17
19.	Mike DiFelice	5.0	12.2	–	16
	Gerald Williams	10.1	6.7	–	16
21.	Russ Johnson	11.3	4.0	–	15
	Kevin Stocker	6.0	8.1	–	15
23.	Quinton McCracken	8.4	6.0	–	14
24.	Steve Cox	11.0	2.1	–	13
	Bobby Smith	6.1	6.5	–	13

Single-Season Win Shares

	Player	Year	WS
1.	Fred McGriff	1999	24
2.	Rolando Arrojo	1998	17
	Ben Grieve	2001	17
4.	Fred McGriff	2000	16
	Greg Vaughn	2000	16
6.	Greg Vaughn	2001	15
7.	Roberto Hernandez	1999	14
	Gerald Williams	2000	14
9.	Fred McGriff	1998	13
	Jose Canseco	1999	13
	Dave Martinez	1999	13
	Albie Lopez	2000	13
	Fred McGriff	2001	13

Texas Rangers

(includes Washington Senators, 1961-71)

Total Win Shares

	Player	Bat	Fld	Pit	WS
1.	Frank Howard	193.5	13.3	–	208
2.	Ivan Rodriguez	114.8	92.1	–	206
3.	Rafael Palmeiro	180.7	17.3	–	199
4.	Juan Gonzalez	167.8	13.6	–	183
5.	Toby Harrah	132.5	38.9	–	173
6.	Jim Sundberg	75.4	83.6	–	159
7.	Ruben Sierra	127.6	20.9	–	147
8.	Charlie Hough	–	–	145.3	146
9.	Buddy Bell	95.4	39.1	–	134
10.	Rusty Greer	116.7	12.7	–	130
11.	Mike Hargrove	98.1	8.1	–	107
12.	Julio Franco	90.7	13.8	–	105
13.	Pete O'Brien	81.2	20.9	–	103
14.	Ken McMullen	76.3	24.7	–	102
15.	Jeff Burroughs	80.3	9.1	–	90
	Fergie Jenkins	0.0	–	89.0	90
17.	Kenny Rogers	0.0	–	85.7	86
18.	Will Clark	74.0	6.6	–	81
	Bump Wills	49.6	31.2	–	81
20.	Larry Parrish	71.7	8.0	–	80
21.	Ed Brinkman	27.2	48.3	–	76
22.	Jeff Russell	0.0	–	74.7	75
23.	Al Oliver	66.4	7.3	–	74
	Dean Palmer	60.4	12.2	–	74
25.	3 tied with				73

Single-Season Win Shares

	Player	Year	WS
1.	Frank Howard	1968	38
2.	Alex Rodriguez	2001	37
3.	Frank Howard	1969	34
	Ruben Sierra	1989	34
5.	Jeff Burroughs	1974	33
6.	Toby Harrah	1975	32
7.	Juan Gonzalez	1993	31
	Rafael Palmeiro	1993	31
	Rafael Palmeiro	1999	31
10.	Frank Howard	1970	30
	Julio Franco	1989	30

Toronto Blue Jays

Total Win Shares

	Player	Bat	Fld	Pit	WS
1.	Dave Stieb	0.0	0.0	211.1	210
2.	Tony Fernandez	132.3	69.6	–	203
3.	Lloyd Moseby	113.6	45.5	–	159
4.	George Bell	122.2	21.2	–	143
5.	Carlos Delgado	126.8	10.8	–	137
6.	Ernie Whitt	73.1	52.3	–	124
7.	Jim Clancy	–	–	122.2	122
8.	Jesse Barfield	88.7	31.8	–	121
9.	Jimmy Key	–	–	119.0	119
10.	Roberto Alomar	90.1	28.5	–	118
11.	John Olerud	98.4	14.1	–	112
12.	Joe Carter	92.1	16.8	–	109
13.	Tom Henke	–	–	103.4	104
14.	Pat Hentgen	0.0	–	101.8	102
15.	Willie Upshaw	83.2	13.0	–	97
16.	Rance Mulliniks	78.4	17.3	–	95
17.	Kelly Gruber	67.2	27.3	–	93
18.	Fred McGriff	83.0	8.3	–	91
19.	Damaso Garcia	49.4	35.5	–	87
20.	Devon White	58.9	27.7	–	86
21.	Duane Ward	–	–	81.2	82
22.	Shawn Green	63.1	13.8	–	77
	Shannon Stewart	65.1	12.6	–	77
24.	Juan Guzman	0.0	–	76.8	75
25.	2 tied with				74

Single-Season Win Shares

	Player	Year	WS
1.	John Olerud	1993	37
2.	Carlos Delgado	2000	36
3.	Roberto Alomar	1992	34
4.	Roger Clemens	1997	32
5.	Fred McGriff	1989	30
	Roberto Alomar	1993	30
7.	Paul Molitor	1993	29
8.	Jesse Barfield	1986	28
9.	Dave Winfield	1992	27
10.	Lloyd Moseby	1984	26
	Jesse Barfield	1985	26
	George Bell	1987	26
	Fred McGriff	1990	26

Arizona Diamondbacks

Total Win Shares

	Player	Bat	Fld	Pit	WS
1.	Luis Gonzalez	78.4	11.6	–	90
2.	Randy Johnson	0.0	–	77.8	78
3.	Jay Bell	56.0	18.7	–	74
4.	Steve Finley	41.7	17.7	0.2	60
5.	Matt Williams	38.2	17.2	–	55
6.	Tony Womack	22.7	16.8	–	40
7.	Damian Miller	18.3	18.4	–	37
8.	Brian Anderson	0.0	–	32.0	32
	Curt Schilling	0.0	–	31.6	32
10.	Omar Daal	0.7	–	28.2	29
11.	Byung-Hyun Kim	0.0	–	25.3	26
12.	Travis Lee	17.5	6.4	–	24
13.	David Dellucci	18.5	4.1	–	23
	Andy Fox	17.6	6.0	–	23
15.	Andy Benes	0.1	–	21.8	22
16.	Erubiel Durazo	18.6	2.4	–	21
	Gregg Olson	0.6	–	20.7	21
	Kelly Stinnett	11.1	10.6	–	21
19.	Greg Colbrunn	18.0	2.0	–	20
20.	Craig Counsell	9.9	8.6	–	19
	Greg Swindell	0.0	–	19.2	19
22.	Devon White	13.9	4.5	–	18
23.	Tony Batista	11.4	4.6	–	16
	Mark Grace	13.6	2.4	–	16
25.	2 tied with				15

Single-Season Win Shares

	Player	Year	WS
1.	Luis Gonzalez	2001	37
2.	Luis Gonzalez	2000	27
3.	Luis Gonzalez	1999	26
	Randy Johnson	1999	26
	Matt Williams	1999	26
	Randy Johnson	2000	26
	Randy Johnson	2001	26
8.	Steve Finley	1999	24
	Curt Schilling	2001	24
10.	Jay Bell	1999	23

Atlanta Braves

(includes Boston Braves, 1876-1952 and Milwaukee Braves, 1953-65)

Total Win Shares

	Player	Bat	Fld	Pit	WS
1.	Hank Aaron	559.4	67.2	–	629
2.	Kid Nichols	11.4	0.5	429.0	440
3.	Eddie Mathews	373.8	57.2	–	434
4.	Warren Spahn	7.4	–	395.4	405
5.	Phil Niekro	0.0	–	337.4	336
6.	Dale Murphy	230.1	45.1	–	277
7.	Herman Long	144.2	94.5	–	238
8.	Tom Glavine	0.7	–	236.7	236
9.	Fred Tenney	187.7	32.2	0.0	221
10.	Greg Maddux	0.0	–	215.0	216
11.	Rabbit Maranville	111.1	93.2	–	205
12.	Wally Berger	167.6	32.8	–	202
	Hugh Duffy	156.5	44.9	–	202
14.	Jim Whitney	42.6	1.6	155.3	200
15.	Vic Willis	0.0	0.2	193.2	193
16.	John Smoltz	3.2	–	185.2	189
17.	Tommy Holmes	153.6	34.1	–	188
18.	Chipper Jones	165.7	19.3	–	186
19.	John Clarkson	3.2	0.0	180.9	183
20.	Billy Nash	125.0	56.0	0.2	180
21.	Tommy Bond	7.5	0.2	170.5	179
22.	Johnny Logan	107.6	66.8	–	176
	Jack Stivetts	34.3	2.8	138.7	176
24.	Del Crandall	91.7	73.9	–	167
25.	Joe Adcock	146.4	19.4	–	166

Single-Season Win Shares—1900-2001

	Player	Year	WS
1.	Hank Aaron	1963	41
2.	Eddie Mathews	1953	39
3.	Hank Aaron	1959	38
	Eddie Mathews	1960	38
	Hank Aaron	1969	38
6.	Eddie Mathews	1959	37
7.	Bill James	1914	36
	Wally Berger	1933	36
9.	Hank Aaron	1957	35
	Hank Aaron	1960	35
	Hank Aaron	1961	35
	Terry Pendleton	1992	35

Chicago Cubs

Total Win Shares

	Player	Bat	Fld	Pit	WS
1.	Cap Anson	338.1	40.6	0.7	381
2.	Billy Williams	304.7	44.9	–	350
3.	Ryne Sandberg	249.7	93.6	–	346
4.	Ernie Banks	264.9	67.1	–	332
5.	Ron Santo	254.5	67.0	–	321
6.	Gabby Hartnett	211.9	108.1	–	319
7.	Stan Hack	250.5	65.7	–	316
8.	Mark Grace	233.0	35.5	–	269
9.	Jimmy Ryan	213.6	43.7	7.3	265
10.	Three Finger Brown	1.8	0.0	233.9	237
11.	Frank Chance	213.3	22.3	–	236
12.	Phil Cavarretta	204.6	24.9	–	230
13.	Sammy Sosa	198.9	28.0	–	227
14.	Charlie Root	0.8	–	220.8	223
15.	Joe Tinker	122.5	99.5	–	222
16.	Bill Hutchison	3.7	0.0	216.4	220
17.	Johnny Evers	161.3	56.7	–	218
	Wildfire Schulte	178.0	38.0	–	218
19.	Billy Herman	150.9	61.2	–	214
20.	Fergie Jenkins	2.3	–	199.8	203
21.	Bill Nicholson	179.6	23.2	–	202
22.	Larry Corcoran	11.7	0.8	177.0	190
23.	Bill Dahlen	120.3	61.6	–	183
24.	Clark Griffith	9.0	0.2	173.4	182
25.	Hippo Vaughn	3.0	–	170.8	174

Single-Season Win Shares—1900-2001

	Player	Year	WS
1.	Rogers Hornsby	1929	42
	Sammy Sosa	2001	42
3.	Ron Santo	1967	38
	Ryne Sandberg	1984	38
5.	Fergie Jenkins	1971	37
	Ryne Sandberg	1991	37
7.	Three Finger Brown	1909	36
	Pete Alexander	1920	36
	Ron Santo	1964	36
10.	Three Finger Brown	1906	35
	Frank Chance	1906	35
	Hack Wilson	1930	35
	Sammy Sosa	1998	35

Cincinnati Reds

Total Win Shares

	Player	Bat	Fld	Pit	WS
1.	Pete Rose	386.0	72.4	–	458
2.	Johnny Bench	255.3	99.6	–	356
3.	Barry Larkin	228.9	92.1	–	320
4.	Bid McPhee	206.8	98.7	–	305
5.	Frank Robinson	245.4	32.4	–	278
6.	Tony Perez	231.6	37.1	–	270
7.	Dave Concepcion	146.9	124.3	0.0	269
8.	Joe Morgan	218.2	45.2	–	262
9.	Edd Roush	207.3	44.5	–	252
10.	Vada Pinson	192.8	50.2	–	244
11.	Tony Mullane	24.0	3.3	198.8	225
12.	Heine Groh	167.6	50.9	–	219
13.	Eppa Rixey	0.4	–	208.9	211
14.	Dolf Luque	8.1	0.0	195.6	204
	Bucky Walters	10.2	0.0	193.8	204
16.	George Foster	171.9	26.6	–	199
17.	Ted Kluszewski	160.8	18.5	–	179
18.	Paul Derringer	0.0	–	174.6	176
19.	Frank McCormick	150.3	23.9	–	174
20.	Ken Griffey Sr.	149.9	20.1	–	170
21.	Eric Davis	142.0	25.4	–	167
	Frank Dwyer	4.5	0.2	163.3	167
23.	Dan Driessen	142.8	19.5	–	161
24.	Noodles Hahn	0.2	0.0	156.2	158
25.	Will White	7.3	0.0	149.6	157

Single-Season Win Shares—1900-2001

	Player	Year	WS
1.	Joe Morgan	1975	44
2.	Cy Seymour	1905	42
3.	Frank Robinson	1962	41
4.	Joe Morgan	1973	40
5.	Dolf Luque	1923	39
	Joe Morgan	1972	39
7.	Bucky Walters	1939	38
8.	Heine Groh	1917	37
	Pete Rose	1969	37
	Johnny Bench	1972	37
	Joe Morgan	1974	37
	Joe Morgan	1976	37

Colorado Rockies

Total Win Shares

	Player	Bat	Fld	Pit	WS
1.	Larry Walker	114.7	22.3	–	137
2.	Dante Bichette	99.7	22.2	–	122
3.	Vinny Castilla	66.1	30.0	–	97
4.	Andres Galarraga	85.1	9.5	–	95
5.	Todd Helton	78.6	12.9	–	93
6.	Ellis Burks	50.6	13.5	–	64
7.	Neifi Perez	19.5	38.0	–	58
	Eric Young	40.0	18.2	–	58
9.	Pedro Astacio	0.0	–	44.5	45
10.	Bruce Ruffin	0.2	–	43.3	44
11.	Curtis Leskanic	0.8	–	40.6	41
	Steve Reed	0.2	–	40.7	41
13.	Walt Weiss	19.6	19.8	–	40
14.	Darren Holmes	0.0	–	37.1	36
15.	Kevin Ritz	0.0	–	32.9	34
16.	Jeff Cirillo	22.0	10.8	–	33
	Jerry Dipoto	0.0	–	33.0	33
18.	Armando Reynoso	0.0	–	30.6	31
19.	Charlie Hayes	22.0	8.5	–	30
	Jeff Reed	17.7	12.0	–	30
21.	Joe Girardi	10.0	17.2	–	27
22.	John Thomson	0.0	–	25.8	26
23.	Brian Bohanon	0.3	–	23.8	24
24.	Jose Jimenez	0.1	–	22.9	23
	Jamey Wright	0.0	–	23.3	23

Single-Season Win Shares

	Player	Year	WS
1.	Larry Walker	1997	32
2.	Todd Helton	2000	29
3.	Ellis Burks	1996	28
4.	Todd Helton	2001	26
5.	Andres Galarraga	1996	25
	Larry Walker	2001	25
7.	Larry Walker	1999	24
8.	Andres Galarraga	1993	23
	Dante Bichette	1995	23
	Vinny Castilla	1996	23

Florida Marlins

Total Win Shares

	Player	Bat	Fld	Pit	WS
1.	Gary Sheffield	91.3	8.6	–	100
2.	Cliff Floyd	72.1	5.6	–	77
3.	Jeff Conine	64.8	11.2	–	76
4.	Charles Johnson	29.3	35.0	–	64
5.	Luis Castillo	37.1	17.3	–	55
6.	Kevin Brown	0.0	–	48.9	49
	Robb Nen	0.0	–	48.7	49
8.	Mike Lowell	37.0	10.7	–	48
9.	Derrek Lee	36.1	6.5	–	43
	Preston Wilson	32.9	9.7	–	43
11.	Kevin Millar	38.2	3.8	–	42
12.	Edgar Renteria	24.8	16.4	–	41
13.	Kurt Abbott	21.8	12.2	–	33
	Antonio Alfonseca	0.0	–	34.4	33
15.	Mark Kotsay	23.6	7.7	–	32
16.	Pat Rapp	0.0	–	30.3	31
17.	Ryan Dempster	0.0	–	30.6	30
	Alex Fernandez	0.0	–	30.2	30
19.	Greg Colbrunn	24.1	5.0	–	29
20.	Mike Redmond	12.4	14.1	–	27
	Devon White	21.5	5.1	–	27
22.	Chuck Carr	12.7	12.9	–	26
	Al Leiter	0.0	–	25.8	26
	Terry Pendleton	19.0	6.7	–	26
25.	Alex Gonzalez	15.1	10.4	–	25

Single-Season Win Shares

	Player	Year	WS
1.	Gary Sheffield	1996	34
2.	Kevin Brown	1996	26
	Cliff Floyd	2001	26
4.	Moises Alou	1997	23
	Kevin Brown	1997	23
6.	Gary Sheffield	1997	22
7.	Bobby Bonilla	1997	21
	Charles Johnson	1997	21
9.	Jeff Conine	1995	20
	Mike Lowell	2000	20
	Preston Wilson	2000	20
	Mike Lowell	2001	20
	Kevin Millar	2001	20

Houston Astros

Total Win Shares

	Player	Bat	Fld	Pit	WS
1.	Craig Biggio	268.5	74.1	–	342
2.	Jeff Bagwell	290.9	25.2	–	318
3.	Jose Cruz	231.7	39.9	–	273
4.	Cesar Cedeno	209.5	42.7	–	253
5.	Jimmy Wynn	202.6	30.1	–	232
6.	Bob Watson	174.5	17.7	–	194
7.	Joe Morgan	144.9	32.1	–	176
	Terry Puhl	143.7	32.7	–	176
9.	Bill Doran	124.9	43.2	–	168
10.	Doug Rader	96.4	38.1	–	134
11.	Larry Dierker	0.1	–	131.3	132
	Joe Niekro	1.0	–	130.5	132
13.	Ken Caminiti	90.6	36.8	–	127
14.	Kevin Bass	103.5	22.8	–	126
15.	Glenn Davis	106.5	15.0	–	120
16.	Don Wilson	0.3	–	107.3	108
17.	J.R. Richard	0.3	–	103.1	106
18.	Nolan Ryan	0.0	–	106.0	105
	Dave Smith	0.3	–	104.1	105
20.	Rusty Staub	90.9	12.8	–	104
21.	Ken Forsch	0.1	–	100.6	100
	Mike Scott	0.0	–	100.0	100
23.	Enos Cabell	78.6	20.5	–	98
24.	Denny Walling	76.1	17.5	–	95
25.	Craig Reynolds	44.8	46.6	0.0	91

Single-Season Win Shares

	Player	Year	WS
1.	Jeff Bagwell	1996	41
2.	Craig Biggio	1997	38
3.	Jeff Bagwell	1999	37
4.	Jimmy Wynn	1969	36
5.	Craig Biggio	1998	35
6.	Cesar Cedeno	1972	33
7.	Jimmy Wynn	1968	32
	Craig Biggio	1992	32
	Craig Biggio	1996	32
	Jeff Bagwell	1997	32
	Lance Berkman	2001	32

Los Angeles Dodgers

(includes Brooklyn Dodgers, 1884-1957)

Total Win Shares

	Player	Bat	Fld	Pit	WS
1.	Zack Wheat	316.4	56.8	–	373
2.	Duke Snider	282.7	53.0	–	337
3.	Pee Wee Reese	203.9	111.3	–	314
4.	Willie Davis	204.1	65.7	–	270
5.	Gil Hodges	227.0	34.0	–	261
6.	Don Drysdale	7.0	–	250.9	258
7.	Jackie Robinson	201.8	55.0	–	257
8.	Jim Gilliam	178.4	68.2	–	247
9.	Don Sutton	0.0	–	237.4	238
10.	Dazzy Vance	0.0	–	229.4	229
11.	Ron Cey	170.8	52.8	–	223
	Steve Garvey	190.4	33.6	–	223
13.	Carl Furillo	174.4	42.4	–	217
14.	Maury Wills	139.4	74.0	–	215
15.	Roy Campanella	137.6	68.3	–	207
16.	Dixie Walker	173.2	33.5	–	206
17.	Brickyard Kennedy	10.2	0.0	186.0	196
18.	Sandy Koufax	0.0	–	193.5	194
19.	Adonis Terry	37.2	5.4	149.2	192
20.	Pedro Guerrero	162.3	21.5	–	185
	Bill Russell	102.2	83.9	–	185
22.	Davey Lopes	134.4	45.9	–	180
23.	Nap Rucker	0.6	–	175.7	177
24.	Burleigh Grimes	7.4	–	162.7	169
25.	2 tied with				168

Single-Season Win Shares—1900-2001

	Player	Year	WS
1.	Duke Snider	1954	39
	Mike Piazza	1997	39
3.	Jackie Robinson	1951	38
4.	Duke Snider	1953	37
5.	Dazzy Vance	1924	36
	Jackie Robinson	1949	36
	Duke Snider	1955	36
	Tommy Davis	1962	36
9.	Harry Lumley	1906	35
	Zack Wheat	1924	35
	Sandy Koufax	1966	35
	Pedro Guerrero	1985	35

Milwaukee Brewers
(includes Seattle Pilots, 1969)

Total Win Shares

Player	Bat	Fld	Pit	WS
1. Robin Yount	317.3	103.1	–	423
2. Paul Molitor	268.1	44.9	–	313
3. Cecil Cooper	184.5	16.6	–	202
4. Jim Gantner	93.5	69.2	0.2	163
5. Don Money	119.1	28.8	–	148
6. Ben Oglivie	129.0	17.2	–	147
7. Gorman Thomas	102.1	23.5	–	127
8. B.J. Surhoff	72.3	41.6	–	114
9. George Scott	93.8	12.3	–	106
10. Jeff Cirillo	75.3	27.1	–	104
11. Greg Vaughn	89.1	13.7	–	102
12. Sixto Lezcano	84.5	16.4	–	101
Charlie Moore	58.0	39.7	–	101
Jim Slaton	0.0	–	102.1	101
15. Teddy Higuera	–	–	99.5	100
16. Jeromy Burnitz	78.2	15.3	–	93
17. Mike Caldwell	–	–	89.7	90
18. John Briggs	70.5	10.1	–	80
Rob Deer	68.1	13.2	–	80
Dave Nilsson	67.3	12.3	–	80
21. Jose Valentin	45.2	31.5	–	78
22. Moose Haas	–	–	76.9	77
23. Bill Wegman	–	0.0	75.9	76
24. Tommy Harper	57.3	11.6	–	70
Dave May	50.6	18.3	–	70

Single-Season Win Shares

Player	Year	WS
1. Robin Yount	1982	39
2. Robin Yount	1989	34
3. Tommy Harper	1970	33
Robin Yount	1983	33
5. Robin Yount	1988	31
6. Paul Molitor	1982	30
Paul Molitor	1991	30
Fernando Vina	1998	30
9. Cecil Cooper	1982	29
Paul Molitor	1987	29

Montreal Expos

Total Win Shares

Player	Bat	Fld	Pit	WS
1. Tim Raines	230.3	36.3	–	268
2. Gary Carter	153.5	86.9	–	239
3. Andre Dawson	168.8	47.8	–	216
4. Tim Wallach	137.6	72.1	0.2	211
5. Steve Rogers	0.0	–	182.3	182
6. Vladimir Guerrero	106.1	13.6	–	119
7. Bob Bailey	91.8	18.5	–	110
8. Warren Cromartie	84.3	22.4	–	106
Dennis Martinez	0.0	–	106.4	106
10. Marquis Grissom	68.8	33.9	–	103
Larry Walker	82.6	20.5	–	103
12. Ron Fairly	82.8	11.7	–	94
13. Larry Parrish	70.0	21.1	–	92
Rusty Staub	82.5	8.6	–	92
15. Rondell White	64.8	25.3	–	91
16. Moises Alou	70.0	18.2	–	89
17. Andres Galarraga	71.8	12.8	–	85
18. Bryn Smith	0.0	–	82.7	83
19. Mike Lansing	50.9	31.3	–	82
20. Tim Burke	0.0	–	78.2	79
Ellis Valentine	66.2	13.9	–	79
22. Chris Speier	38.7	37.0	–	76
23. Delino DeShields	58.0	16.3	–	74
24. Hubie Brooks	58.6	13.1	–	73
25. Steve Renko	3.1	0.0	70.2	72

Single-Season Win Shares

Player	Year	WS
1. Tim Raines	1985	36
2. Tim Raines	1987	34
3. Rusty Staub	1971	32
Tim Raines	1984	32
Tim Raines	1986	32
6. Gary Carter	1982	31
7. Rusty Staub	1970	30
Gary Carter	1980	30
Gary Carter	1984	30
Marquis Grissom	1993	30

New York Mets

Total Win Shares

	Player	Bat	Fld	Pit	WS
1.	Tom Seaver	0.0	–	265.7	266
2.	Darryl Strawberry	174.8	20.4	–	195
3.	Howard Johnson	140.6	28.0	–	169
4.	Jerry Koosman	0.0	–	163.3	163
5.	Dwight Gooden	2.1	–	151.8	154
6.	Edgardo Alfonzo	109.4	33.9	–	144
7.	Keith Hernandez	126.3	15.5	–	142
8.	Cleon Jones	116.2	25.4	–	141
9.	Ed Kranepool	110.1	19.9	–	132
	Mookie Wilson	101.5	30.2	–	132
11.	Bud Harrelson	67.2	63.8	–	130
12.	Jerry Grote	59.0	57.9	–	116
13.	Kevin McReynolds	99.2	14.3	–	114
14.	Lee Mazzilli	87.4	15.9	–	104
15.	Sid Fernandez	0.6	–	99.8	101
16.	Jon Matlack	0.1	–	96.9	99
17.	Wayne Garrett	67.3	30.7	–	97
18.	John Franco	0.0	–	94.6	94
	Mike Piazza	76.9	17.2	–	94
20.	Rusty Staub	82.9	11.3	–	93
21.	Dave Magadan	80.6	10.6	–	91
22.	John Stearns	56.9	31.8	–	89
23.	John Olerud	77.1	9.7	–	87
24.	Tommie Agee	62.1	23.5	–	86
25.	2 tied with				83

Single-Season Win Shares

	Player	Year	WS
1.	Howard Johnson	1989	38
2.	Edgardo Alfonzo	2000	36
3.	John Olerud	1998	34
4.	Keith Hernandez	1984	33
	Gary Carter	1985	33
	Dwight Gooden	1985	33
7.	Tom Seaver	1969	32
	Tom Seaver	1971	32
9.	Kevin McReynolds	1988	31
10.	Cleon Jones	1969	30
	Darryl Strawberry	1987	30
	Darryl Strawberry	1988	30
	Bernard Gilkey	1996	30
	Robin Ventura	1999	30

Philadelphia Phillies

Total Win Shares

	Player	Bat	Fld	Pit	WS
1.	Mike Schmidt	378.3	88.3	–	467
2.	Ed Delahanty	266.7	37.5	–	305
3.	Richie Ashburn	222.3	68.2	–	289
4.	Robin Roberts	4.2	–	272.0	277
5.	Steve Carlton	3.2	–	275.1	276
6.	Sherry Magee	238.1	35.4	–	274
7.	Pete Alexander	2.8	–	236.2	238
8.	Roy Thomas	193.6	39.3	0.2	233
9.	Del Ennis	187.1	28.6	–	215
10.	Dick Allen	191.7	19.1	–	211
11.	Johnny Callison	177.1	32.2	–	209
12.	Gavy Cravath	169.7	17.5	–	188
	Chuck Klein	164.9	23.4	–	188
14.	Greg Luzinski	165.3	18.2	–	184
15.	Puddin' Head Jones	125.7	51.5	–	179
16.	John Titus	153.0	23.4	–	177
17.	Cy Williams	147.8	27.4	–	176
18.	Sam Thompson	148.0	18.3	–	166
19.	Billy Hamilton	146.2	19.1	–	165
20.	Von Hayes	132.1	24.2	–	158
	Fred Luderus	137.9	20.4	–	158
22.	Darren Daulton	113.6	39.3	–	154
23.	Larry Bowa	79.0	72.9	–	151
24.	Garry Maddox	106.1	44.2	–	150
25.	Tony Taylor	100.2	47.7	–	148

Single-Season Win Shares—1900-2001

	Player	Year	WS
1.	Pete Alexander	1916	44
2.	Pete Alexander	1915	43
3.	Dick Allen	1964	41
4.	Pete Alexander	1917	40
	Steve Carlton	1972	40
6.	Mike Schmidt	1974	39
7.	Sherry Magee	1907	38
8.	Mike Schmidt	1980	37
	Mike Schmidt	1982	37
10.	Sherry Magee	1910	36

Pittsburgh Pirates

Total Win Shares

Player	Bat	Fld	Pit	WS
1. Honus Wagner	468.4	130.8	0.6	598
2. Paul Waner	328.6	57.5	–	388
3. Roberto Clemente	316.4	59.5	–	377
4. Willie Stargell	339.1	31.4	–	370
5. Max Carey	240.5	86.5	–	329
6. Arky Vaughan	230.1	68.8	–	299
7. Fred Clarke	233.6	49.1	–	282
8. Pie Traynor	192.5	79.6	–	274
9. Wilbur Cooper	8.9	–	242.3	250
10. Tommy Leach	173.2	74.2	–	247
11. Babe Adams	7.6	–	234.1	243
12. Lloyd Waner	168.7	66.4	–	235
13. Bill Mazeroski	105.2	112.4	–	219
14. Sam Leever	2.7	0.0	209.1	212
15. Bob Friend	0.9	–	205.3	205
16. Dave Parker	170.9	29.3	–	202
17. Barry Bonds	173.0	26.6	–	201
18. Ralph Kiner	174.8	19.5	–	194
19. Deacon Phillippe	3.0	0.0	178.7	183
20. Al Oliver	146.4	33.8	–	181
21. Ginger Beaumont	136.8	30.8	–	168
22. Andy Van Slyke	134.7	31.9	–	167
23. Gus Suhr	140.0	21.1	–	161
24. Vern Law	5.8	0.0	153.3	157
Ed Morris	0.2	0.1	156.5	157

Single-Season Win Shares—1900-2001

Player	Year	WS
1. Honus Wagner	1908	59
2. Honus Wagner	1905	46
Honus Wagner	1906	46
4. Honus Wagner	1907	44
5. Honus Wagner	1904	43
6. Honus Wagner	1909	42
7. Barry Bonds	1992	41
8. Arky Vaughan	1935	39
9. Honus Wagner	1901	37
Ralph Kiner	1949	37
Dave Parker	1978	37
Barry Bonds	1990	37
Barry Bonds	1991	37

St. Louis Cardinals

Total Win Shares

Player	Bat	Fld	Pit	WS
1. Stan Musial	538.7	66.8	0.0	604
2. Rogers Hornsby	319.5	42.8	–	361
3. Lou Brock	281.3	40.3	–	320
4. Bob Gibson	6.0	–	313.3	317
5. Enos Slaughter	240.6	45.5	–	285
6. Ozzie Smith	168.8	106.6	–	273
7. Ted Simmons	187.5	60.2	–	246
8. Ken Boyer	183.7	63.1	–	245
9. Curt Flood	144.9	75.1	–	221
10. Joe Medwick	186.6	27.3	–	215
11. Jim Bottomley	195.0	18.8	–	214
12. Ray Lankford	173.2	35.8	–	211
13. Red Schoendienst	130.7	78.8	–	210
14. Jesse Haines	0.2	0.0	206.0	206
15. Frankie Frisch	132.6	62.8	–	196
16. Bob Caruthers	59.6	3.5	126.6	191
17. Johnny Mize	166.6	13.0	–	180
18. Tip O'Neill	141.5	26.1	9.4	177
19. Marty Marion	77.8	95.5	–	173
20. Willie McGee	130.3	39.1	–	169
21. Keith Hernandez	151.0	18.8	–	168
22. Harry Brecheen	1.4	–	160.5	163
Dizzy Dean	0.6	–	163.6	163
24. Bill Sherdel	5.2	0.0	156.3	162
25. Dave Foutz	30.4	3.4	128.4	161

Single-Season Win Shares—1900-2001

Player	Year	WS
1. Rogers Hornsby	1922	47
2. Stan Musial	1948	46
3. Stan Musial	1946	44
4. Rogers Hornsby	1921	41
Joe Torre	1971	41
Mark McGwire	1998	41
7. Joe Medwick	1937	40
Stan Musial	1949	40
9. Stan Musial	1943	39
Stan Musial	1951	39

San Diego Padres

Total Win Shares

	Player	Bat	Fld	Pit	WS
1.	Tony Gwynn	353.4	45.1	–	398
2.	Dave Winfield	153.8	17.9	–	172
3.	Gene Richards	104.4	14.5	–	120
4.	Nate Colbert	98.0	13.3	–	112
5.	Trevor Hoffman	0.8	–	109.4	110
6.	Ken Caminiti	91.5	16.3	–	108
7.	Garry Templeton	51.6	53.1	–	105
8.	Terry Kennedy	72.7	29.5	–	102
9.	Randy Jones	0.0	–	98.0	98
10.	Gene Tenace	71.7	14.6	–	86
11.	Eric Show	0.5	–	84.5	83
12.	Bip Roberts	63.3	17.3	–	82
13.	Steve Finley	65.6	14.3	–	80
14.	Johnny Grubb	65.6	9.1	–	75
	Benito Santiago	40.2	34.3	–	75
16.	Carmelo Martinez	60.8	13.1	–	74
17.	Phil Nevin	61.7	9.8	–	72
18.	Andy Benes	0.2	–	70.5	71
19.	Tim Flannery	46.0	21.4	–	70
20.	Andy Ashby	0.0	–	68.7	69
21.	Ed Whitson	0.0	–	68.1	68
22.	Wally Joyner	60.8	5.6	–	66
	Kevin McReynolds	49.9	16.0	–	66
24.	Roberto Alomar	44.8	18.0	–	64
25.	2 tied with				59

Single-Season Win Shares

	Player	Year	WS
1.	Tony Gwynn	1997	39
2.	Ken Caminiti	1996	38
3.	Tony Gwynn	1984	35
4.	Dave Winfield	1979	33
5.	Gary Sheffield	1992	32
6.	Jack Clark	1989	31
	Phil Nevin	2001	31
8.	Tony Gwynn	1989	30
	Greg Vaughn	1998	30
10.	Tony Gwynn	1986	29
	Tony Gwynn	1987	29
	Ryan Klesko	2001	29

San Francisco Giants

(includes New York Giants, 1883-1957)

Total Win Shares

	Player	Bat	Fld	Pit	WS
1.	Willie Mays	525.1	101.3	–	626
2.	Mel Ott	474.0	51.6	–	528
3.	Christy Mathewson	11.9	0.2	413.0	425
4.	Willie McCovey	337.5	23.4	–	363
5.	Barry Bonds	305.0	16.7	–	322
6.	Carl Hubbell	0.5	–	303.3	305
7.	Amos Rusie	8.3	0.3	274.9	283
8.	Bill Terry	245.6	32.2	–	278
9.	Mickey Welch	13.2	0.4	260.7	275
10.	Larry Doyle	222.5	45.4	–	269
11.	Juan Marichal	0.7	–	257.9	260
12.	Mike Tiernan	219.4	31.0	0.0	251
13.	George Burns	206.2	31.9	–	239
14.	Roger Connor	203.9	23.3	–	228
15.	Will Clark	204.5	17.0	–	222
16.	Travis Jackson	137.1	74.0	–	211
17.	Ross Youngs	180.8	25.6	–	206
18.	George Davis	152.9	48.4	–	202
19.	Art Fletcher	115.0	82.7	–	197
20.	George Van Haltren	156.5	32.3	1.3	190
21.	Bobby Bonds	160.0	27.7	–	187
22.	Art Devlin	126.7	57.0	–	183
23.	Tim Keefe	2.1	0.0	179.8	181
24.	Orlando Cepeda	163.9	15.5	–	179
25.	Hal Schumacher	3.0	0.0	174.0	176

Single-Season Win Shares—1900-2001

	Player	Year	WS
1.	Barry Bonds	2001	54
2.	Barry Bonds	1993	47
3.	Will Clark	1989	44
4.	Willie Mays	1965	43
5.	Joe McGinnity	1904	42
6.	Willie Mays	1962	41
7.	Joe McGinnity	1903	40
	Rogers Hornsby	1927	40
	Willie Mays	1954	40
	Willie Mays	1955	40
	Willie Mays	1958	40

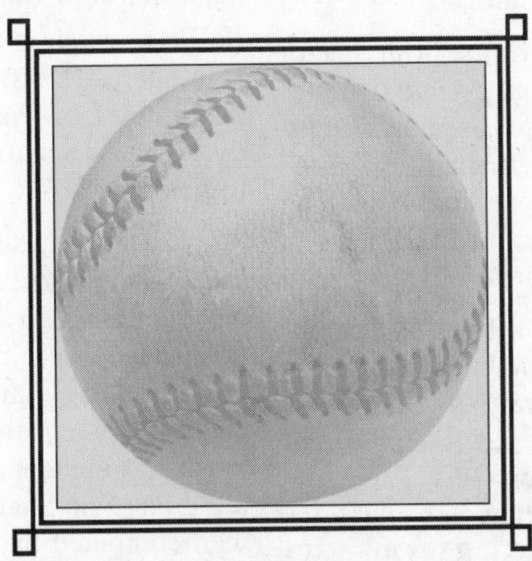

Miscellaneous

The following charts are presented as a sort of potpourri of data that can be generated when using the Win Shares method. Expanded versions of a few of the charts will be available in an "electronic book" version (as a downloadable Adobe PDF file), and can be purchased via the STATS, Inc. website (www.stats.com).

The first sample section lists the yearly and career Win Shares for some of the top players in history, as well as for a group that earned 50 career Win Shares apiece. The last part of this first section lists the career totals for the top 300 players of all time. The sum of batting, fielding and pitching Win Shares will not always round to the total Win Shares credited for a given season, since the partials are rounded in accordance with the circumstances of the appropriate team(s).

Next, we list the batting Win Shares generated by a group of 12 of the leading hitters in history. We include the Runs Created (RC), Outs Made (Outs) and Marginal Runs (MR) in the yearly breakdown, as well as the player's seasonal age as of June 30. The Marginal Runs are the claim points generated and are rounded to the nearest integer in the charts. The career Win Shares per 100 outs are computed by adjusting the actual outs by a ratio of team offensive innings to batting outs each season and then summing them. Offensive innings are determined by getting the team's pitcher innings, adding its road losses, subtracting its home wins, and then multiplying the resulting sum by three to obtain a fractional innings total. The total career adjusted outs are listed in parentheses.

The Year of Birth charts break down the Win Shares generated by players at various stages of their careers. The players listed produced a minimum of 150 career Win Shares if they were born between 1930 and 1950, 100 if they were born between 1951 and 1958, or one if their year of birth was 1959.

Next, we list the leading players by year and league in terms of batting, pitching and fielding Win Shares. The fielding charts are broken down by position and include estimated innings prior to 1987 and actual innings thereafter. Multiple players are listed for outfielders, as well as for more recent seasons at all positions.

The Runs Scored and Home Run Factor chart displays the numbers that go into computing those park factors. They're based on weighting the computed season's figures at four and the surrounding four seasons at one apiece, as long as there are no park breaks. For 2001 factors, only the 1999-2001 seasons are used.

The Offensive/Defensive Team Splits describe much of the information that's involved in dividing the team's Win Shares between the offense and defense (pitching and fielding combined), including Park Factor (PF), Park Run Adjustment (PA), Expected Runs Scored (ExR), Expected Opponent Runs (XOR), Offensive Credits (OffC) and Defensive Credits (DefC). ExR, XOR, OffC and DefC are presented in rounded integer form. The Offensive Percentage (Off%) is the ratio of offensive to total credits, which is then multiplied by three times the team wins to determine Offensive Win Shares (OWS). The Defensive Win Shares (DWS) is the difference between Total and Offensive Win Shares. The ratio of total credits to total Win Shares is listed in the Cost column.

Much of this information is repeated in the next chart, the breakdown for 2001 teams, dividing Win Shares among batting, pitching and fielding. But this one includes the percentage of defensive Win Shares that is credited to pitchers (PitPct), which is then applied to the defensive Win Shares (DefWS) to obtain the total distributed to hurlers (PitWS) only. The difference between DefWS and PitWS is the amount credited to fielders (FldWS).

The way those fielding Win Shares are divided among the various positions is detailed in the Fielding Wins Allocation chart. The claim percentage at each position is listed, as well as the resulting claim points and Win Shares. The claim points equal the product of the position's intrinsic weight and the claim percentage minus .200. The Win Shares allotted to each position is then computed by multiplying the team's total fielding Win Shares by the ratio of position claim points to total team fielding claim points.

We then include pitching worksheets for a sampling of teams that were either very good (minimum 102 wins) or very bad (maximum .250 winning percentage). The basic stats of each team's pitchers are listed, as are the claim points and Win Shares they ultimately earned.

Finally, we list the difference (Diff) between Actual (ActDP) and Expected Double Plays (ExpDP) by team from 1950 through the 2001 campaign.

Career Summaries for Top 40 Players

Babe Ruth

Year	Bat	Field	Pitch	Sum	WS
1914	0.17	–	0.74	0.91	1
1915	6.43	–	16.87	23.31	23
1916	4.64	–	31.96	36.60	37
1917	6.01	–	30.40	36.41	36
1918	24.65	2.48	12.67	39.80	40
1919	33.51	1.98	7.94	43.43	43
1920	47.88	3.27	0.17	51.31	51
1921	47.69	4.98	0.00	52.67	53
1922	25.02	3.58	–	28.60	29
1923	48.48	6.23	–	54.71	55
1924	41.67	2.94	–	44.61	45
1925	11.64	1.47	–	13.11	13
1926	42.60	2.63	–	45.22	45
1927	40.47	4.06	–	44.52	45
1928	42.69	2.16	–	44.85	45
1929	30.64	1.75	–	32.39	32
1930	36.48	1.23	0.79	38.50	38
1931	36.29	1.55	–	37.84	38
1932	34.16	1.64	–	35.80	36
1933	27.62	0.83	0.49	28.94	29
1934	18.21	1.82	–	20.03	20
1935	1.81	0.13	–	1.95	2
Totals	608.76	44.72	102.04	755.52	756

Ty Cobb

Year	Bat	Field	Pitch	Sum	WS
1905	2.66	1.26	–	3.92	4
1906	13.21	2.79	–	15.99	16
1907	37.38	3.64	–	41.02	41
1908	34.02	2.07	–	36.09	36
1909	39.88	4.14	–	44.01	44
1910	40.02	5.39	–	45.41	45
1911	41.28	6.04	–	47.32	47
1912	36.52	3.58	–	40.10	40
1913	27.71	3.34	–	31.05	31
1914	23.59	2.27	–	25.85	26
1915	41.56	6.39	–	47.95	48
1916	35.28	4.78	–	40.06	40
1917	40.37	5.52	–	45.89	46
1918	28.68	1.84	0.07	30.59	31
1919	28.18	3.46	–	31.64	32
1920	16.19	3.52	–	19.71	20
1921	21.97	3.70	–	25.67	26
1922	25.75	3.23	–	28.98	29
1923	20.31	3.38	–	23.70	24
1924	22.78	4.72	–	27.51	27
1925	22.34	2.50	0.34	25.18	25
1926	9.92	0.52	–	10.44	10
1927	19.66	2.40	–	22.06	22
1928	10.20	2.29	–	12.49	12
Totals	639.44	82.77	0.41	722.62	722

Honus Wagner

Year	Bat	Field	Pitch	Sum	WS
1897	7.77	1.44	–	9.21	9
1898	17.27	4.38	–	21.65	22
1899	20.43	5.23	–	25.65	26
1900	30.22	3.73	0.16	34.10	34
1901	30.03	6.81	–	36.84	37
1902	28.85	5.97	0.46	35.29	35
1903	27.50	7.65	–	35.15	35
1904	38.09	4.94	–	43.03	43
1905	36.75	9.60	–	46.35	46
1906	34.20	11.32	–	45.52	46
1907	36.42	7.67	–	44.09	44
1908	49.21	9.74	–	58.96	59
1909	33.07	9.38	–	42.45	42
1910	21.98	8.19	–	30.17	30
1911	23.18	7.16	–	30.34	30
1912	23.61	11.83	–	35.44	35
1913	11.93	6.21	–	18.14	18
1914	10.02	8.83	–	18.85	19
1915	16.23	7.00	–	23.22	23
1916	13.19	3.92	–	17.11	17
1917	3.86	0.87	–	4.73	5
Totals	513.83	141.84	0.62	656.29	655

Hank Aaron

Year	Bat	Field	Pitch	Sum	WS
1954	10.28	2.44	–	12.73	13
1955	25.40	3.71	–	29.11	29
1956	26.66	3.42	–	30.09	30
1957	32.11	3.14	–	35.25	35
1958	27.85	3.82	–	31.67	32
1959	35.42	2.09	–	37.50	38
1960	31.91	2.65	–	34.56	35
1961	29.74	5.53	–	35.26	35
1962	30.11	4.03	–	34.14	34
1963	37.19	3.53	–	40.73	41
1964	29.76	2.86	–	32.62	33
1965	26.58	4.18	–	30.75	31
1966	24.60	2.49	–	27.09	27
1967	29.97	3.86	–	33.83	34
1968	27.75	4.03	–	31.79	32
1969	33.32	4.48	–	37.80	38
1970	21.19	3.26	–	24.45	25
1971	30.39	2.13	–	32.52	33
1972	19.56	1.71	–	21.26	21
1973	18.15	2.07	–	20.22	20
1974	11.49	1.81	–	13.31	13
1975	9.02	0.02	–	9.04	9
1976	4.82	0.01	–	4.83	5
Totals	573.27	67.27	–	640.54	643

Willie Mays

Year	Bat	Field	Pitch	Sum	WS
1951	14.22	5.07	–	19.29	19
1952	3.56	1.65	–	5.22	5
1954	31.36	8.87	–	40.23	40
1955	34.81	5.00	–	39.81	40
1956	22.91	4.29	–	27.20	27
1957	29.82	3.90	–	33.72	34
1958	33.40	6.11	–	39.51	40
1959	27.07	5.28	–	32.34	32
1960	32.60	5.21	–	37.81	38
1961	29.02	4.84	–	33.87	34
1962	34.08	6.70	–	40.78	41
1963	33.19	4.71	–	37.90	38
1964	31.19	7.00	–	38.18	38
1965	34.99	8.11	–	43.11	43
1966	30.06	6.62	–	36.68	37
1967	15.67	5.27	–	20.93	21
1968	25.94	4.49	–	30.43	30
1969	14.07	2.60	–	16.67	17
1970	21.59	2.54	–	24.13	24
1971	24.74	2.71	–	27.44	27
1972	10.52	1.60	–	12.11	12
1973	3.19	1.58	–	4.78	5
Totals	538.00	104.14	–	642.14	642

Cy Young

Year	Bat	Field	Pitch	Sum	WS
1890	0.00	–	7.63	7.63	8
1891	0.00	–	27.95	27.95	28
1892	0.00	–	43.92	43.92	44
1893	0.00	–	35.54	35.54	35
1894	0.00	–	39.07	39.07	39
1895	0.00	–	36.69	36.69	37
1896	2.23	0.02	40.52	42.77	43
1897	0.00	0.01	27.74	27.74	28
1898	1.97	–	32.21	34.17	34
1899	0.00	–	35.32	35.32	35
1900	0.00	–	22.28	22.28	22
1901	0.00	–	40.44	40.44	41
1902	0.00	–	38.47	38.47	38
1903	4.02	–	33.75	37.77	38
1904	0.64	–	34.14	34.78	35
1905	0.00	–	28.13	28.13	28
1906	0.00	–	12.98	12.98	13
1907	0.00	–	26.88	26.88	27
1908	0.00	–	27.33	27.33	27
1909	0.00	–	20.15	20.15	20
1910	0.00	–	9.81	9.81	10
1911	0.00	–	4.12	4.12	4
Totals	8.86	0.03	625.07	633.96	634

Tris Speaker

Year	Bat	Field	Pitch	Sum	WS
1907	0.00	0.14	–	0.14	0
1908	0.99	1.16	–	2.15	2
1909	26.24	7.67	–	33.91	34
1910	27.26	6.45	–	33.70	34
1911	21.21	5.92	–	27.14	27
1912	41.57	9.90	–	51.47	51
1913	31.04	4.50	–	35.54	36
1914	36.48	8.90	0.00	45.39	45
1915	28.15	8.29	–	36.44	36
1916	36.54	4.35	–	40.90	41
1917	29.77	7.45	–	37.21	37
1918	20.44	6.15	–	26.59	27
1919	19.15	7.75	–	26.90	27
1920	33.12	5.77	–	38.89	39
1921	22.05	5.18	–	27.24	27
1922	26.47	3.14	–	29.61	30
1923	30.36	5.08	–	35.44	35
1924	17.79	2.80	–	20.58	21
1925	20.93	3.98	–	24.91	25
1926	20.97	7.44	–	28.41	29
1927	17.46	3.89	–	21.34	21
1928	3.77	2.08	–	5.86	6
Totals	511.74	118.01	0.00	629.75	630

Stan Musial

Year	Bat	Field	Pitch	Sum	WS
1941	2.74	0.36	–	3.10	3
1942	23.82	4.57	–	28.39	28
1943	33.07	5.71	–	38.78	39
1944	33.13	4.78	–	37.91	38
1946	40.86	3.16	–	44.02	44
1947	21.75	3.01	–	24.76	25
1948	42.37	3.86	–	46.23	46
1949	34.82	5.35	–	40.16	40
1950	28.74	2.85	–	31.59	32
1951	34.96	3.81	–	38.77	39
1952	32.80	4.41	0.00	37.20	37
1953	30.11	3.35	–	33.46	33
1954	28.47	2.09	–	30.56	30
1955	25.86	2.96	–	28.83	29
1956	23.74	2.53	–	26.28	26
1957	28.37	1.82	–	30.19	30
1958	18.74	2.46	–	21.20	21
1959	6.94	1.23	–	8.17	8
1960	11.56	1.65	–	13.21	13
1961	10.91	2.99	–	13.90	14
1962	16.56	2.53	–	19.09	19
1963	8.37	1.25	–	9.62	10
Totals	538.69	66.75	0.00	605.44	604

Eddie Collins

Year	Bat	Field	Pitch	Sum	WS
1906	0.00	0.14	–	0.14	0
1907	0.00	0.07	–	0.07	0
1908	9.00	2.37	–	11.37	11
1909	34.74	7.79	–	42.53	43
1910	29.80	9.26	–	39.07	39
1911	29.21	6.11	–	35.32	35
1912	30.05	6.12	–	36.17	36
1913	33.15	5.84	–	38.99	39
1914	37.12	5.81	–	42.93	43
1915	31.96	7.75	–	39.72	40
1916	23.73	6.86	–	30.59	31
1917	25.74	5.79	–	31.53	32
1918	12.18	3.41	–	15.60	16
1919	20.63	6.01	–	26.65	27
1920	29.75	8.75	–	38.50	38
1921	14.97	5.80	–	20.77	21
1922	17.42	5.14	–	22.56	23
1923	18.94	4.62	–	23.56	24
1924	21.61	3.19	–	24.80	25
1925	18.42	3.38	–	21.81	22
1926	14.75	2.73	–	17.47	17
1927	9.58	1.73	–	11.31	11
1928	0.84	0.01	–	0.85	1
1929	0.00	–	–	0.00	0
1930	0.00	–	–	0.00	0
Totals	463.60	108.71	–	572.31	574

Mickey Mantle

Year	Bat	Field	Pitch	Sum	WS
1951	12.13	0.84	–	12.97	13
1952	28.43	3.97	–	32.40	32
1953	22.09	3.68	–	25.78	26
1954	32.45	3.67	–	36.12	36
1955	34.14	6.85	–	40.99	41
1956	43.79	4.84	–	48.64	49
1957	46.06	5.05	–	51.11	51
1958	35.68	3.80	–	39.48	39
1959	25.63	4.12	–	29.74	30
1960	31.27	4.59	–	35.87	36
1961	42.96	4.93	–	47.89	48
1962	30.92	1.77	–	32.69	33
1963	13.07	1.29	–	14.36	14
1964	30.53	2.92	–	33.45	34
1965	14.43	1.44	–	15.86	16
1966	16.65	1.46	–	18.12	18
1967	23.70	1.62	–	25.32	25
1968	23.04	1.22	–	24.26	24
Totals	506.97	58.06	–	565.03	565

Walter Johnson

Year	Bat	Field	Pitch	Sum	WS
1907	0.00	–	3.94	3.94	4
1908	0.13	–	19.58	19.71	20
1909	0.00	–	12.49	12.49	12
1910	0.00	–	35.60	35.60	36
1911	0.14	–	30.76	30.90	31
1912	3.01	–	44.12	47.14	47
1913	3.83	0.02	50.28	54.13	54
1914	2.20	0.00	35.44	37.65	38
1915	2.21	0.01	39.34	41.56	42
1916	1.74	–	34.49	36.23	36
1917	3.21	–	25.48	28.69	29
1918	3.25	0.14	34.95	38.34	38
1919	0.17	0.00	26.74	26.91	27
1920	1.13	0.00	9.05	10.18	10
1921	0.90	–	22.32	23.22	23
1922	0.00	–	20.96	20.96	21
1923	0.00	–	17.02	17.02	17
1924	1.57	–	27.86	29.43	29
1925	4.99	–	21.47	26.46	26
1926	0.00	–	14.90	14.90	15
1927	1.81	–	3.10	4.91	5
Totals	30.29	0.17	529.89	560.35	560

Ted Williams

Year	Bat	Field	Pitch	Sum	WS
1939	29.52	2.70	–	32.22	32
1940	27.34	2.48	0.12	29.94	30
1941	39.62	2.26	–	41.88	42
1942	41.50	4.58	–	46.07	46
1946	45.11	4.00	–	49.11	49
1947	41.11	3.36	–	44.47	44
1948	36.78	2.69	–	39.47	39
1949	36.62	3.33	–	39.94	40
1950	17.86	1.55	–	19.41	19
1951	30.37	3.34	–	33.71	34
1952	1.05	0.05	–	1.10	1
1953	8.80	0.42	–	9.21	9
1954	27.32	1.95	–	29.27	29
1955	20.59	2.86	–	23.46	23
1956	22.51	2.44	–	24.95	25
1957	35.24	2.65	–	37.89	38
1958	23.53	1.39	–	24.91	25
1959	7.71	0.96	–	8.67	9
1960	19.86	1.05	–	20.91	21
Totals	512.43	44.05	0.12	556.60	555

Pete Rose

Year	Bat	Field	Pitch	Sum	WS
1963	14.48	4.72	–	19.19	19
1964	6.77	5.71	–	12.48	12
1965	22.32	4.90	–	27.22	27
1966	18.08	7.14	–	25.22	25
1967	19.45	4.71	–	24.16	24
1968	28.37	3.93	–	32.30	32
1969	34.38	2.88	–	37.25	37
1970	23.30	5.47	–	28.77	29
1971	23.76	4.24	–	28.00	28
1972	28.59	3.25	–	31.84	32
1973	29.43	4.12	–	33.55	34
1974	22.73	4.10	–	26.83	27
1975	27.26	3.27	–	30.53	31
1976	25.07	4.58	–	29.65	30
1977	19.97	3.15	–	23.13	23
1978	22.77	4.27	–	27.05	27
1979	24.61	2.56	–	27.17	27
1980	14.23	3.14	–	17.36	17
1981	14.97	1.81	–	16.78	17
1982	14.19	2.62	–	16.80	17
1983	4.92	2.19	–	7.10	7
1984	7.12	1.30	–	8.43	8
1985	12.29	1.28	–	13.56	14
1986	2.72	0.49	–	3.21	3
Totals	461.77	85.83	–	547.61	547

Rickey Henderson

Year	Bat	Field	Pitch	Sum	WS
1979	8.72	0.87	–	9.59	10
1980	27.41	6.52	–	33.93	34
1981	22.92	4.09	–	27.02	27
1982	25.58	2.58	–	28.16	28
1983	27.18	2.93	–	30.10	30
1984	27.01	1.12	–	28.13	28
1985	32.41	5.27	–	37.68	38
1986	20.86	5.34	–	26.20	26
1987	18.09	1.99	–	20.08	20
1988	26.14	2.07	–	28.22	28
1989	26.00	3.51	–	29.51	30
1990	35.25	3.61	–	38.86	39
1991	22.83	1.67	–	24.50	25
1992	23.33	1.77	–	25.10	25
1993	23.44	1.40	–	24.84	25
1994	9.18	1.33	–	10.51	11
1995	18.30	0.74	–	19.04	19
1996	13.96	2.02	–	15.98	16
1997	13.88	1.11	–	14.99	15
1998	18.05	2.20	–	20.25	20
1999	14.68	1.63	–	16.31	16
2000	7.14	1.63	–	8.77	8
2001	11.34	0.91	–	12.26	12
Totals	473.71	56.32	–	530.03	530

Mel Ott

Year	Bat	Field	Pitch	Sum	WS
1926	1.72	0.22	–	1.94	2
1927	3.25	0.47	–	3.72	4
1928	17.35	2.26	–	19.60	20
1929	26.86	3.97	–	30.84	31
1930	23.60	4.47	–	28.06	28
1931	21.88	4.32	–	26.20	26
1932	30.75	1.94	–	32.69	33
1933	26.47	4.84	–	31.31	31
1934	33.92	3.79	–	37.71	38
1935	30.28	4.24	–	34.52	35
1936	33.43	2.88	–	36.31	36
1937	28.50	3.21	–	31.71	32
1938	31.50	4.18	–	35.68	36
1939	26.28	1.13	–	27.42	28
1940	21.22	2.52	–	23.74	24
1941	24.92	0.78	–	25.70	26
1942	32.98	2.39	–	35.36	35
1943	15.68	0.76	–	16.44	16
1944	23.61	1.11	–	24.72	25
1945	19.83	1.80	–	21.63	22
1946	0.00	0.28	–	0.28	0
1947	0.00	–	–	0.00	0
Totals	474.04	51.56	–	525.59	528

Barry Bonds

Year	Bat	Field	Pitch	Sum	WS
1986	10.72	3.92	–	14.64	15
1987	16.27	5.67	–	21.94	22
1988	23.20	2.72	–	25.92	26
1989	19.29	3.77	–	23.07	23
1990	32.50	4.23	–	36.73	37
1991	33.24	3.27	–	36.51	37
1992	37.77	3.01	–	40.78	41
1993	44.02	2.70	–	46.72	47
1994	22.71	2.14	–	24.85	25
1995	34.60	1.47	–	36.06	36
1996	37.32	1.67	–	38.99	39
1997	34.48	1.95	–	36.43	36
1998	31.53	2.30	–	33.83	34
1999	18.07	1.21	–	19.28	19
2000	30.00	1.67	–	31.67	32
2001	52.22	1.65	–	53.87	54
Totals	477.95	43.34	–	521.28	523

Frank Robinson

Year	Bat	Field	Pitch	Sum	WS
1956	23.37	2.63	–	26.00	26
1957	23.49	3.18	–	26.67	27
1958	15.96	3.56	–	19.52	20
1959	23.56	1.71	–	25.27	25
1960	21.22	2.13	–	23.35	23
1961	29.20	5.27	–	34.47	34
1962	36.27	4.47	–	40.74	41
1963	20.39	2.82	–	23.21	23
1964	28.45	4.27	–	32.73	33
1965	23.49	2.34	–	25.84	26
1966	38.01	2.72	–	40.73	41
1967	27.53	1.95	–	29.48	30
1968	21.49	2.34	–	23.83	24
1969	28.78	3.49	–	32.26	32
1970	23.00	3.00	–	26.00	26
1971	20.11	2.48	–	22.59	23
1972	12.17	2.00	–	14.17	14
1973	25.08	0.60	–	25.68	26
1974	18.77	0.02	–	18.79	18
1975	6.00	–	–	6.00	6
1976	1.48	0.02	–	1.49	1
Totals	467.82	50.99	–	518.82	519

Joe Morgan

Year	Bat	Field	Pitch	Sum	WS
1963	1.10	0.12	–	1.22	1
1964	0.00	0.44	–	0.44	0
1965	25.13	5.19	–	30.31	30
1966	17.09	1.56	–	18.65	19
1967	23.36	3.16	–	26.51	26
1968	1.67	0.07	–	1.74	2
1969	19.14	4.99	–	24.13	24
1970	18.88	4.76	–	23.64	24
1971	22.64	6.60	–	29.23	29
1972	32.58	6.78	–	39.36	39
1973	33.51	7.00	–	40.51	40
1974	30.95	5.94	–	36.90	37
1975	36.24	7.76	–	44.00	44
1976	32.65	4.21	–	36.86	37
1977	24.20	6.19	–	30.38	30
1978	13.96	3.32	–	17.29	17
1979	14.10	3.96	–	18.05	18
1980	15.92	5.18	–	21.10	21
1981	10.65	3.70	–	14.35	14
1982	24.32	4.47	–	28.79	29
1983	14.93	4.00	–	18.93	19
1984	10.89	1.55	–	12.44	12
Totals	423.89	90.94	–	514.84	512

Rogers Hornsby

Year	Bat	Field	Pitch	Sum	WS
1915	0.23	0.12	–	0.35	0
1916	25.25	3.02	–	28.27	28
1917	30.59	7.01	–	37.60	38
1918	14.71	3.52	–	18.23	18
1919	23.02	3.41	–	26.43	26
1920	33.45	4.91	–	38.36	38
1921	35.90	5.21	–	41.12	41
1922	42.86	3.97	–	46.83	47
1923	23.87	1.59	–	25.46	26
1924	34.51	3.90	–	38.41	38
1925	32.99	2.48	–	35.47	36
1926	18.21	3.18	–	21.40	21
1927	33.75	6.04	–	39.80	40
1928	30.93	1.71	–	32.64	33
1929	35.65	5.88	–	41.53	42
1930	2.08	0.62	–	2.70	3
1931	18.07	2.05	–	20.12	20
1932	0.91	0.20	–	1.12	1
1933	4.39	0.42	–	4.81	4
1934	1.08	0.09	–	1.17	1
1935	0.00	0.08	–	0.08	0
1936	0.15	0.01	–	0.16	0
1937	1.11	0.17	–	1.27	1
Totals	443.70	59.63	–	503.33	502

Nap Lajoie

Year	Bat	Field	Pitch	Sum	WS
1896	4.84	0.45	–	5.29	5
1897	18.15	2.67	–	20.82	21
1898	21.52	4.01	–	25.53	26
1899	15.85	3.18	–	19.04	19
1900	17.30	5.04	–	22.34	22
1901	36.28	5.67	–	41.95	42
1902	17.40	4.09	–	21.49	22
1903	25.95	5.29	–	31.24	31
1904	35.38	5.65	–	41.02	41
1905	10.98	2.90	–	13.88	14
1906	24.96	8.11	–	33.07	33
1907	22.44	9.14	–	31.58	32
1908	22.07	10.38	–	32.46	32
1909	20.70	6.15	–	26.86	27
1910	40.41	6.19	–	46.60	47
1911	11.94	1.86	–	13.80	14
1912	17.72	4.02	–	21.74	22
1913	16.69	6.11	–	22.80	23
1914	4.92	2.33	–	7.25	7
1915	10.57	1.27	–	11.84	12
1916	2.69	1.40	–	4.09	4
Totals	398.76	95.91	–	494.67	496

Lou Gehrig

Year	Bat	Field	Pitch	Sum	WS
1923	1.96	0.06	–	2.01	2
1924	0.70	0.03	–	0.73	1
1925	12.21	2.56	–	14.77	15
1926	27.72	2.74	–	30.46	30
1927	41.45	2.63	–	44.09	44
1928	39.36	2.51	–	41.87	42
1929	28.97	2.84	–	31.81	32
1930	37.27	1.62	–	38.89	39
1931	34.28	1.74	–	36.02	36
1932	35.80	2.47	–	38.27	38
1933	33.81	2.21	–	36.02	36
1934	38.84	2.62	–	41.46	41
1935	31.87	2.46	–	34.34	34
1936	34.88	3.15	–	38.02	38
1937	34.34	1.53	–	35.87	36
1938	23.05	1.75	–	24.80	25
1939	0.00	0.09	–	0.09	0
Totals	456.51	33.02	–	489.52	489

Carl Yastrzemski

Year	Bat	Field	Pitch	Sum	WS
1961	9.53	2.70	–	12.24	12
1962	17.13	3.97	–	21.11	21
1963	24.33	4.28	–	28.61	29
1964	16.04	4.20	–	20.23	20
1965	18.66	2.05	–	20.71	21
1966	18.06	3.40	–	21.46	21
1967	38.18	4.01	–	42.19	42
1968	35.75	3.29	–	39.03	39
1969	22.30	3.63	–	25.92	26
1970	33.42	2.61	–	36.02	36
1971	17.35	3.50	–	20.85	21
1972	16.54	1.95	–	18.49	19
1973	20.66	3.20	–	23.86	24
1974	21.76	2.64	–	24.40	24
1975	16.03	3.52	–	19.55	20
1976	15.82	2.47	–	18.29	18
1977	19.50	4.38	–	23.87	24
1978	16.26	2.28	–	18.55	19
1979	11.68	1.47	–	13.15	13
1980	9.40	0.89	–	10.29	10
1981	6.66	0.65	–	7.31	7
1982	12.31	0.37	–	12.68	13
1983	8.64	0.04	–	8.69	9
Totals	426.00	61.49	–	487.49	488

Kid Nichols

Year	Bat	Field	Pitch	Sum	WS
1890	0.82	0.00	42.18	43.00	43
1891	0.00	–	39.33	39.33	39
1892	0.72	0.22	46.99	47.94	48
1893	0.87	0.00	39.20	40.06	40
1894	1.80	0.01	35.15	36.96	37
1895	0.11	0.00	33.93	34.04	34
1896	0.00	0.04	32.86	32.89	33
1897	1.89	–	39.41	41.30	41
1898	0.99	0.00	42.60	43.60	44
1899	0.00	–	31.34	31.34	31
1900	0.00	–	18.42	18.42	18
1901	4.15	0.25	27.63	32.03	32
1904	0.00	–	27.07	27.07	27
1905	0.00	0.00	11.56	11.56	11
1906	0.00	–	0.00	0.00	0
Totals	11.36	0.53	467.67	479.56	478

Pete Alexander

Year	Bat	Field	Pitch	Sum	WS
1911	0.00	–	33.95	33.95	34
1912	0.00	–	24.23	24.23	24
1913	0.00	–	27.44	27.44	27
1914	0.00	–	26.17	26.17	26
1915	0.00	–	43.32	43.32	43
1916	2.29	–	41.95	44.25	44
1917	0.51	–	39.11	39.63	40
1918	0.00	–	2.21	2.21	2
1919	0.00	–	25.65	25.65	26
1920	1.71	–	34.46	36.17	36
1921	1.27	–	20.15	21.42	22
1922	0.00	–	18.44	18.44	18
1923	0.00	–	26.62	26.62	27
1924	0.01	–	13.76	13.77	14
1925	0.00	–	20.00	20.00	20
1926	0.58	–	14.90	15.48	16
1927	0.33	–	28.17	28.50	28
1928	0.74	–	18.28	19.02	19
1929	0.00	–	9.81	9.81	10
1930	0.00	–	0.00	0.00	0
Totals	7.46	–	468.61	476.07	476

Mike Schmidt

Year	Bat	Field	Pitch	Sum	WS
1972	0.32	0.42	–	0.74	1
1973	6.74	3.41	–	10.15	10
1974	30.10	8.62	–	38.72	39
1975	22.06	5.82	–	27.87	28
1976	27.97	7.52	–	35.49	35
1977	26.95	5.80	–	32.75	33
1978	17.74	5.15	–	22.89	23
1979	26.71	6.62	–	33.32	33
1980	30.69	6.71	–	37.40	37
1981	25.85	3.66	–	29.51	30
1982	30.82	5.82	–	36.64	37
1983	28.00	7.13	–	35.13	35
1984	20.88	4.84	–	25.72	26
1985	23.71	2.53	–	26.24	26
1986	26.60	4.55	–	31.14	31
1987	19.48	6.62	–	26.09	26
1988	11.56	2.52	–	14.08	14
1989	2.13	0.58	–	2.71	3
Totals	378.30	88.33	–	466.63	467

Eddie Mathews

Year	Bat	Field	Pitch	Sum	WS
1952	15.45	3.32	–	18.77	19
1953	34.78	4.03	–	38.81	39
1954	28.16	4.44	–	32.60	33
1955	31.08	2.66	–	33.73	34
1956	26.50	2.52	–	29.03	29
1957	29.47	3.30	–	32.77	33
1958	19.56	4.47	–	24.03	24
1959	32.07	4.40	–	36.46	37
1960	34.98	2.91	–	37.88	38
1961	28.65	3.95	–	32.60	33
1962	21.29	4.50	–	25.79	26
1963	25.46	5.09	–	30.55	31
1964	17.17	2.93	–	20.10	20
1965	16.92	5.20	–	22.11	22
1966	12.25	3.47	–	15.71	16
1967	12.43	1.53	–	13.96	14
1968	1.19	0.25	–	1.44	2
Totals	387.41	58.95	–	446.36	450

Sam Crawford

Year	Bat	Field	Pitch	Sum	WS
1899	2.79	1.14	–	3.93	4
1900	9.56	2.79	–	12.35	12
1901	23.53	0.59	–	24.13	24
1902	20.23	3.14	–	23.38	23
1903	22.54	2.71	–	25.25	25
1904	18.10	2.69	–	20.79	21
1905	32.61	3.15	–	35.76	36
1906	20.44	2.74	–	23.17	23
1907	31.53	4.51	–	36.05	36
1908	29.77	2.40	–	32.17	32
1909	26.30	6.20	–	32.50	32
1910	20.10	2.84	–	22.94	23
1911	29.87	2.31	–	32.18	32
1912	22.20	1.73	–	23.93	24
1913	25.24	2.09	–	27.33	27
1914	27.97	2.91	–	30.87	31
1915	24.37	3.35	–	27.72	28
1916	11.65	1.17	–	12.82	13
1917	0.00	0.25	–	0.25	0
Totals	398.81	48.72	–	447.52	446

Reggie Jackson

Year	Bat	Field	Pitch	Sum	WS
1967	1.07	0.48	–	1.55	2
1968	21.84	3.40	–	25.24	25
1969	37.98	2.62	–	40.60	41
1970	13.87	3.07	–	16.94	17
1971	27.80	4.07	–	31.87	32
1972	23.46	2.96	–	26.42	26
1973	29.31	2.48	–	31.79	32
1974	27.68	2.34	–	30.02	30
1975	23.99	3.12	–	27.11	27
1976	23.22	2.17	–	25.39	25
1977	25.20	2.21	–	27.42	27
1978	19.94	2.76	–	22.70	23
1979	20.37	2.79	–	23.15	23
1980	29.72	1.32	–	31.04	31
1981	8.12	1.36	–	9.49	10
1982	20.64	1.66	–	22.30	22
1983	3.89	0.36	–	4.25	4
1984	9.64	0.06	–	9.69	10
1985	16.75	0.91	–	17.67	18
1986	13.48	0.03	–	13.50	13
1987	5.79	0.23	–	6.02	6
Totals	403.76	40.39	–	444.16	444

Al Kaline

Year	Bat	Field	Pitch	Sum	WS
1953	0.36	0.05	–	0.42	1
1954	4.21	2.90	–	7.11	7
1955	28.71	2.25	–	30.96	31
1956	23.35	2.90	–	26.25	26
1957	15.30	4.61	–	19.91	20
1958	18.66	4.14	–	22.80	23
1959	22.66	4.59	–	27.25	27
1960	12.24	4.81	–	17.05	17
1961	24.52	4.78	–	29.30	29
1962	16.44	2.63	–	19.07	19
1963	22.55	2.39	–	24.94	25
1964	21.31	3.04	–	24.35	24
1965	18.07	1.83	–	19.90	20
1966	27.83	2.64	–	30.48	31
1967	26.85	3.41	–	30.27	30
1968	15.98	1.95	–	17.93	18
1969	14.07	2.55	–	16.62	17
1970	16.52	2.10	–	18.62	19
1971	19.69	1.87	–	21.56	22
1972	12.29	1.50	–	13.78	14
1973	5.95	1.63	–	7.57	8
1974	15.29	–	–	15.29	15
Totals	382.86	58.57	–	441.43	443

Eddie Murray

Year	Bat	Field	Pitch	Sum	WS
1977	20.19	0.61	–	20.80	21
1978	25.19	2.60	–	27.79	28
1979	22.24	2.66	–	24.91	25
1980	23.89	1.67	–	25.56	26
1981	19.09	2.10	–	21.19	21
1982	25.38	3.36	–	28.74	29
1983	28.33	2.68	–	31.01	31
1984	30.57	2.89	–	33.46	33
1985	25.65	2.52	–	28.17	28
1986	17.98	1.54	–	19.52	20
1987	17.44	2.50	–	19.93	20
1988	19.12	1.38	–	20.50	21
1989	18.31	3.14	–	21.45	21
1990	28.94	1.70	–	30.64	31
1991	12.66	2.71	–	15.37	16
1992	18.54	1.01	–	19.54	20
1993	14.08	1.26	–	15.34	15
1994	8.09	0.34	–	8.43	9
1995	15.75	0.33	–	16.08	16
1996	6.04	0.02	–	6.06	6
1997	0.13	–	–	0.13	0
Totals	397.62	37.01	–	434.63	437

Jimmie Foxx

Year	Bat	Field	Pitch	Sum	WS
1925	0.70	0.00	–	0.70	1
1926	0.68	0.40	–	1.08	1
1927	4.94	0.58	–	5.52	6
1928	17.11	4.73	–	21.84	22
1929	30.02	3.65	–	33.68	34
1930	29.99	3.69	–	33.68	34
1931	21.34	2.89	–	24.22	24
1932	36.71	3.58	–	40.29	40
1933	37.49	3.23	–	40.72	41
1934	29.37	2.58	–	31.95	32
1935	26.32	3.56	–	29.87	30
1936	22.65	3.01	–	25.66	26
1937	19.26	4.21	–	23.47	23
1938	32.68	1.13	–	33.80	34
1939	28.58	1.64	0.18	30.40	30
1940	20.97	3.36	–	24.33	24
1941	17.23	2.43	–	19.65	20
1942	4.53	0.81	–	5.35	5
1944	0.00	0.19	–	0.19	0
1945	5.92	0.51	1.90	8.33	8
Totals	386.47	46.18	2.08	434.73	435

George Brett

Year	Bat	Field	Pitch	Sum	WS
1973	0.00	0.15	–	0.15	0
1974	6.60	2.75	–	9.34	9
1975	19.80	5.31	–	25.11	25
1976	28.09	4.77	–	32.86	33
1977	22.43	6.82	–	29.25	29
1978	17.55	5.29	–	22.85	23
1979	27.08	5.72	–	32.80	33
1980	31.47	4.55	–	36.02	36
1981	11.74	2.22	–	13.96	14
1982	22.37	4.28	–	26.65	27
1983	22.25	1.83	–	24.08	24
1984	10.88	2.88	–	13.76	14
1985	32.27	4.98	–	37.25	37
1986	15.82	3.37	–	19.18	19
1987	13.77	1.51	–	15.28	15
1988	25.04	1.05	–	26.09	26
1989	15.45	1.79	–	17.25	17
1990	24.24	1.83	–	26.06	26
1991	7.96	0.11	–	8.07	8
1992	10.99	0.30	–	11.29	11
1993	5.72	–	–	5.72	6
Totals	371.52	61.52	–	433.03	432

Cal Ripken Jr.

Year	Bat	Field	Pitch	Sum	WS
1981	0.00	0.40	–	0.40	0
1982	15.58	7.52	–	23.10	23
1983	25.05	10.27	–	35.32	35
1984	26.97	9.74	–	36.71	37
1985	17.11	8.25	–	25.36	25
1986	18.07	9.67	–	27.74	28
1987	13.01	6.59	–	19.60	20
1988	20.12	5.26	–	25.38	25
1989	15.52	10.05	–	25.57	26
1990	12.72	7.00	–	19.72	20
1991	26.53	7.17	–	33.70	34
1992	12.39	8.50	–	20.89	21
1993	10.72	6.23	–	16.94	17
1994	11.56	6.49	–	18.05	18
1995	8.02	7.74	–	15.76	16
1996	14.76	7.58	–	22.34	22
1997	11.94	6.03	–	17.97	18
1998	9.28	4.09	–	13.37	13
1999	10.42	1.38	–	11.79	12
2000	5.14	3.16	–	8.30	8
2001	5.84	3.30	–	9.14	9
Totals	290.74	136.43	–	427.16	427

Christy Mathewson

Year	Bat	Field	Pitch	Sum	WS
1900	0.01	–	0.25	0.26	0
1901	0.00	–	20.85	20.85	21
1902	0.22	0.15	21.68	22.05	22
1903	0.00	–	37.18	37.18	37
1904	1.37	–	33.07	34.43	34
1905	2.02	–	37.45	39.47	39
1906	2.05	–	17.62	19.67	20
1907	0.00	–	28.99	28.99	29
1908	0.00	–	38.60	38.60	39
1909	1.80	–	32.05	33.85	34
1910	1.83	–	28.45	30.28	30
1911	0.00	–	31.89	31.89	32
1912	1.30	–	29.63	30.94	31
1913	0.00	–	29.75	29.75	30
1914	0.93	–	17.91	18.84	19
1915	0.34	–	4.35	4.69	5
1916	0.71	–	3.27	3.97	4
Totals	12.58	0.15	412.97	425.70	426

Paul Waner

Year	Bat	Field	Pitch	Sum	WS
1926	23.34	5.12	–	28.46	28
1927	30.29	5.34	–	35.63	36
1928	29.19	4.81	–	34.00	34
1929	23.48	6.34	–	29.83	30
1930	22.32	3.10	–	25.43	26
1931	20.84	4.75	–	25.59	26
1932	27.61	4.01	–	31.62	32
1933	24.57	3.47	–	28.04	28
1934	26.73	3.38	–	30.10	30
1935	17.81	4.09	–	21.90	22
1936	28.27	3.73	–	32.00	32
1937	23.65	4.12	–	27.78	28
1938	11.72	3.02	–	14.74	15
1939	12.59	1.72	–	14.31	14
1940	6.22	0.49	–	6.71	7
1941	8.22	1.28	–	9.50	9
1942	9.75	1.08	–	10.83	11
1943	8.79	0.89	–	9.69	10
1944	4.41	0.35	–	4.76	5
1945	0.00	–	–	0.00	0
Totals	359.81	61.11	–	420.92	423

Robin Yount

Year	Bat	Field	Pitch	Sum	WS
1974	3.51	4.31	–	7.82	8
1975	10.18	3.97	–	14.15	14
1976	4.59	8.92	–	13.51	14
1977	11.28	4.56	–	15.84	16
1978	12.71	5.84	–	18.55	19
1979	6.50	7.63	–	14.13	14
1980	18.67	6.67	–	25.34	25
1981	13.38	6.40	–	19.77	20
1982	32.36	6.25	–	38.61	39
1983	25.72	6.85	–	32.56	33
1984	21.92	4.87	–	26.79	27
1985	14.26	2.02	–	16.28	16
1986	18.64	4.02	–	22.67	23
1987	22.66	3.54	–	26.20	26
1988	23.15	8.17	–	31.33	31
1989	29.51	4.03	–	33.54	34
1990	15.39	2.86	–	18.25	18
1991	11.94	3.57	–	15.51	16
1992	14.81	5.26	–	20.07	20
1993	6.17	3.37	–	9.54	10
Totals	317.34	103.13	–	420.47	423

Dave Winfield

Year	Bat	Field	Pitch	Sum	WS
1973	2.98	0.37	–	3.35	3
1974	15.74	1.19	–	16.93	17
1975	16.81	2.71	–	19.51	20
1976	21.62	3.10	–	24.73	25
1977	21.48	2.28	–	23.77	24
1978	25.97	2.33	–	28.30	28
1979	29.72	3.24	–	32.96	33
1980	19.49	2.71	–	22.20	22
1981	13.20	2.34	–	15.54	16
1982	18.03	2.04	–	20.06	20
1983	19.54	2.63	–	22.17	22
1984	24.65	1.69	–	26.34	26
1985	17.50	3.25	–	20.76	21
1986	13.94	2.91	–	16.85	17
1987	15.80	2.02	–	17.82	18
1988	29.20	1.96	–	31.16	31
1990	12.10	1.07	–	13.17	13
1991	15.45	2.05	–	17.49	17
1992	26.15	0.57	–	26.72	27
1993	9.09	0.58	–	9.67	10
1994	4.90	0.02	–	4.92	5
1995	0.00	–	–	0.00	0
Totals	373.36	41.06	–	414.42	415

Paul Molitor

Year	Bat	Field	Pitch	Sum	WS
1978	8.05	3.76	–	11.81	12
1979	20.03	6.35	–	26.38	26
1980	14.79	3.86	–	18.64	19
1981	7.29	1.03	–	8.32	8
1982	26.08	3.81	–	29.89	30
1983	17.00	6.16	–	23.16	23
1984	0.00	0.37	–	0.37	0
1985	16.32	4.32	–	20.64	21
1986	11.02	3.12	–	14.14	14
1987	27.02	1.56	–	28.58	29
1988	24.60	2.56	–	27.16	27
1989	22.30	4.66	–	26.97	27
1990	16.70	2.22	–	18.92	19
1991	29.06	0.56	–	29.62	30
1992	27.78	0.61	–	28.40	28
1993	29.00	0.37	–	29.37	29
1994	18.69	0.12	–	18.81	19
1995	11.63	–	–	11.63	12
1996	17.49	0.38	–	17.86	18
1997	13.12	0.12	–	13.24	13
1998	9.49	0.14	–	9.63	10
Totals	367.46	46.08	–	413.54	414

Tim Keefe

Year	Bat	Field	Pitch	Sum	WS
1880	0.54	–	10.27	10.81	11
1881	2.91	0.00	20.11	23.01	23
1882	4.38	0.28	19.40	24.06	24
1883	2.78	0.23	66.48	69.49	70
1884	6.26	0.27	40.56	47.08	47
1885	0.32	0.00	41.99	42.31	42
1886	0.34	0.00	37.99	38.34	38
1887	1.43	0.02	37.61	39.05	39
1888	0.00	0.00	35.48	35.48	35
1889	0.00	–	26.71	26.71	27
1890	0.00	–	18.60	18.60	19
1891	0.13	–	3.50	3.63	4
1892	0.00	–	23.93	23.93	24
1893	0.22	–	9.97	10.20	10
Totals	19.30	0.81	392.60	412.71	413

Warren Spahn

Year	Bat	Field	Pitch	Sum	WS
1942	0.00	–	0.00	0.00	0
1946	0.00	–	8.67	8.67	9
1947	0.00	–	32.27	32.27	32
1948	0.00	–	14.48	14.48	14
1949	0.00	–	23.73	23.73	24
1950	0.00	–	20.71	20.71	21
1951	0.00	–	25.47	25.47	26
1952	0.00	–	21.74	21.74	22
1953	0.00	–	30.55	30.55	31
1954	0.04	–	23.29	23.33	23
1955	0.84	–	17.80	18.64	19
1956	0.09	–	23.81	23.90	24
1957	0.00	–	21.53	21.53	22
1958	4.68	–	23.11	27.79	28
1959	0.07	–	23.29	23.36	23
1960	0.00	–	16.08	16.08	16
1961	1.59	–	22.90	24.49	25
1962	0.00	–	23.16	23.16	23
1963	0.07	–	21.93	22.01	22
1964	0.00	–	0.89	0.89	1
1965	0.00	–	7.18	7.18	7
Totals	7.37	–	402.59	409.96	412

Career Summaries for Players With 50 Win Shares

Chuck Crim

Year	Bat	Field	Pitch	Sum	WS
1987	–	–	12.10	12.10	12
1988	–	–	11.43	11.43	11
1989	–	0.00	11.38	11.38	11
1990	–	–	6.90	6.90	7
1991	–	–	4.16	4.16	4
1992	–	–	2.48	2.48	2
1993	–	–	0.43	0.43	0
1994	0.00	–	3.28	3.28	3
Totals	0.00	0.00	52.15	52.15	50

Ted Lepcio

Year	Bat	Field	Pitch	Sum	WS
1952	5.35	2.82	–	8.17	8
1953	1.49	2.48	–	3.97	4
1954	5.79	3.84	–	9.64	10
1955	1.69	1.66	–	3.35	3
1956	5.76	2.53	–	8.29	8
1957	4.71	1.54	–	6.25	6
1958	0.74	1.31	–	2.05	2
1959	4.32	2.26	–	6.57	6
1960	0.89	1.00	–	1.89	2
1961	0.31	0.76	–	1.07	1
Totals	31.05	20.21	–	51.26	50

Ron Coomer

Year	Bat	Field	Pitch	Sum	WS
1995	1.91	0.53	–	2.44	2
1996	3.96	1.02	–	4.98	5
1997	11.27	2.83	–	14.10	14
1998	3.49	2.83	–	6.31	6
1999	4.59	3.16	–	7.75	8
2000	6.07	3.14	–	9.20	9
2001	4.10	2.31	–	6.40	6
Totals	35.37	15.82	–	51.19	50

Mike Ryba

Year	Bat	Field	Pitch	Sum	WS
1935	0.18	–	1.31	1.48	1
1936	0.00	0.16	1.26	1.42	1
1937	1.10	0.03	6.96	8.10	8
1938	–	–	0.24	0.24	0
1941	0.00	–	7.06	7.06	7
1942	0.00	0.18	2.47	2.64	3
1943	0.00	–	9.30	9.30	9
1944	0.00	–	9.03	9.03	9
1945	0.60	–	10.28	10.87	11
1946	0.33	–	0.63	0.96	1
Totals	2.20	0.37	48.53	51.10	50

Gene Baker

Year	Bat	Field	Pitch	Sum	WS
1953	0.00	0.05	–	0.05	0
1954	9.70	3.97	–	13.67	14
1955	10.51	5.61	–	16.12	16
1956	6.89	4.48	–	11.36	11
1957	5.39	3.16	–	8.56	8
1958	0.74	0.34	–	1.08	1
1960	0.00	0.17	–	0.17	0
1961	0.00	0.07	–	0.07	0
Totals	33.24	17.85	–	51.09	50

Hipolito Pichardo

Year	Bat	Field	Pitch	Sum	WS
1992	–	–	7.70	7.70	8
1993	–	–	10.28	10.28	10
1994	–	–	4.80	4.80	5
1995	0.00	–	5.38	5.38	5
1996	–	–	4.49	4.49	4
1997	–	–	4.76	4.76	5
1998	0.00	–	5.79	5.79	6
2000	0.00	–	6.41	6.41	6
2001	–	–	1.34	1.34	1
Totals	0.00	–	50.95	50.95	50

F.P. Santangelo

Year	Bat	Field	Pitch	Sum	WS
1995	2.64	0.53	–	3.17	3
1996	10.94	6.77	–	17.71	18
1997	6.55	3.91	–	10.46	10
1998	3.94	2.02	–	5.96	6
1999	8.84	1.31	–	10.15	10
2000	0.41	0.89	–	1.30	1
2001	1.30	0.88	–	2.18	2
Totals	34.62	16.32	–	50.93	50

Clyde Kluttz

Year	Bat	Field	Pitch	Sum	WS
1942	3.13	1.84	–	4.97	5
1943	1.17	2.84	–	4.01	4
1944	4.45	2.83	–	7.28	7
1945	4.63	3.66	–	8.29	9
1946	2.10	2.39	–	4.48	4
1947	5.27	3.24	–	8.51	8
1948	1.36	4.01	–	5.36	5
1951	5.27	0.49	–	5.76	6
1952	0.54	1.72	–	2.25	2
Totals	27.91	23.01	–	50.92	50

Roy Mahaffey

Year	Bat	Field	Pitch	Sum	WS
1926	0.00	–	0.24	0.24	0
1927	0.21	–	0.00	0.21	0
1930	0.00	–	5.88	5.88	6
1931	0.00	–	12.96	12.96	13
1932	0.00	–	10.19	10.19	10
1933	0.00	–	6.99	6.99	7
1934	0.11	–	5.20	5.31	5
1935	0.00	–	9.09	9.09	9
1936	0.00	–	0.00	0.00	0
Totals	0.32	–	50.54	50.87	50

Atlee Hammaker

Year	Bat	Field	Pitch	Sum	WS
1981	–	–	0.00	0.00	0
1982	0.00	–	6.70	6.70	7
1983	0.00	–	13.45	13.45	13
1984	0.11	–	2.24	2.35	2
1985	0.00	–	5.78	5.78	6
1987	0.00	–	9.26	9.26	9
1988	0.00	–	6.04	6.04	6
1989	0.68	–	3.45	4.13	4
1990	0.00	–	2.67	2.67	3
1991	0.00	–	0.00	0.00	0
1994	–	–	0.30	0.30	0
1995	–	–	0.00	0.00	0
Totals	0.79	–	49.90	50.69	50

Bob Bruce

Year	Bat	Field	Pitch	Sum	WS
1959	–	–	0.00	0.00	0
1960	0.00	–	6.30	6.30	6
1961	0.00	–	1.08	1.08	1
1962	0.38	–	8.61	8.99	9
1963	0.00	–	7.49	7.49	8
1964	0.00	–	18.18	18.18	18
1965	0.00	–	8.24	8.24	8
1966	0.00	–	0.00	0.00	0
1967	0.00	–	0.17	0.17	0
Totals	0.38	–	50.07	50.44	50

Barry Foote

Year	Bat	Field	Pitch	Sum	WS
1973	0.91	–	–	0.91	1
1974	7.15	7.42	–	14.58	15
1975	0.00	5.72	–	5.72	6
1976	2.21	4.93	–	7.14	7
1977	0.90	1.05	–	1.95	1
1978	0.00	0.72	–	0.72	1
1979	7.13	3.70	–	10.82	11
1980	1.88	3.33	–	5.20	5
1981	0.55	2.62	–	3.17	3
1982	0.00	0.18	–	0.18	0
Totals	20.73	29.68	–	50.40	50

Mark Williamson

Year	Bat	Field	Pitch	Sum	WS
1987	–	–	9.56	9.56	10
1988	–	–	3.52	3.52	4
1989	–	–	12.18	12.18	12
1990	–	–	9.29	9.29	9
1991	–	–	3.89	3.89	4
1992	–	–	2.45	2.45	2
1993	–	–	4.32	4.32	4
1994	–	–	5.16	5.16	5
Totals	–	–	50.36	50.36	50

Fred Valentine

Year	Bat	Field	Pitch	Sum	WS
1959	0.28	0.07	–	0.35	0
1963	0.99	0.13	–	1.12	1
1964	2.06	0.75	–	2.81	3
1965	0.47	0.26	–	0.73	1
1966	21.35	2.89	–	24.24	24
1967	15.25	2.53	–	17.78	18
1968	2.60	0.70	–	3.30	3
Totals	43.00	7.33	–	50.32	50

Jack Gleason

Year	Bat	Field	Pitch	Sum	WS
1877	0.00	0.00	–	0.00	0
1882	9.86	2.41	–	12.27	12
1883	13.46	0.69	–	14.15	14
1884	16.86	3.09	–	19.95	20
1885	0.00	0.04	–	0.04	0
1886	2.59	1.31	–	3.90	4
Totals	42.78	7.54	–	50.31	50

Davy Force

Year	Bat	Field	Pitch	Sum	WS
1876	1.01	1.46	–	2.47	2
1877	3.93	3.77	–	7.69	8
1879	0.59	4.67	–	5.26	5
1880	0.00	3.28	–	3.28	3
1881	0.00	4.81	–	4.81	5
1882	3.30	4.15	–	7.45	7
1883	1.33	4.11	–	5.44	6
1884	2.22	5.64	–	7.85	8
1885	1.44	1.48	–	2.92	3
1886	0.00	3.11	–	3.11	3
Totals	13.81	36.49	–	50.29	50

Matt Keough

Year	Bat	Field	Pitch	Sum	WS
1977	–	–	0.94	0.94	1
1978	–	–	12.18	12.18	12
1979	–	–	3.39	3.39	3
1980	–	–	17.94	17.94	18
1981	–	–	8.84	8.84	9
1982	–	–	1.55	1.55	2
1983	–	–	0.77	0.77	1
1985	0.00	–	0.05	0.05	0
1986	0.74	–	3.84	4.58	4
Totals	0.74	–	49.50	50.25	50

Herm McFarland

Year	Bat	Field	Pitch	Sum	WS
1896	0.00	0.27	–	0.27	0
1898	1.97	0.44	–	2.41	3
1901	16.15	5.14	–	21.28	21
1902	9.27	1.28	–	10.54	10
1903	12.57	3.10	–	15.68	16
Totals	39.95	10.23	–	50.18	50

Tim Hulett

Year	Bat	Field	Pitch	Sum	WS
1983	0.00	0.06	–	0.06	0
1984	0.00	0.20	–	0.20	0
1985	7.86	3.55	–	11.42	11
1986	3.89	4.00	–	7.89	8
1987	0.00	1.89	–	1.89	2
1989	3.98	1.03	–	5.01	5
1990	3.98	1.90	–	5.87	6
1991	0.00	0.83	–	0.83	1
1992	4.08	1.79	–	5.86	6
1993	4.37	3.37	–	7.73	8
1994	1.13	2.08	–	3.21	3
1995	0.00	0.15	–	0.15	0
Totals	29.28	20.85	–	50.13	50

Kevin Millwood

Year	Bat	Field	Pitch	Sum	WS
1997	0.00	–	2.95	2.95	3
1998	0.00	–	9.73	9.73	10
1999	0.00	–	22.16	22.16	22
2000	0.00	–	10.05	10.05	10
2001	0.00	–	5.22	5.22	5
Totals	0.00	–	50.11	50.11	50

Other players with exactly 50 Win Shares:

Atkinson, Al (1884-1887)
Baldwin, James (1995-2001)
Bradley, Tom (1969-1975)
Brame, Erv (1928-1932)
Brown, Lew (1876-1884)
Cain, Sugar (1932-1938)
Clarke, Nig (1905-1920)
Clines, Gene (1970-1979)
Cruz, Deivi (1997-2001)
Downey, Tom (1909-1915)
Fermin, Felix (1987-1996)
Fette, Lou (1937-1945)
Heep, Danny (1979-1991)
Henry, Doug (1991-2001)
Heredia, Gil (1991-2001)
Howard, Del (1905-1909)
Jacklitsch, Fred (1900-1917)
Jenkins, Geoff (1998-2001)
Jordan, Ricky (1988-1996)
King, Eric (1986-1992)
LaGrow, Lerrin (1970-1980)
Leach, Terry (1981-1993)
Littell, Mark (1973-1982)
May, Derrick (1990-1999)
Mlicki, Dave (1992-2001)
Neis, Bernie (1920-1927)
Powell, Jake (1930-1945)
Sexson, Richie (1997-2001)
Smith, Dwight (1989-1996)
Taylor, Harry (1890-1893)

Batting/Fielding/Pitching Breakdowns for Top 300 Players

Player	Bat	Field	Pitch	Sum	WS
Babe Ruth	608.76	44.72	102.04	755.52	756
Ty Cobb	639.44	82.77	0.41	722.62	722
Honus Wagner	513.83	141.84	0.62	656.29	655
Hank Aaron	573.27	67.27	–	640.54	643
Willie Mays	538.00	104.14	–	642.14	642
Cy Young	8.86	0.03	625.07	633.96	634
Tris Speaker	511.74	118.01	0.00	629.75	630
Stan Musial	538.69	66.75	0.00	605.44	604
Eddie Collins	463.60	108.71	–	572.31	574
Mickey Mantle	506.97	58.06	–	565.03	565
Walter Johnson	30.29	0.17	529.89	560.35	560
Ted Williams	512.43	44.05	0.12	556.60	555
Pete Rose	461.77	85.83	–	547.61	547
Rickey Henderson	473.71	56.32	–	530.03	530
Mel Ott	474.04	51.56	–	525.59	528
Barry Bonds	477.95	43.34	–	521.28	523
Frank Robinson	467.82	50.99	–	518.82	519
Joe Morgan	423.89	90.94	–	514.84	512
Rogers Hornsby	443.70	59.63	–	503.33	502
Nap Lajoie	398.76	95.91	–	494.67	496
Lou Gehrig	456.51	33.02	–	489.52	489
Carl Yastrzemski	426.00	61.49	–	487.49	488
Kid Nichols	11.36	0.53	467.67	479.56	478
Pete Alexander	7.46	–	468.61	476.07	476
Mike Schmidt	378.30	88.33	–	466.63	467
Eddie Mathews	387.41	58.95	–	446.36	450
Sam Crawford	398.81	48.72	–	447.52	446
Reggie Jackson	403.76	40.39	–	444.16	444
Al Kaline	382.86	58.57	–	441.43	443
Eddie Murray	397.62	37.01	–	434.63	437
Jimmie Foxx	386.47	46.18	2.08	434.73	435
George Brett	371.52	61.52	–	433.03	432
Cal Ripken Jr.	290.74	136.43	–	427.16	427
C. Mathewson	12.58	0.15	412.97	425.70	426
Paul Waner	359.81	61.11	–	420.92	423
Robin Yount	317.34	103.13	–	420.47	423
Dave Winfield	373.36	41.06	–	414.42	415
Paul Molitor	367.46	46.08	–	413.54	414
Tim Keefe	19.30	0.81	392.60	412.71	413
Warren Spahn	7.37	–	402.59	409.96	412
Monte Ward	158.74	77.04	174.16	409.94	409
Willie McCovey	379.41	27.11	–	406.52	408
Pud Galvin	10.21	0.47	389.91	400.59	403
Fred Clarke	335.67	64.22	–	399.88	400
Tony Mullane	47.01	5.79	348.08	400.88	399
Tony Gwynn	353.40	45.05	–	398.46	398
George Davis	296.70	100.19	0.00	396.89	398
John Clarkson	11.65	0.23	384.25	396.14	396
Wade Boggs	319.32	74.16	0.15	393.63	394
Bill Dahlen	248.89	143.35	–	392.23	394
Lefty Grove	0.00	–	391.86	391.86	391
Old Hoss Radbourn	33.03	3.35	354.24	390.62	391
Tim Raines	336.12	52.71	–	388.84	390
Jesse Burkett	335.17	52.94	0.39	388.49	389
Tom Seaver	0.15	–	389.40	389.54	388
Joe DiMaggio	325.83	60.50	–	386.33	387
Rod Carew	331.95	53.43	–	385.38	384
Charlie Gehringer	295.32	87.27	–	382.59	383
Cap Anson	338.09	40.63	0.68	379.39	381
Zack Wheat	322.09	58.09	–	380.19	380
Luke Appling	268.03	108.63	–	376.66	378
Roberto Clemente	316.42	59.50	–	375.93	377
Al Simmons	305.36	69.03	–	374.40	375
Yogi Berra	267.50	104.70	–	372.20	375
Phil Niekro	0.00	–	375.32	375.32	374
Billy Williams	329.10	44.92	–	374.03	374
Harmon Killebrew	337.08	35.04	–	372.12	371
Willie Stargell	339.13	31.39	–	370.53	370
Gaylord Perry	0.19	–	368.44	368.64	369
Carlton Fisk	254.70	113.46	–	368.16	368
Steve Carlton	3.28	–	366.94	370.22	366
Frankie Frisch	258.02	106.68	–	364.70	366
Roger Connor	322.33	40.25	–	362.58	363
Darrell Evans	294.94	67.29	–	362.23	363
Eddie Plank	5.04	–	354.85	359.89	361
Rusty Staub	322.78	35.34	–	358.13	358
Harry Heilmann	325.09	30.86	–	355.96	356
Arky Vaughan	275.64	80.18	–	355.82	356
Johnny Bench	255.26	99.59	–	354.85	356
Brooks Robinson	248.08	106.48	–	354.56	356
Goose Goslin	305.42	49.36	–	354.78	355
Dan Brouthers	329.27	25.50	0.00	354.77	355
Ed Delahanty	311.08	42.51	–	353.59	355
Mickey Welch	22.88	0.41	330.08	353.37	354
Sherry Magee	305.80	46.62	–	352.42	354
Duke Snider	296.84	54.84	–	351.68	352
Roger Clemens	0.53	–	349.36	349.89	352
Lou Whitaker	265.58	87.20	–	352.79	351
Max Carey	254.02	94.78	–	348.80	351
Tony Perez	299.05	47.57	–	346.62	349
Lou Brock	300.29	49.00	–	349.29	348
Dwight Evans	293.59	51.86	–	345.45	347
Ryne Sandberg	249.67	93.66	–	343.33	346
Bobby Wallace	201.47	114.20	29.92	345.58	345
Roberto Alomar	258.18	86.88	–	345.07	345
G. Van Haltren	256.37	47.78	40.48	344.63	344
Mark McGwire	323.07	20.03	–	343.10	342
Craig Biggio	268.48	74.13	–	342.61	342
Dick Allen	312.37	29.50	–	341.87	342
Andre Dawson	278.90	62.21	–	341.11	340

Player	Bat	Field	Pitch	Sum	WS
Jimmy Sheckard	272.40	66.41	–	338.82	339
Bert Blyleven	0.00	–	338.58	338.58	339
Robin Roberts	5.17	–	332.88	338.04	339
Johnny Mize	310.05	26.85	–	336.89	338
Gary Carter	214.66	123.88	–	338.55	337
Bob Caruthers	90.71	6.02	240.16	336.89	337
Billy Hamilton	287.53	49.00	–	336.53	337
Jim McCormick	18.72	1.29	314.68	334.70	334
Rafael Palmeiro	300.33	34.30	–	334.63	334
Nolan Ryan	0.00	–	332.30	332.30	334
Joe Cronin	235.32	97.79	–	333.11	333
Willie Keeler	284.55	48.52	–	333.07	333
Ernie Banks	264.95	67.13	–	332.07	332
Will Clark	303.58	25.74	–	329.32	331
Bobby Grich	236.41	94.14	–	330.55	329
Richie Ashburn	255.94	73.81	–	329.75	329
Tommy Leach	232.54	96.07	–	328.61	328
Sam Rice	268.73	54.21	2.11	325.05	327
Dave Parker	281.68	42.65	–	324.33	327
Ozzie Smith	187.17	139.84	–	327.01	325
Reggie Smith	274.40	51.92	–	326.32	325
Gabby Hartnett	215.90	109.71	–	325.61	325
Ron Santo	255.50	68.84	–	324.34	324
Enos Slaughter	275.39	49.56	–	324.96	323
Fergie Jenkins	2.31	–	319.19	321.50	323
Willie Davis	243.08	78.29	–	321.37	322
Red Ruffing	30.70	0.02	289.79	320.51	322
Harry Hooper	268.28	53.08	0.27	321.64	321
Graig Nettles	228.95	92.00	–	320.94	321
Vada Pinson	251.25	69.38	–	320.63	321
Barry Larkin	228.93	92.09	–	321.02	320
Don Sutton	0.00	–	318.81	318.81	319
Alan Trammell	225.08	92.59	–	317.67	318
Jake Beckley	278.86	37.89	0.00	316.75	318
Jeff Bagwell	290.90	25.15	–	316.05	318
Bob Gibson	5.99	–	313.30	319.29	317
Greg Maddux	0.07	–	315.84	315.91	317
Fred McGriff	288.39	27.77	–	316.15	316
Stan Hack	250.47	65.67	–	316.14	316
Jack Clark	289.05	26.35	–	315.40	316
Jimmy Ryan	252.20	55.52	7.31	315.02	316
Ted Simmons	242.35	72.99	–	315.34	315
Norm Cash	279.26	34.50	–	313.76	315
Joe Torre	258.28	55.12	–	313.40	315
Eppa Rixey	0.81	–	310.48	311.29	315
Pee Wee Reese	203.91	111.29	–	315.19	314
Edd Roush	255.69	58.28	–	313.98	314
Bill Dickey	217.88	94.95	–	312.83	314
Ken Griffey Jr.	262.57	51.13	–	313.70	313
Jose Cruz	261.72	48.81	–	310.53	313
Joe Medwick	267.41	44.40	–	311.81	312
Ted Lyons	5.78	0.00	305.30	311.08	312
Jim Palmer	0.42	–	310.41	310.83	312
Willie Randolph	213.31	97.44	–	310.76	312
Keith Hernandez	277.26	35.03	–	312.28	311
Orlando Cepeda	283.18	27.21	–	310.39	310
Early Wynn	14.75	–	293.45	308.21	309
Frank Thomas	302.04	5.97	–	308.01	308
Harold Baines	283.87	23.59	–	307.47	307
Bid McPhee	206.83	98.75	–	305.58	305
Jimmy Wynn	260.61	44.61	–	305.22	305
Jim O'Rourke	258.69	45.00	1.34	305.03	305
Al Oliver	259.93	44.38	–	304.31	305
Joe Kelley	252.24	51.65	–	303.88	305
Carl Hubbell	0.54	–	303.34	303.88	305
Nellie Fox	192.97	111.74	–	304.71	304
Bobby Bonds	259.26	42.68	–	301.94	302
Rabbit Maranville	158.89	142.90	–	301.79	302
Ken Singleton	271.42	30.05	–	301.47	302
Buddy Bell	214.17	87.98	–	302.14	301
Home Run Baker	235.05	65.34	–	300.39	301
Dennis Eckersley	0.00	–	298.15	298.15	301
Brian Downing	253.23	44.92	–	298.15	298
Billy Herman	219.04	77.13	–	296.16	298
Frank Howard	272.15	24.12	–	296.26	297
Mickey Vernon	262.46	34.25	–	296.71	296
Three Finger Brown	3.75	0.03	292.71	296.49	296
Cesar Cedeno	242.92	52.21	–	295.12	296
Brett Butler	239.38	57.53	–	296.91	295
Hugh Duffy	234.49	59.34	–	293.82	295
Joe Jackson	262.82	29.94	–	292.75	294
Dale Murphy	242.74	49.27	–	292.01	294
Kid Gleason	93.15	49.20	149.16	291.50	294
Luis Aparicio	170.57	122.82	–	293.39	293
Amos Rusie	8.27	0.27	284.73	293.28	293
Vic Willis	0.00	0.18	292.54	292.71	293
George Sisler	260.24	24.59	8.33	293.16	292
Dave Foutz	107.99	19.73	164.98	292.70	292
Bob Feller	0.70	–	291.71	292.42	292
Red Faber	2.08	–	289.15	291.23	292
Kiki Cuyler	242.95	47.74	–	290.70	292
Elmer Flick	257.44	32.48	–	289.93	291
Fielder Jones	222.28	67.41	–	289.68	290
George Burns	241.26	46.94	–	288.20	290
Tommy John	0.00	–	289.51	289.51	289
Larry Doyle	237.51	50.25	–	287.76	289
Bob Elliott	237.47	51.39	–	288.86	287
Bob Johnson	250.76	36.64	–	287.40	287
Jack Quinn	5.55	0.07	281.60	287.23	287
Ed Konetchy	247.13	39.13	0.88	287.15	287

Player	Bat	Field	Pitch	Sum	WS
Jack Powell	3.77	0.02	282.60	286.39	287
Toby Harrah	226.51	58.17	–	284.67	287
Amos Otis	215.35	72.50	–	287.85	286
Burleigh Grimes	10.69	–	275.61	286.30	286
Chili Davis	262.91	22.16	0.29	285.36	285
Jack Stivetts	46.50	4.05	234.18	284.73	285
Mark Grace	246.65	37.90	–	284.55	285
Elmer Smith	158.97	28.90	96.22	284.09	285
Heinie Manush	245.01	38.90	–	283.91	285
Sal Bando	230.15	52.38	0.02	282.55	283
Charlie Buffinton	26.47	2.00	253.21	281.68	283
Minnie Minoso	239.69	41.84	–	281.52	283
Boog Powell	257.54	24.56	–	282.10	282
Jim Rice	244.20	35.59	–	279.79	282
Kirby Puckett	223.79	58.41	–	282.20	281
Bobby Doerr	196.40	85.68	–	282.08	281
Ron Cey	220.28	60.24	–	280.52	280
Fred Lynn	227.85	51.90	–	279.75	280
Bert Campaneris	178.51	101.13	0.00	279.64	280
Tony Fernandez	179.08	99.43	–	278.51	280
Earl Averill	223.87	54.54	–	278.41	280
Ken Boyer	211.13	70.18	–	281.31	279
Steve Garvey	237.15	42.55	–	279.70	279
Lave Cross	166.37	113.26	–	279.63	278
Dixie Walker	234.91	44.23	–	279.14	278
King Kelly	225.68	50.83	1.88	278.39	278
Bill Terry	245.65	32.19	–	277.83	278
Joe Sewell	188.17	89.89	–	278.05	277
Lou Boudreau	187.45	89.34	–	276.79	277
Bobby Murcer	233.52	41.09	–	274.62	277
Gary Sheffield	245.71	29.23	–	274.94	276
Jim Whitney	51.22	1.80	222.15	275.16	275
Mickey Cochrane	193.62	81.26	–	274.88	275
Jimmy Collins	183.22	89.41	–	272.63	274
Pie Traynor	192.47	79.56	–	272.04	274
Clark Griffith	15.24	0.29	257.46	273.00	273
Rocky Colavito	234.01	36.85	1.14	272.00	273
Adonis Terry	41.34	5.50	224.83	271.67	273
Jose Canseco	253.71	17.72	0.00	271.44	272
Heine Groh	201.51	69.63	–	271.14	272
Cy Seymour	167.97	43.98	58.38	270.33	272
Joe Judge	234.79	30.82	–	265.62	270
Dave Concepcion	146.86	124.29	0.00	271.15	269
Joe McGinnity	2.16	0.21	267.98	270.34	269
George Foster	230.00	39.33	–	269.33	269
Ron Fairly	232.69	36.36	–	269.05	269
Dave Bancroft	164.05	103.43	–	267.48	269
Jim Kaat	4.09	–	268.16	272.25	268
Tony Phillips	211.19	56.73	–	267.92	268
Larry Doby	221.95	45.88	–	267.82	268

Player	Bat	Field	Pitch	Sum	WS
Johnny Evers	198.08	69.55	–	267.62	268
Eddie Yost	222.45	45.65	–	268.10	267
Hank Greenberg	240.55	26.13	–	266.68	267
Bobby Bonilla	228.68	37.13	0.00	265.80	267
Bill Freehan	175.38	89.61	–	264.99	267
Wilbur Cooper	9.77	–	257.18	266.94	266
Clyde Milan	209.93	55.03	–	264.96	266
Harry Stovey	232.15	34.13	0.14	266.42	265
Bobby Veach	219.07	47.00	0.06	266.13	265
Herman Long	160.88	104.78	–	265.67	265
Ed Walsh	5.60	0.05	259.35	265.00	265
Vern Stephens	191.44	73.18	–	264.63	265
Chet Lemon	200.43	63.25	–	263.68	265
Edgar Martinez	250.67	13.19	–	263.86	264
Hal Newhouser	2.65	–	260.79	263.44	264
Silver King	11.21	0.04	253.11	264.37	263
Gil Hodges	229.25	34.40	–	263.66	263
Don Mattingly	233.14	30.20	–	263.35	263
Roy White	227.53	35.33	–	262.86	263
Jake Daubert	228.42	33.96	–	262.37	263
Augie Galan	223.49	38.09	–	261.58	263
Juan Marichal	0.68	–	260.46	261.14	263
Waite Hoyt	1.45	–	263.07	264.52	262
Don Baylor	244.80	17.11	–	261.91	262
Red Schoendienst	165.83	95.35	–	261.18	262
Jack Glasscock	170.10	89.94	0.09	260.13	261
Jim Fregosi	198.34	61.63	–	259.97	261
Whitey Ford	3.03	–	255.57	258.61	261
Roy Thomas	215.67	44.67	0.20	260.54	260
Ken Griffey Sr.	226.25	32.59	–	258.84	259
Guy Hecker	66.17	3.53	188.02	257.73	259
Paul O'Neill	213.65	41.65	0.00	255.30	259
Jim Bottomley	232.75	26.12	–	258.87	258
Larry Gardner	179.42	79.07	–	258.49	258
Joe Tinker	144.82	113.53	–	258.35	258
Bucky Walters	18.17	5.67	234.37	258.21	258
Don Drysdale	7.02	–	250.85	257.87	258
Gus Weyhing	2.61	0.15	254.99	257.75	258
Buddy Myer	192.02	65.61	–	257.64	258
Rick Monday	212.88	43.81	–	256.69	258
Jackie Robinson	201.75	55.03	–	256.78	257
Jim Bunning	0.21	–	256.47	256.69	257
Gary Matthews	224.43	32.13	–	256.56	257
Carl Mays	18.84	–	237.07	255.91	256
Hoyt Wilhelm	0.00	–	255.55	255.55	256
Luis Tiant	3.07	–	250.30	253.37	256
George Mullin	33.24	0.05	222.33	255.62	255
Mike Piazza	206.43	48.03	–	254.45	255
Dummy Hoy	206.14	48.91	–	255.04	254
Wally Joyner	226.23	28.87	–	255.10	253
Maury Wills	168.15	82.37	–	250.52	253

Ty Cobb

Year	Age	RC	Outs	MR	WS
1905	18	14	118	5	2.66
1906	19	56	259	35	13.21
1907	20	132	405	102	37.38
1908	21	113	407	85	34.02
1909	22	139	381	110	39.88
1910	23	137	329	112	40.02
1911	24	172	354	136	41.28
1912	25	147	334	117	36.52
1913	26	99	272	77	27.71
1914	27	80	241	62	23.59
1915	28	153	402	120	41.56
1916	29	123	355	96	35.28
1917	30	144	379	116	40.37
1918	31	90	269	70	28.68
1919	32	100	315	75	28.18
1920	33	81	302	52	16.19
1921	34	120	340	86	21.97
1922	35	121	355	88	25.75
1923	36	106	399	69	20.31
1924	37	119	443	75	22.78
1925	38	111	272	83	22.34
1926	39	47	171	31	9.92
1927	40	102	343	68	19.66
1928	41	58	249	34	10.20
Totals			7694		639.44
			(7970)		8.02
					Per 100 Outs

Hank Aaron

Year	Age	RC	Outs	MR	WS
1954	20	61	362	32	10.28
1955	21	112	445	76	25.40
1956	22	111	446	77	26.66
1957	23	126	434	93	32.11
1958	24	111	430	78	27.85
1959	25	142	434	108	35.42
1960	26	117	445	84	31.91
1961	27	124	441	89	29.74
1962	28	134	428	98	30.11
1963	29	146	451	113	37.19
1964	30	114	411	83	29.76
1965	31	117	416	84	26.58
1966	32	114	460	78	24.60
1967	33	123	439	90	29.97
1968	34	95	463	65	27.75
1969	35	127	410	94	33.32
1970	36	109	381	75	21.19
1971	37	120	348	92	30.39
1972	38	84	349	56	19.56
1973	39	93	286	67	18.15
1974	40	58	258	37	11.49
1975	41	57	379	26	9.02
1976	42	31	220	14	4.82
Totals			9136		573.27
			(9074)		6.32
					Per 100 Outs

Willie Mays

Year	Age	RC	Outs	MR	WS
1951	20	75	353	45	14.22
1952	21	18	100	10	3.56
1954	23	139	394	104	31.36
1955	24	146	418	110	34.81
1956	25	106	436	71	22.91
1957	26	134	429	98	29.82
1958	27	138	415	103	33.40
1959	28	123	416	89	27.07
1960	29	122	439	90	32.60
1961	30	133	423	97	29.02
1962	31	146	456	107	34.08
1963	32	127	434	96	33.19
1964	33	126	427	93	31.19
1965	34	138	400	106	34.99
1966	35	115	412	83	30.06
1967	36	74	375	47	15.67
1968	37	92	379	68	25.94
1969	38	66	303	43	14.07
1970	39	97	352	67	21.59
1971	40	94	320	70	24.74
1972	41	41	201	26	10.52
1973	42	23	174	10	3.19
Totals			8056		538.00
			(8003)		6.72
					Per 100 Outs

Babe Ruth

Year	Age	RC	Outs	MR	WS
1914	19	1	8	0	0.17
1915	20	22	65	17	6.43
1916	21	18	103	11	4.64
1917	22	22	90	16	6.01
1918	23	74	225	59	24.65
1919	24	121	296	98	33.51
1920	25	192	305	163	47.88
1921	26	208	353	172	47.69
1922	27	107	287	80	25.02
1923	28	193	341	161	48.48
1924	29	178	348	144	41.67
1925	30	71	265	44	11.64
1926	31	167	330	137	42.60
1927	32	176	368	141	40.47
1928	33	165	376	132	42.69
1929	34	138	343	105	30.64
1930	35	176	363	140	36.48
1931	36	178	339	145	36.29
1932	37	147	303	118	34.16
1933	38	121	326	91	27.62
1934	39	88	263	63	18.21
1935	40	12	61	7	1.81
Totals			5758		608.80
			(5890)		10.34
					Per 100 Outs

Stan Musial

Year	Age	RC	Outs	MR	WS
1941	20	11	27	9	2.74
1942	21	97	328	71	23.82
1943	22	129	424	96	33.07
1944	23	134	382	104	33.13
1946	25	151	405	119	40.86
1947	26	117	428	77	21.75
1948	27	176	400	141	42.37
1949	28	154	417	115	34.82
1950	29	136	374	101	28.74
1951	30	147	385	114	34.96
1952	31	125	402	93	32.80
1953	32	144	407	106	30.11
1954	33	141	430	103	28.47
1955	34	120	405	84	25.86
1956	35	109	439	72	23.74
1957	36	119	349	89	28.37
1958	37	93	336	63	18.74
1959	38	48	271	24	6.94
1960	39	56	250	34	11.56
1961	40	67	278	40	10.91
1962	41	93	308	64	16.56
1963	42	46	259	26	8.37
Totals			7704		538.69
			(7688)		7.01
					Per 100 Outs

Honus Wagner

Year	Age	RC	Outs	MR	WS
1897	23	50	162	31	7.77
1898	24	98	422	56	17.27
1899	25	129	383	87	20.43
1900	26	150	330	115	30.22
1901	27	133	365	100	30.03
1902	28	117	366	88	28.85
1903	29	127	338	94	27.50
1904	30	129	324	103	38.09
1905	31	136	356	106	36.75
1906	32	117	347	91	34.20
1907	33	121	349	96	36.42
1908	34	131	381	107	49.21
1909	35	114	354	88	33.07
1910	36	99	398	65	21.98
1911	37	110	327	81	23.18
1912	38	111	388	76	23.61
1913	39	61	299	37	11.93
1914	40	61	424	30	10.02
1915	41	78	442	47	16.23
1916	42	56	318	34	13.19
1917	43	25	178	12	3.86
Totals			7251		513.83
			(7430)		6.92
					Per 100 Outs

Ted Williams

Year	Age	RC	Outs	MR	WS
1939	20	153	394	111	29.52
1940	21	138	386	100	27.34
1941	22	170	285	143	39.62
1942	23	160	350	131	41.50
1946	27	165	350	136	45.11
1947	28	160	359	129	41.11
1948	29	160	331	128	36.78
1949	30	174	395	136	36.62
1950	31	97	240	71	17.86
1951	32	145	373	109	30.37
1952	33	4	6	3	1.05
1953	34	34	56	29	8.80
1954	35	117	266	94	27.32
1955	36	101	218	80	20.59
1956	37	104	275	78	22.51
1957	38	143	271	119	35.24
1958	39	102	299	76	23.53
1959	40	46	215	27	7.71
1960	41	84	222	64	19.86
Totals			5291		512.40
			(5246)		9.77
					Per 100 Outs

Mickey Mantle

Year	Age	RC	Outs	MR	WS
1951	19	57	262	35	12.13
1952	20	111	386	82	28.43
1953	21	95	331	69	22.09
1954	22	125	391	95	32.45
1955	23	135	369	105	34.14
1956	24	173	355	142	43.79
1957	25	155	312	131	46.06
1958	26	138	379	108	35.68
1959	27	110	400	79	25.63
1960	28	118	401	86	31.27
1961	29	156	360	126	42.96
1962	30	114	262	93	30.92
1963	31	46	125	36	13.07
1964	32	116	339	90	30.53
1965	33	65	282	44	14.43
1966	34	68	250	50	16.65
1967	35	82	347	58	23.70
1968	36	79	348	57	23.04
Totals			5899		506.97
			(5854)		8.66
					Per 100 Outs

Frank Robinson

Year	Age	RC	Outs	MR	WS
1956	20	114	436	76	23.37
1957	21	110	439	71	23.49
1958	22	97	419	60	15.96
1959	23	117	405	81	23.56
1960	24	102	357	73	21.22
1961	25	127	397	91	29.20
1962	26	152	428	115	36.27
1963	27	88	377	60	20.39
1964	28	123	418	90	28.45
1965	29	112	437	76	23.49
1966	30	141	430	109	38.01
1967	31	108	349	84	27.53
1968	32	74	327	53	21.49
1969	33	117	391	87	28.78
1970	34	94	347	67	23.00
1971	35	85	357	58	20.11
1972	36	52	274	33	12.17
1973	37	100	410	68	25.08
1974	38	83	380	55	18.77
1975	39	25	94	17	6.00
1976	40	8	56	4	1.48
Totals			7528		467.82
			(7483)		6.25
					Per 100 Outs

Tris Speaker

Year	Age	RC	Outs	MR	WS
1907	19	0	16	0	0.00
1908	20	9	94	3	0.99
1909	21	93	393	64	26.24
1910	22	104	367	77	27.26
1911	23	103	350	71	21.21
1912	24	162	365	128	41.57
1913	25	116	347	88	31.04
1914	26	123	420	94	36.48
1915	27	106	413	75	28.15
1916	28	135	350	108	36.54
1917	29	111	354	83	29.77
1918	30	81	332	55	20.44
1919	31	87	368	55	19.15
1920	32	146	371	110	33.12
1921	33	116	339	82	22.05
1922	34	111	280	84	26.47
1923	35	154	387	117	30.36
1924	36	99	339	65	17.79
1925	37	110	279	80	20.93
1926	38	107	404	69	20.97
1927	39	94	375	58	17.46
1928	40	27	150	13	3.77
Totals			7093		511.7
			(7338)		6.97
					Per 100 Outs

Mel Ott

Year	Age	RC	Outs	MR	WS
1926	17	9	37	6	1.72
1927	18	21	121	10	3.25
1928	19	86	305	58	17.35
1929	20	155	376	115	26.86
1930	21	134	359	94	23.60
1931	22	104	353	73	21.88
1932	23	143	389	109	30.75
1933	24	105	430	73	26.47
1934	25	144	403	109	33.92
1935	26	130	411	94	30.28
1936	27	140	377	107	33.43
1937	28	120	393	86	28.50
1938	29	134	373	102	31.50
1939	30	106	290	81	26.28
1940	31	105	395	71	21.22
1941	32	110	383	78	24.92
1942	33	124	398	93	32.98
1943	34	71	299	48	15.68
1944	35	97	289	72	23.61
1945	36	90	320	62	19.83
1946	37	0	66	0	0.00
1947	38	0	4	0	0.00
Totals			6771		474.04
			(6792)		6.98
					Per 100 Outs

Eddie Collins

Year	Age	RC	Outs	MR	WS
1906	19	0	13	0	0.00
1907	20	1	19	0	0.00
1908	21	44	255	25	9.00
1909	22	118	394	91	34.74
1910	23	110	415	81	29.80
1911	24	122	331	93	29.21
1912	25	126	383	92	30.05
1913	26	123	376	94	33.15
1914	27	129	403	101	37.12
1915	28	128	413	97	31.96
1916	29	97	416	66	23.73
1917	30	100	434	69	25.74
1918	31	54	261	35	12.18
1919	32	91	393	58	20.63
1920	33	131	420	92	29.75
1921	34	89	372	51	14.97
1922	35	99	443	58	17.42
1923	36	101	391	65	18.94
1924	37	118	407	79	21.61
1925	38	97	301	67	18.42
1926	39	74	269	50	14.75
1927	40	49	160	33	9.58
1928	41	5	23	3	0.84
1929	42	0	7	0	0.00
1930	43	0	1	0	0.00
Totals			7300		463.60
			(7531)		6.16
					Per 100 Outs

Year of Birth Charts for Selected Players

Young (Yng) is the player's Win Shares through the 24th year after the year of birth.
Prime (Prm) is his Win Shares from the 25th to the 29th year after the year of birth.
Post Prime (Pst) is his Win Shares from the 30th to the 34th year following his YOB.
Final (Fin) is his Win Shares in or after the 35th year following his year of birth.
Total (Tot) is the player's total Win Shares for his career.
B, F and P are the player's career percentage of Batting, Fielding and Pitching Win Shares.

Year of Birth: 1930

Player	Yng	Prm	Pst	Fin	Tot	B	F	P
Groat, D.	5	75	112	33	225	57	43	–
Kuenn, H.	40	109	68	6	223	80	20	–
Friend, B.	27	80	87	13	207	0	–	100
Skowron, B.	13	73	73	24	183	89	11	–
Crandall, D.	42	86	45	6	179	54	46	–
Moon, W.	20	92	61	2	175	86	14	–
Law, V.	16	67	44	30	157	4	0	96

Year of Birth: 1931

Player	Yng	Prm	Pst	Fin	Tot	B	F	P
Mays, W.	104	171	194	173	642	84	16	–
Mantle, M.	148	205	145	67	565	90	10	–
Mathews, E.	125	161	132	32	450	87	13	–
Banks, E.	49	143	75	65	332	80	20	–
Boyer, K.	14	118	113	34	279	75	25	–
Bunning, J.	0	81	100	76	257	0	–	100
Jackson, L.	9	79	89	48	225	0	–	100
Virdon, B.	14	82	61	0	157	66	34	–

Year of Birth: 1932

Player	Yng	Prm	Pst	Fin	Tot	B	F	P
Wills, M.	0	42	123	88	253	67	33	–
Held, W.	0	78	69	6	153	72	28	–

Year of Birth: 1933

Player	Yng	Prm	Pst	Fin	Tot	B	F	P
Colavito, R.	35	133	99	6	273	86	14	0
Roseboro, J.	1	75	82	23	181	59	41	–
Siebern, N.	2	104	65	0	171	88	12	–
Francona, T.	18	95	29	23	165	87	13	–

Year of Birth: 1934

Player	Yng	Prm	Pst	Fin	Tot	B	F	P
Aaron, H.	139	183	157	164	643	89	11	–
Kaline, A.	108	117	123	95	443	87	13	–
Clemente, R.	42	98	146	91	377	84	16	–
Cash, N.	0	108	108	99	315	89	11	–
Aparicio, L.	49	87	87	70	293	58	42	–
Maris, R.	30	126	67	0	223	87	13	–
White, B.	17	97	95	0	209	86	14	–
Allison, B.	0	102	94	7	203	85	15	–
Pascual, C.	28	99	44	4	175	2	–	98
Wagner, L.	10	66	78	1	155	90	10	–
Landis, J.	29	96	26	0	151	73	27	–

Year of Birth: 1935

Player	Yng	Prm	Pst	Fin	Tot	B	F	P
Robinson, F.	98	154	153	114	519	90	10	–
Gibson, B.	5	80	133	99	317	2	–	98
Alou, F.	12	81	108	40	241	85	15	–
Perry, J.	15	45	72	73	205	1	0	99
Taylor, T.	27	75	51	45	198	67	33	–
Koufax, S.	26	100	68	0	194	0	–	100
McDaniel, L.	36	61	40	49	186	0	–	100

Year of Birth: 1936

Player	Yng	Prm	Pst	Fin	Tot	B	F	P
Killebrew, H.	48	120	147	56	371	91	9	–
Howard, F.	13	95	151	38	297	92	8	–
Drysdale, D.	91	117	50	0	258	3	–	97
Mazeroski, B.	69	84	61	5	219	48	52	–
Gonzalez, T.	9	86	81	7	183	82	18	–

Year of Birth: 1937

Player	Yng	Prm	Pst	Fin	Tot	B	F	P
Robinson, B.	58	129	110	59	356	70	30	–
Cepeda, O.	98	98	98	16	310	91	9	–
Marichal, J.	16	133	96	18	263	0	–	100
Buford, D.	0	67	118	9	194	81	19	–
Haller, T.	1	87	87	4	179	67	33	–
Cuellar, M.	0	25	85	63	173	0	–	100
Boyer, C.	29	80	51	0	160	58	42	–
Tresh, T.	0	121	39	0	160	81	19	–

Year of Birth: 1938

Player	Yng	Prm	Pst	Fin	Tot	B	F	P
McCovey, W.	49	127	129	103	408	93	7	–
Williams, B.	35	138	141	60	374	88	12	–
Perry, G.	1	67	125	176	369	0	–	100
Pinson, V.	109	120	71	21	321	78	22	–
Fairly, R.	43	90	74	62	269	86	14	–
Kaat, J.	33	80	65	90	268	2	–	98
Flood, C.	57	117	47	0	221	66	34	–
Cardenas, L.	31	81	80	7	199	53	47	–
Alou, M.	13	51	105	10	179	82	18	0
Mincher, D.	9	77	76	0	162	90	10	–

Year of Birth: 1939

Player	Yng	Prm	Pst	Fin	Tot	B	F	P
Yastrzemski, C.	62	143	126	157	488	87	13	–
Niekro, P.	0	46	100	228	374	0	–	100
Brock, L.	24	130	120	74	348	86	14	–
McAuliffe, D.	38	119	78	6	241	75	25	–
Callison, J.	86	110	45	0	241	83	17	–
Pappas, M.	76	67	67	0	210	0	0	100
Carty, R.	0	70	59	80	209	93	7	–
Davis, T.	85	53	43	26	207	88	12	–
Osteen, C.	23	76	87	15	201	2	0	98
Northrup, J.	0	55	89	17	161	83	17	–

Year of Birth: 1940

Player	Yng	Prm	Pst	Fin	Tot	B	F	P
Stargell, W.	21	109	143	97	370	92	8	–
Santo, R.	95	154	75	0	324	79	21	–
Davis, W.	82	91	117	32	322	76	24	–
Torre, J.	70	108	119	18	315	82	18	–
Tiant, L.	11	81	78	86	256	1	–	99
Oliva, T.	28	132	76	9	245	89	11	–
Lolich, M.	25	64	108	27	224	0	–	100
Harper, T.	21	67	104	12	204	82	18	–
Tovar, C.	0	76	96	6	178	79	21	0
Menke, D.	44	75	57	0	176	74	26	–

Year of Birth: 1941

Player	Yng	Prm	Pst	Fin	Tot	B	F	P
Rose, P.	58	147	152	190	547	84	16	–
Powell, B.	74	116	86	6	282	91	9	–
Freehan, B.	50	117	93	7	267	66	34	–
McCarver, T.	48	86	42	28	204	67	33	–
Hunt, R.	39	85	67	0	191	79	21	–
Wood, W.	6	54	117	13	190	0	–	100
Stottlemyre, M.	33	91	53	0	177	1	–	99

Year of Birth: 1942

Player	Yng	Prm	Pst	Fin	Tot	B	F	P
Perez, T.	10	135	112	92	349	86	14	–
Allen, D.	109	131	98	4	342	91	9	–
Wynn, J.	58	130	115	2	305	85	15	–
Campaneris, B.	46	102	99	33	280	64	36	0
Fregosi, J.	105	118	33	5	261	76	24	–
Koosman, J.	0	71	73	96	240	0	–	100
Horton, W.	43	96	60	34	233	92	8	–
Bailey, B.	55	65	65	4	189	80	20	–
Reed, R.	1	45	53	82	181	1	–	99
McMullen, K.	39	102	32	2	175	76	24	–
McNally, D.	38	85	45	0	168	0	–	100
McDowell, S.	58	96	12	0	166	0	0	100
Kessinger, D.	8	73	64	14	159	52	48	–

Year of Birth: 1943

Player	Yng	Prm	Pst	Fin	Tot	B	F	P
Morgan, J.	76	118	188	130	512	82	18	–
Jenkins, F.	35	135	84	69	323	1	–	99
John, T.	41	70	58	120	289	0	–	100
White, R.	13	140	98	12	263	87	13	–
May, L.	14	108	79	24	225	90	10	–
Cardenal, J.	42	82	80	8	212	80	20	–
Petrocelli, R.	47	123	35	0	205	67	33	–
Johnson, D.	29	95	44	3	171	71	29	–
Piniella, L.	0	63	46	55	164	82	18	–
Millan, F.	4	78	70	0	152	61	39	–

Year of Birth: 1944

Player	Yng	Prm	Pst	Fin	Tot	B	F	P
Seaver, T.	44	140	106	98	388	0	–	100
Carlton, S.	29	108	100	129	366	1	–	99
Staub, R.	104	124	96	34	358	90	10	–
Nettles, G.	3	90	122	106	321	71	29	–
Bando, S.	24	143	104	12	283	81	19	0
Scott, G.	40	90	82	4	216	86	14	–
Niekro, J.	15	32	36	106	189	1	–	99
Blair, P.	54	94	34	1	183	65	35	–
Rader, D.	20	87	59	0	166	73	27	–
Belanger, M.	11	66	73	12	162	36	64	–
Lyle, S.	12	62	66	21	161	1	–	99
Briggs, J.	48	78	33	0	159	88	12	–
McGraw, T.	5	72	44	37	158	1	–	99
Sanguillen, M.	2	90	65	0	157	67	33	–
Patek, F.	6	69	66	9	150	52	48	–

Year of Birth: 1945

Player	Yng	Prm	Pst	Fin	Tot	B	F	P
Carew, R.	53	110	135	86	384	86	14	–
Smith, R.	68	128	96	33	325	84	16	–
Sutton, D.	48	93	75	103	319	0	–	100
Palmer, J.	36	109	126	41	312	0	–	100
Monday, R.	62	94	69	33	258	83	17	–
Lopes, D.	0	41	118	81	240	77	23	–
McRae, H.	0	44	97	89	230	95	5	–
Bowa, L.	0	54	79	46	179	51	49	–
Wise, R.	35	72	62	9	178	3	–	97
Messersmith, A.	29	88	52	0	169	1	–	99
Holtzman, K.	45	80	32	0	157	0	–	100

Year of Birth: 1946

Player	Yng	Prm	Pst	Fin	Tot	B	F	P
Jackson, R.	85	147	129	83	444	91	9	–
Oliver, A.	28	110	104	63	305	85	15	–
Bonds, B.	78	133	88	3	302	86	14	–
Murcer, B.	49	140	82	6	277	85	15	–
Watson, B.	13	107	104	12	236	91	9	–
Tenace, G.	8	97	108	18	231	82	18	–

Player	Yng	Prm	Pst	Fin	Tot	B	F	P
Hunter, C.	61	117	28	0	206	2	0	98
Fingers, R.	13	68	66	41	188	1	–	99
Rudi, J.	15	101	53	4	173	85	15	–
Torrez, M.	17	55	67	20	159	0	–	100

Year of Birth: 1947

Player	Yng	Prm	Pst	Fin	Tot	B	F	P
Fisk, C.	2	95	98	173	368	69	31	–
Evans, D.	11	116	103	133	363	81	19	–
Bench, J.	107	146	88	15	356	72	28	–
Ryan, N.	24	102	73	135	334	0	–	100
Cruz, J.	15	58	116	124	313	84	16	–
Singleton, K.	16	119	138	29	302	90	10	–
Otis, A.	53	115	94	24	286	75	25	–
Hebner, R.	52	89	62	16	219	86	14	–
Boone, B.	0	46	65	99	210	49	51	–
Munson, T.	46	108	52	0	206	70	30	–
Money, D.	39	82	62	14	197	74	26	–
Bumbry, A.	0	48	92	29	169	80	20	–
Garber, G.	0	39	57	64	160	0	–	100
Tekulve, K.	0	16	67	76	159	0	0	100

Year of Birth: 1948

Player	Yng	Prm	Pst	Fin	Tot	B	F	P
Harrah, T.	20	114	108	45	287	80	20	–
Cey, R.	2	115	106	57	280	79	21	–
Garvey, S.	16	110	97	56	279	85	15	–
Concepcion, D.	15	102	103	49	269	54	46	0
Foster, G.	14	89	111	55	269	85	15	–
Hough, C.	0	48	36	149	233	0	–	100
Chambliss, C.	24	78	87	32	221	87	13	–
Kingman, D.	21	57	71	46	195	90	10	0
Russell, B.	32	66	61	26	185	55	45	–
Rivers, M.	12	93	68	12	185	79	21	–
Cash, D.	42	100	23	0	165	64	36	–
Grubb, J.	1	78	49	29	157	89	11	–

Year of Birth: 1949

Player	Yng	Prm	Pst	Fin	Tot	B	F	P
Schmidt, M.	11	158	172	126	467	81	19	–
Grich, B.	55	119	110	45	329	72	28	–
Simmons, T.	77	127	89	22	315	77	23	–
Baylor, D.	29	98	77	58	262	93	7	–
Baker, D.	43	77	99	26	245	83	17	–
Cooper, C.	4	68	127	42	241	92	8	–
Reuschel, R.	30	89	42	79	240	0	–	100
Hendrick, G.	15	101	94	27	237	84	16	–
Buckner, B.	34	65	81	46	226	83	17	–
Hargrove, M.	0	107	90	15	212	90	10	–
Maddox, G.	36	101	56	10	203	72	28	–
Blue, V.	54	96	40	12	202	0	–	100
Mayberry, J.	63	90	46	0	199	90	10	–
Garner, P.	0	70	84	41	195	68	32	–
Reuss, J.	31	57	73	33	194	1	–	99
Oglivie, B.	9	57	97	31	194	87	13	–
Thornton, A.	1	87	60	38	186	94	6	–
Rogers, S.	15	79	86	2	182	0	–	100
Zisk, R.	17	106	55	0	178	90	10	–
Gamble, O.	27	83	59	8	177	92	8	–
Dempsey, R.	2	34	62	60	158	49	51	0

Year of Birth: 1950

Player	Yng	Prm	Pst	Fin	Tot	B	F	P
Downing, B.	11	78	70	139	298	85	15	–
Griffey Sr., K.	13	104	83	59	259	87	13	–
Matthews, G.	44	98	96	19	257	87	13	–
Luzinski, G.	50	121	76	0	247	93	7	–
White, F.	5	58	71	77	211	49	51	–
Speier, C.	73	66	43	24	206	55	45	–
DeCinces, D.	0	76	89	40	205	77	23	–
Alexander, D.	22	51	52	67	192	0	–	100
Guidry, R.	0	72	63	39	174	–	0	100
Hooton, B.	39	81	39	5	164	0	–	100
Orta, J.	33	75	42	10	160	86	14	–
Bochte, B.	5	73	53	28	159	86	14	–
Matlack, J.	63	65	28	0	156	0	–	100
Forsch, B.	9	61	43	41	154	5	–	95
Thomas, G.	3	56	76	17	152	83	17	–

Year of Birth: 1951

Player	Yng	Prm	Pst	Fin	Tot	B	F	P
Winfield, D.	40	132	105	138	415	90	10	–
Evans, D.	41	74	120	112	347	85	15	–
Blyleven, B.	122	79	68	70	339	0	–	100
Parker, D.	36	141	71	79	327	87	13	–
Bell, B.	63	94	96	48	301	71	29	–
Cedeno, C.	139	105	51	1	296	82	18	–
Madlock, B.	46	98	77	21	242	84	16	–
Gossage, G.	30	85	75	33	223	0	–	100
Sundberg, J.	22	93	65	20	200	47	53	–
Burroughs, J.	76	82	38	0	196	91	9	–
Driessen, D.	34	80	63	2	179	87	13	–
Flanagan, M.	1	67	47	43	158	–	–	100
Burleson, R.	25	95	21	11	152	49	51	–
Cowens, A.	14	78	46	0	138	75	25	–
Leonard, D.	14	89	22	8	133	–	–	100
Ashby, A.	6	39	42	31	118	59	41	–
Stennett, R.	67	50	1	0	118	56	44	–
Dent, B.	34	63	19	0	116	40	60	–
Minton, G.	0	22	53	36	111	2	–	98
Thomas, D.	44	43	22	0	109	65	35	–
Gullett, D.	80	22	0	0	102	0	–	100
Ruthven, D.	16	59	25	0	100	1	–	99

Year of Birth: 1952

Player	Yng	Prm	Pst	Fin	Tot	B	F	P
Lynn, F.	59	100	89	32	280	81	19	–
Porter, D.	60	92	66	4	222	73	27	–
Smalley, R.	23	84	66	8	181	70	30	–
Mumphrey, J.	11	61	75	13	160	80	20	–
Collins, D.	22	54	49	8	133	82	18	–
Whitt, E.	1	12	64	49	126	58	42	–
Knight, R.	0	49	62	12	123	74	26	–
Denny, J.	24	40	59	0	123	0	–	100
Moreno, O.	5	81	33	0	119	62	38	–
Reynolds, C.	1	58	42	14	115	51	49	0
Remy, J.	32	55	26	0	113	58	42	–
Gross, G.	51	29	27	6	113	84	16	0
Ford, D.	30	59	21	0	110	85	15	–
Krukow, M.	0	44	54	11	109	2	–	98
Andujar, J.	6	31	69	2	108	0	–	100
Forster, T.	57	19	31	0	107	4	0	96
Gross, W.	0	59	45	0	104	81	19	0
Lamp, D.	0	40	38	25	103	0	–	100

Year of Birth: 1953

Player	Yng	Prm	Pst	Fin	Tot	B	F	P
Brett, G.	96	133	109	94	432	86	14	–
Hernandez, K.	41	120	133	17	311	89	11	–
Rice, J.	64	116	91	11	282	87	13	–
Tanana, F.	86	43	60	52	241	0	–	100
Candelaria, J.	49	54	51	28	182	0	–	100
Parrish, L.	28	74	70	4	176	83	17	–
Sutter, B.	39	84	42	3	168	0	–	100
Gantner, J.	2	45	68	48	163	57	42	0
Lezcano, S.	45	92	22	0	159	84	16	–
Quisenberry, D.	0	55	92	10	157	0	–	100
Rhoden, R.	36	33	76	10	155	5	–	95
Armas, T.	8	62	45	16	131	75	25	–
Herndon, L.	10	60	58	2	130	80	20	–
Richards, G.	21	92	9	0	122	88	12	–
Hassey, R.	0	44	45	26	115	62	38	–
Ward, G.	0	31	70	13	114	77	23	–
Cromartie, W.	14	82	10	5	111	80	20	–
DeJesus, I.	18	67	21	0	106	59	41	–
Moore, C.	27	45	31	0	103	59	41	–

Year of Birth: 1954

Player	Yng	Prm	Pst	Fin	Tot	B	F	P
Dawson, A.	40	132	83	85	340	82	18	–
Carter, G.	73	129	111	24	337	63	37	–
Smith, O.	20	69	122	114	325	57	43	–
Randolph, W.	61	97	94	60	312	69	31	–
Eckersley, D.	70	60	67	104	301	0	–	100
Martinez, D.	28	50	36	119	233	0	–	100
Washington, C.	57	66	59	12	194	84	16	–
Thompson, J.	52	87	26	0	165	89	11	–
Stanley, B.	28	77	42	2	149	–	–	100
Kemp, S.	34	91	14	0	139	87	13	–
Tudor, J.	0	40	79	16	135	0	–	100
Honeycutt, R.	5	49	36	40	130	0	–	100
Knepper, B.	36	34	49	5	124	1	–	99
McGregor, S.	20	74	27	0	121	–	–	100
Moreland, K.	0	44	65	6	115	81	19	–
Manning, R.	49	50	15	0	114	70	30	–
Landreaux, K.	7	75	32	0	114	77	23	–
Hernandez, W.	17	25	66	1	109	1	–	99

Year of Birth: 1955

Player	Yng	Prm	Pst	Fin	Tot	B	F	P
Yount, R.	85	144	130	64	423	75	25	–
Clark, J.	67	97	116	36	316	92	8	–
Lemon, C.	78	100	78	9	265	76	24	–
Wilson, W.	29	108	71	29	237	71	29	–
Morris, J.	24	78	76	47	225	0	–	100
Smith, L.	1	83	61	45	190	88	12	–
Darwin, D.	5	48	58	71	182	0	–	100
Murphy, D.	17	104	52	0	173	78	22	–
Reardon, J.	3	60	60	34	157	0	–	100
Jones, R.	50	58	31	0	139	77	23	–
Mazzilli, L.	61	53	20	0	134	85	15	–
Bannister, F.	17	64	46	1	128	0	–	100
Clancy, J.	13	63	46	6	128	0	–	100
Leonard, J.	15	56	48	8	127	84	16	–
Harris, G.	0	7	51	50	108	1	–	99
Whitson, E.	11	39	37	20	107	0	–	100
Smith, D.	0	37	56	13	106	0	–	100
Scott, M.	0	11	86	8	105	0	–	100
Rawley, S.	14	46	42	0	102	0	–	100
Smith, B.	0	27	56	17	100	0	–	100
Heath, M.	6	42	46	6	100	56	44	–

Year of Birth: 1956

Player	Yng	Prm	Pst	Fin	Tot	B	F	P
Murray, E.	100	142	113	82	437	91	9	–
Molitor, P.	57	82	116	159	414	89	11	–
Murphy, D.	50	139	92	13	294	83	17	–
Parrish, L.	49	98	73	28	248	59	41	–
Guerrero, P.	11	134	88	13	246	90	10	–
Templeton, G.	92	68	47	2	209	58	42	–
Welch, B.	30	61	77	20	188	0	0	100
Puhl, T.	74	71	31	0	176	81	19	–
Herr, T.	4	91	70	5	170	69	31	–
Sutcliffe, R.	17	64	54	18	153	0	–	100
Wilson, M.	2	80	65	4	151	76	24	–
Kennedy, T.	9	88	49	4	150	67	33	–
Brooks, H.	3	63	72	11	149	78	22	–
Oberkfell, K.	30	66	42	3	141	72	28	–
Leibrandt, C.	7	36	64	31	138	0	–	100
Sanderson, S.	28	43	34	33	138	0	–	100

Player	Yng	Prm	Pst	Fin	Tot	B	F	P
Wynegar, B.	78	51	7	0	136	61	39	–
Redus, G.	0	44	57	19	120	85	15	–
Bernazard, T.	7	74	36	0	117	71	29	–
Oester, R.	10	69	33	0	112	58	42	–
Soto, M.	17	88	4	0	109	1	–	99
Mulliniks, R.	12	49	41	6	108	77	23	–
Law, V.	1	57	47	3	108	69	31	0
Davis, J.	0	67	39	0	106	52	48	–

Year of Birth: 1957

Player	Yng	Prm	Pst	Fin	Tot	B	F	P
Whitaker, L.	61	116	110	64	351	75	25	–
Butler, B.	4	80	120	91	295	81	19	–
Wallach, T.	4	94	101	49	248	67	33	0
Lansford, C.	71	84	74	15	244	82	18	–
Gibson, K.	17	90	82	29	218	89	11	–
Stieb, D.	39	104	63	4	210	0	0	100
Smith, L.	6	81	70	41	198	0	–	100
Pena, T.	8	84	57	26	175	42	58	–
Candiotti, T.	0	21	74	63	158	0	–	100
Ray, J.	2	88	63	0	153	68	32	–
Jones, D.	0	2	59	85	146	0	–	100
Stewart, D.	6	36	77	22	141	0	–	100
Horner, B.	63	73	4	0	140	84	16	–
Hubbard, G.	31	79	30	0	140	53	47	–
Henke, T.	0	28	69	43	140	0	–	100
Orosco, J.	2	69	27	40	138	1	0	99
Griffin, A.	27	60	43	4	134	38	62	–
Boddicker, M.	0	60	69	3	132	–	–	100
Durham, L.	18	93	15	0	126	88	12	–
Bedrosian, S.	1	62	46	10	119	0	–	100
Robinson, D.	32	35	46	3	116	6	0	94
Black, B.	0	55	47	13	115	0	–	100
Gladden, D.	0	41	57	16	114	77	23	0
Upshaw, W.	4	82	21	0	107	85	15	–
Ojeda, B.	5	54	37	8	104	0	–	100

Year of Birth: 1958

Player	Yng	Prm	Pst	Fin	Tot	B	F	P
Henderson, R.	99	142	147	142	530	89	11	–
Boggs, W.	15	162	124	93	394	81	19	0
Trammell, A.	78	132	81	27	318	71	29	–
Gaetti, G.	11	88	70	80	249	65	35	0
McGee, W.	11	100	74	39	224	79	21	–
Hershiser, O.	0	74	63	73	210	1	0	99
Doran, B.	3	111	78	1	193	74	26	–
Hayes, V.	15	98	64	0	177	83	17	–
Scioscia, M.	24	74	70	0	168	57	43	–
Henderson, D.	12	50	90	8	160	77	23	–
Fletcher, S.	1	66	60	21	148	57	43	–
Thon, D.	30	50	60	7	147	64	36	–
Hurst, B.	2	68	74	0	144	0	–	100
O'Brien, P.	2	84	52	3	141	78	22	–
Righetti, D.	21	79	34	3	137	0	–	100
Slaught, D.	4	40	54	32	130	69	31	–
Ramirez, R.	30	41	42	0	113	55	45	–
Petry, D.	43	51	14	0	108	0	–	100
Higuera, T.	0	59	41	0	100	–	–	100

Year of Birth: 1959

Player	Yng	Prm	Pst	Fin	Tot	B	F	P
Raines, T.	68	153	110	59	390	86	14	–
Sandberg, R.	35	128	146	37	346	73	27	–
Baines, H.	57	100	81	69	307	92	8	–
Phillips, T.	14	52	107	95	268	79	21	–
McReynolds, K.	3	113	81	5	202	82	18	–
Moseby, L.	48	99	30	0	177	72	28	–
Bell, G.	4	105	62	0	171	86	14	–
Barfield, J.	24	96	46	0	166	77	23	–
Bass, K.	2	89	46	11	148	82	18	–
Morgan, M.	7	23	66	40	136	1	–	99
Moore, M.	8	64	55	6	133	0	–	100
Nixon, O.	0	12	58	57	127	62	38	–
Gullickson, B.	44	43	36	3	126	0	–	100
Bradley, P.	1	92	31	0	124	88	12	–
Jacoby, B.	0	77	43	0	120	76	24	–
Eisenreich, J.	4	2	59	43	108	81	19	–
Thompson, M.	0	46	50	10	106	77	23	–
Webster, M.	0	71	33	1	105	78	22	–
Worrell, T.	0	54	16	35	105	0	0	100
Backman, W.	14	66	22	0	102	73	27	–
Dotson, R.	49	41	4	0	94	–	–	100
Pena, A.	15	37	31	8	91	0	–	100
Gedman, R.	17	62	11	0	90	53	47	–
Burke, T.	0	49	37	0	86	0	–	100
Davis, M.	18	64	3	0	85	84	16	–
Harper, B.	2	6	72	3	83	76	24	–
Gott, J.	13	31	33	2	79	0	–	100
Walker, G.	12	65	2	0	79	90	10	–
Uribe, J.	0	49	29	0	78	46	54	–
Boyd, O.	6	45	22	0	73	0	–	100
Burns, B.	53	18	0	0	71	–	–	100
Cox, D.	4	49	14	4	71	0	–	100
Rasmussen, D.	1	47	21	0	69	1	–	99
Niedenfuer, T.	24	40	5	0	69	0	–	100
Foley, T.	2	39	22	3	66	52	48	0
LaPoint, D.	19	38	9	0	66	0	–	100
Hesketh, J.	0	26	25	7	58	0	–	100
Wynne, M.	8	40	10	0	58	69	31	–
Bielecki, M.	0	9	34	14	57	0	–	100
Reynolds, R.	1	40	15	0	56	80	20	–
Sheets, L.	0	40	12	0	52	92	8	–
Williamson, M.	0	14	31	5	50	–	–	100
Patterson, B.	0	1	24	23	48	2	–	98
Dayley, K.	7	23	16	0	46	1	–	99
Carman, D.	0	38	6	0	44	0	–	100

Player	Yng	Prm	Pst	Fin	Tot	B	F	P
Petralli, G.	2	20	22	0	44	71	29	–
Hudson, C.	9	33	0	0	42	0	–	100
Horton, R.	0	37	2	0	39	0	0	100
Ortiz, J.	2	12	21	2	37	41	59	–
Jeltz, S.	0	26	11	0	37	35	65	–
Nipper, A.	2	34	0	0	36	0	–	100
Atherton, K.	6	28	1	0	35	0	–	100
McMurtry, C.	16	15	1	0	32	0	–	100
Francona, T.	8	21	3	0	32	79	20	0
Aguayo, L.	7	22	1	0	30	60	40	–
Terry, S.	0	12	17	0	29	2	–	98
McClendon, L.	0	2	24	1	27	81	19	–
Jeffcoat, M.	2	7	17	0	26	1	–	99
Havens, B.	14	9	1	0	24	0	–	100
Little, B.	9	15	0	0	24	58	42	–
Bilardello, D.	9	7	6	0	22	27	73	–
Holton, B.	0	16	6	0	22	0	–	100
Perry, P.	0	16	4	0	20	3	–	97
Bordi, R.	0	19	0	0	19	0	–	100
Brown, M.	1	18	0	0	19	83	17	–
Beard, D.	14	1	0	0	15	–	–	100
Straker, L.	0	13	0	0	13	–	–	100
Johnson, D.	0	0	13	0	13	–	–	100
Wellman, B.	1	9	3	0	13	20	80	–
Tingley, R.	0	0	6	4	10	21	79	–
Winn, J.	0	10	0	0	10	0	–	100
Jones, M.	5	4	0	0	9	–	–	100
Heathcock, J.	2	7	0	0	9	0	–	100
Best, K.	0	8	0	0	8	–	–	100
Frobel, D.	2	6	0	0	8	62	38	–
Kepshire, K.	0	8	0	0	8	0	–	100
Rincon, A.	8	0	0	0	8	0	–	100
Brown, M.	5	2	0	0	7	–	–	100
Ainge, D.	7	0	0	0	7	1	99	–
Johnson, B.	6	0	0	0	6	31	69	–
Eufemia, F.	0	6	0	0	6	–	–	100
Fimple, J.	5	0	0	0	5	38	62	–

Player	Yng	Prm	Pst	Fin	Tot	B	F	P
Gordon, D.	0	5	0	0	5	–	–	100
Nelson, R.	4	0	0	0	4	70	30	–
Clutterbuck, B.	0	2	2	0	4	–	–	100
Hernandez, L.	3	1	0	0	4	73	27	–
Stefero, J.	1	3	0	0	4	59	41	–
Lozado, W.	0	4	0	0	4	79	21	–
Meier, D.	0	3	0	0	3	51	49	–
Adams, R.	2	1	0	0	3	26	74	–
Noce, P.	0	3	0	0	3	14	86	–
Robbins, B.	3	0	0	0	3	–	–	100
Williams, M.	0	3	0	0	3	–	–	100
Babitt, S.	3	0	0	0	3	60	40	–
Shipanoff, D.	0	3	0	0	3	0	–	100
Walker, T.	0	3	0	0	3	53	47	–
Creel, K.	0	2	0	0	2	–	–	100
Sanchez, A.	1	1	0	0	2	82	18	–
Jones, A.	0	2	0	0	2	–	–	100
Pena, B.	0	2	0	0	2	19	81	–
Gerber, C.	0	2	0	0	2	6	94	–
Keener, J.	2	0	0	0	2	–	–	100
Dodson, P.	0	2	0	0	2	88	12	–
Arnold, T.	0	2	0	0	2	–	–	100
Blocker, T.	0	2	0	0	2	15	85	0
Heinkel, D.	0	2	0	0	2	0	–	100
Hinshaw, G.	2	0	0	0	2	83	17	–
Adduci, J.	0	2	0	0	2	69	31	–
Nelson, J.	2	0	0	0	2	33	67	–
Dunbar, T.	0	1	0	0	1	82	18	–
Madison, S.	0	0	1	0	1	17	83	–
Brown, M.	0	1	0	0	1	–	–	100
Krawczyk, R.	0	1	0	0	1	–	–	100
Kelly, B.	0	1	0	0	1	–	–	100
Allen, R.	0	1	0	0	1	91	9	–
Barkley, J.	0	1	0	0	1	–	–	100
Hensley, C.	0	1	0	0	1	–	–	100
Isales, O.	1	0	0	0	1	95	5	–
Milner, B.	1	0	0	0	1	100	0	–

Batting Leaders by League and Season

Year	Lg	Player, Team	RC	Out	WS
1876	NL	Ross Barnes, ChN	113	184	17.43
1877	NL	Deacon White, Bos	75	163	14.22
1878	NL	Paul Hines, Prv	62	165	13.37
1879	NL	Paul Hines, Prv	98	263	18.16
1880	NL	George Gore, ChN	82	206	19.46
1881	NL	Cap Anson, ChN	95	206	19.87
1882	NL	Dan Brouthers, Buf	94	222	18.41
1882	AA	Pete Browning, Lou	82	179	16.63
1883	NL	Dan Brouthers, Buf	115	266	22.24
1883	AA	Harry Stovey, Phi	120	293	23.43
1884	NL	Paul Hines, Prv	120	342	22.84
1884	UA	Fred Dunlap, STL	159	264	32.77
1884	AA	Charley Jones, Cin	141	324	24.15
1885	NL	Roger Connor, NYG	130	286	28.33
1885	AA	Dave Orr, NY	100	292	26.34
1886	NL	Roger Connor, NYG	134	313	33.11
1886	AA	Henry Larkin, Phi	138	385	26.56
1887	NL	Sam Thompson, Det	152	342	25.26
1887	AA	Tip O'Neill, StL	192	292	31.70
1888	NL	Jimmy Ryan, ChN	133	367	28.99
1888	AA	Harry Stovey, Phi	128	378	23.41
1889	NL	Dan Brouthers, Bos	138	304	26.07
1889	AA	Tommy Tucker, Bal	158	331	28.52
1890	NL	George Pinckney, Bro	129	335	23.55
1890	PL	Pete Browning, Cle	135	309	22.37
1890	AA	Cupid Childs, Syr	121	323	27.11
1891	NL	Billy Hamilton, Phi	156	348	32.59
1891	AA	Dan Brouthers, Bos	152	316	27.72
1892	NL	Dan Brouthers, Bro	149	391	29.53
1893	NL	Ed Delahanty, Phi	163	376	23.33
1894	NL	Hugh Duffy, Bos	203	312	28.01
1895	NL	Jesse Burkett, Cle	168	332	30.45
1896	NL	Ed Delahanty, Phi	162	305	28.70
1897	NL	Willie Keeler, Bal	153	337	28.32
1898	NL	Ed Delahanty, Phi	137	369	30.37
1899	NL	Ed Delahanty, Phi	164	348	36.51
1900	NL	Elmer Flick, Phi	145	351	31.00
1901	AL	Nap Lajoie, Phi	169	313	36.28
1901	NL	Jesse Burkett, StL	153	378	35.15
1902	AL	Ed Delahanty, Was	130	295	29.16
1902	NL	Honus Wagner, Pit	117	366	28.85
1903	AL	Nap Lajoie, Cle	101	331	25.95
1903	NL	Frank Chance, ChC	116	299	28.71
1904	AL	Nap Lajoie, Cle	129	351	35.38
1904	NL	Honus Wagner, Pit	129	324	38.09
1905	AL	Sam Crawford, Det	96	407	32.61
1905	NL	Cy Seymour, Cin	147	371	37.91
1906	AL	George Stone, StL	127	391	33.66
1906	NL	Honus Wagner, Pit	117	347	34.20
1907	AL	Ty Cobb, Det	132	405	37.38
1907	NL	Honus Wagner, Pit	121	349	36.42
1908	AL	Ty Cobb, Det	113	407	34.02
1908	NL	Honus Wagner, Pit	131	381	49.21
1909	AL	Ty Cobb, Det	139	381	39.88
1909	NL	Honus Wagner, Pit	114	354	33.07
1910	AL	Nap Lajoie, Cle	135	385	40.41
1910	NL	Sherry Magee, Phi	131	369	33.57
1911	AL	Ty Cobb, Det	172	354	41.28
1911	NL	Wildfire Schulte, ChC	127	435	27.92
1912	AL	Tris Speaker, Bos	162	365	41.57
1912	NL	Heinie Zimmerman, ChC	128	368	30.10
1913	AL	Home Run Baker, Phi	125	381	33.72
1913	NL	Gavy Cravath, Phi	117	357	25.89
1914	AL	Eddie Collins, Phi	129	403	37.12
1914	NL	George Burns, NYG	108	405	27.99
1914	FL	Benny Kauff, Ind	143	376	32.13
1915	AL	Ty Cobb, Det	153	402	41.56
1915	NL	Gavy Cravath, Phi	114	389	30.24
1915	FL	Benny Kauff, Bro	112	325	29.95
1916	AL	Tris Speaker, Cle	135	350	36.54
1916	NL	Zack Wheat, Bro	94	400	26.54
1917	AL	Ty Cobb, Det	144	379	40.37
1917	NL	Rogers Hornsby, StL	95	369	30.59
1918	AL	Ty Cobb, Det	90	269	28.68
1918	NL	Heine Groh, Cin	80	348	22.67
1919	AL	Babe Ruth, Bos	121	296	33.51
1919	NL	George Burns, NYG	97	380	27.79
1920	AL	Babe Ruth, NYY	192	305	47.88
1920	NL	Rogers Hornsby, StL	123	394	33.45
1921	AL	Babe Ruth, NYY	208	353	47.69
1921	NL	Rogers Hornsby, StL	151	385	35.90
1922	AL	George Sisler, StL	141	375	27.82
1922	NL	Rogers Hornsby, StL	179	400	42.86
1923	AL	Babe Ruth, NYY	193	341	48.48
1923	NL	Jack Fournier, Bro	119	349	25.15
1924	AL	Babe Ruth, NYY	178	348	41.67
1924	NL	Rogers Hornsby, StL	161	334	34.51
1925	AL	Harry Heilmann, Det	142	377	27.77
1925	NL	Rogers Hornsby, StL	158	320	32.99
1926	AL	Babe Ruth, NYY	167	330	42.60
1926	NL	Paul Waner, Pit	118	368	23.34
1927	AL	Lou Gehrig, NYY	182	395	41.45
1927	NL	Rogers Hornsby, NYG	139	389	33.75
1928	AL	Babe Ruth, NYY	165	376	42.69
1928	NL	Rogers Hornsby, Bos	133	323	30.93
1929	AL	Babe Ruth, NYY	138	343	30.64
1929	NL	Rogers Hornsby, ChC	178	395	35.65

Year	Lg	Player, Team	RC	Out	WS
1930	AL	Lou Gehrig, NYY	182	393	37.27
1930	NL	Hack Wilson, ChC	171	395	31.48
1931	AL	Babe Ruth, NYY	178	339	36.29
1931	NL	Bill Terry, NYG	122	400	26.03
1932	AL	Jimmie Foxx, Phi	188	379	36.71
1932	NL	Lefty O'Doul, Bro	129	381	31.51
1933	AL	Jimmie Foxx, Phi	165	371	37.49
1933	NL	Wally Berger, Bos	110	371	30.83
1934	AL	Lou Gehrig, NYY	170	374	38.84
1934	NL	Mel Ott, NYG	144	403	33.92
1935	AL	Lou Gehrig, NYY	145	366	31.87
1935	NL	Arky Vaughan, Pit	141	319	32.02
1936	AL	Lou Gehrig, NYY	181	381	34.88
1936	NL	Mel Ott, NYG	140	377	33.43
1937	AL	Lou Gehrig, NYY	167	372	34.34
1937	NL	Joe Medwick, StL	163	408	36.85
1938	AL	Jimmie Foxx, Bos	172	373	32.68
1938	NL	Mel Ott, NYG	134	373	31.50
1939	AL	Ted Williams, Bos	153	394	29.52
1939	NL	Johnny Mize, StL	138	386	30.93
1940	AL	Ted Williams, Bos	138	386	27.34
1940	NL	Johnny Mize, StL	137	407	30.86
1941	AL	Ted Williams, Bos	170	285	39.62
1941	NL	Dolph Camilli, Bro	121	387	27.43
1942	AL	Ted Williams, Bos	160	350	41.50
1942	NL	Mel Ott, NYG	124	398	32.98
1943	AL	Charlie Keller, NYY	108	387	31.51
1943	NL	Stan Musial, StL	129	424	33.07
1944	AL	Stan Spence, Was	113	421	28.59
1944	NL	Stan Musial, StL	134	382	33.13
1945	AL	Snuffy Stirnweiss, NYY	114	469	26.87
1945	NL	Phil Cavarretta, ChC	115	330	28.11
1946	AL	Ted Williams, Bos	165	350	45.11
1946	NL	Stan Musial, StL	151	405	40.86
1947	AL	Ted Williams, Bos	160	359	41.11
1947	NL	Johnny Mize, NYG	137	415	29.01
1948	AL	Ted Williams, Bos	160	331	36.78
1948	NL	Stan Musial, StL	176	400	42.37
1949	AL	Ted Williams, Bos	174	395	36.62
1949	NL	Stan Musial, StL	154	417	34.82
1950	AL	Larry Doby, Cle	120	356	25.86
1950	NL	Earl Torgeson, Bos	122	427	28.98
1951	AL	Ted Williams, Bos	145	373	30.37
1951	NL	Stan Musial, StL	147	385	34.96
1952	AL	Larry Doby, Cle	111	386	28.80
1952	NL	Stan Musial, StL	125	402	32.80
1953	AL	Al Rosen, Cle	143	424	36.74
1953	NL	Eddie Mathews, Mil	146	414	34.78
1954	AL	Mickey Mantle, NYY	125	391	32.45
1954	NL	Duke Snider, Bro	140	410	34.56
1955	AL	Mickey Mantle, NYY	135	369	34.14

Year	Lg	Player, Team	RC	Out	WS
1955	NL	Willie Mays, NYG	146	418	34.81
1956	AL	Mickey Mantle, NYY	173	355	43.79
1956	NL	Duke Snider, Bro	118	413	27.28
1957	AL	Mickey Mantle, NYY	155	312	46.06
1957	NL	Hank Aaron, Mil	126	434	32.11
1958	AL	Mickey Mantle, NYY	138	379	35.68
1958	NL	Willie Mays, SF	138	415	33.40
1959	AL	Mickey Mantle, NYY	110	400	25.63
1959	NL	Hank Aaron, Mil	142	434	35.42
1960	AL	Mickey Mantle, NYY	118	401	31.27
1960	NL	Eddie Mathews, Mil	123	417	34.98
1961	AL	Mickey Mantle, NYY	156	360	42.96
1961	NL	Hank Aaron, Mil	124	441	29.74
1962	AL	Mickey Mantle, NYY	114	262	30.92
1962	NL	Frank Robinson, Cin	152	428	36.27
1963	AL	Tom Tresh, NYY	100	394	25.08
1963	NL	Hank Aaron, Mil	146	451	37.19
1964	AL	Mickey Mantle, NYY	116	339	30.53
1964	NL	Dick Allen, Phi	130	452	34.92
1965	AL	Tony Oliva, Min	112	420	28.54
1965	NL	Willie Mays, SF	138	400	34.99
1966	AL	Frank Robinson, Bal	141	430	38.01
1966	NL	Willie McCovey, SF	118	367	32.40
1967	AL	Carl Yastrzemski, Bos	148	409	38.18
1967	NL	Roberto Clemente, Pit	115	395	32.22
1968	AL	Frank Howard, Was	109	452	36.74
1968	NL	Willie McCovey, SF	109	390	32.17
1969	AL	Reggie Jackson, Oak	138	413	37.98
1969	NL	Willie McCovey, SF	140	352	37.30
1970	AL	Carl Yastrzemski, Bos	145	407	33.42
1970	NL	Willie McCovey, SF	129	368	31.45
1971	AL	Bobby Murcer, NYY	119	375	34.45
1971	NL	Joe Torre, StL	136	429	38.43
1972	AL	Dick Allen, CWS	123	374	37.59
1972	NL	Joe Morgan, Cin	118	420	32.58
1973	AL	Reggie Jackson, Oak	112	409	29.31
1973	NL	Willie Stargell, Pit	126	376	34.04
1974	AL	Jeff Burroughs, Tex	111	419	30.92
1974	NL	Joe Morgan, Cin	119	387	30.95
1975	AL	John Mayberry, KC	122	410	30.81
1975	NL	Joe Morgan, Cin	137	354	36.24
1976	AL	Rod Carew, Min	112	453	28.16
1976	NL	Joe Morgan, Cin	126	344	32.65
1977	AL	Rod Carew, Min	155	402	35.29
1977	NL	George Foster, Cin	129	447	28.32
1978	AL	Jim Rice, Bos	141	490	32.63
1978	NL	Dave Parker, Pit	126	404	32.74
1979	AL	Ken Singleton, Bal	120	427	28.01
1979	NL	Dave Winfield, SD	125	433	29.72

Year	Lg	Player, Team	RC	Out	WS
1980	AL	George Brett, KC	119	298	31.47
1980	AL	Reggie Jackson, NYY	117	371	29.72
1980	AL	Rickey Henderson, Oak	121	453	27.41
1980	NL	Mike Schmidt, Phi	126	415	30.69
1980	NL	Keith Hernandez, StL	119	431	25.43
1980	NL	Andre Dawson, Mon	99	428	23.78

Year	Lg	Player, Team	RC	Out	WS
1981	AL	Rickey Henderson, Oak	84	321	22.92
1981	AL	Dwight Evans, Bos	92	306	22.48
1981	AL	Cecil Cooper, Mil	75	309	20.78
1981	NL	Mike Schmidt, Phi	91	258	25.85
1981	NL	George Foster, Cin	76	308	21.78
1981	NL	Andre Dawson, Mon	80	290	20.49

Year	Lg	Player, Team	RC	Out	WS
1982	AL	Robin Yount, Mil	135	461	32.36
1982	AL	Dwight Evans, Bos	127	455	27.01
1982	AL	Cecil Cooper, Mil	119	466	26.93
1982	NL	Mike Schmidt, Phi	113	395	30.82
1982	NL	Dale Murphy, Atl	120	455	28.11
1982	NL	Pedro Guerrero, LA	108	419	26.08

Year	Lg	Player, Team	RC	Out	WS
1983	AL	Eddie Murray, Bal	122	427	28.33
1983	AL	Wade Boggs, Bos	121	400	27.69
1983	AL	Rickey Henderson, Oak	110	395	27.18
1983	NL	Pedro Guerrero, LA	111	434	28.02
1983	NL	Mike Schmidt, Phi	115	420	28.00
1983	NL	Dale Murphy, Atl	124	436	26.69

Year	Lg	Player, Team	RC	Out	WS
1984	AL	Eddie Murray, Bal	121	427	30.57
1984	AL	Rickey Henderson, Oak	102	384	27.01
1984	AL	Cal Ripken Jr., Bal	114	465	26.97
1984	NL	Tony Gwynn, SD	112	434	30.10
1984	NL	Keith Hernandez, NYM	105	400	29.58
1984	NL	Ryne Sandberg, ChC	126	459	28.87

Year	Lg	Player, Team	RC	Out	WS
1985	AL	Rickey Henderson, NYY	135	398	32.41
1985	AL	George Brett, KC	135	388	32.27
1985	AL	Don Mattingly, NYY	133	475	29.68
1985	NL	Tim Raines, Mon	119	415	32.03
1985	NL	Pedro Guerrero, LA	110	353	30.84
1985	NL	Willie McGee, StL	120	421	30.65

Year	Lg	Player, Team	RC	Out	WS
1986	AL	Wade Boggs, Bos	128	396	30.66
1986	AL	Don Mattingly, NYY	134	467	29.98
1986	AL	Joe Carter, Cle	116	487	24.62
1986	NL	Tim Raines, Mon	116	405	28.72
1986	NL	Mike Schmidt, Phi	114	411	26.60
1986	NL	Keith Hernandez, NYM	104	398	26.20

Year	Lg	Player, Team	RC	Out	WS
1987	AL	Alan Trammell, Det	129	413	28.27
1987	AL	Wade Boggs, Bos	139	376	28.06
1987	AL	Mark McGwire, Oak	125	411	27.88
1987	NL	Jack Clark, StL	124	309	31.55
1987	NL	Tim Raines, Mon	124	372	29.27
1987	NL	Darryl Strawberry, NYM	121	401	27.71

Year	Lg	Player, Team	RC	Out	WS
1988	AL	Jose Canseco, Oak	137	461	36.16
1988	AL	Dave Winfield, NYY	117	403	29.20
1988	AL	Mike Greenwell, Bos	127	424	27.42
1988	NL	Will Clark, SF	125	433	34.30
1988	NL	K. McReynolds, NYM	100	405	27.88
1988	NL	Darryl Strawberry, NYM	101	426	27.71

Year	Lg	Player, Team	RC	Out	WS
1989	AL	Ruben Sierra, Tex	125	459	29.68
1989	AL	Robin Yount, Mil	124	438	29.51
1989	AL	Fred McGriff, Tor	113	427	28.21
1989	NL	Will Clark, SF	141	409	41.12
1989	NL	Kevin Mitchell, SF	125	402	35.40
1989	NL	Howard Johnson, NYM	129	425	34.84

Year	Lg	Player, Team	RC	Out	WS
1990	AL	Rickey Henderson, Oak	123	357	35.25
1990	AL	Cecil Fielder, Det	122	435	28.14
1990	AL	Mark McGwire, Oak	100	424	24.85
1990	AL	George Brett, KC	107	392	24.24
1990	AL	Jose Canseco, Oak	93	373	23.72

Year	Lg	Player, Team	RC	Out	WS
1990	NL	Barry Bonds, Pit	125	390	32.50
1990	NL	Lenny Dykstra, Phi	119	413	30.01
1990	NL	Eddie Murray, LA	116	402	28.94
1990	NL	Ryne Sandberg, ChC	121	451	26.90
1990	NL	Brett Butler, SF	105	466	24.00

Year	Lg	Player, Team	RC	Out	WS
1991	AL	Frank Thomas, CWS	138	405	33.19
1991	AL	Jose Canseco, Oak	117	448	29.78
1991	AL	Paul Molitor, Mil	132	469	29.06
1991	AL	Danny Tartabull, KC	111	348	26.75
1991	AL	Cal Ripken Jr., Bal	124	469	26.53

Year	Lg	Player, Team	RC	Out	WS
1991	NL	Barry Bonds, Pit	124	395	33.24
1991	NL	Will Clark, SF	118	406	31.38
1991	NL	Ryne Sandberg, ChC	124	442	28.43
1991	NL	Bobby Bonilla, Pit	111	432	27.63
1991	NL	Fred McGriff, SD	101	403	23.34

Year	Lg	Player, Team	RC	Out	WS
1992	AL	Frank Thomas, CWS	127	421	32.36
1992	AL	Roberto Alomar, Tor	117	419	29.38
1992	AL	Mark McGwire, Oak	103	362	27.97
1992	AL	Paul Molitor, Mil	118	448	27.78
1992	AL	Dave Winfield, Tor	109	431	26.15

Year	Lg	Player, Team	RC	Out	WS
1992	NL	Barry Bonds, Pit	130	350	37.77
1992	NL	Andy Van Slyke, Pit	112	436	28.96
1992	NL	Terry Pendleton, Atl	113	471	28.71
1992	NL	Darren Daulton, Phi	108	365	27.07
1992	NL	Craig Biggio, Hou	96	470	26.83

Year	Lg	Player, Team	RC	Out	WS
1993	AL	John Olerud, Tor	144	372	34.11
1993	AL	Frank Thomas, CWS	136	400	31.79
1993	AL	Juan Gonzalez, Tex	129	384	29.16
1993	AL	Paul Molitor, Tor	135	451	29.00
1993	AL	Rafael Palmeiro, Tex	127	443	26.96

Year	Lg	Player, Team	RC	Out	WS
1993	NL	Barry Bonds, SF	160	388	44.02
1993	NL	Gregg Jefferies, StL	111	386	26.93
1993	NL	Lenny Dykstra, Phi	127	468	26.72
1993	NL	Matt Williams, SF	104	433	23.62
1993	NL	David Justice, Atl	113	445	23.46

Year	Lg	Player, Team	RC	Out	WS
1994	AL	Frank Thomas, CWS	117	283	25.06
1994	AL	Albert Belle, Cle	112	281	22.15
1994	AL	Paul O'Neill, NYY	96	259	20.59
1994	AL	Kirby Puckett, Min	94	322	19.29
1994	AL	Paul Molitor, Tor	102	317	18.69

Year	Lg	Player, Team	RC	Out	WS
1994	NL	Jeff Bagwell, Hou	113	279	28.06
1994	NL	Barry Bonds, SF	103	284	22.71
1994	NL	Craig Biggio, Hou	93	311	20.94
1994	NL	Fred McGriff, Atl	95	303	20.55
1994	NL	Mike Piazza, LA	80	292	18.22

Year	Lg	Player, Team	RC	Out	WS
1995	AL	Edgar Martinez, Sea	150	347	31.64
1995	AL	Frank Thomas, CWS	130	369	27.62
1995	AL	Tim Salmon, Cal	133	378	26.04
1995	AL	Albert Belle, Cle	121	403	25.42
1995	AL	Chuck Knoblauch, Min	118	395	23.11

Year	Lg	Player, Team	RC	Out	WS
1995	NL	Barry Bonds, SF	127	383	34.60
1995	NL	Craig Biggio, Hou	112	418	24.38
1995	NL	Barry Larkin, Cin	109	356	24.07
1995	NL	Reggie Sanders, Cin	109	363	23.87
1995	NL	Eric Karros, LA	101	409	22.36

Year	Lg	Player, Team	RC	Out	WS
1996	AL	Mark McGwire, Oak	134	306	27.86
1996	AL	Alex Rodriguez, Sea	148	418	27.54
1996	AL	Mo Vaughn, Bos	149	453	27.38
1996	AL	Rafael Palmeiro, Bal	142	462	27.09
1996	AL	Albert Belle, Cle	145	442	26.83

Year	Lg	Player, Team	RC	Out	WS
1996	NL	Jeff Bagwell, Hou	148	417	38.62
1996	NL	Barry Bonds, SF	159	382	37.32
1996	NL	Gary Sheffield, Fla	144	387	32.65
1996	NL	Ken Caminiti, SD	136	398	30.89
1996	NL	Mike Piazza, LA	119	389	28.16

Year	Lg	Player, Team	RC	Out	WS
1997	AL	Frank Thomas, CWS	150	369	38.70
1997	AL	Ken Griffey Jr., Sea	147	451	30.80
1997	AL	Edgar Martinez, Sea	127	394	26.48
1997	AL	David Justice, Cle	117	356	25.18
1997	AL	Tim Salmon, Ana	130	440	24.84

Year	Lg	Player, Team	RC	Out	WS
1997	NL	Tony Gwynn, SD	138	402	37.47
1997	NL	Barry Bonds, SF	132	403	34.48
1997	NL	Mike Piazza, LA	136	380	32.26
1997	NL	Craig Biggio, Hou	147	445	30.79
1997	NL	Jeff Bagwell, Hou	141	432	29.42

Year	Lg	Player, Team	RC	Out	WS
1998	AL	Albert Belle, CWS	151	445	34.86
1998	AL	Ken Griffey Jr., Sea	135	476	24.83
1998	AL	Frank Thomas, CWS	120	455	24.58
1998	AL	Edgar Martinez, Sea	125	398	24.14
1998	AL	Juan Gonzalez, Tex	129	445	23.77

Year	Lg	Player, Team	RC	Out	WS
1998	NL	Mark McGwire, StL	165	369	39.51
1998	NL	Sammy Sosa, ChC	141	479	31.78
1998	NL	Barry Bonds, SF	140	419	31.53
1998	NL	John Olerud, NYM	127	385	29.46
1998	NL	Craig Biggio, Hou	140	459	28.92

Year	Lg	Player, Team	RC	Out	WS
1999	AL	Manny Ramirez, Cle	151	373	31.27
1999	AL	Rafael Palmeiro, Tex	147	408	30.76
1999	AL	Derek Jeter, NYY	145	437	30.67
1999	AL	Jason Giambi, Oak	136	414	28.34
1999	AL	Roberto Alomar, Cle	141	425	26.99

Year	Lg	Player, Team	RC	Out	WS
1999	NL	Jeff Bagwell, Hou	157	427	34.97
1999	NL	Chipper Jones, Atl	144	415	31.66
1999	NL	Mark McGwire, StL	146	393	28.89
1999	NL	Vladimir Guerrero, Mon	133	444	24.89
1999	NL	Brian Giles, Pit	129	381	24.31

Year	Lg	Player, Team	RC	Out	WS
2000	AL	Jason Giambi, Oak	162	357	35.62
2000	AL	Carlos Delgado, Tor	162	390	34.72
2000	AL	Frank Thomas, CWS	165	415	33.26
2000	AL	Alex Rodriguez, Sea	136	404	28.85
2000	AL	Edgar Martinez, Sea	133	397	28.16

Year	Lg	Player, Team	RC	Out	WS
2000	NL	Barry Bonds, SF	130	349	30.00
2000	NL	Jeff Kent, SF	136	426	29.75
2000	NL	Edgardo Alfonzo, NYM	129	388	29.07
2000	NL	Gary Sheffield, LA	131	363	28.72
2000	NL	Sammy Sosa, ChC	138	435	28.20

Year	Lg	Player, Team	RC	Out	WS
2001	AL	Jason Giambi, Oak	156	368	35.81
2001	AL	Alex Rodriguez, Tex	149	460	31.43
2001	AL	Ichiro Suzuki, Sea	135	475	30.66
2001	AL	Roberto Alomar, Cle	139	415	30.43
2001	AL	Jim Thome, Cle	133	386	29.44

Year	Lg	Player, Team	RC	Out	WS
2001	NL	Barry Bonds, SF	180	330	52.22
2001	NL	Sammy Sosa, ChC	166	408	39.16
2001	NL	Luis Gonzalez, Ari	163	431	32.51
2001	NL	Shawn Green, LA	135	454	32.11
2001	NL	Gary Sheffield, LA	117	376	28.32

Pitching Leaders by League and Season

Year	Lg	Player, Team	IP	ERA	WS
1876	NL	George Bradley, StL	573.0	1.23	51.20
1877	NL	Jim Devlin, Lou	559.0	2.25	58.27
1878	NL	Tommy Bond, Bos	532.2	2.06	58.62
1879	NL	Pud Galvin, Buf	593.0	2.28	57.53
1880	NL	Jim McCormick, Cle	657.2	1.85	49.71
1881	NL	Jim Whitney, Bos	552.1	2.48	35.93
1882	NL	Old Hoss Radbourn, Prv	474.0	2.09	44.10
1882	AA	Will White, Cin	480.0	1.54	50.93
1883	NL	Old Hoss Radbourn, Prv	632.1	2.05	51.15
1883	AA	Tim Keefe, NY	619.0	2.41	66.48
1884	NL	Old Hoss Radbourn, Prv	678.2	1.38	83.12
1884	UA	Bill Sweeney, Bal	538.0	2.59	44.43
1884	AA	Guy Hecker, Lou	670.2	1.80	62.24
1885	NL	John Clarkson, ChN	623.0	1.85	58.41
1885	AA	Ed Morris, Pit	581.0	2.35	55.97
1886	NL	Lady Baldwin, Det	487.0	2.24	51.98
1886	AA	Dave Foutz, StL	504.0	2.11	52.26
1887	NL	John Clarkson, ChN	523.0	3.08	49.89
1887	AA	Elmer Smith, Cin	447.1	2.94	51.49
1888	NL	Charlie Buffinton, Phi	400.1	1.91	43.85
1888	AA	Silver King, StL	585.2	1.64	66.26
1889	NL	John Clarkson, Bos	620.0	2.73	60.38
1889	AA	Silver King, StL	458.0	3.14	42.37
1890	NL	Bill Hutchison, ChN	603.0	2.70	54.21
1890	PL	Silver King, Chi	461.0	2.69	44.48
1890	AA	Scott Stratton, Lou	431.0	2.36	44.77
1891	NL	Bill Hutchison, ChN	561.0	2.81	49.10
1891	AA	Sadie McMahon, Bal	503.0	2.81	39.47
1892	NL	Kid Nichols, Bos	453.0	2.84	46.99
1893	NL	Amos Rusie, NYG	482.0	3.23	39.95
1894	NL	Amos Rusie, NYG	444.0	2.78	54.80
1895	NL	Pink Hawley, Pit	444.1	3.18	39.89
1896	NL	Cy Young, Cle	414.1	3.24	40.52
1897	NL	Kid Nichols, Bos	368.0	2.64	39.41
1898	NL	Kid Nichols, Bos	388.0	2.13	42.60
1899	NL	Vic Willis, Bos	342.2	2.50	38.95
1900	NL	Joe McGinnity, Bro	343.0	2.94	29.39
1901	AL	Cy Young, Bos	371.1	1.62	40.44
1901	NL	Vic Willis, Bos	305.1	2.36	33.28
1902	AL	Cy Young, Bos	384.2	2.15	38.47
1902	NL	Jack Taylor, ChC	324.2	1.33	30.40
1903	AL	Cy Young, Bos	341.2	2.08	33.75
1903	NL	Joe McGinnity, NYG	434.0	2.43	40.45
1904	AL	Jack Chesbro, NYA	454.2	1.82	51.80
1904	NL	Joe McGinnity, NYG	408.0	1.61	42.30
1905	AL	Rube Waddell, Phi	328.2	1.48	34.98
1905	NL	Christy Mathewson, NYG	338.2	1.28	37.45
1906	AL	Al Orth, NYA	338.2	2.34	33.67
1906	NL	Three Finger Brown, ChC	277.1	1.04	35.30
1907	AL	Ed Walsh, CWS	422.1	1.60	36.80
1907	NL	Orval Overall, ChC	268.1	1.68	31.89
1908	AL	Ed Walsh, CWS	464.0	1.42	46.62
1908	NL	Christy Mathewson, NYG	390.2	1.43	38.60
1909	AL	Frank Smith, CWS	365.0	1.80	29.91
1909	NL	Three Finger Brown, ChC	342.2	1.31	35.82
1910	AL	Jack Coombs, Phi	353.0	1.30	36.02
1910	NL	Three Finger Brown, ChC	295.1	1.86	29.34
1911	AL	Ed Walsh, CWS	368.2	2.22	30.88
1911	NL	Pete Alexander, Phi	367.0	2.57	33.95
1912	AL	Walter Johnson, Was	369.0	1.39	44.12
1912	NL	Christy Mathewson, NYG	310.0	2.12	29.63
1913	AL	Walter Johnson, Was	346.0	1.14	50.28
1913	NL	Christy Mathewson, NYG	306.0	2.06	29.75
1914	AL	Walter Johnson, Was	371.2	1.72	35.44
1914	NL	Bill James, Bos	332.1	1.90	35.32
1914	FL	Claude Hendrix, Chi	362.0	1.69	36.35
1915	AL	Walter Johnson, Was	336.2	1.55	39.34
1915	NL	Pete Alexander, Phi	376.1	1.22	43.32
1915	FL	Dave Davenport, STL	392.2	2.20	33.58
1916	AL	Walter Johnson, Was	369.2	1.90	34.49
1916	NL	Pete Alexander, Phi	389.0	1.55	41.95
1917	AL	Eddie Cicotte, CWS	346.2	1.53	35.15
1917	NL	Pete Alexander, Phi	388.0	1.83	39.11
1918	AL	Walter Johnson, Was	326.0	1.27	34.95
1918	NL	Hippo Vaughn, ChC	290.1	1.74	26.93
1919	AL	Eddie Cicotte, CWS	306.2	1.82	32.11
1919	NL	Hippo Vaughn, ChC	306.2	1.79	30.27
1920	AL	Jim Bagby, Cle	339.2	2.89	32.16
1920	NL	Pete Alexander, ChC	363.1	1.91	34.46
1921	AL	Red Faber, CWS	330.2	2.48	37.02
1921	NL	Burleigh Grimes, Bro	302.1	2.83	29.11
1922	AL	Red Faber, CWS	352.0	2.81	31.04
1922	NL	Wilbur Cooper, Pit	294.2	3.18	24.83
1923	AL	Urban Shocker, StL	277.1	3.41	24.77
1923	NL	Dolf Luque, Cin	322.0	1.93	38.97
1924	AL	Walter Johnson, Was	277.2	2.72	27.86
1924	NL	Dazzy Vance, Bro	308.1	2.16	35.57
1925	AL	Herb Pennock, NYY	277.0	2.96	23.31
1925	NL	Pete Donohue, Cin	301.0	3.08	26.48
1926	AL	George Uhle, Cle	318.1	2.83	31.72
1926	NL	Ray Kremer, Pit	231.1	2.61	24.23
1927	AL	Ted Lyons, CWS	307.2	2.84	28.87
1927	NL	Jesse Haines, StL	300.2	2.72	28.17
1928	AL	Lefty Grove, Phi	261.2	2.58	27.44
1928	NL	Dazzy Vance, Bro	280.1	2.09	32.00
1929	AL	Lefty Grove, Phi	275.1	2.81	28.31
1929	NL	Red Lucas, Cin	270.0	3.60	24.39

Year	Lg	Player, Team	IP	ERA	WS
1930	AL	Lefty Grove, Phi	291.0	2.54	37.08
1930	NL	Dazzy Vance, Bro	258.2	2.61	25.77
1931	AL	Lefty Grove, Phi	288.2	2.06	41.83
1931	NL	Ed Brandt, Bos	250.0	2.92	26.13
1932	AL	Lefty Grove, Phi	291.2	2.84	32.94
1932	NL	Lon Warneke, ChC	277.0	2.37	30.98
1933	AL	Mel Harder, Cle	253.0	2.95	23.83
1933	NL	Carl Hubbell, NYG	308.2	1.66	33.33
1934	AL	Lefty Gomez, NYY	281.2	2.33	30.76
1934	NL	Dizzy Dean, StL	311.2	2.66	37.46
1935	AL	Wes Ferrell, Bos	322.1	3.52	30.23
1935	NL	Dizzy Dean, StL	325.1	3.04	31.14
1936	AL	Lefty Grove, Bos	253.1	2.81	28.56
1936	NL	Carl Hubbell, NYG	304.0	2.31	36.88
1937	AL	Lefty Gomez, NYY	278.1	2.33	28.90
1937	NL	Jim Turner, Bos	256.2	2.38	27.05
1938	AL	Red Ruffing, NYY	247.1	3.31	23.64
1938	NL	Bill Lee, ChC	291.0	2.66	28.05
1939	AL	Bob Feller, Cle	296.2	2.85	31.74
1939	NL	Bucky Walters, Cin	319.0	2.29	34.50
1940	AL	Bob Feller, Cle	320.1	2.61	33.69
1940	NL	Bucky Walters, Cin	305.0	2.48	32.01
1941	AL	Thornton Lee, CWS	300.1	2.37	32.01
1941	NL	Whit Wyatt, Bro	288.1	2.34	27.66
1942	AL	Tex Hughson, Bos	281.0	2.59	27.86
1942	NL	Mort Cooper, StL	278.2	1.78	28.77
1943	AL	Spud Chandler, NYY	253.0	1.64	27.48
1943	NL	Mort Cooper, StL	274.0	2.30	28.51
1944	AL	Dizzy Trout, Det	352.1	2.12	38.12
1944	NL	Bucky Walters, Cin	285.0	2.40	30.30
1945	AL	Hal Newhouser, Det	313.1	1.81	37.04
1945	NL	Hank Wyse, ChC	278.1	2.68	24.15
1946	AL	Hal Newhouser, Det	292.2	1.94	32.84
1946	NL	Howie Pollet, StL	266.0	2.10	27.04
1947	AL	Hal Newhouser, Det	285.0	2.87	24.28
1947	NL	Warren Spahn, Bos	289.2	2.33	32.27
1948	AL	Hal Newhouser, Det	272.1	3.01	27.31
1948	NL	Johnny Sain, Bos	314.2	2.60	28.21
1949	AL	Mel Parnell, Bos	295.1	2.77	31.36
1949	NL	Warren Spahn, Bos	302.1	3.07	23.73
1950	AL	Art Houtteman, Det	274.2	3.54	25.33
1950	NL	Robin Roberts, Phi	304.1	3.02	25.61
1951	AL	Early Wynn, Cle	274.1	3.02	23.59
1951	NL	Sal Maglie, NYG	298.0	2.93	27.75
1952	AL	Bobby Shantz, Phi	279.2	2.48	32.70
1952	NL	Robin Roberts, Phi	330.0	2.59	31.81
1953	AL	Virgil Trucks, StL-CWS	264.1	2.93	25.38
1953	NL	Robin Roberts, Phi	346.2	2.75	35.03
1954	AL	Early Wynn, Cle	270.2	2.73	24.27
1954	NL	Robin Roberts, Phi	336.2	2.97	30.99
1955	AL	Billy Pierce, CWS	205.2	1.97	23.05
1955	NL	Robin Roberts, Phi	305.0	3.28	23.67
1956	AL	Early Wynn, Cle	277.2	2.72	27.48
1956	NL	Don Newcombe, Bro	268.0	3.06	25.22
1957	AL	Jim Bunning, Det	267.1	2.69	26.29
1957	NL	Warren Spahn, Mil	271.0	2.69	21.53
1958	AL	Billy Pierce, CWS	245.0	2.68	22.09
1958	NL	Warren Spahn, Mil	290.0	3.07	23.11
1959	AL	Hoyt Wilhelm, Bal	226.0	2.19	23.23
1959	NL	Vern Law, Pit	266.0	2.98	24.07
1960	AL	Jim Bunning, Det	252.0	2.79	19.54
1960	NL	Lindy McDaniel, StL	116.1	2.09	25.03
1961	AL	Whitey Ford, NYY	283.0	3.21	22.36
1961	NL	Warren Spahn, Mil	262.2	3.02	22.90
1962	AL	Hank Aguirre, Det	216.0	2.21	22.29
1962	NL	Bob Purkey, Cin	288.1	2.81	25.75
1963	AL	Dick Radatz, Bos	132.1	1.97	23.82
1963	NL	Dick Ellsworth, ChC	290.2	2.11	32.18
1964	AL	Dean Chance, LAA	278.1	1.65	31.67
1964	NL	Don Drysdale, LA	321.1	2.18	26.40
1965	AL	Sam McDowell, Cle	273.0	2.18	25.36
1965	NL	Sandy Koufax, LA	335.2	2.04	33.19
1966	AL	Jim Kaat, Min	304.2	2.75	26.19
1966	NL	Sandy Koufax, LA	323.0	1.73	35.12
1967	AL	Joe Horlen, CWS	258.0	2.06	22.95
1967	NL	Jim Bunning, Phi	302.1	2.29	24.76
1968	AL	Denny McLain, Det	336.0	1.96	33.08
1968	NL	Bob Gibson, StL	304.2	1.12	36.36
1969	AL	Denny McLain, Det	325.0	2.80	28.94
1969	NL	Bob Gibson, StL	314.0	2.18	32.29
1970	AL	Sam McDowell, Cle	305.0	2.92	29.73
1970	NL	Bob Gibson, StL	294.0	3.12	26.02
1971	AL	Wilbur Wood, CWS	334.0	1.91	33.36
1971	NL	Fergie Jenkins, ChC	325.0	2.77	34.66
1972	AL	Gaylord Perry, Cle	342.2	1.92	39.04
1972	NL	Steve Carlton, Phi	346.1	1.97	40.38
1973	AL	John Hiller, Det	125.1	1.44	30.54
1973	NL	Tom Seaver, NYM	290.0	2.08	29.04
1974	AL	Gaylord Perry, Cle	322.1	2.51	29.55
1974	NL	Phil Niekro, Atl	302.1	2.38	28.32
1975	AL	Jim Palmer, Bal	323.0	2.09	31.33
1975	NL	Randy Jones, SD	285.0	2.24	28.32
1976	AL	Jim Palmer, Bal	315.0	2.51	27.32
1976	NL	Phil Niekro, Atl	270.2	3.29	21.20
1977	AL	Jim Palmer, Bal	319.0	2.91	28.74
1977	NL	Bruce Sutter, ChC	107.1	1.34	26.84
1978	AL	Ron Guidry, NYY	273.2	1.74	31.18
1978	NL	Phil Niekro, Atl	334.1	2.88	30.29
1979	AL	Jim Kern, Tex	143.0	1.57	24.88
1979	NL	Phil Niekro, Atl	342.0	3.39	23.64

Year	Lg	Player, Team	IP	ERA	WS
1980	AL	Mike Norris, Oak	284.1	2.53	25.17
1980	AL	Doug Corbett, Min	136.1	1.98	24.04
1980	AL	Larry Gura, KC	283.1	2.95	22.47
1980	NL	Steve Carlton, Phi	304.0	2.34	28.61
1980	NL	Jerry Reuss, LA	229.1	2.51	20.70
1980	NL	Rick Camp, Atl	108.1	1.91	20.32

Year	Lg	Player, Team	IP	ERA	WS
1981	AL	Steve McCatty, Oak	185.2	2.33	18.06
1981	AL	Rollie Fingers, Mil	78.0	1.04	17.35
1981	AL	Jack Morris, Det	198.0	3.05	15.62
1981	NL	Tom Seaver, Cin	166.1	2.54	16.92
1981	NL	F. Valenzuela, LA	192.1	2.48	16.72
1981	NL	Steve Carlton, Phi	190.0	2.42	16.17

Year	Lg	Player, Team	IP	ERA	WS
1982	AL	Dave Stieb, Tor	288.1	3.25	25.07
1982	AL	Dan Quisenberry, KC	136.2	2.57	21.53
1982	AL	Dan Spillner, Cle	133.2	2.49	20.59
1982	NL	Steve Carlton, Phi	295.2	3.10	25.33
1982	NL	Joe Niekro, Hou	270.0	2.47	24.60
1982	NL	Steve Rogers, Mon	277.0	2.40	24.03

Year	Lg	Player, Team	IP	ERA	WS
1983	AL	Dan Quisenberry, KC	139.0	1.94	27.84
1983	AL	Dave Stieb, Tor	278.0	3.04	24.41
1983	AL	Rich Dotson, CWS	240.0	3.23	21.18
1983	NL	Mario Soto, Cin	273.2	2.70	24.56
1983	NL	John Denny, Phi	242.2	2.37	22.50
1983	NL	Jesse Orosco, NYM	110.0	1.47	20.06

Year	Lg	Player, Team	IP	ERA	WS
1984	AL	Dave Stieb, Tor	267.0	2.83	25.31
1984	AL	Willie Hernandez, Det	140.1	1.92	24.03
1984	AL	Dan Quisenberry, KC	129.1	2.64	23.66
1984	NL	Bruce Sutter, StL	122.2	1.54	22.96
1984	NL	Dwight Gooden, NYM	218.0	2.60	18.13
1984	NL	Rick Rhoden, Pit	238.1	2.72	18.01

Year	Lg	Player, Team	IP	ERA	WS
1985	AL	Bret Saberhagen, KC	235.1	2.87	24.43
1985	AL	Dave Stieb, Tor	265.0	2.48	24.43
1985	AL	Charlie Leibrandt, KC	237.2	2.69	23.49
1985	NL	Dwight Gooden, NYM	276.2	1.53	32.65
1985	NL	John Tudor, StL	275.0	1.93	27.08
1985	NL	Orel Hershiser, LA	239.2	2.03	22.60

Year	Lg	Player, Team	IP	ERA	WS
1986	AL	Roger Clemens, Bos	254.0	2.48	28.79
1986	AL	Teddy Higuera, Mil	248.1	2.79	24.92
1986	AL	Mike Witt, Cal	269.0	2.84	22.52
1986	NL	Mike Scott, Hou	275.1	2.22	26.78
1986	NL	F. Valenzuela, LA	269.1	3.14	21.01
1986	NL	Rick Rhoden, Pit	253.2	2.84	19.47

Year	Lg	Player, Team	IP	ERA	WS
1987	AL	Roger Clemens, Bos	281.2	2.97	27.71
1987	AL	Frank Viola, Min	251.2	2.90	24.22
1987	AL	Jimmy Key, Tor	261.0	2.76	23.44
1987	NL	Orel Hershiser, LA	264.2	3.06	20.60
1987	NL	Tim Burke, Mon	91.0	1.19	19.68
1987	NL	Bob Welch, LA	251.2	3.22	19.32

Year	Lg	Player, Team	IP	ERA	WS
1988	AL	Frank Viola, Min	255.1	2.64	24.94
1988	AL	Mark Gubicza, KC	269.2	2.70	24.34
1988	AL	Teddy Higuera, Mil	227.1	2.45	22.19
1988	NL	Orel Hershiser, LA	267.0	2.26	24.62
1988	NL	Danny Jackson, Cin	260.2	2.73	21.78
1988	NL	Greg Maddux, ChC	249.0	3.18	19.96

Year	Lg	Player, Team	IP	ERA	WS
1989	AL	Bret Saberhagen, KC	262.1	2.16	28.31
1989	AL	Bert Blyleven, Cal	241.0	2.73	22.21
1989	AL	Mark Gubicza, KC	255.0	3.04	19.11
1989	NL	Orel Hershiser, LA	256.2	2.31	20.56
1989	NL	Greg Maddux, ChC	238.1	2.95	19.51
1989	NL	Mark Davis, SD	92.2	1.85	18.92

Year	Lg	Player, Team	IP	ERA	WS
1990	AL	Roger Clemens, Bos	228.1	1.93	28.15
1990	AL	Chuck Finley, Cal	236.0	2.40	22.59
1990	AL	Dave Stewart, Oak	267.0	2.56	21.22
1990	AL	Bobby Thigpen, CWS	88.2	1.83	20.47
1990	AL	Dennis Eckersley, Oak	73.1	0.61	19.26

Year	Lg	Player, Team	IP	ERA	WS
1990	NL	Doug Drabek, Pit	231.1	2.76	20.29
1990	NL	Frank Viola, NYM	249.2	2.67	19.57
1990	NL	Ed Whitson, SD	228.2	2.60	18.78
1990	NL	Rob Dibble, Cin	98.0	1.74	17.13
1990	NL	Ramon Martinez, LA	234.1	2.92	17.08

Year	Lg	Player, Team	IP	ERA	WS
1991	AL	Roger Clemens, Bos	271.1	2.62	25.47
1991	AL	Kevin Tapani, Min	244.0	2.99	21.20
1991	AL	Mark Langston, Cal	246.1	3.00	20.13
1991	AL	Tom Candiotti, Cle-Tor	238.0	2.65	20.11
1991	AL	Jim Abbott, Cal	243.0	2.89	20.10

Year	Lg	Player, Team	IP	ERA	WS
1991	NL	Tom Glavine, Atl	246.2	2.55	23.14
1991	NL	Dennis Martinez, Mon	222.0	2.39	17.88
1991	NL	Mitch Williams, Phi	88.1	2.34	17.72
1991	NL	Jose Rijo, Cin	204.1	2.51	17.41
1991	NL	Greg Maddux, ChC	263.0	3.35	17.02

Year	Lg	Player, Team	IP	ERA	WS
1992	AL	Roger Clemens, Bos	246.2	2.41	26.01
1992	AL	Mike Mussina, Bal	241.0	2.54	24.08
1992	AL	Kevin Appier, KC	208.1	2.46	20.47
1992	AL	Jack McDowell, CWS	260.2	3.18	19.71
1992	AL	Charles Nagy, Cle	252.0	2.96	19.47

Year	Lg	Player, Team	IP	ERA	WS
1992	NL	Greg Maddux, ChC	268.0	2.18	27.37
1992	NL	Bob Tewksbury, StL	233.0	2.16	21.18
1992	NL	Doug Drabek, Pit	256.2	2.77	19.70
1992	NL	Mike Morgan, ChC	240.0	2.55	19.43
1992	NL	Tom Glavine, Atl	225.0	2.76	19.17

Year	Lg	Player, Team	IP	ERA	WS
1993	AL	Kevin Appier, KC	238.2	2.56	26.96
1993	AL	Jeff Montgomery, KC	87.1	2.27	22.32
1993	AL	Randy Johnson, Sea	255.1	3.24	22.15
1993	AL	David Cone, KC	254.0	3.33	21.27
1993	AL	Jimmy Key, NYY	236.2	3.00	21.10

Year	Lg	Player, Team	IP	ERA	WS
1993	NL	Jose Rijo, Cin	257.1	2.48	25.46
1993	NL	Greg Maddux, Atl	267.0	2.36	25.28
1993	NL	John Wetteland, Mon	85.1	1.37	21.45
1993	NL	Tom Glavine, Atl	239.1	3.20	20.11
1993	NL	Steve Avery, Atl	223.1	2.94	19.19

Year	Lg	Player, Team	IP	ERA	WS
1994	AL	David Cone, KC	171.2	2.94	19.82
1994	AL	Mike Mussina, Bal	176.1	3.06	18.43
1994	AL	Roger Clemens, Bos	170.2	2.85	16.40
1994	AL	Randy Johnson, Sea	172.0	3.19	15.45
1994	AL	Pat Hentgen, Tor	174.2	3.40	14.96

Year	Lg	Player, Team	IP	ERA	WS
1994	NL	Greg Maddux, Atl	202.0	1.56	25.96
1994	NL	Bret Saberhagen, NYM	177.1	2.74	16.04
1994	NL	Danny Jackson, Phi	179.1	3.26	13.50
1994	NL	Doug Drabek, Hou	164.2	2.84	13.19
1994	NL	Marvin Freeman, Col	112.2	2.80	13.18

Year	Lg	Player, Team	IP	ERA	WS
1995	AL	Randy Johnson, Sea	214.1	2.48	21.89
1995	AL	Kenny Rogers, Tex	208.0	3.38	20.84
1995	AL	Mike Mussina, Bal	221.2	3.29	20.19
1995	AL	David Cone, Tor-NYY	229.1	3.57	18.89
1995	AL	Tim Wakefield, Bos	195.1	2.95	18.52

Year	Lg	Player, Team	IP	ERA	WS
1995	NL	Greg Maddux, Atl	209.2	1.63	29.87
1995	NL	Tom Glavine, Atl	198.2	3.08	19.89
1995	NL	Hideo Nomo, LA	191.1	2.54	16.73
1995	NL	John Smoltz, Atl	192.2	3.18	16.62
1995	NL	Mark Wohlers, Atl	64.2	2.09	16.46

Year	Lg	Player, Team	IP	ERA	WS
1996	AL	Pat Hentgen, Tor	265.2	3.22	24.00
1996	AL	Ken Hill, Tex	250.2	3.63	22.39
1996	AL	Charles Nagy, Cle	222.0	3.41	21.23
1996	AL	Roger Clemens, Bos	242.2	3.63	19.52
1996	AL	Kevin Appier, KC	211.1	3.62	19.33

Year	Lg	Player, Team	IP	ERA	WS
1996	NL	Kevin Brown, Fla	233.0	1.89	25.86
1996	NL	John Smoltz, Atl	253.2	2.94	25.70
1996	NL	Greg Maddux, Atl	245.0	2.72	22.55
1996	NL	Tom Glavine, Atl	235.1	2.98	21.38
1996	NL	Trevor Hoffman, SD	88.0	2.25	20.25

Year	Lg	Player, Team	IP	ERA	WS
1997	AL	Roger Clemens, Tor	264.0	2.05	31.66
1997	AL	Randy Johnson, Sea	213.0	2.28	23.06
1997	AL	Justin Thompson, Det	223.1	3.02	20.51
1997	AL	Andy Pettitte, NYY	240.1	2.88	20.32
1997	AL	Pat Hentgen, Tor	264.0	3.68	19.30

Year	Lg	Player, Team	IP	ERA	WS
1997	NL	Pedro Martinez, Mon	241.1	1.90	26.36
1997	NL	Greg Maddux, Atl	232.2	2.20	25.71
1997	NL	Kevin Brown, Fla	237.1	2.69	23.07
1997	NL	Curt Schilling, Phi	254.1	2.97	21.60
1997	NL	Darryl Kile, Hou	255.2	2.57	21.16

Year	Lg	Player, Team	IP	ERA	WS
1998	AL	Roger Clemens, Tor	234.2	2.65	25.04
1998	AL	Pedro Martinez, Bos	233.2	2.89	20.94
1998	AL	Kenny Rogers, Oak	238.2	3.17	18.60
1998	AL	David Wells, NYY	214.1	3.49	17.86
1998	AL	Jamie Moyer, Sea	234.1	3.53	17.70

Year	Lg	Player, Team	IP	ERA	WS
1998	NL	Kevin Brown, SD	257.0	2.38	25.37
1998	NL	Greg Maddux, Atl	251.0	2.22	24.94
1998	NL	Tom Glavine, Atl	229.1	2.47	23.31
1998	NL	Curt Schilling, Phi	268.2	3.25	22.38
1998	NL	Al Leiter, NYM	193.0	2.47	21.09

Year	Lg	Player, Team	IP	ERA	WS
1999	AL	Pedro Martinez, Bos	213.1	2.07	26.89
1999	AL	Derek Lowe, Bos	109.1	2.63	18.72
1999	AL	Jamie Moyer, Sea	228.0	3.87	17.62
1999	AL	Mariano Rivera, NYY	69.0	1.83	17.37
1999	AL	Brad Radke, Min	218.2	3.75	17.15

Year	Lg	Player, Team	IP	ERA	WS
1999	NL	Randy Johnson, Ari	271.2	2.48	26.18
1999	NL	Mike Hampton, Hou	239.0	2.90	24.19
1999	NL	Kevin Millwood, Atl	228.0	2.68	22.16
1999	NL	Billy Wagner, Hou	74.2	1.57	20.50
1999	NL	Kevin Brown, LA	252.1	3.00	19.19

Year	Lg	Player, Team	IP	ERA	WS
2000	AL	Pedro Martinez, Bos	217.0	1.74	28.86
2000	AL	Derek Lowe, Bos	91.1	2.56	18.64
2000	AL	David Wells, Tor	229.2	4.11	17.96
2000	AL	Mike Mussina, Bal	237.2	3.79	17.54
2000	AL	Mariano Rivera, NYY	75.2	2.85	16.50

Year	Lg	Player, Team	IP	ERA	WS
2000	NL	Randy Johnson, Ari	248.2	2.64	25.87
2000	NL	Greg Maddux, Atl	249.1	3.00	24.27
2000	NL	Tom Glavine, Atl	241.0	3.40	21.19
2000	NL	Kevin Brown, LA	230.0	2.58	19.84
2000	NL	Mike Hampton, NYM	217.2	3.14	18.40

Year	Lg	Player, Team	IP	ERA	WS
2001	AL	Joe Mays, Min	233.2	3.16	22.23
2001	AL	Mike Mussina, NYY	228.2	3.15	20.17
2001	AL	Roger Clemens, NYY	220.1	3.51	18.69
2001	AL	Mariano Rivera, NYY	80.2	2.34	18.67
2001	AL	Freddy Garcia, Sea	238.2	3.05	18.35

Year	Lg	Player, Team	IP	ERA	WS
2001	NL	Randy Johnson, Ari	249.2	2.49	25.70
2001	NL	Curt Schilling, Ari	256.2	2.98	23.88
2001	NL	Javier Vazquez, Mon	223.2	3.42	20.51
2001	NL	Greg Maddux, Atl	233.0	3.05	19.59
2001	NL	Darryl Kile, StL	227.1	3.09	17.83

Defensive Win Shares Leaders by League and Season—Catcher

Year	Lg	Player, Team	G	Inn	WS
1876	NL	John Clapp, StL	61	552.0	3.60
1877	NL	Lew Brown, Bos	55	494.0	4.13
1878	NL	Pop Snyder, Bos	58	527.0	4.68
1879	NL	Pop Snyder, Bos	80	716.0	7.07
1880	NL	Silver Flint, ChN	67	601.0	4.35
1881	NL	Charlie Bennett, Det	70	625.0	4.74
1882	NL	Charlie Bennett, Det	65	574.0	5.06
1882	AA	Pop Snyder, Cin	70	628.0	5.10
1883	NL	Doc Bushong, Cle	63	572.0	4.27
1883	AA	Bill Holbert, NY	68	633.0	6.29
1884	NL	Buck Ewing, NYG	80	644.0	5.59
1884	UA	George Baker, STL	68	609.0	5.14
1884	AA	Pop Snyder, Cin	65	578.0	7.06
1885	NL	Buck Ewing, NYG	63	532.0	3.90
1885	AA	Doc Bushong, StL	85	753.0	6.38
1886	NL	Charlie Bennett, Det	69	567.0	5.41
1886	AA	Doc Bushong, StL	106	945.0	7.44
1887	NL	Tom Daly, ChN	64	563.0	6.08
1887	AA	Kid Baldwin, Cin	96	823.0	4.55
1888	NL	Buck Ewing, NYG	78	675.0	4.73
1888	AA	Wilbert Robinson, Phi	65	606.0	5.07
1889	NL	Buck Ewing, NYG	97	849.0	6.22
1889	AA	Jack Boyle, StL	80	640.0	4.35
1890	NL	Charlie Bennett, Bos	85	742.0	5.76
1890	PL	Duke Farrell, Chi	90	792.0	7.79
1890	AA	Jack O'Connor, CoC	106	845.0	5.39
1891	NL	Chief Zimmer, Cle	116	1021.0	6.86
1891	AA	Morgan Murphy, Bos	104	853.0	6.98
1892	NL	Chief Zimmer, Cle	111	971.0	6.86
1893	NL	John Grim, Lou	92	806.0	4.15
1894	NL	Duke Farrell, NYG	104	932.0	7.35
1895	NL	Deacon McGuire, Was	132	1079.0	6.23
1896	NL	Ed McFarland, StL	80	683.0	5.11
1897	NL	John Warner, NYG	110	935.0	7.90
1898	NL	Lou Criger, Cle	82	712.0	6.32
1899	NL	Ed McFarland, Phi	94	824.0	6.13
1900	NL	Ed McFarland, Phi	93	776.0	5.15
1901	AL	Billy Sullivan, CWS	97	842.0	6.46
1901	NL	Malachi Kittridge, Bos	113	998.0	6.81
1902	AL	O. Schreckengost, 2 tms	71	657.0	6.35
1902	NL	Johnny Kling, ChC	112	997.0	6.18
1903	AL	Lou Criger, Bos	96	860.0	7.09
1903	NL	Pat Moran, Bos	107	924.0	7.00
1904	AL	Deacon McGuire, NYA	97	871.0	6.44
1904	NL	Johnny Kling, ChC	104	909.0	5.47
1905	AL	O. Schreckengost, Phi	114	1012.0	8.33
1905	NL	Red Dooin, Phi	107	946.0	6.23
1906	AL	O. Schreckengost, Phi	89	743.0	6.25
1906	NL	Johnny Kling, ChC	96	844.0	5.77
1907	AL	O. Schreckengost, Phi	99	870.0	9.25
1907	NL	Red Dooin, Phi	94	794.0	6.04
1908	AL	Boss Schmidt, Det	121	1072.0	5.98
1908	NL	Red Dooin, Phi	132	1143.0	8.72
1909	AL	Ira Thomas, Phi	84	736.0	5.89
1909	NL	George Gibson, Pit	150	1328.0	8.95
1910	AL	Jack Lapp, Phi	63	517.0	4.33
1910	NL	George Gibson, Pit	143	1291.0	8.27
1911	AL	Ira Thomas, Phi	103	784.0	6.71
1911	NL	Chief Meyers, NYG	128	998.0	5.56
1912	AL	John Henry, Was	63	515.0	4.80
1912	NL	Jimmy Archer, ChC	118	974.0	5.37
1913	AL	Ray Schalk, CWS	125	1038.0	7.37
1913	NL	Bill Killefer, Phi	118	952.0	9.65
1914	AL	Ray Schalk, CWS	125	1032.0	7.33
1914	NL	Bill Killefer, Phi	90	774.0	6.34
1914	FL	Walter Blair, Buf	128	993.0	8.76
1915	AL	Ray Schalk, CWS	134	1148.0	6.39
1915	NL	Frank Snyder, StL	142	1172.0	7.78
1915	FL	Bill Rariden, New	142	1261.0	10.67
1916	AL	Ray Schalk, CWS	124	1072.0	9.40
1916	NL	Hank Gowdy, Bos	116	961.0	7.51
1917	AL	Ray Schalk, CWS	139	1227.0	10.05
1917	NL	Bill Killefer, Phi	120	1047.0	8.53
1918	AL	Steve O'Neill, Cle	113	956.0	6.23
1918	NL	Bill Killefer, ChC	104	911.0	6.95
1919	AL	Ray Schalk, CWS	129	1065.0	6.61
1919	NL	Bill Killefer, ChC	100	895.0	7.29
1920	AL	Ray Schalk, CWS	151	1313.0	10.37
1920	NL	Mickey O'Neil, Bos	105	804.0	5.63
1921	AL	Ray Schalk, CWS	126	1081.0	7.00
1921	NL	Walter Schmidt, Pit	111	983.0	6.77
1922	AL	Ray Schalk, CWS	142	1240.0	11.24
1922	NL	Bob O'Farrell, ChC	125	1074.0	9.56
1923	AL	Muddy Ruel, Was	133	1114.0	8.66
1923	NL	Frank Snyder, NYG	112	943.0	7.20
1924	AL	Muddy Ruel, Was	147	1267.0	8.56
1924	NL	Zack Taylor, Bro	93	737.0	7.57
1925	AL	Muddy Ruel, Was	126	1016.0	8.41
1925	NL	Frank Snyder, NYG	96	750.0	7.77
1926	AL	Luke Sewell, Cle	125	1115.0	6.40
1926	NL	Bob O'Farrell, StL	146	1223.0	8.97

Year	Lg	Player, Team	G	Inn	WS
1927	AL	Mickey Cochrane, Phi	123	1036.0	7.38
1927	NL	Gabby Hartnett, ChC	126	1081.0	8.08
1928	AL	Mickey Cochrane, Phi	130	1117.0	6.10
1928	NL	Gabby Hartnett, ChC	118	976.0	8.72
1929	AL	Mickey Cochrane, Phi	135	1169.0	8.93
1929	NL	Jimmie Wilson, StL	119	956.0	5.59
1930	AL	Mickey Cochrane, Phi	130	1060.0	9.48
1930	NL	Gabby Hartnett, ChC	136	1213.0	9.76
1931	AL	Bill Dickey, NYY	125	1082.0	6.64
1931	NL	Jimmie Wilson, StL	110	900.0	7.94
1932	AL	Mickey Cochrane, Phi	137	1177.0	11.24
1932	NL	Earl Grace, Pit	114	921.0	7.15
1933	AL	Rick Ferrell, 2 tms	137	1212.0	6.99
1933	NL	Gabby Hartnett, ChC	140	1175.0	7.53
1934	AL	Rick Ferrell, Bos	128	1069.0	7.22
1934	NL	Gabby Hartnett, ChC	129	1083.0	10.72
1935	AL	Bill Dickey, NYY	118	990.0	7.84
1935	NL	Gabby Hartnett, ChC	110	932.0	7.35
1936	AL	Luke Sewell, CWS	126	1076.0	8.38
1936	NL	Gus Mancuso, NYG	138	1176.0	8.59
1937	AL	Bill Dickey, NYY	137	1198.0	9.77
1937	NL	Al Lopez, Bos	102	892.0	7.00
1938	AL	Rudy York, Det	116	999.0	6.97
1938	NL	Al Todd, Pit	132	1122.0	8.31
1939	AL	Bill Dickey, NYY	126	1085.0	7.76
1939	NL	Harry Danning, NYG	132	1126.0	8.42
1940	AL	Rollie Hemsley, Cle	117	973.0	8.76
1940	NL	Harry Danning, NYG	131	1165.0	7.76
1941	AL	Bill Dickey, NYY	104	830.0	6.44
1941	NL	Mickey Owen, Bro	128	982.0	8.01
1942	AL	Birdie Tebbetts, Det	97	807.0	6.26
1942	NL	Mickey Owen, Bro	133	1092.0	7.72
1943	AL	Paul Richards, Det	100	881.0	7.21
1943	NL	Ray Mueller, Cin	140	1174.0	10.95
1944	AL	Frankie Hayes, Phi	155	1322.0	8.56
1944	NL	Ray Mueller, Cin	155	1346.0	8.04
1945	AL	Frankie Hayes, 2 tms	151	1237.0	8.00
1945	NL	Ken O'Dea, StL	91	714.0	7.03
1946	AL	Buddy Rosar, Phi	117	998.0	6.33
1946	NL	Ray Mueller, Cin	100	884.0	6.16
1947	AL	Buddy Rosar, Phi	102	895.0	6.99
1947	NL	Bruce Edwards, Bro	128	1103.0	7.19
1948	AL	Jim Hegan, Cle	142	1215.0	9.27
1948	NL	Del Rice, StL	99	797.0	6.35
1949	AL	Jim Hegan, Cle	152	1229.0	10.45
1949	NL	Roy Campanella, Bro	127	1109.0	6.75
1950	AL	Jim Hegan, Cle	129	1099.0	9.68
1950	NL	Wes Westrum, NYG	139	1153.0	9.96
1951	AL	Yogi Berra, NYY	141	1237.0	9.19
1951	NL	Roy Campanella, Bro	140	1234.0	8.33
1952	AL	Yogi Berra, NYY	140	1249.0	8.58
1952	NL	Del Rice, StL	147	1159.0	8.64
1953	AL	Sammy White, Bos	131	1091.0	7.96
1953	NL	Roy Campanella, Bro	140	1192.0	8.54
1954	AL	Jim Hegan, Cle	137	1148.0	9.67
1954	NL	Del Crandall, Mil	136	1143.0	9.12
1955	AL	Sherm Lollar, CWS	136	1102.0	9.20
1955	NL	Roy Campanella, Bro	121	1060.0	7.27
1956	AL	Yogi Berra, NYY	135	1178.0	7.30
1956	NL	Ed Bailey, Cin	106	934.0	6.66
1957	AL	Yogi Berra, NYY	121	1024.0	8.80
1957	NL	Roy Campanella, Bro	100	873.0	6.42
1958	AL	Yogi Berra, NYY	88	786.0	6.55
1958	NL	Del Crandall, Mil	124	1077.0	8.11
1959	AL	Sherm Lollar, CWS	122	993.0	8.07
1959	NL	Del Crandall, Mil	146	1268.0	9.68
1960	AL	Sherm Lollar, CWS	123	972.0	7.46
1960	NL	Hal Smith, StL	124	910.0	8.80
1961	AL	Earl Battey, Min	131	1155.0	7.41
1961	NL	John Roseboro, LA	125	1007.0	7.46
1962	AL	Earl Battey, Min	147	1239.0	8.08
1962	NL	Johnny Edwards, Cin	130	1108.0	8.74
1963	AL	Earl Battey, Min	146	1213.0	9.04
1963	NL	Johnny Edwards, Cin	148	1241.0	9.82
1964	AL	Elston Howard, NYY	146	1322.0	10.47
1964	NL	Johnny Edwards, Cin	120	1063.0	8.96
1965	AL	Bill Freehan, Det	129	1084.0	7.71
1965	NL	Tom Haller, SF	133	1089.0	7.20
1966	AL	Bill Freehan, Det	132	1171.0	7.98
1966	NL	John Roseboro, LA	138	1120.0	8.19
1967	AL	Bob Rodgers, Cal	134	1081.0	6.35
1967	NL	Tim McCarver, StL	130	1154.0	9.64
1968	AL	Bill Freehan, Det	138	1207.0	10.06
1968	NL	Johnny Bench, Cin	154	1315.0	9.20
1969	AL	Bill Freehan, Det	120	1033.0	6.91
1969	NL	Randy Hundley, ChC	151	1291.0	10.16
1970	AL	George Mitterwald, Min	117	1025.0	8.17
1970	NL	Johnny Bench, Cin	139	1170.0	9.46
1971	AL	Bill Freehan, Det	144	1241.0	6.64
1971	NL	Manny Sanguillen, Pit	135	1178.0	9.16
1972	AL	Ed Herrmann, CWS	112	873.0	7.06
1972	NL	Duffy Dyer, NYM	91	842.0	9.26
1973	AL	Thurman Munson, NYY	142	1246.0	7.45
1973	NL	Joe Ferguson, LA	122	1088.0	8.24
1974	AL	Glenn Borgmann, Min	128	934.0	7.70
1974	NL	Johnny Bench, Cin	137	1137.0	7.94

Year	Lg	Player, Team	G	Inn	WS
1975	AL	Brian Downing, CWS	137	1203.0	7.89
1975	NL	Steve Yeager, LA	135	1192.0	7.93
1976	AL	Jim Sundberg, Tex	140	1209.0	9.14
1976	NL	Johnny Bench, Cin	128	1062.0	7.51
1977	AL	Jim Sundberg, Tex	149	1242.0	10.96
1977	NL	Gary Carter, Mon	146	1270.0	7.81
1978	AL	Jim Sundberg, Tex	148	1305.0	10.48
1978	NL	Gary Carter, Mon	152	1314.0	7.95
1979	AL	Jim Sundberg, Tex	150	1288.0	10.32
1979	NL	Gary Carter, Mon	138	1202.0	10.87
1980	AL	Rick Cerone, NYY	147	1271.0	8.94
1980	NL	Gary Carter, Mon	149	1315.0	11.10
1981	AL	Jim Sundberg, Tex	98	859.0	5.52
1981	NL	Gary Carter, Mon	100	846.0	6.83
1982	AL	Bob Boone, Cal	143	1214.0	8.41
1982	NL	Gary Carter, Mon	153	1357.0	10.63
1983	AL	Lance Parrish, Det	131	1090.0	9.54
1983	NL	Gary Carter, Mon	144	1258.0	10.51
1984	AL	Lance Parrish, Det	127	1087.0	7.97
1984	NL	Tony Pena, Pit	146	1265.0	9.23
1985	AL	Bob Boone, Cal	147	1194.0	8.36
1985	NL	Gary Carter, NYM	143	1254.0	11.04
1986	AL	Rich Gedman, Bos	134	1141.0	9.48
1986	NL	Jody Davis, ChC	145	1274.0	8.03
1987	AL	Ernie Whitt, Tor	131	1032.0	7.54
1987	NL	Mike Scioscia, LA	138	1147.2	8.67
1988	AL	Andy Allanson, Cle	133	1149.1	7.93
1988	NL	Tony Pena, StL	142	1189.1	9.14

Year	Lg	Player, Team	G	Inn	WS
1989	AL	Bob Boone, KC	129	1083.0	9.62
1989	AL	Terry Steinbach, Oak	103	823.0	5.78
1989	AL	Lance Parrish, Cal	122	1053.1	5.61

Year	Lg	Player, Team	G	Inn	WS
1989	NL	Mike Scioscia, LA	130	1063.0	7.88
1989	NL	Tony Pena, StL	134	1086.1	7.41
1989	NL	Damon Berryhill, ChC	89	764.1	7.09

Year	Lg	Player, Team	G	Inn	WS
1990	AL	Lance Parrish, Cal	131	1098.0	10.22
1990	AL	Tony Pena, Bos	142	1186.0	9.75
1990	AL	Carlton Fisk, CWS	116	970.0	8.11

Year	Lg	Player, Team	G	Inn	WS
1990	NL	Darren Daulton, Phi	139	1115.0	7.91
1990	NL	Mike Scioscia, LA	132	1069.0	6.60
1990	NL	Joe Oliver, Cin	118	943.0	5.98

Year	Lg	Player, Team	G	Inn	WS
1991	AL	Lance Parrish, Cal	111	912.2	8.16
1991	AL	Tony Pena, Bos	140	1156.2	8.08
1991	AL	B.J. Surhoff, Mil	127	1055.0	5.64

Year	Lg	Player, Team	G	Inn	WS
1991	NL	Tom Pagnozzi, StL	139	1156.1	9.59
1991	NL	Benito Santiago, SD	151	1305.1	8.31
1991	NL	Craig Biggio, Hou	139	1175.1	5.44

Year	Lg	Player, Team	G	Inn	WS
1992	AL	Ivan Rodriguez, Tex	116	982.2	8.73
1992	AL	Pat Borders, Tor	137	1160.2	7.33
1992	AL	Sandy Alomar Jr., Cle	88	729.2	7.09

Year	Lg	Player, Team	G	Inn	WS
1992	NL	Joe Oliver, Cin	141	1200.0	6.99
1992	NL	Kirt Manwaring, SF	108	874.1	6.61
1992	NL	Tom Pagnozzi, StL	138	1189.0	6.55

Year	Lg	Player, Team	G	Inn	WS
1993	AL	Ron Karkovice, CWS	127	1038.2	11.60
1993	AL	Dave Valle, Sea	135	1131.1	8.50
1993	AL	Chris Hoiles, Bal	124	1040.0	6.84

Year	Lg	Player, Team	G	Inn	WS
1993	NL	Rick Wilkins, ChC	133	1077.1	10.21
1993	NL	Kirt Manwaring, SF	130	1090.2	9.97
1993	NL	Mike Piazza, LA	146	1243.1	8.83

Year	Lg	Player, Team	G	Inn	WS
1994	AL	Terry Steinbach, Oak	93	754.1	6.50
1994	AL	Ivan Rodriguez, Tex	99	837.2	5.58
1994	AL	Chris Hoiles, Bal	98	838.2	5.14

Year	Lg	Player, Team	G	Inn	WS
1994	NL	Benito Santiago, Fla	97	786.2	6.93
1994	NL	Joe Girardi, Col	93	757.0	5.75
1994	NL	Kirt Manwaring, SF	97	829.1	5.29

Year	Lg	Player, Team	G	Inn	WS
1995	AL	Ivan Rodriguez, Tex	127	1065.0	9.42
1995	AL	Dan Wilson, Sea	119	1017.0	9.35
1995	AL	Ron Karkovice, CWS	113	867.0	5.92

Year	Lg	Player, Team	G	Inn	WS
1995	NL	Joe Girardi, Col	122	1044.1	6.75
1995	NL	Charles Johnson, Fla	97	844.2	5.95
1995	NL	Mike Piazza, LA	112	941.0	5.23

Year	Lg	Player, Team	G	Inn	WS
1996	AL	Ivan Rodriguez, Tex	146	1222.2	11.56
1996	AL	Dan Wilson, Sea	135	1130.0	6.71
1996	AL	Charlie O'Brien, Tor	105	801.0	6.35

Year	Lg	Player, Team	G	Inn	WS
1996	NL	Charles Johnson, Fla	120	998.0	9.65
1996	NL	Javy Lopez, Atl	135	1112.2	8.05
1996	NL	Tom Pagnozzi, StL	116	974.2	7.18

Year	Lg	Player, Team	G	Inn	WS
1997	AL	Ivan Rodriguez, Tex	143	1201.0	11.35
1997	AL	Dan Wilson, Sea	144	1202.0	9.07
1997	AL	Benito Santiago, Tor	95	819.1	7.04
1997	AL	Charlie O'Brien, Tor	69	592.1	6.51
1997	AL	Mike Matheny, Mil	121	929.2	6.42

Year	Lg	Player, Team	G	Inn	WS
1997	NL	Charles Johnson, Fla	123	1076.2	11.07
1997	NL	Jason Kendall, Pit	142	1218.0	8.70
1997	NL	Brad Ausmus, Hou	129	1032.2	6.39
1997	NL	Mike Piazza, LA	139	1199.1	6.36
1997	NL	Javy Lopez, Atl	117	951.0	5.76

Year	Lg	Player, Team	G	Inn	WS
1998	AL	Ivan Rodriguez, Tex	139	1197.1	11.02
1998	AL	Darrin Fletcher, Tor	121	971.1	6.17
1998	AL	Terry Steinbach, Min	119	1007.0	5.98
1998	AL	Jorge Posada, NYY	99	792.0	5.80
1998	AL	Sandy Alomar Jr., Cle	111	930.0	5.65

Year	Lg	Player, Team	G	Inn	WS
1998	NL	Javy Lopez, Atl	128	1092.1	8.43
1998	NL	Mike Piazza, 3 tms	140	1190.0	8.20
1998	NL	Charles Johnson, 2 tms	131	1143.2	8.11
1998	NL	Jason Kendall, Pit	144	1253.1	6.58
1998	NL	Brad Ausmus, Hou	124	1054.1	6.28

Year	Lg	Player, Team	G	Inn	WS
1999	AL	Ivan Rodriguez, Tex	141	1208.1	11.95
1999	AL	Brad Ausmus, Det	127	1080.2	7.73
1999	AL	John Flaherty, TB	115	990.2	6.68
1999	AL	Charles Johnson, Bal	135	1093.0	5.91
1999	AL	Terry Steinbach, Min	96	811.2	5.17

Year	Lg	Player, Team	G	Inn	WS
1999	NL	Mike Lieberthal, Phi	143	1191.1	6.36
1999	NL	Mike Redmond, Fla	82	652.2	6.16
1999	NL	Tony Eusebio, Hou	98	764.2	5.49
1999	NL	Eddie Perez, Atl	98	758.0	5.48
1999	NL	Henry Blanco, Col	86	693.1	5.44

Year	Lg	Player, Team	G	Inn	WS
2000	AL	Brad Ausmus, Det	150	1231.1	10.54
2000	AL	Jorge Posada, NYY	142	1182.0	8.47
2000	AL	Ben Molina, Ana	127	1092.0	8.43
2000	AL	Ivan Rodriguez, Tex	87	736.1	6.24
2000	AL	Einar Diaz, Cle	74	624.2	4.77

Year	Lg	Player, Team	G	Inn	WS
2000	NL	Mike Matheny, StL	124	1031.2	10.34
2000	NL	Henry Blanco, Mil	88	732.1	6.84
2000	NL	Mike Lieberthal, Phi	106	896.0	6.22
2000	NL	Jason Kendall, Pit	147	1280.2	5.84
2000	NL	Damian Miller, Ari	97	805.2	5.10

Year	Lg	Player, Team	G	Inn	WS
2001	AL	Einar Diaz, Cle	134	1114.2	7.12
2001	AL	A.J. Pierzynski, Min	110	901.2	6.92
2001	AL	Dan Wilson, Sea	122	941.0	6.90
2001	AL	Ivan Rodriguez, Tex	106	855.1	6.19
2001	AL	Ramon Hernandez, Oak	135	1131.2	5.86

Year	Lg	Player, Team	G	Inn	WS
2001	NL	Brad Ausmus, Hou	127	1056.2	10.05
2001	NL	Mike Matheny, StL	121	1002.0	7.69
2001	NL	Benito Santiago, SF	130	1080.0	7.34
2001	NL	Charles Johnson, Fla	125	1061.0	7.34
2001	NL	Damian Miller, Ari	121	978.0	5.95

Defensive Win Shares Leaders by League and Season—First Base

Year	Lg	Player, Team	G	Inn	WS
1876	NL	Herman Dehlman, StL	64	577.0	1.36
1877	NL	Jumbo Latham, Lou	59	543.0	1.03
1878	NL	Chub Sullivan, Cin	61	548.0	1.51
1879	NL	Joe Start, Prv	65	600.0	1.59
1880	NL	Cap Anson, ChN	81	697.0	2.06
1881	NL	Cap Anson, ChN	84	738.0	1.70
1882	NL	Dan Brouthers, Buf	84	737.0	2.03
1882	AA	Charlie Comiskey, StL	77	674.0	1.57
1883	NL	Dan Brouthers, Buf	97	851.0	1.95
1883	AA	Harry Stovey, Phi	93	824.0	1.86
1884	NL	John Morrill, Bos	91	824.0	2.32
1884	UA	J. Schoeneck, 3 tms	105	906.0	2.52
1884	AA	Dave Orr, NY	110	956.0	2.79
1885	NL	Roger Connor, NYG	110	983.0	2.21
1885	AA	Jim Field, 2 tms	94	853.0	1.85
1886	NL	Roger Connor, NYG	118	1017.0	2.71
1886	AA	Milt Scott, Bal	137	1191.0	3.50
1887	NL	Cap Anson, ChN	122	1085.0	2.95
1887	AA	Tommy Tucker, Bal	136	1173.0	3.51
1888	NL	Roger Connor, NYG	133	1173.0	2.98
1888	AA	Tommy Tucker, Bal	129	1136.0	2.18
1889	NL	Cap Anson, ChN	134	1219.0	2.47
1889	AA	Dave Foutz, Bro	134	1148.0	3.15
1890	NL	Tommy Tucker, Bos	132	1173.0	2.85
1890	PL	Roger Connor, NY	123	1094.0	4.19
1890	AA	Harry Taylor, Lou	118	1080.0	2.78
1891	NL	Roger Connor, NYG	129	1159.0	2.81
1891	AA	Charlie Comiskey, StL	141	1211.0	3.89
1892	NL	Dan Brouthers, Bro	152	1355.0	4.11
1893	NL	Jake Beckley, Pit	131	1167.0	2.56
1894	NL	Roger Connor, 2 tms	120	1052.0	2.31
1895	NL	Jake Beckley, Pit	129	1141.0	2.70
1896	NL	Patsy Tebeau, Cle	122	1080.0	2.95
1897	NL	Perry Werden, Lou	131	1120.0	2.50
1898	NL	Dan McGann, Bal	145	1248.0	2.94
1899	NL	Jake Beckley, Cin	134	1170.0	2.99
1900	NL	Jake Beckley, Cin	140	1221.0	2.05
1901	AL	Frank Isbell, CWS	137	1199.0	2.95
1901	NL	John Ganzel, NYG	138	1212.0	2.65
1902	AL	Frank Isbell, CWS	133	1191.0	3.02
1902	NL	Fred Tenney, Bos	134	1197.0	2.56
1903	AL	John Anderson, StL	133	1164.0	2.92
1903	NL	Jack Doyle, Bro	139	1214.0	3.02
1904	AL	Candy LaChance, Bos	157	1406.0	3.19
1904	NL	Fred Tenney, Bos	144	1259.0	2.80
1905	AL	Harry Davis, Phi	150	1370.0	3.81
1905	NL	Fred Tenney, Bos	148	1325.0	3.93
1906	AL	Tom Jones, StL	143	1253.0	3.31
1906	NL	Jim Nealon, Pit	154	1358.0	2.78
1907	AL	Jiggs Donahue, CWS	157	1406.0	4.10
1907	NL	John Ganzel, Cin	143	1231.0	2.34
1908	AL	George Stovall, Cle	132	1196.0	3.45
1908	NL	Ed Konetchy, StL	154	1367.0	3.34
1909	AL	Frank Isbell, CWS	101	912.0	2.68
1909	NL	Kitty Bransfield, Phi	138	1262.0	2.55
1910	AL	George Stovall, Cle	132	1196.0	2.64
1910	NL	Jake Daubert, Bro	144	1307.0	3.08
1911	AL	Hal Chase, NYA	124	1121.0	3.06
1911	NL	Jake Daubert, Bro	149	1332.0	3.57
1912	AL	Stuffy McInnis, Phi	153	1357.0	2.40
1912	NL	Fred Luderus, Phi	146	1304.0	3.78
1913	AL	Stuffy McInnis, Phi	148	1292.0	2.70
1913	NL	Dots Miller, Pit	150	1360.0	2.42
1914	AL	Chick Gandil, Was	145	1293.0	3.40
1914	NL	Ed Konetchy, Pit	154	1357.0	3.46
1914	FL	Harry Swacina, Bal	158	1362.0	3.64
1915	AL	Wally Pipp, NYY	134	1184.0	2.42
1915	NL	Fred Luderus, Phi	141	1264.0	3.03
1915	FL	Ed Konetchy, Pit	152	1350.0	4.44
1916	AL	Wally Pipp, NYY	148	1311.0	2.96
1916	NL	Ed Konetchy, Bos	158	1406.0	3.97
1917	AL	Wally Pipp, NYY	155	1411.0	3.13
1917	NL	Ed Konetchy, Bos	129	1180.0	2.67
1918	AL	George Sisler, StL	114	1033.0	2.52
1918	NL	Fred Merkle, ChC	129	1163.0	3.84
1919	AL	Chick Gandil, CWS	115	1012.0	2.46
1919	NL	Ed Konetchy, Bro	132	1173.0	2.56
1920	AL	Wally Pipp, NYY	153	1353.0	3.13
1920	NL	Charlie Grimm, Pit	148	1330.0	4.60
1921	AL	Stuffy McInnis, Bos	152	1339.0	3.79
1921	NL	Charlie Grimm, Pit	150	1385.0	3.75
1922	AL	Earl Sheely, CWS	149	1337.0	3.32
1922	NL	Charlie Grimm, Pit	154	1376.0	3.62
1923	AL	Earl Sheely, CWS	156	1388.0	2.64
1923	NL	Charlie Grimm, Pit	152	1340.0	3.03
1924	AL	Joe Hauser, Phi	146	1287.0	3.56
1924	NL	Charlie Grimm, Pit	151	1353.0	2.98
1925	AL	Lou Gehrig, NYY	120	994.0	2.56
1925	NL	Bill Terry, NYG	126	1088.0	2.81
1926	AL	Lou Gehrig, NYY	155	1361.0	2.74
1926	NL	Wally Pipp, Cin	155	1358.0	3.96

Year	Lg	Player, Team	G	Inn	WS
1927	AL	Phil Todt, Bos	139	1199.0	3.22
1927	NL	Bill Terry, NYG	150	1341.0	3.50
1928	AL	Lu Blue, StL	154	1372.0	2.85
1928	NL	Del Bissonette, Bro	155	1396.0	2.65
1929	AL	Jimmie Foxx, Phi	142	1251.0	3.27
1929	NL	George Kelly, Cin	147	1310.0	3.13
1930	AL	Jimmie Foxx, Phi	153	1356.0	3.69
1930	NL	Bill Terry, NYG	154	1361.0	3.32
1931	AL	Joe Kuhel, Was	139	1215.0	2.82
1931	NL	Earl Sheely, Bos	143	1219.0	3.05
1932	AL	Jimmie Foxx, Phi	141	1264.0	3.34
1932	NL	Bill Terry, NYG	154	1369.0	3.51
1933	AL	Jimmie Foxx, Phi	149	1307.0	3.22
1933	NL	Buck Jordan, Bos	150	1335.0	3.16
1934	AL	Lou Gehrig, NYY	153	1353.0	2.62
1934	NL	Gus Suhr, Pit	151	1323.0	3.25
1935	AL	Zeke Bonura, CWS	138	1217.0	2.82
1935	NL	Bill Terry, NYG	143	1263.0	3.63
1936	AL	Lou Gehrig, NYY	155	1385.0	3.15
1936	NL	Buddy Hassett, Bro	156	1403.0	3.12
1937	AL	Jimmie Foxx, Bos	150	1335.0	4.21
1937	NL	Elbie Fletcher, Bos	148	1327.0	2.87
1938	AL	Hank Greenberg, Det	155	1346.0	2.97
1938	NL	Elbie Fletcher, Bos	146	1253.0	2.72
1939	AL	Joe Kuhel, CWS	136	1213.0	2.68
1939	NL	Frank McCormick, Cin	156	1394.0	3.46
1940	AL	Rudy York, Det	155	1375.0	3.38
1940	NL	Frank McCormick, Cin	155	1395.0	2.99
1941	AL	Joe Kuhel, CWS	151	1361.0	3.48
1941	NL	Frank McCormick, Cin	154	1367.0	3.45
1942	AL	Rudy York, Det	152	1363.0	3.95
1942	NL	Frank McCormick, Cin	144	1321.0	3.16
1943	AL	Joe Kuhel, CWS	153	1364.0	3.33
1943	NL	Elbie Fletcher, Pit	154	1368.0	2.48
1944	AL	Mike Rocco, Cle	155	1401.0	3.22
1944	NL	Frank McCormick, Cin	153	1368.0	3.15
1945	AL	George McQuinn, StL	136	1165.0	3.01
1945	NL	Frank McCormick, Cin	151	1329.0	3.05
1946	AL	Hank Greenberg, Det	140	1233.0	3.82
1946	NL	Frank McCormick, Phi	134	1161.0	2.64
1947	AL	George McQuinn, NYY	142	1250.0	3.00
1947	NL	Stan Musial, StL	149	1321.0	3.01
1948	AL	Mickey Vernon, Was	150	1304.0	3.12
1948	NL	Johnny Mize, NYG	152	1328.0	2.24
1949	AL	Mickey Vernon, Cle	153	1346.0	3.40
1949	NL	Gil Hodges, Bro	156	1403.0	2.70
1950	AL	Luke Easter, Cle	128	1119.0	2.47
1950	NL	Eddie Waitkus, Phi	154	1376.0	2.93

Year	Lg	Player, Team	G	Inn	WS
1951	AL	Mickey Vernon, Was	137	1214.0	2.65
1951	NL	Ted Kluszewski, Cin	154	1381.0	3.72
1952	AL	Mickey Vernon, Was	153	1391.0	3.44
1952	NL	Whitey Lockman, NYG	154	1349.0	3.10
1953	AL	Mickey Vernon, Was	152	1345.0	2.76
1953	NL	Steve Bilko, StL	154	1340.0	3.01
1954	AL	Mickey Vernon, Was	148	1324.0	2.72
1954	NL	Gil Hodges, Bro	154	1392.0	3.64
1955	AL	Vic Power, KCA	144	1257.0	2.60
1955	NL	Gil Hodges, Bro	139	1215.0	2.46
1956	AL	Vic Wertz, Cle	133	1050.0	2.46
1956	NL	Bill White, NYG	138	1225.0	3.46
1957	AL	Vic Power, KCA	113	944.0	2.68
1957	NL	Ed Bouchee, Phi	154	1363.0	2.71
1958	AL	Bob Boyd, Bal	99	790.0	2.10
1958	NL	Stan Musial, StL	124	1029.0	2.46
1959	AL	Vic Power, Cle	121	1073.0	3.47
1959	NL	Gil Hodges, LA	113	929.0	2.15
1960	AL	Vic Power, Cle	147	1286.0	3.45
1960	NL	Joe Adcock, Mil	136	1208.0	2.38
1961	AL	Norm Cash, Det	157	1401.0	3.23
1961	NL	Gordy Coleman, Cin	150	1230.0	3.02
1962	AL	Norm Cash, Det	146	1285.0	3.16
1962	NL	Orlando Cepeda, SF	160	1352.0	2.83
1963	AL	Norm Cash, Det	142	1233.0	2.63
1963	NL	Bill White, StL	162	1462.0	2.57
1964	AL	Norm Cash, Det	137	1148.0	2.43
1964	NL	Bill White, StL	160	1416.0	3.95
1965	AL	Norm Cash, Det	139	1174.0	2.59
1965	NL	Wes Parker, LA	154	1378.0	3.99
1966	AL	Norm Cash, Det	158	1375.0	2.17
1966	NL	Bill White, Phi	158	1364.0	2.95
1967	AL	Harmon Killebrew, Min	160	1343.0	2.88
1967	NL	Orlando Cepeda, StL	151	1324.0	2.36
1968	AL	Tom McCraw, CWS	135	1166.0	2.36
1968	NL	Donn Clendenon, Pit	155	1391.0	2.83
1969	AL	Don Mincher, Sea	122	1041.0	2.41
1969	NL	Joe Torre, StL	144	1252.0	3.38
1970	AL	Mike Hegan, Mil	139	1116.0	2.46
1970	NL	Wes Parker, LA	161	1443.0	3.19
1971	AL	Jim Spencer, Cal	145	1249.0	2.88
1971	NL	Nate Colbert, SD	153	1370.0	2.81
1972	AL	Dick Allen, CWS	143	1182.0	2.86
1972	NL	Nate Colbert, SD	150	1362.0	3.04
1973	AL	John Mayberry, KC	149	1299.0	2.84
1973	NL	Lee May, Hou	144	1225.0	2.49
1974	AL	George Scott, Mil	148	1322.0	2.05
1974	NL	Steve Garvey, LA	156	1405.0	3.36

Year	Lg	Player, Team	G	Inn	WS
1975	AL	Carl Yastrzemski, Bos	140	1179.0	3.28
1975	NL	Steve Garvey, LA	160	1449.0	3.52
1976	AL	George Scott, Mil	155	1368.0	3.09
1976	NL	Steve Garvey, LA	162	1462.0	3.83
1977	AL	Jason Thompson, Det	158	1420.0	2.37
1977	NL	Steve Garvey, LA	160	1406.0	3.18
1978	AL	Chris Chambliss, NYY	155	1365.0	3.25
1978	NL	Dan Driessen, Cin	151	1282.0	2.77
1979	AL	Eddie Murray, Bal	157	1399.0	2.66
1979	NL	Bill Buckner, ChC	140	1212.0	2.89
1980	AL	Bruce Bochte, Sea	133	1137.0	2.65
1980	NL	Pete Rose, Phi	162	1378.0	3.14
1981	AL	Eddie Murray, Bal	99	885.0	2.10
1981	NL	Steve Garvey, LA	110	957.0	2.50
1982	AL	Eddie Murray, Bal	149	1284.0	3.36
1982	NL	Steve Garvey, LA	158	1367.0	3.21
1983	AL	Eddie Murray, Bal	153	1363.0	2.68
1983	NL	Bill Buckner, ChC	144	1204.0	2.65
1984	AL	Pete O'Brien, Tex	141	1238.0	3.16
1984	NL	Steve Garvey, SD	159	1319.0	3.44
1985	AL	Pete O'Brien, Tex	159	1346.0	3.38
1985	NL	Keith Hernandez, NYM	157	1380.0	4.02
1986	AL	Don Mattingly, NYY	160	1413.0	3.33
1986	NL	Glenn Davis, Hou	156	1348.0	3.31
1987	AL	Pete O'Brien, Tex	158	1300.0	4.08
1987	NL	Andres Galarraga, Mon	146	1274.2	3.43
1988	AL	Pete O'Brien, Tex	155	1307.1	4.06
1988	NL	Glenn Davis, Hou	151	1341.1	3.25

Year	Lg	Player, Team	G	Inn	WS
1989	AL	Nick Esasky, Bos	153	1322.1	3.30
1989	AL	Rafael Palmeiro, Tex	147	1236.1	3.25
1989	AL	Pete O'Brien, Cle	154	1331.0	3.04

Year	Lg	Player, Team	G	Inn	WS
1989	NL	Eddie Murray, LA	159	1418.2	3.14
1989	NL	Mark Grace, ChC	142	1240.1	3.13
1989	NL	Glenn Davis, Hou	156	1377.2	3.03

Year	Lg	Player, Team	G	Inn	WS
1990	AL	Rafael Palmeiro, Tex	146	1255.2	3.19
1990	AL	Fred McGriff, Tor	147	1299.0	2.77
1990	AL	Kent Hrbek, Min	120	1021.0	2.30

Year	Lg	Player, Team	G	Inn	WS
1990	NL	Mark Grace, ChC	153	1315.1	3.95
1990	NL	Andres Galarraga, Mon	154	1318.1	3.00
1990	NL	Will Clark, SF	153	1338.1	2.29

Year	Lg	Player, Team	G	Inn	WS
1991	AL	Wally Joyner, Cal	141	1238.0	3.19
1991	AL	John Olerud, Tor	135	1126.1	3.09
1991	AL	Mark McGwire, Oak	152	1262.2	2.86

Year	Lg	Player, Team	G	Inn	WS
1991	NL	Mark Grace, ChC	160	1404.1	4.13
1991	NL	Will Clark, SF	144	1234.1	2.92
1991	NL	Eddie Murray, LA	149	1301.1	2.71

Year	Lg	Player, Team	G	Inn	WS
1992	AL	John Olerud, Tor	133	1095.2	2.81
1992	AL	Don Mattingly, NYY	143	1223.2	2.69
1992	AL	Rafael Palmeiro, Tex	156	1382.2	2.46

Year	Lg	Player, Team	G	Inn	WS
1992	NL	Mark Grace, ChC	157	1414.0	3.94
1992	NL	Jeff Bagwell, Hou	159	1401.1	2.76
1992	NL	Eric Karros, LA	143	1201.1	2.53

Year	Lg	Player, Team	G	Inn	WS
1993	AL	Rafael Palmeiro, Tex	160	1395.1	3.71
1993	AL	Wally Joyner, KC	140	1194.0	3.26
1993	AL	John Olerud, Tor	137	1205.1	2.54

Year	Lg	Player, Team	G	Inn	WS
1993	NL	Jeff Bagwell, Hou	140	1229.2	2.63
1993	NL	Kevin Young, Pit	135	1056.2	2.58
1993	NL	Mark Grace, ChC	154	1350.1	2.50

Year	Lg	Player, Team	G	Inn	WS
1994	AL	Rafael Palmeiro, Bal	111	976.2	2.51
1994	AL	John Olerud, Tor	104	900.0	2.17
1994	AL	Don Mattingly, NYY	97	836.2	2.17

Year	Lg	Player, Team	G	Inn	WS
1994	NL	Hal Morris, Cin	112	964.1	2.02
1994	NL	Eric Karros, LA	109	930.1	1.93
1994	NL	Jeff Bagwell, Hou	109	945.2	1.91

Year	Lg	Player, Team	G	Inn	WS
1995	AL	Rafael Palmeiro, Bal	142	1238.0	2.95
1995	AL	Tino Martinez, Sea	139	1195.2	2.75
1995	AL	Don Mattingly, NYY	125	1038.0	2.55

Year	Lg	Player, Team	G	Inn	WS
1995	NL	Fred McGriff, Atl	144	1240.2	3.88
1995	NL	Andres Galarraga, Col	142	1229.1	2.43
1995	NL	Eric Karros, LA	143	1271.2	2.42

Year	Lg	Player, Team	G	Inn	WS
1996	AL	Tino Martinez, NYY	151	1305.2	3.47
1996	AL	Rafael Palmeiro, Bal	159	1418.2	2.92
1996	AL	Scott Stahoviak, Min	114	902.2	2.28

Year	Lg	Player, Team	G	Inn	WS
1996	NL	Eric Karros, LA	154	1391.1	3.43
1996	NL	Mark Grace, ChC	141	1218.0	2.64
1996	NL	Fred McGriff, Atl	158	1401.0	2.55

Year	Lg	Player, Team	G	Inn	WS
1997	AL	Tino Martinez, NYY	150	1309.1	3.57
1997	AL	Jeff King, KC	150	1291.0	3.36
1997	AL	Rafael Palmeiro, Bal	155	1356.0	3.00
1997	AL	Tony Clark, Det	158	1383.2	2.83
1997	AL	Paul Sorrento, Sea	139	1057.2	2.07

Year	Lg	Player, Team	G	Inn	WS
1997	NL	Mark Grace, ChC	148	1291.0	3.14
1997	NL	Eric Karros, LA	162	1447.2	2.93
1997	NL	J.T. Snow, SF	156	1333.1	2.31
1997	NL	John Olerud, NYM	146	1236.1	2.11
1997	NL	David Segui, Mon	125	1071.2	2.10

Year	Lg	Player, Team	G	Inn	WS
1998	AL	David Segui, Sea	134	1143.1	3.25
1998	AL	Rafael Palmeiro, Bal	159	1378.1	2.97
1998	AL	Tino Martinez, NYY	142	1215.0	2.49
1998	AL	Carlos Delgado, Tor	141	1256.2	2.39
1998	AL	Jeff King, KC	112	944.1	2.17

Year	Lg	Player, Team	G	Inn	WS
1998	NL	John Olerud, NYM	157	1337.0	4.03
1998	NL	Mark Grace, ChC	156	1390.1	3.42
1998	NL	Rico Brogna, Phi	151	1272.2	3.11
1998	NL	Todd Helton, Col	146	1208.0	2.97
1998	NL	Jeff Bagwell, Hou	147	1311.1	2.80

Year	Lg	Player, Team	G	Inn	WS
1999	AL	Tino Martinez, NYY	158	1342.0	5.18
1999	AL	Tony Clark, Det	132	1147.2	2.02
1999	AL	Carlos Delgado, Tor	147	1305.0	1.97
1999	AL	Jim Thome, Cle	111	953.2	1.95
1999	AL	Jason Giambi, Oak	142	1208.2	1.80

Year	Lg	Player, Team	G	Inn	WS
1999	NL	John Olerud, NYM	160	1385.2	3.57
1999	NL	Rico Brogna, Phi	157	1352.1	3.38
1999	NL	J.T. Snow, SF	160	1344.1	2.98
1999	NL	Travis Lee, Ari	114	869.0	2.47
1999	NL	Todd Helton, Col	156	1310.0	2.38

Year	Lg	Player, Team	G	Inn	WS
2000	AL	John Olerud, Sea	158	1358.2	3.93
2000	AL	Tino Martinez, NYY	154	1290.2	2.77
2000	AL	Ron Coomer, Min	124	1064.2	2.67
2000	AL	Jason Giambi, Oak	124	1064.1	2.53
2000	AL	Jim Thome, Cle	107	923.0	2.40

Year	Lg	Player, Team	G	Inn	WS
2000	NL	Todd Helton, Col	160	1349.0	3.63
2000	NL	Todd Zeile, NYM	151	1270.0	3.62
2000	NL	Eric Karros, LA	153	1331.2	2.73
2000	NL	Derrek Lee, Fla	147	1133.0	2.50
2000	NL	Jeff Bagwell, Hou	158	1362.0	2.29

Year	Lg	Player, Team	G	Inn	WS
2001	AL	Tino Martinez, NYY	149	1293.1	3.99
2001	AL	Doug Mientkiewicz, Min	148	1269.1	2.90
2001	AL	Carlos Delgado, Tor	161	1438.2	2.51
2001	AL	Scott Spiezio, Ana	105	791.2	2.44
2001	AL	John Olerud, Sea	158	1347.2	2.03

Year	Lg	Player, Team	G	Inn	WS
2001	NL	Todd Helton, Col	157	1370.0	3.59
2001	NL	Todd Zeile, NYM	149	1273.1	3.54
2001	NL	Travis Lee, Phi	156	1351.2	3.04
2001	NL	Jeff Bagwell, Hou	160	1414.2	2.42
2001	NL	Mark Grace, Ari	135	1111.0	2.39

Defensive Win Shares Leaders by League and Season—Second Base

Year	Lg	Player, Team	G	Inn	WS
1876	NL	Ed Somerville, Lou	64	606.0	3.68
1877	NL	George Wright, Bos	58	521.0	2.71
1878	NL	Jack Burdock, Bos	60	544.0	3.66
1879	NL	Jack Burdock, Bos	84	753.0	3.62
1880	NL	Fred Dunlap, Cle	85	760.0	3.60
1881	NL	Davy Force, Buf	51	469.0	3.28
1882	NL	Jack Burdock, Bos	83	731.0	3.83
1882	AA	Cub Stricker, Phi	72	635.0	3.73
1883	NL	Jack Farrell, Prv	95	848.0	5.02
1883	AA	Joe Gerhardt, Lou	78	710.0	4.58
1884	NL	Fred Pfeffer, ChN	112	997.0	4.82
1884	UA	Fred Dunlap, STL	100	881.0	5.22
1884	AA	Joe Gerhardt, Lou	106	963.0	6.88
1885	NL	Fred Pfeffer, ChN	109	984.0	4.82
1885	AA	Pop Smith, Pit	106	980.0	6.65
1886	NL	Joe Gerhardt, NYG	123	1055.0	5.28
1886	AA	Bid McPhee, Cin	140	1243.0	5.20
1887	NL	Fred Pfeffer, ChN	123	1089.0	6.78
1887	AA	Bid McPhee, Cin	129	1139.0	6.35
1888	NL	Fred Pfeffer, ChN	135	1186.0	6.23
1888	AA	Bid McPhee, Cin	111	1030.0	6.11
1889	NL	Fred Pfeffer, ChN	134	1224.0	5.87
1889	AA	Bid McPhee, Cin	135	1192.0	8.88
1890	NL	Bid McPhee, Cin	132	1189.0	7.39
1890	PL	Joe Quinn, Bos	130	1137.0	6.80
1890	AA	Jack Crooks, CoC	134	1152.0	4.82
1891	NL	Danny Richardson, NYG	114	1023.0	7.01
1891	AA	Cub Stricker, Bos	139	1220.0	6.55
1892	NL	Bid McPhee, Cin	144	1288.0	7.22
1893	NL	Bid McPhee, Cin	127	1133.0	7.60
1894	NL	Monte Ward, NYG	136	1192.0	6.20
1895	NL	Cupid Childs, Cle	119	1042.0	5.92
1896	NL	Cupid Childs, Cle	132	1168.0	8.56
1897	NL	Heinie Reitz, Bal	128	1107.0	7.02
1898	NL	Bobby Lowe, Bos	145	1282.0	6.49
1899	NL	Bobby Lowe, Bos	148	1302.0	6.23
1900	NL	Claude Ritchey, Pit	123	1110.0	6.40
1901	AL	Kid Gleason, Det	135	1186.0	5.77
1901	NL	Claude Ritchey, Pit	139	1232.0	5.63
1902	AL	Hobe Ferris, Bos	134	1197.0	6.36
1902	NL	Bobby Lowe, ChC	117	1095.0	6.14
1903	AL	Hobe Ferris, Bos	139	1232.0	5.93
1903	NL	Claude Ritchey, Pit	137	1216.0	7.15
1904	AL	Hobe Ferris, Bos	156	1392.0	6.87
1904	NL	Johnny Evers, ChC	152	1337.0	8.32
1905	AL	Hobe Ferris, Bos	140	1256.0	6.13
1905	NL	Billy Gilbert, NYG	115	1025.0	6.16
1906	AL	Nap Lajoie, Cle	130	1197.0	6.65
1906	NL	Claude Ritchey, Pit	151	1337.0	7.32
1907	AL	Nap Lajoie, Cle	128	1135.0	8.94
1907	NL	Johnny Evers, ChC	151	1319.0	7.39
1908	AL	Nap Lajoie, Cle	156	1413.0	10.34
1908	NL	Otto Knabe, Phi	151	1353.0	7.17
1909	AL	Eddie Collins, Phi	152	1376.0	7.71
1909	NL	Johnny Evers, ChC	126	1154.0	5.98
1910	AL	Eddie Collins, Phi	153	1396.0	9.26
1910	NL	Dave Shean, Bos	148	1311.0	7.12
1911	AL	Eddie Collins, Phi	132	1188.0	6.11
1911	NL	Otto Knabe, Phi	142	1249.0	6.18
1912	AL	Morrie Rath, CWS	157	1409.0	9.46
1912	NL	Dick Egan, Cin	149	1350.0	5.70
1913	AL	Nap Lajoie, Cle	126	1120.0	6.11
1913	NL	George Cutshaw, Bro	147	1328.0	6.49
1914	AL	Eddie Collins, Phi	152	1337.0	5.81
1914	NL	Miller Huggins, StL	147	1286.0	6.04
1914	FL	Jack Farrell, Chi	155	1403.0	6.32
1915	AL	Eddie Collins, CWS	155	1399.0	7.75
1915	NL	George Cutshaw, Bro	154	1389.0	7.43
1915	FL	Frank LaPorte, New	146	1342.0	5.64
1916	AL	Eddie Collins, CWS	155	1407.0	6.86
1916	NL	George Cutshaw, Bro	154	1401.0	6.51
1917	AL	Eddie Collins, CWS	156	1418.0	5.79
1917	NL	Larry Doyle, ChC	128	1095.0	4.38
1918	AL	Joe Gedeon, StL	123	1102.0	5.47
1918	NL	George Cutshaw, Pit	126	1130.0	4.41
1919	AL	Del Pratt, NYY	140	1263.0	6.98
1919	NL	Morrie Rath, Cin	138	1247.0	7.03
1920	AL	Eddie Collins, CWS	153	1371.0	8.75
1920	NL	Pete Kilduff, Bro	134	1208.0	6.63
1921	AL	Bucky Harris, Was	154	1383.0	7.74
1921	NL	Johnny Rawlings, 2 tms	146	1252.0	4.92
1922	AL	Aaron Ward, NYY	152	1336.0	6.58
1922	NL	Frank Parkinson, Phi	139	1238.0	5.41
1923	AL	Aaron Ward, NYY	152	1363.0	8.47
1923	NL	Sammy Bohne, Cin	96	834.0	5.27
1924	AL	Aaron Ward, NYY	120	1037.0	5.94
1924	NL	Frankie Frisch, NYG	143	1244.0	6.77
1925	AL	Bucky Harris, Was	144	1275.0	6.29
1925	NL	Hughie Critz, Cin	144	1278.0	7.69
1926	AL	Max Bishop, Phi	119	945.0	6.54
1926	NL	Hughie Critz, Cin	155	1381.0	8.70

Year	Lg	Player, Team	G	Inn	WS
1927	AL	Charlie Gehringer, Det	121	1086.0	5.39
1927	NL	Frankie Frisch, StL	153	1362.0	11.06
1928	AL	Max Bishop, Phi	125	1091.0	6.27
1928	NL	Freddie Maguire, ChC	138	1252.0	8.04
1929	AL	Ski Melillo, StL	141	1219.0	7.19
1929	NL	Rogers Hornsby, ChC	156	1381.0	5.88
1930	AL	Charlie Gehringer, Det	154	1352.0	8.19
1930	NL	Frankie Frisch, StL	123	1123.0	7.54
1931	AL	Ski Melillo, StL	151	1311.0	7.21
1931	NL	Freddie Maguire, Bos	148	1293.0	7.54
1932	AL	Tony Lazzeri, NYY	133	1187.0	6.66
1932	NL	Rabbit Maranville, Bos	149	1304.0	6.84
1933	AL	Charlie Gehringer, Det	155	1397.0	8.33
1933	NL	Hughie Critz, NYG	133	1198.0	10.69
1934	AL	Charlie Gehringer, Det	154	1361.0	7.04
1934	NL	Hughie Critz, NYG	137	1196.0	8.56
1935	AL	Charlie Gehringer, Det	149	1318.0	7.11
1935	NL	Billy Herman, ChC	154	1394.0	7.86
1936	AL	Charlie Gehringer, Det	154	1359.0	6.98
1936	NL	B. Whitehead, NYG	153	1353.0	8.44
1937	AL	Jackie Hayes, CWS	143	1236.0	8.48
1937	NL	B. Whitehead, NYG	152	1346.0	9.12
1938	AL	Joe Gordon, NYY	126	1129.0	6.42
1938	NL	Billy Herman, ChC	151	1362.0	8.96
1939	AL	Joe Gordon, NYY	151	1333.0	6.95
1939	NL	Lonny Frey, Cin	124	1114.0	7.11
1940	AL	Joe Gordon, NYY	155	1373.0	7.43
1940	NL	Lonny Frey, Cin	150	1365.0	7.66
1941	AL	Jimmy Bloodworth, Was	132	1198.0	6.32
1941	NL	Lonny Frey, Cin	145	1300.0	7.05
1942	AL	Jimmy Bloodworth, Det	134	1204.0	7.31
1942	NL	Lonny Frey, Cin	140	1249.0	7.06
1943	AL	Joe Gordon, NYY	152	1384.0	8.40
1943	NL	Lonny Frey, Cin	144	1292.0	7.92
1944	AL	Snuffy Stirnweiss, NYY	154	1390.0	8.92
1944	NL	Woody Williams, Cin	155	1397.0	8.55
1945	AL	Eddie Mayo, Det	124	1090.0	7.43
1945	NL	Don Johnson, ChC	138	1200.0	6.92
1946	AL	Bobby Doerr, Bos	151	1340.0	10.44
1946	NL	Red Schoendienst, StL	128	1144.0	7.26
1947	AL	Bobby Doerr, Bos	146	1268.0	7.79
1947	NL	Emil Verban, Phi	155	1328.0	8.37
1948	AL	Snuffy Stirnweiss, NYY	141	1208.0	7.56
1948	NL	Danny Murtaugh, Pit	146	1250.0	7.15
1949	AL	Bobby Doerr, Bos	139	1253.0	8.68
1949	NL	Red Schoendienst, StL	138	1210.0	8.56
1950	AL	Jerry Priddy, Det	157	1395.0	11.03
1950	NL	Red Schoendienst, StL	143	1254.0	7.58
1951	AL	Bobby Avila, Cle	136	1201.0	7.52
1951	NL	Jackie Robinson, Bro	150	1255.0	8.95
1952	AL	Nellie Fox, CWS	151	1347.0	9.24
1952	NL	Red Schoendienst, StL	142	1232.0	7.81
1953	AL	Bobby Avila, Cle	140	1225.0	8.83
1953	NL	Red Schoendienst, StL	140	1210.0	7.69
1954	AL	Bobby Avila, Cle	141	1215.0	8.19
1954	NL	Davey Williams, NYG	142	1239.0	8.05
1955	AL	Nellie Fox, CWS	154	1361.0	8.67
1955	NL	Red Schoendienst, StL	142	1238.0	6.12
1956	AL	Nellie Fox, CWS	154	1382.0	7.84
1956	NL	Johnny Temple, Cin	154	1342.0	6.25
1957	AL	Nellie Fox, CWS	155	1388.0	8.15
1957	NL	Don Blasingame, StL	154	1412.0	8.87
1958	AL	Nellie Fox, CWS	155	1382.0	7.77
1958	NL	Bill Mazeroski, Pit	152	1340.0	8.87
1959	AL	Nellie Fox, CWS	156	1408.0	7.96
1959	NL	Charlie Neal, LA	151	1360.0	9.39
1960	AL	Marv Breeding, Bal	152	1257.0	7.46
1960	NL	Bill Mazeroski, Pit	151	1350.0	9.03
1961	AL	Chuck Schilling, Bos	158	1389.0	8.93
1961	NL	Bill Mazeroski, Pit	152	1334.0	8.16
1962	AL	Jerry Kindall, Cle	154	1357.0	8.29
1962	NL	Bill Mazeroski, Pit	159	1418.0	11.64
1963	AL	Bobby Richardson, NYY	150	1356.0	8.14
1963	NL	Bill Mazeroski, Pit	138	1262.0	9.97
1964	AL	Jerry Adair, Bal	153	1367.0	9.09
1964	NL	Bill Mazeroski, Pit	162	1442.0	8.94
1965	AL	Jerry Adair, Bal	157	1412.0	9.43
1965	NL	Bill Mazeroski, Pit	127	1104.0	7.47
1966	AL	Bobby Knoop, Cal	161	1405.0	8.23
1966	NL	Bill Mazeroski, Pit	162	1454.0	10.76
1967	AL	Horace Clarke, NYY	140	1290.0	8.11
1967	NL	Tito Fuentes, SF	130	945.0	6.17
1968	AL	Horace Clarke, NYY	139	1222.0	8.29
1968	NL	Felix Millan, Atl	145	1307.0	6.73
1969	AL	Horace Clarke, NYY	156	1383.0	7.05
1969	NL	Felix Millan, Atl	162	1435.0	7.85
1970	AL	Dave Johnson, Bal	149	1305.0	7.95
1970	NL	Tommy Helms, Cin	148	1199.0	7.18
1971	AL	Dick Green, Oak	143	1261.0	9.72
1971	NL	Felix Millan, Atl	141	1262.0	8.16
1972	AL	Jack Brohamer, Cle	132	1167.0	6.74
1972	NL	Dave Cash, Pit	97	874.0	7.50
1973	AL	Bobby Grich, Bal	162	1414.0	10.91
1973	NL	Felix Millan, NYM	153	1375.0	7.89
1974	AL	Bobby Grich, Bal	160	1440.0	8.14
1974	NL	Ted Sizemore, StL	128	1155.0	8.67

Year	Lg	Player, Team	G	Inn	WS
1975	AL	Bobby Grich, Bal	150	1340.0	8.94
1975	NL	Rennie Stennett, Pit	144	1275.0	8.44
1976	AL	Bobby Grich, Bal	140	1232.0	7.33
1976	NL	Manny Trillo, ChC	156	1410.0	9.06
1977	AL	Bump Wills, Tex	150	1319.0	7.85
1977	NL	Davey Lopes, LA	130	1090.0	7.80
1978	AL	Bump Wills, Tex	156	1322.0	7.56
1978	NL	Manny Trillo, ChC	149	1278.0	8.13
1979	AL	Willie Randolph, NYY	153	1329.0	7.81
1979	NL	Ted Sizemore, ChC	96	808.0	6.07
1980	AL	Damaso Garcia, Tor	138	1191.0	7.13
1980	NL	Manny Trillo, Phi	140	1255.0	7.25
1981	AL	Lou Whitaker, Det	108	921.0	4.95
1981	NL	Tom Herr, StL	103	922.0	4.60
1982	AL	Julio Cruz, Sea	151	1312.0	8.15
1982	NL	Glenn Hubbard, Atl	144	1268.0	8.28
1983	AL	Frank White, KC	145	1255.0	8.58
1983	NL	Johnny Ray, Pit	151	1275.0	8.99
1984	AL	Willie Randolph, NYY	142	1261.0	7.13
1984	NL	Ryne Sandberg, ChC	156	1363.0	9.46
1985	AL	Willie Randolph, NYY	143	1244.0	7.92
1985	NL	Glenn Hubbard, Atl	140	1167.0	9.14
1986	AL	Frank White, KC	151	1268.0	7.71
1986	NL	Ron Oester, Cin	151	1336.0	7.56
1987	AL	Frank White, KC	152	1279.1	7.64
1987	NL	Bill Doran, Hou	162	1399.2	7.75
1988	AL	Frank White, KC	148	1186.1	8.08
1988	NL	Jose Lind, Pit	153	1319.0	7.09

Year	Lg	Player, Team	G	Inn	WS
1989	AL	Frank White, KC	132	1059.1	7.01
1989	AL	Harold Reynolds, Sea	151	1298.1	6.61
1989	AL	Johnny Ray, Cal	130	1157.1	6.49

Year	Lg	Player, Team	G	Inn	WS
1989	NL	Jose Oquendo, StL	156	1360.2	7.84
1989	NL	Ryne Sandberg, ChC	155	1339.1	7.60
1989	NL	Willie Randolph, LA	140	1240.2	7.10

Year	Lg	Player, Team	G	Inn	WS
1990	AL	Jody Reed, Bos	119	984.2	6.80
1990	AL	Harold Reynolds, Sea	160	1406.1	6.63
1990	AL	Scott Fletcher, CWS	151	1321.1	6.19

Year	Lg	Player, Team	G	Inn	WS
1990	NL	Jose Lind, Pit	152	1275.1	8.54
1990	NL	Ryne Sandberg, ChC	154	1315.0	6.93
1990	NL	Robby Thompson, SF	142	1167.0	5.84

Year	Lg	Player, Team	G	Inn	WS
1991	AL	Harold Reynolds, Sea	159	1402.1	7.19
1991	AL	Roberto Alomar, Tor	160	1420.2	6.96
1991	AL	Chuck Knoblauch, Min	148	1240.1	6.90

Year	Lg	Player, Team	G	Inn	WS
1991	NL	Ryne Sandberg, ChC	157	1374.2	8.15
1991	NL	Jose Lind, Pit	149	1242.1	7.47
1991	NL	Juan Samuel, LA	152	1317.2	6.41

Year	Lg	Player, Team	G	Inn	WS
1992	AL	Jody Reed, Bos	142	1256.0	7.99
1992	AL	Carlos Baerga, Cle	160	1434.0	6.97
1992	AL	Chuck Knoblauch, Min	154	1339.2	6.64

Year	Lg	Player, Team	G	Inn	WS
1992	NL	Ryne Sandberg, ChC	157	1379.1	8.26
1992	NL	Jose Lind, Pit	134	1190.2	7.14
1992	NL	Robby Thompson, SF	120	1051.0	5.41

Year	Lg	Player, Team	G	Inn	WS
1993	AL	Scott Fletcher, Bos	116	982.1	6.92
1993	AL	Jose Lind, KC	136	1152.2	6.58
1993	AL	Roberto Alomar, Tor	151	1305.1	6.35

Year	Lg	Player, Team	G	Inn	WS
1993	NL	Mark Lemke, Atl	150	1299.2	9.25
1993	NL	Jody Reed, LA	132	1134.2	7.64
1993	NL	Craig Biggio, Hou	155	1352.2	7.10

Year	Lg	Player, Team	G	Inn	WS
1994	AL	Jody Reed, Mil	106	931.1	6.49
1994	AL	Roberto Alomar, Tor	106	873.1	5.04
1994	AL	Mark McLemore, Bal	96	816.0	4.85

Year	Lg	Player, Team	G	Inn	WS
1994	NL	Mark Lemke, Atl	103	899.0	6.44
1994	NL	Craig Biggio, Hou	113	979.2	4.86
1994	NL	Carlos Garcia, Pit	98	855.0	3.76

Year	Lg	Player, Team	G	Inn	WS
1995	AL	Carlos Baerga, Cle	134	1165.0	6.65
1995	AL	Luis Alicea, Bos	132	1150.2	6.17
1995	AL	Roberto Alomar, Tor	128	1126.2	5.31

Year	Lg	Player, Team	G	Inn	WS
1995	NL	Mark Lemke, Atl	115	967.1	7.05
1995	NL	Mike Lansing, Mon	127	1105.1	6.59
1995	NL	Bret Boone, Cin	138	1214.1	5.90

Year	Lg	Player, Team	G	Inn	WS
1996	AL	Roberto Alomar, Bal	141	1217.2	7.33
1996	AL	Fernando Vina, Mil	137	1165.2	6.44
1996	AL	Mark McLemore, Tex	147	1279.1	6.31

Year	Lg	Player, Team	G	Inn	WS
1996	NL	Mark Lemke, Atl	133	1166.1	7.43
1996	NL	Mike Lansing, Mon	159	1368.0	7.16
1996	NL	Delino DeShields, LA	154	1315.1	6.58

Year	Lg	Player, Team	G	Inn	WS
1997	AL	Roberto Alomar, Bal	109	896.2	6.00
1997	AL	Damion Easley, Det	137	1161.2	5.13
1997	AL	Chuck Knoblauch, Min	153	1316.2	4.81
1997	AL	Scott Spiezio, Oak	146	1256.0	4.71
1997	AL	Tony Fernandez, Cle	109	840.1	4.32

Year	Lg	Player, Team	G	Inn	WS
1997	NL	Craig Biggio, Hou	160	1384.1	7.46
1997	NL	Mike Lansing, Mon	144	1234.0	7.06
1997	NL	Bret Boone, Cin	136	1115.1	6.81
1997	NL	Mark Lemke, Atl	104	849.2	6.44
1997	NL	Eric Young, 2 tms	154	1327.1	6.37

Year	Lg	Player, Team	G	Inn	WS
1998	AL	Chuck Knoblauch, NYY	149	1292.2	7.52
1998	AL	Roberto Alomar, Bal	144	1236.1	6.66
1998	AL	Jose Offerman, KC	152	1325.1	6.11
1998	AL	Miguel Cairo, TB	148	1233.0	6.06
1998	AL	Damion Easley, Det	140	1179.1	6.04

Year	Lg	Player, Team	G	Inn	WS
1998	NL	Fernando Vina, Mil	158	1382.2	8.79
1998	NL	Quilvio Veras, SD	131	1126.0	8.68
1998	NL	Bret Boone, Cin	156	1358.0	6.65
1998	NL	Mike Lansing, Col	153	1275.0	6.48
1998	NL	Tony Womack, Pit	152	1316.0	6.08

Year	Lg	Player, Team	G	Inn	WS
1999	AL	Roberto Alomar, Cle	156	1306.1	7.85
1999	AL	Randy Velarde, 2 tms	156	1358.1	6.04
1999	AL	Mark McLemore, Tex	135	1158.2	5.59
1999	AL	Damion Easley, Det	147	1229.0	5.51
1999	AL	Miguel Cairo, TB	117	994.0	5.43

Year	Lg	Player, Team	G	Inn	WS
1999	NL	Craig Biggio, Hou	155	1351.1	8.73
1999	NL	Pokey Reese, Cin	146	1222.2	8.58
1999	NL	Bret Boone, Atl	151	1296.2	7.86
1999	NL	Edgardo Alfonzo, NYM	158	1380.2	7.44
1999	NL	Quilvio Veras, SD	119	1003.0	5.65

Year	Lg	Player, Team	G	Inn	WS
2000	AL	Randy Velarde, Oak	122	1032.0	6.53
2000	AL	Ray Durham, CWS	151	1303.1	5.92
2000	AL	Mark McLemore, Sea	129	1091.1	5.85
2000	AL	Damion Easley, Det	125	1069.2	5.79
2000	AL	Roberto Alomar, Cle	155	1309.1	5.60

Year	Lg	Player, Team	G	Inn	WS
2000	NL	Jeff Kent, SF	150	1258.0	7.03
2000	NL	Pokey Reese, Cin	133	1129.0	6.73
2000	NL	Jay Bell, Ari	145	1243.2	6.47
2000	NL	Edgardo Alfonzo, NYM	146	1240.2	6.44
2000	NL	Mark Grudzielanek, LA	148	1284.2	5.80

Year	Lg	Player, Team	G	Inn	WS
2001	AL	Ray Durham, CWS	150	1294.1	7.13
2001	AL	Frank Menechino, Oak	136	1160.2	7.06
2001	AL	Roberto Alomar, Cle	157	1324.0	6.94
2001	AL	Bret Boone, Sea	156	1370.0	6.55
2001	AL	Alfonso Soriano, NYY	156	1384.1	6.42

Year	Lg	Player, Team	G	Inn	WS
2001	NL	Fernando Vina, StL	151	1299.1	6.12
2001	NL	Jeff Kent, SF	140	1171.0	6.12
2001	NL	Marlon Anderson, Phi	140	1210.2	5.84
2001	NL	Eric Young, ChC	147	1244.2	5.47
2001	NL	Edgardo Alfonzo, NYM	122	1026.1	5.39

Defensive Win Shares Leaders by League and Season—Third Base

Year	Lg	Player, Team	G	Inn	WS
1876	NL	Joe Battin, StL	63	572.0	3.82
1877	NL	Bob Ferguson, Har	56	500.0	2.63
1878	NL	Ezra Sutton, Bos	59	535.0	3.09
1879	NL	Ned Williamson, ChN	70	640.0	4.53
1880	NL	George Bradley, Prv	57	497.0	3.62
1881	NL	Ned Williamson, ChN	76	677.0	4.71
1882	NL	Ned Williamson, ChN	83	747.0	4.92
1882	AA	Hick Carpenter, Cin	80	721.0	3.84
1883	NL	Ezra Sutton, Bos	93	812.0	4.78
1883	AA	Arlie Latham, StL	98	873.0	5.55
1884	NL	Ezra Sutton, Bos	110	1001.0	5.84
1884	UA	Yank Robinson, Bal	71	669.0	5.17
1884	AA	Arlie Latham, StL	110	985.0	9.02
1885	NL	Ned Williamson, ChN	113	997.0	5.80
1885	AA	Arlie Latham, StL	109	981.0	5.76
1886	NL	Tom Burns, ChN	112	1012.0	5.46
1886	AA	Frank Hankinson, NY	136	1182.0	8.27
1887	NL	Art Whitney, Pit	119	1072.0	7.40
1887	AA	Arlie Latham, StL	132	1170.0	7.77
1888	NL	Billy Nash, Bos	105	975.0	6.43
1888	AA	Billy Shindle, Bal	135	1183.0	9.91
1889	NL	Billy Nash, Bos	128	1126.0	7.11
1889	AA	Billy Shindle, Bal	138	1191.0	8.49
1890	NL	Tom Burns, ChN	139	1237.0	7.09
1890	PL	Billy Nash, Bos	129	1122.0	9.24
1890	AA	Charlie Reilly, CoC	137	1192.0	9.18
1891	NL	Arlie Latham, Cin	135	1180.0	6.32
1891	AA	Pete Gilbert, Bal	139	1217.0	6.75
1892	NL	Billy Nash, Bos	135	1190.0	8.21
1893	NL	Billy Nash, Bos	128	1143.0	7.08
1894	NL	Billy Nash, Bos	132	1165.0	7.11
1895	NL	Lave Cross, Phi	125	1059.0	8.67
1896	NL	Charlie Irwin, Cin	127	1103.0	7.28
1897	NL	Jimmy Collins, Bos	134	1185.0	8.17
1898	NL	Bobby Wallace, Cle	141	1238.0	9.30
1899	NL	Jimmy Collins, Bos	151	1330.0	10.88
1900	NL	Jimmy Collins, Bos	141	1236.0	8.52
1901	AL	Jimmy Collins, Bos	138	1210.0	7.03
1901	NL	Harry Wolverton, Phi	93	845.0	5.75
1902	AL	Lave Cross, Phi	137	1216.0	7.59
1902	NL	Tommy Leach, Pit	134	1183.0	7.30
1903	AL	Jimmy Collins, Bos	130	1172.0	7.29
1903	NL	Ed Gremminger, Bos	140	1229.0	6.86
1904	AL	Lee Tannehill, CWS	153	1368.0	9.37
1904	NL	Tommy Leach, Pit	146	1288.0	9.29
1905	AL	Lee Tannehill, CWS	142	1308.0	8.58
1905	NL	Art Devlin, NYG	153	1350.0	8.08
1906	AL	Lee Tannehill, CWS	99	915.0	8.07
1906	NL	Art Devlin, NYG	148	1298.0	8.73
1907	AL	Bill Bradley, Cle	139	1234.0	7.29
1907	NL	Art Devlin, NYG	140	1252.0	6.63
1908	AL	Lee Tannehill, CWS	136	1213.0	8.58
1908	NL	Art Devlin, NYG	157	1402.0	8.49
1909	AL	Home Run Baker, Phi	146	1318.0	5.47
1909	NL	Art Devlin, NYG	143	1294.0	7.66
1910	AL	Home Run Baker, Phi	146	1349.0	6.89
1910	NL	Art Devlin, NYG	147	1282.0	6.89
1911	AL	Home Run Baker, Phi	148	1355.0	7.31
1911	NL	Eddie Zimmerman, Bro	122	1106.0	6.43
1912	AL	Larry Gardner, Bos	143	1284.0	7.66
1912	NL	Buck Herzog, NYG	140	1220.0	9.00
1913	AL	Jimmy Austin, StL	142	1302.0	5.07
1913	NL	Mike Mowrey, StL	131	1118.0	5.69
1914	AL	Larry Gardner, Bos	153	1368.0	7.91
1914	NL	Red Smith, 2 tms	150	1368.0	8.20
1914	FL	Tex Wisterzil, Bro	149	1301.0	8.62
1915	AL	Ossie Vitt, Det	151	1349.0	9.45
1915	NL	Heine Groh, Cin	131	1191.0	7.27
1915	FL	Mike Mowrey, Pit	151	1337.0	5.34
1916	AL	Ossie Vitt, Det	151	1376.0	11.39
1916	NL	Mike Mowrey, Bro	144	1293.0	7.58
1917	AL	Home Run Baker, NYY	146	1310.0	5.93
1917	NL	H. Zimmerman, NYG	149	1277.0	7.55
1918	AL	Eddie Foster, Was	127	1199.0	6.73
1918	NL	Ollie O'Mara, Bro	121	1087.0	5.78
1919	AL	Larry Gardner, Cle	139	1245.0	7.31
1919	NL	Heine Groh, Cin	121	1087.0	5.90
1920	AL	Larry Gardner, Cle	154	1377.0	9.18
1920	NL	Heine Groh, Cin	144	1280.0	6.21
1921	AL	Larry Gardner, Cle	152	1354.0	7.54
1921	NL	Jimmy Johnston, Bro	150	1332.0	5.48
1922	AL	Bob Jones, Det	119	1016.0	5.86
1922	NL	Babe Pinelli, Cin	156	1385.0	7.30
1923	AL	Willie Kamm, CWS	149	1334.0	7.45
1923	NL	Bernie Friberg, ChC	146	1298.0	7.78
1924	AL	Willie Kamm, CWS	145	1298.0	6.26
1924	NL	Bernie Friberg, ChC	142	1316.0	7.28
1925	AL	Willie Kamm, CWS	152	1365.0	7.15
1925	NL	Pie Traynor, Pit	150	1340.0	9.47
1926	AL	Willie Kamm, CWS	142	1228.0	8.63
1926	NL	Chuck Dressen, Cin	123	1055.0	7.24

Year	Lg	Player, Team	G	Inn	WS
1927	AL	Ossie Bluege, Was	146	1304.0	8.03
1927	NL	Pie Traynor, Pit	143	1262.0	8.94
1928	AL	Willie Kamm, CWS	155	1367.0	7.45
1928	NL	Freddy Lindstrom, NYG	153	1339.0	8.32
1929	AL	Joe Sewell, Cle	152	1348.0	8.28
1929	NL	Pinky Whitney, Phi	154	1348.0	7.69
1930	AL	Marty McManus, Det	130	1117.0	6.96
1930	NL	Wally Gilbert, Bro	150	1323.0	6.81
1931	AL	Ossie Bluege, Was	152	1361.0	6.12
1931	NL	Sparky Adams, StL	138	1220.0	5.91
1932	AL	Willie Kamm, Cle	148	1318.0	8.91
1932	NL	Pinky Whitney, Phi	151	1355.0	6.06
1933	AL	Jimmy Dykes, CWS	151	1323.0	6.43
1933	NL	Pie Traynor, Pit	154	1362.0	5.33
1934	AL	Bill Werber, Bos	130	1143.0	6.09
1934	NL	Stan Hack, ChC	109	879.0	4.41
1935	AL	Bill Werber, Bos	123	1120.0	5.71
1935	NL	Johnny Vergez, Phi	148	1263.0	4.91
1936	AL	Odell Hale, Cle	148	1303.0	6.61
1936	NL	Lew Riggs, Cin	140	1225.0	6.16
1937	AL	Harlond Clift, StL	155	1352.0	7.34
1937	NL	Stan Hack, ChC	150	1348.0	5.77
1938	AL	Harlond Clift, StL	149	1273.0	6.66
1938	NL	Stan Hack, ChC	152	1362.0	6.73
1939	AL	Ken Keltner, Cle	154	1344.0	7.83
1939	NL	Cookie Lavagetto, Bro	149	1335.0	6.49
1940	AL	Harlond Clift, StL	147	1292.0	6.06
1940	NL	Bill Werber, Cin	143	1272.0	6.77
1941	AL	Ken Keltner, Cle	149	1304.0	8.38
1941	NL	Bill Werber, Cin	107	996.0	7.30
1942	AL	Ken Keltner, Cle	151	1351.0	6.55
1942	NL	Pinky May, Phi	107	836.0	4.56
1943	AL	Bill Johnson, NYY	155	1415.0	8.29
1943	NL	Pinky May, Phi	132	1117.0	5.07
1944	AL	Mark Christman, StL	145	1320.0	8.92
1944	NL	Whitey Kurowski, StL	146	1275.0	5.77
1945	AL	George Kell, Phi	147	1342.0	7.23
1945	NL	Steve Mesner, Cin	148	1302.0	8.93
1946	AL	George Kell, 2 tms	131	1207.0	5.30
1946	NL	Lee Handley, Pit	102	882.0	4.05
1947	AL	Hank Majeski, Phi	134	1209.0	5.47
1947	NL	Frankie Gustine, Pit	156	1355.0	5.76
1948	AL	Johnny Pesky, Bos	141	1231.0	5.15
1948	NL	Frankie Gustine, Pit	118	983.0	5.26
1949	AL	Johnny Pesky, Bos	148	1313.0	6.69
1949	NL	Bob Elliott, Bos	130	1160.0	5.21
1950	AL	Al Rosen, Cle	154	1368.0	7.00
1950	NL	Puddin' Head Jones, Phi	157	1394.0	5.67
1951	AL	Al Rosen, Cle	154	1377.0	5.07
1951	NL	Puddin' Head Jones, Phi	147	1301.0	4.87
1952	AL	Hector Rodriguez, CWS	113	952.0	4.75
1952	NL	Puddin' Head Jones, Phi	147	1322.0	5.80
1953	AL	Al Rosen, Cle	154	1355.0	5.66
1953	NL	Puddin' Head Jones, Phi	147	1258.0	6.08
1954	AL	Jim Finigan, Phi	136	1154.0	4.30
1954	NL	Puddin' Head Jones, Phi	141	1232.0	6.10
1955	AL	Andy Carey, NYY	135	1219.0	5.18
1955	NL	Ken Boyer, StL	139	1070.0	4.37
1956	AL	Al Rosen, Cle	116	990.0	3.91
1956	NL	Ken Boyer, StL	149	1279.0	5.24
1957	AL	Frank Malzone, Bos	153	1365.0	5.86
1957	NL	Don Hoak, Cin	149	1326.0	5.00
1958	AL	Frank Malzone, Bos	155	1379.0	5.78
1958	NL	Ken Boyer, StL	144	1291.0	7.72
1959	AL	Frank Malzone, Bos	154	1364.0	5.80
1959	NL	Ken Boyer, StL	143	1241.0	5.96
1960	AL	Brooks Robinson, Bal	152	1356.0	7.08
1960	NL	Ken Boyer, StL	146	1260.0	7.77
1961	AL	Clete Boyer, NYY	141	1202.0	7.23
1961	NL	Ken Boyer, StL	153	1359.0	5.73
1962	AL	Clete Boyer, NYY	157	1402.0	7.99
1962	NL	Ken Boyer, StL	160	1435.0	5.36
1963	AL	Brooks Robinson, Bal	160	1424.0	7.00
1963	NL	Ron Santo, ChC	162	1457.0	5.81
1964	AL	Brooks Robinson, Bal	163	1456.0	6.32
1964	NL	Ron Santo, ChC	161	1424.0	6.86
1965	AL	Clete Boyer, NYY	147	1255.0	6.99
1965	NL	Ron Santo, ChC	164	1472.0	5.81
1966	AL	Max Alvis, Cle	157	1414.0	5.56
1966	NL	Ron Santo, ChC	152	1355.0	5.05
1967	AL	Brooks Robinson, Bal	158	1410.0	7.15
1967	NL	Ron Santo, ChC	161	1447.0	7.22
1968	AL	Brooks Robinson, Bal	162	1443.0	6.93
1968	NL	Ron Santo, ChC	162	1447.0	6.57
1969	AL	Brooks Robinson, Bal	156	1376.0	6.96
1969	NL	Doug Rader, Hou	154	1328.0	5.77
1970	AL	Graig Nettles, Cle	154	1310.0	8.65
1970	NL	Doug Rader, Hou	154	1390.0	6.58
1971	AL	Graig Nettles, Cle	158	1419.0	9.76
1971	NL	Ron Santo, ChC	149	1305.0	4.94
1972	AL	Graig Nettles, Cle	150	1342.0	7.07
1972	NL	Doug Rader, Hou	152	1365.0	6.17
1973	AL	Graig Nettles, NYY	157	1381.0	7.39
1973	NL	Darrell Evans, Atl	146	1315.0	6.69
1974	AL	Aurelio Rodriguez, Det	159	1380.0	7.06
1974	NL	Mike Schmidt, Phi	162	1435.0	8.62

Year	Lg	Player, Team	G	Inn	WS
1975	AL	Graig Nettles, NYY	157	1399.0	6.60
1975	NL	Darrell Evans, Atl	156	1371.0	7.67
1976	AL	Graig Nettles, NYY	158	1438.0	7.13
1976	NL	Mike Schmidt, Phi	160	1428.0	7.52
1977	AL	George Brett, KC	135	1179.0	6.82
1977	NL	Mike Schmidt, Phi	149	1317.0	5.74
1978	AL	Graig Nettles, NYY	159	1404.0	6.70
1978	NL	Darrell Evans, SF	155	1379.0	6.04
1979	AL	Buddy Bell, Tex	147	1238.0	6.43
1979	NL	Mike Schmidt, Phi	157	1338.0	6.58
1980	AL	Doug DeCinces, Bal	142	1219.0	7.36
1980	NL	Mike Schmidt, Phi	149	1320.0	6.71
1981	AL	John Castino, Min	98	880.0	4.37
1981	NL	Art Howe, Hou	98	818.0	4.22
1982	AL	Buddy Bell, Tex	145	1252.0	6.43
1982	NL	Tim Wallach, Mon	156	1406.0	5.95
1983	AL	Gary Gaetti, Min	154	1338.0	6.44
1983	NL	Mike Schmidt, Phi	153	1346.0	7.12
1984	AL	Wade Boggs, Bos	156	1353.0	7.93
1984	NL	Tim Wallach, Mon	160	1390.0	8.54
1985	AL	Gary Gaetti, Min	156	1262.0	6.32
1985	NL	Tim Wallach, Mon	154	1330.0	8.34
1986	AL	Gary Gaetti, Min	156	1345.0	7.37
1986	NL	Terry Pendleton, StL	156	1371.0	8.50
1987	AL	Gary Gaetti, Min	150	1293.1	5.37
1987	NL	Tim Wallach, Mon	150	1307.1	6.92
1988	AL	Kelly Gruber, Tor	156	1314.0	6.72
1988	NL	Tim Wallach, Mon	153	1344.0	7.55

Year	Lg	Player, Team	G	Inn	WS
1989	AL	Jack Howell, Cal	142	1211.0	7.28
1989	AL	Steve Buechele, Tex	145	1153.1	7.00
1989	AL	Wade Boggs, Bos	152	1339.1	5.87

Year	Lg	Player, Team	G	Inn	WS
1989	NL	Ken Caminiti, Hou	160	1414.2	8.09
1989	NL	Terry Pendleton, StL	161	1390.0	7.45
1989	NL	Tim Wallach, Mon	153	1357.1	5.21

Year	Lg	Player, Team	G	Inn	WS
1990	AL	Gary Gaetti, Min	151	1291.0	6.42
1990	AL	Kevin Seitzer, KC	152	1257.2	6.30
1990	AL	Robin Ventura, CWS	147	1210.0	4.67

Year	Lg	Player, Team	G	Inn	WS
1990	NL	Tim Wallach, Mon	161	1425.2	7.46
1990	NL	Ken Caminiti, Hou	149	1249.1	5.09
1990	NL	Charlie Hayes, Phi	146	1236.2	4.77

Year	Lg	Player, Team	G	Inn	WS
1991	AL	Mike Pagliarulo, Min	118	913.1	5.42
1991	AL	Gary Gaetti, Cal	152	1339.2	5.23
1991	AL	Kelly Gruber, Tor	111	977.1	4.88

Year	Lg	Player, Team	G	Inn	WS
1991	NL	Terry Pendleton, Atl	148	1283.2	6.48
1991	NL	Ken Caminiti, Hou	152	1308.2	5.93
1991	NL	Charlie Hayes, Phi	138	1043.2	4.95

Year	Lg	Player, Team	G	Inn	WS
1992	AL	Robin Ventura, CWS	157	1395.1	7.11
1992	AL	Gregg Jefferies, KC	146	1288.1	4.77
1992	AL	Leo Gomez, Bal	137	1221.2	4.18

Year	Lg	Player, Team	G	Inn	WS
1992	NL	Terry Pendleton, Atl	158	1389.0	6.26
1992	NL	Gary Sheffield, SD	144	1247.2	5.74
1992	NL	Tim Wallach, Mon	85	700.2	4.27

Year	Lg	Player, Team	G	Inn	WS
1993	AL	Wade Boggs, NYY	134	1122.2	5.22
1993	AL	Robin Ventura, CWS	155	1367.0	4.99
1993	AL	B.J. Surhoff, Mil	121	1013.2	4.24

Year	Lg	Player, Team	G	Inn	WS
1993	NL	Terry Pendleton, Atl	161	1392.2	6.72
1993	NL	Jeff King, Pit	156	1366.2	5.67
1993	NL	Ken Caminiti, Hou	143	1237.0	5.14

Year	Lg	Player, Team	G	Inn	WS
1994	AL	Robin Ventura, CWS	108	930.0	4.07
1994	AL	Scott Cooper, Bos	104	882.0	3.97
1994	AL	Gary Gaetti, KC	85	708.1	3.50

Year	Lg	Player, Team	G	Inn	WS
1994	NL	Matt Williams, SF	110	965.1	3.80
1994	NL	Bobby Bonilla, NYM	107	917.2	3.51
1994	NL	Charlie Hayes, Col	110	955.1	3.48

Year	Lg	Player, Team	G	Inn	WS
1995	AL	Travis Fryman, Det	144	1275.0	7.54
1995	AL	Tim Naehring, Bos	124	1077.2	3.94
1995	AL	Wade Boggs, NYY	117	935.0	3.83

Year	Lg	Player, Team	G	Inn	WS
1995	NL	Charlie Hayes, Phi	141	1255.0	4.68
1995	NL	Terry Pendleton, Fla	129	1129.1	3.87
1995	NL	Ken Caminiti, SD	143	1226.0	3.73

Year	Lg	Player, Team	G	Inn	WS
1996	AL	Robin Ventura, CWS	150	1274.1	5.49
1996	AL	Travis Fryman, Det	128	1116.1	4.97
1996	AL	Dave Hollins, 2 tms	144	1226.1	4.57

Year	Lg	Player, Team	G	Inn	WS
1996	NL	Vinny Castilla, Col	160	1374.0	8.50
1996	NL	Ken Caminiti, SD	145	1274.0	6.89
1996	NL	Shane Andrews, Mon	123	939.0	5.14

Year	Lg	Player, Team	G	Inn	WS
1997	AL	Jeff Cirillo, Mil	150	1294.1	6.46
1997	AL	Cal Ripken Jr., Bal	162	1401.0	6.02
1997	AL	Travis Fryman, Det	153	1331.2	5.81
1997	AL	Matt Williams, Cle	151	1284.2	4.97
1997	AL	Scott Brosius, Oak	107	825.2	4.37

Year	Lg	Player, Team	G	Inn	WS
1997	NL	Scott Rolen, Phi	155	1337.0	5.91
1997	NL	Vinny Castilla, Col	157	1372.0	4.88
1997	NL	Edgardo Alfonzo, NYM	143	1117.0	4.77
1997	NL	Kevin Orie, ChC	112	901.0	4.56
1997	NL	Gary Gaetti, StL	132	1075.1	4.44

Year	Lg	Player, Team	G	Inn	WS
1998	AL	John Valentin, Bos	153	1325.2	7.03
1998	AL	Robin Ventura, CWS	161	1380.2	6.18
1998	AL	Scott Brosius, NYY	150	1312.2	5.87
1998	AL	Travis Fryman, Cle	144	1266.0	4.51
1998	AL	Cal Ripken Jr., Bal	161	1365.1	4.09

Year	Lg	Player, Team	G	Inn	WS
1998	NL	Jeff Cirillo, Mil	149	1307.2	7.16
1998	NL	Scott Rolen, Phi	159	1419.0	5.82
1998	NL	Shane Andrews, Mon	147	1232.0	5.75
1998	NL	Vinny Castilla, Col	162	1422.2	4.84
1998	NL	Edgardo Alfonzo, NYM	144	1232.2	4.65

Year	Lg	Player, Team	G	Inn	WS
1999	AL	Scott Brosius, NYY	132	1150.2	5.91
1999	AL	John Valentin, Bos	111	952.1	5.57
1999	AL	Troy Glaus, Ana	153	1344.0	4.18
1999	AL	Todd Zeile, Tex	155	1354.1	4.09
1999	AL	Joe Randa, KC	156	1355.1	3.85

Year	Lg	Player, Team	G	Inn	WS
1999	NL	Robin Ventura, NYM	160	1356.0	8.16
1999	NL	Matt Williams, Ari	153	1358.0	6.81
1999	NL	Jeff Cirillo, Mil	155	1338.1	6.25
1999	NL	Aaron Boone, Cin	136	1110.0	5.02
1999	NL	Scott Rolen, Phi	112	962.1	4.21

Year	Lg	Player, Team	G	Inn	WS
2000	AL	Tony Batista, Tor	154	1367.0	6.06
2000	AL	Troy Glaus, Ana	156	1373.0	5.50
2000	AL	Scott Brosius, NYY	134	1150.1	5.15
2000	AL	Corey Koskie, Min	139	1164.1	5.10
2000	AL	Travis Fryman, Cle	154	1346.1	4.84

Year	Lg	Player, Team	G	Inn	WS
2000	NL	Jeff Cirillo, Col	155	1321.0	5.29
2000	NL	Adrian Beltre, LA	138	1200.1	5.26
2000	NL	Robin Ventura, NYM	137	1110.2	4.81
2000	NL	Scott Rolen, Phi	128	1080.0	4.39
2000	NL	Mike Lowell, Fla	136	1191.1	4.13

Year	Lg	Player, Team	G	Inn	WS
2001	AL	Eric Chavez, Oak	149	1300.2	6.11
2001	AL	Corey Koskie, Min	150	1308.0	5.75
2001	AL	Scott Brosius, NYY	120	1076.2	5.74
2001	AL	David Bell, Sea	134	1128.0	5.07
2001	AL	Joe Randa, KC	137	1195.2	3.79

Year	Lg	Player, Team	G	Inn	WS
2001	NL	Scott Rolen, Phi	151	1329.1	6.43
2001	NL	Robin Ventura, NYM	139	1141.1	5.84
2001	NL	Jeff Cirillo, Col	137	1165.0	5.48
2001	NL	Mike Lowell, Fla	144	1250.2	4.65
2001	NL	Placido Polanco, StL	103	810.0	4.29

Defensive Win Shares Leaders by League and Season—Shortstop

Year	Lg	Player, Team	G	Inn	WS
1876	NL	George Wright, Bos	68	618.0	3.17
1877	NL	Davy Force, StL	50	457.0	3.31
1878	NL	George Wright, Bos	59	537.0	4.76
1879	NL	George Wright, Prv	85	776.0	5.65
1880	NL	Arthur Irwin, Wor	82	745.0	5.95
1881	NL	Jack Glasscock, Cle	79	705.0	5.08
1882	NL	Jack Glasscock, Cle	83	746.0	5.60
1882	AA	Bill Gleason, StL	79	688.0	3.84
1883	NL	Jack Glasscock, Cle	93	820.0	6.26
1883	AA	Chuck Fulmer, Cin	92	831.0	5.28
1884	NL	Davy Force, Buf	105	942.0	5.61
1884	UA	Walter Hackett, Bos	103	909.0	4.92
1884	AA	Tom McLaughlin, Lou	94	860.0	8.00
1885	NL	Monte Ward, NYG	111	988.0	6.55
1885	AA	Germany Smith, Bro	108	953.0	7.93
1886	NL	Monte Ward, NYG	122	1050.0	7.11
1886	AA	Pop Smith, Pit	98	861.0	7.35
1887	NL	Monte Ward, NYG	129	1113.0	8.68
1887	AA	Bill White, Lou	132	1182.0	7.24
1888	NL	Arthur Irwin, Phi	122	1102.0	7.79
1888	AA	Frank Fennelly, 2 tms	127	1170.0	9.58
1889	NL	Jack Glasscock, Ind	132	1134.0	8.60
1889	AA	Ollie Beard, Cin	141	1243.0	12.25
1890	NL	Bob Allen, Phi	133	1195.0	12.83
1890	PL	Monte Ward, Bro	128	1152.0	9.07
1890	AA	Phil Tomney, Lou	108	983.0	8.26
1891	NL	Herman Long, Bos	139	1231.0	9.71
1891	AA	Tommy Corcoran, Phi	133	1171.0	10.71
1892	NL	Germany Smith, Cin	139	1225.0	12.32
1893	NL	Germany Smith, Cin	130	1167.0	10.54
1894	NL	Hughie Jennings, Bal	128	1114.0	9.41
1895	NL	Bill Dahlen, ChN	129	1128.0	11.70
1896	NL	Hughie Jennings, Bal	130	1152.0	11.99
1897	NL	Hughie Jennings, Bal	116	1034.0	9.24
1898	NL	Tommy Corcoran, Cin	153	1350.0	11.07
1899	NL	Tommy Corcoran, Cin	123	1078.0	8.43
1900	NL	Bones Ely, Pit	130	1140.0	10.02
1901	AL	Billy Clingman, Was	137	1172.0	8.72
1901	NL	Bill Dahlen, Bro	129	1138.0	8.40
1902	AL	Bobby Wallace, StL	131	1173.0	9.21
1902	NL	Herman Long, Bos	107	959.0	7.38
1903	AL	Bobby Wallace, StL	135	1194.0	8.36
1903	NL	Bill Dahlen, Bro	138	1204.0	9.34
1904	AL	Freddy Parent, Bos	155	1387.0	9.14
1904	NL	Joe Tinker, ChC	140	1239.0	10.13
1905	AL	George Davis, CWS	151	1391.0	7.38
1905	NL	Joe Tinker, ChC	149	1346.0	10.01
1906	AL	Terry Turner, Cle	147	1304.0	12.72
1906	NL	Honus Wagner, Pit	137	1215.0	11.26
1907	AL	Bobby Wallace, StL	147	1282.0	7.72
1907	NL	Mickey Doolan, Phi	145	1273.0	9.26
1908	AL	George McBride, Was	155	1391.0	9.31
1908	NL	Joe Tinker, ChC	157	1428.0	12.73
1909	AL	Donie Bush, Det	157	1396.0	8.72
1909	NL	Joe Tinker, ChC	143	1271.0	10.43
1910	AL	George McBride, Was	154	1353.0	8.43
1910	NL	Mickey Doolan, Phi	148	1342.0	10.27
1911	AL	Donie Bush, Det	150	1364.0	9.75
1911	NL	Mickey Doolan, Phi	145	1299.0	10.80
1912	AL	George McBride, Was	152	1349.0	8.85
1912	NL	Honus Wagner, Pit	143	1321.0	11.83
1913	AL	Buck Weaver, CWS	151	1302.0	12.42
1913	NL	Art Fletcher, NYG	136	1209.0	9.05
1914	AL	George McBride, Was	156	1381.0	11.20
1914	NL	Rabbit Maranville, Bos	156	1405.0	13.35
1914	FL	Mickey Doolan, Bal	145	1252.0	10.78
1915	AL	George McBride, Was	146	1295.0	9.47
1915	NL	Buck Herzog, Cin	153	1326.0	10.43
1915	FL	Ernie Johnson, STL	152	1372.0	9.93
1916	AL	George McBride, Was	139	1253.0	10.82
1916	NL	Dave Bancroft, Phi	142	1268.0	10.88
1917	AL	Ray Chapman, Cle	156	1412.0	9.90
1917	NL	Art Fletcher, NYG	151	1338.0	12.67
1918	AL	R. Peckinpaugh, NYY	122	1101.0	8.06
1918	NL	Art Fletcher, NYG	124	1099.0	9.34
1919	AL	R. Peckinpaugh, NYY	121	1090.0	8.09
1919	NL	Art Fletcher, NYG	127	1140.0	8.67
1920	AL	Wally Gerber, StL	154	1359.0	8.72
1920	NL	Dave Bancroft, 2 tms	150	1379.0	10.06
1921	AL	Everett Scott, Bos	154	1356.0	12.71
1921	NL	Rabbit Maranville, Pit	153	1404.0	10.73
1922	AL	Everett Scott, NYY	154	1382.0	11.18
1922	NL	Rabbit Maranville, Pit	138	1221.0	9.65
1923	AL	Wally Gerber, StL	154	1373.0	11.20
1923	NL	Rabbit Maranville, Pit	141	1284.0	8.35
1924	AL	R. Peckinpaugh, Was	155	1345.0	13.09
1924	NL	Glenn Wright, Pit	153	1382.0	9.41
1925	AL	Joe Sewell, Cle	153	1349.0	9.39
1925	NL	Glenn Wright, Pit	153	1351.0	9.54
1926	AL	Joe Sewell, Cle	154	1364.0	9.68
1926	NL	Tommy Thevenow, StL	156	1386.0	11.41

Year	Lg	Player, Team	G	Inn	WS
1927	AL	Mark Koenig, NYY	122	1099.0	7.40
1927	NL	Travis Jackson, NYG	124	1084.0	7.81
1928	AL	Joe Sewell, Cle	137	1188.0	6.80
1928	NL	Hod Ford, Cin	149	1311.0	11.14
1929	AL	Red Kress, StL	146	1284.0	8.33
1929	NL	Charlie Gelbert, StL	146	1281.0	9.85
1930	AL	Joe Cronin, Was	154	1348.0	11.10
1930	NL	Rabbit Maranville, Bos	138	1241.0	8.85
1931	AL	Joe Cronin, Was	155	1375.0	12.05
1931	NL	Charlie Gelbert, StL	130	1154.0	8.22
1932	AL	Joe Cronin, Was	141	1258.0	9.33
1932	NL	Dick Bartell, Phi	154	1384.0	8.66
1933	AL	Billy Rogell, Det	155	1386.0	11.31
1933	NL	Billy Jurges, ChC	143	1209.0	9.31
1934	AL	Billy Rogell, Det	154	1357.0	8.52
1934	NL	Arky Vaughan, Pit	149	1322.0	10.06
1935	AL	Billy Rogell, Det	150	1354.0	9.92
1935	NL	Leo Durocher, StL	142	1228.0	11.51
1936	AL	Frankie Crosetti, NYY	151	1372.0	8.07
1936	NL	Dick Bartell, NYG	144	1276.0	10.10
1937	AL	Luke Appling, CWS	154	1345.0	9.23
1937	NL	Dick Bartell, NYG	128	1140.0	9.18
1938	AL	Joe Cronin, Bos	142	1224.0	9.08
1938	NL	Arky Vaughan, Pit	147	1328.0	8.86
1939	AL	Frankie Crosetti, NYY	152	1338.0	9.91
1939	NL	Billy Myers, Cin	151	1360.0	8.35
1940	AL	Lou Boudreau, Cle	155	1356.0	11.59
1940	NL	Marty Marion, StL	125	1048.0	6.97
1941	AL	Phil Rizzuto, NYY	128	1109.0	9.29
1941	NL	Pee Wee Reese, Bro	151	1342.0	8.78
1942	AL	Phil Rizzuto, NYY	144	1283.0	11.28
1942	NL	Pee Wee Reese, Bro	151	1358.0	11.67
1943	AL	Luke Appling, CWS	155	1386.0	8.75
1943	NL	Eddie Miller, Cin	154	1386.0	10.20
1944	AL	Vern Stephens, StL	143	1282.0	9.12
1944	NL	Marty Marion, StL	144	1257.0	10.67
1945	AL	Vern Stephens, StL	144	1284.0	6.98
1945	NL	Buddy Kerr, NYG	148	1318.0	8.34
1946	AL	Johnny Pesky, Bos	153	1341.0	10.33
1946	NL	Marty Marion, StL	145	1268.0	10.89
1947	AL	Phil Rizzuto, NYY	151	1312.0	11.11
1947	NL	Marty Marion, StL	141	1262.0	10.58
1948	AL	Vern Stephens, Bos	155	1379.0	8.12
1948	NL	Pee Wee Reese, Bro	149	1339.0	9.06
1949	AL	Vern Stephens, Bos	155	1376.0	9.18
1949	NL	Granny Hamner, Phi	154	1380.0	10.71
1950	AL	Phil Rizzuto, NYY	155	1352.0	11.32
1950	NL	Granny Hamner, Phi	157	1403.0	9.17

Year	Lg	Player, Team	G	Inn	WS
1951	AL	Chico Carrasquel, CWS	147	1277.0	10.56
1951	NL	Granny Hamner, Phi	150	1333.0	8.90
1952	AL	Pete Runnels, Was	147	1325.0	9.33
1952	NL	Roy McMillan, Cin	154	1355.0	9.00
1953	AL	Billy Hunter, StL	152	1322.0	10.68
1953	NL	Johnny Logan, Mil	150	1312.0	10.86
1954	AL	Chico Carrasquel, CWS	155	1375.0	10.00
1954	NL	Al Dark, NYG	154	1362.0	9.51
1955	AL	George Strickland, Cle	128	1071.0	8.44
1955	NL	Roy McMillan, Cin	150	1293.0	9.40
1956	AL	Luis Aparicio, CWS	152	1287.0	7.92
1956	NL	Roy McMillan, Cin	150	1327.0	10.62
1957	AL	Gil McDougald, NYY	121	1042.0	7.44
1957	NL	Roy McMillan, Cin	151	1241.0	7.93
1958	AL	Luis Aparicio, CWS	145	1262.0	9.18
1958	NL	Chico Fernandez, Phi	148	1285.0	8.02
1959	AL	Luis Aparicio, CWS	152	1335.0	7.22
1959	NL	Ernie Banks, ChC	154	1385.0	8.68
1960	AL	Luis Aparicio, CWS	153	1358.0	9.14
1960	NL	Maury Wills, LA	145	1226.0	7.83
1961	AL	Tony Kubek, NYY	145	1266.0	9.20
1961	NL	Maury Wills, LA	148	1305.0	8.79
1962	AL	Zoilo Versalles, Min	160	1414.0	10.19
1962	NL	Dick Groat, Pit	161	1428.0	8.72
1963	AL	Ron Hansen, CWS	144	1269.0	10.50
1963	NL	Dick Groat, StL	158	1371.0	8.57
1964	AL	Ron Hansen, CWS	158	1428.0	10.67
1964	NL	Leo Cardenas, Cin	163	1454.0	8.58
1965	AL	Luis Aparicio, Bal	141	1291.0	7.96
1965	NL	Maury Wills, LA	155	1399.0	10.18
1966	AL	Jim Fregosi, Cal	162	1428.0	8.87
1966	NL	Leo Cardenas, Cin	160	1424.0	9.67
1967	AL	Rico Petrocelli, Bos	141	1246.0	9.22
1967	NL	Dal Maxvill, StL	148	1258.0	7.96
1968	AL	Bert Campaneris, Oak	155	1366.0	8.63
1968	NL	Dal Maxvill, StL	151	1263.0	9.79
1969	AL	Leo Cardenas, Min	160	1449.0	10.50
1969	NL	Dal Maxvill, StL	131	1056.0	10.01
1970	AL	Leo Cardenas, Min	160	1404.0	9.61
1970	NL	Bobby Wine, Mon	159	1292.0	8.62
1971	AL	Mark Belanger, Bal	149	1277.0	9.37
1971	NL	Bud Harrelson, NYM	140	1257.0	10.21
1972	AL	Bert Campaneris, Oak	148	1337.0	9.60
1972	NL	Larry Bowa, Phi	150	1300.0	7.26
1973	AL	Freddie Patek, KC	135	1114.0	9.54
1973	NL	Bill Russell, LA	162	1489.0	8.86
1974	AL	Bucky Dent, CWS	154	1313.0	8.74
1974	NL	Dave Concepcion, Cin	160	1382.0	9.96

Year	Lg	Player, Team	G	Inn	WS
1975	AL	Bucky Dent, CWS	157	1402.0	10.21
1975	NL	Dave Concepcion, Cin	130	1110.0	9.92
1976	AL	Mark Belanger, Bal	153	1339.0	10.70
1976	NL	Dave Concepcion, Cin	150	1326.0	10.27
1977	AL	Rick Burleson, Bos	154	1365.0	11.06
1977	NL	Dave Concepcion, Cin	156	1326.0	10.72
1978	AL	Rick Burleson, Bos	144	1305.0	11.42
1978	NL	Ozzie Smith, SD	159	1315.0	10.38
1979	AL	Rick Burleson, Bos	153	1306.0	11.75
1979	NL	Dave Concepcion, Cin	148	1298.0	9.29
1980	AL	Rick Burleson, Bos	155	1345.0	9.47
1980	NL	Ozzie Smith, SD	158	1410.0	10.03
1981	AL	Alan Trammell, Det	105	902.0	6.48
1981	NL	Ozzie Smith, SD	110	986.0	6.13
1982	AL	Alfredo Griffin, Tor	162	1389.0	8.95
1982	NL	Ozzie Smith, StL	139	1257.0	10.38
1983	AL	Cal Ripken Jr., Bal	162	1452.0	10.27
1983	NL	Dale Berra, Pit	161	1432.0	10.77
1984	AL	Cal Ripken Jr., Bal	162	1439.0	9.74
1984	NL	Ozzie Smith, StL	124	1073.0	7.62
1985	AL	Tony Fernandez, Tor	160	1407.0	9.93
1985	NL	Ozzie Smith, StL	158	1412.0	10.54
1986	AL	Cal Ripken Jr., Bal	162	1437.0	9.67
1986	NL	Ozzie Smith, StL	144	1290.0	9.27
1987	AL	Greg Gagne, Min	136	1079.0	9.29
1987	NL	Ozzie Smith, StL	158	1356.1	10.21
1988	AL	Walt Weiss, Oak	147	1241.0	9.74
1988	NL	Ozzie Smith, StL	150	1330.0	7.69

Year	Lg	Player, Team	G	Inn	WS
1989	AL	Cal Ripken Jr., Bal	162	1433.1	10.05
1989	AL	Felix Fermin, Cle	153	1311.0	9.18
1989	AL	Tony Fernandez, Tor	140	1243.0	9.10

Year	Lg	Player, Team	G	Inn	WS
1989	NL	Kevin Elster, NYM	150	1208.1	10.14
1989	NL	Jose Uribe, SF	150	1215.2	7.73
1989	NL	Shawon Dunston, ChC	138	1159.1	7.09

Year	Lg	Player, Team	G	Inn	WS
1990	AL	Ozzie Guillen, CWS	159	1361.1	9.08
1990	AL	Tony Fernandez, Tor	161	1384.0	8.41
1990	AL	Alvaro Espinoza, NYY	150	1209.1	7.45

Year	Lg	Player, Team	G	Inn	WS
1990	NL	Barry Larkin, Cin	156	1344.0	9.80
1990	NL	Spike Owen, Mon	148	1194.1	8.09
1990	NL	Alfredo Griffin, LA	139	1153.2	6.35

Year	Lg	Player, Team	G	Inn	WS
1991	AL	Omar Vizquel, Sea	138	1134.1	8.73
1991	AL	Alvaro Espinoza, NYY	147	1197.0	7.62
1991	AL	Greg Gagne, Min	137	1067.2	7.18

Year	Lg	Player, Team	G	Inn	WS
1991	NL	Barry Larkin, Cin	119	1032.0	9.17
1991	NL	Tony Fernandez, SD	145	1262.2	8.18
1991	NL	Dickie Thon, Phi	146	1277.0	7.22

Year	Lg	Player, Team	G	Inn	WS
1992	AL	Greg Gagne, Min	141	1146.1	8.79
1992	AL	Cal Ripken Jr., Bal	162	1440.0	8.50
1992	AL	Gary DiSarcina, Cal	157	1376.1	6.79

Year	Lg	Player, Team	G	Inn	WS
1992	NL	Ozzie Smith, StL	132	1156.1	8.66
1992	NL	Barry Larkin, Cin	140	1207.2	8.48
1992	NL	Jay Bell, Pit	159	1411.1	7.81

Year	Lg	Player, Team	G	Inn	WS
1993	AL	Omar Vizquel, Sea	155	1330.2	9.05
1993	AL	Greg Gagne, KC	159	1331.0	9.00
1993	AL	John Valentin, Bos	144	1221.2	7.89

Year	Lg	Player, Team	G	Inn	WS
1993	NL	Jay Bell, Pit	154	1349.0	9.90
1993	NL	Ozzie Smith, StL	134	1138.1	8.23
1993	NL	Royce Clayton, SF	153	1328.2	7.93

Year	Lg	Player, Team	G	Inn	WS
1994	AL	Cal Ripken Jr., Bal	112	986.2	6.49
1994	AL	Greg Gagne, KC	106	922.0	6.44
1994	AL	Gary DiSarcina, Cal	110	982.0	5.67

Year	Lg	Player, Team	G	Inn	WS
1994	NL	Jay Bell, Pit	110	943.2	6.56
1994	NL	Barry Larkin, Cin	110	960.1	6.08
1994	NL	Wil Cordero, Mon	109	968.2	5.16

Year	Lg	Player, Team	G	Inn	WS
1995	AL	Omar Vizquel, Cle	136	1187.0	7.80
1995	AL	Cal Ripken Jr., Bal	144	1250.0	7.74
1995	AL	Benji Gil, Tex	130	1100.2	6.44

Year	Lg	Player, Team	G	Inn	WS
1995	NL	Kevin Stocker, Phi	125	1073.1	7.55
1995	NL	Jose Vizcaino, NYM	134	1119.2	7.13
1995	NL	Walt Weiss, Col	136	1140.2	6.91

Year	Lg	Player, Team	G	Inn	WS
1996	AL	Alex S. Gonzalez, Tor	147	1316.0	10.11
1996	AL	Mike Bordick, Oak	155	1338.0	7.94
1996	AL	David Howard, KC	135	1109.0	7.48

Year	Lg	Player, Team	G	Inn	WS
1996	NL	Greg Gagne, LA	127	1126.2	10.60
1996	NL	Barry Larkin, Cin	151	1242.1	6.81
1996	NL	Royce Clayton, StL	113	997.2	6.53

Year	Lg	Player, Team	G	Inn	WS
1997	AL	Jay Bell, KC	149	1271.0	7.45
1997	AL	Alex S. Gonzalez, Tor	125	1102.1	7.36
1997	AL	Derek Jeter, NYY	159	1417.0	7.14
1997	AL	Mike Bordick, Bal	153	1335.1	7.09
1997	AL	Nomar Garciaparra, Bos	153	1344.1	6.77

Year	Lg	Player, Team	G	Inn	WS
1997	NL	Royce Clayton, StL	153	1287.1	7.71
1997	NL	Edgar Renteria, Fla	153	1328.2	7.60
1997	NL	Mark Grudzielanek, Mon	156	1368.1	6.77
1997	NL	Jose Vizcaino, SF	147	1221.0	6.67
1997	NL	Jeff Blauser, Atl	149	1235.0	6.09

Year	Lg	Player, Team	G	Inn	WS
1998	AL	Alex S. Gonzalez, Tor	158	1398.1	8.68
1998	AL	Omar Vizquel, Cle	151	1316.0	8.33
1998	AL	Mike Bordick, Bal	150	1238.1	7.20
1998	AL	Gary DiSarcina, Ana	157	1370.2	6.85
1998	AL	Alex Rodriguez, Sea	160	1389.1	6.38

Year	Lg	Player, Team	G	Inn	WS
1998	NL	Neifi Perez, Col	162	1385.2	9.55
1998	NL	Rey Ordonez, NYM	151	1289.0	8.04
1998	NL	Chris Gomez, SD	143	1191.1	7.92
1998	NL	Ricky Gutierrez, Hou	141	1147.2	7.75
1998	NL	Jose Valentin, Mil	139	1060.2	6.51

Year	Lg	Player, Team	G	Inn	WS
1999	AL	Mike Bordick, Bal	159	1355.0	9.39
1999	AL	Miguel Tejada, Oak	159	1377.1	7.54
1999	AL	Deivi Cruz, Det	155	1300.1	7.31
1999	AL	Nomar Garciaparra, Bos	134	1171.2	7.17
1999	AL	Rey Sanchez, KC	134	1128.2	6.92

Year	Lg	Player, Team	G	Inn	WS
1999	NL	Rey Ordonez, NYM	154	1316.2	9.67
1999	NL	Neifi Perez, Col	157	1369.2	8.87
1999	NL	Barry Larkin, Cin	161	1372.2	8.27
1999	NL	Mike Benjamin, Pit	93	730.2	6.37
1999	NL	Jose Hernandez, 2 tms	137	1054.0	6.08

Year	Lg	Player, Team	G	Inn	WS
2000	AL	Alex Rodriguez, Sea	148	1285.0	8.38
2000	AL	Rey Sanchez, KC	143	1198.0	7.95
2000	AL	Jose Valentin, CWS	141	1212.1	7.77
2000	AL	Cristian Guzman, Min	151	1307.0	7.09
2000	AL	Miguel Tejada, Oak	160	1400.1	6.95

Year	Lg	Player, Team	G	Inn	WS
2000	NL	Neifi Perez, Col	162	1402.2	10.94
2000	NL	Rich Aurilia, SF	140	1193.0	7.19
2000	NL	Tony Womack, Ari	143	1244.0	6.35
2000	NL	Edgar Renteria, StL	149	1258.0	6.33
2000	NL	Pat Meares, Pit	126	1075.0	5.00

Year	Lg	Player, Team	G	Inn	WS
2001	AL	Alex S. Gonzalez, Tor	154	1374.1	9.85
2001	AL	Miguel Tejada, Oak	162	1431.1	7.65
2001	AL	Omar Vizquel, Cle	154	1320.2	6.80
2001	AL	Rey Sanchez, KC	100	851.0	6.60
2001	AL	Derek Jeter, NYY	150	1312.1	5.87

Year	Lg	Player, Team	G	Inn	WS
2001	NL	Orlando Cabrera, Mon	162	1406.2	13.47
2001	NL	Rey Ordonez, NYM	148	1226.1	9.27
2001	NL	Rich Aurilia, SF	149	1313.0	7.21
2001	NL	Edgar Renteria, StL	137	1153.1	6.78
2001	NL	Jimmy Rollins, Phi	157	1388.1	6.72

Defensive Win Shares Leaders by League and Season—Outfield

Year	Lg	Player, Team	G	Inn	WS
1876	NL	Jack Remsen, Har	69	606.0	4.12
1876	NL	Paul Hines, ChN	64	567.0	3.77
1876	NL	Johnny Ryan, Lou	64	586.0	3.23
1877	NL	Orator Shaffer, Lou	60	558.0	3.16
1877	NL	Bill Crowley, Lou	58	525.0	2.84
1877	NL	Jim O'Rourke, Bos	60	548.0	2.84
1878	NL	Jack Remsen, ChN	56	515.0	2.32
1878	NL	Charley Jones, Cin	61	548.0	2.22
1878	NL	Abner Dalrymple, Mil	61	547.0	2.08
1879	NL	Orator Shaffer, ChN	72	664.0	4.05
1879	NL	Charley Jones, Bos	83	753.0	3.84
1879	NL	Paul Hines, Prv	85	776.0	3.63
1880	NL	Abner Dalrymple, ChN	86	775.0	4.64
1880	NL	Paul Hines, Prv	75	706.0	4.44
1880	NL	George Gore, ChN	74	701.0	4.30
1881	NL	George Gore, ChN	72	620.0	3.97
1881	NL	Hardy Richardson, Buf	79	732.0	3.66
1881	NL	Paul Hines, Prv	78	716.0	2.89
1882	NL	Abner Dalrymple, ChN	84	764.0	3.86
1882	NL	Joe Hornung, Bos	84	749.0	3.67
1882	NL	Paul Hines, Prv	82	744.0	3.50
1882	AA	Joe Sommer, Cin	80	721.0	4.63
1882	AA	Jimmy Macullar, Cin	76	705.0	3.13
1882	AA	Jud Birchall, Phi	74	662.0	2.92
1883	NL	George Gore, ChN	92	810.0	5.45
1883	NL	Paul Hines, Prv	89	807.0	4.45
1883	NL	Joe Hornung, Bos	98	860.0	4.19
1883	AA	Hugh Nicol, StL	84	791.0	4.49
1883	AA	Pop Corkhill, Cin	85	750.0	3.70
1883	AA	Charley Jones, Cin	90	803.0	3.48
1884	NL	Paul Hines, Prv	108	1004.0	4.95
1884	NL	Cliff Carroll, Prv	113	1036.0	4.42
1884	NL	Jim Lillie, Buf	114	982.0	4.04
1884	UA	Dave Rowe, STL	92	828.0	3.95
1884	UA	Bill Harbridge, Cin	80	688.0	3.61
1884	UA	Mike Slattery, Bos	96	862.0	3.35
1884	AA	Curt Welch, Tol	107	946.0	6.37
1884	AA	Hugh Nicol, StL	87	833.0	6.08
1884	AA	Steve Brady, NY	110	980.0	4.83
1885	NL	Jim Fogarty, Phi	88	748.0	7.00
1885	NL	George Gore, ChN	109	997.0	5.75
1885	NL	Abner Dalrymple, ChN	113	1016.0	4.43
1885	AA	Curt Welch, StL	112	1002.0	5.51
1885	AA	Hugh Nicol, StL	111	1002.0	4.71
1885	AA	Pete Browning, Lou	112	1002.0	4.61
1886	NL	Ed Andrews, Phi	104	922.0	5.53
1886	NL	George Gore, ChN	118	1034.0	5.07
1886	NL	Sam Thompson, Det	122	1104.0	4.82
1886	AA	Curt Welch, StL	138	1229.0	6.93
1886	AA	Tip O'Neill, StL	138	1229.0	5.59
1886	AA	Chicken Wolf, Lou	123	1108.0	4.87
1887	NL	Jim Fogarty, Phi	123	1073.0	5.15
1887	NL	Dick Johnston, Bos	127	1101.0	4.91
1887	NL	George Gore, NYG	111	963.0	4.88
1887	AA	Curt Welch, StL	123	1069.0	8.36
1887	AA	Pop Corkhill, Cin	128	1099.0	7.42
1887	AA	Pete Browning, Lou	134	1171.0	5.21
1888	NL	Jim Fogarty, Phi	117	1060.0	7.09
1888	NL	Dick Johnston, Bos	135	1225.0	5.54
1888	NL	Ed Andrews, Phi	124	1119.0	5.05
1888	AA	Pop Corkhill, 2 tms	135	1228.0	6.94
1888	AA	Curt Welch, Phi	135	1209.0	6.93
1888	AA	Tommy McCarthy, StL	131	1174.0	6.42
1889	NL	Jimmy McAleer, Cle	110	965.0	6.01
1889	NL	Dick Johnston, Bos	132	1146.0	5.71
1889	NL	George Gore, NYG	120	1057.0	5.08
1889	AA	Charlie Duffee, StL	132	1182.0	7.36
1889	AA	Pop Corkhill, Bro	138	1205.0	5.30
1889	AA	Curt Welch, Phi	125	1094.0	5.09
1890	NL	Walt Wilmot, ChN	139	1237.0	7.84
1890	NL	Bug Holliday, Cin	131	1191.0	5.98
1890	NL	Cliff Carroll, ChN	136	1237.0	5.93

Year	Lg	Player, Team	G	Inn	WS
1890	PL	Jimmy Ryan, Chi	118	1034.0	6.52
1890	PL	Hugh Duffy, Chi	137	1219.0	6.12
1890	PL	Mike Griffin, Phi	115	1014.0	4.85
1890	AA	Jim McTamany, CoC	125	1098.0	5.86
1890	AA	Farmer Weaver, Lou	127	1155.0	5.14
1890	AA	Charlie Hamburg, Lou	133	1206.0	4.80
1891	NL	Steve Brodie, Bos	133	1167.0	5.77
1891	NL	Jimmy Ryan, ChN	117	1051.0	4.83
1891	NL	Mike Griffin, Bro	134	1205.0	4.32
1891	AA	Dummy Hoy, StL	141	1223.0	7.60
1891	AA	Curt Welch, Bal	113	985.0	5.30
1891	AA	Tip O'Neill, StL	129	1105.0	4.85
1892	NL	Jimmy McAleer, Cle	149	1285.0	9.25
1892	NL	Mike Griffin, Bro	127	1120.0	6.79
1892	NL	Hugh Duffy, Bos	146	1264.0	5.49
1893	NL	Steve Brodie, 2 tms	132	1140.0	5.78
1893	NL	Elmer Smith, Pit	128	1111.0	5.56
1893	NL	Joe Kelley, Bal	125	1065.0	4.97
1894	NL	G. Van Haltren, NYG	137	1199.0	6.90
1894	NL	Frank Shugart, StL	122	1080.0	5.32
1894	NL	Eddie Burke, NYG	136	1209.0	5.12
1895	NL	Jimmy McAleer, Cle	131	1116.0	7.29
1895	NL	Steve Brodie, Bal	131	1126.0	5.86
1895	NL	Jake Stenzel, Pit	129	1110.0	5.04
1896	NL	Jimmy McAleer, Cle	116	1049.0	6.24
1896	NL	Bill Lange, ChN	121	1067.0	6.11
1896	NL	Steve Brodie, Bal	132	1168.0	5.77
1897	NL	G. Van Haltren, NYG	129	1122.0	6.61
1897	NL	Billy Hamilton, Bos	126	1109.0	5.60
1897	NL	Dummy Hoy, Cin	128	1076.0	5.38
1898	NL	Hugh Duffy, Bos	152	1340.0	7.10
1898	NL	Bill Lange, ChN	111	984.0	5.51
1898	NL	Ducky Holmes, 2 tms	135	1160.0	5.17
1899	NL	Kip Selbach, Cin	140	1204.0	7.02
1899	NL	Joe Kelley, Bro	143	1180.0	6.61
1899	NL	Hugh Duffy, Bos	147	1272.0	6.09
1900	NL	Billy Hamilton, Bos	136	1187.0	6.35
1900	NL	Chick Stahl, Bos	135	1178.0	5.51
1900	NL	Fred Clarke, Pit	104	882.0	5.34

Year	Lg	Player, Team	G	Inn	WS
1901	AL	Jimmy Barrett, Det	135	1178.0	8.16
1901	AL	Dummy Hoy, CWS	132	1173.0	5.43
1901	AL	Chick Stahl, Bos	131	1152.0	5.29
1901	NL	Elmer Flick, Phi	138	1208.0	6.08
1901	NL	Roy Thomas, Phi	129	1150.0	5.28
1901	NL	Fred Clarke, Pit	127	1160.0	5.01
1902	AL	Fielder Jones, CWS	135	1203.0	6.56
1902	AL	Jimmy Barrett, Det	136	1191.0	5.56
1902	AL	Emmett Heidrick, StL	109	1007.0	5.39
1902	NL	Jimmy Sheckard, Bro	123	1092.0	5.34
1902	NL	Ginger Beaumont, Pit	130	1182.0	5.20
1902	NL	John Dobbs, 2 tms	122	1109.0	5.06
1903	AL	Fielder Jones, CWS	136	1220.0	4.75
1903	AL	Patsy Dougherty, Bos	139	1251.0	4.70
1903	AL	Harry Bay, Cle	140	1244.0	4.49
1903	NL	Jimmy Sheckard, Bro	139	1221.0	6.38
1903	NL	Sam Mertes, NYG	137	1208.0	5.72
1903	NL	Cy Seymour, Cin	135	1136.0	5.43
1904	AL	Fielder Jones, CWS	149	1335.0	7.28
1904	AL	Dave Fultz, NYA	90	793.0	4.83
1904	AL	Emmett Heidrick, StL	130	1179.0	4.77
1904	NL	Cy Seymour, Cin	130	1166.0	7.06
1904	NL	Fred Odwell, Cin	126	1129.0	6.15
1904	NL	Sam Mertes, NYG	147	1300.0	5.71
1905	AL	Fielder Jones, CWS	153	1387.0	8.79
1905	AL	Socks Seybold, Phi	133	1159.0	5.46
1905	AL	Danny Hoffman, Phi	118	1085.0	4.98
1905	NL	Roy Thomas, Phi	147	1343.0	7.56
1905	NL	Jimmy Slagle, ChC	155	1407.0	7.36
1905	NL	Sherry Magee, Phi	155	1399.0	4.72
1906	AL	Fielder Jones, CWS	144	1304.0	6.50
1906	AL	Charlie Hemphill, StL	154	1347.0	5.37
1906	AL	Wid Conroy, NYA	97	851.0	5.10
1906	NL	Cy Seymour, 2 tms	151	1322.0	6.70
1906	NL	Jimmy Slagle, ChC	127	1153.0	6.48
1906	NL	Jimmy Sheckard, ChC	149	1349.0	5.18
1907	AL	Fielder Jones, CWS	154	1368.0	8.57
1907	AL	Joe Birmingham, Cle	130	1134.0	5.20
1907	AL	Ed Hahn, CWS	156	1396.0	4.89

Year	Lg	Player, Team	G	Inn	WS
1907	NL	Roy Thomas, Phi	121	1066.0	5.49
1907	NL	Tommy Leach, Pit	111	945.0	5.44
1907	NL	Sherry Magee, Phi	139	1223.0	5.20
1908	AL	Joe Birmingham, Cle	121	1084.0	7.61
1908	AL	Fielder Jones, CWS	149	1377.0	6.82
1908	AL	Josh Clarke, Cle	131	1223.0	4.65
1908	NL	Fred Osborn, Phi	152	1364.0	5.74
1908	NL	Cy Seymour, NYG	155	1411.0	5.64
1908	NL	Fred Clarke, Pit	151	1395.0	4.43
1909	AL	Tris Speaker, Bos	142	1278.0	7.67
1909	AL	Sam Crawford, Det	139	1275.0	5.92
1909	AL	Bob Ganley, 2 tms	94	825.0	5.13
1909	NL	Solly Hofman, ChC	153	1377.0	6.60
1909	NL	Fred Clarke, Pit	152	1402.0	6.43
1909	NL	Tommy Leach, Pit	138	1294.0	5.27
1910	AL	Tris Speaker, Bos	140	1269.0	6.45
1910	AL	Ty Cobb, Det	137	1221.0	5.39
1910	AL	Rube Oldring, Phi	134	1265.0	4.54
1910	NL	Bill Collins, Bos	151	1354.0	7.68
1910	NL	Tommy Leach, Pit	131	1195.0	6.34
1910	NL	Jimmy Sheckard, ChC	143	1287.0	5.62
1911	AL	Ty Cobb, Det	146	1234.0	6.04
1911	AL	Tris Speaker, Bos	138	1193.0	5.92
1911	AL	Joe Birmingham, Cle	102	907.0	5.65
1911	NL	Rebel Oakes, StL	151	1360.0	6.88
1911	NL	Dode Paskert, Phi	153	1373.0	6.27
1911	NL	Fred Snodgrass, NYG	149	1333.0	5.57
1912	AL	Tris Speaker, Bos	153	1346.0	9.90
1912	AL	Clyde Milan, Was	154	1377.0	6.98
1912	AL	Duffy Lewis, Bos	154	1343.0	5.13
1912	NL	Max Carey, Pit	150	1373.0	5.81
1912	NL	Jimmy Sheckard, ChC	146	1291.0	5.68
1912	NL	Tommy Leach, 2 tms	97	857.0	4.72
1913	AL	Clyde Milan, Was	154	1396.0	5.59
1913	AL	Howard Shanks, Was	109	952.0	4.73
1913	AL	Danny Moeller, Was	153	1396.0	4.58
1913	NL	Dode Paskert, Phi	120	1097.0	5.89
1913	NL	Fred Snodgrass, NYG	133	1206.0	5.51
1913	NL	Zack Wheat, Bro	135	1199.0	5.25
1914	AL	Tris Speaker, Bos	156	1409.0	8.90
1914	AL	Shano Collins, CWS	154	1391.0	5.26
1914	AL	Bobby Veach, Det	145	1317.0	4.92
1914	NL	Tommy Leach, ChC	136	1217.0	6.92
1914	NL	Chief Wilson, StL	154	1382.0	6.35
1914	NL	Les Mann, Bos	123	922.0	4.49
1914	FL	Charlie Hanford, Buf	155	1387.0	8.95
1914	FL	Benny Kauff, Ind	154	1365.0	6.32
1914	FL	Dutch Zwilling, Chi	154	1406.0	5.69
1915	AL	Tris Speaker, Bos	150	1328.0	8.29
1915	AL	Ty Cobb, Det	156	1398.0	6.39
1915	AL	Clyde Milan, Was	151	1362.0	5.99
1915	NL	Hi Myers, Bro	153	1390.0	6.50
1915	NL	Zack Wheat, Bro	144	1363.0	6.04
1915	NL	Possum Whitted, Phi	119	1056.0	5.30
1915	FL	Chet Chadbourne, KC	152	1359.0	6.41
1915	FL	Dutch Zwilling, Chi	148	1342.0	5.88
1915	FL	Rebel Oakes, Pit	153	1358.0	5.86
1916	AL	Happy Felsch, CWS	141	1291.0	6.26
1916	AL	Clyde Milan, Was	149	1349.0	5.27
1916	AL	Bobby Veach, Det	150	1370.0	5.04
1916	NL	Max Carey, Pit	154	1420.0	7.81
1916	NL	Cy Williams, ChC	116	1042.0	6.22
1916	NL	Zack Wheat, Bro	149	1344.0	5.38
1917	AL	Tris Speaker, Cle	142	1283.0	7.45
1917	AL	Happy Felsch, CWS	152	1369.0	7.02
1917	AL	Duffy Lewis, Bos	150	1339.0	5.59
1917	NL	Max Carey, Pit	153	1394.0	6.20
1917	NL	Cy Williams, ChC	136	1168.0	5.18
1917	NL	Benny Kauff, NYG	153	1394.0	5.13
1918	AL	Tris Speaker, Cle	128	1137.0	6.15
1918	AL	Clyde Milan, Was	124	1190.0	5.54
1918	AL	Amos Strunk, Bos	113	1025.0	4.83
1918	NL	Max Carey, Pit	126	1140.0	6.66
1918	NL	Hi Myers, Bro	107	977.0	6.56
1918	NL	Dode Paskert, ChC	121	1105.0	5.52
1919	AL	Tris Speaker, Cle	134	1202.0	7.75
1919	AL	Happy Felsch, CWS	135	1160.0	6.18
1919	AL	Ping Bodie, NYY	134	1193.0	6.06

Year	Lg	Player, Team	G	Inn	WS
1919	NL	Carson Bigbee, Pit	124	1128.0	7.07
1919	NL	Edd Roush, Cin	133	1231.0	6.69
1919	NL	Benny Kauff, NYG	134	1208.0	4.40
1920	AL	Bobby Veach, Det	154	1385.0	6.94
1920	AL	Happy Felsch, CWS	142	1235.0	6.35
1920	AL	Baby Doll Jacobson, StL	154	1355.0	6.09
1920	NL	Hi Myers, Bro	152	1411.0	8.06
1920	NL	Edd Roush, Cin	139	1273.0	5.52
1920	NL	Max Carey, Pit	129	1170.0	5.28
1921	AL	Baby Doll Jacobson, StL	142	1235.0	5.26
1921	AL	Sam Rice, Was	141	1236.0	5.19
1921	AL	Tris Speaker, Cle	128	1062.0	5.18
1921	NL	Max Carey, Pit	139	1292.0	6.65
1921	NL	Carson Bigbee, Pit	146	1313.0	5.26
1921	NL	Ray Powell, Bos	149	1297.0	4.59
1922	AL	Baby Doll Jacobson, StL	137	1194.0	5.27
1922	AL	Ken Williams, StL	153	1391.0	5.08
1922	AL	Whitey Witt, NYY	138	1224.0	5.04
1922	NL	George Burns, Cin	156	1379.0	6.65
1922	NL	Max Carey, Pit	155	1369.0	5.66
1922	NL	Hi Myers, Bro	152	1346.0	4.63
1923	AL	Babe Ruth, NYY	148	1313.0	6.17
1923	AL	Johnny Mostil, CWS	143	1255.0	5.53
1923	AL	Whitey Witt, NYY	144	1317.0	5.33
1923	NL	Jigger Statz, ChC	154	1367.0	8.18
1923	NL	Max Carey, Pit	153	1376.0	6.38
1923	NL	Edd Roush, Cin	137	1252.0	5.27
1924	AL	Baby Doll Jacobson, StL	152	1327.0	6.36
1924	AL	Al Simmons, Phi	152	1345.0	5.82
1924	AL	Ira Flagstead, Bos	144	1263.0	5.34
1924	NL	Max Carey, Pit	149	1339.0	7.67
1924	NL	Jigger Statz, ChC	131	1185.0	6.65
1924	NL	Edd Roush, Cin	119	1063.0	4.25
1925	AL	Al Simmons, Phi	153	1349.0	8.60
1925	AL	Goose Goslin, Was	150	1288.0	5.72
1925	AL	Ira Flagstead, Bos	144	1214.0	5.19
1925	NL	Edd Roush, Cin	134	1179.0	6.09
1925	NL	Max Carey, Pit	130	1122.0	5.18
1925	NL	Curt Walker, Cin	141	1273.0	5.03
1926	AL	Tris Speaker, Cle	149	1300.0	7.44
1926	AL	Johnny Mostil, CWS	147	1322.0	6.00
1926	AL	Al Simmons, Phi	147	1325.0	5.91
1926	NL	Kiki Cuyler, Pit	157	1379.0	6.84
1926	NL	Taylor Douthit, StL	138	1221.0	6.14
1926	NL	Paul Waner, Pit	139	1234.0	5.12
1927	AL	Alex Metzler, CWS	134	1176.0	6.10
1927	AL	Earle Combs, NYY	152	1317.0	6.01
1927	AL	Bibb Falk, CWS	145	1269.0	5.26
1927	NL	Jigger Statz, Bro	122	1114.0	7.25
1927	NL	Taylor Douthit, StL	125	1112.0	6.34
1927	NL	Lloyd Waner, Pit	150	1313.0	5.67
1928	AL	Fred Schulte, StL	143	1263.0	6.48
1928	AL	Johnny Mostil, CWS	131	1164.0	5.81
1928	AL	Bing Miller, Phi	133	1152.0	4.31
1928	NL	Taylor Douthit, StL	154	1415.0	8.69
1928	NL	Lloyd Waner, Pit	152	1336.0	7.34
1928	NL	Paul Waner, Pit	131	1168.0	4.47
1929	AL	Fred Schulte, StL	116	1007.0	7.29
1929	AL	Mule Haas, Phi	139	1245.0	5.75
1929	AL	Al Simmons, Phi	142	1290.0	5.51
1929	NL	Lloyd Waner, Pit	151	1361.0	7.90
1929	NL	Paul Waner, Pit	143	1289.0	6.24
1929	NL	Ethan Allen, Cin	137	1172.0	5.28
1930	AL	Tom Oliver, Bos	154	1357.0	6.09
1930	AL	Mule Haas, Phi	131	1144.0	5.92
1930	AL	Sammy West, Was	118	935.0	5.90
1930	NL	Johnny Frederick, Bro	142	1211.0	7.46
1930	NL	Jimmy Welsh, Bos	110	950.0	5.55
1930	NL	Kiki Cuyler, ChC	156	1389.0	5.53
1931	AL	Sammy West, Was	127	1085.0	7.36
1931	AL	Tom Oliver, Bos	148	1316.0	5.99
1931	AL	Earl Averill, Cle	155	1290.0	5.15
1931	NL	Wally Berger, Bos	156	1380.0	8.13
1931	NL	Lloyd Waner, Pit	153	1385.0	7.31
1931	NL	Paul Waner, Pit	138	1208.0	4.61
1932	AL	Joe Vosmik, Cle	153	1369.0	8.03
1932	AL	Sammy West, Was	143	1257.0	6.60
1932	AL	Earl Averill, Cle	153	1369.0	6.42

Year	Lg	Player, Team	G	Inn	WS
1932	NL	Lloyd Waner, Pit	131	1173.0	6.08
1932	NL	Kiddo Davis, Phi	133	1203.0	5.62
1932	NL	Wally Berger, Bos	134	1220.0	5.13
1933	AL	Earl Averill, Cle	149	1281.0	7.11
1933	AL	Fred Schulte, Was	142	1248.0	6.74
1933	AL	Al Simmons, CWS	145	1295.0	5.14
1933	NL	Wally Berger, Bos	136	1230.0	4.97
1933	NL	Mel Ott, NYG	152	1268.0	4.84
1933	NL	Chick Fullis, Phi	151	1337.0	4.73
1934	AL	Earl Averill, Cle	154	1311.0	6.22
1934	AL	Doc Cramer, Phi	152	1296.0	5.51
1934	AL	Sammy West, StL	120	1057.0	4.87
1934	NL	Kiddo Davis, 2 tms	109	920.0	5.96
1934	NL	Jack Rothrock, StL	154	1344.0	4.97
1934	NL	Lloyd Waner, Pit	139	1195.0	4.92
1935	AL	Al Simmons, CWS	126	1066.0	6.34
1935	AL	Ben Chapman, NYY	138	1206.0	6.18
1935	AL	Mel Almada, Bos	149	1300.0	6.16
1935	NL	Ethan Allen, Phi	156	1316.0	7.28
1935	NL	Lloyd Waner, Pit	121	1056.0	6.20
1935	NL	Terry Moore, StL	117	1040.0	5.37
1936	AL	Doc Cramer, Bos	154	1336.0	8.96
1936	AL	Ben Chapman, 2 tms	133	1140.0	5.76
1936	AL	Joe DiMaggio, NYY	138	1255.0	4.88
1936	NL	Johnny Cooney, Bro	130	1120.0	6.40
1936	NL	Augie Galan, ChC	145	1257.0	6.10
1936	NL	Wally Berger, Bos	133	1214.0	4.52
1937	AL	Mike Kreevich, CWS	138	1162.0	8.13
1937	AL	Joe DiMaggio, NYY	150	1346.0	6.11
1937	AL	Doc Cramer, Bos	133	1142.0	5.21
1937	NL	Vince DiMaggio, Bos	130	1129.0	6.14
1937	NL	Lloyd Waner, Pit	123	1051.0	5.24
1937	NL	Gene Moore, Bos	148	1327.0	4.70
1938	AL	Doc Cramer, Bos	148	1257.0	6.74
1938	AL	Joe DiMaggio, NYY	145	1262.0	5.68
1938	AL	Mike Kreevich, CWS	127	1090.0	5.38
1938	NL	Harry Craft, Cin	151	1348.0	6.79
1938	NL	Vince DiMaggio, Bos	149	1346.0	5.92
1938	NL	Carl Reynolds, ChC	125	1105.0	5.55
1939	AL	Barney McCosky, Det	145	1272.0	8.02
1939	AL	Mike Kreevich, CWS	139	1234.0	7.41
1939	AL	Joe DiMaggio, NYY	117	1010.0	6.23
1939	NL	Enos Slaughter, StL	149	1276.0	5.17
1939	NL	Harry Craft, Cin	134	1206.0	5.10
1939	NL	Terry Moore, StL	121	1024.0	5.05
1940	AL	Mike Kreevich, CWS	144	1273.0	8.66
1940	AL	Barney McCosky, Det	141	1213.0	5.68
1940	AL	Roy Weatherly, Cle	135	1181.0	4.51
1940	NL	Dixie Walker, Bro	136	1246.0	6.42
1940	NL	Terry Moore, StL	133	1158.0	5.34
1940	NL	Harry Craft, Cin	109	939.0	4.73
1941	AL	Barney McCosky, Det	122	1018.0	5.93
1941	AL	Joe DiMaggio, NYY	139	1240.0	5.16
1941	AL	Mike Kreevich, CWS	113	1018.0	4.75
1941	NL	Pete Reiser, Bro	133	1173.0	7.68
1941	NL	Terry Moore, StL	121	1095.0	6.08
1941	NL	Vince DiMaggio, Pit	151	1306.0	6.05
1942	AL	Dom DiMaggio, Bos	151	1331.0	8.61
1942	AL	Doc Cramer, Det	150	1357.0	6.97
1942	AL	Barney McCosky, Det	154	1393.0	5.92
1942	NL	Enos Slaughter, StL	151	1302.0	5.07
1942	NL	Stan Musial, StL	135	1100.0	4.57
1942	NL	Vince DiMaggio, Pit	138	1223.0	4.47
1943	AL	Doc Cramer, Det	138	1277.0	5.95
1943	AL	Stan Spence, Was	148	1311.0	5.51
1943	AL	Thurman Tucker, CWS	132	1196.0	5.16
1943	NL	Tommy Holmes, Bos	152	1373.0	7.46
1943	NL	Stan Musial, StL	155	1415.0	5.71
1943	NL	Vince DiMaggio, Pit	156	1363.0	5.65
1944	AL	Johnny Lindell, NYY	149	1305.0	6.28
1944	AL	Thurman Tucker, CWS	120	1084.0	6.24
1944	AL	Doc Cramer, Det	141	1283.0	4.79
1944	NL	Buster Adams, Phi	151	1377.0	5.30
1944	NL	Jim Russell, Pit	149	1322.0	5.23
1944	NL	Johnny Barrett, Pit	147	1289.0	5.13
1945	AL	Milt Byrnes, StL	125	1106.0	5.55
1945	AL	Mike Kreevich, 2 tms	121	1064.0	5.45
1945	AL	Roy Cullenbine, 2 tms	150	1340.0	5.34

Year	Lg	Player, Team	G	Inn	WS
1945	NL	Carden Gillenwater, Bos	140	1267.0	7.67
1945	NL	Andy Pafko, ChC	140	1224.0	6.45
1945	NL	Goody Rosen, Bro	141	1235.0	6.16
1946	AL	Dom DiMaggio, Bos	142	1234.0	6.86
1946	AL	Joe DiMaggio, NYY	131	1162.0	4.69
1946	AL	Stan Spence, Was	150	1335.0	4.46
1946	NL	Carl Furillo, Bro	112	794.0	5.21
1946	NL	Enos Slaughter, StL	156	1364.0	4.14
1946	NL	Dain Clay, Cin	120	1087.0	3.99
1947	AL	Dom DiMaggio, Bos	134	1165.0	6.18
1947	AL	Sam Chapman, Phi	146	1302.0	5.96
1947	AL	Catfish Metkovich, Cle	119	1034.0	4.58
1947	NL	Tommy Holmes, Bos	147	1258.0	4.95
1947	NL	Enos Slaughter, StL	142	1219.0	4.45
1947	NL	Terry Moore, StL	120	1062.0	4.40
1948	AL	Dom DiMaggio, Bos	155	1379.0	6.44
1948	AL	Joe DiMaggio, NYY	152	1316.0	5.28
1948	AL	Dale Mitchell, Cle	140	1198.0	4.61
1948	NL	Ralph Kiner, Pit	154	1274.0	4.69
1948	NL	Carl Furillo, Bro	104	890.0	4.63
1948	NL	Hal Jeffcoat, ChC	119	1028.0	3.85
1949	AL	Dom DiMaggio, Bos	144	1284.0	5.54
1949	AL	Sam Chapman, Phi	154	1361.0	5.30
1949	AL	Hoot Evers, Det	123	1054.0	5.25
1949	NL	Bobby Thomson, NYG	156	1374.0	6.53
1949	NL	Richie Ashburn, Phi	154	1392.0	6.38
1949	NL	Stan Musial, StL	156	1356.0	5.33
1950	AL	Irv Noren, Was	121	1060.0	5.95
1950	AL	Dom DiMaggio, Bos	140	1202.0	5.80
1950	AL	Joe DiMaggio, NYY	137	1185.0	4.36
1950	NL	Richie Ashburn, Phi	147	1300.0	6.78
1950	NL	Bobby Thomson, NYG	149	1263.0	5.66
1950	NL	Andy Pafko, ChC	144	1296.0	4.56
1951	AL	Irv Noren, Was	126	1119.0	5.93
1951	AL	Jim Busby, CWS	139	1137.0	5.05
1951	AL	Dom DiMaggio, Bos	146	1337.0	4.77
1951	NL	Richie Ashburn, Phi	154	1385.0	6.36
1951	NL	Lloyd Merriman, Cin	102	866.0	5.36
1951	NL	Willie Mays, NYG	121	1091.0	5.07

Year	Lg	Player, Team	G	Inn	WS
1952	AL	Jim Busby, 2 tms	144	1263.0	6.67
1952	AL	Jim Rivera, 2 tms	141	1230.0	5.69
1952	AL	Dave Philley, Phi	149	1335.0	5.68
1952	NL	Hank Sauer, ChC	151	1310.0	6.31
1952	NL	Richie Ashburn, Phi	154	1382.0	6.20
1952	NL	Hal Jeffcoat, ChC	95	705.0	4.79
1953	AL	Jim Busby, Was	150	1323.0	7.93
1953	AL	Jim Rivera, CWS	156	1404.0	7.65
1953	AL	Tom Umphlett, Bos	136	1190.0	7.15
1953	NL	Richie Ashburn, Phi	156	1370.0	6.64
1953	NL	Bill Bruton, Mil	150	1331.0	6.33
1953	NL	Duke Snider, Bro	151	1356.0	5.08
1954	AL	Larry Doby, Cle	153	1400.0	7.43
1954	AL	Jim Busby, Was	155	1383.0	5.94
1954	AL	Minnie Minoso, CWS	146	1333.0	4.71
1954	NL	Willie Mays, NYG	151	1337.0	8.87
1954	NL	Richie Ashburn, Phi	153	1365.0	7.98
1954	NL	Bill Bruton, Mil	141	1288.0	5.52
1955	AL	Jimmy Piersall, Bos	147	1214.0	9.53
1955	AL	Mickey Mantle, NYY	145	1249.0	6.83
1955	AL	Jim Rivera, CWS	143	1172.0	4.64
1955	NL	Duke Snider, Bro	146	1329.0	5.56
1955	NL	Bill Bruton, Mil	149	1349.0	5.40
1955	NL	Richie Ashburn, Phi	140	1236.0	5.21
1956	AL	Jimmy Piersall, Bos	155	1327.0	9.32
1956	AL	Jim Busby, Cle	133	1150.0	6.25
1956	AL	Mickey Mantle, NYY	144	1223.0	4.84
1956	NL	Duke Snider, Bro	150	1369.0	6.57
1956	NL	Bill Virdon, 2 tms	154	1282.0	5.44
1956	NL	Bill Bruton, Mil	145	1276.0	5.22
1957	AL	Jimmy Piersall, Bos	151	1283.0	7.18
1957	AL	Mickey Mantle, NYY	139	1270.0	5.05
1957	AL	Bill Tuttle, Det	128	1098.0	4.67
1957	NL	Richie Ashburn, Phi	156	1402.0	7.27
1957	NL	Duke Snider, Bro	136	1216.0	6.25
1957	NL	Bill Virdon, Pit	141	1264.0	5.85
1958	AL	Jim Landis, CWS	142	1285.0	4.98
1958	AL	Harvey Kuenn, Det	138	1214.0	4.71
1958	AL	Jimmy Piersall, Bos	125	976.0	4.55

Year	Lg	Player, Team	G	Inn	WS
1958	NL	Curt Flood, StL	120	1020.0	6.90
1958	NL	Bill Virdon, Pit	143	1210.0	6.79
1958	NL	Willie Mays, SF	151	1337.0	6.11
1959	AL	Jim Landis, CWS	148	1374.0	7.77
1959	AL	Minnie Minoso, Cle	148	1292.0	4.66
1959	AL	Willie Tasby, Bal	137	1195.0	4.62
1959	NL	Bill Virdon, Pit	144	1279.0	6.41
1959	NL	Willie Mays, SF	147	1300.0	5.28
1959	NL	George Altman, ChC	121	1034.0	4.58
1960	AL	Al Kaline, Det	142	1299.0	4.81
1960	AL	Mickey Mantle, NYY	150	1333.0	4.59
1960	AL	Bill Tuttle, KCA	148	1288.0	4.46
1960	NL	Willie Mays, SF	152	1371.0	5.21
1960	NL	Curt Flood, StL	134	944.0	4.44
1960	NL	Wally Moon, LA	127	1049.0	3.95
1961	AL	Jackie Brandt, Bal	136	1233.0	4.99
1961	AL	Bill Bruton, Det	155	1345.0	4.99
1961	AL	Mickey Mantle, NYY	150	1317.0	4.93
1961	NL	Vada Pinson, Cin	153	1362.0	8.95
1961	NL	Hank Aaron, Mil	154	1385.0	5.49
1961	NL	Frank Robinson, Cin	150	1273.0	5.27
1962	AL	Albie Pearson, LAA	160	1419.0	5.32
1962	AL	Bill Bruton, Det	145	1274.0	5.16
1962	AL	Lenny Green, Min	156	1335.0	5.03
1962	NL	Curt Flood, StL	151	1335.0	9.18
1962	NL	Willie Mays, SF	161	1397.0	6.70
1962	NL	Bill Virdon, Pit	156	1367.0	6.23
1963	AL	Albie Pearson, LAA	148	1337.0	4.42
1963	AL	Tom Tresh, NYY	144	1303.0	4.30
1963	AL	Carl Yastrzemski, Bos	151	1350.0	4.28
1963	NL	Curt Flood, StL	158	1411.0	6.64
1963	NL	Johnny Callison, Phi	157	1413.0	6.26
1963	NL	Willie Davis, LA	153	1242.0	5.40
1964	AL	Jackie Brandt, Bal	134	1181.0	6.42
1964	AL	Jimmie Hall, Min	137	1194.0	5.51
1964	AL	Mike Hershberger, CWS	134	1112.0	4.41
1964	NL	Curt Flood, StL	162	1445.0	8.69
1964	NL	Willie Davis, LA	155	1405.0	7.44
1964	NL	Willie Mays, SF	155	1369.0	6.97

Year	Lg	Player, Team	G	Inn	WS
1965	AL	Jose Cardenal, Cal	129	1143.0	5.13
1965	AL	Ken Berry, CWS	156	1151.0	5.05
1965	AL	Jimmie Hall, Min	141	1221.0	4.71
1965	NL	Willie Mays, SF	151	1362.0	8.11
1965	NL	Willie Davis, LA	141	1294.0	6.74
1965	NL	Roberto Clemente, Pit	145	1325.0	4.97
1966	AL	Tommie Agee, CWS	159	1455.0	7.65
1966	AL	Ted Uhlaender, Min	100	890.0	4.64
1966	AL	Tony Oliva, Min	159	1434.0	4.37
1966	NL	Curt Flood, StL	159	1433.0	8.32
1966	NL	Willie Mays, SF	150	1396.0	6.62
1966	NL	Willie Davis, LA	152	1373.0	5.44
1967	AL	Tommie Agee, CWS	152	1308.0	6.43
1967	AL	Reggie Smith, Bos	144	1296.0	5.58
1967	AL	Paul Blair, Bal	146	1269.0	5.07
1967	NL	Vada Pinson, Cin	157	1414.0	5.75
1967	NL	Adolfo Phillips, ChC	141	1184.0	5.64
1967	NL	Willie Mays, SF	134	1170.0	5.27
1968	AL	Jose Cardenal, Cle	153	1388.0	6.37
1968	AL	Mickey Stanley, Det	130	1176.0	5.31
1968	AL	Reggie Smith, Bos	155	1386.0	5.00
1968	NL	Curt Flood, StL	149	1328.0	7.26
1968	NL	Roberto Clemente, Pit	131	1192.0	5.21
1968	NL	Adolfo Phillips, ChC	141	1114.0	4.89
1969	AL	Paul Blair, Bal	150	1294.0	8.10
1969	AL	Lou Piniella, KC	129	1106.0	4.71
1969	AL	Jim Northrup, Det	143	1265.0	4.59
1969	NL	Curt Flood, StL	152	1339.0	7.90
1969	NL	Tommie Agee, NYM	146	1324.0	6.71
1969	NL	Bobby Bonds, SF	155	1397.0	5.62
1970	AL	Paul Blair, Bal	128	1092.0	6.60
1970	AL	Amos Otis, KC	159	1463.0	5.94
1970	AL	Reggie Smith, Bos	145	1258.0	5.86
1970	NL	Bobby Tolan, Cin	150	1336.0	7.05
1970	NL	Tommie Agee, NYM	150	1362.0	6.14
1970	NL	Pete Rose, Cin	159	1365.0	5.47
1971	AL	Amos Otis, KC	144	1283.0	6.81
1971	AL	Paul Blair, Bal	138	1186.0	4.85
1971	AL	Dave May, Mil	142	1247.0	4.51

Year	Lg	Player, Team	G	Inn	WS
1971	NL	George Foster, 2 tms	132	1082.0	5.28
1971	NL	Bobby Bonds, SF	154	1379.0	5.18
1971	NL	Willie Davis, LA	157	1406.0	4.56
1972	AL	Paul Blair, Bal	139	1105.0	5.27
1972	AL	Cesar Tovar, Min	139	1197.0	4.91
1972	AL	Bobby Darwin, Min	142	1200.0	4.73
1972	NL	Willie Davis, LA	146	1300.0	6.52
1972	NL	Al Oliver, Pit	138	1261.0	4.73
1972	NL	Rick Monday, ChC	134	1121.0	4.70
1973	AL	Paul Blair, Bal	144	1166.0	6.94
1973	AL	Mickey Stanley, Det	157	1403.0	6.00
1973	AL	Bill North, Oak	138	1240.0	5.66
1973	NL	Willie Davis, LA	146	1298.0	5.74
1973	NL	Garry Maddox, SF	140	1238.0	4.83
1973	NL	Dusty Baker, Atl	156	1396.0	4.83
1974	AL	Amos Otis, KC	143	1310.0	7.03
1974	AL	Paul Blair, Bal	151	1339.0	5.53
1974	AL	Bill North, Oak	138	1204.0	5.35
1974	NL	Bake McBride, StL	144	1225.0	6.15
1974	NL	Cesar Cedeno, Hou	157	1350.0	6.13
1974	NL	Jimmy Wynn, LA	148	1324.0	5.65
1975	AL	Fred Lynn, Bos	144	1265.0	6.00
1975	AL	Bill North, Oak	138	1230.0	5.82
1975	AL	Ken Henderson, CWS	137	1237.0	5.19
1975	NL	Al Oliver, Pit	153	1357.0	6.07
1975	NL	Cesar Geronimo, Cin	148	1182.0	5.49
1975	NL	Garry Maddox, 2 tms	110	948.0	5.24
1976	AL	Ron LeFlore, Det	132	1158.0	5.78
1976	AL	Mickey Rivers, NYY	136	1255.0	5.25
1976	AL	Juan Beniquez, Tex	141	1157.0	5.16
1976	NL	Garry Maddox, Phi	144	1229.0	5.84
1976	NL	Bill Buckner, LA	153	1330.0	4.19
1976	NL	Al Oliver, Pit	106	951.0	4.16
1977	AL	Chet Lemon, CWS	149	1331.0	6.02
1977	AL	Mickey Rivers, NYY	136	1223.0	5.68
1977	AL	Amos Otis, KC	140	1230.0	5.51
1977	NL	Dave Parker, Pit	158	1471.0	6.65
1977	NL	Omar Moreno, Pit	147	1194.0	5.48
1977	NL	Cesar Cedeno, Hou	137	1240.0	5.46
1978	AL	Amos Otis, KC	136	1218.0	6.27
1978	AL	Mickey Rivers, NYY	138	1246.0	5.94
1978	AL	Fred Lynn, Bos	149	1345.0	5.91
1978	NL	Omar Moreno, Pit	152	1345.0	6.84
1978	NL	Andre Dawson, Mon	153	1356.0	6.30
1978	NL	Garry Maddox, Phi	154	1285.0	6.24
1979	AL	Chet Lemon, CWS	147	1291.0	6.38
1979	AL	Fred Lynn, Bos	143	1262.0	6.09
1979	AL	Rick Bosetti, Tor	162	1417.0	5.90
1979	NL	Tony Scott, StL	151	1349.0	7.20
1979	NL	Omar Moreno, Pit	162	1493.0	7.07
1979	NL	Andre Dawson, Mon	153	1388.0	6.41
1980	AL	Dwayne Murphy, Oak	158	1457.0	10.04
1980	AL	Willie Wilson, KC	159	1459.0	7.30
1980	AL	Rickey Henderson, Oak	157	1418.0	6.52
1980	NL	Omar Moreno, Pit	162	1458.0	7.75
1980	NL	Garry Maddox, Phi	143	1204.0	5.95
1980	NL	Dale Murphy, Atl	154	1384.0	5.86
1981	AL	Willie Wilson, KC	101	922.0	4.24
1981	AL	Dwayne Murphy, Oak	106	980.0	4.17
1981	AL	Rickey Henderson, Oak	107	989.0	4.09
1981	NL	Andre Dawson, Mon	103	934.0	4.51
1981	NL	Ken Griffey Sr., Cin	99	843.0	3.95
1981	NL	Tony Scott, 2 tms	99	898.0	3.81
1982	AL	Lloyd Moseby, Tor	145	1163.0	6.39
1982	AL	Willie Wilson, KC	135	1200.0	5.44
1982	AL	Al Bumbry, Bal	147	1307.0	4.57
1982	NL	Andre Dawson, Mon	147	1311.0	5.63
1982	NL	Omar Moreno, Pit	157	1393.0	5.56
1982	NL	Ruppert Jones, SD	114	1009.0	4.52
1983	AL	George Wright, Tex	161	1418.0	7.35
1983	AL	Chet Lemon, Det	145	1270.0	6.05
1983	AL	Lloyd Moseby, Tor	147	1284.0	5.32
1983	NL	Eddie Milner, Cin	139	1201.0	5.93
1983	NL	Mookie Wilson, NYM	148	1335.0	5.70
1983	NL	Andre Dawson, Mon	157	1373.0	5.25
1984	AL	Kirby Puckett, Min	128	1146.0	9.20
1984	AL	Lloyd Moseby, Tor	156	1401.0	6.85
1984	AL	Willie Wilson, KC	128	1143.0	6.84

Year	Lg	Player, Team	G	Inn	WS
1984	NL	Kevin McReynolds, SD	143	1263.0	7.28
1984	NL	Dale Murphy, Atl	160	1407.0	6.97
1984	NL	Tim Raines, Mon	160	1411.0	5.35
1985	AL	Kirby Puckett, Min	161	1422.0	6.52
1985	AL	Lloyd Moseby, Tor	152	1382.0	6.51
1985	AL	Jesse Barfield, Tor	154	1398.0	6.14
1985	NL	Eddie Milner, Cin	135	1102.0	5.75
1985	NL	Willie McGee, StL	149	1300.0	5.26
1985	NL	Kevin McReynolds, SD	150	1345.0	5.22
1986	AL	Gary Pettis, Cal	153	1376.0	6.04
1986	AL	Willie Wilson, KC	155	1379.0	5.80
1986	AL	Rickey Henderson, NYY	146	1301.0	5.34
1986	NL	Kevin Bass, Hou	155	1351.0	6.26
1986	NL	Willie McGee, StL	121	1047.0	5.31
1986	NL	Mitch Webster, Mon	146	1283.0	4.66
1987	AL	Jesse Barfield, Tor	158	1340.1	6.74
1987	AL	Willie Wilson, KC	143	1222.1	5.56
1987	AL	Ken Williams, CWS	115	955.2	5.04
1987	NL	Milt Thompson, Phi	146	1114.1	6.00
1987	NL	Barry Bonds, Pit	145	1153.1	5.67
1987	NL	Andy Van Slyke, Pit	150	1239.2	4.80
1988	AL	Robin Yount, Mil	158	1380.1	8.17
1988	AL	Kirby Puckett, Min	158	1349.2	6.04
1988	AL	Joe Carter, Cle	156	1366.2	5.33
1988	NL	Gerald Young, Hou	145	1280.0	5.77
1988	NL	Andy Van Slyke, Pit	152	1324.2	5.47
1988	NL	John Shelby, LA	140	1212.0	5.04
1989	AL	Devon White, Cal	154	1365.2	6.16
1989	AL	Kirby Puckett, Min	157	1329.1	5.80
1989	AL	Dave Henderson, Oak	149	1298.1	5.73
1989	AL	Cecil Espy, Tex	133	1004.1	5.16
1989	AL	Cory Snyder, Cle	125	1076.1	4.98
1989	NL	Gerald Young, Hou	143	1252.2	7.39
1989	NL	Tony Gwynn, SD	157	1378.2	4.40
1989	NL	Milt Thompson, StL	147	1218.1	4.29
1989	NL	Brett Butler, SF	152	1293.1	4.26
1989	NL	Andy Van Slyke, Pit	123	1065.0	4.23
1990	AL	Lance Johnson, CWS	148	1183.2	5.27
1990	AL	Dave Henderson, Oak	116	982.1	4.86
1990	AL	Roberto Kelly, NYY	160	1389.2	4.70
1990	AL	Gary Pettis, Tex	128	1032.0	4.65
1990	AL	Ken Griffey Jr., Sea	151	1332.2	4.54
1990	NL	Lenny Dykstra, Phi	149	1287.2	5.17
1990	NL	Billy Hatcher, Cin	131	1080.2	5.09
1990	NL	Joe Carter, SD	150	1308.0	5.05
1990	NL	Dave Martinez, Mon	108	849.1	4.55
1990	NL	Barry Bonds, Pit	150	1287.0	4.23
1991	AL	Devon White, Tor	156	1384.0	11.51
1991	AL	Lance Johnson, CWS	158	1333.0	7.50
1991	AL	Kirby Puckett, Min	152	1306.0	6.86
1991	AL	Ken Griffey Jr., Sea	152	1271.2	5.50
1991	AL	Joe Carter, Tor	151	1335.1	5.21
1991	NL	Ron Gant, Atl	148	1293.1	6.91
1991	NL	Brett Butler, LA	161	1409.0	6.23
1991	NL	Marquis Grissom, Mon	138	1183.0	5.21
1991	NL	Otis Nixon, Atl	115	872.1	4.37
1991	NL	Ray Lankford, StL	149	1217.1	3.94
1992	AL	Brian McRae, KC	148	1283.1	6.38
1992	AL	Devon White, Tor	152	1307.0	6.31
1992	AL	Kirby Puckett, Min	149	1274.2	6.31
1992	AL	Lance Johnson, CWS	157	1364.0	5.70
1992	AL	Mike Devereaux, Bal	155	1396.0	5.44
1992	NL	Marquis Grissom, Mon	157	1402.1	8.01
1992	NL	Darrin Jackson, SD	153	1357.1	6.21
1992	NL	Andy Van Slyke, Pit	154	1373.2	5.66
1992	NL	Ray Lankford, StL	153	1369.0	5.54
1992	NL	Otis Nixon, Atl	111	962.0	5.50
1993	AL	Brian McRae, KC	153	1345.1	6.90
1993	AL	Lance Johnson, CWS	146	1238.0	5.63
1993	AL	Chad Curtis, Cal	151	1314.1	5.37
1993	AL	Billy Hatcher, Bos	130	1106.1	4.72
1993	AL	Devon White, Tor	145	1265.2	4.46
1993	NL	Marquis Grissom, Mon	157	1357.0	10.03
1993	NL	Otis Nixon, Atl	116	998.2	6.64
1993	NL	Chuck Carr, Fla	139	1180.2	6.54
1993	NL	Lenny Dykstra, Phi	160	1422.1	5.64
1993	NL	Larry Walker, Mon	132	1145.0	5.34
1994	AL	Lance Johnson, CWS	103	899.0	5.17
1994	AL	Brian McRae, KC	110	978.2	4.53
1994	AL	Turner Ward, Mil	99	836.0	4.35
1994	AL	Bernie Williams, NYY	107	938.2	4.01
1994	AL	Brady Anderson, Bal	109	964.0	3.35
1994	NL	Marquis Grissom, Mon	109	979.2	7.94
1994	NL	Roberto Kelly, 2 tms	110	939.2	3.86
1994	NL	Chuck Carr, Fla	104	880.0	3.76
1994	NL	Ryan Thompson, NYM	98	855.2	3.65
1994	NL	Moises Alou, Mon	106	922.1	3.42

Year	Lg	Player, Team	G	Inn	WS
1995	AL	Bernie Williams, NYY	144	1274.2	6.30
1995	AL	Jim Edmonds, Cal	139	1190.1	5.27
1995	AL	Albert Belle, Cle	142	1265.0	4.59
1995	AL	Kenny Lofton, Cle	114	974.0	4.38
1995	AL	Otis Nixon, Tex	138	1221.0	4.26
1995	NL	Marquis Grissom, Atl	136	1158.2	7.55
1995	NL	Brian McRae, ChC	137	1213.0	5.09
1995	NL	David Justice, Atl	120	1035.1	4.49
1995	NL	Ray Lankford, StL	129	1116.0	4.40
1995	NL	Raul Mondesi, LA	138	1204.2	4.36
1996	AL	Rich Becker, Min	146	1187.2	6.29
1996	AL	Kenny Lofton, Cle	152	1334.0	6.18
1996	AL	Bernie Williams, NYY	140	1232.0	4.64
1996	AL	Darryl Hamilton, Tex	147	1266.1	4.53
1996	AL	Ernie Young, Oak	140	1113.2	4.51
1996	NL	Marquis Grissom, Atl	158	1380.0	6.84
1996	NL	Ray Lankford, StL	144	1242.0	6.17
1996	NL	F.P. Santangelo, Mon	124	812.0	5.85
1996	NL	Steve Finley, SD	160	1416.2	5.03
1996	NL	Brian Jordan, StL	136	1138.1	4.97
1997	AL	Gerald Williams, Mil	154	1317.0	6.62
1997	AL	Brian L. Hunter, Det	162	1422.2	5.82
1997	AL	Ken Griffey Jr., Sea	153	1332.2	4.90
1997	AL	Jim Edmonds, Ana	115	967.0	4.79
1997	AL	Marquis Grissom, Cle	144	1250.2	4.66
1997	NL	Rondell White, Mon	151	1339.0	8.18
1997	NL	Andruw Jones, Atl	147	972.0	6.04
1997	NL	Raul Mondesi, LA	159	1390.0	5.04
1997	NL	Kenny Lofton, Atl	122	1047.1	5.02
1997	NL	Sammy Sosa, ChC	161	1416.2	3.97
1998	AL	Darren Lewis, Bos	152	1312.0	6.65
1998	AL	Jim Edmonds, Ana	153	1312.2	5.76
1998	AL	Kenny Lofton, Cle	154	1321.2	5.32
1998	AL	Quinton McCracken, TB	153	1315.0	5.24
1998	AL	Chad Curtis, NYY	148	1165.2	4.85

Year	Lg	Player, Team	G	Inn	WS
1998	NL	Andruw Jones, Atl	159	1372.2	9.48
1998	NL	Doug Glanville, Phi	158	1398.0	6.44
1998	NL	Carl Everett, Hou	123	1047.0	4.61
1998	NL	Devon White, Ari	144	1219.1	4.53
1998	NL	Steve Finley, SD	157	1335.1	4.25
1999	AL	Darren Lewis, Bos	130	1124.2	6.73
1999	AL	Bernie Williams, NYY	155	1354.2	6.58
1999	AL	Garret Anderson, Ana	153	1342.1	5.59
1999	AL	Troy O'Leary, Bos	157	1359.2	5.50
1999	AL	Chris Singleton, CWS	127	1097.2	5.11
1999	NL	Andruw Jones, Atl	162	1447.1	9.83
1999	NL	Steve Finley, Ari	155	1347.2	7.58
1999	NL	Mike Cameron, Cin	146	1260.2	6.95
1999	NL	Doug Glanville, Phi	148	1267.2	5.14
1999	NL	Darryl Hamilton, 2 tms	134	1085.1	4.46
2000	AL	Carl Everett, Bos	126	1063.2	6.01
2000	AL	Chris Singleton, CWS	145	1202.2	5.00
2000	AL	Bernie Williams, NYY	137	1170.0	4.94
2000	AL	Darin Erstad, Ana	136	1187.0	4.92
2000	AL	Garret Anderson, Ana	148	1308.1	4.81
2000	NL	Andruw Jones, Atl	161	1430.1	8.91
2000	NL	Ken Griffey Jr., Cin	141	1227.1	6.83
2000	NL	Tom Goodwin, 2 tms	143	1138.0	6.53
2000	NL	Doug Glanville, Phi	150	1275.1	5.03
2000	NL	Steve Finley, Ari	148	1283.2	4.90
2001	AL	Torii Hunter, Min	147	1295.1	7.90
2001	AL	Darin Erstad, Ana	146	1269.1	7.64
2001	AL	Mike Cameron, Sea	149	1272.1	7.55
2001	AL	Carlos Beltran, KC	152	1324.0	5.90
2001	AL	Johnny Damon, Oak	154	1350.1	5.27
2001	NL	Andruw Jones, Atl	161	1435.1	8.26
2001	NL	Juan Pierre, Col	154	1257.2	6.59
2001	NL	Doug Glanville, Phi	150	1310.2	5.89
2001	NL	Richard Hidalgo, Hou	144	1235.0	5.54
2001	NL	Steve Finley, Ari	131	1110.2	5.23

Park Run and Home Run Factors—2001

	Hm	HmG	Hm Fact	Rd	RdG	Rd Fact	Pk Fact
Angels							
Run:	4682	486	9.63	4272	486	8.79	1.0960
HR:	1110	486	2.28	993	486	2.04	1.1178
Orioles							
Run:	2752	320	8.60	3312	328	10.10	0.8517
HR:	608	320	1.90	712	328	2.17	0.8753
Red Sox							
Run:	4664	486	9.60	4495	482	9.33	1.0291
HR:	991	486	2.04	1061	482	2.20	0.9263
Indians							
Run:	5293	482	10.98	5214	490	10.64	1.0320
HR:	1228	482	2.55	1012	490	2.07	1.2336
White Sox							
Run:	3276	324	10.11	3096	324	9.56	1.0581
HR:	880	324	2.72	700	324	2.16	1.2571
Tigers							
Run:	3164	324	9.77	3236	324	9.99	0.9778
HR:	516	324	1.59	760	324	2.35	0.6789
Royals							
Run:	5297	485	10.92	4637	486	9.54	1.1447
HR:	1119	485	2.31	1067	486	2.20	1.0509
Twins							
Run:	4785	486	9.85	4522	485	9.32	1.0560
HR:	976	486	2.01	1089	485	2.25	0.8944
Yankees							
Run:	4616	481	9.60	4768	486	9.81	0.9782
HR:	1159	481	2.41	1018	486	2.09	1.1503
Athletics							
Run:	4632	486	9.53	4983	485	10.27	0.9276
HR:	1085	486	2.23	1115	485	2.30	0.9711
Mariners							
Run:	2868	324	8.85	3348	324	10.33	0.8566
HR:	588	324	1.81	728	324	2.25	0.8077
Devil Rays							
Run:	3890	404	9.63	3921	405	9.68	0.9945
HR:	817	404	2.02	855	405	2.11	0.9579
Rangers							
Run:	5643	490	11.52	5415	482	11.23	1.0251
HR:	1353	490	2.76	1310	482	2.72	1.0160
Blue Jays							
Run:	5076	490	10.36	4518	482	9.37	1.1052
HR:	1127	490	2.30	1155	482	2.40	0.9598

	Hm	HmG	Hm Fact	Rd	RdG	Rd Fact	Pk Fact
Diamondbacks							
Run:	4717	486	9.71	4393	486	9.04	1.0738
HR:	1270	486	2.61	1103	486	2.27	1.1514
Braves							
Run:	4239	486	8.72	4274	486	8.79	0.9918
HR:	983	486	2.02	1008	486	2.07	0.9752
Cubs							
Run:	4480	486	9.22	4767	486	9.81	0.9398
HR:	1090	486	2.24	1166	486	2.40	0.9348
Reds							
Run:	3140	324	9.69	3200	324	9.88	0.9812
HR:	760	324	2.35	736	324	2.27	1.0326
Rockies							
Run:	6702	486	13.79	4413	486	9.08	1.5187
HR:	1620	486	3.33	1030	486	2.12	1.5728
Marlins							
Run:	4259	481	8.85	4756	490	9.71	0.9123
HR:	887	481	1.84	1009	490	2.06	0.8955
Astros							
Run:	4389	405	10.84	3957	405	9.77	1.1092
HR:	1186	405	2.93	1013	405	2.50	1.1708
Dodgers							
Run:	4146	486	8.53	4969	486	10.22	0.8344
HR:	1119	486	2.30	1207	486	2.48	0.9271
Brewers							
Run:	3116	324	9.62	3068	324	9.47	1.0156
HR:	888	324	2.74	736	324	2.27	1.2065
Expos							
Run:	4791	486	9.86	4348	486	8.95	1.1019
HR:	1030	486	2.12	928	486	1.91	1.1099
Mets							
Run:	3988	486	8.21	4541	487	9.32	0.8800
HR:	950	486	1.95	1092	487	2.24	0.8718
Phillies							
Run:	4505	486	9.27	4580	486	9.42	0.9836
HR:	999	486	2.06	1055	486	2.17	0.9469
Pirates							
Run:	3024	324	9.33	3036	324	9.37	0.9960
HR:	600	324	1.85	712	324	2.20	0.8427
Padres							
Run:	4304	486	8.86	5158	486	10.61	0.8344
HR:	1033	486	2.13	1181	486	2.43	0.8747
Giants							
Run:	2784	324	8.59	3404	324	10.51	0.8179
HR:	584	324	1.80	936	324	2.89	0.6239
Cardinals							
Run:	4650	489	9.51	4647	482	9.64	0.9863
HR:	1196	489	2.45	1170	482	2.43	1.0076

Offensive/Defensive Team Splits

American League—2000

Team	PF	PA	ExR	XOR	OffC	DefC	Off%	OWS	DWS	Cost
Anaheim	1.025	1.012	872	872	411	457	.473	116.4	129.6	3.53
Baltimore	0.910	0.958	822	818	367	330	.526	116.8	105.2	3.14
Boston	1.024	1.011	872	875	338	585	.367	93.5	161.5	3.62
Cleveland	1.054	1.025	875	880	495	522	.487	131.4	138.6	3.77
Chicago	1.059	1.027	879	887	521	510	.506	144.1	140.9	3.62
Detroit	0.932	0.969	834	833	389	439	.470	111.5	125.5	3.49
Kansas City	1.090	1.041	895	893	414	427	.492	113.7	117.3	3.64
Minnesota	1.106	1.049	902	895	279	480	.367	76.0	131.0	3.67
New York	1.003	1.001	846	849	431	477	.475	123.9	137.1	3.48
Oakland	0.912	0.959	814	820	524	433	.547	149.4	123.6	3.51
Seattle	0.832	0.922	786	792	498	424	.540	147.5	125.5	3.38
Tampa Bay	0.997	0.999	859	851	287	452	.388	80.3	126.7	3.57
Texas	1.085	1.039	891	884	385	370	.510	108.5	104.5	3.55
Toronto	1.046	1.021	873	874	407	421	.492	122.5	126.5	3.32

National League—2000

Team	PF	PA	ExR	XOR	OffC	DefC	Off%	OWS	DWS	Cost
Arizona	1.030	1.014	820	822	366	496	.424	108.2	146.8	3.38
Atlanta	0.984	0.992	795	803	397	506	.439	125.2	159.8	3.17
Chicago	0.893	0.950	785	776	356	276	.564	109.9	85.1	3.24
Cincinnati	1.096	1.045	852	855	382	534	.417	106.3	148.7	3.59
Colorado	1.615	1.287	1033	1034	431	674	.390	95.9	150.1	4.49
Florida	0.909	0.958	770	769	331	372	.471	111.6	125.4	2.97
Houston	1.137	1.064	865	859	488	362	.574	124.0	92.0	3.94
Los Angeles	0.846	0.928	751	753	408	416	.495	127.7	130.3	3.19
Mliwaukee	0.954	0.979	810	806	319	399	.444	97.2	121.8	3.28
Montreal	0.995	0.998	806	798	319	312	.506	101.6	99.4	3.14
New York	0.886	0.947	764	771	410	434	.486	137.0	145.0	2.99
Philadelphia	1.047	1.022	835	826	274	425	.392	76.4	118.6	3.58
Pittsburgh	0.982	0.992	814	807	370	339	.522	108.1	98.9	3.42
San Diego	0.823	0.917	754	752	360	328	.523	119.3	108.7	3.02
San Francisco	0.827	0.919	738	746	541	387	.583	169.8	121.2	3.19
St. Louis	1.002	1.001	798	806	472	454	.510	145.3	139.7	3.25

Categories: Park Factor (PF), Park Adjustment (PA), Expected Runs Scored (ExR), Expected Opposition Runs (XOR), Offensive Credits (OffC), Defensive Credits (DefC), Offensive Percentage (Off%), Offensive Win Shares (OWS), Defensive Win Shares (DWS), Cost of a Win Share in terms of runs (Cost)

American League—2001

Team	PF	PA	ExR	XOR	OffC	DefC	Off%	OWS	DWS	Cost
Anaheim	1.096	1.044	821	818	264	513	.340	76.4	148.6	3.45
Baltimore	0.852	0.932	736	727	304	276	.524	99.1	89.9	3.07
Boston	1.029	1.013	798	800	357	470	.431	106.1	139.9	3.36
Cleveland	1.032	1.015	795	800	484	395	.551	150.3	122.7	3.22
Chicago	1.058	1.027	801	802	382	424	.474	118.0	131.0	3.23
Detroit	0.978	0.990	779	771	319	296	.519	102.8	95.2	3.10
Kansas City	1.145	1.067	846	837	289	414	.411	80.1	114.9	3.61
Minnesota	1.056	1.026	803	806	353	459	.435	111.0	144.0	3.18
New York	0.978	0.990	775	783	401	477	.457	130.2	154.8	3.08
Oakland	0.928	0.967	760	771	489	526	.482	147.4	158.6	3.32
Seattle	0.857	0.934	728	745	549	506	.520	181.0	167.0	3.03
Tampa Bay	0.995	0.997	784	774	264	289	.478	88.8	97.2	2.98
Texas	1.025	1.012	797	793	476	237	.668	146.2	72.8	3.25
Toronto	1.105	1.049	836	836	332	517	.391	93.9	146.1	3.54

National League—2001

Team	PF	PA	ExR	XOR	OffC	DefC	Off%	OWS	DWS	Cost
Arizona	1.074	1.034	791	797	406	535	.432	119.2	156.8	3.41
Atlanta	0.992	0.996	758	761	335	514	.394	104.1	159.9	3.22
Chicago	0.940	0.972	734	738	395	420	.485	128.0	136.0	3.09
Cincinnati	0.981	0.991	763	755	338	298	.532	105.3	92.7	3.21
Colorado	1.519	1.242	943	938	433	520	.454	99.5	119.5	4.35
Florida	0.912	0.959	731	728	362	363	.499	113.8	114.2	3.18
Houston	1.109	1.051	801	807	431	458	.485	135.2	143.8	3.19
Los Angeles	0.834	0.923	704	707	392	331	.542	139.9	118.1	2.80
Milwaukee	1.016	1.007	771	764	339	355	.488	99.6	104.4	3.40
Montreal	1.102	1.048	799	792	254	392	.394	80.4	123.6	3.17
New York	0.880	0.944	720	721	267	383	.412	101.2	144.8	2.64
Philadelphia	0.984	0.992	755	757	353	432	.450	116.1	141.9	3.05
Pittsburgh	0.996	0.998	757	747	264	277	.488	90.7	95.3	2.91
San Diego	0.834	0.923	703	702	423	255	.624	147.9	89.1	2.86
San Francisco	0.818	0.915	703	707	434	327	.570	153.9	116.1	2.82
St. Louis	0.986	0.994	746	753	426	461	.480	134.0	145.0	3.18

Divisions Among Batting, Pitching and Fielding Win Shares—2001

American League

Team	WS	OffWS	DefWS	PitPct	PitWS	FldWS
Anaheim	225	76.3851	148.6149	.686	101.9253	46.6896
Baltimore	189	99.0931	89.9069	.660	59.3363	30.5707
Boston	246	106.1291	139.8709	.705	98.5589	41.3120
Cleveland	273	150.3118	122.6882	.727	89.2390	33.4492
Chicago	249	117.9617	131.0383	.691	90.5038	40.5345
Detroit	198	102.7728	95.2272	.653	62.2111	33.0161
Kansas City	195	80.1305	114.8695	.628	72.1442	42.7252
Minnesota	255	110.9678	144.0323	.673	96.9419	47.0904
New York	285	130.1658	154.8342	.723	111.9025	42.9317
Oakland	306	147.3626	158.6374	.714	113.2536	45.3838
Seattle	348	181.0410	166.9590	.680	114.5115	52.4475
Tampa Bay	186	88.8357	97.1643	.646	62.7744	34.3900
Texas	219	146.1857	72.8143	.635	46.2581	26.5562
Toronto	240	93.9205	146.0796	.683	99.6998	46.3797

National League

Team	WS	OffWS	DefWS	PitPct	PitWS	FldWS
Arizona	276	119.1523	156.8477	.686	107.5676	49.2801
Atlanta	264	104.1145	159.8855	.710	113.5176	46.3678
Chicago	264	127.9847	136.0153	.711	96.6772	39.3381
Cincinnati	198	105.2624	92.7376	.697	64.6089	28.1288
Colorado	219	99.4641	119.5359	.654	78.2055	41.3304
Florida	228	113.7812	114.2188	.683	78.0105	36.2083
Houston	279	135.1704	143.8296	.684	98.3969	45.4327
Los Angeles	258	139.9269	118.0731	.691	81.5990	36.4740
Milwaukee	204	99.5991	104.4009	.666	69.5180	34.8829
Montreal	204	80.3524	123.6476	.688	85.0800	38.5676
New York	246	101.2292	144.7708	.692	100.1816	44.5892
Philadelphia	258	116.0502	141.9498	.685	97.1835	44.7663
Pittsburgh	186	90.7113	95.2887	.677	64.5097	30.7790
San Diego	237	147.8908	89.1092	.682	60.7807	28.3284
San Francisco	270	153.9477	116.0523	.689	79.9495	36.1028
St. Louis	279	134.0006	144.9994	.672	97.4772	47.5222

Fielding Wins Allocation Chart—2001

American League

Team	FldWS	C	1B	2B	3B	SS	OF	Total
Angels	46.69	.577	.727	.498	.409	.397	.667	
Claim Points		14.33	6.32	9.54	5.02	7.09	27.09	69.38
Win Shares		9.64	4.26	6.42	3.38	4.77	18.23	46.69
Orioles	30.57	.432	.317	.440	.553	.510	.505	
Claim Points		8.82	1.40	7.68	8.47	11.16	17.69	55.22
Win Shares		4.88	0.78	4.25	4.69	6.18	9.79	30.57
Red Sox	41.31	.397	.471	.480	.426	.428	.453	
Claim Points		7.49	3.25	8.96	5.42	8.21	14.67	48.00
Win Shares		6.44	2.80	7.71	4.67	7.06	12.63	41.31
Indians	33.45	.536	.446	.572	.370	.525	.356	
Claim Points		12.77	2.95	11.90	4.08	11.70	9.05	52.45
Win Shares		8.14	1.88	7.59	2.60	7.46	5.77	33.45
White Sox	40.53	.430	.455	.558	.338	.512	.546	
Claim Points		8.74	3.06	11.46	3.31	11.23	20.07	57.87
Win Shares		6.12	2.14	8.02	2.32	7.87	14.06	40.53
Tigers	33.02	.449	.556	.504	.561	.355	.428	
Claim Points		9.46	4.27	9.73	8.66	5.58	13.22	50.93
Win Shares		6.13	2.77	6.31	5.62	3.62	8.57	33.02
Royals	42.73	.525	.376	.549	.568	.743	.609	
Claim Points		12.35	2.11	11.17	8.83	19.55	23.72	77.73
Win Shares		6.79	1.16	6.14	4.85	10.74	13.04	42.73
Twins	47.09	.659	.585	.270	.571	.475	.601	
Claim Points		17.44	4.62	2.24	8.90	9.90	23.26	66.36
Win Shares		12.38	3.28	1.59	6.32	7.02	16.50	47.09
Yankees	42.93	.361	.608	.435	.592	.401	.400	
Claim Points		6.12	4.90	7.52	9.41	7.24	11.60	46.78
Win Shares		5.61	4.49	6.90	8.63	6.64	10.65	42.93
Athletics	45.38	.462	.486	.568	.577	.494	.501	
Claim Points		9.96	3.43	11.78	9.05	10.58	17.46	62.25
Win Shares		7.26	2.50	8.58	6.60	7.72	12.73	45.38
Mariners	52.45	.607	.464	.518	.575	.516	.674	
Claim Points		15.47	3.17	10.18	9.00	11.38	27.49	76.68
Win Shares		10.58	2.17	6.96	6.16	7.78	18.80	52.45
Devil Rays	34.39	.461	.451	.453	.497	.416	.497	
Claim Points		9.92	3.01	8.10	7.13	7.78	17.23	53.16
Win Shares		6.42	1.95	5.24	4.61	5.03	11.14	34.39
Rangers	26.56	.771	.518	.453	.443	.551	.340	
Claim Points		21.70	3.82	8.10	5.83	12.64	8.12	60.20
Win Shares		9.57	1.68	3.57	2.57	5.57	3.58	26.56
Blue Jays	46.38	.528	.538	.684	.511	.661	.503	
Claim Points		12.46	4.06	15.49	7.46	16.60	17.57	73.64
Win Shares		7.85	2.55	9.75	4.70	10.45	11.07	46.38

Fielding Wins Allocation Chart—2001

National League

Team	FldWS	C	1B	2B	3B	SS	OF	Total
Diamondbacks	49.28	.483	.585	.634	.527	.529	.596	
Claim Points		10.75	4.62	13.89	7.85	11.84	22.97	71.92
Win Shares		7.37	3.17	9.52	5.38	8.12	15.74	49.28
Braves	46.37	.451	.420	.553	.330	.546	.599	
Claim Points		9.54	2.64	11.30	3.12	12.46	23.14	62.19
Win Shares		7.11	1.97	8.42	2.33	9.29	17.25	46.37
Cubs	39.34	.538	.438	.482	.488	.435	.438	
Claim Points		12.84	2.86	9.02	6.91	8.46	13.80	53.90
Win Shares		9.37	2.08	6.59	5.04	6.17	10.07	39.34
Reds	28.13	.632	.486	.452	.486	.362	.424	
Claim Points		16.42	3.43	8.06	6.86	5.83	12.99	53.60
Win Shares		8.61	1.80	4.23	3.60	3.06	6.82	28.13
Rockies	41.33	.367	.689	.411	.598	.474	.646	
Claim Points		6.35	5.87	6.75	9.55	9.86	25.87	64.25
Win Shares		4.08	3.77	4.34	6.14	6.35	16.64	41.33
Marlins	36.21	.677	.595	.494	.599	.451	.452	
Claim Points		18.13	4.74	9.41	9.58	9.04	14.62	65.50
Win Shares		10.02	2.62	5.20	5.29	4.99	8.08	36.21
Astros	45.43	.694	.512	.440	.509	.499	.557	
Claim Points		18.77	3.74	7.68	7.42	10.76	20.71	69.08
Win Shares		12.35	2.46	5.05	4.88	7.08	13.62	45.43
Dodgers	36.47	.666	.496	.472	.503	.433	.380	
Claim Points		17.71	3.55	8.70	7.27	8.39	10.44	56.06
Win Shares		11.52	2.31	5.66	4.73	5.46	6.79	36.47
Brewers	34.88	.554	.498	.592	.389	.436	.489	
Claim Points		13.45	3.58	12.54	4.54	8.50	16.76	59.37
Win Shares		7.90	2.10	7.37	2.67	4.99	9.85	34.88
Expos	38.57	.231	.396	.421	.357	.686	.496	
Claim Points		1.18	2.35	7.07	3.77	17.50	17.17	49.03
Win Shares		0.93	1.85	5.56	2.96	13.76	13.50	38.57
Mets	44.59	.281	.598	.479	.553	.567	.465	
Claim Points		3.08	4.78	8.93	8.47	13.21	15.37	53.84
Win Shares		2.55	3.96	7.39	7.02	10.94	12.73	44.59
Phillies	44.77	.470	.587	.524	.636	.489	.529	
Claim Points		10.26	4.64	10.37	10.46	10.40	19.08	65.22
Win Shares		7.04	3.19	7.12	7.18	7.14	13.10	44.77
Pirates	30.78	.284	.605	.424	.518	.570	.470	
Claim Points		3.19	4.86	7.17	7.63	13.32	15.66	51.83
Win Shares		1.90	2.89	4.26	4.53	7.91	9.30	30.78
Padres	28.33	.533	.308	.458	.549	.318	.398	
Claim Points		12.65	1.30	8.26	8.38	4.25	11.48	46.31
Win Shares		7.74	0.79	5.05	5.12	2.60	7.02	28.33
Giants	36.1	.619	.423	.609	.273	.597	.447	
Claim Points		15.92	2.68	13.09	1.75	14.29	14.33	62.06
Win Shares		9.26	1.56	7.61	1.02	8.31	8.33	36.10
Cardinals	47.52	.644	.354	.542	.681	.591	.531	
Claim Points		16.87	1.85	10.94	11.54	14.08	19.20	74.48
Win Shares		10.76	1.18	6.98	7.37	8.98	12.25	47.52

Team Worksheets for Pitchers

1892 Boston Beaneaters

Tm RA/9 vs. Cutoff: 4.37259 vs. 7.2463264

Pitcher	W-L	IP	Sv	ERA	CP	WS
Nichols, C.	35-16	453.0	0	2.84	217.40	46.99
Stivetts, J.	33-16	415.2	3	3.03	185.86	40.17
Staley, H.	24-9	299.2	0	3.03	132.07	28.55
Clarkson, J.	8-7	145.2	0	2.35	71.45	15.44
Viau, L.	1-0	9.0	0	0.00	7.41	1.60
Clarkson, A.	1-0	7.0	0	1.29	5.30	1.15
Kelly, M.	0-0	6.0	0	1.50	2.33	0.50
Team	102-48	1336.0	3	2.86	621.82	134.40

1899 Cleveland Spiders

Tm RA/9 vs. Cutoff: 8.9145565 vs. 9.9145565

Pitcher	W-L	IP	Sv	ERA	CP	WS
Hughey, J.	4-29	283.0	0	5.41	91.21	8.89
Knepper, C.	4-22	219.2	0	5.78	66.23	6.45
Schmit, C.	2-16	138.1	0	5.86	31.88	3.11
Carsey, K.	1-8	77.2	0	5.68	26.39	2.57
Hill, B.	3-6	72.1	0	6.97	16.41	1.60
Sudhoff, W.	3-8	86.1	0	6.98	16.25	1.58
Harper, J.	1-4	37.0	0	3.89	15.93	1.55
Bates, F.	1-18	153.0	0	7.24	11.30	1.10
Stivetts, J.	0-4	38.0	0	5.68	9.03	0.88
Lochhead, H.	0-0	3.2	0	0.00	3.04	0.30
Wilson, H.	0-1	8.0	0	9.00	0.48	0.05
Colliflower, H.	1-12	98.0	0	8.17	0.00	0.00
Maupin, H.	0-3	25.0	0	12.6	0.00	0.00
McAllister, S.	0-2	16.0	0	9.56	0.00	0.00
Kolb, E.	0-1	8.0	0	10.1	0.00	0.00
Team	20-134	1264.0	0	6.37	288.15	28.08

1904 New York Giants

Tm RA/9 vs. Cutoff: 3.0673032 vs. 5.1534557

Pitcher	W-L	IP	Sv	ERA	CP	WS
McGinnity, J.	35-8	408.0	5	1.61	178.09	42.30
Mathewson, C.	33-12	367.2	1	2.03	139.21	33.07
Taylor, L.	21-15	296.1	0	2.34	92.81	22.04
Wiltse, G.	13-3	164.2	3	2.84	49.73	11.81
Ames, R.	4-6	115.0	3	2.27	32.79	7.79
Dunn, J.	0-0	4.0	1	4.50	0.04	0.01
Milligan, B.	0-1	25.0	2	5.40	0.00	0.00
Elliott, C.	0-1	15.0	0	3.00	0.00	0.00
Bowerman, F.	0-0	1.0	0	9.00	0.00	0.00
Team	106-46	1396.2	15	2.17	492.67	117.02

1906 Chicago Cubs

Tm RA/9 vs. Cutoff: 2.4698679 vs. 4.497470

Pitcher	W-L	IP	Sv	ERA	CP	WS
Brown, M.	26-6	277.1	3	1.04	120.72	35.30
Pfiester, J.	20-8	250.2	0	1.51	83.88	24.53
Reulbach, E.	19-4	218.0	3	1.65	78.61	22.99
Lundgren, C.	17-6	207.2	2	2.21	63.27	18.50
Taylor, J.	12-3	147.1	0	1.83	48.52	14.19
Overall, O.	12-3	144.0	1	1.88	44.79	13.10
Beebe, F.	7-1	70.0	1	2.70	16.40	4.80
Wicker, B.	3-5	72.1	0	2.99	6.10	1.78
Harper, J.	0-0	1.0	0	0.00	0.43	0.12
Team	116-36	1388.1	10	1.75	462.72	135.30

1912 Boston Red Sox

Tm RA/9 vs. Cutoff: 3.5947137 vs. 5.9154444

Pitcher	W-L	IP	Sv	ERA	CP	WS
Wood, J.	34-5	344.0	1	1.91	171.44	40.41
O'Brien, B.	20-13	275.2	0	2.58	96.98	22.86
Bedient, H.	20-9	231.0	2	2.92	87.42	20.60
Collins, R.	13-8	199.1	0	2.53	80.57	18.99
Hall, C.	15-8	191.0	2	3.02	65.61	15.46
Bushelman, J.	1-0	7.2	0	4.70	1.76	0.42
Van Dyke, B.	0-0	14.1	0	3.14	1.64	0.39
Pape, L.	1-1	48.2	1	4.99	1.24	0.29
Smith, D.	0-0	3.0	0	3.00	0.97	0.23
Cicotte, E.	1-3	46.0	0	5.67	0.00	0.00
Hageman, C.	0-0	1.1	0	27.0	0.00	0.00
Team	105-47	1362.0	6	2.76	507.64	119.65

1927 New York Yankees

Tm RA/9 vs. Cutoff: 3.8793476 vs. 6.275898

Pitcher	W-L	IP	Sv	ERA	CP	WS
Moore, W.	19-7	213.0	13	2.28	115.90	23.49
Hoyt, W.	22-7	256.1	1	2.63	114.98	23.30
Pennock, H.	19-8	209.2	2	3.00	82.86	16.79
Shocker, U.	18-6	200.0	0	2.84	80.85	16.38
Ruether, D.	13-6	184.0	0	3.38	60.70	12.30
Pipgras, G.	10-3	166.1	0	4.11	46.38	9.40
Shawkey, B.	2-3	43.2	4	2.89	18.41	3.73
Thomas, M.	7-4	88.2	0	4.87	14.44	2.93
Giard, J.	0-0	27	0	8.00	0.00	0.00
Beall, W.	0-0	1.0	0	9.00	0.00	0.00
Team	110-44	1389.2	20	3.20	534.52	108.32

1931 Philadelphia Athletics

Tm RA/9 vs. Cutoff: 4.1264648 vs. 6.6951604

Pitcher	W-L	IP	Sv	ERA	CP	WS
Grove, L.	31-4	288.2	5	2.06	171.73	41.83
Earnshaw, G.	21-7	281.2	6	3.67	114.55	27.90
Walberg, R.	20-12	291.0	3	3.74	99.04	24.12
Mahaffey, R.	15-4	162.1	2	4.21	53.20	12.96
Rommel, E.	7-5	118.0	0	2.97	48.61	11.84
Hoyt, W.	10-5	111.0	0	4.22	34.91	8.50
McDonald, H.	2-4	70.1	0	3.71	15.04	3.66
Krausse, L.	1-0	11.0	0	4.09	3.48	0.85
Shores, B.	0-3	16.0	0	5.06	0.00	0.00
Peterson, J.	0-1	13.0	0	6.23	0.00	0.00
Carter, S.	0-0	2.1	0	19.3	0.00	0.00
Team	107-45	1365.1	16	3.47	540.54	131.66

1935 Boston Braves

Tm RA/9 vs. Cutoff: 5.7654138 vs. 6.7654138

Pitcher	W-L	IP	Sv	ERA	CP	WS
Smith, B.	8-18	203.1	5	3.94	62.13	8.87
Frankhouse, F.	11-15	230.2	0	4.76	44.90	6.41
Cantwell, B.	4-25	210.2	0	4.61	41.53	5.93
Brandt, E.	5-19	174.2	0	5.00	24.10	3.44
MacFayden, D.	5-13	151.2	0	5.10	20.83	2.97
Blanche, A.	0-0	17.1	0	1.56	9.59	1.37
Betts, H.	2-9	159.2	0	5.47	9.03	1.29
Mangum, L.	0-0	4.2	0	3.86	1.01	0.14
Benton, L.	2-3	72.0	0	6.88	0.00	0.00
Brown, B.	1-8	65.0	0	6.37	0.00	0.00
Rhem, F.	0-5	40.1	0	5.36	0.00	0.00
Team	38-115	1330.0	5	4.93	213.11	30.43

1953 Brooklyn Dodgers

Tm RA/9 vs. Cutoff: 4.4913087 vs. 6.487382

Pitcher	W-L	IP	Sv	ERA	CP	WS
Erskine, C.	20-6	246.2	3	3.54	94.17	19.96
Labine, C.	11-6	110.1	7	2.77	59.40	12.59
Milliken, M.	8-4	117.2	2	3.37	43.03	9.12
Meyer, R.	15-5	191.1	0	4.56	41.32	8.76
Hughes, J.	4-3	85.2	9	3.47	41.28	8.75
Roe, P.	11-3	157.0	0	4.36	40.49	8.58
Loes, B.	14-8	162.2	0	4.54	36.47	7.73
Wade, B.	7-5	90.1	3	3.79	33.23	7.04
Podres, J.	9-4	115.0	0	4.23	32.48	6.88
Black, J.	6-3	72.2	5	5.33	16.69	3.54
Moore, R.	0-1	8.0	0	3.38	2.14	0.45
Branca, R.	0-0	11.0	0	9.82	0.00	0.00
Mickens, G.	0-1	6.1	0	11.4	0.00	0.00
Palica, E.	0-0	6.0	0	12.0	0.00	0.00
Team	105-49	1380.2	29	4.10	440.69	93.42

1954 Cleveland Indians

Tm RA/9 vs. Cutoff: 3.1958666 vs. 5.3656559

Pitcher	W-L	IP	Sv	ERA	CP	WS
Wynn, E.	23-11	270.2	2	2.73	92.72	24.27
Garcia, M.	19-8	258.2	5	2.64	89.69	23.48
Lemon, B.	23-7	258.1	0	2.72	88.18	23.08
Houtteman, A.	15-7	188.0	0	3.35	49.75	13.02
Mossi, D.	6-1	93.0	7	1.94	49.09	12.85
Narleski, R.	3-3	89.0	13	2.22	44.07	11.54
Feller, B.	13-3	140.0	0	3.09	43.54	11.40
Newhouser, H.	7-2	46.2	7	2.51	26.81	7.02
Chakales, B.	2-0	10.1	0	0.87	7.16	1.87
Hoskins, D.	0-1	26.2	0	3.04	5.43	1.42
Santiago, J.	0-0	1.2	0	0.00	0.49	0.13
Hooper, B.	0-0	34.2	2	4.93	0.33	0.09
Tomanek, D.	0-0	1.2	0	5.40	0.00	0.00
Team	111-43	1419.1	36	2.78	497.27	130.16

1961 New York Yankees

Tm RA/9 vs. Cutoff: 3.79629 vs. 5.6519785

Pitcher	W-L	IP	Sv	ERA	CP	WS
Ford, W.	25-4	283.0	0	3.21	94.82	22.36
Arroyo, L.	15-5	119.0	29	2.19	94.45	22.27
Stafford, B.	14-9	195.0	2	2.68	72.36	17.06
Terry, R.	16-3	188.1	0	3.15	62.51	14.74
Coates, J.	11-5	141.1	5	3.44	41.58	9.80
Sheldon, R.	11-5	162.2	0	3.60	39.80	9.39
Daley, B.	8-9	129.2	0	3.96	23.06	5.44
Reniff, H.	2-0	45.1	2	2.58	18.71	4.41
Ditmar, A.	2-3	54.1	0	4.64	3.14	0.74
Clevenger, T.	1-1	31.2	0	4.83	2.05	0.48
James, J.	0-0	1.1	0	0.00	0.84	0.20
Turley, B.	3-5	72.0	0	5.75	0.00	0.00
McDevitt, D.	1-2	13.0	1	7.62	0.00	0.00
Downing, A.	0-1	9.0	0	8.00	0.00	0.00
Duren, R.	0-1	5.0	0	5.40	0.00	0.00
Maas, D.	0-0	0.1	0	54.0	0.00	0.00
Team	109-53	1451.0	39	3.46	453.31	106.91

1962 New York Mets

Tm RA/9 vs. Cutoff: 5.9664335 vs. 6.9664335

Pitcher	W-L	IP	Sv	ERA	CP	WS
Craig, R.	10-24	233.1	3	4.51	52.96	8.94
Jackson, A.	8-20	231.1	0	4.40	50.74	8.57
Hook, J.	8-19	213.2	0	4.84	39.39	6.65
MacKenzie, K.	5-4	80.0	1	4.95	19.79	3.34
Moorhead, B.	0-2	105.1	0	4.53	17.82	3.01
Miller, B.L.	1-12	143.2	0	4.89	16.67	2.82
Cisco, G.	1-1	19.1	0	3.26	7.89	1.33
Hunter, W.	1-6	63.0	0	5.57	6.84	1.15
Anderson, C.	3-17	131.1	4	5.35	5.62	0.95
Foss, L.	0-1	11.2	0	4.63	2.60	0.44
Miller, B.G.	2-2	20.1	1	7.08	1.60	0.27
Daviault, R.	1-5	81.0	0	6.22	0.73	0.12
Hillman, D.	0-0	15.2	1	6.32	0.11	0.02
Mizell, W.	0-2	38.0	0	7.34	0.00	0.00
Jones, S.	0-4	23.1	0	7.71	0.00	0.00
Moford, H.	0-1	15.0	0	7.20	0.00	0.00
Labine, C.	0-0	4.0	0	11.3	0.00	0.00
Team	40-120	1430.0	10	5.04	222.76	37.62

1962 San Francisco Giants

Tm RA/9 vs. Cutoff: 4.2485747 vs. 5.9798841

Pitcher	W-L	IP	Sv	ERA	CP	WS
Sanford, J.	24-7	265.1	0	3.43	84.51	19.44
Marichal, J.	18-11	262.2	1	3.36	84.27	19.39
O'Dell, B.	19-14	280.2	0	3.53	75.12	17.28
Pierce	16-6	162.1	1	3.49	56.54	13.01
Miller, S.	5-8	107.0	19	4.12	36.47	8.39
Bolin, B.	7-3	92.0	5	3.62	32.69	7.52
Larsen, D.	5-4	86.1	11	4.38	24.47	5.63
Duffalo, J.	1-2	42.0	0	3.64	5.64	1.30
McCormick, M.	5-5	98.2	0	5.38	5.25	1.21
Perry, G.	3-1	43.0	0	5.23	4.21	0.97
Garibaldi, B.	0-0	12.1	1	5.11	1.86	0.43
LeMay, D.	0-1	9.1	1	7.71	0.00	0.00
Team	103-62	1461.2	39	3.79	411.02	94.56

1970 Baltimore Orioles

Tm RA/9 vs. Cutoff: 3.4936881 vs. 5.3398013

Pitcher	W-L	IP	Sv	ERA	CP	WS
Palmer, J.	20-10	305.0	0	2.71	95.62	24.98
McNally, D.	24-9	296.0	0	3.22	82.85	21.64
Cuellar, M.	24-8	297.2	0	3.48	68.81	17.97
Richert, P.	7-2	54.2	13	1.98	39.88	10.42
Hardin, J.	6-5	145.1	1	3.53	29.37	7.67
Phoebus, T.	5-5	135.0	0	3.07	28.40	7.42
Watt, E.	7-7	55.1	12	3.25	26.13	6.82
Hall, D.	10-5	61.1	3	3.08	24.21	6.32
Lopez, M.	1-1	60.2	0	2.08	19.23	5.02
Drabowsky, M.	4-2	33.1	1	3.78	7.62	1.99
Leonhard, D.	0-0	28.1	1	5.08	0.00	0.00
Beene, F.	0-0	6.0	0	6.00	0.00	0.00
Team	108-54	1478.2	31	3.15	422.12	110.26

1984 Detroit Tigers

Tm RA/9 vs. Cutoff: 3.9528689 vs. 5.7311296

Pitcher	W-L	IP	Sv	ERA	CP	WS
Hernandez, W.	9-3	140.1	32	1.92	115.43	24.03
Petry, D.	18-8	233.1	0	3.24	74.92	15.60
Morris, J.	19-11	240.1	0	3.60	66.38	13.82
Lopez, A.	10-1	137.2	14	2.94	64.04	13.33
Wilcox, M.	17-8	193.2	0	4.00	45.16	9.40
Berenguer, J.	11-10	168.1	0	3.48	44.86	9.34
Bair, D.	5-3	93.2	4	3.75	26.85	5.59
Rozema, D.	7-6	101.0	0	3.74	23.82	4.96
Scherrer, B.	1-0	19.0	0	1.89	9.10	1.89
O'Neal, R.	2-1	18.2	0	3.38	6.55	1.36
Monge, S.	1-0	36.0	0	4.25	4.92	1.03
Mason, R.	1-1	22.0	1	4.50	4.35	0.91
Abbott, G.	3-4	44.0	0	5.93	0.00	0.00
Willis, C.	0-2	16.0	0	7.31	0.00	0.00
Team	104-58	1464.0	51	3.49	486.38	101.25

1990 Oakland Athletics

Tm RA/9 vs. Cutoff: 3.5233517 vs. 5.2612314

Pitcher	W-L	IP	Sv	ERA	CP	WS
Stewart, D.	22-11	267.0	0	2.56	94.42	21.22
Eckersley, D.	4-2	73.1	48	0.61	85.69	19.26
Welch, B.	27-6	238.0	0	2.95	80.13	18.01
Nelson, G.	3-3	74.2	5	1.57	43.51	9.78
Sanderson, S.	17-11	206.1	0	3.88	39.95	8.98
Honeycutt, R.	2-2	63.1	7	2.70	33.70	7.57
Burns, T.	3-3	78.2	3	2.97	23.37	5.25
Moore, M.	13-15	199.1	0	4.65	16.53	3.71
Klink, J.	0-0	39.2	1	2.04	15.81	3.55
Young, C.	9-6	124.1	0	4.85	11.18	2.51
Chitren, S.	1-0	17.2	0	1.02	9.33	2.10
Harris, R.	1-0	41.1	0	3.48	9.16	2.06
Norris, M.	1-0	27.0	0	3.00	7.49	1.68
Bitker, J.	0-0	3.0	0	0.00	1.75	0.39
Otto, D.	0-0	2.1	0	7.71	0.00	0.00
Team	103-59	1456.0	64	3.18	472.02	106.08

1998 New York Yankees

Tm RA/9 vs. Cutoff: 4.053891 vs. 6.4511685

Pitcher	W-L	IP	Sv	ERA	CP	WS
Wells, D.	18-4	214.1	0	3.49	85.52	17.86
Cone, D.	20-7	207.2	0	3.55	80.64	16.84
Rivera, M.	3-0	61.1	36	1.91	68.52	14.31
Pettitte, A.	16-11	216.1	0	4.24	60.83	12.70
Hernandez, O.	12-4	141.0	0	3.13	59.98	12.52
Mendoza, R.	10-2	130.1	1	3.25	56.67	11.83
Irabu, H.	13-9	173.0	0	4.06	55.13	11.51
Lloyd, G.	3-0	37.2	0	1.67	25.72	5.37
Stanton, M.	4-1	79.0	6	5.47	20.75	4.33
Holmes, D.	0-3	51.1	2	3.33	19.38	4.05
Nelson, J.	5-3	40.1	3	3.79	17.83	3.72
Buddie, M.	4-1	41.2	0	5.62	6.03	1.26
Bruske, J.	1-0	9.0	0	3.00	4.69	0.98
Tessmer, J.	1-0	8.2	0	3.12	4.67	0.98
Bradley, R.	2-1	12.2	0	5.68	2.25	0.47
Borowski, J.	1-0	9.2	0	6.52	0.93	0.19
Banks, W.	1-1	14.1	0	10.1	0.00	0.00
Jerzembeck, M.	0-1	6.1	0	12.8	0.00	0.00
Erdos, T.	0-0	2.0	0	9.00	0.00	0.00
Team	114-48	1456.2	48	3.82	569.55	118.93

1999 Atlanta Braves

Tm RA/9 vs. Cutoff: 4.0441875 vs. 6.5118217

Pitcher	W-L	IP	Sv	ERA	CP	WS
Millwood, K.	18-7	228.0	0	2.68	100.69	22.16
Maddux, G.	19-9	219.1	0	3.57	76.50	16.84
Smoltz, J.	11-8	186.1	0	3.19	75.15	16.54
Rocker, J.	4-5	72.1	38	2.49	71.15	15.66
Glavine, T.	14-11	234.0	0	4.12	65.73	14.47
Remlinger, M.	10-1	83.2	1	2.37	54.96	12.10
McGlinchy, K.	7-3	70.1	0	2.82	34.97	7.70
Seanez, R.	6-1	53.2	3	3.35	33.39	7.35
Mulholland, T.	4-2	60.1	1	2.98	25.32	5.57
Springer, R.	2-1	47.1	1	3.42	21.31	4.69
Chen, B.	2-2	51.0	0	5.47	5.61	1.23
Bergman, S.	1-0	6.1	0	2.84	3.97	0.87
Perez, O.	4-6	93.0	0	6.00	2.97	0.65
Speier, J.	0-0	28.2	0	5.65	2.55	0.56
Ebert, D.	0-1	8.0	1	5.63	0.29	0.06
Cortes, D.	0-0	3.2	0	4.91	0.15	0.03
Hudek, J.	0-1	16.2	0	6.48	0.00	0.00
Bowie, M.	0-1	4.0	0	13.5	0.00	0.00
Cather, M.	1-0	2.2	0	10.1	0.00	0.00
Wohlers, M.	0-0	0.2	0	27.0	0.00	0.00
Stull, E.	0-0	0.2	0	13.5	0.00	0.00
Winkelsas, J.	0-0	0.1	0	54.0	0.00	0.00
Team	103-59	1471.0	45	3.65	574.73	126.49

2001 Seattle Mariners

Tm RA/9 vs. Cutoff: 3.8518772 vs. 5.9662104

Pitcher	W-L	IP	Sv	ERA	CP	WS
Garcia, F.	18-6	238.2	0	3.05	89.01	18.35
Moyer, J.	20-6	209.2	0	3.43	74.81	15.43
Sele, A.	15-5	215.0	0	3.60	65.74	13.56
Rhodes, A.	8-0	68.0	3	1.72	57.90	11.94
Sasaki, K.	0-4	66.2	45	3.24	57.22	11.80
Abbott, P.	17-4	163.0	0	4.25	45.37	9.35
Nelson, J.	4-3	65.1	4	2.76	40.70	8.39
Pineiro, J.	6-2	75.1	0	2.03	35.59	7.34
Franklin, R.	5-1	78.1	0	3.56	25.83	5.33
Charlton, N.	4-2	47.2	1	3.02	22.75	4.69
Halama, J.	10-7	110.1	0	4.73	17.15	3.54
Paniagua, J.	4-3	66.0	3	4.36	17.11	3.53
Tomko, B.	3-1	34.2	0	5.19	3.65	0.75
Fuentes, B.	1-1	11.2	0	4.63	2.51	0.52
Stark, D.	1-1	14.2	0	9.20	0.00	0.00
Team	116-46	1465.0	56	3.54	555.37	114.51

Actual and Expected Double Plays—1950-2001

1950 American League

Team	ActDP	ExpDP	Diff
Red Sox	181	189.8	-8.8
Indians	160	155.4	4.6
White Sox	181	185.2	-4.2
Tigers	194	177.6	16.4
Yankees	188	162.8	25.2
Athletics	208	198.8	9.2
Browns	155	190.9	-35.9
Nationals	181	186.9	-5.9

1950 National League

Team	ActDP	ExpDP	Diff
Braves	146	157.1	-11.1
Dodgers	183	159.8	23.2
Cubs	169	191.4	-22.4
Reds	132	150.3	-18.3
Giants	181	152.7	28.3
Phillies	155	148.9	6.1
Pirates	165	175.3	-10.3
Cardinals	172	168.6	3.4

1951 American League

Team	ActDP	ExpDP	Diff
Red Sox	184	182.5	1.5
Indians	151	157.1	-6.1
White Sox	176	161.7	14.3
Tigers	166	181.7	-15.7
Yankees	190	155.1	34.9
Athletics	204	189.2	14.8
Browns	179	201.9	-22.9
Nationals	148	168.3	-20.3

1951 National League

Team	ActDP	ExpDP	Diff
Braves	157	168.1	-11.1
Dodgers	192	162.4	29.6
Cubs	161	178.2	-17.2
Reds	141	153.0	-12.0
Giants	175	156.0	19.0
Phillies	146	149.4	-3.4
Pirates	178	187.8	-9.8
Cardinals	187	185.5	1.5

1952 American League

Team	ActDP	ExpDP	Diff
Red Sox	181	177.9	3.1
Indians	141	152.4	-11.4
White Sox	158	147.9	10.1
Tigers	145	168.6	-23.6
Yankees	199	165.2	33.8
Athletics	148	167.0	-19.0
Browns	176	161.7	14.3
Nationals	152	159.4	-7.4

1952 National League

Team	ActDP	ExpDP	Diff
Braves	143	156.6	-13.6
Dodgers	169	144.1	24.9
Cubs	123	144.9	-21.9
Reds	145	156.2	-11.2
Giants	175	156.4	18.6
Phillies	145	138.0	7.0
Pirates	167	174.6	-7.6
Cardinals	159	155.7	3.3

1953 American League

Team	ActDP	ExpDP	Diff
Red Sox	173	169.2	3.8
Indians	197	168.1	28.9
White Sox	144	164.0	-20.0
Tigers	149	184.7	-35.7
Yankees	182	161.8	20.2
Athletics	161	172.7	-11.7
Browns	165	173.9	-8.9
Nationals	173	148.5	24.5

1953 National League

Team	ActDP	ExpDP	Diff
Dodgers	161	141.0	20.0
Cubs	141	162.4	-21.4
Redlegs	176	160.9	15.1
Braves	169	151.2	17.8
Giants	151	167.8	-16.8
Phillies	161	135.5	25.5
Pirates	139	173.0	-34.0
Cardinals	161	168.6	-7.6

1954 American League

Team	ActDP	ExpDP	Diff
Orioles	152	160.8	-8.8
Red Sox	163	178.2	-15.2
Indians	148	133.8	14.2
White Sox	149	142.6	6.4
Tigers	131	155.0	-24.0
Yankees	198	159.9	38.1
Athletics	163	179.8	-16.8
Nationals	172	166.9	5.1

1954 National League

Team	ActDP	ExpDP	Diff
Dodgers	138	149.4	-11.4
Cubs	164	170.3	-6.3
Redlegs	194	163.6	30.4
Braves	171	158.9	12.1
Giants	172	158.6	13.4
Phillies	133	134.2	-1.2
Pirates	136	175.6	-39.6
Cardinals	178	177.2	0.8

1955 American League

Team	ActDP	ExpDP	Diff
Orioles	159	165.7	-6.7
Red Sox	140	160.3	-20.3
Indians	152	141.2	10.8
White Sox	147	151.0	-4.0
Tigers	159	149.7	9.3
Athletics	174	182.6	-8.6
Yankees	180	153.9	26.1
Nationals	170	177.9	-7.9

1955 National League

Team	ActDP	ExpDP	Diff
Dodgers	156	143.3	12.7
Cubs	147	159.5	-12.5
Redlegs	169	149.1	19.9
Braves	155	168.3	-13.3
Giants	165	162.4	2.6
Phillies	117	127.2	-10.2
Pirates	175	173.1	1.9
Cardinals	152	155.0	-3.0

1956 American League

Team	ActDP	ExpDP	Diff
Orioles	142	156.8	-14.8
Red Sox	168	178.4	-10.4
Indians	130	135.0	-5.0
White Sox	160	148.7	11.3
Tigers	151	157.0	-6.0
Athletics	187	183.3	3.7
Yankees	214	171.2	42.8
Nationals	173	198.4	-25.4

1956 National League

Team	ActDP	ExpDP	Diff
Dodgers	149	138.1	10.9
Cubs	141	154.2	-13.2
Redlegs	147	158.0	-11.0
Braves	159	151.3	7.7
Giants	143	147.8	-4.8
Phillies	140	132.4	7.6
Pirates	140	149.7	-9.7
Cardinals	172	158.4	13.6

1957 American League

Team	ActDP	ExpDP	Diff
Orioles	159	151.1	7.9
Red Sox	179	186.2	-7.2
Indians	154	162.8	-8.8
White Sox	169	160.2	8.8
Tigers	151	141.9	9.1
Athletics	162	166.4	-4.4
Yankees	183	165.5	17.5
Senators	159	182.5	-23.5

1957 National League

Team	ActDP	ExpDP	Diff
Dodgers	136	139.7	-3.7
Cubs	140	155.0	-15.0
Redlegs	139	140.1	-1.1
Braves	173	168.3	4.7
Giants	180	164.9	15.1
Phillies	117	119.9	-2.9
Pirates	143	150.7	-7.7
Cardinals	168	158.8	9.2

1958 American League

Team	ActDP	ExpDP	Diff
Orioles	159	138.8	20.2
Red Sox	172	189.7	-17.7
Indians	171	161.9	9.1
White Sox	160	159.2	0.8
Tigers	140	148.2	-8.2
Athletics	166	170.1	-4.1
Yankees	182	169.0	13.0
Senators	163	177.8	-14.8

1958 National League

Team	ActDP	ExpDP	Diff
Cubs	161	171.4	-10.4
Redlegs	148	152.6	-4.6
Dodgers	198	170.8	27.2
Braves	152	157.6	-5.6
Phillies	136	141.2	-5.2
Pirates	173	159.3	13.7
Giants	156	164.1	-8.1
Cardinals	163	169.5	-6.5

1959 American League

Team	ActDP	ExpDP	Diff
Orioles	163	142.5	20.5
Red Sox	167	164.2	2.8
Indians	138	140.5	-2.5
White Sox	141	150.5	-9.5
Tigers	131	128.5	2.5
Athletics	156	156.4	-0.4
Yankees	160	157.4	2.6
Senators	140	156.4	-16.4

1959 National League

Team	ActDP	ExpDP	Diff
Cubs	142	148.8	-6.8
Reds	157	145.0	12.0
Dodgers	154	151.0	3.0
Braves	138	147.5	-9.5
Phillies	132	134.2	-2.2
Pirates	165	142.9	22.1
Giants	118	136.7	-18.7
Cardinals	158	157.6	0.4

1960 American League

Team	ActDP	ExpDP	Diff
Orioles	172	151.4	20.6
Red Sox	156	169.6	-13.6
Indians	165	153.6	11.4
White Sox	175	168.7	6.3
Tigers	138	142.4	-4.4
Athletics	149	159.4	-10.4
Yankees	162	165.4	-3.4
Senators	159	165.2	-6.2

1960 National League

Team	ActDP	ExpDP	Diff
Cubs	133	159.0	-26.0
Reds	155	142.5	12.5
Dodgers	142	135.6	6.4
Braves	137	142.4	-5.4
Phillies	129	137.1	-8.1
Pirates	163	140.5	22.5
Giants	117	131.9	-14.9
Cardinals	152	139.1	12.9

1961 American League

Team	ActDP	ExpDP	Diff
Orioles	173	149.9	23.1
Red Sox	170	172.1	-2.1
Indians	142	153.7	-11.7
White Sox	138	158.0	-20.0
Tigers	147	130.4	16.6
Athletics	160	180.2	-20.2
Angels	154	171.0	-17.0
Twins	150	151.5	-1.5
Yankees	180	150.2	29.8
Senators	171	170.0	1.0

1961 National League

Team	ActDP	ExpDP	Diff
Cubs	175	171.7	3.3
Reds	124	142.9	-18.9
Dodgers	162	146.7	15.3
Braves	152	166.0	-14.0
Phillies	179	173.8	5.2
Pirates	189	165.5	23.5
Giants	126	136.0	-10.0
Cardinals	165	170.6	-5.6

1962 American League

Team	ActDP	ExpDP	Diff
Orioles	152	142.6	9.4
Red Sox	152	157.9	-5.9
Indians	168	154.6	13.4
White Sox	153	152.5	0.5
Tigers	114	125.2	-11.2
Athletics	131	160.3	-29.3
Angels	153	164.8	-11.8
Twins	173	145.1	27.9
Yankees	151	147.4	3.6
Senators	160	156.9	3.1

1962 National League

Team	ActDP	ExpDP	Diff
Cubs	171	183.1	-12.1
Reds	144	149.6	-5.6
Colt .45s	149	153.0	-4.0
Dodgers	144	156.0	-12.0
Braves	154	151.8	2.2
Mets	167	184.7	-17.7
Phillies	167	162.0	5.0
Pirates	177	160.8	16.2
Giants	153	142.2	10.8
Cardinals	170	154.7	15.3

1963 American League

Team	ActDP	ExpDP	Diff
Orioles	157	146.1	10.9
Red Sox	119	137.3	-18.3
Indians	129	132.9	-3.9
White Sox	163	143.1	19.9
Tigers	124	136.0	-12.0
Athletics	131	154.7	-23.7
Angels	155	163.7	-8.7
Twins	140	127.5	12.5
Yankees	162	138.1	23.9
Senators	165	167.4	-2.4

1963 National League

Team	ActDP	ExpDP	Diff
Cubs	172	150.8	21.2
Reds	127	122.6	4.4
Colt .45s	100	123.8	-23.8
Dodgers	129	135.4	-6.4
Braves	161	146.2	14.8
Mets	151	171.1	-20.1
Phillies	147	154.5	-7.5
Pirates	195	163.3	31.7
Giants	113	133.6	-20.6
Cardinals	136	131.8	4.2

1964 American League

Team	ActDP	ExpDP	Diff
Orioles	159	142.2	16.8
Red Sox	123	149.3	-26.3
Indians	149	150.7	-1.7
White Sox	164	130.5	33.5
Tigers	137	144.1	-7.1
Athletics	152	162.4	-10.4
Angels	168	163.8	4.2
Twins	131	137.2	-6.2
Yankees	158	150.3	7.7
Senators	145	152.6	-7.6

1964 National League

Team	ActDP	ExpDP	Diff
Cubs	147	172.7	-25.7
Reds	137	120.2	16.8
Colt .45s	124	137.4	-13.4
Dodgers	126	129.6	-3.6
Braves	139	139.9	-0.9
Mets	154	166.4	-12.4
Phillies	150	133.4	16.6
Pirates	179	163.8	15.2
Giants	136	138.9	-2.9
Cardinals	147	140.8	6.2

1965 American League

Team	ActDP	ExpDP	Diff
Orioles	152	143.8	8.2
Red Sox	129	151.0	-22.0
Angels	149	159.2	-10.2
Indians	127	124.9	2.1
White Sox	156	144.9	11.1
Tigers	126	130.8	-4.8
Athletics	142	147.0	-5.0
Twins	158	141.8	16.2
Yankees	166	154.5	11.5
Senators	148	153.1	-5.1

1965 National League

Team	ActDP	ExpDP	Diff
Cubs	166	171.3	-5.3
Reds	142	136.2	5.8
Astros	130	142.8	-12.8
Dodgers	135	130.5	4.5
Braves	145	147.4	-2.4
Mets	153	172.1	-19.1
Phillies	153	151.4	1.6
Pirates	189	162.1	26.9
Giants	124	130.6	-6.6
Cardinals	152	145.1	6.9

1966 American League

Team	ActDP	ExpDP	Diff
Orioles	142	139.1	2.9
Red Sox	153	158.8	-5.8
Angels	186	165.0	21.0
Indians	132	130.7	1.3
White Sox	149	146.7	2.3
Tigers	142	142.0	0.0
Athletics	154	157.0	-3.0
Twins	118	121.8	-3.8
Yankees	142	156.5	-14.5
Senators	139	137.9	1.1

1966 National League

Team	ActDP	ExpDP	Diff
Braves	139	142.9	-3.9
Cubs	132	164.1	-32.1
Reds	133	132.0	1.0
Astros	126	136.7	-10.7
Dodgers	128	129.3	-1.3
Mets	171	180.0	-9.0
Phillies	147	155.5	-8.5
Pirates	215	166.1	48.9
Giants	131	136.0	-5.0
Cardinals	166	147.6	18.4

1967 American League

Team	ActDP	ExpDP	Diff
Orioles	144	138.8	5.2
Red Sox	142	132.7	9.3
Angels	135	140.1	-5.1
Indians	138	127.9	10.1
White Sox	149	146.2	2.8
Tigers	126	127.9	-1.9
Athletics	120	130.8	-10.8
Twins	123	124.3	-1.3
Yankees	144	163.1	-19.1
Senators	167	156.2	10.8

1967 National League

Team	ActDP	ExpDP	Diff
Braves	148	140.5	7.5
Cubs	143	149.5	-6.5
Reds	124	130.8	-6.8
Astros	120	139.1	-19.1
Dodgers	144	151.3	-7.3
Mets	147	154.2	-7.2
Phillies	174	143.2	30.8
Pirates	186	179.3	6.7
Giants	149	141.6	7.4
Cardinals	127	133.6	-6.6

1968 American League

Team	ActDP	ExpDP	Diff
Orioles	131	129.8	1.2
Red Sox	147	144.1	2.9
Angels	156	137.6	18.4
Indians	130	114.1	15.9
White Sox	152	161.1	-9.1
Tigers	133	122.0	11.0
Twins	117	133.5	-16.5
Yankees	142	158.1	-16.1
Athletics	136	131.9	4.1
Senators	144	158.3	-14.3

1968 National League

Team	ActDP	ExpDP	Diff
Braves	139	132.1	6.9
Cubs	149	148.9	0.1
Reds	144	162.5	-18.5
Astros	129	143.2	-14.2
Dodgers	144	140.9	3.1
Mets	142	132.5	9.5
Phillies	163	156.1	6.9
Pirates	162	162.6	-0.6
Giants	125	130.8	-5.8
Cardinals	135	123.8	11.2

1969 American League

Team	ActDP	ExpDP	Diff
Orioles	145	132.0	13.0
Red Sox	178	170.7	7.3
Angels	164	144.9	19.1
Indians	153	149.2	3.8
White Sox	163	182.0	-19.0
Tigers	130	133.9	-3.9
Royals	114	139.9	-25.9
Twins	177	158.4	18.6
Yankees	158	150.0	8.0
Athletics	162	153.6	8.4
Pilots	149	169.8	-20.8
Senators	159	168.2	-9.2

1969 National League

Team	ActDP	ExpDP	Diff
Braves	114	121.7	-7.7
Cubs	149	152.6	-3.6
Reds	158	159.5	-1.5
Astros	136	137.8	-1.8
Dodgers	130	138.5	-8.5
Expos	179	172.1	6.9
Mets	146	126.4	19.6
Phillies	157	161.6	-4.6
Pirates	169	154.9	14.1
Padres	140	166.4	-26.4
Giants	155	151.7	3.3
Cardinals	144	135.8	8.2

1970 American League

Team	ActDP	ExpDP	Diff
Orioles	148	132.3	15.7
Red Sox	131	144.2	-13.2
Angels	169	145.4	23.6
Indians	168	160.0	8.0
White Sox	187	196.7	-9.7
Tigers	142	155.9	-13.9
Royals	162	151.1	10.9
Brewers	142	158.0	-16.0
Twins	130	137.2	-7.2
Yankees	146	159.1	-13.1
Athletics	152	136.4	15.6
Senators	173	176.3	-3.3

1970 National League

Team	ActDP	ExpDP	Diff
Braves	118	137.3	-19.3
Cubs	146	146.1	-0.1
Reds	173	161.3	11.7
Astros	144	160.3	-16.3
Dodgers	135	142.0	-7.0
Expos	193	172.8	20.2
Mets	136	120.0	16.0
Phillies	134	136.7	-2.7
Pirates	195	176.5	18.5
Padres	159	169.2	-10.2
Giants	153	159.0	-6.0
Cardinals	159	167.3	-8.3

1971 American League

Team	ActDP	ExpDP	Diff
Orioles	148	131.5	16.5
Red Sox	149	151.3	-2.3
Angels	159	163.0	-4.0
Indians	159	171.9	-12.9
White Sox	128	154.2	-26.2
Tigers	156	163.0	-7.0
Royals	178	158.5	19.5
Brewers	152	154.4	-2.4
Twins	134	147.6	-13.6
Yankees	159	164.4	-5.4
Athletics	157	124.6	32.4
Senators	170	163.4	6.6

1971 National League

Team	ActDP	ExpDP	Diff
Braves	180	159.4	20.6
Cubs	150	157.7	-7.7
Reds	174	156.5	17.5
Astros	152	147.7	4.3
Dodgers	159	148.6	10.4
Expos	164	181.0	-17.0
Mets	135	131.2	3.8
Phillies	158	167.9	-9.9
Pirates	164	163.2	0.8
Padres	144	160.5	-16.5
Giants	153	144.2	8.8
Cardinals	155	171.0	-16.0

1972 American League

Team	ActDP	ExpDP	Diff
Orioles	150	127.3	22.7
Red Sox	141	153.3	-12.3
Angels	135	144.3	-9.3
Indians	157	155.9	1.1
White Sox	136	143.3	-7.3
Tigers	137	139.8	-2.8
Royals	164	153.6	10.4
Brewers	145	145.3	-0.3
Twins	133	144.7	-11.7
Yankees	179	165.7	13.3
Athletics	146	134.6	11.4
Rangers	147	161.2	-14.2

1972 National League

Team	ActDP	ExpDP	Diff
Braves	130	140.3	-10.3
Cubs	148	153.6	-5.6
Reds	143	133.2	9.8
Astros	151	143.1	7.9
Dodgers	145	135.9	9.1
Expos	141	160.0	-19.0
Mets	122	122.7	-0.7
Phillies	142	147.0	-5.0
Pirates	171	140.5	30.5
Padres	146	148.1	-2.1
Giants	121	138.9	-17.9
Cardinals	146	141.9	4.1

1973 American League

Team	ActDP	ExpDP	Diff
Orioles	184	155.1	28.9
Red Sox	162	153.6	8.4
Angels	153	155.0	-2.0
Indians	174	179.3	-5.3
White Sox	165	180.2	-15.2
Tigers	144	152.9	-8.9
Royals	192	195.0	-3.0
Brewers	167	174.1	-7.1
Twins	147	159.5	-12.5
Yankees	172	168.0	4.0
Athletics	170	140.5	29.5
Rangers	164	180.9	-16.9

1973 National League

Team	ActDP	ExpDP	Diff
Braves	142	162.0	-20.0
Cubs	155	164.1	-9.1
Reds	162	150.8	11.2
Astros	140	147.0	-7.0
Dodgers	166	136.4	29.6
Expos	156	167.3	-11.3
Mets	140	135.1	4.9
Phillies	179	162.0	17.0
Pirates	156	166.4	-10.4
Padres	152	158.9	-6.9
Giants	138	148.1	-10.1
Cardinals	149	137.4	11.6

1974 American League

Team	ActDP	ExpDP	Diff
Orioles	174	165.5	8.5
Red Sox	156	154.0	2.0
Angels	150	166.0	-16.0
Indians	157	165.9	-8.9
White Sox	188	170.4	17.6
Tigers	155	169.9	-14.9
Royals	166	167.4	-1.4
Brewers	168	166.4	1.6
Twins	164	164.4	-0.4
Yankees	158	164.0	-6.0
Athletics	154	143.4	10.6
Rangers	164	156.0	8.0

1974 National League

Team	ActDP	ExpDP	Diff
Braves	161	139.5	21.5
Cubs	141	167.9	-26.9
Reds	151	136.4	14.6
Astros	161	164.0	-3.0
Dodgers	122	126.7	-4.7
Expos	157	158.6	-1.6
Mets	150	146.6	3.4
Phillies	168	161.4	6.6
Pirates	154	156.7	-2.7
Padres	126	172.2	-46.2
Giants	153	153.7	-0.7
Cardinals	192	153.3	38.7

1975 American League

Team	ActDP	ExpDP	Diff
Orioles	175	150.1	24.9
Red Sox	142	146.5	-4.5
Angels	164	148.3	15.7
Indians	156	152.0	4.0
White Sox	155	178.3	-23.3
Tigers	141	159.1	-18.1
Royals	151	152.3	-1.3
Brewers	162	167.2	-5.2
Twins	147	162.3	-15.3
Yankees	148	138.6	9.4
Athletics	140	132.3	7.7
Rangers	173	166.7	6.3

1975 National League

Team	ActDP	ExpDP	Diff
Braves	147	164.1	-17.1
Cubs	152	175.4	-23.4
Reds	173	144.6	28.4
Astros	166	168.4	-2.4
Dodgers	106	113.8	-7.8
Expos	179	175.2	3.8
Mets	144	141.6	2.4
Phillies	156	144.3	11.7
Pirates	147	145.1	1.9
Padres	163	163.4	-0.4
Giants	164	156.5	7.5
Cardinals	140	149.6	-9.6

1976 American League

Team	ActDP	ExpDP	Diff
Orioles	157	152.2	4.8
Red Sox	148	145.6	2.4
Angels	139	150.7	-11.7
Indians	159	144.4	14.6
White Sox	155	166.7	-11.7
Tigers	161	172.2	-11.2
Royals	147	151.8	-4.8
Brewers	160	150.0	10.0
Twins	182	163.7	18.3
Yankees	141	137.2	3.8
Athletics	130	141.3	-11.3
Rangers	142	145.2	-3.2

1976 National League

Team	ActDP	ExpDP	Diff
Braves	151	156.7	-5.7
Cubs	145	156.5	-11.5
Reds	157	138.8	18.2
Astros	155	158.6	-3.6
Dodgers	154	141.4	12.6
Expos	179	181.6	-2.6
Mets	116	119.0	-3.0
Phillies	148	127.4	20.6
Pirates	142	149.5	-7.5
Padres	148	160.2	-12.2
Giants	153	165.3	-12.3
Cardinals	163	160.5	2.5

1977 American League

Team	ActDP	ExpDP	Diff
Orioles	189	156.0	33.0
Red Sox	162	147.7	14.3
Angels	137	143.8	-6.8
Indians	145	143.3	1.7
White Sox	125	144.1	-19.1
Tigers	153	160.9	-7.9
Royals	145	142.1	2.9
Brewers	165	166.4	-1.4
Twins	184	169.5	14.5
Yankees	151	139.5	11.5
Athletics	136	151.6	-15.6
Mariners	162	164.4	-2.4
Rangers	156	146.1	9.9
Blue Jays	133	168.0	-35.0

1977 National League

Team	ActDP	ExpDP	Diff
Braves	127	154.9	-27.9
Cubs	147	163.8	-16.8
Reds	154	135.0	19.0
Astros	136	142.5	-6.5
Dodgers	160	135.1	24.9
Expos	128	146.1	-18.1
Mets	132	125.0	7.0
Phillies	168	150.4	17.6
Pirates	137	129.7	7.3
Padres	142	162.9	-20.9
Giants	136	147.0	-11.0
Cardinals	174	146.7	27.3

1978 American League

Team	ActDP	ExpDP	Diff
Orioles	166	153.9	12.1
Red Sox	171	158.6	12.4
Angels	136	140.6	-4.6
Indians	142	155.2	-13.2
White Sox	130	151.9	-21.9
Tigers	177	154.8	22.2
Royals	153	132.6	20.4
Brewers	144	160.5	-16.5
Twins	171	165.9	5.1
Yankees	134	134.3	-0.3
Athletics	145	141.3	3.7
Mariners	174	177.0	-3.0
Rangers	140	155.2	-15.2
Blue Jays	163	163.6	-0.6

1978 National League

Team	ActDP	ExpDP	Diff
Braves	126	143.1	-17.1
Cubs	154	170.3	-16.3
Reds	120	138.4	-18.4
Astros	109	128.0	-19.0
Dodgers	138	136.5	1.5
Expos	150	142.2	7.8
Mets	160	145.0	15.0
Phillies	156	128.8	27.2
Pirates	133	130.9	2.1
Padres	171	149.8	21.2
Giants	118	129.1	-11.1
Cardinals	155	148.0	7.0

1979 American League

Team	ActDP	ExpDP	Diff
Orioles	161	138.1	22.9
Red Sox	166	165.8	0.2
Angels	172	150.8	21.2
Indians	149	155.7	-6.7
White Sox	142	172.4	-30.4
Tigers	184	157.4	26.6
Royals	160	157.9	2.1
Brewers	153	162.7	-9.7
Twins	203	183.6	19.4
Yankees	183	166.0	17.0
Athletics	137	178.4	-41.4
Mariners	170	182.2	-12.2
Rangers	151	161.5	-10.5
Blue Jays	187	183.3	3.7

1979 National League

Team	ActDP	ExpDP	Diff
Braves	139	155.0	-16.0
Cubs	163	167.1	-4.1
Reds	152	142.7	9.3
Astros	146	130.4	15.6
Dodgers	123	140.9	-17.9
Expos	123	133.5	-10.5
Mets	168	154.5	13.5
Phillies	148	149.0	-1.0
Pirates	163	138.8	24.2
Padres	154	160.2	-6.2
Giants	138	158.2	-20.2
Cardinals	166	154.1	11.9

1980 American League

Team	ActDP	ExpDP	Diff
Orioles	178	161.8	16.2
Red Sox	206	185.6	20.4
Angels	144	154.3	-10.3
Indians	143	166.9	-23.9
White Sox	162	178.4	-16.4
Tigers	165	163.6	1.4
Royals	150	162.1	-12.1
Brewers	189	170.0	19.0
Twins	192	180.7	11.3
Yankees	160	158.4	1.6
Athletics	115	138.1	-23.1
Mariners	189	184.2	4.8
Rangers	169	173.6	-4.6
Blue Jays	206	191.3	14.7

1980 National League

Team	ActDP	ExpDP	Diff
Braves	156	146.7	9.3
Cubs	149	171.7	-22.7
Reds	144	132.7	11.3
Astros	145	133.1	11.9
Dodgers	149	133.9	15.1
Expos	126	138.5	-12.5
Mets	132	133.1	-1.1
Phillies	136	151.3	-15.3
Pirates	154	139.2	14.8
Padres	157	162.3	-5.3
Giants	124	146.7	-22.7
Cardinals	174	158.7	15.3

1981 American League

Team	ActDP	ExpDP	Diff
Orioles	114	106.6	7.4
Red Sox	108	111.1	-3.1
Angels	120	112.3	7.7
Indians	91	105.8	-14.8
White Sox	113	105.6	7.4
Tigers	109	105.1	3.9
Royals	94	92.3	1.7
Brewers	135	120.4	14.6
Twins	103	119.2	-16.2
Yankees	100	88.7	11.3
Athletics	74	89.1	-15.1
Mariners	122	117.4	4.6
Rangers	102	109.2	-7.2
Blue Jays	102	105.0	-3.0

1981 National League

Team	ActDP	ExpDP	Diff
Braves	93	99.6	-6.6
Cubs	103	109.6	-6.6
Reds	99	90.4	8.6
Astros	81	83.6	-2.6
Dodgers	101	90.9	10.1
Expos	88	81.5	6.5
Mets	89	93.9	-4.9
Phillies	90	104.6	-14.6
Pirates	106	96.4	9.6
Padres	117	118.0	-1.0
Giants	102	107.2	-5.2
Cardinals	108	103.4	4.6

1982 American League

Team	ActDP	ExpDP	Diff
Orioles	140	144.8	-4.8
Red Sox	172	167.2	4.8
Angels	171	173.0	-2.0
Indians	129	156.6	-27.6
White Sox	173	170.3	2.7
Tigers	165	154.9	10.1
Royals	140	148.4	-8.4
Brewers	185	162.0	23.0
Twins	162	147.6	14.4
Yankees	158	146.4	11.6
Athletics	140	155.6	-15.6
Mariners	158	150.0	8.0
Rangers	169	177.3	-8.3
Blue Jays	146	152.8	-6.8

1982 National League

Team	ActDP	ExpDP	Diff
Braves	186	150.7	35.3
Cubs	110	147.7	-37.7
Reds	158	139.8	18.2
Astros	154	132.2	21.8
Dodgers	131	138.1	-7.1
Expos	117	117.1	-0.1
Mets	134	155.4	-21.4
Phillies	138	136.7	1.3
Pirates	133	143.8	-10.8
Padres	142	131.1	10.9
Giants	125	148.1	-23.1
Cardinals	169	157.4	11.6

1983 American League

Team	ActDP	ExpDP	Diff
Orioles	159	153.6	5.4
Red Sox	168	163.6	4.4
Angels	190	199.4	-9.4
Indians	174	170.3	3.7
White Sox	158	154.3	3.7
Tigers	142	140.0	2.0
Royals	178	168.9	9.1
Brewers	162	163.2	-1.2
Twins	170	167.3	2.7
Yankees	157	149.9	7.1
Athletics	157	154.5	2.5
Mariners	159	173.2	-14.2
Rangers	151	163.5	-12.5
Blue Jays	148	151.0	-3.0

1983 National League

Team	ActDP	ExpDP	Diff
Braves	176	154.6	21.4
Cubs	164	167.4	-3.4
Reds	121	141.0	-20.0
Astros	165	142.5	22.5
Dodgers	132	135.7	-3.7
Expos	130	134.0	-4.0
Mets	171	162.0	9.0
Phillies	117	142.4	-25.4
Pirates	165	140.3	24.7
Padres	135	136.2	-1.2
Giants	109	144.8	-35.8
Cardinals	173	157.9	15.1

1984 American League

Team	ActDP	ExpDP	Diff
Orioles	166	164.3	1.7
Red Sox	128	163.5	-35.5
Angels	170	162.0	8.0
Indians	163	157.9	5.1
White Sox	160	153.5	6.5
Tigers	162	137.7	24.3
Royals	157	158.2	-1.2
Brewers	156	164.6	-8.6
Twins	134	145.4	-11.4
Yankees	177	159.3	17.7
Athletics	159	150.6	8.4
Mariners	143	166.8	-23.8
Rangers	138	145.0	-7.0
Blue Jays	166	147.6	18.4

1984 National League

Team	ActDP	ExpDP	Diff
Braves	153	157.5	-4.5
Cubs	137	149.4	-12.4
Reds	116	137.5	-21.5
Astros	160	142.5	17.5
Dodgers	146	153.4	-7.4
Expos	147	127.9	19.1
Mets	154	136.6	17.4
Phillies	112	136.9	-24.9
Pirates	142	136.4	5.6
Padres	144	127.0	17.0
Giants	134	162.5	-28.5
Cardinals	184	161.2	22.8

1985 American League

Team	ActDP	ExpDP	Diff
Orioles	168	166.3	1.7
Red Sox	161	175.4	-14.4
Angels	202	165.4	36.6
Indians	161	168.7	-7.7
White Sox	152	153.0	-1.0
Tigers	152	143.6	8.4
Royals	160	168.7	-8.7
Brewers	153	155.5	-2.5
Twins	139	153.5	-14.5
Yankees	172	137.6	34.4
Athletics	137	149.1	-12.1
Mariners	156	181.8	-25.8
Rangers	145	160.0	-15.0
Blue Jays	164	144.5	19.5

1985 National League

Team	ActDP	ExpDP	Diff
Braves	197	191.7	5.3
Cubs	150	164.2	-14.2
Reds	142	135.3	6.7
Astros	159	144.6	14.4
Dodgers	131	143.0	-12.0
Expos	152	146.3	5.7
Mets	138	130.3	7.7
Phillies	142	159.7	-17.7
Pirates	127	160.6	-33.6
Padres	158	135.3	22.7
Giants	134	143.0	-9.0
Cardinals	166	145.5	20.5

1986 American League

Team	ActDP	ExpDP	Diff
Orioles	163	151.0	12.0
Red Sox	146	142.9	3.1
Angels	156	144.2	11.8
Indians	148	170.4	-22.4
White Sox	142	149.5	-7.5
Tigers	163	152.4	10.6
Royals	153	156.7	-3.7
Brewers	146	138.5	7.5
Twins	168	155.9	12.1
Yankees	153	149.1	3.9
Athletics	120	149.5	-29.5
Mariners	191	189.4	1.6
Rangers	160	161.6	-1.6
Blue Jays	150	149.4	0.6

1986 National League

Team	ActDP	ExpDP	Diff
Braves	181	179.3	1.7
Cubs	147	155.8	-8.8
Reds	160	148.5	11.5
Astros	108	112.1	-4.1
Dodgers	118	145.9	-27.9
Expos	132	142.3	-10.3
Mets	145	136.2	8.8
Phillies	157	150.8	6.2
Pirates	134	159.4	-25.4
Padres	135	138.6	-3.6
Giants	149	139.1	9.9
Cardinals	178	139.8	38.2

1987 American League

Team	ActDP	ExpDP	Diff
Orioles	174	160.4	13.6
Red Sox	158	154.4	3.6
Angels	162	138.7	23.3
Indians	128	155.5	-27.5
White Sox	174	156.3	17.7
Tigers	147	148.5	-1.5
Royals	151	169.7	-18.7
Brewers	155	147.1	7.9
Twins	147	145.9	1.1
Yankees	155	147.5	7.5
Athletics	122	143.4	-21.4
Mariners	150	154.3	-4.3
Rangers	148	158.0	-10.0
Blue Jays	148	139.6	8.4

1987 National League

Team	ActDP	ExpDP	Diff
Braves	170	174.9	-4.9
Cubs	154	160.1	-6.1
Reds	137	131.6	5.4
Astros	113	127.0	-14.0
Dodgers	144	148.0	-4.0
Expos	122	128.1	-6.1
Mets	137	144.0	-7.0
Phillies	137	145.3	-8.3
Pirates	147	144.8	2.2
Padres	135	149.8	-14.8
Giants	183	145.3	37.7
Cardinals	172	154.7	17.3

1988 American League

Team	ActDP	ExpDP	Diff
Orioles	172	170.8	1.2
Red Sox	123	139.7	-16.7
Angels	175	176.9	-1.9
Indians	131	154.4	-23.4
White Sox	177	173.4	3.6
Tigers	129	138.5	-9.5
Royals	147	156.3	-9.3
Brewers	146	142.1	3.9
Twins	155	134.8	20.2
Yankees	161	156.0	5.0
Athletics	151	139.5	11.5
Mariners	168	148.3	19.7
Rangers	145	162.7	-17.7
Blue Jays	170	159.4	10.6

1988 National League

Team	ActDP	ExpDP	Diff
Braves	138	149.5	-11.5
Cubs	128	148.9	-20.9
Reds	131	131.5	-0.5
Astros	124	126.8	-2.8
Dodgers	126	127.9	-1.9
Expos	145	130.8	14.2
Mets	127	113.8	13.2
Phillies	139	147.6	-8.6
Pirates	128	132.8	-4.8
Padres	147	128.9	18.1
Giants	145	127.1	17.9
Cardinals	131	143.3	-12.3

1989 American League

Team	ActDP	ExpDP	Diff
Orioles	163	164.6	-1.6
Red Sox	162	156.5	5.5
Angels	173	158.2	14.8
Indians	126	147.9	-21.9
White Sox	176	158.8	17.2
Tigers	153	181.6	-28.6
Royals	139	151.6	-12.6
Brewers	164	161.7	2.3
Twins	141	148.4	-7.4
Yankees	183	169.9	13.1
Athletics	159	134.7	24.3
Mariners	168	165.9	2.1
Rangers	137	148.3	-11.3
Blue Jays	164	159.9	4.1

1989 National League

Team	ActDP	ExpDP	Diff
Braves	124	124.9	-0.9
Cubs	130	132.5	-2.5
Reds	108	133.0	-25.0
Astros	121	126.1	-5.1
Dodgers	153	120.3	32.7
Expos	126	136.5	-10.5
Mets	110	107.1	2.9
Phillies	136	145.6	-9.6
Pirates	130	133.7	-3.7
Padres	147	132.0	15.0
Giants	135	123.6	11.4
Cardinals	134	139.2	-5.2

1990 American League

Team	ActDP	ExpDP	Diff
Orioles	151	152.9	-1.9
Red Sox	154	164.9	-10.9
Angels	186	180.9	5.1
Indians	146	155.4	-9.4
White Sox	169	152.6	16.4
Tigers	178	172.9	5.1
Royals	161	156.5	4.5
Brewers	152	166.3	-14.3
Twins	161	159.7	1.3
Yankees	164	166.8	-2.8
Athletics	152	135.0	17.0
Mariners	152	157.4	-5.4
Rangers	161	162.1	-1.1
Blue Jays	144	149.2	-5.2

1990 National League

Team	ActDP	ExpDP	Diff
Braves	133	145.9	-12.9
Cubs	136	142.9	-6.9
Reds	126	126.1	-0.1
Astros	124	121.7	2.3
Dodgers	123	117.7	5.3
Expos	134	122.0	12.0
Mets	107	111.0	-4.0
Phillies	150	142.2	7.8
Pirates	125	123.4	1.6
Padres	141	125.8	15.2
Giants	148	149.2	-1.2
Cardinals	114	135.5	-21.5

1991 American League

Team	ActDP	ExpDP	Diff
Orioles	172	166.4	5.6
Red Sox	165	158.1	6.9
Angels	156	160.8	-4.8
Indians	150	155.8	-5.8
White Sox	151	146.4	4.6
Tigers	171	176.0	-5.0
Royals	141	156.7	-15.7
Brewers	176	160.9	15.1
Twins	161	151.0	10.0
Yankees	181	159.9	21.1
Athletics	150	156.5	-6.5
Mariners	187	161.5	25.5
Rangers	138	164.4	-26.4
Blue Jays	115	138.7	-23.7

1991 National League

Team	ActDP	ExpDP	Diff
Braves	122	123.5	-1.5
Cubs	120	136.5	-16.5
Reds	131	121.0	10.0
Astros	129	127.3	1.7
Dodgers	126	126.8	-0.8
Expos	128	134.5	-6.5
Mets	112	121.2	-9.2
Phillies	111	128.6	-17.6
Pirates	134	129.2	4.8
Padres	130	119.5	10.5
Giants	151	133.3	17.7
Cardinals	133	123.1	9.9

1992 American League

Team	ActDP	ExpDP	Diff
Orioles	168	148.6	19.4
Red Sox	170	168.2	1.8
Angels	172	166.3	5.7
Indians	176	158.2	17.8
White Sox	134	161.9	-27.9
Tigers	164	168.6	-4.6
Royals	164	156.5	7.5
Brewers	146	141.1	4.9
Twins	155	149.8	5.2
Yankees	165	165.9	-0.9
Athletics	158	144.1	13.9
Mariners	170	176.3	-6.3
Rangers	153	160.4	-7.4
Blue Jays	109	138.8	-29.8

1992 National League

Team	ActDP	ExpDP	Diff
Braves	121	127.7	-6.7
Cubs	142	150.2	-8.2
Reds	128	124.6	3.4
Astros	125	127.8	-2.8
Dodgers	136	145.9	-9.9
Expos	113	135.0	-22.0
Mets	134	136.7	-2.7
Phillies	128	131.3	-3.3
Pirates	144	144.2	-0.2
Padres	127	131.0	-4.0
Giants	174	135.1	38.9
Cardinals	146	128.0	18.0

1993 American League

Team	ActDP	ExpDP	Diff
Orioles	171	162.8	8.2
Red Sox	155	147.3	7.7
Angels	161	155.7	5.3
Indians	174	162.3	11.7
White Sox	153	146.5	6.5
Tigers	148	162.6	-14.6
Royals	150	151.0	-1.0
Brewers	148	149.6	-1.6
Twins	160	165.2	-5.2
Yankees	166	170.9	-4.9
Athletics	161	165.3	-4.3
Mariners	173	159.3	13.7
Rangers	145	162.7	-17.7
Blue Jays	144	146.6	-2.6

1993 National League

Team	ActDP	ExpDP	Diff
Braves	146	133.1	12.9
Cubs	162	157.9	4.1
Reds	133	141.4	-8.4
Rockies	149	168.0	-19.0
Marlins	130	143.7	-13.7
Astros	141	129.4	11.6
Dodgers	141	154.9	-13.9
Expos	144	147.9	-3.9
Mets	143	146.7	-3.7
Phillies	123	129.1	-6.1
Pirates	161	154.4	6.6
Padres	129	137.7	-8.7
Giants	169	131.4	37.6
Cardinals	157	152.1	4.9

1994 American League

Team	ActDP	ExpDP	Diff
Orioles	103	93.6	9.4
Red Sox	124	110.4	13.6
Angels	110	111.9	-1.9
Indians	119	118.7	0.3
White Sox	91	80.5	10.5
Tigers	90	117.4	-27.4
Royals	102	104.8	-2.8
Brewers	130	116.3	13.7
Twins	99	112.2	-13.2
Yankees	122	113.1	8.9
Athletics	105	103.4	1.6
Mariners	102	115.3	-13.3
Rangers	106	114.5	-8.5
Blue Jays	105	97.1	7.9

1994 National League

Team	ActDP	ExpDP	Diff
Braves	85	98.1	-13.1
Cubs	110	108.1	1.9
Reds	91	92.5	-1.5
Rockies	117	125.5	-8.5
Marlins	111	106.3	4.7
Astros	110	107.1	2.9
Dodgers	104	105.8	-1.8
Expos	90	89.1	0.9
Mets	112	106.9	5.1
Phillies	96	95.4	0.6
Pirates	131	121.6	9.4
Padres	82	97.3	-15.3
Giants	113	106.3	6.7
Cardinals	119	113.5	5.5

1995 American League

Team	ActDP	ExpDP	Diff
Orioles	141	125.4	15.6
Red Sox	151	142.5	8.5
Angels	120	125.0	-5.0
Indians	142	135.1	6.9
White Sox	131	142.9	-11.9
Tigers	143	162.8	-19.8
Royals	168	151.9	16.1
Brewers	186	168.7	17.3
Twins	141	144.4	-3.4
Yankees	121	127.5	-6.5
Athletics	151	141.8	9.2
Mariners	108	133.1	-25.1
Rangers	156	149.1	6.9
Blue Jays	131	139.7	-8.7

1995 National League

Team	ActDP	ExpDP	Diff
Braves	113	122.5	-9.5
Cubs	115	134.2	-19.2
Reds	140	119.1	20.9
Rockies	146	151.8	-5.8
Marlins	143	133.9	9.1
Astros	120	141.1	-21.1
Dodgers	120	115.5	4.5
Expos	119	127.1	-8.1
Mets	125	127.3	-2.3
Phillies	139	130.3	8.7
Pirates	138	144.8	-6.8
Padres	130	129.0	1.0
Giants	142	136.4	5.6
Cardinals	156	133.7	22.3

1996 American League

Team	ActDP	ExpDP	Diff
Orioles	173	167.2	5.8
Red Sox	152	174.1	-22.1
Angels	156	169.9	-13.9
Indians	156	157.2	-1.2
White Sox	145	150.9	-5.9
Tigers	157	196.9	-39.9
Royals	184	152.5	31.5
Brewers	180	167.6	12.4
Twins	142	143.5	-1.5
Yankees	146	154.2	-8.2
Athletics	195	180.0	15.0
Mariners	155	153.3	1.7
Rangers	150	161.9	-11.9
Blue Jays	187	150.0	37.0

1996 National League

Team	ActDP	ExpDP	Diff
Braves	143	137.9	5.1
Cubs	147	151.1	-4.1
Reds	145	147.8	-2.8
Rockies	167	186.5	-19.5
Marlins	187	161.1	25.9
Astros	130	151.9	-21.9
Dodgers	143	133.3	9.7
Expos	121	136.4	-15.4
Mets	163	150.3	12.7
Phillies	145	133.5	11.5
Pirates	144	164.4	-20.4
Padres	136	140.4	-4.4
Giants	165	146.7	18.3
Cardinals	139	136.8	2.2

1997 American League

Team	ActDP	ExpDP	Diff
Angels	140	150.0	-10.0
Orioles	148	148.9	-0.9
Red Sox	179	172.9	6.1
Indians	159	167.8	-8.8
White Sox	131	135.0	-4.0
Tigers	146	158.8	-12.8
Royals	168	150.1	17.9
Brewers	171	150.8	20.2
Twins	170	157.6	12.4
Yankees	156	151.5	4.5
Athletics	170	195.0	-25.0
Mariners	143	151.8	-8.8
Rangers	155	164.8	-9.8
Blue Jays	150	133.9	16.1

1997 National League

Team	ActDP	ExpDP	Diff
Braves	136	124.0	12.0
Cubs	117	139.4	-22.4
Reds	129	131.1	-2.1
Rockies	202	189.8	12.2
Marlins	167	146.8	20.2
Astros	169	150.2	18.8
Dodgers	104	122.2	-18.2
Expos	150	140.2	9.8
Mets	165	154.4	10.6
Phillies	134	138.3	-4.3
Pirates	149	162.7	-13.7
Padres	132	169.3	-37.3
Giants	157	157.7	-0.7
Cardinals	156	145.2	10.8

1998 American League

Team	ActDP	ExpDP	Diff
Angels	146	149.4	-3.4
Orioles	144	155.8	-11.8
Red Sox	128	132.9	-4.9
Indians	146	160.8	-14.8
White Sox	161	158.0	3.0
Tigers	164	166.4	-2.4
Royals	172	157.9	14.1
Twins	135	139.3	-4.3
Yankees	146	131.0	15.0
Athletics	155	148.0	7.0
Mariners	139	139.2	-0.2
Devil Rays	178	165.2	12.8
Rangers	140	147.7	-7.7
Blue Jays	131	135.2	-4.2

1998 National League

Team	ActDP	ExpDP	Diff
D'backs	125	143.8	-18.8
Braves	139	131.6	7.4
Cubs	107	147.9	-40.9
Reds	142	135.7	6.3
Rockies	193	174.7	18.3
Marlins	177	178.8	-1.8
Astros	144	147.4	-3.4
Dodgers	154	150.6	3.4
Brewers	192	160.2	31.8
Expos	127	148.7	-21.7
Mets	151	143.5	7.5
Phillies	131	149.7	-18.7
Pirates	161	145.9	15.1
Padres	155	140.8	14.2
Giants	157	156.1	0.9
Cardinals	160	160.7	-0.7

1999 American League

Team	ActDP	ExpDP	Diff
Angels	156	165.3	-9.3
Orioles	191	171.5	19.5
Red Sox	132	132.4	-0.4
Indians	154	168.5	-14.5
White Sox	149	154.9	-5.9
Tigers	156	158.8	-2.8
Royals	188	180.0	8.0
Twins	150	147.5	2.5
Yankees	132	143.7	-11.7
Athletics	166	163.8	2.2
Mariners	182	181.8	0.2
Devil Rays	198	193.9	4.1
Rangers	169	167.2	1.8
Blue Jays	165	162.5	2.5

1999 National League

Team	ActDP	ExpDP	Diff
D'backs	132	132.6	-0.6
Braves	127	134.6	-7.6
Cubs	135	142.1	-7.1
Reds	139	128.1	10.9
Rockies	189	186.2	2.8
Marlins	150	167.2	-17.2
Astros	175	148.0	27.0
Dodgers	137	152.7	-15.7
Brewers	146	160.5	-14.5
Expos	125	149.7	-24.7
Mets	147	142.3	4.7
Phillies	144	145.7	-1.7
Pirates	179	162.7	16.3
Padres	151	136.5	14.5
Giants	155	150.7	4.3
Cardinals	163	158.1	4.9

2000 American League

Team	ActDP	ExpDP	Diff
Angels	182	172.0	10.0
Orioles	151	159.9	-8.9
Red Sox	120	143.2	-23.2
Indians	147	168.8	-21.8
White Sox	190	163.3	26.7
Tigers	172	165.3	6.7
Royals	185	178.1	6.9
Twins	155	143.8	11.2
Yankees	132	139.6	-7.6
Athletics	164	174.9	-10.9
Mariners	176	156.8	19.2
Devil Rays	170	172.1	-2.1
Rangers	162	175.7	-13.7
Blue Jays	176	168.7	7.3

2000 National League

Team	ActDP	ExpDP	Diff
D'backs	138	128.7	9.3
Braves	137	145.5	-8.5
Cubs	139	149.0	-10.0
Reds	156	145.6	10.4
Rockies	176	166.3	9.7
Marlins	144	162.3	-18.3
Astros	150	149.3	0.7
Dodgers	151	150.0	1.0
Brewers	186	172.9	13.1
Expos	151	162.4	-11.4
Mets	121	140.3	-19.3
Phillies	136	136.5	-0.5
Pirates	168	185.1	-17.1
Padres	155	152.8	2.2
Giants	173	150.2	22.8
Cardinals	148	135.2	12.8

2001 American League

Team	ActDP	ExpDP	Diff
Angels	142	152.8	-10.8
Orioles	137	149.7	-12.7
Red Sox	129	141.2	-12.2
Indians	137	151.3	-14.3
White Sox	149	154.8	-5.8
Tigers	164	176.3	-12.3
Royals	204	170.0	34.0
Twins	118	130.3	-12.3
Yankees	132	127.9	4.1
Athletics	151	141.3	9.7
Mariners	137	122.0	15.0
Devil Rays	144	144.5	-0.5
Rangers	167	166.9	0.1
Blue Jays	184	169.6	14.4

2001 National League

Team	ActDP	ExpDP	Diff
D'backs	148	122.8	25.2
Braves	133	137.1	-4.1
Cubs	113	129.6	-16.6
Reds	136	158.6	-22.6
Rockies	167	163.7	3.3
Marlins	174	159.5	14.5
Astros	138	143.0	-5.0
Dodgers	138	136.3	1.7
Brewers	156	168.0	-12.0
Expos	139	147.9	-8.9
Mets	132	126.4	5.6
Phillies	145	142.2	2.8
Pirates	168	174.3	-6.3
Padres	127	140.9	-13.9
Giants	170	150.6	19.4
Cardinals	156	144.5	11.5

About the Authors

Bill James, who lives in Lawrence, Kansas, is the author of three children and the father of more than three baseball books, including the recent *Bill James Historical Baseball Abstract*. Well, the co-author of three children; his wife, Susan McCarthy, helped with those; that was just the kind of arrangement they had. Mr. James has worked with STATS, Inc. for many years on countless different projects.

Jim Henzler is a senior editor at STATS, Inc. He initially provided statistical support for ESPN, and has contributed to numerous STATS books as a writer, programmer and editor. Before joining STATS in 1995, he had stints as a reporter and producer for a regional media network, as well as an actuary. He resides in O'Fallon, Missouri, with his wife Cortina and sons Gerard and Philip.

About STATS, Inc.

STATS, Inc., a News Corporation company, is affiliated with—and is the official statistics provider to—FOX Sports. STATS collects and disseminates most, if not all, of the information found within these pages, in addition to the statistics you might find on your favorite website. STATS, Inc. is the nation's leading sports information and statistical analysis company, providing detailed sports services for a wide array of consumer and commercial clients.

As one of the elite companies in sports, STATS provides the most detailed, up-to-the-minute sports information to professional teams, print and broadcast media, software developers and interactive service providers around the country. STATS' network of trained sports reporters records the details of more than 3,800 sporting events across the four major sports annually. Some of our major clients include FOX Sports, the Associated Press, Lycos, *The Sporting News*, ESPN.com, Yahoo!, Electronic Arts, MSNBC, SONY, Topps, WGN Sports and YES Network.

STATS Publishing, a division of STATS, Inc., produces eight pro sports annuals, including the *Major League Handbook*, *The Scouting Notebook*, the *Pro Football Handbook*, the *Pro Basketball Handbook* and the *Hockey Handbook*. The annuals now are available in a PDF e-book format on our website (www.stats.com), as well as the traditional book form. In 1998, STATS introduced two baseball encyclopedias, the *All-Time Major League Handbook* (second edition updated through 1999) and the *All-Time Baseball Sourcebook*. Together they combine for more than 5,000 pages of baseball history. Also, original articles by STATS authors appear three times per week in the Insider section of ESPN.com. All of our publications and additional editorial content deliver STATS' expertise to fans, scouts, general managers and media across the country.

In addition, STATS Fantasy Sports is at the forefront of the fantasy sports industry. We develop fantasy baseball, football, basketball, hockey, golf and auto racing games for a host of sites. We also feature the first historical baseball simulation game created specifically for the Internet—Diamond Legends. No matter what time of year, STATS Fantasy Sports has a fantasy game to keep even the most passionate sports fan satisfied.

Information technology has grown by leaps and bounds in the last decade. STATS will continue to be at the forefront as a supplier of the most up-to-date, in-depth sports information available.

For more information on our products, or on joining our reporter network, contact us via:

Internet — www.stats.com
http://biz.stats.com

Toll Free in the USA at 1-800-63-STATS (1-800-637-8287)

Outside the USA at 1-847-470-8798

Or write to:

STATS, Inc.
8130 Lehigh Ave.
Morton Grove, IL 60053